Reference and Information Services

BECKENHAM LIBRARY

London Borough of Bromley Library Service

The Standard

Finnish–English   English–Finnish Dictionary

The Standard
Finnish–English
English–Finnish
Dictionary

AINO WUOLLE

Holt, Rinehart and Winston   Eastbourne

Werner Söderström Osakeyhtiö   Helsinki

© Aino Wuolle and
Werner Söderström Osakeyhtiö 1978 and 1981

Holt, Rinehart and Winston Ltd
St. Anne's Road, Eastbourne, East Sussex, BN21 3UN

Holt, Rinehart and Winston 1986

First Holt, Rinehart and Winston edition 1986

British Library Cataloguing in Publication Data

The Standard Finnish dictionary.
1. Finnish language—Dictionaries—English
2. English language—Dictionaries—Finnish
494'.541321   PH279

ISBN 0-03-910704-3

Printed and bound in Finland

TO THE USER OF THE DICTIONARY

In order to save space frequent use has been made of parentheses in the dictionary.

An alternative which can be used in place of the foregoing word or expression has been given in parentheses ( ). Parentheses are also used after verbs for the prepositions used in conjunction with them.

Words (or parts of words) enclosed in square brackets [ ] may be omitted without the meaning being changed. Additionally, words and references which clarify the meaning are sometimes given within these brackets.

Parentheses are also used to save space as in the following cases:

luku number; etc . . .
. . . **-kausi** term; (**~maksu** terminal fee; **~todistus** terminal report)
-kirja reader

Those adverbs which can easily be formed from the corresponding adjectives using the ending -ly are usually omitted (note, for example, **automaattinen** automatic(al), adv. automatically). Neither have all the nouns with the suffix -ness which may be formed from the corresponding adjectives been included. For example **pehmeys** softness, etc. means that a substantive may also be formed from the other equivalents of **pehmeä** in the same manner.

A list of irregular verbs is included in the back of the dictionary.

"The Concise Oxford Dictionary" has been used as a model for English orthography. Consequently, forms with the endings -ize, -ization (e.g. civilize, civilization) have been used, even though parallel forms in -ise and -isation are common in England.

ABBREVIATIONS USED IN THE DICTIONARY

a. adjective
adv. adverb
alat. vulgar
Am. American
anat. anatomy
ark. colloquial
biol. biology
bot. botany
dipl. diplomacy
ed. previous
elok. movies
Engl. England
et. primarily
fem. feminine
fil. philosophy
fys. physics
fysiol. physiology
geol. geology
geom. geometry
halv. disparagingly
harv. rarely
henk. of a person
hist. historical
ilm. aeronautics
ilmat. meteorology
inf. infinitive
intr. intransitive
kaupp. commerce
keitt. culinary
kem. chemistry
kiel. linguistics
kirjanp. bookkeeping
kirjap. printing
kirk. church
koll. collective word
ks. see
kuv. in a metaphorical sense
leik. playfully
lentok. aviation
liik. business
luonn. natural science
l. v. nearest equivalent
lyh. abbreviation
lääk. medicine
maant. geography
mat. mathematics
mek. mechanics
mer. nautical

min(er). mineralogy
mus. music
nyk. nowadays
parl. parliament
pilk. mockingly
pl. plural
pol. politics
prep. prepositions
pron. pronoun
psyk. psychology
puh. when speaking (of)
puhek. colloquial
puut. horticulture
raam. Bible
rad. radio
rak. construction
raut(at.) railway
run. poetic
s. noun (substantive)
seur. following word
Skotl. Scottish
sot. military
sähk. electrical
t. or
taid., tait. art
tav. usually
teatt. theatre
tekn. technology
tiet. scientific
tr. transitive
tähttit. astronomy
urh. sports
usk. religion
v. verb
valok. photography
valt. government
vanh. archaic
vir. in official style
voim. gymnastics
vrt. compare
yhd. in combinations
yl. usually, usual
zo. zoology

a.p. = a person
sb., sb's = somebody,
   somebody's
sth = something

The following abbreviations are used for the different case forms of the Finnish indefinite pronouns joku 'somebody' and jokin 'something'

jku = joku, jkin = jokin (nominative); jkta = jotakuta, jtk = jotakin (partitive)

jkn = jonkun, jnk = jonkin (genitive)

jkssa = jossakussa, jssk = jossakin (inessive)

jkh = johonkuhun, jhk = johonkin (illative)

jksta = jostakusta, jstk = jostakin (elative)

jklla = jollakulla, jllak = jollakin (adessive)

jklle = jollekulle, jllek = jollekin (allative)

jklta = joltakulta, jltak = joltakin (ablative), etc.

PRONUNCIATION

Consonants

g	this is hard, as in **goat**
h	is invariably pronounced, after both consonants and vowels
ng	as in singer, not as in finger (that is, without the g-sound)
r	this is rolled in the front of the mouth
s	is always hard, as in so

Vowels and diphthongs

aa	is a long **a**, as in far (no **r**-sound)
ah	is a short version of **aa**: between a in bat and u in but
æ	as **a** in bat
æœ	is a long ae sound
ew	is a rounded form of **ee**
igh	as in **high**
ur	as in fur (no **r**-sound)

In Finnish, the stress always falls on the first syllable of a word.

A

aakko|sellinen alphabetic [al].
-set alphabet; *kuv.* ABC,
elements. **-sjärjestys**
alphabetic [al] order. **-staa**
arrange in alphabetic [al]
order. **-sto** alphabet.
aallokko swell; surf; *merellä
käy kova* ~ the sea is very
rough, there is a heavy sea.
aallon|harja crest of a wave.
-murtaja breakwater, mole.
-pituus wavelength; *31 metrin
-pituudella* in the 31 metre
band. **-pohja** trough [of a
wave].
aallotar water-nymph.
aalto wave; billow; *(vyöry-)*
roller; *lyhyillä aalloilla* on
short wave [s]; *25 metrin
-pituudella* on 25 metres.
aaltoi|leva *(meri)* surging,
rolling; swaying; *(tukka)*
wavy. **-lla** undulate, *(tukka)*
wave; *(järvi ym.) -lee* there
are big waves. **-lu** heaving,
surge [of the sea], swell;
(esim. maan) undulation.
aalto|levy corrugated iron.
-liike wave-motion. **-mainen**
wavy, wave-like; undulating.
-pahvi corrugated cardboard.
-viiva wavy line.
aamiai|nen breakfast; *(lounas)*
lunch; *-sen aikaan* at
breakfast-time; *syömme -sta
kello 8* we have b. at 8; *he
ovat -sella* they are at b.,
they are eating breakfast.
aamiaistunti lunch hour.
aamu morning; *-lla* in the m.;
kesäkuun 1 päivänä ~lla on
the morning of the 1st of
June; *maanantai ~na* on
Monday m.; *eräänä ~na* one
m.; *koko ~n* all m.; *tänä
~na* this m.; *~lla varhain* in
the early m.; *varhain
seuraavana ~na* early next m.

-hartaus morning worship.
-hetki: ~ *kullan kallis* the
early bird catches the worm.
-hämärä morning twilight,
dawn. **-isin** in the morning.
-juna early train. **-kirkko**
morning service, matins.
-kylmä cool of a morning,
morning freshness. **-nkoitto**
dawn, daybreak. **-päivä**
forenoon, morning; *kello 10
~llä* at 10 [o'clock] in the
morning; *(~puku* šaketti
morning coat). **-rusko** aurora,
the red sky at dawn. **-takki**
dressing gown, *Am.m.*
bathrobe. **-uninen** sleepy in
the morning. **-yö:** ~*stä* after
midnight, in the small hours.
aapinen ABC-book, spelling
book.
aari *(mitta)* are (= 100 sq.
metres).
aaria *mus.* aria.
aarniometsä primeval forest.
aarre treasure; hoard. **-aitta**
treasury. **-löytö** treasure trove.
aarteen|etsijä treasure-seeker.
-kaivaja digger for treasures.
aarteisto treasury, treasure-house.
aasi donkey, *et. kuv.* ass, *kuv.*
dunce.
Aasia Asia; *Vähä* ~ Asia
Minor. **a-lainen** *a. & s.*
Asiatic, Asian.
aasimainen ass-like.
aasin|ajaja donkey-driver.
-tamma she-ass.
aate idea; *(aatos)* thought.
aateli noble birth, *(-sto)*
nobility. **-nen** noble, . . . of
noble family.
aatelis|arvo nobility. **-kartano**
manor. **-mies** nobleman.
-nainen noblewoman, lady of
rank. **-suku** noble family.
-sääty nobility.
aatelis|to nobility, *(päärit)* the

peerage. **-vaakuna** coat of arms, armorial bearings. **aatel|iton** not of noble birth, commoner. **-oida** raise to the nobility, knight; *kuv.* ennoble. **-uus** nobleness, nobility. **aate|maailma** world of ideas. **-piiri** sphere of ideas. **-rikas** rich in ideas **-rikkaus** richness of ideas. **-toveri** congenial spirit, fellow [pacifist etc.]; *(kannattaja)* supporter. **-virtaus** current of thought. **aatos** thought; idea. **aatteelli|nen** idealistic; ideal, non-real, *(esim. yhdistys)* non-profit-making; *(ylevä)* high-minded. **-suus** idealism. **aatto, -ilta** eve; *jnk ~na* on the eve of... **aava** *a.* open, wide; *(laaja)* vast, extensive; *~lla merellä* on the open sea *(t.* high seas). **aave** ghost, spectre, spook; *(-näky)* apparition, phantom. **-mainen** ghostlike, ghostly, eerie. **-maisuus** ghostliness. **aavikko** vast plain; *(hiekka-)* desert; waste; *(ruoho-)* prairie; *ks. aro.* **aavis|taa** have a presentiment, have a feeling, foresee; *(epäillä)* suspect; *(odottaen)* anticipate; *-tin sitä* I thought as much; *enpä osannut silloin ~* little did I think then; *kukapa olisi voinut ~* who would have thought it. **-tamaton** unforeseen, unexpeeted. **-tamatta** unexpectedly; *mitään pahaa ~* suspecting no evil. **aavistus** presentiment; *paha ~* foreboding, misgiving; *minulla ei ollut ~takaan siitä, että* I had no idea that... **abbedissa** abbess. **Abessinia** Abyssinia, Ethiopia. **a-lainen** *a. & s.* Abyssinian. **abnormi** abnormal. **-suus** abnormality. **abortti** abortion; *laiton ~* criminal a. **absolutis|mi** *(raittius)* total abstinence. **-ti** total abstainer, teetotaller. **absoluuttinen** absolute.

abstra|holda, **-ktinen** abstract. **adjektiivi** adjective. **adjutantti** aide [-de-camp] *(lyh.* A.D.C), *jkn* to; adjutant. **adoptio** adoption. **adoptoida** adopt. **adressi** greetings card; *suru ~ (l.v.)* remembrance card. **Adrianmeri** the Adriatic [Sea]. **adventisti** Seventh-day Adventist. **adventti** Advent. **adverbi** adverb. **-aali(nen)** adverbial. **aforismi** aphorism. **Afrikka** Africa. **-lainen** *a. & s.* African. **agaatti** agate. **agen|tti** *liik., kiel.* agent. **-tuuri** agency [-business]; representation. **agio** *liik.* agio, [exchange] premium. **agit|aatio** agitation. **-aattori** agitator. **-oida** agitate. **agraari** agrarian. **agressiivinen** aggressive. **agronomi** agriculturist, agronomist. **ahavoi|tua** get weather-beaten. **-tunut** weather-beaten; tanned. **ahdas** narrow, *(tila, asunto)* cramped; *(kaita)* strait; *(rajoittunut)* limited; *(tiukka)* tight; *täällä on ~ta* there is very little space here, we are cramped for space, *(paljon väkeä)* it (the room) is [very] crowded, *puhek.* it's a tight fit here; *asua ahtaasti* live in overcrowded conditions; *olla ahtaalla* be in [financial] straits, be hard pressed [for money], *puhek.* be hard up; *joutua ahtaalle* get into difficulties (into a tight corner); *sanan ahtaammassa merkityksessä* in the strict sense of the word. **-mielinen** narrow-minded; strait-laced. **-mielisyys** narrow-mindedness. **ahde** *(mäen~)* slope, hillside. **ahdinko** crush, crowd[ing]; *(pula)* straits, difficulty; *~on asti täynnä väkeä* packed (crowded) with people. **-tila** straits, distress, straitened circumstances; *(pula)* predicament.

ahdist|aa press; *(puristaa)* pinch; be tight: *kuv.* harass, beset, attack, oppress, *(kysymyksillä, m.)* heckle; *(esim. kaupustelija)* importune; *henkeäni* ~ I am short of breath; *kenkä* ~ the shoe pinches; *mieltäni* ~ I am anxious (distressed, oppressed with anxiety); *-ava tunne* feeling of oppression. **-aja** pursuer. **-ella** molest, harass. **-us** oppression, anxiety; torment, agony; vexation; *(hengen-)* difficulty in breathing; *-tuksen alainen* oppressed, distressed, troubled.

aher|rus striving; bustle; toil[ing]. **-taa** work hard; *(raataa)* toil; *kuv.* hammer away.

ahjo forge; *kuv.* seat, nest.

ahker|a diligent, industrious, hard-working; busy; *(oppilas, m.)* studious. **-aan, -asti** diligently, busily; hard; *(usein)* frequently. **-oida** work hard, be busy [at work]; exert oneself, take pains; ~ *edistyäkseen* strive to make progress. **-uus** diligence, industry.

ahkio [dog] sleigh.

ahma glutton, *Am.* wolverine. **-ista** devour; eat voraciously. **-tti** glutton, gormandizer.

ahmia eat ravenously; gormandize; gorge (oneself with); *m. kuv.* devour; feast one's eyes on, gloat over.

ahnas voracious, ravenous; gluttonous; greedy.

ahne greedy; *(halukas)* eager, *jnk* for; *rahan* ~ greedy for money. **-htia** be greedy, *jtk* for; *(haluta)* covet; have a craving (for). **-us** greed[iness], avidity; *(petomaisuus)* voracity; *(saituus)* avarice; *rahan* ~ love of money, greed for money.

aho clearing, glade.

ahrain fish gig.

ahtaa stow; ~ *täyteen* pack full; stow, cram, *jtk* with.

ahtaa|ja stevedore. **-minen** stowage, stowing.

ahtau|s narrowness; tightness; cramped conditions; *mer.* stowage; *tilan* ~ lack of space (of room); *asuntojen* ~ overcrowding, cramped housing accommodation. **-utua** narrow; crowd.

ahtojää pack-ice, ice pack.

ahven perch, bass.

ai oh! oh dear!

aidake rail[ing]; *(oikeussalin)* bar.

aidan|pano fencing **-seiväs** fence-post, stake.

aidata fence [in]; enclose [by a fence].

aie intention; intent; purpose; *(tuuma)* plan; *olin aikeissa lähteä* I intended to leave, I was going to (about to) leave; *tappamisen aikeessa* with intent to kill.

aiemmin *ks. aikaisemmin.*

Aigeianmeri the Aegean [Sea].

aihe *(syy)* reason, cause; *(kirjoituksen ym.)* subject, theme, topic; *(taulun)* motif; *(itu)* germ; *jstk* ~*esta* on a subject; *ei ole* ~*tta jhk* there is no reason to; *sinulla ei ole* ~*tta . .* you have no cause (no occasion) to . .; *naurun* ~ cause for laughter, *(esine)* object of mirth; *antaa* ~*tta jhk* give rise to; give ground for; *vrt. aiheuttaa.*

aihee|llinen well-founded; justifiable, *(suositeltava)* advisable. **-ton** groundless. *(perätön)* unfounded; unjustified; uncalled for; ~ *muistutus* unjustifiable (uncalled-for) remark; ~ *hälytys* false alarm; *oli täysin* ~ *(m.)* lacked any justification. **-ttomasti** without a *(t. any)* reason (cause). **-ttomuus** groundlessness.

aihetodiste circumstantial evidence.

aiheu|ttaa cause, bring about, give rise to; *(johtaa)* lead to, result in; *(tuottaa)* produce; create; *. .-tti keskustelua* — provoked (called forth) a discussion; *jnk* *-ttama* caused by, due to, called forth by. **-ttaja**

originator; *(syy)* cause; source. **-tua** be caused, be occasioned by, be induced by, be due to; *vrt. -ttaa; (syntyä)* come (rise) from, originate in; *mistä tämä -tuu?* what causes this? what is the cause of this? what is this due to? *siitä -tuu hänelle suuria kustannuksia* that will cause him a lot (a great deal) of expense.

aika 1. *s.* time; *(ajankohta)* hour, moment; *(-kausi)* day[s], time[s]; period; age; *(toimisto- ym)* [office] hours; *sadan vuoden ~* [a period of] a hundred years; *lepo~* a period of rest; *Neiti Aika* speaking clock; *onko sinulla ~a* .. can you spare me a moment .. ; *~a on runsaasti* there is plenty of time,.. *niukasti* time is short; *kun minulla on ~a* when I get (have) time; *tilata ~* make an appointment (with); *meidän ~namme* in our times; *uusi ~* the new age, *(hist.)* modern times; *minun on ~ lähteä* it is time for me to leave; *jnk ~na* during; *minun ~nani* in my time; *kuningatar Elisabetin ~na* in the age (the reign) of Queen Elizabeth; *~ ajoin* at times, from time to time; at intervals; *jksk ~a* for some time, for a while; *jnk ~a* some time, for a time; *sillä ~a* meanwhile, [in the] meantime; *sillä ~a kun* while; *mihin ~an* [at] what time? *kello 8 ~an* [at] about 8 o'clock; *samaan ~an* at the same time; *siihen ~an* at that time; *ei pitkään ~an* not for a long time; *jo oli ~kin* it was about time; *~naan* in due time, *(yhteen aikaan)* at one time, *(ajoissa)* in time; *~nani asuin siellä* at one time I used to live there; *vrt. aikoinaan; kaikella on ~nsa* there is a time for everything; *entisinä aikoina* in the old days; *kaikkina aikoina* at all times; *aikoja*

siihen long ago, *kuhden viikon ajan* for two weeks; *ajan mittaan* with [the progress of] time, in [the] course of time; *ajan pitkään, ajan oloon* in the long run; *tulla ajoissa (junalle ym.)* catch [the train] ; *saada ~an ks. aikaansaada.*

aika 2. *adv.:* ~ *hyvä* pretty *t.* fairly good, *(huononpuoleinen)* rather good; ~ *paljon* [quite] a lot, a good deal; ~ *tavalla* a lot, a great deal; ~ *veitikka* a proper rascal.

aikaan|saada bring about, accomplish, *(aiheuttaa)* cause; effect; *(tuottaa)* produce; lead to; ~ *ihmeitä* work wonders; ~ *vahinkoa* do damage. **-saannos** achievement, accomplishment, *(teko)* deed. **aikaa|säästävä** time-saving. **-viepä** time-consuming, *(hidas)* slow.

aikaihminen adult, grown-up. **aikai|lla** delay; lag, loiter; *-li vastatessaan* hesitated before answering, was slow to reply. **-lu** delay. **-nen** early; *jkn ~* of the time of .. ; dating from. **-semmin** earlier; previously, formerly. **-sempi** earlier; previous. **-simmin** earliest. **-sin** early; ~ *aamulla* early in the morning,. at an early hour. **-sintaan** at the earliest. **-suus** earliness. **aika|järjestys** chronological order; *a-tyksessä (m.)* chronologically. **-kauppa** *liik.* contract for future delivery. **-kausi** period; *hist.* age, era, epoch. **-kauskirja (-lehti)** periodical, magazine, journal. **-kautinen** periodic[al]. **-kirja** chronicle; ~*t (m.)* annals, records. *raam.* [the Books of the] Chronicles. **-lainen** contemporary; *hänen -laisensa* his contemporaries. **-luokka** *kiel.* tense. **-merkki** time-signal. **-mitta** tempo. **aika|mies** adult, grown-up man. **-moinen** [fairly] big, siz[e]able, considerable; ~ *nainen!* some woman!

aika|muoto tense. **-määrä** term. **-taulu** time-table: *Am.* schedule; *~n mukainen* scheduled; appointed. **-uttaa** *sot.* time. **-yksikkö** unit of time.

aikoa intend, be going to; *(suunnitella)* plan; *hän aikoo kauppiaaksi* he intends to become a merchant; *aiottu matkani* my proposed journey; *aioin juuri lähteä* I was just about to leave; *aikomatta(an)* unintentionally, without intention.

aikoinaan *(kerran)* at one time, once; *~ hän* in his day (in his time) he ..

aikomus intention; purpose; *(tuuma)* plan; *vahingoittamisen aikomuksessa* with intent to cause damage; *minulla on ~* .. I intend to .., it is my intention to ..; *aikomuksetta* unintentionally.

aikuinen grown-up, adult; *sen ~ tapa* a custom of that time; *kivikauden ~* of *(t.* belonging to) the Stone Age.

aikuiskasvatus adult education.

aimo fair-sized: good. proper, thorough.

aina always; invariably; constantly; ever; *hän ~ vain lukee* he keeps on reading; *~ tähän asti* up to the present time; *~ siitä asti* ever since: *~ sieltä saakka* all the way from; *~ sen mukaan kuin* according as.

ainainen perpetual, continual, constant; *ainais-* permanent.

aina|kaan: *ei ~* at least not, at any rate not. **-kin** at least, *(vähintään)* at the [very] least; *(joka tapauksessa)* at any rate, anyhow.

aine matter, stuff, *kem.* substance; *(tarve-)* material; *(oppi-)* subject; *(-kirjoitus)* composition, essay.

aineelli|nen material; temporal; *~ etu* material benefit. **-staa** give substance to. **-stua** materialize. **-suus** materialism.

aineen|koetus testing of materials. **-mukainen:** *~ luettelo* general index. **-vaihdunta** metabolism;

(~taudit metabolic diseases.)

aineeton immaterial.

aineisto *(ainekset)* material. *(kirjan, m.)* subject-matter.

aine|kirjoitus composition. **-osa** component, constituent [part] **-osanen** particle.

aines material, stuff; matter; *(-osa)* element; *ainekset* material[s]; *(ruokalajin)* ingredients; *kansan parhaat ainekset* the pick of the people; *hänessä on ~ta jksk* he has got the makings of .. in him.

aine|sana material noun. **-yhdiste** compound. **-yhdistelmä** combination of subjects.

aini|aaksi for ever, for all time. **-aan** [for] always, eternally.

ainoa only; sole; *~ poika* only son; *~ perillinen* sole heir; *joka ~ (a.)* every single; *(s.)* every single one; *ei ~kaan (a.)* not a single; *(s.)* not a single one, no one; *tämän ~n kerran* [for] this once. **-laatuinen** unique. **-laatuisuus** uniqueness. **-staan** only; merely, solely; *ei ~ vaan myös* not only but also .. **ainutkertainen** *(vertaa vailla)* unique, unparalleled; *ks.* kertakaikkinen.

airo oar; *(lyhyt)* scull. **-nhanka** rowlock. **-nlapa** blade of an oar. **-nveto** stroke [of an oar].

airut messenger, herald; *(juhlassa)* usher: *run. m.* harbinger.

aisa shaft; pole; *(nuotan)* wing; *panna aisoihin* put in the shafts, *(valjastaa)* harness; *pitää aisoissa* keep in check, keep within bounds, curb; *pysyä aisoissa* keep oneself in check, restrain oneself.

aisti sense; *(maku)* taste; *aisti*-sensory. **-a** perceive, sense. **-hairahdus** illusion. **-harha** hallucination. **-kas** tasteful, *(tyylikäs)* stylish, elegant; *erittäin ~ (t. -kkaasti)* in excellent taste; *hän on ~* she has style. **-kkuus** tastefulness, good taste; elegance. **-llinen**

sensual, *(aisti-)* sensuous.
-llisuus sensuality. -mus
perception; sensation. -ton
tasteless. -ttomuus lack of
taste. -viallinen: *-vialliset*
people with sensory defects.
-viallisuus sensory defect.
aita fence, *(pensas-)* hedge;
(pysty)) paling; *urh.* hurdle;
(et. rakennusaikana) hoarding;
(kaide) railing. -amaton
unfenced, not fenced [in].
-aminen fencing [in]. -juoksu
hurdles, hurdling; *400 m.* ~
400 metres hurdles. -us
enclosure; *(karjapiha)* pen,
Am. corral.
aitio box.
aito true, genuine; real. -hopea
real silver, sterling silver. -us
genuineness.
aitta shed [for provisions],
storehouse; *(vilja-)* granary;
koota ~*an* garner.
aituri *urh.* hurdler, *(hevonen)*
jumper.
aivan quite; altogether; very;
(täysin) fully, perfectly;
wholly, entirely; *(ihan)*
exactly; *(juuri)* just; ~ *alusta*
(asti) from the very
beginning; ~ *heti* at once,
right away; ~ *huono* really
bad, altogether bad; ~ *hyvin*
perfectly well; ~ *ilman apua*
without any help whatever; ~
keskellä right in the middle;
~ *kuin* [just] as if; ~ *liian*
kallis much too dear; ~ *niin!*
exactly! quite right! that's it!
~ *pian* very soon; ~ *sama*
mies the very [same] man;
~ *terve (m.)* in perfectly
good health; ~ *äsken* just
now, a moment ago.
aivas|taa sneeze. -taminen
sneezing. -tus sneeze. -tuttaa:
minua ~ I feel like sneezing.
aivo *ks. aivot.* -halvaus stroke,
apoplexy. -kalvontulehdus
meningitis. -kasvain brain
tumour. -koppa brain-pan.
-kuori cerebral cortex. -pesu
brain-washing. -t brain (brains
tav. äly); *isot* ~ cerebrum;
pienet ~ cerebellum. -tauti
disease of the brain. -tärähdys
concussion [of the brain].

vamma brain injury. -vlenti
brain drain. -verenvuoto
cerebral h[a]emorrhage.
ajaa *tr.* drive; *(kuljettaa)*
convey, carry, take; *(riistaa)*
hunt; *intr.* drive; ride [a
bicycle; in a car, in a train];
go [by car, by train],
(autolla, m.) motor; *(kuv.,*
aatetta) advocate, champion;
~ *jkn asiaa (lak.)* plead a
p.'s cause in court; ~ *kilpaa*
race [a p.]; ~ *jku kumoon*
knock (run) down; ~ *läpi*
push (force) through; ~ *parta*
shave; ~ *pois* drive away; ~
takaa chase, pursue; *mitä hän*
~ *takaa* what is he driving
at? ~ *ulos* turn .. out,
send sb. packing; ~ *yhteen*
collide; ~ *yli* run over; *hän*
ajoi minut asemalle he took
me to the station [in his
car]; *hän ajoi autonsa* he ran
his car into [a stone, a tree].
ajaja driver; *(auton m.)*
chauffeur; *kuv.* champion,
advocate.
ajall|aan, -ansa in time; at the
right time; *sana* ~ a word in
season.
ajalli|nen temporal, *(maallinen)*
mundane -suus temporalness,
temporal life.
ajan|hukka loss of time; waste
of time. -jakso period; epoch.
-kohta point [of time],
moment in *(t. of)* time; ~*an*
nähden sopiva timely; *tuona*
kriitillisenä ~*na* at that
critical juncture. -kohtainen ..
of current interest, topical; ~
kysymys (m.) question of the
day. -kohtaislähetys current
affairs programme. -kulu
pastime; ~*ksi* to pass the
time. -lasku calendar, style;
vanhaa ~*a* old style. -mittaan
in [the] course of time, in
the long run. -mukainen up
to date, modern. -mukaistaa
bring .. up to date,
modernize. -mukaisuus
modernity. -ottaja time-keeper.
-pitkään in the long run.
-puute lack of time. -viete
pastime; *(*~*kirjallisuus* light
reading).

ajatel|la think (about, of); *(harkita)* consider; *ajattele ehdotustani* [Please] think about my proposal; *hän ajatteli lapsuusaikaansa* she was thinking about her childhood days; *ajattelehan kustannuksia* [just] think of the cost! *en voisi ~ kaan tehdä sellaista* I shouldn't think of doing such a thing! *~ hyvää jksta* think highly (well) of sb.; *ajattele asiaa!* think the matter over! *jtk tarkemmin -lessani* on second thoughts, on further consideration; *tulla -leeksi* happen to think (of); *kuinka tulit sitä -leeksi?* what made you think of that? what put the idea into your mind? *ajattelepas, jos . .* just fancy if; *ajattelepas, jos tekisin sen* suppose (supposing) I were to do it; *ajattelematta* without thinking, thoughtlessly; *älä enää sitä ajattele* put that out of your mind! dismiss that from your thoughts! *ei -tavissakaan* [it is] out of the question, it is not to be thought of; *~ uudestaan (kahdesti)* think twice. **-ma** aphorism; maxim. **-tava** worth thinking about, *(ajateltavissa oleva)* conceivable, imaginable. **ajaton** timeless, dateless; *(sopimaton)* inopportune. **ajattaa** have . . carted (hauled, taken), away *pois; ~ partansa* have oneself shaved, have a shave. **ajattele|maton** thoughtless, heedless, inconsiderate, indiscreet [word, *sana*]; *(kevytmielinen)* light-headed; hasty. **-mattomasti** inconsiderately, without consideration. **-mattomuus** lack of consideration, indiscretion, thoughtlessness. **-minen** thinking, consideration; *sen pelkkä ~kin* the mere thought of it; *se antoi minulle -misen aihetta* it set me thinking. **-vainen** thinking, reflective, thoughtful. **ajatte|lija** thinker. **-lu** thinking;

thought, reflection; *(mietiskely)* meditation. **ajatuksellinen** pertaining to thought; logical. **ajatuksen|juoksu** train of thought. **-vapaus** freedom of thought. **ajatus** thought; idea; reflection, *Engl. m.* reflexion; *(merkitys)* meaning; *(mielipide)* opinion; *ajatuksiin vaipunut* absorbed in thought; *tein sen ajatuksissani* I did it absent-mindedly *(t.* without thinking). **-aika:** *antaa jklle ~a* allow sb. time for consideration. **-kanta** standpoint, point of view. **-kyky** faculty of thought. **-maailma** world of ideas. **-peräinen** abstract. **-ponnistelu** mental effort. **-suunta** trend of ideas. **-tapa** way of thinking. **-tenlukija** mind-reader. **-tenvaihto** exchange of ideas. **-toiminta** mental activity. **-viiva** dash. **-voima** power of thought. **-yhtymä** association of ideas. **ajautua** drift; be driven; *(rantaan)* be stranded. **ajelehti|a** be adrift, drift; float; *-va laiva* a derelict ship. **aje|lla** ride, drive; *(pää, parta)* shave [off, *paljaaksi*]. **-lu** drive, ride; *lähteä ~lle* go for a drive (a ride), go motoring. **aje|ttua** swell [up], become swollen. **-ttuma** swelling. **-tus:** *on ajetuksissa* is swollen. **ajo** driving; *(metsästys)* chase, hunt [ing]; *(jälkiä myöten)* track [ing]; *(kuorman)* hauling, haulage. **-hiekka** drift-sand. **ajoissa** *ks. aika; tulla ~* be in time. **ajoittaa** *urh.* time; *(löytö ym)* date. **ajoitt|ain** at times; occasionally. **-ainen** occurring at intervals; periodical; *(satunnainen)* occasional; *(uusiutuva)* recurrent. **ajo|jahti** *(poliittinen ym)* witch hunt. **-jää** drift-ice. **-kaista** lane. **-kielto:** *. . on -kiellossa* [the road] is closed to traffic. **-kki** vehicle. **-koe**

driving test. **-koira** hound
(*esim*. foxhound). **-kortti**
driving licence; *menettää ∼nsa*
be disqualified from holding a
d. l. **-maksu** (*taksi- ym*) fare.
-metsästys hunt, chase. **-mies**
driver. **-neuvo** vehicle,
conveyance. **-nopeus** driving
rate, speed; *sallittu ∼* speed
limit. **-palkka** (*tavaran*)
haulage. **-retki** drive, ride.
ajos abscess.
ajo|tie drive; (*katu*) roadway.
-valot headlights.
ajuri cab driver, cabman.
-asema cab-stand.
ajuruoho thyme.
akaasia acacia.
akana husk; *∼t* chaff.
akateemi|kko academician. **-nen**
academic [al]; *∼ oppiarvo*
university degree; *saavuttaa ∼*
oppiarvo graduate, take one's
degree; *on -sesti sivistynyt*
has had a university
education.
akatemia academy.
akileija columbine.
akka old woman. **-mainen**
[old-] womanish; unmanly.
-maisuus [old-] womanishness;
cowardice. **-valta** petticoat
rule; *olla -vallan alla* be
henpecked.
akku accumulator. **-paristo**
storage battery.
akkuna window; *vrt. ikkuna.*
akkusatiivi accusative [case].
akordi chord; *liik.* arrangement.
akryyli acryl.
akseli *fys. ym.* axis (*pl.* axes);
mek. shaft, (*pyörän*) axle.
-väli (*auton*) wheel-base.
aksiisi excise, inland revenue.
-nalainen excisable, liable to
excise.
aktiivi *kiel.* active [voice].
-nen active. **-suus** activeness,
activity.
aktivoida activate.
aktuaari registrar; (*vakuutus-*)
actuary.
akustiikka acoustics, acoustic
qualities.
akvaario aquarium, tank.
akvarelli water-colour
[painting]. **-väri** water-colour.
ala area, (*tila*) space, (*alue*)

territory, (*ammatti-*)
occupation; trade, profession;
(*toimi-*) field, sphere, line;
(*haara*) branch; (*laajuus*)
extent; *laaja ∼ltaan* large in
extent; *elokuva- ∼lla* in the
film industry; *tieteellisellä*
∼lla within the field (domain)
of science; *voittaa ∼a* gain
ground; *pysyä ∼llaan* keep
within one's province,
(*kurissa*) keep quiet; *asia ei*
kuulu minun ∼ani this is not
in my line. **-arvoinen** inferior,
not up to the standard.
-arvoisuus inferiority, inferior
quality. **-hanka** lower oarlock.
-huone *Engl. parl.* the House
of Commons. **-huuli** lower lip.
-ikäinen *a.* under age; *s.*
minor. **-ikäisyys** minority.
alai|nen: *jnk ∼* subject to..;
käsittelyn ∼ ..under
consideration; *rangaistuksen ∼*
subject (liable) to punishment;
veron ∼ liable to duty; *hänen*
alaisensa (*virkamiehet*) his
subordinates; *saattaa* (*jnk*)
-seksi subject (to); *joutua jnk*
-seksi be subjected (to), be
exposed (to), (*naurun*) become
an object of ridicule; *hän*
joutui saman kohtalon -seksi
he suffered (met with) the
same fate. **-suus** subordination.
ala|jaotus subdivision. **-juoksu**
(*joen*) lower course. **-kerros,**
-kerta (*pohja-*) ground floor;
-kerrassa (*m.*) downstairs.
-kkain under each other, one
below another. **-kuloi|nen**
melancholy, .. in low
spirits; *tehdä a-seksi* depress,
discourage. **-kuloisesti** in a
downcast manner, dejectedly.
-kuloisuus low spirits,
melancholy. **-kunto:** *-kunnossa*
not quite well; *tunsin olevani*
a-ssa I felt out of sorts, I
felt bad. **-kuntoisuus** low
condition. **-kuu** the waning
moon. **-kynsi:** *joutua*
alakynteen be defeated
(beaten); *jouduin alakynteen*
(*hänestä*) he got the better of
me, I came off the loser.
-leuka lower jaw; mandible.
-luokka lower class; (*rahvas*)

the lower classes.
-luokkalainen pupil of a lower
form. **-luomi** lower [eye]lid.
-maa lowland. **-maailma**
underworld.
alamai|nen *s.* subject;
(kansalainen) national; *a.*
subservient, humble,
submissive, *jklle* to. **-suus**
subjection; subserviency;
(uskollinen) allegiance.
ala|mittainen under size; below
standard, inferior. **-mäki**
[downward] slope; *-mäkeä*
downhill.
alanko low-lying land,
lowland [s]. **-maalainen** *s.*
Netherlander.
Alankomaat the Netherlands.
ala|osa lower part, lower
portion, bottom. **-osasto**
subdivision. **-otsikko** subhead
-[ing]. **-puoli** lower side
(part); bottom, foot; *-puolella,*
-lle under [neath]; on, onto
the lower side; beneath;
below. **-puolinen** lower,
bottom. **-puolisko** lower half.
-pää lower end. **-raajat** lower
extremities (limbs). **-reuna**
lower edge; bottom, foot [of
the page, *sivun*]. **-ruumis**
lower part of the body.
alas down; downward [s]; ~
portaita down the stairs,
downstairs; *jokea* ~ down the
river; *mäkeä* ~ downhill:
laskea ~ let down, lower;
mennä ~ descend.
alasin anvil.
alas|päin downward [s], down.
-suin upside down; *kaataa* ~
upset, overturn.
alas|ti: *olla* ~ be naked;
riisuutua ~ undress, strip [to
the skin] . **-tomuus**
nakedness; nudity; bareness.
-ton naked; *tait.* nude;
(paljas) bare, uncovered;
undressed.
alati always, constantly; *(yhä)*
ever-; ~ *vaihteleva*
ever-changing; *~vihreä*
evergreen.
ala|va low [-lying]. **-viite**
footnote. **-vuus** lowness; low
situation. **-ääni** low tone;
alaäänet the lower register.

albumi album.
alem|ma(ksi) lower, lower
down, farther down. **-muus**
lower position; *(huonommuus)*
inferiority; *hinnan* ~ the
lower price; *-muuden tunne*
inferiority feeling; **(~kompleksi**
inferiority complex). **-paa**
[from] farther down. **-pana**
farther down, lower down;
(kirjoituksessa) below; ~
mainittu .. mentioned
(stated) below. **-pi** lower;
under; *(virassa ym)* inferior,
subordinate.
alempi|arvoinen *ks. ed.;* ..
of lower rank. **-palkkainen**
lower paid.
alene|minen sinking; drop,
decrease; *hintojen* ~ fall
(decline) in prices. **-va** falling,
dropping; *suoraan ~ssa*
polvessa in direct descent.
alennus *(hinnan-)* reduction [in
price], cut; *(myynti-)*
discount; *(virka-)* degradation;
antaa ~ta allow a discount; *5*
%:n ~ *sovitusta hinnasta* a
reduction of 5 % on the
price agreed upon; *myydä*
alennuksella sell at a
discount. **-lippu** reduced-fare
ticket. **-merkki** *mus.* flat.
-myynti sale. **-tila** state of
abasement, degradation.
alen|taa lower, reduce; bring
down, cut; *kuv.* degrade,
debase; ~ *hintaa* reduce a
price [by .. %]; ~ *arvoa*
(m.) depreciate, *(rahan)*
devalue, *(henkilön)* disparage,
belittle; ~ *itsensä* humble
oneself; ~ *sotamieheksi*
degrade to the ranks; ~
äänensä lower (drop) one's
voice; *alennettuun hintaan* at
a reduced price. **-tava**
degrading, debasing. **-tua** *ks.*
aleta; kuv. condescend, to,
jhk. **-tuvainen** *kuv.*
condescending. **-tuvaisuus**
condescension.
aleta fall, go down; sink,
drop; *(vähetä)* decrease; *hinta*
alenee the price falls (goes
down, drops); *lukumäärä*
alenee (m.) there is falling
off in the number.

Algeria Algeria. **a-lainen** Algerian.

alhaa|lla [low] down, down below; low; ~ *vasemmalla* bottom left; *pysyä* ~ remain low. **-lta,** ~ **päin** from below (beneath).

alhai|nen low; *kuv.* mean, vile; *-simmillaan (kuv.)* at its lowest mark, at the lowest ebb; *(oli -sta) sukua .. of* modest origin, (he came) from a humble family. **-so** populace, the hoi polloi. **-suus** lowness, *kuv.* baseness, meanness.

ali- *vrt. ala-.* **-arvioida** underrate, underestimate. **-arviointi** underestimation. **-hankkija** subcontractor. **-hinta:** *myydä ~an* sell below cost price. **-johtaja** sub-director. **-käytävä** underpass, *Engl. m.* subway [crossing]. **-luutnantti** *meriv.* sublieutenant. **-lääkäri** assistant physician (surgeon). **-mmainen** lower, *vrt. alin.* **-mmaksi** lowest [down], farthest down. **ali|n** lowest; undermost; ~ *hinta* lowest price, bottom price. **-nen** lower. **-nna** lowest, nethermost; *kaikkein* ~ underneath everything [else].

alin|omaa constantly, perpetually, continually. **-omainen** perpetual, continual.

ali|paino(inen) underweight, short weight. **-palkattu** underpaid. **-päällystö** *sot.* non-commissioned officers, *meriv.* petty officers. **-ravitsemus** undernourishment, malnutrition. **-ravittu** undernourished, underfed.

alis|taa *(jnk ratkaistavaksi ym)* submit to sb.'s decision, refer (to); subordinate, subject (to); ~ *jtk valtaansa* subdue; subjugate; *-teinen lause* subordinate clause. **-tua** submit (to); *(taipua)* yield; resign oneself, *(mukaantua)* reconcile oneself [to one's fate, *kohtaloonsa*]. **-tumaton** unsubmissive; unyielding. **-tuminen** submission (to); *(nöyryys)* resignation. **-tuvainen**

submissive. **-tuvalsesti** submissively, with resignation. **-tuvaisuus** submissiveness.

alitaju|inen subconscious. **-nta** the subconscious [mind].

alitse under, below.

alittaa be (fall) below, fall short of; *(tarjous)* underbid.

alitui|nen perpetual, continual; *(lakkaamaton)* incessant, continuous; *-sesti* constantly.

ali|työllisyys underemployment. **-upseeri** non-commissioned officer, *meriv.* petty officer. **-vuokralainen** subtenant.

alkaa begin, start, commence, *(ryhtyä)* set about, enter upon; *(saada alkunsa)* originate, *jstk* in; *(joesta)* have its source; ~ *toimintansa (m.)* opens; ~ *tulla kylmä* it is getting cold; *jnk alkaessa* at the beginning of . .; *alkamaisillaan* about to begin.

alkaen: *jstk* ~ since; from . . on, [as] from; *(esim. jnk voimaantulosta)* with effect from; *siitä (ajasta)* ~ ever since [that time]; *tästä* ~ *(lähtien)* henceforth, from now on.

alka|ja beginner; originator, author. **-jaiset** opening [ceremony]. **-jaispuhe** opening address.

alkali *ks. emäs.* **-nen** alkaline.

alka|maton not [yet] commenced; unopened. **-minen** beginning, commencement, start[ing]; *odottaa puheen -mista* wait for the speech to begin.

alkeelli|nen primitive; *(alku-)* primary; *(alkeis-)* elementary. **-suus** primitiveness.

alkeet elements, rudiments; ABC.

alkeis- elementary. **-hiukkanen** elementary particle. **-kirja** elementary book, primer. **-koulu** preparatory school; *(Engl. kansakoulun ~)* infant school. **-kurssi** elementary course. **-opetus** primary education. **-tiedot** elementary knowledge; *hänellä on hyvät* ~ *historiassa* he is well

grounded in history.
alkemi|a alchemy. **-sti** alchemist.
alkio embryo.
alkoholi alcohol; *~n vaikutuksen alaisena* under the influence of a. **-juoma** alcoholic drink. **-liike** liquor store. **-nhimo** dipsomania. **-pitoinen** alcoholic. **-pitoisuus** percentage of alcohol. **-smi** alcoholism. **-sti** alcohol addict, alcoholic. **-ton** non-alcoholic; *~ juoma* soft drink.
alkovi (*komero*) alcove.
alku beginning, start, outset, commencement; (*synty*) origin, rise; *~aan* originally; primarily; *aluksi, alussa* at first, to begin with; *jnk alussa* at the beginning of; *alusta pitäen* from the very beginning; from the first; *alusta loppuun* from beginning to end; *saada ~nsa* originate, *jstk* in, from; arise, spring (from), (*joki*) rise, have its origin (source) in; *panna alulle* start; *päästä ~un* get started.
alku- initial, original. **-aika** beginning; *jnk -aikoina* in the early days of .. **-aine** element. **-aste** initial stage. **-asukas** native; *-asukkaat* aborigines, natives. **-eläin** protozoon (*pl.* -zoa). **-erät** *urh.* qualifying heats. **-ihminen** primitive man. **-isin:** *olla ~ jstk* be derived from, derive its origin from, originate in. **-(j)aan** originally. **-juoksu** headwaters. **-juuri** origin; source, root. **-kantainen** primitive. **-kesä** [the] early part of [the] summer; *~stä* in early summer. **-kieli** original [language]. **-kirjain** initial [letter]; *-kirjaimet* initials. **-lause** preface. **-liite** prefix. **-lima** protoplasm. **-lähde** *kuv.* source. **-nopeus** initial velocity, (*ammuksen*) muzzle v. **-perä** origin; source. **-peräinen** original, (*väärentämätön*) authentic; *~ kappale* (*kirjoitus*) original. **-peräisesti** originally. **-peräisyys** originality. **-puoli**

first part, beginning; *ensi viikon -puolella* early next week. **-puolisko** first half. **-sointu** alliteration. **-soitto** prelude, overture **-tekijä** *mat.* prime number. **-tila** original state. **-tutkinto** preliminary examination.
alkuun|panija initiator, originator; (*pahan*) instigator.
alku|valmistelut preparatory measures, preliminaries. **-viikko:** *alkuviikosta* at the beginning of the week. **-voima** primitive strength. **-yö** early part of the night.
alla (*jnk*) under, beneath; (*alempana*) below; *joulun ~* [just] before Christmas; *~ oleva (seuraava)* .. given , (stated) below; *~päin oleva* downcast, dejected. **-mainittu** .. mentioned below.
allas trough; (*pesu- ym.*) basin; (*uima-*) pool; *WC~* pan.
alle under; below, underneath; *~ 20 asteen* below 20 degrees; *~ 16-vuotias* under 16 [years of age]; *jäädä auton ~* be run over by a car.
allegoria allegory.
allekirjoi|ttaa sign [one's name to]; *~ kirje* sign a letter. **-ttaja** signer: (*~valtio* signatory power). **-ttaminen** signing. **-ttanut** the undersigned. **-tus** signing; (*nimi-*) signature.
allergi|a allergy. **-nen** allergic.
alleviivata underline; *kuv.* emphasize.
alli long-tailed duck.
alligaattori *zo.* alligator.
allikko (vesi-) pool, puddle; *joutua ojasta ~on* fall out of the frying pan into the fire, go from bad to worse.
almanakka calendar, almanac.
almu alms (*pl.* alms). **-nantaja** almsgiver. **-npyytäjä** beggar.
aloite intiative; (*eduskunta-*) private member's bill; *jkn aloitteesta* on a p.'s initiative; *omasta aloitteestaan* of one's own accord; *tehdä ~ jhk* take the initiative (in .. -ing). **-kyky, ~isyys** initiative, enterprise.

aloi|ttaa begin, initiate, ks.
alkaa; korttip. lead; begin
[by .. -ing, .. -malla]; start,
lead off; set up; ~
neuvottelut open (enter into)
negotiations. **-tteentekijä**
initiator. **-ttelija** beginner.
alokas beginner; sot. recruit,
(varusmies) conscript;
(oppipoika) apprentice; ottaa
alokkaita recruit.
alppi alp; Alpit the Alps.
-aurinko (hoito) sun ray
treatment; (~lamppu sun
lamp). **-hiihto, -lajit** alpine
ski-ing. **-jono** chain of alps.
-kasvisto alpine flora. **-kauris**
Alpine ibex, steinbock.
-kiipeilijä Alpine climber,
Alpinist. **-maa** alpine country.
-maja chalet. **-ruusu**
rhododendron. **-sauva**
alpenstock.
alta from under .., from
below (beneath); (alitse)
under; pois ~! get out of the
way! ~ valkoinen white
underneath. **-päin** from
underneath (beneath, below).
altis (taipuvainen) willing;
inclined, disposed (to);
(vastaanottavainen) susceptible,
liable, sensitive (to); (harras)
devoted; vaaralle ~ exposed
to danger, endangered; panna
alttiiksi (jllek) expose (to),
imperil; risk [one's life];
joutua alttiiksi jllek be [come]
exposed to .., meet with;
olla alttiina lie open (to).
-taa lääk. predispose.
alttari altar. **-liina** altar-cloth.
-palvelus altar service, liturgy.
-taulu altarpiece.
alttiiksi|antava (uhraava)
self-sacrificing, self-effacing.
-antavaisuus sacrifice,
self-effacement.
alt|tiisti willingly, readily,
devotedly. **-tius** willingness,
inclination; liability, jllek to;
~ (esim. taudille) suscep-
tibility, predisposition
(to); (antaumus) dedi-
cation.
altto mus. alto. **-viulu** viola.
-ääni alto.
alue (ala) area; territory;

(seutu) region; (piiri) district;
kuv. = ala; kaupungin ~ella
within the city [limits];
tehtaan ~ factory grounds.
-ellinen territorial; regional.
-enluovutus cession of
territory. **-vesi:** aluevedet
territorial waters.
aluksi ks. alku.
alullepano initiative, starting.
alumiini aluminium, Am. -inum.
aluna alum. **-inen** aluminous.
alun|perin, -pitäen from the
first, originally.
alus (laiva) vessel, craft (pl. =
sg.). **-hame** underskirt,
petticoat, slip. **-housut**
underpants, drawers.
-kasvillisuus ground vegetation,
(alakasvos) undergrowth. **-maa**
dependency, possession,
(siirto-) colony. **-paita**
[under] vest.
alussa ks. alku; vuosisadan ~
at the beginning (in the early
part) of this century.
alusta base; foundation, (auton)
chassis; rak. bed [ding];
mount, (teline) stand; (lasin
ym.) coaster; mat.
alus|taa (taikina) knead, mix;
(aine) outline; ~ keskus-
telukysymys introduce a
subject for discussion. **-taja**
opening speaker, introducer.
-talainen tenant; -talaiset
tenantry. **-tava** preliminary;
provisional, tentative; ~t työt
preparations, preparatory
work. **-tavasti** preliminarily;
provisionally, tentatively. **-tus**
(kysymyksen) introduction.
alus|vaate undergarment;
-vaatteet underwear,
underclothes, (naisen, m.)
lingerie; -vaatteisillaan in
one's underclothes.
amanuenssi l. v. assistant.
amatsoni amazon.
amatööri amateur.
Ambomaa Ovamboland.
ambulanssi, -auto ambulance.
amerikatar American woman.
Amerikka America.
amerikkalai|nen American.
-sittain in American fashion.
-staa Americanize. **-stua** be
- [come] Americanized. **-suus**

Americanism.
ametisti amethyst.
amfetamiini amphetamine.
amfiteatteri amphitheatre.
amiraali admiral **-nlaiva**
[admiral's] flagship.
ammat|eittain by occupation.
-illinen occupational;
professional, trade.
ammatin|harjoittaja person
engaged in a trade (a
profession). **-valinta:** *-valinnan
ohjaus* vocational guidance.
ammatti occupation, *(käsityö)*
trade, craft, *(henkinen)*
profession; business;
ammatiltaan by trade, by
profession. **-ala** trade;
profession; speciality.
-diplomaatti career diplomat.
-entarkastaja factory inspector,
inspector of working conditions.
-kateus trade rivalry.
-kirjallisuus professional
literature. **-kokemus**
professional experience. **-koulu**
vocational school, trade
school. **-koulutu|s:** *a-ksen
saanut* [professionally]
qualified. **-kunta** craft, trade;
hist. guild; (**~laitos** guild
system). **-lainen** craftsman,
skilled workman; *urh.*
professional. **-laisuus**
professionalism. **-liitto** trades
union; *~jen keskusjärjestö*
Trades Union Congress
(T.U.C.). **-mainen** professional.
-mies craftsman, skilled
workman; *(tuntija)* expert,
specialist. **-muusikko**
professional musician. **-opetus**
vocational education.
-salaisuus trade secret.
-sanasto specialist *(t.*
technical) terminology.
-taidoton unskilled. **-taito**
[professional] skill,
craftsmanship. **-taitoinen**
skilled, trained. **-tauti**
occupational disease. **-tiedot**
professional knowledge. **-toveri**
colleague. **-työ** skilled work.
-työläinen skilled worker.
-urheilija professional.
-yhdistys trade union
[branch[, [local branch of]
t.u.; (**~järjestelmä**

trade-unionism; **~liike** t.u.
movement). **-ylpeys**
professional pride.
amme tub, vat; *kylpy~* bath.
ammentaa scoop, ladle;
(veneestä m.) bail [a boat];
kuv. procure, obtain, acquire;
~ runsaista lähteistä draw
from rich sources.
ammoi|n long ago. **-nen** very
ancient; *jo -sista ajoista* from
time immemorial.
ammollaan: *olla ~* be wide
open; *suu ~* gaping, agape;
katsella suu ~ gawp.
ammoniakki ammonia.
ammotta|a gape, be wide open,
(esim. kuilu) yawn; *-va haava*
gaping wound.
ammua low, moo.
ammu|nta shooting; fire. **-s**
shot; *ammukset* ammunition.
-skella shoot, keep on
shooting.
ampaista shoot; dash.
ampeeri ampere.
ampiai|nen wasp **-spesä** wasp's
nest. **-spisto** sting [of a
wasp].
ampu|a shoot (at); *(laukaista)*
fire (at); *(nuoli ym)*
discharge, *(ohjus ym)* launch;
~ kuoliaaksi shoot dead, gun
down; *~ laukaus* fire a shot.
-ja shot, marksman.
ampulli amp [o]ule.
ampuma|-ase gun; *-aseet*
firearms. **-haava** bullet wound.
-harjoitus rifle-practice,
target-practice. **-hiihto**
biathlon. **-kilpailu** shooting
competition. **-linja** line of
fire.**-matka** range; *~n päähän,
päästä* within r. **-rata**
rifle-range. **-taito** skill in
shooting, marksmanship. **-taulu**
target.
amputoida amputate.
amuletti amulet.
analogi|a analogy. **-nen**
analogical; analogous (to).
analysoida analyse.
analyy|si analysis *(pl. -yses).*
-tikko analyst. **-ttinen**
analytic [al].
ananas pineapple.
anarki|a anarchy. **-sti** anarchist.
anast|aa seize, lay hold of;

(valtaa, valtaistuin) usurp;
(jkn osuus) appropriate;
(valloittaa) annex; ~ *jklta jtk*
(m.) dispossess sb. of **-aja**
usurper. **-us** usurpation;
appropriation; annexation.
anatomi anatomist. **-a** anatomy.
-asali dissecting-room. **-nen**
anatomical.
Andit the Andes.
ane indulgence. **-kauppa** sale
of indulgences. **-kauppias**
pardoner. **-kirja** letter of
indulgence.
anemia an[a]emia; *(näivetys-)*
pernicious a.
angervo meadowsweet; *puut.*
spir[a]ea.
angiina *l. v.* tonsillitis.
anglikaaninen Anglican.
anglosaksinen *a. & s.*
Anglo-Saxon.
ani: ~ *harvoin* extremely
seldom, very rarely.
anis *(kasvi)* anise, *(mauste)*
aniseed.
anjovis anchovy.
ankar|a severe, stern; *(tiukka)*
strict; *(voimakas)* strong;
(tuima) violent, vehement;
(kova) hard; acute, sharp,
intense; ~ *kilpailu* keen
competition; ~ *kuri* rigid
(rigorous) discipline; ~
kuumuus intense heat; ~
pakkanen severe (bitter)
frost; ~ *taistelu* tough
struggle, hard fight; *tehdä*
~*mmaksi* aggravate. **-asti**
severely; ~ *kielletty* strictly
forbidden. **-uus** severity,
rigour; strictness; intensity.
ankea dismal, dreary, cheerless;
~ *aika* time of anxiety.
ankerias eel.
ankka duck, *(koiras)* drake;
(sanomal.) false report, hoax,
canard.
ankkuri anchor; *olla* ~*ssa* ride
at anchor; ~*ssa oleva*
anchored; *laskea* ~ drop
anchor; *nostaa* ~ weigh
anchor. **-kela** capstan.
-kettinki chain-cable. **-paikka**
anchorage; roadstead. **-touvi**
mooring cable.
ankkuroida anchor; ~ *laiva*
(m.) moor a ship.

anniske|lla retail intoxicants,
-lu [retail] sale of
intoxicants; *(~oikeus* licence
to sell intoxicants; *~ravintola*
on-licence restaurant).
annos portion, *(kortti- ym.)*
ration; *(lääkettä)* dose *(m.*
kuv.); (ruokapöydässä) serving,
puhek. helping; *annoksittain*
(ravint.) à la carte. **-tella**
ration out, apportion.
ano|a ask, *jklta jtk* sb. for . .,
petition; request; *(rukoillen)*
implore, entreat; ~ *apua* ask
for help; ~ *asian lykkäämistä*
apply for a postponement; ~
eläkettä petition for a pension.
anodi anode.
ano|ja petitioner; applicant.
-mus request; petition;
(hakemus) application;
anomuksesta on request;
hänen -muksestaan at his
request (at the r. of Mr X);
(~kirjelmä written application;
~lomake application form).
anoppi mother-in-law.
ansa snare, trap; *mennä* ~*an*
be trapped; *kuv.* fall into a
trap.
ansait|a earn, *(olla jnk*
arvoinen) deserve, merit, be
worthy of; *ei -se* you're
welcome *(et. Am.),* [oh,] not
at all; ~ *rahaa* earn money
[by . .-ing], *(rikastua)* make
money, earn good money;
kirja ei -se lukemista the
book is not worth reading;
hyvin -tu well-earned;
well-deserved. **-sematon**
unmerited. **-sematta(an)**
undeservedly, without
deserving it.
ansari greenhouse. **-kasvi**
hothouse plant.
ansas *rak.* truss.
ansio *(siveellinen)* merit[s];
(työ-) earnings; income;
(virka-) qualification; ~*t ja*
haitat merits and demerits,
advantages and disadvantages;
hänen ~*staan* thanks to him;
lukea jkn ~*ksi* give sb. the
credit for; ~*n mukaan*
according to one's deserts; *se*
oli hänen koulunsa ~*ta* his
school deserves the credit for

. .; ~*tta* undeservedly; ~*ttani* without my deserving it. **-itu**|a: *a-nut mies* a man of merit; *hän on a-nut isänmaan palveluksessa* he has distinguished himself in the service of his country. **-kas** meritorious, deserving, praiseworthy. **-kkaasti** with merit, with credit. **-kkuus** meritoriousness; merit. **-luettelo** [list of] qualifications, curriculum vitae. **-lähde** source of income. **-mahdollisuus** means of earning a livelihood. **-merkki** medal. **-puoli** good side, merit. **-ton** without merit [s], undeservedly; (*ansaitsematon*) unmerited. **-ttomasti** undeservedly. **-tulo** earned income. **-työ** work for wages, gainful employment; ~*ssä* gainfully employed. **-äiti** working mother.

antaa give; (*ojentaa*) hand [over], (*edelleen*) pass on; (*sallia*) let, allow; (*lahjoittaa*) present; (*suoda*) afford, render; (*luottaa*) yield; (*käsitys ym.*) convey; (*asetus, määräys*) issue, make out [an order]; ~ *apua* render help; *annoin korjata* (*korjautin*) *sen* I had it repaired; *annoin hänen ymmärtää* I gave him to understand; *ikkuna* ~ *pohjoiseen* the window faces north; *anna minun olla!* leave me alone!

antaja giver, donor.

antau|**muksellinen** devoted, dedicated. **-mus** devotion; dedication.

antautu|a give oneself up, *m. sot.* surrender (to), capitulate; yield oneself [prisoner, *vangiksi*]; (*ryhtyä*) enter [upon], enter into, take up; (*harrastuksella*) devote oneself to; ~ *jllek alalle* enter a profession; ~ *jnk valtaan* yield to [despair], abandon oneself to [sorrow]. **-minen** surrender; capitulation; (*alistuminen*) submission. **-misehdot** terms of surrender.

anteeksi: ~! excuse me! I beg your pardon! [I am] sorry! ~, *en kuullut* I beg your pardon! *anna* ~! forgive me! *suoda* ~ (*m.*) make allowance (for); excuse; *pyytää* ~ *jklta* apologize to a p. (for), make one's excuses (to). **-annettava** pardonable, excusable. **-antamaton** unpardonable, inexcusable, indefensible. **-antamus** forgiveness. **-antava** forgiving; indulgent. **-antavasti** forgivingly. **-pyydellen** with many apologies, apologetically. **-pyyntö** excuse; apology. **-pyytelevä** apologetic.

anteli|**aisuus** open-handedness; liberality, generosity. **-as** open-handed, generous, liberal.

antenni *rad.* aerial.

antibioottinen, ~ *aine* antibiotic.

antiikki *s.* antiquity. **-esine** antique, curio. **-kauppa** antique dealer's. **-nen** *a.* antique.

antiikva roman type.

antikristus Antichrist.

antikvaari|**nen** (*kirjakauppa*) second-hand [book-shop]; *ostaa -sesta kirjakaupasta* buy [a book] second-hand.

antilooppi antelope.

antimet yield; gifts.

anti|**podi** *maant. (pl.)* antipodes. **-septinen** antiseptic.

anto (*setelien*) issue of notes. **-isa** productive, rich; *kuv.* rewarding. **-isuus** productiveness. **-lainaus** lending. **-päivä** date of issue.

antologia anthology.

antrasiitti anthracite.

antropologi|a anthropology. **-nen** anthropological.

antur|a sole. **-oida** sole, (*uudelleen*) re-sole.

Antverpen Antwerp.

aortta aorta.

apa|**attinen** apathetic. **-tia** apathy.

apea dejected, depressed.

Apenniinit the Apennines.

apeus dejectedness, low spirits.

apila clover, (~*n lehti*) trefoil.

apina monkey; (*hännätön*) ape. **-mainen** apish; monkeyish.

apokryfinen apocryphal.

apostoli apostle; *M en teor the* Acts [of the Apostles].

apostrofi apostrophe.

apotti abbot.

appelsiini orange. **-hillo** [orange] marmalade. **-nkuori** orange-peel.

appi father-in-law. **-vanhemmat** parents-in-law.

aprikoosi apricot.

aprilli|narri April fool. **-päivä** All Fools' day.

apteekkari [pharmaceutical *t.* dispensing] chemist, pharmacist; *Am.* druggist.

apteekki *Engl.* chemist's [shop], pharmacy; *Am.* drugstore; *(sairaalan, laivan)* dispensary. **-apulainen** dispenser. **-tavara** pharmaceutical preparation [s].

apu help; aid, assistance; succour; *(hyöty)* use, avail; *(parannus)* remedy; *(pelastava)* rescue; *(avustus)* relief; *(tuki)* support; *siitä ei ollut ~a* it did not help, it had no effect, it was of no avail; *jnk avulla* by [the] aid of, by means of, by; *jkn (henk.) avulla* with the help of; *hänen avullaan* with his assistance, assisted by him; *kiitoksia avusta* thanks for your [kind] help; *avutta* unaided. **-joukot** reinforcements; auxiliary troops. **-jäsen** auxiliary member. **-kassa** relief fund. **-keino, -neuvo** expedient, means, medium. **-koulu** *l.v.* school for retarded children. **-lainen** assistant, helper; *päivä~* daily help.

apulais|johtaja assistant manager. **-pappi** curate.

apu|lähde resource. **-mies** handy-man; assistant. **-raha** grant, subsidy; *(opinto-)* scholarship. **-ri** helper; hand. **-sana** *kiel.* particle. **-verbi** auxiliary [verb].

Arabia Arabia. **a-lainen** *s.* Arab; *a.* Arabian; Arabic. **a-n kieli** Arabic.

arabi|maat the Arab countries. **-ystävällinen** pro-Arab.

arast|aa *ks. aristaa;* shun;

shrink (from); *~ työtä ohun* work, be work-shy. **-elematon** not timid, unshy. **-ella** *ks. arkailla.*

arbuusi *ks. arpuusi.*

areena arena.

arenti *ks. vuokra.*

aresti custody, *sot.* guardroom; *panna ~in* lock up.

Argentiina Argentina, the Argentine. **a-lainen** *a.* Argentine; *s.* Argentinean.

arina [fire-] grate. **-kivi** hearthstone.

aris|taa, -tella be shy, be timid; *(vältellä)* shirk; *jalkojani ~ my* feet feel tender.

aristo|kraattinen aristocratic [-al]. **-kratia** aristocracy.

arit|meettinen arithmetical. **-metiikka** arithmetic.

arjalainen *a. & s.* Aryan.

arka sensitive, *jllek* to; *(hellä)* tender, sore; *(varova)* careful; *(pelokas)* timid, timorous, faint-hearted; *(ujo)* shy; *~ kohta (kuv.)* tender spot; *~ kunniastaan* jealous of one's honour; *~ kylmettymiselle* susceptible to colds.

arkai|lematon unshrinking, bold. **-lematta** unshrinkingly, boldly; *(kursailematta)* with perfect ease, unconcernedly. **-lija** coward. **-lla** be timid, be shy; be overcautious; hesitate; *en -le sanoa totuutta* I do not shrink from telling the truth. **-lu** shyness, timidity; hesitation; diffidence.

arkais|mi archaism. **-tinen** archaic.

arka|luonteinen delicate; *(ihmisestä)* sensitive. **-luonteisuus** delicacy; sensitiveness. **-mainen** faint-(chicken-) hearted; cowardly. **-maisuus** lack of courage. **-tunteinen** sensitive; considerate. **-tunteisuus** delicacy [of feeling], sensitiveness.

arkeologi arch[a]eologist. **-a** arch[a]eology.

arki week-day.

arki- *(yhd.)* everyday. **-elämä** everyday life. **-huone** *ks. olo-.*

arva

-ilta week-day evening. -kieli colloquial language; -kielessä colloquially. -nen everyday, commonplace. -olot everyday conditions (affairs); -oloissa käytettäväksi for everyday use. -puku informal dress, everyday clothes, (miehen, m.) lounge suit. -päivä week-day, workday. -päiväinen everyday; kuv. commonplace, humdrum.-päiväisyys ordinariness; humdrum character. -ruoka everyday fare, homely fare. -sin on week-days.

arkisto records, archives, files. -ida file. -kaappi filing cabinet. -nhoitaja record-keeper, archivist.

arki|toimet daily occupations, daily routine. -työ daily work. -vaatteet everyday clothes.

arkki sheet [of paper]; raam. ark.

arkki|herttua archduke. -hiippakunta archbishop's diocese. -piispa archbishop.

arkkiteh|ti architect. -toninen architectural. -tuuri architecture.

arkku chest; (matka-) trunk; (ruumis-) coffin; (merimiehen) locker; (sillan) caisson.

arktinen arctic.

arkuus tenderness, soreness; sensitiveness; (pelokkuus) diffidence, timidity.

armahdus pardon; (yleinen) amnesty. -oikeus right of pardon, prerogative of mercy.

armah|taa have mercy, jkta on; pity; (antaa armoa) pardon; (säästää) spare; Jumala -takoon (meitä) God have mercy on us. -tavainen merciful; compassionate. -tavaisuus compassion, mercifulness, forbearance.

armas a. dear, beloved; (suloinen) sweet, charming; s. sweetheart, beloved, darling.

armeija army. -kunta army corps.

armeliaisuus mercifulness; charity. -laitos charitable institution. -murha, -kuolema euthanasia. -työ act of charity.

armelias merciful, charitable.

armias: auta ~ good gracious! armo grace; (laupeus) mercy, clemency, sot m. quarter; ~a! mercy! have mercy on me! ~sta out of mercy; Jumalan ~sta by the grace of God; olla jkn ~illa be at the mercy of; päästä (jkn) ~ihin find favour with; ~n vuonna .. in the year of grace .. -istuin throne of grace. -ittaa: armoitettu puhuja a speaker by the grace of God. -lahja usk. gift of grace. -leipä bread of charity. -llinen gracious; merciful. -llisesti graciously, mercifully. -nanomus petition for pardon. -naika days of grace. -nisku coup de grace, finishing blow. -nosoitus mark (token) of favour. -ton merciless, pitiless; unmerciful, ruthless, uncharitable. -ttomuus mercilessness, -vuosi year of grace.

aro steppe; Am. prairie.

aromi flavour, aroma.

arpa lot; lottery ticket; lyödä ~a cast (draw) lots; ~ on heitetty the die is cast; ~ lankesi hänelle the lot fell upon him; arvalla by lot. -jaiset lottery.

arpajaisvoitto [lottery] prize.

arpa|kuutio (-noppa) die (pl. dice). -lippu lottery ticket, raffle ticket. -peli gamble; game of chance.

arpeutu|a cicatrize, scar. -minen scar formation.

arpi scar; tiet. cicatrix (pl. cicatrices). -nen scarred.

arpo|a draw lots: jk esine sell in a raffle, raffle .. away.

arpuusi water-melon.

arsenikki arsenic.

artikkeli kiel. ym. article.

artikla article.

artisokka: maa- ~ Jerusalem artichoke; latva-~ globe a.

arvaamaton incalculable; inestimable, invaluable; (odottamaton) unforeseen, unlooked-for.

arvai|lla guess. -lu: pelkkää ~a mere guesswork.

arvata *guess, jtk at; (arvioitaan)*
anticipate, foresee; surmise; ~
oikeaan guess right, hit it;
arvaamalla by guessing, by
way of conjecture; *arvaamatta
(odottamatta)* unexpectedly,
unawares; *arvaahan vielä* have
another guess; *arvaan, että* ..
I expect ..

arva|tenkin, -ttavasti
presumably, probably; very
likely.

arvelevainen hesitating; cautious.

arvella think, *jstk* of, about;
(luulla) suppose; *(katsoa)*
consider; *(empiä)* hesitate; ~
parhaaksi deem it best;
keneksi minua arvelet whom
do you take me for;
vähääkään arvelematta without
the slightest hesitation.

arvelu thought, opinion;
surmise. **-ttaa:** .. ~ *minua* ..
fills me with apprehension, ..
makes me feel uneasy; *minua
-tti lähteä* I was quite
reluctant to leave. **-ttava**
precarious, risky; *(epäilyttävä)*
doubtful, suspicious;
-ttavuus precariousness, hazard;
seriousness, gravity.

arvi|o appraisal, estimate,
valuation, estimation; ~*lta* at
a rough estimate,
approximately, roughly
[speaking]. **-hinta** estimated
value.

arvioi|da estimate, evaluate,
appraise; assess; ~ *alhaiseksi*
value at a low price; *-tu* ..
hintaiseksi valued at £ ..; ~
liian pieneksi underestimate,
underrate; ~ *liian suureksi*
overestimate, overrate. **-nti**
[e]valuation, estimation,
assessment; *(esim. ohjelman)*
etukäteis- briefing (TV-
briefing); *vrt. arvostelu.*

arvio|kauppa: *-kaupalla* at
random; approximately.
-laskelma estimate, calculation.
-mies valuer, appraiser.
-nmukainen approximate,
rough.

arvo value; worth *(et. kuv.);*
(merkitys) importance,
consequence; *(-kkuus)* dignity;
prestige; *(virka-)* rank, title,

(oppi) degree; *(arvonanto)*
esteem, regard; ~*ltaan*
suurempi of greater value:
antaa, panna ~a jllk value
[highly], attach great value
to .., appreciate; set great
store by; *pitää suuressa
arvossa* hold in high esteem,
esteem [a p.] highly; *se ei
ole sinun ~llesi sopivaa* it is
beneath your dignity, it is
unworthy of you; *tavaroita
. .:n ~sta* goods to a value
of .. **-asema** rank, station.
-aste rank; *kohota ~issa* rise
in rank, be promoted. **-esine:**
~*et* valuables. **-henkilö**
dignitary; ~*t (m.)* notables.
-inen worth . .; *(ansaitseva)*
worthy; *5 punnan* ~ *(m.)*
valued at £ 5; *näkemisen* ~
worth seeing; *vähemmän* ~
of lesser value; *työ on
tekemisen* ~ the work is
worth the trouble; *hän on
saanut -isensa vastustajan* he
has met his match. **-isa**
honoured, esteemed, worthy;
dear; ~ *herra!* Dear Sir, . .;
~ *kirjeenne* your esteemed
letter; ~*t vieraat!*
distinguished guests!

arvoi|tuksellinen enigmatic
-[al], puzzling, problem-
atic[al]. **-tuksellisuus**
puzzling, nature, myste-
riousness. **-tus** riddle;
puzzle, enigma; *puhua -tuksin*
speak in riddles.

arvo|järjestys order of
precedence. **-kas** worthy;
dignified; *(kallis)* valuable, ..
of [high] value. **-kkaasti** with
dignity, in a dignified
manner. **-kkuus** dignity;
valuableness, *(arvo)* worth,
value. **-kirje** registered letter.
-luokka grade, class. **-lähetys**
registered postal matter.
-maailma *l.v.* set of values
-merkki badge [of rank];
(hiha-) chevron; *a-merkit*
marks of rank.

arvon|alennus decrease of (in)
value, depreciation. **-anto**
respect, esteem, regard.

arvo|nimi title. **-nmukainen**
fitting, proper, due. **-nnousu**

rise (increase) in value,
increment.
arvonta draw[ing] of lots,
raffle.
arvo|paperi security; stock;
(**~kauppa** stock-broking;
~ **pörssi** stock exchange).
-sana *(koulussa)* mark;
*suorittaa tutkinto hyvin
arvosanoin* pass an
examination with credit
(distinction). **-ssapidetty**
respected, esteemed, valued.
-ssapito: *jnk* ~ respect, regard
for. **-staa** appreciate, value.
arvoste|leminen criticizing;
criticism; judgment. **-leva**
critical; fault-finding. **-lija**
critic, reviewer. **-lla** criticize;
judge; *(arvioida)* estimate;
mikäli voin ~ as far as I
can judge; ~ *muita itsensä
mukaan* judge others by
oneself; ~ *väärin* misjudge.
-lu criticism, critique; *(kirjan)*
review; *hyvät ~t (m.)* good
notices, a good press; *sai
hyvän (huonon) ~n* was
favourably (unfavourably)
reviewed; (**~kyky** judg[e]ment,
discrimination; **~kykyinen** ..
having discrimination;
judicious; **~kyvytön**
undiscriminating;
~kyvyttömyys lack of
judg[e]ment; **~peruste:** *a-et*
basis of estimation, criteria of
evaluation).
arvo|ton valueless, .. of no
value, worthless;
(ansaitsematon) unworthy; ~
näyte sample of no value.
-ttomuus worthlessness;
insignificance. **-valta** authority;
prestige. **-valtainen** authori-
tative.
asbesti asbestos.
ase weapon; *(työ-)* tool; *ilma-*
~ air arm; *aseet* arms;
~ihin! to arms! *~issa* under
arms; ~ *kädessä* weapon in
hand; *nousta ~isiin* take up
arms (against); *riisua ~ista*
disarm; *tahdoton* ~ tool.
-ellinen armed.
aseen|kantaja armour-bearer.
-käyttö use of arms.
aseeton unarmed; *(riisuttu*

aseista) disarmed.
aseharjoitus training in the use
of arms.
aseistakieltäytyjä conscientious
objector, draft resister.
aseistariisunta disarmament.
aseis|tautua arm oneself. **-tus**
armament[s].
ase|kuntoinen ... fit for
military service, able-bodied.
-laji branch of service, arm.
-lepo truce; armistice; *vrt.
tulitauko.*
asema site, location; position;
rautat. ym. station, *Am. m.*
depot; *(tila, -nne)* state,
situation; *(yhteiskunn.)* status;
kaupungin ~ the site of the
town; *sinun ~ssasi* in your
place; *korkeassa ~ssa oleva*
.. of high standing (position);
asettua asemiin take up positions;
pysyä asemissaan remain at
their posts. **-alue** station
grounds. **-kaava** plan;
(**~suunnittelu** town-planning).
-laituri platform. **-piha** railway
yards. **-piirros** [ground-]plan.
-päällikkö station-master. **-silta**
platform. **-sota** trench warfare.
asemesta: *jnk* ~ instead of, in
place of.
asen|ne attitude; *ottaa jk* ~
adopt an a.; *vrt. seur.* **-noitua**
take a stand (position, view).
-taa instal[l], fit [up]; mount;
~ *taloon vesijohdot* lay on
water [to a house]. **-taja**
fitter, mechanic; *(sähkö-)*
electrician. **-nus** installation,
fitting.
asento position, posture,
(teennäinen) pose; *(ryhti)*
carriage; *~!* attention! *ottaa*
~ come to attention.
ase|palvelus military service;
kutsua a-ukseen call up **-puku**
hisl. armour. **-seppä** armourer;
gunsmith. **-takki** combat
jacket, tunic, coat of uniform.
-tehdas arms factory. **-teollisuus**
armaments industries *(pl.).*
asete *liik.* draft.
asetel|la arrange, adjust; *-tava*
adjustable. **-ma** *(taulu)* still
life.
asetta|a place, put, set, lay; ~
kello set a clock; ~ *ehdokas*

put up (run) a candidate; ~
ehdoksi make it a condition
(that ..); ~ *entiselleen* restore;
~ *komitea* appoint a
committee; ~ *paikalleen* place
in position, *(takaisin)* replace;
~ *vekseli* make a draft, draw
a bill (on a p.); ~ *virkaan*
install [in office]. **-ja**
(vekselin) drawer.

asettu|a place (station) oneself,
take one's stand; *(pysyvästi)*
settle down; *(lauhtua)* abate,
subside; calm; ~ *asumaan jhk*
settle [down] in (at) a place,
take up one's residence at; ~
ehdokkaaksi present oneself as
a candidate for, run for; ~
jllek kannalle take up a
position [in a matter];
pakkanen -u the cold is
breaking; *tuska -i* the pain
was relieved.

asetus decree, *(laki)* statute;
statutory regulation. **-kokoelma**
statute-book.

asetyleeni acetylene.

ase|varasto store of arms;
arsenal. **-varikko** arms depot.
-varustelut armaments. **-veli**
companion in arms.
-velvollinen .. liable to
military service; *s.* conscript,
national serviceman.

asevelvollisuus conscription,
national service [duty];
suorittaa ~ do one's military
service.

asevoima armed might; ~*lla* by
force of arms.

asfaltoida coat with asphalt.

asfaltti asphalt, bitumen.
-päällysteinen asphalt, tarmac,
Am. black-top [road]. **-huopa**
asphalt roofing. **-tie** paved
road.

asia matter, thing, affair;
(toimitettava) errand, message;
(toimi-, liike-) business;
concern; *(juttu)* case, cause;
~*an!* to business! *mennä
suoraan ~an* go straight to
the point; ~ *ei kuulu hänelle*
it is no business of his; ~*in
näin ollen* under the
circumstances; ~*sta toiseen* by
the way; *itse ~ssa* in [point
of] fact; *mitä ~a Teillä on*

what can I do for you?
käydä asioilla run errands; go
shopping; *sinun ~si on
päättää* it is up to you to
decide; *rauhan* ~ the cause
of peace; *valtakunnan ~t*
affairs of state; *se on hänen
~nsa* that's his business (his
worry.)

asiaa|harrastava: ~*t* those
interested [in the matter].
-nkuuluma|ton irrelevant, not
to the point; *a-ttomat* those
not concerned. **-nkuuluva**
pertinent [to the matter],
relevant; due, appropriate.
-npuuttuminen intervention.

asiain|hoitaja chargé d'affaires.
-kulku course of events. **-tila**
state of affairs, state of
things.

asiakas customer; client. **-piiri**
circle of customers, clientèle.

asiakirja document, deed; *lak.
m.* instrument; ~*t* papers,
(seuran) proceedings.

asialli|nen *a.* businesslike,
matter-of-fact, *(käytännöllinen)*
down-to-earth, *(asiaan
kuuluva)* pertinent; matter-of-
fact; *kysymys oli hyvin* ~
(was) very much to the point.
-sesti to the point; in a
matter-of-fact way. **-suus**
pertinence; businesslike
character.

asiamies [authorized] agent;
representative; *(valtuutettu)*
proxy, *(asianajaja)* attorney.

asianajaja lawyer; solicitor,
attorney, *(oikeudessa, Engl.)*
barrister; *kääntyä* ~*n puoleen*
consult a lawyer. **-nammatti**
legal profession.

asianajo pleading. **-toimisto**
solicitor's office, law practice.

asian|haara circumstance;
riippuu -haaroista [well,] that
depends .. **-harrastus** interest,
jhk in. **-laita** case; situation;
vrt. asiaintila; jos näin on ~
if such be the case; ~ *on
aivan toinen* the matter is
entirely different. **-mukainen**
due, proper; fitting.
-mukaisesti duly, in due form.
-mukaisuus fitness, propriety.
-omainen the [party *t.* person]

concerned; *(-mukainen)* due, proper; *kaikille -omaisille* to all whom it may concern. **-omistaja** *(kantaja)* the plaintiff. **-osainen** *-osaiset* parties concerned. **-tila** state of things, situation. **-tuntemus** [expert] knowledge; informed opinion. **-tunteva** competent; expert; ~*lta taholta kerrotaan* well-informed sources state .. - **-tuntija** expert, specialist, *jnk* in; authority (on).

asia|paperi *ks. -kirja.* **-poika** errand boy, office boy. **-ton** irrelevant; *(epäolennainen)* immaterial; *(aiheeton)* unjustified. **-ttomasti** without sufficient cause; unjustifiably.

asioi|da transact (do) business. **-misto** agency. **-tsija** agent.

askar|e work; job, duty; *koti-~et* household chores. **-rella** busy oneself, be busy; ~ *kotitoimissa* be busy about the house. **-ruttaa** occupy. **-telu** hobby crafts, hobbies; ~*huone* hobbies room.

askeetti, -nen ascetic.

askel step, pace; *(jälki)* footstep; *(pitkä)* stride; ~ *~eelta* step by step; *joka ~eella* at every step. **-ma** *(askel)* step.

aspi *(salparauta)* hasp.

aspiriini aspirin.

assimil|aatio assimilation. **-oitua** *(yhtäläistyä)* be assimilated (with).

Assyria Assyria. **a-lainen** Assyrian.

aste degree; grade; *(arvo- ym.)* rank; *(kehitys-)* stage; *(korkeus-)* level; ~ *~elta* step by step, by degrees; *10 ~en pakkanen* 10 degrees (C.) below freezing-point; *alhaisella ~ella* on a low level (plane). **-ikko** scale; *et. kuv.* gamut; *-ikolla varustettu* graduated; *(~levy* protractor).

asteittai|n gradually, by degrees. **-nen** gradual; progressive. **-suus** gradation.

astella step, pace; walk, stroll.

asteri *bot.* aster.

astevaihtelu consonantal gradation.

asti: *jhk* ~ *(ajasta)* till, until; *(paikasta)* as far as, [up] to *ks. saakka.*

astia vessel; container; *(tynnyri)* cask; *(ruoka-)* dish. **-inpesukone** dish [-] washer. **-kaappi** *(ruokahuoneen)* sideboard; cupboard; *(keittiön)* dresser. **-mitta** cubic measure. **-pyyhe** drying-cloth. **-sto** set, service.

astinlauta carriage-step, *(auton)* running-board; *kuv.* stepping stone.

astma asthma. **-atikko, -attinen** asthmatic.

astro|logi astrologer. **-logia** astrology. **-nomia** astronomy.

astua step; *(käydä)* tread, go, walk; ~ *alas* step down, descend; alight (from); ~ *esille* step forward; ~ *jhk* step (get) into; enter [a p.'s service, *jkn palvelukseen*]; *(nousta)* ascend; ~ *huoneeseen* enter a room; ~ *laivaan* go on board; ~ *maihin* land, go ashore; ~ *jkn sijalle* take a p.'s place; *astukaa sisälle* come in, please! ~ *virkaan* take office; enter office; ~ *voimaan* come into force, take effect.

astuin step.

astunta stepping, treading; *(käynti)* gait; step, pace; walk. **astu|skella** step along, wander. **-ttaa** *(esim. tamma)* have (a mare) served. **-tus** service.

asu appearance; *(muoto)* form, shape; *(puku)* dress; *urheilu-* ~ sportswear.

asua *intr.* live, reside; *(tilapäisesti)* stay; *tr.* inhabit, occupy (a house); *hän asuu veljensä luona* he lives at his brother's; *voit* ~ *luonani* you can stay with me, I can accommodate you [for two days, *kaksi päivää*]; ~ *vuokrahuoneessa* live in lodgings; *pitää .. asumassa* lodge a p.; *jkn asuma* inhabited by; *tiheään asuttu* densely populated.

asuin|huone living-room. **-kumppani** room-mate. **-paikka** place of residence, domicile,

ab e d e, **rakennue**
dwelling-house. **-sija**
dwelling-place, habitation.
asujaimisto population,
inhabitants.
asukas inhabitant; *(kaupungin,
m.)* resident. **-luku** population.
asukki boarder; lodger;
(hoidokas) inmate.
asumalähiö suburb, *(yhden
järjestön ym. suunnittelema)*
housing estate, *(puutarha-
kaupunki)* garden city.
asumaton uninhabited;
unoccupied, vacant; *(autio)*
waste.
asumis|jätteet residential waste.
-tiheys residential density.
asumus dwelling; lodging,
quarters. **-ero** separation.
asunno|nmuutos change of
residence. **-ton** houseless,
homeless.
asunto residence, dwelling;
(vuokrahuone) lodgings, living
quarters; home; accommo-
dation; *voitteko antaa
minulle asunnon viikoksi* can
you accommodate me for a
week? **-alue** residential area.
-kanta housing. **-la** dormitory.
-olot housing conditions.
-osake flat; *ks. seur.*
-osakeyhtiö house-owning
company, build-and-buy
company. **-pula** housing
shortage. **-vaunu** caravan,
trailer.
asustaa dwell, reside; stay.
asusteet clothing; *(lisä-)*
accessories; *urheilu~*
sportswear.
asusteliike clothing store.
asu|ttaa populate; colonize;
settle [in a place]. **-ttava**
habitable, fit to live in; *~ksi
kelpaamaton* unfit for
habitation. **-ttu** inhabited;
harvaan ~ sparsely populated.
asutus settlement, colonization.
-alue settled area. **-keskus**
population centre.
Ateena Athens. **a-lainen** *a. &
s.* Athenian.
ateis|mi atheism. **-ti** atheist.
-tinen atheistic.
ateljee studio.
ateri|a a meal; *(vauvan)* feed; *~n*

aihaan **at mealtime;** *olla ~lla*
be having one's meal;
(pöydässä) be at table. **-oida**
have a meal, eat.
Atlantti the Atlantic Ocean.
atleetti athlete. **-nen** athletic.
atomi atom. **-kausi** atomic age.
-kärki *(ohjuksen)* atomic
[war]head. **-käyttöinen**
atom-powered. **-oppi** atomic
theory. **-paino** atomic weight.
-pommi atom [ic] bomb.
-voimala nuclear power station.
attentaatti attempt upon a p.'s
life, attempted assassination.
(pommi-) bomb outrage.
attribuutti *kiel.* attribute.
audienssi audience.
auer haze.
aueta open; become unfastened,
become untied, come loose;
(esim. napista) come undone;
(puhjeta) unfold; *(levitä)*
spread.
aukaista open; *(lukosta)*
unlock; *~ solmu* untie
(unfasten) a knot.
aukea *a.* open; *s.* plain. **-ma**
open place; *(metsän)* glade;
(kirjan) double page; *keski~
~* centre pages, centre spread.
auki open; *kiertää ~* unscrew;
untwine; *repiä ~* tear (rip)
open; *virka on ~* the post is
vacant. **-o** open place, square.
-oloaika: *konttorin ~* office
hours; *pankin ~* banking
hours.
aukko opening, aperture *(m.
valok.)*; gap; *(esim. rintaman)*
break, breach; blank.
aukoa open [again and again]:
unfold, unwind.
auktoriteetti authority.
aula assembly hall.
aul|is liberal, generous,
bounteous; willing, ready;
auliisti (m.) freely. **-ius**
generosity, liberality;
willingness.
auma, -ta rick, stack.
aura, -ta plough, *Am.* plow.
auringon- *(yhd.)* .. of the sun;
solar. **-jumala** sun-god. **-kukka**
sunflower. **-lasku** sunset,
sundown. **-lämpö** heat of the
sun. **-nousu** sunrise. **-paahde**
blaze of the sun. **-paahtama**

tanned, sunburnt. **-paiste** sunshine. **-paisteinen** sunny. **-palvoja** sun-worshipper. **-palvonta** sun-worship. **-pilkku** sunspot. **-pimennys** eclipse of the sun. **-pisto** sunstroke. **-säde** sunbeam. **-valo** sunlight.

aurinko sun; *auringon noustessa* at sunrise; *auringon valaisema* sunlit. **-inen** sunny. **-kello** sun-dial. **-kunta** solar system. **-kylpy** sun-bath; *ottaa ~ä (m.)* sun-bathe, take a sun-bath, sun oneself. **-vuosi** solar year.

auskult|antti *(koulussa) l. v.* student teacher attending classes. **-oida** attend classes as an observer.

Australia Australia. **a-lainen** *a. & s.* Australian.

autereinen hazy.

auti|o waste, desolate; uninhabited; *~ksi jätetty* deserted, abandoned; *(~maa* desert). **-oittaa** lay waste; depopulate. **-us** desolateness, desolation.

auto [motor-]car, *et. Am.* auto [mobile]; *(vuokra-)* taxi; *ajaa ~a* drive; *ajaa ~lla* travel (go) by car, motor; *menin sinne ~lla* I went there by car. **-asema** taxi stand. **-asentaja** motor mechanic. **-gangsteri** hit-and-run driver. **-hurjastelija** reckless motorist, road-hog, *Am.* speedster. **-ilija** motorist. **-ilu** motoring. **-jono** line of cars. **-kolari** car crash. **-korjaamo** motor-car repair shop, garage. **-koulu** driving school. **-kuljetus** road haulage. **-kuorma** lorry *(Am.* truck) load. **-lautta** car ferry. **-liikenne** motor traffic. **-matka** car drive *(pitempi:* trip).

automaatio automation. **automaatti** *(itsetoimiva koje)* automaton; slot-machine, vending-machine, *(firman). ruoka-~* food machine; *makeis-~* candy m.; *raha-* coin m. **-kivääri** automatic rifle. **-nen** automatic [al]. **-puhelin** dial telephone. **-sesti** automatically.

-vaihteisto automatic transmission.

automatisoi|da automate, *(puhelin)* automatize. **-nti** automatization, automation.

automerkki make (of car).

auton|ajaja driver; *vrt. seur.* **-alusta** chassis *(pl. = sg)* **-katsastaja** motor vehicle examiner. **-katsastus** [annual] motor vehicle inspection. **-kuljettaja** *(henkilö-)* chauffeur; *(vuokra-)* taximan; bus-driver. **-kori** [motor]car body. **-myyjä** car salesman.

autonomi|a autonomy. **-nen** autonomous.

autonomistaj|a car owner; *-ien lukumäärä* car-ownership.

auto|onnettomuus motor [-car] accident.

autoritaarinen authoritarian.

auto|talli, -vaja garage. **-tie** motor road. **-varas** car thief, joy-rider. **-vuokraamo** car hire firm, car rental agency.

auttaa help; assist, aid; lend a [helping] hand; *(tukea)* support; *(korjata)* remedy; *(hyödyttää)* be of use; *auttaisitteko ..* I wonder if you could help me? *on helposti autettavissa* that's easily remedied (put right); *se ei auta asiaa* that won't do any good, that won't help matters; *minun ei auta viipyä* it won't do for me to stay; *minun ei auta muu kuin totella* I cannot but obey.

autta|ja helper; *(avustaja)* assistant. **-maton** past (beyond) help; irreparable; incurable; incorrigible. **-mattomasti** beyond help; *~ menetetty* irrecoverable, irretrievable. **-mattomuus** incurability. **-minen** helping, aiding. **-va** *(joltinen)* passable, fair. **-vainen** helpful, ready (willing) to help. **-vaisuus** helpfulness. **-vasti** tolerably, fairly; *hän puhuu englantia ~* he speaks English fairly well.

autuas blissful; blessed.

autuu|s blessedness, bliss, beatitude; *usk.* salvation. **-ttaa** save; make blessed, beatify.

avaamaton unopened, *(kh ju)* uncut; closed.

avaimenreikä keyhole.

avain key, *jnk* of, to; *(ulko-oven)* latchkey; *(salakielen ym.)* key [to the code, to the puzzle]; *säilykepurkin* ~ tin-opener. **-kimppu** bunch of keys. **-lapsi** latch-key child.

avajais|et opening [ceremony], inauguration. **-puhe** opening address.

avanne *lääk.* fistula.

avanto hole in the ice. **-uimari** winter bather.

avar|a wide; vast; extensive; *(leveä)* broad; *(tilava)* spacious; .. *vaikuttaa ~lta* gives a feeling of space. **-taa** widen, expand; extend. **-tua** widen [out], expand.

avaruus wideness; volume; *tähti.* [outer, *ulko-*] space; *avaruudessa* in space; *ampua avaruuteen* launch into space. **-alus** spacecraft. **-aika** the Space Age. **-asema** space station. **-matka** space flight. **-mies** space-man, astronaut, *(venäläinen)* cosmonaut. **-puku** space-suit. **-raketti** space rocket. **-tekniikka** space technology. **-tiede** space research.

avata open; *(käärö)* unwrap; *(hana)* turn on; *rad., sähk.* switch on; *(lukko)* unlock; *(päästää irti)* unfasten; *(solmu)* untie, undo; *(napista)* unbutton, *(haka)* unhook; *(hihna)* unstrap, *(solki)* unbuckle; *(pullo, m.)* uncork; *(julkinen rakennus ym.)* inaugurate; ~ *liike* establish a business; ~ *jkn silmät (kuv.)* disenchant; *milloin pankki avataan?* when does the bank open?

ava|us opening *jne.;* (~*puhe* opening address). **-utua** open, unfold.

avio marriage; *avio-* marital, matrimonial. **-ehto** marriage settlement. **-elämä** married life. **-ero** divorce. **-este** impediment [to marriage]. **-lapsi** legitimate child.

avioliitto marriage; matrimony; *mennä* ~*on* marry [a p. *jkn kanssa*]; *purkaa* ~ dissolve a marriage; *a-liiton edellinen* premarital; *a-liiton ulkopuolinen* extramarital, .. [born] out of wedlock; *ovat onnellisessa -liitossa* have a happy married life. **-lainsäädäntö** marriage laws. **-neuvoja** marriage counsellor. **-neuvola** marriage guidance centre, matrimonial advice bureau. **-neuvonta** marriage guidance. **-romaani** story of married life.

avio|llinen matrimonial; conjugal; marital. **-lupaus** promise of marriage. **-mies** husband; married man. **-onni** matrimonial happiness. **-pari** married couple. **-puoliso** marriage partner, *lak.* spouse; ~*t* husband and wife. **-rikos** adultery. **-suhde** marital status. **-sääty** married state; matrimony. **-ton** illegitimate. **-vaimo** [wedded] wife.

avoimesti openly; frankly.

avoin open; *(virasta)* vacant; ~ *luotto* blank credit; ~ *valtakirja* unlimited power of attorney; ~ *virka (m.)* vacancy.

avo|jalkainen barefoot[ed]. **-jaloin** barefoot. **-kaulainen** *(puvusta)* low[-necked]. **-kätinen** open-handed. **-meri** open sea; *-merellä* on the high sea[s]. **-mielinen** open [-hearted], frank, candid. **-mielisyys** open-heartedness, frankness, candour. **-nainen** open. **-päin(en)** bare-headed. **-silmin** with open eyes; open-eyed. **-suin** with one's mouth open; agape. **-sylin** with open arms. **-takka** fireplace. **-vesi** open water; *ensi avovedellä* [per] first open water *(lyh. f. o. w.)*.

avu *(hyve)* virtue; *(ominaisuus)* [good] quality, *(ansio)* merit.

avu|ksi, -lla *ym. ks.* apu.

avuli|aisuus helpfulness. **-as** helpful; obliging; willing to help.

avullinen *olla jklle* ~ *(jssk)*

help, assist a p. (in ..-ing).
avun|anto assistance, help, aid; *lak.* aiding and abetting. **-huuto** cry for help. **-pyyntö** request for help. **-pyytäjä** beggar. **-tarve:** *olla -tarpeessa* be in need of help. **-tarvitsija** .. needing help, needy.
avus|taa *(auttaa)* assist, aid, help; *(kannattaa)* support; *(valtiosta)* subsidize; *(juhlassa, ohjelmassa ym.)* assist, co-operate (in), lend one's services (at); ~ *sanomalehteä* contribute to a newspaper; ~ *teatterissa* take part in a play; *hänen -taessaan* with his

co-operation. **-taja** helper; assistant; *(sanomalehden)* contributor (to); *(lähetystössä)* attaché; *toimia jkn ~na (lak.)* hold a brief for. **-tus** support; help, assistance; *(hätä-)* relief; *(-osuus)* contribution, subscription; *(vuotuinen ym. raha-)* allowance, *(apuraha)* grant; *(valtion tukipalkkio)* subsidy. **-retkikunta** relief expedition. **-toimi(nta)** relief action (operations); *vrt. pelastus-.*
avu|ton helpless; incapable. **-tta** without help, unassisted. **-ttomuus** helplessness.

B

Baabelin torni the tower of Babel.

baari bar. **-kaappi** drink cupboard.

babylonialainen *a. & s.* Babylonian.

Baijeri Bavaria. **b-lainen** *a. & s.* Bavarian.

bakeliitti bakelite.

bakteer|i bacterium, *pl.* bacteria; *-eja tappava* bactericidal, antibacterial. **-iton** abacterial. **-iviljelys** bacterial culture.

bakterio|logi bacteriologist. **-logia** bacteriology. **-loginen** bacteriological.

baletti ballet. **-tanssijatar** ballet-dancer, ballerina. **-tyttö** chorus girl.

Balkan Balkan; *∼in maat* the Balkans.

balladi ballad, lay.

ballistinen ballistic.

balsam|i balsam; *et. kuv.* balm. **-oida** embalm.

Baltian maat the Baltic countries.

bambu *(-ruoko)* bamboo.

banaali banal, commonplace.

banaani banana.

baptisti Baptist.

barbaari barbarian. **-nen** barbarous, barbaric. **-suus** barbarism.

barokki baroque.

barrikadi barricade.

barytoni, -laulaja baritone.

basaari bazaar.

basilli bacillus *(pl.* bacilli). **-kauhu** bacteria scare. **-nkantaja** [germ] carrier.

baskeri beret.

baskilainen *a. & s.* Basque.

basso, -laulaja, -ääni bass. **-viulu** bass, double bass.

bataatti sweet potato.

batisti batiste, cambric.

beduiini Bedouin.

Belgia Belgium. **b-lainen** *a. & s.* Belgian.

ben(t)siini petrol; *Am.* gasol|ine, -ene, *puhek.* gas. *(et. puhdistus-)* benzine. **-asema** petrol station, filling station. **-säiliö** petrol tank.

bentsoli *kem.* benzene, benzol.

Berliini Berlin. **b-läinen** *s.* inhabitant of Berlin, Berliner; *a.* Berlin.

Bernin alpit Bernese Alps.

bernhardilaiskoira St. Bernard [dog].

betoni concrete. **-laatta** panel of precast concrete.

biisami musk-rat.

biisonihärkä bison, buffalo.

bilanssi balance-sheet.

biljardi billiards. **-keppi** [billiard] cue. **-peli** [game of] billiards.

biljoona *Engl.* billion, *vrt. miljardi.*

biokemia biochemistry.

biologi biologist. **-a** biology. **-nen** biological.

Biskaijan lahti the Bay of Biscay.

Boden-järvi Lake of Constance.

blanko *liik.* [in] blank. **-tunnuste** blank acceptance.

blokki *(valtio-)* bloc.

bofoori Beaufort *(esim. 6 ∼a* strong breeze; *8 ∼a* fresh gale).

boheemi Bohemian.

boikotoida, boikotti boycott.

boksi digs, diggings.

boksiitti bauxite.

bolševi|kki Bolshevik. **-smi** Bolshevism. **-stinen** Bolshevist -[ic].

boori *kem.* boron. **-happo** boric acid. **-salva** boracic ointment. **-vesi** boracic acid solution.

bordelli brothel.
Bospori the Bosp[h]orus.
Brasilia Brazil. **-lainen** *a. & s.*
 Brazilian.
bravuuri *mus.* bravura. **-numero**
 star turn.
Bretagne Brittany.
Britannia Britain.
Britein saaret the British Isles.
brittiläi|nen *a.* British. *s.*
 Briton; *b-läiset (m.)* the
 British.
brokadi brocade.
bromi *kem.* bromine.
bronkiitti bronchitis.
brošyyri brochure, leaflet.
brutaalinen *(raaka)* brutal.
brutto gross. **-arvo** gross value.
 -paino gross weight. **-tulo**
 gross income; *(-tuotto)* gross
 proceeds.
Bryssel Brussels.
budhalai|nen *a.* Buddhist[ic]
 s. Buddhist. **-suus** Buddhism.

budjetoida budget for, prepare
 (draw up) a budget.
budjetti budget. **-esitys** budget
 [proposals]. **-vuosi** financial
 (fiscal) year.
bufetti refreshment room.
buldogi bulldog.
bulevardi boulevard, avenue.
Bulgaria Bulgaria. **b-lainen** *a.*
 & s. Bulgarian.
bulla *(paavin)* bull.
bulvaani *kuv.* dummy, straw
 man.
bumerangi boomerang.
bunkkeri concrete dugout,
 pill-box.
buuata boo.
buuri Boer. **-sota** Boer war.
byrokr|aattinen bureaucratic.
 -atia bureaucracy, red tape.
bysanttilainen Byzantine.
Böömi Bohemia. **b-läinen** *a. &*
 s. Bohemian.

C

Celsius *ks. lämpömittari.*
cembalo harpsichord.
Chile Chile. **c-läinen** *a. & s.*
 Chilean.
cif c.i.f. (cost, insurance and
 freight).

D

daalia dahlia.
daami [lady-, girl-] partner; *korttip.* queen; *hieno* ~ elegant lady.
dalmatialainen *a. & s.* Dalmatian *(m. d-nkoira).*
damaski|**t** gaiters. **-teräs** Damascus steel.
damasti *(kangas)* damask.
Damokleen miekka sword of Damocles.
Dardanellit the Dardanelles.
darvinis|**mi** Darwinism. **-tinen** Darwinian.
datiivi *kiel.* dative.
debet debit. **-puoli** debit side.
debyytti debut.
deeki|**s**: *mennä -kselle* go to the dogs; *olla -ksellä* be down on one's luck.
deflaatio deflation, disinflation.
degeneroitua degenerate.
dekaani dean.
dekkari *puhek.* whodunit.
deklinaatio declension; inflection.
delfiini *zo.* dolphin.
delta delta, estuary.
dementoida deny.
demobilisoida demobilize *(puhek.* demob).
demo|**kraatti** democrat; *(~nen* democratic). **-kratia** democracy. **-kratisoida** democratize.
demoni demon. **-nen** demoniac.
demonstratiivinen *kiel.* demonstrative.
demoralisoida demoralize.
denaturoi|**da** denature; *-tu sprii* methylated spirits.
deodorantti deodorant; antiperspirant.
desi|**gramma** decigramme. **-litra** decilitre. **-maali** decimal. **-metri** decimetre.
desinf|**ektio** disinfection. **-ioida** disinfect. **-ioimisaine** disinfectant.
despootti despot. **-nen** despotic.
determinatiivinen *kiel.* determinative.
devalv|**aatio** devaluation. **-oida** devalue.
diadeema diadem.
diagnoosi *lääk.* diagnosis; *tehdä* ~ diagnose. **-ntekijä** diagnostician.
diagrammi diagram, graph.
diakoni deacon. **-ssa** deaconess; *(~laitos* deaconess institution).
dialogi dialogue.
diapositiivi (kuva) colour transparency *(t.* slide).
diatermia diathermy.
dieetti diet. **-nen** dietetic.
diesel|**käyttöinen** diesel-operated (-propelled). **-moottori** d. engine.
diftongi diphthong.
diiva *(operetti- ym)* prima donna; *~maiset eleet* airs and graces **-illa** act the prima donna.
dikta|**attori** dictator. **-torinen** dictatorial. **-tuuri** dictatorship.
dilli dill.
diplomaatti diplomat [ist]. **-ala:** *hän on ~lla* he is in the diplomatic service. **-kunta** diplomatic corps.
diplom|**aattinen** diplomatic; *d-ttiset suhteet* d. relations **-atia** diplomacy.
diplomi diploma. **-insinööri** graduate engineer, diploma engineer.
diskantti *mus.* treble; descant.
diskont|**ata** *pankk.* discount.
diskontto discount. **-korko** discount rate, *(keskuspankin)* bank rate. **-liike** discount business.
diskoteekki discotheque.
divisioona division.
dogi *ks. buldogi; tanskan~*

Great Dane.
dogm|atiikka dogmatics. **-i** dogma.
dokumenttielokuva documentary film.
dollari dollar *(lyh. $)*. **-laina** dollar loan. **-nseteli** dollar bill.
dominikaani (-munkki) Dominican [friar], Black Friar.
domino domino; *(-peli)* dominoes.
dominoi|da dominate; *-va (määräämishaluinen)* domineering.
doorilainen Doric, Dorian.
dosentti *l.v.* senior lecturer, docent, *Am.* assistant

professor.
draama drama. **-llinen** dramatic.
dramaattinen dramatic [al].
dramat|isoida dramatize. **-urgi** dramaturg[e].
dreeni drain.
dresyyri training.
dritteli cask.
dromedaari *zo.* dromedary.
džonkki junk.
duetto *mus.* duet.
duralumiini duralumin, hard aluminium.
duuri *mus.; C~* C major.
dynaaminen dynamic.
dynamii|kka dynamics. **-tti** dynamite; *räjäyttää -tilla* dynamite; **(~mies** dynamiter).

E

eboniitti ebonite, vulcanite.
edelle *(eteen)* ahead; *jkn* ~
ahead of, in front of, *(ennen)*
before . ., *(sivuitse)* past . .;
päästä ~ get ahead (of).
edelleen further; furthermore,
moreover; *(eteenpäin)* on,
onward [s], ahead; *(yhä)* still;
lue ~ read on! go on
[reading]! ~ *toimitettavaksi*
to be forwarded; *jksk aikaa*
~ for a while longer; ~*(kin)*
tehdä jtk continue to do sth.,
go on (keep on) doing sth.;
on ~ *voimassa* continues in
force, is still valid.
edelli|nen previous, foregoing;
(lähinnä ~*)* preceding;
pre[war *sodan*-]; ~ —
jälkimmäinen the former —
the latter; *-senä päivänä* the
day before; *-senä iltana* on
the previous evening;
viimeisen ~ the last but one;
sunnuntain ~ *yö* Saturday
night.
edelly|ttää presuppose; *(olettaa)*
assume, presume; postulate;
(varmana asiana) take . . for
granted; *-ttäen, että* provided
[that], granted that; *tämä* ~
että this preconceives [the
idea] that; *hänen -tetään*
tulevan it is understood that
he will come; *kuten nimikin*
(jo) ~ as the name implies;
edellyttäkäämme . . let us
assume. **-tys** presupposition;
(ehto) [pre]condition,
prerequisite; *(tarvittava*
ominaisuus) qualification; *sillä*
-tyksellä, että provided [that],
on condition that; *lähtien jstk*
-tyksestä assuming that; *luoda*
-tykset jllek create the
necessary conditions for;
meillä on kaikki -tykset
onnistua we have every

chance of succeeding.
edellä *prep., postp.* ahead of,
in front of; *adv.* before;
(yllä) above; *kelloni on (viisi*
minuuttia) ~ my watch is
[five minutes] fast; *on jksta,*
jkta ~ *(parempi)* has the
advantage of, is ahead of;
aikaansa ~ ahead of the
times; *mene sinä* ~ you go
first; *pää* ~ head first
(foremost). **-kävijä** predecessor;
precursor, forerunner; *(~kansa*
pioneer nation). **-käypä,**
-käyvä preceding; previous.
-mainittu . . mentioned
(stated) above, aforesaid,
(yllä) above-mentioned. **-oleva**
foregoing, previous; preceding.
edeltäjä predecessor.
edeltä|käsin, -päin beforehand,
in advance; ~ *määrätty*
predestined. **-vä** preceding.
edeltää precede.
edem|mäksi farther on;
(kauemmaksi) farther off.
-pänä farther on; *(kauempana)*
farther off. **-pää** from farther
off.
edentää remove farther.
edes *(ainakin)* at least; even;
ei ~ not even. **-mennyt**
(vainaja) deceased, late.
-ottamus doing; undertaking.
-päin forth, forward;
(edelleen) further; *ja niin* ~
(jne.) and so forth, and so
on, etc. (= et cetera).
edessä in front (of); ahead
(of); before; in the front;
sellainen tehtävä on ~*ni* such
a task awaits me; *meillä on*
vaikeuksia ~*mme* there are
difficulties ahead.
edestakaisin to and fro, back
and forth; *(matkasta)* there
and back.
edestä *(-päin)* from the front

(of); ~ *otettu kuva* a front view (of); ~ *auki (oleva)* open at the front; *minun ~ni (sijastani)* in my place, instead of me.

edesvastuu responsibility; *olla ~ssa jstk* be responsible (answerable) for; *~n uhalla (lak.)* under penalty of the law. **-llinen** responsible. **-llisuus** responsibility. **-ntunne** sense of responsibility. **-ton** irresponsible. **-ttomuus** irresponsibility.

edetä advance, proceed, move on, pass on; progress; *(loitota)* draw away; *sotajoukko etenee* the army advances (pushes forward); *kuinka pitkälle asia on edennyt* how far has the matter progressed.

edisty|ksellinen progressive. **-minen** advance, progress, headway; improvement.

edistys progress *ks. ed.; (uudistus)* reform. **-askel** step forward; *~eet* progress *(sg.)*, strides. **-mielinen** progressive. **-työ** reform work.

edis|tyä [make] progress; advance, proceed; get on; *(parantua)* improve; ~ *(maailmassa)* get on in the world; *pitkälle -tynyt* far advanced; *oppilas on -tynyt hyvin* the pupil has made good progress; ~ *huonosti* make little progress, be backward; ~ *suuresti (jllak alalla) m.* make great strides in .. **-täjä** promoter, furtherer. **-täminen** promotion, advancement; *myynnin ~* sales promotion. **-tämiskeino** means of furthering. **-tää** further, promote, advance; *(vaurastuttaa)* improve; contribute to [the welfare of, *jnk hyvinvointia*]; *(kello)* be fast, gain.

edulli|nen advantageous, *(hyödyllinen)* useful; *(tuottava)* profitable, remunerative; *(suotuisa)* favourable; *(ulkonäkö)* prepossessing; *(puollettava)* advisable; ~ *kauppa* [good] bargain; ~

tarjous (m.) liberal offer; *on Suomelle taloudellisesti -sta* it is in Finland's economic interest (to, that); *olla jkta -semmassa asemassa* have the advantage over. **-semmin** to greater advantage, more profitably. **-sesti** to [one's] advantage, profitably. **-suus** advantage [ousness]. profitableness.

eduskunta [national] parliament; *e- kunnan jäsen* member of [the] parliament, deputy. **-aloite** bill. **-ehdokas** candidate for parliament. **-katsaus** parliamentary report. **-laitos** system of representation. **-talo** Parliament building. **-vaalit** general election.

edus|mies representative; *lak.* proxy, attorney. **-ta** place in front (of), front; *jnk ~lla, -lle* in front of; *(lähellä, -lle)* [close] by; *paidan ~* shirt front; *Helsingin ~lla* off H. **-taa** represent; stand for.

edustaja representative; *(ilmentymä)* exponent; *(valtuutettu)* delegate; *(kansan-)* member of the parliament, *(puolestapuhuja)* spokesman; *~in huone (U.S.A.)* House of Representatives. **-kamari** *(Ranskan)* Chamber of Deputies. **-kokous** meeting of delegates. **-npaikka** seat [in the parliament].

edusta|jisto representatives. **-va** *a.* representative [of]; *(huomattava)* distinguished. **-vuus** representativeness.

edustus representation. **-kulut** entertainment expenses. **-to** representation, *(jnnek lähetetty)* mission. **-velvollisuus:** *-llä on paljon e-suuksia ..* has to entertain a great deal.

eebenpuu ebony.

eekkeri acre (0.405 ha).

eeppinen, eepos epic.

eetteri ether.

eettinen ethical.

Egypti Egypt. **e-läinen** *a. & s.* Egyptian.

ehdit: *kun ~* when you get

time (an opportunity); *ks.*
ehtiä.

ehdo|kas candidate; *asettaa jku
-kkaaksi jhk* put sb. up as a
candidate for, nominate a p.
for; *asettuu -kkaaksi* will
stand as a (*esim.* Liberal)
candidate; (~**lista** list of
candidates). **-kkuus** candidacy,
candidature.

ehdollepano nomination.

ehdolli|nen conditional;
~ *tuomio* suspended sentence
(judgment); *sai -sen tuomion
(m.)* was given a conditional
discharge, *(nuoresta Engl.)*
was put on probation. **-staa**
condition.

ehdonalai|nen conditional;
laskea -seen vapauteen release
on parole (Am.), *vrt. ed.*

ehdoton unconditional;
absolute; positive; categorical;
~ *kuuliaisuus* implicit
obedience; ~ *raittius* total
abstinence; .. *täytyy
ehdottomasti* it is imperative
that ..

ehdo|ttaa propose; suggest;
(tehdä esitys) move; ~
hyväksyttäväksi recommend ..
for adoption. **-ttaja** proposer;
mover. **-ttomasti** absolutely;
positively; ~ *paras (m.)*
decidedly (unquestionably) the
best. **-ttomuus** absoluteness;
positiveness. **-tus** proposal, *et.
Am.* proposition; suggestion;
(kokouksessa, m.) motion;
tehdä ~ make (submit) a
proposal; *hyväksyä* ~ accept
a p.; *hänen ehdotuksestaan* at
his suggestion.

ehe|ys wholeness; soundness;
unity; *(koskemattomuus)*
integrity. **-yttäminen** *m.*
integration. **-yttää** make
whole; unite. **-ä** whole, sound;
unbroken, undamaged, intact;
~ *kokonaisuus* a harmonious
whole.

ehjä = *ed.; ehjin nahoin*
[escape] unhurt, unscathed,
[get off] with a whole skin.

ehkä perhaps, maybe;
(mahdollisesti) possibly; *hän
sanoi* ~ *tulevansa* she said
she might come; *ehken*

menekään perhaps I shan't
go; ~*pä niin on* I suppose
so.

ehkäi|semätön unchecked,
unrestrained. **-sevä** *(ennakko-)*
preventive. **-sevästi:** *vaikuttaa
~ jhk* have a preventive
(checking) effect on. **-styä** be
checked (restrained, arrested).
-stä check; restrain; *(estää)*
prevent, hinder; impede,
obstruct; *(hankaluuttaa)*
hamper; ~ *kasvussaan* stunt;
~ *kehitystä* arrest the
development; ~ *jkh tuumat*
thwart sb.'s plans.

ehkäisy checking; prevention;
(raskauden) contraception.
-keino preventive [means];
method of contraception.
-pilleri contraceptive pill *(t.*
tablet), the Pill. **-väline**
contraceptive. **-tulli** prohibitive
duty.

ehost|aa *(»meikata»)* make up.
-us make-up.

ehtimiseen again and again;
constantly; ~ *kysellä* keep
asking.

ehtiä have time, find time;
(tulla ajoissa) arrive in time;
en ehdi I have no time; *en
ehdi tulla* I can't manage to
come; *ehdittekö puhua hetken
kanssani?* can you spare me
a minute? *kun ehdin siihen
asti* when I get that far; ~
junalle catch a train, be in
time for the train.

ehto condition; *(sopimuksessa)*
stipulation, provision; *ehdot
(liik.)* terms; *millä ehdoilla* on
what terms? *ehdoin tahdoin*
deliberately, intentionally;
ehdoitta unconditionally; *ei
millään ehdolla* on no
condition (account); *sillä
ehdolla, että* on condition
that; *panna ehdoksi* make it
a condition [that]; *saada
ehdot (koulussa)* be moved up
conditionally.

ehtoo evening, night. **-llinen**
kirk. Holy Communion, the
Lord's Supper; the Eucharist;
jakaa -llista administer
Communion; *käydä -llisella*
partake of Holy Communion.

ehtoollis|kalkki chalice,
Communion cup. **-leipä**
sacramental bread, the host.
-vieras communicant. **-viini**
sacramental wine.

ehtotapa *kiel.* conditional
[mood].

ehty|minen running dry, drying
[up]. **-mätön** *kuv.*
inexhaustible, unfailing. **-ä**
stop giving milk; *kuv.* be
exhausted, run dry.

ehyt *ks. eheä.* **-laitainen** *bot.*
entire.

ei no; *(en, et, ei jne.)* not; *ei*
— *eikä* neither — nor; *ei*
hänkään ole sen parempi nor
is he any better; *eiköhän ole*
parasta wouldn't it be best;
hän on sisaresi, eikö olekin?
she is your sister, isn't she?
ethän ole väsynyt your aren't
tired, are you? ~ *kukaan*
nobody; no one; ~ *mikään* no,
none; nothing; *ei-kenenkään*
maa no-man's-land;
ei-sosialistinen non-Socialist.

eikä *(enkä, etkä, emmekä jne)*
and . . not; *(hän ei mennyt)*
emmekä mekään nor *(t.*
neither) did we.

eikö *ks. ei.*

eilen yesterday; ~ *aamulla*
yesterday morning; *vrt. eilis-.*

eili|nen [. . of] yesterday; ~
sanomalehti yesterday's paper;
-sestä lukien beginning with
yesterday; *-sestä viikko*
yesterday week.

eilis|aamu ~*na* yesterday
morning. **-ilta** ~*na* yesterday
evening, last night. **-iltainen**
yesterday evening's; ~ *tapaus*
the event last night. **-päivä**
yesterday; ~*n* of yesterday.

einestuotteet cooked foods.

ei- |sosialistinen *ks. ei* **-toivottu**
unwanted.

eittä|mättä undeniably, beyond
dispute. **-mättömyys**
incontestability. **-mätön**
indisputable, incontestable.

eittää deny; dispute, contest.

ekologi|a ecology. **-nen** ecologic
- [al].

eksy|ksissä, -ksiin astray; *on* ~
is lost. **-minen** losing one's
way; erring. **-nyt** stray. **-ttävä**

misleading; ~ *yhdennäköisyys*
(m.) bewildering likeness. **-ttää**
lead . . astray, mislead;
eksytetty . . led astray,
misguided; ~ *jäljiltä* put off
the scent.

eksyä go astray, get lost, lose
one's way; *(hairahtua)* err; ~
totuudesta stray (wander,
deviate) from the truth; ~
yksityisseikkoihin lose oneself
in details.

ekumeeninen [o]ecumenic[al].

elanto living, livelihood; *vrt.*
elatus.

elatus subsistence, maintenance,
sustenance; *(elanto)* living,
livelihood; *ansaita elatuksensa*
make a living (by *-lla*). **-apu**
maintenance money.
-velvollisuus duty of
maintenance.

ele gesture; *(kasvojen)*
expression.

eleetön expressionless;
(vaatimaton) unassuming,
demure.

elefantti elephant. **-tauti**
elephantiasis.

elegia *run.* elegy.

ele|htiä gesticulate. **-kieli** gesture
language, sign language.

elektro|di electrode. **-lyysi**
electrolysis. **-ni** electron;
(~*putki* electronic valve,
electron tube). **-niikka**
electronics.

elellä live; ~ *huolettomana*
lead a carefree life.

elementti prefabricated unit;
(betoni-) precast concrete
block.

elenäytelmä dumb show,
pantomime, *vrt. pantomiimi.*

eli or.

eliitti élite.

eli|mellinen organic. **-metön**
inorganic. **-mistö** organism,
system.

eliminoida eliminate.

elin organ; body; *elimet (m.)*
system; *hallinto* ~ governing
body.

elin|aika lifetime; *-ajaksi* for
life. **-aikainen** . . for life,
lifelong. **-ehto** vital condition.
-ikä lifetime; *-iäksi* for life.
-ikäinen, -kautinen lifelong; ~

vanki life prisoner, prisoner for life.
elinkeino source of livelihood; occupation, trade, industry. **-elämä** economic life. **-vapaus** freedom of trade and industry.
elin|korko [life] annuity. **-kustannukset** cost of living. **-kustannusindeksi** c. of l. index. **-kykyinen** viable. **-kysymys** question of vital importance. **-neste** life fluid. **-tapa** manner (mode) of living. **-tarvike:** *-tarvikkeet* provisions, foodstuffs; (~**kortti** ration card; ~**pula** scarcity of food).
elintaso standard of living. **-kilpailu** keeping up with the Joneses,/ *(häikäilemätön)* rat race.
elin|toiminto vital function. **-voima** vital power, vitality. **-voimainen** .. full of vitality, vital; vigorous; robust. **-voimaisuus** vitality.
eliö organism.
elje: *elkeet* pranks, tricks.
ellei *(ellen, ellet jne.)* if not, unless; ~ *heitä olisi ollut* .. if it had not been for them .., but for them ..
ellip|si ellipse. **-tinen** elliptic [al].
ellott|aa: *minua* ~ I feel sick, I have a feeling of nausea. **-ava** sickening, nauseating.
elo life; *(vilja)* corn, *Am.* grain; *(sato)* crop; *olla* ~*ssa* be alive; ~*ssa oleva* living; *jäädä* ~*on* survive [a p.]; ~*on jääneet* the survivors, those surviving; *àntaa* ~*a* invigorate. **-hopea** mercury, quicksilver.
eloi|sa lively, full of life, sprightly, vivacious; *(esim. kuvaus)* vivid; animated. **-sasti** in a lively manner, vivaciously, vividly. **-suus** liveliness, animation, vivacity.
elo|juhla harvest festival. **-kuu** August.
elokuva film, [motion] picture; ~*t* cinema, the pictures, *Am.* the movies. **-esitys** cinema show. **-kamera** cine-camera, movie camera. **-kone** *(-heitin)*

cinema projector. **-osa** screen role. **-ta** film. **-taide** cinematographic art. **-teatteri** cinema, picture theatre *(t.* house).
elollinen living; organic.
elon|kipinä spark of life. **-korjuu** harvest [ing]. **-leikkuukone** harvester. **-merkki** sign of life. **-päivät** days of [one's] life; *jos minulle -päiviä suodaan* .. if I am spared ..
elos|telija fast man; rake, rip (an old rip). **-tella** lead a loose life. **-telu** dissipation, loose living.
elo|ton lifeless; inanimate; inert; *(ilmeestä ym)* vacant. **-ttomuus** lifelessness. **-virna** *bot.* vetch.
elpy|minen revival; *(m. kaupan)* recovery. **-ä** revive, recover; *(toipua)* pick up, rally.
eltaantu|a turn rancid. **-nut** rancid.
elukka beast, animal, creature.
elvy|ke stimulus, incentive. **-tys** revival; restoration; recovery. **-ttää** animate, enliven, stimulate, quicken; restore [to life], revive, *(esim. hukkunut)* resuscitate.
elähdyttä|ä enliven, invigorate, stimulate; *aatteen -mä* inspired by an idea. **-vä** life-giving, animating, inspiring.
elähtänyt past one's prime, passé [e], worn-out [through dissipation].
eläimelli|nen animal; *(raaka)* bestial, brutal, brutish. **-syys** bestiality, brutality.
eläimistö the animal world; *zo.* fauna.
eläin animal; beast; *(luontokappale)* creature. **-kunta** animal kingdom. **-laji** species of animal. **-lääketiede** veterinary science. **-lääkäri** veterinary surgeon *(lyh.* vet). **-oppi** zoology. **-rata** zodiac. **-rutto** cattle plague. **-rääkkäys** cruelty to animals. **-satu** fable. **-suojelu(s)** protection of animals; (~**yhdistys** society for the prevention of cruelty to animals). **-tarha** zoological

garden [s] *(lyh.* zoo).
-tenkasvattaja breeder of
animals. **-tiede** zoology.
-tieteellinen zoological.
-tieteilijä zoologist.
eläk|e pension; *asettua -keelle*
retire on a pension; *joutua
-keelle* be pensioned [off];
-keelle siirtyminen retirement;
-keellä oleva pensioned,
retired; *-keeseen oikeutettu*
entitled to a pension. **-ikä:**
lähestyy ~ä .. is nearing
retirement. **-ikäinen** of
pensionable age. **-kassa**
pension society. **-läinen**
pensioner. **-vakuutus** old-age
pension insurance.
eläköön hurrah! *~ ..* long live
. . . **-huuto** cheer; *kolminkertainen ~ jllek* three cheers
for *. . .*
elämi|nen living; *-sen taito* art
of living; *-sen oikeus* right to
live.
elämys experience; *se oli ~!* it
was quite an e.
elämä life *(pl.* lives); *(melu)*
noise; *koko ~ni aikana*
during all my time, all my
life [long]; *~ä kokenut ..*
who has seen a great deal of
life, experienced; *-än
kyllästynyt* tired (sick) of life.
-kerralli|nen biographical; *e-set
tiedot* curriculum vitae. **-kerta**
biography, life; *oma ~*
autobiography; *-kerran
kirjoittaja* biographer.
elämän|halu will to live; zest
for life. **-haluinen** *(ks. ed.)
hän on ~ (m.)* she loves life.
-ilo joy of living. **-iloinen**
high-spirited, cheerful. **-juoksu**
kuv. race. **-katsomus** outlook
on life, view of life, life
attitude. **-kohtalo** lot in life,
fate. **-kokemus** experience [of
life]. **-kulku** course of life.
-kumppani *ks.* -toveri. *
-kutsumus calling, vocation.
-myönteinen positive. **-nautinto**
enjoyment of life. **-ohje**
maxim, rule of life. **-taistelu**
struggle for life. **-tapa** way of
life, way of living; *-tavat*
living habits. **-tarina** life
story. **-tehtävä** aim of life,

purpose in life. **-tie** course of
life. **-toveri** life-companion.
-työ life-work. **-ura** career.
-vaiheet events of life; career.
-vesi elixir of life. **-viisaus**
philosophy of life.
elämöidä be noisy, make a
noise.
elät|täjä *(perheen)* bread-winner,
supporter. **-tää** *(ylläpitää)*
support, maintain, provide
for; *~ itsensä jllak* support
oneself by, earn one's living
by; *hänellä on perhe
-ettävänä* he has a wife and
family to keep; *olla jnk
-ettävänä* depend on sb. [for
support].
eläv|yys liveliness, animation;
vivacity. **-ä** living; *(eläin)*
live; *(vilkas)* lively; animated,
vivid; *~ltä, ~nä* alive; *~t ja
kuolleet* the living and the
dead; *se (tapaus) on vielä
~nä mielessäni* it is still
fresh in my mind. **-ästi**
vividly, in a lively manner.
-öittää animate; inspire. **-öitys**
elok. animation.
eläyty|minen *l.v.* (deep *t.* vivid)
insight. **-ä:** *~ jhk* put one's
soul into; *(jkn tunteisiin)*
enter into (sb.'s feelings).
elää live; *(olla elossa)* be
alive; *(elättää itsensä)* support
oneself; *~ jstk, jllak* live,
subsist on [fruit], live on
[one's salary], live by (..
-ing, *jtk tekemällä); eläessään*
when he was alive; *~
onnellista elämää* lead a
happy life; *~ yli aikansa*
outlive one's (its) time; *hän
eli .. -vuotiaaksi* he lived to
the age of; *joka ~, näkee* he
who lives will see.
emakko sow.
emal|ji, -joida enamel.
emi *bot.* pistil.
emigrantti emigrant.
emi|lehti carpel. **-ö**
gyn [o]ecium.
emo dam.
empi|minen hesitation. **-vä**
hesitating, hesitant. **-ä**
hesitate; be doubtful, be in
two minds; *-mättä* without
[any] hesitation.

emul|gaattori emulsifying agent.
-goida emulsify. **-sio** emulsion.
emä dam. **-karhu** she bear.
-ksinen basic, alkaline. **-laiva**
mother ship; *(lentokoneiden)*
aircraft carrier. **-lammas** ewe.
-lippu counterfoil, *Am.* stub.
-maa mother country.
emän|nyys household
management; housewifery;
duties of a hostess. **-nöidä**
manage the household, keep
house; act as a hostess.
-nöitsijä housekeeper.
emäntä hostess, lady of the
house; *(perheen-)* housewife;
(esim. koiran) mistress;
(vuokra-) landlady; *emännän*
velvollisuudet duties of a
hostess. **-koulu** rural
homemaking school.
emäs *kem.* base, alkali.
en, et, ei, emme, ette, eivät
not; *(vastauksissa)* no; *ks. ei.*
emätin *anat.* vagina.
endokrinologia endocrinology.
enemmistö majority; the
greater part (of); *hän sai 10*
ääntä ~n he gained a m. of
10 votes. **-hallitus** majority
government. **-päätös** majority
resolution.
enem|myys greater amount,
preponderance. **-män** more;
kolme kertaa ~ three times
as much; *~ kuin* more than,
(yli, m.) upwards of [*esim.*
. . . 300 miles]; *pitää*
jstk ~ kuin .. like sth.
better than, prefer sth. to;
tarjota ~ kuin jku outbid a p.
ei -pää kuin no more than; *~*
tai vähemmän more or less.
-pi more; further, *hintojen ~*
nousu a further rise in
prices; *-pää en minä voi* I
can do no more; *ei -pää*
eikä vähempää neither more
nor less; *älkäämme puhuko*
siitä -pää don't let us talk
any more about it; *sen -mittä*
without any more ado; [he
got up and left] just like
that; *-mältä osalta* for the
most part; *-män arvoinen*
worth more, of greater value.
enen|eminen increase. **-evä**
increasing; *yhä ~* ever-i.

energia energy, power.
enetä increase; grow; rise.
englanni|nkielinen [. . in]
English; *~ sanomalehti* an
English-language newspaper.
-npeninkulma mile. **-tar**
Englishwoman *(pl.* -women).
Englanti England; *vrt. Iso*
Britannia; Englannin kanaali
the [English] Channel; *E-n*
suurlähetystö the British
Embassy; *e~ (kieli)* English;
englannin kielellä in English;
englannin opettaja teacher of
English.
englantilai|nen *a.* English. *s.*
Englishman, Englishwoman;
-set Englishmen, English people;
(koko kansa) the English, the
British. **-s-amerikkalainen**
Anglo-American.
enimmäis|hinta top price.
-määrä maximum.
enim|mäkseen most commonly,
mostly, for the most part;
chiefly. **-män** most; *~*
tarjoava the highest bidder.
enin most; *~ kaikista* most of
all; *enimmät heistä* most of
them; *enimmät äänet* the
most votes, the majority of
votes. **-tään** at [the] most.
eniten most; *pidän tästä ~* I
like this best [of all]; *~*
rahaa [he has] the most
money.
enkeli angel. **-mäinen** angelic.
ennakko *(-maksu)* advance
[money]; *maksaa ~a* pay in
advance. **-arvio** budget. **-ehto**
precondition. **-esitys**
(kutsuvieraille) preview.
-ilmoitus prior notice.
-laskelma preliminary
calculation.
ennakkoluulo prejudice, bias.
-inen prejudiced, bias[s]ed.
-isesti with prejudice. **-suus**
prejudice. **-ton** unprejudiced,
unbias[s]ed. **-ttomasti** withouτ
prejudice. **-ttomuus** freedom
from prejudice.
ennakko|maksu advance
payment. **-mielipide**
preconceived opinion. **-näytös**
preview. **-odotu|s:** *vastasi -ksia*
came up to expectations.
-osto advance booking; *Am.*

reservation. **-tapaus** precedent.
-tieto advance information.
-tilaus advance subscription.
-varaus advance booking.
-vero advance amount of tax.
ennako|ida foreshadow; *(arvata
-lta)* anticipate. **-lta**
beforehand, in advance; ~
määrätty predestined,
foreordained; *maksaa* ~ pay
in advance; *odottaa* ~
expect; anticipate. **-npidätys**
(veron) pay-as-you-earn
(P.A.Y.E), tax at the source;
vrt. pidätys.
ennal|laan, -leen as before;
unchanged; *saattaa -leen*
restore [to its former
condition]. **-talaskematon**
unforeseeable. **-tamääräys**
predestination.
enne omen, portent, augury.
ennemmin earlier;
(mieluummin) rather; ~ *tai
myöhemmin* sooner or later.
ennen *prep.* before, previous
to; *adv.* before [now];
previously; *(mieluummin)*
rather; ~ *aikaan, muinoin*
formerly, in the old days; ~
aikojaan too early,
prematurely; ~ *kaikkea* above
all; first of all; ~ *pitkää*
before long, by and by; *sitä*
~ before that, before then; ~
kuin before; [not] until; *ei
kestänyt kauan* ~ *kuin hän
tuli* it was not long before
he came; ~ *kuulumaton*
unheard of; *tässä oli* ~ *talo
(m.)* there used to be a
house here. **-aikainen**
premature; untimely [death,
kuolema], overhasty
[conclusion, *johtopäätös*].
-aikaisesti prematurely. **-kuin**
ks. ennen.
ennestään *ks. entuudestaan;
tiesin sen* ~ I already knew
it.
ennus|merkki omen,
[premonitory] sign. **-taa**
predict, foretell, forecast;
prophesy; *(et. pahaa)*
forebode; foreshadow; *(jklle
korteista ym)* tell a p.'s
fortune; *se* ~ *(ei ennusta)
hyvää hänelle* it augurs well

(it bodes no good) for him.
-taja prophet; seer; *(povari)*
fortune-teller. **-taminen**
foretelling, prophesying. **-te**
forecast; *lääk.* prognosis *(pl.*
-oses). **-tus** prophecy,
prediction.
ennä|ttää have time;
(saavuttaa) reach; arrive,
jnnek at, in; ~ *ennen jkta*
get ahead of, forestall,
anticipate a p.; *-tätkö tulla
(m.)* can you manage (find
time) to come? *-titkö junaan?*
were you in time for the
train? did you catch the
train? **-tyksellinen** record,
unprecedented. **-tys** record;
(saavutus) achievement; *lyödä*
~ break (beat) a r.;
ennätysvauhtia at r. speed.
eno [maternal] uncle.
ensi first; *(tuleva)* next;
(aikaisin) earliest; ~ *aluksi* to
begin with; ~ *hetkestä asti*
from the first, from the very
beginning; ~ *kerralla* next
time; ~ *kerran* [for] the first
time; ~ *kerran, kun* the first
time (I saw her . .); ~ *käden
tiedot* first-hand knowledge; ~
sijassa in the first place; ~
työkseni luin . . the first
thing I did was to read . .;
~ *viikolla* next week; ~
vuonna next year. **-apu** first
aid; (~**asema** first-aid
station). **-arvoinen** *(tärkeä)*
vital, of the first importance.
-asteinen *(alku-)* primary.
-esiintyjä *(fem.)* debutante.
-esiintyminen debut. **-ilta** first
night. **-kertainen;** ~ *rikkomus*
first offence. **-kertalainen**
beginner, first-timer; first
offender *vrt. ed.* **-kesäinen** . .
[of] next summer. **-ksi** [at]
first, firstly; primarily; ~ —
toiseksi first [ly] — second
-[ly]; ~*kin* in the first
place, first and foremost, for
one thing; *(aluksi)* to begin
with. **-luokkainen** first-class,
first-rate; prime. **-mmäi|nen**
first; foremost, principal; *e-set
kaksi* the first two; *e-stä
kertaa* [for] the first time; ~
mitä näin . . the first thing I

saw; *hän nai -sen, joka tielle osuu* she'll marry the first [man] that comes.

ensin first, in the first place; at first; *ei ~kään* not at all; not in the least; *ei ~kään liian aikaisin* none too soon; ~ *mainittu* [the] first mentioned; [the] former. **-nä(kin)** first, firstly, in the first place; for one thing; *(aluksi)* to begin with; *(alkujaan)* originally.

ensi|rakastaja *teatt.* juvenile lead. **-sijaisesti** in the first place, primarily.

ent|eellinen ominous. **-eillä** forebode, foretoken.

enti|nen former, ex-, one-time; *(aikaisempi)* earlier, previous; ~ *kuningas* ex-king; *-seen aikaan* in the old days, in past times; *-stä parempi* better than [ever] before; *-seen tapaan* [in the same way] as before; *hinnan vähennys -sestään* a further fall in price; *on varjo -sestään* (she) is a shadow of her former self.

entis|aika olden times; past [times]; *~an (m.)* in the past, in days gone by. **-aikainen** old, ancient. **-elleen: jäädä** ~ remain unchanged; *saattaa* ~ restore, re-establish. **-ellään** as before, unchanged. **-estään** further. **-tys, -täminen** restoration. **-tää** restore.

entisyy|s past; *ulottuu pitkälle -teen* extends (goes) far back in time.

entsyymi enzyme.

entuudesta(an) in advance; *(ennen)* previously; *vrt. ennestään, vanhastaan.*

entä: ~ *hän* what about him? ~ *jos* what if ..? suppose [I were to go, *menisin*]; ~ *sitten* so what? what then!

enää more, further; *(kauemmin)* longer; *ei* ~ no more, no longer; *ei koskaan* ~ never more, never again.

epidemia epidemic.

epilogi epilogue.

episodi episode.

epistola epistle.

epuuttaa withdraw, take back, cancel.

epä|aistikas .. in bad taste. **-asiallinen** unbusinesslike. **-demokraattinen** undemocratic. **-edulli|nen** disadvantageous, unfavourable; unprofitable; *jklle* ~ *(m.)* to sb.'s disadvantage; *olla e-sessa asemassa* be at a disadvantage; *vaikuttaa e-sesti jhk* have an unfavourable influence on. **-edullisuus** disadvantage [ousness]; unprofitableness. **-hedelmä** accessory fruit. **-hieno** ill-mannered, unpolished, discourteous; ungentlemanly, unladylike; *(karkea)* rude. **-hienous** rudeness; indelicacy. **-huomio** oversight, slip; *~ssa* inadvertently, by oversight, absent-mindedly.

epähygieeninen insanitary.

epäilem|inen doubting. **-ättä** no doubt, without any doubt, undoubtedly, doubtless; unquestionably. **-ätön** undoubted, unquestionable, indubitable; unmistakable.

epäilevä suspicious, distrustful; sceptical; *olla ~llä kannalla* be doubtful (be in doubt) about .. **-isyys** suspiciousness, distrust [fulness].

epäilijä doubter; sceptic.

epäil|lä doubt; *(jkta jstk)* suspect (a p. of); *(ei luottaa)* distrust, be suspicious of; *(epäröidä)* hesitate; *alkaa* ~ *jkta* become suspicious of a p.; *häntä -lään murhasta* he is suspected of murder; *-en häntä valehtelijaksi* I suspect him to be (him of being) a liar; *en epäile, etteikö* I have no doubt that ..; *epäillen* with suspicion; doubtfully; *-tynä jstk* on suspicion of having (+ pp.) **-tävä** doubtful, dubious; suspicious.

epäily|(s) doubt; suspicion; *(arvelu)* misgiving; scruple; *epäilyksen alainen* suspect [ed], *s.* suspect; *saattaa epäilyksen alaiseksi* bring .. under suspicion; *siitä ei ole ~täkään* there is no doubt about that. **-ttävyys** suspiciousness; doubtfulness. **-ttävä** suspicious, suspect; doubtful; ~ *kunnia* dubious distinction. **-ttää** make .. doubtful; *minua* ~ I have my doubts (about); *asia* ~ *minua* the matter looks suspicious to me, I am doubtful about the matter.

epä|inhimillinen inhuman. **-isänmaallinen** unpatriotic. **-itsekkyys** unselfishness. **-itsekäs** unselfish; altruistic. **-itsenäinen** .. lacking in independence, dependent on others, not self-reliant. **-johdonmukainen** inconsistent. **-johdonmukaisuus** inconsistency. **-jumala** idol (~**nkuva** idol; ~**npalvoja** idolater; ~**npalvonta** worship of idols, idolatry). **-järjesty|s** disorder, confusion; disarray; *puhek.* mess: *e-ksessä* in disorder, out of order; *saattaa e-kseen* disarrange. **-kelpo** good-for-nothing. **-kiitollinen** ungrateful. **-kohta** fault, defect; drawback; *epäkohdat (m.)* bad conditions, ills, abuses, *(valituksen aiheet)* grievances, *(yhteiskunnalliset, m.)* social evils. **-kohteliaisuus** discourtesy, impoliteness. **-kohtelias** impolite, discourteous, rude, ill-mannered. **-kunnioittava** disrespectful. **-kunto** disorder; *joutua* ~*on* go wrong, get out of gear, break down; *olla -kunnossa* be out of [working] order. **-kuntoinen** .. out of order; useless; bad, poor. **-kypsä** unripe; *kuv.* immature. **-käytännöllinen** unpractical, *Am.* impractical. **-käytännöllisyys** lack of practical sense. **-lojaali** disloyal; ~ *kilpailu* unfair competition. **-looginen** illogical. **-lukuinen** innumerable. **-lukuisuus** countless number. **-luonnollinen** unnatural. **-luotettava** unreliable, untrustworthy. **-luotettavuus**

unreliability, untrustworthiness. **epä|luottamus** lack of confidence (in), distrust (of);. **-lause** vote of censure (on); *antaa* ~ *(m.)* pass a vote of no-confidence in sb. **epäluulo** suspicion; distrust; *joutua* ~*n alaiseksi jstk* be suspected of. **-inen** suspicious; distrustful. **-sesti** with suspicion, suspiciously. **-isuus** suspiciousness, distrust [fulness]. **epä|metalli** metalloid. **-miehekäs** unmanly. **-miellyttävyys** unpleasantness, disagreeableness. **-miellyttävä** unpleasant, disagreeable, displeasing, unattractive, distasteful. **-mieltymys** dissatisfaction (with sb., at sth.). **-mieluinen** undesirable; unwelcome, unwanted; *ks. ed.* **-mieluisasti** reluctantly, unwillingly. **-mieluisuus** unpleasantness. **-mukainen** not uniform, irregular, asymmetric [al]. **-mukava** uncomfortable; inconvenient. **-mukavuus** discomfort, inconvenience. **-muodostuma** deformity, malformation. **-muotoinen** deformed, misshapen. **-murtoluku** improper fraction. **-määräi|nen** indefinite, undetermined, indeterminate; nondescript; *(häilyvä)* vague, hazy, *(sanonta, m.)* woolly; uncertain; *e-seksi ajaksi* indefinitely. **-määräisyys** indefiniteness, vagueness, uncertainty. **-naisellinen** unwomanly, unfeminine. **-normaali(nen)** abnormal. **epäoikeudenmukai|nen** unjust, unfair, wrongful. **-suus** injustice; unfairness. **epä|oikeutettu** unjustified; unjustifiable. **-oikeutus** unjustifiableness. **epäolennai|nen** unessential; immaterial; *-set seikat* unessentials. **-suus** immateriality. **epäonni** bad luck. **-stua** fail, not succeed, have no success, be unsuccessful. **-stuminen** failure. **-stunut** unsuccessful;

-stuneesti unsuccessfully, without success; ~ *yritys (m.)* failure.

epä|orgaaninen inorganic. **-puhdas** unclean; *kem. ym* impure. **-puhtaus** uncleanness; impurity. **-pätevä** unqualified, imcompetent. **-realistinen** unrealistic. **-rehellinen** dishonest; deceitful, false; ~ *peli* foul play. **-rehellisyys** dishonesty. **-ritarillinen** unchivalrous. **-ritarillisuus** lack of chivalry.

epäröi|dä hesitate, be undecided, be irresolute, be in doubt, waver; *-den* hesitatingly. **-minen** hesitation, indecision, indetermination, hesitancy, wavering. **-mättä** unhesitatingly, without hesitation. **-vä** hesitating, wavering, doubtful; irresolute, undecided.

epä|selvyys indistinctness; obscurity. **-selvä** not clear, indistinct; *(sekava)* hazy, confused; obscure; *(jota ei voi lukea)* illegible. **-siisteys** untidiness. **-siisti** untidy; *(likainen)* dirty; *(huolimaton)* slovenly, sloppy, *(siivoton)* bedraggled. **-sikiö** monster. **-siveellinen** immoral. **-sointu** discord [ant note]; disharmony. **-sointuinen** discordant, dissonant. **-sopu** disagreement, discord; *olla epäsovussa* be at variance, disagree [with]. **-sopuinen** .. at variance, .. on bad terms; *ks. ed.* **-sosiaalinen** antisocial. **-sovinnainen** unconventional **-suhde, -suhta** disproportion. **-suhtainen** disproportionate; .. out of proportion. **-suopea** ill-disposed (towards); unkind; *(arvostelu ym.)* harsh, severe **-suopeus** averseness. **-suora** indirect; ~ *esitys* indirect speech. **-suosio** disfavour, disgrace; *joutua ~on* fall into disfavour; *(yleisön) ~ssa oleva* unpopular. **-suosiollinen** unfavourably disposed (towards), unfavourable. **-suosiollisuus** unfavourableness. **-suotuisa** unfavourable,

unpropitious; disadvantageous. **-suotuisuus:** *sään* ~ the unfavourable weather. **-symmetrinen** asymmetric [al]. **-säännöllinen** irregular. **-säännöllisyys** irregularity. **-säätyinen:** ~ *avioliitto* mésalliance.

epä|tahti: *-tahdissa* out of time; out of step. **-taiteellinen** inartistic. **-taloudellinen** uneconomic; uneconomical. **-tarkka** inaccurate, inexact; *kelloni on* ~ my watch keeps bad time. **-tarkkuus** inaccuracy. **-tasainen** uneven; *(jako)* unequal; ~ *luku* odd number. **-tasaisuus** unevenness, inequality. **-tavallinen** unusual, uncommon. **-terve** morbid. **-terveellinen** unhealthy, *(ruoka)* unwholesome. **-terveellisyys** unhealthiness, unwholesomeness. **-tietoinen** uncertain; dubious, doubtful.

epä|tietoisuus uncertainty; suspense, doubt; doubtfulness. **-todellinen** unreal; untrue to life. **-todennäköinen** unlikely, improbable. **-toivo** despair, desperation; despondency; *~n partaalla* on the verge of despair; *saattaa ~on* drive .. to desperation. **-toivoinen** desperate, despairing; *olla* ~ *(jnk suhteen)* despair of. **-toivoisuus** hopelessness, desperateness. **-toverillinen** uncompanionable. **-tyydyttävä** unsatisfactory. **-täsmällinen** inexact; unpunctual. **-täydellinen** incomplete; imperfect. **-täydellisyys** incompleteness; imperfection. **-usko** disbelief; *raam.* unbelief. **-uskoinen** unbelieving; incredulous, sceptical. **-uskottava** incredible. **-vakainen** unsteady, unstable; *(ihmisestä)* inconstant; *(vaihteleva)* changeable, variable. **-vakaisuus** unsteadiness, instability; changeableness; fickleness. **-varma** uncertain, not sure; *(turvaton)* insecure; doubtful; *(käsi)* unsteady; ~ *itsestään* unsure of oneself. **-varmuu|s**

uncertainty; insecurity; *e -den tunne* feeling of insecurity (uncertainty). **-viisas** imprudent., unwise, inadvisable; ill-advised. **-virallinen** unofficial. **-vire:** ~*essä* out of tune. **-yhdenmukainen** incongruous. **-yhtenäinen** disconnected; incoherent.

epäys refusal, denial. **epäystävälli|nen** unfriendly, unkind. **-sesti** unkindly. **-syys** unkind [li]ness, unfriendliness. **epäämä|ttömyys** indisputability. **-tön** indisputable, incontestable, unquestionable; *(-ttömän selvä)* unmistakable.

erakko hermit, recluse. **-elämä** secluded life. **-maja** hermitage.

ereh|dys mistake; *(epähuomiosta joht.)* oversight, slip; error; *erehdyksestä* by mistake, as a result of a mistake, inadvertently. **-dyttävä** misleading, *(petollinen)* deceptive, fallacious. **-dyttää** mislead; deceive, delude. **-tymättömyys** infallibility. **-tymätön** infallible; unerring. **-tyväinen** liable to err, fallible. **-tyväisyys** liability to err, fallibility. **-tyä** make a mistake, be mistaken (about), be wrong; *ellen -dy* if I am not mistaken; ~ *oikeasta ovesta* mistake the door; ~ *tiestä* take the wrong road; ~ *henkilön suhteen (kuv.)* misjudge a p.; ~ *laskuissa* misreckon, count up wrong; ~ *sanomaan* make a slip of the tongue ~ *välimatkasta* miscalculate the distance; *ei voi erehtyä..* there is no mistaking (what ought to be done, *oikeasta menettelystä*).

erheellinen misleading; erroneous, incorrect.

eri separate; *(-lainen)* different; ~ *syistä* for various reasons; ~ *maksusta* against extra payment; *olla ~ mieltä* disagree, *jkn kanssa* with, *jstk* about, on; *se on kokonaan ~ asia* it is quite another matter. **-arvoisuus** inequality. **-kielinen**

.. speaking a different language. **-koinen** separate; *(-tyinen)* particular, special; *(poikkeava)* extraordinary; *(omituinen)* peculiar; *-koisen sopiva* particularly suited, singularly adapted.

erikois|ala special line, speciality; ~*ni on ..* I specialize in .. **-artikkeli** *(sanomal.)* feature. **-asema** privileged position. **-esti** particularly, .. in particular, especially; *(nimenomaan)* specially, expressly. **-etu** [special] privilege. **-harrastus** special interest, hobby. **-kieli** jargon. **-kirjeenvaihtaja** special correspondent. **-laatuinen** [of] extraordinary [character], special. **-leima** peculiar characteristics. **-luettelo** special catalogue; specifications. **-luokka** special unit (in an ordinary school). **-lupa** special licence, special leave. **-lääkäri** specialist, special. **-opinnot** special studies. **-seikka** particular. **-taa** specialize. **-tapaus** separate case, *(poikkeus-)* exceptional case; *kussakin -tapauksessa* in each individual case. **-tarjous** special offer. **-tua** specialize (in). **-tuntemus** expert knowledge. **-tuntija** specialist (in), expert (on). **-uus** peculiarity; peculiar character; special feature.

erikokoi|nen: *(ovat) -sia* unequal in size, of different (various) sizes.

erikseen separately; individually; *(syrjään)* aside. **eri|laatuinen** dissimilar; heterogeneous; *-laatuiset aineet* different kinds of substances. **-lainen** different (from), dissimilar (to); *aivan ~ kuin tämä* entirely unlike (different from) this. **-laisesti** in various ways; *(toisin)* differently, in a different way, otherwise. **-laistua** become different; differentiate. **-laisuus** dissimilarity (to), difference. **erilleen** apart; asunder; *joutua* ~ *jstk* become separated (detached) from; *(toisistaan,* *m.)* drift apart; *panna* ~ set apart, put aside; *päästä* ~ *jstk* get rid of.

erill|inen separate; detached; ~ *tapaus* isolated case; ~ *huoneisto* self-contained flat. **-isosasto** *sot.* detachment. **-israuha** separate peace. **-ään** apart; *asua* ~ live apart; *he asuvat* ~ they have separated; *pysyä* ~ *jstk* keep aloof from.

eri|mielinen .. divided in opinion, .. not at one; *he ovat -mielisiä (m.)* they do not agree. **-mielisyy|s** difference of opinion, disagreement; *on olemassa e-ttä siitä, miten* opinions differ as to how .. **-muotoi|nen:** *e-sia* .. differing (varying) in shape, irregular.

erinomai|nen excellent, splendid, capital, fine **-sen** particularly; exceedingly, extremely; ~ *kaunis (m.)* most beautiful. **-sesti** excellently, very well; *voin* ~ I'm fine, I feel fine. **-suus** excellence.

erinäi|nen: *e-siä,* **-set** certain, some; *'e-siä kertoja* [quite] a number of times.

erinäköi|nen unlike [in appearance], dissimilar (to). **-syys** dissimilarity.

eri|oikeus privilege. **-painos** offprint, excerpt. **eripurai|nen** divided, disagreeing; .. at variance, .. at odds. **-suus** disagreement, discord; friction.

eriseurai|nen separatistic. **-suus** separatism.

eriskummalli|nen curious, strange; peculiar; queer, odd; extraordinary; bizarre; ~ *henkilö* eccentric. **-suus** strangeness, peculiarity; queerness, oddness, oddity.

erisnimi proper noun.

eristin insulator.

eristyneisyys isolation.

eristys isolation; *tekn.* insulation; (~**aine** insulating material; ~**nauha** insulating tape).

eris|täytyä keep aloof, keep apart, keep oneself to oneself.

-tää separate [from others], *m. kem.* isolate; *sähk., fys.* insulate; *(sulkea pois)* cut off; exclude.

erisuuntai|nen diverging, divergent. **-suus** divergence.

erisuurui|nen .. of different size[s]. **-suus** inequality [of size].

eritaso|liittymä, -risteys interchange; *ks. ali-, ylikäytävä.*

erite excretion, *(sisä-)* secretion.

eritellä analyse; *(erottaa)* set apart, separate; *(luetella)* specify.

eritoten particularly, especially; in particular; notably.

erittely analysis *(pl.* -yses); specification.

erittyä *fysiol.* be secreted.

erittäin very, exceedingly; in particular; *kukin* ~ each one separately (individually); ~ *hyvin* extremely well; ~ *kiintoisa (m.)* highly interesting. **-kin** *ks. ed.;* in particular; chiefly; *ks. semminkin.*

erittää *fysiol.* excrete, secrete.

erityi|nen particular, [e]special; *(eri)* separate, specific; *ei mitään -stä* nothing [in] particular. **-sesti** especially, particularly; *(varta vasten)* specially. **-skoulu** school for handicapped children. **-sluokka** special unit for handicapped children.

eritys *fysiol.* excretion, *(sisä-)* secretion. **-elin** secretory organ.

eritä part; differ; *mielipiteet eriävät* opinions differ; *eriävät mielipiteet* disagreement, divergence (division) of opinion.

eriuskolainen *a.* heterodox; *s.* dissenter, nonconformist.

erivapautu|s exemption; *kirk.* dispensation; *antaa jklle* ~ exempt a p. from; *-ksen saanut* exempt[ed].

erivärinen .. of a different colour.

eriyttää differentiate.

eriyty|ä become differentiated; *-nyt* differentiated.

eriävä separable; *(poikkeava)*

differing, diverging; different;
.. esitti ~n mielipiteen ..
expressed a dissenting
(dissentient) opinion.

ero parting, separation; (avio-)
divorce; (erotus) difference,
distinction; disparity [in age,
ikä-]; (virka-) discharge;
(eroaminen) resignation,
retirement; ~n hetki the hour
of parting; antaa ~ jklle
discharge, dismiss; ottaa ~
retire, resign; leave [one's
job]; hän on saanut ~n
miehestään she has divorced
her husband; päästä ~on jstk
get rid of.

eroa|maton inseparable.
-**mattomuus** inseparability.

eroavai|nen separable;
(erilainen) different. -**suus**
difference, divergence;
dissimilarity; discrepancy,
disparity.

ero|hakemus resignation; jättää
~ hand in one's r. -**(jais)juhla**
farewell. -**nhetki** hour of
parting. -**nnut** retired,
(puolisosta) divorced. -**npyyntö**
resignation.

eroottinen erotic.

eroraha severance pay.

ero|ta part, jksta from, jstk
with; separate (from); (ottaa
avioero) divorce [one's
husband t. wife], get a
divorce, (asumusero) separate;
(olla erilainen) differ from;
diverge; ~ kirkosta leave the
Church; ~ koulusta leave
school; ~ jstk (liitosta ym.)
withdraw from, resign one's
membership of; ~ työpaikasta
leave one's job; ~ virasta
resign, (asettua eläkkeelle)
retire; virasta eronnut retired;
he ovat eronneet they are
divorced. -**todistus** leaving
certificate, report [on
leaving school].

erotiikka sex; (eroottisuus)
eroticism.

erottaa separate, part;
(irrottaa) detach; (osata
erottaa) distinguish; (virasta,
työpaikasta) dismiss,
discharge, arkik. fire, sack; ~
koulusta expel from school,

(jksk ajaksi) suspend; hän ei
voi ~ hyvää pahasta he
cannot distinguish between
good and evil; en voi
silmilläni mitään ~ I
am unable to discern
anything.

erott|amaton inseparable;
(viranhaltijasta) irremovable.
-**amattomuus** inseparability.
-**aminen** separation, parting;
(toimesta) removal, dismissal;
(koulusta) expulsion; kuv.
discernment. -**autua** (näkyä)
stand out [clearly]; vrt.
erottua. -**elu** (tavaran) sorting;
(rotu- ym.) discrimination,
segregation.

ero|ttua (näkyä) be discerned
(distinguished), stand out;
(erota) differ from. -**tuomari**
referee, (tennis ym.) umpire.
-**tus** difference, distinction;
inequality; disparity;
erotukseksi jstk as distinct
(distinguished) from; ilman
~ta without distinction;
indiscriminately; ~**kyky**
discrimination). -**vuoro:** ~ssa
oleva retiring.

erä (tili-) item, entry; (määrä)
amount; (ainetta) quantity;
(tavara-) lot, consign-
ment, (osuus) share;
urh. heat, (tennis) set,
(nyrkk.) round, (jääkiekkoilu)
period; (maksu-) instalment,
part-payment; vähin erin in
small quantities, a little at a
time; tällä ~ä this time, for
the time being, for now.

erämaa wilderness, (korpi) the
wilds; (autiomaa) desert.

erän|kävijä hunter. -**käynti**
hunting, woodcraft.

eräs a. one, (tietty) a certain;
s. a [certain] person,
somebody; eräät muut certain
other people; eräänä päivänä
one day; tässä eräänä päivänä
the other day; eräässä
tapauksessa in one instance.

eräänlainen .. of a certain
kind; some kind of,
something of a .. ; e-laiset
ihmiset certain [kinds of]
people; vrt. jonkinlainen.

erään|tymispäivä day (date) of

maturity. **-tyä** mature, become due, fall due; *-tynyt* payable, *(vekseli)* mature; *-tynyt korko* accrued interest.
esi- *(yhd.)* pre-. **-historiallinen** prehistoric.
esiin forward; forth, out; *astua* ~ come forward, step forth; *pistää* ~ project, *(ulos)* stick out. **-huuto** call; *teatt. m.* curtain-call. **-pistävä** projecting, protruding. **-tuoda** *(lausua)* state, express. **-tyjä** performer. **-tyminen** appearance; *(käytös)* behaviour, bearing; occurrence; *(sokerin)* ~ *veressä* the presence of .. in the blood; *päättävä* ~ firm action, determined stand taken (by a p.).
esiintymis|kelpoinen presentable. **-tapa** *(seurustelu-)* manners. **-tottumus** experience of appearing in public.
esiintymä deposit.
esiintyä make one's appearance, appear; present oneself; *(käyttäytyä)* conduct oneself; *(jonakin)* pose (as), *(toimia)* act; *(sattua)* occur, happen; *(esiintyy, tavataan)* is met with, is found; ~ *edukseen* make a favourable impression; ~ *julkisesti* appear in public; ~ *jssk osassa* appear as .., act *(perform)* the part of; *saattaa* ~ *seikkoja, jotka* .. things may turn up that; *esiintyy selvemmin* stands out more clearly.
esi|isä ancestor; *~t (m.)* forefathers, forbears. **-kartano** ante-chamber. **-kaupunki** suburb. **-kko** cowslip, primrose. **-koinen** *a.* firstborn [child].
esikois|oikeus [right of] primogeniture; *raam. ym* birthright. **-teos** first work. **-uus** primogeniture; birthright.
esi|kristillinen pre-Christian. **-kunta** *sot.* staff; *-kunnassa* on the *s.;* (*~upseeri* staff officer). **-kuva** *(malli)* pattern, model, example; prototype; *(ihanne)* paragon; *ottaa jku ~kseen*

take a p. as a pattern (an example); *hyveen* ~ paragon (pattern, model) of virtue; *brittiläisen ~n mukaan* on the British model. **-kuvallinen** exemplary. **-kuvallisuus** exemplariness. **-lehti** *(liimaamaton)* fly-leaf. **-liina** apron; pinafore, *(lasten, leik.)* pinny; *kuv.* chaperon. **-liite** *kiel.* prefix.
esille forward, forth, out; to the front; *vrt. esiin; ottaa* ~ take (bring) out, produce; *(käsiteltäväksi)* bring up; *panna* ~ put out; *päästä* ~ stand out [clearly], be brought out, *(menestyä)* get on; *kysymys tulee* ~ the question will come up; *jättää (kaikki) esille* leave things about.
esillä on hand, *(käsillä)* at hand, ready; *(nähtävänä)* on view; ~ *oleva (tapaus)* the present case, *(asia)* the matter in hand (*t.* under consideration); .. *oli* ~ .. had been set out; *kysymys on* ~ the question is up for discussion, *(oikeudessa)* the question is before the court.
esi|lukija reader. **-maku** foretaste (of). **-merkillinen** exemplary. **-merkki** example, *jstk* of; instance; *(valaiseva)* illustration; *(lasku-)* problem, sum; *kuvaava* ~ *(tapaus)* a case in point; *esimerkiksi (esim.)* for instance, for example *(lyh. e. g.)*; *-merkin vuoksi* by way of an example; *näyttää jklle hyvää ~ä* set sb. an example; *olla ~nä* serve as an example. **-miehyys** leadership, chairmanship. **-mies** superior; *(johtaja)* chief; principal; *(työnjohtaja)* foreman.
esine object; thing; *(kauppa-)* article; *olla jnk ~enä* be the object of, be subjected to .. **-ellinen** concrete.
esi|opinnot preparatory studies. **-puhe** preface. **-rippu** curtain. **-rukous** intercessory prayer, intercession. **-taistelija** champion.

esitel|lä present; *(vieras ym)* introduce. **-mä** lecture; discourse (on). **-möidä** give (deliver) a lecture, lecture; read a paper (on). **-möitsijä** lecturer, reader of a paper.

esit|telijä introducer; presenter [of a case], person reporting on a case; civil servant who prepares matter for discussion and refers it to minister for decision. **-tely** presentation, introduction; **(~lehti(nen)** leaflet, brochure, prospectus). **-täjä** proposer; introducer; *(sekin kirjeen)* bearer. **-täytyä** introduce oneself.

esittää put forward, set forth, present; *(mainita)* give, state; express; *(näyttää)* produce, show; *(jku toiselle)* introduce to; *(esittelijänä)* refer .. [for decision]; *(puhe ym)* deliver; *(kiitos, anteeksipyyntö)* extend, offer; *(soitosta ym)* execute, render; ~ *(kysymys) keskusteltavaksi* propose (bring up) .. for discussion; ~ *kysymys* put a question to a p.; ~ *maksettavaksi* present .. for payment; ~ *mielipiteenään* advance the opinion that; ~ *näytelmä* perform (produce) a play; ~ *jtk osaa* play (t. act) a part; ~ *soittoa* perform [on the piano]; ~ *todisteita* submit evidence; ~ *vastalauseensa* raise a protest against; ~ *väärin* misrepresent; *edellä esitetyn nojalla* on the basis of what has been stated; *ketä kuva ~?* who [m] does the picture represent?

esitys presentation; *(kokouksen)* motion; *(näytös)* performance; *(puheen)* delivery; *(soiton ym)* execution; *vrt. tulkinta.* **-lista** agenda. **-taito** interpretative ability, [art of] description. **-tapa** way of presenting; rendering, *(suullinen)* delivery; *(kirj. ym)* style.

esi|vaalit primary [election]. **-valta** the authorities, the government. **-vanhemmat** ancestors, forbears.

eskaaderi squadron; fleet.

eskadroona [cavalry] troop.

eskimo Eskimo *(pl. -s).*

Espanja Spain. **e-lainen** *a.* Spanish; *s.* Spaniard. **e-n kieli** Spanish. **e-ntauti** Spanish influenza. **e-tar** Spanish woman.

esplanadi esplanade, avenue.

essee *(tutkielma)* essay.

este obstacle, obstruction; hindrance; impediment; *(pidäke)* check, restraint; *urh.* hurdle, fence; *vrt. aita, -juoksu; minulle sattui ~ I* was prevented from appearing (attending); *laillinen ~* lawful excuse; *~ttä ilmoittamatta* without explaining one's absence; *~en sattuessa Teille* in case you are prevented.

esteelli|nen having a lawful excuse; *(jäävi)* disqualified; incompetent. **-syys** incapacity, incompetence.

esteettinen [a] esthetic.

estee|ttömyys liberty; *(~todistus* licence). **-ttömästi** without impediment, unchallenged. **-tön** free; .. at liberty; ~ *todistaja* competent witness.

este|juoksu steeplechase. **-llä** [try to] hinder, raise difficulties; *(etsiä tekosyitä)* make excuses. **-ly** *(anteeksipyytävä)* excuse; *(tekosyy)* pretence, pretext; *(vastaväite)* objection. **-ratsastus** steeplechase.

estetiikka [a] esthetics.

esto *psyk.* inhibition. **-ton** uninhibited, free.

estyä be hindered, be prevented; *hänen matkansa estyi* he was prevented from making the trip.

estäminen prevention, obstruction *jne.*

estää prevent, hinder; *(olla esteenä)* block, obstruct, impede; preclude; *(lakkauttaa)* check; suppress; ~ *lankeamasta* prevent from falling; ~ *liikennettä* block (obstruct) the traffic; ~ *tekemästä jtk (m.)* keep a p. from [doing] a th., hold .. back.

etana slug; *(kuori-)* snail; *~n*

vauhdilla at a snail's pace.
etappi stage; *vrt. seur.* **-tie**
sot. supply line.
eteen to the front; *(tiellä)* in
the way; *(esille)* forward; *jnk,*
jkn ~ in front of . . . ,
before, at the front of;
pysähdyin ikkunan ~ I
stopped at the window; *älä*
mene ~i don't get in my
way; *katsoa ~sä* look ahead
(m. kuv.); ~ *katsomatta*
without looking ahead. **-päin**
ahead; on, forward [s],
onward [s]; *siirtykää* ~ move
along please, pass along (the
car, *vaunussa);* (*~pyrkivä*
ambitious, aspiring).
eteinen [entrance-]hall;
vestibule; *(porstua)* porch.
etelä south; *~ssä* in the south;
~stä from the south, from a
southerly direction; *~än* to
the south, southward [s], *jstk*
[to the] south of; *~mmälssä,*
-ksi farther [to the] south.
Etelä|-Amerikka South
America. **e-amerikkalainen**
South-American. **-Eurooppa**
southern Europe.
etelä|inen southern; south;
southerly; *-isin* southernmost.
-maalainen *a.* southern; *s.*
inhabitant of the south.
E~manner Antarctica. **-myrsky**
southerly gale. **-napa** South
pole; *~seudut* antarctic
regions, the Antarctic. **-osa**
southern part, south. **-puoli**
south side; *jnk -puolella, -lle*
[to the] south of . .
-rannikko south coast. **-tuuli**
south wind, southerly wind.
-valtiot *(U.S.A)* the Southern
States, the South; *E-valtioiden*
asukas Southerner.
etene|minen advance, progress,
(edistyminen) advancement,
headway. **-misliike** *sot.*
advance.
etenkin in particular,
especially, above all; *vrt.*
etupäässä; ~ *kun* especially
as, all the more [so] as.
ete|vyys proficiency, [great]
ability; *(taito)* skill. **-vä**
proficient, able; prominent,
distinguished, [pre-]eminent;

(mainio) excellent; *~mpi*
superior [to *kuin*]; *on*
muita paljon ~mpi is far
superior to the others; excels
the others. **-vämmyys**
superiority; eminence. **-västi**
in an able manner, ably;
excellently.
ethän *ks. -han, -hän;* ~ *mene*
sinne you are not going
there, are you?
etiikka *(siveysoppi)* ethics.
etiketti etiquette; *(nimilippu)*
label.
etikka vinegar. **-happo** acetic
acid. **-kurkku** pickled
cucumber.
Etiopia Ethiopia. **e-lainen** *a. &*
s. Ethiopian.
etnografi|a ethnography. **-nen**
ethnographic.
etruskilainen *a. & s.* Etruscan.
etsa|ta etch. **-us** etching.
etsi|jä seeker, searcher.
-kkoaika visitation. **-minen**
seeking, search [ing], quest.
etsimätön unsought [-for].
etsin *valok.* view-finder.
etsintä search, *(ratsia)* raid.
etsintäkuulu|ttaa post a p. as
wanted [by the police]; *-tettu*
wanted by the police.
etsiske|llä search for, hunt. **-ly**
search, hunt, inquiry.
etsivä detective; *yksityis* ~
Am. private eye; ~ *poliisi* d.
force.
etsi|ä look for, seek; search
(for); be on the lookout for;
(kirjasta, luettelosta) look up
(in); ~ *käsiinsä* hunt out,
seek out, *(rikollinen)* hunt
down; *ketä etsit?* who [m] are
you looking for; *etsimässä,*
-mään jtk in search (in quest)
of.
ette you don't; ~ *saa* you
must not.
ettei *(etten, ettet jne)* [so]
that . . not, so as not to . .
; *siltä varalta* ~ in case.
että that; *sekä hän* ~ *minä*
both he and I, he as well as
I; *siksi* ~ because.
etu advantage; profit; interest;
(hyöty) benefit; *se on minulle*
suureksi eduksi it is of great
advantage (benefit) to me; *on*

eduksi *jllek* is to the advantage of, is beneficial (profitable) to; *se olisi asialle eduksi* the matter would benefit (profit) by that; *valvoa ~aan* look after one's own interest; *omaa ~ani silmälläpitäen* in my own interest; *on Ranskan ~jen mukaista* it lies in the French interests; *muuttua edukseen* change for the better; *asia päättyi sinun eduksesi* the case was decided in your favour.

etu- front; *tiet.* anterior.

etu | **ajo-oikeus** priority, *Am.* right of way. **-ala** foreground; *~lla* in the f.; *astua ~lle* come to the front (the fore). **-anti** advance [-money]. **-hammas** front tooth; *tiet.* incisor. **-huone** anteroom. **-ilija** pusher, climber. **-illa** *(jonossa ym)* jump the queue.

Etu-Intia India.

etu | **istuin** front seat. **-jalka** front leg, foreleg. **-joukko** vanguard. **-järjestö** *l.v.* union. **-kansi** *(laivan)* foredeck. **-kumara:** *~ssa* bent forward. **-käpälä** front paw. **-käteen** beforehand, in advance; *~ maksettu* paid in advance; *prepaid; antaa ~* advance; *~ sovittu* [previously] agreed upon; prearranged; *~ kiittäen* thanking you in anticipation. **-lasti:** *~ssa* down by the head. **-liite** *kiel. ks. esi-*. **-lukko** padlock. **-lyhty** headlight. **-mainen** first, foremost; the forward [one]. **-masto** foremast. **-matka** start; *saada ~ jstk* get the start of; *10 yardin ~* a lead of 10 yards. **-merkintö** *mus.* signature. **-mus** front. **-nenä:** *olla jnk ~ssä* be at the head of .., lead; *asettua jnk ~än* place oneself at the head of, assume the leadership of; *jku ~ssä ..* leading the way. **-nimi** first name, Christian name. **-oikeudeton** unprivileged. **-oikeus** privilege; right of precedence, priority; *(hallitsijan ym)* prerogative.

-oikeutettu privileged; preferential; *e-tetut osakkeet* preference shares, preferred stock. **-osa** front [part]. **-permantopaikka** seat in the stalls. **-puoli** front; face; *(rahan)* obverse; *jnk etupuolella* at the front of, in front of; *tiet.* anterior (to). **-purje** foresail. **-pyörä** front wheel; (**-veto** front-wheel drive). **-pää** front; *~ssä* at the head (of); *(erittäin)* chiefly, mainly, principally. **-rivi** front rank; front (first) row; *~ssä (kuv.)* in the forefront; *~n miehet (kuv.)* leading men. **-rauhanen** prostate. **-ryhmä** interest group. **-sija** preference; precedence, priority; *asettaa jku ~lle* place .. first. **-sivu** front [side]; front page. **-sormi** forefinger, index [finger]. **-tavu** prefix.

etuus advantage.

etu | **vartio** outpost, advance guard; (**-kahakka** outpost skirmish; **-palvelus** picket duty). **-varustus** entrenchment; breastwork, bulwark.

etymologi | **a** etymology. **-nen** etymologic [al].

etäi | **nen** distant, remote. **-simpänä** farthest away, most distant. **-syys** distance; remoteness; *3 mailin etäisyydellä jstk* at a distance of 3 miles from. **-syysmittari** rangefinder, *tekn.* telemeter.

etää | **lle** far [away], far off. **-ltä** from [a] far, from a distance. **-mmällä** at a greater distance, farther [away]. **-ntyä** draw [farther] away.

eukko old woman.

eunukki eunuch.

Eurooppa Europe. **e-lainen** *a. & s.* European.

evakuoida evacuate; *evakko* evacuee; *vrt. siirtoväki.*

evankeli | **nen** evangelical. **-lioida** evangelize. **-sluterilainen** Evangelical-Lutheran. **-sta** evangelist. **-umi** gospel.

eversti colonel. **-luutnantti** lieutenant-colonel.

evp. *(eronnut vakinaisesta*

palveluksesta) retired from active service.
evä fin. **-llinen** finned, finny. **-jalka** flipper.
eväs: *eväät* box lunch, sandwiches, provisions; *vrt. seur.* **-kori** lunch- (tea-) basket. **-laukku** lunch-box,

(sotilaan) haversack. **-tys** *kuv.* instruction, directive; *(~keskustelu* preliminary discussion). **-tää** provide [with] food; *kuv.* instruct, brief.
evätä refuse, *(hylätä)* reject; ~ *pyyntö* decline a request.

F

fagotti *mus.* bassoon.
fajanssi glazed earthenware, faience.
fakiiri fakir.
faktori *kirjap.* foreman.
fak|turoida, -tuura invoice.
falangi phalanx.
falsetti *mus.* falsetto.
fanaat|ikko fanatic. -tinen fanatical. -tisuus fanaticism.
fanfaari fanfare.
fantas|ia fantasy; fancy. -tinen fantastic.
farao Pharaoh.
fariinisokeri brown sugar.
farisealai|nen *s.* Pharisee; *a.* Pharisaic [al]. -suus Pharisaism.
farmakologi pharmacologist.
farmari farmer. -auto estate car, *Am.* station wagon. -housut jeans.
farma|seutti dispenser. -seuttinen pharmaceutical. -sia pharmacy.
farmi farm.
farssi *(ilveily)* farce.
fasaani pheasant.
fasadi *(etupuoli)* front, facade, face.
fasisti *pol.* Fascist.
fasetti *(hiottu pinta)* facet.
fatalisti fatalist. -nen fatalistic.
feminiini, -nen feminine.
fenkoli *(-mauste)* fennel.
fenoli phenol.
feodaali *hist.* feudal. -järjestelmä, -laitos feudal system, feudalism.
fermaatti *mus.* fermata, pause.
fermentti *kem.* ferment.
fetissi *(taikaesine)* fetish.
fetsi fez.
fiasko fiasco, failure.
fideikomissi *l.v.* entailed estate.
fiikus india-rubber tree.
fiksu *ark.* clever, bright.
filantrooppi philanthropist. -nen philanthropic.

filee fillet, tenderloin.
Filippiinit Philippine Islands.
filmata film, shoot:
filmi film. -kamera cine-camera, *Am.* movie camera. -kasetti film cartridge. -rulla roll of film; film cartridge. -tähti film star.
filologi philologist. -a philology. -nen philological.
filosofi philosopher. -a philosophy; ∼n kandidaatti cand. phil., Bachelor of Arts (B.A.); ∼n maisteri mag. phil., Master of Arts (M.A.); -antohtori Doctor of Philosophy (Ph. D.). -nen philosophic [al].
filtraatti *kem.* filtrate.
finaali *mus.* finale; *urh.* final [s].
finanssi financial; ∼t finances. -mies financier. -tiede finance.
finiitti- *kiel.* finite.
finni pustule, pimple; ∼t (m.) spots.
Firenze Florence.
firma firm.
fisteli *lääk.* fistula.
flaami Fleming; ∼n kieli Flemish. -lainen *a.* Flemish.
Flanderi Flanders.
flanelli flannel.
flegmaattinen phlegmatic.
floretti foil.
fluor|i fluoride [s], *(alkuaine)* fluorine. -oida fluoridate.
flyygeli *mus.* grand piano.
foinikialainen Ph[o]enician.
folio *(alumiini- ym)* foil. -koko folio.
fone|ettinen *kiel.* phonetic. -tiikka phonetics.
forelli brown trout.
formaliini *kem.* formalin.
fosfaatti *kem.* phosphate.
fosfori *kem.* phosphorus. -happo phosphoric acid.

fraasi *(puhetapa)* phrase.
frakki dress coat. **-pukuinen** .. in evening dress.
fraktuura Gothic type.
frangi franc.
fregatti frigate.
frekvenssi frequency.
fresko fresko *(pl. -es)*.
friisi *(otsikko)* frieze. **-läinen** Frisian.
frotee terry cloth. **-pyyhe** Turkish towel.
fuksi freshman.

futuuri *kiel.* future [tense].
fuuga fugue.
fuusio fusion, *liik.* merger. **-ida** merge.
fysi|ikka physics. **-kaalinen** physical; ~ *hoito* physio-therapy.
fysiologi physiologist. **-a** physiology. **-nen** physiologic[al].
fyysi|kko physicist. **-nen** physical.
Färsaaret the Faroe Islands.

G

Galilea Galilee. g-lainen
  Galilean.
galleria gallery.
Gallia Gaul. g-lainen a. Gallic.
  s. Gaul.
gallupkysely Gallup poll.
galva|aninen fys. galvanic.
  -noida galvanize.
gamma: ~säteily g. radiation.
gaselli gazelle.
gastronomi gastronome.
geeni gene.
gemssi chamois.
generaattori generator.
genetiivi kiel. genitive,
  possessive [case].
Geneve Geneva; ~n järvi Lake
  of Geneva.
Genova Genoa. g-lainen
  Genoese.
geodeetti geodesist. -nen
  geodesic.
geologi geologist. -a geology.
  -nen geologic[al].
geometri|a geometry. -kko
  geometrician. -nen
  geometric[al].
gepardi cheetah.
germaani Teuton. -nen a.
  Teutonic, Germanic.
Gibraltarin salmi the Strait[s]
  of Gibraltar.
giljotiini guillotine.
glaseehansikkaat kid gloves.
glykoosi (rypälesokeri) glucose.
glyseriini glycerine.
glögi l.v. mulled wine.
gobeliini gobelin tapestry.

golf (-peli) golf; ~in pelaaja
  golfer. -housut plusfours.
  -kenttä golf links.
golf virta the Gulf-stream.
Golgata Calvary.
gondoli gondola; ~n kuljettaja
  gondolier.
gonggongi gong.
gootti Goth. -lainen Gothic.
  -laistyyli Gothic style.
Gotlanti, g-lainen Got[h]land.
graafinen graphic; ~ kuvio
  diagram, diagrammatic
  drawing, graphic representation.
grafiitti miner. graphite, black
  lead, plumbago.
gramma gramme, Am. gram.
gramofoni gramophone. Am.
  m. phonograph. -levy
  [gramophone] record, disc.
granaatti (kivi) garnet. -omena
  pomegranate.
graniitti granite.
gratinoi|da: -tuna au gratin.
greippi grapefruit.
grilla|ta grill, [spit-]roast;
  barbecue; -ttu pihvi steak.
grilli ks. paahdin; ulko~ (Am.)
  barbecue grill.
grogi whisky and soda, Am.
  highball.
groteski grotesque.
grynderi l.v. developer.
Grönlanti Greenland.
gynekologi gyn[a]ecologist. -a
  gyn[a]ecology.
Göteborg Gothenburg.

H

Haag The Hague.
haahka eider. **-nuntuva,** **~peite** eiderdown.
haaksirikko shipwreck. **-inen** [ship]wrecked. **-utua** be shipwrecked; *h-tunut alus* wreck.
haalari dungarees, overalls. **-työntekijä** blue-collar worker.
haale|a tepid, lukewarm. **-ta** cool [off]. **-us** tepidity.
haalia *(koota)* gather, scrape together, bring .. together, rustle up, *(värvätä)* drum up.
haalis|taa *(väriä)* bleach. **-tua** *(väreistä)* fade, become faded; *-tunut* faded, discoloured. **-tuneisuus** faded condition.
haamu ghost, apparition. **-kirjoittaja** ghost writer.
haapa aspen.
haara branch; *(oksa)* bough; *(joen ym)* fork; *(suunta)* direction; *~t* legs; *eri haaroille* in different directions. **-antua** *ks. -utua.* **-asento** standing astride. **-inen** branched; *kaksi ~* two-branched. **-konttori, -liike** branch [office]. **-kynttilä** branched candle. **-osasto** branch. **-pääskynen** swallow. **-rata** branch line. **-utua** branch *(us. off, out)*, ramify. **-utuma** branch, *(et. pieni)* ramification. **-utumiskohta** fork; *(kahtia)* bifurcation.
haaremi harem.
haarikka tankard.
haarniska armour.
haarukka fork; *(-purje)* gaff.
haasia drying-hurdle.
haaska carcass; *~t (m.)* carrion. **-aja** wasteful person. **-antua** be wasted. **-ta** waste; squander. **-us** wasting, waste; squandering.
haasta|a speak; *lak.* summon;

(kuv. & otteluun) challenge; *~ jku oikeuteen* bring an action against, sue a p.; *~ todistajaksi* call (summon) as a witness; *~ riitaa* pick a quarrel. **-ttella** interview. **-ttelija** interviewer. **-ttelu** interview.
haaste *lak.* writ, [writ of] summons; *kuv.* challenge; *antaa jklle ~* serve a writ on sb. **-lla** talk, chat [together], have a chat.
haava 1. wound; *(leikkuu-)* cut; *(ammottava)* gash; *(sääri-, maha- ym)* ulcer. **2.:** *tällä ~a* this instant, *(nykyään)* at present; *yhtä ~a* simultaneously.
haava|inen sore. **-side** dressing; gauze bandage. **-utuma** sore; ulcer. **-voide** ointment, salve.
haave fancy, fantasy, illusion. **-ellinen** dreamy; fanciful, fantastic. **-ellisesti** dreamingly, in a dreamy manner. **-ellisuus** dreamy (romantic) disposition. **-ilija** dreamer. **-illa** [day-] dream. **-ilu** [day-] dreaming, reverie. **-kuva** vision, illusion. **-mielinen** dreamy; sentimental.
haavi [hoop] net, *(perhos-)* butterfly net.
haavoi|ttaa wound; inflict a wound, *jkta* on; *~ kuolettavasti* wound fatally. **-ttua** be wounded, *jhk* in; *-ttuneet* the wounded. **-ttumaton** invulnerable. **-ttumattomuus** invulnerability. **-ttuva** vulnerable. **-ttuvaisuus** vulnerability.
haeskella search, seek, hunt (for).
haettaa: *haetti sen minulla* had me bring it, sent me for it.
hahmo shape, figure, form;

(ääriviivat) outline; *jnk ~ssa*
in the guise (shape) of ..;
ihmisen ~ssa in human guise.
-tella sketch, outline; trace
[out]. **-ttua** take shape.
hahtuva tuft; flock; *(pilven)*
wisp of cloud.
hai shark.
haihat|ella day-dream; *-televa*
erratic; fanciful. **-telija**
dreamer, utopian. **-telu**
[vapid] day-dreaming;
(häälyminen) shilly-shallying,
toing and froing; *nuoruuden*
~t vagaries of youth.
haih|duttaa evaporate, vaporize;
kuv. dispel; *~ jkn haaveet*
disillusion. **-dutus** evaporation.
-tua evaporate, [be]
volatilize [d]; *(hälvetä)* be
dispersed, be scattered; *suru*
-tuu sorrow is dispelled; *~*
muistista be obliterated from
memory; *sumu -tuu* the fog
is lifting (clearing); *~ kuin*
tuhka tuuleen vanish into thin
air. **-tumaton** nonvolatile.
-tuminen evaporation;
exhalation. **-tuva(inen)** volatile;
ethereal; *kuv.* fleeting,
passing, fugitive, evanescent.
-tuvaisuus volatility; *kuv.*
fugitiveness.
haikala *ks.* hai.
haikara heron, *(katto-)* stork.
haike|a sad; poignant. **-us**
sadness; poignancy.
haiku *(tuprut)* puff, whiff.
hailakka pale, faded.
haili Baltic herring.
haima *anat.* pancreas. **-neste**
pancreatic juice.
hairah|dus error, fault; slip;
nuoruuden ~ a youthful
indiscretion. **-duttaa** lead ..
astray, mislead. **-tua** commit
an error (indiscretion); err;
be misled.
hais|kahtaa smell, *jltk* of; *kuv.*
savour of. **-ta** smell, *jltk* of;
~ hyvältä smell good, have a
sweet smell; *~ pahalta* smell
bad, have an offensive smell,
(löyhkätä) stink; *~ palaneelta*
smell of burning. **-taa** smell;
(vainuta) scent; *-toin heti*
käryn I smelled a rat. **-tella**
sniff, *jtk* at. **-ti** [sense of]

smell. **-unäätä** skunk.
haitalli|nen injurious, harmful,
noxious; *(turmiollinen)*
detrimental; deleterious; *~*
vaikutus (m.) adverse effect;
terveydelle ~ injurious to
health. **-suus** injuriousness,
harmfulness.
haitata inconvenience; [give]
trouble; *(ehkäistä)* hamper,
impede; *(vahingoittaa)* hurt; *ei*
se haittaa (mitään) that won't
do any harm, it does not
matter! never mind! *työtä*
haittaavat puutteet the work
suffers from defects; *huono*
sää haittasi kilpailua the bad
weather spoilt (marred) the
match.
haitta disadvantage, drawback;
trouble; *(vahinko)* injury,
harm; detriment; *(esim.*
vamma) handicap; *olla jklle*
haitaksi put sb. to
inconvenience, give a p.
trouble. **-aste** degree of
disability. **-puoli** drawback.
-vaikutus ill-effect, injurious
effect.
haituva down, *vrt. seur.*
haiven *(karva)* hair, down;
(kasvissa) floss, *(persikan ym)*
fur; *vrt.* hahtuva.
haja *ks.* hajalla, -lle.
hajaannus dissolution,
disintegration; *(eripuraisuus)*
split, division, *usk. ym*
schism. **-tila** state of
dissolution; *~ssa oleva*
disorganized, disintegrated.
hajaan|nuttaa cause to scatter
(to disintegrate), cause a split
(a division). **-tua** break up,
dissolve; *(eri tahoille)* scatter,
disperse; *kokous -tui* the
meeting broke up; *äänet*
-tuivat the votes were
scattered. **-tuminen** breaking
up, dissolution.
haja|lla: *olla ~* lie [scattered]
about, be spread out; *~an*
oleva scattered, dispersed;
hiukset ~ with one's hair
brushed out (hanging down);
sääret ~ with one's legs
astride. **-lle:** *mennä ~* break
up, go apart; *(rikki)* go to
pieces; *ottaa ~* take .. apart,

take .. to pieces; *laskea,
päästää* ~ *(sot.)* disband,
demobilize. **-mielinen**
absent-minded; preoccupied.
-mielisyys absent-mindedness.
-n: *hujan* ~ *lattialla* lying
about on the floor. **-nainen**
scattered; *(puhe ym)*
incoherent; disconnected;
desultory. **-naisuus**
incoherence, disconnectedness;
(esim. opintojen) desultoriness.
-reisin astride. **-sijoitus**
decentralization **-taitteisuus**
astigmatism. **-tapaus** isolated
case. **-ääni** stray vote.
hajoa|maton indissoluble.
-minen breaking [up],
dissolution; disintegration;
scattering, dispersion; *kem.*
decomposition. **-mistila** state
of decomposition; *kuv.* state
of dissolution (of disintegration).
hajonta dispersion.
hajo|ta break up, dissolve.
-ttaa disperse, scatter; *(parl.
ym)* dissolve; *(repiä alas)* tear
down, demolish; *(kone)* take
to pieces; ~ *ainesosiinsa*
break up, decompose; ~
kokous break up a meeting;
~ *maan tasalle* level (raze) to
the ground; ~ *vihollinen*
scatter the enemy; ~
voimiaan dissipate one's
strength. **-ttajalinssi** concave
lens. **-ttaminen, -tus** *(esim.
parl.)* dissolution; dispersal.
haju smell; odour, *(hyvä)*
scent; *(löyhkä)* stink, foul
smell. **-aine** scent. **-aisti** sense
of smell. **-elin** organ of smell.
-hermo olfactory nerve. **-herne**
sweet pea. **-inen:** *jnk* ~ ..
with a (having a) .. smell;
miellyttävän ~
pleasant-smelling. **-lukko**
drain-trap. **-pihka** asaf[o]etida.
-staa *(parfymoida)* scent.
-suola smelling-salts, sal
volatile. **-ton** odourless; *on* ~
has no smell. **-ttomuus**
absence of odour. **-vesi** scent,
perfume. **-voide** pomade. **-öljy**
essence.
haka 1. hook; clasp; bolt; *ovi
on haassa* the door is

hooked. **2.** pasture [ground],
(pieni) paddock. **-nen** hook;
(sinkilä) staple; *-set (sulkeet)*
[square] brackets; *panna -siin*
hook, *(sulkeisiin)* put (enclose)
in brackets; *päästää -sista*
unhook. **-neula** safety-pin.
-risti, ~**lippu** swastika.
hakata hew; *(kiveä ym)* cut;
(pilkkoa) chop; ~ *maahan*
hew down; ~ *metsää* fell
trees; ~ *poikki* cut off, chop
off, *(oksia)* lop.
hake|a seek, look, *jtk* for;
search (for); *(käsiinsä)* hunt
.. up, look .. up; *(noutaa)*
fetch; *(virkaa ym)* apply for;
(oikeustietä) sue for; ~
lohdutusta seek consolation
in; ~ *muutosta päätökseen*
appeal the case; ~
saatavaansa sue .. [for a
debt]; ~ *jtk (ilmoittamalla)*
advertise for; *tulen -maan
sinua* I'll call (come round)
for you, I'll pick you up.
-misto index. **-mus** application
[for a job]; *(anomus)*
petition; *hylätä* ~ refuse an
application; *jättää* ~ make an
a.; (~**lomake** application form).
hakija applicant; *(pyrkijä)*
aspirant; candidate (for).
hakkai|lla *jkta* flirt with, pay
court to, make love to. **-lu**
flirting, flirtation.
hakkaus cutting, hewing;
(metsän) felling timber,
logging.
hakkauttaa have .. hewn (cut
down, felled).
hakkelus chopped meat.
hakku pick, pickaxe.
hakkuu logging, felling.
hako sprig of spruce (of pine).
-teillä off course, off the
track.
haksahdus blunder.
haku search, quest; *olla työn
haussa* be in search of work,
be looking for work; *mennä
puun* ~*un* go for wood. **-aika**
period of application.
-kelpoinen qualified (for).
-kelpoisuus qualification [s].
-paperit written application.
-sana headword. **-teos**
reference book.

halailu necking, hugging.
halata embrace, hug; *(haluta)* desire; long, yearn (for).
halava *(-puu)* bay willow.
haljeta split, cleave; crack, burst; *nauraa ~kseen* split one's sides [with laughter], burst with laughter; *sydän halkeaa* the heart breaks; *haljennut lasi* a cracked glass.
halkai|sematon unsplit. **-sija** *mat.* diameter; *mer.* jib. **-sta** cleave, split; slit.
halke|ama split, cleft, *(rako)* crevice, chink; *(pienempi)* crack; *tiet.* fissure; *(et. jäätikössä)* crevasse. **-illa** crack; *(iho ym)* chap.
halki through; *(yli)* across; *(kahtia)* in two; *(rikki)* asunder; *mennä ~* split, crack; *~ aikojen* through the ages; *~ elämäni* all [through] my life; *~ torin* across the marketplace; *~ vuoden* throughout the year; *puhua asiat ~* speak plainly, tell sb. in so many words. **-leikkaus** longitudinal section. **-nainen** cracked, cleft; broken. **-o: huuli~** cleft lip.
halko stick of [fire]wood, log; *halot* firewood. **-a** cleave, split; *(paloittaa)* cut up. **-kauppias** dealer in firewood. **-pino** pile of firewood. **-syli** *l.v.* cord of wood. **-tarha** wood-yard. **-vaja** wood-shed.
halla frost; *~n panema* damaged by frost, *(vikuuttaa))* nipped by frost. **-narka** sensitive to frost. **-nkestävä** frost resistant, hardy. **-yö** frosty night, night of frost.
hallava pale grey.
halli hall, *(kauppa-)* market hall; *(hylje)* grey seal.
hallinnollinen administrative; governmental.
hallinta *lak.* occupancy, tenancy; *jkn hallinnassa* under a p.'s control; *~an ottaminen* taking possession [+ seizin]. **-oikeus** right of possession.
hallinto administration; management. **-alue** administrative district. **-elin**

governing body. **-kustannukset** costs of administration. **-neuvosto** supervisory board,
hallit|a rule; *(kuningas ym)* reign (over); govern; control; dominate; *hän -see englanninkieltä* he has [a good] command of *(t.* he commands) the English language; *~ tilannetta* control the situation; *~ omaisuuttaan* be in control of one's property; *~ valtakuntaa* rule (govern) a state; *Yrjö VI:n -essa* during the reign of George VI; *hän ei hallinnut osaansa (tunteitaan)* he did not master his part (his feelings). **-seva** ruling *jne;* [pre]dominating; on *~lla paikalla* has a commanding position.
hallitsija ruler; sovereign; monarch. **-nvaihdos** change of ruler. **-suku** reigning house, ruling family; dynasty.
hallitus government; cabinet; *(esim. Nixonin)* [the Nixon] administration; *(yhtiön)* [board of] directors; *Suomen ~* the Finnish government; *Saigonin ~* the Saigon regime; *h-tuksen jäsen* cabinet-member; *mennä h-tukseen* enter the government; *muodostaa (uusi) ~* build a new government; *h-tuksesta (kruunusta) luopuminen* abdication. **-aika** reign, rule. **-järjestelmä** system of government; régime. **-kaupunki** seat of the government. **-kausi:** .. *-n -kautena* in the reign of. **-mielinen:** *~lehti* a paper supporting the government. **-muoto** [form of] government; *(valtiosääntö)* constitution. **-pula** cabinet crisis. **-puolue** party in power. **-suunta** government policy.
hallussa: *jkn ~* in a p.'s possession, *vrt. haltu.*
halonhakkaaja woodcutter.
halpa cheap, inexpensive; *kuv.* humble; *ostaa halvalla* buy cheap (at a low price, at a bargain); *halvalla* cheaply;

halp

myydä halvemmalla kuin
undercut a p.
-arvoinen .. of little value;
humble, lowly. **-arvoisuus** low
value; humbleness. **-hintainen**
cheap, inexpensive; ~
näytäntö performance at
popular prices. **-korkoinen:** ~
laina low-interest loan.
-mainen mean, base, ignoble;
(halveksittava) despicable.
-mielinen base-minded, mean.
-mielisyys baseness. **-sukuinen**
.. of humble origin.
halpuus cheapness; humbleness;
hinnan ~ lowness of the
price, the low price.
halstar|i gridiron. **-oida** broil.
haltija 1. occupant, holder;
possessor, owner; *~lle asetettu*
made payable to bearer; *viran*
~ holder of an office. **2.**
(-tar) fairy; *(paha)* goblin,
(maahinen) gnome; *(henki)*
genius *(pl.* genii), guardian
spirit.
haltio: *olla ~issaan* be
exultant, be in an ecstasy [of
joy] ; *joutua ~ihinsa* go into
ecstasies; *ks. -itua.* **-issaolo**
ecstasy. **-ittaa** thrill; make ..
wild with enthusiasm. **-itua**
become exalted, become
highly enthusiastic. **-ituminen**
exaltation.
haltu: *pitää hallussaan* have in
one's possession, occupy,
hold; *(hoidossaan)* keep in
one's care; *jkn ~un* into a
p.'s possession (keeping);
antaa jkn ~un hand over to,
deliver; commit to the care
of, entrust to, *(käsiin)* leave
in the hands of; *ottaa ~unsa*
take possession of;
(huolekseen) take over, take
charge of; *Jumalan ~un* God
be with you!
halu desire (for), *(kaipuu)*
longing (for), *(toivo)* wish;
(taipumus) tendency, bent,
inclination; *(himo)* lust;
(mieli-) eagerness; *~lla, ~sta*
with pleasure, willingly;
hänellä ei ole ~a lukea he
does not like to read;
minulla on hyvä ~ .. I have
a good mind to ... **-inen:**

jnk ~ desirous of, eager (to
do sth.); in the mood, in a
humour for. **-kas** willing; ready;
disposed, inclined (to);
erittäin ~ eager, anxious (to),
desirous; ~ *ostaja* prospective
buyer; *halukkain silmin* with
longing glances. **-kkaasti**
willingly, readily, gladly;
(himokkaasti) covetously.
-kkuus willingness, readiness;
eagerness.
halu|ta wish, want, desire; feel
inclined; *(kielt. & kys.)
lauseissa)* care for; *-aisin
tietää* I should like to know;
-atteko kupin teetä would you
like a cup of tea? ~
mieluummin prefer; *-aisin
mieluummin* I would rather
have (a cup of tea); *hän
tekee niinkuin -aa* he does as
he pleases; *aivan kuten -at*
just as you wish (choose);
mitä -atte? what do you
want? *haluttu* desired;
haluttua tavaraa goods in
great demand. **-ton** unwilling;
reluctant, disinclined;
(välinpitämätön) listless,
apathetic; *olen* ~ *menemään
sinne (m.)* I dislike to go
there, I don't want to go
there. **-ttomuus** unwillingness,
disinclination, listlessness,
apathy.
halva|antua be paralysed;
-antunut paralysed. **-ta**
paralyse. **-us** paralysis;
(-kohtaus) stroke, apoplexy,
(aivoveritulppa) cerebral
thrombosis.
halvek|sia despise, disdain;
scorn, look down upon. **-sija**
scorner (of). **-siminen**
contempt (for), disdain (of);
disrespect (of). **-sittava**
contemptible, despicable.
-sittavuus despicableness. **-siva**
scornful, contemptuous.
halvemmuus lower price.
halven|taa disparage; belittle;
(hintaa) cheapen, reduce.
-taminen disparagement,
detraction; reduction;
oikeuden ~ contempt of
court. **-tava** disparaging,
derogatory.

halveta cheapen, become cheaper.
hama: ~*an* unto; ~*sta* ever since.
hamara back (of an axe, a knife).
hame skirt; *(puku)* dress. **-kangas** dress-material.
hammas tooth *(pl.* teeth); *(rattaassa)* cog; ~*tani särkee* I have toothache; *vetää pois* ~ extract a tooth; *(vauva) saa hampaita* is cutting teeth; *hampaiden puhkeaminen* teething; *hampaiden oikominen* orthodontics; *ajan* ~ the ravages of time; *on joka miehen hampaissa (kuv.)* is on everyone's tongue. **-harja** toothbrush. **-jauhe** tooth-powder. **-kiille** dental enamel. **-kirurgi** dental surgeon. **-kivi** tartar. **-kuoppa** tooth-socket; alveolus. **-laitainen** *bot.* dentate. **-luu** dentine. **-lääketiede** dentistry; dental science. **-lääkäri** dentist; *-n ammatti* dentist's profession, dentistry. **-mätä** caries. **-pihdit** [dental] forceps. **-pora** dentist's drill. **-proteesi** denture. **-puikko** toothpick. **-rata** rack railway. **-ratas** gearwheel, cogwheel. **-rivi** row of teeth. **-särky** toothache. **-taa** tooth, indent. **-tahna** toothpaste. **-teknikko** dental technician, dental mechanic. **-tenkiristys** gnashing of teeth. **-tikku** toothpick. **-vesi** liquid dentifrice. **-ydin** pulp. **-äänne** *kiel.* dental.
hampaan|juuri root of a tooth. **-kolo** cavity [in a tooth]; *·minulla on jtk* ~*ssa häntä vastaan* I have an old score to settle with him. **-puhkeaminen** teething; dentition. **-täyte** filling.
hampaaton toothless.
hampaisto teeth; *(et. teko-)* denture.
hamppu hemp. **-köysi** hempen rope.
hamstrata hoard.
-han, -hän why; *onkohan hän kotona* I wonder if he is at home; *siellähän sinä olet*

why, there you are!
sinullahan on auto you have got a car, haven't you?
tunnethan hänet you know him, don't you?
hana tap; faucet; *(pyssyn)* hammer, cock.
hangata rub; chafe, gall; *kenkä hankaa* the shoe chafes; ~ *kirkkaaksi* rub up, polish.
hangoitella: ~ *vastaan* struggle against .., make resistance; be refractory.
hanhen|kynä quill. **-maksa(pasteija)** goose-liver (paste). **-marssi** single file. **-paisti** roast goose. **-poika** gosling.
hanhi goose *(pl.* geese), *(koiras-)* gander. **-lauma** flock of geese.
hanka(in) rowlock, oarlock.
hankal|a difficult; troublesome; inconvenient; ~ *käsitellä* awkward [to handle], cumbersome. **-asti** with difficulty. **-oittaa** render .. more difficult; hamper. **-uus** difficulty, trouble; inconvenience.
hankauma chafed place; abrasion.
hankaus rub[bing]; *(kitka)* friction *(m. kuv.).* **-äänne** spirant, fricative.
hankautua be rubbed, be chafed.
hanke plan, project; design; undertaking; *(valmistus)* preparation; *(aie)* intention, intent; *(vehkeily)* design; *olla hankkeessa lähteä* prepare to go, get ready to leave.
hanki crust of [frozen] snow, crust[ed snow]; *(kinos)* snowdrift; ~ *kantaa* the snow bears.
hankinta procuring, acquiring, acquisition; *kaupp.* delivery; *hankinnan laiminlyöminen* nondelivery. **-aika** date of delivery. **-kykyinen** capable [of delivering], strong. **-sopimus** delivery contract. **-tarjous** offer for delivery, tender.
hankki|a get, procure; *(varustaa)* provide, supply,

furnish (with), *kaupp.* deliver; *(itselleen)* acquire; obtain, secure; ~ *apua* find help; ~ *jklle auto* get a taxi for; ~ *lupa* secure a permit; obtain permission; ~ *rahoja (m.)* raise money; ~ *tietoja jstk* obtain information about; *hän on -nut omaisuuden* he has made a fortune; *hän hankkii (ansaitsee) hyvin* he gets good money by it; *hankkii sadetta* it looks like rain. **-ja** *kaupp.* supplier, *(ruoka-)* purveyor, caterer. **-utua** prepare oneself, get ready (for).

hanko fork, pitchfork.

hansa|kaupunki Hanse town. **-liitto** the Hanseatic league.

hansikas glove. **-kauppa** glover's.

hanuri accordion.

hapahko sourish, somewhat sour.

hapan sour; *kem.* acid; *happamen näköinen* sour-looking, surly; *olla ~ (kuv.)* sulk; *happamia, sanoi kettu* sour grapes [said the fox]. **-imelä** sour-sweet. **-kaali** sauerkraut. **-leipä** sour [black] bread.

haparoida grope, *jtk* after, for; fumble (for).

hapa|ta turn sour. **-ttaa** sour; leaven. **-tus** souring; *m. kuv.* leaven.

hape|ton free from oxygen. **-ttaa** *kem.* oxidize. **-ttua** [become] oxidize[d]. **-ttumaton** inoxidizable. **-tus** oxidization.

happa|maton unleavened. **-muus** sourness; acidity. **-neminen** turning sour.

happi *kem.* oxygen. **-kaasu** oxygen [gas]. **-laite** oxygen apparatus. **-nen:** *runsas ~* rich in oxygen. **-säiliö** oxygen container.

happo acid. **-inen** [containing] acid. **-isuus** acidity; *liika ~* hyperacidity. **-marja** barberry.

hapsi: *hapset* hair.

hapsottaa ks. *harottaa.*

hapsut tassels.

hapuil|la grope, fumble, *jtk* for; ~ *sanoja* fumble for words, be at a loss for a word; *-len* by feeling one's (its) way; *-eva* fumbling, groping; uncertain; *kuv.* tentative.

hara *(karhi)* harrow; ~*llaan* spread out.

harakan|pesä *kuv.* ramshackle house. **-varpaat** scrawl, »hen scratches».

harakka magpie.

harata harrow.

hara|va, -voida rake.

harha s. = *seur.; vrt. -luulo; yhd.* mis-. **-aistimus** delusion, hallucination.

harhaan astray; *ampua ~* miss [the mark]; *astua ~* make a false step, stumble, *(portaissa)* miss a stair; *johtaa ~* lead astray, mislead; *osua ~* miss; ~ *osunut* misdirected. **-johdettu** misguided, misled. **-johtava** misleading, delusive. **-nuttaa** mislead. **-tua** lose oneself; *-tunut* gone astray.

harha|askel false step, lapse, mistake. **-illa** stray, wander [about]; *(samoilla)* rove, roam. **-isku** misdirected blow, miss. **-kuva** distorted picture; *ks. seur.* **-kuvitelma** illusion. **-laskelma** miscalculation. **-luoti** stray bullet. **-luulo** wrong idea; illusion, delusion; *(eksymys)* error; ~*n vallassa* labouring under a delusion. **-näky** optical illusion. **-oppi** heresy. **-oppinen** *a.* heretical; *s.* heretic. **-oppisuus** heresy. **-päätelmä** fallacy. **-tie** wrong way, wrong path; *johtaa -teille* lead astray; *joutua -teille* get on the wrong track. **-usko** false opinion, misbelief. **-uttaa** mislead.

harja brush; *(vuoren ym)* ridge; *(aallon, linnun)* crest, comb; *(huippu)* top; *(hevosen)* mane.

harjaan|nus practice; exercise. **-nuttaa** train. **-tua** become trained, have practice (in); *-tunut* trained; practised, experienced, skilled. **-tumaton** untrained, unpractised, inexperienced. **-tuneisuus** training; experience.

harja|hirsi ridge pole. **-ksinen** bristly. **-nne** ridge. **-nnostajaiset** topping- out celebrations (after reaching roof level of building).
harjas bristle; *nostaa harjakset* bristle up.
harjata brush; ~ *pois* b. off.
harjoi|tella practise; *(näytelmää, osaa)* rehearse; ~ *kirjoitusta* practise writing; ~ *soittamaan pianoa* practise on the piano; ~ *jssak ammatissa* be learning a trade. **-telma** *taid.* study; sketch. **-ttaa** practise, exercise; carry on, pursue; do; *(jtk pahaa, m.)* commit; *(harjaannuttaa)* train, drill; rehearse; ~ *jtk ammattia* carry on (follow) a trade; ~ *kauppaa* carry on (do, transact) business, *(jnk)* engage in a trade, deal (in); ~ *opintoja* pursue [one's] studies; ~ *sotamiehiä* drill soldiers; ~ *vilppiä* practise cheating; ~ *väkivaltaa* commit an outrage, use violence. **-ttaja:** *jnk* ~ person engaged in ..; instructor, trainer. **-ttamaton** untrained, unpractised. **-ttava:** *tointaan* ~ *lääkäri* a practising doctor, practitioner. **-ttelija** learner of a trade; apprentice. **-ttelu** training, practice; (~**aika** period of training).
harjoitus practice, exercise; training; *(ase-)* drill; *teatt.* rehearsal. **-tehtävä** exercise; *mat.* example, sum.
harju ridge; *geol.* eskar.
harjus *zo.* grayling.
harki|nta deliberation, consideration; reflection; *tarkan -nnan jälkeen* on mature deliberation, on reflection *t.* close consideration; (~**kyky** judg[e]ment). **-ta** consider, deliberate, think [it] over, reflect upon; ponder, *(punnita)* weigh [in one's mind]; ~ *parhaaksi* consider (deem) it best; ~ *tarkemmin* think .. over, reconsider; *asiaa -ttuani* after thinking the matter over, on second thoughts; *olla*

-ttavana be under consideration; *-tseva* reflecting; prudent, circumspect. **-tsematon** unconsidered; inconsiderate; heedless, rash. **-tsemattomasti** without considering, heedlessly. **-ttu** premeditated, deliberate; *hyvin* ~ well-considered; *huonosti* ~ ill-advised, ill-judged. **-tusti** deliberately, with deliberation.
harkki drag; grapnel.
harkko bar; [gold, silver] ingot, bullion; *(rauta-)* pig. **-rauta** pig-iron.
harmaa grey, *Am.* gray. **-haikara** heron. **-hapsinen** grey-haired. **-nkirjava** mottled grey. **-ntua** turn grey. **-päinen** greyhaired; grizzled.
harma|htava greyish, grizzly. **-us** greyness.
harmi annoyance, vexation; trouble; displeasure; *olla* ~*ssaan* feel vexed. **-llinen** annoying, vexatious, provoking; *sepä -llista* how annoying! what a nuisance! **-llisuus** vexatiousness; annoyance. **-stua** be annoyed, be vexed, feel indignant *(jklle* with, *jhk* at). **-stuminen** indignation, resentment. **-tella** fret (about). **-ton** harmless. **-ttaa** annoy, vex; *(ärsyttää)* provoke; *minua -tti* I was annoyed at [him *t.* his saying so]. **-ttomuus** harmlessness.
harmonia harmony.
harmoni harmonium. **-kka** accordion.
harott|aa: *-ava tukka* straggling hair.
harp|ata stride; *(loikata)* leap.
harpikko set of drawing instruments.
harppaus stride; leap.
harppi [pair of] compasses; dividers.
harppu harp.
harppu|una, -noida harpoon.
harpun|kieli harp string. **-soittaja** harpist.
harras devoted; warm, fervent; *usk. ym* devout; *(kiihkeä)* ardent; ~ *kuulija* earnest listener; ~ *rukous* fervent prayer; ~ *toivomus* ardent

wish. **-taa** take an interest,
be interested (in); ~ *urheilua*
go in for sports; ~ *kansan
parasta* devote oneself to
(look after) the best interests
of the people; *asiaa -tavat* all
those interested; *alkaa ~ jtk*
become interested in, take to.
-te hobby. **-telija** amateur,
dilettante. **-tus** interest, *jhk*
in; *(erikois-, m.)* hobby;
kirjalliset -tukset literary
pursuits; *hänellä on laaja
~piiri* his interests range
widely.
harsia baste, tack.
harso gauze, *(kasvo-)* veil
-kangas gauze. *(suru- ym)*
crepe.
harta|asti earnestly; ardently,
devoutly; with great interest.
-udenharjoitus devotions.
hartaus devotion; earnestness;
warmth, fervour. **-hetki**
prayers, devotions. **-kirja**
religious book. **-kirjallisuus**
devotional literature. **-kokous**
prayer-meeting.
hartei|lla on [one's] shoulders.
-lta: *karistaa vastuu ~an*
shuffle off responsibility.
harteva *ks. hartiakas.*
harti|a shoulder; *siirtää vastuu
toisten -oille* shift the blame
to other shoulders.
hartia|huivi shawl. **-kas** broad
-shouldered.
hartsata rosin.
hartsi resin; *(kova)* rosin.
-mainen resinous.
harva sparse, not dense; *(~t)*
few; *(tukka m.)* thin; *(kangas)*
loose, coarse; ~ *se päivä*
nearly every day; *olla ~ssa*
be scarce, be rare; *puut ovat
~ssa* the trees are far apart;
sellaisia miehiä on ~ssa (m.)
such men are few and far
between; *~an (hitaasti)*
slowly; *~an asuttu* sparsely
(thinly) populated; *~kseen*
slowly; at long intervals; now
and then; *(yksitellen)* one by
one.
harvainvalta oligarchy.
harva|kudontainen coarsely
woven. **-lukuinen** .. few
(small) in number; ~ *yleisö*

the *(t. a)* small attendance.
-lukuisuus small number,
paucity. **-puheinen** taciturn,
uncommunicative; ~ *mies* a
man of few words. **-puheisuus**
taciturnity.
harve|neminen thinning [out].
-nnus thinning [out]; *kirjap.*
spacing out. **-ntaa** make ..
thinner; *(metsää ym)* thin;
kirjap. space [out]. **-ta** get
thinned, thin [out];
(lukumäärältään) be reduced
in number.
harvinai|nen rare, uncommon,
unusual; infrequent; *-sen suuri*
unusually (exceptionally) large.
-suus rareness, rarity;
infrequency; *(esine)* rare thing.
curiosity.
har|voin seldom, rarely; ~
tapahtuva [of] infrequent
[occurrence]; *harvemmin* less
commonly, less frequently.
-vuus thinness; scarcity.
hasis hash[ish].
hassahtava not in his (her)
right senses, not all there,
dotty, cracked.
hassu silly, foolish; crazy, mad.
-nkurinen funny, comical,
droll; ludicrous. **-nkuriisuus**
ludicrousness, funniness. **-sti**
foolishly; *ks. hullusti.* **-tella**
act the fool, play the fool;
play about. **-ttelu** foolery,
clowning. **-us** foolishness.
hatar|a flimsy, poorly
constructed, unsubstantial;
ramshackle [house]; *kuv.*
vague; *(löyhä)* loose; ~ *muisti*
poor memory; ~ *puolustus*
flimsy excuse; *~t tiedot*
superficial knowledge. **-uus**
flimsiness; looseness;
vagueness; *(heikkous)* poorness.
hattara wisp of cloud, cloudlet.
hattu hat; *nostaa ~aan* raise
one's hat; *panna ~ päähänsä*
put on one's hat. **-kauppa**
(naisten) milliner's, *(miesten)*
hatter's. **-rasia** hatbox. **-tukki**
[hat-] block.
hatun|koppa crown of a hat.
-lieri brim of a hat. **-tekijä**
hatter.
haudan|kaivaja grave-digger,
sexton. **-ryöstäjä** grave-robber.

-takainen: ~ *elämä* life beyond.
haudata bury, inter.
haud|e *(kääre)* compress; *(lämmin)* fomentation; *(puuro-)* poultice; *(vesi)* bath. **-ella** bathe [with hot water]; apply hot fomentations (to). **-onta** bathing; fomentation; *(munien)* brooding, *(koneessa)* incubation. **-uttaa** *(ruokaa)* stew.
hauislihas biceps.
haukahtaa yelp.
haukata bite, take a bite; snap (at).
hauki pike; *(nuori)* pickerel.
haukka hawk; falcon.
-metsästys hawking, falconry.
-metsästäjä falconer.
haukkoa: ~ *henkeään* gasp [for breath], pant; ~ *ilmaa* gasp for air.
haukku bark[ing]. **-a** bark, *jkta* at, *(kimakasti)* yelp, *(ulvoen)* bay; *kuv.* abuse; ~ *pataluhaksi* haul sb. over the coals, heap abuse (upon); *koirat -ivat kuin hullut* the dogs barked their heads off. **-masana:** ~*t* abuse, invective. **-manimi** nickname.
hauko|tella yawn. **-tus** yawn[ing]. **-tuttaa** make .. yawn; *minua* ~ I feel like yawning.
haukunta bark[ing]; yelp[ing].
hauli: ~*t* shot, *(isot)* buckshot. **-kko** shotgun; fowling-piece.
haura|s brittle; fragile, *kuv. ym* frail. **-us** brittleness, fragility.
haureelli|nen lewd. **-suus** lewdness, licentiousness.
haureus lewdness, immorality; *raam.* adultery.
hauska pleasant, pleasurable, delightful; jolly; amusing; ~ *kuulla* I am [very] glad (pleased) to hear it; *meillä oli hyvin* ~*a* we had a good time; *pidä* ~*a* have a nice time, enjoy yourself; ~*a joulua* merry Christmas! **-nnäköjnen** good-looking, handsome. **-sti** pleasantly, agreeably.
hausku|ttaa amuse, entertain.

-tus amusement, diversion, entertainment.
hauskuus pleasure, enjoyment; *(huvi)* amusement, fun, merriment.
hauta grave; tomb; *haudan hiljaisuus* deathlike silence; *Pyhä* ~ the Holy Sepulchre. **-amaton** unburied. **-antua** be buried (in). **-holvi** [burial] vault, tomb; crypt.
hautajais|et funeral *(-issa* at), burial. **-puhe** funeral oration. **-saatto** funeral procession.
hauta|kammio sepulchre. **-kappeli** cemetery chapel; *(ensim. sairaalan)* mortuary; *(krypta)* crypt. **-kirjoitus** inscription on a tombstone. **-kivi** tombstone, gravestone, headstone [on sb.'s grave]. **-kumpu** [burial] mound. **-patsas** monument.
hautaus burial, interment. **-apu** aid towards funeral expenses; (~**kassa** burial fund). **-kustannukset** funeral expenses. **-maa** cemetery, *(vanhempi)* burial-ground. **-menot** burial service, funeral rites. **-toimisto** undertaker's, firm of undertakers, *Am. m.* mortician.
hautautua be buried (in).
hautoa bathe, apply [hot] compresses to; foment; *(linnuista)* sit on eggs, brood; *(esille)* hatch; ~ *kostoa* harbour thoughts of revenge; ~ *mielessään* brood (on, over), ponder (over).
hautoma|aika brooding time, incubation period. **-koje** incubator.
hautua *lääk.* be fomented, be bathed; *(ruoka)* steam, stew, *(tee)* draw.
havah|duttaa wake, [a]rouse. **-tua** awake, wake up. **-tuminen** awakening.
Havaijin saaret the Hawaiian Islands.
havainno|itsija observer. **-llinen** graphic; clear, lucid **-llistaa** make clear; illustrate. **-llisuus** clearness, clarity.
havainto perception; *(huomio)* observation; finding. **-kyky**

perceptive faculty. **-opetus**
[teaching by] object-lessons.
-virhe error in observation.
-välineet audio-visual aids.

havait|a observe; perceive;
(huomata) notice, note, see,
become aware of; discover;
realize; *-tiin tarpeelliseksi* was
found necessary. **-tava**
perceptible; noticeable.

havit|ella desire; *(tavoitella)*
aspire (to, after), hanker
(after, for), be after [sb.'s
money]. **-telu** aspiration (for).

havu: *kuusen ~t* spruce twigs.
-metsä coniferous forest.
-nneula needle [of fir]. **-puu**
conifer.

he they; *heidät, heitä* them;
heille to them; for them;
heiltä from them; *heistä* of
(t. about) them.

Hebridit the Hebrides.

hede *bot.* stamen. **-kukka**
staminate *(t.* male) flower.

hedelmä fruit; *~t* fruit;
(joskus) fruits; *~stä puu
tunnetaan* a tree is known by
its fruit. **-hyytelö** jelly.
-kauppa fruit shop, [the]
fruiterer's. **-kauppias** fruiterer.
-llinen fertile, *kuv. m.*
fruitful; *(maaperä)* rich,
productive. **-llisyys** fruitfulness,
fertility. **-nkorjuu** fruit harvest.
-nraakile unripe fruit. **-puu**
fruit-tree. **-puutarha** orchard.
-salaatti fruit salad. **-sokeri**
fructose. **-säilykkeet** preserved
fruit, tinned *(Am.* canned)
fruit. **-ttömyys** infertility;
sterility. **-tön** infertile;
unfruitful; *(maa m.)* barren;
kuv. fruitless. **-viljelys**
fruit-growing.

hedelmöi|dä bear fruit. **-minen**
fructification; *(viljan)*
blossoming. **-ttää** fertilize;
fecundate; *kuv.* inspire,
stimulate; *h-ävä (kuv.)*
inspiring, fruitful. **-tyminen,**
-tys *zo., bot.* fertilization,
(naisesta) conception. **-tyä** be
fertilized, *(naisesta)* conceive.

hegemonia hegemony.

hehke|ys bloom, blossom,
(uhkeus) luxuriance. **-ä**
blooming, fresh.

hehku blow, *kuv. m.* ardour,
fervour. **-a** glow; *(esim.
raudasta)* be red-hot; *hänen
kasvonsa -ivat vihasta* his
face glowed (was flushed)
with anger. **-lamppu**
incandescent lamp (bulb). **-ttaa**
heat to incandescence, bring
.. to a red heat; *tiet.* ignite;
-tettu viini mulled wine. **-va**
glowing; *(esim. rauta)* red-hot;
kuv. burning, ardent, fiery;
(hiilet) live. **-vasti** glowingly;
ardently.

hehtaari hectare (2.471 acres).

hehtolitra hectolitre (26.42
gallons).

hei hallo! hello! *Am.* hi!

heid|än their; theirs. **-ät** *ks.
he; jos näen ~* if I see them.

heijas|taa throw back; reflect;
(säteillä) radiate. **-te** *lääk.*
reflex, jerk. **-tin** reflector;
(pimeässä, tiellä käyt.)
luminous badge. **-tua** be
reflected. **-tuma** reflex.

heijastus reflection, reflex. **-koje**
projector. **-kulma** angle of
reflection. **-liike** reflex action.

heike|ntyä *ks. heiketä.* **-ntää**
weaken; *(ruum. m.)* debilitate,
enfeeble; *(huonontaa)* impair.
-tä weaken, grow weaker;
lose strength; abate, die
down; decrease; *tuuli
heikkenee* the wind is
dropping.

heikkeneminen weakening;
decline; *(tuulen ym)*
abatement.

heikko weak; *(ääni ym)* faint;
(voimaton) feeble, infirm;
(hento) frail, delicate; slight;
(kehno) poor; *heikompi jkta
(kyvyiltään)* inferior to; *~
puoli* failing, shortcoming,
weak point; *~ terveys*
delicate (weak, poor) health;
~ tuuli light wind; *heikot
perusteet* slender grounds.
-hermoisuus neurasthenia.
-lahjainen .. of limited
intelligence. **-mielinen** moron.
-mielisyys moronism.
-näköinen weak(poor)-sighted.
-näköisyys poor sight.
-rakenteinen of slender
build. **-tahtoinen** weak-minded.

heikko|us weakness; feebleness, infirmity; *(et. äkillinen)* faintness; *(hentous)* frailty; *(luonteenvika)* weak point, foible, failing; *yleinen* ~ general debility. **-virta** low-voltage current.
heikommuus inferiority.
heikon|taa, -tua *ks. heikentää*
heikäläinen one of them.
heila girl- (boy-)friend, sweetheart.
heilah|della sway, swing; fluctuate; *fys.* oscillate. **-dus** swing; *(heilurin)* oscillation. **-taa** sway, swing. **-telu** oscillation; fluctuation.
heilimöidä *(ruis)* be in flower.
hei|lle *ks. he; kirjoitin heille* I wrote them [a letter]. **-ltä** *ks. he.*
heilua swing, *(huojua)* sway, rock *(m. mer.); (heilurin tap.)* oscillate.
heiluri pendulum; ~*n lyönti* stroke of a p. **-liike** oscillation.
heiluttaa swing, sway; rock; *(kättä)* wave; *(häntää)* wag; whisk.
heimo tribe; *(Skotl.)* clan; *(zo. bot. ym)* family; *(rotu)* race. **-kuntaisuus** tribalism. **-lainen** kinsman; *(suku-)* relative; *-laiset* kinsfolk. **-laisuus** kinship. **-npäällikkö** tribal chief, chieftain. **-sota** tribal war.
heimoushenki spirit of kinship.
heinikko grass; *(niitty)* meadow.
heinä hay; *(ruoho)* grass; *olla* ~*ssä* be hay-making, make hay. **-hanko** hay-fork, pitchfork. **-kasvi** grass. **-kuu** July. **-lato** haybarn. **-mies** haymaker. **-niitty** hayfield. **-nteko** haymaking; *(~aika* haymaking time, mowing time). **-nuha** hay fever. **-ruko** haystack, hayrick. **-seiväs** haypole. **-sirkka** grasshopper; *(iso)* locust. **-suova** stook of hay.
heisimato tapeworm.
heistä *ks. he.*
heitellä throw, fling; toss [a ball, *palloa*]*;* ~ *sinne tänne* throw about; *olla jnk*

heiteltävänä be a plaything of . .
heitte|ille: *jättää* ~ abandon, *(uhri, m.)* leave the scene of the accident. **-lehtiä** toss, *(auto, l.v.)* skid, swerve.
heittiö scoundrel, rascal.
heitto throw, fling, cast[ing], toss. **-ase** missile. **-istui|n** ejector-seat; *pelastautui -men avulla (m.)* managed to eject his catapult seat. **-keihäs** javelin. **-merkki** apostrophe. **-pussi** pushover. **-vapa** spinning rod. **-vuoro** throw.
heittäytyä throw oneself; *(syöksyä)* plunge (into); *(antautua)* give oneself up [to despair]; ~ *(juomaan yms.)* indulge in [drink], take to . .
heittää throw; cast; fling; toss; *(singota)* hurl; ~ *arpaa* cast lots, *(rahalla)* toss up; ~ *henkensä* draw one's last breath, pass away; ~ *hyvästi jklle* take leave of; ~ *jkta kivellä päähän* throw a stone at a p.'s head; ~ *mielestään* dismiss; ~ *pois* throw away, dispose of, discard; ~ *sikseen* let be, let alone, *(toivo)* abandon; ~ *vetensä* make (pass) water.
heitä *ks. he; en nähnyt* ~ I didn't see them.
heiveröinen very slender, weak [-looking], puny.
heksametri hexametre.
hekuma voluptuousness, lust. **-llinen** voluptuous, lascivious.
hekumoi|da indulge in sensual pleasure, indulge oneself (in); *(jllak)* gloat over, revel in. **-tsija** voluptuary; sensualist.
hela ferrule; ~*t* mountings, *(oven ym)* fittings.
helakan|punainen scarlet. **-sininen** bright blue, clear blue.
helatorstai *(t.-lauantai)* Ascension Day.
heleys brightness, clearness.
heleä bright, clear. **-ääninen** clear-voiced.
Helgolanti Heligoland.
helikopteri helicopter. **-satama, -asema** heliport, helidrome.
heli|nä tinkle; jingle. **-stellä**

jingle, tinkle; jangle. **-stin**
rattle; *(kolmio)* triangle. **-stä**
clink; jingle, tinkle; *olla*
-semässä be up against it, be
at one's wits' end; *-sevä*
vaski sounding brass.
helk|kyä ring, sound;
(kielisoittimesta) twang. **-ytellä**
twang; ~ *hiljaa harppuaan*
touch one's harp. **-ytys**
twang [ing].
hella range, stove; *sähkö~*
(m.) electric cooker.
helle heat, hot weather. **-aalto**
heat wave. **-kypärä** [sun- *t.*
tropical] helmet.
helleeni Hellene. **-nen** Hellenic.
hellitellä fondle, pet; coddle.
hellittä|mättömyys persistency,
perseverance. **-mätön**
persistent; persevering; *(luja)*
firm; insistent; untiring.
helli|ttää loosen, slacken, relax;
(päästää) let go; ease [up];
(antaa perään) yield; ~
otteensa let go (release) one's
hold. **-tä** come loose, loosen,
slacken, relax; *(antaa perään)*
give way, yield.
helliä [fondly] cherish; fondle.
helluntai Whitsuntide; *~n*
aikana at W. **-lainen** *usk.*
Pentecostal. **-päivä** Whit
Sunday.
hell|yttää soften, make ..
relent; ~ *itkemään* move to
tears. **-yys** tenderness;
affection.
hellä tender; affectionate; *(arka*
m.) sore; *jalkani tuntuu ~ltä*
my foot is tender. **-kätinen:**
hän on ~ he has a gentle
touch (a light hand).
-sydäminen tender-hearted.
-sydämisyys tender-heartedness.
-tunteinen tender; sensitive.
-tunteisuus tenderness;
sensitiveness. **-varainen** gentle;
careful; *(hieno-)* considerate.
-varoin gently; *(varovasti)*
with care.
helma hem; *(syli)* lap; *luonnon*
~ssa out in the open. **-synti**
besetting sin.
helmeillä *(juoma)* sparkle;
bubble.
helmenpyynti pearl fishery.
helmi pearl; *(lasi-, puu- ym.)*

bead. **-kana** guinea-fowl
(-hen). **-kirjailu** bead-work.
-kuu February. **-nauha** pearl
necklace, string of pearls;
[string of] beads. **-simpukka**
pearl-oyster. **-taulu** abacus.
-äinen mother-of-pearl.
-äisnappi pearl button.
helottaa shine.
helpo|sti easily; readily;
without difficulty; *mitä*
-immin with greatest ease; ~
sulava easily digested,
digestible; ~ *tunnettava*
recognizable. **-ttaa** make
easier, facilitate; *(huojentaa)*
ease; *(kipua)* soothe, relieve;
~ *hintaa* moderate the price;
sade ~ the rain is lessening;
tuska ~ the pain is abating.
-ttua be facilitated; be
relieved; abate. **-tus** relief;
alleviation, remission; *(hinnan)*
reduction; *-tuksen huokaus* a
sigh of relief.
helppo easy; *(halpa)* cheap,
low; *päästä helpolla* get off
easily. **-heikki** cheapjack.
-hintainen *et. kuv.* cheap, *vrt.*
huokea-. **-käyttöinen** easy to
operate, handy. **-pääsyinen**
easy of access, easily
accessible. **-tajuinen** easy to
understand, *(kansan-)* popular.
-us ease, easiness, facility.
helskyttää [make a] clatter,
rattle; jingle.
heltei|nen sultry, hot. **-syys**
sultriness.
heltta wattle; *(sienien ym)* gill.
helty|mätön unrelenting,
inexorable, unmoved. **-ä**
soften, relent; ~ *itkemään* be
moved to tears.
helve|tillinen infernal, hellish.
-tinkone infernal machine. **-tti**
hell.
hely trinket; spangle.
helä|dys ring; clang. **-dyttää**
[cause to] ring; sound;
(harppua) twang. **-tää** ring,
clang; sound; *(kilahtaa)* clink.
hemaiseva gorgeous, stunning.
hemmot|ella spoil; pamper,
coddle. **-telu** coddling,
overindulgence.
hempe|ys sweetness, charm,
loveliness; *(vienous)* gentleness.

-ä sweet, charming; gentle. **-ämielisyys** tenderness [of heart] , soft-heartedness; sentimentality.

hemppo linnet.

hempukka bird, doll, *halv.* tart, *Am.* broad.

hengelli|nen spiritual; ~ *sääty* the clergy. **-syys** spirituality.

hengen|ahdistus difficulty in breathing. **-heimolainen** soulmate, kindred spirit. **-heimolaisuus** congeniality of mind, affinity (between). **-hätä** mortal terror. **-lahjat** intellectual gifts. **-pelastus** lifesaving, rescue. **-pitimiksi** to keep body and soul together. **-ravinto** spiritual food. **-rikos** capital crime. **-vaara** deadly peril; *oli* ~*ssa* his life was in danger, he was in mortal danger. **-vaarallinen** perilous, highly dangerous; *(sairaus)* grave, *(tila)* critical. **-veto** breath. **-viljely** intellectual culture.

henge|ttömyys lifelessness. **-tär** genius *(pl.* genii). **-tön** lifeless, dead; .. lacking spirit.

hengi|ttää breathe; *(esim. kasveista)* respire; ~ *sisään* breathe in, inhale; ~ *ulos* breathe out, exhale. **-tys** breathing, respiration; breath; *sisään* ~ inspiration; *(~elimet* respiratory organs; ~*laite* respirator; ~*tiet* respiratory tract; ~*vaikeus* difficulty in breathing).

hengäh|dys breath, gasp; *(~ -tauko* breathing spell.). **-tää** take breath.

hengäs|tyminen shortness of breath, breathlessness. **-tyttää** make breathless. **-tyä** get out of breath, become breathless.

henke|vyys esprit; *(vilkkaus)* animation. **-vä** animated, *(keskustelu)* .. on a high level; bright-minded; spirituel; *(kasvot)* soulful. **-västi** in an animated manner.

henkeäsalpaava breathtaking.

henki *(elämä)* life; *(henkilö)* person; *(ilma)* air; *(hengitys)* breath; *henkeni edestä* for my life; *henkeä*

kohti per head; *ajan* ~ the spirit of the time; *pyhä* ~ the Holy Spirit; *jäädä* ~*in* survive; *(olla, pysyä, päästä)* *hengissä* (be, keep, escape) alive; *ottaa (jku) hengiltä* do away with, *sl.* bump off; *pelätä henkeään* go in fear of one's life; *pidättää henkeään* hold one's breath; *vetää henkeä* take [a deep] breath; *vetää henkeensä* inhale; *henkensä kaupalla* at the risk of his life. **-hieverissä:** *olla* ~ have only a spark of life left.

henkiin|herättäminen restoration [to life]; resuscitation; *kuv.* revival. **-jäänyt** *a.* surviving. *s.* survivor.

henki|kirja census list. **-kirjoittaja** registrar. **-kirjoitus** census. **-lääkäri** personal physician.

henkilö person; ~*t (näytelmän)* cast. **-auto** [passenger] car. **-idä** personify; impersonate. **-itymä** personification. **-ityä** be personified. **-kohtainen** personal; individual. **-kohtaisesti** personally, in person. **-kohtaisuu|s:** *mennä -ksiin* become personal, make personal remarks. **-kunta** staff, personnel, employees. **-liikenne** passenger traffic. **-llinen** personal. **-llisyys** identity; *näyttää toteen h-syytensä* establish one's i.; *(~todistus* i. card).

henkilö|npalvonta personality cult. **-puhelu** personal call. **-tiedot** personal details, biographical data.

henki|maailma spirit [ual] world. **-nen** mental; intellectual; ~ *työ* intellectual work; *-sen työn tekijä* non-manual worker, white-collar worker; *viisi* ~ *toimikunta* a committee of five. **-olento** spirit. **-patto** *a.* outlawed; proscribed; *s.* outlaw. **-raha** poll-tax, capitation. **-reikä** air-hole, vent-hole. **-rikos** felonious *(t.* criminal) homicide. **-syys** spirituality; intellectuality.

-toreet: *olla -toreissa* be breathing one's last. -torvi windpipe, trachea. -vakuuttaa insure. -vakuutus life insurance, life assurance; *ottaa* ~ insure one's life, take out a life-insurance policy; (~yhtiö life-insurance company). -vartija, -vartio body-guard, life guard. -ystävä close friend, bosom friend. -ä breathe.
henkäi|stä breathe, draw breath; gasp. -sy breath; gasp.
henkäys breath; *(tuulen)* puff, whiff; *tuulen* ~ breath of air, puff of wind.
hennoa have the heart to ..
hento delicate, *(-kasvuinen)* slender; *(pieni)* tiny; weak. -mielinen tender- (soft-) hearted. -rakenteinen [.. of] slender [build]. -us delicacy, tenderness; slenderness.
hepen|et frills, finery, gewgaws; *parhaissa -issä* in full fig.
heppu, -li *sl.* bloke, guy.
heprea Hebrew; *oli ~a minulle* .. was Greek to me. -lainen *a.* Hebraic, Hebrew; *s.* Hebrew.
hera whey. -htaa trickle; *vesi* ~ *kielelleni* my mouth begins to water. -inen wheyey.
hereillä awake; ~ *oleva* waking.
heristää: ~ *nyrkkiä jklle* shake one's fist at ..
herjaa|ja reviler, blasphemer. -va abusive; libellous.
herjata abuse, revile; *(jtk pyhää)* blaspheme.
herjaus abuse, revilement; *lak.* libel. -kirjoitus libel[lous article]. -puhe abusive speech. denunciation. -sana abusive (insulting) word.
herjetä cease, stop, *jstk* .. -ing.
herkeä|mättä incessantly, without intermission (*t.* stopping). -mätön incessant, unceasing; *(alituinen)* steady; continuous.
herkis|tyä become sensitive. -tää sensitize.
herkku delicacy, dainty; *(-pala)* titbit, *Am.* tidbit; *herkut (m.)* goodies. -pala dainty bit,

titbit. -sieni mushroom. -silava bacon. -suu gourmet.
herkkyys sensitiveness (to), sensitivity.
herkkä sensitive, *jllek* to; *(taipuvainen)* apt, inclined (to); *(vastaanottavainen)* susceptible (to); *(vaikutteille)* impressionable; *hyvin* ~, *yli-* ~ highly strung; ~ *loukkaantumaan* easily offended, [too] quick to take offence; ~ *uni* light sleep. -itkuinen easily moved to tears. -kuuloinen .. with a keen sense of hearing. -tunteinen sensitive, easily affected, impressionable. -tunteisuus sensibility. -uninen *s.* light sleeper. -uskoinen credulous; unsuspecting, *(helppo pettää)* gullible. -uskoisuus credulity.
herkulli|nen delicious, choice. -suus deliciousness, daintiness.
herku|tella eat well; *(jllak)* feast upon ... -ttelija gourmet. -ttelu sumptuous fare; gormandizing.
hermo nerve; *käydä jkn ~ille* get on sb.'s nerves. -jännitys nerve strain. -keskus nerve centre. -kimppu bundle of nerves. -lääkäri nerve specialist. -romahdus nervous breakdown. -sairas neuropath[ic]; *(neurootikko)* neurotic. -sairaus *ks. -tauti.* -sota war of nerves. -sto nervous system. -stollinen nervous, neurological.
hermostu|a get nervous; *-nut* nervous; irritable. -minen nervous irritability, *m.* frayed nerves, tense nerves. -neisuus nervousness. -ttaa set [one's] nerves on edge; irritate; *-ttava* trying to the nerves, *(tärisyttävä)* nerve-racking.
hermo|särky neuralgia. -tauti nervous disorder, neurological disease. -väre spasm.
herne pea; ~en *palko* pea-pod. -kasvi leguminous plant. -keitto pea soup.
herpaantu|a go limp, slacken. -maton unweakened.
herpaista unnerve; weaken;

(halvata) paralyse *(m. kuv.).*

herra gentleman, man; *(isäntä)* master; *(nimen ed.)* Mr [äänt. mistö]; *(puhuttelusana)* Sir; ~n *rukous* the Lord's Prayer; ~n *tähden!* for goodness' (heaven's) sake! *hyvät ~t!* Dear Sirs, Gentlemen; *elää herroiksi* live like a lord; *olla oma ~nsa* be one's own master.

herrain|vaatteet men's clothing. **-vaatehtimo** men's outfitters.

herras|kartano manor house, country house. **-mies** gentleman. **-nainen** gentlewoman. **-tella** live like a lord. **-väki** people of good family; gentry, *(harvemmin)* gentlefolk, *(palvelijan puh.)* master and mistress.

herruus authority; superiority; domination; *(ylivalta)* supremacy.

hertta *(maa)* hearts. **-kortti** heart. **-kuningas** king of hearts.

herttai|nen sweet, nice; lovable, pleasant. **-suus** sweetness; pleasantness.

herttua duke. **-kunta** duchy, dukedom. **-llinen** ducal. **-tar** duchess.

heru|a trickle; *(tihkua)* ooze [out].

hervo|ta *ks. herpaantua; (irtautua)* fall inert, drop. **-ton** limp, inert; numb. **-ttomasti** limply, inertly. **-ttomuus** limpness.

herännäi|nen pietist. **-syys** pietism.

herä|te impulse; stimulus. **-ttää** wake [up], [a]waken; *kuv.* arouse; call forth; ~ *epäilyksiä* arouse suspicion; ~ *eloon* revive; ~ *kauhua* inspire .. with awe (terror); ~ *kuolleista* raise from the dead; ~ *jk kysymys* raise a question; ~ *toiveita* raise hopes; *-ttäkää minut kello 7* please, call me at seven; *älä -tä vauvaa* don't wake the baby.

herätys waking; *kuv.* awakening, *usk.* revival. **-kello** alarm-clock. **-kokous** revival

meeting. **-saarnaaja** revivalist preacher.

herä|tä wake [up], awake; *herätessä(än)* on waking [up]; *en herännyt ajoissa* I overslept; *onko vauva jo -nnyt* has the baby waked (woken) yet? *herää kysymys* the question arises (whether). **-äminen** awakening.

hetale fringe; shred.

hete spring; morass, swamp.

heti instantly, immediately; at once, directly, in a minute; ~ *(kohta) kun* as soon as; ~ *paikalla (m.)* this very moment, straight away. **-mmiten** [as] soon [as possible], at the first opportunity.

hetiö *bot.* the stamens.

hetkelli|nen momentary; temporary; *(haihtuva)* transitory. **-sesti** momentarily; *(hetkeksi)* for a moment (a while). **-syys** short duration, momentariness; transitoriness.

hetki moment, instant; while; *hetkeksi* for a while; ~ *hetkeltä* every moment; ~ *on lyönyt* the hour has struck; *oikealla hetkellä* at the right moment; *tällä hetkellä* [at] this [very] moment; at present, at the moment, for the time being; *viime hetkessä* at the last minute; only just in time; *on hetken lapsi* lives for the moment, is a spontaneus person; *onnen hetket* happy hours. **-nen** *s.* little while; ~ *(olkaa hyvä)!* just a moment (a minute)! one moment, please! **-täin** at [odd] times, by fits and starts.

hetula *zo.* whalebone.

hevillä easily, readily; *ei* ~ *(m.)* only with difficulty.

hevo|nen horse; *voim.* side-horse; *-sen selässä* on horseback; *nousta -sen selkään* mount a horse; *astua -sen selästä* dismount; *pudota -sen selästä* fall off a horse.

hevosen|harja [horse's] mane. **-hoitaja** groom. **-kengittäjä** farrier, blacksmith. **-kenkä** horseshoe.

hevos|jalostus horse-breeding (-raising). **-kaakki** hack, jade. **-kauppias** horse-dealer. **-mies** horseman. **-näyttely** horse-show. **-rotu** breed of horses. **-siittola** stud. **-suka** curry-comb. **-urheilu** horse-racing, the turf. **-voima** horse-power (= h.p.); *130 ~inen moottori* a 130 horse-power engine.

hiaisin *(partaveitsen)* strop.

hidas slow; leisurely; *(myöhäinen)* tardy, *(~televa)* dilatory; *~ tekemään työtä* slow [at one's work]; *hitain askelin* slowly, at a slow pace. **-ajatuksinen** slow of thought, dull-witted. **-kulkuinen** slow. **-luontoinen** phlegmatic. **-oppinen** slow to learn. **-taa** slow down, retard; *-tettu (elok.)* slow-motion. **-telija** laggard. **-tella** be slow, delay, linger; loiter. **-telu** slowness; loitering; dawdling. **-tua** become slow[er], slow up; be delayed; *vauhti -tuu* the speed slackens. **-tus** delay[ing], retardation; *~lakko* slow-down, *ks. jarrutus-.* **-tuttaa** slow down, slow up; *~ askeleitaan* slacken one's pace.

hieho heifer.

hiekka sand; *(karkea)* gravel; *valua ~an* come to nothing. **-aavikko** [sandy] desert, sands. **-harju** sandy ridge. **-inen** sandy. **-jyvänen** grain of sand. **-kivi** sandstone. **-kuoppa** sand-pit. **-käytävä** gravel path. **-laatikko** *(lasten)* sand pit. **-maa** sandy soil. **-paperi** sand-paper. **-pohja** sandy bottom. **-ranta** sandy beach, sands. **-särkkä** sand-bank.

hiekoittaa sand.

hieman [just] a little; somewhat; slightly.

hieno fine; chic, elegant, finely dressed; *(ohut)* thin; delicate; *(maku ym)* exquisite, choice; *(ylevä)* noble; *(-stunut)* refined; *~ käytös* good manners; *~ nainen* gentlewoman; *~n hieno* very fine, exquisite; *~n näköinen* of distinguished appearance;

~ssa seurassa in polite society. **-hipiäinen ..** with a soft skin, fine-complexioned. **-makuinen** fine-tasting, delicious. **-mekaanikko** precision-tool maker. **-ntaa** grind fine; powder, pulverize; crush; *(murentaa)* crumble. **-piirteinen** fine-featured. **-pyykki** delicates. **-rakeinen** fine-grained. **-rakenteinen** finely built. **-stelija** snob; *(keikari)* fop, dandy. **-stella** show off, give oneself airs. **-stelu** showing off; snobbery, snobbishness. **-sti** finely; elegantly; delicately; *~ sivistynyt* highly cultured. **-sto** the smart set, smart people, people of fashion, Society. **-stua** become refined; *-stunut* refined, polished; *(esim. maku)* subtle. **-stuneisuus** refinement; *liika ~* over-refinement. **-takeet** cutlery. **-tunteinen** considerate, thoughtful of others, tactful. **-tunteisuus** delicacy [of feeling], considerateness, consideration. **-us** fineness, delicacy; elegance; thinness. **-varainen** considerate, delicate.

hiero|a rub; *lääk.* massage; *(rikki)* grate; *~ kauppaa* bargain (for), try to come to terms (with sb.): *~ rauhaa* negotiate for peace. **-ja** masseur, *(nais-)* masseuse. **-makoje** massage machine. **-nta** massage; rubbing. **-ttaa** have .. massaged. **-utua** rub, chafe, gall.

hiertymä abrasion, chafed spot.

hiertää chafe, abrade.

hies|tyä be covered with perspiration; *-tynyt* perspiring, sweaty.

hiesu silt.

hiet|a [fine] sand. **-ikko** [stretch of] sands.

hievah|taa move, stir, budge; *-tamatta* immovably, firmly; *paikaltaan -tamatta* without stirring [from the spot], without budging.

hiha sleeve. **-inen:** *lyhyt~* short-sleeved. **-llinen ..** with sleeves. **-naukko** arm-hole,

-nsuu wristband; *(käänne)*
cuff. **-ton** sleeveless.
hihi|ttää giggle, titter. **-tys**
giggling, snicker, snigger.
hihk|aista let out a yell. **-aisu**
yell. **-ua** yell; scream; shriek.
hihna strap, [leather] band,
(kapea) thong; *(kone-)* belt;
(kiväärin) sling; *talutus ~*
lead; *vrt. kytkeä, taluttaa.*
-kuljetin belt conveyor.
-käyttöinen belt-driven. **-pyörä**
pulley.
hiidenkirnu pothole.
hiihto skiing *(m.* ski'ing.
ski-ing). **-hissi** ski lift. **-housut**
ski trousers. **-joukot** skiborne
troops. **-keli** *hyvä ~* good
skiing. **-kisat** winter games.
-puku ski [ing] suit. **-retki**
skiing trip. **-urheilu** skiing.
-varusteet skiing outfit;
(pukineet) ski wear.
hiih|täjä skier. **-tää** ski; *mennä*
-tämään go skiing.
hiilestää coal.
hiili *(kivi-)* coal; *(puu-)*
charcoal; *kem.* carbon; *hiilet*
coals, *(hehkuvat)* embers;
ottaa ~ä bunker, coal. **-hanko**
poker.
hiilihappo carbonic acid,
(dioksidi) carbon dioxide.
-inen carbonated; *(vesi)*
aerated. **-jää** dry ice.
hiili|hydraatti carbohydrate.
-kaivos coal-mine, colliery.
-kerros coal stratum, coal-bed.
-murska slack; *(-rata)*
cinder-track. **-paperi** carbon
paper. **-piirustus** charcoal
drawing. **-säiliö** coal-bin;
(laivan) bunker. **-vety**
hydrocarbon.
hiil|los embers, dying fire, live
coals. **-lyttää** char, carbonize.
-tyminen carbonization. **-tyä**
be [come] charred; *-tynyt*
charred.
hiipi|ä sneak; *(huoneeseen m.)*
slip, steal, *(pois)* slink away;
-vä sneaking, lurking, *(tauti)*
insidious.
hiippa mitre. **-kunta** diocese,
bishopric.
hiipua fade; die down.
hiiren|korva *koivu on ~lla* the
birch is budding. **-pyydys**

mouse-trap.
hiiri mouse *(pl.* mice). **-haukka**
buzzard. **-lavantauti** mouse
typhus.
hiisi troll; *mitä hiidessä* what
the dickens!
hiisk|ahdus sound; whisper. **-ua**
ei ~ sanaakaan not breathe a
word, not tell a soul.
hiiva yeast. **-sieni** yeast fungus.
hiiviskellä sneak about, lurk
about.
hiki perspiration, sweat; *olla*
hiessä be in a sweat, be
perspiring [all over], *(ikkuna)*
be steamed. **-helmi** bead of
sweat. **-hihna** sweat-band.
-huokonen pore. **-nen** sweaty.
-rauhanen sweat gland. **-syys**
sweatiness.
hikoi|lla perspire, sweat. **-lu**
perspiration, sweat [ing].
hiljaa quiet [ly], still; softly;
~! be quiet! *~ hyvä tulee*
gently *[does it]!* take it easy!
ajakaa ~ drive slowly; *kulkea*
~ go slowly, travel at a slow
pace; *olla ~* keep quiet;
(ääneti) be silent; *puhua ~*
speak softly (in a soft *t.* low
voice).
hiljai|nen low; *(rauhallinen)*
quiet, still; *(äänetön)* silent,
taciturn; *liik.* dull; *~ aika*
(liik.) dead season; *-sella*
tulella over a slow fire. **-suus**
stillness, quiet [ness]; silence;
(äänen) lowness; *vaatia -suutta*
ask for silence.
hilja|kkoin recently, lately, of
late. **-kseen, -lleen** slowly, at
a leisurely pace; without
hurrying. **-n, -ttain** recently;
not long ago.
hilje|mmin more slowly; in a
lower voice. **-neminen**
subsidence, abatement. **-ntyä**
quiet [en] down; *vrt. -tä.*
-ntää quiet [en], still; calm;
(ääntä ym) subdue, muffle,
hush, *(virittää -mmäksi)* tone
down; *~ vauhtia* slacken the
speed, slow down, slow up.
-tä become quiet, become
calm; *(asettua)* subside, abate;
vauhti -nee the speed slackens.
hilkka hood, cap.
hilleri *zo.* polecat.

hilli|ke check, *jllek* upon; restraint. **-ntä** restraint, control. **-tty** restrained, controlled; composed; *(väri)* subdued, quiet; *-tyllä äänellä* in, a quiet voice; *hänen esiintymisensä oli ~ä* he appeared composed.

hilli|ttömyys lack of restraint; unruliness. **-ttömästi** unrestrainedly. **-tä** check, restrain; repress, suppress, curb; *(hallita)* master, control; calm; hold back; *-tse mielesi* control your temper! control yourself! *~ nauruaan (m.)* refrain from laughing. **-tön** unchecked, unrestrained, ungovernable, uncontrollable, unmanageable; *(raju)* unruly, wild.

hillo jam; preserve. **-ta** make jam; preserve.

hilpeys cheerfulness, gaiety, mirth, merriment.

hilpeä cheerful, merry, gay, jolly; *(eloisa)* animated, lively, brisk; *(pirteä)* bright; *~llä mielellä* in high spirits, in a gay mood.

hilse dandruff. **-illä** scale off, peel [off]; *iho -ilee* the skin is peeling.

Himalaja the Himalayas.

himmen|nin *valok.* diaphragm. **-tymätön** unobscured, undimmed. **-ntyä** become dark[er], become [more] obscure, grow dim; *(metalli)* tarnish. **-ntää** dim; darken, obscure; blur; *(auton valot)* dip the lights; *valok.* stop down, screen off; *(kuv. loistollaan)* eclipse, outshine. **-tä** *ks.* **-ntyä**; *(kalveta)* fade. **-ys** dimness, obscurity; dullness.

himmeä dim; obscure; *(kiilloton)* lustreless, dull, *(tummunut)* tarnished, *(pinta)* matt; *~n kiiltävä* dull-lustre [satin]; *~ksi hiottu lasi* ground glass.

himo lust (for); desire (for); craving, greed, thirst (for); *(alkoholin)* addiction to drink. **-inen** covetous; greedy (for); addicted to. **-ita** feel a desire (for), covet; desire; have a craving (for). **-kas** greedy. **-ruoka** favourite dish.

hina|aja tug [boat]. **-ta** tow, have .. in tow; *ottaa -ttavaksi* take .. in tow.

hinaus towing, towage. **-köysi** towline, towrope; trail rope.

hindulai|nen *a. & s.* Hindu. **-suus** Hinduism.

hinkalo bin; *(lehmän)* stall.

hinku|a whoop. **-yskä** whooping-cough.

hinnan|alennus price reduction (cut); *suuri ~* slashed price[s]. **-ero** difference in price, margin. **-lasku** fall (decline) of prices. **-nousu** rise (advance, increase) in price[s]; *(äkillinen)* boom.

hinnasto price-list, catalogue.

hinnoi|tella, -ttaa fix the price, set a price (on), price [at £ 3]. **-ttelu** fixing of prices.

hinta price; rate; *(joskus)* figure; *(jhk) ~an* at [3sh.], at the price of; *mistä hinnasta* at what price? *hinnasta mistä hyvänsä* at any price, at all costs; *matkalipun ~ fare.* **-ilmoitus** quotation. **-inen** *viiden markan ~* costing five marks; *minkä ~ on ..* what is the price of? how much is ..? *halpa ~* low-priced. **-lappu** [price-] label. **-luettelo** price list, catalogue. **-luokka** price range. **-politiikka** prices policy. **-sota** price [-cut] war. **-sulku** freezing of prices. **-säännöstely:** *~n alainen* price-controlled. **-tarjous** quotation. **-taso** price level.

hinte|lyys slimness, delicate build. **-lä** slender, slim; lanky.

hio|a grind; *(lasia ym)* cut; *(teroittaa)* sharpen, whet; *~ kirkkaaksi* polish. **-ke** mechanical pulp.

hioma|kone grinding-machine. **-ton** unground; uncut; *kuv.* unpolished, crude. **-ttomuus** dullness, *kuv.* lack of polish.

hiomo *(puu-)* mechanical pulp mill.

hios|taa cause perspiration; *-tava (ilma)* sultry. **-tua** get

sweaty.
hiota perpire, sweat.
hiottu ground, cut; sharpened; *kuv.* smooth, polished.
hioutu|a be ground; *(kulua)* wear smooth; become polished. **-neisuus** polish.
hipaista touch .. lightly, graze; *(ohimennen)* brush past, skim by.
hipat party, celebration; spree, fling, [wild] blast.
hipiä skin; complexion. **-inen:** *tumma* ~ dark-complexioned.
hipoa almost touch, verge on.
hippa touch-last; *olla* ~*silla* play tag.
hirmu|hallitsija tyrant; despot. **-hallitus** reign of terror. **-inen** dreadful, frightful, terrible; horrible. **-isen** dreadfully, frightfully. **-isuus** dreadfulness, frightfulness. **-lisko** dinosaur. **-myrsky** hurricane, *Am.* tornado, *(Itä-Aasiassa)* typhoon. **-työ** atrocity. **-valta** tyranny, despotism; terrorism. **-valtainen** tyrannical, despotic; terroristic. **-valtias** tyrant, despot.
hirnu|a neigh, whinny. **-nta** neighing, whinnying.
hirsi log; beam, balk; *hirret* timber; *joutua hirteen* be hanged. **-maja** log cabin. **-puu** gallows. **-rakennus** log house, timbered house.
hirssi millet.
hirtehi|nen gallows-bird. **-spila** grim humour.
hirtto|nuora halter. **-paikka** the gallows.
hirttäytyä hang oneself.
hirttää hang, execute by hanging.
hirven|ajo deer-stalking, elk-hunting. **-liha** venison. **-nahka** deerskin. **-sarvensuola** volatile salt. **-sarvet** antlers.
hirveä dreadful, terrible; awful; heinous; ~*n näköinen* hideous [-looking].
hirvi elk, *(koiras)* stag, hart; *Am.* moose. **-eläin** deer.
hirvi|ttävyys horribleness. **-ttävä** horrible, horrid, grievous, hideous. **-ttää** terrify; *minua* ~ I am scared. **-tä** dare,

venture. **-ö** monster; (~**mäinen** monstrous).
hissi lift; *Am.* elevator. **-aukko** lift-well.
historia history. **-llinen** historical; ~ *aika* historic times; ~ *hetki* a historic moment. **-nkirjoittaja** historian, historiographer. **-nkirjoitus,** historiography. **-ntakainen** prehistoric. **-ntutkija** historian. **-ntutkimus** historical research.
histo|riikki history; *(yleiskatsaus)* survey. **-rioitsija** historian.
hita|asti slowly; ~ *vaikuttava* slow [-acting]; ~ *mutta varmasti* slow but sure. **-us** slowness; sluggishness, *(velttous)* sloth; *fys.* inertia.
hitsa|ta weld. **-aja** welder. **-us** welding.
hitto [the] devil; ~ *soikoon* hang it! [well,] I'll be blowed; *hitosti* like blazes; *hitonmoinen (mies)* a devil of a fellow.
hitu|nen a little (a tiny) bit; particle; *ei* ~*stakaan* not a bit, not a whit.
hiukai|sta: *minua* ~*see* I feel hungry [for something salty].
hiukan a little, a bit, a trifle, *(jonkinverran)* somewhat; ~ *parempi (m.)* slightly better; ~ *liian tumma (m.)* a shade too dark.
hiukka(nen) particle; grain; *h-sen* a little, a bit, a trifle.
hiuksen|halkominen hairsplitting. **-hieno:** ~ *ero* a very fine distinction. **-verta** a hair's breadth.
hius hair; *hiukset (tukka)* hair; ~*ten leikkuu* hair-cut, *(tasoitus)* trimming. **-huokoinen** capillary. **-huokoisuus** capillarity, capillary attraction. **-karva** hair; ~*n verta* a hair's breadth; *hänen henkensä oli* ~*n varassa* his life hung by a hair, it was touch and go [with him]. **-kiinne, -lakka** hair spray. **-laite** coiffure, *puhek.* hair-do. **-marto** scalp; *punastua* ~*a myöten* blush to the roots of one's hair.

-nauha [hair-]ribbon. -neula hairpin. -palmikko plait. -pilli *anat.* capillary. -solki hair slide. -suoni capillary [vessel]. -vesi hair tonic, hair lotion. -voide hair cream. -väri hair dye.

hiutale flake.

hive|llä touch gently; stroke; *ääni -lee korvia* the voice delights the ear; *se -lee hänen turhamaisuuttaan* it flatters (tickles) his vanity. hiven: ~ *en verran* a trifle, a bit. -aineet trace elements.

hivutta|a (*kalvaa*) wear away, consume; -*ttava* wasting. -utua (*eteenpäin*) shuffle along, (*alas*) slither down.

-hko, -hkö: *vanhahko* rather old; *pienehkö* smallish.

hohde shimmer, gleam; lustre; sheen.

hohkai|nen porous; spongy. -suus porosity, porousness.

hohkakivi pumice [-stone].

hoho|ttaa guffaw, roar with laughter. -tus horse-laugh, guffaw.

hoht|aa shine, gleam, shimmer; (*säteillä*) radiate; *taivas* ~ *punaisena* there is a red glow in the sky; -*avan valkoinen* glistening white.

hohtimet pincers.

hohtokivi brilliant; ~*llä koristettu* .. set with brilliants.

hoi hollo[a]! *mer.* ahoy!

hoidokki ward; inmate.

hoike|ntaa make [more] slender, make a p. look slimmer. -ta become more slender, get thinner.

hoikka slender, slim; thin; (*hoilakka*) lank. -säärinen thin-legged.

hoikkuus slenderness, slimness; thinness.

hoilata *ark.* yell, shout, *Am.* holler.

hoiper|rella stagger, reel; totter; -*teli alas portaita* (he) staggered down the steps.

hoippu|a totter; (*huojua*) sway; -*va käynti* unsteady walk.

hoita|a take care of, look after, see to; attend [to a matter]; (*hoivata*) tend, nurse; (*johtaa*) manage, run; *lääk.* treat; ~ *huonosti* take bad care of; mismanage; neglect; ~ *sairasta* nurse a patient; ~ *jkn taloutta* keep house for; *ottaa* ~*kseen* take charge of; *hänellä on* .. *hoidettavanaan* he is in (he has) charge of. -ja keeper, caretaker; (*esim. pesän*) administrator; (*lapsen, sairaan*) nurse. -jatar nurse. -maton uncared for; (*esim. ulkoasu*) unkempt. -mattomuus lack of [proper] care; neglect.

hoito care; attendance; management; (*lapsen ym*) nursing; *lääk.* treatment, therapy; (*hallinto*) administration. -henkilökunta nursing (*t.* medical)staff. -la, -laitos home, institution; -*laitoksessa* in care. -menetelmä method of treatment, cure. -tapa [course of] treatment, *vrt. ed.*

hoiva care; *ottaa jku hoiviinsa* take care (charge) of. -ta nurse, tend, take good care of; (*suojata*) shelter. -ton unprotected.

hokea say again and again.

hokki calk; (*kengän*) spike.

hoks|ata grasp, tumble to (sth.); *on -aavainen* is quick- (ready-) witted.

holhooja guardian. -hallitus regency.

holho|ta take care of; be a guardian (of). -tti ward. -us guardianship; *on -uksen alainen* .. has been declared incapable of managing his (her) own affairs.

holkki holder; *tekn.* sleeve.

hollan|ninkieli Dutch. -nitar Dutchwoman. H-ti Holland. -tilainen *a.* Dutch. *s.* Dutchman.

holti|ton irresponsible. -ttomuus irresponsibility.

holvata arch, vault.

holvi vault. -hauta vault, tomb. -kaari arch. -katto vaulted roof. -käytävä arcade, archway. -mainen vaulted.

home mould; mildew. -htua become mouldy. -htunut, -inen

mouldy, mildewed; musty.
-sieni mould fungus.
homma duty, care [s]; *(touhu)*
bustle; *(yritys)* undertaking;
olla ~ssa be busy; *paljon ~a*
much to do, a great deal on
one's hands. **-kas** busy, active.
-ta be busy; bustle; *(järjestää)*
arrange; *(hankkia)* get,
procure; *mitä siellä -taan?*
what is going on there?
homo|geeninen homogeneous.
-genisoida homogenize.
-seksuaalisuus homosexuality.
honka [tall] pine. **-puu**
redwood.
hono|tus nasal voice quality.
-ttaa talk through the nose.
hontelo lank [y], scraggy,
gangling.
hopea silver; *~t* silver [ware].
-haapa white poplar. **-hapset**
silver hair. **-harkko** ingot of
silver. **-hela** silver mounting.
-häät silver wedding. **-nharmaa**
silver-grey. **-nhohtoinen** [. .
with a] silvery [sheen]. **-raha**
silver coin. **-seppä** silversmith.
-tavarat silver [articles],
silverware.
hopeinen silver.
hopeoida silver-plate.
hoppu haste, hurry, scurry.
hoputtaa urge . . on, hurry . .
on; hustle.
horisontti horizon.
horjah|dus stumbling, stumble;
kuv. false step. **-taa** stagger;
(kompastua) stumble.
horju|a stagger, totter; *kuv.*
vacillate, waver, falter; *~*
päätöksessään be irresolute;
kielenkäyttö -u usage varies;
hänen terveytensä -u her
health is giving way *(t.*
declining). **-maton** unshaken;
immovable; unwavering.
-mattomuus firmness,
steadfastness. **-ttaa** cause . . to
totter; shake, sway *(m. kuv.);*
kuv. cause to waver,
(suunnastaan) deflect a p.
from his course. **-va** tottering;
wavering; *(päättämätön)*
undecided; *(epävakaa)*
unsteady, unstable; *(terveys)*
uncertain, failing. **-vuus**
unsteadiness; indecision,

vacillation.
horkka ague; *puhek.* the
shivers.
hormi flue.
hormoni hormone.
horna abyss, the bottomless pit.
horros torpor, stupor, lethargy;
(kevyt) doze, drowse.; *olla*
talvihorroksissa lie dormant,
hibernate. **-tila** *(uni-)* trance;
coma. **-uni** lethargic sleep.
horsma willow herb.
hortensia hydrangea.
hosua lay about one; *(lyödä)*
strike; *~ käsillään (m.)* throw
one's arms about; gesticulate;
~ pois jtk fight off .
hotelli hotel. **-nomistaja** hotel
proprietor. **-poika** buttons,
page boy, *Am.* bell boy,
bellhop.
hotkia gorge, gulp, wolf down.
houkk|a, -io *s.* fool, idiot,
dupe.
houku|tella allure; entice,
inveigle (into); *(kiusata)*
tempt; *(kehotella)* persuade; *~*
(mielistelemällä) coax; *~ jku*
puhumaan draw a p. into
talk; **-tteleva** tempting,
attractive, beguiling. **-tin**
allurement, enticement;
attraction. **-ttelu** alluring,
tempting. **-tus** allurement;
temptation; *kuv.* lure; (**~lintu**
decoy; *kuv. m.* decoy-duck;
~ääni call note).
hourai|lla be delirious, wander;
(raivoten) rave; *-leva*
delirious. **-lu** delirium,
wandering.
houre: *~et* ravings, delirium;
kuv. fancies. **-kuva**
hallucination.
hourupäinen crazy, mad, out
of one's mind.
housun|kannattimet [a pair of]
braces, *Am.* suspenders.
-lahje trouser-leg. **-prässit** trouser
creases. **-tasku** trouser [s]
pocket.
housupuku trouser *(Am.* pants)
suit.
housut [pair of] trousers,
pants; *(alus-)* drawers;
(naisten) underpants, *(pikku-)*
panties, *(esim. villa-)* knickers;
(polvi-) shorts, breeches; *tehdä*

housuihinsa foul one's pants; *olla jkn housuissa (kuv.)* be in sb.'s shoes.

hovi court; *~ssa* at court. **-hankkija** purveyor to H.M. the King (Queen). **-herra** courtier. **-marsalkka** master of the royal household. **-mestari** butler; *(ravintolassa)* head-waiter. **-mies** courtier. **-nainen** lady-in-waiting. **-narri** court jester. **-neiti** maid of honour. **-niiaus** curtsey. **hovi**|**oikeus** Court of Appeal. **-poika** page. **-runoilija** poet laureate. **-saarnaaja** court chaplain. **-suru** court mourning.

huhmar mortar.

huhtikuu April.

huhu rumour; *~na kerrotaan* it is rumoured. **-illa** rumour.

huija|**ri** swindler; cheat. **-ta** swindle; cheat; *sl.* diddle. **-us** swindle, swindling; cheating.

huikea *(tavaton)* huge.

huiken|**nella** be fickle; be reckless. **-televainen** fickle, flighty; gay, fast. **-televaisuus** fickleness, flightiness; gaiety, gay life.

huilu flute. **-niekka** fluteplayer, flutist.

huima *(hurja)* reckless, wild; *~ yritys* a daring attempt; *(hinta) nousee ~sti* sky-rockets. **-ava** giddy, dizzy; *~ ero* vast difference; *~ summa* fantastic sum; *~a vauhtia* at a breakneck speed; *~n korkealla* at a dizzy height. **-päinen** daring, dashing; foolhardy. **-päisyys** daring, recklessness; foolhardiness. **-pää** daredevil, madcap. **-ta** make .. dizzy; *päätäni ~a* I feel giddy (dizzy). **-us** giddiness, dizziness; *lääk.* vertigo.

huipen|**taa** *kuv.* bring to a head; *hän -si sanottavansa kolmeen kohtaan* he made three points. **-tua** *kuv.* culminate (in), reach its climax.

huippu top, peak, *(vuoren, m.)* summit; *(kärki)* apex; *hulluuden ~* the height of folly;

kaiken huipuksi on top of everything else; *kohota ~unsa* reach its culmination, culminate; *tornin ~* spire; *valtansa huipulla* at the height of one's power. **-hinta** top price. **-kohta** peak, climax, culmination, acme; *saavuttaa ~nsa* reach a maximum, reach its peak. **-kuormitus** peak load. **-kurssi** peak quotation. **-nopeus** top speed. **-taso** top level; *~n kokous* summit conference. **-urheilija** top-ranking athlete. **H-vuoret** Spitzbergen.

huiputtaa fool, dupe, cheat, *sl.* diddle.

huiskin: *~ haiskin* helter-skelter, pell-mell.

huisku *(pöly-)* feather duster. **-ttaa** wave, *(huiskauttaa)* swish.

huitoa fling, wave [one's arms about], fight with one's arms, *(jkta kepillä)* lay about .. with a stick.

huivi scarf, head scarf, *(hartia-)* shawl.

hukassa: *olla ~* be lost, *(kadoksissa)* be missing; *olemme ~* we are undone.

hukata lose; *(turhaan)* waste; *aikaa hukkaamatta* without loss of time, without delay.

hukka *(turmio)* destruction, ruin; *(tappio)* loss, waste.

hukkaan in vain, to no purpose; *~ joutunut* lost; *~ mennyt* wasted, useless, fruitless; *mennä ~* be wasted, be in vain.

hukkua be lost, get lost; *(veteen)* drown, be drowned.

hukutta|**a** drown. **-utua** drown oneself.

huligaani hooligan, rough, rowdy, *Am.* hoodlum.

hulin|**a** hullabaloo; *mennä ~ksi* end in general disorder. **-oida** be unruly, riot. **-ointi** disorderly conduct, disturbance.

hulivili madcap, gay (happy-go-lucky) fellow.

huljuttaa wash, rinse (off); swill [to and fro].

hullaan|**tua** go mad; *~ jhk* become infatuated with a p.; *-tunut* mad on, mad about,

Am. crazy about; *olla -tunut jkh (m.)* love a p. to distraction.

hullu *a.* mad, crazy; insane; *s.* lunatic; *elokuva* ~ film fan; *ulkoilu* ~ fresh-air fiend; *tulla ~ksi* go mad, go off one's head; *hän ei ole ~mman näköinen* he is not at all bad-looking; *ei olisi ~mpaa* it wouldn't be such a bad idea; *tästä ei tule ~a hurskaammaksi* I cannot make head or tail of this.

hullunkuri|nen extremely funny; absurd, bizarre; *(lystikäs)* ludicrous, droll, comical. **-suus** ludicrousness, drollery; absurdity.

hullunmylly *kuv.* bedlam, hurly-burly.

hullu|sti wrong [ly], the wrong way, amiss; *hänen kävi* ~ things went badly with him; *sepä oli* ~ too bad! **-tella** play the fool. **-ttelija** madcap, practical joker. **-ttelu** folly, frolic, gay pranks, clowning. **-tus** foolishness; *-tuksia!* nonsense! don't be silly! *se olisi ~ta* it would be madness.

hulluus madness, insanity; *(mielettömyys)* foolishness, folly.

hulmah|dus flutter. **-taa** flutter, *(tuli)* flare up.

hulmuta flutter, fly, *(tukka ym)* wave.

hulpio selvage, selvedge.

hulttio wastrel, waster, good-for-nothing [fellow]. **-mainen** worthless, good-for-nothing.

humaaninen humane.

humahdus whir[r], whiz.

humala hop; *(juopumus)* [state of] intoxication; *olla ~ssa* be drunk, be intoxicated, *(lievästi)* be tight. **-inen** *a.* intoxicated; *a & s.* drunk. **-päissään** under the influence [of drink]. **-salko** hop pole.

humal|isto hop-garden, hopfield. **-luttaa** intoxicate, make .. drunk. **-tua** get intoxicated, get drunk, *jstk* with.

humanis|mi humanism. **-tinen:**

-tiset aineet (yliop.) Arts subjects, the humanities.

humi|na murmur [ing], humming, *(korvien)* buzzing. **-sta** murmur, hum; *(tuuli, m.)* whisper, sigh.

hummeri lobster.

humoristinen humorous.

humpuuki humbug.

humu *(pauhu)* rumble, din; *elämän ~ssa* in the whirl (bustle) of life; *elää ~ssa ja sumussa* lead a fast life.

hunaja honey. **-inen** [.. of] honey; *kuv.* honeyed. **-kenno** honeycomb.

hunnin|ko: *joutua -golle* go to rack and ruin; *on -golla* is down and out; *(asiasta)* is in a bad way.

hunnit *hist.* the Huns.

hunnuttaa veil.

huntu veil.

huoah|dus sigh; breath. **-taa** sigh; *(henkäistä)* get one's breath; ~ *helpotuksesta* give a sigh of relief.

huoata sigh; *(valittaen)* groan.

huohottaa pant, breathe heavily.

huojen|nus relief, ease; *(hinnan)* reduction. **-taa** ease, lighten; ~ *ehtoja* modify the terms; ~ *hintaa* lower (reduce) the price; ~ *sydäntään* unburden one's heart, get .. off one's chest, talk one's troubles out. **-tua** become easier; be relieved; *(hinta)* get cheaper; go down, fall.

huoju|a rock; *(heilua)* swing, sway; *-vin askelin* with tottering steps. **-ttaa** rock; shake, swing, sway.

huoka|ista sigh; ~ *syvään* heave a deep sigh. **-us** sigh.

huokea cheap; low; *myydä ~sta* sell cheap, sell at a low price; ~*t ehdot* easy terms. **-hintainen** cheap; ~ *painos (m.)* popular edition. **-hintaisuus** cheapness, popular price.

huokeus *(hinnan)* cheapness.

huoko|inen porous, spongy. **-isuus** porosity. **-nen** *anat.* pore.

huokua exhale; *kuv.* breathe.

huolehti|a take care (of), look

after, attend to; see to;
(toimittaa) arrange; *(olla
huolissaan)* be anxious, worry
(about); ~, *että* .. see to it
that. **-vaisuus** solicitude.
huolelli|nen careful; *(siisti)*
neat; *(viimeistelty)* elaborate;
-sesti carefully, with care;
thoroughly. **-suus** carefulness,
care.
huolen|alainen distressing,
alarming; *(huolestunut)* .. full
of care, anxious. **-pito** care;
charge.
huole|stua get anxious, get
worried; *-tunut* anxious,
concerned, uneasy; worried;
oltiin -tuneita jstk concern
was felt about . . .
-tuneesti anxiously, with
anxiety; *katsahti häneen* ~
gave him a worried look.
-tuneisuus anxiety. **-tuttaa**
make .. anxious, alarm;
-tuttava alarming.
huole|ti unconcerned [ly];
(turvallisesti) safely;
confidently; *ole* ~ set your
mind at rest; don't worry!
-ton free from care [s],
care-free, non-caring;
light-hearted, happy-go-lucky;
unconcerned, careless. **-ttaa**
worry; make .. uneasy; *jk* ~
minua I am worried about.
-ttomasti unconcernedly;
carelessly, negligently.
-ttomuus unconcern; freedom
from care, carelessness.
huol|i care; worry; anxiety;
(huolellisuus) carefulness; *olla
~ssaan (jstk)* feel anxious,
worry (about); *ottaa jtk
-ekseen* undertake to .., take
.. in hand; *pitää -ta jstk*
take charge of, look after,
look to [it that], attend to,
(esim. perheestään) provide
for, *(itsestään, m.)* shift for
oneself; *jätä se minun -ekseni*
leave it to me. **-ia** care
(about), mind (about); *älä -i*
never mind! *älä -i mennä* you
had better not go; *en -i sitä*
I don't care to have it, I
don't want it.
huoli|maton careless; needless;
(leväperäinen) negligent;

slipshod, slapdash, slovenly
[work], sloppy. **-matta** *(jstk*
~) in spite of, despite,
notwithstanding; *siitä seikasta
~, että* .. *(m.)* irrespective of
(apart from) the fact that; .
siitä ~ *(sittenkin)* none the
less, nevertheless, for all that;
hänen vioistaan ~ *pidämme
hänestä* for all his faults, we
like him. **-mattomuus**
carelessness; negligence. **-nta**
liik. forwarding; *(~liike f.*
agency). **-tsija** forwarding *(t.*
shipping) agent. **-tella** take
pains (with); *-teltu* neat,
elaborate, carefully finished,
(miehen ulkoasu) well-groomed.
huollettava *s.* dependant.
huol|taa take care of; *(auto
ym)* service; *(elättää)* provide
for, support. **-taja** supporter,
(perheen) breadwinner,
(holhooja) guardian; *olla jkn
~na* have the custody of.
-tamo garage.
huolto care; welfare; *(palvelu)*
service; servicing; *sot. ym.*
maintenance, supply; *sot.*
logistics; *huollon varassa*
on national assistance;
lähettää auto ~on
send the car in for service.
-alue trust territory. **-alus**
supply ship. **-apu** public
welfare. **-asema** service
station, garage, *Am.*
gas[oline] station. **-joukot**
logistical troops, *Engl.* army
service corps. *Am.*
maintenance and supply
troops. **-konttori** welfare
department. **-laitos** [welfare]
institution. **-muodot** supportive
(t. welfare) services. **-työ:**
yhteiskunnallinen ~ welfare
work. **-työntekijä** social
welfare worker. **-yhteydet** *sot.*
supply lines. **-yksikkö** supply
unit.
huoma: *jättää jkn ~an* leave
in a p.'s care (charge); *uskoa
jkn ~an* entrust to ..
huomaama|ton unnoticeable,
imperceptible; inconspicuous;
(ei huomattu) unnoticed;
(tarkkaamaton) inattentive. **-tta**
unnoticed; *(epähuomiossa)*

inadvertently; *se jäi minulta*
~ I overlooked it. **-ttomasti**
imperceptibly; inconspicuously.
-ttomuus imperceptibility;
inattention; *(epähuomio)*
oversight; blunder.
huomaavai|nen attentive;
considerate, *(kohtelias)* polite.
-suus attention, attentiveness.
huoma|ta notice, observe, note,
become aware of, perceive;
catch sight of; discover,
detect; *kuv.* see, find; *huomaa*
note; *huom.* N.B. (= *nota
bene)*; ~ *erehdyksensä* realize
one's mistake; *jäädä -amatta*
pass unnoticed, be overlooked,
(jklta) escape a p.'s notice; *ei*
~ overlook, take no notice
(of). **-ttava** noticeable,
perceptible; *(selvästi)* marked;
(melkoinen) considerable;
(etevä) outstanding, prominent;
remarkable, notable,
noteworthy; *(näkyvä)*
conspicuous; ~ *henkilö (m.)* a
distinguished person; ~
parannus a decided
improvement; *~ssa määrin* in
(t. to) a noticeable degree;
olla ~lla sijalla occupy a
prominent place. **-ttavasti**
perceptibly, noticeably,
appreciably, markedly,
considerably. **-ttavuus**
conspicuousness, prominence.
-ttu prominent; *kohota ~un
asemaan* rise to distinction.
huomau|ttaa point out, remark;
(muistuttaa) remind. **-tus**
remark; comment.
huomen *(aamu)* morning; *~na*
tomorrow; *hyvää ~ta* good
morning! **-aamu:** *~na*
tomorrow morning. **-ilta:** *~na*
tomorrow night (evening).
huominen *a.* tomorrow's, [. .
of] tomorrow; *huomiseen* till
tomorrow.
huomio attention, notice;
(havainto) observation; *~n
arvoinen* worth noticing; *ottaa
~on* take into consideration,
pay attention to, bear in
mind; consider; allow for,
make allowance for; *ottaen
~on* in view of, considering,
in consideration of, having

regard to; *jättää ~on
ottamatta* pay no attention to,
disregard, ignore; *pyydän tulla
~on otetuksi* I should like to
be considered; *herättää ~ta*
arouse attention, attract
notice, *(tavatonta ~ta)* create
a sensation; *kiinnittää ~ta
(~nsa) jhk* give attention to,
take notice of, *(jkn huomio)*
call (draw) attention to; *älä
kiinnitä häneen ~ta* pay no
attention to him.
huomi|oida observe. **-oitsija**
observer, commentator.
huomio|kyky [power of]
observation. **-onotettava** . .
worthy of consideration;
considerable. **-taherättävä**
striking, conspicuous;
sensational.
huomispäivä tomorrow.
huone room; ~ *kadulle
(pihalle) päin* front (back)
room; *tilata* ~ reserve a
room [at a hotel]. **-enlämpö**
room temperature. **-entaulu**
catechism. **-isto** flat, *et. Am.*
apartment.
huonekalu piece of furniture;
~t furniture. **-kangas**
upholstery material. **-kauppias**
furniture dealer. **-sto** [suite
of] furniture.
huone|kasvi house plant.
-kumppani room-mate. **-kunta**
household; house; *(perhe)*
family.
huono bad; *(kehno)* poor;
(paha) wicked, *(kurja)*
wretched; ~ *kohtelu (m.)*
rough treatment, ill-usage;
~lla menestyksellä with little
success, with poor results;
~lla tuulella in a bad humour
(mood); ~ *puoli* weak point,
drawback; ~ *terveys* poor
health, ill-health; *~ssa
kunnossa* in bad condition;
olla ~na sairaana be very ill.
-kuuloinen hard of hearing.
-kuuloisuus [partial] deafness.
-laatuinen of poor quality,
inferior. **-maineinen** . . of bad
reputation; notorious,
disreputable. **-maineisuus** bad
reputation, notoriety,
disrepute. **-mmuus** inferiority;

(laadun) inferior quality. **-mpi** worse; inferior (to); *-mpaan päin* for the worse.
-muistinen; *on* ~ has a bad memory, is forgetful. **-nlainen** rather poor. **-nnus** deterioration.

huonont|aa make .. worse, impair. **-ua** deteriorate, get worse. **-uminen** deterioration.

huono|näköinen weak-sighted. **-onninen** unlucky, ill-fated (-starred). **-päinen** unintelligent, not bright; *on* ~ has a poor head [for mathematics *etc*]. **-sti** badly, ill, poorly; *asiat ovat* ~ things are bad (in a bad way, in a sad state); *hänen oli käydä* ~ he very nearly came to a sad end, he had a narrow escape.

huono|ta get worse; deteriorate; *-nemaan päin* on the decline. **-tuulinen** moody. **-tuulisuus** bad temper. **-us** badness; poorness; *(tavaran)* inferior quality. **-vointinen** indisposed, unwell. **-vointisuus** indisposition.

huopa felt; *(-peite)* blanket, *(esim. matka-)* rug. **-hattu** felt hat. **-kynä** felt pen.

huor|a harlot, prostitute; whore. **-in:** *tehdä* ~ commit adultery. **-uus** adultery.

huosta possession; *(hoito)* care, charge; custody; *ottaa ~ansa* take charge of.

huotra scabbard.

huovata back the oars, back water; *soutaa ja* ~ shilly-shally.

hupa|ilu comedy, farce. **-isa** jolly, amusing. **-isuus** pleasantness, jolliness.

hupakko scatterbrained [girl].

hupeneminen decrease; vanishing.

hupi fun; *~hahmo* figure of f.

hupsu *a.* foolish, silly; crazy, idiotic; *s.* simpleton, dunce. **-tella** play the fool. **-us** foolishness.

huristaa speed, fly, let go at a good speed.

hurja wild; *(hillitön)* unrestrained; *(raivokas)* furious, frantic, violent.

-nrohkea foolhardy. **-päinen** fierce, ferocious; *(pelkäämätön)* reckless. **-päisyys** ferocity; recklessness. **-pää** madcap; *(yltiö-)* fanatic.

hurjaste|lija madcap; *auto~* dangerous driver. **-lla** lead a wild life. **-lu** wild life, *(elostelu)* dissolute life; *(auto-ym)* reckless driving.

hurj|istua become furious, fly into a rage; *h-tunut* frenzied, infuriated. **-uus** wildness, recklessness; fury.

hurma ecstasy, rapture; fascination [of speed, *vauhdin*]. **-antua** be [come] fascinated (charmed, infatuated). **-ava** charming. **-henki** fanatic. **-henkinen** fanatic [al]. **-henkisyys** fanaticism. **-ta** charm, fascinate, captivate, enrapture. **-us** charm; enchantment, fascination.

hurme gore. **-inen** gory.

hurmio ecstasy. **-itua** go into ecstasies (raptures); *vrt. huuma, -ta.*

hurraa hurrah! **-huuto** cheer, *jklle* for; *-huudot* cheering.

hurrata cheer [a p., *jklle*].

hursk|as pious, *(harras)* devout; *s.* devotee. **-astella** make a show of piousness; *~televa* sanctimonious. **-astelu** sanctimoniousness; bigotry. **-aus** piety; saintliness.

hursti sacking; burlap.

husaari hussar.

huti|loida do .. carelessly; scamp, bungle; *-loiva* slovenly, careless, slipshod. **-lus** careless fellow.

huudah|dus exclamation, *(-sana)* interjection. **-taa** exclaim, cry out, call out; ~ *ilosta* cry out for joy, give a cry of delight.

huuh|della rinse [out]; wash; *(esim. W.C.)* flush. **-donta** rinsing; rinse; *kullan* ~ panning for gold.

huuhkaja eagle-owl.

huuhtelu rinse, wash; *lääk.* irrigation; *(esim. W.C:n)* flushing. **-ruisku** douche.

huuhto|a rinse [out], wash; ~

kultaa pan for gold; ~ *pois*
wash off (away). **-utua** *(yli
laidan)* be washed overboard.
huuli lip; *(sutkautus)* quip,
[wise]crack, witticism; *heittää
huulta* banter, joke; *painaa
~lleen* press to one's lips.
-harppu mouth-organ,
harmonica. **-kukkainen** *bot.*
labiate. **-nen:** *paksu~*
thick-lipped. **-parta** moustache.
-puikko lip-stick. **-puna**
lip-stick; *panna ~a* put on l.
-voide lip salve. **-äänne** *kiel.*
labial [sound].
huuma *(ilon, voiton)* ecstasy.
-antua *(et. iskusta)* be
stunned; be stupefied; *~ntunut
(m.)* dazed, dizzy. **-ta** stun;
stupefy; *(urheilija ym.)* dope;
intoxicate; *menestyksen -ama*
intoxicated by success; *onnen
-ama* drunk with happiness;
riemun -ama giddy *(t.*
transported) with joy.
huumaus daze, *kuv.*
intoxication; *lääk.* [light]
an[a]esthesia; *riemun ~* an
ecstasy of delight. **-aine** drug,
narcotic, *sl.* dope; *~en
käyttäjä* drug addict (abuser),
(et. heroiinin) junkie; *~en
myyjä* drug peddler; *~en
vaikutuksen alaisena* under the
influence of drugs, high [on
pot ym].
huume *ks. ed.; ~itten käyttäjät*
narcotic addicts. **-laki**
narcotics act.
huumori humour. **-ntaju** sense
of humour; *on ~inen* has a
s. of h.
huur|re white frost, hoarfrost,
rime. **-teinen** .. white (rimed)
with frost.
huuru vapour, steam.
huut|aa call [out], shout, yell,
shriek; ~ *apua* call for help;
~ *jkta avuksi* call a p. to
one's aid; ~ *jku kuninkaaksi*
proclaim .. king. **-ava** *kuv.*
glaring, flagrant; *(hätä)* crying.
huuto cry, call, shout; yell;
(huutokaupassa) bid;
ihmettelyn ~ a cry of
astonishment; *päästä ~on*
come into vogue; *olla
huonossa huudossa* have a

bad reputation; *joutua
huonoon ~on* fall into
disrepute; *saattaa huonoon
~on* bring discredit on.
-kauppa auction, public sale;
-kaupan toimittaja auctioneer;
myydä -kaupalla sell by
auction, auction off; *ostaa jtk
-kaupasta* buy at an auction;
(~kamari auction rooms).
-matka: *~n päässä* within
call. **-merkki** exclamation
mark. **-torvi** megaphone.
-äänestys acclamation.
huveta dwindle; decrease,
shrink; *hupeni puoleen* was
reduced to [one] half.
huvi pleasure, fun; *(huvitus)*
amusement, entertainment; *~n
vuoksi* for [the] fun [of the
thing]; *omaksi ~kseen* for
one's own pleasure. **-ala**
entertainment industry, show
business. **-kausi** season.
huvila villa, cottage, bungalow,
country-house. **-kaupunki**
garden suburb. **-yhdyskunta**
suburban community.
huvi|lennätys joy flight. **-linna**
pleasure palace. **-maja**
summer-house. **-matka**
pleasure-trip. **-matkailija**
excursionist. **-näytelmä**
comedy. **-puisto** amusement
park. **-pursi** luxury yacht.
-retkeilijä excursionist. **-retki**
excursion; *tehdä* ~ go on an
e. **-tella** amuse oneself, enjoy
oneself; celebrate; *-ttelimme
perusteellisesti (puhek.)* we
had a high old time.
-tilaisuus entertainment. **-ttaa**
amuse, divert; interest;
(hauskuttaa) entertain; *minua
-tti* I was amused at *(t. by)*
.. **-ttava** amusing,
entertaining. **-ttelu** amusement;
merry-making; *~nhaluinen*
fond of amusement,
pleasure-loving. **-tus**
amusement, entertainment,
diversion; pleasure. **-vero**
entertainment duty, *Am.*
amusement tax.
hyasintti hyacinth.
hydraulinen hydraulic.
hyeena hyena.
hygi|eeninen hygienic; sanitary.

-enia hygiene.
hyi fie! ~ *häpeä* for shame!
hyinen icy.
hykertää: ~ *käsiään* rub one's
hands.
hylje seal.
hylkeen|nahka sealskin. **-pyynti**
sealing. **-pyytäjä** sealer. **-rasva**
seal blubber.
hylki|ä despise; reject; *vettä*
-vä water-repellent. **-ö**
good-for-nothing, wastrel;
yhteiskunnan ~ social outcast.
hylky refuse, waste; *mer.*
wreck; *joutua hylyksi* become
a wreck. **-joukko** dregs, scum.
-puu waste timber. **-tavara**
defective goods, rejects; *mer.*
wreckage; *(maihin ajautunut)*
stranded goods, *(vedessä*
uiskenteleva) flotsam [and
jetsam].
hylk|ääminen rejection;
abandonment, desertion;
refusal, declining (of an
offer); *ehdotti esityksen*
h-mistä moved the rejection
of the proposal. **-äävä:** ~
päätös rejection.
hylly shelf *(pl.* shelves);
(junassa ym) rack. **-kaappi**
cupboard. **-kkö** shelves,
shelving. **-stö** *(yhdistelmä)*
storage unit.
hyllyä shake, *(maa)* quake.
hylsy [cartridge] case.
hylättävä unacceptable, .. to
be condemned.
hylätä reject; *(jättää)* forsake,
leave, abandon, desert; *(ei*
tunnustaa) disown; *(evätä)*
refuse, decline; *(esim.*
äänestyslippu) cancel; *(jk*
kelvottomana) discard; *(maali,*
urh.) disallow; *(syyte)* dismiss;
~ *kutsu* decline an invitation;
~ *pyyntö* refuse a request; ~
tarjous reject an offer; ~ *jku*
tutkinnossa fail [to pass] a p.,
sl. Engl. plough; *(anomus ym)*
hylättiin was turned down;
(lääkärintark ym.) reject; ~
vaimonsa desert one's wife;
tunsi itsensä hylätyksi had a
feeling of rejection.
hymi|nä murmur [ing]; *laulun*
~ humming of a tune;
(tuulen) sighing. **-stys** *kuv.*

[songs of] praise; eulogy.
hymni hymn; anthem.
hymy smile; *(teennäinen)*
smirk. **-huuli:** ~*n* with a
smile on one's lips, smilingly.
-illä smile (at, on); *(typerästi)*
simper, smirk, *(leveästi)* grin,
smile all over one's face;
(ivallisesti) sneer (at); *(kuv.,*
suosia) smile [up]on. **-ilyttää**
make .. smile; *(huvittaa)*
amuse. **-kuoppa** dimple.
hymähtää smile [slightly],
(ivallisesti) sneer at.
hypellä jump, hop, skip; frisk.
hypistellä: ~ *jtk (sormin)*
finger at, fiddle with.
hypno|osi hypnosis.
-ottinen hypnotic. **-tismi**
hypnotism. **-tisoida** hypnotize.
hypoteekki mortgage. **-laina**
mortgage loan.
hypotee|si hypothes|is, *pl.* -es.
-ttinen hypothetic [al].
hyppiä jump, hop; skip.
hyppy jump, leap, bound.
(veteen ym) plunge. **-ri**
take-off [board *t.* platform].;
(~mäki ski jump). **-sellinen** a
pinch (of).
hyppä|ys jump; leap, bound;
yhdellä -yksellä at a bound.
hypäh|dys bound. **-tää** bound;
give a jerk; ~ *pystyyn* jump
to one's feet, start up.
hypätä jump; leap, spring; ~
asiasta toiseen skip from one
subject to another; ~ *veteen*
plunge into the water; ~
yhdellä jalalla hop on one
leg; ~ *(sivun) yli* skip [a
page].
hyrin|ä hum[ming], buzz[ing].
-stä hum, buzz.
hyrrä [spinning-]top. **-liike**
gyration. **-tä** gyrate.
hyrsky surge, spray. **-tä** surge.
hyrähtää *(itkuun)* burst out
crying.
hyräillä hum, croon.
hyssyttää hush; ~ *lasta uneen*
lull a child to sleep.
hysteerinen hysteric [al].
hytistä shiver [with cold].
hytkyä shake, rock.
hytkähtää [give a] jump;
(vavahtaa) start, give a start;
sydämeni hytkähti my heart

stood still.
hytti cabin; *(loisto-)* stateroom.
-paikka berth.
hytty|nen mosquito *(pl. -es)*,
gnat; *siivilöidä -siä* strain at a
gnat; *-sen purema*
mosquito-bite. **-sverkko**
mosquito-net.
hyve virtue. **-ellinen** virtuous.
-ellisyys virtue, virtuousness.
hyvi|lleen, -llään *(jstk)*
delighted, pleased (with, at).
hyvin well; *(sangen)* very;
(kovin) very much; ~
järjestelty well-organized,
well-arranged; ~ *kiinnostunut*
much *(t.* greatly) interested
(in); ~ *tehty* well-made; well
done [!]; ~ *moni heistä* a
great many of them; ~ *paljon*
very much, a great deal; ~
paljon kirjoja plenty of books,
lots of books. **-ansaittu**
well-deserved (-earned).
-hoidettu well cared for,
well-kept, *(esim. puisto)* neatly
kept; *(esim. tukka, parta)*
well-groomed. **-kasvatettu** well
brought up; *(sivistynyt)*
well-bred. **-kin** quite, rather.
-varustettu well-stocked.
hyvinvointi well-being; health;
(aineellinen) prosperity. **-valtio**
(huolto-) welfare state.
-yhteiskunta [the] affluent
society.
hyvinvoipa *(varakas)*
prosperous, well-to-do.
hyvi|ttää make up (to sb. for),
make good, compensate (for);
make amends for; *(tileissä)*
credit; *(maksaa takaisin)*
reimburse; ~ *jkn tiliä* credit
[an amount] to a p.'s
account, credit a p.'s account
(with). **-tys** compensation *(m.
raha-)*; recompense; *(tileissä)*
crediting; *(alennus)* allowance;
-tykseksi jstk as compensation
for, in return for; *antaa ~tä
(m.)* rehabilitate a p.; *vaatia
~tä* demand satisfaction for.
hyvyys goodness; kindness;
tämän maailman ~ the good
things of this world.
hyvä *a.* good; kind; *s.* good,
welfare; *(etu)* benefit; ~ *herra
(kirjeessä)* Dear Sir; *~t*

herrat Dear Sirs, *Am.*
Gentlemen! ~ *on!* good! all
right! *no ~!* very well! well
then! *ole, olkaa ~* please
(harvoin tarjottaessa); *ole ~
(tässä saat,* jtk annettaessa)
here you are! there you are!
*(Kiitoksia paljon! —) ole ~
(pidä ~näsi)* you're welcome!
[Oh,] not at all! *ole ~ ja
sulje ikkuna* shut the window,
please *(t.* will you?) *olkaa ~
ottakaa leipää* will you have
some bread? *ei oikein ~ä
(kuulu)* (How are you? —) not
too well, I am afraid; *ei ~llä
eikä pahalla* neither by fair
means nor foul; *~llä syyllä*
with good reason; *~llä
tuulella* in good humour, in a
good mood; *~n aikaa* a good
while; *~n joukon yli 100* well
over a hundred; *~n matkaa*
quite a long way, quite a
distance; *pitää ~nään* put up
with; *pidä ~näsi* you are
welcome to it! *sillä ~* there
is no more to be said; *~ä
matkaa* [have] a pleasant
journey! **-enteinen** auspicious,
propitious. **-huuto** cheer,
acclamation.
hyväi|llä caress, fondle; pet;
-levä (m.) gentle, soft. **-ly**
caress[es]; *(~sana* term of
endearment).
hyväksi: *jnk (jkn)* ~ for ..,
for the benefit (the good) of;
hänen -kseen in his favour,
for his good; *hyväksemme
(liik.)* to our credit; *nähdä ~*
see fit. **-käyttö** utilization;
exploitation.
hyväksy|jä *(vekselin)* acceptor.
-minen, -mys approval,
approbation; acceptance;
(myöntymys) consent;
(vekselin, m.) endorsement;
acknowledgement; *(äänekäs)*
applause. **-ttävyys**
acceptability. **-ttävä** acceptable.
-västi approvingly; *nyökkäsi ~
(m.)* gave a nod of approval.
-ä approve (of); *(kutsu ym.)*
accept; *(tutkinnossa)* pass;
(tunnustaa) recognize,
acknowledge; sanction;
(jäseneksi ym.) admit; ~

ehdot accept the terms; ~
laki adopt a law; *hänet -ttiin
(tutkinnossa)* he passed [the
examination]; *häntä ei -tty* he
failed [in] the examination;
ei ~ (m.) disapprove (of);
ehtoja ei voida ~ (m.) the
terms are unacceptable;
lakiehdotus -ttiin the bill was
passed.

hyvä|kuntoinen in good
condition. **-lahjainen** talented.
-luontoinen good- (sweet-)
tempered. **-luontoisuus** good
nature. **-maineinen..** of good
repute (reputation). **-nahkainen**
kuv. good-natured.

hyvänen: ~ *aika!* goodness
[me]! my goodness! good
heavens!

hyvän|hajuinen sweet-scented
(-smelling); fragrant, aromatic.
-laatuinen *(kasvain)* benign,
nonmalignant. **-nlaatuisuus**
benignancy. **-lainen** fairly
good; fair, middling.
-makuinen .. of good flavour,
palatable; *on ~* tastes good.
-suopa benevolent, benign;
kindly disposed. **-suopuus**
goodwill, kindliness.

hyvänsä: *kuka ~* anybody,
(jokainen joka) whoever; *kuka
~ heistä* any one of them;
mitä ~ whatever; anything;
mitä ~ hän tekeekin ..
whatever he does; *hän
näyttää sietävän mitä ~* he
seems to stand anything;
olipa sen laita miten ~ be it
as it may, however it may
be; *mitä laatua ~* of any
kind.

hyvän|tahtoinen kind,
benevolent; well-meaning.
-tahtoisesti kindly; ~
lähettänette minulle would you
please (would you be good
enough to) send me ..
-tahtoisuus kindness,
benevolence, goodwill.
-tapainen well-behaved
(-mannered). **-tekeväinen**
charitable. **-tekeväisyys**
charity; charitableness;
(~*laitos* charitable *(t.* charity)
institution; ~**myyjäiset** charity
bazaar). **-tekijä** benefactor;

(~tär) benefactress.
Hyväntoivonniemi the Cape of
Good Hope.
hyväntuuli|nen good-humoured,
cheerful. **-suus** good humour.
hyvä|onninen fortunate.
-oppinen quick to learn.
-palkkainen well-paid. **-päinen**
clever, quick-witted, bright.
-stellä take leave of a p., bid
a p. farewell. **-sti** good-bye!
(illalla good night); *arkik.* bye
bye; (~**jättö** parting;
farewell).**-sydäminen**
kind-hearted. **-sydämisyys**
kind-heartedness, kindness.
-tekoinen well made, .. a
good make. **-tuloinen** *(toimi)*
lucrative, remunerative; *hän
on ~* he has a good income.
-työ kind *(t.* charitable) deed;
hyvät työt good works.
hyvää|tarkoittava well-meaning.
-tekevä beneficial.
hyydyttää [cause to] congeal,
coagulate.
hyytelö jelly. **-ityä** [turn to]
jelly. **-mäinen** jelly-like,
gelatinous.
hyyty|minen congelation; *(veren
ym)* clotting, coagulation. **-ä**
congeal; *(maksottua)*
coagulate, clot; *(hyytelöstä
ym)* set; *-nyt* congealed,
jellied, *(veri ym)* clotted,
coagulated.
hyödyk|e commodity. **-sikäyttö**
utilization.
hyödylli|nen useful, .. of
benefit, .. of [great] use;
profitable. **-syys** usefulness,
utility, use; profitability;
(~*periaate* utilitarian principle).
hyödy|ttää benefit, profit, be
of use (to); *mitä se ~* what
is the use [of it]? what
good is it? *se ei -tä mitään*
it is no use, it is of no
avail; *ei -ttäisi* it would serve
no purpose. **-ttömyys**
uselessness, futility;
fruitlessness. **-ttömästi**
uselessly, to no purpose. **-tön**
useless, .. of no use (avail);
(hukkaan mennyt) fruitless,
futile; *on ~tä yrittää* it is no
use trying.
hyökkäys attack, assault (on);

(rynnäkkö) charge; *(maahan)*
invasion; *(-retki)* raid (on).
-haluinen aggressive. **-kanta:**
olla -kannalla take the
offensive. **-sota** war of
aggression. **-suunnitelma** plan
of attack. **-vaunu** tank.
hyökkää|jä aggressor; assailant,
attacker; *(maahan-)* invader;
urh. forward, *(jääkiekk.)* attack
man. **-mättömyyssopimus**
non-aggression pact. **-vä**
attacking *jne.;* aggressive.
hyöky surge; swell. **-aalto** tidal
wave; *(tyrskyt)* breakers.
hyökätä attack; assault [a p.
jkn kimppuun]; *(maahan ym)*
invade; *(syöksyä)* rush, dash;
~ *jkn kimppuun (m.)* fall
upon a p.; ~ *ovelle* make for
the door; *poliisi hyökkäsi
mielenosoittajia vastaan* the
police charged the
demonstrators.
hyönteinen insect.
hyönteis|myrkky insecticide.
-syöjä insect-eater; *a.*
insectivorous. **-tiede**
entomology. **-tieteellinen**
entomological. **-tutkija**
entomologist.
hyöri|nä flurry, bustle; hurry.
-ä be busy; bustle.
hyöty use; benefit; *(etu)*
advantage; *(voitto)* profit;
käyttää hyödykseen make use
of, utilize, *(riistää)* exploit;
olla hyödyksi be useful, be
helpful, be of use (of value);
se ei ole kenellekään hyödyksi
it is no good (it is of no
use) to anyone. **-ajoneuvo**
commercial vehicle. **-kuorma**
payload. **-mansikka** strawberry.
-näkökohdat utilitarian
considerations. **-suhde** *tekn.*
efficiency.
hyötyä benefit, profit (by);
(voittaa) gain (by); ~ *jstk
(m.)* derive advantage (benefit)
from.
hyöt|ää force. **-ö** forcing.
hädintuskin narrowly, just; with
a narrow margin; *hän
pelastui* ~ he had a narrow
escape, he escaped by the
skin of his teeth.
hädissään: *olla* ~ *jstk* be

distressed (alarmed) about.
hädänalainen distressed;
destitute, needy; ~ *asema*
distress.
häijy bad, malicious, evil; *(et.
lapsesta)* naughty. **-nilkinen**
malicious, malevolent.
-nilkisyys maliciousness,
malice. **-ys** malice, ill will.
häikäilemä|ttä unscrupulously,
regardless of others;
inconsiderately. **-ttömyys**
unscrupulousness; lack of
consideration. **-tön**
unscrupulous; inconsiderate;
(julkea) arrogant; .. *on* ~ ..
has no scruples.
häikäi|llä have consideration
(for); have scruples (about ..
-ing); *(empiä)* hesitate; boggle
at. **-ly** consideration;
hesitation, scruples.
häikäis|tä dazzle. **-evä** dazzling,
kuv. brilliant. **-ysuoja** *(auton)*
sun-shield.
häil|yä swing, sway; *(horjua)*
waver; *-yvä* wavering,
faltering; *(epävakaa)*
inconstant, fickle.
häipy|minen vanishing; *rad.*
fading, *elok. m.* fade-out.
-mätön ineffaceable, indelible.
-vä *(kestämätön)* fugitive,
transitory. **-ä** vanish; fade
[out]; *vrt. hälvetä.*
häiri|intymätön undisturbed.
-intyä be disturbed; *h-tynyt*
disturbed. **-tsevästi**
disturbingly; *vaikuttaa* ~ have
a disturbing effect. **-tä**
disturb; interfere (with);
(vaivata) [cause]
inconvenience, trouble; *rad.*
jam; *-tty lepo (m.)* broken
rest.
häiriö disturbance; disorder;
(haitta) inconvenience; *rad.*
interference, atmospherics. **-tön**
undisturbed; *rad.* interfer-
ence-free.
häiv|e, -ähdys trace (of a
smile, *hymyn);* shade.
häkel|tyä get confused, get
flurried; *hän ei -tynyt* he was
not put out.
häkil|ä, -öidä hackle.
häkki *(linnun ym)* cage;
(kana-) coop; *panna ~in*

cage; coop in.
häkä carbon monoxide; *kuolla
~än* be asphyxiated. **-myrkytys**
carbon monoxide poisoning.
häli|nä noise, tumult, hubbub,
clamour, *(turha)* fuss; *mikä ~*
what a to-do! **-stä** make a
noise, clamour; *-sevä* noisy,
clamorous.
hälve|neminen dispersion. **-ntää**
dispel, disperse. **-tä** be
dispelled; disappear, fade
[away]; *sumu -nee* the mist
is clearing.
häly commotion, stir,
excitement; *kyllä tästä ~
nousee* this will create a
sensation; *pitää suurta ~ä
jstk* make a great fuss about
.. **-tin** alarm *(esim.* burglar
a.). **-ttää** give the alarm,
sound the alarm; alert [the
police].
hälytys alarm; *väärä ~* false
alarm. **-ajoneuvo** emergency
vehicle. **-laite** alarm [system];
vrt. hälytin. **-tila, -valmius**
alert.
hämi: *olla ~llään* be
embarrassed; *saattaa ~lleen*
embarrass, disconcert sb.
-llinen *(-llään oleva)* ks.
ed.; (ujo) shy, self-conscious,
ill at ease.
hämmen|nys embarrassment,
bewilderment, perplexity; *olla
-nyksissä* be confused, be
disconcerted; *käsitteiden ~*
confusion of ideas. **-nyttävä**
bewildering, *(ajatusta)*
distracting. **-tymätön**
undisturbed, *(henk.)*
unperturbed. **-tyä** *(henk.)*
be [come] confused
(bewildered, perplexed); *olin
-tynyt heidän seurassaan* felt
embarrassed (abashed) in
their presence. **-tää** mix, stir;
kuv. confuse; upset; *vrt. ed.*
hämmin|ki confusion; disorder;
-gin vallassa (m.) flustered.
hämmäs|tys surprise,
astonishment, amazement;
suureksi -tyksekseni to my
great surprise, to my
astonishment. **-tyttävä**
surprising, amazing,
astounding. **-tyttää** surprise;

astonish, amaze. **-tyä** be
astonished, be surprised (at);
be amazed; be taken aback.
hämy twilight, *(ilta-)* dusk.
-inen dusky, dim.
hämähäkinseitti cobweb,
spider's web, *(hieno kuin ~)*
gossamer.
hämähäkki spider.
hämär|tää darken, grow dusky;
alkaa ~ it is getting dark;
silmiäni ~ my eyes are
growing dim. **-yys** dimness,
darkness; obscurity.
hämärä *a.* dark; dim, obscure;
dusky; hazy; *s.* dusk, twilight;
(aamu-) the grey dawn; *~
aavistus* vague idea; *hämärin
sanoin* in veiled language; *~n
peitossa* shrouded in mystery.
-peräinen shady; obscure.
-peräisyys shadiness; obscurity.
-sokeus night blindness. **-sti**
dimly, faintly, vaguely.
hämä|tä, -ys bluff.
hämäännyttää confuse, perplex,
puzzle, disconcert.
hän he, *fem.* she; *hänet, häntä*
him, *fem.* her; *hänelle* to
(for) him, her; *häneltä* from
him, her; *hänestä* of (about)
him, her.
-hän ks. *-han.*
hänen his; *fem.* her, hers.
hännys tail. **-takki** swallowtail
coat, tails; *-takissa* in [full]
evening dress. **-telijä**
sycophant. **-tellä:** *~ jkta*
cringe before, fawn upon,
curry favour with.
hännä|llinen tailed. **-tön** tailless.
häntä tail; *(ketun)* brush; *ks.
hän.*
häpeissään: *olla ~ jstk* be
ashamed of.
häpeä shame, disgrace;
dishonour; *(hyi) ~!* for
shame! *~kseni* to my shame;
on ~ksi jklle is a disgrace
to; *joutuu ~än* is put to
shame; *saattaa ~än* bring
shame upon, disgrace. **-llinen**
shameful, disgraceful;
infamous, ignominious; *~
juttu (m.)* scandalous affair.
-llisyys shamefulness,
disgracefulness. **-mättömyys**
shamelessness, effrontery;

impudence, brazenness. **-mätön** shameless, brazen, unashamed. **-paalu** pillory. **-pilkku** stain, taint, blot.
häpäi|sevä insulting; defamatory. **-stä** disgrace; dishonour; *(jtk pyhää)* profane; *(loukata)* violate; *(lippua)* desecrate.
härkä ox *(pl. oxen)*; *(nuori)* steer. **-jyvä** ergot. **-päinen** pigheaded, obstinate. **-päisyys** obstinacy. **-taistelija** bullfighter. **-taistelu** bull fight.
härmä white frost, rime, *bot.* mildew.
härnätä tease, chaff.
härski *ks. eltaantunut.*
härän|häntä(liemi) oxtail (soup). **-liha** beef. **-paisti** joint *(t.* sirloin) of beef. **-rinta** brisket of beef.
häthätää in a hurry, hastily.
hätiköi|dä be in [too great] a hurry, *(työssä)* scamp; *tehdä -mällä* scamp, *(pilata)* boteh sth. **-ty** rash; [over]hasty, precipitate; ~ *työ* a botched piece of work; *älä tee -jä johtopäätöksiä* don't jump to conclusions.
hätistää chase away, shoo [away].
hätkäh|dyttää startle; *-dyttävä* startling. **-tää** start, give a start.
hätyy|tellä *(esim. tyttöjä)* molest. **-ttää** harass, assail; molest; *(esim. velan takia)* press (.. for payment of a debt).
hätä distress; *(pula)* trouble; *(vaara)* danger; *(huoli)* anxiety; *(kiire)* hurry; *hädän tullen* in the hour of need; *ei* ~ *lakia lue* necessity knows no law; *mikä* ~*nä?* what is wrong? what's the trouble? what is the matter [with you]? *ensi* ~*än* to tide a p. over, for the time being; *rientää* ~*än* hasten to the rescue. **-apu** relief. **-huuto** cry of distress.
hätäi|lemättömyys calm[ness], composure. **-lemätön** calm, composed, collected. **-llä** hurry [too much]; act rashly; be

anxious; *älä -le* don't worry! *(älä kiirehdi)* take your time. **-ly** hurrying; fussing; anxiety. **-nen** hasty, hurried; impatient; anxious; ~ *silmäys* a hurried (a cursory) glance. **-syys** haste, hastiness, hurry; impatience.
hätä|jarru emergency brake. **-kaste** emergency christening. **-keino** emergency measure; makeshift, expedient. **-kello** alarm-bell. **-merkki** distress signal. **-pikaa** in a hurry. **-satama** port of distress, *kuv.* haven of refuge. **-tila:** ~*ssa* in case of need, in an emergency, *(äärimmäisessä)* in case of extreme urgency. **-valhe** white lie; fib. **-vara** makeshift. **-varjelus** self-defence. **-äkärsivä** distressed, destitute.
hätään|tyä become alarmed; *-tynyt* alarmed, anxious; startled; *-tyi suunniltaan* got scared out of his (her) wits.
häveli|äisyys modesty, diffidence. **-äs** modest; bashful, coy, diffident.
häve|ttää make .. feel ashamed; *minua* ~ I am ashamed (of). **-tä** be (feel) ashamed (of); *etkö häpeä* are you not ashamed [of yourself]? *häpeämättä* shamelessly, unblushingly.
hävinnyt: *(kadonnut)* lost, missing.
hävi|ttäjä destroyer, *ilm.* fighter. **-ttää** destroy; *(autioksi)* lay .. waste, devastate; ravage; *(tyystin)* annihilate; *(varoja)* misappropriate; ~ *juurineen* destroy root and branch, root out; eradicate; ~ *maan tasalle* level to the ground, raze; ~ *omaisuutensa* run through one's fortune; ~ *sukupuuttoon* exterminate.
hävitys destruction, ruin; devastation; ravage[s]; *(joskus)* havoc. **-sota** war of extermination.
hävi|tä disappear, vanish; *(pelissä ym)* lose; incur (suffer, sustain) a loss; ~

kaupassa lose in a transaction; ~ *näkyvistä (m.)* pass out of sight. **-ämätön** indestructible; ineffaceable, indelible.

häviö ruin; destruction; *(kukistuminen)* fall, downfall; *(tappio)* loss; *(taistelussa)* defeat; *joutua ~lle* lose; meet with defeat; *joutua ~ön* be ruined; *saattaa ~ön* ruin.

hävy|ttömyys shamelessness; effrontery, impudence; insolence. **-tön** shameless; impudent, insolent.

häväistys insult, affront; violation. *(jkn pyhän)* profanation; blasphemy. **-juttu** scandal. **-kirjoitus** libel, lampoon. **-puhe** slander.

hää|joukko bridal party. **-lahja** wedding present.

häälyä hover; waver.

hää|matka honeymoon trip. **-menot** wedding ceremony, marriage service. **-puku** wedding dress.

häämöttää be dimly visible; loom; be [dimly] outlined.

hääriä bustle, be busy.

hää|t wedding; *häissä* at a w. **-tavat** marriage customs.

häätää evict; turn out.

häätö eviction. **-oikeus** right to evict.

hökkeli hovel, hut; shack.

höl|kkä jog-trot. **-kyttää** *(juosta* ~) jog [along].

höllen|tyä get loose [r], slacken; relax. **-tää** make .. loose [r], loosen; slacken.

höll|yys looseness, slackness; *kuv.* laxity. **-ä** loose.

höllä suinen babbling.

hölmis|tys amazement, stupefaction. **-tyttää** amaze, puzzle, dumbfound. **-tyä** be [come] amazed (dumbfounded, stupefied).

hölmö [silly] fool, simpleton, *kuv. m.* idiot.

hölty|minen loosening; relaxation. **-ä** get loose, work loose, loosen.

hölynpöly nonsense; *puhua ~ä* talk nonsense, drivel; *puhdasta ~ä!* [pure] nonsense!

höper|tyä *(vanhuuttaan)* become senile, grow childish; *-tynyt* in his dotage.

höperö muddled [in the head], cracked [up]; *vanha ~* old fool, dotard.

höpistä mumble; *(laverrella)* prattle.

höpsiä talk nonsense, drivel; *älä höpsi!* don't be silly!

höristää: ~ *korviaan* prick up one's ears.

hörppiä drink noisily, *sl.* slurp.

hörö: *korvat ~ssä* with ears pricked up.

höyhen feather. **-huisku** feather-duster. **-inen** feathered. **-patja** feather mattress. **-puku** plumage. **-saaret** Land of Nod. **-sarja** feather-weight. **-tää** pluck; *kuv.* lick, give .. a good licking. **-töyhtö** plume.

höylä plane. **-nlastut** shavings. **-penkki** carpenter's bench. **-tä** plane; dress. **-ämö** planing works.

höyry steam, vapour; *täyttä* ~ä at full steam; *muuttaa (-ttua) ~ksi* evaporate. **-jyrä** steam roller. **-kaappi** vapour-bath. **-kattila** boiler. **-kone** steam-engine. **-laiva** steamer, steamship; *(~liikenne* steamship traffic). **-pilli** hooter. **-stää** *tekn.* vaporize. **-ttää, -tä** steam. **-veturi** steam-engine. **-voima** steam-power. **-ävä** steamy, steaming.

höys|te seasoning, flavour [ing]; *(mauste)* spice; relish *(m. kuv.)*. **-teinen** seasoned, flavoured; spiced. **-tämätön** unspiced, unseasoned. **-tää** spice, season; enrich; *vahvasti -tetty* highly seasoned; *kuv.* spiced; interspersed [with stories etc.]

höyty web, fane [of a feather]; down.

I

iankaiken for ever [and ever].
iankaikki|nen eternal;
everlasting. **-sesti** eternally, for
ever. **-suus** eternity.
idealis|mi idealism. **-ti** idealist.
idempänä farther east.
iden|tifioida identify. **-ttinen**
identical.
ideologi|a ideology. **-nen**
ideological.
idiootti idiot.
idylli idyll. **-nen** idyllic.
idänpuoleinen eastern, east.
idät|tää [make] sprout,
germinate. **-ys** germination.
ien gum; *ikenet* gums, *tiet.*
gingivae.
ies yoke; *panna ikeeseen* yoke,
put a yoke on; *karistaa
yltään* ~ throw off the yoke.
ihai|lija admirer; (~*posti* fan
mail). **-lla** admire; have [a
great] admiration (for);
ihaillen admiringly. **-ltava**
admirable. **-lu** admiration.
ihan *ks. aivan;* ~ *uusi*
perfectly (entirely) new; *se on*
~ *mahdotonta* it is utterly
(absolutely) impossible.
ihana lovely, delightful, fine;
glorious, marvellous,
wonderful; *iki-*~ (*m.*)
exquisite. **-sti** beautifully.
ihanne ideal.
ihannoi|da idealize. **-nti**
idealization.
ihanteelli|nen ideal;
(*aatteellinen*) idealistic.
-smielinen idealistic. **-suus**
idealism.
ihanuus loveliness; gloriousness,
glory; *ihanuudet* lovely
(delightful) things.
ihast|ua be charmed (with),
become delighted (*jhk* with,
jstk at); be taken with; *on
-unut (rakastunut) jkh* is
sweet on, has a crush on. **-us**

delight; enchantment. **-uttaa**
delight; fascinate; charm;
-uttava charming, lovely.
ihka(sen): ~ *uusi* brand new.
ihme wonder; marvel; (*-työ*)
miracle; ~*ekseni* to my
astonishment; ~*en hyvin*
wonderfully well, extremely
well, splendidly; ~*kös, jos* ..
no wonder if; *kuin* ~*en
kautta* as by a miracle; *mitä*
~*essä* .. *!* what on earth [do
you mean?]; *miten* ~*essä* ..?
how did you ever [manage
to do that?]; *tehdä* ~*itä*
work wonders, perform
miracles.
ihmeelli|nen wonderful,
marvellous, (*yliluonnollinen*)
miraculous; (*kummallinen*)
odd, strange; *-stä kyllä*
curiously enough, strange to
say. **-syys** wonderfulness;
curiousness; *-syydet* curiosities,
marvels, wonders.
ihmeidentekijä miracle-worker.
ihmeitätekevä wonder-working.
ihme|lapsi infant prodigy.
-lääkäri [miraculous] healer;
(*puoskari*) quack. **-maa**
wonderland. **-tellä** wonder,
marvel (at); be surprised,
astonished (at); *ei ole
-ttelemistä* .. it is no
wonder that .. . **-teltävä**
wonderful, surprising,
astonishing; ~ *yhdennäköisyys*
striking likeness; *-teltävän
hyvin* remarkably well; *ei ole
*~*ä* is not to be wondered at.
-ttely wonder [ing];
astonishment, surprise. **-tys:**
täynnä ~*tä* filled with
wonder. **-tyttää** fill (strike) ..
with wonder; astonish; *se ei
minua ensinkään -tytä* it does
not surprise me in the least.
-työ miracle.

ihminen man (*pl.* men), human
being, *puhek.* human;
(*henkilö*) person; *ihmiset*
people; *Ihmisen Poika* the
Son of Man.
ihmis|apina anthropoid [ape].
-arka shy, timid. **-arvo** human
dignity; (~**inen** *elämä* a
worthwhile existence *t.* life).
-asunto human habitation.
-elämä life, life of man.
-hahmo human guise. **-henki**
[human] life; ~**en** *menetys*
loss of life. **-ikä** lifetime.
-joukko crowd [of people].
-kunta mankind, humanity.
-luonto human nature.
-oikeudet human rights.
-olento human creature.
-rakkaus love of mankind.
-ravin|to: *-noksi kelpaamaton*
not fit [for man] to eat.
-ruumis human body. **-suhteet**
human relations. **-suku**
mankind, the human race
(species). **-syöjä** cannibal;
(*tiikeri ym*) man-eater. **-tavat**
[good] manners. **-tiede**
anthropology. **-tuntemus**
knowledge of human nature.
-tuntija [a good] judge of
people. **-tyä** learn manners;
become civilized. **-viha**
misanthropy. **-vihaaja**
misanthrope. **-ystävä**
philanthropist. **-ystävällinen**
philanthropic; humane,
charitable; humanitarian.
-ystävällisyys philanthropy,
humanitarianism.
ihmisyys humanity; humaneness.
iho skin; (*hipiä*) complexion.
-inen (*yhd.*) -skinned,
complexioned; *hieno*~ with
delicate skin. **-huokonen** pore.
-jauhe face powder. **-karva**
hair; *haitalliset* ~*t* superfluous
hair; *-karvojen poistoaine*
depilatory. **-maali** paint,
make-up; (*punainen*) rouge.
-mato blackhead.
ihon|alainen subcutaneous.
-siirto skin grafting. **-väri**
complexion. **-värinen**
flesh-coloured.
iho|paita vest. **-saippua** toilet
soap. **-tauti** skin disease;
(~**lääkäri** dermatologist; ~**oppi**

dermatology). **-ttuma** eczema,
eruption; rash. **-voide** face
cream, cold cream.
ihra [animal] fat; *sian* ~
(*puhdistettu*) lard.
iilimato leech (*m. kuv.*).
ikenet gums; ~ *irvissä*
grinning [ly].
iki- (*yhd.*) (*vanha*) primeval;
(*ylen*) over-; (*iäinen*) eternal;
(*iäksi*) ever-. **-ihastunut**
overjoyed. **-ilo** everlasting
joy. **-liikkuja** perpetual motion
machine. **-maailmassa:** *en* ~
not for the whole world
[would I ..]. **-muistettava**
never-to-be-forgotten.
-muistoinen immemorial;
-muistoisista ajoista from time
i. **-nen:** *joka* ~ every single
[one]. **-nä:** *ei* ~ never, not
for anything; not for the life
of me! *en* ~*ni ole sellaista
roskaa kuullut* never in all
my life have I heard such
nonsense! *kuka* ~ whoever;
niin paljon kuin ~ *voin* as
much as I possibly can. **-oma**
very own. **-päivä:** *ei*
ikipäivinä never in the world.
-uni eternal sleep. **-vanha**
ancient, very old, (*tapa ym*)
time-honoured.
ikkuna window; (*sivusta*
avattava) casement-w., (*työntö-,*
Engl.) sash-w.; (*hytin*)
porthole; ~*n ääressä* at the
w.; *saanko avata* ~*n* do you
mind if I open the w.?
katso ulos ~*sta* look out of
the w. **-komero** window
recess. **-lauta** window-sill,
(*-penkki*) window ledge.
-luukku shutter. **-nkehys**
window frame. **-npieli** window
jamb. **-nsomistaja**
window-dresser. **-ruutu**
[window-]pane. **-verho** curtain.
ikoni icon.
ikui|nen eternal, everlasting;
(*alituinen*) perpetual, (*pysyvä*)
permanent. **-sesti** for ever,
eternally. **-staa** perpetuate;
immortalize. **-suus** eternity.
ikä age; (*elämä*) life; (*elinikä*)
lifetime; *iäksi* for ever; for
ever; *eli 80 vuoden* ~*än* lived
to be 80 [years old]; *koko*

~*nsä* all his life, his whole life long; *10 vuoden iässä* at the age of 10 [years]; *parhaassa iässään* in his prime, in his best years; *nuorella iällä* early in life. **-aste** stage of life. **-erotus** difference in age. **-inen:** *minun ikäiseni* [of] my age; *10 vuoden* ~ 10 years of age, aged 10 [years], *(attrib.)* ten-year-old; *ikäisekseen* for his age; *50 vuoden* ~ *mies* a man of fifty. **-järjes|tys:** *i-tyksessä* according to age. **-kausi** period of life. **-lisä** *l.v.* seniority bonus. **-loppu** worn with years, decrepit. **-luokka** age class. **-mies** elderly man. **-neito** spinster. **-raja** age limit. **-toveri** age-mate. **-vuosi:** *kolmanella ikävuodellaan* in his third year.

ikävysty|minen boredom, ennui. **-nyt** bored; weary (of). **-ttävä** boring; dull; tiresome; ~ *ihminen* bore. **-ttää** weary; bore. **-ä** get tired, get weary (of); *lopen -nyt* bored to death.

ikävyy|s tedium, tediousness; trouble; *joutua -ksiin* get into trouble; *aiheuttaa -ksiä (m.)* cause difficulties; *nyt saamme -ksiä* we are in for it (in for trouble).

ikävä *a.* tedious, tiresome, dull, uninteresting; unpleasant; *s.* tedium, boredom; *(mielipaha)* regret; *(kaipaus)* longing; *kuinka ~ä* what a pity! how sad! ~*kseni* to my regret; *minun tulee sinua* ~ I shall miss you; ~ *kyllä* regrettably, unfortunately; *on* ~ *kuulla, että* .. I am sorry to hear that ..

ikävöidä long, yearn (for), *(kaivata)* miss; ~ *kotiin* be homesick; *ikävöity* longed for, wished for.

ikään: *niin* ~ likewise, also. **-kuin** as though; as it were; ~ *en tietäisi* as if I didn't know.

ikäänty|ä grow old; *-nyt* advanced in age (years); *-minen* aging.

ilahdutt|aa gladden, cheer [up]; *minua* ~ *kuulla, että* I am delighted (pleased, glad) to hear that; *-ava* pleasing, joyful.

ilakoi|da be in high spirits, make merry, frolic. **-nti** merry-making.

iljanne sheet of ice.

ilje|ttävyys nauseousness; loathsomeness. **-ttävä** disgusting, loathsome, sickening; nauseous, repulsive. **-ttää** fill .. with disgust, nauseate, sicken; *minua* ~ I am disgusted (with, at), it sickens me (to). **-tys** loathing, nausea. **-tä** *(tehdä jtk)* have the face (the impudence) to ..

ilkamoi|da jest, banter; make fun of. **-nti** jesting, bantering, *(epäkunnioittava)* flippancy. **-va** bantering, facetious, *(pilkkaava)* mocking.

ilkeys wickedness; malice; *ilkeyksissään* out of malice, out of spite.

ilkeä bad, wicked, evil; vicious, malicious; *(haju ym)* loathsome, nasty; *(et. lapsi)* naughty. **-mielinen** evil-minded; malevolent. **-mielisyys** malice, spite. **-sti** maliciously.

ilki|alaston stark naked. **-mys** villain, rascal. **-teko, -työ** evil deed; outrage. **-valta** mischief, outrage [s]; disorderly conduct; *harjoittaa ~a* do mischief. **-valtainen** mischievous, outrageous; *(esim. nuorisojoukko)* disorderly [crowd]. **-valtaisuu|s:** *-det* outrages, mischief. **-ö** *ks. ilkimys.*

ilkku|a scoff (at), jeer (at), mock; *-va* mocking, gibing, derisive. **-ja** scoffer, mocker.

illalli|nen supper; *-sen aikaan* at supper-time, at dinner-time (klo 19—21); *olla -sella* have supper; ~ *on pöydässä* supper is served.

illan|suussa towards evening. **-vietto** evening entertainment, social evening.

illastaa have [one's] supper.

illemmällä later in the evening.

ilma air; *(sää)* weather; *(vatsassa)* flatus, wind; *on kaunis* ~ the weather is fine, it is a beautiful day; *tuntua* ~*ssa (kuv.)* be in the air.

ilmaan|tua appear, make one's appearance, *kuv.* emerge, turn up, arise; *kun sopiva tilaisuus -tuu* as opportunity arises. **-tuminen** appearance.

ilma|hyökkäys air-raid. **-hälytys** air-raid alarm, alert.

ilmailu aviation, flying.

ilmai|nen free, free of charge, gratuitous; *-seksi (m.)* for nothing.

ilmais|ematon unexpressed. **-eminen** disclosure. **-in** indicator. **-ta** reveal, disclose; *(paljastaa)* expose; *(osoittaa)* show, indicate; *(lausua)* express; *kuten hän asian -i* as he put it; ~ *itsensä* reveal (betray) oneself; ~ *läsnäolonsa* make one's presence known; ~ *salaisuus (m.)* divulge a secret, *jklle (m.)* let a p. into a secret; *verbi -ee toimintaa* the verb denotes action; *jtk -eva* expressive of, indicative of.

ilmaisu manifestation; *(ilmaus)* expression; utterance; *saa* ~*nsa jssk* finds expression in. **-keino** means of expression. **-tapa** mode (manner) of expression.

ilma|johto overhead line. **-kartoitus** aerial mapping. **-kehä** atmosphere; ~*n paine* atmospheric pressure. **-kelpoinen** airworthy. **-kerros** air layer, aerial region. **-kirje** air letter. **-kivääri** airgun. **-kuljetusjoukot** airborne troops. **-kuoppa** air-pocket. **-laiva** air-ship.

ilman without; ~ *aikojaan* for no reason at all, for [the] fun [of the thing]; ~ *muuta* without any more ado; offhand, straightway, right off; *(hän nousi) ja lähti* ~ *muuta pois* and left just like that; *hyväksyn* ~ *muuta* I accept without question; ~ *häntä olisi voinut käydä hullusti* but for him things might have

gone wrong; *jäädä* ~ go without; *olla* ~ do without.

ilman|ala climate; *totuttaa, tottua* ~*an* acclimatize, become acclimatized. **-herruus** air supremacy. **-kostutin** humidifier. **-muutos** change of weather. **-paine** atmospheric pressure. **-pitävä** air-tight. **-pitävästi** hermetically. **-puhdistuslaite** air filter. **-suunta** point of the compass, cardinal point. **-vaihto** ventilation.

ilma|pallo balloon. **-patsas** air column. **-piiri** atmosphere. **-pommitus** air raid. **-posti** *ks. lento-*. **-puntari** barometer, weather-glass. **-purjehdus** aerial navigation. **-rata** elevated railway; *(köysi-)* cableway. **-rengas** pneumatic tyre. **-silta** airlift. **-rosvous** *(kaappaus)* air piracy, hijacking. **-sota** aerial warfare.

ilmasto climate; *tottua* ~*on* acclimatize oneself. **-ida:** *-itu* air-conditioned. **-inti** air-conditioning. **-llinen** climatic. **-oppi** climatology. **-suhteet** climatic conditions.

ilma|taistelu aerial battle. **-teitse** by air. **-tiede** meteorology. **-tiehyt** air-channel. **-tieteellinen** meteorological. **-tiivis** airtight; *-tiiviisti pakattu* vacuum packed. **-tila** airspace; *lentok.* air territory. **-ton** void [of air]. **-torjunta** air raid defence; *(~tykki* anti-aircraft gun). **-tyynyalus** hovercraft.

ilmaus expression; *(merkki)* sign, evidence; *taudin* ~ *(m.)* symptom; *voiman* ~ manifestation of strength.

ilma|va; *(tilava)* spacious, roomy. **-vaivat** flatulence. **-valokuva** aerial photograph. **-virta** current of air. **-voimat** *sot.* air force[s]. **-vuus** airiness.

ilme expression; look, air. **-etön** expressionless; vacant, inexpressive. **-ikkyys** expressiveness. **-ikäs** expressive; full of expression.

-inen obvious; apparent, plain, evident; manifest. **-isesti** obviously, evidently, clearly. **-isyys** obviousness, plainness. **-kieli** play of features. **-nemismuoto** [form of] manifestation. **-ntää** express.
ilmestymi|nen appearance. **-späivä** date of publication.
ilmestys revelation; *(näky)* vision. **-kirja** The Revelation.
ilmestyä appear; *(julkaisuista, m.)* be published, be issued, come out; ~ *näkyviin* come in [to] sight, *jstk* emerge (from).
ilme|tty veritable; ~ *isänsä* the very image of his father, a chip off the old block. **-tä** appear; *(osoittauttua)* prove, turn out; *(käydä ilmi)* be revealed; become evident; *tästä -nee, että* from this it is apparent that; *-ni, että hän oli* he turned out to be; *saattaa ~ seikkoja* things may turn up [that ..]; *tileissä -ni vajaus* the accounts showed a deficit.
ilmi: *käydä ~* be evident, be seen, *jstk* from; transpire, emerge; *tulla, joutua ~* be brought to light, be discovered; *tuoda ~* reveal; express; *saattaa ~* bring .. to light; reveal. **-antaa** inform (against a p.), report (a p., for). **-antaja** informer. **-anto** information; *jkn -annon nojalla* on the i. of .. **-elävä** living, life-like; .. in the flesh. **-kapina** open rebellion. **-liekki** full blaze; *-liekissä* all ablaze; *puhjeta ~in* burst into flame, *(kuv.)* flare up. **-sota:** *-sodassa keskenään* at open war with each other. **-tulo** discovery; detection.
ilmiö phenom|enon, *pl.* -ena. **-mäinen** phenomenal.
ilmoi|ttaa inform (a p. of, *jklle jtk)*, notify; make known, let .. know; *(juhlallisesti)* announce; *(sanomalehdessä)* advertise; *liik. m.* advise; *(esim. poliisille)* report (to); ~ *eroavansa* resign from,

(yhdistyksestä) withdraw one's membership (of); ~ *nimensä* give one's name, tell a p. one's name; ~ *uutinen varovasti* break the news; *hän -tti olevansa kirjan tekijä* he declared himself to be the author; *täten -tetaan, että* notice is hereby given that *.. -ttaja* informant; *(sanomal.)* advertiser. **-ttamaton** unannounced; unstated. **-ttaminen** notifying *jne;* announcement; *(sanomalehd.)* advertising, *(julisteilla)* bill-posting.
-ttautua report [oneself]; *(kilpailuun ym)* enter [one's name] for; ~ *hakijaksi* put in an application (for); ~ *tutkintoon* enter [oneself] for an examination.
ilmoittautumi|nen announcement; entrance. **-svelvollisuus** duty to report.
ilmoitus announcement; notice; notification; *(tieto)* information; *(sanomalehd.)* advertisement; *(lausuma)* statement; *panna ~ lehteen* insert an advertisement in a paper; *saada ~ jstk* receive notice of; *ilman edelläkäypää ~ta* without previous notice; *~ten liimaaminen kielletty* stick no bills! **-osasto** advertisement section. **-taulu** advertising board, notice board. **-teline** hoarding, *Am.* billboard. **-toimisto** advertising agency.
ilo joy; delight; pleasure; *(riemu)* rejoicing; ~ *kseni* to my delight; ~ *lla* with pleasure; ~ *sta* with joy, for joy. **-huuto** cry (shout) of joy.
iloi|nen gay, cheerful, merry; *(mielissään)* delighted, pleased (at); *olin ~ siitä* I was [so] glad [of that, to hear that]; *-sta joulua* Happy Christmas; ~ *veitikka* a jolly fellow (chap). **-suus** cheerfulness, gaiety. **-ta** be glad (at, about), rejoice (at, in), [have] delight (in), be delighted, be happy (about); *-tsen tulostanne*

(etukäteen) I am looking forward to your arrival. **ilo|kaasu** laughing gas, nitrous oxide. **-mieli:** ~*n* cheerfully, gladly, with pleasure. **-mielinen** gay, cheerful. **ilon|aihe** cause for rejoicing. **-kyynelet** tears of joy. **-pito** merrymaking, amusement. **ilo|sanoma** good news. **-stua** be delighted (at, with). **-ton** joyless, cheerless. **-ttelu** merriment, jollity. **-ttomuus** cheerlessness. **-tulitus** fireworks. **-tyttö** streetwalker, prostitute.

ilta evening; *illalla* in the e.; *(eilisiltana)* yesterday e., last night; *(maanantai)~na* on Monday evening, on the e. of [June 1st]; *tänä ~na* tonight; *illempänä* later in the e.; *hyvää ~a* good evening! **-aurinko** evening sun, setting sun. **-hämy** twilight. **-isin** in the evening[s]. **-juna** night train. **-kirkko** evening service. **-koulu** night school. **-kutsut** evening party. **-ma(t)** social evening, evening entertainment. **-myöhä:** ~*llä* late in the evening. **-puoli** afternoon; *-puolella* towards evening. **-puku** evening dress. **-päivä** afternoon; ~*llä* in the a.; *tiistai~nä* on Tuesday a. **-rukous** evening prayer. **-rusko** sunset glow. **-uninen** sleepy in the evening. **-yö:** ~*stä* towards midnight.

ilve prank, antic[s]. **-htijä** jester, wag. **-htiä** jest; play tricks (on); make fun of. **-ilijä** jester; clown. **-illä** *(ilkamoida)* banter; act the clown. **-ily** *(näytelmä)* farce. **ilves** lynx.

imar|rella flatter. **-telija** flatterer. **-telu** flattery. **imeltää** sweeten. **ime|lyys** sweetness; *kuv.* blandness. **-lä** sweet; ~ *hymy* bland smile; ~*t sanat* sugary words. **ime|ttäjä** wet nurse. **-ttäväinen** *ks. nisäkäs.* **-ttää** nurse, suckle, breast-feed. **-tys** breast feeding. **-väinen** suckling,

infant. **-väiskuolleisuus** infant mortality. **-yttää** impregnate, saturate. **-ytyminen** absorption. **-ytyä** be absorbed, soak (into); *(tunkeutua)* penetrate. **-ä** suck; ~ *sisäänsä* absorb, take up, *(kuv. m.)* imbibe; ~ *kuiviin* drain.
immuuni immune (against, to). **-us** immunity.
imper|atiivi imperative [mood]. **-fekti** past tense, imperfect.
impi maid[en], virgin.
improvisoida improvise.
imu suction. **-ke** mouthpiece; [cigar-, cigarette-] holder. **-kuppi** suction pad. **-kyky** power of absorption. **-kykyinen:** ~ *aine* absorbent. **-neste** lymph. **-paperi** blotting-paper. **-pumppu** suction pump. **-ri** blotting-pad, blotter. **-roida** vacuum. **-suoni** lymph vessel.
indefiniitti- indefinite.
indeksi index; *-luku* i. number.
indikatiivi indicative [mood].
indo|eurooppalainen *a. & s.* Indo-European. **I~kiina** Indo-China.
induktio *fys.* induction.
infinitiivi infinitive.
inflaatio inflation. **-kierre** inflationary spiral.
inflatorinen inflationary.
influenssa influenza *(lyh. flu).*
informoida inform, give .. information (on, about).
inhimilli|nen human; *(ihmisystävällinen)* humane. **-sesti** humanly, humanely; ~ *katsoen* humanly speaking. **-styä** become more humane. **-syys** humaneness, humanity.
inho disgust (at, for), loathing (for), detestation, abhorrence (of). **-ta** detest, abhor, abominate, loathe, have a loathing for. **-ttaa:** *minua ~ jk* I loathe. **-ttava** detestable, abominable, loathsome, hideous; disgusting. **-ttavuus** detestableness; repulsiveness.
inistä whimper, whine.
inkivääri ginger.
inkvisitio inquisition.
innoi|ttaa inspire; *-ttava* inspiring. **-tus** inspiration.

inno|kas eager, enthusiastic; keen; ardent; *(innostunut)* interested; *(uuttera)* zealous; ~ *keskustelu (m.)* animated conversation. **-kkuus** eagerness, enthusiasm; keenness, ardour, zeal.

innos|taa inspire [with enthusiasm], animate, enliven. **-tua** become greatly interested (in), get enthusiastic (about), become inspired (by); ~ *liiaksi* get excited. **-tuneesti** eagerly, enthusiastically, with great interest. **-tunut** interested (in), enthusiastic (over, about); keen (on). **-tus** interest (in); enthusiasm (for, about). **-tuttaa** rouse a p.'s enthusiasm, make ... interested.

innoton half-hearted; uninterested.

insinööri engineer, graduate in engineering. **-tiede** engineering. **-upseeri** engineer officer.

inspiraatio inspiration.

intendentti superintendent, *(museon)* curator.

inter|jektio interjection. **-naatti(koulu)** boarding school. **-noida** intern. **-rogatiivi-** interrogative.

Intia India; ~*n valtameri* the Indian Ocean; ~*n-Pakistanin sota* the Indo-Pakistan [i] war. **intiaani** Red *(t.* American) Indian. **-vaimo** squaw.

intialainen *a. & s.* Indian.

into eagerness, keenness; enthusiasm; ardour, zeal; fervour; *olla innoissaan* be enthusiastic, be excited. **-himo** passion. **-himoinen** passionate. **-himoisesti** passionately; with emotion. **-himoton** dispassionate.

intoi|lija enthusiast; zealot. **-lla** be enthusiastic; *(liiaksi)* be overzealous. **-lu** enthusiasm.

intomielinen enthusiastic, zealous.

intoutua be filled with enthusiasm; ~ *liiaksi* be over-enthusiastic.

intransitiivinen intransitive.

inttää insist [upon]; ~ *vastaan* argue against; contradict.

invalidi disabled person, *(sota-)* disabled soldier; *(sairas, raihnainen)* invalid. **-soida** disable; *-soitunut* disabled. **-teetti** disability; ~*aste* degree of d.

ionosfääri ionosphere.

irlannitar Irishwoman.

Irlanti Ireland; *(valtio)* Republic of Ireland, Eire; *Pohjois-* ~ Northern Ireland. **i-lainen** *a.* Irish; *s.* Irishman; *i-laiset* the Irish.

irrall|aan loose; *olla* ~ be loose, be unfastened; *(eläin ym)* be at large. **-een** *ks. irti;* *päästää* ~ let .. loose, loosen; *(vapaaksi)* release, *(esim. koira)* let .. off the lead, unleash. **-inen** loose; detached, separate; disconnected, isolated; *(suhde)* irregular.

irro|ta loosen, be unfastened, come loose, come off. **-tettava** detachable. **-ttaa** loosen, unfasten, detach; *(solmu ym)* untie; unbind; undo; disconnect; remove, free; ~ *otteensa* let go one's hold; *-tettava* detachable. **-ttautua** disengage oneself, free oneself.

irstai|lija libertine, debauchee. **-lla** lead a dissolute (a loose) life. **-lu** debauchery; dissipation. **-suus** dissoluteness. **irstas** loose, dissolute, licentious.

irtai|misto movables. **-n** loose; ~ *omaisuus* personal estate (property), movable property.

irtautu|a come loose, become unfastened, loosen. **-maton** undetachable; fixed, firm.

irti loose; *ottaa kaikki* ~ *jstk (kuv.)* make the most of; *päästä* ~ become (get) unfastened, *(liikkuessa)* work loose; *päästää* ~ unfasten, loosen, let loose, let go [one's hold]; *(eläin ym)* unloose, unleash, *(koira)* let off the lead, unchain; *tuli on* ~*!* fire! *sanoa* ~ give notice, *(velka)* call in; *hänet on sanottu* ~ he has been given notice; *sanoa* ~ *sopimus* cancel a contract, *(et. valtiol.)*

denounce a treaty; *sanoutua* ~ give notice of leaving. **-sanominen** notice. **-sanomis|aika** [period of] notice; *3 kuukauden i-ajalla* subject to 3 months' notice.

irto|kaulus [loose] collar. **-kukat** cut flowers. **-lainen** vagrant, vagabond, layabout. **-laisuus** vagrancy. **-laisväestö** drifters, people on the loose. **-nainen** loose, unfastened; separate; *(vapaa)* free; *(kävely ym)* slack, limber. **-numero** single copy. **-pohja** insole. **-ripset** false lashes. **-seinä** movable partition; screen. **-takki:** ~ *ja housut* odds.

irvi: *~ssä suin* grinning [ly]. **-hammas** mocker. **-kuva** distorted picture, caricature. **-stys** grin; grimace. **-stää** grin; make faces (a face), *jklle* at.

irvokas grotesque, burlesque.

iskelmä [musical *t.* song] hit, pop tune. **-laulaja** pop singer, crooner.

iske|vä sharp, incisive. **-ytyä:** fasten on to; *(esim. auto)* crash into; *(mieleen)* be imprinted on the mind. **-ä** strike, hit hard, deliver a blow; knock; bump; *(tutustua)* pick up; ~ *jkta (m.)* deal a p. a blow, hit out (at a p.); ~ *haava* inflict a wound; ~ *naula jhk* drive a nail into; ~ *kiinni jhk* grab, clutch; ~ *kyntensä jhk* pounce upon, *(linnusta)* swoop [down] upon; ~ *maahan* knock down; ~ *päänsä jhk* bump (knock) one's head against; ~ *silmää jklle* wink at; *on iskenyt silmänsä jhk* has his eye on; ~ *suonta* let *(t.* draw) blood; ~ *tulta* strike a light, *(kuv.)* flash; ~ *yhteen* come to blows, *(autot)* collide, crash; *(mielipiteet)* clash; *salama iski puuhun* the tree was struck by lightning.

iskias sciatica.

isku blow, stroke; knock; impact; *(puukon)* stab; *raskas* ~ *(kuv.)* hard blow, severe shock; *yhdellä ~lla* at one *(t. a)* blow; all at once. **-joukko**

striking-force. **-nvaimennin** shock absorber. **-ri** firing pin. **-sana** catchword, slogan.

islannitar Icelandic woman.

Islanti Iceland. **i-lainen** *a.* Icelandic; *s.* Icelander; *islannin kieli* Icelandic.

iso big, large; *Iso-Britannia* Great Britain; ~ *kirjain* capital [letter]. **-hko** fairly big (large). **-isä** grandfather; *~n isä* great g. **-kasvuinen** tall. **-kokoinen** large-sized. **-nlainen** siz[e]able, .. of considerable size. **-purje** mainsail. **-rokko** smallpox. **-ruutuinen** large-checked. **-töinen** laborious.

isotooppi isotope.

iso|täti great aunt. **-vanhemmat** grandparents. **-varvas** big toe. **-äiti** grandmother.

israelilainen *a. & s.* Israeli *(pl.* -s); *hist. raam.* Israelite.

istahtaa sit down [for a while]; *(lintu ym)* perch.

istua sit; be seated; *ks. istuutua;* *(oikeus ym)* sit, be in session; *(lintu)* be perched; ~ *valveilla (odottaen jkta)* sit up [for a p.]; *hyvin istuva* .. of good fit; *(tapa ym) istuu lujassa* has deep roots. **-llaan** in a sitting position, sitting. **-lleen:** *nousta* ~ sit up.

istuin seat; chair; *piispan* ~ bishop's throne.

istuk|as *(-oksa)* cutting, slip. **-ka** placenta, *tekn.* chuck, socket.

istuma|kylpy hip bath. **-lakko** sit-down strike. **-paikka** seat; *-ssa on 500 ~a* [the hall] can seat 500 people (has a seating capacity of 500). **-työ** sedentary work.

istunto session. **-kausi** term. **-sali** [session] hall.

istuskella sit about.

istu|ttaa plant; set; *(tauti)* inoculate [with a disease]. **-tus** planting; plantation; *(~puikko* dibble). **-utua** sit down; take a seat, seat oneself; *istuutukaa!* take a seat, please! sit down, please!

isyys fatherhood; paternity.

isä father; *(lapsen puh.)* dad -[dy]. **-llinen** fatherly, paternal. **-llisyys** fatherliness. **-meidän** the Lord's Prayer, Our Father.
isänmaa native country. **-llinen** patriotic. **-llisuus** patriotism. **-nkavaltaja** traitor [to one's native land]. **-nrakkaus** patriotism. **-nystävä** patriot.
isän|istö [board of] directors; *(laivan-)* shipowners. **-yys** management; *(valta)* dominion; *(isännän tehtävät)* duties as host. **-öidä** be the master, be in charge, *(juhlassa)* act as host. **-öitsijä** [general] manager.
isänperintö patrimony.
isäntä master, head of the house; *(vieraitten)* host; *(maatalon)* farmer; *(vuokra-)* landlord; *(työnantaja)* employer; *ravintolan* ~ restaurant proprietor. **-eläin**, **-kasvi** host. **-väki** master and mistress; host and hostess.
isä|puoli stepfather. **-tön** fatherless. **-ukko** dad [dy], the old man.
Italia Italy. **i-lainen** *a.* & *s.* Italian. **i-n kieli** Italian.
italiatar Italian woman.
itar|a stingy, close [-fisted], niggardly, miserly. **-uus** stinginess, niggardliness.
itikka insect.
itiö *bot.* spore.
itke|ttynyt: *hän oli -ttyneen näköinen* her face was tear-smudged; *-ttyneet silmät* tearful eyes. **-ttää** make .. cry, cause to weep; *minua* ~ I feel like crying. **-ä** cry, weep, *jtk* over; ~ *ilosta* weep for (with) joy; ~ *kovaa kohtaloaan (m.)* bewail one's sad fate; ~ *katkerasti (m.)* cry one's heart out; *hän ei voinut olla -mättä* she could not help weeping.
itku crying, weeping. **-silmin** with tearful eyes; amid tears. **-virsi** dirge, lamentation.
itse *s.* self; *pron.* myself, yourself, himself, herself, itself; oneself; ourselves, yourselves, themselves; *näin*

hänet ~ I saw him myself, I myself saw him; *saanko puhutella herra N:ää itseään* may I speak to Mr. N. himself; ~*kseen* by oneself, *(puhua ym.)* .. to oneself; ~*ssään* [in] itself, .. as such; ~*stään* of itself, *ks. hakus,; hänen* ~*nsä tähden* for his (her) own sake; ~ *puolestani* as fas as I am concerned; I for my part; *hän ei ole oma* ~*nsä* he is not himself; *hän on* ~ *rehellisyys* he is the soul of honesty; *en saanut ketään uskomaan* ~*äni* I couldn't get anyone to believe me. **-aiheuttama** self-caused, self-inflicted.
itseensä|sulkeutunut uncommunicative, reserved. **-tyytyväinen** self-satisfied, complacent.
itse|hallinnollinen autonomous. **-hallinto** self-government. **-hillintä** self-control, self-command. **-keskeinen** self-centred, egocentric. **-kieltämys** self-denial. **-kkyys** selfishness, egotism; egoism. **itsekohtai|nen** subjective; *kiel.* reflexive. **-suus** subjectivity.
itse|kritiikki self-criticism. **-kukin** each one. **-kunnioitus** self-respect. **-kylläinen** self-sufficient. **-käs** selfish, egoistic, self-seeking. **-luottamus** self-confidence (-reliance). **-merkitsevä** self-recording. **-murha** suicide; *tehdä* ~ commit s.; *(~yritys* suicidal attempt). **-murhaaja** suicide. **-määräämisoikeus** [right of] self-determination.
itsensä|alentaminen self-abasement. **-elättävä** self-supporting.
itsenäi|nen independent; self-governing, autonomous, sovereign; *saada -sen valtion asema* reach statehood. **-styä** become independent; *vasta -stynyt* newly independent (emancipated).
itsenäisyys independence. **-pyrinnöt** struggle for independence. **-päivä**

Independence Day.
itse|oikeutettu .. as a matter of course; *(virkansa perusteella)* ex officio.
-opiskelu private study.
-oppinut self-educated. **-palvelu** self-service. **-petos** self-deception.
itsepintai|nen persistent; stubborn. **-suus** persistence. stubbornness.
itsepuolustus self-defence.
-päinen stubborn; obstinate, headstrong; self-willed.
-päisesti obstinately, wilfully.
-päisyys stubbornness, obstinacy, insistence. **-rakas** conceited, self-satisfied.
-rakkaus conceit, self-importance.
itsestään of itself, by itself; spontaneously; of one's own accord; ~ *selvä* self-evident; *on* ~ *selvää* it goes without saying; ~ *syntyvä* spontaneous; ~ *virittyvä* self-winding.
itse|suggestio auto-suggestion.
-suojeluvaisto instinct of self-preservation. **-sytytys** spontaneous combustion.
-syytös self-reproach. **-tarkoitus** end in itself. **-tehostus** self-assertion. **-tiedoton** unconscious. **-tietoinen** self-assertive (-important).
-tietoisuus self-assertion (-importance). **-toimiva** self-acting, automatic.
-tuntemus self-knowledge.
-tunto self-esteem. **-tutkistelu** self-examination. **-valaiseva** luminous. **-valtainen** *(oma-)* arbitrary; *(yksin-)* autocratic.
-valtaisuus arbitrariness.
-valtias autocrat; sovereign.
-valtius autocracy; absolutism.
-varma self-confident (-assured). **-varmuus** [self-]assurance.
itu shoot, *(m. perunan)* sprout.
itä east; *idässä, -stä* in, from the e.; *aurinko nousee idästä* the sun rises in the e.; *~än (päin)* to the e., eastwards;

Itä-Suomi eastern Finland; *idempänä* father [to the] east.
Itä-Eurooppa eastern Europe.
-eurooppalainen East-European.
itä|inen eastern, east. **-isin** easternmost; *itäisimpänä* farthest east.
Itä|-Intia the East Indies.
i-lainen East Indian.
itä|koillinen east-north-east.
-maalainen *s.* Oriental. **-maat** the Orient, the East. **-mainen** oriental, Eastern.
Itämerenmaat the Baltic countries.
Itämeri the Baltic.
itämi|nen sprouting, germination. **-saika** time of germination; *(taudin)* incubation period.
itä|osa eastern part; *Suomen ~ssa* in the east of Finland.
-puoli east side; *jnk -puolella* [to the] east of, eastward of.
-raja eastern frontier.
-rannikko east coast.
Itä-Saksa East Germany, the Democratic Republic of Germany.
itätuuli east (easterly) wind.
Itävalta Austria. **i-lainen** Austrian.
itävyys germinative capacity.
itää germinate, sprout.
iva mockery; derision; irony; *joutua ~n esineeksi* become the butt of ridicule (an object of derision); *kohtalon ~* irony of fate. **-aja** mocker, scoffer.
-huuto jeer, hoot. **-hymy** sneer. **-kuva** caricature.
ivalli|nen mocking; derisive; ironic [al]; sarcastic; *-sesti* scornfully, ironically. **-suus** scornfulness; sarcasm.
iva|mukailu parody, *jstk* on.
-nauru derisive laughter. **-runo** satire. **-sana** gibe, taunt.
ivata scoff, jeer (at); deride, ridicule.
iäi|nen eternal, everlasting.
-syys eternity.
iäksi for life, for ever.
iäkäs aged; advanced in years.
iäti eternally, for ever.

J

ja and; *vrt. edespäin.*

jaa yes; *(-ääni)* ay *(pl. ayes).*

jaala yawl.

jaari|tella prate [on] about (sth. *jstk*). **-tus** babbling; *turhaa -tusta* idle talk, nonsense.

Jaava Java. **j-lainen** *a. & s.* Javanese.

jae *raam.* verse; *kem.* fraction.

jae|lla distribute; *(esim. muonaa)* serve out; ~ *käskyjä* issue orders. **-ttava** *mat.* dividend. **-ttavuus** divisibility. **-ttu** divided; *tuli -tulle kolmannelle sijalle* was joint third.

jahka as soon as; *(kun)* when.

jahti yacht.

jakaa divide (into *jhk*, by *jllk*, *(halkoa)* split [up]; *(jkn t. jdenk kanssa)* share; *(usealle)* distribute, portion out, *(maata)* parcel out; *korttip.* deal; *(palkinnot)* give away; *(postia)* deliver; ~ *kahtia* divide in two, halve; ~ *luokkiin* divide into classes, classify; ~ *osuus, tehtävä* allot, assign; ~ *tasan* divide equally.

jaka|ja divider; distributor; *mat.* divisor. **-maton** undivided. **-us** parting; *kammata hiukset -ukselle* part one's hair. **-utua** be divided, divide; fall into [. . parts]. **-utuma** distribution. **-utumaton** undivided.

jake|lija distributor. **-lu** distribution, dealing out; *(postin)* delivery.

jakkara footstool.

jakku jacket. **-puku** suit, suit costume.

jako division; sharing; distribution. **-avain** adjustable spanner; monkey-wrench.

-inen: *kaksi* ~ bipartite. **-lasku** division. **-mielitauti** schizophrenia. **-osuus** dividend. **-taulu** *sähk.* switchboard.

jaks|aa be able to, have strength enough to; *(voin jne.)* can; *miten -at* how are you? *en -a tehdä sitä* it is too much for me, I can't manage it; *en -a enempää* I can do no more, I cannot go on any longer; *huusi minkä -oi* shouted at the top of her voice; *löi minkä -oi* hit as hard as he could; *en -a hänen kanssaan* he has exhausted my patience, I can't do with him.

jakso succession, sequence; series; cycle *(m. sähk.)*; *(ajan)* period; *(vaihe)* phase; *(osa)* section; *yhteen ~on* in [unbroken] succession; at a stretch. **-ittain** serially; *(ajan-)* periodically. **-ittainen** periodic [al]. **-luku** frequency, cycles [per second].

jalan on foot. **-jälki** footprint; *(saappaan)* bootprint. **-kulkija** pedestrian, walker. **-kulkutunneli** subway. **-rinta** instep, metatarsal arch. **-sija** footing, foothold; *saada* ~ gain a footing (a foothold).

jalas runner; *(keinutuolin)* rocker; *(lentok.)* skid.

jalava elm.

jalka leg, *(-terä)* foot *(pl. feet)*; *(lasin)* stem; *(lampun ym)* stand; base; *panna kengät ~ansa* put on one's shoes; *riisua jalasta* take off; *10 jalan pituinen* ten feet long; *auttaa jaloilleen (kuv.)* set . . on his feet [again]; *jkn ~in juurassa* at a p.'s feet. **-inen:** *neli~* four-footed. **-isin** on foot, afoot; *kulkea* ~

walk; leg it. **-käytävä**
footway, pavement, *Am.*
sidewalk. **-lamppu** standard
lamp. **-lista** skirting board.
-matka walking-tour, hike.
jalkapallo, -ilu football. **-ilija**
football-player, footballer.
-joukkue football team. **-kenttä**
football ground. **-ottelu**
football match.
jalka|patikassa on foot; *leik.*
on Shank's mare. **-pohja** sole.
-puu stocks. **-terä** foot. **-tuki**
instep support, *vrt. tuki.*
-vaimo mistress, concubine.
-vaivainen footsore.
-väensotilas infantryman. **-väki**
infantry.
jalkei|lla: *olla* ~ be up [and
about], be on one's feet. **-lle:**
päästä ~ be able to get up.
jalkine: ~*et* footwear; boots
and shoes. **-korjaamo** shoe
repair shop. **-liike** shoe shop.
jalko|jenhoito pedicure. **-pää:**
vuoteen ~ foot of a bed.
jalo noble *(m. metallista);*
high-minded, *(ylevä)* lofty,
sublime, high.
jaloi|tella take a walk, stretch
one's legs; *mennä -ttelemaan*
go for a stroll. **-ttelu** walk.
jalokaasu noble (inert) gas.
jalokivi precious stone, jewel,
gem; ~*korut* jewellery.
-kauppias jeweller. **-sormus**
ring set with jewels.
jalo|luontoinen . . of noble
nature. **-mielinen**
noble-minded, generous,
liberal, magnanimous.
-mielisyys noble-mindedness,
generosity; magnanimity.
jalopeura lion.
jalo|puu precious wood,
hardwood [s]. **-rotuinen**
thoroughbred [horse],
pedigree [dog etc].
jalos|taa ennoble; *(kasveja ym)*
cultivate, improve, *(puita)*
graft, *(rotua, m.)* breed; ~
raaka-ainetta refine, work up,
process. **-te** processed (worked
up) product. **-tua** be [come]
ennobled, refined *jne.*
-tumaton unrefined,
unimproved. **-tus** ennobling;
refining; working up; (~**aste**

degree of working up; ~**laitos**
manufacturing plant).
jalo|sukuinen [. . of] noble
[family], high-born. **-sukuisuus**
noble birth (lineage). **-us**
nobleness.
jalus|ta stand, pedestal; base.
-tin stirrup.
jana segment of a line.
jankko subsoil.
jankuttaa harp on the same
string, nag.
jano thirst; *minun on* ~ I am
thirsty. **-inen** thirsty. **-ta** thirst
(for, after). **-ttaa:** *minua* ~ I
feel thirsty.
jao|llinen divisible (by); *tasan*
~ divisible evenly [by 5].
-llisuus divisibility. **-sto**
section, division. **-tella** divide;
apportion. **-ton** indivisible; ~
luku prime number. **-ttomuus**
indivisibility.
Japani Japan **j-lainen** *a. & s.*
Japanese *(m. pl.)* **j-n kieli**
Japanese.
japanitar Japanese woman.
jarru brake; *kuv.* drag. **-laitteet**
brake equipment. **-mies**
brakeman. **-ttaa** brake, put on
the brake, apply the brake;
kuv. obstruct. **-ttaja** *kuv.*
obstructionist.
jarrutus braking, *kuv.*
obstruction. **-lakko** go-slow,
slow-down, work-to-rule.
-politiikka policy of
obstruction.
jarru|raketti retro-rocket. **-valo**
stop light.
jasmiini jasmine, jessamine.
jaspis jasper.
jatkaa continue; proceed, go
on, keep on [. . -ing]; carry
on; *(tauon jälk.)* resume;
(pidentää) lengthen, extend;
(panna jatkos) add a piece
to, *tekn.* join, scarf; ~
lukemista read on, go on
reading; ~ *matkaa(nsa*
continue, proceed on one's
journey; ~ *työtä* go on
working, go on with one's
work; . . *hän jatkoi* he went
on to say, he continued by
saying . .
jatke extension.
jatko continuation; sequel;

(pidennys) extension; *(lisäys)* addition; *kirja on ~a jhk* the book is a sequel to; *~a seuraa* to be continued. **-aika** *urh.* extra time, *(ravintolassa)* extension. **-johto** extension flex. **-kertomus** serial story. **-kurssi** extension course, follow-up course. **-s** lengthening piece; *(liitos)* seam, joint.

jatku|a be continued; *(kestää)* continue, last, be going on, go on; *(ulottua)* extend, run; *keskustelun -essa* in the course of the conversation. **-maton** discontinuous. **-minen** continuation; extension; *(kestäminen)* continuance. **-va** continued, continual; *(yhtä mittaa ~)* continuous, uninterrupted; constant; *~ kättentaputus (m.)* prolonged applause. **-vasti** continually, *(herkeämättä)* continuously, without interruption; *lisääntyy ~* continues to increase. **-vuus** continuity; permanence.

jauha|a grind; *(myllyssä, m.)* mill; *~ samaa asiaa* harp on the same string. **-ttaa** have .. ground. **-tus** milling, grinding.

jauh|e grist; powder; *(~liha* minced meat). **-ennus** pulverization. **-entaa** pulverize, powder. **-inkivi** millstone.

jauho *(~t)* meal; *(hieno, et. vehnä)* flour. **-inen** mealy; floury. **-mainen** mealy, floury; farinaceous. **-velli** gruel.

Jeesus Jesus; *-lapsi* the Child J.

jengi gang.

jenkki yankee. **-tukka** crew cut.

jesuiitta Jesuit.

jo already; *tiedän sen ~* I already know it; *~ silloin* as early as that; *~ lapsena* even as a child; *~ nyt* by now; *näyttää ~ nyt ilmeiseltä* already it seems clear [that] *~ vuonna 1920* as early as 1920; *~ko olet lounastanut?* have you had lunch already?

jodi iodine. **-suola** iodized salt.

joen|haara fork of a river. **-suu** mouth of a river; *(laaja)* estuary. **-uoma** river bed.

jogurtti yoghurt.

johan: *~ nyt!* nonsense! indeed! *~ nyt jotakin* well, I declare! well, well! really? you don't say so? *~ olet sen nähnyt* you have seen it, haven't you?

johda|nnainen *kiel.* derivative. **-nnos** *kiel.* derivation. **-nto** introduction; *-nnoksi* as an (by way of) i. **-ttaa** lead, conduct; *(opastaa)* guide; *~jtk (jkn) mieleen* remind .. of, suggest [.. to a p.]. **-tus** guidance; *(kirjan)* introduction.

johdettava: *helposti ~* easily led, tractable.

johdin conductor; [electric] wire; *kiel.* suffix; *anat.* duct. **-auto** trolley bus.

johdonmukai|nen consistent; *-sesti* logically, consistently. **-suus** consistency.

johdosta *(jnk)* in consequence of, on account of, because of, owing to; *tämän ~* because of this.

johonkin somewhere.

johtaa lead, *mus., fys.* conduct; *(suunnata)* direct; *(olla etunenässä)* head, lead the way; *(opastaa)* guide; *(liikettä ym)* manage; *kiel. ym* derive; *~ alkunsa jstk* derive its origin from, *(sukujuurensa)* trace one's descent back to; *~ huomio toisaalle* divert someone's attention; *~ puhetta* occupy (be in) the chair, preside; *~ työtä* superintend the work; *tie ~ .. the road runs to ..*

johtaja leader; *(liikkeen ym)* manager, *(johtokunnan jäsen)* director; *Am. m.* president; *(laitoksen ym)* head, superintendent, principal; *(päällikkö)* chief, *(koulun)* headmaster, head; *jkn ~na ollessa* under a p.'s management (leadership). **-ntauti** manager sickness. **-tar** manageress; *(koulun)* head [mistress]; *(sairaalan)* matron.

johta|minen leading *jne; fys.* conduction; *kiel.* derivation.

-va: ~ *asema (m.)* managerial position.

johto leadership, direction, lead; *(liikkeen ym)* management; *(johdatus)* guidance; *(vesi- ym)* pipe, conduit, *(sähkö-)* wire; *(liitäntä-)* cord, flex; *(puhelin-ym)* line; *jkn johdolla* under the direction of; *opiskella jkn johdolla* study under; *olla johdossa (urh.)* lead, *(jnk)* head .., have charge of [affairs]; *mennä ~on (kilpailussa ym)* take the lead; *ryhtyä ~on* assume the leadership, take over. **-aate** leading principle. **-aihe** *mus.* leitmotif. **-elin** governing body. **-henkilö(t)** executive [s]. **-kunta** [board of] management, trustees, council; *(koulun)* school board; *(yhdistyksen)* executive committee; *-kunnan kokous* board meeting. **-lanka** *kuv.* clue. **-pääte** suffix. **-päätös** conclusion, inference; *tehdä ~* draw (reach, form) a conclusion, conclude, infer, deduce. **-tähti** guiding star.

joht|ua: ~ *jstk* be caused by; come from, arise from *(t.* out of), be due to; *(saada alkunsa)* originate in; *(seurata)* follow, be a consequence of; ~ *jkn mieleen* come into a p.'s mind, occur to a p.; *ajatus -ui mieleeni* the idea suggested itself to me; *sana -uu latinasta* the word is derived from Latin; *mistä -uu, että ..* why is it that? *tästä -uu, että ..* from this it follows that; *-uiko se siitä että ..* was it because ..

joiden whose, .. of which, ~ *avulla* with whose help, by aid of which.

joidenkin: ~ *mielestä* in the opinion of some.

joka 1. *indef. pron.* every, each; *(kaikki)* all; ~ *kerran kun* whenever, each time; ~ *paikassa* everywhere; ~ *puolella* on every side, all around; ~ *päivä* every day, daily; ~ *tapauksessa* at all

events; ~ *toinen* every other *(t.* second); ~ *kolmas vuosi* every three years. **2.** *relat. pron.* which, *(henkilöstä)* who; that; *(jää usein kääntämättä, esim.: onko tämä kirja, jota tarkoitat?* is this the book you mean? *mies, jonka kanssa puhuit eilen* the man you spoke to yesterday ..); *jonka, joiden (gen.)* whose, .. of which; *jonka johdosta* as a result of which; *jota whom,* which; *ne, jotka* .. those who ... **-hetkinen** hourly. **-inen** *a.* every, *(kukin)* each; *s.* every one, each [one]; ~ *ken* .. *(m.)* whoever; ~ *meistä* each of us; we all, all of us. **-kesäinen** .. [recurring] every summer. **-päiväinen** everyday; daily; *(kulunut)* commonplace, ordinary; trite; ~ *lehti* daily [paper]; *-päiväisessä puheessa* colloquially. **-viikkoinen** weekly. **-vuotinen** yearly, annual.

jokel|lus babble, crowing, baby-talk. **-taa** babble, gurgle, crow.

joki river; *(puro)* stream; *joen varrella* on the river, *(talo)* by the r.; *jokea ylös (alas)* upstream, downstream. **-alue** [river] basin. **-alus** river-craft. **-laakso:** *Reinin ~* the Rhine valley. **-liikenne:** *harjoittaa ~ttä* ply a river.

jokin some, any; *s. pron.* something, anything; *joksikin aikaa* for a *(t.* some) time; ~ *päivä sitten* a day or two ago; *onko sinulla jotakin sanottavaa* have you anything to say? *joissakin suhteissa* in some respects.

joki|uoma river-bed. **-varsi** riverside. **-äyriäinen** crayfish. **-äyräs** bank [of a river].

joko 1. already? ~ *hän on tullut* has he come already? *(jokohan)* I wonder whether he has come already; ~ *postinkantaja on käynyt?* has the postman already been? **2.** ~ — *tai(kka)* either .. or ..

jokseenkin fairly, *(lähes)* almost.

joku s. somebody, someone; *(kys. laus.)* anybody, anyone; *a.* some; any; *jotkut* some [people]; ~ *heistä* one of them; *jotkut heistä* some of them; *jotkut harvat (heistä)* a few [of them]. **-nen** a few, some.

jollainen [such] as, the like of which.

jollei if not, unless.

jolloin when; at which [time]; ~ *kulloin* once in a while. **-kin** some time.

joltinen(kin) tolerable, passable, fair; *(jonkinlainen)* a certain; *joltisella varmuudella* with reasonable certainty.

jompikumpi one or the other, *(kumpi tahansa)* either; ~ .. *-sta (-stä)* one of ..

jonkalainen ks. jollainen.

jonkin: ~ *verran* ks. verran.

jonkinlai|nen some kind of, .. of some sort, a sort of; something of a .. *teki -sen vaikutuksen* made some sort of impression; *kuulin jos -sta* I heard all sorts of things.

jonne where; *paikka* ~ *he aikoivat muuttaa* the place they intended to move to.

jono line, queue. *sot. (pari-)* file, *(vuori-)* range, *(jakso)* succession; *seisoa ~ssa* stand in a line (a queue). **-ttaa** queue [up].

jopa *(vieläpä)* even; [or] indeed; ~*han nyt* you don't say [so]! indeed! well, well!

Jordania Jordan. **j-lainen** Jordanian.

jos if; in case; provided that; supposing that; ~ *jo(ta)kin* all sorts of things; ~ *kohta* even if; even though; ~ *tapaisin hänet, puhuisin hänelle* if I met him, I would speak to him. **-kin** even if, even though, although. **-kus** sometimes, at times; ~ *tulevaisuudessa* some time in the future. **-pa** if; ~ *hän pian tulisi* if only he would come soon! ~ *hän tulisi* I wish she would come; ~ *hän ei tulekaan* what if he doesn't come?

jossa where. **-kin** somewhere, [in] some place or other; *(kys.)* anywhere.

josta ks. joka; about which; *asia* ~ *soitin* the matter I telephoned about.

jota: ~ — *sitä* the — the. **-kin** something; *luulee olevansa* ~ .. thinks he is somebody; *vrt. jokin.* **-kuinkin** fairly. **-vastoin** while, whereas.

joten [and] so, and thus. **-kin** fairly; rather; ~ *samanlainen, -sia* much the same. **-kuten** somehow; in some way. **-sakin** fairly, *(likimain)* something like; ~ *entisellään* much as before.

jotkut some.

jott|a in order that, so that; in order to (+ inf.); ~ *saisin* so as to get. **-ei** in order that .. not, so as not to, *(joskus)* lest.

jouduttaa hasten, hurry, *(työtä)* speed up; accelerate; *(hoputtaa)* urge .. on; ~ *askeleitaan (m.)* quicken one's steps.

jouhi: *jouhet* [horse]hair. **-patja** [horse]hair mattress.

joukko crowd, multitude, mass, *(järjestynyt)* body, troop, *sot. m.* force; *(iso)* host; *joukot (sot.)* forces, troops; ~ *talonpoikia* a number of peasants; *joukossa among* [st], *(-mme)* among us, in our midst; *kuulua .. ~on* belong to .., be numbered among ..; *joukolla* in a body, in force; *suurin joukoin* in great numbers, *koko joukon* a great deal; *joukon jatkona* to swell the number. **-anomus** monster petition. **-jenkuljetusalus** troopship. **-kokous** mass meeting. **-liike** mass movement. **-murha** wholesale murder; massacre. **-osasto** unit. **-sidontapaikka** regimental aid post, *Am.* first aid station. **-tiedotusvälineet** ks. *-viestimet.* **-tuotanto** mass production. **-viestimet** mass media [of communication].

joukkue *urh.* team; *sot.* platoon; troop; body; *(rikos-)*

band, gang.
joukoittain in great numbers, in masses.
joulu Christmas; ~*na* at C.; *viettää* ~*a* celebrate C., *(jossak.)* spend C. (at, in). **-aatto** Christmas Eve; ~*na* on C.E. **-juhla** Christmas festival. **-kuu** December. **-kuusi** Christmas-tree. **-lahja** Christmas present. **-lehti** Christmas publication. **-loma** Christmas holidays. **-npyhät** Christmas [tide]; *j-n pyhinä* during C. **-pukki** Santa Claus, Father Christmas. **-päivä** Christmas Day; *toinen* ~ Boxing Day.
jousen|jänne bowstring. **-käyttö** bowing. **-veto** stroke of the bow.
jousi bow *(m. mus.); (-pyssy)* cross-bow; *(joustin)* spring; *jouset (mus.)* strings. **-ammunta** archery. **-kvartetti** string quartet [te]. **-mies** archer. **-patja** spring mattress. **-soitin** stringed instrument. **-ttaa** spring. **-vaaka** spring balance.
joust|aa be elastic *jne*. **-amaton** inelastic. **-ava** elastic, springy, resilient; *(henk.)* flexible; *hän kävelee* ~*sti (m.)* there is a spring in his step. **-avuus** elasticity, resilience; flexibility. **-tin** spring.
joutaa have time, find time; *en jouda tulemaan* I cannot [spare the time to] come; ~*ko tämä sinulta* can you spare this?
joutav|a idle, useless, needless; ~ *asia* trifle, bagatelle, mere nothing; ~ *jaaritus* empty talk, idle chatter; ~*n pieni* trifling, trivial; *-ia! rubbish! nonsense!* **-uus** triviality, futility.
jouten disengaged; *olla* ~ be free; *(toimetonna)* be idle, be doing nothing;~ *ollessa* at leisure.
joutil|aisuus inactivity. **-as** free, at leisure; inactive, unoccupied, at liberty; *kulkea -aana* idle [away one's time], dawdle.

jouto|aika free time, leisure; spare time, time off. **-hetki** leisure hour, spare moment. **-käynti** *ks. tyhjä-*. **-päivä** day off.
joutsen swan. **-laulu** swan-song.
joutu|a get, fall, come (into), get (to); be involved in; *(kohteeksi)* come under [criticism etc]; *(jklle)* fall to; *joutukaa* make haste, hurry up! ~ *epäkuntoon* get out of [working] order; ~ *kiinni* be caught; ~ *jkn korviin* reach a p.'s ears; ~ *jkn käsiin* fall into the hands of; ~ *näkemään* happen to see; ~ *sairaalaan* be taken to (*t.* enter) hospital; ~ *sotaan (maasta)* be involved in war; ~ *jnk uhriksi* fall victim to; ~ *vaikeuksiin* get into (get involved in) difficulties; ~ *vankilaan* be sent to prison, land in jail (gaol); ~ *velkaan* incur debts; *jouduin paikalle ajoissa* I arrived there in time; (*. . yritin sanoa), mutta P. -i ennen* but P. anticipated me; *-i epätoivoon* was driven to despair; *minne hän on -nut?* what has become of him?
joutui|n quickly. **-sa** quick, speedy, rapid, prompt. **-suus** swiftness, promptness, quickness, speediness.
jugoslaavi Yugoslav.
Jugoslavia Yugoslavia.
juhannu|s Midsummer; *juhannuksena* at M. **-aatto** Midsummer ['s] eve. **-kokko** Midsummer bonfire.
juhla festival; celebration; *kirkollinen ym)* feast; *(huvi)* entertainment, party; *viettää jnk . . -vuotisjuhlaa* celebrate the . . th anniversary of . . **-asu** festival attire. **-ateria** banquet. **-hetki** great occasion. **-ilo** festivity. **-kulkue** [festival] procession.
juhlalli|nen solemn; grand. **-suus** solemnity; *-suudet* ceremonies, festivities.
juhla|menot ceremonies; *-menojen ohjaaja* master of c. **-näytäntö** gala performance.

-puhe festival oration, speech for the occasion. **-puku** full dress, evening dress; *sot.* full-dress uniform. **-päivä** festival [day]; red-letter day; *(pyhä)* holiday, holy day. **-päivälliset** banquet, gala dinner. **-sali** great hall, *(koulun)* assembly hall. **-tilaisuus** social *(t. festive)* occasion. **-tunnelma** festival spirit. **-valaistus** illumination, *(julkisivun)* flood lighting.

juhli|a celebrate; go out [to parties], be celebrating; *voittajaa -ttiin* the winner was fêted, the winner was given a terrific reception; ~ *muistopäivää* celebrate the anniversary of, commemorate . . . **-ja** *(vapun* May day) celebrant. **-nta** celebration [s], tribute [s]; *(nuorison)* high jinks. **-staa** solemnize.

juhta beast of burden, draught animal.

jukuripäinen pig-headed.

julis|taa declare; *(virall.)* proclaim; announce; ~ *oppia* preach a doctrine; ~ *sota* declare war (on); ~ *tuomio* pronounce sentence; ~ *virka avoimeksi* advertise a vacancy. **-te** placard, poster, bill; *seinä~* wall sticker. **-tus** [public] notice; declaration, proclamation; *(-kirja)* manifesto *(pl. -es).*

juljeta have the impudence (the effrontery) to . .

julkai|sematon not made public, unpublished. **-seminen** publication; announcement. **-sija** publisher. **-sta** make public; *(kirja ym)* publish; *(kihlaus ym)* announce; *(laki ym)* promulgate. **-su** publication; ~*t (seuran)* transactions, proceedings.

julke|a insolent, arrogant; *(esim. vääryys)* gross; *(hävytön)* impudent, brazen; *miten ~a!* what cheek! how cheeky (beastly) [of him]! that was pretty cool! ~ *roisto* a cool customer. **-us** impudence, effrontery.

julki: *lausua* ~ express

[publicly]; *tulla* ~ get (become) known; *tuoda* ~ disclose; *nyt salat ~!* out with it! *he ovat* ~ *kihloissa* their engagement has been announced. **-lausuma** declaration, communiqué.

julki|nen public; open; ~ *mielipide* public opinion; ~ *sana* the press. **-pano** public notice. **-sesti** publicly, in public, openly. **-sivu** front, facade, frontage; *(talon)* ~ *on . . päin . .* faces, fronts (upon), *(esim. etelään)* fronts south; *vrt. päin.* **-staa** make known (public); release. **-suus** publicity; *saattaa -suuteen* bring before the public, make public; *-suuden henkilö* public figure, *(julkkis)* celebrity, pop figure.

julma cruel; ferocious, fierce.

julm|istua become infuriated, be enraged. **-uri** tyrant; *(hirviö)* beast. **-uus** cruelty, *(petomainen)* ferocity.

jumala god; *J-n kiitos* thank God! *jos J* ~ *suo* God willing; *J ~a pelkäävä* God-fearing; ~*n selän takana ks. selkä.*

jumalais|olento deity, divinity. **-taru** myth.

jumalalli|nen divine. **-suus** divineness.

jumalan|hylkäämä God-forsaken **-kieltäjä** atheist. **-kieltämys** atheism. **-kuva** image of God; *(epä-)* idol. **-palvelus** [divine] service. **-pelko** fear of God. **-pilkka** blasphemy. **-pilkkaaja** blasphemer.

jumala|tar goddess. **-ton** godless, ungodly; irreligious; wicked. **-ttomuus** godlessness, ungodliness.

jumali|nen godly; religious, devout. **-suus** piety.

jumal|oida idolize; adore, worship. **-olento** deity.

jumaluus divinity. **-opillinen** theological.

jumaluus|oppi theology; *-opin tohtori* Doctor of Divinity. **-oppinut** theologian.

juna train; *ajaa ~ssa* travel (go) by t.; *mennä ~lla* take

the t., catch a t.; *nousta ~an*
get into the t.; *poistua ~sta*
get off the t. **-ilija** train guard,
Am. conductor. **-laituri**
platform. **-lautta** train ferry.
-nkuljettaja train driver.
-nvaihto change of train.
-onnettomuus railway accident.
-vuoro train service.
junkkari young rascal.
junt|ata ram; drive [piles]. **-ta**
ram, pile-driver; *(esim.
sotilas-)* junta, junto.
juoda drink; ~ *lasi pohjaan*
drain one's glass [to the
bottom]; *ratkesi juomaan*
took to drink.
juok|sennella run about. **-seva**
flowing; current; *(nestemäinen)*
liquid, fluid;. ~ *tili* current
account; *~t asiat* current
matters, routine business; *~t
menot* running expenses. **-sija**
runner; *(-hevonen)* trotter.
juoksu run [ning]; flow [ing];
course; *100 metrin* ~
100-metre event; *täyttä ~a* at
full speed. **-aika** heat;
(koira)lla on ~ (the bitch) is
in season, she has come on
heat. **-hauta** trench. **-jalka:** *~a*
running, at a run. **-kilpailu**
running race. **-poika** errand
boy, office boy. **-solmu**
slip-knot. **-tin** *(maidon)* rennet,
(metallin) flux. **-ttaa** make . .
run, *(nestettä)* draw,
(vähitellen) drain off; *(maitoa)*
curdle.
juolah|taa: *mieleeni -ti* it
occurred to me, it struck me,
it entered my mind.
juolavehnä couch-grass.
juolukka bog whortleberry.
juoma drink, beverage. **-himo** craving
for drink, addiction to drink.
-lasi drinking-glass, *(jalaton)*
tumbler. **-nlaskija** cup-bearer.
-raha tip, gratuity; *antaa jklle
~a* tip a p.; *tässä on ~a* :
this is for you. **-ri** drunkard,
hard drinker. **-veikko** fellow
toper.
juomingit drinking-bout, spree,
binge, booze [-up].
juoni intrigue, plot, design;
(kepponen) trick; *näytelmän* ~

plot of a play; *virittää ~a*
lay plots, intrigue. **-kas**
plotting, scheming, crafty.
-kkuus craft [iness], guile.
-tella plot. **-ttelija** schemer,
plotter. **-ttelu** plotting;
intrigues, machinations *(pl.)*.
juont|aa *(ohjelma)* compère;
juurensa jstk derive its origin
from. **-aja** compère,
announcer, *(tietokilpailun)*
quiz-master. **-ua** spring, arise
(from); date [from the 14th
century].
juopa gulf, breach.
juopo|tella drink; *sl.* booze.
-ttelija drinker; tippler. **-ttelu**
sl. boozing.
juoppo *s.* drinker, drunk,
drunkard; *a.* addicted to
drink. **-hulluus** delirium
tremens. **-lalli** habitual
drunkard, toper, sot. **-us**
drunkenness, hard drinking,
insobriety.
juopu|a become intoxicated, get
drunk. **-mus** intoxication;
drunkenness.
juoru gossip. **-akka** gossip,
scandalmonger. **-kello** gossip-
monger. **-nhaluinen** gossipy.
-ta gossip; *(kannella)* tell
tales. **-teitä** by the grape-vine.
juosta run; *(virrata)* flow; ~
tiehensä run away.
juotava *a.* drinkable, fit to
drink; *s.* drink; *anna minulle
~a* give me something to
drink.
juote *tekn.* solder.
juo|tin soldering-iron. **-tos**
soldered joint.
juottaa make . . drink;
(metallia) solder; ~ *(hevosta
ym)* water.
juotto watering; soldering.
-paikka watering place.
-vasikka fattened calf.
juov|a a streak, stripe. **-ainen**
streaked; striped; *kelta~* . .
with yellow streaks (stripes).
-ikas *ks. ed.; (puu)* veined,
grained; ~ *kangas* striped
material. **-ittaa** stripe, streak.
juovu|s *-ksissa (oleva)*
intoxicated, drunk; ~ *päissään*
under the influence of drink.
-ttaa intoxicate, make drunk.

-**tusjuoma** intoxicant.
jupakka squabble, altercation.
jupista murmur, mutter; grumble.
juridinen judicial, juridical.
juro sullen, surly, sulky; morose, unsociable. -**ttaa** be in the sulks, sulk. -**us** sullenness, sulkiness.
jutella talk, chat.
juttelu talk, chat. -**nhaluinen** talkative, chatty.
juttu story, tale, *(kasku)* anecdote; *(oikeus-)* case, lawsuit; *hieno (mainio)* ~ a fine thing! *ikävä* ~ a sad business, an unpleasant affair; *se on pikku* ~ that's nothing (a small matter); *siinä koko* ~ that's all there is to it; *se on toinen* ~ that's [quite] another matter.
juurakko root-stock, rhizome.
juure|kset [edible] roots.
-**llinen** rooty. -**notto** *mat.* extraction of a root. -**ton** rootless. -**ttomuus** rootlessness.
juuri 1. *adv.* just; *(täysin)* fully, quite; *(äsken)* newly, freshly; *ei* ~ *mitään* scarcely anything; ~ *nyt* right now; *ei* ~ *niin paljon* not quite so much; *riittää* ~ *ja* ~ barely suffices; ~ *sillä hetkellä* at that very moment; *olin* ~ *kertomaisillani* .. I was on the point of telling; *ei ollut* ~ *ketään liikkeellä* there was no one much about.
juuri 2. *s.* root; *(vuoren ym)* foot; *kiskoa* ~*neen* pull up by the roots, uproot; *jnk juurella* at the foot of; *puun juurella* at the root of a tree; *(jnk) jalkain juuressa* at [a p.'s] feet; *hävittää* ~*neen* destroy root and branch. -**harja** scrubbing-brush. -**kas** beet [root]. -**kasvi** edible root; (~**viljelys** cultivation of root-crops). -**kori** wicker-basket. -**mukula** corm, *(m. varsi-)* tuber. -**sana** root-word. -**vesa** sucker.
juur|ruttaa root; *kuv. (mieleen)* imprint [on a p.'s mind], impress [on a p.]. -**tajaksaen** circumstantially, at length, in

detail.
juur|tua take root *(m. kuv.),* root, spring roots; *kuv.* become ingrained; ~ *lujaan (kuv.)* be firmly established (fixed), become rooted; *syvälle* -*tunut* deep [ly] rooted.
juusto cheese. -**aine** casein. -**kupu** cheese-cover. -**mainen** cheesy, caseous. -**maito** curdled milk. -**utua** curdle.
juutalainen *s.* Jew; *a.* Jewish.
juutalais|kortteli Jewish quarter, ghetto. -**nainen** Jewess. -**uus** Judaism. -**vaino** Jew-baiting. -**viha** anti-Semitism.
juutti jute.
juuttua stick, *jhk* in.
jyke|vyys heaviness; sturdiness. -**vä** sturdy, robust; massive, stout.
jylh|ä wildness; desolateness. -**ä** wild, rugged, rough; *(synkkä)* gloomy.
jyli|nä, -stä *ks. jyri|nä, -stä.*
Jyllanti Jutland.
jymy rumble, din, roar. -**vaikutus** sensational effect.
jymäh|dys boom, bang; thud; detonation. -**tää** boom; thud.
jymäyttää *(puijata)* fool, take .. in.
jyri|nä rumble, thunder, *(ukkosen jyrähdys)* clap (peal, roll) of thunder. -**stä** thunder.
jyrk|entää make steeper; *kuv.* make more radical. -**etä** become steep [er]; *kuv.* become [more] radical. -**kyys** steepness; *kuv.* sharpness; radicalism.
jyrkkä steep, precipitous; sharp, abrupt *(m. kuv.);* *(ankara)* strict; ~ *ero* sharp distinction (contrast); ~ *uudistus* radical reform; ~ -*vasemmistolainen* pronounced left-winger; ~ *vastaus* categorical answer; *ryhtyä jyrkkiin toimenpiteisiin* adopt rigorous measures. -**piirteinen** [very] marked, pronounced, sharply defined. -**sanainen** sharply worded.
jyrkä|nne bluff, precipice. -**sti** steeply; sharply, strictly; categorically; *kieltää jtk* ~ deny flatly; *mitä jyrkimmin*

most decidedly, most emphatically.
jyrsi|jä rodent. **-n** (*terä*) cutter. **-nkone** *tekn.* milling-machine. **-ä** gnaw, *jtk* at.
jyrä roller; (*höyry-*) steamroller. **-hdys** [peal of] thunder. **-htää** thunder. **-tä** roll.
jysk|e noise; crash; (*tykkien . ym*) boom, (*koneen*) pounding, thud. **-yttää** pound, *jtk* on; thump; (*sydän*) throb.
jysäh|dys thud, thump. **-tää** thump, bump, (*pudota*) fall down with a thud.
jyvä grain; ~*t* (*vilja*) corn, *Am.* grain; *päästä ~lle jstk* get wise to. **-aitta** granary. **-hinkalo** bin. **-nen** granule. **-sin** (*pyssyn*) bead, front sight.
jähme|piste solidifying point. **-ttyä** solidify; (*kangistua*) become stiff; *hän -ttyi kauhusta* he was paralysed with terror, his blood froze. **-ys** solidity; stiffness, rigidity.
jähmeä solid; (*kankea*) stiff.
jäidenlähtö breaking-up of ice.
jäinen icy, .. of ice.
jäkkärä: *aho* ~ cudweed.
jäkälä lichen.
jälje|kkäin one after another (the other). **-lle** left; (*yli*) over; *jäädä* ~ (*muista*) be left behind, fall behind; (*tähteeksi*) be left [over], remain. **-llä** left; (*yli*) over; *hänellä ei ole rahaa* ~ he has no money left; ~ *oleva(t)* remaining, the rest (of).
jäljen|nös copy; reproduction; *-nöksen oikeaksi todistaa .. * certified by .. , certified correct, certified to be a true copy. **-tää** copy; reproduce.
jälje|ssä after, behind; *olla* ~ (*kuv.*) be behindhand [with one's work], (*m. maksuissa*) be in arrears; *kelloni käy* ~ my watch loses, my watch is [5 minutes] slow; *olla ajastaan* ~ be behind the times. **-stä** after; (~**päin** afterwards, subsequently). **-ttömiin** leaving no trace. **-tön** trackless; traceless.
jälji|tellä imitate, copy; (*matkia*) mimic; ape; *-ttelevä*

imitative. **-telmä** imitation; (*petoll. tark.*) counterfeit.
jäljitte|lemätön inimitable. **-lijä** imitator, mimic. **-ly** imitation; mimicry; (~**taito** mimicry).
jälji|ttää track, trace. **-tys** tracking.
jälkeen after; (*taakse*) behind; *toinen toisensa* ~ one after another; *jättää ~sä* leave [behind], (*kilpailussa ym*) outdistance, outstrip; *jonka* ~ after which, whereupon; *sen* ~ *kun* after; *tämän* ~ upon this; *sodan* ~ (*siitä alkaen*) [he has lived in L.] since the war. **-jättämä** left [behind]; ~ *omaisuus* estate (property) left. **-jäänyt** backward; (*eloon*) surviving; ~ *teos* posthumous work; *-jääneet* those left behind, the survivors. **-päin** afterwards; later. **-tuleva** coming; ~*t sukupolvet* generations to come.
jälke|inen subsequent, *jnk* to; *jnk* ~ after .., following ..; *sodan* ~ post-war. **-läinen** descendant; (*toimessa*) successor; *-läiset* descendants, offspring.
jälki trace; track; (*jalan-*) footprint, (*merkki*) mark; imprint, impression; *jälkeäkään jättämättä* leaving no trace; *olla jnk (jkn)* ~ *jäljillä* be on the track (trail) of; (*koira*) get the scent; *päästä jäljille* (*kuv.*) get a clue; *seurata jkn ~ä* track a p., (*kuv.*) follow in the steps of; *kulkee isänsä ~ä* follows in his father's footsteps; *joutua jäljiltä* get off the track; (*koira*) lose scent; *hänen jäljilleen ei ole päästy* he has not been traced.
jälki|hoito after-care (-treatment). **-istunto:** *jättää ~on* keep in; *jäädä ~on* be kept after school. **-joukko** rear [-guard]; *-joukossa* in the rear. **-katsaus** retrospect; *luoda* ~ *jhk* review, look at .. in retrospect. **-kesä** Indian summer. **-kirjoitus** postscript (*lyh.* P.S.). **-lasku**

after-reckoning. **-liite** *kiel.* suffix. **-maailma** after-world, posterity. **-maku** aftertaste. **-mmäinen** latter; ~ *osa (kirjan)* second part; *edellinen* .. ~ the former .. the latter. **-näytös** *kuv.* sequel. **-painos** reprint; ~ *kielletään* all rights reserved. **-polvi**: *-polvet* future generations, posterity. **-puolisko** latter part, second half. **-ruoka** sweet, dessert; ~ *lusikka* dessert spoon. **-sato** *kuv.* aftermath [of war]. **-seuraus** after-effect. **-syntyinen** posthumous. **-säädös** will; (~**lahjoitus** legacy, bequest). **-tauti** complication. **-vaatimus**: *-vaatimuksella* cash on delivery *(lyh. C.O.D.).* **-vaikutus** after-effect. **-viisaus** wisdom after the event, hindsight.

jälleen again, .. once more; re-; *asettaa ~ paikalleen* replace; *elvyttää ~* revive; *voittaa, saavuttaa ~* regain. **-asutus** resettlement. **-elpyminen** revival. **-myyjä** retailer, retail dealer. **-myynti** retail. **-näkeminen** meeting [again], reunion. **-rakennus** reconstruction. **-vakuuttaa** reinsure.

jänis hare; *(matkustaja)* stowaway. **-emo** she-hare. **-koira** harrier, beagle. **-tää** *kuv.* show the white feather, funk.

jänne tendon; sinew; *(jousessa)* string; *mat.* chord. **-side** ligament. **-väli** span.

jänni|te tension, *(sähk. m.)* voltage. **-ttyneesti** tensely, with strained attention, intently. **-ttyä** be stretched; be strained; tighten; *-ttynyt (m.)* tense, excited. **-ttävä** *kuv.* exciting, thrilling. **-ttää** strain; stretch; *(pingottaa)* tighten; ~ *jousi* draw a bow; ~ *jtk äärimmilleen* strain .. to breaking-point; ~ *liikaa* overstrain; *älä -tä!* take it easy! **-tys** tension, strain; *(odotus)* suspense; *(kiihtymys)* excitement; (~**romaani** thriller, suspense story).

jännäri thriller, »whodunit». **jänte|vyys** muscularity, vigour. **-vä** muscular, vigorous, springy. **jänterä** thick-set; sturdy. **jänö** bunny. **järeä** coarse; rough; *(tykistö)* heavy. **-tekoinen** crude, coarse. **järi|stys** shaking, quaking, quake. **-stä** shake, quake; *(vapista)* tremble. **-syttää** cause to quake (to tremble). **järjelli|nen** reasonable; ~ *olento* rational being. **-syys** reasonableness; rationality. **järjen|juoksu** line (train) of thought. **-mukainen** rational. **-mukaisuus** rationality. **-vastainen** unreasonable. **järjeste|lijä** organizer. **-llä** put in order, arrange; adjust; *(säännellä)* regulate; ~ *asioitaan* settle one's affairs. **järjestelmä** system. **-llinen** systematic; planned. **-llisesti** systematically. **-llistää** systematize. **-llisyys** system. **-tön** unsystematic. **järjestely** arrangement; regulating; organizing; ~*t (m.)* measures, adjustments; ~*n alaisena* under process of organization. **-kyky** organizing ability. **-raide** *-raiteet* shunting tracks. **järjestykse|llinen** orderly. **-npito** maintenance of [law and] order. **-nvalvoja** peace officer, *ks. järjestysvalta.* **järjesty|minen** organization. **-mättömyys** lack of organization. **-mätön** unorganized. **-nyt** organized. **järjesty|s** order; *(vuoro)* succession, sequence; *(-aisti)* orderliness; *panna -kseen* put .. in order, arrange; *valvoa ~tä* keep (maintain) order; *luetella -ksessä* enumerate in succession; *-tyksen mies* orderly person. **-aisti** sense of order. **-luku** ordinal. **-mies** *(huvitilaisuudessa)* usher, attendant. **-numero** running number. **-rikos** breach of the peace. **-sääntö** regulation[s]. **-valta** the police. **järjes|tyä** get into order;

(järjestöksi) organize, get organized; ~ *riviin* line up; *-tykää riviin!* fall in! **-täjä** arranger, organizer; *(koulussa)* monitor. **-täminen** putting in [to] order, arrangement, organization. **-tämätön** not arranged, unregulated. **-tänsä:** *kaikki* ~ every one [without exception]. **-täytyä** organize; *(kokous)* come to order. **-tää** put (set) in order, adjust, settle; arrange, organize, stage [a demonstration, *mielen-osoitus*]; *Am. m.* fix; ~ *asiansa kuntoon* settle one's affairs; ~ *huone* put things straight in a room. **-tö** organization.

järje|ttömyys unreasonableness, absurdity. **-tön** unreasonable; irrational; *(mieletön)* senseless, absurd; nonsensical; *puhua -ttömiä* talk nonsense.

järkei|llä reason, argue; philosophize. **-stää** rationalize. **-susko** rationalism.

järke|vyys reasonableness, common sense. **-vä** sensible, reasonable; ~ *harkinta* sober judgment; *hän on* ~ he has his head screwed on the right way; *hän oli kyllin* ~ . . *-kseen* he had the [good] sense to . .

järki reason; sense, understanding; *joutua järjiltään* go out of one's mind; *oletko järjiltäsi* have you taken leave of your senses? *saattaa jku ~insä* bring . . to his senses; *tulla ~insä* come to one's senses; *täydessä järjessään* in charge of one's faculties; *siinä ei ole mitään järkeä* it doesn't make sense. **-avioliitto** marriage of convenience. **-ihminen** sensible person. **-olento** rational being. **-peräinen** rational; ~ *maanviljelys* scientific farming. **-syy** rational argument.

järkkymä|ttömyys immovability. **-tön** immovable; firm, steadfast.

järkkyä shake; tremble; *(horjua)* falter.

järky|ttyneisyys agitation. **-ttyä**

be upset, upset oneself. **-ttää** *(paikaltaan)* dislodge, *kuv.* upset, unsettle; ~ *mieltä* agitate; *-ttävä* agitating, shocking, upsetting. **-tys** shock.

järkähtämä|ttömyys immovableness; firmness; inflexibility. **-tön** unshaken, immovable; firm; *(taipumaton)* inexorable; *(pettämätön)* unfailing.

järsiä crop, nibble.

järvi lake; *on hauskaa olla järvellä* it's fun being out in a boat. **-alue** lake district. **-kalastus** fresh-water fishing. **-rikas** rich in lakes.

jäsen member; *(raaja)* limb; *(nivel)* joint; *ottaa ~eksi* admit as a member, *(merkitä)* enrol (in). **-inen:** *5- ~* valiokunta a committee of five; *vahva ~* strong-limbed. **-kortti** membership card. **-maksu** membership fee. **-määrä** membership. **-nellä** analyse; *(aine)* outline. **-tely** analysis; *(aineen)* outlining. **-yys** membership. **-äänestys:** *alistaa j-tykseen* put to the vote *(compel a ballot)* [among the members].

jäte remnant, residue; waste; *ks. jätteet.* **-huolto** refuse *(Am.* garbage) disposal. **-kasa** refuse heap. **-paperi** waste paper. **-tuote** waste product. **-vesi** waste water; effluent, sewage.

jätkä *(tukki-)* lumber|man, -jack; loafer.

jätte|et refuse, rubbish, *Am.* garbage; *(tähteet)* leavings, table scraps; offal; *-iden hävittäminen* refuse disposal.

jättiläinen giant.

jättiläis- gigantic. **-askel** gigantic stride; . . *edistyy ~in* is making tremendous progress. **-kokoinen** gigantic, enormous. **-mäinen** gigantic, giantlike. **-nainen** giantess.

jättäytyä surrender [oneself], resign oneself (to, into); ~ *jälkeen* fall behind.

jättää leave; *(antaa)* deliver, hand over; *(~ sisään)* hand in, present; *(lähteä pois, m.)*

quit; *(luopua)* give up;
(virasta) retire from;
(perintönä) leave .. to sb.; ~
asiakirja jhk hand in, submit;
file, lodge [a complaint]; ~
jälkeensä leave [behind],
älkimaailmalle) hand down;
~ *oman onnensa nojaan* leave
.. to [his] fate, *(selviytymään
omin päin)* leave to [his,
their] own resources; ~ *pois*
leave out, omit, exclude; ~
sanomatta leave .. unsaid; ~
sikseen give up, drop; ~ *jtk
tekemättä* leave a th. undone,
fail to do a th; *jätettiin
kolmanneksi (urh.)* was beaten
into third place.
jätättää: *kello* ~ the clock is
slow, the watch loses.
jäykis|te stiffening; *~kangas*
buckram. **-tyä** be [come] stiff,
stiffen; *(jähmettyä)* become
petrified (paralysed). **-tää** make
stiff, stiffen.
jäykkyys stiffness, rigidity; *kuv.
m.* constraint, formality.
jäykkä stiff, rigid; *(taipumaton)*
inflexible, unbending;
stubborn; ~ *oppimaan* slow
to learn. **-kouristus** lock-jaw,
tetanus. **-luonteinen** stubborn.
-niskainen stiff-necked,
obstinate.
jäytää gnaw (at); *kuv.* prey
upon, undermine.
jää ice; *olla ~ssä* be frozen,
be covered with ice; *~ssä
oleva* frozen [up], *(satama,
laiva)* ice-bound; *hän putosi
jäihin* he fell through the ice.
-dyttää freeze; ice. **-dytys**
(syvä-) quick-freezing.
jäädä remain, stay; stop; ~
huomaamatta escape notice; ~
ilman be left without; ~
istumaan remain sitting; ~
kesken be left unfinished,
remain uncompleted; ~ *pois*
stay away; ~ *päivälliselle* stay
for dinner; ~ *tulematta* fail
to appear (to arrive); ~ *yöksi*
stay overnight; *asia jäi
sikseen* the matter was
dropped, it came to nothing.
jää|este ice obstruction. **-etikka**
glacial acetic acid.
jäähdy|tellä cool off. **-tin, -ttäjä**

cooler; refrigerator; *(auton)*
radiator. **-ttämö** refrigerating
plant. **-ttää** cool, chill;
refrigerate. **-tys** cooling;
refrigeration; (**~huone**
refrigerating room;
cold-storage chamber; **~kaappi**
refrigerator; **~laitos** cooling
plant).
jäähile: *~et* frostwork.
jäähtyminen cooling [down].
jäähtyä cool, get cool.
jäähy: *~llä (urh.)* on the
penalty bench, in the penalty
box.
jäähyväis|et parting; farewell;
jättää ~ take one's leave.
-juhla farewell entertainment.
-käynti farewell visit. **-lahja**
parting gift. **-näytäntö** farewell
performance.
jää|juoma iced drink. **-kaappi**
refrigerator, »fridge». **-karhu**
polar bear. **-kausi** Ice Age,
glacial epoch. **-kautinen**
glacial. **-kenttä** field of ice.
-kiekkoilu ice-hockey. **-kylmä**
ice-cold, icy; *~sti* icily.
jääkäri light infantryman.
jää|lautta *(ajelehtiva)* [ice]
floe. **-lohkare** block of ice.
-meri polar sea; *Pohjoinen J~*
the Arctic Ocean; *Eteläinen
J~* the Antarctic Ocean.
jäämistö estate [of a deceased
person], »property left (by
jkn), (kirjallinen) remains.
jään|lähtö breaking-up of
[the] ice. **-murtaja** ice-breaker.
jäänne relic, rudiment; survival.
jäännös remainder *(m. mat.)*,
the rest; *(jäte)* remnant;
kirjanp. balance; *maalliset
jäännökset* mortal remains.
-erä remainder, remnants; old
stock. **-pala** remnant. **-varasto**
remaining stock.
jää|palloilu bandy [-ball]. **-peite**
coating of ice; *(-kalotti)*
icecap. **-peitteinen** covered
with ice. **-puikko** icicle.
jäärä|päinen stubborn. **-pää**
mule, bullhead; *(vanhoillinen)*
diehard.
jää|röykkiö mass of ice, ice
pack. **-sohjo** sludge; slush.
-suhteet ice conditions.
jäätelö ice, ice[-]cream. **-tikku,**

-tötterö ice-cream stick (cone).
jäätikkö sheet of ice, ice field;
(vuorilla) glacier.
jäätymispiste freezing-point.
jäätymätön unfrozen;
non-freezing.
jääty|**ä** freeze; ~ *kiinni
maahan* f. to the ground; *-nyt*
frozen.
jäätä|**ä** convert into ice, freeze;
chill; *-vä* chilling; *-vä kylmyys*
icy cold, *(kuv.)* icy coldness.
jää|**tön** free from ice; open.

-vuori iceberg.
jäävi *a.* disqualified; not legally
competent. **-tön:** ~ *todistaja*
unchallengeable witness. **-ys**
legal incapacity.
jäävä|**tä** challenge the validity
of; *(todistaja)* take exception
to; disqualify sb. [from acting
as a witness]. **-äminen**
disqualification. **-ämätön**
unchallengeable.
jörö sullen, sulky. **-jukka** sulky
fellow.

K

kaaderi cadre.
kaakao cocoa. **-papu** cacao bean. **-puu** cacao-tree.
kaakattaa cackle, cluck, *(ankka)* quack.
kaakeli [glazed] tile, Dutch tile. **-uuni** tiled stove.
kaakko south-east. **-inen** southeast [erly].
kaakku *ks. kakku.*
kaali cabbage. **-nkupu** cabbage head.
kaame|a ghastly, gruesome, grisly, uncanny. **-us** ghastliness. **-kaan -kään:** *ei hänkään* not even he; *hän ei tullut, etkä sinäkään* he did not come, nor did you; *et sinä tullut~* you did not come after all; *. . tuleeko hän~* [I don't know] whether he will come either.
kaaos chaos.
kaapata *mer.* capture, *(et. lentokone)* hijack, *Am.m.* skyjack.
kaapeli -köysi cable. **-sähke** cable, *Am.* cablegram. **-televisio** cable television.
kaapia scrape; *(hevosesta)* paw.
kaapp|arilaiva privateer. **-aus** capture; *(vallan-)* coup; *(lentokoneen)* hijacking (of a plane, of planes).
kaappi cupboard,. *Am.* closet; *(vaate-)* wardrobe; *(kirja-)* bookcase; *(ruokahuoneen)* sideboard; *(koriste-)* cabinet. **-juoppo** bedroom drinker. **-kello** grandfather clock.
kaapu gown, *(munkin)* frock; *(viitta)* cloak.
kaare|illa bend, curve. **-utua** arch, be arched. **-va** bent, curved; arched. **-vuus** curve, curvature, arched form, arch.
kaari curve; *rak. ym.* arch; *et. tiet.* arc; *(jousen)* bow; *kaaressa* in a curve. **-asteikko**

protractor. **-holvi** arched vault. **-ikkuna** arched window. **-lamppu** arc-lamp. **-pyssy** [cross-]bow. **-silta** arch bridge. **-viiva** curved line.
kaarna bark, rind.
kaar|re *(tien-)* bend, curve. **-roke** *(puvun)* yoke. **-ros** bend; turn. **-taa** bend, turn a curve; *(auto äkkiä, m.)* swerve; *(tehdä kierros)* make a circuit, go round.
kaarti guards. **-lainen** guardsman.
kaarto bend; *(lankaa)* skein. **-liike** *sot.* [out]flanking attack.
kaartua curve; wind; *(holviksi)* arch.
kaasu gas; *lisätä ~a (autossa)* accelerate; *vähentää ~a* throttle down. **-hana** gas-tap. **-johto** gas pipe, *(pää-)* g. main. **-kammio** gas chamber. **-kello** gasometer. **-laitos** gas-works; *-laitoksen asentaja* gas-fitter. **-liekki** gas-jet. **-liesi** gas-range (cooker). **-mainen** gaseous. **-mittari** gas-meter. **-myrkytys** gas poisoning; *saada ~* be gassed. **-naamari** gas-mask. **-poletti** gas-meter disc. **-poljin** *(auton)* accelerator [pedal]. **-säiliö** gasholder, gas reservoir, gas tank. **-ttaa** gasify, convert into gas; *(huone)* fumigate; *(tappaa)* gas. **-tin** carburettor, **-valaistus** gas lighting.
kaataa overturn; *(vene, lasi ym)* upset; *(maahan)* fell; *(iskemällä)* knock down, strike down; *(nestettä)* pour, *(läikyttää)* spill: *~ kahvia (kuppeihin)* pour out coffee; *~ hallitus* bring down (overthrow) the government; *~ puu* fell (cut down) a tree; *satoi kaatamalla* it was

kaat   112

pouring, the rain came down in sheets.
kaato|allas sink. **-paikka** refuse tip, dumping-ground, rubbish dump. **-sade** downpour, cloudburst.
kaatu|a fall; be upset, be overturned, overturn, *(veneestä)* capsize; *(suistua)* fall down, collapse; ~ *kuolleena maahan* drop dead; ~ *taistelussa* be killed in action; *loukkaantui -essaan* was injured in a fall. **-matauti** epilepsy; *(~nen* epileptic).
kaava pattern, model; *mat.* formula. **-illa** outline; *kuv. m.* figure, forecast, envisage. **-ke** form. **-mainen** formal; stiff; set [in one's ways]. **-maisuus** formalism, formality, stiffness.
kaavio scheme, diagram. **-mainen** schematic. **-kuva** diagrammatic drawing, diagram.
kabaree cabaret.
kabinetti *(hallitus)* cabinet; *(huone)* small private room.
kade envious; *hänen kävi kateeksi* he envied [me my success]. **-hdittava** enviable.
kadeh|tia envy; *(ei suoda)* [be] grudge; *hän -ti ystävänsä menestystä* he envied his friend's success, *vrt. ed.*
kadetti cadet. **-koulu** Military Academy.
kadoksi|in: *joutua* ~ be lost; disappear; *olla -ssa* be missing.
kado|ta disappear; be lost; *(haihtua)* vanish; *minulta katosi hattu* I lost my hat; ~ *näkyvistä (m.)* pass out of sight; *kauneus katoaa* beauty fades. **-ttaa** lose; *-tettu (usk.)* damned, lost. **-tus** damnation, doom.
kadun|kulma street corner. **-lakaisija** street sweeper. **-lasku** paving. **-puoleinen:** ~ *huone* room facing the street, front room. **-risteys** street crossing.
kaduttaa: *minua* ~, *että* .. I regret that ..

kaha|kka skirmish. **-koida** skirmish, fight.
kahdeksan eight. **-kertainen** eightfold. **-kulmainen** octagonal. **-kulmio** octagon. **-kymmentä** eighty. **-nes** eighth [part]; *(~nuotti* quaver).
-toista eighteen. **-tuntinen:** ~ *työpäivä* eight-hour day.
kahdeksas [the] eighth. **-kymmenes** [the] eightieth. **-toista** [the] eighteenth.
kahden: *me* ~ we two by ourselves; *olemme* ~ *kesken* we are alone, we are by ourselves; *olla* ~ *vaiheilla* be in two minds. **-kertainen** double, twofold. **-keskinen** confidential. **-laatuinen** .. of two kinds. **-maattava:** ~ *vuode* double bed. **-puoleinen** mutual. **-taa** double. **-tua** [be] double [d].
kahdeskymmenes [the] twentieth. **-osa** twentieth.
kahdes|ti twice; ~ *viikossa* twice a week; ~ *kuussa ilmestyvä* biweekly. **-toista** [the] twelfth.
kahdis|taa double. **-tua** [be] double [d].
kahdestoista [the] twelfth. **-osa** twelfth [part].
kahi|na rustle, *(hameen)* swish -[ing]; *(nujakka)* scuffle. **-nointi** *(kadulla)* rioting. **-sta** rustle.
kahla|aja wader. **-amo** ford. **-ta** wade. **-uspaikka** fording place, ford.
kahle|et irons, *et. kuv.* fetters, shackles; *(siteet)* bonds; *-issa* in irons; fettered; *panna -isiin* put in irons. **-htia** chain; fetter, shackle; ~ *(esim. vuoteeseen)* confine to .. **-koira** watch-dog.
kahmaista grab, grasp.
kahna|ta rub; chafe. **-us** rubbing; *kuv.* rub; *-uksetta* without a hitch, without friction.
kahta: ~ *parempi* doubly good, twice as good; ~ *innokkaammin* with redoubled zeal. **-alla** on two sides. **-alle** in two different directions. **-lainen** two sorts (kinds) of

. .; dual. **-laisuus** duality.
kahtia in two [parts[, in half.
-jako division in [to] two
[equal parts].
kahva handle, *(miekan)* hilt,
(nuppi) knob.
kahveli *mer.* gaff.
kahvi coffee; *keittää ~a* make
c.; *olla ~lla jkn luona* have
c. (at . .'s, with sb.).
-aamiainen breakfast with
coffee. **-kalusto** coffee set.
-kannu coffee-pot. **-kestit**
coffee party. **-kupillinen** cup
of coffee. **-kuppi** coffee-cup.
-la café, coffee bar, cafeteria.
-leipä buns, cakes (to serve
with coffee). **-nkeitin** coffee
percolator, c.-maker. **-nkorvike**
coffee substitute. **-nporot**
coffee grounds. **-nselvike**
clarifier. **-pannu** coffee-pot.
-pensas coffee-shrub.
kai perhaps, probably, *(ehkä,*
m.) maybe; *minun ~ täytyy*
mennä I suppose I must go.
kaide *(kaiteet)* balustrade,
banisters, *(sillan)* railing,
parapet; *(pirta)* reed. **-puu**
handrail; *~t* banisters.
kaihdin curtain; *(alas*
vedettävä) blind; *(ulko-)*
canvas blind.
kaihi cataract; *(viher-)*
glaucoma.
kaiho longing; yearning. **-isa**
longing, wistful; languishing.
-mielisyys wistfulness;
melancholy. **-ta** long (for,
after), yearn (for), pine,
languish (for).
kaihtaa shun; avoid.
kaiken|kokoinen . . of all
sizes. **-lainen** all kinds (sorts)
of; . . of every description.
kaiketi probably, presumably;
(varmaankin) surely.
kaikin|puolin in every respect.
-puolinen universal, general.
(yleis-) all-round.
kaikkein very, . . of all; *~*
enimmän most of all; *~*
kaunein rakennus the most
beautiful building; *~ suurin*
the very largest, the biggest
of all. **-pyhin** the holy of
holies.
kaikkeus universe, cosmos.

kaikki all; *(jokainen)* every;
(koko) whole entire; *s.* all,
everything; *~ kaikessa* the
whole world (to, *jklle)*; *~,*
mitä minulla on all [that] I
have; *me ~* we all, all of
us; *ota ~!* take the [whole]
lot! *siinä ~* that is all, that
is the long and the short of
it; *kaiken aikaa* all the time,
all along; *kaiken päivää* all
day long; *kaiket päivät* for
days on end; *kaikkea muuta*
kuin . . anything but; *tehdä*
kaikkensa do all in one's
power, do one's utmost;
kaikkea vielä! nonsense! *~en*
aikojen (suurin the greatest
. .) ever, *(tilaisuus)* the chance
of a lifetime.
kaikki|aan in all, taken all
together, all told; *vieraita oli*
~ 130 the visitors totalled
130; *kerta ~ (ei)* just (not).
-alla everywhere; *(missä*
tahansa) anywhere; throughout
[Europe], *(maailmassa, m.)*
all over the world, the world
over; *vähän ~* here, there
and everywhere.
kaikki|näkevä all-seeing.
-ruokainen omnivorous.
-tietävyys omniscience. **-tietävä**
omniscient. **-valtias** almighty,
omnipotent; all-powerful.
-valtius omnipotence. **-voipa**
almighty, omnipotent.
kaiku echo; resonance. **-a**
echo, resound; reverberate;
jnk sävelten -essa to the
strains of; *naurun -essa* amid
peals of laughter. **-luotaus**
echo-sounding. **-pohja**
sound [ing]-board. **-va** echoing;
sonorous; loud.
kaima namesake.
kainalo armpit; . . *~ssa* . .
under his (her) arm; *pistä*
kätesi ~oni take my arm.
-kuoppa armpit. **-sauva** crutch.
kaino shy,bashful, coy.
kainos|telematon unconstrained.
-tella be shy, be embarrassed;
lainkaan -telematta quite at
one's ease. **-telu** bashfulness;
timidity.
kainous bashfulness, shyness.
kaipaus longing; regret.

kaira drill, auger; *(salomaa)* backwoods. **-nreikä** bore-hole. **-ta** drill.

kaisl a club-rush, *(järvi-)* bulrush. **-ikko** bulrushes.

kaista *(ajo-)* lane, *sot.* sector. **-le** strip. **-päinen** foolish, cracked. **-pää** madcap, fool.

kaita *a.* narrow; *v.* tend. **-filmikamera** cine camera; 8 (16) mm. movie camera. **-liina** table-runner.

kaits|elmus Providence. **-ija** *(vartija)* guardian, *(puiston)* attendant. keeper, *(paimen)* shepherd; *lasten* ~ baby-sitter.

kaiutin loud-speaker; *(~laitteet* amplifiers). **-ttaa** *(säveltä)* strike up a song.

kaiva|a dig, *(joskus)* delve; *(hampaita ym)* pick; *(myyrä ym)* burrow; *(etsien)* dig out, excavate; *(haudasta)* exhume, disinter; *(tunneli)* drive, cut; ~ *maata jnk alta (kuv.)* undermine; ~ *maahan* bury, dig in. **-nto** canal.

kaiva|ta long (for); miss; *(tarvita)* require, need; *(olla vailla)* lack; *kaipaa korjausta* needs mending (fixing); *me olemme -nneet sinua* we have missed you; ~ *katkerasti* miss sorely; **-ttu** longed for; *kauan -ttu* long-needed.

kaiva|ttaa have .. dug; ~ *ruumis maasta* have a body disinterred (exhumed). **-us** excavation. **-utua:** ~ *maahan (sot.)* dig in.

kaivella pick; *mieltäni kaivelee* it frets me, it worries me ..

kaiver|rus engraving; inscription. **-ruttaa** have .. engraved. **-taa** engrave; inscribe. **-taja** engraver.

kaivinkone excavator.

kaivo well; *etsiä* ~ dowse; *kaivaa* ~ sink a w.; *nostaa vettä ~sta* draw water from a w. **-nkatsoja** water-diviner.

kaivos mine; pit; *(avo-)* opencast mine. **-alue** mining area (district). **-aukko** pithead. **-insinööri** mining engineer. **-kuilu** [mine-]shaft. **-mies** miner; collier. **-onnettomuus** mine disaster. **-pölkky** pit

prop. **-teollisuus** mining [industry]. **-työ** mining.

kajah|dus, -taa clang, ring.

kajas|taa shimmer; loom; be reflected; *päivä* ~ the day is breaking (dawning). **-tus** shimmer, gleam; *(päivän)* dawn.

kajota touch; *kuv.* touch upon.

kajuutta cabin.

kakara *leik.* kid, *halv.* brat.

kakistella: ~ *kurkkuaan* clear one's throat.

kakko|nen two; *korttip.* deuce.

kakku cake. **-lapio** cake slice. **-lautanen** cake dish. **-paperi** cake doily. **-vuoka** baking tin.

kaksi two; ~ *kertaa* twice, two times; ~ *sen vertaa* twice as much; *kahden puolen jtk* on both sides of; *kahden hengen (huone* double room, *auto* two-seater). **-jakoinen** bipartite. **-jalkainen** two-legged; biped. **-kerroksinen** two-storey [ed]; *(bussi)* double-decker. **-kielinen** bilingual. **-kymmentä** twenty. **-mielinen** ambiguous, equivocal. **-mielisyys** ambiguity; double entendre. **-naamai|nen** two-faced; ~ *peli* double-dealing, duplicity; *pelata -sta peliä* double-cross. **-nainen** twofold; dual. **-naisuus** duality. **-neuvoinen** hermaphrodite. **-toista** twelve.

kaksin|kerroin: *kääntää* ~ fold .. double. **-kertainen** double, twofold; ~ *ikkuna* double-glazed window. **-kertaistaa** double. **-kertaistua** [be] double [d]. **-kertaisuus** doubleness. **-naiminen** bigamy. **-nos** doubling; duplication. **-peli** *(tennis)* singles. **-puhelu** duologue. *(keskustelu)* dialogue. **-taistelija** duel [l] ist. **-taistelu** duel; single combat.

kaksi|näytöksinen .. in two acts. **-o** two-room flat [let]. **-osainen** .. in two parts, *(-niteinen)* .. in two volumes. **-piippuinen** double-barrelled. **-rivinen** *(takki)* double-breasted. **-raiteinen** double-track. **-sataa** two hundred. **-selitteinen**

ambiguous. **-suuntainen** two-way [traffic]. **-tahtimoottori** two-stroke engine. **-taso** biplane. **-tavuinen** dissyllabic. **-teräinen** two-(double-)edged. **-toista** twelve. **-ttain** in twos, two by two, two at a time; in couples. **-vaiheinen** two-phase. **-valjakko** carriage and pair. **-vuotias** two years old; ~ (lapsi ym) a two-year-old [child]. **-vuotinen** biennial, (kurssi) two-year. **-ääninen** two-part.

kaksois|elämä double life. **-kappale** duplicate; replica. **-kerake** double consonant. **-leuka** double chin. **-olento** double. **-piste** colon. **-sisar, -veli** twin sister (brother). **-ääntiö** diphthong.

kakso|nen twin; -set twins.

kaktus cactus (pl. m. cacti).

kala fish; kuin ~ kuivalla maalla like a fish out of water; mennä ~an go fishing; olla ~ssa be out fishing; pyytää kaloja catch fish. **-haavi** landing-net. **-halli** fishmarket. **-inen, -isa** .. abounding in fish. **-kauppias** fishmonger. **-kukko** bread with pork and muikku (fish) cooked inside. **-lampi** fish-pond. **-lokki** common gull. **-mies** fisherman.

kalan|istutus planting of fish, fish-breeding. **-kutu** spawning. **-maiti** soft roe, milt. **-maksaöljy** cod-liver oil. **-poikaset** fry. **-pyydykset** fishing tackle. **-pyynti** fishing. **-ruoto** fish-bone. **-saalis** catch [of fish]. **-viljely** fish-breeding.

kala|onni fisherman's luck. **-porras** fish ladder.

kalast|aa fish, catch fish. **-aja** fisherman; (urheilu-) angler.

kalastus fishing; fishery, catching of [herring etc.]. **-alus** fishing craft. **-kausi** fishing season. **-tarvikkeet** fishing tackle. **-urheilu** fishing.

kala|säilykkeet tinned (Am. canned) fish. **-sääski** osprey. **-talous** fishing industry. **-vedet** fishing ground, (suuret)

fisheries. **-velka:** on vanhoja -velkoja maksettavanaan has old scores to settle. **-verkko** fishing net.

kalenteri calendar; ~vuosi c. year.

kalevan|miekka Orion. **-tuli** summer lightning.

kali kem. potash, potassium oxide.

kaliberi calibre.

kalifi caliph.

Kalifornia California. **k-lainen** a. & s. Californian.

kalikka stick, billet.

kali|na, -sta rattle, clatter; (hampaista) chatter. **-stella** rattle, clatter; clank, jangle.

kalium potassium.

kalja beer.

kaljaasi (m. kaleeri) galley.

kalju bald; (paljas) bare. **-päinen** bald [-headed]. **-päisyys** baldness.

kalke rattling, clatter; vasaran ~ hammering.

kalkio|ida trace. **-paperi** carbon paper; (läpinäkyvä) tracing-paper.

kalkita (maata) lime; (seinää ym) whitewash.

kalkkarokäärme rattle-snake.

kalkki 1. lime; (sammuttamaton) quick-lime; sammutettu ~ slaked l.; **2.** (malja) chalice, cup. **-kivi** limestone; (~louhos quarry). **-laasti** mortar. **-maalaus** fresco. **-nen** limy. **-pitoinen** calcareous. **-utua** be calcified, calcify. **-utuminen** calcification; suonten ~ arteriosclerosis. **-uuni** lime kiln. **-väri** lime-wash, whitewash.

kalkkuna turkey. **-kukko** turkey cock. **-npaisti** roast turkey.

kalku|tella pound, hammer. **-tus** clatter; (vasaran) pounding, hammering.

kallell|aan, -een tilted, .. at an angle, .. on one side; olla ~ lean, incline, (esim. hattu) be tilted.

kalleus 1. expensiveness, costliness; **2.** (esine) valuable.

kalliinajanlisä cost-of-living increment (allowance).

kallio rock; (et. ranta-) cliff.

kall   116

-inen rocky. **-maalaus** rock painting. **-perusta, perä** bedrock. **-seinämä** rock-face. **K~vuoret** the Rocky Mountains.
kallis dear; expensive; *kalliista hinnasta* at a high price, dear, dearly; *se voi käydä sinulle kalliiksi* you may have to pay for it dearly. **-arvoinen** precious, valuable, costly; .. of [great] value, priceless. **-arvoisuus** costliness; high value. **-hintainen** expensive, dear, costly.
kallis|taa 1. *(hintaa)* raise, increase the price (of); **2.** lean, incline; ~ *korvansa jllek* lend an ear to. **-tua 1.** rise [in price]; *hinta -tuu* the price is going up; **2.** lean, incline; *(laiva)* [give a] list, heel. **-tuma** inclination, tilt; *(laivan)* heel, list, *(keinuessa)* lurch. **-tuminen 1.** *(hintojen)* rise in prices; **2.** *m. kuv.* leaning, inclination.
kallo skull, cranium. **-nmurtuma** skull fracture, fractured skull.
kalm|a death. **-ankalpea** deathly pale. **-isto** graveyard.
kalori calorie.
kalossi galosh.
kalotti skull-cap; *(jää-)* icecap.
kalpa sword; *(miekkailu-)* épée.
kalpe|a pale, pallid; *käydä ~ksi* turn pale. **-us** pallor, paleness.
kalsea *(sää)* raw, chilly *(m. kuv.)*, bleak.
kals|kahdus clang. **-kahtaa** clank. **-ke** clatter, clanking; *aseiden ~* clash of arms.
kaltai|nen like; *olla jnk ~* be like; resemble; *saman ~* similar (to); *he ovat toistensa -sia* they are [much] alike.
kaltev|a leaning, inclined [plane, *pinta*], slanting; sloping. **-uus** inclination, declivity; .. *-n asteen -uudella* at an angle of .. degrees.
kaltoin: *kohdella ~* treat cruelly.
kalu thing, article; object; *(siitin)* penis; *mennyttä ~a* lost, gone for good.

kalus|taa furnish, fit up. **-tamaton** unfurnished. **-to** *(huone-)* furniture; *(kiinteä)* fixtures; *(kalut)* implements; equipment, outfit; *(~luettelo* inventory; *~vaja* tool shed). **-tus** furnishing [s].
kalvaa gnaw *(m. kuv.)*; *kenkä ~* the shoe rubs (chafes); *(loukkaus) kalvoi hänen mieltään* .. still rankled in his mind.
kalvakka wan, pale.
kalveta turn pale; *hän kalpeni kauhusta* she went white with fear.
kalvo film; *anat., bot.* membrane; pellicle. **-mainen** filmy, membranous.
kalvosin cuff. **-nappi:** *-napit* cuff-links.
kama junk.
kamal|a ghastly; dreadful, frightful. **-uus** ghastliness, dreadfulness.
kamana lintel.
kamara surface; *(kuori)* crust; *isänmaan ~* native soil.
kamari chamber. **-herra** chamberlain. **-musiikki** chamber music. **-neiti** lady's maid, waiting maid, *(prinsessan ym)* maid in waiting. **-palvelija** valet. **-rouva** lady in waiting.
Kambodša Cambodia; **k-lainen** Cambodian.
kamee *(-koriste)* cameo.
kameleontti chameleon.
kameli camel; *(yksikyttyräinen)* dromedary. **-nkarva** camel hair.
kamferi camphor.
kamiina stove, heater *(esim. oil-heater)*.
kammata comb; ~ *tukkansa (m.)* do one's hair.
kammio chamber; room; *(koppi)* cell; *(sydän-)* ventricle; *munkin ~* monk's cell.
kammo dread; horror, *(inho)* abhorrence. **-ta** dread. **-ttaa:** *se minua ~* it fills me with dread; *-ttava* dreadful; uncanny.
kampa comb, *(tiheä)* tooth comb. **-aja** hairdresser, hair stylist. **-amo** hairdresser's.

-lanka worsted [yarn].
kampanja campaign.
kampata trip [sb. up].
kampaus hairstyle, hairdo; *pesu ja* ~ shampoo and set. **-neste** setting lotion.
kampela flat-fish, flounder.
kamppai|lla struggle (against). **-lu** struggle, combat.
kampurajalka club-foot.
kamreeri chief accountant.
kana hen, *(lajina)* domestic fowl; ~*t (m.)* poultry; *paistettua* ~*a* roast chicken.
Kanaali: *Englannin* ~ the [English] Channel.
Kanada Canada. **k-lainen** *a. & s.* Canadian.
kana|haukka goshawk. **-häkki, -koppi** hen-coop. **-la** poultryhouse; poultry farm. **-lintu** gallinaceous bird.
kanan|hoito poultry-rearing (-farming). **-liha** *kuv.* goose pimples. **-muna** [hen's] egg. **-poika** chicken, broiler.
kanaria|lintu canary. **K-n saaret** the Canary Islands.
kanava channel; *(kaivettu)* canal; *anat., m.* meatus. **-kangas** canvas. **verkko** canal system, network of canals.
kanavoi|da canalize. **-nti** canalization.
kandidaatti candidate.
kaneli cinnamon. **-nkuori** cinnamon bark.
kanerva heather. **-kangas** heath, *(suuri)* moor.
kangas 1. material, stuff, [woven] fabric, *(villainen)* cloth; *kankaat* textiles. **2.** *(-maa)* moor, heath. **-kantinen** .. bound in cloth. **-kauppa** draper's [shop]. **-kenkä** cloth shoe. **-malli** sample of cloth. **-pala** piece of cloth. **-puut** handloom.
kangas|taa loom. **-tus** mirage.
kangertaa stumble in one's speech; *(änkyttää)* stammer, stutter.
kangis|taa stiffen. **-tua** stiffen; become stiff; *kaavoihin -tunut* set in one's ways, fixed in one's habits, *(ahdasmielinen)* hidebound.
kaniini rabbit. **-nkoppi, -tarha**

rabbit hutch. **-nnahka** cony.
kankea stiff, rigid; *(kylmästä)* numb [with cold]; *(esim. käännös)* wooden. **-jalkainen** stiff-legged.
kankeus stiffness, rigidity.
kanki bar. **-rauta** bar (rod) iron.
kankuri weaver.
kannalta *ks. kanta.*
kannanmuutos change of one's attitude; *(hallituksen)* change of policy.
kannas neck of land, isthmus.
kannatin support, prop. **-pylväs** supporting pillar, buttress.
kanna|ttaa 1. *(tukea)* support *(m. kuv.)*, sponsor; second; back [up] *(pitää ylhäällä)* hold up, carry; **2.** *(olla tuottava)* pay, be profitable; *(ansaita)* be worth; *jää* ~ the ice bears; *liike* ~ the business pays well; *minun ei -ta ostaa autoa* I cannot afford [to buy] a car; *siitä ei -ta puhuakaan* it's no use even speaking about that; *sinun ei -ta mennä sinne* it is not worth your while going there; *asiaa* ~ *ajatella* the matter deserves consideration; *-tan edellistä puhujaa* I agree with the previous speaker; *-tetaan!* I second it! **-tettava** worthy of support. **-ttaja** supporter, adherent; *(aatteen, m.)* advocate. **-ttamaton** unremunerative, unprofitable, uneconomic. **-ttava** paying, profitable. **-ttavuus** profitableness. **-tus** support; approval.
kanne case; *(syyte)* action; *(valitus)* complaint; *nostaa* ~ *jkta vastaan* bring a legal action against, prosecute.
kannella tell tales, bear tales; *koul. sl.* peach against.
kannellinen provided with a lid, covered; *(laiva)* decked.
kannike *(ripa)* handle; *(-nauha)* sling.
kannikka crust [of bread].
kannu jug, pitcher; *(tee- ym)* pot; *(esim. viini-)* flagon; ~*ja on valettu innokkaasti* there has been a great deal of

speculation about . .. **-nvalaja**
pilk. dabbler in politics.
kannus spur; *kannuksen pyörä*
rowel. **-taa** spur on, *kuv.*
stimulate, incite; *-tava*
encouraging, stimulating. **-tin**
spur, *kuv. m.* stimulus.
kanootti canoe.
kansa people, *(-kunta)* nation;
Suomen ~ the Finnish
people; *yhteinen* ~ *(rahvas)*
the common people; *siellä oli
paljon* ~*a* there were a lot of
people.
kansain|liitto the League of
Nations. **-vaellus** migration of
peoples. **-välinen** international.
-välisyys internationality.
-yhteisö [the British]
Commonwealth [of Nations].
kansakoulu primary school,
elementary school.
kansa|kunta nation. **-lainen**
national; citizen; *(saman
maan)* fellow-citizen;
fellow-countryman.
kansalais|kokous mass meeting.
-luottamus *vanh.* civil rights.
-oikeudet civil rights. **-sota**
civil war. **-taa** naturalize.
-tieto civics. **-tua** become
naturalized. **-uus** citizenship.
-velvollisuudet civic duties.
kansallinen national.
kansallis|eepos national epic.
-kiihko nationalism.
-kiihkoilija nationalist;
chauvinist. **-kiihkoinen**
nationalist; chauvinistic.
-kokous national convention.
-laulu national anthem.
-mielinen *a. & s.* nationalist.
-mielisyys national spirit;
nationalism. **-omaisuus**
national wealth. **-puku**
national dress, regional
costume. **-päivä** national day.
-ruoka national dish. **-sankari**
national hero. **-sosialismi**
Nazism. **-sosialisti** national
socialist, Nazi. **-taa**
nationalize. **-taminen**
nationalization. **-tunne** national
spirit. **-uus** nationality.
kansan|auto people's car.
-edustaja member of the
parliament, *Am. l.v.*
congressman. **-eläke** national

old-age pension. **-eläkelaitos**
National Pensions Office.
-heimo tribe. **-huoltoministeriö**
Ministry of Supply *(t.* Food).
-johtaja popular leader.
-joukko crowd. **-juhla** popular
festival. **-kerros** stratum *(pl.*
strata) of population. **-kieli**
vernacular. **-kiihottaja** agitator,
demagogue. **-kokous** mass
meeting. **-konsertti** popular
concert. **-korkeakoulu** people's
college, adult education
college. **-laulu** folk song.
-luokka class. **-mies** man of
the people. **-murha** genocide.
-nousu [up]rising. **-omainen**
popular, *puhek.* folksy.
-omaisuus simplicity,
democratic ways. **-opetus**
education of the people.
-opisto people's college.
-paljous multitude. **-perinne**
folklore. **-puhuja** stump orator.
-puisto public park. **-rintama**
popular front. **-runo** rune,
traditional poem. **-runous** folk
poetry; *k-uden tutkija*
folklorist. **-satu** folk-tale.
-suosio popularity. **-tajuinen**
popular; *tehdä k-uiseksi*
popularize. **-tajuisuus**
simplicity. **-taloudellinen**
economic; politico-economic.
-talous(tiede) economics,
national economy. **-tanhu**
folk-dance, country dance.
-tasavalta people's republic.
-tulo national income. **-tuote**
national product. **-valistus**
public education.
kansanvalta democracy. **-inen**
democratic. **-isuus** democracy.
kansan|villitsijä demagogue.
-äänestys referendum,
plebiscite.
kansa|tiede ethnology.
-tieteellinen ethnological.
kansi lid, cover; *(laivan)* deck;
(kirjan) cover; binding; *kannet
(kansio)* folder, file; *kannella*
on deck; *kannesta kanteen*
from cover to cover.
-kuvatyttö cover girl. **-lasti**
deck cargo. **-lehti** cover.
-matkustaja deck passenger.
kansio file, *(kannet)* folder.
-ida file.

kansleri chancellor.
kansli|a [secretarial] offices.
   -sti government clerk.
kansoittaa populate.
kanssa with, together with.
   -ihminen fellow-man
   (-creature). **-käymi|nen**
   dealings, communication
   [between people]; *olla k-sissä
   jkn kanssa* associate with a
   p. **-perilli|nen** coheir; *k-set
   (m.)* joint heirs.
kanta *(suhtautumis-)* attitude,
   stand; standpoint; *(näkö-)*
   point of view; *(raha- ym)*
   standard; *(auto-, lintu- ym)*
   population; *(~osa, tyvi)* base;
   (kengän) heel; *(naulan)* head;
   (kuitin, lipun) counterfoil,
   stub; *(varsi)* stalk; *asettua
   jllek kannalle* take a stand
   (a position) [in a matter];
   tältä kannalta katsoen from
   this point of view; *juridiselta
   kannalta* from a juridical
   aspect; *sivistys on korkealla
   kannalla* the standard of
   education is high; *asiain
   nykyisellä kannalla* as matters
   stand now; *pysyä kannallaan*
   stand one's ground.
kantaa carry, *kuv. m.* bear; ~
   hedelmää bear fruit; ~
   seuraukset take the
   consequences; ~ *veroja* levy
   taxes; *jää* ~ the ice bears;
   niin kauas kuin silmä ~ as
   far as eye can reach; *ääni* ~
   kauas the voice carries far.
kanta|-asiakas regular
   [frequenter]. **-isä** progenitor.
   -ja porter; *lak.* plaintiff;
   (hautajaisissa) pallbearer.
   -kaupunki down-town section.
   -kirja pedigree book. **-lippu**
   counterfoil, stub. **-maton:**
   silmän k-ttomiin beyond the
   range of vision, out of sight.
   -muoto original (basic) form.
   -mus load. **-pää** heel; *kiireestä
   ~hän* from top to toe.
   -pääoma initial capital. **-sana**
   root-word, radical. **-sormus**
   signet ring. **-utua:** ~ *jkn
   korviin* reach a p.'s ears.
   -vieras regular visitor
   (frequenter). **-vuus** carrying
   capacity; *kuv.* scope. **-äiti**

kuv. mother.
kantele Finnish zither, kantele.
kante|lija talebearer, telltale.
   -lu talebearing, blabbing; *lak.*
   complaint.
kanto stump, stub; *(veron)*
   collection. **-inen:** *on .. -n* ~
   has a carrying capacity of ..
   -matka range. **-raketti** carrier
   (*t.* booster) rocket. **-siipialus**
   hydrofoil ship. **-tuoli** sedan
   [-chair].
kanttori precentor, cantor.
kanuuna gun; cannon *(pl. =
   sg).*
kaoliini kaolin, china-clay.
kapakala dried fish.
kapak|ka pub *(lyh.* = public
   house); restaurant; *Am.*
   saloon; *(~kierros* pub crawl).
   -oitsija public-house *(Am.*
   saloon-)keeper.
kapalo|ida swaddle. **-lapsi** baby,
   infant.
kapasiteetti capacity.
kapea narrow. **-raitainen**
   narrow-striped. **-raiteinen**
   narrow-gauge.
kapeikko narrow pass,
   (pullonkaula) bottleneck.
kapellimestari orchestral
   conductor, band-leader.
kapeus narrowness.
kapina rebellion, revolt,
   insurrection; *sot., mer.*
   mutiny; *nousta ~an* rise in
   rebellion. **-henki** spirit of
   rebellion. **-llinen** *a.* rebellious,
   insurgent; *s.* rebel, insurgent;
   mutineer.
kapine thing, object; *~et*
   things.
kapinoi|da rebel, revolt,
   mutiny. **-tsija** rebel.
kapiot trousseau.
kapitalis|mi capitalism. **-ti**
   capitalist.
Kap|kaupunki Cape Town.
   -maa the Cape [Province].
kappa coat, cloak; *(mitta, l.
   v.)* gallon.
kappalainen curate; *(hovi- ym)*
   chaplain.
kappale piece, bit; *(esine)*
   object; *(tekstissä)* paragraph;
   section; *(kirjaa ym)* copy; *fys.*
   body: *(näytelmä)* play; *2
   shillingiä* ~ 2 sh. apiece, 2

sh. each; *saan maksun ~elta* I am paid by the piece; *hajosi ~iksi* went to pieces; *kirjaa on 5 ~tta* there are 5 copies of the book. **-ittain** by the piece. **-tavara** piece goods. **-työ** piece-work.

kappeli chapel.

kapris capers.

kapsahtaa *(pudota)* plump [down]; ~ *jkn kaulaan* hug.

kapse clatter; *kavion ~* c. of hoofs.

kapseli capsule.

kapteeni captain; *(kauppalaivan)* master.

kapula stick; *(viesti-)* baton; *(suu-)* gag.

kara *tekn.* spindle.

karaatti carat.

karah|taa *-ti punaiseksi* blushed suddenly; ~ *pystyyn* jump up.

karahvi decanter, *(vesi-)* carafe.

karais|ta harden, temper; inure; *(terästää)* steel. **-tua** become hardened; *-tunut* hardened, *(kylmää kestämään)* inured to cold.

karamelli sweet; *~t* sweets, bonbons, *Am.* candy.

karanteeni quarantine.

karata run away; *sot.* desert; *(vankilasta ym)* escape; *(rakastunut pari)* elope; ~ *jkn kimppuun* rush at.

karavaani caravan.

karbidi carbide.

karbolihappo carbolic acid.

kardemumma cardamom.

kardiaaniakseli *(auton)* drive *(propeller)* shaft.

kardinaali cardinal.

karehtia ripple; *kuv.* play.

karhe|a rough; ~ *ääni* hoarse (husky, rasping) voice. **-us** roughness; hoarseness.

karhi, -ta harrow.

karhu bear. **-makirje** dunning letter. **-najo** bear-hunting. **-npentu** [bear] cub. **-ntalja** bearskin. **-ta** dun.

kari rock; *(-kko)* reef; *(matalikko)* shallow; *ajaa ~lle* run aground, strike a rock; *irrottaa ~lta* refloat.

karikkeet [forest] litter.

karikkoinen rocky, reefy.

karilleajo running aground, grounding.

karis|ta fall off, drop off. **-taa** shake [off]; ~ *harteiltaan vastuu* shuffle off responsibility.

karitsa lamb.

karja livestock, *(nauta-)* cattle. **-aura** *Am.* cow-catcher.

karjaista roar.

karja|kko dairymaid, milkmaid, *(mies-)* cowman.

Karjala Karelia; *~n kannas* the Karelian Isthmus.

karjalainen Karelian.

karja|lauma herd [of cattle]. **-nhoito** livestock rearing, animal husbandry, cattle-farming. **-nkasvattaja** livestock farmer, stockbreeder. **-näyttely** cattle show. **-piha** farmyard. **-rotu** breed of cattle. **-talous** animal husbandry.

karju boar. **-a** roar; bawl.

karkaaminen running away; flight; escape; *sot.* desertion; *(parin)* elopement.

karkai|sta harden; *(päästää)* temper; *vrt. karaista;* ~ *luontonsa* steel one's heart. **-su-uuni** hardening furnace.

karkaus|päivä Leap Year Day. **-vuosi** leap-year.

karkea coarse, *(pinta)* rough; *kuv.* rude, harsh; ~ *työ* rough work; *~n työn tekijä* unskilled workman; ~ *pila* coarse joke; ~ *virhe* grave error. **-karvainen** *(koira)* wire-haired. **-käytöksinen** ill-mannered, unmannerly. **-piirteinen** coarse-featured. **-puheinen** rough-tongued. **-puheisuus** coarseness of speech. **-tekoinen** roughly made.

karkeisseppä blacksmith.

karkelo dance, *(leikki)* play. **-ida** dance.

karkeus coarseness, roughness.

karko|ttaa drive away; turn out; *(koulusta ym)* expel; *kuv.* dispel; *(ulkomaalainen)* deport, expel; *(mielestään* banish from one's mind. **-tus** banishment, expatriation; deportation; *(koulusta ym)* expulsion; (~**paikka** place of exile).

karku: *lähteä* ~*un* run away; *päästä* ~*un* [manage to] escape; get away; *täyttä* ~*a* at full gallop. **-lainen, -ri** runaway; *sot.* deserter; *vankikarkuri* escaped prisoner. **-retki** flight; *(harha-askel)* escapade.

karm|aiseva spine-chilling. **-ea** grisly, gruesome; harsh, bitter.

karm|ia feel raw; *selkääni -ii sitä ajatellessani* it gives me the shivers to think of it.

karmosiini, -punainen crimson.

karnevaali carnival.

karpalo cranberry.

karppi *zo.* carp.

karsa|asti askew; *kuv.* unkindly. **-s** unkind; *katsoa -in silmin* look askance (at), regard with disapproval, be unfavourably disposed towards. **-staa** squint. **-stus** distortion, *(silmien)* squint. **-us** wryness; averseness.

karsia *(oksia)* lop [off], prune; *(poistaa)* strike .. out, eliminate; *kirjoitusta on paljon karsittu* the article has been severely edited.

karsina pen.

karsinta pruning, lopping, *(tasoittaminen)* trimming; elimination. **-kilpailu** trial. **-kurssi** elimination course. **-ottelu** qualifying (eliminating) match.

karski harsh, stern, rough, gruff, *(reima)* brisk. **-us** harshness, sternness.

karsta *(villa-)* card; *(noki)* soot, *lääk.* crust. **-ta** card.

kartano estate; *(piha)* yard. **-nomistaja** estate-owner.

kartan|piirtäjä cartographer. **-piirustus** map-drawing, mapping, cartography.

kartasto atlas.

kartelli *liik.* cartel.

kartio cone. **-mainen** conical.

kartoi|ttaa map; draw a map of, [make a] chart. **-tus** mapping.

kartonki paper board; *(-rasia)* carton.

kartta map, *(kaupungin)* street-map; *(meri-)* chart.

karttaa avoid [. .-ing], evade; *(pysyä loitolla)* keep [away] from; *hän* ~ *seuraa* he keeps to himself, he shuns company.

kartta|laukku map-case. **-luonnos** sketch map.

karttaminen avoidance.

karttapallo globe.

kartteleva evasive; *ihmisiä* ~ shy of people; *työtä* ~ workshy.

karttu *(maila)* bat; stick.

karttu|a grow, increase; accumulate; *hänelle -u ikää* he is getting on in years; *-nut korko* the interest accrued. **-isa** ample, abundant. **-minen** increase.

kartuttaa increase, augment, add to; heap [up], pile [up], accumulate; ~ *tietojaan* improve one's knowledge.

karu barren, sterile; *(kuiva)* arid, *(paljas)* bare.

karuselli roundabout, merry-go-round.

karuus barrenness, sterility.

karva hair; *oikeassa* ~*ssaan (kuv.)* in its true colours; *(turkista)* lähtee karvoja the fur is coming out, *(koirasta . .)* the dog is shedding (losing) fur. **-inen** hairy. **-isuus** hairiness. **-lakki** fur cap. **-lankamatto** hair carpet. **-npoistoaine** depilatory, hair remover. **-peite** fur. **-peitteinen** covered with hair, hairy, hirsute.

karvas bitter; *se oli* ~*ta nieltävää* it was a bitter pill to swallow; ~ *kokemukseni on ollut* my harsh experience has been .. manteli bitter almonds. **-pippuri** black pepper. **-suola** Epsom salt [s]. **-tella** smart; *mieltäni -telee* it vexes me [to think that ..].

karvaton hairless.

karvaus bitterness, acridity.

karviaismarja gooseberry. **-pensas** gooseberry bush.

kas look! look here; why, [there he is!] ~ *niin* now then! well! ~ *tässä (saat)* here you are! ~ *vain* just look! well, I never! why [,did you ever!] ~, *asia on*

niin, että .. you see, ..
kasa stack, heap, pile; *(joukko)*
mass, lot. **-antua** accumulate;
(lumi, hiekka) drift. **-antuma**
accumulation.
kasakka Cossack.
kasari saucepan.
kasarmi barracks. **-majoitus**
quartering in barracks.
kasata heap [up], pile [up];
accumulate, amass.
kasetti casette, *valok.*
cartridge.
kaskelotti *(-valas)* sperm-whale.
kaski 1. *(-maa)* burnt-over
clearing; *polttaa kaskea ks.*
kulottaa **2.** *(päähine)* helmet.
kasku anecdote, story.
kasoittain in heaps, heaps of ..
Kaspianmeri the Caspian Sea.
kassa cash; *(myymälän)*
paydesk, *(konttorin)* pay-office;
(rahasto) funds. **-alennus** cash
discount. **-holvi** strong-room.
-kaappi safe, strong box.
-kappale, **-magneetti** box-office
draw. **-kirja** cash-book. **-kone**
cash register. **-kuitti** cash
receipt, sales slip. **-lipas**
cash-box. **-nhoitaja** *(pää-)*
cashier. **-säästö** cash in hand.
-tili cash account. **-vaillinki**
deficit. *(kavallus)* defalcation.
kassi *(kanto-)* shopping-bag,
tote bag; *(verkko-, muovi-)*
string (plastic) bag.
kast|aa wet; *(kastella)* water;
(upottaa) dip, immerse; *kirk.*
baptize, christen; *hänet -ettiin*
Kaarloksi he was christened
Charles. **-aja:** *Johannes ~*
John the Baptist.
kastanja, **-nruskea** chestnut.
kastanjetit castanets.
kaste dew; *~ kirk.* baptism,
(lapsen) christening. **-helmi**
dewdrop. **-inen** dewy.
kaste|lla *(suihkulla ym)*
sprinkle, spray [with water];
(märäksi) wet; *(kosteaksi)*
moisten; *(viljelysmaata)*
irrigate; *-lin jalkani* my feet
got wet; *lapsi -lee* the baby
wets its bed.
kastelu *(kukkien ym)* watering;
sprinkling [with water];
(viljelysmaan) irrigation. **-laitos**
system of irrigation. **-vaunu**

street-sprinkler.
kaste|malja font. **-mato**
earthworm. **-todistus** certificate
of baptism. **-toimitus** baptism.
kasti caste. **-jako**, **-laitos** caste
system.
kastike sauce, dressing, *(kirpeä,*
m.) ketchup; *(liha-)* gravy.
-kauha sauce-ladle, gravy
spoon. **-malja** sauce boat.
kastua become wet, get wet; *~*
likomäräksi get drenched, get
soaked [to the skin].
kasukka chasuble.
kasva|a grow; *(lisääntyä)*
increase; *~ isoksi* grow up;
~ korkoa yield interest; *~*
umpeen (haavasta) heal over;
-va nuoriso the rising
generation; *ruohoa -va*
grass-grown. **-in** growth; *lääk.*
tumour. **-ttaa** *(viljaa ym)*
grow, raise; *(et. lapsia)* bring
up; rear; *(tiedollisesti)*
educate; *(karjaa)* breed;
raise; *~ partaa* grow a beard.
-ttaja grower; *(karjan ym)*
breeder; *(nuorison)* educationist,
pedagogue. **-ttava** educative.
-tti foster-child; *(~poika*
foster-son).
kasvatuksellinen educational.
kasvatus upbringing, rearing,
raising, *(eläinten, m.)*
breeding, *(viljely)* growing;
(tiedollinen) education;
training. **-isä** foster-father.
-järjestelmä educational
system. **-laitos** reform *(Engl.*
approved) school, training
school. **-opillinen**
pedagogic[al]. **-neuvola** child
guidance clinic. **-oppi**
pedagogy. pedagogics.
kasvi plant. **-aine** vegetable
matter. **-heimo** plant family.
-huone greenhouse, hothouse.
-kokoelma collection of plants;
herbarium. **-kset** vegetables.
-kunta vegetable kingdom.
-lava hotbed, forcing-bed.
-llisuus vegetation. **-maailma**
vegetable world. **-maantiede**
botanic geography. **-neste** sap.
-njalostus plant improvement.
-nkumppani companion from
childhood. **-o** flora. **-opillinen**
botanic[al]. **-oppi** botany.

kasvis|rasva vegetable fat.
-ravinto vegetable food.
-ruokalaji vegetable dish.
-syöjä vegetarian; *(eläin)*
herbivore. **-to** flora.
kasvitarha kitchen garden.
-nviljely horticulture.
kasvi|tiede botany. **-tieteellinen**
botanic [al]. **-tieteilijä** botanist.
kasvojen|hieronta face massage.
-ilme expression of the face.
-piirteet features.
kasvopyyhket *(paperi)* facial
tissue.
kasvot face; *harv.* countenance.
kasvu growth; *(lisääntyminen)*
increase; *hoikka ~ltaan* of
slender build. **-ikäinen** *(nuori)*
adolescent. **-kausi** period of
growth. **-voima** growing power.
kataja juniper. **-nmarja** juniper
berry; *(~viina* gin).
katal|a a mean, base, vile,
ignoble. **-uus** meanness,
baseness.
katarri catarrh.
katastrof|aalinen catastrophic. **-i**
catastrophe.
kate cover [ing]; *liik.* cover.
katederi teacher's desk.
katedraali cathedral.
kateelli|nen envious, *jklle* of;
jealous (of). **-suus** envy,
jealousy.
kateenkorva thymus [gland],
(ruokalaji) sweetbread.
kateu|s envy; *-desta* out of
envy (jealousy).
katgutti catgut.
katinkulta mica.
katiska fish trap.
katkai|sin *tekn.* switch. **-sta**
break; break off; *(leikata)* cut
off; *(kiskomalla)* tear off; *~*
puhe interrupt a speech; *~*
viholliselta paluumatka cut off
the enemy's retreat; *~ virta*
(sähk.) switch off (cut off)
the current; *~ välinsä jkn*
kanssa sever (break off)
connections with ..
katkarapu shrimp.
katkea|ma break, breach; *lääk.*
fracture. **-maton** unbroken;
uninterrupted; continuous.
-minen breaking; rupture.
katkelma *(kirjasta)* fragment.
-llinen fragmentary.

katker|a bitter; *~ mieli*
resentment; *~ pala* bitter pill;
~t sanat harsh words. **-o** *bot.*
gentian. **-oittaa** embitter; *~*
jkn mieltä (muisto ym) rankle
in . .'s mind. **-oitua** be [come]
embittered. **-uus** bitterness.
katke|ta break, be cut off;
snap; *(keskeytyä)* be
interrupted; *minulta -si käsi* I
broke my arm; *neuvottelut*
-sivat the talks broke down.
katko|a a break off, cut. **-nainen**
broken, fragmentary; *(sekava)*
disconnected, incoherent.
-naisuus brokenness;
incoherence. **-viiva** broken line.
katku smell.
kato *(viljan)* failure of crops;
viljasta tuli ~ the crops
failed. **-amaton** imperishable;
unfading; ineffaceable.
-amattomuus imperishableness.
-aminen disappearance;
vanishing. **-ava(inen)**
perishable; transitory.
-avaisuus perishableness,
transitoriness.
katodi cathode.
katoli|nen a. & s. [Roman]
Catholic. **-suus** Catholicism.
katon|harja ridge of a roof.
-pano, -peiteaine roofing.
-räystäs eaves.
katos roof, canopy; *(vaja)*
shed, *(kylkiäinen)* lean-to.
katovuosi bad year.
katsahtaa [have a] look, [take
a] glance (at).
katsanto sight; *ensi katsannolta*
at first sight. **-kanta** point of
view, viewpoint. **-tapa** way of
looking at things.
katsas|taa inspect, survey; *sot.*
review. **-taja** inspector. **-tus**
inspection; *mer.* survey;
(~todistus registration
certificate; *vrt. auton-).*
katsaus review, *(yleis-)* survey;
(silmäys) look, glance; *luoda*
~ jhk survey.
katse look, glance; *(kiinteä)*
gaze; *irrottaa ~ensa jstk* take
one's eyes off, look away
from; *kohdata jkn ~* meet a
p.'s eye. **-lija** spectator,
onlooker, looker-on. **-lla** look,
jtk at; regard, *(tarkaten)*

watch; *(olla katselijana)* look on, be looking on; ~ *jkta epäluuloisesti* eye (view) .. with suspicion; ~ *ulos ikkunasta* look out of the window; ~ *ympärilleen* look about one, look round. **-lmus** survey; *sot.* review.
katso|a look (at), *(pitkään)* gaze (at), watch; *(pitää jnak)* consider; regard as, look upon as; *(huolehtia)* see to it that .. ; ~ *hyväksi* see fit; ~ *viisaaksi* deem (think) it wise; *anna minun* ~ let me have a look [at it]; *katso ohjetta sivulla* .. ! for instructions see page .. ; *katso vain ettet (vilustu)* mind you don't (catch cold), be careful not to .. ; *-kaamme* let us see; *tee kuten parhaaksi -t* do as you think best.
katso|en: *jhk* ~ in view of, considering; *tarkemmin* ~ looking [at the matter] more closely. **-ja** spectator; (**~lava** stand for spectators). **-matta:** *jhk* ~ regardless of, irrespective of the. **-mo** *vrt. ed.;* auditorium, house; *pää* ~ grand stand; *täysi* ~ full house.
kattaa *(pöytä)* lay [the table]; *(talo)* roof; *(peittää)* cover; *valmiiksi katettu* ready laid; *pöytä on katettu* dinner (lunch) is served.
katteeton *(šekki)* dud, not covered; *(lupaus)* empty.
kattila pot; *(kala-)* fish-kettle; *(hillo-)* jam pot; *(höyry-)* boiler. **-huone** boiler-house. **-kivi** fur.
katto roof; *(sisä-)* ceiling; *(vaunun ym)* top; *(suoja)* shelter. **-huopa** roofing felt. **-ikkuna** skylight. **-parru** beam, rafter. **-teline** *(auton)* roof rack. **-tiili** tile. **-tuoli** roof truss. **-valaisin** ceiling light.
katu street; *(valtaväylä)* thoroughfare; *(puisto-)* avenue; *(ajotie)* roadway; *kadulla* in the street; *N:n kadun varrella* in *(Am.* on) N. street; *kadun toisella puolella* across the street; *kadun mies* the man

in the street.
katua repent, *jtk* [of] sth.; regret; be sorry (for).
katu|kahvila pavement (kerbside) café. **-kaupustelija** street vendor, hawker. **-kiveys** paving. **-kivi** paving stone. **-koroke** [safety] island. **-käytävä** pavement; *Am.* sidewalk. **-lamppu** street lamp.
katum|aton unrepentant, impenitent. **-us** repentance; penitence; *-uksen tekijä* penitent; *-uksen teko* penance; (**~päivä** day of penance).
katu|nainen street-walker. **-oja** gutter. **-poika** street arab, guttersnipe. **-sulku** road block; barricade.
katuvainen repentant, remorseful.
kauan long, [for] a long time; *(jo)* ~ *sitten* long ago; *niin* ~ *kuin* as long as; while; *miten* ~ *siitä on* how long ago was it? (.. *kun)* how long is it since ..?
kauas far [away]. **-kantava** *kuv.* far-reaching. **-kantoinen:** ~ *tykki* long-range gun.
kauem|maksi further [off]. **-min** longer; *elää jkta* ~ survive a p. **-paa** from further away; *en voi viipyä* ~ *kuin* I cannot stay for more than [two days]. **-pana** further away.
kauha ladle; *(nosturin)* lifting bucket. **-kuormaaja** loader.
kauhe|a terrible, awful; dreadful, frightful, horrible; *~n* terribly. **-us** dreadfulness.
kauhis|taa strike .. with terror; *-tava* terrifying, appalling, ghastly. **-tua** be terrified, be stricken with terror; *-tuin (m.)* I was scared. **-tus** terror, horror. **-tuttaa** terrify; *minua ~jk* I am appalled (shocked) at ..
kauhtana caftan; *(papin)* gown, cassock.
kauhtua *(väristä)* fade.
kauhu horror; terror, fright; *~kseni* to my horror; *~n tasapaino* balance of terror. **-kakara** enfant terrible, young savage. **-kertomus** atrocity *(t.*

horror) story.
kauimpana furthest away.
kaukaa from far away, from [a]far, from a great distance; *(syytä) ei tarvitse etsiä* ~ is not far to seek.
kaukai|nen distant; remote; far-away; ~ *sukulainen* distant relation. **-suus** remoteness.
kaukalo trough.
kaukana far [away], far off, a long way off, at a great distance, in the distance; ~ *oleva* distant; ~ *siitä* far from it; ~ *toisistaan* wide *(t. far)* apart.
Kaukasia Caucasia. **k-lainen** *a. & s.* Caucasian.
Kaukasusvuoret the Caucasus.
kauko|itä the Far East. **-juna** long-distance train. **-kirjo|itin** teleprinter; *välittää k-ittimella* teletype. **-näköinen** long-sighted, *kuv.* far-sighted. **-näköisyys** far-sightedness; foresight; **-objektiivi** telephoto lens. **-ohjaus** remote control. **-puhelu** trunk call, *Am.* long-distance call; *(maaseutu-)* toll call. **-putki** telescope. **-valot** high *(t.* headlight) beam.
kaula neck; *(kurkku)* throat; ~*ni on kipeä* I have a sore throat; *huivi* ~*ssa* with a scarf round one's neck. **-aukko** neckline; *puvussa on iso* ~ the dress has a low neckline. **-hihna** collar. **-huivi** scarf *(pl. m.* scarves). **-inen:** *pitkä* ~ long-necked. **-koru** necklace. **-liina** scarf *(pl. m.* scarves), neckerchief. **-nauha** necklace, necklet. **-panta** collar. **-puuhka** [fur] boa, fur. **-rauhanen** jugular gland.
kauli|a roll. **-n** rolling pin.
kauluks|ennappi [collar] stud. **-inen:** *korkea* ~ *(puvusta)* high-necked.
kauluri *(paidan)* collar band.
kaulus collar; *kova (pehmeä)* ~ stiff (soft) c. **-nappi** collar stud.
kauna grudge, ill will, resentment; *kantaa* ~*a jklle* have a grudge against, bear a p. a grudge.

kauneuden|aisti sense of (eye for) beauty. **-hoito** beauty treatment; *(~aine* cosmetic).
kauneus beauty, loveliness. **-kilpailu** beauty contest. **-salonki** beauty parlour.
kaunis beautiful; handsome, good-looking; *(joskus)* fair; *(ihana)* lovely; fine; *ilma on* ~ it is fine; ~ *juttu (pilk.)* a fine (pretty) business!
-muotoinen well-shaped (-modelled), shapely. **-sanainen** well-worded. **-staa** embellish, beautify; *(koristaa)* adorn. **-telematon** unembellished; ~ *totuus* the plain [unvarnished] truth. **-tella** *kuv.* colour. **-tua** improve in looks, become more beautiful. **-tus** embellishment; adornment. **kauno|kirjailija** writer of fiction. **-kirjallinen** literary. **-kirjallisuus** [imaginative] literature, belles lettres; *(romaani-)* fiction. **-kirjoitus** penmanship; calligraphy. **-luistelu** *ks.* taito-. **-luku** elocution. **-puheinen** eloquent. **-puheisuus** eloquence, oratory. **-puhuja** orator. **-sielu** [a]esthete; idealist. **-taiteet** the fine arts. **-tar** beauty; belle.
kaupaksi|käymätön unsalable, unmarketable. **-käypä** salable, marketable.
kaupalli|nen commercial; mercantile; ~ *avustaja* commercial attaché. **-staa** commercialize. **-suus** commercial character.
kaupan|hieronta bargaining. **-hoitaja** manager [of a shop]. **-käynti** trading (in, *jllk)*; business. **-päällisiksi** into the bargain; for good measure; *antaa jtk* ~ *(m.)* throw .. in.
kaup|ata, -itella offer for sale. *(kadulla)* peddle.
kauppa trade; commerce; business; *(osto-)* bargain; *(myymälä)* shop, *Am.* store; *(liiketoimi)* transaction, deal; *(et. huon. merk.)* traffic; *kotimaan (ulkomaan)* ~ home (foreign) trade; *hieroa* ~*a* bargain; *käydä* ~*a* do (carry

on, transact) business (with), trade (with); *harjoittaa (esim. turkis)* ~a do business in, deal in [furs]; *Venäjän* ~*mme on laaja* we do a lot of trade with Russia; *päättää* ~ close a deal; *mennä kaupaksi* sell well; *tarjota kaupaksi* offer for sale, put up for sale; *on kaupan* is for (on) sale; *tein hyvän kaupan* I made a [good] bargain. **-ala:** *ruveta* ~*lle* go into business. **-apulainen** shop-assistant, salesman, -woman. **-arvo** market value. **-edustaja** commercial traveller. **-halli** market-hall. **-hinta** selling (*osto-* purchase) price. **-huone** commercial firm (house). **-kamari** Chamber of Commerce. **-katu** shopping street. **-kaupunki** commercial city. **-kirja** deed of purchase. **-kirje** business letter. **-kirjeenvaihto** commercial correspondence. **-koju** stall. **-korkeakoulu** School of Economics. **-koulu** commercial school. **-kumppani** trade (trading) partner. **-la** market town, urban district, *Am.* township. **-laiva** merchant ship, merchantman. **-laivasto** merchant fleet, mercantile marine. **-liike** business. **-lippu** merchant flag. **-maantiede** commercial geography. **-matkustaja** [commercial] traveller, travelling salesman. **-mies** tradesman, trader. **-ministeri** minister of commerce; *Engl.* President of the Board of Trade. **-neuvos** councillor of commerce (Finnish title). **-neuvottelut** trade talks. **-opisto** commercial college. **-oppi** business science. **-politiikka** trade policy. **-puoti** shop, *Am.* store. **-puutarha** market garden, *Am.* truck farm. **-sopimus** trade agreement (pact, treaty). **-suhteet** trade relations. **-summa** purchase-money. **-tase** balance of trade, foreign-trade balance. **-tavara** commodity;

~*t (m.)* merchandise, goods. **-tori** market [-place], market square. **-tuttava** business friend. **-vaihto** turnover. **-vajaus** trade deficit. **-yhteydet** trade links (connections). **-yhtiö** [trading] company, firm.

kauppias merchant, tradesman; dealer (in, *jnk); (myymälän omistaja)* shopkeeper, *Am.* storekeeper.

kaupungin|hallitus city government. **-johtaja** city manager. **-lääkäri** city medical officer. **-oikeudet** town charter. **-osa** part (quarter) of a town. **-talo** town (city) hall. **-valtuusto** town council. **-valtuutettu** town councillor, *Am.* city council man.

kaupungistu|a be [come] urbanized. **-minen** urbanization.

kaupunki town; *(suuremi)* city; *Helsingin* ~ the town of H.; *lähteä* ~*in (kaupungille)* go [in]to town; *matkustaa* ~*in* go up to town. **-kunta** municipality, township. **-lainen** town resident; *-laiset* townspeople. **-laistua** become urbanized. **-laisväestö** town (urban) population. **-talo** town house.

kaupuste|lija *(huumausaineiden ym)* peddler; pedlar, hawker. **-lla** hawk, peddle.

kaura oats. **-hiutaleet** oat flakes. **-jauho** oatmeal. **-puuro** [oatmeal] porridge. **-suurimot** rolled (hulled) oats. **-velli** oatmeal gruel.

kauris [mountain] goat; *vrt. metsä~; Kauriin kääntöpiiri* the Tropic of Capricorn.

kausi period, age; *(huvi- ym)* season. **-alennus** seasonal discount. **-juoppo** spree drinker. **-lippu** season ticket. **-luonteinen** seasonal.

kautsu caoutchouc; gum elastic, natural rubber.

kautta through, by [means of]; *Helsingin* ~ via H., by way of H.; *toista* ~ by another route; *meidän* ~*mme* through us, through our mediation; ~ *maailman* throughout the

world. -altaan thoroughly,
altogether, all over; ~ kypsä
ripe throughout. -kulku
passage through; (~juna
through train; ~tavara transit
goods).

kavah|taa (pystyn) start up;
(taapäin) shrink back; ~ jtk
boggle at, (varoa) beware
[of]; hän -ti unestaan he
awoke with a start.

kavala treacherous, deceitful,
false, (juoni) underhand;
(sala-) insidious.

kavaljeeri chivalrous man: hist.
cavalier; (tanssi-) partner.

kaval|lus embezzlement,
misappropriation, defalcation;
maan ~ treason. -taa betray;
(varoja) embezzle. -taja
traitor, jnk to; (varojen)
embezzler, defaulter. -uus
treacherousness, perfidiousness,
falseness, fraudulence.

kave|ntaa narrow; (pukua) take
in. -ntua, -ta narrow (m. off t.
down); (kärki) taper [off].

kaveri chum, pal; fellow, Am.
guy.

kaviaari caviar [e].

kavio hoof. -nkapse pounding
of hoofs.

kavuta climb, clamber;
scramble [up the hill,
vuorelle [.

kehdata not be ashamed; have
the face [to].

kehitellä develop; elaborate.

kehitty|mättömyys undeveloped
state. -mätön undeveloped.
-neisyys advanced state,
development. -nyt developed,
advanced; mature.

kehi|ttyä develop, jksk into,
-ttää develop (m. valok.);
(lämpöä ym) generate;
(parantaa) improve; ~ auki
unwind.

kehitys development, (tiet. m.)
evolution; (edistys) progress.
-alue development area. -apu
development aid. -aste stage
of development. -kulku stage
(process) of development.
-kykyinen capable of
development, likely to
develop. -kykyisyys capacity to
develop. -maa emergent t.

[newly] developing country.
-oppi theory of evolution.
-vammainen (vajaamielinen)
mentally handicapped
(deficient). -vammaisuus
mental deficieney, mental
subnormality.

kehkeytyä develop; arise.

kehno bad, poor; ~ mies a
mean fellow; ~t vaatteet
shabby clothes. -us badness,
poorness.

keho body.

keho|ttaa urge, tell, advise [a
p. to], (rohkaista) encourage;
(taivuttaa) persuade. -tus
exhortation, request, (rohkaisu)
encouragement; jkn -tuksesta
at a. p.'s suggestion.
-tushuuto cry of encouragement.

kehruu spinning. -kone
spinning jenny.

kehrä wheel; disc. -sluu
malleolus. -tä spin; (kissasta)
purr. -varsi spoke; (värttinä)
spindle. -äjä spinner; (-lintu)
nightjar. -ämö spinning mill.

kehto cradle. -laulu lullaby.

kehu|a praise; (kerskata) boast
(of), brag (about); -matta
without boasting; ei ole
-mista nothing to boast of.
-skelija blusterer, swaggerer,
braggart. -skella bluster,
swagger.

kehy|s frame, framework;
(reuna) border; -kset (kuv.)
limits. frame[work].

kehä circle; periphery; (leikki-)
pen; (ympärys) circumference.
-antenni frame aerial. -kalvo
anat. iris. -kukka marigold.
-llinen peripheral. -nmuotoinen
circular. -tie ring road.
-tuomari referee.

keidas oasis (pl. oases).

keihäs spear; lance; urh.
javelin. -mies sot. lancer. -tää
spear.

keihään|heitto urh.
javelin-throw. -kärki
spearhead. -varsi shaft of a
spear.

keijukainen fairy, elf.

keikahtaa rock, tumble,
(kumoon) tip over, topple
over.

keikai|lla show off; behave like a dandy. **-lu** foppishness; *(pöyhkeily)* snobbishness.
keikari fop, dandy; snob. **-mainen** foppish, dandyish.
keikka job.
keikkua swing, rock, *(vene, m.)* toss; *(tasapainoilla)* balance.
keikuttaa swing, rock; ~ *tuolia* tilt a chair; ~ *päätään* toss one's head.
keila [ten]pin, skittle [pin]. **-ilija** bowler. **-illa** play skittles, Am. bowl. **-ilu** Am. bowling, tenpins. **-nmuotoinen** conical. **-pallo** skittle-ball; bowling ball. **-peli** Am. tenpins. **-rata** skittle-alley, Am. bowling-alley.
keille ks. kenelle.
keimai|lija coquette, flirt. **-lla** flirt. **-lu** coquetry; flirtation.
keino means, way; expedient; *jollakin* ~*in* in some way; *tällä* ~*in* by this means; ~*lla millä hyvänsä* by hook or by crook; *viimeisenä* ~*na* as a (in the) last resort. **-emo** incubator. **-siemennys** artificial insemination. **-tekoi|nen** artificial; *k-set helmet* imitation pearls. **-tella** speculate (in); ~ *itselleen jtk* get sth. by cunning. **-ttelija** speculator; *(sota-ajan)* profiteer. **-ttelu** speculation.
keinu swing. **-a** swing; *(laiva)* roll, *(huojua)* sway; *(laudalla)* seesaw; *(tuolissa ym)* rock. **-hevonen** rocking-horse. **-ttaa** swing; rock. **-tuoli** rocking-chair.
keisari emperor. **-kunta** empire. **-leikkaus** caesarean section. **-llinen** imperial. **-nna** empress. **-nvihreä** Paris green.
keit|e decoction. **-in** cooker, cooking apparatus; *kahvin* ~ coffee-maker. **-os** boiling; concoction.
keittiö kitchen. **-astiat** kitchen utensils. **-kasvitarha** kitchen garden. **-kone** ks. yleiskone. **-liesi** [kitchen] range. **-mestari** chef. **-nportaat** back stairs.
keitto boiling, cooking; *(liemi)* soup. **-astiat** cooking utensils.

-kirja cookery-book, cook-book. **-komero** kitchenette. **-koulu** cookery-school. **-levy** hot-plate. **-taito** culinary art, cookery.
keittäjä cook.
keit|tää *(vedessä)* boil; *(valmistaa ruokaa)* cook; ~ *kahvia, teetä* make coffee (tea); *kovaksi -etty* hard-boiled; *ei kypsäksi -etty* underdone.
keitä ks. kuka.
kekkerit feast; celebration.
keko rick, stack; *kantaa kortensa* ~*on* add one's mite to the pile. **-sokeri** loaf sugar.
kekseli|äisyys inventiveness, power (capacity) of invention. **-äs** [.. of an] inventive [turn of mind]; *(neuvokas)* resourceful; ingenious.
keksi *(vene-)* boat-hook; *(leivos)* biscuit; cracker.
keksi|jä inventor. **-ntö** invention. **-ä** invent, devise, *(havaita)* detect, find [out]; discover; *en voi* ~ .. *(m.)* I can't think of ..
kekäle firebrand; ~*et* embers.
kela reel; *sähk.* coil; *(laivan)* winch, capstan. **-ta** reel [in, up], wind up; coil.
keli going; state of the roads; ~ *on huono* the going is bad. **-rikko** bad state of the roads.
kelju unpleasant, *(kiero)* crooked, fishy; *kuinka* ~*a!* how annoying!
kelkka toboggan, sledge; *kääntää* ~*nsa (kuv.)* reverse one's policy, change horses [in midstream]. **-illa** toboggan. **-ilu** bobsleigh [ing], bobsled [ding], *(ohjas-)* tobogganing. **-mäki** toboggan slide.
kellari cellar. **-kerros** basement.
kellastu|a [turn] yellow; *paperi on -nut* the paper has yellowed [with age, *vanhuuttaan*].
keller|tää be tinged with yellow; *-tävä* tinged (shot) with yellow, yellowish.
kello clock; *(tasku- ranne-)* watch; *(soitto-)* bell; ~*n*

rannehihna watch strap, *(metallinen)* w. bracelet; ~ *10* at ten o'clock; *kello on viittä vailla (yli) kuusi* it is five [minutes] to (past) six; *paljonko* ~ *on* what time is it? what is the time? [Excuse me, but] could you tell me what time it is? *soittaa* ~*a* ring the bell; *käy kuin* ~ runs like clockwork; *täsmällisesti kuin* ~ with clockwork precision, like clockwork; *katsoa* ~*sta aika* tell the time. **-laite** clockwork. **kellon|avain** clock key. **-jousi** watch spring. **-kieli** clapper. **-koneisto** works of a clock (watch). **-kuori** watch-case. **-lasi** watch-glass. **-lyömä:** ~*llä* on the stroke of the hour. **-osoitin** hand [of a clock]. **-perät** watch-chain. **-pidin** watch-stand. **-soittaja** bell-ringer. **-soitto** tolling [of bells], bell-ringing.
kello|seppä watchmaker. **-sepänliike** watchmaker's [shop]. **-taulu** dial. **-torni** belfry.
kellu|a float, *(valuutta, m.)* fluctuate. **-ke** pontoon, *lentok.* float; *(koru)* drop.
kelmeä pale.
kelmu film, *(eräs laatu)* cellophane.
kelpaa|maton useless; *(lippu ym)* not valid; *(ei sopiva)* unfit [for use, *käytettäväksi*]; *asuttavaksi* ~ unfit for habitation;; *syötäväksi* ~ not fit to eat; *tehdä -mattomaksi* incapacitate (for). **-mattomuus** uselessness, unfitness. **-va** valid; *(virkaan)* qualified (for); *(sopiva)* fit; *käytettäväksi* ~ fit for use.
kelpo decent; excellent; ~ *lailla* quite a lot, considerably; ~ *mies* a fine fellow. **-inen** fit (for), *(pätevä)* valid; *(virka-)* qualified [for a post]. **-isuus** qualifications; validity; (~**vaatimukset** required qualifications).
keltai|nen yellow; *-sen ruskea* fawn [-coloured].
kelta|kuume yellow fever.

-multa yellow ochre; **-narsissi** daffodil. **-nokka** *kuv.* freshman. **-sieni** chanterelle. **-sirkku** yellowhammer. **-tauti** jaundice.
kelttiläinen *a.* Celtic; *s.* Celt.
keltuainen yolk.
kelvata do, be good enough, be fit (for); *(lippu ym)* be valid; *se ei kelpaa* that won't do; *se ei kelpaa mihinkään* it is no good; *kelpaako tämä?* will this do? *sitä kelpasi katsella* it was worth looking at.
kelvo|llinen fit, good, *jhk* for; proper, *(henkilöstä)* capable, competent. **-llisuus** fitness; *(henkilön)* ability, competence. **-ton** worthless, useless, good-for-nothing; *julistaa -ttomaksi* declare invalid, invalidate. **-ttomasti** not properly, incompetently. **-ttomuus** worthlessness, unfitness.
kemia chemistry. **-llinen** chemical; ~ *pesu (kuiva)* dry cleaning; *pesettää -llisesti* have . . dry-cleaned.
kemikaali: ~*t* chemicals. **-kauppa** *ks. rohdos-*.
kemisti [scientific] chemist.
kemut celebration, party; *hienot* ~ a marvellous feast.
ken who? *(se joka)* he (she) who, whoever.
kene|lle who, [to] whom; ~ *sen annoit?* who did you give it to. **-ltä:** ~ *tuon sait?* who did you get that from? **-nkään:** *ei* ~ nobody's; *ei* ~ *maa* no man's land.
kengittää shoe.
kenguru kangaroo.
kengän|antura sole. **-kiilloke** shoe polish. **-kiillottaja** shoeblack. **-kärki** toe. **-nauha** [shoe] lace.
kenkä shoe; *(varsi-)* boot; *kengät jalassa* with shoes on; *panna kengät jalkaan* put on one's shoes; *riisua kengät* take off one's shoes. **-in** *(kepin)* ferrule. **-kauppa** shoe-shop. **-lusikka** shoe horn. **-muste** blacking. **-pari** pair of shoes. **-raja** worn-out shoe.

-**tehdas** [boot and] shoe
factory. -**voide** shoe polish,
shoe cream.
kenno honeycomb; *sähk.* cell.
keno: *pää* ~*ssa* with one's
head thrown back.
kenraali general. -**harjoitus**
dress-rehearsal. -**kuvernööri**
governor-general. -**luutnantti**
lieutenant-general. -**majuri**
major-general.
kenties maybe, perhaps.
kenttä field. -**keittiö** field
kitchen, mobile kitchen.
-**kiikari** field-glass[es],
binocular[s]. -**sairaala** field
hospital. -**tykistö** field
artillery. -**tykki** field-gun
(-piece). -**urheilu** ks. yleis-
-**vuode** camp bed.
kepeä light.
kepittää beat, cane; *(kasveja)*
stake.
keppi stick; *(ruoko-)* cane;
antaa jklle ~*ä* give .. a
whipping. -**hevonen**
hobby-horse; *kuv.* fad.
-**kerjäläi|nen:** *joutua k-seksi* be
reduced to beggary.
kepponen trick, practical joke;
tehdä (jklle) ~ play a trick
(on).
kerake consonant.
kera(lla) with.
keramiikka pottery, ceramics.
kerettiläi|nen *s.* heretic; *a.*
heretical. -**syys** heresy.
kerho club; *(opinto- ym)* circle.
kerinpuut reel.
keripukki scurvy.
keri|tsimet *(lampaan)* shears.
-**tä** 1. cut, clip; *(lampaista)*
shear; 2. *(ehtiä)* arrive in
time; *en kerkiä* I have no
time.
keriä wind [into a ball],
(kiertää) coil; ~ *auki* unwind.
kerjuu begging; *käydä* ~*lla* go
begging. -**kirje** begging letter.
kerjäläi|nen beggar. -**spoika**
beggar boy. -**ssauva** beggar's
staff.
kerjätä beg, *jtk* for.
kerkeä quick, prompt, ready.
kerma cream *(m. kuv.).* -**inen**
creamy. -**kannu**, -**kko** cream
jug. -**nvärinen** cream-coloured.
-**vaahto** whipped cream.

kermoa skim off the cream.
kernaa|sti willingly, readily;
with pleasure; -*mmin* rather.
kerra|kseen: *riittää* ~ it's
enough for now. -**llaan** at a
time. -**n** once; ~ *päivässä*
once a day; *tämän* ~ this
time, *(ainoan* ~*)* just this
once; *vielä* ~ once more;
viimeisen ~ for the last time;
oli(pa) ~ .. *(sadussa)* once
upon a time there was ..
-**nkin** for once, *(vihdoin)* at
last. -**ssaan** entirely,
altogether; perfectly; simply;
~ *mahdoton* utterly
impossible; ~ *mainio* just
splendid, *ei* ~ *mitään*
absolutely nothing. -**sto** set of
underwear.
kerrata repeat; *koul. ym* revise;
(pääkohdittain) recapitulate.
kerroin coefficient.
kerroksi|nen *(yhd.)* -storeyed,
-storied; *viisi* ~ a five-storey
[building]. -**ttain** in layers.
kerronta narration.
kerros layer, *(maa-)* stratum
(pl. strata); *rak.* stor[e]y;
toisessa kerroksessa on the
second floor. -**hyppy** high
dive; -*hypyt* high diving.
-**sänky** bunk bed. -**taa** deposit
in layers, stratify. -**talo** block
of flats. -**tu|a** be stratified;
-*nut* stratified. -**tuma** stratum
(pl. strata); deposit.
kerrottava *mat.* multiplicand.
kersantti sergeant.
kerskai|leva boastful;
vainglorious. -**lija** boaster,
braggart. -**lla** boast, brag (of,
about); swagger; *puhek.*
swank; -*llen* boastfully.
kersk|ata, -**ua**, -**uri** *ks. ed.*
kerta time; *(kierto-)* turn; ~
kaikkiaan once for all; ~
kaikkiaan ihana just lovely; ~
kaikkiaan ei definitely not; ~
kerralta every time; ~
toisensa jälkeen time and
again, time after time; *kaksi*
~*a niin suuri* twice as big;
kolme ~*a* three times [three
is nine]; *moneen* ~*an*
repeatedly, many times; *tällä*
~*a* this time; for now; *ei*
~*akaan* not *(t.* never) once.

[oh,] not at all; *jnk kestäessä* during; *kuinka kauan luulet kestäväsi* how long will you be able to hold out; *matka ~ viikon* the trip takes a week; *se ei kestä kauan* it won't take long.
kesy tame; domestic. **-ttäjä** [-]tamer. **-ttämätön** untamed; *(hevonen)* unbroken. **-ttää** tame; *(kotieläimiä)* domesticate. **-tön** untamed; wild. **-yntyä** become tame (domesticated).
kesä summer; *~llä* in [the] summer; *viime ~nä* last s., *(ensi)* next s.; *kaiken ~ä* all [the] s.; *viettää ~ä* spend the s. **-asunto** *(komea)* summer residence. **-helle:** *-helteellä* in the summer heat. **-huvila** summer villa (cottage). **-inen** summery, summer. **-isin** in [the] summer. **-kausi** summertime, summer season. **-kuu** June. **-käyttö:** *~ön* for summer wear. **-loma** summer holidays (vacation). **-mökki** country cottage. **-puku** summer dress (suit). **-päivä** summer ['s] day; *(~nseisaus* summer solstice). **-sijainen** [summer] substitute. **-sydän:** *~nä* at the height of summer. **-vieras** summer guest. **-yliopisto** university summer course.
ketju chain; *sot.* line, cordon. **-kirje** snowball letter. **-kolari** multiple collision, *(iso)* mass pile-up. **-polttaja** chain-smoker.
ketkä *ks. kuka.*
keto field. **-orvokki** wild pansy.
kette|ryys agility, nimbleness. **-rä** agile, nimble, alert.
kettinki chain, cable.
kettu fox. **-mainen** foxy, foxlike; cunning.
ketun|ajo fox-hunt[ing]. **-häntä** foxtail, brush. **-leipä** *bot.* wood sorrel. **-poika(nen)** fox-cub.
ketä *ks. kuka:* *~ tarkoitat?* who do you mean? *ei ~än* nobody, no one.
keuhko lung; *~t* lungs, *(teuraseläinten)* lights. **-katarri** bronchitis. **-kuume, -tulehdus**

pneumonia. **-pussintulehdus** pleurisy. **-putki** bronch|us, *pl.* -i; *-putken tulehdus* bronchitis. **-syöpä** lung cancer. **-tauti** pulmonary tuberculosis; *(~parantola* sanatorium).
keula bow [s]; *~n puolella* ahead, afore. **-kansi** foredeck. **-kuva** figure-head. **-masto** foremast. **-matkustaja** foredeck passenger. **-osa** prow. **-purje** foresail. **-vannas** stem.
keve|nnys relief, alleviation. **-ntyä** *ks. kevetä; -tynein mielin* with a feeling of relief. **-ntää** lighten, ease; relieve; *~ sydäntään* unburden oneself (to). **-tä** become lighter, be lightened; be relieved. **-ys** lightness; ease. **-ä** light; easy; *ottaa asiat ~ltä kannalta* take things easy; *~llä mielellä* light at heart, in buoyant spirits.
kevyt light [in weight]; *vrt. ed.* **-aseinen** light-armed. **-jalkainen** light of foot. **-kenkäinen:** *~ nainen* lady of easy virtue. **-mielinen** frivolous; *(irstas)* wanton, loose, fast. **-mielisyys** frivolity; wantonness. **-sarja** lightweight class.
kevai|nen springlike; spring; vernal; *~ sää* spring weather. **-sin** in [the] spring.
kevät spring; *keväällä* in the s., in s.; *tänä keväänä* this s. **-aika** springtime. **-ilma** *(sää)* spring [like] weather. **-juhla** spring fête. **-kesä:** *~llä* in early summer. **-kylvö** spring sowing. **-lukukausi** spring term. **-päivä** spring day; *(~ntasaus* vernal equinox). **-talvi** early spring. **-tulva** spring flood. **-tuulahdus** vernal *(t.* spring) breeze.
kide crystal. **-rakenteinen** crystalline. **-sokeri** granulated sugar, caster sugar.
kidnappaus kidnapping, abduction.
kidukset gills.
kidu|ttaa torture; *(kiusata)* torment; *~ lihaansa* mortify one's flesh; *-ttava* excruciating, racking. **-tus**

torture.
kieha|htaa boil up; *hänen
verensä -hti* his blood boiled.
-uttaa bring to the boil,
parboil.
kiehkura coil, ringlet, *(kutri)*
lock, curl.
kiehtoa captivate, fascinate.
kiehu|a boil; *-van kuuma (m.)*
piping hot. **-mispiste** boiling
point. **-ttaa** boil.
kiekko disk; *urh.* discus; *jää~*
puck; *savi~* clay pigeon.
kiekon|heitto discus-throw.
-heittäjä discus-thrower.
kieku|a crow. **-minen**
crow[ing]; *kukon* ~ cock's
crow.
kiele|ke *(kallion)* projecting
rock, projection. **-llinen**
linguistic; *-lliset vaikeudet
(m.)* language difficulties.
kielen|kärki point of the
tongue. **-käyttö** [linguistic]
usage; language. **-kääntäjä**
translator. **-puhdistaja** purist.
-tuntija linguist. **-tutkija**
philologist. **-tutkimus**
philological research.
kiele|vyys garrulity; glibness.
-vä garrulous, voluble, glib.
kieli *anat.* tongue; *(puhuttu)*
language, tongue; *(soittimen)*
string, chord; *millä kielellä* in
what language; *kielestä
toiseen* from one language
into another. **-kello** *kuv.*
telltale. **-kuva** metaphor.
-kysymys language question.
-mies linguist. **-minen**
tale-bearing. **-nen:** *suomen~* in
Finnish, *(henkilöstä)*
Finnish-speaking; *englannin~
sanomalehti* an
English-language newspaper.
-niekka language adept.
-opillinen grammatical.
-opinnot linguistic studies;
harjoittaa -opintoja study
languages. **-oppi** grammar.
-soitin stringed instrument.
-taistelu language feud. **-taito**
knowledge of languages,
linguistic abilities. **-taitoinen**
on ~ .. speaks many foreign
languages, *(erittäin ~)* has a
great command of languages,
is an accomplished linguist.

-taju [natural] language sense.
-tiede philology. **-tieteellinen**
philological, linguistic.
-tieteilijä philologist, linguist.
-virhe mistake, error [in
language].
kieliä tell tales [out of
school]; *älä kieli!* don't blab!
don't let on.
kielo lily of the valley.
kieltei|nen negative. **-sesti** in
the negative, negatively. **-syys**
negative attitude.
kielten|opettaja teacher of
languages. **-sekoitus** confusion
of tongues.
kielto prohibition, ban (on,
*jnk); refusal, denial. **-laki**
prohibition. **-lause** negative
sentence. **-sana** negative.
-tavara contraband.
kieltä|minen forbidding; denial;
negation. **-mättä** undeniably,
unquestionably. **-mätön**
undeniable; indisputable,
incontestable; unchallenged.
-ymys abstinence (from);
self-denial, self-effacement.
-ytyminen refusal. **-ytyä**
refuse; decline; *(luopua)* give
up; *(pidättyä)* abstain, refrain
(from); ~ *hyväksymästä* refuse
to accept; ~ *tarjouksesta*
decline (turn down) an offer.
-vä negative: ~ *vastaus (m.)*
refusal.
kieltää *(ei sallia)* forbid;
prohibit; *(ei myöntää)* deny;
vrt. kieltäytyä; ~ *jklta jtak*
refuse a p. sth; ~ *lapsensa*
disown; *kielsi jyrkästi
(sanoneensa)* denied flatly
(categorically) [that he had
said so]; *ei voi ~, että* ..
it cannot be denied that;
kielletty prohibited; *on
ankarasti kielletty* is strictly
forbidden; *pääsy kielletty* no
admittance.
kiemur|a coil, curl; *(mutka)*
bend. **-rella** *(esim. mato)*
wriggle *(m. kuv.); (tie ym)*
wind, twist; *(tuskissa)* writhe;
(joki) meander; *-televa (m.)*
tortuous.
kieppua swing; *(roikkua)*
dangle.
kieriskellä wallow, roll about.

kieri|ttää, -ä roll.
kiero not straight; wry, twisted; crooked, distorted; *(esim. lauta)* warped; *katsoa ~on* squint, have a cast in one's eye; *~ menettely* crooked conduct; *~peli* foul play. **-illa** scheme; palter (with sth.). **-silmäinen** squint-eyed. **-silmäisyys** squint. **-us** crookedness; distortion. **-utua** become warped (distorted), *henk.* become perverted (twisted).
kierre *(ruuvin)* thread, worm; *(langan)* twist; *(pallon)* spin. **-kaihdin** blind. **-llä** circle (round), circulate; *(kuljeksia)* wander about; *kuv.* evade; beat about the bush; *-llen kaarrellen* in a roundabout way, *(vältellen)* evasively; *kiertelemättä* straight out. **-portaat** winding stairs.
kierros round, circuit; turn; *(pyörän ym)* revolution; *(kiertotie)* detour; *(kilparadalla)* lap, *(erä)* round, *(satelliitin)* orbit.
kierto circulation, round; cycle; *(pyörintä)* rotation. **-ajelu** sightseeing tour. **-kirje** circular [letter]. **-koulu** *vanh.* ambulatory school. **-kulku** circulation. **-kysely** questionnaire; *lähettää ~* send [round] an inquiry. **-liike** rotary motion, rotation. **-matka** round trip (tour). **-palkinto** challenge cup. **-portaat** winding stair[s], spiral staircase. **-teitse** in a roundabout way. **-tie** detour, circuitous route. **-tähti** planet.
kiertue touring company; *hän on maaseutu~ella* he is touring the countryside.
kier|tyä twist, wind, get twisted; coil; *~ vääräksi* become distorted. **-tävä** itinerant, circulating, travelling; ambulatory. **-tää** turn, twist; wind; *intr.* circle, rotate, go around; *(tehdä mutka)* make a detour; *(veri ym)* circulate; *(lakia ym)* evade; *(veroja)* dodge, evade; *~ auki* unscrew, unwind; *~*

hihansa ylös roll up one's sleeves; *~ kaasu pienemmälle* turn down the gas; *~ kätensä jkn kaulaan* put one's arms round a p.'s neck; *(satelliitti) ~ Maata* circles (orbits) [round] the Earth; *~ samaa rataa* go round and round, go round in the same groove, *(ajatuksista, m.)* be obsessed (with an idea); *hän -si kysymykseni* he avoided (dodged) my question; *hän -si mäen* he went round the hill; *maa ~ auringon ympäri* the earth revolves round the sun; *panna jk -tämään* pass round. **-ukka** spiral, coil; *(ehkäisy-väline)* diaphragm, intrauterine device (IUD). **-teinen** spiral.
kieto|a wind, twine; *(kääriä)* wrap up; *kuv.* involve (in); *auki* unwrap; *~ jku pauloihinsa* catch .. in one's toils, ensnare. **-utua** wind; become entangled *(kuv. in-volved)* in, [be] intertwine[d].
kihara *s.* curl, lock; *a* curly, wavy. **-tukkainen** curly-haired.
kihar|rin curler. **-tua** curl, wave.
kihelmöidä itch; tingle.
kihistä fizz, sizzle; *(vilistä)* be alive (with), be teeming (with).
kihl|a *mennä -oihin jkn kanssa* get engaged to; *olla -oissa* be engaged [to be married]. **-attu** engaged [to be married]; *s.* fiancé, *fem.* fiancée.
kihla|jaiset betrothal party. **-kortti** announcement of [the] engagement. **-kunta** jurisdictional district [in rural areas]. **-sormus** engagement ring. **-us** engagement. **-utua** become engaged (to); *-utuneet* the engaged couple.
kihokki *bot.* sundew.
kihomato pinworm.
kihota trickle; ooze [out]; *vesi kihoaa kielelleni* my tongue waters.
kihti gout.
kiidättää hurry, speed.
kiihdy|ke stimulus. **-ksissä** in a state of excitement. **-ttää**

excite, inflame; *(nopeuttaa)* accelerate; speed up; *(sotaa)* escalate.

kiihke|ys *ks. kiihko.* **-ä** impetuous, violent; hot, ardent, passionate; ~ *keskustelu* a heated discussion.

kiihko impetuosity; fury, heat; mania. **-ilija** zealot, fanatic, *usk. m.* bigot. **-isänmaallinen** chauvinistic. **-kansallinen** nationalist. **-mielinen** fanatical. **-mielisyys** fanaticism. **-ton** dispassionate.

kiiho|ke stimulus. *pl.* -li; *kuv. m.* incentive, incitement. **-ttaa** excite; agitate; *(yllyttää)* stir up, incite; *(virkistää)* stimulate; ~ *hermoja* excite (irritate) the nerves; ~ *mielikuvitusta* excite the imagination; ~ *ruokahalua* whet the appetite; *-ttava* stimulating. **-ttaja** agitator. **-ttua** *ks. kiihtyä.* **-ttuvaisuus** excitability. **-tus** agitation; stimulation; (~**aine** stimulant; ~**puhe** inflammatory speech; ~**työ** agitation).

kiihty|mys excitement; agitation. **-vyys** *fys.* acceleration.

kiihty|ä get excited, become agitated; *(tulistua)* flare up; *(yltyä)* increase [in violence]; *-neessä mielentilassa* in an agitated frame of mind; *-vä liike (fys.)* accelerated motion; *tuuli -y (m.)* the wind is getting up.

kiikari field-glasses; binoculars; *(teatteri-)* opera-glasses. **-kivääri** rifle with telescopic sight.

kiikastaa: *mistä ~?* where does the shoe pinch? where's the rub?

kiikkerä easily rocked, unsteady.

kiikki: *joutua ~in* get into a fix (a pinch), be cornered.

kiikku, -a swing. **-lauta** seesaw.

kiikuttaa swing, rock.

kiila wedge; *(kankaasta)* gusset. **-ta** wedge [in]; *(esim. auto)* cut in.

kiille mica.

kiillo|ke polish. **-ton** dull;

lustreless. **-ttaa** polish; *(metallia, m.)* burnish; *(vahalla)* wax. **-tus** polishing; (~**aine** polish; ~**vaha** polishing wax; ~**voide** [shoe-]polish).

kiilto lustre; gloss; polish. **-kuva** *l.v.* sticker. **-mato** glow-worm. **-nahka** patent leather, lacquered leather. **-pintainen** glossy; glazed.

kiiltä|vyys glossiness; lustre, brilliancy. **-vä** shiny; glossy; *(kirkas)* bright.

kiiltää shine, glisten; glitter, gleam.

kiilua glimmer; glow, glint.

kiima rut, *(naaraalla)* heat, estrous cycle. **-aika** mating time; *vert. juoksuaika.*

Kiina China. **k-lainen** *a. & s.* Chinese *(pl. = sg.)* **k-n kieli** Chinese. **k-nkuori** cinchona bark. **k-tar** Chinese woman.

kiinne|kohta hold. **-laastari** adhesive *(t.* sticking) plaster. **-laina** mortgage loan.

kiinni fast; *(suljettu)* closed, shut; *joutua ~* be caught [-ing. *jstk*]; *liimata ~* gum on [to]; *ommella ~* sew on; *ottaa ~* catch, *(vangiksi, ym.)* capture; *panna ~* close; *pitää ~* hold on [to], *(jstk, m.)* keep hold of, *(kuv.)* adhere to, stick to; *saada ~* catch up [with]; *lehdet ovat ~ toisiisaan* the leaves stick to each other; ~ *veti!* it's a deal! **-ke** fastening. **-ttää** fasten, *jhk* [on] to, fix *(m. valok.),* attach (to); *lak.* mortgage; *(laiva)* moor; *(koukulla)* hook, *(liimalla)* stick [on], *(naulalla)* nail, *(neulalla)* pin, *(postimerkki)* affix; ~ *huomiota jhk* pay *(t.* direct) attention to; ~ *katseensa jhk* fix one's eyes on; ~ *mieltä* interest. **-tys** fastening; *lak.* mortgage; (~**kohta** hold, attachment).

kiinnos|taa interest; *se ei -ta minua* I am not interested [in it], I take no interest in it. **-tava** interesting. **-tua** become interested in, take an interest in; *-tunut* interested.

-tus interest; *herättää ~ta* arouse (stimulate) [a p.'s] i. in.

kiint|eistö real estate. **-eys** firmness, solidity. **-eä** firm; fixed; *(jähmeä)* solid; *(tarkkaavaisuus)* close; *(tilaus)* firm; *~t hinnat* fixed prices; *hinnat pysyivät -einä* prices remained firm. **-iö** quota.

kiinto|jää solid ice. **-nainen** fixed. **-pallo** captive balloon. **-tähti** fixed star.

kiinty|mys attachment, devotion (to), fondness (for). **-ä** become attached (to); *-nyt jkh (m.)* devoted to, fond of.

kiipeli fix, dilemma.

kiipijä climber *(m. kuv.).*

kiiras|torstai Maundy Thursday. **-tuli** purgatory.

kiire hurry, haste; rush; *minulla on kova ~* I am in a great hurry, I am extremely busy; *asialla on ~* the matter is urgent; *ei ole ~ttä* there is no hurry; *~essä* in a hurry, hurriedly; *lähtö~essä* in the hurry *(t.* scurry) of leaving. **-ellinen** urgent, pressing, hasty; *(pikainen)* speedy, prompt; *k-llisesti* hurriedly. **-ellisyys** *(asian)* pressing nature, urgency. **-esti** in haste, hastily, quickly. **-htiä** hurry, hasten; make haste; *(työtä)* expedite, hurry on; *-hdi!* hurry up! come on! buck up! *-hdi hitaasti!* take your time! **-immiten** as quickly as possible. **-inen** hurried, rushed; *-iset askeleet* hurried steps; *-iset tehtävät* pressing business; *olin niin ~ että* I was in so much of a hurry, I was so busy [that].

kiiruhtaa hurry, hasten, make haste.

kiiruna [rock] ptarmigan.

kiiski ruff.

kiisseli thickened fruit juice.

kiista controversy, dispute, *(riita)* quarrel, strife. **-kirjoitus** polemic[al] article. **-naihe** bone of contention. **-nalainen** disputed, contested, controversial; *~ kysymys* the question at issue (in dispute).

kiist|aton ks. kiistämätön. **-ellä**

argue, dispute; *(asiasta) ~än (vielä) kiivaasti .. is* [still] hotly argued about. **-ämätön** indisputable, undisputed, incontestable, unchallenged; *on ~tä .. is* beyond dispute.

kiistää dispute, *(kieltää)* deny; *~ väite* challenge the truth of a statement.

kiisu pyrites.

kiite|llä thank; *(ylistää),* praise, commend. **-ttävyys** praiseworthiness. **-ttävä** praiseworthy, laudable; *(arvosana)* excellent.

kiitolinja-auto freight-liner, long-distance lorry.

kiitolli|nen grateful; thankful; *~ maaperä* good ground; *~ tehtävä* a rewarding task; *~ yleisö* a grateful public, *(esim. teatt.)* an appreciative audience; *olen Teille hyvin ~* I am very much obliged to you (for). **-suuden|velka** debt of gratitude; *olla k-velassa (jklle)* be indebted to .. **-suus** gratitude; *-suudella (m.)* gratefully, with thanks.

kiito|rata runway. **-ratsastus** flat race. **-tavara** express goods.

kiitos thanks; *(ylistys)* praise; *kiitoksia paljon* many thanks, thank you very *(t.* so) much; *Jumalan ~* thank God; *ei ~* no, thank you; *kyllä, ~* yes, please; *~ hyvää* (t. *hyvin)* very well, thank you; fine, thanks; *kiitokseksi jstk* in return for. **-jumalanpalvelus** thanksgiving service. **-kirje** letter of thanks.

kiittämä|ttömyys ingratitude. **-tön** ungrateful.

kiittää thank, *jstk* for; *(ylistää)* praise; *kiitä onneasi* you may thank your [lucky] stars! *kiitän sydämestäni* thank you ever so much! *minun on kiittäminen häntä* I am indebted to him (for).

kiit|jää speed, fly; *~ ohi* speed by; *(ohi)-ävä hetki* fleeting moment.

kiivailla be zealous, *(jkta vastaan)* declaim against.

kiivas violent, vehement;

(henkilöstä) quick-tempered (-headed); irascible; hot; *kiivaat sanat* sharp words. **-luontoinen** hot-tempered (-blooded), of violent temper. **-tua** lose one's temper, get into a temper. **-tus** burst of temper.

kiivaus violence; hot temper.

kiivetä climb; *vrt. kavuta;* ~ *puuhun* climb a tree; ~ *tikapuita* climb [up] a ladder.

kikattaa giggle, titter.

kikka *(niksi)* gimmick.

kilahtaa clink, tinkle.

kili|nä, -stä jingle, tinkle, clink, jangle. **-stää** jingle; ~ *laseja* clink (touch) glasses.

kilj|ahdus yell, squeal. **-ua** yell; roar; *(aasi)* bray. **-unta** yelling, roar[ing].

kilo|(gramma) kilogram[me]. **-haili** sprat. **-metri** kilometre. *Am.* -meter; *(~patsas* kilometre stone). **-watti** kilowatt.

kilpa contest; *juosta, ajaa ~a* run (ride) a race; *(jkn kanssa)* race a p. **-ajo** horse race; *(~hevonen* racehorse; *~rata* race-course). **-auto** racer, racing car. **-autoilija** racing driver. **-autoilu** car racing. **-hakija** rival applicant, competitor. **-ileva** competing, rival.

kilpai|lija competitor; rival; *urh. m.* entrant. **-lla** compete (with sb.), for *jstk.*

kilpailu competition; contest; *urh. m.* event, *(kilpailut)* match, meeting, tournament; *(nopeus-)* race; *kuv.* rivalry. **-kelvoton** disqualified. **-kielto** suspension; *julistaa ~on* suspend. **-kyky** competitiveness. **-kykyinen** competitive, able to compete. **-sarja** series of events.

kilpa|juoksija runner, sprinter; *(hevonen)* race-horse. **-juoksu** [running] race; *(~rata* running-track). **-kenttä** [athletics] field, ground, *kuv.* arena. **-kosija** rival suitor. **-purjehdus** regatta. **-rata** race-track. **-ratsastus** horse-race. **-silla:** *olla -silla*

compete [with one another]; *haastaa -sille* challenge .. [to a contest]. **-soutu** boat-race. **-urheilu** competitive sports. **-varustelu** armaments race, arms race.

kilpi shield; *(vaakuna-)* escutcheon; coat of arms; *(kyltti)* sign[board], *(esim. autossa)* [number-] plate. *(ovessa)* door-plate. **-konna** tortoise; *(meri-)* turtle; *(~nkuori* tortoise-shell). **-kuva** device. **-rauhanen** thyroid gland.

kilpisty|ä rebound; *yritys -i jhk* failed, broke down (because of).

kilta guild.

kiltti good-natured, good, kind.

kilv|an *ks.* **kilpaa. -oitella** contend; *(jtk saadakseen)* strive for. **-oittelu** striving; *vrt. seur.* **-oitus** struggle, effort[s]; *raam.* fight.

kimakka shrill; *vrt.* **kimeä.**

kimalainen bumble-bee.

kimal|lus glimmering, glittering. **-taa** glimmer, glitter, sparkle.

kime|ys shrillness. **-ä** shrill, high-pitched; piercing.

kimmo|inen elastic, springy, resilient. **-isuus** elasticity. **-ta** be elastic; *(takaisin)* rebound, bounce back; *(luoti)* ricochet. **-ton** inelastic.

kimo roan.

kimpaantua flare up.

kimpale chunk, piece; lump.

kimppu bunch; bundle, cluster; *käydä (jkn) ~un* attack; *he olivat kimpussani* they were on me.

-kin also, too; *(vieläpä)* even.

kina squabble, wrangle. **-stella, -ta** argue; bicker, quarrel.

kiniini quinine.

kinkku ham.

kinnas mitten; *viitata kintaalla* snap one's fingers (at).

kinnerjänne Achilles tendon.

kinos [snow-]drift.

kintereillä: *jkn ~ at* a p.'s heels.

kinttu leg, *(eläimen)* hock.

kioski kiosk, stall.

kiperä *kuv.* complicated, tricky, sticky, knotty.

kipeä ill; *et. attr.* sick; *(arka)* sore; ~ *jalka* sore foot; ~ *kohta (m. kuv.)* tender spot; ~ *tarve* urgent (pressing) need; *tehdä* ~*tä* hurt. **-sti** sorely; *sitä kaivataan* ~ it is badly needed.
kipin kapin helter skelter; straight away.
kipin|ä spark *(m. kuv.)*. **-öidä** emit sparks, spark.
kippi (auto) tip-up lorry, *Am.* dump truck.
kippis cheers!
kippura: *mennä* ~*an* curl.
kipsi gypsum; plaster [of Paris]; *panna* ~*in* put in plaster. **-jäljennös** plaster cast. **-nen** [. . of] plaster. **-nvalaja** plasterer. **-side** plaster cast *(t.* jacket).
kipu pain. **-rahat** damages; smart money.
kirahvi giraffe.
kire|ys strain, tenseness; *(rahamarkkinain)* stringency. **-ä** tight, *(köysi)* taut; *et. kuv.* tense; *(kova)* strict; *raha on* ~*llä* money is tight (scarce); ~*t välit* strained relations.
kiri spurt.
kiris|tys strain; *(rahan)* extortion, *(uhkauksin)* blackmail; *(~yritys* attempt at blackmail). **-tyä** tighten; *kuv.* become strained; *asema -tyy yhä* the situation is growing more and more critical. **-täjä** extortioner, blackmailer. **-tää** tighten; *(puristaa)* be too tight; ~ *ehtoja* make stipulations more stringent; ~ *hampaitaan* gnash one's teeth; ~ *jklta lupaus* wring a promise from; ~ *rahoja* extort money, blackmail; ~ *tietoja* extract information (from).
kirja book; *(paperia)* quire; *ilmestyä* ~*na* appear in book form; *viedä kirjoihin* enter [in a book]; *pitää* ~*a jstk* keep accounts; *olla huonoissa kirjoissa* be in [. .'s] bad books. **-aja** registrar. **-aminen** booking, entry; *(kirjeen)* registration. **-hylly** book-shelf.
kirjai|lija writer, author;

(~**nimi** pen name; ~**tar** authoress). **-lla** write, be a writer; *(ommella)* embroider; *kullalla -ltu* embroidered with gold. **-mellinen** literal; *k-llisesti* literally, to the letter. **-misto** alphabet. **-n** letter; *isoilla -milla* in capitals, in upper case; *pienet -met* lower case.
kirja|kaappi bookcase. **-kauppa** book-shop. **-kauppias** bookseller. **-ke** type. **-kieli** literary language. **-llinen** literary; *(kirjoitettu)* written; ~ *anomus* application in writing; ~ *tutkinto* written examination.
kirjallisuuden|arvostelija literary critic. **-arvostelu** review. **-historia** history of literature.
kirjallisuus literature. **-luettelo** bibliography, [list of] references. **-viite** recommended literature.
kirjaltaja typographer.
kirja|myymälä *(esim. asemalla)* bookstall. **-nen** booklet.
kirjan|kansi cover; binding. **-kustantaja** publisher. **-merkki** book-mark. **-nimi** title [of a book]. **-oppinut** scribe. **-painaja** printer. **-pito** book-keeping; *yksin-, kaksinkertainen* ~ book-keeping by single (double) entry. **-pitäjä** book-keeper, accountant. **-päällys** jacket. **-päätös** closing of the books. **-sidonta** bookbinding. **-sitoja** bookbinder. **-sitomo** bookbinding business.
kirja|paino printing office; *(~taito* [art of] printing; typography). **-rengas** book-club. **-sin** type. **-sivistys** book-learning. **-toukka** bookworm.
kirjasto library. **-nhoitaja** librarian.
kirja|ta *(kirje ym)* register; *(viedä kirjaan)* book. **-us** registration; booking.
kirjav|a multi-coloured, many-coloured, variegated, *(sekalainen)* heterogeneous, varied; *kuv. m.* miscellaneous;

140

~n korea gaudy; ~ seura
motley crowd; ~ silkkikangas
(m.) printed silk; ~t vaiheet
varying fortunes; mustan ja
valkoisen ~ black and white.
-uus diversity [of colours].
kirje letter. -ellinen .. by
letter; written. -ellisesti by
letter.
kirjeen|kantaja postman.
-kirjoittaja letterwriter. -saaja
addressee. -vaihtaja
correspondent. -vaihto
correspondence; olla
-vaihdossa correspond (with);
(~toveri pen friend, pen pal;
correspondent).
kirje|itse by letter. -kortti
postcard. -kuori envelope.
-kurssi postal course.
-kyyhkynen homing pigeon.
-lippu note. -lmä letter,
[written] communication, lak.
writ. -opisto correspondence
school. -painin paperweight.
-paperi letter (note-) paper.
-vaaka letter-balance. -velka:
olla (jklle) ~a owe a letter
to ..
kirjoa embroider.
kirjoi|ttaa write; (lehtiin)
contribute to; ~ koneella type;
koneella -tettu (teksti)
typescript; ~ käsin write [by
hand]; käsin -tettu
hand-written; ~ lasku make
out a bill; ~ muistiin make
a note of, write down; ~
musteella write in ink; ~
nimensä jhk sign; ~
puhtaaksi make a clean (a
fair) copy; -tin saadakseni
kirjan I wrote for the book;
-tan kirjeen hänelle I will
write him a letter (a letter
to him); miten se -tetaan?
how do you spell it? tätä
-tettaessa at the time of
writing. -ttaja writer.
-ttamaton unwritten; blank.
-ttautua (jhk) put one's name
down, be enrolled, enter one's
name, register [esim. at the
university].
kirjoitus writing; article.
-harjoitus writing exercise.
-kirjai|n written character;
-min kirjoitettu cursive. -kone

typewriter; kirjoittaa ~ella
type. -kouristus writer's
cramp. -neuvot writing set.
-pöytä writing-table, desk.
-salkku brief-case. -taito art
of writing. -tapa manner (t.
style) of writing. -tarvikkeet
stationery, writing materials.
-vihko copy book. -virhe
mistake in spelling, clerical
error.
kirjolohi rainbow trout.
kirjonta embroidery.
kirjopyykki coloureds.
kirjuri clerk.
kirkai|sta [give a] scream,
shriek. -su scream; shriek.
kirkas clear; bright; (kiiltävä)
shiny; run. limpid; ~ päivä
(m.) sunny day. -taa make
bright, brighten; clarify;
(valaista) make clear; usk.
transfigure. -tua become clear,
(esim. sää) clear up, (kasvot
ym) brighten [up]; -tunut
(kuv.) transfigured. -värinen
bright-coloured. -ääninen
clear-voiced.
kirkkaus clearness; brightness.
kirkko church; kirkossa
(jumalanpalveluksessa) at c.
(muuten) in the c.; käydä kirkossa go to c. -herra rector,
vicar, parson; (~nvirasto
church registry office).
-historia church history. -isä:
~t Fathers of the Church.
-juhla church festival. -kansa
church-goers. -konsertti church
concert. -käsikirja [book of]
ritual, Engl. Prayer Book.
-laki canon law. -laulu
(veisuu) congregational
singing. -maa churchyard.
-musiikki sacred music.
-neuvosto vestry. -vuosi
canonical year.
kirkolli|nen ecclesiastical,
church. -skokous synod,
Church Assembly. -vero
church tax.
kirkon|isäntä churchwarden.
-kello church-bell. -kirjat
church (t. parish) register;
olla -kirjoissa jssak be
registered in [the parish of].

-kirous ban, excommunication; *julistaa -kir, -kesseen* excommunicate. **-kylä** village [with a church]. **-menot** church service; ritual. **-penkki** pew. **-torni** church tower, *(huippu)* steeple. **-vahtimestari** verger.

kirkossakävijä church-goer.

kirku|a shriek, scream; yell. **-na** screech, *(lokin ym)* squawk.

kirm|ailu frolicking. **-ata** frolic.

kirnu, -ta churn. **-piimä** buttermilk.

kiro|illa swear, use bad language. **-ta** curse; *-ttu* damned, confounded. **-us** curse; *(kirosana)* swear-word.

kirpeys bitterness, pungency.

kirpeä bitter, pungent, *kuv. m.* trenchant.

kirppu flea.

kirsi frost in the ground.

kirsikka cherry. **-puu** cherry-tree.

kirstu *ks. arkku; (ruumis-)* coffin.

kirurgi surgeon. **-a** surgery. **-nen** surgical.

kirva plant-louse *(pl. -lice)*.

kirveen|isku blow with an axe. **-terä** head of an axe.

kirve|llä smart; *-levin sydämin* with an aching heart. **-ly** smarting [pain].

kirves axe, *Am. m.* ax; *iskeä kirveensä kiveen (kuv.)* be wide of the mark. **-mies** carpenter.

kirvo|ittaa loosen, relax; release. **-ta:** ~ *kädestä* slip out of one's hand [s].

kisa play; ~*t* games. **-illa** play; frolic. **-kenttä** playground; athletic field.

kiskaista snatch; ~ *itsensä irti* wrench oneself away, break away (from).

kisko bar, *(rata-)* rail; ~*ilta suistuminen* derailment. **-auto** rail-car. **-ttaa** lay rails.

kisk|oa pull, jerk, tug; ~ *jkta hihasta* pull .. 's sleeve (.. by the sleeve); ~ *irti* tear off; ~ *korkoa* practise usury; ~ *tiikaa (maksua)* overcharge, *(nylkeä)* fleece; ~ *pois hammas* extract (pull out) a

tooth. **-uri** *(koron-)* usurer; *(~korko* usurious interest; *~vuokra* extortionate rent).

kissa cat. **-mainen** feline, catlike. **-nkello** hare-bell. **-nnaukujaiset** caterwaul[ing]. **-npoikanen** kitten.

kisälli journeyman.

kita jaws *(pl.)*. **-kieleke** uvula. **-laki** [hard] palate; *pehmeä* ~ soft palate; *(~halkio* cleft palate). **-risa** adenoids.

kitara guitar; *soittaa* ~*a* play the g. **-nsoittaja** guitarist.

kitata cement; putty.

kite|inen crystalline. **-yttää, -ytyä** crystallize. **-ytyminen** crystallization.

kitistä *(esim. ovi)* creak; *(lapsi ym)* squeak, whine.

kitka friction.

kitkerä bitter, acrid; harsh.

kitkeä weed, pull up weeds; *(pois)* weed out; ~ *maata* weed the garden.

kitsas niggardly, stingy; *(pikkumainen)* mean. **-telija** niggard. **-tella** be niggardly, be stingy. **-telu** stinginess.

kitsaus niggardliness, parsimony.

kitti cement, *(ikkuna-)* putty.

kitu|a suffer pain; linger, languish. **-kasvuinen** stunted. **-uttaa:** *elää* ~ scrape a precarious living.

kiuas bathhouse stove.

kiukku crossness; anger; *olla kiukuissaan* fume. **-inen** cross, angry, irate. **-päinen** ill-tempered; irascible.

kiuku|stua get angry. **-tella** be in a tantrum, be peevish. **-ttelija** crosspatch.

kiulu pail.

kiuru lark, skylark.

kiusa annoyance, vexation; nuisance, bother, bore; ~*lla* out of spite; ~*llani* to spite .., to get even with ..; *tehdä* ~*a* tease. **-aja** tempter. **-antua** be annoyed, be vexed (with). **-antunut** worried, irritated. **-llinen** troublesome, vexatious, irksome; *sepä -llista* how annoying! what a nuisance! **-nhenki** tormentor, pest. **-nkappale** nuisance. **-ntekijä** teaser, mischief-maker.

-ta torment, harass, *(vaivata)* annoy, trouble, worry; *(ärsyttää)* vex; tease; *(viekoitella)* tempt; *jnk -ama* tormented with .., annoyed by .. **-us** temptation; *johdattaa -ukseen* lead into t.; *joutua -ukseen* be tempted (to).

kiusoitella tease, chaff.

kiva jolly good, jolly nice, funny; ripping, *et. Am.* cute; *~a! fine!; meillä oli ~a* we had great fun.

kivahtaa snap, *jklle* at.

kiven|ammunta blasting. **-hakkaaja** stone-cutter. **-heitto** stone's throw. **-kova** hard as stone, stony. **-louhinta** quarrying.

kivennäi|nen *a. & s.* mineral. **-slähde** mineral spring, spa. **-stiede** mineralogy. **-svesi** mineral water.

kives *anat.* testicle.

kivetty|mä fossil. **-ä** be petrified, turn into stone; fossilize; *kauhusta -neenä* petrified with terror.

kive|tä pave [with stones]; *laakakivillä -tty* metalled with flagstones. **-ys** [stone] paving, pavement.

kivi stone; *kivestä tehty* [.. of] stone, made of stone, earthenware. **-astiat** stoneware, earthenware. **-hiili** coal; (~alue coal-field; ~kaivos coal-mine, colliery; ~kerros coal-bed). **-jalka** stone foundation. **-kausi** the Stone Age. **-kko** stony soil. **-kunta** mineral kingdom. **-kynä** slate-pencil. **-laatta** slab [of stone], flagstone. **-lohkare** block of stone; boulder. **-louhos** quarry. **-murska** crushed stone, rubble. **-muuri** stone wall. **-nen** stone; *~ maaperä* stony soil. **-painos** lithograph. **-pora** rock-drill. **-reunus** *(käytävän)* kerb. **-ruukku** earthenware jar, crock. **-rikko** *bot.* saxifrage. **-röykkiö** heap of stones.

kivis|tys ache, pain. **-tää** ache; *päätäni ~ (kovasti)* I have a [racking] headache.

kivi|talo stone house, *(tiili-)* brick house. **-taulu** stone tablet, *(lasten)* slate. **-ttää** pelt with stones; *~ kuoliaaksi* stone to death. **-työmies** stone-mason. **-veistämö** stone-masonry. **-öljy** petroleum, rock oil.

kivu|lloinen ailing, sickly; *on hyvin ~* is an invalid. **-lloisuus** ill-health. **-ton** painless.

kivääri rifle; gun. **-nlaukaus** report [of a gun]. **-nluoti** bullet. **-npiippu** rifle barrel. **-tuli** rifle fire.

klarinetti clarinet.

klassi|kko classic; classicist. **-llinen, -nen** classical, classic.

klikki clique.

klinikka clinic; hospital.

klišee cut, printing-block; *kuv.* cliché.

kloori chlorine.

kloroformi chloroform.

klosetti lavatory, toilet, W.C., *(vessa)* loo. **-paperi** toilet tissue.

knalli bowler.

-ko, -kö if, whether; *saitko sen?* did you get it? *hänkö sen sai?* was it he who got it? *kysy, tuleeko hän* ask whether he will come [along].

kodi|kas cosy, snug, homely. **-kkuus** cosiness. **-nhoitaja** home aid. **-nhoito** household management, homecraft. **-ton** homeless; *-ttomat lapset* waifs and strays, deprived children.

koe trial; *(kokeilu)* experiment, test *(m. koul.); kokeeksi* on trial, on probation, *(tavarasta)* on approval. **-aika** *[period of]* probation. **-ajaa** test. **-ajo** trial *(t. test)* run. **-erä** trial heat. **-kaniini** guinea pig. **-kirjoitus** written test. **-lento** test flight. **-lentäjä** test pilot. **-poraus** exploratory drilling. **-putki** test tube; (~lapsi test-tube baby).

koet|ella try; *~ jkn kärsivällisyyttä* try a p.'s patience; *~ voimiaan (jkn kanssa)* pit oneself against .. **-inkivi** touchstone, *kuv. m.* test, criterion.

koett|aa try [out]; attempt,

endeavour, *(joskus)* seek; *(jnk laatua)* test, *(esim. maistaa)* sample; ~ *onneaan* try one's luck; ~ *parastaan* do one's best; ~ *pukua* try on a dress (suit); ~ *valtimoa* feel the pulse. **-elemus** trial, ordeal.

koe|tus trial, test; *(puvun)* fitting; *panna koetukselle* put to the test; *kestää* ~ stand the test. **-vuosi** year of probation.

kofeiini caffeine.

koha|hdus stir. **-uttaa:** ~ *olkapäitään* shrug one's shoulders.

kohdakkoin in the near future; *ks. piakkoin.*

kohdata meet; encounter; *(sattumalta)* run across, come across; *kuv.* meet with; *häntä kohtasi onnettomuus* he met with an accident, he had (he was involved in) an accident; *sopia kohtaamisesta* make an appointment.

kohd|e *kiel. ym* object; *sot.* objective, *(tutkimuksen)* subject. **-ella** treat; ~ *huonosti* treat badly, ill-treat. **-en** toward [s], to; *tässä kohden* at this place, *(asiassa)* on this point, *(suhteessa)* in this respect.

kohdis|taa direct; turn; ~ *huomionsa jhk* direct one's attention to [wards]; ~ *sanansa jklle* adress one's remarks to .. **-tua** be directed, be turned (to, towards); apply to, *(esim. tutkimus)* be concerned with, *(vahinko)* affect; *epäilys -tui: häneen* suspicion fell on him.

kohentaa *(parannella)* touch up, furbish up; ~ *tulta* poke the fire; ~ *pielusta* shake [up] a cushion.

kohi|na rush, roar. **-sta** murmur; *(pauhata)* roar.

kohju hernia. **-vyö** truss.

kohme: *olla ~essa* be numb, be stiff with cold. **-lo** hangover. **-ttua** grow stiff (numb) with cold; *-ttunut* numb.

koho *(ongen ym)* float; *käsi ~lla* with one's arm raised.

-aminen rising, *(virassa)* promotion. **-illa** swell, heave. **-kas** soufflé. **-kohta** *kuv.* highlight. **-kuva** relief.

kohota rise; increase, go up; *(hinnat, m.)* advance; *lentok.* ascend, climb; *(korkeampaan asemaan)* be promoted *(esim.* to the position of a manager); ~ *jnk yli* surpass; *kuume -aa* (his, her) fever is going up. **-ttaa** raise; *(nostaa)* lift up; elevate; *(arvoa ym)* enhance; *mieltä -ttava* elevating, [soul-] inspiring; *vrt. korottaa.* **-uma** elevation; protuberance.

kohta 1. *adv.* soon; *(heti)* at once, directly, straight away; *heti* ~ on the spot, immediately. **2.** *s.* point; place; *(kappale)* paragraph, section *(m. laissa)*; *(kirjoituksessa, m.)* passage; *omalta kohdaltani* as far as I am concerned; *sain sen kohdalleen* I got it put straight; *osua kohdalleen* hit the mark; *kohdalleen osuva* well put; *kaikissa kohdin* on every point, in every respect.

kohtaan toward [s]; to; *olla ystävällinen jkta* ~ be kind to

kohtalai|nen medium; moderate; fair, passable; *-sen* fairly; *-sen hyvä (m.)* reasonably good; *-sen suuri ..* of medium size, fairly big. **-suus** mediocrity.

kohtalo fate, lot; destiny. **-kas** fateful, *(kuolettava)* fatal. **-toveri** companion in misfortune.

kohtaus meeting; *(sovittu)* appointment; *teatt.* scene, *elok. TV (m.)* footage; *(taudin)* attack; fit. **-paikka** meeting-place, rendezvous.

kohte|liaasti politely. **-liaisuus** politeness, courtesy; compliment; (**~käynti** courtesy call). **-lias** polite, courteous. **-lu** treatment, usage; *huono* ~ mistreatment.

kohti: *jtk* ~ toward [s], *-wards* *itää* ~ to [wards] the east; *kotia* ~ homewards; *10 markkaa henkilöä* ~ 10 marks

each (*t.* per person). **-suora**
perpendicular; *(pysty)* vertical;
-suoraan (m.) at right angles
(to).
kohtu womb, uterus.
kohtuulli|nen moderate,
reasonable; fair; ~ *elämässään*
temperate in one's way of
life; ~ *toimeentulo* a decent
living; *-seen hintaan* at a
reasonable price, at moderate
cost; *kuten -sta olikin* as was
only fair (reasonable). **-uus**
moderation.
kohtuu|s moderation;
reasonableness, justice; *se on
oikeus ja* ~ it is only just;
-della ei voi enempää vaatia
more cannot reasonably be
demanded; *-den rajoissa*
within reason. **-hinta:** *~an* at
a moderate price, fairly
cheap. **-ton** unreasonable,
unfair; immoderate; *(liiallinen)*
exorbitant, excessive; *(esim.
vuokra)* extortionate; *käyttää
-ttomasti (alkoholia ym)*
overindulge in . .
kohu sensation, rumpus,
hullabaloo; *siitä nousi* ~ it
created a sensation. **-ta:**
maailma -aa jstk the world is
in an uproar about.
koi [clothes] moth; *(aamun)*
dawn.
koilli|nen north-east. **-stuuli**
north-east [erly] wind.
koinsyömä moth-eaten.
koipi shank, leg.
koira dog; *(ajo-)* hound; *siihen
on* ~ *haudattuna* there is
something behind this, *puhek.*
I smell a rat.
koiran|heisipuu guelder-rose.
-ilma beastly weather.
-kasvattaja dog-breeder. **-koppi**
kennel. **-kuje** dog's (*t.* dirty)
trick. **-leuka** practical joker,
wag. **-pentu** pup [py]. **-pommi**
toy torpedo. **-putki** wild
chervil. **-uinti:** *uida ~a*
dog-paddle.
koira|näyttely dog show. **-pari**
brace of dogs. **-rotu** breed of
dogs. **-tarha** kennels. **-vero**
dog-licence.
koiras male; *(linnusta)* cock.
-karhu he-bear. **-kettu** dog

fox. **-kissa** tom-cat.
koiravaljakko dog team.
koiruus: *tehdä jklle koiruutta*
play a dirty trick on . .
koittaa: *päivä* ~ the day
breaks; *päivän koittaessa* at
dawn, at daybreak.
koit|ua: *siitä ei koidu mitään
hyvää* no good will come of
that; *siitä -uu kuluja* it will
involve expense; *minulle -ui
menoja* I incurred expense
[through this]; *se -uu hänelle
kunniaksi* it will redound to
his credit.
koivikko birch grove,
birchwood.
koivu birch. **-inen** birch.
-nmahla birch sap. **-nvarpu**
birch twig.
koje apparatus; instrument;
(laite) appliance; device;
(vekotin) gadget; *~et*
apparatus; equipment. **-lauta**
dashboard, instrument panel.
koju *(kauppa-)* stall, booth;
(makuu-) bunk, berth; *(maja)*
cabin.
kokaiini cocaine.
kokardi cockade.
koke|a experience; suffer, meet
with; undergo; ~ *verkko*
examine [and empty] a net.
-ellinen experimental. **-ilija**
experimenter. **-illa** try [sth.
out on], make experiments,
experiment, *jllak* on, with;
antaa jkn ~ give . . a chance
to try; *-iltavaksi* on trial; ~
autoa give the car a trial
run (spin). **-ilu**
experiment [ation], trial;
(~nluonteinen tentative,
experimental). **-las** candidate;
aspirant.
kokema|ton inexperienced.
-ttomuus inexperience.
koke|mus experience; *-muksesta*
from e.; *oppia -muksesta*
learn by e.; *katkerasta
-muksesta tiedän* I know out
of my own bitter (harsh) e.;
(~peräinen empiric [al]). **-nut**
experienced; *. . on kovia* ~
. . has endured many
hardships.
kokka bow. **-puhe** joke,
witticism. **-puu** bowsprit.

kokkar|e lump; *(myky)* dumpling; *(maa-)* clod. **-oitua** get lumpy; *kem.* coagulate.
kokkeli *(muna-)* scrambled eggs.
kokki cook.
kokko *(-tuli)* bonfire, midsummer pyre.
koko 1. *a.* whole, the whole (of), entire; *adv.* rather; fairly; ~ **päivän** *(m.)* all day long; ~ **talven** all the winter; ~ **joukon** a good deal, *(puhek.)* quite a lot; ~ **joukon parempi** considerably better; ~ **Helsinki** all H., the whole of H.; ~ **hyvä** fairly good, *(huonohko)* rather good; ~ **maailmassa** throughout the world, all over the world. **2.** *s. (suuruus)* size; *(ruumiin)* stature; *(mitat)* dimensions; *(tilavuus)* volume; **pientä** ~*a* .. of small size. **-aminen** collection; *(koneen)* assembling. **-elma** collection.
kokoi|lija collector. **-lla** collect; gather. **-nen:** *jnk* ~ [of] the size of ..; **minun -seni** of my size; **eri -sia** of various sizes.
koko|jyväleipä whole-meal bread. **-kuva** full-length portrait. **-käännös** about-turn; **tehdä** ~ turn about, turn round. **-lattiamatto** wall-to-wall carpet [ing]. **-naan** wholly, entirely, completely, totally; ~ **toinen** quite another. **-nainen** whole, entire, total; **-naista 10 vuotta** all of ten years.
kokonais- overall, total. **-luku** *mat.* whole number, integer. **-määrä** total amount. **-ratkaisu** *ks.* nippu-. **-summa** [sum] total; **voitto nousee** .. ~*an* the profits total .. ~ **-tulo** gross income. **-uus** entirety, totality; whole; **-uudessaan** in its entirety, as a whole, altogether; **ehjä** ~ an integrated whole. **-vaikutelma** general impression. **-valtainen** all-inclusive.
kokonuotti semibreve.
kokoomus composition, *fys.* consistency. **-hallitus** coalition government. **-puolue** conservative (coalition, union) party.

kokoon together; up; *kutsua* ~ call together; *kääriä* ~ roll up; *panna* ~ put together, *(laatia)* compose, draw up, *tekn.* assemble; *taittaa* ~ fold up; ~ *pantava* collapsible, folding [seat, tuoli]. **-kutsuminen** convocation, calling [together]. **-pano** composition. **-pantu** composed, made up (of); **olla** ~ *jstk* consist of. **-tua** assemble, meet; come together, gather. **-tuminen** *m.* get-together. **-työnnettävä** folding, collapsible.
kokous meeting; assembly, conference; *(kansainvälinen)* congress; *(esim. koulutoverien)* reunion; *kutsua* **kokoukseen** summon a meeting, convene. **-paikka** meeting-place, *(huone, sali)* assembly room (hall).
koksi coke.
kola|htaa bump; **pääni -hti seinään** I bumped my head against the wall. **-ri** *(auto-)* collision, crash. **-uttaa** knock, strike.
kolea raw, bleak, chilly.
kolehti collection; *kantaa* ~*a* take a collection. **-haavi** collection bag.
kolera cholera.
kolesteroli cholesterol.
kolh|aista knock, hit. **-aisu** bruise. **-ia** batter; damage.
kolhoosi kolkhoz, collective farm.
kolhu knock; **elämän** ~*t* buffetings of life; *vrt.* **kolhaisu**.
kolibakteeri colon bacillus.
kolibri humming-bird.
kolikko [large] coin.
koli|na noise; clatter. **-sta** make a noise; clatter. **-stella:** ~ *ovea* rattle the door.
kolja *zo.* haddock.
kolkata *sl.* clobber, *(tappaa)* bump off.
kolkka corner; *(seutu)* parts.
kolkko gloomy, dismal, dreary; *(kaamea)* gruesome; *(kolea)* raw; *(autio)* desolate.
kolku|ttaa knock, rap (at), *(hiljaa)* tap; **ovelle -tettiin** there was a knock at the door. **-tus** knock [ing].

kollaasi *ks. kooste.*
kollationoida collate.
kolle|ga colleague. **-ginen**
  collegiate. **-gio** college;
  (opettaja-) teachers' council.
kollektiivinen collective.
kolli package, piece [of
  goods]. **-kissa** tom-cat.
kolm|annes third [part]; *kaksi*
  ~ta two thirds. **-as** [the]
  third; *pää -antena jalkana*
  helter-skelter; *kolmanneksi*
  third [ly]; *(~kymmenes* [the]
  thirtieth; *~osa* [one-] third).
  -asti three times. **-astoista**
  [the] thirteenth.
kolme three; *~na kappaleena*
  in triplicate; *me ~* we three,
  the three of us. **-kymmentä**
  thirty. **-nlainen** . . . . . of
  three kinds. **-sataa** three
  hundred. **-sti** three times.
  -toista thirteen.
kolmi- three-, tri-, triple; *jakaa*
  ~a divide into three parts.
  -haarainen three-branched.
  -jako tripartition. **-jalka**
  tripod. **-kerroksinen**
  three-storey [ed]. **-kko** trio.
  -kulma triangle. **-kulmainen**
  triangular. **-kymmenvuotinen**
  of thirty years [duration]; *~*
  sota the Thirty Years' War.
  -liitto Triple Alliance. **-loikka**
  triple jump. **-mastolaiva**
  threemaster. **-nainen** threefold,
  treble, triple. **-naisuus** [the]
  Trinity. **-nkertainen** threefold;
  triple, treble; three-ply.
  -nkertaisesti threefold, trebly.
  -kertaistua treble, be trebled.
  -o triangle; *~n muotoinen*
  triangular. **-osainen** consisting
  of three parts; *(kirja)* . . in
  three parts, *(näytelmä)* in
  three acts. **-pyörä** *(polku-)*
  tricycle. **-päiväinen** lasting
  three days. **-sen:** *~ vuotta*
  about three years. **-sin** in a
  group of three; *menimme*
  sinne ~ the three of us went
  there. **-sivuinen** three-sided,
  trilateral. **-sointu** triad,
  common chord. **-särmäinen**
  triangular. **-tavuinen**
  trisyllabic; *~ sana* trisyllable.
  -ulotteinen three-dimensional.
  -vuotias *a.* three years old;

atr. & s. three-year-old.
  -vuotinen lasting three years,
  triennial. **-yhteinen** triune.
kolmo|is- triple; *(~kappale*
  triplicate). **-nen** three, *(pelissä,*
  m.) trey. **-set** triplets.
kolo hole; cavity, hollow.
kolonna column
koloratuuri coloratura.
kolo|ttaa ache. **-tus** ache, pain.
kolpakko tankard.
kolttonen trick, prank.
kolvi soldering-iron.
kome|a fine, grand; splendid,
  magnificent; stately, imposing;
  (hauskannäköinen)
  good-looking. **-illa** make a
  display, parade, show off. **-ilu**
  show, parade, ostentation.
komen|nella push around, order
  about. **-nus** command;
  jkn-nuksesta at a p.'s c.;
  (~kunta command,
  detachment).
koment|aa command; be in
  command of; *-ava kenraali*
  the general in c. **-aja**
  commander.
komento command; *(järjestys)*
  order; *jkn komennossa* under
  command of. **-sana** word of
  command. **-silta** bridge. **-torni**
  conning tower.
komero built -in cupboard
  (vaate- wardrobe), *Am. m.*
  closet; recess, alcove.
komeus magnificence,
  stateliness, state, splendour.
komi|ssaari commissioner,
  (poliisi-) inspector; *(Neuv.*
  Ven.) commissar. **-tea**
  committee.
kommellus mishap; slip.
komment|aari, -oida comment
  (on). **-oija** commentator.
kommunikea communiqué.
kommunis|mi communism. **-ti**
  communist. **-tinen**
  communist [ic].
kompa quip. **-kysymys** tricky
  question. **-runo** epigram. **-sana**
  sarcasm.
kompara|atio comparison. **-tiivi**
  comparative [degree].
kompassi compass. **-neula**
  compass needle.
kompas|tua stumble (against,
  over). **-tus** stumbling; *(~kivi*

stumbling-block).
kompensoida compensate.
kompleksi complex.
komposti compost.
komppania company.
kompromissi compromise.
kompuroida crawl, scramble.
konditionaali conditional [mood].
konditoria confectioner's, pastry shop.
kone machine; engine; *höyry* ~ steam engine; ~*et* machinery.
koneelli|**nen** mechanical. **-sesti** by machine, mechanically. **-staa** mechanize.
koneen|**hoitaja, -käyttäjä** machine-(engine-)man, *mer.* engineer, machinist.
kone|**huone** (*laivan*) engine-room. **-insinööri** mechanical engineer. **-isto** machinery; (*pienempi*) mechanism; (*kellon*) works. **-kirjoittaja** typist. **-kirjoitus** typing. **-kivääri** machine-gun. **-käyttöinen** mechanically operated. **-mainen** mechanical. **-mestari** engineer. **-oppi** science of machinery, [general] engineering practice. **-paja** engineering shop (works). **-pelti** bonnet, *Am.* hood. **-pistooli** sub-machine gun. **-rikko** breakdown. **-seppä** mechanic. **-tehdas** machine factory. **-teollisuus** engineering [industry]. **-tykki** A-gun. **-työ** machine work; *se on* ~*tä* it is machine-made. **-vika** engine failure, breakdown. **-öljy** engine oil.
konferenssi conference (on).
Kongo the Congo. **k-lainen** *a. & s.* Congolese.
kongressi congress.
konjakki brandy.
konjugaatio conjugation.
konjunk|**tiivi** subjunctive [mood]. **-tio** conjunction. **-tuuri** *ks. suhdanne.*
konkreettinen concrete; palpable.
konkurssi bankruptcy, failure; *tehdä* ~ become bankrupt. fail. **-pesä** bankrupt's estate. **-rikos** fraudulent bankruptcy.
konna scoundrel, villain; *zo.*

toad. **-mainen** villainous, knavish. **-nkoukku** dirty trick. **-ntyö** villainous deed, knavery.
konossementti bill of lading (B/L).
konsepti rough draft; (*puhujan*) notes.
konsertti concert, recital; *pitää* ~ give a c. **-flyygeli** concert grand. **-matka** concert tour. **-sali** concert hall.
kon|**servatorio** conservatoire. **-sistori** consistory; (*yliop.*) council. **-sonantti** consonant.
konstaapeli policeman, constable; *yli*~ police sergeant.
konsti trick. **-kas** intricate; complicated; tricky.
konstruoida construct.
konsu|**laatti** consulate. **-lentti** counsellor, adviser; *maatalous* ~ agricultural expert. **-li** consul; (~**nvirasto** consulate).
konsultti consultant.
kontata crawl, creep.
kontra|**amiraali** rear-admiral. **-basso** double-bass.
kontrahti contract, agreement; *tehdä* ~ [make a] contract (for).
kontrolli|**i** control; supervision. **-oida** control, check.
kontta: *kontassa* numb with cold.
kontti knapsack; container.
konttokurantti account current.
konttori office. **-aika** office hours; ~*na* in (during) business hours. **-apulainen** office employee, clerk. **-henkilökunta** office staff. **-huoneisto** office [premises]. **-neiti** woman clerk. **-paikka** office job, clerical job. **-päällikkö** office manager. **-sti** clerk.
kontu homestead; *koti ja* ~ hearth and home.
koodi code.
kookas big, large; (*-kasvuinen*) tall.
kookos|**matto** coconut matting. **-palmu** coconut palm. **-pähkinä** coconut.
koo|**lla** assembled. **-lle:** *tulla* ~ come (*t.* get) together, assemble; *kutsua* ~ convene, summon.

koomi|kko comedian. **-llinen** comic [al].

koommin: *ei sen* ~ never since.

koossa: *pitää (pysyä)* ~ hold .. together; ~ *pysyvä* coherent.

kooste collage.

koostu|a be composed (of), consist (of). **-mus** composition.

koota collect, gather; *(kone ym)* assemble; amass; *(varastoon)* lay up, store up, hoard up; ~ *ajatuksensa* collect one's thoughts, pull oneself together; ~ *rahaa (hankkia)* raise money, *vrt. rahankeräys; kootut teokset* complete works.

kope|a haughty, arrogant, overbearing. **-illa** be haughty, ride a high horse; *-ileva* arrogant, high and mighty. **-ilu** arrogance, haughtiness.

kopeloida grope after, fumble; *(omavaltaisesti)* tamper with.

kopeus haughtiness, arrogance.

kopina stamp [ing], tramp; pattering.

kopio copy; *valok.* print; *valo~* photocopy. **-ida** copy, *(käsin, m.)* transcribe; *valok.* print; *vien filmit -itavaksi* I'll take the films to be printed.

kopistella make a noise; rattle (with); ~ *lunta kengistään* shake the snow off one's shoes.

kopla *(varas- ym)* band, gang.

koppa basket; *(hatun)* crown.

koppava haughty, high and mighty.

koppelo wood-grouse, hen capercaillie.

koppi cell; *urh.* catch; *sain kopin käteeni* I caught the ball.

kopu|ttaa knock, rap (at). **-tus** knock, rap.

koraali choral [e], hymn.

koraani [the] Koran.

korahdus rattle.

koralli coral. **-npunainen** coral. **-riutta** coral reef.

kore|a fine; showy; garish; *~t värit* gaudy colours. **-illa** *(jllak)* show off, make a show (a parade) of; *(pukeutua*

koreilevasti) overdress, dress up. **-ilu** ostentation, show -[iness]; vanity; (**~nhalu** love of fine clothes, vanity; **~nhaluinen** vain, fond of show).

korento cowlstaff.

koreus *(koristus)* show, finery; *(hienous)* elegance; smartness.

kori basket, *(kala-, pullo-)* crate; *(auton)* [car] body. **-huonekalut** wicker furniture.

kori|na rattle. **-sta** have a rattle in one's throat.

koripallo basket-ball.

koris|taa decorate, adorn *(m. kuv.); (hattua, pukua jllak)* trim; *(ruokia)* garnish. **-tamaton** unadorned. **-tautua** dress up, adorn oneself.

koriste ornament; *(hatun, puvun)* trimming; *(koru)* trinket. **-ellinen** decorative. **-esine:** *~et* fancy goods; bric-a-brac, knick-knacks. **-kasvi** ornamental plant. **-lematon** *kuv.* natural, artless, unaffected. **-lla** decorate; ornament; deck [out]. **-lu** decoration. **-maalari** decorator.

koristus ornament; adornment; *(koru)* finery; *(huoneen ym)* decoration.

kori|teos wickerwork. **-tuoli** cane (wicker) chair.

korjaa|maton not repaired; uncorrected. **-mo** repair shop, *(auto-, m.)* garage.

korja|ta repair, *Am.* fix; *(parsia ym)* mend; correct, put right; rectify, amend; *(koe)* mark; *(huoneisto)* do up; ~ *epäkohta* redress a grievance; ~ *pois* clear away, remove; ~ *puku* alter a dress; ~ *ruoka pöydästä* clear the table; ~ *sato* harvest [the crop], reap the harvest; ~ *tekstiä* revise, edit; *viedä -ttavaksi* take .. to be repaired; *.. ei ole -ttavissa* is irreparable, is beyond repair; *-ttu painos* revised edition **-us** repair [s]; correction; *(muutos)* alteration; *-uksen alaisena* under repair; *huoneisto on -uksen alaisena* the flat is being [re]decorated; *.. on*

-uksen tarpeessa .. needs doing up; (~**arkki** proof sheet; ~**luku** proof-reading; ~**mies** repair man, mechanic; ~**paja** repair-shop; ~**vedos** proof). **-uttaa** have .. repaired. **-utua** be repaired; be remedied.

korjuu: *hyvässä* ~*ssa* in safe keeping.

korkea high; (*puu ym*) tall; elevated; *kuv.* lofty, exalted; *(jnk) korkein määrä* maximum; *elää* ~*an ikään* live to a great age, reach an advanced age. **-arvoinen** .. of high rank (position). **-kantainen** *(kengästä)* high-heeled. **-kaulainen** high-necked. **-kirkollinen** High Church. **-korkoinen** high-interest. **-koulu** institute of university standing, college, School (*esim.* S. of Economics). **-lentoinen** high-flown. **-lla** high [up]; *sijaita* ~ lie high, have a high situation. **-lle** high [up], to a height. **-lta** from a [great] height. **-mpi** higher; superior; *-mmalle* higher [up], to a greater height. **-paine** high pressure, *ilmat.* anti-cyclone, high pressure. **-suhdanne** boom. **-sukuinen** high-born.

korkei|n highest, topmost; supreme; ~ *hinta* top price; ~ *määrä* greatest amount, maximum; ~ *oikeus* Supreme Court; *on -mmillaan* is at its peak. **-ntaan** at most, .. at the outside.

korkeus height; altitude; *(äänen)* pitch; *veden* ~ level of water, *(merenpinnan)* sea level; *Teidän Korkeutenne* Your Highness. **-hyppy** high jump. **-mittari** altimeter.

korkita cork.

korkki cork, *(pullon, m.)* stopper, bottle top. **-matto** linoleum. **-ruuvi** corkscrew. **-vyö** cork belt.

korko *(kengän)* heel; *(raha-)* interest; *kiel.* stress; *5 %* ~*a vastaan* at 5 % interest; *kasvaa* ~*a korolle* bear

compound interest; ~*a kasvava* interest-bearing; *lainata* ~*a vastaan* lend at interest; *tuottaa* ~*a* yield interest. **-kanta** rate of interest. **-kartta** relief map. **-kuva** relief. **-merkki** accent. **-tappio** loss of interest. **-tulo** income from interest.

korkuinen: *metrin* ~ one metre high (in height); *minun korkuiseni* .. of my height.

kornetti cornet.

koroillaeläjä person of independent means.

koro|ke platform, *(puhuja-, m.)* rostrum; dais; *(pienempi)* stand, podium; *(katu-)* [safety] island; (~**keskustelu** panel discussion). **-llinen** *ks. painollinen*; ~ *laina* loan at interest.

koron|kiskonta usury. **-kiskuri** usurer.

koros|taa stress, emphasize, lay stress on; *(esim. kauneutta)* highlight; dais; *(pienempi)* stress, emphasis; *hienoinen vieras* ~ a slight foreign accent.

koroton *kiel.* unstressed; *liik.* free of interest.

koro|ttaa raise; *(lisätä)* increase, heighten, *(hintaa, m.)* advance; enhance; *(jhk arvoon)* promote; *hänet -tettiin everstiksi* he was promoted colonel; ~ *äänensä* raise one's voice, speak up. **-tus** rise, increase; (~**merkki** *mus.* sharp).

korpi backwoods; wilderness. **-lakko** wildcat (*t.* unofficial) strike.

korppi raven. **-kotka** vulture.

korppu rusk. **-jauho** [golden] breadcrumbs.

korpraali lance corporal.

korrehtuuri proof.

korrelaatti *kiel.* antecedent.

korroosio corrosion.

korruptio corruption.

korsi culm, straw, stem of grass; *kantaa kortensa kekoon* do one's bit, add one's mite to the pile.

Korsika Corsica. **k-lainen** *a. & s.* Corsican.

korskea haughty.

korsku|a, -nta snort.

korsu dugout.

korte *bot.* horse-tail.

kortinpelaaja card-player.

kortisoni cortisone.

kortisto files, card-index.

kortteli *(taloryhmä)* block.

kortti card; *(leipä ym)* rationing-card; *peli ~* playing-card; *pelata ~a* play cards; *panna kaikki yhden kortin varaan* put all one's eggs in one basket. **-järjestelmä** card-index [system]. **-pakka** pack of cards, *Am.* deck. **-peli** card-game. **-temppu** card-trick.

koru ornament, trinket; *(riipus)* pendant; *~t* jewellery. **-kieli** flowery (florid) language. **-lause** high-sounding phrase; *tyhjät ~et* empty phrases (words), balderdash. **-lipas** trinket box, jewellery case. **-ompelu** fancy needle-work, embroidery. **-painos** de luxe edition. **-sähke** greetings telegram. **-tavara** fancy goods, trinkets. **-ton** simple; artless; unaffected. **-ttomuus** simplicity.

korva ear; *hyvä (sävel) ~ a* good ear for pitch; *antaa jkta korville* box (cuff) sb.'s ears; *kallistaa ~nsa jllek* lend an ear to; *olla pelkkänä ~na* be all ears; *velassa korviaan myöten* over head and ears in debt; *hän ei ota kuuleviin korviinsa* he turns a deaf ear to ..

korvaamaton irreplaceable; irreparable; *(mahdoton saada takaisin)* irrecoverable.

korva|-aukko aural orifice. **-kuulo** hearing; *~n mukaan* [play] by ear. **-käytävä** auditory meatus. **-lehti** auricle. **-llinen:** *kynsiä ~llistaan* scratch one's ear. **-lääkäri** otologist, ear specialist. **-nnipukka** ear lobe. **-nsuhina** buzzing in the ear. **-nsuojus** ear shield, ear protector, *(talvella)* ear muff. **-rengas** ear-ring. **-sieni** Gyromitra esculenta. **-särky** ear-ache.

korva|ta compensate, *(asettaa*

sijalle) replace (with, by), substitute (for); balance; *~ tappio jklle* compensate a. p. for loss, make up a loss; *~ vahinko* make good a damage; *-amme Teidän kustannuksenne* we will refund (reimburse) your expenses; *ei ole -ttavissa* is impossible to replace.

korvatillikka box (cuff) on the ear.

korvau|s compensation; remuneration; indemnity; *-kseksi jstk* as a compensation for: *(hän tekee sen) ~ta vastaan* [he will do it] for a consideration. **-svaatimus** claim [for damages].

korventaa singe, scorch.

korviasärkevä ear-splitting, *(-huumaava)* deafening.

korvike substitute; *isän ~* father s. *(t.* surrogate).

kosi|a propose, *jkta* to. **-ja** suitor. **-nta** proposal [of marriage]. **-skella** court, woo *(m. kuv., yleisöä ym);* *~ jkn suosiota* court a p.'s favour.

koska when? [at] what time? *(sentähden että)* because, as, since; *~an* ever; *ei ~an* never.

koske|a touch; *(tarkoittaa)* refer to, concern, apply to; *(kipeästi)* hurt; *se koski minuun kipeästi (kuv.)* it gave me pain; *se ei koske minua* that does not concern me; .. *koski pikkuasioita ..* related to minor details. **-maton** untouched, intact; *(loukkaamaton)* inviolable. **-mattomuus** inviolability; *dipl.* immunity; *alueellinen ~* territorial integrity.

koskenlask|ija rapids-shooter. **-u** shooting the rapids.

koske|tella touch; *kuv.* touch upon, treat (of). **-tin** key; *sähk.* contact; *seinä~ ks. pistorasia.* **-ttaa** touch, *kuv.* touch upon. **-ttimisto** keyboard. **-tus** touch *(m. mus.);* contact; *joutua -tuksiin jkn, jnk kanssa* get (come) into contact with; *vähäisimmästä -tuksesta* at the

least touch, on the slightest
manipulation; (~**kohta** point
of contact). **-va:** *jtk* ~
regarding, as regards.
koski rapids; *(putous)*
water-fall.
kosme|ettinen: *k-ttiset aineet*
cosmetics. **-tologi** beauty
specialist, cosmetician.
kosminen cosmic.
kosmopoliitti cosmopolitan.
kosmoskynä copying pencil.
kosolti copiously, .. in
abundance.
kosta|a avenge; *(jklle jk)*
revenge oneself on a p. for,
take revenge on a p. for; ~
hyvä pahalla repay good with
evil.
koste|a damp; moist, humid.
-ikko *(keidas)* oasis. **-us**
dampness, humidity; moisture;
suojeltava -udelta keep dry.
kosto revenge, vengeance;
(-toimet) retaliation. **-nhalu,**
-nhimo desire for revenge.
-nhimoinen vindictive,
revengeful. **-toimenpiteet**
(valtion) reprisals; retaliatory
measures.
kostu|a get damp, get moist;
ei siitä paljon kostu there is
little to be gained by that.
-ttaa moisten, damp[en].
kota [Laplander's] hut, tepee;
bot. capsule.
kotelo case, container;
(pistoolin) holster; *zo.*
chrysa|lis *(pl.* -lides). **-itua** be
encapsulated. **-koppa** *zo.*
cocoon.
koti home; ~*ni (m.)* my place;
kodissani in (at) my home.
-apulainen home help. **-aresti**
~*ssa* under house arrest.
-askareet household duties,
housework. **-eläin** domestic
animal. **-elämä** home life.
-etsintä house search. **-hartaus**
family worship. **-ikävä**
home-sickness.
kotiin home; *jäädä* ~ stay at
h.; *tulla* ~ come h.; *jättää*
jtk ~ leave .. at home.
-kanto delivery. **-kutsuminen**
recall. **-lähetys** delivery. **-päin**
homeward [s]. **-tulo** return
home, home-coming.

koti|kaupunki home town.
-kieli language of [one's]
home. **-kissa** house-cat; *kuv.*
stay-at-home. **-kudonnainen**
hand-woven [goods],
(kansallinen) folkweave.
-kutoinen hand-woven; ~
kangas (m.) homespun. **-liesi**
[domestic] hearth; fireside.
kotilo *zo.* gastropod.
koti|lääkitys household remedy;
self-medication. **-lääkäri** family
doctor. **-maa** home country,
homeland; ~*n* .. domestic,
home, inland; ~*n uutiset*
home news. **-mainen** native;
home, domestic; ~ *teollisuus*
home industry; **-maista**
(suomalaista) valmistetta .. of
Finnish make. **-markkinat**
home market. **-matka** journey
home; way back; ~*lla* on the
way home; ~*lla oleva (et.*
laiva) homeward bound. **-mies**
(lastenkaitsija) baby-sitter.
-opettaja [private] tutor.
-opettajatar governess. **-paikka**
place of residence; domicile.
-rauhanrikkominen *l.v.*
invasion of privacy. **-rouva**
housewife. **-seutu** home area.
-takki smoking jacket. *(naisen)*
house-dress (-coat). **-talous**
home economics; (~**opettaja**
home economist;
~**opettajaopisto** college for
teachers of home economics).
-tarkastus house search;
toimittaa ~ *jssk* search a
house. **-tarve** household use.
-tehtävä homework, task.
-tekoinen home-made.
-teollisuus hand[i]craft,
homecrafts, home industries.
-uttaa disband; demobilize.
-utua come (arrive) home;
(tottua olemaan) make oneself
at home, feel at home;
become acclimatized; ~
kieleen be accepted in a
language. **-väki** *-väkeni* my
people, my family.
kotka eagle. **-nnenä** aquiline
nose. **-npesä** eagle's nest.
-npoika eaglet, young eagle.
-nsilmä eagle eye.
kotkata clinch.
kotko|ttaa, -tus cluck; cackle.

kotletti cutlet, chop.
koto home; ~a from h. **-inen**
homelike, cosy; .. on -sta it
is quite like home, it is nice
and comfortable; ~ sävel a
breath of home. **-isin:** ~ jstk
a native of ..; hän on ~
..sta he is (he comes) from
..; se ei ollut paljon mistään
~ it did not amount to
much. **-na** at home; ~ni at
home, in my home; hän ei
ollut ~ ajoissa he was not
home in time; ole kuin ~si!
make yourself at home!
kottarainen starling.
kottikärryt wheelbarrow.
kotva: ~n aikaa a while.
koukata hook; snatch; sot. out-
flank; (jääkiekk.) hook.
kouker|o flourish, curlicue.
-oinen winding, sinuous. **-rella**
wind, meander.
koukis|taa bend, bow. **-tua**
bend; become crooked (bent);
~maahan stoop down.
koukkaus (äkkikäännös, esim.
auton) swerve; urh. hooking.
koukku hook; (ripustin)
hanger; koukussa bent,
crooked. **-inen** crooked;
curved, bent. **-nenäinen**
hook-nosed. **-selkäinen**
round-shouldered, bowed.
koulu school; käydä ~a attend
s.; ~ssa in (t. at) s.; mennä
~un go to s.; olla (luvatta)
poissa ~sta play truant, stay
away from school. **-aine**
school subject. **-ateria** school
lunch. **-esimerkki** typical
example; object-lesson.
-hallitus National Board of
Education. **-ikä** school age.
-kasvatus education, schooling.
-kirja school-book. **-koti**
approved school, community
home, Am. reform school,
training school. **-kunta** school.
-lainen pupil, school-boy, -girl.
-laitos school system. **-laiva**
training ship. **-maksu** school
fee [s].
koulu|johtaja head [master],
principal. **-johtajatar**
head [-mistress]. **-käynti**
attending school, school
attendance. **-käynyt** educated;

trained. **-opettaja**
school-teacher, schoolmaster,
(~tar) schoolmistress.
koulu|nuoriso school-children,
those of school age. **-painos**
school edition. **-pakko**
compulsory school attendance.
-poika schoolboy. **-radio**
school broadcasting (~ohjelma
school programme). **-ratsastus**
dressage. **-sivistys** school
education. **-talo** school
building. **-tieto** book learning.
-todistus school report. **-toveri**
schoolfellow, schoolmate. **-ttaa**
educate; train; (taimia) prick
out (t. off), transplant; (tettu
sairaanhoitaja trained (Am.
graduate) nurse. **-ttaja**
instructor. **-tus** education,
schooling; training. **-tyttö**
schoolgirl. **-vuosi** school year.
koura fist, [hollow of the]
hand; kovin kourin with a
firm hand; jnk kourissa in
the grip of. **-antuntuva**
palpable, tangible. **-ista** grasp,
kuv. grip. **-llinen** handful.
kouris|taa: sydäntäni ~ .. it
wrings my heart (to). **-tus**
convulsion; cramp;
-tuksenomainen spasmodic,
convulsive.
kouru channel; (katto-) gutter;
(lasku-) spout.
kova hard; (ankara) severe;
strict; stern; harsh, unfeeling;
(äänestä) loud; ~ isku heavy
(hard) blow; ~ jano, nälkä
severe thirst (hunger); ~t
kannet (kirjan) boards; ~
kilpailu severe (keen)
competition; ~ kuumuus
intense heat; ~ myrsky
[strong] gale, storm; ~ onni
hard luck; ~ raha hard cash,
coin; ~ tuuli strong wind; ~
vauhti great (high) speed;
~ksi keitetty hard-boiled; ~lla
äänellä in a loud voice,
loud [ly]; ~n linjan mies
hard-liner; (oppia) ~ssa
koulussa [learn] the hard
way; hän on kokenut kovia
he has endured many
hardships; jos ~lle ottaa if it
comes to a pinch. **-kour|ainen**
heavy-handed; rough; pidellä

k-aisesti handle roughly. **-kumi** vulcanite. **-levy** hardboard, *(puolikova)* medium board. **-kuoriainen** beetle. **-naamainen** hard-faced. **-osainen** unlucky, hapless. **-pintainen** *kuv.* hard-boiled. **-päinen** thick-headed, dull-witted. **-pää** blockhead. **-sin** whetstone; hone. **-sti** severely, heavily, very much; *tehdä työtä (yrittää)* ~ work (try) hard; ~ *mielissään* greatly pleased, very [much] pleased. **-sydäminen** hard-hearted, uncharitable. **-vatsainen** constipated. **-ääninen** loud, noisy; *vrt. kaiutin.*

kove|mmin harder *jne.;* louder; *puhua* ~ speak louder. **-ntaa** make harder, make heavier, *(esim. ehtoja)* harden; *(lisätä)* increase.

kover|a hollow; concave. **-taa** hollow [out], scoop out, gouge [out]. **-uus** concavity.

kove|ta harden, become hard; become solid. **-ttaa** harden *(m. kuv.)* **-ttua** *ks. koveta;* *(paatua)* become callous. **-ttuma** *(kädessä ym)* callus, induration.

kovike *(-kangas)* buckram.

kovin very; *(ylen)* extremely, exceedingly; *ei ~kaan suuri* not particularly big.

kovistaa *(jkta)* bring pressure to bear upon .., press; *(nuhdella)* take .. to task.

kovuus hardness; severity; *(äänen)* loudness.

kraatteri crater.

kranaat|ti shell; *(käsi-)* hand-grenade. **-inheitin** mortar.

krapu *ks. rapu; Kravun kääntöpiiri* the Tropic of Cancer.

krapula hangover. **-ryyppy** hair of the dog.

krassi nasturtium, *(vihannes-)* garden cress.

kravatti *ks. solmio.*

kreditiivi letter of credit.

Kreeta Crete.

kreikan kieli Greek.

Kreikka Greece. **k-lainen** *s. & a.* Greek; *a.* Grecian; **k-laiskatolinen kirkko** [the

Greek] Orthodox Church.

kreivi count; *Engl.* earl ~*n aikaan* in the nick of time. **-kunta** *Engl.* county. **-tär** countess.

krematorio crematory.

Kreml the Kremlin.

kreppi crepe, crêpe. **-nailon** crepe nylon, stretch nylon. **-paperi** crepe paper.

kretonki cretonne; *(kiilto-)* chintz.

kriikuna bullace.

kriisi crisis *(pl.* crises).

kriit|illinen, -tinen critical.

krike|tti cricket; *-tin pelaaja* cricketer.

Krim the Crimea; ~*n sota* the Crimean war.

kriminnahka Persian lamb.

krinoliini crinoline.

kristalli crystal; cut glass. **-nkirkas** crystal [-clear], crystalline.

kristi|kunta Christendom. **-llinen** Christian. **-llisyys, -noppi** Christianity. **-nusko** Christian faith; *kääntyttää ~on* convert to Christianity.

Krist|us Christ; *ennen -uksen syntymää* before C. (B.C.); *jälkeen -uksen syntymän* anno Domini (A.D.).

kriteeri criter|ion *(pl.* ia).

kritiikki criticism; critique.

kroketti croquet. **-nuija** mallet.

krokotiili crocodile.

kromi chromium. **-keltainen** chrome yellow. **-tettu** chromium-plated.

kronikka chronicle.

kronometri chronometer.

krooninen chronic.

kruuna|amaton uncrowned. **-jaiset** coronation [ceremony] **-ta** crown; *hänet -ttiin kuninkaaksi* he was crowned king. **-us** coronation.

kruunu crown; *(aatelis-)* coronet; *(katto-)* chandelier, *(kristalli-)* lustre; *luopua ~sta* abdicate; ~ *vai klaava* heads or tails.

kruunun|perillinen successor to the throne. **-perimys** succession [to the throne]. **-prinssi, -prinsessa** Crown Prince (Princess). **-tavoittelija**

claimant to the throne,
pretender. **-vouti** bailiff.
kud|e weft; *panna kangas
kuteelle* loom a web. **-elma**
woven fabric. **-in** knitting.
-onn|ainen textile [fabric];
-aiset textiles. **-os** woven
fabric; weave, texture; *anat.*
tissue.
kuha pike-perch. **-nkeittäjä**
[golden] oriole.
kuherrus cooing. **-kuukausi**
honeymoon.
kuhertaa coo.
kuhilas [corn] shock.
kuhista *(vilistä)* swarm.
kuhmu bump, lump. **-inen**
bumpy, *(lommoinen)* buckled.
kuhn|ailla loiter, lag; dawdle;
-aileva loitering, dilatory,
sluggish. **-uri** *zo.* drone; *vrt
seur.* **-us** sluggard.
kuih|duttaa wear away, wear
down. **-tua** wither [away],
wilt; *(ihmisistä)* pine [away];
-tunut withered, faded.
kuikka black-throated diver,
Am. arctic loon.
kuilu cleft, gorge; *(syvä)* abyss,
chasm; *(hissin)* shaft; *(kuv.
esim. luottamus~)* gap.
kuin as; like; *(komp. jälj.)*
than; *(ikäänkuin)* as if, as
though; *niin suuri* ~ as big
as; *kolme kertaa enemmän* ~
three times as many as;
toisenlainen ~ different from;
hän ei muuta ~ *itki* she did
nothing but weep. **-ka** how;
~ *ikävää!* what a pity! ~
niin? why? how so? ~ *voit? how*
are you? ~ *hän koettikin*
however he tried, no matter
how much he tried; *vaikka
suuttuisin* ~ however cross I
get; *sehän on tarkoituksesi,
vai~?* that's what you mean,
isn't it?
kuiska|aja *teatt.* prompter. **-illa**
whisper. **-ta** whisper; *teatt.
ym* prompt; *-ten* in a
whisper. **-us** whisper.
kuisti porch. **-kko** veranda [h].
kuita|ta receipt; *-ttu* receipted;
-taan (maksetuksi) paid;
received [with thanks]; *asia
on on sillä -ttu* that squares
(settles) the matter.

kuiten|kaan: *ei* ~ not ..
however, not .. anyway; *(hän
lupasi) eikä* ~ *tullut* .. and
yet he did not come. **-kin**
however; *(sittenkin)* still,
[and] yet; *(siitä huolimatta)*
nevertheless, for all that;
kiitoksia ~ thank you just
the same.
kuitti receipt, acknowledgement
[in writing]; *nyt olemme
kuitit* now we are quits.
kuitu fibre, *Am.* fiber.
-kangas non-woven fabric. **-levy**
[wood] fibreboard, fibre
[-building] board, wallboard,
(eristys-) insulating board.
kuiv|a dry *(m. kuv.); (seutu)*
arid; ~ *ruoka* solid food; *-in
jaloin* with [my] feet dry;
päästä ~lle (maalle) reach dry
land; *kuin kala ~lla maalla*
like a fish out of water;
juosta -iin run dry, be
drained; *kiehua -iin* boil dry;
joki on -illaan the river has
dried up. **-aa:** *suutani* ~ my
mouth feels parched.
kuiva|kiskoinen dry,
uninteresting, dull. **-ta** dry;
(ojittamalla) drain; *(pyyhkiä)*
wipe. **-telakka** dry-dock. **-ttaa**
dry; *(ojittamalla)* drain;
(lihaa) cure. **-tus** drying;
draining.
kuivaus|laite dryer. **-linko** spin
dryer. **-teline**, **-hylly** *(astiain)*
draining board.
kuiv|ettua dry [up], become
parched; *(jäsen ym)* wither,
atrophy. **-ua** become dry; dry;
(joki ym) dry up; *(ehtyä)* run
dry. **-uus** dryness; *(kuiva sää)*
drought.
kuja lane; alley [way]. **-nne:**
muodostaa ~ *(kadulle)* line
[the street].
kuje prank; trick, lark;
~et trickery. **-illa**
banter, be up to tricks (to
mischief). **-ilu** tricks, mischief;
(~nhaluinen mischief-loving).
kuka who; *ketkä* who *(pl.);
keitä siellä oli?* who was
there? ~ *siellä* who is there?
who is it? *olipa* ~ *tahansa*
whoever it may be; ~ *heistä*
which of them? **-an** anybody,

any one; *ei ~* no one; nobody; *ei ~ heistä* none of them; *~ muu* anybody else.

kukallinen flowered; flowery.

kukin everybody, everyone, each; *~ heistä* each [one] of them; *he lähtivät ~ taholleen* they went their several ways.

kuki|nta flowering, bloom. **-nto** blossom, inflorescence.

kukis|taa subdue; subjugate; *(kapina)* suppress, quell; *(kaataa)* overthrow; *(voittaa)* vanquish. **-tua** be overthrown; fall; *-tunut* overthrown. **-tuminen** fall, overthrow.

kukittaa strew with flowers, *(koristaa)* adorn with flowers.

kukka flower, blossom; *olla kukassa* be in bloom (flower); *puhjeta ~an* burst *(t.* come) into blossom. **-kaali** cauliflower. **-kauppa** florist's, flower shop. **-kauppias** florist. **-kimppu** bunch of flowers, bouquet. **-laite** basket of flowers. **-maa** flower-bed. **-näyttely** flower show.

kukkaro purse; *jos ~ sallii* if I can afford it; *se on liikaa minun kukkarolleni* it is beyond my pocket.

kukka|ruukku flower-pot. **-seppele** wreath; garland. **-vihko** bunch of flowers, bouquet.

kukkas|kieli flowery language. **-viljelys** floriculture.

kukk|ea flourishing; fresh, rosy; *on ~eimmillaan* is in full bloom. **-ia** flower, bloom, *(et. hedelmäpuista)* blossom; *.. -ivat ..* are out.

kukko cock. **-kiekuu** cock-a-doodle-doo. **-poikanen** cockerel. **-taistelu** cock-fight.

kukkua cuckoo; *käki kukkuu* the cuckoo is calling.

kukkul|a hill; *valtansa -oilla* at the height of one's power. **kukkura:** *~llaan* brimful; *kaiken ~ksi* to crown the lot. **-inen** *(lusikka)* heaped.

kukois|taa bloom, *kuv.* flourish, prosper, thrive; *-tava* blooming, *kuv.* thriving, flourishing. **-tus** bloom[ing], *kuv. m.* prime; *(~kausi*

period of prosperity; golden age).

kukon|harja cockscomb. **-kannus** cockspur. **-laulu** crow of a cock; *~n aikaan* at cock-crow,

kulaus draught, gulp, pull [at the bottle].

kulho bowl, basin; [deep] dish.

kulissi scene, *(sivu-)* wing; *~t takana* behind the scenes.

kulje|ksia wander [about]; roam, rove; stroll, ramble; *-skeleva* wandering.

kuljetta|a transport; carry, convey, haul. **-ja** *(auton)* driver; *(junan)* train driver.

kuljetus transport[ation], carriage, conveyance, hauling; *(maantie-)* road haulage; *~ maksetaan perillä* carriage forward; *~ ovelta ovelle* door-to-door transport. **-hihna** conveyor belt. **-kirja** consignment note. **-kustannus** cost of transport. **-lentokone** transport airplane. **-liike** *(yhtiö)* carriers, haulage company. **-maksu** transport charges; carriage, freight. **-välineet** means of transport.

kulkea go; walk; *(matkata)* travel; *(kuljeskella)* stroll, ramble; *(~ohi)* pass; *~ jalan* go on foot, walk; *~ toista kautta (tietä)* take another road; *katu -ee idästä länteen* the street runs east and west; *laiva -ee A:n ja B:n väliä* the steamer plies between A. and B.; *kuljettu matka* the distance covered. **-eutua** be carried; drift. **-ija** wanderer; vagabond.

kulku going; course; run; *(läpi-)* passage; *joen ~* the course of the river; *junain ~ on muuttunut* the train schedules have been changed; *tapausten ~* the course of events; *asian ~ oli seuraava* it happened in the following way. **-e** procession. **-kauppias** pedlar, huckster. **-kelpoinen** fit for traffic; *(joki)* navigable. **-kelvoton** impassable, untrafficable. **-laitos** communications; *(~*

ministeriö Ministry of Transport.). **-nen** sleigh-bell. **-neuvo(t)** [means of] conveyance. **-nopeus** speed. **-puhe** idle talk; *(kuulema)* hearsay. **-ri** tramp; vagabond, vagrant. **-tauti** epidemic. **-vuoro(t)** service. **-väylä** passage, thoroughfare, navigable waterway; *(liike-)* traffic route.

kullan|himo thirst for gold. **-huuhdonta** gold-washing. **-kaivaja** gold-digger. **-keltainen** golden. **-muru** dear, darling, ducky. **-tekijä** alchemist. **-teko** alchemy. **-värinen** golden, gold-coloured.

kullata gild; *kullattu* gilt, [silver] overlaid with gold.

kulloin|enkin at a (at any) given time. **-kin** at each time; at the time.

kulma angle; *(nurkka)* corner; *katsoa ~insa alta* frown, scowl (at). **-hammas** canine. **-inen** *(yhd.)* -angled; -cornered. **-karvat** eyebrows. **-kivi** corner-stone. **-rauta** angle-iron. **-talo** corner house. **-us** corner. **-viivoitin** set square.

kulmi|kas angular. **-o** *(yhd.)* -gon; *kuusi ~* hexagon. **-ttain** cornerwise.

kulo forest fire; *~ntorjunta* fighting of forest fires. **-ttaa** burn over. **-valkea** *kuv.* wildfire. **-varoitus** forest fire warning.

kulta gold; *kuv.* darling, sweetheart; *~seni (m.)* love, sweetie, honey; *lapsi ~* dear child! **-aika** golden age. **-ehto** gold clause. **-harkko** gold ingot. **-häät** golden wedding. **-inen** gold, golden. **-jyvä** grain of gold. **-kaivos** gold-mine. **-kala** gold-fish. **-kanta** gold standard; *luopua -kannasta* go off the g. s. **-kello** gold watch. **-kuume** gold-fever. **-mitali** gold medal. **-pitoinen** .. containing gold. **-pitoisuus** gold content. **-raha** gold coin. **-sankainen** gold-rimmed. **-seppä** goldsmith; *(myymälä)* jeweller's. **-silaus** gilding.

-sormus gold ring. **-us** gilding; gilt. **-vitjat** gold chain.

kulttuuri culture; civilization. **-elämä** cultural life. **-historia** history of culture (civilization).

kulu: *ajan ~ksi* to pass the time.

kulu|a be worn, wear [away]; *(ajasta)* pass, go by, elapse; *(tulla käytetyksi)* be used up; *~ loppuun* wear out, become worn out; *~ umpeen* draw to a close, *(päättyä)* expire; *kuta pitemmälle yö -i* as night drew on; *siihen -u aikaa* it takes time. **-essa:** *aikojen ~* in the course (process) of time; *matkan ~* during the trip; *vuoden ~* within a year; *(tämän vuoden)* in the course of this year. **-minen** wear [and tear].

kulunki cost; expense; *kulungit* expenditure. **-tili** expense account.

kulunut worn-out, shabby, threadbare; *kuv.* hackneyed, stale, well-worn; *viimeksi ~ vuosi* the past year.

kulut cost[s], expenses; *(omat)* kulunne your charges; *kuluista välittämättä* regardless of cost.

kulu|ttaa consume; *(vaatteita)* wear; *(käyttää)* use; *(et. rahaa)* spend, expend, *jhk* on; *(aikaa)* pass, spend; *~ hukkaan* waste; *~ loppuun* wear out; use up, exhaust. **-ttaja** consumer; *~valistus* consumer guidance. **-ttava** *(työ)* exhausting. **-ttua** after; *tunnin ~* in an hour ['s time]; *vuoden ~* after a year, a year from now. **-tus** consumption; use; *(kuluminen)* wear [and tear]; *(~osuuskunta* consumers' co-operative society; *~pinta* [tyre] tread *~tavarat* consumer goods; *kesto~* durable consumer goods. **-va:** *~ kuu* the current month, this month; *~ vuosi* the current year.

kumah|dus dull sound; boom. **-taa** boom, *(kello)* toll.

kumar|a bent, bowed; round-shouldered. **-rus, -taa**

bow. **-tua** bow [down], stoop [down]; *(äkkiä)* duck.
kumea dull, hollow.
kumi rubber, *(pyyhe-, m.)* india-rubber; gum. **-hansikas** rubber glove. **-kangas** rubber cloth. **-liima** gum; rubber glue.
kumina caraway.
kumi|nauha elastic; rubber band. **-nen** [.. of] rubber. **-pallo** rubber ball. **-pihka** gum resin. **-pohja** rubber sole. **-puu** rubber tree. **-rengas** *(pyörän)* tyre, *Am.* tire. **-saappaat** rubber-boots. **-tossu** rubber-soled shoe, gym shoe.
kumma: ~ *kyllä* oddly (curiously, strangely) enough; ~*ko*, *jos* .. no wonder if; *mitä* ~*a sinä puhut* what ever are you talking about? *sepä* ~*a* how odd! how strange! **-ksua, -stella** be surprised, be astonished (at), wonder (at). **-llinen** curious; strange, odd, queer; *-llisen* curiously, peculiarly. **-llisuus** strangeness, oddness. **-stua** be surprised, be astonished (at). **-tus** astonishment, amazement. **-tuttaa** surprise, astonish, fill with wonder.
kummi godfather, godmother; sponsor; *olla jkn* ~*na* stand sponsor for ..
kumminkin yet, nevertheless.
kummi|nlahja christening present. **-poika** godson. **-setä, -täti** *ks. kummi.* **-tytär** goddaughter.
kummi|tella haunt [a house, *talossa*]; *tässä talossa -ttelee* this house is haunted. **-tus** ghost; spook; (~*juttu* ghost-story).
kummuta: ~ *esiin* well forth (out, up).
kumoam|aton irrefutable. **-inen** annulment.
kumo|llaan upside down, overturned, *(vene)* capsized. **-on:** *ajaa (joku)* ~ knock down, run down; *kaataa* ~ upset, overturn; *mennä* ~ turn over; *purjehtia* ~ capsize; *äänestää* ~ vote down.
kumo|ta cancel, annul, nullify,

(laki) repeal, revoke, *(väite)* refute; ~ *päätös* overrule a decision; ~ *uutinen* deny a piece of news; ~ *vaali* declare an election invalid. **-uksellinen** *a.* subversive, *a. & s.* revolutionary. **-us** overthrow, *(vallan-)* revolution.
kumpi which [of the two]? ~ *on vanhempi* which is the older one? ~ *tahansa* either [one], whichever [you like]; *kumman haluat* which [one] do you want? **-kaan:** *ei* ~ *heistä* neither of them. **-kin** each [of the two]; *(molemmat)* both; *kummallakin puolen* on either side, on both sides; ~ *on yhtä hyvä* one is as good as the other; *yksi kumpaakin lajia* one of each kind.
kumppa|ni companion; *(liike-)* partner; *N. ja* ~ N. & Co. **-nus:** *he ovat -nukset* they are [close] companions, *ark.* they are chums. **-nuus** fellowship; *(liike-)* partnership.
kumpu hill, knoll, hillock.
kun when; as; ~ *sitä vastoin* whereas; ~ *taas* while, whereas; *sillä aikaa* ~ while; ~ *olin tullut kotiin* .. after reaching home, on getting home.
kuningas king. **-kunta** kingdom. **-mielinen** royalist. **-mielisyys** royalism. **-suku** line of kings; royal family.
kuningatar queen.
kuninkaalli|nen royal, regal; *-set (henkilöt)* royalty.
kuninkaan|kruunu royal crown. **-linna** royal castle. **-poika** royal prince.
kuninkuus royalty, kingship.
kunnalli|nen municipal; [local] council, corporation; ~ *koulu* council school; ~ *asuintalo* council house.
kunnallis|asetus local-government act. **-hallinto** local government. **-koti** *(vanhain-)* local authority home. **-tekniikka** public utilities. **-vaalit** local government elections. **-verot** *Engl.* rates. *Am.* local taxes.

kunnan|lääkäri Medical Officer of Health. **-valtuusto** local government council, municipal council. **-virkailija** local government officer.

kunnas hill [ock], knoll.

kunnes till, until; ~ *toisin ilmoitetaan* until further notice.

kunnia honour; glory; *jnk (jkn)* ~ksi in honour of; *hänen* ~kseen (m.) to his credit; *se on hänelle* ~ksi it does him credit; *kautta* ~ni upon my honour! *pitää* ~ssa hold in respect, honour; *tehdä* ~a salute, *(kiväärillä)* present arms; ~a *loukkaava* libellous, slanderous; *(suorittaa jtk)* ~lla [perform a task] creditably; *sain kuulla* ~ni *häneltä* he gave me a piece of his mind. **-asia** matter (point) of honour. **-jäsen** honorary member. **-kas** glorious; illustrious; ~ *rauha* an honourable peace. **-kierros** lap of honour. **-kirja** diploma. **-komppania** guard of honour. **-konsuli** honorary consul. **-kuja:** *muodostaa* ~ form a guard of honour, be lined up [in the street]. **-laukaus** salute; *ammuttiin 21* ~ta a 21-gun s. was fired. **-legioona** Legion of·Honour. **-llinen** honourable; honest, decent; ~ *mies (m.)* a man of honour. **-llisuus** honourableness; . honesty, respectability. **-maininta** honourable mention. **-merkki** decoration; *saada* ~ be decorated.

kunnian|arvoinen venerable; worthy. **-arvoisuus** venerableness. **-himo** ambition; ambitiousness. **-himoinen** ambitious. **-loukkaus** libel; *(suullinen)* slander. **-osoit|us** honour, homage; *suurin k-uksin* with great honours. **-teko** *sot.* salute; *seistä* ~asennossa *(haudalla ym)* stand to attention, *(sot.)* stand at the salute. **-tunto** sense of honour.

kunnia|paikka place (seat) of honour. **-palkinto** highest

honours. **-portti** triumphal arch. **-porvari** honorary citizen. **-päivä** day of glory. **-sana** word of honour; ~lla on one's [word of] honour, *(sot.)* on parole. **-tohtori** doctor h. c. (honoris causae); *hänet vihittiin* ~ksi he received the honorary degree of Ph.D., D.Ph[il.] *ym.* **-ton** infamous; dishonourable. **-ttomuus** infamy, dishonour. **-vartio** guard of honour. **-velka** debt of honour. **-vieras** guest of honour. **-virka** honorary office.

kunnioi|tettava honoured, respected, esteemed. **-ttaa** honour; esteem; respect; *(juhlia)* do homage to. **-ttava** respectful; ~sti with respect, *(liik.)* yours faithfully, *(tutummalle)* yours sincerely, *Am.* respectfully yours, very truly yours. **-tus** respect, esteem, regard; *(syvä)* reverence, veneration; *-tuksen osoitus* homage, tribute; *kaikella -tuksella* with due respect.

kunnolli|nen good, decent; respectable; *(oikea)* proper. **-sesti** ably; properly.

kunnon: ~ *ateria* a square meal; ~ *mies* a fine (decent) fellow. **-ssa** *ks. kunto;* (~**pito** maintenance, upkeep).

kunnos|taa recondition, do up; repair, adjust, put in order, overhaul. **-tautua** distinguish oneself, make one's mark.

kunnoton good-for-nothing; wretched, worthless.

kunpa if only! ~ *hän tulisi!* I wish she would come!

kunta local authority [area], municipality, urban *(maalla* rural) district; *Am. m.* township; ~ *maksaa* the local authorities pay; *kunnan palveluksessa oleva* local government employee.

kunto *(tila)* condition, state; order; *urh.* form; *hyvässä kunnossa* in good condition, in good shape (repair), *(terve)* fit, *(urh.)* in good form; *mainiossa kunnossa* splendidly fit, *(urh.)* in fine (excellent) form; *huonossa kunnossa* in bad condition, in bad repair, out of repair, *(urh.)* off form; *en tunne olevani kunnossa* I don't feel [quite] up to the mark; *laittaa ~on* put in [working] order, put right; *pitää kunnossa* keep in good repair; *hänellä ei ole kunnon nuttua* he has not a decent coat. **-isuus** condition, fitness; *(~luokka* fitness class, *(paras)* highest category). **-koulu** keep-fit school. **-pyörä** exercise [bi]cycle. **-uttaa** rehabilitate. **-utus** rehabilitation.

kuohah|dus agitation; *vihan ~* fit of anger. **-taa** boil; *(kiivastua)* flare up.

kuohi|las eunuch. **-ta** castrate.

kuohkea loose, light, mellow; *vrt.* **möyheä.**

kuohu foam; *(hyrsky)* surge; *kevät~t (joen)* spring spate. **-a** surge; *(kiehua)* boil [over]; *(juomasta)* effervesce. **-kerma** whipped cream. **-s:** *olla -ksissa* be agitated, be worked up. **-ttaa:** *~ mieliä* stir up emotion. **-va** foaming; bubbling, sparkling.

kuokk|a hoe; *(~vieras* uninvited guest, gate-crasher). **-ia** hoe [up weeds].

kuola slobber, slaver. **-imet** bit. **-lappu** bib. **-ta** slobber, dribble.

kuolema death; *(poistuminen)* decease; *~n kielissä* at the point of death, at death's door; *en ~kseni voi* .. I cannot for the life of me ..

kuoleman|pelko fear of death. **-rangaist|us** capital punishment; *k-uksen uhalla* under pain (penalty) of death. **-sairas** mortally ill (sick). **-sairaus** fatal illness. **-synti** deadly sin. **-syy** cause of death; *~n tutkimus* [coroner's] inquest. **-tapaus** [case of] death. **-tuomio** death-sentence; *(allekirjoittaa)* ~ sign a death-warrant. **-tuottamus** [involuntary] manslaughter.

kuolema|ton immortal. **-ttomuus** immortality.

kuole|ttaa deaden; *vrt.* *puuduttaa; (laina ym)* amortize; *(maksaa)* pay off; *(asiakirja)* cancel, declare invalid. **-ttava** deadly; mortal, fatal, lethal. **-ttavasti** mortally, fatally. **-tus** *(lainan ym)* amortization, paying off; *vrt.* *puudutus; (~laina* loan repayable by instalments; *~rahasto* sinking fund). **-utua** become numb (insensitive). **-vainen** *a. & s.* mortal. **-vaisuus** mortality; *vrt.* *kuolleisuus.*

kuoliaaksi: *ampua ~* shoot .. dead; *lyödä ~* strike .. dead, slay; *paleltua ~* freeze to death.

kuolin|haava mortal wound. **-ilmoitus** obituary *(t.* death) notice. **-isku** mortal blow. **-kamppailu** death-struggle. **-kello** passing-bell. **-naamio** death-mask. **-pesä** estate of a deceased person. **-päivä** *(muisto)* anniversary of a p.'s death. **-todistus** death certificate. **-vaate** shroud. **-vuode** death-bed.

kuolio *lääk.* gangrene, necrosis; *joutua ~on (lentok.)* stall.

kuolla die; pass away, expire; *~ jhk (tautiin)* die of (from); *(luonnollinen kuolema)* die a natural death; *~ haavoihinsa* die from one's wounds; *~ sukupuuttoon* die out; *kuolemaisillaan* dying, at the point of death.

kuolleisuus death-rate, mortality.

kuollut dead; deceased; *kuolleena syntynyt* still-born; *oli kuolleessa pisteessä* had reached deadlock, was at a stalemate; *nousta kuolleista* rise from the dead; *on ~ is dead, (perf.)* has died; *K~meri* the Dead Sea; *Kuolleen meren kääröt* the D.S. scrolls.

kuolon|enkeli angel of death. **-hiljaisuus** dead silence. **-kalpea** deathly pale. **-tuska** mortal agony.

kuomu hood, [collapsible] top.

kuona slag, *m. kuv.* dross.

kuono muzzle; nose; *(kärsä)* snout. **-inen:** *tylppä~* blunt-nosed. **-karvat** whiskers. **-koppa** muzzle; *varustaa -kopalla* muzzle.

kuontalo [unkempt] mop of hair.

kuopia dig, burrow; ~ *maata (hevonen)* paw the ground.

kuoppa pit; *(pieni)* hole; *(poskessa)* dimple; *(syvennys)* hollow; *kuopalla olevat posket* hollow cheeks. **-inen** *(tie)* bumpy; *(merimatka, tie)* rough. **-silmäinen** hollow-eyed.

kuopus youngest child.

kuore *zo.* smelt.

kuori 1. *(kirkon)* chancel, choir. **2.** *(munan ym)* shell; *(hedelmän)* peel, fruit skin; hull, husk; crust; *(puun)* bark; *(kellon)* case; *(perunan)* peel, jacket; *keittää perunat ~neen* boil potatoes in their skins; *kovan kuoren alla (kuv.)* under (his) hard exterior. **-a** peel, *(omena, m.)* pare, *(muna ym)* shell; hull, *(viljaa)* husk, *(puu)* bark, *(maitoa)* skim [the cream off the milk]; **-ttu maito** skim milk **-ainen** beetle. **-kerros** *lääk.* cortex. **-maton** unpeeled; *(maito)* unskimmed, whole [milk]. **-utua** hatch out.

kuorma load; *(taakka)* burden; *purkaa* ~ unload. **-aja, -in** loader. **-auto** [motor] lorry, *Am.* truck; *(umpi-)* motor van. **-hevonen** draught-horse. **-sto** transport [column]. *Am.* baggage; *(huolto)* service corps. **-ta** load. **-us** loading.

kuormi|ttaa load, charge. **-tus** load [ing] (**~kyky** load capacity).

kuoro choir; *(oopperan ym)* chorus. **-lainen** member of a choir. **-laulu** choral singing. **-njohtaja** leader of a choir. **-poika** choir-boy.

kuorru|ttaa *keitt.* ice. **-tus** icing.

kuorsa|ta snore. **-us** snoring, snore.

kuosi pattern, design; *(muoti)* fashion; style; *tämä on viimeistä ~a* this is the newest style (latest fashion).

-kas elegant; fashionable, stylish. **-kkuus** stylishness.

kuovi *zo.* curlew.

kupari copper. **-kaivos** coppermine. **-lanka** copper wire. **-nen** [. . of] copper. **-piirros** copperplate. **-raha** copper [coin].

kupata cup.

kuper|a convex. **-keikka** somersault; *heittää ~a* turn a somersault. **-uus** convexity.

kupillinen cupful, a cup of . .

kupla bubble.

kupletti comic song.

kupo sheaf *(pl.)* sheaves).

kupoli cupola, dome.

kuponki coupon.

kuppari cupper.

kuppatauti syphilis. **-nen** syphilitic.

kuppi cup. **-kunta** clique. **-la** [coffee] bar, café.

kupsahtaa: *kaatua* ~ tumble down, *(pyörtyneenä)* keel over; *kuolla* ~ kick the bucket.

kupu *(linnun)* crop, craw; *(lampun)* shade; *(kaalin)* head; *(kupoli)* dome; *(hatun)* crown. **-kaali** cabbage. **-katto** cupola, dome.

kura mud; mire. **-inen** muddy; miry. **-isuus** muddiness. **-suojus** mudguard. **-ta** dirty, soil.

kureliivi corset, stays.

kuri discipline; *ruumiillinen* ~ corporal punishment; *pitää ~ssa* hold in check; *pitää kovaa ~a* maintain strict discipline; *totella* ~a toe the line; *~llaan* for a joke, for fun; out of mischief.

kuriiri courier; *~postissa* by diplomatic bag.

kurikka club.

kurimus maelstrom, whirlpool.

kurin|alainen disciplined. **-pidollinen** disciplinary. **-pito** discipline; *(~rikkomus* breach of d.). **-pitäjä** [strict] disciplinarian.

kurista croak; *(vatsa)* rumble.

kuris|taa strangle; *tekn.* throttle; *rintaani* ~ I feel choked. **-tus** strangling; *(~läppä* throttle; *~tauti* croup).

kuri|ton undisciplined; unmanageable, unruly. **-ttaa** discipline; *(lyödä)* thrash, whip; *kuv.* chastise. **-ttomuus** want of discipline, indiscipline.

kuritus [corporal] punishment; *kuv.* chastisement. **-huone** convict prison, *(-rangaistus)* imprisonment [with hard labour], *Am.* penitentiary; *(~vanki* convict).

kurja miserable, wretched; pitiable; ~ *ilma* nasty weather.

kurjen|miekka iris. **-polvi** *bot.* crane's-bill, geranium.

kurjuus misery, wretchedness; *(köyhyys)* poverty, destitution.

kurki crane; *(auran)* handles. **-hirsi** ridge-pole.

kurkis|taa peep; peer, have a look. **-tusreikä** peep-hole.

kurkku 1. *(kasvi)* cucumber. **2.** *anat.* throat; ~*ni on kipeä* I have a sore throat; *täyttä ~a* at the top of one's voice; *kiljuivat täyttä ~a* screamed their heads off; *itku kurkussa* on the verge of tears. **-ajos** quinsy **-mätä** diphtheria. **-ääni** guttural sound; *kiel.* guttural.

kurkottaa stretch [one's neck to see ..], reach out (for, *jtk ottaaksesen);* crane [forward, out of the window]; ~ *päätänsä ym* stretch up [one's head, one's arm].

kurkun|kansi epiglottis. **-pää** larynx.

kurlata gargle.

kurn|ia: *vatsaani -ii* my stomach is rumbling. **-uttaa** croak.

kuro|a gather, pucker [up]. **-utuma** stricture, strangulation.

kurpitsa gourd, pumpkin.

kurppa woodcock.

kursai|lematon unceremonious, free and easy. **-lla** stand on ceremony, *(turhia)* be unduly formal; *-lematta* without [any] ceremony. **-lu** ceremony.

kursi|ivi italics. **-voida** italicize, print in italics.

kurssi course; *(kauppa-)* [rate of] exchange, rate; *päivän ~in* at the current rate of exchange; *virallisen ~in* at the official rate; *mikä on punnan ~* what is the rate of exchange for the pound. **-ilmoitus** quotation. **-kirjat** set books. **-lainen** person attending a course. **-nalennus** fall in rate. **-nnousu** advance in rate. **-tappio** loss on exchange. **-vaihtelu** exchange fluctuation.

kurttu *(ihossa)* wrinkle; *(vaatteessa ym)* crease; *olla kurtussa* be wrinkled; *mennä ~un* get wrinkled, *(otsa)* pucker up. **-inen** wrinkled; *(puku ym)* creased, crumpled.

kurvikas *leik.* curvaceous.

kustannus expense, cost; *k-ukset* charges, expenditure; *jnk k-uksella* at the cost (expense) of; *jnk välittömät k-ukset* prime cost; *kirja ilmestyy S:n k-uksella* the book is published by S. **-arvio** [cost] estimate. **-hinta:** ~*an* at cost. **-liike** publishing firm. **-oikeus** copyright, publishing rights.

kustan|taa pay for, , pay the cost of; defray the expenses of; *(kirja)* publish; *sen voin itselleni* ~ I can afford that; *-nan sinulle päivällisen* I shall treat you to dinner. **-taja** *(kirjan)* publisher. **-tamo** publishing house.

kuta: ~ .. *sitä* the .. the. **-kuinkin** fairly, tolerably; ~ *toivoton* rather hopeless.

kutea spawn.

kuten as, like; ~ *ennen* as before; ~ *isäsi* like your father ..; ~ *haluat* as you like, [you can do the job] how you like, the way you like; ~ *(oli) sovittu* as agreed upon.

kuti: *ei pidä ~aan* does not hold good.

kuti|ava ticklish. **-na** itch [ing]. **-sta** tickle, itch.

kutis|taa shrink. **-tua** shrink: *(vähiin)* dwindle; *lääk. ym* contract; *-tunut* shrunk, shrunken **-tumisvara** allowance for shrinkage.

kutittaa tickle.

kutku tickling, tickle;

itch[ing]. -ta feel ticklish; itch.

kuto|a weave; *neuloa* knit. -ja weaver; *(käsin)* handloom weaver; *(sukan)* knitter.

kutoma|kone [machine] loom, *(neuloma)*- knitting machine. -teollisuus textile industry.

kutomo textile mill.

kutri lock, curl.

kutsu invitation; call; *(määräävä)* summons: ~t party; *pitää* ~t give a party. -a call; *(virallisesti)* summon; *(vieraaksi)* invite, ask [to dinner etc.]; ~ *sisälle* ask sb. in; ~ *kotiinsa* invite sb. home; ~ *koolle (kokous)* convene; ~ *lääkäri* call in a doctor; ~ *nimeltä* call .. by name; ~ *takaisin* call .. back, recall; *-in hänet luokseni* I invited him to my house, I asked him to come and see me. -kortti invitation card. -maton uninvited. -merkki call-sign. -mus calling, vocation; ~*tietoisuus* sense of mission. -nta enrolment for military service, draft [call]. -ääni *(eläimen)* mating call.

kutteri cutter.

kutu spawning. -aika spawning time.

kuu moon; *(-kausi)* month; *tässä* ~*ssa* [during] this month; ~*n kehä* lunar halo; ~*hun lasku* moon landing; ~*hunlaskeutumisalus* lunar module.

Kuuba Cuba; k-lainen Cuban.

kuuden|kertainen sixfold; sextuple. -nes sixth [part].

kuudes [the] sixth. -kymmenes [the] sixtieth. -toista [the] sixteenth.

kuukausi month; *12 puntaa k-udessa* £ 12 a month; *kolmeksi k-udeksi* for three months. -julkaisu monthly [publication]. -määrä: *-määriä, -määriin* for months. -palkka monthly salary. -raha monthly allowance. -ttain monthly, every month.

kuukauti|nen monthly; *-set* menses, menstruation.

kuula *(luoti)* bullet; *työntää* ~*a* put the shot.

kuula|kas, -kka transparent; limpid. -kkuus transparency; limpidness.

kuula|kärkikynä ballpoint pen. -laakeri ball-bearings. -ntyöntö shot-put.

kuule|ma hearsay; ~*n mukaan* according to h. -mma according to what I have heard, for all I know; *häntä ei* ~ *hyväksytty* I hear he did not pass.

kuuliai|nen obedient; dutiful. -suudenvala oath of allegiance. -suus obedience.

kuulija hearer, listener; ~*t* = seur. -kunta audience.

kuul|la hear; *(saada tietää)* learn, be told; *-ehan!* look here! I say! *jkn -len* in a p.'s hearing; ~ *väärin* mishear *(esim.* I misheard him to say ..); *hän -ee huonosti toisella korvalla* he is deaf in one ear; *oletko -lut hänestä (häneltä)?* have you had any news of (from) him? *olin kuulevinani* I thought I heard; *hän ei ollut kuulevinaan* he pretended not to hear.

kuulo hearing. -aisti [sense of] hearing. -elin organ of hearing. -hermo auditory nerve. -inen: *hyvä* ~ with good hearing. -ke *rad.* headphone, receiver. -koje hearing aid. -kuva *rad.* radio sketch. -matka: ~*n päässä* within earshot (hearing). -puhe hearsay. -staa sound. -torvi *(puhelimen)* receiver, *(-koje)* ear trumpet; *(lääkärin)* stethoscope. -vika hearing loss. -vikainen hard of hearing.

kuultaa be dimly visible; ~ *läpi* be translucent.

kuultokuva transparency, slide.

kuulu far-famed.

kuulu|a be heard; be audible; *(jklle, jhk)* belong to; [ap]pertain to; *(joihinkin)* be among; *-i laukaus* a shot was heard; *-n heidän joukkoonsa* I am one of them; *se ei k. asiaan* it is irrelevant (is beside the point); *asia ei k. minuun* the matter does not concern me; *mitä -u?* how's life, how are you getting on, *(kuinka voitte)* how are you? *anna ~* go ahead! *puhe oli näin -va* the speech ran as follows; *hän -u olevan rikas* he is said to be rich, they say he is a rich man. **-isa** famous, well-known; noted, famed (for), renowned; celebrated, illustrious; *(surullisen)* notorious. **-isuus** renown; fame; *(pah. merk.)* notoriety; *(-sa henkilö)* celebrity. **-maton** inaudible; *(ennen-)* unheard-of, unprecedented; *-mattomissa* out of hearing. **-miset** news. **kuuluotain** moon probe. **kuulus|taa** *(tiedustella)* inquire, make inquiries (after, for). **-tella** examine *(m. kokelasta)*, interrogate, *(todistajaa ym)* question; *(läksyä)* hear. **-telu** examination, hearing [of witnesses]. **kuulu|ttaa** announce, make known; advertise; *(avioliittoon)* publish the banns; *(julistaa)* proclaim, declare; *heidät -tettiin viime pyhänä* their banns were announced last Sunday. **-ttaja** *rad. ym* announcer. **-tus** announcement; advertisement; notice; *(avioliittoon)* banns; *ottaa ~* [ask to] have one's banns called. **-va** audible; *(jhk ~)* belonging to, [ap]pertaining to; *hänelle ~ (tuleva)* due to him. **-vuus** audibility; *rad.* reception. **kuuma** hot; *~ vyöhyke* torrid zone; *meni kaupaksi kuin kuumille kiville* sold like hot cakes. **-verinen** hot-blooded, hot-tempered. **-vesisäiliö** hot-water reservoir. **kuume** fever; *on ~essa (m.)* has a temperature; *mitata ~* take a p.'s temperature. **-houre** delirium. **-inen** feverish. **-käyrä** temperature curve. **-reuma** infectious arthritis. **-mittari** clinical thermometer. **-ntaa** heat [up].

-ta become hot; become heated. **kuum|oittaa**: *poskiani ~* my cheeks are burning. **-uus** heat. **kuunari** schooner. **kuunne|lla** listen (to); *(luentoa)* attend; *(oppituntia)* sit in [on a lesson[; *(salaa)* eavesdrop, *(puhelinta)* tap [the telephone wires]; *hänen puhelintaan -ltiin* his telephone was tapped; *kuuntele tarkemmin* be more attentive. **-lma** radio play (sketch). **kuun|pimennys** eclipse of the moon. **-sirppi** crescent. **kuuntelija** listener. **kuuntelu** listening (to). **-lupa** radio licence. **kuuperä** lunar soil. **kuuri** regimen, *(lääke-)* course. **kuura** hoarfrost, [white] frost. **kuuro 1.** deaf; **2.** *(sade)* . shower; *~ jkn rukouksille* deaf to the entreaties of; *kaikua ~ille korville* fall on deaf ears; *~jen koulu* deaf school. **-mykkä** *a.* deaf and dumb. **-us** deafness. **-utunut** deafened. **kuusama** *bot.* honeysuckle. **kuusen|havut** spruce twigs. **-käpy** spruce cone. **kuusi 1.** *(puu)* spruce, fir. **2.** *(luku)* six. **-kko** spruce wood. **-kulmainen** hexagonal. **-kulmio** hexagon. **-kymmentä** sixty. **-kymmenvuotias** *s.* sexagenarian. **-peura** fallow **-puu** *liik.* whitewood. **-toista** sixteen. **kuutamo** moonlight, moonshine; *~lla* in the moonlight; *on kirkas ~* there is a bright moon. **-ilta** moonlight night. **-maisema** moonlit landscape. **kuutio** cube. **-mainen** cubic[al]. **-metri** cubic metre. **-sisällys** cubic content. **-tilavuus** cubic capacity. **kuva** picture, image; figure *(lyh.* fig.); *otin hänestä ~n* I took a photograph (a photo *t.* snapshot) of her. **-aja** portrayer; *valok.* camera-man. **-amataiteet** the fine arts. **-amaton** indescribable, .. beyond description. **-annollinen** figurative; metaphorical.

-arvoitus rebus. **-ava** descriptive; *(jllek ~)* characteristic of. **-elma** tableau *(pl. -x); näytelmässä on 8 ~a* the play has 8 scenes.
kuvailla describe; set forth, portray; *kuvaileva* descriptive.
kuvainpalvonta image worship.
kuva|kieli imagery, metaphorical language. **-kirja** picture-book. **-kudos** tapestry. **-laatta** block, cut. **-lehti** pictorial, illustrated magazine. **-llinen** illustrated. **-nauha** videotape; *ottaa ~lle* videotape. **-nauhuri** videotape recorder. **-nheitin** projector. **-nkaunis** pretty as a picture. **-nveisto,** ~taide sculpture. **-nveistäjä** sculptor. **-patsas** statue. **-pinta, -ruutu** television screen. **-postikortti** picture post-card. **-staa** reflect, mirror. **-stin** looking-glass, mirror. **-stua** be reflected; *(ilmetä)* be manifested; *~ selvästi jtk vastaan* stand out clearly (against).
kuva|ta describe; depict, portray; *(esittää)* represent; *elok.* film, photograph; *(olla kuvaava)* be characteristic of; *~ matkaansa* describe (give an account of) one's trip; *~ sanoin ja kuvin* portray in words and pictures. **-taide** visual arts. **-teos** illustrated work. **-tus** fright. *~s* description; *elok.* photography *(selostus)* account; [re]presentation.
kuve waist, loins; *kantaa miekkaa kupeellaan* carry a sword at one's side.
kuvernööri governor.
kuvio figure. **-inti** pattern. **-llinen** figured, patterned; printed. **-ton** unfigured, plain
kuvi|tella imagine, figure to oneself; *en voi ~ ..* I cannot imagine (conceive of, envisage, picture) [myself doing .. *tekeväni*]; *-teltu* imaginary, fancied, fictitious. **-telma** fancy; daydream; illusion. **-tettu** illustrated. **-ttaa** illustrate. **-tteellinen** imaginary. **-ttelu**

imagination; *se on pelkkää ~a* it is idle fancy; *(~kyky* imaginative power). **-tus** illustration [s] .
kuvo|ttaa: *minua ~* I feel sick. **-tus** nausea.
kvartetti quartet [te].
kvartsi quartz.
kveekari Quaker, Friend.
kybernetiikka cybernetics.
kyetä be able (to), be capable [of -ing]; *en kykene* I cannot, I am not up to [-ing].
kyhmy boss, knob; *anat.* nodule, protuberance. **-inen** bumpy, knotty; nodular.
kyhä|elmä article; *(vähäpätöinen)* scribble. **-ilijä** *halv.* scribbler. **-illä** *(kirjoittaa)* write, scribble; draw. **-tä** *(kokoon)* draw up, construct.
kykene|mättömyys *(jhk)* inability, incapacity, incompetence; *(sukup.)* impotence. **-mätön** incapable [of -ing], unable (to), incompetent; incapacitated; *saattaa -mättömäksi jhk* incapacitate .. for. **-vä** able (to), capable [..-ing]; competent; *~sti* ably, capably.
kyky ability, capacity (for); capability, aptitude; *sielun kyvyt* faculties [of the mind]; *parhaan ~ni mukaan* to the best of my ability.
kyljys chop, cutlet.
kylki side, flank; *kyljellään on* its side; *kyljittäin, kyljessä* alongside. **-luu** rib. **-rakennus** wing.
kylkiäinen *(kaupan mukana)* free gift, *(vaja)* lean-to.
kyll|iksi, -in enough; sufficiently; *-in suuri* big enough; *saada -ikseen* have enough. **-yys** fullness; plenty.
kyllä yes; *(tosin)* certainly; indeed; *~ kai* I think so; probably; *~, kiitos* yes, please! *niinpä ~* quite so! yes, indeed! *minä ~ tulen* I will certainly (I'll be sure to) come. **-inen** satisfied. **-isyys** repletion.
kylläste impregnant.

kyllästy|mys satiety; surfeit.
-mättömyys insatiability.
-mätön insatiable. **-nyt:** ~ *jhk*
tired of, sick of. **-ttää** satiate;
sicken; *(ikävystyttää)* bore . .
to death.

kylläs|tyä get tired, tire (of);
olen lopen -tynyt jhk I am
sick to death of, I am fed
up with. **-tää** saturate;
impregnate; *-tetty, -tämätön*
impregnated, not i.

kylme|ntää make . . cool [er],
cool. **-ttyminen** cold. **-ttyä**
catch [a] cold; *-ttynyt*
chilled; *on* ~ has a [bad]
cold. **-tä** become cold, cool.

kylmyys cold, coldness.

kylmä cold; chilly; *(ihmisestä)*
cold, frigid; *minun on* ~ I
am (I feel) cold; *on* ~
ulkona it is cold outside;
kylmi|llään, -lleen unheated.
-hkö rather cold, cool.
-kiskoinen cold, chilly.
-kuljetusauto cold-storage van.
-narka sensitive to cold,
(kasvi) not hardy. **-nhaava**
chilblain. **-nvihat** gangrene.
-verinen cold-blooded; *(tyyni)*
cool. **-verisesti** in cold blood;
coolly. **-verisyys**
cold-bloodedness; coolness,
self-possession.

kylp|eä bathe; *(ammeessa)* have
a bath; *kylvin eilen (saunassa)*
I was in the sauna yesterday.
-ijä bather.

kylpy bath; *(järvi- ym)* bathe.
-amme bath, [bath-]tub.
-huone bathroom. **-kausi**
bathing season. **-laitos** baths.
(rannalla) bathing place. **-lakki**
bathing cap. **-lä** health resort,
spa. **-paikka** bathing-resort,
spa. **-pyyhe** bath towel. **-ranta**
[bathing] beach. **-suola**
bath-salts. **-takki** bath-robe.
-vaippa bathing wrap.

kyltymätön insatiable.

kylve|ttäjä bath attendant. **-ttää**
bath.

kylvää sow; ~ *eripuraisuutta*
sow [the seeds of]
dissension; *minkä ihminen* ~,
sen hän myös niittää a man
reaps what he sows.

kylvö sowing. **-aika** sowing

season. **-kone** sowing machine,
seed-drill. **-mies** sower.
-siemen seed.

kylä village; *(pieni)* hamlet;
mennä (jkn luokse) ~*än* pay
a visit (to), call upon. **-illä:**
olla -ilemässä be on a visit
(to), be visiting a p. **-ily**
visit[ing]. **-kunta** village
[community]. **-läinen** villager.

kymmen: ~*iä tuhansia* tens of
thousands; *muutamia* ~*iä*
some thirty or forty.

kymmen|en ten; ~ *tuhatta* ten
thousand. **-es,** ~*osa* tenth
[part]. **-ittäin** by the dozen;
dozens, scores (of).
-järjestelmä decimal system.
-kertainen tenfold. **-kulmio**
decagon. **-kunta** about ten,
some ten; ~ *vuotta* ten years
or so. **-luku:** . . *-luvulla* in
the [nineteen-]tens.
-murtoluku decimal fraction.
-ottelu *urh.* decathlon. **-vuotias**
ten years old (of age), *(attr.)*
ten-year-old. **-vuotisjuhla** tenth
anniversary, decennial
celebration. **-vuotiskausi**
ten-year period.

kymmenys decimal;
kymmenykset tithes. **-luku**
decimal. **-pilkku** decimal
point. **-vaaka** decimal balance.

kymppi ten.

kyniä pluck.

kynnys threshold. **-matto**
doormat.

kynsi nail; *(eläin-)* claw;
(petolinnun) talon; *(taistella)*
~*n hampain* [fight] tooth and
nail; *pitää kiinni* ~*n hampain*
hold on [to . .] with hook
and claw; *iskeä kyntensä*
pounce [upon *jhk*]; *joutua
jkn* ~*in* get into sb.'s
clutches; *jos vain kynnelle
kykenen* if I am able to
stand up. **-ajos** felon, whitlow.
-enhoito manicure. **-harja**
nail-brush. **-lakka** nail polish.
-laukka garlic. **-rauta** nail
cleaner. **-sakset** nail-scissors
(-clippers). **-viila** nail file. **-ä**
scratch.

kynttelikkö *(katto)* chandelier,
(pöytä-) candela|brum *(pl.*
-bra).

kynttilä candle; *(ohut)* taper.
-**njalka** candlestick. -**npäivä**
Candlemas. -**npätkä** candle-end.
-**nsydän** candle wick. -**nvalo**
candlelight. -**sakset** snuffers.
kyntää plough, *Am.* plow.
kyntö|aika ploughing time.
-**mies** ploughman.
kynä pen; *(lyijy-)* pencil;
(sulka) quill. -**ilijä** writer;
halv. scribbler. -**kotelo**
pencil-case. -**nteroitin** [pencil]
sharpener. -**nterä** [pen] nib.
-**nvarsi** penholder. -**nveto**
stroke of a pen. -**sota**
polemic. -**teline** penrack.
-**veitsi** penknife.
Kypros Cyprus; *kyproslainen*
Cypriot.
kyps|entää mature; *(leipää)*
bake. -**yminen** maturation.
kypsymä|ttömyys immaturity.
-**tön** unripe, not ripe; *et kuv.*
immature.
kyps|yttää ripen, mature. -**yys**
ripeness; *et. kuv.* maturity.
-**yä** ripen, mature. -**ä** ripe,
mature; *(paistunut)* baked;
well done; *paisti ei ole* ~
the roast is underdone; ~*ksi*
keitetty well done.
kypärä helmet.
kyse: ~*essä oleva asia* the
matter in question, the matter
concerned (involved, at issue);
henki on ~*essä* it is a
question of life and death;
kun on ~*essä* .. when it is
a question of, when it comes
to .. -**en|alainen** questionable;
pitää -alaisena [call in]
question; *on -alaista (m.)* it
is doubtful [whether]. -**inen**
.. in question. -**liäs**
inquisitive.
kyse|llä ask, *(tiedustella)*
inquire (for, about);
interrogate; -*lin häneltä tietä*
I asked him the way. -**ly**
inquiry; interrogation;
(~*lomake* questionnaire).
kyssäkaali kohlrabi.
kysymy|s question; query;
inquiry; *tehdä* ~ put a
question (to); *se ei tule*
-*kseenkään* it is out of the
question; *asia josta on* ~ the
matter in question; *mistä on*

~ what is it all about? what
is the matter? -*ksen ollessa*
jstk in the case of; *tämä*
herättää -ksen this raises
(poses) the question (of);
Berliinin ~ the Berlin
problem. -**slause** interrogative
sentence. -**smerkki**
question-mark; query. -**ssana**
interrogative.
kysyntä demand, *jnk* for; ~ *ja*
tarjonta demand and supply;
~ *on suuri* there is a great
demand for ..
kysyvä inquiring; *kiel.*
interrogative.
kysy|ä ask; inquire; *(vaatia)*
require; ~ *jklta* ask a p.
about, inquire of a p. about;
~ *lupaa* ask permission; ~
neuvoa ask a p.'s advice,
consult a p.; *voidaan* ~ it is
pertinent to ask [whether];
hän -i minua he asked (he
inquired) for me; *hän -i*
vointiani he inquired after
me; *sitä tavaraa ei -tä* there
is no demand for that article,
that article is not in demand;
se -y aikaa it takes time; *se*
-*y kärsivällisyyttä* it requires
patience; *teitä -tään* you are
wanted [on the telephone].
kyteä smoulder [on] *(m. kuv.)*
kytk|eytyä *kuv.* be associated
with, be linked to. -**eä** *tie*
[up] (to), *(koira)* put on the
lead, *tekn.* connect, couple;
(ketjuun) chain up; -*ettynä*
(sähk.) on; *(hihnaan)* on a
lead. -**in** coupling; *sähk.*
switch; *(auton)* clutch. -**yt** *tie*
[chain], *(hihna)* leash; *panna,*
päästää -yestä unleash.
kyttyrä hump, hunch. -**selkä**
hunchback. -**selkäinen**
hunchbacked, humpbacked.
kyvy|kkyys ability. -**käs** able,
capable. -**ttömyys**
incompetence. -**tön** incapable
(of -ing), unable (to);
incompetent.
kyyditys *(koululaisten)* busing;
(muilutus) abduction.
kyydit|ä drive, *vrt. ed,;* ~ *jnnek ja*
tappaa take .. for a ride.
kyyhky|nen dove, pigeon.
-**slakka** dovecote.

kyyhöttää huddle.
kyykistyä crouch, squat.
kyykky: *olla kyykyssä* [be] squat [ting]; *laskeutua ~yn* squat [down].
kyykäärme viper, adder.
kyynel tear. **-einen** tearful. **-kaasu** tear-gas. **-kanava** tear-duct. **-silmä:** *-silmin* with eyes filled with tears. **-tyä** fill with tears; water.
kyyni|kko cynic. **-llinen** cynical. **-llisyys** cynicism.
kyynär|pää elbow; *käytellä -päitään* elbow one's way. **-varsi** forearm. **-ä** ell.
kyyr|istyä squat, *m. urh.* crouch; *(pelosta)* cower. **-y:** *käydä selkä ~ssä* walk bent (bowed).
kyyti ride, *(peukalo-)* lift; *aika ~ä* at a good speed; *yhtä ~ä* at a stretch, at one sitting. **-hevonen** post-horse. **-maksu** fare. **-mies** driver. **-väli** stage.
kyömynenä Roman nose.
käden|käänne: *-käänteessä* in [less than] no time, in the twinkling of an eye. **-liike** gesture. **-lyönti:** *vahvistaa jtk -lyönnillä* shake hands on .. **-puristus** handshake. **-sija** handle, *(nuppi)* knob. **-väännö** wrist-wrestling.
kädestä|katsoja palmist. **-katsominen** palmistry.
käen|kaali *bot.* wood-sorrel. **-piika** *zo.* wryneck.
käher|rys waving; wave; *(~pihdit* curling-irons (-tongs). **-täjä** hair-dresser. **-tää** wave, curl.
käh|eys hoarseness. **-eä** hoarse, *(ääni, m.)* husky. **-istä** wheeze; hiss.
kähmiä *(rahaa)* cash in.
kähveltää pinch, pilfer, filch.
käki cuckoo.
käly sister-in-law.
kämmekkä *bot.* orchid.
kämmen palm, flat of the hand.
kämppä [log] cabin.
känsä callosity, callus, *(varpaan)* corn. **-inen** callous. **-laastari** corn plaster.
käpertyä curl up, roll up; *(kurtistua)* shrivel; *kuv.* draw

up, *(itseensä)* be wrapped up in oneself.
käppyrä: *olla ~ssä* be curled up; be shrivelled (shrunk).
käpy cone. **-rauhanen** pineal gland.
käpälä paw. **-mäki:** *lähteä -mäkeen* take to one's heels; bolt.
käris|tä sizzle, sputter. **-tää** fry, frizzle, broil.
kärj|ekäs pointed. **-etön** not pointed, blunt. **-istyä** *kuv.* become acute (critical); be aggravated. **-istää** make [more] critical, bring to a head; sharpen, heighten; *-istäen voi sanoa* to put it very strongly, to put it at its crudest.
kärkevä *(moite)* pointed. *(pureva)* incisive, cutting, sharp.
kärki point *(m. kuv.):* geom. *ym* apex *(pl.* apices): *(kielen ym)* tip; *(pää)* end; *(ivan)* edge; *niemen kärjessä* at the end of the cape; *olla kärjessä (urh.)* head [a race]; *mennä kärkeen* take the lead. **-joukko** vanguard. **-piste** apex.
kär|kkyä hang about (after sth.), be after sth, *(jklta)* bother a p. for; *~ tietoja* hang about hoping to get news. **-käs** desirous (of), greedy (for); *~ uutisille* eager for news; **-kkäin silmin** with greedy eyes.
kärppä stoat, *(talvella)* ermine.
kärpä|nen fly; *(harrastus)* hobby; *keräily~* the collecting bug; *tehdä -sestä härkänen* make mountains out of molehills.
kärpännahka ermine.
kärpäs|haavi fly-net. **-läiskä, -lätkä** fly-flap, swatter. **-paperi** fly-paper. **-sieni** fly agaric.
kärryt cart; *(esim. kotti-)* barrow.
kärsimys suffering; affliction. **-näytelmä** passion-play. **-viikko** Holy Week.
kärsi|mättömyys impatience. **-mätön** impatient. **-vä** suffering, afflicted. **-vällinen** patient, forbearing. **-vällisyys**

patience, forbearance.
kärsiä suffer; *(kestää)* endure,
go through; *(sietää)* bear,
stand; *(suvaita)* tolerate; ~
janoa suffer from thirst; ~
kustannukset bear the cost; ~
puutetta suffer want, *(jnk)*
have to go without; ~
rangaistus undergo
punishment; pay the penalty;
~ *vahinkoa* suffer damage
(by), suffer a loss; *en voi ~
häntä* I cannot bear (stand)
him.
kärsä snout; *(norsun)* trunk.
kärttää *(jklta jtk)* pester,
bother [a p. for]; beg.
kärtyi|nen cross; peevish;
petulant. **-syys** crossness;
petulance.
kärven|tyä get scorched;
become singed. **-tää** scorch,
(tukkaa ym) singe.
käry [smoky] smell; *ruoan* ~
smell of cooking. **-tä** smell;
reek; *lamppu -ää* the lamp is
smoking.
käräjä|juttu lawsuit. **-t** Assizes,
district court session; *kansan*~
Popular Assembly.
käräjöi|dä carry on a lawsuit;
ruveta -mään (jkn kanssa)
take legal proceedings against,
go to law with. **-nti** litigation.
käsi hand; ~ *kädessä* h. in h.;
ottaa jkta kädestä take .. by
the h.; *elää kädestä suuhun*
live from h. to mouth; *joutua
jkn* ~*in* fall into the hands
of; *saada jtk* ~*insä* get hold
of; lay one's hands on;
joutua toisiin ~*in* change
hands; *käydä* ~*ksi* attack,
(tehtävään) get down to, get
to grips with; *päästä* ~*ksi
jhk* get hold of; get at; ~*llä*
at hand; ~*llä oleva asia* the
matter in hand; *aika on* ~*ssä*
the time has come, the time
is on; *saada jtk* ~*stään*
get a th. off one's hands;
suoralta kädellä offhand,
straight off; *käteen jäävä
palkka* take-home pay. **-ala**
[hand-]writing, hand; *hänellä
on selvä* ~ he writes a
legible hand; *(*~**ntutkimus**
graphology). **-kirja** handbook,

manual, guide. **-kirjasto**
reference library. **-kirjoitus**
manuscript *(lyh. M. S.)*;
(elokuva-) script. **-kkäin** hand
in hand. **-koukku, -kynkkä:**
-koukussa arm-in-arm, with
arms linked. **-kranaatti**
hand-grenade. **-kähmä**
hand-to-hand fight, scuffle;
joutua ~*än* come to blows.
-laukku hand-bag.
käsin by hand; ~ *tehty* made
by h., hand-made; ~
kosketeltava tangible, palpable;
täältä ~ from this direction.
-kirjoitettu written by hand.
-kudottu hand-woven.
-maalattu hand-painted.
käsine glove.
käsi|noja *(tuolin)* arm; *(kaide)*
hand-rail. **-puoli** *a.* one-armed;
tarttua jkta -puolesta take ..
by the arm. **-puu** hand-rail.
-puuhka muff. **-pyyhe** towel.
-raha deposit. **-rattaat**
handcart. **-raudat** handcuffs;
panna rautoihin handcuff.
-rysy rough-and-tumble.
käsi|te concept, idea. **-tellä**
treat; *(käsin)* handle,
manipulate; *(kosketella, kuv.)*
deal with, treat of;
(tietokoneella ym) process;
ottaa -teltäväksi take up [for
discussion]; *asianne on -telty*
your matter has been
considered; *mahdoton (t.
vaikea) käsitellä*
unmanageable; *mitä kirja
-ttelee?* what does the book
deal with? what is the book
about .?
käsiteollisuus handicrafts industries.
käsitesekaannus confusion of
ideas.
käsitettävä comprehensible;
intelligible.
käsitteellinen abstract.
käsittely treatment;
management, handling; *parl.*
reading, discussion; ~*n
alaisena* under consideration.
käsittämä|ttömyys
incomprehensibility. **-tön**
incomprehensible,
unintelligible; inconceivable.
käsi|ttää comprehend;

understand, grasp; *(huomata)* realize; *(sisältää)* comprise, include; *(minun)* ~kseni according to my opinion, as far as I can see; *minun järkeni ei sitä -tä* I can't make sense of it, it passes my comprehension, it is beyond me; *huoneisto* ~ *4 huonetta* the flat has (consists of) four rooms; ~ .. *alueen* covers an area of ..; ~ *30 % Suomen viennistä* accounts for 30 % of Finnish exports; *koko maan -ttävä* country-wide. **-tys** comprehension; idea; view; *(mielipide)* opinion; *hänellä ei ole siitä* ~*täkään* he has no idea of it; *-tykseni mukaan* in my view; *olin siinä -tyksessä* I was under the impression [that]; *(~kanta* standpoint; ~**kyky** [power of] comprehension).

käsituliaseet small arms.

käsityö handwork, handicraft, *(naisten)* needlework; *on* ~*tä* is hand-made. **-koulu** school of needlework. **-laukku** workbag. **-läinen** artisan, craftsman.

käsi|varsi arm. **-voima** handpower; strength of arm; *käy* ~*lla* is worked by hand. **-välitteinen** operator-connected.

käske|ä order, command; *(kutsua)* invite; ~ *jkn tehdä jtk (m.)* tell .. to do sth.; *minut -ttiin sisälle* I was told (invited) to come in; *-mätön* unbidden, unasked; *-vä* commanding, imperious, authoritative.

käsky order [s], command; *usk.* commandment; *kenen* ~*stä on* whose orders? **-kirje** edict. **-läinen** *halv.* underling, stooge. **-nalainen** *a. & s.* subordinate. **-nalaisuus** subordination. **-nhaltija** governor. **-tapa** *kiel.* imperative [mood]. **-valta** authority, command.

kätei|nen cash; *-sellä* [in] cash, in ready money; *maksaa -sellä* pay cash; *myönnämme 3 %:n alennuksen -sellä maksettaessa* we allow 3 %

for cash. **-salennus** cash discount. **-smaksu** down payment. **-svarat** cash in hand.

kätellä *(jkta)* shake hands (with).

kätev|yys handiness, dexterity. **-ä** handy, *(näppärä, m.)* deft, dexterous, clever with one's hands; *-ästi* deftly; easily.

kätilö midwife *(pl. -wives)*.

kätke|ytyä hide, conceal oneself; be hidden in. **-ä** hide, conceal, *jklta* from; *(varastettua tavaraa)* receive; *-tty iva* covert (hidden) sarcasm.

kätkyt cradle.

kätkö hiding-place; cache; *olla* ~*ssä* be hidden; *panna* ~*ön* hide [away].

kätten|päällepaneminen laying on of hands. **-taputus** applause.

kättely shaking hands.

kätyri tool, cat's paw.

käve|llä walk, take a walk; *(kuljeskella)* stroll. **-ly** walk, stroll; *lähteä* ~*lle* go for a walk; *olla* ~*llä* be out taking a walk; *(~kansi* promenade deck; ~**katu** pedestrian street; ~**keppi** walking-stick; ~**matka** walk; ~**paikka** walk; promenade; ~**puku** coat and skirt, suit; ~**retki** walking tour, hike).

käv|ijä visitor; caller; *ahkera* ~ *jssak* frequenter (of); *teatterissa* ~ theatre-goer. **-äistä** *(jssak)* pay a [short] visit to; *(jkn luona)* drop in [to see], drop in on a p.

käydä go; *(kone)* work; *(juoma)* ferment; *(astua)* tread; *(lääkäri, postinkantaja ym)* call; ~ *jksk* become, grow, get; ~ *jssk* visit, call at a place; *hän kävi täällä tänään* he was (he called) here to-day; *hän kävi luonani* he came to see me; *oletteko käynyt Lontoossa* have you been to London? *onko postin-kantaja (jo) käynyt?* has the postman been? ~ *laatuun* do; ~ *läpi* go through, *(tarkastaa, m.)* look over; *se ei käy päinsä* that won't do;

ei käy (kelpaa)! that won't wash! *käyden* at a walk, *(jalan)* on foot; *käykää sisälle* come in! step in! *miten asian on käynyt* how has it turned· out? what was the outcome? *miten hänen käy* what will become of him! *hänen kävi hyvin* he did very well, *(paremmin kuin . .n)* he fared better than . .; *kävi miten kävi* come what may, for better or for worse; *kelloni ei käy* my watch is not going, my watch has stopped; *kello käy kahta* it is past one.

käy|minen *(nesteen)* fermentation. **-mälä** lavatory, toilet, *(vessa)* loo. **-mätön** *(juoma)* unfermented.

käynnis|tin starter. **-tää** start.

käynti visit, call; *(kävely)* walk, gait, step; *olla käynnissä* be running, be in operation; *panna ~in* start [up], set . . going; *on täydessä käynnissä (kuv.)* is in full swing; *tunnen hänet käynnistä* I know him by his gait. **-inpano** starting. **-kortti** [visiting-] card, *Am.* calling card; *jättää ~nsa jklle* leave a card on . .

käypä *(raha ym)* current, *(hinta ym)* going; *(tavara)* marketable.

käyristyä become crooked *(t.* curved); bend.

käyrä *a.* crooked, curved; *s.* curve, diagram, graph. **-selkäinen** round-shouldered. **-torvi** horn.

käyskennellä wander; stroll.

käyte ferment.

käytetty used; second-hand; *ostaa ~nä* buy s.-h.

käytettäv|ä: *-issä oleva* available, . . at hand; *olla jkn ~nä* be at sb.'s disposal; *antaa jkn ~ksi* place at a p.'s disposal; *~näni olleet lähteet* the sources I have had access to.

käyttä|mätön unused, not in use; *(esim. huone)* spare. **-ytyminen** behaviour, conduct. **-ytymis-** behavioural. **-ytyä**

behave [oneself], conduct oneself.

käyttää use, make use of, employ; apply; exercise, *(esim. vaikutusvaltaa)* exert; *(pukua)* wear; *(kuluttaa)* consume, *(aikaa)* spend; *(konetta)* run, operate, work, drive; *~ hyvin* put to good use, *(mahdollisimman hyvin)* make the most of; *~ hyväkseen* make use of, utilize, avail oneself of; take advantage of, exploit; *~ loppuun* use up, *(kuluttaa)* wear out; *~ tilaisuutta* seize the opportunity; *~ väärin* misuse, abuse; *minä en voi sitä ~ (m.)* I have no use for it; *vrt. käyte|ttävä, -tty.*

käyttö use, utilization, employment; wear; operation. **-arvo** utility value. **-hihna** driving belt. **-inen:** *diesel~* diesel-operated (-propelled); *atomi~* atom-powered. **-jousi** mainspring. **-kelpoinen** useful, serviceable, fit for use. **-kelvoton** useless, unfit for use, unserviceable. **-kunto:** *-kunnossa* in working order. **-kustannukset** running costs. **-ohjeet** directions [for use]. **-oikeus** right to use; enjoyment. **-varat** liquid assets. **-voima** motive power, *(esim. auton)* propelling power.

käytännölli|nen practical; handy; *-sesti katsoen* practically [speaking]. **-syys** practicalness, *(henkilön)* good practical sense; *~ syistä* for practical reasons.

käytän|tö practice; *(käyttö)* use; *(tapa)* custom, usage; *-nössä* in practice; *-nössä mahdollinen (toteuttaa)* practicable; *-nössä mahdoton* impracticable; *ottaa ~ön* adopt, introduce, bring into use; *soveluttaa ~ön* put into practice; *tulla ~ön* come into use; *joutua pois -nöstä* go out of use, fall into disuse; *poistaa -nöstä* abolish.

käytävä corridor, passage; *(puiston ym)* walk, path.

käytös behaviour, conduct;

manners; *huono* ~ bad behaviour, misbehaviour. **-tapa** manners.

käämi coil. **-ä** spool, wind up. **-kään** ks. *-kaan.*

käänne turn; *(mutka)* bend, curve; *(muutos)* change; *(taudin)* crisis, turning-point; *(puvun)* lapel, *(housunlahkeen)* turn-up, *(hihan)* cuff; *sai uuden käänteen* took a new turn; ~ *parempaan* change for the better. **-kohta** turning-point; *muodosti ~n* marked a t.-p. **-llä** turn over. **-ttävä** *(esim. takki)* reversible.

käännynnäinen convert.

käänny|ttää *usk.* convert; ~ *takaisin* turn away. **-tys** conversion.

käännös turn; *(kielellinen)* translation; ~ *oikeaan (komennuksena)* right turn *(t. face)!* *täys*~ about turn! **-harjoitus** translation exercise. **-kirjallisuus** translated literature. **-toimisto** translation bureau. **-virhe** error in translation.

käänteentekevä epoch-making.

käänty|mys conversion. **-nyt** *usk. a.* converted; *s.* convert.

kään|tyä turn; *usk.* be converted; ~ *kristinuskoon (m.)* become a Christian, embrace Christianity; ~ *oikealle* turn [off] to the right; ~ *jkn puoleen* turn to (approach) a p., *(esim. lääkärin)* consult [a physician]; ~ *parempaan päin* take a turn for the better; ~ *syrjään* turn aside, strike off; *asia -tyi toisin* the matter took a different turn; *onni on -tynyt* the luck has turned (changed); *tauti on -tynyt pelottavaksi* the illness has taken an alarming turn; *tuuli on -tynyt* the wind has changed (shifted). **-täjä** translator. **-tää** turn; *(taittaa)* fold; *kiel.* translate; *usk.* convert; ~ *jkn huomio jhk* draw a p.'s attention to; ~ *jllek kielelle* translate into; ~ *kaulus pystyyn* turn up one's

collar; ~ *pois* turn away, *(ajatukset)* distract, *(katse)* avert; ~ *selkänsä jklle* turn one's back on; ~ *toisaalle* divert; *käännä!* P.T.O. (please turn over), *Am.* over.

kääntö|filmi reversal film. **-piiri** tropic. **-puoli** reverse side, back; *jatkuu -puolella* continued overleaf; *kirjoittaa nimensä (šekin) -puolelle* endorse. **-silta** swing bridge, *rautat.* turntable.

kääpiö dwarf, pygmy. **-mäinen** dwarfed. **-sarja** bantam weight.

kääpä fungus growth.

käär|e wrapper; *lääk.* compress, *(side)* bandage, dressing; *kylmä* ~ cold compress; *panna ~eseen* bandage; *hänellä on pää ~essä* he has a bandage round his head; *(~paperi* wrapping paper). **-inliina** shroud. **-iytyä** wrap oneself up (in). **-iä** wind, twine; wrap [up]; *(kokoon)* fold up; ~ *auki* unwrap; ~ *hihat ylös* roll up (tuck up) one's sleeves; ~ *paperiin* wrap [up] in paper.

käärme snake; serpent. **-enlumooja** snake-charmer. **-enmyrkky** venom. **-enpurema** *s.* snake-bite. **-mäinen** snake-like, snaky.

käärö bundle, *(paketti)* parcel, package; *(rulla)* roll; *panna ~ön* bundle up, make up into a bundle (a parcel).

köh|inä [dry] cough. **-ä** cough.

kököttää squat; *istua ~ kotona* sit at home and mope.

köli keel.

Köln Cologne.

kömmähdys blunder, faux pas, bloomer; *Am.* boner.

kömpe|lyys clumsiness. **-lö** clumsy, ham-handed; *kuv.* awkward; *~sti tehty* bungled.

kömpiä crawl, shuffle [along].

köntistyä stiffen, grow numb with cold.

köpittää stump [along].

körttiläinen pietist.

köyden|punoja rope-maker. **-pätkä** rope-end. **-veto** *urh.* tug of war.

köyh|dyttää reduce to poverty, impoverish. **-tyä** become poor; *(perin)* be reduced to beggary; *-tynyt* impoverished. **-yys** poverty; want.

köyhä poor; *(puutteessa oleva)* indigent, needy; ~*t* the poor, the destitute. **-aatteinen** poor (lacking) in ideas. **-inhoito** relief of the poor. **-listö** proletariat. **-napu** public assistance, poor relief. **-sisältöinen** poor (meagre) in content.

köykkyselkäinen bowed.

köykäinen light.

köynnös *(viini-)* vine; *(koriste-)* garland, festoon. **-kasvi** creeper, climbing plant, climber.

köyr|istää bend, bow; arch. **-y:** *kulkea selkä ~ssä* walk bent.

köysi rope, cord, *mer. m.* line; *vetää yhtä köyttä* pull together. **-luuta** mop, swab. **-portaat** rope ladder. **-rata** cable railway, cableway. **-stö** rigging, tackle.

köyttää [tie with a] rope; tie, secure [with a rope], lash, *jhk* [on] to.

Kööpenhamina Copenhagen.

L

laadinta drawing up, preparation, *(sanakirjan ym)* compilation.

laadullinen qualitative.

laah|ata drag [along with]; trail; *(perässään)* tow. **-autua** be dragged [along]. **-uksenkantaja** train-bearer. **-us** train; *(~nuotta* trawl). **-ustaa** drag, trail; *käydä ~* drag one's feet, shuffle along.

laaja extensive; wide, vast; large, *kuv.* comprehensive; *sanan laajimmassa merkityksessä* in the broadest (widest) sense of the word; *~lle levinnyt* widespread. **-kangas** *elok.* wide screen. **-kantoinen** far-reaching. **-kantoisuus** wide scope. **-kulmaobjektiivi** wide-angle lens. **-lti** widely, extensively; *~ tunnettu* widely known, known far and wide.

laajen|eva expanding. **-nus** expansion, extension, enlargement; dila[ta]tion. **-taa** widen, expand; extend, enlarge; *anat. ym* dilate; *~ valtaansa* extend one's power. **-tua** widen, extend, expand; *fys.* distend, dilate; *-tunut* enlarged, dilated, distended. **-tuma** *anat.* dila[ta]tion. **-tuminen** *sydämen ~* enlargement of the heart. **-tumiskyky** expansive power.

laaj|eta expand, spread; become dilated; *vrt. -entua.* **-uinen** *5 mailin ~* 5 miles wide, 5 miles in width (in extent); *teos on 400 sivun ~* the work comprises 400 pages. **-uus** width; extent; extensiveness, comprehensiveness; range *(esim. tietojen)* scope; *koko -uudessaan* in its whole extent.

laaka|kivi flagstone, slab.

-paino offset.

laakea flat; level; *(laaja)* wide.

laakeri 1. laurel, bay. **2.** *tekn.* bearing; *niittää laakereita* win laurels; *seppelöidä ~lla* crown with laurels. **-nlehti** bayleaf. **-seppele** laurel wreath.

laakio plateau, table-land.

laakso valley; *run.* vale, dale.

laama *zo.* llama.

laapis lunar caustic.

laari bin.

laastar|i plaster. **-ilappu** piece (strip) of plaster, plaster band. **-oida** plaster.

laatia draw up; prepare; compose; *(esim. sanakirja)* compile; make [out], work out; *~ kontrahti* draw up a contract; *~ lakeja* make laws; *~ jkn nimelle* make out in the name of; *~ pöytäkirja (valmiiksi;* write up) take down the minutes; *~ suunnitelma (m.)* work out a plan; *lausunto oli hyvin laadittu* the report was well formulated (worded).

laatikko box; *(iso, pakka-)* case, *(harva)* crate; *(veto-)* drawer; *(pakka-, m.)* chest; *(ruoka)* casserole [dish].

Laatokka Lake Ladoga.

laatta plate, slab; *(kaakeli-)* tile; *vrt. levy; muisto ~* plaque, tablet, *Am.* marker; *(seinässä)* wall plaque. **-kiveys** flagstone pavement.

laatu quality; *kaupp. m.* brand; *(laji)* kind, sort; *laadultaan hyvää)* [.. of] good quality; *paras ~aan* the best of its kind; *yksityistä ~a* of a private nature; *käydä ~un* do. **-ero** difference in kind. **-inen:** *minkä ~* of what kind? **-kuva** genre picture. **-sana** adjective. **-tavara** quality goods. **-tuote**

quality product. **-unkäypä** passable.

laava lava.

laboratorio laboratory.

labyrintti labyrinth; maze.

ladata load; charge.

ladella place in a row (in rows), *kuv.* rattle off, reel off, enumerate.

lad|elma composition. **-onta** type-setting.

laguuni lagoon.

lahde|ke, -lma bay; *(pieni)* cove.

lahja gift, present; *(avustus)* contribution; *(-kkuus)* talent; *antaa ~ksi* give as a present, make. . a present of. ., present. with; *saada ~ksi* get as *(t.* for) a present, be presented with. **-inen:** *runsas~* richly endowed. **-kappale** presentation copy. **-kas** talented, gifted; intelligent. **-kirja** deed of gift. **-kkuus** talent (for). **-kortti** gift voucher (token). **-näytäntö** benefit [performance]. **-paketti** gift parcel. **-pakkaus** gift wrapping. **-palkkio** bonus, gratuity. **-ton** not talented. **-ttomuus** lack of talent.

lahje *(housun)* leg.

lahjoa bribe; corrupt; *puhek.* grease . .'s palm.

lahjoi|ttaa present [a p. with, a th. to]; give, bestow (upon); donate; *(et. laitokselle, koululle)* endow; *hän -tti 100 dollaria . .n rakentamiseen* he contributed £ 100 towards the building of. **-ttaja** donor. **-tus** donation; presentation.

lahjo|maton incorruptible. **-mattomuus** incorruptibility. **-nta** bribery. **-ttav|a:** *-issa.* . open to bribes, corruptibility.

lahjus bribe.

lahko *luonn.* order; *usk.* sect, denomination. **-lainen** sectarian; *Engl.* nonconformist, dissenter. **-laisuus** sectarianism.

lahna bream.

laho *a.* decayed; rotten; *s.* decay; *kuiva ~* dry rot. **-ta** [become] decay[ed], rot. **-us** decayed state.

lahti bay, *(iso, meren-)* gulf; *(lahdeke)* cove; *lahden pohjassa* at the head of the bay.

laide side, edge; *(laivan)* gunwale.

laidun pasture, pasturage; *(pieni)* paddock, *(laaja)* grazing ground; *olla laitumella* be out to grass, be grazing; *päästää laitumelle* put out to grass. **-taa** pasture, graze.

laiha thin, *(m. lihasta)* lean; spare; *(kehno)* meagre, scanty; *~ maa* poor soil, barren soil.

laih|duttaa make. . thinner, reduce [in weight]; *hän ~ (puhek.)* she is slimming (reducing). **-dutus** slimming; *»~kuurilla»* on a s. diet.

laiho standing crop.

laih|tua get thin[ner], lose weight, reduce; *-tunut* thin, *(lopen)* emaciated; *-duin 5 kiloa* I lost 5 kilos. **-uus** thinness, leanness.

laikku fleck, patch, spot.

lailla: *aika ~* a good deal; *millä ~* in what way (manner)? *tällä ~* in this way, thus.

lailli|nen lawful; legal; *(pätevä)* valid; *(oikea)* legitimate; *~ este* lawful impediment; *lawful excuse [esim.* for non-appearance]; *~ perillinen* legitimate heir; *tulee -seen ikään* comes of age; *-sessa järjestyksessä* in due order. **-staa** legitimate; *-stettu* registered. **-suus** lawfulness, legality; legitimacy.

laime|a weak, *liik. m.* dull, *(veltto)* slack, languid, *(välinpitämätön)* indifferent, lukewarm; *~ yritys* feeble (lame) attempt. **-ntaa** weaken; lessen; *(juomaa)* dilute. **-ta** become weak[er], weaken, lose its strength, *(olut ym)* go flat; *kuv. m.* slacken, flag. **-us** weakness, feebleness.

laimin|lyödä neglect; *(jättää tekemättä)* fail [to do sth.]; *~ hyvä tilaisuus* miss a good opportunity. **-lyönti** neglect, failure [to do sth.]; omission; negligence. **-lyöty**

neglected, uncared for.
laina loan; *on ~ssa* is [out]
on loan; *antaa ~ksi* lend,
give a p. the loan of; *saada
~ksi* have sth. on loan,
obtain as a loan; *saanko. .
~ksi?* may I have the loan
of. .? **-höyhenet** *kuv.* borrowed
plumes. **-kirjasto** lending-
library, circulating library.
lainalainen bound (regulated)
by law.
laina|lause quotation. **-nantaja**
lender. **-nottaja** borrower.
-sana loan-word. **-summa**
amount of loan. **-ta** lend,
Am. loan; *(ottaa lainaksi)*
borrow, *jklta* from; *(kirjasta
ym)* quote, cite. **-tavara**
borrowed property. **-us** loan;
lending; borrowing; *(kirj.)*
quotation; *(~liike* lending
business; *~merkit* quotation
marks, inverted commas).
laine wave, billow. **-htia**
billow; undulate.
-lainen: *tämän ~* of this kind;
kahden ~ of two kinds;
huonon ~ rather bad;
tamperelainen from Tampere,
inhabitant of T.; *SAK-~*
SAK-connected (*t.* associated).
lain|haku action for debt.
-huudatus legal confirmation
of possession, registration,
legalization [of purchase].
lainkaan: *ei ~* not at all, not
in the least.
lain|kohta passage, paragraph
[in a section of law].
-kuuliainen law-abiding.
-kuuliaisuus obedience to the
law **-käyttö** application of
law. **-laatija** legislator.
-mukainen according to law,
lawful. **-opillinen** juridical,
judicial, legal, law. **-oppi** *ks.*
oikeustiede. **-oppinut** jurist.
-rikkoja lawbreaker. **-rikkomus**
breach of the law. **-suoja|ton**
s. outlaw; *julistaa l-ttomaksi*
outlaw, proscribe.
-säädännöllinen legislative.
-säädäntö legislation,
law-making; *(~valta* legislative
power). **-säätäjä** legislator.
-vastainen contrary to law;
illegal. **-voima** legal force;

saada ~ become legal,
become valid.
laipio *mer.* bulkhead.
laippa flange.
laiska lazy; idle; indolent.
-nlinna easy chair. **-nläksy**
punishment lesson. **-npäivät**
easy life. **-nvirka** sinecure;
soft job.
laisk|iainen *zo.* sloth. **-otella** be
lazy, idle [away one's time].
-ottelu dawdling. **-uri** idler,
drone, loiterer. **-uus** idleness,
laziness.
laita 1. *(sivu)* side, edge;
(reuna) brim; *laitoja myöten
täynnä* brimful; *metsän
laidassa* at the edge of the
woods; *yli laidan* overboard.
2. *(asian-)* state [of affairs];
niin on ~ that's how it is,
such is the case; *miten hänen
~nsa on* how is he? *hänen
~nsa on huonosti* he is in a
bad way; *kuinka on ~si?*
how is it with you? how are
you? *minun ~ni on samoin*
it's the same with me.
-kaupunki outskirts of the
town; *(~lainen* suburban).
-vastai|nen= *l-sta* by (on) the
wind.
laitattaa have. . made
(prepared, repaired); *~
kuntoon* have. . put in order,
have. . fixed.
laite appliance, device;
apparatus; *(vekotin)* gadget;
laitteet equipment, apparatus,
(esim. valaistus) fittings.
laiton illegal, unlawful; illicit.
laitos establishment, institution;
institute; *tekn.* plant. **-tua** be
institutionalized.
laitta|a make; prepare;
(järjestää) arrange; *(korjata)*
repair, mend, *Am.* fix; *~
ruokaa* cook, prepare food; *~
päivällinen (valmiiksi)* get the
dinner ready. **-utua** *(kuntoon)*
get ready; *~ tiehensä* make
off.
laitteisto equipment; apparatus;
outfit; facilities (for).
laittomuus illegality,
unlawfulness; wrongfulness.
laituri quay, pier, *(lastaus-)*
wharf *(pl. ~s, -rves), (et.*

uiva) landing-stage, *(pieni)* jetty; *rautat. ym* platform; ~*lla,* ~*ssa* at the quay; *laskea* ~*in* dock.

laiva ship; *(alus)* vessel; *(höyry-)* steamer; liner; *(kirkon)* nave; ~*an,* ~*ssa* on [ship]board; *astua, nousta* ~*an* go on board [a ship], board a ship; embark; *viedä* ~*an* take. . on board. **-aja** shipper. **-annousu** embarkation. **-kulku** navigation. **-laituri** quay. **-liike(nne)** steamship service. **-linja** [steamship] line. **-lääkäri** ship's doctor. **-maksut** shipping dues. **-matka** voyage. **-miehistö** [ship's] crew. **-mies** seaman.

laiva|hylky wreck. **-isäntä** shipowner [s]. **-kansi** deck. **-kapteeni** captain, *(kauppalaivan, m.)* master. **-lasti** shipload, cargo. **-päällystö** ship's officers. **-rakennus** shipbuilding, naval architecture. **-rakentaja** shipbuilder [s], *(insinööri)* naval engineer. **-runko** hull. **-selvittäjä** shipbroker [s]. **-selvitys** clearance. **-varustaja, -varustamo** shipowner [s]. **-veistämö** shipyard.

laiva|paperit ship's papers. **-poika** ship-boy, cabin-boy. **-päiväkirja** log-book. **-silta** landing-stage. **-sto** fleet; *(merivoimat)* navy; (~*asema* naval station; ~*tukikohta* naval base).

laiva|ta ship, dispatch. **-tarvikkeet** ship's stores. **-telakka** shipbuilding yard, dock. **-us** shipment, shipping; (~*satama* port of shipment; ~*sopimus* shipping contract, charterparty). **-vene** ship's boat, launch. **-vuoro** steamship service; ~*t* sailings. **-väki** ship's company. **-väylä** channel. **-yhteys** steamship connection.

laivu|e flotilla; *ilm.* squadron. **-ri** master; skipper.

laji kind, sort, *(merkki)* make, brand; *luonn.* species; *urh.* event, sport. **-ke** variety. **-tella** sort [out], assort, grade.

-telma assortment; *(valikoima)* selection.

lakais|ta sweep; **-ematon** unswept.

lakana sheet. **-kangas** sheeting.

lakastua wither [away], fade.

laka|ta 1. cease, *jstk* [from] -ing, stop (-ing); leave off [smoking etc.]; *on -nnut satamasta* it has stopped (ceased) raining, the rain has stopped; ~ *ilmestymästä* cease to appear; ~ *työstä* stop (cease) working, stop work; **2.** lacquer, varnish; *(sinetöidä)* seal.

lakea level; *(aava)* open.

lakeija footman, lackey.

lakeus plain.

laki 1. law, act, statute; *säätää lakeja* make laws, enact laws; *laissa säädetty* established by law. **2.** *(korkein kohta)* top, crown, summit. **-asiaintoimisto** lawyer's office. **-ehdotus** bill; *hyväksyä* ~ pass a b. **-kieli** legal language. **-kirja** code of laws, statute-book. **-mies** lawyer. **-määräinen** fixed (prescribed) by law, lawful, legal. **-määräys** provision in a law. **-pykälä** section of an act. **-sana** legal term. **-sääteinen** statutory. **-tiede** science of law; jurisprudence; *opiskella* ~*ttä* read law. **-tieteellinen** juridical.

lakka lacquer, varnish; *(kirje-)* sealing-wax; *(marja)* [arctic] cloudberry. **-puikko** stick of sealing-wax.

lakkaa|maton incessant, unceasing; uninterrupted. **-matta** without stopping, without intermission, ceaselessly, continuously.

lakkau|ttaa stop; *(esim. sanomalehti)* suppress; *(määräraha ym)* withdraw; *(ei jatkaa)* discontinue, suspend; *(poistaa)* abolish; ~ *maksut* suspend payment; ~ *työt (tehtaassa)* shut down. **-tus** withdrawal; suppression; suspension; abolition.

lakki cap.

lakko strike; *olla lakossa* be on s.; *ryhtyä* ~*on* go [out]

on s. (*jstk syystä* in protest against .); *lopettaa* ~ call off a s. **-avustus** strike pay. **-illa** strike. **-lainen** striker. **-tila:** *julistaa* ~*an* declare a strike. **-vahti** strike picket.
lako: *lyödä* (*laihot*) ~*on* lay [crops] flat; *olla laossa* lie flat, be beaten down.
lakonrikkuri strike-breaker, blackleg, rat, *Am. m.* scab.
lakoninen laconic; concise.
lakritsi liquorice.
lama: *mieleni on* ~*ssa* I am depressed; *kauppa on* ~*ssa* trade is slack (dull). **-annus** depression. **-kausi** period of depression. **-antua** become paralyzed; grow dull, slacken. **-uttaa** paralyze; (*esim. isku*) stun; (*lannistaa*) dishearten, discourage; depress.
lammas sheep (*pl.* sheep); (*liha*) mutton. **-koira** sheep-dog, collie. **-lauma** flock of sheep. **-mainen** sheepish. **-paisti** leg of mutton, (*paistettu*) roast mutton. **-tarha** [sheep]fold.
lammikko pond, pool.
lampaan|hoito sheep-farming (-breeding). **-kyljys** mutton chop. **-lapa** shoulder of mutton. **-liha** mutton, (*karitsan*) lamb. **-nahka** sheepskin. **-villa** sheep's wool.
lampetti sconce, bracket candlestick.
lampi pond; (*esim. metsä-*) small lake, (*vuoristo-*) tarn.
lamppu lamp; (*hehku-*) bulb. **-öljy** *ks.* palo-.
lampun|jalka lamp-stand. **-kupu** lamp-globe. **-lasi** lamp-chimney. **-sydän** wick. **-valo** lamplight. **-varjostin** lamp-shade.
langaton wireless.
lange|nnut fallen, (*maksettavaksi*) due, (*vekseli*) mature. **-ta** fall, have a fall; (*kompastua*) stumble; (*hairahtua*) lapse into; (*maksettavaksi*) fall (become) due, mature; (*jkn tehtäväksi*) devolve upon; ~ *jkn hyväksi* fall to. **-ttaa** (*tuomio*) pronounce sentence, pass

judg[e]ment.
lanka thread; (*puuvilla-*) cotton; (*villa- ym*) yarn; (*metalli-*) wire. **-kerä** ball of yarn (thread). **-rulla** reel [of cotton], spool. **-vyyhti** skein of yarn.
lankeem|us fall; *ylpeys käy -uksen edellä* pride goes before a fall.
lankku plank, *liik.* deal.
lanko brother-in-law.
lanne loin, (*lonkka*) hip; *kädet lanteilla* with hands on [one's] hips, with one's arms akimbo.
lannis|taa (*jkn mieli*) discourage, dishearten, crush a p.'s spirit; (*jkn valta*) subdue, overcome. **-tua** be discouraged; *mieleni -tui* I became disheartened, I lost heart. **-tumaton** indomitable, undaunted.
lannoi|te fertilizer. **-ttaa** manure; fertilize. **-tus** manuring; (~*aine* fertilizer.)
lanta manure, dung; (*linnun ym*) droppings. **-tadikko** dung-fork, manure fork.
lantio pelvis.
lantti coin.
lanttu swede *Am.* rutabaga.
lapa shoulder, (*airon*) blade. **-luu** shoulder-blade. **-mato** broad tapeworm. **-nen** mitten.
lape flat; *lappeellaan* flatwise (*airo*) at rest.
lapikas boot.
lapio spade, shovel. **-ida** shovel.
lappalai|nen *s.* Laplander, Lapp; *a.* Lappish, Lapp. lander's hut, tepee. **-snainen -skoira** Lapp dog. **-skota** Lap-Lapp woman. **-spuku** Laplander's dress.
Lappi Lapland; *lapin kieli* Lappish, Lapp.
lappu piece, bit; (*laastari- ym*) pad; (*paikka*) patch; (*kangas-, m.*) shred; (*paperi-*) [paper] slip; (*hinta- ym*) label; *silmä~* eye patch. **-liisa** [woman] traffic warden, parking attendant, *Am.* meter maid.
lapselli|nen childish, puerile; (*lapsen kaltainen*) childlike;

(yksinkertainen) naïve. **-suus** childishness.

lapsen|hoitaja nurse. **-lapsi** grandchild. **-leikki** child's play. **-murha** infanticide. **-rattaat** children's push chair. **-tyttö** nurse-maid. **-usko** childhood faith. **-vaunut** perambulator, *(lyh.)* pram; *Am.* baby carriage.

lapse|ton childless. **-ttomuus** childlessness.

lapsi child *(pl.* children); *(syli-)* baby, infant; *lapsena ollessani* when a child; *lapsesta asti,* from *(t.* since) childhood; *ottaa lapsekseen* adopt; *~lle sallittu* for children also; *~lta kielletty* for adults only. **-halvaus** infantile paralysis, polio [myelitis]. **-lauma:** *hänellä on suuri ~* he has a large family. **-lisä** child allowance. **-puoli** stepchild. **-rakas** fond of children. **-vuode** childbed, childbirth; *(~kuume* puerperal fever).

lapsuuden|koti childhood home. **-ystävä** friend of one's childhood.

lapsuus childhood; *(varhainen)* infancy; *lapsuuteni aikana* in my childhood days. **-ikä** childhood.

laputtaa *(tiehensä)* beat it, make oneself scarce; *ala ~!* off you go!

lasi glass; *~ vettä* a g. of water. **-astia** glass dish; *~t* glassware. **-kaappi** glass case. **-kuitu** fibreglass. **-kupu** glass cover. **-llinen** glassful; glass. **-maalaus** stained glass. **-mainen** glassy. **-mestari** glazier. **-nen.** . [made] of glass, glass. **-nhionta** glass-grinding. **-nleikkaaja** glass cutter. **-npuhaltaja** glass blower. **-nsirpale:** *~et* broken bits of glass, glass fragments. **-ruutu** pane [of glass]. **-tavara** glassware. **-te** glaze. **-tehdas** glassworks. **-ttaa** glaze. **-ttaja** glazier. **-tus** glazing. **-tölkki** glass jar. **-villa** glass wool.

laske|a *tr. (alas)* lower; let down; *(asettaa)* lay; *(päästää)* let, *(irti)* let go; *mat.* count, calculate, compute, reckon, *(mukaan)* include; *(arvioida)* estimate; *intr. (aleta)* fall, go down, decrease, drop; *(aurinko)* set; *(joki)* empty, discharge [itself] (into); *~ kauppaan* put on the market; *~ koskea* shoot the rapids; *~ kulut* calculate the expenses; *~ leikkiä* joke, jest; *~ lippu* lower a flag, strike one's colours; *~ maihin* land, *(matkustaja)* put ashore; *~ mukaan* include, count. . in, reckon among; *~ päässään* figure (work out) in one's head; *~ seppele jkn haudalle* lay a wreath on a p.'s grave; *~ jku sisälle* let. . in, admit; *~ vettä kylpyammeeseen* run the bath water; *~ väärin* miscalculate, miscount; *~ yhteen* add [up], add together; *hinta on -nut* the price has dropped (gone down); *joki -e mereen* the river empties (discharges) into the sea; *-ttu (arvioitu)* expected, calculated. **-lma** calculation; estimate; *erehtyä -lmissaan* miscalculate; *ottaa -lmissaan huomioon* take into account. **-lmallinen** calculating. **-lmoida** calculate. **-maton** incalculable. **-nta** calculation, calculus. **-nto** arithmetic. **-tella** reel off; *(suksilla)* ski downhill; *~ omiaan* stretch the truth; *~ sukkeluuksia* crack jokes. **-ttelurinne** slalom *(t.* ski) slope. **-uma** *(veren)* sedimentation rate; *(radioaktiivinen ~)* fall-out. **-utua** go down, descend; *(painua)* sink; *(rakennus ym)* settle; *(tulla alas)* get down, come down, alight; *(lentokone)* land; touch down; *~ pitkälleen* lie down; *~ pohjaan (sakka)* settle.

laskiai|nen Shrovetide. **-spulla** Shrove bun. **-stiistai** Shrove Tuesday.

laskimo| vein. **-veri** venous blood.

laskos fold, pleat; tuck; *(vasta-)* box-pleat; *laskoksissa* *oleva* folded; pleated. **-taa** fold; pleat.

lasku *(maksettava)* bill, note, *Am.* check; *(faktuura)* invoice; *(tili-)* account; *(laskelma)* calculation; *ottaa ∼issa huomioon* take into account, make allowance for [delay, *viipyminen*]; *laatia ∼* make out a bill; *merkitkää se minun ∼uni* charge it to my account; *omaan ∼un* on his (her) own account; *ostaa ∼un* buy on credit. **-esimerkki** problem, sum, example. **-haara** *(joen)* outlet. **-kausi** period of decline; *liik. m.* recession. **-kone** calculating machine. **-opillinen** arithmetical. **-oppi** arithmetic. **-porras** gangway. **-putki** wastepipe, *lääk.* drain. **-pää:** *hänellä on hyvä ∼* he has a good head for arithmetic. **-sana** numeral, number. **-silta** drawbridge. **-suhdanne** downward trend, recession, *vrt. lamakausi.* **-suunta** *liik.* decline, fall [in prices]. **-tapa:** *neljä ∼a* the four rules of arithmetic. **-teline** landing gear. **-ttaa** *liik.* invoice. **-varjo** parachute; *hypätä ∼llä* parachute, *(pelastautua)* escape [unscathed] by p., bale out; *(∼hyppääjä* parachutist; *∼joukot* paratroops). **-vesi** low water. **-viivoitin** slide rule. **-virhe** error in calculation, miscalculation.

lasta splint; *(muurarin)* trowel; *keitt. ym* spatula. **-ta** load, lade; *laiva on ∼ttavana* the ship is loading (taking in freight); *∼ttu laden.* **-us** loading; *(∼laituri* quay, wharf; *∼työntekijä* dock-labourer; stevedore).

lasten|hoitaja children's nurse. **-hoito** care of children. **-huolto** child welfare. **-huone** nursery. **-kaitsija** baby-sitter. **-kasvatus** bringing up [of] children, upbringing, rearing of children. **-koti** children's home. *(orpo-)* orphanage. **-lääkäri** p[a]ediatrician. **-seimi** day nursery. **-suojelu** child

welfare. **-tarha** kindergarten, nursery school. **-tauti** children's disease. **-vaunut** *ks. lapsen-.*

lasti load; *(laivan)* cargo; *täydessä ∼ssa* fully loaded. **-laiva** cargo (freight) steamer. **-npurkaus** unloading. **-ruuma** hold.

lastoittaa put in splints.

lastu chip, *(höylän)* shaving. **-levy** [wood] particle board, chipboard. **-villa** wood-wool, *Am.* excelsior.

lata|amaton unloaded, *(akku)* uncharged. **-us** charging, *(aseen)* loading.

latina, -lainen Latin.

latkia lap [up].

lato barn, shed.

lato|a *(kasaan)* pile [up], *(päällekkäin)* stack; heap, pack, stow; *kirjap.* set [up], put in type, compose; *∼ riviin* place in a row. **-ja** type-setter, compositor. **-makone** type-setting machine. **-mo** composing-room. **-mus** set matter.

lattea flat, *kuv.* insipid.

lattia floor; *panna ∼* floor. **-luukku** trap-door. **-nkiillotuskone** floor polisher. **-vaha** floor polish.

latu track; trail.

latuskajalka flat-foot.

latv|a top; *(joen)* upper course, headwaters. **-apurje** topsail. **-oa** top, *(oksia)* poll.

latvialainen Latvian.

lauantai Saturday.

laudanpätkä end of [a] board.

laudatur honours [course].

laudoi|ttaa board, line with boards; *(panelilla)* wainscot. **-tus** boarding; wainscot[ing].

laueta go off, *(räjähtäen)* explode; *jännitys laukesi* the tension relaxed.

lauh|a mild; temperate. **-duttaa** appease, soothe; *(jäähdyttää)* cool [off]; *tekn.* condense. **-kea** temperate; mild; *(säyseä)* meek. **-keus** mildness; gentleness, meekness. **-tua** be appeased, soften, relent; *sää ∼tuu* the weather is getting milder; *pakkanen ∼tuu* the

cold is abating.
laukai|sta fire [off], discharge,
(ohjus ym) launch; *(jännitys)*
relieve, ease, relax. **-sualusta**
(ohjuksen) launching pad.
laukata gallop.
laukaus shot; *(pamahdus)*
report. **-tenvaihto** shooting,
exchange of shots.
laukka gallop; *(lyhyt)* canter;
täyttä ~a at full gallop.
laukku bag; *(koulu-, m.)*
satchel; *(kartta- ym)* case.
laul|aa sing; *(lintu, m.)* warble;
puhtaasti ks. t.; ~ jkn ylistystä
sing a p.'s praises. **-aja(tar)**
[professional] singer. **-ajaiset**
[vocal] concert. **-elma** song, air.
-ella sing, *(hyräillä)* hum.
laulu song; air, melody, tune;
(oppiaineena ym) singing.
-juhla choral festival. **-kirja**
song-book. **-kuoro** choir,
choral society. **-lintu**
song-(singing-) bird, songster.
-llinen vocal. **-nopettaja**
singing-master (-mistress).
-npätkä snatch of song.
-näytelmä musical, musical
comedy. **-rastas** song-thrush.
-seura glee club. **-taide** art of
singing, vocal art. **-tunti**
singing lesson. **-ääni**
singing-voice.
lauma herd, *(et. lammas-, m.*
kuv.) flock; drove; swarm,
host, *(esim. susi-)* pack;
(hunni- ym) horde; *keräytyä*
laumoihin flock together;
laumoittain in flocks, in
crowds. **-eläin** gregarious
animal. **-vaisto** the herd
instinct.
laupeuden|sisar sister of
charity. **-työ** act of charity.
laup|eus mercy, mercifulness,
charity. **-ias** merciful,
charitable; *~ samarialainen*
the good Samaritan.
lause sentence, *(lyhyt)* clause.
-enjäsennys analysis [of a
sentence]. **-enosa** part of
sentence. **-jakso** period. **-korko**
sentence stress. **-opillinen**
syntactic. **-oppi** syntax. **-parsi**
idiom, idiomatic expression;
phrase. **-tapa** phrase. **-yhdistys**
complex sentence. **-yhteys**

context.
lausu|a utter, say; state; *(ilmi)*
express; *(ääntää)* pronounce;
(runo) recite, read poetry; *~*
ajatuksensa jstk give one's
opinion about. **-ja** reciter,
elocutionist. **-ma** utterance,
statement. **-nta** pronunciation;
(runon) poetry reading,
recitation; *(~ilta* recital;
~taide art of elocution). **-nto**
statement; *(virall.)* report;
opinion.
lauta board; *lyödä jku laudalta*
displace, cut. . out. **-kunta**
board, committee, commission;
lak. jury. **-mies** juryman,
juror, lay member of a court.
-nen plate; *lentävä ~* flying
saucer; *-set (mus.)* cymbals.
-sliina [table] napkin.
lauta|ta *(yli)* ferry; *tukkeja*
float. **-tarha** timber *(Am.*
lumber) yard. **-vuoraus**
[weather] boarding; wainscot.
lauteet platform in a sauna.
lautt|a ferry [-boat]; raft; *juna-*
~ train ferry. **-asilta** floating
bridge. **-aus** floating; *(~väylä*
waterway for timber-floating).
-uri ferryman.
lava platform, *(katsoja-)* stand,
(näyttämö) stage; *(kukkas-)*
bed; *(lasinalainen)* cold frame,
(lämmin) hotbed.
lavantauti typhoid fever.
lavas|taa stage. **-taja** stage *(t.*
scenic) designer. **-teet** set[s].
-tus staging, stage decor,
[stage] scenery.
lavea wide; extensive;
(seikkaperäinen) circumstantial,
exhaustive; *~sti (m.)* at great
length.
laventeli lavender.
laver|rella, -rus jabber, babble;
älä -tele asiasta don't blab.
-telija chatterbox.
laveri [sleeping] bunk.
lavetti gun-carriage.
lavitsa bench.
legenda legend.
legioona legion.
lehah|taa flit, *ohi* by; *~*
lentoon take wing; *hänen*
kasvonsa -tivat punaisiksi her
face flushed.
lehd|etön leafless, bare. **-istö**

foliage; *(sanoma-)* the press;
(~**tilaisuus** press conference).
-**ittyä** put forth leaves.
lehmus lime, linden, *Am.*
basswood.
lehmä cow. -**kauppa**, *-kaupat*
log-rolling, deal [between
political parties]. -**nliha** beef.
lehteillä leaf [in a book].
lehteri gallery.
lehtevä leafy, rich in foliage.
lehti leaf *(pl.* leaves);
(sanoma-) [news]paper;
(avaimen) bit; *puu on
lehdessä* the tree is in leaf;
puhjeta lehteen burst into
leaf. -**kaali** kale. -**kasvi** foliage
plant. -**kuja** avenue. -**kulta**
gold-leaf (-foil). -**kuusi** larch.
-**maja** arbour, bower. -**metsä**
broad-leaved deciduous
wood [land]. -**mies** journalist.
-**myymälä** news-stand,
book-stall. -**mäinen** leaflike.
-**puu** broad-leaved deciduous
tree. -**saha** fret-saw. -**salaatti**
lettuce. -**täi** plant-louse *(pl.*
-lice). -**vihreä** chlorophyll. -**ö**
[writing] pad, *(piirustus-)*
drawing pad, sketch-block.
lehto grove, coppice, copse.
-**kerttu** garden warbler.
-**kurppa** woodcock.
-**pöllö** tawny owl.
lehtori *l. v. (koul.)* senior
teacher, *(yliop.)* lecturer.
lehvä spray, twig.
leija kite. -**illa** hover, float;
soar.
leijona lion, *(naaras)* lioness.
-**nkita** *bot.* snapdragon.
leik|ata cut; *(esim. puku)* cut
out; *(paistia ym)* carve;
(saksilla, m.) clip; *(lyhyeksi)*
crop; *(hedelmäpuita)* prune;
lääk. operate, *jku* on;
(puhkaista) lance; *geom.*
intersect; *(tukka, tasoittaa)*
trim, *(kynnet)* cut, pare; ~
poikki, pois cut off; *(lyhyeksi)*
-**attu** [cut] short, *(tukka, m.)*
closely cropped. -**e** *(lehti-)*
[press] cutting, *(liha-)* steak;
(~**kirja** scrap-book). -**ellä** cut,
clip; *(pieneksi)* cut up;
(ruumiita) dissect.
leikilli|nen joking, jocular,
playful, humorous. -**syys**

humour [ousness], jocularity.
leikin|laskija joker. -**lasku**
joking, jest. -**teko** child's play;
elämä ei ole ~*a* life is no
joke; *se on hänelle vain* ~*a*
for him it is the easiest
thing.
leikitellä play (with).
leikk|aaja cutter, *(elon)* reaper;
elok. editor -**aus** cutting; cut,
incision; *lääk.* operation; *elok.*
editing; *(poikki~)* section;
(koriste-) carving; (~**piste**
[point of] intersection;
~**pöytä** operating-table; ~**sali**
operating-room, -theatre).
-**auttaa** *(tukkansa)* have one's
hair cut, have a haircut,
(hyvin lyhyeksi) have a close
crop.
leikkele *ks. leike;* ~*et* cold
cuts. -**liike** delicatessen shop
(store)
leikki game; *(pila)* joke, jest,
fun; *leikillä(än)* in fun, in
play, by way of a joke; ~
sikseen joking apart; *siitä on*
~ *kaukana* it is no joking
matter; *kääntää leikiksi* turn. .
into a joke; *laskea* ~*ä* joke,
jest, make fun [of a p.];
lasketko ~*ä? (narraatko)* are
you kidding?. -**kalu** toy.
plaything; (~**kauppa** toyshop).
-**kehä** play pen. -**kenttä**
playground. -**puhe** joke, jest.
-**sota** sham fight. -**syys**
playfulness. -**sä** playful. -**toveri**
playmate, play-fellow. -**ä** play,
be at play; ~ *sotaa* play
at being soldiers,
play war-games.
leikkokukat cut flowers.
leikkuu *(elon)* harvest. -**aika**
reaping time. -**kone** *(tukan)*
clippers; *(elon-)* harvester.
-**lauta** cutting-board. -**mies**
harvester, reaper. -**puimuri**
combine harvester.
leili flagon.
leima stamp; *(sinetti)* seal;
painaa ~*nsa jhk* leave its
mark (stamp) on; ~*a antava*
characteristic. -**amaton**
unstamped.
leimah|dus flash; flash of
lightning. -**taa** flash, flare; ~
ilmituleen burst into flame [s],

(kuv.) blaze up, flare up.
leima|maksu stamp-duty.
-merkki [revenue]stamp.
-paperi stamped paper. **-sin**
[rubber] stamp, stamper, die;
(~**väri** stamping ink). **-ta**
stamp, *jksk* as, *(petturiksi
ym)* brand as; *oli jnk -ama
(kuv.)* bore the imprint of,
was marked by. **-uttaa** have..
stamped. **-vero** stamp-duty.
leimu, -ta flame, blaze; *-ava*
flaming, *(kuv.)* burning,
glowing, fiery.
leini gout, rheumatism.
leinikki *bot.* buttercup.
leipo|a bake; ~ *kakku* make
(kypsentää bake) a cake. **-mo**
bakery, baker's [shop].
leipuri baker. **-liike** bakery,
baker's business; pastry shop.
leipä bread; loaf *(pl.* loaves);
ansaita ~nsä earn one's
living; *lyödä leiville* be worth
while, pay. **-kori** bread-basket.
-kortti bread ticket. **-myymälä**
baker's [shop]. **-puu**
bread-fruit tree; *kuv.* means
of livelihood. **-työ** daily
bread and butter stint,
day-to-day job. **-viipale** slice
of bread. **-vilja** food grain.
leiri camp, encampment;
asettua ~in encamp. **-elämä**
camping; *viettää ~ä* camp.
-ntä camping; (~**alue** camping
site *t.* ground). **-paikka**
camping place. **-tuli** camp
fire. **-ytyä** encamp.
leivin|jauhe baking powder;
-lauta pastry board. **-uuni**
baking oven.
leiviskä *kuv.* talent.
leivo [sky]lark.
leivonnai|nen: *-set* pastries.
leivos pastry, cake. **-lapio** cake
slice. **-pihdit** cake tongs.
leivän|kuori crust of bread.
-muru breadcrumb. **-pala** piece
(bit) of bread. **-puute** scarcity
of bread.
leivätön breadless.
lejeerinki *tekn.* alloy.
lekkeri [small] keg.
lekotella bask [in the sun].
lelli|kki, -poika pet, favourite.
-tellä coddle, pamper; ~
pilalle spoil by coddling.

-ttely pampering, fondling.
lelu toy, plaything.
lemmekäs amorous.
lemmen|juoma love potion,
philtre. **-laulu** love-song.
-seikkailu love-affair.
lemmi|kki darling; favourite;
bot. forget-me-not; (~**eläin**
pet). **-skellä** make love. **-skely**
love-making, *(halailu)* cuddling,
Am. necking. **-tty** beloved;
sweetheart.
lempe|ys mildness; leniency;
kohdelle liialla -ydellä
overindulge. **-ä** mild, sweet;
gentle; (~**luontoinen** gentle,
sweet-tempered).
lempi love. **-ajatus** pet idea.
-harrastus hobby. **-lapsi**
favourite [child]. **-nimi** pet
name. **-runoilija** favourite
poet. **-ä** love; make love.
lemu, -ta smell; stink.
leninki dress, frock.
lenkki loop; *(kiinnitys-)*
fastening; *lähteä lenkille* go
for a run (a walk).
lenn|ellä fly about, hover.
-okas winged, eloquent, lofty.
-okki model aeroplane.
lennon|johtaja air control
officer. **-johto** airfield control.
lennätin telegraph. **-kuva**
telephoto. **-lanka** telegraph
wire. **-toimisto** telegraph
office. **-tieto** telegraphic
message.
lento flight; *lähteä ~on* take
wing; *nousta ~on (kone)* take
off; *ampua lennosta* shoot..
on the wing. **-aika** flying
time. **-ase** air arm. **-emäntä**
air hostess, *Am.* air
stewardess. **-hiekka** driftsand.
-hyökkäys aerial attack,
(-pommitus) air-raid. **-kala**
flying fish. **-kenttä** airfield,
airport, aerodrome.
-kirje: ~*enä* by airmail.
lentokone aeroplane, plane,
aircraft *(pl.* = *sg.), Am,*
airplane. **-suoja** hangar.
-mekaanikko air mechanic.
lento|lehti leaflet **-linja** air-line
(-route), aerial service. **-lippu**
flight ticket. **-matka** trip by air
flight. **-näytös** flying display.
-onnettomuus air crash

(accident). **-pallo** volleyball.
-pommi [aerial] bomb. **-posti**
airmail; ~*tse* by a. **-suukko:**
heittää ~blow a kiss. **-teitse**
by air. **-tukialus**
aircraft-carrier. **-tukikohta** air
base. **-tähti** shooting star,
meteor. **-vuoro** flight, aerial
service. **-yhtiö** air line.
lentue flight.
lentäjä flyer, airman, aviator,
(ohjaaja) pilot.
lentää fly; *(matkustaa
lentokoneella, m.)* go (travel)
by air.
leopardi leopard.
lepakko bat.
lepattaa flutter, *(liekki)* flicker;
(räpytellä) flap.
leper|rellä, -tely babble, gurgle.
lepinkäinen *zo.* shrike.
lepo rest, *(rauha)* quiet; *mennä
levolle* go to bed; *levossa* at
rest; ~! *(sot.)* at ease. **-asento**
resting position. **-hetki** hour
of rest. **-koti** convalescent
home. **-paikka** resting-place.
-päivä day of rest. **-sohva**
couch, divan. **-tasanne** landing.
-tuoli easy chair.
lepp|eä, -oisa mild, sweet;
gentle, placid.
leppymä|ttömyys implacability.
-tön implacable, unappeasable,
relentless, irreconcilable.
leppyä be conciliated
(appeased); *(sopia)* be
reconciled (with).
leppä alder. **-kerttu** ladybird.
-lintu redstart.
lepra leprosy.
lepuu|ttaa rest; *-ttava* restful.
lepyttää conciliate, propitiate;
appease.
lerppa: *olla lerpallaan* hang
loose, slouch. **-huulinen** with
drooping lips.
leseet bran.
lesemätön *(jauho)* whole meal.
leskenlehti *bot.* coltsfoot.
leskeys widowhood, *(miehen)*
widowerhood.
leski widow; *(-mies)* widower;
jäädä leskeksi (naisesta) be
left a widow, be widowed.
-kuningatar Queen dowager.
-mies widower.
lesti: ~*t* shoe-trees; *panna* ~*lle*

(venyttää) tree; *pysyä* ~*ssään*
stick to one's last.
lestyjauhot sifted flour.
letka|us gibe, *(vastaus)* retort;
a dig [at me, *minulle*].
-uttaa make a sarcastic
remark, taunt.
letku hose; tube, tubing.
letti plait.
letukka hussy.
leuka chin; *(-pieli)* jaw.
-kuoppa dimple. **-lappu** bib.
-luu jawbone.
leukoija stock.
leuto mild; ~ *ilmasto*
temperate climate. **-us**
mildness.
leve|ntää broaden, widen. **-tä**
broaden, widen [out]. **-ys**
breadth, width; (~**aste** [degree
of] latitude; ~**piiri** parallel).
leveä broad, wide. **-harteinen**
broad-shouldered, square-built.
-lierinen wide-brimmed.
-raiteinen broad-gauge.
levi|kki circulation. **-ttää**
spread, spread out; *(laajentaa)*
extend; *kuv. m.* propagate,
disseminate; ~ *perättömiä
huhuja* spread (circulate) false
reports. **-tä** spread; *(ulottua)*
extend; *sanomalehti -ää
laajalle* the newspaper has a
large circulation; *laajalle -nnyt*
widely distributed, widespread.
-äminen spread[ing], *(esim.
kasvin)* propagation.
levolli|nen calm, unperturbed;
composed, self-possessed. **-suus**
calmness; coolness, composure;
equanimity.
levo|ton restless; uneasy (about,
for a p.), anxious (about);
olla ~ *jstk (m.)* worry about;
saattaa -ttomaksi make. .
uneasy, fill. . with anxiety;
-ttomat ajat turbulent times.
-tto|muus restlessness;
uneasiness; anxiety;
disturbance; *-muutta herättävä*
alarming, disquieting.
levy plate, *(ohut metalli-)*
sheet, *(kova- ym.)* board, *(iki-
ym)* lacquered board, *vrt.
kuitu- ym; (et. pyöreä)* disk;
(pöydän) top, *(irto-)* leaf;
(ääni-) record, disc; *ottaa
(laulaa, soittaa)* ~*lle* record.

-inen: *metrin* ~ one metre wide (in width). **-ke** plaque. **-seppä** sheet-iron worker, tinsmith. **-soitin** record player; (~**automaatti** jukebox). **-ttää** record. **-tys** recording.

levä 1. *olla* ~*llään* be spread [out]; *siivet* ~*llään* with widespread wings. **2.** *bot.* alga *(pl.* algae).

leväh|dys rest; (~**hetki** breathing-spell). **-tää** rest [oneself], take a rest.

leväperäi|nen negligent, neglectful. **-syys** negligence.

levä|tä rest, have a rest; repose; *olen* ~*nnyt kyllikseni* I have had a good rest; *-tköön rauhassa* may he rest in peace.

leyhytellä fan.

liata dirty, soil; smear; mess [up], make a mess of; *(housunsa, lapsesta)* foul.

Libanon the Lebanon; *l-ilainen* Lebanese.

liberalisoi|da liberalize. **-nti** liberalization.

liehakoi|da fawn upon; ~ *jkn suosioon* (m.) curry favour with, insinuate oneself into a p.'s good graces; *-va* fawning. **-tsija** fawner; flatterer.

liehi|tellä make much of, pay court to. **-ttely** exaggerated attentions.

liehu|a flutter, flap, *(lippu)* fly; *-vin lipuin* with colours flying. **-ttaa** make.. flutter; wave.

lieju slime, mud, mire, ooze. **-inen** muddy, miry. **-maa** miry ground; *(hyllyvä)* quagmire. **-pohja** mud [dy] bottom.

lieka tether; *panna* ~*an* tether.

liek|ehtiä flame, blaze, flash. **-inheitin** flame-thrower. **-ki** flame; *olla* ~*en vallassa* be ablaze.

liemi soup; »*liemessä*» in the soup, in a spot. **-kauha** soup scoop. **-lautanen** soup plate. **-malja** tureen. **-ruoka** liquid food.

lienee may; *hän* ~ *tullut* he has probably come; ~*kö se totta* I wonder whether it is true.

lieri brim. **-ö** cylinder. **-ömäinen** cylindrical.

liero worm.

liesi range, (electric) cooker.

liete silt; *(maatuma)* alluvium; *lietteet* sludge. **-hiekka** alluvial sand.

lietsoa blow; *kuv.* fan the flame of, foment; ~ *uutta rohkeutta* inspire new courage.

liettualainen, -nkieli Lithuanian.

lieve hem, *(reuna)* border; *jnk liepeillä* close to, on the outskirts of. **-ilmiö** fringe phenomenon.

lieven|nys relief, ease; alleviation. **-tyä** become less severe, be relieved, ease (up *t.* off). **-tää** relieve, allay; *(rangaistusta)* mitigate, reduce; relax; *-tävät asianhaarat* extenuating circumstances; ~ *ehtoja* moderate (modify) the terms.

lievetakki frock-coat.

lievike relief.

lievi|mmin: ~ *sanoen* to say the least of it, to put it at its mildest. **-ttää** ease; soothe. **-tys** relief, ease.

liev|yys slightness; lightness, leniency. **-ä** mild; slight; *(rangaistus ym)* light; lenient.

liha flesh; *(teuras-)* meat; ~*a syövä (eläimistä)* carnivorous; *hyvässä* ~*ssa* well fed. **-inen** fleshy; meaty. **-kappale** cut of meat, *(iso)* chunk of meat. **-karja** beef (store) cattle. **-kauppa** butcher's [shop]. **-kauppias** butcher. **-ksinen** muscular. **-ksisto** muscular system. **-ksitulo** *usk.* incarnation. **-liemi** broth, clear soup; (~**kuutio** stock cube). **-llinen** carnal, fleshly. **-mehuste** beef extract. **-muhennos** stewed meat. **-mylly** mincing machine. **-nkidutus** asceticism. **-nsyöjä** *zo.* carnivore. **-nvärinen** flesh-coloured. **-piirakka** meat pie. **-pyörykkä** meat ball. **-ruoka** *(-laji)* meat course, meat [dish]. **-säilykkeet** tinned (canned) meat.

lihas muscle. **-kudos** muscular tissue. **-säie** muscular fibre.

-toiminta muscular action.
-voima muscular strength.
lihav|a fat, *(henk., m.)* stout,
corpulent. **-ahko** inclined to
stoutness, somewhat stout.
-uus fatness; stoutness,
corpulence.
liho|a gain [weight]; *hän -i 7
kiloa* he gained (put on) 7
kilos. **-ttaa** make. . fat;
(syöttämällä) fatten.
liiaksi too much, too; *~kin*
more than enough, enough
and to spare; *syödä ~*
overeat; *veloittaa ~*
overcharge.
liialli|nen excessive;
superfluous, surplus;
(kohtuuton) inordinate; *~
kohteliaisuus* excessive
(exaggerated) politeness. **-suus**
excess [iveness]; extravagance;
superfluity; *mennä -suuksiin*
go to extremes.
liian too; *~ suuri* too big
(large); excessive; *~kin hyvin*
only too well; *~ herkkä,
kohtelias (m.)* oversensitive,
overpolite.
liidellä float, soar.
liietä: *liikeneekö sinulta 20
markkaa* can you spare me
twenty marks; *liikenemään
asti* [enough and] to spare.
liika *a (tarpeeton)* superfluous,
surplus; excess [ive]; *se on
~a* it is too much; *maksaa
~a* pay too much; *syödä ~a*
overeat; *minä olen täällä ~a*
I am one too many here.
-asutus overpopulation.
liikah|dus movement. **-duttaa**
[cause to] move, stir. **-taa**
move, stir, *(hievahtaa)* budge;
-tamatta without stirring,
motionless.
liika|herkkyys over-sensitiveness.
-herkkä over-sensitive, highly
strung. **-hienostus** over-refinement. **-kuormitus** overload.
-lihavuus obesity. **-maksu**
overpayment; *ottaa ~a*
overcharge. **-määrä** excess
[amount]; surplus. **-nainen**
superfluous; surplus;
(liiallinen) excessive. **-naisuus**
superfluity; superabundance.
-nimi by-name, nickname.

-paino overweight, excess
weight. **-rasitus** overstrain,
over-exertion. **-tuotanto**
over-production. **-varvas** corn.
-väestö surplus population,
overspill.
liike motion, movement;
(kauppa-) business, [business]
firm, concern, *(myymälä)*
shop; *käden~ (m.)* gesture;
lopettaa ~ wind up business;
panna liikkeelle set . . going (in
motion), *(kuv. koota)* muster
up; start; *liikkeessä* in
motion, *(raha ym)* in
circulation; *laskea liikkeeseen*
issue, put in circulation **-aika:**
~na during business hours.
-ala: *antautua ~lle* adopt a
business career, go into
business. **-apulainen**
shop-assistant. **-asia** business
matter; *-asioissa* on business;
olla -asioissa jkn kanssa
transact (do) business with.
-elämä business [life]; *~ on
lamassa* business is dull
(slack). **-hermo** motor nerve.
-htiä stir, move about, *sot.*
manoeuvre. **-huoneisto** business
premises. **-kannallepano**
mobilization. **-kanta:** *asettaa
-kannalle* mobilize. **-keskus**
business centre. **-kirje** business
letter. **-kumppani** partner;
ottaa ~ksi take. . into
partnership. **-laajuus** range of
movement. **-laskenta**
accountancy. **-maailma** world
of business. **-matka** business
trip. **-mies** business [-]man;
(~mäinen businesslike).
-nainen business woman. **-nevä**
available, spare; surplus.
liikenne traffic; service;
välittää ~ttä run, ply
[between A. and B.]. **-este**
obstacle to traffic; *~en takia*
on account of the traffic
being blocked **-häiriö**
disruption of traffic. **-kone**
passenger plane. **-kulttuuri**
road manners. **-kuolema**
death-toll on the roads. **-laitos**
public transport [service].
-lentäjä commercial pilot.
-merkki traffic sign.
-onnettomuus traffic accident.

-poliisi constable on
point-duty. -rikkomus traffic
violation, motoring offence.
-seisaus traffic jam. -säännöt
traffic regulations. -turvallisuus
traffic safety. -valo traffic
light. -väline means of
conveyance. -väylä traffic
route, (katu) thoroughfare.
-yhteys connection [s]. -ympyrä
[traffic] roundabout (t. Am.
circle).
liikennöi|dä run [a line, linjaa,
to jnnek], maintain traffic,
operate [between. . and. .].
-tsijä traffic contractor. -tävä
trafficable.
liikenteenjakaja divisional
island.
liike|pankki commercial bank.
-pula business crisis. -pääoma
working capital. -salaisuus
trade secret. -suhteet business
connections; olla -suhteissa
jkh have business relations
(with), be connected with.
-talo commercial house.
firm. -toimi [business]
transaction. -toiminta business
activity. -toimisto office.
-tuttava business acquaintance,
b. friend; (asiakas) customer;
client. -vaihto turnover;
(~vero purchase tax). -voima
motive power, propelling power. -voitto profit. -yhteys ks.
-suhteet. -yritys business
enterprise.
liikkeellepaneva motive; kuv.
impelling.
liikkeellä about, on the move;
huhuja on ~ rumours are
going around, (voimia. .)
forces are at work.
liikkeen|harjoittaja business
man, shopkeeper. -hoitaja
manager of a business.
liikkeeseenlasku issue.
liikkiö ham.
liikku|a move, stir; (hievahtaa)
budge; (olla liikkeessä) be in
motion; be in circulation;
(huhu ym) be afloat; be
current. -matila space to
move, elbow-room. -maton
immobile, motionless.
-mattomuus immobility. -va
moving; mobile; ~ kalusto

(rautat.) rolling stock. -vaisuus
mobility.
liikunta movement; [physical]
exercise. -kasvatus physical
training. -kyky ability to
move. -vapaus freedom of
movement.
liiku|skella move about. -tella
move; (käsitellä) handle;
-teltava movable. -ttaa move
(m. kuv.), stir (m. kuv.); kuv.
touch; (koskea) concern; se ei
-ta minua it does not concern
me, it is no business of
mine; -ttava moving, touching;
-ttunut moved, touched. -tus
emotion.
liima glue. -inen gluey. -nauha
gummed tape. -ta glue; ~ jhk
(m.) stick, paste, paste. . up
(in, on). -us gluing. -väri
distemper.
liina (-vaate) linen; (pää-) head
scarf; pöytä~ table-cloth.
-inen linen. -vaate: -vaatteet
linen; (~kaappi linen
cupboard). -öljy linseed oil.
liioin: ei ~ not. . either,
neither.
liioi|tella exaggerate, overdo; ~
osassaan (näyttelijästä)
overact; -teltu exaggerated;
extravagant. -ttelu exaggeration.
liipais|in trigger. -ta pull the
trigger.
liister|i paste. -öidä paste;
gum, stick.
liite (kirjaan) appendix;
(asiakirjaan) supplement;
(kirjeeseen) enclosure. -kohta
joint, junction. -kuva plate.
liitin (paperi-) paper clip.
liitolento gliding. -kone glider.
liitos joint; join, seam; (jatkos)
scarf; aueta liitoksistaan burst
seams. -alue l.v. suburban
area. -paperi gummed tape.
liitto alliance; league, union;
federation; (sopimus) treaty;
olla liitossa jkn kanssa be
allied with; tehdä ~ enter
into an alliance. -hallitus
federal government. -kansleri
[Federal] Chancellor. -kunta
league; [con]federation.
-lainen allied. -utua form
(enter into) an alliance; ally
themselves; join forces, be

leagued together (against),
gang up (on, against).
-utumaton non-aligned. **-utunut**
allied; *-utuneet* the allies.
-tasavalta federal republic.
liitt|yä join; attach oneself to;
(jäseneksi) become a member
of; enter; ~ *puolueeseen* join
a party; *hänen nimensä -yy. .*
his name is associated with;
siihen -yy kustannuksia it
involves expense; *-yen
(edelliseen puhujaan)* in
agreement with.
liittää join; enclose [in a
letter, *kirjeeseen*]; attach;
(lisäksi) add; *(yhteen)* unite;
(osana kokonaisuuteen)
incorporate.
liitu chalk. **-kallio** chalk cliff.
-palanen piece of chalk.
-paperi enamelled paper.
liitän|näisjäsen associate
member. **-täjohto** cord, flex.
liitää glide; float, soar.
liivate gelatine.
liivi(t) waistcoat, *Am.* vest;
(naisen) [elastic] corset;
(kapeat) girdle, suspender
(Am. garter) belt, *(lasten)*
under-bodice, *(kansallispuvun
ym)* bodice; *housu~*
panti-girdle.
liivihame petticoat dress.
lika dirt; filth. **-antua** get
dirty, become soiled, soil;
(esim. vesi) be polluted. **-inen**
dirty, soiled; unclean, impure,
filthy. **-isuus** dirtiness;
impurity, unclean[li]ness.
-kaivo cesspool. **-pilkku** spot
of dirt. **-sanko** slop bucket.
-vesi *(pesu- ym)* slops;
sewage. **-viemäri** sewer.
likei|nen intimate. **-syys**
intimacy; *vrt. läheinen, -syys.*
liki near, close [to]. **-arvo**
approximate value. **-main**
approximately, very nearly;
(noin) about; *ei ~kaan* not
nearly, nothing like. **-määrin**
approximately, roughly.
-määräinen approximate,
rough. **-näköinen** near-(short-)
sighted.
likis|tyä be jammed, get
squeezed. **-tää** *(jkn kättä)*
squeeze; jam; *(olla ahdas)*

pinch.
liko: *olla liossa* [be]
soak[ing]; *panna ~on* put to
soak, *kuv.* risk. **-märkä**
soaked, wet through.
likvidoida liquidate.
likööri liqueur.
lilja lily.
lima mucus, phlegm; *(esim.
kalan)* slime. **-inen** slimy;
mucous. **-kalvo** mucous
membrane.
limittäin [with edges]
overlapping; *olla ~* overlap.
limonaati lemonade.
limppu [round] loaf.
lingota sling; fling, hurl;
(pyykkiä) spin-dry.
linja line; *koul.* course.
-auto bus; *(kauko-)* coach;
(~pysäkki bus stop). **-jako**
l.v. division into lines *(tason
mukaan;* streams), choice of
line (course). **-laiva** liner.
linkkitorni television
transmission tower.
linkkuveitsi clasp-knife.
linko sling; *pyykki~* spin dryer.
linna castle; *(palatsi)* palace;
(vankila) prison; *(linnoitus)*
fortress; *istua ~ssa* be
imprisoned, be in prison. **-ke**
fort. **-mainen** palatial.
linnan|herra lord of the castle.
-kirkko palace chapel. **-piha**
castle yard. **-päällikkö**
commandant. **-rouva** chatelaine.
linnaväki *sot.* garrison.
linnoi|ttaa fortify. **-tus**
fortification; *(linna)* fortress,
citadel, stronghold; *(~laitteet*
fortifications).
linnun|laulu song of birds.
-muna bird's egg. **-pelätti**
scarecrow. **-pesä** bird's nest.
-poika young bird, fledgling.
L~rata the Milky Way,
galaxy. **-silmä:** *~llä nähty(nä)*
a bird's-eye view of. . **-tie:**
~tä as the crow flies.
linnus|taa fowl. **-taja** fowler.
linoli, -matto linoleum.
linssi lens.
lintsata play truant, cut
[lessons, a lesson].
lint|ta: *kengät ovat -assa* the
shoes (heels) are worn down
one side.

lintu bird. **-häkki** bird-cage.
-kauppias poulterer; *(häkki-)*
bird-fancier. **-koira** bird dog,
pointer, setter. **-lauta** bird
table. **-nen** birdie. **-parvi** flock
of birds. **-pyssy** fowling-piece.
-tiede ornithology. **-tieteilijä**
ornithologist.
lio|ta soak, get soaked. **-ttaa**
soak.
lipas box, case. **-to** chest of
drawers; *(kirjoitus-)* desk.
lipeä lye. **-kala** [dried] codfish
soaked in lye solution.
-kielinen glib-tongued. **-kivi**
caustic soda.
lippa peak. **-lakki** peaked cap.
lippo landing-net, scoop-net.
lippu flag, banner, standard,
colours; *(piletti)* ticket;
(äänestys-) ballot paper;
(paperi-) slip; *nostaa ~ (mer.)*
hoist one's flag; *laskea ~*
lower (strike) one's flag.
-kangas bunting. **-kunta**
company. **-laiva** flagship.
-myymälä ticket-office
(-window), *teatt.* box-office.
-tanko flagstaff, flag pole.
lipsah|dus slip [of the tongue].
-taa *(luiskahtaa)* slip; *se -ti
huuliltani* it slipped out, it
[just] escaped me.
lipun|kantaja standard-bearer.
-myyjä booking-clerk.
liputtaa flag; *tänään liputetaan*
the flags are flying today [in
honour of.. *jkn kunniaksi*];
liputettu decorated with flags.
liristä purl, ripple.
lirkuttaa *(mielistellä)* coax.
lisensiaat|ti: *lääketieteen ~*
Licentiate in Medicine.
lisenssi licence; *~lla on (t.
under)* l.
lisko lizard; *(herneen)* l.v. pod.
Lissabon Lisbon.
lista 1. *rak.* lath, *(piena)*
moulding. **2.** list, catalogue,
Am. catalog; register.
lisä addition; increase; *tämän
~ksi* besides this, in addition
to this; *ehdotan ~ksi I*
further propose; *kaksi ~ä* two
more; *halutteko ~ä teetä*
would you like some more
tea? *ota vähän ~ä!* have
some more! **-aine** *(ruoan)*

additive. **-arvovero**
value-added tax *(lyh.* VAT).
-edut fringe benefits. **-joki**
tributary. **-ke** appendage,
appendix. **-kulu** extra expense.
-laite accessory [equipment].
-lehti supplement; special
edition. **-maksu** additional
charge, *rautat.* excess fare.
-merkitys secondary meaning.
-munuaiset adrenal glands.
-nimi nickname. **-osa**
accessory part. **-rakennus**
extension, annex [e]. **-tauti**
complication. **-tieto** further
information; *~ja antaa..* for
further particulars apply to. .
-tulo extra income. **-tä** add,
jhk to; *(enentää)* increase,
bring. . up to; heighten;
(esim. ponnistuksia) intensify;
(täydentää) supplement;
augment; *haluan vielä ~ I*
wish to add [that]. **-varuste**
(auton ym) accessory, extra;
~et optional equipment. **-vero**
additional tax, surtax. **-voimat**
reinforcements. **-ys** addition;
increase; *(kasvu)* growth;
palkan ~ increase (rise) of
salary. **-äntyminen** increase;
(esim. solun) multiplication;
(suvun) propagation,
reproduction. **-änt|yä** increase;
multiply; *(esim. ihmiset)*
reproduce themselves, *(eläin)*
breed; *yhä -yvä liikenne* the
steadily increasing (growing)
traffic.
litis|tyä be flattened. **-tää**
flatten [down], squash.
litra litre (1.76 pints), *Am.*
liter.
litteä flat.
liturgia liturgy.
liue|ntaa, -ta dissolve.
liukas slippery; *(ovela)* smart.
-kielinen glib. **-tua** slip, lose
one's footing.
liukene|maton insoluble. **-va**
soluble.
liukkaus slipperiness.
liuku|a slide; slip; glide; *ks.
luisua.* **-hihna** conveyor belt;
assembly line; *kuin ~lta* in a
steady stream. **-objektiivi**
zoom lens. **-portaat** escalator,
moving staircase. **-rata** chute;

slide.
liuo|s solution. **-tin** solvent,
(esim. öljyn) emulgator. **-ttaa**
dissolve.
liuska *(paperi- ym)* slip, strip,
(siru) piece; chip; *anat.*
lobule. **-kivi** slate.
liuske slate, *(kiteinen)* schist.
liuta crowd, swarm.
livahtaa slip; ~ *jkn käsistä* s.
through. . 's fingers; ~
karkuun escape, slip away; ~
kuin koira veräjästä get away
with it.
liveri livery. **-pukuinen** liveried.
liver|rys warble, twitter. **-tää**
trill; *(linnusta)* warble, chirp.
live|ttää: *jalkaa* ~ it is
slippery. **-tä** slip.
livistää bolt, make off, *sl.*
hook it.
loata soil, dirty, mess. . up.
logaritmi logarithm.
logiikka logic.
lohdu|llinen comforting,
consoling; *on -llista ajatella.*.
it is a comfort to think. .
-ton inconsolable, disconsolate.
-ttaa comfort, console.
-ttautua *(jllak)* console oneself
with, take comfort in.
-ttomuus disconsolateness. **-tus**
comfort; consolation, solace;
laiha ~ cold comfort;
*(~***palkinto** consolation prize).
lohen|poika young salmon.
-punainen salmon-coloured.
-pyynti catching salmon.
lohi salmon *(pl. = sg.).*
-käärme dragon. **-nen**
abounding in salmon. **-pato**
salmon-weir. **-perho** salmon-fly.
-portaat salmon-ladder.
lohjeta split, cleave; be broken
off, split off.
lohk|aista break off; *(erottaa)*
separate, detach; *(halkoa)*
split. **-are** block, boulder. **-o**
sector; section; *(esim.
keuhkon)* lobe. **-oa** separate;
partition; *(paloittaa)*
dismember. **-ominen** *(tilusten)*
partitioning of landed
property.
lohtu consolation, solace.
loihtia conjure; *(lumota)* cast
a spell on; *(esiin)* conjure up
loik|ata leap, bound, jump; *pol.*

defect. **-kaus** leap, bound.
-kia leap, bound; spring.
loikoilla loll, lie out-stretched;
sprawl.
loimi *(hevos-)* blanket;
(kankaan) warp.
loimu blaze, flare. **-koivu** flamy
birch. **-ta** blaze.
loinen parasite.
lois|eläin, -kasvi parasitic
animal (plant).
loiskah|dus splash; plunge.
-taa splash; ~ *mereen* splash
down.
loisk|e splash [ing] ; lap [ping] .
-ua, -utella splash.
loist|aa shine; *(säteillä)* beam;
~ *tiedoillaan* excel in; *hänen
silmänsä -ivat ilosta* her eyes
gleamed with joy; ~
kirkkaammin kuin jk
outshine. **-ava** shining, *m.*
kuv. bright; *kuv.* splendid,
magnificent, glorious (*~n
älykäs ym)* brilliant. **-e** shine;
light; lustre; *(säihky)* sparkle.
-elamppu fluorescent lamp.
-elias resplendent; *(upea)*
splendid, grand; *(pramea)*
showy, gorgeous; *(ylellinen)*
luxurious; sumptuous.
loisto brilliancy; splendour;
magnificence, grandeur;
(ylellisyys) luxury; show;
(majakka) beacon; *koko
~ssaan* in all its glory. **-auto**
luxury car. **-juna** de-luxe
train. **-kausi** flourishing
period, heyday, golden age.
-painos de-luxe edition.
loito|lla far away, far off; at
a distance; *pitää jkta* ~ keep
a p. at a distance (at arm's
length); *pysyä* ~ *(jstk)* keep
one's distance, stand aloof
(from). **-mma|lla, -lle** farther
away *(t.* off). **-ntaa** remove
(bring) farther away; *(sot.
joukkoja)* disengage. **-ntaminen**
sot. disengagement. **-ta** draw
away; drift farther away.
loit|sia conjure, practise magic;
(lumota) enchant; *(manata)*
call up. **-sija** magician;
sorcerer. **-su** incantation;
spell, charm; (*~***luku** charm,
magic formula. **-runo** magic
verse).

loiva gently sloping; *(esim. katto)* slanting.
lojaali loyal.
lojua loll.
loka mud, dirt; *vetää ~an (kuv.)* drag in the dirt. **-inen** muddy. **-kuu** October. **-suojus** mudguard, *(auton)* wing.
lokero compartment; *(kaapin)* pigeon-hole; *(talle-)* safe-deposit box.
lokikirja [ship's] log.
lokki gull; sea-gull.
lokomobiili traction-engine.
loksu|a, -ttaa *(kengistä)* fit loosely, flap [up and down] *(hampaista)* be loose; clack.
loma *(väli)* gap; interval; *(kesä- ym)* holidays, vacation; *sot.* leave, furlough; *(virkavapaus)* leave [of absence]; *jnk ~ssa, ~sta* between; *työn ~ssa* between working hours; *~lla* on leave; *hän on ~lla* he is away on holiday *(pitkällä:* for his holidays); *~ni on kesäkuussa* I have my holiday in June; *päästää ~lle (sot.)* furlough; *minulla on 3 tuntia ~a* I have three hours off. **-hetki** moment of leisure; *~nä* in spare hours. **-ilija** holiday-maker. **-ke** form, *Am.* blank. **-kurssi** vacation course, *(kesä-)* summer school. **-kylä, -leiri** holiday village (camp). **-matka** holiday tour. **-päivä** day off; holiday, day of recreation. **-uttaa** furlough, lay off.
lomit|se between, from among. **-taja** vacation replacement, holiday assistant.
lommo dent; *~ille painunut* [completely] buckled.
lompakko wallet, *Am. m.* billfold, pocket-book.
lonkero *(rönsy)* runner; *zo.* arm, tentacle.
lonkka hip; haunch. **-luu** hipbone. **-särky** sciatica.
Lontoo London. **l-lainen** *s.* Londoner; *a.* London.
logiikka logic.
loogi(lli)nen logical.
looši *(seuran)* lodge; *ks. aitio.*
lootus lotus, Chinese water-lily.

lopen quite, altogether; *~ kulunut* [completely] worn out, *(puheenparsi)* hackneyed; *~ väsynyt* tired out, dead tired, worn out, *sl.* dead beat.
lopetta|a end; finish, conclude, close; *(lakata)* stop; *(koulunsa)* leave, complete; *(eläin)* put down, put to sleep, destroy; *~ liike* discontinue (close) a business; *~ maksut* suspend payment; *~ toimintansa* cease its activities, *(yhtiö)* go out of business, *(tehdas)* close down; *~ tupakoiminen* leave off (give up, stop) smoking. **-jaiset** closing festivity, breaking up.
loppiai|nen Epiphany. **-saatto, -späivä** Twelfth-night.
loppu end, close, finish; conclusion, termination; *(jäännös)* rest, remainder; *tehdä ~ jstk* put an end to; *(jnk) lopulla* towards the end of; *lopulta* in the end, finally; *lopussa* at an end; over; *jnk lopussa* at the end of; *varat ovat lopussa* the funds are exhausted; *kaikki on lopussa* all is finished; *lopussa kiitos seisoo* all is well that ends well; *se on hänen ~nsa* that will be the end of him. **-a** end, *jhk* in; come to an end; *(lakata)* cease, stop; *(päättyä)* terminate; *olla -maisillaan* be drawing to a close; *häneltä -ivat rahat* he ran out of money, his money gave out; *viini -i* the wine ran out; *sodan loputtua* after the end of the war. **-erä** final [heat]. **-ikä** the rest of one's life. **-kilpailu** final. **-kiri** spurt. **-lause** concluding sentence, conclusion. **-liite** suffix. **-ma|ton** endless, interminable, never-ending; *l-ttomiin* indefinitely, endlessly. **-näytös** final act, closing scene. **-puoli** latter part; *jnk -puolella* toward the end of. **-pää** [tail-] end. **-sanat** closing words, epilogue. **-sointu** rhyme. **-summa** total amount.

-suora *kuv.* homestretch; *~lla* in the final straight. **-tili:** *antaa* pay off. **-tulos** final outcome, end result. **-tutkinto** final examination.

loppuun to an (to the) end; *palaa ~* burn out; *puhua ~* speak to the end, conclude; *saattaa ~* bring . . . to completion (to an end), carry. .through, complete. **-käsitelty** concluded. **-myydä** sell off, sell out, clear stock. **-myynti** clearance sale. **-myyty** sold out, out of stock; *(kirja)* out of print.

lopuksi finally; at last, in the end; *loppujen ~ (kuitenkin)* after all.

lopu|llinen final, ultimate; definitive; *~ voitto (m.)* decisive victory. **-lta** at last; in the end, finally, eventually, ultimately. **-ssa** *ks. loppu.* **-ton** endless, interminable; infinite.

lorista gurgle, bubble, purl.

loru idle talk, babble; *~a* nonsense! **-ta** jabber, talk nonsense.

lossi ferry.

loti|na, -sta splash, swash, squelch.

lotja barge, lighter.

louh|ia quarry, *(ampumalla)* blast. **-ikko** [jagged] rocks. **-os** quarry, stone-pit.

loukata hurt *(m. kuv.),* injure; *(solvata)* insult, offend; *(esim. lakia)* violate, infringe; *~ jkn oikeutta (m.)* encroach upon a p.'s rights; *se loukkaa korvaa* it offends the ear; *se loukkasi minua* it gave me offence, *(kunniaani, ylpeyttäni)* it piqued (wounded) my pride. **loukkaa|maton** inviolable. **-mattomuus** inviolability; integrity. **-ntua** be hurt *(m. kuv.),* be injured; *kuv.* take offence (at), be offended; resent, feel resentment; take sth. as a personal affront; *helposti -ntuva* quick to take offence. **-va** insulting. **loukkaus** offence, insult, affront; *~ tunteitani vastaan* an outrage to my feelings; *oikeuksieni ~* an infringement

of my rights. **-kivi** stumbling-block.

loukko corner, nook; cranny.

loukku trap; *(hamppu-)* brake.

lounai|nen south-west [erly], south-western. **-stuuli** south-west wind, south-wester.

lounas lunch, luncheon; *vrt. lounainen.* **-taa** lunch; *voisimmeko ~ yhdessä* could we have lunch together? can you meet me for lunch? **-tauko** lunch break.

lovi score, dent; notch; *(aukko)* gap; *leikata ~* notch; *langeta loveen* fall into a trance.

lude bed-bug.

luen|noida lecture [certain subjects], *jstk m.* on; give a lecture. **-noitsija** lecturer. **-to** lecture; *käydä -noilla* attend lectures; *(~sali* lecture room, auditorium).

luet|ella enumerate, give [a list of]; *~ järjestyksessä* give. . in order; *~ yksityiskohtaisesti (m.)* specify. **-tava** .. worth reading, readable; *s.* reading; *minulla ei ole mitään ~a* I have nothing to read. **-telo** list; catalogue; *merkitä (esim. jäsen) ~on* enrol. **-teloida** list. **-telointi** listing; enrolment.

luhistua fall in, tumble down; be shattered; collapse; *(suunnitelma)* come to nothing, fall through.

luhti loft.

luihu insinuating; sly.

luikerrella wriggle.

luimistaa *(hevosesta)* flatten his (her) ears.

lui|nen [.. of] bone. **-seva** bony, scrawny.

luis|kahtaa slip. **-taa** slide; *(solua)* glide; *(sujua)* run; *työ ~* the work is progressing [well]. **-telija** skater. **-tella** skate. **-telu** skating.

luistin [ice] skate. **-rata** skating rink.

luisu *(auton)* skidding.

luisua glide, slip; *(auto)* skid; slither [off the road]; *(alaspäin, kuv.)* go downhill.

luja firm; strong, stout;

(vankka) steady; *(kestävä)* durable; *(jyrkkä)* decided, resolute; *(järkähtämätön)* steadfast; stable; ~*a fast*, at high speed, *(kovalla äänellä)* loud; *pysyä* ~*na* stand firm, be steadfast, persevere; *olla* ~*ssa* be securely (firmly) fixed. **-luonteinen** firm, determined; strong-minded. **-rakenteinen** strongly built; sturdy, solid. **-sti** firmly, securely; hard *jne*. **-tahtoinen** strong-willed. **-tekoinen** of solid make, *(kestävä)* hard-wearing.

luji|lla: *olla* ~ have a hard time, be hard pressed (hard put to it); *pitää* ~ keep a firm hand over; *panna -lle* press hard; *se otti -lle* it was a tough job.

lujitt|aa make.. firmer; *kuv.* strengthen, cement. **-ua** grow firmer; *kuv.* be strengthened (fortified), grow [more] stable; *(esim. vastarinta)* stiffen.

lujuus firmness; strength; steadiness; steadfastness.

luke|a read; *(opiskella)* study; *(laskea)* count; ~ *kirjasta* read in a book; ~ *rukous* say a prayer; ~ *jnk ansioksi, jstk johtuvaksi* attribute (ascribe).. to; *kaikki siihen luettuna* all included; *tästä päivästä lukien* from this day *tammik. 1. päivästä lukien* [as] from January 1; *hänen päivänsä ovat luetut* his days are numbered. **-ma** reading. **-ma|ton** innumerable; countless, untold; *l-ttomia kertoja* times without number. **-minen** reading. **-misto** reader. **-neisuus** wide reading. **-nut** well-read, erudite. **-utua** count oneself, *jhk* among, *(kuulua)* be among.

lukija reader. **-kunta** [circle of] readers.

lukio *(Suomessa)* sixth, seventh and eighth forms of secondary school, *Engl.* sixth form [s], sixth form college, *Am.* senior high school. **-luokat** *ks. ed.*

lukit|a a lock [up]. **-sematon** unlocked.

lukkari precentor.

lukkiintua jam, be jammed.

lukko lock; latch; *(aseen)* breech; *lukon kieli* latch; *panna ~on* lock; *avata* ~ unlock; *lukon takana* under lock and key; *lukossa* locked, *(korva)* blocked. **-laite** locking device. **-neula** safety-pin. **-seppä** locksmith.

luku number; figure; *(kirjan)* chapter; *luvultaan..* in number; *luvut (opinnot)* studies; *ottaa* ~*un* take into account, *(huomioon)* allow for; *rahti* ~*un otettuna* including the freight; ~*un ottamatta* excluding.., with the exception of; *pitää* ~*a jstk* keep an account of; *jkn* ~*un* for account of; *1800-luvulla* in the 19th century, in the eighteenth-hundreds; *1920-luvulla* in the 1920's. **-halu** taste for study. **-inen:** *kuusi*~ a six-figure [phone number]; *suuri*~ large [in number]. **-isa** numerous; *olla* ~*mpi kuin..* outnumber, be superior in numbers to.. **-järjestys** timetable, schedule. **-kammio** study. **-kappale** reading passage. **-kausi** term; *Am.* semester; (~*maksu* term fee; ~*todistus* term report). **-kirja** reader. **-lasit** reading glasses. **-määrä** number; ~*ltään..* in number; *on* ~*ltään* numbers.. **-sali** reading-room. **-sana** numeral. **-suunnitelma** plan of study. **-taidoton** *(ja kirjoitus-)* illiterate. **-taito** ability to read, literacy. **-taitoinen** able to read, *(ja kirjoitus-)* literate. **-tie:** *antautua* ~*lle* go in for an academic career. **-vuosi** school year, academic year.

lume(ilmiö) delusion.

lumen|luonti snow clearing. **-tulo** snowfall.

lumeton snowless.

lumi snow; *sataa lunta* it is snowing; *peittyä lumeen* be snowed up; *lumen peittämä* covered with snow, snowbound. **-aura** snow plough. **-este** stoppage (block) owing to snow. **-hiutale** snowflake. **-kenkä** snowshoe. **-kiitäjä** snowcat. **-kinos** snowdrift. **-kko** weasel. **-lapio** snow shovel. **-linna** snow castle. **-mies** snowman. **-myrsky** snowstorm, blizzard. **-nen** snowy. **-pallo** snowball. **-peitteinen** covered with snow, *(vuori)* snow-capped. **-pyry** whirling (driving) snowstorm; *kovassa ~ssä* in driving snow. **-räntä** sleet. **-sade** fall of snow. **-sohjo** slush. **-sokea** snowblind. **-sota** snowball fight. **-ukko** snowman. **-valkea** snow-white. **-vyöry** avalanche.

lumme water-lily.

lumo: *olla jnk ~issa* be charmed by; *joutua jnk ~ihin* fall under..'s spell; *päästää ~ista* break the spell. **-ava** charming, fascinating. **-ta** enchant, bewitch; charm; *-ttu* enchanted; spellbound. **-us** enchantment; spell; *(-voima)* charm.

lumppu rag. **-ri** rag-and-bone man.

lunas|taa redeem *(m. usk.)*; buy.. out; *(vekseli)* pay, honour, meet; *~ matkalippu* buy a ticket; *~ pantista* take out of pawn; *~ velkakirja* redeem a promissory note. **-taja** redeemer. **-tus** redemption; *(-maksu) (kirjeen)* surcharge, *(leima-)* stamp fee.

lunnaat ransom.

luntata *l.v.* cheat.

luo to.

luoda create; *~ katseensa jhk* look at, glance at; *~ katseensa maahan* look down; *~ lunta* shovel (shift, clear) snow; *~ nahkansa* shed its skin; *~ valoa jhk* shed (throw) light on; *kuin luotu jhk* cut out for.

luodata sound.

luode north-west; *(pakovesi)* ebb; low tide, low water; *~ ja vuoksi* ebb and flow. **-tuuli** north-west [erly] wind.

luodinkestävä bullet-proof.

luoja creator; *L~* the Creator.

luoki|tella, -ttaa classify; grade.

-tus classification, grading.

luokka class; *Am. koul.* grade, *Engl. m.* form; category; *luokanvalvoja* class-teacher, form-master; *jäädä luokalle* not be moved up; *on omaa ~ansa* is in a class by itself. **-erotus** class distinction. **-huone** classroom. **-taistelu** class struggle. **-tietoinen** class-conscious. **-toveri** classmate.

luokse to; *~ni* to me; *otti hänet ~en* took him in. **-pääsemätön** inaccessible, unapproachable. **-päästävä** accessible,.. easy of access, approachable.

luola cave, grotto; *(eläimen)* den, lair; hole. **-ihminen** cave -man. **-tutkimus** speleology.

luomakunta creation.

luomi *(silmä-)* eyelid; *(ihossa)* birth-mark, mole.

luominen *(maailman)* creation; *lumen ~* clearing of snow.

luomis|historia the creation story. **-kyky, -voima** creative ability (power).

luomus creation.

luona: *jnk ~* near [to], close to; by, close by; *asua jkn ~* live (stay) with a p.; *syödä päivällistä jkn ~* dine with.. **luonne** character; personality; disposition; *luonteeltaan* by nature; of a [military, social etc.] nature. **-htia** characterize. **-näyttelijä** character actor. **-vikainen** *a.* psychopathic *s.* psychopath. **-vika(isuus)** disorder of character, psychopathy.

luonnis|taa, -tua: *-tuu hyvin* is a success, turns out well.

luonnolli|nen natural; *(teeskentelemätön)* unaffected, unstudied; *~ asia* a matter of course; *-sta kokoa (oleva)* life-size. **-sesti** naturally; of course; certainly. **-suus** naturalness.

luonnon|este physical impediment; *ellei ~itä satu* [wind and] weather permitting.. **-historia** natural history. **-ihana** beautiful,.. of great natural beauty; *~lla*

paikalla beautifully situated; ~
paikka a beauty-spot. **-ilmiö**
natural phenomenon. **-kansa**
primitive people. **-kauneus**
natural beauty, scenic beauty.
-kuvaus description of nature.
-laatu disposition, turn of
mind. **-lahja** gift of nature,
talent. **-laki** law of nature;
~en mukaisesti in the course
of nature. **-oppi** physical
science [s]. **-pakko** physical
necessity.
-parannus nature healing *(t.*
cure). **-raikas** fresh;
unaffected, unsophisticated.
-rikkaus natural wealth,
(-varat) n. resources. **-suojelija**
conservationist. **-suojelu**
[nature] conservation; *(~alue*
[nature] preserve). **-tiede**
natural science; *-tieteiden*
tohtori Doctor of Science (D.
Sc.). **-tieteellinen** pertaining to
natural science, natural
history *(attr.).* **-tieteilijä**
naturalist, [natural] scientist.
-tila natural state. **-tuote**
natural product. **-tutkija**
naturalist. **-varai|nen:** *l-sena* in
the wild state. **-vastainen.** .
contrary to nature. **-voima:**
~t forces of nature, the
elements.
luonnos sketch, [rough] draft.
-kirja sketch-book. **-taa** sketch,
draw in outline.
luonnostaan naturally, by
nature, from its nature.
luonno|ton unnatural;
abnormal; *(teennäinen)*
affected. **-ttomuus**
unnaturalness; abnormality.
luontai|nen natural;
(synnynnäinen) innate,
inherent; *se on hänelle -sta*
(m.) it comes natural to him.
-setu *ks. luontois-.* **-shoito**
nature cure.
luonteen|kasvatus
character-building. **-kuvaus**
character drawing. **-laatu**
temperament, disposition,
temper. **-lujuus** strength of
character. **-omainen,**
-ominaisuus characteristic.
-piirre trait [of character],
character feature.

luonne|inen: *on syytöksen* ~ is
in (of) the nature of an
accusation. **-va** natural;
(vapaa) unconstrained, easy
[-going]. **-vuus** naturalness;
ease.
luonto nature; *luonnossa*
(tavarana) in kind. **-inen:** *sen*
~ of such a nature
(character); *hyvä* ~
good-natured, good-tempered.
-isetu payment in kind, *m.*
fringe benefits. **-kappale**
creature.
luopio renegade, turncoat,
(uskon-) apostate, backslider.
luopu|a give up, abandon;
relinquish; desist (from);
(tavasta) leave off; ~
aikeestaan give up (abandon,
desist from) one's purpose; ~
kilpailusta give up the
contest, drop out of the race;
~ *kruunusta* abdicate; ~
taistelusta give up [the
fight]; ~ *uskostaan* renounce
one's faith; ~ *virastaan* resign
[one's office]. **-minen**
withdrawal, retirement;
kruunusta ~ abdication. **-mus**
(uskosta) apostasy; *(petollinen)*
desertion, defection.
luostari *(nunna-)* convent;
(munkki-) monastery; *mennä*
~in enter a convent. **-kammio**
cell. **-laitos** monasticism.
-lupaus: *tehdä* ~ take the
vow [s]. **-nesimies** prior, father
superior. **-npiha** *(t.* **-käytävä)**
cloister. **-veli** friar, monk.
luota: *jnk (jkn)* ~ from; *lähteä*
jkn ~ leave. **-antyöntävä**
forbidding.
luotain *(esim. kaiku-)* sounder;
kuu~ moon probe.
luotaus sounding.
luotei|nen north-west [erly];
north-western. **-stuuli**
northwest [erly] wind. **-sväylä**
northwest passage.
luotetta|va reliable; trustworthy,
dependable; *(varma)* safe; *~t*
lähteet ilmoittavat
well-informed sources state;
olen kuullut ~lta taholta I
have it on good authority, I
am responsibly told, I am
reliably informed. **-vuus**

reliability, trustworthiness.
luoti bullet; *(kellon)* weight;
(muurarin ym) plumb; *mer.*
lead. **-lanka** plumb-line. **-suora**
vertical. **-viiva** vertical line.
luoto rock; *(matalikko)* shoal;
(-saari) rocky islet.
luoton|antaja lender; creditor.
-anto lending. **-tarve** demand
for credit.
luotsa|ta pilot. **-us** piloting,
pilotage.
luotsi pilot. **-asema** pilot
station. **-maksu** pilotage fee.
luotta|a *(jhk)* trust, have
confidence in; depend upon,
rely on; count upon; *en luota
häneen* I do not trust him;
ei luota omiin kykyihinsä
mistrusts his (her) own
powers; ~ *Jumalaan* put one's
trust in God; *siihen voit ~*
depend upon it! ~ *sokeasti
jhk* have blind confidence in;
-en lupaukseenne trusting to
your promise. **-mukse|llinen**
confidential; *l-llisesti* in
[strict] confidence. **-mus**
confidence (in), trust (in),
reliance (on); ~*ta herättävä. .*
inspiring confidence; ~*ta
nauttiva* [highly] trusted;
-muksen puute mistrust, lack
of confidence; (~**lause** vote of
confidence; ~**mies** trustee,
(pää-) shop-steward; ~**toimi**
position of trust). **-vainen**
trusting, trustful, confident;
-vaisesti (m.) with confidence.
luotto *liik.* credit; *luotolla on
c.; myöntää ~a* give c.; *trust
a p.; hänellä on ~a* he
enjoys c. **-kortti** credit card.
-laitos credit company.
-tietotoimisto mercantile
agency.
luova creative.
luovia tack.
luovu|ttaa surrender, give up;
yield; *(alue)* cede; *(antaa)*
deliver; relinquish; hand over,
make over; *(siirtää)* transfer;
lak. m. convey; *(rikollinen)*
extradite; *(šakki ym)* resign.
-ttamaton inalienable. **-tus**
surrender, cession; delivery,
transfer, conveyance.
luovuus creativity, creative

ability.
lupa permission, leave;
(käyttö-) licence; *(myöntymys)*
consent; *(loma)* holiday; *antaa*
~ grant permission, permit;
jkn luvalla with (by)
permission of. .; *omin lupinsa*
on one's own authority;
without permission; *onko
täällä ~ polttaa* is smoking
allowed here? may I smoke
here? *tekijän luvalla* with
permission of the author;
tänään on ~a koulusta there
is no school today, we have
a holiday today. **-ava**
promising. **-kirja** licence.
-päivä holiday. **-us** promise;
(juhlallinen) vow; *antaa ~*
make a promise. **-utua**
promise; *(esim. maksamaan)*
pledge [£20]; *(suostua)*
consent to; *olen jo -utunut
muualle* I have a previous
engagement.
luppakorva lop-eared.
lupsakka jovial.
lurjus rascal, scoundrel, knave.
lusikallinen spoonful.
lusikka spoon. **-ruoka** liquid
food. **-uistin** spoon-bait.
luterilai|nen *a. & s.* Lutheran.
-suus Lutheran doctrine,
Lutheranism.
lutikka bug, bedbug.
lutka slut, hussy.
luu bone.
luudanvarsi broomstick.
luu|jauhot bone-dust. **-kudos**
bone (osseous) tissue.
luukku *(ikkuna-)* shutter;
(uunin) door; *(laivan)* hatch.
luulevainen suspicious,
distrustful.
luulla think, believe; suppose;
(luulotella) imagine; ~ *jkta
toiseksi* take (mistake) a p.
for; *miksi minua luulet?* what
do you take me for? *hän
luulee olevansa jtk* he thinks
he is somebody; *luulisin niin*
I should think so.
luulo belief; thought; *tein sen
siinä ~ssa, että. .* I did it
under the impression that;
vastoin ~a contrary to
expectation. **-sairas**
hypochondriac. **-sairaus**

imaginary illness;
hypochondria. **-tella** imagine,
fancy; *(uskotella itselleen)*
persuade oneself. **-teltu**
imaginary, fancied. **-ttelu**
imagination, fancy.
luultava probable, likely; *on
~a, että hän tulee* he is
likely to come; *se ei ole ~a*
it is improbable. **-sti**
probably, presumably; in all
probability; *tapaan hänet ~
kaupungissa* I am likely to
meet him in town.
luumu plum; *(kuivattu, m.)*
prune. **-puu** plum-tree.
luunmurtuma fracture.
luuranko skeleton. **-inen** *zo.*
vertebrate.
luusto bones, skeleton, frame.
luuta broom.
luutnantti lieutenant.
luu|ton boneless. **-tua** ossify.
-valo gout. **-ydin** bone
marrow.
luva|llinen permissible; allowed;
(laillinen) lawful. **-ta** promise;
(juhlallisesti) pledge [oneself];
vow; *(sallia)* allow; *se lupaa
hyvää* it promises well; *-ttu
maa* promised land. **-ton** not
allowed; illicit; *-ttomasti*
without permission.
lyhde sheaf *(pl. sheaves).*
lyhenn|elmä abstract, summary;
~jstk condensed from. **-ys**
abbreviation; abridgment;
(~ote extract).
lyben|tää shorten, curtail;
(sana) abbreviate; *(teosta)*
abridge; *(typistää)* cut short,
(häntää) dock; *(velkaa)* pay
off; *-tämättä* in full. **-tämätön**
unabridged.
lyhetä grow shorter, shorten.
lyhty lantern; *(katu-)* lamp;
(auton ym) headlight. **-pylväs**
lamp-post.
lyhye|nläntä stumpy, stubby.
-sti briefly, in brief, in short.
lyhyt short; brief; *loppua lyhy-
een (äkisti)* come to a sudden
end. **-aalto** short-wave; *(ula)*
VHF. **-aikainen.**. of short
duration, *(esim. laina)*
short-term; *(hetkellinen)*
transitory. **-ikäinen** short-lived;
vrt. ed. **-jännitteinen**

(ihmisestä) not capable of
sustained effort. **-kasvuinen**
short of stature, undersized,
stumpy. **-näköinen**
short-sighted, *(liki-, m.)*
near-sighted. **-sanainen** curt,
short; *(suppea)* succinct.
-tavarat haberdashery, odds
and ends, *Am.* notions.
-tukkainen short-haired.
lyhyys shortness; briefness,
brevity.
lyijy lead. **-inen** lead; leaden.
-kynä pencil. **-nharmaa**
lead-coloured, leaden. **-paino**
lead weight. **-tää** lead.
-valkoinen lead paint, white
lead. **-vesi** lead lotion.
lykkäy|s postponement;
(vara-aika) respite. **-tyä** be
postponed; lie over.
lykätä push; *(kuv.,
tuonnemmaksi)* postpone, put
off; defer; *(siirtää)* adjourn;
(ratkaistavaksi) refer, *jkn* to;
~ syy jkn niskoille lay the
blame on.
lymyillä hide oneself, lie low,
keep in hiding.
lynkata lynch.
lypsy milking. **-inen**; *hyvä ~
lehmä* a good milker. **-karja**
dairy-stock. **-kone** milking
machine. **-lehmä** milker.
lypsää milk; *intr.* yield milk.
lyriikka lyric poetry.
lyseo lycée, secondary school,
state grammar school.
lysoli lysol.
lysti *s.* amusement; fun. **-käs**
amusing; jolly; droll; funny.
lysähtää collapse, flop down.
lyyhistyä collapse.
lyyra lyre.
lyyri|kko lyric poet. **-(lli)nen**
lyric [al].
lyödä strike, hit, beat *(m.
sydämestä); (läimäyttää)* slap;
~ maahan knock down; *~
rahaa* coin money; *~ rikki*
break, *(esim. ikkuna)* smash;
~ ennätys (m.) break a
record; *~ kortti pöytään* play
a card; *~ naula (jhk)* drive a
nail (into); *~ päänsä seinään*
knock (bump) one's head
against the wall; *~ takaisin*
hit back; beat back, repulse;

kello on lyönyt 12 the clock
has struck 12; *aallot löivät
yli kannen* the waves swept
over the deck; *liekit lyövät
ulos ikkunoista* the flames are
bursting out from the
windows; *heidät lyötiin
(voitettiin)* they were beaten.
lyöjä *urh.* batsman.
lyömäsoitin percussion
instrument.
lyönti blow; stroke *(m.urh.)
lyönnilleen kello 12* on the
stroke of 12.
lyöttä|ytyä *(jkn seuraan)* join;
~ *yhteen* combine, join
forces, *(us. pah. merk.)* band
(gang) together. **-ä** *(rahaa)*
mint, coin; *(mitali)* strike,
have a medal struck [in
honour of. .].
lähde spring, fountain [-head];
kuv. ym source; *lähteet
(kirjan)* references. **-kirjallisuus**
works of reference.
lähei|nen near, close; *(lähellä
oleva)* adjacent, near-by;
(tuttavallinen) intimate; ~
sukulainen near (close)
relation; ~ *ystävä* close
(intimate) friend; *he ovat -stä
sukua* they are closely related.
-syys nearness; vicinity,
neighbourhood; *aivan jnk
-syydessä* in the immediate
vicinity of, in close
proximity to.
lähe|kkäin near (close to) each
other. **-lle** near; close to. **-llä**
near, *jtk* [to], close (to);
close by, near by; at a short
distance; *tässä ~* near here; ~,
oleva neighbouring, near-by.
-ltä from near (close) by, at
close quarters; from close
range; ~ *ja kaukaa* from far
and near; *se koskee häntä
aivan* ~ it concerns him most
closely. **-mmin** nearer, closer;
ajatella asiaa ~ think the
matter over. **-mpi** *ks. ed.;*
selonteko a more detailed
account; ~*ä tietoja antaa.* .
for further particulars apply
to. . . **-nnellä** approach;
(tungetella) make advances to;
~ *totuutta* come near to the
truth; *hän -ntelee 50:tä* he is

approaching *(t.* getting on
for) 50. **-ntää** bring nearer *(t.*
closer to). **-s** nearly; *(melkein)*
almost; *ei* ~*kään* not nearly,
nothing like [so, *niin*]; ~
200 henkeä nearly 200 people.
-styä approach, draw near.
lähe|te *(raha-)* remittance;
(~keskustelu preliminary
debate [preceding referral of
bill to committee]. **-tin**
transmitter, sender.
lähetti *sot.* orderly,
(toimistossa) office boy (girl),
messenger; *kirk.* missionary;
(šakkip.) bishop. **-läs** envoy,
(suur-) ambassador.
lähett|yvillä: *jnk* ~ somewhere
near. ., in the neighbourhood
of. . . **-äjä** sender; *kaupp.*
consigner.
lähet|ttää send; send off,
dispatch; *kaupp. m.* consign;
(et. rahaa) remit; *(edelleen)*
send on, forward, *(pöydässä)*
pass on; ~ *ohjelmaa (rad.)*
be on the air; ~ *takaisin*
send back, return; *-än
sinulle.* . I'll let you have.
lähetys dispatch; *kaupp.*
consignment; *rad.*
transmission; *kirk.* mission.
-aika broadcasting time.
-asema broadcasting station,
transmitter, *kirk.* mission
station. **-saarnaaja** missionary.
-työ missionary work.
lähetystö legation, *(suur-)*
embassy; *(henkilöryhmä)*
delegation, deputation.
-sihteeri secretary of legation.
lähetä approach, draw near;
near; *(esim. viivat)* converge.
lähi|aika: *-aikoina* at an early
date, shortly; *aivan -aikoina*
in the immediate future. **-itä**
the Middle East. **-kuva** *valok.*
close-up, close shot. **-main** *ks.*
liki-; on ~ approximates; *ei*
~*kaan* not nearly, far from.
-mmä|inen *s.* neighbour,
fellowman; *l-isen rakkaus*
charity. **-n** *a.* nearest, closest;
(-nnä seuraava) next; ~
naapuri (m.) next-door
neighbour; ~ *ympäristö*
immediate neighbourhood.
-nnä nearest; next; *(ensi*

sijassa) mainly, in the first place; ~ *edellinen.* . immediately preceding; ~ *paras* the next (the second) best; ~ *seuraava* the [very] next,. . immediately following. **-omaiset** next of kin. **-pitäjä** neighbouring parish. **-seutu,** **-stö** vicinity, neighbourhood. **-tulevaisuus:** *-suudessa* at an early date, in the near future. **-valot** *(auton)* dipped *(Am.* dimmed) lights.

lähtemätön ineffaceable; indelible.

läht|eä go; *(jnnek)* leave (for), depart; *(matkaan)* start, set out; *(irti)* come off; come loose; *(esim. väri)* come out; ~ *ajelulle, kävelylle* go for a drive (a walk); ~ *juoksemaan* start to run; ~ *jkn luota* leave; ~ *matkalle* set out (start) on a journey; *(tahra)* *-ee bensiinillä* it will come off with petrol; *hän on -enyt Englantiin* he has left for England; *hänen lähdettyään* after his departure; *minun on lähdettävä* I must be off, *puhek.* got to be going; *juna* *-ee pian* the train will leave soon; *-emäisillään* about to leave; *-evät junat* departures. **-ien:** *jstk* ~ since; *joulusta* ~ [ever] since Christmas; *siitä* ~ since [then], ever since; *tästä* ~ from now on, henceforth; *mistä* ~ ? since when? *ensi maanantaista* ~ [as] from next Monday.

lähtö departure; start[ing]; *ilm.* take-off, *urh.* start; *ennen ~ä* before leaving; *olla lähdössä* be about to leave. **-aika** time of departure. **-isin:** *olla ~ jstk* derive one's (its) origin from, come from, originate in. **-kohta** starting-point. **-laskenta** count-down. **-merkki** starting signal. **-passi:** *antaa jklle ~t (erottaa)* give. . the sack; *saada ~t* get the sack, be sacked *(Am.* fired). **-päivä** date of departure. **-teline** *urh.* starting block. **-valmis** ready to leave. **-viiva** starting post.

läik|kyä splash; *(maahan ym)* spill, be spilled. **-yttää** splash; *(maahan)* spill.

läimäy|s *(piiskan)* crack, lash; *(kädellä)* slap, smack. **-ttää** slap, smack; *(hevosta)* lash.

läisk|e crack[s]; smack[s]; *(läike)* splash.

läiskä blot, stain, smear.

läjä heap, *(pinottu)* pile; *panna* ~*än* heap [up]; pile [up].

läkkipelti tin plate.

läksy lesson; *lukea ~nsä* learn (prepare) one's lesson[s], do one's home-work. **-ttää** lecture, take a p. to task. **-tys** lesson; rating, rebuke.

läkähtyä choke; suffocate.

lämmetä become warm[er], get warm, warm up; *hän lämpeni (puhuessaan)* he warmed to his subject.

lämmin *a.* warm; *(kuuma)* hot; *s.* warmth; ~ *ruoka* hot dish; *lämpimät terveiset* warm (cordial) greetings; *hänellä on* ~ *he* is warm; *minun tuli* ~ I got warm; *viisi astetta ~tä* five degrees above freezing point (above zero). **-sydäminen** warm-hearted. **-vesisäiliö** hot-water cistern.

lämmi|tellä warm oneself. **-ttäjä** *vanh.* stoker, *(veturin)* fireman. **-ttämätön** unheated. **-ttää** warm, warm up; *(kuumentaa)* heat; *(höyrykattilaa)* fire; ~ *uunia* heat an oven. **-tys** heating; *(~laite* heating apparatus). **-tä** get warm, warm up; *sauna lämpiää* the sauna is getting warm, we are heating the s.

lämmön|johtaja conductor of heat. **-nousu** slight fever.

lämpi|myys warmth. **-mästi** warmly; *aurinko paistaa* ~ the sun is warm. **-ö** *(teatterin)* foyer.

lämpö warmth; *fys.* heat; *(-tila)* temperature; *lämmöllä* with warmth, with enthusiasm; *lämmön lasku* fall in temperature. **-aalto** heat wave. **-aste** degree of heat, degree above zero. **-halvaus** heat-stroke. **-hoito** [radiant] heat. **-inen** warm. **-johto**

central heating system.
-kaappi warming cupboard,
(laboratorion ym) incubator.
-mittari thermometer;
Celsiuksen ~ the centigrade
(t. Celsius) t. **-määrä**
temperature. **-patteri** radiator.
-tila temperature. **-yksikkö**
thermal unit.
länget collar, hames.
länkisäärinen bow-legged.
lännenfilmi Western
länsi west; *lännestä* from the
west; *länteen päin* (to)
towards the west,
westward[s]; *(jstk)* west of;
länteen menevät junat trains
going west; *aurinko laskee
länteen* the sun sets in the
west; *tuulee lännestä*
the wind is in the west.
L-Eurooppa Western
Europe. **-eurooppalainen** West
European. **L-Intia** the West
Indies. **-intialainen** West
Indian. **-maat** the West.
-mainen western, occidental.
-osa western part. **-puoli** west
side; *jnk ~tse* west of. .
-rannikko west coast.
L~Saksa West Germany.
-tuuli west[erly] wind. **-vallat**
the Western Powers.
läntinen western, west;
(suunnasta) westerly.
läpeensä throughout, all
through, thoroughly.
läpi *s.* hole; *adv.* through; ~
vuoden [all] the year round;
~ *yön* throughout the night;
käydä ~ pass through; *(kuv.)*
go through, undergo,
(tarkastaa) go over, look
over. **-kotaisin** thoroughly,
throughout. **-kulkeva.** . going
through; *~t junat* through
trains. **-kulku** passage through;
transit; ~ *(t. -ajo) kielletty*
no thoroughfare. **-kuultamaton**
opaque. **-kuultava** translucent;
transparent. **-kuultavuus**
translucence; transparency.
-käydä *ks. käydä.* **-käytävä**
passage. **-leikkaus**
[cross-]section. **-matka** journey
through. **-mitaten** in diameter.
-mitta diameter. **-murto**
break-through; *sot. m.* breach

[in the enemy's line]. **-märkä**
wet through, drenched,
soaked. **-näkymätön** not
transparent; opaque. **-näkyvä**
transparent. **-pääsemätön**
impassable; impenetrable.
-pääsy passage through; *ks.
-kulku.* **-tunkema:** *jnk* ~
instinct with, *(aatteen)* ~
imbued with, [the book is]
shot through with . .
-tunkematon impenetrable.
-tunkeva penetrating; *(huuto
ym)* piercing. **-valaisu**
fluoroscopy.
läppä valve; *(kellon)* clapper.
läpäi|semätön impenetrable,
impermeable; impervious, *jtk*
to. **-stä** penetrate; pierce;
(mennä läpi) go through,
pass; *et. fys.* permeate;
(tutkinto) pass, get through.
läpättää beat, *(sydämestä, m.)*
palpitate.
läski pork; fat of pork.
läsnä present; *(paikalla)* on the
spot; *olla läsnä (jssk)* be
present (at), attend. .; *minun
~ ollessani* in my presence;
kaikkien ~ ollessa in the
presence of all. **-oleva:** *~t*
those present. **-olo** presence.
lättä|hattu teddy-boy. **-jalkainen**
flat-footed.
lätäkkö pool, puddle.
lävis|tin [paper] perforator,
punch [ing apparatus]. **-täjä**
mat. diagonal. **-tää** pierce
[through]; *(pistää läpi)* prick
[through]; *tekn.* perforate;
puncture;. punch; *(esim.
tikarilla)* stab.
lävitse through.
läähä|ttää pant; breathe
heavily; *(haukkoa ilmaa)* gasp.
-tys pant [ing].
lääke medicine; *(parannuskeino)*
remedy. **-aineet**
pharmaceuticals. **-kasvi**
medicinal plant. **-määräys**
prescription. **-oppi**
pharmacology. **-pullo** medicine
bottle. **-hoito** medication.
-tiede [science of] medicine;
-tieteen kandidaatti Bachelor
of M. *(lyh.* B. M.); *-tieteen
ylioppilas* medical student.
-tieteellinen medical.

lääkinnällinen medicinal.
lääkintä treatment, cure.
-aliupseeri medical NCO.
-henkilökunta medical staff.
-huolto medical service. **-olot**
(terveydenhoidolliset) sanitary
conditions. **-upseeri** medical
officer. **-voimistelija**
physiotherapist. **-voimistelu**
physiotherapy.
lääkintöhallitus National Board
of Health.
lääki|tä medicate. **-tys**
medication.
lääkäri physician; doctor;
(virka- ym) medical officer;
(kirurgi) surgeon; ~n hoidossa
under medical treatment.
-kirja doctor book. **-kunta** the
medical profession. **-napu**
medical aid; *etsiä* ~*a* seek
medical aid, consult a doctor.
-nhoito medical treatment.
-npalkkio doctor's fee.
-ntarkastus, -ntutkimus medical
examination. **-ntodistus**
medical certificate.
lääni administrative district;
department; *(maakunta)*
province. **-nhallitus** provincial
government. **-tys** fief; (~**laitos**
feudal system, feudalism).
lääppi|ä paw; *hän ei pidä*
-misestä she doesn't like
being pawed about; *ole*
-mättä! cut it out!
läävä cow-shed.
lönky|ttää trot, jog. **-tys**
jog-trot.
lörp|pö *s.* babbler, chatterbox;
a. garrulous. **-ötellä** babble,
blab. **-ötys** babble, idle talk.

löydös find; finding.
löyhentää loosen; slacken, relax.
löyhkä stink, stench. **-tä** stink;
-ävä stinking, malodorous,
fetid.
löyh|tyä get loose, come loose;
loosen, slacken. **-ytellä** fan.
-yys looseness; slackness.
löyhä loose, *(höllä)* slack; *kuv.*
lax; *(suhde)* irregular; *löyhin*
perustein on flimsy grounds;
(..llä) on ruuvi ~llä has a
screw loose.
löyly steam; *heittää* ~*ä* throw
water on hot stones (in
Finnish sauna). **-nlyömä**
cracked; *hän on hiukan* ~ he
is not all there. **-ttää** dust a
p.'s jacket, give. .a [good]
thrashing. **-tys** thrashing.
löysä loose; ~ *panos* blank
cartridge; ~ *vatsa*
diarrh[o]ea; ~*ksi keitetty*
soft-boiled; *ohjakset ovat* ~*llä*
the reins are slack; *ottaa*
asiat löysin rantein take
things easy.
löyt|yä be found, be
discovered; *ehkä se vielä* -*yy*
perhaps it will turn up. **-äjä**
finder; discoverer. **-ää** find;
(keksiä) discover; *(jnnek)* find
one's way (to); *on*
löydettävissä is to be found;
en löydä sopivaa sanaa I am
at a loss for the right word.
löytö find; discovery. **-lapsi**
foundling. **-palkka** reward.
-retkeilijä explorer. **-retki**
exploring expedition, voyage
of discovery. **-tavaratoimisto**
lost property office.

M

maa earth; *(vastak. vesi)* land; *(valtakunta)* country *(m. maaseutu); (-npinta)* ground; *~lla* in the country; *~lle* [in]to the country; *jkn ~lla* on sb.'s land; *~lla ja merellä* (by) land and sea; *~mme* our country, this land of ours; *~n päällä* on the earth; *pudota ~han* fall to the ground; *nousta, astua maihin* go ashore, disembark; *uida maihin* swim ashore; *maissa* ashore, on shore; *kuuden maissa* [at] about six o'clock; *~ta omistava* land-owning; *~ta omistamaton* landless. **-alue** territory; area [of land]; *(tilus)* domain.

maadoittaa *ks. maattaa.*
maaginen magic[al].
maahan|hyökkäys invasion. **-muuttaja** immigrant. **-muutto** immigration. **-tulolupa** entry permit, visa. **-tuonti** import[ation].

maaherra [district] governor.
maailma world; *~lle* out into the wide world; *ennen ~ssa* in the old days, in olden times. **-llinen** worldly.
maailman|avaruus space. **-ennätys** world record. **-historia** history of the world. **-kaikkeus** [the] universe. **-kansalainen** cosmopolitan. **-katsomuksellinen** ideological. **-katsomus** attitude to life, outlook on life, ideology. **-kauppa** international trade. **-kaupunki** metropolis. **-kieli** universal *(t. world)* language. **-kuulu** world-renowned. **-loppu** end of the world. **-maine** world-wide fame. **-matkaaja** globetrotter. **-mestari** world champion. **-mestaruus** world championship. **-mies, -nainen**
man (woman) of the world. **-näyttely** world fair. **-pyörä** Ferris wheel. **-rauha** world peace. **-sota** world war. **-valta** world-power. **-ympäripurjehdus** circumnavigation of the world.

maa|johto earth, ground [connection]. **-joukkue** [inter]national team. **-kaasu** natural gas. **-kartano** country estate. **-kiinteistö** landed property. **-krapu** *leik.* landlubber. **-kunnallinen** provincial. **-kunta** province.

maalaamaton unpainted.
maalai|nen rustic, country, provincial; *s.* peasant; *-set* country people, peasantry.
maalais|elämä country life, rural life. **-kunta** rural district, rural local authority area **-liitto** agrarian party. **-mainen** rustic. **-nuoriso** young people in the country. **-olot** country conditions. **-talo** farm-house. **-tua** become countrified, rusticate. **-väestö** rural population.
maalari painter; *(taiteilija)* artist. **-mestari** master painter.
maala|ta paint; *~ uudelleen* repaint, paint over; *keltaiseksi -ttu* painted yellow; *-ttu!* wet paint! **-uksellinen** picturesque. **-us** painting, picture; *(~taide* art of painting; *~teline* easel). **-uttaa:** *~ kuvansa* have one's picture painted.
maali 1. *(väri)* paint; 2. *(pilkka)* target; *urh.* goal; winning-post, finish; *~ssa urh.* at the finish; *hän saapui ~in toisena* he came in second. **-inammunta** target-practice. **-kamera** photo-finish camera.
maaliskuu March.
maali|suora the home stretch.

-taulu target. **-vahti**
goalkeeper. **-viiva** finishing
line, goal line.
maallikko s. layman; a. lay;
maallikot the laity. **-saarnaaja**
lay preacher.
maalli|nen earthly, mundane;
temporal; *(vastak. kirkollinen)*
secular. **-smielinen**
worldly-minded. **-stunut**
secularized.
maaltapako rural depopulation,
migration from country to
town.
maa|mies farmer; (**~koulu**
school of agriculture). **-myyrä**
zo. mole. **-nalainen**
underground, subterranean; ~
rautatie [the] Underground,
the Tube, Am. the Subway.
maanantai Monday.
maan|järistys earthquake, earth
tremor. **-kavallus** treason.
-kavaltaja traitor [to one's
country]. **-kiertäjä** tramp,
vagabond, vagrant, bum.
-kuulu far-famed, widely
known. **-laatu** soil. **-mies**
[fellow] countryman,
compatriot. **-mittari** surveyor.
-mittaus surveying; (**~tiede**
geodesy). **-moukka** country
bumpkin, rustic. **-omistaja**
landowner. **-omistus**
landownership. **-osa** continent.
-pako exile; *ajaa ~on* banish
[from a country], exile.
-pakolainen exile. **-pakolaisuus**
exile, banishment.
-petoksellinen treasonable.
-petos [high] treason. **-pinta**
surface of the earth.
-puolustus defence [of the
country]. **-siirtokone** earth
mover. **-suru** national
mourning. **-teitse** by road.
maantie high road, main road.
-gangsteri *(auto)* hit-and-run
driver. **-kuljetus** road haulage.
-rosvo highwayman.
maan|tiede geography.
-tieteellinen geographical.
-tieteilijä geographer. **-tuote**
product of the soil. **-vaiva**
scourge; *kuv.* public nuisance.
-vieremä landslide. **-viljelijä**
farmer.
maanviljelys farming;

agriculture. **-kalut** agricultural
implements (tools). **-koulu**
agricultural school. **-näyttely**
agricultural fair. **-oppi**
agronomy; agriculture. **-työ**
farm work.
maanvuokra [ground-]rent. **-aja**
tenant, lessee.
maa|omaisuus landed property,
land. **-orja** serf. **-orjuus**
serfdom. **-ottelu** international
match. **-pallo** globe; ~*n*
puolisko hemisphere. **-palsta**
parcel of land. **-perä** soil,
ground, earth; *valmistaa ~ä*
jllek prepare the ground for.
-pihka bitumen. **-pähkinä**
groundnut, peanut.
maaseutu country [side [;
maaseudulla in the country,
in rural areas. **-kaupunki**
provincial town. **-lainen**
provincial,.. from the country.
-lehti provincial newspaper.
-väestö rural population.
maasilta viaduct.
maasta|muutto emigration.
-vienti export [ation].
maasto terrain, ground. **-auto**
jeep. **-juoksu** cross-country
race. **-utua** take cover. **-vaunu**
cross-country vehicle.
maasäl|pä feldspar.
maata lie; *(nukkua)* sleep;
panna ~ lie down, *(yöksi)* go
to bed; ~ *sairaana* be down
[with *jssak taudissa*], be laid
up (with). **-meno:** ~*n aika*
bedtime, time to go to bed.
maa|talo farmhouse.
-taloudellinen agricultural.
maatalous agriculture, farming.
-ministeriö ministry of
agriculture. **-näyttely**
agricultural show. **-tiede:** *m-*
ja metsätieteiden kandidaatti
Bachelor of Agriculture and
Forestry. **-tuote** farm product.
maatiaisrotu: ~*a* of a native
stock (breed).
maa|tila farm; *(suuri)* [landed]
estate; (**~nomistaja** owner of
a farm (an estate). **-tilkku**
patch of land. **-ton** landless.
maattaa *tekn.* earth.
maatua decay, moulder.
maa|työ agricultural work.
-työläinen farm labourer

(worker, hand). **-vara** road clearance. **-voimat** land forces.
made burbot.
madella crawl. creep; *kuv.* cringe (before).
madonna, -nkuva madonna.
madonsyömä worm-eaten.
magneetti magnet. **-nen** magnetic. **-neula** magnetic needle. **-suus** magnetism.
magneetto magneto.
magnet|ofoni tape recorder, recording machine. **-oida** magnetize.
maha stomach. **-haava** gastric ulcer. **-lasku:** *tehdä ~* belly-land. **-laukku** stomach. **-neste** gastric juice. **-syöpä** cancer of the stomach.
mahdolli|nen possible; potential; *(tuleva)* prospective; *hyvin -sta* very likely; *mikäli -sta* if possible; *niin pian kuin -sta* as soon as possible, at [my, your] earliest convenience; *minulle ei ole -sta (m.)* I am not in a position to. .; *kaikilla -silla keinoilla* by every possible means; *~ panna toimeen* feasible, practicable; *tehdä -seksi* render possible, (jklle) enable [a p. to]; **-simman** *hyvin* in the best possible way, as well as possible; *-simman halvalla* at the lowest possible price [s]. **-sesti** possibly; *~ olen väärässä* I may be wrong. **-suus** possibility; chance; *on pieni ~ there* is a slight chance [that]; *-suuden mukaan* as far as possible; *minulla ei ole muuta -suutta* I have no other choice; *elämäni ~* the chance of a lifetime.
mahdo|ton impossible; *(mieletön)* absurd; *aivan ~ta* utterly impossible; *~ ajatella* unthinkable; *~ lukea* illegible; *~ saada takaisin* irrecoverable; *~ toteuttaa* impracticable; *~ tuntea* unrecognizable; *~ ymmärtää* unintelligible; *-ttoman suuri* enormous, huge; *vaatia -ttomia* demand the impossible. **-ttomuus**

impossibility.
mahduttaa make. . go in.
mahla sap.
mahonki mahogany.
mahtaa *(voida)* be able to; *hän ~ olla kaunis* she must be pretty; *mitä hänestä ~ tulla* I wonder what will become of him; *ei mahda mitään* there is nothing to be done about it, it can't be helped.
mahta|illa show off; *-ileva,* high and mighty, *(määräilevä)* domineering. **-va** powerful, high, mighty; *(suuri)* great; *maailman ~t* the great ones of the earth. **-vuus** mightiness; greatness; *vrt. seur.*
mahti power; might. **-pontinen** bombastic. **-pontisuus** bombast, grandiloquence.
mahtua have room; go in [to]; *astiaan mahtuu 5 litraa* the vessel holds 5 litres; *saliin mahtuu. .* the hall has a seating capacity of. . [people]; *sinne ei mahdu kovin monta henkeä* there is not room for very many people there.
maihin. . to land. **-lasku** landing. **-nousu** landing, disembarkation; *~alus,* *~alukset* landing craft.
maila bat; *(tennis)* racket; *(golf-)* club; *(esim. kroketti-)* mallet; *(jääkiekko-)* stick.
maili mile.
main: *niillä ~* thereabouts,. . or so.
maine reputation; *(kuuluisuus)* fame, renown; *on hyvässä (huonossa) ~essa* has a good (bad) reputation; *huono ~* disrepute; *saattaa huonoon ~eseen* bring discredit on; *saavuttaa ~tta* win fame. **-eton** undistinguished. **-ikas** celebrated, renowned, famous, illustrious. **-ikkuus** renown, celebrity, illustriousness.
-mainen, -mäinen -like; *poika~* boyish.
mainingit [ground-]swell, rolling sea.
maininta mention[ing];

quotation.

mainio excellent, fine, splendid; ~! fine! excellent! *jaksan ~sti* I am very well, I feel first-rate, I am doing splendidly.

maini|ta mention; *(tuoda esiin)* give, state, say; *(esimerkki)* quote; ~ *jku nimeltä* mention. . by name, name; *jättää -tsematta* not- mention, pass over in silence; *minulta jäi -tsematta* I omitted to mention; *muita -tsematta* to say nothing of the others; *-ttakoon* it may (should) be mentioned. **-ttava**. worth mentioning, noteworthy; *ei ~a (m.)* nothing to speak of. **-ttu** the said. ., *(edellä).*. mentioned before *(t. above).*

mainonta advertising; publicity.

mainos advertisement. **-juliste** poster, bill, sticker. **-kilpi** advertising sign; *(-teline)* billboard, hoarding. **-lehtinen** advertising leaflet. **-mies** publicity man. **-pala** advertising snippet (spot). **-taa** advertise. **-temppu** publicity stunt. **-toimisto** advertising agency. **-tus** advertising; publicity. **-valot** advertising lights, neon signs.

mairi|tella flatter; cajole; *-tteleva* flattering. **-ttelu** flattery, cajolery.

maisema landscape, scenery. **-kortti** picture postcard. **-maalari, -maalaus** landscape painter (painting).

maiskuttaa smack [one's lips]; ~ *kieltään* click one's tongue.

maissi maize, *Am.* corn. **-hiutaleet** corn flakes. **-jauhot** cornflour.

maistaa taste; *(koettaa)* sample.

maisteri ks. *filosofian ~.* **-narvo** university degree of mag. phil. (of Master of Arts). **-nvihkiäiset** conferment of masters' degrees, degree ceremony.

maistraatti administrative council [of a town].

maist|ua taste; ~ *hyvältä* taste good (nice), have a nice taste; *miltä tuo -uu?* what

does that taste like?

maiti milt. **-aisneste** latex.

maito milk; *lasi ~a* a glass of m. **-hammas** milk-tooth, deciduous tooth. **-happo** lactic acid. **-kannu** milk-can, *(kaadin)* milk-jug. **-kauppa** milkshop, dairy. **-pullo** *(lapsen)* feeding-bottle. **-pystö** milk can. **-rupi** infantile eczema. **-talous** dairy industry; *(~tuotteet)* dairy produce).

maitse by land.

maitt|aa: *hänelle ei maita ruoka* he has no appetite; *-ava* appetizing, palatable.

maja cottage, cabin, hut. **-illa** lodge, stay (at a p.'s), *Am.* room (at).

majakanvartija lighthouse keeper.

majakka lighthouse, light; beacon. **-laiva** lightship.

maja|paikka quarters, lodgings. **-talo** inn.

majava, -nnahka beaver.

majestee|tillinen majestic. **-tti** majesty; *Teidän ~nne* Your Majesty; *Hänen ~nsa kuningas* His Majesty, the King; *(~rikos* lese-majesty).

majoi|ttaa accommodate, *puhek.* put [a p.] up; lodge; *sot.* billet [on, *jkn luo*], quarter. **-ttua** take lodgings. **-tus** accommodation; quartering.

majoneesi mayonnaise.

majuri major, *ilmav.* squadron leader.

makaroni macaroni.

makasiini storehouse, *(kiväärin)* magazine.

make|a sweet; ~ *nauru* a good laugh. **-iset** sweets, confectionery, *Am.* candy. **-iskauppa** sweet shop, confectioner's, *(koulun)* tuckshop; *Am.* candy store. **-us** sweetness. **-uttaa** sweeten. **-uttamisaine** sweetening [agent].

makkara sausage.

makrilli mackerel.

maksa liver.

maks|aa pay, *jstk* for; *(olla hintana)* cost; ~ *kallis hinta* pay dear; ~ *kustannukset* pay (defray) the expenses; ~ *lasku, velka (m.)* settle a bill

(a debt); ~ *vähitellen* pay in instalments; *mitä se* ~? how much is it? what is the price? *-an tavarat saadessani* the goods will be paid for on delivery; *ei -a vaivaa* it is not worth the trouble; *-oi mitä -oi* at all costs; *-ettava Helsingissä* payable at H. **-aja** payer. **-ama|ton** unpaid, unsettled, owing; ~ *kirje* unstamped letter; *m-ttomat saatavat* outstanding claims.
maksa|ruoho stonecrop, sedum **-tauti** liver complaint.
maksimimäärä maximum [amount].
maksoittua coagulate, clot.
maksu payment; *(koulu-, pysäköinti- ym)* fee; *(ajo-)* fare; *(palkka)* pay; *(veloitus)* charge; *(suoritus)* settlement; ~*t (m.)* dues; ~*ksi jstk* in payment (settlement) of; ~*n laiminlyöminen* non-payment; ~*tta* free of charge. **-aika:** *lainan* ~ *on 10 vuotta* the loan is repayable over ten years; *3 kk. -ajalla* on 3 months' credit. **-ehdot** terms (conditions) [of payment]; *edullisilla -ehdoilla* on favourable terms. **-erä** instalment; *(tilissä)* item. **-kyky** ability to pay; solvency. **-kykyinen** solvent. **-kyvyttömyys** insolvency. **-kyvytön** insolvent. **-määräys** order for payment. **-osoitus** money order, draft. **-päivä** date of payment, *(palkan)* pay-day. **-tapa** mode of payment. **-tase** balance of payments. **-ton**. free of charge, gratuitous. **-valmius** liquidity. **-väline:** *laillinen* ~ legal tender.
maku taste; flavour; *se ei ole minun* ~*uni* it is not to my taste; *kullakin on oma* ~*nsa* tastes differ. **-aisti** [sense of] taste. **-asia:** *se on* ~ it is a matter of taste. **-inen:** *minkä* ~ *se on* what does it taste like? **-pala** titbit, delicacy.
makulatuuri waste paper.
makuu: *mennä* ~*lle* retire, go to bed; *(lepäämään)* lie down

[for a rest]; *olla* ~*lla* be in bed; be lying down. **-haava** bedsore. **-halli** sun balcony, solarium. **-huone** bedroom. **-paikka** *(laivassa ym)* berth. **-sali** dormitory. **-säkki** sleeping bag. **-vaunu** sleeping-car, *Am.* sleeper.
malajilainen *a. & s.* Malay[an].
maleksi|a hang around, loiter [about]; loaf. **-ja** loafer, loiterer.
Malesia Malaysia.
malja bowl, *raam.* chalice; cup; *(jkn kunniaksi)* toast; ~*nne* your health! here's to you! *esittää jkn* ~ propose a p.'s health; *juoda jkn* ~ drink to the health of, toast a p. **-kko** bowl; *(kukka-, m.)* vase.
malka beam.
mallas malt. **-juoma** malt drink, beer.
malli pattern, *(tait. ym, koneen)* model, *(piirros ym)* design; *(näyte)* specimen, sample; *olla* ~*na (tait.)* pose for an artist; *jkn* ~*n mukaan* according to a pattern, on the *(esim.* British) model; *tehdä jnk* ~*n mukaan* model. . (after, on, upon); *uusinta* ~*a* of the latest pattern *t.* style *(esim. auto* model *t.* make). **-kelpoinen** exemplary. **-koulu** model school. **-npiirtäjä** [pattern-] designer. **-npiirustus** [pattern-] designing. **-nukke** lay figure, *(ompelu-)* dummy. **-tapaus** a case in point. **-tila** model farm. **-tilkku** sample.
Mallorca Majorca.
malmi ore. **-kaivos** ore mine. **-pitoinen** ore-bearing. **-rumpu** gong. **-suoni** vein of ore, lode.
maltalainen Maltese.
malti|llinen calm, collected, self-possessed; *(kohtuullinen)* moderate; sober; level-headed. **-llisuus** calmness, composure, moderation. **-ton** impatient. **-ttomuus** impatience; immoderation.
maltta|a have patience; ~ *mielensä* compose oneself; stop to think. **-maton** hasty, impatient.

maltti presence of mind; composure, self-possession; *menettää ~nsa* lose one's head (one's temper); *säilyttää ~nsa* keep one's temper, control oneself.

malva *bot.* mallow.

mammona mammon.

mammutti mammoth. **-petäjä** sequoia.

mana: *~lle mennyt* deceased. **-la** abode[s] of the dead. Hades.

mana|aja sorcerer; *henkien ~ (pois)* exorcist. **-ta** drive out, exorcise; *(kirota)* curse; *~ esiin* conjure up, call forth (*t.* up). **-us** conjuration.

mandariini mandarin; *(hedelmä)* mandarin[e], *(amerikk.)* tangerine.

mandaatti(alue) mandated territory.

mandoliini mandolin[e].

maneeri manner[ism].

maneesi riding-school.

maneetti *zo.* jelly-fish.

mangaani manganese.

manifesti manifesto.

mankel|i, -oida mangle.

mankua whine.

mannaryynit semolina, *Am.* farina.

mannekiini mannequin, [fashion] model.

manner mainland **M~eurooppa** the Continent [of Europe]. **-ilmasto** continental climate. **-jalusta** continental shelf. **-maa** continent. **-mainen** continental.

mansikka strawberry; *aho~* wild s.; *oma maa ~, muu maa mustikka* east, west, home is best **-maa** strawberry bed.

manteli almond. **-puu** almond tree.

mantere *ks. manner.*

manttaali assessment unit for land [tax].

mantteli cloak; *(virka-)* robe; *(sotilaan)* greatcoat.

manööveri manoeuvre, *Am.* maneuver.

mappi *(asiakirja-)* file.

marakatti guenon, *kuv.* monkey.

maratonjuoksu Marathon race.

margariini margarine, *puhek.*

marge.

marginaali margin.

marhaminta halter.

marianpäivä Lady Day, Annunciation Day.

marihuana marijuana.

marista be peevish.

marionetti puppet.

marja berry; *mennä ~an* go berrying. **-hillo** jam. **-kuusi** yew. **-mehu** fruit juice. **-staa** pick berries.

markiisi marquis, marquess; *(verho)* sun blind, awning. **-tar** marchioness, *(ei Engl.)* marquise.

markka mark; *Suomen ~a* Finnmarks.

markkina|arvo market value. **-hinta** market price. **-katsaus** market survey. **-koju** market stall (stand).

markkin|at market; fair; *-oilla* on (in) the market; *tuoda -oille* put on the market. **-oida** market. **-ointi** marketing.

marmelaati jelly sweets, *(hillo)* jam, *(appelsiini-)* marmalade.

marmori marble. **-kuva** marble bust (statue). **-levy** marble slab, *(esim. pöydän)* marble top. **-nen** marble.

marmoroida marble.

Marokko Morocco.

marraskuu November.

mars: *~ matkaan!* off you go!

marsalk|ka marshal; *(juhlissa, m.)* usher. **-ansauva** marshal's baton.

marseljeesi the Marseillaise.

marsipaani marchpane, marzipan.

marssi march; *lähteä ~in* m. away (*t.* off). **-a** march. **-järjestys** marching order. **-käsky** marching orders.

marsu guinea-pig.

marttyyri martyr. **-kuolema** a martyr's death; *kärsiä ~* suffer martyrdom. **-us** martyrdom.

masen|nus depression, low spirits; *olla ~nuksissa* be depressed. **-taa** discourage, dishearten; *-tava (m.)* depressing. **-tua** be disheartened, be discouraged; *-tunut* depressed. **-tumaton**

indomitable.
maskotti mascot.
maskuliini masculine.
massa mass; bulk; *(paperiym)* pulp; ~*t* the masses.
masto mast. **-nhuippu** mast-head.
masuuni blast furnace.
matal|**a** low; *(vedessä)* shallow; (~**hyökkäys** *ilm.* ground attack; ~**kantai**|**nen:** *-set kengät* flat shoes; ~*korkoinen* low-interest; *vrt. ed;* ~**paine** low pressure, *ilmat.* depression, low; ~**suhdanne** depression; ~**vesi** low tide, low water). **-ikko** shoal, shallow; *olla -ikolla* be aground. **-uus** lowness; shallowness.
mate|**leva** *kuv.* servile, cringing. **-levaisuus** servility. **-lija** reptile. **-lu** cringing, crawling.
matema|**atikko** mathematician. **-attinen** mathematical. **-tiikka** mathematics.
materialis|**mi** materialism. **-ti** materialist. **-tinen** materialist -[ic].
matinea matinee.
matka journey, *(lyhyempi)* trip; *(kierto- ym)* tour; *(meri-)* voyage; *(jnk yli)* passage, crossing; *(etäisyys)* distance; *(tie)* way; ~*lla* on the way; ~*lla jhk* on the way to, en route to, *(laivasta)* bound for; *minne* ~? where are you going; *jnk* ~*n päässä* at a distance of; *sinne on pitkä* ~ it is a long way off; *sinne on tunnin* ~ it is an hour's journey from here; *hän on matkoilla* he is away from home, he is [away] on a trip, *(ulkomailla)* he is abroad. **-apuraha** travel grant [for study], travelling scholarship. **-arkku** trunk. **-eväs** provisions [for a journey]. **-huopa** travelling rug.
matkai|**lija** traveller; *(huvi-)* tourist; (~**yhdistys** tourist association). **-lla** travel, journey.
matkailu tourism; touring, travel [ling]. **-auto** touring car. **-halu** wanderlust. **-keskus** tourist centre.
matka|**kertomus** report [of a journey]. **-kirjoituskone** portable typewriter. **-kreditiivi** letter of credit. **-kustannukset** travelling expenses. **-kuvaus** travel sketch, *(kirja)* book of travel [s]. **-laukku** suitcase, travelling-bag. **-lippu** ticket; *-lipun hinta* fare, passage money. **-mies** traveller. **-muisto** souvenir. **-njohtaja** tour conductor, guide, *Engl. m.* courier. **-opas** guide [-book]. **-puku** travelling-dress (suit). **-radio** portable radio, transistor set. **-rahat** fare, passage-money, *(korvaus)* travelling allowance. **-reitti** route.
matka|**seurue** party of tourists. **-šekki** travellers' cheque. **-suunnitelma** itinerary.
matkatavara, ~*t* luggage, *Am.* baggage; ~*in säilytys (huone)* cloakroom. **-säiliö, -tila** *(autossa)* boot, *Am.* trunk. **-toimisto** luggage office; weighing desk. **-hylly** rack. **-vaunu** luggage van (wagon).
matka|**toimisto** travel bureau, travel agent [s]. **-toveri** travelling companion, fellow traveller.
matki|**a** imitate; mimic **-mistaito** imitative ability.
matkus|**taa** travel, journey; *(jnnek)* go (to); *hän* ~ *Amerikkaan* he is going to America; *milloin -tatte* when are you leaving? *hän on -tanut Lontooseen* he has left for London; *Suomessa -taessani* when travelling in (when touring) Finland.
matkustaja traveller; *(juna-, laiva- ym)* passenger. **-kone** passenger plane. **-koti** lodging-house. **-laiva** passenger boat (ship, steamer). **-liikenne** passenger traffic.
matkus|**tella** travel; *paljon -tellut* [widely] travelled. **-tus** travelling; (~**kielto** ban on travel).
mato worm, *(toukka)* maggot. **-kuuri** worming. **-lääke** vermifuge.

matonkude carpet rag.
matrikkeli register, roll[s];
panna ~*in* register, enrol[l].
matruusi seaman; sailor.
matto carpet, *(pieni)* rug;
kynnys~ door-mat; *vrt.*
kokolattia-.
mauk|as savoury, appetizing,
tasty, palatable. **-kuus**
tastiness, deliciousness.
maurilainen *a.* Moorish; *s.*
Moor.
maustaa season, spice.
mauste spice *(m. kuv.)*,
seasoning, flavour[ing],
condiment. **-kasvi** aromatic
herb. **-neilikka** clove. **-pippuri**
Jamaica pepper, allspice.
mau|ton tasteless *(m. kuv.)*;
unsavoury; *kuv...* in bad
taste. **-ttomuus** tastelessness;
lack of taste.
me we; *meidät, meitä* us;
meille to us, for us; *vrt. hän,*
he.
medaljonki *(kaulassa*
kannettava) locket.
meedio [spiritual] medium.
mehe|vyys juiciness. **-vä** juicy
(m. kuv.); succulent; ~
kuvaus rich (spicy) account.
mehikasvi succulent plant.
mehiläi|nen bee; *-sen pisto*
bee-sting.
mehiläis|hoitaja bee-keeper.
-hoito bee-keeping. **-kenno** cell
[of a honeycomb].
-kuningatar queen bee. **-pesä**
beehive.
mehu juice. **-kas** juicy. **-linko,**
-npuristin juice extractor. **-ste**
extract.
meidän our; ours; ~
kanssamme with us.
meijeri dairy, *Am.* creamery.
-kkö dairy|woman, -maid. **-sti**
dairyman.
meikäläinen one of us.
meirami marjoram.
meisseli chisel.
meistää punch.
mekaani|kko mechanic,
mechanician. **-nen** mechanical;
-set lelut mechanical *(t.*
clockwork) toys.
meka|niikka mechanics. **-nisoida**
mechanize.
mekastaa romp, make a noise.

meklari broker.
Meksiko Mexico; ~*n lahti*
Gulf of M.; **m-lainen** *a. & s.*
Mexican.
mela paddle.
melkein almost, nearly; ~
isompi almost bigger; ~ *liian*
hyvä almost too good; ~
musta almost black; ~ *500*
henkeä nearly 500 people;
~*pä toivoisin* I almost wish;
~ *yhtä iso (m.)* much the
same size (as).
melko fairly; ~ *paljon* a good
deal (of). **-inen** considerable;
substantial, sizable; *-isella*
menestyksellä quite
successfully; *-isella*
varmuudella with reasonable
certainty; *-ista enemmän* much
more. **-sesti** considerably.
mella|kka riot, disturbance, *m.*
street violence, clash. **-koida**
riot. **-koitsija** rioter. **-staa**
(esim. lapset) be noisy, romp.
-stelu *(kadulla)* disturbance,
disorderly conduct.
mellottaa refine, *(putlata)* puddle.
melo|a paddle, canoe, scull.
-nta canoeing.
melodinen melodious.
meloni melon.
melske clamour; uproar,
turmoil. **-inen** turbulent.
meltorauta malleable iron.
melu noise; *kadun* ~ noise
from the traffic; *pitää* ~*a*
jstk raise a row; *paljon* ~*a*
tyhjästä much ado about
nothing. **-ava, -isa** noisy,
boisterous. **-ta** make a noise,
be noisy.
meneh|tyä perish, *jhk* with;
succumb [to a disease];
break [down] under; ~
häpeästä be overwhelmed with
shame; ~ *janoon* die of
thirst; *väsymyksestä*
-tymäisillään ready to drop
with fatigue, utterly exhausted.
meneillään in progress.
menekki sale[s], market;
tavaroilla on hyvä ~ the
goods sell readily, the goods
are in demand; *ei ole* ~*ä*
there is no market for, there
is little sale for. **-kirja** best-
seller.

menestykselli|nen successful.
-syys success [fulness].

menes|tys success; *saavuttaa*
~tä succeed, achieve (meet
with) success; *huonolla*
-tyksellä with little success;
(näytelmästä) tuli ~.. went
down well. **-tyä** succeed, be
successful; be a success;
(viihtyä) thrive; *(vaurastua)*
prosper; *hän -tyy hyvin* he is
doing well, he is getting on
nicely; *-tyi (onnistui)*
paremmin came off the better.

mene|tellä act, proceed; deal
[with a matter, *jssk asiassa*];
(käyttäytyä) conduct oneself;
näin -tellen in (by) doing so;
-ttelit oikein niin sanoessasi
you did right to say so; *se*
-ttelee näinkin it will do this
way, too. **-telmä** procedure;
method.

menettely practice, action;
hänen ~nsä the way he
acted. **-tapa** manner of
proceeding; course of action;
policy.

mene|ttää lose; *(tuhlata)* waste;
lak. forfeit; *(jättää*
käyttämättä) miss [an
opportunity, *tilaisuus*]; *~*
henkensä lose one's life; *~*
maineensa (»kasvonsa») lose
face; *julistaa jk -tetyksi*
declare a th. forfeited. **-tys**
loss.

menneisyys [the] past.

mennessä: *kello yhteen ~* by
one o'clock; *tähän ~* till
now, up to now, up to the
present, so far.

menninkäinen earth sprite,
gnome.

mennyt gone, *(aika)* past; *~*
aika (kiel.) past tense; *~*
vuosi the past year; *menneinä*
vuosina in past years, in
years gone by; *hän on ~tä*
miestä he is undone; *~tä*
kalua lost [forever]; *se on*
ollut ja ~ it is past and
gone; let bygones be bygones;
olkoon menneeksi very well,
then!

menn|ä go; *~ ohi* pass, pass
over, *(jkn ohi)* pass a p.; *~*
pois go away, leave, depart;

~ jnk yli (esim. kadun) cross,
vrt. ylittää; menetkö sinne?
are you going there? *siihen*
menee paljon aikaa it takes
(requires) much time; *-en*
tullen on the way there and
back.

meno *(kulku)* course; *(raha-)*
expense; *~t* expenses,
expenditure; *(juhla-)*
ceremonies; *tulot ja ~t*
income and expenditure; *~ ja*
paluu there and back, *(-lippu)*
return ticket, *Am.* two-way
ticket; *entistä ~aan* on the
old lines; *yhteen ~on* at a
stretch, at a sitting, without
a check; *olin juuri ~ssa ulos*
I was just about to go out.
-arvio estimate of expenditure.
-erä item of expenditure.
-lippu single ticket; *(~ ja*
paluu) return t. **-matka** the
journey there; the way there.
-puoli debit side.

meren|alainen submarine.
-kulkija seafarer, navigator.
-kulku navigation, seafaring.
-käynti [heavy] sea, rough
sea [s]; *on kova ~* there is a
heavy roll of the sea. **-lahti**
bay, gulf. **-neito** sea-nymph,
mermaid. **-pinta** surface of
the sea; *-pinnan yläpuolella*
above sea-level. **-pohja**
sea-bed, sea floor. **-rannikko**
sea coast, sea-board;
-rannikolla at the seaside, on
the coast. **-takainen** overseas,
transmarine. **-tutkimus**
oceanography. **-vaha**
meerschaum.

meri sea; *lähteä ~lle* go to
sea; *olla ~llä* be at sea;
lähteä merelle (laiva) put to
sea; *aavalla merellä* out at sea,
on the high seas; *~tse* by
sea. **-antura** *zo.* sole.

meridiaani meridian.

meri|eläin marine animal.
-hirviö sea monster. **-hätä**
peril at sea; *-hädässä* in
distress. **-ilmasto** maritime
climate. **-jalkaväki** marines.
-kadetti naval cadet. **-kapteeni**
sea captain, master. **-karhu**
sea-dog. **-kartta** chart. **-kauppa**
maritime trade. **-kelpoinen**

seaworthy. **-kipeä** seasick.
-kortti chart. **-koulu**
navigation school. **-kuntoisuus**
seaworthiness. **-kylpylä** seaside
resort. **-levä** seaweed. **-liikenne**
navigation. **-maisema**
(maalaus) seascape. **-matka**
voyage; passage, crossing.
-merkki buoy; light buoy; *vrt.*
reimari; (maalla) sea-mark;
beacon. **-metso** cormorant.
-mies sailor, seaman; (~**koti**
sailors' home; ~**solmu** reef
knot, square knot. **-ministeri**
Engl. First Lord of the
Admiralty, *Am.* Secretary of
the Navy. **-ministeriö** *Engl.*
Admiralty, *Am.* Navy
Department. **-näköala** sea
view. **-onnettomuus** disaster at
sea. **-pelastus** life-saving,
salvage. **-peninkulma** nautical
mile. **-pihka** amber. **-puolustus**
naval defence. **-rosvo** pirate,
buccaneer; (~**radio** pirate
radio). **-rosvous** piracy. **-sairas**
seasick. **-sankari** naval hero.
-satama seaport. **-selitys** sea
protest. **-sota** naval war [fare];
(~**koulu** naval academy).
-sotilas naval seaman; *(jalka-,*
-tykkimies) marine. **-suola** sea
salt. **-taistelu** naval battle.
-tauti seasickness. **-teitse, -tse**
by sea, by water. **-tähti**
starfish. **-upseeri** naval officer.
-vahinko sea damage, average.
-vakuutus marine insurance.
-valta naval (sea, maritime)
power. **-vartiosto** coastguard.
-vesi seawater, salt water.
-voima: ~*t* navy, naval
troops, *(jalkaväki)* marines.
-väki navy.
merkata mark.
merkeli marl.
merkilli|nen remarkable;
(kummallinen) peculiar,
strange; extraordinary; *-stä*
kyllä strangely (oddly) enough.
-syys remarkableness.
peculiarity; *(-nen esine)*
curiosity.
merkinanto signalling.
-järjestelmä signal code.
merki|ntä note, annotation,
(tili-) entry. **-tsevä** significant;
(jtk ilmaiseva) expressive,

indicative, suggestive (of).
-ttävä noteworthy, notable;
remarkable, outstanding, *ks.*
seur. **-tyksellinen** significant;
(tärkeä) important. **-tyksetön**
insignificant, of no account.
-tys meaning, sense; *(tärkeys)*
significance, importance;
ahtaammassa -tyksessä in a
narrower sense; *tällä on*
vähän ~tä this is of little
consequence; (~**oppi**
semantics).
merki|tä *(panna merkki)* mark
(usein off); *(muistiin)* write
down, make a note of;
(tarkoittaa) mean, signify;
(ilmaista) indicate, denote;
liik. subscribe [for shares,
osakkeita]; ~ *kirjaan* enter
[in the books], make an
entry; ~ *luetteloon* list,
catalogue, record, enter.. on
the list, *(jäseneksi)* enrol; ~
nimensä jhk sign one's name;
~ *jk (avustus)summa*
contribute (subscribe) a sum
(to); *se ei -tse mitään* it
does not matter; *-tty mies* a
marked man.
merkki mark, sign, token,
indication; *(esim. auto~)*
make; *jnk merkiksi* as a sign
(token) of; *antaa ~ (jstk)*
give the signal (for), *(laivalle)*
signal a ship; *panna merkille*
notice, [take] note [of];
merkillepantava noteworthy,. .
worth noticing; *on*
merkillepantavaa it should be
noted. **-kieli** sign language.
-mies outstanding man, man
of note (distinction). **-päivä**
memorable day. **-tapaus**
noteworthy event. **-teos**
outstanding work; standard
work. **-tuli** beacon.
merta fish-trap, [lobster .*t.*
crayfish] pot; *nyt on piru*
merrassa the fat is in the
fire.
mesenaatti patron.
mesi nectar; honey. **-marja**
arctic bramble.
messi mess room.
Messias Messiah.
messinki, -nen brass.
messu mass; ~*t* fair. **-halli**

exhibition hall. **-kasukka**
chasuble. **-puku** vestment. **-ta**
chant, intone; *katol.* say mass.
mestari master; *(jssk taidossa)*
expert, adept (in); *urh.*
champion; *mus.* maestro.
-llinen masterly; *-llisesti* in a
m. way. **-näyte** specimen of
skilled work, *(-teko)*
master-stroke. **-teos**
masterpiece.
mestaruus mastery; *urh.*
championship. **-kilpailut**
championship [s].
mesta|ta behead; guillotine. **-us**
execution; (~**lava** scaffold;
~**pölkky** block).
metalli metal. **-arvo** *(rahan)*
intrinsic value. **-lanka** wire;
(~**verkko** wire netting, *hieno*
wire gauze). **-nen** metal. **-raha**
coin. **-rasia, -tölkki** tin, *Am.*
can. **-seos** alloy. **-teollisuus**
metal industry.
metel|i row, uproar; *(mellakka)*
riot. **-öidä** make a noise (a
racket); riot.
meteor|i meteor. **-ologi**
meteorologist.
metku trick; dodge.
metri metre, *Am.* meter.
-järjestelmä metric system.
-mitta metric measure.
metsi|kkö wood; coppice. **-ttyä**
revert to forest. **-ttää** afforest.
metso capercaillie, wood grouse.
metsä wood, woods, woodland,
(iso) forest; ~*n peittämä*
forested, wooded; *lähteä ~lle*
go hunting. **-inen**
[well-]wooded. **-kana** grouse.
-karju wild boar. **-kauris**
roe-deer. **-lampi** woodland
pond. **-lintu** wild fowl. **-maa**
woodland. **-maisema** woodland
scene. **-mies** hunter;
woodsman.
metsän|haaskaus deforestation.
-hakkuu cutting, felling,
-hoitaja certified forester,
forest officer. **-hoito** forestry.
-istutus afforestation. **-raja**
timber-line. **-reuna** edge
of the wood. **-riista** game.
-vartija forester, *Am.* forest
ranger.
metsä|palo forest-fire.
-peitteinen wooded. **-polku**

trail, forest-path.
metsästys hunting. **-aika**
hunting (-shooting) season.
-kivääri sporting gun. **-koira**
sporting dog, hound. **-laki**
game act. **-lupa** shooting
licence. **-maat** hunting
ground [s]. **-maja** hunting-
(shooting-) box.
metsäs|täjä hunter. **-tää** hunt,
(kiväärillä) shoot, *Am.* hunt;
olla -tämässä be [out]
hunting (shooting).
metsä|talous forestry economics.
-tiede forestry. **-työmies** forest
worker, lumberjack. **-työmaa**
lumbering *(t.* logging)
site. **-tön** woodless,.. devoid
of forest [s]. **-varat** forest
resources.
miedontaa dilute.
miehe|kkyys manliness. **-käs**
manly; masculine.
miehi|nen male; masculine; ~
väestö male population;
kymmen~.. consisting of ten
men. **-stö** men; *mer., lentok.*
crew; *neljä ~ön kuuluvaa*
four crew. **-ttää** man,
(anastaa) occupy. **-tys**
occupation; (~**joukot** troops of
occupation).
miehuuden|ikä manhood.
-voima virility.
miehuulli|nen manly,
courageous, brave. **-suus**
bravery, valour; manliness.
miehuus manhood; manliness;
parhaassa miehuuden iässä in
one's prime.
miekan|isku sword-cut; ~*tta*
without striking a blow. **-terä**
edge (blade) of a sword.
miekka sword. **-ilija** fencer.
-illa fence. **-ilu** fencing;
(~**nopettaja** fencing-master;
~**taito** [art of] fencing,
swordsmanship). **-kala**
sword-fish.
miele|inen pleasing, agreeable;
minun -iseni.. to my liking,
to my taste.
mielekäs meaningful; *ei ole*
~*tä* there is no sense in...
mielell|ään willingly, with
pleasure, gladly; *haluaisin -äni*
I should like to; *olisin ~äni*
tavannut hänet I would like

to have seen him.
mielen|häiriö mental
disturbance; ~*ssä* while
mentally disordered. **-kiinnoton**
uninteresting. **-kiinto** interest;
herättää ~*a* arouse (stimulate)
interest, interest [a p.];
yleistä ~*a herättävä.* . of
general interest. **-kiintoinen**
interesting. **-laatu** turn of
mind; disposition. **-liikutus**
emotion. **-lujuus** strength of
mind. **-maltti** presence of
mind. **-muutos** change of
mind; *usk. ym* change of
heart. **-osoittaja** demonstrator.
-osoituksellinen demonstrative.
-osoitus demonstration. **-rauha**
peace of mind. **-terveys**
mental health. **-tila** state of
mind. **-vika** mental
derangement. **-vikainen** *a.*
mentally deranged, insane.
-vikaisuus insanity. **-ylennys**
usk. edification.
miele|ttömyys absurdity; folly.
-tön. . out of one's senses;
senseless; foolish, crazy; ~
hinta absurd (fantastic) price;
~ *ilosta* delirious with joy.
mieli mind; *(mielentila)* frame
of mind, mood; *mielestäni* in
my opinion, to my mind, in
my view; *onko hän mielestäsi
kaunis* do you consider her
beautiful; *olen sitä mieltä,
että.* . I am of the opinion
that; *olen eri mieltä* I
disagree, I take a different
view (of); *olla samaa mieltä
kuin* agree with; *olla* ~*ssään
jstk* be delighted (at, with),
be pleased (with); *hyvällä
mielellä* in good spirits; *tehdä*
~ wish, have a mind to;
panna mieleensä remember,
take note of; *pitää mielessä*
keep (bear) in mind; *sinun
~ksesi* to please you; *tehdä
jklle* ~*ksi* humour a p.; ~*n
määrin* as much as one
pleases, at will; *olla jklle
mieleen* please; *tulee mieleen*
comes to mind; *siinä mielessä
kuin* in the sense that; *tässä
mielessä* with this in mind.
-aine favourite subject. **-ala**
mood, humour. **-halu** desire;

appetite. **-harmi** worry;
annoyance, vexation. **-harrastus**
hobby. **-hyvin** willingly, gladly,
with pleasure. **-hyvä** pleasure,
delight; satisfaction; *tuotti
minulle* ~*ä* it gave me
pleasure, it pleased me.
-johde impulse; *omituinen* ~
whim, caprice, quirk; *hetken
-johteesta toimiva* impulsive;
äkillisestä -johteesta on the
spur of the moment. **-kuva**
idea, [mental] image.
-kuvituksekas imaginative.
-kuvituksellinen fantastic,
fanciful, imaginary.
-kuvitukseton unimaginative.
-kuvitus imagination, fancy.
-lause motto. **-nen** *(yhd.)*
-minded; *ystävällis*~ kindly
disposed. **-paha** regret;
displeasure; *(-harmi)*
resentment, annoyance; ~*kseni
kuulin.* . I was sorry to hear
. . **-pide** opinion, view;
(~*tutkimus* opinion survey,
public-opinion poll). **-puoli** *a.*
insane, demented; *s.* lunatic,
madman. **-puolisuus** insanity.
-ruoka favourite dish. **-sairaala**
mental hospital, home for
mental cases. **-sairas** mentally
ill; *s.* mental patient. **-sairaus**
mental disorder (disease).
mielis|televä fawning; flattering.
-tellä *(jkta)* fawn upon, try to
ingratiate oneself with; *-tellen
(salavihkaa) voittaa jkn
luottamus* insinuate oneself
into the confidence of. **-tyä**
ks. mieltyä.
mieli|suosio: ~*lla* willingly, of
one's free will. **-tauti** mental
disease; ~*en erikoislääkäri*
psychiatrist; (~*oppi*
psychiatry). **-teko** desire,
craving. **-tietty** sweetheart.
-työ favourite occupation.
-valta discretion; *(~isuus)*
arbitrariness; *olla jkn -vallassa*
be left to a p.'s discretion.
-valtainen arbitrary;
high-handed.
mielle conception, idea.
-yhtymä association of ideas.
mielly|ttävyys pleasantness;
charm. **-ttävä** pleasing;
pleasant, agreeable, attractive,

lik[e]able. **-ttää** please; catch
a p.'s fancy; appeal (to),
attract; *se ei -tä minua (m.)*
I do not like it.
mieltenkuohu excitement,
agitation.
mielty|mys liking; *(kiintymys)*
affection (for), attachment
(to). **-ä** *(jhk)* take to, become
fond of; *on -nyt jhk (m.)* has
a liking for.
mieltä|järkyttävä agitating,
shocking. **-ylentävä** elevating,
uplifting.
mielui|mmin preferably; *kävelen*
~ I prefer to walk. **-nen, -sa**
welcome; ~ *tehtävä* a
pleasant (an agreeable) task.
mieluummin rather, sooner;
preferably; *jään ~ kotiin* I
prefer to stay at home, I
would rather stay at home.
miero: *joutua ~n tielle* be
reduced to begging.
mies man *(pl.* men); *(avio-)*
husband; *miehissä (kaikki)* to
the last man, all together; in
force; *miesten ~* a splendid
fellow, one in a thousand; *5
shillinkiä mieheen* 5 sh. each;
onko sinussa ~tä siihen? are
you man enough for that?
-henkilö man, male. **-hukka**
losses, casualties. **-kohtainen**
personal. **-kuoro** male choir.
-luku number [s]; *suurempi ~*
superior n.; *vihollinen oli
-luvultaan meitä paljon
voimakkaampi* the enemy
greatly outnumbered us.
-lukuinen numerous. **-muistiin**
in living memory. **-mäinen**
manly, masculine; *(naisista)*
mannish. **-palvelija** valet;
butler. **-polvi** generation.
-puoli *(suvun)* spearside.
-puolinen male, masculine.
-tenhuone *puhek.* gents.
-voima *(-vahvuus)* man-power.
-väki men, *ark.* menfolk.
miete thought, reflection; idea;
olla mietteissään be lost in
thought. **-lmä** aphorism.
mieti|ntö report. **-skellä**
meditate, *jtk* on; ponder (on),
(hautoa) brood (on, over);
-skelevä contemplative,
meditative. **-skely** meditation;

contemplation.
mieto weak; mild; ~ *viini*
light wine.
mietti|minen contemplating *jne.*
-misaika time for consideration. **-vä** thoughtful,
reflective.
miettiä think, *jtk* about, of;
reflect (on), consider,
think over; *(tuumailla)*
contemplate.
migreeni migraine.
mihin where? ~ *aikaan* at
what time? ~ *tuota
käytetään?* what's that for?
-kään: *hänestä ei ole* ~ he's
good for nothing.
miilu charcoal-pit.
miina mine; *(jalkaväki-)*
antipersonnel m.; *ajaa ~an*
strike a m. **-laiva**(*-nlaskija*)
mine-layer. **-nraivaaja**
mine-sweeper. **-vyöhyke**
mine-field.
miinoittaa mine, *(laskea
miinoja)* lay mines.
miinus minus, less.
mikro|aaltouuni micro-wave
oven; **-auto** [go-]kart. **-bi**
microbe. **-filmi** microfilm.
-foni microphone, *(puhelin~)*
mouthpiece. **-housut** hot pants.
-skooppi microscope; *(~nen*
microscopic, *(pieni)*
microscopical).
miksi why? for what reason?
wherefore? ~*pä ei* why not.
mikä which; what; ~ *kirja*
what book? which book? ~
niistä? which of them? ~ *nyt
on (hätänä)* what's the
matter? what's wrong? ~
kaunis taulu what a beautiful
picture! *~hän tämä on* I
wonder what this is; *mistä
syystä* for what reason?; . .
kuin se mikä. . [her coat is
as long] as the one [I am
wearing]; *~pä siinä (voin
mennäkin)* I don't mind [if I
go].
mikäli as far as, in so far as;
(jos) if; ~ *tiedän* as *(t.* so)
far as I know, for all I
know.
mikään any; anything; *ei* ~
no; nothing; *ei millään
ehdolla* not for anything, on

no account.
Milano Milan.
miliisi militia; militiaman.
militantti militant.
milj|ardi milliard, *Am.* billion.
-oona million; ~ *miestä* a m.
men; *kaksi* ~*a* two million
[people], *(puntaa)* £ 2
million; (~**mies** millionaire).
millainen what kind (sort) of,
of what kind; ~ *hän on*
what is he like? ~ *mies*
what kind of [a] man?
milli|gramma milligramme.
-metri millimetre.
milloin when? [at] what time?
(jolloin) when; ~ — ~ now
— now, sometimes —
sometimes; ~ *missäkin* now
here, now there; ~ *tahansa*
at any time, no matter when;
whenever [you wish]. **-kaan**
ever; *ei* ~ never.
milläänkään: *hän ei ollut* ~ he
did not turn a hair.
miltei almost; ~ *samankokoisia*
much the same size.
mimiikka play of expressions.
miner|aali mineral. **-alogia**
mineralogy.
miniatyyri miniature.
minim|aalinen minimal. **-i**
minimum [price, *hinta*]. **-oida**
minimize.
ministeri [government] minister; *Engl.* cabinet minister. **-stö**
government, cabinet. **-ö**
ministry; *Engl. m.* office
(esim.: Home O., *sisäasiain*
~: War O., *sota~);*
department.
minkki mink. **-turkki** mink
coat.
minkä which; . . ~ *haluat*
which [ever] you like, the
one you like; *(kysymyksenä)*
which [of these] do you
want? ~ *takia* for what
reason? why? *(relat.)* for
which reason, because of
which.
minkä|lainen *ks.* millainen.
-näköinen: ~ *mies oli?* what
did the man look like?
-tähden why? for what
reason? **-än|lainen:** *ei ollut*
-laista mahdollisuutta there
was no chance whatever.

minne where? where to? ~
matka where are you going
(t. off to)? *~päin* in what
direction? which way? **-kään:**
ei ~ nowhere.
minttu mint.
minua, minut *ks.* minä.
minun my; mine; ~ *kanssani*
with me; ~ *takiani* because
of me, for my sake; *vrt.*
minä.
minuutti minute; *minuutilleen*
to the minute. **-osoitin** *m.*
long hand.
minä I; *psyk.* the ego; *minua,*
minut me; *minulle* to me;
liian paljon minulle too much
for me; *minusta* in my
opinion, to me; *minusta hän*
on oikeassa I think he is
right.
mirhami myrrh.
mirri pussy[-cat], puss.
mis|sä where? ~ *hyvänsä*
anywhere, *konj.* wherever; ~
maassa? in what country? *ei*
~än nowhere; *siellä jos ~än*
there if anywhere. **-tä** from
where? from what place? ~
tulet where do you come
from? ~ *sen tiedät* how do
you know that? ~ *olet sen*
löytänyt where did you find
it? *ei ~än* [from] nowhere;
ei ~än hinnasta not. . at any
price.
misteli *bot.* mistletoe.
mitali medal; *~n toinen puoli*
kuv. the reverse of the m.
mitata measure [out]; gauge;
(maata) survey; *(askelin)* pace
off [a distance]; ~ *runsaasti*
give good measure.
mitellä: ~ *voimiaan jkn kanssa*
measure one's strength against.
miten how? in what way? *oli*
~ *oli* be that as it may;
tiedän ~ *hänet saan käsiini* I
know how to find him; ~
ihana taulu! what a beautiful
picture! ~ *kuten* somehow or
other. **-kä** *(mitä sanoitte)*
sorry, what did you say? I
beg your pardon? **-kään:** *ei* ~
in no way; by no means! on
no account! *jos* ~ *voin* if I
possibly can.
mitoittaa dimension.

mitta measure; measurement; *mitan mukaan tehty* made to measure (to order), *Am.* custom [-made]; *ottaa jksta ~* take a p.'s measurements, measure a p. [for a suit etc.]; *ottaa toisistaan ~a (kuv.)* take their measure; *täyttää ~ (kuv.)* be up to standard; *ajan ~an* in the long run; *vuoden ~an* in the course of the year; *maksaa samalla mitalla* pay sb. in his own coin. **-amaton** immeasurable. **-asteikko** scale. **-illa** *kuv.: ~ lattiaa* pace; *(jkta katseellaan)* size. . up. **-inen** [5 metres] in length; *olla sanansa ~* be as good as one's word. **-kaava** measure; scale; *suuressa ~ssa* on a large scale. **-lasi** graduated glass. **-nauha** tape measure. **-puku** suit made to measure, *Am.* custom-made suit. **-puu** [foot-]rule, *m. kuv.* yardstick; *kuv.* standard. **-ri** *(yhd.)* -meter; gauge; *kaasu~* gas-meter; *sade~* rain-gauge. **-suhde** proportion; *-suhteet* dimensions. **-us** measurement; measuring; *(~oppi* geometry). **-yksikkö** measuring unit.

mitä what; *(superl. vahv.)* most; *~ kuuluu* what news? *(kuinka voitte)* how are you? *paras ~ tiedän* the best [that] I know; *~ — sitä* the — the; *~ pikemmin sitä parempi* the sooner the better; *~ mielenkiintoisin kirja* a most interesting book; *~ varovaisimmin* with the utmost care; *~pä siitä* it doesn't matter! never mind!

mität|tömyys insignificance; unimportance. **-öidä** cancel. **-ön** insignificant, inconsiderable trifling, trivial; *(kelpaamaton)* not valid, invalid; [null and] void; *~ summa* trifling sum; *-tömän pieni* negligible [quantity, *määrä*]; *julistaa -ttömäksi* annul, cancel, nullify.

mitään anything; *ei ~* nothing. **-sanoma|ton** uninformative;

m-ttomat kasvot (ilmeettömät) poker face.

modaalinen modal.

modisti milliner.

moduuli module, *mat.* modulus.

moinen such; *oletko moista kuullut?* did you ever hear the like of that?

moite blame, censure; reproof.

moit|ittava blameworthy, blamable, reprehensible;. . open to blame (criticism). **-teenalai|nen** *ks. ed.; saattaa m-seksi* compromise. **-teeton** blameless; irreproachable; faultless. **-teettomuus** blamelessness. **-tia** blame, *jstk* for; find fault with; criticize; *(nuhdella)* reproach; *~ testamenttia* dispute a will. **-timishaluinen** fault-finding.

mokkatakki suede coat.

mokoma: *en ole ~a kuullut* I never heard anything like it; *kaikin mokomin* by all means, don't mention it; *hän tahtoi kaikin mokomin tietää* he insisted on knowing.

molekyyli molecule.

molemm|at both; *me ~* b. of us, the two of us; *-in puolin* on b. sides, on either side (of). **-inpuolinen** mutual; reciprocal.

molli *mus.* minor.

momentti *lak.* subsection, clause, item.

monen|kertainen manifold; multiple. **-keskinen** multilateral. **-lainen** *-laisia.* . of many kinds,. . of various kinds, many kinds of. ., a great variety of. . **-laisuus** diversity. **-muotoinen** multiform.

mones: *kuinka ~* which [in order]? *~ko päivä tänään on* what date is it today? **-ti** many a time, many times; often.

mongolilainen *s.* Mongol [ian]; *a.* Mongol.

moni many [a]; *~ mies* many a man; *(monta miestä)* many men; *moneen vuoteen* for years; *monen monta kertaa* over and over again, *(puhek.)* heaps of times; *monin verroin*

far,.. by far; *monet* many,
several. **-avioinen** polygamous.
-avioisuus polygamy. **-arvoinen**
pluralistic. **-kansallinen**
multinational, *(sopimus)*
multilateral. **-kielinen** multi-
lingual; ~ *henkilö* polyglot.
-kko, -kollinen plural. **-kulmio**
polygon. **-lapsinen** *perhe* a
large family. **-lukuinen**
numerous. **-miljoonikko**
multimillionaire. **-muotoinen:**
on ~ (it) takes many forms..
-mutkainen complicated,
complex; ~ *kysymys* an
intricate question. **-mutkaisuus**
complicated nature,
complexity, intricacy. **-nainen**
various, diversified, manifold,
varied. **-naisuus** [great]
variety, diversity; multiplicity.
-nkertainen multiple.
-nkertaistaa manifold, multiply
[many times over]. **-numeroinen:** ~ *luku* number
of several figures (digits).
-puolinen many-sided;
versatile, diversified.
-puolisuus many-sidedness;
versatility. **-sanainen** wordy,
verbose. **-sanaisuus** wordiness,
verbosity. **-staa** *(kojeella)*
duplicate. **-ste** duplicate.
monistus [office] duplicating,
(valokopioimalla ym)
reprography. **-kone** duplicator.
-laitteet reprography facilities.
moni|tahoinen many-faceted.
-tahokas polyhedron.
-tavuinen polysyllabic. **-tuinen:**
monen -tuista kertaa ever so
many times. **-tyydyttymättömät**
rasvahapot polyunsaturates.
-vaiheinen eventful. **-vuotinen**
many years'; *(kasvi)*
perennial; ~ *ystävyys* a
friendship of many years'
standing. **-väri-** multicolour.
-värinen multicoloured.
-ääninen: ~ *laulu* part-song;
laulaa -äänisesti sing in parts.
mono|grammi monogram. **-kkeli**
eye-glass, monocle. **-logi**
monologue. **-poli** monopoly.
monsuuni monsoon.
monta many; ~ *kertaa* many
(several) times. **-ko?** how
many?

moottori motor, engine.
-ajoneuvo motor vehicle.
-kelkka snowmobile. **-pyörä**
motor-cycle. **-pyöräily**
motor-cycling. **-saha** motor
saw, *Am.* chain saw. **-tie**
motorway, *Am.* motor
(express) highway, freeway; *(4
-kaistainen)* dual carriageway.
-vene motorboat. **-vika** engine
trouble, breakdown; *autoon
tuli* ~ the car broke down
[on the way].
moottoroida motorize.
mopo moped.
mopsi pug [-dog].
moraali morals, *(opetus)* moral,
(esim. sotajoukon) morale.
-nen moral. **-ton** immoral,..
of loose morals.
moreeni moraine.
morf|iini morphia, morphine.
-inisti morphine addict.
mormoni Mormon, Latter-day
Saint.
morsian bride; *(kihlattu)*
fiancée.
morsius|huntu bridal veil. **-lahja**
wedding present. **-neito**
bridesmaid. **-pari** bride and
bridegroom. **-puku**
wedding-dress.
mosaiikki mosaic [work].
Mosambik Mozambique.
moskeija mosque.
Moskova Moscow.
motelli motel.
motiivi *(perustelu)* motive.
moukari sledge-hammer.
-nheitto hammer-throw.
moukka lout; boor. **-mainen**
loutish, boorish; unmannerly.
muassa: *muun* ~ among other
things, inter alia; *eräs syy oli
muun* ~ one reason, among
many, was. .
muhamettilai|nen *a.*
Mohammedan, Moslem,
Muslim; *s.* Mohammedan,
Moslem. **-suus**
Mohammedanism; Islam.
muhen|nos stew; *vrt. seur.* **-taa**
stew; *-nettu.* . cooked in white
sauce.
muhke|a stately, imposing;
grand, impressive. **-us**
stateliness, magnificence.
muhvi muff.

muija old woman.

muinai|nen old, ancient; *-sina aikoina* in ancient (olden) times; *muistella -sia* recall memories of the past.

muinais|aika antiquity, ancient times. **-aikainen** antique. **-esine** antique. **-jäännös** relic [of antiquity]. **-löytö** arch[a]eological find. **-muisto** ancient monument. **-suomalainen** *a.* old Finnish; *s.* ancient Finn. **-taru** ancient tradition, legend. **-tiede** arch[a]eology. **-tieteellinen** arch[a]eologic[al]. **-tieteilijä** arch[a]eologist. **-uus** antiquity.

muinoin: *ennen* ~ in days long past, in olden times.

muis|taa remember, recollect, recall; *-kseni* as far as I can remember, to the best of my recollection, if my memory does not fail me; *en -ta tavanneeni* I don't remember having met; *en -ta nimiä* I have a bad (poor) memory for names; *en -ta hänen nimeään* I can't think of his name [at the moment]; *-tettakoon* it should be kept in mind that.. **-tamaton** forgetful, oblivious. **-tella** recollect, recall, call [back] to mind, think back [to a period]. **-telma** recollection, reminiscence; ~*t* (*m.*) memoirs. **-tettava** memorable. **-ti** memory; *kaksi* ~*in* (*lask.*) carry two; *merkitä* ~*in* write down; *pitää* ~*ssa* bear in mind; ~*sta* from memory; *minun* ~*ni aikana* within my recollection. **-tiinpano** note; *tehdä* ~*ja* make (take) notes.

muisti|kirja note-book. **-lehtiö** memory pad. **-lista** memo. (*t.* shopping) list, check list. **-o** memoran|dum, (*pl.* -da). **-virhe** slip of the memory.

muisto memory; (*-esine*) souvenir, keepsake; ~*ksi* as a remembrance; *jnk* (*jkn*) ~*ksi* in commemoration of; *lapsuuden* ~*t* recollections of childhood; *viettää jtk* ~*a* commemorate [an event]. **-esine** souvenir, memento.

-hetki, -jumalanpalvelus memorial service. **-juhla** memorial festival, commemoration; *viettää 100-vuotis*~*a* commemorate the centenary (of). **-kirja** album. **-lahja** souvenir, parting gift. **-levyke** plaque. **-merkki** memorial. **-mitali** commemorative medal. **-patsas** statue, monument. **-puhe** commemoration speech, memorial address. **-päivä** anniversary. **-raha** medal. **-rikas** memorable. **-runo** commemorative poem. **-sanat** obituary. **-taulu** memorial tablet.

muistu|a: *-u mieleeni* I remember. **-ttaa** remind (of), (*yhtäläisyytensä kautta*) resemble; (*huomauttaa*) remark (on, upon), point out, call [a p.'s] attention to; (*moittien*) reprove, (*vastaan*) object (to); *onko Teillä mitään -ttamista* have you any objections. **-tus** reminder; (*huomautus*) remark, comment; (*nuhde*) reproof, reprimand; (*vastaväite*) objection.

muka supposed[ly], alleged[ly]; *hän on* ~ *sairas* he says (*t.* he pretends) he is ill; *hän on* ~ *varakkaampi* he is supposed to be wealthier; *sitä* ~*a kuin* in proportion as.

mukaan: *jnk* ~ according to, by; *laskunne* ~.. *päivältä* (*m.*) as per your invoice of.. ; *painon* ~ by weight; *sen* ~ *kuin* [according] as, in so far as; *sen* ~ *mitä hän sanoo* according to what he says; *tarpeen* ~ as needed, as required; *lukea* ~ include; ~ *luettuna* including.., inclusive of; *ottaa* ~ take along, take.. with one; *ota minut* ~ take me with you; *tule* ~! come along! **-satempaava** captivating, compelling; gripping; *puhe oli* ~ *the* speech carried the hearers away (along). **-tua** accommodate oneself, adapt oneself (to); adjust oneself.

muka|elma imitation;

(muunnelma) adaptation. **-illa**
imitate; adapt. **-inen** *(jnk)*. .
in accordance with; consistent,
compatible (with); *olla jnk ~
(m.)* be in keeping with,
agree with, coincide with.
-isesti *(jnk)* according to, in
accordance (conformity) with,
sen ~ accordingly.
mukana with; *~ seuraava*
accompanying, enclosed,
attached; *~ni tulevat*. . I shall
be accompanied by; *olla jssk
~ (läsnä)* be present at;
minulla ei ole rahaa ~ni I
have no money with me;
tuoda ~an bring along, *(kuv.)*
bring in its train,
(seurauksena) entail, involve.
mukau|ttaa *(jhk)* suit. . (to),
gear. . (to). **-tua** adapt
oneself, adjust oneself (to),
(esim. pol. järjestelmään)
conform; *(noudattaa)* comply
(with); *ks. mukaantua.*
-tumaton not adaptable,
unaccommodating. **-tumiskyky**
adaptability, ability to adapt
oneself. **-tuva** adaptable,
accommodating; compliant.
-tuv(ais)uus adaptability,
compliance.
mukav|a comfortable, nice,
(sopiva) convenient, handy;
(hauska) pleasant. **-uus**
comfortableness, comfort, ease,
convenience; *nykyajan
mukavuuksin varustettu* with
every modern convenience;
(~laitos toilet, lavatory, public
convenience.)
muki mug.
mukiin: *menee ~* will do.
-menevä passable; fairly good,
tolerable; not bad.
mukiloida belabour, beat up, mug.
mukula *(juuri)* corm, *(varsi-,
m.)* tuber; *(lapsi)* kid. **-kivi**
cobblestone.
mulatti mulatto.
mulko|illa roll one's eyes;
glare, stare, glower (at).
-silmäi|nen . . with protruding
eyes.
mullata cover, earth over,
(perunaa) earth up.
mullikka heifer, *(sonni ~)* bull
calf.

mullin: *~ mallin* upside down,
topsy-turvy.
mullis|taa turn upside down;
overthrow, upset; *(kokonaan,
m.)* revolutionize. **-tava**
revolutionizing. **-tus** upheaval;
revolution.
multa soil, earth; *muuttua
mullaksi* moulder, turn into
dust. **-sieni** truffle.
mumista mumble; mutter.
mummo old woman; *(isoäiti)*
grandmother, *(mummi)* granny.
muna egg; *tiet.* ovum *(pl.
ova)*. **-kas** omelet[te]. **-kokkeli**
scrambled eggs. **-kuppi** egg
cup. **-lukko** padlock.
-nkeltuainen yolk [of egg].
-nkuori eggshell. **-nvalkuainen**
white [of egg]; *tiet.* albumen,
vrt. valkuaisaine. **-sarja** ovary.
-solu egg cell. **-ta:** *~ itsensä*
put one's foot in it, make a
blunder. **-us** blunder; howler.
muni|a lay eggs; *hyvä -maan
(kanasta)* a good layer.
-tusmuna nest-egg.
munkki monk; *(leivos)*
doughnut. **-kunta** monastic
order. **-likööri** Benedictine.
-luostari monastery.
munuai|nen kidney. **-skivi**
kidney-stone, renal calculus.
-srasva suet. **-stauti** kidney
disease. **-stulehdus** nephritis.
muodikas fashionable, stylish;
up-to-date.
muodolli|nen formal. **-suus**
formality, form; *ilman
-suuksia* without ceremonies,
informal [ly]; *pelkkä ~* a
mere formality.
muodon|muutos change in
form, transformation. **-vaihdos**
metamorphosis.
muodos|taa form; fashion,
shape; *(hallitus)* build; *(tehdä)*
constitute; make up;
(perustaa) establish; *~
toisenlaiseksi* remodel; *12
henkilöä ~ valamiehistön* a
jury consists (is composed) of
12 people. **-tella** fashion,
shape, *(laatia)* formulate.
-telma *sot.* formation. **-tua** be
formed; be composed, *jstk* of;
~ jksk become, turn into,
(esim. tavaksi) grow into;

niin, ettei -tu savua so that no smoke is produced; *vesi -tuu höyryksi* water is transformed (converted) into steam. **-tuma** formation. **muodo|ton** shapeless; deformed, misshapen. **-ttomuus** shapelessness; deformation. **muok|ata** work up; *(viljellä)* till, prepare [the soil], break up; *(nahkaa)* dress, curry. **-kaamaton** untilled; ~ *maaperä* unprepared (unbroken) ground. **-kaus:** *maan* ~ tilling.

muona food, provisions. **-nhankkija** caterer. **-mies** farm labourer. **-varat** provisions. **muoni|ttaa** supply with provisions, victual. **-tus** provisioning; catering.

muoti fashion, style; *olla muodissa* be the fashion, be in vogue; *jäädä muodista* go out of fashion; *määrää muodin* sets the fashion. **-kuva** fashion-plate. **-lehti** fashion-paper (-magazine). **-liike** ladies' outfitters, *(hattu-)* milliner's. **-näytös** mannequin show. **-salonki** fashion house. **-sana** vogue word. **-taiteilija** fashion designer, *(liike)* couturier. **-tavarat** fashionable articles, ladies' wear.

muoto form, shape; *muodon vuoksi* for form's sake, pro forma, *(näön)* for the sake of appearances; *ei millään ~a* by no means, under no circumstances; *älä millään ~a* for goodness' sake don't; *muodoltaan samanlainen* similar in form; *asia saa sen kautta aivan toisen muodon* that gives the matter an entirely different aspect. **-illa** design, *(laatia)* formulate; *hyvin -iltu* well designed, *(puhe)* well-worded. **-ilu** design. **-inen** *(jnk)* in the form (shape) of. **-kuva** portrait, likeness; *(~maalari* portrait painter). **-oppi** morphology. **-puoli** deformed, shapeless, irregular. **-seikka** matter of form. **-valmis** perfect in form, finished.

muotti mould; *tekn.* die, matrix.

muovai|lla mould, model, shape; *(kirjallisesti)* adapt, revise; *(sovitella)* modify, *(muodostella)* formulate. **-lu** modelling.

muova|ta shape, mould, give shape to. **-utua** shape (form) itself; *-utuva* plastic.

muovi plastic; *~pussi* p. bag.

murahtaa growl, snarl.

muratti ivy.

murea crisp; *(esim. liha)* tender.

mureh|duttaa grieve. **-tia** grieve *(jkta* for, *jtk* at, over); *(olla huolissaan)* be anxious, worry.

mure|ke stuffing; *(liha-)* forcemeat. **-leipä** crisp bread.

muren|taa crumble, *m. kuv.* crush; ~ *hienoksi* reduce to powder. **-tua** crumble [away]; *(rapautua)* disintegrate.

murha murder. **-aja** murderer. **-mies** murderer, assassin; cut-throat. **-poltto** arson. **-ta** murder; *(sala-)* assassinate; *-ava arvostelu* crushing criticism. **-yritys** attempt on a p.'s life, attempted murder.

murhe grief, sorrow, *(huoli)* care; *olla ~issaan jstk* be grieved, grieve (about). **-ellinen** sad, sorrowful, melancholy. **-ellisuus** sadness. **-enlaakso** vale of tears. **-mieli:** *~n* with sadness in one's heart. **-näytelmä** tragedy.

muri|na, -sta growl, snarl.

murjo|a maul; *maailman -ma* ill-used by the world. **-ttaa** mope.

murju hovel, shack.

murmeli marmot.

murre dialect.

murros break [ing]. **-ikä** [age of] puberty; *~iässä* at puberty. **-ikäinen** pubertal adolescent. **-kausi** crisis, critical period.

murska: *lyödä ~ksi* dash. . to pieces, smash [up]; *mennä ~ksi* go to pieces. **-ta** crush; shatter; break; ~ *jkn toiveet* shatter a p.'s hopes.

mursu walrus.

murt|aa break; *puhuu -aen englantia* speaks English with a foreign accent, *(huonosti)* speaks halting English; ~ *ovi* break a door open, force a door; ~ *rintama* break through [the enemy's] lines; *vesi mursi padon* the water burst the dam; *se mursi hänen terveytensä* it ruined his health. **-autua** break *(jhk into, jkn läpi through)*. **-ee|llinen** dialect [al]; *puhuu -llisesti* speaks [a] dialect. **-eellisuus** provincialism.
murto breaking, *jhk* into; *(-varkaus)* house-breaking, *(näyteikkuna-)* smash-and-grab raid. **-luku** fraction. **-maahiihto** cross-country ski-ing. **-osa** fraction. **-vakuutus** burglary insurance. **-varas** burglar, house-breaker. **-varkaus** burglary. **-yritys** attempted burglary.
murtu|a break, *(pato ym)* burst; *(luu)* be fractured; *hän -i (kuv.)* he collapsed, he broke down; *-nut* broken, *(terveys)* shattered, *(luu, m.)* fractured. **-ma** break, breach, *(luun)* fracture. **-maton** unbroken; unbreakable.
muru crumb.
museo museum.
muser|taa crush *(m. kuv.); (esim. hedelmä)* squash, mash; *-tava* overwhelming, *(arvostelu)* crushing. **-tua** be crushed; be overwhelmed; be struck all of a heap.
musikaalinen musical.
musiikki music. **-arvostelu** musical criticism. **-kauppa** music shop, music-seller's. **-opisto** college (academy) of music, conservatoire. **-oppi** music.
muskettisoturi musketeer.
muskotti nutmeg, nutmeg-tree, mace.
musliini muslin.
musta black; ~ *hevonen* dark horse; ~ *pörssi* b. market; *~n pörssin kauppias* b.-marketeer (market dealer); *~lla listalla* black-listed; ~ *taulu* blackboard; *~n ruskea*

b. brown. **-aminen** *kuv.* mud-slinging. **-ihoinen** black, dark-skinned. **-lainen** gipsy, Romany. **-naan:** ~ *väkeä* packed with people. **-pukuinen** dressed in black. **-rastas** blackbird. **-sukkainen** jealous (of). **-sukkaisuus** jealousy. **-ta** blacken, *kuv.* smear. **-tukkainen** black-haired. **-valkoinen** black and white.
muste ink; *~ella* in ink; *~essa oleva* [all] inky. **-kala** octopus; cuttlefish. **-kumi** ink eraser. **-lma** bruise, *(silmä mustana)* a black eye; *on -lmilla* is black and blue. **-pullo** ink-bottle, inkstand. **-ta** blacken, grow black; *(maailma) -ni silmissäni* everything went black for me. **-tahra** ink blot.
mustikka bilberry, whortleberry, *Am,* blueberry.
mustua grow (turn) black, blacken; *(hopeasta)* tarnish.
muta mud, mire. **-inen** muddy. **-kylpy** mud bath. **-pohja** mud bottom.
mutista mumble, mutter.
mutka bend, curve; detour; *~t (kuv.)* ins and outs; *tien ~ssa* at a bend of the road; *muitta mutkitta* without further (any more) ado, straight away. **-inen** winding, tortuous. **-llinen** *kuv.* complicated, involved, intricate. **-ton** plain, simple.
mutki|kas winding; *m. kuv.* sinuous, tortuous; *se tekee asian -kkaaksi* that complicates matters. **-stua** *kuv.* become more complicated. **-tella** wind [in and out]; *(joesta)* meander; *-tteleva (m.)* serpentine.
mutta but; ~ *kumminkin* still, yet.
mutteri nut. **-avain** spanner.
mutustaa munch.
muu *(joku, jokin, mikään ~)* [somebody, something, anything] else; *(toinen)* other, *(epäm. art. varust.)* another; *(jäljelläoleva)* the rest [of]; *kaikki ~t* all the others, everybody else; *me ~t* the

rest of us; *~lla tavalla* otherwise; *millä ~lla(kaan) tavalla* how else [can I. .]; *mitä ~ta* what else? *ei kukaan ~ kuin hän (m.)* no one but he, no one besides him; *en voi ~ta kuin* I cannot but; *hän ei tee ~ta kuin itkee* she does nothing but cry; *ilman ~ta ks. ilman; en anna ilman ~ta periksi* I won't give in as easy as all that; *älä ~ta sano* you said it! **-alla** elsewhere, somewhere else; *enemmän kuin missään ~* more than anywhere else. **-alle** *ks. ed.* **-alta** from elsewhere. **-an** a, an, a certain.

muukalai|nen *s.* stranger; *(ulkomaalainen)* foreigner, alien; *a.* foreign; alien. **-slegioona** foreign legion.

muuli mule. **-najaja** muleteer.

muulloin at another time; *joskus ~* some other time.

muumio mummy.

muun|lainen. . of another (of a different) kind. **-nella** *(sovitella)* adapt; *(lieventäen)* modify; *(vaihdella)* vary. **-nelma** adaptation; *mus.* variation. **-nos** modification; *luonnont.* variety; *(kertomuksen)* version. **-taa** transform; convert, *jksk* into. **-taja** transformer.

muurahai|nen ant. **-shappo** formic acid. **-skeko** ant hill.

muurain cloudberry.

muura|ri mason, bricklayer. **-ta** do masonry work, wall [up]. **-us** brickwork, masonry; *(~lasta* trowel).

muuri wall; *(uuni)* fireplace.

muus|a muse. **-ikko** musician.

muutama some, a few; *~t* some, a few; *~t ihmiset* some people; *~n kerran* a few times; *~n päivän* [for] a few days.

muute: *muutteeksi* for a change. **-lla** change, alter; shift [one's position, *asentoaan*].

muut|en otherwise, or [else], else, *(sen lisäksi)* besides; *(ohimennen)* incidentally; *~*

vain for no special reason; *kuinkas ~* naturally. **-oin** *ed.; jotenkin ~* in some other way; for that matter.

muutos change, alteration; *(vaihtelu)* variation; *(lain)* amendment; *(järjestelmän ym)* change-over; *~ parempaan päin* a change for the better.

muutt|aa move; *(asuntoa)* move [house]; *(siirtää)* remove; *(toisenlaiseksi)* change, alter, turn, *jksk* into; transform; *tekn. ym* convert; *(linnuista)* migrate; *~ maahan, maasta* immigrate, emigrate; *~ mielensä* change one's mind, *(kantansa)* shift one's ground; *~ pois (m.)* leave; *~ rahaksi* convert into money, *(käteiseksi)* cash; *~ taloon* move into a house, move in; *muutamme ensi' viikolla* we are moving house next week; *~ vaatteita* change [one's clothes]; *N:ään matkustavien on muutettava junaa. . .ssa* passengers for N. change at. .; *kaulusta pitää vähän ~* the collar must be altered a little; *se ~ asian* that alters the case; *se ei muuta asiaa* that makes no difference.

muutto moving, removal; *(lintujen)* migration. **-lintu** migratory bird, migrant. **-mies** removal man. **-kuorma** vanload [of furniture]. **-vaunut** furniture van.

muuttu|a change, alter, be changed; turn [into[; *et. tekn.* be converted; *(vaihdella)* vary; *~ muodoltaan* change [in] form; *~ huonommaksi* change for the worse; *hän on suuresti -nut* he is much changed. **-maton** unchangeable, unalterable; *(entisellään)* unchanged. **-va** changeable, variable.

myhäi|llä smile [contentedly]. **-ly** self-satisfied (smug) smile.

mykerökukkainen composite.

mykis|tyä fall silent; be dumbfounded [with amazement, *hämmästyksestä*]. **-tää** silence.

mykiö lens.

mykkä dumb; *(joskus, kuv.)* mute, tongue-tied; ~ *filmi* silent [film].

myller|rys tumult. **-tää** stir up, throw into confusion.

mylly mill. **-nkivi** millstone. **-nratas** mill-wheel. **-teollisuus** milling industry.

mylläri miller.

mylv|iä bellow; *myrsky -ii* the tempest is roaring (howling).

München Munich.

myrkky poison; *(et. käärmeen)* venom; *lääk.* toxin. **-hammas** fang. **-kaasu** poison gas. **-käärme** poisonous snake. **-sieni** toadstool.

myrkylli|nen poisonous, venomous. **-syys** poisonous qualities; *kuv.* venom.

myrky|ttää poison. **-tys** poisoning; *(~oire* toxic symptom). **-tön** non-poisonous.

myrsky [strong] gale, *(yleisemmin, kuv.)* storm, tempest; ~ *n kourissa* caught in a storm; ~*n enne* a sign of an approaching gale. **-inen, -isä** stormy, tempestuous, *(suosio)* thundering. **-keskus** storm centre. **-npuuska** squall. **-sää:** ~*llä* in stormy weather. **-tuuli** gale. **-tä** storm; *-ää* a storm is raging; *-ävä* turbulent, storm-tossed [sea, *meri*]. **-varoitus** gale-warning.

myrtti myrtle.

myski musk.

myssy cap; *(nauha-)* bonnet, *(teekannun)* cosy.

myst|eeri mystery. **-iikka** mysticism. **-ikko** mystic. **-illinen** mystical; *(salaperäinen)* mysterious.

mytologia mythology.

mytty bundle; *mennä ~yn* come to nothing, fall through.

myy|dä sell [at, *jhk hintaan*]; *(panna menemään)* dispose of; ~ *halvalla, kalliilla* sell cheap (dear); ~ *loppuun* sell out (off), clear one's stock; ~ *tukuittain* sell in lots; *helposti myytävä* saleable; *myytävänä* for sale, *et. Am.* on sale. **-jä** seller, salesman, *lak.* vendor. **-jäiset** bazaar, sale of work. **-jätär** saleswoman, shopgirl.

-mälä shop, *Am.* store; *(~apulainen* shop-assistant; ~*pöytä* counter; ~*nhoitaja* shop manager; ~*varas* shop-lifter).

myynti sale, sales; selling; *(liikevaihto)* turnover. **-hinta** selling price. **-koju** stall. **-osasto** sales department. **-palkkio** commission. **-päällikkö** sales manager. **-taito** salesmanship. **-tarjous** tender, offer.

myyrä *(pelto-)* vole; *(maa-)* mole.

myöhem|min later [on]; afterwards; subsequently; *vuotta* ~ a year later; the following year. **-pi** later, subsequent.

myöhä late; ~*än illalla* late in the night; ~*än yöhön* till late at night; *olla* ~*ssä* be late, *(juna ym)* be overdue. **-inen** late. **-isintään** at the latest. **-styminen** being late; delay. **-styä** be late, *jstk, jltk* for; miss, come [too] late; *(viivästyä)* be delayed; ~ *junasta* miss the train; *juna -styi . . minuuttia* the train was late by.. minutes; *hän on -stynyt maksuissaan* he is behind-hand (in arrears) with his payments. **-än** late.

myönnyty|s admission; concession; *(helpotus)* allowance; *tehdä -ksiä* make concessions.

myöntei|nen affirmative; *-sesti* in the affirmative; *odottaen -stä vastausta* hoping for a favourable reply.

myönty|mys consent, assent; *hän nyökäytti päätään -myksen merkiksi* he nodded assent; *vaikeneminen on -myksen merkki* silence is a sign of consent. **-mätön** unyielding. **-väinen** compliant, yielding; accommodating; *(liian)* indulgent, permissive. **-väisyys** yielding disposition; submissiveness; compliance (with).

myön|tyä consent, *jhk* to; assent, give one's consent (to); *(suostua)* agree (to), accept. **-tää** admit, concede, *(tunnustaa)* recognize, acknowledge; *(antaa)* grant, *(esim. alennusta)* allow; ~ *laina* grant a loan; ~ *eläke* grant a pension to; *hän -si sen todeksi* he admitted (acknowledged, owned) [that] it was true; *jos aika* ~ if time permits.

myös also,. . too; *(-kin)*. . as well; *ei ~kään*. . not. . either; *ei. ., eikä ~kään* not. ., nor. .; *en minä sitä saanut, etkä ~kään sinä* I did not get it, neither *(t.* nor) did you.

myöten along; *antaa* ~ *(suostua)* give in, yield; *polviaan* ~ up to one's knees, knee deep; *sitä* ~ so far, thus far; *sitä* ~ *kuin* in proportion as.

myötä [along] with; ~ *tai vastaan* for or against; ~ *mäkeä* downhill; ~ *seuraava* accompanying; enclosed, attached. **-illä** accompany. **-ily** accompaniment. **-inen** favourable; propitious; ~ *onni* [good] luck, good fortune; ~ *tuuli (m.)* fair wind. **-jäiset** dowry, marriage portion. **-käyminen** success; *m- ja vastoinkäymisessä* in weal and woe, *(vihkikaavassa)* for better for worse. **-mielinen** sympathetic; *olla* ~ *jklle* be favourably disposed towards; *suhtautua -mielisesti jhk* sympathize with, be in sympathy with. **-mielisyys** favourable attitude, sympathy. **-päivään** clockwise, with the sun. **-tunto** sympathy; *ilmaista ~nsa* sympathize (with). **-tuntoinen** sympathetic (towards). **-tuntolakko** sympathy strike. **-tuuli** fair wind, favourable wind; *purjehtia -tuuleen* sail before the wind. **-vaikuttaa:** ~ *jhk* contribute to, conduce to. **-vaiku|tus** cooperation; *jkn -tuksella* with the c. of. .

mädä|nnyttää cause to rot, decompose. **-nnäisyys** rottenness, putridity; *kuv.* depravity. **-ntyä, -tä** decay,

rot [away], putrefy.

mäen|lasku tobogganing; *(mäkihyppy)* ski jump. **-rinne** hillside, slope. **-törmä** bluff.

mäki hill, *(kumpu)* knoll; *laskea mäkeä* toboggan. **-hyppy** ski jump. **-hyppääjä** ski jumper. **-kelkka** bobsleigh. **-nen** hilly.

mäkärä buffalo gnat.

mämmi Finnish Easter dish, made of rye meal and malted.

männikkö pine wood.

männyn|havu: ~*t* pine twigs; *(~öljy* pine-needle oil).

mänty pine, Scotch fir; *(puulaatu)* pine, redwood. **-metsä** pine forest.

mäntä *tekn.* piston, plunger.

märeh|tijä *zo.* ruminant. **-tiä** chew the cud; *tiet. & kuv.* ruminate.

märk|iminen suppuration. **-ivä** suppurative, purulent. ~*iä* suppurate. **-yys** wetness; moisture. **-ä** *a.* wet; *s.* pus; *vuotaa ~ää* discharge; *(~inen* purulent, discharging; *~pesäke* abscess; *~vuoto* purulent discharge).

märssy *mer.* top.

mäski mash.

mässä|tä gorge oneself, eat [and drink] to excess, gormandize. **-ys** eating [and drinking] excessively. **-äjä** gormandizer.

mäsä: *lyödä ~ksi* smash; *mennä ~ksi* go to pieces.

mäti roe; *laskea ~nsä* spawn.

mätkähtää flop [down].

mätä *a.* rotten; decayed; *koul. sl.* lousy; *s.* rot, decay; *(märkä)* pus; ~ *muna* bad egg. **-haava** ulcer; *kuv.* rankling sore. **-kuu** *l.v.* dog days. **-neminen** rotting, decay; putrefaction. **-nemistila** state of decomposition.

mätäs hummock, tussock.

mäyrä badger. **-koira** dachshund, badger-dog.

määkiä bleat.

määre qualifier; adjunct, attribute, qualification.

määri|tellä determine, fix; *(lähemmin)* specify. **-telmä** definition. **-ttelemätön**

undefined; indefinable. **-ttää** determine; *(tauti)* diagnose.

määrä amount; quantity; *(luku-)* number; *(summa)* sum; *(aste)* degree, extent; *(suhde)* proportion; *suuri ~ kirjoja* a great number (a lot) of books; *jossakin määrin* to some (to a certain) extent, in some measure (degree); *suuressa määrin* to a great extent, *(huomattavassa)* to a considerable extent; *suurin määrin* in great numbers, in great quantities; *olla ~* be to; *heidän oli ~ tavata* they were to meet; *(laivan) on ~ saapua* is due [at 1 o'clock]; *~ltään..* for [£ 10], to the amount of; *~ltään rajoitettu* limited in quantity. **-aika** fixed time; *~na* at the appointed time; *-ajan kuluessa* within the fixed (prescribed) period; *~ kului umpeen* deadline was reached; *~ on käsillä* the time is on. **-aikainen** held (occurring) at stated intervals; *(säännöllinen)* regular. **-hetki:** *-hetkellä* at exactly the appointed time (the predetermined moment). **-illä** order [sb.] about; *-ilevä* domineering. **-npää** goal; *vrt. seur.* **-paikka** [place of] destination. **-päivä** day set, date fixed. **-raha** grant, allowance, *(valtion)* appropriation.; *myöntää ~* make a g., authorize *(äänestämällä* vote) a sum for... **-tietoinen** purposeful, purposive; *-tietoisesti* with a sense of purpose. **-tietoisuus** purposefulness, [consistency of] purpose.

määr|ätty fixed; specified; *(tietty)* certain. **-ätä** determine; fix; *(käskeä)* order, direct, *(laki, m.)* provide, lay down, prescribe; *lääk.* prescribe; *(nimittää)* appoint; assign; *kiel.* qualify, modify; *~ ehdot* lay down (dictate) the terms; *~ hinta* fix the price [at.. *jksk*]; *~ päivä* set a date (a day) for; *vaikuttimet, jotka -äsivät hänen toimintansa* the motives governing his action; *niinkuin laki -ää* as the law directs; *laissa -ätty* prescribed (provided) by law; *tarkoin -ätty* definite. **-ätön** boundless.

määräys *(käsky)* order [s], instruction, direction; *(virkaan-)* appointment; *(lääke-)* prescription; *(lain ym)* provision, regulation; *kiel. ks. seur.; tein ~ten mukaisesti* I did as directed; *-äyksestä on* sb.'s orders (instructions). **-sana** *ks. määre.* **-valta** right of determination, authority; *hänellä on ehdoton ~* he is in absolute control.

määrää|mätön undetermined, indefinite. **-vä** determining, determinative; *vrt. määräilevä; ~ artikkeli* definite article; *~ tekijä (ratkaiseva)* decisive factor.

möhkäle chunk, lump.

möh|iä, -äys fumble, bungle.

mökki cottage, hut. **-läinen** cottager. **-pahanen** hovel; *hänen -pahasensa* his shack of a habitation.

mökä hullabaloo.

möly roar [ing]; bawling.

mönjä red lead.

mörkö bugbear, bogey.

möyhe|ntää *(maata)* break up, loosen [up]. **-ä** loose, fluffy, porous

N

naakka jackdaw, daw.
naali arctic fox.
naama face; *vasten* ~*a* to one's
face. **-ri** mask.
naamiais|et masked ball,
masquerade. **-puku** fancy dress.
naamio mask; *riisua* ~ unmask,
(~*nsa*) throw off the mask.
-ida mask, *kuv. m.* disguise;
teatt. make up; *sot.*
camouflage. **-inti** *sot.*
camouflage.
naapuri neighbour. **-maa**
neighbouring country. **-sopu**
neighbourliness; *hyvässä*
-sovussa on friendly terms.
-sto neighbourhood; vicinity.
naara drag, grapnel.
naaras female. **-hirvi** doe.
-kissa, **-koira** she-cat (-dog).
-leijona lioness. **-susi** she
wolf. **-tiikeri** tigress.
naarata drag, *jtk* for.
naarmu, **-ttaa** scratch. **-inen**
scratched.
naatit tops.
naava hanging moss, tree
lichen.
nafta (*vuoriöljy*) naphtha,
petroleum. **-liini** naphthalene.
-lähde oil well.
nahanmuokkaus leather-dressing,
currying.
nahistua get leathery.
nahjus sluggard, laggard;
drifter. **-mainen** sluggish, slow.
-tella be slow, lag [behind].
nahka skin, (*parkittu*) leather.
-hihna leather strap. **-inen** [. .
of] leather, leathern.
-kantinen . . bound in leather.
-kotelo leather case. **-mainen**
leathery, leatherlike. **-selkäinen**
(*kirja*). . with a leather back.
-tavarat leather goods. **-tehdas**
leather factory; tannery.
-teollisuus leather industry.
naida marry; get married,

(*joskus*) wed.
naiivi naïve, naive.
naima|este impediment to
marriage. **-haluinen** anxious to
get (keen on getting) married.
-ikä marriageable age,
marrying age. **-ikäinen** . . of
marriageable age. **-ilmoitus**
matrimonial advertisement.
-lupa marriage licence.
-tarjous proposal of marriage.
-ton unmarried, single.
-ttomuus unmarried state;
(*miehen*) bachelorhood.
naimi|nen marriage; *-sen*
kautta by m.; *mennä -siin*
(*jkn kanssa*) marry. ., get
married (to); *mennä uusiin*
-siin marry again, remarry;
joutua hyviin -siin marry well,
make a good match,
(*rikkaisiin*) marry money.
-skauppa match; *-skauppojen*
välittäjä (*kuv.*) match-maker.
nainen woman (*pl.* women);
hyvät naiset ja herrat! Ladies
and Gentlemen!. . *naisineen*. .
and their ladies.
naisasia women's rights;
(*äänioikeus-*) woman suffrage.
-liike feminist movement,
(*naisten vapautus-*) women's
liberation movement, Women's
Lib.
naiselli|nen womanly, feminine.
-suus womanliness, femininity.
naisen|nimi woman's name.
-puku woman's dress. **-ääni**
female voice.
nais henkilö woman, female.
-istua (*esim. yliopisto*) become
feminized. **-kirjailija** woman
writer. **-kuoro** women's choir.
-lääkäri woman doctor.
-maailma feminine world.
-mainen effeminate. **-opettaja**
woman teacher. **-puolinen**
female, woman; *kiel.*

feminine. **-pääosa:** ~*n esittäjä* leading lady. **-sukupuoli** female sex.
naisten|huone ladies' room. **-hurmaaja** *puhek.* lady-killer. **-lehti** women's magazine. **-pukimo** ladies' outfitters. **-satula** side-saddle. **-tauti** women's disease; (~*lääkäri* gyn[a]ecologist; ~**oppi** gyn[a]ecology). **-vihaaja** woman-hater, misogynist.
nais|työläinen woman worker. **-voimistelu** women's gymnastics. **-väki** womankind, women [folk]. **-ylioppilas** woman student.
naittaa marry sb. [off], *jklle* to.
nakertaa gnaw.
nakkimakkara [Frankfurt] sausage.
naks|ahdus snap, click. **-ahtaa** [give a] snap, click. **-uttaa** (*esim. kellosta*) tick.
naku|ttaa knock. **-tus** knocking, tap [ping], (*vasaran*) hammering.
naljailu joking, teasing.
nalkuttaa nag.
nalli detonator, percussion cap.
namuset sweets.
napa pole; (*pyörän*) hub, nave; *anat.* navel. **-jää** polar ice. **-nuora** umbilical cord. **-piiri** polar circle; *pohjoinen* ~ arctic c.; *eteläinen* ~ antarctic c. **-retkeilijä** polar explorer. **-retki(kunta)** polar expedition. **-seutu** polar region. **-tanssija** belly-dancer.
napina grumbling.
napinreikä buttonhole.
napista grumble, murmur.
napittaa button [up].
Napoli Naples.
nappi button; *päästää napista* unbutton; *aueta napista* come undone, come unbuttoned. **-rivi** row of buttons.
nappula pin, peg. **-takki** duffle-coat.
napsah|dus, -taa snap; click.
napsia pick at; (*ampua*) pick off.
napu|ttaa knock, *jhk* at; (*kevyesti*) tap; *joku* ~ (*oveen*) there is a knock [at the

door]. **-tus** knock[ing]; tap.
narah|dus, -taa creak.
nari|sta creak; (*kitistä*) squeak; grate; *-sevat kengät* squeaky shoes.
narko|maani drug (narcotic) addict, drug abuser; junkie (*et. heroinisti*). **-osi** [general] an [a]esthesia. **-ottinen:** ~ *aine* narcotic.
narr|ata cheat; take in; (*vetää nenästä*) fool, dupe. **-i** fool; clown; *pitää ~naan* make a fool of; (~**mainen** foolish; foppish).
narsissi narcissus; *kelta~* daffodil.
narsku|a crunch; (*narista*) creak. **-ttaa:** ~ *hampaitaan* grind (grate) one's teeth.
narttu bitch.
naru string, cord.
naseva . . to the point, telling, smart.
naskali awl; (*pojan-*) young scamp, young rascal.
nasta tack; stud; (*paino-*) drawing-pin; (*jää-*) spike; *sl.* (*kiva*) jolly good. **-hammas** pivot crown. **-rengas** [steel-] studded tyre.
natista: ~ *liitoksissaan* creak at the joints.
natrium *kem.* sodium.
natsa stub, butt.
natsi Nazi.
naudan|liha beef. **-paisti** [joint of] beef; roast beef.
nauha ribbon; tape; band; (*koriste-, m.*) braid, (*kengän ym*) lace. **-kenkä** laced shoe. **-ruusuke** bow.
nauh|oittaa [tape-] record, (*etukäteen*) prerecord. **-oite, -oitus** taped recording. **-uri** tape recorder.
naukua mew.
naula 1. nail; (*piikki*) spike; (*kengän*) hobnail; (*naulakon*) peg; **2.** (*paino*) pound (*lyh. lb.*); *osua ~n kantaan* hit it, hit the nail on the head. **-kko** coat-rack. **-nkanta** nail head. **-ta** nail, *jhk* on [to], to. . .
nauli|ta nail, *jhk* to; *kuv.* fix; *paikalleen* **-ttuna** rooted to the spot.

naur|aa laugh, *jllek, jklle* at;
(hihittää) giggle; ~ *partaansa*
snigger, snicker, laugh up
one's sleeve, chuckle to
oneself; *en voi olla -amatta* I
cannot help laughing; *oin
makeasti* I had a good laugh.
-ahtaa give a laugh. **-attaa**
make. . laugh; amuse; *mikä
sinua* ~ what do you find so
amusing? **-ettava** ridiculous;
ludicrous; *älä tee itseäsi ~ksi*
don't make yourself ridiculous.
nauris turnip.
nauru laughter, *(naurahdus)*
laugh; *herättää* ~*a* cause
amusement; *se ei ole mikään*
~*n asia* it is no laughing
matter. **-hermo:** *kutkuttaa*
~*jani* it tickles me. **-**
nalai|nen: *joutua n-seksi*
make a fool of oneself,
become a laughing-stock;
saattaa jku n-seksi make a p.
look ridiculous. **-npuuska**
paroxysm of laughter.
-nremahdus burst of laughter.
nauta cattle; *sata* ~*a* 100 head
of cattle. **-karja** cattle.
nautinno|llinen enjoyable, full
of enjoyment. **-nhimo** love of
pleasure. **-nhimoinen**
pleasure-loving, self-indulgent.
nautinta usage. **-oikeus**
usufructuary right, right of
enjoyment.
nautinto enjoyment; pleasure;
antautua ~*ihin* overindulge
[oneself]. **-aineet** stimulants.
nauttia enjoy; *(lääkettä ym)*
take; ~ *jstk* enjoy a th., take
pleasure in, delight in; ~
arvonantoa enjoy high esteem,
stand in high esteem; ~
eläkettä have (get) a pension;
~ *opetusta jssak* receive
instruction in; *nautittava*
enjoyable, *(n-ksi kelpaava)* fit
to eat (drink).
navakka: ~ *tuuli* fresh wind.
navetta cow-house, cow-shed.
ne they; ~ *jotka*. . those who;
niiden their; theirs; *niissä
tapauksissa (joissa)* in those
cases [in which], in cases
[where]; *niitä näitä* this and
that.
neekeri negro; ~*t* negroes,

blacks, *(Afrikassa)* Africans;
(värilliset) coloured people.
-nainen negress, negro woman.
nefriitti(kivi) jade.
negatiivi, -nen negative.
neilikka pink, *(iso)* carnation;
(mauste-) cloves.
neit|i *(nimen edessä)* Miss. **-o,**
~nen [young] girl; *run.*
maid [en]. **-seellinen** virginal.
-syt virgin; ~ *Maria* the
Virgin Mary; *(~matka* maiden
voyage; ~*puhe* maiden
speech). **-syys** virginity.
neli gallop; ~*ä* at a gallop.
-jalkainen a. four-footed; *s. &
a.* quadruped. **-kko** firkin
(8—9 gallons). **-kulmainen**
four-cornered, four-square.
-kulmio quadrangle. **-kätinen**
four-handed. **-lehtinen**
four-leaved. **-nkertainen**
fourfold, quadruple.
-nkertaistaa quadruple.
-nkontin on all fours. **-npeli**
(tennis) double [s]; *seka~*
mixed doubles; *(golf ym)*
foursome. **-näytöksinen**. . in
four acts. **-pyöräinen**
four-wheeled. **-skulmainen**
square. **-stys** full speed;
gallop. **-stää** gallop. **-taitekoko**
quarto. **-ttäin** four at a time.
-vuotias *a.* four years old,
attrib. four-year-old; ~ *lapsi*
a child of four. **-ääninen**
four-part.
neliö square *(m. mat.)*;
korottaa ~*ön* square. **-jalka,**
-metri square foot (metre).
-mitta square measure.
neljä four; *jakaa* ~*än osaan*
quarter. **-kymmentä** forty.
-nneksi in the fourth place,
fourthly. **-nnes** fourth [part],
quarter; *kello on* ~*tä yli
kaksi* it is a quarter past
two; *(~tunti* a quarter of an
hour). **-s** [the] fourth. **-sataa**
four hundred. **-skymmenes**
[the] fortieth. **-sosa** quarter;
(~nuotti crotchet).
-sti four times. **-stoista** [the]
fourteenth. **-toista** fourteen.
nelo|nen four. **-set** quadruplets.
nenä nose; *(kärki)* point; ~*n
selkä* bridge of the nose;
aivan ~ni edessä under my

[very] nose; *puhua ~änsä*
talk through one's nose; *vetää
~stä* fool. **-kkyys**
impertinence. **-käs** impertinent,
pert, saucy; *-kkäästi* saucily.
-liina handkerchief. **-luu** nasal
bone. **-njuuri** base of the
nose. **-npää** tip of the nose.
-nvarsi ridge of the nose.
-verenvuoto nosebleed [ing].
-äänne nasal.
neonvalo neon sign.
nero genius. **-kas** (*laite,
keksintö ym*) ingenious; *~
mies* a man of genius; *~
ajatus* a brilliant idea. **-kkuus**
ingenuity, ingeniousness;
(*nero*) genius. **-nleimaus** stroke
of genius.
neste liquid; fluid. **-kaasu**
bottled gas, liquid gas. **-mitta**
measure of capacity. **-mäinen**
liquid. **-yttää, -ytyä** condense,
liquefy.
netto net. **-hinta, -paino,
-voitto** net price (weight,
profits).
neula needle, (*nuppi-*) pin.
-kotelo needle-case. **-nen**
needle. **-nkärki** point of a
needle, pin point. **-npisto**
stitch; prick of a needle (a
pin); *kuv.* pinprick. **-nsilmä**
eye of a needle; *kuv.* needle's
eye. **-tyyny** pincushion.
neule knitting. **-kangas** jersey.
-puikko knitting needle. **-puku**
knitted dress, jersey dress. **-pusero** jumper, sweater.
-teollisuus knitwear industry.
-vaatteet knitwear.
neulo|a sew; (*puikoilla*) knit;
vrt. ommella. **-nnaiset**
knitwear.
neutr|aloida neutralize. **-i**
neuter. **-oni** neutron.
neuroo|si neurosis. **-tikko,
-ttinen** neurotic.
neuvo advice (*pl. = sg.*);
(*keino*) way [out], expedient;
se oli hyvä ~ it was a good
piece of advice; *~a antava*
advisory; *kysyä ~a jklta* ask
a p.'s advice, consult a p.;
kenen ~sta on whose advice?
ei ole muuta ~a there is no
other way, I have no choice.
neuvo|a advise, counsel;

(*sanoa*) tell; (*tietä ym*) show.
-ja adviser; counsellor;
consultant; *karjanhoidon ~*
expert in stock-raising. **-kas**
resourceful; inventive. **-kkuus**
resourcefulness. **-la** (*lasten*)
child health centre. **-nantaja**
adviser, counsellor. **-nta**
counselling; advice; *ammatti-
~* vocational guidance;
(*~asema* consulting centre). **-s,
-mies** councillor. **-sto** council,
board.
Neuvosto|liitto the Union of
Soviet Socialist Republics, *lyh.*
U.S.S.R., the Soviet Union.
n-tasavalta Soviet republic.
neuvo|tella (*jkn kanssa jstk*)
consult [a p. about]; discuss,
confer (with); negotiate; *~
rauhanehdoista* negotiate [the]
terms of peace; *-tteleva jäsen*
consulting member. **-ton**
irresolute, indecisive; at a
loss [what to do], in a state
of indecision. **-ttelija**
negotiator. **-ttelu** consultation,
conference; negotiation; *olla
~issa* carry on negotiations
(talks); *ryhtyä ~ihin* open
negotiations (with); (*~pöytä*
negotiating table; *~ratkaisu*
negotiated settlement).
neva marsh, swamp, fen.
nid|e, -os binding, (*osa*)
volume. **-ottu**: *~ kirja*
paperback; *~na* in paper
covers, limp.
niel|aista gulp down; swallow,
(*esim. peto*) devour. **-aisu**
gulp. **-lä** swallow (*m. kuv.*);
(*ahnaasti*) wolf [down], *vrt.*
nielaista; (*varoja ym*) swallow
up, absorb; *~ solvaus* swallow
(pocket) an insult; *katosi kuin
maan -emänä* vanished as if
swallowed up by the earth;
kaikki -evä (*intohimo*)
[all-]devouring.
nielu throat; *anat.* pharynx.
-risa tonsil.
niemi cape; promontory,
(*kallio-*) headland. **-maa**
peninsula; *Intian ~* the
Indian subcontinent.
nieriä char; *puro~* brook trout.
nietos drift [of snow].
nihkeä damp, moist.

nii|ata, -aus curtsey.
niidet heddle.
niikseen: *jos ~ tulee* if it comes to that, come to that.
Niili the Nile.
niin so; *(siten)* thus; *(vastauksissa, esim. ~ olen)* so I am; yes, I am; *~ että.*. so that; *~ hyvä kasvatus* such a good education, so good an education; *~ kai* presumably; [yes,] I daresay; *~ kauan kuin* as long as; *~ kuin* as [he does]; *~ kuin isänsä, hän on.*. like his father, he is. .; *~ kuin haluan* [I wear my hair] how *(t. the way)* I like; *tee ~kuin sanon* do as I tell you; *niinkö?* is that so? really? *~ ollen* such being the case; *oli ~ tai näin* either way; *~ päin* that way; *~ sanottu* so-called; *aivan ~, niinpä ~* exactly, quite so; certainly! *eikö ~* isn't that so? *sitä sinä tarkoitat, eikö ~* you mean that, don't you? *ei niinkään pieni* not so [very] small; *~ hän kuin muutkin* he as well as the others; *~ (ainakin) toivon* I hope so. **-ikään** likewise; also;. . too.
niini bast.
niinmuodoin consequently, accordingly; thus, then.
niisi *ks. niidet.*
niiskuttaa snuffle.
niistää blow [one's nose].
niitata, niitti rivet.
niitto mowing, cutting. **-kone** mowing machine, mower. **-niitty** meadow. **-maa** meadowland.
niittää mow; mow down; *vasta niitetty* new-mown.
nikama vertebra *(pl. -e).*
nikkel|i nickel; *(~kaivos* nickel mine). **-öidä** nickel-plate.
nikotiini nicotine.
niko|ttaa: *minua ~* I have the hiccups. **-tus** hiccup [ing].
niksi trick; gimmick.
nilja|inen, -kas slimy; *(liukas)* slippery.
nilkka ankle. **-imet** gaiters. **-sukat** ankle socks, bobby-socks, *Am. m.* anklets.

nilkuttaa limp, hobble.
nilviäinen mollusc.
nimelli|nen nominal. **-sarvo** nominal value, face value; *myydä ~sta* sell at par (at face value); *vain ~* in name only.
nimen|huuto roll call; *pitää ~* call the roll, call the names. **-muutto** change of name. **-omaan** expressly, specially,. . in particular. **-omainen** express, explicit.
nime|tä [mention by] name, *(ehdokas)* nominate. **-tön** nameless; anonymous; *~ sormi* ring-finger. **-äminen** nomination, naming.
nimi name, *(kirjan)* title; *nimeni on.*. my name is, I am called. .; *nimeltään.*. by [the] name of, called. .; *tuntea nimeltä* know by name; *jnk ~ssä, nimessä* on behalf of; *antaa jklle ~ jkn mukaan* name. . after; *nimittää asioita niiden oikealla nimellä* call a spade a spade. **-ke** title; *(otsikko)* heading. **-kilpi** sign; nameplate. **-kirja** register, roll. **-kirjain:** *-kirjaimet* initials. **-kirjoitus** signature; autograph. **-kko:** *jkn ~* named after. .; adopted. **-kortti** [visiting-]card. **-kristitty** nominal Christian. **-lehti** title-page. **-lippu** label; *varustaa -lipulla* label. **-lista** list of names. **-luettelo** list of names; roll; *(aakkosellinen)* index of names. **-merkki** pseudonym. **-nen** by the name of. ., called. ., *(esim. kirja)* entitled. .; *minkä ~* by (of) what name? **-osa** title-role. **-päivä** nameday. **-sana** *kiel.* noun.
nimismies head of the constabulary, rural police chief, *Am. l.v.* sheriff.
nimitellä *(haukkua)* call. . names.
nimistö terminology, nomenclature.
nimi|ttäin namely *(lyh. viz.);* that is; *olin ~ sairaana* I was ill, you see. **-ttäjä** *mat.*

denominator. **-ttää** name;
(kutsua) call; term; *(virkaan)*
appoint; *(ehdokkaaksi)*
nominate; ~ *jkn mukaan*
name after. **-tys** name, term;
designation; *(virka)*
appointment. **-ö** title; (~**sivu**
title-page).
nipin: ~ *napin* barely, only
just; by a narrow margin;
hän pelastui ~ *napin (m.)* he
had a narrow escape.
nipisti|n *(pinne)* clip, *(-met)*
tweezers, pincers.
nipistää pinch; nip [off,
poikki].
nippu bundle; bunch. **-ratkaisu**
package deal.
nipu|kka tip; *(kärki)* point.
-ttaa make up into bundles,
bundle.
nirso fastidious, choosey.
niska nape of the neck;
kosken ~ssa above the
waterfall; *lykätä syy jkn*
niskoille lay the blame on a
p.'s shoulders; *vääntää ~t*
nurin (jltk) wring. .'s neck.
niskoi|tella be refractory; be
insubordinate. **-ttelu**
insubordination, refractoriness.
nisä teat. **-käs** mammal.
nito|a stitch, sew; *(sitoa)* bind.
-makoje stapler.
nitraatti nitrate.
niuk|alti, -asti scantily,
sparingly; *minulla on* ~ *rahaa*
I am short of money. **-entaa**
reduce, curtail; cut down.
niukk|a scanty; scarce; ~ *mitta*
short measure; ~ *toimeentulo*
scanty (bare) living; ~
ravinto poor (meagre) fare.
-uus scantiness; scarcity.
nivel joint; articulation; *bot.*
node; *(rengas)* link. **-jalkainen**
arthropod. **-raitiovaunu**
articulated tramcar. **-reuma**
rheumatoid arthritis. **-tää**
articulate.
nivoutua *(toisiinsa)* inter|twine,
-twist.
nivus|et groin. **-taive, -tyrä**
inguinal bend (hernia).
Nizza Nice.
no well! now! ~ *niin!* well!
all right! so there!
Nobel-kirjailija Nobel

prize-winning writer, Nobel
laureate.
noeta soot, make sooty.
noidannuoli lumbago.
noin about, *Am. m.* around;
circa; ~ *3 tai 4 (m.)* some
three of four; ~ *paljon* so
much; ~ *kaunis kuva* such a
fine picture; ~ *kello kaksi*
[at] about two o'clock; ~ *iso! (m.)*
that big! *kas* ~ there now!
that's it!
noita magician, sorcerer. **-akka**
witch. **-vaino** persecution of
witches, *kuv.* witch hunt.
noit|ua cast a spell (on);
bewitch. **-uus** witchcraft,
sorcery.
noja support, prop, *(pohja)*
ground; *kuv.* basis; *jnk ~lla*
by virtue of, on the strength
of; *minkä ~lla* on what
ground[s]? *pää käden ~ssa*
resting one's head against
one's hand; *jäädä oman*
onnensa ~an be left to one's
fate. **-puut** *voim.* parallel
bars. **-ta** lean, recline, *jhk*
against, on; ~ *keppiin*
support oneself with a stick.
-tuoli armchair; easy-chair.
-utua lean; *-utuu (perustuu)* is
based (founded) on; *jhk*
-utuen on the strength of;
hän -utui lausunnossaan lakiin
he based his statement on
the law.
nokare pat [of butter].
noki soot; *(viljan)* blight, smut;
olla noessa be sooty. **-luukku**
soot-hole. **-nen** sooty. **-pilkku**
smut, smudge. **-valkea**
chimney fire.
nokka bill, *(et. petolinnun)*
beak; *(astian)* spout, lip;
(auton ym) nose; *autot*
törmäsivät yhteen nokat
vastakkain the cars crashed
head on; *pistää ~nsa jhk*
stick one's nose into; *ottaa*
nokkiinsa take offence (at).
-huilu recorder. **-kolari**
head-on collision. **-viisas**
impertinent.
nokkel|a quick [-witted],
ready-minded, clever; ~
sanainen ready with an
answer. **-uus** resourcefulness;

(puheessa) ready wit.
nokkia peck, *jtk* at.
nokko|nen nettle. **-skuume**
nettle-rash, hives.
nola|ta snub, discomfit; take a
p. down [a peg or two]; ~
itsensä put one's foot in it, .
make a fool of oneself. **-us**
snubbing.
nolla nought, nil, *(asteikossa)*
zero; *(puhelinnumerossa)* 0
[*äänt.* ou]; ~*n arvoinen* of
no value at all; *hän on
täydellinen* ~ he is a nobody;
lämpömittari on ~*ssa* the
thermometer is at zero;
kolmella pisteellä ~*a vastaan*
by three points to nought.
-piste zero.
nolo baffled, embarrassed,
discomfited; ~ *asema* an
awkward position; *sai* ~*n
lopun* came to a sorry ·
(ignominious) end; *oli* ~*n
näköinen* looked blank
(foolish). **-stua** be baffled.
-ttaa: *minua -tti* I felt cheap.
-us discomfiture.
nominatiivi nominative [case].
nopea fast; rapid [growth,
kasvu], swift; quick, prompt;
(kiireellinen) speedy; ~
palvelu speedy service.
-kulkuinen fast. **-mmin** faster,
more quickly; *en halua ajaa*
~ I don't want to go any
faster. **-sti** fast; rapidly;
speedily, quickly. **-älyinen**
quick of understanding,
sharp-witted.
nopeus speed; rapidity;
swiftness, quickness; . .
nopeudella tunnissa at the
speed *(t.* rate) of. . per hour;
lisätä nopeutta accelerate;
tuulen ~ wind velocity.
-mittari speedometer. **-rajoitus**
speed limit, restriction of
speed.
nopeuttaa speed up.
noppa die *(pl.* dice). **-peli** dice.
nopsa agile, nimble. **-jalkainen**
swift-footed.
norja lithe, supple.
Norja Norway. **n-lainen** *a.* &
s. Norwegian. **n-n kieli**
Norwegian.
norjentaa make [more] supple.

norkko *bot.* catkin.
normaali normal; standard.
-koko regular size. **-koulu**
normal school, teacher-training
secondary school. **-olot:**
-oloissa under normal
conditions. **-proosa** standard
prose. **-raiteinen**
standard-gauge. **-staa**
normalize.
normi norm.
norppa ringed seal.
norsu elephant. **-nluu** ivory.
nost|aa raise; lift [up]; *(esim.
rahaa)* draw; *(maasta)* take
up, pick up; *(kojeella)* hoist;
~ *hintaa* raise the price; ~
kapina raise a rebellion; ~
purjeet hoist sail; ~ *pystyyn*
set. . up, *(auttaa jaloilleen)*
help. . to one's feet. **-attaa**
rouse, raise; *(synnyttää)* cause,
call forth; produce.
nosto|kanki lever. **-koje**
hoisting apparatus. **-kurki**
crane. **-mies** [a] conscript
who has either not yet served
his period of military service
or has completed his periods
of active and reserve service.
-silta vertical-lift bridge,
(yl. lasku-) drawbridge.
-väki *l.v.* auxiliary reserve.
nosturi crane; *(laivan)* winch.
nota|ari notary; *julkinen* ~ n.
public. **-riaattiosasto** trust
department.
noteera|ta quote; *-taan
pörssissä* has a noting on
'change. **-us** quotation;
(valuutan) rate [of exchange].
notk|ea pliant; supple; agile;
(taipuisa) flexible. **-eus** agility,
suppleness. **-istaa** bend; ~
polviaan bend the knee.
-istua bend, get bent.
notko hollow, dell. **-selkäinen**
sway-backed.
notkua *(taipua)* bend; sag.
noudattaa observe; *(käskyä)*
obey; ~ *esimerkkiä* follow [a
p.'s] example; ~ *kutsua*
accept an invitation; ~ *lakia*
keep (obey, observe) the laws;
~ *jkn neuvoa* follow (take) a
p.'s advice; ~ *jkn pyyntöä*
comply with a p.'s request; ~
sääntöä ym keep a rule; ~

varovaisuutta be careful, observe caution; *verbi* ~ *subjektin persoonaa ja lukua* the verb agrees with its subject in person and number.

noukkia pick; *(koota)* gather.

nousta rise, arise; get up; *(seisomaan, m.)* stand up; *(bussiin)* get into; *(hinta, m.)* increase; ~ *jhk määrään* amount to, *(luku-, m.)* number; ~ *hevosen selkään* mount a horse; ~ *(ilmaan, lentokone)* take off; ~ *laivaan* go on board; ~ *pystyyn* get up, stand up; ~ *pöydästä* rise from table; ~ *valtaistuimelle* ascend the throne; ~ *vuorelle* ascend (climb) a mountain; ~ *yli* exceed [a sum, *jnk summan*]; *aurinko nousee idästä* the sun rises in the east; *hinnat nousevat* prices will go up; *hän nousee aikaisin* he gets up (he rises) early; *siitä voi* ~ *riita* a quarrel may arise about it, a dispute may ensue over it; *nouseva polvi* the rising generation.

nousu rise; ascent; *(maan, m.)* [upward] slope; *(hintojen, m.)* increase, advance; *ilm.* take-off; *(kansan-)* [up]rising; *vuorelle* ~ ascent of a mountain; ~*(suunna)ssa* on the increase. **-kas** upstart, parvenu; (~**mainen** upstart). **-suhdanne** boom. **-suunta** upward trend. **-vesi** rising tide, flood [-tide]; *on* ~ the tide is rising (coming in); *korkein* ~ high tide, high water.

nouta|a fetch; bring; call for; *lähettää -maan* send for; *tulla -maan* come for; *voitko tulla minua -maan* can you call for me? *onko hän käynyt sen -massa* has he been for it? has he been to get it? *noudetaan* to be called for.

novelli short story; *(pienoisromaani)* novelette. **-kokoelma** collection of short stories.

nuha [common] cold, cold in the head, *lääk.* rhinitis;

minussa on ~ I have [caught] a cold. **-kuume** feverish cold.

nuhde reproach; reproof; admonition [s]. **-lla** reproach [sb. with, *jstk*]; reprove, *(torua)* rebuke; remonstrate (with a p. about); *(varoitellen)* admonish. **-saarna** sermon, lecture.

nuhr|aantua get smudged. (soiled). **-uinen** bedraggled.

nuhtee|ton irreproachable, above reproach, blameless. **-ttomuus** blamelessness.

nuija club; hammer; *(esim. kroketti-)* mallet.

nuiji|a hammer, *(esim. kuoliaaksi)* club; *puheenjohtaja n. pöytään (päätöksen)* the chairman brought the hammer down [on the decision].

nujakka rough-and-tumble.

nujertaa break; crush; suppress.

nukahtaa fall asleep, go to sleep; ~ *hetkiseksi* have a nap, drop off, have a snooze.

nukka nap, *(sametin ym)* pile. **-matto** [thick] pile carpet. **-vieru** threadbare; shabby, seedy-looking.

nukke doll. **-hallitus** puppet government. **-kaappi** doll's *(Am.* doll) house. **-teatteri** puppet-show *(t.* theatre).

nukku|a sleep, be asleep; *(vaipua uneen)* fall asleep, go to sleep; *mennä -maan* go to bed; ~ *sikeästi* sleep soundly; ~ *liian pitkään* oversleep; *menen (säännöllisesti) aikaisin -maan* I keep early hours; *olla -vinaan* feign sleep. **-malähiö** dormitory town. **-matti** sandman.

nuku|ksissa asleep. **-ttaa** *lääk.* an[a]esthetize; *minua* ~ I feel sleepy; *minua alkoi* ~ I got sleepy. **-tus** *lääk.* [general] an[a]esthesia; (~**aine** general an[a]esthetic; ~**lääkäri** an[a]esthetist).

nulikka scamp, young rascal.

numero number *(lyh.* No., *pl.* Nos.), figure; *(suuruus-)* size; *(sanomalehd.)* copy, issue; *(ohjelman)* act, item; *(auton, rekisteri-)* number plate. **-ida**

number. **-imaton** unnumbered.
-inen *(yhd.)* in .. figures; *viisi-
~ luku* a five-figure
number. **-järjestys** numerical
order. **-levy** number plate;
(puhelimen) dial.
nummi moor; *(kangas)* heath.
nunna nun. **-luostari** convent.
nuo those.
nuoho|oja chimney-sweep. **-ta**
sweep.
nuokkua nod; *(lerppua)* droop;
hang down.
nuolaista lick; *älä nuolaise
ennenkuin tipahtaa* don't
count your chickens before
they are hatched.
nuolen|kärki arrow-head.
-pääkirjoitus cuneiform.
nuoli arrow; *et. kuv.* shaft;
(heitto-) dart; *nuolen
nopeudella* swift as an arrow.
-viini quiver.
nuolla lick.
nuora string, twine, cord;
(kuivaus- ym) line. **-llatanssija**
tight-rope walker. **-npunoja**
rope-maker. **-npätkä** piece of
rope. **-tikkaat** rope-ladder.
nuore|hko rather young,
youngish. **-kas** youthful; *~
ikäisekseen* young for one's
years. **-kkuus** youthfulness.
-mpi younger; *(virassa ym)*
junior; *K. ~ K.* Junior *(lyh.
Jun., Jr)*; *hän on minua
vuotta ~ (m.)* he is a year
my junior; *15 vuotta -mmat
lapset* children under 15
[years]; *hän näyttää -mmalta
kuin mitä hän on (m.)* he
does not look his years.
-nnus rejuvenation. *(~leikkaus*
r. operation). **-ntaa** make. .
younger, rejuvenate. **-ntua** get
younger, grow young again,
be rejuvenated.
nuori young; juvenile;
(kasvuikäinen) adolescent;
nuoret young people,
youngsters, the young;
nuorena when young, in my
(his) youth, early in life; *~
henkilö (lak.)* minor. **-herra**
master. **-kko** bride. **-so** youth;
(nuoret) young people;
(~kirjallisuus juvenile
literature; *~rikollisuus* juvenile

delinquency; *~vankila Engl.*
borstal).
nuor|tea youthful; supple. **-tua**
ks. nuorentua.
nuorukai|nen youth, young
man. **-sikä** adolescence.
nuoruuden|aika days of youth,
early life. **-erehdys** youthful
indiscretion. **-into** youthful
ardour. **-rakkaus** early love,
early attachment. **-ystävä**
school-day friend; *~ni* friend
of my youth.
nuoruus youth; *~ ja hulluus*
youth will have its fling, boys
will be boys.
nuosk|a(ilma) thaw; mild
weather. **-ea:** *~ lumi* damp
(t. wet) snow.
nuotio camp fire.
nuotta seine. **-kalastus** seine
fishing.
nuotti note; *(sävel)* tune;
melody; *nuotit* music; *soittaa
suoraan nuoteista* play
[music] at sight. **-avain** clef.
-laukku music case. **-paperi**
music-paper. **-teline**
music-stand. **-viiva** line of a
staff. **-viivasto** staff *(pl.*
staves).
nupi, -naula tack.
nuppi *(kepin ym)* head, knob;
button; *(kellon)* crown. **-neula**
pin.
nuppu bud; *olla nupulla* be in
bud.
nupukivi cobblestone.
nureksia complain, grumble.
nurin inside out; *(kumoon)*
over; *~ niskoin* head over
heels, headlong; topsy-turvy;
~ päin inside out, upside
down; *kääntää ~* turn. .
inside out; turn upside down;
reverse; *mennä ~* overturn,
(liike) fail.
nuri|na grumbling. **-sta**
grumble; complain.
nurinkuri|nen. . all wrong,
perverted, *(mieletön)*
preposterous. **-sesti** the wrong
way, absurdly. **-suus** absurdity.
nurja wrong; *kuv.* adverse; *~
puoli* wrong side; *~ katse*
cross look; *~t olot* adverse
conditions; *neuloa ~a* purl.
-mielinen averse, ill-disposed.

-mielisyys unfriendliness; illwill.
nurkka corner; *(kulma)* angle; *(soppi)* nook. **-kunta** clique. **-us** corner.
nurku|a grumble; complain; *-matta* without a word of complaint. **-maton** uncomplaining.
nurmi grass; *(-kko)* lawn.
nutipää hornless.
nuttu coat; jacket.
nuttura bun [of hair], chignon.
nuuhkia sniff, snuff (at).
nuusk|a snuff. **-anruskea** snuff-coloured. **-arasia** snuff-box. **-ata** take snuff. **-ia** sniff (at) *kuv.* pry [into]; *(selville)* ferret out. **-ija** spy.
nyhtää tear, pull [out]; *(kulmakarvoja ym)* pluck.
nykeröenenä snub nose; pug nose; *(~inen* snub-nosed).
nykiä jerk; twitch; pull (at); *(kalasta)* bite; nibble; *nykii* I have a bite; *nykien* by fits and starts; *nykivä* jerky; *nykiminen (hermostunut)* twitch, spasm [s], tic.
nyky: *tätä ~ä* nowadays. **-aika** the present [time]; our time [s]; *~na* nowadays, at the present time, in these days; *-ajan keksinnöt* modern inventions. **-aikai|nen** present-day; *(uuden-)* modern, up-to-date; *n-sesti* modernly [furnished]. **-aikaistaa** modernize. **-englanti** modern English. **-hetki:** *-hetkeen asti* up to the present [time], to date. **-inen** present, present-day; *(vallitseva)* prevailing, existing, current; *~ asiaintila* the present state of affairs. **-isellään** as it is now; *(muuttamatta)* unchanged. **-isin** at [the] present [time], today, *ks. nykyään.* **-isyys** the present. **-kieli** modern language. **-maailma** the world of today. **-musiikki** contemporary music. **-olot** existing conditions; *-oloissa* under the e. c. **-polvi** present generation. **-päivä:** *-päivien Pariisi* the Paris of our day; *-päivien Englanti* contemporary England. **-tärkeä.** . of current interest,

topical, of contemporary concern. **-ään** at present; nowadays, currently, these days.
nykäi|stä jerk [at a p.'s sleeve, *jkta hihasta*]; pull. **-sy** jerk; tug, pull; twitch; *yhdellä ~llä* at one go.
nylk|eä skin, flay; *kuv.* fleece, *(kiskoa)* overcharge. **-yhinta** extortionate price.
nyplä|tä *(pitsiä)* make lace. **-ys** bobbin lace-making; *(~tyyny* lace-pillow).
nyppiä pick; *(esim. kulmakarvoja)* pluck.
nyppy *(ihossa)* pimple.
nyrjäh|dys sprain. **-dyttää** sprain; *(väännähdyttää)* twist. **-tää:** *jalkani -ti* I sprained my foot.
nyrkinisku blow with the fist.
nyrkkei|lijä boxer, pugilist. **-llä** box. **-ly** boxing; *(harjoitus-)* sparring; *(~hansikas* boxing-glove; *~kehä* ring; *~ottelu* boxing-match; prize fight).
nyrkki fist; *puristaa kätensä ~in* clench one's fist; *~in puristettu käsi* clenched hand; *puida ~ä* shake one's fist (at). **-oikeus** mob law. **-sääntö** rule of thumb.
nyrp|eä sullen, surly, glum, morose; *(äreä)* cross; *olla ~* [be in a] sulk. **-istää:** *~ nenäänsä jllek* turn up one's nose at.
nyst|ermä, -yrä node, nodule.
nyt now; *~ heti* right away; at once; *~ kun.* . now that. .
nyt|kiä, -kähdellä twitch, jerk.
nyttemmin now, nowadays.
nyyhky|ttää sob. **-tys** sob; sobbing.
nyytti bundle. **-kestit** Dutch party *(t.* treat).
nyök|käys nod. **-yttää** nod; *~ päätään* n. one's head. **-ätä** nod; *~ hyväksymisen merkiksi* nod assent.
nyöri string, cord; twine. **-ttää** lace; tie up.
näennäinen seeming, apparent; ostensible.
näet you see, you know; *vrt. nimittäin.*

nähden: *jhk* ~ in view of, considering; in respect of; *siihen* ~ *että* in view of the fact that; *ikäänsä* ~ for his age; *(maan asema) kuuhun* ~ in relation to the moon; *meihin* ~ *paremmassa asemassa* in a favourable position compared with us. **nähdä** see; *(erottaa)* discern; *(huomata)* find; ~ *parhaaksi* see fit; *minun* ~*kseni* as far as I can see; *muiden nähden* in the presence of others; *hänet nähdessäni* at the sight of him; *ei olla näkevinään* pretend not to see, cut. . dead; *olin näkevinäni* I thought I saw; *nähtäväksi jää* it remains to be seen. **nähtä|vyys** sight; *katsella (kaupungin ym)* -*vyyksiä* see the sights [of the town], go sightseeing. **-vä** worth seeing; *(näkyvä)* visible; ~*ksi (liik.)* oñ approval. **-västi** seemingly, apparently; *(ilmeisesti)* evidently.
näi|hin: ~ *aikoihin* about this time; ~ *asti* until now. **-llä:** ~ *main* hereabouts.
näin in this way, like this; so; thus; ~ *korkea* so high, that high; ~ *ollen* under the [se] circumstances; ~ *paljon* this much, so much; ~ *pitkälle* thus far; ~ *hän selitti asian* that's the way he explained it. **-muodoin** thus, this being the case.
näive|ttyä wither [away]; -*ttynyt (m.)* dried up, shrunken.
näke|minen sight; *sen pelkkä* ~ the mere s. of it. **-miin** see you later, see you soon, *(joskus)* so long. **-mys** view[s] , outlook. **-mä:** *ensi* ~*ltä* at first sight. **-mätön** unseeing; *(ei nähty)* unseen.
näkijä *(näkyjen* ~*)* visionary; seer; *(silmin* ~*)* eye-witness.
näkinkenkä mussel; *(kuori)* shell.
näkkileipä crispbread, hard [rye] bread.
näky sight; vision; *nähdä* ~*jä* have visions. **-mä** view. **-mättömyys** invisibility. **-mätön**

invisible. **-vyys** visibility; *TV:n* ~*alue* TV coverage area. **-vä** visible; -*vissä* in view; *on* -*vissä* is in sight, is visible; *jkn* -*vissä* within sight of; *kadota* -*vistä* pass out of sight, disappear from sight; *hän hävisi* -*vistäni* I lost sight of him; *tulla* -*viin* come into view; come into sight, appear; *saada jtk* -*viinsä* catch sight of.
näkyä be seen, be visible; appear; *(erottua)* be discerned; *näkyy olevan..* appears to be; *tästä näkyy (,että)* it can be seen from this [that]; *talo ei näy tänne* the house cannot be seen from here; *tahraa ei näy* the stain does not show; *seuraukset alkavat* ~ the consequences begin to show themselves.
näkö [eye]sight, vision; *(ulko-)* appearance, looks; *näöltä(än)* in appearance; *tuntea näöltä* know by sight; *näön vuoksi* for the sake of appearance; *hänellä on heikko* ~ his eyesight is poor. **-aisti** [sense of] sight. **-aistimus** visual perception. **-ala** view; scene; *kuv.* prospect, outlook; *(kokonais-)* panorama; *. . josta on* ~*. .* -*lle* overlooking. .; *(~***kortti** picture post-card; ~**vaunu** panoramic car).
-harha optical illusion. **-hermo** optic nerve. **-inen:** *jnk* ~ like *.., ..*-looking; *minkä* ~ *se on* what does it look like? how does it look? *hän on isänsä* ~ he looks like his father, he bears a resemblance to his father; *kuva on (mallin)* ~ it's a good likeness; *he ovat hyvin toistensa* -*isiä* they are very much alike. **-ispainos** facsimile. **-isyys** likeness; *vrt. yhden* ~. **-kanta** [point of] view; *siltä* -*kannalta katsoen* from that point of view. **-kenttä** *fys.* field of vision, visual field. **-kohta** point of view, point, consideration; aspect. **-kulma** visual angle. **-kuulo** speech reading. **-kyky**

visual capacity, eyesight. **-piiri**
range of vision, horizon;
poissa ~stä out of sight.
-puhelin picture phone. **-torni**
outlook tower.
nälkiin|tyä be starved; *-tynyt*
starving, starved, famished.
nälkä *s.* hunger; *minun on,*
tulee ~ I am (I am getting)
hungry; *nähdä ~ä* hunger;
kuolla ~än starve to death.
-inen hungry. **-kuolema**
starvation. **-palkka**
starvation wages. **-vuosi** year
of famine.
nälviä carp (at).
nälänhätä famine.
nämä these; *näinä päivinä* one
of these days; any day now.
nänni nipple.
näper|rellä tinker (with, at),
potter about (with). **-tely**
tinkering; finicky job.
näpiste|lijä pilferer. **-llä** pilfer,
filch. **-ly** pilfering; *lak.* petty
larceny; *~yn taipuvainen*
light-fingered.
näppy **-lä** pimple, pustule.
näppäi|llä pluck; *-lysoittimet*
plucked instruments. **-mistö**
keyboard, *(urkujen)* manual.
-n key.
näppär|yys handiness, dexterity.
-ä handy, dexterous, deft;
clever [with one's fingers];
(kekseliäisyyttä osoittava)
ingenious.
näp|säyttää flip, snap [one's
fingers], flick.
näreikkö cluster of young
spruces or firs.
närhi jay.
närkäs|tys resentment;
indignation. **-tyttää** offend,
annoy; cause irritation. **-tyä**
become indignant (at; with a
p.); *(loukkaantua)* take offence.
jstk at; *-tyin hänen*
käytöksestään I resented his
behaviour.
närästys heartburn; acid
dyspepsia.
näveri gimlet.
näykkiä nag (at); snap.
näyte specimen; *(kaupp. ym)*
sample; *(todiste)* proof;
näytteeksi jstk as a sample;
as a proof of; *näytteillä* on

view, on display; *panna*
näytteille exhibit, display, put
on public show. **-ikkuna** show
window. **-kaappi** *(lasikko)*
show case. **-kappale** sample,
specimen.
näytel|lä show; *(panna*
nähtäväksi) display; *teatt.*
play, act; *(esittää)* present; *~*
jkn osaa appear as, play
(act) the part of; perform; *~*
tärkeätä osaa jssk play an
important part (role) in;..
-tiin 20 kertaa.. had a run
of 20 nights. **-mä** play;
drama; show; *(joskus)*
spectacle; *~n henkilöt*
characters in a play, cast;
(~esitys performance;
~kappale play; *~kirjailija*
playwright, dramatist;
~kirjallisuus dramatic
literature; *~llinen* dramatic;
~musiikki incidental music;
~taide dramatic art).
näyte|numero sample copy.
-tilkku sample.
näytteille|panija exhibitor. **-pano**
exhibition, display.
näyttelijä actor; *ruveta ~ksi* go
on the stage. **-seurue**
theatrical company. **-tär**
actress.
näyttely exhibition, fair,
(karja-, kukka-) show; *Am.*
exposition. **-alue** exhibition
grounds. **-esine** exhibit.
-huoneisto showrooms.
näyttämö *teatt.* stage; *kuv.* of
scene, theatre *(esim.* t. of
war, *sota~)*; *sovittaa ~llä*
esitettäväksi dramatize.
-koristeet, -laitteet scenery,
stage décor. **-llepano** staging.
-llinen scenic. **-nmuutos**
change of scene;
scene-shifting. **-taide** scenic
art. **-tottumus** stage experience.
näyttäy|tyä show oneself
(itself); appear; *(näkyä)* be
seen; *hän ei -tynyt (täällä)* he
did not show up.
näyt|tää *tr.* show; *intr.* appear;
seem; *(olla näköinen)* look,
have the appearance of;
-ettäessä upon presentation,
(pankk.) at sight; *~ toteen*
prove; demonstrate the truth

nöyr

of; *hän ~ olevan sairas* he
seems (appears) to be ill,
(sairaalta) he looks ill; *~
siltä kuin. .* it looks as
though; *minusta ~ siltä,
että. .* it seems to me that. .;
~ tulevan sade it looks like
rain; *hänestä ~ tulevan hyvä
laulajatar* she shows promise
of becoming a good singer.
-tö *lak.* substantiation, proof.
näyt|äntö performance; show;
(~kausi theatrical season). **-ös**
show; display; *teatt.* act;
kolminäytöksinen [a play] in
three acts.
nään|nys: *olla näännyksissä* be
exhausted. **-nyttää** exhaust;
prostrate. **-tymys** exhaustion.

-tyä grow faint, *jhk* with;
become exhausted; *(taakan
alle)* sink [under a burden];
~ nälkään starve [to death].
näärännäppy sty.
näätä [pine-]marten.
nöyhtä fluff.
nöyr|istellä be servile; *(jklle)*
cringe, truckle (to), fawn
upon; *-istelevä* servile. **-istely**
servility. **-tyä** humble oneself,
grow humble. **-yys** humility,
humbleness. **-yytää** humiliate,
humble. **-yytys** humiliation;
kärsiä ~ be humiliated. **-ä**
humble; lowly [in spirit],
meek; *(alistuvainen)*
submissive; *(kuuliainen)*
obedient.

O

oas thorn, *(pieni)* prickle.
obduktio autopsy.
objekti object. **-ivi** indirect object; *valok.* lens. **-ivinen** objective. **-lasi** slide.
obligaatio bond, debenture; *~t (m.)* stocks. **-laina** bond [ed] loan.
odotella be waiting (for).
odote|ttavissa: *muuta ei ollut ~* what else could you expect. **-ttu** expected; *kauan ~* long-expected; *heitä oli paljon ~a vähemmän* their number was far short of expectation. **-tusti** according to expectations, as expected.
odotta|a wait (for, for sb. to) *(jnk tapahtuvan)* expect; *(toivoen)* look forward (to); hope (for); *(aavistaa)* foresee; *odota vähäsen* wait a bit! *-kaa hetkinen'* just a moment, please! *~ kauan* wait a long time; *odotan kirjettä* I am expecting a letter; *antaa jkn ~ keep sb.* waiting; *-en vastaustanne* awaiting your [early] reply; *jäädä -valle kannalle* await developments; *on odotettavissa* is to be expected; *sitä odotinkin* that's what I expected, I thought as much; *emme tiedä, mikä meitä ~* we do not know what is in store for us; *vastausta ei tarvinnut kauan ~* the answer was not long in coming; *kuten saattoi ~kin* as might have been expected. **-maton** unexpected, unlooked-for. **-matta** unexpectedly; *(vastoin luuloa)* contrary to [all] expectation [s]. **-va** waiting; expectant [mother, *äiti* [; *jäädä ~lle kannalle* wait and see, adopt an attitude of

waiting.
odotus waiting; expectation, anticipation, *(jännitys)* suspense; *vastaa odotuksia* comes up to [a p.'s] expectations. **-aika** time of waiting, waiting period. **-sali** waiting-room.
ohda|ke thistle. **-kkeinen** *kuv.* thorny.
ohe|en by; *(mukaan)* with; *liittää ~* enclose. **-inen:** *-isena* enclosed; herewith. **-istaa** enclose; *-istettu, m.* appended, attached. **-lla** with, along with; *(lisäksi)* besides; *jonka ~* besides which; *sen ~* besides [that], in addition [to that]; *tämän ~* besides [this], moreover.
ohen|taa [make] thin[ner], thin down. **-tua** become (grow) thinner, thin; *-tunut (ilma)* rarefied.
ohessa [close] by; *tien ~ (ohesta)* by the wayside (roadside).
ohi by, past, *(lopussa)* over; *~ kulkiessani* when passing by; *päästää ~* let . . pass, allow . . to pass; *se menee ~* it will pass; *kaikki vaara on ~* all danger is past *(t.* over). **-kiitävä** fleeting. **-kulkeva** . . passing by. **-kulkija** passer-by. **-kulku** passing by; *(~tie* bypass). **-marssi** march-past. **-matka:** *~lla* when passing by. **-menevä** passing; *kuv.* transient, transitory; *~ä laatua* of a temporary nature. **-mennen** in passing; *~ sanoen* by the way.
ohimo temple. **-luu** temporal bone.
ohi|tse by; *kulkea ~* pass. **-ttaa** pass, *(auto)* overtake; *ryhtyä -ttamaan* carry on to

overtake. **-tus** overtaking;
(**~kielto** no overtaking).
ohj|aaja leader, *(neuvoja)*
instructor; *(auton)* driver,
chauffeur; *teatt.* & *elok.*
director; *(lentokoneen)* pilot.
-aamo *lentok.* cockpit;
(nosturin) cab.
ohjaks|et reins; *vrt. suitset; -issa
oli. . (kuv.). .* was at the
helm; *tiukentaa -ia* tighten
one's hold.
ohjat|a lead, guide; direct;
conduct; *(laivaa)* navigate;
steer; *(autoa)* drive; *lentok.*
pilot; *-tava* guided. **-tavuus**
manoeuvrability; control [of a
car].
ohjaus guidance, direction,
(opintojen) tuition; *tekn.*
control, steering. **-hytti** *lentok.*
cockpit. **-kyky;** *menetti ~nsä*
lost control (of). **-laitteet**
steering gear, *lentok.*
controls. **-pyörä** steering
wheel; *olla ~ssä* be at the
wheel. **-sauva** control stick.
-tanko *(polkupyörän)*
handle-bars. **-virhe** navigational
error.
ohje direction, instruction;
(sääntö) rule, precept;
(ruoka-) recipe; *dipl.* directive;
ääntämis~(et) guide to the
pronunciation; *sinulle ~eksi*
for your guidance; *antaa ~ita*
instruct [a p.]; *~iden
mukaisesti* as directed. **-hinta**
recommended price.
ohjelm|a programme, *Am.*
program; *(puolueen, m.)*
platform; *illan ~* the
programme for the evening.
-allinen: *~ illanvietto* social
gathering with entertainment.
-isto repertoire, repertory.
-oida program [me]. **-ointi**
programming.
ohje|nuora guiding principle.
-sääntö regulations, rule [s],
sot. m. order [s]; *(esim.
kaupungin, yhtiön antama)*
bylaw; *-säännön vastainen*
contrary to rules and
regulations.
ohjus missile; *mannerten
välinen ~* intercontinental m.;
torjunta ~ anti-missile m.

-alus missile-launching vessel.
-tiede rocketry.
ohra barley. **-jauhot** barley
flour. **-jyvät** barley. **-ryynit**
pearl barley.
ohukas small pancake.
ohut thin; *(ilmasta)* rarefied; *~
takki (m.)* light coat; *(ilmasta)
kulunut* worn thin; *ohuessa
puvussa* thinly dressed.
-kuorinen thin-skinned. **-suoli**
small intestine.
ohuus thinness, *(ilman)* rarity.
oieta straighten [out]; unbend;
(esim. tukka) come uncurled.
oikai|sta straighten; *(korjata)*
correct; rectify, put right;
take sb. up [for -ing, *jstk*];
(pitkälleen) stretch oneself, lie
down; *~ metsän läpi* take a
short cut through the woods.
-su correction.
oikea right; true, *(aito)*
genuine; *(-mielinen)* just;
(virheetön) correct; *(todellinen)*
real; *(asianmukainen)* due,
proper; *~lla* on the right
[hand], at the right; *~lle* to
the right; *olla ~ssa* be right;
olet ~ssa you are [quite]
right; *~an aikaan* at the
right time; opportunely; *~lla
hetkellä lausuttu* well-timed,
[a word] in season; *~ puoli,
sivu* right side, *(laivan)*
starboard; *jnk ~lla puolella*
on the right side of, to the
right of; *~lla puolellani* on
my right; *hänen oikea
kätensä (kuv.)* his right-hand
man. **-kielisyys** grammatical
correctness, correct language.
-kätinen right-handed.
-mielinen just, upright.
-mielisyys justice, integrity.
-mmin more correctly; *~
sanoen* to put it more
exactly. **-npuoleinen**
right-hand, . . on the right; *~
liikenne* right-hand traffic.
-oppinen orthodox. **-peräinen**
authentic. **-peräisyys**
authenticity; *todistaa jnk ~*
authenticate. **-staan** really;
properly; *(todellisuudessa)* in
reality, in point of fact.
-uskoinen orthodox.
oikein right, rightly; correctly;

(todella) really; *(hyvin)* very; *(sangen)* quite; ~ **päin** the right side up *(t. out)*; the right way; **onko** ~, **että**.. is it right that..? **onko se** ~ **totta** is it really true? **teit** ~ **kun tulit** you did right to come; **aivan** ~ quite so; **menetellä** ~ act in the right way, do [the] right [thing]; ~**ko totta?** really? **se oli sinulle** ~ that served you right! **-kirjoitus** spelling; (~**virhe** spelling error).

oikeisto the Right. **-lainen** *a.* right-wing; *s.* right-winger.

oikeude|llinen legal, juridical; judicial; *naisen* ~ *asema* the legal status of women; **-llisesti** *pätevä* valid in law, legal.

oikeudenkäynti lawsuit; action, [legal] proceedings; *(käsittely)* trial; *panna alulle* ~ bring an action, take proceedings (against), go to law. **-avustaja** counsel. **-järjestys** procedure. **-kulut** court fees, costs. **-laitos** judiciary. **-tietä** by legal proceedings.

oikeuden|käyttö administration of law; jurisdiction. **-loukkaus** violation of justice. **-mukainen** just; *(oikea)* rightful, legitimate; *(kohtuullinen)* fair; *ollakseni täysin* ~ *in all fairness* [to, *jklle*] **-mukaisesti** justly, with justice. **-mukaisuus** rightfulness, justness; justice. **-omistaja** assignee. **-palvelija** officer of the court, bailiff. **-tunto** sense of justice.

oikeudeton lawless; contrary to justice.

oikeus right, *jhk* to; justice; *(-istuin)* court [of justice]; ` *(etu-)* privilege; *millä oikeudella?* by what right? *päästä oikeuksiinsa* come into one's own; *saattaa jku oikeuksiinsa* restore a p. to his rights; *pitää kiinni oikeuksistaan* stick up for one's rights; *tehdä jklle oikeutta (kuv.)* do justice to; *hänellä ei ole oikeutta..* he has no right to, he has no

authority to..; *oikeutta myöten* in justice, by rights; *oikeuden istunto* session of the court; *vedota korkeampaan oikeuteen* appeal to a court of higher instance; *minulla on* ~ *puolellani* I have a just cause. **-apu** legal aid. **-asia** legal matter, case; (~**mies** Ombudsman). **-aste:** *ensimmäinen* ~ court of first instance. **-istuin** court, lawcourt. **-juttu** case, lawsuit. **-kansleri** attorney general. **-laitos** judicial system. **-lääketiede** forensic medicine. **-lääketieteellinen** medicolegal. **-ministeri** minister of justice. **-murha** judicial murder. **-oppinut** jurisprudent. **-piiri** jurisdiction. **-tie:** ~*tä* by legal means; *periä* ~*tä* sue. **-tiede** jurisprudence, law; *-tieteen kandidaatti* Bachelor of Laws, LL.B. **-turva:** *(kaikille) sama* ~ equality of justice. **-valtio** constitutional state.

oikeu|ttaa entitle, *jhk* to, justify; *-tettu (jhk)* entitled to; *-tetut vaatimukset* just (rightful, legitimate) claims; *huomautus oli* ~ the remark was justified. **-tus** justification; authority.

oikku whim, caprice; *luonnon* ~ a freak of nature; *oikut (m.)* whimsies, quirks. **-illa** be whimsical, be capricious.

oiko|a set right, rectify; *(suoraksi)* straighten; ~ *jäseniään* stretch oneself. **-lukija** proof-reader. **-luku** proof-reading. **-sulku** short circuit. **-tie** short cut; *mennä* ~*tä* take a s. c.

oiku|kas, -llinen capricious, whimsical. **-llisuus** capriciousness; whimsicality. **-ttelu** whims, caprices.

oinas wether.

oire *(esim. taudin)* symptom; *(merkki)* sign. **-ellinen** symptomatic.

oivalli|nen excellent; fine; splendid, first-rate. **-suus** excellence; splendidness.

oival|llus insight. **-taa** see, perceive, recognize; *-lan sen*

täydellisesti I am fully aware of that.
oja ditch; *(lasku-)* drain; *vrt. allikko.*
ojen|nus straightening; *(rivin)* alignment; *(nuhteet)* reproof, reprimand; *(~nuora* guiding principle). **-taa** extend, hold out; *(pitkäksi)* stretch out; *(antaa)* hand, *(edelleen)* pass, *(kurottaa)* reach; *(nuhdella)* rebuke; *~ jklle (lahja)* present. . with; *-netuin käsin* with outstretched arms. **-tautua** *(suoraksi)* stretch oneself. **-tua** straighten; *hän ei ota ~kseen* he is incorrigible.
oji|ttaa ditch; *(sala-)* drain. **-tus** ditching, draining, *(sala-)* underground drainage.
ojossa: *käsi ~* with one's hand outstretched.
oka thorn, spine, prickle. **-inen** prickly, thorny.
okra ochre.
oksa branch; *(haara)* bough; *(pieni)* twig, sprig; *(esim. kukkiva)* spray; *(laudassa)* knot, snag. **-inen** branchy; *(laudasta ym)* knotty. **-s** *puut.* scion. **-saha** pruning saw. **-staa** graft, bud. **-stus** grafting; *(~vaha* grafting wax). **-ton** clear [of knots].
okse|nnus vomiting; vomit. **-nnuttaa:** *minua ~* I feel sick. **-ntaa** vomit, throw up.
oksia prune; trim.
oksidi oxide.
oktaani octane.
oktaavi *mus.* octave.
okulaari eye-piece.
olankohautus shrug.
oleelli|nen essential; material. **-sesti** essentially; substantially. **-suus** essential nature.
olemassa|oleva existing, existent. **-olo** existence; *(esiintyminen)* occurrence; *taistelu ~sta* struggle for existence.
ole|maton non-existent. **-mattomuus** non-existence; nullity. **-mus** being; *(luonne)* nature; substance; *olemukseltaan* in essence; intrinsically. **-nnainen**

essential; material, substantial; *(sisäinen)* inherent, intrinsic; *~ osa (m.)* essence. **-nnaisesti** *m.* in essence. **-nnoida** personify, impersonate, embody. **-nnoituma** personification, embodiment. **-nto** being, creature; person.
oleske|lla stay; sojourn; *(asua)* live, reside. **-lu** stay; sojourn, visit [to, *jssk*]; *(~lupa* sojourn permit, residence visa).
ole|ttaa suppose; *(edellyttää)* presume; assume; *olettaen, että* . . on the presumption that; *oletetaan kaksi pistettä, A ja B* given two points, A and B; *oletettu* hypothetical. **-ttamus** supposition, presumption, assumption; *tiet.* hypothesis. **-va** existing; *(vallitseva)* prevailing.
olevinaan: *olla ~* be haughty, ride the high horse; *he olivat ~.* . they made believe (made out) that they were. .
oliivi olive. **-öljy** olive oil.
olinpaikka whereabouts.
olio being; creature.
olipa: *~ niin tai näin* either way.
olisi *ks. olla; ~npa tiennyt* I wish I had known.
oljen|keltainen straw-coloured. **-korsi** straw; *tarttua -korteen* clutch (catch) at a straw.
olka shoulder. **-in** shoulder-strap; *-imet* braces, *Am.* suspenders. **-kivi** console, bracket. **-nauha** shoulder-strap. **-pää** shoulder. **-varsi** upper arm.
olki straw; *oljet* straw. **-hattu** straw hat. **-katto** thatched roof. **-lyhde** bundle of straw.
olkoon: *~ niin (mutta)* that may be so (,but); *~ sää millainen tahansa* whatever the weather is like.
olla be; *(pystyssä)* stand; *(pitkällään)* lie; *(olemassa)* exist; *(esiintyä)* occur; *(sijaita)* be situated; *(olla tehty jstk, koostua)* be [made] of; consist of; *minulla on, oli* I have, I had; *pöydällä on kirjoja* there are books on the table; *olipa (asia) kuinka*

tahansa be that as it may; *olkoonpa, että* granting that; *olkoonpa se kuinka hyvä tahansa* no matter how good it is; *minusta on kuin. .* it seems to me as if; *olin putoamaisillani* I was about to fall, I was on the point of falling, I nearly fell; *~ vastaamatta* fail to answer; *en voi ~ nauramatta* I cannot help laughing; *päätin ~ menemättä* I decided not to go; *hän ei ollut tietävinään* he pretended not to know; *olla (kokouksessa ym) mukana* attend [a meeting]; *kotona ollessani* while at home; *hänen täällä ollessaan* while [he was] here, during his stay here; *mikä sinun on* what is the matter with you? *minun on paha ~* I feel uncomfortable; *minun oli se maksettava* I had to pay it; *sinun olisi oltava* you ought to (you should) be. .

ollenkaan. . at all; *ei ~* not in the least, not in the slightest degree.

olletikin particularly, notably, the more so as.

olo existence; *(oleskelu)* stay; *~t* conditions, circumstances; state of things (of affairs); *hyvissä ~issa* in easy circumstances; *näissä ~issa* in *(t.* under) these circumstances; *sellaisissa ~issa* under such conditions; *~jen tuntemattomuus* unfamiliarity with the conditions. **-huone** lounge, sitting-room, living-room. **-muoto** form of existence. **-suhde:** *-suhteet* circumstances, conditions; *hän voi -suhteisiin nähden hyvin* he is as well as can be expected under the circumstances; *-suhteiden pakosta* by force of circumstances. **-tila** state, condition.

oluen|panija brewer. **-pano** brewing.

olut beer, *(varasto-)* lager. **-panimo** brewery. **-ravintola**

beerhouse.

olympiakisat Olympic games.

oma own; *onko tämä teidän ~nne* is this yours? *kenen ~ tämä on* who[m] does this belong to? *saanko sen ~kseni* may I have it for my own? *hänellä on ~ talo* he has a house of his own; *ota sinä tuo kirja, minä otan ~ni* you take that book, I will take mine; *~ kiitos* self-praise; *olemalla ~ itsemme* by being ourselves; *-llä on ~ lehmä ojassa. .* has an axe to grind; *omin neuvoin, omin päin* on one's own, of one's own accord, by oneself; *olla omiansa jhk* be suited, be adapted for, be appropriate; *omiaan ks. t.; päästä omilleen* break even. **-apu** self-help. **-ehtoinen** spontaneous. **-elämäkerta** autobiography. **-hyväinen** self-satisfied, [self-]complacent. **-hyväisyys** self-satisfaction, conceit.

omai|nen close relative, relation; *(lähi)* -iset next of kin. **-suus** property; *et. lak.* estate; *(varallisuus)* wealth; *(~rikos* crime involving property; *~tase* balance-sheet; *~vero* property tax).

oma|kohtainen subjective; *(henkilö-)* personal. **-kotitalo** [small] single-family house. **-ksua** adopt; *~ jk aate* embrace an idea, *(asia)* espouse a cause, *(mielipide)* adopt a view. **-kuva** self-portrait. **-kätinen. .** by one's own hand,. . in one's own hand [writing]. **-kätisesti** with one's own hand. **-laatuinen** peculiar. **-leimainen** characteristic. **-narvontunto** self-respect. **-nkädenoikeus** mob law; *harjoittaa o-oikeutta* take the law into one's own hands.

omantunnon|arka overscrupulous; *(aseistakieltäytyjä)* conscientious objector. **-asia** matter of conscience. **-vaivat** pangs *(pistot* pricks) of conscience *vrt. tunnon-.*

omanvoiton|pyynti selfishness,

self-interest. **-pyyntöinen**
self-seeking.
oma|peräinen original,
(itsenäinen) independent.
-peräisyys originality. **-päinen**
self-willed, wilful. **-ta** own;
hold, possess, have. **-tekoinen**
home-made. **-toimisesti** on
one's own. **-tunto** conscience;
huono ~ bad (guilty) c.; hyvä
~ clear c.; hyvällä
omallatunnolla in good c.
-valoinen self-luminous.
-valtainen arbitrary. **-valtaisuus**
arbitrariness. **-varainen**
self-sufficient; independent.
-varaisuus [economic]
self-sufficiency, autarky.
omeletti omelet [te].
omena apple. **-hillo** stewed
apples. **-puu** apple-tree. **-sose**
apple sauce. **-torttu** apple
tart. **-viini** cider.
omiaan: on ~ jhk is of a
nature to, lends itself to; on
~ osoittamaan goes to show;
tämä on tuskin ~.. this is
hardly likely to..; panna ~
stretch the facts, embroider
[the truth].
ominai|nen characteristic, jllek,
jklle of; peculiar (to); olla
jklle -sta (m.) mark,
distinguish a p. **-slämpö**
specific heat. **-spaino** specific
gravity. **-spiirre** characteristic;
jnk ~ (m.) a feature of.
-suus quality, property; jssak
-suudessa in the capacity of.
omintakei|nen independent;
(alkuperäinen) original. **-suus**
independence; originality.
omis|taa own, possess, have;
(jklle, jhk tarkoitukseen)
dedicate; ~ aikansa jllek
devote one's time to; ~
huomiota jllek give a matter
one's attention; ~ omakseen
acknowledge; ~ hyvä terveys
enjoy good health. **-taja**
owner, proprietor; (haltija)
possessor; holder. **-tautua**
(jllek) devote oneself to.. **-tus**
possession; ownership; (jklle)
dedication; (~oikeus right of
possession, proprietary rights;
~sanat dedication).
omitui|nen strange, queer, odd;

extraordinary; ~ ihminen a
queer person; minulla oli ~ olo
I felt queer; -sta kyllä oddly
(strangely, curiously) enough.
-suus peculiarity; strangeness,
oddness, queerness; oddity;
eccentricity.
ommel seam; lääk. suture. **-la**
sew; do needlework; (puku,
m.) make; ~ kiinni (esim.
nappi) sew on; (haava) stitch,
suture.
ompe|lija, ~tar needlewoman,
dressmaker. **-limo** dressmaker's
business.
ompelu sewing, needlework.
-kehys embroidery frame.
-kone sewing-machine. **-lipas**
work-box. **-rihma** sewing
cotton, thread. **-seura** sewing
circle. **-silkki** sewing-silk.
ongelma puzzle; problem.
-llinen problematic, puzzling,
involved.
ongen|koukku fish-hook. **-siima**
[fishing-]line. **-vapa** fishing-
rod.
onginta angling, line-fishing.
onkalo cavity, hollow.
onki hook and line,
[fish]hook; (kalastaa ongella)
catch on hook and line;
tarttua onkeen (kala) bite,
kuv. swallow the bait; saada
onkeensa hook. **-a** m. kuv.
angle (for), Am. fish [with
hook and line]. **-ja** angler.
-mato angling worm.
onnekas lucky; successful.
onnelli|nen happy; lucky
[chance sattuma]; fortunate.
-sesti happily jne.; hän saapui
~ perille he arrived safely
(safe and sound). **-staa**
make.. happy; bless, jllak
with. **-suus** happiness.
onnen|kauppa hazard; oli ~a it
was a matter of luck. **-onkija**
fortune-hunter; adventurer.
-poika lucky fellow. **-potkaus**
lucky stroke, stroke of good
fortune. **-päivä** lucky day.
-toivo|tus congratulation;
o-tukset best wishes, good
wishes; (syntymäpäivän
johdosta) many happy returns
of the day.
onnetar Lady Luck.

onneton unhappy; unfortunate, unlucky.

onnettomuus misfortune; *(-tapaus)* accident; disaster; *(pienempi)* mishap, misadventure; *(turmio)* calamity; *(onnellisuuden vastakohta)* unhappiness. **-paikka** scene of the accident. **-päivä** fatal day.

onni luck; fortune; *(menestys)* success; *(onnellisuus)* happiness; *onneksi* fortunately, luckily [enough]; *paljon onnea!* best wishes; *(sulhaselle)* congratulations, *(morsiamelle)* I wish you every happiness; *vrt. toivottaa; huono ~* bad luck; *onnen poika* lucky man, lucky fellow.

onnis|taa: *häntä -ti* he had luck. **-tua** be successful, succeed, meet with success; *(asioista)* be a success; *~ tekemään jtk* succeed in doing, manage to do sth.; *~ keksimään (esim. ratkaisu)* hit [up]on; *onnistui mainiosti. .* was a great success,. . came off very well; *ei -tunut. .* was (. . proved) a failure. **-tuminen** success. **-tunut** successful, *(sattuva)* apt, appropriate.

onni|tella congratulate, *jkta jstk* a p. upon; *vrt. toivottaa.* **-ttelu** congratulation; *(~kortti* greetings card; *~sähke* greetings telegram.).

ontelo *s.* cavity, hollow.

ontto hollow; *kuv.* empty.

ontu|a limp, walk lame, be lame, *kuv.* halt. **-minen** limp [ing]. **-va** lame, limping.

oodi run. ode.

oopiumi opium.

ooppera opera. **-laulaja,** *~tar* opera-singer. **-musiikki** operatic music.

opaali *min.* opal. **-nvärinen** opalescent.

opas guide *(m. -kirja).* **-koira** guide dog [for the blind], *Am.* Seeing Eye dog. **-taa** guide; *(näyttää tietä)* show. . the way; *(johtaa)* lead, conduct; direct; *(neuvoa)*

instruct; *(sisään)* show in, *(tutustuttaa)* introduce into. **-tin** signal. **-tus** guidance; direction; instruction.

operetti musical comedy, operetta, light opera.

ope|tella learn, be learning; *(harjoitella)* practise. **-ttaa** teach; instruct (sb. in); *(harjoittaa)* train; *~ hevosta* break a horse; *opetettu* trained, *(siistiksi, koira)* house-trained, *(temppuja tekemään)* performing. **-ttaja** teacher; *(mies-, m.)* master; instructor; *(koti-)* tutor; *(~kokelas* student teacher; *~kunta* teaching staff; *~nvirka* teaching post; *~tar* woman teacher; schoolmistress). **-ttajisto** staff of teachers. **-ttamaton** untrained, untaught, *(hevonen)* unbroken. **-ttavainen** instructive.

opetus teaching; instruction, training; lesson, moral; *(kansan-)* education; *antaa jklle ~ta jssk* give. . instruction in, teach. . **-aine** subject [taught]. **-elokuva** educational film, *(dokumentti-)* documentary [film]. **-lapsi** disciple. **-menetelmä** method of teaching. **-ministeri** minister of education. **-olot** educational conditions. **-runo** didactic poem. **-suunnitelma** curriculum. **-taito** teaching ability. **-toimi** education. **-tunti** lesson, class, period. **-välineet** educational equipment.

opillinen scholastic; theoretical; *~ sivistys* education, book-knowledge, scholarship.

opin|ahjo seat of learning. **-halu** eagerness to learn. **-haluinen** eager to learn; studious. **-käynyt** trained. **-näyte** *l.v.* test.

opinto, *opinnot* study, studies; *harjoittaa ~ja* study; *olla työssä kustantaakseen ~nsa* pay one's way through an outside job, work one's way through [the course etc.]. **-aika** years of study, college years. **-aine** subject, study. **-kerho** study circle. **-kirja**

study report book. **-laina** loan for study expenses. **-matka** study trip; *olla ~lla* travel for purposes of study. **-neuvonta** educational guidance. **-suunnitelma** plan of studies, *(tietyssä aineessa)* syllabus. **-toveri** fellow-student.

opiske|lija student; *(yliopistossa)* university student, undergraduate. **-lla** study, pursue studies; read; *-len (maan) kieltä* I am learning the language [of the country]. **-lu** study; *(~aika: o-nani* in my undergraduate days).

opisto institute; school, college; academy.

oppi doctrine; *(oppineisuus)* learning; *(tieto)* knowledge; *ottaa ~a jstk* learn by, take a lesson from; *olla (jklla) opissa* be learning a trade with. ., serve one's apprenticeship; *se oli hänelle opiksi* it was a lesson to him; *~a ikä kaikki* [we] live and learn.

oppi|a learn, acquire, pick up; *~ tekemään jtk* learn how to; *~ pahoille tavoille* acquire bad habits; *~ tuntemaan* get to know;. . *voi ~* can master [this method, a language etc.]; *~kseen, ~kseni* so as to learn. **-aine** subject; branch of study. **-arvo** academic degree; *saavuttaa ~* take one's degree, graduate. **-isä** master, teacher. **-jakso** course. **-kirja** text-book. **-koulu** secondary school, *Am.* high school. **-laitos** educational institution; school. **-las** pupil; *(ammatti-)* apprentice. **-lause** dogma. **-maton** uneducated, unlettered, untutored; *(luku- ja kirjoitustaidoton)* illiterate; ignorant. **-mattomuus** lack of education, ignorance. **-neisuus** learning, scholarship, erudition. **-nut** *a.* learned, *(korkeasti-)* scholarly; *s.* learned man. **-poika** apprentice. **-sali** lecture-room (-hall). **-sanasto** [technical] terminology. **-sopimus**

indenture [s].

-suunta school. **-tunti** lesson; *(koulu-, m.)* class. **-tuoli** chair. **-vainen** ready to learn, docile. **-vaisuus** readiness to learn. **-velvollisuus** compulsory education. **-vuosi** year of apprenticeship.

oppositio opposition; *~halu* love of o. **-puolue(et)** the Opposition.

opt|iikka optics. **-ikko** optician. **-inen** optic [al].

optimisti optimist. **-nen** optimistic [al].

oraakkeli oracle. **-mainen** oracular.

oranki *zo.* orang-outang.

ora|pihlaja hawthorn. **-tuomi** sloe, blackthorn.

oras shoot, sprout; *on oraalla* has sprouted, has come up. **-taa** sprout, shoot up, spring up.

orava squirrel.

orgaaninen organic.

organis|aatio organization. **-atorinen** organizational. **-mi** organism. **-oida** organize.

ori stallion. **-varsa** colt.

orja slave; *olla jnk (pahan tavan) ~* be a slave to, overindulge in; *alkoholin (narkoottisten aineiden) ~* drink (drug) addict; *tehdä työtä kuin ~* slave, drudge. **-kauppa** slave-trade. **-kauppias** slave-trader. **-llinen** slavish. **-nruusu** short-pedicelled rose. **-ntappura** = *ed;* *(~inen* thorny; *~kruunu* crown of thorns). **-työ** slave labour. **-tar** female slave.

orjuu|s slavery, servitude; bondage; *-den lakkauttaminen* abolition of slavery. **-ttaa** enslave. **-tus** enslavement.

orkesteri orchestra; *sovittaa ~lle* orchestrate. **-njohtaja** orchestral conductor. **-soitto** orchestral music.

orkidea orchid.

orpo *a.* orphan [ed], *(turvaton)* forlorn; *s.* orphan; *jäädä orvoksi* be orphaned. **-kassa** orphan fund. **-koti** orphanage. **-lapsi** orphan child. **-us**

orphanhood.
orsi rafter; *(kana- ym)* perch,
roost.
ortodoksi, -nen [Greek]
Orthodox.
orvaskesi epidermis.
orvokki violet, *(puutarha-, ym)*
pansy.
osa part *(m. kirjan)*; portion;
(osuus) share; *(suhteellinen)*
proportion; *(kokonaisuuden)*
component; *(kirjan)* volume;
(rooli) role, rôle; *(kohtalo)*
fate; lot; ~*ksi* partly;
partially, in part; ~*ltani* for
my part; *(omalta)* ~*ltaan*
vaikuttaa jhk contribute to;
suurelta ~*lta, suureksi* ~*ksi*
in large part, largely, to a
great extent; *ottaa* ~*a jhk*
take part in, participate in,
(suruun) sympathize with; ~*a*
ottaen *(suruun)* with my
sympathy; *tulla jkn* ~*ksi* fall
to a p.'s lot; *saada jtk*
~*kseen* meet with, *(kokea)*
experience, gain [favour,
suosiota], attract [notice,
huomiota]. **-aika (-päivä)**
part-time. **-aottavainen**
sympathizing. **-inen** *(yhd.)*..
in.. parts,.. in.. volumes.
-jako cast [ing]. **-kas** partner;
(osakkeenomistaja) shareholder,
Am. stockholder; *(osaomistaja)*
part-owner.
osake share, Am. stock;
osakkeet (m.) stock [s]. **-anti**
issue of shares. **-enemmistö**
share majority. **-huoneisto** flat
in house-owning company.
-keinottelija speculator in
stock; *(lasku-)* bear; *(nousu-)*
bull. **-kirja** share certificate.
-markkinat stockmarket.
-merkintä subscription for
shares. **-pankki** joint-stock
bank. **-pääoma** share capital.
-yhtiö limited company *(lyh.*
Ltd), joint-stock company,
Am. [stock] corporation,
incorporated company (Inc.)
osakkeenomistaja shareholder,
stockholder.
osakkuus partnership.
osakunta students' union.
osalli|nen *a.* participant,
concerned, interested (in); *s.*

party, partner (in); ~ *jhk*
(m.) a party to; *päästä -seksi*
share in, become a
participant in.. **-stua** *(jhk)*
participate, take part (in),
attend [a meeting,
kokoukseen], be accessory to
[a crime, rikokseen],
(tahattomasti) be involved in;
-stuva committed, engaged,
participatory. **-minen**
participation. **-suus**
participation; part, share;
(rikokseen) complicity.
osa|maksu part payment;
(maksuerä) instalment. **-määrä**
mat. quotient. **-nen** small
part; particle. **-nottaja**
partaker, participator. **-notto**
participation (in); *(suruun)*
sympathy; *lausua* ~*nsa* express
one's s.; (~**maksu**
subscription). **-puilleen** about.
-puoli party. **-päivätyö:** ~*tä*
tekevä part-time worker.
osasto department; section;
(vuode-) ward; *(jaosto)*
division; *(sotilas-)* body,
detachment, [group]; *(yksikkö)* unit;
(rautatievaunun) compartment.
-nhoitaja *(sairaan-)* ward
sister, head-nurse. **-päällikkö**
chief of a department,
departmental manager.
osata be able to; *(tuntea)*
know; *osaa (voi)* can; *hän
osaa englantia* he knows
English; *hän osaa uida hyvin*
he can swim well; ~
jonnekin find one's way to;
~ *käyttäytyä* know how to
behave; ~ *maaliin* hit the
mark; *oikein osattu* that's a
good hit; *hän ei osaa.. (m.)*
he does not know how to..
osa|ton without a [ny] share
in; *jäädä -ttomaksi (jstk)* be
left without sth. **-toveri**
companion in misfortune.
-valtio [confederate] state;
Am. tav. State. **-voitto** *liik.*
percentage of profit.
osingonjako payment of
dividends.
osinko *liik.* dividend; *jakaa* ~*a*
pay a d. **-lippu** coupon.
osittai|n partly, partially, in
part. **-nen** partial. **-smaksu**

partial payment, instalment.
osoite address. **-kalenteri**
directory. **-lippu** label;
(sidottava) tag, tie-on label.
-paikka destination. **-toimisto**
address and information
service.
osoitin *(kellon)* hand; pointer.
osoi|ttaa show, display; ·
(sormella) point (at);
(ilmaista) indicate; *(tuoda
esiin)* express; *(todistaa)*
prove; demonstrate, denote;
(kirje ym) address; ~ *jkta
(joukosta)* point. . out; ~
huomiota pay attention (to);
~ *mieltään* demonstrate; show
one's feelings; *tämä ~
selvästi.*. this proves clearly;
*hän -tti minut tänne,
luoksenne* he directed me
here, he referred me to you;
kuten sen nimikin ~ as its
name implies; *jtk -ttava (m.)*
indicative of. . **-ttaja** *mat.*
numerator. **-ttau|tua** show
oneself, show itself; ~ *jksk*
prove, turn out [to be,
olevan]; *se o-tui oikeaksi* it
proved correct; it proved
true; *se o-tui tarpeettomaksi*
it proved unnecessary;
jälkeenpäin o-tui it appeared
afterwards. **-tus** evidence,
proof; *(ilmaus)* expression;
(merkki) sign, indication,
token.
ost|aa buy [at. . *jhk hintaan*],
purchase; *(tyhjiin)* buy up; ~
jtk itselleen buy oneself a
th., buy sth. for oneself. **-aja**
buyer, purchaser; *(asiakas)*
customer; *(~piiri* circle of
customers).
osteri oyster. **-npyynti**
oyster-fishing.
osto buying; purchase. **-halu**
demand. **-haluinen** willing
(inclined) to buy. **-hinta** cost
price, prime cost; *(hinnalla* at
cost price; *alle -hinnan* below
cost. **-kyky** purchasing power.
-kykyinen able to buy.
-pakko: *ilman ~a* without
obligation to buy. **-s**
purchase; *käydä -ksilla* do
one's shopping, be out
shopping; *lähteä -ksille* go

[out] shopping; *(~keskus*
shopping centre; *(~laukku*
shopping bag).
osu|a hit, strike; ~ *maaliin* hit
the mark; ~ *oikeaan* strike
home; hit the nail on the
head; *laukaus ei osunut* the
shot missed [the mark]; *arpa
osui minulle* I won the draw;
katse osui häneen [his] eyes
fell on her; *he osuivat yhteen*
they chanced to meet. **-ma**
hit; *saada ~* score a hit;
(~tarkkuus accuracy of aim).
osuus share; *(osa)* part,
portion; *(panos)* stake. **-kassa**
cooperative fund. **-kauppa**
cooperative shop *(Am.* store).
-kunta co-operative society.
-meijeri co-operative dairy.
-toiminnallinen co-operative.
-toiminta co-operation; *(~liike*
co-operative movement).
osuva. . to the point,
appropriate, apt; *(huomautus)*
pertinent.
osviitta hint; pointer.
otaksu|a suppose; assume;
(varmaksi) take. . for granted.
-ma supposition, assumption.
-ttava presumable; *(luultava)*
probable. **-ttavasti** presumably,
supposedly.
Otava Charles's Wain, the
Plough, *Am.* the [Big *t.*
Great] Dipper.
ote hold, *(luja)* grip, grasp;
(kirjasta ym) extract. **-lla**
fight, *urh.* contend, compete.
otolli|nen acceptable, *(sovelias)*
convenient, proper,
appropriate; ~ *vastaus*
acceptable answer; *-seen
aikaan* at a favourable
(opportune) moment. **-suus**
opportuneness; convenience.
otos sample.
otsa forehead, *run.* brow; *~nsa
hiessä* by the sweat of one's
face; ~ *rypyssä* with knitted
brows, frowning. **-ke** heading;
(nimiö) title. **-koriste, -ripa**
diadem, tiara. **-luu** frontal
bone. **-tukka** fringe.
otsik|ko heading, headline,
head, title; *rak.* pediment; *jnk
-on alla* under the title of,
entitled; *julkaista suurin -oin*

splash. **-oida** head.

ottaa take; *(pois)* take away (from); take off, remove; *(esim. rahaa pankista)* draw [money from the bank]; ~ *esille* bring out, produce, *(kysymys)* bring up; ~ *huostaansa* take charge of; ~ *kiinni jstk* catch hold of, seize, grasp; ~ *käsiteltäväksi* take up [for consideration, for discussion]; ~ *laina* raise a loan; ~ *maksua* charge; ~ *osaa (kongressiin ym)* attend; ~ *pois (jklta jtk)* take .. away from, *(lupa ym)* withdraw, *(ajokortti)* suspend, *(yltä)* take off; ~ *tehdäkseen jtk* undertake [to do] a th.; take on [a work, *työ*]; ~ *jtk vakavasti, totisesti* take.. seriously, take.. in earnest; ~ *vastaan* receive, *(hyväksyen)* accept; *hän ei ottanut sitä uskoakseen* he would not believe it.

ottelu fight, contest, encounter; *(peli)* match.

otto *(tililtä ym)* withdrawal. **-lapsi** adopted child. **-poika, -tytär** adopted son (daughter).

-vanhemmat adoptive parents.

otus *(riista)* game; *(elukka)* beast.

oudo|ksua think (consider).. strange. **-nnäköinen**.. of an unusual (a strange) appearance, queer [-looking], odd [-looking]. **-stuttaa** surprise.

outo unfamiliar; *(harvinainen)* unusual; strange, odd; peculiar. **-us** oddness, strangeness; unfamiliarity.

ovel|a shrewd; *(kekseliäs)* clever, smart; subtle. **-uus** shrewdness, cunning.

oven|kamana door frame. **-pieli** door-post. **-ripa** door handle, *(pyörä)* door-knob. **-suu:** *seisoa ~ssa* stand at the door. **-vartija** door-keeper; janitor; *(hotellin)* porter.

ovi door; *ovesta* through the d.; *ovella* at the d.; *on ovella (kuv.)*.. is imminent; *ovella ovelle* from door to door. **-aukko** door-way. **-kello** door-bell; ~ *soi* there is a ring at the door. **-raha** admission [fee]. **-verho** door curtain.

P

-pa, -pä *(loppuliite): jospa (kunpa) tietäisin* if I only knew; *sanopa minulle* just tell me; *lähdetäänpä* let's go; *enpä tiedä* oh, I don't know.

paaduttaa harden [one's heart, *sydämensä*].

paah|de heat [of the sun]. **-din** grill, roaster, *(leivän)* toaster, *(varras-)* [rotating] spit roaster; rotisserie. **-taa** *(kuumentaa)* heat; *(korventaa)* be blazing hot, scorch; *keitt.* grill, [spit-]roast, barbecue; *(leipää)* toast. **-toleipä** toast. **-topaisti** roast beef.

paali *(pakka)* bale, pack.

paalu pile; pole. **-juntta** piledriver. **-rakennus** pile-dwelling. **-ttaa** drive piles (into); *(tontti, raja)* stake [out *t.* off]. **-tus** piling, pile-work. **-varustus** palisade.

paanukatto shingle roof.

paari ~t stretcher, litter; *(ruumis-)* bier. **-nkantaja** stretcher-bearer. **-vaate** [funeral] pall.

paarma gadfly.

paasata rant.

paasi rock face, *(laakea)* flat rock.

paasto fast. **-naika** *kirk.* Lent. **-najan:** *3. ~ sunnuntai* third Sunday in Lent. **-ta** fast.

paatu|a be [come] hardened; *-nut (m.)* unrepentant, obdurate, inveterate. **-mus, -neisuus** hardness [of heart], obduracy.

paavi pope. **-llinen** papal, pontifical; popish. **-nistuin** papal chair, Holy See. **-nvaali** papal election. **-nvalta** papacy.

padota dam [up].

paeta flee; *(päästä pakoon)* escape; *(lähteä pakoon)* take to flight; *~ velkojiaan* run

away from one's creditors; *~ vihollisen tieltä* flee before the enemy.

paha *a.* bad; evil; *(ilkeä)* wicked, *(et. lapsesta)* naughty; *(vaikea)* severe, serious; *s.* evil; *puhua, ajatella ~a jksta* speak (think) ill of a p.; *olla pahoillaan jstk* be sorry [about], *(valittaa)* regret; *panna ~kseen* take it ill, take offence (at), *(kovin)* take it as a personal affront, take a thing to heart; *tehdä ~a jklle* [do a p.] harm, hurt, *(esim. ruoka)* disagree (with); *~a aavistamaton* unsuspecting; *~n päivän varalle ks. vara; on ~sta* will have a bad effect; *hänellä on ~ mielessä* he is up to mischief; *~n ilman lintu (kuv.)* bird of ill omen. **-enteinen** ominous. **-maineinen** notorious. **-maineisuus** notoriety.

pahan|hajuinen bad-smelling, evil- (foul-)smelling, malodorous. **-ilkinen** spiteful, wicked; malicious. **-ilkisyys** malice, spite. **-kurinen** mischievous; unruly. **-laatuinen** *lääk.* malignant. **-laatuisuus** malignancy. **-suopa** ill-disposed; malevolent. **-suopaisuus** ill will, malevolence. **-tapainen** ill-mannered; wicked. **-tekijä** evil-doer, malefactor; *(rikoksen-)* offender. **-teko** evil deed, misdeed; *(ilkivalta)* mischief. **-ntuulinen** bad-tempered,. . in a bad temper.

pahasti *ks. pahoin.*

pahas|tua take it ill, be offended, take offence at; *jollette -tu (m.)* if you don't mind.

pahe vice. **-ellinen** profligate; vicious, depraved. **-ellisuus** immorality.

paheksu|a disapprove (of), view with disfavour, find fault with, *(ankarasti)* deprecate; *-va katse* a glance of reproof. **-nta** disapproval, disapprobation.

pahe|mmin worse. **-mpi** worse; *sen* ~ so much the w. [for him, *hänelle*]; unfortunately. **-nnus** offence; reproach; *~ta herättävä* offensive; scandalous, shocking; *herättää ~ta* give offence. **-ntaa** make.. worse, aggravate; *(huonontaa)* impair. **-ntua** get (grow) worse, be aggravated; *(pilaantua)* be spoiled; *vrt. pilaantua.*

pahin [the] worst; *pahimmassa tapauksessa* if the worst comes to the worst.

pahka lump, node, protuberance; *(puussa ym)* gnarl, gall.

pahnat litter, straw.

pahoi|llaan *olla* ~ be sorry (about), regret.

pahoin badly; *(joskus)* ill; ~ *sairaana* seriously ill; *pelkään* ~, *että..* I am very much afraid that.. **-pidellä** maltreat; assault. **-pitely** maltreatment; *lak.* assault [and battery]; *(lasten)* baby bashing (battering). **-vointi** nausea: *tuntea ~a* feel sick, **-voipa** unwell, indisposed.

pahoi|tella be sorry (for, about), regret, deplore. **-ttaa** *(jkn mieltä)* give offence to, hurt [a p.'s feelings]. **-ttelu** regret.

pah|olainen the Evil One, the devil. **-us** good heavens! darn it! *pahuksen kärpäset* those damned (confounded) flies! **-uus** badness, wickedness, evil.

pahvi [paste]board, cardboard. **-kantinen** *(kirja)* bound in boards. **-rasia** cardboard box, carton.

paidan|kaulus shirt collar. **-nappi** shirt-button; *(irtonainen)* stud. **-rinta** shirt-front.

paikalla at the place, *(itse ~)* on the spot; *(heti)* there and then; immediately, at once, outright; ~ *(paikan päällä) tapahtuva tarkastus* on-site inspection; *~an seisova..* standing still; stationary; *(esim. vesi)* stagnant.

paikallinen local.

paikallis|juna stopping train. **-leima** *kuv.* local colour. **-puudutus** *lääk.* local an[a]esthesia. **-taa** localize, *(paikantaa)* locate; *-tunut* localized. **-tuntemus** local knowledge. **-vaisto** sense (bump) of locality. **-väri** local colour.

paikalta from the place; *poistua* ~ leave [the place *t.* scene, *us.* of the accident].

paikan|hakija applicant. **-määräys** *kiel.* adverb of place. **-nimi** place-name. **-taa** locate. **-välitystoimisto** employment agency.

paikata patch [up]; *(korjata)* mend, repair; *(hammas)* fill, stop.

paikka 1. place; *(tila)* room; *(seutu)* locality; *(kohta)* spot, point; *(sijaitsemis-)* site, situation *(m. palvelus-)*; *(toimi)* position, post, job; *parl. ym.* seat; **2.** patch; *hakea ~a* apply for a job; *on paikallaan* it is proper, it is quite in order; *paikoillaan* in position; *pysyä paikoillaan* stay in place; *asettaa paikoilleen* put in position; *työntää paikoiltaan* displace; *pitää ~nsa* hold good; *se pitää ~nsa* that is so, quite right; *kaupunki on ihanalla paikalla* the town is beautifully situated; *vrt. paikalla.* **-kunnallinen** local. **-kunta** place, locality; neighbourhood, region, parts. **-kunta|lainen** *p-laiset* local people *(t.* residents). **-lippu** seat ticket. **-nsapitämätön** not valid, untenable. **-nsapitävä** tenable; accurate, correct;.. *on* ~.. holds good. **-varaamo** booking-office.

paikkeilla about.

paikoi|n in places; *niillä* ~

something like that,
thereabouts. **-tellen, -ttain** in
[some] places; *(siellä täällä)*
here and there. **-ttaa** park.
-tusalue parking lot.
paimen herdsman; *(yhd.)* **-herd**
(esim. lammas~ shepherd).
-koira sheepdog; *skotlannin~*
collie; *saksan~* Alsatian. **-runo**
pastoral [poem]. **-taa** tend;
et. kuv. shepherd. **-tolainen**
nomad.
paina|a press; *kirjap. & tekn.*
print; *intr.* weigh; ~ *alas*
(m.) force down [prices,
hintoja]; *painettuna* in print;
astia ~ *paljon* the vessel
weighs a great deal, the vessel
is heavy; ~ *mieleen(sä)*
imprint on one's mind,
impress on a p.; *se ajatus* ~
minua that thought weighs on
my mind; *mikä häntä (hänen
mieltään)* ~? what is on her
mind? what is worrying her?
huolten -ma weighed down by
cares, care-worn. **-jai|nen**
nightmare; **-smainen**
nightmarish. **-llus:** *pelkällä
napin -lluksella* at the push
(press) of a button. **-ttaa**
have.. printed. **-tus** printing;
impression. **-utua** press
oneself; *(hellästi jtk vastaan)*
nestle [against, close to];
(toisiinsa) huddle together. **-va**
heavy; weighty; *(tärkeä)*
pressing, momentous; ~*t syyt*
weighty (grave) reasons. **-vuus**
weight [iness].
paine pressure, *kuv. m.* stress.
-ilma compressed air. **-keitin**
pressure cooker.
paini wrestling. **-a** wrestle. **-ja**
wrestler. **-ottelu**
wrestling-match. **-skella** wrestle;
grapple, struggle.
paino weight; *(taakka)* load;
(kirja-) printing press; *(sana-)*
stress, *(korostus, kuv.)*
emphasis; *ilmestyä* ~*sta*
appear in print; ~*ssa* in
[the] press; *panna* ~*a
(sanoihinsa)* lay emphasis on,
emphasize [one's words];
panna jhk suurta ~*a* attach
great weight (importance) to.
-arkki printed sheet. **-inen:**

jnk ~.. weighing.. **-kanne**
action for libel [against a
newspaper]. **-kas** emphatic.
-kirjain block letter. **-kkaasti**
with emphasis; emphatically,
forcibly. **-kkuus** emphasis.
-kone printing press. **-kunto:**
-kunnossa ready for the press.
-kustannukset cost of printing.
-laki *fys.* law of gravity. **-lasti**
ballast, *kuv.* burden. **-llinen**
stressed. **-muste** printing ink.
-nappi press-stud, *Am.* snap
fastener. **-nasta** drawing-pin.
-nnosto weight-lifting.
-nvähennys loss of weight.
-paikka place of printing.
-piste centre of gravity.
painos edition; impression;
uusi ~ *(korjaamaton)* printing;
eri ~ reprint; *parannettu* ~
(kuv.) improved version. **-staa**
press [sb. to do sth.], put
pressure on, bring pressure to
bear on; *(ahdistaa)* oppress,
weigh on sb.'s mind; ~ *jkta
vastaamaan* press sb. for an
answer; **-stava** oppressive;
sultry. **-stunut** depressed. **-stus**
pressure; *harjoittaa* ~*ta* bring
pressure [to bear] on a p.;
(~**ryhmä** pressure group). **-ton**
weightless, imponderable, *kiel.*
unstressed. **-staa** stress.
-ttomuu|s: *p-den tila*
weightlessness, zero gravity.
-tuote: *-tuotteet* printed matter
(t. papers). **-valmis** ready for
the press. **-vapaus** freedom of
the press. **-virhe** misprint;
~*iden luettelo* errata. **-voima**
gravity, force of gravitation.
-vuosi year of publication.
-yksikkö unit of weight.
painu|a sink; settle; droop;
(laskea) drop; *(veden alle)*
submerge; *(kokoon)* collapse;
~ *mieleen* imprint (fix) itself
in the mind; ~ *muistiin* be
impressed on the memory;
pää -neena with drooping
head. **-ksissa** *(mieliala)*
depressed; *(käheä)* hoarse.
-ma depression.
paise boil, abscess.
paiskata throw, fling;
(singahduttaa) hurl, toss,
send.. flying; ~ *(ovi)* kiinni

slam [the door], shut [the door] with a bang.
paist|aa 1. (*loistaa*) shine; 2. *tr.* roast, (*uunissa, m.*) bake; (*pannussa*) fry; (*paahtaa*) grill; (*tulella*) broil; *liiaksi -ettu* overdone. **-atella:** ~ *päivää* bask in the sun, sun oneself. **-e** shine, glare.
paisti roast; (*-pala*) joint [of beef etc.]. **-npannu** frying-pan. **-nrasva** cooking-fat. **-nuuni** oven.
paist|okelmu [transparent] baking wrap. **-os** baked dish, pie. **-ua** be roasted, be roasting *jne.; hyvin -unut* well (*t.* evenly) baked, (*liian vähän*) underbaked, underdone.
paisu|a swell; (*laajeta*) expand; *-u ylpeydestä* swells with pride; *-nut* swollen. **-ma** swelling. **-ttaa** swell; *kuv.* exaggerate.
paita shirt; (*naisen*) vest. **-hihasillaan** in one's shirt-sleeves. **-kangas** shirting.
paitsi except, excepting, except for; apart from; (*joskus*) save; but; (*jnk lisäksi*) besides; *jota* ~ besides which; *kaikki* ~ *kolme* all but three.
paitsio *urh.* offside.
paja (*sepän*) smithy; (*työ-*) workshop.
pajatso clown, buffoon; (*peli-*) coin machine.
paju willow, osier. **-kuoppa** wicker basket. **-lintu** willow warbler. **-nköysi:** *syöttää -nköyttä* draw the long bow, pull [sb.'s] nose, kid.
pakahtua burst; break; *olin* ~ *nauruun* I nearly burst [my sides] with laughter; *sydämeni oli* ~ I thought my heart would break.
pakana heathen, pagan. **-kansa** heathen people. **-llinen** heathen, pagan. **-maailma** heathendom.
pakanuus heathenism, paganism.
pakarat buttocks.
pakas|taa freeze. **-e:** ~*et* frozen foods. **-ettu** frozen; ~ *kala* [prepacked] frozen fish. **-tin** freezer.
paka|ta pack; *-ten täynnä* packed (with), chock-full; ~ *tavaransa* pack [up] one's things; *kauniisti -ttuna* decoratively wrapped up.
paketti parcel, packet; (*pikku-*) small package; *kuv.* (= *nippu*) package; *lahja* ~ gift parcel; *panna* ~*in* wrap .. up. **-auto** [delivery] van. **-laiva** packet boat. **-osoitekortti** address card [accompanying a parcel]. **-paperi** wrapping [paper]. **-posti** parcel post. **-ratkaisu** package deal. **-toimisto** parcels office.
paki|na chat, talk; (*sanomalehden*) causerie. **-noida** [have a] chat (with). **-noitsija** causerie writer, columnist. **-sta** chat.
Pakistan: ~*in hallitus* the Pakistani government. *p~ilai|nen* Pakistani; *p-set* the Pakistanis.
pakka bundle, pack; (*kangasta*) roll. **-huone** [customs] warehouse.
pakka|nen cold, frost; *on* ~ it is freezing. **-saste** degree of frost. **-skausi** cold period. **-slokero, -ssäilö** freezer. **-sneste** antifreeze. **-ssää** sub-zero weather.
pakkaus packing; package. **-laatikko** packing case, box.
pakko compulsion, constraint; (*tarve*) necessity; (*väkivalta*) force; *käyttää* ~*a* use force; *hänen oli* ~ *lähteä* he was compelled (forced) to leave, he had to leave, he was obliged to go; *pakosta* from necessity, under compulsion. **-huutokauppa** compulsory auction. **-keino** coercion, force. **-lasku** *ilm.* forced landing, emergency landing. **-lomauttaa** lay off. **-lunastaa** purchase compulsorily, expropriate. **-lunastus** compulsory purchase; expropriation (*m.* = *pakko-otto*). **-mielle** obsession. **-paita** strait-jacket. **-syöttö** forced feeding. **-toimen|pide:** *ryhtyä p-piteisiin* resort to force, (*äärimmäisiin* to extremes). **-työ** hard

labour, penal servitude; (~**leiri**
forced labour camp). -**verottaa**
levy tribute on, raise a levy.
pako flight; escape; *ajaa ~on*
put. . to flight; *lähteä ~on*
take to flight; *päästä ~on*
escape. -**illa** keep in hiding;
avoid. -**kaasu** exhaust fumes.
-**kauhu** panic; *yleisö joutui
~n valtaan* the audience was
panic-stricken. -**lainen** refugee;
(pakeneva) fugitive.
pakolais|hallitus government in
exile. -**kysymys**, -**leiri** refugee
problem (camp).
pakolli|nen compulsory;
enforced, obligatory. -**sesti** by
compulsion, forcibly.
pako|paikka [place of] refuge;
shelter. -**putki** exhaust pipe.
-**retki** flight. -**stakin:** ~ *on. .*
there is (are) bound to be. .
pako|te -*tteet* sanctions. -**ton**
unconstrained; free, voluntary.
-**ttaa** force, compel, constrain;
(saada) make; bring [oneself
to do a th. *itsensä jhk*];
(metallia) beat, emboss;
(särkeä) ache; ~ *jku
tunnustamaan* force (wring) a
confession from a p.; -*ttava*
compulsive, imperative; -*ttava
tarve* urgent need; -*ttavat syyt*
compelling reasons. -**tus**
compulsion; *(kipu)* ache, pain.
pakovesi ebb, low tide.
paksu thick; dense;
(ruumiiltaan) stout; ~ *takki
(m.)* a heavy coat; ~ *sumu*
thick (dense) fog. -**inen:**
kahden tuuman ~ two inches
thick (in thickness). -**kuorinen**
thick-skinned; *(esim. muna)*
thick-shelled. -**nahkainen**
thick-skinned. -**ntaa** make. .
thicker, thicken. -**pohjainen**
(-anturainen) thick-soled,
heavy-soled. -**päinen**
thick-headed, thick-witted.
-**suoli** large intestine. -**ta**
become thicker, thicken. -**us**
thickness *jne.*
▶ala bit, piece; *(esim. liha-)*
cut [of meat], *(paksu)* chunk;
(saippua) tablet; *(esim.
sokeri-)* lump; ~ ~*lta* piece
by piece, bit by bit,
piecemeal.

pala|a burn; *(olla tulessa)* be
on fire; ~ *loppuun* burn out;
~ *poroksi* burn down; *mieleni
~ sinne* I long (yearn) to go
there; -*nut bussi (ym)*
burnt-out bus. -**minen** burning;
kem. combustion.
pala|nen bit, [little] piece;
fragment; lump [of sugar].
-**peli** jig-saw puzzle. -**sokeri**
lump sugar.
palat|a return, come back, get
back; recur [to a p.,
mieleen]; revert [to the
subject, *aineeseen*]; *(astua
jälleen)* re-enter; ~ *työhönsä*
resume one's work, go back
to one's work; *kotiin -tuani*
after my return home, when
I am back home.
palatsi palace. -**mainen** palatial.
palauttaa return; restore;
send. . back; ~ *ennalleen*
restore [to its former
condition], reestablish; ~
mieleen recall, call to mind;
~ *jkn kunnia* rehabilitate a p.
palava burning; ardent; ~
innostus glowing enthusiasm;
~ *rukous* fervent prayer; ~*t
aineet* combustibles.
pale|lla be cold, be freezing;
feel chilly. -**lluttaa** freeze.
-**ltua** freeze; *poskeni ovat
-ltuneet* my cheeks are
frost-bitten; -*ltunut* frozen,
injured by frost. -**ltuma**
frostbite.
Palestiina Palestine; *p~lainen
a.* Palestine, Palestinian; *s.*
Palestinian.
paletti *(värilasta)* palette.
palikka stick; *(leikki-)* brick.
paljas bare, uncovered; naked;
(kalju) bald; *(pelkkä)* mere; ~
taivas open sky; *paljaalla
silmällä* with the naked eye;
paljain päin, *jaloin*
bare-headed, barefoot [ed]; ~*ta
lorua* sheer nonsense.
-**jalkainen** barefoot [ed]; *kuv.*
born and bred (in). -**taa**
uncover, bare; *kuv.* lay. .
bare, expose; *(jnk laatu)*
show. . up [for what it is];
(muistopatsas) unveil;
(ilmaista) reveal, disclose;
(miekka) draw; *vaatia jkta*

-*tamaan aikeensa* call for a show-down. **-tua** be exposed; be revealed. **-tus** exposure; *(muistopatsaan)* unveiling; *(ilmituonti)* disclosure.
palje: *palkeet* bellows.
paletti sequin.
paljo|n much, many; *(et. myönt. laus.)* a lot of; plenty of; *(komp. edessä, m.)* far [better, *parempi*]; *aika ~* quite a lot (of); *aivan liian ~* far too much, too many by far; *~ko* how much? *(.. kello on?)* what is the time? *~ puhuva* meaning [look, *katse*]. **-us** quantity, great number [s]; volume, mass, multitude.
palkan|korotus wage increase, pay rise; salary increase; *sain -korotuksen (Am.)* I had a raise. **-nauttija** salaried person; wage-earner. **-pidätys** stoppage; *(veron-)* tax deduction; *ks. pidätys.*
palka|ta hire; engage [a p. for]. **-ton** unsalaried, unpaid. **-ttomasti** without pay; without a reward. **-ttu** salaried, paid.
palkinnonsaaja prize-winner.
palkinto prize; *(korvaus)* reward; *saada ~* win (be awarded) a prize; *~jen jako* prize-giving. **-lautakunta** judging committee. **-obligaatio** government bond, *Engl.* premium bond. **-palli** *urh.* winners' rostrum. **-tuomari** judge.
palkita reward; *(kilpailussa)* award a prize (to); *(hyvittää)* recompense, repay; *~ paha hyvällä* requite evil with good.
palkka salary, *(ruum. työstä)* wages; pay; *(palkinto)* reward; earnings; *(palkinto)* reward; *sama ~ ks. sama.* **-asteikko** wage-scale. **-ehdot** terms of employment. **-kiista** pay dispute. **-lainen** hired man, hireling. **-luokka** wage *(t. salary)* class. **-lista** payroll; wages-sheet. **-neuvottelut** pay talks. **-politiikka** pay policy. **-pussi** pay-packet. **-ratkaisu** wage settlement. **-sopimus** wage agreement. **-soturi**

mercenary. **-taso** level of wages. **-työläinen** wage earner, worker. **-us** wages, salary; payment **-vaatimu|s** pay claim, wage claim (demand); *ilmoittaa -ksensa* state [the] salary required.
palkki beam, baulk.
palkkio *(lääkärin, asianajajan ym)* fee; *(hyvitys-)* bonus; *(tekijä-)* royalty; *(korvaus)* reward.
palko pod, legume. **-kasvi** leguminous plant.
palkollinen servant, hired man.
pallas *zo.* halibut.
palle hem, border.
pallea diaphragm, midriff.
pallero toddler; *~ikäisille* for toddlers.
palli stool.
pallo ball; *(kuula)* bowl; *mat.* sphere. **-illa** play ball. **-ilu** playing ball. **-kartta** globe. **-nmuotoinen** spherical, globular. **-npuolisko** hemisphere. **-peli** ball game. **-salama** ball lightning.
palmi|kko, -koida plait.
palmu palm. **-sunnuntai** Palm Sunday.
palo fire; *(suuri, m.)* conflagration. **-auto** fire-engine. **-haava** burn; *(veden, höyryn aiheuttama)* scald. **-hälytys** fire-alarm.
paloi|tella cut up; *(jakaa)* divide.. up; *(tonteiksi)* parcel out. **-ttelu** cutting up; partitioning.
palo|kalusto fire-fighting equipment. **-katselmus** fire inspection. **-kello** fire-alarm. **-kunnantalo** fire-station. **-kunta** fire-brigade; fire service. **-kuntalainen** fireman. **-muuri** fire-proof wall.
palon|sammutus, -torjunta fire-fighting; *(~harjoitus* fire-drill).
palo|pommi incendiary bomb. **-posti** hydrant, fireplug. **-puhe** inflammatory speech. **-päällikkö** fire chief. **-ruisku** fire-engine. **-sotilas** fireman. **-tikkaat** fire-escape. **-torni** fire-station tower. **-vahinko** damage by fire. **-vakuuttaa**

insure against fire. **-vakuutus** fire-insurance; (~**yhtiö** fire-insurance company). **-viina** spirits. **-öljy** paraffin [oil], *Am.* kerosene.

palst|a parcel [of land], plot, site; *(kirjan ym)* column. **-akorrehtuuri** galley proof. **-atila** small farm. **-oittaa** parcel [out], divide into lots.

palttaa hem.

palsternakka parsnip.

palttina linen.

palttu black-pudding; *antaa ~a jllle* not care a fig (a hoot) about. .

palturi: *puhua ~a* talk nonsense.

paluu return. **-lippu:** *meno- ja ~* return *(Am.* round-trip) ticket. **-matka** return journey; way back; *lähteä ~lle* start back, start for home. **-posti:** *~ssa* by return [of post]. **-tie** way back.

palvata cure.

palve|levainen obliging, eager to help. **-lija** servant; (~*tar*) domestic [servant], maid; *kirkon ~* minister of the church. **-lla** serve; attend on *(asiakasta* to); *(pöydässä)* wait on; *(Jumalaa)* worship; *miten voin ~* how can I help you; *valmiina (teitä) -lemaan* at your service; *joko Teitä ~an?* are you being attended to? **-lu** service; (~**ammatti** service occupation; ~**raha** tip; ~**talo** block of service flats, *Am.* apartment hotel).

palvelu|s service; employment; duty; *ilmoittautua -kseen* report to duty; *-ksesta vapaa(na)* off duty; *-kseen halutaan* situations vacant, *Am.* help wanted; *olla jkn -ksessa* be in a p.'s service (employ), be employed by a p.; *ottaa jku -kseensa* take. . into one's employment, engage; *tehdä jklle ~* do (render) a p. a service, do a p. a favour; **-kseenastumismääräys** draft card.

palvelus|koira working dog.

-kunta staff of servants. **-paikka** situation, place. **-todistus** testimonial. **-tyttö** maid. **-väki** servants.

palvo|a worship; adore. **-ja** worshipper. **-nta** worship; adoration.

pamah|dus bang; *vrt. seur.* **-taa** *(ovi)* bang; *laukaus -ti* a gun was fired, *(kuului)* a report was heard.

pamfletti pamphlet.

pamppailla throb, beat.

pamppu truncheon, staff; *(puhek., esim. teollisuus~)* tycoon.

paneeli panel[ling], wainscot[ing]. **-keskustelu** *ks. koroke-.*

pane|tella slander; backbite, malign; *-tteleva* slanderous. **-ttelu** slander.

panimo brewery.

pankin|johtaja [bank] manager. **-kamreeri** bank accountant. **-ryöstö** bank robbery.

pankki bank;. . *on rahaa pankissa. .* has money in the b.; *ottaa rahaa pankista* withdraw from the b.; *panna ~in* deposit at the bank; *hoitaa ~asiansa jssk* bank at (in). **-iri** banker; ~*liike* banking-house. **-kirja** bankbook, passbook. **-korko** bank rate of interest. **-liike** banking. **-osake** bank share. **-saldo** bank balance. **-siirto** bank giro service. **-talletus** deposit. **-tili** bank account. **-valtuusmies** supervisor of government bank [appointed by parliament]. **-virkailija** bank official, bank clerk.

panna 1. *(asettaa)* put, set, place; *(tav. pitkälleen)* lay; *(jku tekemään jtk)* get (a p. to . .), make (a p.. .), cause (a p. to do sth.); ~ *kiinni* fasten; *(sulkea)* close; ~ *alkuun* initiate; introduce [a habit, *tapa*], *(kuv.)* launch; *olutta* ~ brew beer; ~ *sanomalehteen* put (insert) in a newspaper; ~ *toimeen* execute, effect, carry out; ~ *vastaan* raise objections; ~ *ylleen, päähänsä* put on; *mitä* *aiot ~ yllesi* what are you going to wear? *panee arvelemaan* makes one hesitate.

panna 2. *s.* ban, excommunication; *julistaa ~an* excommunicate; *(kieltää)* prohibit, ban.

pannu pan; pot; *(höyrykattila)* boiler; *kahvi ~* coffee-pot; *vesi~* kettle. **-huone** boiler-room, boiler-house. **-kakku** [thick] pancake, batter pudding; *siitä tuli ~* it fell flat.

pano *(pankkiin)* deposit.

panos contribution, *(pelissä)* stake; *(pyssyn)* charge; round. **-taa** charge, load.

panssari armour. **-auto** armoured car. **-levy** armour-plate. **-paita** coat of mail. **-torjuntaraketti** anti-tank rocket. **-torjuntatykki** anti-tank gun. **-vaunu** tank.

panssaroi|da armour; *-tu* armoured, ironclad.

pantata pawn.

pantomiimi dumb show. **-taiteilija** mimer.

pantteri panther, leopard.

pantti pawn; pledge; *(kiinteistö-)* mortgage; *(takuu)* security; *(leikeissä-* forfeit; *lunastaa ~* redeem a pledge; *antaa, jättää pantiksi* pledge, leave as a pledge, lodge as a security; *panen pääni pantiksi!* I'll stake my head [on it]! **-kuitti** pawn-ticket. **-laina** pawn-money; *(~konttori* pawnbroker's office; *~laitos* pawnshop; *~liike* pawnbroking). **-leikki** game of forfeits. **-vanki** hostage; *ottaa -vangiksi* seize as a hostage.

paperi paper; *panna ~lle* commit to p., write down. **-arkki** sheet of paper. **-kauppa** stationer's [shop]. **-kauppias** stationer. **-kone** paper machine. **-kori** waste-paper basket. **-lippu** slip of paper. **-massa** *ks. -vanuke.* **-nen** [. .of] paper. **-nvalmistus** paper manufacture. **-palanen** bit (scrap) of paper. **-pussi** paper bag. **-puu** pulp

wood. **-raha** paper money, paper currency. **-tehdas** paper mill. **-teollisuus** paper industry. **-vanuke** paper pulp. **-veitsi** paperknife.

paperoida paper.

papiksivihkiminen ordination.

papiljotti curler, curling-pin.

papillinen clerical; priestly.

papin|todistus extract from the church register; *(syntymä-)* birth certificate. **-vaali** church election. **-virka** ministry.

pappi clergyman, pastor; chaplain, *(ei anglikaanisen kirkon)* minister; *(et. katol.)* priest. **-la** rectory, vicarage, *Skotl.* manse. **-smies** clergyman, ecclesiastic. **-sseminaari** theological college, seminary. **-ssääty** clergy; *(katol.)* the holy orders.

papu bean; *(herne)* pea.

papukaija parrot; *laulu~ ks. undulaatti.*

paraati parade; *(ohimarssi)* march-past; *ottaa vastaan ~* take the salute. **-puku** *sot.* full-dress uniform.

paradoksaalinen paradoxical.

parafiini paraffin wax. **-öljy** *(puhdistettu)* [medicinal] paraffin.

parafoida initial.

para(h)iksi just right; *~ pitkä, suuri* [just] the right length (size); *se on hänelle ~* it serves him right; *tulin kotiin ~ illalliselle* I came home just in time for dinner.

par|aikaa, -aillaan just; just now; *~ kestävä (pidettävä) . .* now in progress; *vrt. parhaillaan.*

parakki hut.

parane|maton *(taudista)* incurable. **-minen** recovery.

paran|nella *ks. parantaa; (esim. kirjaa)* revise, edit, *(taideteosta ym)* retouch, touch up. **-nus** improvement; betterment; *usk.* repentance; *lääk.* cure; *(henko-)* remedy; *tehdä ~* become a reformed character; *(~keino* remedy, cure). **-taa** improve; ameliorate, amend; *(tauti)* cure, heal; *(poistaa vika)* remedy; ~ *tapansa* mend one's ways; ~ *tietojaan* improve one's knowledge; *se ei -na asiaa* it does not help (improve) matters; *-nettavissa (oleva)* curable; remediable. **-taja** healer; *yhteiskunnan* ~ reformer. **-tola** sanator|ium *(pl. -ia)*. **-tua** get better, improve; *(toipua)* recover, get well, *(esim. haava)* heal; *ks. parata.* **-tumaton** incorrigible, *(tauti)* incurable. **-tuminen** improvement; recovery.

paras best; *tehdä parhaansa* do one's best, try one's [very] best; *parhaansa mukaan* to the best of one's ability; *katsoa parhaaksi* think it best; *sinun olisi ~(ta) lähteä* you had better go; *en parhaalla tahdollanikaan voinut* no matter how hard I tried I could not; *parhaassa tapauksessa* at best.

par(ast)aikaa just now (then).

para *ks. -ntua; toivottavasti -net pian* I hope you soon get well again.

paratiisi paradise. **-lintu** bird of paradise.

paratyyfus paratyphoid.

paremmanpuoleinen fairly good.

parem|min better; *hän ei käsitä tätä sen ~ kuin minäkään* he does not understand it any more than I do. **-muus** superiority, superior (better) quality. **-pi** better; *(laadultaan)* superior; *(muutos) -paan päin* [a change] for the better; *pitää jtk (jtk muuta) -pana* prefer .. (to); *-pana pidettävä* preferable (to); *sen, sitä ~* so much the better; *olla ~* be superior (to), surpass; *(~osainen.. in better circumstances,.. better off, well off).

parh|aastaan mostly, for the most part; chiefly. **-aillaan** just now, [just] at the time; *hän ~ lounasti* he was having lunch. **-aimmillaan** at one's (its) best. **-aimmisto** élite; the flower (of). **-aiten** best.

pari *(kenkä- ym)* pair;

(muuten) couple; *avio~* married couple; ~ *päivää* a couple of days, a day or two; *kaksi ~a hansikkaita* two pairs of gloves; *missä on tämän hansikkaan ~* where is the other glove; *ihmisten ~ssa* among people; *kaksi kenkää (jotka ovat) eri ~a* two odd shoes.

pari | **arvo** par value, face value. **-kurssi** ~*in* at par.

Pariisi Paris. **p-lainen, p-tar** Parisian.

parikymmentä a score of. ., about twenty.

parila gridiron; grill.

parillinen.. forming a pair; *(tasainen)* even [number, luku].

pariloi|da broil, roast; *-tu (m.)* barbecued [steak *pihvi*].

pari|nen: *-sen viikkoa* a couple of weeks. **-ovi** double door, folding door. **-puoli** odd. **-sataa** about two hundred. **-skunta** married couple. **-sto** *fys.* battery. **-tella** copulate, *(eläimestä, m.)* mate. **-ton** odd. **-ttaa** mate; procure. **-ttain** in pairs, in couples; two by two. **-ttaja** procurer, *(nainen)* procuress, bawd. **-ttelu** copulation. **-utua** pair [off], mate. **-utumisaika** mating season. **-valjakko** span [of horses].

parja|ta defame; slander; malign; *-ttu* much-maligned. **-us** slander, abuse; *(~kirjoitus* libel, libellous article).

parka *a.* poor; *s.* poor fellow; *(naisesta, lapsesta)* poor thing.

parkai|sta cry out; [give a] scream; shriek. **-su** cry; scream, shriek.

parketti parquet. **-lattia** parquet floor.

parkita tan.

parkki *(kuori)* bark; *(laiva)* barque. **-happo** tannic acid, tannin. **-intua** be tanned *(kuv.* hardened).

parku screaming; howl [ing]. **-a** bawl, *(kirkua)* scream, *(ulvoa)* howl.

parlamen|taarikko parliamentarian. **-taarinen**

parliamentary. **-tarismi**
parliamentarianism. **-tti**
parliament; *-tin jäsen* member
of parliament *(lyh.* M.P.):
(**~rakennus** parliament
building; *Engl.* Houses of
Parliament).
parodi|a, -oida parody.
paroni baron. **-tar** baroness.
parra|kas bearded. **-najo**
shaving; a shave; (**~kone**
safety-razor, electric shaver;
~välineet shaving outfit).
-nkasvu growth of beard.
-nsänki stubble.
parras brink, verge *(et. kuv.);*
edge; *(astian)* brim; *(aluksen)*
rail; *jyrkänteen partaalla* on
the brink (edge) of a
precipice; *olla haudan*
partaalla have one foot in
the grave; *perikadon partaalla*
on the verge of ruin. **-valo**
footlight; *joutua ~on (kuv.)*
come into the limelight.
parraton beardless.
parru small square timber; *~t*
(liik.) balks, beams.
parsa asparagus.
parsi|a darn; *(korjata)* mend.
-nlanka darning-cotton,
(villainen) darning-wool.
-nneula darning-needle.
parta beard; *ajaa ~(nsa)* shave.
-saippua shaving-soap. **-suti**
shaving-brush. **-vaahdoke**
shaving-cream. **-veitsi** razor.
-vesi shaving lotion.
partio *sot.* patrol. **-johtaja**
scout-master. **-lainen** scout.
-puku scout uniform. **-poika**
boy scout. **-päällikkö** chief
scout. **-retki** excursion; *sot.*
commando raid [behind the
enemy lines]. **-tyttö** girl
guide, *Am.* girl scout. **-työ**
scouting.
parti|saani guer[r]illa. **-siippi**
participle. **-tuuri** score.
parturi barber. **-liike** barber's
shop.
parveilla *(esim. kaloista)* shoal;
(mehiläisistä) swarm; *(linnuista*
ym) flock.
parveke balcony; *teatt.* circle;
ylin ~ gallery. **-paikka** seat
in the balcony (circle
t. gallery), *vrt. seur.*

parvi 1. swarm; *(lintu- ym)*
flock; *(kala-)* shoal, school;
(joukko) crowd; *(teatt.) ks.*
ed.; ensi~ dress circle. **2.**
(ullakko) garret, attic.
pasaatituuli trade-wind.
pasianssi patience.
pasma *(lanka-)* skein.
passata *(jkta)* fetch and carry
for, wait [hand and foot] on.
(korttip.) pass.
passi passport; *antaa ~ (jklle)*
issue a p. (to).
passiivi passive [voice].
-muoto passive [form]. **-nen**
passive. **-suus** passivity.
passi|maksu passport fee.
-ntarkastus examination of
passports. **-pakko** compulsory
passport system. **-toimisto**
passport office, alien office.
-ttaa send.
pastelli pastel. **-maalaus** pastel
drawing. **-väri** pastel colour.
pastilli lozenge, pastil[le].
pastori pastor, parson,
minister; *(esim. kirjeessä,*
nimen ed.) Rev. *(lyh. =*
reverend).
pastöroida pasteurize.
pasuuna trombone.
pata pot; *(-kortti)* spade,
(-maa) spades. **-juoppo** chronic
drinker. **-kortti** spade. **-lappu**
kettle-holder. **-rouva** queen of
spades. **-suti** scourer.
pataljoona battalion.
pata|paisti braised joint.
-rumpu kettledrum. **-ässä** ace
of spades.
pateettinen high-flown,
(liikuttava) pathetic.
patent|inhaltija patentee. **-oitu**
patented.
patentti patent; *saada, ottaa ~*
jllek obtain (take out) a p.
for.. **-anomus** application for
a patent. **-kirja** letters patent.
-lääke patent (proprietary)
medicine. **-toimisto** patent
agency. **-virasto** patent office.
patikkaretki hiking tour.
patja mattress. **-kangas**
tick[ing]. **-npäällinen** tick.
pato dam; barrage; *(suoja-)*
dike, dyke, embankment.
patologi pathologist. **-a**
pathology. **-nen** pathologic[al].

pato|luukku sluice [-gate].
-utua be dammed; *-utunut*
(esim. tunne) pent-up, repressed.
patriarkka patriarch.
patriisi patrician.
patruuna cartridge. **-vyö**
cartridge-belt.
patsas statue; *(pylväs)* pillar;
column; *(puu-)* post.
patteri *sot.* battery; *(lämpö-)*
radiator.
patti spavin; *(šakkip.)*
stalemate.
patukka truncheon, staff.
pauh|ata roar; rumble. **-ina, -u**
roll; rumble; din, noise.
paukah|dus bang, *(pamaus)*
report. **-taa** *ks. pamahtaa;* ~
kiinni shut with a bang.
pauke noise, din; *tykkien* ~
roar (booming) of guns,
cannonade.
paukku|a crack; *(ryskää)* crash;
on -va pakkanen it is bitterly
cold. **-panos** blank cartridge.
paukuttaa *(ovia ym)* bang,
slam; ~ *käsiään* clap one's
hands.
paul|a *(nyöri)* string, *(kengän
ym)* lace; *(ansa)* snare, trap;
saada jku -oihinsa get a p.
in one's toils; *(~kenkä* laced
shoe.). **-oittaa** lace up; tie up.
paussi rest, pause.
paviaani *zo.* baboon.
paviljonki pavilion.
pedaali *(poljin)* pedal.
pedago|gi educationalist. **-giikka**
pedagogy, pedagogics.
pegamoidi leatherette.
pehku(t) litter.
pehme|ntää make.. soft [er],
soften. **-tä** soften, become
soft[er]; *(heltyä)* relent. **-ys**
softness *jne.* **-ä** soft; *(hento)*
tender; *~t kannet (kirjan)*
limp covers; *tehdä* ~ *lasku*
soft-land; ~ *maa* loose soil.
pehm|ike cushion, pad. **-ittää**
soften; *kuv. (piestä)* lick,
beat. **-itä** soften. **-ustaa**
cushion, pad, upholster. **-uste**
padding.
pehtori steward, bailiff.
peijakas darn it!
peikko [hob]goblin, troll,
(mörkö) bugbear.
peilata *mer.* take the bearings.

peili looking-glass; mirror.
-kirkas glassy [surface, *pinta*].
-kuva mirror image;
reflection. **-lasi** plate glass.
peipponen chaffinch.
peite cover [ing], coat, cloak;
(vuode-) quilt; *(untuva-)*
eiderdown, downie; *(huopa)*
blanket.
peite|llä cover [up]; conceal,
hide; *(lapsi)* tuck up [in bed] ;
~ *jkn vikoja* gloss over. .'s
faults; *peittelemättä* unreser-
vedly; *(suoraan)* in plain words,
straight out.
peitenimi code name.
peitsi spear; lance, pike.
peitte|inen: *lumi*~ covered
with snow, snow-covered.
-lemätön undisguised, plain;
(avomielinen) unreserved,
frank.
pei|tto cover [ing]; *vrt. peite;
olla jnk peitossa* be covered
(by *t.* with). **-ttyä** become
covered (with); be wrapped
[up] (in); be coated (with).
-ttää cover, cover up;
(verhota) envelop; *kuv.*
disguise, cloak; *tekn.* coat; ~
jk näkymästä hide.. from
view; *se* ~ *menot* it covers
the expenses.
pekoni bacon.
pelaaja player.
pelargoni geranium.
pelas|taa save; *(vaarasta ym)*
rescue [from drowning,
hukkumasta], *(tavaraa)*
salvage. **-taja** rescuer. **-tautua**
save oneself. **-tua** be saved;
escape; be delivered (from).
pelastus rescue (from); *mer. ym*
salvage; *(vapahdus)* salvation.
-armeija Salvation Army.
-keino [means of] rescue.
-köysi life-line. **-laite**
life-saving apparatus. **-miehistö**
mer. lifeboat crew, *(tavaran)*
salvage men. **-rengas** *(-poiju)*
life-buoy; *vrt. -vyö.* **-toiminta,**
-työ rescue work (operations),
(tavaran) salvage work. **-vene**
lifeboat. **-vyö** life-belt,
cork jacket. **-yhtiö** salvage
company.
pelata play; *(uhkapeliä)*
gamble; ~ *korttia* play cards;

menettää pelaamalla gamble away.

peli game; *(leikki)* play; *(ottelu)* match; *panna ~in* stake. **-erä** round. **-himo** passion for gambling.

pelikaani *zo.* pelican.

peli|kortti [playing-] card. **-kumppani** partner. **-luola** gaming club, gambling hall (den). **-markka** chip, counter. **-nappula** man, piece. **-seura** card party. **-velka** gambling debt. **-voitto** winnings at cards.

pelkistää *kem.* reduce.

pelkkä mere, nothing but; *(puhdas)* pure; sheer; *minulla on ollut ~ä iloa hänestä* he has brought me nothing but joy; *~ä pötyä* sheer nonsense.

pelk|o fear, dread; apprehension; *(pelästys)* fright; *jnk pelosta* for fear of; *olla peloissaan* be afraid, be frightened, *(jnk puolesta)* be afraid for, be anxious about; *herättää ~a jkssa* inspire. . with fear. **-uri** coward; *(~mainen* cowardly; *~maisuus* cowardliness). **-uruus** cowardice.

pelkästään merely, only; simply; *~ jo. . syystä* if for no other reason than. .

pelkää|mättä without fear, fearlessly. **-mätön** fearless.

pellava flax; *(liina)* linen. **-inen** flax [en]; linen. **-lanka** linen thread. **-nsiemen** flax seed, *lääk.* linseed. **-pää** flaxen-haired child. **-tehdas** linen factory. **-tukka** flaxen hair. **-öljy** linseed oil.

pelle, **-illä** clown, lark about. **-ily** larking.

pelo|kas timid, timorous; fearful, apprehensive. **-kkuus** timidity. **-naihe** cause for alarm. **-nsekainen** mingled with fear; *-tella* give. . a fright; *ei antanut itseään ~* refused to be intimidated. **-ton** undaunted, undismayed, fearless, intrepid.

pelott|aa frighten, scare; *(säikähdyttää)* startle; *(tekemästä jtk)* deter (from +

-ing); *(synnyttää pelkoa jkssa)* inspire. . with fear, intimidate, *(kunnioituksen sekaista)* fill with awe, *(kauhistuttaa)* terrify; *minua ~* I am afraid, I feel frightened, I dread [to go there, *mennä sinne*]; *-ava* frightening; terrifying.

pelottelu scaring, intimidation. **-ase**, **-keino** deterrent.

pelottomuus fearlessness.

pelti *(levy)* plate, *(ohut)* sheet *(esim. rauta~* sheet-iron); *(uunin)* damper. **-katto** galvanized iron roof. **-rasia** tin, *Am.* can. **-seppä** tinsmith, sheet-iron worker.

pelto field; *(-maa)* cultivated ground; *ajaa jku pellolle* turn. . out; *heittää pellolle (kuv.)* chuck [it] out. **-hiiri** [striped] fieldmouse. **-kana** partridge. **-maa** arable land. **-pyy** *ks. -kana* **-tilkku** patch.

peluri gambler.

peläs|tys fright. **-tyttää** frighten, scare. **-tyä** be (get) frightened, be scared, take fright; *-tynyt* frightened, scared; startled.

pelätä fear; be afraid, *jtk* of; *~ henkeään* be (go) in fear of one's life; *hän pelkäsi putoavansa* he was afraid of falling; *on pelättävissä, että. .* it is to be feared that; *älä pelkää* don't be frightened! *pelkäänpä, että niin on* I am afraid so; *(kahden miehen) pelätään kuolleen* are feared dead.

penger bank, embankment, *(pato)* dike; *(~mä)* terrace; *rata~* railway embankment. **-mä** terrace. **-mäinen** terraced. **-rys** embankment. **-tää** bank up, embank; terrace.

peni|kka *(koiran)* puppy, pup; *(karhun, leijonan ym)* cub; *(~mainen* puppyish; *~tauti* distemper). **-koida** whelp.

peninkulma 10 kilometres, league.

penisilliini penicillin.

penkki bench, seat; *(kirkon-)* pew. **-rivi** row [of benches], *(kohoava)* tier [of seats]. **-urheilija** sports fan.

penkoa rummage (in), *(tonkia)*

grub (in), (esim. taskuja)
fumble (in).

penni penny (pl. pence,
pennies). **-tön** penniless.

pensai|kko thicket [of bushes],
bush; brushwood, (matala)
scrubland. **-nen** bushy.

pensas bush; shrub. **-aita** hedge.

penseä lukewarm, half-hearted.

pens|seli brush. **-lata** paint
[the throat, kurkkua].

pentu cub, (koiran) pup [py],
(kissan) kitten; halv. (lapsesta)
brat; saada ~ja bring forth
young, whelp.

perata (puutarhaa ym) weed,
(kuokalla) hoe [up]; (raivata)
clear; (marjoja) pick over,
(karviais-) top and tail;
(kaloja) clean, gut.

pereh|dyttää (jhk) make. .
acquainted (familiar) with;
initiate into. **-tymätön** (jhk)
unfamiliar with, not
conversant with; asiaan ~
(m.) uninitiated. **-tynyt** (jhk)
[well] acquainted with,
familiar with, [well] versed
in, well up on, steeped in.
-tyä become familiar with, get
acquainted with, (päästä
perille) get into.

perfekti perfect [tense].

pergamentti parchment. **-käärö**
roll of parchment.

pergamiini greaseproof paper.

perhe family; household;
~ittäin by families; hyvästä
~estä of good family, well
connected; nelihenkinen ~ a
family of four. **-asiat** family
affairs. **-ellinen:** ~ mies man
with a family, family man.
-elämä family life.

perheen|emäntä housewife.
-huoltaja breadwinner. **-isä**
father of a (the) family.
-jäsen member of the family;
asua ~enä kodissa live with
the family.

perhe|hauta family tomb.
-huolet domestic trouble.
-kasvatus l. v. homemaking.
-kunta family; household.
-onni domestic happiness.
-piiri family circle. **-riita**
domestic quarrel. **-suhteet**
family circumstances. **-syyt:**

-syistä for family reasons.
-tuttava family friend.

perho (onki-) fly. **-nen**
butterfly, (yö-) moth.

perhos|onki fly-hook. **-uinti**
butterfly stroke.

peri|aate principle; -aatteesta
on p.; -aatteen mies a man
of principle. **-aatteellinen**. . of
principle; ~ kysymys question
of principle. **-aatteellisesti** in
principle; on principle; olen
~ samaa mieltä I agree in p.
-aatteeton unprincipled.

perijä inheritor, (nainen)
inheritrix; heir, jnk to. **-tär**
(rikas) heiress.

peri|kato ruin; destruction;
joutua ~on be ruined; ~on
tuomittu doomed. **-ksi:** antaa
~ yield, give in. **-kunta** heirs.
-kuva prototype, (malli)
paragon, model. **-kuvallinen**
typical.

perille to the destination;
there; ~ saakka all the way
there; ajaa asia ~ carry
(push) the matter through;
saapua ~ reach one's
destination, arrive; päästä jstk
~ find out; en voi päästä
tuosta ~ I can't make that
out; ~ toimittamaton
undelivered.

perilli|nen heir, vrt. perijä;
kuoli ilman -stä died without
issue.

perillä at one's destination;
there; milloin olemme ~
when are we there? olla ~
jstk be familiar with; hän on
~ niistä asioista he is well
informed on such matters;
asioisiin ~ olevien lähteiden
mukaan according to informed
sources.

perimmäinen hindmost;
farthest, utmost, extreme.
perimys inheritance. **-järjestys**
succession.

perimä|tapa established custom.
-tieto tradition. **-tön**
uncollected; unclaimed.

perin thoroughly; (ylen)
extremely; exceedingly; ~
harvoin very rarely; ~ tärkeä
highly important. **-juurin**
thoroughly, radically, root and

branch.

perin|ne tradition. **-näinen**
traditional. **-näistapa**
traditional custom. **-näistieto**
tradition.

perinnölli|nen hereditary;
(peritty) inherited. **-syys**
heredity; *(~tiede* genetics).

perinnönjako division of
inheritance.

perinnö|tön disinherited; *tehdä
-ttömäksi* disinherit.

perinpoh|jainen thorough;
(seikkaperäinen) circumstantial,
detailed. **-jaisuus** thoroughness.
-jin thoroughly, radically;. . in
detail, minutely.

perinteellinen traditional;
conventional.

perintä *(maksun)* collection.

perintö inheritance; legacy;
jättää ~nä jklle leave to;
luopua perinnöstä renounce
one's inheritance; *saada
perinnöksi* inherit; *tila on
mennyt ~nä isältä pojalle* the
farm has passed (descended)
from father to son. **-kaari**
laws of inheritance. **-osa,
-osuus** share of an
inheritance. **-tila** family estate.
-vero inheritance tax.

peri|synti original sin.
-vihollinen arch enemy. **-ytyä**
be inherited, *(perinne)* be
handed down, pass [from
father to son]; *(tauti)* -ytyy is
hereditary, can be transmitted
(from. . to. .); *-ytyy (jltk
ajalta)* goes back to; *-ytyvä
(m.)* heritable.

periä inherit, come into [a
fortune, *suuri omaisuus*];
(kantaa) collect; levy [taxes,
veroja]; *(oikeuden kautta)*
recover [damages,
vahingonkorvausta].

perjantai Friday; *~na* on F.

perk|aamaton uncleaned;
(puutarha) unweeded; *vrt.
perata.* **-aus** cleaning *jne.;
(maan)* clearing. **-eet** *(kalan)*
guts.

perkele the devil.

permanto floor; *teatt. etu~*
stalls; *taka~* pit. **-paikka**
stall, seat in the stalls; seat
in the pit.

perna spleen, milt. **-rutto**
anthrax.

Persia Persia. **p-lainen** *a. & s.*
Persian.

persikka peach. **-puu** peach-tree.

persilja parsley.

perso greedy, extremely fond
(of); *puhek.* a pig for
[ice-cream etc].

personoida personify.

persoona person. **-llinen**
personal. **-llisuus** personality;
ks. henkilökohtaisuus.
-pronomini personal pronoun.
-ton impersonal. **-ttomuus**
impersonality.

perspektiivi perspective.

peru inheritance.

peruk|ka out-of-the-way corner;
Pohjan -koilla in the Far North.

Peru Peru. **p-lainen** *a. & s.*
Peruvian.

peruna potato *(pl. -es).* **-jauhot**
potato flour. **-lastut** chips.
-maa potato field, *(pieni)*
potato patch. **-nistutus** potato
planting. **-nnosto** potato
lifting. **-rutto** potato blight.
-sose mashed potatoes.

perunkirjoitus inventory of a
deceased person's estate.

perus|aine primary matter,
elemental substance.
-aineenvaihdunta basic
metabolic rate. **-ajatus**
fundamental idea. **-asento**
attention; *seisoa -asennossa*
stand at a. **-edellytys** essential
condition. **-kallio** ground-rock.
-kirja charter. **-kivi** foundation
stone. **-koulu** »basic school»,
l. v. comprehensive school
(covering 4 years of primary
and 5 of secondary
education). **-korjaus** primary
repairs. **-luku** cardinal
number. **-piirre** fundamental
characteristic; essential
feature. **-pääoma** initial
capital. **-syy** primary cause.
-sävel key-note.

perusta foundation; base; *kuv.*
basis.

perus|taa found; establish;
(panna alulle) set up, start;
(nojata) base (on); *~
professorinvirka* create a
university chair; *ei siitä*

kukaan -ta nobody cares about that; *-tava kokous* constitutive meeting; *vrt. perustella.* **-taja** founder. **-te** ground, basis; *(syy)* reason, argument; *sillä ~ella, että* on the ground that; *tällä ~ella* on this basis; *millä ~illa?* on what grounds? **-teellinen** thorough [-going]; *(syvällinen)* profound. **-teellisuus** thoroughness. **-teeton** groundless; unfounded. **-telematon** unaccounted for. **-tella** give reasons for, state arguments for, account for; make out a case for; *tarkoin -teltu* closely argued; *-telee (jtk)* hyvin makes out a good case for; *onko -teltua, että Suomi..* is there a case for Finland [.. -ing]; *heidän asiansa oli heikosti -teltu* they put forward a weak case. **-telu** argument, line of argument. **-tua** *(jhk)* be founded (based) on.

perustus foundation, base; groundwork; *kuv.* basis; *laskea ~ jllek* lay the foundation of, found; *paloi perustuksiaan myöten* burnt to the ground. **-kustannukset** initial expenses. **-laillinen** constitutional. **-lainvastainen** unconstitutional. **-laki** constitution [act], basic law; *(~valiokunta* constitutional committee).

peruukki wig.

peruu|ttaa back, reverse [a car, *auto*]; *kuv.* revoke, call off; *(tehdä mitättömäksi)* cancel; *~ hakemus* withdraw an application; *~ sanansa* take back one's word; *~ tilaus* cancel an order; *~ (uutinen) sanomalehdessä* deny. **-ttamaton** irrevocable. **-ttamattomasti** irrevocably; positively [the last time; *viimeinen kerta*]. **-tua** be cancelled; *kauppa on -tunut* the deal is off. **-tus** withdrawal; cancellation, annulment; *(~peili* driving mirror; *~vaihde* reverse, reversing gear).

perä rear, back [end], tail end; *(aluksen)* stern; *(pyssyn)* butt; *~n puolella* astern (of); *pitää ~ä* steer; *huhussa ei ole ~ä* the rumour has no foundation. **-aukko** anus. **-hytti** aft[er] cabin. **-isin:** *olla ~ (jstk)* come from, derive from, originate in, *(ajalta)* date from; *~ Ranskasta* of French origin. **-kansi** quarter deck. **-kkäin** one after another; *(yhtä mittaa). .* in succession; *kolmena päivänä ~* on three successive days, for three days running (in succession). **-kkäinen** consecutive, successive. **-lasti:** *~ssa* overloaded by the stern. **-lle** to the rear, towards the back; *huoneen ~* to the far end of the room. **-llä** in the rear; in the background. **-mies** mate; *ensimmäinen ~* first mate, first officer. **-moottori** outboard motor. **-npitäjä** steersman, helmsman. **-puikko** suppository. **-pukamat** piles, h[a]emorrhoids. **-ruiske** enema. **-ruisku** enema syringe. **-sin** rudder, helm, steering gear; *olla -simessä (m. kuv.)* be at the helm. **-ssä** in the rear, *(laivan)* aft; *(jäljessä)* after; behind. **-stä** after; behind; *jonka ~* after which, whereupon; *(~päin* afterwards; later). **-suoli** rectum. **-ti** quite, altogether; *(täysin)* wholly; extremely; *~ turmeltunut* utterly corrupted, rotten to the core. **-ttäinen** successive, consecutive. **-ttömyys** groundlessness. **-tysten** one after another. **-tön** groundless; baseless; unfounded; *osoittautui -ttömäksi* proved groundless. **-valo** *(auton)* backlight, tail-light. **-vannas** stern-post. **-vaunu** trailer. **-yttää** back. **-ytyä** back [out of, *jstk*]; *sot.* retreat, fall back; *~ tarjouksestaan* withdraw one's offer, pull out. **perään** behind; *antaa ~* give way; give in, yield, submit (to); *katsoa jnk ~* look after. **-antavainen** compliant.

-antavaisuus compliance.
-tyminen backing out; *sot.*
retreat. **-tyä** *sot.* retreat.
pese|ttää have.. washed, have..
cleaned. **-ytyä** wash [oneself],
have a wash.
pesijä washerwoman, laundress.
pesimis|aika nesting-time.
-pönttö bird house, bird box.
pesi|ytyä *kuv.* establish itself
(in), gain a hold (on). **-ä**
nest.
pessimistinen pessimistic.
pest|ata engage, hire; *sot.*
recruit. **-aus** engagement; *sot.*
enlistment. **-autua**
(sotapalvelukseen) enlist;
(laivaan) ship (on board. .). **-i**
hire; *ottaa* ~ enlist.
pestä wash; ~ *astioita* wash
dishes, wash up; ~ *auto* give
the car a wash [-down]; ~
kätensä wash one's hands
(kuv. of. .); ~ *lattia* mop,
(harjalla scrub) the floor; ~
pyykkiä wash, do [the]
washing, launder; *-vä*
washable; *onko tätä helppo*
~? does this *(t.* will it)
launder well?.
pesu wash[ing]. **-aine** *(jauhe)*
washing powder, detergent.
-allas wash-basin; *(keittiön)*
sink. **-istuin** bidet. **-karhu** *zo*
raccoon. **-kone**
washing-machine, washer. **-la,**
-laitos laundry; *(itsepalvelu-)*
launderette; *(kemiall.)* the
cleaners. **-nkestävä** washable;
fast [colour, *väri*]. **-sieni** ·
sponge. **-vaatteet** washing.
-vati washbasin.
pesä nest *(m. kuv.);*
(maanalainen) lair, hole;
(kuolin-) estate; *(liesi)* grate;
(esim. paheen) hotbed. **-ero**
settlement of property
[between husband and wife].
-ke *(taudin)* nest, seat of
disease, *lääk.* focus;
konekivääri~ machine-gun
nest. **-muna** nest-egg. **-njako**
distribution of an estate
[among the heirs]. **-nselvittäjä**
administrator; executor.
-nselvitys winding up of a
deceased person's estate.
-paikka nest, seat; *(et.*

paheiden) hotbed, sink [of
vice]. **-pallo** Finnish baseball.
petku|ttaa cheat, swindle, take
in; fool, trick, pull a p.'s leg.
-ttaja cheat, swindler; *(toisena*
esiintyvä) impostor. **-tus**
cheating, swindle; fraud.
peto [wild] beast. **-eläin** beast
of prey, predator. **-lintu** bird
of prey.
petolli|nen deceitful, false,
treacherous; fraudulent;
(asioista, m.) deceptive,
delusive [hope, *toivo*]. **-suus**
deceitfulness, falseness;
fraudulence.
peto|mainen brutal. **-maisuus**
brutality.
petos deceit, deception,
betrayal, fraud; *(vilppi)*
treachery; *petoksella* by
cheating.
petroli: *valo~* ks. *paloöljy.*
petsata *(puuta)* stain.
petturi traitor; betrayer.
petty|mys disappointment;
(turhauma) frustration; *tuottaa*
jklle ~ *(m.)* let.. down. **-ä**
be disappointed; be frustrated;
~ *jnk suhteen* be mistaken
(in, as to, about); **-nyt**
disappointed; **-neet** *toiveet*
thwarted (frustrated) hopes.
pettä|mätön unfailing; *(varma)*
infallible. **-vä** deceitful;
deceptive, fallacious.
pettää deceive; *(kavaltaa)*
betray; *(ystävä)* let.. down;
(johtaa harhaan) delude; ~
kaupassa cheat.. in a
bargain; ~ *jkn luottamus* play
a p. false; ~ *sanansa* break
(go back on) one's word;
hänen rohkeutensa petti his
courage deserted (failed) him;
hänen laskunsa pettivät he
miscalculated; *perustus petti*
the foundation gave way.
peuhata romp, be boisterous.
peukalo thumb; *hänellä on* ~
keskellä kämmentä his fingers
are all thumbs; *pidä* ~*a*
pystyssä! thumbs up! **-ida**
tamper (with). **-inen**
Hop-o'-my-Thumb; *zo.* wren.
-kyyti: thumbed ride; [give,
get] a lift; *pyytää* ~*ä* thumb
a lift. **-sääntö** rule of thumb.

peukku *ks. peukalo; pitää* ~*a* cross one's fingers, keep one's fingers crossed.

peura [wild] reindeer; *Am.* caribou; *laukon*~ white-tailed deer.

piakkoin soon, shortly; at an early date.

pian soon, in a little while; ~ *sen jälkeen* shortly after [that]; *niin* ~ *kuin* as soon as.

piano [upright] piano; *soittaa* ~*a* play the piano. **-kappale** piece for the piano. **-konsertti** piano recital. **-nkieli** piano string. **-nkosketin** key. **-nsoittaja** piano player, pianist. **-nvirittäjä** piano tuner. **-sovitus** arrangement for the piano. **-tuoli** piano stool.

pidellä hold [a p. by, *jkta jstk*]; *(käsitellä)* handle, *(kohdella)* treat; ~ *pahoin* ill-treat, treat cruelly, use. . roughly.

pide|nnys extension, prolongation; *(lykkäys)* respite. **-ntää** lengthen; extend; *(et. ajasta)* prolong. **-tä** become longer, lengthen; be prolonged.

pidi|ke holder, catch, clamp. **-n** *(yhd.)* -holder; *lampun* ~ lamp socket.

pidot banquet; feast.

pidä|ke clog; *kuv.* bar, *psyk.* control, restraint; *vapautua* **-kkeistä** break loose from all restraint. **-tellä** hold back; *henkeään* **-tellen** with bated breath. **-tyväinen** abstemious; reserved. **-ttyväisyys** abstinence; continence, restraint; *kuv.* reserve. **-ttyä** restrain oneself, check oneself; contain oneself; ~ *jstk* refrain from, abstain from [drinking, *juomasta*], *(esim. väkivalt. teosta)* withhold one's hand; *esiintyä* **-ttyvästi** keep one's distance. **-ttyä, -täytyä** *(äänestämästä)* abstain [from voting]. **-ttää** hold back, keep back; restrain; *(vangita)* arrest, detain, take. . into custody; *(ei antaa, ei maksaa)* withhold; *(oikeus jhk)* reserve; ~ *henkeään* hold one's

breath; ~ *nauruaan* keep back one's laughter, refrain from laughing; *en voinut* ~ *nauruani (m.)* I could not help laughing; *jkn tuloista* stop. . out of sb.'s income; ~ *virantoimituksesta* suspend. . from office; *kaikki oikeudet p-tetään* all rights reserved; *-tettynä* in detention. **-tys** arrest, detention, *(veron ym* stoppage; *-tykset [esim.* social insurance contribution] stoppages. (**~kyky** continence [of urine etc.]).

piehtaroida roll [about], tumble [about]; wallow, welter.

pieli post, *(oven)* doorpost, *(ikkunan ym.)* jamb; *oven pielessä* at the door; *mennä pieleen* go wrong, go off the rails, go to the devil, go phut.

piena fillet, moulding; lath.

pien|ehkö rather small, smallish. **-eliö** micro-organism. **-eneminen** diminution. **-enevä** diminishing. **-ennys** reduction; decrease. **-entyä, -etä** decrease [in size], diminish, become smaller. **-entää** make. . smaller; *(vähentää)* diminish, cut down [expenses, *kuluja*], reduce; *(vaatekappale)* take in; *(alentaa)* lower, lessen; *(paloitella)* cut up, chop.

pieni small; little; *pienen* ~ tiny, minute; ~ *lapsi* little child, baby; ~ *muutos* slight change; *pienet rahat* change; *se on* ~ *asia* it it a trifling matter; *pienempi* smaller; *(joskus)* lesser, minor; *(vähempi)* less; *pienin* smallest, least; *pienemmässä määrin* to a less extent. **-kasvuinen** small [in stature]. **-kokoinen** small-sized. **-ruutui-nen** small-checked, fine-checked.

pien|jännite *sähk.* low tension. **-kuluttaja** small-scale consumer.

piennar *(pellon)* edge.

pienois|bussi minibus. **-kivääri** small-bore rifle. **-koko** miniature; ~*a* in m. **-kuva** miniature. **-malli** scale model.

pien|okainen baby, little one.

-tenlastenkoulu infant school (*lastentarha*) nursery s. **pien|teollisuus** small [-scale] industry. **-tila** small-holding. **-viljelijä** small farmer, smallholder.
pienuus smallness, small size.
piestä whip, lash; flog; (*lyödä*) beat; ~ *jku pahanpäiväiseksi* beat.. black and blue.
piha yard; ~*lla* in the y. **-maa** [court]yard; (*koulun, m.*) playground. **-npuoleinen:** ~ *huone* room facing the courtyard.
pihdit [pair of] tongs; (*laaka-ym*) pliers; (*katko-*) nippers; *lääk. ym* forceps.
pihistä fizz, sizzle.
pihistää pinch.
pihka resin, gum; *olla* ~*ssa jkh* (*kuv.*) have a crush on, be sweet on. **-antua** *kuv.* get stuck (on). **-inen** resinous, pitchy.
pihlaja rowan[-tree], mountain ash. **-nmarja** rowan-berry.
pihti *ks. pihdit*. **-liike** *sot.* pincer movement.
pihvi beefsteak.
pii flint, silicon; *kova kuin* ~ flinty. **-happo** silicic acid. **-kivi** flint.
piika hired girl.
piikitellä taunt.
piikki thorn, (*pieni*) prickle, (*esim. siilin*) spine; (*ampiaisen*) sting; (*-langan*) barb; (*haravan ym*) prong; (*kamman*) tooth; (*naula*) spike; (*pistosana*) prick, fling, taunt. **-kampela** turbot. **-kenkä** spiked shoe. **-korko** stiletto heel. **-lanka** barbed wire; (~**aita** barbed-wire fence; ~**este** barbed-wire entanglement). **-nen** thorny, prickly. **-sika** porcupine. **-syys** prickliness.
piil|eksiä hide, lie in hiding, lie hidden, (*esim. rikollinen*) lie low. **-lä** be hidden, be concealed; *siinä -ee suuri vaara* a great danger lurks there; *-evä* (*lääk.*) latent.
piilo hiding-place; *olla* ~*ssa* be hidden, be in hiding, hide; *mennä* ~*on* hide; *panna* ~*on*

hide [away]. **-kamera** candid camera. **-lasit** contact lenses.
-paikka hiding-place, (*eläinten, m.*) covert; (*kätkö*) secret place; (*sopukka*) recess, cranny. **-silla:** *olla* ~ play hide-and-seek. **-tajunta** the unconscious. **-ttaa** hide, conceal; (*esim. pakolaista*) shelter. **-utua** hide, *jklta* from.
piilu hatchet.
piimä sour milk, (*kirnu-*) buttermilk.
piina torture; agony, torment. **-llinen** painful, (*kiusallinen*) embarrassing, awkward. **-penkki** rack.
piinty|ä become fixed [in a habit]; *-nyt* inveterate; confirmed.
piipittää cheep, chirp.
piippu pipe; (*kiväärin*) barrel. **-hylly** pipe-rack; *teatt.* gallery. **-tupakka** pipe tobacco.
piipun|pesä pipe bowl. **-polttaja** pipe smoker. **-varsi** pipe stem.
piirakka, piiras pie; pasty; (*marja-*) tart.
piiri circle; (*rengas*) ring, *geom. ym* circumference; (*alue*) district; (*ulottumis-*) scope, range; *asettua* ~*in jkn ympärille* form a circle around. .; *hienoissa piireissä* in elegant circles; *koko maan* ~*n käsittävä* global; *leviää kansan* ~*in* spreads among the people. **-kunta** district. **-leikki** round game. **-lääkäri** district physician. **-ttää** besiege (*m. kuv.*), lay siege to; (*ympäröidä*) surround; (*estääkseen ulospääsyn*) blockade. **-tys** siege; *lopettaa* ~ raise the siege; (~**tila** state of siege).
piir|re feature, (*luonteen-, m.*) trait; *suurin piirtein* on the whole, by and large. **-ros** drawing, design; sketch; diagram. **-to** score, mark, (*viiva*) line; (*esim. kynän*) stroke. **-tyä** be delineated; (*jtk vastaan*) be outlined against. **-täjä** drawer; (*ammatti-*) designer, draughtsman. **-tää** draw; design; (*luonnostaa*) outline, sketch; ~ *viiva* draw

(trace) a line; *-retty elokuva* animated film.

piiru mark, *(kompassin)* point; *(puu)* spar, pole.

piirustaa draw.

piirustus drawing; design; sketch. **-hiili** charcoal. **-lauta** drawing-board. **-lehtiö** sketch block. **-liitu** crayon; pastel. **-nasta** drawing pin. **-sali** art room. **-taito** draughtsmanship.

piisami musk-rat.

piiska whip. **-auto** radio patrol car. **-nisku** lash with the whip. **-nsiima** lash. **-ta** whip, *(mattoja)* beat.

piispa bishop. **-llinen** episcopal. **-nistuin** see, bishop's throne. **-nsauva** crosier.

piitata concern oneself, trouble oneself (about); *siitä minä vähän piittaan* I don't care a rap! I don't give a damn!

piittaamat|on unconcerned [about other people's feelings]. **-tomuus** lack of consideration.

pika: *tuota ~a* instantly, at once, in no time.

pikai|nen quick, rapid; speedy; prompt; *~ luonne* quick (hot, hasty) temper. **-stua** lose one's temper, flare up. **-stus** rashness; *-stuksissa (lak.)* without premeditation. **-isuus** quickness; hastiness.

pika|jakelu special delivery. **-juna** express [train], fast train, non-stop train. **-juoksija** sprinter. **-kirje** express letter. **-kirjoittaja** stenographer; *kone- ja ~* shorthand-typist, *Am.* stenographer. **-kirjoitus** shorthand, stenography. **-kivääri** light machine-gun, rapid-fire rifle. **-kurssi** crash course. **-käynti** lightning visit. **-luistelu** speed skating. **-luistin** racing skate. **-lähetti** express messenger; courier. **-marssi** forced march. **-moottori** speedboat.

pikantti piquant; cute.

pika|oikeus drumhead court martial. **-posti:** *~ssa* by special delivery. **-puhelu** priority call. **-päinen** hot-headed; rash.

pikari cup; goblet.

pika|tavara express goods; *(~toimisto* express delivery office). **-tie** clearway, expressway. **-tuli** rapid firing. **-tykki** rapid-fire gun. **-viesti** express message, *urh.* sprint relay. **-vihainen** quick to take offence, touchy, irascible. **-vihaisuus** quick temper.

pikee *(kangas)* piqué.

pikemmin quicker, sooner; *(~kin)* rather; *~ kuollut kuin elävä* more dead than alive.

piki pitch; *(suutarin-)* cobbler's wax. **-intyä** *kuv.* get sweet, get stuck (on). **-lanka** waxed thread, wax thread.

pikimmin: *mitä ~* as soon as possible, at an early date.

piki|musta pitch black; jet black [hair, *tukka*]. **-nen** pitchy.

pikkelsi pickles.

pikku little, tiny. **-asia** trifle, trifling matter. **-auto** [passenger *t.* private] car; taxi. **-joulu** *l.v. (esim. firman)* Christmas staff party. **-kauppias** small tradesman. **-kaupunki** small town; country town. **-leivät** biscuits, cookies. **-mainen** mean; overparticular. **-maisuus** meanness. **-piru** imp. **-raha** [small] change. **-ruinen** tiny, minute, *Skotl.* wee. **-seikka** trifle; minor point. **-serkku** second cousin. **-sormi** little finger. **-tavarat** small wares, haberdashery, fancy goods. **-tunnit** small hours. **-vanha** precocious. **-varvas** little toe.

pila *(leikki)* joke, jest; fun; *mennä ~lle* be ruined; *vrt. seur.; on ~lla* is spoilt; *tehdä ~a jstk* make fun of; *piloillaan* for *(t. as)* a joke, for the fun of the thing, jestingly. **-antua** be ruined; *-tunut* damaged, *(liha ym)* tainted, *(hedelmä)* decayed; *on -tunut* has gone bad; *helposti p-tuva* perishable. **-antumaton** unspoilt, undamaged; in good condition. **-hinta** *ks. pilkka-.* **-illa** banter, chaff; make fun (of sb.). **-juttu** anecdote. **-kuva**

cartoon, caricature. **-lehti**
comic paper. **-npäiten** for
[the] fun [of it]. **-nteko**
joking; fooling. **-piirros**
caricature, (et. poliittinen)
cartoon. **-piirtäjä** caricaturist,
cartoonist. **-puhe** joking.
pilari pillar; column. **-sto**
colonnade.
pilata spoil; (turmella) ruin;
mar; (vahingoittaa) damage;
~ (lapsi) hemmottelemalla
spoil [a child].
piletti ticket; ks. lippu.
pilkah|dus glimpse; toivon ~ a
glimmer of hope. **-taa**
(välähtää) glimmer, (esille)
peep out; näin. .n -tavan
esille I caught a glimpse of.
pilkalli|nen mocking, derisive;
(ivallinen) scornful, sneering,
ironical. **-suus** derisiveness.
pilkata scoff; mock (at), deride;
~ Jumalaa blaspheme;
Jumalaa pilkkaava
blasphemous.
pilkistää peep [out].
pilkka 1. ridicule; mockery;
scoffing, derision; (leikki) jest,
fun; pitää jkta ~naan make
fun of, make a fool of;
joutua pilkan esineeksi
become a laughing-stock (an
object of derision). **2.**
(merkki) blaze; (maali) target;
osua keskelle ~a hit the
bull's eye. **-aja** scoffer,
mocker; (Jumalan-)
blasphemer. **-anammunta**
target-practice. **-hinta**
ridiculously low price;
-hinnasta at a great bargain;
for a song. **-huuto** sneer, jeer,
hoot. **-kirves** joker, wag.
-nauru derisive (scornful)
laugh [ter]. **-nimi** nickname.
-runo lampoon. **-sana** taunt,
gibe.
pilkki|onginta ice fishing.
-onkija ice fisherman.
pilkkoa split; (puita) chop;
maa on pilkottu the country
has been dismembered.
pilkkopimeä a. pitch dark; s.
pitch darkness.
pilkku dot; speck; (täplä) spot;
(välimerkkinä) comma; i:n ~
dot over i; pilkulleen exactly

[the same size, yhtä suuret],
to a T. **-kuume** typhus.
pilku|llinen dotted, spotted.
-ttaa dot; punctuate [a
sentence, lause].
pillahtaa: ~ itkuun burst out
crying.
pillas|tua run away, bolt;
-tunut hevonen runaway
[horse].
pilleri pill.
pilli (vihellys-) whistle;
(juoma-) straw; (tehtaan)
hooter. **-stö** (urku-) pipes.
-tää: itkeä ~ snivel, blubber.
pilttuu stall, box.
pilven|hattara speck of cloud.
-peittämä overclouded. **-piirtäjä**
skyscraper.
pilve|ttyä cloud over. **-tön**
cloudless, unclouded.
pilvi cloud; olla pilvessä be
overclouded, be cloudy, be
overcast; (sodanaikainen)
over, become overcast; ~ä
hipova. . reaching to the
skies, sky-high. **-linna** castle
in the air. **-nen** cloudy, dull
[day, päivä] ; overcast.
pime|nnys (auringon, kuun)
eclipse; (sodanaikainen)
black-out. **-ntää** darken;
obscure; kaupunki on
pimennettynä there is a
black-out in the town. **-tä**
grow dark, [be] darken[ed];
(himmetä) be obscured. **-ys**
darkness, dark; obscurity. **-ä**
a. dark; kuv. obscure; s.
dark[ness]; ~n tullen at
nightfall, with the fall of
darkness; ~n tultua (m.) after
dark; ~ turvin under cover
of night; ~ssä in the dark.
pimittää darken, obscure; dim;
(tulojansa) withhold
information on one's income;
(jklta rahaa) cheat; (uutinen)
-tettiin was kept [in the]
dark.
pimu bird, birdie, Am. baby,
chick, doll.
pinaatti spinach.
pingo|tin (kangaspuissa) temple.
-ttaa stretch; strain, tighten
[a rope, köyttä] ; (esim.
opiskellessa) overdo it; älä
-ta! slack off a bit! **-tettu**

stretched, taut. **-ttua** be
stretched; tighten; *(jännittyä)*
grow tense; *-ttunut* strained,
tense. **-tus** strain, tension.
pingviini *zo.* penguin.
pinkka stack, pile; bundle.
pinko, -ja swot, grind.
pinna‖llinen superficial, surface,
kuv. m. shallow. **-nmitta**
square measure. **-nmuodostus**
topography.
pinna‖ri *ark.* shirker. **-ta** shirk,
(tunnilta) cut [a class], play
truant [from school].
pinne *(liitin)* clip; *olla
pinteessä* be in a fix, be in
a tight place.
pinnis‖tellä exert oneself. **-tys**
tension; strain. **-tää** strain;
exert; ~ *kaikki voimansa*
exert all one's strength, strain
every nerve.
pinnoi‖ttaa *(rengas)* retread. **-te**
surfacing, coating.
pino, -ta stack, pile.
pinsetit tweezers, small forceps.
pinta surface; *(taso)* plane;
kuv. exterior; *pinnalta katsoen*
on the surface, on the face
of it; *maan* ~ *(m.)* the face
of the Earth; *pitää* ~*nsa* hold
out, hold one's ground. **-ala**
area. **-kiilto** veneer, gloss.
-käsittely finish, surface
coating. **-liitäjä** hovercraft.
-puolinen superficial, shallow;
~ *tutustuminen kirjaan* a
cursory reading of the book.
-puolisuus superficiality. **-vesi**
surface-water.
pioneeri engineer, sapper.
-joukot the Engineers.
pioni peony.
pipar‖juuri horse-radish. **-kakku**
gingerbread biscuit. **-minttu**
peppermint.
pippur‖i pepper; *(~nen*
peppery). **-oida** pepper.
pirahdus sprinkle; *sateen* ~ a
sprinkle (spurt) of rain.
piris‖tys stimulation; *(~pilleri*
pep-pill). **-tyä** brighten up,
cheer up. **-tää** refresh,
stimulate; liven.. up; *-tävä
(sää)* bracing.
pirskeet *sl.* feast, spree, wild
blast.
pirskottaa sprinkle.

pirst‖ale splinter; ~*et (m.)*
debris; *(esim. armeijan)*
scattered remnant [of an
army]. **-oa** break to shivers,
smash; *(hajottaa)* shatter;
(valtakunta) dismember;
(riitojen) -oma divided by.
-ominen, -onta *(maatilojen)*
land fragmentation. **-outua**
break into shivers, [be]
shatter [ed].
pirta *[weaver's]* reed.
pirte‖ys liveliness, briskness. **-ä**
lively, spirited, alert, agile,
puhek. (esim. potilas) perky.
pirtti living-room [in Finnish
farm-house]; log cabin.
piru devil. **-llinen** devilish,
diabolical. **-llisuus** devilry;
devilishness.
pisama freckle. **-inen** freckled.
pisar‖a drop. **-oida** drip;
(sateesta) sprinkle. **-oittain** in
drops, drop by drop.
piste point *(m. kilpailu-);*
(välimerkki) full stop, period;
(pilkku) dot; *(tutkinnossa,
koul.)* mark; *hän sai 45* ~*ttä*
he scored 45 points. **-lakko**
selective strike. **-lasku**
reckoning by points.
piste‖liäs *kuv.* cutting;
sarcastic. **-llä** sting; *(neulalla
ym)* prick; *kuv.* be sarcastic.
piste‖määrä [number of]points,
marks; score. **-viiva** dotted
line. **-voitto** points victory;
saada ~ win on points.
pistin *(hyönteisen)* sting; *sot.*
bayonet.
pisto sting, prick; *(ompelu-)*
stitch; *hän sai* ~*n sydämeensä*
his conscience pricked him.
-haava puncture wound, stab.
-kas slip, cutting. **-koe**
random sample, sample test.
-kosketin plug, *Am. m.* jack.
pistooli pistol.
pisto‖rasia wall socket; *kytkeä*
~*an* put the plug in the
socket, plug in. **-s** *(hyönteisen
ym)* sting, bite; *(injektio)*
injection, shot; *(kyljessä)* a
stitch (a stabbing pain) in
the side. **-sana** sarcastic
remark; sarcasm, gibe. **-tulppa**
plug.
pist‖äytyä: ~ *jkn luona* drop

in (pop in, look in) [to see a p.], *Am.* stop in (*t.* by), drop by. **-ää** *(neulalla ym)* prick; stick *(m. pistää jhk); (hyönteisestä)* sting, bite; *(panna)* put; ~ *esiin* project, jut out, *(reiästä)* stick out; ~ *kuoliaaksi* stab to death; ~ *lauluksi* strike up a song; ~ *lävitse* pierce through; ~ *silmään* be conspicuous; *pistin sormeeni* I pricked my finger; *päähäni pisti.* . it occurred to me; *-ävä* cutting, sarcastic, *(esim. haju)* pungent.

pitki|**n:** ~ *jtk* along; ~ *vuotta* throughout the year; ~ *matkaa* all the way through; ~ *ja poikin* throughout [the length and breadth of]. **-ttyä** be prolonged (protracted, drawn out). **-ttäin** lengthways, lengthwise, longitudinally. **-ttäinen** lengthwise; longitudinal. **-ttää** lengthen; extend; prolong; *(viivyttää)* delay.

pitko long wheat loaf, bun loaf.

pitkulainen oblong, elongated.

pitkä long; *(ihmisestä ym)* tall; *~n ajan, ~ksi aikaa* for a long time; *ei ~än aikaan* not for a long time; *-stä aikaa* after a long time, after all this time; ~ *elokuva* feature film; *sinne on* ~ *matka* it is a long way off; *ennen ~ä* before long; *vuoden ~än* in the course of the year; *mennä liian ~lle* go too far; *näyttää ~ä nenää jklle* cock a snook at, thumb one's nose at; *panna ~kseen* lie down; *~lleko?* how far? **-aikainen.** . of long duration; ~ *laina* long-term loan; *vrt. -llinen.* **-hkö** rather long, longish, *(henkilö)* fairly tall. **-ikäinen** long-lived. **-ikäisyys** longevity. **-jännitteinen** sustained. **-karvainen** long-haired. **-kasvuinen** tall. **-koipinen** long-legged. **-lle** far; *aika on kulunut* ~ the time is far advanced; ~ *päässyt* advanced. **-llinen** long; lengthy; prolonged; lingering

[*illness, sairaus*]; *onni ei ollut* ~ the happiness was short-lived. **-llisyys** long duration. **-llä** far. **-llään:** *olla* ~ be lying down, lie outstretched. **-lti** far, a long way; *(esim. puhua* ~) at [great] length; *onko sinne* ~ is it far off? **-matkainen:** *vieras* a guest from far away. **-mielinen** long-suffering, forbearing. **-mielisyys** forbearance. **-nlainen** fairly long; ~ *matka* quite a distance; ~ *puhe* a rather lengthy speech. **-nomainen** oblong, elongated. **-npyöreä** oval. **-näköinen** long-sighted. **-perjantai** Good Friday. **-piimäinen** long-winded, long-drawn-out. **-siima** trawl line. **-sti** at great length. **-styä** grow tired [of waiting, *odotukseen*], be fed up, get bored (with); *-styttävä* boring. **-vartinen** long-handled; *(saapas)* long-legged. **-veteinen** long-winded, lengthy, *(ikävä)* tedious. **-veteisyys** tediousness. **-vihainen** unforgiving; slow to forget.

pitkään far; *katsoa* ~ *jtk* take a good (*t.* long) look at; *puhua* ~ speak at great length; *hän nukkuu* ~ *aamuisin* he is a late riser.

pito|**inen** *(yhd.)* containing. .; *(esim.) malmi~* ore-bearing. **-isuus** *(yhd.)* percentage of. .; *kulta~* gold content. **-vaatteet** everyday clothes.

pitsi lace. **-nnypläys** [bobbin] lace-making.

pitui|**nen:** *jnk* ~. . long,. . in length; *minun -seni mies* a man of my height; *sormen* ~ of a finger's length; *sen* ~ *se* that's the end of the story; *viiden jalan* ~ *seiväs* a fivefoot pole, a pole measuring five feet.

pituus length; *(ihmisen ym)* height; *pitkin pituuttaan* [at] full length; *kasvaa pituutta* grow in height. **-akseli** longitudinal axis. **-aste** [degree of] longitude. **-hyppy** long jump. **-mitta** linear

measure, long measure.
-suunta: ~*an* lengthwise,
longitudinally.
pitäen: *siitä* ~ ever since;
since then.
pitäjä parish, *Am.* county.
-läinen parishioner.
pitäisi should; ought to; *vrt.
ed; (hän työskentelee liian
ahkerasti,) vaikka sanon, ettei
hänen* ~ though I tell her
not to.
pitää keep; hold; *(säilyttää)*
retain, maintain, *(jnak)*
consider, regard (as), look
upon (as); ~ *jstk* like, have
a liking for; ~ *jstk enemmän
kuin. .-sta* prefer .. to ..; ~
autoa keep a car; ~ *jkta
kädestä* hold.. by the hand;
~ *kiinni jstk* keep hold of,
(kuv.) keep to, stick to,
adhere to, *(muodollisuuksista)*
stand on form; ~ *kokous*
hold a meeting ~ *lupauksensa*
keep one's promise; ~ *puhe*
make (deliver) a speech; ~
päivälliset give a dinner party
[for, *jkn kunniaksi*]; ~
ravintolaa run a restaurant
[business]; ~ *yhtä* agree;
hänestä pidetään paljon he is
very popular; *pidin paljon
kirjasta (m.)* I enjoyed the
book very much; *kenenä
minua pidät* whom do you
take me for? *astia ei pidä
vettä* the vessel does not hold
water; *hänen piti tulla jo
eilen* he was to come
yesterday; *sinun pitäisi* you
ought to; *minun olisi pitänyt
mennä* I should have gone;
minun ~ *mennä* I must go, I
have to go, I must be off;
mitä pidät tästä? how do you
like this? what do you think
of this? *jarrut eivät pitäneet*
the brakes failed to grip;
pitäkää passinne esillä! have
your passports ready!
piukka tight; *(köysi, m.)* taut.
plagi|aatti plagiarism. **-oida**
plagiarize.
plaketti plaque.
planeetta planet.
platina platinum.
platoninen platonic.

pleksilasi perspex.
pluskvamperfekti pluperfect
[tense].
plusmerkki plus sign.
plyysi *(-kangas)* plush.
pohatta magnate.
pohdi|nta discussion. **-skelu**
speculation.
pohja bottom; foundation, basis
(et. kuv.); (kanta) base;
(antura) sole; *jnk* ~*lla* at the
bottom, *kuv. m.* at the root
of, *(perusteella)* on the
ground (basis) of; ~*ltaan*
fundamentally, at bottom;
pohjiaan myöten thoroughly;
paloi ~*an got* burnt [at the
bottom]; *sydämen* ~*sta* from
the bottom of one's heart;
with all one's heart; *juoda*
~*an* drain [one's glass];
maljat ~*an!* bottoms up!
sininen risti valkoisella ~*lla* a
blue cross on a white field.
-hinta rock-bottom price.
-kerros substratum;
(rakennuksen) ground floor,
Am. first floor; *(kellari-)*
basement. **-lainen**
Ostrobothnian. **-lasti** ballast.
-llinen *(kengän)* loose sole.
-maali priming.
Pohjan|lahti the Gulf of
Bothnia. **-maa** Ostrobothnia,
East Bothnia. **-meri** the North
Sea.
pohjantähti pole star.
pohja|nuotta trawl. **-palkka**
basic salary *(t. pay).* **-piirros**
ground plan, plan. **-raha**
subscription. **-rahasto** initial
fund. **-sakka** sediment; *(viinin
ym)* dregs, lees; *(kahvin ym)*
grounds. **-sävel** key-note. **-ta**
intr. reach bottom; *maal.*
prime, ground; ~ *kenkiä* sole
(resole) shoes. **-tiedot**
foundation;. . *lla on hyvät* ~
jssk.. is well grounded in. .
-ton bottomless, fathomless.
-tuuli north (northerly) wind.
-uttaa: ~ *kenkänsä* have one's
shoes resoled. **-utua:** ~ *jhk*
be based on. **-vesi** ground
water; *(laivassa)* bilge-water.
-virta undercurrent. **-väri**
ground colour.
pohje calf *(pl.* calves).

pohjimm|ainen . . [situated] nearest to the bottom; lowest; *-aisena* at the [very] bottom; *-iltaan* basically.

pohjoi|nen *a.* northern, north; *s.* [the] north; *-seen päin* to[wards] the north; northwards; *-seen menevät junat* trains going north.

Pohjois-|Amerikka North-America; **p-lainen** North-American. **-Eurooppa** Northern Europe; **(p~lainen** North-European). **-kalotti** the Scandinavian shield.

pohjois|in northernmost; *-impana* farthest [in the] north. **-koillinen, -luode** north-northeast (-west). **-maalainen** *a.* Nordic; *s. (l.v.)* northerner. **-maat** the Nordic countries. **-mainen** northern, Nordic; *P~ Neuvosto* the Nordic Council. **-napa** North pole; **(~retkeilijä** arctic explorer; **~retki, -kunta** arctic expedition). **-osa** northern part. **-puoli** north side; *jnk -puolella* [to the] north of, on the north side of. **-suomalainen** North-Finnish. **-tuuli** north[erly] wind.

pohjola the North.

pohju|kaissuoli duodenum **-kka** bottom; *lahden -kassa* at the bottom of the bay. **-staa** ground; *(maalilla)* prime.

pohtaa winnow.

pohtia deliberate (upon), discuss, *(harkita)* think. . over, consider.

poiju buoy.

poika boy, lad; *(jkn ~)* son; *vrt. poikanen.* **-koulu** boys' school. **-lapsi** male child; baby boy. **-mainen** boyish. **-maisuus** boyishness; *(-kuje)* boyish trick. **-mies** bachelor; single man. **-nen** little boy; lad [die [; *(eläimen)* young *(pl. = sg.); mustarastaan ~ a* fledgling blackbird; *vrt. pentu.* **-nulikka** young rascal, scamp. **-puoli** stepson.

poiketa turn off, turn aside; deviate, digress, diverge (from), *(erota)* differ; *~ aineesta* digress from the subject; *~ suunnastaan* deviate from its course; *~ jkn luo(na)* drop in [to see a p.]; *laiva poikkeaa jhk* the steamer calls (touches, puts in) at; *jstk poiketen* as distinct (distinguished) from. .

poikia bring forth young, produce young; *(lehmä)* calve; *(hevonen)* foal; *(lammas)* lamb; *(sika)* farrow; *(kissa)* have kittens, *(villieläin)* have cubs.

poiki|ttain crosswise, transversely; across [the road, *tiellä*]. **-ttainen** crosswise, transverse.

poikke|ama deviation; *fys.* deflection, *tähtit.* declination. **-ava** divergent; deviant; *tavallisuudesta ~* exceptional, abnormal,. . out of the ordinary. **-avuus** divergence; deviation. **-uksellinen** exceptional; *p-llisesti* exceptionally, by way of an exception. **-us** exception; *(miltei) -uksetta* [almost] without exception, [almost] invariably.

poikkeus|laki emergency law. **-tapaus** exceptional case; *p-tapauksessa (m.)* exceptionally. **-tila** state of emergency.

poikki off; *jnk ~* across; *hakata, leikata ~* cut off; cut in two; *keppi on ~* the stick is broken. **-juova** transverse stripe *(t.* line). **-katu** cross street; *toinen ~ vasemmalla* the second turning on the left. **-leikkaus** cross-section, transverse section. **-nainen** broken. **-parru** cross beam, cross-bar. **-puu** cross-piece, cross-bar. **-teloin** across [the road, *tiellä*]; *asettua ~ (kuv.)* set one's face against [it], oppose. **-tie** crossroad. **-viiva** cross-line; *mat.* transversal.

poikue litter; *(linnun)* brood, hatch.

poimi|a pick [up], *(valita)* pick out, *(keräillä)* gather; *(tähkäpäitä)* glean; *(otteita)* extract. **-nto** *kirj.* extract, excerpt; *~ja (m.)* gleanings

(from).
poimu fold; *(laskos)* pleat, *(pienempi)* tuck; *(kure)* gather. **-inen** pleated. **-ttaa** pleat, tuck, *(rypyttää)* gather; *(esim. verhot)* drape.
pois away, off; *jäädä ~* 'stay away, fail to appear, absent oneself; *jättää ~* omit, leave out, *(esim. tupakka)* leave off smoking; *lähteä ~* go away, leave; *sormet ~!* hands off! *sano ~!* fire away! **-päin** away; *ja niin ~* and so forth; *kääntää katseensa ~ (m.)* avert one's eyes.
poissa away, absent; *olla ~* be away [from home, *kotoa*], be absent (from); *jkn ~ ollessa* in a p.'s absence. **-oleva** absent; *~t* those a. **-olo** absence; nonattendance, nonappearance; *loisti ~llaan* was conspicuous by its (his, her) absence.
pois|**taa** remove; eliminate; *(sulkea pois)* exclude; *(käytännöstä)* withdraw [from use], do away with; abolish [slavery, *orjuus*]; *(tileistä)* write off; *(vähentää)* deduct; *(pyyhkiä)* strike out *(t. off)*, delete; *(tahra, m.)* take out. **-to** liik. depreciation [charge], *~t* depreciation; *(~putki* exhaust pipe). **-tua** go away, leave; *(junasta ym)* get off [the train]; *(vetäytyä)* withdraw; *~ paikkakunnalta* leave the locality.
pojan|**poika** grandson. **-tytär** granddaughter.
pokaali [prize] cup.
pokeri poker.
pokkuroida bow and scrape [before.. *jklle*], kowtow (to).
polemiikki controversy; polemic.
poletti [gas-meter] disc *(t. disk)*; *(vastamerkki t.-lippu)* check.
poliisi police; *(-mies)* policeman, *koll.* police. **-asema** police-station, police-office. **-koira** police dog. **-konstaapeli** [police] constable. **-laitos** the police, police force. **-mestari** Chief Constable. **-tutkinto** police-court examination.

-viranomaiset police authorities. **-voima** police force.
polii|**tikko** politician. **-ttinen** political.
poliklinikka out-patient department *(t.* service), *Am.* Clinic.
politiikka politics; *(et. henkilön, puolueen noudattama)* policy.
politi|**koida** take part in politics, talk politics. **-koitsija** [petty] politician. **-soida** politicize.
poljen|**ta** tramp[ing], stamping *jne.* **-to** rhythm.
polj|**in** treadle; *(soittokoneen, auton)* foot pedal, *(polkupyörän)* pedal; *-ettava* treadle [sewing machine, *ompelukone*].
polkea trample; tread [on the pedal], *(tömistäen)* stamp [one's foot, *jalkaansa*]; *(polkupyörää ym)* pedal; *kuv.* tread down, trample on; *~ jalkoihinsa* trample under foot; *~ jnk hintaa* force down the price of; *~ paikallaan* mark time; *~ rikki* crush under one's feet; *~ tahtia* beat time with one's foot.
polkka polka.
polku path *(m. kuv.)*, footpath. trail; *kuv.* track. **-hinta** very low price; *vrt. pilkka-; myydä -hinnasta (esim. ulkomaille)* dump. **-myynti** dumping.
polkupyörä bicycle, *puhek.* bike; *ajaa ~llä* ride a bicycle, cycle. **-ilijä** [pedal]cyclist. **-ily** cycling. **-tie** bicycle track. **-retki** cycling tour.
polku|**ratas** tread-wheel. **-sin** pedal.
pollari bollard; *(sl.* = *poliisi)* cop.
poloinen poor; *(kurja)* wretched, unlucky.
polskuttaa splash.
polt|**e** sharp pain; ache. **-in** burner; *(~rauta* branding-iron; marking-iron; *merkitä ~raudalla* brand).
poltt|**aa** burn; *(kuumalla vedellä)* scald; *(korventaa)*

scorch; *(tupakkaa)* smoke; *(ruumis)* cremate; *(esim. haava)* cauterize; *(intr. kirveltää)* smart; ~ *pohjaan* [let. .] burn; ~ *poroksi* burn. . to the ground; ~ *posliinia* fire; ~ *tiiliä* bake; ~ *viinaa* distil spirits; *auringon -ama* sunburnt; *nokkonen* ~ the nettle stings; *vatsaani* ~ I have a [sharp] pain in my stomach; *-ava kysymys* a burning question; *-ava jano* a burning (parching) thirst. **-imo** distillery.

poltto burning; *(palaminen)* combustion; *(polte)* pain; *(synnytys)poltot* labour pains. **-aine** fuel; *ottaa ~tta* refuel. **-hautaus** cremation. **-lasi** burning glass. **-merkki** brand. **-moottori** internal-combustion engine. **-neste** liquid fuel. **-piste** focus, focal point. **-puut** firewood, fuelwood. **-rovio** ks. *rovio.* **-sprii** methylated spirits. **-turve** peat. **-uhri** burnt offering. **-väli** focal distance. **-öljy** fuel oil.

polve|**illa** wind, zigzag. **-lta** bend, angle, loop. **-utua** *(jstk)* descend from, be descended from, derive [its (one's) origin] from; trace one's family back to. **-utuminen** descent. **-utumisuppi** theory of evolution.

polvi knee; *(mutka)* bend; *(suku-)* generation; *olla ~llaan* kneel; *suoraan alenevassa polvessa* in direct descent. **-housut** shorts, short trousers; *(~en alapuolelle kiinnitetyt)* [knee-]breeches. **-lumpio** knee-cap. **-nivel** knee-joint. **-stua** kneel [down].

polyyppi *zo.* polyp; *(kasvain, m.)* polypus.

pomeranssinkuori orange-peel.

pommi bomb; *kuv.* bombshell; *~en purkaminen* bomb disposal. **-attentaatti** bomb outrage. **-hyökkäys** bombing raid. **-kone** bomber. **-nkestävä** bomb-proof. **-nsirpale** bomb splinter (fragment). **-suoja** bombproof shelter. **-ttaa**

bombard *(m. kuv.)*, shell, *(ilmasta)* bomb. **-tus** bombardment, shelling, *(ilma-)* bombing.

pomo boss, *puhek.* big gun, *(esim. teollisuus~)* tycoon.

poni pony.

ponnahdus bound, spring. **-lauta** *m. kuv.* springboard, diving board; *(~hypyt* springboard diving).

ponnahtaa bound, spring; ~ *auki* fly (spring) open; ~ *pystyyn* spring up; ~ *takaisin* rebound.

ponne|**kas** emphatic, strong. **-kkaasti** with emphasis, emphatically. **-kkuus** stress, emphasis; force. **-ton** lame, feeble.

ponni|**staa** exert [oneself], strain; make an effort; *(pyrkiä)* struggle, strive; *urh.* take off; ~ *eteenpäin* strive forward; ~ *kaikkensa* exert all one's strength; ~ *vastaan* make resistance. **-stautua** ~ *pystyyn* struggle to one's feet. **-stella** struggle, *(jtk vastaan, m.)* try hard not to. . **-stus** exertion, effort, strain[ing]; *urh.* take-off; *omien ~tensa tuloksena* by his own efforts; *(~lauta* springboard, take-off board).

ponsi *bot.* anther; *(paino)* stress, emphasis; *siinä ei ole pontta eikä perää* there is neither rhyme nor reason in it; *antaa pontta puheelleen* emphasize one's words; . . *asetti seuraavat ponnet.* . made the following points. **-ehdotus** proposed *(t.* draft) resolution. **-lause** resolution.

pontev|**a** vigorous, forcible; *(tarmokas)* energetic. **-uus** vigorousness, vigour; energy.

pontikka moonshine. **-tehdas** illicit still.

ponttoni pontoon.

popliini poplin.

poppamies magician; medicine-man.

poppeli poplar.

pora drill; bore. **-kone** boring (drilling) machine; *~en terä* bit. **-ta** drill; bore. **-us**

boring, bore; (~**reikä** borehole).

pore, -illa bubble.

porkka ski stick, ski pole.

porkkana carrot.

pormestari *Am. & Engl.* mayor; *(Hollannissa ym)* burgomaster; *Cityn yli~* Lord Mayor.

porno porn. **-grafia** pornography. **-grafinen** pornographic.

poro 1. *(sakka)* sediment, dregs; *(esim. kahvin)* grounds; *polttaa ~ksi* lay. . in ashes. **2.** *(eläin)* reindeer. **-erotus** round-up (for marking reindeer). **-mies** herder. **-nliha** reindeer meat.

poro|peukalo *a.* ham-fisted; *s.* bungler. **-porvarillinen** petty bourgeois.

porras step; stair; *(-silta)* footbridge; *portaat* [flight of] stairs, staircase, *(et. ulko-)* steps; *portaita ylös, alas* up-(down)stairs. **-käytävä** staircase. **-taa** terrace; *kuv.* stagger; scale (up *t.* down).

porsaan|kyljys pork chop. **-reikä** *kuv.* loophole.

pors|as pig. **-ia** farrow.

porstua [entrance] hall.

port|aat ks. porras. **-aikko** staircase.

portieeri *(hotellin)* receptionist.

portinvartija gate-keeper, porter.

portteri porter.

portti gate, gateway; *portista* through the gate. **-käytävä** gateway.

portto harlot, whore; prostitute.

Portugali Portugal. **p-lainen** *a. & s.* Portuguese *(pl. = sg.).* **p-n kieli** Portuguese.

portviini port.

porukka crowd, gang.

porvari bourgeois; citizen; *vanh.* burgess. **-llinen** bourgeois, middle-class. **-luokka** middle class. **-ssääty** estate of burgesses. **-sto** bourgeoisie.

poseerata pose.

posetiivi barrel-organ.

positiivi *kiel.* positive. **-nen** positive.

poski cheek. **-hammas** molar. **-luu** cheekbone. **-parta**

[side-]whiskers, sideboards, *Am.* sideburns. **-pää** cheek-bone.

posliini china[ware], porcelain. **-astiasto** china set; dinner set, tea set *jne.* **-maalaus** porcelain painting. **-nen** [. . of] china. **-tehdas** china factory. **-teollisuus** porcelain manufacture.

possessiivi|nen *kiel.* possessive. **-pronomini** possessive pronoun.

posti post, *et. Am.* mail; *panna ~in* post; *vien kirjeen ~in* I'll take a letter to the post; *tänään ei tule ~a* there is no post today; *ensi ~ssa* by the next post. **-auto** post-office van. **-ennakko** C.O.D. (= cash on delivery). **-hallitu|s** Post-Office Department; *p-ksen pääjohtaja* Postmaster-General. **-juna** mail train. **-kortti** postcard. **-laatikko** post-box, letter-box; *Am.* mail-box; *Engl. m.* pillar-box. **-laitos** postal system *(t.* services). **-laiva** mail-boat. **-leima** postmark. **-lokero** post-office box (P.O.B.). **-luukku** letter-box. **-lähetys** postal matter. **-maksu** postage; *~t* postal charges, postage rates; *~tta* free of postage. **-merkki** [postage] stamp; *varustaa -merk(e)illä* stamp; *(~kokoelma* collection of stamps). **-mestari** postmaster. **-myynti** mail order business. **-nhoitaja** postmaster(-mistress). **-nkantaja** postman. **-nkanto** delivery. **-nkuljetus** forwarding by post. **-numero** post code. **-osoite** postal address. **-osoitus** postal order. **-paketti** parcel; *~na* by parcel post. **-siirto** Post Office Giro: (*~tili* postal giro account). **-säkki** mail bag. **-säästöpankki** post-office savings bank. **-talo** *(pää-)* General Post-Office. **-taksa** postage rates. **-toimisto** post-office; *pää~* General P.-O. *(lyh.* G. P. O.). **-tse** by post, by mail. **-ttaa** post, *Am. tav.* mail. **-vaunu** mail van. **-vaunut** *vanh.* stage-coach. **-virkailija** post-office clerk.

-yhteys postal communication.
potaska potash.
potea *(jtk)* be ill (with), suffer (from).
potenssi *mat.* power, degree; *korottaa ~in* raise to a power, *(toiseen)* square.
potilas patient.
potk|aista kick; *(ampuma-aseesta, m.)* recoil. **-ia** kick. **-u** kick; *onnen ~* stroke of good luck; *antaa ~t* sack; *saada ~t* be fired; *(~housut* rompers; *~kelkka* kick sledge; *~lauta* scooter; *~pallo* football). **-uri** *(laivan ym)* screw, propeller; *ilm.* air-screw; *~n akseli* screw shaft; *~n siipi* blade [of a propeller].
poukama inlet, bay, cove, creek.
pouta dry weather. **-inen** rainless. **-sää** dry weather.
pov|ari fortune-teller. **-ata** tell fortunes [by the cards, *korteista*]; *~ jklle* tell sb. his fortune, *(kädestä, m.)* read a p.'s hand.
povi bosom, breast. **-nen:** *pyöreä ~* curvaceous, full-bosomed. **-tasku** inside pocket.
Praha Prague.
praktiikka practice.
prame|a ostentatious, showy. **-illa** show off, parade [one's finery] ; *~ uudessa hatussa* sport a new hat. **-ilu** ostentation, show [iness]. **-us** pomp, display, show.
predikaa|tti *kiel.* predicate. **-tintäyte** predicate complement.
preeria prairie.
preesens *kiel.* present [tense].
preludi prelude.
preparaatti preparation; specimen.
prepositio *kiel.* preposition.
presbyteeri(nen) Presbyterian.
presidentin|linna presidential residence. **-vaali** presidential election. **-virka** office of president, presidency.
presidentti president. **-ehdokas** presidential candidate. **-kausi** presidency.
pressu tarpaulin.

Preussi Prussia.
priima first-class; *(et. ruokatavarasta)* prime; *(erinomainen)* fine, choice; *~ laatu(a)* prime quality.
prikaati brigade.
priki brig.
primadonna prima donna; leading lady.
prins|essa princess. **-si** prince; *(~puoliso* prince consort).
probleema problem.
profee|tallinen prophetic. **-tta** prophet.
professori professor [of, in, *jnk aineen*]. **-nvirka** professorship, [professor's] chair.
profiili profile.
progressiivinen progressive; *~ tulovero* graded income tax.
prok|uristi managing clerk. **-uura** procuration, proxy; *merkitä ~lla* sign per pro.
promemoria memorandum.
promootio conferment of degrees, degree ceremony, *Am. m.* commencement.
pronomini *kiel.* pronoun.
pronssi Bronze. **-kausi** Bronze Age. **-nen** [.. of] bronze.
proomu barge, lighter.
proosa prose. **-llinen** prosaic.
propagand|a propaganda; *tehdä ~a (jnk puolesta)* carry on p. for. **-istinen** propagandist [ic].
prosen|tti per cent, %; *viiden prosentin korolla* at five per cent interest; *-tteina (jstk)* in terms of percentage, [expressed] as per cent of. **-luku**, **-määrä** precentage. **-tuaalinen** percentage, per cent.
prosessi *lak.* lawsuit.
prospekti prospectus.
prostit|uoitu prostitute. **-uutio** prostitution.
proteesi prosthesis, *(raaja, m.)* artificial limb (leg, arm), *(hammas-)* denture.
protestantti Protestant. **-nen** Protestant. **-suus** Protestantism.
protestoida protest (against), lodge a protest.
protokolla minutes, *dipl.* protocol.
protoni proton.
proviisori *l.v.* head dispenser,

qualified chemist.
provo|kaattori provocateur.
-kaatio provocation. **-soida**
provoke.
präss|it *(housun)* trouser
creases. **-ätä** press.
psalmi psalm. **-nkirjoittaja**
psalmist.
psykiatri psychiatrist. **-a**
psychiatry. **-nen** psychiatric.
psyko|analysoida psychoanalyse.
-analyysi psychoanalysis.
-analyyttinen psychoanalytic.
-logi psychologist. **-logia**
psychology. **-loginen**
psychological.
psyko|osi psychosis. **-paatti(nen)**
psychopath(ic). **-terapia**
psychotherapy.
psyyk|e psyche, soul, mind.
-kinen psychic, mental.
pudistaa shake [one's head,
päätänsä] ; *(jtk jstk)* shake ..
off. .; ~ *hihastaan (kuv.)*
produce sth. off-hand (off the
cuff); ~ *ies niskoiltaan* throw
off the yoke.
pudo|ta fall [down], drop;
(suistua) tumble [down]; ~
hevosen selästä be thrown
from one's horse, fall off
one's horse; *minulta putosi jk*
I dropped something; *-tessaan*
in falling; *olla putoamaisillaan*
be on the point of falling, be
about to fall. **-ttaa** drop, let. .
fall.
puhal|lettava inflatable. **-lin**
tek. blower, *mus.* wind
instrument; *-timet* the wind,
puu~ woodwind.
puhallus blow[ing]. **-lamppu**
blow-lamp. **-soitin** wind
instrument.
puhaltaa blow; ~ *jtk ilmaa*
täyteen blow up, inflate; ~
sammuksiin blow out.
puhdas clean; pure [air, *ilma;*
heart, *sydän*] ; *(puhtautta*
harrastava) cleanly; ~
omatunto clear conscience; ~
voitto clear profit, *(netto-)*
net profit; ~ *paperi*
(kirjoittamaton) blank paper;
kirjoittaa puhtaaksi make a
clean (fair) copy; *puhua*
suunsa puhtaaksi speak one's
mind, speak out. **-henkinen**

pure. **-kielinen** *(oikea-)*
correct. **-kielisyys** correct
language; purism. **-oppinen**
orthodox. **-rotuinen**
pure-blooded; *(eläimistä)*
thoroughbred; ~ *hevonen*
thoroughbred. **-sydäminen** pure
in heart.
puhdetyö(t) spare-time
activities, hobby crafts.
puhdis|taa clean, cleanse,
purify *(m. kuv.);* clear;
(siivota) clear up, tidy up;
(kirkastaa) polish; *tekn.*
refine; *kuv.* purge (from); ~
rikkaruohoista weed; ~ *syystä*
clear. . of a charge. **-tautua**
kuv. clear oneself [of guilt,
syystä], be exonerated [from
a charge, *syytöksestä*] ; *vrt.*
seur. **-tua** become clean
(pure), be purified; *kuv.* be
cleared [of . . *jstk*]; *-tunut*
purified. **-tus** cleaning,
cleansing, purification;
(poliittinen) purge; (**~aine**
cleanser; detergent; **~jauhe**
cleansing powder).
puhe speech, address; *(juhla-,*
m.) oration; *(puhelu)* talk,
chat; *~essa ja kirjoituksessa*
in speech and in writing, in
spoken and written language; *~*
pitää ~ make a speech, give
an address; *johtaa ~tta*
preside; *ottaa (jk) ~eksi* bring
up, introduce [a subject];
tulla ~eksi come up [in
conversation]; *siitä asiasta*
~en ollen speaking of that;
*~ena oleva.. * in question,. .
under discussion; *antautua*
~isiin jkn kanssa enter into
conversation with a p.;
päästää jku ~illeen grant
(give). . an interview; *siitä ei*
ole ~ttakaan that is out of
the question. **-elin** organ of
speech.
puheen|aihe subject of
conversation, topic; *on*
yleisenä ~ena is the talk of
the town. **-alainen** . . in
question,. . under discussion.
-johtaja chairman, *et. Am.*
president; *olla ~na* be in the
chair, preside, take the chair;
hänen ~na ollessaan under

his chairmanship; ~*n äänen ratkaistessa* by exercise of the chairman's vote. **-parsi** phrase, *(sanantapa)* saying; *(jllek kielelle ominainen)* idiom. **-sorina** hum [of voices]. **-vuoro: *teillä on* ~** it is your turn to speak; *saivat 3 minuutin* ~*ja* (speakers) could not have the floor for more than 3 minutes.

puhe|kieli spoken language; conversational [English, Finnish *jne.*], *(arki-)* colloquial language; *-kielessä* colloquially. **-kyky** faculty (power) of speech; *saada* ~*nsä takaisin* recover one's speech. **-liaisuus** talkativeness, loquacity. **-lias** talkative, loquacious.

puhelimitse by telephone, on the telephone.

puhelin telephone, *puhek.* phone; *puhelimessa!* speaking! *puhua puhelimessa jkn kanssa* speak to . . on the telephone; *älä sulje* ~*ta* hold on, hold the line. **-johto** telephone line. **-koppi** call-box, telephone box. **-keskus** telephone exchange. **-koje** telephone [apparatus]. **-lanka** telephone wire. **-luettelo** telephone directory. **-numero** telephone number; *valita* ~ dial a number. **-soitto** telephone call. **-torvi** receiver. **-välittäjä** telephone operator. **-yhteys** telephone connection; *päästä -yhteyteen* get through (to).

puhe|lla talk (with, to), *(pakinoida)* chat; ~ *jkn kanssa* have a talk with, talk, chat, converse (with). **-lu** talk; *(keskustelu)* conversation; *(puhelin-)* [phone] call; telephone conversation; *lopettaa* ~ hang up, ring off. **puhe|miehistö** presiding officers. **-mies** *(eduskunnan)* Speaker; (~ *Mao)* Chairman;.. *oli jkn -miehenä* acted as spokesman for. **-näytelmä** drama. **-näyttämö** [dramatic] stage. **-taito** oratory; rhetoric. **-tapa** manner of speaking; mode of

expression. **-tekniikka** technique of speech, elocution. **-torvi** speaking-tube; *kuv.* mouthpiece. **-valta** right to speak; *hänellä ei ole* ~*a asiassa* he has no voice in the matter. **-vapaus** liberty of speech. **-vika** speech defect, impediment in [one's] speech. **-ääni** [speaking] voice.

puhjeta burst; *(aueta)* open; *(kukista)* burst into flower, blossom [out], come out; *(alkaa)* break out; ~ *itkuun* burst out crying; *nuppu puhkeaa* the bud opens; *(ruusut) ovat puhjenneet* are out; *sota puhkesi* the war broke out; *sodan puhjetessa* at the outbreak of war; *rokko puhkeaa (tulirokossa ym)* the rash comes out; *rengas puhkesi* a tyre was punctured, one of the tyres went flat; ~ *sanomaan* burst out, exclaim.

puhk|aista *(tunkea läpi)* break through; *(lävistää)* pierce [through], puncture [a tyre, *rengas*]; *lääk.* lance [a boil, *paise*]. **-i** through; *lyödä* ~ knock a hole in; *(ulkoa)* knock in; *(sisältä)* knock out; *mennä* ~ burst open, *(kumi)* blow out.

puhkuisuus *lääk.* flatulence.

puhtaaksi: ~*kirjoitettu teksti* a fair (clean) copy. **-kirjoittaja** copyist, copying clerk. **-kirjoitus** copying.

puhtaanapito *(katujen)* street cleansing. **-laitos** municipal cleansing department.

puhtaasti cleanly, purely; *laulaa* ~ keep in tune, sing in *(vastak.* out of) tune.

puhtaus cleanness; *m. kuv.* purity; cleanliness.

puhu|a speak, *jklle* to, *jstk* of, about; talk; *(sanoa)* say; ~ *itsekseen* talk to oneself; ~ *jnk, jkn puolesta* speak for; speak in favour of; *jstk* -**mattakaan** *(saati)* let alone; *-mattakaan siitä, että.*. to say nothing of *(t.* not to mention) the fact that. .; *olen kuullut siitä* -**ttavan** I have heard about it, I have heard it mentioned; *hän ei tahdo kuulla siitä -ttavan(kaan)* he will have none of it; *jstk -en* on the subject of; *realistisesti -en* in realistic terms; *-tteko englantia?* do you speak English? *älkäämme puhuko enää siitä* we will say no more about it. **-ja** speaker; *(kauno-)* orator; (~**lava** platform; rostrum). **-ma|ton** speechless, tongue-tied; *mennä p-ttomaksi* become speechless, lose one's tongue. **-tella:** ~ *jkta* speak to (with) a p., address a p.; *miksi häntä ~an* how does one address him? **-ttelu** address; (~**sana** term of address).

puhveli buffalo.

puida thresh, *kuv.* thrash.

puijata trick, cheat, *sl.* diddle.

puikahtaa ks. *pujahtaa*.

puikkelehtia thread one's way [through, *jnk läpi*], thread [in and out].

puikkia: ~ *tiehensä* make off.

puikko pin, *(neule-)* knitting needle; *(tikku)* stick *(m. esim. lakka-)*; *(lääke-)* suppository.

puima|kone threshing-machine. **-la** threshing floor.

puinen wooden,. . of wood.

puista|ttaa: *minua* ~ I shudder, *(et. kylmästä)* I am shivering; *minua* ~ *sitä ajatellessani* I shudder to think of it, I shudder at the thought. **-tus** shudder.

puistikko [small] garden, small park.

puisto park; *(iso, esim. koulun, sairaalan)* grounds. **-istutus** public garden. **-katu, -tie** avenue. **-nvartija** park attendant, park-keeper.

puite: *puitteet* frame, framework; *(ikkunan)* casement, sash; *jnk puitteissa (kuv.)* within the framework (limits) of.

pujah|taa slip, slide; *(tiehensä)* slip away; *siihen on -tanut virhe* an error has crept in there.

pujo|a, -s splice. **-liivi** pullover, slipover.

pujott|aa thread (through); ~ *neulaan* thread a needle; ~ *helmiä lankaan* string beads. **-elu(hiihto)** slalom.

pukama lump, *(paise)* boil.

puke|a dress; clothe *(m. kuv.);* ~ *ylleen* put on [a dress, *puku*]; *vrt. pukeutua;* ~ *ajatuksensa sanoiksi* clothe (couch) one's thought in words; *hattu -e häntä* the hat is very becoming to her; *jhk puettu* dressed in; *miten tyttö oli puettu (m.)* what did she wear? *jksks puettu* dressed [up] as, *(eksyttäkseen)* disguised as. **-maton** undressed. **-utua** dress [oneself], put on one's clothes, get dressed; ~ *koreisiin* dress up, make oneself smart; *naiseksi -utunut mies* a man dressed up as a woman; *miten olit p-tunut?* what did you wear? **-utumispöytä** dressing-table. **-va** becoming. **puki|met** dress; *täysissä -missa* fully dressed. **-ne** article of clothing, garment.

pukinnahka goatskin, buckskin.

pukki billy-goat, buck; *(teline)* trestle; horse. **-silta** trestle-bridge.

puku dress; *(miehen)* suit; *(naisen, m.)* gown, frock; *(et. historiallinen, kansallinen)* costume; *(vaatteet)* clothes, garments; *run. ym* attire, apparel, garb. **-huone** dressing-room. **-inen** *(yhd.)* dressed in . .; *suru~* [dressed] in mourning, wearing mourning. **-kangas** suiting; *(hame-)* dress-material. **-neulomo** dress-maker's [establishment]. **-näytelmä** costume piece. **-näytös** mannequin show. **-pussi** mothproof bag. **-tanssiaiset** fancy-dress ball.

pula shortage [of, *jnk*]; *(pulma)* predicament, pinch, mess, fix; *(liike- ym)* crisis; *joutua ~an* get into difficulties, get into a tight place; *jättää ~an* leave in the lurch; *olla ~ssa* be in a pinch; *pahassa ~ssa* in a sad

plight, in sore straits. **-aika,
-kausi** depression, recession,
slump.
pulisongit [side-] whiskers,
sideboards, *Am.* sideburns.
pulittaa *puhek.* fork out.
puliukko *puhek.* meths drinker.
pulkka pulka, Laplander's sled.
pull|ea plump, chubby. **-eus**
plumpness, chubbiness.
pullis|taa distend;
(puhaltamalla) inflate;
(paisuttaa) swell. **-tua** distend,
expand; bulge, swell [out]; ~
esiin protrude. **-tuma** swelling,
bulge, protuberance.
pullo bottle, *(pieni, esim.
tasku-)* flask; *olla ~llaan*
bulge. **-kori** crate [for
bottles]. **-mainen**
bottle-shaped. **-nkapseli** bottle
top *(t.* cap). **-nkaula**
bottleneck. **-ntulppa** stopper.
-ruokinta: *aloittaa* ~ put the
baby on the bottle. **-ttaa**
bulge out, *(panna pulloon)*
bottle.
pullukka *(tyttö)* dumpling,
(nainen) tubby woman.
pulma difficulty, dilemma;
problem. **-llinen** difficult, hard
[to solve]; complicated;
puzzling; ~ *asema* awkward
position. **-llisuus** difficulty;
awkwardness; complexity.
pulpahtaa well up, come up;
spring, well [forth, *esille*].
pulpetti desk.
pulputa well [up, forth];
gurgle, bubble [up]; *(virrata)*
flow.
pulska fine-looking; *(komea)..
of fine physique, fine.
pulssi pulse.
pultti bolt, pin, peg.
pulveri powder.
pumm|ata sponge. **-i** bum.
pumppu pump. **-laitos** pumping
plant.
pumpuli cotton; *vrt. puuvilla.*
pumpunmäntä pump piston.
pumputa pump; ~ *tyhjäksi*
pump.. out.
puna red; *(helakka)* scarlet;
(poski-) rouge. **-hilkka** Little
Red Riding-Hood. **-inen** red;
-isella (musteella) in red ink;
-isen ruskea red [dish] brown,

auburn [hair, *tukka*]; ~ *lanka
(kuv.)* main thread; *kuin* ~
vaate like a red rag; *hänen
kasvonsa lehahtivat -isiksi* she
went red in the face. **-juuri**
beetroot. **-kampela** plaice.
-keltainen orange, reddish
yellow. **-kettu** red fox. **-kka**
red-faced, ruddy, florid. **-kkuus**
ruddiness. **-multa** red ochre.
-nahka redskin. **-nenäinen**
red-nosed. **-poskinen..** with
red (rosy) cheeks,
rosy-cheeked. **-rintasatakieli**
robin [redbreast]. **-silmäinen**
red-eyed. **-sinervä** violet. **-stua**
blush, flush, redden, colour.
-stus blush. **-ta** redden;
colour.. red, stain.. red;
(ihomaalilla) paint.. red.
-tauti dysentery. **-tukkainen**
red-haired. **-tulkku** *zo.*
bullfinch. **-viini** red wine,
claret.
puner|rrus red glow. **-taa** have
a shade of red [in it];
-tava.. tinged with red,
reddish.
punkki mite, tick.
punnerrus *urh.* press. **-puu**
balancing bar.
punni|ta weigh; *kuv.* weigh [in
one's mind], ponder, think..
over, consider; ~ *(jklle)
hedelmiä* weigh out [a pound
of] fruit (for); ~ *sanojaan*
weigh one's words; *tarkoin
asiaa -ttuani* on mature
deliberation. **-tus** weighing.
punnus weight.
punoa twist; *(kiertää)* twine,
(yhteen) intertwine, interlace;
~ *juonia* intrigue, plot; ~
köyttä make rope, *(pujoa)*
splice.
punoi|ttaa be red, be flushed;
-ttavat posket rosy (flushed)
cheeks; *taivas* ~ the sky is a
glowing red.
puno|s twist; twine; *(nyöri)*
cord; *kehittää -ksesta* untwist.
-utua get twisted; twine;
keskustelu -utui pitkäksi the
discussion became long
drawn-out.
punssi punch.
punta pound [sterling]; *2* ~*a*
£ 2. **-blokki** sterling area.

puntari steelyard.
puntavaluutta sterling.
puntti bundle.
puola spool; bobbin; *(pyörän)*
spoke; *(tikapuissa)* rung.
Puola Poland. **p-lainen** *a.*
Polish; *s.* Pole. **p-n kieli**
Polish.
puola|puu *(tikkaissa)* rung,
round; *~t (voim.)* wall bars.
-ta spool, wind.
puoleen: *kääntyä jkn ~* turn
to; *neuvoa kääntymään jkn ~*
refer a p. to.. **-savetäva**
attractive.
puole|inen: *jnk ~* situated on
the.. side;. *järven~ (ikkuna)..*
looking [out] towards the
lake, *(huone)* facing the lake;
kadun (pihan) ~ huone front
(back) room; *hyvän~* fairly
good; *pienen~* on the small
side. **-ksi** half; *~ läpikuultava*
semi-transparent; *onnistuin
vain ~* I succeeded only in
part; *~ leikillään* half in fun.
-lla *tällä ~ jtk* on this side
of; *olla jkn ~* be on the
side of; *olen ehdotuksen ~* I
am in favour of the proposal;
olla voiton ~ have the upper
hand. **-lle** *tälle ~* to this
side (of), over here; *mennä
vihollisen ~* go over to the
enemy; *saada jku ~en win..*
over. **-lta** *joka ~* from every
side; from every angle; *äidin
~* on the mother's side; *jkn
~ (taholta)* on the part of, at
the hands of; *~ päivin* at
noon. **-n:** *toisella ~ (jtk)* on
the other side (of), beyond. .;
kahden ~ on either hand,
(jtk) on either side of. **-sta**
(edestä) for; *(nimessä)* on
behalf of; *muodon ~* as to
(as regards) form; *omasta ~ni*
for my part, as far as I am
concerned; *sekä ~ että
vastaan* both for and against;
~ ja vastaan puhuvat seikat
pros and cons.
puoli *s.* side; *(puolikas)* half;
(osa) part; *(seutu)*
neighbourhood; *(lak.,
asianosainen)* party; *a.* half;
*vrt. puolella, -lle, -lta, -n; ~
vuotta* half a year; *kaksi ja*

~ mailia two miles and a
half, two and a half miles;
kello ~ yhdeksän at half past
eight; *saat puolet siitä* you
will get half of it; *puolta
isompi (kahta)* twice as large;
puolta vähemmän less by [a]
half; *hyvä ~* good point,
(etu) advantage; *heikko, paha
~* drawback, disadvantage;
asiassa on toinenkin ~ there
are two sides to the matter;
asiaa voidaan katsoa eri ~lta
there is more than one way
to look at the matter; *harkita
asiaa ~n ja toisin* consider
the matter from all angles;
toiselta puolen on the other
hand; *pitää jkn puolta* take a
p.'s side, stand up with,
(puolustaa) stand up for;
pitää ~ansa hold one's own,
stand one's ground; *vetää
puoleensa* attract. **-aika** half;
(väli-) half-time. **-alaston**
half-naked. **-apina** lemur.
-automaattinen semi-automatic.
-avoin half open. **-jumala**
demigod. **-kas** half. **-kasvuinen**
half-grown. **-kengät** shoes.
-ksi half; *panna ~* halve.
-kuollut half dead. **-kuu** half
moon; crescent; *~nmuotoinen*
crecent-shaped. **-kypsä** half
ripe; halfbaked; *(liha ym)*
underdone, *Am.* rare. **-lippu**
half-fare ticket. **-llaan** half
filled (with), half full. **-lleen**
half full. **-matkassa** half-way.
-nainen half done,
half-finished; **-naiset**
toimenpiteet half measures.
-naisuus *kuv.* half-heartedness.
-nen: *-sen vuotta* about half a
year. **-nuotti** half note,
minim. **-pallo** hemisphere.
-pimeä *s.* semidarkness. **-piste**
semicolon. **-pohja** [half-] sole.
-pohjata sole, resole. **-pukeissa**
half-dressed, in dishabille.
-päivä noon, noontide; *ennen
~ä* before noon, *lyh.* a.m.
(ante meridiem); *jälkeen
puolenpäivän* after noon *(lyh.*
p. m.). **-sivistynyt**
half-educated, semicivilized.
-sko half. **-so** spouse;
(miehen) wife, *(naisen)*

husband; *(kuningattaren ym)*
consort. **-sokea** half-blind;
partially blind. **-sotilaallinen**
para-military. **-sukka** sock.
-tanko: *liput olivat -tangossa*
flags were flown at half-staff
(-mast). **-tekoinen** half done.
-tie: ~*hen*, ~*ssä* half-way,
midway. **-toista** one and a
half, a.. and a half. **-totuus**
half-truth. **-ttaa** halve; divide
into halves. **-ttain** half, by
halves. **-valmis** half finished.
-valmiste semimanufactured
article; ~*et* half-finished
goods. **-verinen** half-breed,
(hevonen) half-bred. **-virallinen**
semiofficial. **-vuosittain**
semiannually. **-vuotias** six
months old. **-vuotinen**
half-yearly; semiannual.
-väkisin half forcibly. **-väli**
middle; ~*ssä* in the middle
(of); *(matkaa)* half-way (from),
midway (between); *kesäkuun*
~*ssä (m.)* in mid-June;
1930-luvun ~*ssä* in the middle
nineteen-thirties. **-ympyrä**
semicircle. **-ympyräinen**
semicircular. **-yö** midnight; ~*n*
aikaan at m., about m.
-ääneen in an undertone,
under one's breath.

puol|taa *(suosittaa)* recommend;
(kannattaa) support; speak in
favour (in support) of;
(puolustaa) defend; ~
anomuksen hyväksymistä
favour the granting of a
request; *-tava lausunto*
favourable opinion. **-taja**
supporter; *(jnk asian ajaja)*
advocate. **-tolause**
recommendation.

puolue|ton impartial;
unbias [s]ed; uncommitted,
disinterested, *(valtio)* neutral;
fair; *-ttomasti* impartially.
-ttomuus impartiality;
neutrality; (~*politiikka* policy

of neutrality).
puolue|edut party interests.
-henki party spirit. **-kanta**
(jkn) [a p.'s] political views.
-kiihko party zeal, partisan
spirit. **-kokous** [party]
congress, *Am*, convention.
-kuri party discipline. **-lainen**
member of a party; *(jkn)*
follower, supporter. **-ryhmä**
faction. **-taistelu** party conflict.
-toveri fellow party-member.
puolukka red whortleberry.
puolus|taa defend; *(suojella)*
safeguard; *(lieventää)* be an
excuse (for); *(pitää jkn*
puolta) stand up for; ~
erehdystään excuse one's
mistake; ~ *kantaansa*
maintain one's position; ~
oikeuksiaan defend (stand up
for) one's rights; ~
vaatimuksiaan vindicate one's
claims; *-tettavissa oleva*
excusable, justifiable, *(esim.*
sot.) defensible. **-taja**
defender; *urh.* [full] back.
-tautua defend oneself;
(sitkeästi) stand out [against
the enemy, *vihollista vastaan*];
excuse oneself [by.. -ing, *jllak*],
plead.. as an excuse. **-tella**
(anteeksipyydellen) apologize
(for).

puolustus defence; excuse;
vedota jhk puolustukseksi
plead.. as an excuse (for);
hänellä ei ollut mitään
sanottavaa p-tukseksi he had
nothing to say for himself.
-ase weapon of defence.
-asema position of defence.
-asianajaja counsel for the
defence. **-järjestelmä** [system
of] defences. **-kanta:** *pysyä*
-kannalla be on the defensive.
-keino means of defence.
-kirjoitus apology. **-kyvytön**
incapable of defence,
defenceless. **-laitos** defence
forces. **-laitteet** defence works.
-liitto defensive alliance.
-ministeri minister of defence.
-ministeriö ministry of
defence. **-puhe** [speech for
the] defence. **-sota** defensive
war. **-toimi:** *ryhtyä* ~*in* take
defence action. **-voima:** ~*t*

defence forces, armed forces.
puomi boom; bar, barrier; *voim.* [balance] beam.
puoska|ri quack [doctor]. **-roida** practise quackery.
puoti shop, *Am.* store.
purai|sta bite; *(koirasta, m.)* snap, jkta at. **-su** bite.
pure|ksia chew. **-ma** bite. **-nta** bite, occlusion. **-skella** chew, masticate; *(rouskutella)* munch. **-skelu** chewing, mastication. **-utua** *jhk* sink its teeth in, *sot.* dig itself in. **-va** biting; sharp; incisive, mordant; ~ *iva* caustic satire; ~ *pakkanen* bitter cold.
puris|taa press, *(kokoon)* compress, squeeze; *(venistää)* jam; *(olla tiukka)* be [too] tight; ~ *jkn kättä* shake hands with; ~ *rintaansa vastaan (m.)* clasp to one's breast; *kenkä* ~ the shoe pinches (is too tight); *siitä se kenkä ~kin* that's where the shoe pinches. **-tin** press; *(ruuvi-)* clamp. **-tua** be pressed, get squeezed, get jammed, *(kokoon)* be compressed, constrict. **-tus** pressing; pressure; *(kokoon-)* compression; *(likistys)* squeeze, jam.
puritaani Puritan.
purje sail; *nostaa ~(et)* set sail; *vähentää ~ita* shorten sail; *täysissä ~issa* [in] full sail. **-ala** spread of canvas. **-alus** sailing-boat *(t.* vessel).
purjehdus sailing, navigation, *(huvi-)* yachting; *Välimeren* ~ Mediterranean cruise. **-kausi** sailing-season. **-kelpoinen** *(väylä)* navigable; *(alus)* seaworthy. **-retki** yachting trip.
purjeh|tia sail; *lähteä -timaan (veneellä)* go for a sail; *(laivasta)* set sail; ~ *väärällä lipulla* sail under false colours. **-tija** sailor; *(huvi-)* yachtsman.
purje|kangas canvas. **-laiva** sailing ship (vessel). **-lanka** twine. **-lento** gliding, soaring; *(~kone* sailplane, glider). **-tuuli** fair wind. **-vene** sailing-boat; yacht.

purjosipuli leek.
purk|aa undo, *(esim. ommel)* unpick, take out; *(talo ym)* pull down, demolish; *(kone ym)* dismantle; *(osiinsa)* take apart, take to pieces; *(lasti ym)* unload, discharge; unpack; unbox; ~ *avioliitto* dissolve a marriage; ~ *kauppa* cancel a deal; ~ *kihlaus* break off an engagement; ~ *kuorma (autosta)* unload [a lorry]; ~ *sopimus* annul (cancel, dissolve) a contract; ~ *kiukkunsa jkh* take it out on; ~ *miina, pommi* defuse; ~ *pahaa tuultaan, sisuaan* vent one's anger (spleen); ~ *sydäntään* unburden one's heart; ~ *jtk, joka painaa mieltä* get a th. off one's chest; ~ *jtk toimintaan* act. \ out. **-amaton** indissoluble. **-aminen** *(rakennuksen)* demolition; *(lastin)* unloading; *(kaupan ym)* cancellation; *(liiton ym)* dissolution; *(pommin ym)* disposal. **-aus** discharge; *(raju)* outburst; *(tulivuoren)* eruption; *vihan* ~ outburst of hate; *(~paikka* port of discharge).
purkaut|ua come undone; *(joki ym)* discharge; *(kauppa ym)* be cancelled; *(kihlaus ym)* be broken off; *(tulivuori)* erupt; *(tulivuori) -uu (m.)* .. is discharging; *joki -uu mereen* the river empties (discharges) into the sea; *ajatukset -uivat säveliksi* the thoughts found expression in music; *katkeruus -ui sanoiksi* bitterness burst into words. **-uminen** *sähk.* discharge. **-utumistie** *psyk.* outlet.
purkki *(lasi-)* jar; *(pelti-)* tin, can.
purnata grouse, grumble.
puro brook, stream. **-nieriä** brook char. **-taimen** brown trout.
purppur|a, -ainen purple.
purra bite; *(pureskella)* chew; ~ *hammasta* set one's teeth.
pursi craft, vessel; *(huvi-)* yacht. **-mies** boatswain. **-seura**

yacht club.

purskah|dus: *naurun* ~ burst (peal) of laughter. **-taa:** ~ *itkuun* burst into tears; ~ *nauruun* burst into laughter.

purs|kua spurt out, gush out. **-otin** squeezer. **-ottaa** squeeze out. **-uta** *(tihkua)* trickle; *(esiin, hitaasti)* ooze out; *pursuaa yli laitojen* runs over, overflows; *-uva elinvoima* sparkling (bubbling) vitality.

purtilo trough.

purukumi chewing-gum.

pusero blouse; *(paidan mallinen)* shirt; *(neule-)* jumper.

puser|rin press, squeezer. **-rus:** *-ruksissa oleva* squeezed (jammed) in; *joutua -ruksiin* get jammed. **-taa** press, *(kokoon)* compress; squeeze; *(likistää)* jam; pinch; ~ *mehu jstk* press (squeeze) the juice out of; ~ *rikki* crush. **-tua** get squeezed, *kuv. (esiin)* burst [from her lips], *(kokoon)* constrict [with fear].

pusk|ea butt; *(sonnista)* toss, *(haavoittaen)* gore; *(iskeä)* ram [into, *jhk*]; ~ *työtä* work hard; ~ *päänsä seinään* ram (knock) one's head against the wall. **-utraktori** bulldozer. **-uri** *rautat.* buffer; *(auton)* bumper; *taka*~ rear b.; (**~valtio** buffer state).

pussi bag; *zo. ym* pouch; *anat. & bot.* sac. **-eläin** marsupial. **-lakana** fitted sheet. **-tauti** *(siko-)* mumps.

puti|puhdas: *hänet ryöstettiin -puhtaaksi* he was robbed of every penny he had.

putka jail; lock-up; *joutua ~an* land in jail, be locked up.

putki *(johto)* pipe; tube; *(radio-)* valve, *Am.* tube; *(talon) putket* plumbing; *varustaa (talo) ~lla* plumb, *(uusilla)* replumb. **-johto** piping, pipe, conduit. **-lo** *(tuubi)* tube. **-mainen** tubular. **-posti** pneumatic dispatch. **-sto** piping, pipe layout. **-työläinen** plumber. **-vastaanotin** *rad.* valve set.

putous *(vesi-)* falls, waterfall.

puu tree; *(-aine)* wood; *(poltto-)* firewood; *(tarve-)* timber; *puhua ~ta heinää* talk nonsense, drivel; *joutua puille paljaille* be left penniless (empty-handed); *oli kuin ~sta pudonnut* was struck all of a heap. **-aine** wood; *~et* timber. **-astia** wooden vessel, wooden dish; **-dus:** *on puuduksissa* is numb, is asleep. **-duttaa** *lääk.* an [a] esthetize. **-dutus** local an [a] esthesia; (*~aine* local an [a] esthetic).

puuh|a *ks. homma; hänellä on liian paljon ~a* he is too busy, he has too many things on his hands; *olla ~ssa* be busy, be occupied. **-akas** active, busy; *(yritteliäs)* enterprising. **-ata** be busy; bustle; *(jnk hyväksi)* work for.

puu|hiili charcoal. **-hioke** mechanical pulp.

puuhka muff; *(kaula-)* fur collar, boa.

puu|jalka *-jalat* tilts. **-jaloste:** *~et* woodworking products. **-kaasu** producer gas. **-kaasutin** wood gas producer. **-kenkä** wooden shoe; clog, sabot.

puukko [sheath-] knife. **-tappelu** knife-fight.

puukottaa stab [with a knife], knife.

puu|laatikko wooden box (case); *(säle-)* crate. **-laji** kind of wood, *(kasvava)* species of tree. **-leikkaus** wood carving. **-lusikka** wooden spoon. **-lämmitys** heating with wood.

puuma puma.

puu|massa *ks. -vanuke.* **-merkki** mark.

puun|hakkaaja wood-cutter. **-jalostusteollisuus** wood-working (-processing) industries.

puu|piirros woodcut. **-pino** pile of wood. **-raja** timber line. **-rakennus** *ks. -talo.*

puuro porridge; cooked cereal; *(joskus, m.)* pudding.

puuseppä joiner; *(kirvesmies)* carpenter; *(huonekalu-)* cabinet-maker.

puusepän|liike carpenter's

business. **-oppilas** carpenter's apprentice. **-työ** carpentry, joinery. **-verstas** joinery shop.
puusk|a gust [of wind]; *(tovi)* spell; *(kohtaus)* bout, attack. **-ainen** gusty, squally. **-assa: kädet** ~ with hands on hips. **-ittain** in spells, by fits and starts; at intervals. **-ittainen** gusty; fitful; paroxysmal.
puu|sprii wood-spirit, methyl alcohol. **-talo** wooden house; *(valmisosista koottava)* prefabricated house.
puutarha garden; *(hedelmä-)* orchard; *suunnitella (ja laittaa)* ~ lay out a garden. **-kalu** garden tool. **-kasvi** garden plant. **-kaupunki** garden city. **-koulu** gardening school. **-maa** garden-plot. **-mansikka** strawberry. **-neuvoja** gardening instructor. **-nhoito** gardening, horticulture. **-näyttely** gardening exhibition, flower show. **-ruisku** garden syringe. **-sakset** pruning (lopping) shears. **-tuotteet** garden produce. **-työ**
puutarhuri gardener.
puutavara timber [products], *Am.* lumber; *kova* ~ hardwood, *pehmeä* ~ softwood. **-ala, -kauppa** timber (*Am.* lumber) trade. **-kauppias** timber merchant. **-liike** timber business.
puute lack, want; deficiency; *(vähyys)* shortage; *(puutteellisuus)* defect; *(heikko puoli)* shortcoming, failing; *(menetys)* deprivation; *tilan* ~ lack of space; *olla jnk puutteessa* lack; be in need of; *kärsiä* ~*tta* suffer want; *opettajista on* ~ there is a shortage of teachers; *paremman puutteessa* in the absence of anything better.
puu|teollisuus timber industry. **-teokset** wooden goods. **-ton** treeless, bare.
puuter|i [face-] powder; *(~huisku* powder-puff; *~rasia* compact). **-oida** powder.
puutostauti deficiency disease.
puutteelli|nen defective,

imperfect; *(riittämätön)* inadequate, insufficient; ~ *sanavarasto* a limited vocabulary. **-suus** defectiveness; *(puute)* lack, deficiency, defect.
puutteenalai|nen needy, destitute. **-suus** need, poverty, destitution.
puuttu|a be lacking, be deficient, be wanting [in, *jtk*]; *(olla kateissa)* be missing; *minulta -u jtk* I lack. .; *se vielä -isi* well, I never! *kun sanoja -u* when words fail; ~ *asiaan* interfere (intervene) in a matter; ~ *puheeseen* interrupt, break in; ~ *yksityiskohtiin* go into details; *summasta -i yksi dollari* the sum was one dollar short; *-va* deficient; missing; *-va halu* lack of interest. **-minen** lack [ing]; absence.
puutua grow numb, go numb, get stiff.
puu|työ woodwork. **-vanuke** wood-pulp. **-veistos** wood carving.
puuvilla cotton. **-inen** [. . of] cotton. **-istutus** cotton plantation. **-kangas** cotton material. **-lanka** cotton thread, [sewing] cotton. **-nsiemenkakku** cotton-cake. **-npensas** cotton-plant. **-tehdas** cotton mill.
puvusto wardrobe.
pyhiin|vaellus pilgrimage; *(~paikka* place of pilgrimage; shrine). **-vaeltaja** pilgrim.
pyhimys saint; *julistaa pyhimykseksi* canonize. **-kehä** halo. **-taru** legend.
pyhi|ttää sanctify; *(vihkiä)* dedicate, consecrate; ~ *lepopäivä* keep the sabbath; observe Sunday; *jkn muistolle -tetty* sacred to the memory of; *tarkoitus* ~ *keinot* the end justifies the means. **-täminen:** *lepopäivän* ~ Sunday observance. **-tys** sanctification.
pyhyys holiness; sanctity; *(esim. muiston)* sacredness; *pyhyyden loukkaus* sacrilege;

lain ~ sanctity of law.
pyhä *a.* holy; sacred; *s.*
(*-päivä*) holy day, feast[day];
(*loma-*) holiday; (*sunnuntai*)
Sunday; ~ *henki* the Holy
Spirit; ~ *lehmä* (*kuv.*) sacred
cow; *kaikkein pyhin* the holy
of holies; ~ *Yrjö* St (Saint)
George. **-aatto** eve of a
holiday.
pyhäin|jäännös relic. **-päivä** All
Saints' Day.
pyhä|isin on Sundays. **-kkö**
sanctuary; shrine. **-koulu**
Sunday school. **-päivä**
feast-day, holy day;
(*sunnuntai*) Sunday. **-sti:**
luvata ~ solemnly promise;
vannoa ~ take a solemn
oath, vow. **-vaatteet** *leik.*
Sunday best.
pyjama pyjamas, *Am.* pajamas.
pykälä (*lovi*) notch; dent; nick;
(§) section; paragraph;
(*sopimuksessa ym*) clause.
-inen notched; indented,
jagged. **-merkki** section-mark.
pykälöidä notch, indent.
pylväi|kkö, -stö colonnade;
(*kuistin tapainen*) portico.
pylväs pillar; column; (*patsas*)
post. **-käytävä** colonnade.
-pyhimys stylite. **-rivi** row of
pillars, colonnade. **-sänky**
fourposter.
pyramidi pyramid.
Pyreneet the Pyrenees;
Pyreneiden niemimaa the
[Iberian] Peninsula.
pyrintö aspiration;
endeavour[s], effort[s];
(*tarkoitus*) aim.
pyristellä struggle; (*kala*)
flounder; (*siivillä*) flutter.
pyrki|jä aspirant; candidate.
-mys endeavour[s], effort[s];
aspiration; (*suunta*) tendency;
rauhan -mykset efforts to
achieve peace.
pyrkiä strive (for); (*koettaa*)
try, endeavour, seek [to do a
th., *jtk tekemään*], aim (at);
(*tavoitella*) aspire (to); ~
kouluun apply for admission
to a school, (*korkeakouluun*)
seek entrance to the
university; ~ *jhk päämäärään*
strive for an end, aim at. .;

~ *rantaan* try to reach land;
~ *sisälle* try to get in; ~
täydellisyyteen aim at (aspire
to) perfection; *hinnat -vät*
nousemaan prices tend to
rise; *mihin hän -i?* what is
he driving at? *mihin sillä*
pyrit? what are you aiming at
by that?
pyrkyri climber, careerist.
pyrstö tail. **-tähti** comet.
pyry, -ilma whirling (driving)
snow; *pyryssä* in whirling
snow. **-ttää** whirl [about];
(*ulkona*) ~ there is a whirling
snowstorm (a flurry of snow).
pyrähtää flutter; ~ *lentoon* fly
away, take wing.
pyssy gun; rifle; *ks. kivääri.*
pysty erect. **-asento** upright
(erect) position. **-kaulus**
stand-up collar. **-myynti** sale
of standing timber. **-mätön**
incompetent, incapable.
-nenäinen snub-nosed. **-päinen**
. . with one's head erect.
-ssä: ~ (*oleva*) upright,
erect; *kaulus* ~ with one's
collar turned up; *nenä* ~
with one's nose in the air;
tukka ~ with one's hair
standing on end; *pitää* ~
(*kuv.*) keep up, sustain,
maintain; *pysyä* ~ stand,
(*jaloillaan*) keep on one's feet,
keep one's balance. **-suora** *a.*
& *s.* vertical; ~*an,* ~*ssa*
vertically.
pystyttää put up, erect; set up;
pitch (*a tent, teltta*); ~
muistopatsas jklle erect a
monument (a statue) to. .
pysty|viiva vertical [line]. **-vä**
able, *jhk* to; capable (of),
competent. **-yn** into an
upright position; up; *asettaa*
~ put. . upright; put. . on
end; *auttaa* ~ help a p. to
his feet; *nostaa* ~ set. . up,
stand. . up; *nousta* ~ get up,
stand up, rise; *tie nousi* ~
insurmountable obstacles
arose; *panna* ~ (*liike*) start,
(*juhlat*) throw a party.
pysty|ä be able (to), be
capable (of . .-ing); (*terä*) cut;
ei ~ (*ei tehota*) have no
effect on; *häneen ei p.*

imartelu he is not susceptible to flattery; *hän ei p. siihen* he is not capable of doing it; *hän ei p. tehtävään* he is not equal to the task; *näytä, mihin -t* prove yourself! *niin hyvin kuin -n* as well as I can.

pystö: *maito~* [large] milk can.

pysy|tellä keep [away, *poissa*]; ~ *loitolla* keep aloof. keep one's distance, stand off; ~ *sisällä* stay in, keep indoors; *hinta on -tellyt. . markassa* the price has remained steady at. . marks. **-tfää** keep; *(entisellään)* maintain, keep. . unchanged; ~ *voimassa* retain [in force]. **-vä** permanent; *(luja)* fixed, stable; enduring, lasting; *jäädä ~ksi* remain permanent. **-v(äis)yys** lasting quality, permanence.

pysyä stay; *(jäädä)* remain; *(pysytellä)* keep (to); *jos sää pysyy tällaisena* if it stays like this; ~ *asiassa* keep (stick) to the subject, keep to the point; ~ *erillään jstk* stand (hold oneself) aloof from, keep away from; ~ *huoneessaan* keep to one's room; ~ *jyrkkänä* persist, persevere; ~ *kiinni jssak* stick to; ~ *koossa* hold together, cohere; ~ *lujana* remain firm, *(päätöksessään)* stick to one's resolve; ~ *paikoillaan* stay in one's place, keep in position; ~ *pinnalla* keep afloat, *(kuv.)* keep on the top; ~ *rauhallisena* keep cool, remain calm; ~ *sanassaan* keep one's word, stand by one's promise; ~ *tasoissa jkn kanssa* keep up with, *(rinnalla)* keep pace with; ~ *totuudessa* keep (adhere) to the truth; ~ *virassaan* remain in office; ~ *voimassa* remain in force; ~ *vuoteessa* keep to one's bed, stay in bed.

pysäh|dys stop, halt; standstill; *(liikenteessä)* block; *(keskeytys)* pause; *on -dyksissä* is at a standstill;

liikenne oli -dyksissä lumiesteiden takia the traffic was blocked by snowfall; *(~paikka* stopping-place). **-dyttää** stop, *kuv.* set a stop to; *vrt. pysäyttää.* **-tyä** stop, halt; draw up; come to a standstill (to a stop); *(lakata)* cease; *(kesken)* break off [in the middle of a sentence, *keskellä lausetta*]; ~ *äkkiä* stop short, stop dead.

pysä|kki stop, stopping-place. **-köidä** park. **-köimispaikka** car park. **pysäköinti** parking; ~ *kielletty* no parking, no waiting; *pysäköinnin valvoja* parking (car-park) attendant; traffic warden. **-maksu** parking fee. **-mittari** parking meter. **-paikka** car park, *(bussien)* coach park. **pysäyttää** stop; bring to a standstill, *(esim. liikenne, m.)* hold up; *(hillitä)* check, arrest; *(hevonen)* rein in, pull up [one's horse]; *(kone, m.)* cut [the engine] off; ~ *(filmin) liike* freeze the action.

pyy hazel-grouse; *parempi ~ pivossa kuin kymmenen oksalla* a bird in hand is worth two in the bush. **pyyde** *(pyrkimys)* aspiration, ambition; interest; *(halu)* desire. **-llä** ask; keep asking; ~ *jkta jäämään* urge. . to stay. **-ttäessä** *ks. pyytää.* **pyydys** trap, *(ansa)* snare. **-tys** catching; *(ansoilla)* trapping; *linnun~* bird-catching (snaring). **-tää** catch; *(ansoilla)* trap, snare.

pyyhe towel; *kylmät pyyhkeet* a cold rub-down; *kosteus~* facial blotter. **-kangas** towelling. **-kumi** eraser. **pyyhinliina** towel.

pyyhk|iä wipe; mop; *(pois)* wipe off, *(jtk kirjoitettua)* strike out, cross out, delete, *(esim. velka)* cancel; *(kuivata)* dry; ~ *kyynelensä* dry (wipe away) one's tears. **-äistä** wipe; *(lakaista)* sweep; *aalto -äisi hänet mereen* the wave

washed him overboard.
pyykinpesu washing.
pyykittää mark boundaries,
demarcate.
pyykki 1. *(pesu)* wash[ing];
pestä ~ä wash, do the
washing. **2.** *(raja-)* boundary
stone *(t.* mark), landmark.
-nuora clothes-line. **-poika**
clothes peg *(Am.* c.-pin).
-päivä washing day.
pyyle|vyys plumpness,
corpulence. **-vä** plump,
[rather] stout.
pyynti *(kalan ym)* catching,
(metsästys) hunting.
pyyntö request; *(anomus)*
petition; *pyynnöstä* on
request, on application, *(jkn)*
at a p.'s request.
pyyteetön disinterested.
pyytää ask, request; *(hartaasti)*
beg; *(pyytämällä ~)* entreat,
urgently request; *(pyydystää)*
catch; *~ jklta jtk* ask.. for;
~ apua ask [a p.] for help;
~ jku lounaalle invite sb. to
lunch; *pyydämme Teitä..* we
would ask you to;
(lähetetään) pyydettäessä on
(by) request; on application;
pyytämättä unasked, without
being asked; *(kutsumatta)*
uninvited.
pyökki beech.
pyöre|ys roundness. **-ä** round,
rounded, *(joskus)* rotund;
circular; *(mitään sanomaton)*
non-committal; woolly; *~ (iso)
summa* round sum; *silmät
-inä* wide-eyed; *-in luvuin* in
round figures; *~sti* roughly.
pyöri|ntä rotation; revolving
jne. **-stää** round, round off.
-ttää roll; wheel [a hoop,
vannetta]; et. tekn. rotate;
(kiertää) turn. **-ä** *(kiertää)*
revolve. rotate; turn; *(vieriä)*
roll; circulate (round..);
circle; *(esim. hyrrä)* spin;
sana -i kielelläni the word is
on the tip of my tongue;
maailma -i silmissäni my
head is spinning; *-vä* rotating;
rotary; *vrt. kiertää.* **-äinen** *zo.*
porpoise.
pyörre whirl; *(vedessä)* eddy,
(iso) whirlpool; vortex;

taistelun pyörteessä in the
tumult of battle;
maailmansodan pyörteessä in
the maelstrom of world war;
vallankumouksen pyörteessä in
the throes of revolution;
*joutui tahtomattaan
tapahtumien pyörteeseen* was
caught up in events. **-myrsky**
tornado, cyclone; *vrt. hirmu-.*
-tuuli whirlwind.
pyörry|ksissä be in a faint (a
swoon). **-ttää:** *minua, päätäni
~* I feel giddy (dizzy), my
head is swimming; *päätä
-ttävä* dizzy. **-tys** giddiness,
dizziness; *lääk.* vertigo.
pyörty|mys swoon, faint. **-ä**
faint, swoon, pass out; *-nyt*
fainted.
pyöry|kkä *(liha- ym)* [meat]
ball. **-lä** circle.
pyörä wheel; *(polku-)* bicycle;
pyörillä varustettu wheeled;
panna jkn pää ~lle bewilder;
*menestys saattoi hänen päänsä
~lle* success went to his
head. **-hdys** swing, turn; *tekn.
ym* revolution. **-htää** *(ympäri)*
swing round. **-ilijä** cyclist.
-illä [ride a] bicycle, cycle.
-ily cycling. **-inen:** *kaksi~*
two-wheeled.
pyörän|akseli axle; *(koneessa)*
shaft. **-jälki** wheel track,
(syvä) rut. **-napa** hub. **-puola**
spoke. **-rengas** tyre, tire.
-vanne rim [of a wheel].
pyörästö gearing.
pyörö|kaari round arch.
-näyttämö revolving stage. **-ovi**
revolving door.
pyöveli executioner.
pähkinä nut; hazel-nut; *kova ~
(kuv.)* a hard nut to crack.
-nkuori nutshell. **-nsärkijä**
nut-cracker. **-puu** hazel,
hickory.
pähkähullu stark mad.
päihde, -aine intoxicating agent
(huume) drug.
päih|dys: *olla -dyksissä* be
intoxicated, be drunk. **-dy|ttää**
intoxicate; *p-ttävät juomat*
intoxicants. **-tymys**
intoxication. **-tyä** become
intoxicated, get drunk; *-tynyt*
intoxicated, drunk, *(lievästi)*

tipsy, tight.
päihittää beat, *(hakata)*
clobber, *koul. sl.* wallop.
päin in the direction of..,
towards, to; *etelään ~*
to[wards] the south,
southwards; *ikkuna on etelään
~* the window faces south,..
pihalle ~ gives on [to] the
courtyard; *mihin ~* in what
direction? which way? *mistä
~* from what direction? *juosta
~ jtk* run against; *~
kasvojani* to my face. **-en:**
kaksi ~ two-headed. **-nkään:** *ei
sinne ~* nothing of the kind.
-nsä: *käy ~* may be done, is
possible; is proper, is fitting;
ei käy ~ että menet sinne it
won't do for you to go
there. **-nvastai|nen** opposite,
contrary (to); *~ järjestys*
reverse order; *p-seen suuntaan*
in the opposite direction;
mikään ei todista p-ista there
is no evidence to the
contrary. **-nvastoin** on the
contrary; *ja ~* and vice
versa; *asia on aivan ~* it is
just the opposite (the
reverse), it is just the other
way; *~ kuin* contrary to,
unlike; *vrt. sitä vastoin.*
-ssään: *olla ~* be drunk.
-stikkaa head first, headlong.
päitset headstall, halter.
päive|ttyä get sunburnt, get
tanned; *-ttynyt* sunburnt. **-tys**
sunburn, sun tan.
päivi|neen: *vaatteineen
päivineen* clothes and all. **-sin**
by day, in the daytime. **-tellä**
l.v. bemoan, complain (of).
päivittäi|n daily, day by day;
matkustaa ~ työhönsä (lähiöstä)
commute between home and
work. **-nen** daily.
päivyri wall *(t. table)* calendar.
päivys|tys duty. **-täjä:** *olla ~nä*
be on duty. **-tää** be on duty
[for the day]. **-tävä:** *~
apteekki* pharmacy on duty,
rota pharmacy; ~ lääkäri
doctor on call.
päivä day; *(aurinko)* sun; *~llä*
by day, in the day-time; *~ssä*
a day, per day; *kaksi kertaa
~ssä* twice a day, twice

daily; *3 dollaria ~ssä* three
dollars a day; *elokuun 4. ~nä*
on the fourth of August;
kirjeenne huhtikuun 7. ~ltä
your letter of April 7th; *joka
~* every day, daily; *~
päivältä* day by day, day
after day; *~stä toiseen* from
day to day; *eräänä ~nä* one
day; *tässä eräänä ~nä* the
other day; *jonakin ~nä
(tulevaisuudessa)* some day;
näinä päivinä one of these
days; *kaiken ~ä* all day long;
~t pitkät day in, day out;
edellisenä ~nä the day
before; *tähän ~än mennessä*
till now, up to date; *(en ole
nähnyt häntä) kahteen ~än* [I
have not seen him] for two
days; *monesko ~ tänään on?*
what date is it today? *hyvää
~ä (e.p.p.)* good morning!
(j.p.p.) good afternoon!
(usein m.) hello, how are you?
(= hauska tutustua) how do
you do? **-hoito** *(lasten)* day
care. **-juna** day train.
-järjes|tys programme *(t.
order)* of the day, *(lista)*
agenda; *viime aikoina
p-tykseen tulleet asiat* matters
which have recently come to
the fore. **-kausi:** *~a* day in,
day out; for many days.
-kirja diary; *(luokan)* register;
kirjanp. journal, daybook;
kirjoittaa ~an enter sth. in
one's diary, *(koul.)* mark the
register. **-koti** day nursery.
-käsky order of the day.
-lehti daily [paper]. **-lleen:** *~
kaksi vuotta* two years to a
day, exactly two years. **-llinen**
dinner; *syödä -llistä* dine;
milloin syötte -llistä? what
time do you have dinner?
päivällis|aika dinner-time.
-kutsut dinner-party. **-pöytä**
dinner-table. **-uni** after-dinner
nap. **-vieras** guest [at
dinner], guest for dinner;
diner.
päivä|läinen day-labourer.
-matka day's journey. **-määrä**
date.
päivän|kakkara ox-eye daisy,
marguerite. **-koitto** dawn,

daybreak (*p-koitteessa* at d.).
-kohtainen topical; *on* ~
has been much in the news.
-kysymys question of the day.
-paahtama sunburnt. **-paiste**
sunshine. **-polttava.** . of
current (of topical) interest;
~ *kysymys* burning question
of the day. **-puoleinen.** .
situated on the sunny side,
sunny. **-seisaus** solstice. **-selvä**
clear as day, evident, obvious.
-tasaaja equator. **-tasaus**
equinox. **-valo** daylight; ~*ssa*
by d.; *tulla* ~*on* come to
light; *saattaa* ~*on* bring to
light. **-varjo** sunshade, parasol.
päivä|näytäntö matinee. **-palkka**
day's wages, daily pay;
-palkalla by the day.
-palkkalainen day-labourer.
-peite bedspread, counterpane,
coverlet. **-raha** daily
allowance. **-sakko** daily
fine[s]. **-sydän** middle of the
day, noon, midday; ~*nä* at
noon, at midday. **-työ** day's
work; day-to-day job; *olla*
~*ssä* work by the day;
(~**läinen** day-labourer). **-tä**
date; *kirje on -tty maaliskuun
1 p:nä* the letter is dated
March 1st;. . *-tty kirjeenne*
your letter of [March 1st]; ~
myöhemmäksi, aikaisemmaksi
postdate, antedate. **-ys** date.
-ämätön undated.
pälkä|htää: päähäni *-hti* it
occurred to me, it entered
my head. **-hässä** in a
dilemma; *auttaa jku -hästä*
help a p. out.
pälyillä gaze [suspiciously],
peer [to either side], glance
[furtively], give . . sidelong
glances.
päntätä: ~ *päähänsä* grind
away [at Latin, *latinaa*].
päre (*katto-*) shingle; (*kori-*)
splint. **-katto** shingle roof.
-koppa splint basket.
pärinä rattle; (*herätyskellon
ym*) buzzing; (*torven*) blaring;
rumpujen ~ beating of drums.
-stä buzz; (*rämistä*) rattle.
pärjätä do well (in), get on;
manage [well], cope (with);
pärjäätkö ilman apua? can you

manage without help?
pärsky|ttää, -ä spatter, splash.
pässi ram. **-npää** *kuv.*
blockhead.
pätem|isentarve desire (need)
to assert oneself. **-ättömyys**
imcompetence, incapacity;
disqualification; invalidity.
-ätön incompetent, incapable;
(*kelpaamaton*) invalid; *julistaa
-ättömäksi* declare invalid (*t.*
null and void).
päte|vyys competence, ability;
qualifications; (~**vaatimus**
qualifications required). **-vä**
competent; capable; qualified;
(*kelpaava*) valid; (*pitävä*)
tenable; ~ *virkaan* qualified
for the position; ~*t syyt*
good grounds; *ei* ~*ä syytä* no
just cause; ~ *este* valid
excuse.
päteä be valid; hold good; *ei
päde enää* is not valid (in
force) any longer.
pätkä stump, end.
pää head; (*loppu*) end; (*kärki*)
point; (*latva*) top; *hattu* ~*ssä*
with one's hat on; *ottaa
hattu* ~*stä* take off one's hat;
pahalla ~*llä* in a bad humour
(temper); *alla päin* in low
spirits;. . *-lla on hyvä* ~ is
brainy; *menestys nousi hänelle*
~*hän* success went to his
head; *saada* ~*hänsä* get [it]
into one's head; *pöydän* ~*ssä*
at the head (at the end) of
the table; *jkta* ~*tään pitempi*
(*kuv.*) head and shoulders
above. .
pää|aine main (*t.* major)
subject; *opiskella jtk* ~*enaan
Am.* major in. . **-aines** chief
ingredient. **-ajatus** leading
idea. **-asia** main thing; main
point; ~*ssa* in the main,
mainly. **-asia|llinen** principal,
main, chief; (*oleellinen*)
essential; **-llisesti** chiefly,
principally; predominantly,
primarily; (*enimmäkseen*)
mostly, for the most part.
-elinkeino principal (main)
industry. **-esikunta** general
staff. **-harjoitus** dress
rehearsal. **-henkilö** principal
character; hero, heroine. **-hine**

head-dress. **-hyve** cardinal virtue. **-hänpiintymä** fixed idea. **-hänpisto** notion, idea; *(oikku)* whim. **-ilmansuunnat** cardinal points. **-jakso** *zo.* phylum, *bot.* division. **-johtaja** general manager, director general. **-johto** main. **-joukko** main body. **-kallo** skull, cranium. **-katsomo** grand stand. **-katu** main (principal) street. **-kaupunki** capital; (~**lainen** inhabitant of the capital). **-kieli** principal language. **-kirja** ledger. **-kirjoitus** leading article, leader, *(toimituksen)* editorial. **-kohdittain:** *selostaa ~ jtk* give the main points of; give an outline of. . **-kohta** main point. **-konsuli** consul general. **-konttori** head-office. **-laki** crown of the head. **-lause** principal sentence (clause). **-liike** head business. **-liina** head scarf.
päälle: *jnk ~ on. .,* on top of. ., *(yli)* over, above; ~ *päätteeksi* over and above that; moreover, besides. **-kirjoitus** heading, title. **-kkäin** one on top of another (the other); (~**menevä,** ~**meno** overlapping).
päälli|kkyys command; leadership. **-kkö** chief, *Skotl. ym* chieftain; *(liikkeessä, m.)* head, principal; *sot.* commander, *(linnan)* commandant; *(laivan)* ship's master. **-mmäinen** topmost, uppermost. **-nen** covering; *(huonekalun)* cover; spread; *(tyynyn)* tick, *(irto-)* case, slip; *-sin puolin* superficially. **-ällys** coat[ing], cover; *(-paperi)* wrapper; *(kirjan, suojus-)* [dust-]jacket. **-kenkä** overshoe. **-lakana** top sheet. **-mies** foreman; *puhek.* boss. **-paperi** wrapping-paper. **-puoli** top side; outer side, outside. **-takki** overcoat, greatcoat. **-te** coating, covering; *(tien)* surface, top. **-tää** cover, coat (with); *(esim. julkisivu)* face (with). **-tö** officers. **-vaatteet** outer garments, outdoor

clothes.
pää|llä: *jnk ~ on. .,* on top of; *(yläpuolella)* above. ., *(yli)* over. **-ltä:** *riisua ~än* take off [one's clothes]; ~ *katsoen* externally, in outward appearance, *(ensi näkemältä)* on the face of it; *moni on kakku ~ kaunis. .* fine feathers do not always make fine birds. **-päin** *ks. ed.*
pää|luokka *kiel.* voice. **-luottamusmies** shop steward. **-maali** aim, object, goal. **-maja** headquarters. **-mies** head; *lak.* client; principal. **-ministeri** prime minister, premier. **-määrä** aim, object; goal; *saavuttaa ~nsä* gain one's ends; *ilman ~ä* aimlessly, with no point in view; (~**tön** aimless, purposeless). **-nahka** scalp. **pään|alus** pillow; cushion. **-nyökkäys** nod. **-särky** headache. **-tie** neckline. **-vaiva** bother, trouble; *nähdä ~a (jstk)* bother one's head (about).
pääoma capital; *kiinteä ~* fixed c.; *muuttaa ~ksi* capitalize; convert into capital. **-nomistaja** capitalist. **-npako** flight of capital. **-nsijoitus** investment. **-tili** capital *(t.* stock) account. **pää|osa** main part, bulk (of); *teatt.* leading role, the lead. **-ovi** main entrance, front door. **-paino:** *panna ~ jhk* lay the main stress on, attach primary importance to. **-periaate** leading principle. **-perillinen** principal heir. **-piirre** main feature; *-piirteittäin* in broad outline, in a general way. **-rakennus** main building; *(tilan)* farmhouse. **-rata** main line, trunk line. **pääri** peer. **päärm|e, -ätä** hem. **päärynä** pear. **-nmuotoinen** pear-shaped. **-puu** pear-tree. **pää|sana** headword. **-sihteeri** secretary-general. **-sisällys** essence, substance. **-sisäänkäytävä** main entrance. **pääsiäi|nen** Easter; *-senä* at E.

-sjuhla Easter festival; (juutalaisten) Passover. **-slammas** paschal lamb. **-slilja** daffodil. **-sloma** Easter holiday. **-smuna** Easter egg. **-späivä** Easter Sunday; toinen ~ Easter Monday.

pääskynen swallow.

päässä: jnk matkan ~ at a distance of;. . away; kilometrin ~ jstk (m.) one kilometre from. . **-lasku** mental arithmetic.

päästä 1. v. get; (saapua jhk) arrive at t. in; (jstk, m.) escape; pääseekö hän mukaan can he come along? (saako) may he come along? ~ jnnek get into, (jäseneksi, oppilaaksi) be admitted to; ~ jstk (pois) get out of, (esim. sairaalasta) be discharged; ~ eroon jstk get rid of; ~ helpolla get off easily; ~ käsiksi jhk get at, (esim. ongelmaan) get to grips with; ~ lähtemään get away; ~ sisälle get in; ~ sopimukseen arrive at (come to) an agreement; ~ tuloksiin reach results; varomaton sana pääsi hänen suustaan an incautious word escaped him; (kengännauha) pääsi auki came undone; tuskin oli hän päässyt sitä sanomasta, kun. . he had scarcely uttered that when. .; siitä ei pääse mihinkään there is no escaping (getting away from) that; pääseekö sinne autolla? can you get there by car? pääsin (sinne) menemästä I did not need to go, I escaped going [there]; mieluummin pääsisin siitä I'd rather not [do that]; ~kseen vaivasta to avoid (to be spared) trouble; pyydän ~ tästä can I be excused?

päästä 2. after; tunnin ~ (m.) in an hour; jnk matkan ~ at (t. from) a distance of. .

päästäinen zo. shrew.

päästää let go, (irti) release, let loose, (irrottaa) unfasten, disengage (from); (sairaalasta ym) discharge; (terästä)

temper; ~ auki open, undo, (napeista) unbutton, (nyöri) untie, unlace; ~ huuto utter a cry, give a scream, cry out; ~ irti (kätensä) release one's hold; ~ käsistään let go, (esim. tilaisuus) let slip; ~ jku sisälle let. . in, admit; ~ vapaaksi release, set. . free; ~ yliopistoon admit. . to the university; ~ jku vähällä, helpolla let. . off easily; päästä minut let me go! päästä meidät pahasta (raam.) deliver us from evil.

päästö|todistus school-leaving certificate. **-tutkinto** school-leaving examination.

pääsy (jhk) access to; admission [in]to, admittance to; vapaa ~ entrance free; ~ (asiattomilta) kielletty no admittance [except on business]; (paikkaan) on helppo ~ (the place) is easily accessible. **-kortti** admission card. **-lippu** ticket [of admission]. **-maksu** admission, entrance fee. **-tutkinto** entrance examination. **-vaatimukset** entrance requirements.

pää|syy main (chief) reason. **-sääntö** principal rule. **-tarkoitus** main purpose, chief object.

pää|tehtävä principal task. **-tekijä** chief factor. **-teos** principal work.

pääte|llä draw conclusions (from), conclude, infer; jstk -llen judging by. . **-lmä** deduction, conclusion. **pääteos** principal work.

päätepiste end point.

päätoiminen full-time.

päätoimittaja editor-in-chief.

päätty|minen termination, conclusion; (loppu) end, close; (umpeenkuluminen) expiration, expiry. **-misaika** [time of] expiration. **-mätön** unfinished; mat. recurring [decimal].

päättyä end, terminate; be

concluded, close; come to an end; *(kulua umpeen)* expire; *(lakata)* cease; ~ *jhk* end with, end (terminate) in; ~ *huonosti* turn out badly; ~ *onnellisesti* turn out well, prove successful, be a success, *(kertomus ym)* have a happy ending; *tauti -i kuolemaan* the illness proved fatal; *kokous -i* the meeting came to an end, the meeting closed; *hakuaika -y huomenna* the time set for application expires to-morrow. **päättä|jäiset** breaking up [of school], *Am.* commencement. **-mätön** *(tili)* unbalanced; *(ratkaisematon)* not [yet] decided; *(epäröivä)* undecided, irresolute. **-väinen** resolute, determined. **-väisyys** resolution, determination. **päät|tää** end, bring.. to an end (to a close); conclude, terminate; *(valmiiksi)* finish, complete; *(tili)* make up, close; *(tehdä päätös)* decide, determine; make up one's mind; ~ *asia* decide a question, settle a matter; ~ *jtk jstk* conclude, infer from; ~ *tili* strike a balance, balance an account; *asia on -etty* the matter is settled; *hän on -tänyt saattaa työn loppuun* he has made up his mind (he is determined) to finish the work; *-tävät elimet* deciding bodies; *siitä -täen* judging from that; *kaikesta -täen* evidently, apparently. **päätuote** principal (main) product. **pääty** gable. **-kolmio** tympanum; pediment. **päätyä** [finally] come to, end [up] in; ~ *jhk tulokseen* arrive at a result. **päätäpahkaa** headlong, precipitately; head over heels. **päätöksentekijä** decision-maker. **päätön** headless; *kuv.* foolish, mad, senseless, absurd; *puhua päättömiä* talk nonsense. **päätös** decision; *lak.* judgment, *(rikosasiassa)* sentence. *(valamiehistön)* verdict;

(arviomiesten ym) award; *(päätelmä)* conclusion; *antaa* ~ *asiassa (lak.)* pronounce (give, render a) verdict; rule [that. .]; *(kokouksessa) tehty* ~ the resolution passed; *panna päätöksensä toimeen* carry one's resolution into effect; *saattaa päätökseen* bring to a conclusion, complete; *tehdä* ~ decide, determine, resolve; make up one's mind; *tulla jhk päätökseen* come to a decision. **-lasku** proportion, rule of three. **-lauselma** resolution. **-valta** authority (power) to decide. **-valtainen:** ~ *jäsenluku* quorum. **pää|vahti, -vartio** main guard. **-vaikutin** chief motive, mainspring. **-vastuu** main responsibility. **-voitto** the first prize. **-vuokralainen** principal tenant. **-äänenkannattaja** leading organ. **pöhö** [o]edema. **-ttymä** swelling. **-ttyä** swell; *-ttynyt* swollen, puffy. **pöhkö** *a.* nuts; *joku* ~ *(Am.)* some kind of a nut. **pöker|rys** stupefaction; *-ryksissä* stupefied, dazed. **pölkky** log, *(alasin ym)* block. **-pää** blockhead, dunce. **pöllähdys, -tää** puff. **pöllö** owl. **pöly** dust; *olla ~ssä* be covered with d., be dusty. **-hiukkanen** particle of dust. **-inen** dusty. **-kapseli** *(pyörän)* hub-cap. **-nimuri** vacuum cleaner. **-riepu** duster. **-ttyä** get dusty. **-sokeri** icing sugar. **-ttää** dust; *(nostaa p-ä)* raise (stir up) the dust; *bot.* pollinate. **-tys** *bot.* pollination. **pönkittää** prop [up]. **pönkkä** prop; support; strut. **pönttö** can, tin; *(linnun)* bird-house; *(poliisin)* box; *leik. (puhujan)* pulpit; *vrt. allas.* **pörrö|inen** ruffled up, rumpled; tousled, dishevelled; *(takkuinen)* shaggy. **-ttää** ruffle, rumple; *(tupeerata)* back-comb.

pörssi stock exchange; *(Ranskassa ym)* bourse. **-hinta** exchange price. **-keinottelija** speculator on the exchange. **-noteeraukset** stock exchange quotations. **-välittäjä** stockbroker, jobber.

pötkiä: ~ *pakoon* take to one's heels, run for it; ~ *tiehensä* bolt, make off.

pötkö stick.

pöty [stuff and] nonsense; *(roska)* rubbish. **-puhe** nonsense.

pöyh|eä puffy; fluffy. **-istellä** *kuv.* strut, swagger. **-iä:** ~ *pielus* shake up a cushion.

pöyhk|eillä be cocky, ride the high horse; *-eilevä käynti* swaggering gait. **-eys** conceit; arrogance, haughtiness. **-eä** conceited, high and mighty, swanky, *puhek.* stuck-up.

pöyristytt|ää horrify, appal; *-ävä* appalling, horrifying, revolting.

pöytä table; *pöydän ääressä* at the table; *istua ~än* sit down to dinner (lunch etc.); *ruoka on pöydässä* dinner (lunch etc.) is served; *panna pöydälle asia* table a question. **-astia:** ~*t* tableware. **-astiasto** dinner (lunch, breakfast) set. **-hopeat** table silver. **-keskustelu** conversation at table; table-talk.

pöytäkirja minutes; report of the proceedings; record; *pitää ~a* take down the minutes; *merkitä ~an* enter in the minutes, record; *~n ote* extract from the minutes; *~n pitäjä* keeper of the minutes; *tarkistaa ~* verify (check) the minutes.

pöytä|laatikko drawer. **-levy** top of the table; *(irto-)* leaf. **-liina** table-cloth. **-rukous** grace; *lukea ~* say g. **-tavat** table manners. **-toveri** partner at table.

R

raadanta toiling; drudgery.
raadella tear.. to pieces; lacerate; *kuv.* tear.
raaha|ta drag, trail. **-utua** be dragged along [by the train, *junan alla*].
raais|taa brutalize, coarsen. **-tua** be (become) brutalized.
raaja limb; ~*t (m.)* extremities. **-rikko** *s.* cripple. **-rikkoinen** crippled, maimed, disabled.
raaka 1. *(laivan)* yard. **2.** raw; crude *(m. kuv.)*; *(kypsymätön)* green [fruit, *hedelmä*], unripe, not ripe; *(käytökseltään)* rude, coarse; brutal. **-aine,** ~**et** raw material. **-kumi** crude rubber. **-lainen** barbarian. **-laisteko** barbaric action, inhuman deed. **-laisuus** barbarism. **-mainen** brutal; *(karkea)* coarse, rude. **-maisuus** brutality. **-purje** square sail. **-silkki** raw silk; shantung. **-sokeri** raw (unrefined) sugar. **-tuotanto** primary production. **-tuote** unrefined product. **-öljy** crude oil.
raakile green fruit; omenan ~ green apple.
raakkua *(varis)* caw; *(korppi)* croak.
raakuus rawness, crudity; rudeness, coarseness; brutality.
raama|ttu the Bible, the Scriptures. **-tullinen** biblical.
raamatun|historia Bible history. **-kohta** Bible passage. **-käännös** translation of the Bible, Bible translation. **-lause** biblical quotation.
raapai|sta scratch; graze; ~ tulta strike a light. **-su** scratch.
raape|kumi ink eraser. **-vesi** ink remover.
raapia scratch, *(joskus)* claw,

(kaapia) scrape.
raapu|ttaa erase, rub out. **-tus** **-(kohta)** erasure.
raast|aa tear, pull; *(laahata)* drag [along]; *(vihanneksia ym)* grate. **-e:** *juusto~* grated cheese. **-in(rauta)** grater.
raastu|pa courtroom. **-vanoikeus** magistrates' court, *Am.* municipal court.
raata|a toil, drudge; *puhek.* slave away, *(esim. koulussa)* grind away [at one's studies]. **-ja** drudge.
raate|leva rapacious [beast, *eläin*], predatory. **-lu** laceration.
raati council. **-huone** town hall, city hall. **-mies** magistrate.
raato carcass.
raavaanliha beef.
raavas *ark.* grown-up; robust; *koll.* cattle.
radikaali, -nen radical; *nuoret* ~*t* the r. young.
radio radio, wireless [set]; ~*ssa* on the radio, on (over) the air; *hän esiintyy* ~*ssa huomenna* he will be on the air tomorrow; *aukaista (sulkea)* ~ switch on (off) the radio; ~ *soi* the radio is on *(pauhaa..* at full blast); *hakea* ~*sta jk asema* tune in to..; *vääntää* ~ *hiljemmäksi* turn down; *tulokset ilmoitetaan* ~*-ssa* the results will be announced on the radio. **-aktiivinen** radioactive; ~ *laskeuma* r. fall-out; ~ *säteily* nuclear radiation. **-aktiivisuu|s** radioactivity; *r-den valvonta* radiation control. **-asema** broadcasting station. **-esitelmä** broadcast talk.
radioi|da broadcast; radio *(imp. & pp.* **-ed)**. **-nti** broadcasting. **-tse** by radio.

radio|kuunnelma radio play.
-laite radio set; *-laitteet* r. equipment. **-luotain** radiosonde, radiometeorograph. **-lupa** wireless licence. **-lähetin** radio transmitter. **-lähetys** radio transmission; broadcast; *lopettaa* ~ go off the air. **-nkuuntelija** listener. **-ohjelma** broadcast programme; *lähettää ~a* be on the air. **-peilaus** radio location. **-puhelin** radio telephone. **-putki** valve, *Am.* tube. **-sähköttäjä** radio operator. **-selostaja** radio commentator. **-suunnin** [radio] direction finder. **-vastaanotin** radio set, *(matka-)* transistor set. **-yhtiö** broadcasting corporation.
rae hailstone; *(jyvänen)* grain, granule; *rakeet, rakeita* hail; *sataa rakeita* it is hailing. **-kuuro** hail-shower, hailstorm.
raha money; *(lantti)* coin; *(valuutta)* currency; *~t* money; funds; *puhtaana ~na* in ready money, *(käteisenä)* in cash; *lyödä ~a* coin, mint; *muuttaa ~ksi* convert into money, realize; *olla rahoissaan* have some cash; *olla vähissä rahoissa* be short of money; *saada vastinetta ~lleen* get one's money's worth. **-ansio** earnings. **-apu, -avustus** pecuniary aid. **-arpajaiset** lottery with money prizes. **-arvo** monetary value. **-asiat** money matters; finances; *-lla on huonot* ~ is financially embarrassed.
raha|-automaatti coin machine. **-huolet** money worries. **-järjestelmä** monetary system. **-kanta** monetary standard, standard of currency. **-kas** moneyed. **-ke** *(kaasu-)* gas-meter disk. **-kirje** letter containing money. **-kokoelma** collection of coins. **-kukkaro** purse. **-kysymys** question of money. **-lahja** money gift. **-laina** loan of money. **-laitos** financial institution. **-llinen** pecuniary, monetary; financial; ~ *etu* pecuniary advantage.

-llisesti financially. **-lähetys** remittance. **-markkinat** money-market. **-mies** financier, capitalist. **-määrä** amount of money.
rahan|ahne greedy of money. **-arvo** money value; ~*n aleneminen* inflation, drop in the value of money. **-keräys** collection; *panna toimeen* ~ start a c., have a whip-round. **-lyönti** coining [of money]; minting. **-niukkuus** scarcity of money. **-puute** lack of money. **-saanti** supply of money. **-sijoitus** investment. **-tarve** demand for capital. **-vaihtaja** money-changer. **-vaihto** money exchange. **-väärentäjä** counterfeiter.
raha|paja mint. **-palkinto** money prize. **-palkka** wages. **-pula** money difficulties; *olla ~ssa* be short of money, be [hard] pressed for money, be hard up. **-pussi** purse. **-sakko** fine. **-staa** collect. **-staja** collector, cashier; *(linja-auton)* conductor. **-sto** *(pohja-)* fund, *(lahjoitettu, m.)* foundation; *(valtion kassa)* treasury; *(~nhoitaja* treasurer). **-stus** collection. **-summa** sum [of money]. **-taloudellinen** financial. **-talous** finances; monetary policy. **-tiede** numismatics. **-toimi** finances; *(~kamari* municipal finance department). **-toimisto** finance office. **-ton** impecunious, penniless, *sl.* [stony-]broke. **-valta** plutocracy. **-varainhoitaja** treasurer. **-varat** means, funds, financial resources. **-yksikkö** monetary unit, unit of currency.
rahdata freight, *(laiva)* charter.
rahina rattle, *lääk.* rales.
rahkasuo sphagnum bog.
rahoi|ttaa finance. **-ttaja** financier.
raht|aaja charterer, freighter. **-aus** chartering, freighting; *(-kirja* charter party (C/P).
rahti *(laiva)* freight; *(maa-)* carriage, *Am.* freight; rate; ~ *maksetaan perillä* freight [to

be charged] forward, carriage forward; ~ *maksettu(na)* carriage paid, *(meri-)* freight [pre]paid. **-kirja** way-bill, consignment note; *mer.* bill of lading *(lyh.* B/L); *lentok.* air waybill. **-laiva** cargo ship, freighter. **-liike** carrying trade. **-maksu** freight [charge] *vrt. rahti;* ~*tta* freight prepaid, carriage paid. **-tavara** freight; *lähettää* ~*na* send by goods train, send as ordinary freight.

rahtu bit; a little; *ei* ~*akaan* not a bit, not in the least. **-nen:** *-sen parempi* a little [bit] better, a trifle better; ~ *suolaa* a pinch of salt; ~ *pippuria* a little pepper; *unen*~ a wink of sleep.

rahvaanomainen vulgar, *(talonpoikais-)* peasant, rustic.

rahvas common people, *(maalais-)* countryfolk; *(massat)* hoi polloi.

raidallinen striped.

raide track; line; *suistua raiteilta* be derailed, go off the rails. **-leveys** gauge. **-vaihde** switch.

raidoittaa stripe; streak.

raihnai|nen sickly, ailing; decrepit [with age]; ~ *henkilö* invalid; *vanha ja* ~ aged and infirm. **-suus** weakness, decrepitude.

raik|as fresh; *(viileä)* cool; *(heleä)* clear, bright; *(sää, m.)* crisp. **-kaus** freshness; coolness.

raiku|a clang, ring, *(kaikua)* resound; *-va* ringing; *suosionosoitusten -essa* amid loud applause.

railakas brisk, jaunty, carefree; ~ *ilta* a convivial evening.

railo crack; *(avattu)* channel in the ice.

raina film strip; *(kuultokuva)* slide, transparency.

raion rayon.

raippa rod; *(piiska)* whip; lash; *antaa raippoja* flog, whip. **-rangaistus** whipping, flogging.

raisk|ata ruin, destroy; *(nainen)* rape. **-aus** rape.

rais|u frisky; boisterous, romping. **-uus** wildness, boisterousness.

raita 1. stripe; streak. **2.** *bot.* [goat-] willow. **-inen** striped; streaked, streaky.

raiteinen *(yhd.)* -track; *yksi-, (kaksi-)* single- (double-) track; *kapea*~ narrow-gauge.

raitio|tie tramway, *Am.* streetcar line; (~**liikenne** tramcar traffic; ~**pysäkki** tram stop). **-vaunu** tram[car], *Am.* streetcar; *ajaa* ~*lla* go by tram, take the tram; *nousta* ~*un* get into a tram; *poistua* ~*sta* get off a tram.

raitis fresh, *(viileä)* cool; *(ei juopunut)* sober, *(ehdottoman* ~) teetotal, *s.* teetotaller; *haukkaamassa* ~*ta ilmaa* taking the air. **-henkinen** soberminded. **-taa** freshen; *kuv.* sober. **-tua** be refreshed; become sober, become an abstainer.

raittiisti coolly *jne.; tuulee* ~ there is a cool (an invigorating) breeze.

raittius freshness; *(väkijuomiin nähden)* temperance, teetotalism. **-aate** [cause of] temperance. **-juoma** non-alcoholic drink, soft drink. **-liike** temperance movement. **-mies** total abstainer, teetotaller.

raiv|aamaton uncleared; ~ *ala* unbroken ground. **-ata** clear; *kuv.* pioneer; ~ *tieltä(än)* clear.. out of the way, do away with; ~ *tie metsän läpi* cut a road through the forest; ~ *tietä (kuv.)* pave the way, open the way (for); break new ground; *hän on -aava tiensä (menestykseen)* he will forge ahead. **-aus** clearing; (~**traktori** bulldozer; ~**työ** *kuv.* pioneer work).

raivo rage, fury; *(mieletön)* frenzy; *olla* ~*issaan* be in a rage, be furious, *jstk* at. **-hullu** *a.* raving mad; *s.* violent lunatic. **-isa** furious, frantic, mad. **-kkuus** fury; violence. **-npurkaus** outburst of rage. **-stua** fly into a

passion, become furious.
-stu|ttaa make. . furious,
drive. . mad, infuriate, enrage;
-ttava maddening. **-ta** rage;
(olla vallalla) run riot, be
rampant. **-tar** fury. **-tauti**
rabies, hydrophobia.
raja limit, bound; *(maiden ym)*
boundary [line], border;
(valtiollinen) frontier;
kaupungin ~*t* town
boundaries, *Am.* city limits;
~*nsa kaikella* one must draw
the line somewhere; *olla jnk*
~*lla* border (on); *jnk* ~*lla*
oleva bordering (on),
adjoining; *jnk rajoissa* within
the limits of; *pysyä*
kohtuuden rajoissa keep
within the bounds of
moderation; *tulojensa rajoissa*
within one's income; *mennä*
~*n yli* cross the frontier;
panna ~ *jllek* put a limit to;
vrt. rajoittaa. **-arvo** *mat.*
limit. **-hinta** [price-] limit.
-kahakka border skirmish.
-kaupunki frontier town.
-kkain bordering each other
~ *oleva(t)* adjoining,
contiguous; *olla* ~ adjoin
[each other]. **-maa** border
-[land]. **-nloukkaus** frontier
infringement. **-pyykki** boundary
stone, *kuv.* landmark. **-riita**
frontier controversy. **-selkkaus**
frontier incident. **-seutu**
frontier, border. **-tapaus**
borderline case. **-ton**
unlimited, unbounded;
(ääretön) boundless; endless;
infinite; *hänen riemunsa oli*
~ his joy knew no bounds.
-ttomasti without bounds,
beyond measure,
unrestrictedly. **-ttomuus**
boundlessness; infinity.
-vartio(sto) frontier guard.
-viiva boundary line, line of
demarcation.
rajoi|ttaa border; limit, restrict,
confine [one's activity to,
toimintansa jhk]; *Suomea*
~ *idässä Neuvostoliitto* the
U.S.S.R. borders Finland to
the east; **-tettu** limited;
restricted; *(ehdollinen)*
qualified. **-ttamaton** unlimited,

unrestricted; absolute. **-ttava**
restrictive. **-ttua** *(jhk)* border
[up]on, *kuv.* restrict (confine)
oneself (to); *(asioista)* be
limited (to). **-ttuneisuus**
limitation[s]; narrow outlook.
-tus limitation, restriction;
limit; *eräin -tuksin* subject to
certain reservations
(qualifications); *-tuksitta*
freely, without restrictions.
raju violent, vehement;
(hillitön) ungovernable, unruly.
-ilma storm; ~ *on tulossa* a
storm is brewing. **-us**
violence, vehemence; fury.
rakas dear, beloved; *(läheinen)*
intimate; *rakkaani* love,
honey, ducky, sweetie. **-taa**
love; *-tava* loving,
affectionate; *-tettu* beloved,
sweetheart. **-taja** lover. **-tajatar**
mistress. **-tavaiset** lovers. **-tella**
make love, *jkta* to. **-telu**
love-making. **-tettava** amiable;
lovable. **-tettavuus** amiability;
lovableness. **-tua** fall in love,
jkh with; *-tunut.* . in love
(with).
rakeinen granular.
rakenne structure; construction;
on rakenteilla is under (is in
course of) construction. **-lma**
structure.
rakennus building; *(komea)*
edifice; *(kokoonpano)*
structure; construction. **-aika**
building time. **-aineet** building
materials. **-elementti** building
unit. **-insinööri** building
engineer. **-jätteet** rubble.
-kustannukset cost of building.
-lautakunta Board of Works.
-levy [fibre] building board.
-mestari [master-] builder.
-palikka brick. **-ryhmä** group
of buildings. **-sarja** kit
(do-it-yourself kit). **-taide**
architecture. **-taiteellinen**
architectural. **-telineet**
scaffolding. **-tyyli** [style of]
architecture. **-työläinen**
building worker.
-työmaa building site.
raken|nuttaa have. . built
(erected, constructed). **-taa**
build; construct; *(pystyttää)*
erect; ~ *jälleen* rebuild,

reconstruct, re-erect; ~ *jtk jnk varaan (kuv.)* build. . (found. .) upon; *-netut alueet* built-up areas. **-taja** builder. **-tamaton:** ~ *tontti* vacant lot. **-taminen** building. **-tava** constructive [work, *työ*]. **-teellinen** structural. **-teilla** under construction. **-teinen:** *solakka* ~ of slender body build. **-tua:** ~ *jllek* be founded (based) upon.

raketti rocket; missile; *~aseet* missiles; *raketinheitin* rocket launcher, bazooka. **-merkki** signal rocket.

rakkaasti affectionately, tenderly.

rakkauden\|tunnustus declaration of love. **-työ** deed of charity.

rakkaudeton loveless, devoid of love.

rakkaus love (of; for *t.* towards a p.); *(uskollinen)* devotion (to); *rakkaudesta* for love, *(jkh)* out of love for. **-asia, -juttu** love-affair. **-avioliitto** love-match. **-kirje** love-letter. **-romaani** love story. **-seikkailu** love-affair.

rakki, -koira cur.

rakkine [the] thing, contraption.

rakko *(virtsa- ym)* bladder; *(ihossa)* blister; *tyhjentää ~nsa* relieve oneself, pass water; *hänen kätensä olivat rakoilla* his hands were blistered.

rakkula blister, vesicle. **-inen** blistery.

rako slit; chink; slot; *(seinässä ym)* crack; cleft; *jättää raolleen* leave. . ajar. **-valkea** log fire.

raksahtaa crack, snap; click.

raksi strap; *(silmukka)* sling; *(takin ym)* tag.

raksuttaa *(kello)* tick.

rakuuna dragoon.

ralla\|ttaa troll. **-tus** trolling.

ralli rally.

rampa crippled; *(ontuva)* lame; *tehdä rammaksi* maim; *jäi rammaksi loppuiäkseen* remained a cripple for the rest of his life. **-utua** be crippled, be disabled, be maimed.

ramppi front of the stage; *(-valot)* footlights. **-kuume** stage fright.

rangais\|ta punish; *(kurittaa)* correct, discipline. **-tava** punishable, penal. **-tus** punishment; *(et. sakko)* penalty; *kielletty -tuksen uhalla* prohibited under penalty; *(~aika* term [of punishment]; *kärsiä r-nsa loppuun* serve one's sentence; *~laitos* penal institution *~potku* penalty kick; *~siirtola* penal colony; *~vanki* convict).

rankai\|sematon unpunished. **-sematta** with impunity; unpunished. **-su** punishment; *(~toimenpide* punitive measure).

rankasti heavily; *sataa ~* it is raining hard, it is pouring.

rankka heavy; profuse. **-sade** heavy rain, downpour.

ranne wrist. **-hihna** *(suksisauvan)* hand-strap; *ks. kello.* **-kello** wrist watch. **-rengas** bracelet.

rannikko coast; shore. **-asukkaat** coastal inhabitants. **-kalastus** inshore fishing. **-kaupunki** seaside town. **-laiva** coasting-vessel, coaster. **-laivasto** coastal defence fleet. **-puolustus** coastal defence. **-rata** coast line. **-seutu** coastal region, coast. **-tykistö** coast artillery. **-vartiosto** [body of] coast-guards. **-väestö** maritime population.

Ranska France; *~n (m.)* French; *~n Saksan (sota)* Franco-German.

ranska, *~n kieli* French. **-lainen** *a.* French; *s.* French\|man, -woman; *-laiset* the French. **-laisystävällinen** pro-French. **-nleipä** French roll. **-ntaa** translate into French. **-tar** Frenchwoman.

ranta shore; *(hiekka-)* beach; *(äyräs)* bank; *run.* strand; *meren rannalla* on the seashore, at the seaside; *ajautua rannalle* be washed ashore; *kautta ~in* circuitously. **-hietikko** sands;

beach. **-kaistale** strip of shore
-kallio cliff. **-käärme** grass
snake. **-pato** sea-wall. **-penger**
bank. **-törmä** *(jyrkkä)* bluff.
-viiva coast-line.
rao|llaan ajar. **-ttaa** open.. a
little.
rapa dregs; *(kura)* mud;
(sohjo) slush; *(lika)* dirt. **-kivi**
rough red granite, »rapakivi»
porphyry. **-kko** mud hole.
raparperi rhubarb.
rapata plaster, [face with]
roughcast.
rapautua weather, disintegrate.
rapi|na rustle; *(esim. kynän)*
scratching. **-sta** rustle,
(sateesta, m.) patter. **-suttaa**
rustle.
raportti report, statement;
antaa ~ (jstk) report (upon).
rapp|aaja plasterer. **-aus**
plastering, facing, *(karkea)*
roughcast.
rappeu|tua fall into decay;
(rakennus) become dilapidated;
(rotu, ihminen) degenerate;
-tunut *(rakennus ym)*
dilapidated, tumbledown,.. out
of repair, *(siveellisesti)*
degenerate. **-tuneisuus** state of
decline; dilapidated state;
degeneracy.
rappio decline, decay; ruin;
olla ~lla (esim. viljelys) be in
a neglected condition,
(rakennus) be dilapidated; *hän
on kokonaan ~lla* he has
gone to the dogs. **-alkoholisti**
meths drinker, dosser. **-tila**
[state of] decay, decline;
(siveellinen) degeneracy;
decadence.
rapsi rape.
rapsodia rhapsody.
rapu crayfish, *Am.* crawfish.
rasah|dus, -taa rustle.
rasavilli *a.* boisterous, wild; *s.*
mischief [-maker], *(tyttö)*
tomboy.
rasia box; case; *marja~* punnet.
rasi|te encumbrance, *(-oikeus)*
easement, way leave. **-ttaa**
strain; *(painaa)* burden, weigh
down; *lak.* encumber; ~
itseään liiaksi overstrain
oneself, overtax one's strength,
overwork; *~(jkta) liiaksi* be

too great a strain (upon);
verojen ~ttama burdened with
taxes. **-ttava** strenuous, trying;
(raskas) burdensome. **-ttua**
strain oneself; ~ *liiaksi*
be [come] overworked
(overwrought), overstrain
oneself; **-ttunut** strained;
overwrought. **-tus** exertion;
strain, stress; *lak.*
encumbrance; charge; *liika~*
overstrain, overexertion; *olla
jklle -tuksena* be a burden to.
raskaasti heavily; severely;
(sikeästi) soundly.
raskas heavy; *(esim. tyyli)*
ponderous; weighty; ~
liikuttaa cumbersome;
raskaalla mielellä in low
spirits, heavy-hearted; ~ *rikos*
serious crime; ~ *syytös* grave
(serious) charge; ~ *tykistö*
heavy artillery; ~ *uni* sound
(deep, heavy) sleep; *on
raskaana* is pregnant; *tulla
raskaaksi* become pregnant.
-mielinen melancholic.
-mielisyys melancholy, *lääk.*
melancholia. **-sarja** *urh.*
heavy-weight class.
raskaudentila pregnancy.
raskau|s weight, heaviness;
gravity; *lääk.* pregnancy. **-ttaa**
lak. aggravate; *(vaivata)*
burden, oppress; *-ttava seikka*
aggravating circumstance.
rastas thrush, *(räkätti)* fieldfare.
rasti tick; *urh.* checkpoint;
merkitä ~lla tick off, check
off.
rasva fat; *(kone-)* lubricating
grease; *olla ~ssa* be greasy.
-aine fat, fatty substance.
-happo fatty acid; *monityy-
dyttymättömät -hapot*
polyunsaturates. **-inen** fat
[meat, *liha*]; greasy; *(iho)*
oily. **-isuus** fatness; greasiness.
-kerros layer of fat. **-nahka**
oiled leather. **-nmuodostus**
accumulation of fat. **-rauhanen**
fat gland. **-sydän** fatty
degeneration of the heart. **-ta**
grease; *(öljytä)* oil, *(koneita,
m.)* lubricate; *(voidella)*
smear. **-tahra** grease spot,
smear. **-tyven** dead calm. **-us**
greasing; oiling, lubrication.

rata track; *(rautatie-, m.)* line; *kuv.* course; *(taivaankappaleen)* orbit; *(ammuksen)* trajectory; *ampua (raketti) radalleen* put into orbit; *asettua radalleen (avaruudessa)* go into orbit; *kulkee ~ansa (avaruudessa)* is orbiting. **-kierros** lap. **-kisko** rail.

ratamo greater plantain.

rata|osa [railway] section. **-penger** railway embankment. **-piha** [railway] station. **-pölkky** [railway] sleeper, *Am.* cross-tie. **-urheilu** *ks. kenttä-.* **-vaihde** [railway] points. **-vartija** linesman.

ratas wheel.

ratifioida ratify.

rationalisoida rationalize; improve efficiency.

rati|na, -sta crackle.

ratkai|sematon unsettled, undecided; unsolved, unresolved; ~ *ottelu* draw. **-seva** decisive; conclusive; *~lla hetkellä* at the critical (decisive) moment; *tehdä ~ päätös* make up one's mind definitely. **-sta** decide, settle, determine; *(selvittää)* solve; resolve; *(ristisanatehtävä)* work; ~ *kysymys* settle (decide) a question; ~ *riita* settle a controversy; ~ *tehtävä (mat. ym)* work out; *teidän tehtäväksenne jää* ~ it is for you to decide; *~vissa oleva* solvable,.. capable of solution; *vaikeasti ~va..* hard to solve; *kysymys on -sematta* the question is [still] open. **-su** decision, settlement; solution; *(asia) joutuu ~un* will come up for decision; *päästä ~n asiassa* get the matter settled, reach a decision; *(~valta* power to determine; authority).

ratk|eama rip. **-eta** rip [open]; come unstitched; *(tulla ratkaistuksi)* be settled; ~ *itkuun* burst out crying; ~ *juomaan* take to drink; ~ *saumasta* burst at the seam. **-oa** rip [up]; *(sauma)* take out, unpick.

ratsain on horseback.

ratsas|taa ride [a horse]; *-tava (m.)* mounted. **-taja** rider; *(merkki)* tab; *taitava* ~ *(m.)* skilled horseman; *(~patsas* equestrian statue).

ratsastus riding. **-housut** riding breeches. **-kilpailu** horse-race. **-puku** riding outfit. **-rata** [race] track. **-retki** ride. **-saappaat** riding boot. **-taito** horsemanship. **-urheilu** equestrian sports.

ratsia round-up, raid.

ratsu mount, *run.* steed, charger; *(šakki-)* knight. **-hevonen** riding-horse. **-mestari** cavalry captain. **-mies** rider; *sot.* cavalry-man, trooper. **-palvelija** groom. **-piiska** whip, crop. **-poliisi** mounted policeman. **-väki** cavalry.

rattaat wag[g]on, *(kaksipyöräiset)* cart; *(vaunut)* carriage.

ratti *(ohjauspyörä)* wheel; *ratissa* at the w. **-juoppo** drunken driver. **-juoppous** driving under the influence of alcohol, drunken driving.

ratto pleasure. **-isa** gay, jolly; *meillä oli ~a* we had a jolly good time (a lot of fun). **-poika** playboy.

raudikko chestnut.

raudoi|ttaa mount.. with iron; *-tettu (m.)* reinforced with iron. **-tus** iron mountings, iron fittings; reinforcement.

raueta weaken, lose strength; *(jäädä sikseen)* be dropped; ~ *tyhjiin* come to nothing, fall through; *antaa asian ~* drop the matter; *asia raukesi* the matter was dropped; *voimat raukeavat* the strength is failing.

rauha peace; *(tyyneys)* quiet[ness]; *~n aikana* in time[s] of peace; *tehdä ~* conclude (make) peace; *hieroa ~a* negotiate peace; *jättää jku ~an* leave.. in peace; *let.. alone; palauttaa ~n kannalle* put on a peacetime footing; *~ssa (m.)* at peace [with, *jkn kanssa*]. **-isa**

peaceful; quiet. **-llinen**
peaceful; calm, unperturbed,
undisturbed, still, tranquil;
-llista tietä peaceably; by
peaceful means; *pysyä -llisena*
keep one's peace. **-llisuus**
peacefulness, calm [ness],
tranquillity. **-naate** pacifism;
r-aatteen ajaja pacifist. **-naika**
time of peace; (*~inen*
peacetime). **-nehdot** terms of
peace.

rauhanen gland.
rauhan|häiritsijä disturber of
the peace, mischief-maker.
-neuvottelu(t) peace
negotiations. **-omainen**
peaceful. **-politiikka** policy of
appeasement. **-rikkoja**
disturber of the peace.
-rikkomus breach of the
peace. **-sopimus** peace treaty.
-tarjous peace offer. **-tekijä**
peacemaker. **-teko** conclusion
of peace. **-tuomari** justice of
the peace. **-turvajoukot** peace
corps, peace-keeping force.
rauhaskudos glandular tissue.
rauha|ton restless; (*huolestunut*)
uneasy; *-ttomat ajat* unsettled
(troubled) times. **-ttomuus**
unrest, restlessness; *sattuu
r-muuksia* disturbances occur.
rauhoite *lääk.* tranquillizer.
rauhoi|ttaa calm, quiet, soothe,
appease; set [a p.'s mind] at
rest; (*vaikuttaa vakuuttavasti*)
reassure; (*riistaa*) protect
[game] by law; *~ maa*
pacify a country; *-ttava*
soothing, (*lääke*) sedative;
(*vakuuttava*) reassuring,
(*lohdullinen*) comforting. **-ttua**
calm oneself; calm down;
compose oneself. **-tus**
pacification; (*riistan*)
protection [of game]; (*~aika*
close season; *~ lääke*
tranquillizer).
rauk|aista make.. feel faint;
minua -aisee I feel tired. **-ea**
faint, languid; fatigued.
-eaminen (*asian, sopimuksen*)
falling through, dropping. **-eus**
faintness; languor, lassitude.
raukka *s.* poor creature, poor
thing, poor fellow; (*pelkuri*)
coward, dastard; *a.* poor;

lapsiraukat poor children.
-mainen cowardly, dastardly.
-maisuus cowardice.
rauni|o ruin; (*ihmis-*) wreck;
olla ~ina lie in ruins. **-oittaa**
lay in ruins, ruin. **-oläjä** heap
of ruins.
rausku *zo.* ray, skate.
rauskuttaa crunch.
rauta iron; *raudat (pyydys-)*
trap; (*kahleet*) irons; *panna
rautoihin* put in irons. **-betoni**
reinforced concrete,
ferro-concrete. **-esirippu** iron
curtain. **-inen** [.. of] iron; *~
tahto* will of iron; *~ terveys*
iron constitution. **-isannos**
iron ration. **-kaivos** iron
mine. **-kanki** iron bar.
-kauppa ironmonger's [shop],
hardware store. **-kauppias**
ironmonger, dealer in
hardware. **-kausi** Iron Age.
-koura iron hand. **-lanka**
wire; (*~aita* wire fence;
~verkko wire netting, (*hieno*)
wire gauze). **-levy** iron plate,
sheet iron. **-malmi** iron ore.
-pelti sheet iron; (*paksu*) iron
plate. **-pitoinen** iron-bearing.
-ristikko iron grating;
(*vankilan*) bars. **-romu**
scrap-iron. **-sänky** iron
bedstead. **-tammi** holm oak.
-tavara hardware,
ironmongery. **-tehdas**
ironworks. **-teitse** by rail.
-teollisuus iron industry.
rautatie railway, *Am.* railroad.
-asema railway station. **-kisko**
rail. **-liikenne** railway traffic
(*t.* service). **-linja** railway line.
-läinen railway employee.
-matka railway journey.
-onnettomuus railway accident.
-raide railway track. **-ravintola**
railway restaurant, refreshment
room. **-silta** railway bridge.
-solmu junction. **-vaunu**
[railway] carriage, coach,
Am. railroad-car; (*tavara-*)
wag[g]on, (*avo-*) truck.
-verkko network of railway
lines. **-virkamies** railway
official. **-ylikäytävä** level
crossing.
ravata trot.
ravi (*hevosen*) trot; *ajaa ~a*

trot [one's horse]. **-kilpailut** trotting race.

ravin|ne nutrient. **-teinen:** *niukka* ~ of low food value.

ravinto food, nourishment; nutriment. **-aine** nutritive substance; nutrient; ~*et* foodstuffs. **-arvo** nutritive value. **-järjestys** diet.

ravintola restaurant. **-henkilökunta** restaurant staff. **-lasku** bill. **-liike** restaurant business. **-nemäntä** manageress of a restaurant. **-nisäntä** restaurant proprietor. **-vaunu** dining car.

ravintoloitsija restaurant-keeper.

ravintorasva edible fat.

ravirata trotting track.

ravis|taa shake; *(sekoittaa)* shake up; *(pois)* shake off. **-tella** *kuv.* shake up. **-tua** get leaky; *-tunut* leaky.

ravit|a feed; nourish; *kuv.* foster; *(ylläpitää)* support: *(tyydyttää)* satisfy; *-tu (kylläinen)* satisfied. **-semus** nutrition; nourishment. **-seva** nourishing, nutritious. **-sevuus** nutritiousness.

raviurheilu trotting.

ravustaa catch crayfish.

reaali|aine modern subject. **-koe** general knowledge examination. **-koulu** modern school. **-linja** modern *(t.* non-classical) side.

re|agoida react [to *jhk;* against, *jtk vastaan*]. **-aktio** reaction; (~**käyttöinen** jet-propelled; *ks. suihku).*

realistinen realistic.

reelinki railing.

refer|aatti *(selostus)* report; *(yhteenveto)* summary. **-oida** report; give a summary of. .

refleksiivinen *kiel.* reflexive.

reformaattori reformer. **-oitu:** ~ *kirkko* Reformed Church.

rehelli|nen honest; square; *(suora)* straight, forthright, sincere; ~ *peli (kuv.)* fair play. **-sesti** honestly, squarely; *menetellä* ~ play fair. **-syys** honesty, integrity; ~ *maan perii* honesty is the best policy.

rehen|nellä put on airs; show

off; swagger; *-televä* swaggering, blustery, overbearing. **-telijä** braggart, swaggerer. **-tely** showing off.

rehe|vyys luxuriant growth, luxuriance. **-vä** flourishing, luxuriant, lush; *(esim. rikkaruohot)* rank. **-västi** luxuriantly. **-vöityminen** overfertilization [through water pollution]. **-vöityä** be overfertilized.

rehot|taa flourish, luxuriate; *paheet -tavat* evil is rife.

rehti upright, fair and square, straightforward, *vrt. reilu.* **-ys** uprightness, rectitude.

rehtori headmaster; principal; *(yliopiston) Am.* president, *Engl.* vice-chancellor, *Skotl. ym* rector. **-nvirka** headmastership, principalship.

rehu feed, animal feedstuffs, *(et. korsi-)* fodder, *(heinä-)* forage. **-kakku** feeding cake, oil cake. **-staa** forage.

rehvastella bluster, swagger.

rei'ittää perforate, punch.

reikä hole; *(aukko)* opening, aperture; gap; *(rako)* slot. **-inen** perforated. **-kortti** punch[ed] card. **-meisti** punch. **-ompelu** hemstitch.

reilu straightforward, reliable; *(kunnon)* proper; ~ *ateria* a good square meal; ~ *kaveri* a decent (jolly good) fellow; ~ *käytös* sporting conduct; ~ *peli* fair play.

reima brisk; bouncing.

reimari spar-buoy.

Rein the [river] Rhine.

reipas brisk, active, lusty; vigorous; *(rivakka)* alert; *reippaassa tahdissa* at a rapid pace. **-tua** regain one's strength, improve in health, become stronger. **-tuttaa** invigorate, refresh, cheer up.

reipp|aasti briskly, promptly, in a spirited manner; vigorously. **-ailla, -ailu** *ks. ulkoilla.* **-aus** briskness; alertness.

reisi thigh; *(lampaan)* leg of mutton. **-luu** thigh-bone. **-paisti** *(naudan)* round of beef, *(sian)* ham. **-valtimo** femoral artery.

reitti course, route; *(väylä)* channel; *(matka-)* itinerary.
reivata take in sail.
reiällinen.. with holes [in it]; perforated.
reki sleigh, sledge, *(us. pieni)* sled; *ajaa reellä* [go by] sleigh. **-keli** sleighing; *mainio* ~ good sleighing.
rekister|i register; *(luettelo)* list, roll; *(kirjoissa ym)* index; (~**kilpi** number plate; ~**tonni** register [ed] ton). **-öidä** register, record; book, *(nimiluetteloon)* enrol [l]. **-öimismaksu** registration fee.
rekka-auto articulated lorry.
rekki *voim.* [horizontal] bar.
relatiivi *s. & a.* relative. **-lause, -pronomini** relative clause (pronoun).
rele, -oida relay.
remahdus: *naurun* ~ burst (peal) of laughter.
remburssi *liik.* documentary credit, *Am.* letter of credit.
remontti repairs; *ks. korjaus.*
rempallaan: *asiat ovat* ~ things are in a bad way (shape).
rem(p)seä free and easy, jaunty.
remu noise, clamour; uproar; *(riemu)* boisterous merriment. **-ava** [very] noisy, rowdy. **-ta** be noisy.
renessanssi the Renaissance; *(kirjall.)* the Revival of Learning.
rengas ring; *(ketjussa ym)* link; *(auton)* [car] tyre, *Am.* tire. **-kirja** loose-leaf book. **-mainen** ring-shaped. **-matka** circular tour, round trip. **-rikko** puncture. **-tuma** *liik.* ring, pool.
renki hired man, hired hand; farm hand.
renkutus jingle.
rento limp, slack, relaxed; [free and] easy, easy-going. **-us** slackness, *(tapojen)* easy ways. **-uttaa, -utua** relax.
renttu disreputable fellow, [useless] layabout, lout. **-mainen** seedy-looking.
rentukka *bot.* marsh marigold.
repale rag. **-inen** ragged, tattered.

repe|ytyä tear, be torn. **-ämä** rent, tear; *lääk. ym* rupture.
repiä tear; rip [open, *auki*]; *et. kuv.* rend; *(rikki)* tear up, tear to pieces; *(irti)* tear off, tear out; ~ *auki* rip up, tear open; ~ *rakennus* pull down a building; *repivä (esim. arvostelu)* destructive.
repliikki repartee, rejoinder, *teatt.* lines, *(loppu-)* rag.
report|aasi report; coverage (of). **-teri** reporter.
repostella *jtk* handle (use) roughly, manhandle.
reppu knapsack, rucksack.
repu|t: *saada* ~ fail [in an examination], muff an examination, *sl.* be ploughed. **-ttaa** fail, flunk.
repäi|sevä thrilling, drastic. **-stä** tear, *(irti)* tear out, tear off; ~ *rikki* tear to pieces, tear asunder; ~ *kätensä (esim. naulaan)* tear open one's hand.
reseda *bot.* mignonette.
resepti *lääk.* prescription; *(keitto- ym)* recipe.
reservi reserve, the reserve [s]. **-läinen** reservist. **-upseeri** officer of (in) the reserve.
resiina [railway] inspection trolley, hand-car.
reti roadstead; *on* ~*llä* is lying in the roads.
retiisi radish.
retikka black radish.
retkahtaa flop down.
retkei|lijä excursionist; *(päivän)* day-tripper; *(jalan)* hiker, walker; *(tutkimus-)* explorer. **-llä** make excursions; *(jalan)* hike; *(samoilla)* ramble. **-ly** excursion [s], outing [s]; *(jalan, m.)* rambling, hiking; (~**maja** hikers' *t.* youth hostel).
retki trip; *(huvi-)* picnic, outing, excursion; *(kävely-)* walking tour; *(tutkimus- ym)* expedition; *tehdä* ~ go for a picnic; make a trip (an excursion) (to). **-kunta** expedition.
retkottaa hang loose, flap; *maata* ~ loll, sprawl.
retku *ks. renttu.*
rettel|ö trouble, difficulties, *(selkkaus)* dispute, tangle;

(~**haluinen** .. looking for trouble). **-öidä** make trouble; *(ahdistellen)* worry sb. **-öitsijä** trouble-maker.

retuperä: *olla ~llä* be in a neglected (a run-down) condition.

retusoida retouch, touch.. up.

retuuttaa drag [along], lug.

reuma *ks. nivel~*.

reum|aattinen rheumatic. **-atismi** rheumatism, *(kivut)* rheumatics.

reuna edge, border, margin *(m. kirjan); (lasin ym)* brim; *reunoja myöten täynnä* brimful; *vuotaa yli reunojen* run over, overflow; *jyrkänteen ~lla* on the brink (edge) of the precipice; *metsän ~ssa* at the edge (skirt) of the woods. **-inen** -edged, -bordered. **-merkintä, -muistutus** marginal note. **-pitsi** lace edging.

reunus edge, margin; border; *(takan)* mantelshelf. **-nauha** tape; trimming. **-taa** edge, border; *(esim. katua)* line; *(koristella)* trim.

revalvoi|da revalue upward, upvalue. **-nti** upward revaluation.

revanssi revenge.

reve|htymä rupture. **-tä** rend, tear; ~ *kahtia* be torn in two.

reviiri *(eläimen)* territory.

revolveri revolver.

revontulet aurora borealis, northern lights, *(etelässä)* aurora australis.

revä|htää rupture; *(silmät) -htivät suuriksi* flew wide open.

rieha|antua become boisterous (unmanageable). **-kas, -kka** boisterous, romping.

riehua rage; ~ *tarpeekseen (esim. myrsky)* spend its fury; ~ *valloillaan* be rampant, *(esim. himot)* have free reins, run wild.

riekale rag, shred, tatter; *kulua ~iksi* be worn to rags (to tatters). **-inen** tattered.

riekko *zo.* willow grouse, *Am.* willow ptarmigan.

riemas|tua rejoice, *(suuresti)* be

carried away with joy. **-tus** [great] rejoicing, exultation, jubilation. **-tuttaa** make.. exultant, delight.

riemu joy, delight; rejoicing; *(ilonpito)* merriment. **-huuto** cry of joy. **-isa** joyful, joyous. **-ita** rejoice (at, in); exult (at, in, over); **-itseva** exultant, jubilant. **-juhla** celebration, festival, *(esim. 50-vuotis-)* jubilee. **-kaari** triumphal arch. **-kas** joyful; exultant. **-päivä** day of rejoicing. **-saatto** triumphal procession. **-vuosi** year of jubilee.

rienata blaspheme.

rien|to: *riennot* interests, aspirations, ambitions, activities; *(~askel: edistyä ~askelin* make great strides. **-tää** hurry; hasten; *(kiitää)* speed; *aika* ~ time flies.

riepottaa *(eläimestä)* worry, *(myrskystä)* rip through.

riepu rag, cloth.

riesa nuisance.

rieska flat, thin barley loaf.

rie|tas impure; indecent, obscene, lewd. **-ttaus** impurity; *vrt. ed.*

rihkama frippery, finery, baubles, gewgaws, knick-knacks; *(kama)* trash. **-kauppa** fancy goods (small-ware) shop. **-kauppias** haberdasher.

rihla|t rifling, grooves. **-ta** rifle.

rihma thread; yarn; *(nyöri)* string. **-rulla** reel of thread *(t.* cotton).

riidan|aihe cause of quarrel, bone of contention. **-alainen** subject to dispute. disputed... at issue; disputable. **-alaisuus** disputableness. **-halu** quarrelsomeness. **-haluinen** quarrelsome. **-ratkaisija** arbitrator, referee.

riidaton undisputed, uncontested.

riidellä quarrel, have a row; *(kinastella)* squabble, wrangle, bicker.

riihi drying-house.

riikin|kukko peacock; *-kukon naaras* peahen.

riimi rhyme.

riimu headstall, *(-nvarsi)* halter.

-kirjoitus runic inscription.
-kivi runic stone.
riipai|sta *kuv.* cut . . to the quick; *sydäntäni -si* it wrung my heart; *-seva* heart-rending, harrowing.
riipiä strip [. . off].
riippu|a hang, be suspended from; hang loose; *kuv.* depend (on); *-en siitä, (on) ko* . . depending [up]on whether. . **-lukko** padlock.
-maton independent, *(valtio, m.)* sovereign; *(taloudellisesti, m.)* self-supporting. **-matta** *(jstk)* regardless of, irrespective of [whether, *-ko, -kö*]; *toisistaan ~* independently [of each other]. **-matto** hammock.
-mattomuus independence.
-valaisin suspended lamp.
-silta suspension bridge.
-vainen dependent (on); *(päätös on) ~ hyväksynnästä* subject to approval. **-vaisuus** dependence (on); *(~suhde* interdependence, correlation).
riipu|s *(koru)* pendant; *olla -ksissa* droop, hang down; *pää -ksissa* with drooping head. **-ttaa** [let] hang.
riisi rice; *(paperi-)* ream.
-puuro boiled rice, rice porridge. **-suurimot** rice. **-tauti** rickets. **-tautinen** rickety.
-vanukas rice pudding.
riista game. **-maa** hunting-ground[s] ; preserve.
-nsuojelu protection of game; *(~alue* game preserve).
-nvartija gamekeeper.
riis|to exploitation. **-täjä** *(työläisten ym.)* exploiter.
-täytyä wrench (tear) oneself away; *~ irti (hevonen, ym)* break loose. **-tää** deprive [a p. of], *(esim. kuoleman kautta)* bereave (of); *(ryöstää)* rob; take [away], dispossess (of); *(temmata)* wrench, tear; *(nylkeä)* exploit; *~ jklta henki* take a p.'s life; *-tetyt* the [dispossessed and] exploited.
riis|ua *(vaatteet)* undress; take off [one's dress, *pukunsa*]; *~ alastomaksi* strip; *~ aseista* disarm; *~ valjaista* unharness

a horse; *~ kengät jalastaan* take off one's shoes. **-unta** undressing *jne.; aseista ~* disarmament. **-uutua** undress [oneself], take off one's clothes.
riita quarrel, *(meteli)* row; *(kiista)* dispute, controversy; *(eripuraisuus)* disagreement; *(kina)* squabble, wrangle; *(suku-)* feud; *haastaa ~a* kick up a row, pick a quarrel (with); *joutua ~an ks. riitaantua; riidassa* at variance, not on good terms (with); *olla riidassa (m.)* be at odds (with). **-antua** fall out (with); have a disagreement (with). **-inen, -isa** quarrelsome; *-iset suhteet* strained relations. **-isuus** difference[s], disagreement; strife; controversy. **-juttu** civil action, suit. **-kapula** bone of contention. **-kirjoitus** controversial article. **-kohta** point of controversy. **-kysymys** controversy; matter in dispute.
-puoli *lak.* party. **-raha:** *panna ~ kahtia* split the difference.
riite thin coat of ice.
riittoisa *on ~* . . goes a long way, [it will] last long.
riittä|mättömyys insufficiency, inadequacy. **-mätön** insufficient, inadequate. **-vyys** sufficiency; adequacy. **-vä** sufficient; adequate; *~n suuri* large enough, sufficiently large; *~t todisteet* sufficient evidence, ample proof. **-västi** sufficiently; enough.
riittää be enough, be sufficient, suffice; *jo ~* that's enough, that will do; *mikäli tilaa ~* as far as there is room, as far as space allows; *siihen minun voimani eivät riitä* it is beyond my strength; *~kö ruokamme?* will our food last? *~kö öljy yli talven?* is there [enough] oil to last out the winter?
riiva|ta: *jnk -ama* possessed by. .
riivinrauta grater.
rikas rich (in); *(vauras)* wealthy, opulent. **-aatteinen**

rich in ideas. **-sisältöinen.**.
rich in meaning. **-taa** *tekn.*
concentrate, dress. **-tua** get
rich, make a fortune.
-tuminen getting rich.
-tuslaitos concentrating plant.
-tuttaa enrich.
rike offence, misdemeanour.
rikka dust particle; cinder; *et.
raam.* mote; *rikat* sweepings;
refuse, *Am.* garbage; *minulla
on ~ silmässä (tav.)* I have
something in my eye; *ei
panna ~a ristiin* not lift a
finger. **-kuilu** refuse (*Am.*
garbage) chute. **-lapio** dustpan.
-läjä rubbish heap. **-ruoho**
weed. **-säiliö** dustbin, litter
bin.
rikkaus wealth, riches *(pl.),*
kuv. richness, *(runsaus)*
abundance (of).
rikki 1. broken, *(palasina)* in
pieces; *(kulunut)* worn
through, worn out; *lyödä ~*
break [to pieces]; smash;
mennä ~ break [to pieces].
rikki 2. *kem.* sulphur, *Am,*
sulfur. **-dioksidi** sulphur
dioxide. **-happo** sulphuric acid.
-kiisu iron pyrites. **-kukka**
flowers of sulphur. **-lähde**
sulphur spring.
rikkinäi|nen broken; *~ ihminen*
an inwardly disintegrated
person. **-syys** broken
condition; *(hajaannus)*
division, disunion.
rikki|pitoinen sulphurous. **-vety**
hydrogen sulphide. **-viisas**
[too] smart, too clever,
puhek. smart Aleck.
rikko|a break *(m. kuv.);*
(loukata) violate, infringe;
trespass (against); *~ lakia*
violate a law, commit a
breach against the law; *~
sanansa* break one's word; *~
jkta vastaan* offend against,
do.. an injury, wrong; *~
välinsä jkn kanssa* break off
one's relations with; *sopimus
on rikottu* the agreement has
been broken. **-ja:** *jnk ~*
transgressor of. ., violator
of. .; *lain ~* law-breaker.
-maton *kuv.* inviolate.
-mattomuus inviolability.

-minen *(jnk)* breach, violation,
transgression, infringement;
sopimuksen ~ breach of
contract; *lupauksen ~ (et.
avio-)* breach of promise.
-mus offence; *lak., m.*
misdemeanour; *urh.* foul.
-utua get broken, break; *kuv.*
be broken off.
rikkuri strike-breaker; blackleg.
rikoksen|tekijä criminal. **-uusija**
recidivist.
rikolli|nen *a.* criminal; *s.*
criminal; culprit. **-suus** crime,
delinquency; criminality.
rikos crime, criminal offence;
(törkeä) felony; *tehdä ~*
commit a crime. **-asia, -juttu**
criminal case. **-lainsäädäntö**
criminal legislation. **-laki**
penal law [s]. **-oppi**
criminology. **-poliisi** criminal
investigation department
(C.I.D.). **-toveri** accomplice.
rima lath, batten, *urh.* bar.
rimpuilla tug and pull,
struggle, wriggle; *~ vastaan*
make resistance, resist.
rimputtaa strum.
rinkilä ring- (or loop-) shaped
bun (biscuit).
rinnakkai|n abreast; side by
side. **-nen** parallel. **-sehdotus**
alternative proposition. **-selo**
co-existence. **-sluokka** parallel
course.
rinna|lla: *jnk, jkn ~* side by
side with, abreast of,
(vieressä) by, by [a p.'s]
side, beside, *(ohella)* along
with, *(tasalla)* on a level
with, *(verrattaessa)* [as]
compared with; *pysytellä jkn
~* keep up with, keep pace
with. **-lle** *ks. ed.; asettaa.*.
jnk ~ place.. at the side of,
(vertaiseksi) put.. on a level
with; *päästä jkn ~ (urh.)*
draw level with. **-n** *ks.* **-kkain**
~ *(jnk kanssa)* abreast [of].
rinnanympärys chest measure.
rinnas|taa place.. on a level
(with), consider equal (to);
draw a parallel between; *et.
kiel.* co-ordinate;.. *ei voida ~
jhk..* cannot compare with;
-tettu co-ordinate [clause,
lause]. **-tus** parallel;

co-ordination.
rinne slope; hillside,
mountainside; descent, declivity.
rinnus *(paidan)* front.
rinta breast; *(-kehä)* chest;
(povi) bosom; *(jalan)* instep;
painaa ~ansa vastaan clasp to
one's breast. **-kehä** chest,
thorax. **-koru** brooch. **-kuva**
half-length picture; *(veisto-)*
bust. **-käänne** lapel. **-lapsi**
[breast-fed] infant, suckling.
-lasta breastbone. **-liha**
(teuraseläimen) brisket. **-liivit**
brassiere, *(tav. lyh.)* bra.
rintama front; *~lla* at the f.;
*asettua yhteiseen ~an (jtk
vastaan)* form a united front
(against). **-hyökkäys** frontal
attack. **-mies** *(entinen)*
ex-service man. **-palvelus**
service at the front. **-sotilas**
front-line soldier.
rinta|neula brooch. **-peri|llinen**
direct heir; *r-lliset (m.)* issue.
-sokeri barley sugar. **-tasku**
breast pocket. **-tilkku**
(esiliinan) bib. **-uinti**
breast-stroke [swimming]. **-va**
full-bosomed. **-varustus**
parapet; breastwork. **-ääni**
chest-note.
ripa handle; *tekn.* rib.
ripe|ys quickness; briskness. **-ä**
quick, prompt; brisk; alert.
ripillepääsy confirmation.
ripilläkäynti [partaking of]
Communion.
ripi|ttäytyä confess. **-ttää** hear
a p.'s confession, confess;
kuv. lecture, take. . to task.
-tys confession; *kuv.* talking
to, lecture.
ripottaa strew; sprinkle;
scatter; *~ sokeria jhk*
sprinkle. . with sugar.
rippeet remnant[s], rests,
(kuulon, näön) residual
[hearing, vision]; *vrt. tähteet.*
rippi confession; *(ehtoollinen)*
[Holy] Communion; *käydä
ripillä* go to Communion;
päästä ripille be confirmed.
-isä confessor; *(katol. kirk.)*
father confessor. **-kirkko**
Communion service. **-koulu**
confirmation school. **-lapsi**
first communicant. **-vieras**

communicant.
ripsi 1. *(-kangas)* rep. **2.**
(silmä-) [eye]lash. **-väri**
mascara.
ripsu fringe. **-a** whisk [off,
away].
ripuli diarrh[o]ea.
ripus|taa hang [up]; *(ulos)*
hang out; *~ jhk (m.)* suspend
from; *~ kaulaansa* hang. .
round one's neck; *~ naulaan*
hang. . on a nail. **-tin** *(vaate-)*
dress-hanger, clothes-hanger.
risa *(nielu-)* tonsil; *(kita-)*
adenoid.
risah|dus, -taa rustle.
risainen ragged, tattered;
(kulunut) worn out, frayed.
risa|tauti scrofula. **-tautinen**
scrofulous.
risiiniöljy castor oil.
riski risk; *ottaa ~* run a risk,
take the risk (of . .-ing).
ristei|lijä cruiser. **-llä** cruise;
maassa -lee rautateitä the
country is traversed by
railways. **-ly** cruise.
riste|ys crossing; junction; *(m.
~asema); tien -yksessä* at the
crossroads, at junctions. **-yttää**
cross-[breed], cross-fertilize.
-ytys cross[ing].
risti cross *(m. kuv.); mus.*
sharp; *(-kortti)* club, *(maa)*
clubs; *kirjap.* dagger; *panna
kätensä ~in* clasp one's
hands; *kädet ~ssä* with folded
hands, *kuv.* without lifting a
finger; *jalat ~ssä* with legs
crossed; *ei ~n sielua* not a
living soul. **-aallokko**
cross-swell, choppy sea. **-holvi**
groined vault. **-huuli** hare-lip.
ristiin crosswise; *mennä ~*
cross; *~ rastiin menevä*
interlacing, criss-cross [lines];
edut menevät ~ interests
conflict; *puhua ~* contradict
oneself. **-naulinta** crucifixion.
-naulita crucify; *-naulitun
kuva* crucifix.
risti|kirkko cruciform church.
-kko *(rauta- ym)* grating,
grille, *(säle-)* lattice, trellis;
(kalterit) bars. **-kkäin**
crosswise, across. **-kukkainen**
cruciferous. **-kuulustella**
cross-examine, cross-question.

-**kuulustelu** cross-examination.
-**käytävä** *(kirkon)* cross-aisle; *(luostarin)* cloister. -**luu** *anat.* sacrum. -**mänimi** Christian name, first name.

ristin|merkki sign of the cross; *tehdä* ~ make the sign of the cross, cross oneself. -**muotoinen** cross-shaped, cruciform.

risti|pisto cross-stitch. -**retkeilijä** crusader. -**retki** crusade.

ristiriita conflict, disagreement; *(erilaisuus)* discrepancy; *olla ristiriidassa jnk kanssa* conflict with, clash with, be in contradiction to, be out of harmony with; *joutua ~an* get into conflict, come into collision (with). -**inen** conflicting; contradictory; ~ *aika* time of conflict; *-iset tiedot* contradictory reports. -**isuus** contradiction; *(sovittamattomuus)* incompatibility, incongruence; *(epäjohdonmukaisuus)* inconsistency.

risti|sanatehtävä crossword [puzzle]. -**selkä** sacrum, small of the back. -**side:** *lähettää -siteenä* send by book-post, send as printed matter. -**siitos** crossbreeding, interbreeding. -**tuli** cross-fire. -**veto** draught.

risti|ä *(kastaa)* christen, baptize; ~ *kätensä* clasp one's hands; -**ttiin..** *-ksi* was christened [John]. -**äiset** christening.

-**isu:** ~*t* twigs, brushwood. -**kimppu** fag [g]ot. -**kko** thicket, brushwood.

ritari knight; *lyödä ~ksi* dub.. a knight. -**kunta** order [of knighthood]. -**laitos** chivalry. -**llinen** chivalrous, *kuv. m.* gallant; *-llisesti* gallantly. -**llisuus** chivalry. -**merkki** decoration. -**sääty** [order of] knighthood.

itsa sling, catapult, *Am.* slingshot.

-**iuduttaa** consume; wear away, waste.

-**iuhtaista** jerk; snatch; ~ *itsensä irti* break away (from), break loose.

riuku pole.

riutta reef; *(särkkä)* bank.

riutu|a pine away; languish, *(kulua)* waste [away]; *-nut (vanhuuttaan)* worn with age; *näyttää -neelta* look wan. -**minen, -mus** pining away; decline.

rivakka brisk, energetic.

rivi line; row *(esim. talo~* row of houses); *(mies-, m.)* rank; *asettua ~in* line up, draw up in line; *kahdessa ~ssä* two deep; *lukea ~en välistä* read between the lines; ~*en välissä (sanojen alla) oleva* implied. -**mies** common soldier. -**stö** *sot.* column. -**talo** terrace [d] house *(t.* bungalow).

rivo indecent, obscene, lewd. -**puheinen** coarse-mouthed. -**us** indecency, obscenity.

rodullinen racial.

rohdos: *rohdokset* drugs *(m. huume);* pharmaceuticals. -**kauppa** chemist's, drugstore. -**kauppias** chemist, druggist.

rohjeta dare, venture, *(ottaa vapaus)* take the liberty (to).

rohkai|sta encourage; *(tehdä rohkeaksi)* embolden; ~ *jkn mieltä* inspire.. with courage, infuse courage (into); *uutinen -si meitä* the news bucked us up; ~ *mielensä* gather up courage; *-seva* encouraging. -**stua** *ks. ed.;* take heart, pluck up [one's] courage, buck up. -**su** encouragement.

rohke|a courageous, brave; *(uskalias)* bold, undaunted, *puhek.* plucky; *(~puheinen* outspoken). -**us** courage; bravery; boldness, *puhek.* pluck; *(moraalinen)* fortitude; *menettää -utensa* lose heart; *-utta!* buck up!

rohmuta hoard.

rohti|a *(pellavia)* dress, comb [flax]. -**met** tow.

rohto medicine, drug.

rohtu|a get chapped. -**ma** chap.

roihu blaze; flare. -**ta** flame [up], blaze [up].

roikale lout.

roikkua hang [down]; *(heilua)* dangle.

roima sturdy, bouncing.

roina rubbish.
roisk|ahtaa splash, spatter. **-e**
splash[ing]; spray; (~**suojus**
splash guard, mud flap). **-ua**
splash; *hänen takkiinsa -ui. .*
her coat was spattered with. .
-uttaa splash.
roisto scoundrel, knave, villain;
rascal. **-mainen** knavish,
villainous. **-maisuus** villainy.
roju rubbish.
rokko pock; *(iso-)* smallpox.
rokonarpi pock-mark.
roko|ttaa vaccinate, inoculate
(against). **-te** vaccine. **-tus**
vaccination; (~**pakko**
compulsory vaccination;
~**todistus** certificate of
vaccination).
romaani novel. **-kirjailija**
novelist. **-kirjallisuus** fiction.
romaaninen Romance, *tait.*
Romanesque.
romah|duksellinen
catastrophic[al]. **-dus**
breakdown, collapse; *liik.*
crash, failure. **-taa** come
down with a crash, crash
down; tumble down; ~
maahan collapse; *toivo -ti*
hope[s] fell flat, hope was
dashed; *hänen terveytensä -ti*
her health broke down.
Romania Roumania. **r-lainen** *a.*
& s. Roumanian.
roman|ssi romance. **-tiikka**
romanticism. **-tikko**
romanticist, writer (painter) of
the romantic school. **-ttinen**
romantic.
rommi rum.
romu rubbish, lumber; junk.
-kamari lumber-room. **-kauppa**
junk shop, *(myynti)* scrap
dealing. **-kauppias** scrap
dealer. **-rauta** scrap-iron. **-ttaa**
scrap, break up. **-ttua** be
wrecked; *(auto) -ttui* became
(t. is now) a write-off.
rooli part, role, rôle.
Rooma Rome.
roomalai|nen *a. & s.* Roman.
-skatolinen Roman Catholic.
ropo *raam.* mite; *(rahanen)*
penny, groat, farthing.
roska rubbish, trash *(m. kuv.);*
litter; ~*t (jätteet)* refuse,
garbage; *puhua* ~*a* talk

nonsense. **-inen** untidy,
littered. **-kirjallisuus** trashy
literature, garbage *(kuv.).*
-kuilu rubbish chute. **-laatikko,**
-pönttö dustbin, *(kadulla)*
litter bin. **-läjä** scrap heap.
-mylly garbage disposal.
-npolttouuni incinerator. **-väki**
rabble, mob, riff-raff.
rosmariini rosemary.
rosoi|nen rough, rugged;
uneven. **-suus** roughness;
unevenness.
rosvo robber, bandit, brigand.
-joukko gang of robbers.
-juttu *kuv.* blood-curdling
story. **-radiolähetys** pirate
broadcast. **-retki** plundering
(looting) expedition; raid;
tehdä ~ä jnnek raid a place.
-ta rob; loot, plunder. **-us**
robbery; looting, pillage.
rotan|myrkky rat-poison.
-pyydys rat-trap.
rotev|a robust; sturdy;
(~**jäseninen** large-limbed;
~**kasvuinen** strongly built).
-uus robustness.
rotko gorge, ravine, chasm,
cleft.
rotta rot. **-koira** ratter.
rottinki rattan, cane.
rotu race, breed, stock,
strain; *hyvää ~a*
(oleva) . . of good stock. **-eläin**
pedigree animal, thoroughbred.
-ennakkoluulo race prejudice.
-erottelu racial segregation.
-hevonen thoroughbred,
bloodhorse. **-hygienia** eugenics.
-inen: *jnk* ~ of. . breed; of. .
race. **-karja** pedigree cattle.
-karsinoimaton desegregated.
-karsinointi racial segregation.
-kiihkoilija racist. **-kiihkoilu**
racism. **-sekoitus** mixture of
breeds, *(ihmisistä)* mixture of
races. **-syrjintä** racial
discrimination. **-tunnus** racial
characteristic. **-viha** race
hatred.
rouh|e: ~*et* crushed grain,
grits. **-ia** grind . . [coarse];
(kiviä ym) crush; *(malmia)*
stamp. **-in** *(-kone)* crusher.
rousku|a, -ttaa crunch.
routa frost [in the ground].
-inen frozen.

rouva married woman; *(vaimo)* wife; *(puhutteluna)* madam; ~ N. Mrs *(äänt.* misiz) N. **-sväki** ladies.

rovasti »rovasti», *l.v. Engl.* canon.

rovio pyre; *polttaa ~lla* burn .. at the stake.

rubiini ruby.

ruhjevamm|a bruise, contusion; *sai -oja* sustained bruises.

ruhjo|a maim; *(mustelmille)* bruise; *(murskata)* crush; *kuoli auton -mana* was crushed under a car. **-utua** be maimed.

ruho *(teuraan)* carcass.

ruhtinaalli|nen princely. **-sesti** in a princely manner; royally.

ruhtinas prince. **-kunta** principality. **-suku** princely house.

ruhtinatar princess.

ruiku|**ttaa, -tus** whine, whimper.

ruis rye. **-jauho(t)** rye-meal; *(seulottu)* rye-flour. **-kaunokki** cornflower.

ruisk|**ahtaa** spurt, squirt; spout. **-e** *lääk.* injection.

ruisku *(kastelu- ym)* sprayer; *lääk. ym.* syringe; *(palo-)* fire-engine. **-kannu** watering-pot(-can). **-ta** squirt; *(voimakkaana suihkuna)* spout. **-ttaa** *(kastella ym)* spray; *(paloruiskulla)* play the hose (on); *lääk.* inject; syringe. **-tus** *(puutarhan ym)* spraying; *lääk.* injection; *(~aine* spray; *~laite* sprayer).

ruis|**leipä** rye bread. **-pelto** rye-field. **-rääkkä** *zo.* corn-crake.

rujo malformed, shapeless.

ruka|ta regulate [a watch].

rukiinjyvä grain of rye. **-tähkä** ear *(t.* head) of rye.

rukka *ks.* raukka.

rukka|**nen** mitten; *antaa jklle -set* refuse a p. ['s offer of marriage], turn a p. down.

rukki spinning-wheel.

ruko [hay]cock.

rukoi|**lla** pray [to God, *Jumalaa*]; *(hartaasti pyytää)* implore, entreat, beseech; ~ *jkn puolesta* pray for; ~ *armoa* beg for mercy; ~ *iltarukouksensa* say one's

evening prayer; *-levasti* pleadingly, imploringly.

rukous prayer; supplication. **-hetki** hour of prayer. **-huone** chapel, meeting-house. **-kirja** prayer-book. **-nauha** rosary. **-päivä** *l.v.* intercession day.

ruletti roulette.

rulla roll; roller; *(lanka- ym)* reel. **-luistimet** roller skates. **-portaat** escalator. **-puu** bobbin wood. **-ta** *ilm.* taxi. **-tuoli** wheel chair, invalid chair.

ruma ugly, unattractive, *(ei kaunis)* plain, *Am.* homely; ~ *ilma* bad weather, *(puhek.)* nasty weather; ~ *juttu* ugly affair. **-sti** in an ugly (disagreeable) manner; *siinä hän teki* ~ that was mean of him.

rumentaa make.. ugly; *(arpi ym)* disfigure, cause cosmetic disadvantage.

rummu|**ttaa** drum, beat a drum; bang [on the piano]. **-tus** drumming, beating of drums.

rumpali drummer.

rumpu drum; *(silta)* culvert. **-kalvo** *ks. täry-.* **-palikka** drumstick.

rumuus ugliness.

runko stem; *(puun ym)* trunk; *(laivan ym)* hull; *(kehä)* frame [work], skeleton; *(auton)* frame; *lentok.* fuselage. **-ruusu** standard rose. **-tie** arterial road *(t.* highway), trunk road.

runnella mangle, mutilate; maul; *(hävittää)* ravage; *taudin runtelemat kasvot* a face marked with the ravages of disease.

runo poem; *(Kalevalan)* rune; *~ja* poems, *koll.* poetry. **-elma** poem. **-ilija** poet; *(~lahja* poetic gift, gift of poetry; *~tar* poetess). **-illa** write poetry. **-ilu** [writing of] poetry. **-jalka** foot. **-kieli** poetical language. **-listen** poetic, poetical; ~ *vapaus* poetic licence. **-llisesti** poetically. **-llisuus** poetic quality. **-mitallinen** metrical. **-mitta** metre; *-mitalla..* in verse. **-niekka** versifier; rhymer. **-nlaulaja** rune-singer. **-nlausunta** poetry reading. **-pukuinen**. . in verse form. **-ratsu** Pegasus, winged horse. **-suoni** poetic vein. **-tar** muse. **-teos** poetical work; *(-kappale)* piece of poetry. **-us** poetry; (~**oppi** poetics).

runs|aasti. . in abundance, plenty [of. .],. . in plenty; amply;. . in profusion; ~ *10 puntaa* well over £ 10, a good £ 10; ~ *30 dollaria* 30-odd dollars; ~ *kuvitettu* richly illustrated; ~ *rahaa* plenty of money; ~ *tietoja (m.)* a wealth of information; *mitata* ~ give a good measure. **-as** abundant, copious, plentiful, ample, large; *(liikanaisen)* profuse; *-ain määrin* in ample measure, amply; *-ain käsin* liberally; ~ *mitta* an ample (a generous) measure; ~ *sato* a rich harvest, a bumper crop; *viipyi -aan tunnin* stayed [well] over an hour; (~**kätinen** liberal, generous; open-handed; ~**lukuinen** numerous). **-audensarvi** cornucopia. **-aus** abundance, plenty; profusion; wealth.

ruoan|jätteet leavings [of food], scraps. **-käry** smell of cooking. **-laittaja** cook. **-laitto** cooking, cookery; (~**taito** art of cookery). **-sulatus** digestion; (~**elimet** digestive organs; ~**häiriö** indigestion; ~**kanava** alimentary canal). **-tähteet** scraps, remnants [of food]. **-valmistuskone** [food] mixer.

ruohikko grass; *(ruohokenttä)* lawn.

ruoho grass. **-inen** grass-grown, grassy. **-kasvi** herb. **-kenttä** lawn. **-nkorsi** stem (stalk) of grass; **-nleikkuu** cutting of grass; mowing the lawn; (~**kone** lawn-mower). **-sipuli** chives. **-ttua**: *on -ttunut* is grown over [with weeds etc.].

ruoka food; *. . on ruoalla* is having lunch, dinner; *tässä ravintolassa on hyvä* ~ the cooking is good at this

restaurant; ~ *ei pysy potilaan sisällä* the patient cannot retain any food. **-aika** meal-time; ~*an* at meal-time. **-aine**: ~*et* food, foodstuffs. **-annos** serving, portion of food; *sot.* ration. **-astia** dish. **-halu** appetite. **-haluttomuus** poor appetite.

ruokai|lija boarder. **-lla** have one's meals, eat [one's meals]; *(olla ruoalla)* be at table. **-lu** eating; (~**huone** dining-room, *laitoksen* lunch-room; ~**välineet** table cutlery).

ruoka|järjestys diet. **-kaappi** food cupboard; pantry. **-la** eating-house; *(tehtaan)* canteen. **-laji** dish; course. **-lappu** bib. **-leipä** [plain] bread. **-lepo** after-dinner nap. **-lista** bill of fare, menu. **-lusikka** table-spoon. **-lusikallinen:** ~ *jtk* a table-spoonful of. . **-multa** mould, top soil. **-myrkytys** food poisoning. **-pöytä** dining-table; *-pöydässä* at table. **-rahat** cost of board. **-ryyppy** appetizer. **-sali** dining-room. **-säiliö** pantry; larder. **-tavara(t)** foodstuffs. **-tavaramyymälä** provision store, *(iso valintamyymälä)* supermarket. **-torvi** [o]esophagus. **-tunti** lunch break. **-valio** diet. **-varasto** stock of provisions. **-varat** provisions, food supplies. **-vieras** boarder; *(ravintolan ym)* customer, diner. **-öljy** table oil.

ruokinta feeding, feed.

ruokki razorbill[ed auk].

ruokkia feed.

ruoko reed; *(sokeri-, bambu-)* cane. **-keppi** cane. **-pilli** reed. **-sokeri** cane sugar.

ruoko|ta clean, clean out; dress; ~ *hevosta* groom a horse. **-ton** untidy, filthy; *(säädytön)* improper; obscene. **-ttomuus** uncleanliness; obscenity.

ruop|ata dredge. **-paaja** dredge[r]. **-paus** dredging.

ruori rudder; helm, wheel. **-mies** helmsman, steersman.

-ratas steering-wheel.
ruoska whip; *kuv.* scourge.
-nsiima lash, thong. -nsivallus lash with a whip.
ruoskia flog; whip.
ruoste rust; *(vasken-)* verdigris; *(viljan, m.)* blight; *olla ~essa* be rusty; *~en syömä* corroded [by rust]. -inen rusty. -pilkku rust spot.
ruostu|a rust, become (get) rusty; *~ kiinni* rust up. -maton stainless [steel, *teräs*]. -nut rusty, corroded.
ruoti rib. -a bone.
ruoto *(kalan)* bone; *(sulan)* shaft. -inen bony.
ruotsalai|nen *s.* Swede; *a.* Swedish. -ssyntyinen. . of Swedish birth. -stua become Swedish.
Ruotsi Sweden; *r~ (kieli)* Swedish; *r-a puhuva* Swedish-speaking.
ruotsin|kielinen Swedish [-speaking], Swedish-language [newspaper, *lehti*]. -taa translate into Swedish.
ruotsitar Swedish woman.
rupa|ttaa, -tella chat. -ttelu chat [ting], small talk.
rupi scab, *(kuori)* crust; scurf. -nen scabby. -sammakko toad.
rupla rouble.
rusakko brown hare.
rusentaa crush *(m. kuv.)*.
rusikoida handle. . roughly, maul; batter.
rusina raisin. -kakku fruit-cake.
rusk *ks. syksy.*
ruskea brown. -silmäinen brown-eyed. -tukkainen brown-haired; *s. fem.* brunette.
ruske|htava brownish. -ttua get sunburnt, get tanned. -tus tan.
ruskistaa *keitt.* brown.
rusko red[ness], glow. -hiili brown coal, lignite. -levä brown algae *(pl.)*. -ttaa: *taivas ~* there is a red glow in the sky.
ruskuainen *(munan-)* yolk.
rusto cartilage, gristle. -mainen cartilaginous. -ttua form cartilage.
ruti|kuiva dry as dust. -köyhä penniless. -vanhoillinen

ultraconservative.
rutistaa squeeze, crush; *(rypistää)* crumple.
rutto the plague; pestilence; *ruton saastuttama* plague-stricken. -paise *kuv.* plague-spot.
ruudinkeksijä: *hän ei ole mikään ~* he is no genius.
ruudu|kas, -llinen checked; *(paperi)* square-ruled.
ruuhi flat-bottom rowboat, punt.
ruuhka *(liikenne-)* traffic jam (block). -aika rush hour[s]. -antua be jammed.
ruukku pot; crock; *ruukun sirpale* crock. -kasvi potted plant.
ruukun|tekijä potter. -teko potmaking, pottery.
ruuma hold.
ruumiilli|nen bodily, corporal; physical; *~ työ* manual work; *-sen työn tekijä* manual worker. -sesti bodily; physically. -staa embody, incarnate. -stua be embodied; become incarnate. -stuma embodiment.
ruumiin|avaus post-mortem [examination], autopsy. -harjoitus physical exercise. -kulttuuri physical training. -liikunta exercise. -lämpö [body] temperature. -mukainen tight-fitting. -osa part of the body, member. -poltto cremation. -rakenne constitution, physique. -siunaus funeral service, burial rites. -tarkastus personal search; *-lle toimitettiin ~* was physically searched, *(tunnustellen)* was frisked *[esim. for a gun]*, *(riisumalla)* was stripped and searched. -vamma [bodily] injury. -vika physical defect, deformity. -voimat bodily strength.
ruumiiton incorporeal, immaterial.
ruumis corpse, *(keho)* body. -arkku coffin. -auto hearse. -huone mortuary. -myrkytys ptomaine poisoning. -paarit bier. -saarna funeral sermon. -saatto funeral procession.

-**vaunut** hearse.
ruuna gelding.
ruusu rose; *(vyö-)* shingles.
-**inen** rosy. -**kaali** Brussels
sprouts. -**ke** rosette; bow.
-**nen:** *prinsessa R~* the
Sleeping Beauty. -**nmarja** hip.
-**nnuppu** rose-bud. -**npunainen**
rose-red, rose-coloured. -**papu**
scarlet runner. -**pensas**
rose-bush. -**puu** rosewood.
-**tarha** rose-garden. -**vesi** rose
water. -**öljy** attar of roses.
ruutana *zo.* crucian [carp].
ruuti gunpowder, powder.
-**tehdas** gunpowder factory.
ruutu *(ikkuna- ym)* pane;
(neliö) square; *(malleissa ym)*
check; *korttip.* diamonds;
hypätä ~a play hopscotch.
-**kortti** diamond. -**kuningas**
king of diamonds.
ruuvata screw; *~ auki, ~ irti*
unscrew; *~ (kansi) kiinni*
screw the lid on.
ruuvi screw; *(-lla) on päässään
~ irti* has a s. loose; *kiristää
~a* tighten a s. -**avain**
[screw-] wrench; spanner.
-**kierre** worm, thread. -**mutteri**
nut. -**pihdit** clamp. -**puristin**
vice, clamp. -**taltta**
screw-driver.
ruveta begin, start, set about;
take to [drink, *juomaan),*
take up [a trade, *jhk
ammattiin*], go in for; *~ jksk*
become. .; *~ englantia
opiskelemaan* take up the
study of English; *~ jkn
palvelukseen* enter a p.'s
service; *~ riitelemään* start
quarrelling, *Am. m.* -eling
ryhdikkyys erect (good)
carriage. -**käs** erect. -**stäytyä**
pull oneself up, *kuv.* pull
oneself together. -**ttömyys** poor
carriage; *kuv.* lack of
backbone, lack of character.
-**tön.** . with a poor carriage,
slouching; *kuv...* with no
backbone, spineless.
ryhmi|ttyä group themselves,
form groups; *(autosta)* get in
lane, get into the proper
lane. -**ttää** group, classify. -**tys**
grouping.
ryhmy|inen knotty; knobby.

-**sauva** cudgel.
ryhmä group; *(joukko)* body;
(pensaita ym) clump; cluster;
(puolue-) faction; *(luokka)*
category; *sot.* squad. -**kunta**
group; clique, set. -**lento**
formation flight. -**sana**
collective noun. -**työ** group
work; teamwork.
ryhti *(ruumiin)* carriage,
bearing; *siveellinen ~* moral
strength, morale.
ryhtyä begin, start, set about;
take up (sth.), go in for;
undertake (to), set to, take to
[-ing]; enter into
[conversation, *keskusteluun*];
embark on [an enterprise,
yritykseen], engage in
[speculation, *keinotteluun*];
(turvautua) resort to; *~ (jtk
tehtävää) hoitamaan (toisen
jälkeen)* take over; *~
neuvotteluihin* enter into
negotiations; *~ toimenpiteisiin*
take steps, take measures;
~ työhön set to work, get to
work; tackle (get to grips
with) a job; *~ uudelleen*
resume [work, *työhön*]; *~
väkivaltaan* resort to violence.
ryijy [Finnish] rug.
rykelmä pile; conglomeration.
rykiä clear one's throat,
(yskiä) cough.
rykmentti regiment.
rykäistä *ks. rykiä.*
rymi|nä rumble, din. -**stä**
rumble.
rynnis|tys attack, [on] rush;
kuv. drive; *(ponnistus)*
exertion. -**tää** attack, rush; *~
eteenpäin* press forward.
rynnä|kkö attack, assault,
charge; *vallata -köllä* [take
by] storm; *ryhtyä ~ön* launch
an attack; *(~kivääri* assault
rifle). -**tä** [make an] attack,
charge; *(syöksyä)* rush, dash.
ryntäys rush, run [on the
banks, *pankkeihin*].
rypeä wallow; *~ paheissa* w.
in vice.
rypis|tymätön *(kankaasta)*
crease-resisting. -**tyä** get
crumpled; *(et. kangas)* crease;
-tynyt crumpled, crushed. -**tää**
crumple, *(kangasta)* crease;

(esim. otsaa) wrinkle; ~ *kulmiaan (m.)* knit one's brows, *(vihaisesti)* frown.

ryppy wrinkle; crease; *(poimu)* pucker, gather; *(vako)* furrow; *otsa rypyssä (m.)* with his brow knitted; with a frown. **-inen** *(puku ym)* creased, crumpled; *(otsa)* wrinkled.

rypsi turnip rape.

rypy|ttää gather, pucker. **-tys** gathering.

rypäle *(viini-)* grape. **-mehu** grape juice. **-sokeri** grape sugar; glucose. **-terttu** cluster of grapes.

rysk|e crash. **-yttää** pommel, pound [away] [at the door, *ovea*], ◀hump.

rysty(nen) knuckle.

rysä fyke.

rysähtää crash.

ryteikkö tangle [of fallen trees].

rytmi rhythm. **-llinen** rhythmic [al].

rytäkkä tumult, uproar, hubbub.

rye|ttyä get soiled. **-ttää** soil.

ryyni *ks. suurimo.*

ryyp|iskellä drink; *ark.* booze, tipple. **-py** drink, dram. **-päistä** sip; *(yhtenä kulauksena)* toss off. **-ätä** drink.

ryysy rag; ~*t* rags, tatters. **-inen** ragged; tattered. **-läinen** ragamuffin.

ryömi|ä crawl; creep. **-imiskaista** slow lane, crawler lane. *Am.* creeper lane.

ryöp|py shower; *(räiske)* spray; *parjausten* ~ *(kuv.)* torrent of abuse. **-ytä** *(lentää)* whirl, fly [about].

ryöstää rob (a p. of); *(mukiloida ja* ~*)* mug; plunder, loot, pillage, sack; *(ryöstellä)* maraud; *(siepata)* kidnap, abduct.

ryöstö robbery, *(mukilointi)* mugging; plunder [ing], pillage, depredation [s]; *(sieppaus)* kidnapping, abduction. **-käyttö, -viljely** ruthless exploitation, overexploitation. **-metsästys:** *harjoittaa* ~*tä* exhaust the stock of game. **-murha** murder and robbery. **-retki**

looting expedition, foray. **-saalis** booty, spoils. **-yritys** attempted robbery.

ryövä|ri robber. **-ys** robbery; robbing.

rähi|nä racket; *(esim. humalaisten)* brawl. **-nöidä** make a disturbance. **-nöinti** disorderly conduct. **-sijä** brawler. **-stä** brawl.

rähjä *a. (kurja)* wretched; miserable; *ukko*~ poor old man.

rähmä [mucous] secretion.

räike|ys glaringness; glare; *(värin)* gaudiness. **-ä** glaring; *(väristä, m.)* gaudy, garish, harsh; gross [injustice, *vääryys*]; flagrant [crime, *rikos*]; ~ *vastakohta* sharp (striking) contrast.

räisk|e *(roiske)* spray; *(pauke)* crackle. **-yttää** spatter; sprinkle. **-yä** splash, spatter; *(rätistä)* crackle; *(säkenöidä)* sparkle; *-yvän iloinen* ready to jump for joy, exuberant. **-äle** pancake.

räjähdys explosion, blast; *(paukahdus)* detonation. **-aine** explosive. **-kaasu** explosive gas. **-mäinen** explosive; *ks. väestönkasvu.* **-panos** explosive charge. **-vamma** blast injury.

räjäh|tämätön unexploded; ~ *pommi (»suutari»)* dud. **-tää** explode; *(ilmaan)* blow up.

räjäy|ttää explode, *(ilmaan)* blow up. **-tys** blasting.

räkä snot. **-inen** snotty.

räkättirastas fieldfare.

räme pine bog. **-ikkö** swampy tract, morass. **-inen** swampy; marshy.

rämeä cracked.

rämi|nä racket, *(auton)* rattle, clatter. **-stin** rattle. **-stä, -syttää** rattle.

rämpiä flounder, wade.

rämä ramshackle; rickety old [chair, *tuoli-*]. **-päinen** reckless.

ränni water spout, drainpipe.

ränsistyä [fall into] decay; become dilapidated.

räntä wet snow; sleet. **-inen** slushy.

räpistellä flounder, flap about.

räpy|lä *(uima-)* web; *urh.*

baseball mitt; (~**jalkainen**
web-footed). **-tellä** flap, flutter.
-ttää flap [its wings,
siipiään], flutter; ~ *silmää*
blink. **-tys:** *siipien* ~
wing-beat.
rästi arrears; *olla* ~*nä* be in
a. **-kanto** collection of [taxes
in] arrears.
räti\|nä, -stä crackle.
rätti rag, cloth.
rävä\|htää: ~ *auki* fly open.
-yttää: *silmää -yttämättä*
without blinking.
räyh\|ätä make a disturbance;
brawl. **-ääjä** brawler.
räystäs eaves. **-kouru** gutter.
rääkkäys ill-treatment.
rääky\|nä caw [ing]; croak [ing].
-ä caw; croak.
rääkätä torture; torment; *kuv.*
murder [a foreign language,
vierasta kieltä].
rääsy rag. **-inen.** . in rags,
ragged; tattered.
räätäli tailor. **-mestari** master

tailor. **-nammatti:** *harjoittaa*
~*a* be in the tailoring
business. **-nliike** tailoring
business.
röhkiä grunt.
röhönauru horse-laugh, guffaw.
röijy jacket; *(villa- m.)*
cardigan.
rökittää *sl.* wallop.
rönsy *bot.* runner.
röntgen\|hoito roentgen (X-ray,
x-ray) treatment. **-kuva**
roentgenogram, X-ray [film].
-laitteet roentgen equipment
(*t.* facilities). **-ologi**
radiologist. **-säde:** *-säteet*
roentgen rays, X-rays.
röyh\|elö frill. **-istää:** ~
rintaansa be puffed up [with
pride].
röyhke\|ys insolence; arrogance;
impudence. **-ä** insolent;
arrogant, *(hävytön)* impudent,
cheeky.
röyht\|äistä, -äys belch, burp.
röykkiö pile, heap.

S

saada get, obtain; receive; *(lupa)* be allowed, be permitted; *(apuv.)* may, *(voi)* can; *(jku tekemään jtk)* make. ., get. . to; manage [to prevent, *estetyksi*]; *(saavuttaa)* gain, win, acquire, secure [a seat, *istuinpaikka*]; ~ *aikaan* bring about, effect, perform, cause; accomplish; ~ *hoitoa* receive (be given) treatment; ~ *hyötyä (ym)* derive benefit from, profit by; ~ *jku luopumaan jstk (m.)* persuade a p. to give up sth; ~ *lupa* get permission; ~ *ostajia* find purchasers; ~ *tauti* contract an illness; ~ *tietää* get to know, learn [from, *jklta; of t.* about *jstk*], be informed [of, *jstk*], be told, hear, gather; ~ *tunnustusta (osakseen)* gain *(t.* win) recognition; ~ *vamma* suffer an injury; ~*t mennä* you may go; *hän sai lähteä sinne* he was allowed to go there; *se sai minut nauramaan* it made me laugh; *sain odottaa* I had to wait, I was kept waiting; *kysyin saisinko. .* I asked if I might. .; *saisinko tulitikun?* may I trouble you for a match? *saisinko vähän voita* will you pass the butter, please? *saisinko puhutella. .* I wonder if I could speak to. .? *saanko polttaa* do you mind if I smoke? *saanko avata ikkunan* would you mind if I opened the window? *kirjeenne saatuani* on receiving (on receipt of) your letter; *ei ole saatavissa* is not to be had, is not available.

šaahi shah.

saaja receiver, recipient; *(tavaralähetyksen, m.)* consignee; *(kirjeen)* addressee.

saakka *(jhk)* up to, as far as, *(ajasta)* until, till, [up] to; *joulusta* ~ [ever] since Christmas; *tähän* ~ thus far; until (till) now, up to now, hitherto; *alusta* ~ from the very beginning; *kotiin* ~ *(m.)* all the way home; *loppuun* ~ to the end; *aivan viime aikoihin* ~ until quite recently.

saaliin|himo rapacity, rapaciousness. **-himoinen** rapacious; voracious.

saalis prey; *(ryöstö- ym)* booty, spoils; *(et. kalan)* catch, haul; *(metsästäjän)* bag, kill; *joutua jnk saaliiksi* fall a prey to. **-taa** prey, *kuv.* hunt, angle for; *olla -tamassa* be on the prowl; *elää -tamalla* live [up] on prey.

saama|mies creditor. **-ton** inefficient, incapable; unenterprising. **-ttomuus** inefficiency; lack of enterprise.

saanti: *kalan* ~ catch of fish; *veden* ~ water supply.

saapas boot; *saappaat jalassa* with boots on; *saappaan varsi* boot-leg. **-pari** pair of boots. **-pihti** bootjack.

saapu|a arrive (at, in), come (to), get [there, *sinne*]; *(lähestyä)* approach; *(s-ville)* appear; ~ *kaupunkiin* arrive at (in) the town, get to the town, reach the town; ~ *maahan* enter a country; *milloin juna -u Helsinkiin* when is the train due to arrive in H.? when does the train get to H.? *odotan hänen -van (tiistaina)* I am expecting her on. .; *saavu|ttaessa, -ttua(ni). .* on [my] arrival at (in). . **-minen**

arrival; *(maahan)* entry.
-mispäivä day of arrival.
-villa present; *olla* ~ be
present (at), attend. ., be
there, be on the spot. **-ville:**
tulla ~ appear [before the
court, *oikeuteen*], put in an
appearance, present oneself;
puhek. turn up, show up.
saarelainen islander.
saari island, *run.* isle; *saaressa*
on an island. **-asema** insular
position. **-ilmasto** insular
climate. **-nen:** *runsas*~ studded
with islands. **-ryhmä** group of
islands· **-sto** archipelago,
skerries; (~**lainen**
islander). **-valtakunta** island
kingdom *(t.* state).
saarna sermon; message;
(ripitys) lecture; *pitää* ~
deliver a sermon. **-aja**
preacher; *(vankilan ym)*
chaplain. **-nuotti** sermonizing
tone. **-ta** preach. **-tuoli** pulpit.
saarni ash. **-(pui)nen** ash [en].
saar|ros blockade; *olla*
saarroksissa be surrounded, be
encircled; *(satama ym)* be
blockaded. **-taa** surround,
encircle; *sot.* block. **-to**
blockade; *julistaa* ~*on* declare
a blockade (on); *saarron*
murtaja blockade-runner;
(~**liike** flank movement;
~**politiikka** policy of
encirclement).
saasta filth; impurity; taint.
-inen filthy, impure, unclean,
foul. **-isuus** filth; foulness;
sordidness.
saast|e *vrt.* **-uke;** pollution. **-ua**
be polluted (contaminated).
-uke pollutant; *teollisuus-*
-ukkeet industrial effluents *(t.*
wastes). **-uminen, -uneisuus**
(ilman, veden) pollution,
(esim. ruoan) pollution,
-uttaa pollute, contaminate;
(tartuttaa) infect, taint. **-utus**
contamination, taint.
saatana Satan. **-llinen** Satanic,
diabolic [al].
saatav|a *s.* claim; balance due
(to), balance in one's favour;
~*t (m.)* debts; *Teidän* ~*nne*
meiltä your account against
us; *ulkona olevat* ~*t*

outstanding debts, credits due;
-ana available. **-issa** available,
obtainable, handy, at hand;. .
on runsaasti ~ there is a
plentiful (an ample) supply
of. .
saati(kka) all the more so,
(puhumattakaan) let alone, to
say nothing of, not to
mention; ~ *sitten* much less
[so]; ~ *sitten hän* to say
nothing of him.
saatt|aa 1. *(seurata)*
accompany, go with. ., see [a
p. home, *kotiin*], *(laivalle ym)*
see . . off; *(suojaten)* escort;
mer. convoy; *(opastaen)*
conduct. **2.** *(kyetä)* be able
(to), be capable of [-ing];
may; ~ *niin olla* it may be
so; *hän on -anut tulla* he
may have come; *en saata*
tehdä sitä (m.) I am unable
to do it; I cannot bring
myself to do it; *sellaista* ~
tapahtua such things will *(t.*
may) happen. **3.** get, induce
[a p. to do a th., *jku*
tekemään jtk], make [a p.
laugh, *jku nauramaan*]; ~
aikaan bring about, cause, ~
paljon pahaa aikaan do a
great deal of harm; ~
epätoivoon drive. . to despair;
~ *kosketukseen (jkn kanssa)*
bring into contact with; ~
jkn tietoon bring to the
notice of (to a p.'s notice *t.*
attention); *tämä (toimenpide)*
-oi maan sotaan this involved
the country in war; *-aisi*
might. **-aja** companion; escort.
-o *(kulkue)* procession;
(~**väki:** *väkeä oli paljon*
there was a great crowd to
see. . off). **-ue** escort;
(ylhäisen henkilön) suite;
(laiva-) convoy.
saavi tub.
saavu|ttaa reach; achieve;
attain; *(saada kiinni)*
overtake, catch up with;
(voittaa) gain, win, acquire;
(saada) obtain; ~
maisterinarvo take (attain)
the degree of mag. phil. *(t.*
M. A.); ~ *menestystä* win
success; ~ *jk pistemäärä*

score.. points; ~ *tarkoituksensa* gain one's end, attain one's purpose; ~ *hyvät tulokset* arrive at good results; ~ *voitto* win (gain) a victory; *-tettu taito* the skill attained; *(jkn) -tettavissa* within [a p.'s] reach; *-tettavissa oleva* attainable, obtainable. **-ttamaton** unattainable,.. beyond reach,.. out of reach. **-tus** attainment, achievement, accomplishment; *(tulos)* result.

sabot|aasi sabotage; *harjoittaa ~a* commit [acts of] s. **-oida** sabotage.

sadankomitea Committee of 100.

sada|nnes hundredth [part]. **-s** [the] hundredth.

sada|tella curse; swear (at). **-ttelu** cursing; swearing.

sade rain; shower *(esim. luoti~* shower of bullets); *sateella* in the rain, when it rains. **-aika, -kausi** rainy season, the rains. **-ilma** rainy weather *(-lla* in). **-kuuro** shower [of rain]. **-lla:** *satelee* it is raining. **-mittari** rain-gauge. **-määrä** rainfall. **-pilvi** rain cloud. **-pisara** raindrop. **-ryöppy** heavy shower of rain, downpour. **-takki** raincoat, waterproof, mac, mackintosh.

sadin trap; snare; *joutua satimeen* be trapped, *(kuv.)* be caught [in a trap].

sadoittain hundreds of. .,.. in hundreds.

sadonkorjuu harvest [ing].

saeta get (grow) thicker, thicken.

safiiri sapphire.

saha saw; *(-laitos)* sawmill. **-jauhot** sawdust. **-kone** sawing-machine. **-laitainen** toothed, *bot.* serrate [d]. **-laitos** sawmill. **-nterä** saw blade. **-pukki** saw [ing]-horse. **-reunainen** *(esim. veitsi)* serrated. **-ta** saw; ~ *poikki* saw off. **-tavara** sawn timber, sawn goods, *Am.* lumber. **-teollisuus** sawmill (timber *t. Am.* lumber) industry.

-tukki saw log.

sahrami, safrani saffron.

sahviaani morocco [leather].

saippua soap; *(-pala)* cake of soap. **-astia -kuppi** soap-dish. **-inen** soapy. **-kotelo** soap box. **-kupla** soap-bubble. **-tanko** bar of soap. **-vaahto** soap-lather. **-vesi** [soap-] suds.

saippuoida soap; lather.

saira|la hospital; infirmary; *(pienempi)* nursing home; *(laivan ym)* sick-bay; *otettiin ~an* was admitted to hospital; *(~lääkäri* house-surgeon, -physician). **-lloinen** sickly; ailing, infirm; *(patologinen)* morbid; *hän on ~* she has bad (weak) health; *(-lloisuus* sickliness, ill health. **-nhoitaja** [hospital] nurse, *(kurssinkäynyt)* trained *(Am.* graduate) nurse, registered nurse (R.N.); *-oppilas* student nurse. **-nhoito** nursing; *(~opisto* School of Nursing). **-nsija** bed.

sairas sick; *(et. predikatiivina)* ill; *(esim. kudos)* diseased; pathological, morbid; *(huonovointinen)* indisposed, unwell; *s.* sick person, *(potilas)* patient; *olla sairaana* be ill, be sick; *tulla sairaaksi* fall ill, get ill (sick), be taken ill; *ilmoittautua sairaaksi* report sick. **-huone** sickroom. **-kassa** sick-fund. **-kertomus** case record. **-koti** nursing home. **-käynti** home visit, [professional] call. **-lento** ambulance flight. **-loma** sick-leave. **-luettelo** sick-list. **-mielinen**.. sick in mind, mentally disordered. **-sali** ward.

sairas|taa be ill, *et. Am.* be sick; *(potea)* [be] suffer[ing], *jtk* from. **-tella** be in poor health, be sickly, be ailing. **-tua** be taken ill (with), fall ill, get ill; contract, catch [an illness, *jhk tautiin*]; *hän on -tunut flunssaan* he has caught (he is down with) the flu.

sairas|vaunu ambulance. **-voimistelija** *ks. lääkintä-*. **-vuode** sick-bed.

sairaus illness, sickness; *(tauti)* disease. **-eläke** sickness pension. **-tapaus** case of illness. **-vakuutus** [national] health insurance.

sait|a stingy, miserly, mean; tight-fisted. **-uri** miser, *ark,* screw. **-uus** stinginess, miserliness.

saivar|rella split hairs; be pedantic. **-telija** hair-splitter. **-telu** hair-splitting.

SAK *l.v.* T.U.C. *~-lainen* affiliated to the SAK.

sakaali jackal.

sakara point[ed end]; *(kuun)* horn.

sakariini saccharine.

saka|risto, -sti vestry; *(katol. kirk.)* sacristy.

šakata checkmate.

saketti morning coat.

sake|a thick; *(tiheä)* dense. **-us** thickness; thick consistency.

sakki gang, crowd.

šakki chess; *pelata ~a* play c. **-lauta** chess-board. **-matti** [check-]mate. **-nappula** chessman. **-peli** [game of] chess. **-tehtävä** chess problem.

sakka sediment, dregs, *(kahvin)* grounds; *kem.* precipitate, deposit. **-utua** deposit a sediment.

sakko fine; penalty; *sakon uhalla* on pain of a fine; *tuomita ~ihin ks. seur.*

sakottaa fine; impose a fine [of..] upon a p.

sakramentti sacrament.

Saksa Germany; *Saksan.. (m.)* German; *~n liittotasavalta* the Federal Republic of Germany (Federal Germany, West Germany); *~n demokraattinen tasavalta* the German Democratic Republic.

saksa *(kieli)* German. **-lainen** *a. & s.* German. **-laisranskalainen** Franco-German. **-laistua** become Germanized.

saksan|hirvi red deer, *(uros)* stag. **-kieli** [the] German [language]. **-kielinen** [.. in] German. **-kuusi** European silver fir. **-paimenkoira** Alsatian, German shepherd.

-pähkinä walnut. **-taa** translate into German.

saksatar German woman.

sakset [pair of] scissors; *(suuremmat)* shears.

saksofoni saxophone.

sala *(yhd.)* secret; *on ~ssa* is hidden, Is concealed; is latent; *pitää ~ssa* keep.. secret; hold back; *~ssa pidettävä (kahdenkeskinen)* confidential. **-a** secretly, in secret, in secrecy (privacy); *(piilotellen)* surreptitiously; on the sly; *isältään ~* without his father's knowledge. **-ammattilaisuus** shamateurism.

salaatti salad; *(lehti-)* lettuce. **-kastike** salad dressing. **-kuppi** salad bowl. **-lusikat (haarukat)** salad servers.

sala|-ampuja sniper. **-hanke** plot; frame-up; *olla -hankkeissa* plot, conspire (against). **-illa** conceal. **-inen** secret; hidden, concealed; underhand; clandestine; *(yksityinen)* [private and] confidential; *~ palvelu* Secret Service. **-isuus** secret; *julkinen ~* open s. **-juoni** intrigue; plot, conspiracy. **-kapakka** *Am.* speakeasy. **-kari** submerged rock. **-kauppa** illegal trade. **-kavala** insidious; treacherous; *~ menettely (m.)* underhand practices. **-kavaluus** insidiousness. **-kieli** code. **-kihlat:** *olla -kihloissa* be secretly engaged (to). **-kirjain** cipher. **-kirjoitus** cipher [ing].

salakka bleak.

sala|kuljettaja smuggler. **-kuljetus** smuggling; *(~laiva* smuggler; *~tavara* contraband goods). **-kuuntelija** eavesdropper; *rad.* pirate listener. **-kuuntelu** listening without a licence, *(puhelimen)* tapping; *(~laitteet* bugging device). **-kähmäinen** underhand; clandestine. **-kähmäisyys** stealthiness. **-käytävä** secret passage. **-laatikko** secret drawer. **-liitto** conspiracy, plot. **-liittolainen** conspirator. **-lyhty** dark lantern.

salama [flash of] lightning; ~ *iski puuhun* a tree was struck by lightning; *kuin* ~ *kirkkaalta taivaalta* like a bolt from the blue. **-nisku** stroke of lightning. **-nleimahdus** flash of lightning. **-nnopea**. . quick (swift) as lightning. **-nnopeasti** with lightning speed. **-valo** *valok.* flash-light.
salamanteri *zo.* salamander.
sala|merkki cipher. **-metsästys** poaching. **-metsästäjä** poacher.
salamoi|da flash; *salamoi* it is lightening; *hänen silmänsä -vat* his eyes flashed fire, his eyes flashed [with anger].
sala|murha assassination. **-murhaaja** assassin. **-myhkäinen** secretive. **-myhkäisyys** secretiveness. **-nimi** assumed name; *(kirjailijan)* pseudonym, nom de plume; *nimellä* under a pseudonym. **-oja** [underground] drain. **-ojittaa** drain. **-ovi** secret door. **-peräinen** mysterious; secretive. **-peräisyys** mysteriousness, mystery. **-poliisi** detective. **-poltto** *(viinan)* illicit distilling, *Am.* moonshining. **-seura** secret society. **-siittiö** *bot.* cryptogam.
ala|ta keep. . secret; conceal, keep [from, *jklta*]; ~ *totuus* hide the truth, keep the truth back, withhold the truth; *hän ei sitä -nnut* he made no secret of it. **ala|tarkoitus** hidden purpose. **-tie:** *-teitse* through secret channels. **-tieteet** occult sciences.
alava brittle willow.
ala|vehkeilijä plotter. **-vehkeily** plotting; machination [s].
-vihjaus insinuation. **-vihkaa** furtively, in secret; on the quiet. **-vihkainen** furtive, stealthy.
aldo balance.
ali drawing-room; *(konsertti-ym)* hall, assembly hall; *(sairaalan)* ward.
alisyylihappo salicylic acid.

salkku briefcase, portfolio, document case; executive case.
salko pole; *(tanko)* staff.
salkuton. . without portfolio.
salli|a permit, allow; give. . permission; let; *jos aika -i* if time permits; *jos -tte* if you don't mind. **-mus** fate, destiny; *(kaitselmus)* Providence.
salmi sound; strait [s]; *Calais'n salmi* the Straits of Dover.
salmiakki sal ammoniac.
salo backwoods, the wilds. **-maa** backwoods, hinterland.
salonki drawing-room; *(esim. laivan)* saloon; *(kirjallinen ym)* salon; *kauneus~* beauty parlour. **-kivääri** small-bore rifle.
salpa bolt; *(telki)* bar; *on salvassa* is bolted, is barred; *lukon ja salvan takana* under lock and key. **-rauta** *(aspi)* hasp. **-utua** be bolted; be blocked up, be obstructed.
salpietari saltpetre, potassium nitrate. **-happo** nitric acid.
salskea *(mies)* tall and spare, upstanding.
salva *(voide)* salve, ointment.
salvaa put up [the framework of] [a house, *taloa*].
salvata bolt; bar; *pelko salpasi kieleni* I was speechless with fear; *salpaa hengen jklta* takes away one's breath; *henkeä salpasi* breathing was impeded.
salvia sage.
salvos timberwork.
sama [the] same; identical; ~*a kokoa* (m.). . of a size; ~ *mies* the same man, the very man; ~*an aikaan kuin*. . at the same time as. .; simultaneously with; *olla* ~*a mieltä kuin* agree with; *olen aivan* ~*a mieltä* I fully agree; ~*sta työstä* ~ *palkka* equal pay for equal work. **-lla** at that very moment; *(-an aikaan)* at the same time; *(sen ohessa)* besides; ~ *kertaa* at one and the same time; ~ *kuin* at the same time as. ., *(sillä välin)* while; ~ *tavalla* in the same way, in like

manner, alike; similarly; *vrt. samoin.*

saman|aikainen contemporaneous, simultaneous (with); *olla ~ kuin* coincide with. **-aikaisuus** coincidence. **-arvoinen.** . of the same value,. . of equal value; *~ kuin* equal to. . **-arvoisuus** equality. **-henkinen** congenial. **-ikäinen.** . of the same age. **-kaltainen.** . of the same kind (as), similar (to), like. **-kaltaisuus** similarity. **-keskinen** concentric. **-kokoinen.** . [of] the same size, similarly sized (as); *~ kuin.* . as large as. ., equal in size to. . **-laatuinen** similar; alike. **-lainen.** . of the same kind, similar (to); *ne ovat kaikki -laisia* they are all the same; they are all alike; *minunkin on ostettava ~* I must buy one [like that], too. **-laisuus** resemblance, similarity. **-luontoinen.** . of the same nature; similar. **-merkityksinen** . . equivalent in meaning (to), *kiel.* synonymous (with). **-mielinen** like-minded. **-muotoinen.** . of the same form (shape), similar [in shape]. **-niminen.** . of (with) the same name. **-näköinen** similar [in appearance], like; *he ovat hyvin -näköisiä* they are very much alike, they strongly resemble each other. **-pituinen.** . of the same length. **-sukuinen** related, allied. **-suuntainen.** . going in the same direction,. . to the same effect; *~ ehdotus* a proposition along the same lines. **-tapainen** similar,. . much the same. **-tekevä** all the same; *se on ~ä* it makes no difference, it is all the same [to me].

samapalkkaisuus equal pay.

sama|ssa at that very moment; *vrt. samalla.* **-staa** identify (with); equate (with). **-ten** likewise;. . the same; *(hauskaa joulua!. .) samaten* [merry Christmas!. .] the same to

you! *hän teki ~* he did the same; *ja hän ~* and he likewise *(t.* as well).

same|a thick; turbid, cloudy; *(himmeä)* obscure; *kalastaa ~ssa vedessä* fish in troubled waters. **-ntaa** make. . muddy; *kuv.* trouble, cloud [a p.'s happiness, *jkn onnea*]; *(himmentää)* darken. **-ntamaton** undisturbed, untroubled. **-ntua, -ta** get muddy, become turbid; *kuv.* become clouded; *-ntunut (auton ikkuna)* fogged-up.

sametti velvet; *~jäätelö* soft ice. **-mainen** velvety. **-nen** [. . of] velvet.

sameus muddiness, turbidity; cloudiness.

sammakko frog; *sammakonpoikanen* tadpole. **-mies** frogman.

sammal moss. **-ikko** moss. **-lus** lisping, lisp. **-oitua** become covered with moss, become mossy (overgrown with moss). **-peitteinen** moss-covered. **-taa** lisp.

sammenmäti caviar[e].

sammio vat, basin.

sammu|a go out; be extinguished; *kuv. puheh.* pass out; *(hiipua)* die down; *(jano)* be quenched; *(suku)* become extinct; *-va (katse)* fading; *aikoja -nut rakkaus* a love long dead. **-ksissa:** *on ~* has gone out. **-maton** unquenchable [thirst, *jano*]. **-tin** fire extinguisher. **-ttaa** put out, extinguish; *kuv.* quench; *(kaasu)* turn off, *(sähkö, radio)* switch off; *~ janonsa* quench one's thirst; *~ kynttilä* put out *(puhaltamalla:* blow out) a candle; *~ savuke* stub out *(polkemalla:* stamp out) a cigarette; *-tettu kalkki* slaked lime. **-ttamaton** unextinguished; *~ kalkki* quick-lime. **-tus** putting [the fire] out, extinguishing; fire fighting; *(~kalusto* fire-extinguishing apparatus; *~laite* fire extinguisher).

samoi|lla ramble, rove, roam.

-lu rambling.
samoin in the same way (manner); likewise,. . the same; *kiitos*, ~ thanks! [the] same to you!. . *ja* ~ *olin minäkin*. . and so was I.
samota ramble, roam.
sampi sturgeon.
samppanja champagne.
samuus sameness; identity.
sana word; (*sanoma*) message; (*oppi-*) term; ~*sta* ~*an* word for word, (~*n mukaisesti*) literally, verbatim; ~*lla sanoen* in a word, (*lyhyesti*) in short, to put the matter in a nutshell; *pitää* ~*nsa* keep one's word, be as good as one's word; ~*nsa pitävä mies* an man of his word; (*antaa*) ~ ~*sta* tit for tat; *lähettää* ~ send word; *toisin sanoin* in other words; *ylistävin sanoin* in terms of [high] praise; *sanoin ja kuvin* in text and pictures; *sanoin kuvaamaton* indescribable, beyond words.
-harkka: *joutua* ~*an* have words (with). **-inen** (*yhd*.): *jyrkkä* ~ sharply worded.
-jalka bracken. **-järjestys** word order; *suora* (*käänteinen*) ~ normal (inverted) w. o.
-kiista dispute, controversy.
-kirja dictionary; *katsoa* ~*sta* look up in a d.; ~*n tekijä* lexicographer, compiler of a dictionary. **-käänne** phrase; phrasing. **-leikki** play upon words, pun. **-llinen** verbal.
luettelo list of words, vocabulary. **-luokka** part of speech. **-muoto** wording.
anan|lasku proverb; ~*n tapaan* proverbially; *S*~*t* (*raam.*) Proverbs. **-mukainen** literal.
-mukaisesti literally, word for word. **-mukaisuus** literalness, exactness. **-parsi** saying; ayword; *on tullut -parreksi* has become proverbial.
saattaja messenger; herald.
tapa expression; saying.
tuoja messenger. **-vaihto** exchange of words; *kiivas* ~ (*m.*) altercation. **-valta** voice; *-llä*) *ei ole* ~*a asiassa* has o say in the matter. **-vapaus**

liberty (freedom) of speech.
-vuoro turn [to speak]; *vrt. suunvuoro*.
sana|ristikko crossword.
-runsaus abundance of words.
-seppä coiner of words. **-sota** dispute, controversy, war of words; *olla* ~*silla* have a heated argument. **-sto** vocabulary, glossary; (*oppi-*) terminology; nomenclature.
-sutkaus witticism. **-tarkka** literal. **-ton** speechless, tongue-tied; *tulla -ttomaksi* be dumbfounded (nonplussed).
-tulva flow (torrent) of words.
-valmis. . quick at repartee.
-valmius ready wit. **-varasto** vocabulary.
sandaali sandal.
saneeraus redevelopment; (*talon*) re-fitting; (*slummin*) slum clearance.
sane|lla dictate; ~ *vala* administer an oath (to). **-lu** dictation; *kirjoittaa* ~*n mukaan* write down from dictation, take dictation, (*esim. kirje*) take down a letter; (~*kone* dictaphone, ~*ratkaisu* dictate).
sangallinen. . with a handle.
sangen very; ~ *hyvin* perfectly well; ~ *paljon* a good deal, a great many.
saniainen fern.
sanitääri first aid assistant.
sanka (*ripa*) handle; (*kukkaron ym*) frame; *silmälasien sangat* frame of spectacles.
sankari hero. **-aika** the heroic age. **-kuolema** death of a hero; *sai* ~*n* died a hero's death. **-llinen** heroic. **-llisesti** heroically. **-llisuus** heroism.
-npalvonta hero-worship. **-tar** heroine. **-työ** heroic deed.
sankaruus heroism.
sankka thick, dense.
sanko pail, bucket.
sannikas sandal.
sannoittaa sand.
sano|a say; tell; (*nimittää*) call; (*lausua*) state, express; ~ *jäähyväiset* bid farewell; *voitteko* ~, *missä*. . can you tell me where. .? *niin* ~*kseni* so to speak, as it were;

-kaamme *(50)* [let us] say [fifty]; sanaakaan *-matta* without saying (uttering) a word; sano minun *-neen* mark my words! lyhyesti *-en* in short; toisin *-en* that is to say; on *-mattakin selvää* it goes without saying, it is a matter of course; sanotaan it is said, they say [that. .]; hänen *-taan olevan. .* he is said to be. .; niin *-ttu* so-called; ei ole *-ttu, että. .* it does not follow that; ei *-ttavassa määrin* not in any degree worth mentioning, not appreciably. **-ma** message; news; tidings.

sanoitt|aa: *jkn -ama* words by.

sanomalehden|myyjä newsvendor. **-toimittaja** editor [of a newspaper]. **-toimitus** editorial staff of a newspaper.

sanomalehdistö the press.

sanomalehti newspaper, paper. **-ala** journalism. **-ilmoitus** [newspaper] advertisement. **-katsaus** press review. **-leike** press cutting. **-mies** journalist, pressman. **-myymälä** newsagent's; *(kadulla)* news-stand. **-paperi** newsprint; *(painettu)* newspaper. **-poika** newsboy. **-uutinen** newspaper item.

sano|maton unspeakable, unutterable, inexpressible; *-mattoman kaunis* exceedingly beautiful, beautiful beyond description. **-nta** expression; *tiet.* term; *(tyyli)* style; *arkinen* ~ colloquial phrase; (~**tapa** mode of expression, phrase). **-ttava:** *mitä sinulla on* ~*a* what have you got to say? *ei* ~*sti* nothing to speak of. *-utua:* ~ *irti* give notice, *(esim. jstk politiikasta)* dissociate oneself from; ~ *irti (virasta)* resign from.

santa sand, *(sora)* gravel.

santarmi gendarme.

santelipuu sandalwood.

sao|staa *kem.* precipitate. **-stua** be precipitated, settle. **-stus** precipitation. **-ta** get thicker, thicken.

saparo tail, *(hius-)* pigtail.

sapatti Sabbath.

sapekas. . full of gall,. . full of bitterness; *(myrkyllinen)* venomous, virulent.

sapeli sabre; sword.

sapettaa gall; stir up a p.'s anger.

sappi gall; bile; *se kuohuttaa sappeani* that makes me boil with rage; *purkaa sappeansa* vent one's anger (spleen). **-kivi** gallstone. **-rakko** gallbladder. **-tauti** gallbladder disease.

sapuska grub.

sara *bot.* sedge.

sarake column.

sarana hinge. **-istuin** tip-up seat. **-tuoli** folding chair.

saras|taa dawn; *päivän -taessa* at dawn, at daybreak. **-tus** dawn.

sardiini sardine.

sarja series; set; *(jakso)* succession; *(rivi)* line; *kevyt, raskas* ~ light-(heavy-)weight class. **-filmi** [TV] series. **-julkaisu** serial publication. **-kukkainen** umbelliferous. **-kuva** comic strip, strip cartoon; ~*t* comics, (~**lehti** comic book). **-numero** serial number. **-tuotanto** serial production.

sarka 1. *(pelto-)* plot, strip; **2.** *(kangas)* frieze, homespun.

sarveis|aine keratin. **-kalvo** cornea. **-kerros** horny layer.

sarve|llinen horned. **-ton** hornless.

sarvi horn; *(hirven ym)* antler. **-karja** horned cattle. **-kuono** rhinoceros, *(lyh.)* rhino. **-mainen** horny, corneous. **-päinen** horned, *(hirvistä ym)* antlered.

sata a *(t.* one) hundred; *satoja vuosia* [for] hundreds of years; *satoja kertoja* hundreds of times; *useita satoja miehiä* many hundreds of men, several hundred men; *viisi~a* five hundred.

sataa rain *(m. kuv.)*; ~ *vettä* it is raining; ~ *lunta* it is snowing, snow is falling; ~ *rankasti* it is raining heavily; ~ *kaatamalla* it is pouring, the rain is pelting down;

satoi(pa) tai paistoi rain or shine; *äsken satanut lumi* freshly fallen snow.

sata|-asteinen centigrade. **-kertainen** hundredfold; *satakertaisesti* a hundredfold. **-kieli** nightingale. **-kunta** about a hundred, a hundred or so. **-luku:** *kahdeksansataaluvulla* in the ninth century.

satama harbour, port; *et. kuv.* haven; *poiketa ~an* call at a port; *saapua ~an* make harbour; put into a port; *lähteä ~sta* sail from a port. **-allas** [wet-]dock. **-järjestys** harbour regulations. **-kapteeni** captain of the port, harbour-master. **-kaupunki** [sea]port. **-konttori** harbour-master's office. **-laituri** quay. **-maksut** harbour-dues, port charges. **-nsuu** entrance to a port. **-rata** harbour railway. **-työläinen** dock-worker; docker, longshoreman. **-viranomaiset** port authorities.

sata|määrin in (by) hundreds; *niitä oli siellä* ~ there were hundreds [and hundreds] of them. **-vuotias**. . a hundred years old; *s.* centenarian. **-vuotinen** centennial, centenary.

satavuotis|juhla centenary, centennial [celebration]. **-muisto:** *viettää (jkn)* ~*a* celebrate the hundredth anniversary (the centenary) of. .

sateen|kaari rainbow. **-suoja** shelter from the rain; = *seur.* **-varjo** umbrella.

sateeton rainless.

sateinen rainy; ~ *päivä (m.)* wet day.

satelliitti satellite; *sää~* meteorological s.

satiini *(silkki-)* satin; *(puuvilla-)* sateen.

satiiri satire. **-kko** satirist. **-nen** satiric [al].

sato yield; crop, harvest *(m. kuv.).* **-isa** high-yielding, *(runsas)* plentiful, abundant. **-isuus** productiveness; fertility. **-toiveet** harvest prospects.

sattu|a happen, chance;

(tapahtua) occur, come about; take place, come to pass; *(osua)* hit [the mark, *maaliin];* *(jkn osalle)* fall [to a p., to a p.'s lot]; *jalkani -i kiveen* I hit (I knocked) my foot against a stone; *kivi -i häntä päähän* the stone struck him on the head; *polveeni -i* I hurt my knee; *se -i häneen kipeästi* it hurt his feelings deeply; *kaikki, mitä eteeni -u* everything that comes my way; *jos hyvin -u* if all goes well; *sepä -i hyvin* why, that was lucky! *jos hän -isi tulemaan* if she should come; *joulupäivä -u tiistaiksi* Christmas day falls on a Tuesday; ~ *yhteen* coincide; *satuimme yhteen* we happened to meet; *esteen -essa* in case of hindrance; *sodan -essa* in the event of war; *-neesta syystä* for certain reasons, owing to unforeseen circumstances. **-ma** chance; *(tapaus)* incident; *jättää (kaikki)* ~*n varaan* leave [things] to chance, let chance decide; *on ~n varassa.* . it is a mere chance [if. .]; *onnellinen* ~ a lucky chance. **-malta** by chance, by accident, accidentally; *aivan* ~ quite by accident; *hän oli* ~ *siellä* he happened to be there. **-manvarainen** accidental, fortuitous, haphazard.

sattuva . . to the point, telling; striking [example, *esimerkki];* *(sopiva)* apt, appropriate; *huomautus oli* ~ the remark struck home; *vastaus oli erinomaisen* ~ the answer was very much to the point, the answer hit the nail on the head. **-sti** to the point.

satu fairy-tale; *(kertomus)* story, tale. **-kirja** book of fairy-tales, story-book. **-kuningas** legendary king.

satula saddle; *heittää jku ~sta (m.)* unhorse, unseat a p.; *ilman ~a* bareback. **-loimi** saddle-cloth. **-seppä** harness-maker. **-vyö**

[saddle-]girth.
satuloida saddle.
satu|maa(ilma) fairyland,
wonderland. **-mainen** fabulous,
fantastic.
satunnai|nen accidental, chance
[meeting, *kohtaaminen*];
casual, fortuitous; *(tilapäinen)*
temporary; *-set menot*
incidental expenses; *-set
pikkutyöt* odd jobs. **-sesti**
accidentally, incidentally,
occasionally.
satu|näytelmä dramatized
fairy-tale. **-prinssi** fairy prince.
satuttaa *(loukata)* hurt; ∼
itsensä hurt oneself.
saukko otter.
sauma seam; *(liitos)* joint. **-ta**
seam; *(puusepän)* joint. **-ton**
kuv. smooth.
saun|a sauna [bath]. **-ottaa**
bath. **-ottaja** attendant in
sauna.
sauva staff; stick; rod;
(marsalkan) baton; *(taika-)*
wand; *(piispan)* crosier.
sauvoa pole; punt.
saven|valaja potter. **-valanta,
-valu** pottery.
savi clay. **-astia:** ∼*t*
earthenware, stoneware,
pottery. **-kukko** toy ocarina.
-kuoppa clay-pit. **-kyyhkynen**
clay pigeon. **-maa** clayey soil;
loam. **-maja** mud hut;
(savitiilistä tehty) adobe. **-nen**
clayey. **-puoli** ringworm, tinea.
-ruukku crock; earthenware
pot. **-tavarat, -teokset**
earthenware, pottery, ceramics.
savu smoke. **-hattu** cowl. **-inen**
smoky. **-kanava** [smoke] flue.
savuke cigarette; *savukkeen
pätkä, sytytin c.* butt *(t.* end),
c. lighter; *haluatteko
savukkeen* will you have a
c.? **-kotelo** cigarette case.
-rasia packet *(Am.* pack) of
cigarettes.
savun|haju, -katku smell of
smoke. **-harmaa** smoky grey,
smoke-coloured.
savu|naamari smoke-helmet.
-patsas column of smoke.
-piippu chimney; smokestack,
(laivan ym) funnel. **-pilvi**
cloud of smoke. **-pommi**

smoke-bomb (-ball). **-silli**
smoked herring, kipper.
savus|taa smoke; *(palvata)*
cure; *(huone)* fumigate; *-tettu*
smoked, *(liha)* smoke-dried.
savu|ta smoke; *(levittäen pahaa
hajua)* reek. **-ton** smokeless.
-torvi chimney. **-ttaa** smoke.
-ttua get smoky. **-verho**
smoke-screen.
se it; that; the; *se kirja,
jonka ostin. .* the book [that]
I bought; *se, joka* he (she)
who, whoever; *se, mikä* that
which; *se siitä!* that's that!
sen parempi so much the
better; *se on* that is *(lyh.*
i.e.); *sen ajan. .* of that
period; *sen johdosta, että*
owing to the fact that; *sen
jälkeen* after that, afterwards,
subsequently, thereafter,
thereupon, since; *sen jälkeen
kun* since, after; *sen lisäksi*
in addition [to that]; *sen
sijaan* instead [of that]; *sen
tähden, sen vuoksi* therefore,
for that reason, consequently;
siinä kaikki! that's all! *siihen
aikaan* at the (that) time;
sille taholle that way; *sillä
hetkellä* at the time; *sinä
vuonna* that year; *vrt. siitä,
sillä, sitä, ne, niitä jne.*
sea|ssa: *jnk* ∼ among. ., in the
midst of. **-sta:** *jnk* from
among. .
seemiläinen s. Semite; a.
Semitic.
seepra *zo.* zebra.
seerumi serum.
sees, -teinen clear, bright;
serene. **-tyä** clear up; brighten.
seideli tankard, mug.
seikka circumstance, *(sattunut)*
incident; *(asia)* thing; matter;
se ∼*, että* the fact that;
nämä seikat (m.) these points,
these considerations.
seikkai|lija adventurer;
(∼*luonne* adventurous spirit;
∼*tar* adventuress). **-lla** *lähteä
s-lemaan* go out in search of
adventure. **-lu** adventure;
(∼*kas* adventurous; ∼*nhalu*
love of adventure; ∼*nhaluinen*
adventure-loving, adventurous).
seikka|peräinen detailed,

minute, circumstantial.
-peräisesti in detail, minutely,
circumstantially. **-peräisyys**
fullness of detail; minuteness;
circumstantiality, particularity.
seimi manger, *(talliasetelma)*
crèche; *lasten~* day nursery,
crèche.
seinä wall; *lyödä päänsä ~än
(kuv.)* run one's head against
a wall; *panna ~ä vastaan*
drive sb. into a corner; *päin
seinä* all wrong. **-kosketin** *ks.
pistorasia.* **-maalaus** wall
painting, mural painting. **-mä**
wall. **-pallo** *(peli)* squash.
-paperi wallpaper. **-peili** wall
mirror. **-pylväs** pilaster.
-valaisin wall light; bracket
lamp, sconce. **-verho** tapestry.
seireeni siren.
seis stop! *voim.* stand! *sot.*
halt!
seisaa|llaan standing. **-lleen:**
nousta ~ stand up, rise [to
one's feet].
seisah|dus stop[ping], stoppage,
halt; standstill; *(esim.
liikenteessä)* block; *et. kuv.*
stagnation; *joutua -duksiin*
come to a standstill,
(liikenteestä) be blocked, be
held up; *on -duksissa* is at a
standstill, *(tehdas, kone ym)*
is not running. **-duttaa** stop;
bring . . to a stand [still]; *~
hevonen* stop, pull up [a
horse]. **-taa, -tua** stop, come
to a stop; come to a
standstill.
seisake halt.
seiso|a stand; be at a
standstill; *nousta -maan* stand
up, rise; *jäädä -maan* remain
standing; *panna (esim. tehdas)
-maan* put out of operation;
kelloni seisoo my watch has
stopped. **-mapaikka** standing
place, standing-room. **-skella**
stand about. **-ttaa** stop.
seitsemän seven. **-kymmentä**
seventy. **-nes** seventh [part].
-toista seventeen.
seitsemäs [the] seventh.
-kymmenes [the] seventieth.
-osa [one *t.* a] seventh.
-toista [the] seventeenth.
seitsen|haarainen sevenbranched.

-kertainen sevenfold. **-kymmen**|-
luku: *-luvulla* in the seventies.
-kymmenvuotias *a.* . . seventy
years old; *s.* a man
of seventy, a septuagenarian.
seitsikko septet.
seitti cobweb, [spider's] web.
seiväs pole; *(aidan, m.)* stake.
-hyppy pole vault. **-tää** stake,
(lävistää) pierce.
sekaan: *jnk ~* among; *panna
(jhk) ~* mix. . with. **-nus**
confusion, disorder; *puhek.*
mix-up. **-nuttaa** confuse. **-tua**
meddle [in other people's
business, *toisten asioihin*],
interfere (with *t.* in);
(sekoittua) mix; *(kuv.)* get
mixed up (with), be
implicated [in an affair,
juttuun], be involved (in); *~
puhuessaan* be [come]
confused, lose the thread.
-tuminen interference,
meddling (with); intervention
(in).
seka-avioliitto mixed marriage.
sekai|nen mixed; *(sekava)*
confused, *(sotkuinen)* tangled;
muddled; *(samea)* muddy;
hiekan~ mixed with sand.
-sin all mixed up; in
confusion, jumbled together,
upside down; *tilit ovat ~*
accounts are not in order;
on päästään hiukan ~ [he]
is not all there, he is dotty.
seka|kuoro mixed choir. **-lainen**
mixed; miscellaneous; various;
-laisia kuluja sundry expenses,
sundries. **-melska** mess,
medley, muddle. **-muoto(inen)**
hybrid. **-päinen** muddle-headed.
-rotu mixed breed. **-rotuinen**. .
of mixed breed, cross-bred;
(ihmisistä). . of mixed blood.
-sikiö hybrid; cross. **-sorto**
confusion, disorder; chaos.
-sortoinen disordered; chaotic.
-sotku jumble, mess, *(puhe)*
gibberish. **-tavara** sundry
wares, sundries; *(~kauppa*
general shop, general store).
-työmies unskilled workman.
-va confused; muddled [in
the mind]; *(hajanainen)*
incoherent; *(sotkuinen)*
tangled; involved; *-vin tuntein*

with mixed feelings. **-vasti** in
a confused manner;
incoherently. **-vuus** confusion,
confused state.
sekki, šekki cheque, *Am.*
check; *10 dollarin* ~ a c. for
10 dollars. **-tili** cheque *(Am.*
checking) account. **-vihko** c.
book.
sekoi|tin mixer. **-ttaa** mix
[up], *(joskus)* blend;
(hämmentää) stir; *(sotkea)* stir
up, muddle [up]; *(lisätä)* mix
in, put in; *(erehdyksestä jhk)*
mistake.. for, *(toisiinsa)* mix
up; ~ *kortit* shuffle the
cards; ~ *käsitteet* confuse the
ideas; ~ *suunnitelmat* upset
the plans. **-ttamaton** unmixed;
(aito) pure, genuine. **-ttua**
mix, *jhk* with; blend;
intermix, intermingle. **-tus**
mixture; mix; *(tee-, ym)*
blend; admixture.
seksi sex. **-kkyys** sexiness. **-käs**
sexy.
sektori sector.
sekunda second-rate; seconds.
sekundantti second.
sekunti second. **-kello**
stop-watch. **-osoitin**
second-hand.
sekä and: ~ .. *että* both ..
and,.. as well as ..
selailla turn over the leaves
[of a book], leaf [in a
book].
selin *ks.* selkä.
'seli|tettävä. . to be explained;
-tettävissä oleva explicable,
explainable; *asia on helposti
-tettävissä* the matter can
easily be accounted for *(t.* is
easily explained). **-ttämätön**
inexplicable; *(ei -tetty)*
unexplained;.. not cleared up.
-ttää explain, account for;
(tulkita) interpret; *(selvittää)*
make out; *(esim. jtk. teoriaa)*
expound; *hän -tti olevansa
halukas* he declared himself
willing (to); *tämä* ~ *sen,
että.* . this accounts for the
fact that. .; ~ *jk
olemattomaksi* explain. . away;
~ *väärin* misinterpret,
misconstrue; ~ *syynsä (m.)*
give one's reasons; *-ttävä*

explanatory. **-tys** explanation;
(-ttävä lausunto) statement;
comment; ~, *selitykset
(ratkaisu)* key [to a
problem], *(kuvan, kuvion)*
legend; *selitykseksi* as an *(t.* by
way of) explanation.
selja elder.
seljetä clear up; brighten;
(ilma) alkaa ~ it is clearing
up, it is getting brighter.
selke|ys clearness, clarity;
distinctness; lucidity. **-ä** clear,
bright; *(selvä)* distinct; *vrt.*
selvä.
selkka|us *(rettelö)* trouble,
difficulty; *(riita)* conflict,
clash; *(sotku)* tangle; *joutua
-ukseen viranomaisten kanssa*
get into trouble with the
authorities.
selko clearness; *(tieto)*
information; *ottaa* ~ *jstk* find
out, inform oneself (about);
inquire into; *saada* ~*a jstk*
find out; *tehdä* ~*a jstk* give
an account of; account for;
hankkia tarkka ~ *jstk* make
a close inquiry about. .
-selä|lleen, -llään wide open;
avata ovi ~ open the door
wide.
selkä back; *(järven-)* open
lake; *(vuoren)* ridge; *antaa*
~*än jklle* beat, spank, dust a
p.'s jacket; *saada* ~*änsä* be
beaten; *kääntää* ~*nsä jklle*
turn one's back on *(t.* to);
istua selin jhk sit with one's
back towards. .; *selälleen,
-llään* on one's back, *(auki)*
wide open; *kaatua selälleen*
fall backwards; *jkn selän
takana (m. kuv.)* behind a
p.'s back; *Jumalan selän
takana* at the back of
beyond. **-inen** -backed. **-liha**
(teuraan) sirloin. **-mys** back.
-nikama vertebra *(pl.* -e).
-noja back rest, [seat] back.
-pii: ~*täni karmi* a tingle ran
down my spine; ~*tä karmiva*
spine-chilling. **-puoli** back;
rear. **-rangaton** spineless,
invertebrate. **-ranka** backbone
(m. kuv.); spine, spinal
column. **-rankainen** *a. & s.*
vertebrate. **-reppu** knapsack,

rucksack. **-sauna** whipping, thrashing; *antaa ~ (m.)* spank. **-uinti** back-stroke. **-ydin** spinal cord.

sellai|nen such,. . like that;. . of that kind; *~ mies* that sort of man; *~sta ei olisi tapahtunut.* . such a thing would not have happened; *ei mitään -sta* nothing of the kind; *-sessa tapauksessa* in such a case; *ihailen -sia henkilöitä* I admire people like that; *-sta sattuu* such things will happen; *-senaan* as such, as it stands; *ja sen -sta* and what have you.

selleri: *lehti ~* celery; *juuri~* celeriac.

selli *(koppi)* cell.

sello *mus.* [violon]cello. **-nsoittaja** [violon]cellist.

sellofaani film, *(eräs laatu)* cellophane.

sellu|loidi celluloid. **-loosa** cellulose, chemical pulp; *(~tehdas* cellulose mill; *~teollisuus* cellulose industry; *~vanu* cellulose wadding.

selonteko account (of), report (on), *(selvitys)* exposition, description; explanation.

selos|taa give an account of, report (on); describe; *~ jtk laajasti (lehdessä ym)* give wide coverage to. **-taja** reporter, *(esim. radio-)* commentator. **-tus** report, *(esim. urh.)* commentary. *(~vihkonen* prospectus, leaflet).

selusta back; *sot.* rear; *hyökätä ~an* attack. . in the rear.

selve|nnys [further] light (on); *pyytäisin ~tä tähän kohtaan* I should like to have this point [further] clarified. **-ntää** make. . clear[er], make. . plain[er], clarify; *(valaista)* illustrate. **-tä** *(seljetä)* clear up; *(selvitä)* become clear[er]; clarify.

selvi|ke *(kahvin)* clarifier. **-lle:** *käydä ~* become clear (evident); *tutkimuksesta kävi ~ että.* . the investigation showed that; *edelläolevasta on käynyt ~* it will be clear

from the foregoing; *päästä ~ jstk* find out. **-llä:** *olla jstk ~* be clear on, be well informed (about); *olen siitä täysin ~* it is perfectly clear to me. **-ttämätön** unexplained; *~ kysymys* unsolved *(t.* open) question. **-ttää** clear up, clarify; *(vyyhti)* disentangle; *(järjestää)* adjust, settle; *(selittää)* explain; *(tehdä selväksi)* make clear, bring. . home [to a p., *jklle*]; *mer.* clear; *liik.* liquidate, wind up; *(ratkaista)* solve; *~ kantansa* make one's position clear; *~ kuolinpesä* wind up a deceased person's estate; *~ asia oikeudessa* settle a matter in the court; *~ raha-asiat* straighten out (settle) one's affairs. **-tys** clearing up; adjustment, settlement; *(laivan)* clearing; *(rikosten)* detection; *antaa ~ jstk* give an account of; *hankkia ~tä asiaan* look further into the matter. **-tysmies** *(kuolinpesän)* administrator, executor, *(konkurssipesän)* liquidator. **-tä** *(seljetä)* clear up, brighten; *(tulla selväksi)* become clear; *(päästä)* get off [with 2 months, *2 kk rangaistuksella*], escape [alive, *hengissä*]; *(päihtymyksestä)* sober up; *(tointua)* recover; *asia -si* the matter was cleared [up]; *hänelle -si* it dawned on him, he realized (that); *~ tyrmistyksestään* recover from one's amazement. **-ytyä** *(suoriutua)* come off [well, hyvin], get out of [a fix, *pulasta*], cope with [a task, *tehtävästä*]; pull through [an illness, *taudista*]; clear [a fence, *aidasta*]; *~ hengissä* escape alive; *~ voittajana* come off victorious; *~ vaikeuksista* get over difficulties. **-ö** axiom.

selvyys clearness; clarity; distinctness; *(käsialan)* legibility; *(järjen)* lucidity.

selvä clear; distinct, plain; *(ilmeinen)* obvious;

unmistakable; *(raitis)* sober; *(järjenjuoksu)* lucid; ~ *totuus* the plain [unvarnished] truth; ~*t todistukset* clear proof, manifest evidence; ~ *valhe* evident lie; ~*ä puhetta* plain talk; *itsestään* ~ self-evident; *on itsestään* ~*ä* it goes without saying; *pitää (itsestään)* ~*nä* take. . for granted; *ottaa* ~ *jstk* find out, inform oneself on (about); ascertain, *(tutkia)* inquire into; *saada* ~ *jstk, jk selville* find out; make out, discover, detect; *en saa tästä* ~*ä (kirjoituksesta ym)* I can't make this out; *tehdä* ~*ä jstk* account for; *hänelle kävi* ~*ksi, että* he realized that; *hän ilmaisi asiansa hyvin* ~*sti* he was quite explicit [about the matter]. **-järkinen** clear-thinking (-headed). **-kieli:** *tulkita -kielelle* decode, decipher. **-näkijä** clairvoyant. **-näköinen** clear-sighted. **-näköisyys** clear-sightedness; clairvoyance. **-piirt|einen** clear-[cut], [sharply] defined; pronounced, marked; *s-eisesti* in a clear-cut manner. **-piirteisyys** distinctness [of outline], clear-cut character. **selä|ke** *keitt.* fillet, undercut. **-llään** on one's back. **-ttää** *urh.* force into a fall. **-nne** *(vuoren)* ridge.
sementti cement; *kiinnittää sementillä* cement.
seminaari teachers' training college; *(pappis-)* seminary; *(yliop.)* seminar. **-lainen** trainee in education, student teacher.
semminkin particularly; ~ *kun* all the more because, the more so as.
semmoi|nen *ks. sellainen;* *-senaan* as such; as it is.
senaa|tti senate. **-ttori** senator.
sen|aikuinen. . dating from that time,. . of that time;. . at that time. **-ikäinen.** . of that age. **-jälkeen** after that; afterwards; *ks. se.* **-kaltainen** such,. . of such nature.
senkin; ~ *roisto* you

scoundrel; ~ *pelkuri* what a coward you are!
senkka *puhek.* sedimentation rate (ESR).
senmukai|nen consistent with. . **-sesti** accordingly, in conformity therewith.
sensaatio sensation. **-lehdistö** yellow press. **-mainen** sensational. **-uutinen** sensational piece of news.
sens|ori censor. **-uroida** censor. **-uuri** censorship; ~*n avaama* opened by censor.
sen|tapainen such,. . like that, *(saman-)* similar; *jotakin -tapaista* something like that, something to that effect.
sentimentaali|nen sentimental. **-suus** sentimentality.
senttimetri centimetre, *Am.* -meter.
sen|tähden, -vuoksi for that reason, therefore, because of that; ~ *että.* . because. .
sentään yet, still; for all that; *(mutta)* hän *ei* ~ *voinut sitä tehdä* yet he could not [bring himself to] do it; *tulithan* ~*!* you did come after all!
seos mixture, mix; *(metalli-)* alloy.
seota mix, blend (with); *(henkisesti)* get confused, *(järki)* become mentally disordered.
sepeli, -kivi road metal, macadam; *päällystää* ~*llä* macadamize.
sepel|kyyhkynen ring-dove, wood-pigeon. **-valtimo** coronary artery; *(~tukos* coronary thrombosis).
sepi|te, -telmä [piece of] composition. **-ttää** make, *(keksiä)* make up, invent, coin [words, *sanoja*]; *(panna kokoon)* put together; *(kirjoittaa)* write, compose.
seppel|e wreath, garland. **-öidä** decorate with wreaths; festoon, garland; ~ *laakereilla* crown. . with laurels.
seppä blacksmith; smith; *ei kukaan* ~ *syntyessään* no one is a born artisan; *oman onnensa* ~ the architect of one's own fortune.

sepus|taa make up, fabricate, forge [lies, *valheita*]; (*»keittää kokoon»*) concoct; (*keksiä*) invent; (*kyhäillä*) scribble. **-taja** scribbler. **-tus** scribble.

sepä: ~ *kummallista* that's strange! how curious! ~ *se* that's [just] it! exactly!

serbia|lainen *a. & s.* Serbian; *s.* Serb; **-n kieli** Serbian, Serb.

serenadi serenade.

serkku cousin; *he ovat serkukset* they are cousins; *hän on äitini* ~, ~*ni poika* he is my first cousin once removed.

serpentiinit ticker-tape, streamers, confetti.

seteli [bank-]note, *Am.* bill; 5 *punnan* ~ a five-pound note. **-nanti** note issue, issue of bank-notes. **-pankki** bank of issue. **-raha** paper money (currency).

setripuu cedar.

setä [paternal] uncle.

seul|a sieve, strainer; (*hiekka-ym*) screen; (~*tutkimus* screening test [s]). **-oa** sift; *kuv.* pick out, separate (. . from); *hän ei -o sanojaan* he does not choose his words.

seura company; (*yhdistys*) society; (*huvi-*) party, assembly; *olla jkn* ~*ssa* be in a p.'s company; be accompanied by; *pitää* ~*a* (*jklle*) keep a p. company, entertain [the guests]; ~*a karttava* unsociable, uncompanionable; ~ *rakastava* (*eläin*) gregarious; *vrt. seurallinen*; ~*n vuoksi* for company; (*jku*) ~*naan* with [*esim.* a dog] for company.

seuraa|ja successor. **-mus** consequence. **-va** following, ensuing; subsequent, succeeding; (*ensi*) next; ~*na päivänä* the next day, [on] the following day, the day after; ~*na oli. .* next came. .; *oli* ~*nlainen* was as follows. **-vasti** as follows, in the following way (*t.* terms = -*vin sanoin*); thus; *kuuluu* ~

runs a follows.

seura|elämä social life; *ottaa osaa* ~*än* move in society. **-ihminen** sociable person; society man (woman). **-koira** pet dog. **-kunnallinen** congregational. **-kunta** parish, (*jumalanpalveluksessa*) congregation. **-kuntalainen** parishioner. **-lainen** companion; (*saattaja*) escort. **-leikki** parlour game. **-llinen** sociable, companionable. **-llisuus** sociability. **-matka** group (*t.* conducted) tour. **-mies:** *hän on hauska* ~ he is very good company. **-nainen** lady's companion. **-narka** averse to society; unsociable. **-nhaluinen** sociable. **-näytelmä** amateur play. **-piiri** circle of friends; ~*t* society.

seura|ta follow; (*mukana*) accompany; (*virassa ym*) succeed; (*noudattaa*) observe; (*olla seurauksena*) be a consequence of, ensue from; (*katseellaan*) watch; ~ *aikaansa* keep abreast of the times; ~ *esimerkkiä* (*m.*) follow suit, follow [a p.'s] lead; ~ *jkn neuvoa* (*m.*) take (act on) a p.'s advice; *-a neuvoani* take my advice! ~ *ohjeita* follow [the] instructions; *tästä -a, että* it follows that; *hakemusta tulee* ~ *selvitys.* . the application should be accompanied by an account of. .; *hänen mukanaan -a hänen vaimonsa* he will be accompanied by his wife. **-us** consequence; issue; ~*uksena jstk* as a result of; *siitä oli -uksena.* . it resulted in. .; *vastata -uksista* take the consequences; *sillä -uksella että* with the result that. .

seurue (*seura*) party, company; (*ylhäisen henkilön*) suite, entourage; *kymmenhenkinen* ~ a party of ten. **-stella** associate (with), keep company (with); (*poika ja tyttö*) go together, (*vakituisesti*) go steady with; *he -stelevat paljon* they

spend a lot of time in each
other's company. **-stelu**
associating [with people],
social life, social intercourse;
(nuorten) courtship; *antautua
~un jkn kanssa* take up with;
(**~sääntö** social etiquette;
~taito social talents; **~tapa**
manners [of polite society]).

seutu region; area; *(lähi-)*
neighbourhood, vicinity;
(paikka) locality; *(piiri)*
district; tract; *näillä seuduin* in
this neighbourhood, in these
parts. **-villa:** *jnk ~* in the region
of. ., near. .; *(ajasta)* [at]
about.

sfinksi sphinx.

sh = s *tai* š.

shekki cheque, *ks. sekki.*

Siam *ks. Thaimaa.*

siamilainen *a. & s.* Siamese.

sian|hoito pig-breeding. **-ihra**
lard. **-kyljys** pork chop. **-liha**
pork. **-liikkiö** ham. **-nahka**
pigskin. **-paisti** roast pork.
-puolukka bearberry. **-saksa**
jargon, gibberish. **-sorkka:**
-sorkat pig's feet. **-syltty**
brawn.

side band, tie, bond *(et. kuv.);*
(kääre) bandage; *(kirjan)*
binding *(m. suksi-); panna
siteeseen* tie up, *(lääk.)*
bandage, dress. **-aine:** *~et*
[surgical] dressings. **-harso**
gauze. **-kalvo** conjunctiva.
-kudos connective tissue. **-sana**
conjunction. **-tarpeet** bandaging
materials.

sido|nta binding; bandaging.
-ttaa: *~ haava* have a wound
dressed (bandaged); *~ kirja*
have a book bound [in
leather, etc]. **-ttu** *(kirja)*
bound, hardbound; *kuv.* tied
[up].

siedettä|vyys tolerableness. **-vä**
tolerable, bearable; *~sti*
tolerably [well].

siekai|lla hesitate; have
scruples (about); *-lematta*
unhesitatingly.

sie|llä there; at that place; *~
täällä* here and there; *~
ylhäällä* up there; *~ oli
paljon ihmisiä* there were a
lot of people there; (**~olo**

stay there). **-ltä** from there;
~ täältä from different
(various) quarters; (**~päin**
from that direction).

sielu soul; *(mieli)* mind. **-kas**
soulful. **-kellot** passing bell.
-kkuus soulfulness. **-llinen**
mental, psychic [al]. **-messu**
requiem.

sielun|elämä mental life. **-hoito**
care of souls, pastoral care.
-kyky: *-kyvyt* mental faculties;
-llä oli kaikki -kyvyt tallella..
was in charge of his
faculties. **-paimen** shepherd of
the fold, pastor. **-rauha** peace
of mind. **-ravinto** spiritual
food. **-tila** mental state. **-tuska**
mental agony. **-vaellus**
transmigration of souls;
(**~oppi** doctrine of
reincarnation). **-vihollinen** the
arch-enemy.

sielu|tiede psychology.
-tieteellinen psychological.
-tieteilijä psychologist. **-ton**
soulless.

siema|ista gulp [down]. **-us**
gulp; pull [at the bottle,
pullosta]; *täysin -uksin* in
deep draughts; to the full.

siemen seed; *(taudin, m. kuv.)*
germ; *(tähkäpäässä)* grain [of
seed]; *(appelsiinin ym)* pip.
-aihe *bot.* ovule. **-etön**
seedless. **-kauppa** seedsman's
shop. **-kauppias** seedsman.
-kota capsule. **-neste** semen.
-tyä [run to] seed. **-vilja**
seed-corn (-grain).

sienestää gather mushrooms, go
mushrooming.

sieni fungus *(pl. -gi), (tav.
herkku-)* mushroom, *(myrkky-)*
toadstool; *(pesu-)* sponge.
-muhennos mushrooms in
white sauce. **-mäinen** spongy,
lääk. fungoid.

siepata snatch, grab; *(tarttua)*
catch, seize; *(henkilö)* kidnap,
abduct; *(anastaa)* lay hold of;
(matkalla) intercept [a letter,
kirje].

sieppo fly-catcher.

siera whetstone.

sierain nostril.

sierettyä get rough; *(halkeilla)*
get chapped, chap.

sieto(kyky) tolerance.
sietämä|ttömyys unbearableness, intolerableness. **-tön** unbearable; insufferable, intolerable; unendurable; excruciating [pain, *tuska*].
sietää bear, endure, stand; *(suvaita)* tolerate; put up with; *sitä ~ miettiä* it is worth thinking over; *hänen terveytensä ei sitä siedä* his health will not permit it; *vatsani ei siedä kahvia* coffee does not agree with me at all; *sietäisit saada selkääsi* you deserve a beating; *(asiaa) sietäisi tutkia* it does bear examination.
sievis|tellä *tr.* embellish; *intr.* be affected. **-tely** embellishment; affectation.
siev|oinen nice; handsome [fortune, *omaisuus*]. **-yys** prettiness; handsomeness. **-ä** pretty, attractive; handsome, *Am. m.* cute.
sifoni(pullo) siphon.
sifonki chiffon.
sihi|nä hiss [ing], wheeze. **-stä** hiss.
sihteeri secretary. **-ntoimi** secretaryship. **-stö** secretariat.
siihen there; *~ asti* up to that time, until (till) then; *(paikasta)* thus far, so far, [up] to that point; *ei ole ~ aikaa* there is no time for that.
siika lavaret.
siili hedgehog.
siilo silo.
siima line; *(ruoskan)* lash.
siimes shade, shadow.
siintää be dimly seen (visible).
siinä in that, in it, therein; *(siellä)* there; *~ kaikki* that's all; *~ määrin* to such an extent, so much so (that); *~ olet oikeassa* you are right about that; *~ teet oikein* you're right in doing so; *~ syy* that's why; *~pä se* that's just it!
siipi wing; *tekn.* blade, *(tuulimyllyn, m.)* vane; *~ensä suojaan* under one's wings; *~en väli* wing span. **-karja** poultry; *(~nhoito* poultry-farming) **-rakennus**

wing. **-ratas** paddle-wheel.
-rikko.. with clipped wings, with a broken wing.
siirappi syrup, sirup, *Engl. m.* treacle. **-mainen** syrupy.
siirr|ettävä movable, [trans]-portable; *liik.* transferable. **-ännäinen** transplant.
siirto removal, transfer; *(peli-)* move; *(elimen)* transplantation; *(tileissä)* [amount] brought forward, *(alareunassa)* carried forward; *(vekselin)* endorsement. **-kirja** deed of transfer. **-kunta** settlement. **-la** colony.
siirtolai|nen emigrant, *(maahanmuuttava)* immigrant; colonist; settler. **-slaiva** emigrant ship. **-stulva** flow of emigrants. **-suus** emigration, *(maahanmuutto)* immigration.
siirtolapuutarha allotment garden.
siirtolippu transfer ticket.
siirtomaa colony. **-tavara** colonial produce; *~t* groceries; *(~kauppa* grocer's [shop], *Am.* grocery). **-politiikka** colonial policy.
siirto|työläiset foreign labour. **-väki** displaced population; evacuees *(pl.)*.
siirty|minen removal; shift [ing], change-over; *(kokouksen ym)* postponement. **-mä** transition; *(~kausi* transition[al] period). **-vä** movable.
siir|tyä move; shift; *(toiselle, toisaalle)* be transferred (to); *(lykkäytyä)* be postponed; *(toiseen maahan)* emigrate; immigrate; *~ paikaltaan* move [from its place], stir, be dislodged; *~ toiselle paikkakunnalle* move to another locality; *~ puhumaan jstk* proceed to [talk about], turn to [another matter]; *~ syrjään* step aside; *~ toisiin käsiin* change hands; *~tyy isältä pojalle* is handed down from father to son. **-täjä** *(vekselin)* endorser. **-tää** move, *(pois)* remove; transfer; transport, *(esim. tekn.)* transmit; shift; *(elin)* transplant, *(kudosta, m.)* graft;

kirjanp. carry forward *(t. over); (luovuttaa)* make. . over; *lak. m.* convey, assign; hand over; *(vekseli ym)* endorse; *(paikaltaan)* dislodge; *(tunkea syrjään)* displace; ~ *kello eteenpäin* put forward, *(taaksepäin)* put back; ~ *luokalta* move. . up; ~ *jk summa (kirjoissa)* carry a sum over *(t.* forward), bring a sum forward; ~ *tuonnemmaksi* put off, postpone, *(esim. maksupäivää)* defer; ~ *verta* transfuse blood; ~ *vuoria (kuv.)* move mountains.

siis thus, so; therefore, consequently, accordingly; ~ *sinä ymmärrät* then you understand; *olin* ~ *oikeassa* so I was right.

siist|eys tidiness; clean [li] ness. **-i** tidy, neat; *(puhdas)* clean; cleanly; *(siivo)* decent. **-imätön** *(esim. huone)* untidy, not tidied up; untrimmed. **-iytyä** tidy oneself up. **-iä** tidy [up], clean [up]; put things straight [in a room]; *vrt. sijata.*

siit|epöly pollen. **-in** penis. **-os** breeding; *(~ori* stud-horse). **-tiö** spermatozoon *(pl.* -zoa). **-tää** beget, *(eläin)* breed; *avioliitossa -etty (lak.)* conceived in wedlock; ~ *jälkeläisiä (m.)* procreate [offspring].

siitä 1. of it, of that, about it, about that; from it; ~ *kun* since; ~ *johtuu, että* hence it is *(t.* follows) that; ~ *en tiedä mitään* I know nothing of that (about it); *kerro minulle kaikki* ~! tell me all about it! ~ *on jo kymmenen vuotta* ten years have passed since [then]; *joko* ~ *on kauankin* was it long ago? *hän aukaisi laukun ja otti* ~*. .* she opened the bag and took out. .; *~kin huolimatta* even so; *se* ~ [well,] that's that.

siitä 2. *v.* be begotten; *(eläimistä)* breed, be bred *(m. kuv.); (saada alkunsa)* be produced.

siive|käs, -llinen winged; ~ *sana* household word. **-nkärki** wing tip. **-tön** wingless.

siivil|ä strainer. **-öidä** strain, pass. . through a strainer.

siivittää *run.* lend wings to.

siivo *a. (säädyllinen)* decent; *(hyväntahtoinen)* good-natured; *s. (kunto)* condition, state; *(järjestys)* order; *(huono s.)* disorder; *voi sitä ~a (puhek.)* what a mess! **-amaton** untidy,. . in disorder. **-oja** charwoman, *(hotellin)* chambermaid, *(sairaalan ym)* cleaner, *(laivan)* [cabin] stewardess. **-sti** decently; *(hiljaa)* quiet [ly]; *pysyä* ~ keep quiet, behave oneself. **-ta** clean; put. . in order, tidy [up]; ~ *perinpohjin (m.)* give. . a thorough cleaning; ~ *huoneensa* do one's room. **-ton** untidy; unkempt [hair, tukka]; *(rähjäinen)* messy, bedraggled; *(säädytön)* indecent. **-ttomuus** untidiness; indecency. **-us** cleaning, house-cleaning; *(säädyllisyys)* decency; *(~takki* overall).

sija room, space; *(paikka)* place; *kiel.* case; *jnk ~an* instead of, in place (in lieu) of, *(korvaukseksi)* in return for; *sen ~an* instead of that, *(sitä vastoin)* on the other hand; *sen ~an, että* instead of [-ing]; *kun sen* ~ whereas; *sinun ~ssasi* in your place, *(sinuna)* if I were you; *ensi ~ssa* in the first place, first and foremost; *asettaa jnk ~an* substitute. . for; *asettaa ensi ~lle* place. . first, give. . precedence; *se antaa ~a muistutuksille* it leaves room for criticism; *hänellä on huomattava* ~ he holds a prominent position [among,. . joukossa]; *mennä sijoiltaan* be dislocated; *on sijoiltaan* is out of joint. **-inen** substitute, deputy, stand-in (for); *(esim. lääkärin* locum [tenens]; *olla jkn -isena* act as a p.'s substitute, deputize (for); *-sena toimiva (m.)* acting. **-nti**

site, location.
sijais hallitus regency. **-kärsimys** vicarious suffering. **-opettaja** substitute teacher. **-uus** *ks. viran ~*
sijaita be situated, be located, lie, stand, be.
sijamuoto case.
sijata do [one's bed].
sijoiltaanmeno dislocation.
sijoi|ttaa place, locate; *(jhk tilaan)* accommodate [fit]; *liik.* invest; *(pankkiin)* deposit; *(myydä)* dispose of; *~ joukkoja (sot.)* station troops; *~ vartio* post sentries; *~ jku luokseen yöksi* accommodate (put up) a p. for the night. **-ttua** place oneself, *urh.* be placed; *(pysyvästi)* settle. **-tus** *(rahan)* investment; *(~paikka* location, site).
sika pig, *(ruokana, m.)* pork; *et. kuv.* swine *(pl. = sg.); ostaa ~ säkissä* buy a pig in a poke. **-la** piggery. **-humala;** *~ssa* dead drunk. **-mainen** swinish; *kuv. m.* beastly, dirty [trick, *teko*], bloody [lie, *valhe*]. **-maisuus** swinishness.
sikari cigar. **-imuke** cigar-holder. **-kotelo** cigar-case. **-laatikko** cigar-box; box of cigars. **-npolttaja** cigar-smoker. **-npätkä** cigar-stump.
sikermä group, cluster.
sike|ys heaviness; soundness. **-ä** heavy [sleep, *uni*]; *olla ~ssä unessa* be fast *(t. sound)* asleep. **-ästi** soundly.
sikinsokin pell-mell, topsy-turvy, upside down, in a mess.
siki|ävä(inen) prolific, fecund. **-ö** f[o]etus; *(alkio)* embryo; *~t (jälkeläiset)* offspring, progeny; *kyykäärmeitten ~t* generation of vipers; *(~oppi* embryology).
siko|lätti pigsty. **-paimen** swineherd. **-tauti** mumps, parotitis.
sikseen: *jättää jk ~* drop; abandon, give up; *jäädä ~* be dropped; *asia saa jäädä ~* the matter may rest there, we will drop the matter; *matka jäi ~* the trip did not materialize; the trip was

abandoned.
siksi therefore, for that reason, because *(t.* on account of) of that; *(niin)* so; *(siinä määrin)* to such a degree, to such an extent; *~ kun(nes)* till, until; *~ pitkä* so long, of such length [that]; *jos ~ tulee* if it comes to that, come to that; *se on ~ liian pieni* it is too small for that [purpose].
sikuri, -salaatti chicory.
sikä|li in that, in the respect that; *~ kuin* in so far as, in as much as; according as; *~ mikäli* to the extent that.., to that extent.. **-läinen..** there,.. at (of) that place; living (residing) there; **-läiset** *olot (m.)* the local conditions.
silakka Baltic herring.
silat harness.
sila|ta plate; *~ kullalla* plate with gold, gild; **-ttu** [gold-] plated. **-us** plating; *et. kuv.* varnish; *loppu~ (kuv.)* finishing [touches].
sile|ys smoothness; evenness. **-ä** smooth; *(kiiltävän)* sleek [hair, *tukka*]; *(tasainen)* even; *(~karvainen* smooth-haired).
silikaatti silicate.
silinteri *ks. sylinteri; (-hattu)* silk hat, *(kokoon painettava)* opera hat.
sili|tellä smooth down; smooth out; *(sivellä)* stroke. **-ttäjä** ironer, *(pesijä ja ~)* laundress. **-ttää** smooth [out], *(esim. tukkaa)* smooth down; flatten [out]; *(sivellä)* stroke; *(silitysraudalla)* iron; press. **-tys** ironing; *(~kone* electric ironer; calender; *~lauta* ironing-board; *~rauta* flat-iron, iron; *säätö-* automatic iron; *höyry-* steam iron).
silkin|hieno silky. **-viljelys** silk culture, sericulture.
silkka pure, sheer; *~ totuus* the plain truth; *~a pötyä* utter nonsense.
silkki silk. **-huivi** silk scarf. **-kangas** silk material; *-kankaat (m.)* silk-stuffs, silks. **-kutomo** silk-weaving mill. **-lanka** silk [thread]. **-mato**

silkworm. **-mäinen** silk-like,
silky. **-nauha** silk ribbon. **-nen**
[. . of] silk. **-paperi**
tissue-paper. **-perhonen**
silk-moth. **-pukuinen** . .
[dressed] in silk. **-vuori** silk
lining. **-äispuu** mulberry [tree].
sill'aikaa [in the] meantime,
meanwhile; ~ *kun* while.
sillan|arkku bridge support,
abutment. **-korva** head of a
bridge. **-pää,** ~**asema**
bridgehead.
silleen: *jäädä* ~ remain as it
is, remain unchanged; *asia jäi*
~ it was left at that; *jättää*
~ let the matter rest.
silli herring; *tiukassa kuin* ~*t*
tynnyrissä packed like
sardines. **-npyynti** catching
[of] herring. **-nsaalis** catch of
herring. **-parvi** school of
herring. **-salaatti** salad of
pickled herring and
vegetables; *kuv.* jumble, mess.
šillinki shilling.
silloi|n then, at that time, at
the time; ~ *tällöin* now and
then, now and again, at
times. **-nen**. . at (of) that
time;. . then prevailing,. . then
existing; ~ *pääministeri* the
then Prime Minister; ~ *aika*
that time, those times; *-sissa*
oloissa in the circumstances
as they then were.
silloittaa bridge, span [a river,
joki].
sillä for; because, as; with it;
mitä ~ *tarkoitat?* what do
you mean by that (it)? ~
lailla in that way, like that,
(*huud.*) that's the way! ~
välin [in the] meantime.
-hän for that reason; ~ *hän*
teki sen that's why he did it.
silmi|kko mesh; *vrt. silmu;*
(*kypärän*) vizor. **-koida** *puut.*
bud. **-nnähtävä** apparent,
obvious, manifest; (*ilmeinen*)
evident. **-nnäkijä** eye-witness.
-ttömästi violently, beyond
reason; ~ *rakastunut* over
head and ears in love; ~
suuttunut beside oneself with
rage. **-tön** (*sokea*) blind;
(*häikäilemätön*) ruthless;
violent; ~ *säikähdys* panic

fright; ~ *raivo, viha* blind
rage (hate).
silmu (*kasvin*) bud. **-kka** loop,
(*esim. ansan, hirttonuoran*)
noose; (*neule-*) stitch;
(*kiemura*) coil; (*verkon*) mesh;
(*pieni*) eyelet.
silmä eye (*m. neulan ym*);
(*verkon*) mesh; (*kutimen*)
stitch; ~ *kovana* intently; ~*t*
suurina wide-eyed; ~*stä* ~*än*
face to face; *katsoa vaaraa*
~*stä* ~*än* face danger; *pitää*
jtk ~*llä* keep an eye on,
watch, supervise; see to [it
that, *että*]; *jtk* ~*lläpitäen*
having regard to, taking into
consideration; *vasten silmiä* to
one's face; *jnk silmien edessä*
under a p.'s eyes; *kadota jkn*
silmistä disappear out of a
p.'s sight; *minun silmissäni* in
my view; ~ *juoksee; ks.*
silmäpako. **-hermo** ophthalmic
nerve. **-illä** have a glance (a
look) at, glance over; look
at, view, survey;
pintapuolisesti -illessä when
glancing. . over [superficially].
-inen: *sini*~ blue-eyed. **-istä**
(*jtk*) take a look at;
hätäisesti ~ *jtk* give.. a
hasty glance. **-kulma** corner
of the eye. **-kuoppa**
eye-socket. **-lasit** [eye-]glasses,
spectacles; (*suoja-*) goggles.
-läpito watching [over],
superintendence, supervision,
surveillance. **-luomi** eyelid.
-lääkäri eye specialist,
ophthalmologist. **-mitalla** by
[the] eye. **-muna** eyeball.
-määrä (*tarkoitus*) aim, object;
olla ~*nä* (*m.*) have in view.
-neula needle.
silmän|isku wink[ing].
-kantama eyeshot.
-kantama|ton: *s-ttomiin* out of
sight. **-kääntäjä** conjurer;
(~**temppu** conjuring trick).
-lume eyewash; ~*eksi* to
delude; ~*tta* bluff. **-luomiväri**
eye shading. **-palvelija**
eye-servant. **-rajausväri** eye
liner. **-ruoka** feast for
the eyes; ~*a* (*m.*) a sight for
sore eyes. **-räpäyksellinen**
instantaneous. **-räpäys** moment,

instant; -räpäyksessä in a moment, in the twinkling of an eye, instantly, in no time at all; (~valokuva snapshot).
-tekevä: ~t top people, VIPs; kaikki ~t everyone of note.
-valkuainen white of the eye.
-vilkutus winking.

silmä|pako ladder. Am. run.
-puoli one-eyed [person].
-ripset eyelashes; vrt. ripsi.
-tauti eye disease. -terä pupil; kuv. apple of one's eye.
-tikku: olla jkn ~na be an eye-sore to. -tyksin, -tysten face to face, eyeball to eyeball; olla ~ jnk kanssa be confronted (faced) with.
-vamma eye lesion. -ys look, glance; (silmäily) survey; luoda ~ jhk [take a] glance at; ensi -yksellä at [the] first glance, at first sight.
-änpistävä conspicuous; striking; olla ~ stand out.

silo|inen smooth. -ttaa smooth; (paperia ym) calender. -ttelu smoothing, finish.

silpiä hull.

silpo|a mutilate, maim; (kuv., esim. valtakunta) dismember.
-herne garden-pea. -utua be mutilated.

silppu chopped straw; roughage; (ape) mash. -kone chaff-cutter.

silputa chop, cut up.

silta ,bridge; (raitiovaunun ym) platform; vrt. laituri; polttaa sillat takanaan burn one's boats.

silti however; yet, still; (siitä huolimatta) even so, nevertheless, for all that; se on ihmeellistä mutta ~ totta it is strange, and yet it is true.

siluetti silhouette, (esim. kaupungin) skyline.

sima (-juoma) mead. -suinen mellifluous, honey-tongued.

simpanssi zo. chimpanzee.

simpukankuori mussel shell.

simpuk|ka zo. mussel, clam, scallop; sieniä -oissa scalloped mushrooms.

simputtaa l.v. bully.

sinapin|siemen mustard seed;

raam. grain of mustard seed.

sinappi mustard. -tölkki mustard-pot.

sine|lmä bruise. -rtävä bluish.

sine|tti seal; (~lakka sealing-wax; ~sormus signet-ring). -töidä seal, affix a seal (to).

sinfonia symphony. -konsertti symphony concert.

sing|ahtaa hurtle; fly [out]. -ota hurl, fling, (m. intr.) hurtle.

sini 1. [the] blue; blue colour; 2. mat. sine. -happo prussic acid. -harmaa bluish grey. -jäljennös blue print. -kettu blue fox. -musta blue-black. -nen blue. -piika wood-nymph. -pukuinen . dressed in blue. -punainen violet, (vaaleampi) lilac. -raitainen blue-striped. -silmäinen blue-eyed. -valkoinen blue and white. -vihreä bluish green. -vuokko hepatica.

sinkauttaa hurtle, hurl.

sinkilä staple.

sinkkaus dovetail.

sinkki zinc. -levy zinc plate. -pelti sheet zinc. -valkea zinc white. -voide zinc ointment.

sinko recoilless rifle. -illa fly [around]. -utua be hurled.

sinne there; ~ mentäessä on the way t.; ~ tänne here and there, up and down, hither and thither. -päin in that direction, that way; (suunnilleen) thereabouts; jotakin ~ something like that; ei ole ~kään it is nothing of the kind. -tulo arrival [there].

sinooperi cinnabar.

sinunlaisesi: ~mies a man like you.

sinutella be on Christian-name terms (with).

sinä you; sinun your; yours; ~kö sen teit? was it you who did it?

sinänsä as it is, as such.

sionistinen: ~ liike Zionist movement, Zionism.

sipai|sta graze; brush; -si seinää glanced against the

wall; ~ *jkta korvalle* give sb.
a box on the ear.
Siperia Siberia; ~*n rata*
Trans-Siberian railway.
s-lainen *a.* & *s.* Siberian.
sipsu|ttaa trip. **-tus** trip[ping],
mincing walk.
sipuli onion; *(kukka-)* bulb.
-kasvi bulbous plant, bulb.
sireeni 1. *bot.* lilac; **2.** *(sumu-
ym)* siren.
siri|stellä: ~ *silmiään* screw up
one's eyes [in the sun].
-ttää: *sirkka* ~ the cricket is
chirping.
sirkka *zo.* cricket. **-lehti**
seed-leaf, cotyledon.
sirkkelisaha circular saw.
sirkku, -nen *zo.* bunting.
sirkus circus.
sirku|ttaa chirp, twitter,
chirrup. **-tus** chirp[ing],
twitter, chirrup.
siro *(hieno)* graceful, delicate;
(solakka) slender. **-muotoinen**
well-shaped (-formed), well *(t.*
beautifully) modelled.
-rakenteinen. neatly built,
shapely; *(esim. laiva)..* of
graceful lines. **-tekoinen** neatly
made, neat.
siro|tella strew, sprinkle.
-telusikka sifter. **-tesokeri**
castor sugar. **-ttaa** strew,
sprinkle; *(hajottaa)* scatter
[about].
sirous gracefulness, neatness.
sirpale splinter; *(palanen)*
fragment. **-enkestävä**
splinter-proof.
sirppi sickle.
sirri *zo.* sand-piper.
siru chip, fragment; splinter.
sisar sister. **-ellinen** sisterly.
-enpoika nephew. **-entytär**
niece. **-puoli** step-sister,
half-sister. **-us** *tiet.* sibling; *he
ovat -ukset* they are sisters
(t. brothers); *(pojasta ja
tytöstä)* they are brother and
sister; *(-piiri* family circle).
-uus sisterhood.
sisempi inner, interior.
Sisilia Sicily. **s-lainen** *a* & *s.*
Sicilian.
sisilisko lizard.
sisi|mmäinen, -n innermost,
inmost; *-mmässään (he..)* in

their inmost hearts.
sisko sister.
sissi gue[r]rilla, *(meri-)*
freebooter. **-joukko** irregulars.
-päällikkö chief of a guerrilla
band. **-sota** guerrilla war[fare].
sisu perseverance; grit, *puhek.*
guts; *paha* ~ headstrong
disposition; *purkaa ~aan* give
vent to one's anger. **-kas**
persistent; headstrong.
-npurkaus fit of temper.
sisus, -ta the inside, the
interior; *sisukset (puhek.)*
innards; *sisuksiani kaivelee..*
(sth.) gnaws at my innards.
-taa *(kalustaa)* furnish;
(vuorilla) line. **-tamaton**
unfurnished; not lined. **-te**
lining. **-tus** fittings;
furnishings; *(kiinteä)* fixtures;
(huonekalut) furniture;
(-taiteilija interior decorator).
sisä *ks.* **-llä, -ltä** *jne.* **-asia:** ~*t
(pol.)* internal affairs.
-asiainministeri Interior
Minister; *Engl.* Home
Secretary. **-asiainministeriö**
Ministry of the Interior;
Engl. Home Office. **-elin**
internal organ. **-eritys** internal
secretion; *(~rauhanen*
endocrine gland). **-inen** inner,
internal, *et. kuv.* inward;
interior; intrinsic [value,
arvo], inherent [quality,
ominaisuus]; *hänen* ~
minänsä his inner man.
-kkäin one within
the other. **-kkö** housemaid,
Am. chamber-maid.. **-korva**
internal ear. **-kuva** interior
[view]. **-lle** inside; *käydä* ~
go in, enter. **-llinen** inner;
internal. **-llisesti** internally;
inwardly; ~ *(nautittavaksi)* for
internal use. **-llissota** civil
war. **-llyksetön** meaningless;
empty. **-llys** contents; *(aihe)*
subject-matter; *hän kirjoitti
kirjeen, jonka* ~ *oli seuraava
(m.)* he wrote a letter to this
effect; *jnk pääasiallinen* ~ the
substance of..; *(~luettelo*
table of contents). **-llyttää**
include; incorporate. **-llä** in,
within, inside; *(huoneessa)*
indoors. **-llökäs** full of

meaning *(t. information).*
-lmys: *-lmykset* entrails,
viscera; bowels; *poistaa*
-lmykset clean; *(kaloista)* gut;
(linnuista) draw. **-ltyä** be
included, be contained, be
comprised (in); form a part
of; *-ltyykö se sopimukseen
(m.)* does that enter into the
agreement; *tähän summaan ei
-lly vuokraa* this sum does
not include the rent. **-ltä**
from the inside, from within,
(huoneesta, m.) from indoors;
(-puolelta) [on the] inside.
-ltää contain; include; *(astia)*
hold; *(käsittää)* comprise; *se
~ suuren vaaran it* involves
great danger; *hänen sanansa
-lsivät myös sen, että. .* his
words also implied that. . **-ltö**
contents. **-luku** reading.
-lähetys home mission. **-maa**
interior of the country; *~ssa*
inland; *~han* inland, up
country; *~n ilmasto* inland
climate. **-meri** inland sea.
-moottori *(vene)* inboard
motor-boat. **-oppilas** boarder.
-oppilaitos boarding-school.
-osa inner part, the interior
(of). **-poliittinen:** *~ kysymys*
question of internal politics.
-politiikka domestic politics;
Suomen ~ the internal policy
of Finland. **-puoli** the inside,
the interior; *jnk -puolella*
inside, within. **-rengas** *(auton)*
tube; *-renkaaseen kuuluva
(kuv.)* insider. **-renkaaton**
tubeless. **-seinä** inside wall.
-ssä: *jnk ~* in. ., within. .,
inside. . *jnk ~* out of.
-tasku inside pocket. **-tauti**
internal disease; *(~lääkäri*
specialist in internal diseases,
Am. internist).
sisävesi: *sisävedet* inland
waters. **-kalastus** fresh-water
fishing. **-liikenne** inland
navigation.
sisään into; *ikkunasta ~* in
through the window; *päästää
jku ~* admit; *astukaa ~* come
in, please! **-jättö** handing in,
Am. filing. **-kirjoitus**
enrol [l]ment; *(~maksu*
entrance fee). **-käytävä**

entrance. **-painunut** sunken,
hollow. **-päin** inward [s], in;
~ kääntynyt (luonne)
introverted; *s.* introvert.
-pääsy admission, admittance;
~ on vapaa admission free.
-tulo entry.
siten thus; so; in that way;
(sen kautta) by that means,
thereby.
sitke|ys toughness; *kuv.*
perseverance, persistence. **-ä**
tough; *(nesteestä)* viscous,
sticky; *kuv.* persevering,
dogged, tenacious; *sen henki
on ~ssä* it is hard to kill;
(~henkinen tough-lived;
~syinen stringy). **-ästi** toughly,
persistently.
sitkis|tyä, -tää toughen.
sito|a bind *(m. kuv.)*; *(solmita)*
tie [up]; *(kiinnittää)* fasten
(to); *(haava)* bandage, dress;
(kirja) bind; *(itsensä jkh)* tie
oneself to; *~ jhk kiinni* tie,
fasten to; *~ jkn silmät*
bandage a p.'s eyes, blindfold
a p.; *en halua ~ itseäni* I
don't want to be tied down,
(lupauksilla) to bind myself
with promises; *tauti -i hänet,
vuoteeseen* the disease
confined her to her bed;
-matta Teitä without
obligation on your part.
-maton unbound. **-mo** bindery.
-umus obligation, engagement,
commitment; *(sopimus)*
agreement, contract; *(velka-)*
liability. **-utua** bind oneself,
engage oneself (to); commit
oneself (to); *(ottaa
tehdäkseen)* undertake to; *~tä
hankkimaan* contract to
deliver; *~ maksamaan* pledge. .
-utumaton uncommitted;
non-aligned. **-va** binding,
conclusive [proof, *todiste*],
firm [offer, *tarjous*]; *(aine)*
solidifying.
sitra zither.
sitruuna lemon. **-happo** citric
acid. **-mehu** lemon juice.
-nkuori lemon rind. **-npuristin**
lemon-squeezer. **-viipale** slice
of lemon.
sittemmin afterwards,
subsequently, later [on].

sitt   340

sitten then; *(sen jälkeen)* after that; afterwards; ~ *joulun* since Christmas; *aikoja* ~ long ago; *vuosia* ~ years ago; *kuka hän* ~ *on* who is he then? *mitä* ~ *tapahtui?* what happened next? **-kin** however, yet, still; *(siitä huolimatta)* nevertheless, for all that, after all; *hän on rikas, mutta* ~ *onneton* he is rich, yet he is unhappy; *vioistaan huolimatta hän on* ~ notwithstanding *(t.* with all) his faults he is. . **-kään:** *hän ei* ~ *tullut* he did not come after all.
sittiäinen dor.
sitä it; the; ~ *ennen* before that; ~ *paitsi* besides, in addition [to that], moreover; ~ *parempi* so much the better; ~ *suuremmalla syyllä, kun.* . all the more because, with all the more reason as, the more so because; ~ *vastoin* on the contrary, by contrast, conversely; *kun* ~ *vastoin* while, whereas.
siun|ata bless; *Jumala -atkoon sinua* God bless you! ~ *ruoka* say grace. **-auksellinen** blessed,. . full of blessings. **-aus** blessing.
sival|lus slap; lash. **-taa** slap; *(huitaista)* lash; *(lyödä)* strike (at), deal a p. a blow.
sivee|llinen moral; ~ *kysymys* question of morals; *-llisessä suhteessa* morally, from a moral point of view. **-llisyys** morality; morals *(~käsite* conception of morality; *~rikos* sexual crime; outrage against public decency). **-ttömyys** immorality; obscenity. **-tön** immoral; unchaste, *(julkaisu)* obscene.
sive|llin brush; *(hieno, m.)* hair pencil; *-ltimen veto* stroke of the brush. **-llä** stroke; apply, *jhk* to; *(levittää)* spread, *(voita jhk)* butter.
siveys chastity; virtue. **-käsite** moral concept. **-opillinen** ethical. **-oppi** ethics. **-saarnaaja** moralizer, sermonizer.

siveä chaste, virtuous; *(puhdas)* pure.
siviili civilian; *puhek.* . in civvy street. **-avioliitto** civil marriage; *mennä ~on* be married at a registry office. **-henkilö** civilian. **-ilmailu** civil flying. **-oikeus** civil law. **-puku:** *-puvussa (ark.)* in one's civvies; *vrt. seur.* **-pukuinen.** . in civilian *(t.* plain) clothes,. . in mufti. **-rekisteri** civil register. **-sääty** marital status. **-väestö** civilian population.
sivis|tyksellinen educational, cultural. **-tymättömyys** lack of education (culture). **-tymätön** uneducated, uncultured; *(tavoiltaan)* ill-bred, unmannerly. **-tyneistö** educated class. **-ty|nyt** educated, cultured; civilized; well-bred; *s-neessä seurassa* in polite society; ~ *maailma* civilized world, civilization.
sivistys *(koulu-)* education; civilization; *(kulttuuri)* culture. **-elämä** cultural life. **-historia** cultural history. **-kieli** *l.v.* cultural language; *suuret -kielet* the (most) important languages of the civilized world. **-laitos** educational institution. **-maa, -maailma** civilized country, world. **-olot** educational conditions. **-pyrkimykset** educational pursuits. **-sana** international word. **-sanakirja** dictionary of international words, phrases and quotations. **-taso** standard of education. **-valtio** civilized state.
sivistyä become civilized (educated).
sivu 1. *s.* side; *(kirjan)* page; *(siipi)* wing. 2. *(ohi)* by, past; *kulkea jnk* ~ pass [by]; *ks. sivu|lla, -lle, -lta.* **-aja** geom. tangent. **-asia** minor point, side issue. **-elinkeino** subsidiary trade, secondary occupation. **-haara** *(suvun)* collateral branch. **-henkilö** subordinate character. **-huone** adjoining room. **-itse** by, past. **-joki** tributary. **-katu** side

street. **-kulkija** passer-by.
-kuva side view. **-lause**
subordinate clause. **-liike**
branch. **-lla** on (by) the side
(of); aside. **-lle** to the side
(of); aside; (~**päin** to the
side; outwards). **-llinen**
outsider; *-lliset* those not
concerned. **-lta** from the side;
avasin kirjani ~ 20 I
opened my book at page 20.
sivu|maku extraneous flavour,
peculiar taste; *(lisä-)* smack.
-mennen in passing; ~ *sanoen*
by the way; incidentally.
-merkitys secondary meaning.
-myymälä branch shop. **-määrä**
number of pages. **-osa**
supporting part. **-ovi** side
door. **-raide** side-track, siding.
-rata branch [line]. **-seikka**
minor point, unessential
[point]. **-ssa** on (at) the side;
aside. **-sta** from the side; *s.*
flank; (~**hyökkäys** flank
attack).
sivuta be tangent to, touch;
(ennätystä) equal; *kuv.* touch
[upon].
sivu|tarkoitus ks. taka-ajatus.
-tehtävä subordinate part. **-tie**
byway. **-toimi** secondary
occupation, side-line. **-tulot**
extra income. **-tuote**
by-product. **-tusten** side by
side. **-tuuli** side wind, cross
wind.
sivuu|ttaa pass [by], go by;
overlook; *(syrjäyttää)*
supersede, supplant; ~
kysymys pass over (disregard)
a question; ~ *vaitiololla* pass
over in silence; *keski-iän
-ttanut. .* past middle age.
sivu|vaikutus side effect. **-vaunu**
side-car.
skaala scale.
skandaali scandal.
skandinaavi(nen) Scandinavian.
Skandinavia Scandinavia.
skeptikko sceptic.
sketsi sketch.
skootteri scooter.
skorpioni *zo.* scorpion.
skotlannitar Scots|woman *(pl.
-women).*
Skotlanti Scotland; **s-lainen** *s.*
Scot, Scots|man *(pl. -men); a.*

Scotch, Scottish; *skotlannin
kieli (murre)* Scotch, Scots.
slaavilainen *s.* Slav; *a.*
Slav[on]ic.
slovakki Slovak.
sloveeni Slovene, Slovenian.
slummi slum. **-utua** be reduced
to a slum.
smaragdi emerald.
smirgeli emery. **-paperi** emery
paper.
smoking, smokki dinner-jacket,
Am. tuxedo *(pl. -s, -es).*
sodan|aihe cause of war.
-aikainen wartime. **-edellinen**
pre-war. **-haluinen** war-minded;
warlike, bellicose. **-julistus**
declaration of war. **-jälkeinen**
post-war. **-käynti** warfare.
-lietsoja warmonger. **-uhka**
threat of war.
sohia poke, *jtk* at.
sohjo ks. *lumi~, jää~.*
sohva sofa; settee; *(lepo-)*
divan, *Am.* couch.
soi|da ring; *(kuulua)* sound;
(kaikua) resound; clang;
(esim. kirkonkelloista) peal,
chime, toll; *kello soi* the bell
is ringing, *(ovikello)* there is
a ring at the door. **-din:**
ampua soitimelta shoot
[birds] at mating-time.
soihdunkantaja torch-bearer.
soihtu torch. **-kulkue** torchlight
procession.
soija soy. **-kastike** soy[a]
sauce. **-papu** soybean.
soik|ea oval. **-io** oval; *mat.*
ellipse.
soikko tub.
soima|ta reproach, reprove;
scold, rebuke. **-us** reproach,
reproof, reprimand.
soinen swampy, marshy.
soin|nillinen *kiel.* voiced. **-niton**
kiel. voiceless. **-nukas**
sonorous; melodious; ~ *ääni
(m.)* rich voice, full-sounding
voice. **-nukkuus** sonorousness,
melodiousness. **-nuton**
tuneless, toneless, flat. **-nuttaa**
tune; *(yhteen)* bring. . into
accord. **-ti** ring, clang; tone.
-tu sound, ring, tone;
harmony, accord. **-tua** sound,
ring; *(kaikua)* resound; ~
yhteen harmonize, chime in,

(esim. värit) tone in well with. **-tuoppi** harmonics. **-tuva** sonorous; melodious.
soiro batten, *(kapea)* scantling.
soitannollinen musical.
soitanto music.
soitin [musical] instrument. **-kauppa** music-dealer's, music-store. **-kauppias** music-dealer. **-musiikki** instrumental music. **-nus** instrumentation. **-taa** instrument.
soitt|aa *(kelloa)* ring [the bell]; *(soittimella)* play; *(puhaltaa)* blow [a horn, torvea]; *(jklle puhelimessa)* telephone, puhek. phone sb., ring sb. up, *Am.* call sb. [up]; *(valita numero)* dial a number; *(hoitajaa ym.)* ring for; *(pianoa, viulua)* play the piano (the violin); ~ *suutansa* jabber [away]. **-aja** player; musician; *(soittokunnassa)* bandsman.
soitto music; *(soittaminen)* playing; *(kellon)* ring; peal [ing], toll [ing]; *puhelin-* ~ call. **-kappale** piece of music. **-kello** bell. **-kone** musical instrument. **-kunta** band; *(orkesteri)* orchestra. **-lava** bandstand. **-niekka**, **-taiteilija** musician. **-rasia** musical-box. **-taituri** virtuoso. **-tunti** music-lesson.
sokais|ta blind *(m. kuv.)*; *(häikäistä)* dazzle. **-tua** be blinded, be dazzled; *(hullaantua)* be infatuated.
soke|a blind *(m. kuv.)*; *(kuv. = ehdoton)* implicit; *hänen toinen silmänsä on* ~ he is blind in one eye; *hän tuli* ~*ksi* he went blind, *(sodassa)* was blinded [in the war]. **-ainkirjoitus** braille. **-ainkoulu** school for the blind.
sokel|lus cluttering, slurred speech. **-taa** clutter, *(kuin juopunut)* talk thick.
sokeri sugar. **-astia** sugar-basin. **-herne** string-pea. **-juurikas** sugar-beet. **-kakku** sponge cake. **-keko** loaf of sugar. **-leipomo** confectioner's. **-leipuri** confectioner. **-mainen**

sugary, saccharine. **-pala** lump of sugar. **-pihdit** sugar-tongs. **-pitoinen**, . containing sugar. **-pitoisuus** percentage of sugar, sugar-content. **-ruoko** sugar-cane. **-tauti** diabetes. **-tautinen** diabetic. **-tehdas** sugar refinery.
sokeroida sugar, sweeten.
soke|us blindness. **-utua** go blind.
sokkanaula cotter-pin.
sokkelo labyrinth, maze. **-inen** labyrinthine.
šokki shock. **-hoito** shock treatment. **-tila:** ~*ssa* in shock.
sokko blindman; *(-leikki)* blindman's buff. **-lento** instrument flying. **-silla:** *olla* ~ play hide and seek.
sola pass, *(ahdas)* gorge, defile.
solahtaa slide, slip.
sola|kka slender, slim. **-kkuus** slenderness, slimness.
solidaarinen loyal. **-suus** solidarity.
soli|na, **-sta** tinkle, babble.
solis|lihas subclavian muscle. **-luu** clavicle, collar-bone.
solisti soloist.
solkata: ~ *suomea* speak broken *(t.* halting) Finnish.
solki buckle; *(haka-)* clasp; *(nipistin)* clip; *panna solkeen* buckle [up]; *päästää soljesta* unbuckle. **-kenkä** buckle shoe.
solm|ia tie; *(sitoa)* bind; *(suhde)* establish, set up; ~ *liitto* enter into alliance (with); ~ *avioliitto* enter into matrimony; ~ *rauha* conclude peace, make peace. **-io** tie, necktie; *(~neula* tie-pin).
solmu knot *(m. mer.)*; *olla* ~*ssa* be tied in a knot; *panna* ~*un* tie in a knot; *päästää* ~*sta* untie. **-ke** bow [-tie]. **-kohta** [railway-]junction. **-staa** crochet.
solu cell.
solua slide, glide, slip.
solu|ketto cell membrane. **-kudos** cellular tissue. **-lima** cytoplasm. **-neste** cell sap. **-njakautuminen** cell division. **-oppi** cytology. **-ttaa** make. . glide, *kuv.*, **-ttautua** infiltrate.

-tuma nucleus [of a cell]. **-tus** *kuv.* infiltration.
solv|aaja slanderer. **-aava** insulting, slanderous. **-ata** insult, offer an insult (to); *(parjata)* abuse; slander. **-aus** insult, affront; abuse; slander.
soma pretty, sweet, nice, *(sorja)* dainty, neat, *Am.* cute.
somist|aa adorn, decorate; trim, *Am.* fix. . up; *kukin* *-ettu* decked with flowers. **-aja** *(ikkunan)* window-dresser.
sommi|tella put. . together, compose [a letter, *kirje*]; *(laatia)* draw up; *(piirustus ym.)* design. **-ttelu** composition; *(luonnos)* draft; design.
sompa ring [on ski stick].
somuus prettiness, neatness, daintiness.
sonaatti *mus.* sonata.
sondi *lääk.* probe, bougie.
sonetti sonnet.
sonni bull.
sonta dung; muck.
sooda soda; *(puhdistettu)* bicarbonate of soda. **-vesi** soda-water.
soolo solo. **-laulaja** soloist. **-osa** solo. **-tanssija** solo dancer.
soopeli, -nnahka sable.
soper|rus mutter[ing], murmur. **-taa** mumble, mutter, murmur; *(tapailla sanoja)* falter; *(änkyttää)* stammer.
sopeu|ttaa *(jhk)* adapt. . to, gear. . to. **-tua** accommodate oneself, *jhk* to, adapt oneself (to); become adjusted to, *(alistua)* reconcile onseself to; *-tuva* adaptable.
sopi|a fit; suit; *(olla sovussa)* agree; *(et. väreistä)* match; *(tehdä s-mus)* make an agreement, agree (on, upon, about); *(tehdä sovinto)* become reconciled; *(riita ym)* settle, make it up (with); *takki sopii hyvin (hänelle)* the coat fits [him] well,. . is an excellent fit;. . *sopii huonosti.* . fits badly,. . is a bad fit; *minulle ei -nut* it did not suit me, it was not convenient for me; *musta sopii hänelle* black suits (is

becoming to) her; *he eivät sovi keskenään* they do not get on [with each other], they don't hit it off; *kahvi ei sovi minulle* coffee does not agree with me; ~ *jhk, jksk* be fit[ted] *t.* suited for; *en sovi opettajaksi* I am not cut out to be a teacher;. . *ei sovi hienolle naiselle* it does not become a lady (to); ~ *tapaamisesta* make an appointment, arrange to meet sb.; ~ *yhteen* fit in with, *(väreistä ym)* match, go together, go with, *(henkilöistä)* suit each other, *(pari)* be well matched; *sovittuun hintaan* at the price agreed upon; *sovittuun aikaan* at the appointed time; *sopii mainiosti* [that] suits me fine! *jos se sopii sinulle* if that's all right by you; *autoon sopii viisi henkeä* the car accommodates five persons. **-maton** unfit, not fit (for); unsuitable (for), inappropriate; inconvenient; *(ajan puolesta)* untimely, ill-timed; improper [behaviour, *käytös*]; *(säädytön)* indecent; *hänen arvolleen* ~ unworthy of him. **-mattomuus** unfitness, unsuitability, inconvenience; impropriety; indecency.
sopimu|s agreement, *(kirjallinen)* contract; *valt.* pact, *(esim. rauhan-)* treaty; *(välipuhe)* arrangement; *-ksen kohta* stipulation; *tehdä* ~ make a contract, enter into an agreement; *hieroa* ~*ta* negotiate; *päästä -kseen* reach (arrive at) an agreement, come to terms; *-ksen mukaisesti* according to agreement, as agreed upon; *yhteisestä -ksesta* by common consent; *(~kirja* [formal] contract; deed).
sopiva suitable, fit (for); suited, fitted (for); *(mukava)* convenient; *(asianmukainen)* appropriate, proper; *(arvolle ym)* [be]fitting; *(säädyllinen)* decent; *(ajan puolesta)*

opportune, timely, well-timed;
(*edullinen*) expedient; *ei ole*
~*a* (*m.*) it is not proper
(good form); it is not
becoming [for a lady] (to);
~*n aikaan* at a convenient
time, opportunely; ~*lla tavalla*
in a suitable manner, in
some suitable way, suitably;
niinkuin ~*ksi näette* as you
see fit; *siihen* ~ *nauha* a
ribbon to match it;
tarkoitukseen ~ suited
(adapted) for the purpose;
juuri minulle ~ just the thing
for me. **-isuus** suitability,
suitableness; appropriateness;
fitness; propriety; *-isuuden
rajoissa* within the bounds of
propriety.
soppi corner, nook; recess.
sopraano soprano. **-osa** soprano
[part].
sopu harmony, concord;
(*ykseys*) unity; good
fellowship; *olla sovussa jkn
kanssa* be on good terms
with. **-hinta** reasonable price.
-isa peaceable; (*sävyisä*)
accommodating, compliant.
-isuus peaceableness, easy
temper. **-ottelu** fix.
sopukka corner, nook, recess;
(*kätkö*) cranny.
sopuli *zo.* lemming.
sopu|sointu harmony, accord,
unison; (*yhtäpitävyys*)
conformity; *olla -soinnussa* be
in harmony, harmonize (with);
be in keeping (with).
-sointuinen harmonious,
harmonic. **-suhta** symmetry;
proportion. **-suhtainen**
well-proportioned;
symmetric [al]. **-suhtaisuus**
symmetry.
sora gravel, grit. **-htaa**
(*vihloen*) grate, jar [upon a
p.'s ears]. **-inen** gravelly.
-kielisyys rhotacism. **-kuoppa**
gravel pit. **-tie** gravel road.
-ääni discordant note (*m.
kuv.*).
sore|a graceful; pretty,
handsome. **-us** gracefulness;
handsomeness.
sori|na (*esim. puheen*) murmur,
hum [of conversation]. **-sta**

murmur.
sorkka [cloven] hoof;
(*vasaran*) claw; *sian sorkat*
pig's trotters. **-rauta** crowbar,
(*et. varkaan*) jemmy, *Am.*
jimmy. **-tauti**: *suu- ja* ~
foot-and-mouth disease.
sorkkia poke; (*tonkia*) grub,
root; tamper (with); ~
puutarhassa potter [and
totter] in the garden.
sormeilla finger (at).
sormen|jälki finger-print. **-liike**:
yhdellä -liikkeellä at a flick
of the finger. **-pää** finger-tip.
sormi finger; *osoittaa
sormellaan* point one's finger
(at); point. . out; *katsoa* (*jtk*)
läpi ~*en* wink (at); turn a
blind eye to. **-aakkoset**
manual alphabet. **-harjoitus**
five-finger exercise. **-kas**
[knitted] glove. **-tuntuma**: *-lla*
instinctively; roughly.
sormus ring. **-tin** thimble;
(~*kukka* foxglove).
sorr|ettu, -onalainen oppressed,
subjugated.
sorsa wild duck, mallard.
-npoika duckling, young duck.
-poikue brood of wild ducks.
-stus duck shooting.
sort|aa oppress; keep. . in
subjection; (*polkea*) trample. .
under foot; tyrannize over.
-aja oppressor. **-o** oppression;
(~*järjestelmä*, ~*valta* regime
of violence; ~*kausi* period of
oppression). **-ua** fall [down],
tumble down, crash to the
ground; (*luhistua*) collapse,
(*esim. seinä*) fall in, (*esim.
maa*) give way; (*menehtyä*)
succumb (to); ~ *taakkansa
alle* sink (break down) under
one's burden; ~ *huonoille
teille* get (fall) into bad ways;
-unut (*ääni*) broken.
sortsit shorts.
sorv|aaja turner. **-ata** turn [in
a lathe]; *taitavasti -attu*
(*kuv.*) well-turned. **-i**
[turning-]lathe.
sose mash; *peruna*~ mashed
potatoes; *omena*~ apple
sauce. **-keitto** purée.
sosiaali|avustus social security

benefit. **-demokraatti** social democrat. **-demokratia** social democracy. **-huolto** social services. **-ministeri** Minister for the Social Services. **-nen** social. **-politiikka** social policy. **-toimisto** social security office. **-turva** social security.

sosialis|mi socialism. **-oida** socialize; nationalize. **-ti** socialist. **-tinen** socialist [ic].

sosiologi social scientist. **-a** sociology, social science.

sota war; *(sodankäynti)* warfare; *(taistelu)* fight [against.. *jtk vastaan*]; *nyt on ~* there is a war on; *käydä ~a* wage war (on); *rotta~* war on rats; *~a käyvä* belligerent; *olla sodassa (jkta vastaan)* be at war (with); *sodan sattuessa* in the event of war. **-aika** war time. **-ase** weapon of war. **-harjoitus** manoeuvres; military exercises. **-historia** military history. **-huuto** warcry, battlecry. **-inen**, **-isa** war-like; militant. **-isuus** warlike disposition. **-joukko** army, troops. **-juoni** stratagem. **-kanta:** *-kannalla* on a war-footing; *asettaa -kannalle* mobilize; *olla -kannalla (kuv.)* be at enmity, be at daggers drawn [with]. **-kelpoinen.** . fit for war service. **-kieltotavara** contraband of war. **-kirjeenvaihtaja** war correspondent. **-kirves** battle-axe. **-korkeakoulu** [General] staff college. **-korvaus** reparations, war indemnity. **-kulut** war expenses. **-laina** war loan. **-laitos** *(maan)* army, navy and air force. **-laiva** war-ship. **-laivasto** navy. **-laki** martial law. **-marsalkka** Field Marshal. **-mies** soldier; *(tavallinen, m.)* private, *Am.* enlisted man, G.I.; *(kortti-)* jack, knave. **-ministeri** minister of war; *Engl.* Secretary of State for War, *Am.* Secretary of War. **-ministeriö** *Engl.* War Office.

-neuvottelu council of war. **-näyttämö** theatre of war. **-oikeus** court martial. **-palvelus** military service; *kutsua -palvelukseen* call up; *olla -palveluksessa* be in the services. **-polku** war-path. **-ponnistus** war effort. **-päällikkö** military commander, general. **-ratsu** charger, steed. **-retki** military expedition, campaign. **-rikollinen** war criminal. **-saalis** war booty, spoils of war; *(voitto-)* trophy. **-sankari** military hero. **-satama** fortified port, naval base. **-taito** art of war; strategy. **-tarvikkeet** war material, war supplies, munitions. **-tarviketeollisuus** munitions industries. **-tiede** military science. **-tila** state of war. **-toimet** military operations. **-vahinko** war damage. **-vammai|nen** disabled soldier *(t.* ex-serviceman); *-set (m.)* the war-disabled. **-vanke|us** captivity; *joutui -uteen* was taken prisoner of war. **-vanki** prisoner of war *(lyh.* POW). **-varustukset** armament [s]. **-velka** war debt. **-veteraani** veteran. **-voima** *(sotilaallinen ~)* military power. **-vuodet** the war years. **-väki** soldiers, troops; military forces; *-väen otto* recruiting.

sotia wage war, make war (against), war (against); *(taistella)* fight (against); *(olla ristiriidassa)* conflict with, jar with; *sotii järkeä vastaan* is contrary to reason.

sotienvälinen inter-war. **sotilaalli|nen** military, *(sotilaalle ominainen)* soldierly. **-sesti** in a military manner.

sotilas soldier; *(vakinaisessa väessä)* regular; *(šakki-)* pawn. **-ammatti** the military profession. **-arvo** military rank. **-asiamies** military attaché. **-diktatuuri** military dictatorship. **-henkilö** military man, soldier. **-ilmailu** military aviation. **-karkuri** deserter. **-koti** soldiers' canteen.

-koulutus military training.
-lentokone army plane.
-lentäjä airman. **-liitto** military
alliance. **-lääkäri** army (naval,
air-force) medical officer.
-mestari *l. v.* warrant- officer.
-pukuinen. . in uniform,
uniformed. **-sairaala** military
hospital. **-soittokunta** military
band. **-ura** military career.
-valta military rule,
militarism. **-valtio** militaristic
state.
sotisopa fighting equipment;
(haarniska) armour.
sotk|ea *(sekoittaa)* mix; *kuv.*
(polkea) tread; *häntä ei saa*
~ *(juttuun)* he must not get
involved (mixed up) in; ~
mielessään (kaksi henkilöä)
mistake a p. for another; ~
taikinaa knead the dough; ~
vyyhti tangle a skein. **-eutua**
get entangled, *jhk* in;
(sekaantua) be involved (in);
(hämmentyä) become confused,
get stuck, lose the thread. **-u**
tangle; *(sekamelska)* jumble,
muddle, mess. **-uinen**
[en]tangled *(m. kuv.)*
muddled; *(mutkikas)* involved,
intricate, complicated.
šottis schottische.
soturi warrior.
soudella row; *lähteä*
soutelemaan go for a row, go
out in a boat.
sout|aa row; *(pientä venettä,*
m.) scull; *souda kovemmin*
pull harder. **-aja** rower,
oarsman. **-u** rowing; *(~kilpailu*
boat-race; *~retki* boat-trip,
rowing-trip; *~urheilu* rowing,
boating; *~vene* rowboat,
rowing-boat).
soveli|aisuus suitability;
propriety. **-as** suitable, fit
(for); appropriate, proper;
(mukava) convenient.
sovel|luttaa apply, *jhk* to; *ks.*
-taa. **-lutus** adaptation. **-taa**
apply, adapt (to), fit (to); ~
käytäntöön adapt. . to use,
put . . in practice; *-lettavissa*
oleva applicable; *-lettu tiede*
applied science. **-tua** *(jhk)* be
suited (adapted) to, suit . ., be
suitable [for, *jklle*], fit [the

occasion, *tilaisuuteen*], be
appropriate; *(ajan ym*
puolesta) be convenient; *-tuu*
jhk (on omiaan) lends itself
to. **-tumaton**. . unsuitable
(for); inapplicable (to); not
suited, unfitted (for). **-tuva**
suitable (for), applicable (to),
adapted (to *t.* for). **-tuvuus**
suitability; *(~koe* aptitude
test).
sovinnai|nen conventional.
-stapa conventionality,
convention. **-suus**
conventionalism.
sovinnolli|nen conciliatory;
(rauhallinen) peaceable. **-suus**
conciliatory disposition;
peaceableness.
sovinnonhieroja peacemaker.
sovinto reconciliation; *(sopu)*
harmony, amity; *(järjestely)*
settlement, adjustment; *tehdä*
~ *be[come]* reconciled, make
it up; come to an
arrangement; *olla sovinnossa*
(keskenään) be on good
terms; *selvittää asia*
sovinnossa settle a matter
amicably. **-kuolema** expiatory
death. **-oikeus** arbitration
court; *jättää -oikeuden*
ratkaistavaksi submit. . to
arbitration. **-politiikka** policy
of appeasement. **-tuomari**
arbitrator. **-tuomio** arbitration.
-uhri expiatory sacrifice.
sovi|tella adjust, adapt [to, *jnk*
mukaan); (riitaa) mediate,
conciliate. **-telma** *mus.*
arrangement. **-ttaa** suit, adapt,
accommodate [to, *jnk*
mukaan]; (toisiinsa, yhteen)
fit in, combine; *(jhk)* build
into, incorporate into;
(sovitella) adjust; arrange;
(hyvittää) make amends for,
usk. ym. atone for, expiate;
(riitapuolet) conciliate;
(välittää) mediate (between);
~ *paikoilleen* fit. . in, fit. .
into its place, put (place). .
in position; ~ *pianolle*
arrange for the piano; ~
puku fit on (try on) a suit
(a dress); *-ttava* conciliatory.
-ttamaton irreconcilable; *(esim.*
rikos) unexpiated,

(anteeksiantamaton) unforgivable. **-ttelija** mediator, *(työriidan, m.)* conciliator. **-ttelu;** *(työriidan ym)* conciliation, mediation; (~**ehdotus** proposal for settlement). **-ttu** agreed [upon], appointed, fixed. **-tus** adaptation; *usk. ym.* atonement, expiation; *(puvun)* fitting; *mus.* arrangement.

speditööri forwarding agent [s].

spektri spectrum *(pl.* -ra).

spekuloida speculate.

spinetti *mus.* spinet.

spiraali spiral.

spiritismi spiritualism. **-ti** spiritualist. **-tinen** spiritualistic; ~ *istunto* seance.

spitaalitauti leprosy. **-nen** leper.

spontaaninen spontaneous.

sprii spirit.

stadion stadium.

standardi standard. **-oida** standardize.

standartti standard *(lyh.* std).

statiivi tripod.

statisti supernumerary, [stage] extra; *olla* ~*na* have a walk-on part.

stereo: ~*laitteet* stereo equipment. **-foninen:** ~ *äänentoisto* stereophony; ~ *äänilevy* stereo disc. **-tyyppi,** ~**laatta** stereotype. **-typoida** stereotype.

terili sterile.

teriloida sterilize. **-nti** sterilization.

tilisti stylist. **-nen** stylistic.

tipendi scholarship; grant, student award, bursary. **-aatti** scholarship student; [Fulbright etc.] grantee.

toalainen *a.* stoic [al]; *s.* stoic.

trategi strategist. **-nen** strategic.

tratosfääri stratosphere.

treptokokki streptococc|us *(pl.* -i). **-mysiini** streptomycin.

trutsi *zo.* ostrich.

truuma *lääk.* goitre, *Am.* goiter.

trykniini strychnin [e].

ubjekti subject. **-tiivinen** subjective. **-iivisuus** subjectivity.

ublimoida sublimate.

ubstantiivi noun, substantive.

-nen substantive, substantival.

subventio [state] subsidy. **-oida** subsidize.

suden|korento dragon-fly. **-kuoppa** pitfall. **-pentu** wolf-cub.

suggeroida influence. . by suggestion. **-stio** suggestion; ~*lle altis* suggestible.

suhahdus whiz [z]. **-taa** whiz [z] [by, *ohi*], whistle, swish.

suhdanne, -nteet *(t.* market) conditions; *-nteille herkkä* cyclically sensitive; *alhainen* ~ depressed state of the market; *nouseva* ~ favourable trend; (~**jakso** trade cycle; ~**taantuma** recession; ~**vaihtelut** economic fluctuations). **-ton** disproportionate,.. out of proportion; *(liiallinen)* excessive.

suhde relation, proportion; relationship, *mat.* ratio; *suhteet (m.)* connexions, connections; *suhteessa jhk* in relation (to), in proportion (to); *eräässä suhteessa* in one respect; *monessa suhteessa* in many respects; *tässä suhteessa* in this respect (regard); *samassa suhteessa* in proportion. **-luku** ratio. **-toiminta** public relations, PR activity; (~**virkailija** PR officer).

suhditus *tait.* conditioning.

suhi|na *(tuulen)* sigh [ing], murmur [ing]; whiz [zing]; *(korvien)* buzzing in the ears. **-sta** sigh, murmur; whistle.

suhta proportion.

suhtau|tua *mat.* be to.. [as.. is to.. *niinkuin.* .], be in a ratio of [3 to 2]; ~ *jhk* take an attitude, take a stand [in a matter, towards a question]; *miten hän siihen -tui* how did he respond? what was his reaction? ~ *suopeasti (jhk)* be favourably inclined (towards). **-tuminen** stand, attitude; reaction.

suhteellinen proportional, proportionate; relative, comparative; ~ *vaalitapa*

proportional representation;
-llisen hyvä relatively
(comparatively) good. **-llisesti**
in proportion (to),
proportionately. **-llisuus**
proportion; (~**teoria** theory of
relativity). **-n:** *jnk ~* in
regard to, regarding, *(jtk
koskien)* concerning, as to;
sen ~ (m.) on that subject;
as far as that is concerned.
-ton disproportionate,.. out of
[all] proportion; *-ttoman
suuri* disproportionately large.
-ttomuus disproportion, lack
of proportion.
suhteuttaa proportion, *jhk* to.
suhuäänne sibilant.
suihku jet, *(voimakas)* spout;
(roiske) spray; *(kylpy- ym)*
shower. **-huone** shower bath.
-kaivo, -lähde fountain.
-(lento)kone jet plane. **-ta**
spurt, spout. **-ttaa** spurt,
spout; *puut.* spray.
suikale strip, band.
suin|kaan: *ei ~* by no means,
on no account; *(ei
tosiaankaan)* certainly not,
surely not. **-kin** *(vain)* only;
(mahdollisesti) possibly; *jos ~
(on) mahdollista* if at all
possible; *niin pian kuin ~* as
soon as possible, at your
earliest convenience.
suinpäin headlong, head over
heels.
suipen|taa make.. narrower,
make.. pointed. **-tua** become
narrower, narrow [off]; taper.
suippo narrow; *(suippeneva)*
tapering; *(terävä)* pointed.
-kaari pointed arch. **-kärkinen**
pointed, peaked.
suistaa hurl, throw; *~ kiskoilta*
derail.
suisto, -maa estuary, delta.
suistua fall, tumble down; *~
kiskoilta* be derailed, leave
the rails; *~ hevosen selästä*
fall off one's horse; *~ tieltä
(auto)* run off the road, leave
the road, *(luisua)* slither off
the road; *auto alkoi
heittelehtiä ja suistui tieltä*
the car began to swerve and
bounced off the road.
suits|et bridle. **-ittaa** [put the]

bridle (on).
suitsu|ttaa burn incense. **-tus**
incense; (~**astia** censer).
sujauttaa slip (in, into).
suju|a: *miten työ sujuu* how
are you getting on with the
work? *~ hyvin* progress well,
(esim. asiat) go well, *(onnistua)* be a success. **-t** quits. **-va**
fluent; easy; *~ kynä* fluid
pen. **-vuus** fluency; ease, flow.
suka *(hevos-)* currycomb.
sukan|neulomakone
stocking-frame (-loom). **-suu**
top of a stocking. **-terä** foot
of a stocking. **-varsi** stocking
leg.
sukel|lus dive; *olla -luksissa* be
submerged; *mennä -luksiin*
submerge; (~**kello** diving bell;
~**kypärä** diver's helmet; **-laite**
(kevyt) aqualung [apparatus];
~**vene** submarine). **-taa** dive;
(sukellusveneestä, m.)
submerge; *(syöksyä)* plunge
[into]. **-taja** diver; (~**npuku**
diving dress, diver's suit).
-tautua: *~ esiin* emerge.
sukeu|tua *(johtua)* ensue, arise;
(kehittyä) develop [into];
väittely -tui vilkkaaksi a
lively discussion ensued.
sukia *(hevosta)* curry.
sukka stocking; *(miehen,
puoli-)* sock; *koll. m.* hose.
-housut tights, panti-hose.
-nauha [stocking] suspender,
Am. garter *(Engl. säären
ymp. kiinnitettävä)*; (~**ritaristo**
Order of the Garter). **-puikko**
knitting-needle. **-sillaan** in
one's stockings.
sukkela quick; swift; *(älykäs)*
clever, bright. **-sanainen**
quick-witted, quick-tongued,
(vastauksissa).. quick at
repartee. **-älyinen** ready-witted;
on ~ has quick wits.
sukkeluus cleverness, ready wit;
(pila) witty remark, witticism,
joke.
sukkula shuttle; *~n muotoinen*
spindle-shaped.
suklaa chocolate; cocoa. **-levy**
slab of chocolate. **-nruskea**
chocolate.
suksi ski. **-sauva** ski-stick. **-side**
[ski] binding. **-voide** ski wax.

suku family; kin; *(-kanta)* strain, stock; *(-perä)* extraction, lineage; ancestry; *(syntyperä)* birth; *(hallitsija-)* house; *bot. & zo.* genus; *kiel.* gender; *olla ~a jklle* be related to; *kaukaista, läheistä ~a jklle* a distant (a near) relation of; *ylhäistä ~a. .* of noble birth; *omaa ~a H.* born H.; *hän on omaa ~a. .* her maiden name is. . **-kartano** family estate; *lak.* entail. **-kieli** related language. **-kirja** pedigree, genealogy. **-kunta** generation. **-lainen** relative, relation; *(harvemmin)* kinsman, -woman; *-laiset (m.)* kindred; *lähimmät -laiset* next of kin; *hän on -laiseni (m.)* he is a connection (connexion) of mine. **sukulais|kansa** kindred people. **-side:** *-siteet* family ties. **-suhde** relationship, family connection. **-uus** relationship. **suku|luettelo** genealogy. **-nimi** family name, surname. **-perä** descent, lineage, parentage. **-polvi** generation. **-puoli** sex; *(~elimet* genitals; *~nen* sexual; *~ kanssakäyminen* sexual intercourse; *~ viehätys* sex appeal; *~tauti* venereal disease; *~valistus* information on sexual matters; *~vietti* sex instinct; *~yhteys* sexual intercourse). **suku|puu** genealogical tree, family tree. **-puutto** extinction; *hävittää ~on* exterminate; *kuolla ~on* become extinct; *~on kuollut* extinct. **-rutsaus** incest. **-selvitys** [account of] ancestry. **-taulu** genealogical table. **-tutkimus** genealogy. **-vika** family weakness. **-yhtäläisyys** family likeness. **-ylpeys** ancestral pride. **sula** melted, molten; *(juokseva)* liquid, fluid; *(jäätymätön). .* not frozen; *(pelkkä)* sheer; *on ~ (= suoja)* it is thawing; *~ maa* unfrozen ground; *~ vesi* open water; *~ voi* melted butter; *se on ~a hulluutta* it is sheer madness; *se on ~ mahdottomuus* it is utterly (absolutely) impossible; *sulimmat kiitokseni* my most sincere thanks. **sulaa** melt; *(metall. ym)* fuse; *(liueta)* dissolve; *(ruoasta)* be digested; *~ yhteen (esim. väreistä)* blend (melt) into each other; *lumi on sulanut* the snow has melted [away]. **sula|ke** sähk. fuse; *-kkeen palaminen* blow-out; *polttaa ~* blow a fuse. **-maton** *(ruoasta)* indigestible; undigested. **-mispiste** melting-point. **-tejuusto** cream cheese, cheese spread. **-ttaa** melt; *(rautamalmia)* smelt; *(ruokaa)* digest, *kuv.* put up with, stomach; *(oppimansa)* take in; *~ toisiinsa* fuse, amalgamate, *(tehden samankaltaisiksi)* assimilate. **-tto** smelting works, smelting house, smeltery. **-tus** *(jääkaapin)* defreezing; *(~pannu* melting-pot; *~uuni* smelting furnace; *-utua* fuse, merge, *(et. väreistä)* blend; *~ jhk* become merged (incorporated) in. **-va** melting; *(ruoasta)* digestible; *(nuortea)* supple; *(siro)* graceful; *vaikeasti ~* indigestible. **-vuus** suppleness; grace [fulness]. **sulf|aatti** sulphate, *Am.* sulfate. **-iitti** sulphite, *Am.* sulfite. **sulha|nen** fiancé; *(vihille menevä)* bridegroom. **-spoika** best man, groomsman. **sulje|ttu** closed; *~ järjestys* close order; *joutua -tuksi (esim. kaivokseen)* be trapped in. **sulka** feather; *(iso)* plume. **-kynä** quill. **-pallo** shuttlecock, *(-peli)* badminton. **-sato** moulting [season]; *olla -sadossa* moult. **-töyhtö** plume. **sulke|a** close, shut, shut up; *(esteillä)* bar, obstruct; block [up]; *~ kaasu-, vesihana* turn off the gas (the water); *~ radio* switch off the radio; *~ jku jstk* shut a p. out; *~ pois* exclude, rule out, *(estää)* debar from; *~ jkn huomioon* recommend. . for a p.'s consideration; *~ kirje* seal a

letter; ~ *piiriinsä* comprise,
embrace; ~ *satama* close the
harbour; ~ *syliinsä* fold in
one's arms, hug, embrace;
sulkisitteko ikkunan? would
you mind closing the
window? **-et** [*haka-* square]
brackets; *-issa* in brackets, in
parenthesis; *-isiin pantu*
bracketed. **-misaika**
closing-time. **-utua** close, shut;
(*lukon taakse*) lock oneself in
(into one's room, *huonee-*
seensa); ~ *kuoreensa*
withdraw into one's shell
(into oneself); *-utunut*
uncommunicative; reticent,
reserved.
sulku sluice; (*kanavan-*) lock,
flood-gate; (*pato*) dam; (*katu-*)
barricade; (*este*) obstruction,
block[ing]; *panna* ~ *jllek* put
a stop to; *sulun vartija*
lock-keeper. **-laitos** lock.
-maksu lockage. **-merkki**
parenthesis, bracket. **-pallo**
(*ilmatorjunta-*) barrage
balloon. **-portti** lockgate.
-telakka dock. **-tuli** *sot.*
barrage, curtain-fire. **-viiva**
barrier line.
sullo|a pack, stuff, cram,
bundle (into). **-utua** crowd,
pack.
sulo *s.* charm, grace. **-inen**
sweet; lovely; charming,
delightful, pleasing. **-isuus**
sweetness, loveliness; charm.
-sointu sweet melody. **-stuttaa**
sweeten. **-tar** : *-ttaret* the
Graces. **-ton** . . without charm,
graceless. **-tuoksuinen**
sweet-scented, fragrant. **-us**
sweetness; charm, grace.
sulttaani sultan.
suma drive [of logs], [log-]
jam.
sume|a misty; hazy; fogged-up.
-ilematta without [any]
scruples. **-ntaa** shroud . . in
mist; darken, obscure; *kuv.*
dim, cloud [a p.'s mind, *jnk*
järki]. **-ntua** become misty.
summa sum; (*määrä*) amount;
(*kokonais-*) [sum] total;
nousta jhk ~*an* amount to.
-kauppa wholesale purchase;
-kaupalla in the lump, in

bulk. **-mutikassa** at random.
summeri *tekn.* buzzer.
summittai|n wholesale;
summarily. **-nen** summary.
sumppu (*kala-*) fish-chest
(-well).
sumu fog; mist; (*auer*) haze.
-inen foggy, misty; nebulous.
-isuus fogginess, mistiness.
-merkki fog-signal.
-peitteinen. . shrouded
(wrapped) in fog. **-sireeni,**
-torvi fog-horn.
sunnuntai Sunday. **-numero**
Sunday issue (number). **-sin**
on Sundays.
suntio verger.
suo swamp, marsh, bog; fen.
suoda grant; afford, allow;
bestow (on); give; *soisin, että*
niin olisi I wish it were so;
suokaa anteeksi! excuse me!
jos Jumala suo God willing;
hän ei suonut minulle
silmäystäkään he did not
vouchsafe me a glance; *hän*
ei suo itselleen lepoa he
allows himself no rest;
hänelle suotiin kunnia.. he
had the honour (of -ing);
hänelle suotiin lämmin
vastaanotto he was given a
warm welcome; *olla suomatta*
[be]grudge a p. sth.
suoda|tin filter; (~*savuke*
filter-tipped cigarette). **-ttaa**
filter. **-tus** filtration; (**-paperi**
filter paper).
suodin filter.
suodos filtrate.
suoja 1. shelter; (*turva*)
protection; *sot.* cover;
(*pakopaikka*) refuge; ~*n puoli*
(*mer.*) leeward; (*jnk*) ~*ssa*
under the shelter of, (*jkn*)
under a p.'s protection; *ottaa*
suojiinsa take . . under one's
protection, take. . under one's
wing; *mennä* ~*an* find (take)
shelter; *olla* ~*ssa jltk* be
sheltered from, be protected
from. 2. *a.* (*leuto*) mild; *s.*
(*-sää, -ilma*) thaw; *on* ~ it is
thawing. **-inen** sheltered.
-koroke street island (refuge).
-kypärä crash helmet. **-lasit**
[protective] goggles. **-muuri**
defensive wall. **-npuoli** *mer.*

leeward, lee side. **-paikka** shelter. **-peite** tarpaulin. **-puku** overalls; boiler-suit.

suoja|ta shield; guard, safeguard (against), protect (against, from); *-ttu* sheltered. **-tie** pedestrian crossing, *(iso)* zebra crossing. **-toimenpide** protective measure. **-ton** unprotected; defenceless. **-tti** protegé, *fem.* protegée. **-tulli** protective duty. **-utua** protect, [safe]guard oneself (against), find shelter from, *sot.* take cover. **-väri** protective colouring, mimicry.

suoje|lija protector; patron. **-lla** protect (against, from); *-leva (varjella)* preserve from; [safe]guard; *~ksemme itseämme ikäviltä yllätyksiltä* to guard ourselves against unpleasant surprises; *-leva* protective; *(lääk.)* prophylactic. **-lu** *ks. seur.;* (**~alue** protectorate; *vrt. riistan-),*

suojelus protection; defence; safeguard; patronage. **-enkeli** guardian angel. **-kunta** civil guard. **-pyhimys** patron saint.

suojus shield, guard, protector; shelter; cover[ing]; *(kotelo)* case, casing, *(-kaihdin)* screen; *(kirjan päällys)* jacket; *polven~* knee-pad. **-lehti** *bot.* bract. **-tin** guard, protector, pad.

suola salt, *(karkea)* rock salt. **-amaton** unsalted. **-astia** salt-cellar. **-happo** hydrochloric acid. **-inen** salt, salty; *~ vesi* salt water. **-kala** salt[ed] fish. **-kurkku** pickled cucumber, *(pieni)* gherkin. **-liha** salt[ed] meat. **-liuos** saline solution. **-pitoinen** . containing salt, saliferous. **-ta** salt; salt down, cure; *~ttu (m.)* corned. **-ton** saltless, unsalted; *~ vesi* fresh *(t. sweet)* water. **-vesi** salt water; brine.

suoli intestine, bowel; gut. **-jänne** catgut. **-mato** intestinal worm. **-sto** intestines, bowels, guts; (**~taudit**) intestinal disorders).

suomaa marshland, marshy land.

suomalai|nen *a.* Finnish; *s.* Finn. **-ssyntyinen**. . of Finnish extraction (descent). **-staa** make. . Finnish; *~ nimensä* adopt a Finnish name. **-sugrilainen** Finno-Ugric.

suomen|kielinen [. . in] Finnish; *(suomea puhuva)* Finnish-speaking; *~ sanomalehti* a Finnish-language newspaper. **S-lahti** the Gulf of Finland. **-mielinen** pro-Finnish. **-mielisyys** pro-Finnish attitude (views). **-nos** translation into Finnish; *-nnoksena* as a Finnish translation, in Finnish. **-sukuinen**. . related to the Finns, Finnic. **-taa** translate into Finnish. **-taja** translator [into Finnish].

Suomi Finland; *Suomen kansa* the Finnish people; *s~ (suomen kieli)* Finnish, the Finnish language; *suomeksi* in Finnish.

suomia *(piestä)* whip, thrash, *kuv.* criticize [severely].

suomu scale; lamina. **-inen** scaly. **-peite** scaly covering. **-s:** *-kset* scales. **-staa** scale.

suomuurain [arctic] cloudberry.

suonen|isku bleeding, letting of blood. **-sykintä** pulse, pulsation. **-veto** cramp.

suoni *anat.* blood vessel, *(laskimo, lehden)* vein; *(malmi-)* seam; *nopea ~ rapid* pulse. **-kohju** varicose vein [s].

suonkuivatus reclaiming (draining) of swamp [s].

suopa soft soap.

suope|a favourable; kind, well-disposed; *-in silmin* favourably. **-amielinen** favourably disposed (inclined) (towards). **-us** favour, propitiousness, kind[li]ness; goodwill.

suo|peräinen swampy, boggy. **-pursu** marsh tea.

suopunki lasso.

suor|a straight; *(tukasta, piikki-)* lank; right [angle, *kulma*], *(välitön)* direct; *kuv.* straight [in one's dealings], straightforward, forthright; frank; *s. (viiva)* straight line;

~ *lähetys* live broadcast; ~ *puhe* plain (*t.* straightforward) language; ~ *toiminta* direct action; ~*a päätä* straight, directly, right away; ~*lta kädeltä* off hand, straight [off], out of hand, (*lausuttu*) off-the-cuff; *-in sanoin* in plain terms, straight out; *-in tie* the shortest route; *seisoa* ~*na* stand straight, stand erect, *kuv.* not bow [in the storm]. **-aan** straight, direct (to); (*vilpittömästi*) frankly, openly; ~ *sanoen* frankly speaking, to tell the truth; *käydä* ~ *asiaan* come straight to the point; *kirjoittakaa meille* ~*!* write to us direct! ~ *verrannollinen* directly proportional.

suora|kaide rectangle; *-kaiteen muotoinen* rectangular. **-kulmainen** right-angled [triangle, *kolmio*]; rectangular. **-luontoinen** straightforward, upright. **-nainen** direct, immediate [cause, *syy*]; (*todellinen*) actual; (*selvä*) plain, downright [lie, *vale*]. **-naisesti** directly. **-puheinen** outspoken, plain-spoken, frank. **-sanainen** in prose; prose. **-ssa** straight; erect. **-staan** downright; simply; (*ehdottomasti*) absolutely, positively; *ellei* ~ if not; not to say. .; *hän ei sitä* ~ *sanonut, mutta* he did not exactly say so but. . **-sukainen** straightforward, plain-spoken, forthright. **-sukaisuus** straightforwardness, outspokenness. **-viivainen** rectilinear.

suori|a *mer.* clear [a ship, *laiva*]. **-staa** straighten [out], rectify; ~ *vartalonsa* straighten up. **-stautua** draw oneself up, stretch oneself [to one's full height]. **-ttaa** perform; do, make; execute [an order, *tilaus*]; carry out, carry through, effect; (*ratkaista*) solve; (*selvittää*) settle; (*maksaa*) pay; defray [the expenses, *kustannukset*]; (*tutkinto ym*) pass; ~

asevelvollisuutensa serve one's time as conscript; ~ *kurssi* take a course, (*loppuun*) follow a course through; ~ *laskuesimerkki* do (work out, solve) a problem; ~ *maksu* pay, make payment; *jäädessä -ttamatta* in case of non-payment, failing payment; ~ *tehtävä* perform (execute) a task; ~ *tilaus* execute an order; ~ *tutkinto* pass (take) an examination, (*loppu-*) sit for one's finals; ~ *velka* pay (settle) a debt, meet [one's] liabilities; *hän on -ttanut suurenmoisen elämäntyön* he has performed (done, accomplished) a magnificent life's work. **-ttamaton** unexecuted *jne.*; (*maksamaton*) unpaid, unsettled; outstanding. **-tus** performance; (*maksu*) payment; settlement; (*aikaansaannos*) achievement; *laskunne -tukseksi* in settlement of your account; (~*koe* performance test; ~*kyky* performance.; ~*kykyinen* efficient; ~*tila* liquidation; *joutua s-an* go into liquidation; *liike on s-ssa* the business is being wound up; ~*yhteiskunta* meritocracy). **-utua** get along, manage; cope with [a task, *tehtävästä*]; ~ *hyvin tutkinnosta* do well in an examination; ~ *vaikeuksista* overcome [the] difficulties; ~ *voittajana jstk* come off the winner; *hän -utui voittajana väittelystä* he got the better of his opponent in the debate.

suortuva tress; curl, lock.

suoruus straightness, directness; frankness.

suosi|a favour; patronize; (*kannattaa*) support; *-ttu* popular,. . in favour; *-tuin* most favoured [nation, *kansa*]; *kaikkien -ma* the favourite of everybody. **-ja** patron. **-kki** favourite; (~*iskelmät* pop songs; · ~*järjestelmä* favouritism).

suosio favour; (*yleisön*) popularity; *olla* (*suuressa*)

~*ssa* be in [high] favour, be [very] popular; *olla jkn ~ssa* be in a p.'s good graces, *(esim. oppilaiden, yleisön)* be popular with; *päästä yleisön ~on* gain popularity; *osoittaa jklle ~taan* applaud; *saavutti ~ta* went down well, met with applause. **-llinen** favourable, kindly disposed; *jkn -llisella avulla* with a p.'s kind assistance; *jkn -llisella luvalla* by courtesy of. . **-llisesti** favourably, with favour. **-llisuus** favourable benevolence.

-n|huuto *-huudot* acclamation. **-nmyrsky** storm (burst) of applause; *esitys nostatti ~n* the performance brought down the house. **-nosoi|tus** favour; *-tukset* applause.

uosi|tella, -ttaa recommend [a p. for a position, *jkta jhk toimeen*]; *-teltava*. . to be recommended; advisable. **-ttaja** reference; *olen maininnut Teidät ~na* I have mentioned you as a r. **-ttelu** recommendation. **-tuimmuus** preferential treatment. **-tus** recommendation; *-tukset* references; *jkn -tuksesta* on a p.'s recommendation; *(~kirje* letter of introduction).

ostu|a consent, agree (to); assent (to); *(hyväksyä)* accept; ~ *myönnytyksiin* grant (agree to) concessions; ~ *jkn pyyntöön* grant (comply with) p.'s request; ~ *tarjoukseen* accept an offer; ~ *jkn toivomuksiin* gratify a p.'s wishes. **-mus** consent (to); acceptance; *(hyväksymys)* approval; *antaa -muksensa jhk* consent, give one's consent to, assent to; *jkn -muksella* with a p.'s consent *(permission)*. **-tella** persuade, induce [a p. to do sth.]. **ttaa** *ks. ed.; saada jku etuksi puolellensa* win a p. over [to one's side]. **-ttelu** *tonien ~jen jälkeen* after much persuasion; *(~kyky* power of persuasion). **-vainen** illing, inclined (to); *(valmis)*

ready. **-vaisuus** willingness, readiness.

suotav|a desirable,. . to be desired, advisable; *erittäin ~a* highly desirable. **-uus** desirability.

suotta *(turhaan)* in vain, to no purpose; *(syyttä)* unnecessarily; *se on ~* it is useless.

suotui|sa favourable, propitious; *(edullinen)* advantageous; *(sopiva)* convenient; suitable. **-suus** favourableness; advantageousness.

suova *(heinä)* stack. **-ta** stack.

supa|ttaa, -sta whisper.

super|fosfaatti superphosphate **-latiivi** superlative. **-vallat** super powers.

supi 1. ~*suomalainen* pure (genuine, true) Finnish; purely Finnish. **2.** *zo* raccoon. **-koira** raccoon dog.

supi|na, -sta whisper; mumble.

supis|taa reduce; *(rajoittaa)* limit, restrict; *(vähentää)* cut down, cut, curtail; *(tekstiä ym)* abridge, *lääk. ym* contract, constrict; ~ *kustannuksia* cut down expenses, retrench; ~ *murtoluku* cancel a fraction; ~ *sanottavansa lyhyeen* be brief, cut it short; *-tetussa muodossa* in a condensed form. **-tava** restrictive; *(esim. kasvovesi)* astringent. **-telma** summary, resumé, abstract; ~ *jstk (m.)* condensed from. . **-tua** *(esim. lihas)* contract; be reduced (to), be limited, be restricted (to); *hänen ansionsa -tuvat hyvin vähiin* he has few if any merits. **-tus** reduction; restriction; curtailment; *mat.* cancellation. **-tuva(inen)** contractile; contracting.

suppe|a concise, succinct, brief; *(liian)* incomplete, uninformative; *(täsmällinen)* terse. **-asti** concisely, briefly. **-us** conciseness; condensed form.

suppilo funnel. **-mainen** funnel-shaped.

suppu: *vetää suunsa ~un* purse up one's lips.

sure|minen mourning, grief.
-ttaa grieve, give pain (to).
-ttava sad, grievous.

suri|na buzz[ing], hum[ming];
(esim. mehiläisen) drone. **-sta**
buzz, hum; (kone) whir,
drone.

surkas|tua (kasvussaan) be
checked in its growth,
be[come] stunted; (lakastua)
wither [away]; (näivettyä)
atrophy. **-tuma** rudiment.

surk|ea sad, deplorable, dismal;
(kurja) miserable, wretched;
(surkuteltava) lamentable,
pitiful; ~ssa tilassa in a sad
state; loppua ~sti [begin with
a bang and] end with a
whimper. **-eus** sadness;
miserableness; pitifulness.

surku: minun tulee jkta ~ I
feel pity for. **-hupaisa**
tragicomic. **-tella** pity, be
sorry (for); (valittaa) regret,
deplore. **-teltava** pitiful,
pitiable; (valitettava)
regrettable, deplorable,
lamentable. **-teltavuus**
pitifulness; miserableness.
-ttelu pity[ing], commiseration.

surma death; saada ~nsa be
killed, meet one's death. **-najo**
fatal drive. **-nisku** death-blow.
-nsilmukka ilm. looping the
loop; tehdä ~ loop the loop.
-ta slay; put. . to death;
(tappaa) kill; (joukoittain)
massacre. **-uttaa** have. . slain
(killed).

surra grieve (at, for), be
grieved (at); regret; mourn
(for, over); ~ jkta mourn
[the loss of] a p.; ~
joutavia worry over nothing
(over trifles).

suru sorrow; grief, (-aika)
mourning; (huoli) worry;
~kseni to my sorrow, to my
great regret; kuulin ~kseni
(m.) I was grieved to hear;
ilossa ja ~ssa in weal and
woe. **-aika** [period of]
mourning. **-harso** mourning
veil, (kangas) mourning crêpe.
-llinen sad, sorrowful; grieved;
-llisen kuuluisa notorious.
-llisuus sadness, mournfulness.
-marssi funeral march. **-mielin**

with a heavy heart. **-mielinen**
sad [at heart], melancholic.
-mielisyys sadness [of heart];
melancholy. **-nvalittelu**
condolence. **-nvoittoinen**
[rather] sad, melancholy.
-puku mourning; olla -puvussa
wear mourning; pukeutua ~un
go into mourning. **-pukuinen**. .
in mourning. **-reunainen:** ~
paperi mourning paper.
-saattue funeral procession.
-talo house of mourning.
-ton. . free from care,
care-free; (välinpitämätön)
unconcerned; (maailmallinen)
worldly [-minded]. **-ttomuus**
freedom from care;
light-heartedness; unconcern.

surv|aista thrust. **-in** pestle. **-oa**
crush, pound.

susi wolf (pl. wolves); kuv. sl.
dud; ~ lammasten vaatteissa
a wolf in sheep's clothing.
-lauma pack of wolves.

suti brush, scourer.

sutkaus sally [of wit],
witticism, quip.

suu mouth; (aseen ym.)
muzzle; (aukko) opening,
aperture; (sataman) entrance;
(lasku-) outlet; (kannun) lip;
syödä ~ hunsa eat [up]; ~
kiinni be quiet! hold your
tongue! shut up! pudota
suulleen fall on one's face;
joen ~ssa at the mouth of
the river; oven ~ssa at the
door; illan ~ssa towards
evening; ~hunpantava(a) ark.
grub; ~sta ~hun menetelmä
the kiss of life,
mouth-to-mouth resuscitation.
-della, -delma kiss. **-hinen**
(soittimen) mouthpiece.
-kappale mouthpiece, nozzle.
-kapula gag. **-kko** kiss. **-kopu:**
pitää ~a bandy words, (jstk)
wrangle (about). **-lake** nozzle.
-laki plate; (~halkio cleft
palate). **-las** garrulous,
loquacious; talkative. **-laus**
garrulousness. **-llinen** oral;
verbal [message, sanoma].
-llisesti orally; by word of
mouth. **-nliike** movement of
the lips.

suunnan|muutos pol. change o

policy. **-osoitin** ks. *vilkku.*

suunn|ata direct (towards); *(tähdätä)* aim (at), point (at); *(kääntää)* turn [one's eyes to, towards]; level [accusations at, *syytöksiä*]; *(kulku|nsa)* direct one's steps to [wards], make for, head for; *(esim. laiva)* steer to [wards]; *(esim. ajatukset toisaalle)* divert. **-a|ton** enormous, immense, vast, huge; colossal; *kasvaa s-ttomaksi* grow [to] enormous [size]; ~ *määrä velkoja (m.)* no end of debts. **-attomuus** enormity, immensity, vastness, hugeness. **-ikas** *geom.* parallelogram. **-illeen** about; *(arviolta)* approximately; *(noin)* something like, some [60 people, *60 henkeä*], much [the same, *sama*[; *(lähes)* nearly; ~ *niin* something like that. **-istaa** *urh.* orienteer. **-istautua** get one's bearings, orient oneself. **-istautuminen** orientation. **-istus** *urh.* orienteering. **-itella** plan; design, project; outline, map out [one's work, *työnsä*]; lay out, draw up.

suunnitelma plan, scheme; project (for); *(luonnos)* design, draft. **-llinen** methodical, systematical; planned [beforehand]; laid out on a regular plan. **-llisesti** according to plan. **-llisuus** methodicalness. **-nmukainen** ks. *-llinen.* **-talous** planned economy. **-ton**.. without a regular plan.

suunnitt|eilla under consideration, [in process of] being planned;.. *on* ~ plans are in being to.. **-elu** planning.

suun|pieksijä gabbler, windbag. **-soitto** idle talk, gabble.

suunta direction, way, course; *(taho)* quarter; *(mielipide- ym.)* trend [of opinion], tendency, drift; *joka suunnalta* from all directions; *jnk ~an* in the direction (of); *jotakin siihen ~an* something to that effect; *käy samaan ~an (m.)*

follows along the same lines; *kääntyä toiseen ~an (m.)* take another course; *joutua pois oikealta suunnalta* get off one's course; *katsoa molempiin suuntiin* look both ways; *oli suunniltaan* .. was beside himself (herself). **-numero** code *(t.* routing) number. **-us** *(t.* routing) line; policy. **-utua** be directed, *jhk* towards, at; *(tähdätä)* aim (at); *(kääntyä)* turn (towards); tend (towards). **-viitta** *(auton)* [direction] indicator. **-viiva** line; *seuraan näitä -viivoja* I shall proceed on *(t.* along) these lines.

suunti|a take the bearings. **-mislaite** direction finder, radio compass.

suun|täysi mouthful. **-vuoro** chance to speak; *en saanut ~a* I did not get a word in edgeways.

suu|ontelo oral cavity. **-pala** morsel; bite. **-paltti** chatterbox. **-pieli** corner of the mouth. **-puhe** hearsay.

suure *mat.* quantity. **-hko** rather big, fairly large; largish, sizeable. **-llinen** grandiose, [.. on a] grand [scale]. **-mpi** greater; larger, bigger; *olla jtk* ~ *(m.)* exceed [in number], be in excess [of, *kuin*].

suuren|moinen grand, magnificent, splendid, great; imposing. **-moisesti** in grand style, grandly, splendidly. **-moisuus** grandeur, magnificence, splendour. **-nella** magnify; *(liioitella)* exaggerate. **-nus** enlargement; magnification; *(~lasi* magnifying glass). **-nuttaa** have.. enlarged. **-taa** enlarge, widen; magnify *(m. kuv.)*; *(lisätä)* increase, raise. **-televainen**.. disposed to exaggerate. **-telu** exaggeration. **-tua** become larger (bigger); enlarge; *(lisääntyä)* increase; grow; *(laajeta)* widen, extend.

suure|sti greatly, highly; [very] much; *(melkoisesti)* considerably; *pahoittelen* ~ I

deeply regret (that). **-ta** increase [in size].
suurherttua Grand Duke. **-kunta** Grand Duchy. **-tar** Grand Duchess.
suuri great [honour, *kunnia; calamity, onnettomuus*]; *(iso)* big, large; high; *(laaja)* wide, extensive; *suureksi osaksi* to a great extent, largely; ~*n määrin* in great numbers, in great quantities; ~ *määrä* a large number; *suuret kustannukset* high costs. **-arvoinen**. . of high (great) value, very valuable. **-lukuinen** numerous. **-lukuisuus:** *niiden* ~ their great number [s]. **-luuloinen** pretentious.
suurimo: ~*t* grits, groats, hulled grain; *riisi*~*t* rice; *kaura*~*t* rolled oats.
suuri|n greatest, largest, biggest; ~ *osa* the greater part, the main part, the majority; *-mmaksi osaksi* for the most part, mostly, chiefly; *mitä -mmalla tarkkuudella (m.)* with extreme care; *-mmillaan* at its height. **-ruhtinas** Grand Duke; (~**kunta** Grand Duchy). **-ruutuinen** large-checked. **-sananainen** grandiloquent; *vrt. seur.* **-suinen** blustering,. . who talks big; *(kerskaileva)* boastful, bragging. **-suuntainen**. . on the grand level, grandiose,. . outlined on a large scale. **-töinen** laborious.
suur|jännite *sähk.* high tension. **-kaupunki** big city; metropolis; (~**lainen** inhabitant of a big city, metropolitan). **-lakko** general strike. **-lähettiläs** ambassador; *kiertävä* ~ roving a.; ~*tasolla* on an ambassadorial level. **-mestari** grand master. **-mies** great man. **-myymälä** *ks. tavaratalo.* **-piirteinen** large-minded, broad-minded; *(esim. suunnitelma)* [. . on a] grand [scale]. **-politiikka** high politics. **-pujottelu** giant slalom. **-riista** big game. **-risti** Grand Cross. **-siivous** general

[house-] cleaning. **-syömäri** big eater. **-teollisuus** large-scale industry. **-tilallinen** owner of a large farm. **-tuotanto** large-scale production. **-työ** great achievement.
suurui|nen: *jnk* ~ of the size of; *sadan markan* ~ *summa* a sum amounting to a hundred marks.
suurus thickening; *(aamiainen)* breakfast. **-taa** thicken.
suuruuden|hullu megalomaniac. **-hulluus** megalomania, illusion of grandeur.
suuruus greatness; bigness, largeness; magnitude; *(koko)* size; *(laajuus)* wideness, extent; *huoneen* ~ *(m.)* the dimensions of the room; *tuntematon* ~ unknown celebrity *(t.* quantity). **-luokka** order [of magnitude]. **-suhde** proportion.
suurvalta great power.
suutahtaa become angered, flare up.
suutari shoemaker, cobbler; *(kala)* tench; *(puhek., räjähtämätön ammus)* dud.
suute|lo kiss. **-lu** kissing.
suutin nozzle, *(pölynimurin, m.)* tool.
suuttu|a become (get, grow) angry, *jstk* at, *jkh* with a p.; be [come] annoyed (at; with a p.), *Am. puhek.* get mad (at a p.); *hän -u helposti* he is quick to take offence; *siitä -isi kuka tahansa (m.)* that is enough to vex a saint. **-mus** anger; *(harmi)* indignation. **-nut** angry, *jstk* at, *jkh* with a p., exasperated (at, about), *Am. puhek.* mad (at); annoyed (at; with a p.); *olla* ~ *(m.)* be in a huff.
suutu|s: *olla -ksissaan* be angry, be indignant [at, *jstk*]. **-ttaa** make. . angry, anger, rouse a p.'s anger; *(ärsyttää)* vex, provoke, annoy.
suuvesi mouth-wash.
suvait|a tolerate, stand, put up with; *(alentua)* condescend (to); *hän ei suvainnut vastata* he did not deign (condescend)

to answer; *jos -sette* if you please. **-sematon** intolerant. **-semattomuus** intolerance. **-sevainen** tolerant. **-sevaisuus** tolerance.
suvanto dead-water, still water.
suvereeni sovereign. **-suus** sovereignty.
suvi *(kesä)* summer.
suvu|llinen *biol.* sexual. **-njatkaminen** propagation. **-ton** asexual, sexless. **-ttomuus** sexlessness.
Sveitsi Switzerland. **s-läinen** *a. & s.* Swiss *(pl = sg.).*
syankalium potassium cyanide.
syden|polttaja charcoal-burner. **-poltto** charcoal burning.
sydämelli|nen hearty, cordial, heartfelt [congratulation]; kind; ~ *tervehdykseni (m.)* my kindest regards. **-syys** heartiness, cordiality.
sydämen|asia affair of the heart; *ottaa ~kseen* have. . much at heart. **-muotoinen** heart-shaped. **-siirto** cardiac transplantation. **-tuska** heartache. **-tykytys** heartbeat; *(nopea)* palpitation.
sydäme|ttömyys heartlessness. **-tön** heartless.
sydämistyä become angry (exasperated); fly into a passion.
sydän heart; *(puun)* pith; *(pähkinän, siemenen ym)* kernel, *(keskus)* core *(m. kuv.); (kynttilän)* wick; *laskea jk jkn sydämelle* enjoin upon a p.; *on jkn sydämellä* is near. .'s heart; *koko sydämestäni* with all my heart; *olla ~ kurkussa* have one's heart in one's mouth. **-ala** pit of the stomach, epigastrium. **-eteinen** auricle. **-halvaus** heart failure. **-juuri:** *~a myöten kauhistunut* shocked to the roots of one's being. **-kammio** ventricle [of the heart]. **-kesä** middle of the summer; midsummer; *~llä* at midsummertime, at the height of summer. **-keuhkokoje** heart-lung machine. **-kohtaus** heart attack. **-käpy** darling. **-lihas**

myocardium. **-läppä** cardiac valve. **-maa** backwoods. **-päivä** midday. **-suru** heartache. **-talvi** depth of winter, midwinter. **-tauti** heart disease. **-täsärkevä** heartbreaking. **-veri** heart['s]-blood; *(~tulppa* coronary thrombosis, myocardial (cardiac) infarction). **-vika** [organic] heart disease. **-yö** midnight; *~llä* at m.
syinen fibrous.
sykerö *(hius-)* knot.
sykintä beat[ing], pulsation.
sykkiä beat, pulsate; throb.
sykkyrä kink; *mennä ~än* kink, become kinky; *(sotkeutua)* get tangled.
syksy autumn, *Am.* fall; *~llä* in [the] autumn; *viime ~nä* last autumn; *(metsä, puut) ~n väriloistossa. .* fired by autumn tints. **-inen** autumn-like, autumnal.
sykä|hdys beat, throb. **-hdyttää** make. . beat (throb); *minua -dytti* I was thrilled. **-htää** throb; start; *sydämeni -hti* my heart jumped [at the sight, *sen nähdessäni*]. **-ys** impulse.
sylei|llä embrace; hug. **-ly** embrace.
syli 1. arms, *(helma)* lap; **2.** *(-mitta)* fathom, six feet; *(halko-, l. v.)* cord; *sulkea ~insä* clasp in one's arms; *ottaa ~insä* take. . on (in) one's lap. **-koira** lap-dog. **-kummi** godmother [who holds the baby at its christening]. **-lapsi** baby, infant. **-llinen** armful.
sylinteri cylinder. **-mäinen** cylindric[al].
sylkeä spit; expectorate.
sylki spittle; *tiet.* saliva; *(yskös)* sputum, expectoration. **-rauhanen** salivary gland.
sylky spitting. **-astia** spittoon.
syltty brawn.
sylys armful.
symbaali cymbal.
symbol|i symbol. **-iikka** symbolism. **-inen** symbolic [al]. **-(is)oida** symbolize.
symmetri|a symmetry. **-nen** symmetrical.

symp|aattinen sympathetic; *(miellyttävä)* attractive. **-atia** sympathy.

synagooga synagogue.

syndikaatti syndicate.

synkis(tyt)tää make gloomy, cast a gloom over; darken.

synkkyys gloom[iness], dreariness, bleakness; melancholy.

synkkä gloomy, dreary; *(kalsea)* bleak; *(pimeä)* dark; *(jylhä)* desolate; moody, sullen; *synkät ajatukset* gloomy (black) thoughts; *synkät pilvet* dark (lowering) clouds. **·-mielinen** melancholic. **-mielisyys** *lääk.* melancholia.

synkronoida synchronize.

synnilli|nen sinful. **-syys** sinfulness.

synnin|päästö absolution. **-tekijä** sinner. **-tunnustus** confession [of sins]. **-tunto** contrition, consciousness of one's sins.

synni|ttömyys freedom from sin. **-tön.** . free from sin, sinless.

synnyin|maa native country. **-seutu** native place, *(-paikka)* birth-place.

synnynnäinen innate, inherent, inborn, inbred; congenital [defect, *vika*]; *hän on ~ sotilas* he is a born soldier.

synny|ttäjä parturient, woman in labour; [expectant] mother. **-ttää** give birth to, be delivered of; *kuv.* give rise to, bring about, cause, arouse, create, call forth, produce, *(kehittää)* generate [heat, *lämpöä*]; *~ epäilystä* arouse suspicion; *voima ~ liikettä* energy produces motion. **-tys** delivery, childbirth; *(~laitos* maternity hospital; *~lääkäri* obstetrician; *~oppi* obstetrics; *~tuskat* labour [pains], pangs of childbirth).

synonyymi synonym. **-nen** synonymous.

synte|ettinen synthetic [al]. **-tisoida** synthe|size, -tize.

synti sin; *tehdä ~ä* sin. **-enanteeksianto** forgiveness (remission) of sins.

-inlankeemus the Fall [of man]. **-luettelo** list of sins. **-nen** *a.* sinful; *s.* sinner. **-pukki** scapegoat. **-syys** sinfulness. **-taakka** burden of sin.

synty birth; *(alkuperä)* origin, rise; *~jään suomalainen* Finnish by birth. **-inen** *(yhd.): suomalais~* .. of Finnish descent (extraction). **-isin** by birth; *(omaa sukua)* born, née; *~ venäläinen* Russian-born.

syntymä birth. **-aika** date of birth. **-kaupunki** native city (town). **-merkki** birth-mark, mole. **-paikka** place of birth. **-päivä** birthday; *parhaat onnitteluni ~si johdosta!* many happy returns! **-todistus** birth certificate. **-tön** unborn. **-vuosi** year of birth.

synty|nyt born. **-perä** origin, descent, birth; *~ltään saksalainen* of German extraction; *alhaista ~ä.* . of humble origin. **-peräinen** native; *~ amerikkalainen* a n. of America. **-sana** magic word. **-vyys** birth-rate; *-vyyden säännöstely* birth control.

synty|ä be born; be brought forth; be produced; *(saada alkunsa)* originate, arise, come into being, spring up; *-nyt vuonna.* . born in. .; *milloin hän on -nyt* when was he born? *-essään* at his birth, when he was born; *heille -i poika* a son was born to them; *-i tappelu* a fight came about, there was a fight; *-i kiusallinen vaitiolo* there was a painful silence, a painful silence ensued; *-i vihollisuus* enmity sprang up; *siitä voi ~ riita* that may give rise to a quarrel; *syntyykö siitä mitään* will anything come **õf** that?

sypressi cypress.

syrji|ntä discrimination. **-ttäin** edge|ways, -wise. **-ä** discriminate (against).

syrjä edge, border; margin; *(sivu)* side; *~än* aside; out of the way; *jäädä ~än* be ignored; be disregarded;

panna ~*än* put (lay) aside, put by; ~*ssä* aloof; *pysytellä* ~*ssä* keep at a distance (from), stand aloof (aside); *vetäytyä* ~*än* withdraw (from). **-askel** side step. **-hyppäys** *(poikkeama)* digression (from); *(esim. avioliitossa)* escapade. **-inen** out-of-the-way, outlying; *(etäinen)* remote, distant. **-isyys** out-of-the-way location; remoteness. **-katu** back street. **-kaupunki** outskirts [of the town]. **-kulma** outlying part (of). **-silmäys** sidelong glance. **-tysten** edge to edge. **-tä** edge, trim. **-yttää** oust; set aside; supersede, *(tullen itse tilalle)* displace, supplant.
sysi charcoal; *menköön syteen tai saveen* for good or ill, for better or worse. **-miilu** charcoal-pit. **-musta** coal-black, jet-black.
sysiä keep pushing, hustle, poke.
systemaattinen systematic [al].
sysä|tä push, shove; give.. a push; thrust; *(tyrkätä)* poke; ~ *kumoon* push (knock).. over, upset; ~ *luotaan* push.. away, *(kuv.)* repulse, rebuff. **-ys** push; *(työntö)* thrust; *kuv.* impetus, encouragement, impulsion; *antaa jklle* ~ prompt [a p. to..]; *-yksittäin* by fits and starts.
sytty|minen ignition; *(puhkeaminen)* outbreak. **-mätön** uninflammable. **-väinen** inflammable. **-ä** kindle, be kindled *(m. & et. kuv.)*; light, *(tuleen)* catch fire, take fire; ignite; *(leimahtaa)* burst into flames, blaze up; *(puhjeta)* break out; *talo on -nyt palamaan* the house has caught fire; *tulipalo on -nyt* a fire has broken out; *sota -i* the war broke out; *hänen vihansa -i* his anger was kindled; *puut -vät helposti* wood kindles (lights) easily.
syty|ke kindling. **-tin** *(ammuksen)* fuse, primer, *(savukkeen)* lighter. **-ttävä** inspiring, stirring. **-ttää** light, kindle *(m. kuv.)*, *(tuleen)* set

fire to, set.. on fire; *(panos ym)* fire; *tekn.* ignite; ~ *tuli* light a fire; ~ *talo tuleen* set a house on fire; ~ *piippunsa* light one's pipe; ~ *tulitikku* strike a match; ~ *sähkövalo* switch on the light. **-tys** ignition; *(~laite* igniting apparatus, igniter; ~**lanka** fuse; ~**tulppa** sparking *(Am.* spark) plug).
syven|nys depression; *(seinä-)* recess, niche, alcove. **-tyä** get engrossed in, become absorbed in, go deep into; *mietteisiinsä -tyneenä* lost in meditation, deep in thought. **-tää** make.. deeper, deepen.
syv|etä become deeper, deepen. **-yinen:** *10 jalan* ~ 10 feet deep *(t.* in depth). **-yys** depth; deep; *(kuilu)* abyss; (~**pommi** depth-charge).
syvä deep; *kuv.* profound; ~ *lautanen* soup plate; *kulkea* ~*ssä (laiva)* draw deep; ~*ssä unessa* sound asleep. **-llekäypä** *kuv.* deep, thorough-going. **-llinen** deep, profound; *(perusteellinen)* thorough. **-llisyys** depth; profundity. **-mietteinen** deep, profound. **-mietteisyys** profoundness, depth of thought. **-nmerenkalastus** deep-sea fishing. **-nne** deep place; hollow. **-paino** photo-gravure. **-satama** deep-water harbour. **-ys** draught.
syy 1. cause, *jhk* of; reason (for), occasion; *(peruste)* ground; *(vika)* fault; *mistä* ~*stä* for what reason? on what ground [s]? why? *siitä* ~*stä* for that reason, because of that, on that account; ~*stä, täydellä* ~*llä* with good reason; ~*stä tai toisesta* for some reason or other; ~*ttä* without a (any) reason, without cause; ~ *on hänessä* he is to blame, *(minussa)* it is my fault, I am to blame; *ilman omaa* ~*tään* through no fault of his own; *esittää* ~ *jhk* state the reason for; *ottaa jk* ~*kseen* bear the blame; *panna, lukea (jk) jkn*

~ksi lay the blame on a p.'s shoulders, blame a p. for, attribute (a th.) to. .; *onko ~tä* is there [good] reason to. .? *(perusteltua)* is there a case for (. . -ing)? *on hyvä ~* there is [good] reason to. ., there is a good case for (. . -ing); *minulla on ~tä.* . I have reason to. .

syy 2. *(kuitu)* fibre; filament.

syyh|elmä itch, *(kotieläimillä)* mange. **-y** itch. **-yttää** itch; *(kyhnyttää)* rub, scratch. **-yä** itch.

syylli|nen *a.* guilty; *s.* culprit, offender, the guilty person; *-seksi todistettu* convicted, *jhk* of. **-styä** *jhk* make oneself guilty of; commit [a crime etc]. **-syys** guilt; *kieltää -syytensä* deny one's guilt, plead not guilty.

syylä wart.

syyn|alainen guilty. **-takeeton** irresponsible; *hän on ~* he is not responsible (not accountable) for his actions. **-takeettomuus** irresponsibility. **-takeinen** responsible. **-takeisuus** responsibility.

syy|peräinen causal. **-pää** guilty; *olla ~ jhk* be guilty of, be to blame for.

Syyria Syria; **s-lainen** *a. & s.* Syrian.

syys|kesä late summer, latter part of the summer. **-kuu** September. **-kylvö** autumn sowing. **-lukukausi** autumn term. **-myöhä:** *~llä* late in the autumn. **-päivä** autumn day; *(~ntasaus* autumnal equinox). **-talvi** early winter.

syysuhde causality.

syyte indictment; *(oikeusjuttu)* action; prosecution; *nostaa ~ jkta vastaan* bring an action against, take legal proceedings against; *joutua syytteeseen* be prosecuted (for). **-kirjelmä** bill of indictment. **-tty** defendant, the accused.

syytteen|alainen. . charged (with),. . accused (of); *olla -alaisena* be under an indictment; *panna -alaiseksi* indict.

syy|ttäjä accuser; *lak.* prosecutor; *yleinen ~* state prosecutor, *Am.* prosecuting attorney. **-ttää** accuse, *jkta jstk* a p. of, charge (with), make (lodge) a charge (against sb. for); *lak. m.* prosecute (for); *(moittia)* blame, lay the blame (on); *syyttäkää itseänne* you have yourself to blame; *hän ~ huonoa terveyttään* he gives ill health as an excuse; *hän -tti tietämättömyyttään (m.)* he pleaded ignorance; *-tettynä jstk* on a charge of; *hän loi minuun syyttävän katseen* he glanced at me reproachfully. **-ttömyys** innocence; *vakuuttaa -ttään* protest one's innocence. **-ttömästi** innocently.

syyttää *(solvauksia ym)* heap *(t.* shower) abuse upon a p.; *(savua, saastetta)* emit, belch [forth], spew.

syy|tön free from guilt, guiltless (of); *(viaton)* innocent; *lak.* not guilty; *julistaa -ttömäksi* acquit; *-ttömäksi julistaminen* acquittal. **-tös** accusation, charge.

syö|dä eat; *(eläimistä, m.)* feed (on); *(aterioida)* have one's meals; *(kalasta)* take; *~ aamiaista (ym)* have breakfast; *~ liiaksi* overeat; *~ sanansa* break (go back on) one's word. **-jätär** gorgon; ogress.

syöksy rush; *ilm.* dive. **-hammas** tusk. **-kypärä** crash helmet. **-lasku** *urh.* downhill [race]. **-pommitus** dive bombing. **-ä** rush, dash; throw oneself; plunge [into the water, *veteen*]; topple [into a ravine, *kuiluun*]; *(tulla syöstyksi)* be thrown; fall; *lentok. auto ym.* crash; *lentokone -i pellolle* the aeroplane crashed down on to the field.

syöm|inki banquet, feast. **-älakko:** *ryhtyä ~on* go on hunger-strike. **-ätön:** *olla -ättömänä* go without eating, fast.

syöpy|ä eat [its way] into; *(kemiallisesti)* corrode, be[come] corroded (eroded); *(mieleen)* be impressed on a p.'s mind; *(esim. tavat)* become ingrained; *syvälle -nyt* deep-rooted, deep-seated, inveterate.

syöpä cancer, carcinoma. **-kasvain** cancerous growth, malignant tumour.

syöpäläiset vermin.

syöstä throw; plunge [the country into war, *valtakunta sotaan*]; ~ *jkn kimppuun* fall upon; ~ *tulta* spit (emit) fire; ~ *vallasta* overthrow; ~ *valtaistuimelta* dethrone; *vrt. syytää.*

syöstävä shuttle.

syö|tti bait; *(houkutus)* decoy; *panna syöttejä koukkuihin* bait the hooks. **-ttäjä** *urh.* feeder. **-ttää** feed *(m. tekn.): (lihottaa)* fatten; *(tennis)* serve; ~ *hevoselle heiniä* feed hay to the horse; feed the horse on hay; ~ *juttu jklle* make.. swallow a story.

syöttö feeding; *urh. (tennis)* service; *(jalkap.)* pass; *jatkuvalla syötöllä* in a steady stream, non-stop. **-elukka, -karja** cattle kept for fattening. **-laite** feeder. **-putki** feed-pipe. **-vasikka** fatted calf.

syötävä *a.* eatable, edible [mushroom, *sieni*]; *s.* food, eatables, something to eat; ~*ksi kelpaamaton* uneatable, inedible; *onko sinulla mitään* ~*ä* have you anything to eat?

syövy|ttää corrode, *(esim. vesi)* erode; *(etsata)* etch; *ruosteen -ttämä* affected by rust; *vesi -tti kannaksen poikki* the water cut (wore) a channel through the neck of land; *-ttävä* corrosive, caustic. **-tys** corrosion; etching; *(~aine* corrosive, caustic; ~**neula** etching needle.).

säde ray; beam; *mat.* radius; *toivon* ~ a ray (gleam) of hope;.. *-n säteellä* within a radius of. **-htiä** radiate, emit rays. **-hoito** radiotherapy, irradiation. **-kehä** halo. **-tys**

[ir]radiation.

säe *(rivi)* line; *(runon)* verse.

säen spark.

säes|tys accompaniment. **-täjä** accompanist. **-tää** accompany.

sähi|nä hiss[ing], wheeze. **-stä** hiss, wheeze.

sähke telegram, wire; *(kaapeli-)* cable; ~*itse* by wire. **-osoite** telegraphic address.

sähkö electricity; ~*llä käyvä* electrically operated. **-aita** electrified fence. **-asentaja** electric fitter, electrician. **-hoito** electrotherapy. **-inen** electric, electrical;.. charged with electricity. **-insinööri** electrical engineer. **-isku** electric shock. **-istys** electrification. **-istää** electrify. **-johto** electric wire; *(liitäntä-)* cord, flex; *-johdot* wiring. **-juna** electric train. **-kello** electric clock; *(soitto-)* electric bell. **-koje** electrical appliance. **-käyttöinen** electrically driven, run by electricity. **-laite: -laitteet** electric fittings. **-laitos** electric [power-]plant, electricity works. **-lamppu** electric lamp, *(hehku-)* electric bulb. **-lanka** electric wire. **-lasku** electricity bill. **-liesi** electric cooker (range, stove). **-lennätin** telegraph. **-liike** electric outfitters. **-lämmitys** electric heating. **-mittari** electricity meter. **-moottori** electric motor. **-oppi** electricity. **-parranajokone** electric shaver. **-rata** electric railway.

sähkösanoma telegram, wire. **-lomake** telegraph form. **-maksu** charge for telegram. **-nauha** tape. **-taksa** telegraph rates. **-toimisto** telegraph office.

sähkö|teitse by wire. **-tekniikka** electrical engineering. **-teknikko** electrician. **-ttäjä** [telegraph] operator; *mer.* radio officer, *puhek.* sparks. **-ttää** telegraph, wire, *(kaapelitse)* cable. **-tuoli** electric chair. **-tuuletin** electric fan. **-tys** telegraphy. **-valaistus** electric lighting. **-valo** electric

light. **-vatkain** [electric]
mixer, whisker, *(pieni)*
hand-held mixer. **-virta** electric
current. **-voima** electric power,
(vesi-) hydroelectric power.
säie *(syy)* fibre, *(köyden)*
strand, *(lanka)* filament.
säihky sparkle; lustre. **-ä** flash;
(säkenöidä) sparkle; *(säteillä)*
beam; glow; *hänen silmänsä
-ivät* her eyes were sparkling,
(tulta) her eyes flashed fire.
säi|kkyä shy, *jtk* at; be
frightened (at). **-kyttää**
frighten, scare; *(hätkähdyttää)*
startle. **-kähdy|s** fright; shock;
selvisi -ksellä got off with a
fright, was none the worse
[for the accident]. **-käh|tää**
be scared, *jtk* by, at; take
fright, be frightened; *en
milloinkaan ole niin s-tänyt* I
never had such a fright.
säiliö tank, cistern, *(suuri)*
reservoir. **-auto** tank truck,
road tanker. **-idä** store. **-laiva**
tanker. **-vaunu** tank car.
säilyke tinned *(Am.* canned)
goods. **-hedelmät** tinned fruit.
-rasia tin, *Am.* can; *~n
avaaja* tin-opener. **-tehdas**
canning factory. **-tölkki**
preserving jar, *(lasi-, m.)* glass
jar.
säily|ttää keep, store; preserve,
conserve [ancient relics,
muinaisaarteita]; retain,
maintain, sustain [friendly
relations with]; *~ järjestys*
maintain order; *~ tulevia
tarpeita varten* preserve (keep,
store) for future needs; *~
malttinsa* retain (keep) one's
composure; *~ jku (rakkaassa)
muistossa* treasure a p.'s
memory. **-tys** preservation,
conservation; maintenance;
(pankissa) [open] safe-deposit;
vietiin -tykseen went into
store; *(~aine* preservative;
~huone store-room, *(ruoan)*
pantry; *~keino* preservative,
means of preservation;
~lokero safe, *(matkatavaran)*
luggage locker). **-ä** be
preserved; *(pahentumatta)*
keep; be maintained, be
retained; *(varjeltuna)* be

safeguarded (against); *(kestää)*
last, endure; *(säästyä)* be
spared, escape [destruction,
tuholta]; *~ hengissä* escape
alive, survive; *~ nuorekkaana*
preserve one's youthful
appearance; *hyvin -nyt* well
preserved; in a good state of
preservation.
säilä blade [of a sword];
(miekk.) sabre.
säilö: *jättää ~ön
(matkatavara)* leave at the
left-luggage counter, *(esim.
turkki)* leave in storage;
varmassa ~ssä in safe
keeping; *poliisin ~ssä* in
custody. **-ä** preserve.
säkeistö stanza.
säken|e spark. **-öidä** sparkle;
scintillate; **-öivä** sparkling.
säkillinen a sack [full], *jtk* of,
bagful.
säkki sack; *(pussi)* bag; *panna
suu ~ä myöten* cut one's coat
according to one's cloth.
-kangas sacking; sackcloth.
-pilli bagpipe.
säkä *(eläimen)* withers.
säle splint[er], slat, lath. **-aita**
paling, fence. **-ikkö**
lattice [-work], trellis [-work],
(metalli-, koriste-) grille-work.
-kaihdin Venetian blind.
sälpä *miner.* spar.
sälyttää burden, load; *~ jtk
jkn niskoille (kuv.)* impose
[duties] on a p., saddle a p.
with.
sälöillä splinter.
sämpylä [French] roll.
sängyn|katos canopy. **-peite**
(päällys-) counterpane,
bedspread. **-pylväs** bedpost.
sänki stubble.
sänky bed, bedstead. **-huopa**
blanket. **-vaatteet** bedding;
bed-clothes.
sänti|lleen *ks.* täsmälleen.
-llinen punctual; regular;
(tarkka) exact, precise. **-llisyys**
punctuality, precision.
säppi latch; clasp; *panna ~in*
latch.
säpsäh|tää give a start, be
startled (at), start; **-din** *(kun
hän..)* he gave me a start. .
säpäle splinter, shiver; *on ~inä*

is [all] in pieces; *mennä*
~*iksi* be smashed to pieces
(*puhek.* to smithereens).
säristä rattle, crack.
särkeä break, (*murskata*)
smash, *et. kuv.* shatter;
päätäni särkee my head is
aching, I have a headache; ~
ovi break [down] a door; ~
jnk suunnitelmat ruin (spoil)
a p.'s plans.
särki *zo.* roach.
särkkä (*hiekka-*) ridge of sand,
dune; (*vedessä*) [sand-]bank.
särky ache, pain.
särky|mätön umbreakable.
-tabletti *puhek.* pain-killer.
-vyys fragility. **-vä** fragile,
brittle.
särky|ä break, be broken;
(*pirstaksi*) go to pieces, be
shattered, (*haljeta*) crack;
burst; (*musertua*) be crushed;
~*nyt ääni* cracked voice; ~*nyt
onni* wrecked (shattered)
happiness; *heidän välinsä -i*
their relations were severed.
särmi|käs angular; jagged. **-ö**
prism; (~*mäinen* prismatic).
särmä edge. **-inen** angular;
(*yhd.*) -edged. **-isyys** angularity.
särähtää give a crack[ing
sound], crack.
särö crack, fissure, (*vika*) flaw.
-inen cracked.
sätei|llä radiate, *kuv. m.* beam;
-levän iloinen radiant
(beaming) with joy. **-ly**
radiation, *kuv.* radiance;
(~*suojaus* protection against
radiation; ~*ttää* irradiate;
~*tys* irradiation; **-valvonta**
radiation control). **-täinen**
radial; radiate.
sätky|nukke marionette, puppet.
-tellä struggle [to get free],
(*esim. kala*) flounder [in the
net, *verkossa*]; (*kiemurrella*)
wriggle. **-ttely** wriggling.
sätkä hand-rolled cigarette.
-kone roll-your-own-cigarette
machine.
sättiä scold, upbraid.
sävel tone; (*sävelmä*) tune,
melody. **-askel** tone. **-asteikko**
[musical] scale. **-järjestelmä**
tonality. **-korkeus** pitch. **-kulku**
intonation. **-laji** key. **-lys**

[musical] composition. **-mä**
piece of music, melody, air.
-taide [art of] music.
-taiteilija musician. **-täjä**
composer. **-tää** compose; (*jk*)
set.. to music, write [the]
music (for).
sävy (*äänen ym*) tone;
(*vivahdus*) tint, touch; (*säväys*)
flavour; ~*ltään tummempi*
darker in tone; *määrätä jnk*
~ set the tone (for). **-isyys**
quiet disposition; tractability,
docility, gentleness. **-isä**
even-tempered; tractable,
manageable, docile; meek,
mild.
säväh|tää flinch; *hänen
sydämensä -ti* her heart
jumped; *katsomo -ti* the
audience thrilled; *-ti
punaiseksi* blushed suddenly.
säynävä *zo.* ide.
säyse|ys gentleness; quietness.
-ä gentle; quiet; meek;
(*mukautuva*) compliant;
(*hyväntapainen*) well-behaved.
sää weather; *kauniilla* ~*llä* in
fine weather; *olipa* ~
millainen tahansa in any
weather; ~*n salliessa* weather
permitting.
säädylli|nen decent; (*sopiva*)
proper, decorous;
(*kunniallinen*) respectable.
-syys decency, propriety; tact;
respectability; *loukata -syyttä*
outrage public decency.
säädy|ttömyys indecency,
impropriety; immodesty. **-tön**
indecent, improper, immodest;
(*sivistymätön*) unseemly,
unmannerly.
säädös edict, decree; (*laki-*)
statute, act, provision of the
law.
sää|ennuste weather forecast.
-havainto meteorogical
observation. **-kartta** weather
chart. **-katsaus** weather report.
sääli pity (for), compassion;
minun on ~ *häntä* I pity
him, I feel sorry for him; *on*
~ *häntä* he is to be pitied;
~*stä häntä kohtaan* out of
pity for him; *olisi* ~ *lähteä*
it would be a pity to go;
~*ttä* pitilessly, without pity.

-mättömyys uncharitableness, lack of pity; hardness. **-mättömästi** pitilessly, mercilessly; cruelly. **-mätön** pitiless, uncharitable; *(armoton)* unmerciful, merciless; ruthless, relentless; ~ *kohtalo* unmerciful (hard, cruel) fate. **-ttävyys** pitifulness; miserableness. **-ttävä** pitiful, piteous, pitiable; *(henkilöstä, m.)*.. to be pitied; *(kurja)* miserable, wretched. **-ttää** arouse pity; *hän* ~ *minua* I pity him, I feel sorry for him. **-väinen** pitying,.. full of pity; compassionate. **-väisyys** pity, compassion. **-ä** pity, take pity, *jkta* on, feel pity (for); *(armahtaa)* have mercy (on); *(säästää)* spare; **-västi** pityingly; with pity; **-kää** *meitä* have compassion (pity) on us.

säämiskä chamois, shammy leather.

sään|ennustaja weather prophet. **-muutos** change of weather. **säännellä** regulate, adjust. **säännölli|nen** regular; *(järjestystä noudattava)* orderly; *-sissa oloissa* under normal conditions; *asiain* ~ *meno* due course of things; *-sin väliajoin* at regular intervals. **-sesti** regularly; as a rule; normally. **-syys** regularity; normal state. **säännön|mukainen** regular; normal; *(asianmukainen)* due. **-vastainen**.. contrary to the rule [s]; ~ *peli t. isku* foul. **säännö|s** regulation; provision [of the law]. **-stellä** regulate; *(elintarvikkeita ym)* ration. **-stely** rationing; ~*n alainen* rationed. **-ttömyys** irregularity. **-tön** irregular; *(tavallisuudesta poikkeava)* abnormal. **sääntö** rule; *(säännös)* regulation; *on yleisenä* ~*nä* it is a generally accepted rule; *säännöt (yhdistyksen)* rules of orders, constitution [and standing orders]; ~*jen mukainen*.. in accordance with the rules. **-määräinen** statutory. **-perintö** entail.

sääoppi meteorology.
sääri leg; shank; *(pohje)* calf. **-luu** shin-bone, tibia.
säärys, -tin gaiter, legging.
sääski gnat; *(hyttynen)* mosquito. **-harso** mosquito-net. **-parvi** swarm of mosquitoes.
sääste|liäs economizing. **-llä** economize, *jtk* with; be sparing (of); ~ *(voima)varojaan* husband one's resources.
sääs|tyä be saved, be left over; *(tulla varjelluksi)* be spared, be preserved (from); escape [infection, *tartunnalta*]. **-täväinen** economical; thrifty; sparing, chary [of words, *sanoissaan*]; careful [with one's money]. **-täväisyys** economy; thrift [iness]. **-tää** save; *(säälitellen)* spare; *(olla säästeliäs)* economize; *(koota)* save up, *(varata)* reserve, keep; ~ *voimiaan* conserve one's energies; ~ *jku huolista* spare a p. concern; *ei -tä ylistystään* is not sparing with praise; *-täen* economically; sparingly; *-tä henkeni!* spare my life! *vaivojaan -tämättä* sparing no pains. **-tö** saving[s]; *(jäännös)* balance; *panna* ~*ön* save [up]; (~*liekki* pilot light *t.* burner); ~*lipas* savings box, money-box; ~*pankki* savings bank; ~*tili* savings account; ~*varat* savings).
säästöön|panija depositor. **-pano** *(talletus)* deposit.
sää|suhteet weather conditions. **-tiedotus** weather report.
säätiö foundation; endowment.
sääty *(asema)* station, position; *(luokka)* class; *(arvo)* rank; *(valtio-)* estate. **-ennakkoluulo** class prejudice. **-erotus** class distinction. **-henkilö** person of rank.
säätää prescribe; *(määrätä)* direct; *tekn.* regulate, adjust; ~ *lakeja* make *(t.* enact) laws; *ihminen päättää, Jumala* ~ man proposes, God disposes; *kuten laki* ~ as the law directs; *lain säätämässä järjestyksessä* in the order

prescribed by law; *säädettävä* adjustable, [automatically] controlled; *säädetty nopeus* regulation speed.

säätö regulation, adjustment.

-laite adjuster, control device; *rad.* tuning device; *-laitteet* controls. **-vipu** control lever.

söpö *Am.* cute; *eikö hän ole ~?* isn't she a darling?

Š

ks. **S**

T

taaj|a thick, dense; *-oissa riveissä* in close ranks; *-aan asuttu* densely (thickly) populated. **-ama** densely populated community. **-aväkinen** ks. ed. **-uus** denseness; *tekn. ym* frequency.

taakka burden; load; *(paino)* weight.

taakse *(jnk)* behind. ., *(tuolle puolen)* beyond; *asettua jkn ~ (kuv.)* back; *katsoa ~en* look back, look behind one. **-päin** backward [s], back; *ajassa ~ ulottuva* retrospective; *(~meno* going backward, backward movement, *kuv. m.* decline).

taannehti|a retroact. **-va** retroactive, *vrt.* takautuva.

taannoi|n not a very long time ago. **-nen** past, bygone; recent.

taan|nuttaa set back; keep back, *(estää)* impede. **-tua** suffer a set-back; *(huonontua)* decline; *olla -tumassa* be on the decline. **-tuminen** retrogression. **-tumuksellinen** reactionary. **-tumus** reaction, set-back, *(taloudellinen)* recession, *(huononeminen)* decline; *(~suunta* reactionary tendency). **-tuva** retrogressive, declining.

taapert|aa toddle, *(hanhi)* waddle. **-aja** toddler.

taara tare; dead weight.

taas again; *(uudelleen)* anew, afresh; *(kerta vielä)* once more; *(sitä vastoin)* on the other hand; *kun ~* while; whereas. **-kin** again, once more.

taata guarantee, *(harvemmin)* warrant; *(mennä takuuseen)* give (furnish) a guarantee; *(varmistaa)* ensure; *sen takaan* I guarantee that; I assure you that; *en voi ~ tiedon*

todenperäisyyttä I cannot vouch for the truth of the statement;. . *takasi hänelle toimeentulon.* . assured him a livelihood.

taateli date. **-palmu** date-palm.

taattu guaranteed, warranted; *(turvattu)* safe; *(luotettava)* reliable, trustworthy.

taatusti assuredly;. . *ovat ~ oikeita* are guaranteed (warranted) genuine.

tabletti tablet.

tabu taboo.

tadikko fork.

tae 1. *(sepän-)* blacksmith's work. **2.** *(vakuus)* guarantee, guaranty; *antaa takeita jstk* guarantee; *hankkia takeet* provide sureties; *henki-vakuutus voi olla lainan takeena* a life-insurance policy can serve as security for a loan.

taem|maksi, -pana farther back, farther behind.

tafti taffeta.

taha|llaan on purpose, purposely; *(aikomuksella)* intentionally; *(harkiten)* deliberately. **-llinen** intentional; *(harkittu)* deliberate, purposeful, wilful [murder, murha]. **-nsa** ever; *kuinka paljon ~* however much, no matter how much; *kuka ~* anybody, *(jokainen joka)* whoever; *olkoon hän kuka ~* whoever he may be, no matter who he is; *mikä ~* whichever, whatever; *missä ~* anywhere, [in] any place; *minne ~ hän meneekin.* . wherever he goes. .; *olipa se miten hyvä ~* however good it is, be it ever so good. **-ton** unintentional, unpremeditated; involuntary.

tahdas paste.

tahdi|kas tactful, discreet. **-kkuus** tact[fulness], discretion. **-ton** tactless; indiscreet, inconsiderate. **-ttomuus** tactlessness, lack of tact.

tahdon|ilmaus manifestation of will. **-lujuus, -voima** strength of will, will-power; volition. **-ponnistus** effort of will.

tahdoton involuntary; ~ *välikappale jkn käsissä* a mere tool in the hands of.

tahko (*-kivi*) grindstone, whetstone. **-kone** grinding-machine. **-ta** grind.

tahm|a coating. **-ainen** sticky, (*kieli*) coated. **-ea** sticky, viscid, viscous. **-eus** stickiness, viscidity.

tahna paste.

taho (*suunta*) direction, quarter; *joka ~lta* from every quarter; *jkn (henkilön) ~lta* [*esim.* unkind treatment] at the hands of. **-kas:** *moni~* polyhedron.

tahra stain, spot, (*esim. muste-*) blot (*kaikki m. kuv.*); (*et. rasva-*) smear; (*maali-ym.*) daub; *kuv. m.* blemish, taint, flaw. **-amaton** unstained, unsoiled. **-antua** become stained (soiled). **-inen** stained. **-npoistoaine** stain remover.

tahra|ta stain, soil, *kuv. m.* taint; (*liata*) dirty; smear; ~ *maineensa* disgrace oneself. **-ton** spotless; untainted, unblemished, *kuv. m.* immaculate.

tahti time; *mus. m.* measure, bar; (*nopeus*) tempo; (*kävely-*) step; *tahdissa* in time; in step; *lyödä, viitata ~a* beat time; *pysyä tahdissa* keep time; *soiton tahdissa* in time with the music; *joutua pois tahdista* get out of time (of step). **-jako** measure. **-kello** metronome. **-laji** time. **-viiva** bar-line. **-puikko** baton.

tahto will, (*toivomus*) wish; *hyvä* ~ good will; good intention[s]; *hänen viimeinen ~nsa* his last wish; *viedä ~nsa perille* get one's way, have one's [own] way; *omasta tahdostaan* of one's own accord. **-a** want; wish, desire; (*olla halukas*) be willing (to + inf.); (*tehdä mieli*) like; (*aikoa*) intend; *tahdon* (*m.*) I will; ~ *lisää* want some more; *-en tai -mattani* whether I will or no[t], whether I wanted or not; *-mattani* unintentionally, not meaning to [do it]; *-isin, että jäisit* I should like you to stay; *tahtoisitteko antaa minulle.* . [would you] please give me. ., may I trouble you for. .; *-isin ennemmin jäädä kotiin* I would rather stay at home; *hän tietää mitä hän ~o* (*m.*) he knows his own mind; *jos tahdot* if you like, if you wish [it]; *tee miten tahdot* do as you like (please, wish, want)! [you can] suit yourself! *puut eivät tahdo palaa* the firewood won't burn.

tai or; *olipa suuri ~ pieni* be it large or small, whether great or small.

taide art. **-aarre** art treasure. **-arvo** artistic value. **-esine** work of art. **-historia** history of art. **-kauppa** art dealer's. **-kauppias** art dealer. **-kokoelma** art collection. **-koulu** art school. **-lasi** art glass. **-maalari** artist, painter. **-museo** art gallery. **-nautinto** artistic enjoyment. **-näyttely** art exhibition. **-ompelu** art needlework. **-teollisuus** arts and crafts, crafts and design. **-teos** work of art.

taido|kas skilful; elaborate; *-kkaasti tehty* beautifully made. **-kkuus** skill; elaborateness. **-nnäyte** specimen of skill. **-ton** unskilful.

taika magic, witchcraft; (*lumous*) charm, spell. **-esine** fetish. **-huilu** magic flute. **-isku:** *kuin ~sta* as if by magic, like magic. **-kalu** charm, talisman, amulet. **-keino:** *~lla* by magic. **-sauva** magic wand. **-temppu**

conjuring trick. **-usko(isuus)** superstition. **-uskoinen** superstitious. **-varpu** divining(dowsing)-rod. **-voima** magic [power].

taikina dough; *(ohukais- ym.)* batter; *(tahdas)* paste. **-mainen** doughy. **-marja** alpine currant.

taikka *ks. tai.*

taik|oa conjure, use magic, practise witchcraft. **-uri** magician, sorcerer, wizard; *(temppujen tekijä)* conjurer. **-uus** magic; *(noituus)* witchcraft, sorcery.

taimen trout.

taimi seedling, *(vesa)* sprout, *(puun)* sapling. **-lava** [garden-] frame, nursery bed, seed bed. **-sto, -tarha** nursery.

tainnos: *olla tainnoksissa* be unconscious; *mennä tainnoksiin* faint, *(»sammua»)* pass out. **-tila** [state of] unconsciousness.

taipale stretch [of road], distance; *(matka)* way; *lähteä ~elle* set out, set off [on a journey]; *olla ~ella* be on the road; *elämän ~* course of life.

taipu|a bend; *(koukistua)* bow; curve; turn [down, *alas*]; *(mukautua)* comply [with a p.'s wishes, *jkn tahtoon*]; *(alistua)* submit (to); *(antaa perään)* give way, yield (to); *(suostua)* give in; agree (to); *kiel.* be inflected, *(verbi)* be conjugated, *(subst.)* be declined; *~ kohtaloonsa* resign oneself to one's fate; *hän ei -nut tekemään sitä* he could not be persuaded (prevailed upon) to do it. **-isa** flexible, pliable, pliant [nature, *luonne*]; *(notkea)* lithe; supple. **-isuus** flexibility, pliability. **-maton** inflexible; *et. kuv.* unyielding, unbending; immovable; intractable, inexorable; *kiel.* indeclinable. **-matto|muus** inflexibility; *hänen -muutensa* his uncompromising nature.

taipu|mus inclination (to), aptitude (for); *(lahjat)* talent (for); tendency; *-mukset (m.)*

leanings; *~ jhk tautiin* predisposition to a disease; *hänellä on ~ta laiskuuteen* he is inclined to laziness; *olla ~ta jhk (m.)* feel drawn to; *hänellä on soitannollisia -muksia* she has musical talent. **-vainen** disposed, inclined (to), *(halukas)* willing, ready; *(altis)* prone, liable (to); *olla ~ jhk (m.)* feel inclined to. **-vaisuus** disposition, inclination; willingness, readiness; tendency (to), leaning (towards).

taiste|lija fighter, combatant. **-lla** fight (with, against), battle (against); contend [with difficulties, *vaikeuksia vastaan*]; *(kamppailla)* struggle; *~ jtk vastaan (m.)* combat [diseases, *tauteja vastaan*].

taistelu fight; struggle; *(sota-)* battle; action; *~ elämästä ja kuolemasta* life-and-death struggle; *ryhtyä ~un* engage the enemy. **-halu** desire to fight. **-haluinen** *.* combative; militant. **-harjoitus** manoeuvre. **-henki** fighting spirit; morale. **-joukot** combat troops. **-järjestys** order of battle. **-kaasu** war gas. **-kenttä, -tanner** battlefield. **-kinnas** gauntlet. **-koske|tus:** *joutua -tukseen* establish contact (with). **-laiva** battleship. **-rintama** line of battle, *(sota-)* front. **-toveri** companion-in-arms. **-voimat** fighting forces. **-välineosasto** ordnance department.

taitaa *(osata)* know; *(kyetä)* be able (to); *(apuverbi)* is likely (to); *hän ~ useita kieliä* he has command (complete mastery) of several languages; *~ (niin) olla* it may be so, I think so; *(Onko hän täällä? —) Ei taida olla* I think not.

taita|maton unskilful, unskilled, incompetent, *(tottumaton)* inexperienced; *(kömpelö)* clumsy, a poor hand, poor (at); *jtk ~* not familiar with, knowing no. ., ignorant of; *(jtk)* kieltä ~ unable to speak. . **-mattomuus** lack of skill, incompetence; inexperience, clumsiness. **-va** skilful, skilled [in one's trade, *ammatissaan*], proficient; *(näppärä)* clever (at), handy; *(mestari)* expert (in, at); ~ *ammattimies* an able craftsman; *olla ~ jssk (m.)* be [very] good at. . **-vasti** skilfully, with skill; capably; cleverly. **-vuus** skill; [great] ability, proficiency; dexterity; expertness.

taite *(laskos)* fold; *uuden ajan taitteessa* at the dawn of a new era; *vuosisadan taitteessa* at the turn of the century.

taiteelli|nen artistic. **-sesti** artistically. **-suus** artistic quality, artistry.

taiteen|arvostelija art critic. **-harrastaja** amateur in art; *(-ystävä)* lover of art. **-suosija** patron of art. **-tuntija** connoisseur [of art].

taiteilija artist. **-luonne:** *hän on ~* he has an artistic temperament. **-nero** artistic genius. **-nimi** stage name. **-tar** [woman] artist.

taite|katto curb roof, mansard roof. **-kohta** turning-point. **-lehtinen** folder.

taito skill; *(kyky)* ability; *puhek.* know-how, *(tieto)* knowledge; *(hyvä)* proficiency (in); *kielen ~* knowledge of a language; *taidolla* skilfully, with skill. **-inen:** *hän on suomenkielen ~* he knows Finnish, he speaks Finnish; *hän on kirjoitus~* he can write. **-lento** stunt flying. **-lentäjä** stunt airman. **-luistelu** figure skating. **-parsinta** invisible mending. **-voimistelija** equilibrist, acrobat.

taittaa break; *(kääntää)* fold; *kirjap.* make up [into pages]; ~ *kokoon* fold up; ~ *valoa* refract the light.

taitto *kirjap.* make-up, making up; *(kuvalehden)* lay-out. **-vedos** page proof. **-vika** *lääk.* error of refraction.

taittu|a break [off], be broken; *(valosta)* be refracted. **-ma** break. **-minen** *(valon)* refraction.

taitur|i virtuoso; master; *viulu~* virtuoso on the violin. **-illinen** masterly, skilful. **-uus** virtuosity; mastery; *(taito)* skill; ~, *jolla se suoritettiin* its masterly execution.

taivaa|llinen heavenly; celestial; *ei tuon -llista* nothing whatever.

taivaan|kansi firmament. **-kappale** heavenly body. **-napa** zenith. **-ranta** horizon. **-sininen** azure, skye-blue. **-vuohi** *zo.* common snipe.

taivaaseenastuminen ascension.

taival *ks.* taipale; *katkaisi (100 km)* taipaleen covered a distance of. . **-taa** journey; wander.

taivas sky, skies; heaven; *kehua maasta taivaaseen* praise to the skies; *pudota taivaalta* drop from the skies; *taivaan ja maan luoja* maker of heaven and earth. **-alla, -alle** in the open air, out of doors.

taive bend; fold.

taivu|tella try to persuade; ~ *jkta tuumiinsa* try to influence a p. in favour of one's plans. **-ttaa** bend; *(kaarelle)* bow; *kuv.* induce, persuade; *kiel.* inflect, *(verbejä)* conjugate, *(nomineja)* decline; ~ *jku tekemään jtk* persuade (induce) a p. to do sth.; *-tettu* curved. **-ttelu** *kuv.* persuasion. **-tus** bending; *kiel.* inflexion, inflection, *(nominien)* declension, *(verbien)* conjugation; (~**luokka** class; declension; ~**muoto** inflexion [al form]; ~**pääte** inflexion).

taju consciousness; *olla ~issaan* be conscious; *palata ~ihinsa* recover consciousness, come round; *huumorin~* sense of humour. **-nta** consciousness; *(käsitys)* conception, comprehension, apprehension. **-ta** realize, grasp, comprehend, apprehend; *(esim. soitantoa)*

have a taste for; *hän -si
aseman heti ensi silmäyksellä*
he grasped (took in) the
situation at a glance. **-ton**
unconscious, senseless,
insensible. **-ttava**
comprehensible; intelligible.
-ttomuus unconsciousness.
taka- *(yhd.)* back, rear; hind.
takaa from behind; from the
back (rear); *voimainsa ~* with
all one's strength; *ajaa ~*
pursue; *omasta ~* on one's
own; *.. on jtk omasta ~* is
self-supporting in.. **-ajaja**
pursuer. **-ajo** pursuit; chase.
takaaja guarantor; *olla jkn
~na* stand surety (security)
for.
taka-ajatus ulterior thought *(t.
motive)*. **-ala** background.
takaapäin from the back, from
behind; *sot.* in the rear.
taka|hammas back tooth;
molar. **-inen:** *talon ~ pelto*
the field behind the house;
rajan-.. situated beyond the
frontier; *atlantin~* transatlantic.
takaisin back; *(verbien yht.
usein)* re-; *maksaa ~* pay
back, repay, refund,
reimburse, *(kostaa)* retaliate;
saada ~ get back, recover;
regain; *tulla ~* come back,
return; *tulen heti ~* I shall
be back presently. **-kutsu**
recall. **-maksu** repayment,
reimbursement, refund[ing].
taka|isku set-back; *(moottorin)*
back kick. **-istuin** back seat.
-jalka hind leg; *nousta
-jaloilleen* rear. **-kohtainen**
kiel. relative. **-listo** hinterland.
-lukossa double locked. **-maa**
remote district. **-na** behind; at
the back; *hänellä on ~an..*
he is backed by..; *mitä siinä
on ~* what is at the bottom
of that? **-osa** back. **-ovi** back
door, rear entrance. **-paju:**
jäädä ~lle be left behind, get
behindhand; *olla ~lla* be
backward, be behind [in
one's work, *työssään*].
-pajuinen backward;
underdeveloped. **-perin**
backward[s]; *viikko ~* a
week ago *(t.* back). **-peroinen**

wrong, backward, absurd,
perverted. **-peroisesti** the
wrong way. **-peroisuus**
perverseness. **-piha** back yard.
-portti rear entrance; back
door *(m. kuv.); kuv.* loophole.
-puoli back; *(kääntö-)* reverse
side; *(ihmisen)* seat, posterior,
behind, *(eläimen)* hind
quarters. **-pyörä** back (rear)
wheel. **-raajat** hind legs.
-raivo back of the head,
occiput. **-rivi** back row. **-sivu**
back page. **-talvi** return of
winter, winter weather in
spring. **-tasku** hip-pocket.
taka|us security, surety,
guarantee; *(oikeus-)* bail; *vrt.
takuu; mennä -ukseen jkn
puolesta, jstk (oikeudessa)* go
bail for; *olla jklle -uksessa*
stand surety for; *saada laina
-usta vastaan* obtain a loan
on security; *hänet vapautettiin
~ta vastaan* he was released
on bail. **-mies** surety, security.
-sitoumus guarantee. **-summa**
guarantee.
takau|(tu)ma *elok.* flashback.
-tuva retrograde; *maksetaan
~sti* will be back-dated
[to *.. jstk lähtien*].
taka|valo rear *(t.* tail) light.
-varikko confiscation, seizure;
ottaa ~on confiscate, seize.
-varikoida *ks. ed.;
(sotilastarkoituksiin)*
commandeer.
taker|tua get stuck, stick (in),
fasten (in *t.* to); *~ kurkkuun*
stick in the throat; *hänen
takkinsa -tui koneen rattaisiin*
his coat caught in the wheels
of the engine; *kertaakaan
-tumatta (kuv.)* without once
getting stuck; *~ halukkaasti
(jkn virheeseen)* leap at.
takia: *jnk ~* for..the sake of,
(vuoksi) because of, on
account of; *sen ~* for that
reason, *(johdosta)* in
consequence of that; *hänen
~an* for his sake, on his
account; *sairauden ~* owing
to illness; by reason of
illness.
takiainen bur [r] *(m. kuv.)*,
burdock.

takila rig [ging], tackle; *riisua* ~ strip (dismantle) a ship.

takimmainen hindmost,. . farthest back,. . farthest behind.

takinkaulus coat collar.

takka fireplace; hearth. **-valkea:** *~n ääressä* by the fireside.

takki coat; *(lyhyt, m.)* jacket.

takkirauta pig iron.

takku shag; *olla takussa* be shaggy, be tangled. **-inen** shaggy, tangled. **-isuus** shagginess.

tako|a *(rautaa)* forge; *(vasaroida)* hammer; *(hakata)* beat; *(nyrkeillä)* pound, pommel; ~ *silloin kun rauta on kuumaa* strike while the iron is hot; *taottava* malleable. **-mateos** article of wrought iron. **-mo** forge. **-rauta** wrought iron.

taksa rate [s], tariff; *halvan ~n aikana* when the cheap rate is on.

taksi taxi [-cab], cab; *mennä ~lla* go by t., take a t.; *tilata* ~ call a t., phone for a t. **-asema** taxi-(cab-) rank, *Am.* taxi-stand. **-mies** taxi-driver.

taksoi|ttaa assess (at), rate; estimate. **-tus** assessment; (~**lautakunta** assessment committee; ~**mies** assessor).

takt|iikka tactics; policy. **-ikko** tactician. **-ikoida** manoeuvre. **-illinen** tactical.

takuu guarantee *vrt. takaus; antaa* ~ furnish a g.; *~ta vastaan* on security; *kellosta on* ~ there is a guarantee on the watch.

tali tallow. **-kynttilä** tallow candle. **-rauhanen** sebaceous gland. **-tiainen** great tit.

talja *mer.*. [lifting] block; *(vuota)* pelt, *run.* fleece.

talkki talc; talcum powder.

talkoot work party, *(esim. rakennus-)* house-building bee.

tallata trample, tread (on, upon), tread. . down; ~ *jalkoihinsa* trample under foot.

talle|lla left. **-lokero** safe deposit box. **-ntaa** preserve; *(ääninauhalle t.* **-levylle)**

record. **-ssa:** *hyvässä* ~ in safe keeping. **-ttaa** *(pankkiin)* deposit; *vrt. tallentaa; ~ jtk jkn huostaan* lodge with sb. **-ttaja** depositor. **-tus** deposit; (~**korko** interest rate on deposits; ~**tili** deposit account; ~**todistus** deposit receipt).

talli stable. **-renki** groom, stable | man (-boy).

tallustaa tramp; *(vaivalloisesti)* trudge [along, *eteenpäin*], plod [on].

talo house, *(iso, kerros-)* block of flats, *Am.* apartment block; *(maa-)* farm. **-llinen** [owner-] farmer.

talon|emäntä housewife, lady of the house. **-isäntä** *(vuokra-)* landlord; *(talollinen)* farmer, peasant proprietor. **-mies** caretaker, *et. Am.* janitor. **-omistaja** house-owner. **-poika** peasant; farmer. **-poikainen** country [-], peasant, rustic.

talonpoikais|kieli rustic speech. **-talo** farm [-house]. **-vaimo** peasant woman. **-väestö** peasantry; agricultural population; farmers.

taloudelli|nen economic; financial; *(säästäväinen)* economical. **-sesti** economically. **-suus** economy.

talouden|hoitaja manager, steward, *(nainen)* housekeeper. **-hoito** economy; management; *vrt. seur.* **-pito** housekeeping.

talous economy; *(yksityinen)* household, house; *pitää taloutta* keep house. **-apulainen** domestic help. **-arvio** budget. **-askare:** *~et* domestic duties. **-elämä** economy; economic life. **-huoli:** *~huolet* household cares. **-kalu** household utensil. **-kone** household appliance; *(yleis-)* mixer. **-koulu** housekeeping school. **-käsineet** *tav.* rubber gloves. **-lama** depression. **-mies** economist. **-opettaja** home economist. **-oppi** economics. **-politiikka** economic policy. **-pula** economic crisis. **-rahat** household allowance.

-raken|nus: *-nukset* offices.
-sprii *l.v.* methylated spirits.
-tavarat household articles
(goods). **-tiede** economics.
-tieteellinen economic.
-tieteilijä economist. **-työ**
housework. **-yhteisö** economic
community; *Euroopan* ~ the
Common Market, EEC.
talteen: *panna* ~ put away,
store [up]; *ottaa* ~ take care
of, keep; ~ *otettu* found.
taltata, taltta chisel.
taltioida *(nauhalle)* record.
talttu|a abate, subside, go
down; *(kesyttyä)* be tamed.
-maton untamable, tameless.
taltuttaa *(tyynnyttää)* quiet[en],
calm, make. , subside; *(hillitä)*
check; tame.
talu|ttaa lead [by the hand,
kädestä]; *koiria on -tettava*
hihnassa dogs must be led.
-tushihna dog lead. **-tusnuora**
leading-string; *kulkea (naisen)*
~ssa be tied to a woman's
apron-strings.
talvehtia winter, spend (pass)
the winter; *(säilyä)* survive
[the winter] ; *t-iva (kasvi)*
hardy.
talvi winter; *talvella* in [the]
w., during the w.; *viime*
talvena last w. **-asunto** winter
residence; winter quarters.
-kausi winter; winter season;
-kaudet throughout the winter.
-nen wintry, winter.
-olympialaiset Winter
Olympics. **-omena** winter
apple. **-pakkanen** severe cold;
-pakkasilla during the cold
spells in winter. **-puku** winter
dress. **-puutarha** conservatory.
-päivä winter ['s] day;
(~nseisaus) winter solstice).
-rengas snow tyre. **-sin** in
winter, in the winter-time.
-säilö: *panna ~ön* put away
for the winter; *~ssä* in
winter storage. **-takki** winter
coat. **-tamineet** winter clothes,
winter outfit. **-tela:** *panna*
-teloille lay up for the
winter; *olla -teloilla* be laid
up for the winter [season].
-uni winter sleep, hibernation;
maata -unessa hibernate.

-urheilu winter sports.
tamburiini tambourine.
tamineet equipment; outfit.
tamma mare. **-varsa** filly.
tammenterho acorn.
tammi oak; *ks. -peli.* **-kuu**
January. **-lauta** draughtboard.
-nen oak,. . of oak, oaken.
-peli draughts, *Am.* checkers.
-puu oak.
tanakka thick-set, sturdy;
(jäykkä) rigid, *(vahva)* heavy,
strong; steady; substantial
[meal, *ateria*]. **-rakenteinen**
[person] of heavy body-build.
tanhu [folk] dance.
tankata refuel; *(änkyttää)*
stammer; *(vatvoa)* keep saying
or asking; nag; *(päähänsä)*
pound into one's head.
tankki tank; *täyttää* ~ refuel;
täyttäkää ~ fill her up. **-laiva**
tanker. **-vaunu** tank car.
tanko pole; rod; *(sauva)* staff;
(saippua- ym) bar, *(lakka-*
ym) stick.
tanner field; *(maa)* ground.
Tanska Denmark. **t-lainen** *a.*
Danish; *s.* Dane. **t-n kieli**
Danish. **t-tar** Danish woman.
tanssi, *~t* dance. **-a** dance;
mennä -maan go dancing;
~taanko? shall we dance?
-aiset dance, *(suuremmat)*
ball; *koulu~ (Am.)* prom.
-aispuku ball dress. **-askel**
dance step. **-ja, -jatar** dancer.
-koulu dancing-school. **-lava**
dance hall. **-mestari** expert
dancer. **-nopettaja** dancing
master *(fem.* mistress). **-sali**
ballroom. **-sävelmä** dance
tune. **-ttaa** *(jkta)* dance with.
tantieemi percentage of (share
in) profits.
taonta forging.
tapa manner, way, fashion;
custom, *(tottumus)* habit;
usage, *(käytäntö)* practice;
mode; *tähän ~an* in this way
(manner), thus, like this, this
way; *suomalaiseen ~an* in
Finnish fashion; *sillä tavalla*
in that way, thus, so; *tavalla*
tai toisella some way or
other, in one way or another;
ei millään tavoin by no
means; *kaikin tavoin* in every

[possible] way; *minulla on ∼na.* . I usually. .; *minulla oli ∼na* I used to. .; *oliko sinulla ∼na.* . used you to. .? *on ∼na* it is customary, it is the custom (of *jkn); heillä on ollut ∼na* their practice has been; *kuten on ∼na sanoa* as the saying is; *ottaa tavaksi* make a habit of (. . -ing); *tulla tavaksi* become a habit; *olen ottanut tavaksi nousta aikaisin* I make it a rule to rise early; *tavaksi tullut* customary, established; *∼ni mukaan* true to my habit; *paha ∼* bad habit; *hienot tavat* refined (polished) manners; *hyvät tavat* good manners; *(se) on vastoin hyviä tapoja* it is bad form; *tavan takaa* every now and then, time after time.

tapah|tua happen, occur, take place; *(sattua)* come to pass, come about; *-tui mitä -tui* whatever happens, come what may; *on -tunut onnettomuus (m.)* there has been an accident; *siten -tuu hänelle oikeus* in that way justice will be done to him. **-tuma** occurrence, event; incident, happening; *(∼paikka* scene; *∼sarja* series of events).

tapailla *(hapuilla)* grope (after, for); fumble (for); *∼ sanoja* be at a loss for words.

tapai|nen like. ., of. . kind; *tämän ∼* of this kind (sort); *jotakin saman -sta* something like that, *(puheesta)* something to that effect; *se on hänen -staan* it is [just] like him.

tapain|kuvaus *maal.* genre. **-turmelus** depravity.

tapamuoto *kiel.* mood.

tapaninpäivä Boxing day.

tapaturma accident; *minulle sattui ∼* I had (I met with) an accident. **-inen** accidental. **-isesti** in an accident; *kuoli ∼sesti (m.)* was accidentally killed. **-laukaus** shooting accident; *se oli ∼* the gun went off accidentally. **-vakuutus** accident insurance.

tapaukseton uneventful.

tapau|s case, instance; event; *(tapahtuma)* occurrence; *siinä -ksessa, että (hän ei saavu)* in case [he does not come]; *siinä -ksessa* in that case; *parhaassa -ksessa* at best; *ei missään -ksessa* under no circumstances, on no account; *(arvostella) kunkin -ksen mukaan* from case to case, on its own merits. **-selostus** case report.

tapella fight; be at blows.

tapet|it wallpaper; *panna ∼* hang (put up) w., *(uudet)* repaper, redecorate. **-oida** paper.

tappaa kill; *(ottaa hengiltä)* put. . to death, *(surmata)* slay.

tappara battle-axe.

tappe|lija fighter. **-lu** fight; *(nujakka)* scuffle, rough-and-tumble; *(mellakka)* riot; joutua *∼un* come to blows, get to fighting; *(∼kukko* fighting-cock, game-cock; *∼nhalu|inen* full of fight, pugnacious; *näyttää t-iselta* show fight; *∼pukari* rowdy, swashbuckler, biawler, ruffian).

tappi *(veneen ym)* plug, *(tynnyrin)* tap, *(tulppa)* stopper, plug, *(esim. saranan)* pin; *(liitoksen)* tenon.

tappio defeat; loss; *∼t* losses, *(sot. m.)* casualties; *kärsiä ∼* suffer defeat, be defeated, *(kauppassa)* suffer (incur) a loss; joutua *∼lle* be beaten, be conquered, be defeated; *(myydä) ∼lla* [sell] at a loss; *∼ta tuottava* losing [concern, liike]; *saada ∼ta (m.)* lose (on, by); *olla ∼lla* have the worst of it, be the loser. **-llinen**. . involving loss, losing. **-mieliala** defeatism. **-tili** loss account.

tappo killing; *lak.* [voluntary] manslaughter. **-raha** bounty, *jstk* on. **-rahat** tow.

tappurat tow.

tapuli pile [of timber]; *(kello-)* campanile.

taputtaa tap, *(lujemmin)* clap; *(hyväillen)* pat; *∼ käsiään* applaud.

tarha enclosure; *(piha)* yard, cattle-yard, *Am.* corral; *(pieni)* pen; *(kettu- ym)* farm. **-käärme** *ks. ranta-*. **-us** *(minkki- ym)* farming.

tariffi tariff; *(rautatie-, ym)* schedule, list of rates; *palkka~* rate of wages.

tarin|a a tale, story, narrative. **-oida** talk, chat; *(kertoa)* tell [stories].

tarjeta stand the cold.

tarjoi|lija waiter; *(laivassa ym)* steward; *(baari-)* barman, bartender. **-lijatar** waitress; stewardess; barmaid; *vrt. ed.* **-lla** serve, wait [at table, *pöydässä*]; *(kiertää t-llen)* hand around; ~ *jklle* wait [up]on; *-llaan kerman kera* is served with cream. **-lu** service; serving, waiting [at table]; *juhla-, merkkipäivä- ym)* catering. **-lupöytä** *(ruokahuoneen)* sideboard; *(ravintolan)* counter, *(baari)* bar.

tarjo|kas volunteer; *(pyrkijä)* candidate. **-lla** on offer; *nykyisin* ~ *oleva* .. available at present; *ehdotuksia on* ~ *useampia* many suggestions have been put forth. **-lle: panna** ~ *(ruokia)* set out. **-na:** *vaara on* ~ danger is at hand; *oli* ~ *vaara että.* . there was immediate danger that.. **-nta** supply; *kysyntä ja* ~ demand and s. **-oja** bidder; *enimmin (vähimmin)* ~ the highest (lowest) b. **-ta** offer, *jstk* for; *(huutokaupassa ym)* bid; *(kestitä)* treat [a p. to a glass of wine, *jklle lasi viiniä*]; *(pöytätoverille)* pass [some bread, *leipää*]; ~ *enemmän kuin jku* outbid a p.; ~ *vähemmän* underbid [a p.]; ~ *myytäväksi* offer.. for sale; ~ *palveluksiaan jklle* offer (tender).. one's services; ~ *jklle päivällinen* invite a p. [out] to dinner; treat a p. to dinner; *hän -si kaikille lasillisen* he stood everybody drinks; *-si tilaisuuden.* . afforded an opportunity (to). **-tin** tray; salver. **-us** offer,

tender; *(huutokauppa-)* bid; *(ehdotus)* proposal, proposition; *pyytää -uksia* invite tenders; *tehdä* ~ *jstk* make an offer [of an article, *myytäessä;* for. ., *ostettaessa*]. **-utua** offer (to), volunteer [to do sth.; for a task]; ~ *auttamaan jkta* offer one's services to, offer to help; *kun tilaisuus -utuu* when an opportunity arises (presents itself).

tarkalleen exactly; precisely.

tarkas|taa examine; inspect [a factory, *tehdas*]; *(käydä läpi)* look over, go through; *(esim. jnk tuoreus, kokoomus)* test; *(esim. laskuja)* check; *(kirjallisesti)* revise; *kirjanp. audit; sot.* review; *(tarkata)* observe [closely], watch [closely]; ~ *passit* examine the passports; ~ *matkatavarat* examine (search) the luggage; *merkitä -tetuksi* check off; *vrt. tarkastella.* **-taja** inspector; *(joissakin laitoksissa)* controller, comptroller; *sot.* inspecting officer; *(koulun, m.)* superintendent; supervisor; *maidon* ~ inspector (tester) of milk. **-tamaton** unexamined; uninspected; untested; unverified. **-tella** examine, *(silmäillä)* survey; look (at); consider; study; *asiaa voidaan* ~ *monelta kannalta* the matter may be viewed from many angles; *lähemmin -teltaessa* on closer consideration; *-teltavana* under examination. **-telu** critical examination; scrutiny. **-ti** accurately; closely; carefully; *kuunnella* ~ listen attentively; *pitää* ~ *kiinni* adhere strictly [to the rules etc.]; *(kello) käy* ~ keeps exact time. **-tus** examination; inspection; *sot.* review; *(valvonta)* supervision, control; *(etsintä)* search; *(~asema* control, checkpoint; *~kertomus* report [of inspection]; *tilin~* auditor's report; *~matka* inspection tour).

tark|ata watch [closely]; observe; *tarkatkaa, mitä sanon* heed (listen carefully to) what I say; *tarkkaa, että saat kunnon tavaraa* mind [that] you get good quality; *-kaavasti* attentively.
tarke|kirjoitus phonetic transcription. **-mmin** more accurately *jne.;* ~ *asiaa ajateltuani* after reconsidering the matter; *katso* ~ look more closely; *(puhumme asiasta)* ~.. in more detail. **-ntaa** *valok.* focus.
tarkis|taa adjust; *(laskuja ym)* check; *(jnk vahvistamiseksi)* verify; *(et. kirjallisesti)* revise; *-tettu painos* revised edition. **-tamaton** unchecked; unrevised. **-tus** adjustment; checking, *(kirjallinen)* revision.
tarkk|a accurate; exact; precise; *(tiukka)* close; *(ankara)* strict; *(huolellinen)* careful; detailed, particular; *(säästäväinen)* economical; *(varma)* sure; *(terävä)* sharp, keen; ~ *aika* exact time; ~ *korva* accurate ear, keen ear; ~ *jäljennös* exact copy; ~ *tutkimus* close inquiry; *olla* ~ *kunniastaan* be jealous of one's honour; *pitää* ~*a huolta jstk* take good care of, be careful (be very particular) about; *pitää* ~*a lukua jstk* keep [a] strict account of; *ei se niin* ~*a ole*.. it does not matter so much [if..]. **-aamaton** inattentive. **-aamattomuus** inattentiveness, inattention. **-a-ampuja** sharpshooter. **-aan** *ks. tarkasti; katsoa jtk* ~ look at.. closely; *kuunnella* ~ listen attentively. **-aavainen** attentive; *(valpas)* watchful, heedful; observant; *-vaisesti* attentively; *hyvin -vaisesti* with keen attention, intently. **-aavaisuus** [close] attention; attentiveness.
tarkkai|lija observer. **-lla** watch, observe. **-lu** watch, observation; supervision. **-n** TV monitor.
tarkka|kuuloinen.. with keen

hearing. **-näköinen** sharp-(keen-) eyed; *kuv.* discerning. **-näköisyys** *kuv.* keen-sightedness, discernment. **-piirteinen** sharply defined.
tarkkuus accuracy, exactness, exactitude; precision; strictness; keenness; *10 asteen t-uudella* to within (with an accuracy of) 10 degrees. **-kello** chronometer. **-työ** precision work.
tarkoi|n closely, *vrt. tarkasti;* ~ *asiaa harkittuani* upon mature deliberation. **-ttaa** mean; have.. in view; *(aikoa)* intend; ~ *jkn parasta* have a p.'s welfare in mind; ~ *totta* be in earnest, mean it seriously; *en saa selville, mitä tämä* ~ *(m.)* I am unable to make out the meaning of this; *ketä sinä -tat* who[m] do you mean? *mitä sillä -tatte* what do you mean by that? *numerot tarkoittavat..* the figures denote *(t.* refer to).. **-ttamaton** unintentional, undesigned. **-tuksellinen** intentional; purposeful, deliberate. **-tuksellisesti** intentionally, purposely, on purpose.
tarkoituksenmukai|nen adapted (suited) to its purpose,.. serving the purpose; appropriate, expedient;.. *on hyvin* ~ is very much to the purpose; *on* ~ answers (serves) the purpose. **-sesti** [in a manner well adapted] to the purpose; suitably. **-suus** fitness [for the purpose], appropriateness; expediency; (~**syistä** for expediency).
tarkoitukse|ton purposeless, pointless.. without point; aimless; *(hyödytön)* useless; *se olisi ~ta* it would serve no purpose. **-ttomuus** lack of purpose, purposelessness.
tarkoitu|s purpose; *(päämäärä)* object, aim; *(aie)* intention; *(ajatus)* meaning; **-ksella** intentionally, advisedly; *mihin -kseen* for (to) what purpose? *missä -ksessa* with what intention? with what end in

tarm																													376

view? for what purpose? *siinä
-ksessa* for that purpose, to
that end; *oppimis -ksessa*
with a view to (with the
object of) learning; *(meni)
hyvään -kseen* to a good
cause; *hyvässä -ksessa* with
good intentions; *hänen -ksensa
oli. .* he intended to. .; *-kseni
ei ollut. .* I did not mean to,
I had no intention of (. .
-ing). **-sperä** object, aim.
tarmo energy; vigour. **-kas**
energetic; active. **-kkaasti**
energetically, vigorously; with
energy. **-kkuus** energy, vigour.
-ton. . lacking energy; inert,
lethargic. **-ttomuus** lack of
energy.
tarpee|ksi sufficiently; *(kyllin)*
enough [money, *rahaa*]; ~
iso large enough; *jtk on* ~
there is enough of. ., . .
suffices; *enemmän kuin* ~
more than enough, enough
and to spare. **-llinen**
necessary, *jklle* for a p.,
needful; *(tarvittava)* required,
requisite; *(asianmukainen)*
due; *(välttämätön)*
indispensable; *olla* ~ *(m.)* be
needed, be wanted. **-llisuus**
necessity; *(tarve)* need. **-n:**
olla ~ be needed, be
necessary; ~ *vaatiessa* when
necessary, when required. **-ton**
unnecessary, needless;
(aiheeton) uncalled-for;
(hyödytön) useless; *(liika)*
superfluous; undue; *-ttoman*
unnecessarily; *tehdä -ttomaksi
(työväkeä)* cause redundancy.
-ttomuus needlessness.
tarpoa plod; ramble.
tarra- self-fastening. **-kuva**
sticker.
tarr|ata grasp, clutch, grab [a
th.], seize [a p. by the
collar, *jnk kaulukseen*], lay
hold of. **-autua:** ~ *kiinni jhk*
fasten [up]on, cling to.
tarttu|a grasp; *(lujasti)* clutch,
grip, *(äkkiä)* grab; catch,
snatch (at); seize, catch hold
of; bite [at the hook,
koukkuun]; *(kiinnittyä jhk)*
stick (to, in), get stuck (in),
lodge (in); *(taudista)* be

infectious, *(kosketuksen
kautta)* be contagious; be
transmitted (by); ~ *aseisiin*
take up arms; ~ *asiaan*
intervene, interfere (in); ~
kurkkuun stick in the throat,
(jkta) grasp a 'p. by the
throat, clutch a p.'s throat; ~
jkn käteen take *(lujasti:*
seize) a p.'s hand; ~ *työhön*
set to work; *tauti -i minuun
hänestä* I caught the disease
from her. **-va** infectious,
(kosketuksen kautta)
contagious.
tartu|nta infection; *(kosketus-)*
contagion; *levittää ~a* spread
infection; *saada* ~ catch the
infection, catch the disease;
(~aine contagious matter;
~tauti infectious disease).
-ttaa infect [sb. with],
transmit sth. to; *jnk -ttama*
infected with.
taru legend; *(sankari-)* saga;
(jumalais-) myth; *todellisuus
on ~a ihmeellisempi* fact is
stranger than fiction. **-henkilö**
legendary character. **-mainen**
fabulous. **-nomainen** legendary;
mythical.
tarve need, want;
(välttämättömyys) necessity;
(vaatimus) requirement;
*tarpeet (= tarveaineet) ks.
tarvike; tarpeen vaatiessa,
tullen* when necessary, if
required; as necessity arises;
omaa ~tta varten for one's
own use; *olla jnk tarpeessa*
have need of, be in
want of, need; *olla
tarpeen vaatima* be needed,
be necessary; *saada
tarpeekseen jstk* have enough
of; *täyttää jk* ~ supply (meet,
satisfy) a need; *toimittaa
luonnolliset tarpeensa* obey
the call of nature. **-aineet**
material [s]. **-kalu** implement;
tool. **-puut** timber.
tarvi|ke: -kkeet requisites;
material [s], supplies, *(lisä-)*
accessories, *(varusteet)*
equipment, outfit, material [s],
supplies.
tarvi|s: *ei ole* ~ *sinun tehdä
sitä* it is not necessary for

you to do it, you need not do it. **-ta** need, be in need (in want) of, have need of; require; ~ *kipeästi jtk* need. . badly; be in urgent need of; *-ttaessa* when needed, if necessary. **-tsevainen** needy. **-ttava** necessary;. . required; *siihen ~t varat* the requisite funds.

tasa: *jnk ~lla, ~lle* on a level with; *(samassa viivassa)* flush with; *ajan ~lla* up to date; *saattaa ajan ~lle* bring. . up to date, update; *kehityksen ~lla* abreast of developments; *pysyä jnk ~lla* keep up with; *hän ei ole tilanteen ~lla* he is not equal to the occasion. he is not able to cope with the situation; *olla tehtävänsä ~lla* be equal to one's task. **-antua** become steady, acquire steadiness.
'asa'-arvo equality. **-arvoinen** equal. **-arvoisuus** equality. **-astuja** ambler. **-inen** even; level, flat; *(sileä)* smooth; *(yhdenmukainen)* uniform; steady; ~ *vauhti* even *(t.* uniform) speed. **-isesti** evenly, smoothly. **-isuus** evenness *jne.* **-jako** equal division, equal distribution (of). **-kurssi** par [of exchange]. **-lla, -lle** *ks. tasa.* **-luku** even number. **-lämpöinen** *zo.* warm-blooded. **-n** evenly, equally; *(tarkalleen)* just, exactly; *jakaa* ~ divide (distribute). . equally, *(esim. kustannukset)* share. . equally, go halves; *pelata* ~ draw; ~ *ei käy onnen lahjat* Fortune's gifts are not equally divided; *ottelu päättyi* ~ the match ended in a draw. **-nko** plain, *(-maa)* flat country; *(ylä~)* plateau.
asapaino balance, equilibrium; *~ssa* [well] balanced; *pysyä ~ssa* keep one's balance; *joutua pois ~sta* be thrown off balance; *valtiollinen* ~ balance of power. **-illa** balance oneself (on). **-inen** balanced, well-adjusted.
-taituri acrobat, *(trapetsi-)* trapeze artist. **-tila**

equilibrium. **-ton** unbalanced. **-ttaa** [counter] balance. **-ttelu** *pol. m.* trimming.
tasa|paksu. . of even thickness. **-peli** draw. **-pinta** plane; level. **-pohjainen** flat-bottomed. **-puolinen** impartial, fair, unbias [s]ed, *(ohjelma)* balanced. **-puolisuus** impartiality, fairness. **-suhtainen** well-proportioned, symmetrical.
tasata divide into equal parts, divide evenly (equally) (among, between), distribute evenly (among).
tasavalta republic. **-inen**, **-lainen** republican. **-isuus** republicanism.
tasa|vertainen equal. **-virta** direct currect. **-väkinen** equally matched; *he ovat -väkiset* they are equal [in strength].
tase *liik.* balance, statement of accounts. **-tili** balance sheet.
tasku pocket; *pistää ~un(sa)* pocket. **-ase** pocket pistol. **-kello** pocket watch. **-kirja**, **-romaani** paperback. **-koko**, *~inen* pocket size. **-lamppu** torch, *Am.* flashlight. **-matti** pocket-flask. **-raha** pocket-money; *(naisen)* pin-money. **-sanakirja** pocket dictionary. **-varas** pickpocket. **-varkaus:** *tehdä* ~ pick [sb.'s] pocket.
taso plane; *(korkeus-)* level; *(esim. työn)* standard; *olla samalla ~lla* be on a level (with), be on the same level; *poliittisella ~lla* on the political plane.
tasoi|ttaa make. . [more] even, even; level [the ground, *maata*]; *(silittää)* smooth [out, down]; *(leikaten)* trim [the hair, *tukka*]; *(kuv. = tehdä samanlaiseksi)* equalize; *(summa)* round [it off], *(tili)* balance; ~ *tietä (kuv.)* pave the way (for). **-tus** levelling; trimming; *urh.* odds *(~merkki mus.* natural).
tasoylikäytävä level-crossing.
tassu paw.
tataari Tartar.

tattari buckwheat.
tatti boletus.
tatuoi|da, -nti tattoo.
taudin|kohtaus attack of illness.
-oire symptom [of disease].
-pesä seat of the disease.
tauko pause; interval; *mus.*
rest. **-amaton** incessant,
uninterrupted, continuous.
taula German tinder,
touchwood.
taulu picture; *(maalaus)*
painting; *(esim. koulun)*
board; *(taulukko)* table;
(kellon) dial. **-kko** table;
(graafinen) graph. **-koida**
tabulate, draw up a table.
-kokoelma collection of
pictures, picture-gallery.
-nkehys picture frame.
tauo|ta cease, stop [. . -ing];
come to a stop; *taukoamatta*
without stopping; without a
break; continually. **-ton**
non-stop.
tausta background. **-peili**
(auton) driving mirror,
rear-view mirror.
tauti disease; *(sairaus)* illness,
sickness, malady; complaint;
disorder; *kuolla jhk ~in* die
of *(t.* from); *mitä ~a hän*
potee what is he suffering
from? **-suus** morbidity,
sickness rate. **-vuode** sick-bed.
tavalla, tavat *ks. tapa.*
tavallaan in a manner, in a
way; in a fashion, in a
manner of speaking; *(jossakin*
määrin) to a certain extent;
omalla ~ in his (her, their)
own way; *hän kertoi sen*
omalla ~ (m.) he gave his
own version of it.
tavalli|nen usual; ordinary;
(usein esiintyvä) frequent;
common; *(yleinen)* general; ~
mies: the average man; ~
sotamies common soldier;
private; *-set ihmiset* ordinary
people; *-sessa puvussa* in
informal dress; *-seen tapaan*
as usual; *-sissa oloissa* under
ordinary *(t.* normal)
conditions; *kuten -sta* as
usual, as is customary; *-sta*
suurempi unusually
(exceptionally) large; *-sta*

enemmän more than usual.
-sesti usually, commonly;
(yleensä) generally;
(säännöllisissä oloissa)
ordinarily. **-suus** commonness;
frequency; *-suuden mukaan* as
usual; *-suudesta poikkeava. .*
out of the ordinary,
extraordinary; *-suudesta*
poiketen contrary to one's
usual practice.
tavan|mukainen, -omainen
customary, usual, habitual,
accustomed; *-omaiset aseet*
conventional arms. **-takaa**
time and again, every little
while.
tavara goods, *(et. yhd.)* ware
(esim. tinware), wares;
(kauppa-) merchandise;
article [s]; *(omaisuus)*
property; *(tuotanto-)* product;
~t (m.) [personal] effects,
belongings. **-erä** parcel, lot.
-juna goods train,
freight-train. **-katos** goods
shed. **-käärö** parcel, package.
-laji line (kind) of goods.
-leima trade-mark. **-liikenne**
goods traffic. **-luettelo**
inventory. **-lähetys**
consignment, shipment of
goods. **-merkki** trademark,
(-laji) brand. **-nvaihto**
exchange of commodities,
trade. **-näyte** sample, *(malli)*
pattern. **-säiliö, -tila** *(auton)*
boot, *Am.* trunk. **-talo**
department store; *(halpa)*
discount house, self-service
department store. **-teline**
(pyörän) luggage carrier,
(auton katolla) roof-rack.
-toimisto goods *(et. Am.*
freight)* office. **-varasto** stock
on hand, store of goods.
-vaunu goods waggon, luggage
van, *Am.* freight car.
tava|ta 1. meet; *(sattua yhteen)*
come across, run into, happen
upon; *(yllättää)* come upon;
(pahanteosta ym) catch;
saisinko ~. . can I see *(t.*
speak to). .? *toivon tapaavani*
Teidät pian I hope to see you
soon; *en ole koskaan häntä*
tavannut I have never met
her; *on -ttavissa (kotonaan)* is

at home; *hänet -ttiin
varkaudesta* he was caught
stealing. **tavata 2.** *(kirjain kirjaimelta)*
spell.
tava|ton unusual, uncommon;
extraordinary;
(poikkeuksellinen) exceptional;
(kuulumaton) unheard-of;
-ttoman unusually [large,
suuri], exceedingly [beautiful,
kaunis], extremely [difficult,
vaikea]; ~ *hinta* excessive
price; *meillä oli -ttoman
hauskaa* we enjoyed ourselves
greatly (immensely); *niitä oli
-ttoman paljon (m.)* there
were ever so many of them.
-ttomasti unusually *jne.*
tavaus spelling. **-virhe** mistake
in spelling.
tavoin in .. way, like ..; *millä
~?* in what way? how?, *ks.
tapa.*
tavoi|te aim, object; *(esim.
myynti-)* target. **-tella** try to
catch; aspire (after), be after;
~ *kuuta taivaalta* reach for
the moon; ~ *mainetta* aspire
to fame; ~ *rikkautta* strive
for riches; *-teltava* desirable,
covetable; *-teltu kaunotar* a
sought-after beauty. **-ttaa**
catch [a ball], catch up with,
overtake [a p.]; *(auto)* catch
[a bus], find [a taxi], *(jku
kotoa t. puhelimella)* reach;
(koettaa ~) try to get hold
of, *(jkn katsetta)* try to
catch; ~ *menettämänsä aika*
make up for lost time;
*(samoja lukuja) ei tänä
vuonna -teta.* `will not be
attained this year; *lähti
-ttamaan rikollista* left in
pursuit of the [escaped]
criminal. **-ttelija** claimant (to),
vallan ~t seekers after power.
-ttelu *(jnk)* pursuit (of).
tavu syllable; *jakaa ~ihin*
divide into syllables. **-inen.** [
of. . syllables; *moni~*
polysyllabic.
te you; *teille* to you, for you;
teitä you; *onko tämä Teidän*
is this yours? (. . *hattunne.*.
your hat?)
teatteri theatre; *~ssa* at the t.;

käydä ~ssa go to the t. **-ala:**
ruveta ~lle go on the stage.
-arvostelija dramatic critic.
-arvostelu dramatic criticism.
-kappale play. **-kärpänen:** *-lla
on ~ (haluaa näyttelijäksi).*.
is stage-struck. **-kiikari**
opera-glasses. **-koulu** dramatic
school. **-lava** stage. **-mainen**
theatrical. **-njohtaja** theatre
manager. **-näytäntö**
[theatrical] performance;
show. **-ohjelma** programme;
(juliste) play-bill. **-seurue**
touring company. **-ssakävijä**
theatre-goer, playgoer. **-talo**
theatre. **-yleisö** theatre-going
public, *(katsomo)* audience.
tee tea; *keittää ~tä* make tea;
juomme ~tä kello neljä we
have tea at four; *voitteko
tulla ~lle?* could you come to
tea? **-illallinen** high tea.
-kannu tea-pot. **-kuppi** teacup.
-kutsut tea-party. **-lusikallinen**
teaspoonful. **-lusikka** teaspoon.
teema *mus.* theme, motif;
(verbin) principal parts [of a
verb].
teennäi|nen affected; unnatural;
artificial; *(pakkoinen)* forced.
-sesti affectedly; in an
affected manner. **-syys**
affectation.
teepensas tea shrub.
teerenpisama freckle.
teeri black grouse; *(koiras)*
blackcock, *(naaras)* grey-hen.
teesken|nellä pretend [to be
ill], feign [ignorance], affect
[friendship], simulate; make
believe; assume an air (a
look) of [innocence,
viattomuutta]; *(esiintyä
t-nellen)* be affected; *-nelty*
affected; feigned.
-telemättömyys unaffectedness,
artlessness. **-telemätön**
unaffected; unfeigned; artless;
(vilpitön) sincere. **-televä**
affected; *(ulkokullattu)*
hypocritical. **-telijä** hypocrite.
-tely affectation, pretence,
make-believe.
teettää have. . made; ~ *uusi
takki* have a new coat made.
tee|tölkki tea caddy. **-vati**
saucer.

tehdas factory, mill, works.
-alue factory grounds.
-kaupunki manufacturing town.
-laitos manufacturing plant,
factory. **-mainen:** ~ *valmistus*
factory production. **-maisesti**
on an industrial scale *(t.
basis).* **-seutu** manufacturing
district. **-tavara** manufactured
goods (articles). **-tuote** factory
product. **-työ** factory work;..
on ~*tä* is factory-made.
-työläinen factory worker.
-valmisteet manufactured
goods.
tehdä do; make [a coat,
takki; a p. happy, *jku
onnelliseksi*]; *(suorittaa)*
perform, accomplish, execute,
carry out; *(jtk pahaa)*
commit; *(laatia)* draw up; ~
jksk render, make; ~ *hyvää*
do good; be beneficial; *se
tekee hyvää hänelle* it does
him good; ~ *ihmeitä* work
wonders; ~ *kauppa* make
(conclude) a bargain; ~ *rikos*
commit a crime; ~ *jk työ* do
a piece of work, do a job;
~ *kysymys* ask. . a question,
put a question (to); ~ *matka*
make a journey; ~ *merkintöjä*
take notes; ~ *työtä* work; ~
velvollisuutensa do one's duty;
ottaa ~*kseen* undertake (to);
mitä se tekee? what does it
matter? what of that?;..
tekee (yhteensä) 15 sh. it
makes 15 sh., that'll be 15
sh.; *teit oikein kun menit
sinne* you did right in going
there; *mitä minun on tehtävä?*
what am I to do? *onko
mitään tehtävissä?* is there
anything to be done [about
it]? *minulla on paljon
tekemistä* I have much to do;
olla tekemäisillään jtk be
about to. .; *olla tekevinään*
pretend to. .
teho effect, action, *(koneen)*
capacity, output; efficiency;
[effective] power; ~*a
tavoitellen* [she did it] for
effect. **-kas** effective, efficient.
(~ava) impressive. **-kkaasti**
effectively. **-kkuus**
effectiveness, efficiency,

efficacy. **-osasto** *ks. -staa.*
-sekoitin liquidiser, *Am.*
electric blender. **-staa** render..
more effective; heighten,
intensify; *(esim. valvontaa)*
tighten up; *(korostaa, esim.
tausta)* set off, serve as a
foil to; highlight; *-stetun
hoidon osasto* intensive-care
unit. **-ste:** *ääni~et* sound
effects. **-stus** intensification;
setting off; *itse~*
self-assertion. **-ta** be effective,
have (produce, exert) an
effect (on), act (on); have the
desired effect; *(miellyttää)*
impress;.. *-si voimakkaasti.*.
was very impressive. **-ton**
ineffective, ineffectual, *(kem.
ym.)* inactive; *olla* ~ *(m.)* be
of no effect. **-ttomuus**
ineffectiveness, inefficiency.
tehtaan|hinta maker's *(t.
factory)* price. **-isännöitsijä**
factory superintendent. **-piippu**
chimney stack.
tehtailija manufacturer, factory
owner.
tehtävä task; *(velvollisuus)*
duty, *(virka-)* function;
commission; *(elämän- ym)*
mission [in life]; *(lasku- ym)*
problem; *(koulu-)* lesson;
antaa jklle jk ~ set a p. a
task, assign [a task] to;
antaa jk jkn ~*ksi* commission
a p. to, charge a p. with;
täyttää ~*nsä* perform one's
task, fulfil one's duty; *minun
~ (nä)ni on.* . it is my
business to; *ryhtyä hoitamaan
(uutta)* ~*ä* take over [a job];
hoitaa tehtäviään discharge
one's duties (responsibilities).
teidän your; yours.
teikäläinen one of you, one of
your people; ~ *ajatustapa*
your way of thinking.
teilata *kuv.* destroy.
teini sixth-former, *Am.*
senior-highschool pupil.
-ikäinen *l. v.* teen-ager,
a. teen-aged.
teippi [adhesive] tape.
teititellä address [a p.]
formally, not be on
Christian-name terms.
tek|aista do (make). . in haste,

make hastily; *(keksiä)* make up, fabricate, invent; *tekaistu* trumped up [story, *juttu*], fictitious. **-eillä** in [course of] preparation; *on* ~ is being made (prepared), is under construction, in course of preparation; *mitä on* ~ *(m.)* what is up? **-ele** [unpretentious] piece of work. **-e**|**minen** doing *jne.; joutua t-misiin jkn kanssa* come into contact with; *sillä ei ole mitään t-mistä* ..*n kanssa* it has nothing to do with; *olla -misissä jkn kanssa* have dealings with; *en halua olla missään t-misissä hänen kanssaan (m.)* I am through with him. **-e**|**mätön** undone; *tehtyä ei t-mättömäksi saa* what is done cannot be undone. **-eytyä:** ~ *jksk* pretend to be. ., sham [illness, *sairaaksi*], feign, affect [ignorance, *tietämättömäksi*]. **-ijä** maker; *(kirjan-) author; mat. ym* factor; *tärkeä* ~ an important factor; *työ* ~*änsä kiittää* a workman is known by his work; *(*~*noikeus* copyright. ~**npalkkio** author's remuneration, *(prosentti)* royalty.
tekn|**iikka** technics, technology, engineering, *(tekotapa)* technique. **-ikko** technician; technologist. **-illinen** technical; ~ *korkeakoulu* Institute *(t.* School) of Technology, technical *(t.* technological) university; ~ *opisto* college of advanced technology; ~ *koulu* technical school. **-nen** *ks. ed.*
teko deed, act; *(työ)* work; *(menettely)* action; *(saavutus)* achievement; *hyvät teot* good actions, *(raam.)* good works; *paha* ~ evil deed; *tavata jku itse teosta* catch. . in the act, catch. . red-handed; *sanoin ja teoin* in word and deed; *suomalaista* ~*a* of Finnish make. **-hammas** false tooth; *-hampaat* denture. **-hengitys** artificial respiration; *vrt. suu.*

-jäsen artificial limb. **-kuitu** man-made fibre; synthetic fibre. **-kukka** artificial flower. **-kuu** satellite. **-nahka** imitation leather. **-palkka** pay, charge [for making. .]; *paljonko otatte* ~*a* how much do you charge for your work? **-pyhyys** hypocrisy. **-pyhä** hypocritical; *s.* hypocrite. **-silkki** artificial silk; rayon. **-silmä** artificial eye. **-syy** pretext; subterfuge; *etsiä -syitä* try to find excuses, resort to evasions; *sillä* ~*llä, että hän oli sairas* on the pretext that he was ill, under the pretext (the pretence) of being ill. **-tapa** method of preparation; technique. **-tukka** false hair.
tekst|**ata** print [by hand], write in print; *-atut kirjaimet* block letters. **-i** text; *(paino*~*)* print; *(filmin)* caption, *vrt. seur. (sanat)* wording; *(päivän* ~ *(raam.)* lesson. **-itys** *elok., TV* subtitles.
tekstiili textile; *ks. kutoma-.*
tela roller, roll, cylinder: *telat (laivan)* stocks, slipway; *laskea teloilta* launch; *lähteä teloiltaan* leave the slipway, be launched. **-ketju** caterpillar tread; *(*~**traktori** caterpillar tractor). **-kka** dock, shipyard. *tulla* ~*an* dock. **-koida** dock. **-kointi** docking. **-pölkyt** stocks.
tele|**objektiivi** telephoto lens. **-skooppi** telescope.
telepatia telepathy.
televisio television, TV, *(koje)* t. set; *puhek. (telkkari)* the telly, the box; ~*ssa on* television; *katsella* ~*ta* watch television. **-ida** televise. **-kuuluttaja** television announcer. **-lähetin** t. transmitter. **-lähetys**, **-puhe** t. broadcast. **-nkatselija** televiewer, watcher of TV. **-toiminta** t. broadcasting.
teline stand, rack; *(kehys-)* frame; ~*et (rakennus-)* scaffolding; *(voim.)* apparatus. **-harjoitukset** [gymnastic] exercises on apparatus.
teljetä bolt, bar; ~ *jku jhk*

shut sb. (into), lock up.
telki bar; bolt; ~*en takana*
under lock and key.
telkkä goldeneye.
telmiä romp, be boisterous.
teloi|**ttaa** execute. **-ttaja**
executioner. **-tus** execution.
teltta tent; *(suuri)* marquee;
pystyttää ~ pitch a tent.
-katos canopy; canvas cover.
-sänky camp bed.
temmata pull; wrench;
(nykäistä) jerk; ~ *jkn käsistä*
snatch. . from a p.'s hands; ~
mukaansa (kuv.) carry [the
audience] with one, sweep
(carry) [the reader] along.
temmel|**lys** tumult; turmoil;
(~kenttä arena). **-tää** *(esim.
myrsky)* rage; ~ *vapaasti*
have free rein[s], run high.
temp|**aus** pull; jerk; *urh.*
snatch; *kuv.* drive; *mainos~*
publicity stunt. **-autua** *(irti)*
wrench oneself away (from),
break loose; ~ *mukaan* be
carried away. **-oa** jerk, pull.
temppeli temple. **-herra** Knight
Templar.
temppu trick; dodge; *rohkealla
tempulla* by a bold stroke.
-ilu trickery.
tenava kid, tot.
tendenssi tendency, trend, drift;
(kirjan ym.) purpose.
-näytelmä [a] play with a
message.
tenho *(-voima)* enchantment,
glamour, charm, fascination;
~ava glamorous. **-ta** enchant,
charm, fascinate.
tennis *(-peli)* [lawn-] tennis;
pelata ~tä play t. **-halli**
indoor tennis-court [s]. **-kenttä**
tennis-court. **-kilpailu** tennis
tournament.
tenori, -laulaja tenor. **-ääni**
tenor voice; *(-osa)* tenor
[part].
tentti examination, *puhek.*
exam; *suorittaa* ~ pass an e.;
pitää ~ conduct an e. **-ä**
examine [sb. in .., on his
knowledge of] ; *(jtk jklle)* be
examined by.
tenä: *tehdä ~ä* resist, offer
resistance.
teolli|**nen** industrial. **-staa**

industrialize. **-suudenharjoittaja**
industrialist.
teollisuus industry, *us.*
industries. **-elämä** industrial
life. **-kaupunki** industrial
(manufacturing) town. **-keskus**
industrial centre. **-lait**|**os**
manufacturing establishment,
industrial plant; *-okset*
industries. **-mies** industrialist.
-pomo tycoon, captain of
industry. **-seutu** industrial
area. **-tuotteet** manufactured
products (goods).
teologi theologian. **-nen**
theological.
teonsana *kiel.* verb.
teoree|**tikko** theorist. **-ttinen**
theoretic [al].
teoria theory.
teos work; *(tuote)* product,
production; *(kirja, m.)* volume.
teosofi theosophist. **-a**
theosophy. **-nen** theosophic [al].
tepastella *(lapsesta)* toddle.
tepsi|**ä** be effective, have an
effect; *ne sanat -vät* the
words produced the desired
effect;. . *ei -nyt* had no effect
[on him].
terap|**eutti** therapist. **-ia**
therapy.
terha|**kka** brisk, lively;
vigorous; *(vanhus)* hale and
hearty, spry; *-kasti* briskly,
boldly. **-kkuus** spirit;
briskness; enterprise.
teriö *bot.* corolla.
termi *(oppisana)* term.
termiitti termite.
terminologia terminology.
termos thermos. **-kannu**
vacuum pitcher. **-pullo**
thermos [flask], vacuum flask.
-taatti thermostat.
ternimaito beestings.
teroittaa sharpen; *(esim. kynää,
m.)* point; *(hioa)* grind;
(mieleen) impress on a p.,
imprint on a p.'s memory.
terrori, -smi terrorism. **-sti**
terrorist. **-soida** terrorize.
-teko terrorist outrage.
terssi *mus.* third.
terttu cluster, *tiet.* raceme.
terva tar. **-inen** tarry. **-npoltto**
tar-burning. **-pääskynen** swift.
-skanto resinous stump, *kuv.*

(adj.).. sound to the core. **-ta**
tar; give.. a coating of tar.
terv|e healthy; *(predikatiivina)*
well; sound [in body and
mind], *(-järkinen)* sane; *olla
~enä* be healthy, be well, be
in good health; *tulla ~eksi*
recover, be cured; *~
arvostelukyky* sound judgment;
~ järki common sense; *~ellä
pohjalla* on a sound basis;
terve! hello! *(lähtiessä)*
cheerio, *(maljasi)* cheers; *~
tuloa* nice you could come!
(joskus) welcome. **-eellinen**
healthy, healthful, wholesome;
(hyväätekevä) beneficial,
salutary. **-eellisyys** healthiness.
-eesti soundly; sanely.
terveh|dys greeting; salutation;
(sotilas-) salute; *(joulu- ym)*
compliments of the season;
(~käynti call, courtesy call;
mennä t-käynnille jkn luo pay
one's respects to; *~puhe*
address of welcome, words of
welcome). **-tiä** greet, *sot.*
salute; *(kädestä)* shake hands
with; *(kumartaa)* bow,
(nyökäyttää) nod, *(nostaa
hattua)* raise one's hat (to);
~ jkta iloiten greet.. with
joy; *käydä -timässä jkta* pay
sb. a visit, call on a p.; *käy
-timässä* come and see me!
look me up! *hän ei -di
minua kadulla (m.)* he cuts
me in the street. **-dyttäminen**
(esim. talouselämän) putting
the economy on a sound
basis, reorganization,
[economic] reconstruction.
-tyminen recovery. **-tyä**
recover, get well.
tervei|set regards,
(kunnioittavat) compliments,
respects; *-siä.. -lle*
remember me to; *sano -siä
jklle* give my kind regards
(to); *parhain -sin* with kindest
regards; *rakkaat ~ -lta* love
from..
terve|järkinen sane,.. sound in
mind. **-tuliaiset** welcome.
-tuliaispuhe welcoming speech.
-tullut welcome; *lausua jku
-tulleeksi* bid a p. w. **-tuloa:**
~ .. you are welcome [at

t. in Helsinki, at this
occasion]; *vrt. terve.*
-yde|llinen hygienic; sanitary;
-lliset olot sanitary conditions.
terveyden|hoito care of the
health; hygiene; *(yleinen)*
public health [measures];
(~lautakunta board of
health). **-huolto** public health;
(kansallinen) National Health
Service. **-tila** [state of] health.
terveys health; *huono ~* bad
health, ill-health; *terveydeksi
your health!* here's to you!
juoda jkn terveydeksi drink to
a p.'s health. **-lähde** mineral
spring, spa. **-opillinen**
hygienic. **-oppi** hygiene. **-side**
sanitary towel. **-sisar** public
health nurse. **-suola** salts.
-syy: *-syistä* for health
reasons. **-vesi** medicinal water.
terä blade; *(koneissa ym)*
cutter, bit, *(reuna)* [cutting-]
edge; *(hampaan)* crown;
(kynän) nib; *bot.* corolla;
aurinko loistaa täydeltä ~ltä
the sun is shining in full
splendour. **-ase** sharp-edged
weapon.
teräks|enharmaa steel-grey.
-inen.. of steel *(m. kuv.),*
steel.
terälehti *bot.* petal.
teräs steel. **-betoni** reinforced
concrete. **-kynä** steel pen.
-kypärä steel helmet. **-köysi**
steel cable, wire rope. **-lanka**
steel wire. **-piirros** steel
engraving. **-täytyä** steel oneself
[against, *vastaan*]. **-tää** steel,
harden. **-villa** steel wool.
terä|vyys sharpness, keenness,
edge, *(kuv. m.)* acumen. **-vä**
sharp, keen [intellect, *äly*];
(kärjekäs) pointed; acute
[angle, *kulma*]; *(pureva)*
cutting, biting, trenchant,
mordant; *~ huomautus* sharp
(caustic) remark; *~ katse*
sharp (piercing) look; *~ kieli*
a sharp tongue; *~ tyttö* a
sharp (clever) girl; *(luokan)
-vin oppilas* the brightest
pupil; *~ vastaus* sharp retort,
(sukkela) witty answer; *~t
laskokset* knife pleats.
terävä|järkinen keen- (sharp-)

witted, acute, astute. **-järkisyys**
sharpness. **-kulmainen**
acute-angled. **-kärkinen**
pointed. **-näköinen**
keen-sighted, *kuv*.
sharp-sighted. **-näköisyys**
keen-sightedness; discernment.
-päinen clever, intelligent,
(fiksu) brainy; acute, shrewd.
testamen|tata bequeath, leave
[by will]. **-tintekijä** testator,
fem. testatrix.
-tintoimeenpanija executor [of
a will]. **-tti** will; *et raam.*
testament; *kuolla ilman ~a*
die intestate; *(~lahjoitus*
legacy; *~määräys* stipulation
in a will).
test|ata, -i test.
teuras|karja beef cattle,
slaughter-cattle. **-taa** slaughter.
-taja butcher. **-tamo**
slaughter-house, abattoir. **-tus**
slaughter; *kuv.* butchery,
(joukko-) massacre. **-uhri**
sacrifice.
Thai-maa Thailand; **t~lainen**
Thai.
tiainen titmouse.
tie road; way; *(kulkutie)*
passage, pathway; *kysyä ~tä*
ask sb. the way; *olla jkn
~llä* stand in a p.'s way, be
in the way; *pois ~ltä!* get out
of the way! *hän meni toista
~tä* he took another road,
(matkusti) he went by another
route; *rauhallista ~tä* by
peaceful means; *mennä
~hensä* take oneself off; *mene
~hesi!* go away! *minun olisi
paras laittautua ~heni* I had
better make tracks; *kulkea
omaa ~tään (kuv.)* take a
line of one's own.
tiede science. **-akatemia**
academy of science [s]; *Engl.*
the Royal Society. **-kunta**
department, faculty. **-mies** *(et.
luonnontieteilijä)* scientist.
tiedoksianto notification, notice.
tiedollinen instructional.
tiedon|antaja informant. **-anto**
information, communication,
notice, *(selostus)* report;
(esim. päivittäinen) bulletin;
(~toimisto inquiry office).
-haara branch of knowledge.

-haluinen. . eager to learn,
studious.
tiedostaa *psyk.* recognize.
tiedote announcement,
statement; bulletin,
communiqué, *(lehdistölle, m.)*
handout.
-ttomuus unconsciousness,
insensibility.
tiedo|ttaa make known; notify
[a p. *jklle*]; announce, report.
-tus notification, notice,
report, communication;
announcement; *(~palvelu*
intelligence [service];
~tilaisuus l.v. press
conference; *~väline* medium;
~välineet [mass] media [of
communication]).
tiedus|taa *ks. -tella; ~ asuntoa
ym (m.)* look about for. .
-telija *(vakoilija)* scout. **-tella**
inquire [about. ., concerning. .
jtk asiaa], make inquiries;
sot. reconnoitre; *~ jkta*
inquire *t.* ask for *(jkn vointia
after)*; *~ jkn mielipidettä* ask
a p.'s opinion, consult a p.;
~ tietä ask the way. **-telu**
inquiry; *sot.* reconnaissance,
reconnoitring; *(~lento*
reconnaissance flight; *~osasto*
intelligence department; *~retki*
reconnoitring expedition).
tiehyt duct, canal, channel.
tiehöylä road scraper.
tien|haara *(et. kuv.)* parting of
the ways. **-mutka** curve (bend)
of the road.
tien|oo neighbourhood; tract,
region; *näillä -oin* in these
parts, in this neighbourhood;
kello viiden -oissa about 5
o'clock.
tien|raivaaja *kuv.* pioneer.
-raivaus clearing the way;
kuv. pioneer work. **-rakennus**
road building, road making;
(~suunnitelma road project).
-risteys crossing of roads,
crossroads, junction. **-vieri**
roadside, wayside; *~llä* by the
side of the road, along the
road. **-viitta** signpost.
tie|puolessa by the wayside.
-sulku road block; *vrt. katu-*.

tieteelli|nen scientific. **-sesti** scientifically. **-syys** scientific character (nature). **tieteen|haara** branch of science. **-harjoittaja** man of science, scientist. **tieteillä** pursue scientific studies. **tieteisromaani** science fiction book. **tieten** knowingly, consciously; ~ *tahtoen* wilfully and knowingly; of set purpose; intentionally; *minun* ~*i* with my knowledge. **-kin** of course; naturally. **-kään:** *eipä* ~ of course not, certainly not. **tieto** knowledge; *(ilmoitus)* information; notice; intelligence; *tiedot* information; data; *lähemmät tiedot* particulars; *antaa tiedoksi* make.. known; *antaa* ~ *jstk* notify, inform of, give notice of, let.. know; *saada* ~ *(jstk)* be informed of, receive information of; *saattaa jtk jkn* ~*on* bring to a p.'s knowledge; *tulla* ~*on* become known, *(esim. salaisuus)* get out; *tulla jkn* ~*on* come to a p.'s notice; *hankkia* ~*ja* gather information (about); *saamamme tiedon mukaan* according to information received; *vastoin parempaa* ~*aan* contrary to his better judgment; *pitää omana* ~*naan* keep.. to oneself. **-inen** conscious, *jstk* of; *olla* ~ *jstk* have knowledge of, know about, be aware of; *täysin* ~ *(jstk)* fully conscious of; *-isena siitä, että* knowing that..; *pitää.. -isena* keep a p. informed (of), keep.. posted. **-isesti** consciously. **-isuus** consciousness; knowledge. **-jenkäsittely** data processing. **-kilpailu** quiz [programme]. **-kirja** instructional book. **-kone** computer. **-liikennesatelliitti** communications satellite. **-puolinen** theoretical. **-rikas..** of wide knowledge, knowledgeable. **-sanakirja**

encyclopedia. **-toimisto** *(uutis-)* news agency. **tietous** knowledge; lore *(esim. folklore, bird lore).* **tie|tty** known; a certain, a given; *se on* ~ of course, certainly; *tietyssä mielessä* in a certain sense; *pitää* ~*nä* take for granted. **-ttävä:** *tehdä* ~*ksi* make known. **-ttävästi** so *(t. as)* far as is known; for all we know, to the best of my (our) knowledge. **tiety|mätön** *(epävarma)* uncertain; *kadota t-mättömiin* disappear without leaving a trace. **-sti** of course; certainly! *(luonnollisesti)* naturally. **tietyö** road-making. **-läinen** road labourer. **tietäjä** soothsayer, seer. **tietämys** knowledge. **tietä|mättä:** ~*ni* unknowingly, without my knowledge; *tieten tai* ~*än* wittingly or unwittingly. **-mättömyys** ignorance (of). **-mätön** ignorant, unaware (of), unacquainted (with), in the dark (about). **tietää** know; have knowledge of; be aware, be conscious of; *(merkitä)* mean, signify; ~*kseni* as *(t.* so) far as I know, for anything I know; *ei minun* ~*kseni (m.)* not to my knowledge, not that I know of; *saada* ~ learn [from, *jklta*], be informed (of; by a p.), gather, (from a p.); *haluaisimme* ~ we should like to know; *hän ei ole tietävinään minusta* he ignores me, he takes no notice of me; *hän ei ole siitä* ~*kseenkään* he acts as if he knew nothing about it; *mitä tämä* ~ what does this mean (signify)? *tiesinhän sen* I knew as much. **tie|tön** pathless, trackless. **-verkko** network of roads, road system. **tihe|ikkö** thicket. **-ntää** make.. thicker (denser); ~ *käyntejään* visit.. more frequently. **-tä** become thick[er], thicken,

grow denser. **-ys** thickness,
density, denseness; *(lukuisuus)*
frequency. **-ä** thick, dense
[fog, *sumu*]; close, *(kirjoitus)*
cramped; *(usein tapahtuva)*
frequent; *~än* thickly, densely
[populated, *asuttu*]; *tuhka-*
~än in rapid succession, thick
and fast; *tietoja saapui ~än*
reports arrived at frequent
intervals; *niitä on ~ssä* they
are close together.
tihku|a ooze, exude; trickle;
seep [through]; *julkisuuteen,*
m.) dribble, filter [through
the town, *kaupungille*]. **-sade**
drizzle.
tihrusilmäinen blear-eyed.
tihutyö evil deed, outrage.
Tiibet Tibet. **t-iläinen** Tibetan.
tiikeri tiger, *(naaras)* tigress.
-npentu tiger cub.
tiilen|poltto brick-making.
-punainen brick red. **-värinen**
brick-coloured.
tiili brick; *(katto-)* tile. **-katto**
tile [d] roof. **-kivi** brick.
-rakennus brick building.
-tehdas brickyard, brick-works.
-uuni brick kiln.
tiine pregnant, big with young;
(hevonen) with foal, *(lehmä)*
with calf.
tiinu tub.
tiira *zo.* tern.
tiirikka picklock; *avata lukko*
tiirikalla pick a lock;
tiirikalla aukeamaton
burglar-proof.
tiistai Tuesday; *~na* on T.
tiiviisti tight [ly], close [ly];
mennä ~ kiinni shut tight.
tiivis tight; *(kangas)* tightly
(closely) woven; *(tiheä)* dense,
compact; *(veden-, ilmanpitävä)*
water-(air-)tight. **-te** packing,
gasket; *(uute)* extract. **-telmä**
summary, abstract; *~ jstk*
condensed from.. **-tys**
tightening, *tekn.* packing;
(höyryn) condensation; *(~aine*
packing; **-lista**
[window-]stripping; *~rengas*
washer). **-tyä** tighten, become
tight; *(kaasuista ym)* be
condensed, condense. **-tää**
tighten; *(täyttää)* stop [up],
(esim. saumoja) caulk; *tekn.*

pack; *(ikkuna)* seal up; *fys.*
condense.
tiiviys tightness; closeness;
denseness, density;
compactness.
tikanheitto darts.
tikapuut ladder, stepladder.
tikari dagger; *(pieni)* stiletto.
tikata stitch; *(peitettä)* quilt.
tiki|ttää tick. **-tys** tick [ing].
tikka woodpecker. **-peli** darts.
tikkaat stepladder, ladder.
tikki *(pelissä)* trick, *lääk.*
stitch. **-takki** quilted coat.
tikku *(esim. sormesta)* splinter;
(isompi) stick; *ei ole pannut*
~a ristiin has not lifted a
finger. **-karamelli** lollipop.
tila room, space; *(sijoitus-)*
accommodation; *(olo-)* state,
condition; *(asema, yhteiskunn.*
ym) status; *(maa-)* estate,
(pieni) farm; *~a vievä, ottava*
bulky, voluminous; *ensi ~ssa*
at the first opportunity, at
your (my) earliest convenience,
(paluupostissa) by return [of
post]; *tehdä ~a jklle* make
room for;.. *vie paljon ~a..*
takes up a great deal of
space (of room); *~ ei salli*
space does not permit;
sairaan ~ the patient's
condition; *valtasi toisen ~n*
was placed second; *asettaa jtk*
jnk ~lle substitute sth. for,
replace.. by; *tulla jkn ~lle*
take a p.'s place, supersede a
p.; *salissa on ~a 500*
hengelle the hall
accommodates (seats) 500
people.
tilaaja subscriber (to). **-määrä**
number of subscribers.
tilais|uus occasion; *(tarjoutuva)*
opportunity, chance;
(virallinen, m.) function;
(esim. juhla-) social occasion;
-uuden sattuessa when
occasion offers; *käyttää -uutta*
seize (avail oneself) of an
opportunity; *pääställä ~*
käsistään miss (waste) an
opportunity; *tässä -uudessa* on
this occasion.
tilallinen farm-owner, farmer;
estate-owner.
tilan|ahtaus lack *(t.* limitation)

of space (of room), cramped conditions. **-hoitaja** steward, bailiff, manager of an estate.

tilan|ne situation; *(asema)* position; *olla -teen herrana* have the situation well under control; *-teen tasalla* equal to the occasion; *aina -teen mukaan* according to the circumstances. **-netiedotus** communiqué.

tilan|omistaja ks. *tilallinen*. **-puute** lack of space.

tilapäi|nen occasional, casual; *(väliaikainen)* temporary, provisional. **-sesti** temporarily, for the time being. **-sruno** poem for a special occasion. **-styöt** odd jobs.

tilasto statistics. **-llinen** statistical. **-tiede** statistics. **-tieteilijä** statistician.

tilata order, *jklta* from; *(lehtiä ym)* subscribe (to); *(paikka)* book, reserve; *~ aika* make an appointment [with a doctor, a hairdresser etc.]; *~ jstk liikkeestä (m.)* place an order [with a firm] for. .

tilaton: *~ väestö* landless population.

tilaus order; *(sanomalehden)* subscription (to); *tilauksen mukaan tehty* made to order, *(puku)* made to measure, *Am.* custom-made; *hankkia (lehden) tilauksia* collect subscriptions (for); *toimittaa ~* carry out (execute, fill) an order; *tilauksessa* on order. **-hinta** subscription; **-hinnat** subscription rates. **-lento** charter flight. **-lista** order sheet, *(aikakauslehden)* subscription list. **-maksu** subscription. **-pukimo** tailor. **puku** *Am.* custom-made suit.

tava|a spacious, roomy. **-uus** cubic contents, cubic capacity; *(kappaleen)* capacity, volume; *~mitta* measure of capacity, cubic measure).

tihi zo. waxwing.

ti|li account *(lyh. a|c)*; *tehdä ~ jstk* give (render) an account of, account for; *avata ~* open an account (with); *maksaa ~in* pay on account; *merkitä*

jkn ~in enter in *(t. on)* a p.'s account, put. . down to a p.'s account; *pitää ~ä* keep accounts; *tehdä ~ jkn kanssa* settle (square) one's accounts with; *vaatia jkta ~lle jstk* call sb. to account for, take sb. to task for. **-asema** balance. **-kirja** account-book. **-llepanokortti** paying-in form. **-mies** accountant. **-npito** keeping of accounts. **-npitäjä** accountant. **-npäätös** closing (balancing) of the books; *(kuv. ym)* balance sheet. **-ntarkastaja** auditor, *(valantehnyt)* chartered accountant; *~in lausunto* auditors' report. **-ntarkastus** audit, auditing [of accounts]. **-nteko** reckoning; *t-teon päivä* day of r. **-pussi** pay packet. **-päivä** pay-day. **-ttää** render an account, account for. **-tys** [statement of] accounts. **-vapaus** discharge; *myöntää ~* grant d. **-velvollinen** responsible. **-vuosi** financial year, fiscal year.

tilk|e: *tilkkeet* oakum. **-itä** caulk; make tight, stop.

tilkka drop.

tilkku scrap, *(paikka)* patch. **-peitto** patchwork quilt.

tillittää *(itkeä)* blubber.

tilukset estate; *(maa)* land [s].

timantti diamond; *(lasinleikkaajan)* glazier's diamond.

timotei timothy [-grass].

tina tin; *~ ja lyijyseos* pewter. **-kaivos** tin mine. **-kalut** tinware. **-levy** tin-plate. **-paperi** tinfoil. **-sotamies** tin soldier. **-ta** tin; *(sisältä)* line with tin. **-us** tinning; tin lining.

tinka: *viime tingassa* at the last moment.

tinkimisvara margin (allowance) for reduction.

tinki|mättömästi unconditionally, unreservedly. **-mätön** unconditional; absolute, unreserved; *(rajaton)* unqualified. **-ä** a bargain [. . down to, *jhk hintaan*]; haggle; *~ hinnasta (myyjänä)*

take off; -*mättä*
unconditionally, without
reserve.
tinneri thinner; ~*n*
nuuhkiminen t.-sniffing.
tip|ahtaa drop. **-oittain** in
drops, drop by drop.
tipotiessään: *on* ~ has
disappeared without a trace;
is gone for good.
tippa drop; *tipat* drops. **-leipä**
[sugared] [May-day] fritter.
-pallo drop bottle.
tippu|a drop, drip. **-kivi**
stalactite, (*kohoava*) stalagmite.
tippuri gonorrh[o[ea.
tiputtaa drop; *veteen -etaan
muutamia tippoja.* . a few
drops of. . are added to the
water.
tiputus *lääk.: suoneen* ~
intravenous drip. **-pullo**
medicine dropper.
tirkis|tellä, -tää peep, peer.
-tysreikä peep-hole.
Tiroli the Tyrol; *t-laishattu*
alpine hat.
tirsku|a, -nta giggle, titter.
tiski counter.
tisla|aja distiller. **-ta** distil. **-us**
distillation; (~**astia** retort;
~**koje** still).
titaani Titan; (*metalli*) titanium.
tiu score; twenty.
tiuhaan in quick succession,
thick and fast.
tiuk|asti tightly; closely;
(*kiinteästi*) firmly, steadily,
fixedly; *pitää jtk* ~ *silmällä*
keep a sharp eye on. **-ata**
(*vaatia*) demand; insist upon
[getting]; ~ *jklta jtk* (*m.*)
press. . for. **-entaa** tighten
[up], (*kuria, m.*) make. .
more strict (more rigid); ~
otettaan tighten one's hold.
-ka tight; (*kova*) hard, keen
[competition, *kilpailu*];
(*tarkka*) close; (*kudos*) tightly
(closely) woven; (*ankara*)
strict [discipline, *kuri*],
severe; ~ *nuttu* tight [-fitting]
coat; ~ *ohjelma* crowded
programme; ~ *valvonta* rigid
supervision, strict control; *kun
~ tulee* if it comes to a
pinch, at a pinch, when the
crunch comes; *raha on -alla*

money is short; *joutua -alle*
get into a tight place; *panna
jku -alle* press. . hard;
(~**katseinen** stern-looking).
-kuus tightness; strictness *jne.*
tiuku [small] bell.
tiusk|aista, -ata speak sharply,
snap (at). **-aisu** harsh
speaking, snap.
toalettipaperi toilet paper ·(*t.*
tissue).
todella really; truly; *todellako!*
really? indeed? you don't say
so? **-kin** really, indeed.
todelli|nen real, (*oikea*) true;
(*tosi-*) veritable; *-set
olosuhteet* actual conditions.
-suus reality; *-suudessa* in
reality, in fact, actually;
(~**kuvaus** picture of real life;
~**pohja:** *siltä puuttuu t.* it is
not based on reality).
toden|mukainen truthful.
-mukaisuus truthfulness,
veracity. **-näk|öinen** probable,
likely; ~ *syy* the most
probable cause; *on hyvin
-öistä* there is every
likelihood [that. .]. **-näköisesti**
probably; *hyvin* ~ (*m.*) in all
probability. **-näköisyys**
probability; likelihood;
(~**laskelma** probability
calculus). **-peräinen** real, (*tosi*)
true, veracious; (*oikea-*)
authentic. **-peräisyys** reality;
truth [fulness]; accuracy;
kieltää jnk ~ deny the
accuracy of; *varmentaa
ilmoituksen* ~ authenticate.
-taa verify; **-teolla** really,
actually, truly; (*tosissaan*) in
earnest.
tode|ta find, note, ascertain;
establish [the truth of],
verify; (*esim. taudin
aiheuttaja*) identify; (*väite*)
-ttiin vääräksi was found to
be false; *puhuja totesi* the
speaker stated (indicated). .
todis|taa prove; witness [a p.'s
signature, *jkn allekirjoitus*],
testify (to), give evidence (of),
bear witness (to); *mat. m.*
demonstrate; ~ *oikeaksi*
certify [the correctness of],
verify; *oikeaksi -tettu
jäljennös* certified copy; ~ *jku*

syylliseksi jhk convict. . of; ~
testamentti attest a will; ~
jkta vastaan bear testimony
against; *se ~ hyvää makua* it
is indicative of good taste;
todistaja -ti, että. . the
witness testified that;
*tapaturmaa ei kukaan ollut
-tamassa* there was no witness
to the accident; *mikä oli
-tettava* which was to be
proved. **-taja** witness; *kutsua
~ksi* call in evidence;
kuulustella -tajia hear
witnesses, take the evidence;
olla jnk tapahtuman ~na
witness an occurrence; *~in
lausunto* testimony, evidence.
-tamaton uncertified;
unverified; unproved. **-te**
proof, evidence; *ks. tosite.*
-telu argumentation. **-tettavasti**
as can be proved,
demonstrably. **-tus** proof (of),
testimony; *et. lak.* evidence;
(kirjallinen) certificate;
(palvelus-) testimonial; *(koulu-)*
school report; *on -tuksena
jstk* bears witness to, testifies
to; *~aineisto* evidence;
(~jäljennös copy of a
testimonial; *~kappale* [piece
of] evidence; exhibit;
~kelpoinen: t. henkilö
competent witness; *~voima*
weight of evidence; *jllak on
suuri ~* . . is powerful
evidence).
tohtia dare.
tohtor|i doctor; *lääketieteen ~
d.* of medicine *(lyh.* M. D.).
-inarvo doctor's degree,
doctorate; *saavuttaa ~* take
one's doctor's degree.
-inväitöskirja doctoral thesis
(Am. dissertation).
tohveli slipper. **-sankari**
henpecked husband.
toimeen|paneva executive.
-panija executor. **-panna**
execute, carry out;
(järjestää) arrange; make
[improvements, *parannuksia*] .
-pano execution,
putting into effect; *(~valta*
executive power). **-tulo** living,
livelihood, subsistence;
toimeentuloon riittävä palkka

a living wage; *(~lähde* source
of livelihood).
toime|kas active; busy;
(yritteliäs) enterprising.
-kkuus activity. **-ksiantaja**
client; principal.
-ksi|anto commission; *jkn
-annosta* by order of. **-liaisuus**
activity. **-lias** active. **-npide**
measure; step; *(teko)* action;
(menettely) procedure; *ryhtyä
-npiteisiin* take measures, take
steps (to), take [a matter] in
hand, take action (on a
matter), *tarmokkaisiin
-npiteisiin (m.)* adopt vigorous
measures; *ei anna aihetta
mihinkään -npiteisiin* does not
call for any action. **-ton** idle;
inactive; *(ilman tointa)*
unemployed; *olla ~na (m.)* be
idle, do nothing; *~ jäsen*
passive member. **-ttomuus**
idleness; inactivity.
toimi occupation, employment;
(paikka) position, situation,
post; job; *(virallinen)* office;
(askare) business; affair;
function; *käytännöllisen
elämän toimet* practical
affairs; *antaa jtk jkn toimeksi*
entrust a p. with; charge. .
with; *astua toimeen* enter
upon one's duties; *(jkn
jälkeen)* take over; *ottaa
toimekseen* undertake; *panna
toimeen* put into effect, carry
out; *ryhtyä toimeen* take
action; take measures (to),
(työhön) set to work; *saada
toimekseen* be charged with
[. . -ing], be commissioned (to);
toimeksi saanut by order;
tulla toimeen manage, get
along, get on [with, *jkn
kanssa*]; *tulee hyvin toimeen*
is doing well; *tulla toimeen
ilman jtk* do without; *jkn
toimesta* through a p.,
through a p.'s agency.
toimi|a work, operate;
function; be in operation, be
in action, act; *(jssk asiassa)*
go about a th.; *~ jnak* act
[as host, *isäntänä*] , *(esim.
elimistä)* function (as); *~
komitean jäsenenä* serve on
a committee; *~ lääkärinä*

practise medicine; ~ *sen
mukaan* act accordingly; ~
jssk mukana take an active
part in; ~ *jkn hyväksi* work
for a p. (on a p.'s behalf);
~ *jkn neuvon mukaan* act
upon a p.'s advice; *kone -i
hyvin* the machine works
(runs) well; *-va jäsen* active
member. **-aika** term of
office. **-ala** line [of
business]. **-henkilö**
functionary; *vrt. johto-*.
-kausi period of office.
-kunta committee. **-lupa**
concession; (*~alue*
concession). **-nimi** firm.
-nnallinen functional.
toiminnanjohtaja executive
director.
toiminta action, function[ing];
operation; activity; activities;
olla toiminnassa (laitos) be in
operation, be in action,
(kone, m.) be running. **-ala**
sphere of activity, field of
action. **-halu** eagerness to
work. **-haluinen**.. willing to
work. **-kertomus** report.
-kyvytön incapacitated. **-ohje**
instruction, direction;
directive. **-periaate** policy.
-säde range of action. **-tapa**
mode of action. **-tarmo**
energy; vigour. **-tarmoinen**
energetic, vigorous. **-terapia**
occupational therapy. **-vapaus**
liberty of action. **-vuosi** *(tili-)*
financial year.
toimipaikka post; *t-paikan
osoite* business address.
toimisto office; bureau. **-aika**
office hours. **-apulainen** office
employee. **-päällikkö** office
manager, head clerk. **-tilat,
-huoneisto** office premises.
toimitsija functionary.
toimi|ttaa do, perform; carry
out [a task, *tehtävä*]; *liik.
(perille)* deliver, *(hankkia)*
supply; *(sanomalehteä ym.)*
edit; *(huolehtia)* arrange, see
to, attend to; *(virkatehtäviä)*
discharge [the duties of..];
(laatia) compile [a dictionary,
sanakirja]; ~ *asia* do an
errand; ~ *jumalanpalvelus*
conduct (officiate at) a

service; ~ *mielipidetutkimus*
take a poll [on a matter]; ~
painosta publish, issue; ~
jklle sana give a p. a
message; ~ *takaisin* restore,
return [a th. to its owner,
omistajalleen]; ~ *tilaus*
execute an order; *vaali
-tetaan huomenna* the election
will take place (will be held)
tomorrow; *valmiina -tettavaksi*
ready for delivery. **-ttaja**
editor; *esim. uutis~* news
editor *t.* broadcaster;
(ohjelman) producer; *(joskus)*
correspondent; *(sanakirjan)*
compiler. **-tus** performing,
execution; function,
ceremony; *liik.* delivery,
(lähetys) dispatch;
(sanomalehden) editorial staff,
(-konttori) editorial office;
-tukset (seuran) proceedings;
(~aika term of delivery;
~johtaja manager, managing
director; *~kunta* editorial
committee; *~mies* executor;
~ministeriö caretaker
government; *~palkkio*
commission; *~sihteeri*
sub-editor); *~tuttaa:* ~
tutkimus cause an
investigation to be made. **-va**
acting, active *(m. tulivuori);*
operative. **-valta** authority.
toinen *a.* another, *(muu)* other;
(järjestyslukuna) second; *s.*
another [one], the other; ~
teistä one of you; ~ *tai* ~
one or the other; ~ *toisensa
jälkeen* one after the other,
one after another; ~ *toistaan*
each other, one another;
toisilleen to each other, to
one another; *toiset* the others,
other people; *kaikki toiset
(m.)* all the rest; *joka* ~
päivä every other day; *joku*
~ someone else, somebody
else; *jonakin toisena päivänä*
some other day; *hän tuli
toiseksi (urh.)* he finished
(came in) second, he was the
runner-up; *toisella tavalla
kuin*.. differently from, in a
different way from; *olla toista
mieltä* be of a different
opinion; *toisella puolella* on

the other side of, beyond; *toiselle puolelle* to the other side (of), across; *toiselta puolen. . toiselta puolen* on the one hand. . on the other hand; *toisen kerran* another time, the second time, for the second time; *jonkun toisen (gen.)* someone else's; *se on aivan toista* it is quite another thing, it is a very different matter.

tointua recover, *jstk* from; recover consciousness, come round, come to.

toip|ilas convalescent; (*~aika* convalescence; *~koti* convalescent home). **-ua** recover [from an illness, *taudista*]; *hän on toipumassa (m.)* he is convalescing, he is mending, he is picking up [quickly, *nopeasti*]. **-uminen** recovery.

toisaa|lla somewhere else, elsewhere. **-lle** in another direction; somewhere else; *kääntyä ~* take another direction; *suunnata (esim. ajatukset) ~* divert. **-lta** from another direction, from somewhere else; on the other hand; *etsiä jtk ~* look for. . elsewhere.

ois|arvoinen secondary; *~ kysymys* question of s. importance, secondary matter. **-eksi** secondly; in the second place; *~ paras* second (next) best. **-enlaatuinen, -enlainen. .** of another (a different) kind (*t.* sort), different (from). **oisin** otherwise, differently, in a different way; *~ kuin* unlike; *järjestää ~* rearrange; *~ sanoen* in other words, that is to say; *ellei ~ ilmoiteta* unless informed to the contrary. **-aan** sometimes; now and then, occasionally; at times. **-to** variation, variant. **tois|kertainen** *~ rikos* second offence. **-luokkainen** second-class (-rate). **-paikkakuntalainen** non-resident. **-puolinen** one-sided. **toissa** *~ päivänä* the day

before yesterday; *~ vuonna* the year before last.

tois|taa repeat; (*yhä uudelleen*) reiterate; *~ pääkohdittain* recapitulate. **-taiseksi** for the present, for the time being, for now; so far; until further notice; *vielä ~* as yet; *lykättiin ~* was deferred [indefinitely]; *hänen ~ paras teoksensa* his best work yet (*t.* hitherto). **-tamiseen** [for] a second time, [over] again, once again, once more. **-tanta** repetition. **-te** another time; (*joskus ~*) some other time; *tulkaa ~kin* come again! **-to** repetition. **-tua** be repeated, repeat itself, recur, occur again. **-tuva** repeated; *~sti* repeatedly.

toito|ttaa blow [a trumpet etc], toot [on] a horn; (*töräyttää*) hoot; *~ maailmalle* noise abroad, blazon forth. **-tus** tooting.

toive hope; wish; *huonot ~et* poor prospects, poor outlook; *antaa (jklle) ~ita jstk* hold out hopes (of), lead. . to expect; *~eni on täyttynyt* I've got my wish; *~ita herättävä* hopeful; *siitä on hyviä ~ita* it promises well; *paranemisesta ei ole ~ita* there is no hope of recovery; *. . ei vastaa ~ita . .* falls short of expectation; *yli ~iden* beyond expectation. **-ajattelu** wishful thinking. **-ikas** hopeful; promising. **-ikkuus** hopefulness.

toivio|retkeläinen pilgrim. **-retki** pilgrimage.

toivo hope; *jnk ~ssa* in the hope of; *heittää kaikki ~* give up hope; *kaikki ~ on mennyttä* there is no hope.

toivo|a hope (for), wish; *~ parasta* hope for the best; *jkn parasta* wish a p. well; *-en jtk* in the hope of; *-en, että* hoping that, in the hope that; *~ suuria (odottaa)* expect much; *kävi niinkuin -inkin* it went according to my wishes; *hän -i, vaikkei toivoa ollut* he hoped against hope; -isin tietäväni I wish I knew. **-minen** hoping; sen suhteen on paljon -misen varaa it leaves a great deal to be desired, it leaves plenty of room for improvement. **-mus** wish; desire; lausua -muksena, että express a desire (the hope) that; täyttää jkn ~ fulfil (comply with) a p.'s wish; -muksenne mukaisesti in compliance with your wishes. **-npilkahdus** gleam of hope. **-ton** hopeless; desperate. **-ttaa** wish; ~ jklle onnea wish a p. good luck (t. happiness), express one's best wishes to, (onnitella) congratulate a p. (upon); -tan onnea (ennen tenttiä) best of luck, (syntymäpäivänä) many happy returns! ~ jklle hyvää yötä say good night to a p.; ~ tervetulleeksi bid. . welcome. **-ttava** desirable,. . to be desired; on ~a it is to be hoped (that). **-ttavasti** we hope [you will come, tulette], it is to be hoped [that. .], (vastauksissa = sitä toivon) I hope so; ~ en I hope not. **-ttavuus** desirability. **-ttomasti** hopelessly, desperately. **-ttomuus** hopelessness; despair. **-ttu** desired; hoped-for, wished-for.

tokaista blurt out; (väliin) throw in.

toki: eihän ~ oh, no! surely not! eihän hän ~ liene mennyt you don't mean that he has gone! sano ~ meille do tell us; sekin on ~ jotakin still that is something.

tokka dock.

tokko whether, if; en tiedä, ~ I don't know whether; ~pa vain! I wonder!

toksiini toxin.

tola: on oikealla ~lla is on the right track; asiat eivät ole oikealla ~lla something is wrong.

tolkku sense; saada ~a jstk make sense out of. ., make. . out; en saa tästä mitään ~a I cannot make this out, this is all Greek to me.

tolku|ton confused, senseless; (jota ei ymmärrä) unintelligible; puhua -ttomia talk nonsense. **-ttomuus** confusion; lack of sense.

tollo, tolvana fool; (tyhmyri) ignoramus, dunce.

tomaatti tomato. **-kastike** tomato sauce. **-sose** tomato ketchup.

tomppeli dolt, fool; (aasi) ass. **-mainen** silly, foolish.

tomu dust; (vainajan) ashes, remains; ~ksi to dust. **-inen** dusty. **-maja** mortal clay. **-pilvi** nostatti -pilven raised a cloud of dust. **-sokeri** icing sugar. **-ta** be dusty. **-ttaa** dust.

Tonava the Danube.

tonkia root up, dig, grub.

tonni ton; 2000 ~n alus two-thousand-tonner. **-kala** tunny. **-luku** tonnage. **-sto** tonnage.

tontti [building-]site, Am. building lot. **-vero** land tax.

tonttu brownie.

topaasi topaz.

topakk|a resolute, domineering, puhek. gutsy; on ~ has a mind of her own. **-uus** self-assertion.

toppaus padding; quilting.

tora quarrel; wrangle, squabble. **-hammas** fang; (norsun ym) tusk. **-illa, -ta** quarrel; bicker, squabble. **-isa** quarrelsome.

torakka cockroach.

tori market-place; (aukio) square; mennä ~lle go to the market. **-hinta** market price. **-kauppa** market trade, marketing.

torju|a ward off, fend off; avert; (ei hyväksyä) reject; (tuholaisia) destroy; psyk. repress; ~ hyökkäys repel (repulse, beat off) an attack; ~ isku ward off a blow; ~ luotaan (ajatus) dismiss a thought from one's mind; ~ luotaan (jku) turn away, (tarjous) turn down, (pitää loitolla) keep. . at a distance; luotaan -va (luonne) forbidding; ~ syytös deny an accusation; ~ vaara avert a danger; ~ väite refute an argument. **-minen** warding off *jne*. **-nta** = *ed.;* rejection; *(tuholaisten)* destruction; *palon~* fire-fighting; *(~hävittäjä ilm.* interceptor; *~ohjus* anti-missile missile).

torkah|dus nap, doze. **-taa** take a nap, doze off.

torkkua be drowsy.

torni tower; *(suippo, kirkon)* steeple; spire; *(pieni, m. panssari-)* turret; *(šakki-)* rook. **-haukka** kestrel.

-nhuippu spire. **-pääsky** swift.

torpedo torpedo. **-ida** torpedo. **-vene** torpedo-boat.

torppa *Skotl. & Engl.* croft. **-ri** tenant [farmer], leaseholder, crofter.

torstai Thursday. **-sin** on Thursdays.

torttu cake; *(hedelmä-)* tart; *tortut* pastries.

toru|a scold; *~ jkta (m.)* give. . a scolding. **-t** scolding; rebuke.

torven|soittaja trumpeter. **-toitotus** blast of a trumpet.

torvi horn; trumpet; *anat. ym* pipe, tube; *(kannun)* spout; *auton ~* car horn. **-mainen** tubular. **-soitin** brass instrument. **-soittokunta** brass band.

tosi *s.* truth; *a.* true, veritable; *olla ~ssaan* be serious *(t.* in earnest); mean it seriously; *käydä toteen* come true, come to pass, be fulfilled; *näyttää toteen* prove [the truth of], demonstrate [the truth of], *(lak.)* substantiate; *osoittautua todeksi* prove [to be] true; *toden totta* truly, in truth; *toden teolla* really; *puhua totta* speak the truth; *totta puhuakseni* to tell the truth; *totta puhuen* strictly speaking; *ihanko totta* really? *vrt. totta.* **-aan** indeed; *pyydän ~ anteeksi* I do apologize [for coming, *että tulin*]; *onpa ~kin* it certainly is; yes, indeed; *en ~kaan tiedä* I'm sure, I don't know; *ei ~kaan ole niin helppoa* is isn't all that easy. **-asia** fact; *tapahtunut ~* fait accompli.

-asiallinen actual, real,. . founded on fact. **-asiallisesti** in fact, actually, in effect. **-n.** . it is true; *hänellä on talo, ~ pieni, mutta. .* he has a house, a small one to be sure, but. . **-seikka** fact. **-ssaan:** *olla aivan ~* be in earnest, mean it [quite] seriously, mean business. **-tapaus** true event. **-tarve** actual need. **-te** voucher; *tosittee|ksi, -na* for reference.

tosikko *puhek.* sober-sides.

tossut *(vauvan)* bootees, *(kumi-)* sneakers, sandshoes, gym shoes.

totaalinen: *~ sota* total *(t.* all-out) war.

totali|saattori totalizator, *puhek.* tote; *~veikkaus* tote-betting. **-taarinen** totalitarian.

totella obey; *(seurata)* follow; answer [the helm, *peräsintä*], respond to; be obedient to.

toteu|ttaa carry out, put into effect, realize [a plan, an ambition, *suunnitelma, aikomus*]; *(saattaa loppuun)* fulfil, accomplish, carry through; *(panna toimeen)* put into practice; *mahdollinen ~* practicable; realizable. **-ttaminen** realization; *itsensä ~* self-fulfilment. **-tua** come true; materialize, be realized, be fulfilled; come off, work out. **-tumaton** unfulfilled. **-tuminen** realization, materialization.

toti|nen serious, grave, earnest. **-sesti** truly, in very truth. **-suus** seriousness, earnestness.

totta: *eikö ~ ks. (eikö) niin; ~kai* certainly! [yes,] indeed! of course! oh yes! *~han sinä tulet* you will come, won't you? *niin ~ kuin elän* as sure as I am alive today; *niin ~ kuin Jumala minua auttakoon* so help me God.

tottele|maton disobedient; insubordinate; *olla ~ jkta kohtaan* be disobedient to, disobey a p. **-mattomuus** disobedience; insubordination. **-vainen** obedient, dutiful. **-vaisuus** obedience.

tottu|a become accustomed to, get used to, accustom oneself to; *olla -nut jhk* be used (accustomed) to; *-nut purjehtija* experienced (trained) yachtsman; *-neella kädellä* with a trained hand; *totuttuun tapaan* in the usual (customary) manner. **-maton** unaccustomed, *(jhk)* unused to, not used to; unfamiliar with. **-mattomuus** unfamiliarity (with), inexperience. **-mus** custom, habit; *(harjoitus)* practice; *vanhasta -muksesta* from force of habit; *~ta aiheuttava (lääke ym)* addictive. **-neesti** in an experienced manner, *(taitavasti)* skilfully.

totu|nnainen conventional. **-ttaa** accustom, make.. accustomed (to); make.. familiar (with); *(karaista)* inure. **-ttautua** [try to] accustom oneself; get used to; *(jhk tapaan)* get into the habit [of smoking etc.].

totuude|llinen, -nmukainen truthful, veracious. **-nmukaisuus** truthfulness, veracity. **-nrakkaus** [love of] truth.

totuus truth; *hän sai kuulla totuuden* he was told the [whole] truth; *katkera ~ a* home truth.

touhu bustle; fuss; *(kiire)* flurry. **-kas** busy; bustling; *(palvelushaluinen)* officious. **-ta** be busy; bustle [about].

toukka larva *(pl. -e)*; *(et. perhosen)* caterpillar, *(et. kovakuoriaisen)* grub; *(juustossa ym)* maggot. **-aste** larval stage.

touko [spring] sowing. **-aika** sowing season. **-kuu** May.

touvi hawser.

toveri comrade; *(kumppani)* companion; mate; *opettaja~* fellow teacher; *koulu~* schoolmate, schoolfellow; *ylioppilas-~* fellow student. **-henki** fellowship. **-llinen** companionable, comradely, *puhek.* matey. **-llisuus** sociability, camaraderie. **-piiri** *(ystävä-)* circle of friends.

toveruus comradeship, fellowship; companionship.

traagi|nen tragic [al]. **-suus** tragicalness; *sen ~ (m.) the* tragedy of it.

traani whale-oil, train-oil.

trag|edia, -iikka tragedy.

trakooma trachoma.

traktaatti tract, *(sopimus)* treaty.

traktori tractor, *(tela-)* caterpillar t.

transistoroi|da transistorize; *kokonaan -tu* all-transistorized.

transitiivinen *kiel.* transitive.

trapetsi trapeze. **-taiteilija** t. artist.

trasseli cotton waste.

tratta *liik.* draft.

treen|ata train. **-aus** training.

trigonometria trigonometry.

trikiini trichina *(pl. -e).*

trikoo knitwear, jersey, tricot. **-puku** knitwear *(t.* jersey) suit (dress). **-tavarat** knitwear. **-t** tights, *Am.* leotards.

trimmata *(loistokuntoon)* condition; *(moottori)* tune up.

Troija Troy. **t-lainen** *a. &. s.* Trojan.

trokari *(viina-)* bootlegger.

trooppinen tropical.

tropiikki tropics.

trotyyli trinitrotoluene, TNT.

trubaduuri troubadour.

trukki truck (fork t., loading t.).

trumpetti trumpet.

trusti *liik.* trust, combine.

tsaari Tsar, Czar. **-tar** Tsarina, Czarina.

tšekkiläinen *a. &. s.* Czech.

Tšekkoslovakia Czechoslovakia. **t-lainen** *a. & s.* Czechoslovak.

tuberkkelibasilli tubercle bacillus.

tuberkuloo|si tuberculosis. **-ttinen** tuberculous, tubercular.

tuhan|nes thousandth, *(-osa)* thousandth [part] (of). **-nesti** a thousand times. **-sittain** by (in) thousands, by the thousand; *~ ihmisiä* thousands of people.

tuhat a (one) thousand; *yksi mahdollisuus tuhannesta* one chance in a thousand; *tuhansissa kodeissa* in thousands of homes; ~ *ja yksi yötä* Arabian Nights. **-jalkainen** myriapod; *(juoksu-)* centipede. **-kertainen** thousandfold. **-määrin:**. . *oli* ~ there were thousands [and thousands] of. . **-taituri** jack of all trades. **-vuotinen:** ~ *valtakunta* millennium.

tuher|taa dabble; *(tuhria)* daub. **-taja** bungler, dauber.

tuhis|ta hiss; *(sieraimiinsa)* sniff, snuffle.

tuhka ashes; *kuin ~ tuuleen* as ashes before the wind; *kaupunki on ~na* the town is laid in ashes. **-kuppi** ash-tray. **-nharmaa** ash-grey, ashen. **-rokko** measles. **-tiheään** in rapid succession, very frequently.

tuhkimo Cinderella.

tuhl|aaja spendthrift; *(~poika* the prodigal son). **-aavainen** wasteful, extravagant. **-aavaisuus** wastefulness, extravagance. **-ata** squander; *(haaskata)* waste; ~ *rahaa turhuuksiin* spend money recklessly; ~ *lahjoja jklle* lavish presents on; ~ *aikaa* waste time. **-aus** extravagance.

tuhm|a naughty; *vrt. tyhmä.* **-uus** naughtiness.

tuho ruin, *(esim. jnk valtakunnan)* fall; *(hävitys)* destruction, havoc; ravage; *(täydellinen)* annihilation; *(vahinko)* damage; *tehdä ~a* cause destruction, play havoc [among, with *jssk*]; *alkoholi oli hänen ~nsa* drink was his undoing; *tulvan ~t* damage by the flood; *~a tuottava* destructive, ruinous. **-aseet** weapons of [mass] destruction. **-eläin, -hyönteinen, -lainen** pest. **-isa** disastrous, destructive; calamitous; *(kuolettava)* fatal (to). **-isuus** disastrous character; destructiveness. **-laismyrkky** pesticide. **-laistyö** sabotage. **-polttaja** incendiary. **-poltto** arson, incendiarism.

tuhota destroy, ruin; *(autioittaa)* lay waste,

devastate; *(vahingoittaa)* damage; *(viimeiseen mieheen)* annihilate; *(kuv. usein)* wreck [a p.'s happiness, *jkn onni*], undo.

tuho|tulva flood. **-työ** work of destruction; devastation, damage. **-utua** be destroyed, be ruined, perish; *(et. laiva)* be wrecked.

tuhr|aantua get dirty, get soiled. **-ata, -ia** soil.

tuhto [rower's] seat, thwart.

tuijo|ttaa stare, gaze (at); *(vihaisesti)* glower, glare (at); *(rakastuneesti)* make eyes at, ogle. **-tus** staring, stare.

tuike twinkling, twinkle.

tuike|a sharp; *(ankara)* stern; grim; **-us** sharpness; sternness.

tuiki quite; altogether; *(ylen)* extremely; ~ *kelvoton* utterly worthless; ~ *mahdoton* simply (absolutely) impossible; ~ *tarpeellinen.* . of utmost necessity.

tuikkia twinkle, glimmer, gleam.

tuim|a sharp; grim; *(ankara)* severe; stern, hard; ~ *katse* sharp (grim) look; ~ *pakkanen* severe (biting, bitter) cold. **-uus** sharpness; severity, grimness.

tuisku [driving] snowstorm; blizzard. **-ta** be whirling; be flying; *lumi -aa* the snow is blowing about; *umpeen -nnut* snowed up, blocked with snow [-drifts].

tuiterissa tiddly, tipsy.

tuittu|päinen hot-tempered; ill-tempered, *(äkäinen)* cross, irascible. **-päisyys** hot (quick) temper. **-pää:** ~ *tyttö* ill-tempered girl, *vrt. ed.*

tukah|duttaa suffocate; smother, stifle, keep back, repress; ~ *kapina* suppress (quell, put down) a rebellion; ~ *tulen valta* smother (extinguish, put out) a fire; *-dutettu huuto* stifled cry; *-dutettu kiukku* repressed anger. **-duttaminen** smothering *jne.;* suppression, repression. **-duttava** suffocating; sultry, sweltering [heat, *kuumuus*]; *(painostava)* oppressive. **-tua** be smothered, be stifled *jne.*

tukal|a hard, difficult, *(kiusallinen)* awkward, embarrassing; ~*ssa asemassa* in an awkward situation, in difficulties. **-uus** difficulty; *(pula)* embarrassment.

tukan|kuivauslaite hair-dryer. **-leikkuu** hair-cut[ting]; (~**kone** clippers).

tukea support *(m. kuv.),* give support (to); prop [up]; *(vahvistaa)* strengthen, sustain; *(esim. valtio)* subsidize; *jkn tukemana* supported by; backed by.

tukeh|dus suffocation. **-duttaa** choke, suffocate; *vrt. tukahduttaa;* asphyxiate. **-tua** be suffocated, die from suffocation.

tukev|a steady, firm; stable; *(vahva)* heavy; substantial [meal, *ateria*]; *(tanakka)* sturdy; ~*sti paikoillaan* firmly (securely) in position. **-atekoinen**. . of solid make, stout. **-uus** steadiness, firmness, stoutness, heavy (strong) quality.

tuki support; *(kuv. esim. perheen)* mainstay; *(pönkkä)* prop, strut; *(esim. -sidos)* brace, *(jalan alla)* instep (metatarsal arch) support; *antaa tukea jllek* give support to, support; *jnk tueksi* in support of. **-aiset** *leik. ks. -palkkio.* **-kohta** *sot.* base. **-mies** *jalkap.* half-back.

tukinuitto timber (log) floating. **tuki|palkkio** subsidy; *(hinta-)* price support. **-pylväs** supporting pillar; *kuv.* mainstay. **-rauta** clamp.

tukistaa: ~ *jkta* pull a p.'s hair.

tukka hair. **-laite** coiffure, hair style, *puhek.* hair-do. **-nuottasilla:** *olla* ~ *(kuv. = kiistellä)* be at loggerheads.

tukkeutua become blocked (obstructed), *(putki, m.)* be clogged, *(liikenne)* be blocked.

tukki log; beam *(m. kangas-);* *(kiväärin)* stock.

tukkia stop, stop up; *(sulkea)* shut [up]; *(esim. liikenne)*

block [up]; *(tulpalla)* plug [up]; *(estää)* obstruct; ~ *reikä* stop (plug) a hole, *(vuoto)* stop a leak.

tukki|lainen lumberjack. **-lautta** raft. **-puu** timber. **-suma** jam of logs. **-työ** logging. **-työläinen** lumberjack. **-yhtiö** lumber company.

tukko *(tukku)* bunch, *(esim. hius-)* tuft; *(heinä- ym)* wisp; *(side)* dressing; *harso~* swab; *vrt. vanu~; sormi~* finger stall; *olla tukossa* be blocked, be obstructed.

tukku bunch; *(seteleitä)* wad; *ostaa tukussa* buy wholesale. **-hinta** wholesale price. **-kauppa** wholesale [trade]. **-kauppias** wholesale dealer, [wholesale] merchant. **-osto** bulk buying.

tukos *lääk.* occlusion.

tukuittain wholesale.

tuleentua ripen.

tuleh|dus inflammation; (~**peräinen** inflammatory). **-duttaa** cause inflammation. **-tua** become (get) inflamed; *-tunut* inflamed.

tulema *mat.* answer.

tulen|arka inflammable; ~ *aine* combustible. **-arkuus** inflammability. **-johto** fire control. **-kestävä** fireproof; *(liekin-)* flameproof; ~ *lasi* heat-resisting glass; ~ *tiili* firebrick; ~ *vuoka* oven-proof dish, ovenware. **-lopettami|nen:** *antaa t-skäsky* issue a cease-fire. **-vaara** fire risk; danger of fire.

tuleva coming; future; *(seuraava)* next; *(aiottu)* prospective; ~ *elämä* the life to come; ~*lla viikolla* next week; ~*t sukupolvet* (m.) generations to come; *(säästää)* *tulevien päivien varalta* [put. . by] for a rainy day; *mitä minulle on* ~*a* what is due to me; ~*n kuun 1. päivänä* on the first of next month.

tulevaisuu|s future; *sen on* ~ *osoittava* time will show, only time can tell, this is a problem for the future; *-den näkymät* outlook, prospects

[for the future]; -den *suunnitelmat* plans for the future.
tuli fire; *(valo)* light; *tulessa* afire, aflame; *on tulessa* is on fire, *(ilmi-)* is ablaze; *mennä vaikka tuleen jkn puolesta* go through fire and water for sb.; *avata* ~ open fire (on); *vastata tuleen* return the fire; *ei ottanut tulta (kuv.)* did not catch on.
tuli|aiset [home-coming] present [s]. **-ja** comer.
tuli|ase fire-arm. **-kaste** baptism of fire. **-kivi** brimstone. **-koe** ordeal by fire. **-kuuma** red-hot. **-linja** firing line. **-mmainen:** *tuhat -mmaista* confound it! **-nen** fiery; *(palava)* burning; hot; *(kiihkeä)* passionate, ardent; hot-headed; ~ *kiire* great haste; *-sen kuuma* burning hot; *koota -sia hiiliä jkn pään päälle* heap coals of fire on a p.'s head; *kuin -silla hiilillä* like a cat on hot bricks. **-palo** fire; *(roihu, m.)* conflagration. **-patsas** raam. pillar of fire. **-peräinen** volcanic. **-pesä** furnace. **-punainen** fiery red, scarlet. **-rokko** scarlet fever. **-sesti** hotly, passionately, ardently. **-staa** *(höyryä)* superheat. **-stua** lose one's temper, get excited, flare up. **-suus** fiery *(t.* hot) temper. **-taistelu** gun battle. **-tauko** cease-fire. **-terä** brand new. **-tikku** match; *(~laatikko* match-box). **-ttaa** fire (at). **-vuori** volcano.
tulkin|nanvarainen open to [various] interpretations. **-ta** interpretation.
tulkita interpret; *(salakirjoitus)* decipher, *(koodi)* decode; *(selittää)* expound, explain; ~ *väärin* misinterpret, misconstrue, put a false construction on.
tulkki interpreter.
tulla come; *(päästä)* get [there, sinne], *(saapua)* arrive (at, *iso paikka:* in); *(jksk)* become, get, grow; *tulee (pitää)* has to, shall, must;

jnk, jkn tulisi. . should,. . ought to; *kun talvi tuli* when the winter came (set in); ~ *iloiseksi* be glad (pleased), be [come] delighted; ~ *ajatelleeksi jtk* happen (come) to think of; ~ *sanoneeksi* happen to say, let slip; ~ *takaisin* come back, return; *tulen heti takaisin* I shall be back presently; *toinen bussi tulee pian* there will be another bus soon; *minun tuli jano, nälkä* I got (I became) thirsty (hungry); *tulee kylmä* it is getting cold; *minun tuli kylmä* I became cold, I began to feel cold; *mitä minuun tulee* as far as I am concerned, for my part; *mitä siihen asiaan tulee* as for that, for that matter, as regards that; *tuletko mukaan* are you coming [along]? *sanokaa, että hän tulisi kello 10* tell him to call at 10 o'clock; *siitä ei tule mitään* it will come to nothing; *mikä pojasta tulee* what is the boy [going] to be; *hänestä tuli kirjailija* he became an author; *hänestä tulisi kelpo sotilas* he would make a good soldier; *kotiin tullessani* when I got (arrived) home; *mikä sinun tuli (on)* what is the matter with you; *tulisitteko (teatteriin yms.)* would you like to come to. ., could you come to. .; *hän tulee isäänsä* he takes after his father. *se tulee olemaan vaikeata* it will be difficult; *tuleeko siitä mitään?* will it come to anything? *kaupasta ei tule mitään* the deal is off.
tull|aamaton uncustomed. **-ata** clear, examine at the custom-house; *onko teillä jotakin tullattavaa* have you anything to declare? **-aus** customs examination.
tulli customs; *(maksu)* duty; *maksaa ~a* pay duty (on); *silkin* ~ *on korkea* there is a heavy duty on silk. **-asema** customs. **-kamari** customs office; custom-house. **-käsittely**

ks. -*tarkastus.* -**laitos** the Customs. -**leima** custom-house stamp. -**maksu** duty; ~*tta* free of duty. -**muuri** tariff wall. -**nalainen** dutiable, subject (liable) to duty. -**nhoitaja** customs officer. -**politiikka** tariff policy. -**puomi** toll-bar. -**selvitys** customs clearance. -**sopimus** tariff treaty. -**taksa** customs tariff. -**tarkastus** customs examination. -**ton,** -**vapaa** free of (exempt from) duty, duty-free. -**tulot** customs revenue. -**vapaus** exemption from duty. -**varasto** bonded warehouse; ~*ssa* in bond. -**virkamies** custom-house officer, customs official.

tulo coming; arrival; *(sisään)* entrance; *(raha-)* income, *(et. valtion)* revenue; *mat.* product; ~*t* income, receipts, *(jstk kertyvät)* proceeds; returns; *(palkka)* earnings; ~*t ja menot* income and expenditure; *hänellä on .. ~ja vuodessa* he is making .. a year; *hänellä ei ole muita ~ja kuin palkkansa* he has no income other than his salary; ~*a tuottava* profitable, remunerative; *on* ~*ssa* is coming, is on the way; is drawing near, is approaching. -**arvio** estimate of income; *t-ja menoarvio* budget. -**asteikko** income scale *(t.* bracket). -**erä** item of income; sum received. -**kas** newcomer. -**ksellinen** productive,.. yielding results, successful. -**kseton**.. without result [s]; unsuccessful; *(turha)* of no avail. -**luokka** income bracket. -**lähde** source of income. -**njako** income distribution. -**politiikka** incomes policy. -**puoli** debit side.

tulos result; *(loppu-)* outcome, issue; *(seuraus)* consequence; *mat.* answer; *tiet. m.* finding; *tuloksetta* without result, to no purpose; *antaa hyvä ~* bring good results, yield a good return; *saavuttaa hyvä ~* obtain a good result; *keskustelun tuloksena oli, että*

the discussion resulted in .. ; *vaalin tulokset* election returns. -**tase** profit and loss account. -**taulu** scoreboard.

tulovero income tax.
tulppa plug; stopper, bung.
tulppaani tulip.

tulv|a flood, *(suuri)* deluge; *kuv. m.* influx, torrent, flow; *olla* ~*n vallassa* be flooded, be inundated; ~*naan* in torrents; ~*illaan* brimming (with); *joki on* -*illaan* the river has overflowed its banks. (~*alue* flooded area). -**anaika** season of floods. -**avahinko** damage by flood. -**avesi** flood. -**ia** *(esim. joki)* overflow [its banks]; break (burst) its banks, flood; flow; *(jhk, kuv.)* pour into; *joet -ivat* the streams flooded; *hänelle -ii kirjeitä* he is flooded with letters.

tuma nucleus *(pl.* nuclei).
tumma dark. ~ *puku* dark suit. -**hko** darkish. -**ihoinen** dark-skinned; dusky, swarthy. -**npunainen** dark red. -**tukkainen** dark-haired. -**verinen** dark, *(naisesta, m.)* brunette.

tumme|ntaa darken. -**ta** darken, become (grow) dark [er].
tummuus darkness.
tumpata stub out.
tunaroida bungle, fumble.
tunge|ksia [be] crowd [ing], throng, *(parveilla)* mill around. -**tella** *kuv.* intrude, obtrude oneself [upon, *jkn seuraan*]. -**ttelevainen** intrusive, obtrusive; importunate. -**ttelevaisuus** intrusiveness, obtrusiveness. -**ttelija** intruder, importunate person. -**ttelu** intrusion, obtrusion.

tungos crowd, throng; [traffic] congestion; crush; *tungokseen asti täynnä* crowded, packed (with), overcrowded, jammed [with people].

tunke|a press, force, *jhk* into; crowd; *(pieneen tilaan)* jam, squeeze into; ~ *läpi* penetrate; force one's way through, break through;

(nestemäisistä aineista)
permeate; ~ *tieltään* force. .
aside; displace; ~ *takaisin*
force (press). . back. **-illa** *ks.*
tungetella. **-utua** force one's
way, push; *(jkn seuraan)*
intrude; *(lävitse)* penetrate;
edge one's way through; ~
eteenpäin press forward, push
on; ~ *toisen alueelle (m.*
kuv.) encroach [up]on
another's land (property etc.);
~ *väliin (esim. auto)* cut in;
vihollinen -utui maahan the
enemy invaded the country.
tunkio rubbish-heap.

tunkki jack; *nostaa tunkilla*
jack up [the car].

tunne feeling, *(m. = liikutus)*
emotion; sense; sensation [of
heat, of pain]; *syyllisyyden* ~
sense of guilt. **-arvo**
sentimental value. **-elämä**
emotional life. **-ihminen:** *on*
~ is emotional, is a
spontaneous person.
tunneittain hourly, by the hour.
tunneli tunnel; *(jalankulku-)*
subway.
tunnelm|**a** sentiment;
atmosphere; *(mielentila)* mood;
~ *oli korkealla* spirits ran
high; *yleinen* ~ public
sentiment. **-allinen** . full of
feeling, moving. **-oida** be
sentimental.
tunne|**peräinen** emotional. **-syyt**
reasons of sentiment;
-syistä for sentimental reasons.
tunne|**ttu** well-known; known
[for, *jstk*], noted, famed; *(us.*
pahassa merk.) notorious;
kansainvälisesti ~ *(m.)*
internationally acknowledged;
hän on ~ *hyvänä puhujana*
he is known to be a good
speaker; *jos se tulee -tuksi* if
it becomes known; if is gets
about; *tehdä nimensä -tuksi*
make a name for oneself;
kuten ~*a* as is well known;
-tumpi, -tuin better (best)
known. **-tusti** known to be
[good, *hyvä*], [generally]
accepted (as), *(joskus)*
admittedly.
tunnis|**taa** identify; recognize.
-tus identification.

tunnolli|**nen** conscientious. **-suus**
conscientiousness.
tunnon|**rauha:** *sai* ~*n* [his]
conscience was at rest
(peace). **-tarkka** conscientious,
scrupulous. **-tarkkuus**
conscientiousness,
scrupulousness, meticulousness.
-vaivat pangs of conscience,
remorse, compunction.
tunno|**ton** unscrupulous;
(tajuton) unconscious;
insensible; *tehdä -ttomaksi*
render insensible. **-ttomuus**
insensibility; unscrupulousness.
tunnus [distinctive] mark,
sign; emblem; *(kilpi)* badge;
(-sana) password, watchword.
-kuva symbol. **-lause** motto.
-merkillinen characteristic;
typical. **-merkki** [distinctive]
mark, sign; distinctive feature,
characteristic. **-sana** *sot.*
password; *(erikois-)* parole;
(isku-) watchword, slogan.
-sävel signature tune. **-taa**
confess; make a confession;
(jtk uskoa) profess; *(myöntää)*
admit; own [up to];
acknowledge, *(valtio)* recognize
[officially]; ~ *rikoksensa*
confess one's crime; ~ *itsensä*
syylliseksi (oikeudessa) plead
guilty; ~ *vastaanottaneensa*
acknowledge the receipt of; ~
vekseli accept a bill; ~ *väriä*
follow suit, *kuv.* show one's
colour. **-taja** *(vekselin)*
acceptor; *jnk uskon* ~
adherent to a faith. **-te**
(vekselin-) acceptance. **-tella**
feel [about] (for); *(hapuilla)*
feel one's way, fumble (for);
kuv. see how the land lies,
sound [a p.]; ~ *jkn*
mielipidettä (jstk) sound a p.
(about, as to). **-telu:** ~*t*
(kuv.) exploratory contacts;
tehdä ~*ja (m.)* put out
feelers. **-tuksellinen**
confessional. **-tus** confession
(m. usk.); usk. creed;
(hyväksymys, m. valtion)
recognition; appreciation;
-tukseksi hänen ansioistaan in
recognition of his merits;
saada ~*ta* win recognition;
~*ta ansaitseva.* . worthy of

recognition; ~ta antava (kiitollinen) appreciative. **-tähti** sign.

tunte|a feel; (tietää) know; (olla tuttu) know, be acquainted (with); (jku jksk) recognize; tunnen hänet I know him; tunsin hänet heti I knew him (I recognized him) at once; ~ äänestä know (recognize) a p. by his voice; en ollut ~ sinua I could hardly recognize you; oppia -maan get (come) to know; ~ iloa feel joy; ~ itsensä onnelliseksi, sairaaksi feel happy (ill); tehdä tunnetuksi make known.

tunteelli|nen emotional; (ylen) sentimental; (herkkä) sensitive. **-suus** sentimentality; emotionalism; sensitiveness.

tuntee|ton unfeeling, unemotional. **-ttomuus** lack of feeling, insensibility.

tunteilla be emotional, be sentimental.

tunte|maton unknown; unfamiliar; (vieras) strange; ~ henkilö a stranger [to me, minulle]; seutua ~ unfamiliar with the neighbourhood; matkustaa ~na travel incognito; -mattoman sotilaan hauta the unknown warrior's tomb. **-mattomuus** (jnk) unfamiliarity (with). **-mus** knowledge (of); familiarity (with).

tunti hour; (opetus-) lesson; 45 minuutin ~ 45-minute period; antaa tunteja give lessons (in), (tutkintoa varten) coach (sb. in); (10 mk) tunnilta ten marks an hour; tunnin ~ hour; tunnin matka an hour's journey.

tuntija (jnk) expert (in), connoisseur (of); judge [of horses etc.].

tunti|kausi: ~a for hours [and hours]. **-lasi** hour-glass, sandglass. **-nen:** .. lasting.. hours, .. hours'; 8-~ työpäivä eight-hour day. **-nopeus** speed per hour. **-opettaja** part-time teacher. **-osoitin** hour hand. **-palkka** wages per hour;

(tehdä työtä) -palkalla [be paid] by the hour. **-palkkio** charges (fee) per hour.

tunto feeling, touch; (tunne) sensation [of]; (oma-) conscience; (taju) consciousness. **-aisti** tactile sense. **-elin** tactile organ. **-hermo** sensory nerve. **-levy** (sotilaan) identity disk. **-merkki** mark of identification; distinctive mark; (paikan) landmark; -merkit [personal] description. **-sarvi** antenna, tentacle.

tuntu|a feel [soft, pehmeältä]; be [refreshing, virkistävältä]; be felt, make itself felt, (esim. haju) be noticeable; (näyttää) seem, appear; -u hyvälle it feels good; -u pahalta (mielessäni) I feel uncomfortable; minusta -u it seems to me [as if, kuin]. **-ma:** pysyä ~ssa (urh.) hang on.

tunturi mountain, fell, fjeld.

tuntuva perceptible; (huomattava) considerable, marked. **-sti** perceptibly; considerably; ~ enemmän a good deal more, much more.

tuo that; subst. that one; ~lla tavoin like that; ~ssa there; ~ssa talossa in that house; ~n ~stakin again and again, time and again.

tuoda bring; (jnnek, esim. tapa) introduce; (noutaa) fetch; (kuljettaa) carry; (perille) deliver; ~ esille express; ~ ilmi disclose; ~ maahan import; ~ mukanaan bring.. with one, (kuv.) bring in its train.

tuohi birch bark. **-kontti** knapsack of birch-bark.

tuoja bearer [of a message, sanan-]; (maahan-) importer.

tuokio a [little] while; a moment; a minute; tuossa ~ssa in [less than] no time, in a moment, this minute, right away. **-kuva** glimpse; (valo-) snapshot.

tuokkonen [birch-bark] basket; (pahvi-) carton, (marja-) punnet.

tuoksina tumult.
tuoksu good (sweet) smell, scent, odour; fragrance; aroma. **-a** smell [good, *hyvältä*], be fragrant.
tuoli chair; seat; *(selkänojaton)* stool; **-n käsinoja** arm [of a chair]. **-rivi** row [of chairs]; *porrastetut* ~*t* tiers of seats.
tuolla [over] there; ~ *alhaalla* down there; ~ *puolen* beyond; ~ *ulkona* out there.
tuollainen *a.* such,. . like that, such a [man, *mies*];. . of that kind; *s.* such a one.
tuolta from there.
tuomari judge *(m. palkinto-);* justice; *Engl. m.* magistrate; *urh.* umpire, *jalkap.* referee; *(riidanratkaisija)* arbitrator; *(oikeust.kand.)* Bachelor of Laws, L L. B. **-ntoimi** office of a judge.
tuomaskuona basic slag.
tuomi bird-cherry.
tuomio judg[e]ment; *(rikosjutuissa)* sentence; *(lautakunnan, m. yl.)* verdict; *(yl. merkit.)* doom, condemnation; *(esim. palkintotuomarin)* award; *langettaa* ~ pronounce judg[e]ment; *viimeinen* ~ the last judg[e]ment. **-istuin** court [of justice]; tribunal; forum. **-kapituli** Chapter. **-kirkko** cathedral. **-kunta** judicial district. **-päivä** day of judg[e]ment, doomsday. **-rovasti** dean; *(~kunta** deanery). **-valta** judicial power; jurisdiction.
tuomiset [home-coming] presents.
tuomi|ta *(rikollinen)* sentence; *(arvostella)* judge; condemn *(m. kuv.); (etuja jklle)* adjudge; award; ~ *kuolemaan* sentence. . to death; ~ *sakkoihin* fine [a p.], impose a fine [of. . upon a p.]; ~ *jku syylliseksi* convict a p. (of), *(lautakunta)* pass a verdict of guilty upon; ~ *jku vankeuteen* sentence. . to [three years', *elinkautiseen: life*] imprisonment; *-ttu* condemned, *(jhk kohtaloon)*

doomed [to failure, *epäonnistumaan*]; *-tseva* ready to judge, censorious; condemnatory. **-ttava**. . to be condemned, condemnable.
tuommoinen such,. . like that.
tuonela realm of the dead, Hades.
tuonne [over] there. **-mmaksi** farther that way; farther away; *lykätä* ~ postpone, put off. **-mpana** farther away (off); *(myöhemmin)* later on, *(alla)* below. **-päin** that way, in that direction.
tuonti import, importation; *(-tavarat)* imports. **-kielto** import embargo, ban on [the] import (of). **-liike** import firm. **-rajoitus** import restriction. **-tavarat** imported goods, imports. **-tulli** import duty. **-vero** *(ylimääräinen)* import surcharge. **-voittoisuus** unfavourable balance of trade.
tuoppi stoup, tankard.
tuore fresh; *(kostea)* moist, *(rapea)* crisp; *(äskeinen)* recent; ~*et uutiset* the latest news; ~ *leipä* fresh [ly] baked; ~ *puutavara* unseasoned timber; *se on hänellä ~essa muistissa* it is still fresh in his mind, he retains a lively recollection of it. **-mehu** juice. **-us** freshness.
tuo|ssa there. **-sta** from there; *(asiasta)* of that.
tuotanto production; *(määrään nähden)* output. **-komitea** Works Council *(t. Committee)*. **-kustannukset** cost of production. **-kyky** productive capacity. **-linja** assembly line. **-määrä** output.
tuote product; *(kalu)* article; *tuotteet (m.)* produce. **-esittelijä** demonstrator.
tuott|aa produce; yield; *(aiheuttaa)* cause; ~ *hedelmää* bear fruit; ~ *häpeää* bring disgrace [up]on; ~ *kunniaa jklle* be a credit to; ~ *ulkomailta* import from abroad; ~ *vahinkoa* cause damage; ~ *voittoa*. . yields a profit, *(liike, m.).* . is a paying concern; *se* ~

vaikeuksia it presents difficulties; ~ *hyvän sadon* gives a good yield (return);.. *-i hyvän hinnan* fetched a high price; *se ei -anut minulle mitään iloa* it gave me no pleasure, I derived no pleasure from it. **-aja** producer. **-amaton** unproductive; unprofitable. **-ava** productive; *(tuloja-)* profitable, remunerative, paying. **-avuus** productivity, productiveness; profitableness. **-elias** productive, *(kirjailija)* prolific. **-o** yield, returns; *(voitto)* profit; *vrt. tuotanto.* **-oisa** *ks. tuottava.*

tupa hut, cottage, cabin; *(huone)* living-room [in a farmhouse]. **-antulijaiset** house-warming. **-jumi** furniture beetle.

tupakan|haju smell of tobacco. **-polttaja** smoker. **-poltto** smoking; *hän on lopettanut -polton* he has left off smoking, he is an ex-smoker; ~ *kielletty* no smoking. **-tuhka** tobacco ashes.

tupakka tobacco; *panna tupakaksi* have a smoke. **-kauppa** tobacconist's. **-kauppias** tobacconist. **-kukkaro** tobacco pouch. **-mies** smoker. **-tehdas** tobacco factory. **-vaunu** smoking-carriage; *(-osasto)* smoking-compartment.

tupakoi|da smoke. **-maton** *s.* non-smoker. **-nti** smoking.

tupat|a force, press, push; *-en täynnä* chock-full (of).

tupeeraus *(hiusten)* back-combing, back-brushing.

tuppautua: ~ *jnnek, jkn seuraan* intrude.

tuppi *m. tiet.* sheath; *(miekan, m.)* scabbard; case, casing. **-suu** silent person; *olla ~na* not say a word.

tupru|ta whirl, blow about; puff; *lumi -aa* the snow is whirling about. **-tella** *(piippuaan)* puff [at one's pipe].

tupsahtaa: *tulla* ~ come unexpectedly.

tupsu tassel; tuft. **-lakki** tasselled cap.

turbaani turban. **-päinen** turbaned.

turbiini turbine.

turha unnecessary, needless; *(hyödytön)* useless,.. of no use, futile, vain; ~ *pelko* groundless fear; ~ *työ* useless (wasted) work; ~ *vaiva* vain efforts, lost labour; ~*t toiveet* vain hopes; *tehdä ~ksi* baffle, frustrate;.. *osoittautui ~ksi.* . proved fruitless (futile, in vain). **-an** in vain, to no purpose; *(suotta)* unnecessarily. **-mainen** vain, *(pöyhkeilevä)* vainglorious. **-maisuus** vanity. **-nkaino** prudish; ~ *ihminen* a prude. **-npäiten** unnecessarily. **-npäiväinen** futile, *(mitätön)* trifling, trivial. **-npäiväi|syys** futility; *t-syyksiä* trifles. trifling matters. **-ntarkka** too particular, overparticular; fussy; *(nirso)* fastidious; pedantic; ~ *henkilö* pedant. **-u(tu)ma** *psyk.* frustration.

turhuus vanity; futility.

turilas cockchafer.

turkis: *turkikset* furs, *(muokkaamattomat)* pelts, skins. **-eläin** fur-bearing animal. **-kaulus** fur collar. **-kauppa** fur trade; *(myymälä)* furrier's [shop]. **-kauppias** furrier. **-lakki** fur cap. **-metsästäjä** trapper. **-reunusteinen** fur-trimmed. **-sisuste** fur lining. **-sisusteinen** fur-lined. **-takki** fur coat. **-tarhaus** fur- (mink etc) farming.

turkki *(eläimen)* fur, coat, *(nyljettynä)* pelt; *(takki)* fur coat.

Turkki Turkey. **t-lainen** *a.* Turkish; *s.* Turk.

turkkuri furrier.

turkoosi turquoise.

turma ruin, destruction.

turme|lematon unspoilt, unspoiled, undamaged. **-lla** spoil; *(vahingoittaa)* damage, do damage (to), injure; mar; harm, hurt; *(tuhota)* ruin, destroy; *(moraalisesti)* deprave; ~ *terveytensä* ruin one's health. **-ltua** be spoiled, be[come] damaged. **-ltumaton** unspoilt, undamaged; uncorrupted. **-ltunut** spoilt, damaged; *(moraalisesti)* corrupt. **-lus** *(tapain ym.)* depravity, demoralization; *(rappio)* decay, decline.

turmio ruin; *syöksyä* ~*on* plunge headlong to destruction; *se vei hänet* ~*on* it was his undoing. **-llinen** pernicious, noxious; injurious, harmful; *(-ta tuottava)* ruinous, destructive. **-llisuus** pernicious (detrimental) character; harmfulness; destructive effect[s].

turna|**jaiset** tournament, tourney. **-us** tournament.

turpa muzzle; *(sian ym.)* snout.

turpe|**a** bloated; swollen; turgid; *(huuli)* thick. **-us** bloated condition.

turruttaa make numb, render insensible, *kuv.* [be]numb.

turska cod.

turt|**a** numb, insensible. **-ua** become numb; *kuv.* be dulled; become apathetic.

turturikyyhky turtle-dove.

turva *(suoja)* shelter; *(suojelus)* protection; *(-paikka)* refuge; *(-llisuus)* security, safety; ~*ssa* in safety, safe, secure (against *t.* from); *olla* ~*ssa jltk* be safe (safeguarded) from, be protected from; *ottaa jku turviinsa* take.. under one's protection; *vanhuuteni* ~ the support (mainstay) of my old age. **-kokous** *Euroopan* ~ Conference on European Security. **-llinen** safe; *(varma)* secure. **-llisesti** safely, securely; *(luottamuksella)* with confidence. **-llisuus** safety, security; *(~kokous ks. turva-; ~neuvosto* Security Council). **-paikka** place of safety, haven [of refuge]; *(~oikeus: pyytää t-oikeutta* apply for political asylum). **-säilö** protective custody. **-ta** protect, secure (from), safeguard, guard (against); *(luottaa)* trust (in a p., to a th.); *(vakuuttaa)*

ensure; ~ *jkn lupauksiin* trust to a p.'s promises. **-ton** unprotected, defenceless; ~ *tila* exposed condition. **-tti** ward, protegé, *fem.* protegée. **-ttomuus** defencelessness; *(epävarmuus)* insecurity. **-ttu** secure, protected. **-utua** resort to, have recourse to, fall back upon; turn to; ~ *lääkäriin* seek medical assistance; *jhk t-tumatta* without resort to. **-vyö** safety belt, seat belt.

turve turf; sod; *(suo-)* peat. **-pehku** moss litter. **-suo** peat bog (moor).

turvo|**s**: *olla -ksissa* be swollen. **-ta** swell. **-tus** swelling, oedema.

tusin|**a** a dozen *(lyh. doz.)*; *kaksi* ~*a* two dozen. **-akaupalla** by the dozen. **-oittain** dozens of. .

tuska pain; *(hätä)* agony, distress, anguish; *(kidutus)* torment; *kärsiä tuskia* suffer pain; ~*a lievittävä lääke* painkiller. **-illa** be impatient; *(olla levoton)* be anxious, be restless. **-inen** .. filled with agony; restless. **-llinen** painful; agonizing [doubt, *epätieto*]. **-llisuus** painfulness. **-nhiki** cold sweat. **-nhuuto** cry of agony. **-stua** become (get) impatient. **-stuttaa** make. . impatient; irritate; *t-ttava* irritating, vexatious. **-ton** painless. **-ttomuus** painlessness.

tuskin hardly, scarcely; *hän* ~ *paranee* he will hardly (he is not likely to) recover; ~ *mitään* scarcely anything; ~ *milloinkaan* hardly (scarcely) ever; *olin* ~ *päässyt perille, kun* scarcely had I arrived when; ~ *nähtävä* barely visible.

tuskitella fret (over), vex oneself.

tušši India ink, drawing ink.

tutista shake; tremble; *tutiseva (m.)* doddering.

tutka radar.

tutkain point; *potkia* ~*ta vastaan* kick against the pricks.

tutki|**a** examine; investigate,

study; test; explore [arctic regions, the possibilities etc.]; ~ *jtk asiaa* look, inquire [into a matter]; *lak. m.* hear; interrogate [a prisoner]; *tiet.* do research work [on, *jtk*]; *-va katse* searching (scrutinizing) look. **-elma** study, treatise, paper (on). **-ja** investigator; *(tiedemies)* scientist; research-worker; *(kuulustelija)* examiner; (~**lautakunta** *(vero-)* tax-appeal board). **-maton** unexamined,. . not investigated; *(maa-alue)* unexplored; *(jota ei voi tutkia)* inscrutable; impenetrable [mystery, *salaisuus*]. **-mattomuus** inscrutability. **-mus** examination; investigation (of, into), study, research; *(esim. alueen)* exploration, inquiry [into, *jnk asian*]; *(oikeudellinen)* trial; *suorittaa -muksia* make (carry out) investigations; (~**laitos** research institute; ~**matkailija** explorer; ~**pöytäkirja** records of an investigation; ~**retki** exploring expedition; ~**työ** research work). **-ntavanki** prisoner committed for trial; *~na* in custody pending trial). **-nto** examination; *-nnon suorittanut* qualified; (~**lautakunta** board of examiners; ~**vaatimukset** examination requirements). **-skella** study; meditate (on); consider. **-vasti** searchingly, inquiringly.

tuttava *s.* acquaintance; *vanha ~ni* an old a. of mine. **-llinen** familiar, intimate; *liian ~ too (t. unduly)* familiar; *olla -llisissa väleissä* be on intimate terms. **-llisuus** familiarity, intimacy. **-piiri** *(jkn)* circle of [one's] acquaintances, [one's] friends. **tutta|vuus** acquaintance; *(läheinen)* intimacy; *solmia ~* strike up an acquaintance; *ehdotan lähempää -vuutta* I suggest we use our Christian names; (~**suhteet** influential

acquaintances).

tutti baby's dummy, *(pullon suulla)* nipple. **-pullo** feeding bottle.

tuttu familiar, acquainted (with); *(tunnettu)* known; *on ~a jklle* is familiar to a p.; *oletteko ~ja* are you acquainted? do you know each other? *hyvän päivän ~* a speaking acquaintance.

tutunomainen familiar.

tutus|tua become acquainted (with), make [a p.'s] acquaintance; *(perehtyä)* become familiar (with); ~ *jhk lähemmin* come to know a p. better. **-tumistarjous** introductory offer. **-tuttaa** acquaint, familiarize (a p. with), *(m. esittää)* introduce (a p. to), *(perehdyttää)* initiate (into).

tuudi|tella, -ttaa lull [to sleep]; *(keinuttaa)* rock. **-ttautua** *(luuloon)* lull oneself [into believing. .].

tuuh|ea bushy, tufty; *(tiheä)* thick; *(lehtevä)* leafy; (~**tukkainen . .** with thick hair). **-eus** bushiness; leafiness.

tuulahdus breath of wind.

tuulen|henki breath of wind; breeze. **-puoli** windward; weather side. **-puuska** gust [of wind], squall. **-suoja** shelter [from the wind]; *mer.* lee; *olla ~ssa* be sheltered from the wind. **-tupa** castle in the air.

tuulet|in *(sähkö-)* electric fan; ventilator. **-taa** air, give. . an airing; *(huonetta)* ventilate. **-tua** become aired; be ventilated. **-us** airing; ventilation; (~**laitteet** ventilation system; ~**teline** airing rack).

tuuli wind; *(heikko)* breeze; *(ankara)* gale; *(myrsky)* storm; *kuv.* mood, humour; *käy kova ~* there is a strong wind, it is very windy; ~ *on etelässä* the wind is in the south, it is blowing from the south, there is a southerly wind; *tuulen puolella* [to] windward (of); *tuulen voima, nopeus* wind force, velocity; *hyvällä tuulella* in a good humour (temper); *kun olen sillä tuulella* when I am in the mood [for it], when the mood takes me; *tuulesta temmattu.* . with no foundation [whatever]. **-ajo:** *olla ~lla* drift with the wind, be adrift; *joutua ~lle* be cast adrift *(m. kuv.).* **-hattu** fickle person, weathercock. **-kangas** wind-proof material. **-kannel** Aeolian harp. **-lasi** *(auton)* windscreen, *Am.* windshield; *~n pyyhkijä* w. wiper. **-mittari** wind-gauge. **-moottori** windmill pump. **-mylly** windmill. **-nen** windy; gusty; *(t-lle altis)* exposed to the wind. **-pussi** *ilm.* wind sock, wind sleeve. **-spää** squall, gust, *kuv.* whirlwind. **-viiri** weathervane; weathercock.

tuulla blow; *tuulee* it is windy, there is a lot of wind [today]; *alkaa ~* a wind is getting up, *(voimistuu)* the wind is rising; *alkoi ~* a wind got up.

tuum|a 1. thought, idea; *-asta toimeen* no sooner said than done; *yksissä -in jkn kanssa* together with a p. **2.** *(-mitta)* inch *(lyh.* in). **-ailla, -ata, -ia, -iskella** think; ponder, reflect (upon); *(aikoa)* plan; *mitä asiasta -aat?* what do you think of it?

tuumamitta inch-measure.

tuupata push, give. . a push.

tuupertua: *~ maahan* slump (sink) to the ground, drop [with fatigue, *väsymyksestä*].

tuup|pia push; jostle; *(hiljaa, esim. kylkeen)* nudge, poke; *(juoksijat) -pivat toisiaan* jostled (elbowed) each other.

tyhjen|nys emptying, evacuation. **-tymätön** inexhaustible. **-tyä** become empty, be emptied, be exhausted. **-täminen** *(kaupungin ym)* evacuation. **-tävä** *kuv.* exhaustive, thorough. **-tää** empty; *et. kuv.* exhaust [a supply, *varasto*]; *(asukkaista ym)* vacate [a building], evacuate [a town];

(postilaatikko ym) clear; *(kallistamalla)* tip out; *~ lasi* empty (drain) a glass; *~ pöytä (ruoista)* clear the table; *~ vesi veneestä* bail out a boat.

tyhj|iö vacuum, void. **-yys** emptiness; void, blank.

tyhjä empty; vacant [seat, *istuin*]; blank [page, *sivu*], bare; *(jtk vailla)* devoid of; *(joutava)* idle, vain; *~ jstk* empty of [meaning], void of [fish]; *~ksi poimittu* picked bare; *tyhjin käsin* empty-handed; *tyhjin suin* empty; *tyhjillään oleva* empty, vacant; *~ arpalippu* blank; *~ paristo* exhausted battery; *~ksi hakattu (metsä)* stripped bare; *~ä puhetta* idle (empty) talk; *~n takia* for nothing; *tehdä ~ksi* foil, thwart, cross [a p.'s plans, *jkn suunnitelmat*]. **-käynti** *tekn.* idle motion, idling; *käydä ~ä* idle, be idling. **-npäiväinen** trifling, insignificant. **-npäiväisyys** triviality; *(joutava asia)* trifle, trifling matter. **-ntoimittaja** idler, loafer, loiterer, good-for-nothing.

tyhm|yri stupid fellow, simpleton. **-yys** stupidity; folly; foolishness, silliness; *puhua -yyksiä* talk nonsense; *älä tee -yyksiä* don't make a fool of yourself. **-ä** stupid; foolish, silly; *(kovapäinen)* dense, dull, thick-headed; *(epäviisas)* unwise; *hän ei ole mikään ~ mies (m.)* he is no fool; *(~nrohkea* foolhardy; *~nylpeä* snobbish; *~sti* stupidly *jne.; tein ~sti, kun* it was stupid of me to. .).

tykin|ammus shell. **-kuula** cannon-ball. **-lavetti** gun-carriage.

tykistö artillery. **-tuli** artillery fire.

tykki gun, *(harvemmin)* cannon; *~en jyske* booming of cannon, gun-fire. **-mies** gunner. **-tuli** gun-fire. **-vaunut** gun-carriage. **-vene** gunboat.

tykkänään wholly, altogether.

tyky|ttää pulsate; beat;

(kiivaasti) throb, palpitate. **-tys** pulsation, beat [ing]. **tykö:** *jkn ~* to; *~nä ks. luona.*
tylli *(kangas)* tulle.
tylpistää make.. blunt [er], blunt.
tylppä blunt. **-kulmainen** obtuse-angled. **-kuonoinen** blunt-nosed, pug-nosed. **-kärkinen** blunt [-ended].
tyls|entää make.. [more] dull, dull. **-istyä** *kuv.* become [mentally] dull. **-istää** *kuv.* make.. [mentally] dull. **-yttää** blunt. **-yys** bluntness; *kuv.* dullness; stupor, apathy. **-ä** dull-edged; blunt; *kuv.* dull; *(saamaton)* inert; *(~mielinen* idiot; *~mielisyys* idiocy).
tyl|y unkind; *(karkea)* harsh, *(töykeä)* gruff, brusque; *~ vastaus* curt (brusque) reply. **-yys** unkindness, harshness, brusqueness.
tymp|eys flatness, staleness, *(vastenmielisyys)* distaste, disgust. **-eytyä** *(jhk)* take a dislike to, get sick of, become disgusted with. **-eä** flat, stale, insipid. **-äisevä** disgusting; nauseating, sickening. **-äistä** disgust; be repulsive [to a p.]; *(ikävystyttää)* bore; *jk -äisee minua* I am thoroughly disgusted with, I have a distaste for. **-ääntyä** be fed up, *jhk, jkh* with.
tynkä stump, stub.
tynnyri barrel; cask; *(pieni)* keg. **-nala** *l.v.* acre *(oik.* 1.22 acres). **-ntekijä** cooper. **-nteko** cooperage. **-nvanne** hoop [of a barrel].
typer|yys foolishness; stupidity. **-ä** foolish; stupid; *älä ole ~* don't be silly!
typis|tää dock [the tail, *häntä*], cut short, crop; *(lyhentää)* abridge; *(-tellä)* mutilate, maim.
typpi *kem.* nitrogen. **-bakteerit** nitro-bacteria. **-happo** nitric acid. **-lannoite** nitrogenous fertilizer. **-pitoinen** nitrogenous.
typykkä poppet, girl [ie]; *(pimu)* bird, birdie, dame.
typö: *~ tyhjä* quite (absolutely)

empty; completely deserted.
tyranni tyrant. **-mainen** tyrannical. **-soida** tyrannize (over); browbeat, bully. **-us** tyranny.
tyreh|dyttää stop; *(ehkäistä)* check; staunch [the flow of blood, *verenvuoto*]. **-tyä** stop; be checked; *hänen runosuonensa -tyi* his poetic vein dried up.
tyr|kkiä push, jostle *(tönäistä)* poke, *(kyynärpäällä)* nudge. **-kyttää** press (sth. on sb.), obtrude (on), *(mielipiteitä)* impose [one's views on], ply sb. with [arguments, drink]; *~ kaupaksi* [try to] foist sth. (on to sb.). **-kätä** push, *(lujemmin)* shove; poke [sb. in the side, *jkta kylkeen*].
tyrmis|tys consternation. **-tyttää** stupefy, dumbfound; *t -ttävä* staggering. **-tyä** become petrified, become motionless [with terror, *kauhusta*]; *-tynyt (m.)* thunderstruck, stupefied.
tyrmä dungeon; jail, gaol. **tyrmä|tä** knock.. out. **-ys** knock-out.
Tyroli the Tyrol. **t-lainen** *a.* & *s.* Tyrolese *(pl. = sg.).*
tyrsky surge, surf; *~t* breakers.
tyrä hernia. **-vyö** truss.
tyttären|poika grandson. **-tytär** granddaughter.
tyttö girl. **-ikä** girlhood. **-koulu** girls' school. **-lapsi** [baby] girl. **-mäinen** girlish. **-mäisyys** girlishness. **-nen** little girl. **-nimi** maiden name; *-nimeltään* nee, born.
tytär daughter. **-puoli** step-daughter. **-yhtiö** affiliated company, subsidiary.
tyven *a.* & *s.* calm; *~en puoli* lee [side].
tyvi base; proximal part; butt [end]. **-laho** butt *(t.* root) rot.
tyydy|ttämätön unsatisfied; *(jota ei voi t-ttää)* insatiable. **-ttävä** satisfactory; *(arvosana, m.)* fair. **-ttää** satisfy; gratify [a wish, *halu*]; *(olla tyydyttävä)* give satisfaction; *~ tarve* satisfy (supply, meet) a demand. **-tys** satisfaction, gratification.

tyyli style. **-kkyys** good style,
stylishness. **-käs** stylish;
chic; .. *on* ~ .. has style.
-llinen stylistic. **-nen:**
suomalais~ .. in [the]
Finnish style. **-niekka** stylist.
-puku picture frock. **-tellä:**
-telty (tait.) stylized. **-tön.** .
without style.

tyyn|esti calmly, quietly;
suhtautua jhk ~ take a th.
calmly. **-eys** calmness, calm;
tranquillity; *(mielen-, m.)*
composure. **-i** *a.* calm;
tranquil; placid; *(hiljainen)*
quiet; *(ei hämmentynyt)*
composed; *s.* calm; *-ellä*
mielellä in a calm state of
mind; with equanimity; *-ellä*
(ilmalla) in calm weather;
-essä vedessä suuret kalat
kutevat still waters run deep;
Tyynimeri the Pacific
[Ocean].

tyynni: *kaikki* ~ all [of it],
every bit of it, *(jok'ainoa)*
every single one [of them].

tyyn|nyttää calm, quiet; soothe;
(lasta) hush; *-nytti mieliä*
reassured the public. **-tyä**
calm oneself, calm down;
become calm *(m. meri);*
(tuuli) abate, subside.

tyyny cushion; *(vuode-)* pillow.
-liina pillow case.

tyypillinen typical (of); ~
esimerkki typical example, a
case in point.

tyyppi type; *ei ole minun ~äni*
[he] is not my type; *sen*
~set [people] of that type.

tyyssija retreat; *(ahjo)* seat;
nest.

tyystin carefully; thoroughly;
altogether.

tyyten wholly, entirely.

tyyty|mättömyys dissatisfaction,
discontent, displeasure (with);
t-myyden aiheet grievances.
-mätön dissatisfied,
discontented (with), displeased;
disgruntled; *-mättömät (m.)*
the malcontents. **-väinen**
satisfied, contented (with),
content, pleased (with).
-väisyys contentment,
satisfaction (with). **-ä** *(jhk)* be
satisfied (content) with,

content oneself with;
(mukautua) acquiesce in; ~
kohtaloonsa resign oneself to
one's fate; ~ *vähään* content
oneself with little.

työ work, labour; *(-paikka)*
job, employment; *(tehtävä)*
task; *(teko)* deed, act; *saada*
~tä find work; *tehdä ~tä*
work; *minulla on paljon ~tä*
I have got a great deal of
work; *onko sinulla paljon*
~tä? do you have much
work? *ryhtyä ~hön* set to
work; *ensi ~kseni* .. the first
[thing] I did was to; ~
miehen kunnia work ennobles
man; *olla ~ssä* be at work,
(jklla) be employed by; *onko*
tämä sinun ~täsi is this your
work (your doing)? *hienoa*
~tä fine workmanship; *~tä*
karttava work-shy; *~tä*
säästävä (kone) labour-saving;
~ *tekevä* working, labouring.
-aika time of work; working
hours. **-ala** line, branch; field
of work. **-ansio** earnings.

työehtosopimus agreement on
wages and conditions of
employment, *Am.* collective
agreement. **-neuvottelut**
collective bargaining.

työ|hevonen workhorse, cart
horse. **-huone** work[ing-]room;
(verstas) workshop;
(tiedemiehen) study;
(taiteilijan) studio.
-ikäinen .. of working age.
-into eagerness to work.
-kalu tool; instrument; *~t*
(m.) implements, kit; *(~kaappi*
tool chest; *~vaja* tool shed).
-kenttä sphere (field) of
activity. **-kyky** working
capacity. **-kykyinen** fit for
work. **-kyvyttömyys** disability
[for work]. **-kyvytön** .
incapacitated [for work];
disabled. **-leiri** labour camp.
-llistää employ. **-llisyys**
employment. **-lupa** work
permit. **-läinen** worker; *vrt.*
työmies ym; -läiset (m.)
workpeople.

työläs laborious, arduous; *(vaikea)*
hard, heavy, tough,
troublesome. **-tyä** get tired

(of).

työmaa work-place; job-site; *(rakennus-)* building site.
työmarkkina|järjestöt labour market organizations. **-suhteet** industrial relations. **-t** labour market.
työmies workman, worker, working man; labourer.
työn|antaja employer. **-haluinen.** . willing to work. **-jako** division of labour. **-johtaja** foreman, overseer, *Am.* boss. **-johto** supervision of work. **-puute** scarcity of work. **-seisaus** stoppage of work, shut-down. **-sulku** lock-out. **-tekijä** worker, working man (woman), labourer *(esim.* farm l.). **-teko** working, work. **-tutkimus** work study, time and motion study. **-täyteinen** busy.
työn|tyä push oneself; be pushed (forced, driven). **-tää** push, thrust; *(pakottaa)* force, drive; ~ *takaisin* force back, repel; ~ *vesille* shove off.
työntö|kärryt wheelbarrow, push-cart. **-ovi** sliding door. **-tuoli** wheel chair.
työnvälitys employment exchange. **-toimisto** employment agency.
työ|näyte specimen of work. **-paikka** work place; employment, situation, job. **-olot** working conditions. **-paja** workshop. **-palkka** wages, pay; *(-kustannus)* cost of labour; *(teko-)* cost of making. ., charges. **-palvelu** labour conscription. **-puku** working clothes. **-päivä** work-day, working day. **-pöytä** work table; writing-table. **-rauha** industrial peace. **-ryhmä** [working] team. **-riita**, **-selkkaus** labour dispute.
työsken|nellä work, be working; be at work; be employed. **-tely** working; work.
työ|sopimus working agreement. **-stökone** machine tool. **-suhde:** *olla kiinteässä -suhteessa* work on a permanent basis. **-taakka** burden of work. **-taistelu** industrial action; *ryhtyä ~un*

take i. a. **-takki** overall. **-tapaturma** occupational accident (injury). **-teho** efficiency. **-teliäisyys** industry, industriousness. **-teliäs** industrious, hard-working; diligent. **-tilaisuus** job opportunity, vacant job. **-todistus** testimonial, character. **-toveri** fellow worker; *(esim. tiedemiehen)* co-worker, collaborator. **-ttömyys** unemployment; *(~avustus* unemployment benefit, the dole; *~tilanne* state of unemployment; *~työt* relief work; *~vakuutus* unemployment insurance). **-tuomioistuin** Industrial Relations Court. **-tätekevät** working people. **-tön** unemployed,. . out of work. **-valiokunta** executive committee. **-velvollinen** labour conscript. **-voima** labour, workers; *~n puute* shortage of labour. **-vuoro** shift.
työväen|kysymys labour question. **-liike** labour movement. **-luokka** working class. **-opisto** workers' evening school. **-puolue** *Engl.* the Labour Party. **-suojelu** industrial welfare; *(~laki Engl.* Factory Acts). **-yhdistys** workers' association.
työväestö workpeople.
työväki working men, workers, *(tehtaan, m.)* hands.
tähde remnant, *ks. tähteet.*
tähde|llinen important; pressing. **-llisyys** importance.
tähden = *takia; minun tähteni* for my sake; *tämän* ~ for this reason, therefore.
tähden|lento shooting star. **-muotoinen** star-shaped.
tähdentää emphasize, lay stress on, stress.
tähd|etön starless. **-istäennustaja** astrologer. **-istö** constellation.
tähdätä aim, *jhk* at, take aim; *(olla suunnattuna)* be aimed, be directed (at).
tähkä head, ear; *(kukintomuotona)* spike. **-pää** head; *t-päiden poimija* gleaner.

tähteet remains [of food], left-overs.

tähti star; *kirjap.* asterisk; *taivas on tähdessä* it is starlight. **-kirkas** starlit, starry. **-kuvio** constellation. **-lippu** the star-spangled banner, the stars and stripes. **-sumu** nebula. **-taivas** starry sky. **-tiede** astronomy. **-tieteellinen** astronomical. **-tieteilijä** astronomer. **-torni** [astronomical] observatory. **-yö** starlit night; ~*ssä*, ~*nä* by starlight.

tähtä|in sight; *-imen jyvä* bead; *hänellä on jtk -imessä (kuv.)* he has.. in view; *katsoa jtk pitkällä -imellä* take a long view of; *pitkän -imen* long-term [programme etc]. **-ys** sighting, aiming; *pitkällä -yksellä* taking the long view; (~*laite* sight[s]).

tähys|tellä look. **-tys** lookout; observation; *lääk.* -scopy *(esim.* bronchoscopy); ~*torni* lookout [tower]. **-täjä** lookout, observer. **-tää** keep a lookout, be on the lookout, scout about (for).

tähän here; ~ *asti* this far, thus far, *(ajasta)* so far, hitherto, until now; ~ *(päivään) mennessä* up to the present [time], to date.

täi louse *(pl.* lice).

täkäläinen. in (at) this place, local.

tällainen. like this,.. of this kind; such.

tällöin now; *(silloin)* then; at that time.

tämä this, this one; *tähän aikaan päivästä* at this time of the day; *tällä puolen* on this side of; ~*n kuun 6.* *päivänä* on the 6th of this month; ~*n jälkeen* after this; *10 vuotta* ~*n jälkeen* 10 years hence; ~*n verran* this much; *tänä iltana* tonight; *tässä kohden* at this point, *(äsiassa)* on this point; *tätä tietä* this way.

tämän|päiväinen today's,.. [of] today. **-tapainen**.. of this kind (sort).

tänne here. **-mmäksi** farther this way. **-päin** this way, in this direction.

tänään today; ~ *aamupäivällä* this morning; ~ *on tiistai* today is Tuesday.

täpl|ikäs spotted, spotty, *(pilkullinen)* dotted, speckled [with black etc]. **-ä** spot; speck.

täpär|yys: *ajan* ~ the limited time; *hänen asemansa* ~ his critical position. **-ä** short; ~ *paikka* a near thing; ~ *pelastus* a narrow escape; *hänen henkensä oli* ~*llä* he escaped by the skin of his teeth; *aika on* ~*llä* time is short; *voitti* ~*sti* won by a narrow margin, barely won; *se oli* ~*llä* it was a hairbreadth escape (a close shave).

täpö: ~ *täysi*, ~ *täynnä* crammed; crowded, packed [with people, *ihmisiä*], chock-full.

täri|nä shaking; *(esim. ajopelien)* jolting; *(täristys)* tremor. **-stä** shake, *(esim. ajopelit)* jolt; *(vapista)* tremble. **-syttää** shake; *kuv.* shock; *t-ttävä* shocking, shattering.

tärke|ys importance; *(painavuus)* weight. **-ä** important; *(merkityksellinen)* significant; *(oleellinen)* essential; urgent; *hyvin* ~ of great importance, *(ensiarvoisen)* of vital importance; *pitää* ~*nä (m.)* consider.. of importance, attach importance to; *minun on* ~*tä tietää* it is important for me to know.

tärk|kelys starch. **-ki** starch; (~*paita* starched shirt).

tärpätti turpentine. **-öljy** oil of turpentine.

tärvel|lä spoil; ruin, destroy. **-tyä** be spoiled; be ruined.

tärykalvo ear-drum, tympanic membrane.

täryyttää: *ajaa* ~ bump [along the road].

täräh|dys shock; *lääk.* concussion [of the brain];

(räsähdys) clash, crack. **-tää** clash; *(täristä)* shake; *maa -ti* the ground shook (trembled); *hänen päänsä -ti seinään* he knocked his head against the wall; *-tänyt dotty,*. . [a bit] cracked.

täsmentää define [. . further]; specify.

täsmäll|een exactly, precisely; *(määräajalleen)* punctually: ~ *kello 1 (m.)* at one o'clock sharp; *hän saapui ~ (sovittuun aikaan)* he kept his appointment [exactly], he was on time. **-inen** exact, precise, accurate; *(säntillinen)* punctual; *(tiukka)* strict; ~ *kuin kello* as regular as clockwork. **-istää** define. **-isyys** exactness, precision, accuracy; punctuality.

täsmätä agree; tally.

tässä here; at this, in this; ~ *saat (jtk annettaessa)* here you are! *vrt. tämä.*

tästedes henceforth; from now on.

tästä from this; of this, about this; *(täältä)* from here; ~ *johtuu, seuraa.*. hence (from this) it follows (that); ~ *lähtien* from now on, henceforth; *en tiedä ~ mitään* I know nothing about this.

täten in this way (manner); thus; herewith, by this means; ~ *ilmoitetaan, että.*. this is to give notice that.., it is hereby announced that..

täti [maternal *t.* paternal] aunt; *äidin t. isän ~* great-aunt.

täydelleen completely; utterly; *vrt. täysin.*

täydelli|nen complete; perfect; *(täysi)* full; entire; *(ehdoton)* absolute; ~ *nimi* full name, [one's] name in full; ~ *pimeys* total (complete) darkness. **-sesti** perfectly; completely, entirely; *(täysin)* fully, wholly; ~ *lyöty* completely (utterly, totally) defeated. **-styä** perfect oneself, reach perfection. **-stää** perfect; complete. **-syys** perfection; perfectness; completeness;

-syyden huippu the pink of perfection.

täyden|nys completion; *jkn -nykseksi* to supplement. .; *(~osa l.v.* supplement). **-tää** complete, make.. complete, make up [the number, *lukumäärä*]; *(liittää t-nykseksi)* supplement; *(varastoja)* replenish; *täydentävä* complementary, supplementary [to, *jtk*].

täynnä full [of, *jtk*]; filled (with); *(tupaten ~)* crowded, crammed, packed (with); *sali oli ~ viimeistä sijaa myöten* the hall was filled to capacity.

täys|aikainen *ks. täysi-.* **-automaattinen** fully automatic.

täysi full; *(täydellinen)* complete; perfect; *(koko)* whole; ~ *syy* every reason; *täydellä syyllä* justly, rightly; *täydellä syyllä voidaan sanoa* it can be said with good reason; *täydessä kunnossa* in good repair; *oli ~ työ.*. it was hard work, it was all he could do to. .; *merkitä täyteen* subscribe in full. **-aikainen** full-term, mature. **-arvoinen** *(raha)* standard. **-hoito** board and lodging; *olla -hoidossa* board [with a p., *jkn luona*]. **-hoitola** boarding-house. **-hoitolainen** boarder. **-ikäinen.**. of age; *lak.* major; *tulla -ikäiseksi* come of age. **-ikäisyys** majority, age. **-kasvui|nen** grown-up, adult *(m. subst.);* full-grown; *tulla -seksi* grow up. **-kuu** full moon. **-lukuinen** fully attended. **-lukuisuus** full numbers. **-mittainen.**. up to [the] standard.

täysin fully; *(aivan)* quite; *(kokonaan)* entirely, wholly, totally; ~ *kehittynyt* fully developed; ~ *levännyt* thoroughly rested; ~ *maksettu* paid in full; ~ *valmis* completely finished, completed; ~ *yhtä hyvä* just *(t.* fully) as good; *ottaen ~ huomioon* with full regard to. **-oppinut** master (of), expert (in). **-palvellut** emeritus [professor].

täysi|näinen full. **-näisyys** fullness. **-painoinen**. . of full weight, *kuv.* of high standard. **-pitoinen** up to [the] standard. **täysistunto** plenary session. **täysi|valtainen** invested with full powers, fully authorized; ~ *ministeri* minister plenipotentiary. **-valtaisuus** full powers, full authority. **täys|järkinen** sane,. . in full possession of one's senses. **-korjaus:** *asunnossa tehtiin* ~ the flat was completely refitted. **-käännös** about turn; ~ *oikeaan* right-about face! *teki (poliittisen) t-nöksen* reversed his policy. **-maito** whole milk. **-mittainen**. . of full length (*t.* size), *kuv.* up to the standard. **-osuma** direct hit. **-työllisyys** full employment. **-vakuutus** (*auton*) comprehensive [motor-car] insurance. **-valmiste** finished product. **-verinen** thoroughbred [horse]. **-villa(inen)** pure wool. **täyte** filling (*m. hammas-*); (*esim. vanu-*) padding; *keitt.* stuffing, dressing; *kuv.* makeweight. **-aine** filling. **-en:** *kaataa* (*ym.*) ~ fill [with, *jtk*]. **-kynä** fountain-pen. **-läinen** (*vartaloltaan*) plump, full-bodied, (*ääni ym.*) rich, mellow. **-paino** makeweight. **-sana** expletive. **-vaalit** by-election.

täyt|ymys fulfilment; realization. **-yä** get (become) filled (with), fill (with); (*toteutua*) be fulfilled, be realized, come true. **-ymätön** unfulfilled. **-äminen** filling. **-ämätön** unfilled; unfulfilled; ~ *lupaus* a promise which was not kept.

täyttää fill, fill up; (*reikä*) stop, (*eläin, m. ruoaksi*) stuff, (*lomake*) fill in (*t.* out); *kuv.* fulfil, *et. Am.* fulfil; (*toimittaa*) carry out, execute; ~ *tänään* he turns [*esim.* forty] today; *hän* ~ *30 vuotta ensi kuussa* he will be thirty next month; *30 vuotta t-äneet*

those over thirty; ~ *hammas* fill (stop) a tooth; ~ *käsky* perform an order, execute (carry out) an order; ~ *lomake* (*m.*) complete; ~ *lupaus* (*m.*) keep one's promise; ~ *sitoumuksensa* honour one's engagements, fulfil one's obligations; ~ *tarpeet* meet the needs; ~ *kaikki vaatimukset* come up to the requirements, meet [all] the requirements, ~ *vajaus* cover the deficit; ~ *velvollisuutensa* discharge (do) one's duty; *se* ~ *koko sivun* it fills (takes up) an entire page.

täyt|yä have to, be obliged to; *minun -yy* I must, I have to; *täytyykö sinun mennä?* must you go? do you have to go? have you [got] to go? *minun -yi* I had to; *hänen on -ynyt käydä siellä aikaisemmin* he must have been there before. **täytäntö** fulfilment; *panna ~ön* carry. . into effect, execute; *mennä ~ön* be fulfilled, be realized, come true.

täytäntöön|paneva executive. **-pano** execution, carrying into effect; (*lain ym.*) enforcement [of the law]; **(~viranomainen** executive authority).

täällä here, in (at) this place. **-olo:** *~ni, ~si jne.* my (your) stay here.

täältä from here, from this place; *koska lähdet* ~ when are you leaving [this place]?

töher|rys daub[ing]. **-tää** scrawl, (*maalilla*) daub.

töhriä daub, smear.

töintuskin narrowly; only just; ~ *pelastui* had a near escape, (he) narrowly escaped [drowning, *hukkumasta*].

tökerö awkward; *tehdä ~sti* botch, bungle.

tökätä (*kyynärpäällä*) nudge.

tölkinavaaja tin opener.

tölkittää tin, *Am.* can.

tölkki jar; pot; (*säilyke-*) tin, *Am.* can.

tölli hut, cabin, shack.

töllistellä gape (at).

tömi|nä *(jymy)* rumble; thumping; stamping. **-stellä** stamp [one's feet]. **-stä** rumble.

tönäistä, töniä bump (into, against), jostle; *älä töni* don't push [me]!

tönö cabin, shack.

töppö|häntä bobtail. **-korvainen** crop-eared.

törke|ys coarseness; grossness. **-ä** *(karkea)* coarse; rude; *(vakava)* grave; gross [insult, loukkaus]; ~ *laiminlyönti* gross negligence; ~ *rikos* *(lak.)* felony; ~ *vale* gross lie; ~ *virhe* grave error, big mistake; ~ *vääryys* gross *(glaring)* injustice.

törky dirt, filth; *(roju)* rubbish; trash; *(jätteet)* refuse, garbage.

törmä bank; *jyrkkä* ~ bluff, *(rinne)* steep hillside.

törmä|tä: ~ *jhk* run into, *(esim. auto)* crash into; hit (dash, strike) against; ~ *vastakkain (kuv.)* clash; ~ *yhteen* collide, crash [into each other]; *auto -si puuhun* the car crashed into a tree. **-ys** bump; crash, collision.

törröttää stick out, stand out.

törä|hdys blast [of a horn], *(auton)* hoot, honk. **-yttää:** ~ *torvea* blow a horn, *(auton)* hoot the car horn. **-htää** blare.

tötterö cone.

töyhtö *(linnun päässä)* crest; *(tupsu)* tuft. **-hyyppä** lapwing.

töyke|ys brusqueness, rudeness. **-ä** harsh; brusque; unobliging, discourteous, gruff.

töykkiä jostle.

töyräs bluff.

töyssäh|dellä bump along [the road]. **-tää** bounce.

töytäistä [give. . a] push, shove.

U

udar udder.

udella inquire [about;.. of a p.], question, sound [a p. about, *jtk*], be inquisitive.

uhalla *ks. uhka.*

uhanalainen threatened, exposed.

uhata threaten (with), menace; *uhaten* threatening [ly]; *uhkaava vaara* impending danger; *aseella uhaten, uhattaessa* at gunpoint.

uhi|tella be defiant. **-ttelu** defiance; bravado.

uhka threat, menace; *(vaara)* risk, hazard; *(uhma)* defiance, spite; *uhalla* out of [mere] spite; *kaiken uhallakin* at all costs; *jnk uhalla* at the risk of, *(sakon ym)* on pain (under penalty) of [£ 10]; *henkeni uhalla* at the risk of losing my life; *olla ~na jllek* be a threat to. **-ava** threatening, menacing, impending, imminent. **-illa** threaten. **-peli** gambling; *~n harjoittaja* gambler. **-rohkea** daring, rash, reckless; *(tyhmän-)* foolhardy. **-rohkeus** daring, rashness. **-us** threat, menace. **-vaatimus** ultimatum. **-yritys** hazardous (risky) undertaking; [bold] venture.

uhke|a splendid, magnificent, grand; *(komea)* gorgeous; *(rehevä)* luxuriant. **-us** magnificence; splendour.

uhkua brim over (with), flow (with); abound (in); *hän uhkuu iloa* she is exuberant with joy.

uhma defiance. **-ikä** the obstinate age. **-ileva** defiant. **-illa** *ks. uhmata* **-ilu** defiance. **-mieli** [spirit of] defiance. **-mielinen** defiant (to, towards); refractory. **-ta** defy; *(vaaraa ym)* brave, challenge;

-ten jtk in defiance of. .

uhra|ta sacrifice; lay down [one's life, *henkensä*]; *(omistaa)* devote [one's time to, *aikansa jhk*]; *(rahaa)* spend, go to the expense [of £ 100], go to great expense; *uhraamalla ihmishenkiä (m.)* at the sacrifice of human life. **-us** sacrifice. **-utua** sacrifice oneself; give oneself up (to), devote oneself (to). **-utuvainen** self-sacrificing. **-utuvaisuus** self-sacrifice.

uhri sacrifice, *(poltto- ym.)* offering; *(saalis)* victim, prey; *joutua jnk ~ksi* fall a victim to, *(tapaturman)* suffer an accident. **-eläin** sacrificial animal, victim. **-karitsa** sacrificial lamb; *virheetön ~* unblemished l.

uida swim; bathe; *(kellua)* float; *mennä uimaan* go swimming (for a swim); *menen uimaan* I am going to have a swim.

uikuttaa moan, wail; *(vikistä)* whine.

uima|-allas swimming-pool. **-halli** [indoor] swimming-bath [s]. **-housut** swimming trunks. **-huone**, **-koppi** bathing hut (cubicle). **-hyppy** [fancy] dive. **-jalka** web-foot. **-kalvo** web. **-kilpailu** swimming contest. **-la**, **-laitos** public swimming-baths. **-liike** [swimming] stroke. **-näytös** swimming display. **-opetus** instruction in swimming. **-puku** bathing costume (suit). **-rakko** *(kalan)* sound. **-ranta** bathing beach. **-ri** swimmer. **-taidoton** non-swimmer; *on ~* cannot swim. **-taito** [art of] swimming. **-taituri** expert swimmer. **-tyyny** swimming

float.
uimuri *tekn.* float.
uinahtaa drop asleep, snooze.
uinti swimming; *uinnin*
  opettaja s. instructor. **-matka**
  swim. **-tyyli** style [of
  swimming].
uinua slumber.
uiskennella swim; *(kellua)* float.
uistin spoon-bait; *soutaa ~ta*
  fish with a s.-b.
uittaa float.
uitto *(tukkien)* timber floating.
  -kouru timber slide. **-mies**
  timber-(log-)floater. **-yhtiö**
  [timber] floating company.
ujellus whistle, *(suihkukoneen)*
  scream.
ujo *(tukkier)* shy, timid; coy;
  (hämillinen) self-conscious.
ujostele|maton unshy, at one's
  ease, unconstrained.
ujo|stella be shy, feel
  embarrassed [in the presence
  of..]; *-stelematta* without
  blushing, unconcerned [ly],
  unabashed; *älkää -stelko
  minua* never mind me!
  -stuttaa: *häntä u-tti* she felt
  shy. **-us** shyness, bashfulness.
ukki grandpa.
ukko old man. **-mainen** senile.
  -nen thunder [and lightning];
  ~ käy it is thundering; *on
  -sta ilmassa* there is a
  thunderstorm brewing, *(kuv.)*
  trouble is brewing; *~ iski
  puuhun* the lightning struck a
  tree.
ukkosen|johdatin lightning
  conductor *(Am.* rod). **-jyrinä**
  thunder. **-jyrähdys** clap (peal)
  of thunder.
ukkos|kuuro thundery shower.
  -pilvi thunder-cloud. **-sade**
  thunder shower.
ukonilma thunderstorm.
Ukraina the Ukraine.
ulappa the open sea;
  (valtameren, m.) the high seas.
ula(radio) ultra-short wave,
  V. H. F.
uli|na yelp [ing]. **-sta** yelp;
  (ulvoa) howl.
ulj|as gallant, *(rohkea)* brave,
  valiant; *(komea)* stately
  [carriage, *ryhti*], splendid;
  (ylevä) noble. **-uus** gallantry,

bravery; stateliness.
ulko- *(yhd.)* outer, exterior;
  (-puolinen) outside, outward,
  external; *~a* from outside,
  from the outside; on the
  outside; *oppia ~a* learn by
  heart (by rote), memorize,
  commit. . to memory. **-asia:**
  ~t foreign affairs;
  *(~***inministeri** minister for
  foreign affairs; *Engl.* Foreign
  Secretary, *Am.* Secretary of
  State; *~***inministeriö** Ministry
  of Foreign Affairs; *Engl.*
  Foreign Office, *Am.* State
  Department; *~***invaliokunta**
  Foreign Affairs Committee).
ulko|asu [outward, external]
  appearance. **-grilli** *Am.*
  barbecue. **-huone** outbuilding;
  (käymälä) privy. **-illa**
  (patikoida) hike; *hän -ilee
  paljon* he is an outdoor
  person *(t.* type).
ulkoilu outdoor activities.
  -tta|a: *~ koiraa* take the dog
  for a walk; *koirien -minen
  kielletty* no dogs allowed.
ulko|ilma [the] open air; *~ssa*
  out of doors, outdoors;
  *(~***kokous** open-air meeting).
  -kaihdin sun-blind, awning.
  -kohtainen objective.
  -kohtaisuus objectiveness,
  objectivity. **-korva** external
  ear. **-kullattu** hypocritical; *~
  ihminen* hypocrite. **-kultaisuus**
  hypocrisy. **-kuori** outer shell;
  the exterior. **-laitamoottori** *ks.*
  perä-. **-luku** learning by heart,
  rote-learning. **-lähetys** *TV*
  outside broadcast. **-läksy**
  lesson [to be] learnt by
  heart.
ulkomaa foreign country;
  u-mailla, -lle abroad; *u-mailta*
  from abroad; *~n uutiset*
  foreign news. **-lainen**
  foreigner, *lak.* alien; *-laiset*
  (m.) foreign people. **-nkauppa**
  foreign trade. **-nmatka** journey
  (trip) abroad; *hän on ~lla* he
  is [travelling] abroad.
  -nvaluutta foreign exchange.
ulko|mainen foreign. **-ministeri**
  ks. ulkoasiain-. **-muistista** by
  heart, from memory. **-muoto**
  appearance, looks, exterior;. *~*

pettää appearances are deceptive; *muodoltaan* in appearance. **-na** out [in the rain, *sateessa*]; outside, out of doors, outdoors; *on* ~ is out, has gone out; (~**liikkumiskielto** curfew; *kaupungissa on* ~ the town is under a c.; ~ *kumottiin* the c. was lifted).

ulko|nainen external, outward; *-naisesti* externally, *lääk.* for external use. **-nema** projection, projecting part. **-neva** . . standing out, projecting, prominent [cheekbone, *poskiluu*]. **-näkö** *ks. -muoto*; *-näöstä päättäen* to judge from appearances, by the looks of him (her); *tuntea jku -näöltä* know . . by sight. **-osa** outer part, the outside (of). **-ovi** outer door; street door, *(pienen talon)* front door. **-politiikka** foreign policy. **-puoli** [the] outside, exterior; *-puolella* outside, *(pinnalla)* on the outside, *(jnk)* beyond . .; *-puolelta* from outside; *ulko- ja sisäpuolelta* outside as well as inside, within and without. **-puolinen** outer, outward; external; *(sivullinen)* s. outsider. **-reuna** outer (outside) edge. **-saaristo** outer (outlying) islands. **-salla** out of doors. **-työ** outdoor work. **-valta** foreign power. **-varustus** outer fortification.

ullakko garret, attic, loft. **-kamari** garret room.

ulo|ke projection, *(kallion)* ledge. **-mmaksi** farther out. **-mpana** farther out (off, away).

ulos out; *(ulkopuolelle)* outside; *(ulkoilmaan)* out of doors, outdoors; *(-käynti)* exit; ~! get out! *ajaa* ~ turn out; *viedä*. . ~ take. . out. **-ajo** turning out. **-hengitys** breathing out, expiration. **-käytävä** way out; exit. **-marssi** walk-out. **-mitata** distrain (on a p.), put in the bailiffs. **-otto** distraint; *sähk.* outlet; *-oton alainen* distrainable; (~**mies**

distrainer). **-päin** outward [s]; out. **-pääsy** way out *(m. kuv.)*. **-taa** evacuate [the bowels]; *en ole -tanut* my bowels have not moved [today]. **-tava** purgative. **-te,** *~et* excrement, faeces, *lääk. m.* stools. **-tus** defecation, *vrt. ed.;* (~**aine** laxative, purge).

ulott|aa extend, stretch. **-ua** reach, extend, stretch; cover [a wide field, *laajalle*]; *(jstk jhk, m.)* range [from. . to]; ~ *kauas menneisyyteen* go far back in time; ~ *laajalle (m.)* be extensive; *en ulotu sinne* it is beyond my reach. **-uma:** *~n päässä* within reach *(esim. tykin* range) of. **-uvuus** dimension [s], extent, range. **-uvi|lla, -lle** within reach of; *(helposti) käden* ~ within easy reach; *vihollistulen* ~ within range of enemy fire.

ulpukka yellow water-lily.

ulsteri ulster.

ulvo|a howl; roar *(m. myrsky)*. **-nta** howl [ing]; *(sireenin)* hoot [ing].

ummeh|tuneisuus stuffiness; mustiness; *kuv.* staleness. **-tunut** close, stuffy *(maku)* musty, stale; *ahtaat, -tuneet olot* stifling conditions.

umme|ssa: *silmät* ~ with closed eyes, with one's eyes shut. **-tus** constipation.

ummikko person who speaks only his own language.

ummistaa close, shut [one's eyes to, *silmänsä jltk*].

umpeen up; *kasvaa* ~ *(haavasta)* heal [over]; *kulua* ~ expire; *luoda* ~ fill up (in); *vuoden ~sa* throughout the year. **-kulunut** expired.

umpi: *ummessa silmin* with one's eyes shut; *tie on ummessa* the road is blocked [by snow]. **-auto** closed car. **-erite** internal secretion. **-kuja** blind alley; *kuv.* deadlock, impasse; *ovat ajautumassa ~an* are heading for a deadlock; *joutua ~an* come to a dead end. **-kuuro** stone-deaf. **-lippu:** *äänestää -lipuin* ballot. **-lisäke**

appendix. **-mielinen**
uncommunicative, *(varovainen)*
reserved. **-mielisyys**
uncommunicative disposition,
reticence. **-mähkäinen**. . made
at random, haphazard,
. random; *(likimääräinen)*
rough. **-mähkään** at random;
haphazardly. **-nainen** closed;
(katettu) covered. **-oida**
preserve [by sterilizing at
100—120 C°]. **-solmu**
overhand knot; hard knot.
-suolentulehdus appendicitis.
-suoli c [a] ecum; *-suolenlisäke*
appendix; *-suolen leikkaus*
operation for appendicitis.
-täynnä full to bursting.
-vaunu *(-auto)* closed
car; saloon.

umppu bud.

undulaatti budgerigar, *lyh.*
budge, budgie.

une | **ksia** dream (of, about).
-liaisuus sleepiness,
drowsiness; somnolence. **-lias**
sleepy, drowsy; lethargic. **-lma**
dream; daydream, reverie.
-lmoida dream. **-nhorros** doze;
(tainnos) stupor; *-nhorroksissa*
dazed with sleep. **-nnäkö**
dream. **-nselitys** interpretation
of dreams. **-ton** sleepless.
-ttaa: *minua* ~ I feel sleepy;
-ttava soporific. **-ttomuus**
sleeplessness, insomnia.

unho *ks. unohdus;* ~(*la*) limbo.
uni sleep; *(unennäkö)* dream;
~*ssani* in my sleep; *nähdä
unta* dream; *minä näin unen*
I had a dream; *olla unessa*
be asleep, be sleeping; *en
saanut unta* I could not get
to sleep; *en saanut unen
rahtustakaan silmiini* I didn't
sleep a wink. **-keko**
sleepyhead, lie-abed; *seitsemän*
~*a* the seven sleepers. **-kirja**
book of dreams. **-kko** poppy.
-lääke sleeping pill *(t.* tablet).
-nen sleepy; *raskas*~ a heavy
(sound) sleeper. **-ssa:** *kävellä*
~*an* walk in one's sleep;
(~*kävijä* sleep-walker,
somnambulist; **-käynti**
sleep-walking; somnambulism;
~*saarnaaja* trance preacher).
-tauti sleeping-sickness.

univormu uniform. **-pukuinen**
uniformed.

Unkari Hungary. **u-lainen** *a. &
s.* Hungarian. **u-n kieli**
Hungarian.

unoh | **dus** oblivion; *joutua,
jäädä -duksiin* be forgotten,
fall (sink) into oblivion. **-taa**
forget; *-din kirjani kotiin* I
left my book at home, I
forgot to bring my book
[with me]. **-tua** be forgotten;
~ *ajatuksiinsa* lose oneself in
thought; *se -tui mielestä* it
escaped my memory, I forgot
it; *se -tui kotiin* I left it at
home. **-tumaton**
never-to-be-forgotten,
unforgettable. **-tumattomuus**

unssi ounce *(lyh. oz.).*

untuva down. **-inen** downy;
fluffy. **-patja** bed of down.
-peitteinen downy. **-peite** *ark.*
downie.

uoma bed *(esim.* river-bed),
channel; *palata vanhaan*
~*ansa (kuv.)* get into the old
rut again.

upe | **a** stately, splendid,
imposing, magnificent. **-us**
magnificence, stateliness,
splendour.

upo | **kas** crucible; melting-pot.
-ksiin: *ampua* ~ sink. **-ksissa**
under [the] water, submerged.
-ksista: *nousta* ~ emerge. **-ta**
sink; *(laivasta, m.)* go down,
founder. **-ttaa** sink; *(kastaa)*
dip; immerse; *(metall., puus.)*
inlay; ~ *kultaan* set in gold;
~ *laiva (avaamalla
pohjaventtiili)* scuttle a ship;
jhk -tettu (pienempi) kuva
inset, *(kartta)* inset map.
-ttaminen *(nesteeseen)*
immersion. **-tus** sinking. **-uusi**
brand new, spanking new.

uppiniskai | **nen** insubordinate,
(esim. eläin, yskä) refractory;
obstinate. **-suus**
insubordination, stubbornness.

uppo | **ama** *mer.* displacement.
-rikas immensely (enormously)
rich.

upseeri [commissioned] officer.
-kunta the officers. **-narvo**
rank of an officer; *saada* ~
receive one's commission. **-sto**

ks. -kunta.

ura *(elämän-)* career; *(suunta)* course; *(väylä)* channel; *minkä* ~n *valitset* what profession (what career) are you going to choose? *vanhaa* ~ansa along the beaten track. **-auurtava** pioneering.

uraani uranium.

urakka contract; *kuv. (tehtävä)* stint; *urakalla* by contract; *antaa työ urakalle* give.. out on contract; *ottaa urakalle* undertake.. on contract. **-palkka:** *saada* ~a be paid by the piece (by the job). **-tarjo|us** tender for a contract; *pyytää u-uksia* invite tenders. **-työ** contract work, piece-work.

urakoitsija contractor.

uranuurtaja pioneer; *olla jnk* ~*(na)* pioneer.

urhea brave; valiant; *(peloton)* intrepid; ~ *puolustus* gallant (brave) defence.

urhei|lija sportsman; athlete. **-lla** go in for sports (athletics).

urheilu athletics; *(laajemmin)* sport. **-asu(steet)** sportswear. **-auto** sports car. **-halli** field house. **-harjoitukset** athletic exercises. **-henki:** *(reilu)* ~ sportsmanship. **-hullu** sport fanatic. **-kalastus** sport fishing, angling. **-katsaus** sports review. **-kenttä** athletic ground[s], sports ground (field). **-kilpailut** sports meeting. **-laji** sport; event. **-lentäjä** private pilot. **-liitto** athletic association. **-maailma** sporting world. **-opisto** physical-training college. **-puku** sports suit. **-seura** athletic club. **-sukellus** skin-diving. **-sukeltaja** skin-diver. **-uutinen** sporting news.

urheus bravery, valour; courage.

urho hero *(pl. -es).* **-kas** heroic. **-kkuus** heroism. **-ollinen** brave, valiant; *(rohkea)* bold; courageous. **-ollisuus** bravery.

urkinta spying, espionage.

urkki|a *(selville)* search out, spy [out]; *(nuuskia)* pry

(into). **-ja** spy.

urku|harmoni harmonium. **-jensoittaja** organ-player. **-jensoitto** organ music. **-konsertti** organ recital. **-parveke** organ loft. **-pilli** organ pipe. **-ri** organist.

uros male, *(-peura ym)* buck.

urotyö heroic deed; feat, exploit.

urpu catkin.

urut organ.

use|a many [a]; ~*t* many, several, *(eri)* various, *(lukuisat)* a great many, a [great] number (of); *useita kertoja* many times, many a time; ~*mmin* more often; *useimmat* most; *useimmissa tapauksissa* in most cases, in the majority of cases; *useita vuosia* [for] several years. **-asti** often. **-immin, -immiten** most often, most frequently; *(enimmäkseen)* mostly.

usein often, frequently; ~ *tapahtuva* frequent, [occurring] at frequent intervals. **-kin** often enough, ever so often.

uskali|aisuus boldness, daring. **-as** bold, daring, audacious; *(uskallettu)* hazardous, risky; venturesome. **-kko** daredevil.

uskal|lus daring, boldness; courage. **-taa** dare, venture; *(panna alttiiksi)* risk, hazard; *hän ei -la tehdä sitä* he dare not do it, he does not dare to do it; *-latko kysyä häneltä?* dare you ask him? *en -tanut kysyä häneltä* I didn't dare [to] ask him; *hän -si..* (= *kehtasi)* he had the face to.. *-tautua* venture, run the risk [of.. -ing]; *minne kukaan ei -taudu* where nobody dares to venture.

usko belief (in); *usk. m.* faith; *hyvässä* ~*ssa* in good faith, bona fide; *olin siinä* ~*ssa, että..* I was under the impression that.. **-a** believe (in); *(luottaa)* trust (in); *(huostaan)* [en]trust a p. with, *(itsensä)* trust oneself to; *(tehtäväksi)* entrust [a

task] to; *(salaisuus)* confide
[a secret to]; *ei ~ (m.)*
disbelieve; *~ todeksi* believe. .
to be true, give credit
(credence) to; *~ hyvää, pahaa
jksta* believe well (ill) of a
p.; *en usko häntä* I don't
believe him *(t.* what he says);
sitä en usko I do not think
so; *et voi ~, kuinka. .* you
cannot imagine how. . **-llinen**
faithful; loyal, true (to);
(kiintynyt) devoted; *~
alamainen* loyal subject; *~
kannattaja* staunch supporter.
-llisuudenvala oath of
allegiance. **-llisuus** faithfulness,
fidelity, loyalty; *(alamaisen)*
allegiance. **-maton** incredible,
unbelievable. **-mattomuus**
incredibility. **-mus** belief.
usko|asia matter of faith.
-kappale article of faith;
dogma. **-lahko** sect. **-lause**
dogma.
uskonnolli|nen religious. **-suus**
religiousness, piety.
uskonnon|opetus religious
instruction. **-vapaus** religious
freedom. **-vastainen**
anti-religious.
uskonno|ton irreligious.
-ttomuus irreligion.
uskon|oppi dogmatics, *(kristin-)*
Christian doctrine. **-puhdistaja**
reformer. **-puhdistus**
reformation. **-sankari**
champion of faith. **-sota**
religious war.
uskonto religion; *(kouluaineena)*
religious knowledge, Christian
doctrine. **-filosofia** philosophy
of religion. **-kunta**
denomination.
uskon|tunnustus confession of
faith, creed. **-vaino** religious
persecution.
usko|tella make. . believe
(that), pretend; *~ olevansa
(m.)* imagine that one is, kid
oneself (that); *(toisille) (m.)*
try to pass oneself off as;
(lehti) -ttelee lukijoilleen . .
leads its readers to believe;
*hänelle voi ~ melkein mitä
tahansa* he will believe almost
anything; *kuka on -tellut
sinulle sellaista* who ever put

that into your head? *sitä voit
~ toisille!* tell that to the
marines! **-ton** unfaithful (to),
disloyal, false, untrue. **-ttava**
credible; *(todennäköinen)*
plausible, likely; *tuskin ~a*
not very likely; scarcely
credible. **-ttavuus** credibility;
likelihood. **-ttelu** make-believe,
[self-]suggestion. **-ttomuus**
unfaithfulness, faithlessness;
disloyalty. **-ttu** *a.* trusted; *s.*
intimate, confidant, *fem.*
confidante; *~ mies* trustee;
ottaa jku -tukseen take sb.
into one's confidence. **-utua**
(jklle) confide in a p. *(sth.
to. .).* **-vainen** *a.* religious; *s.*
believer; *-vaiset (m.)* religious
people.
usuttaa set [the dog] on sb.;
(toistensa kimppuun) set. . at
strife, set. . by the ears.
usva fog, mist. **-inen** misty.
-isuus haziness; mistiness.
utare udder.
uteli|aisuus curiosity;
inquisitiveness. **-as** curious;
(kyseliäs) inquisitive; *~
tietämään. .* anxious (eager) to
know. .
utu mist. **-inen** misty. **-kuva**
illusive image.
uudelleen anew, afresh; *(taas)*
again, once more; *rakentaa ~*
rebuild; *istuttaa ~* transplant;
muodostaa ~ remodel,
reorganize, *(hallitus)* build a
new government. **-järjestely**
reorganization; *(hallituksen)*
Cabinet reshuffle.
uuden|aikainen modern,
up-to-date; *(huon. merk)*
new-fangled; *(kuosista)*
fashionable. **-aikaistaa**
modernize. **-aikaisuus**
modernity. **-kuosinen**
fashionable. **-lainen** . of a
new kind (type).
uudenvuoden|aatto New Year's
Eve. **-kortti** New Year card.
-onnittelu(t) New Year
greetings, good wishes for the
New Year. **-päivä** New Year's
Day. **-valvojaiset:** *olla
u-jaisissa* watch the old year
out.
uudestaan = *uudelleen: yhä ~*

over and over again,
repeatedly; *alkaa* ~ begin
(start) afresh, make a new
start; resume; *istuttaa* ~
transplant.
uudesti|synnyttää regenerate.
-syntyminen rebirth,
regeneration. **-syntyä** be born
again, be regenerated.
uudin curtain; *uutimet (m.)*
hangings, draperies, *Am.*
drapes.
uudis|asukas settler, colonist.
-asutus settlement. **-raivaus**
newly cleared land; *suorittaa*
~*työtä (kuv.)* break new
ground. **-rakennus** new
building.
uudis|taa renew, innovate;
(kerrata) repeat; *(parantaen)*
renovate; *(järjestää uudestaan)*
reorganize; reconstruct; ~
vanha tapa revive an old
custom; ~ *vekseli* renew
(prolong) a bill of exchange;
vrt. uusia. **-taja** innovator.
-tua be renewed, be repeated;
be revived; recur. **-tus**
renewal; *(parannus)* reform;
innovation; (~*hanke* proposed
reform; ~*työ* reform work).
-viljelys newly cultivated land.
uuhi ewe.
uuma waist.
uumenet interior; *maan* ~ the
bowels of the earth.
uuni *(paistin-)* oven;
(lämmitys-) stove; *(sulatus-
ym)* furnace; *(kuivaus- ym)*
kiln; *(takka)* fireplace.
-koukku poker. **-kuiva**
oven-dried.
uupu|a become exhausted; grow
tired, become fatigued, tire;
uupuu (puuttuu) is lacking.
-maton indefatigable;
unwearying, untiring, tireless;
unflagging [zeal, *into*].
-mattomuus indefatigability.
-mus exhaustion, prostration,
fatigue. **-nut** exhausted; tired
[out], weary, fatigued, worn
out; *lopen* ~ dead tired.
uuras industrious. **-taa** be
busy; work hard (at); toil;
minun on -tettava I must put
my nose to the grindstone.
-tus hard work, toil.

uurna urn; *vaali*~ ballot box.
uur|re groove, furrow. **-ros**
(pykälä) notch. **-taa** groove,
furrow; *(naarmuttaa)* score;
(kovertaa) hollow [out]; cut
[a channel, *ura*]. **-teinen**
grooved, furrowed.
uus|asiallinen: ~
rakennustaide functional
architecture. **-hopea** German
silver, silver-plated ware.
uusi new; novel; *(veres)* fresh;
aivan ~ brand new; ~ *aika*
modern times; *Hyvää uutta
vuotta!* Happy New Year!
mitä uutta what news? *mennä
~in naimisiin* remarry; *tämä
~ onnettomuus (entisten
lisäksi)* this additional
misfortune. **-a** renew; *(korjata)*
renovate; *(kerrata)* repeat;
(vaihtaa) replace; *(kunnostaa)*
recondition; *-ttu (painos)*
[completely] revised. **-kuu**
new moon. **-nta** renewal;
repetition; modernization;
rad., TV repeat, *teatt.* re-run;
(~*painos* new impression;
~*rikos* repeated offence).
-utua be renewed; be
repeated; repeat itself; recur,
occur again; *(palata)* return;
tauti u-tui the disease
recurred, the patient had a
relapse; *säännöllisesti -utuva.* .
recurrent. **-utuminen** *(taudin)*
recurrence.
Uusi Seelanti New Zealand.
uuskolonialismi neocolonialism.
uuskreikka modern Greek.
uusnatsilaisuus neo-Nazism.
uuti|nen [piece of] news; news
item; *ikäviä -sia* sad news,
sad tidings. **-skatsaus** *TV*
newscast, *(filmi)* newsreel.
-slähetys news broadcast, news
transmission. **-ssulku** news
embargo.
uutisten|hankinta reporting.
-hankkija reporter.
uutis|tiedotus news bulletin.
-toimisto news agency.
-toimittaja news editor *(t.*
broadcaster). **-välineet** news
media. **-välähdys** news flash.
uutos, uuttaa extract.
uutter|a industrious, assiduous;
painstaking. **-uus** industry,

assiduity.
uut|ukainen: *uuden* ~
brand-new. **-uus** newness;
novelty; *uutuuden viehätys* the
charm of novelty; *uutuuksia*
novelties.
uuvu|s: *olla -ksissa* be tired

[out], be exhausted, be
fatigued, be dead tired. **-ttaa**
exhaust, tire [out], wear out,
fatigue; *-ttava* wearying. **-tus**
exhaustion; prostration;
(~**taistelu** war of attrition).

V

vaahdota foam, froth; *(saippua)* lather; *(juoma, m.)* effervesce.
vaahtera maple.
vaahto foam; froth; scum; *(et. saippua-)* lather. **-inen** foamy, frothy; foaming. **-kumi** foam rubber. **-muovi** foam [plastic]. **-päinen** foam-crested. **-sammutin** foam [fire-] extinguisher.
vaaja *(kiila)* wedge.
vaaka balance, *(talous-)* scales *(pl.);* weighing machine; *kallistaa vaa'an jnk eduksi* tips the scale in favour of; *jk painaa vaa'assa* weighs heavy in the balance. **-asento** horizontal position. **-kuppi** scale. **-lauta:** *on -laudalla* is at stake. **-suora** horizontal; level; *~an* horizontally.
vaaksa span.
vaakuna [coat of] arms; armorial bearings. **-kilpi** coat of arms. **-tiede** heraldry. **-tieteellinen** heraldic.
vaalea light; pale; *(ihon, tukan väri)* fair; *~ puku* light-coloured dress; *~ tukka (m.)* blond[e] hair. **-nharmaa** light (pale) grey. **-npunainen** pink. **-nsininen** light (pale) blue. **-tukkainen** fair [-haired]. **-verikkö** blonde. **-verinen** fair, blond, *(naisesta)* blonde.
vaale|ntaa make.. pale, make light[er]; bleach. **-ta** *(henkilöstä)* turn pale; *(haalistua)* fade, be discoloured. **-us** lightness; paleness; light colour; fairness.
vaali *(~t)* election; *vrt. valinta.*
vaalia take [great, good] care of; *(esim. muistoa)* cherish; *(hoivata)* nurse [tenderly].
vaali|ehdokas candidate [for an election]. **-huoneisto** polling

station. **-juliste** election poster. **-julistus** appeal to the voters. **-kausi** election time. **-kelpoinen** eligible. **-kelpoisuus** eligibility. **-kelvoton** ineligible. **-kiihotus** electioneering; *harjoittaa ~ta* electioneer. **-laki** election laws. **-lause** motto. **-liitto** election agreement. **-lippu** ballot-paper, voting-paper. **-lista** election list, *Am.* ticket. **-luettelo** register of voters. **-oikeutettu** entitled to vote. **-petos** rigged election; *harjoittaa ~ta* rig an (the) election. **-piiri** electoral district, constituency. **-ruhtinas** Elector. **-saarna** probationary sermon. **-taistelu** election campaign. **-tapa** electoral system. **-tappio:** *kärsiä ~* be defeated in an election. **-tulos** election returns (figures). **-uurna** ballot box.
vaan but.
vaania lurk, prowl, *(väijyksissä)* lie in ambush (for).
vaappua rock, swing, sway [to and fro]; *(käydessä)* waddle.
vaara 1. danger, peril; *(uhka)* risk, hazard, jeopardy; *olla ~ssa* be in danger, be endangered; *olla ~ssa menettää* run the risk of losing; *joutua ~an* get into danger; *on ~na jllek* is a danger to; *~ ohi (merkki)* [the] all clear. **2.** [wooded] hill. **-llinen** dangerous; perilous; *(uskallettu)* hazardous, risky; *(kriittinen)* critical. **-llisuus** dangerousness, dangerous nature (character). **-nalainen** dangerous;.. exposed to danger; *(uhattu)* threatened; *on ~ (m.)* involves danger; *saattaa v-alaiseksi* expose.. to danger,

endanger, imperil. **-ntaa**
endanger, risk, hazard. **-ton**
not dangerous, devoid of
danger; harmless, safe; *tehdä
-ttomaksi (pommi)* defuse.
-ttomuus freedom from
danger; harmlessness.
-vyöhy|ke danger zone;
»v-kkeessä» at risk.
vaari 1. grandfather, grandpa.
vaari 2. *ottaa ~ jstk* pay
attention (to), pay heed (to),
heed; *pitää ~ jstk* see to it
[that. .], look after [one's
own interests], mind.
vaarna plug; peg.
vaate cloth; *(-aine)* material,
stuff; *vaatteet* clothes,
clothing; dress. **-harja** clothes
brush. **-htimo** ready-made
outfitters; *herrain ~*
gentlemen's outfitters. **-huone**
clothes closet. **-kaappi**
wardrobe. **-kappale** article of
clothing, garment. **-kerta** set
of clothes; *(vaihto-)* change of
clothes. **-komero** [built-in]
wardrobe, *Am. m.* clothes closet.
vaateli|aisuus pretentiousness.
-as pretentious; exacting;
(röyhkeän) presumptuous.
vaate|naulakko coat-rack,
clothes rack. **-parsi** dress.
-ripustin *(vaatepuu)* [coat]
hanger. **-säilö** cloakroom, *Am.*
checkroom. **-ttaa** clothe;
(pukea) dress. **-tus** clothing;
(~liike clothing store;
~teollisuus clothing industry).
-varasto stock of clothing;
(puku-) wardrobe.
vaati|a demand; claim;
(omakseen) lay claim to;
(vaatimalla ~) insist (on);
(tehdä tarpeelliseksi) call for,
require; *~ maksua* demand
payment, *~ (elämältä) paljon*
expect a lot of life; *(tämä
työ) -i häneltä paljon* places
great demands on him;
vaadittaessa on demand;
olojen -ma necessitated
(required) by the
circumstances; *siihen
vaaditaan aikaa* it takes
(requires) a great deal of
time; *jos tarve vaatii* if
necessary, if need be;

onnettomuus vaati 10 uhria
ten lives were lost in the
accident; *vaadittava* required.
-maton modest, unpretentious,
unassuming; simple.
-mattomuus modesty. **-mus**
demand, claim; *(pyyde)*
pretension; *(tutkinto-)*
requirement; *ajan -mukset* the
requirements of the times;
hänellä on suuret -mukset
he is exacting in his
demands, he demands a great
deal [of *jklta*]; *asettaa
-muksia liian korkealle* don't
require so much; *esittää ~*
enter (put in) a claim;
täyttää (tutkinto-) -mukset
satisfy the examiners; *hänen
-muksestaan* in response to
his demand, at his request.
-va(inen) exacting. **-vaisesti** in
an exacting manner,
pretentiously. **-vaisuus**
pretentiousness.
vaatturi tailor. **-liike** tailoring
business.
vadelma raspberry. **-hillo**
raspberry jam.
vael|lus wandering; *(vaeltelu)*
rambling; stroll [ing]; *(joukko-)*
migration; *elämän~* way
(pilgrimage) through life. **-taa**
wander; stroll; roam; *(käydä,
m. kuv.)* walk; *-tava*
wandering; migratory [people,
kansa], itinerant [musician,
soittoniekka]; *-tava ritari*
knight-errant.
vaha wax. **-inen** [.. of] wax.
-kangas oil-cloth. **-kuva** wax
figure. **-kynttilä** wax candle.
-ntapainen waxy, wax-like.
-paperi wax[ed] paper. **-ta**
wax. **-tulppa** *(korvassa)* plug
of wax. **-us** waxing.
vahdinvaihto change of guard.
vahingoi|ttaa injure, damage;
harm; hurt; do damage (to);
mar; *ruosteen -ttama* affected
by rust. **-ttua** be injured, be
hurt, *(vioittua)* be damaged,
suffer [damage]. **-ttumaton**
undamaged; unhurt, uninjured;
(henkilöstä m.) safe and
sound, unscathed.
vahingolli|nen injurious,
harmful, noxious; detrimental.

-suus injuriousness, harmfulness.

vahingon|ilo malicious pleasure. **-iloinen** malicious, spiteful. **-korvaus** compensation, indemnification; *lak.* damages; *vaatia ~ta* claim damages; (~**vaatimus** claim for damages, compensation claim). **-laukaus** shooting accident; *se oli ~* the shot went off accidentally. **-teko** [doing] damage.

vahinko damage; harm, loss, injury; (*onnettomuus*) misfortune, misadventure; *aiheuttaa ~a* cause damage, do harm; *vahingossa* by accident, (*huomaamatta*) unawares, inadvertently; *mikä ~* what a pity! *on ~, että* it is too bad that, it is a pity that; ~ *vain, että* it is too bad that, (*sen pahempi*) unfortunately. .; *olla vahingoksi* be to [a p.'s] disadvantage; *oma ~si!* the loss is yours.

vahti watch; guard; look-out; (*vartija*) watchman; *olla vahdissa, -palveluksessa* (*mer.*) be on watch, have the watch; *vrt. vartio.* **-a** [keep] watch over, keep guard; *voisitteko ~* will you watch (over . .). **-koira** watch dog. **-mestari** [hall] porter; attendant; (*kirkon*) verger, (*koulun*) janitor. **-miehistö** watch. **-paraati** [parade of] soldiers mounting guard. **-vuoro** watch; *olla ~ssa* have the watch.

vahva strong, (*luja*) firm; (*kestävä*) durable, sturdy; thick; heavy; (*ateria, m.*) substantial; ~ *kangas* heavy cloth, strong (durable) material; ~ *usko* firm (staunch, unwavering) belief. **-rakenteinen** strongly built. **-sti** strongly, firmly. **-virta** power current.

vahvennus *sot.* reinforcement [s].

vahvis|taa strengthen; (*varmentaa*) confirm; corroborate; verify; ratify [a treaty, *sopimus*]; reinforce (*m.* *tekn.*); ~ *nimikirjoituksellaan* certify. . with one's signature; attest; ~ *jkta uskossa* strengthen (fortify) a p. in his faith; ~ *valalla* attest. . on oath, confirm. . by oath; ~ *ääntä ym* (*sähk.*) amplify; *-tava lääke* tonic. **-tamaton** unconfirmed; unverified. **-tua** be [come] strengthened, grow in strength, gain strength; (*saada v-tusta*) be confirmed. **-tus** strengthening; confirmation; (*hyväksymys*) sanction; (*lisä-*) reinforcement; *huhuun ei ole saatu ~ta* the rumour has not been confirmed; *jnk -tukseksi* in corroboration (confirmation) of.

vahv|uinen: *jnk ~* of the thickness of; *minkä ~* how thick? of what thickness? *2000 miehen ~ joukko* a troop 2000 strong. **-uus** strength.

vai or; *sinäkö ~ minä* you or I; ~ *niin* is that so? [oh,] I see! indeed! really? ~ *niin, et siis voi tulla* so you can't come; *hänhän on opettaja, ~ onko?* she is a teacher, isn't she?

vai|entaa silence, hush. . up. **-eta** become silent, cease [speaking etc.]; (*olla vaiti*) be silent, keep silence (about), keep. . quiet, conceal. .; *äänet vaikenivat* the sounds became hushed, the sounds died away; *vaieten* in silence, silently.

vaih|de *rautat.* switch, *Engl. m.* points; (*auton*) gear; (*muutos*) change; *-teen vuoksi* for a change, for the sake of variety; *vuosisadan -teessa* at the turn of the [19th to the 20th] century; (~**laatikko** gearbox). **-della** alternate; vary between. . and (from. . to), range (from. . to); fluctuate; *-dellen* alternately.

vaihde|mies pointsman. **-ttavuus** (*rahan*) convertibility. **-tanko** gear lever. **-vuodet** menopause.

vaihdo|kas changeling. **-s** change.

vaihe phase; *(aste)* stage *(m. raketin); (elämän-)* vicissitude; *tässä* ~*essa* at this stage *(t. juncture); jnk* ~*illa* about; *niillä* ~*illa* something like that; *vuoden 1930* ~*illa* in 1930 or thereabouts, somewhere about 1930; *kaikissa elämän* ~*issa* in all vicissitudes of life, in all phases of life, through thick and thin; *olla kahden* ~*illa* be in two minds, hesitate. **-ikas** eventful; chequered, *Am.* checkered. **vaih|taa** change; *(keskenään)* exchange, *puhek.* swap; *rautat.* switch; *(esim. paristo)* replace; ~ *ajatuksia* exchange ideas; ~ *junaa* change trains; ~ *omistajaa* change hands; ~ *parempaan* exchange.. for a better one; ~ *rahoja* change money; ~ *vaatteita* change, *(esim. iltapuku ylle)* c. into evening dress; ~ *vahti* relieve the guard; *voitteko* ~ *punnan?* can you give me change for a pound? ~ *(autossa)* ykkösestä kakkoseen change over from first to second gear *(t.* speed). **-televa(inen)** changeable, variable, varying, varied; inconstant; *(oikullinen)* fickle, flighty; *-televalla onnella* with varying success; ~ *sää* changeable (unsettled) weather. **-televaisuus** changeableness, variability. **-telu** variation, variety, fluctuation; *(vuorottelu)* alternation; ~*n vuoksi* for a change; *(*~*väli* range of variation). **vaihto** changing, change; exchange, interchange; *(uuteen)* replacement. **-arvo** exchange value. **-avain** monkey wrench. **-ehto, -ehtoinen** alternative. **-ehtoisesti** alternatively; interchangeably. **-kauppa** barter [ing]; *tehdä* ~*a* barter. **-kelpoinen** interchangeable. **-kurssi** [rate of] exchange. **-lämpöinen** cold-blooded. **-pyörä, -ratas** gear. **-raha** [small] change. **-suhde:** *ulkomaankaupan -suhteet*

terms of trade. **-virta** alternating current. **-väline** medium of exchange. **vaihtua** change, be [come] changed, *jhk* into; shift. **vaijeri** cable. **vaikea** difficult, hard; *(vakava)* serious; severe; tough, *puhek.* knotty, tricky; ~ *asema* awkward (precarious) position; ~*t ajat* hard times, times of distress; ~ *tehtävä* difficult task, *puhek.* sticky proposition; *hänen ei ollut* ~*(ta) päästä ulos (m.)* he had no difficulty in getting out. **-laatuinen** severe; *vrt. pahan-*. **-nlainen** rather difficult. **-pääsyinen** . difficult of access,.. not [easily] accessible. **-selkoinen** hard to understand, abstruse. **-sti** [only] with difficulty; seriously [wounded, *haavoittunut*], badly; ~ *ratkaistava*.. difficult (hard) to solve. **-tajuinen**.. hard (difficult) to understand. **vaikeneminen** silence. **vaiker|oida** moan, groan; *(valittaa)* complain. **-rus** moan [ing], groan [ing]. **vaike|us** difficulty; *(koettelemus)* hardship; *olla* -*uksissa* be in trouble (in difficulties); *edessäni on (paljon)* -*uksia* I have difficulties to face, I am confronted by many difficulties; *saattaa* -*uksiin* involve.. in difficulties. **-uttaa** render (make) [more] difficult, hamper. **-utua** become [more] difficult. **vaikka** [al]though; *(*~ *kohta)* even if, even though; ~ *kuinka paljon* any amount; ~ *kuinkakin pieni* however small; ~ *koska* [at] any time; ~ *kuka* anybody, no matter who; ~ *minne* no matter where; ~ *kohta oli vahva mies; ei jaksanut* strong though he was he could not..; *saat* ~ *kolme* you can have as many as three; *(koska lähdetään?—)* ~ *heti* now if you like; *(minkä*

valitset?—) ~ *tämän* let's say this [one]; *yksi menetelmä, ~pa hyväkin, ei riitä* a single method, albeit good, does not suffice; ~ *mikä olisi* whatever happens.
vaikku ear-wax, cerumen.
vaiku|te impulse; *saada -tteita jklta* be influenced by. **-telma** impression; *minulla on se ~, että* I am under the impression that. **-tin** motive. **-ttaa** have [a, an. .] effect, exercise an effect (on); take effect; influence; *(koskea)* affect; act (on); *(myötä-)* contribute, be conducive, conduce (to); ~ *jltak* seem, strike [a p.] as being, give the impression of being. ., make a [n]. . impression; ~ *siltä kuin* it seems as if; *palkkojen nousu* ~ *hintoihin* wage increases react on prices; ~ *päätökseen* influence (affect) the decision; *sen -ttavat monet seikat* it is caused by various circumstances. **-ttava** effective; impressive; *(pelkästään)* ~ *tekijä* influential (potent) factor. **-ttavuus** effectiveness. **-tukseton**. . without [any] effect (influence); ineffective. **-tus** effect, *jhk* upon; influence (on, upon, over); action; *olla jnk -tuksen alainen* be under the influence of, be influenced by [a p.]; *jäädä ilman ~ta* fail to make an effect; *teki edullisen -tuksen* created a favourable impression; *pula-ajan -tukset* the consequences of the depression; *(~piiri* sphere of influence; **-tapa** mode of action; *~valta* influence, *jkh* [up]on; *~valtainen* influential).
vai|lla, -lle without; *olla jtk ~* lack; *jäädä jtk vaille* be left without; *hiukan vaille 100 markkaa* a little short of 100 marks; *kello on neljännestä ~ 1* it is a quarter to one; *jäi vastausta vaille* remained unanswered.
vaillinai|nen incomplete; *(puutteellinen)* defective,

imperfect. **-suus** incompleteness; defectiveness, imperfection.
vaillinki *(raha-)* deficit.
vaime|a *(ääni)* muffled, subdued. **-nnus** moderation; alleviation; damping. **-ntaa** moderate, *(ääni)* muffle. **-ntua, -ta** quieten [down]; be alleviated; *(myrsky)* abate, die down, *(ääni)* die away.
vaimo wife *(pl. wives).*
vain only, [nothing] but; merely; *(pelkästään). .* alone; ~ *hiukkasen (m.)* just a little; ~ *vähän toivoa jäljellä* but little hope left; *mitä vain* anything.
vainaja [the, a] deceased; *isä~ni* my late (my deceased) father.
vainio field.
vaino persecution. **-harha** delusion of persecution; *(~luuloisuus* paranoia). **-hullu** paranoiac. **-lainen** foe. **-ta** persecute; *nämä muistot -sivat häntä* these memories haunted him.
vainu scent; *tarkka ~ keen* s. **-koira** sleuth-hound. **-ta** scent *(m. kuv.), (koirasta, m.)* pick up the scent of. .
vaippa cloak; *(kaapu)* cape, gown; *tekn.* mantle, casing; *(peite)* cover; *(vauvan)* napkin, *et. Am.* diaper.
vaipu|a sink *(m. kuv.);* drop [with fatigue, *uupuneena maahan*]; *(jhk pahaan)* lapse (into); *ajatuksiin -neena* deep *(t.* lost) in thought.
vaisto instinct; *tyyli~* sense of style. **-mainen** instinctive. **-maisesti** instinctively, by instinct; *toimia* ~ *(m.)* act on instinct. **-nvarainen** instinctive; intuitive. **-ta** sense.
vaisu faint, feeble; dull.
vaiteli|aisuus taciturnity; reticence. **-as** taciturn; silent; reticent, uncommunicative.
vaiti silent; *olla* ~ be silent, observe silence; *ole* ~ be quiet! *käske häntä olemaan ~ (ark.)* tell him to shut up. **-ollen** in silence. **-olo** silence; *(~velvollinen.* . bound to

secrecy; ~**velvollisuus**
professional confidentiality).
vaiva trouble; bother, worry,
annoyance; *(kipu)* pain; ~*tta*
without difficulty; **nähdä**
(paljon) ~*a* take [much]
trouble, take [great] pains
(with); *ei säästänyt vaivojaan*
he spared no pains (no
efforts); *olla jklle* ~*ksi* give. .
trouble, put. . to
inconvenience; ~*lla hankittu,*
saatu hard-earned, hard-won;
ei maksa ~*a* it is not worth
while. **-antua** *ks. vaivautua;*
-tunut self-conscious, ill at
ease. **-inen** *kuv.* miserable,
wretched; *s.* invalid, cripple;
~ *summa* paltry sum. **-iskoivu**
dwarf birch. **-isuus** misery,
wretchedness.
vaivalloi|nen troublesome;
(vaikea) hard, difficult;
(kiusallinen) trying,
wearisome; *(suuritöinen)*
laborious; arduous; onerous;
hyvin ~ *(m.)* involving much
trouble (difficulty). **-suus**
troublesomeness; laboriousness;
great difficulty.
vaivan|näkö trouble. **-palkkio:**
sain sen ~*na* I got it for my
trouble.
vaiv|ata trouble, give [a p.]
trouble, bother, worry,
inconvenience [a p.];
(kiusata) harass, vex; ~
taikinaa knead the dough; ~
itseään liiaksi overstrain
oneself; ~ *päätään jllak*
trouble one's head about; ~
silmiään strain one's eyes;
hänen käytöksensä -aa minua
his conduct annoys (vexes)
me; *häntä -aa päänsärky* he
is suffering from headache;
(yleensä) he is subject to
headaches; *mikä sinua -aa*
what is the matter with you?
what is wrong [with you]?
anteeksi, että -asin sorry to
have bothered you. **-aton**
(helppo) easy. **-attomasti**
without [any] trouble
(difficulty); easily. **-autua**
[take] trouble, take the
trouble [of . . -ing], trouble
oneself; *älä -audu!* please

don't bother; *-autunut*
(hämillinen) embarrassed. **-oin**
with difficulty; *(tuskin)* barely;
vain ~ only with great
difficulty.
vaja shed; *(kylkiäinen)* lean-to,
vajaa short, not full; ~ *mitta*
short measure; ~*t puolet*
rather less than half.
-kuntoinen, -kykyinen handicapped. **-liikkeinen** *(pakko-)*
spastic. **-lukuinen** numerically
incomplete, not fully attended.
-mielinen mentally deficient
(subnormal, handicapped).
-mielisyys mental subnormality
(deficiency). **-mittainen** short,. .
not up to the required size,
undersized; not up to
standard. **-painoinen** short
[-weight]. **-ravitsemus**
malnutrition. **-työllisyys**
underemployment.
vajanainen deficient.
vaja|us shortage, *(vaillinki)*
deficit. **-vainen** imperfect,
defective. **-vaisuus**
defect[iveness], imperfection,
deficiency.
vajo|ta sink, *jhk* in [to]; fall;
(laiva, m.) founder; ~
syvyyteen go down, *(pohjaan)*
go to the bottom. **-ttaa** sink;
hanki ~ the snow surface
does not bear.
vakaa firm, stable; steadfast;
steady; *vakain tuumin* wilfully.
-ja inspector of weights and
measures. **-nnuttaa** strengthen;
settle; establish, stabilize.
-ntua become firm (stable),
(sää) become settléd, *(hinnat)*
steady; *kuv. (henk.)* settle
down; *v-tunut mies* a staid
man. **-ntumaton** unsettled.
vakanssi vacancy.
vaka|umuksellinen . . baséd on
conviction. **-umus** conviction;
assurance; *v-mukseni on.* . I
am fully convinced (that);
kuolivat -umuksensa puolesta
died for their conviction[s].
-us testing [of weights and
measures]. **-uttaa** consolidate;
stabilize.
vakava serious, grave; *(luja)*
firm, steady, stable; ~ *asema*
secure position; *ottaa asia*

~*lta kannalta* take a th.
seriously; *(aivan) vakavissaan*
in [dead] earnest. **-henkinen**
earnest, serious. **-nlaatuinen**
serious.
vakavarai|nen reliable, solid
[firm, *liike*], well-established;
(maksukykyinen) solvent,
[financially] sound. **-suus**
solvency, sound financial
position.
vakav|asti seriously; ~ *puhuen*
s. speaking, to be serious.
-uus earnestness, seriousness;
stability, firmness, steadiness.
vakiin|nuttaa establish [. .
firmly]. **-tua** become
established [in use,
käytäntöön]; **-tunut** [well-]
established, set, *(mielipide)*
fixed, settled; *vrt. vakaantua.*
vakinai|nen regular; *(pysyvä)*
permanent; standing; *(menot
ym.)* ordinary; ~ *virka*
regular (permanent) position;
~ *sotaväki* regular army,
standing army; ~ *palvelus
(sot.)* active service. **-staa**
(työsuhde) decasualize. **-suus**
permanence.
vakio *mat.* constant. **-ida**
standardize. **-koko** stock size.
-laatu standard quality.
-varuste(et) standard
equipment.
vakituinen permanent.
vakka bushel; ~ *kantensa
valitsee* birds of a feather
flock together, like will to
like; *(~juttu* spying
affair; *~satelliitti* intelligence
satellite; *~toiminta* espionage).
vakosametti corduroy.
vakuu|s security, guarantee.
-ttaa insure; assure [a p.
that. . *jklle*]; protest [one's
innocence, profess
[friendship]; *(selittää)* declare;
saada -ttuneeksi convince [a
p. of]; ~ *jnk varalta* insure

against; *-ttamalla* ~ affirm,
earnestly assure. **-ttamaton**
uninsured. **-ttautua** convince
oneself (of, about), assure
oneself (of), make sure
(about), ascertain. **-ttava**
convincing. **-ttelu** assurances,
protestations. **-ttua** become
conviced, *jstk* of; that. .
vakuutus assurance; *(palo- ym)*
insurance; *(selittävä)*
declaration; *lak.* affidavit;
affirmation; *vakuutuksen
ottaja* policy-holder, the
insured [person]. **-arvo**
insurable value; *(-summa)*
insurance. **-asiamies** insurance
agent. **-kirja** insurance policy.
-maksu insurance premium.
-yhtiö insurance company.
vala oath; *(pyhä lupaus)* vow;
vannoa ~ take (swear) an
oath; *vahvistaa ~lla* confirm
by oath; *väärä* ~ perjury;
tehdä väärä ~ perjure oneself.
valaa cast; *(muodostella)*
mould; *(kaataa)* pour; *tiet.
(parafiiniin)* embed; ~ *eloa
jhk* instil (infuse) spirit into;
~ *kynttilöitä* mould (dip)
candles; ~ *tinaa* seek omens
[for the New Year] by
melting down tin (lead) and
dropping it in cold water.
valaan|pyynti whaling; *(~laiva*
whaler). **-rasva** whale (train)
oil; *(ihra)* -blubber.
valaehtoi|nen ~ *todistus (l.v.)*
affidavit; *vakuuttaa -sesti*
declare under oath.
valai|sematon unlighted. **-seva**
luminous, *kuv.* illustrative
(of), elucidating; *kirkkaasti* ~
bright. **-sin** lighting (electric
light) fixture, lamp.
valais|ta light, light up,
illuminate; *kuv.* illustrate [by,
with *jllak*], throw (shed) light
[on the matter, *asiaa*],
elucidate; *huone oli hyvin -tu*
the room was well lighted
(well lit up); *ehkä voin* ~
sinua tässä asiassa perhaps I
can enlighten you on this
point.
valaistus light *(m. kuv.)*,
lighting; illumination; *kuv.*
illustration. **-aine** illuminant.

-laitteet *(sähkö-)* electric light fittings.
valaja founder.
valakka gelding.
vala|liitto confederation.
-liittolainen confederate. **-llinen** sworn;. . on oath; ~ *todistus (m.)* affidavit; *kuulla -llisesti* examine. . under oath.
-miehistö jury. **-mies** juryman, juror. **-nta** casting. **-ntehnyt** sworn, *(tilintarkastaja)* chartered. **-pattoinen** perjured, forsworn.
valas whale.
valeasuinen. . in disguise.
valeh|della lie, tell a lie; *-televa* lying, mendacious. **-telija** liar.
vale|helmi false (imitation) pearl. **-hyökkäys** feigned attack. **-kuolema** apparent death, suspended animation. **-kuollut** apparently dead, in a state of suspended animation. **-kuva** mock appearance. **-liike** sham manoeuvre.
valella pour [water upon, *jtk vedellä*], sprinkle (with).
vale|nimi false name, assumed name. **-parta** false beard. **-puku** disguise. **-pukuinen** disguised,. . in disguise.
valhe lie, untruth, falsehood; *~enpaljastuskoje* lie detector. **-ellinen** false; *(ei tosi)* untrue,. . not true. **-ellisuus** falsehood.
valikoi|da choose; *(huolellisesti)* select, pick out. **-ma** selection, choice, assortment.
valimo foundry.
valin|kauha *kuv.* melting pot. **-nainen** optional. **-nanvara** choice, option.
valinta selection, choice; *muuta valinnan varaa ei ole* there is no other choice *(t.* alternative). **-myymälä** *(iso)* supermarket. **-vapaus** [right of] choice, [right of] option.
valio|joukko select [ed] body, picked troop, the élite [of. .]. **-kunta** committee, *parl., m.* commission.
valis|taa enlighten; *(sivistää)* educate; illuminate. **-tua** become enlightened. **-tunut**

enlightened. **-tus** enlightenment; *(sivistys)* education; *-tuksen aika (hist.)* the Age of Enlightenment; (~**työ** educational work).
valit|a choose; *(vaalissa)* elect; *(huolellisesti)* select; pick [out]; *hänet -tiin presidentiksi* he was elected President; ~ *jäseneksi* elect a p. member [of a society]; *-tavaksi kelpaava* eligible; *-tu* (woman) of one's choice; *-uin sanoin* in well-chosen words; ~ *uudelleen* re-elect.
valitetta|va deplorable, regrettable; unfortunate; *on* ~*a* it is to be regretted [that. .]. **-vasti** unfortunately; ~ *en voi tulla* I regret being unable to come.
valitsija voter; ~*t = seur.* **-kunta** electorate; *(vaalipiiri)* constituency. **-miehistö, -mies** electoral college. **-mies** elector.
vali|ttaa complain (of, about; to a p. about); *(voihkia)* moan, groan; bewail; *(surkutellen)* regret, deplore; be sorry; *(surua)* condole [with a p. *jkn*]; appeal [against] [a judgment, *tuomiosta*], lodge a complaint, [lodge a] protest [against an appointment *nimityksestä*]; ~ *jksta* make a complaint against a p.; *-ttaen suruanne* with my sympathy; ~ *korkeampaan oikeuteen* appeal to a higher court; *-ttava* complaining; *-tti syvästi* expressed his deep regret (that. .) **-ttelu** regret. **-tus** complaint; complaining; lament; *(vetoomus)* appeal; (~**aika** time for appeal; ~**huuto** cry of distress; ~**oikeus** right of appeal; ~**virsi** lamentation).
valja|at harness; *on -issa* is harnessed; *päästää -ista* unharness. **-kko** team. **-staa** *(m. koskesta)* harness; put the harness on.
valjeta grow (become) light [er]; *(sarastaa)* dawn, *(kirkastua)* brighten [up].

valju bleak; *(kalpea)* pale, pallid.
valkai|sematon unbleached. **-sta** bleach; *(kalkita)* whitewash.
valkama haven; harbour.
valkea *a.* white; *s. (tuli)* fire, *(valo)* light.
valkeus whiteness, *(valo)* light.
valko|hehku white heat.
-ihoinen *a.* white [-skinned]; *s.* white. **-inen** white; ~ *verisolu* white blood cell, leukocyte. **-kangas** *elok.* screen. **-pippuri** white pepper. **-pukuinen** .. dressed in white. **-sipuli** garlic. **-tukkainen** white-haired. **-viini** white wine. **-vuokko** wood anemone.
valkuai|nen white; albumen. **-saine** protein.
vallalla: ~ *oleva* prevailing, prevalent.
vallan quite. **-kin** particularly [when, as, since *kun, koska*].
vallan|alainen dependent (on); subject (to). **-alaisuus** dependence; subordination; subjection [to..'s rule]. **-anastaja** usurper. **-himo** greed for power, mania for power. **-himoinen.** . greedy for power. **-kaappaus** coup [d'état]. **-kumouksellinen** *a. & s.* revolutionary. **-kumous** revolution; *(~hanke* revolutionary plan; *~mies* revolutionary). **-perijä** heir to the throne; *olla lähin ~* stand next in succession. **-perimys** succession; *(~oikeus* right of succession). **-pitäjä:** *~t* those in power, [the] holders of power.
vallas|luokka upper class. **-nainen** lady of rank.
valla|ta occupy; *(liittää valtakuntaansa)* annex; *(tunteesta puh.)* overcome, overwhelm; *(mieli, -kuvitus)* capture; ~ *laiva* capture a ship; ~ *maata viljelykselle (t. mereltä)* reclaim land; ~ *takaisin* recapture; *kauhun valtaamana* seized (stricken) with terror, overcome by dread; *ajatus valtasi mieleni* the thought preoccupied my mind. **-ton** unruly;

undisciplined; ungovernable. **-ttomuus** unruliness, unruly nature; *(v-ton teko)* mischief.
valli embankment, bank; *(suoja-)* dyke; *sot.* rampart. **-hauta** *(vesi-)* moat.
vallit|a dominate; rule, reign; *(olla v-sevana)* be predominant, predominate, *(yleisenä)* prevail; *rauha -see maassa* there is peace in the country, peace reigns in the country. **-seva** prevailing, prevalent; *(hallitseva)* [pre]dominant, [pre]dominating; *-sevat olot* the prevailing (existing) conditions.
valli|ttaa entrench. **-tus** entrenchment, rampart.
valloi|llaan, -lleen on the loose, vrt. *valta.*
valloi|ttaa conquer *(m. kuv.);* capture; take possession of; *kuv. m.* captivate. **-ttaja** conqueror. **-ttamaton** unconquered; *(jota ei voi v-ttaa)* unconquerable, impregnable. **-tus** conquest *(m. kuv.);* capture; *(~retki* invasion; *~sota* war of conquest).
valmen|nus training. **-taa** train. **-taja** trainer. **-tautua** train; be studying for [a profession, *ammattiin*].
valmis ready, prepared, *jhk* for; *(valmistettu)* finished, completed; *hänellä on se valmiina* he has finished it; *rakennus on valmiina* the building is completed; *valmiina ostettu ready-made* [coat, *takki*]; *saada jk valmiiksi* get a th. finished (done), complete, finish a th. **-matka** [all-]inclusive tour, package tour.
valmis|taa prepare; make; *(tehdasmaisesti)* manufacture; *(tuottaa)* produce; *(valmiiksi)* finish, complete; ~ *tilaa jllek* make room for. **-taja** maker, manufacturer; producer. **-tamaton** *(edeltä)* not prepared beforehand. **-tamatta** without preparation; *puhua ~* speak extempore. **-tautua** get ready

(for), prepare [oneself], make preparations (for). **-tautumaton** unprepared (for). **-tava** preparatory; preliminary; ~ *koulu* preparatory school.
valmiste preparation; *(tehdas-)* manufacture, make; *on ~illa* is in [course of] preparation, *(talo)* under construction. **-lla** prepare. **-lu(t)** preparations, preliminaries. **-vero** excise.
valmis|tua be finished, be completed; get ready (for); *vasta -tunut opettaja* newly qualified teacher; *(talon) -tuttua* on completion [of the house]. **-tumaton** unprepared. **-tus** preparation; manufacture; *(valmiiksiteko)* finishing, completion; (~**hinta** factory price; ~**kustannukset** cost of production); ~**tapa** method of production).
valmius readiness; preparedness.
valo light; *(valaistus)* lighting; *kynttilän ~ssa* by candlelight; *jkn ~ssa (kuv.)* in the light of; *saattaa epäedulliseen ~on* put. . in an unfavourable light; *saattaa huonoon ~on* bring discredit on. **-hoito** artificial sun treatment. **-hämy** *tait.* chiaroscuro. **-ilmiö** optical phenomenon. **-isa** light; luminous; [well] lighted; clear; *(luonne)* positive; ~*t toiveet* bright prospects. **-isuus** light; luminousness; brightness. **-juova-ammus** tracer bullet. **-keila** spotlight. **-kopio,** ~**ida** photocopy.
valokuva photograph, photo; *(tuokio-)* snapshot. **-aja** photographer. **-amo** [photographer's] studio. **-ta** photograph, take a photo [graph] (of). **-uksellinen** *(v-ukseen sopiva)* photogenic. **-uttaa** have. . photographed; ~ *itsensä* have one's photo (one's picture) taken.
valokuvaus photography. **-kone** camera. **-levy** photographic plate. **-liike** sellers of photographic materials, photo shop. **-tarpeet** photographic material.
valo|mainos illuminated advertisement, neon sign. **-merkki** light signal.
valon|heitin searchlight, *(julkisivun)* floodlight; *(auton)* headlight. **-herkkä** sensitive to light; *(paperi ym)* sensitized.
valo|-oppi optics. **-pilkku** bright spot. **-piste** *sähk.* outlet. **-puoli** bright side.
valos cast [ing].
valo|ton *(pimeä)* dark. **-ttaa** *valok.* expose, *kuv.* throw (shed) light on. **-tus** exposure; (~**mittari** exposure meter). **-voima** illuminating power; *(sähkölampun)* candle-power.
val|pas watchful, wakeful; alert, vigilant; *olla valppaana* be [on the] alert. **-ppaus** watchfulness; alertness, vigilance.
valssata *tekn.* roll.
valssi 1. *(tela)* roller. **2.** *(tanssi)* waltz; *tanssia* ~*a* waltz. **-tahti** waltz-time.
valta power (over); rule, domination; *(mahti)* might; *(toimi-)* authority; *hänellä on* ~ *tehdä se (m.)* it is in his power to do it; *päästä* ~*an* come (rise) to power; *saattaa* ~*nsa alaiseksi* subject, subdue, subjugate; *joutua jnk* ~*an (tunteen)* be overcome (overwhelmed) by; *olla vallalla* prevail; *päästä vallalle* become prevalent; *olla valloillaan* have free reins, run riot, run wild, *(raivota)* rage; *vallassa oleva puolue* the party in power. **-antulo:** *Hitlerin* ~ H.'s take-over. **-istuin** throne; *nousta -istuimelle* ascend the throne; *hänen -istuimelle noustessaan* at his accession; (~**puhe** speech from the throne; ~**sali** room of state).
valta|katu main street. **-kirja** power (letter) of attorney; *(lähettilään)* credentials; ~**lla** by proxy. **-kunnallinen** national, nation-wide.
valtakunnanoikeus: *asettaa syytteeseen -oikeudessa* impeach.
valta|kunta realm; *(valtio)*

state; *(kuningas-)* kingdom.
-merentakainen oversea[s];
transatlantic. **-meri** ocean;
(~laiva ocean-going steamer).
-osa majority, the bulk (of);
~ltaan predominantly. **-taistelu**
struggle for power. **-tie** main
road, high road.
valtaus capture; occupation;
annexation; *(kaivos-)* claim.
-joukot occupation troops.
valta|va huge, enormous;
immense; tremendous; ~
enemmistö an overwhelming
(a vast, the great) majority.
-vuus hugeness, enormousness.
-väylä main channel.
valti|as ruler, master. **-atar**
mistress; sovereign. **-kka**
sceptre, Am. **-ter. -mo** artery
tunnustella jkn ~a feel a p.'s
pulse.
valtio state; *(hallitus)*
government; *valtion.. (m.)*
state [school, *koulu*],
government [bond,
obligaatio]; *~n kustannuksella*
at public expense; *~n*
virkailija government employee,
public *(t.* civil) servant.
-johtoinen state-controlled.
-kalenteri official yearbook.
-keikaus coup. **-liitto** union
([con]federation) [of states].
-llinen state,.. of state;
government; national; public;
-lliset vaalit general election.
-mies statesman; *(~taito*
statesmanship; *~ura* political
career). **-muoto** system of
government; constitution.
-neuvosto cabinet, *(joskus)*
government [building].
altion|hoitaja administrator,
regent. **-kirkko** state *(t.*
established) church. **-laina**
government loan. **-pankki**
national bank. **-päämies** head
of [a] state. **-tulot** public
revenue *(sg.).* **-varat**
government funds. **-velka**
national debt. **-vero** state tax.
-virka: *-virassa* in public
service. **-virkamies:** *on ~ ks.*
ed.
altio|-oppi political science.
-petos high treason.
altiopäivä|mies member of

[the] parliament. **-t** Diet,
parliament.
valtio|salaisuus state secret.
-sihteeri undersecretary of
state. **-sääntö** constitution.
-taito statecraft. **-tiede**
political science; *-tieteellinen*
tiedekunta Faculty of Political
and Social Sciences. **-valta**
government; state *(t.* national)
power.
valtiovarain|ministeri minister
of finance; *Engl.* Chancellor
of the Exchequer, *Am.*
Secretary of the Treasury.
-ministeriö ministry of
finance; *Engl.* Treasury.
valtio|vierailu State visit.
-viisas diplomatic. **-viisaus**
kuv. diplomacy.
valtoi|n loose, free; *-(me)naan*
at large; unhindered; *(hiukset)*
hanging down, *(lapset)*
running loose, *(hillittömänä)*
on the loose.
valtti trump. **-ässä** ace of
trumps.
valtuus authority, power[s];
antaa jklle täydet valtuudet
invest a p. with full
power[s]; *täysillä valtuuksilla*
varustettu fully authorized;
ylittää valtuutensa exceed
one's authority. **-kirja** letter
of credence, credentials.
-kunta delegation. **-mies**
(kaupungin) town (city)
councillor. **-sto** town council,
(kunnan) local council.
valtuu|ttaa authorize, empower;
-tettu a. authorized,
empowered; *s.* authorized
agent, proxy; delegate. **-tus**
authorization, warrant.
valu|a flow; run [down, over],
flow [out], *(kynttilä)* gutter;
~ *virtanaan* pour [down];
sade -i virtanaan it was
pouring [down]. **-rauta** cast
iron. **-ri** foundry-worker. **-teos**
cast[ing]. **-teräs** cast steel.
valuutta currency. **-keinottelu**
speculation in foreign
currency. **-kurssit** rates of
exchange. **-markkinat** foreign
exchange market. **-rajoitukset**
currency restrictions.
valve: *olla ~illa* be awake.

-uttaa awaken, arouse. **-utua** wake up; *v-tunut* awakened, wide-awake; *(valistunut)* enlightened.

valvo|a be awake; be wakeful; watch [by a p.'s bedside, *jkn vuoteen ääressä*]; *(kokeissa)* invigilate; *(katsoa)* see (look) to it [that, *että*], look after, take care of; *(johtaen)* superintend, supervise, have charge of; ~ *jkn etuja* look after (attend to) sb.'s interests; ~ *järjestystä* maintain order; ~ *myöhään iltaisin* stay up late; keep late hours; ~ *saataviaan (konkurssissa)* lodge a claim [in bankruptcy]. **-ja** supervisor; *(kokeiden)* invigilator. **-nta** control; custody, charge; *(yli-)* supervision, superintendence; *jkn -nnaan alaisena* under the supervision of, under control of.

vamma injury, *lääk. m.* lesion; *saada* ~ be injured, be hurt. **-inen** handicapped, *(invalidi)* disabled. **-uttaa, vammoittaa** injure.

vampyyri vampire.

vanadiini vanadium.

vanamo linnaea, *Am.* twinflower.

vanavesi wake; *jkn vanavedessä* in the wake of *(t.* track) of, *(joskus)* in the backwash of.

vandaali *hist.* Vandal.

vaneri plywood; *(viilu)* veneer.

vangin|puku prison clothes. **-vartija** jailer, prison warder.

vangit|a arrest, take.. into custody; *(panna vankilaan)* imprison, put.. in prison; *olla -tuna* be under arrest; be in prison. **-seminen** arrest; capture; imprisonment. **-semismääräys** warrant [for arrest].

vanha old; ancient; *(iäkäs)* aged; ~ *aika* ancient times, antiquity; ~ *tekijä (kuv.)* an old hand; *~lla iällään* when old, at an advanced age, late in life; *elää hyvin ~ksi* live to a great age; *vanhempi* older; *vanhempi sisareni* my

elder sister; *vanhempi liikekumppani* senior partner; *hän on kaksi vuotta minua vanhempi (m.)* he is two years older than I, he is two years my senior; *kahtatoista vuotta vanhemmille* for children over 12 years [of age]; *vanhin* oldest; *(perheen) vanhin poika* the eldest son. **-htava** *puhek.* [slightly] dated. **-hko** elderly, rather old. **-inkoti** old people's home, home for the aged. **-naikainen** old-fashioned, .. out of date. **-naikaisuus** old-fashioned character. **-piika** old maid, spinster. **-poika** bachelor. **-staan** of old.

vanhem|mat parents; *-pain neuvosto* parents' committee; *-pain rakkaus* parental love. **-muus** seniority.

vanhe|ntua grow old, *(velka ym.)* come within the statute of limitations; *-ntunut* antiquated, *(sana, sanonta)* archaic, *puhek.* [out-]dated, *(käytännöstä jäänyt)* obsolete. **-ta** age, grow (get) old[er]; *(käytännöstä)* become obsolete, become antiquated; *-neva* ag[e]ing.

vanhoilli|nen *a.* & *s.* conservative; *s.* stick-in-the-mud. **-suus** conservatism.

vanhurs|kas righteous, just. **-kaus** righteousness, justness. **-kauttaa** justify. **-kauttaminen** justification.

vanhus old man (woman); *vanhukset* old people, aged people, the old.

vanhuuden|heikko decrepit. **-heikkous** decrepitude; senility. **-höperö** senile. **-turva** prop of one's declining years. **-vaivat** infirmities of old age.

vanhuus oldness; *(korkea ikä)* old age. **-eläke** old-age pension.

vanilja vanilla. **-kastike** vanilla sauce. **-tanko** vanilla stick. **-sokeri** vanilla sugar.

vankasti firmly, steadily; *syödä* ~ have a good (a proper) meal.

vankeinhoito prison welfare.
vankeus imprisonment; *(et. sota-)* captivity; *tuomittiin kuudeksi kuukaudeksi vankeuteen* was sentenced to six months' imprisonment. **-aika** prison term.
vanki prisoner; *(rikos-)* convict; *olla ~na* be imprisoned, be in prison (in jail); *ottaa vangiksi* take. . prisoner; *joutua vangiksi* be captured, be taken prisoner. **-koppi** cell. **-la** prison, jail; *sl.* nick; *joutua ~n* be sent to prison; *(~njohtaja* governor *t.* warden of a prison). **-leiri** prison camp.
vankka firm, steady; *(tukeva)* solid; *~ ateria* substantial meal; *~ pohja* solid (firm) foundation; *~ ruumiinrakenne* robust (sturdy) frame. **-tekoinen** strongly built.
vankkumaton unflinching, staunch.
vankkurit wag[g]on.
vannas *(veneen-)* stem; *(auran-)* ploughshare.
vanne hoop; *(rauta-, m.)* band; *(pyörän)* rim.
vanno|a swear; take an oath, swear to it [that. .]; *enpä mene -maan* I can't swear to it. **-ttaa** *(jkta)* take a p.'s oath; *(pyytää hartaasti)* implore, entreat, beseech. **-utua:** *v-tunut vihamies* sworn enemy.
vanttera thick-set, robust, sturdy.
vanu cotton wool; *(täyte-)* wad[ding]. **-a** felt up, felt. **-kas** pudding. **-ke** pulp. **-ttaa** full. **-tukko, -tuppo** swab (pledget, ball) of cotton, *(esim. korvassa)* cotton-wool plug.
vapa rod.
vapaa free; *(ilmainen, m.)* gratuitous, exempt [from taxes, *veroista*]; *(joutilas)* disengaged; vacant [seat, *paikka*]; unattached; *(käytös)* unconstrained; *~na* at liberty; *~lla (vaihde)* in neutral; *~lla jalalla* at large; *päästää ~ksi* set. . free, release, liberate; *~*

toimi vacant situation; *~sta tahdostaan* of his (her) own free will, of his (her) own accord; *kaksi päivää ~ta* two days off; *~ näköala* wide *(t.* open) view; *sai ~t kädet* was given a free hand. **-aika** spare time, leisure. **-ajattelija** free-thinker. **-ehtoinen** voluntary; *~ aine* optional subject. **-ehtoisesti** voluntarily, of one's own free will, of one's own accord. **-ehtoisuus** voluntariness, free will. **-herra** baron. **-herratar** baroness. **-kauppa** free trade. **-kaupunki** free city. **-kirje** franked letter; *(~oikeus* franking privilege). **-kirkko** free church. **-kirkollinen** free-church. **-lippu** free ticket, complimentary ticket. **-mielinen** liberal. **-mielisyys** liberalism. **-muurari** freemason; *(~us* freemasonry). **-oppilas** non-paying pupil. **-paini** free-style wrestling. **-pyörä** free wheel, coaster. **-päivä** day off, holiday. **-satama** free port. **-sti** freely; free [of charge], *(maksutta, m.)* gratis; *~ laivassa* free on board (f. o. b.); *saat ~* you are at liberty to . . **-uinti** free-style swimming. **-valtio** free state.
vapahdus salvation; deliverance. **-taa** *usk.* save; *(päästää)* deliver. **-taja** Saviour.
vapaudenrakkaus love of freedom.
vapaus freedom, liberty; *ottaa (jk) ~* take the liberty [of. . -ing], venture to. .; *ottaa vapauksia jnk suhteen* take liberties with. **-sota** war of independence. **-taistelija** champion of liberty. **-taistelu** struggle for liberty.
vapau|ttaa free (from), set free, release, liberate; *(pelastaa)* deliver; *(taakasta ym)* relieve (of), rid (of); *(veroista ym)* exempt (from); *lak.* acquit; *~ vankilasta* release. . from prison; *-ttava tuomio* acquittal. **-tua** be freed, be released; get free; get rid of; be exempted

from; *(itsenäistyä)* be
emancipated; *en voi ~ siitä
ajatuksesta* I cannot get the
thought out of my mind;
kaasua -tuu gas is liberated
(set free). **-tus** liberation,
release, discharge; exemption
(from); acquittal; emancipation.

vapi|sta tremble; *(väristä)*
shiver; *(et. kammosta)*
shudder; *(täristä)* shake;
quake; *~ pelosta* tremble with
fear; *-seva* trembling;
tremulous; *-sevalla äänellä* in
a trembling voice,
tremulously. **-suttaa** make. .
tremble.

vappu, vapunpäivä the first of
May, May Day.

vara reserve; *parantamisen ~*
room for improvement;
kutistumis~ allowance for
shrinkage; *~t* means, ks.
*hakus.; minulla ei ole ~a
siihen* I cannot afford it, it
is beyond my pocket;
rakentaa jnk ~an build upon;
jättää. . jnk ~an let. . depend
upon; *panna kaikki yhden
kortin ~an* ks. *kortti; ~lla* in
readiness, ready; *jnk ~lta* in
case of. .; to provide against;
pahan päivän ~lle against a
rainy day; *kaiken ~lta* just in
case; *kaikkien
mahdollisuuksien ~lta* for any
emergency; *siltä ~lta, että. .*
[just] in case. ., in the event
that. .; *pitää ~nsa* take care.

vara- spare; emergency; vice-.
-amiraali vice-admiral.
-inhoitovuosi financial year.
-joukko reserve troop. **-jäsen**
deputy member. **-kas** wealthy,
rich; well-to-do,. . well off.
-kkuus wealth[iness]. **-konsuli**
vice-consul. **-kuningas** viceroy.
-llisuus wealth; means;
(~suhteet circumstances). **-mies**
reserve; deputy; *olla ~miehenä*
deputize (for). **-nto** reserve
fund. **-osa** spare part.
-puheenjohtaja vice-chairman.
-puhemies deputy speaker.
-pyörä spare wheel. **-rahasto**
reserve fund. **-rehtori** *(koulun)*
vice-principal, assistant
headmaster. **-rengas** spare

tyre. **-rikko** bankruptcy,
failure; *(-tila)* insolvency;
tehdä ~ go bankrupt, fail;
-rikon partaalla on the verge
of bankruptcy. **-rikkoinen**
bankrupt; insolvent.

varas thief *(pl.* thieves).
-joukkue gang of thieves.
-lähtö false start.

varast|aa steal; commit a theft;
~ jkn taskusta (m.) pick a
p.'s pocket; *hän -ti (urh.)* he
jumped the gun; *hän
(näyttelijä) -ti koko näytelmän*
she stole the show; *hän -ti
hetken levon* she snatched a
moment of rest. **-ella** practise
theft, thieve; *(näpistellä)* pilfer.

varasto store, stock;
(tarveaine-) supply; *(-huone)*
storehouse; *(ammus- ym)*
depot; *kuv. m.* fund; *~t (m.)*
supplies; *~ssa* in stock, in
store; *kerätä ~on* stockpile,
(rohmuta) hoard; *panna ~on*
store, put in storage; *pitää
~ssa* keep in stock, stock.
-aitta storehouse. **-huone**
store-room, storage room;
warehouse. **-ida** store, store
up, stock; lay in *(t.* down).
-maksu storage. **-nhoitaja**
stock-keeper, *(-mies)*
warehouseman. **-myymälä**
»Cash and Carry» shop. **-olut**
lager.

varat means, resources; funds;
assets; *~ ja velat* assets and
liabilities; *varainsa mukaan*
according to one's means;
omilla varoillaan at one's
own expense; *elää yli
varojensa* live beyond one's
means; *huonoissa varoissa. .*
of modest means, badly off.

varata reserve; *(panna syrjään)*
put aside, set apart; allow
[plenty of time, *runsaasti
aikaa*]; *~ huone (m.)* engage
a room; *~ paikka* reserve a
seat, *(laivan ym)* book a
berth; *~ jklle tilaisuus* give a
p. an opportunity; *-ttu (m.)*
taken; *~ itselleen aikaa* take
time off.

vara|ton. . without means,
impecunious, *(köyhä)* poor.
-ttomuus lack of means;

poverty. **-tuomari** *l.v.* Master of Laws, LL. M. **-uloskäytävä** emergency exit. **-uksellinen** qualified. **-uksellisuus** reserve. **-ukseton** unreserved. **-us** reserve, reservation; proviso; *-uksetta* without reserve; *-uksin* with reservations; *eräin -uksin* subject to certain reservations (*t.* provisos). **-utua** be prepared, get ready [for *jhk*]. **-vuode** spare (*t.* extra) bed.

varhai|n early, at an early hour. **-nen** early; *-sessa vaiheessa* at an early stage, early on. **-skypsä** precocious.

varietee variety. **-teatteri** music hall.

varikko depot.

variksenpelätti scarecrow.

varis crow.

vari|sta fall off, come down; *(lehdistä)* drop; *(hajalleen)* be scattered; *puusta -see lehtiä (m.)* the tree sheds leaves. **-staa** shed, *(pudistaa)* shake.

varje|lla protect, *jltk* from, against; preserve, keep (from); guard (against); *Herra -lkoon sinua* the Lord keep thee; *taivas -lkoon!* good heavens! *v-tava kosteudelta* keep dry. **-lu(s)** protection; keeping.

varjo shadow; *(siimes)* shade; *kuv.* pretext, *(verho)* cloak; *jnk ~lla* under pretence (cover) of, *(esim. ystävyyden)* under the cloak (veil, semblance) of friendship; *asettaa ~on* throw into the shade. **-aine** contrast medium. **-inen, -isa** shady, .. affording shade. **-kuva** silhouette; shadow. **-mainen** shadow-like; shadowy. **-puoli** dark side; disadvantage, drawback. **-staa** shade; *kuv.* overshadow, *(seurata salaa)* shadow; *puut -stavat katua* trees shade the street. **-stin** shade; screen.

vark|ain stealthily; *(luvattomasti)* surreptitiously; *(salaa)* secretly. **-aus** theft; stealing; *lak.* larceny; *saatiin kiinni -audesta* was caught stealing; *(~juttu* case of stealing).

varm|a sure, certain;

(turvallinen) secure [foundation, *pohja*], safe [investment, *sijoitus*]; *(luotettava)* reliable; *(esim. mielipide)* firm, decided, definite, fixed; *~ asiastaan* sure of one's ground; *~ esiintyminen* firm (decided) attitude, *(esiintymistapa)* air of assurance; *~ itsestään* sure of oneself, self-confident; *hankkia ~ tieto jstk* make sure about, ascertain; *ole ~ siitä* depend upon it; *oletko ~ siitä?* are you sure about it? *minusta tuntuu ~lta* I feel certain [that..]; *olla jstk hyvin ~* be definite (positive) about; *voit olla ~ avustani* you may count on my aid. **-aan:** *ette ~kaan ole* I don't think you have. .; *en ~kaan* I am afraid I.. **-aankin** [very] probably, very likely, I expect.., I suppose.. *(otaksuttavasti)* presumably; *se on ~ hän* it must be he, I suppose it is he. **-asti** surely; definitely; [most] certainly, to be sure; *en voi ~ sanoa* I cannot say for sure (for certain); *hän tulee ~* he is sure to come; *uskon aivan ~, että..* I firmly believe that, I am confident that, I am fully convinced that; *milloin hän on ~ kotona?* when is one sure to find him at home? **-ennus** confirmation, certification; corroboration. **-entaa** certify, *(vahvistaa)* confirm, *(lak m.)* countersign. **-istaa** confirm; *(lujittaa)* strengthen; *(todistaa)* certify, verify; *tekn. (ase)* put.. at safety, half-cock. **-istautua** *jstk* make sure (of, that..). **-istin** safety catch. **-istua** be confirmed, be [further] strengthened; assure oneself; *~kseni* so as to make sure [that, *jstk*]. **-istus** confirmation; protection (against). **-uus** certainty; sureness; assurance; security; safety; *hankkia ~ jstk* make sure about, find out.. for certain; *(vain) varmuuden*

vuoksi for safety's sake,
[just] to be on the safe side;
(~**lukko** safety lock; ~**varasto**
stockpile).

varo|a look out, *jtk* for, be on
one's guard (against), be
careful (with, about); ~ *jtk*
tekemästä take care (be
careful) not to do a th.;
varokaa take care! look out!
watch out! beware [of the
dog, *koiraa*], mind [the step,
porrasta].

varoissa: *hyvissä* ~ well off,
(melko) comfortably off.

varoi|ttaa warn [of *jstk;*
against a p.]; ~ *jkta*
tekemästä jtk warn sb. not
to.., caution sb. against (..
-ing), dissuade a p. from;
-*ttava esimerkki* an example
which serves as a warning.
-**tus** warning, caution;
(nuhteleva) admonition;
(~**huuto** shout of warning;
~**laukaus** warning shot; ~**taulu**
caution board).

varo|keino precaution,
precautionary measure; *ryhtyä*
~*ihin* take precautions.
-**maton** incautious, imprudent,
heedless, *(puheessa)* indiscreet;
(ajattelematon) inconsiderate,
thoughtless. -**mattomuus**
incautiousness,
inconsiderateness. -**vainen**
cautious; careful; *(valpas)*
watchful; *(järkevä)* prudent;
ole ~ be careful! take care!
look out! -**vaisuus**
cautiousness, caution;
carefulness, care; *on*
noudatettava suurta v-suutta
great care should be taken,
great caution must be
exercised; (~**toimenpide**
precaution). -**vasti** with care.
-**venttiili** safety valve.

varpaisillaan on tiptoe; *kävellä*
~ *(m.)* tiptoe.
varpata *mer.* warp.
varppi *mer.* warp, towline.
varpu [bare] twig. -**nen**
sparrow. -**shaukka**
sparrow-hawk.
varrantti *liik.* bonded
warehouse.
varras spit.

varre|lla *(vieressä)* on, by, by
the side of; *(kuluessa)* during;
elämäni ~ in the course of
my life; *joen* ~ [situated] on
a river; *matkan* ~ during the
journey, on the way; *vuosien*
~ in the process (course) of
years, down the years;
Unioninkadun ~ in Union
street. -**llinen**.. provided with
a handle; *bot...* with a stem.
-**lta:** *jnk* ~ [from] along
the..; *havaintoja elämäni* ~
observations gathered in the
course of my life.
varsa foal; *(ori)* colt; *(tamma)*
filly.
varsi handle; arm; *bot.* stalk,
(vahvempi) stem; *tekn. m.*
bar, shaft, *(poran)* brace,
(kirveen) helve; *hento*
varreltaan.. of slender build.
-**kenkä** boot.
varsi|n quite; *(hyvin)* very;
(erinomaisen) exceedingly,
extremely; ~ *hyvin* perfectly
well, very well; ~ *hyvä*
fair [ly good]. -**nainen**..
proper; essential; *(todellinen)*
true, actual; *(vakinainen)*
ordinary; *sanan -naisessa*
merkityksessä in the proper
(strict) sense of the word.
-**naisesti** really, actually.
varsin|kaan particularly. -**kin**
particularly, especially [as,
since, *kun*].
vartalo trunk, body; figure,
stature; *kiel.* stem, radical.
-**kuva** full-length picture.
varta vasten specially,
purposely, for the particular
purpose [of..-ing].
varteen: *ottaa* ~ take into
consideration (into account),
heed; pay attention to,
consider; *otan tarjouksen* ~ I
will consider the offer.
-**otettava**.. worthy of
consideration.
varten *(tähden)* on account of,
because of; *(jklle)* for; *mitä*
~ wherefore? why? for what
reason? *sitä* ~ for that
reason, therefore, because of
that; *sitä* ~, *että*.. in order
to.
vartija watchman, *(esim.*

puiston) attendant, keeper; *sot.* guard, sentry; *lakko~* picket.

varti|o guard; *(-aika)* watch; *(partio-)* patrol; *olla ~ssa* be on guard duty, stand sentry. **-oida** watch, guard, keep guard over; *-oituna* guarded, under guard, under escort. **-oimaton** unguarded.

vartio|laivue convoy. **-paikka** post; *-paikallaan* at one's p. **-palvelus** guard duty. **-sto** guard; *(saattue)* escort. **-torni** watch-tower. **-tupa** guard-room. **-väki** guard; *(linnan)* garrison.

varttua grow, grow up; *(kehittyä)* develop (into); *~ miheheksi* grow into manhood, grow to be a man; *varttunut* grown up, *(kypsynyt)* mature.

varui|llaan on one's guard; *(valppaana)* on the alert; *ole -llasi* look out! watch out! be careful!

varus|huone armoury. **-kunta** garrison. **-mestari** armourer. **-mies** conscript [in active service]; *Engl.* national serviceman, *Am.* draftee.

varus|taa fit [out]; equip; provide, furnish, supply, *jllak,* with; *(linnoittaa)* fortify; *-tettu* equipped (with); *hyvin -tettu* well equipped (with); well supplied, *(kaupp.)* well stocked. **-tamo** *ks. laivan~* **-tautua** equip oneself, fit oneself out (for); *sot.* arm. **-tautuminen** *sot.* arming, [re]armament. **-te:** *~et* equipment, outfit. **-telu** *(sota-)* [re]armament. **-tus** equipment, outfit; *(linnoitus)* fortifications, *(puolustus-)* defences; *(~ohjelma* armament programme; *~teollisuus* armaments industries). **-väki** garrison.

varvas -toe.

vasa *(hirven)* elk calf.

vasalli vassal. **-us** vassalage. **-valtio** vassal state.

vasama bolt, arrow.

vasar|a hammer; *(puinen)* mallet; *~n kalke* pounding of hammers. **-oida** hammer, *jtk* at; *(jatkuvasti)* hammer away.

vaseliini vaseline.

vasemma|lla on the left [side, hand], *jnk* of, at the left, to the left (of); *mer.* on the port (larboard) side, to port; *hänen ~ puolellaan* on his left. **-lle** to the left (of), *mer.* to port. **-npuoleinen** left [-hand]; *~ liikenne* left-hand traffic.

vasemmisto the Left. **-lainen** *a.* left-wing; *s.* left-winger, leftist. **-puolue** leftist party. **-sanomalehti** left-wing paper.

vasempaan [to the] left; *käännös ~* left turn.

vasen left; *~ puoli, sivu* left [hand] side, *(laivan)* port, larboard; *vasemmalla puolellani* on my left. **-kätinen** left-handed.

vasikan|liha veal. **-nahka** calfskin, calf. **-paisti** veal joint, roast veal.

vasikka calf *(pl. calves).*

vaskenkarvainen copper-coloured.

vaski copper; *kuin helisevä ~* as sounding brass. **-tsa** blindworm.

vasta 1. *(sauna-)* whisk of birch twigs [used in sauna].

vasta 2. *(ei ennen kuin)* only, but, not until; *(äsken)* just now, a while ago; *~ leivottu* freshly baked; *~ nyt* only now, not until now [did I hear, *sain kuulla*]; *sepä ~ on jotakin!* why, that is something! *~kin* in the future; *käykää ~kin* call again.

vastaaja defendant; *(avioerojutussa)* respondent.

vasta-|alkaja beginner, novice. **-alkava** budding [poet, *runoilija*];*.. on ~.. is a* beginner.

vastaamaton unanswered; *tarkoitustaan ~* unsuited, inexpedient.

vastaan against; *(kohti)* towards; *lak., urh* versus *(lyh. v., esim.* A. v. B.*); taistella jtk ~* fight against; *(hyvä)* *lääke nuhaa ~* a remedy for colds; *hän tuli meitä ~* he met us, *(vastaanottamaan)* he came to meet us; *panna jtk ~* oppose, object to; *minulla* *ei ole mitään sinne menemistä* ~ I have nothing against going there; *onko sinulla mitään sitä* ~ have you any objections [to it]? do you mind? *tarkastella jtk valoa* ~ hold a th. up to the light; *selkä seinää* ~ with one's back to the wall; *10 äänellä yhtä* ~ by 10 votes to one. **-hangoittelu** opposition. **-otin** receiver, [receiving] set. **-ottaa** receive; *(hyväksyen)* accept; *maksettava -otettaessa* to be paid on receipt, cash (collect) on delivery *(lyh. C.O.D.).* **-ottaja** receiver, recipient; *(kirjeen)* addressee, *(tavaran)* consignee. **-ottavainen** susceptible (to). **-otto** receipt; *(henkilöiden)* reception; *(lääkärin ~aika)* consulting hours; *tilata* ~ make an appointment [with a doctor]; *(~apulainen* receptionist). **-sanomaton** indisputable. **-sanomatta** without protest.

vastaava corresponding; *~t (liik.)* assets; *tarkoitustaan* ~ .. which serves the purpose; *~nlainen* similar; *~sti* correspondingly; respectively. **vasta|ehdokas** rival candidate. **-ehdotus** counter-proposition. **-hakoinen** reluctant; unwilling. **-hakoisesti** reluctantly; against the grain, against one's will. **-hakoisuus** reluctance; unwillingness, disinclination. **-hyökkäys** counter-attack. **-inen** future, *(tuleva)* coming, prospective; *(v-kkainen)* contrary, opposed (to); *-isen varalle* for the future, for a rainy day; *tiistain -isena yönä* Monday night; *lain* ~ contrary to law, unlawful; *uskonnon~* antireligious. **-isku** counterblow. **-isuus** future. **-kaiku** response; *herätti ~a* struck responsive chords. **-kirja** pass-book, bank-book. **vastakkai|n** against (opposite) each other; *(silmätysten)* facing each other; *kuulustella* ~ confront [a witness with another]. **-nen** opposite,

contrary [to]; *-set mielipiteet* conflicting (differing) opinions; *-sessa järjestyksessä* in reverse order; *-sessa tapauksessa* if the contrary be true; *oli aivan* ~ was in direct contradiction (to). **-suus** contrast; contradiction, antagonism, discrepancy; *tietojen* ~ the conflicting reports. **-svaikutus** contrasting effect.

vasta|kohta *(jnk)* contrast, the opposite (of), the reverse of; *(jyrkkä)* antithesis; *~na jllek* in contrast to; *jnk täydellinen* ~ the exact opposite of; *olla räikeänä ~na jllek* stand in sharp contrast to. *~ksi* [as a present] in return. **-laskos** box pleat; inverted pleat. **-lause** protest. **-leivottu** freshly baked, new-baked, *kuv.* new-fledged. **-lypsetty:** ~ *maito* milk straight from the cow. **-merkki** check. **-myrkky** antidote, antitoxin. **-mäki** ascent, rise; upward slope; *-mäkeä* uphill. **-nainut** newly married; *-naineet (m.)* the newly-weds. **-näyttelijä:** *olla jkn ~nä* play opposite sb. **-paino** counterbalance; *jnk ~ksi* to counterbalance. . **-palvelu|s** return service; *tehdä jklle* ~ return a p. a service, reciprocate; *-kseksi* in return (for). **-pelaaja** opponent; *(toveri)* partner. **-puoli** opposite side; opposing party. **-puolue** the [party in] opposition. **-päinen.** . situated (. . lying) opposite, opposite. **-päivään** counter-clockwise, against the sun. **-päätä** opposite, *jtk* [to]. .; *(kadun toisella puolella)* across the street; *toisiamme* ~ *(m.)* facing each other, vis-à-vis. **-rakka|us:** *hän ei saanut v-utta* his love was not returned (reciprocated). **-rinta** resistance (to), opposition (to); *asettua ~an* put oneself in opposition (to); *tehdä ~a* offer resistance, resist, oppose; *(~liike* resistance movement). **-ssa** against; *olla* *jkta* ~ meet a p. [at the station, *asemalla*]. **-syntynyt** newborn. **-syytös** counter-accusation.

vastata answer [a p. *jklle;* the demands, *vaatimuksia;* for *jstk*]; reply (to); give an answer; *(vierailuun, äänimerkkiin ym)* return; *(olla edesvastuussa)* answer for, be responsible (answerable) for; *(olla jnk mukainen)* correspond to (with), *(olla jnk veroinen)* equal; ~ *kysymykseen* answer (reply to) a question; ~ *tarkoitustaan* answer (serve) its purpose; ~ *tarvetta* meet the requirements; ~ *jkn tervehdykseen* return a p.'s greeting; *joutua vastaamaan jstk* be called to account for, be made responsible for; *laadun tulee* ~ *hintaa* the quality must correspond to the price.

vasta|tehty newly-made. **-ttavat** *liik.* liabilities. **-tullut** *a.* newly arrived; *s.* newcomer, new arrival. **-tusten** facing each other. **-tuuli** contrary (adverse) wind; *-tuulessa* in a head wind; *meillä oli* ~ we had the wind against us.

vastaus answer, *jhk* to, reply (to); *(joskus)* rejoinder; *(terävä)* retort; *vastaukseksi jhk* in reply to, in answer to [your letter], *(tekoon)* in response to; *odottaa ~ta* expect an answer; *~ta pyydetään* a reply is requested, *(kortissa)* R.S.V.P.; *~ta ei tullut* there was no reply.

vasta|vaikutus counteraction. **-vakoilu** counter-espionage. **-valittu** newly-elected. **-vallankumous** counter-revolution. **-vierailu** return call. **-virta:** *~an* against the current, upstream. **-vuoroinen** reciprocal. **-vuoroisuus** reciprocity. **-väite** objection (to); argument (against). **-väittäjä** opponent. **vastedes** in the future, henceforth.

vasten against; ~ *silmiä* to one's face. **-mielinen** repulsive, repugnant; obnoxious; *(epämiellyttävä)* displeasing, disagreeable, unpleasant;.. *on minulle* ~ I have a dislike for. **-mielisesti** unwillingly, reluctantly; against one's will. **-mielisyys** *(jtk kohtaan)* dislike (of), distaste (for), antipathy (for, to, against); aversion (to); repugnance (against); *(esim. hajun, tehtävän)* repulsiveness.

vastike substitute; *(korvaus)* compensation; *jnk vastikkeeksi (sijaan)* in return for, in exchange for.

vastikään a while (a moment) ago; *(äskettäin)* only recently.

vastine counterpart; *(esim. sanan)* equivalent; counterword: *lak.* plea, rejoinder; *saada ~tta rahalleen* get value for one's money; get one's money's worth.

vastoin against, contrary to; in contrast to; ~ *jkn tahtoa* against a p.'s wishes; ~ *luuloa, odotusta* contrary to expectations. **-käyminen** adversity, misfortune; hardship. **vastuksellinen** troublesome; difficult; trying.

vastus hardship; difficulty; *(vaiva)* trouble, bother; *sähk.* resistance, *(-kela)* r. coil, *(-laite)* resistor; *olla vastuksena* be a nuisance. **-taa** resist, oppose, make (offer) resistance; *(olla vastaan)* object (to); *asettua jtk vastustamaan* set oneself against, set oneself in opposition to; *ehdotustani -tettiin* my proposal met with opposition. **-taja** opponent; adversary, antagonist; *jnk* ~ *(usein)* anti-. **-tamaton** irresistible. **-tamattomuus** irresistibility. **-tamishalu** spirit of opposition. **-tus** resistance, opposition; *saada osakseen ~ta* meet with opposition; *(~kyky* power of resistance; *~kykyinen*.. able to resist, resistant).

vastuu responsibility; risk; *meidän ~llamme* at our risk; *olla ~ssa* be responsible (answerable, accountable) (for); *ottaa ~* assume (shoulder) the responsibility, admit responsibility (for); *yhteinen ~* joint responsibility; *ks. karistaa.* **-llinen** responsible,.. involving responsibility. **-nalainen** responsible, *jstk,* for, answerable, accountable [to *jklle,* for *jstk*]. **-nalaisuus** responsibility. **-ntunne** sense of responsibility. **-ton** irresponsible. **-tuntoinen** responsible. **-vapaus** freedom from responsibility. **-velvollisuus** liability.

vati dish; *(esim. pesu-)* basin. **vatka|in** beater, whisker, *(sähkö-)* mixer. **-ta** whisk, *(munia, m.)* beat, *(kermaa, m.)* whip, *(voita)* work.

vatsa stomach; *tiet.* abdomen. *(maha)* stomach; *tyhjin vatsoin* with an empty belly; *tyhjentää ~* purge. **-haava** *ks. maha-.* **-happo:** *liikaa ~ja* hyperacidity of the stomach. **-kalvo** peritoneum; *~ntulehdus* peritonitis. **-katarri** catarrh of the stomach. **-laukku** stomach. **-nkipu** stomach ache; *tiet.* abdominal pain. **-ontelo** abdominal cavity. **-tauti** stomach complaint.

watti watt.

vauhdi|kas brisk; *(eloisa)* vivacious; *(nopea)* quick; *-kkaasti* briskly; with verve. **-kkuus** briskness; speed. **-llinen:** *~ hyppy* flying jump.

vauhk|o shy, skittish. **-oontua** shy (at). **-ous** shyness, skittishness.

vauhti speed, rate, velocity; *kovaa ~a* at a great speed; *suurinta ~a* at top speed; *päästä ~in* get into full speed *(t. kuv.* full swing); *ottaa ~a* take a running start. **-hirmu** roadhog. **-pyörä** fly-wheel.

vaunu carriage, *Am.* car; *(rautatie-, m.)* coach, *(tavara-)* truck, waggon, *(umpinainen)* goods waggon. **-nlasti** waggon load. **-nosasto** compartment. **-npeite** tarpaulin. **-silta** platform.

vaura|s well-to-do,.. well off, affluent, wealthy; *~ yhteiskunta* the affluent society. **-stua** become prosperous, prosper, get on in the world, make one's pile. **-us** prosperity; wealth, affluence.

vaurio damage. **-ittaa** damage, injure. **-itua** suffer damage, be damaged.

vauva baby.

vavahtaa [give a] start.

vavist|a *ks. vapista.* **-us** tremor, shiver; shudder.

vedellä *ks. vetää; ei se vetele* that won't do, it will never do.

veden|alainen *a. & s.* submarine; *(kari ym)* sunken, submerged. **-haltija** water-sprite. **-jakaja** watershed, divide. **-korkeus** water-level. **-neito** water-nymph, naiad. **-paisumus** flood, deluge; *raam.* the Flood. **-pinta** surface [of the water]. **-pitävä** waterproof; *(astioista ym)* watertight. **-puhdistuslaitos** water-purifying plant, sewage disposal plant. **-puute** scarcity of water. **-saanti** water supply. **-suojelu** water conservation.

vedos *kirjap.* proof; *palsta~* galley p., *taitto~* page p.

vedota appeal, *jkh* to; *(puolustukseksensa)* plead [one's youth, *nuoruuteensa*]; *~ henkilökohtaisesti jkh* make a personal appeal to; *vetoamalla siihen, että..* on the plea that. .

vedättää have.. hauled.

vegetaari vegetarian.

vehje *(koje)* device, apparatus; *(vekotin)* gadget; *vehkeet (juonet)* intrigues, plots, machinations.

vehkei|lijä plotter, schemer; conspirator. **-llä** plot; conspire (against), intrigue (against); *-levä* scheming, designing. **-ly** plotting, intrigues.

vehma|s luxuriant, rank; lush.

-us luxuriance, rankness, richness.

vehnä wheat. **-jauho(t)** wheat flour. **-njyvä** grain of wheat. **-nen** wheat bread. **-nleseet** wheat bran.

vehre|ys verdancy. **-ä** verdant.

veijari rascal, sly dog. **-romaani** picaresque novel.

veikata bet; *(kupongilla)* do the pools.

veik|eys mischievousness. **-eä** mischievous, *(esim. hattu, nukke)* cute. **-istely** coquetry.

veikkaaja pools punter.

veikkaus betting; *jalkap.* football pools; *voittaa v-uksessa* win on the f. p. **-kuponki** pools coupon. **-voitto** pools prize.

veikko mate, fellow, *Am.* guy; *(veli)* brother.

veisata sing [hymns].

veistellä whittle; cut.

veisto woodwork, handicraft, *(koulussa, m.)* carpentry. **-kuva, -s** piece of sculpture. **-taide** sculpture.

veistämö *(laivan-)* [ship] yard.

veistää carve, cut; *(veistellä)* whittle, chip [away, *pois*]; *(hakata)* hew; ~ *marmoriin* hew in marble.

veisu song. **-u** singing [of hymns], chanting.

veitikka *leik.* rascal, rogue; *pikku* ~ you little rogue; ~ *silmäkulmassa* with a twinkle in his eye. **-mainen** roguish; mischievous. **-maisuus** roguishness.

veitsen|kärki point of a knife. **-pisto** stab. **-terä** knife-blade; *olla ~llä (kuv.)* hang by a thread.

veitsi knife. *(pl.* knives).

veiv|ata crank [up] [a car, *autoa*], grind [an organ, *posetiivia*]. **-i** *ks. kampi.*

vekara kid, *(poika-)* urchin.

vekkuli jolly fellow; wag.

vekotin gadget.

vekseli bill [of exchange] *(lyh.* B/E); draft; *asettaa* ~ draw a bill [for. .] on sb., draw an amount on sb. [at six months]; *lunastaa* ~ discharge (honour) a bill; *langennut* ~

bill due. **-nasettaja** drawer. **-nhyväksyjä** acceptor of a bill, drawee. **-nsaaja** payee [of a bill].

vela|ksi on credit. **-llinen** debtor. **-ton.** free from debt,. . out of debt; *(kiinnittämätön)* unencumbered.

velho magician, sorcerer, wizard; *(-vaimo)* sorceress, witch.

veli brother *(pl. ks. kieliopp.)* **-kulta** *ks. vekkuli.* **-puoli** half-brother, stepbrother.

veljei|llä fraternize, hobnob, rub shoulders (with). **-ly** fraternization.

veljelli|nen brotherly, fraternal. **-sesti** fraternally, like brothers.

veljen|malja toast of friendship. **-murha** fratricide. **-poika** nephew. **-tytär** niece.

velje|kset brothers; *he ovat -ksiä* they are brothers. **-skansa** sister nation. **-skunta** brotherhood, fraternity; order. **-srakkaus** brotherly love.

veljeys brotherhood, fraternity; brotherliness.

velka debt; *velat (liik.)* liabilities; *olla jklle velassa* be in debt (to), owe sb. [£ 10]; *us. kuv.* be indebted to; *velaksi* on credit; *joutua ~an ks. seur.* **-antua** get (run) into debt; contract (incur) debts; *v-tunut* involved in debt. **-inen.** . in debt. **-kirja** promissory note. **-pää** guilty, *jhk* of. **-taakka** burden of debt. **-vaatimus** claim.

velko|a demand (ask for) [the] payment of; *(vaatia)* claim; *(karhuta)* dun; *koetti* ~ *saataviaan* tried to recover his outstanding debts. **-ja** creditor; *~in kuulustelu* hearing of creditors.

velli gruel, porridge.

vello|a: -va (meri) storm-tossed.

veloittaa charge [. . to a p.'s account, *jnk tiliä*], debit [a p. with]; ~ *liiaksi* overcharge; ~ *tiliä* draw on (debit) an account.

veltos|taa make. . slack, slacken; *(heikentää)* weaken. **-tua** become slack; slacken;

-tunut slack[ened], weakened, effeminate.

veltto slack, inert; languid, indolent; *(hervoton)* limp; *veltot lihakset* flabby (flaccid) muscles. **-us** slackness, languor, inertia.

velvoi|te obligation. **-ttaa** bind, oblige [sb. to], put (place) sb. under an obligation; ~ *jku jhk (käskeä)* enjoin. . upon a p., charge (with); ~ *jku maksamaan sakkoa* impose a fine of. . on. .; *-ttava* binding, obligatory. **-tus** obligation.

velvolli|nen duty-bound, obliged, under obligation (to). **-suudentunto** sense of duty. **-suudentuntoinen** faithful, dutiful; conscientious.

velvollisuu|s duty; *-det (m.)* responsibilities; *tehdä -tensa* do one's duty; *laiminlyödä -tensa (m.)* fail in one's duty; *-den täyttäminen* fulfilment of one's duty; *-tensa unohtava* forgetful of one's duty, negligent.

venakko Russian woman.

vene boat, *(soutu-)* rowboat, rowing boat. **-ily** [motor] boating. **-kunta** [a boat's] crew. **-laituri** landing stage. **-laulu** barcarole. **-retki** boating excursion. **-vaja** boathouse.

Venetsia Venice; **v-lainen** Venetian.

vento: ~ *vieras a.* absolutely strange, utterly unknown [to me]; *s.* an absolute (a complete) stranger.

venttiili ventilator; *(läppä)* valve.

veny|mätön inelastic. **-tellä:** ~ *itseään* stretch oneself; *puhua -tellen* drawl. **-ttää** stretch [out], draw out, expand; *(liiaksi, kuv.)* protract. **-tys** stretching; *(~lujuus* tensile strength). **-vä** elastic *(m. kuv.)*, resilient; *(sitkeä)* stringy; ~ *termi* a sweeping term. **-vyys** elasticity. **-ä** stretch, stretch out; become protracted; *(olla v-vä)* be elastic; *kokous -i pitkäksi* the meeting became long-drawn-out; *hänen*

kasvonsa -ivät pitkiksi her face fell.

venäh|dys strain. **-dyttää** strain [a tendon, *jänne*].

Venäjä Russia; ~*n-Suomen* Russo-Finnish; *v~ (kieli)* Russian.

venäjänkielinen Russian.

venälä|nen *a. & s.* Russian. **-stää** Russianize.

veranta veranda [h]; porch.

verbi verb. **-muoto** verb form.

veren|himo bloodthirstiness. **-himoinen** bloodthirsty. **-hukka** loss of blood. **-imijä** bloodsucker. **-kierto** circulation; *(~elimet* circulatory system). **-luovuttaja** blood donor. **-myrkytys** blood-poisoning. **-paine** blood pressure. **-pisara** *(kukka)* fuchsia. **-siirto** blood transfusion. **-syöksy** pulmonary h[a]emorrhage. **-tahraama** blood-stained. **-tungos** congestion [of the brain, *aivoissa*]. **-vuodatus** bloodshed. **-vuoto** bleeding, h[a]emorrhage; *(~tauti* h[a]emophilia; *~tautinen* bleeder). **-vähyys** lack of blood; *lääk.* an[a]emia.

veres fresh; *saatiin kiinni vereseltään* was caught red-handed. **-tää** *kuv.* refresh [one's memory, *muistiaan*], brush up [one's English]; *-tävä (silmä)* bloodshot.

vere|tön bloodless; *lääk.* an[a]emic; *(kalpea)* pale, pallid. **-vyys** abundance of blood; high colour. **-vä** full-blooded, *(punakka)* ruddy [-cheeked].

verhiö *bot.* calyx.

verho cover[ing]; *kuv.* cloak; *(ovi-, ikkuna-)* curtain; ~*t (m.)* draperies; *savu~* smoke screen. **-ilija** upholsterer. **-illa** upholster, do upholstering; drape (with). **-lehti** *bot.* sepal. **-ta** cover; wrap up (in), *(sisältä)* line (with); envelop; *(pukea)* clothe; *(suojata)* screen; *salaperäisyyteen -ttu* wrapped (shrouded) in mystery. **-utua** cover oneself (with), be[come] enveloped (in, with), be shrouded (in).

veri blood; *on veressä* is [all] bloody, is blood-stained; *~ssään* bleeding; *~in syöpynyt* deeply-rooted; *se on hänellä ~ssä* it runs in his blood, it is inherent in him; *herättää pahaa verta* arouse indignation. **-heimolainen** blood-relation. **-heimolaisuus** relationship by blood, consanguinity. **-hera** serum. **-koe** blood test. **-koira** *ks. vihi-.* **-löyly** massacre, carnage. **-nahka** cutis. **-nen** bloody, sanguinary [battle, *taistelu*]; gory. **-neste** blood plasma. **-näyte** blood sample. **-palttu** *(m. ohukkaat)* blood pancake(s). **-pisara** drop of blood. **-punainen** blood-red, crimson. **-sesti** bloodily; *kostaa ~* take a bloody revenge (on). **-solu** blood cell. **-stää** be bloodshot. **-suoni** vein; *anat.* blood-vessel; (*~sto* vascular system; *~tauti: sydän- ja v-taudit* cardiovascular diseases). **-syys** bloodiness. **-tahra** blood stain. **-tulppa** embolus; blood clot, thromb|us (*pl. -i*), thrombosis; *sydän~* coronary thrombosis. **-työ** bloody deed. **-yskä** h[a]emoptysis.

verka cloth. **-inen** [.. of] cloth.

ver|kalleen slowly, slow, at a slow rate; leisurely. **-kkainen** slow, easy-going.

verkko net, network; (*hämähäkin ym*) web; *kuv.* toils. **-aita** wire-netting fence. **-kalvo** retina. **-kassi** string bag. **-keinu** hammock. **-mainen** net-like, reticular.

verkko|pallo *ks. tennis.* **-silmä** compound eye.

verkosto network.

vermutti vermouth.

vernissa, -ta varnish.

vero tax (on); (*kunnallis-*) [local] rate; (*et. tavara-*) duty; (*vieraalle vallalle*) tribute; *~a maksava* tax-paying; *hän maksoi . ~a* he paid £ .. in taxes. **-asteikko** scale of taxation. **-helpotus** tax relief.

-inen equal; *jkn (jnk) ~* a p.'s equal, as good as, a match for; *olla jnk ~ (m.)* be equal to, equal ..; *pitää jnk -isena* put.. on a level with, consider.. as good as. **-ilmoitus** [income-]tax return; (*~kaavake* income-tax form). **-kuitti** tax receipt. **-lautakunta** assessment committee. **-lippu** income-tax demand note, *Am.* tax bill. **-merkki** revenue stamp.

veron|alainen taxable [property, *omaisuus*],.. liable to taxation. **-huojennus** modification (reduction) of taxes. **-kantaja** tax-collector. **-kanto** collection of taxes. **-kavallus** cheating the income tax, (*-pakoilu*) tax evasion. **-kiertäjä** tax dodger. **-maksaja** taxpayer. **-maksukyky** ability to pay one's taxes. **-palautus** tax refund. **-pidätys** tax deduction; *ks. pidätys; v-tyksen jälkeen* after taxes.

vero|taakka burden of taxes. **-tettava** taxable. **-ton..** exempt from taxes, tax-free. **-ttaa** tax, lay (impose) a tax (upon, on); assess [sb. at..]; *~ liikaa* overtax.

verotus taxation. **-arvo** taxable value. **-järjestelmä** system of taxation. **-peruste(et)** basis of taxation.

vero|vapaus exemption from taxes. **-velvollinen** *s.* taxpayer; *a..* liable to taxation. **-virasto** tax department; *Engl. l.v.* Board of Inland Revenue. **-äyri** tax unit, tax rate.

verran: *jonkin ~* to some extent (degree), in some measure (degree); *tämän ~* this much; *metrin ~* about one metre.

verrannolli|nen proportional; (*suhteellinen*) relative; *kääntäen ~* inversely proportional. **-suus** proportion [ality].

verranto proportion; analogy.

verra|ta compare, *jhk* with; *jhk -ten* compared with, in comparison with (*t.* to); *on -ttavissa jhk (m.)* is comparable to, is equal to; *ei ole -ttavissa tähän* is not to be compared to this,.. cannot compare with this. **-ten** comparatively. **-ton** incomparable,.. beyond comparison, unequalled, unparalleled, unrivalled; *(arvaamaton)* invaluable; *-ttoman kaunis* of matchless beauty. **-ttain** comparatively, relatively. **-ttava:** *jhk ~ comparable to.* **-ttomasti** incomparably, pre-eminently; by far [the best, *paras*]; immeasurably; *~ parempi* better by far, vastly superior (to).

verry|tellä limber up. **-ttelypuku** [athletic] training suit, track suit.

verso shoot. **-a** sprout, shoot forth; *(nousta)* spring up.

verstas workshop, shop.

vert|a *(määrä)* extent, amount; *jonkin verran* to some (to a certain) extent; somewhat, a little [earlier, *aikaisemmin*]; *minkä verran* to what extent? how much? *monta ~a* many times; *saman verran* [just] as much; *sen verran* so much, that much; *vetää vertoja jklle* be equal to, be a match for; *~ansa vailla (oleva)* incomparable, unequalled. **-ailla** compare; make (draw) comparisons (between), draw parallels; *(tarkistaa)* check; *-aileva* comparative. **-ailu** comparison; *~n vuoksi* for the sake of c.; *kestää ~n jnk kanssa* bears comparison with; *(~aste, ~muoto* degree of comparison). **-ainen** *a.* & *s.* equal; *(kaltainen)* like; *s.* match; *on jkn ~* is a match for; *hänen ~aisensa (miehet)* his equals, *(kyvyiltään)* men of his calibre; *vrt. veroinen.*

verta|uksellinen allegoric[al]; metaphorical. **-us** comparison; *raam.* parable; *puhua -uksin* speak figuratively; *(~kohta* point of comparison: *~kuva* symbol; *~kuvallinen* allegoric[al], symbolic[al]; *~ maksu* token payment).

vertavuotava bleeding.

veruke pretext, *(puolustelu)* excuse; *(välttely)* evasion, subterfuge; *hakea verukkeita* seek pretexts (excuses).

veräjä [wicket-]gate; *päästä kuin koira ~stä* get away with it.

vesa shoot, sprout, *(suvun)* scion; *(haara)* offshoot; *(lapsi)* kid.

vesi water; *~ssä silmin* with tears in one's eyes; *laskea ~lle (alus)* launch; *veden alla oleva* submerged; *olla veden varassa* be afloat, swim; *sai veden herahtamaan kielelleni* made my mouth water; *olla ~llä* be out in a boat; *lasi vettä* a glass of water. **-eläin** aquatic animal. **-hana** water tap, *Am.* faucet. **-hauta** moat; *urh.* water-jump. **-huolto** water supply. **-höyry** water vapour, steam.

vesijohto water main, water pipes; *hist.* aqueduct; *talossa on ~* there is water laid on to the house; *~ ja saniteettilaitteet* modern plumbing. **-laitos** waterworks. **-liike** plumber's [business]. **-putki** water pipe. **-vesi** tap water.

vesi|kasvi water plant. **-katto** roof. **-kauhu** hydrophobia, rabies. **-kko** [European] mink. **-klosetti** water closet, W.C. **-lasi:** *myrsky ~ssa* a storm in a tea-cup. **-lastissa** waterlogged. **-leima** watermark. **-lintu** *koll.* waterfowl; aquatic bird. **-liukoinen** water-soluble. **-liuos** aqueous solution (of ..). **-llelasku** launching. **-lukko** *ks. haju-.* **-lätäkkö** puddle. **-mäinen** water-like, watery. **-määrä** volume of water. **-oikeus** *lak.* water rights court. **-pallo(peli)** water polo. **-parannus** hydrotherapy; *ks. kylpylä.* **-patsas** column of water. **-peräinen** wet; marshy. **-pisara** drop of water. **-pallo** water polo. **-poika** total abstainer; *on ~* is on the wagon. **-posti** hydrant. **-putous**

waterfall, falls, cataract, *(pieni)* cascade. **-pöhö** [o]edema. **-raja** waterline. **-rakko** water-blister. **-rokko** chicken-pox. **-sanko** water bucket. **-stö** lake and river system, watercourse. **-suihku** jet of water. **-säiliö** [water] reservoir, tank. **-taso** hydroplane. **-tie** waterway, water route, sea route; *-teitse* by water, by sea. **-ttää** water down. **-vaaka** spirit level. **-voima** water-power, hydraulic power. **-väri** water-colour; (~**maalaus** water colour).

vessa *puhek.* loo.

vesuri billhook.

vetel|ehtijä loafer, slacker, layabout. **-ehtiä** loiter, idle, loaf [about], dawdle, lounge [about], slack. **-ys** sluggard. **-yys** looseness; slackness. **-ä** *(velli)* thin; *(hyytelö & kuv.)* floppy, *kuv.* sloppy; slack, indolent; ~ *ote* flabby handshake; *kävellä* ~*sti* slump, slouch; *älä istu* ~*ssä asennossa* don't slouch.

veteraani veteran.

veti|nen watery; wet. **-stellä** *(itkeä)* snivel.

veto draught; *(vetäisy)* pull; *(esim. kynän)* stroke; *(vetäminen)* traction; *(veikka)* bet; *lyödä* ~*a* [make a] bet, wager; *kellosta on* ~ *loppunut* the clock has run down, the watch wants winding up. **-hihna** strap; *(koneen)* belt. **-inen** draughty; *kahden litran* ~.. holding two litres; *laiva on 1000 tonnin* ~ the ship has a capacity of 1000 tons. **-isuus** cubic capacity, [gross, net] tonnage. **-juhta** draught animal. **-ketju** fastener, zipper; zip; *kiinnitetään* ~*lla* [the dress] zips *[esim.* down the back]; *vetää* ~ *kiinni* zip.. up **-numero** attraction.

veto-oike|us [right of] veto; *käytti -uttaan* exercised the veto, vetoed [the decision].

vetoomus appeal.

vetovoima pull; *fys.* gravitational pull, gravity; *(viehätys)* [power of]

attraction.

vettyä become watery, be soaked.

veturi engine, locomotive. **-nkuljettaja** engine-driver, *Am.* engineer; train-driver. **-lämmittäjä** fireman, stoker.

vety *kem.* hydrogen. **-pommi** hydrogen *(lyh.* H-)bomb. **-superoksidi** hydrogen peroxide.

vetä|istä pull [quickly], give.. a sudden pull; draw [a line, *viiva*]; *(siepata)* snatch. **-isy** [quick] pull; jerk. **-ytyminen** withdrawal, *sot. m.* retreat. **-ytyä** withdraw (from); retire (from); draw back; *sot.* retreat, fall back; ~ *pois jstk* pull out; ~ *syrjään* retire, step aside; ~ *velvollisuudesta* shirk a duty, evade one's responsibility; ~ *yksityiselämään* retire into private life.

vetää pull, *jstk* at; draw; *(kuormaa)* haul; *(laahata)* drag; *mer.* tug; *(sisältää)* hold; ~ *hammas jklta* pull out (extract) a tooth; ~ *kello* wind up a clock (a watch); ~ *lippu alas* lower (haul down) a flag; ~ *lippu tankoon* raise (hoist, put up) a flag; *suonta* ~ I have got a cramp; ~ *yhtä köyttä* pull together; ~ *yllensä* pull.. on; *astia* ~ *5 litraa* the vessel holds 5 litres; *ikkunasta* ~ there is a draught from the window; *savutorvi ei vedä* the chimney does not draw.

vialli|nen faulty, defective, imperfect. **-suus** faultiness, defectiveness; imperfect condition; *(ruumiin)* deformity.

via|ton innocent; *(asia)* harmless. **-ttomuus** innocence.

viedä take; *(kuljettaa)* carry, convey; *(johtaa)* lead (to, into); bring; *(riistää)* deprive [a p. of]; *(vaatia)* require; ~ *jkn aikaa* take up sb.'s time; ~ *kirjaan* enter; ~ *maasta* export; ~ *pois* take (carry).. away, remove;.. *vie paljon aikaa* takes (requires) a great deal of time; *tämä vie jhk (kuv.)* will result in..

viehe lure.

viehke|ys charm, grace [fulness]. **-ä** charming, graceful, attractive.

viehä|ttyä be charmed, be fascinated. **-ttävä** charming; lovely; attractive. **-ttää** charm, fascinate. **-tys** charm, grace; attraction; (~kyky, ~voima power to charm, attractiveness).

viejä bearer [of a message]; (maasta-) exporter.

viek|as cunning, sly; shrewd, crafty. **-kaus** cunning, shrewdness, craftiness; viekkaudella by cunning.

viekoi|tella [al]lure, entice; ~ jklta jtk (m.) cheat a p. out of [his money]; -tteleva tempting. **-tus** allurement, enticement; (kiusaus) temptation.

vielä still, yet; (lisäksi) more; further; only, as late as; ~ eilen only yesterday; ~ 60-luvulla as late as the 1960's; ~ enemmän still (even, yet) more; ~ kerran once more; ~ mitä nothing of the kind; ei ~ not yet; ei aivan ~ not quite yet; ~ on huomattava it is further to be noticed; haluatko ~ vähän teetä would you like some more tea? onko ~ teetä? is there any more tea? ~ nytkin even now, even today; ~ 500 dollaria another 500 dollars. **-pä** (-kin) even; (lisäksi) furthermore, besides.

viemäri drain; sewer; (keittiön, m.) sink; (kylpyammeen, ym.) plug-hole. **-järjestelmä, viemäröinti** sewerage, system of sewers. **-putki** drain-pipe, sewer. **-vesi** waste water, sewage.

Wien Vienna; wienerleipä Danish pastry. **wieniläinen** a. Viennese, Vienna; s. Viennese.

vieno mild, gentle; soft. **-us** mildness, gentleness.

vienti (maasta-) export; (kirjaan) entry; Suomen vuotuinen ~ the annual exports of Finland. **-kauppa** export trade. **-kielto** export

ban. **-liike** export business. **-lupa** export licence. **-palkkio** export bonus. **-tavarat** exports. export goods. **-tulli** export duty. **-voittoinen**: ~ kauppatase favourable balance of trade.

vieraan|tua become estranged. **-tuminen** estrangement; alienation. **-varainen** hospitable. **-varaisuus** hospitality.

vierai|lija visitor, guest. **-lla** visit [a p., a place]; be on a visit (to), pay (sb.) a visit; (käydä) call (on). **-lu** visit; (pitempi) stay [with a p.]; (~aika visiting hours; ~käynti call; ~näytäntö special performance; antaa ~ give a special performance; ~puku afternoon dress). **-silla, -sille** on a visit; . meni -sille. . went to see (call on) [the Joneses].

vieras a. strange, (tuntematon) unknown, jklle to; (ulkomainen) foreign [language, kieli]; s. guest, visitor; (muukalainen) stranger; ~ mies (todistaja) witness; vieraalla maalla in a foreign country, abroad; . on jklle ~ta. . is unfamiliar (foreign) to. .; meillä oli vieraita we had company. **-huone** guest room, spare room. **-kielinen**. . in a foreign language. **-kirja** guest-book, visitors' book. **-käynti** visit, (lyhyt) call. **-maalainen** a. foreign; s. foreigner, alien. **-peräinen**. . of foreign origin. **-taa**: ~ jkta be shy of. .

vieraus strangeness.

vier|een: jnk ~ by. ., beside. ., (aivan) close by; viereeni by me, by my side, next to me. **-einen**. . close by, nearby, next [door, ovi]; adjacent; ~ huone next room. **-ekkäin** next to each other; side by side.

viere|llä: tien ~ by the side of the road. **-ssä**: jnk ~ beside. ., by the side of, next to. **-stä** from the side of, from close by. **-tysten** side by

side.
vieri side; ~ *vieressä* close
[together]. **-nkivi** boulder.
-skellä roll. **-tse:** *jnk* ~ by. .,
past. . **-ttää** roll; ~ *syy jkn
niskoille* lay the blame on. .
-ä roll; *vuosien -essä* over the
years.
vier|oa shun; *seuraa -ova. .*
unsociable. **-oittaa** estrange
(from), alienate; *(tavasta)*
break sb. of a habit; *(vauva)*
wean; *v-ttaminen (pahasta)
tavasta* habit-breaking. **-oitus**
weaning, *vrt. ed.* '**-oksua** ks.
vieroa; *työtä v-suva* work-shy.
viertotie causeway.
vierus|kulma *mat.* adjacent
angle. **-ta:** *jnk* ~*lla* by the
side of. **-toveri:** ~*ni (m.)* the
man (woman) [sitting] next
to me, [the lady] on my left
(right).
vieräh|tää roll; *(kulua)* pass;
kyynel -ti hänen poskelleen a
tear trickled down her cheek.
viesti message, tidings; *(sana)*
word. **-joukkue** relay team.
-joukot Signal Corps. **-kapula**
baton. **-njuoksu** relay race.
-ntä signalling;
communications; *(~välineet*
media of communication).
-ttää signal. **-tys** signalling.
-upseeri signals officer.
vietellä allure, entice (into);
(nainen) seduce: *(kiusata)*
tempt.
viette|lijä *(naisen)* seducer.
-lijätär temptress. **-lys**
allurement, temptation.
vietti instinct, urge; *psyk. m.*
drive.
vietto celebration.
viettäv|yys slope; declivity. **-ä**
sloping, slanting, downhill.
viettää 1. *(juhlallisesti)*
celebrate; *(kuluttaa)* spend,
pass; ~ *jnk muistoa* celebrate
the memory of. .,
commemorate; ~ *säännöllistä
elämää* lead a regular life;
häät vietettiin siellä the
wedding took place there. **2.**
(laskeutua) slope [downward],
descend, incline, *(esim. katto)*
slant.
viha hatred (of, towards sb.),

run. hate; *(-mielisyys)* enmity;
(suuttumus) anger; *purkaa
~ansa jkh* vent one's anger,
take it out (on); *se pisti
~ksi* it angered (annoyed)
me; *olla vihoissaan* be angry,
jklle with a p., *jstk* at;
joutua jkn vihoihin incur a
p.'s displeasure, fall into a
p.'s disfavour; *heillä oli
vanhaa ~a* they had an old
grudge (an old quarrel);
unohtaa vanhat ~t bury the
hatchet. **-inen** angry, *jklle*
with a p., *jstk* at; annoyed
(at), angered; *Am. m.* mad
(at); ~ *koira* fierce dog.
-isuus anger. **-mielinen** hostile
(to), inimical; *(valtiolle)*
subversive. **-mielisesti** hostilely,
in a hostile manner.
-mielisyys hostility, hostile
attitude (towards); animosity
(towards, for). **-mies** enemy,
foe; *hankkia itselleen -miehiä*
make enemies. **-nkauna**
grudge; spitefulness, rancour.
-npurkaus outburst of anger
(wrath).
vihan|nekset vegetables.
-nesliemi vegetable soup.
-noida be green. **-nuus**
verdure, green[ness]. **-ta**
green, verdant; *(~rehu* green
fodder).
viha|päissään in a fit of anger.
-stua get angry, become
exasperated (annoyed); *v-tunut
(m.)* irate, enraged. **-stuttaa**
make. . angry, *(suututtaa)*
exasperate, *(raivostuttaa)*
enrage. **-ta** hate; *(kammota)*
detest; *-ttava* hateful, odious,
detestable.
vihdoin at last; at length;
(lopuksi) finally, in the end,
ultimately, eventually; ~
viimein at long last. **-kin** at
last.
viheliäi|nen miserable,
wretched. **-syys** miserableness,
wretchedness.
vihel|lys whistle; *(~pilli*
whistle). **-tää** whistle;
(paheksuen) hiss, *jklle* [at] a
p., at sb.
viher|alue(et) green spaces.
-iöidä be green, be verdant.

-kaihi *lääk.* glaucoma. **-tävä** greenish.

vihi: *saada ~ä jstk* get wind (scent) of, get an inkling of. **-koira** bloodhound, sleuth.

vihille: *mennä ~* be married.

vihj|ailla, -aista, -ata *(jklle jtk)* give sb. a hint (an intimation), hint to a p., drop sb. a hint; *vihjailetko, etten puhu totta?* are you suggesting that I am not telling the truth? **-aus, -e** hint, intimation; *puhek.* tip; *(viite)* reference.

vihki|minen wedding; *(jhk tarkoitukseen)* dedication; inauguration; *toimittaa ~ (avioliittoon)* officiate at a p.'s marriage. **-mys** dedication, consecration. **-mäkaava** marriage formula. **-mätodistus** marriage certificate. **-mätön** unmarried. **-sormus** wedding-ring. **-vesi** holy water. **-ytyä** dedicate oneself (to).

vihkiä *(avioliittoon)* marry, join in marriage; *(jhk tarkoitukseen)* dedicate (to); *(esim. rakennus)* inaugurate; *(pyhittää)* consecrate; *(et. papiksi)* ordain; *(maisteriksi ym.)* confer the degree of [mag. phil.] upon; *kirkkoa vihittäessä* at the dedication (consecration) of the church; *vihitty vaimoni* my wedded wife. **-iset** wedding [ceremony], marriage ceremony; dedication; inauguration; consecration.

vihko book *(kirjoitus-)* notebook; *(esim. koulu-)* exercise book. **-nen** leaflet, brochure.

vihl|aista cut, *(repiä)* rend; *päätäni -aisee* I have a shooting pain in my head. **-oa** *ks. ed.; grate* [upon sb.'s ears, *korvia*], *(hampaita)* hurt; *sydäntä -oi* my heart was wrung (by. .).

vihma, -sade drizzle.

vihne awn.

vihoi|tella be angry, be annoyed, fume (at); *(haava)* become inflamed, begin to hurt. **-ttaa** make angry; offend.

viholli|nen enemy. **-sjoukot** hostile (enemy) troops. **-smaa** hostile country. **-suus** hostility; enmity; *alkaa, lopettaa -suudet* commence (suspend) hostilities.

vihoviimeinen the very last; *(huonoin)* the poorest [imaginable].

vihre|ys greenness; verdure. **-ä** green; *näyttää ~tä valoa (kuv.)* give the go-ahead; *panna ~n veran alle* sweep under the rug.

vihta whisk of birch twigs [used in sauna].

vihtrilli *kem.* vitriol.

vihuri gust of wind, flurry; *(myrsky)* gale. **-rokko** German measles, rubella.

viidakko jungle.

viiden|neksi fifthly. **-nes** fifth [part].

viides [the] fifth. **-kymmenes** [the] fiftieth. **-ti** five times. **-toista** [the] fifteenth.

viihd|e light entertainment; *(~musiikki* light music, pop music). **-yke** diversion. **-yttäjä** *(viihdetaiteilija)* entertainer. **-yttää** quiet[en], soothe; *(pientä lasta)* lull; *(hauskuttaa)* divert. **-ytys** diversion, amusement; *etsiä ~tä (lohtua)* seek solace (in).

viihty|isyys cosiness, comfort. **-isä** cosy. **-mys** comfort; contentment. **-mättömyys** dissatisfaction. **-vyys** *(työssä)* job satisfaction.

viihtyä get on, get along [well]; *(kasvi)* thrive; *~ hyvin (m.)* feel at home, enjoy one's stay (in, at); *~ huonosti* be uncomfortable, not feel at home, get on [poorly].

viikari young rascal, scamp.

viikate scythe. **-mies:** *tuonen ~* Death.

viikinki viking. **-alus** viking boat. **-retki** viking raid.

viikko week; *viikon* [for] a week; *kaksi ~a (m.)* a fortnight; *tällä viikolla* [during] this week; *~ sitten* a week ago; *viikon päästä* a week from now, this day week, after a week, *(viikon* *kuluessa)* in (within) a week; *viikoksi* for a week;.. *viikolta, viikossa.*. a week,.. per week; *kerran viikossa* once a week, weekly; *en ole nähnyt häntä ~on* I have not seen him for a week. **-inen.**. lasting [for].. weeks; *tämän ~* this week's. **-katsaus** weekly review. **-kaupalla** for weeks. **-kausi** a week's time; *-kauden* [for] a week; *~a* for weeks [and weeks]. **-kertomus** weekly report. **-lehti** weekly [paper]. **-palkka** weekly wages.

viikoittai|n weekly; every week. **-nen** weekly.

viikon|loppu week-end. **-päivä** day of the week; *(arki-)* weekday.

viiksi: *viikset* moustache; *(kissan ym)* whiskers. **-niekka** *a.*.. wearing a moustache, mustachioed.

viikuna fig. **-nlehti** fig leaf. **-puu** fig tree.

viila file. **-aja** filer. **-penkki** bench vice. **-ta** file; *~ poikki* file off.

viile|ntää cool. **-tä** cool [down].

viilettää speed, fly [past, *ohi*].

viile|ys coolness. **-ä** cool.

viili processed sour whole milk.

viilokki fricassee.

viilto incision, slash, [long] cut. **-haava** incised wound.

viilt|ää slash, cut; incise; *(halki)* slash, slit; *~ auki* cut (rip) open. **-ävä** *(kipu)* shooting [pain], *(ääni)* harsh.

viilu veneer.

viima strong wind; cold wind; draught, current of air.

viime last; *~ aikoina* recently, lately, of late; *(aivan) ~ aikoihin saakka* until [quite] recently; *~ kädessä* ultimately; *~ tingassa* at the last moment (minute); *~ vuonna* last year; *~ vuosina* in recent years, in the last few years. **-aikainen** recent. **-in** finally; *vrt. vihdoin.* **-inen** last; *(myöhin)* latest; *(loppu-)* final; *(äärimmäinen)* extreme; *~ numero (lehden)* current number, latest issue;

toivomus last wish; *-isen edellinen* the last but one; *-iseen asti* to the [very] last, to the utmost; *-iseen mieheen* to the last man; *-isen kerran* [for] the last time; *-iset tiedot* [the] latest news, last-minute news; *tulla -isenä* come (arrive) last, be the last one to arrive; *-isten kymmenen vuoden aikana* during the last ten years. **-inkin** at last. **-isillään** on one's last legs, *(raskaana)* near her time.

viimeis|tellä put (give) the finishing touches (to); *(kirjallista työtä)* revise. **-tely** finishing, finishing touch [es], [final] revision. **-tään.**. at the latest, not later than..

viimeksi last; lastly. **-mainittu.**. mentioned last, last-mentioned; *(jälkimmäinen)* the latter.

viime|vuotinen.. of last year, last year's. **-öinen;** *~ halla* the frost last night, last night's frost.

viina spirits; *(väkijuoma)* liquor; alcohol; *sl.* booze; *~an menevä* addicted to drink. **-pannu** still. **-npolttaja** distiller [of spirits]; *(pontikan)* moonshiner.

viini 1. wine; **2.** *(nuoli-)* quiver; *viljellä ~ä* cultivate vines; grow grapes. **-happo** *kem.* tartaric acid. **-kauppa** wine business. **-kauppias** wine-merchant, vintner. **-kellari** wine cellar. **-kivi** tartar. **-köynnös** [grape-]vine. **-lasi** wineglass. **-marja** currant. **-nkorjaaja** vintager. **-nkorjuu** harvesting of grapes. **-nviljelijä** wine-grower. **-nviljelys** wine-growing, viticulture. **-pullo** wine bottle. **-rypäle** grape. **-sato** vintage; *vuoden 1970 ~a* of the v. of 1970. **-tarha** vineyard. **-tarhuri** vine-dresser.

viinuri waiter.

viipale slice; *(silava-, ym)* rasher; *(paksu)* hunk.

viipymättä without [a moment's] delay, without loss of time; immediately.

viipy|ä delay; linger; *(pysähtyä)* stay, stop [at, in a place *jssak;* with a p. *jkn luona*], stay on [after the others, *toisten mentyä*]; *(viivästyä)* be delayed; *(olla hidas)* be slow; dwell on [the details, *yksityiskohdissa*]; *-i hetken ennenkuin .* . it took a moment before. *.; en viivy kauan* I shan't be long; *hän -i siellä yön* he stayed (stopped) there overnight.
viiri streamer, pennant; standard. **-kukko** weathercock.
viiriäi|nen *zo.* quail.
viiru streak.
viisaasti wisely *jne.; menetellä ~* act wisely, use discretion.
viisas *a.* wise; clever; *(järkevä)* judicious; in one's right mind, sane; *olisi viisainta lähteä* it would be a wise thing to go; we had better go; *~ten kerho* brains trust; *~ten kivi* philosophers' stone. **-telija** hair-splitter. **-tella** try to be smart; be splitting hairs; *-televa* [over]smart. **-telu** hair-splitting; sophistry. **-tua** become wise[r]; get more sense; *vahingosta -tuu* experience is a great teacher, once bitten, twice shy; *hän ei ole siitä -tunut* she is none the wiser [for it].
viisaus wisdom; cleverness; judiciousness.
viisi five; *välitän ~ siitä* I don't care [a bit *t.* a hoot]. **-kerroksinen** five-storey [ed]. **-kko** quintet [te]. **-kulmio** pentagon. **-kymmentä** fifty.
viisikymmen|vuotias. . fifty years old; [a man] of fifty. **-vuotisjuhla** fiftieth anniversary.
viisi|nkertainen fivefold. **-näytöksinen**. . in five acts. **-ottelu** pentathlon. **-sataa** five hundred. **-toista** fifteen. **-vuotias**. . five years old (of age), five-year-old [child], [a child] of five. **-vuotinen** five years',. . of five years' duration. **-vuotiskausi** period of five years. **-vuotissuunnitelma** five-year plan.

viisto oblique; *(kalteva)* slanting; *~ssa, ~on* obliquely, diagonally, askew; *riippua ~ssa* hang awry (crooked); *leikata kangas ~on* cut the cloth on the bias; *hioa, leikata ~on (tekn.)* bevel. **-us** obliqueness; slant.
viisumi visa; *hankkia ~ (m.)* get one's passport visaed. **-pakko:** *on ~* a visa is obligatory.
viita|ta point, *jhk* at, to; point out [the defects, *puutteisiin*], indicate; *(kädenliikkeellä)* beckon, motion; *(tarkoittaa)* refer (to); *(tähdätä)* allude (to); hint (at); *(koulussa)* hold (put) up one's hand; *~ hyvästiksi jklle* wave good-bye to a p.; *-ten viime kirjeeseenne* referring to your last letter; *-ttuun suuntaan* in the direction indicated; *hän viittasi minua istumaan* he signed (motioned) to me to take a seat; *kaikki viittaa siihen, että .* . everything indicates that, everything points to. .
viite reference; suggestion.
viitisenkymmentä about fifty, some fifty, fifty or so.
viitoi|ttaa stake out; *(esim. tie)* mark out; *mer.* buoy [a fairway, *väylä*]; *hänen -ttamiaan suuntaviivoja* on the lines laid down by him.
viito|nen five. **-set** quintuplets.
viitsiä care to; *en viitsinyt* I couldn't be bothered to. .
viitta 1. cloak; *(kaapu)* gown; *(hartia-)* cape. **2.** stake; *(tien-)* signpost; *mer.* spar-buoy, buoy.
viitt|ailla allude, *jhk* to, make allusions (to), hint (at); *(ilkeästi)* insinuate (that. .). **-ailu** allusion [s], insinuation [s]. **-aus** allusion (to), hint (at), intimation; *puhek.* tip; *(sala-)* insinuation; *(ehdotus)* suggestion; *(esim. sanakirjassa)* cross-reference. **-eellinen** suggestive. **-oa** make signs to; motion. **-oilla** gesticulate. **-oilu** gesticulation. **-omakieli** sign language.
viiv|a line; *(vetäisy)* stroke:

(ajatus-) dash. **-ata** rule; ~ *yli* strike out; *-attu* ruled. **-aamaton** unruled. **-oitin** ruler. **-oittaa** rule, line.

viivy|tellä delay; *(jnk tekemisessä)* be long [in . . -ing]; *(aikailla)* linger; loiter; *-ttelemättä* without delay. **-ttely** delay. **-ttää** delay, retard; *(pidättää)* detain, take up [a p.'s] time; *en tahdo ~ sinua kauemmin* I won't keep you longer. **-tys** delay.

viivä|hdys short stay. **-htää** stay, stop [at a place for a while, *jssak hetkinen*], tarry. **-stys** delay; *hänen -stymisensä* his being late. **-styttää** *ks.* viivyttää. **-styä** be late, be delayed.

vika fault; *(puute)* defect, deficiency; *(rikkouma)* flaw; ~*(a)* *näössä* defective sight; *missä ~ on?* where is the trouble? what is wrong [with it]? ~ *on minussa* it is my fault, I am to blame; *kenen ~ se oli?* whose fault was it? *koneessa on jokin ~* there is something wrong with the machine; *lasissa on ~* there is a defect (a flaw) in the glass; *siihen ei tullut mitään ~a* no harm was done to it. **-antua** be damaged, be injured; suffer [damage]; *v-tumaton* undamaged. **-pisto** miss. **-pää** guilty (of).

viki|nä squeak[ing]. **-stä** squeak; whine, whimper.

vikkel|yys quickness; swiftness. **-ä** quick; swift.

vikla sandpiper.

vikoilla find fault.

vikuri restive, intractable.

vikuutt|aa damage, do damage (to); injure; *hallan -ama* nipped by frost.

vilah|dus, vilaus glimpse; *(välähdys)* flash; *nähdä ~ jstk* glimpse. .; *näin hänet vilaukselta* I caught a glimpse of him; *-duksessa* in a flash. **-taa** flash, twinkle; ~ *ohi* glance past, flit by.

vili|nä commotion; bustle. **-stä** swarm; *jssak -see jtk.* . is teeming with, is alive with. .

vilja corn, *Am.* grain; *(laiho)* crop[s]. **-aitta** granary. **-kasvi** cereal. **-laji** cereal, variety (kind) of grain. **-lti** in large quantities, in abundance, profusely, in profusion. **-pelto** cornfield. **-sato** grain crop[s]. **-va** fertile, fruitful; *(runsas)* rich. **-varasto** stock (supply) of corn (grain). **-vuus** richness [of the soil], fertility.

vilje|lemätön. . not cultivated, uncultivated, untilled, waste. **-lijä** tiller; *(et. yhd.)* grower; *teen ~* tea-planter. **-llä** cultivate; grow; raise; *(muokata)* till [the soil]; *(esim. helmiä, bakteereja)* culture;. . *eivät tahdo kasvaa viljeltyinä*. . are difficult to grow in cultivation. **-ly(s)** cultivation, tillage; *(et. yhd.)* culture *(esim. puutarha~* horticulture); *ottaa -lykseen* bring. . under cultivation; *(~kasvi* cultivated plant; *~kelpoinen* arable; *~maa* agricultural land, farmland).

vilkai|sta glance (at), [take a] look (at); *(silmäillä)* look over [quickly]; *-sen lehteä* I'll glance through the paper. **-su** glance, look.

vilkas lively, vivacious, animated, sprightly; vivid [imagination, *mielikuvitus*]; active, busy; ~ *kysyntä* keen (brisk) demand; ~ *liikenne* busy (heavy) traffic. **-liikenteinen** busy; crowded [street, *katu*]. **-tua** become [more] lively, get new life, become enlivened. **-tuttaa** make. . [more] lively; enliven, animate; *(uudelleen)* revive. **-verinen** sanguine; lively.

vilkk|aasti in a lively way (manner), with animation, with verve; vividly; actively; *osoittaa ~ suosiotaan jllek* applaud. . heartily, acclaim [the winner, *voittajalle*]. **-aus** liveliness, vivacity, animation, spirit, life; *liikenteen ~* the busy traffic.

vilkku *(auton)* indicator [light]; *(-lyhty)* signalling lamp. **-a** twinkle, blink;

(värähdellä) flicker; *(välähtää)*
flash. **-loisto** beacon. **-valo**
winking (flashing) light.
vilku|illa glance [around,
ympärilleen], *(salavihkaa)*
glance furtively, steal a glance
(at); *(syrjäsilmällä)* leer (at).
-ttaa blink; wink [at a. p.,
silmää jklle]; *(huiskia)* wave.
-tus blinking; winking; wave,
waving.
villa wool; *~t (villapeite)*
fleece. **-inen** wollen, [.. made
of] wool; *(-peitteinen)* woolly;
painaa -isella (kuv.) gloss. .
over; hush up. **-kangas**
woollen cloth *(t. material),*
wool. **-kankainen** woollen.
-kehräämö woollen mill.
-koira poodle. **-käsine** woollen
glove. **-lanka** woollen yarn,
worsted, wool. **-paita** woollen
shirt; sweater; *(esim.
merimiehen)* jersey. **-sukka**
woollen stocking *(lyhyt:* sock).
-takki cardigan, sweater.
-tavarat woollen goods,
woollens. **-teollisuus** wool
industry. **-va** woolly.
villi *a.* wild, savage [tribe,
heimo]; *s.* savage; *pol.*
independent; *~t eläimet (m.)*
wild life. **-ihminen** savage.
-intyminen *(eläinten, kasvien)*
running wild. **-intyä** run wild;
(vain ihmisistä) become
uncivilized; *v-tyneet lapset*
young savages. **-kaali** henbane.
-kissa wild-cat. **-kko** madcap.
-peto wild beast. **-ruusu**
dog-rose, wild rose. **-sika**
[wild-]boar. **-tsijä** instigator.
-tys agitation; *viimeinen,
uusin* ~ the latest craze. **-tä**
(esim. kapinaan) stir up,
instigate, excite; *huvitteluhalu
on -nnyt nuorisomme* a
craving for pleasure has taken
hold of our youth. **-viini**
Virginia creeper. **-ys** wildness;
savageness, savagery.
vilpi|llinen deceitful, false,
fraudulent; *(epärehellinen)*
dishonest. **-llisyys**
deceitfulness; falseness;
fraudulence. **-stellä** be
deceitful; cheat. **-ttömyys**
sincerity; candour, frankness.

-tön sincere; *(avomielinen)*
candid, frank; *(suora)*
straightforward; *(rehellinen)*
honest, upright; *-ttömin mielin*
in good faith, bona fide.
vilpo|inen cool; *(raitis)* fresh.
-isuus coolness; freshness. **-la**
veranda [h], *Am.* porch.
vilppi deceit, double-dealing,
fraud; *harjoittaa ~ä* cheat.
vilske bustle, flurry.
vilu chill [iness]; cold; *minun
on* ~ I am cold, I feel cold.
-inen cold. **-npuistatus,
-nväristys** fit of shivering.
-nväreet cold shivers. **-stua**
catch [a] cold; *hän on
v-tunut* he has a cold.
-stuminen [catching] cold,
exposure to cold; *hyvä lääke
v-mista vastaan* a good cure
for colds. **-ttaa:** *minua* ~ I
feel cold.
vilvoi|tella cool [oneself], cool
off. **-ttaa** cool [.. off].
vimma fury, frenzy, rage;
saattaa vimmoihinsa make. .
furious, infuriate, enrage;
vihan ~ssa in a fit of anger,
in a rage.**-stua** fly into a
passion, become infuriated.
-ttu furious, frantic, frenzied;
kuin ~ *(m.)* like hell.
ving|ahdus squeal; creak[ing];
squeak. **-ahtaa** *(viulu ym)*
squeak. **-uttaa:** ~ *viulua*
scrape the fiddle.
vinha *(nopea)* swift, fast; *~a
vauhtia* at a furious
(headlong) speed.
vinku|a *(viuhua)* whistle, *(luoti)*
whiz; *(hengitys)* wheeze;
(viulu ym) squeak; *tuuli
vinkuu* the wind is howling
(whistling). **-na** howling;
wheezing.
vinkkuraviiva zigzag line.
vino oblique, slanting; inclined;
distorted [mouth, *suu*]; *~ssa*
on one side, askew, *(esim.
hattu)* at an angle; *jotain on
~ssa* something is wrong;
~lla (painettu) in italics.
-kirja|sin italic [type];
v-similla in italics. **-kulmainen**
oblique-angled. **-neliö** *mat.*
rhomb. **-silmäinen**
oblique-eyed, slant-eyed. **-us**

obliqueness, obliquity, bias; *(kasvojen)* distortion.
vintiö villain; rascal.
vintti 1. *(ullakko)* loft, attic;
2. *(kaivon)* [bucket] pole.
-koira greyhound.
vintturi windlass, winch, jack.
vinyyli vinyl.
vioi|ttaa damage, injure. **-ttua** be damaged, suffer damage; be injured, suffer an injury; *näkö -ttui* sight was impaired. **-ttuma** injury; lesion.
vipu lever.
viralli|nen official; ~ *syyttäjä* public prosecutor; ~ *vastaväittäjä* ex-officio opponent. **-suus** official character.
viraltapano removal from office, discharge.
viran|hakija applicant (for). **-haltija** holder of an office. **-omainen** [proper] authority. **-omaiset** the authorities. **-sijainen** substitute; deputy; *vrt. sijainen*. **-sijaisuus** deputyship; *hoitaa jkn v-suutta* act as a substitute for. **-toimitus** performance of the duties of one's office; *olla v-tuksessa (m.)* be on duty, attend to one's duties; *v-tuksen ulkopuolella* off duty; *pidättää v-tuksesta* suspend.
vira|sto office, *(valtion)* civil service department. **-ton .** out of office.
vire tune; *vireessä (mus.)* tuned; *(pyssy)* cocked; *panna ~ille* introduce, bring up; *~illä oleva kysymys* the question under discussion; *oli parhaassa ~essään* in his best form; *en päässyt oikein ~eseen* I couldn't get into the right mood. **-ys** energy, vigour; alertness; *henkinen ~* mental agility. **-ä** alert, spry, mentally active (agile).
virhe fault; error; *(erehdys)* mistake, *(törkeä)* blunder, *(tahdoton, esim. kirjoitus-)* slip; *tehdä ~itä* make mistakes; commit errors. **-ellinen** faulty; erroneous, incorrect; *(väärä)* wrong; *(epätarkka)* inaccurate; *v-llisesti* incorrectly,

wrong [ly]. **-ellisyys** faultiness; incorrectness; inaccuracy. **-ettömyys** faultlessness, correctness; accuracy. **-etön** faultless; flawless; *(oikea)* correct; accurate; *(erehtymätön)* infallible. **-lähde** source of error. **-piste** penalty point. **-päätelmä** fallacy.
viri|ke fuel; *(kiihoke)* incitement; stimulus; impetus; *antaa ~ttä jllek* stimulate; *add -fuel* to. **-ttäjä** *mus.* tuner. **-ttää** *mus.* tune [up]; *rad.* tune in [to Lahti *ym*]; *valok.* wind on; *(ansa)* set; *(ase)* cock; ~ *tuli* light (kindle) a fire; ~ *laulu* strike up a song; ~ *alemmaksi* tune. . down; ~ *salajuonia* intrigue (against); ~ *pauloja (kuv.)* lay snares for. **-tys** tuning. **-tä** light, take fire; *et. kuv.* be kindled; ~ *jälleen* flame up again; be revived; *-si vilkas keskustelu* an animated discussion ensued.
virka office; *asettaa ~an* instal [1]. . in office, *(entiseen ~an)* reinstate in one's post; *astua ~an* take office; *olla virassa* hold (fill, occupy) an office; *panna viralta* remove. . from office, discharge, depose; *sillä ei ole mitään ~a* it is no good; *~a toimittava (v.t.)* acting. **-aika** office hours. **-anasettajaiset** inauguration. **-anastujaisesitelmä** inaugural lecture. **-arvo** official rank. **-asema** official position. **-asia** official matter; *-asioissa* on official business. **-ero** discharge; *hän sai ~n* he was granted a discharge, his resignation was accepted.
virkahtaa put in [a word], utter.
virka|heitto dismissed [officer]. **-huone** office [-room]. **-ikä** time in office, period of service; *(korkeampi)* seniority in office. **-ilija** employee; official, functionary; *(esim. yhdistysten)* officer; *~t* salaried persons, *(johto-)* executives. **-into** zeal in office. **-intoinen** [over]zealous

[in the performance of one's duties], officious. **-kirje** official letter. **-loma** vacation; ~lla on vacation, on leave. **-matka** official journey; hän on ~lla he is away on official business. **-mies** official; (hallituksen) civil servant; (~hallitus caretaker government; ~kunta body of civil servants; officials; ~ura official career). **-nainen** professional (t. career) woman. **-nimitys** appointment. **-puku** uniform. **-pukuinen**. . in uniform, uniformed. **-syyte** action [against an official].
virkata crochet.
virka|tehtävä official duty; hoitaa -tehtäviään discharge (perform) the duties of one's office. **-todistus** (papin-) [official] extract from parish register. **-toveri** colleague. **-ura** career. **-valta** bureaucracy; puhek. red tape. **-valtainen** bureaucratic. **-valtaisuus** bureaucracy. **·vapa|us** leave [of absence]; (-loma) vacation; nauttii v-utta is on leave, (sairauden takia) is on sick-leave. **-veli** colleague; fellow [clergyman, doctor ym]. **-virhe** official misconduct (malpractice). **-vuosi** year of service. **-ylennys** promotion; (~peruste basis for promotion).
virke kiel. [complex] sentence.
virk|eys liveliness; vigour, vitality. **-eä** lively, spirited, animated; brisk; spry, puhek. (esim. potilas) perky; (elinvoimainen) vigorous; ~llä mielellä (m.) in a spirited mood; vrt. vireä. **-istys** refreshment; recreation; relaxation; (esim. puiston) ~arvo amenity value; (~matka recreation trip). **-istyä** refresh oneself, recuperate, gather new strength, recover strength; be [re]invigorated. **-istää** refresh; invigorate, stimulate: puhek. buck up; **-istävä** refreshing, invigorating.
virkkaa utter, say.
virkku brisk; spry; alert.

virkkuu crocheting. **-neula** crochet hook.
virma (hevonen) frisky. **-juuri** bot. valerian.
virna bot. vetch.
virnis|tellä grin, grimace, make a wry face; (ivallisesti) sneer, leer. **-tys** grin; grimace.
Viro Esthonia. **v-lainen** a. & s. Esthonian. **v-n kieli** Esthonian.
virota (henkiin) revive, be revived; (tainnoksista) recover consciousness, be resuscitated.
virran|jakaja distributor. **-katkaisin** sähk. switch.
virrata stream, flow; (juosta) run; (valua, esim. sateesta) pour, come pouring [down]; ~ sisälle pour into [the city, kaupunkiin].
virsi hymn. **-kirja** hymn-book.
virstanpylväs milestone, landmark.
virta current (m. sähkö-); (joki) stream; kuv. flow; torrent; vuotaa ~naan flow in streams; (esim. veri haavasta) gush out in streams. **-hepo** hippopotamus, hippo. **-piiri** circuit. **-us** current, stream; kuv. m. tendency. **-viivainen** stream-line [d].
virtsa urine. **-aminen** urination; -amisvaivat difficulties in u. **-happo** uric acid. **-putki** urethra. **-myrkytys** ur[a]emia. **-pakko** frequency of urination. **-rakko** [urinary] bladder. **-ta** urinate, ark. pee. **-tietulehdus** urinary infection.
virtuoosi virtuos|o (pl. -os, -i).
viru|a lie, be lying; ~ pitkällään lie outstretched; ~ sairasvuoteessa be bedridden; ~ vankilassa languish in prison. **-ttaa** (huuhtoa) rinse [out]. **-tus** rinsing, rinse.
virvatuli will-o'-the wisp, ignis fatuus.
virvel|i fishing rod with reel, Am. rod and reel. **-öidä** spin (for).
virvilä lentil.
virvoi|ttaa refresh, invigorate; (henkiin) revive, resuscitate. **-tus** refreshment; (~juoma soft drink, mineral water).

virvokk|eet, -eita refreshments.

visa curly birch. **-inen.** . of curly birch; ~ *kysymys* a knotty question. **-koivu** curly birch.

viseer|ata visa. **-aus** visaing.

viser|rys twitter[ing], chirp[ing]. **-tää** twitter. chirp, chirrup.

viskaali public prosecutor.

visk|ain *(vesi-)* bailer. *(viljan)* fan. **-ata** throw; fling; *(kevyesti)* toss; chuck; ~ *syytös jkta vastaan* hurl an accusation against a p. **-ellä** throw about.

viski whisky.

vismutti bismuth.

vispilä beater; whisk.

vissi ks. *tietty.*

visu stingy, niggardly. **-sti** carefully; closely, strictly.

visva purulent discharge.

vitamiini vitamin; C~ vitamin C. **-npuute** lack of vitamins. **-pitoinen** vitaminous. **-rikas** high-vitamin, rich in vitamins. **-valmiste** vitamin preparation.

vitaminoida vitaminize.

viti lumi powdery snow. **-valkoinen** snow-white.

vitja: ~t chain.

vitka|lleen slowly, tardily. **-llinen** slow, tardy, dilatory. **-stella** be slow, be sluggish; lag [behind], hang back, loiter; *v-telematta* without delay, without hesitation. **-stelu** delay.

vitsa twig; *antaa* ~*a* spank; give sb. a beating (whipping, thrashing).

vits|ailija joker; punster. **-ailla** joke, crack jokes, jest.

vitsaus *kuv.* plague, scourge.

vitsi joke, jest; *ymmärsi* ~*n* saw (got) the point. **-käs** witty; funny.

viuhka fan.

viuh|ina, -ua whistle, whiz.

viulu violin; fiddle; *maksaa* ~*t* pay the piper. **-laatikko** violin case. **-niekka** violinist. **-njousi** [violin] bow. **-nkieli** [violin] string. **-nsoittaja** violin player; fiddler. **-nsoitto** playing the violin. **-taiteilija** violinist.

vivah|dus shade, tinge; touch; nuance; *synonyymienkin merkityksissä on usein* ~*eroja* even synonyms often have different shades of meaning. **-taa** have a shade (a tinge, a touch) of, be tinged with.

vohkia *sl.* pinch.

vohla kid.

vohveli wafer; waffle.

voi! oh! ah! oh dear! *(valitettavasti)* alas; ~ *kun minulla olisi.* . I wish I had. .

voi butter.

voida *(kyetä)* be able (to), be capable [of. .-ing], *(olla tilaisuudessa)* be in a position (to); *(terveyden puolesta)* be, feel; *voi* can, *(saattaa)* may; *ei voi* cannot, is not able to, is unable to, is incapable of [. .-ing]; *voi olla niin* it may be so; *voi olla (ehkä)* maybe; *olen tehnyt voitavani* I have done all in my power, I have done my utmost, I have done my best; *sille ei voitu mitään* there was nothing to be done about it; *kuinka voitte?* how do you feel? *voin hyvin* I am well, I feel well, *(oikein hyvin)* I am quite well, I am all right; *voidaan sanoa* it may be said; *hän ei ole voinut sanoa niin* he cannot have said so; *hän sanoi voivansa tulla* he said he could come.

voide ointment; *(kasvo- ym.)* cream; *on hyvässä voiteessa* is well greased (oiled). **-lla** grease; *(öljytä)* oil; *(konetta, m.)* lubricate; *(suksia)* wax; *kuv.* anoint.

voihkia moan, groan.

voi|kimpale pat of butter. **-kukka** dandelion. **-leipä** buttered slice of bread, open sandwich, *(kaksois-)* sandwich; *(~pöytä* cold table, buffet table; hors d'oeuvres).

voima strength; force; power; *(mahti)* might; vigour; *(-peräisyys)* intensity; *esimerkin* ~ force of example; *henkinen* ~ mental power, strength of mind; *olla* ~*ssa* be in force, be valid, hold good; *tarjous on* ~*ssa*

the offer stands; *ollen* ~*ssa.* .
-*sta lähtien* with effect from . . ;
astua, tulla ~*an* come into
force, become valid, take
effect; *saattaa* ~*an* bring into
force, bring (put) into effect;
olla hyvissä voimissa be in
good condition; *se käy yli*
~*ini* it is too much for my
strength; *kaikin voimin* as
hard as one can (could);
radio soi täydellä voimalla
the radio was on at full
blast. **-anpano** putting
(bringing, carrying) into force
(into effect); (*lain*)
enforcement. **-antulo** coming
into force.
voimailu strength sports.
voima|kas strong; (*-llinen*)
powerful; forcible; (*valtava*)
mighty; (*-peräinen*) intense;
vigorous; (*ravinnosta*)
substantial; ~ *isku* powerful
(heavy) blow; ~ *mielipide*
strong (powerful) opinion; ~
puhe forceful (emphatic)
speech; ~ *väri* strong
(intense) colour; ~*sanainen*
strongly worded. **-kkaasti**
strongly; powerfully. **-kkuus**
strength; power [fulness];
vigour; force [fulness];
intensity. **-kone** engine; motor.
-laitos *tekn.* power-station.
power plant; (*vesi-*)
hydroelectric plant. **-llinen**
powerful, forceful, mighty,
potent. **-llisuus** power [fulness];
might [iness].
voiman|koetus test of strength.
-lisäys increase of strength.
-lähde source of strength.
-ponnistus exertion; effort.
-siirto [power] transmission.
voima|paperi kraft paper.
-peräinen intensive, intense.
-peräistää intensify. **-peräisyys**
intensity. **-sana** strong word,
swear-word. **-ssaoleva** . in
force, valid; (*vallalla-*)
prevailing. **-ssaolo** validity;
kontrahdin ~*aika* the term of
the contract. **-suhteet** relative
strength. **-ton** powerless,. .
without strength (power),
lacking [in] strength (vigour);
feeble. **-ttomuus** powerlessness;

lack of strength (of power, of
vigour); weakness; infirmity.
-varat resources. **-virta** power
current. **-yksikkö** unit of
power.
voimis|telija gymnast. **-tella** do
gymnastic (physical) exercises.
voimistelu physical training,
gymnastics, *lyh.* gym. **-kenkä**
puhek. gym shoe, *Am.*
sneaker. **-nopettaja** physical
training master (mistress).
-puku gymnastics suit. **-sali**
gymnasium. **-väline:** ~*et*
gymnastic appliances (*koll.*
apparatus)
voimistua be strengthened,
strengthen, become stronger,
gain strength.
voinen buttery.
vointi state of [one's] health,
condition; (*terveys*) health;
(*kyky*) ability; ~*ni mukaan* to
the best of my ability.
voi|paperi greaseproof paper,
sandwich paper.
-sula melted butter. **-taikina**
[puff] paste.
voitava: ~*ni* all I can.
voitelu greasing; oiling;
lubrication; (*kuninkaitten*)
anointment; *viimeinen* ~
extreme unction. **-aine**
lubricant, grease. **-kannu** oil
can. **-kuppi** oil cup. **-öljy**
lubricating oil.
voito|kas, -llinen victorious.
-kkuus victoriousness.
voiton|himo greed for gain;
cupidity. **-himoinen** greedy for
gain, profit-seeking. **-hurma,**
-huuma flush of victory. **-jako**
profit-sharing. **-jumalatar**
goddess of victory. **-merkki**
trophy. **-puoli:** *olla -puolella*
be winning, have the
advantage (over); *päästä*
-puolelle get the upper hand,
gain the advantage (over).
-riemu triumph. **-riemuinen**
triumphant. **-varma** . sure of
victory.
voitt|aa win [a game, *peli;* in,
on, *jssk*]; (*esim. vaaleissa*
paikkoja) gain; (*vastustaja ym.*)
conquer, beat; *et. kuv.*
overcome [an illness, *tauti*];
gain [time, *aikaa*]; get the

better of; *(olla etevämpi)* be superior to, surpass, *(ylittää)* exceed; *(ansaita)* profit (by), derive profit (from); ~ *taistelu* gain a victory; ~ *palkinto* win (take) the prize, carry off the prize; *hän -i ensimmäisen palkinnon (m.)* he was awarded the first prize; ~ *itsensä* conquer oneself; ~ *korttipelissä* win at cards; ~ *lukumäärältään* be superior to. . in numbers, exceed in number; ~ *jku puolelleen* win. . over to one's side; ~ *ujoutensa* overcome one's shyness; *ansiot -avat puutteet* the merits outweigh the defects; *mitä siinä on voitettavissa* what is to be gained by that; *tämä ~ kaikki edelliset* this surpasses all previous ones; *aikaa ~kseen* [in order] to gain time. **-aja** victor; conqueror; *(et. kilpailuissa)* winner. **-amaton** unconquered; unsurpassed; *(jota ei voiteta)* invincible, unconquerable; *(et. esteistä)* insurmountable, insuperable. **-amattomuus** invincibility.

voitto victory; *(loistava)* triumph; *(liike-)* profit[s], gain; return, proceeds; *(arpajais- ym.)* prize; *myydä voitolla* sell at a profit; *saada, saavuttaa ~ jksta* gain (win) a victory (over); *on voitolla* has the upper hand; *päästä voitolle* be victorious, *(esim. riidassa)* have the best of it, *(mielipide)* prevail; *vie voiton jstk* surpasses, is superior to; *saada ~a jstk* derive profit from, make a profit out of; *tuottaa ~a* yield a profit; *~a tuottava* profitable. **-isa** victorious. **-kaari** triumphal arch. **-kulku** triumphal march. **-kulkue** triumphal procession. **-osuus** share in the profits. **-saalis** trophy.

voivo|tella wail, moan, complain (of). **-tus** wail[ing], moan[ing], lamentation.

vokaali vowel. **-nmukaus** vowel

mutation. **-äänne** vowel sound.
volframi tungsten.
voltti somersault, *sähk.* volt.
vonkua howl.
vouhottaa fuss.
vouti bailiff; overseer.
vuodattaa shed; pour [out].
vuode bed; *(sänky)* bedstead; *vuoteessa* in bed; *sijata ~* make a bed, *olla vuoteen omana* be laid up, be bedridden, keep *(t.* be confined to) one's bed; *panna lapsi vuoteeseen* put a child to bed. **vuoden|aika** season. **-tulo** [the year's] crop, crops. **-vaihde** turn of the year. **vuode|nuttu** bed jacket. **-peite** quilt; *(päivä-)* bedspread, counterpane. **-sohva** convertible sofa. **-vaatteet** bedclothes, bedding. **vuohen|maito** goat's milk. **-nahka** goatskin. **vuohi** goat; she-goat, nannygoat. **vuoka** baking *(t.* cake) tin; *(tulenkestävä)* casserole dish, fireproof pan. **vuokko** anemone. **vuokra** rent, *(autosta ym.)* hire, *(maasta)* lease; *antaa ~lle* let (to); *~lla* on hire, *(maa)* on lease. **-aika** lease. **-aja** tenant; lessee; *(talonisäntä)* landlord. **-auto** taxi; *~n kuljettaja (m.)* taximan. **-huone** rented room; *asua (kalustetussa) ~essa* live in lodgings. **-huoneisto** rental *(t.* rented) flat (apartment). **-isäntä** landlord. **-kasarmi** tenement-house, *(kerrostalo)* block · of flats. **-lainen** tenant; lessee, *(arentimies)* leaseholder; *(asukki)* lodger. **-lautakunta** housing committee. **-maa** rented land. **-sopimus** lease; contract. **vuokra|ta** rent, *(esim. auto)* hire; *(toiselle)* let, rent, hire [out], *(alivuokralaiselle)* sublet; ~ *itselleen huone (m.)* take a room; ~ *laiva* charter a ship; *-ttavana* to let, *(auto ym.)* for hire. **-tila** leasehold, *(pieni)* small holding. **-tilallinen** tenant farmer. **-ton** rent-free. **vuoksi 1.** *(jnk)* for the sake

of, on account of, because
of; in consequence of;
(puolesta) on behalf of; *jkn* ~
for a p.'s sake; *jonka* ~
wherefore, for which reason;
sen ~ because of that, for
that reason; *huvin* ~ for fun.
vuoksi 2. *(meri-)* high tide,
high water, flood[-tide]; ~
ja luode tide, ebb and flow.
vuol|aasti swiftly, rapidly;
(runsaasti) copiously; in
torrents. **-as** fast-flowing,
swift; ~ *virta (m.)* strong
current; *kyyneleet valuivat
-aana virtana* tears were
flowing freely.
vuol|eksia whittle, *jtk* at. **-la**
carve, *jtk* at; cut, chip (away).
vuolukivi steatite, soap-stone.
vuon|a, -ia lamb.
vuono fiord, *Skotl.* firth.
vuor|aamaton. . not lined;. .
without weatherboards. **-ata**
line; *(laudoilla)* put [the]
weatherboards on; *(vanulla)*
wad.
vuoren|harja mountain ridge.
-huippu mountain top,
summit, peak. **-peikko**
mountain sprite. **-seinämä**
mountain[side], rock-face.
-varma dead certain.
vuori 1. *(sisuste)* lining.
vuori 2. mountain; *(pieni)* hill;
(kallio, m. geol.) rock; *voi~*
butter surplus. **-ilmasto**
mountain climate. **-insinööri**
mining engineer. **-jono** range
of mountains. **-kauris**
steinbock, ibex. **-kide** rock
crystal. **-malmi** rocky ore.
-nen mountainous, hilly.
-neuvos »councillor of mining»
(title in Finland). **-saarna** the
Sermon on the Mount.
vuoristo mountains,
mountainous country.
-kiipeilijä mountaineer.
-kiipeily [mountain] climbing,
mountaineering. **-lainen**
mountaineer; highlander. **-rata**
(huvipuiston) switchback, *(iso)*
mountain railway.
vuori|teollisuus, -työ mining
[industry]. **-öljy** rock oil,
petroleum.
vuoro turn; *(työ-)* shift;

(tanssi-) figure; ~*n mukaan,
perään* in turn; *kukin* ~*llaan*
each in his turn; *nyt on
teidän* ~*nne (m.)* you are
next.. **-aikainen** intermittent.
-in alternately, by turns; ~..,
~. . sometimes. ., sometimes. .;
now. ., now. . **-ittain** in turn;
alternately, by turns;
(vaihtovuoroin) in shifts.
-ittainen alternating. **-järjestys:**
v-tyksessä in turn. **-kausi** day
and night, day, twenty-four
hours; *kaikkina -kauden
aikoina* at all hours.
-keskustelu, -puhelu dialogue.
-kone air liner. **-laiva** regular
steamer, liner. **-lento**
scheduled flight. **-staan** in
turn. **-tella** take turns, take it
in turns (to); alternate [with
each other]; occur alternately.
-tellen by turns, in turn;
. . and . . alternately.
-ttelu alternating, alternation;
(esim. yön ja päivän)
interchange. **-työ** shift work.
-vaikutus interaction, interplay.
-vesi tide. **-viljelys** rotation of
crops.
vuosi year; ~ *sitten* a year
ago; *(jo)* ~*a* for years; *joka*
~ every year, yearly,
annually; ~ *vuodelta* year by
year, year after year; *tänä
vuonna* [during] this year;
vuonna 1950 in [the year]
1950; ~*en varrella* in the
course of years; *vuodessa* in
a year, per year, per annum;
kerran vuodessa once a year;
kolmatta vuotta [for] more
than two years; *eilen oli
kulunut tasan* ~ *siitä, kun.*.
yesterday marked exactly one
year since. . **-juhla** annual
celebration, anniversary.
-katsaus yearly review. **-kausi**
a year's time; ~*a,* ~*in* for
years, for many years, *puhek.*
for ages; *(ei)* ~*in* for years.
-kerta a year's issues, annual
volume; *(viini-)* vintage;
vanhat -kerrat back-volumes.
-kertomus annual report;
hyväksyä ~ adopt the report.
-kokous annual meeting.
-kymmen decade, [period of]

ten .years. **-luku** year. **-luokka** age class. **-maksu** annual subscription (fee); yearly premium. **-neljännes** quarter. **-palkka** yearly salary. **-päivä** anniversary. **-rengas** annual ring. **-sata** century. **-sataisjuhla** centenary. **-tilaaja** yearly (annual) subscriber. **-ttain** annually, yearly; every year. **-tuhat** a thousand years, millennium; *-tuhansia* for thousands of years. **-tulot** yearly income. **-tuotanto** annual output (production). **-voitto** annual profit.

vuota hide, *(lampaan ym.)* pelt.
vuot|aa leak, be leaky; *(virrata)* flow; *(nenä)* run; ~ *verta* bleed; *vene* ~ the boat leaks (has a leak, has sprung a leak); *silmäni -avat* my eyes are watering. **-ava** leaking, leaky, *(nenä)* running.
vuoti|as *(yhd.)*. . years old,. . years of age, aged. .; *kaksi~ lapsi (m.)* a child of two, a two-year-old child. **-nen** *(yhd.).* . years', lasting. . years.
vuoto leak, leakage; *(märän ym.)* discharge; *(veren)* bleeding; *saada* ~ *(mer.)* spring a leak.
vuotuinen annual, yearly.
vyyhdinpuut reel.
vyyhti skein; *sotkuinen* ~ *(kuv.)* a bad tangle. **-ä** reel, wind up.
vyö belt, girdle; waist-band; *(leveä, kangas-)* sash. **-hyke** zone; *(alue)* belt; *~raja* zonal boundary; *~tariffi* zone tariff; *kuuma* ~ torrid zone, tropics. **-ruusu** shingles.
vyöry slide, *(et. lumi-)* avalanche. **-ä** roll, slide [down, *alas*].
vyö|ttää gird [up]. **-täiset**, **-tärö** waist.
väentungos crowd of people.
väestö population; inhabitants. **-nkasvu** increase (growth) of population; *räjähdysmäinen* ~ population explosion. **-nlaskenta** census. **-nsiirto** displacement of population. **-nsuoja** air-raid shelter. **-nsuojelu** air raid precautions

(lyh. A. R. P.); civil defence. **-ntiheys** density of population. **-politiikka** population policy. **-tilasto** vital statistics.
vähe|ksyä belittle, disparage; *(halveksia)* despise. **-mmistö** minority; *(~hallitus* minority government). **-mmyys** inferiority in numbers. **-mmän** less; *siellä oli* ~ *kuin 10 henkeä* there were fewer than ten people; ~ *arvoinen* of less value; *sitäkin* ~ so much the less. **-mpi** less; *(pienempi)* smaller; *-mmässä määrin* in a less degree. **-neminen** decrease, falling off. **-nnettävä** *mat.* minuend. **-nnys** deduction, cut, curtailment; *(~lasku* subtraction).
-ntymätön undiminished, unabated [interest, *mielenkiinto*]; undiminishing, unabating [zeal, *into*]. **-ntyä** decrease, diminish. **-ntäjä** *mat.* subtrahend. **-ntää** lessen, diminish; reduce [. . by one half, *jk puolella*]; decrease; cut [down], curtail; *(poistaa)* deduct (from), take off; *mat.* subtract, take. . from; *(arvoa ym.)* detract from; ~ *jkn palkasta* deduct from a p.'s salary; ~ *vauhtia* reduce (lessen, diminish, slacken) the speed, *(esim. juna)* slow down; *kun 7:stä -nnetään 4, jää 3* seven less *(t.* minus) 4 is 3. **-tä** lessen, grow less, diminish [in number], decrease; *olla -nemässä* be on the decrease (the decline).
vähi|mmin least; *kaikkein* ~ least of all; ~ *tarjoava* the lowest bidder.
vähimmäis- minimum. **-palkka** minimum wage.
vähi|n least; *(pienin)* smallest; ~ *määrä* minimum, smallest quantity; *ei ~täkään* not [in] the least, not in the slightest [degree]; *ei ole ~täkään epäilystä* there is no doubt whatever. **-ntään** at least, at the [very] least; *(ei alle)* not less than. . **-tellen** little by little; gradually, by degrees; *(ajan oloon)* by and by. **-ten**

[the] least; *ei* ~ not least;
..-lla oli ~ *virheitä.*. had the
fewest mistakes. **-ttäin** in
small quantities, retail; *myydä*
~ retail, sell [by] retail;
ostaa ~ buy retail. **-ttäinen**
gradual.
vähittäis|hinta retail price.
-kauppa retail business.
-kauppias retail dealer,
retailer. **-maksu** instalment;
~*lla* by instalments; *ostaa*
~*lla* buy on hire-purchase
terms; (~**järjestelmä**
hire-purchase system). **-myynti**
retail sale.
vähyys smallness; *(niukkuus)*
scarcity; shortage;
(vähälukuisuus) fewness.
vähä little; *ei* ~*äkään* not [in]
the least; ~*n päästä* at
frequent intervals, every little
while; *olla vähissä* be scarce;
vähisä varoissa in narrow
circumstances; *olla* ~*llä* come
[very] near [.. -ing],
narrowly escape; *olin* ~*llä*
myöhästyä junasta I very
nearly (I all but) missed my
train; ~*ltä piti, ettei hän*
hukkunut he came very near
drowning, he was within a
hair's breadth of drowning;
päästä ~*llä* escape (get off)
easily; ~*t siitä* never mind
[about that]! no matter!
~*äkään epäilemättä* without
the slightest hesitation.
Vähä-Aasia Asia Minor.
vähä|arvoinen. of little
value;.. of minor importance.
-eleinen unassuming. **-inen**
small; *(-pätöinen)* slight,
minor; *ei -isintäkään*
aavistusta not the remotest
(the least) idea. **-lukuinen**.
few in number. **-lukuisuus**
small number; *osanottajien* ~
the small attendance.
-mielinen *s.* imbecile.
-mielisyys imbecility.
vähä|n a little, little; *(hiukan)*
a [little] bit, a trifle; *(jnk*
verran) some; *(harvat)* few; ~
aikaa a short time, a little
while; ~ *parempi* a little (a
trifle, slightly) better; ~ *rahaa*
little money, *(jnk verran)* a

little money; *haluaisin* ~ *lisää*
teetä I should like some
more tea;.. *(vain)* ~, *jos*
ollenkaan little if any; *jäseniä*
oli liian ~ there were too
few members. **-osainen,**
-väkinen underprivileged.
-puheinen. of few words;
uncommunicative, taciturn.
-puheisuus taciturnity;
reticence. **-pätöinen** slight,
trivial, trifling [sum, *summa*];
(-arvoinen). of little
importance, unimportant,
insignificant; ~ *asia* trifle.
-pätöisyys slightness, trivial
nature; unimportance,
insignificance. **-varainen**. of
small means,.. of modest
means. **-varaisuus** lack of
means. **-verinen** an [a]emic.
-verisyys an [a]emia.
väijy|s: *olla -ksissä* lie in
ambush, lie in wait (for). **-tys**
ambush, ambuscade. **-ä** lie in
ambush (for), lie in wait
(for); *(vaania)* lurk;
(odotellen) watch [for an
opportunity, *tilaisuutta*]; ~
jkn henkeä seek a p.'s life.
väi|kkyä glimmer, gleam,
glitter; ~ *jkn mielessä* loom
before a p.; *huulilla -kkyi*
ivallinen hymy a sneer
hovered about her lips.
väis|tyä give way, yield; *(astua*
syrjään) step (move) aside;
withdraw (from), recede; ~
jkn, jnk tieltä get out of a
p.'s way, give place to; ~
väkivallan tieltä yield to
force; *minä en -ty*
askeltakaan I will not yield
an inch. **-tämätön**
unavoidable, inevitable. **-tää**
parry, fend off, ward off [a
blow, *isku*]; *(auto)* give way;
(välttää) avoid; *(mutkitellen)*
dodge, evade; *(kumartumalla)*
duck; ~ *vaara* evade the
danger.
väi|te statement, assertion,
claim; allegation; *(väittelyssä)*
argument; *lak.* plea; *pysyä*
väitteessään maintain one's
point. **-tellä** dispute, argue
(about), debate (on); ~
tohtoriksi defend one's

doctoral thesis. **-telmä** proposition; thesis. **-tetty** alleged. **-ttely** dispute, debate, argument. **-ttää** claim; state, declare; *(varmuudella)* assert, maintain; allege; ~ *vastaan* object (to), contradict, *(asettaa kyseenalaiseksi)* challenge. **-tös** claim; (~**kirja** doctoral thesis, academic dissertation; ~**tilaisuus** public defence of a thesis).

väkev|yys strength, power; intensity. **-ä** strong; powerful. **-öittää** *kem.* concentrate.

väki people, *puhek.* folks; *(miehet)* men; *kokouksessa oli vähän, paljon väkeä* the meeting was poorly (well) attended. **-joukko** crowd; mass of people, multitude. **-juoma** intoxicant; ~*t (m.)* hard liquor, alcohol [ic drinks]. **-lannoite** fertilizer. **-luku** population. **-näinen** forced, constrained. **-näisesti** in a constrained manner, affectedly. **-pakko** compulsion; *-pakolla* by force, violate; *-pyörä* pulley. **-rehu** concentrates, concentrated food *(Am.* feed). **-rikas** populous. **-rynn|äkkö** assault; *valloittaa v-äköllä* [take by] storm. **-sin** by force, forcibly. **-vallantekijä** perpetrator of an outrage. **-vallanteko** act (deed) of violence, outrage. **-vallaton** non-violent.

väkivalta violence; *tehdä ~a* commit violence, use violence. (against), commit an outrage (upon), violate; *(naiselle)* rape; *väkivalloin* by violence, by force. **-inen** violent; *-isin keinoin* by means of violence; ~ *kuolema* violent death; *saada ~ kuolema (m.)* die by violence; *lempeää ~a käyttäen* using gentle compulsion; *ei ollut ulkoisen -vallan merkkejä* there were no outward signs of violence. **-isesti** violently. **-isuus** violence; *v-suudet* [deeds of] violence. **-politiikka** policy of violence. **-rikokset** crimes of violence.

väki|viina spirits, alcohol. **-voima** ~*lla* by sheer force.

väkä barb. **-inen** barbed. **-nen** *(koukku)* hook.

väli space [between . .], interval *(m. ajasta); (aukko)* gap; *(etäisyys)* distance; ~*t (suhteet)* relations; terms; *olla hyvissä väleissä jkn kanssa* be on good terms with, get on well with; *joutua huonoihin väleihin jkn kanssa* fall out with; *selvittää ~nsä jkn kanssa* settle up with; *vähän ~ä* at frequent intervals; *every little while; jätä riittävästi ~ä* leave sufficient [blank] space; *ei sillä ~ä* it makes no difference; *mennä, tulla ~in* intervene, *(sekaantua)* interfere.

väli- intermediate. **-aika** intervening time, interval *(m. teatt.),* intermission; *lyhyin -ajoin* at short intervals. **-aikainen** temporary; provisional; ~ *hallitus* interim government. **-aikaisesti** temporarily; provisionally; for the time being; pro tempore *(lyh.* pro tem.); *hoitaa virkaa* ~ fill a position pro tem. **-aikaisuus** temporary nature; provisional character. **-aikamerkki** interval signal. **-aste** intermediate stage; transition stage. **-ensel|vittely, -vitys** showdown; settlement. **-erät** *urh.* semi-finals. **-ilmansuunta** intercardinal point.

väliin between; *(joskus)* sometimes; *jättää ~* skip; *tokaista ~* interpose; *tulla ~* intervene. **-tulo** intervention.

väli|kansi steerage. **-kappale** means, medium; *(ase)* instrument, tool. **-katto** ceiling. **-kirja** contract, agreement. **-kkö** passage, corridor. **-kohtaus** incident; intermezzo. **-korva** middle ear. **-kysymys** interpellation; *tehdä* ~ interpellate. **-käsi** intermediary, go-between; *olla pahassa -kädessä* be between the devil and the deep sea. **-lasku** intermediate landing, stop; *tehdä* ~ stop [over], make a stop[-over]; *ilman*

~*a* non-stop. **-lehti:** *-lehdillä
varustettu* interleaved. **-lle**
(*jnk*) between. . **-llinen**
indirect. **-llisesti** indirectly. **-llä**
between; ~ *oleva*
intervening,. . lying (situated)
between; *sinun pitäisi tehdä
jotakin muuta* ~ you should
do something else in between.
-matka distance; (*pieni*) space;
pienen ~*n päässä täältä* [at]
a short distance from here.
Välimeri the Mediterranean.
väli|merkki punctuation mark;
panna -merkit punctuate.
-mies arbitrator; mediator.
-muoto intermediate form;
transition. **-n:** *sillä* ~ [in
the] meantime. **-ne** (*keino*)
means; medi|um (*pl.* -a); (*ase*)
implement, appliance; ~*et*
(*m.*) equipment, apparatus.
-neistö equipment, facilities
(for). **-nen** (*jnk*).. lying
(situated) between;
(*keskinäinen*) mutual;
valtioitten ~ interstate.
välin|pitämättömyys
indifference; negligence.
-pitämättömästi indifferently,
with indifference. **-pitämätön**
indifferent, unconcerned;
uninterested; (*huolimaton*)
negligent; (*vain muodon
vuoksi jtk tekevä*) perfunctory.
väli|näytös interlude. **-pala**
[in-between] snack; *haukata*
~*a* have a s. **-pitsi** lace
insertion. **-puhe** agreement;
understanding; (*ehto*)
stipulation. **-päätös** temporary
judgment. **-rauha** truce. **-rikko**
breach, rupture, rift. **-ruoka**
intermediate course. **-sarja**
welterweight. **-seinä** partition;
erottaa ~*llä* partition off.
-sisuste interlining. **-ssä**
between; *kirjan* ~ between
the leaves of the book;
kahden tulen ~ between two
fires. **-stä** (*jnk*) [from]
between; (*toisinaan*)
sometimes. **-ttäjä** mediator;
(*välikäsi*) intermediary; *liik.*
agent, middleman, broker;
toimia ~*nä* (*m.*) act as a
go-between. **-ttävä** *kuv.*
mediatory. **-ttää 1.** (*siirtää*)

transmit, convey; *rad. m.*
relay; (*toimia välittäjänä*) act
as an intermediary (in);
(*sovittaa*) mediate;
(*neuvotellen*) negotiate;
(*järjestää*) arrange [a loan for
a p. *laina jklle*], (*uutisia ym*)
supply, (*puheluja*) connect;
(*hankkia*) provide. **2.** (*huolia*)
care, *jksta* for a p., *jstk*
about; mind; (*ottaa
huomioon*) pay attention (to);
~ *liikennettä* carry on traffic,
run, ply [between. ., *jnk
välillä*]; *hän* ~ *kiinteistöjä* he
is a real-estate agent; *hän -tti
minulle huoneiston* he found
a flat for me; *olla -ttämättä
jstk* (*m.*) disregard; ~ *viisi
jstk* not care twopence about;
ei välitä kysyä does not care
(take the trouble) to ask; *älä
välitä minusta* don't mind
me! *älä välitä siitä* never
mind [that]! **-ttömyys**
immediateness, directness;
spontaneity. **-ttömästi**
immediately, directly;
spontaneously. **-tunti** break,
recess.
välitys mediation; agency; *mek.*
transmission; *kuv.* medium;
tiedon~ news service; *hänen
-tyksellään* through him,
through his mediation, by his
good offices; *jnk v-tyksellä*
through the medium (agency)
of. **-ehdotus** proposal for
settlement. **-liike** agency. **-mies**
intermediary, mediator.
-palkkio brokerage,
commission. **-pyörä**
transmission gear. **-toimisto**
agency; broker's office.
-tuomari arbitrator. **-tuomio**
arbitration; award. **-yritys**
attempt at mediation.
välit|ön immediate; direct;
(*vaistomainen*) spontaneous;
(*luonteva*) natural, unaffected;
jnk -tömässä läheisyydessä in
close proximity to; *-tömät
verot* assessed taxes. **-tömästi**
immediately; spontaneously.
väli|vaihe intermediate stage.
-verho curtain.
välj|entää make loose [r],
loosen; enlarge. **-etä** become

loose[r]; widen. **-yys**
looseness; *(reiän ym)* calibre.
-ä loose; wide; *(vaatteista, m.)* loose-fitting.
väljäh|tyä become flat (stale); *-tynyt* flat, stale, insipid.
väl|ke gleam[ing]; glitter[ing]; brilliance. **-kkyä** gleam; glitter; glimmer; *(leimahtaa)* flash; *(säteillä)* sparkle. **-kyntä** TV flicker.
välskäri army surgeon.
väl|tellä evade. **-ttyä** escape; *(virhe)* olisi *v-ynyt* would have been avoided [if. .]; *ei voi* ~ *ajatukselta, että. .* one cannot avoid thinking that. .
välttämä|ttä necessarily; *haluta* ~ insist on [doing sth.], be determined [to know, *tietää*]. **-ttömyys** inevitability; unavoidableness; necessity; *v-myyden pakosta* of necessity. **-ttömästi** inevitably; necessarily; *(pakosta)* perforce. **-tön** inevitable, unavoidable; *(tarpeellinen)* necessary; *(jota ilman ei voi olla)* indispensable; essential; *(pakottava)* imperative; *on jnk* ~ *edellytys* is essential to. .
välttävä passable; tolerable; *(arvosanana ym)* fair; fairly good.
välttää avoid; *(onnistua välttämään)* escape; *(vältellä)* evade, elude; *(pysyä loitolla)* keep away from; ~ *jkn kohtaamista* [try to] avoid meeting a p.; *~ksenne väärinkäsityksiä* to provide against misunderstanding.
välä|hdys flash; *(vilahdus)* glimpse. **-htää** flash; *mieleeni -hti* it struck me. **-yttää** give glimpses (slants) [on. . *jtk*].
vänrikki second lieutenant.
väre ripple; *(vilun)* ~*et* shiver[s]. **-illä** ripple; shimmer; *(kuumuudesta)* quiver; *(hymy ym)* hover.
-karvat *anat.* cilia.
väri colour; *(väritys)* colouring; *(-vivahdus)* hue, tint; *(maali)* paint; *(värjäys-)* dye; *korttip.* suit. **-aine** colouring agent, pigment. **-aisti** sense of colour. **-kkyys** richness of

colour, colourfulness. **-kkäästi** in rich colours. **-kuva** coloured picture, *(kuulto-)* colour slide. **-kynä** coloured pencil; *(liitu-)* crayon, pastel. **-käs** colourful, rich in colour, [richly] coloured. **-laatikko** colour box. **-liitu** crayon. **-linen** coloured. **-loiste** brilliancy of colour[s]; *ks. · syksy*. **-malli** sample of colour. **-nauha** [typewriter] ribbon. **-nen** *(yhd. -coloured; ruohon~* grass-coloured,.. of the colour of grass. **-npitävä** fast-coloured.
värinä shiver[ing], quiver[ing]; trembling; tremor; vibration; *(välkyntä, TV)* flicker; *lääk.* fibrillation.
väri|paino colour-print[ing]. **-sokea** colour-blind. **-sokeus** colour-blindness.
väris|tys shiver, shudder; *(vapistus)* tremor. **-tä** shiver, quiver; *(vapista)* tremble; shake; ~ *kylmästä* shiver with cold; *-evä (ääni ym)* tremulous.
väri|sävy colour shade, tint. **-tehdas** dye factory; *(maali-)* paint factory. **-tön** uncoloured. **-ttää** colour; *kuv.* embellish. **-ttömyys** lack of colour. **-tys** colouring, coloration, colour. **-tyyny** inking pad. **-tön** colourless. **-valokuvaus** colour photography. **-vivahdus** shade, tinge, tint, hue.
värj|äri dyer. **-ätä** dye; *(tukka, m.)* tint; *(puuta, lasia ym. & tiet.)* stain; *(värittää)* colour; *tätä kangasta on helppo* ~ this material dyes well. **-äys** dyeing. **-äyttää** have. . dyed. **-äämätön** undyed. **-äämö** dye-works.
värjöttää be shivering, shiver.
värttinä distaff. **-luu** radius.
värv|ätä enlist; recruit; *(asiakkaita)* drum up; ~ *ääniä* canvass for votes. **-äys** enlistment. **-äytyä** enlist. **-ääjä** recruiting-sergeant; *äänten* ~ canvasser for votes.
väräh|dellä vibrate. **-dys** vibration; quiver, tremble;

(**~liike** vibratory motion, vibration; **~luku** frequency).
-dyttää cause. . to vibrate.
-tely vibration. **-tää** quiver, tremble; vibrate.
väräj|ää *(prees. 3 pers.) ks. ed.; -ävä* quivering *jne.*, vibrant; *liikutuksesta -ävällä äänellä* in a voice trembling with emotion.
västäräkki wagtail.
väsy|ksissä *ks. väsynyt.* **-mys** tiredness, weariness, fatigue; *(uupumus)* exhaustion; *-myksen tunne* tired feeling.
-mättömyys tirelessness, indefatigability. **-mättömästi** with untiring zeal, tirelessly, indefatigably. **-mätön** untiring, tireless, indefatigable; unflagging. **-neesti** wearily.
-nyt tired, *jhk* of, weary (of); fatigued; *(uupunut)* exhausted, tired out; *(raukea)* languid.
-s: *olla -ksissä* be (feel) tired.
-ttävyys wearisomeness; tiresomeness. **-ttävä** tiring, fatiguing, exhausting; *(kyllästyttävä)* tiresome. **-ttää** tire, fatigue; *(uuvuttaa)* tire out, wear out, exhaust; *minua ~ I* am (I feel) tired. **-ä** tire, get tired (weary), *jhk* of [. . -ing]; become fatigued; become exhausted; *olen -nyt siihen (m.)* I am sick of it.
väsähtää get [a little] tired; be overcome by weariness.
vätys good-for-nothing [fellow].
vävy son-in-law.
väylä channel, passage; fairway; course.
vääjäämätön undeniable; indisputable; *(peruuttamaton)* irrevocable.
vään|ne turn, twist. **-nellä** turn and twist; be twisting. **-nys:** *kasvot tuskasta -nyksissä* his face distorted by pain.
-telehtiä *(tuskissaan)* writhe; *hän v-lehti naurusta* he was convulsed with laughter. **-tyä** turn; *(kiertyä)* twist, get twisted. **-tää** turn; twist; wind; *(muodottomaksi, m. kuv.)* distort; *(kangella ym)* prise; *~ auki* turn on [the valve, *venttiili*], prise open [a

box, *laatikko*]; *~ kiinni* turn off; *~ pienemmälle* turn down [the gas, *kaasu*]; *~ poikki* twist. . off; *~ vesi vaatteista* wring out the clothes.
-töpuserrin *(pyykin)* wringer.
vääpeli sergeant 1st class.
väären|nys forgery; falsification; fake; adulteration; *konkr. m.* counterfeit. **-täjä** forger; *(rahan)* counterfeiter. **-tämätön** unadulterated; *(oikea)* genuine, real; *(alkuperäinen)* authentic.
-tää falsify; forge; *(rahaa, m.)* counterfeit; *(jtk sekoittamalla)* adulterate; *~ jkn nimi* forge a p.'s signature.
väärin wrong, wrongly, the wrong way; wrong; *(erheellisesti)* incorrectly, erroneously; *(verbien yht. usein)* mis-; *arvostella ~* misjudge; *kirjoittaa ~* misspell; *käsittää ~* misunderstand; *käyttää ~* abuse, misuse; *laulaa ~* sing out of tune; *muistaa ~* not remember. . correctly; *ellen muista ~* if I remember right[ly]; *tehdä ~* do wrong, *(jklle)* offend against a p.; *kelloni käy ~* my watch is wrong. **-käsitys** misunderstanding; misconception. **-käyttö** *(esim. alkoholin, luottamuksen)* abuse (of); misuse [of one's office, *virka-aseman*]. **-käytös** *(varojen)* misappropriation; *-käytökset* irregularities, malpractices. **-pelaaja** cheat, card-sharper. **-päin** the wrong way, wrong; *(ylösalaisin)* upside down.
vääris|tellä twist [the meaning of, *jnk merkitystä*], distort; *(esittää väärin)* misrepresent, put a false construction on, misconstrue; *(tulkita väärin)* misinterpret. **-tely** misrepresentation, perversion [of facts]. **-tyminen** *(äänen, rad.)* distortion. **-tyä** get (become) crooked (twisted), become distorted; *-tynyt* twisted, warped, distorted.
-tää make. . crooked; *(taivuttaa)* bend; *(kiertää)*

twist, *(kieroksi)* distort; *kuv.*
pervert, distort.
vääryydellinen wrongful, unjust.
vääryys crookedness; *kuv.*
injustice [to a p., *jkta
kohtaan*], wrong; iniquity;
vääryydellä by unjust (unfair)
means, wrongfully, wrongly,
unjustly; *vääryydellä saatu
(m.)* ill-gotten; *kärsiä vääryyttä*
suffer injury, be wronged;
tehdä vääryyttä jklle wrong a
p.; do sb. an injustice.
väärä *(koukistunut)* crooked;
(taipunut) bent; *(väännetty)*
twisted; *(ei oikea)* wrong,
incorrect, faulty, false [pride,
ylpeys]; *(epäoikeudellinen)*
wrongful, unfair, untrue;
(subst. ed. usein) mis-; ~
laskelma miscalculation; ~
ilmianto false information;
~ *kurkku; niellä jtk ~än
kurkkuun* swallow. . the wrong

way; ~ *kuva* wrong (false,
distorted) picture; ~ *oppi*
false doctrine; heresy; ~ *raha*
counterfeit money, false coin;
~ *tieto: olet saanut vääriä
tietoja* you have been
misinformed; ~ *todistus* false
testimony; ~*t sääret* bandy
legs; ~ *tulkinta*
misrepresentation; ~ *tuomio*
unjust sentence; *olla* ~*ssä* be
[in the] wrong, be mistaken,
be at fault; *kävellä (selkä)*
~*ssä* walk bent, stoop [as
one walks]; *osoittaa* ~*ksi*
prove. . [to be] false,
disprove [a statement, *väite*],
refute [a charge, *syytös*];
menin ~*än bussiin* I took (I
got into) the wrong bus.
-mielinen unrighteous, unjust.
-oppinen heretic [al]. **-säärinen**
bandy-legged, bow-legged.

Y

ydin marrow; *(kasvin)* pith; *kuv. m.* core, heart; *asian ~ (tav.)* the substance (the essence, the gist) of the matter; *se koskee luihin ja ytimiin* that cuts one to the quick. **-aine** medullary substance. **-ajatus** fundamental idea. **-ase** nuclear weapon; *(~koe* nuclear test; *~koekielto* nuclear test ban). **-fysiikka** nuclear physics. **-kohta** gist; heart; *(pää-)* essential point. **-kärki** *(ohjuksen)* nuclear warhead. **-luu** marrowbone. **-miilu** nuclear pile *(t.* reactor). **-sulkusopimus** nuclear non-proliferation treaty. **-taisteluvälineet** nuclear weapons.
yhdeksikkö nine.
yhdeksän nine. **-kertainen** ninefold. **-kymmentä** ninety. **-kymmenvuotias** *s.* nonagenarian. **-nes** ninth [part]. **-sataa** nine hundred. **-toista** nineteen.
yhdeksäs [the] ninth. **-kymmenes** [the] ninetieth. **-toista** [the] nineteenth.
yhden|aikainen simultaneous (with). **-kokoinen.** . of equal size;. . *ovat -kokoisia.* . are of a size, are equally large. **-lainen.** . of the same kind.
yhdenmukai|nen uniform; symmetric [al]; consistent; analogous; *ne ovat keskenään -set (m.)* they conform to each other. **-sesti** uniformly; in accordance (with). **-staa** standardize, bring into line. **-suus** uniformity; conformity; symmetry; analogy.
yhden|näköinen similar [in appearance].. . *like; vrt. saman-.* **-näköisyys** similarity of appearance; *heidän*

y-syytensä their resemblance to each other. **-suuntainen** parallel. **-suuntaisesti** parallel; *kulkea ~* run parallel. **-tekevä.** . just (all) the same; *se on ~ä* it makes no difference, it does not matter, it is all the same [to me], it is immaterial [whether. .]; *kaikki on hänelle ~ä* he is indifferent to everything. **-tyminen** integration. **-tyä** be [come] integrated. **-tää** integrate. **-vertainen.** . on a level,. . on a par; *(tasa-)* equal; equally good; *he ovat -vertaisia* they are equals. **-vertaisuus** equality.
yhdessä together; *toimia ~* co-operate, collaborate, act in concert; *kaikki ~ (m.)* in a body.
yhdestoista [the] eleventh; *yhdennellätoista hetkellä* at the e. hour.
yhdis|te *kem.* compound. **-tellä** combine. **-telmä** combination; [two-(three-)piece] set; *pusero-ja villatakki~* twin set. **-tys** association; *(seura)* society. **-tyä** be united, unite; combine; join; *Yhdistyneet Kansakunnat (Y.K.)* United Nations (U.N.). **-tää** unite, *jhk* to, with; unify; combine; connect; *(liittää yhteen)* join (to, with), attach (to); link up, link together; *(Haaga) -tettiin Helsinkiin* was incorporated into Helsinki; *Itävalta -tettiin Saksaan v. 1938* Austria was annexed by Germany in 1938; *-tetty* kilpailu Nordic Combined.
yhdyn|näinen compound [word]. **-tä** *(sukupuoli-)* coitus, sex act.
yhdys|elämä life together.

-kunta community. **-linja** *sot.*
line of communication. **-mies**
contact man. **-sana** compound
[word]. **-side** [connecting]
link, bond (between), tie.
-upseeri liaison officer.
Y-vallat the United States,
lyh. the U.S. [A.]. **-viiva**
hyphen; *liittää ~lla* hyphen.
yht|aikaa at the same time
[as, *kuin*], simultaneously
(with); *kaikki ~ (m.)* all at
once; *tapahtua ~* coincide.
-aikainen simultaneous,
coincidental.
yhteen together; *juottaa ~* join
by soldering; *kuuluua ~* belong
together; *laskea ~* add up,
add together; *liittää ~* join
[.. together], unite,
(kiinnittää) fasten. . together,
(kuv.) link; *ottaa ~* clash,
come to blows, join battle
with; *sattua ~* coincide,
(tavata) happen to meet;
sopia ~ go [well] with, *jnk
kanssa; ~ kertaan* once. **-ajo**
collision. **-kuuluva.** . belonging
together, associated.
-kuuluvuus solidarity; *y-uuden
tunne* feeling of togetherness.
-laskettu added [up]; *~
summa* sum total. **-lasku**
addition; *(-laskeminen)* adding
up; *(~tehtävä* sum).
-liittyminen union; coalition.
-otto clash, encounter;
confrontation. **-sattuma**
coincidence. **-sopimaton**
incompatible, inconsistent
(with). **-sulattaminen** fusion.
-sä altogether, in all; put
tehden ~. . making a total
of. **-törmäys** collision, crash.
-veto summary, abstract,
resumé; *esittää ~na*
summarize.
yhtei|nen common,. . in
common; joint [responsibility,
vastuu]; *~ ilo* general
rejoicing; *~ kansa* the
common people; *~ ystävämme*
our mutual friend; *-sin
ponnistuksin* with united
(concerted) efforts. **-sesti** in
common, jointly;
together.
yhteis|henki [spirit of]
solidarity; community spirit.
-hyvä common good, public
welfare. **-kasvatus**
co-education. **-koulu** mixed
[secondary] school,
co-educational school.
-kunnallinen social; *~ asema*
social status; *~ vaara* social
menace.
yhteiskunnanvastainen antisocial.
yhteiskunta society; community.
-asema social position. **-elämä**
community life. **-järjestys**
social order. **-kerros** stratum
(pl. strata) of society. **-luokka**
social class. **-olot** social
conditions. **-oppi** civics.
-rakenne social structure.
-tiede social science, sociology.
yhteis|laukaus volley, salvo;
ampua ~ fire a volley. **-laulu**
community singing. **-majoitus**
dormitory accommodation.
-markkinat: *Euroopan ~* the
Common Market, EEC.
-mitallinen *mat.*
commensurable. **-määrä** total
amount. **-omaisuus** common
property. **-rahasto** joint security.
-toimi|nta co-operation; joint
(united, concerted) action;
team-work; *olla y-nnassa jkn
kanssa* co-operate with. **-tunne**
fellow-feeling; feeling of
solidarity. **-työ** joint work,
team-work; co-operation,
collaboration; *(~haluinen,
~kykyinen* co-operative).
-verotus joint taxation.
-voimat: *~voimin* with united
forces. **-ymmär|rys** mutual
understanding; *päästä
y-rykseen* come to an
understanding (to terms). **-yys**
community; *omaisuuden ~*
joint ownership. **-ö**
community.
yhtenäi|nen uniform; consistent;
homogeneous; *(sarja ym.)*
connected, *(jatkuva)*
continuous. **-skoulu**
comprehensive school. **-stää**
co-ordinate; unify. **-syys**
uniformity, consistency;
coherence; unity.
yhtenään continuously;
constantly.
yhtey|s connection *(Engl. m.*

connexion); association; *(teksti-)* context; *(kulku-)* communication, service; *(kosketus)* contact; *(suhde)* relation; fellowship, unity; *olla -dessä jnk kanssa* be connected with, have a connection with, *(esim. kirjeenvaihto-)* communicate with, *(esim. liike-)* have [business] connections with; *sen -dessä* in connection (in conjunction) with that; *joutua lähempään -teen jkn kanssa* get into closer contact (touch) with, become more closely connected (associated) with; *asettua -teen jkn kanssa* communicate with, get into touch with; *pitää -ttä* maintain communication, keep in contact (with); *katkaista vihollisen yhteydet* cut off the enemy's communications; *pyhäin ~* communion of saints. **-ttää** assimilate.

yhtiö company, *Am.* corporation. **-järjestys** articles of association. **-kokous** meeting of shareholders, *(vuosi-)* annual general meeting. **-kumppani** partner; *ruveta jkn ~ksi* enter into partnership with.

yhtye *mus.* band.

yhtymä union; *liik.* concern, combine. **-kohta** point of contact; *(esim. rautateiden)* junction; *(kahden viivan)* point of convergence.

yhtyä unite, be united; combine; join [each other]; join [the party, *seuraan;* in the praise of.. *ylistämään jtk*]; *(mielipiteeseen)* agree with; *~ lauluun* join in the singing; *~ lausuntoon* endorse (concur in) a statement; *tiemme yhtyvät* our ways meet; *pankit yhtyvät* the banks merge.

yhtä equally; [just] as good as, *hyvä kuin; ~ aikaa* at once, at he same time; simultaneously [with, *kuin*]; *~ helposti* just as easily, with equal ease; *~ kaikki* even so, still; *~ suuri (m.)..* equal in

size,.. of equal size; *~ suuri kuin..* as large as.., [of] the same size as.., equal to.. in size. **-jaksoinen** continuous; *(keskeytymätön)* unbroken. uninterrupted. **-jaksoisesti** continuously; without a break. **-jaksoisuus** continuity; unbroken sequence.

yhtäkkiä suddenly, all of a sudden, all at once; abruptly; *pysähtyä ~* stop short, come to a sudden standstill.

yhtä|**läinen**.. of the same kind, similar; *(sama)* identical; *~ äänioikeus* equal suffrage. **-läisesti** in the same manner, in like manner, similarly. **-läisyys** resemblance, similarity; *(~merkki* equation sign). **-lö** *mat.* equation. **-mittaa** *(alituisesti)* continually, constantly. **-mittainen** unbroken, uninterrupted; continuous. **-pitämättömyys** discrepancy. **-pitämätön..** not in agreement (with); incompatible. **-pitävyys** agreement, conformity. **-pitävä** *(jnk kanssa)* in accordance with, consistent with, compatible with; *ne ovat -pitäviä* they agree (are in agreement). **-pitävästi** uniformly, in conformity (with).

yht|**äällä, -äänne** in one direction. **-ään** any; *ei ~* not at all, not a bit, not any [better, *parempi*].

yhä *(vielä)* still; *(alituisesti)* ever, continually; *~ enemmän* more and more; *~ eneneva* ever-increasing, ever-growing; *~ harvemmin* more and more rarely; *~ kasvava* continually (constantly) growing; *~ paremmin* better and better; *~ uudelleen* over and over again, again and again, repeatedly; *on ~ kohoamassa* continues to rise. **-ti** ever, continually, perpetually.

ykkönen one.

ykseys unity.

yksi one; a; *(ainoa)* only, sole; a single; *~ ja sama* one and the same; *~ ja toinen* a few

people; *yhden hengen huone*
single [bed]room; *yhdestä
suusta* with one voice,
unanimously; *yhtenä miehenä*
to a man; *olivat yhtä mieltä*
were of the same opinion,
[they] agreed (on, about
sth.); ~*n tein* at the same
time; ~*ssä neuvoin jkn
kanssa* jointly with.. .; ~
*kaikkien ja kaikki yhden
puolesta* all for each and
each for all, jointly and
severally; *ei yhdessäkään
talossa* not in a single house.
-avioinen monogamous.
-avioisuus monogamy.
-jumalaisuus monotheism.
-kamarijärjestelmä one-chamber
system. **-kantaan**
monotonously. **-kerroksinen**
one-storey [ed]. **-kielinen ..** in
one language only;
(henkilöstä ..) speaking one
language only. **-kkö** unit; *kiel.*
singular; (~*hinta* price per
unit; ~*muoto* singular form,
singular). **-köllinen** singular.
-lö individual. **-löllinen**
individual; individualistic.
-löllisyys individuality.
-mielinen unanimous; ~
mielipide consensus of
opinion; *he ovat y-mieliset
(siitä, että)* they are agreed
that.. **-mielisesti** unanimously,
by common consent; *toteavat
~ agree in stating.* **-mielisyys**
unanimity; *(sopu)* unity,
concord; ~ *on voimaa* united
we stand, divided we fall;
päästä y-syyteen jstk come to
an agreement (an
understanding) about, agree
upon; *varsin suuri ~ vallitsee
siitä, että* there is general
agreement that. .
yksin alone; by oneself;
(ainoastaan) only; ~ *senkin
hän tietää* he knows even
that; *hän ~ sen tietää* he
alone knows it; *hänestä ~
riippuu* it depends on him
alone; *hän teki tämän aivan
~ (ilman apua)* he did it
single-handed, she did it on
her own. **-huoltajaperhe**
one-parent family.

yksineuvoinen unisexual.
yksinkertai|nen simple,
uncomplicated; *(ei
moninkertainen)* single;
(vaatimaton) plain [dinner,
päivällinen); *(henkilöstä)*
simple-minded; *(lapsellinen)*
naïve; *kirjanp.* [book-keeping]
by single entry. **-sesti** simply;
plainly. **-staa** simplify.
-staminen simplification. **-suus**
simplicity; plainness.
yksin|laulu solo singing; solo.
-lento solo flight. **-oikeus**
exclusive rights, monopoly;
-omaan exclusively, solely; ~
siitäkin syystä if only for
that reason, for that reason
alone. **-omainen** exclusive;
sole. **-puhelu** soliloquy;
monologue. **-tanssi** solo
dancing. **-valta** autocracy;
monarchy. **-valtainen**
autocratic. **-valtias** autocrat;
monarch, sovereign.
yksi|näinen lonely; solitary
[place, *paikka)*; *(syrjäinen)*
secluded; *(naimaton)* single; ~
äiti unmarried mother.
-näisyys loneliness, solitude;
isolation; seclusion; *y-syyden
tunteen valtaama* engulfed by
a sense of loneliness. **-nään**
alone, by oneself;
unaccompanied; on one's own;
matkustin sinne -näni I went
there on my own; *aivan ~*
all alone. **-näytöksinen** one-act
[play, *näytelmä]*. **-oikoinen**
uncomplicated. **-puolinen**
one-sided; unilateral.
-puolisuus one-sidedness.
-rivinen *(takki)* single-
breasted. **-selitteinen**
unambiguous. **-stään** alone; *jo
~ vuokra* the rent alone. *jo*
-suuntainen: ~ *liikenne*
one-way traffic. **-taso**
monoplane. **-tavuinen** of one
syllable, monosyllabic. **-tellen**
one at a time; one by one.
-toikkoinen monotonous;
unvaried. **-toikkoisuus**
monotony; sameness. **-toista**
eleven. **-totinen** serious.
-ttäinen, -ttäis- single,
individual. **-tyinen** private;
(erikoinen) special, individual.

yksityis|alue: *-alueelle
tunkeutuminen (kuv.)* invasion
of privacy. **-asia** private
(personal) matter; *se on
kunkin ~ (m.)* that is
everybody's own affair.
-asunto private dwelling. **-auto**
private car. **-elämä** private
life; *~n suoja* safeguarding of
privacy. **-henkilö** private
person. **-kohdittain** in detail,
minutely. **-kohta** detail,
particular; item; *mennä
-kohtiin* enter *(t.* go) into
details. **-kohtainen** detailed;
minute, circumstantial.
-kohtai|sesti in detail;
minutely, circumstantially;
y-semmin in greater detail.
-koulu private school. **-käyttö:**
~ varten for personal use.
-omaisuus private property.
-opettaja private teacher,
tutor, coach. **-seikka** detail.
-sihteeri private secretary.
-tapaus individual case. **-tunti**
private lesson. **-yritteliäisyys**
private enterprise. **-yrittäjä**
entrepreneur.

yksi|vakainen grave, serious.
-vuotias one year old; *~ lapsi*
one-year-old child, child of
one. **-vuotinen** one-year
[course, *kurssi*],.. lasting one
year; *~ kasvi* annual [plant].
-värinen. of one colour;
plain [material, *kangas*],
-ääninen one-part [song]; *~
laulu* singing in unison. **-ö**
[one-room] flatlet.

yleensä in general, generally;
as a rule; *~ katsoen* taken
as a whole; on the whole.

ylei|nen general; *~ mielipide*
public opinion; *~ sääntö*
general (universal) rule; *~ tie*
public highway; *tulla -seen
käyttöön* come into general
use; *-sessä käytössä* in
common use; *on -sesti
tunnettua* it is common
knowledge.

yleis|avain master key.
-esikunta general staff. **-esti**
generally, in general;
universally; *~ ottaen (puhuen)*
by and large, generally
(broadly) speaking; *~*

tavattava. . of common (of
frequent) occurrence.
-eurooppalainen pan-European.
-hyödyllinen. . for the public
good; for purposes of public
utility. **-inhimillinen:** *y-lliseltä
näkökannalta (katsoen)* from
the point of view of
humanity. **-katsaus** [general]
survey (of). **-kieli** standard
(sivistynyt: polite) language.
-kokous general assembly.
-kone *(keittiön)* food mixer.
-kustannukset overhead costs,
overheads. **-kuva** overall view
(of). **-käsitys** general idea.
-lakko general strike.
-luontoinen general. **-lääke**
universal remedy; panacea.
-lääkäri general practitioner.
-maailmallinen universal. **-nero**
universal genius. **-piirre**
general feature. **-pätevyys**
universal applicability. **-pätevä**
generally applicable,. . of
universal application. **-radio**
broadcasting company, *Engl.*
the British Broadcasting
Corporation *(lyh.* BBC).
-silmäys survey, *jhk* of; *luoda
~ jhk* survey. ., make a
survey of. **-sivistys** all-round
education. **-tajuinen** popular.
-tiedot general knowledge.
-tyminen: *autojen ~* the
increasing frequency of cars.
-tyä become [more] common
(frequent). **-tää** generalize.
-urheilija athlete. **-urheilu**
Engl. athletics, *Am.*
track-and-field sports,
track [and field];
(**~kilpailut** athletics
meeting; **~maaottelu** athletics
international). **-vaikutelma**
general impression. **-yys**
frequency, commonness;
universality.

yleisö [the] public; *(teatteri-
ym.)* audience; *suuri ~* the
general public. **-menestys**
public success;.. *lla oli suuri
~* .. was a great success.
-määrä attendance. **-nosasto**
letters to the editor.

ylelli|nen luxurious;
extravagant; sumptuous [meal,
ateria]; *viettää -stä elämää*

lead a luxurious life, live extravagantly. **-syys** luxury; extravagance; (~**tavarat** luxuries.

ylemmyys superiority. **ylem|mä(ksi)** higher [up], farther up; (yli) above; muita ~ above the rest. **-pi** upper, top. **-pänä** higher [up], farther up; above. **-pää** from higher (farther) up.

ylen extremely, exceedingly; (sangen) very; highly; ~ määrin abundantly, (liikaa) excessively; ~ onnellinen exceedingly happy, overjoyed. **-katse** contempt, scorn. **-katseellinen** scornful, contemptuous, disdainful. **-katseellisesti** scornfully, slightingly; with an air of superiority. **-katsoa** despise; disdain; (väheksyä) look down upon, slight, hold cheap; -katsoen with scorn, with contempt. **-määrin** ks. ylen; hänellä on ~ töitä he is snowed under with work. **-määräinen** excessive;.. beyond measure; y-isen kohtelias overpolite; y-isen työn rasittama (m.) worn out with overwork.

ylennys promotion, advancement, (palkan-) rise, increase [of salary]; (~**peruste** basis for promotion). **ylen|palttinen** abundant, profuse; excessive. **-palttisuus** superabundance, excess. **-syöminen** overeating. **ylentää** raise; elevate; (virassa) promote; hänet ylennettiin kapteeniksi he was promoted captain; tulla ylennetyksi be promoted, obtain (win) promotion. **ylettö|myys** immoderation, exorbitance; excess [iveness]. **-mästi** immoderately; beyond measure, excessively. **yletä** rise [in rank, arvossa], be promoted. **yletön** (kohtuuton) immoderate, unreasonable; (liiallinen) excessive; extravagant; vaatia ylettömiä make unreasonable (exorbitant) demands.

ylev|yys loftiness, sublimity; nobleness. **-ä** lofty, high; exalted, sublime; (~**mielinen** high-minded, noble-minded, magnanimous; noble; ~**mielisyys** high-mindedness, noble-mindedness, magnanimity.

ylhäi|nen noble; high-born; (korkea) high, lofty. **-ssukuinen**. . of high (of noble) birth. **-ssukuisuus** noble birth. **-syys** highness; hänen -syytensä His Excellency. **-sö** the upper classes, (ylimystö) aristocracy.

ylhää|lle up; high. **-llä** [high] up; hyvin ~ at a great height (altitude); tuolla ~ up there; (kuvassa) oikealla ~ top right. **-ltä** from above; from the top.

yli over; above; more than; ~ koko. . all over [the world]; summa oli ~. . the sum exceeded. . (was in excess of. .); joen ~ vievä silta the bridge across the river; käy ~ ymmärrykseni is beyond my comprehension. **-aika** overtime. **-aistillinen** supersensual. **-ajo** running over. **-arvioida** overestimate, overrate. **-arviointi** overestimation.

yli|herra overlord. **-herruus** supremacy, dominance. **-hinta:** ~an [buy. .] at a fancy price. **-hoitaja** (johtava) director of nursing service, Engl. m. matron. **-huomenna, -huominen** the day after tomorrow. **-ihminen** superman. **-ikäinen** superannuated,. . over age,. . above the prescribed age. **-inhimillinen** superhuman. **-insinööri** chief engineer. **-johtaja** [deputy] director general. **-johto** sot. high command. **-jäämä** surplus; excess. **-jäänyt** remaining, residual,. . left over. **-kansallinen** supranational. **-kansoittunut** overpopulated. **-kansoitus** overpopulation. **-kersantti** Senior Sergeant. **-kulku** crossing; passage [over]; (~**silta** flyover, overpass). **-kuormittaa**

overload. **-kuormitus**
overload[ing]. **-käytävä** *(taso-)*
level crossing. **-luoden:**
ommella ~ overcast.
-luonnollinen supernatural.
-luonnollisuus supernatural
character. **-lääkäri** chief *(t.*
head) physician, chief surgeon.
-maallinen superterrestrial;
transcendental. **-malkaan** as a
rule, generally; on the whole.
-malkainen general;
(lähentelevä) approximate,
rough; *(sattumanvarainen)*
haphazard, casual; *-malkaisesti*
generally, in a general way,
in a summary fashion.
-malkaisuus casual (summary)
character. **-menokausi** *ks.
siirtymä-.* **-mielinen** arrogant.
presumptuous. **-mielisyys**
arrogance; presumptuousness;
haughtiness. **-mmilleen:** *nousta*
~ reach its greatest height
(intensity), reach its climax.
-mmillään at its highest, at
its greatest height; at its
peak. **-muistoi|nen:** *y-sista
ajoista* from time immemorial.
-mmäinen *ks. ylin;* ~ *pappi*
high priest. **-myksellinen**
aristocratic. **-mys** aristocrat.
-mystö aristocracy. **-määräinen**
extra, extraordinary; special;
~ *juna* special train. **-n**
uppermost, topmost, top
[storey, *kerros*]; *(korkein)*
highest, *kuv.* supreme, chief;
~ *johto* supreme command.
-nen *a.* upper; *s. (ullakko)*
loft, attic. **-nnä** uppermost, at
the top, highest. **-nopeus**
speeding. **-olkainen**
supercilious; nonchalant.
-opettaja senior teacher.
yliopisto university *(-ssa* at);
college; *kirjoittautua ~on*
matriculate. **-kaupunki**
university town. **-llinen**
academic [al], university.
-opinnot university studies.
-piirit academic circles.
-sivistys university education.
ylioppilas university student;
undergraduate; *oikeustieteen* ~
law student; *y-laana ollessani
(m.)* during my college years;
päästä y-laaksi qualify for

entrance to a university.
-kirjoitukset written
examination for entrance to a
university. **-koti** students'
hostel. **-kunta** students' union.
-lakki student's cap. **-todistus**
higher school certificate.
-tutkinto higher school
examination; *suorittaa* ~
Engl. pass the examination
for the G.C.E. (General
Certificate of Education) at A
(Advanced) level.
yli|ote advantage; *saada* ~ get
the upper hand, *jksta* of.
-paino excess weight; *~maksu*
charge for excess luggage.
-painoinen overweight.
-päällikkö commander-in-chief.
-päällikkyys supreme
command. **-päänsä** on the
whole; generally, in general;
tietääkö hän ~ *mitään* does
he know anything at all.
-pääsemätön insurmountable,
insuperable.
ylis|tys praise; *(~laulu* song of
praise; *~puhe* eulogy). **-tää**
praise, *(jkta, m.)* eulogize,
extol, sing the praises of;
(kirkastuttaa) glorify; *(runossa,
laulussa)* celebrate. . in song;
~ *pilviin asti* praise. . to the
skies.
yli|tarjonta oversupply.
-tarkastaja chief inspector.
ylitse over; across. **-kuohuva**
gushing. **-vuotava** overflowing;
exuberant.
ylittää exceed; surpass;
(valtuus) overstep; *(katu ym)*
cross; ~ *sallittu nopeus*
exceed the speed limit; *älä
ylitä tietä* don't cross the
road; *(hän) ylitti itsensä*
excelled himself.
yli|tuomari chief justice.
-tuotanto over-production. **-tys**
(tilin) overdraft; *(meren)*
crossing. **-työ** overtime work;
tehdä ~tä work overtime.
-valotettu overexposed. **-valta**
supremacy. **-valvoja** supervisor,
superintendent. **-valvonta**
supervision, superintendence.
-viinuri head waiter. **-voima**
superior power, superior
force; *väistyä ~n tieltä* yield

to superior numbers; *taistella (suurta) ~a vastaan* fight against [overwhelming] odds. **-voimainen** superior [in force, in strength, in numbers]; overpowering; *käydä jklle y-aiseksi* become too much for a p., overwhelm a p.; *suru oli hänelle ~* she was overcome by grief; *y-isin ponnistuksin* by superhuman efforts; *y-isesti* predominantly; *y-aisesti paras* by far the best. **-vääpeli** Master Sergeant.

ylkä bridegroom.

ylle on; *pukea ~nsä* put on [one's clothes]; dress [oneself], get dressed.

yllin kyllin enough and to spare.

ylly|ke incitement, incentive; *antaa ~ttä* encourage, give impetus to. **-ttäjä** inciter, instigator. **-ttää** incite; urge; egg on; instigate [sb. to crime, *jkta rikokseen*]. **-tys** inciting, incitement; agitation.

yllä above; *(päällä)* on, upon; *kuten ~ on sanottu* as stated (as mentioned) above; *(olla ~(än)* wear. **-esitetty**.. given (stated, cited) above. **-kkötarkastus** raid. **-mainittu** above-mentioned. **-oleva** the above. **-pito** maintenance, support; upkeep; sustenance; *(~kustannukset* cost of maintenance). **-pitää** maintain, support; keep up; sustain; *~ järjestystä* maintain (keep, preserve) order.

yllä|ttyä be surprised, be taken by surprise. **-ttää** surprise, take.. unawares (by surprise); *~ jku varastamasta* catch a p. stealing; *yö -tti meidät* we were overtaken by night. **-tyksellinen** surprising; startling. **-tys** surprise; *(~hyökkäys* surprise attack).

ylp|eillä be proud, *jstk* of, take pride (in). **-eys** pride; haughtiness. **-eä** proud, *jstk* of; haughty; *puhek.* high and mighty, stuck-up.

yltiö fanatic. **-harras** bigoted. **-isänmaallinen** chauvinistic. **-isänmaallisuus** chauvinism.

-päinen fanatic [al]. **-päisyys** fanaticism. **-pää** fanatic.

ylt'|yleensä all over. **-ympäri** all over [the floor, *lattiaa*], everywhere.

yltyä increase [in violence]; *(pakkasesta ym)* get more intense, grow in intensity; *tuuli yltyy* the wind in rising.

yltä [from] above; at (from) the top; *(pois)* off; *riisua ~än* take off [one's clothes]; *~ päältä* wholly, altogether, all over. **-kyllin** more than enough, enough and to spare, plenty (of); an abundance (of); *rahaa on ~* money is plentiful. **-kylläinen** profuse, plentiful; *(runsas)* copious, abundant; *(ylen ravittu)*.. more than satisfied, surfeited. **-kylläisyys** abundance; *(vauraus)* affluence.

yltää reach; *~ jhk saavutukseen* achieve a result.

ylväs proud, lordly; *(jalo)* noble. **-telijä** boaster. **-tellä** pride oneself (on); *(kerskailla)* boast (of); *~ hienoilla vaatteillaan* parade one's fine clothes. **-tely** boasting; swanking.

ylä upper; superior, higher. **-hanka** windward. **-huone** *(Engl. parl.)* the Upper House, the House of Lords. **-huuli** upper lip. **-ilma:** *yläilmoissa (kuv.)* in higher spheres. **-juoksu** upper course, headwaters. **-kansi** upper deck. **-kerros, -kerta** upper stor[e]y, top stor[e]y; *yläkerrassa* on the top floor, upstairs. **-leuka** upper jaw. **-luokka** *(koulun)* higher form. *Am.* upper grade. **-luokkalainen** pupil in (of) a higher class (form, grade). **-maa** highlands; upland[s]. **-mäki** ascent, rise; uphill road; *-mäkeä* uphill. **ylänkö** highlands, uplands; *(~maa* high *t.* elevated land). **ylä|osa** upper part, top; *(~ton* topless). **ylä|pinta** upper surface, top. **-puolella** *(jnk)* above; *on kaiken kiitoksen ~* is beyond praise; *pöydän ~ (m.)* over

the table. **-puolelle** above.
-puolelta [from] above. **-puoli**
upper side, top. **-pää** upper
end, top. **-reuna** upper edge.
-ruumis upper part of the
body, trunk. **-tasanko** plateau,
tableland. **-vä** elevated.
ylös up, upwards; *jtk* ~ up a
th. **-alaisin** upside down, the
wrong side up; *(mullin
mallin)* topsy-turvy; *(kumoon)*
over; *kääntää* ~ *(m.)* upset.
-nousemus resurrection. **-päin**
upwards; (~**kääntynyt** . turned
up, bent upwards).
ymmä|lle: *joutua* ~ become
perplexed, become bewildered;
saattaa ~ perplex, bewilder,
disconcert. **-llä** perplexed,
bewildered, confused; *olla* ~
(m.) be at a loss [what to
do]; (~**olo** perplexity,
confusion).
ymmär|rettävyys intelligibility.
-rettävä intelligible,
comprehensible; *helposti* ~
easy to understand, readily
understandable. **-rettävästi**
intelligibly; understandably.
-rys understanding;
intelligence; intellect;. reason;
täyttä ~*tä vailla* non compos
mentis. **-tämys** understanding;
sympathy; *-tämyksen puute*
lack of understanding.
-tämättömyys lack of
judg[e]ment, lack of
[common] sense;
(ajattelemattomuus)
indiscretion. **-tämätön**
injudicious, unwise;
(ajattelematon) indiscreet;
(tyhmä) foolish; *on* ~ lacks
understanding. **-täväinen**
understanding; sensible.
-täväisyys [good] sense,
sensibleness. **-tää** understand,
(käsittää) comprehend; grasp,
realize; *(tajuta)* see; *en* ~*tänyt,
mitä hän sanoi (m.)* I did
not catch what he said;
minun ~*kseni* as far as I
understand [the matter], as
far as I can see; ~ *väärin*
misunderstand; get a wrong
(a mistaken) idea [of,
about]; *en voinut* ~
(kirjoitusta) I could not make

it out; *minun annettiin* ~ I
was given to understand.
ymppäys grafting.
ympy|riäinen round, circular.
-rä circle; (~**nmuotoinen**
circular).
ympäri [a]round, about; ~
maata all over the country;
~ *vuoden* throughout (all
through) the year; *kääntyä* ~
turn round, *(esim. auto tiellä)*
make a U-turn; ~*llä oleva.* .
lying about (around),
surrounding; *katsella* ~*lleen*
look about one; *kerääntyä jkn*
~*lle* gather (flock) around a
p.; *kaupungin* ~*llä on vuoria*
the city is surrounded by
hills. **-leikkaus** circumcision.
-lle, -llä *ks. ympäri.*
-purjehdus circumnavigation.
-stö environment;
surroundings; setting; *(lähistö)*
neighbourhood, vicinity,
environs; (~**nsuojelija**
conservationist, environ-
mentalist; ~**nsuojelu**
environmental control *(t.*
protection, the Environment).
-vuorokautinen round-the-
clock.
ympärys circumference; *(kehä)*
periphery; *rinnan, vyötäisten*
~ chest (waist) measurement.
-mitta *ks. ed.*
ympäröidä surround; enclose,
encircle; envelop; ~ *jk aidalla*
fence in.
ympätä *(oksastaa)* graft (on).
ynistä *(lehmä)* low, moo.
ynnä and; [together] with;
mat. plus; ~ *muuta (ym)* et
cetera, etc.
ynse|ys disobligingness;
unfriendliness. **-ä** disobliging,
unobliging; unkind[ly],
ill-disposed (towards).
ypö: ~ *yksin* utterly alone.
yritteli|äisyys [spirit of]
enterprise. **-äs** enterprising.
yrittäjä enterpreneur.
yri|ttää attempt, try, make an
effort, endeavour; ~ *parastaan*
do one's best, take pains,
(kaikin voimin) go all out;
anna minun ~ let me have a
try (a go)! *ei yrittänyttä
laiteta* there's no harm in

trying. **-tys** attempt; ·
(pyrkimys) effort, endeavour;
trial; *(liike-)* undertaking,
enterprise; *ensi yrityksellä* at
the first attempt; *uhkarohkea*
~ [bold] venture; *pako~*
attempt at flight, attempted
escape; *(~demokratia*
industrial democracy).
yrmeä cross [-grained], morose.
yrtti herb.
ysk|iä cough. **-ä** cough;
ymmärrän ~n I can take the
hint; *(~nkaramelli* cough-drop,
cough lozenge). **-ös**
expectoration, sputum.
ystävys: *y-vykset* friends,
puhek. chums. **-tyä** make
friends, become friendly, *jkh*
with, befriend a p.
ystävyydenosoitus token of
friendship.
ystävyys friendship; *(läheinen)*
close friendship, intimacy;
~- ja avunantosopimus Pact of
Amity, Co-operation and
Support. **-ottelu** friendly game.
-side tie (bond) of friendship.
-suhde friendly relations.
ystävä friend; *erota ystävinä*
part friends; *hän on hyvä*
~ni he is a good (a great)
friend of mine. **-llinen** kind,
kindly; friendly; amicable,
affable; *saksalais~*
pro-German. **-llisesti** kindly,
in a friendly manner.
-llismielinen friendly. **-llisyys**
kind [li] ness, friendliness,
gentleness. **-piiri** circle of
friends. **-tär** [woman, girl]
friend.

ytime|kkyys *kuv.* pithiness;
terseness. **-käs** *kuv.* pithy;
terse. **-ttömyys** *kuv.* lack of
pithiness, staleness. **-tön** *kuv.*
insipid, stale, flat.
yö night; *yöllä* at (by) night,
in the night; *yötä päivää* day
and night; *olla yötä* spend
(pass, stay) the night [at a
place, with sb.]; *jäädä yöksi*
stay (stop) overnight, stop for
the night; *hyvää yötä* good
night! **-astia** chamber [-pot].
-hoitaja night nurse.
-juna night train. **-kausi:**
yökaudet night in and night
out. **-kerho** night-club. **-kylmä**
night frost. **-lamppu** bedside
lamp. **-lepo** night's rest.
-llinen nightly, nocturnal.
-maja doss house, casual
ward;~night shelter. **-nuttu**
dressing-gown. **-paita** *(naisen)*
night-gown, *puhek.* nighty.
-perhonen moth. **-puku**
night-dress, pyjamas, *Am.*
pajamas. **-puu:** *mennä ~lle* go
to bed.
yöpyä stay (stop) overnight;
(olla yötä) spend (pass) the
night (at).
yö|pöytä bedside table. **-sija**
lodging for the night; *antaa*
~ put sb. up for the night.
-sydän midnight; *~nä* in the
dead of night. **-työ**
night-work. **-uni** night's sleep.
-vartija night-watchman.
-valvonta vigil. **-vartio**
night-watch. **-vieras** guest for
the night. **-vuoro** night-shift;
~ssa (m.) on night duty.

Ä

äes, -tää harrow.

ähky *lääk.* colic.

äidilli|nen motherly, maternal. **-sesti** in a motherly way; with motherly affection. **-syys** motherliness.

äidin|ilo a mother's joy, maternal joy. **-kieli** mother (*t.* native) tongue. **-maito** mother's milk; *ä-maidolla ruokittu* breast-fed. **-perintö** maternal inheritance. **-rakkaus** mother love. **-vaisto** maternal instinct.

äijä old man.

äitel|yys [cloying] sweetness. **-ä** [sickly] sweet, cloying, *kuv.* mawkish.

äiti mother; *äidin puolelta* on the mother's side. **-enpäivä** Mother's day. **-puoli** stepmother. **-vainaja** deceased mother. **-ys** motherhood, maternity; (~avustus maternity benefit; ~huolto maternity welfare; ~kasvatus, ~opetus mothercraft).

äke|ys vehemence; crossness. **-ä** (*kiivas*) vehement; (*äreä*) cross, crusty; angry.

äkilli|nen sudden, abrupt [departure, *lähtö*]; precipitate; (*hätäinen*) hasty, (*taudista*) acute. **-sluontoinen** acute. **-syys** suddenness, abruptness.

äkisti suddenly, all of a sudden.

äkki|arvaamaton unforeseen, unlooked-for; (*odottamaton*) unexpected. **-arvaamatta** unexpectedly; when least expected; unawares, all of a sudden. **-jyrkkä** precipitous, abrupt, steep; *on ~ (m.)* descends abruptly. **-jyrkänne** precipice. **-käänne** sharp (sudden, abrupt) turn; (*mutka*) sharp bend (curve). **-näinen**

hasty, hurried; (*äkillinen*) sudden; abrupt. **-näisyys** suddenness. **-pikaa** suddenly; hurriedly. **-pikainen.** . short-tempered; rash; (*-arvaamaton*) sudden. **-pikaisuus** quick temper; *ä-suudessa* in a rash moment. **-rynnä|kkö:** *vallata ä-köllä* take by storm. **-syvä** precipitous, steep; *on ~* . . it gets deep suddenly here. **äkkiä** suddenly, abruptly; *pysähtyä ~* stop short; *tule ~!* come quickly!

äks|y ill-tempered, cross; (*hillitsemätön*) unmanageable; (*eläin*) vicious, fierce. **-yllä** be fierce, be unmanageable. **-yys** fierceness; unmanageableness.

äkä|inen angry, cross; fierce; ill-tempered. **-isyys** anger; exasperation; fierceness. **-mystyä** become fierce (furious). **-pussi** shrew, vixen. **-pää:** *äkäpäissään* in a fit of anger.

älkää do not, don't; *älkäämme* let us not, don't let us. .; *älköön luulko, että.* . he should not think that. .

ällis|tellä gape. **-tys** amazement, astonishment. **-tyttää** amaze, dumbfound; stun. **-tyä** be dumbfounded, be taken aback; be amazed; *-tynyt (m.)* astounded, thunderstruck.

äly wit, brains; intelligence; acumen, astuteness. **-kkyys** intelligence; (~koe intelligence test; ~luku, ~osamäärä intelligence quotient). **-kkäästi** intelligently. **-käs** intelligent; clever, bright, quick-witted; *erittäin ~* [very] highly intelligent. **-llinen** intellectual. **-mystö** intelligentsia. **-niekka**

wit, intellectual; *(älymystöön kuuluva)* high-brow. **-peräinen** intellectual. **-pää** superbrain, *vrt. -niekka.* **-ttömyys** lack of intelligence. **-tä** understand, comprehend; *(käsittää)* realize, grasp; catch [the meaning of]. **-tön** unintelligent.
ilä do not, don't; ~ *huoli* never mind! *~hän nyt!* you don't say so!
ilähtää yelp, give a yelp; whine.
immä old woman.
impäri pail, bucket. **-llinen** pailful, bucketful.
inky|ttää, -tys stammer, stutter.
äpärä *a.* illegitimate; *s.* bastard.
ire|ys crossness; grumpiness; peevishness. **-ä** cross; grumpy, gruff, sullen, ill-tempered.
irhennellä show fight.
äristä growl; *(murista)* snarl.
ärjy|ntä roar[ing]. **-ä** roar; *(ihmisestä, m.)* yell, shout.
ärjäistä shout, at, *jklle.*
ärsy|ke stimulus, irritant. **-ttyä** become irritated; *vrt. ärtyä.* **-ttää** irritate; provoke; *(kiusoittaa)* tease. **-tys** irritation.
ärty|inen, -isä irritable, touchy; fretful, peevish, petulant. **-isyys** irritability. **-mys** irritation. **-vä** irritable. **-vyys** irritability. **-ä** become (be) irritated; get inflamed.
ärähtää snap (at), *(koira)* snarl.
äske|inen recent; *(entinen)* former. **-n** just [now]; a while ago; *vasta juuri* ~ only just now, only a moment ago; ~ *mainittu* .. just mentioned. **-ttäin** recently, lately, of late; ~ *tapahtunut* recent; *(~en* recent).
ässä ace; *risti~* ace of clubs.
äveri|äisyys wealth. **-äs** rich, wealthy.
äyri öre; *kuv.* a penny.
äyriäinen crustacean; *(rapu)* crayfish.
äyräs bank; brink; edge; *joki on tulvinut yli äyräittensä* the river has overflown (broken) its banks.
äyskäri baler, scoop.
ääne|en(sä) aloud. **-kkyys**

loudness, noisiness. **-kkäästi** loud[ly]. **-käs** loud, noisy. **-llinen** vocal.
äänen|kannattaja mouthpiece; *(lehti)* organ. **-eristys** sound insulation. **-murros:** *hänellä on* ~ his voice is breaking. **-paino** stress. **-sävy** tone [of voice]. **-toisto** sound reproduction. **-vahvistin** amplifier. **-vaimennin** silencer, *Am.* muffler. **-värinsäätö** tone control.
äänes|tys voting, vote; *(lippu-,)* ballot voting; *salainen* ~ secret ballot; *toimittaa* ~ take a vote; *ensimmäisessä -tyksessä* at the first ballot; *(~alue* voting district; *~koju* polling booth; *~lippu* ballot-paper; *~luettelo* register of voters; the vote; *~paikka* polling station; *~prosentti* *oli korkea-*there was a heavy (70%) poll). **-täjä** voter. **-tää** vote; *(toimittaa ä-tys)* take a vote; *(lipuilla)* ballot; ~ *jstk* put sth. to the vote; ~ *jnk puolesta* vote for, *jkta* give one's vote to; ~ *tyhjää* vote blank; *käydä -tämässä* go to the polls, cast one's vote; *pidättyminen -tämästä* abstention.
ääne|ti silently, in silence; *olla* ~ be silent, keep silence. **-ttömyys** silence. **-ttömästi** silently; without a sound, noiselessly. **-tön** silent; soundless; *(hiljainen)* still; tacit [consent, *myöntymys*].
ääni sound; *(puhe-, laulu-)* voice; *(sävel, merkki-)* tone; *(äänestys-)* vote; *mus.* part; *(kuoronjohtaja) antoi äänen* gave the note; *hän on aina äänessä* he talks all the time; *160:llä äänellä 30:a vastaan* by 160 votes to 30; *hän sai 70 ääntä* he polled 70 votes. **-aalto** sound wave; *ks. ääntä-.* **-ala** range [of voice], register. **-elokuva** sound film, talking film. **-eristetty** sound-proof. **-huuli** vocal cord. **-kerta** *(urkujen)* register. **-laji** tone [of voice]. **-levy** record,

disc. **-merkki** sound signal.
-määrä number of votes.
-nauha recording tape. **-nen**
(yhd.) kaksi~ .. for two
voices, two-part. **-oikeus** right
to vote, the vote; the
franchise; *yleinen ~* universal
suffrage; *naisten ~* woman
suffrage; *-oikeuden vasta
saaneet nuoret* newly
enfranchised youngsters.
-oikeutettu. . entitled to vote.
-oppi acoustics. **-radio** sound
broadcasting. **-rasia** sound
box. **-rauta** tuning-fork. **-te,**
-tys recording. **-tehosteet**
sound effects. **-valli:** *murtaa
~* break the sonic barrier.
-valta voice. **-valtainen**
qualified to vote.
äänne sound. **-llä** utter sounds,
articulate. **-merkki** phonetic
symbol. **-oppi** phonetics.
ään|nähdys [slight] sound; *ei
~täkään* not a (not the
slightest) sound. **-nähtää** utter
(breathe) a sound.
äänteen|mukainen phonetic.
-mukaisesti phonetically.
-mukaisuus: *oikeinkirjoituksen
~* the phonetic spelling.
-mukaus vowel modification
(mutation).
äänten|enemmistö majority of
votes. **-keräily** canvassing for
votes, vote-catching. **-lasku**
counting of votes.
äänt|iö vowel. **-yä** be
pronounced. **-äminen, -ämys**
pronunciation.
ääntämis|merkintä phonetic
transcription. **-ohje:** *~et* key
to. the pronunciation.
-sanakirja pronouncing
dictionary. **-virhe** error in
pronunciation.
ääntä: *~ nopeampi* supersonic;

~ hitaampi subsonic.
-vaimentava sound-absorbing.
ääntää pronounce; *(äännellä)*
articulate; *~ väärin*
mispronounce.
ääreen: *jnk ~* beside. ., at (by)
the side of; *istuutua pianon
~* sit down at the piano.
ääre|llinen finite. **-llisyys**
finiteness. **-ssä:** *ikkunan ~* by
the window; *pöydän ~* at the
table. **-stä:** *(esim. löytää)*
beside, by; *ei poistunut
hetkeksikään sairasvuoteen ~*
never left the bedside for a
moment. **-ttömyys** endlessness;
infinity, infiniteness;
immensity, vastness. **-tön**
infinite; endless; *(rajaton)*
boundless; *(suunnaton)*
immense, vast, huge,
enormous; *äärettömän.* .
infinitely [small, *pieni*],
immensely [large, *suuri*],
extremely [difficult, *vaikea*].
ääri limit, bound; *(reuna)*
edge; brim; *~ään myöten
täynnä* brimful, *(sali ym)*
filled to capacity; *kaikilta
maailman ~ltä* from all parts
of the world; *maailman ~in*
to the ends of the world.
-mmilleen to the utmost, to
the limit. **-mmillään:** *on ~*
has reached its climax.
-mmäinen extreme, utmost;
ä-äisen extremely,. . in the
extreme. **-mmäisyys**
extreme [ness]; *ä-syyteen asti*
to the utmost; *mennä
ä-syyksiin* go to extremes;
(~ainekset lunatic fringe;
~mies extremist; *~puolue*
extremist party; *~toimenpide*
extreme measure, extremity).
-viiva contour; outline *(m.
kuv.); ~t* contours, outline.

Ö

öi|nen nightly, nocturnal; *öiseen aikaan* in the night [-time], at night. **-sin** in the night, at night.

öljy oil; *(kivi-, vuori-)* petroleum, naphtha; *valaa ~ä tuleen* add fuel to the fire. **-inen** oily. **-johto** oil pipe. **-kakku** oil-cake. **-kamiina** oil heater. **-kangas** oil-cloth. **-kannu** oil can. **-keitin** oil-stove. **-lautta, -läikkä** slick of oil, oil slick. **-lähde** oil-spring, oil well. **-lämmitys** oil-fire central heating. **-maalaus** oil painting. **-maali** oil paint; *(-väri)* oil colour. **-mäinen** oily. **-mäki** *raam.* the Mount of Olives. **-notto** **-porauslautta** (t.**-torni**) oil rig. refuelling. **-npuhdistamo** oil refinery. **-pitoinen.** . containing oil. **-puu** olive-tree, olive. **-säiliö** oil-tank, oil reservoir. **-tahra** oil stain. **-takki** oilskin. **-tynnyri** oil drum. **-tä** oil, lubricate. **-vaate:** *-vaatteet* oilskins. **-väri** oil colour.

öylätti wafer, host.

SÄÄNNÖTTÖMIEN VERBIEN LUETTELO

Perusmuoto	Imperfekti	Partis. perfekti	
abide	abode, abided	abode, abided	viipyä, jäädä; sietää
arise	arose	arisen	nousta, saada alkunsa
awake	awoke, awaked	awaked, awoke	herätä, herättää
be	was	been	olla
bear	bore	borne, born(syntynyt)	kantaa, synnyttää
beat	beat	beaten	lyödä, voittaa
become	became	become	tulla jksk
beget	begot	begotten	siittää, synnyttää
begin	began	begun	alkaa, aloittaa
behold	beheld	beheld	nähdä
bend	bent, bended	bent	taivuttaa, taipua
bereave	bereft, bereaved	bereft, bereaved	riistää
beseech	besought	besought	pyytää hartaasti
beset	beset	beset	ahdistaa
bet	bet, betted	bet, betted	lyödä vetoa
bid	bade, bid	bidden, bid	käskeä, tarjota, lausua
bind	bound	bound	sitoa
bite	bit	bitten, bit	purra
bleed	bled	bled	vuotaa, vuodattaa verta
bless	blessed, blest	blessed, blest	siunata
blow	blew	blown	puhaltaa, tuulla
break	broke	broken	taittaa, rikkoa, murtua, mennä rikki, särkyä
breed	bred	bred	kasvattaa; siittää aiheuttaa
bring	brought	brought	tuoda
broadcast	broadcast	broadcast	radioida
build	built	built	rakentaa
burn	burnt, burned	burnt, burned	palaa, polttaa
burst	burst	burst	haljeta, murtaa
buy	bought	bought	ostaa
can (prees.)	could	—	voi, osaa
cast	cast	cast	heittää, valaa
catch	caught	caught	ottaa (saada) kiinni, pyydystää
chide	chid	chidden, chid	nuhdella
choose	chose	chosen	valita
cleave	cleft, clove, cleaved	cleaved, cloven	halkaista

cling	clung	clung	takertua, pitää tiukasti kiinni
clothe	clothed	clothed, clad	vaatettaa, pukea
come	came	come	tulla
cost	cost	cost	maksaa, olla hintana
creep	crept	crept	ryömiä
crow	crew, crowed	crowed	kiekua
cut	cut	cut	leikata
dare	dared, durst	dared	uskaltaa
deal	dealt	dealt	käydä kauppaa, jakaa
dig	dug	dug	kaivaa
do (he does)	did	done	tehdä
draw	drew	drawn	vetää, piirtää
dream	dreamt, dreamed	dreamt, dreamed	nähdä unta, uneksia
drink	drank	drunk	juoda
drive	drove	driven	ajaa
dwell	dwelt	dwelt	asua
eat	ate	eaten	syödä
fall	fell	fallen	pudota, langeta
feed	fed	fed	syöttää, ruokkia
feel	felt	felt	tuntea
fight	fought	fought	taistella
find	found	found	löytää
flee	fled	fled	paeta
fling	flung	flung	singota
fly (m. paeta)	flew	flown	lentää
forbear	forbore	forborne	pidättyä jstk
forbid	forbade, forbad	forbidden	kieltää
forecast	forecast(ed)	forecast(ed)	ennustaa
foresee	foresaw	foreseen	aavistaa
forget	forgot	forgotten	unohtaa
forgive	forgave	forgiven	antaa anteeksi
forsake	forsook	forsaken	hylätä
freeze	froze	frozen	jäätyä, paelluttaa, pakastaa
get	got	got, (U.S.A. m.) gotten	saada, tulla jksk, päästä jhk
gird	girded, girt	girded, girt	vyöttää
give	gave	given	antaa
go (he goes)	went	gone	mennä, matkustaa
grind	ground	ground	jauhaa
grow	grew	grown	kasvaa, viljellä, tulla jksk
hang	hung	hung	riippua, ripustaa
	hanged	hanged	hirttää
have (he has)	had	had	olla jklla, omistaa
hear	heard	heard	kuulla
heave	heaved, hove	heaved, hove	nostaa, huoata
hew	hewed	hewn, hewed	hakata
hide	hid	hidden, hid	kätkeä

hit	hit	hit	iskeä, lyödä, osua
hold	held	held	pitää, vetää (astioista)
hurt	hurt	hurt	vahingoittaa, loukata
keep	kept	kept	pitää, säilyttää
kneel	kneeled, knelt	kneeled, knelt	polvistua
knit	knitted, knit	knitted, knit	kutoa, neuloa
know	knew	known	tietää, tuntea, osata
lade	laded	laden	lastata
lay	laid	laid	panna, laskea
lead	led	led	johtaa, taluttaa
lean	leaned, leant	leaned, leant	kallistua, nojata
leap	leapt, leaped	leapt, leaped	hypätä
learn	learned, learnt	learned, learnt	oppia
leave	left	left	jättää, lähteä
lend	lent	lent	lainata jklle
let	let	let	sallia, vuokrata
lie	lay	lain	maata, olla, sijaita
light	lighted, lit	lighted, lit	sytyttää, valaista
lose	lost	lost	kadottaa, menettää
make	made	made	tehdä, valmistaa
may (prees.)	might	—	saa, saattaa
mean	meant	meant	tarkoittaa
meet	met	met	tavata
mistake	mistook	mistaken	erehtyä
mow	mowed	mowed, mown	niittää
must (prees.)	(had to)	—	täytyy
ought (to)	—	—	pitäisi
outdo	outdid	outdone	viedä voitto
overcome	overcame	overcome	voittaa
overdo	overdid	overdone	liioitella
overhear	overheard	overheard	(salaa) kuulla
partake	partook	partaken	ottaa osaa
pay	paid	paid	maksaa
put	put	put	panna
quit	quitted, quit	quitted, quit	lähteä
read	read [red]	read [red]	lukea
rend	rent	rent	repiä
repay	repaid	repaid	maksaa takaisin
rid	ridded, rid	ridded, rid	vapauttaa
ride	rode	ridden	ratsastaa
ring	rang	rung	soida, soittaa
rise	rose	risen	nousta
run	ran	run	juosta
saw	sawed	sawn, sawed	sahata
say	said	said	sanoa
see	saw	seen	nähdä
seek	sought	sought	hakea, etsiä
sell	sold	sold	myydä
send	sent	sent	lähettää
set	set	set	asettaa, panna
sew	sewed	sewn, sewed	ommella
shake	shook	shaken	pudistaa, vapista

shall (prees.)	should	—	pitää, fut. apuverbi
shave	shaved	shaved, shaven	ajaa parta
shear	sheared	shorn, sheared	keritä
shed	shed	shed	vuodattaa
shine	shone	shone	loistaa, paistaa
shoe	shod	shod	kengittää
shoot	shot	shot	ampua
show	showed	shown, showed	näyttää, osoittaa, näkyä
shrink	shrank	shrunk, shrunken	kutistua, -taa
shut	shut	shut	sulkea, sulkeutua
sing	sang	sung	laulaa
sink	sank	sunk, sunken	vajota, upota, upottaa
sit	sat	sat	istua
slay	slew	slain	surmata
sleep	slept	slept	nukkua
slide	slid	slid, slided	liukua
sling	slung	slung	heittää, lingota
slink	slunk	slunk	hiipiä
slit	slit	slit	viiltää, halkaista
smell	smelt, smelled	smelt, smelled	haista, haistaa
smite	smote	smitten	lyödä
sow	sowed	sown, sowed	kylvää
speak	spoke	spoken	puhua
speed	sped, speeded	sped, speeded	kiiruhtaa, kiitää
spell	spelt, spelled	spelt, spelled	tavata, kirjoittaa
spend	spent	spent	viettää, kuluttaa
spill	spilt, spilled	spilt, spilled	kaataa, läikyttää
spin	spun, span	spun	kehrätä
spit	spat	spat	sylkeä
split	split	split	halkaista, haljeta
spoil	spoilt, spoiled	spoilt, spoiled	pilata
spread	spread	spread	levitä, levittää
spring	sprang, sprung	sprung	hypätä
stand	stood	stood	seisoa
steal	stole	stolen	varastaa
stick	stuck	stuck	pistää, tarttua t. pitää kiinni
sting	stung	stung	pistää
stink	stank, stunk	stunk	löyhkätä
strew	strewed	strewed, strewn	sirotella
stride	strode	strode, stridden	astua (pitkin askelin)
strike	struck	struck, (adj.) stricken	lyödä, tehdä lakko
string	strung	strung	pujottaa, jännittää
strive	strove	striven	pyrkiä

swear	*swore*	*sworn*	vannoa
sweep	*swept*	*swept*	lakaista
swell	*swelled*	*swollen*	ajettua, paisua
swim	*swam*	*swum*	uida
swing	*swung*	*swung*	heiluttaa, heilua, keinua
take	*took*	*taken*	ottaa, viedä
teach	*taught*	*taught*	opettaa
tear	*tore*	*torn*	repiä
tell	*told*	*told*	sanoa, kertoa, käskeä
think	*thought*	*thought*	ajatella, luulla
thrive	*throve,* *thrived*	*thriven,* *thrived*	viihtyä, menestyä
throw	*threw*	*thrown*	heittää
thrust	*thrust*	*thrust*	työntää
tread	*trod*	*trodden*	astua, polkea
undergo	*underwent*	*undergone*	kärsiä, kestää
understand	*understood*	*understood*	ymmärtää
undertake	*undertook*	*undertaken*	ottaa tehdäkseen
undo	*undid*	*undone*	avata, tuhota
upset	*upset*	*upset*	kaataa, järkyttää
wake	*woke, waked*	*waked,* *woken*	herätä, herättää
wear	*wore*	*worn*	**olla yllään, kulua**
weave	*wove*	*woven, wove*	kutoa
wed	*wedded*	*wedded, wed*	naida
weep	*wept*	*wept*	itkeä
wet	*wet, wetted*	*wet, wetted*	kastella
will (prees.)	*would*	—	tahtoo, fut. apu- verbi
win	*won*	*won*	voittaa
wind	*winded,* *wound*	*winded,* *wound*	kiertää, kiemur- rella, vetää (kello)
withdraw	*withdrew*	*withdrawn*	vetää pois, pois- tua
withhold	**withheld**	*withheld*	pidättää, olla antamatta
withstand	*withstood*	*withstood*	vastustaa, kestää
work	*worked,* *wrought*	*worked,* *wrought*	tehdä työtä, työskennellä, aikaansaada
wring	*wrung*	*wrung*	vääntää
write	*wrote*	*written*	kirjoittaa

Edelläoleva luettelo sisältää paitsi varsinaisia säännöttömiä kan-
taverbejä myös joukon sanakirjassa esiintyviä yhdysverbejä sekä
ns. vaillinaiset apuverbit

TAVUJAKO

Koska sanakirjan uudessa painoksessa tavutuksesta on ladonta-teknisistä syistä luovuttu, annettakoon tässä englanninkielisten sanojen tavutuksesta muutamia yleisohjeita:

Ääntämisellä on ratkaiseva merkitys, ei kirjoitustavalla. Tärkeitä tekijöitä ovat vokaalin pituus ja tavun painollisuus.

Esim. Painollinen tavu (lyhyt vokaali): ag ony, char acter, feath er
      »   » (pitkä   »): ba by, pa tron, le gal, i vory

Painoton tavu: an i mal, dec o rate, pop u lar

Konsonanttiyhdistelmät ym.: fa ther, feath er, laugh ter
   con scious, se lec tion, ques tion
   so cial pi geon (poikkeuksia fash ion, fas cism)

Kahdennettu konsonantti ym: at tempt, ap ply, emp ty, punc tual

J:nä ääntyvän i:n edellä: sen ior, un ion, opin ion, al ien
   (mutta du bious, te dium)

Konsonantti +l (tai r) sananloppuisen e:n edellä: i dle, fum ble, jun gle, li tre

Lyhyiden sanojen jakamista on vältettävä, myöskään ei mielellään eroteta imperfektin ja partisiipin päätteitä.

aika: *vanha hyvä* ~ the good old days.
aikaraja time-limit, deadline
aina: ~ *kun* whenever.
ajastin timer.
ajatolla(h) ayatollah.
ajo|kortti *Am.* driver's license. **-rata**
carriageway, *Am.* roadway.
akillesjänne Achilles tendon
akupunktuuri acupuncture.
alanumero *(puhelin-)* extension.
alennus *m.* price cut.
alennus- *m.* cut-price.
alku *(taudin)* onset.
aloitekykyinen ... having initiative;
hän on ~ he has i.
alppihiihto Alpine skiing.
altis: *vaikutuksille* ~ impressionable.
altistaa *m.* expose.
altistus exposure.
aluesuunnittelu regional planning.
amanuenssi *lääk.* houseman, house
officer, *Am.* intern.
ammattikurssi vocational course.
ammus *m.* round of ammunition.
antiikkikauppa *m.* antique shop.
aprillipila April fool ['s joke].
apuhoitaja practical nurse.
apukoulu *m.* special school.
armomurha euthanasia.
armonanomus *m.* appeal for clemency.
artikkeli: *epämääräinen* ~ indefinite
article; *määräinen* ~ definite a.
arvaamaton *m.* unpredictable.
arvolisävero value-added tax *(lyh.*
VAT).
arvosana *Am.* grade.
asiantuntemus *m.* expertise.
asia|sisältö factual content. **-virhe** error
of fact.
aste: *(koulun) ala-* *(ylä-)* ~ lower
(upper) level (forms, grades).
astianpesuneste washing-up liquid.
astronautti astronaut.

audiovisuaali|nen: *-set apuvälineet*
audiovisual aids.
aurinkoenergia solar energy.
avain: *avaimet käteen -periaate*
turn-key basis.
avio-onni married happiness.
avoliitto *l. v.* common-law marriage,
cohabitation, consensval union.
avu *m.* asset.
blini blin, blintz[e].
briljantti brilliant.
bruttokansantuot gross national
product *(lyh.* GNP).
edellinen: *viimeistä* ~ *m.* next to the
last.
edes: *hän ei* ~ *pyytänyt minua
istuutumaan (m.)* he didn't so much as
ask me to sit down.
edustava *(tyylikäs)* presentable.
edustusjoukkue representative team.
ehtiä: ~ *junalle (m.)* make the train.
ekumenia ecumenism.
elementti *m.* prefabricated component
(element); section. **-rakentaminen**
prefabrication, prefabricated
contruction.
empatia empathy.
energia|lähde source of energy, energy
source. **-nsäästötoimet** energy
conservation measures.
energinen energetic.
epilep|sia epilepsy. **-tikko, -tinen**
epileptic.
epä|hygieeninen unhygienic,
unsanitary. **-metalli** *m.* nonmetal.
-poliittinen non-political.
erehdys: *inhimillinen* ~ human error.
erittyä *m.* be excreted.
erityisopetus special education.
esimiesasema supervisory position.
esitellä *(tuotteita)* show, display;
(laitetta, m.) demonstrate.
esit|tää *-tävät taiteet* performing arts.

esteettömyystodistus m. certificate of no marriage impediment.

eteinen (sydämen) atrium.

etäispääte terminal.

evp.: eversti evp. NN Colonel NN (ret.).

evästys m. briefing.

fasis|mi fascism. **-tinen** fascist[ic].

fossiili fossil. **-nen:** ~ polttoaine fossil fuel.

grafiikka graphic arts, graphics.

grafologi graphologist. **-a** graphology.

haara m. crotch.

haihattelija m. visionary.

hallimestaruuskilpailut indoor championships.

halpa m. low-cost.

-han, -hän: ... mutta hänhän onkin upporikas [he can afford a trip around the world,] but then he is loaded.

hankausjauhe scouring powder; abrasive.

harjoi|ttelija m. trainee. **-tusaine** practical subject.

helluntailaisuus Pentecostalism, the Pentecostal movement.

henkilöllisyystodistus m. certificate of identification.

henkiparannus spriritual healing.

heroiini heroin.

hienomekaniikka precision mechanics.

hiu|kan, -kkasen m. a little bit.

homoseksuaali(nen) a. & s. homosexual; a. puhek. gay.

huh whew!

huippu|kokous summit meeting (conference), puhek. summit. **-kunto** top form.

humala: juoda itsensä ~an get drunk.

humalainen attr. drunken.

hymykampanja campaign of smiles.

hyödyntää exploit, utilize.

hyötöreaktori breeder reactor.

hölk|kä (kunto-) jogging. **-ätä** jog.

idea idea.

ientulehdus gingivitis.

intensiivinen intensive, intense.

islamilainen a. Islamic; vrt. muhamettilainen.

itseoppinut m. self-taught.

jakomielitautinen a. & s. schizophrenic.

jo: [hän on asunut täällä] ~ kymmenen vuotta ... for ten years now.

johtamistaito managerial skill;

leadership.

joko: ~ hän on tullut? (m.) has he come yet?

joukko|kokous m. rally. **-oppi** set theory.

jälki-istunto detention.

järjestelmäkamera system camera.

järjestyspoliisi l. v. patrol police.

jää|halli ice-rink. **-tanssi** ice dancing.

kahdenvälinen bilateral.

kahviaamiainen m. continental breakfast.

kaikki: ~en aikojen (m.) all-time (record, ennätys).

kaljuuntua lose one's hair, go bald.

kampaamo m. hairdressing salo[o]n, h. parlour.

Kamputsea Cambodia, Kampuchea.

kamputsealainen a. & s. Cambodian. Kampuchean.

kana m., vars. Am. [domestic] chicken.

kandidaatti m. bachelor.

kannustin m. incentive.

kantokahva carrying handle.

kapitalistinen capitalist[ic].

karenssiaika waiting time.

kasettinauhuri cassette [tape] recorder.

katse: heidän ~ensa kohtasivat their eyes met.

kattojärjestö umbrella organization.

kauko|-ohjaus m. telecontrol. **-ohjattu** remote-control[led], remotely controlled.

kaupallisuus m. commercialism.

kauppias m. stockist.

keilahalli bowling alley.

keskenmeno lääk. spontaneous abortion.

keskus|järjestö central organization, [con]federation. **-liitto** central union, [con]federation.

kestoaika duration [time].

kesäsijainen m. summer replacement.

kielitaju m. instinct of the language.

kierroslukumittari rev[olution] counter, tachometer.

kierrä|ttää tekn. recycle. **-tys** recycling.

kiihottaa m. arouse.

-kin vrt. -han, -hän (lis.).

kinofilmi [perforated] 35-mm film. **-kamera** 35-mm [miniature] camera.

kirjakieli m. standard language; suomen ~ (m.) standard Finnish.

kirja|ta: -ttuna by registered post.

kodin|hoitaja homemaker. **-koneet**

home appliances.

kolmivuotinen *m.* three-year, of three years.

kommandiittiyhtiö limited partnership.

konepaja *m.* machine shop.

konttorikone business machine, office m.

korkea|oktaaninen high-octane. **-tasoinen** high-level; of [a] high standard.

korkopolitiikka interest rate policy.

kuitu *(ravinnossa, m.)* roughage.

kulissientakainen behing-the-scenes, backstage.

kulkeutua *m.* find one's way.

kuntourheilu conditioning sport[s].

kuolemanjälkeinen: ~ *elämä* the afterlife.

kuoronjohtaja *m.* choirmaster.

kuorruttaa *(kalaa, lihaa ym.)* glaze.

kutsukilpailu invitation[al] event (competition, tournament).

kuulovammainen . . . with impaired hearing, *attr.* hearing-impaired; *lievästi (vaikeasti)* ~ [a child] with a mild (severe) hearing impairment.

kuulovika *m.* impaired hearing, hearing impairment.

kuumahierre thermomechanical pulp.

kuusinkertainen *ks.* kuudenkertainen.

kuvanauhuri *m.* TV recorder, video r.

lahonsuoja-aine wood preservative.

lama depression.

lapsenomainen childlike.

laskin calculator; *elektroni*~ electronic c.; *tasku*~ pocket c.

lastenvaatteet children's wear.

lehmäkauppa *m.* horse-trade *(-kaupat m.* horse-trading).

lento|kelpoinen airworthy. **-liikenne** air traffic.

lesbolainen *a. & s.* lesbian.

levyjarrut disc (disk) brakes.

liennytys détente.

lifta|ri hitchhiker. **-ta** hitchhike.

liikenne: *ajoneuvo*~ vehicular traffic; *joukko*~ mass transit; *julkinen* ~ public transit.

liikenne|laitos: *Helsingin* ~ Helsinki Transport. **-silmä** road sense. **-turvallisuus** *m.* road safety.

liikuntavammainen . . . with a motor handicap.

lirkuttaa *m.* wheedle.

lisäarvovero value-added tax *(lyh.* VAT).

litistä squelch.

lumimies Abominable Snowman.

-luokkalainen former, *Am.* grader *(esim.* sixth- ~).

luontaistuotekauppa health food store.

lähekkäin *m.* close together.

lämmitysöljy heating oil.

lämpö|saaste thermal pollution. **-voimala** thermal power station.

maailmanmarkkinahinta world price.

maannousu uplift.

maastoajoneuvo all-terrain vehicle.

maatalouspolitiikka agricultural policy, farm p.

mahtua: *ei mahdu ovesta* [the piano] won't go through the door.

mainos: *TV-* ~ TV commercial.

maksu: *kurssi*~ course fee; *tutkinto*~ examination f.

maolai|nen Maoist. **-suus** Maoism.

massaurheilu mass sports.

matka|iluala the travel business. **-njärjestäjä** tour operator.

meluntorjunta noise control.

meteorologia meteorology.

metrijärjestelmä: *siirtyä* ~*än* change over to the metric system, go metric; ~*än siirtyminen* metrication.

metsäteollisuus forest[-based] industry.

mielisairaanhoitaja mental nurse.

mikroprosessori microprocessor.

miljardi a (one) thousand million, *Am.* billion.

miljoonakaupunki city with (of) a million [or more] inhabitants. millionaire city.

moni: *meitä on moneksi* it takes all kinds (sorts) [to make a world].

moni|käyttöinen, -toimi- multipurpose. **-puoluejärjestelmä** multiparty system.

muikku *l. v.* vendace.

muistikatko memory gap.

muotitietoinen fashion-conscious..

murskavoitto crushing (devastating) victory.

murtovesi brackish water.

musikaali musical [comedy].

myymälä|auto mobile shop. **-varkaus** shop-lifting.

naapuruussuhteet neighbourly relations.

naarmuuntumaton scratchproof.

naispappeus the ordination of women (*t.* women's ordination) [as priests (*t.* to the priesthood)].

nallipyssy cap pistol, cap gun.

nestekaasu *m.* liquefied petroleum gas (*lyh.* LPG).

niputtaa *kuv.* lump (together).

niska: *päästä ~n päälle (kuv.)* get the upper hand (of).

niskatuki headrest.

nivel|bussi articulated bus. **-side** ligament.

noidankehä vicious circle.

nollakasvu no-growth.

näkövammainen visually impaired.

objektiivisuus objectivity.

olennaisuus essentiality, essential nature.

omavarainen: *~ jnk suhteen* self-sufficient in sth.

omistusoikeus *m.* ownership (of), title (to), property (in).

onnenkauppa *m.* lottery (marriage is a l.).

osatekijä contributory factor.

osuus *m.* proportion.

pahanhajuinen: *~ hengitys* bad breath, mouth odour.

pakko|avioliitto shotgun marriage. **-loma** paid leave.

paljastaa *(salaisuus ym. m.)* divulge.

palka|llinen paid, . . . with pay. **-ton** unpaid, . . . without pay.

palkinto *(kilpailussa voitettu, m.)* trophy; award.

palkka|liukuma wage slide, w. drift. **-taso:** *alhaisen -tason maat* low-wage countries.

palo|ntorjunta *m.* fire prevention, f. control. **-suojelu** fire protection.

palstatila: *antoi runsaasti ~ a* [the paper] gave wide coverage (to).

pankkiryöstö bank robbery.

pariluistelu pair skating.

perhesiteet family ties.

pessaari pessary; cap, diaphragm.

pessimis|mi pessimism. **-ti** pessimist.

pesuominaisuudet laundering qualities.

piennar *(tien)* verge, *Am.* shoulder.

piirtoheitin overhead projector.

pinnoittaa *(rengas) m.* recap.

pitkäaikainen *(kauan jatkunut t. kestänyt)* long-standing.

poliisilaitos *m.* police department.

postinumero *Am.* zip code.

promille part per thousand; *veren alkoholipitoisuus ylitti 0,8 ~ a* the proportion of alcohol in the blood exceeded 80 milligrammes per 100 millilitres of blood.

prosentti: *paino~, tilavuus~* per cent by weight (by volume); *~yksikkö* percentage point.

provisio commission. **-palkkainen** paid on a commission basis.

puhel|invaihde [telephone] switchboard. **-unvälittäjä** *m.* telephonist.

punainen: *~ verisolu* red blood cell, erythrocyte.

puolapuut *m.* stall bar, wall rack.

puolustaja *jääkiekk.* defenceman.

puolustus|asianajaja *m.* defence counsel, d. lawyer. **-haara** service [of the armed forces].

puunsuoja-aine wood preservative.

pyrkiä: *~ rauhaan, neuvotteluihin* seek peace (negotiations).

pystykorva: *suomen~* Finnish spiz.

pysäköintirikkomus parking offence.

pyörä|tie cycle track, *Am.* bikeway. **-tuoli** wheelchair.

päivyst|ys: *m.* on-call duty; *lääkäri~* duty doctor service; *~korvaus* on-call allowance. **-ävä:** *~ lääkäri* *m.* duty doctor.

päällystää *(tie)* pave, surface.

pääomavirta capital flow.

pääte *(etäis-)* terminal.

päätty|ä: *hakuaika -y. . .* (m.) closing date [for applications]. . .

radiopuhelin *(pieni)* walkie-talkie.

rakennus|elementti *m.* building element (component), construction e. (c.). **-liike** building firm. **-urakoitsija** building contractor.

ratkaisematon *m.* outstanding.

rehevöityminen eutrophication.

retkipyörä touring bicycle.

rikkomus *m.* infringement, infraction (*m. urh.*).

rikosrekisteri criminal record. **-toimisto** c. record[s] office.

riski: *ottaa ~ (m.)* take a chance.

rivimie|s *m.* rank-and-filer; *-het* the rank and file.

rullalauta skateboard.

ruostesuojaus rust-proofing, r.

protection.
ruotia *kuv.* scrutinize; criticize.
ryhmä *m.* team. **-edut** sectional
interests.
rytminen: ~ *voimistelu (nais-)* modern
gymnastics, Moderne Gymnastics.
rästi: *vero~t* back taxes; *vuokra~t*
arrears of rent, back rent.
ryöstökalastus overfishing.
sala-ammattilainen shamateur.
samalla: ~ *kertaa (m.)* at once.
sarjafilmi *m.* [TV] serial.
se: ~ *että* the fact that.
seisokki shut-down.
sepelvaltimotauti coronary disease.
SEV the Council for Mutual Economic
Assistance, CMEA, Comecon.
sitoa: *indeksiin sidottu* index-tied.
siistata de-ink.
sisään|käynti, -käytävä *m.* way in.
sorvaaja *m.* lathe operator.
sotilasjuntta military junta.
strategia strategy.
stressaava stressful.
stressi stress.
stuertti steward.
suihkumoottori jet engine.
suku: *omaa ~a H. (m.)* née H.
sukupuolivalistus *m.* sex education.
suoramainonta direct mail advertising.
suositushinta recommended price.
suunta|merkki turn[ing] indication,
direction signal. **-vilkku** direction
indicator, *Engl. m.* trafficator.
syrjäsilmä: *nähdä, katsoa ~llä* see
(look) out of the corner of one's eye.
syyntakeeton *m.* non compos mentis.
syöttää *(jalkap., jääkiekk.)* pass.
särkylääke analgesic, pain-killing drug.
taluttaa *(eläintä)* walk, *(polkupyörää,*
m.) push, wheel.
talvihorros hibernation.
tarjo|ta: *eniten -ava* the highest bidder.
tasan: *pelata ~ (m.)* tie; [*peli oli*] ~ *3–3*
three all.
tasapaino|aisti sense of balance
(equilibrium). **-häiriö(t)** disturbance
of equilibrium, disequilibrium.
tasapeli *m.* tie.
taskulaskin pocket calculator.
teknologi|a technology. **-nen**
technological.
tekojäärata artificial ice-rink.
Teneriffa Tenerife.

teollisuushalli advance factory.
teologia theology.
terveys|kasvatus health education.
-keskus health centre.
tie: ~ *tä!* gangway!
tiedekunta: *lääketieteellinen* ~ *(m.)*
school of medicine, medical school;
oikeustieteellinen ~ *(m.)* law school.
tiedotustilaisuus *(sisäinen)* information
meeting.
tilinauha pay slip.
toimihenkilö *m.* salaried employee; *~t*
(m.) salaried staff.
toimitusaika *m.* date of delivery,
delivery date.
toisin: *ellei* ~ *ilmoiteta (m.)* unless
noted (stated) otherwise.
toisinajatteleva dissident; *~t (m.)*
those who do not conform.
tonni: *metrinen* ~ *(1000 kg)* tonne,
metric ton.
tosiasia: *hänet asetettiin tapahtuneen*
~n eteen he was presented with a fait
accompli.
tosin: *en* ~ *ole varma* I'm not sure,
though.
toteuttaa: *mahdollinen* ~ *(m.)* feasible.
transistori transistor.
transsendenttinen: ~ *mietiskely*
transcendental meditation.
tuhlata *(rahaa)* splash out.
tukiopetus remedial instruction.
tulliasema *m.* customs post.
tunnusmerkki *(kuv.)* hallmark.
tuntipalkka *m.* hourly rate.
tuotantoväline(et) means of
production.
tuotevastuu product liability.
turhautu|a become frustrated. **-nut**
frustrated.
turvatoime(npitee)t security (safety)
precautions; *ankariin turvatoimiin*
ryhdyttiin strict s. precautions were
taken.
työ: *käydä ~ssä* go out to work; *omaa*
~tä tekevä self-employed.
työ|kokemus work experience,
employment e. **-moraali** work ethic.
-paikka: *-paikat (= työläiset)* shop
floor; [*luottamusmiesten menettelyä ei*
hyväksytty] *työpaikoilla* on the s. f.
-paikkasuhteet, -suhdeasiat labour
relations.
työsuojelu|asiamies safety officer.

-valtuutettu safety delegate, s. representative.

työtaakka *m.* work-load.

työttömyys: *kausi~* seasonal unemployment; *kitka~* frictional u.; *rakenne~* structural u.; *suhdanne~* cyclical u. **-aste** rate of unemployment, u. r.

työ|turvallisuus safety at work, s. of labour, industrial s. **-viikko** working week; *tekevät lyhennettyä -viikkoa* are on short-time working. **-voima** *m.* labour force, work force (*~ministeri* minister of labour (of employment)).

työ|yhteisö working community. **-ympäristö** working environment, w. surroundings.

ulko|ministeri *m.* foreign minister. **-suomalainen** Finnish expatriate.

unilääke *m.* hypnotic.

uros *vrt. koiras.*

uusiutu|maton *(energialähde ym.)* non-renewable. **-va** renewable.

vaa'ankieliasema: *on ~ssa* holds the balance.

vaaka|lauta: *on -laudalla (m.)* hangs in the balance.

vai: *~ niin (m.)* I see.

vaihde: *neljä ~tta eteen ja peruutus~* four forward gears (speeds) and reverse; *ykkös~* low gear. **-pyörä** multispeed bicycle.

vaihtaa *(auton vaihde)* change *(Am.* shift) gear; *~ kakkoseen (m.)* c. into second g.

-vaihteinen: *kolmi~ polkupyörä, vaihdelaatikko* three-speed bicycle (gearbox).

vaihto-oppilas exchange student.

vaihtuvuus *(työvoiman, henkilökunnan)* turnover.

vakuut|taa: *hän -ti että* he gave an assurance that.

-valmisteinen: *venäläis~* Russian-made.

vamma: *selviytyä vammoitta* escape unhurt.

vapaa|-aika: *-ajan ongelma* leasure-time problem.

vapautusrintama liberation front.

varaslähtö: *ottaa ~* jump the gun *(m. kuv.).*

vastaanotto: *hänellä on ~ neljästi viikossa* he holds four surgeries a week.

vastaava: *löytää koulutustaan ~a työtä* find a job commensurate with one's education (training).

vesiensuojelu water conservation.

vesistö *m.* waterway.

vieraskielinen: *attr.* foreign-language.

viimei|nen: *-sen edellinen (m.)* next to the last.

viransijaisuus: *sai opettajan -den* got a substitute teaching position.

virhelyönti *(konekirj.)* typing error.

voimanosto power lifting.

vuodesohva *m.* sofa bed.

vuoristorata *(huvipuiston) Am.* roller coaster.

vyörengas radial-ply tyre.

vähittäismaksujärjestelmä *Am.* installment plan.

väistämättömyys inevitability.

välipal|a: *syödä -oja* eat between meals.

ydin|energia nuclear energy. **-voimala** nuclear power plant.

yhteyt|tää *m.* photosynthesize. **-täminen** *(viherkasvien)* photosynthesis.

yleensä: *miksi hän ~ (= ollenkaan) tuli tänne?* why did he come here in the first place?

yleisurheilumaaottelu *m.* international athletics match.

ystävyysseura friendship society.

yösija *m.* overnight accommodation.

älkää: *älköön kukaan luulko että* let no one think that.

ääneneristys *m.* sound-proofing.

äänieristetty sound-proofed.

The Standard

English–Finnish Dictionary

The Standard
English–Finnish
Dictionary

olt, Rinehart and Winston   Eastbourne

erner Söderström Osakeyhtiö   Helsinki

TO THE USER OF THE DICTIONARY

In order to facilitate the finding of words, this dictionary adheres to strict alphabetical order. Thus, each word is to be looked up at its correct place, in alphabetical order, even if it is a compound or derivative.

The tilde (~) indicates the entire heading word or the entire preceding entry word, a hyphen (-) indicates the entire first part of the entry word up to the vertical line. If the heading word has no vertical line a hyphen is also used to correspond to the entire word when they are to be written together. The tilde followed by a hyphen (~-) is thus used when both parts of the compound are connected with a hyphen, e.g. **motor** s. moottori, etc. **-car** . . . (= motor-car). **-ist** . . . (= motorist). **-man** . . . (= motorman).

Parentheses have often been used in order to save space. An alternative which can be used instead of the preceding word or phrase is given in normal parentheses( ). Brackets [ ] are used to indicate words or parts of words which may be omitted without changing the meaning as well as for words which clarify the meaning further. Additionally, parentheses have been used in the following instances:

> **prohibit** v. kieltää etc. . . . **-ion**
> s. kielto; kieltolaki; (**-ist** s.
> kieltolain kannattaja). **-ive,**
> **-ory** a. kieltävä etc.

Here, then, **-ist** = prohibitionist, **-ive** = prohibitive.

Proper names are also included in the dictionary, so that, among other reasons, the derivatives based on proper names are listed under the base word.

PRONUNCIATION

The pronunciation of English words is given after the entries. The basic model followed is based on the system developed by D. Jones. This system, which uses the symbols of the international phonetic alphabet, is commonly used in English textbooks and dictionaries for foreigners.

AMERICAN ORTHOGRAPHY

Since in most cases this dictionary uses British orthography only, it is important that users familiarize themselves with the examples below which illustrate American orthography compared with that used in Britain:

British	American	
ae	e	etiology, hemoglobin, hemorrhage
	ae tai e	egis, eon, anemia, anesthetic
oe	e	fetus, esophagus, h[a]emorrhage, an[a]emia, f[o]etus.)
our	or	armor, candor, color, favor, fervor, harbor, honor, humor, labor, neighbor, odor, rumor, splendor, tumor, valor, vapor, vigor
ll or l	l	canceled, equaled, traveled, traveling, marvelous
l or ll	ll	enroll, enthrall, install, instill, enrollment, fulfillment, installment, fulfill, skillful, willful
pp	p	kidnaped, -ing: worshiped, -ing
tt	t	carbureted, carbureter, sulfureted
re	er	center, goiter, liter, meager, meter, reconnoiter, saltpeter, scepter, theater (but acre, massacre, ogre)
c	s	defense, expense, offense, pretense
x or ct	ct	connection, inflection, reflection
ize or ise	ize	apologize, realize

ABBREVIATIONS USED IN THE DICTIONARY

a. adjective (adjectival)
adv. adverb
alat. vulgar
Am. American
anat. anatomy
a p., a p.'s a person (someone),
   a person's (someone's)
apuv. auxiliary
art. article
a th., a thing (something)
attr. attribute
auto. automobile
biol. biology
Cambr. (at) Cambridge
ed. previous
elok. cinema
eläint. zoology
Engl. British
epäm. indefinite
erisn. proper noun
eräänl. a kind of
et. particularly
fil. philosophy
fon. phonetics
fys. physics
geol. geology
geom. geometry
halv. disparagingly
harv. rarely
hist. history
ilm. aviation
imp. preterite
imperat. imperative
inf. infinitive
int. interjection
intr. intransitive
jk someone (subj.)
jkn someone's (poss.)
jkta someone (obj.)
jonkin something (obj.)
jnnk to somewhere
jssk jossakin etc.
kasv. botany
kaupp. commerce
keitt. cooking
kem. chemistry
kestom. progressive form
kiel. linguistics, grammar
kirjanp. bookkeeping

kirjap. printing
kirk. ecclesiastical term
koll. collective, collectively
komp. comparative
konj. conjunction
korttip. card game
koul. schoolchildren's term
krik. cricket
ks. see
kuv. metaphorically
lak. legal term
lastenk. children's language
lat. Latin
leik. playfully
lentok. aviation
liik. business language
lukus. number
l. v. nearest equivalent
lyh. abbreviation, abbreviated
lääk. medicine
m. also
mat. mathematics
mek. mechanics
mer. nautical
meteor. meteorology
miekk. fencing
miner. mineralogy
mus. music
määr. definite
nyk. nowadays
Oxf. (at) Oxford
parl. parliament
p., pers. person
pass. passive
pilk. mockingly
pl. plural
pol. politics
pp. past participle
ppr. present participle
pred. predicative
pref. prefix
prep. preposition
pres. present
pron. pronoun
psyk. psychology
puhek. colloquial
raa. Biblical
rad. radio
rak. construction

rauta. railway
refl. reflexive
relat. relative
run. poetic language
s. substantive, noun
sb. somebody
seur. next
sg. singular
s., sh. shilling(s)
Skotl. Scottish
sl. slang
sot. military term
sth. something
sup. superlative
sähk. electricity
t. or
tav. usually

teatt. theatre
tekn. technical
tiet. scientific
tietok. computers
tr. transitive
täht. astronomy
urh. sports
us. often
usk. religion
v. verb
valok. photography
valt. state
vanh. archaic, old fashioned
vrt. cf.
yhd. compound
yliop. university

A

A, a [ei] *s.* a-kirjain; nuotti, sävel a; *A*
= automatic; *A gun* konetykki; *AA* =
anti-aircraft; *A 1* ensiluokkainen.
Lyh.: **A.A.** *automobile Association;
Alcoholics Anonymous;* **A. B.**
able-bodied seaman; **ABM**
anti-ballisitic missile torjuntaohjus; **a.
c.** *alternating current;* **a/c** *account* tili;
acc. *account;* **A. D.** ['ei 'di:] *(Anno
Domini)* jälkeen Kristuksen
(syntymän), jKr.; **A. D. C.**
aide-de-camp adjutantti; **ad, advt**
advertisement; **ad lib.** *(ad libitum)*
mielin määrin, vapaasti; **AEA** *Atomic
Energy Authority;* **AEC** *atomic
Energy Commission;* **Ala.** *Alabama;*
Alas. *Alaska;* **A level** ks. *advanced;*
a.m. *(ante meridiem) before noon* e.
p. p.; **A. M. S.** *Army Medical Service;*
anon. anonymous; **A. P.** *Associated
Press;* **ANZAC** *Australian-New
Zealand Army Corps;* **Apr.** *April;* **A.
R. A.** *Associate of the Royal
Academy;* **Ariz.** *Arizona;* **Ark.**
Arkansas; **A. R. P.** *Air Raid
Precautions* väestönsuojelu; **Asst**
Assistant; **A T S.** *Auxiliary
Territorial Service;* **Aug.** *August;* **A.
V.** *Authorized Version;* **avdp**
avoirdupois; **Ave.** *avenue.*
1. [ə] *pref.* (vanh.) *afoot* jalan; *[the
house] is abuilding* on rakenteilla.
2. [ə, painollisena ei] t. **an** [ən, æn]
epäm. *art. (a man, an apple, an hour);
they are of a size* ne ovat
samankokoiset; *twice a week* kahdesti
viikossa; *£ 40 a year* 40 puntaa
vuodessa.
back [ə'bæk] *adv.* taaksepäin; *be
taken* ~ nolostua.
bacus ['æbəkəs] *s.* helmi, laskutaulu.
baft [ə'ba:ft] *adv.* (laivan)
peräpuolella, -lle; *prep.* takana,

taakse.
abandon [ə'bændən] *v.* jättää, hylätä;
luopua jstk; *s.* huolettomuus,
riehakkuus; *he* ~*ed himself to despair*
hän lankesi epätoivoon, antautui
toivottomuuden valtaan. **-ed** [-d] *a.*
hylätty; turmeltunut, rietas. **-ment** *s.*
jättäminen, luovuttaminen; hylättynä
olo.
abase [ə'beis] *v.* alentaa, nöyryyttää.
-ment *s.* alennus(tila), nöyryytys.
abash [ə'bæʃ] *v.* saattaa hämille t.
häpeämään; ~*ed* hämillään (oleva).
-ment *s.* hämminki.
abate [ə'beit] *v.* vähentää, lieventää,
alentaa (hinta); vähentyä, heikentyä;
tyyntyä. **-ment** *s.* lievennys, helpotus.
abattoir ['æbətwa:] *s.* teurastamo.
abb|acy ['æbəsi] *s.* apotinarvo. **-ess**
['æbis] *s.* abbedissa. **-ey** ['æbi] *s.*
(apotti)luostari; luostarikirkko; *the
A~* = *Westminster A~.*
abbot ['æbət] *s.* apotti.
abbrevia|te [ə'bri:vieit] *v.* lyhentää.
-tion [-'eifn] *s.* lyhennys, lyhenne.
ABC ['eibi:'si:] *s.* aakkoset; ensi
alkeet; *ABC States* Argentina, Brazil,
Chile.
abdic|ate ['æbdikeit] *v.* luopua
(kruunusta). **-ation** [-'keifn] *s.*
kruunustaluopuminen.
abdom|en ['æbdəmən] *s.* vatsa. **-inal**
[æb'dɔminl]*a.* vatsan-; ~ *cavity*
vatsaontelo.
abduct [æb'dʌkt] *v.* ryöstää siepata,
kidnapata. **-ion** [æb'dʌkʃn] *s.*
sieppaus, ryöstö.
abeam [ə'bi:m] *adv.* poikittain (mer.).
abed [ə'bed] *adv.* vuoteessa.
Aber|deen [æbə'di:n] *erisn.* **-donian**
[-'əunjən] *s.* Aberdeenin asukas.
aberra|nt [æ'berə)nt] *a.* harhaileva,
harhaan joutunut. **-tion** [æbə'reiʃn] *s.*

eksyminen harhautuminen; säännöttömyys.

abet [ə'bet] v. yllyttää, auttaa; aid and ~ avustaa (rikoksessa). **-tor** [-ə] s. yllyttäjä; avustaja.

abeyance [ə'be(i)əns] s.: is in ~ on toistaiseksi ratkaisematta; fall into ~ jäädä käytännöstä, lakata olemasta voimassa.

abhor [əb'hɔ:] v. inhota, kammota. **-rence** [əb'hɔr(ə)ns] s. inho. **-rent** [əb'hɔr(ə)nt] a. inhottava, vastenmielinen.

abid|e [ə'baid] abode, abode, v. odottaa; kärsiä, sietää, kestää; viipyä, jäädä; ~ by pitää kiinni jstk, pysyä jssk. **-ing** a. pysyvä, kestävä.

ability [ə'biliti] s. kyvykkyys, kyky; (et. pl.) henkiset kyvyt; ~ to pay maksukykyisyys.

abject ['æbdʒekt] a. alhainen, kurja, viheliäinen. **-ion** ['dʒekʃn] s. alennustila; viheliäisyys.

abjure [əb'dʒuə] v. luopua valallisesti (jstk), hylätä, kieltää.

ablaze [ə'bleiz] adv. ilmitulessa.

able ['eibl] a. kykenevä, pystyvä, kyvykäs; be ~ to kyetä, voida (tehdä jtk). ~bodied voimakas; a.-b. seaman ylimatruusi.

ablution [əb'lu:ʃn] s. pesu.

ably ['eibli] adv. kykenevästi, taitavasti.

abneg|ate ['æbnigeit] v. kieltää itseltään; luopua (uskosta). **-ation** [-'geiʃn] s. kieltäminen.

abnormal [æb'nɔ:m(ə)l] a. epänormaali, (säännönmukaisesta) poikkeava. **-ity** [-'mæliti] s. abnormiuus, poikkeavuus, säännöttömyys.

aboard [ə'bɔ:d] adv. & prep. laivassa, -aan; [close, hard] ~ vieressä, -een: welcome ~! tervetuloa laivaan (lentokoneeseen, Am. junaan, bussiin)!

abode [ə'bəud] v. imp. & pp. ks. abide; s. oleskelupaikka, asumus; take up one's ~ asettua asumaan.

abolish [ə'bɔliʃ] v. poistaa, lakkauttaa. **-ment** s. poistaminen, (et. orjuuden) lakkauttaminen. **-ist** [-ist] s. neekeriorjuuden vastustaja.

A-bomb ['eibɔm] ks. atomic.

abomina|ble [ə'bɔminəbl] a. inhottava, iljettävä, hirveä. **-te** [-eit] v. inhota. **-tion** [-'neiʃn] s. inho, kammo; inhottava asia; hold sth. in ~ inhota.

aborigin|al [æbə'ridʒ|ənl] a. alkuperäinen, alku-, kanta-. **-es** [-ini:z] s. pl. alkuasukkaat.

abort [ə'bɔ:t] v. surkastua; epäonnistua. **-ion** [ə'bɔ:ʃn] s. raskaudenkeskeytys, abortti; keskenmeno (spontaneous ~); criminal ~ laiton a.; (~ist sikiönlähdettäjä). **-ive** [-tiv] a. keskenaikainen; surkastunut; epäonnistunut.

abound [ə'baund] v. olla runsaasti, yltäkyllin, tulvillaan (jtk in, with); the lake ~s in fish järvessä on runsaasti kalaa, järvi on kalaisa.

about [ə'baut] prep. ympäri, -llä, -lle; läheisyydessä; noin, paikkeilla, suunnilleen, jokseenkin; -sta, -stä; adv. ympäri; melkein; we were talking ~ him puhuimme hänestä; I told him ~ it kerroin hänelle siitä; how ~ you entä sinä? what ~ going for a walk mitä arvelet, menisimmekö kävelylle; [there were papers] lying ~ on the floor hujan hajan lattialla, pitkin lattiaa; I have no money ~ me minulla ei ole rahaa mukanani; ~ four kello neljän tienoissa; right ~ [turn]! täyskäännös oikeaan! be ~ to aikoa; he was ~ to go hän oli lähtemäisillään, juuri lähdössä; bring ~ saada aikaan; it came ~ tapahtui; he will soon be [up and] ~ again hän on pian taas jalkeilla; rumours are ~ that huhutaan, että; he went a long way ~ hän teki pitkän mutkan; I've had just ~ enough nyt olen saanut tarpeekseni; I'm ~ sick of this alan saada kyllikseni tästä; it's ~ time to.. on korkea aika..

above [ə'bʌv] prep. & adv. yläpuolella, -lle, yllä; yli; ~ all ennen kaikkea; that is ~ me se käy yli ymmärrykseni; be ~ a th. pitää itseään liian hyvänä jhk; over and ~ päälle päätteeksi;.. mentioned ~ edellä t. yllä mainittu; the ~ edellä mainittu; as stated ~ kuten yllä on mainittu; ~ the clouds pilvien yläpuolella; ~ 21 years of age 21 vuotta täyttänyt. **~-board** *adv. & a.* avoimesti, rehellisesti; avoin, rehellinen.

abra|de [ə'breid] *v.* raapia, hangata. **-sion** [ə'breiʒn] *s.* hankaaminen; hiertymä.

Abraham ['eibrəhæm] *erisn.*

abreast [ə'brest] *adv.* rinnatusten, rinnan; ~ *of (with)* jnk tasalla; ~ *of the times* aikansa tasalla.

abridg|e [ə'bridʒ] *v.* lyhentää, supistaa. **-(e)ment** *s.* lyhentäminen; lyhennelmä.

abroad [ə'brɔːd] *adv.* ulkomailla, -lle; liikkeellä; laajalti, laajalle; *from* ~ ulkomailta; *go* ~ matkustaa ulkomaille; *there is a rumour* ~ huhutaan.

abrogate ['æbrəgeit] *v.* poistaa, kumota.

abrupt [ə'brʌpt] *a.* (äkki)jyrkkä; äkillinen; katkonainen; töykeä. **-ness** *s.* jyrkkyys; katkonaisuus; töykeys.

abscess ['æbsis] *s.* märkäpesäke, ajos.

abscissa [æb'sisə] *s.* abskissa.

abscond [əb'skɔnd] *v.* paeta (rangaistusta), livistää.

absence ['æbsns] *s.* poissaolo; puute; ~ *of mind* hajamielisyys; *leave of* ~ loma; *in the* ~ *of* jkn poissaollessa, jnk puutteessa.

absent ['æbsnt] *a.* poissa oleva; puuttuva; hajamielinen; *v.* [æb'sent]: ~ *oneself* poistua, pysyä poissa. **-ee** [æbsn'tiː] *s.* poissaoleva. **-ly** *adv.* hajamielisesti. **~-minded** *a.* hajamielinen. **~-mindedness** *s.* hajamielisyys.

absinth(e) ['æbsinθ] *s.* koiruoho, absintti.

absolute ['æbsəluːt] *a.* absoluuttinen; täydellinen; ehdoton, rajoittamaton, rajaton, kiistaton; silkka. **-ly** *adv.* ehdottomasti jne.; kerrassaan, peräti; aivan niin. **-ness** *s.* ehdottomuus.

absolution [æbsə'luːʃn] *s.* synninpäästö.

absolut|ism ['æbsəlu:tizm] *s.* rajaton valta, itsevaltius; absolutismi. **-ist** [-ist] *s.* absolutismin kannattaja (valt.).

absolve [əb'zɔlv] *v.* julistaa vapaaksi, vapauttaa (*from*).

absorb [əb'sɔːb] *v.* imeä itseensä,

(kem.) absorboida; sulattaa itseensä; omaksua (tietoja); viedä kokonaan, kiehtoa. **-ed** [-d] *a.* kiinnostunut, syventynyt; ~ *in thought* syviin ajatuksiin vaipunut. **-ent** [-ənt] *a. & s.* imukykyinen (aine); ~ *cotton* vanu. **-ing** *a.* kiehtova, erittäin kiintoisa.

absorption [əb'sɔːpʃn] *s.* absorptio, imeytyminen; syventyminen, syventyneisyys.

abstain [əb'stein] *v.* pidättyä. **-er** [-ə] *s.* ehdottoman raitis (us. *total* ~), raittiusmies.

abstemious [æb'stiːmiəs] *a.* pidättyväinen, kohtuullinen.

abstention [əb'stenʃn] *s.* pidättyminen (et. äänestämästä).

abstinen|ce ['æbstinəns] *s.* pidättyminen, pidättyvyys, kohtuullisuus; raittius. **-t** [-ənt] *a.* pidättyvä, kohtuullinen.

abstract ['æbstrækt] *a.* abstrakti, käsitteellinen; vaikeatajuinen; *s.* yhteenveto; *v.* [æb'strækt] erottaa, abstrahoida; tehdä yhteenveto (jstk); (puhek.) varastaa. **-ed** [-id] *a.* hajamielinen. **-ion** [æb'strækʃn] *s.* abstraktio, abstrakti käsite; hajamielisyys.

abstruse [æb'struːs] *a.* vaikeatajuinen; hämärä.

absurd [əb'sɔːd, -'zə:d] *a.* järjetön; mahdoton; naurettava. **-ity** [-iti] *s.* järjettömyys, mahdottomuus.

abundan|ce [ə'bʌndəns] *s.* runsaus, yltäkylläisyys; *in* ~ runsaasti. **-t** [-ənt] *a.* runsas, yltäkylläinen. **-tly** *adv.* runsaasti, yllin kyllin; ~ *clear* täysin selvää.

abus|e [ə'bjuːs] *s.* väärinkäyttö; solvaus, loukkaus; *v.* [ə'bjuːz] käyttää väärin; herjata, solvata; *streams of* ~ herjausten tulva; *drug* ~ *r* huumeiden käyttäjä; ~ *s* epäkohdat. **-ive** [-siv] *a.* herjaava, kiroileva; ~ *language* kiroilu.

abut [ə'bʌt] *v.* olla rajakkain, rajoittua (*upon* jhk). **-ment** *s.* tukipilari, tuki.

abysmal [ə'bizməl] *a.* pohjaton.

abyss [ə'bis] *s.* kuilu, pohjaton syvyys, horna.

Abyssinia [æbi'sinjə] *erisn.* Abessinia.

acacia [ə'keiʃə] *s.* akaasia(puu).

academi|c [ækə'demik] *a.*

akateeminen; oppinut; sovinnainen, teoreettinen; s. yliopistomies, akateeminen kansalainen; pl. teoreettiset keskustelut. **-cal** [-l] a. akateeminen; s.: ~s akateeminen puku. **-cian** [ǝkæǝ'mi∫n] s. akateemikko, akatemian jäsen.

academy [ǝ'kædǝmi] s. akatemia; taiteellinen t. kirjallinen seura; opisto, koulu.

accede [æk'si:d] v. tulla jhk, astua (virkaan), liittyä jhk; suostua (to jhk); ~ to the throne nousta valtaistuimelle.

accelera|te [æk'selǝreit] v. kiihdyttää, jouduttaa; kiihtyä. **-tion** [-'rei∫n] s. kiihtyvä nopeus. **-tor** [-ǝ] s. (auton) kaasupoljin.

accent ['æksnt] s. paino, korko(merkki), korostus; murtaminen, vieraanvoittoisuus; v. [æk'sent] korostaa, painottaa; ~ed painollinen. **-uate** [æk'sentjueit] v. korostaa; tähdentää. **-uation** [-'ei∫n] s. painottaminen.

accept [ǝk'sept] v. ottaa vastaan; suostua, hyväksyä; tunnustaa (vekseli). **-able** [-ǝbl] a. hyväksyttävä; tervetullut, otollinen; the terms are not ~ to them he eivät voi hyväksyä ehtoja. **-ance** [-(ǝ)ns] s. vastaanottaminen, hyväksyminen, suostumus; tunnustaminen, tunnuste. **-ation** [-'tei∫n] s. (sanan) tavanomainen merkitys. **-ed** [-id] pp. yleisesti hyväksytty t. tunnustettu. **-or** [-ǝ] s. vekselin tunnustaja.

access ['ækses] s. pääsy (to); sisäänkäytävä; have ~ to päästä jkn puheille, olla käytettävissä; ~ to credit luoton saanti; the place is easy of ~ paikkaan on helppo päästä. **-ary** [æk'sesǝri] s. rikostoveri; ks. accessory. **-ibility** [-i'biliti] s. helppopääsyisyys. **-ible** [æk'sesǝbl] a. helppopääsyinen, luoksepäästävä; (helposti)lähestyttävä; altis (to jllk); ~ to all m. kaikkien saatavissa; ~ to the public yleisölle avoin. **-ion** [æk'se∫n] s. pääsy (to jhk), valtaistuimelle nousu (m. ~ to the throne). **-ory** [æk'sesǝri] a. lisä-, sivu-; s. rikostoveri; (et. pl.) asusteet, lisätarvikkeet, -osat.

acciden|ce ['æksid(ǝ)ns] s. (kiel.)

muoto-oppi. **-t** [-nt] s. sattuma; tapaturma, onnettomuus; by ~ sattumalta; vahingossa; he had an ~ hänelle sattui tapaturma; was killed in an ~ kuoli tapaturmaisesti. **-tal** [-'dentl] a. satunnainen, tilapäinen; tapaturmainen; ~ly = by accident.

acclaim [ǝ'kleim] v. tervehtiä suosionhuudoin; s. suosionhuudot.

acclamation [æklǝ'mei∫n] s. (tav. pl.) suosionhuudot; huutoäänestys.

acclimati|zation [ǝklaimǝtai'zei∫n] s. mukautuminen (ilmastoon). **-ze** [ǝ'klaimǝtaiz] v. mukauttaa t. mukautua ilmastoon.

acclivity [ǝ'kliviti] s. rinne, nousu.

accolade ['ækǝleid] s. ritariksilyönti.

accommodat|e [ǝ'kɔmǝdeit] v. sovittaa (to jnk mukaan); tehdä mieliksi jklle; majoittaa; ~ sb. with hankkia, toimittaa jklle jtk; ~ oneself to mukautua, sopeutua jhk; [the hostel] can ~ 30-ssa on tilaa kolmellekymmenelle; can you ~ me for the night voitteko järjestää minulle yösijan. **-ing** a. avulias; sopuisa, mukautuva. **-ion** [-'dei∫n] s. sovittaminen; majoitus, -tilat; sopimus; hotel ~ hotellihuone(et); ~ bill apuvekseli; ~ ladder (laivan) köysiportaat.

accompan|iment [ǝ'kʌmp(ǝ)nimǝnt] s. säestys. **-ist** [-nist] s. säestäjä.

accompan|y [ǝ'kʌmp(ǝ)ni] v. saattaa; säestää, myötäillä; [he will be] -ied by his wife [hän saapuu] vaimonsa seurassa; the ~ing figure siihen liittyvä (t. oheinen) kuva.

accomplice [ǝ'kʌmplis, ǝ'kɔm-] s. rikoskumppani.

accomplish [ǝ'kɔmpli∫] v. saattaa päätökseen, suorittaa; toteuttaa. **-ed** [-t] pp. & a. loppuunsuoritettu; monitaitoinen, taitava **-ment** s. toteuttaminen, päätökseen saattaminen; (hieno) suoritus; pl. (seuraelämän) taidot.

accord [ǝ'kɔ:d] v. olla yhtäpitävä, olla sopusoinnussa; suoda, myöntää, antaa; s. yhtäpitävyys, sopusointu; with one ~ yksimielisesti; of one's ow ~ omasta halusta, vapaaehtoisesti, itsestään. **-ance** [-(ǝ)ns] s. yhtäpitävyys; in ~ with jnk

mukaisesti. **-ing** *adv.: ~ to* jnk
mukaan; *~ as* sikäli kuin. **-ingly** *adv.*
sen mukaisesti, niin ollen, siis.
accordion [əˈkɔːdjən] *s.* harmonikka,
hanuri.
accost [əˈkɔst] *v.* (lähestyä ja)
puhutella.
account [əˈkaunt] *v.* pitää jnak; *(~ for)*
tehdä tili jstk; selittää; *s.* tili, lasku;
selonteko, selitys; arvo, merkitys;
etu; *call to ~* vaatia jku tilille; *keep~s*
pitää kirjanpitoa; *open an ~ with*
avata tili jssak; *put down to a p.'s ~*
merkitä jkn laskuun; *take into ~* ottaa
lukuun t. huomioon; *turn to ~* käyttää
hyödykseen; *by all ~s* kaikesta
päätellen; *of no ~* merkityksetön; *on
one's own ~* omaan laskuun, omalla
vastuulla; *[buy...] on ~* tiliin; *on ~ of*
jnk johdosta; *on that ~* siitä syystä; *on
no ~* ei millään muotoa; *he is much
~ed of* häntä pidetään suuressa
arvossa; *that ~s for* itse selittää asian.
-ability [-əˈbiliti] *s.* vastuu. **-able** [-əbl]
a. vastuussa *(for* jstk), syyntakeinen,
tilivelvollinen, selitettävissä oleva.
-ant [ənt] *s.* kirjanpitäjä;
tilintarkastaja.
ccredit [əˈkredit] *v.* akkreditoida,
valtuuttaa (lähettilääksi); ks. *credit sb.
with*.
ccretion [əˈkriːʃn] *s.*
yhteenkasvaminen, -kasvu.
ccrue [əˈkruː] *v.* aiheutua, koitua; *the
interest ~d* karttunut korko.
ccumula|te [əˈkjuːmjuleit] *v.* koota,
kasata, kartuttaa, kasaantua, karttua.
-tion [-ˈleiʃn] *s.* kokoaminen; kasa;
paljous; kasaantuminen, kertyminen.
-tor [-ə] *s.* akku, akkumulaattori.
ccura|cy [ˈækjurəsi] *s.* täsmällisyys,
tarkkuus; paikkansapitävyys; *~ of
aim* osumatarkkuus. **-te** [-rit] *a.*
täsmällinen, tarkka; oikea.
ccursed [əˈkɔːsid] *a.* kirottu,
inhottava.
ccusation [ækju(ː)ˈzeiʃn] *s.* syytös.
ccusative [əˈkjuːz(ə)tiv] *s. & a.*
akkusatiivi(-).
ccusatory [əˈkjuːzət(ə)ri] *a.* syyttävä.
ccuse [əˈkjuːz] *v.* syyttää *(of* jstk); *the
~d* syytetty.
ccustom [əˈkʌstəm] *v.* totuttaa *(to
~hk); ~ oneself* tottua; *be ~ed to* olla

tapana. **-ed** [-d] *a.* tavallinen,
totunnainen, tottunut.
ace [eis] *s.* ässä; ykkönen; tähtiajaja,
ilmasankari *(air~); within an ~ of
death* kuolemaisillaan.
acerbity [əˈsɔːbiti] *s.* katkeruus,
karvaus, kirpeys.
acet|ic [əˈset|ik] *a.* etikka-; *~ acid*
etikkahappo. **-one** [ˈæsitəun] *s.*
asetoni. **-ylene** [-iliːn] *s.* asetyleeni.
ache [eik] *s.* särky, kipu; *v.* särkeä,
pakottaa, kivistää.
achieve [əˈtʃiːv] *v.* suorittaa loppuun;
saada aikaan; saavuttaa. **-ment** *s.*
saavutus, (hieno) suoritus.
Achilles [əˈkiliːz] *erisn.; heel of ~*
akilleenkantapää, arka kohta; *~
tendon* akillesjänne.
acid [ˈæsid] *a.* hapan, karvas; *s.* happo;
Am. sl. = LSD. **-ity** [əˈsiditi] *s.*
happamuus; liikahappoisuus. **-ulous**
[əˈsidjuləs] *a.* hapahko.
ack-ack [ˈækˈæk] *s.: ~ gun =*
anti-aircraft gun.
acknowledg|e [əkˈnɔlidʒ] *v.* tunnustaa,
myöntää; ilmoittaa
vastaanottaneensa. **-(e)ment** *s.*
tunnustus; kiitos; kuitti; *in ~ of*
kiitollisuuden osoitukseni,
tunnustukseni jstk.
acme [ˈækmi] *s.* huippu.
acne [ˈækni] *s.* näppylä-, finnitauti.
acolyte [ˈækəlait] *s.* apulainen; noviisi.
acorn [ˈeikɔːn] *s.* tammenterho.
acoustic [əˈkuːstik] *a.* kuulo-. **-s** [-s] *s.
pl.* akustiikka.
acquaint [əˈkweint] *v.* tutustuttaa;
ilmoittaa; *be ~ed with* tuntea jku, olla
perehtynyt jhk; *~ oneself with*
tutustua. **-ance** [-(ə)ns] *s.* tuttavuus;
tuttava; *make sb.'s ~* tutustua jkh.
acquiesce [ækwiˈes] *v.* alistua, tyytyä,
suostua *(in* jhk). **-nce** [-ns] *s.*
alistuvuus; suostumus. **-nt** [-nt] *a.*
alistuva, myöntyväinen.
acquire [əˈkwaiə] *v.* hankkia; voittaa,
saavuttaa; oppia; *~d* hankittu. **-ment**
s. (hankittu) tieto t. taito, *pl.* taidot,
avut.
acquisi|tion [ækwiˈziʃn] *s.*
hankkiminen, hankinta; hankittu
omaisuus; voitto saalis; *he is a distinct
~ [to the team]* arvokas lisä. **-tive**
[æˈkwizitiv] *a.* voitonhaluinen;

acqu

(~ness s. voiton-, rahanhimo).

acquit [ə'kwit] v. vapauttaa; julistaa syyttömäksi; ~ *oneself of* suorittaa jtk, suoriutua jstk. **-tal** [-l] s. syyttömäksi julistaminen.

acre ['eikə] s. eekkeri (n. 4 000 m²). **-age** [-ridʒ] s. pinta-ala.

acrid ['ækrid] a. katkera, karvas, kirpeä. **-ity** [ə'kriditi] s. katkeruus, pisteliäisyys.

acrimon|ious [ækri'məunjəs] a. katkera, kirpeä, pisteliäs. **-y** ['ækriməni] s. katkeruus; pisteliäisyys.

acrobat ['ækrəbæt] s. taitoisirkusvoimistelija. **-ic** [-'bætik] a. akrobaattinen; ~s akrobatia.

across [ə'krɔs] adv. ristiin, poikki; prep. poikki, halki; toisella puolella, toiselle puolelle; *ten metres* ~ 10 metriä leveä; *come* ~ kohdata, tavata; *get one's meaning* ~ tulla ymmärretyksi.

acrostic [ə'krɔstik] s. (run.) akrostikon.

act [ækt] s. teko, toimi; asiakirja; asetus, laki; näytös, esitys, (esim. sirkus)numero; v. toimia, menetellä; vaikuttaa; näytellä, esittää; *in the* [*very*] ~ itse teossa; *Acts* [*of the Apostles*] Apostolien teot; ~ *of war* laiton sotatoimi; ~ *out* (psyk.) purkaa (esim. tunteita) toimintaan; ~ *up to* toimia jnk mukaisesti; ~ [*up*]*on* noudattaa jtk, vaikuttaa jhk; **-ing** a. toimiva; väliaikainen, virkaatekevä; s. näytteleminen; ~ *manager* toimitusjohtaja.

action ['ækʃn] s. toiminta, toimi, toimenpide, teko, työ; vaikutus; taistelu (sot.); oikeudenkäynti; *bring an* ~ *against* haastaa oikeuteen; *take* ~ ryhtyä toimiin; *put...out of* ~ tehdä toiminta- t. taistelukyvyttömäksi. **-able** [-əbl] a. syytteeseen oikeuttava.

activate ['æktiveit] v. aktivoida.

activ|e ['æktiv] a. toimiva; toimekas, reipas, vilkas; aktiivinen; ~ *service* aktiivipalvelus; ~ *voice* aktiivi (kiel.); *take an* ~ *part in* osallistua aktiivisesti jhk. **-ity** [æk'tiviti] s. toiminta; vilkkaus; pl. työt, toimet.

act|or ['æktə] s. näyttelijä. **-ress** [-ris] s. näyttelijätär.

actual ['æktjuəl] a. todellinen,

varsinainen. **-ity** [æktju'æliti] s. todellisuus; pl. todelliset olot. **-ize** [-aiz] v. toteuttaa; käsitellä todenmukaisesti. **-ly** adv. itse asiassa; todella; tosiaankin.

actuary ['æktjuəri] s. aktuaari, vakuutusmatemaatikko.

actuate ['æktjueit] v. panna liikkeelle; vaikuttaa.

acuity [ə'kjuəti] s. terävyys.

acumen [ə'kju:mən] s. terävä-älyisyys.

acupuncture ['ækjupʌŋktʃə] s. akupunktio.

acute [ə'kju:t] a. terävä, terävä-älyinen; korkea, kimeä; ankara (tuska ym); (taudista) äkillisluontoinen; ~ *pleasure* suuri, valtava ilo. **-ness** s. terävyys, ankaruus.

adage ['ædidʒ] s. sananparsi, mietelmä

Adam ['ædəm] erisn. Aatami; *I don't know him from* ~ en tunne häntä ulkonäöltäkään.

adamant ['ædəmənt] a. timantinkova, järkkymätön. **-ine** [-'mæntain] a. = ed.

adapt [ə'dæpt] v. sovittaa (*to* jnk mukaan), soveltaa; ~ *oneself to circumstances* mukautua, sopeutua olosuhteisiin; ~ed from jstk mukailtu **-ability** [-ə'biliti] s. mukautuvaisuus. **-able** [-əbl] a. mukautuva, sopeutuva **-ation** [-'teiʃn] s. mukautumiskyky; mukaelma. **-ed** [-id] a. sopiva (*to* jhk **-er** [-ə] s. (sähk.) sovitusliitin, sovitin **-ive** [-iv] a. mukautuva.

add [æd] v. lisätä, liittää; laskea yhtee (m. ~ *up*, ~ *together*); ~ *to* lisätä jtk; ... ~*ed to*... ynnä; ... ~ *s up to*...o yhteensä, (puhek.) merkitsee.

addendum [ə'dendəm] s. (pl. *addend* lisäys.

adder ['ædə] s. kyykäärme; *flying* ~ sudenkorento.

addict [ə'dikt] v.: ~ *oneself to* antautu hk; s. ['ædikt] *morphine* ~ morfinis *drug* (t. *dope*) ~ huumausaineen käyttäjä t. orja, narkomaani. **-ed** [-i a.: *be* ~ *to* olla ylen mieltynyt, altis jhk; ~*to drink* juopotteleva. **-ion** [ə'dikʃn] s. mieltymys, himo *(alcoho* ~ *)*. **-ive** [-iv] a. riippuvuutta aiheuttava (esim. huumausaine).

Addis Ababa ['ædis'æbəbə] erisn.

addition [ə'diʃn] s. lisäys; yhteenlasku; in ~ sen ohessa, lisäksi; in ~ to jnk lisäksi. **-al** [-l] a. lisä-; (~ly lisäksi).

addle ['ædl] a. hedelmätön; mätä; tyhjä, sekava; v. mädäntyä; panna sekaisin; (~-pated sekava(päinen).

address [ə'dres] v. osoittaa (kirje ym); kääntyä jkn puoleen, puhutella, pitää puhe; kohdistaa; ryhtyä jhk (~ oneself to); s. [Am. 'ædres] osoite; puhe; käytöstapa; form of ~ puhuttelumuoto, arvo; pay one's ~es to kosiskella jkta. **-ee** [ædre'siː] s. (kirjeen) saaja.

adduce [ə'djuːs] v. tuoda esiin, esittää.

Adelaide ['ædəleid] erisn. (kaupunki)

Aden ['eidn] erisn.

adenoids ['ædinɔidz] s. nielun kattorisan liikakasvu.

adept ['ædept] a. täydellisesti perehtynyt; s. tuntija, mestari.

adequacy ['ædikwəsi] s. riittävyys. **-ate** [-it] a. riittävä, tarkoitustaan vastaava; (~ly tyydyttävästi).

adhere [əd'hiə] v. olla kiinni (to jssk), kiinnittyä; pitää kiinni, lujasti pysyä (to jssk). **-nce** [-rəns] s. kiinnipysyminen, -pitäminen; uskollisuus. **-nt** [-rənt] s. kannattaja.

adhesion [əd'hiːʒn] s. ks. adherence; kannatus; kiinnike (lääk.); adheesio. **-sive** [-siv] a. tahmea, kiinni pysyvä; ~ plaster kiinnelaastari; ~ tape teippi, liima-, tarranauha.

ad hoc ['ædhɔk] adv. tätä (tarkoitusta) varten.

adieu [ə'djuː] s. jäähyväiset.

adipose ['ædipəus] a. rasva-.

adjacency [ə'dʒeisnsi] s. läheisyys. **-ent** [-nt] a. läheinen; vieremen, rajakkain oleva (to jnk kanssa).

adjectival [ædʒek'taiv(ə)l] a. adjektiivinen. **-e** ['ædʒiktiv] s. adjektiivi, laatusana.

adjoin [ə'dʒɔin] v. olla (jnk) vieressä. **-ing** a. vieremen, raja-, naapuri-.

adjourn [ə'dʒəːn] v. lykätä, siirtää; hajaantua (parl. ym); siirtyä; **-ment** s. lykkääminen, lykkäys; hajaantuminen.

adjudge [ə'dʒʌdʒ] v. tuomita; määrätä. **-ment** s. tuomio.

adjudicate [ə'dʒuːdikeit] v. ks. adjudge; langettaa tuomio.

adjunct ['æ'dʒʌŋ(k)t] s. lisä, liite, apu; avustaja; määre.

adjure [ə'dʒuə] v. vannottaa; pyytämällä pyytää.

adjust [ə'dʒʌst] v. panna kuntoon; järjestää, asettaa kohdalleen; sovitella, soveltaa (to jnk mukaan); tarkistaa, korjata; well-~ed sopeutunut, sopeutuva. **-able** [-əbl] a. sovitettavissa oleva, sopeutuva, -inen; siirrettävä, säädettävä. **-ment** s. järjestely, sovittaminen, säätö, tarkistus.

adjutant ['ædʒut(ə)nt] s. adjutantti; ~ bird intialainen haikara.

adman ['æd|mən] s. sl. mainosmies. **-mass** [-mæs] s. & a. joukkoviestimille altis (väestö).

administer [əd'minist|ə] v. hallita, hoitaa, johtaa, toimittaa; jakaa, antaa; huolehti jstk (to); the oath was ~ed to him häneltä otettiin vala. **-ration** [-'treiʃn] s. hallinto, hoito; jakaminen; antaminen; (oikeuden)käyttö; hallintokausi, hallitus. **-rative** [-rətiv] a. hallinnollinen, hallinto-. **-rator** [-reitə] s. hallintomies; (jnk) hoitaja; hulhooja, selvitysmies.

admirable ['ædm(ə)rəbl] a. ihmeteltävä, ihailtava, erinomainen. -ly ihailtavasti.

admiral ['ædm(ə)r(ə)l] s. amiraali. **-ty** [-ti] amiraalinarvo; the A~ amiraliteetti, meriministeriö; First Lord of the ~ meriministeri.

admiration [ædmə'reiʃn] s. ihailu; she was the ~ of all kaikki ihailivat häntä.

admire [æd'maiə] v. ihailla. **-er** [-rə] s. ihailija. **-ingly** [-riŋli] adv. ihaillen.

admissible [əd'misəbl] a. luvallinen.

admission [əd'miʃn] s. pääsy; pääsymaksu; myönnytys, myöntäminen; gain ~ to päästä jhk.

admit [əd'mit] v. päästää (sisään); ottaa (esim. kouluun, sairaalaan); myöntää; sallia (of jtk); the hall ~s 500 people salissa on tilaa 500:lle; this ~s of no doubt tämä ei jätä sijaa epäilykselle; . . ~ting a finger sormen mentävä. **-tance** [-əns] s. (sisään)pääsy; no ~ except on business pääsy asiattomilta kielletty! **-ted** [-id] a. tunnustettu; (~ly adv.

tunnustetusti, tunnetusti.)

admixture [əd'mikstʃə] s. sekoitus, lisä.

admoni|sh [əd'mɔni|ʃ] v. nuhdella, varoittaa. **-tion** [ædmə'niʃn] s. (lievä) nuhde; varoitus **-tory** [-it(ə)ri] a. varoittava.

ado [ə'du:] s. touhu, hälinä; *without any (further)* ~ pitemmittä puheitta.

adobe [ə'dəubi] s. (auringon kuivaama) savitiili.

adolescen|ce [ædə(u)'lesns] s. nuoruusikä. **-t** [-nt] a. nuoruusiässä oleva; s. nuorukainen, nuori tyttö; ~s nuoret.

adopt [ə'dɔpt] v. ottaa lapseksi; ottaa (*for, as* jksk); omaksua, ottaa käytäntöön; hyväksyä (esitys). **-ed** [-id] a. otto-; *my ~ed country* uusi kotimaani. **-ion** [ə'dɔpʃn] s. lapseksi ottaminen, omaksuminen jne. **-ive** [-iv] a. otto-; ~ *father* kasvatusisä.

adora|ble [ə'dɔ:rəbl] a. hurmaava, ihailtava; *what an ~ baby!* mikä ihana vauva! **-tion** [ædɔ:'reiʃn] s. palvonta, jumalointi.

adore [ə'dɔ:] v. palvoa, jumaloida; rakastaa.

adorn [ə'dɔ:n] v. koristaa, kaunistaa, **-ment** s. koristus, koriste.

adrenal [ə'dri:nl] a.: ~ *glands* lisämunuaiset. **-in** [ə'drenəlin] s. adrenaliini.

Adriatic [eidri'ætik] *erisn.: the ~* [*Sea*] Adrianmeri.

adrift [ə'drift] a. tuuliajolla, -lle.

adroit [ə'drɔit] a. taitava, kätevä, näppärä. **-ness** s. taitavuus

adulation [ædju'leiʃn] s. liehakointi, imartelu.

adult ['ædʌlt, ə'd-] a. & s. aikuinen, täysikasvuinen; ~ *education* aikuiskasvatus.

adulter|ate [ə'dʌltəreit] v. väärentää; sekoittaa (lisäainetta jhk), turmella; ~*d milk* maito, johon on lisätty vettä. **-ation** [-'reiʃn] s. väärentäminen; huonontaminen (jtk lisäämällä). **-er** [-rə] s. avionrikkkoja. **-ess** [-ris] s. avionrikkkoja (nainen). **-ous** [-rəs] a. avionrikkoja-. **-y** [-ri] s. aviorikos.

adumbrate ['ædʌmbreit] v. hahmotella.

advence [əd'vɑ:ns] v. viedä eteenpäin, edistää, korottaa, parantaa; ylentää; maksaa ennakkoa; esittää; edetä,

edistyä; kohota, nousta; s. eteneminen, edistys; yleneminen; (hinnan) nousu; ennakkomaksu; laina; lähentely (us. *pl.);* ~ *money* ennakkomaksu; *in* ~ etukäteen; ~ *guard* etujoukko; ~*d position* eteentyönnetty asema (sot.). **-d** [t] a. kehittynyt, edistynyt; ~ *ideas* uudenaikaiset ajatukset; *the ~ level* (tav. lyh. *A level*) tutkinto *(G.C.E.*-tutkinnon osa), joka oikeuttaa pääsemään yliopistoon ym; ~*studies* korkeammat opinnot; *at an ~ age* korkeassa iässä, iäkkäänä. **-ment** s. edistäminen; (virka)ylennys.

advantage [əd'vɑ:ntidʒ] s. etu (m. tennis), etusija, paremmuus, voitto, höyty; *take ~ of* käyttää hyväkseen; *have an ~ over* olla jkta edullisemmassa asemassa; *turn to ~* käyttää hyödykseen; *to the best* ~ edullisimmin. **-ous** [ædvən'teidʒəs] a. edullinen.

advent ['ædvənt] s. saapuminen; *A* ~ adventti; *Seventh-day A* ~*ist* adventisti. **-itious** [-'tiʃəs] a. satunnainen, tilapäinen.

adventur|e [əd'ventʃə] s. seikkailu; uhkayritys; v. vaarantaa. **-er** [-rə] s. seikkailija; onnenonkija. **-ess** [-ris] s. seikkailijatar. **-ous** [-rəs] a. seikkailunhaluinen; seikkailukas, vaarallinen, uhkarohkea.

adverb ['ædvə:b] s. adverbi. **-ial** [æd'və:bjəl] a. adverbi-.

advers|ary [ædvəs(ə)ri] s. vastustaja. **-e** ['ædvə:s] a.: ~ *to* jnk vastainen; viha-, vihollismielinen; haitallinen; vastakkainen; ~ *fortune* = seur. **-ity** [əd'və:siti] s. vastoinkäyminen, kova onni; onnettomuus.

advert [əd'və:t] v.: ~ *to* viitata jhk.

advertise ['ædvətaiz] v. ilmoittaa (lehdessä ym), mainostaa; ~ *for an assistant* ilmoittaa lehdessä hakevansa apulaista; **-ment** [əd'və:tismənt, Am. '- -'taizmənt] s. ilmoitus; mainos(tus).

advertising ['ædvətaizin] s. ilmoittaminen; mainonta, mainosala; *designer* mainospiirtäjä.

advice [əd'vais] s. neuvot; tiedote; *a piece of* ~ neuvo; *on his* ~ hänen neuvostaan; *take my* ~ noudata neuvoani.

advisable [əd'vaizəbl] *a.* suositeltava, viisas.

advis|e [əd'vaiz] *v.* neuvoa; ilmoittaa antaa tieto, **-ed** [-d] *a.: well-~* harkittu, viisas; *ill-~* harkitsematon. **-edly** [-idli] *adv.* harkitusti, tarkoituksellisesti. **-er** [-ə] *s.* neuvonantaja. **-ory** [-əri] *a.* neuvotteleva, neuvoa antava.

advoc|acy ['ædvəkəsi] *s.* asianajajan toimi; puolustus (oikeudessa). **-ate** [-it] *s.* asianajaja; puoltaja, kannattaja; *v.* [-eit] puol(us)taa, kannattaa, puhua puolesta.

adze [ædz] *s.* talso(kirves).

Aegean [i(:)'dʒi:ən] *a & sb.: the ~* [*Sea*] Aigeianmeri.

aegis ['i:dʒis] *s.: under the ~ of* jkn suojeluksessa.

Aeolian harp [i(:)'əuliən ha:p] *s.* tuulikannel.

aeon ['i:ən] *s.* aioni, maailmankausi.

aerate ['eiəreit] *v.* kyllästää hiilihapolla; hapettaa (anat.).

aerial [ɛəriəl] *a.* ilma-; *s.* antenni (rad.); *~ battle* ilmataistelu; *~ photography* ilmakuvaus; *~ view* ilmavalokuva.

aerie ['ɛəri] *s.* petolinnun pesä.

aero- ['ɛərə-] (yhd.) ilma-. **-batics** [-'bætiks] taitolento. **-drome** [-drəum] lentokenttä. **-dynamics** [-əudai'næmiks] aerodynamiikka. **-lite** ['ɛərəlait] kivimeteoriitti. **-naut** [-'nɔ:t] ilmailija. **-nautics** [-'nɔ:tiks] ilmailu. **-plane** [-plein] lentokone. **-sol** suihkute, aerosoli, sumute. **-stat** [-stæt] ilmapallo.

aesthet|e ['i(:)sθi:t] *s.* esteetikko. **-ic(al)** [i(:)s'θetik, -(ə)l] *a.* esteettinen. **-ics** [i(:)s'θetiks] *s.* estetiikka.

[a]etiology [i:ti'ɔlədʒi] *s.* taudin syyt.

afar [ə'fɑ:] *adv.* kaukana, kauas; *from ~* kaukaa.

affability [æfə'biliti] *s.* ystävällisyys.

affable ['æfəbl] *a.* ystävällinen; kohtelias.

affair [ə'fɛə] *s.* asia, tehtävä, toimi; *~ of honour* kaksintaistelu; *love ~* rakkausjuttu; *current ~s* päivän kysymykset, ajankohtais-.

affect [ə'fekt] *v.* vaikuttaa, koskea, liikuttaa; teeskennellä; *his left lung is ~ed by cancer* hänellä on syöpä

vasemmassa keuhkossa; [*she*] *~s . . .* käyttää mielellään. . . **-ation** [æfek'teiʃn] *s.* teeskentely, teennäisyys. **-ed** [-id] *a.* teennäinen, teeskennelty; sairas (elin); *how is he ~ towards us* miten hän suhtautuu meihin? **-edness** *s.* teennäisyys.

affection [ə'fekʃn] *s.* mielenliikutus; mieltymys, kiintymys; affektio, tauti (lääk.); *our ~s* tunteemme. **-ate** [-it] *a.* rakastava, hellä; *~ly . . .* (kirjeessä) Sinun . .

affianced [ə'faiənst] *a.* kihlattu.

affidavit [æfi'deivit] *s.* valallinen todistus.

affiliate [ə'filieit] *v.* ottaa seuran jäseneksi; liittää; *be ~d with (to)* kuulua jhk (jäsenenä, alaosastona, tytäryhtiönä ym).

affinity [ə'finiti] *s.* sukulaisuus (avioliiton kautta); hengenheimolaisuus, samankaltaisuus; (kem.) affiniteetti.

affirm [ə'fə:m] *v.* vakuuttaa todeksi, vahvistaa, myöntää oikeaksi. **-ation** [æfə'meiʃn] *s.* vakuutus, väite; myöntäminen. **-ative** [-ətiv] *a.* myöntävä; *s.: answer in the ~* vastata myöntävästi.

affix [ə'fiks] *v.* liittää, kiinnittää; liittää.

afflict [ə'flikt] *v.* kiusata, vaivata, koetella. **-ed** [-id] *a.; ~ with* jnk vaivaama, ahdistama, kiusaama. **-ion** [ə'flikʃn] *s.* suru, vastoinkäyminen, onnettomuus, koettelemus.

affluen|ce ['æfluəns] *s.* runsaus, rikkaus, yltäkylläisyys, vauraus. **-t** [-ənt] *a.* tulviva; runsas, yltäkylläinen; *s.* sivujoki; *the ~ society* yltäkylläisyyden yhteiskunta.

afflux ['æflʌks] *s.* tulva.

afford [ə'fɔ:d] *v.* antaa, suoda, tuottaa; *(can-*verbin yht.) olla varaa jhk; liietä; *I cannot ~ it* minulla ei ole varaa siihen.

afforest [æ'fɔrist] *v.* istuttaa metsää jhk. **-ation** [-'teiʃn] *s.* metsän istutus.

affray [ə'frei] *s.* metakka, tappelu.

affront [ə'frʌnt] *v.* loukata, herjata; *s.* loukkaus; *pocket an ~* niellä loukkaus.

Afghan ['æfgæn] *a. & s.* afgaani, afganistanilainen. **-istan** [æf'gænistæn] *erisn.*

afield [əˈfiːld] *adv.: far* ~ etäällä, -lle.

afire [əˈfaiə] *adv.* tulessa

aflame [əˈfleim] *adv.* liekkien vallassa.

afloat [əˈflout] *adv.* veden varassa, pinnalla; merellä; liikkeellä; *be* ~ kelluta; *get a new . . .* ~ panna alulle.

afoot [əˈfut] *adv.* liikkeellä, tekeillä; (vanh.) jalan.

afore [əˈfɔː] *adv. & prep.* keulan puolella, -lle. **-said** *a.* ennen mainittu. **-thought** *a.* harkittu.

afraid [əˈfreid] *pred. a.* peloissaaan: *be* ~ pelätä jtk *(of, that . . .); I'm* ~ I *can't help you* pelkäänpä, että (t. ikävä kyllä) en voi auttaa.

afresh [əˈfreʃ] *adv.* uudelleen.

Africa [ˈæfrikə] *erisn.* Afrikka **-n** [-n] *a. & s.* afrikkalainen (nyk. et. musta).

Afrik|aans [æfriˈkɑːns] *s.* afrikaansin kieli. **-ander** [-ˈkændə] *s.* eteläafrikkal. (nauta)karjarotu. **-aner** [-ˈkɑːnə] *s.* (Et. afr.) afrikaani (buuri).

Afro- [ˈæfrəu-]: ~-*Asian* afroaasialainen.

aft [ɑːft] *adv. & prep.* (laivan) peräpuolella, perään.

after [ˈɑːftə], *adv. & prep.* takana, taakse, jäljessä jälkeen; jälkeenpäin; kuluttua; mukaan; *konj.* sen jälkeen kun; *a.* myöhempi, seuraava; ~ *all* kuitenkin, loppujen lopuksi, sentään; ~ *my heart* mieleiseni; *be* ~ *a th.* tavoitella, pyrkiä jhk; *week* ~ *week* viikko viikolta; *three days* ~ kolme päivää myöhemmin; *in* ~ *years* myöhempinä vuosina; ~ *cabin* perähytti. **~-care** jälkihoito. **~-effect** jälkiseuraus. **-glow** ruskotus. **-math** [-mæθ] *s.* jälkisato (kuv.), seuraukset. **-noon** [-nuːn] *s. & a.* iltapäivä(-). **-thought** myöhästynyt tuuma, ajatus. **-wards** [-wədz] *adv.* myöhemmin, jälkeenpäin.

again [əˈgen, əˈgein] *adv.* uudelleen, jälleen, taas; takaisin; toisaalta; ~ *and* ~ yhä uudelleen; *now and* ~ silloin tällöin; *as much* ~ kaksi kertaa niin paljon; *over* ~ vielä kerran. **-st** [-st] *prep.* vastaan, vastoin; jtk varalta; *a rainy day* pahan päivän varalta; *as* ~ jhk verrattuna; *over* ~ vastapäätä; *run* [*up*] ~ kohdata sattumalta; *he hit his head* ~ *the wall*

hän löi päänsä seinään.

agape [əˈgeip] *adv.* suu ammollaan.

agaric [ˈægərik] *s.* helttasieni.

agate [ˈægət] *s.* akaatti (miner.)

agave [əˈgeivi] *s.* agaave.

age [eidʒ] ikä; elinikä; kausi; ajanjakso, aika; *v.* vanhentua, vanheta; vanhentaa; *of* ~ täysi-ikäinen; *come of* ~ tulla täysi-ikäiseksi; *under* ~ alaikäinen; *ten years of* ~ kymmenen vuotta (vanha); *at the* ~ *of . . .* ikäisenä, -vuotiaana; *what* ~ *is he?* minkä ikäinen (kuinka vanha) hän on? *for his* ~ ikäisekseen; *I have not seen him] for* ~ *s* pitkiin aikoihin; *the Ice A*~ jääkausi; *the Middle Ages* keskiaika. **-d** [-d] *a.* ikäinen; [-id] iäkäs, vanha. **-ing** ks. aging. **-less** [-lis] *a.* ikinuori, ajaton. **-long** *a.* loputtoman pitkä.

agency [ˈeidʒnsi] *s.* toiminta; vaikutus; välitys, agentuuri, toimisto; *through the* ~ *of* jnk, jkn välityksellä, toimesta.

agenda [əˈdʒendə] *s.* esityslista.

agent [ˈeidʒnt] *s.* vaikuttava syy, voima t. aine; agentti; asiamies, edustaja, välittäjä.

agglomera|te [əˈglɔməreit] *v.* kasata kokoon; kasaantua; *a.* [-rit] kasaantunut. **-tion** [-ˈreiʃn] *s.* kasaantuminen, kasa(uma).

agglutinate [əˈgluːtineit] *v.* liimata, agglutinoida.

aggrandizement [əˈgrændizmənt] *s.* suurentaminen.

aggravat|e [ˈægrəveit] *v.* raskauttaa, vaikeuttaa, pahentaa; suututtaa. **-ing** *a.* raskauttava; ärsyttävä, kiusallinen; ~ *circumstances* raskauttavat asianhaarat. **-ion** [-ˈveiʃn] *s.* paheneminen; harmi.

aggrega|te [ˈægrigit] *a.* kokonais-, yhteis-; *s.* joukko, ryhmä, kokonaisuus; *v.* [-eit] koota, yhdistää; *in the* ~ kokonaisuudessaan; ~ *amount* kokonaissumma. **-tion** [-ˈgeiʃn] *s.* keräymä.

aggres|sion [əˈgreʃn] *s.* hyökkäys. **-sive** [-siv] *a.* hyökkäävä, aggressiivinen; hyökkäys-. (**~ness** hyökkäämishalu). **-sor** [-sə] *s.* hyökkääjä, hyökkäävä puoli.

aggrieved [ə'gri:vd] *a.* loukkaantunut.

aghast [ə'gɑːst] *pred. a.* kauhistunut, tyrmistynyt.

agile [ə'ædʒail, Am. -ʒil] *a.* nopsa, ketterä, vilkas. **-ity** [ə'dʒiliti] *s.* ketteryys, notkeus, reippaus.

aging, ageing ['eidʒiŋ] *a.* vanheneva; *s.* vanheneminen.

agio [ædʒi]ou] *s.* kurssiero.

agitat|e ['ædʒiteit] *v.* ravistella (nestettä); tehdä levottomaksi, järkyttää; kiihottaa. **-ion** [-'teiʃn] *s.* levottomuus, mielenliikutus; kiihotus, agitaatio. **-or** [-ə] *s.* kiihottaja, agitaattori.

aglow [ə'glou] *adv. & a.* hehkuva(sti).

agnostic [æg'nɔsti|k] *s.* agnostikko. **-ism** [-sizm] *s.* agnostisismi.

ago [ə'gou] *adv.* sitten; *long ~* kauan sitten; *not long ~* äskettäin.

agog [ə'gɔg] *adv. & pred. a.* innoissaan, jännittynyt; *was ~ for news* odotti innokkaasti (uteliaana) uutisia.

agoniz|e ['ægənaiz] *v.* kiduttaa; olla kuolemantuskassa. **-ing** *a.* tuskallinen.

agony ['ægəni] *s.* (kuoleman)tuska, hätä; kuolinkamppailu.

agrarian [ə'greəriən] *a.* maatalous-, maanomistus-.

agree [ə'gri:] *v.* olla samaa mieltä (*with* jnk kanssa; *on, about* jstk), olla yhtäpitävä, sopia (yhteen); suostua (*to* jhk): sopia (*upon* jstk); noudattaa (kiel.); *I quite ~* olen täysin samaa mieltä; *as ~d upon* kuten oli sovittu; *coffee does not ~ with me* kahvi ei sovellu minulle; *we are all ~d that* olemme kaikki yhtä mieltä siitä, että; *why can't you ~ [together]?* miksi ette tule toimeen keskenänne? **-able** [-riəbl] *a.* miellyttävä, mukava; yhtäpitävä, jnk mukainen (*to*); **-ably** *surprised* iloisesti yllättynyt. **-d** [-d] *a.* sovittu; *~!* hyvä on! **-ment** *s.* sopimus; yhtäpitävyys; sopu; *come to (arrive at t. reach) an ~* päästä sopimukseen, sopia.

agrestic [ə'grestik] *a.* maalais-.

agricultur|al [ægri'kʌltʃ|ər(ə)l] *a.* maanviljelys-, maatalous-. **-e** ['ægrikʌltʃə] *s.* maanviljely(s). **-ist** [-ərist] *s.* maanviljelijä.

aground [ə'graund] *adv.* karilla, (-lle)

run ~ ajaa karille, kariutua.

agu|e ['eigjuː] *s.* horkka. **-ish** [-iʃ] *a.* kuumeinen.

ah [ɑː] *int.* ah! oi! oi! voi!

ahead [ə'hed] *adv.* edellä, -lle; eteenpäin; edessä; *get ~ of* päästä jkn edelle; *go ~!* jatka(kaa)! anna tulla! *v.* edistyä; *look ~* katsoa eteensä; *the years ~* edessä olevat vuodet.

ahoy [ə'hoi] *int.: ship ~* laiva ohoi!

aid [eid] *v.* auttaa; *s.* apu; apulainen; apukeino; *by the ~ of* jnk avulla; *first ~* ensiapu; ks. *hearing ~*.

aide [eid] *s.* (*~ to* jkn) apulainen. **~-de-camp** [-dəkɔːŋ] *s.* adjutantti.

ail [eil] *v.* vaivata; olla sairas. **-ing** *a.* sairaalloinen. **-ment** *s.* sairaus, vaiva.

aim [eim] *v.* tähdätä, suunnata (*at* jhk), tarkoittaa (jtk), pyrkiä (jhk); *s.* maali, pilkka, tähtäys; päämäärä, tavoite; *miss one's ~* ampua harhaan; *take ~* tähdätä. **-less** *a.* päämäärätön, tarkoitukseton.

ain't [eint] (puhek.) lyh. = *am (are, is) not, have (has) not*.

air [ɛə] *s.* ilma, höyry; tuulahdus; ulkonäkö, muoto, ilmeet; laulu, sävelmä; *v.* tuulettaa, kuivata; *A~ Force* ilmavoimat; *~ gun* ilmakivääri, -pistooli; *~ letter* ilmakirje, aerogrammi; *~ service* lento|linja, -vuoro; *~ space* ilmatila; *by ~* lento|teitse, -koneella; *in the open ~* taivasalla; *on the ~* radiossa; *will be on the ~* (rad.) lähettää ohjelmaa, puhuu radiossa; *the secret takes ~* salaisuus tulee ilmi; *clear the ~* puhdistaa ilmaa; *have an ~ of* tuntua t. näyttää jltk; *give oneself ~s* näytellä ylhäistä; *~ one's views* esittää mielipiteitään. **~-base** lentotukikohta. **-bed** ilmapatja. **~-bladder** ilmarakko. **-borne troops** ilmakuljetusjoukot. **-conditioned** ilmastoitu. **~-conditioning** ilmastointi. **-craft** lentokone(et). **-craft-carrier** lentotukialus. **-drome** Am. lentoasema. **-field** lentokenttä. **~-hostess** lentoemäntä. **-ing** *s.* tuulettaminen. **~-lift** ilmasilta. **-less** *a.* ilmaton; tyven. **-line** lentoyhtiö. **-liner** liikennelentokone. **-mail** lentoposti. **-man** lentäjä. **~-minded** ilmailusta kiinnostunut. **-plane** lentokone.

~-pocket ilmakuoppa. **-port** lentokenttä, **-asema** **~-raid** ilmahyökkäys; *a. -r. precautions* (tav. lyh. *A.R.P.*) väestönsuojelu; *a. -r. shelter* väestönsuoja. **-ship** ilmalaiva. **~-sickness** ilmasairaus. **~-strip** (tilapäinen) lentokenttä. **-tight** ilmanpitävä; ehdottoman varma (sl.). **-way** lentoreitti; *~s m.* hengitystiet. **-worthy** lentokelpoinen. **-y** [-i] *a.* ilmava, ilma-, kevyt, huoleton, pinnallinen, tyhjänpäiväinen.

aisle [ail] *s.* (kirkon) sivulaiva, käytävä (Am. m. junassa, teatterissa).

aitch [eitʃ] *s.* h-kirjain.

aitch-bone ['eitʃbəun] *s.* lonkkaluu; reisipala.

ajar [ə'dʒɑː] *adv.* raollaan, -lleen.

akimbo [ə'kimbəu] *adv.: with arms ~* kädet puuskassa.

akin [ə'kin] *pred. a.* sukua; *~ to* (m.) jnk luontoinen, kaltainen.

Alabama [ælə'bæmə] *erisn.*

alacrity [ə'lækriti] *s.* ripeys, hilpeys, aulius.

alarm [ə'lɑːm] *s.* hälytys, hälytysmerkki; levottomuus; *v.* saattaa levottomaksi, pelästyttää; *give the ~* hälyttää; *burglar ~* murtohälytin. **~-clock** herätyskello. **-ed** [-d] *a.* levoton, pelästynyt. **-ing** *a.* hälyttävä, huolestuttava. **-ist** [-ist] *s.* »hätäkello», pelottelija.

alarum [ə'leərəm] *s.* hälytys(laite).

alas [ə'lɑːs] *int.* voi! valitettavasti!

Alaska [ə'læskə] *erisn.*

alb [ælb] *s.* messupaita, alba.

Albania [æl'beinjə] *erisn.* **-n** [-n] *a. & s.* albanialainen, albanian kieli.

albeit [ɔːl'biːit] *konj.* (ei puhek.) vaikkakin.

albino [æl'biːnəu] *s.* albiino.

Albion ['ælbjən] *s.* (vanh. t. run.) Englanti (ja Skotlanti).

album ['ælbəm] *s.* (valokuva- ym) albumi, (äänilevy)kansio.

album|en ['ælbjumin] *s.* valkuaisaine. **-in** [ks. ed.] *s.* albumiini. **-inous** [æl'bjuːminəs] *a.* valkuaispitoinen.

alchem|ist ['ælkimist] *s.* alkemisti, kullantekijä. **-y** ['ælkimi] *s.* alkemia.

alcohol ['ælkəhɔl] *s.* alkoholi. **-ic** [ælkə'hɔlik] *a.* alkoholipitoinen, alkoholi-; *s.* alkoholisti. **-ism** [-izm] *s.* alkoholismi.

alcove ['ælkəuv] *s.* alkovi, (huoneen) syvennys, nurkkaus.

alder ['ɔːldə] *s.* leppä.

alderman ['ɔːldəmən] *s.* ammatinvanhin, neuvosmies.

ale [eil] *s.* (vaalea) olut.

alert [ə'ləːt] *a.* valpas; eloisa, reipas; *s.* hälytys; *v.* hälyttää; *~ .. to* tehdä valppaaksi, varoittaa jstk; *on the ~.* varuillansa. **-ness** *s.* valppaus.

Alexand|er [ælig'zɑːnd|ə], **-ra** [-rə], **-ria** [-riə] *erisn.* **-rine** [-'zændrain] *a. & s.* aleksandrinen (säe), aleksandriini.

alfalfa [æl'fælfə] *s.* (kasv.) sinimailanen.

alga ['ælgə] *s.* (pl. *algae* ['ældʒiː]) levä.

algebra ['ældʒibrə] *s.* algebra.

Algeria [æl'dʒiəriə] *erisn.* **-n** [-n] *a. & s.* algerialainen.

Algiers [æl'dʒiəz] *erisn.* Alger.

alias ['eiliəs] *adv.* toisella nimellä; *s.* väärä nimi, salanimi.

alibi ['ælibai] *s.* alibi, muualla olo; »puolustus»; *prove one's ~* todistaa olleensa muualla.

alien ['eiljən] *a.* vieras, muukalainen; *s.* ulkomaalainen; *enemy ~* vihollismaan kansalainen; *~ office* ulkomaalaistoimisto. **-able** [-əbl] *a.* luovutettavissa oleva. **-ate** [-eit] *v.* vieroittaa, vieraannuttaa; luovuttaa. **-ation** [-'neiʃn] *s.* vieraantuminen; luovuttaminen; *(mental ~)* mielenhäiriö.

alight [ə'lait] *v.* laskeutua (alas, maahan), astua alas; *pred. a.* tulessa; valaistu.

align [ə'lain] *v.* asettaa t. asettua suoraan riviin, ojentaa; *~ oneself with* asettua jkn puolelle. **-ment** *s.* ojennus, rivi; (pol.) ryhmittyminen.

alike [ə'laik] *a.* kaltainen, näköinen; *adv.* samalla tavalla, yhtä lailla; *they are very much ~* he ovat hyvin toistensa näköiset; *rich and poor countries ~* sekä rikkaat että köyhät maat.

aliment|ary [æli'mentəri] *a.* ravitsemus-; *~ canal* ruoansulatuskanava. **-ation** [-'teiʃn] *s.* ravinto, ravitseminen.

alimony ['æliməni] *s.* (eronneen vaimon saama) elatusapu.

Alistair ['ælistə] *erisn.*

alive [ə'laiv] *pred. a.* elossa (oleva), elävä(nä), hengissä; eloisa, vilkas; ~ *to* vastaanottavainen jllek, tietoinen jstk; *be* ~ *with* kuhista; *look* ~ *!* joudu! *keep* .. ~ pitää vireillä; *stay* ~ säilyä hengissä.

alkali ['ælkəlai] *s.* alkali, emäs. **-ine** [-ain] *a.* alkalinen, emäksinen.

all [ɔ:l] *pron. & a. & s.* kaikki, koko; *adv.* kokonaan, aivan; ~ *of them* he kaikki; ~ [*the*] *day* koko päivän; ~ *eyes* pelkkänä silmänä; *that's* ~ *!* siinä kaikki! *is that* ~ *?* siinäkö kaikki? ~ *along* koko matkan, kaiken aikaa; ~ *but* melkein; ~ *in* (puhek.) lopen uupunut, »kuitti»; ~ *in* ~ kaiken kaikkiaan; ~ *in* ~ *to* jkn silmäterä; [*it's*] ~ *one to* yhdentekevää; *go* ~ *out* ponnistaa kaikkensa; ~ *over* yli koko; lopussa; ~ *right* hyvin, oikein, hyvä(ssä kunnossa); hyvä on! ~ *the better* sitä parempi; ~ *the same* siitä huolimatta, yhdentekevää; ~ *told* yhteensä; *after* ~ ks. *after;* *at* ~ lainkaan; *not at* ~ ei ensinkään; ei kestä kiittää; *for* ~ *that* siitä huolimatta; .. *in* ~ yhteensä; [*why ask me to help*] *of* ~ *people* .. juuri (minua); .., *bones and* ~ luineen päivineen; ~ *I want is peace* haluan vain rauhaa; *All Saints' Day* pyhäinpäivä, marraskuun 1. p.

Allah ['ælə] *erisn.*

allay [ə'lei] *v.* hillitä, lievittää.

all-clear *s.* vaara ohi(-merkki).

allegation [æli'geiʃn] *s.* väite.

allege [ə'ledʒ] *v.* väittää; esittää (puolustuksena).

allegiance [ə'li:dʒəns] *s.* (alamaisen) uskollisuus; *oath of* ~ uskollisuudenvala.

allegoric(al) [æle'gɔrik, -(ə)l] *a.* allegorinen, vertauskuvallinen.

allegory ['æligəri] *s.* allegoria, kuvaannollinen esitystapa.

allerg|en ['æledʒən] *s.* herkiste, allergiaa aiheuttava aine. **-ic** [ə'lə:dʒik] *a.* allerginen. **-y** [ælədʒi] *s.* allergia, yliherkkyys.

alleviat|e [ə'li:vieit] *v.* helpottaa, lievittää. **-ion** [-'eiʃn] *s.* helpotus, lievitys.

alley ['æli] *s.* kuja (m. *-way*); (puiston)

käytävä; (keila)rata.

alli|ance [ə'laiəns] *s.* liitto (et. valt.); yhteys. **-ed** [ə'laid, *attr.* 'ælaid] *pp. & a.* liittoutunut; ~ *with* liitossa (jnk valtion kanssa); *the A~* ['ælaid] *Powers* liittoutuneet (1. ja 2. maailmansota). **-es** ['ælaiz] *s. pl.* ks. *ally.*

alligator ['æligeitə] *s.* alligaattori.

alliteration [əlitə'reiʃn] *s.* alkusointu.

allocate ['æləkeit] *v.* antaa, myöntää, jakaa.

allot [ə'lɔt] *v.* jakaa (arvalla), määrätä, myöntää. **-ment** *s.* jakaminen arvalla; osa, osuus, (puutarha)palsta.

all-out *a.* totaalinen.

allow [ə'lau] *v.* sallia, antaa lupa; myöntää (esim. viikkoraha, alennus); antaa jklle ottaa lukuun t. huomioon, varata, poistaa; hyvittää; *she is not* ~*ed out after dark* hän ei saa mennä ulos pimeän tultua; ~ *me to* .. sallikaa minun ..; ~ *£ 100 for expenses* varata 100 puntaa menoihin; ~ *for* ottaa huomioon t. lukuun; ~*ing for* ottaen huomioon; ~ *of* sallia. **-able** [-əbl] *a.* sallittu, luvallinen. **-ance** [əns] *s.* määräraha, (määrä)annos; alennus; *monthly* ~ kuukausiraha; *make* ~ *for* ottaa huomioon; *travelling* ~ matkarahat; *daily* ~ päiväraha.

alloy [ə'lɔi] *v.* seostaa; (kuv.) laimentaa; *s.* ['ælɔi] metalliseos, seostus; ~ *steel* teräslejeerinki.

all-round *a.* monipuolinen, yleis-.

allspice ['ɔ:lspais] *s.* maustepippuri.

all-time *a.* kaikkien aikojen.

allude [ə'lu:d] *v.:* ~ *to* viitata, vihjata jhk.

allure [ə'ljuə] *v.* houkutella, viekoitella; viehättää. **-ment** *s.* houkutus, viehätys.

allu|sion [ə'lu:ʒn] *s.* viittaus, vihjaus. **-sive** [-siv] *a.* vihjaileva, peitetty, epäsuora.

alluvial [ə'lu:vjəl] *a.;* ~ *sand* tulvahieta.

ally [ə'lai] *v.* liittää, yhdistää; *s.* ['ælai] liittolainen; ~ *oneself* liittoutua; *allied to* sukua jllek.

almanac ['ɔ:lmənæk] *s.* almanakka.

almighty ['ɔ:lmaiti] *a.* kaikkivaltias.

almond ['a:mənd] *s.* manteli.

almoner ['a:mənə, Am. 'ælm-] s.
virallinen almujenjakaja; (sairaalan)
sosiaalihoitaja.

almost ['ɔːlməust] adv. melkein, lähes;
~ nothing tuskin mitään.

alms [aːmz] s. (pl. = sg.) almu(t).
~-house (vanh.) vaivaistalo.

aloe ['æləu] s. aloe (kasv.).

aloft [ə'lɔft] adv. korkealla, -lle, ylös;
mastossa, mastoon.

alone [ə'ləun] a. yksin; adv. yksin
(yksin)äni -si, -nsä jne); leave (let) ~
jättää rauhaan, olla sekaantumatta;
let ~ . . jstk puhumattakaan, saati
sitten; let well ~ anna (antaa) asian
olla; you ~ can . . vain sinä voit . .

along [ə'lɔŋ] adv. pitkin; mukana,
mukaan; eteenpäin; prep. pitkin; ~
with (yhdessä) jnk kanssa; I knew it
all ~ tiesin sen alusta alkaen (t.
kaiken aikaa). -side adv. kyljittäin,
vieressä; ~ of jnk vieressä.

aloof [ə'luːf] adv. erillään; a. (m.)
seuraa karttava, välinpitämätön,
varautunut; keep ~ pysytellä syrjässä.
-ness s. välinpitämättömyys.

aloud [ə'laud] adv. ääneen.

alp [ælp] s. alppi; the Alps Alpit.

alpaca [æl'pækə] s. alpakkavilla.

alpenstock ['ælpinstɔk] s. alppisauva.

alpha ['ælfə] s. alfa (-kirjain). -bet
[-bet] s. aakkoset, kirjaimisto.
-betic(al) [-'betik, -(ə)l] a.
aakkosellinen, aakkos-.

alpine ['ælpain] a. alppi-. -ist
['ælpinist] s. alppikiipeilijä.

already [ɔːl'redi] adv. jo; have you had
lunch ~ ? joko olet lounastanut?

Alsace ['ælsæs] erisn. Elsass.

Alsatian [æl'seiʃiən] a. & s.
elsassilainen; saksanpaimenkoira.

also ['ɔːlsəu] adv. myös, -kin; ~-ran
huonosti menestynyt ihminen
(kilpailija ym).

altar ['ɔːltə] s. alttari. ~-cloth
alttarivaate. ~-piece alttaritaulu.

alter ['ɔːltə] v. muuttaa, korjata;
muuttua. -able [-rəbl] a.
muutettavissa oleva. -ation [-'reiʃn] s.
muutos.

altercate ['ɔːltəkeit] v. kiistellä,
riidellä. -tion [-'keiʃn] s. (sana)kiista.

alternat|e [ɔːl'təːnit, Am. 'ɔːl-] a.
vuoroittainen; v. ['ɔːltəneit]
vuorotella, vaihdella; -ing
current vaihtovirta. -ely adv.
vuorotellen.

alterna|tion [ɔːltə'neiʃn] s. vuorottelu,
~ of crops vuoroviljely. -tive
[ɔːl'təːnətiv] a. vaihtoehtoinen; s.
vaihtoehto; I had no ~ minulla ei
ollut valinnan varaa; ~ly
vaihtoehtoisesti.

although [ɔːl'ðəu] konj. vaikka.

alti|meter ['ælti|miːtə, Am. æl'tim-] s.
korkeusmittari. -tude [-tjuːd] s.
korkeus.

alto ['æltəu] s. altto(-osa,-ääni).

altogether [ɔːltə'geðə] adv. täysin,
kokonaan; kaiken kaikkiaan; [it] isn't
~ easy ei ole aivan helppoa.

altruistic [æltru'istik] a. epäitsekäs.

alum ['æləm] s. aluna. -inium
[ælju'minjəm] s. alumiini. -inum
[ə'luːminəm] Am. = ed.

alumni [ə'lʌmnai] s. (sg. alumnus)
entiset oppilaat.

alveolar [æl'viələ] a. hammasvalli-.

always ['ɔːlwez, -weiz] adv. aina.

am [æm, əm, m] be-vbn ind. prees. sg.
1. pers. olen.

amalgam [ə'mælgəm] s.
(elohopea)seos. -ate [-eit] v.
sekoittaa, amalgamoida; sekoittua,
yhdistyä. -ation [-'eiʃn] s.
yhdistäminen, -yminen.

amanuensis [əmænju'ensis] s. kirjuri.

amaryllis [æmə'rilis] s. amaryllis.

amass [ə'mæs] v. kasata, koota.

amateur ['æmətə, -tjuə] s. harrastelija,
amatööri. -ish [-'tə:riʃ] a.
harrastelijamainen.

amaze [ə'meiz] v. hämmästyttää,
ällistyttää; ~d at hämmästynyt jstk;
amazing hämmästyttävä. -ment s.
hämmästys.

amazon ['æməzn] s. amatsoni, kuv.
voimanainen; The A~ Amazon(joki).

ambassa|dor [æm'bæsədə] s.
suurlähettiläs; roving ~ kiertävä s.
-dress [-dris] s. suurlähettiläs
puoliso; naissuurlähettiläs.

amber ['æmbə] s. meripihka; a.
meripihka-; kullanruskea. -gris [-gri:s]
s. harmaa ambra.

ambidextrous ['æmbidekstrəs] a.: [he]
is ~ käyttää vasenta kättään yhtä
hyvin kuin oikeatakin.

ambient ['æmbiənt] *a.* ympäröivä.

ambigu|ity [æmbi'gju(:)iti] *s.* kaksiselitteisyys, epäselvyys. **-ous** [æm'bigjuəs] *a.* kaksiselitteinen, -mielinen, epäselvä.

ambit ['æmbit] *s.* piiri, raja.

ambi|tion [æm'biʃn] *s.* kunnianhimo; kiihkeä halu. **-tious** [-ʃəs] *a.* kunnianhimoinen; ~ *of* kiihkeästi jtk haluava.

ambivalent [əm'bivələnt] *a.* ambivalentti(nen).

amble ['æmbl] *v.* astua tasakäyntiä; *s.* tasakäynti.

ambula|nce ['æmbjul|əns] *s.* ambulanssi, sairaankuljetusauto. **-te** [-eit] *v.* kiertää. **-tory** [-ətəri] *a.* kiertävä; jalkeilla oleva.

ambuscade [æmbəs'keid] *s.* väijytys; *v.* ks. seur.

ambush ['æmbuʃ] *s.* väijytys; *v.* väijyä; hyökätä väijyksistä; *lie in* ~ olla väijyksissä.

ameliora|te [ə'mi:ljəreit] *v.* parantaa, -tua. **-tion** [-'reiʃn] *s.* parantaminen.

amen ['a:'men, ei-] aamen.

amenable [ə'mi:nəbl] *a.* vastuunalainen; mukautuva, taipuvainen, suopea, altis; ~ *to advice* neuvoa kuunteleva.

amend [ə'mend] *v.* parantaa, korjata; parantua. **-ment** *s.* parannus; (lain)muutos, muutosehdotus. **-s** [-z] *s.* korvaus, hyvitys; *make* ~ *for* hyvittää.

amenity [ə'mi:niti] *s.* miellyttävyys; *amenities* (virkistys)mahdollisuudet, palvelut (esim. kirjasto, leikkikenttä); ~ *area* virkistysalue; *for* ~ *purposes* virkistystarkoituksiin.

America [ə'merikə] *erisn.* Amerikka. **-n** [-n] *a.* & *s.* amerikkalaisuus; amerikkalainen kieliomituisuus. **-nize** [-naiz] *v.* amerikkalaistaa, -tua.

amethyst ['æmiθist] *s.* ametisti.

amia|bility [eimjə'biliti] *s.* rakastettavuus. **-ble** ['eimjəbl] *a.* rakastettava; ystävällinen.

amicable ['æmikəbl] *a.* ystävällinen; sovinnollinen.

amid(st) [ə'mid, -st] *prep.* keskellä; joukossa.

amiss [ə'mis] *adv.* & *pred. a.* väärä; väärin; sopimattomasti; *nothing*

comes ~ [*to him*] . . -lle ei mikään mene hassusti; *will not come* ~ ei ole pahitteeksi; *take* ~ panna pahakseen.

amity ['æmiti] *s.* ystävyys, sopu.

Amman [ə'ma:n] *erisn.*

ammonia [ə'mounjə] *s.* ammoniakki.

ammunition [æmju'niʃn] *s.* ampumatarvikkeet, ammukset; ~ *depot* ammusvarikko.

amnesia [æm'ni:zjə] *s.* muistinmenetys.

amnesty ['æmnesti] *s.* yleinen armahdus; *v.* armahtaa.

am(o)eba [ə'mi:bə] *s.* ameeba.

amok [ə'mɔk] *adv.* (m. *amuck*) : *run* ~ raivota hurjana.

among [ə'mʌŋ] *prep.* joukossa, joukkoon, kesken; ~ *other things* muun muassa; ~ *themselves* keskenään; [*one reason*] ~ *many was* muitten muassa oli; *from* ~ joukosta. **-st** [-st] = ed.

amorous ['æmərəs] *a.* rakastunut; lemmekäs, lemmen-.

amorphous [ə'mɔ:fəs] *a.* muodoltaan epämääräinen, hahmoton.

amor|tization [əmɔ:ti'zeiʃn] *s.* kuoletus. **-tize** [ə'mɔ:taiz, Am. 'æmər-] *v.* kuolettaa.

amount [ə'maunt] *s.* summa, määrä; *v.*: ~ *to* nousta jhk; [*a money order*] *to the* ~ *of* . . määrältään; *it* ~*s to the same thing* (se) on aivan sama asia, merkitsee samaa.

amour [ə'muə] *s.* rakkausjuttu.

ampère ['æmpeə] *s.* ampeeri.

amphetamine [æm'fetəmin] *s.* amfetamiini.

amphib|ian [æm'fibiən] *s.* sammakkoeläin. **-ious** [-iəs] *a.* vedessä ja maalla elävä; ~ *tank* amfibipanssarivaunu, maihinnousuvaunu.

amphitheatre [æmfi'θiətə] *s.* amfiteatteri.

ampl|e ['æmpl] *a.* laaja, suuri, runsas, yltäkylläinen. **-ifier** [-faiə] *s.* (äänen)vahvistin.

ampli|fy ['æmplifai] *v.* laajentaa, suurentaa, suurennella; kuvailla laveasti; vahvistaa (ääntä). **-tude** [-tju:d] *s.* laajuus, runsaus; (fys.) värähdyslaajuus.

amply ['æmpli] *adv.* runsaasti.

amp(o)ule ['æmpu:l] *s.* ampulli.

amputate ['æmpjuteit] v. amputoida, katkaista.

amulet ['æmjulit] s. amuletti.

amuse [ə'mju:z] v. huvittaa, hauskuttaa; ~ *oneself* huvitella; ~d *at* (*by*) huvittunut jstk; *amusing* hauska. **-ment** s. huvitus, ajanviete; ~ *park* huvipuisto.

an [æn, ən, n] *epäm. art.*

anachronism [ə'nækrənizm] s. anakronismi, epäajanmukaisuus.

an(a)em|ia [ə'ni:mjə] s. anemia. **-ic** a. aneeminen, vähäverinen.

an(a)esthe|sia [æni:s'θi:zjə] s. puudutus; nukutus (*general* ~). **-tic** [-'θetik] s. puudutus-, nukutusaine. **-tist** [æ'ni:sθitist] s. narkoosilääkäri. **-tize** [æ'ni:sθitaiz] v. puuduttaa, nukuttaa.

anagram ['ænəgræm] s. anagrammi (kirjainleikki).

anal ['ein(ə)l] a. peräaukon.

analges|ia ['ænəl'dʒi:zjə] s. tunnottomuus. **-ic** [-'dʒi:zik] a. & s. kipua lievittävä (lääke).

analog|ical [ænə'lɔdʒik(ə)l] a. analogian mukainen, analoginen. **-ous** [ə'næləgəs] a. analoginen, yhdenmukainen, jtk vastaava. **-ue** ['ænəlɔg] s. vastine, vastaavuus. **-y** [ə'nælədʒi] s. analogia, yhdenmukaisuus.

analy|se ['ænəlaiz] v. analysoida; jäsentää (lause); eritellä. **-sis** [ə'næləsis] s. (pl. *-ses* [-əsi:z]) analyysi; (lauseen) jäsennys; erittely. **-st** [-ist] s. analyytikko; psykoanalyytikko. **-tic(al)** [ænə'litik, -(ə)l] a. analyyttinen.

anarch|ic(al) [æ'na:kik, -(ə)l] a. kumouksellinen. **-ist** ['ænəkist] s. anarkisti.

anarchy ['ænəki] s. anarkia, sekasorto.

anatom|ic(al) [ænə'tɔmik, -(ə)l] a. anatominen. **-ically** adv. anatomisesti. **-ist** [ə'nætəmist] s. anatomi. **-y** [ə'nætəmi] s. anatomia.

ancest|or ['ænsistə] s. esi-isä. **-ral** [æn'sestr(ə)l] a. esi-isiltä peritty; ~ *estate* perintötila. **-ry** [-ri] s. suku, syntyperä.

anchor ['æŋkə] s. ankkuri; v. ankkuroida; *cast* (*weigh*) ~ laskea (nostaa) ankkuri; *ride at* ~ olla

ankkurissa. **-age** [-ridʒ] s. ankkuripaikka.

anchorite ['æŋkərait] s. erakko.

anchovy ['æntʃəuvi, -əvi] s. anjovis.

ancient ['einʃnt] a. (iki)vanha, muinainen; ~ *Rome* antiikin Rooma; *an* A~ *Monument* (säilytettävä) muinaismuisto; *the* ~s antiikin kansat.

ancillary [æn'siləri] a.: ~ *to* jtk edistävä, apu-.

and [ænd, ənd, ən, nd] *konj.* ja; ~ *so forth*, ~ *so on* ja niin edespäin; [*for*] *hours* ~ *hours* tuntikausia.

Andes ['ændi:z] *erisn.; the* ~ Andit.

andirons ['ændaiənz] s. rautatuet (takassa).

Andrew ['ændru:] *erisn.*

anecdote ['ænikdout] s. kasku.

anemone [ə'neməni] s. vuokko; *sea* ~ merivuokko.

anew [ə'nju:] *adv.* uudelleen.

angel ['eindʒl] s. enkeli. **-ic** [æn'dʒelik] a. enkelimäinen, enkeli(n)-.

anger ['æŋgə] s. viha, suuttumus; v. vihastuttaa; *in* [*a moment of*] ~ vihapäissä|än (-ni, -si).

angina [æn'dʒainə] s.: ~ *pectoris* ['pektəris] sydänkouristus.

angle 1. ['æŋgl] s. kulma; nurkka; *at an* ~ vinossa; *at right* ~s suorassa kulmassa; *from a different* ~ toisesta näkökulmasta, toiselta kannalta.

angle 2. ['æŋgl] v. onkia; kalastaa. **-r** [-ə] s. onkimies.

Angli|can ['æŋglikən] a. & s. anglikaani(nen). **-cism** [-sism] s. anglisismi. **-cize** [-saiz] v. englantilaistaa.

angling s. onginta.

Anglo- [æŋglə(u)-] (yhd.) englantilais-. ~**-Indian** s. Intiassa asuva englantilainen. **-phil(e)** [-fail] s. anglofiili. ~ -**Saxon** a. & s. anglosaksi(nen).

Angola [æŋ'goulə] *erisn.* **-n** [-n] a. & s. angolalainen.

angrily ['æŋgrili] *adv.* vihaisesti.

angry ['æŋgri] a. suuttunut, vihainen (*with* jklle; *at, about* jstk); *make* .. ~ suututtaa.

anguish ['æŋgwiʃ] s. tuska, hätä, ahdistus.

angular ['æŋgjulə] *a.* kulmikas, särmikäs; jäykkä. **-ity** [-'læriti] *s.* kulmikkuus.

aniline ['ænilain] *s.* aniliini(väri).

animadver|sion [ænimæd'və:ʃn] *s.* huomautus, moite. **-t** [-'və:t] *v.:* ~ *on* huomauttaa jstk.

animal ['ænim(ə)l] *s.* eläin; *a.* eläimellinen, eläimen; ruumiin; ~ *food* animaalinen ravinto; ~ *spirits* elinvoima, luontainen eloisuus. **-ism** [-izm] *s.* eläimellisyys.

animat|e ['ænimeit] *v.* elähdyttää, innostaa; elävöittää; *a.* [-mit] elävä; ~*d cartoon* piirretty elokuva. **-ed** [-id] *a.* vilkas, eloisa. **-ion** [-'meiʃn] *s.* eloisuus, vilkkaus, pirteys; (elok.) animaatio.

animosity [æni'mɔsiti] *s.* viha(mielisyys), kaunaisuus.

anise ['ænis] *s.* anis(kasvi).

aniseed ['ænisi:d] *s.* anis(mauste), aniksen siemen.

Ankara ['æŋkərə] *erisn.*

ankle ['æŋkl] *s.* nilkka; ~ *socks* nilkkasukat. **-t** [-it] *s.* nilkkarengas.

Ann [æn], **-a** ['ænə], **-e** [æn] *erisn.*

annals ['ænlz] *s. pl.* aikakirjat; vuosikirja.

anneal [ə'ni:l] *v.* mellottaa, karkaista, myöstää; hehkuttaa.

annex [ə'neks] *v.* liittää *(to* jhk); ottaa haltuunsa, annektoida; *s.* ['æneks] (m. ~*e)* lisärakennus; liite. **-ation** [-'seiʃn] *s.* annektointi, anastus, liittäminen.

annihila|te [ə'naiəleit] *v.* tuhota. **-tion** [-'leiʃn] *s.* tuho(aminen).

anniversary [æni'və:səri] *s.* vuosi|päivä, -juhla.

Anno Domini ['ænəu 'dɔminai] *adv.* armon vuonna (tav. lyh. *A. D.)* jKr.

annota|te ['ænə(u)teit] *v.* varustaa huomautuksilla; tehdä muistiinpanoja. **-tion** [-'teiʃn] *s.* huomautus; muistiinpano.

announce [ə'nauns] *v.* ilmoittaa, julistaa, julkaista, julkistaa; kuuluttaa (rad.). **-ment** *s.* tiedotus, ilmoitus. **-r** [-ə] *s.* (radio)kuuluttaja.

annoy [ə'nɔi] *v.* vaivata, kiusata; suututtaa, harmittaa; ~*ed* suuttuksissaan, *at* jstk, *with* jklle; ~*ed*

by jnk vaivaama. **-ance** [-əns] *s.* vaiva, kiusa; harmi **-ing** *a.* kiusallinen, harmillinen.

annual ['ænjuəl] *a.* vuotuinen, vuosi-; jokavuotinen; *s.* yksivuotinen kasvi; vuosikirja. **-ly** *adv.* vuosittain, joka vuosi.

annuity [ə'nju:iti] *s.* elinkorko.

annul [ə'nʌl] *v.* kumota, poistaa, peruuttaa; mitätö|idä, -ntää. **-ment** *s.* peruutus, tyhjäksi tekeminen.

annular ['ænjulə] *a.* rengasmainen.

annulment *s.* kumoaminen.

annunciation [ənʌnsi'eiʃn] *s.: the A ~* Marian ilmestyspäivä, marianpäivä.

anode ['ænəud] *s.* anodi.

anodyne ['ænə(u)dain] *a. & s.* tuskaa lievittävä (lääke).

anoint [ə'nɔint] *v.* (kirk.) voidella. **-ment** *s.* voitelu.

anomalous [ə'nɔmələs] *a.* epäsäännöllinen, poikkeava.

anomaly [ə'nɔməli] *s.* säännöttömyys.

anon [ə'nɔn] *adv.* pian (vanh.); *ever and ~* tuon tuostakin.

anonym|ity [ænə'nimiti] *s.* nimettömyys. **-ous** [ə'nɔniməs] *a.* nimetön, nimeään ilmaisematon; *Alcoholics A~* AA-liike (anonyymit alkoholistit).

anorak ['ænəræk] *s.* anorakki.

another [ə'nʌðə] *pron.* toinen; vielä yksi; *one ~* toinen toistaan; *I should like ~ cup* haluaisin kupin lisää; *not ~ word* ei sanaakaan enää; *one after ~* toinen toisensa jälkeen; *[he may be] ~ Edison* uusi Edison; *one ~* ks. *one.*

answer ['ɑ:nsə] *s.* vastaus; *v.* vastata; olla vastuussa *(for* jhk); *in ~ to* vastaukseena jhk; ~ *back* vastata nenäkkäästi; ~ *the bell* avata ovi; ~*s to the name of* tottelee nimeä; ~ *the phone* vastata puhelimeen; *it did not ~ my hopes* se ei vastannut toiveitani. **-able** [-əbl] *a.* vastuunalainen, vastuussa *(for* jstk).

ant [ænt] *s.* muurahainen; ~*-eater* muurahaiskarhu; ~*-hill* muurahaiskeko.

antagon|ism [æn'tægənizm] *s.* vihamielisyys. **-ist** [-ist] *s.* vastustaja; (~*ic* [-'nistik] *a.* vastustava, vihamielinen). **-ize** [-aiz] *v.* vastustaa; saada jku vastustajakseen.

antarctic [ænt'ɑ:ktik] a. etelänapa-; s.: the A ~ Antarktis, etelänapaseudut, Eteläinen jäämeri (m. the ~ Ocean). **-a** [-ə] erisn.; A~ Etelämanner.

ante- ['ænti] pref. ennen; antenuptial esiavollinen, avioliittoa edeltävä.

antecedent [ænti'si:dnt] a. edelläkäyvä; s. edellä käyvä seikka; (kiel.) korrelaatti; pl. aikaisemmat vaiheet, entisyys.

ante|chamber ['æntitʃeimbə] s. etuhuone. **-date** [-'deit] v. päivätä aikaisemmaksi; edeltää. **-diluvian** [-di'lu:viən] a. vedenpaisumusta edeltävä, perin vanhanaikainen.

antelope ['æntiləup] s. antilooppi.

ante|meridiem [-mə'ridiəm] ks. lyh. a.m. **-natal** ['ænti'neitl] a. syntymää edeltävä; ~ clinic äitiysneuvola.

antenn|a [æn'tenə] s. (pl. -ae [-i:]) tuntosarvi; Am. antenni.

anterior [æn'tiəriə] a. aikaisempi (to kuin); etumainen, etu-. **-ly** (to jnk) edessä.

ante-room ['æntirum] s. etuhuone.

anthem ['ænθəm] s. hymni; national ~ kansallislaulu.

anther ['ænθə] s. (heteen) ponsi.

anthology [æn'θɒlədʒi] s. antologia, runovalikoima.

Anthony ['æntəni] erisn.

anthracite ['ænθrəsait] s. antrasiitti.

anthrax ['ænθræks] s. pernarutto.

anthrop|oid ['ænθrəpɔid] a. ihmismenmuotoinen; s. ihmisapina (m. ~ ape) **-ologic(al)** [-pə'lɒdʒik,-(ə)l] a. antropologinen. **-ology** [-'pɒlədʒi] s. antropologia.

anti|-aircraft ['ænti'εəkrɑ:ft] a.: a.-a. gun ilmatorjuntatykki. **-biotic** [-bai'ɔtik] s. & a. antibiootti(nen aine). **-body** s. vasta-aine.

antic ['æntik] s. (tav. pl.) ilve, temppu.

Antichrist ['æntikraist] s. antikristus.

anticipa|te [æn'tisipeit] v. ennakoida, käyttää ennakolta; ennättää ennen, täyttää (esim. jk toivomus) etukäteen; (osata) odottaa, aavistaa. **-tion** [-'peiʃn] s. odotus, toivo; ennakolta ottaminen; in ~ etukäteen; in ~ of jtk odottaen, jnk varalta. **-tory** [-əri] a. ennakko-.

anti|climax [-'klaiməks] s. antikliimaksi **-clockwise** adv. vastapäivään.

-cyclone s. korkeapaineen alue. **-dote** ['æntidəut] s. vastamyrkky. **~freeze** s. (auto)pakkasneste. **-gen** ['æntidʒən] s. antigeeni. **~missile**: a.-m. defence ohjusten torjunta(järjestelmä); a.-m. missile vastaohjus. **-pathetic(al)** [-pə'θetik, -(ə)l] vastenmielinen. **-pathy** [æn'tipəθi] vastenmielisyys, antipatia. **~-personnel** [-'pə:snel]: a.-p. bombs sirpalepommit. **-podes** [æn'tipədi:z] s. pl. antipodit; vastakkainen kohta maapallolla.

Antilles [æn'tili:z] erisn.: the ~ Antillit.

antiquar|ian [ænti'kwεəriən] a. antikvaarinen, muinaisesineitä koskeva; s. = seur. **-y** ['æntikwəri] s. muinaisesineiden keräilijä.

antiquated ['æntikweitid] a. vanhentunut.

antiqu|e [æn'ti:k] a. antiikki, muinaisaikainen; s. antiikki-, muinaisesine; the ~ antiikki (tyyli). **-ity** [æn'tikwiti] s. antiikin aika, muinaisaika; pl. muinaisjäännökset.

antirrhinum [ænti'rainəm] s. leijonankita (kasvi).

anti-Semit|e ['ænti'si:mait] s. juutalaisvihaaja. **-ic** [-si'mitik] a. antisemiittinen.

anti|septic [ænti'septik] a. & s. antiseptinen aine; s. socal asosiaalinen. **~-tank**: a.-t. gun panssarintorjuntatykki. **-thes|is** [æn'tiθis|is] (pl. -es [-i:z]) vastakohta. **-toxin** vastamyrkky.

antler ['æntlə] s.: ~ s (hirvieläimen) sarvet.

Antwerp ['æntwə:p] erisn. Antverpen.

anus ['einəs] s. peräaukko.

anvil ['ænvil] s. alasin.

anxi|ety [æŋ'zaiəti] s. levottomuus, huoli; kiihkeä halu. **-ous** ['æŋ(k)ʃəs] a. levoton, huolestunut, huolekas; halukas, innokas; be ~ about olla huolissaan jksta; [he is] ~ to [meet you] haluaa välttämättä.

any ['eni] pron. kukaan, mikään, mitään; kuka t. mikä tahansa; joka(inen); adv. lainkaan; in ~ case, at ~ rate ainakin; any number of .. lukemattomia; [come] ~ day you like milloin tahansa; is he ~ better? onko hän parempi (paremmassa kunnossa)? **-body, -one** *pron.* kukaan; joku; kuka tahansa. **-how** *adv.* jollakin tavalla, miten tahansa; joka tapauksessa. **-thing** *pron.* mikään, jokin; mikä tahansa, kaikki; ~ *but* kaikkea muuta kuin; *not for* ~ ei mistään hinnasta; *for* ~ *I know* mikäli tiedän, tietääkseni. **-way** *adv.* jollakin tavalla, jotenkuten; joka tapauksessa, kuitenkin. **-where** *adv.* missään, jossakin; missä tahansa; ~ *else* missään muualla.

Anzac ['ænzæk] *s.* australialainen sotilas; vrt. lyh.

aorta [ei'ɔ:tə] *s.* aortta.

apace [ə'peis] *adv.* (vanh.) joutuisasti, nopeasti.

apart [ə'pɑ:t] *adv.* syrjässä, -ään; erillään, -een; *(500 metres* ~) toisistaan; ~ *from* lukuunottamatta, paitsi; *set* ~ erottaa; *take . .* ~ hajottaa osiin; *tell* [*two people*] ~ erottaa toisistaan; *set* ~ *for* määrätä, varata jhk; *far* ~ harvassa; *joking* ~ leikki sikseen. **-heid** [-heit] *s.* rotuerottelu. **-ment** *s.* huone, (et. Am.) (vuokra)huoneisto; ~ *building* kerrostalo.

apathetic [æpə'θetik] *a.* apaattinen.

apathy ['æpəθi] *s.* apatia, välinpitämättömyys.

ape [eip] *s.* apina; *v.* matkia.

Apennines ['æpinainz] *erisn.: the* ~ Apenniinit.

aperient [ə'piəriənt] *a. & s.* ulostuslääke.

aperture ['æpətʃ(u)ə] *s.* aukko.

apex ['eipeks] *a.* (pl. m. *apices* ['eipisi:z]) huippu, kärki.

aphasia [ə'feiziə, Am. -ʒə] *s.* afaasia.

aphorism ['æfərizm] *s.* mietelause, ajatelma.

apiary ['eipiəri] *s.* mehiläispesä.

apiece [ə'pi:s] *adv.* kappaleelta; jokaiselta, -lle.

aplomb ['æplɔ(ŋ)] *s.* (itse)varmuus.

apocalyp|se [ə'pɔkəlips] *s. : the A* ~ Ilmestyskirja. **-tic** [əpɔkə'liptik] *a.* tuhoa ennustava.

apocryphal [ə'pɔkrifəl] *a.* apokryfinen, hämäräperäinen.

apolog|etic [əpɔlə'dʒetik] *a.* puolust|eleva, -ava; anteeksipyytävä. **-ize** [ə'pɔlədʒaiz] *v.* pyytää anteeksi

(to jklta]. **-y** [ə'pɔlədʒi] *s.* anteeksipyyntö; puolustus.

apo|plectic [æpə'plektik] *a.* apoplektinen, halvaus-. **-plexy** ['æpəpleksi] *s.* halvaus.

aposta|sy [ə'pɔstəsi] *s.* luopuminen (uskosta ym). **-te** [-tit] *s.* luopio.

apos|tle [ə'pɔsl] *s.* apostoli; ks. *act.* **-tolic** [æpəs'tɔlik] *s.* apostolinen, paavin.

apostrophe [ə'pɔstrəfi] *s.* heittomerkki; (poissaolevan) puhuttelu.

apothecary [ə'pɔθikəri] *s.* apteekkari (vanh.).

appal [ə'pɔ:l] *v.* kauhistuttaa; *be* ~ *led at* olla kauhistunut jstk. **-ling** [-iŋ] *a.* kauhistuttava, hirveä.

Appalachian [əpə'leitʃiən]: *the* ~ *Mountains*, ~ *s* Appalakit.

apparatus [æpə'reitəs, Am. -'rætəs] *s.* (pl. ~ *es*) koje(et), laite, laitteet, välineet; elimet.

apparel [ə'pær(ə)l] *s.* puku.

apparent [ə'pær(ə)nt] *a.* silminnähtävä, ilmeinen; näennäinen; *heir* ~ lähin kruununperijä; *as will soon become* ~ kuten pian selviää. **-ly** *adv.* ilmeisesti.

apparition [æpə'riʃn] *s.* ilmestys, näky, aave.

appeal [ə'pi:l] *s.* vetoomus; *v.: ~ to* vedota jhk; kääntyä jkn puoleen; anoa; ~ *against* [*a decision*] valittaa; ~ *to the eye* miellyttää silmää: *it does not* ~ *to me* se ei miellytä minua; ~ *ing* liikuttava, vetoava; miellyttävä; ~ *-ingly* vetoavasti.

appear [ə'piə] *v.* tulla näkyviin; näyttäytyä, esiintyä; ilmestyä; ilmetä, näyttää jltk; saapua, tulla saapuville. **-ance** [-r(ə)ns] *s.* ilmaantuminen, saapuminen, esiintyminen; ulkomuoto, -näkö, todennäköisyys, näennäisyys; *for the sake of* ~ *s* näön vuoksi; *to all* ~ kaikesta päättäen; [*judge*] *by* ~ *s* näön (ulkonaisten seikkojen) mukaan; *keep up* ~ *s* säilyttää (ulkonaisesti) arvokkuutensa ym; *put in an* ~ tulla saapuville, näyttäytyä.

appease [ə'pi:z] *v.* rauhoittaa, lepyttää; tyydyttää. **-ment** *s.: [policy of* ~] sovittelu-, myönnytyspolitiikka.

appella|nt [ə'pelənt] *a.* vetoava; *s.* valittaja. **-tion** [æpe'leiʃn] *s.* nimitys.

append [ə'pend] v. liittää, lisätä. **-age** [-idʒ] s. liite, lisäke. **-icitis** [-i'saitis] s. umpilisäkkeen tulehdus. **-ix** [-iks] s. (pl. m. *-ices* [isi:z]) liite; umpilisäke.

appertain [æpə'tein] v. kuulua *(to* jhk).

appet|ite ['æpitait] s. halu, ruokahalu; himo. **-izer** [-aizə] s. ruokahalun kiihoke. **-izing** [-aiziŋ] a. ruokahalua kiihottava, maukas.

applaud [ə'plɔ:d] v. taputtaa käsiään; hyväksyä.

applause [ə'plɔ:z] s. kättentaputus, aplodit.

apple ['æpl] s. omena; ~ *of discord* riitakapula; ~ *of the eye* silmäterä. **~-cart** : *upset sb.'s a.-c.* pilata jkn suunnitelmat. **~-pie** omenapaistos; *a.-p. order* mallikelpoinen järjestys. **~-sauce** Am. hölynpöly.

appliance [ə'plaiəns] s. laite, koje, väline; *household* ~ s kotitalouskoneet, kodin koneet.

applica|ble ['æplikəbl] *a.* : ~ *to* jhk käytettävissä oleva, sopiva. **-nt** [ənt] s. (paikan ym) hakija; anoja. **-tion** [-'keiʃn] s. päälle asettaminen jne.; käyttäminen, käyttö; soveltaminen; hakemus, anomus; uutteruus, harjaannus; *for external* ~ ulkonaisesti; *on* ~ pyydettäessä.

apply [ə'plai] v. hakea, anoa *(for* jtk); tiedustella, kääntyä (jkn) puoleen *(to);* panna, levittää *(to* jnk päälle, jhk), soveltaa, käyttää; pätea; ~ *the brake* jarruttaa; ~ *oneself to* omistautua, antautua jhk; *this applies to you* tämä koskee teitä; *applied* pp. sovellettu.

appoint [ə'pɔint] v. määrätä, nimittää (virkaan); *at the* ~ *ed time* sovittuun aikaan; *well* ~ *ed* hyvin varustettu. **-ment** s. nimitys; sopimus; sovittu tapaaminen, varattu aika *(with* jkn luona); *pl.* varusteet; *keep an* ~ saapua sovittuun aikaan; *make an* ~ sopia tapaamisesta; *by* ~ sopimuksen mukaan.

apportion [ə'pɔ:ʃn] v. jakaa (suhteellisesti), antaa. **-ment** s. jako.

apposi|te ['æpəzit] *a.* osuva, sattuva; sopiva. **-tion** [-'ziʃn] s. (kiel.) appositio.

apprais|al [ə'preiz(ə)l] s. arviointi. **-e** [ə'preiz] v. arvioida, (hinnoittaa).

appreciable [ə'pri:ʃəbl] *a.* tuntuva, huomattava; *[there was] no* ~ *change* ei olennaista muutosta.

apprecia|te [ə'pri:ʃieit] v. pitää arvossa, antaa arvoa, arvostaa; nousta arvossa. **-tion** [-'eiʃn] s. arvonanto, arvostus, arvio(inti); *in* ~ *of your valuable help* arvokkaasta avustanne kiitollisena. **-tive** [ə'pri:ʃjətiv] *a.* arvostava, kiitollinen.

apprehen|d [æpri'hend] v. (vanh.) käsittää, ymmärtää; pelätä; (lak.) ottaa kiinni. **-sion** [-'henʃn] s. pelko; *be dull (quick) of* ~ omata hidas (nopea) käsityskyky. **-sive** [-'hensiv] *a.* pelokas; *be* ~ *of* pelätä jtk.

apprentice [ə'prentis] s. oppipoika, oppilas; v. panna oppiin. **-ship** s. oppi|aika, -vuodet.

apprise [ə'praiz] v. ilmoittaa.

appro ['æprəu] s. lyh.: *on* ~ nähtäväksi.

approach [ə'prəutʃ] v. lähestyä; kääntyä jkn puoleen, tehdä tarjouksia (kaupp.); s. lähestyminen; tie; pääsy; *difficult of* ~ vaikeapääsyinen, vaikeasti lähestyttävä; .. *can't even* ~ .. ei läheskään vedä vertoja -lle; *[it] was an* ~ *to perfection* lähenteli täydellisyyttä; *make* ~ *es to* lähestyä, lähennellä. **-able** [-əbl] *a.* helppopääsyinen, .. jota on helppo lähestyä.

approbation [æprə'beiʃn] s. hyväksymys.

appropria|te [ə'prəupriit] *a.* sopiva, tarkoituksenmukainen, ominainen; v. [-ieit] ottaa t. anastaa itselleen; määrätä, myöntää (rahaa jhk tarkoitukseen). **-tion** [-i'eiʃn] s. ottaminen, omaksuminen; määrääminen; määräraha.

approval [ə'pru:vl] s. hyväksymys: *[she] nodded her* ~ nyökkäsi suostumuksen merkiksi; *on* ~ nähtäväksi.

approve [ə'pru:v] v. hyväksyä (m. ~ *of);* vahvistaa, **-d** [-d] *a.* hyväksytty; tunnustettu; ~ *school* koulukoti.

approxima|te [ə'prɔksimit] *a.* läheinen; likimääräinen; v. [-eit] olla lähellä; lähentää; lähetä; *~ly adv.* lähes, likimain. **-tion** [-'meiʃn] s. likiarvo; *its an* ~ *to* on lähellä ..

appurtenance [ə'pə:tinəns] *s.* (tav. *pl.*) tarvikkeet; kaikki, mikä kuuluu jhk.

apricot ['eiprikɔt] *s.* aprikoosi.

April ['eipr(ə)l] *s.* huhtikuu; ~ *fool* aprillinarri.

apron ['eipr(ə)n] *s.* esiliina; etunäyttämö; (ilm.) lentokonehallin edusta (lastausta ym varten). ~-**string** esiliinan nauha; *he is tied to his wife's* ~-*strings* hän on tohvelin alla.

apropos ['æprəpəu] *adv.* sopivasti; ~ *of* jstk puhuttaessa.

apse [æps] *s.* alttarikomero.

apt [æpt] *a.* sovelias, tarkoituksenmukainen, omiaan; sattuva, osuva; taipuvainen, altis; pystyvä; ~ *to break* hauras. -**itude** [-itju:d] *s.* taipumus, kyky; pystyvyys; ~ *test* soveltuvuuskoe. -**ness** *s.* soveliaisuus jne.

aqualung ['ækwə-] *s.* sukeltajan paineilmalaitteet.

aqua|rium [ə'kwɛəriəm] *s.* (pl. m. *-ia*) akvaario. -**atic** [ə'kwætik] *a.* vedessä elävä, vesi-. -**educt** ['ækwidʌkt] *s.* vesijohto. -**eous** ['eikwiəs] *a.* vesiperäinen, vetinen, vesi-.

aquiline ['ækwilain] *a.* kotkan-; ~ *nose* kyömynenä.

Arab ['ærəb] *s. & a.* arabialainen; *s.* arabi, arabialainen hevonen. -**ia** [ə'reibjə] *erisn.* -**ian** [ə'reibjən] *a. & s.* arabialainen; ~ *Nights* Tuhat ja yksi yötä. -**ic** [-ik] *a.* arabialainen; *s.* arabian kieli.

arable ['ærəbl] *a.* viljelyskelpoinen.

arbit|er ['ɑ:bitə] *s.* välitystuomari. -**rage** ['ɑ:bitrɑ:ʒ] *s.* välimiesmenettely, arbitraasi.

arbitra|ry ['ɑ:bitr|əri] *a.* mielivaltainen, -**te** [-eit] *v.* ratkaista (välitystuomarina); sovittaa. -**tion** [-'treiʃn] *s.* välitystuomio. -**tor** [-eitə] *s.* välitystuomari.

arboreal [ɑ:'bɔ:riəl] *a.* puu-, puissa elävä.

arb|our, -or ['ɑ:bə] *s.* lehtimaja.

arc [ɑ:k] *s.* kaari; ~ *lamp* kaarilamppu. -**ade** [ɑ:'keid] *s.* kaarikäytävä.

Arcadian [ɑ:'keidjən] *a.* idyllinen, paimen-.

arch 1. [ɑ:tʃ] *s.* kaari, holvi(kaari); *v.* holvata; kaareutua, muodostaa holvi;

köyristää.

arch 2. [ɑ:tʃ] *a.* viekas, veitikkamainen, veikeä.

arch- (yhd.) arkki-, peri-.

arch(a)elog|ical ['ɑ:kiə'lɔdʒik(ə)l] *a.* arkeologinen. -**ist** [ɑ:ki'ɔlədʒist] *s.* arkeologi. -**y** [-ʒi] *s.* arkeologia.

archa|ic [ɑ:'keiik] *a.* muinaisaikainen; vanhahtava, vanhastava. -**ism** ['ɑ:keiizm] *s.* arkaismi.

arch|angel ['ɑ:kein(d)ʒl] arkkienkeli. -**bishop** ['ɑ:tʃ'biʃəp] arkkipiispa. -**duchess** ['ɑ:tʃ'dʌtʃis] arkkiherttuatar. -**duke** ['ɑ:tʃ'dju:k] arkkiherttua.

arched [ɑ:tʃt] *pp. & a.* holvattu; köyristynyt.

archenemy perivihollinen.

archer ['ɑ:tʃə] *s.* jousimies. -**y** [-ri] *s.* jousiammunta.

archetype ['ɑ:kitaip] *s.* perikuva, esikuva.

archipelago [ɑ:ki'peləgəu] *s.* saaristo(meri).

architect ['ɑ:kitekt] *s.* arkkitehti; (kuv.) seppä (~ *of one's own fortunes*). -**ural** [-'tektʃ(ə)rəl] *a.* rakennustaiteellinen. -**ure** [-ʃə] *s.* rakennustaide.

archiv|es ['ɑ:kaivz] *s. pl.* arkisto. -**ist** ['ɑ:kivist] *s.* arkistonhoitaja.

archness ['ɑ:tʃnis] *s.* veitikkamaisuus, veikeys.

archway *s.* holvikäytävä.

arctic [ɑ:ktik] *a.* arktinen, pohjoinen; *the A*~ *Circle* pohjoinen napapiiri; *the A*~ *Ocean* Pohjoinen jäämeri.

ardent ['ɑ:dnt] *a.* palava, kuuma; tulinen, kiihkeä, innokas; ~*ly* hehkuvasti, hartaasti.

ardour, ardor [ɑ:də] *s.* kuumuus; ~ vaaravyöhyke. *into*(mieli).

arduous [ɑ:'djuəs] *a.* vaikea, vaivalloinen, voimia kysyvä.

are 1. [ɑ:, ə] *be*-vbn *ind. prees. pl.*; *they* ~ (lyh. *they're*) he, ne ovat; *we* ~ (me) olemme.

are 2. [ɑ:] *s.* aari.

area ['ɛəriə] *s.* pinta-ala, alue, ala; *danger* ~ vaaravyöhyke.

aren't [ɑ:nt] = *are not.*

argent ['ɑ:dʒ(ə)nt] *s. & a.* (run.) hopea(nvärinen).

Argentin|a [ɑ:dʒən'ti:nə] *erisn.*

Argentiina. **-e** [ˈɑːdʒntain] *a. & s.*
argentiinal inen; *the* ~ Argentiina.
argosy [ˈɑːgəsi] *s.* (run.) laiva.
argot [ˈɑːgəu] *s.* ammatti-, salakieli.
arguable [ˈɑːgjuəbl] *a.: it's* ~ [*whether*]
on kyseenalaista ..
argue [ˈɑːgjuː] *v.* kiistellä, riidellä (*with
sb.* jkn kanssa; *about, on* jstk); sittää
syitä t. perusteita (*for* t. *against*),
väittää, väitellä; osoittaa; ~ *sb. into*
saada uskomaan, taivutella jhk.
argument [ˈɑːgjumənt] *s.* kiista, riita,
peruste, todistelu; pohdinta, väittely;
-ation [-menˈteiʃn] *s.* todistelu;
väittely. **-ative** [-ˈmentətiv] *a.*
väittelynhaluinen.
Argyll [ɑːˈgail] *erisn.*
aria [ˈɑːriə] *s.* aaria.
arid [ˈærid] *a.* kuiva, kuivettunut. **-ity**
[æˈriditi] *s.* kuivuus; hedelmättömyys.
aright [əˈrait] *adv.* oikein.
arise [əˈraiz] *arose* arisen, *v.* nousta;
saada alkunsa; johtua; ilmaantua. **-n**
[əˈrizn] *pp.* ks. arise.
aristoc|racy [ærisˈtɒkrəsi] *s.* ylimystö.
-rat [ˈæristəkræt] *s.* ylimys. **-ratic**
[æristəˈkrætik] *a.* aristokraattinen,
ylimyksellinen (adv. ~ally).
Aristotle [ˈæristɔtl] *erisn.* Aristoteles.
arithmetic [əˈriθmətik] *s.* aritmetiikka,
laskuoppi. **-ian** [-ˈtiʃn] *s.* aritmeetikko.
Arizona [æriˈzəunə] *erisn.*
ark [ɑːk] *s.* (*Noah's* ~ Nooan) arkki;
Ark of the Covenant lii on arkki.
Arkansas [ˈɑːkənsɔː, ɑːˈkænzəs, Am.
m. ˈɑːkənsɔ] *erisn.*
arm 1. [ɑːm] *s.* käsivarsi; varsi; (joen
ym) haara, (tuolin) käsinoja; (takin)
hiha; *keep at* ~ *s length* pitää loitolla;
infant in ~ *s* sylilapsi; *with open* ~ *s*
avosylin; ~ *in arm* käsikoukkua.
arm 2. [ɑːm] *s.* ase (tav. *pl.*); aselaji; *v.*
aseista(utu)a, varusta(utu)a; ks.
arms.
armada [ɑːˈmɑːdə] *s.* suuri
sotalaivasto.
Armageddon [ˈɑːməˈgedn] *erisn.*
Harmagedon.
armament [ˈɑːməmənt] *s.* (tav. *pl.*)
sotavoimat; sota|tarvikkeet,
-varusteet; aseistus; varustelu; ~
industries sotatarviketeollisuus.
armature [ˈɑːmətjuə] *s.* (sähk.)
ankkuri(käämi).

armchair *s.* nojatuoli.
armed [ɑːmd] *a.* aseistettu; ~ *forces*
asevoimat; ~ *neutrality* aseellinen
puolueettomuus.
Armenia [ɑːˈmiːnjə] *erisn.* **-n** [-n] *a. &
s.* armenialainen, armenian kieli.
arm|ful sylillinen. **~-hole** hihanaukko.
armistice [ˈɑːmistis] *s.* aselepo; *A~
Day* marraskuun 11.
armlet [ˈɑːmlit] *s.* käsivarsinauha,
-vanne; pieni lahti.
armor|ial [ɑːˈmɔːriəl] *a.* vaakuna-; ~
bearings (heraldken) tunnuskuva. **-y**
[ˈɑːməri] *s.* vaakunatiede.
armour, armor [ˈɑːmə] *s.* panssari;
haarniska; *v.* panssaroida; ~*ed car*
panssariauto. **~-bearer** aseenkantaja.
~-clad haarniskoitu. **-er** [-rə] *s.*
aseseppä, varusmestari. **-y** [-ri] *s.*
arsenaali, asevarasto.
armpit *s.* kainalokuoppa.
arms [ɑːmz] *pl.* aseet; *small* ~
käsituliaseet; ~ *race* kilpavarustelu;
by force of ~ asevoimin; *take up* ~
tarttua aseisiin; *under* ~ aseissa,
taisteluvalmiina; *coat of* ~ vaakuna.
army [ˈɑːmi] *s.* armeija; sotajoukko,
suuri joukko; ~ *corps* armeijakunta;
A~ Service Corps kuormasto.
aroma [əˈrəumə] *s.* tuoksu, aromi. **-tic**
[ærə(u)ˈmætik] *a.*
voimakastuoksuinen, aromaattinen.
arose [əˈrəuz] *imp.* ks. arise.
around [əˈraund] *adv.* ympäri(llä, -lle);
joka puolella, -lle; *prep.* ympäri.
arouse [əˈrauz] *v.* herättää; kiihottaa
(*s.* arousal).
arraign [əˈrein] *v.* haastaa oikeuteen,
syyttää; moittia.
arrange [əˈrein(d)ʒ] *v.* järjestää,
järjestellä; sopia; sovittaa (mus.); *as
~d* kuten (oli) sovittu, suunniteltu; *I
have ~d for a car to meet you* olen
huolehtinut siitä, että auto on sinua
vastassa. **-ment** *s.* järjestely; sopimus;
sovinto; *pl.* toimenpiteet,
suunnitelmat; sovitus (mus.); *flower
~* kukka|-asetelma, -laite,
kukka-asettelu (taide); *come to an ~*
päästä sopimukseen.
arrant [ˈær(ə)nt] *a.* täysi, täydellinen,
oikea; ~ *nonsense* pelkkää pötyä.
array [əˈrei] *v.* järjestää (joukkoja);
pukea; *s.* taistelujärjestys; (run.) asu;

a fine ~ of.. komea joukko, rivi..

arrear [əˈriə] *s. pl.* maksamaton velka; *~s of correspondence* vastaamattomat kirjeet; *~s of work* tekemättömät työt; *work off ~s* koettaa päästä tasoihin.

arrest [əˈrest] *v.* pysäyttää, ehkäistä; pidättää, vangita; kiinnittää (jkn huomio); *s.* pidättäminen; pysähdys, keskeytys; *under ~* pidätettynä. **-ing** *a.* huomiota herättävä, kiintoisa.

arrival [əˈraivl] *s.* saapuminen, tulo; saapunut henkilö, tulokas, saapuva juna ym; *on my ~* saavuttuani.

arrive [əˈraiv] *v.* saapua, tulla perille *(at, in* jhk); *~ home* saapua kotiin; *~ at a conclusion* päätellä; [*his fan mail proved that] he has ~d* hän on menestynyt.

arroga|nce [ˈærəgəns] *s.* pöyhkeys; röyhkeys, julkeus. **-nt** [-ənt] *a.* ylpeä; röyhkeä, ylimielinen. **-te** [-eit] *v.* vaatia (itselleen).

arrow [ˈærəu] *s.* nuoli **-head** *s.* nuolenkärki.

arse [ɑ:s] *s.* (alat.) takamu|s, -kset, perse, pylly.

arsenal [ˈɑ:sinl] *s.* varikko.

arsenic [ˈɑ:snik] *s.* arsenikki; *a.* [ɑ:ˈsenik] arsenikki-.

arson [ˈɑ:sn] *s.* tuhopoltto.

art 1. [ɑ:t] (vanh.): *thou ~ sinä olet.*

art 2. [ɑ:t] *s.* taide; taito, taitavuus; ammatti; viekkaus, (tav. *pl.;* juoni; *~s and crafts* taideteollisuus; *black ~* magia; *the fine ~s* taiteet; *Master of Arts* (l.v.) filosofian maisteri; *~ student* taideopiskelija; *~ s student* filosofisen tiedekunnan opiskelija.

arter|ial [ɑ:ˈtiəriəl] *a.* valtimo-; *~ road* valtatie. **-iosclerosis** *s.,* verisuonten kalkkiutuminen.

artry [ˈɑ:təri] *s.* valtimo; valtasuoni.

artesian [ɑ:ˈti:zjən] *a.: ~ well* arteesinen kaivo.

artful [ˈɑ:tf(u)l] *a.* viekas, ovela

arthritis [ɑ:ˈθraitis] *s. s.: rheumatoid ~* reuma.

Arthur [ˈɑ:θə] *erisn.*

artichoke [ˈɑ:titʃəuk] *s. ~* latva-artisokka; *Jerusalem ~* maa-artisokka, mukula-a.

article [ˈɑ:tikl] *s.* (sanomalehti- ym) kirjoitus, artikkeli (m. kiel.); tavara;

(sopimuksen) kohta, artikla; kappale, osa; *v.* panna (jkn) oppiin; *serve one's ~s* palvella oppiaikansa

articular [ɑ:ˈtikjulə] *a.* nivel-.

articula|te [ɑ:ˈtikjulit] *a.* nivelikäs; selvä-äänteinen, artikuloitu; *v.* [-eit] niveltää; ääntää selvästi, artikuloida; *~d* m. nivel-; *~ lorry* rekka-auto. **-tion** [-ˈleiʃn] *s.* nivel(liitos), niveltyminen; ääntäminen, artikulaatio.

artifact [ˈɑ:tifækt] *s.* ihmiskäden aikaansaama tuote t. muutos.

artifi|ce [ˈɑ:tifis] *s.* temppu, juoni. **-cial** [-ˈfiʃl] *a.* keinotekoinen, teko-; teennäinen; *~ flowers* tekokukat.

artillery [ɑ:ˈtiləri] *s.* tykistö; *~-man* tykkimies.

artisan [ɑ:ˈti´zæn] *s.* käsityöläinen.

artist [ˈɑ:tist] *s.* taiteilija, taidemaalari. **-e** [ɑ:ˈti:st] *s.,* (tanssi-, laulu- ym) taiteilija. **-ic(al)** [ɑ:ˈtistik, -(ə)l] *a.* taiteellinen. **-ry** [-ri] *s.* taiteellisuus.

artless [ˈɑ:tlis] *a.* yksinkertainen, teeskentelemätön, vilpitön. **-ness** *s.* viattomuus, yksinkertaisuus.

arty [ˈɑ:ti] teennäinen, taiteellisuutta tavoitteleva.

arum [ˈɛərəm] *s.: ~ lily* (puutarha)kalla.

Aryan [ˈɛəriən] *a. & s.* arjalainen.

as [æs, əz] *adv. & konj.* koska, niinkuin; -na, -nä *(~ a child* lapsena); koska; kun; *pron.* kuin; *as.. as* yhtä.. kuin; *twice ~ large ~ this* kaksi kertaa niin iso kuin tämä; *~ far ~* aina.. saakka; *~ far ~ I know* mikäli tiedän; *~ for you* mitä sinuun tulee; *~ it were* niin sanoakseni; *~ if, ~ though* ikäänkuin; *~ to* mitä tulee; *~ well* myös, vrt. *well; ~ yet* tähän mennessä, toistaiseksi; *young ~ I am* vaikka olenkin nuori.

asbestos [æzˈbestəs] *s.* asbesti.

ascend [əˈsend] *v.* nousta, kiivetä; *~ the throne* nousta valtaistuimelle. **-ancy, -ency** [-ənsi] *s.* valta-asema, herruus; etevämmyys. **-ant, -ent** [-ənt] *s.: in the ~* valta-asemassa, nousemassa.

ascension [əˈsenʃn] *s.* nouseminen; *the A~* Kristuksen taivaaseen astuminen; *A~ Day* helatorstai.

ascent [əˈsent] *s.* nouseminen, nousu;

mäki; *the ~ of the mountain* vuorelle nousu.
ascertain [æsəˈtein] *v.* hankkia varma tieto, varmistua jstk, saada selville. **-ment** *s.* selville saaminen.
ascetic [əˈsetik] *a.* askeettinen; *s.* askeetti, **-ism** [-isizm] *s.* askeesi, askeettisuus.
ascorbic [əsˈkɔːbik]: *~ acid* askorbiinihappo.
ascribe [əsˈkraib] *v.: ~ to* lukea jkn ansioksi t. syyksi, pitää seurauksena jstk.
aseptic [əˈseptik] *a.* aseptinen.
ash 1. [æʃ] *s.* saarni; *mountain ~* pihlaja.
ash 2. [æʃ] *s.* tuhka; *lay in ~es* polttaa poroksi; *~-tray* tuhkakuppi; *A~ Wednesday* käärsimysviikon keskiviikko.
ashamed [əˈʃeimd] *a.* häpeissään (oleva); *be ~* hävetä *(of* jtk); *I felt ~ for him* häpesin hänen puolestaan; *you should be ~ of yourself* sietäisit hävetä.
ashen [ˈæʃn] *a.* tuhkanvärinen.
ashore [əˈʃɔː] *adv.* maissa; rantaan, rannalla; *go ~* mennä maihin; *was driven ~* ajautui rantaan.
ashy [ˈæʃi] *a.* tuhka-; tuhan peittämä; tuhkanharmaa.
Asia [ˈeiʃə] *erisn.* Aasia.; *~ Minor* Vähä-Aasia. **-n** [ˈeiʃ(ə)n], **-tic** [eiʃiˈætik] *a. & s.* aasialainen.
aside [əˈsaid] *adv.* sivulle, sivuun, syrjään, syrjässä; *s.* (näyttämöllä) syrjään lausutut sanat; [*the decision] was set ~* kumottiin; *put ~ for* varata jklle; *~ from* paitsi, lukuunottamatta.
asinine [ˈæsinain] *a.* aasimainen.
ask [ɑːsk] *v.* kysyä, kysellä; pyytää; kutsua; vaatia; *he ~ed me the time* hän kysyi minulta, mitä kello oli *(-- the way* kyseli tietä*); ~ about* tiedustella; *~ after* tiedustella (*.. sb.'s health* jkn vointia); *~ for* kysellä; pyytää jtk; *it ~s for attention* se vaatii tarkkaavaisuutta; *you are ~ing for trouble* (t. *for it)* aiheutat itsellesi ikävyyksiä.
askance [əsˈkæns] *adv.* viistoon; *look ~ at* katsoa karsaasti jtk.
askew [əsˈkjuː] *adv.* vinossa, -oon; kallellaan.

asking [ˈɑːskiŋ] *s.* pyytäminen; *I could have it for the ~* saisin sen milloin vain.
aslant [əˈslɑːnt] *adv.* vinossa, -sti.
asleep [əˈsliːp] *adv. & pred. a.* unessa, uneen; nukuksissa; *be ~* nukkua; *fall ~* vaipua uneen, nukahtaa; *fast (sound) ~* sikeässä unessa.
asp [æsp] *s.* = *aspen*; kyy.
asparagus [əsˈpærəgəs] *s.* parsa.
aspect [ˈæspekt] *s.* (ulko)muoto, näkökanta; puoli, sivu; *in this ~* tässä valossa; [*study] every ~ of ..* joka puolelta.
aspen [ˈæspən] *s.* haapa.
asperity [æsˈperiti] *s.* töykeys; ankaruus, tuimuus.
asperse [əˈspəːs] *v.* häpäistä *(sb.'s name).*
asphalt [ˈæsfælt] *s.* asfaltti; *v.* asfaltoida.
asphyxia [æsˈfiksiə] *s.* valekuolema. **-te** [-ieit] *v.* tukehduttaa. **-tion** [-ˈeiʃn] *s.* tukehtuminen.
aspira|nt [æsˈpaiər(ə)nt] *a. s.* pyrkijä, hakija; kokelas. **-te** [ˈæspərit] *s.* aspiraatta. **-tion** [æspəˈreiʃn] *s.* pyrkimys, harras halu.
aspir|e [əsˈpaiə] *v.* pyrkiä *(to become...* jksk), haluta, tavoitella *(after, to* jtk). **-ing** [-riŋ] *a.* korkealle pyrkivä, kunnianhimoinen.
aspirin [ˈæsp(ə)rin] *s.* aspiriini.
ass 1. [æs] *s.* aasi (m. kuv.); *she ~ aasintamma; make an ~ of oneself* tehdä itsensä naurettavaksi.
ass 2. [æs] *s.* (Am. alat.) = *arse.*
assail [əˈseil] *v.* hyökätä, rynnätä kimppuun; ahdistaa. **-ant** [-ənt] *s.* hyökkääjä.
assassin [əˈsæsin] *s.* salamurhaaja. **-ate** [-eit] *v.: he was ~d* hänet murhattiin. **-ation** [-ˈneiʃn] *s.* salamurha.
assault [əˈsɔːlt] *s.* hyökkäys; rynnäkkö; *v.* hyökätä, käydä kimppuun; *~ and battery* pahoinpitely; *~ craft* maihin-nousuvene(et); *~ rifle* rynnäkkö-kivääri; *carry by ~* vallata rynnäköllä.
assay [əˈsei] *s.* (metalli)koe; *v.* suorittaa koe t. analyysi.
assegai [ˈæsigai] *s.* heittokeihäs.
assem|blage [əˈsemblidʒ] *s.* kokoontuminen; kokoelma, joukko. **-ble** [əˈsembl] *v.* koota, kerätä;

kokoontua, kerääntyä. **-bly** [-i] *s.*
kokous; seura; kokoontumismerkki;
~ *hall* (koulun) juhlasali;
kokoonpanohalli; ~ *line* tuotanto-,
kokoonpanolinja; *morning* ~ päivän
avaus (koulussa).

assent [ə'sent] *v.* suostua, myöntyä; *s.*
suostumus, myöntymys;
hyväksyminen; *with one* ~
yksimielisesti.

assert [ə'sə:t] *v.* väittää, vakuuttaa;
vaatia itselleen (oikeuksia); ~ *oneself*
pitää puoliaan. **-ion** [ə'sə:ʃn] *s.* väite,
vakuutus; (jnk) puolustaminen,
tehostaminen. **-ive** [-iv] *a.*
vakuuttava; (itse)varma.

assess [ə'ses] *v.* määrätä (vero),
arvioida. **-ment** *s.* verotus;
arvioiminen. **-or** [-ə] *s.* arviomies.

assets ['æsets] *s. pl.* varat, omaisuus;
sg. **asset** hyödyllinen asia, etu, avu; ~
and liabilities varat ja velat.

asseverate [æ'sevəreit] *v.* vakuuttaa.

assidu|ity [æsi'dju(:)iti] *s.* uutteruus;
-ities liiallinen huomaavaisuus. **-ous**
[ə'sidjuəs] *a.* ahkera, uuttera,
väsymätön; (**~ly** ahkerasti; **~ness**
uutteruus).

assign [ə'sain] *v.* määrätä, antaa (jklle),
osoittaa (jhk); ilmoittaa, sanoa
(syyksi ym); määrätä, uskoa (*sb. to a
task, to do sth*); (lak.) luovuttaa.
-ation [æsig'neiʃn] *s.* (salainen)
kohtaus. **-ee** [æsi'ni:] *s.* uskottu mies.
-ment *s.* määrääminen;
luovutus(kirja); *a tough* ~ vaikea
tehtävä.

assimila|te [ə'simileit] *v.* tehdä t.
sulautua (samankaltaiseksi),
assimiloida, -tua. **-tion** [-'leiʃn] *s.*
yhtäläistyminen; assimilaatio.

assist [ə'sist] *v.* auttaa, avustaa, **-ance**
[-əns] *s.* apu, avustus. **-ant** [-ənt] *a.*
apu(lais)-; *s.* apulainen, avustaja.

assizes [ə'saiziz] *s. pl.* käräjät.

associa|te [ə'səuʃiit] *s.* liiketoveri;
kumppani, työtoveri; (ylimääräinen t.
apu)jäsen; *a.* liittyvä, liittynyt; *v.*
[-ʃieit] yhdistää, liittää; seurustella; *is
~ed with* on yhteydessä jhk, liittyy jhk.
-tion [-si'eiʃn] *s.* yhdistys, seura;
seurustelu; ~ *of ideas* mielleyhtymä;
~ *football* (tavallinen) jalkapallo(ilu).

assort [ə'sɔ:t] *v.* lajitella; sopia yhteen;

~ *ed* hyvin yhteen sopiva. **-ment** *s.*
valikoima, lajitelma.

Ass(o)uan [æsu'æn, 'æs-] *erisn.*

assuage [ə'sweidʒ] *v.*
lievittää   vähentää, vaimentaa.

assum|e [ə'sju:m] *v.* ottaa, omaksua;
anastaa; teeskennellä; otaksua,
olettaa; ~ *the responsibility* ottaa
vastatakseen jstk; *an ~d name* väärä
nimi. **-ing** *a.* suuriluuloinen, pöyhkeä;
~ *that* edellyttäen että. **-ption**
[ə'sʌm(p)ʃn] *s.* ottaminen,
omaksuminen; olettamus;
anastaminen; julkeus; *the A~* Neitsyt
Marian taivaaseenastuminen.

assurance [ə'ʃuərəns] *s.* vakuutus;
vakuus, varmuus; vakaumus;
itsevarmuus; *life* ~ henkivakuutus;
give an ~ vakuuttaa.

assure [ə'ʃuə] *v.* vakuuttaa; saada
vakuuttuneeksi; varmistaa, turvata.
-d [-d] *a.* varma, vakuuttunut;
itsevarma. **-dly** [-ridli] *adv.* varmasti.

Assyria [ə'siriə] *erisn.* **-n** [-n] *a.* & *s.*
assyrialainen.

aster ['æstə] *s.* asteri.

asterisk ['æstərisk] *s.* tähti (kirjap.).

astern [əs'tə:n] *adv.* perässä, -kään,
peränpuolella, -lle; ~ *of* takana.

asthma ['æsmə] *s.* astma,
hengenahdistus, **-tic** [æs'mætik] *a.*
astmaattinen.

astigmatism [əs'tigmətizm] *s.* (silmän)
hajataitteisuus.

astir [əs'tə:] *adv.* liikkeessä, -llä.

astonish [əs'tɔniʃ] *v.* hämmästyttää,
kummastuttaa; *be ~ed at* hämmästyä
jtk. **-ing** *a.* hämmästyttävä. **-ment** *s.*
hämmästys, kummastus.

astound [əs'taund] *v.* saattaa
hämmästyksen valtaan, ällistyttää.

astrakhan [æstrə'kæn] *s.*
astrakaaninahka.

astral [æstr(ə)l] *a.* tähti-.

astray [əs'trei] *adv.* harhateillä, -lle,
harhaan; *go* ~ joutua harhaan.

astride [əs'traid] *adv.* hajareisin.

astringent [əs'trin(d)ʒ(ə)nt] *a.* & *s.*
kutistava (aine), supistava
(kasvosyu).

astrolog|er [əs'trɔlədʒ|ə] *s.* astrologi. **-y**
[-i] *s.* astrologia.

astronaut ['æstrənɔ:t] *s.* astronautti,
avaruusmies.

astronom|er [əs'trɔnəm|ə] s.
tähtitieteilijä. **-ic (-ical)**
[æstrə'nɔmik(ə)l] a. tähtitieteellinen
(m. kuv.). **-y** [-i] s. tähtitiede.

astute [əs'tju:t] a. ovela, terävä, **-ness**
s. terävyys, oveluus.

asunder [ə'sʌndə] a. erillänsä; rikki.

Aswan ['æswɑ:n] ks. *Ass(o)uan.*

asylum [ə'sailəm] s. turvapaikka,
turvakoti; (vanh.) mielisairaala;
(political ~) turvapaikkaoikeus.

at [æt, ət] prep. ilmaisee paikkaa, aikaa,
tilaa, hintaa ym; ~ *home* kotona; ~
my uncle's setäni luona; ~ *the station*
asemalla; ~ *Christmas* jouluna; ~ *two
o'clock* kello kahdelta; ~ *2 shillings*
kahden šillingin hinnasta; ~ *war*
sodassa; ~ *work* työssä; *be* ~ *it* olla
jssk hommassa; *be good* ~ taitava
jssk; . . ~ *that* vielä lisäksi; ~ *times*
joskus; *aim, rush* ~ tähdätä jhk,
hyökätä jtk kohti; *laugh* ~ nauraa
jllek; *clutch* ~ koettaa tavoittaa;
delighted ~ *the idea* ihastunut
ajatukseen.

atavism ['ætəvizm] s. atavismi.

ate [et, Am. eit] imp. ks. *eat.*

athe|ism [eiθiizm] s. ateismi. **-ist** [-ist] s.
jumalankieltäjä. **-istic** [-'istik] a.
ateistinen, jumalaton.

atheneum [æθi'ni(:)əm] s. kirjallinen t.
tieteellinen kerho; lukusali.

Athenian [ə'θi:njən] a. & s.
ateenalainen.

Athens ['æθinz] erisn. Ateena.

athlet|e ['æθli:t] s. (yleis)urheilija;
atleetti; ~ '*s foot* jalkasilsa. **-ic**
[æθ'letik] a. urheilu-. **-ics** [æθ'letiks] s.
pl. (yleis)urheilu.

at-home [ət'həum] s. vastaanotto.

athwart [ə'θwɔ:t] adv. (vinosti)
poikittain; prep. yli, poikki.

Atlantic [ət'læntik] a. & s.: *the* ~
[*Ocean*] Atlantti.

atmospher|e ['ætməsfiə] s. ilmakehä;
ilmapiiri. **-ic(al)** [-'ferik, -(ə)l] a.
ilmakehän, ilma(n)-. **-ics** [-'feriks] s.ʼ
pl. ilmastohäiriöt (rad.).

atoll [ætɔl] s. atolli (riutta).

atom ['ætəm] s. atomi; hiukkanen;
~-*powered* atomikäyttöinen. **-ic**
[ə'tɔmik] a. atomi-; ~ *bomb*
atomipommi; ~ *energy* atomivoima.
-izer [-aizə] s. pirskotin, suihkutin.

atone [ə'təun] v.: ~ *for* sovittaa,
hyvittää jtk. **-ment** s. sovitus; hyvitys;
the A~ Kristuksen sovitustyö.

atro|cious [ə'trəuʃəs] a. hirvittävä,
kammottava. **-sity** [ə'trɔsiti] s.
hirmuteko.

atrophy ['ætrəfi] s. atrofia,
surkastuminen; v. näivettää, -ttyä.

attach [ə'tætʃ] v. kiinnittää; liittää,
yhdistää; vangita, takavarikoida; olla
kiinni jssk, liittyvä, kuulua jhk; ~
much importance to kiinnittää paljon
huomiota, panna paljon painoa jhk;
~*ed you will find* . . oheisena
seuraa . . ; *deeply* ~*ed to* syvästi
kiintynyt jkh; *no blame* ~*es to him*
häneen ei lankea mitään moitetta.

attaché [ə'tæʃei] s. (lähetystön) attašea,
avustaja; *military* ~ sotilasasiamies;
~ *case* (asiakirja)salkku.

attachment [ə'tætʃmənt] s. kiintymys,
mieltymys; kiinnitys(laite), kiinnitin.

attack [ə'tæk] v. hyökätä, käydä
kimppuun; s. hyökkäys; (taudin)
kohtaus; *make an* ~ *(upon)* tehdä
hyökkäys, hyökätä.

attain [ə'tein] v. saavuttaa, saada. **-able**
saavutettavissa oleva. **-der** [-də] s.
(lak.) kunnian ja omaisuuden
menetys (liittyy kuolemantuomioon).
-ment s. saavutus; *pl.* tiedot, taidot.

attaint [ə'teint] v. tuomita kuolemaan
t. lainsuojattomaksi.

attar ['ætə] s.: ~ [*of roses*] ruusu-
esanssi.

attempt [ə'tem(p)t] v. yrittää, koettaa;
s. yritys; ~ *upon sb.'s life* murhayritys.

attend [ə'tend] v. ottaa vaarin, tarkata,
pitää huolta, huolehtia *(to* jstk); olla
läsnä, käydä jssk; (m. ~ *on*) hoitaa
(potilasta), *(to)* palvella (asiakasta
ym); saattaa; ~ *to what I say*
tarkkaa, kuuntele mitä minä sanon;
you are not ~*ing* et ole tarkkaavainen;
~ *upon* palvella; ~ *school* käydä
koulua; *the concert was well* ~*ed*
konsertissa oli paljon väkeä; *success*
~*ed his undertaking* hänen
yrityksensä menestyi; *the method is*
~*ed by some risks* menetelmään liittyy
riskejä; *are you being* ~*ed to?*
palvellaanko teitä? **-ance** [-əns] s.
(jkn) palveleminen, hoitaminen;
läsnäolo *(at* jssk): yleisö(määrä); *be in*

~ olla virantoimituksessa; *a small* ~ harvalukuinen yleisö; *dance* ~ *on* liehitellä jkta. **-ant** [-ənt] *a.* palveleva; liittyvä; *s.* palvelija; *pl.* saattue, seurue; *the* ~ *circumstances* tähän, siihen liittyvät seikat.

atten|tion [ə'tenʃn] *s.* tarkkaavaisuus, huomio; huomaavaisuus, kohteliaisuus; ~ !/[ʃʌn] asento! huomio! *pay* ~ *to* kiinnittää huomiota jhk, huomata, tarkata; *stand at* ~ seistä asennossa **-tive** [-tiv] *a.* tarkkaavainen; huomaavainen.

attenua|te [ə'tenjueit] *v.* ohentaa, miedontaa, heikontaa. **-tion** [-'eiʃn] *s.* (rad.) vaimentaminen.

attest [ə'test] *v.* todistaa; vannottaa.

attic ['ætik] *s.* ullakkohuone, ullakkokerros; *A*~ attikalainen, ateenalainen.

attire [ə'taiə] *v.* pukea, verhota; *s.* puku, asu.

attitud|e ['ætitju:d] *s.* asento; asenne, asennoituminen, suhtautuminen, kanta. **-inize** [-'tju:dinaiz] *v.* esiintyä teennäisesti; *-inizing* poseeraus.

Attlee ['ætli] *erisn.*

attorney [ə'tə:ni] *s.* asiamies; Am. asianajaja; *A* ~ *General* Am. oikeusministeri; *letter (power) of* ~ valtakirja.

attract [ə'trækt] *v.* vetää puoleensa; miellyttää, viehättää; ~ *attention* herättää huomiota. **-ion** [-kʃn] *s.* vetovoima, viehätys(voima). **-ive** [-tiv] *a.* puoleensavetävä, miellyttävä. **-iveness** *s.* viehättävyys.

attributable [a'tribjutəbl] *a.: is* ~ *to* johtuu (voidaan katsoa johtuvan) jstk.

attribute [ə'tribju:t] *v.: ~ to* katsoa jklle kuuluvaksi, kulkea jnk, jkn syyksi t. ansioiksi; *s.* ['ætribju:t] ominaisuus; tuntomerkki; attribuutti; *I* ~ *this to. .* katson sen johtuvan . .sta; *this play has been* ~*d to S.* S:a on pidetty tämän näytelmän tekijänä.

attrition [ə'triʃn] *s.* hankaaminen; *war of* ~ näännytyssota.

attune [ə'tju:n] *v.* saattaa sopusointuun *(to* jnk kanssa); virittää.

auburn ['ɔ:bən] *s.* kullanruskea.

auction ['ɔ:kʃn] *s.* huutokauppa; *v. (~ off)* myydä huutokaupalla **-eer**

[-ʃə'niə] *s.* huutokaupanpitäjä.

audac|ious [ɔ:'deiʃəs] *a.* rohkea, uskalias; häpeämätön, julkea. **-ity** [ɔ:'dæsiti] *s.* (uhka)rohkeus; julkeus.

audib|ility [ɔ:di'biliti] *s.* kuuluvuus. **-le** ['ɔ:dəbl] *a.* kuuluva, selvä. **-ly** kuuluvalla äänellä.

audience ['ɔ:djəns] *s.* kuulijakunta, yleisö; audienssi; *there was a large* ~ yleisöä oli paljon.

audio|metry [ɔ:di'ɔmitri] *s.* kuulonmittaus (audiometrillä). **~-visual** *a.-v.* aids audiovisuaaliset apuvälineet.

audit ['ɔ:dit] *s.* tilintarkastus; *v.* tarkastaa (tilejä). **-ion** [ɔ:'diʃn] *s.* (laulajan ym) koe-esiintyminen. **-or** [-ə] *s.* tilintarkastaja; kuulija. **-orium** [ɔ:di'tɔ:riəm] *s.* luentosali. **-ory** [-(ə)ri] *a.* kuulo-

auger ['ɔ:gə] *s.* kaira.

aught [ɔ:t] *pron.* mitään (vanh.); *for* ~ *I care* minun puolestani.

augment [ɔ:g'ment] *v.* lisätä; kasvaa. **-ation** [-'teiʃn] *s.* lisääminen, lisäys.

augur ['ɔ:gə] *s.* ennustaja; *v.* ennustaa. **-y** ['ɔ:gjuri] *s.* enne.

august [ɔ:'gʌst] *a.* ylevä, korkea.

August ['ɔ:gəst] *s.* elokuu. **-ine** [ɔ:'gʌstin] *erisn.* Augustinus. **-us** [ɔ:'gʌstəs] *erisn.*

auk [ɔ:k] *s.* ruokki.

aunt [ɑ:nt] *s.* täti.

au pair ['əu 'peə] *a.* perheenjäsenen asemassa oleva (apulais)tyttö.

aura ['ɔ:rə] *s.* säteily; aura.

aural ['ɔ:r(ə)l] *a.* korva-.

aureole ['ɔ:riəul] *s.* sädekehä.

aureomycin [ɔ:riə(u)'maisin] *s.* aureomysiini.

aur|icle ['ɔ:rikl] *s.* korvalehti. **-icular** [ɔ:'rikjulə] *a.* korva-.

aurora [ɔ:'rɔ:rə] *s.* aamurusko; ~ *borealis* [bɔri'eilis] revontulet.

auscultation [ɔ:sk(ə)l'teiʃn] *s.* (lääk.) kuuntelu (m. stetoskoopilla).

auspic|e ['ɔ:spis] *s.* enne; *pl.* suojelus; *under favourable* ~*s* hyvin entein; *under the* ~*s of* jkn suojeluksen alaisena. **-ious** [ɔ:s'piʃəs] *a.* hyväenteinen, lupaava, suopea.

Aussie ['ɔ:si] *s.* sl. australialainen sotilas.

auster|e [ɔ:s'tiə] *a.* ankara,

pidättyväinen, jäyhä, karu. **-ity**
[ɔ:s'teriti] s. ankaruus, ankara
itsekuri: ~ [*policy*] tiukka
talouspolitiikka.

Australia [ɔs'treiljə] *erisn.* **-n** [-n] *a.* &
s. australialainen.

Austria ['ɔstriə] *erisn.* Itävalta. **-n** [-n]
a. & *s.* itävaltalainen.

autar|chy ['ɔ:tɑ:ki] s. yksinvalta. **-ky**
[ks. ed] *s.* (taloudellinen)
omavaraisuus.

authentic [ɔ:'θentik] *a.* luotettava,
oikea, aito **-ate** [-eit] *v.* todistaa
aidoksi, laillistaa. **-ity** [-ən'tisiti] *s.*
luotettavuus, aitous.

author ['ɔ:θə] *s.* alkuunpanija, tekijä;
kirjailija. **-ess** [-ris] *s.* tekijä,
kirjailija(tar). **-itarian** [ɔ:θəri'tɛəriən]
a. autoritaarinen. **-itative** [ɔ:'θɔritətiv]
a. arvovaltainen; määräävä, käskevä.
-ity [ɔ:'θɔriti] *s.* auktoriteetti,
arvovalta; valtuus; *those in* ~
vallanpitäjät; *the* -ities viranomaiset;
on good ~ luotettavasta lähteestä.
-ization [ɔ:θərai'zeiʃn] *s.* valtuutus.
-ize ['ɔ:θəraiz] *v.* valtuuttaa. **-ship** *s.*
kirjailijan|toiminta, -ura;
(kirjan)alkuperä.

auto ['ɔ:təu] *s.* Am. = *automobile.*

auto- ['ɔ:təu] (yhd.) itse-. **-biography** *s.*
omaelämäkerta. **-cracy** [ɔ:'tɔkrəsi] *s.*
itsevaltius. **-crat** ['ɔ:təkræt] *s.*
itsevaltias; (~ **-ic** [- -'- -] *a.*
itsevaltainen). **-graph** ['ɔ:təgrɑ:f] *s.*
omakätinen nimikirjoitus; *v.*
kirjoittaa omakätisesti, varustaa
nimikirjoituksellaan. **-gyro, -giro**
[-'dʒaiərəu] *s.* autogiro.

automat ['ɔ:təmæt] *s.*
automaatti(ruokala).

automa|tic [ɔ:tə|'mætik] *a.*
automaattinen, itsetoimiva; ~
weapons konetuliaseet,
automaattiaseet. **-tically**
automaattisesti. **-tion** [-'meiʃn]
automaatio. **-ton** [ɔ:'tɔmət(ə)n] *s.* (pl.
m. *-ta)* s. robotti, automaatti.

automobile ['ɔ:təməbi:l] *s.* (et. Am.)
auto.

autonom|ous [ɔ:'tɔnəməs] *a.*
autonominen, itsenäinen. **-y**
[ɔ:'tɔnəmi] *s.* autonomia, itsehallinto.

autopsy ['ɔ:tɔpsi] *s.* ruumiinavaus.

auto-suggestion *s.* itsesuggestio.

autumn ['ɔ:təm] *s.* syksy; *in the* ~
syksyllä; *last* ~ viime syksynä. **-al**
[ɔ:'tʌmnəl] *a.* syksyinen, syksyn.

auxiliary [ɔ:g'ziljəri] *a.* auttava, apu-; *s.*
auttaja; apuverbi; *pl.* apujoukot.

avail [ə'veil] *v.* hyödyttää; *s.* hyöty; ~
oneself of käyttää hyväkseen; *it was of
no* ~ ei hyödyttänyt, siitä ei ollut
apua. **-ability** [-ə'biliti] *s.* saatavissa
olo. **-able** [-əbl] *a.* saatavissa (oleva).

avalanche ['ævəlɑ:nʃ] *s.* lumivyöry.

avaric|e ['ævəris] *s.* ahneus, saituus.
-ious [-'riʃəs] *a.* ahne, saita.

avenge [ə'ven(d)ʒ] *v.* kostaa jklle (m.
~ *oneself, be* ~ *d on).*

avenue ['ævnju:] *s.* lehtikuja, leveä
katu; (kuv.) tie.

aver [ə'və:] *v.* vakuuttaa.

average ['ævəridʒ] *s.* keskimäärä,
-arvo, -verto; merivahinko; *a.*
keskimääräinen, keskitason; *v.*
määrätä keskiarvo, olla, nousta
keskimäärin (jhk); *on* [*an*] ~, *on the*
~ keskimäärin; *below the* ~ alle
keskitason; *the* ~ *age* keski-ikä.

aver|se [ə'və:s] *a.: ~ to* (t. *from)*
vastahakoinen, haluton. **-sion**
[ə'və:ʃn] *s.* vastenmielisyys; inho; *my
pet* ~ pahinta mitä tiedän.

avert [ə'və:t] *v.* torjua (vaara); kääntää
pois.

aviary ['eiviəri] *s.* lintuhäkki, -huone.

avia|tion [eivi'eiʃn] *s.* ilmailu. **-tor**
['eivieitə] *s.* lentäjä.

avid ['ævid] *a.* ahne, ahnas. **-ity**
['æviditi] *s.* ahneus, ahnaus.

avocado [ævə'kɑ:dəu] *s.*
avokado(hedelmä).

avocation [ævə(u)'keiʃn] *s.*
(sivu)puuha, homma.

avoid [ə'vɔid] *v.* välttää, karttaa. **-able**
[-ədl] *a.* väistettävissä oleva. **-ance**
[-əns] *s.* välttäminen.

avoirdupois [ævədə'pɔiz] *s.* Engl.
kauppapaino(järjestelmä, vrt. *troy).*

Avon ['eivn] *erisn.*

avouch [ə'vautʃ] *v.* vakuuttaa;
vahvistaa; taata; tunnustaa.

avow [ə'vau] *v.* myöntää, tunnustaa. **-al**
[-əl] *s.* tunnustus, myöntäminen. **-ediy**
[-idli] *adv.* tunnustetusti.

avuncular [ə'vʌŋkjulə] *s.* setämäinen.

await [ə'weit] *v.* odottaa.

awake [ə'weik] *awoke,* pp. *awoke* t.

~d, v. herätä, herättää; *pred. a.*
hereillä, valpas; *be ~ to* oivaltaa, olla
täysin tietoinen jstk; *wide ~* valpas. **-n**
[-n] *v.* herättää (tajuamaan jtk *to);*
herätä. **-ning** [-niŋ] *s.* herääminen.
award [ə'wɔ:d] *v.* tuomita jklle; suoda,
antaa; *s.* tuomio; (jklle myönnetty)
palkinto, apuraha ym.
aware [ə'wɛə] *pred. a.* tietoinen,
selvillä; *be ~ of . . (that . .)* olla
tietoinen jstk, tietää, tajuta; *become
~ of* oivaltaa, huomata.
awash [ə'wɔʃ] *adv.* veden rajassa t.
peitossa.
away [ə'wei] *adv.* poissa, pois;
poispäin; *three miles ~* kolmen mailin
päässä; *go ~* mennä pois; *mene
tiehesi! far ~* kaukana; *give ~* (m.)
ilmaista; *make ~ with* ks. *make; work
~ ahertaa; fire ~* anna pamahtaa!
anna kuulua!
awe [ɔ:] *s.* kunnioittava pelko; *v.*
herättää kunnioitusta t. pelkoa jkssa;
stand in ~ of (tuntea kunnioitusta tai)
pelätä jkta. **-struck** *a.* pelon,
kunnioituksen valtaama.
awful [ˈɔːfl] *a.* hirveä, kauhea;
pelottava. **-ly** [ˈɔːfli] *adv.* hirveän,
hirveästi; kauhean (paljon); *I'm ~
sorry* olen kauhean pahoillani.
awhile [ə'wail] *adv.* hetkisen, vähän
aikaa.

awkward [ˈɔːkwəd] *a.* epämukava;
vaikea, hankala, kiusallinen;
kömpelö, hämillinen; kankea; *the ~
age* nulikkaikä; *an ~ customer*
hankala ihminen.
awl [ɔ:l] *s.* naskali.
awning [ˈɔːniŋ] *s.* aurinkokatos,
ulkokaihdin, markiisi.
awoke [ə'wəuk] *imp. & pp.* ks. *awake.*
awry [ə'rai] *adv.* vinossa, vinoon,
kieroon; hullusti.
axe, (et. Am.) **ax** [æks] *s.* kirves; *v.*
poistaa (kuluja ym), lopettaa; *he has
an ~ to grind* hänellä on oma lehmä
ojassa; *get the ~* saada potkut.
axillary [æk'siləri] *a.* kainalo-.
axiom [ˈæksiəm] *s.* aksiooma, aksiomi,
selviö.
axis [ˈæksis] *s.* (pl. *axes* [ˈæksi:z] akseli.
axle [ˈæksl] *s.* (pyörän)akseli. **~-tree** =
ed.
ay, aye [ai] *int.* kyllä; *s.* (pl. *ayes)* jää
myöntävä vastaus; *the ayes have it*
enemmistö on asian puolella.
ayah [ˈaiə] *s.* intialainen lastenhoitaja.
aye [ei] *adv.* aina (Skotl.).
Ayr [ɛə], **-shire** [-ʃiə] erisn.
azalea [ə'zeiljə] *s.* atsalea.
Azores [ə'zɔ:z] erisn.: *the ~* Azorit.
azure [ˈæʒə] *a. & a.* taivaansini(nen).

B

B, b [bi:] s. b-kirjain; nuotti, sävel h; ~ *flat* nuotti b. Lyh.: **b.** *born;* **B. A.** *Bachelor of Arts;* **Bart.** *Baronet;* **B. B. C.** ['bi: bi: 'si:] *British Broadcasting Corporation* Englannin yleisradio; **B.C.** ['bi: 'si:] *before Christ* eKr.; **B.A.** *British Airways;* **B.I.F.** *British Industries Fair;* **Bro(s).** *Brothers* (toiminimissä); **B.Sc.** *Bachelor of Science.*

baa [bɑː] *v.* määkiä; *s.* määkiminen.

Baal ['bei(ə)l] *erisn.*

babble ['bæbl] *v.* jokeltaa, leperrellä; solista; *s.* lepertely; ~ [*out*] *secrets* lörpötellä, laverrella.

babe [beib] *s.* lapsonen; Am. sl. typykkä.

babel ['beibl] *s.* Baabel; sekasorto, (kielten)sekoitus.

baboon [bə'buːn] *s.* paviaani.

baby ['beibi] *s.* pieni lapsi, vauva; sl. kullanmuru, typykkä; ~ *car* pieni auto; *be left holding the* ~ saada kannettavakseen vastuu. **-hood** *s.* varhaislapsuus, vauvaikä. **-ish** lapsellinen. **~-minder** (lapsen, lasten) päivähoitaja. **~-minding** päivähoito. **-sit** olla lapsenkaitsijana t. kotimiehenä. **-sitter** lapsenkaitsija.

Babylon ['bæbilən] *erisn.* **-ian** [-'ləunjən] *a. & s.* babylonialainen.

baccalaureate [bækə'lɔːriit] *s.* kandidaatti; ks. *bachelor.*

bacchanal ['bækənæl] *s.* juomingit.

bachelor ['bætʃlə] *s.* poikamies; bakkalaureus (tav. *B* ~ *of Art.* l. v. hum. kand.). **-hood** *s.* poikamiehen sääty.

bacill|us [bə'siləs] *s.* (pl. *-i* [-ai]) basilli.

back [bæk] *s.* selkä; takaosa, taka-, selkäpuoli; selkänoja; puolustaja (jalkap.); *v.* tukea jkta, olla jkn puolella, kannattaa jkta, lyödä vetoa

jnk puolesta (urh.); peruuttaa, peräyttää, -ytyä; *a.* taka-, vasta-, rästissä oleva; *adv.* takaisin, taaksepäin, takaperin; *at the* ~ *of* jnk takana; *I'll be* ~ *in a moment* palaan kohta; ~ *number* (lehden) vanha numero; ~ *street* syrjäkatu; *two years* ~ kaksi vuotta sitten; ~ *out of* peräytyä, luopua jstk; ~ *up* auttaa, tukea; ~ *water* huovata; *go* ~ *on* rikkoa, pettää; *answer* ~ vastata nenäkkäästi; *get sb.'s* ~ *up* suututtaa; *keep* ~ salata. **~-bencher** (Engl. parl.) takapenkkiläinen. **-bite** *v.* panetella. **-bone** selkäranka; *to the* ~ ytimiä myöten. **~-chat** nenäkäs vastaus. **-cloth, -drop** taustaverho. **-date:** *will be* ~ *d* maksetaan takautuvasti. **-door** salainen, salakavala. **~-formation** takaperoisjohdannainen. **-gammon** eräs lautapeli. **-ground** tausta, taka-ala. **-hand(ed)** rysty-. **-ing** *s.* tuki. **-lash** (kuv.) vihamielinen reaktio. **-log** tekemättömät työt, toimittamattomat (tilaukset ym). **~-pedal** jarruttaa; (kuv.) tehdä täyskäännös. **~-seat** takaistuin. **-slide** luiskahtaa takaisin, luopua. **-slider** luopio. **-stairs** *s.* takaportaat; *a.* = *backdoor.* **-ward** *a.* takaperoinen, takapajulla oleva, jälkeenjäänyt; *adv.* (tav. ~*s*) taaksepäin, takaperin; ~*s and forwards* edestakaisin; (~*ness* jälkeenjääneisyys). **-wash** (kuv.) odottamaton ikävä seuraus. **-water** suvanto. **-woods** korpi, takalistot.

bacon ['beik(ə)n] *s.* pekoni; ~ *and eggs* paistettu pekoni ja muna; *save one's* ~ pelastaa nahkansa.

bacteri|a [bæk'tiəriə] *s. pl.* (sg. *-um*) bakteerit. **-cidal** [-'saidl] *a.* bakteereja tappava. **-ology** [-'ɔlədʒi] *s.*

bakteerioppi, bakteriologia.

bad [bæd] *a. (worse worst)* paha, ilkeä; huono, kelvoton, kehno; pilaantunut; väärä (raha); vahingollinen; sairas; *a* ~ *business (job)* ikävä juttu; ~ *egg* (kuv.) mätämuna; *go* ~ pilaantua; *go to the* ~ mennä hunningolle; *too* ~ vahinko! olipa ikävä(ä)! *not* ~ ei hullumpi, melko hyvä; *not half* ~ ks. *half*; *with* ~ *grace* vastenmielisesti.

bade [bæd, run. beid] *imp.* ks. *bid*.

badge [bædʒ] *s.* merkki (koulun, partio- ym); erikoismerkki, tunnus.

badger [ˈbædʒə] *s.* mäyrä; *v.* ahdistaa.

badly [ˈbædli] *adv.* pahasti jne.; *be* ~ *off* olla huonoissa varoissa; *want sth.* ~ olla kipeästi jnk tarpeessa.

badminton [ˈbædmintən] *s.* sulkapallopeli.

bad-tempered *a.* pahansisuinen.

baffle [ˈbæfl] *v.* tehdä tyhjäksi; saattaa ymmälle, nolata. **-ing** *a.* hämäännyttävä.

bag [bæg] *s.* säkki, pussi; laukku; käsilaukku; metsästyslaukku, saalis; *v.* panna pussiin, »kähveltää», vallata; pullistua; riippua pussina; ~ *and baggage* kimpsuineen kampsuineen. **-gage** [-idʒ] *s.* kuormasto; Am. matkatavarat.

bagel [ˈbeigəl] *s.* donitsin muotoinen (hapan) sämpylä.

bag|gy [ˈbægi] *a.* pussimainen. **-man** kauppamatkustaja. **-pipe(s)** säkkipilli.

Bag(h)dad [bægˈdæd] *erisn.*

bah [bɑː] *int.* johan nyt! pyh!

Bahama [bəˈhɑːmə] *erisn.: the* ~ s Bahama-saaret.

bail 1. [beil] *s.* takaus(mies); *go* ~ [*for*] mennä takuuseen; *v.: he was* ~ed *out* hän pääsi vapaalle jalalle takausta vastaan.

bail 2. [beil] *s.* sanka; *v.* ammentaa; ~ *out a boat* ammentaa vene tyhjäksi; ks. *bale 3*. **-er** [-ə] *s.* viskain, äyskäri.

bailey [ˈbeili] *s.* Old B~ (Lontoon) keskusrikostuomioistuin.

bailiff [ˈbeilif] *s.* oikeudenpalvelija, šeriffin apulainen; tilanhoitaja.

bait [beit] *s.* syötti; *v.* varustaa syötillä, usuttaa koira (tai koiria) eläimen kimppuun; kiusata, härnätä.

baize [beiz] *s.* boijikangas.

bake [beik] *v.* kypsyttää (leipää ym),

paistaa (m. leipoa); polttaa; kypsyä, paistua. **-r** [-ə] *s.* leipuri; ~ 's [*shop*] leipomo, leipämyymälä. **-ry** [-əri] *s.* leipomo.

baking [ˈbeikiŋ] *s.:* ~ *powder* leivinjauhe.

balance [ˈbæləns] *s.* vaaka; tasapaino; bilanssi, saldo, tase; ylijäämä; *v.* olla, pitää tasapainossa, saattaa tasapainoon, tasapainottaa; punnita; päättää (tili); ~ *oneself* pysyä tasapainossa, tasapainotella; ~ *due* saatava(nne); ~ *of payments* maksutase; ~ *of terror* kauhun tasapaino; ~ *of trade* kauppatase; *keep one's* ~ pysyä tasapainossa; *strike a* ~ laatia tase, (kuv.) tehdä kompromissi; *be (hang) in the* ~ olla ratkaisematta; *on* ~ .. kaikki huomioon ottaen, kaiken kaikkiaan; ~ *one's books* tehdä tilinpäätös. **-d** [-t] *a.* tasapainoinen, tasapuolinen. **~-sheet** tase, tiliasema.

balcony [ˈbælkəni] *s.* parveke, (teatt.) toinen parvi.

bald [bɔːld] *a.* kalju, paljas; koristelematon, karu.

baldachin [bɔːldəkin] *s.* korukатos.

balderdash [ˈbɔːldədæʃ] *s.* sekasotku, hölynpöly.

bald|-head, ~-pate *s.* kaljupää. **~-headed** *a.* kaljupäinen; *go at it* b.-h. syöksyä päätä pahkaa jhk. **-ly** *adv.* kaunistelematta, suoraan.

baldric [ˈbɔːldrik] *s.* olkavyö.

Baldwin [ˈbɔːldwin] *erisn.*

bale 1. [beil] *s.* paali; *v.* panna paaliin, paalittaa.

bale 2. [beil] *s.* (run.) tuho.

bale 3. [beil] *v.* (= *bail*) ammentaa; ~ *out* pelastautua laskuvarjon avulla, hypätä (lentokoneesta).

baleful [ˈbeilf(u)l] *a.* turmiollinen.

Balfour [ˈbælfəˌ-uə] *erisn.*

balk, baulk [bɔːk] *s.* palkki, parru, sidehirsi; este; *v.* ehkäistä, estää, tehdä tyhjäksi; laiminlyödä; säikkyä, epäröidä; *she was* ~ed hän pettyi (aikeissaan ym).

Balkan [ˈbɔːlkən] *a.* Balkanin; *erisn.: the* ~ s Balkanin maat.

ball 1. [bɔːl] *s.* pallo; kuula, luoti; kerä; *v.* muodostua palloksi; *meat* ~ liha|pulla, -pyörykkä; ~ *of the eye* silmämuna; ~ *of the foot* päkiä; *keep the* ~ *rolling* pitää (keskustelu ym) vireillä; *have the* ~ *at one's feet* hallita tilannetta; *play* ~ (kuv.) olla valmis yhteistyöhön.

ball 2. [bɔ:l] *s.* tanssiaiset.

ballad ['bæləd] *s.* balladi. **-e** [bæ'la:d] *s.* (kolmiskeistöinen) runo.

ballast ['bæləst] *s.* painolasti.

ball|-bearings kuulalaakeri. ~ **-cartridge** terävä patruuna.

ballerina [bælə'ri:nə] *s.* ballerina.

ballet ['bælei] *s.* baletti. **~-dancer** balettitanssija(tar).

Balliol ['beiljəl] *erisn.*

ballistic [bə'listik] *a.* : ~ *missiles* ballistiset ohjukset.

balloon [bə'lu:n] *s.* ilmapallo; *v.* muodostua palloksi; ~ *up* sotkea.

ballot ['bælət] *s.* salainen äänestys, lippuäänestys; äänestyskuula, suljettu vaalilippu; *v.* äänestää suljetuilla lipuilla; *take a* ~ äänestää; *at the first* ~ ensimmäisessä äänestyksessä; ~ [*for*] äänestää, valita arvalla. **~-box** vaaliuurna. **~-paper** vaalilippu.

ballpoint ~ *pen* kuulakärkikynä.

ball-room *s.* tanssisali.

ballyhoo ['bæli'hu:] *s.* räikeä mainonta; hälinä, meteli.

balm [ba:m] *s.* palsami; lievike. **-y [-i]** *a.* palsami-; sulotuoksuinen, lievittävä.

Balmoral [bæl'mɔrl] *erisn.*

baloney [bə'ləuni] *s.* sl. pöty.

balsa ['bɔ:lsə] *s.* balsa(puu).

balsam ['bɔ:lsəm] *s.* palsami.

Baltic ['bɔ:ltik] *a.* balttilainen; *the* ~ Itämeri.

balust|er ['bæləstə] *s.* pylväs; ~*s* kaiteet. **-rade** [-'treid] *s.* balustradi, reunakaide.

bamboo [bæm'bu:] *s.* bamburuoko, bambu.

bamboozle [bæm'bu:zl] *v.* puijata; hämätä.

ban [bæn] *s.* kielto; (~ *of excommunication*) panna, kirkonkirous; *v.* kieltää; *nuclear test* ~ ydinkoekielto; *a* ~ *on travel* matkustuskielto; *the film was* ~*ned by the censor* sensuuri kielsi filmin.

banai [bə'na:l, 'beinl] *a.* arkipäiväinen, kulunut.

banana [bə'na:nə] *s.* banaani; ~ *skin* banaaninkuori.

band [bænd] *s.* side, nauha; hihna; vanne; vyö; papin kaulus (tav. ~*s*); joukko, joukkue; soittokunta, orkesteri, yhtye; (rad.) taajuusalue, kaista; *v.* liittää, liittyä yhteen (~ *together*); *in the 16-metre* ~ 16 metrin aaltopituudella.

bandage ['bændidʒ] *s.* side, kääre; *v.* sitoa (haava).

band-box pahvi-, hatturasia.

banderole ['bændirəul] *s.* pieni lippu; vyöte, banderolli.

bandit ['bændit] *s.* rosvo, ryöväri.

band|leader, -master *s.* orkesterinjohtaja.

bandoleer, -ier [bændə'liə] *s.* olkavyö, patruunavyö.

band|-saw vannesaha. **-sman** soittaja. **-stand** soittolava. **-wagon**: *jump on the* ~ mennä voittajan puolelle.

bandy ['bændi] *v.* heitellä edestakaisin, sinkautella; *s.* jääpalloilu; *a.* väärä; ~ *words* kiistellä; *the story was bandied about* juttu kiersi suusta suuhun. **~-legged** länkisäärinen.

bane [bein] *s.* surma, turmio, myrkky. **-ful** *a.* turmiollinen.

bang [bæŋ] *v.* läimäyttää, paukutella, iskeä; kolahtaa, pamahtaa; *s.* paukahdus, kolahdus; tärähdys; *go* ~ räjähtää. **-ed**: *she wears her hair* ~ hänellä on otsatukka.

Bangkok [bæŋ'kɔk] *erisn.*

Bangladesh ['bæŋlə'deʃ] *erisn.* **-i [-i]** *a.* & *s.* bangladeshilainen.

bangle ['bæŋgl] *s.* ranne- t. nilkkarengas.

banish ['bæniʃ] *v.* ajaa maanpakoon, karkottaa. **-ment** *s.* maastakarkotus.

banister ['bænistə] *s.* (tav. *pl.*) kaiteet, kaidepuu.

banjo ['bændʒəu] *s.* banjo.

bank 1. [bæŋk] *s.* rantapenger, -törmä, äyräs, (joen)ranta; (tien, radan) penger; (hiekka)särkkä, riutta; *v.* ympäröidä penkereellä, vallittaa, tehdä kaltevaksi; kallistua; kasata, koota, kasaantua (m. ~ *up*).

bank 2. [bæŋk] *s.* pankki; *v.* tallettaa pankkiin, hoitaa pankkiasiansa; ~ *clerk* pankkivirkailija; ~ *rate* diskonttokorko; ~ *on* luottaa jhk. **-er**

s. pankkiiri. **-ing** s. pankkitoiminta; ~ *house* s. pankkiiriliike. **~-note** seteli.

bankrupt ['bæŋkrʌpt] s. & a. vararikkoinen; v. saattaa vararikkoon; *become* ~ tehdä vararikko; ~*'s estate* konkurssipesä. **-cy** [-si] s. vararikko, konkurssi.

banner ['bænə] s. lippu, viiri.

banns [bænz] s. pl. (avio)kuulutus; *put up (publish) the* ~ kuuluttaa; *have one's* ~ *called* ottaa kuulutukset.

banquet ['bæŋkwit] s. juhla-ateria, -päivällinen ; pidot; v. juhlia.

bantam ['bæntəm] a. pienois-; s. (~*weight*) kääpiösarja(n nyrkkeilijä).

banter ['bæntə] s. pilailu; v. kiusoitella, naljailla.

Bantu [bæn'tu:, Am. 'bæntu] s. bantu, -kieli.

baobab ['be(i)əbæb] s. apinanleipäpuu.

baptism ['bæptizm] s. kaste; ~ *of fire* tulikaste. **-al** [bæp'tizm(ə)l] a. kaste-.

bapt|ist [bæptist] s. baptisti; *John the B~* Johannes Kastaja. **-istery** [-(ə)ri] s. kastekappeli, -kirkko. **-ize** [-'taiz] v. kastaa.

bar [bɑː] s. tanko (esim. ~ *of soap*), harkko, poikkipuu; puomi, este; tahtiviiva, tahti; juova; (hiekka)särkkä (joen suulla); aitaus, aidake (oikeussalissa), asianajajan ammatti; tarjoilupöytä, baari; voimistelutanko; rima; pl. ristikko *(prison* ~*s);* v. salvata, teljetä; estää, kieltää *(from* osanotto jhk); juovittaa; *colour* ~ rotuaita; *a* ~ *of chocolate* suklaapötkö; ~ *one* paitsi yhtä; ~*ring* lukuunottamatta, paitsi; *be called to the* ~ päästä asianajajaksi (ks. *barrister).*

barb [bɑːb] s. väkä; v. varustaa väkäsillä; ~*ed wire* piikkilanka; ~*ed wire entanglement (fence)* piikkilankaeste.

Bar|abbas [bə'ræbəs], **-bados** [bɑː'beidəuz], **-bara** ['bɑːbərə] *erisn.*

barbar|ian [bɑː'beəriən] s. barbaari, raakalainen; a. barbaarinen, raaka. **-ic** [bɑː'bærik] a. raakalais-. **-ism** ['bɑːbərizm] s. raakuus, barbaria. **-ity** [-'bæriti] s. raakuus, julmuus. **-ous** ['bɑːbərəs] a. barbaarinen, sivistymätön, raaka(mainen).

barbecue ['bɑːbikjuː] s. suuret parilaat,

ulkogrilli, Am. grillijuhlat; v. pariloida, grillata.

barber ['bɑːbə] s. parturi.

barberry ['bɑːbəri] s. happomarjapensas).

barbiturate [bɑː'bitʃərət] s. barbituraatti.

Barcelona [bɑːsi'ləunə] *erisn.*

barcarole, -lle [bɑːkərəul] s. venelaulu.

bard [bɑːd] s. bardi, (muin. kelttiläinen) runoilija.

bare [beə] a. alaston, paljas, kalju, autio; pelkkä; v. paljastaa; ~ *living* niukka toimeentulo; *lay* ~ paljastaa. **-back(ed)** *adv.* satulatta. **-faced** häpeämätön. **-foot** a. paljasjalkainen; *adv.* paljain jaloin. **~-headed** a. paljaspäinen; *adv.* paljain päin. **-ly** *adv.* töin tuskin, niukasti.

bargain ['bɑːgin] s. sopimus; (hyvä) kauppa; v. hieroa kauppaa, tinkiä; *into the* ~ kaupanpäällisiksi; *a good* ~*ing position* hyvä neuvotteluasema; *I didn't* ~ *for this* tämä ei kuulunut kauppaan, en osannut odottaa tätä.

barge [bɑːdʒ] s. proomu; päällikönvene, loistopursi; v. rynnätä, *(into, against)* törmätä jhk; ~ *in[to]* tuppautua, sekaantua jhk.

baritone, barytone ['bæritəun] s. barytoni(laulaja).

bark 1. [bɑːk] s. kaarna, parkki; v. kuoria.

bark 2. [bɑːk] v. haukkua *(at* jkta); s. haukunta.

bark 3., barque [bɑːk] s. parkkilaiva (run.) laiva, pursi.

barley ['bɑːli] s. ohra; ~ *sugar* rintasokeri.

barm [bɑːm] s. käymisvaahto.

bar|maid tarjoilijatar. **-man** baarimikko, tarjoilija.

barmy ['bɑːmi] a. vaahtoava; sl. hullu.

barn [bɑːn] s. vilja-aitta, lato.

barnacle ['bɑːnəkl] s. siimajalkainen; hanhenkaula; merirokko.

barometer [bə'rɔmitə] s. ilmapuntari.

baron ['bær(ə)n] s. paroni, vapaaherra. **-ess** [-is] s. paronitar. **-et** [-it] s. baronetti; (~*cy* s. baronetin arvo). **-ial** [bə'rəuniəl] a. paronin-.

baroque [bə'rəuk] s. barokki(tyyli); a. barokki.

barque [bɑːk] s. = *bark 3.*

barr

barrack ['bærək] *s.* (tav. *pl.*) kasarmi; parakki; (urh.) »viheltää», pilkata, ivata (pelaajia).

barrage ['bærɑ:ʒ, bæ'rɑ:ʒ] *s.* suuri pato; sulkutuli; ~ *balloon* sulkupallo.

barratry ['bærətri] *s.* käräjänkäynti; merivarkaus.

barrel ['bær(ə)l] *s.* tynnyri, barrel(i), astia; lieriö; (pyssyn) piippu. ~-organ posetiivi.

barren ['bær(ə)n] *a.* hedelmätön; tuottamaton, kuiva; maho; ~ *of results* tulokseton. **-ness** *s.* hedelmättömyys.

barricade [bæri'keid] *s.* katusulku; *v.* sulkea katusululla.

barrier ['bæriə] *s.* este, aita; (asemasillan) veräjä, puomi.

barring *prep.:* ~ *accidents* ellei onnettomuutta satu; vrt. *bar.*

barrister ['bæristə] *s.* asianajaja (jolla on oikeus ajaa asioita oikeudessa).

barrow 1. ['bærəu] *s.* työntökärryt (m. *wheel-* ~); *käsi* kärryt, *-rattaat (esim. luggage-* ~).

barrow 2. ['bærəu] *s.* (hauta)kumpu.

bartender *s.* baarimikko.

barter ['bɑ:tə] *s.* vaihtokauppa; *v.* käydä vaihtokauppaa, vaihtaa.

Bartholomew [bɑ:'θɔləmju:] *erisn.*

barytone ks. *baritone.*

basal ['beisl] *a.* pohja-, perus-.

basalt ['bæsɔ:lt] *s.* basaltti.

bascule ['bæskju:l] *s.:* ~ *bridge* läppäsilta.

base 1. [beis] *a.* alhainen, halpamainen, halveksittava; väärä (raha); ~ *metal* epäjalo metalli.

base 2. [beis] *s.* jalusta, alusta; perusta, pohja; tyvi(osa); (geom.) kanta; (kem.) emäs; (sot.) tukikohta; (urh.) pesä (baseball-pelissä); *v.* perustaa, nojata jhk; *be* ~*d on* perustua jhk; *he is* ~*d on Paris* hän pitää keskuspaikkanaan Pariisia. **-ball** baseball-peli. **-less** *a.* perätön. **-ment** *s.* kivijalka, kellarikerros.

bash [bæʃ] *v.* lyödä lyttyyn, iskeä lujaa; pahoinpidellä; *s.* murskaava isku; *have a* ~ *at* yrittää jtk.

bashful ['bæʃf(u)l] *a.* kaino, ujo, häveliäs.

basic ['beisik] *a.* pohja-, perus-; emäksinen (kem.); *B*~ *English* 800

sanaa käsittävä »perusenglanti».

basil ['bæzil] *s.: sweet* ~ basilika (mauste).

basilica [bə'zilikə] *s.* basilika.

basilisk ['bæzilisk] *s.* basiliski; ~ *glance* paha silmä.

basin ['beisn] *s.* malja, kulho; vati; (vesi)allas; satama-allas; jokialue.

basis ['beisis] *s.* (pl. *bases* [-i:z]) perusta, perustus, pohja.

bask [bɑ:sk] *v.* lämmitellä, paistatella päivää.

basket ['bɑ:skit] *s.* kori, vasu. ~-ball koripallo. **-ful** korillinen. **-ry** [-ri] *s.* korityö.

basque [bæsk, bɑ:sk] *s.* & *a.* (*B*~) baskilainen, baski.

bas-relief ['bɑ:rili:f] *s.* matala korkokuva.

bass 1. [bæs] *s.* meriahven, aurinkoahven.

bass 2. [beis] *a.* basso-, matala; *s.* basso (-ääni, -osa, -laulaja); *double-* ~ kontrabasso (soitin).

bass 3. [bæs] *s.* niini; ~-*wood* s. amerikkal. lehmus.

Bass [bæs] *s.* eräs olutlaatu.

bassinet [bæsi'net] *s.* vauvan kori.

bassoon [bə'su:n] *s.* fagotti.

bast [bæst] *s.* niini.

bastard ['bæstəd] *s.* & *a.* äpärä, avioton (lapsi); sekarotuinen; vale-, väärä. **-y** [-i] *s.* avioton syntyperä.

baste 1. [beist] *v.* harsia kokoon.

baste 2. *v.* valella rasvalla.

baste 3. *v.* piestä.

bastille [bæs'ti:l]; *the B*~ Bastilji.

bastion ['bæstiən] *s.* vallinsarvi.

bat 1. [bæt] *s.* lepakko; *has* ~*s in the belfry* on hassahtanut; [*he is*] ~*s* hullu, höperö (m. *batty*).

bat 2. *s.* maila; lyöjä; *v.* lyödä, olla lyöjänä.

bat 3.: *without* ~*ing an eyelid* silmää räpäyttämättä; [*go off*] *at a rare* ~ hurjaa vauhtia.

batch [bætʃ] *s.* leipomus, uunillinen (leipiä); ryhmä.

bate [beit] *v.* vähentää; pidättää; *with* ~*d breath* henkeä(än) pidättäen.

bath [bɑ:θ, *pl.* -ðz, Am. bæθ, bæðz] *s.* kylpy; kylpyamme; *pl.* kylpylaitos, -paikka, uimahalli; (kem., valok.) haude; *v.* kylvettää; *have a* ~ kylpeä (ammeessa); ~ *chair* pyörätuoli; ~ *the baby* kylvettää vauva.

bathe [beið] v. kylpeä, uida; kostuttaa kastaa; hautoa; s. (ulkoilma)kylpy; [*let's go*] *for a* ~ uimaan; ~ *in perspiration* hiestä märkänä. **-r** [-ə] s. uimari.

bathing ['beiðiŋ] s. kylpeminen, uinti. **~-cabin** uimakoppi. **~-cap** kylpylakki. **~-costume** uimapuku.

bathos ['beiθɔs] s. (tyylin) heilahdus ylevästä t. liikuttavasta naurettavaan.

bath|robe s. kylpytakki, aamutakki. **-room** kylpyhuone. **~-tub** kylpyamme.

bathysphere ['bæθisfiə] s. sukelluspallo.

batiste [bə'ti:st] s. batisti.

baton ['bætɔ:, Am. bə'tɔn] s. patukka; tahtipuikko; (esim. marsalkan) sauva.

batsman s. lyöjä.

battalion [bə'tæljən] s. pataljoona.

batten 1. ['bætn] s. piena, lista; soiro; v. vahvistaa (poikki)pienoilla, listoittaa; ~ *down* tiivistää.

batten 2. ['bætn] v.: ~ [*up*]*on* lihoa (m. hyötyä) jkn kustannuksella.

batter ['bætə] v. lyödä, mukiloida (m. ~ *about*), pahoinpidellä; ampua tykeillä; s. (esim. ohukais)taikina. **-ed** [-d] a. kulunut, kuhmuinen; pahoinpidelty. **-ing-ram** muurinsärkijä. **-y** [-ri] s. patteri; paristo; pahoinpitely (*assault* and ~).

batting s. vanu(levy); (mailalla) lyönti, lyöminen.

battle ['bætl] s. taistelu; v. taistella (*with, against* jtk, jkta vastaan). **~-axe** sotakirves. **~-cruiser** taisteluristeilijä. **-dore** [-dɔ:] pyykkikarttu, sulkapallopelin maila. **~-dress** kenttäpuku. **-field, -ground** taistelukenttä. **-ment** s. (us. *pl.*) sakarahrjainen rintavarustus. **-ship** taistelulaiva.

bauble ['bɔ:bl] s. (joutava) koru, hely, rihkama.

baulk [bɔ:k] v. = balk.

bauxite ['bɔ:ksait] s. bauksiitti.

Bavaria [bə'veəriə] *erisn.* Baijeri. **-n** [-n] a. & s. baijerilainen.

bawd [bɔ:d] s. parittaja. **-y** [-i] a. rivo.

bawl [bɔ:l] v. huutaa; ~ *sb. out* haukkua jkta.

bay 1. [bei] s. laakeri(seppele).

bay 2. [bei] s. merenlahti, poukama.

bay 3. [bei] s. (seinän) osa, uloke; ~ *window* ulokeikkuna.

bay 4. [bei] s. haukunta; v. haukkua; *be at* ~ olla ahdingossa; *bring to* ~ ahdistaa äärimmilleen; *keep…at* ~ pitää (viholliset ym) loitolla.

bay 5. [bei] a. punaisenruskea; s. ruunikko.

bayou [bai'u:] s. rämeinen joen haara.

bayonet ['be(i)ənit] s. pistin; v. lävistää pistimellä.

bazaar [bə'za:] s. itämainen kauppakatu, basaari; myyjäiset.

bazooka [bə'zu:kə] s. (sot.) panssarikauhu.

be [bi:, bi] *was been,* v. olla; olla olemassa; maksaa; käyt. *-ing-*preesensissä (*she is reading*), passiivissa (*the house was built*); *how are you?* kuinka voit(te)? *how much are these apples?* mitä nämä omenat maksavat? *I am to be there at 6* minun on määrä olla siellä kello 6; *you are not to* [*do that*] sinun ei pidä; *his wife to* ~ hänen tuleva vaimonsa; *here you are* kas tässä, tässä saat; *has the postman been?* onko postinkantaja jo käynyt? *I won't* ~ *long* en viivy kauan; *what is he going to be* mikä hänestä tulee? miksi hän aikoo?; *there is a mistake on this page* tällä sivulla on virhe; *there are flowers in the vase* maljakossa on kukkia;

beach [bi:tʃ] s. ranta, kylpyranta; v. laskea rantaan, vetää rannalle. **-comber** [-kəumə] ranta-, satamajätkä. **-head** sillanpääasema.

beacon ['bi:kn] s. merkkituli; pieni majakka, loisto; viitta; v. viitoittaa.

bead [bi:d] s. (lasi-, puu- ym) helmi; kupla, pisara; (kivääirn) jyväsin; *tell one's* ~ s lukea rukouksensa. **-ing** s. helmilista, -koriste. **-y** [-i] a.: ~ *eyes* (pyöreät ja) kiirkkaat silmät.

beadle ['bi:dl] s. (vanh.) suntio.

beagle ['bi:gl] s. jäniskoira; nuuskija.

beak [bi:k] s. nokka; poliisituomari (sl.).

beaker ['bi:kə] s. iso pikari; kaatolasi, muovilasi.

beam [bi:m] s. (niska)hirsi, palkki; (laivan) poikkipuu, laivan (suurin) leveys; (vaa'an) selkä; (auringon ym) säde; v. säteillä; (rad.) säteilykeila, (elektroni)suihku; high ~ kaukovalot; low ~ lähivalot; ~ system suunnattu (radio)lähetys; on her ~ ends (laivasta) kyljellään. (kuv.) ahdingossa. -ing a. säteilevä.

bean [bi:n] s. papu; [I haven't] a ~ penniäkään. -o [-əu] s. (vanh.) kekkerit. ~-stalk pavunvarsi.

bear 1. [beə] s. karhu; pörssikeinottelija (joka käyttää hyväkseen laskusuuntaa): Great B~ (täht.) Iso Karhu.

beat 2. [beə] bore, pp. borne t. born, v. kantaa, tuottaa; synnyttää; kärsiä, kestää, sietää; kannattaa; suuntautua; ~ arms kantaa aseita, olla sotilas; ~ a hand auttaa; ~ a likeness to olla jkn näköinen; ~ sb. company pitää seuraa jklle; ~ witness todistaa; ~ down kukistaa; ~ down upon syöksyä kimppuun; ~ in mind pitää muistissa; it was borne in upon me [that] tulin vakuuttuneeksi siitä; ~ oneself käyttäytyä, esiintyä; ~ away the prize voittaa palkinto; ~ out tukea, vahvistaa; ~ up kestää (against jtk), rohkaista mielensä; ~ upon koskea, tarkoittaa; ~ hard [up] on rasittaa; ~ with suhtautua kärsivällisesti jhk. **-able** [-rəbl] a. siedettävä.

beard [biəd] s. parta; ~ the lion in his den käydä leijonan kimppuun sen omassa luolassa. **-ed** [-id] a. parrakas.

bear|er ['beərə] s. kantaja, (sanan)tuoja, -viejä; haltija. **-ing** s. käyttäytyminen; ryhti; suhde, näkökohta, merkitys; pl. asema, suunta, suuntima; laakeri (tekn.); armorial ~s ks. armorial; [consider it] in all its ~s joka puolelta; lose one's ~s joutua eksyksiin; take the ~s suuntia (mer.); it has no ~ upon the question sillä ei ole mitään tekemistä kysymyksen kanssa.

bearskin s. karhunnahka(lakki).

beast [bi:st] s. eläin, elukka; raaka ihminen; ~ of burden kuormajuhta. **-ly** [-li] a. eläimellinen; inhottava; hirveä, kurja, viheliäinen; adv. hirveän.

beat [bi:t] beat beaten, v. lyödä; piestä; hakata; tomuttaa; vatkata; sykkiä;

olla etevämpi, voittaa, lyödä (back takaisin); takoa; s. lyönti; rummutus; tahdinlyönti, poljento; (poliisin ym) kierros; ~ about the bush kierrellä ja kaarrella; ~ a retreat perääntyä; ~ a way tallata polku; ~ one's brains vaivata päätänsä; ~ the bounds merkitä raja; ~ down the price polkea hintaa; ~ it (sl.) lähteä, luikkia tiehensä; ~ up vatkata; ~ (sb.) up hakata, mukiloida; heart ~ sydämen lyönnit; that ~s everything se vie voiton kaikesta; it ~s me [how] en ymmärrä (kuinka); dead ~ lopen uupunut, »kuitti»; [it's a bit] off my ~ ei aivan minun alaani; B ~ generation (2. maailmansodan jälk.) »lyöty sukupolvi» [beatnik sen edustaja, tav. runoilija, taiteilija]. **-en** [-n] pp. kulunut; uupunut; the ~ track totunnaisuus, vanha rata. **-er** [-ə] s. riistan ajomies; vatkain, vispilä.

beat|ific [bi(:)ə'tifik] autuas. **-fy** [bi'ætifai] v. julistaa autuaaksi, autuuttaa.

beating ['bi:tin] s. selkäsauna.

beatitude [bi(:)ætitju:d] s. autuus; (raam.) the B~s autuaaksijulistamiset (Matt. 6).

beatnik ks. Beat generation.

beau [bəu] s. (pl. -x [-z]) keikari; ihailija.

beautician [bju:'tiʃn] s. kosmetologi.

beauti|ful ['bju:təf(u)l] a. kaunis; ~ly kauniisti; loistavasti. **-fy** [-fai] v. kaunistaa.

beauty ['bju:ti] s. kauneus; kaunotar; pl. beauties m. kauneusarvot; ~ parlour, ~ salon kauneussalonki. **~-spot** luonnon|ihana, -kaunis paikka; kauneuspilkku.

beaver 1. ['bi:və] s. majava.

beaver 2. ['bi:və] s. kypäränsilmikko.

becalm [bi'ka:m] v. tyynnyttää.

became [bi'keim] imp. ks. become.

because [bi'kɔz] adv.: ~ of jnk takia, vuoksi; konj. koska.

beck [bek] s. nyökkäys; he is at sb.'s ~ and call hän tottelee jnk pienintä viittausta. **-on** [-(ə)n] v. viittoa, nyökätä, viittoen kutsua.

becloud [bi'klaud] s. peittää pilvillä.

becom|e [bi'kʌm] became become, v. tulla jksk; sopia (jklle), pukea (jkta);

he became a doctor hänestä tuli lääkäri. **-ing** *a.* pukeva.

bed [bed] *s.* vuode, sänky; sairaansija; puutarhapenkki; (joen)uoma; kerros *v.* istuttaa (us. ~ *out*); kiinnittää, asettaa (~ *down*); mennä makuulle; *go to* ~ mennä nukkumaan *make the* ~ *s* sijata vuoteet; *keep one's* ~ olla vuoteen omana; *got out of* ~ *on the wrong side* nousi väärällä jalalla vuoteesta.

bed|-bug lude. **~-clothes** vuodevaatteet. **-ding** *s.* makuuvaatteet; pahnat. **~-fellow** (vuode)kumppani.

bedeck [bi'dek] *v.* koristaa.

bedevil [bi'devl] *v.* sotkea, panna sekaisin, turmella.

bedim [bi'dim] *v.* himmentää.

bedizen [bi'daizn] *v.* pukea koreaksi.

bedlam ['bedlom] *s.* »hullunmylly»; (vanh.) hullujenhuone.

Bedouin ['bedui] *s.* beduiini.

bed|pan alusastia. **-post** sängynpylväs.

bedraggled [bi'drægld] *a.* likainen, räyhäinen, siivoton.

bed|ridden vuoteen oma(na). **~-rock** kallioperä. **-room** makuuhuone. **-side:** ~ *table* yöpöytä. **-sitter** (= *-sitting-room*) makuu- ja olohuone. **-sore** makuuhaava. **-spread** vuodepeite. **-stead** sänky. **-time** maatapanoaika.

bee [bi:] *s.* mehiläinen; Am. eräänl. talkoot, kilpailu; *he has a* ~ *in his bonnet* hän on jnk pakkomielteen vallassa.

beech [bi:tʃ] *s.* pyökki. **-en** [-n] pyökki-. **-mast** pyökin terho.

beef [bi:f] *s.* härän- t. naudanliha; (pl. *beeves*) häränruho. **-eater** kuninkaallinen henkivartija, *Towern* vartija. **-steak** pihvipaisti.

bee|-hive mehiläispesä, -keko. **~-line** linnuntie; *make a b.-l (for)* mennä suorinta tietä jnnek.

been [bi:n, bin] *pp.* ks. *be; he has* ~ *to* hän on käynyt . . .ssa.

beer [biə] *s.* olut; kalja; *thinks no small* ~ *of* on suuret luulot jstk.

Beersheba [biə'ʃi:bə] *erisn.*

beestings ['bi:stiŋz] *s. pl.* ternimaito.

beeswax ['bi:zwæks] *s.* mehiläisvaha; *v.* kiillottaa (m-vahalla).

beet [bi:t] *s.* juurikas; *red* ~ punajuuri; *white* ~ sokerijuurikas; ~ *sugar* juurikassokeri.

beetle 1. ['bi:tl] *s.* survin, käsijuntta; *v.* nuijia.

beetle 2. ['bi:tl] *s.* kovakuoriainen; *a.* ulkoneva; tuuhea; synkkä; *v.* pistää esiin, riippua; uhata. **~-browed** tuuhea-, synkkäkulmainen.

beetroot *s.* punajuuri.

befall [bi'fɔ:l] *v.* (ks. *fall*) sattua, tapahtua, kohdata.

befit [bi'fit] *v.* sopia.

befogged [bi'fɔgd] *a.* sumun verhoama; (kuv.) hämmentynyt.

before [bi'fɔ:] *adv. & prep.* ennen; edessä, eteen, edelle, edellä; *konj.* ennen kuin, aikaisemmin kuin; mieluummin kuin; ~ *long* ennen pitkää; ~ *the wind* myötätuuleen. **-hand** *adv.* ennakolta, edeltäkäsin; *be* ~ *with* tehdä jtk hyvissä ajoin.

befoul [bi'faul] *v.* tahrata, liata.

befriend [bi'frend] *v.* kohdella jkta ystävänä, auttaa, ystävystyä (jkn kanssa).

beg [beg] *v.* pyytää, anoa, rukoilla; kerjätä; *I* ~ *your pardon* anteeksi, ks. *pardon; I* ~ *to differ* olen eri mieltä; ~ *off* ilmoittaa ettei voi tulla; ~ *the question* olettaa väite todistetuksi, vastata vältellen t. välttää vastaamasta; *it goes begging* kukaan ei halua sitä.

began [bi'gæn] *imp.* ks. *begin.*

beget [bi'get] *begot begotten, v.* siittää, synnyttää, aiheuttaa.

beggar ['begə] *s.* kerjäläinen; (leik.) veikko, veitikka; *v.* tehdä kerjäläiseksi; *it* ~ *s all description* sitä ei voi kuvata sanoin. **-ly** *a.* puutteenalainen, kurja. **-y** [-ri] *s.* (äärimmäinen) puute, kurjuus.

begin [bi'gin] *began begun, v.* alkaa, aloittaa *(she began crying* t. *to cry; the water is* ~ *ning to boil); to* ~ *with* aluksi. **-ner** [-ə] *s.* vasta-alkaja, aloittelija. **-ning** [-iŋ] *s.* alku; *at the* ~ *of* jnk alussa; *in the* ~ alussa; aluksi; *from* ~ *to end* alusta loppuun.

begone [bi'gɔn] *int.* tiehesi!

begonia [bi'gəunjə] *s.* begonia.

begot [bi'gɔt] *imp.* ks. *beget.* **-ten** [bi'gɔtn] *pp.: only* ~ ainosyntyinen.

begrime [bi'graim] v. tahrata.

begrudge [bi'grʌdʒ] v. kadehtia; ei suoda: *we don't ~ you...* suomme sinulle mielellämme...

beguile [bi'gail] v. pettää, viekoitella, houkutella; saada kulumaan, lyhentää (aikaa).

begum ['beigəm] s. (muslimi)ruhtinatar.

begun [bi'gʌn] pp. ks. *begin*.

behalf [bi'hɑ:f] s.: *on ~ of* jkn puolesta, jkn nimissä; *don't be uneasy on my ~* älä ole huolissasi minusta, minun vuokseni.

behav|e [bi'heiv] v. käyttäytyä; (koneesta) toimia, käydä; *~* [*oneself*] käyttäytyä hyvin, olla siivolla; *well-behaved* hyväkäytöksinen. **-iour** [-iə] s. käytös, käyttäytyminen.

behead [bi'hed] v. mestata.

beheld [bi'held] imp. & pp. ks. *behold*.

behest [bi'hest] s. (run.) käsky.

behind [bi'haind] prep. & adv. takana, taakse, jäljessä, jälkeen; s. takapuoli; *fall ~* jäädä jälkeen; *far ~* kaukana takanapäin; *be ~ with* (in) olla jäljessä (opinnoissa ym). **-hand** adv. & a. jäljessä, takapajulla.

behold [bi'hould] beheld beheld, v. nähdä; int. katso! **-en** [-n] a. kiitollisuudenvelassa.

behove [bi'houv], Am. **behoove** [-'hu:v] v.: *it ~s him to*..hänen kuuluu..

beige [beiʒ] s. & a. beige(värinen).

being ['bi:iŋ] s. olemassaolo; olento, olemus; *human ~* ihminen; *in ~* olemassa; *for the time ~* tällä hetkellä, toistaiseksi; *come into ~* syntyä: *bring into ~* aloittaa, aiheuttaa.

Beirut [bei'ru:t] erisn.

belabour [bi'leibə] v. piestä.

belated [bi'leitid] a. myöhästynyt: pimeän yllättämä.

belay [bi'lei] v. kiinnittää (köysi); *~ing-pin* kiinnitysvaarna.

belch [beltʃ] v. röyhtäistä; (*~ forth, ~ out*) syöstä, syyttää (saastetta ym); s. röyhtäisy.

beleaguer [bi'li:gə] v. piirittää.

Belfast [bel'fɑ:st] erisn.

beifry ['belfri] s. kellotorni, -tapuli.

Belgi|an ['beldʒn] a. & s. belgialainen.

-um [-dʒəm] erisn. Belgia.

Belgrade [bel'greid] erisn.

belie [bi'lai] v. olla ristiriidassa; pettää (lupaus ym); *his acts ~d his words* hänen tekonsa ja puheensa olivat keskenään ristiriidassa.

belief [bi'li:f] s. usko.

believe [bi'li:v] v. uskoa (in jhk): luulla, arvella; *~d him* (t. *what he said*) uskoin häntä. **-r** [-ə] s. uskovainen.

belittle [bi'litl] v. vähäksyä, vähätellä.

bell [bel] s. kello, soittokello; kulkunen, tiuku; kellokukka; (mer., pl.) lasi (puolen tunnin vartio); v.: *~ the cat* ottaa suorittaakseen vaarallinen tehtävä; *it rang a ~* se toi mieleen (kaukaisen) muiston; *~-hop* Am. hotellipoika; *~ wether* (lammaslauman) kellokas.

belle [bel] s. kaunotar.

belles lettres [bel'letr] s. kaunokirjallisuus.

belli|cose ['belikəus] a. sotaisa, sodanhaluinen. **-gerency** [bi'lidʒər(ə)nsi] s. sotatila. **-gerent** [bi'lidʒər(ə)nt] a. & s. sotaakäyvä (valtio).

bellow [bi'below] v. mylviä, karjua; s. mylvintä.

bellows ['belouz] s. palkeet.

belly ['beli] s. vatsa, maha; v. pullistua; *-bellied* -mahainen; *~-dancer* napatanssija; *~landing* mahalasku.

belong [bi'loŋ] v.: *~ to* kuulua jklle, jhk; sopia; *it ~s to him* se on hänen (omansa); *we don't feel we ~* tunnemme itsemme ulkopuolisiksi. **-ings** s. pl. omaisuus, tavara.

beloved [bi'lʌvd] pp. rakastettu, armas [attr. m. -vid].

below [bi'lou] prep. alla, alle, alapuolella, -lle; adv. ks. ed.; alas, alakerrassa; maan päällä; tuonnempana (kirjassa), (sivun) alareunassa; *it is ~ him* se ei ole hänen arvonsa mukaista.

belt [belt] s. vyö; hihna; vyöhyke; v. vyöttää; *driving ~* käyttöhihna; *elastic ~* kumiliivi; *hit below the ~* taistella epärehellisesti.

belvedere [belvi'diə] s. näköalatorni.

bemoan [bi'moun] v. valittaa.

bemuse [bi'mju:z] v. huumata.

bench [ben(t)ʃ] s. penkki; tuomioistuin; tuomarikunta; höyläpenkki. **-er** [-ə] Inn of C~·rñn vanhempi jäsen.

bend [bend] bent bent, v. taivuttaa; taipua, koukistaa, -tua; tehdä mutka; jännittää; kumartua; alistua; s. mutka, taive, koukistus; round the ~ (sl.) hullu; ~ forward kumartua eteenpäin; ~ one's steps to suunnata kulkunsa jhk; on ~ed knees polvillaan; ks. bent.

beneath [bi'ni:θ] prep. alla, alapuolella; adv. alapuolella, alhaalla; he thinks it ~ his dignity hänen ei pidä (sitä) arvonsa mukaisena; marry ~ one naida alempisäätyinen.

Benedictine [beni'diktin] s. benediktiinimunkki; b~ [-ti:n] s. benediktiini(likööri).

benediction [beni'dikʃn] s. siunaus (et. jumalanpalv. lopussa).

benefac|tion [beni'fækʃn] s. lahjoitus. **-tor** ['benifæktə] s. hyväntekijä. **-tress** ['benifæktris] s. hyväntekijätär.

benefice ['benifis] s. pastoraatti, papinvirka. **-nce** [bi'nefsns] s. hyväntekeväisyys. **-nt** [bi'nefisnt] a. hyväntekeväinen.

bene|ficial [beni'fiʃl] a. hyväätekevä, terveellinen, hyödyllinen. **-ficiary** [-'fiʃəri] s. avustuksen, lahjoituksen saaja.

benefit ['benifit] s. hyöty, etu; avustus; v. hyödyttää, hyötyä; (by from jstk); ~ performance (concert ym) lahjanäytäntö; for the ~ of jkn hyväksi; derive ~ from hyötyä jstk; maternity ~ äitiysavustus; it wasn't of much ~ siitä ei ollut paljon apua.

Benelux ['benilʌks]: ~ contries Belgia, Alankomaat ja Luxemburg.

benevol|ence [bi'nevələns] s. hyväntahtoisuus. **-ent** [-ənt] a. hyvän|tahtoinen, -suopa; hyväntekeväisyys-

Bengal [beŋ'gɔ:l] erisn. Bengali. **-i** [-i] s. & a. bengalilainen.

benighted [bi'naitid] a. yön yllättämä; (henkisessä) pimeydessä elävä.

benign [bi'nain] a. hyväntahtoinen, suopea; terveellinen (esim. ilmasto); hyvänlaatuinen (tauti). **-ancy** s. hyvänlaatuisuus. **-ant** [bi'nignənt] a.

hyväntahtoinen; ystävällinen, armollinen. **-ity** [bi'nigniti] s. hyvyys, hyväntahtoisuus.

bent [bent] s. taipumus, mielenlaatu; a. sl. rikollinen, epärehellinen; imp. & pp. ks. bend; [he] is ~ on. . -ing on päättänyt (tehdä jtk); he is ~ on mischief hänellä on paha mielessä.

benumb [bi'nʌm] v. jäykistää, tehdä tunnottomaksi, kohmettaa, turruttaa.

benzene ['benzi:n], **benzol** ['benzɔl] s. bentseeni.

benzine ['benzi:n] s. bensiini (puhdistamiseen ym).

bequeath [bi'kwi:ð] v. testamentata.

bequest [bi'kwest] s. (testamentti)lahjoitus, perintö.

bereave [bi'ri:v] ~d~dt. bereft bereft, v. ryöstää, riistää, ottaa pois; ~d sureva; orpo; ~d children orvot. **-ment** s. menetys, suru, kuolemantapaus.

bereft [bi'reft] imp. & pp. ks. bereave; ~ of hope toivoton.

beret ['beret, Am. bi'rei] s. baskeri, baretti.

Berk|eley ['bɑ:kli, Am bə:k-] **-s** [-s] lyh. = seur. **-shire** [-ʃiə] erisn.

Berlin [bə:'lin] erisn. & a. Berliini, berliiniläinen; ~ wool sefiirilanka. **-er** [-'linə] s. berliiniläinen.

Bermudas [bə(:)'mju:dəz] erisn.

Bernese [bə:'ni:z] a. Bernin.

berry ['beri] s. marja; v. marjastaa; go ~ing mennä marjaan.

berserk [bə:sə:k]: go ~ alkaa raivota, riehua.

berth [bə:θ] s. ankkuri-, laituripaikka; makuusija (laivassa ym); paikka, toimi; v. ankkuroida; hankkia makuupaikka (jklle): give a wide ~ to pysytellä etäällä jstk.

Berwick ['berik] erisn.

beseech [bi'si:tʃ] besought besought, v. anoa, rukoilla; ~ing [ly] anova(sti).

beseem [bi'si:m] v. sopia, olla soveliasta jklle. **-ing** a. sopiva.

beset [bi'set] beset beset, v. ympäröidä; ~ by doubts epäilysten ahdistama; [a problem] ~ with difficulties. . joka on hyvin vaikea. **-ting** a.: ~ sin helmasynti.

beside [bi'said] prep. vieressä, -een; jhk verraten; jnk rinnalla; ulkopuolella;

be ~ *oneself* olla suunniltaan; *it is* ~ *the question* ei kuulu asiaan. **-s** [-z] *adv.* sitä paitsi, vielä; *prep.* lisäksi, paitsi; ~ *him* hänen lisäkseen, paitsi häntä.

besiege [bi'si:dʒ] *v.* piirittää; ahdistaa.

besmear [bi'smiə] *v.* tahria.

besmirch [bi'smə:tʃ] *v.* tahrata.

besom ['bi:zəm] *s.* luuta.

besot [bi'sɔt] *v.* tylsistää. **-ted** [-id] *pp. & a.* tylsä, älytön.

besought [bi'sɔ:t] *imp. & pp.* ks. *beseech.*

bespangled [bi'spæŋgld] *a.* paljetein koristettu.

bespatter [bi'spætə] *v.* roiskuttaa (kuraa) jkn päälle.

be|speak [bi'spi:k] *bespoke bespoke(n),* *v.* varata, tilata; osoittaa; [*his manners*] ~ *the gentleman* osoittavat hänet herrasmieheksi. **-spoke** [-'spəuk] *imp. & pp.* tilaustyönä tehty; ~ *tailor* tilauspukimo.

Bess [bes] lyh. = *Elizabeth.*

best [best] *a.* paras; *adv.* parhaiten; *v.* voittaa (puhek.); ~ *man* sulhaspoika; *the* ~ *part of* jnk suurin osa; *at* ~ parhaassa tapauksessa *at its* ~ parhaimmillaan; *it is all for the* ~ se on kaikki parhaaksi; *to the* ~ *of my ability* parhaan kykyni mukaan; *make the* ~ *of a bad business* selittää asiat parhain päin, tyytyä oleviin oloihin; *make the* ~ *of* [*one's time*] käyttää mahdollisimman hyvin; *get the* ~ *of it* suoriutua voittajana; *he likes this* ~ *of all* hän pitää tästä eniten; *the* ~ *thing to do is* parasta, mitä voi tehdä on; *do one's* [*very*] ~ tehdä parhaansa; *in their* ~ pyhävaatteissaan; . . [*runs*] *with the* ~ yhtä hyvin kuin joku toinenkin.

bestial ['bestjəl] *a.* eläimellinen, raaka. **-ity** [besti'æliti] *s.* eläimellisyys.

bestir [bi'stə:] *v.:* ~ *oneself* ryhtyä toimeen, panna töpinäksi.

bestow [bi'stəu] *v.* antaa, lahjoittaa, suoda (*on* jklle); sijoittaa. **-al** [-əl] *s.* antaminen; lahja.

bestrew [bi'stru:] *v.* (*pp.* m. *bestrewn*) sirotella.

bestride [bi'straid] *v.* (ks. *stride*) istua t. seistä hajareisin jnk päällä, ratsastaa.

best-seller menekkikirja.

bet [bet] *s.* veto, vedonlyönti; *v.* lyödä vetoa (*on* jnk puolesta); *I* ~ uskallan veikata, veikkaan (että); *you* ~ *!* sen saat uskoa!

beta ['bi:tə] *s.* beeta (kirjain).

betake [bi'teik] *v.* (ks. *take*); ~ *oneself to* lähteä jhk.

betel [bi:təl]: ~ *nut* betelpähkinä.

Bethany ['beθəni] *erisn.* Betania

bethel ['beθəl] *s.* kappeli, Am. merimieskirkko.

bethink [bi'θiŋk] *v.* (ks. *think*); ~ *oneself* tuumia, muistaa.

betide [bi'taid] *v.* (tav. *konj.*) tapahtua, sattua; *woe* ~ *him* voi häntä!

betimes [bi'taimz] *adv.* ajoissa; varhain.

Bethlehem ['beθlihem] *erisn.*

betoken [bi'təukn] *v.* osoittaa.

betray [bi'trei] *v.* pettää, olla uskoton, ilmiantaa; ilmaista, osoittaa. **-al** [-əl] *s.* petos.

betroth [bi'trəuð] *v.* kihlata. **-al** [-(ə)l] *s.* kihlaus. **-ed** [-ð] *a. & s.* kihlattu.

better ['betə] *a. & adv.* parempi; paremmin; *v.* parantaa, -tua; *like sth.* ~ pitää jstk enemmän; *for the* ~ hyväksi, eduksi; *for* ~ *for worse* myötä- ja vastoinkäymisessä; *get the* ~ *of* voittaa jku; *be* ~ *off* olla paremmissa varoissa; *go one* ~ ylittää tarjous; *you had* ~ *go* sinun olisi parasta lähteä; *so much the* ~ sitä parempi; *you will think* ~ *of it* muutat vielä mielesi; *the* ~ *part* suurin osa; ~ *oneself* parantaa asemansa; *one's* ~ *s* paremmassa asemassa olevat ihmiset; *the* ~ *I know her the more I like her* mitä paremmin opin häntä tuntemaan, sitä enemmän hänestä pidän; . . *(but) I thought* ~ *of it* muutin mieleni. **-ment** *s.* parantaminen.

betting ['betiŋ] *s.* vedonlyönti.

between [bi'twi:n] *prep & adv.* välissä, välillä, väliin; ~ *you and me,* ~ *ourselves* meidän kesken; ~ *us* yhteisesti; *betwixt and* ~ siltä välltä; *in* ~ joukossa, välissä; *houses are few and far* ~ taloja on harvassa.

betwixt [bi'twikst] *prep.* ks. *between.*

Bev|an ['bev(ə)n] *erisn.*

bevel ['bevl] *s.* viistomittain, kulmamitta; särmä; *v.* viistota, leikata viitoksi.

beverage ['bevəridʒ] s. juoma.

bevy ['bevi] s. joukko, parvi.

bewail [bi'weil] v. valittaa, surra.

beware [bi'wɛə] v. (taipumaton) varoa; ~ *of pickpockets* varokaa taskuvarkaita.

bewilder [bi'wildə] s. saattaa hämille t. ymmälle. **-ing** a. hämällyttävä. **-ment** s. hämmennys.

bewitch [bi'witʃ] v. lumota, tenhota, hurmata. **-ing** a. lumoava, viehättävä.

beyond [bi'jɔnd] prep. & adv. toisella puolella, toiselle puolelle, tuolla puolen; yli; paitsi; s.: the ~ tuleva elämä; *it is ~ me* en voi sitä käsittää; ~ *recovery* parantumaton; ~ *words* sanoin kuvaamaton; *at the back of* ~ Jumalan selän takana.

bi- [bai] pref. kaksi-, kaksois-; *bi-monthly* joka toinen kuukausi tapahtuva, kahdesti kuussa ilmestyvä; *bi-weekly* joka toinen viikko ilmestyvä (lehti).

bias ['baiəs] s. vinous; ennakkoluulo; s. herättää ennakkoluuloja *(against* jkta kohtaan); taivuttaa; *a ~ towards* ennakkomieltymys jkh; ~ *band* vinokaista; *cut on the ~* leikata (kangasta) viistoon. **-(s)ed** [-t] a. ennakkoluuloinen, puolueellinen.

biathlon [bai'æθlon] s. ampumahiihto.

bib [bib] s. (lapsen) leukalappu; esiliinan yläosa v. (vanh.) ryypätä; *wine-bibber* viininjuoja.

Bible ['baibl] s. raamattu.

biblical ['biblik(ə)l] a. raamatullinen.

biblio|graphy [bibli'ɔgrəfi] s. bibliografia, kirjallisuusluettelo. **-phile** ['bibliəfail] s. kirjojenystävä.

bibulous ['bibjuləs] a. juopotteleva.

bicarbonate [bai'ka:bənit]: ~ *of soda* natriumbikarbonaatti.

bicentenary [baisen'ti:nəri] a. & s. kaksisataavuotis(juhla)-.

biceps ['baiseps] s. hauislihas.

bicker ['bikə] v. kinastella. **-ing** s. riita.

bicycl|e ['baisikl] s. polkupyörä; v. ajaa polkupyörällä (tav. *cycle).*

bid 1. [bid] bade bidden t. bid bid, v. tarjota (huutokaupassa) käskeä; lausua; ~ *welcome* lausua tervetulleeksi; *it ~ s fair to succeed* se

näyttää onnistuvan; *[do] as you are* ~*[den]* niinkuin sinulle sanotaan; ~ *up* tarjota enemmän.

bid 2. [bid] s. tarjous; yritys; *make a* ~ *for* koettaa saavuttaa. **-der** s. tarjouksentekijä; *the highest* ~ eniten tarjoava. **-ding** s. käsky; tarjoukset.

bide [baid] v.: ~ *one's time* odottaa oikeata hetkeä.

biennial [bai'enjəl] a. kaksivuotinen, -vuotis-; joka toinen vuosi tapahtuva; s. kaksivuotinen kasvi.

bier [biə] s. ruumispaarit.

biff [bif] s. isku, läimäys.

bifocal ['bai'fəuk(ə)l] a.: ~ s kaksiteholasit.

bifurca|te ['baifə:keit] v. haarautua (kahtaanne). **-tion** [-'keiʃn] s. haarautu|minen, -skohta.

big [big] a. iso, suuri; tärkeä; pöyhkeilevä; ~ *bug* »pomo»; *look* ~ olla olevinaan; *talk* ~ olla suuri suustaan.

bigamist ['bigəmist] s. kaksinnaimisissa oleva henkilö.

bigamy ['bigəmi] s. kaksinnaiminen.

bight [bait] s. lahti, poukama.

bigot ['bigət] s. yltiöharras henkilö, kiihkoilija. **-ed** [-id] a. yltiöharras, kiihkoileva. **-ry** [-ri] s. yltiöhartaus, kiihkoilu.

bigwig s. mahtimies, tärkeä henkilö.

bike [baik] s. (puhek.) polkupyörä.

bilateral [bai'læt(ə)rəl] a. kaksipuolinen, molemminpuolinen, kahdenvälinen.

bilberry ['bilb(ə)ri] s. mustikka.

bile [bail] s. sappi; kiukku.

bilge [bildʒ] s. (laivan) pohjakupu; pohjavesi (m. ~*-water);* sl. pöty, palturi.

bilharzia ['bil'ha:zjə] s. bilhartsia.

biliary ['biljəri] a. sappi-.

bilingual [bai'liŋgw(ə)l] a. kaksikielinen.

bilious ['biljəs] a. sappi-, sappitautinen.

bilk [bilk] v. petkuttaa.

bill 1. [bil] s. nokka; (m. *-hook)* vesuri; v.: ~ *and coo* hyväillä.

bill 2. [bil] s. lakiehdotus; lasku; lista, luettelo; mainosjuliste, ohjelma; vekseli; seteli (Am.); v. laskuttaa; ilmoittaa (mainosjulistein), mainostaa

(as jnak); ~ *of carriage (freight)*
rahtikirja; ~ *of exchange* vekseli; ~ *of
fare* ruokalista; ~ *of lading*
konossementti; ~ *of sale* kauppakirja;
stick no ~ s julisteiden kiinnittäminen
kielletty. **-board** ilmoitustaulu.
~-broker vekselinvälittäjä.

billet 1. ['bilit] *s.* majoituslippu,
-paikka; (puhek.) toimi; *v.* majoittaa
(on jkn luo).

billet 2. ['bilit] *s.* pölkky.

billfold lompakko.

billiards ['biljədz] *s.* biljardipeli.

billion ['biljən] *s.* biljoona, Am.
miljardi.

billow ['biləu] *s.* (hyöky)aalto; *v.*
aaltoilla. **-y** [-i] *a.* aaltoileva.

bill|poster, ~ **-sticker** julisteiden
kiinnittäjä.

billy ['bili] *s.* kenttäkattila. ~**goat** *s.*
pukki. ~**-o:** *like* ~ -o vietävästi,
hitosti.

biltong ['biltəŋ] *s.* (auringossa) kuivatut
lihasuikaleet.

bimonthly *ks. bi-*

bin [bin] *s.* laari, hinkalo, pönttö; *litter*
~ roskapönttö.

binary ['bainəri] *a.:* ~ *measure*
kaksijakoinen tahti.

bind [baind] *bound bound, v.* sitoa,
köyttää; kiinnittää; kovettaa;
velvoittaa; olla sitova; pysyä koossa;
s. sidekaari (mus.); ~ *oneself*
sitoutua; ~ *a boy apprentice to a tailor*
panna poika räätälinoppiin; ~ *over*
velvoittaa (et. saapumaan uudestaan
oikeuteen); ~ *up* sitoa; *bound for*
jnnek matkalla; *bound in paper*
nidottu; *ks. bound 3.* **-ing** *a.* sitova; *s.*
nide, kannet. **-weed** kierto (kasv.).

bine [bain] *s.* humalaköynnös.

binge [bindʒ] *s.: on the* ~ juhlimassa.

bingo ['biŋgəu] *s.* bingo (peli).

binnacle ['binəkl] *s.* kompassikaappi.

binocular [bi'nɔkjulə] *s.: [a pair of]* ~ *s*
kiikari.

biochemistry ['baiə(u)'-] *s.* biokemia.

biodegradable ['baiəudi'greidəbl] *a.*
luonnon kiertoon palautuva.

biograph|er [bai'ɔgrəfə] *s.* elämäkerran
kirjoittaja. **-ical** [baiə'græfik(ə)l] *a.*
elämäkerrallinen. **-y** [-i] *s.*
elämäkerta.

biolog|ical [baiə'lɔdʒik(ə)l] *a.*

biologinen. **-ist** [bai'ɔlədʒist] *s.*
biologi. **-y** [bai'ɔlədʒi] *s.* biologia.

biopsy ['baiɔpsi] *s.* (lääk.) koepala.

bioscope ['baiəskəup] *s.* (Et. Afr.)
elokuvateatteri.

bipartite [bai'pɑ:tait] *a.* kaksiosainen.

biped ['baiped] *a. & s.* kaksijalkainen.

biplane ['baiplein] *s.* kaksitaso.

birch [bə:tʃ] *s.* koivu; koivuvitsa; *v.*
antaa vitsaa.

bird [bə:d] *s.* lintu; tipu, pimu; *get the*
~ joutua ulosvihelletyksi, saada
potkut; ~ *of passage* muuttolintu; *a* ~
in the hand is worth two in the bush
parempi pyy pivossa kuin kymmenen
oksalla. ~**-fancier** lintukauppias.
~**-lime** linnunliima. ~'**s-eye:** *have a*
b.-e. view of nähdä jtk
lintuperspektiivissä, saada
yleissilmäys jstk. ~**-nesting** *s.* linnun
munien etsiminen pesistä.

Birmingham ['bə:miŋəm] *erisn.*

birth [bə:θ] *s.* syntymä: synnytys;
poikue; synty, alku; syntyperä; *[she
is] Russian by* ~ syntyperäinen
venakko; *give* ~ *to* synnyttää; ~
control syntyvyyden säännöstely; *m.*
ehkäisy(-). **-day** syntymäpäivä.
~**-mark** syntymämerkki. ~**-rate**
syntyvyys. **-right** esikoisoikeus.

Biscay ['biskei] *erisn.: the Bay of* ~
Biskajan lahti.

biscuit ['biskit] *s.* keksi; laivakorppu;
vaaleanruskea (väri).

bisect [bai'sekt] *v.* leikata kahtia.

bishop ['biʃəp] *s.* piispa; lähetti
(šakkipelissä). **-ric** [-rik] *s.*
piispanistuin.

bismuth ['bizməθ] *s.* vismutti.

bison ['baisn] *s.* biisoni.

bit 1. [bit] *s.* (poran ym) terä;
avaimenlehti; kuolaimet; *v.* panna
kuolaimet hevoselle.

bit 2. [bit] *s.* pala, hitunen; *a* ~ hiukan,
vähän; *a threepenny* ~ kolmen
pennyn raha; ~ *by* ~ vähitellen; *do
one's* ~ tehdä osansa; *not a* ~ ei
hiukkaakaan; *every* ~ *as good* aivan
yhtä hyvä; *wait a* ~ odota hetkinen; *I
gave him a* ~ *of my mind* puhuin
suuni puhtaaksi.

bit 3. [bit] *imp. ks. bite.*

bitch [bitʃ] *s.* narttu, naaras; törkeä
nainen; lutka; *v. (~ up)* sotkea.

bite [bait] *bit, bitten, v.* purra; pistää; syövyttää, syöpyä; tunkeutua; (kalasta) nykiä; tarttua syöttiin; *s.* purema; pisto; suupala; (kalasta) nykäisy; kirpeys, (kuv.) purevuus; terä; ~ *off* puraista, haukata (jstk); ~ *off more than one can chew* yrittää liian suuria; *were you bitten?* puijattiinko sinua? *bitten by the frost* pakkasen purema; *once bitten, twice shy* palanut lapsi karttaa tulta; *biting* pureva.

bitter ['bitə] *a.* karvas; katkera; pureva; *s. pl.* karvasvesi; *to the* ~ *end* viimeiseen saakka; *become* ~ katkeroitua. **~-sweet** *a.* katkeransuloinen; *s.* punakoiso.

bittern ['bitə(:)n] *s.* kaulushaikara.

bitterness *s.* katkeruus, karvaus.

bitts [bits] *s. pl.* paripollarit.

bitum|en ['bitjumin] *s.* maapihka, bitumi. **-inous** [bi'tju:minəs] *a.* bitumi-.

bivalve ['baivælv] *s.* kaksikuorinen simpukka; osteri.

bivouac ['bivuæk] *v. & s.* syöpyä (yöpyminen) taivasalla.

biweekly ks. *bi-*.

bizarre [bi'zɑː] *a.* eriskummallinen.

blab [blæb] *v.* lörpötellä, kieliä.

black [blæk] *a.* musta; tumma(ihoinen); neekeri; musta(ihoinen); musta, laiton; synkkä, *s.* musta; musta väri; musta puku; *v.* mustata; kiillottaa (kenkiä); *beat* ~ *and blue* lyödä sinelmille; *all went* ~ *for me* silmissäni musteni; ~ *art* musta magia; *in sb.'s* ~ *books* jkn epäsuosiossa; *the B*~ *Forest* Schwarzwald; *the* ~ *Country* Engl. (hiili)teollisuusalue; ~ *letter* fraktuura; ~ *market* musta pörssi; ~ *out* pimentää (ikkunat ym). **-amoor** [-əmuə] *s.* murjaani. **-ball** äänestää jäseneksi pyrkivää vastaan. **~-beetle** torakka. **-berry** karhunvatukka. **-bird** mustarastas. **-board** musta taulu. **~-cock** koirasteeri. **-en** [-(ə)n] *v.* mustata, mustua. **-guard** ['blægɑːd] *s.* roisto; *v.* herjata; (~**ly** ritkömainen). **-head** ihomato. **-ing** *s.* kenkämuste. **-ish** [-iʃ] *a.* mustahko. **-leg** huijari; akonrikkuri. **-mail** kiristys; *v.* kiristää

(jklta rahaa). **-mailer** kiristäjä. **~-out** (ikkunoiden) pimennys: *I had a b.-o.* maailma musteni silmissäni. **-ness** *s.* mustuus, pimeys, synkkyys. **-smith** (karkeis)seppä. **-thorn** oratuomi.

bladder ['blædə] *s.* rakko (et. virtsa-, uima- ym); ilmalla täytetty pallo.

blade [bleid] *s.* (kapea) lehti; (veitsen ym) terä, (airon) lapa, (potkurin) siipi; *shoulder~* lapaluu.

blamable ['bleiməbl] *a.* moitittava.

blame [bleim] *v.* moittia; syyttää; *s.* moite; syy, vika; *lay the* ~ *on* syyttää jkta; *I am to* ~ syy on minussa. **-less** *a.* moitteeton, syytön. **-worthy** *a.* moitittava.

blanch [blɑːn(t)ʃ] *v.* valkaista; kalveta; ~ *almonds* kuoria manteleita.

blancmange [blə'mɒnʒ] *s.* kermahyytelö.

bland [blænd] *a.* lempeä, ystävällinen; kohtelias, mairitteleva; leuto, mieto. **-ishment** [-iʃmənt] *s.* (tav. *pl.*) imartelu, mairittelu.

blank [blæŋk] *a.* tyhjä, kirjoittamaton; ilmeetön, sisällyksetön; selvä; pelkkä; *s.* tyhjä paikka; aukko; lomake; tyhjä arpalippu; ~ *cartridge* harjoituspatruuna; ~ *cheque* avoin vekseli; ~ *verse* silosäe; *look* ~ näyttää ällistyneeltä; *his mind was a complete* ~ hänen päänsä tuntui aivan tyhjältä; *my mind went* ~ en muistanut mitään.

blanket ['blæŋkit] *s.* huopa(peite), hevosloimi; (kuv.) vaippa; *a wet* ~ kylmä suihku (kuv.); ~ *term* yleisnimitys.

blankly *adv.* ilmeettömästi; kokonaan, täysin.

blare [blɛə] *v.* toitottaa; *s.* toitotus; kova ääni, pauhina.

blarney ['blɑːni] *s.* mairittelu.

blasé ['blɑːzei] *a.* tympeytynyt.

blasphem|e [blæs'fiːm] *v.* pilkata, herjata; **-ous** ['blæsfiməs] *a.* Jumalaa pilkkaava, herjaava. **-y** ['blæsfimi] *s.* jumalanpilkka.

blast [blɑːst] *v.* tuulenpuuska; toitotus, törähdys; ilmavirta (masuunissa); räjähdys, -panos; *v.* räjäyttää tuhota; *[the wireless] is on at full* ~ soi täydellä voimalla; ~*ed* kirottu. **~-furnace** masuuni, sulatto. **~-off**

(avaruusaluksen ym) laukaisu, lähtö.

blatant ['bleit(ə)nt] *a.* meluava; karkea, räikeä. **-ly** [-li] *adv.* häpeämättä, peittelemättä.

blaze 1. [bleiz] *s.* loimu, roihu, tuli, valo; *v.* loimuta, leimuta, loistaa; *in a* ~ tulessa; *in a* ~ *of colour* väriloistossaan; *to* ~ *s* hemmettiin; *like* ~ *s* vimmatusti; ~ *away* tulittaa jatkuvasti; ~ *up* leimahtaa liekkiin.

blaze 2. [bleiz] *s.* (hevosen) laukki; pilkka (puussa); *v.* pilkoittaa; ~ *a trail* merkitä reitti, (kuv.) raivata uusi tie; *trail* ~ *r* tienviitoittaja.

blaze 3. [bleiz] *v.* (~ *abroad*) kuuluttaa julki.

blazer ['bleizə] *s.* värikäs urheilutakki.

blazing *a.* leimuava, (kuv.) räikeä.

blazon ['bleizn] *s.* vaakunakilpi; *v.* koristaa heraldisesti; julistaa, toitottaa julki (~ *forth*). **-ry** [-ri] *s.* vaakunaoppi; (runsas) koristelu.

bleach [bli:tʃ] *v.* valkaista; vaaleta.

bleak 1. [bli:k] *s.* salakka.

bleak 2. [bli:k] *a.* kylmä, paljas, ankea, synkkä, kolea.

blear ['bliə] *a.* sumea, samea, tihruinen; hämärä. ~**-eyed** sameasilmäinen.

bleat [bli:t] *v.* mäkiää; *s.* määkiminen.

bleb [bleb] *s.* ilmakupla, rakkula.

bled [bled] *imp. & pp.* ks. *bleed.*

bleed [bli:d] *bled bled, v.* vuotaa verta; juosta mahlaa; iskeä suonta; kiristää, nylkeä (kuv.); *.. bled him for £ 500* kiristi väält häneltä 500 puntaa. **-er** [-ə] *s.* verenvuototautinen. **-ing** *s.* verenvuoto; *a.* vertavuotava; väripäästävä.

blemish ['blemiʃ] *v.* rumentaa, pilata; *s.* vika; tahra.

blench [blen(t)ʃ] *v.* säveltää (pelosta), säikkyä; sulkea silmänsä jltk.

blend [blend] *v.* sekoittaa, -ttua; sopia yhteen, sulautua (toisiinsa); *s.* (teeym) sekoitus.

blende [blend] *s.* sinkkivälke.

Blenheim ['blenim] *erisn.; s.* spanielirotu.

bless [bles] ~ *ed* ~ *ed,* harv. *blest blest, v.* siunata; onnellistaa; ylistää; ~ *me!* ~ *my soul!* siunatkoon! hyvänen aika! *well, I'm blest* johan nyt jotakin! *they have been* ~ *ed with ..* heille on

siunautunut .. **-ed** [-id] *a.* siunattu, autuas. **-edness** [idnis] *s.* onnellisuus, autuus. **-ing** *s.* siunaus, armo; (Jumalan) lahja; *what a* ~ *it is* [*that ..*] mikä onni, että ..

blether ['bleðə], **blather** ['blæðə] *s.* lörpöttely, pöty; *v.* jaaritella (joutavia).

blew [blu:] *imp.* ks. *blow.*

blight [blait] *s.* ruoste-, home-, nokisieni; tuho; *v.* turmella, tuhota; *be* ~ *ed* m. raueta tyhjiin. **-y** [blaiti] *s.* kotimaa, Englanti (sot. sl.).

blimp [blimp] *s.* [*Colonel*] *B* ~ patavanhoillinen tyyppi.

blind [blaind] *a.* sokea; näkymätön, vale-; *v.* sokaista, tehdä sokeaksi; *s.* kierrekaihdin, verho; silmänlume; *the* ~ sokeat; ~ *alley* umpikuja; ~ *drunk* kännipäissään; ~ *flying* sokkolento; ~ *window* valeikkuna; *go* ~ sokeutua; *strike* ~ sokaista; *Venetian* ~ *s* sälekaihtimet; *he was* ~ *ed in the war* hän menetti sodassa näkönsä. **-fold** *a. adv.* silmät sidottuina; *v.* sitoa (jkn) silmät. **-man's buff:** *play* ~ olla sokkosilla. **-ness** *s.* sokeus. ~**-worm** vaskitsa.

blink [bliŋk] *v.* räpyttää silmiään, iskeä silmää; siristellä silmiään; ummistaa silmänsä (jltk); *v.* vilkutus; vilke; ~ *ing* (puhek.) kirottu. **-er** [-ə]: ~ *s (pl.)* hevosen silmälaput.

bliss [blis] *s.* ilo; autuus. **-ful** *a.* autuaallinen, autuas.

blister ['blistə] *s.* rakko, rakkula; kupla (puussa ym); vetolaastari; *v.* nostaa t. nousta rakkuloille.

blithe [blaið] *a.* iloinen, hilpeä.

blithering ['blið(ə)riŋ] *a.* laverteleva; ~ *idiot* hölmö.

blitz [blits] *s.* salamahyökkäys; ~ *ed* lentopommituksen tuhoama.

blizzard ['blizəd] *s.* lumituisku, lumimyrsky.

bloat|ed ['bləutid] *a.* paisunut, pöhöttynyt; ~ [*with pride*] pöyhistelevä. **-er** [-ə] *s.* savustettu sill

blob [blɔb] *s.* pilkku, läiskä.

bloc [blɔk] *s.* (valtio)blokki.

block [blɔk] *s.* pölkky; mestauspölkky *(the* ~*)*; hattutukki; (kivi)lohkare, möhkäle; kerrostalo, kortteli; este, liikenneseisaus; kuvalaatta; palikka;

väkipyörä, talja (us. ~ *and tackle*); *v.*
estää, tukkia; muovata (tukilla);
blokeerata; saartaa; ~ *of ice* (Am.)
jääkuutio; ~ *of flats* kerrostalo; *high-*
rise ~ tornitalo; ~ *letters*
painokirjaimet; ~ *in (out)*
hahmotella; ~ *up* sulkea. **-ade**
[blɔ'keid] *s.* saarto; *v.* saartaa; *raise*
the ~ lopettaa saarto; (**~-runner**
saarronmurtaja). **-age** [-idʒ] *s.*
tukkeuma. **-head** pölkkypää. **-house**
paaluvarustus.

bloke [bləuk] *s.* sl. mies, kaveri, heppu.

blond(e) [blɔnd] *a.* vaalea(verinen); *s.*
vaaleaverinen henkilö, vaaleaverikkö
(*blonde*).

blood [blʌd] *s.* veri; suku, rotu,
syntyperä; *v.* totuttaa (koira) vereen;
in cold ~ kylmäverisesti; *his* ~ *is up*
hänen verensä kiehuu; *breed bad* ~
herättää pahaa verta; *let* ~ iskeä
suonta; ~ *feud* verikosto; ~ *group*
veriryhmä; ~ *horse* täysiverihevonen;
~ *picture* verenkuva; *it runs in the* ~
se on suvussa; *young* ~ (vanh.)
keikari. **~-curdling** karmaiseva, verta
hyytävä. **~-guiltiness** verivelka.
-hound vihikoira. **-less** *a.* veretön;
tunteeton, kalpea. **~-letting**
suonenisku. **~-poisoning**
verenmyrkytys. **-shed** verenvuodatus.
-shot verestävä. **~-stained**
verentahraama. **~-sucker** verenimijä.
-thirsty verenhimoinen. **~-vessel**
verisuoni. **-y** [-i] *a.* verinen; julma,
hirveä; (puhek.) kirottu.

▶**bloom** [blu:m] *s.* kukka;
kukoistus(aika), kukkeus, hehkeys;
untuva (persikan ym pinnalla); *v.*
kukkia, kukoistaa; *be in* ~ olla
kukassa. **-er** [-ə] *s.* sl. erehdys. **-ers**
[-əz] *s. pl.* (naisen) leveät
voimisteluhousut. **-ing** *a.* kukoistava;
hiton(moinen).

▶**lossom** [blɔsəm] *s.* (hedelmäpuun
ym) kukka; *v.* puhjeta kukkaan; *in* ~
kukassa; *she* ~ *ed out as* . .hänestä
kehkeytyi . .

▶**lot** [blɔt] *s.* (muste- ym) tahra;
häpeäpilkku, tahra; *v.* tahria, tuhria;
tahrata (maine); kuivata
imupaperilla; ~ *out* pyyhkiä pois;
peittää; tuhota (esim. viholllinen).

▶**lotch** [blɔtʃ] *s.* tahra, näppy. **-ed, -y** *a.*

läiskäinen.

blott|er [blɔtə] *s.* imuri. **-ing-paper** *s.*
im paperi

blouse [blauz] *s.* pusero; (ase)takki.

blow 1. [bləu] *blew blown, v.* puhaltaa;
tuulla; lentää; soittaa (torvea);
räjäyttää (tav. ~ *up*); polttaa
(sulake); olla hengästynyt, läähättää
(puff and ~); sl. tuhlata; *s.* puhallus;
~ *hot and cold* olla horjuva; ~ *a kiss*
heittää lentosuukko; ~ *one's nose*
niistää nenänsä; ~ *one's own trumpet*
kehua itseään; ~ *out* puhaltaa
sammuksiin; *the fuse blew out* sulake
paloi; ~ *over* asettua, mennä ohi; ~
up räjähtää (m. kuv.), räjäyttää;
puhaltaa ilmaa jhk; liioitella; sättiä,
torua; *a storm blew up* nousi kova
tuuli; *[my hat] blew off* lensi päästäni;
[the door] blew open lennähti auki;
when the whistle ~ *s* kun pilli soi; *I'll*
be ~ed if I know en hitto vie tiedä; ~
the expense! viis kuluista; *[go] for a* ~
hengittämään raitista ilmaa.

blow 2. [bləu] *v.* (ks. ed.) puhjeta
kukkaan, kukoistaa.

blow 3. [bləu] *s.* lyönti; kolaus isku; *at*
one ~ yhdellä iskulla; *without a* ~
miekaniskutta; *come to* ~ *s* joutua
käsikähmään.

blower [bləuə] *s.* puhallin, puhaltaja,
sl. puhelin; *organ-* ~ urkujenpolkija.

blow|-fly raatokärpänen. **-lamp**
puhalluslamppu. **~-out** kumin
puhkeaminen; sulakkeen palaminen.
~-up räjähdys.

blown [bləun] *pp.* ks. *blow;* ~ *n up* m.
itseään täynnä.

blowzy [blauzi] *a.* punakka,
huolimattoman näköinen.

blubber [blʌbə] *s.* valaanrasva; *v.*
(itkeä) vollottaa.

bludgeon [blʌdʒn] *s.* nuija,
ryhmysauva.

blue [blu:] *s.* sininen; alakuloinen,
masentunut; tory-puolueeseen
kuuluva, vanhoillinen; *s.* sininen
(väri); (yliopiston) edustusurheilija
(dark ~ Oxfordin, *light ~*
Cambridgen); *a rowing ~*
edustusjoukkueen soutaja; [*dressed*
in ~ sinipukuinen; *look* ~ näyttää
synkältä, masentuneelta; *once in a* ~
moon hyvin harvoin; *a* ~ [*movie*]

säädytön, porno-; *the ~ s* synkkyys,
masennus. **-bell** sinililja, (Skotl.)
sinikello. **-bottle** lihakärpänen.
~-**collar** *worker* haalarityöntekijä.
-jacket merisotilas. ~-**pencil** korjata,
pyyhkiä (sinikynällä). **-print**
sinikopio; suunnitelma,
toimintamalli. **-stocking** sinisukka.

bluff [blʌf] *a.* pystysuora, jyrkkä,
suorasukainen; *s.* jyrkkä törmä,
jyrkänne; hämäys, bluffi; *v.* hämätä.

bluish ['blu:iʃ] *a.* sinertävä.

blunder ['blʌndə] *v.* haparoida (us. ~
along); möhliä, tehdä nolo virhe;
hoitaa huonosti; *s.* törkeä virhe,
munaus, kömmähdys; ~ *upon*
sattumalta löytää jtk. **-buss** [-bʌs]
väkipyssy.

blunt [blʌnt] *a.* tylsä, tylppä;
tunteeton, kylmä (tosiasia);
suorasukainen, töykeä; *v.* tylsyttää;
lieventää, heikontaa. **-ly** suoraan.

blur [blə:] *s.* tahra; hämäryys, epäselvä
kuva; *v.* tuhria; tehdä hämäräksi t.
epäselväksi, sumentaa, samentaa;
~ *red* epäselvä.

blurb [blə:b] *s.* takakansi|mainos,
-teksti.

blurt [blə:t] *v.:* ~ *out* tokaista.

blush [blʌʃ] *v.* punastua *(at* jtk);
hävetä *(for* jkn puolesta); *s.*
puna(stuminen).

bluster [blʌstə] *v.* pauhata, ärjyä;
mahtailla, kerskua; *s.* pauhaaminen;
kerskailu, uhkailu, rehentely.

bo(h) [bəu] *int.:* .. *cannot say* ~ *to a
goose*. .ei (pelosta) saa sanaa
suustaan.

boa ['bə(u)ə]*s.* boakäärme;
kaulapuuhka, kauluri.

boar [bɔ:] *s.* urossika; *wild* ~ karju,
villisika.

board [bɔ:d] *s.* lauta; pelilauta; taulu;
ruoka, täysihoito; lautakunta,
valiokunta, hallitus, laivanlaita;
kartonki, levy; *pl.* näyttämö; *v.*
peittää laudoilla (m. ~ *up).*
laudoittaa; ottaa täysihoitoon, olla
täysihoidossa; ~ *[a ship]* nousta
laivaan, lentokoneeseen ym; asettua
laidatusten toisen laivan kanssa,
entrata (hist.); *above* ~ rehellisesti;
free ~ ilmaiset ateriat; ~ *and lodging*
täysihoito; *B* ~ *of Management* (t.

Directors) johtokunta; *B*~ *of Trade*
kauppaministeriö; *School B*~ koulun
johtokunta; *on* ~ laivassa, -aan, *m.*
lentokonee|ssa, -seen, Am. junassa,
-aan; *go by the* ~ pudota yli laidan,
mennä myttyyn **-er** [-ə] *s.*
täysihoitolainen; sisäoppilas.
-ing-card tarkistuskortti (koneeseen
pääsyä varten). **-ing-school**
sisäoppilaitos.

boast [bəust] *s.* kerskaus, kerskailu; *v.*
(~ of) kerskailla, ylpeillä jllak; [*our
school*] ~ *s a fine swimming-pool* on
ylpeä hienosta uima-altaastaan. **-ful** *a.*
kerskaileva.

boat [bəut] *s.* vene; laiva;
(kastike)kulho; *go* ~ *ing* tehdä
veneretki; *in the same* ~ (kuv.)
samassa veneessä. ~-**hook** keksi.
~-**race** soutukilpailu. **-swain** [bəusn]
pursimies, puosu.

bob [bɔb] *v.* pompahtaa (ylös ja alas),
pomppia; ponnahtaa esiin, tulla esille;
niiata *(~ a curtsy);* leikata tukka; *s.*
(heilurin) paino, luoti; (ongen) koho;
niiaus; nykäys; *ten bob* 10 šillinkiä;
~*bed hair* polkkatukka; ~ *up*
pulpahtaa esiin.

bobbin ['bɔbin] *s.* puola, lankarulla; ~
lace nyplätty pitsi.

bobby ['bɔbi] *s.* poliisi; ~ -*socks (-sox)*
nilkkasukat.

bob|sleigh, -sled (pitkä) kaksoiskelkka.
-tail *s. & a.* töpöhäntä(inen).

bode [bəud] *v.* ennustaa ; ~ *well (ill)*
tietää hyvää (pahaa).

bodice ['bɔdis] *s.* puvun yläosa,
miehusta, (kansallispuvun) liivi.

bodily ['bɔdili] *a.* ruumiillinen,
ruumiin-; *adv.* kokonaisuudessaan,
yhtenä miehenä, henkilökohtaisesti.

bodkin ['bɔdkin] *s.* pujotinneula,
naskali.

body ['bɔdi] *s.* ruumis; keho, vartalo;
(auton ym) kori; pää|osa, -sisällys,
kokoelma, kokonaisuus; -kunta;
joukko; kappale; (viinin) vahva tainu;
in a ~ kaikki yhdessä; *keep* ~ *and
soul together* pysyä hengissä;
diplomatic ~ diplomaattikunta;
heavenly ~ taivaankappale; *legislative*
~ lakiasäätävä elin; *main* ~
pääjoukko. ~-**cloth** hevosloimi.
-guard henkivartija, -vartio.

Boer ['bəuə, 'buə, 'bɔ:] s. & a. buuri

boffin ['bɔfin] s. sl. tiedemies.

bog [bɔg] s. suo, räme; ~ *ged down* jhk vajonnut, paikoilleen juuttunut.

bogey ['bəugi] ks. *bogy*.

boggle ['bɔgl] v. (~ *at*) epäröidä, säikähtää.

boggy ['bɔgi] a. suoperäinen.

bogus ['bəugəs] a. väärä, vale-.

bogy ['bəugi] s. peikko, mörkö.

Bohemia [bəu'hi:mjə] erisn. Böömi. **-n** [-n] a. & s. böömiläinen; boheemi(-).
b-nism [-nizm] s. boheemielämä.

boil 1. [bɔil] s. äkämä, paise.

boil 2. [bɔil] v. kiehua, kuohua; kiehuttaa, keittää; ~ *down* keittää vähiin, (kuv.) tiivistää, -tyä; *it all ~s down to this* asian ydin on tämä; ~ *over with indignation* olla kuohuksissaan; *bring to the ~* kuumentaa kiehumapisteeseen. **-er** [-ə] s. höyrykattila; (keittiön) kuumavesisäilö; ~ *suit* haalarit. **-ing** a. kiehuva; s. kiehuminen; (~-**point** kiehumapiste).

boisterous ['bɔist(ə)rəs] a. myrskyisä, raju; meluava.

bold [bəuld] a. rohkea, uskalias; röyhkeä; voimakas (käsiala ym), selväpiirteinen; *make ~ to, make so ~ as to* rohjeta. **-face:** *in ~* (kirjap.) puolilihavalla. **-ness** s. rohkeus.

bole [bəul] s. runko.

bolero ['bɔlərəu] s. lyhyt liivi t. jakku, bolero.

Boleyn ['bulin] erisn.

bollard ['bɔləd] s. pollari.

Bolshevik ['bɔlʃəvik] s. bolševikki (m. lyh. *Bolshy*).

Bolshevist ['bɔlʃəvist] s. & a. bolševikki(-), bolševistinen.

bolster ['bəulstə] s. pitkä (alus)pielus; täyte; v. (tav. ~ *up*) tukea.

bolt 1. [bəult] s. nuoli; salama; salpa, telki; pultti; v. syöksyä pois, pillastua, rynnätä, livistää; nielaista (nopeasti); hotkia; teljetä; *adv.: sit ~ upright* istua suorana kuin kynttilä; *a ~ from the blue* salama kirkkaalta taivaalta.

bolt 2. [bəult] v. seuloa; tutkia. **-er** [-ə] s. seula.

bolus ['bəuləs] s. (iso) pilleri; (ruoka)pala.

bomb [bɔm] s. pommi; v. pudottaa pommeja, pommittaa; ~ *ing raid* pommihyökkäys.

bombard [bɔm'bɑ:d] v. pommittaa (tykeillä, m. kuv.). **-ier** ['bɔmbə'diə] s. (tykistön) alikersantti. **-ment** s. pommitus.

bombast ['bɔmbæst] s. mahtipontisuus. **-ic** [bɔm'bæstik] a. mahtipontinen.

Bombay [bɔm'bei] erisn.

bomber ['bɔmə] s. pommikone.

bomb|-proof pomminkestävä. **-shell** pommi (kuv.). ~-**sight** pommitustähtäin.

bonanza [bə'nænzə] s. (kuv.) kultakaivos *a ~ year* onnekas vuosi.

bond [bɔnd] s. side; sitoumus, velkakirja; obligaatio; v. (et. pp.) panna tullivarastoon; ~*s* (m.) kahleet; *goods in ~* tullivarastossa olevat tavarat; ~*ed warehouse* tullivarasto. **-age** [-idʒ] s. orjuus. **-(s)man** maaorja.

bone [bəun] s. luu, ruoto: v. poistaa luut, ruotia (kala); sl. vohkia; *bred in the ~* synnynnäinen; *I have a ~ to pick with him* meillä on keskenämme selvitettävää; *[they dismissed him] and made no ~ about it* eivätkä olleet millänsäkään. **-setter** puoskari.

bonfire ['bɔnfaiə] s. kokko.

bonhomie ['bɔnɔmi:] s. rakastettavuus.

bonito [bə'ni:təu] s. tonnikala(laji).

bonnet ['bɔnit] s. (nauhoilla kiinnitettävä) naisen lakki, hilkka; (skotlantil.) venelakki; (auton) konepelti.

bonnie, bonny ['bɔni] a. (Skotl.) kaunis, korea.

bonus ['bəunəs] s. voitto-osuus; lisäpalkkio, (esim. kalliinajan)lisä.

bony ['bəuni] a. luinen, luu-; luiseva.

boo [bu:] v. huutaa paheksuvasti, »buuata».

boob [bu:b] s. höhlä, =. seur.

booby ['bu:bi] s. tomppeli, tyhmeliini. ~-**prize** lohdutuspalkinto (viimeiselle). ~-**trap** »tyhmän loukku»; vaarattomalta näyttävä ansa, pommi ym.

book [buk] s. kirja; lehtiö, vihko; v. viedä kirjoihin, merkitä luetteloon; tilata, varata (paikka, lippu); ~ *club* kirjarengas; ~ *ends* kirjatuet; ~ *token* (kirjakaupan) lahjakortti; *by ~ post*

ristisiteenä; *in* [*sb.'s*] *good (bad)* ~ *s* hyvissä (huonoissa) kirjoissa; *on the* ~ *s* luettelossa; *bring sb. to* ~ vaatia tilille; *fully* ~ *ed up* kaikki paikat varatut. **~-binder** kirjansitoja. **~-case** kirjakaappi. **-ie** [-'buki] *s.* sl. = *bookmaker.* **-ing-clerk** lipunmyyjä. **-ing-office** lippumyymälä, paikkavaraamo. **-ish** *a.* lukuhaluinen, kirjatoukka. **~-keeper** kirjanpitäjä. **~-keeping** kirjanpito; *b.-k. by single (double) entry* yksin(kaksin)-kertainen k. **~-learning** kirjatieto. **~-maker** vedonlyönnin välittäjä. **~-mak(er)** kirjanmerkki. **~-plate** exlibris. **-seller** kirjakauppias. **~-shop (-store)** kirjakauppa. **-stall** kirja- ja lehtikioski. **-worm** kirjatoukka.
boom 1. [bu:m] *s.* puomi.
boom 2. [bu:m] *v.* jyristä, kohista; nousta äkkiä; mainostaa; *s.* jyrähdys, paukahdus; (hintojen) nousu, noususushdanne.
boomerang ['bu:məræŋ] *s.* bumerangi.
boon 1. [bu:n] *s.* suosionosoitus, lahja, siunaus.
boon 2. [bu:n] *a.: a* ~ *companion* hauska veikko.
boor [buə] *s.* moukka. **-ish** [-riʃ] *a.* karkea, moukkamainen.
boost [bu:st] *v.* työntää eteenpäin, vahvistaa; mainostaa, kehua. **-er** [-ə] *s. attr.* lisä-, tehostus-; ~ *rocket* starttiraketti.
boot 1. [bu:t] *s.* (vanh.) etu; *v.* hyödyttää; *to* ~ lisäksi, kaupanpäälliseksi.
boot 2. [bu:t] *s.* (varsi)kenkä, saapas; (auton)tavaratila; *with one's heart in one's* ~ *s* sydän kurkussa; *get the* ~ (sl.) saada potkut; **~-lace** kengännauha.
bootee [bu:ti:] *s.* lapsen tossu, saapikas.
booth [bu:ð] *s.* (myynti- ym) koju; koppi.
boot|**-jack** saapaspihti. **-legger** (alkoholin) salakuljettaja, pirtukauppias.
bootless ['bu:tlis] *a.* hyödytön.
boots [bu:ts] *s.* (hotellin) kengänkiillottaja, hotellipoika.
boot-tree kenkä-, saapaslesti.
booty ['bu:ti] *s.* saalis.

booze [bu:z] *v.* ryypiskellä, juopotella; *s.* juomingit; viina; ~ *r* juoppo.
bopeep [bou'pi:p] *s.* kurkistusleikki.
boracic [bə'ræsik] *a.* boori-.
borax ['bɔ:ræks] *s.* booraksi.
border ['bɔ:də] *s.* reuna, syrjä; reunus; raja, rajamaa *(the B~* Engl. ja Skotl. rajaseutu); *v.* rajoittaa, olla rajana; reunustaa; ~ *upon* rajoittua jhk) lähetä jtk, vivahtaa jhk. **-er** [-rə] *s.* rajaseudun asukas. **-land** (kuv.) rajamaa, -alue. **-line:** ~ *case* rajatapaus.
bore 1. [bɔ] *imp.* ks. *bear.*
bore 2. [bɔ] *v.* porata, puhkaista; ikävystyttää; *s.* (tykin ym) putki, kaliiperi; ikävystyttävä ihminen, harmi; ~ *d to death* lopen ikävystynyt. **-hole** kairausreikä; porakaivo.
boreal ['bɔ:riəl] *a.* pohjoinen.
boredom ['bɔ:dəm] *s.* ikävystyminen.
boric ['bɔ:rik] *a.* boori; ~ *acid* boorihappo.
boring *a.* ikävystyttävä.
born [bɔ:n] *pp.* ks. *bear; a.* syntynyt; synnynnäinen; *he was* ~ *in 1940* hän on syntynyt vuonna 1940. **-e** *pp.* ks. *bear;* kantanut; [*she*] *has* ~ *three children* on synnyttänyt kolme lasta; *it was gradually* ~ *upon me* vähitellen oivalsin.
boron ['bɔ:rɔn, Engl. -rən] *s.* boori.
borough ['bʌrə] *s.* (pikku)kaupunki, kauppala; *municipal* ~ kaupunkikunta; *parliamentary* ~ kaupunkivaalipiiri.
borrow ['bɔrəu] *v.* lainata *(from* jklta).
Borstal [bɔ:stl] *s.:* ~ [*institution*] nuorisovankila.
borzoi ['bɔ:zɔi] *s.* venäjänvinttikoira.
boscage ['bɔskidʒ] *s.* (run.) metsikkö, lehto.
bosh [bɔʃ] (puhek.) *s.* hölynpöly; *int.* pötyä!
bo'sn ['bəusn] ks. *boatswain.*
bosom ['buzəm] *s.* rinta, povi, helma; ~ *friend* sydänystävä.
Bosphorus ['bɔsf(ə)rəs]: *the* ~ Bospori.
boss 1. [bɔs] (puhek.) *s.* päällikkö, pomo; *v.* olla pomona.
boss 2. [bɔs] *s.* kohouma, kuhmu; nuppi; ~ *-eyed* silmäpuoli.
bossy ['bɔsi] *a.* komenteleva.
bo'sun ['bəusn] *s.* puosu, *bo'sn.*

botan|ical [bə'tænik(ə)l] *a.* kasvitieteellinen. **-ist** ['bɒtənist] *s.* kasvitieteilijä. **-ize** ['bɒtənaiz] *v.* tutkia kasveja. **-y** ['bɒtəni] *s.* kasvitiede.

botch [bɒtʃ] *v.* paikata, tehdä kömpelösti, tunaroida, patustaa (m. ~ *up*).

both [bəuθ] *pron.* molemmat; *adv.*: *both...and...sekä...että*; ~ *of them are good* ne ovat molemmat hyviä.

bother ['bɒðə] *v.* kiusa, harmi, vaiva; *v.* kiusata, vaivata; vaivautua; *int.*: ~ *the flies!* pahuksen kärpäset! *don't* ~ *yourself (your head) about it* älä anna sen vaivata päätäsi; *I couldn't be* ~*ed to..*en viitsinyt. . **-ation** [-'reiʃn]: ~! peijakkaan harmillista! **-some** *a.* kiusallinen.

bottle ['bɒtl] *s.* pullo; *v.* säilöä (pulloihin), pullottaa; *too fond of the* ~ *viinaan menevä*: *put* [*the baby*] *on the* ~ aloittaa pulloruokinta; ~ *up* tukahduttaa **~-green** tummanvihreä. **-neck** (kuv.) pullonkaula.

bottom ['bɒtəm] *s.* pohja; perustus; alaosa; (sivun) alareuna, (pöydän) alapää, alin sija; istuin, takamus; *a.* pohjimmainen, alin, viimeinen; *v.* panna pohja (jhk); *perus|taa*, *-tua*, nojautua *(be ~ed upon); at ~* pohjaltaan; *from the ~ of one's heart* sydämen pohjasta; *be at the ~ of* olla jnk takana, syynä; *get to ~ of* päästä perille jstk; *go to the ~* upota; *touch ~* koskettaa pohjaa; *in British ~s* brittiläisissä laivoissa. **-less** *a.* pohjaton.

bougainvillea [bu:gən'viliə] *s.* ihmeköynnös.

bough [bau] *s.* oksa.

bought [bɔ:t] *imp. & pp.* ks. *buy*.

bougie ['bu:ʒi:] *s.* (lääk.) sondi.

boulder [bəuldə] *s.* lohkare, (iso) vierinkivi.

boulevard ['bu:lva:] *s.* bulevardi.

bounc|e ['bauns] *v.* pomppia, poukahtaa, poukahduttaa, kimmahtaa, ponnahtaa; rynnätä; *s.* (pallon) kimmahdus, kimmoisuus: pullistelu; [*catch a ball*] *on the* ~ pompasta. **-er** [-ə] *s.* iso esine ym; emävalhe. **-ing** *a.* tukeva, tanakka.

bound 1. [baund] *s.* (tav. *pl.*) raja; *v.*

rajoittaa; *set* ~ *s to* määrätä rajat jllek; [*keep within*] *the* ~ *s of reason* kohtuuden rajoissa; *there are no* ~ *s to..* .on rajaton; [*F. is*] *-ed on the east by..* (Suomea) rajoittaa idässä. .

bound 2. [baund] *v.* hypätä, loikata; kimmahtaa; pompata; *s.* loikkaus, harppaus.

bound 3. [baund] *imp. & pp.* ks. *bind*; *a.* sidottu; velvollinen *(to) I am not* ~ *to go* minun ei ole pakko lähteä; ~ *to secrecy* vaitiolovelvollinen; *he is* ~ *to win* hän varmasti voittaa; *I'll be* ~ annan pääni pantiksi; *be* ~ *up with* liittyä läheisesti jhk; *my* ~ *en duty* ehdoton velvollisuuteni.

boundary ['baundəri] *s.* raja.

bounder ['baundə] *s.* moukka.

boundless *a.* rajaton.

bount|eous ['baunt|iəs] *a.* = seur. **-iful** [-iful] *a.* antelias, runsaskätinen. **-y** [-i] *s.* anteliaisuus; tukipalkkio.

bouquet ['bukei] *s.* kukkavihko; (viinin) tuoksu.

bourgeois ['buəʒwa:] *a.* porvarillinen; poroporvarillinen; *s.* porvari; poroporvari. **-ie** ['buəʒwa'zi:] *s.* porvarissääty.

bourn 1. [buən] *s.* joki, puro.

bourn(e) 2. [buən] *s.* (run.) määränpää.

Bournemouth ['bɔ:nməθ] *erisn.*

bourse [buəs] *s.* pörssi (ei Engl.).

bout [baut] *s.* kierros; ottelu, kilpailu; (taudin)kohtaus; *drinking*~ juoma-kausi, -kierre.

bovine ['bəuvain] *a.* härän; hidas.

bow 1. [bau] *v.* kumartaa, kumartua, tervehtiä; alistua; taivuttaa, notkistaa; *s.* kumarrus; ~ *assent* kumartaa myöntymyksen merkiksi; *a* ~*ing acquaintance* hyvän päivän tuttava; ~*ed down with care* huolten painama.

bow 2. [bau] *s.* kokka, keula (us. *pl.*); (m. ~-*man*, ~ *oar*) keulasoutaja.

bow 3. [bəu] *s.* kaari, jousi (m. viulun-); nauharuusuke, solmuke, rusetti (~-*tie*); *v.* käsitellä jousta; ~-*window* kaari-ikkuna; *draw the long* ~ suurennella; *within the sound of B*~ *bells* Lontoon Cityssä.

bowdlerize ['baudləraiz] *v.* siivota (tekstiä), sensuroida (turhanpäiten).

bowe

bowel ['bauəl] s. suoli; ~s suolisto; sisus: *have your* ~*s moved?* onko vatsa toiminut?

bower ['bauə] s. lehtimaja, (run.) budoaari, (neitsyt)kammio.

bowie ['bəui] s.: ~-*knife* pitkä metsästyspuukko.

bowl 1. [bəul] s. malja, kulho, piipun pesä; syvänne, syvennys.

bowl 2. [bəul] s. pallo, kuula; *pl.* nurmikeilapeli; *v.* keilata; ~ *along* vieriä; *was* ~*ed out* paloi (pelissä); ~ .. *over* saattaa aivan ymmälle.

bow-legged ['bəu-] *a.* vääräsäärinen.

bowl|er ['bəulə] s. knalli (hattu); keilaaja. **-ing** s. keilailu; (~-*alley* keilarata; ~-*green* keilakenttä).

bow|man [bəu-] jousimies: **-sprit** [bəu-] kaari-ikkuna. ~-**wow** ['bau'wau] *int.* hau-hau; s. »hauva».

box 1. [bɔks] s. puksipuu.

box 2. [bɔks] s. laatikko, rasia, lipas (m. televisio); aitio; osasto (ravintolassa ym); pilttuu, karsina; ajajan istuin; *shooting* ~ metsästysmaja; ~ *office* teatterin lippumyymälä; ~ *off* erottaa väliseinällä; ~ *up* sulkea sisään t. ahtaalle.

box 3. [bɔks] *v.* nyrkkeillä; lyödä; *s.:* ~ *on the ear* korvapuusti.

boxing ['bɔksiŋ] s. nyrkkeily; ~-*weights* nyrkkeilysarjat.

boxing-day tapaninpäivä.

box|-pleat vastalaskos. **-wood** puksipenaus.

boy [bɔi] s. poika; (esim. musta) palvelija; [*oh*] ~ *!* voi veljet! ~ *friend* poikaystävä; ~ *scout* partiopoika. **-hood** s. poikaikä. **-ish** [iʃ] *a.* poikamainen.

boycott ['bɔikɔt] *v.* boikotoida; s. boikotti.

bra [brɑ:] s. (lyh.) rintaliivit.

brace [breis] s. tuki, pönkkä, sidehirsi; poranvarsi; hakanen; pari; *pl.* housunkannattimet; (jalan) tukisidos; hammasraudat (kiinteä oikomislaite); *v.* yhdistää; tukea, vahvistaa; piristää (us. ~ *up);* jännittää; ~ *oneself up* koota voimansa; *bracing air* piristävä ilma. **-let** [-lit] s. rannerengas.

bracken ['bræk(ə)n] s. sananjalka; imarre.

bracket ['brækit] s. (hyllyn, seinälampun) pidin, kannatin, olkakivi, konsoli; *pl.* hakaset, sulkeet; *v.* panna hakasiin; *income* ~ tuloluokka.

brackish ['brækiʃ] *a.* suolapitoinen.

bract [brækt] s. suojuslehti (kasv.)

brad [bræd] s. naula, nasta.

Bradshaw ['brædʃɔ:] *erisn.;* aikataulu (rautat.).

brae [brei] s. (Skotl.) rinne.

brag [bræg] *v.* kerskua; s. kerskailu. **-gart** ['brægət] s. kerskailija.

Brahmin ['brɑ:min] s. bramiini.

braid [breid] s. (koriste)punos, nyöri, palmikko; *v.* punoa; palmikoida.

braille [breil] s. sokeainkirjoitus.

brain [brein] s. aivot; *pl.* äly, (hyvä) pää; *v.* murskata *(a p.* jnk pää); *rack one's* ~ *s* vaivata päätään; ~ *s trust* aivotrusti; ~ *drain* aivovuoto; ~ *wave* neronleimaus, loistava aate. ~-**fag** (aivojen) väsymys. **-less** *a.* älytön. ~-**pan** pääkoppa. **-storm:** ~*ing session* aivoriihi. **-washing** s. aivopesu. **-y** [-i] *a.* hyväpäinen, nokkela.

braise [breiz] *v.* muhentaa.

brake 1. [breik] s. tiheikkö; *m.* = *bracken.*

brake 2. [breik] s. pellavaloukku; *v.* loukuttaa.

brake 3. [breik] s. jarru *v.* jarruttaa; *put on (apply) the* ~ *s* jarruttaa. **-(s)man** jarrumies.

bramble ['bræmbl] s. okainen pensas; karhunvatukka.

bran [bræn] s. leseet.

branch [brɑ:n(t)ʃ] s. oksa; haara; ala; haaraliike, -konttori, -rata; *v.* haarautua (us. ~ *forth, out);* ~ *line* sivurata.

brand [brænd] s. polttorauta; polttomerkki, merkki; tavaramerkki; laatu; palava puunkappale, (kuv.) kekäle, soihtu; *v.* merkitä polttomerkillä, (kuv.) leimata; *is* ~ *ed on my memory* on painunut lähtemättömästi mieleeni **-ing-iron** poltinrauta. **-ish** [-iʃ] *v.* heiluttaa (miekkaa ym). ~-**new** uuden uutukainen.

brandy ['brændi] s. konjakki.

brash [bræʃ] *a.* röyhkeä, äkkipikainen.

brass [brɑ:s] s. messinki; pronssi; vaski;

hävyttömyys; raha; *the* ~ (mus.)
torvet; ~ *band* torvisoittokunta; ~
hat (sl.) korkea upseeri; *get down to* ~
tacks tulla itse asiaan. **-y** [-i] *a.*
messinginkaltainen; häpeämätön,
hävytön.

brassard [bræ'sɑ:d] *s.* käsivarsinauha.

brassière ['bræsiə, Am. brə'ziə] *s.*
rintaliivit (lyh. *bra*).

brat [bræt] *s.* lapsi, kakara.

bravado [brə'vɑ:dəu] *s.* uhmailu,
uhkarohkeus.

brave [breiv] *a.* uljas, urhoollinen,
rohkea; *v.* uhmata; kohdata
rohkeasti. **-ry** [-əri] *s.* urheus,
rohkeus.

bravo ['brɑ:vəu] *int.* hyvä; *s.* (pl. ~*(e)s*)
hyvä-huuto; palkattu murhaaja t.
kätyri.

brawl [brɔ:l] *s.* meteli, rähinä; *v.*
rähistä, metelöidä.

brawn [brɔ:n] *s.* lihakset; (ei Am.)
painosyltty. **-y** [-i] *a.* lihaksekas.

bray [brei] *s.* (aasin) kiljunta; räminä;
v. kiljua; rämistä.

braz|e [breiz] *v.* juottaa yhteen
(messinki- ja sinkkiseoksella). **-en** [-n]
a. messinki-; häpeämätön, röyhkeä
(m. ~*-faced*); ~ *it out* ajaa röyhkeästi
läpi (asia). **-ier** [-iə] *s.* vaskenvalaja;
hiilipannu.

Brazil [brə'zil] *erisn.* Brasilia; ~*-nut*
paara-pähkinä. **-ian** [-jən] *s. & a.*
brasilialainen.

breach [bri:tʃ] *s.* rikkominen; välien
rikkoutuminen; aukko,
läpimurto(kohta), murtuma; *v.*
murtaa (aukko jhk); ~ *of the peace*
yleisen järjestyksen rikkominen; ~ *of
promise* aviolupauksen rikkominen;
[*throw oneself into*] *the* ~ taistelun
tuoksinaan.

bread [bred] *s.* leipä; ~ *and butter*
voileipä. **-crumb** leivänmuru,
korppujauhe. **-fruit** leipäpuun
hedelmä. **-stuffs** vilja, jauhot.

breadth [bredθ] *s.* leveys; ~ *of mind*
avartuneisuus.

breadwinner *s.* perheenhuoltaja.

break [breik] *broke broken, v.* murtaa,
rikkoa, särkeä; taittaa, katkaista;
keskeyttää; raivata; musertaa; saattaa
vararikkoon, räjäyttää (pankki),
tuhota; kesyttää, opettaa (hevonen);

erottaa; murtua, särkyä, mennä rikki
t. poikki; murtautua, tunkeutua;
puhjeta, koittaa; muuttua; (pilvistä)
hajaantua; *s.* murtuminen, murtuma,
aukko; keskeytys, tauko; muutos;
mahdollisuus; päivänkoitto (~ *of
day);* ~ *sb. (oneself) of a habit*
vieroittaa (päästä jstk) tavasta; *his
voice is beginning to* ~ hän saa pian
äänenmurroksen; ~ *even* ks. *even;* ~
loose riuhtaista itsensä irti; ~ *new
ground* raivata maata; ~ *the* [*bad*]
news to ilmoittaa uutinen
hienovaraisesti jklle; ~ *away*
riistäytyä irti; ~ *down* rikkoa, murtaa;
joutua epäkuntoon, särkyä, sortua,
murtua romahtaa; jakaa, eritellä;
jakautua; hajota; ~ *in* murtautua
sisään; puuttua (keskusteluun);
harjoittaa, opettaa (hevonen); ~ *into*
murtautua jhk, puhjeta (nauruun
ym); ~ *off* katkaista, katketa,
keskeyttää; purkaa; ~ *out* puhjeta,
syttyä; *through* murtautua jnk läpi; ~
up hajottaa, hajaantua, hajota,
lopettaa; mennä pirstaleiksi, (jäistä)
lähteä; *school* ~ *s up* loma alkaa; ~
with sb. riitaantua jkn kanssa; *without
a* ~ taukoamatta; *tea* ~ teetauko; *a
lucky* ~ onnenpotkaus; *a clean* ~
(puhek.) täysosuma. **-able** [-əbl] *a.*
särkyvä. **-age** [-idʒ] *s.* särkyminen.
-down (hermo)romahdus; konerikko,
(liikenne- ym) häiriö. **-er** [-ə] *s.*
hyökyaalto; *pl.* tyrskyt. **-fast**
['brekfəst] *s.* aamiainen; *v.* syödä
aamiaista (m. *have* ~). **-neck**
hengenvaarallinen. **-through**
läpimurto. **~-up** hajoaminen;
välirikko; (koulun) päättäjäiset.
-water aallonmurtaja.

bream [bri:m] *s.* lahna.

breast [brest] *s.* rinta; (puvun)
etupuoli, rinnus; (kuv.) sydän; *v.*
ponnistella (aaltoja ym) vastaan,
kohdata rohkeasti; *make a clean* ~ *of*
tunnustaa täysin. ~*-plate*
rintahaarniska. **-stroke** rintauinti.
-work rintavarustus.

breath [breθ] *s.* hengitys; henkäys;
hengenveto, henki; *draw* ~ vetää
henkeä, hengittää; *catch* (*hold*) *one's*
~ pidättää henkeään; *waste one's* ~
tuhlata sanojaan turhaan; *take sb.'s* ~

away hämmästyttää jku sanattomaksi; *take a deep* ~ hengittää syvään; [*they cannot be mentioned*] *in the same* ~ samassa hengenvedossa, yhtaikaa; *out of* ~ hengästynyt; *under one's* ~ kuiskaamalla. **-alyzer** [-əlaizə] *s.:* ~ *test* puhallustesti.

breathe [bri:ð] *v.* hengittää; vetää henkeä, levähtää; huokua, puhaltaa; lausua (hiljaa), hiiskua; antaa (hevosen ym) levätä; ~ *one's last* vetää viimeinen henkäyksensä. **-r** *s.:* go for a ~ mennä kävelylenkille.

breathing ['bri:ðiŋ] *s.* hengitys. **~-space** hengähdysaika.

breath|**less** ['breθlis] *a.* hengästynyt; hiiskumaton, henkeä salpaava. **~-taking** henkeä salpaava.

bred [bred] *imp. & pp.* ks. *breed*.

breech [bri:tʃ] *s.* (ampuma-aseen) sulkukappale, lukko, (putken) perä. **-es** ['britʃiz] *pl.* polvihousut; *she wears the* ~ hän on se, joka määrää. **~-loader** takaa ladattava ampuma-ase.

breed [bri:d] *bred bred v.* siittää; synnyttää, aiheuttaa; kasvattaa, jalostaa (karjan); siitä, syntyä; lisääntyä; *s.* rotu, laji; *well-bred* hyvin kasvatettu, kultivoitu. **-ing** *s.* kasvattaminen; (hieno) kasvatus, hyvä käytös, sivistys.

breeze 1. [bri:z] *s.* paarma.

breez|**e 2.** [bri:z] *s.* vieno tuuli, tuulenhenki, tuulenvire; kina; ~ *in*[*to*] piipahtaa. **-y** [-i] *a.* tuulinen; raikas, vilkas.

Bren *gun* kevyt konekivääri.

brent (-goose) *s.* sepelhanhi.

brethren ['breðrən] *s. pl.* (ks. *brother*) veljet (kuv.)

Breton ['bretn] *s. & a.* bretagnelainen.

brev|**et** ['brevit] *s.* upseerin valtakirja (joka sisältää arvonkorotuksen ilman palkkaa). **-iary** ['bri:viəri] *s.* katol. messukirja. **-ity** [-i] *s.* lyhyys, lyhytaikaisuus.

brew [bru:] *v.* panna (olutta), valmistaa (teetä), hautua; valmistella, hautoa; *s.* juoma; *be* ~*ing* olla tulossa t. tekeillä, hankkia. **-er** [-ə] *s.* oluenpanija. **-ery** ['bruəri] *s.* olutpanimo.

briar ['braiə] *s.* = *brier*; ~ *pipe*

briaaripiippu.

bribe [braib] *s.* lahjus; *v.* lahjoa. **-ry** [-əri] *s.* lahjonta.

bric-a-brac ['brikəbræk] *s.* (joutava) korutavara.

brick [brik] *s.* tiili(kivi); laatta, levy; rakennuspalikka; reilu ihminen, kaveri; *v.* muurata umpeen (m. ~ *up*); *drop a* ~ munata (itsensä). **~-field**, **~-yard** tiilitehdas. **~-kiln** tiiliuuni. **-layer** muurari. **-work** tiilirakenne, muuraus.

bridal [braidl] *a.* morsius-, hää-.

bride [braid] *s.* morsian, nuorikko. **-groom** sulhanen, vastanainut mies. **-smaid** morsiusneito.

bridge 1. [bridʒ] *s.* silta; komentosilta; (nenän) varsi; (viulun) talla; *v.* rakentaa silta, olla siltana (jnk yli). **-head** sillanpää(asema).

bridge 2. [bridʒ] *s.* bridge-peli.

bridle ['braidl] *s.* suitset, ohjakset; *v.* suitsittaa; pitää aisoissa, hillitä; ~ *up* nostaa nokkaansa. **~-path** ratsastuspolku.

brief [bri:f] *a.* lyhyt, lyhytaikainen; suppea; (lak.) lyhyt kirjallinen selonteko, kirjelmä; *v.* antaa tarkat ohjeet t. tiedot (asianajalle), esittää tilannetiedotus (esim. ennen kokousta); *pl.:* ~*s* pikkupöksyt; *in* ~ lyhyesti sanoen; *hold a* ~ *for* edustaa jkta oikeudessa, puhua jkn puolesta. **-case** salkku. **-ing** *s.* ohjeiden (t. käskyjen) jako. **-ly** *adv.* lyhyesti (sanoen). **-ness** *s.* lyhyys.

brier ['braiə] *s.* orjantappurapensas; kellokanerva, ks. *briar*.

brig [brig] *s.* priki (mer.)

brigad|**e** [bri'geid] *s.* prikaati. **-ier** [brigə'diə] *s.* prikaatinkomentaja.

brigand ['brigənd] *s.* (maantie)rosvo.

bright [brait] *a.* loistava, kirkas, valoisa, kiiltävä; eloisa, vilkas, hilpeä, iloinen; älykäs; *adv.* kirkkaasti (m. ~*ly*). **-en** [-n] *v.* tehdä valoisammaksi, valaista, kirkastaa; tehdä iloiseksi; kirkastua, ilostua, piristyä (m. ~ *up*). **-ness** *s.* loisto, valo(isuus), kirkkaus, eloisuus jne.

Bright's disease [braits di'zi:z] *s.* munuaistulehdus.

brill [bril] *s.* silokampela.

brillian|**ce** ['briljəns], **-cy** [-ənsi] *s.*

loisto, loiste. **-t** [-ənt] *a.* säihkyvä, loistava, säteilevä; nerokas, huippuälykäs; *s.* briljantti.
brim [brim] *s.* reuna; lieri; *v.* olla ääriään myöten täynnä; ~ *over* vuotaa yli reunojen. **-ful** *a.* ääriään myöten täynnä (oleva), tulvillaan, piripintaan täytetty.
brimstone ['brimstən] *s.* tulikivi, rikki.
brindled ['brindld] *a.* kailava, juovikas.
brine [brain] *s.* suolavesi.
bring [brin] *brought brought, v.* tuoda, tuoda mukanaan; saada aikaan, aiheuttaa; saada t. saattaa tekemään jtk; *I cannot ~ myself to do it* en saa sitä tehdyksi; ~ *about* aiheuttaa, saada aikaan; ~ *back* palauttaa mieleen; ~ *down* kaataa, syöstä maahan; alentaa (hintaa); ~ *down the house* (teatt.) saada myrskyisät suosionosoitukset; ~ *forth* synnyttää; aiheuttaa; ~ *forward* esittää, siirtää (kirjanp.); ~ *home to* vakuuttaa, tehdä selväksi; ~ *off* saattaa onnelliseen päätökseen; ~ *on* tuoda mukanaan, aiheuttaa; ~ *out* tuoda esille; esittää; julkaista; ~ *over* käännyttää; ~ *round* virvoittaa; kääntää, saada jku muuttamaan mielensä; ~ *through* saada paranemaan; ~ *to a close (an end)* saattaa päätökseen; ~ *to mind* palauttaa mieleen; ~ *to pass* saada aikaan; ~ *under* kukistaa; ~ *up* kasvattaa; antaa ylen; esittää (keskusteltavaksi); ottaa (uudelleen) esille; pysähdyttää äkkiä; ~ *up the rear* olla jälkijoukkona. **-ing** *s.* : ~ *up* kasvatus.
brink [brink] *s.* parras, äyräs; törmä; *on the ~ of* jnk partaalla. **-manship** *s.* (sodan partaalle vievä) jäykkäniskainen politiikka.
briny ['braini] *a.* suolainen.
brisk [brisk] *a.* ripeä, reipas, terhakka; raikas; vilkas (kauppa ym); ~ *up* vilkastuttaa, -tua.
brisket ['briskit] *s.* (teuraan) rinta.
bristl|e [brisl] *s.* harjas; *v.* olla pystyssä; nostaa pystyyn (harjakset); olla täynnä, kihistä (*with* jtk); ~ *up* tuimistua, ärhennellä. **-y** *a.* harjaksinen.
Britain ['britn] *s.* Britannia.

British ['britiʃ] *a.* brittiläinen; *the ~* britit. **-er** [-ə] *s.* britti (Am. ym).
Briton ['britn] *s.* britti.
Brittany ['britəni] *erisn.* Bretagne.
brittle ['britl] *a.* hauras.
broach [brəutʃ] *v.* puhkaista, avata (tynnyri); ottaa puheeksi; ~ *to* kääntyä (kääntää laiva) poikittain tuuleen.
broad [brɔːd] *a.* leveä, laaja, avara; suvaitsevainen; selvä, täysi; yleis-; karkea; *s.* sl. hempukka, naikkonen; *adv.* : *speak ~* puhua leveää murretta; *in ~ daylight* keskellä kirkasta päivää; *in ~ outline* pääpiirtein, karkeasti hahmotellen; ~ *sowing* hajakylvö; *sow ~* kylvää sirotellemalla. **-cast** *v.* (ks. *cast*) radioida; *s.* radiolähetys, -puhe, -esitelmä. **-caster** radiotoimittaja, -selostaja. **-cloth** hieno, musta verka. **-en** [-n] *v.* levittää; levitä, laajeta. **-ly** *adv.* : ~ *speaking* suurin piirtein, yleisesti ottaen. **~-minded** suvaitsevainen, vapaamielinen. **-ness** *s.* leveys. **-side** laivan kylki; täyslaita (sot.). **-sword** lyömämiekka. **-tail** breitschwanz (nahka).
brocade [brə'keid] *s.* brokadi.
broccoli ['brɔkəli] *s.* parsakaali.
brochure ['brəuʃjuə, -'ʃuə] *s.* (esittely)lehtinen, esite, brosyyri.
brogue [brəug] *s.* paksupohjainen urheilukenkä; irlanninvoittoinen englannin kieli.
broil 1. [brɔil] *s.* riita, meteli; *v.* rähinöidä.
broil 2. [brɔil] *v.* pariloida; paahtaa. **-er** [-ə] *s.* broileri, herkkukananpoika.
broke [brəuk] *imp.* ks. *break*; rahaton, »auki» *(stony~)*; ~ *paper* hylkypaperi.
broken ['brəuk(ə)n] *pp.* ks. *break; a.* rikkonainen, särkynyt, murtunut jne; katkonainen, epävarma; huono, vieraanvoittoinen *(~ English)*. **~-hearted** *a.* murtunut.
broker ['brəukə] *s.* kaupanvälittäjä, meklari. **-age** [-ridʒ] *s.* välityspalkkio.
broking ['brəukiŋ] *s.* meklarin ammatti, välitys.
brolly ['brɔli] *s.* = *umbrella*.
brom|ide ['brəumaid] *s.* bromidi. **-ine** [-i(:)n] *s.* bromi.

bronch|ial ['brɒŋkiəl] *a.*
keuhkoputken-. **-itis** [-'kaitis] *s.*
keuhkoputken tulehdus,
keuhkokatarri. **-us** ['brɒŋk|əs] *s.* (pl. *-i*
[-ai]) keuhkoputki.

bronco ['brɒŋkəu] *s.* (villi) hevonen.

bronze [brɒnz] *s.* pronssi; pronssikuva,
-esine, -väri; *v.* värjätä
pronssinväriseksi, pronssata;
päivettää.

brooch [brəutʃ] *s.* rintaneula.

brood [bru:d] *s.* pesue, poikue; (halv.)
jälkeläiset; *v.* hautoa (kuv. ~ *on,
over);* ~ hen hautomakana.

brook 1. [bruk] *s.* puro.

brook 2. [bruk] *v.* sietää (kielt.
lauseessa).

broom [bru:m] *s.* luuta; kultavihma;
jänönpapu. **-stick** luudanvarsi.

broth [brɒθ] *s.* lihaliemi.

brothel ['brɒθl] *s.* bordelli, ilotalo,
porttola.

brother ['brʌðə] *s.* (pl. *-s*, harv. *brethren*
ks. t.) veli; lähimmäinen; ~ *s and
sisters* sisarukset; ~ *s in arms*
aseveikot, sotakaverit. **~-in-law**
lanko. **-hood** *s.* veljeys; veljeskunta.
-ly *a.* veljellinen, veljen.

brougham ['bru(:)əm] *s.* umpivaunut.

brought [brɔ:t] *imp. & pp.* ks. **bring**.

brouhaha ['bru:hɑ:hɑ:] *s.* kohu, hälinä.

brow [brau] *s.* kulmakarva (tav. *pl.);*
otsa; (vuoren) harja; *knit one's* ~ *s*
rypistää kulmiaan (otsaansa). **-beat**
(ks. *beat)* sortaa, tyrannisoida.

brown [braun] *a.* ruskea,
tummaihoinen; *s.* ruskea väri; *v.*
ruskistaa, ruskettua; ~ *bread*
kokojyväleipä; *in a* ~ *study*
mietteisiin vaipunut; ~ *sugar*
fariinisokeri. **-ie** [-i] *s.* tonttu (m.
partiotyttö).

browse [brauz] *v.* jyrsiä, laiduntaa, olla
laitumella; lueskella.

Bruges [bru:ʒ] *erisn.* Brugge.

Bruin ['bru(:)in] *s.* mesikämmen,
Nalle.

bruise [bru:z] *s.* ruhjevamma,
kolhaisuvamma, mustelma; *v.* ruhjoa,
lyödä mustelmille.

brunch [brʌn(t)ʃ] *s.* Am. aamulounas.

brunette [bru:'net] *s.* tummaverikkö.

Brunswick ['brʌnzwik] *erisn.* Braun-
schweig; ~ *line* Hannoverin suku.

brunt [brʌnt] *s.* kovin isku; *bear the* ~
of the battle olla kuumimmassa
tulessa.

brush [brʌʃ] *s.* harja, sivellin; (ketun
ym) häntä; ottelu; pensaikko; *v.*
harjata; sipaista; ~ *aside* sivuuttaa
kevyesti; ~ *by (past)* pyyhkäistä ohi;
~ *up* elvyttää, verestää (tietoja);
siisti(yty)ä. **-wood** p nsaikko,
aluskasvillisuus. **~-work** (taiteilijan)
sivellintekniikka.

brusque [bru:sk]*a.* töykeä, jyrkkä,
tyly.

Brussels ['brʌslz] *erisn.* Bryssel; ~
sprouts ruusukaali.

brutal ['bru:tl] *a.* eläimellinen; raaka,
petomainen. **-ity** [bru:'tæliti] *s.*
petomaisuus, raakuus. **-ize** [-əlaiz] *v.*
tehdä petomaiseksi, raaistaa.

brut|e [bru:t] *a.* eläimellinen; järjetön;
raaka; *s.* järjetön luontokappale;
elukka, raaka ihminen. **-ish** [-iʃ] *a.*
eläimellinen, raaka, epäinhimillinen.

bryony ['braiəni] *s.* koirannauris.

bubble ['bʌbl] *s.* kupla; tyhjä
kuvitelma; *v.* poreilla, pulppuilla,
pulputa; ~ *-gum* palapurukumi.

bubonic [bju:'bɒnik] *a.:* ~ *plague*
paiserutto.

buccaneer [bʌkə'niə] *s.* merirosvo.

Buchan ['bʌkn], **-an** [bju(:)'kænən]
erisn.

Bucharest [bju:kə'rest] *erisn.*

buck [bʌk] *s.* uroskauris, -poro, -jänis
ym; pukki; keikari; Am. sl. dollari;
v.: (hevosesta) hypätä pukkihyppy; ~
[*at]* vastustaa; ~ *up* piristää, rohkaista
(mielensä); *pass the* ~ *to* (sl.) sysätä
vastuu jklle. **-ed** [-t] *a.* rohkaistunut.

bucket ['bʌkit] *s.* sanko, ämpäri;
(tekn.) kauha, ämpäri; *kick
the* ~ potkaista tyhjää, kuolla
kupsahtaa. **~-shop** nurkkatoimisto
(osakekeinottelua varten).

Buckingham ['bʌkiŋəm] *erisn.*

buckle ['bʌkl] *s.* solki; *v.* kiinnittää
soljella; taipua, käyristyä, -tää; ~
[*down] to* ryhtyä (innokkaasti) jhk;
~ *d* m. vääntynyt, lommoinen. **-r** [-ə]
s. (pieni, pyöreä) kilpi.

buckram ['bʌkrəm] *s.* jäykistekangas.

buck|shot karkeat haulit. **-skin** pukin-,
kauriinnahka; *pl.* nahkahousut.
-wheat tattari (kasv.).

bucolic [bju(:)'kɔlik] *a.* maalais-, paimen-; *s.* paimenruno.

bud [bʌd] *s.* nuppu, umppu, silmu; *v.* olla nupulla; kehittyä, puhjeta; ympätä; *in ~* nupullaan; *nip in the ~* tukahduttaa alkuunsa; *~ding* nupullaan, kehittymässä oleva.

Budapest ['bu:də'pest] *erisn.*

Buddh|a [buda] *erisn.* **-ism** ['budizm] *s.* budhalaisuus. **-ist** ['budist] *s.* budhalainen.

buddy ['bʌdi] *s.* Am. kaveri.

budge [bʌdʒ] *v.* liikahtaa, hievahtaa paikaltaan; saada hievahtamaan. **-rigar** [-ərigə:] *s.* (lyh. budg|e, -y) undulaatti, laulupapukaija.

budget ['bʌdʒit] *s.* tulo- ja menoarvio, talousarvio; *v.: ~ for* ottaa mukaan tulo- ja menoarvioon. **-ary** [-əri] *a.* budjetti-.

Buenos Aires ['bwenəs'ai(ə)riz] *erisn.*

buff [bʌf] *s.* (himmeänkeltainen) nahka; ruskeankeltainen väri; jnk alan intoilija; *v.* kiillottaa (säämiskällä); *stripped to the ~* ikosen alasti. **-alo** [-ələu] *s.* puhveli; biisoni.

buffer ['bʌfə] *s.* puskuri (m. kem.); *old ~* vanha hupsu.

buffet 1. ['bʌfit] *s.* isku; *v.* lyödä, iskeä, kolhaista; taistella (jtk vastaan).

buffet 2. ['bʌfit] *s.* astiakaappi, sivupöytä; ['bufei, Am. bə'fei] tarjoilu(pöytä); seisoma-, seisova(pöytä); *~ banquet* seisomaillallinen.

buffoon [bʌ'fu:n] *s.* ilveilijä; *v.* ilvehtiä. **-ery** [-əri] *s.* karkea pila, pelleily.

bug [bag *s.* lude; (leik.) itikka; Am. hyönteinen; (puhek.) basilli; *v.* piilottaa mikrofoni (ym); *(~ a room)* sijoittaa, asentaa (huoneeseen) salakuuntelulaitteet; sl. kiusata; *big ~* pomo, pamppu; *the collecting ~* keräilykärpänen.

bugaboo ['bʌgəbu:] *s.* = seur.

bugbear ['bʌgbeə] *s.* mörkö.

bugger ['bʌgə] *s.* (kuv.) kiusankappale, vintiö *(you little ~!); v.: ~ off!* painu tiehesi!

buggy ['bʌgi] *s.* kevyet rattaat.

bugle ['bju:gl] *s.* merkkitorvi; *v.* toitottaa; *~s* pitkänomaiset lasihelmet. **-r** [-ə] *s.* torvensoittaja.

build [bild] *built built, v.* rakentaa,

pystyttää; muodostaa *(~ a new government); s.* rakenne; ruumiinrakenne; *~ up* muurata umpeen; luoda, kehittää; *~ upon* perustaa, luottaa jhk. **-er** [-ə] *s.* rakennusmestari. **-ing** *s.* rakennus.

built [bilt] *imp. & pp.* ks. *build; solidly ~* hyvin rakennettu; *~-in* seinään upotettu; *~-up area* taajama.

bulb [bʌlb] *s.* (kukka)sipuli; (mittarin)kuula, pullistuma; *electric ~* hehkulamppu. **-ous** [-əs] *a.* sipulinmuotoinen.

Bulgaria [bʌl'gɛəriə] *erisn.* **-n** [-n] *a. & s.* bulgarialainen.

bulge [bʌldʒ] *s.* pullistuma; *v.* työntyä esiin, pullistua; *bulging* (esiin)pullistuva.

bulk [bʌlk *s.* (jnk) suurin osa, pääosa; massa, määrä; koko; lasti; *break ~* purkaa lastia; *in ~* summassa; *~ large in sb.'s eyes* näyttää jkn silmissä suurelta; *~ buying* tukkuosto. **-head** *s.* laipio; väliseinä. **-y** [-i] *a.* iso, tilaa vievä.

bull 1. [bul] *s.* (paavin) bulla.

bull 2. [bul] *s.* sonni, härkä, koiras; (nousuhinnoilla keinotteleva) pörssikeinottelija; *John B~* englantilainen.

bullace ['bulis] *s.* kriikuna.

bull|-dog buldogi. **-doze** raivata; pakottaa (pelottelemalla). **-dozer** raivaustraktori.

bullet ['bulit] *s.* luoti, kuula; *~-proof* luodinkestävä. **-in** [-in] *s.* (virallinen) tiedonanto.

bull|fight härkätaistelu; *(~er* härkätaistelija). **-finch** punatulkku. **-headed** härkäpäinen.

bullion ['buljən] *s.* kulta t. hopea (harkkoina).

bullock ['bulək] *s.* härkä.

bullring härkätaisteluareena.

bull's-eye *s.* (maalitaulun) keskus; pieni pyöreä ikkuna.

bully ['buli] *s.* tyranni, päälläpäsmäri; *v.* sortaa, tyrannisoida, simputtaa, pelotella. **-ing** *s.* pelottelu.

bulrush ['bulrʌʃ] *s.* kaisla; osmankäämi.

bulwark ['bulwək] *s.* vallitus; suoja, turva; (laivan) parras.

bum [bʌm] s. hulttio, maankiertäjä, pummi; »peppu», takapuoli; a. kehno; v. sl. lainailla; ~ around maleksia, viettää kulkurin elämää.

bumble-bee ['bʌmblbi:] s. kimalainen.

bump [bʌmp] s. törmäys, kolahdus; kuhmu; v. törmätä, kolahtaa; ~ of locality paikallisvaisto; ~ off (sl.) panna päiviltä; ~ along the road ajaa täryyttää, töyssytellä. **-er** [-ə] s. täysi lasillinen, runsas (sato).

bumpkin ['bʌm(p)kin] s. maalaistollo.

bumptious ['bʌm(p)ʃəs] a. pöyhkeä, koppava.

bumpy ['bʌmpi] a. kuoppainen, tärskyttävä.

bun [bʌn] s. rusinapulla; hiussykerö.

bunch [bʌn(t)ʃ] s. kimppu; terttu; ryhmä, joukko; v. sitoa kimpuksi; ~ of keys avainnippu.

bundle ['bʌndl] s. mytty, nyytti, käärö, kimppu; v. sulloa t. kääriä mytyksi, kääriä kokoon (~ up); sulloa (esim. autoon); [they] ~d off menivät matkoihinsa, lähtivät tiehensä.

bung [bʌŋ] s. tappi, tulppa; v. sulkea tulpalla, tukkia; ~ed up tukossa.

bungalow ['bʌŋgələu] s. (yksikerroksinen) huvila.

bungle ['bʌŋgl] v. hutiloida, pilata, tunaroida, toheloida; s. tunarointi, tohelointi. **-r** [-ə] poropeukalo, patustaja.

bunion ['bʌnjən] s. vaivaisenluu.

bunk 1. [bʌŋk] s. makuulavitsa, kerrossänky (~ beds); = bunkum.

bunk 2. [bʌŋk] v. karata, luikkia (m. do a ~).

bunker ['bʌŋkə] s. hiilisäiliö (laivassa); este (golfpelissä); (sot.) bunkkeri; v. hiilestää.

bunkum ['bʌŋkəm] s. hölynpöly, palturi.

bunny ['bʌni] s. kani; pupu.

bunting 1. ['bʌntiŋ] s. sirkku.

bunting 2. ['bʌntiŋ] s. lippukangas.

Bunyan ['bʌnjən] erisn.

buoy [bɔi] s. poiju; v. pitää pinnalla; pitää yllä (toivoa ym) (us. ~ up); viitoittaa poijuilla. **-ancy** [-ənsi] s. nostovoima; keveys, joustavuus. **-ant** [-ənt] a. uiva, kelluva; eloisa, joustava, iloinen; (hinnoista) (optimistisen) vakaa.

bur, burr [bə:] s. takertuva siemen; takiainen (m. kuv.); (hammaslääkärin ym) pora.

burberry ['bə:bəri] s. eräänl. sadetakki.

burble [bə:bl] v. pulputa; leperrellä.

burbot ['bə:bət] s. made.

burden ['bə:dn] s. kuorma, taakka; laivan kantavuus; kertosäe; pääsisällys; v. kuormittaa; painaa, rasittaa. **-some** a. raskas; rasittava.

burdock ['bə:dɔk] s. takiainen.

bureau ['bjuərəu] s. (pl. -x [-z] toimisto; kirjoituslipasto. **-cracy** [-'rɔkrəsi] s. virkavalta. **-crat** ['bjuərə(u)kræt] s. byrokraatti. **-cratic** [bjuərə(u)'krætik] a. byrokraattinen, virkavaltainen.

burg [bə:g] s. Am. ark. kaupunki.

burgeon ['bə:dʒn] v. versoa.

burg|ess ['bə:dʒis] s. porvari. **-h** ['bʌrə] s. = borough. **-her** ['bə:gə] s. porvari (ei Engl.)

burgl|ar ['bə:glə] s. murtovaras; ~ alarm murtohälytyslaite. **-arious** [bə:'glɛəriəs] a. (sisään)murto-. **-ary** [-ri] s. murtovarkaus. **-e** ['bə:gl] v. murtautua jhk.

burgomaste [bə:gəmæstə] s. pormestari (Holl. ym.)

burgundy ['bə:g(ə)ndi] s. burgundinviini.

burial ['beriəl] s. hautajaiset; ~ service hautajaistoimitus. **~-ground** hautausmaa.

burin ['bjuərin] s. kaiverrin.

burke [bə:k] v. tukahduttaa, painaa villaisella.

burlap ['bə:ləp] s. säkkikangas.

burlesque [bə:'lesk] a. karkean koominen, irvokas; s. pilaileva kappale; v. tehdä ivamukailu.

burly ['bə:li] a. tukeva, vanttera.

Burm|a ['bə:mə] erisn. **-ese** [bə:'mi:z] a. & s. burmalainen.

burn 1. [bə:n] s. puro.

burn 2. [bən] burnt burnt (joskus ~ed ~ed) v. polttaa, palaa, hehkua; palaa t. polttaa pohjaan; s. palohaava; ~ down palaa, polttaa poroksi; ~ into syöpyä jhk; ~ out palaa loppuun; sth. up polttaa; ~ one's boats polttaa sillat takanaan. **-er** [-ə] s. poltin. **-ing** a. palava, hehkuva; (~-glass polttolasi).

burnish ['bə:niʃ] v. kiillottaa, hangata kiiltäväksi.

burnouse [bə:'nu:s] *s.* burnuusi, huppuviitta.

burnt [bə:nt] *imp. & pp.* ks. *burn*; ~ *offering* polttouhri.

burp [bə:p] *v.* röyhtäistä; röyhtäyttää (vauvaa).

burr [bə:] *s.* sorahdus, sorahtava r-äänne; takiainen ; (lääk.) pora; ks. *bur*.

burrow ['bʌrəu] *s.* kolo, pesä; *v.* kaivaa kolo(ja), möyriä; ~ *into* [*a mystery*] tutkia, kaivella jtk.

bursar ['bə:sə] *s.* rahastonhoitaja; stipendiaatti. **-y** [-ri] *s.* stipendi; (collegen) kassa.

burst [bə:st] *burst burst, v.* haljeta, särkyä; puhjeta; räjähtää; syöksähtää; särkeä, murtaa; *s.* halkeaminen jne.; räjähdys, purkaus, ryöppy; ~ *in, into* rynnätä jhk; ~ *into laughter* purskahtaa nauruun; ~ *out huudahtaa; puhjeta, pillahtaa (crying itkuun); ~ up* ks. *bust; I nearly ~ myself with laughter* olin haljeta (pakahtua) naurusta; ~ *of laughter* naurunpuuska; ~ *of thunder* ukkosen jyrähdys.

bury ['beri] *v.* haudata; kaivaa maahan; peittää; kätkeä; *buried in thought* ajatuksiin vaipunut.

bus [bʌs] *s.* bussi, linja-auto; sl. auto; *v.* kuljettaa bussilla, vrt. *busing: miss the ~* päästää käsistään tilaisuus.

busby ['bʌzbi] *s.* (husaarin) karvalakki.

bush [buʃ] *s.* pensas, pensaikko; (Austr., Afr.) erämaa, salomaa.

bushel ['buʃl] *s.* vakka (8 gallonaa = 36,34 l); *hide one's light under a ~* panna kynttilänsä vakan alle.

bush|**man** ['buʃmən] *s.* uudisasukas (Australian metsissä); B~ (Afr.) bušmanni, pensastolainen. **~-ranger** (australial.) metsärosvo. **-y** [-i] *s.* tuuhea.

busily *adv.:* [*she*] *was ~ engaged in packing* oli kiireisesti pakkaamassa.

business ['biznis] *s.* työ, toimi, asia; liike, -asia, -ala, -toimi; kauppa; ~ *address* toimipaikan osoite; ~ *hours* konttoriaika; ~ *research* suhdannetutkimus; *on ~* liikeasioissa; *a bad ~! ikävä juttu! no admittance except on ~* pääsy asiattomilta

kielletty; *do ~* käydä kauppaa; *get to ~* mennä asiaan; *mind your own ~* älä sekaannu minun asioihini; *that's no ~ of yours* asia ei kuulu sinuun; *it's a teacher's ~ to* opettajan asia(na) on; *I mean ~* puhun vakavissani. ~**-like** *a.* asiallinen, järjestelmällinen. **-man** liikemies.

busing *s.* (lasten) kouluunkuljetus.

busk [bʌsk] *s.* (kureliivin) lastikka.

buskin ['bʌskin] *s. s.* koturni.

busman *s.* bussinkuljettaja; ~ *'s holiday* arkityössä vietetty loma, työloma.

bust [bʌst] *s.* povi; rintakuva; *v.* sl. = *burst;* murskata; *go ~, ~ up* joutua vararikkoon, mennä nurin; *on the ~* hummaamassa. ~**-up** romahdus; riita.

bustard ['bʌstəd] *s.* trappi(lintu).

bustl|**e** ['bʌsl] *v.* touhuta, hyöriä; hääriä; hoputtaa; *s.* touhu, hyörinä, hälinä. **-ing** *a.* touhukas.

busy ['bizi] *a.* (*with, at* jtk) tekemässä, puuhassa (oleva): touhukas; vilkas(liikenteinen); *v.* askarruttaa; *I am very ~* minulla on kiire (t. paljon tekemistä); *I was ~ writing* olin kirjoittamassa; ~ *oneself with* (*in, at, about*) puuhata, toimittaa jtk; [*the line is*] ~ varattu. **-body** tunkeilija; touhuaja, hätikkö. **-ness** *s.* puuhakkuus, monet puuhat.

but [bʌt] *konj.* mutta; vaan; paitsi; kuin; *adv.* vain, ainoastaan; *prep.* paitsi, lukuunottamatta; *all ~* melkein; *I cannot ~ laugh* en voi olla nauramatta; ~ *for your help, I should have failed* ilman apuasi olisin epäonnistunut; *what could he do ~ agree* voiko hän muuta kuin suostua; *the last ~ one* viimeisen edellinen.

butane ['bju:tein] *s.* butaani.

butch [butʃ] *a.* lyhyeksileikattu; maskuliininen.

butcher ['butʃə] *s.* teurastaja, lihakauppias; *v.* murhata (julmalla tavalla); tärvellä. **-y** [-ri] *s.* teurastamo; teurastus (kuv.), verilöyly.

butler ['bʌtlə] *s.* (yksityistalouden) hovimestari.

butt 1. [bʌt] *s.* (iso) tynnyri.

butt 2. [bʌt] *s.* maalitalo (kuv.), ampumavalli; ~*s* ampumarata; ~ *of ridicule* pilan kohde.

butt 3. [bʌt] s. (aseen) paksu pää, tyvi, (pyssyn) perä; (savukkeen) pätkä, tumppi; ~ end tyvi(pää).

butt 4. [bʌt] v. puskea, töytäistä; syöksyä, (into jhk); ~ in sekaantua, puuttua keskusteluun.

butter [ˈbʌtə] s. voi; v. levittää voita (jnk päälle); ~ sb. up mielistellä; know on which side one's bread is ~ed tuntea oma etunsa. **-cup** leinikki. **-fly** (päivä)perhonen; ~ stroke perhosuinti. **-milk** kirnupiimä. **-scotch** toffee. **-y** [-ri] a. voinen; s. ruokasäiliö.

buttock [ˈbʌtək] s.: ~s pakarat, takapuoli.

button [ˈbʌtn] s. nappi, nuppi, nappula; v. napittaa (us. ~ up); ~ed up sulkeutunut; at the push (touch) of a ~ nappia painamalla; [this dress] ~s down the back. . -shaped on napitus (napit) takana. **-hook** s. nappikoukku. **-s** [-z] s. hotellipoika.

buttress [ˈbʌtris] s. tukipylväs, tuki; v. tukea.

buxom [ˈbʌksəm] a. tukeva, pulska.

buy [bai] bought bought, v. ostaa; hankkia (itselleen); s. ostos; ~ off ostaa t. lunastaa vapaaksi; ~ out lunastaa jkn osa (liikkeestä); ~ over lahjoa; ~ up ostaa kokonaan t. tyhjiin. **-er** [-ə] s. ostaja.

buzz [bʌz] v. surista, hyristä, humista; s. surina, sorina; ~ off painua tiehensä. ~ing in the ears korvien humina.

buzzard [ˈbʌzəd] s. hiirihaukka.

buzzer [ˈbʌzə] s. summeri; pilli.

by [ˈbai] prep. lähellä, vieressä, luona, kautta, ohi, ohitse, sivuun; kuluessa,

aikana; ilm. myös keinoa, välikappaletta, mittapuuta ym. (~ listening kuuntelemalla); the church was designed ~ . .on piirtänyt kirkon; lay (put) ~ panna sivuun; [he] was paid ~ the hour sai tuntipalkkaa; ~ day päivällä; ~ the dozen tusinoittain; ~ six o'clock kuuteen mennessä; ~ letter kirjeellisesti; ~ rail rautateitse; little ~ little vähitellen; ~ my honour kunniani kautta; ~ chance sattumalta; ~ far the best kaikkein paras; ~ himself yksinään; ~ name nimeltä; ~ the way sivumennen (sanoen); ~ and ~ ennen pitkää, vähitellen, myöhemmin; ~ and large yleisesti ottaen, suurin piirtein; ~ the ~ sivumennen.

bye [bai]; by the ~ sivumennen (sanoen); bye-bye hyvästi, hei hei! go to bye-byes mennä tutimaan.

by-election täytevaalit

bygone [ˈbaigɔn] a. mennyt, muinainen; s.: let ~s be ~s mikä on ollutta, se on mennyttä.

by-law, bye-law [ˈbailɔː] säännöt, säännöstö, (kunnallis)sääntö.

by-name pilkka-, lisänimi.

by-pass, bypass [ˈbaipɑːs] ohikulkutie; v. kiertää, johtaa jnk ohi; (kuv. m.) ohittaa, jättää huomiotta.

by-product s. sivutuote.

byre [baiə] s. navetta.

by-road s. sivutie.

Byron [ˈbaiər(ə)n] erisn.

bystander s. katselija.

byword s. sananparsi

Byzantine [biˈzæntain] a. & s. bysanttilainen.

C

C, c [si:] s. c-kirjain; nuotti c; Lyh.: **C.** ;(centum) sata, *centigrade* Celsiuksen; **c.** *cent, circa, cubic;* **ca.** *circa;* **Cal.** *California;* **Can.** *Canada;* **Cantab.** *Cantabrigian;* **caps.** *capitals* isoilla kirjaimilla; **Capt.** *Captain;* **CAT** *College of Advanded Technology* teknillinen opisto; **cf.** *confer* vertaa; **c.c.** (**cc.**) = *cu. cm.;* **ch., chap.** *chapter;* **Chron.** *Chronicles* Aikakirjat; **CIA** *Central Intelligence Agency* Yhdysvaltain keskustiedustelupalvelu; **C.I.D.** *Criminal Investigation Department* rikospoliisi; **c. i. f.** *cost, insurance & freight* rahti ja vakuutus hintaan luettuna; **C.-in-C.** *Commander-in-Chief;* **C.I.O.** *Congress of Industrial Organizations* ammattiyhdistysten keskusjärjestö (U.S.A.); **Co.** *Company;* **c/o** *care of* jkn luona (osoitteissa); **C.O.D.** *cash on delivery* jälkivaatimuksella; **Col.** *Colonel* eversti; **Col(o).** *Colorado;* **Conn.** *Connecticut;* **cont.** *[to be] continued;* **CP** *Cape Province, Communist Party,* ks. *cerebral;* **cp.** *compare* vertaa; **cps** *cycles per second* herziä; **cu.** *cubic;* **cwt** *hundredweight.*

cab [kæb] s. (ajurin) rattaat, vuokra-auto *(taxi-~);* (traktorin ym) kuljettajan koppi.

cabal [kə'bæl] s. salajuoni.

cabaret ['kæbərei] s. kabaree.

cabbage ['kæbidʒ] s. kaali; *~ head* kaalinpää.

cabby ['kæbi] s. ajuri, taksimies.

cabin ['kæbin] s. mökki; hytti, kajuutta; *~ class* 2. luokka. **~-boy** laivapoika.

cabinet ['kæbinit] s. kabinetti, hallitus, ministeristö; (esim. levysoittimen) kotelo, suojakansi; *C~ crisis*

hallituspula. **~-maker** taidepuuseppä.

cable ['keibl] s. kaapeli; ankkuriköysi, vahva köysi, vaijeri; (kaapeli) sähke (m. *~ gram); v.* sähköttää; *~-way* köysirata.

cabman s. ajuri, taksimies.

caboodle [kə'bu:dl] *s.: the whole ~* koko roikka.

caboose [kə'bu:s] s. (laivan) keittiö.

cabriolet [kæbriə'lei] s. kabrioletti (nyk. urheiluauto).

cabstand s. taksi-, ajuriasema (m. *cab rank).*

cacao [kə'ka:ou] s. kaakaopuu, -papu; ks. *cocoa.*

cache [kæʃ] s. kätkö; v. kätkeä. **-t** ['kæʃei] s. laatumerkki.

cackel [kækl] v. kotkottaa, kaakattaa; s. kaakatus.

cacophony [kæ'kɔfəni] s. epäsointu.

cactus ['kæktəs] s. (pl. m. *cacti* [-tai] kaktus.

cad [kæd] s. roisto, lurjus, heittiö.

cadaver [kə'deivə] s. (kuolleen) ruumis. **-ous** [kə'dævərəs] a. kalmankalpea.

caddie ['kædi] s. golfinpelaajan mailapoika.

caddish ['kædiʃ] a. konnamainen, alhainen.

caddy ['kædi] s. teerasia.

cadence ['keidns] s. poljento.

cadenza [kə'denzə] s. (loppu)kadenssi.

cadet [kə'det] s. nuorempi poika; kadetti.

cadge [kædʒ] v. hankkia kerjäämällä, kerjätä.

cadmium ['kædmiəm] s. kadmium.

cadre [ka:dr] s. kaaderi, runkohenkilöstö (sot.).

caecum ['si:kəm] s. umpisuoli (pl. *caeca).*

Caesar ['si:zə] s. Caesar; keisari. **-ean**

café   70

[si(:)'zɛəriən] a.; ~ section
keisarileikkaus.
café ['kæfei] s. kahvila; baari.
cafeteria [kæfi'tiəriə] s.
itsepalvelukahvila, kahvio.
caffeine ['kæfiin] s. kofeiini.
caftan ['kæftən] s. kauhtana.
cage [keidʒ] s. häkki; sotavankileiri;
(kaivos)hissin kori; v. sulkea häkkiin.
-y [-i] a. varova(inen),
salamyhkäinen, umpimielinen (adv.
cagily).
cahoots [kə'hu:ts] s.: go ~ panna tasan;
be in ~ with (salaa) pelata yhteispeliä.
Cain [kein] erisn. Kain; raise ~ nostaa
hälinä.
cairn [kɛən] s. kiviröykkiö
(rajamerkkinä ym.). -gorm [-'gɔ:m] s.
savukvartsi.
Cairo ['kaiərəu] erisn. Kairo.
caisson [keis(ə)n] s. uppoarkku;
ammuslaatikko, lavetti; ~ disease
sukeltajantauti.
caitiff ['keitif] s. pelkuri.
cajole [kə'dʒəul] v. mairitella;
houkutella. -ry [-əri] s. imartelu.
cake [keik] s. kakku, leivos, leipä;
(litteä) palanen, levy (~ of soap); v.
tarttua, kovettua, kokkaroitua;
[selling] like hot ~s kun kuumille
kiville.
Calais ['kælei] erisn.
calamit|ous [kə'læmitəs] a. tuhoisa. -y
[-ti] s. (suuri) onnettomuus.
calc|areous [kæl'kɛəriəs] a.
kalkkipitoinen, kalkki-. -ification
[kælsifi'keiʃn] s. kalkkiutuminen. -ify
['kælsifai] v. muuttaa kalkiksi;
kalkkiutua.
calcium ['kælsiəm] s. kalsium.
calcul|able ['kælkjuləbl] a.
arvioitavissa oleva. -ate [-eit] v.
laskea, arvioida; luottaa (upon jhk);
~d tarkoitettu, harkittu, omiaan (to
+ inf). -ating a. laskelmoiva; ~
machine laskukone. -ation [-'leiʃn] s.
lasku, arvio; harkinta. -ator [-eitə] s.
laskin, laskukone. -us [-əs] s. (pl. -i
[-lai]) kivi (lääk.); kalkyyli, laskenta.
Calcutta [kæl'kʌtə] erisn.
caldron ks. cauldron.
Caledonian [kæli'dəunjən] a. & s.
(muinais)skotlantilainen.
calendar ['kælində] s. almanakka;

ajanlasku; ~ month
kalenterikuukausi.
calender ['kælində] s. kiillotuskone,
kalanteri, v. kiillottaa, mankeloida.
calf 1. [kɑ:f] s. (pl. calves [kɑ:vz]
vasikka, (valaan ym) poikanen; ~
love nuoruudenaikainen rakkaus.
calf 2. [kɑ:f] s. (pl. ks. ed.) pohje.
cali|brate ['kælibreit] v. kalibroida.
-bre, -ber ['kælibə] s. kaliiperi.
calico ['kælikəu] s. (pl. ~s, ~es)
puuvillakangas, kalikoo.
California [kæli'fɔ:njə] erisn. -n [-n] a.
& s. kalifornialainen.
caliper, calliper ['kælipə] s.: ~s mitta-,
länkiharppi.
caliph ['kælif, 'kei-] s. kalifi.
calisthenics ['kælis'θeniks] s. pl.
voimistelu.
calk [kɔ:k] s. hokki (hevosen
kengässä); v. hokittaa; = caulk.
call [kɔ:l] v. huutaa, kutsua; nimittää,
sanoa jksk;) käydä (at jssk, on a p.
jkn luona), käväistä; (laivasta)
poiketa jhk; herättää; soittaa
puhelimella; s. huuto, kutsu, kehotus;
kutsu|ääni. -merkki; puhelinsoitto,
puhelu; merkinanto; kutsumus,
vaatimus; vierailu, käynti (pay a ~);
~ sb. names nimitellä, solvata; ~
attention to kiinnittää (jkn) huomio
jhk; ~ back soittaa (t. käydä)
uudelleen; ~ for vaatia, pyytää;
mennä (tulla) hakemaan, noutaa; ~
forth saada aikaan, synnyttää; ~ in
vaatia maksettavaksi; kutsua; ~ in
question asettaa kyseenalaiseksi; ~ off
kutsua pois; peruuttaa; ~ on käydä
tervehtimässä jkta, kehottaa; ~ out
huudahtaa; hälyttää, kehottaa
lakkoon; ~ over [the names] toimittaa
nimenhuuto; ~ to account vaatia
tilille; ~ to mind palauttaa mieleen; ~
up kutsua (sota)palveluskseen; kutsua
esiin, soittaa puhelimella jkle; ~
upon = on; kehottaa jkta (to -maan,
-mään); I didn't feel ~ed upon to. .en
katsonut velvollisuudekseni..; on ~
saatavissa; vaadittaessa maksettava;
within ~ kuulomatkan päässä; put a ~
through yhdistää puhelu jnnek. ~-box
puhelinkioski. ~-boy poika, joka
kutsuu näyttelijät lavalle. -er [-ə] s.
vieras. ~-girl »puhelintyttö». -ing s.

kutsumus, toimi; ~ *card* Am.
nimikortti.
Callaghan ['kæləhən] *erisn.*
calligraphy [kə'ligrəfi] *s.*
kaunokirjoitus.
calliper ks. *caliper*
call|-money vaadittaessa maksettava
laina. **~-note** kutsuääni.
call|osity [kæ'lɔsiti] *s.* känsä, pahka.
-ous ['kæləs] *a.* känsäinen,
kovettunut; kova, tunteeton,
paatunut.
call-over nimenhuuto.
callow ['kæləu] *a.* höyhenetön;
kypsymätön, kehittymätön.
call-up kutsunta.
callus ['kæləs] *s.* kovettuma, känsä.
calm [kɑːm] *a.* tyven, tyyni;
rauhallinen; *v.* tyynnyttää, tyyntyä,
rauhoittaa, -ttua (us. ~ *down*); *s.*
tyven; rauhallisuus, levollisuus.
calor|ie ['kæləri] *s.* kaloria. **-ific** [-'rifik]
a. lämpö-,
column|iate [kə'lʌmnieit] *v.* panetella,
herjata. **-y** ['kæləmni] *s.* panettelu,
herjaus.
calvary ['kælvəri] *s.: C~* Golgata.
calve [kɑːv] *v.* vasikoida, poikia. **-s** *pl.*
ks. *calf.*
Calvinis|m ['kælvinizm] *s.* Kalvinin
oppi. **-t** [-st] *s.* kalvinisti.
calyx ['keiliks] *s.* (pl. m. *calyces)* verhiö
(kasv.).
cam [kæm] *s.* epäkesko, kehrä.
camaraderie [kæmə'rɑːdəri] *s.* hyvä
toveruus.
camber ['kæmbə] *s.* (tien) käyristys,
kuperuus
Cambodia [kæm'bəudjə] *erisn.*
Kamputsea.
Cambrian ['kæmbriən] *a.* kambrinen,
walesilainen.
Cambridge ['keimbridʒ]: ~ *blue*
vaaleansininen.
cambric ['kæmbrik] *s.* hieno palttina,
batisti.
came [keim] *imp.* ks. *come.*
camel ['kæml] *s.* kameli. **-eer** [kæmi'liə]
s. kamelinajaja.
camellia [kə'miːljə] *s.* kamelia.
Camembert ['kæməmbɛə] *s. c.* juusto.
cameo ['kæmiəu] *s.* kamee.
camera ['kæm(ə)rə] *s.* kamera. **~-man**
kuvaaja.

camisole [-səul] *s.* suojusliivi.
camomile ['kæməmail] *s.*
kamomillasaunio, sauramo.
camouflage ['kæmuflɑːʒ] *s.* (sot. ym)
naamiointi; suojaväri; *v.* naamioida.
camp 1. [kæmp] *s.* leiri; *v.* leiriytyä; ~
out asua teltassa; *pitch* ~ leiriytyä;
strike ~ purkaa leiri; *go* ~*ing* mennä
leirille t. telttailemaan.
camp 2. *s. attr.* eksentrinen, räikeä;
naismainen.
campaign [kæm'pein] *s.* sotaretki;
kampanja, tempaus; *v.* olla
sotaretkellä.
campan|ile [kæmpə'niːli] *s.* kellotapuli.
-ula [kəm'pænjulə] *s.* kellokukka.
camp|-bed, **~- chair** telttavuode, -tuoli
camphor ['kæmfə] *s.* kamferi.
camping *s.* leirintä; *camp*[*ing*] *ground*
leirintäalue.
campus ['kæmpəs] *s.* koulun t. collegen
alue.
can 1. [kæn] *s.* kannu; metallirasia,
-tölkki; Am. sl. putka, vankila; *v.*
säilöä; ~*ned meat* lihasäilykkeet;
~*ned music* levytetty, nauhoitettu; *in
the* ~ »purkissa».
can 2. [kæn, kən, kn] *apuv.* ind. prees.;
imp. *could* [kud]; voi(n, -t jne),
osaa(n -t jne); *you* ~ *go* saat mennä;
he ~ *speak French* hän puhuu
ranskaa; *it can't be true* on
mahdotonta, että se olisi totta; *where*
~ *they be?* missä ihmeessä he ovat;
how could you [say so] kuinka saatoit.
Canaan ['keinən] *erisn.* Kanaanin maa.
Canad|a ['kænədə] *erisn.* **-ian**
[kə'neidjən] *a. & s.* kanadalainen.
canal [kə'næl] *s.* kanava; tiehyt; *ear* ~
korvakäytävä. **-ize** ['kænəlaiz] *v.*
kanavoida, (kuv.) ohjailla.
canard [kæ'nɑːd] *s.* perätön uutinen.
canary [kə'nɛəri] *s.* kanarialintu; *the
Canaries (Canary Islands)* Kanarian
saaret.
Canberra ['kænb(ə)rə] *erisn.*
cancel ['kænsl] *v.* pyyhkiä pois,
mitätöidä; peruuttaa, kumota;
~..*out* eliminoida (toisensa). **-lation**
[kænsə'leiʃn] *s.* peruutus,
kumoaminen.
cancer ['kænsə] *s.* syöpä; *the Tropic of
C~* Kravun kääntöpiiri; vrt.
carcinoma. **-ous** [-rəs] *a.* syöpä-.

candelabrum [kændi'lɑ:brəm] s. (pl. -bra) kandelaaberi, haarakynttilänjalka.

candid ['kændid] a. vilpitön, suora; ennakkoluuloton; ~ camera piilokamera.

candidacy ['kændidəsi] s. ehdokkuus.

candida|te ['kændidit] s. hakija, ehdokas, pyrkijä. **-ture** [-ʃə] s. ehdokkuus.

candidly adv. suoraan, avoimesti.

candied ['kændid] a. sokeroitu.

candle ['kændl] s. kynttilä. **~-end** kynttilänpätkä. **-light** kynttilänvalo. **C~mas** kynttelinpäivä. **~-power** normaalikynttilä. **-stick** kynttilänjalka.

candour, candor ['kændə] s. vilpittömyys, suoruus.

candy ['kændi] s. kandisokeri; Am. makeiset; v. päällystää sokerilla, keittää sokerissa; ~ floss hattara (eräänl. tikkukaramelli); candied lemon peel sukkaatti.

cane [kein] s. ruoko; ruoko-, kävelykeppi; v. lyödä, antaa selkään; ~ chair korituoli; ~ sugar ruokosokeri.

canine ['kænain, Am. 'kein-] a. koira(n)-; s. ~ [tooth] kulmahammas.

caning ['keiniŋ] s. selkäsauna.

canister ['kænistə] s. peltirasia; kartessi (m. ~-shot).

canker ['kæŋkə] s. haavauma (et. suussa): ruostesieni (puissa); tuho(toukka): v. tuhota, kalvaa. **-ous** [-rəs] a. jäytävä, kalvava.

cannabis ['kænəbis] s. intialainen hamppu, hasis, marihuana.

cann|ed [kæn|d] a. ks. can 1. **-ery** [-əri] s. säilyketehdas.

cannibal ['kænibəl] s. ihmissyöjä. **-ism** [-izm] s. kannibalismi.

cannon ['kænən] s. (pl. m. sama) tykki. **-ade** [kænə'neid] s. tykkituli **~-ball** tykinkuula. **~-fodder** tykinruoka.

cannot ['kænot] ks. can 2.

cannula ['kænjulə] s. kanyyli.

canny ['kæni] a. ovela, varovainen, säästäväinen.

canoe [kə'nu:] s. kanootti; v. meloa; ~ing melonta.

canon ['kænən] s. kirkollinen säännös; kaniikki (mus. ym) kaanon **-ical**

[kə'nɔnik(ə)l] a. kanoninen. **-ization** [-ai'zeiʃn] s. pyhimykseksi julistaminen. **-ize** [-aiz] v. julistaa pyhimykseksi.

canopy ['kænəpi] s. kunnia-, korukatos; taivaankansi (~ of heaven); v. peittää korukatoksella.

cant 1. [kænt] s. (ammatin ym) erikoiskieli; tekopyhä puhe; v. hurskailla.

cant 2. [kænt] s. kaltevuus, vinous; työntäisy; v. työntäistä kallelleen; kallistaa, olla viistossa.

can't [kɑ:nt] = cannot.

Cantabrigian [kæntə'bridʒiən] a. & s. Cambridgen (ylioppilas).

cantaloup ['kæntəlu:p] s. eräänl. meloni.

cantankerous [kən'tæŋk(ə)rəs] a. riidanhaluinen, ilkeä.

cantata [kæn'tɑ:tə] s. kantaatti.

canteen [kæn'ti:n] s. (tehtaan ym) ruokala, kanttiini; kenttäpullo; pöytäkalulipas t. -laatikko.

canter ['kæntə] s. lyhyt laukka; v. mennä lyhyttä laukkaa.

Canterbury ['kæntəb(ə)ri] erisn.

canticle ['kæntikl] s. ylistysvirsi.

cantilever ['kæntili:və] s.: ~ bridge ulokepalkkisilta.

canto ['kæntəu] s. laulu.

canton ['kænton] s. kantoni, piirikunta; v. ['kæntu:n] s. majoittaa (sotilaita). **-ment** [kən'tu:nmənt] s. majoituspaikka.

canvas ['kænvəs] s. telttakangas, purjekangas; öljyvärimaalaus; purjeet; under ~ teltoissa; täysin purjein.

canvass ['kænvəs] v. pohtia, seuloa; koettaa vaikuttaa (valitsijoihin); kalastaa (ääniä), kerätä (tilauksia); ~ing äänten kalastelu.

canyon ['kænjən] s. kanjoni.

caoutchouc ['kautʃuk] s. kautsu.

cap [kæp] s. lakki, myssy; kansi, päällys (pullon) korkki, suljin; v. kattaa, peittää; kruunata, voittaa; antaa oppiarvo; [percussion] ~ nallihattu; ~ and bells narrinkaapu; set one's ~ at koettaa saada pauloihinsa.

capability [keipə'biliti] s. pystyvyys, kyky.

capable ['keipəbl] a. kykenevä, pystyvä

(of jhk), kyvykäs.

capacious [kə'peiʃəs] *a.* tilava.

capacit|ate [kə'pæsiteit] *v.* tehdä kykeneväksi. **-y** [-i] *s.* tilavuus; vetävyys, kyky, kyvykkyys; teho, kapasiteetti; ominaisuus, asema *(in the ~ of): measure of ~* tilavuusmitta; *filled to ~* täpötäysi.

cap-a-pie [kæpə'pi:] *adv.* kiireestä kantapäähän.

caparison [kə'pærisn] *s.* hevosen tamineet, satulaloimi.

cape 1. [keip] *s.* hartiaviitta, (kampaus)vaippa, kappa.

cape 2. [keip] *s.* niemi; *the C~* Hyväntoivonniemi, Kapmaa (m. = *C~ Province); C~ town* Kapkaupunki.

caper 1. ['keipə] *s.: ~ s* kapris.

caper 2. ['keipə] *s.* hypähdys; kuje; *v.* hypähdellä; kujeilla *(cut ~ s).*

capercai|llie, -lzie [kæpə'keilji] *s.* metso.

capillar|ity [kæpi'læriti] *s.* hiushuokoisuus. **-y** [kə'piləri] *a.* hius-; *s.* hiussuoni.

capital ['kæpit|l] *s.* pääkaupunki; iso kirjain; pääoma; pylväänpää, kapiteeli; *a.* pää-, pääasiallinen, erinomainen, henkeä koskeva, hengen-; *~ goods* pääomahyödykkeet, tuotantotavarat; *~ letter* iso kirjain; *~ levy* omaisuudenluovutusvero; *~ offence* hengenrikos; *~ punishment* kuolemanrangaistus; *~ ship* taistelulaiva t. risteilijä. **-ism** [-əlizm] *s.* kapitalismi. **-ist** [-əlist] *s.* kapitalisti. **-istic** [-ɔ'listik] *a.* kapitalistinen. **-ize** ['kæpitəlaiz] *v.* kirjoittaa isoilla kirjaimilla; muuttaa rahaksi, *(~ on)* käyttää hyödykseen. **-ly** ['kæpitli] *adv.* erinomaisesti.

capitation [kæpi'teiʃn] *s.: ~ tax* henkiraha.

Capitol [kæpitl] (Rooman) Kapitolium, Am. kongressitalo.

capitula|te [kə'pitjuleit] *v.* antautua. **-tion** [-'leiʃn] *s.* antautuminen.

capon ['keipən] *s.* salvokukko.

capri|ce [kə'pri:s] *s.* oikku. **-cious** [kə'priʃəs] *a.* oikullinen; *(~ness* oikullisuus).

Capricorn ['kæprikɔ:n] *s.* Kauris (täht.)

capsicum ['kæpsikəm] *s.*

espanjanpippuri.

capsize [kæp'saiz] *v.* mennä kumoon; kaataa.

capstan ['kæpstən] *s.* käsivintturi.

capsul|ar ['kæpsjulə] *a.* kotelomainen. **-e** [-ju:l] *s.* kapseli; kotelo, (pullon korkin) suojus; siemenkota; *space ~* avaruuskapseli.

captain ['kæptin] *s.* kapteeni; päällikkö; johtaja; *v.* johtaa. **-cy** [-si] *s.* kapteeninarvo.

caption ['kæpʃən] *s.* otsikko; kuvateksti, (filmikuvan) teksti.

captious ['kæpʃəs] *a.* arvosteleva, moitteenhaluinen; saivarteleva.

captiv|ate ['kæptiveit] *v.* saada valtoihinsa, kiehtoa, viehättää. **-e** ['kæptiv] *a.* vangittu, vankina oleva; *s.* vanki; *~ balloon* kiintopallo. **-ity** [kæp'tiviti] *s.* vankeus.

capt|or ['kæptə] *s.* vangiksi ottaja. **-ure** [-tʃə] *s.* vangitseminen, valtaaminen, (laivan) kaappaus; saalis, vanki; *v.* vangita, vallata, kaapata.

Capuchin ['kæpjuʃin] *s.* kapusiinimunkki.

car [kɑ:] *s.* auto, vaunu; Am. rautatievaunu; raitiovaunu (m. *tram~*).

carabineer [kærəbi'niə] *s.* karabinieeri.

carafe [kə'rɑ:f] *s.* karahvi.

caramel ['kærəmel] *s.* poltettu sokeri.

carapace ['kærəpeis] *s.* (kilpikonnan ym) selkäkuori, -kilpi.

carat ['kærət] *s.* karaatti.

caravan ['kærəvæn] *s.* karavaani; asuntovaunu.

caraway ['kærəwei] *s.* kumina.

carbide ['kɑ:baid] *s.* karbidi.

carbine [kɑ:bain] *s.* karbiini.

carbohydrate ['kɑ:bə(u)'haidreit] *s.* hiilihydraatti.

carbolic [kɑ:'bɔlik] *a.: ~ acid* karbolihappo.

carbon ['kɑ:bən] *s.* hiili; hiilipaperi(jäljennös) (m. *~ paper, ~ copy); ~ dating* hiili-ikäys; *~ monoxide* häkä. **-ate** [-it] *s.* karbonaatti. **-ic** [kɑ:'bɔnik] *a.* hiili-; *~ acid* hiilihappo. **-iferous** [-'nif(ə)rəs] *a.* hiilipitoinen. **-ize** [-aiz] *v.* hiiltää.

carbuncle ['kɑ:bʌŋkl] *s.* ajospahka; punainen jalokivi.

carburet ['kɑ:bjuret] *v.* karboroida,

yhdistää hiileen; ~ *ted hydrogen* hiilivety. **-tor, -or, -ter** [-ə] *s.* kaasutin.

carcass, carcase ['ka:kəs] *s.* raato, ruho; runko, rauniot.

carcinoma [ka:si'nəumə] *s.* syöpä; ~ *of the breast* rintasyöpä.

card 1. [ka:d] *s.* karsta; *v.* karstata.

card 2. [ka:d] *s.* (peli-, käynti- ym) kortti; *pl.* korttipeli; *play* ~ *s* pelata korttia; *pack of* ~ *s* korttipakka; *it is on the* ~ *s* se on mahdollista, todennäköistä; *house of* ~ *s* kestämätön suunnitelma ym; ~ *file* (t. *index)* kortisto.

cardamom [ka:dəməm] *s.* kardemumma.

cardboard ['ka:dbɔ:d] *s.* pahvi.

cardiac ['ka:diæk] *a.* sydämen, sydän-.

cardigan ['ka:digən] *s.* neulottu villatakki, neuletakki; ~ *suit* jakkupuku.

cardinal ['ka:dinl] *a.* pääasiallinen, tärkein, pää-, perus-; *s.* kardinaali; ~ *number* perusluku; ~ *points* pääilmansuunnat; ~ *red* kirkkaanpunainen.

cardiogram ['ka:diə(u)græm] *s.* sydänfilmi.

cardio|logist [ka:di'ɔlədʒist] *s.* sydänspesialisti. **-logy** [-i] *s.* sydäntautioppi. **-vascular** *a.:* ~ *diseases* sydän- ja verisuonitaudit.

card-sharper korttihuijari.

care [kɛə] *s.* huoli, murhe; huolellisuus, varovaisuus; huolenpito, hoito; huolto; *v.* huolehtia *(for* jksta); (et. kielt. laus.) välittää (m. ~ *about);* pitää *(for* jksta); (~ *to)* haluta; *worn with* ~ *s* huolten uuvuttama; ~ *of* .. (lyh. *c/o)* jkn luona; *take* ~ *of* pitää huolta, huolehtia jstk, jksta; *take* ~ *!* varo! *take* ~ *not to break* .. varo rikkomasta .. ; *with* ~ varovasti; *I don't* ~ *what he says* on samantekevää mitä hän sanoo; *I couldn't* ~ *less* se on minusta herttaisen yhdentekevää; *for all I* ~ minun puolestani; *would you* ~ *to* .. haluaisit(te)ko ..

careen [kə'ri:n] *v.* kallistaa (laiva); kallistua.

career [kə'riə] *s.* (elämän)ura; virkaura; ammatti; *v.* nelistää; kiitää; *in full* ~ täyttä vauhtia; ~ *s adviser*

ammatinvalinnan ohjaaja. **-ist** [-rist] *s.* kiipijä, karrieristi.

care|free *a.* huoleton. **-ful** *a.* huolellinen, varovainen; säästäväinen. **-less** *a.* huolimaton, välinpitämätön, ajattelematon.

caress [kə'res] *s.* hyväily; *v.* hyväillä.

care|taker *s.* talonvahti, (esim. museon)hoitaja, vahtimestari; (et. Am.) talonmies; ~ *government* toimitusministeristö, virkamieshallitus. **-worn** huolten uuvuttama.

cargo ['ka:gəu] *s.* (pl. ~ *es*, Am. m. ~ *s)* lasti.

Caribbean [kæri'bi:ən] *erisn.: the* ~ *Sea* Karibianmeri.

caribou ['kæribu:] *s.* karibu, peura.

caricatur|e ['kærikə'tjuə] *s.* pilakuva; *v.* karikoida. **-ist** [-rist] *s.* pilapiirtäjä.

caries ['kɛərii:z] *s.: dental* ~ hammasmätä, hampaiden reikiintyminen.

Carlyle [ka:'lail] *erisn.*

carmine ['ka:main] *a. & s.* karmiininpuna(inen).

carnage ['ka:nidʒ] *s.* verilöyly.

carnal ['ka:n(ə)l] *a.* lihallinen; aistillinen. **-ity** [ka:'næliti] *s.* lihallisuus.

carnation [ka:'neiʃn] *s.* (puutarha)neilikka.

carni|val ['ka:ni|vl] *s.* karnevaali. **-vore** [-vɔ:] *s.* lihansyöjä. **-vorous** [ka:'niv(ə)rəs] *a.* lihaa syövä.

carob ['kærəb] *s.* johanneksenleipäpuu.

carol ['kærəl] *s.* laulu, joululaulu; *v.* laulaa iloiten.

Carolina [kærə'lainə] *erisn.: North* ~ (N. C.)

carotid [kə'rɔtid] *s.:* ~ *[artery]* yhteinen päänvaltimo.

carous|al [kə'rauzl] *s.* juomingit. **-e** [kə'rauz] *v.* mässätä, juopotella.

carp 1. [ka:p] *s.* karppi.

carp 2. [ka:p] *v.* pistellä, sättiä *(at* jkta); ~ *ing* pistelijäs.

car-park *s.* paikoitusalue.

Carpathians [ka:'peiθjanz] *s.: the* ~ Karpaatit.

carpent|er ['ka:pintə] *s.* kirvesmies, puuseppä; *v.* salvoa; ~ *'s bench* höyläpenkki. **-ry** [-tri] *s.* puusepäntyö.

carpet ['kɑ:pit] s. matto; v. peittää matolla; *sweep sth. under the* ~ panna vihreän veran alle. ~**-bagger** (Am. pohjoisesta tullut) (poliittinen) onnenonkija, »reppumies».

carriage ['kæridʒ] s. vaunut; rautatievaunu; kuljetus; kuljetusmaksu, rahti; tykinlavetti, alusta, (kirjoituskoneen)vaunu; ryhti, käytöstapa; ~ *forward* rahti maksettava perillä; ~ *paid* rahti maksettu, rahtivapaa; ~ *and pair* parivaljakko. ~**-drive** yksityinen ajotie. ~**-way** ajotie; *dual* ~ kaksiajoratainen tie.

carrier ['kæriə] s. kuljetustoimisto, k:n kantaja; (polkupyörän) tavarateline; (taudin) kantaja; kantoaalto (rad.); ~ *pigeon* viestikyyhkynen.

carrion ['kæriə] s. mätänevä liha; raato, haaska. ~**-eater** haaskansyöjä.

carrot ['kærət] s. porkkana.

carry ['kæri] v. kantaa; kuljettaa; viedä, tuoda; kannattaa; (kirjanp.) siirtää, (mat.) muistiin; sisältää; vallata (linnoitus); ajaa läpi; *[the motion] was carried* meni läpi; ~ *all before one* saada suuri menestys; ~ *the day* voittaa; *he carries himself well* hänellä on hyvä ryhti; ~ *one's point* saavuttaa tarkoituksensa, saada tahtonsa läpi; ~ *away* temmata mukaansa; *be carried away by* joutua jnk lumoihin; ~ *forward* siirtää (kirjanp.); ~ *off* viedä pois, voittaa (palkinto); ~ *it off well* selviytyä kunnialla; ~ *on* jatkaa, harjoittaa (ammattia ym), (puhek.) käyttäytyä omituisesti t. säädyttömästi; kuherrella; ~ *out* panna täytäntöön, suorittaa; ~ *over* = ~ *forward*; ~ *through* viedä läpi, toteuttaa. ~**-cot** (vauvan) kantolaukku. **-ing:** ~ *capacity* kantavuus.

cart [kɑ:t] s. rattaat, kärryt; v. kuljettaa rattailla; ~*-load* kuorma; *put the* ~ *before the horse* tehdä jtk takaperoisesti. **-age** [-idʒ] s. kuljetus, ajo(palkka).

cartel [kɑ:'tel] s. kartelli.

Carthage ['kɑ:θidʒ] erisn. Karthago.

cartilage ['kɑ:tilidʒ] s. rusto.

cartograph|er [kɑ:'trɒf|ə] s. kartanpiirtäjä. **-y** [-i] s.

kartanpiirustus.

carton ['kɑ:tən] s. pahvirasia.

cartoon [kɑ:'tu:n] s. (us. poliittinen) pilakuva; luonnos; v. piirtää pilakuva; *animated* ~ piirretty elokuva. **-ist** [-ist] s. pilapiirtäjä.

cartridge ['kɑ:tridʒ] s. patruuna, panos; rullafilmi; (levysoittimen) äänirasia; Am. kasetti. ~**-paper** kartuusipaperi.

carv|e [kɑ:v] v. leikata (paistia ym), veistää, kaivertaa. **-er** [-ə] s. puunleikkaaja; paistiveitsi; *pl.* paistiveitsi ja -haarukka. **-ing** s. (puu)leikkaus; ~ *knife* paistiveitsi.

cascade [kæs'keid] s. (pieni) vesiputous; v. ryöpytä (putouksena).

case 1. [keis] s. tapaus, asianlaita; tila; sija(muoto); asia, juttu (lak.); *in* ~ jos, siinä tapauksessa että, *(in* ~ *of)* jnk varalta, jnk sattuessa; *just in* ~ kaiken varalta; *in any* ~ joka tapauksessa; *that is not the* ~ asia (asian laita) ei ole niin; *is it the* ~ *that?* onko totta, että? *such being the* ~ niin ollen; *as the* ~ *may be* asiasta (tapauksesta) riippuen; *make out a [good]* ~ *for* perustella . . (hyvin); *make [out] one's* ~ osoittaa olevansa oikeassa; *is there a* ~ *for* . . *-ing* onko perusteltua että . .

case 2. [keis] s. rasia, lipas; laatikko; kotelo, (kellon ym) kuori, päällinen. v. panna koteloon; *upper (lower)* ~ isot (pienet) kirjaimet; *book* ~ kirjakaappi. ~**-hardened** (kuv.) paatunut, kovettunut.

case-history sairaskertomuksen esitiedot.

casein ['keisiin] s. kaseiini.

casemate ['keismeit] s. kasematti (sot.).

casement ['keismənt] s. : ~ *[window]* saranaikkuna.

case|-work henkilökohtainen sosiaalityö. ~**-worker** sosiaalityöntekijä.

cash [kæʃ] s. käteinen raha; kassa; v. vaihtaa t. muuttaa rahaksi; ~ *price* käteishinta; ~ *on delivery* (lyh. *C.O.D.)* jälkivaatimuksella; *out of* ~ ilman rahaa; *pay* ~ maksaa käteisellä; ~ *desk* kassa; ~ *register* kassakone.

cashew ['kæʃu:] : ~ *nut* munuaispuun pähkinä.

cashier 1. [kæ'ʃiə] s. kassanhoitaja.

cash

76

cashier 2. [kə'ʃiə] v. (sot.) erottaa, panna viralta.

cashmere [kæʃ'miə] s. kašmir.

casing ['keisiŋ] s. päällystys, päällys; kotelo, kuori.

cask [ka:sk] s. tynnyri. **-et** [-it] s. (koru)lipas; tuhkauurna; Am. ruumisarkku.

Caspian ['kæspiən] *erisn.: the ~ Sea* Kaspianmeri.

casque [kæsk] s. (vanh.) kypärä.

casserole ['kæsərəul] s. tulenkestävä vuoka; laatikko(ruoka), vuoka.

cassette [kə'set] s. kasetti.

cassock ['kæsək] s. papinkauhtana.

cast [ka:st] *cast cast*, v. heittää, luoda; valaa; määrätä (näyttelijä jhk osaan), jakaa (osat); s. valuteos; osajako, henkilöt (teatt.); muoto, laatu; vivahdus; *she was badly ~* hän oli väärin valittu (osan) esittäjä; *plaster ~* kipsijäljennös; kipsi(side); *~ light on* valaista; *~ a shadow on* luoda varjo(nsa) jhk; *~ one's vote* äänestää; *~ about for* etsiä; *~ aside* hylätä; *~ down* luoda maahan (silmät); *~ in one's lot with* liittää kohtalonsa jhk; *~ off* hylätä, heittää pois; kaventaa, päättää (neuletyö); (irrottaa vene ja) lähteä vesille; *~ on* luoda silmiä (neuletyössä); *~ up* laskea yhteen; *a ~ in the eye* lievä kierosilmäisyys; *~ of features* piirteet; *~ of mind* luonteenlaatu; *look ~ down* olla alakuloisen näköinen; *~-off* hylätty; *~-offs* käytetyt vaatteet.

castanets [kæstə'nets] s. kastanjetit.

castaway ['ka:stəwei] s. hylkiö, haaksirikkoinen.

caste [ka:st] s. kasti; sääty.

castellated ['kæstəleitid] a. sakaramuurein ja tornein varustettu.

caster ks. *castor 1.*

castiga|te ['kæstigeit] v. kurittaa. **-tion** [-'geiʃn] s. kuritus.

Castil|e [kæs'ti:l] *erisn.* Kastilia. **-ian** [kəs'tiliən] *a. & s.* kastilialainen.

casting s. valuteos, -osa; *~ vote* (puheenjohtajan) ratkaiseva ääni. **~-net** käsinuotta.

cast-iron s. valurauta.

castle ['ka:sl] s. linna; torni (šakki.); v. linnoittua, tornittaa (šakki.); *~ in the air (in Spain)* tuulentupa.

castor 1. ['ka:stə] s. sirotustölkki; (esim. tuolin jalan) pyörä, rulla; *~ sugar* sirotesokeri.

castor 2. ['ka:stə] s. majavanhausta; *~ oil* risiiniöljy.

castra|te [kæs'treit] v. kuohita. **-tion** [-'treiʃn] s. kastrointi.

casual ['kæʒuəl] a. satunnainen, tilapäinen; välinpitämätön, huoleton, säännötön; arki-. **-ly** adv. kuin sattumalta, kevyesti, sivumennen. **-ty** [-ti] s. haavoittunut, tapaturman uhri; *c-ties* (sot.) tappiot; *~ list* tappioluettelo.

casuist|ic [kæʒju'istik] a. viisasteleva. **-ry** kasuistiikka.

cat [kæt] s. kissa; *~ suit* haalarit; *~-and-dog* [*life*] eripurainen; *let the ~ out of the bag* ilmaista salaisuus; *like a ~ on hot bricks* kuin tulisilla hiilillä; *not room to swing a ~ in* (on) ahtaat paikat.

cata|clysm ['kætəklizm] s. valtava (luonnon)mullistus. **-comb** [-kəum] s. katakombi. **-lepsy** [-lepsi] s. jäykkyystila. **-logue**, Am. **-log** [-lɔg] s. luettelo; v. luetteloida. **-pult** [-pʌlt] s. katapultti; linko; *~ seat* heittoistuin. **-ract** [-rækt] s. vesiputous; harmaa kaihi.

catarrh [kə'ta:] s. limakalvon tulehdus, katarri.

catastroph|e [kə'tæstrəfi] s. katastrofi, (äkillinen) suuri onnettomuus. **-ic** [-'trɔfik] a. mullistava, romahdusmainen.

catcall ['kætkɔ:l] s. vihellys.

catch [kætʃ] *caught caught*, v. pyydystää, ottaa kiinni, siepata; tarttua, takertua; vangita; olla tarttuva; saada (tauti); tavoittaa, saada kiinni, ehtiä ajoissa jhk; yllättää (*at, in* jssk); käsittää, saada selvää, kuulla; s. saalis, apaja; koppi; hyvä kauppa; juoni; kiinnike, säppi; (mus.) kaanon; *~ sb. napping* tavata nukkumasta; *~ at* kurkottaa, koettaa siepata, tavoitella; *~ [a] cold* vilustua; *~ sb.'s eye* kiinnittää jkn huomio puoleensa; *~ one's breath* haukkoa ilmaa; *~ fire* syttyä; *~ hold of* tarttua jhk; *~ a train* ehtiä junaan; *~ on* tulla muotiin (laulusta ym); *I don't ~ on* en pääse kärryille, en oikein ymmärrä; *~*

out paljastaa, saada kiinni; ~ *up with* tavoittaa jku; *you'll* ~ *it!* joudut ikävyyksiin; ~ *phrase* iskulause; ~ *question* kompakysymys;
~-*as-catch-can* vapaapaini. **-ing** *a.* tarttuva; mieleenjäävä (sävel). **-ment basin** vesialue. **-penny** helppohintainen. **-word** iskusana. **-y** [-i] *a.* mieleenjäävä.

catech|ism ['kætikizm] *a.* katkismus. **-ize** [-aiz] *v.* tehdä kysymyksiä.

categor|ical [kæti'gɔrik(ə)l] *a.* ehdoton. **-y** ['kætigɔri] *s.* kategoria, luokka.

cater ['keitə] *v.:* ~ *for* hankkia muonaa, pitää huolta, huolehtia jstk, palvella jtk. **-er** [-rə] *s.* tarjoilupalveluliike. **-ing** *s.* muonanhankinta; tarjoilupalvelu.

cater|pillar ['kætəpilə] *s.* toukka; telaketju, -traktori. **-waul** [-wɔːl] *v.* naukua.

catfish *s.* monni.

catgut ['kætgʌt] *s.* katgutti, suolilanka.

catharsis [kə'θaːsis] *s.* katharsis.

cathedral [kə'θiːdr(ə)l] *s.* tuomiokirkko.

Catherine ['kæθ(ə)rin] *erisn.* ~-**wheel** *s.* ilotulituspyörä.

catheter ['kæθitə] *s.* katetri.

cathode ['kæθoud] *s.* katodi.

catholic ['kæθəlik] *a.* & *s.* kaikki käsittävä, yleinen; ennakkoluuloton; *C*~ katolilainen; *a.* katolinen. **-ism** [kə'θɔlisizm] *s.* katolisuus.

catkin ['kætkin] *s.* norkko, urpu.

cat|like *a.* kissamainen. ~-**nap** *v.* ottaa nokkaunet.

cat|-o'-nine-tails kattiruoska (mer.). ~'**s-paw** kätyri.

catsup ['kætsəp] *ks. ketchup.*

cattish ['kætiʃ] *a.* kissamainen, ilkeä(mielinen).

cattle ['kætl] *s.* karja, nautakarja; *ten head of* ~ 10 nautaa; ~ *breeding* karjanhoito; ~ *show* karjanäyttely. ~-**lifter** karjavaras.

catty ['kæti] *a. ks. cattish.*

Caucas|ian [kɔː'keiziən] *a.* & *s.* kaukasialainen. **-us** ['kɔːkəsəs] *erisn.* Kaukasus.

caucus ['kɔːkəs] *s.* (vaaleja ym valmisteleva) puoluekokous, vaalikokous.

caudal ['kɔːdl] *a.* häntä-.

caught [kɔːt] *imp. & pp. ks. catch.*

cauldron ['kɔːldr(ə)n] *s.* (iso) kattila.

cauliflower ['kɔliflauə] *s.* kukkakaali.

caulk [kɔːk] *v.* tilkitä.

caus|al ['kɔːz(ə)l] *a.* kausaalinen, syytä ilmaiseva. **-ality** [kɔː'zæliti] *s.* syysuhde. **-ation** [kɔː'zeiʃn] *s.* aiheuttaminen, syy-yhteys.

cause [kɔːz] *s.* syy; aihe, peruste; (oikeus)asia; *v.* aiheuttaa, saada aikaan, olla syynä, aiheena; *there is no* ~ *for anxiety* ei ole aihetta huoleen; *without any* ~ ilman syytä; *make common* ~ *with* toimia yhdessä (jkn) kanssa.

causerie ['kɔuzəri(ː)] *s.* pakina.

causeway ['kɔːzwei] *s.* maantie, pengertie (esim. suoalueen halki).

caustic ['kɔːstik] *a.* syövyttävä; pisteliäs, pureva; *s.* syövytysaine; *lunar* ~ laapis, hopeanitraatti; ~ *soda* lipeäkivi.

cauter|ize ['kɔːtəraiz] *v.* polttaa, syövyttää (pois). **-y** ['kɔːtəri] *s.* poltinrauta; polttaminen.

caution ['kɔːʃn] *s.* varovaisuus; varoitus; *v.* varoittaa; *use* ~ noudattaa varovaisuutta, varoa; *vrt. warn.* **-ary** [-əri] *a.* varoitus-.

cautious ['kɔːʃəs] *a.* varovainen.

caval|cade [kævl'keid] *s.* (juhla-, ratsu)kulkue. **-ier** *s.* ritari, kavaljeeri; *a.* kopea, huoleton; (hist.) kuningasmielinen. **-ry** ['kævlri] *s.* ratsuväki.

cave [keiv] *s.* luola; *v.* kovertaa, ~ *in* painua sisään, vajota, sortua; antaa perään. ~-**man**, ~-**dweller** luolaihminen.

cavern ['kævən] *s.* luola. **-ous** [-əs] *a.* luolamainen, onteloinen.

caviar(e) ['kæviɑː] *s.* kaviaari.

cavil ['kævil] *v.:* ~ *at* arvostella pikkumaisesti, nalkuttaa; *s.* (turha) arvostelu, moite.

cavity ['kæviti] *s.* ontelo; kolo.

cavort [kə'vɔːt] *v.* hypellä, riehakoida.

caw [kɔː] *s.* raakkuminen; *v.* raakkua.

cayenne [kei'en] *s.:* ~ *pepper* cayennepippuri.

cease [siːs] *s.* lakata, lopettaa, loppua; ~-*fire* tulitauko. **-less** *a.* lakkaamaton.

Cecil ['sesl] *erisn.*

cedar ['siːdə] *s.* setri(puu).

cede [siːd] *v.* luovuttaa (alue ym).

ceiling ['si:liŋ] s. (sisä)katto;
(lentokoneen) lakikorkeus; ~ price
enimmäishinta, kattohinta.

celandine ['seləndain] s. keltamo,
mukulaleinikki.

Celebes [se'li:biz] erisn.

celebr|ate ['selibreit] v. viettää
juhlallisesti, juhlia; ylistää; ~ d
kuuluisa. **-ation** [-'breiʃn] s. juhla,
juhliminen; ylistys. **-ity** [si'lebriti] s.
kuuluisuus; kuuluisa henkilö.

celeriac [si'leriæk] s. (juuri)selleri.

celerity [si'leriti] s. nopeus.

celery ['seləri] s. lehtiselleri.

celestial [si'lestiəl] a. taivaan-;
taivaallinen; C~ Empire Kiina; ~
body taivaankappale.

celiba|cy ['selibəsi] s. selibaatti,
naimattomuus. **-te** [-bit] a. & s.
naimaton (henkilö).

cell [sel] s. solu; kammio,
(vanki)koppi; (m. sähk.) kenno, pari;
lokero.

cellar ['selə] s. kellari.

cellist ['tʃelist] s. sellotaiteilija, sellisti.

cello ['tʃeləu] s. sello. **-phane** ['seləfein]
s. sellofaani(laatu).

cellu|lar ['selju|lə] a. solu-. **-loid** [-lɔid]
s. selluloidi. **-lose** [-ləus] s. selluloosa.

Celt [kelt, Am. selt] s. keltti(läinen) **-ic**
[-ik] a. kelttiläinen.

cembalo ['tʃembələu] s. cembalo.

cement [si'ment] s. sementti; sideaine,
kitti; v. sementoida; vahvistaa,
lujittaa.

cemetery ['semitri] s. hautausmaa.

cenotaph ['senətɑ:f] s. (esim.
kaatuneiden) muistomerkki.

censer ['sensə] s. suitsutusastia.

censor ['sensə] s. sensori, tarkastaja;
the C~ (sota)sensuuri; v. sensuroida.
-ious [-'sɔ:riəs] a. moittimishaluinen,
ankara. **-ship** s. painotarkastus,
sensuuri.

censurable ['senʃ(ə)rəbl] a. moitittava.

censure ['senʃə] s. arvostelu, moite; v.
moittia; arvostella.

census ['sensəs] s. väestönlaskenta
(joskus liikenteen); henkikirjoitus.

cent [sent] s. sentti, sentin raha; per
cent sadalta, prosenttia.

centaur ['sentɔ:] s. kentauri.

centen|arian [senti'neəriən] a. & s.
satavuotias. **-ary** [sen'ti:nəri, Am.

'sentnəri] a. satavuotis-; s.
satavuotispäivä, -juhla. **-nial**
[sen'tenjəl] = ed.

centi|grade ['sentigreid] s.
sata-asteinen; ~ thermometer
Celsiuksen lämpömittari. **-metre**
[-mi:tə] s. senttimetri. **-pede** [-pi:d] s.
juoksujalkainen (tuhatjalkainen).

central ['sentr(ə)l] a. keski-, keskus-,
keskeinen; ~ heating
keskuslämmitys. **-ize** [-aiz] v.
keskittää, keskittyä.

centre, center ['sentə] s. keskipiste,
-kohta, -osa, keskus, keskusta; v.
keskittyä, keskittää (on, upon); health
~ terveyskeskus; neuvola; ~ of
gravity painopiste; ~-forward
keskushyökkääjä.

centri|fugal [sen'trifjug(ə)l] a.
keskipakoinen. **-fuge** ['sentrifju:dʒ] v.
sentrifugoida. **-petal** [sen'tripitl] a.
keskihakuinen.

centurion [sen'tjuəriən] s.
sadanpäämies.

century ['sentʃuri] s. vuosisata.

ceramic [si'ræmik] a. keramiikka-. **-s**
[-s] s. keramiikka, savitavarat.

cereal ['siəriəl] s. viljalaji (tav. pl.);
breakfast ~ s (maissi- ym.)hiutaleet.

cere|bellum [seri'beləm] s. pikkuaivot.
-bral ['seribrəl] a. aivo(jen)-; ~ palsy
aivovaurio(isuus), (lyh. CP); CP child
(vajaaliikkeinen) aivovauriolapsi.
-brum ['seribrəm] s. isot aivot.

ceremon|ial [seri'məunjəl] a.
juhlamenoja koskeva; juhlallinen; s.
juhlameno-ohjeet. **-ious** [-jəs] a.
juhlallinen, muodollinen;
kursasteleva. **-y** ['seriməni] s.
juhlamenot, menot; (pyhä) toimitus;
kursailu; Master of C~ies
juhlamenojen ohjaaja; stand upon ~
kursailla; without ~ kursailematta.

cert [sə:t] lyh.: [it's a] [dead] ~
vuorenvarmaa.

certain ['sə:tn] a. varma; tietty,
määrätty; eräs, muuan; for ~ (aivan)
varmasti; make ~ of varmistua jstk **-ly**
adv. varmasti; totta kai, kyllä; ~ not
ei suinkaan, ei tietenkään. **-ty** [-ti] s.
varmuus; varma, kieltämätön asia; for
a ~ varmasti.

certi|ficate [sə(:)'tifikit] s. (kirjallinen)
todistus (esim. death ~); ~ d

[-keitid] tutkinnon suorittanut. **-fy** [ˈsɔːtifai] v. todistaa, vahvistaa; *this is to ~* täten todistetaan ... **-tude** [ˈsɔːtitjuːd] s. varmuus.

cerulean [siˈruːljən] a. taivaansininen.

cerumen [siˈruːmen] s. korvavaha.

cervical [ˈsɔːvik(ə)l] a. kaula-, kohdunkaula(n)-.

cessation [seˈseiʃn] s. lakkaaminen; tauko.

cession [ˈseʃn] v. luovutus.

cesspool [ˈsespuːl] s. likakaivo.

Ceylon [siˈlɔn] *erisn.* (Sri Lanka). **-ese** [siləˈniːz] a. & s. Ceylonin (asukas).

chafe [tʃeif] v. hieroa, hangata, hiertyä; ärsyttää; olla ärtynyt, kärsimätön; s. hankauma, hiertymä.

chaff [tʃɑːf] s. akanat, silppu; roska; kiusoittelu; v. kiusoitella.

chaffer [ˈtʃæfə] v. hieroa kauppaa, tinkiä.

chaffinch [ˈtʃæfin(t)ʃ] s. peippo.

chagrin [ˈʃægrin, Am. ʃəˈgriːn] s. mielipaha; v. tuottaa mielipahaa; ~ed pahoillaan (oleva).

chain [tʃein] s. ketju, kettinki; vitjat; (vuori)jono; sarja; (us. *pl.*) kahleet; v. panna kahleisiin, kytkeä (m. ~ *up*); ~ *reaction* ketjureaktio; **~-armour** rengaspanssari. **~-letter** ketjukirje. **~-smoker** ketjupolttaja. **~-store** haaraliike, myymälä-ketjuun kuuluva liike.

chair [tʃeə] s. tuoli; oppituoli, professorinvirka; puheenjohtajan tuoli; v. kantaa (voittajaa ym) kultatuolissa; ~ *a meeting, be in the ~* olla kokouksen puheenjohtajana. **-man** puheenjohtaja. **-manship** puheenjohtajan virka.

chaise [ʃeiz] s. kääsit.

chalet [ˈʃælei] s. alppimaja.

chalice [ˈtʃælis] s. malja; ehtoolliskalkki.

chalk [tʃɔːk] s. liitu; v. liiduta, merkitä liidulla; *piece of ~* liitupala; ~ *out* hahmotella; ~ *up* merkitä (taululle ym) tulokset; pisteet; panna jkn tiliin. [*it's*] *not true by a long ~* kaukana totuudesta. **-y** [-i] s. liituinen, liidunvalkea.

challenge [ˈtʃælin(d)ʒ] v. haaste; vartiomiehen huuto: »kuka siellä?» v. haastaa (kilpasille ym), esittää haaste,

olla haaste(ena) jhk; uhmata; kiistää, asettaa kyseenalaiseksi; jäävätä; [*a*] *challenging* [*task*] haastava; ~ *cup* kiertopokaali.

chamber [ˈtʃeimbə] s. huone; kamari; kammio (lääk.); ~ *s* (asianajajan) toimisto; ~*-pot* yöastia. **-lain** [-lin] s. kamariherra. **-maid** siivooja (hotellissa ym).

chameleon [kəˈmiːljən] s. kameleontti.

chamois [ˈʃæmwɑː] s. gemssi; ~ [*leather*] [m. ˈʃæmi] säämiskä.

champ [ˈtʃæmp] v. pureskella, rouskuttaa; s. rouskutus.

champagne [ʃæmˈpein] s. samppanja.

champion [ˈtʃæmpjən] s. esitaistelija; mestari; v. taistella (jnk) puolesta; *world ~* maailmanmestari; ~ *horse* palkintohevonen; *that's ~!* loistavaa, hienoa! **-ship** s. mestaruus.

chance [tʃɑːns] s. sattuma; mahdollisuus; todennäköisyys; tilaisuus; onnenkauppa; a. satunnainen; v. sattua; ~ *upon* sattumalta kohdata; *let's ~ it!* koetetaan onneamme! ottakaamme riski! *by ~* sattumalta; *if, by any ~* (jos) ehkä; *game of ~* uhkapeli; *an off ~* (pienen)pieni mahdollisuus; *the ~ s are that he will come* hän luultavasti tulee; *I came on the ~ of finding him* tulin siinä toivossa, että tapaisin hänet; *he stands a* [*good*] ~ *of* .. hänellä on hyvät mahdollisuudet ..

chancel [ˈtʃɑːns|l] s. (kirkon) pääkuori. **-lery** [-ələri] s. kanslerinvirasto, kanslia. **-lor** [-ələ] s. kansleri; (Engl.) suurlähetystön ensimmäinen sihteeri; *Lord* [*High*] ~ lordikansleri (oikeuslaitoksen päällikkö ja ylähuoneen puhemies).

chancery [ˈtʃɑːns(ə)ri] s. lordikanslerin oikeus; *in ~* pää puristuksiinsa toisen (nyrkkeilijän) kainalossa, pinteessä.

chancy [ˈtʃɑːnsi] a. uskallas, uhka-; sattumanvarainen.

chand|elier [ʃændiˈliə] s. kattokruunu. **-ler** [ˈtʃɑːndlə] s. kynttilä- (saippua-ym) kauppias; *ship's ~* laivatarvikkeiden hankkija.

change [tʃein(d)ʒ] v. vaihtaa, muuttaa; muuttua, vaihtua; muuttaa pukua; vaihtaa junaa ym; s. vaihto; muutos, vaihdos; vaihtelu; vaihtoraha,

pikkuraha; (m. ~ *of clothes*)
vaihtovaatekerta; *'C* ~ pörssi; ~ *for
the better (the worse)* tulla t. kääntyä
paremmaksi (huonommaksi); ~
colour muuttaa väriä, punastua,
kalveta; ~ *hands* vaihtaa omistajaa;
~ *places with* vaihtaa paikkaa jkn
kanssa; ~ *up (down)* vaihtaa
suuremmalle (pienemmälle)
vaihteelle; *for a* ~ vaihteeksi; *have
you* ~ *for?* voitteko vaihtaa? *here is
your* ~ tässä on teille rahaa takaisin;
~ *of life* vaihdevuodet. **-able** [-əbl] *a.*
vaihteleva, epävakainen. **-less** *a.*
muuttumaton. **-ling** [-liŋ] *s.*
vaihdokas. **~-over** siirtyminen,
siirtymä.

channel ['tʃænl] *s.* kanava; (joen)
uoma; väylä; tie, ura; *v.* uurtaa;
ohjata, kanavoida (kuv.); *the C* ~
Englannin kanaali.

chant [tʃɑ:nt] *v.* laulaa, messuta; *s.*
psalmilaulu, yksitoikkoinen sävel.
-icleer ['tʃɑ:ntikliə] *s.* kukko.

chao|s ['ke(i)ɔs] *s.* kaaos, sekasorto.
-tic [ke(i)'ɔtik] *a.* sekasortoinen.

chap 1. [tʃæp] *s.* poika, kaveri; *old* ~
vanha veikko, hyvä veli.

chap 2. [tʃæp] *s.* halkeama (ihossa); *v.*
halkeilla, sierettyä; sierettää.

chap 3. *s.:* ~ *s* leuat. **-fallen** allapäin
[oleva].

chapel ['tʃæpl] *s.* kappeli,
rukoushuone.

chaperon ['ʃæpərəun] *s.* (nuoren tytön)
kaitsija, »esiliina», *v.* olla jkn
»esiliinana».

chaplain ['tʃæplin] *s.*
(hovi)kappalainen; *(army, navy, air
force* ~) sotilaspappi.

chapp|ed ['tʃæpt], **-y** ['tʃæpi] *a.*
sierettynyt.

chapter ['tʃæptə] *s.* (kirjan) luku;
tuomiokapituli (n kokous).

char 1. [tʃɑ:] *v.* tehdä siivoustyötä; *s.*
siivooja; sl. tee.

char 2. [tʃɑ:] *v.* hiiltää, -tyä; polttaa t.
palaa puuhiileksi.

character ['kæriktə] *s.* luonne;
tunnusmerkki, leima;
kirjoitusmerkki, kirjain; henkilö;
persoonallisuus; maine.
(palvelus)todistus; ominaisuus; ~
building luonteen kehittäminen; *a*

public ~ julkinen henkilö; *he's quite a*
~ omalaatuinen ihminen; .. *in* ~
ominainen jklle, tyyliin sopiva. **-istic**
[-'ristik] *a.* ominainen,
luonteenomainen, kuvaava; *s.*
tunnusmerkki; omituisuus,
ominaispiirre. **-ize** [-raiz] *v.* kuvata,
luonnehtia; olla (jklle)
luonteenomaista.

charade [ʃə'rɑ:d] *s.* (kuva)arvoitus.

charcoal ['tʃɑ:kəul] *s.* puuhiili.

chare [tʃeə] ks. *char 1.*

charge [tʃɑ:dʒ] *v.* syyttää *(sb. with);*
hyökätä, syöksyä kimppuun; ladata,
täyttää; antaa jklle tehtäväksi;
käskeä, velvoittaa; ottaa maksua,
veloittaa; *s.* syytös; lataus, panos;
hoito, huolenpito, valvonta;
hoidokki, holhotti; hinta,
kustannukset; hyökkäys; ~ .. *to sb.'s
account* merkitä jkn tiliin; *how much
did he* ~ *for it?* paljonko hän otti siitä
maksua (t. pyysi siitä)? ~ *sb. with*
antaa jklle tehtäväksi; [*the
demonstrators*] ~ *d the police*
hyökkäsivät poliisien kimppuun; *be in
(have)* ~ *of* olla (jku, jk)
hoidettavanaan; *in Mary's* ~ Maryn
hoidossa; *give sb. in* ~ luovuttaa
poliisin käsiin; *lay to sb.'s* ~ panna
jkn syyksi; *bring a* ~ *against* syyttää
jkta; *take* ~ *of* ottaa huostaansa,
huolehtia; *free of* ~ ilmaiseksi; [*the
doctor*] *in* ~ hoitava; ~ *s*
kustannukset. **-r** [-ə] *s.* sotaratsu.

charily ['tʃeərili] *adv.* varovasti,
säästäväisesti.

chariot ['tʃæriət] *s.* sota-,
kilpa-ajovaunut.

charisma [kə'rizmə] *s.* armolahja. **-tic**
[kæriz'mætik] *a.* karismaattinen.

charitable ['tʃæritəbl] *a.*
ihmisystävällinen, armelias,
hyväntekeväisyys-.

charity ['tʃæriti] *s.* lähimmäisen
rakkaus, ihmisrakkaus; armeliaisuus,
hyväntekeväisyys (-järjestö,
-yhdistys).

charlatan ['ʃɑ:lət(ə)n] *s.* puoskari,
huijari.

Charlemagne ['ʃɑ:lə'mein, -'main]
erisn. Kaarle Suuri.

Charles [tʃɑːlz] *erisn.* Kaarle; ~'s Wain Otava.

charlotte [ˈʃɑːlət] *s.* (omena)paistos.

charm [tʃɑːm] *s.* loitsu, taika(keino); taikakalu; lumous, viehätys(voima), sulo; *v.* loihtia, taikoa; lumota, tenhota, viehättää, hurmata; *I am* ~*ed to meet you* ihastuttavaa tavata sinut! ~*ed with* ihastunut jhk; *has a* ~*ed life* on haavoittumaton. **-ing** *a.* ihastuttava, viehättävä.

charnel-house [ˈtʃɑːnlhaus] *s.* ruumishuone.

charred *a.* hiiltynyt.

chart [tʃɑːt] *s.* merikartta, -kortti; taulukko, käyrästö, kartta; *v.* kartoittaa; ~*-topper* (mus.) listaykkönen.

charter [ˈtʃɑːtə] *s.* erioikeus(kirja), perustuskirja; rahtauskirja; *v.* antaa erioikeus(kirja); rahdata (laiva), vuokrata; *the Great C*~ Magna Charta; ~*ed accountant* valantehnyt tilintarkastaja; ~*ed plane* tilauslentokone. ~*-party* sertepartia, rahtauskirja.

charwoman [ˈtʃɑːwumən] *s.* siivooja.

chary [ˈtʃɛəri] *a.* pidättyväinen, säästeliäs.

chase 1. [tʃeis] *v.* pakottaa (metallia).

chase 2. [tʃeis] *v.* ajaa takaa, ajaa; *s.* (takaa-)ajo, metsästys; (takaa-ajettu) riista, eläin; *give* ~ *to* ryhtyä ajamaan takaa. **-r** [-ə] *s.* takaa-ajaja; sl. jälkiryyppy, m. kylmä juoma väkevän jälkeen.

chasm [ˈkæzm] *s.* rotko, kuilu.

chassis [ˈʃæsi] *s.* [pl. ˈʃæsiz] (auton) alusta.

chast|e [tʃeist] *a.* siveä, puhdas. **-en** [ˈtʃeisn] *v.* kurittaa; jalostaa, puhdistaa. **-ise** [tʃæsˈtaiz] *v.* rangaista, kurittaa, **-isement** [ˈtʃæstizmənt] *s.* rangaistus, kuritus. **-ity** [ˈtʃæstiti] *s.* siveys, puhtaus.

:hasuble [ˈtʃæzjubl] *s.* messukasukka.

hat [tʃæt] *v.* jutella, rupatella, pakista; *s.* juttelu, rupattelu.

hat|eau [ˈʃætəu] *s.* (pl. -*eaux* [-*ouz*]) linna, herraskartano (Ranskassa). **-elaine** [ˈʃætəlein] *s.* kartanon rouva; käädyt.

hattel [ˈtʃætl] *s.* (tav. *pl.*) irtain omaisuus, tavara.

chatter [ˈtʃætə] *v.* laverrella, lörpötellä; (linnuista) kirskua, räkättää; (hampaista) kalista; *s.* lavertelu, lörpötys; räkätys; kalina. **-box** lörppö.

chatty [ˈtʃæti] *a.* laverteleva.

Chaucer [ˈtʃɔːsə] *erisn.*

chauffeur [ˈʃəufə] *s.* (yksityis)autonkuljettaja.

chauvin|ism [ˈʃəuvinizm] *s.* kansalliskiihko. **-ist** [-ist] *s.* kansalliskiihkoilija.

cheap [tʃiːp] *a.* halpa, huokea; *adv.* halvalla *(get, buy, sell* ~); *feel* ~ olla häpeissään; *hold* ~ halveksia. **-en** [-n] *v.* alentaa, -tua, halventua. **-ly** *adv.* halvalla. **-ness** *s.* halpuus.

cheat [tʃiːt] *v.* pettää, petkuttaa, pelata väärin; luntata; *s.* petos; petkuttaja, huijari, väärinpeluri.

check [tʃek] *s.* (äkillinen) pysähdys, tauko; pidäke, este, hillintä; tarkistus, kontrolli; tarkistusmerkki, rasti; vastamerkki, kassakuitti; Am. šekki; ruutu, ruudullinen kangas; vastoinkäyminen; šakki! *v.* (šakki) šakata; pysähdyttää, ehkäistä, pidättää; tarkistaa (vertailemalla), verrata; viedä (laukku ym) säilytykseen; *keep in* ~ hillitä, pitää kurissa; *without a* ~ yhteen menoon; ~ *in (out)* ilmoittautua saapuessa (lähtiessä); ~ *off* merkitä tarkastetuksi. **-ed** [-t] *a.* ruudullinen. **-er** Am. ks. *chequer*. **-ers** [-əz] *pl.* Am. tammipeli; = *draughts* (Engl.) **-mate** [-ˈmeit] *s.* šakkimatti; ratkaiseva häviö; *v.* tehdä matiksi; tuhota. **-point** tarkastusasema.

Cheddar [ˈtʃedə] *s.* ~ *cheese* cheddarinjuusto.

cheek [tʃiːk] *s.* poski; hävyttömyys; ~ *by jowl* vieri vieressä; *have the* ~ *to* olla otsaa, juljeta. ~**-bone** poskipää. **-y** [-i] *a.* hävytön, röyhkeä.

cheep [tʃiːp] *v.* piipitys; *v.* piipittää.

cheer [tʃiə] *s.* eläköönhuuto, suosionhuuto; iloisuus; kestitys; *pl.* ~*s!* kippis! *v.* ilahduttaa; (~ *up*) rohkaista (mielensä); huutaa eläköötä; ~ *on* yllyttää, innostaa; *of good* ~ rohkealla, iloisella mielellä. **-ful** *a.* hyväntuulinen, iloinen; lahduttava. **-ing** *s.* suosion-, eläköönhuudot. **-io** [-riəu] *int.* hei,

hei! **-less** a. iloton, synkkä. **-y** [-ri] a. iloinen, reipas.

chees|e [tʃi:z] s. juusto; ~**-cake** (m.) kurvikas »seinäkuvatyttö»; ~ *finger* juustotanko; ~**-paring** kitsastelu. **-y** [-i] a. juustomainen; sl. huono.

cheetah ['tʃi:tə] s. gepardi.

chef [ʃef] s. keittiömestari.

Chelsea [tʃelsi] *erisn.*

chemical ['kemik(ə)l] a. kemiallinen; s. kemiallinen aine.

chemise [ʃi'mi:z] s. (naisen) paita.

chemist ['kemist] s. kemisti; apteekkari; ~ *'s* [*shop*] apteekki. **-ry** [-ri] s. kemia.

chemotherapy ['kemə(u)'θerəpi] s. kemoterapia.

cheque [tʃek] s. maksuosoitus, šekki *(for £ 10* kymmenen punnan); *draw a* ~ kirjoittaa sekki. ~**-book** šekkikirja.

chequer ['tʃekə] s.: ~s (pl.) ruutumalli; v. ruuduttaa; ~*ed* ruudukas; kirjava.

cherish ['tʃeriʃ] v. hellästi hoitaa, vaalia, helliä; pitää vireillä; ~ *a hope* elätellä toivoa; *the* ~*ed memory* [*of* ~ *his wife*] rakas muisto.

cheroot [ʃə'ru:t] s. sikarisavuke.

cherry ['tʃeri] s. kirsikka(puu); a. kirsikanpunainen.

cherub ['tʃerəb] s. kerubi. **-ic** [tʃe'ru:bik] a. enkelimäinen.

chervil ['tʃə:vil] s. kirveli.

chess [tʃes] s. šakki(peli). ~**-board** šakkilauta. ~**-man** šakkinappula.

chest [tʃest] s. arkku, kirstu; raha-arkku; rinta, rintakehä; ~ *of drawers* lipasto; ~ *trouble* keuhkovika; *get..off one's* ~ saada sanotuksi, keventää mieltään; *medicine* ~ lääkekaappi.

chesterfield ['tʃestəfi:ld] s. eräänl. sohva t. päällystakki.

chestnut ['tʃesnʌt] s. kastanja; raudikko; vanha vitsi; a. kastanjanruskea.

chevalier [ʃevə'liə] s. ritari.

cheviot ['tʃeviət] s. seviotti.

chevron ['ʃevr(ə)n] s. sotilaan ym hihamerkki (ʌ t. V).

chew [tʃu:] v. pureskella; ~ *upon (over)* miettiä; ~ *the cud* märehtiä (m. kuv.). **-ing-gum** purukumi.

chic [ʃik] a. tyylikäs, hieno.

Chicago [ʃi'ka:gəu] *erisn.*

chicane [ʃi'kein], **-ry** [-əri] s. asian-ajajan juoni, metku, lainvääristely.

chick [tʃik] s. linnunpoika; *the* ~s lapsukaiset.

chicken ['tʃikin] s. kananpoika, (linnun) poikanen; *is no* ~ ei ole enää lapsi. ~**-hearted** raukkamainen. ~**-pox** vesirokko.

chicory ['tʃikəri] s. sikuri; sikuri-salaatti, suppusikuri; vrt. *endive.*

chid [tʃid] *imp.* ks. *chide.*

chide [tʃaid] *chid,* pp. *chidden* t. *chid, v.* nuhdella, torua.

chief [tʃi:f] s. päällikkö, päämies, johtaja; a. pää-, pääasiallinen, tärkein, yli-; *physician-in-*~ ylilääkäri; *in* ~ etenkin. **-ly** *adv.* pääasiassa, etupäässä, **-tain** [-tən] s. päällikkö, päämies.

chiffon ['ʃifɔn] s. šifonki.

chilblain ['tʃilblein] s. kylmänkyhmy.

child [tʃaild] s. (pl. ~*ren* ['tʃildrən] lapsi; *from a* ~ lapsuudesta saakka; *when a* ~ lapsena; *it is* ~ *'s play* se on lastenleikkiä; *with* ~ raskaana. **-bed** lapsivuode; = seur. **-birth** synnytys. **-hood** s. lapsuus. **-ish** a. lapsellinen; lapsen. **-less** a. lapseton. **-like** [-laik] a. lapsenomainen.

Chile ['tʃili] *erisn.* **-an** [-ən] a. & s. chileläinen.

chill [tʃil] s. kylmyys; viileys; a. kylmä, viileä; v. kylmettää, jäähdyttää, viilentää; kylmetä, jäähtyä; *catch a* ~ vilustua. **-iness** s. kylmyys. **-y** [-i] a. kylmä(hkö), kolea, viluinen; kylmäkiskoinen.

chilli, chi i ['tʃili] s. espanjan-, punapippuri.

chime [tʃaim] s. kellonsoitto; v. soida; soittaa kelloja; sointua yhteen; ~ *in* yhtyä puhuttuun, *(with)* sopia yhteen.

chimera [kai'miərə] s. savupiippu, torvi; lampunlasi. ~**-piece** takanreunus. ~**-pot** savupiipun jatkos. ~**-stack** savupiippuryhmä. ~**-sweep(er)** nuohooja.

chimpanzee [tʃimpən'zi:] s. simpanssi (us. lyh. *chimp*).

chin [tʃin] s. leuka; ~**-wagging** juoruilu, lavertelu.

china ['tʃainə] s. posliini, posliiniesineet; a. posliini(nen)-; *C*~ Kiina *the People's Republic of* ~

Kiinan kansantasavalta: ~ *clay* kaoliini; *Chinatown* kiinalaiskortteli; ~ *ware* posliinitavarat.

chine [tʃain] *s.* (eläimen) selkäranka, selkäkappale.

Chinese [ˈtʃaiˈniːz] *a. & s.* (pl. sama) kiinalainen; kiinan kieli; ~ *lantern* kirjava paperilyhty.

chink [tʃiŋk] *s.* kilinä; rako, tirkistysreikä; *v.* kilistä, kalista, kilisyttää; *C*~ (sl.) kiinalainen.

chintz [tʃints] *s.* vahakretonki.

chip [tʃip] *v.* kolhia, kolhaista, lohkaista, veistää, rikkoa; kolhiintua, lohjeta; *s.* pala(nen), sirpale; lastu, säle; kolhaistu kohta, kolo; pelimarkka; ~ *in* keskeyttää; *fish and* ~ *s* paistettu kala ja perunalastut; ~ *ped edges* kolhiintuneet reunat; *he is a* ~ *of the old block* hän on ilmetty isänsä; *have a* ~ *on the shoulder (about)* haastaa riitaa : *when the* ~ *s are down* kun tiukka paikka tulee. **-board** lastulevy. **-munk** [-mʌŋk] *s.* maaorava.

chiro|mancy [ˈkaiərˌomænsi] *s.* kädestä ennustaminen. **-pody** [kiˈropədi] *s.* jalkojenhoito. **-practo** [-ə(u)præktə] *s.* kiropraktikko.

chirp [tʃəːp] *s.* sirkutus, piipitys; *v.* piipittää

chirr [tʃəː] *v.* sirittää. **-up** [ˈtʃirəp] *s.* sirkutus, liverrys; siritys; *v.* sirkuttaa, livertää.

chisel [ˈtʃizl] *s.* taltta; *v.* veistää, hakata taltalla; sl. petkuttaa; ~ *led features* hienot, kauniit piirteet.

chit 1. [tʃit] *s.* tenava.

chit 2. [tʃit] *s.* kirjelippu; (väliaikainen) tunnuste.

chit-chat [ˈtʃit-tʃæt] *s.* rupattelu, juorupuhe.

chivalr|ous [ˈʃivlrəs] *a.* ritari-, ritarillinen. **-y** [-ri] *s.* ritarilaitos; ritaristo; ritarillisuus.

chive [tʃaiv] *s.* ruoholaukka.

chiv(v)y [ˈtʃivi] *v.* hoputtaa; ~ *sb. about* ahdistaa.

hlor|ide [ˈklɔːraid] *s.* kloridi. **-ine** [-iːn] *s.* kloori.

hloro|form [ˈklɔrəfɔːm] *s.* kloroformi; *v.* nukuttaa kloroformilla. **-phyll** [-fil] *s.* lehtiviherä.

hock [tʃɔk] *s.* kiila; *v.* kiilata, tukea

kiiloilla; ~ *-full* täpötäynnä.

chocolate [ˈtʃɔk(ə)lit] *s.* suklaa; kaakao; *a.* suklaanvärinen.

choice [tʃɔis] *s.* valinta; valinnanvara, valikoima; *(a p.'s* ~ *)* jkn valitsema, valittu; *a.* oivallinen, paras, valio-; *which is your* ~ *?* kumman valitset? *he had no* ~ *but* hän ei voinut muuta kuin; *take your* ~ saat valita; *Hobson's* ~ ei valinnan varaa.

choir [ˈkwaiə] *s.* kuoro; kuori; ~ *boy* kuoripoika

choke [tʃəuk] *v.* kuristaa, tukehduttaa; (m. ~ *up*) tukkia; tukehtua, läkähtyä; *s.* kuristusventtiili; ~ *down* niellä; ~ *off* pelottamalla saada jku luopumaan aikeesta; ~ *up* tukkia; ~*d with* täpötäynnä jtk.; ~ *damp* kaivoskaasu. **-r** [-ə] *s.* korkea pystykaulus, (kireä) helminauha ym.

choler|a [ˈkɔlərə] *s.* kolera. **-ic** [-ik] *a.* koleerinen, pikavihainen, äkkipikainen.

cholesterol [kɔlˈestərɔl] *s.* kolestroli.

choos|e [tʃuːz] *chose chosen, v.* valita, valikoida; *[do] as you* ~ niinkuin haluat; *I cannot* ~ *but* go en voi olla menemättä. **-(e)y** [-i] *a.* valikoiva, nirso.

chop 1. [tʃɔp] *v.* hakata; pilkkoa, hienontaa; *s.* isku; kyljys; ~ *about* kääntyä äkkiä; ~ *and change* alinomaa muuttaa (mieltään); ~ *off* hakata irti, katkaista; ~ *up* hienontaa.

chop 2. [tʃɔp] *s.:* ~ *s* leuat, suu.

chop-house *s.* ruokala.

chopp|er [ˈtʃɔpə] *s.* lihakirves. **-ing-block** *s.* hakkuupölkky. **-y** [ˈtʃɔpi] *a.* puuskainen; ~ *sea* ristiaallokko.

chopstick *s.* syömäpuikko.

choral [ˈkɔːr(ə)l] *a.* kuoro-. **-e** [kɔˈrɑːl] *s.* koraali.

chord 1. [kɔːd] *s.* (harpun) kieli; jänne (mat.); *vocal* ~ *s* ks. *cord.*

chord 2. [kɔːd] *s.* akordi (mus.); *common* ~ kolmisointu.

choreograph|er [kɔriˈogrəfə] *s.,* koreografi. **-y** [-i] *s.* koreografia.

chores [tʃɔːz] *s.* (arkipäivän) askareet.

chorister [ˈkɔristə] *s.* kuoropoika, -laulaja

chortle [ˈtʃɔːtl] *v.* nauraa hörähdellä; *s.* hörähtely.

chorus [ˈkɔːrəs] *s.* kuoro; kertosäe, *in*

~ yhteen ääneen.

chose [tʃəuz] *imp.* ks. *choose.* **-n** [-n] *pp.* ks. *choose.*

chow [tʃau] *s.* kiinanpystykorva.

Christ [kraist] *s.* Kristus.

christen ['krisn] *v.* kastaa, ristiä. **C~dom** [-dəm] *s.* kristikunta. **-ing** *s.* kaste, ristiäiset.

Christian ['kristjən] *a.* kristillinen; *s.* kristitty; ~ *name* ristimänimi. **-ity** [kristi'æniti] *s,.* kristin|usko, -oppi; kristikunta. **c~ize** [-aiz] *v.* käännyttää kristinuskoon.

Christmas ['krisməs] *s.* joulu; *Father~* joulupukki; ~ *present* joululahja. **~-box** joululahja, -raha. **~-tree** joulukuusi.

chromatic [krə'mætik]. värikromaattinen.

chrom|e [krəum] *s.* kromi-, kromin|keltainen. **-ium** [-jəm] *s.* kromi; (**~-plated** kromitettu.) **-o-** [-ə(u)-] väri-, **-osome** [-əsəum] *s.* kromosomi.

chronic ['krɔnik] *a.* krooninen; pitkäaikainen; *s.* kroonikko, pitkäaikais|sairas, -potilas.

chronicle ['krɔnikl] *s.* aikakirja, kronikka; *C~s* aikakirjat; *v.* merkitä aikakirjoihin. **-r** [-ə] *s.* kronikoitsija.

chrono|logical [krɔnə'lɔdʒik(ə)l] *a.* kronologinen. **-logy** [krə'nɔlədʒi] *s.* ajanlasku; aikajärjestys. **-meter** [-'nɔmitə] *s.* tarkkuuskello.

chrysal|is ['krisəlis] *s.* (pl. *-ides, ~es*) (hyönteis)kotelo.

chrysanthemum [kri'sænθ(i)məm] *s.* krysanteemi.

chub [tʃʌb] *s.* turpa (eläint.). **-by** [-i] *a.* pullea, pyöreä(poskinen).

chuck 1. [tʃʌk] *v.* heittää, viskata; heittää sikseen, hylätä (m. ~ *up*); taputtaa; *s.* (sl.) antaa matkapassit; ~ *it!* jätä tuo sikseen! **~-er-out** [-ər-] (ravintolan) uloksheittäjä.

chuck 2. [tʃʌk] *s.* (sorvin) kiinnitysistukka; niska(liha).

chuckle ['tʃʌkl] *v.* nauraa itsekseen, hykerrellä; kaakattaa; *s.* naurun hykerrys; kaakatus.

chug ['tʃʌg] *v.:* ~ *along* prutkuttaa.

chum [tʃʌm] *s.* toveri, kumppani; *pl.* kaverukset; *v.:* ~ *with* olla jkn läheinen ystävä, asua yhdessä; ~ *up*

with ystävystyä. **-my** [-i] *a.* »hyvää pataa».

chump [tʃʌmp] *s.* puupölkky; (pölkky)pää; ~ *chop* paksummasta päästä leikattu lampaan kyljys; *off one's* ~ poissa tolaltaan, järjiltään.

chunk [tʃʌŋk] *s.* järkäle, paksu pala.

church [tʃə:tʃ] *s.* kirkko; jumalanpalvelus; seurakunta; *at* ~ jumalanpalveluksessa; *go to* ~ mennä kirkkoon. **~-goer** kirkossakävijä, kirkkovieras. **-warden** *s.* kirkonisäntä. **-y** [-i] *a.* (korkea)kirkollinen. **-yard** hautausmaa.

churl [tʃə:l] *s.* tomppeli, moukka. **-ish** [-iʃ] *a.* moukkamainen; töykeä, pahantuulinen.

churn [tʃə:n] *s.* kirnu; *v.* kirnuta.

chute [ʃu:t] *s.* (viettävä) kouru; liukurata; rikkakuilu.

chutney ['tʃʌtni] *s.* eräänl. kirpeä mauste t. säilyke.

ciao [tʃɑ:ə, Engl. tʃau]*int.* hei!terve!

cicada [si'kɑ:də] *s.* laulukaskas.

cicatr|ix, -ice ['sikatr|iks, -is] *s.* (pl. *-ices*) arpi. **-ize** [-aiz] *v.* arpeutua, arpeuttaa.

cicerone [tʃitʃə'rəuni] *s.* opas.

cider ['saidə] *s.* omenaviini, -juoma.

cigar [si'gɑ:] *s.* sikari; ~*-end* sikarinpätkä.

cigarette [sigə'ret] *s.* savuke. **~-case** savukekotelo. **~-holder** (savuke)imuke.

cilia ['siliə] *s.* värekarvat.

cinch [sintʃ] *s.* sl. helppo tehtävä, varma asia; *v.* varmistua, saada varma ote.

cinchona [siŋ'kəunə] *s.* kiinapuu.

cincture ['siŋtʃə] *s.* vyö.

cinder ['sində] *s.* (~*s*) tuhka; poro, kuona; kivihiilimurska, hiilen siru; ~ *track* hiilimurskarata. **C~ella** [-'relə] *s.* tuhkimo.

cine-camera ['sini-] *s.* kaitafilmikamera. **~-projector** elokuvaprojektori.

cinema ['sinima] *s.* elokuvateatteri. **-tographic** [-mætə'græfik] *a.* elokuva-**cinnabar** ['sinəbɑ:] *s.* sinooperi.

cinnamon ['sinəmən] *s.* kaneli.

cinquefoil ['siŋkfɔil] *s.* hanhikki.

cipher ['saifə] *s.* nolla; numero; salakirjoit|us, -uksen avain; *v.* laskea arvioida (~ *out);* kirjoittaa salakirjoituksella.

circa ['sə:kə] *prep.* noin, suunnilleen, likimain.

circle ['sə:kl] *s.* ympyrä, kehä; piiri; *v.* kiertää; (~ *about, around)* ympyröidä; *dress* ~ ensimmäinen parvi (teatt.); ~ *of friends* ystäväpiiri; *come full* ~ mennä umpeen.

circuit ['sə:kit] *s.* kierros, kiertomatka, -tie, piiri; (tuomarin) käräjämatka; virtapiiri; *short* ~ oikosulku. **-ous** [sə(:)'kju(:)itəs] *a.* kierto-; epäsuora; ~ *route* kiertotie.

circular ['sə:kjulə] *a.* ympyränmuotoinen, pyöreä; kierto-; *s.* kiertokirje (m. ~ *letter);* ~ *saw* pyörösaha; ~ *tour* rengasmatka. **-ize** [-raiz] *v.* lähettää kiertokirjeitä jklle.

circulat|e ['sə:kju|leit] *v.* kiertää; panna kiertämään, levittää; *-ing library* lainakirjasto; *-ing medium* maksuväline. **-ion** [-'leiʃn] *s.* kiertoliike, -kulku; verenkierto; (sanomalehden ym) levikki; *in* ~ liikkeessä, -llä; ~ *of air* ilmanvaihto. **-ory** [-lət(ə)ri] *a.* verenkierto-.

circum|cise ['sə:kəmsaiz] *v.* ympärileikata. **-cision** [-'siʒn] *s.* ympärileikkaus. **-ference** [sə:'kʌmf(ə)rəns] *s.* kehä, ympärys. **-jacent** [-'dʒeisnt] *a.* ympärillä sijaitseva. **-locution** [-lə'kju:ʃn] *s.* kiertely, verukkeet. **-navigate** *v.* purjehtia (esim. maailman) ympäri. **-scribe** [-skraib] *v.* rajoittaa. **-spect** [-spekt] *a.* varovainen; (~**ion** varovaisuus).

circumstan|ce ['sə:kəmstəns, -tæns] *s.* asianhaara, seikka; *pl.* olosuhteet, asiantila; (vain *sg.)* seikkaperäisyys; komeus *(pomp and* ~ *); in* (under) *the* ~ *s* näin ollen; *in easy* ~ *s* hyvissä oloissa. **-tial** [-'stænf(ə)l] *a.* seikkaperäinen, perusteellinen; ~ *evidence* aihetodistus, -tukset (lak.).

circumvent [sə:kəm'vent] *v.* kiertää (m. esim. lakia), pettää, tehdä tyhjäksi. **-ion** [-'venʃn] *s.* pettäminen, petos.

circus ['sə:kəs] *s.* sirkus; ympyräaukio.

cirrus ['sirəs] *s.* (pl. *cirri* [-ai] höyhenpilvi; kärhi (kasv.).

cissy ['sisi] *s.* naismainen mies.

cistern ['sistən] *s.* vesisäiliö.

citadel ['sitədl] *s.* linnoitus.

citation [si'teiʃn] *s.* haaste; lainaus, sitaatti; Am. kunniamaininta.

cite [sait] *v.* haastaa oikeuteen; lainata; mainita (esimerkkinä).

citizen ['sitizn] *s.* kansalainen, (kaupungin) asukas. **-ship** *s.* kansalaisoikeus; kansalaisuus.

citr|ic ['sitr|ik] *a.:* ~ *acid* sitruunahappo. **-us** [-əs] *s.* sitrushedelmä.

city ['siti] *s.* (suuri) kaupunki; *the C~* Lontoon City; *C~ man* liikemies (Cityssä); *C~ of God* Jumalan valtakunta; ~*-bred* kaupungissa kasvanut.

civet ['sivit] *s.* sivettikissa.

civic ['sivik] *a.* kansalais-, yhteiskunnallinen, kunta-. **-s** [-s] *s. pl.* kansalaistieto.

civies ['siviz] *pl. s.* siviilipuku.

civil ['sivil] *a.* yhteiskunnallinen, kansalais-, siviili-; kohtelias; ~ *engineer* tie- ja vesirakennusinsinööri; ~ *marriage* siviiliavioliitto; ~ *rights* kansalaisoikeudet; ~ *rights movement* kansalaisoikeusliike; ~ *servant* valtion virkamies; ~ *war* kansalaissota, sisällissota. **-ian** [si'viljən] *a.* siviili; *s.* siviilihenkilö. **-ity** [si'viliti] *s.* kohteliaisuus. **-ization** [sivilai'zeiʃn] *s.* sivistys, kulttuuri; sivistynyt maailma. **-ize** ['sivilaiz] *v.* sivistää.

civvies ks. *civies; Civvy street* siviilielämä.

clack [klæk] *s.* kalke; palpatus; *v.* kolista; palpattaa.

clad [klæd] ks. *clothe; a.* pukeutunut, -pukuinen.

claim [kleim] *v.* vaatia; väittää; *s.* vaatimus; oikeus (to jhk); väite; (esim. kaivos)valtaus; *lay* ~ *to* vaatia itselleen; *put in a* ~ (for) esittää vaatimus; *stake out a* ~ pyykittää valtausalue. **-ant** [-ənt] *s.* kantaja (lak.).

clairvoyance [klɛə'vɔiəns] *s.* selvänäköisyys.

clam [klæm] *s.* simpukka.

clamant ['kleimənt] *a.* huutava.

clamber ['klæmbə] *v.* kavuta.

clammy ['klæmi] *a.* tahmea, kosteahko, nihkeä.

clam 86

clam|orous ['klæm(ə)rəs] a. äänekäs, meluava. **-our, -or** ['klæmə] s. kova huuto, meteli; v. huutaa, meluta; ~ *for* äänekkäästi vaatia; ~ *against* huutaa julki pahekseumisensa.

clamp [klæmp] s. sinkilä; tukirauta; ruuvipuristin; v. vahvistaa (raudalla), puristaa kiinni; ~ *down on* panna lujille, painostaa.

clan [klæn] s. (Skotl.) klaani, heimo.

clandestine [klæn'destin] a. salainen, luvaton.

clang [klæŋ] s. helähdys; kalke, kalskahdus; raikuminen; v. soida, kalskahtaa, raikua; *drop a* ~ *er* munata itsensä. **-orous** [-gərəs] s. kalskahtava; raikuva. **-our, -or** [-gə] s. kalina, kalske.

clank [klæŋk] s. kalina; v. kalista; kalisuttaa.

clan|nish ['klæniʃ] a. heimo(n)-, sukuylpeä. **-ship** s. heimohenki.

claque [klæk]: *the* ~ palkatut (käsien)taputtajat.

clap [klæp] v. paukuttaa, pamauttaa, läimäyttää; räpyttää; s. kättentaputus, pauke; ~ *of thunder* ukkosenjyrähdys; ~ *eyes on* saada näkyviinsä; ~ *one's hands* taputtaa käsiään; ~ *in prison* heittää vankilaan. **-board** vuorauslauta. **-per** [-ə] s. (kellon) kieli, läppä; räikkä. **-trap** s. vaikutuksen tavoittelu; a. tehoa tavoitteleva.

claret ['klærət] s. punaviini.

clari|fy ['klærifai] v. puhdistaa, kirkastaa; selvittää; selvitä, kirkastua; *-fier* selvike. **-on** [-ən] s. torvi; ~ *call* sotatorvi. **-net** [-net] s. klarinetti. **-ty** [-ti] s. kirkkaus, selkeys.

clash [klæʃ] v. kalista, kalskahtaa; iskeä yhteen, törmätä vastakkain, olla ristiriidassa; s. helinä, kalske, ryske; yhteentörmäys, yhteenotto; ristiriita.

clasp [klɑːsp] s. solki, haka; ote; kädenpuristus, syleily; v. kiinnittää soljella; tarttua, pitää kiinni; syleillä; ~ *sb.'s hand* puristaa jkn kättä; [*with hands*] ~ed ristissä; [*this bracelet*] *won't* ~ ei mene lukkoon. **-knife** linkkuveitsi.

class [klɑːs] s. luokka, opetustunti; kurssi; v. luokitella; (~ *among*)

laskea jhk kuuluvaksi; *middle* ~[*es*] keskiluokka; *in a* ~ *by itself* omaa luokkaansa. **-book** oppikirja. **-fellow, -mate** luokkatoveri.

classi|c ['klæsi|k] a. klassinen, klassillinen; yleisesti tunnustettu, pysyväarvoinen, puhdaslinjainen; s. klassinen kirjailija, klassikko; *pl.: the* ~*s* klassinen (t. antiikin) kirjallisuus; *he reads* ~*s* [*at Oxford*] hän opiskelee antiikin kirjallisuutta ja kieliä. **-cal** [-k(ə)l] a. klassinen. **-cist** [-sist] s. klassisen kirjallisuuden ja kielten tuntija. **-fication** [-fi'keiʃn] s. luokittelu, luokitus. **-fy** [-fai] v. luokitella; *-fied* m. salainen.

class|less luokaton. **-room** luokkahuone. **-y** [-i] a. hieno, tyylikäs.

clatter ['klætə] v. kolista, rämistä; kalisuttaa; s. kalina, räminä.

clause [klɔːz] s. (sivu)lause; (sopimuksen) ehto, klausuuli, momentti.

claustrophobia [klɔːstrə'fəubiə] s. suljetun paikan kammo.

clavicle ['klævikl] s. solisluu.

claw [klɔː] s. kynsi; (ravun ym) saksijalka; sorkka, pihdit (tekn.); v. kynsiä, raapia; tarttua, kahmaista.

clay [klei] s. savi. **-ey** [-i] a. savi-, saviperäinen. **-more** [-mɔː] s. (muinaiskottil.) leveä miekka.

clean [kliːn] a. puhdas; kirjoittamaton; siisti, virheetön, selvä; kaunismuotoinen; täydellinen; *adv.* täydellisesti, aivan, kokonaan; v. puhdistaa, siistiä, kiillottaa; ~ *copy* puhtaaksi kirjoitettu teksti; *I* ~ *forgot about it* unohdin sen täysin; ~ *down* harjata t. pyyhkiä puhtaaksi; ~ *out* puhdistaa, tyhjentää, (sl.) kyniä putipuhtaaksi; *is* ~ *ed out* (puhek.) on rahaton, aivan »auki»; ~ *up* siistiä; hankkia rahaa t. voittoa. **~-cut** teräväpiirteinen. **-er** [-ə] s. siivooja; kemiallinen pesulaitos; *puhdistusaine.* **~-limbed** kaunisjäseninen. **-liness** ['klenlinis] s. puhtaus, siisteys. **-ly** *adv.* puhtaasti jne.; *a.* ['klenli] puhdas, siisti. **-ness** s. puhtaus. **-se** [klenz] v. puhdistaa. **-ser** ['klenzə] s. puhdistusaine. **~-shaven** sileäksi ajeltu. **~-up** puhdistus.

clear [kliə] *a.* kirkas; selvä, selkeä; raikas; puhdas (voitto ym); täysi, kokonainen; esteetön, vapaa *(of* jstk); *v.* tehdä kirkkaaksi, puhdistaa, vapauttaa; raivata, tyhjentää; selviytyä, suoriutua jstk; tuottaa puhdasta voittoa; selvittää (laiva); kirkastua, seljetä; *adv.* selvästi; esteettä, aivan, kokonaan; [*be*] *~ about* selvillä jstk; *get ~ of* selviytyä jstk; *keep ~ of* välttää, olla sekaantumatta; ~ *the table* korjata ruoka pöydästä; ~ *one's throat* kakistella kurkkuaan; ~ *away* viedä pois, tyhjentää; hälvetä; ~ *off* selviytyä jstk, maksaa (velka); hälvetä, laittautua tiehensä; ~ *off* (t. *out*)! ala häipyä! ~ *out* tyhjentää, myydä loppuun; laittautua tiehensä; ~ *up* selvittää, järjestää; kirkastua. **~-ance** [-rəns] *s.* vapautuminen, tyhjentäminen; (laivan)selvitys; vapaa väli; *road ~* maavara; ~ *sale* alennus-, tyhjennysmyynti. **~-cut** selvä, -piirteinen, tarkkarajainen. **~-headed** selväjärkinen. **-ing** *s.* metsänaukea; raivaus; selvitys, clearing (kaupp.). **-ly** *adv.* selvästi, epäilemättä.

cleat [kli:t] *s.* (poikki)piena, lista; (kiinnitys)tappi.

cleavage [ˈkli:vidʒ] *s.* halkeaminen; rako, juopa.

cleave 1. [kli:v] *v.* : ~ *to* riippua kiinni jssk.

cleave 2. [kli:v] *cleft cleft* t. *clove cloven, v.* halkaista; haljeta, lohjeta. **-r** [-ə] *s.* lihakirves.

clef [klef] *s.* nuottiavain.

cleft [kleft] *imp. & pp.* ks. *cleave; s.* halkeama, rako; ~ *palate* suulakihalkio.

clematis [ˈklemətis] *s.* elämänlanka.

clemency [ˈklemənsi] *s.* laupeus, lempeys; lauhkeus.

clench [klen(t)ʃ] *v.* yhteen (t. tarttua) lujasti; ~ *one's teeth* purra hammasta; *with ~ed fists* kädet nyrkissä, nyrkkiä puiden; *a ~ed-fist salute* mustan vallan tervehdys, nyrkkitervehdys; vrt. *clinch.*

clergy [ˈklə:dʒi] *s.* papisto, papit. **-man** [-mən] *s.* (pl. *-men* [-mən]) pappi.

clerical [ˈklerik(ə)l] *a.* papillinen, pappis-; kirjurin, konttori-; ~ *error* kirjoitusvirhe.

clerk [klɑ:k, Am. klə:k] *s.* konttoriapulainen, konttoristi; kirjanpitäjä; kirjuri, notaari; (Am. m.) kauppa-apulainen.

clever [ˈklevə] *a.* näppärä, taitava; lahjakas, älykäs, terävä, nokkela. **-ness** *s.* taitavuus, älykkyys.

clew [klu:] ks. *clue.*

cliché [ˈkli:ʃei] *s.* kulunut lauseparsi, klišee.

click [klik] *v.* naksahtaa, napsahtaa; onnistua; sl. ystävystyä äkkiä; *s.* naksahdus, napsahdus; maiskaus; ~ *one's heels* iskeä kantapäät yhteen.

client [ˈklaiənt] *s.* asiakas; (asianajajan) päämies. **-ele** [klaiən'tel, kli:ən-] *s.* asiakkaat, kävijät, (hotellin) vieraat.

cliff [klif] *s.* kallio; kallioranta, törmä. **-y** [-i] *a.* kallioinen.

climat|e [ˈklaimit] *s.* ilmasto, ilmanala. **-ic** [klai'mætik] *s.* ilmasto(lline)n.

climax [ˈklaimæks] *s.* huippukohta.

climb [klaim] *v.* kiivetä, nousta; *s.* kiipeäminen, nousu. **-er** [-ə] *s.* vuorikiipeilijä, kiipijä (m. kuv.); köynnöskasvi.

clime [klaim] *s.* seutu, ilmanala.

clinch [klin(t)ʃ] *v.* kotkata, niitata; ratkaista, lyödä lukkoon; (nyrkk.) sitoa, *s.* sitominen. **-er** [-ə] *s.* viimeinen, ratkaiseva sana.

cling [kliŋ] *clung clung, v.* takertua, tarttua; tarrautua; pitää tiukasti kiinni *(to* jstk); ~*ing* toisen tukea tarvitseva; vartalonmukainen.

clinic [klinik] *s.* klinikka. **-al** [-(ə)l] *a.* kliininen.

clink [kliŋk] *v.* kilistä(ä); *s.* kilinä, kilahdus; sl. linna, vankila. **-er** [-ə] *s.* klinkkeri.

clip 1. [klip] *s.* nipistin, pinne, (näytepussi- ym) liitin; solki; klipsi; korvakoru; *v.* kiinnittää (esim. papereita) liittimellä.

clip 2. [klip] *v.* leikata, leikellä; typistää; *s.* leikattu pala. **-per** [-ə] *s.* (tav. *pl.*) hiustenleikkuukone; nopea purjelaiva t. lentokone. **-ping** *s.* sanomalehtileike.

clique [kli:k] *s.* nurkkakunta, klikki.

cloak [kləuk] s. viitta, vaippa, verho; v.
verhota, peittää; *under the ~ of
darkness* pimeyden turvin. **~-room**
matkatavara- t. vaatesäilö; toaletti.
clobber [ˈklɔbə] v. hakata, päihittää.
cloche [klɔʃ] s. (lasi)suojus, kupu,
kello(hattu).
clock [klɔk] s. (seinä-, pöytä- ym)
kello; v. ottaa (urheilijalta) aika; *~ in
(out)* leimata saapumis- (t.
lähtö)aikansa kellokorttiin; *it's one
o'~* kello on yksi; *at ten o'~* kello
kymmeneltä; *round the ~*
vuorokauden ympäri. **~-face**
kellotaulu. **-wise** myötäpäivään.
-work s. kellon koneisto; *attr.*
mekaaninen; *like ~* kuin kello, kellon
tarkkuudella.
clod [klɔd] s. multa-(t. savi)kokkare;
moukka. **-hopper** moukka.
clog [klɔg] s. pidäke, taakka, este;
puukenkä; v. ehkäistä, tukkia. **-gy** [-i]
a. tahmea.
cloister [ˈklɔistə] s. pilari-, ristikäytävä,
luostari; *v.: ~ed* eristäytynyt.
close 1. [kləuz] v. sulkea, ummistaa;
lopettaa, päättää; sulkeutua; päättyä;
s. päätös, loppu; *~ about* ympäröidä;
~ down sulkea; *~ in* lähestyä; lyhetä;
~ up sulkea, tukkia; mennä umpeen;
~ with ryhtyä käsikähmään; hyväksyä
(tarjous); *the shop ~s at 6* liike
suljetaan kuudelta; *bring to a ~*
saattaa päätökseen; *~d car* umpiauto;
~d-circuit TV kaapelitelevisio; *~d
[shop]* vain järjestäytyneitä
työntekijöitä käyttävä.
close 2. [kləus] *a.* umpinainen, suljettu;
ahdas; raskas, ummehtunut; salainen,
vaitelias; kitsas; läheinen; tiheä,
tarkka; uuttera; kireä, täpärä; *adv.*
lähellä *(to jtk)*; tarkasti; *~* aidattu ala;
~ attention kiinteä tarkkaavaisuus; *~
combat* käsikähmä; *come to ~ quarters*
joutua käsikähmään; *~ season*
rauhoitusaika; *a ~ shave (call, thing)*
täpärä paikka; *keep ~* pitää salassa;
run sb. ~ seurata jkn kintereillä; *~ at
hand* vieressä, käsillä; *~ by* (aivan)
lähellä; *~ upon* lähes. **~-cropped**
sänkitukkainen. **~-fisted** kitsas.
~-fitting vartalonmukainen, ahdas.
~-hauled hankavastaiseen (merk.).
-ly *adv.* tiiviisti; läheltä; tarkasti;

läheisesti. **-ness** s. tiiviys; ahtaus;
ummehtuneisuus; kitsaus; tarkkuus;
läheisyys.
closet [ˈklɔzit] s. komero (et. Am.);
be ~ed with olla kahdenkeskisessä
neuvottelussa jkn kanssa.
close-up [ˈkləusʌp] s. lähikuva.
closure [ˈkləuʒə] s. sulkeminen;
keskustelun päättäminen.
clot [klɔt] s. kokkare; sl. tomppeli; v.
hyytyä, kokkaroitua; hyydyttää; *blood
~* veritulppa; *~ted cream* juoksutettu
kerma.
cloth [klɔ(:)θ] s. (pl. *cloths* [klɔθs, Am.
klɔðz]) kangas, verka; (pöytä)liina;
bound in ~ kangas(t. klootti)kansissa;
floor-~ lattiariepu; *the ~* papisto.
clothe [kləuð] v. (imp. & pp. *~d* t.
(vanh.) *clad*) pukea, vaatettaa;
verhota.
clothes [kləuðz] s. pl. vaatteet, puku; *~
rack* vaatenaulakko. **~-brush**
vaateharja. **~-horse, -line**
kuivausteline, -nuora. **~-peg, ~-pin**
pyykkipoika. **~-press**
liinavaatekaappi.
cloth|ier [ˈkləuðiə] s. verka-,
kangaskauppias. **-ing** s. vaatteet.
cloud [klaud] s. pilvi; suuri parvi; v.
peittää pilviin; sumentaa; mennä
pilveen (m. *~ over, ~ up*); *in the ~s*
hajamielinen. **-berry** muurain.
~-burst kaatosade. **~-capped**
pilvenkorkuinen. **-ed** *a.* pilvinen. **-less**
a. pilvetön. **-y** [-i] *a.* pilvinen; samea,
hämärä.
clout [klaut] s. riepu; lyönti, kopaus; v.
lyödä.
clove 1. [kləuv] s. mausteneilikka;
(valkosipulin) kynsi; *oil of ~s*
neilikkaöljy.
clove 2. [kləuv] imp. ks. *cleave.* **-n** [-n]
pp. & a. halkinainen; *~ hoof* sorkka;
pukinsorkka.
clover [ˈkləuvə] s. apila; *in ~*
yltäkylläisyydessä; *~ leaf* neliapila (m.
eritasoristeys).
clown [klaun] s. moukka; ilmeilijä,
klovni; pelle; v. pelehtiä, pelleillä,
ilveillä. **-ish** *a.* moukkamainen.
cloy [klɔi] v. kyllästyttää, ällöttää; *~ing*
ällöttävä.
club [klʌb] s. nuija, (esim.
jääkiekko)maila; risti (kortti); kerho;

seura; *v.* iskeä nuijalla; ~ *together* lyöttäytyä yhteen, kerätä (rahaa); ~*s* risti; *the ace of* ~*s* ristiässä. ~**-foot** kampurajalka.

cluck [klʌk] *v.* kotkottaa; *s.* kotkotus.

clue [klu:] *v.* johtolanka, viite.

clump [klʌmp] *s.* ryhmä, rykelmä, möykky; *v.* istuttaa ryhmiin; astua raskaasti.

clumsiness *s.* kömpelyys.

clumsy ['klʌmzi] *a.* kömpelö.

clung [klʌŋ] *imp. & pp.* ks. *cling.*

cluster ['klʌstə] *s.* terttu; parvi, ryhmä; kasaantuma; *v.* kasvaa tertussa; kerääntyä, ryhmittyä.

clutch [klʌtʃ] *v.* tarttua *(at* jhk); ottaa kiinni; *s.* tiukka ote; kytkin (tekn.); *get into the* ~*es of* joutua jkn kynsiin.

clutter ['klʌtə] *s.* epäjärjestys; *v.* (tav. ~ *up)* panna sekaisin, sotkea.

Clyde [klaid] *erisn.*

co- [kəu-] *pref.* yhteis-, kanssa-.

coach [kəutʃ] *s.* (umpi)vaunut, postivaunut; linja-auto, turistiauto, rautatievaunu; (tutkintoon)valmentaja; *v.* valmentaa (tutkintoon ym). **-man** [-mən] ajaja.

coagula|te [kə(u)'ægjuleit] *v.* hyytyä, maksoittua; hyydyttää. **-tion** [-'leiʃn] *s.* hyytyminen.

coal [kəul] *s.* kivihiili; *v.* hiilestää, ottaa hiiliä; *haul (call) over the* ~*s* antaa aimo läksytys. ~**-bed** hiilikerrostuma. ~**-field** hiilikenttä.

coalesce [kə(u)ə'les] *v.* sulautua, liittyä yhteen. **-nce** [-ns] *s.* yhteensulautuminen, yhtyminen.

coalition [kə(u)ə'liʃn] *s.* yhtyminen; kokoomus, liitto.

coal|-mine hiilikaivos. ~**-scuttle** hiililämpäri, -säiliö.

coarse [kɔ:s] *a.* karkea, karhea; raaka ruokoton; yksinkertainen. ~**-grained** karkea(syinen). **-n** [-n] *v.* tehdä, tulla karkeaksi. **-ness** karkeus jne.

coast [kəust] *s.* rannikko; *v.* purjehtia pitkin rannikkoa; laskea mäkeä; ajaa vapaalla. **-al** [-əl] *a.* rannikko-. **-er** [-ə] *s.* rannikkoalus; (lasin ym) alusta, alunen. ~**-guard** rannikkovartiosto. **-line** rantaviiva.

coat [kəut] *s.* takki, päällystakki; (eläimen) turkki, höyhenpeite; kuori, kalvo; päällys(te); *v.* päällystää;

sivellä maalilla; ~ *of arms* vaakuna; ~ *of paint* maalipeite; ~ *and skirt* kävelypuku; *cut one's* ~ *according to one's cloth* panna suu säkkiä myöten. **-ed** [-id] *a.* tahmainen (kieli). **-ee** [-'ti:] *s.* lyhyt takki. ~**-hanger** vaateripustin. **-ing** *s.* (maali- ym) peite, päällyste. ~**-tail(s)** takinlieve.

coax [kəuks] *v.* mielistelemällä taivuttaa, suostutella, taivutella; houkutella.

cob [kɔb] *s.* (tukeva) ratsastushevonen; urosjoutsen; (maissin) lapakko, tähkä.

cobalt ['kəubɔ:lt] *s.* kobolttti.

cobble ['kɔbl] *s.* mukulakivi; *v.* paikata (kenkiä). **-r** [-ə] *s.* kengänpaikkaaja; töhertäjä.

cobra ['kəubrə] *s.* silmälasikäärme.

cobweb ['kɔbweb] *s.* hämähäkinverkko, -seitti.

coca-cola ['kəukə'kəulə] *s.* ks. *coke.*

cocaine [kə'kein] *s.* kokaiini.

cocc|i ['kɔk|ai] *pl.* ks. seur. **-us** [-əs] *s.* kokki (bakteeri).

cochineal ['kɔtʃini:l] *s.* kokenilli.

cock 1. [kɔk] *s.* kukko, koiras(lintu); hana; *v.* nostaa pystyyn, kääntää yläspäin; olla pystyssä; ~ *of the walk* kukko(na) tunkiolla; ~ *one's hat* panna hattu vinoon; ~ *one's ears* höristää korviaan; ~ *one's eys* vilkuttaa silmää; ~ *a gun* virittää pyssyn hana; ~ *sth up* (puhek.) sotkea; ~*-a-doodle-doo* kukkokiekuu; ~*-and-bull story* lastenkamarisatu.

cock 2. [kɔk] *s.* heinäruko; *v.* panna ru'olle.

cockade [kɔ'keid] *s.* kokardi.

Cockaigne [kɔ'kein] *s.* Laiskurila.

cockatoo [kɔkə'tu:] *s.* kakadu.

cock|-chafer turilas. ~**-crow** kukonlaulu, päivänkoitto **-ed** [kɔkt] *a.*: ~ *hat* kolmikolkkahattu. **-erel** ['kɔk(ə)r(ə)l] *s.* kukonpoika. ~**-eyed** kierosilmäinen. ~**-fighting** kukkotappelu. **-horse:** *ride a* ratsastaa polvella ym (lastenk.).

cockle ['kɔkl] *s.* sydänsimpukka; *v.* rypistyä, -tää; *the* ~*s of one's heart* sydämen sopukat. **-shell** simpukankuori; (kuv.) pieni vene, pähkinäkuori.

Cockney ['kɔkni] *s.* (East Endin)

lontoolainen; c ~ accent Lontoon (cockney-) murre s.

cock|pit ['kɔkpit] s. (kukko)taistelukenttä; ohjaushytti (pienessä lentokoneessa); sidontapaikkana käytetty tila sotalaivoissa. **-roach** [-rəutʃ] torakka. **-scomb** [-skəum] kukon harja; keikari. **-sure** itsevarma. **-y** [-i] s. itserakas.

coco ['kəukəu] s. kookospalmu. **-nut** kookospähkinä; ~ matting kookosmatto.

cocoa ['kəukəu] s. kaakao, suklaa.

cocoon [kə'ku:n] s. (silkkiäistoukan) kotelo; kääriä; suojella (esim. muovilla).

cod [kɔd] s. turska (m. ~-fish): ~-liver oil kalanmaksaöljy.

coddle ['kɔdl] v hemmotella; keittää (hiljaisella tulella).

code [kəud] s. lakikokoelma, laki; koodi; v. ilmaista koodikielellä; ~ name peitenimi.

codeine ['kəudi:n] s. kodeiini.

codger ['kɔdʒə] s.: old ~ omituinen ukkeli.

codi|cil ['kɔdisil] s. testamentin lisäys. **-fy** [-fai] v. kodifioida.

co-driver [kəu-] s. kakkosajaja.

co-ed ['kəu'ed] s. yhteiskoulua käyvä tyttö, naisopiskelija.

co-education ['kəuedju'keiʃn] s. yhteiskasvatus. **-al** [-(ə)nl] a. ~ school yhteiskoulu.

coefficient [kə(u)i'fiʃ(ə)nt] s. kerroin (mat.).

coer|ce [kə(u)'ɔ:s] v. pakottaa, hillitä. **-cion** [kə(u)'ɔ:ʃn] s. pakko. **-cive** [-siv] a. pakko-.

coeval [kə(u)'i:v(ə)l] a. samanaikainen, -ikäinen; s. ikätoveri.

coexist [kə(u)ig'zist] v. olla yht'aikaa olemassa. **-ence** [-(ə)ns] s. yhdenaikaisuus; peaceful ~ rauhanomainen rinnakkaiselo. **-ent** [-(ə)nt] a. yhdenaikainen.

coffee ['kɔfi] s. kahvi. ~-grounds kahviporo. ~-pot s. kahvipannu. -kannu. ~-maker kahvinkeitin.

coffer ['kɔfə] s. (raha-)arkku: ~ dam arkkupato.

coffin ['kɔfin] s. ruumisarkku.

cog [kɔg] s. hammas (tekn.)

cogency ['kəudʒnsi] s. vakuuttavuus, todistusvoima.

cogent ['kəudʒnt] a. vakuuttava, painava.

cogged [kɔgd] a. hammas-.

cogita|te ['kɔdʒiteit] v. ajatella, pohtia, **-tion** [-'teiʃn] s. ajatteleminen, pohdinta.

cognate ['kɔgneit] a. samaa sukua t. alkuperää oleva, sukulais-; s. sukulaissana.

cognition [kɔg'niʃn] s. havainto, tieto.

cogniz|ance ['kɔ(g)nizns] s. (lak.) tieto; tuomiovalta; tietopiiri; have ~ of tietää. **-ant** [-nt] a.: ~ of jtk tietävä.

cognomen [kɔg'nəumen] s. lisänimi, sukunimi.

cog-wheel hammaspyörä.

cohabit [kə(u)'hæbit] v. asua yhdessä; olla avoliitossa. **-ation** [-'teiʃn] s. avoliitto.

coheir ['kəu'ɛə] s. toinen t. muu perillinen, perijäkumppani.

coher|e ['kə(u)'hiə] v. pysyä koossa; olla yhtäpitävä (jnk kanssa). **-nce** [-r(ə)ns] s. yhtenäisyys. **-nt** [-r(ə)nt] a. yhtenäinen.

cohesion [kə(u)'hi:ʒn] s. koheesio, kiinnevoima.

coif [kɔif] s. kalotti, hilkka.

coiffure [kwæ'fjuə] s. hiuslaite.

coign [kɔin] s.: ~ of vantage edullinen (tähystys)paikka.

coil [kɔil] v. kiertää (keräksi, vyyhdelle ym), kelata; kiertyä; kiemurrella; s. kiemura, kiehkura; kierukka; (sähk.). kela; käämi.

coin [kɔin] s. (metalli)raha, kolikko; v. lyödä (rahaa): sepittää (sana); pay a p. in his own ~ maksaa samalla mitalla. **-age** [-idʒ] s. rahanlyönti; rahajärjestelmä; [a new] ~ uusi (vasta sepitetty) sana.

coincide [kə(u)in'said] v. sattua samaan aikaan, olla samanaikainen; olla yhtäpitävä. **-nce** [kə(u)'insid(ə)ns] s. yhteensattuma. **-nt** [kə(u)'insid(ə)nt] a. samanaikainen; (~al yhteensattuva, satunnainen).

coiner ['kɔinə] s. vääränrahantekijä; ~ of words sanaseppo.

coitus ['kəuitəs] s. (sukupuoli)yhdyntä.

coke [kəuk] s. koksi; coca-cola.

coker-nut = *coconut.*
colander ['kɔləndə] *s.* lävikkö.
cold [kəuld] *a.* kylmä, viluinen; tunteeton; kylmäkiskoinen; laimea; *s.* kylmyys, pakkanen; vilustuminen, nuha; *be* ~ palella; *I feel* ~ minun on vilu, palelen; *catch* [*a*] ~ vilustua; *that's* ~ *comfort* se on laiha lohtu; *he got* ~ *feet* häntä alkoi jänistää; *left out in the* ~ pulaan jätetty(nä). ~-**blooded** tunteeton; vaihtolämpöinen. -**ish** [-iʃ] *a.* viileä, kylmähkö. ~-**shoulder** kohdella kylmäkiskoisesti. ~-**storage:** *c.*-*s. room* kylmiö.
colic ['kɔlik] *s.* ähky, koliikki.
collabora|te [kə'læbəreit] *v.* tehdä yhteistyötä. -**tion** [-'reiʃn] *s.* yhteistyö, -toiminta (m. sodan aikana vihollisen kanssa). -**tor** [-ə] *s.* työtoveri.
collage [kə'la:ʒ] *s.* kollaasi, koostelma.
collaps|e [kə'læps] *v.* romahtaa, sortua; *v.* sortuminen, luhistuminen; kollapsi (lääk.). -**ible** [-əbl] *a.* kokoon pantava, -käännettävä.
collar ['kɔlə] *s.* kaulus kaulanauha, vitjat; kaulahihna, länget; (tekn.) rengas, laippa; länget; *v.* tarttua kauluksesta, käydä kiinni jkh; sl. kähveltää; (keitt.) sitoa kääryleeksi. ~-**bone** solisluu.
collate [kə'leit] *v.* vertailla, kollationoida.
collateral [kɔ'læt(ə)r(ə)l] *a.* sivu-, syrjä-; välillinen; ~ *security* lisävakuus.
collation [kɔ'leiʃn] *s.* vertailu; kevyt ateria.
colleague ['kɔli:g] *s.* virkaveli, virkatoveri, kollega.
collect 1. ['kɔlekt] *s.* kollehtarukous.
collect 2. [kə'lekt] *v.* koota, kerätä, keräillä; kantaa, periä (maksuja); kerääntyä; noutaa; ~ *oneself* malttaa mielensä; ~ *call* vastapuhelu. -**ed** [-id] *a.* tyyni. -**ion** [kə'lekʃn] *s.* keräys; kokoelma; (verojen ym) kanto, (postilaatikon) tyhjennys; kolehti. -**ive** [-iv] *a.* yhteis-; kollektiivinen; ~ *bargaining* työehtosopimusneuvottelut. -**or** [-ə] *s.* kokooja, keräilijä.
colleg|e ['kɔlidʒ] *s.* kollegio; (Br.

yliop.), Engl. korkeampi oppilaitos, oppikoulu; Am. yliopisto; opisto. -**iate** [kɔ'li:dʒiit] *a.* kollegion; collegen.
collide [kə'laid] *v.* törmätä yhteen; ~ *with* törmätä jhk.
collit ['kɔli] *s.* skotlanninpaimenkoira.
collier ['kɔliə]*s.* hiilikaivosmies. -**y** ['kɔljəri] *s.* hiilikaivos.
collision [kə'liʒn] *s.* yhteentörmäys; ristiriita.
collodion [kə'ləudjən] *s.* kollodium.
colloquial [kə'ləukwiəl] *a.* arkikielinen, puhekielen. -**izm** *s.* puhekielen sanonta. -**ly** *adv.* puhekielessä.
colloquy ['kɔləkwi] *s.* keskustelu, puhelu.
collusion [kə'lu:ʒn] *s.* salainen sopimus (riitapuolen kanssa).
Cologne [kə'ləun] *erisn.* Köln.
Colombia [kə'lʌmbiə] *erisn.* Kolumbia.
colon ['kəulən] *s.* kaksoispiste; paksusuoli.
colonel [kə:nl] *s.* eversti.
colon|ial [kə'ləun|jəl] *a.* siirtomaa(n)-: *s.* siirtomaan asukas. -**ialism** [-jəlizm] *s.* kolonialismi. -**ist** ['kɔlənist] *s.* siirtolainen, uudisasukas. -**ization** [kɔlənai'zeiʃn] *s.* asuttaminen. -**ize** ['kɔlənaiz] *v.* perustaa siirtokunta, asuttaa.
colonnade [kɔlə'neid] *s.* pylväikkö pylväsrivi.
colony ['kɔləni] *s.* siirtokunta, siirtola, siirtomaa.
Colorado [kɔlə'ra:dəu] *erisn.*; ~ *beetle* koloradonkuoriainen.
color|ation [kʌlə'reiʃn] *s.* väritys. -**atura** [kɔlərə'tjuərə, Am. -'tuərə] *a. & s.* koloratuuri(laulajatar).
coloss|al [kə'lɔsl] *a.* valtavan suuri. **C-eum** [kɔlə'siəm] *erisn.* **C-ians** [kə'lɔʃ(ə)nz] *s.* Kolossalaiskirje. -**us** [-səs] *s.* jättiläispatsas.
colour, color ['kʌlə] *s.* väri, väritys; (raikas) ihonväri; (kuv.) luonne, näkö; *pl.* lippu; *v.* värittää; kaunistella; värjääntyä; punastua; *with flying* ~ s loistavasti; *serve with the* ~ s olla sotapalveluksessa; *in its true* ~ s oikeassa valossaan; *off* ~ huonossa kunnossa, alakuloinen; *under* ~ *of* jllak tekosyyllä, jnk varjolla; ~-**bar** rotuaita. -**ed** [-d] *a.*

värillinen, värikäs; kaunisteltu,
liioiteltu; värillinen, neekeri; *Cape
C~s* Etelä-Afrikan sekaroituiset;
cream~ kermanvärinen. **-ful** *a.*
värikäs. **-ing** *s.* väritys, värjäys; ~
matter väriaine.

colt [kəult] *s.* (ori)varsa. **-ish** *a.* varsa-
mainen, vallaton. **-sfoot** leskenlehti.

columbine ['kɔləmbain] *s.* akileija.

Columb|ia [kə'lʌmbiə] *erisn.* **-us** [-bəs]
erisn.

column ['kɔləm] *s.* pylväs, pilari;
palsta, sarake; rivistö; *fifth* ~ viiden
kolonna. **-ist** [-nist] *s.* kolumnisti,
pakinoija.

coma ['koumə] *s.* kooma, tajuttomuus.
-tose [-təus] *a.* tajuton.

comb [kəum] *s.* kampa, suka; (kukon-,
aallon)harja; *v.* kammata, sukia;
haravoida (kuv.); ~ *out* poistaa (jtk
tarpeetonta); *honey* ~ hunajakenno.

combat ['kɔmbət] *s.* taistelu; *v.*
taistella jtk vastaan; *single* ~ taistelu
mies miestä vastaan; ~ *zone*
rintama-alue. **-ant** [-(ə)nt] *a.*
taisteleva; *s.* taistelija. **-ive** [-iv] *a.*
taistelunhaluinen.

combination [kɔmbi'nei∫n] *s.*
yhdistäminen; yhdistys, yhdistelmä;
liitto; *in* ~ *with* yhdessä jnk kanssa.

combine [kəm'bain] *v.* sovittaa yhteen;
yhdistää, -tyä; liittyä yhteen, toimia
yhdessä; *s.* ['kɔmbain] yhtymä;
leikkuupuimuri (m. *~-harvester*).

combus|tible [kəm'bʌstibl] *a.* palava,
tulenarka; *s.* (tav. *pl.*) palava,
tulenarka aine. **-tion** [kəm'bʌst∫n] *s.*
palaminen, polttaminen; ~ *engine*
lämpövoimakone.

come [kʌm] *came come*, *v.* tulla,
saapua; johtua, olla peräisin; tulla
(jklle); *(imp.)* ~ *no!* jouduhan! ~*!*~*!*
no, no! eihän toki; *how* ~*?* mistä tämä
johtuu? miksi? *the life to* ~ tuleva
elämä; ~ *true* toteutua; ~ *undone*
avautua; ~ *what may* käyköön kuinka
tahansa; *he came to see that* hän joutui
havaitsemaan että; *when we* ~ *to
know them better* kun tutustumme
heihin paremmin; ~ *about* tapahtua,
sattua, syntyä; ~ *across* tavata
sattumalta; olla ymmärrettävä; ~
along! tulla mukaan; menestyä; ~
along joudu! ~ *at* tavoittaa, päästä

perille jstk, hyökätä kimppuun; ~
back palata, tulla takaisin; *he came
back a changed man* hän palasi
muuttuneena miehenä; ~ *by* saada
käsiinsä; ~ *down* tulla alas, laskea,
periytyä, *(upon)* moittia, torua, *(with
£ 10)* pulittaa; ~ *for* tulla noutamaan;
~ *in* tulla sisään, tulla (muotiin,
maaliin), päästä (valtaan), kertyä,
(for) saada osakseen; *where do I* ~ *in*
mikä osa minulla on tässä? ~ *into*
(m.) saada haltuunsa (perintö); ~ *off*
irtautua, lähteä; tapahtua, toteutua;
onnistua; *oh,* ~ *off it!* lakkaa jo! älä
viitsi (teeskennellä)! *who came off
best?* kuka voitti? ~ *on* edetä, edistyä;
tulla näyttämölle; alkaa
(odottamatta); ~ *on!* ala tulla!
tulehan! kuulehan! *oh,* ~ *on* älä nyt!
älä viitsi!~ *on* in käy(kää)hän sisälle;
~ *out* ilmestyä, avautua; onnistua;
tulla tietoon; ryhtyä lakkoon;
(tahrasta) lähteä; esiintyä ensi kerran
(seuraelämässä); ~ *round* tulla
tajuihinsa, toipua; pistäytyä
tervehtimässä; ~ *to* tulla tajuihinsa,
nousta jhk (summaan); *[it]* ~*s to this*
merkitsee, että; ~ *to that* jos niikseen
tulee; ~ *up* tulla esiin (t. keskustelun
alaiseksi); ~ *up to* vastata, ulottua,
olla jnk veroinen, lähestyä jkta; ~ *up
with* tavoittaa; tehdä (ehdotus); ~
upon kohdata odottamatta; ~*-at-able*
[-'ætəbl] saavutettavissa oleva,
helppopääsyinen. ~*-back* paluu
(kehään ym). ~*-down* romahdus,
alaspäin meno.

comedian [kə'mi:djən] *s.* koomikko,
komedianäyttelijä (fem. *-dienne*)

comedy ['kɔmidi] *s.* huvinäytelmä.

comely ['kʌmli] *a.* miellyttävä, sievä,
hauskannäköinen.

comestible [kə'mestibl] *s.* (tav. *pl.*)
ruokatavara(t).

comet ['kɔmit] *s.* pyrstötähti.

comfort ['kʌmfət] *v.* lohduttaa; *s.*
lohdutus, huojennus; mukavuus,
aineellinen hyvinvointi; *take* ~
rohkaista mielensä; *[cling to...] for* ~
turvaa etsien; *cold* ~ ks. *cold.* **-able**
['kʌmf(ə)təbl] *a.* mukava, kodikas;
hyvinvoipa; *I am* ~ minun on mukava
olla; *in* ~ *circumstances* hyvissä
oloissa. **-ably** *adv.* mukavasti; ~ *off*

hyvissä varoissa. **-er** [-ə] s. lohduttaja; (lämmin) kaulahuivi; tutti. **-ing** a. lohdullinen, lohduttava. **-less** a. lohduton; ikävä.

comfy ['kʌmfi] a. (puhek.) mukava.

comic ['kɔmik] a. koominen, huvittava; s. koomikko; ~ book sarjakuvalehti; ~ strips, [the] ~ s sarjakuvat. **-al** [-(ə)l] a. koominen, hullunkurinen.

coming ['kʌmiŋ] s. tulo; a ~ man tulevaisuuden mies.

comity ['kɔmiti] s. : ~ of nations kansainvälinen kohteliaisuus.

comma ['kɔmə] s. pilkku; inverted ~ s lainausmerkit.

command [kə'mɑ:nd] v. keskeä, määrätä, komentaa; hallita; herättää (kunnioitusta ym); s. käsky, määräys, komento, komennus; the house ~ s a wide view talosta on laaja näköala; has a good ~ of puhuu (jtk kieltä) hyvin; the officer in ~ komentava upseeri; at your ~ käytettävissänne. **-ant** [kɔmən'dænt] s. (linnan) päällikkö. **-eer** [kɔmən'diə] v. pestata väkisin, takavarikoida sotilastarkoituksiin. **-er** [-ə] s. komentaja, päällikkö; ~-in-chief ylipäällikkö **-ing** a. käskevä; korkealla sijaitseva. **-ment** s. käsky (raam.). **-o** [-əu] s. (pl. ~s) iskujoukko, i-oon kuuluva sotilas.

commemora|te [kə'meməreit] v. viettää jnk muistoa; olla jnk muistomerkkinä. **-tion** [-'reiʃn] s. muistojuhla; in ~ of jkn muistoksi. **-tive** [-rətiv] a. muisto-.

commence [kə'mens] v. alkaa. **-ment** s. alku; (yliop., et. Am.) promootio.

commend [kə'mend] v. ylistää, kiittää; jättää jkn haltuun; ~ itself miellyttää. **-able** [-əbl] a. kiitettävä. **-ation** [kɔmen'deiʃn] s. kiitos.

commensur|able [kə'menʃ(ə)rəbl] a. yhteismitallinen. **-ate** [-ʃərit] a. (jnk) mukainen

comment ['kɔment] s. (selittävä) huomautus, kommentti; v.: ~ upon lausua ajatuksensa jstk, kommentoida. **-ary** [-mənt(ə)ri] s. selitykset, huomautukset; (esim. i urheilu)selostus; selitysteos. **-ate** [-eit] v. (~ on sth.) selostaa. **-ator** [-eitə] s.

(radio-, TV-)selostaja; kommentoija.

commerce ['kɔmə(:)s] s. kauppa.

commercial [kə'mə:ʃ(ə)l] a. kaupallinen, kauppa-; s. (TV) mainos; ~ television mainostelevisio; ~ traveller kauppamatkustaja. **-ize** [-ʃəlaiz] v. kaupallistaa.

commie ['kɔmi] s. (leik., halv.) = communist.

commisera|te [kə'mizəreit] v. sääliä. **-tion** [-'reiʃn] s. sääli.

commissar|iat [kɔmi'sɛəriət] s. intendentuuri. **-y** ['kɔmisəri] s. asiamies; intendentuuriupseeri.

commission [kə'miʃn] s. tehtävä, määräys; upseerin valtakirja; toimi-, valiokunta, komissio; kommissio|kauppa, -palkkio, provisio; v. antaa jklle tehtäväksi, tilata; valtuuttaa; asettaa (laiva) palvelukseen. **-aire** [kəmiʃə'nɛə] s. vahtimestari, portieeri. **-ed** [-d] a.: ~ officer (valtakirjan saanut) upseeri. **-er** [-ə] s. (yli)asiamies; High C~ for Canada Kanadan hallituksen virallinen edustaja Lontoossa.

commit [kə'mit] v. jättää jkn haltuun; passittaa (vankilaan); tehdä (rikos ym); ~ oneself to sitoutua jhk; ~ to memory opetella ulkoa; ~ to writing kirjoittaa, laatia kirjaimisto kielelle: he refused to ~ himself by talking hän varovaisuuden vuoksi ei puhunut mitään. **-ment** s. sitoumus, sitoutuminen. **-tal** [-l] s. vangitseminen; ~ of a crime rikoksenteko. **-ted** a. (asialle) antautunut, harras, m. osallistuva. **-tee** [-i] s. valiokunta, komitea; appoint a ~ asettaa toimikunta; be on a ~ olla komitean jäsenenä.

commod|ious [kə'məudjəs] a. tilava. **-ity** [kə'mɔditi] s. hyödyke, tavara.

commodore ['kɔmədo:] s. kommodori, laivasto-osaston päällikkö.

common ['kɔmən] a. yhteinen; yleinen, julkinen; tavallinen; halpa, arkipäiväinen, alhainen, epähieno; s. yhteismaa, -niitty; ~ cold nuha, vilustuminen; the ~ man kadun mies; ~ market yhteismarkkinat; ~ -or-garden tavallinen; ~ people tavallinen kansa; ~ -room opettajainhuone, seurusteluhuone; ~

weal yhteinen hyvä; *in* ~ yhteisesti, yhteistä; *out of the* ~ tavaton, harvinainen; *it is* ~ *knowledge* on yleisesti tunnettua; *the C~ Market* EEC. **-alty** [-əlti] *s.* yhteinen kansa. **-er** [ə] *s.* aateliton. **-ly** *adv.* tavallisesti; epähienosti, arkisesti. **-place** *s.* arkipäiväinen asia, kulunut lauseparsi; *a.* arkipäiväinen, kulunut. **-s** [-z] *s. pl.* aatelittomat; *the House of C~ s* alahuone. **-wealth** *s.* (liitto)valtio, tasavalta; [*British*] ~ *of Nations* kansainyhteisö.

commotion [kə'məuʃn] *s.* hälinä, epäjärjestys.

communal ['kɔmjun(ə)l] *a.* kunnallinen, kunnan(-), yhteis-, **commune** ['kɔmju:n] *s.* kommuuni; kunta; *v.* [kə'mju:n]: ~ *with* vaihtaa ajatuksia jkn kanssa.

communica|ble [kə'mju:nik|əbl] *a.* viestittävissä oleva; tarttuva (tauti). **-nt** [-ənt] *s.* ehtoollisvieras. **-te** [-eit] *v.* ilmoittaa; siirtää, välittää; tartuttaa, asettua yhteyteen, olla yhteydessä (jnk kanssa); viestittää; käydä ehtoollisella; ~ *itself* välittyä, siirtyä edelleen. **-tion** [-'keiʃn] *s.* tiedonanto, ilmoitus; kanssakäyminen, ajatusten vaihto; (liike-, keskustelu) yhteys; tietoliikenne, tiedonvälitys; ~*s* huoltoyhteydet; ~*s* (*satellite*) tietoliikenne; ~ *cord* hätäjarru. **-tive** [-ətiv] *a.* puhelias, avomielinen.

communion [kə'mju:njən] *s.* yhteys, kanssakäyminen; [*Holy*] *C~* Herran ehtoollinen.

communiqué [kə'mju:nikei] *s.* virallinen tiedonanto, kommunikea.

commun|ism ['kɔmjunizm] *s.* kommunismi. **-ist** [-ist] *s.* kommunisti. **-ity** [kə'mju:niti] *s.,* yhteys, yhteisyys; yhteisö, yhdyskunta; *local* ~ kunta; ~ *centre* l. v. kulttuuritalo; ~ *planning* yhdyskuntasuunnittelu, seutukaavoitus; ~ *singing* yhteislaulu.

commutation [kɔmju(:)'teiʃn] *s.* vaihtaminen, lievennys; ~ *ticket* kausi-, alennuslippu.

commute [kə'mju:t] *v.* vaihtaa, lieventää (rangaistusta); matkustaa säännöllisesti jtk väliä. **-r** [-ə] *s.* kausilipun haltija (joka säännöllisesti matkustaa kodin ja työpaikan väliä).

compact 1. ['kɔmpækt] *s.* sopimus.
compact 2. [kəm'pækt] *a.* tiivis, kiinteä; suppea; *v.* liittää lujasti, yhdistää; *s.* ['kɔm-] puuterirasia.

companion [kəm'pænjən] *s.* toveri, elämäntoveri, kumppani, seuralainen; vastaava kappale, pari; (ritarikunnan) jäsen; ~ *in arms* aseveikko; ~ *in misfortune* kohtalotoveri. **-able** [-əbl] *a.* seurallinen, seuraa rakastava. **-ate** [-it] *s.* toveri-. **-ship** *s.* toveruus, seura.

company ['kʌmp(ə)ni] *s.* seura; vieraat; yhtiö; komppania; (näyttelijä)seurue; *ship's* ~ laivan miehistö; *keep* ~ seurustella; *part* ~ erota.

comparable ['kɔmp(ə)rəbl] *a.* verrattavissa oleva (*with, to*), vertailukelpoinen. **-tive** [kəm'pærətiv] *a.* vertaileva; suhteellinen; *s.* komparatiivi. **-tively** *adv.* suhteellisen, verraten.

compar|e [kəm'pɛə] *v.* verrata, vertailla (m. kiel.); olla verrattavissa; *s.* vertailu; [*as*] ~*d with* verrattuna jhk; . . . *is not to be* ~*d to* ei ole verrattavissa jhk; *beyond* ~ vertaa vailla, verrattomasti. **-ison** [kəm'pærisn] *s.* vertailu; *degrees of* ~ vertailuasteet; *by* ~ suhteellisesti; *in* ~ *with* verrattuna jhk.

compartment [kəm'pɑ:tmənt] *s.* (vaunu)osasto.

compass ['kʌmpəs] *s.* piiri, laajuus; ala, rajat; kompassi; [*pair of*] ~*es* harppi; *v.* ympäröidä; ymmärtää; saada aikaan; *points of the* ~ ilmansuunnat.

compassion [kəm'pæʃn] *s.* sääli; *have* ~ *on* sääliä. **-ate** [-ənit] *a.* sääliväinen, myötätuntoinen.

compati|bility [kəmpætə'biliti] *s.* yhteensopivuus. **-ble** [kəm'pætəbl] *a.:* ~ (*with*) jnk kanssa) yhteensopiva, -soveltuva.

compatriot [kəm'pætriət] *s.* maanmies.
compeer ['kɔmpiə] *s.* vertainen.
compel [kəm'pel] *v.* pakottaa; ~*ling* pakottava; huomiota herättävä, vaikuttava.

compendium [kəm'pendiəm] *s.* suppea yhteenveto.

compensat|e ['kɔmpenseit] *v.* korvata, olla korvauksena; hyvittää. **-ion** [-'seiʃn] *s.* korvaus, hyvitys; *in* ~ *for*

korvauksena jstk. **-ory**
[kəm'pensət(ə)ri] a. hyvittävä,
kompensoiva.
compère ['kɔmpɛə] s. (ohjelman)
kuuluttaja, juontaja; v. kuuluttaa,
juontaa.
compete [kəm'pi:t] v. kilpailla.
compet|ence ['kɔmpit(ə)ns] s.
pätevyys, kelpoisuus; riittävä
toimeentulo. **-ency** [-nsi] s. = ed. **-ent**
[-nt] a. pätevä, laillinen; pystyvä,
kykenevä, kyvykäs. **-ition** [-'tiʃn] s.
kilpailu. **-itive** [kəm'petitiv] a.
kilpa(ilu)-, kilpailukykyinen. **-itor**
[kəm'petitə] s. kilpailija
compilation [kɔmpi'leiʃn] s. kerääminen, laatiminen; kokoomateos.
compile [kəm'pail] v. laatia, kerätä,
toimittaa.
complacen|ce, -cy [kəm'pleisns, -i] s.
mielihyvä; tyytyväisyys. **-t** [-nt] a.
(itse)tyytyväinen.
complain [kəm'plein] v. valittaa; [we
have] nothing to ~ of (about) ei ole
valittamisen aihetta. **-t** [-t] s. valitus,
kanne; tauti, sairaus.
complaisan|ce [kəm'pleizns] s.
hyväntahtoisuus **-t** [-nt] a.
hyväntahtoinen, kohtelias.
complement ['kɔmplimənt] s.
täydennys, (predikaatin) täyte; täysi
määrä; v. täydentää. **-ary** [-'mentəri]
a. täydentävä, komplementti-.
complet|e [kəm'pli:t] a. täydellinen;
kokonainen, täysi; valmis; v. suorittaa
loppuun; lopettaa; täyttää. **-ely** adv.
täysin, kokonaan. **-ion** [-'pli:ʃn] s.
loppuunsaattaminen, lopettaminen,
valmistuminen; täydentäminen.
complex ['kɔmpleks] a. yhdistetty;
monimutkainen; s. yhdistelmä;
kompleksi. **-ion** [kəm'plekʃn] s.
ihonväri, hipiä; (kuv.) luonne. **-ity**
[kəm'pleksiti] s. monimutkaisuus,
moninaisuus, sotku.
complian|ce [kəm'plaiəns] s.
suostuminen; in ~ with jnk
mukaisesti. **-t** [-nt] a. myöntyväinen,
mukautuva.
complica|te ['kɔmplikeit] v. tehdä
monimutkaiseksi, mutkistaa,
vaikeuttaa; ~d monimutkainen,
pulmallinen. **-tion** [-'keiʃn] s.
sekaannus, pulma(llinen seikka);

lisätauti, komplikaatio.
complicity [kəm'plisiti] s. osallisuus
rikokseen.
compliment ['kɔmplimənt] s.
kohteliaisuus; pl. tervehdys, terveiset;
v. [-ment]: ~ sb. on onnitella, lausua
kohteliaisuuksia (jnk johdosta); with
the author's ~ s. tekijän kunnioittavin
terveisin; the ~ s of the season joulu- ja
uudenvuoden tervehdys. **-ary**
[kɔmpli'ment(ə)ri] a. kohtelias;
mairitteleva.
comply fn01[kəm'plai] v. suostua,
mukautua (with jhk).
component [kəm'pəunənt] s. aines, osa
(m. ~ part).
comport [kəm'pɔ:t] v.: ~ oneself
käyttäytyä; ~ with sopia yhteen jnk
kanssa.
compos|e [kəm'pəuz] v. panna kokoon,
laatia, sepittää; säveltää; latoa
(kirjap.); tyynnyttää; sovittaa; ~
oneself rauhoittua. **-ed** [-d] a. tyyni,
rauhallinen; be ~ of koostua jstk. **-er**
[-ə] s. säveltäjä. **-ite** ['kɔmpəzit] a.
yhdistetty. **-ition** [kɔmpə'ziʃn] s.
laatiminen, sepittäminen;
ainekirjoitus, aine; sävellys;
latominen; sommittelu, kokoonpano,
koostumus; luonne. **-itor** [kəm'pəzitə]
s. latoja. **-t** ['kɔmpɔst] s. komposti.
-ure [kəm'pəuʒə] s. mielenmaltti,
tyyneys.
compote ['kɔmpəut] s. hedelmähilloke.
compound 1. [kəm'paund] v. sekoittaa,
yhdistää; sovittaa, sopia; a.
['kɔmpaund] yhdistetty; yhdys-; s.
['kɔm-] yhdistys, yhdiste, yhdyssana;
~ fracture avomurtuma; ~ interest
korkoa korolle, koronkorko.
compound 2. ['kɔmpaund] s. aitaus,
aidattu alue.
comprehen|d [kɔmpri'hend] v.
käsittää, ymmärtää, tajua; sisältää.
-sible [-səbl] a. käsitettävä, tajuttava.
-sion [-ʃn] s. käsityskyky, ymmärrys;
ymmärtämys; ulottuvuus, (laaja) ala.
-sive [-siv] a. laaja; paljon käsittävä t.
sisältävä; ~ faculty ymmärrys; ~
school l. v. yhtenäiskoulu.
compress [kəm'pres] v. puristaa
(kokoon), tiivistää; s. ['kɔmpres] s.
kompressi, haude. **-ed** [-t] a.
tiivistetty; ~ air paineilma. **-ion**

[kəm'preʃn] s. kokoonpuristaminen, tiivistys.

comprise [kəm'praiz] v. sisältää, käsittää.

compromise ['kɔmprəmaiz] s. sovittelu, kompromissi; v. sovittelemalla ratkaista, sopia; saattaa huonoon valoon.

compul|sion [kəm'pʌl|ʃn] s. pakko. **-sive** [-siv] a. pakko-. **-sory** [-s(ə)ri] a. pakollinen, pakko-; ~ *education* oppivelvollisuus.

compunction [kəm'pʌŋ(k)ʃn] s. tunnonvaiva.

compute [kəm'pju:t] v. laskea, arvioida. **-r** [-ə] s. tietokone; ~*ized control* tietokonekontrolli.

comrade ['kɔmrid] s. toveri. **-ship** s. toveruus.

con 1. [kɔn] v. tutkia (m. ~ *over*).

con 2. [kɔn] *lyh.* = *contra; pro and* ~ puolesta ja vastaan; *the pros and* ~*s* puolesta ja vastaan puhuvat seikat.

con 3. *lyh.* = *confidence;* ~ *man* huijari; *I've been* ~*ned* minua on huiputettu.

concatenation [kɔnkæti'neiʃn] s. ketju.

concav|e ['kɔŋkeiv] a. kovera. **-ity** [kɔn'kæviti] s. koveruus.

conceal [kən'si:l] v. salata; kätkeä. **-ment** s. salaaminen; piilopaikka.

concede [kən'si:d] v. myöntää.

conceit [kən'si:t] s. itserakkaus. **-ed** [-id] a. itserakas.

conceivable [kən'si:vəbl] a. ajateltavissa oleva, mahdollinen (uskoa t. kuvitella).

conceive [kən'si:v] v. keksiä, saada (aate); muodostaa itselleen (kuva ym); kuvitella; laatia (suunnitelma); käsittää; hedelmöityä, tulla raskaaksi; ~ *an affection for* ruveta pitämään jksta; *who first* ~*d the idea of* .. kenessä ensin heräsi ajatus ..

concentr|ate ['kɔnsentreit] v. keskittää, -ttyä; väkevöidä (kem.); ~*d fire* keskitys. **-ation** [-'treiʃn] s. keskitys; keskittymiskyky (m. *power of* ~); ~ *camp* keskitysleiri; ~ (t. *con*) *trail* tiivistysjuova (lentokoneen »vana»). **-ic** [kən'sentrik] a. samankeskinen.

concep|t ['kɔnsept] s. käsite. **-tion** [kən'sepʃn] s. käsitys(kyky), ajatus, mielikuva; hedelmöityminen.

concern [kən'sə:n] v. koskea, olla tekemistä jnk kanssa; s. (jkta koskeva) asia; osa(llisuus); huoli, huolestuminen; liike, yhtymä; ~ *oneself about* olla huolissaan jstk; *be* ~*ed* olla levoton, *(in sth.)* olla osallinen jhk, *(with)* käsitellä, koskea jtk; *as (so) far as I am* ~ *ed* mitä minuun tulee; *our first* ~ *should be* meidän tulisi ensi sijassa huolehtia (-sta); *it is no* ~ *of mine* se ei kuulu minuun. **-ed** [-d] a. osallinen; asianomainen; huolestunut; *the parties* ~ asianosaiset. **-ing** *prep.* -sta, -stä, mitä (jhk) tulee.

concert ['kɔnsət] s. konsertti; yhteisymmärrys; v. [kən'sə:t] suunnitella, sopia jstk; *in* ~ with yhdessä; *take* ~*ed action* toimia yhdessä. **-ina** [kɔnsə'ti:nə] s. harmonikka. **-o** [kən'tʃə:təu] s. (pl. ~*s*) konsertto.

concession [kən'seʃn] s. myönnytys; toimilupa(-alue), konsessio. **-aire** [-ʃə'neə] s. toimiluvan haltija.

conch [kɔnk] s. simpukankuori.

concierge [kɔ:(n)si'ɛəʒ] s. portinvartija, ovenvartija.

conciliat|e [kən'silii|eit] v. sovittaa; voittaa, saada puolelleen. **-ion** [-'eiʃn] s. sovinto. **-or** [-eitə] s. välittäjä, rauhanrakentaja. **-ory** [-ət(ə)ri] a. sovittava.

concise [kən'sais] a. suppea, lyhyt. **-ness** s. suppeus.

conclave ['kɔnkleiv] s. konklaavi, salainen kokous.

conclu|de [kən'klu:|d] v. lopettaa, päättää; tehdä, solmia (rauha ym); päätellä *(from* jstk); päättyä; *concluding* loppu-. **-sion** [-ʒn] s. loppu; johtopäätös; *in* ~ lopuksi; ~ *of peace* rauhanteko; *bring to a* ~ saattaa päätökseen; *draw a* ~ tehdä johtopäätös; *try* ~*s* mitellä voimiaan. **-sive** [-siv] a. ratkaiseva.

concoct [kən'kɔkt] v. sekoittaa sepittää, »keittää kokoon». **-ion** [-'kɔkʃn] s. sekoitus; sepustus.

concomitant [kən'kɔmit(ə)nt] a. liittyvä, myötäseuraava, samanaikainen.

concord ['kɔŋkɔ:d] s. sopusointu, sopu. **-ance** [kən'kɔ:dns] s. yhtäpitävyys;

konkordanssi.

concourse ['kɔŋkɔːs] s. (yhteen) kerääntyminen; väentulva; -paljous.

concre|te ['kɔn|kriːt] a. konkreettinen, esineellinen, todellinen; s. betoni, iskos; v. laskea betonilla; [kɔn'kriːt] muodostaa, -tua kiinteäksi massaksi. **-tion** [kɔn'kriːʃn] s. kiinteä, kovettunut massa; kivennäistymä; (lääk.) kiinnikasvama.

concubine ['kɔŋkjubain] s. jalkavaimo.

concur [kɔn'kəː] v. sattua samaan aikaan, vaikuttaa yhdessä, yhteys; olla yhtä mieltä. **-rence** [-'kʌr(ə)ns] s. suostumus; yhteensattuminen. **-rent** [-'kʌr(ə)nt] a. yhtyvä; yhdessä vaikuttava; samanaikainen; yksimielinen; (~ly samanaikaisesti jnk kanssa).

concussion [kɔn'kʌʃn] s. tärähdys [~ *of the brain*] aivotärähdys.

condemn [kɔn'dem] v. tuomita; paheksua; julistaa takavarikoiduksi. **-ation** [kɔndəm'neiʃn] s. tuomitseminen; tuomio.

condensation [kɔndən'seiʃn] s. tiivistäminen; ~ *water* lauhdevesi.

condense [kɔn'dens] s. tiivistää, -tyä; ~*d from* .. supistelma jstk. **-r** [-ə] s. lauhdutin, (sähk.) kondensaattori; kokoojalinssi.

condescen|d [kɔndi'send] v. alentua; suvaita; ~*ing* armollinen. **-sion** [-'senʃn] s. alentuvaisuus.

condign [kɔn'dain] a. täysin vastaava, hyvin ansaittu.

condiment ['kɔndimənt] s. mauste, höyste.

condition [kɔn'diʃn] s. ehto; edellytys; tila, asema; pl. olosuhteet, olot; v. olla ehtona, ehdollistaa; valmentaa hyvään kuntoon; *in good* ~ hyvässä kunnossa; *on no* ~ ei millään ehdolla; *under existing* ~s vallitsevissa olosuhteissa; *is* ~*ed by* riippuvainen jstk. **-al** [-l] a. ehdonalainen, ehdollinen; s. konditionaali (kiel.); *is not* ~ *upon* ei edellytä. **-ing** (urh.) valmennus.

condole [kɔn'dəul] v. valittaa surua (*with* jkn). **-nce** [-ɔns] s. surunvalittelu.

condom ['kɔndəm, 'kʌn-] s. kondomi.

condominium [kɔndə'minjəm] s.

yhteishallintoalue; ~ *apartment* (Am.) osakehuoneisto.

condone [kɔn'dəun] v. antaa anteeksi.

condor ['kɔndɔː] s. kondorikotka.

conduc|e [kɔn'djuːs] v.: ~ *to* johtaa, (osaltaan) vaikuttaa jhk. **-ive** [-iv] a.: ~ *to* jhk johtava, jtk edistävä.

conduct ['kɔndʌkt] s. käytös, menettely(tapa); (liikkeen) johto, hoito; v. [kɔn'dʌkt] johdattaa, saattaa, opastaa; (mus.) johtaa (m. fys.); hoitaa; ~ *oneself* käyttäytyä. **-ed** [-id] a.: ~ *tour* seuramatka. **-ion** [kɔn'dʌkʃn] s. (lämmön ym) johtaminen, -uminen. **-ive** [kɔn'dʌktiv] a. johtava. **-ivity** [kɔndʌk'tiviti] s. johtokyky. **-or** [kɔn'dʌktə] s. (lämmön ym) johde; orkesterinjohtaja; rahastaja (Am. m. junailija); *lightning*-~ ukkosenjohdin. **-ress** [kɔn'dʌktris] s. (nais)rahastaja.

conduit ['kɔndit, Am. -duit] s. putkijohto.

cone [kəun] s. kartio; käpy; (jäätelö)tötterö; ~ *sugar* kekosokeri. **-y** ks. *cony*.

confab ['kɔnfæb] s. & v. lyh. ks. seur.

confabula|te [kɔn'fæbjuleit] v. jutella. **-tion** [-'leiʃn] s. rupattelu, jutustelu.

confection [kɔn'fekʃn] s. (naisten) tyylikäs valmisvaate; makeinen, konvehti. **-er** [-(ə)nə] s. sokerileipuri. **-ery** [-(ə)nri] s. sokerileivokset, makeiset.

confeder|acy [kɔn'fed(ə)rəsi] s. (valtio)liitto. **-ate** [-(ə)rit] a. liittoutunut, liitto-; s. liittoutunut, (sala)liittolainen; rikostoveri; v. [-əreit] yhdistää liitoksi; liittoutua. **-ation** [-ə'reiʃn] s. liitto, valtioliitto.

confer [kɔn'fəː] v. suoda, antaa (*on* jklle); neuvotella; *imperat.* vertaa! (tav. *cf.*) **-ence** ['kɔnf(ə)r(ə)ns] s. neuvottelu. **-ment** [kɔn'fəːmənt] s. (arvon ym) antaminen, suominen.

confess [kɔn'fes] v. tunnustaa; ripittäytyä, ripittää. **-ion** [kɔn'feʃn] s. tunnustus; uskontunnustus; synnintunnustus, rippi. **-ional** [kɔn'feʃənl] a. tunnustuksellinen, tunnustuksenmukainen; s. rippituoli. **-or** [-ə] s. rippi-isä (m. *father*~).

confidant, -e (*fem.*) [kɔnfi'dænt] s.

uskottu.

confid|e [kən'faid] v. luottaa (in), uskoa (to jklle). **-ence** ['kɔnfid(ə)ns] s. luottamus; itseluottamus, -varmuus; - in [strict] ~ luottamuksellisesti; take sb. into one's ~ uskoutua jklle; received a vote of ~ sai luottamuslauseen; vote of no ~ epäluottamuslause; ~ man huijari. **-ent** ['kɔnfid(ə)nt] a. luottavainen; itsevarma; ~ of jstk varma; we are ~ that uskomme varmasti että; ~ ly varmasti. **-ential** [kɔnfi'den∫(ə)l] a. luottamuksellinen; (jkn) luottamusta nauttiva; ~ clerk prokuristi; (~ity [-∫i'æliti] s.: medical c. lääkärin vaitiolovelvollisuus; ~ly adv. luottamuksellisesti; kahden kesken).

configuration [kənfigju'rei∫n] s. muoto, ääriviivat.

confine [kən'fain] v. rajoittaa, sulkea; ~ oneself rajoittua; [I wish] he would ~ himself to the subject että hän pysyisi asiassa; be ~d to one's bed olla vuoteen omana; be ~d synnyttää. **-ment** [kən'fainmənt] s. vankeus, jhk suljettuna oleminen; lapsivuode, synnytys. **-s** ['kɔnfainz] s. pl. rajat.

confirm [kən'fə:m] v. vahvistaa; lujittaa; päästää ripille. **-ation** [kɔnfə'mei∫n] s. vahvistus; konfirmaatio. **-ed** [-d] a. vakiintunut; piintynyt (tapa).

confisca|te ['kɔnfiskeit] v. takavarikoida. **-tion** [-'kei∫n] s. takavarikointi.

conflagration [kɔnflæg'rei∫n] s. suuri tulipalo, palo.

conflict [kɔnflikt] s. ristiriita; selkkaus; v. [kən'flikt] törmätä vastakkain; olla ristiriidassa (with); ~ing ristiriitainen.

confluen|ce ['kɔnfluəns] s. (jokien ym) yhtyminen, yhtymäkohta. **-t** [-ənt] a. yhteenvirtaava.

conform [kən'fɔ:m] v. tehdä jnk mukaiseksi (to); olla yhdenmukainen, mukautua jhk (esim. politiikkaan); [those] who do not ~ (pol.) toisinajattelevat. **-able** [-əbl] a.: ~ to jnk mukainen. **-ist** [-ist] s. Engl. valtiokirkon jäsen. **-ity** [-iti] s. yhdenmukaisuus, sopusointu; in ~ with jnk mukaisesti.

confound [kən'faund] v. saattaa

hämille t. ymmälle; sekoittaa; ~ it! hitto vieköön!; ~ed (puhek.) kiro|tun, -ttu.

confrère ['kɔnfrɛə] s. kollega, (ammatti)toveri.

confront [kən'frʌnt] v. asettaa vastakkain t. kasvokkain; olla vastapäätä; uhmata; kohdata. **-ation** [kɔnfrʌn'tei∫n] s. vastakkain asettaminen, silmätysten oleminen; yhteenotto.

confus|e [kən'fju:z] v. saattaa epäjärjestykseen, sekoittaa; saattaa hämille t. ymmälle. **-ed** [-d] a. hämillään (oleva); sekava. **-ion** [kən'fju:ʒn] sekaannus; hämminki.

confute [kən'fju:t] v. kumota.

congeal [kən'dʒi:l] v. jäädyttää, jähmettää; jähmettyä, hyytyä.

congenial [kən'dʒi:njəl] a. samanhenkinen; (yhteen)sopiva, mieluinen. **-ity** [kəndʒi:ni'æliti] s. samanhenkisyys, hengenheimolaisuus.

congenital [kən'dʒenit(ə)l] s. synnynnäinen, myötäsyntyinen.

conger ['kɔŋgə] s. meriankerias.

congest|ed [kən'dʒestid] a. tungokseen asti täynnä, liian tiheään asuttu; ~ traffic liikennetungos, ruuhka. **-ion** ['-dʒest∫n] s. (veren)tungos, ruuhka, ruuhka; liikakansoitus.

conglomera|te [kən'glɔməreit] v. kasata, kasaantua yhteen; ~d yhteenkasaantunut; s. [-rit] konglomeraatti; = seur. **-tion** [kɔnglɔmə'rei∫n] s. rykelmä, kasauma.

Congo ['kɔŋgəu] erisn.: the ~ Kongojoki. **-lese** [-'li:z] s. & a. kongolainen.

congratula|te [kən'grætju|leit] v. onnitella. **-tion** [-'lei∫n] s. onnentoivotus, onnittelu. **-tory** [-lət(ə)ri] a. onnittelu-.

congrega|te ['kɔŋgrigeit] v. koota yhteen, kokoontua. **-tion** [-'gei∫n] s. seurakunta; kokoontuminen. **-tional** [-'gei∫ənl] a. seurakunta-; kongregationalistinen.

congress ['kɔŋgres] s. kokous, kongressi; C~ Kongressi (Yhdysvaltain parlamentti); C~man Kongressin jäsen.

congur|ence ['kɔŋgruəns] s.
yhtäpitävyys, yhdenmukaisuus. **-ent**
[-ənt] a. yhtäpitävä, yhdenmukainen,
yhtenevä. **-ous** [-əs] a. = *congruent;*
asianmukainen, sopiva.

conic ['kɔnik] a. kartio-. **-al** [-(ə)l] a.
kartionmuotoinen.

conifer ['kəunifə] s. havupuu. **-ous**
[kə(u)'nifərəs] a.: ~ *tree* = ed.

conjecture [kən'dʒektʃə] s. arvaus;
arvelu; v. arvata, arvella.

conjoin [kən'dʒɔin] v. yhdistää, -tyä. **-t**
['kɔndʒɔint] a. yhdistetty.

conjug|al ['kɔn(d)ʒug(ə)l] a. avio-,
aviollinen. **-ate** ['kɔn(d)ʒugeit] v.
taivuttaa (verbejä). **-ation** [-'geiʃn] s.
konjugaatio, taivutus.

conjunc|tion [kən'dʒʌn(k)(ʃ)n] s.
yhdistäminen, yhteys; sidesana,
konjunktio; *in* ~ *with* jnk yhteydessä.
-tiva [kɔndʒʌŋk'taivə] s. (silmän)
sidekalvo. **-tive** [-tiv] a. yhdistävä; s.
yhdistävä konjunktio. **-ture** [-tʃə] s.
tapahtumien yhteensattuma.

conjuration [kɔndʒuə(ə)'reiʃn] s.
manaus.

conjur|e 1. [kən'dʒuə] v. hartaasti
pyytää. **2.** ['kʌn(d)ʒə] v. manata,
loihtia *(up* esille); *-ing tricks*
taikatemput. **-or** ['kʌn(d)ʒərə] s.
taikuri, silmänkääntäjä.

conk [kɔŋk] s. sl. nenä; v. iskeä; ~ *out*
(sl.) joutua epäkuntoon.

con-man ks. *con 3.*

connect [kə'nekt] v. liittää yhteen,
yhdistää, kytkeä; olla yhteydessä,
liittyä. **-ed** [-id] a. yhtenäinen; ~*ed by
marriage* avioliiton kautta sukua; *well*
~*ed* hyvästä perheestä.

Connecticut [kə'netikət] *erisn.*

conne|ction, -xion [kə'nekʃn] s.
yhdistäminen; yhteys, juna(laiva- ym)
yhteys; sukulainen, asiakaspiiri;
(liike)suhde; *in this* ~ tässä
yhteydessä; *in* ~ *with* jnk yhteydessä;
miss the ~ myöhästyä sopivasta
junasta (lentokoneesta ym). **-ctive**
[-ktiv] a. yhdistävä; ~ *tissue*
sidekudos.

conning ['kɔnin] s.: ~ *tower*
komentotorni.

conniv|ance [kə'naivns] s.
leväperäisyys, (äänetön)
hyväksyminen. **-e** [kə'naiv] v.: ~ *at*

ummistaa silmänsä jltk.

connoisseur [kɔni'sɔ:] s.
(taiteen)tuntija.

connotation [kɔnə'teiʃn] s.
sivumerkitys.

connote [kɔ'nəut] v. sisältää, ilmaista
(lisäksi); merkitä.

connubial [kə'nju:bjəl] a. avio(llinen)-.

conque|r ['kɔŋkə] v. valloittaa; voittaa.
-ror [-rə] s. valloittaja, voittaja. **-st**
['kɔŋkwest] s. valloitus; voitto.

consanguinity [kɔnsæŋ'gwiniti] s.
veriheimolaisuus, -sukulaisuus.

conscien|ce ['kɔnʃns] s. omatunto; *in
all* ~ totta puhuen, kaiken kohtuuden
nimessä. **-tious** [kɔnʃi'enʃəs] a.
tunnontarkka, tunnollinen; ~ *objector*
aseistakieltäytyjä.

conscious ['kɔnʃəs] a. tietoinen,
tajuinen. **-ness** s. tajunta, tietoisuus;
she lost ~ hän menetti tajuntansa.

conscrip|t ['kɔnskript] s.
asevelvollinen. **-tion** [kən'skripʃn] s.
asevelvollisuus; sotaväkeenotto.

consecra|te ['kɔnsikreit] v. vihkiä;
pyhittää. **-tion** [kɔnsi'kreiʃn] s.
vihkiminen.

consecutive [kən'sekjutiv] a.
peräkkäinen, toinen toistaan
seuraava; (kiel) seuraus-.

consensus [kən'sensəs] s. yksimielinen
t. yhteinen mielipide (m. ~ *of
opinion*).

consent [kən'sent] v. suostua (*to* jhk);
s. suostumus; *by common* ~
yksimielisesti.

consequen|ce ['kɔns(i)kwəns] s.
seuraus; merkitys; *in* ~ *of* jnk
johdosta; *people of* ~
vaikutusvaltaiset, tärkeät henkilöt; *it
was of no* ~ se ei merkinnyt mitään. **-t**
[-ənt] a. (jstk) johtuva, seuraava. **-tial**
[kɔnsi'kwenʃ(ə)l] a. (jstk) seuraava,
välillinen; suuriluuloinen. **-tly** adv.
niin muodoin, sen tähden.

conserva|tion [kɔnsə'veiʃn] s.
säilyttäminen; *nature* ~
luonnonsuojelu. **-tionist** s.
luonnonsuojelija. **-tism**
[kən'sə:vətizm] s. vanhoillisuus. **-tive**
[kən'sə:v(ə)tiv] a. & s. vanhoillinen,
(pol.) konservatiivi(nen). **-toire**
[kən'sə:vətwa:] s. konservatorio. **-tory**
[kən'sə:vətri] s. kasvihuone,

talvipuutarha; musiikkiopisto.

conserve [kən'sə:v] v. säilyttää, suojella; säilöä.

consider [kən'sidə] v. miettiä, harkita, tarkastella; ottaa huomioon; pitää jnak, katsoa *(oneself* olevansa); *all things* ~*ed* ottaen kaikki asianhaarat huomioon. **-able** [-rəbl] a. huomattava, melkoinen **-ably** huomattavasti, paljon. **-ate** [-rit] a. hienotunteinen; huomaavainen. **-ation** [kənsidə'reiʃn] s. harkinta; hienotunteisuus, huomaavaisuus; (huomioonotettava) seikka, näkökohta, syy; in ~ of ottaen huomioon; *under* ~ harkittavana; *take into* ~ ottaa huomioon; *for a* ~ korvausta vastaan. **-ed** a. harkittu. **-ing** prep. huomioon ottaen, jhk nähden; olosuhteet huomioon ottaen.

consign [kən'sain] v. lähettää; jättää jkn huostaan. **-ee** [kɔnsai'ni:] s. tavaran vastaanottaja. **-ment** s. tavaralähetys.

consist [kən'sist] v.: ~ *of* koostua jstk, käsittää; ~ *in* olla jtk, käsittää; *the study* ~*s of* tutkimus käsittää, tutkimuksen muodostaa. **-ence** [-ns] s. ks. seur. **-ency** [-nsi] s. yhdenmukaisuus; johdonmukaisuus; koostumus, sakeus, tiiviys. **-ent** [-nt] a. yhdenmukainen; johdonmukainen, *(with)* jtk vastaava.

consolation [kɔnsə'leiʃn] s. lohdutus.

console 1. [kən'səul] v. lohduttaa. **console 2.** [*ˈ*kɔnsəul] s. olkakivi.

consolida|te [kən'solideit] v. lujittaa, -tua; yhdistää; vakauttaa; ~*d annuities* = *consols.* **-tion** [-'deiʃn] s. lujittaminen; vakauttaminen.

consols [kən'sɔlz] s. vakautetut valtionobligaatiot.

consonan|ce [*ˈ*kɔnsənəns] s. sopusointu; yhdenmukaisuus. **-t** [-ənt] a.: ~ *with, to* jnk mukainen, sopusointuinen; s. kerake, konsonantti.

consort [*ˈ*kɔnsɔ:t] s. puoliso; *prince* ~ prinssipuoliso; v. [kən'sɔ:t]: ~ *with* seurustella; sopia.

conspectus [kən'spektəs] s. yleiskatsaus.

conspicuous [kən'spikjuəs] a. silmiinpistävä, huomiotaherättävä;

was ~ *by her absence* loisti poissaolollaan.

conspira|cy [kən'spirəsi] s. salaliitto; juoni. **-tor** [-ətə] s. salaliittolainen.

conspire [kən'spaiə] v. tehdä salaliitto; vehkeillä; yhdessä vaikuttaa *(to* jhk).

constab|le [*ˈ*kʌnstəbl] s. (poliisi)konstaapeli; (hist.) linnanpäällikkö; *Chief C~* poliisipäällikkö. **-ulary** [kən'stæbjuləri] s. poliisivoimat.

Constance [*ˈ*kɔnst(ə)ns] *erisn.: Lake* ~ Bodenjärvi.

constan|cy [*ˈ*kɔnst(ə)nsi] s. uskollisuus, kestävyys; muuttumattomuus. **-t** [-(ə)nt] a. muuttumaton, alinomainen; uskollinen; luja, kestävä; s. vakio (matk.); ~*ly* alituisesti.

Constantinople [kɔnstænti'nəupl] *erisn.*

constellation [kɔnstə'leiʃn] s. tähtikuvio.

consternation [kɔnstə(:)neiʃn] s. tyrmistys, hämmästys.

constipation [kɔnsti'peiʃn] s. ummetus.

constituen|cy [kən'stitjuənsi] s. valitsijakunta, vaalipiiri. **-t** [-ənt] a. aineksena oleva; perustuslakia säätävä, valitsija-; s. komponentti, ainesosa (m. ~ *part);* valitsija; päämies.

constitut|e [*ˈ*kɔnstitju:t] v. asettaa, määrätä; perustaa; olla osana t. aineksena, muodostaa. **-ion** [-'tju:ʃn] s. perustaminen; yleisrakenne, konstituutio; valtiosääntö, perustuslaki. **-ional** [-'tju:ʃnl] a. (yleis) rakenteellinen, luontainen; perustuslaillinen; s. (terveys)kävely. **-ive** [-iv] a. perustava; lakiasäätävä.

constrain [kən'strein] v. pakottaa; hillitä, pitää aisoissa, rajoittaa; ~*ed* väkinäinen. **-t** [-t] s. pakko, pakkokeino(t); väkinäisyys.

constrict [kən'strikt] v. vetää kokoon, kutistaa, supistaa; ~*ed* m. rajoittunut. **-ion** [-kʃn] s. kokoonvetäminen; kurouma.

construct [kən'strʌkt] v. rakentaa, konstruoida; laatia, suunnitella. **-ion** [-kʃn] s. rakentaminen; rakenne(lma); konstruktio, lauserakenne; tulkinta; *under* ~ rakenteilla; *put a wrong* ~ *upon* tulkita väärin. **-ive** [-iv] *a.* rakentava; rakenteellinen. **-or** [-ə] *s.* konstruktori, rakentaja.

construe [kən'stru:] *v.* tulkita; kääntää, selittää, analysoida (kieliopillisesti).

consul ['kɔns|l] *s.* konsuli. **-ar** [-julə] *a.* konsulin-. **-ate** [-julit] *s.* konsulaatti, konsulin virasto. **~-general** pääkonsuli.

consult [kən'sʌlt] *v.* kysyä neuvoa, neuvotella; ottaa huomioon; ~ *a dictionary* etsiä, katsoa sanakirjasta; ~ *a doctor* kääntyä lääkärin puoleen; ~*ing hours* vastaanottoaika. **-ant** [-ənt] *s.* neuvonpyytäjä; neuvoa antava, neuvotteleva (lääkäri ym). **-ation** [kɔnsl'teiʃn] *s.* neuvottelu. **-ative** [-ətiv] *a.* neuvoa antava, neuvottelu-.

consume [kən'sju:m] *v.* kuluttaa, käyttää; syödä, nauttia; kalvaa. **-er** [-ə] *s.* kuluttaja; ~ *goods* kulutustavarat; *durable* ~ *goods* kestokulutushyödykkeet; ~ *education* kuluttajanvalistus.

consummate [kən'sʌmit] *a.* täydellinen; *v.* ['kɔnsʌmeit] saattaa täydelliseksi. **-ion** [kɔnsʌ'meiʃn] *s.* täydellistäminen, täyttymys.

consumption [kən'sʌm(p)ʃn] *s.* kulutus; keuhkotauti. **-tive** [-(p)tiv] *a.* & *s.* keuhkotautinen.

contact ['kɔntækt] *s.* kosketus; yhteys; *v.* [kən'tækt] asettua yhteyteen (jkn kanssa), ottaa yhteys jkh; *I made many useful social* ~*s* pääsin yhteyteen moneen minulle hyödyllisen henkilöön; *break* ~ katkaista sähkövirta; ~ *lenses* piilolasit.

contagion [kən'teidʒn] *s.* tartunta. **-ous** [-ʒəs] *a.* tarttuva.

contain [kən'tein] *v.* sisältää; pidättää; hillitä. **-er** [-ə] *s.* astia, säiliö; (liik.) kontti. **-ment** *s.: policy of* ~ (jnk maan) laajenemispyrkimysten estämispolitiikka.

contaminate [kən'tæmineit] *v.* saastuttaa. **-ion** [kɔntæmi'neiʃn] *s.* saastuminen, saaste.

contemn [kən'tem] *v.* halveksia.

contemplate ['kɔntempleit] *v.* tarkastella, mietiskellä; aikoa. **-ion** [-'leiʃn] *s.* mietiskely. **-ive** [kən'templətiv, Am. 'kɔn- - - eitiv] *a.* mietiskelevä.

contemporaneity [kəntemp(ə)rə'ni:iti] *s.* samanaikaisuus. **-ous** [-ə'reinjəs] *a.* samanaikainen.

contemporary [kən'temp(ə)rəri] *a.* nykyajan, tuon ajan; samanaikainen; *s.* aikalainen.

contempt [kən'tem(p)t] *s.* halveksunta, ylenkatse. **-ible** [-əbl] *a.* halveksittava. **-uous** [-juəs] *a.* halveksiva, ylenkatseellinen.

contend [kən'tend] *v.* taistella; väittää.

content 1. ['kɔntent] *s.* tilavuus; -pitoisuus; sisältö. **-s** [-s] *s. pl.* sisällys; *table of* ~ sisällysluettelo.

content 2. [kən'tent] *pred. a.* tyytyväinen; *s.* tyytyväisyys; *v.* tyydyttää; *to one's heart's* ~ mielin määrin; ~ *oneself* tyytyä. **-ed** [-id] *a.* tyytyväinen. **-ment** *s.* tyytyväisyys.

contention [kən'tenʃn] *s.* riita, kiista; väite; *bone of* ~ riitakapula. **-tious** [-ʃəs] *a.* riidanhaluinen; kiistanalainen.

contest [kən'test] *v.* väittää vääräksi, kiistää; taistella, kilpailla (jstk); *v.* ['kɔntest] taistelu; ottelu, kilpailu; ~ *a seat* (parl.) asettua (vasta)-ehdokkaaksi. **-ant** [-ənt] *s.* kilpailija.

context ['kɔntekst] *s.* (lause)yhteys; *in this* ~ tässä yhteydessä.

contiguity [kɔnti'gju(:)iti] *s.* (välitön) kosketus, naapuruus. **-ous** [kən'tigjuəs] *a.* viereinen, naapuri-.

continence ['kɔntinəns] *s.* pidättyvyys; (lääk.) pidätyskyky. **-t** [-ənt] *a.* pidättyvä; *s.* manner(maa); maanosa; *the C* ~ Manner-Eurooppa. **-tal** [-'nentl] *a.* mannermainen, mannermaa(n)-.

contingency [kən'tin(d)ʒnsi] *s.* satunnaisuus; mahdollisuus. **-t** [-nt] *a.* satunnainen, mahdollinen; *s.* määräerä, -osuus, kiintiö (sotilaita, henkilöitä); ~ [*up*]*on* jstk riippuva.

continual [kən'tinjuəl] *a.* jatkuva, alinomainen, lakkaamaton. **-ally** *adv.* yhtämittaa. **-ance** [-əns] *s.* jatkuminen, kestäminen. **-ation** [-'eiʃn] *s.* jatko; pidennys.

continue [kən'tinju:] *v.* jatkaa; pidentää; jatkuvasti tehdä jtk; jatkua, kestää; pysyä, olla edelleen; ~ *d* jatkuva; *to be ~ d* (lyh. *cont.*) jatkoa seuraa; **-ity** [kɔnti'nju:iti] *s.* jatkuvuus; yhtäjaksoisuus. **-ous** [-juəs] *a.* jatkuva, keskeytymätön, yhtäjaksoinen.

contort [kɔn'tɔ:t] *v.* vääntää vääräksi.

contortion [kɔn'tɔ:ʃn] *s.* väänteleminen, väännös; irve. **-ist** [-ist] *s.* käärmeihminen.

contour ['kɔntuə] *s.* ääriviiva.

contra- ['kɔntrə-] *pref.* vasta-. **-band** [-bænd] *a.* salakuljetus-; *s.: ~ [of war]* sotakieltotavara. **-bandist** [-bændist] *s.* salakuljettaja. **-bass** ks. *double-bass.* **-ception** [-'sepʃn] *s.* (hedelmöityksen) ehkäisy. **-ceptive** [-'septiv] *s.* ehkäisyväline.

contract ['kɔntrækt] *s.* välikirja, sopimus; urakka; *v.* [kɔn'trækt] tehdä sopimus, sopia jstk; ottaa urakalla tehdäkseen; saada (tauti); vetää kokoon, kutistaa, -tua; supistaa, -tua; kaventua; *~ debts* velkaantua; *~ the brows* rypistää kulmiaan; *~ ing parties* asianosaiset. **-ile** [kɔn'træktail] *a.* supistuva. **-ion** [kɔn'trækʃn] *s.* kokoonvetäytyminen, supistuminen; supistunut sana. **-or** [kɔn'træktə] *s.* urakoitsija.

contradict [kɔntrə'dikt] *v.* väittää vastaan, kieltää; olla ristiriidassa. **-ion** [-'dikʃn] *s.* vastaväite; ristiriitaisuus; *~ in terms* sanonnan ristiriitaisuus. **-ory** [-(ə)ri] *a.* päinvastainen; ristiriitainen.

contradistinction *s.: in ~ to* erotukseksi jstk, vastakohtana jllek.

contralto [kɔn'træltəu] *s.* kontra-altto.

contraindication *s.* vasta-, kielteissyy.

contraption [kɔn'træpʃn] *s.* laite, vehje, vekotin, vempele.

contrari|ety [kɔntrə'raiəti] *s.* päinvastaisuus, vastakohtaisuus; **-ness** [kɔn'trɛərinis] *s.* uppiniskaisuus. **-wise** ['kɔntrəriwaiz] *adv.* päinvastoin.

contrary ['kɔntrəri] *s.* vastakohta; *a.* päinvastainen, vasta-; [kɔn'trɛəri] uppiniskainen, itsepäinen; *adv.: ~ to* vastoin jtk; *on the ~* päinvastoin; *there is no evidence to the ~* mikään ei todista päinvastaista.

contrast ['kɔntrɑ:st, Am. -træst] *s.* vastakohta; *v.* [kɔn'trɑ:st, Am. -træst] asettaa vastakkain, verrata;

muodostaa vastakohta (jllek), jyrkästi erota *(with* jstk); *by ~* sitä vastoin.

contra|vene [kɔntrə'vi:n] *v.* rikkoa (määräys), kiistää; olla ristiriidassa. **-vention** [-'venʃn] *s.: in ~ of* vastoin.

contribut|e [kɔn'tribju(:)t] *v.* antaa avustuksena; myötävaikuttaa, osaltaan vaikuttaa *(to* jhk). **-ion** [kɔntri'bju:ʃn] *s.* avustus, panos, osuus *(to* jhk); kirjoitus (sanomalehteen ym); pakkovero. **-or** [-jutə] *s.* (et. kirjallinen) avustaja. **-ory** [-jut(ə)ri] *a.* lisä-.

contri|te ['kɔntrait] *a.* katuvainen, särjetty. **-tion** [kɔn'triʃn] *s.* synnintunto; katumus.

contrivance [kɔn'traiv(ə)ns] *s.* keksintö; metku; laite, koje; kekseliäisyys.

contrive [kɔn'traiv] *v.* keksiä; onnistua (järjestämään), saada aikaan; *he ~ed to escape* hänen onnistui paeta. **-r** [-ə] *s.* juonittelija; (hyvä) taloudenpitäjä.

control [kɔn'traul] *s.* (käsky)valta; hallinta, hillintä; valvonta, kontrolli; säätö; tarkistusasema; *pl.* ohjauslaitteet, säätölaitteet; *v.* hallita, hillitä, valvoa; päästä jnk herraksi; tarkistaa (esim. koe); säätää; *assume ~ of* ottaa hallintaansa; *lose ~ of* menettää jnk hallinta; *is out of ~* on ohjauskyvytön; *his car got out of ~* hän menetti auton hallinnan; *price-~led* hintasäännöstelyn alainen.

-lable [əbl] *a.* hallittavissa. **-led** [-d] *pp.* valvottu, kontrolloitu; säännöstelty. **-ler** [-ə] *s.* tarkastaja.

contro|versial [kɔntrə'və:ʃ(ə)l] *a.* riita-, kiista-; kiistanalainen, kiistelty. **-versy** ['kɔntrəvə:si] *v.* väittely, riita; kynäsota. **-vert** ['kɔntrəvə:t] *v.* asettaa kyseenalaiseksi, kiistää.

contum|acious [kɔntju(:)'meiʃəs] *a.* niskoitteleva. **-acy** ['kɔntjuməsi] *s.* niskoittelu. **-ely** ['kɔntju(:)mli] *s.* häväistys, törkeä loukkaus.

contusion [kɔn'tju:ʒn] *s.* ruhje[vamma], kolhaisuvamma.

conundrum [kə'nʌndrəm] *s.* arvoitus.

conurbation [kɔnə:'beiʃn] *s.* asutus- (t. kaupunki)ryhmä.

convalesce [kɔnvə'les] *v.* olla toipilaana. **-nce** [-ns] *s.* toipuminen; toipilasaika. **-nt** [-nt] *a.* toipuva; *s.*

toipilas; ~ home lepokoti.
conven|e [kən'vi:n] v. kutsua kokoon; kokoontua; **-er** [-ə] s. kokoonkutsuja. **-ience** [-jəns] s. sopivuus; mukavuus; [public] ~ käymälä; all modern ~s kaikki nykyajan mukavuudet; at your earliest ~ ensi tilassa; flag of ~ mukavuuslippu; marriage of ~ sovinnaisavioliitto. **-ient** [-jənt] a. sopiva; mukava.
convent ['kɔnv(ə)nt] s. (nunna)luostari. **-ion** [kən'venʃn] s. (puolue- ym) kokous; sopimus; sovinnaistapa. **-ional** [kən'venʃənl] a. sovinnainen; tavanomainen. **-ionality** [kənvenʃə'næliti] s. sovinnaisuus.
converge [kən'və:dʒ] v. lähestyä, lähteä toisiaan, konvergoida. **-nt** [-nt] a. lähenevä; konvergentti.
conversa|ble [kən'və:səbl] a. seuraa rakastava. **-nt** [-'və:s(ə)nt] a.: ~ with perehtynyt jhk, jstk perillä (oleva).
conversation [kɔnvə'seiʃn] s. keskustelu. **-al** [-nl] a. keskustelu(n), puhe-, puhekielen, jokapäiväisessä puheessa käytetty. **-alist** [-nəlist] s. taitava keskustelija.
converse 1. [kən'və:s] v. keskustella.
conver|se 2. ['kɔnvə:s] a. päinvastainen, käänteinen; s. käänteinen suhde, vastakohta; ~ly päinvastoin. **-sion** [kən'və:ʃn] s. muuttaminen; kääntymys.
convert [kən'və:t] v. muuttaa (into jksk), muuntaa; käännyttää; konvertoida; s. ['kɔnvə:t] käännynnäinen. [-ə] (sähk.) s. muuttaja. **-ibility** [-i'biliti] s. (valuutan) vaihdettavuus. **-ible** [-əbl] a. vaihtokelpoinen, vapaaasti vaihdettava; s. auto (jossa alaslaskettava kuomu).
convex ['kɔnveks] a. kupera. **-ity** [kɔn'veksiti] s. kuperuus.
convey [kən'vei] v. kuljettaa, johtaa; toimittaa (perille); ilmaista, johtaa mieleen, antaa (~ an idea) vihjaus. **-ance** [-əns] s kuljetus; ajoneuvo; luovutus(kirja). **-er, -or** [-ə] s.: ~ belt hihnakuljetin, liukuhihna.
convict [kən'vikt] v. todistaa t. tuomita syylliseksi; s. ['kɔnvikt] rangaistuvanki; this ~ ed him [of his

guilt] tämä sai hänet vakuuttuneeksi **-ion** [-'vikʃn] s. syylliseksi todistaminen, tuomitseminen, tuomio; vakaumus; carry ~ olla vakuuttava.
convince [kən'vins] v. saada vakuuttuneeksi, vakuuttaa; convincing vakuuttava.
convivial [kən'viviəl] a. juhla-; rattoisa, hilpeä; ~ companion juomaveikko. **-ity** [-vi'æliti] s. juhlailo.
con|vocation [kɔnvə'keiʃn] s. kokous. **-voke** [kən'vəuk] v. kutsua kokoon.
convol|ution [kən'və'lu:ʃn] s. kierre; poimu. **-vulus** [kən'vɔlvjuləs] s. kierto (kasv.).
convoy ['kɔnvɔi] v. saattaa (vartiona); s. (laiva)saattue.
convul|se [kən'vʌls] v. kouristaa; was ~d with laughter vääntelehti naurusta. **-sion** [-ʃn] s. kouristus. **-sive** [-siv] a. kouristuksentapainen.
cony ['kəuni] s. kaniini.
coo [ku:] s. kujerrus; v. kuhertaa, kujertaa.
cook [kuk] v. keittää; valmistaa ruokaa; kypsyä; s. keittäjä, kokki; what's ~ing? mitä on tekeillä? **-er** [-ə] [-ə] s. (sähkö- ym) keitin, liesi. **-ery** [-əri] s. keittotaito; (~-book keittokirja). **-ie** [-i] s. pikkuleipä; (Skotl.) pulla.
cool [ku:l] a. viileä; rauhallinen; kylmäkiskoinen; (rauhallinen) hävytön; s. viileys; v. jäähdyttää; viilentää; jäähtyä; rauhoittua (m. ~ down). **-er** [-ə] s. jäähdytysastia, jäähdytin. **~-headed** maltillinen, kylmäverinen. **-ly** [-i] adv. viileästi, kylmäkiskoisesti, välinpitämättömästi; häpeämättömästi.
coolie ['ku:li] s. (kiinal.) kuli.
coon [ku:n] s. pesukarhu; (puhek.) neekeri.
co-op [kə(u)'ɔp] s.: the co-op osuuskauppa.
coop [ku:p] v. kanahäkki; v.: ~ up panna häkkiin, sulkea jhk. **-er** [-ə] s. tynnyrintekijä.
co-operat|e [kə(u)'ɔpəreit] v. toimia yhdessä, tehdä yhteistyötä; osaltaan vaikuttaa **-ion** [-'reiʃn] s. yhteistyö, -toiminta; osuustominta. **-ive** [-rətiv]

a. yhteis-, osuus-; osuustoiminnallinen; *s.* osuus|kauppa, -kunta; ~ *society* osuuskunta. **-or** [-ə] *s.* työtoveri.

co-opt [kəu'ɔpt] *v.* valita (täytevaalilla).

co-ordina|te [kəu(u)'ɔ:dineit] *v.* rinnastaa; *a. & s.* [-'ɔ:dnit] rinnastettu, tasavertainen; koordinaatta. **-tion** [-'neiʃn] *s.* rinnastaminen, rinnastus.

coot [ku:t] *s.* nokikana.

cop [kɔp] *s.* poliisi, »jepari», pollari; *v.* siepata kiinni; ~ *it* (sl.) joutua ikävyyksiin.

copartner ['kəu'pɑ:tnə] *s.* osallinen, liiketoveri.

cope 1. [kəup] *s.* kaapu; (taivaan) laki, kupu.

cope 2. [kəup] *v.* selviytyä, suoriutua jstk, olla jnk tasalla *(with).*

Copenhagen [kəupn'heig(ə)n] *erisn.* Kööpenhamina.

coping ['kəupiŋ] *s.* muurinpeite, -harja.

copious ['kəupjəs] *a.* runsas, yltäkylläinen; monisanainen.

copper 1. ['kɔpə] *s.* ks. *cop.*

copper 2. ['kɔpə] *s.* kupari, kuparikolikko; *v.* kuparoida. **~-plate** kuparilevy, -piirros. **-y** [-i] *a.* kupari-, kuparinvärinen.

coppice ['kɔpis], **copse** [kɔps] *s.* nuori metsä, vesakko.

copulat|e ['kɔpjuleit] *v.* paritella. **-ion** [-'leiʃn] *s.* parittelu, yhdyntä.

copy ['kɔpi] *s.* jäljennös; kappale; mallikirjoitus; käsikirjoitus; *v.* jäljentää, jäljitellä; *fair* ~ puhtaaksikirjoitettu teksti; *rough* ~ konsepti. **~-book** kaunokirjoitusvihko. **-ist** [-ist] *s.* puhtaaksikirjoittaja. **-right** kustannusoikeus. **-writer** mainostekstien laatija.

coquet [kəu'ket] *v.* keimailla. **-ry** ['kəukitri] *s.* keimailu. **-te** [kəu'ket] *s.* keimailija. **-tish** [-iʃ] *a.* keimaileva.

coracle ['kɔrəkl] *s.* punottu (vedenpitävällä aineella päällystetty) vene.

coral ['kɔr(ə)l] *s.* koralli; *a.* korallinpunainen.

corbel ['kɔ:bl] *s.* olkakivi.

cord [kɔ:d] *s.* köysi, nuora; (anat.) juoste, jänne, ydin *(spinal ~),* napanuora; syli (mitta); = *corduroy; v.* köyttää; *vocal ~ s* äänihuulet. **-age** [-idʒ] *s.* köysistö.

cordial ['kɔ:diəl] *a. & s.* sydämellinen; sydäntävahvistava (lääke). **-ity** [kɔ:di'æliti] *s.* sydämellisyys.

cordon ['kɔ:dn] *s.* ketju (sot. ym); punos, nauha; *v.*: ~ *off* eristää (alue).

corduroy ['kɔ:dərɔi] *s.* korderoi, vakosametti; ~ *s* vakosamettihousut.

core [kɔ:] *s.* sisin, ydin, sydän (m. tekn.); siemenkota; *v.* poistaa siemenkota; *to the ~* läpikotaisin.

co-respondent ['kɔuris'pɔndənt] *s.* kanssavastaaja (avioerojutussa).

corgi ['kɔ:gi] *s.* (koirarotu).

Corinthian [kə'rinθiən] *a. & s.* korinttilainen; ~ *s* Korinttolaiskirje.

cork [kɔ:k] *s.* korkki; pullontulppa; *v.* sulkea korkilla, korkita (us. ~ *up); ~ jacket* korkkivyö. **-er** [-ə] *s.* mykistävä sana, yliveto. **-ing** *a.* sl. loisto-. **-screw** korkkiruuvi.

corm [kɔ:m] *s.* (juuri-, varsi)mukula.

cormorant ['kɔ:m(ə)r(ə)nt] *s.* merimetso.

corn [kɔ:n] *s.* jyvä; vilja; Am. maissi; *v.* suolata (lihaa); ~ *ed beef* suolattu naudanliha; *Indian* ~ maissi. **~-crake** ruisrääkkä.

corn 2. [kɔ:n] *s.* liikavarvas. **-ea** [-iə] *s.* (silmän) sarveiskalvo.

cornelian [kɔ:'ni:ljən] *s.* karneoli.

corner ['kɔ:nə] *s.* nurkka, kulma; kolkka, soppi; *v.* saattaa ahtaalle (m. *drive into a ~);* ostaa varastoon; (autosta) kaartaa; *[just] make a ~ in* ostaa suuret varastot (jtk tavaraa) hintojen nostamiseksi; *round the ~* kulman takana, (aivan) lähellä. **~-stone** kulmakivi.

cornet ['kɔ:nit] *s.* kornetti (mus.); tötterö.

cornflour, -starch maissijauho. **-flower** ruiskukka.

cornice ['kɔ:nis] *s.* karniisi, reunuslista.

Cornish ['kɔ:niʃ] *a.* cornwallilainen.

cornucopia [kɔ:nju'kəupjə] *s.* runsaudensarvi.

Cornwall ['kɔ:nw(ə)l] *erisn.*

corny ['kɔ:ni] *a.* sl. vanhanaikainen, ikävä, kulunut; sl. kännisärä.

cost

corolla [kəˈrɔlə] s. teriö. **-ry** [-ri] s. luonnollinen seuraus.

corona [kəˈrəunə] s. (täht.) valokehä, korona.

coronary [ˈkɔrənəri] a.: ~ artery sepelvaltimo; ~ thrombosis s-n tukos.

coronation [kɔrəˈneiʃn] s. kruunajaiset.

coron|er [ˈkɔrənə] s. kuolemansyyntutkija. **-et** [-nit] s. aateliskruunu; otsaripa.

corporal [ˈkɔːp(ə)rəl] s. l.v. alikersantti; a. ruumiillinen.

corpora|te [ˈkɔːp(ə)rit] a. järjestynyt; ~ body yhteisö, juridinen henkilö. ~ town kaupunkikunta. **-tion** [-ˈreiʃn] s. yhdyskunta; kaupunginhallitus; Am. osakeyhtiö; ~ [tramways] kunnalliset.

corporeal [kɔːˈpɔːriəl] a. ruumiillinen, aineellinen.

corps [kɔː] s. (pl. = sg. [kɔːz]) joukot, -kunta; army~ armeijakunta; Signal C~ viestijoukot; ~ diplomatique diplomaattikunta.

corpse [kɔːps] s. (kuolleen) ruumis.

corpulen|ce [ˈkɔːpjuləns] s. pyylevyys. **-t** [-ənt] a. pyylevä, lihava.

corpuscle [ˈkɔːpʌsl] s. (veri)solu; keränen; atomi.

corral [kɔˈrɑːl] s. karja-aitaus; v. ajaa aitaukseen.

correct [kəˈrekt] a. oikea; virheetön, moitteeton; v. korjata, oikaista; nuhdella, kurittaa; I stand ~ed tunnustan erehtyneeni. **-ion** [-kʃn] s. korjaus, oikaisu; nuhde. **-itude** [-itjuːd] s. moitteettomuus. **-ive** [-iv] a. ojennus-, parannus-; ~ parannuskeino. **-ly** adv. oikein. **-ness** s. oikeus; säntillisyys. **-or** [-ə] s.: ~ of the press oikolukija.

correla|te [ˈkɔrileit] v. korreloida. **-tion** [kɔriˈleiʃn] s. vastaavuussuhde, korrelaatio.

correspond [kɔrisˈpɔnd] v.: ~ to vastata jtk, olla jnk mukainen; olla kirjeenvaihdossa (with). **-ence** [-əns] s. vastaav(ais)uus, yhdenmukaisuus; kirjeenvaihto. **-ent** [-ənt] s. kirjeenvaihtaja; kirjeenvaihtotoveri; asiamies.

corridor [ˈkɔridɔː] s. käytävä; ~s of power vallankahva.

corrig|enda [kɔriˈdʒendə] s. pl. korjauksia, painovirheitä.

-ible [ˈkɔridʒəbl] a. korjattavissa oleva.

corroborat|e [kəˈrɔbəreit] v. vahvistaa. **-ion** [-ˈeiʃn] s. vahvistus. **-ive** [-(ə)rətiv] a. vahvistava.

corro|de [kəˈrəud] v. syövyttää, **-sion** [-əuʒn] s. syövytys, syöpyminen. **-sive** [-əusiv] a. syövyttävä; s. syövytysaine.

corrugate [ˈkɔrugeit] v. rypistää, -tyä; poimuttaa; ~d iron aaltopelti.

corrupt [kəˈrʌpt] a. turmeltunut; lahjottu; väiristely; v. turmella, pilata; lahjoa; vääristää; pilaantua. **-ibility** [-əˈbiliti] s. lahjottavuus. **-ible** [-əbl] a. lahjottava. **-ion** [kəˈrʌpʃn] s. mätäneminen; lahjonta, korruptio; tapainturmelus, mädännäisyys; virheellinen muoto.

corsage [kɔːˈsɑːʒ] s. (puvun) miehusta, liivi.

corsair [ˈkɔːsɛə] s. merirosvo(laiva).

corset [ˈkɔːsit] s. (kure)liivi, korsetti.

cors(e)let [ˈkɔːslit] s. rintahaarniska.

Corsica [ˈkɔːsikə] erisn. **-n** [-n] a. & s. korsikalainen.

cort|ex [ˈkɔːteks] s. (pl. -ices [-isiːz] kuorikerros, (brain ~) aivokuori. **-isone** [ˈkɔːtizəun] s. kortisoni.

coruscate [ˈkɔrəskeit] v. säkenöidä, kimallella.

cosh [kɔʃ] s. sl. lyijyputki, -patukka; v. iskeä patukalla.

cosher [ˈkɔʃə] ks. kosher.

cosiness [ˈkəuzinis] s. kodikkuus.

cosmetic [kɔzˈmetik] a. & s. kosmeettinen, k. aine.

cosmic [ˈkɔzmik] a. kosminen.

cosmo|naut [ˈkɔzmə(u)nɔːt] s. venäläinen avaruuslentäjä. **-politan** [kɔzməˈpɔlit(ə)n] a. yleismaailmallinen, kosmopoliittinen; s. maailmankansalainen. **-s** [ˈkɔzmɔs] s. maailmankaikkeus.

Cossack [ˈkɔsæk] s. kasakka.

cosset [ˈkɔsit] v. hemmotella, lellitellä.

cost [kɔst, kɔːst] cost cost, v. maksaa, tulla maksamaan, olla hintana; (~ ed, ~ ed) tehdä kustannuslaskelmia, hinnoittaa; s. hinta; kustannus; pl. kustannukset, kulut; ~ accounting kustannuslaskenta; ~ of living index elinkustannusindeksi; ~ price tuotanto- t. tukkuostohinta; at any ~ mihin hintaan hyvänsä; at the ~ of jnk kustannuksella, jhk hintaan; [*I know*] *to my* ~ karvaasta kokemuksesta.

costal ['kɔstl] *a.* kylkiluu(n)-.

costermonger ['kɔstəmʌŋgə] *s.* (vihannes)kaupustelija.

costive ['kɔstiv] *a.* umpitautinen, ummetus-.

costly ['kɔ(:)stli] *a.* kallis(arvoinen).

costume ['kɔstju:m] *s.* (historiallinen, kansallis- ym) puku; kävelypuku; *v.* [kɔs'tju:m] pukea (jhk erikoiseen pukuun). ~-**piece** pukunäytelmä.

cosy ['kəuzi] *a.* mukava; kodikas; *s.* (teekannun ym) peite, myssy.

cot 1. [kɔt] *s.* maja; katos.

cot 2. [kɔt] *s.* lapsen sänky, kevyt vuode; ~ *death(s)* kätkytkuolema.

cote [kəut] *s.* katos, suoja.

coterie ['kəutəri] *s.* nurkkakunta, kuppikunta.

cottage ['kɔtidʒ] *s.* mökki, pieni huvila; ~ *piano* (pieni) pianiino. -**r** [-ə] *s.* mökkiläinen.

cotter ['kɔtə] *s.* (skotlant.) torppari; kiila; ~ *pin* saksisokka.

cotton ['kɔtn] *s.* puuvilla; pumpulilanka, -kangas; *v.:* ~ *on* käsittää, hoksata; ~ [*up*] *to* ruveta pitämään jksta, lyöttäytyä jkn seuraan. ~-**cake** puuvillasiemenkakku. ~-**mill** puuvillatehdas. ~-**wool** vanu (Am. ~-*batting*). -**y** ['kɔtni] *a.* puuvillamainen, villava.

cotyledon [kɔti'li:dn] *s.* sirkkalehti.

couch 1. [kautʃ] *s.* makuusija; leposohva; *v.* ilmaista; (eläimistä) maata (väijyksissä), kyyristyä; ~*ed in insolent terms* röyhkeäin sanoin (ilmaistu, -na); ~ [*a spear*] laskea hyökkäysasentoon.

couch 2. [kautʃ] *s.:* ~ [-*grass*] juolavehnä.

cough [kɔf] *v.* yskiä; kakistella; *s.* yskä.

could [kud, kəd] *imp.* ks. *can.*

council ['kaunsl, -sil] *s.* neuvosto; neuvottelu; johtokunta; ~ *of war* sotaneuvottelu; ~ *house* kunnallinen asuintalo; *local* ~ kunnanvaltuusto. -**lor** [-ə] *s.* neuvosmies; *town-*~kaupunginvaltuutettu.

counsel ['kaunsl] *s.* neuvo; neuvottelu; neuvonantaja;

asianajaja, -t; *v.* neuvoa; *take* ~ neuvotella; *keep one's own* ~ pitää aikeensa salassa. -**ling** *s.* neuvonta. -**lor** [-ə] *s.* neuvonantaja, neuvoja.

count 1. [kaunt] *v.* laskea, luetella; laskea mukaan (m. ~ *in*); pitää jnak; ottaa huomioon; olla tärkeä; *s.* laskeminen; ~ *on (upon)* luottaa jhk; ~ *up* laskea yhteen; *it* ~ *s for much* se merkitsee paljon; *keep* ~ *of* pitää lukua jstk; ~-*down* (raketin) lähtölaskenta.

countenance ['kauntinəns] *s.* kasvot, kasvojen ilme; rohkaisu; *v.* tukea, rohkaista; hyväksyä; *change* ~ muuttaa ilmettä; *keep one's* ~ pysyä vakavana t. rauhallisena.

counter 1. ['kauntə] *s.* pelimarkka, -nappula (tammi-); laskin; myyntipöytä, tiski, kassa(luukku).

counter 2. ['kauntə] *adv.:* ~ *to* vastoin; *a.* vastakkainen, vasta-; *s.* vastaisku; *v.* antaa vastaisku, vastata jhk. -**act** [-'rækt] vaikuttaa t. toimia vastaan, vähentää jnk tehoa, ehkäistä. -**action** [-'rækʃn] vastatoimi(nta), vastustaminen. -**attack** [-rətæk] vastahyökkäys. -**balance** *s.* vastapaino; *v.* olla vastapainona. -**claim** vastavaatimus. -**clockwise** vastapäivään. -**feit** [-fit] *a.* jäljitelty, väärennetty, väärä; *s.* jäljittely, väärennys; *v.* jäljitellä, väärentää. -**feiter** [-fitə] (rahan)väärentäjä. -**foil** (šekin ym) kanta. -**mand** [-ma:nd] *v.* peruuttaa; *s.* peruutus. ~-**move** vastaveto. -**pane** (vuoteen) päiväpeite. -**part** vastine, kaksoiskappale; kollega, virkaveli. -**point** kontrapunkti. -**poise** *s.* tasapaino, vastapaino; *v.* olla vastapainona, pitää tasapainossa. -**sign** *v.* varmentaa nimikirjoituksellaan; *s.* tunnussana. -**vail** korvata; ~*ing* vasta-, tasoitus-.

countess ['kauntis] *s.* kreivitär.

counting-house *s.* konttori.

countless *a.* lukematon.

countrified ['kʌntrifaid)] *a.* maalaistunut.

country ['kʌntri] *s.* maa; maaseutu; seutu; *in the* ~ maalla; *into the* ~ maalle; ~ *house*, ~ *seat* kartano.

-man [-mən] maanmies; maalainen.
-side maaseutu.

county ['kaunti] s. kreivikunta.

coup [ku:] s. kaappaus; (m. ~ *d'état*
[-dei'ta:]) vallankaappaus.

couple ['kʌpl] s. pari (m. avio-);
koirapari, koiranvitjat; v. kytkeä
yhteen, yhdistää; liittyä pariksi; *a ~*
of days pari päivää. **-et** [-it] s. kupletti.
-ing s. kytkin.

coupon ['ku:pɔn] s. kuponki, (korko-
ym) lippu.

courage ['kʌridʒ] s. rohkeus; *take ~*
rohkaista mielensä. **-ous** [kə'reidʒəs]
a. rohkea.

courier ['kuriə] s. matkanjohtaja, opas;
pikalähetti.

course [kɔ:s] s. kulku, (joen) juoksu;
tie, rata, suunta; kurssi; kilpa-ajorata
(m. *race~*;) oppikurssi, luentosarja
(of lectures); (lääke)kuuri; ruokalaji;
menettelytapa, elämäntapa; v. juosta,
kiitää; ajaa (jäniksiä); *in ~ of*
construction rakenteilla; *in ~ of time*
ajan oloon; *~ of events* tapahtumain
kulku; *in due ~* aikanaan; *in the ~ of*
nature luonnon järjestyksen mukaan;
in the ordinary ~ of things tavallisesti,
normaalioloissa; *in the ~ of a year*
vuoden kuluessa; *of ~* tietysti,
luonnollisesti; *it is a matter of ~* se on
itsestään selvää.

court [kɔ:t] s. piha; hovi; tuomioistuin,
oikeus; (tennis- ym) kenttä; v.
liehitellä, kosiskella; tavoitella;
seurustella; *at ~* hovissa; *the C ~ of St*
James's Englannin hovi; *in ~*
oikeudessa; *law ~, ~ of justice*
tuomioistuin, oikeus; *be brought*
before the ~ joutua oikeuteen; *pay ~*
to kosiskella; etsiä jtk, antautua
alttiiksi jllek (*~ disaster*). **~card**
kuvakortti (korttip.).

courteous ['kə:tjəs] *a.* kohtelias.

courtesan [kɔ:ti'zæn] s. kurtisaani.

courtesy ['kə:tisi] s. kohteliaisuus;
suosionosoitus; *by ~ of* jkn
suosiollisella luvalla, jkn
ystävällisesti käyttöön
luovuttama.

courtier ['kɔ:tjə] s. hovimies.

courting s. kosiskelu, seurustelu.

courtly ['kɔ:tli] *a.* kohtelias,
hienokäytöksinen.

court-martial s. sotaoikeus; v. asettaa
sotaoikeuden tutkittavaksi.

court|ship kosiskelu. **-yard** piha.

cousin ['kʌzn] s. serkku; *first ~*
täysserkku; *second ~* pikkuserkku.

cove [kəuv] s. lahdelma, poikama; sl.
kaveri, heppu.

covenant ['kʌvinənt] s. sopimus,
välikirja; liitto (m. raam) **-er** [-ə] s.
(Skotl.) *covenant*-liiton jäsen.

Coventry ['kɔvntri] *erism.: send to ~*
katkaista seurustelu (jkn kanssa).

cover ['kʌvə] v. peittää, kattaa;
verhota, salata; suojata; suorittaa
(matka); kulkea; käsittää, ulottua yli;
korvata, peittää (kustannukset);
selostaa; tähdätä jhk, (tykistä)
kantaa; s. peite; kansi, kirjankansi,
päällinen; (kirje)kuori; kotelo; kate
(liik.); suoja (sot. ym), piilopaikka,
tiheikkö; *~s were laid for six* pöytä oli
katettu kuudelle; *take ~* suojautua;
under ~ of jnk varjolla; *I am ~ed*
minulla on vakuutus; *remain ~ed*
pitää hattu päässä; *the floor was ~ed*
with carpets matot peittivät lattian;
~ing letter saatekirje.

coverage s. selostaminen, reportaasi;
TV~ area katselu-, näkyvyysalue;
give wide ~ to selostaa laajasti.

cover-girl s. kansikuvatyttö.

covert ['kʌvət] *a.* salavihkainen,
peitetty; s. tiheikkö.

cover-up s. salailu, peitteleminen.

covet ['kʌvit] v. haluta, himoita. **-ous**
[-əs] *a.* himoitseva.

covey ['kʌvi] s. (peltopyy)poikue.

cow 1. [kau] s. lehmä; naaras (valas
ym).

cow 2. [kau] v. pelotella, masentaa;
~ed sorrettu, alaspainettu.

coward ['kauəd] s. pelkuri, raukka. **-ice**
[-is] s. pelkuruus. **-ly** [-li] *a.*
raukkamainen; arka.

cow|boy ratsastava karjapaimen.
~-catcher karja-aura.

cower ['kauə] v. kyyristyä (peloissaan).

cow|-herd paimen. **~-hide**
lehmänvuota, l-vuodasta tehty piiska.
~-house navetta.

cowl [kaul] s. (munkin)kaapu, huppu;
(savupiipun) hattu.

co-worker s. työtoveri.

cowslip ['kauslip] s. kevätesikko.

cox [kɔks] *s.* perämies (= *coxswain*); *v.* pitää perää.

coxcomb ['kɔkskəum] *s.* turhamainen narri.

coxswain ['kɔkswein, kɔksn] *s.* (et. kilpasoutu)veneen perämies.

coy [kɔi] *a.* kaino, häveliäs.

coyote ['kɔiəut, kɔi'əuti] *s.* preeriasusi.

cozen ['kʌzn] *v.* pettää.

cozy ['kəuzi] *a.* Am. = *cosy.*

crab [kræb] *s.* taskurapu; eräänl. nosturi; villiomena (m. ~-*apple*); *v.* (puhek.) parjata, moittia. **-bed** [-id] *a.* kärttyinen, pahansisuinen; sotkuinen, vaikeasti luettava (käsiala).

crack [kræk] *s.* halkeama, särö; paukahdus, läimäys; *(funny ~)* sukkeluus; (sisään)murto; *a.* ensiluokan, valio-, loisto-; *v.* säröillä, halkeilla, särkyä, murtua; paukkua; särkeä; läimähdyttää, paukahduttaa; ~ *a joke* veistää sukkeluus; ~ *sth. up* ylistellä; ~ *up* romahtaa, murtua; ~ *a crib* tehdä murto. **-ed** [-t] *a.* säröinen, murroksiosa oleva (ääni); löyhäpäinen, tärähtänyt (m. *crack-brained*). **-er** [-ə] *s.* eräänl. rapea keksi; sähikäinen; paukkukaramelli; [*nut-*] ~ *s* pähkinänsärkijä. **-ing** *a.* hieno, loisto-. **-le** [-l] *v.* rätistä; *s.* rätinä. **-sman** [-smən] *s.* murtovaras.

cradle [kreidl] *s.* kehto (m. kuv.); (maalarin ym) kelkka; *v.* tuudittaa, hyssytellä (sylissään).

craft [krɑːft] *s.* ammatti, käsityö; ammattikunta; taito; alukset, alus; viekkaus; *arts and* ~ *s* taideteollisuus. **-sman** [-smən] *s.* käsityöläinen, ammattitaitoinen työmies. **-smanship** *s.* ammattitaito. **-y** [-i] *a.* viekas.

crag [kræg] *s.* (jyrkkä, rosoinen) kallio. **-gy** [i] *a.* kallioinen; rosoinen.

crake [kreik] *s.* ruisrääkkä (m. *corn-* ~).

cram [kræm] *v.* ahtaa täyteen, sulloa; päntätä päähän(sä). **-mer** [-ə] *s.* (tutkintoon ym)valmentaja.

cramp [kræmp] *s.* suonenveto; sinkilä, ruuvipuristin; *v.* rajoittaa, estää; *writer's* ~ kirjoituskouristus; ~ *ed* ahdas, rajoitettu; liian tiheä t. pieni (käsiala).

crampon ['kræmpən] *s.* jääkenkä.

cranberry ['krænb(ə)ri] *s.* karpalo.

crane [krein] *s.* kurki; nostokurki, nosturi; *v.* ojentaa (kaulaansa), kurkottaa. ~'**s-bill** kurjenpolvi.

cranial ['kreinjəl] *a.* kallon. **-ium** [-jəm] *s.* kallo.

crank [krænk] *s.* kampi; omituinen intoilija (esim. *fresh-air* ~); *v.* vääntää kampea, vääntää käytiin; *a.* kiikkerä; huojuva. **-y** [-i] *a.* oikullinen, omituinen; kiikkerä.

cranny ['kræni] *s.* kolo, piilopaikka.

crap [kræp] *v.* ulostaa; *s.* paska; sl. roska, pöty.

crape [kreip] *s.* (suru)kreppi.

craps [kræps] *s.* eräänl. noppapeli.

crash [kræʃ] *v.* romahtaa, rysähtää; törmätä jhk, syöksyä maahan; (puhek.) tunkeutua kutsumatta jnnek (ks. *gate-* ~ *er*). *s.* romahdus; rysähdys, jyrähdys; yhteentörmäys, kolari, maahansyöksy; *adv.* rysähtäen; ~ *course* teho- t. pikakurssi; ~ *helmet* suojakypärä. ~**-land** tehdä (epäonnistunut) pakkolasku. ~**-landing** ks. ed.

crass [kræs] *a.* karkea, törkeä.

crate [kreit] *s.* sälelaatikko.

crater ['kreitə] *s.* kraatteri.

crave [kreiv] *v.:* ~ *for* kiihkeästi haluta, halata; pyytää.

craven ['kreivn] *s.* pelkuri, raukka; *a.* raukkamainen; *cry* ~ pyytää armoa.

craving ['kreivin] *s.* himo, halu.

craw [krɔː] *s.* (linnun ym) kupu. **-fish** [-fiʃ] = *crayfish.*

crawl [krɔːl] *v.* ryömiä, madella; kihistä; *s.* ryömiminen, mateleminen; (urh.) krooli; *v.* kroolata; *my flesh* ~ *s* pintaani karmii. **-er** [-ə] *s.* matelija; ~ *s* potkuhousut.

crayfish ['kreifiʃ] *s.* jokiäyriäinen, rapu.

crayon ['kreiən] *s.* väriliitu, -piirros.

craze [kreiz] *v.* tehdä mielettömäksi; *s.* kiiho, vimma, (muoti)hulluus, villitys; *the* [*latest*] ~ viimeistä muotia. **-iness** *s.* mielettömyys. **-y** [-i] *a.* mieletön, hullu; hatara, ränsistynyt; ~ *paving* (epäsäännöllinen) laattakiveys; *he is* ~ *about skiing* hän on »hiihtohullu».

creak [kriːk] *v.* narista, kitistä; *s.* narina; ~ *at the joints* natista liitoksissaan. **-y** [-i] *a.* nariseva.

cream [kri:m] *s.* kerma; jälkiruoka; voide; *v.* kermoittua; kuoria kerma; Am. sl. päihittää, antaa selkään; *face ~* kasvovoide; *chocolate ~* suklaakiisseli. **-ery** [-əri] *s.* meijeri. **-y** [-i] *a.* kermankaltainen, -värinen.

creas|e [kri:s] *s.* laskos; ryppy; maaliviiva; *v.* laskostaa; rypistää, -tyä; (**~-resisting** rypistymätön). **-y** [-i] *a.* ryppyinen.

creat|e [kri'eit] *v.* luoda; herättää, aiheuttaa; tehdä, nimittää jksk; perustaa (esim. professorinvirka). **-ion** [-ei∫n] *s.* luominen; luomakunta; (alkuperäinen) luomus, tuote; muotipuku. **-ive** [-iv] *a.* luova; **-ivity** [-'tiviti] *s.* luovuus. **-or** [-ə] *s.* luoja. **-ure** ['kri:t∫ə] *s.* luontokappale; olento; käskyläinen, välikappale.

crèche [krei∫] *s.* lastenseimi, päiväkoti.

creden|ce ['kri:dns] *s.* usko; *letter of ~* suosituskirje; *give ~ to* uskoa. **-tials** [kri'den∫lz] *s.* (lähettilään) valtakirja.

credi|bility [kredə'biliti] *s.* uskottavuus.

-ble ['kredəbl] *a.* uskottava.

credit ['kredit] *v.* uskoa; merkitä jkn hyväksi; *s.* usko, luottamus; ansio, kunnia; luotto, kredit-puoli; *pl.* (filmin) alkutekstit; *~ sb. with* uskoa jkn sanoneen t. tehneen jtk; *one would hardly ~ him with having said so* tuskin uskoisi hänen sanoneen niin; *on ~* velaksi; *letter of ~* kreditiivi; *be a ~ to, do ~ to* olla kunniaksi jklle; *give ~ to* uskoa; *it goes to the ~ of* siitä lankeaa kunnia -lle; *~ squeeze* kireä luottopolitiikka. **-able** [-əbl] *a.* kunniakas, kiitettävä. **-or** [-ə] *s.* velkoja.

credul|ity [kri'dju:liti] *s.* herkkäuskoisuus. **-ous** ['kredjuləs] *a.* herkkäuskoinen.

creed [kri:d] *s.* uskontunnustus.

creek [kri:k] *s.* poukama; Am. pieni joki, puro.

creel [kri:l] *s.* kalakori.

creep [kri:p] *crept crept, v.* ryömiä, madella; hiipiä; (*~ in, into*) pujahtaa; *s.: the ~s* kauhun tunne; *make sb.'s flesh ~* karmaista jkn selkäpiitä. **-er** [-ə] *s.* köynnöskasvi. **-ing** *a: ~ plant =* ed. **-y** [-i] *a.* kammottava.

cremat|e [kri'meit] *v.* polttaa (ruumis). **-ion** [-'mei∫n] *s.* ruumiinpoltto,

polttohautaus. **-ory** ['kremət(ə)ri] *s.* krematorio.

crenellated ['krenileitid] *a.* sakaroilla t. ampuma-aukoilla varustettu.

creole ['kri:oul] *s.* kreoli(tar).

crepe [kreip] *s.* kreppi.

crept [krept] *imp. & pp.* ks. *creep.*

crepuscular [kri pΛskjulə] *a.* hämärä(n)-, hämy-.

crescendo [kri'∫endəu] *adv.* paisuen, paisuttaen (et. mus.)

crescent ['kresnt] *s.* kuunsirppi; puolikuu.

cress ['kres] *s.* krassi, et. vesikrassi.

crest [krest] *s.* (kukon, vuoren, aallon) harja; (kypärän) töyhtö; vaakuna(merkki); *v.* varustaa vaakunalla ym; nousta harjalle. **-fallen** masentunut.

cretaceous [kri'tei∫əs] *a.* liitumainen, liitupitoinen.

Crete [kri:t] *erisn.* Kreeta.

cretin ['kretin] *s.* (lääk.) kretiini.

crevasse [kri'væs] *s.* (jäätikön) halkeama.

crevice ['krevis] *s.* rako, halkeama.

crew 1. [kru:] *s.* laivaväki, miehistö, (soutu)joukkue; joukko; *~ cut* pystytukka.

crew 2. [kru:] *imp.* ks. *crow.*

crib [krib] *s.* pilttuu; jouluseimi (Am. *crèche);* lapsen vuode; plagiaatti, luntti, apukäännös; *v.* sulkea ahtaalle; plagioida. **-bage** [-idʒ] *s.* eräs korttipeli.

crick [krik] *s.* venähdys; *v.* venähdyttää.

cricket 1. ['krikit] *s.* sirkka.

cricket 2. ['krikit] *s.* kriketti(peli); *not ~* ei reilua peliä. **-er** [-ə] *s.* kriketinpelaaja.

cri|ed ks. *cry.* **-er** ['kraiə] *s.* julkinen kuuluttaja.

crime [kraim] *s.* rikos; rikollisuus.

Crimea [krai'miə] *erisn.* Krim.

crimin|al ['kriminl] *a.* rikollinen; rikos-, kriminaali-; *s.* rikoksentekijä, rikollinen; *the ~ code* rikoslaki. **-ality** [-'næliti] *s.* rikollisuus. **-ology** [-'nɔlədʒi] *s.* kriminologia.

crimp [krimp] *v.* kähertää; poimuttaa; *s.* värvääjä.

crimson ['krimzn] *s. & a.* karmosiininpuna(inen); *v.* värjätä karmosiininpunaiseksi; punastua heleäksi.

cringe [krin(d)ʒ] v. kyyristyä; ~ *to* madella jkn edessä, liehakoida; s. liehakointi.

crinkl|e ['kriŋkl] v. rypyttyä, -ttää, poimuttaa; s. poimu; ryppy. **-y** [-i] a. rypytetty, poimuinen; kähärä.

crinoline ['krinəlin, -li:n] s. krinoliini.

cripple ['kripl] s. raajarikko; v. tehdä raajarikoksi, rampauttaa; lamauttaa.

crisis ['kraisis] s. (pl. crises [-i:z] kriisi; (taudin ym) käännekohta.

crisp [krisp] a. murea, rapea, hauras; raikas (ilma), kirpeä; kähärä; v. kähertää, -tyä; paahtaa rapeaksi; Am. *potato* ~ s perunalastut.

criss-cross ['kriskrɔs] a. & adv. ristiin rastiin (kulkeva).

criterion [krai'tiəriən] s. (pl. -ria) kriteeri, (arvostelu)peruste.

critic ['kritik] s. arvostelija. **-al** [-k(ə)l] a. arvosteleva; arveluttava, kriittinen. **-ism** [-isizm] s. arvostelu; moite. **-ize** [-isaiz] v. arvostella; moittia.

critique [kri'ti:k] s. arvostelu, kritiikki.

croak [krouk] v. kurnuttaa; raakkua; puhua käheällä äänellä; sl. kuolla; s. kurnutus; raakkuminen. **-er** [-ə] s. pahanilmanlintu. **-y** [-i] a. raakkuva, käheä.

Croat ['krɔ(u)ət] s. kroaatti. **-ia** [krɔ(u)'eiʃiə] erisn. Kroatia. **-ian** [-'eiʃjən] a. kroatialainen.

crochet ['krouʃei] s. virkkuu(työ); v. virkata.

crock [krɔk] s. saviruukku, ruukunpalanen, -sirpale; vanha koni, autorämä; v.: ~ *up* romahtaa, murtaa (terveys). **-ery** [-əri] s. saviastiat.

crocodile ['krɔkədail] s. krokotiili.

crocus ['kroukəs] s. krookus.

Croesus ['kri:səs] erisn. Kroisos.

croft [krɔft] s. maatilkku; torppa. **-er** [-ə] s. pientilallinen, torppari.

crone [kroun] s. vanha akka.

crony ['krɔuni] s. vanha hyvä ystävä, kaveri.

crook [kruk] s. koukku; mutka; paimensauva; huijari, petkuttaja; v. koukistaa, -tua; *by hook or by* ~ keinolla millä hyvänsä. **-backed** a. kyttyräselkäinen. **-ed** [-id] käyrä, koukkuinen; kiero, epärehellinen.

croon [kru:n] v. hyräillä; s. hyräily. **-er** [-ə] s. (mikrofoniin tunteellisesti laulava) iskelmälaulaja.

crop [krɔp] s. sato, laiho; (linnun) kupu; ratsupiiska; lyhyeksi leikattu tukka; v. leikata, katkaista; jyrsiä (ruohoa); kylvää (with jtk); ~ *well* tuottaa runsasta satoa; ~ *up* tulla ilmi, putkahtaa esiin. **~-eared** töpökorvainen. **-ped** [-t] a. lyhyeksi leikattu. **-per** [-ə] s.: *come a* ~ pudota (päistikkaa); epäonnistua, reputtaa.

croquet ['kroukei] s. krokettipeli; v. krokata.

crosier ['krouʒə] s. piispansauva.

cross [krɔs] s. risti (m. kuv.); risteytys; a. ristikkäinen, risti-; vastakkainen; molemminpuolinen; äkäinen, vihainen (with jklle); v. panna ristiin, vetää risti t. viiva jnk yli; kulkea t. matkustaa jnk poikki, ylittää (tie), mennä ristiin; estää, vastustaa; viivata (sekki); risteyttää; ~ *out* pyyhkiä yli; ~ *examination* ristikuulustelu; ~ *reference* viittaus (saman kirjan) toiseen kohtaan; ~ *road* poikkikatu; ~~*-wind* sivutuuli; *keep one's fingers* ~*ed* l. v. pitää peukkua; ~ *oneself* tehdä ristinmerkki; ~ *one's mind* johtua mieleen; ~ *sb.'s palm* antaa juomarahaa; ~ *sb.'s path* osua jkn tielle; *he has been* ~*ed [in love]* hän on pettynyt. **~-bar** poikkipuu. **~-bow** varsijousi. **-bred** risteytetty. **-breed** sekarotuinen eläin, riste mä. **~-country** murtomaa-, maasto-. **~-cut** oikotie. **~-examine** ristikuulustella. **~-fertilize** ristipölyttää. **~-grained** itsepäinen, häijy.

crossing ['krɔsiŋ] s. jnk ylitys, merimatka; (teiden, tien ja rautatien) risteys, ylikäytävä; [street] ~ suojatie; *level* ~ tasoristeys.

crossly adv. vihaisesti.

cross|patch äkäpussi. **~-purposes:** *be at c.-p.* käsittää toisensa väärin. **~-question** ristikuulustella. **-road** poikkitie; tienhaara. **~-section** läpileikkaus. **~-stitch** ristipisto. **-wise** ristissä, -iin. **-word** ristisanatehtävä, sanaristikko (m. ~ *puzzle*).

crotch [krɔtʃ] s. haara.

crotchet ['krɔtʃit] s. neljännesnuotti;

oikku; haka. **-y** [-i] *a.* oikullinen,
eriskummallinen.

crouch [krautʃ] *v.* kyyristyä,
kyyristellä.

croup [kru:p] *s.* kuristustauti;
(hevosen) lautaset.

croupier ['kru:pjə] *s.* pelipankin
hoitaja.

crow 1. [krəu] *v.* kiekua *(imp.* m. *crew);*
jokeltaa, riemuita, sl. kerskua; *s.*
kiekuminen.

crow 2. [krəu] *s.* varis; *as the ~ flies*
linnuntietä; *~ 's feet* rypyt
silmäkulmissa. **-bar** sorkkarauta.

crowd [kraud] *s.* joukko, lauma,
(väen)tungos; *v.* tunkea, tungeksia;
kerääntyä; ahtaa täyteen, täyttää; *the*
~ joukko, sakki; *in ~ s* laumoittain; *~*
out työntää ulos; *we are ~ed* meillä on
ahdasta. **-ed** [-id] *a.* täpötäynnä
(oleva).

crowfoot ['krəufut] *s.* leinikki.

crown [kraun] *s.* kruunu; seppele;
latva, huippu, päälaki; (hatun) kupu;
hampaanterä, kruunu; engl. raha
(vuoteen 1971: *half a ~* = 2 s. 6 d.);
v. kruunata; seppelöidä; saattaa
huippuunsa; varustaa hammas
kruunulla; *C~ Prince* kruununprinssi;
to ~ all kaiken kukkuraksi.

crozier ks. *crosier.*

cruci|al ['kru:fjəl] *a.* ratkaiseva;
kriittinen. **-ble** ['kru:sibl] *s.*
sulatusastia, upokas; (kuv.) tulikoe.

cruci|fix ['kru:sifiks] *s.* ristiinnaulitun
kuva. **-fixion** [-'fikʃn] *s.*
ristiinnaulitseminen. **-form** *a.*
ristinmuotoinen, risti-. **-fy** [-fai] *v.*
ristiinnaulita.

crud|e [kru:d] *a.* raaka, jalostamaton;
karkea, hienostumaton; *~ oil*
raakaöljy; *~ facts* kylmät tosiasiat.
-ity [-iti] *s.* raakuus, karkeus.

cruel ['kruəl] *a.* julma; sydämetön. **-ty**
[-ti] *s.* julmuus.

cruet ['kru(:)it] *s.* (maustetelineen)
pullo; = seur. **~-stand** mausteikko.

cruise [kru:z] *v.* risteillä; *s.* risteily. **-r**
[-ə] *s.* risteilijä.

crumb [krʌm] *s.* (leivän)muru, leivän
sisus; *v.* murentaa; peittää
korppujauholla. **-le** [-bl] *v.* murentaa;
murentua; ränstyä, luhistua, lahota.

crummy ['krʌmi] *a.* sl. kurja, kehno.

crump [krʌmp] *s.* kova isku.

crumpet ['krʌmpit] *s.* litteä, murea
teeleipä.

crumple ['krʌmpl] *v.* rutistaa, rypistää;
rutistua.

crunch [krʌn(t)ʃ] *v.* narskuttaa,
narskua; rouskuttaa; *s.* narskuminen;
when it comes to the ~ kun tiukka
tulee.

crupper ['krʌpə] *s.* häntävyö;
(hevosen) lautaset.

crusade [kru:'seid] *s.* ristiretki; *v.*
lähteä ristiretkelle. **-r** [-ə] *s.*
ristiretkeläinen.

crush [krʌʃ] *v.* murskata, musertaa;
survoa; tunkea; lannistaa; rutistaa,
rypistää; *s.* tungos; suuret kutsut; *be*
~ed murskaantua; *~ up* hienontaa; . .
does not ~ ei rypisty; *has a ~ on* on
ihastunut jkh. **-ing** *a.* musertava.

Crusoe ['kru:səu] *erisn.*

crust [krʌst] *s.* kuori; (leivän)
kannikka; karsta, rupi; *v.* peittää
kuorella, kuorettua *(~ over); the*
earth's ~ maankuori; *~ on the snow*
hanki. **-acean** [-'eiʃ(ə)n] *s.* äyriäinen.
-y [-i] *a.* paksukuorinen, kova;
kärtyinen, äreä.

crutch [krʌtʃ] *s.* kainalosauva; haara;
pönkkä, tuki.

crux [krʌks] *s.* (pää)pulma, (suurin)
vaikeus.

cry [krai] *v.* huutaa, huudahtaa; itkeä;
tarjota kaupaksi, julistaa; *s.* huuto;
itku, valitus; *~ down* parjata; *~ off*
heittää asia sikseen, perua; *~ out*
huudahtaa; *~ out against* protestoida;
~ out for vaatia; *~ up* ylistää; *~ one's*
heart out itkeä katkerasti; *~ for the*
moon vaatia mahdottomia; *[let her]*
have her ~ out itkeä itkettävänsä; *a*
far ~ pitkä matka (kuv.); *[it's] a far ~*
[from] eroaa suuresti -sta. **~-baby**
itkupilli. **-ing** (kuv.) huutava,
pakottava.

crypt [kript] *s.* holvi (kirkon alla),
krypta. **-ic** [-ik] *a.* salaperäinen,
hämärä. **-o-** [-ɔ(u)-] sala-.

crystal ['kristl] *s.* kide; kristalli; *a.*
kristallinen, kristallinkirkas;
~-gazing ennustaminen
(kristallipallosta). **-line** [-təlain] *a.*
kiteinen; = ed. *a.* **-lize** [-təlaiz] *v.*
kiteyttää, -tyä.

cub [kʌb] s. pentu, poikanen, penikka (m. kuv.); nulikka, nulkki; v. poikia; a ~ [reporter] aloitteleva.

Cuba ['kju:bə] erisn. Kuuba. **-n** [-n] a. & s. kuubalainen.

cubby-hole ['kʌbi-] s. (kuv.) pesä.

cub|e [kju:b] s. kuutio; v. (mat.) korottaa kolmanteen potenssiin. **-ic** [-ik] a. kuutio-. **-icle** [-ikl] s. osasto, koppi (makuusalissa). **-ism** [-izm] s. kubismi.

cuckold ['kʌk(ə)ld] s. aisankannattaja (kuv.).

cuckoo ['kuku:] s. käki; käen kukunta; pl. hölmö; v. kukkua.

cucumber ['kju:kʌmbə] s. kurkku; looked as cool as a ~ näytti rauhalliselta kuin viilipytty.

cud [kʌd] s. märehditty ruoka; chew the ~ märehtiä (m. kuv.).

cuddl|e ['kʌdl] v. syleillä, hyväillä; maata käpertyneenä (~ up); ~ up to painautua jtk lähelle. **-esome** a. hyväilevä. **-y** [-i] a. & s. (sopiva) hyväilyn kohde, pehmeä; ~ bear teddykarhu.

cudgel ['kʌdʒl] s. nuija, ryhmysauva; v. nuijia; ~ one's brains vaivata päätään.

cudweed ['kʌdwi:d] s. ahojäkkärä.

cue [kju:] s. (repliikin) loppusanat, viimeiset vuorosanat (merkkinä seuraavalle); vihje, vihjaus; biljardisauva; hiuspiiska, saparo; take one's ~ from sb. ottaa oppia jksta.

cuff 1. [kʌf] v. lyödä, iskeä; s. isku, korvatillikka.

cuff 2. [kʌf] s. kalvosin, hihankäänne; off the ~ valmistamatta; ~s (m. puhek.) käsiraudat. **~-links** kalvosinnapit.

cuirass [kwi'ræs] s. rintahaarniska.

cuisine [kwi'zi:n] s. keittotaito, keittiö.

cul-de-sac ['kuldə'sæk] s. umpikuja.

culinary ['kʌlinəri] a. keitto-.

cull [kʌl] v. poimia, valita.

culmina|te ['kʌlmineit] p. kohota huippuunsa. **-tion** [-'neiʃn] s. huippu(kohta).

culp|able ['kʌlpəbl] a. rikollinen, rangaistava (~ negligence). **-rit** [-prit] s. rikollinen, syyllinen.

cult [kʌlt] s. kultti, palvonta.

cultivat|e ['kʌltiveit] v. viljellä, kasvattaa; kehittää; sivistää;

harjoittaa; ~d sivistynyt. **-ion** [-'veiʃn] s. (maan)viljely.

cultural ['kʌltʃ(ə)rəl] a. kulttuuri-.

culture ['kʌltʃə] s. viljely(s); sivistys, kulttuuri; v. viljellä (bakteereja ym). **-d** [-d] a. sivistynyt, kultivoitu.

culvert ['kʌlvət] s. pengersilta, rumpu.

cumber ['kʌmbə] v. kuormittaa, olla esteenä. **-some** [-səm] a. vaivalloinen, kömpelö, hankala (käsitellä).

cumbrous ['kʌmbrəs] a. = ed.

cumul|ative ['kju:mjul|ətiv] a. kumulatiivinen, kasaantuva. **-us** [-əs] s. kumpupilvi.

Cunard [kju:'nɑ:d] erisn.

cuneiform ['kju:niifɔ:m] s. nuolenpääkirjoitus.

cunning ['kʌniŋ] a. ovela, viekas; Am. soma, viehkeä; s. oveluus, viekkaus.

cup [kʌp] s. kuppi, pikari; kalkki, kärsimys; malja, pokaali; booli; v. kupata; a ~ of tea kupillinen teetä; ~ one's hands muodostaa kouraksi; in his ~s iloisella tuulella, humalassa. **~-bearer** juomanlaskija. **-board** ['kʌbəd] s. seinäkaappi, astiakaappi; ~ love omanvoitonpyyntöinen rakkaus.

Cupid ['kju:pid] s. lemmenjumala, Cupido.

cupidity [kju:'piditi] s. voitonhimo, ahneus.

cupola ['kju:pələ] s. kupoli; (laivan ym) tykkitorni.

cuppa ['kʌpə] s. sl. = a cup of tea.

cupr|ic, -ous ['kju(:)prik, -rəs] a. kuparipitoinen.

cur [kə:] s. rakki; roisto.

curable ['kjuərəbl] a. parannettavissa (oleva), parantuva.

curacy ['kjuərəsi] s. apulaispapin virka.

curat|e ['kjuərit] s. kirkkoherran apulainen, (us.l.v.) kappalainen. **-ive** [-rətiv] a. parantava. **-or** [kju(ə)'reitə] s. intendentti, hoitaja.

curb [kə:b] s. kuolainvitjat; (kuv.) ohjakset, pidäke; kaivonkehä; ks. kerb; v. suitsittaa; pitää kurissa, hillitä; ~ roof taitekatto.

curd [kə:d] s. juossut maito; pl. kokkarejuusto. **-le** [-l] v. juoksettaa, hyydyttää; juosta, juoksettua; hyytyä, jähmettyä.

cure [kjuə] s. hoito(tapa), parannus, -keino; kuuri; parantuminen; v.

parantaa; säilöä (lihaa ym), suolata; *rest* ~ lepohoito.

curfew ['kə:fju:] *s.* iltasoitto; ulkonaliikkumiskielto; *.. is under a~ .. ssa on u.; impose a ~ on .. *julistaa u. jnnek.

curl|o ['kjuəri|əu] *s.* harvinaisuus, harvinainen taide-esine. **-osity** [-'ɔs(i)ti] *s.* uteliaisuus; (taide-)esine; ~ *shop* antiikkikauppa. **-ous** [-əs] *a.* utelias, tiedonhaluinen; omituinen, kummallinen.

curl [kə:l] *s.* kihara; kiemura; *v.* kähertää; kiertää; kihartua, kiertyä; ~ *of the lip* ivallinen ilme; ~ *up* käpertyä kerälle. **-er** [-ə] *s.* papiljotti.

curlew ['kə:lju:] *s.* isokuovi.

curly ['kə:li] *a.* kihara.

curmudgeon [kə:'mʌdʒn] *s.* kitsastelija; moukka.

currant ['kʌr(ə)nt] *s.* korintti; herukka (*black ~, red ~*).

currency ['kʌr(ə)nsi] *s.* voimassaolo(-aika), käypäisyys, yleisyys; (jnk valtakunnan) raha, valuutta; *gain* ~ levitä; *have short* ~ ovat käytössä vain vähän aikaa; ~ *reserve* valuuttavaranto.

current ['kʌr(ə)nt] *a.* juokseva, kuluva, nykyinen; käypä (raha); yleisessä käytännössä oleva, yleinen; viimeksi ilmestynyt, tuorein, ajankohtainen; sujuva; *s.* virta (m. sähk.); kulku; ~ *account* šekkitili, juokseva tili; ~ *affairs* ajankohtaiset asiat; ~ *expenses* juoksevat menot. **-ly** *adv.* nyt; yleisesti.

curriculum [kə'rikjuləm] *s.* oppikurssi, opinto-ohjelma; ~ *vitae* ['vi:tai] ansioluettelo.

currier ['kʌriə] *s.* nahkuri.

currish ['kə:riʃ] *a.* roistomainen.

curry 1. ['kari] *v.* sukia; muokata, parkita; ~ *favour with* mielistellä.

curry 2. ['kari] *s.* curry (mauste); currylla maustettu ruoka; *v.* maustaa curryjauheella.

curry-comb *s.* suka.

curse [kə:s] *s.* kirous; *v.* kirota, sadatella. **-d** [-id] *a.* kirottu.

curs|ive ['kə:siv] *a.* vino(kirjoitus). **-ory** [-(ə)ri] *a.* pintapuolinen, pääkohdittainen, nopea.

curt [kə:t] *a.* lyhyt, niukkasanainen.

curtail [kə:'teil] *v.* lyhentää; supistaa, vähentää. **-ment** *s.* supistus, rajoitus.

curtain ['kə:tn] *s.* uudin, verho; esirippu; *v.* varustaa verho(i)lla; ~ *off* erottaa, jakaa verhoilla. **~-call** esiinhuuto (teatt.). **~-lecture** kotiripitys. **~-raiser** lyhyt alkunäytelmä.

curts(e)y ['kə:tsi] *s.* niiaus; *v.* niiata; *drop a* ~ niiata.

curvature ['kə:vətʃə] *s.* kaarre, kaarevuus; käyryys (~ *of the spine*).

curve [kə:v] *s.* mutka, kaarre; *v.* käyristää, -tyä; kaartaa, -tua; ~*d* kaareva.

cushion ['kuʃ(ə)n] *s.* pielus, tyyny; pehmike; (biljardipöydän) valli; *v.* varustaa pieluksella; vaimentaa.

cushy ['kuʃi] *a.* sl. helppo.

cusp [kʌsp] *s.* kärki, (kuun ym) sakara.

cuspidor ['kʌspidɔ:] *s.* Am. sylkyastia.

cuss [kʌs] *s.* otus (kuv.). **-edness** [-idnis] *s.* uppiniskaisuus.

custard ['kʌstəd] *s.* munakastike, -vanukas.

custodian [kʌs'təudjən] *s.* (julkisen) rakennuksen hoitaja, valvoja, vartija (~ *of the peace*).

custody ['kʌstədi] *s.* hoito, huosta; vankeus; *protective* ~ turvasäilö; *take into* ~ pidättää; *have the* ~ *of* olla jkn huoltajana.

custom ['kʌstəm] *s.* tapa, tottumus; *pl.* tulli, -laitos; asiakassuhde; ~ *[made] clothes* (m.) tilauksesta valmistetut vaatteet; *withdraw one's custom* katkaista asiakassuhteensa. **~-house** tullikamari; **~-house officer** tullivirkamies.

custom|ary ['kʌstəməri] *a.* tavallinen, tavanomainen; *is it* ~ *for guests to tip .. onko tapana, että (hotelli)vieraat antavat juomarahaa ..lle?* **-er** [-ə] *s.* asiakas; *a queer* ~ kummallinen otus.

cut [kʌt] *cut cut, v.* leikata, haavoittaa, olla terävä, pystyä; hakata, hioa; lyhentää, »saksia»; typistää; alentaa; ei olla näkevinään, olla tervehtimättä (m. ~ *dead*); nostaa (korttip.); *s.* leikkaus, haava, (miekan) pisto, sivallus; uurre; (tukan)leikkuu; pala, viipale; kuosi; alennus, vähennys, supistus; oikotie; *a.* leikattu, hiottu; *(she)* ~ *her finger* leikkasi haavan

sormeensa; ~ *a lecture* jäädä pois
(pinnata) luennolta; ~*s a fine figure*
on komean näköinen; ~*s both ways*
on kaksiteräinen; *it* ~*s no ice* ei tepsi
ollenkaan; ~ *short* keskeyttää äkkiä;
~ *teeth* saada hampaita; ~ *and run*
livistää tiehensä; ~ *across* .. oikaista
jnk poikki; ~ *down* vähentää, alentaa
(kustannuksia); ~ *in* sanoa väliin,
keskeyttää, (autosta) tunkeutua
väliin, kiilata; ~ *it fine* saapua viime
hetkellä; ~ *off* katkaista; ~ *off with a
shilling* tehdä perinnöttömäksi; ~ *out*
leikata (vaatekappale ym), lyödä jku
laudalta; jättää pois; lakata, lopettaa;
~ *that out!* lakkaa jo! *he is* ~ *out for*
hän on kuin luotu (jhk); ~ *up*
paloitella; järkyttää; [*be*] ~ *up about*
järkyttynyt jstk; *a* ~ *above* astetta
parempi; ~ *and dried* täysin valmis;
kaavamainen; ~ *flowers* leikkokukat;
~ *glass* kristallilasi; *a short* ~ oikotie;
~ *prices* alennetut hinnat; *defence* ~*s*
puolustusmenojen supistukset.
cutaneous [kju(:)'teinjəs] *a.* iho(n)-.
cute [kju:t] *s.* nokkela, vitsikäs; soma,
veikeä, sievä.
cuticle ['kju:tikl] *s.* orvaskesi;
kynsivalli; ~ *remover* kynsinauhavesi.
cutlass ['kʌtləs] *s.* (lyhyt) miekka.
cutler ['kʌtlə] *s.* veitsiseppä. **-y** [-ri] *s.*
hienotakeet; ruokailuvälineet,
pöytäkalut.
cutlet ['kʌtlit] *s.* kyljys.
cutt|er ['kʌtə] *s.* leikkaaja; leikkuuase,
-terä; kutteri (mer.). **-ing** *a.* terävä,
pureva; *s.* leikkaus, kaivanto;
sanomalehtileike; pistokas.
cut-throat *s.* murhaaja; *a.* murhaava,
armoton.
cuttlefish ['kʌtlfiʃ] *s.* mustekala.

cyan|ic [sai'ænik] *a.* syaani-. **-ide**
['saiənaid] *s.* syanidi.
cybernetics [saibə:'netiks] *s.*
kybernetiikka.
cyclamen ['sikləmən] *s.* alppiorvokki,
syklaami.
cycl|e ['saikl] *s.* kierto, jakso,
ajanjakso; polkupyörä; *v.* kiertää;
ajaa polkupyörällä; *song* ~ laulusarja.
-ical ['siklik(ə)l] *a.* jaksollinen,
syklinen. **-ing** *s.* pyöräily. **-ist** [-ist] *s.*
pyöräilijä. **-one** [-əun] *s.*
pyörremyrsky. **-ops** [-ɔps] *s.*
kyklooppi.
cygnet ['signit] *s.* nuori joutsen.
cylind|er ['silində] *s.* lieriö, sylinteri.
-rical [si'lindrik(ə)l] *a.* lieriömäinen.
cymbal ['simbl] *s.* : ~*s* lautaset (mus.).
cynic ['sini|k] *a.* kyyninen; *s.* kyynikko.
-al [k(ə)l] *a.* kyyninen, ivallinen. **-ism**
[-sizm] *s.* kyynisyys.
cynosure ['sinəzjuə] *s.* (tav. ~ *of all
eyes, of the world*) huomion kohde.
cypher ['saifə] ks. *cipher.*
cypress ['saipris] *s.* sypressi.
Cypr|iot ['sipriət] *a.* & *s.* kyproslainen.
-us ['saiprəs] *erisn.* Kypros.
cyrillic [si'rilik] *a.* kyrillinen.
cyst [sist] *s.* (lääk.) kysta, rakkula. **-itis**
[-'aitis] *s.* rakkotulehdus. **-oscope**
[-əskəup] *s.* (lääk.) rakontähystin.
cytology [sai'tɔlədʒi] *s.* soluoppi.
czar [zɑː] *s.* tsaari (m. *tsar*). *s.* tsaaritar.
czardas ['zɑːdəs] *s.* csardas.
czarina [zɑː'riːnə] *s.* tsaaritar.
Czech [tʃek] *a.* & *s.* tšekkiläinen; *s.*
tšekki, tšekin kieli.
Czechoslovak ['tʃekə(u)'sləuvæk] *a.* &
s. tšekkoslovakialainen. **-ia** [-'vaːkiə]
erisn. Tšekkoslovakia.

D

D, d [di:] d-kirjain; nuotti d; *D-Day*
maihinnousupäivä (Normandiassa
1944), jnk toiminnan alkamispäivä;
Lyh.: **d.** (= denarius) *penny; died;* **D.**
Dame (arvonimi); **Dak.** *Dakota;*
Dan. *Daniel;* **db, dB** *decibel(s);* **d.c.**
direct current; **D.D.** *Doctor of
Divinity;* **Dec.** *December;* **Del.**
Delaware; **dept.** *Department;* **Deut.**
Deuteronomy; **do.** *ditto;* **doz.** *dozen;*
Dr. *Doctor;* **D.Sc.** *Doctor of Science;*
D.S.O. *Distinguished Service Order;*
D.T. *delirium tremens.*
'd lyh. = *had, would* (et. *I'd, he'd,
they'd*).

dab [dæb] *v.* koskettaa kevyesti,
sipaista, taputtaa; *s.* kevyt lyönti,
taputus, (maali)läiskä.

dabble ['dæbl] *v.* polskutella; *~ in*
harrastella jtk. **-r** [-ə] *s.* harrastelija,
tuhertaja.

dace [deis] *s.* seipi (kala).

dachshund ['dækshund] *s.* mäyrä-
koira.

dad [dæd] *s.* isä, isäukko.

daddy ['dædi] *s.* = ed.; *~-longlegs*
vaaksiainen; lukki.

daemon ks. *demon.*

daffodil ['dæfədil] *s.* keltanarsissi,
pääsiäislilja.

daft [dɑːft] *a.* sekapäinen, hupsu.

dagger ['dægə] *s.* tikari; (kirjap.) risti;
at ~ s drawn sotajalalla; *look ~ s at*
katseellaan lävistää.

dago ['deigəu] *s.* (pl. *-s*) (pilk.)
portugalilainen, espanjalainen t.
italialainen.

dahlia ['deiljə] *s.* daalia.

Dail Eireann ['dɔil 'eərən] *s.* Irlannin
tasavaltsan parlamentin alahuone.

daily ['deili] *a.* jokapäiväinen; *adv.*
päivittäin, joka päivä; *s.* päivälehti; *~
[help]* päiväapulainen.

daintiness *s.* hienous, sirous.

dainty ['deinti] *a.* hieno, sorea, siisti;
herkullinen; liian tarkka, nirso; *s.*
herkkupala.

dairy ['dɛəri] *s.* meijeri. **-ing** *s.*
maitotalous. **-maid** meijerikkö. **-man**
meijeristi; maitokauppias.

dais ['deiis] *s.* koroke.

daisy ['deizi] *s.* kaunokainen, bellis.

Dakota [də'kəutə] *erisn.*

dale [deil] *s.* (run.) laakso.

dalliance ['dæliəns] *s.* rakastelu.

dally ['dæli] *v.* kuluttaa aikaa;
huvitella, leikitellä, rakastella.

Dalmatia [dæl'meifiə] *erisn.* **-n** [-n] *s. &
a.* dalmatialainen; *s.* dalmatiankoira.

dam 1. [dæm] *s.* pato; *v.: ~ up* padota,
hillitä.

dam 2. [dæm] *s.* (eläimistä) emä, emo.

damage ['dæmidʒ] *s.* vahinko; vaurio;
pl. vahingonkorvaus; *v.* vahingoittaa,
turmella.

Damascus [də'mæskəs] *erisn.*

damask ['dæməsk] *a.* damasti-;
ruusunpunainen; *s.* damasti; *v.* kutoa
damastimalliin; *~ rose*
damaskonruusu.

dame [deim] *s.* (naisen) korkea
arvonimi Englannissa; sl. nainen,
typykkä; *D~ Nature* luontoemo.

damn [dæm] *v.* kirota; sadatella; *~ [it]* !
kirottua! **-able** [-nəbl] *a.* kirottu.
-ation [-'neifn] *s.* kadotus; *int.* tuhat
tulimmaista. **-ed** [-d] *a.* kadotettu,
kirottu; *adv.* kirotun.

damp [dæmp] *s.* kosteus; kaivoskaasu;
a. kostea; *v.* kostuttaa; (m. *~en*)
heikentää, laimentaa; *~ down* hillitä,
vaimentaa. **-er** [-ə] *s.* (uunin- ym)
pelti; ilonpilaaja.

damsel ['dæmzl] *s.* neito, tyttö.

damson ['dæmz(ə)n] *s.*
damaskonluumu.

danc|e [dɑ:ns] v. tanssia; s. tanssi; tanssiaiset. **-er** [-ə] s. tanssija, -tar. **~-hall, ~-ing-salon** (Am.)tanssipaikka.

dandelion ['dændilaiən] s. voikukka.

dander ['dændə] s.: get sb. 's ~ up saada kimpaantumaan; get one's ~ up suuttua.

dandle ['dændl] v. kiikuttaa, hypittää.

dandruff ['dændrəf] s. hilse.

dandy ['dændi] s. keikari; sl. eri hieno. **-ish** [-iʃ] s. keikarimainen.

Dane [dein] s. tanskalainen; Great ~ tanskandogi.

danger ['deindʒə] s. vaara; [he] was in ~ of losing his life oli hengenvaarassa; ~ money vaarallisen työn lisä. **-ous** [-rəs] a. vaarallinen.

dangle ['dæŋgl] v. roikkua, riippua; roikuttaa; ~ after juosta (naisen) perässä.

Daniel ['dænjəl] erisn.

Danish ['deiniʃ] a. & s. tanskalainen; tanskan kieli.

dank [dæŋk] a. kostea.

Danube ['dænju:b] erisn.: the ~ Tonava.

Daphne ['dæfni] erisn.; s. näsiä.

dapper ['dæpə] a. siisti, keikarimainen; vikkelä, ketterä.

dapple ['dæpl] v. täplittää; ~d täplikäs. **~-grey** papurikko.

Dardanelles [dɑ:də'nelz] s.: the ~ Dardanellit.

dare [deə] imp. ~d, (joskus) durst, v. uskaltaa, rohjeta; haastaa, uhmata; I ~n't do it en uskalla tehdä sitä; how ~ he say so kuinka hän uskaltaa sanoa niin; he didn't ~ [to] go hän ei uskaltanut mennä; I ~ say luulenpa; I ~ you to do it lyön vetoa, ettet uskalla sitä tehdä. **-devil** s. uskalikko; a. huimapäinen.

daring s. rohkeus, huimapäisyys; a. rohkea.

dark [dɑ:k] a. pimeä, synkkä, tumma; ruskeaihoinen; tietämätön; s. pimeys, hämärä; tietämättömyys; ~ blue tummansininen; (be) in the ~ about jstk tietämätön; before ~ ennen pimeän tuloa; keep sth. ~ pitää salassa; a ~ horse »musta hevonen». **-en** [-n] v. pimentää; synkistää, himmentää; pimetä; synkistyä; he shall never ~ my door hän ei saa

milloinkaan astua kynnykseni yli. **-ly** adv. synkästi; peitellysti. **-ness** s. pimeys; salaisuus, tietämättömyys. **-y, -ey** [-i] s. (halv.) neekeri.

darling ['dɑ:liŋ] s. lemmikki, armas; a. rakas, kallis, lempi-.

darn 1. [dɑ:n] v. parsia; s. parsittu paikka. **-ing-needle** parsinneula.

darn 2. v. kirota; well, I'll be ~ed! pahus soikoon! voi turkanen!

dart [dɑ:t] s. heittokeihäs, nuoli; v. heittää; syöksyä; ~ing eyes vilkkaat silmät; ~s nuolenheitto, tikkapeli. **-board** tikkataulu.

dash [dæʃ] v. heittää, paiskata, murskata; syöksyä, syöksähtää; iskeä; pirskottaa; roiskauttaa; sekoittaa; s. syöksähdys, ryntäys; reipas ote, vauhti; ulkonainen loisto; ajatusviiva; roiskahdus, tilkka, »aavistus»; 100 metres ~ 100 metrin juoksu; cut a ~ tehdä valtava vaikutus; ~ it! pahus soikoon; ~off paiskata paperille; [his hopes] were ~ed raukesivat tyhjiin. **~-board** lokasuojus; (auton) kojelauta. **-ing** a. raju, rohkea; huomiota herättävä, häikäisevä.

dastard ['dæstəd] s. pelkuri. **-ly** [-li] a. raukkamainen.

data ['deitə] s. (sg. datum) tiedot, tosiseikat; ~ processing tietojen-käsittely.

date 1. [deit] s. taateli, -palmu.

date 2. [deit] s. päivämäärä, päiväys; aika, määräaika; (puhek.) »treffit», sovittu kohtaus; heila; v. päivätä; olla peräisin; ajoittaa, iätä; käydä vanhanaikaiseksi; ~ back to, ~ from juontaa alkunsa, olla peräisin jstk; out of ~ vanhanaikainen; up to ~ ajanmukainen; keep sth. up to ~ pitää ajan tasalla; to ~ tähän mennessä; at an early ~ pian. **-d** [-id] a. vanhentunut. **-less** a. ikimuistoinen.

dating s. ajoitus, ikäys.

datum ['deitəm] ks. data.

daub [dɔ:b] v. sivellä; töhertää; s. töherrys. **-er** [-ə] s. töhertäjä.

daughter ['dɔ:tə] s. tytär. **~-in-law** miniä.

daunt [dɔ:nt] v. pelottaa. **-less** [-lis] a. peloton, uljas.

davenport ['dævnpɔ:t] s. eräänl. kirjoituspöytä t. sohva.

David ['deivid], **Davi(e)s** ['deivis] *erisn.*

davit ['dævit] *s.* taavetti (mer.).

Davy ['deivi] *s.: ~ lamp* kaivoslamppu; *~ Jones's locker* meren pohja (hautana).

daw [dɔ:] *s.* ks. *jackdaw.*

dawdle ['dɔ:dl] *v.* kuluttaa aikaa, vetelehtiä. **-r** [-ə] *s.* vetelehtijä.

dawn [dɔ:n] *v.* valjeta, sarastaa; *s.* sarastus, aamunkoitto; *it ~ed upon me* minulle valkeni.

day [dei] *s.* päivä, vuorokausi; aika(kausi); työpäivä; *all [the] ~* koko päivän; *the other ~* tässä eräänä päivänä, pari päivää sitten; *one ~* eräänä päivänä; *some ~* jonakin päivänä; *this ~ week* tästä päivästä viikon perästä; *by ~* päivällä, päiväsaikaan; *by the ~* päiväpalkalla; *by ~* päivältä; *in his ~* aikanaan; *in my school ~s* kouluaikanani; *to a ~* päivälleen; *~ in, ~ out* päivät pääksytysten; *~-to-day* päivittäinen; *let's call it a ~* lopettakaamme tältä päivältä! *win the ~* voittaa; *a six-hour ~* kuuden tunnin työpäivä. **~-boy** päiväoppilas. **-break** päivänkoitto. **~-dream** haaveilu. **-light** *s.* päivänvalo; *~-saving time* kesäaika. **~-nursery** päiväkoti. **~-school** päiväkoulu. **-time** päivä; *in the ~* päiväsaikaan.

daze [deiz] *v.* huumata; *in a ~d state, in a ~* huumaantuneena.

dazzle ['dæzl] *v.* sokaista, häikäistä; *s.* välke.

deacon ['di:kn] *s.* diakoni. **-ess** ['di:kənis] *s.* diakonissa.

dead [ded] *a.* kuollut; eloton, tunteeton; turta, kohmettunut; himmeä; syvä (uni ym); ehdoton, täydellinen; *adv.* kuoleman-, äärimmäisen, ehdottoman; *s.: the ~ of night* ydinsydän; *~ drunk* sikahumalassa; *~ end* umpikuja, umpiperä; *~ heat* ratkaisematon kilpailu; *~ [leaves]* kuihtuneet; *~ [letter]* perilletoimittamaton; *~ shot* mestariampuja; *stop ~* pysähtyä kuin paikalleennaulittuna; *~ against* yrkästi jtk vastaan; *make a ~ set at* nyökätä päättävästi jkn kimppuun; *~ beat* lopen uupunut; *.. hung at ~*

centre oli(vat) kuolleessa pisteessä. **-en** [-n] *v.* vaimentaa, heikontaa; hillitä; tehdä tunnottomaksi. **-line** *s.* (viimeinen) määräaika. **-lock** *s.* täydellinen seisahdus, umpikuja, umpiperä. **-ly** [-li] *a.* kuolettava; hirvittävä; kuoleman-, kalman-; suunnattoman; *adv.* kuoleman-. **-pan** *a.* ilmeetön; *s.* pokeri(naama).

deaf [def] *a.* kuuro; *turn a ~ ear to* ei olla kuulevinaan jtk; *fall on ~ ears* kaikua kuuroille korville. **-en** [-n] *v.* tehdä kuuroksi, huumata; *~ed* kuuroutunut; *~ing* huumaava (melu ym). **~-mute** kuuromykkä. **-ness** *s.* kuurous.

deal 1. [di:l] *s.: ~s* lankut.

deal 2. [di:l] *dealt, dealt* [delt] *v.* jakaa, jaella, antaa; *s.* (korttien) jakaminen, jakovuoro; (puhek.) kauppa; poliittinen ohjelma; *a good ~, a great ~* aika paljon; *~ sb. a blow* antaa isku jklle; *~ [badly, well] by* kohdella (huonosti, hyvin); *~ in* harjoittaa (jnk tavaran) kauppaa, myydä; *~ out* jaella; *~ with* käsitellä jtk; olla tekemisissä (jkn kanssa), kohdella, toimittaa (asia); olla jkn asiakas; *he's easy to ~ with* hänen kanssaan on helppo tulla toimeen; *whose ~?* kuka jakaa (korttip.); *it's a ~!* kiinni veti! *the New D~* ks. *new.* **-er** [-ə] *s.* jakaja; kauppias (esim. *cattle-~, ~ in tobacco).* **-ings** *s. pl.* menettely; kanssakäyminen.

dealt [delt] *imp. & pp.* ks. *deal.*

dean [di:n] *s.* tuomiorovasti; (tav. *rural ~*) lääninrovasti; dekaani.

dear [diə] *a.* kallis, rakas; suloinen, herttainen; (kirjeessä) hyvä; *s.* rakas; *adv.* kalliilla hinnalla; *int.* oh *~, ~ me!* hyvänen aika! *D~ Sir* hyvä herra!; *for ~ life* henkensä edestä; *my ~* kultaseni, rakas ystävä. **-ly** *adv.* hellästi; kalliilla hinnalla. **-y** [-ri], **-ie** *s.* kultaseni.

dearth [də:θ] *s.* puute, pula.

death [deθ] *s.* kuolema, kuolemantapaus; *put to ~* ottaa hengiltä; *at ~'s door* kuoleman partaalla; *be in at the ~* olla mukana riistan tapossa, (kuv.) ratkaisevalla hetkellä; *... to ~* kuoliaaksi, kuolettavasti; lopen. **~-bed**

deb

~-duties perintövero. **-ly** a.
kuoleman(kaltainen)-. **~-rate**
kuolleisuus. **~-roll** kaatuneiden t.
kuolonuhrien luettelo. **~-trap**
surmanloukku. **~-warrant**
kuolemantuomio.

deb [deb] s. (puhek.) = *debutante*.

debacle [dei'bɑːkl] s. mullistus,
romahdus.

debar [di'bɑː] v. sulkea pois jstk. estää
(from).

debase [di'beis] v. alentaa, huonontaa;
halventaa. **-ment** s. alentaminen,
huonontaminen.

debatable [di'beitəbl] a. kiistanalainen.

debate [di'beit] v. väitellä; pohtia; s.
keskustelu; väittely; *debating society*
keskustelukerho.

debauch [di'bɔːtʃ] v. vietellä, turmella;
~ed irstaileva. **-ee** [debɔː'tʃiː] s.
irstailija. **-ery** [-əri] s. irstailu.

debenture [di'ben(t)ʃə] s. velkakirja,
obligaatio.

debilit|ate [di'biliteit] v. heikontaa. **-y**
[-i] s. heikkous.

debit ['debit] s. debet(puoli); v.:
veloittaa.

debonair [debə'nɛə] a. kohtelias,
iloinen.

debris ['debriː] s. pirstaleet, jätteet.

debt [det] s. velka; *get (run) into ~*
velkaantua; *out of ~* velaton; *be in
sb.'s ~* olla velkaa jklle; *National D~*
valtionvelka. **-or** [-ə] s. velallinen.

debug [di'bʌg] v. poistaa
salakuuntelulaitteet; poistaa
(tietokoneen) virheet.

debunk [di'bʌŋk] v. paljastaa, riistää
sädekehä jltk.

debut, début ['deibuː] s.
ensiesiintyminen (seuraelämässä ym).
-ante ['debju(ː)tɑ̃ː(n)t] s. debytantti.

decade ['dekeid] s. vuosikymmen.

decaden|ce ['dekəd(ə)ns] s.
rappeutuminen, rappio. **-t** [-(ə)nt] a.
rappeutunut, dekadentti.

decalogue ['dekələg] s. kymmenen
käskyä.

decamp [di'kæmp] s. lähteä leiristä.

decant [di'kænt] v. dekantoida, kaataa
(hitaasti) toiseen astiaan. **-er** [-ə] s.
viinikarahvi.

decapitate [di'kæpiteit] v. mestata.

decathlon [di'kæθlɔn] s.
kymmenottelu.

decay [di'kei] v. pilaantua; rappeutua,
mädäntyä, kuihtua; s. rappio,
rappeutuminen; mätäneminen; *dental
~* hammasmätä.

decease [di'siːs] s. kuolema; [*the*] *~d*
kuollut, vainaja.

deceit [di'siːt] s. petos. **-ful** a.
petollinen, vilpillinen.

deceive [di'siːv] v. pettää; *I've been ~d
in you* petyin sinuun suhteesi.

decelerate [di:'seləreit] v. hidastaa
vauhtia.

December [di'sembə] s. joulukuu.

decensy ['diːsnsi] s. säädyllisyys.

decennial [di'senjəl] a.
kymmenvuotis-; s.
kymmenvuotispäivä.

decent ['diːsnt] a. säädyllinen, sopiva,
kunnollinen; kohtalainen,
menettelevä; mukava, kunnon *(a ~
fellow)*.

decentralize [di:'sentrəlaiz] v.
desentralisoida, hajauttaa.

decep|tion [di'sepʃn] s. petos;
harhakuva. **tive** [-ptiv] a. pettävä,
petollinen.

decibel ['desibəl] s. desibeli.

decide [di'said] v. päättää, ratkaista. **-d**
[-id] a. varma, päätetty; päättäväinen.
-dly adv. varmasti, epäilemättä.

deciduous [di'sidjuəs] a.: *~ tree*
lehtipuu; *~ teeth* maitohampaat.

decim|al ['desim(ə)l] s. kymmenys;
kymmenmurtoluku; a. desimaali-,
-ate [-meit] v. teloittaa joka
kymmenes, tuhota suureksi osaksi.

decipher [di'saifə] v. tulkita
(salakirjoitus ym).

deci|sion [di'siʒn] s. päätös, ratkaisu;
päättäväisyys; *have you reached
(come to) a ~ yet?* oletko jo
päättänyt? **-sive** [di'saisiv] a.
ratkaiseva, ehdoton, kiistaton;
päättäväinen.

deck [dek] s. (laivan) kansi;
korttipakka; v. koristaa, verhota; *on
~ kannella; ~ chair* kansituoli. **-ed**
[-t] a. kannellinen. **-er** [-ə] s. (yhd.):
ks. double.

declaim [di'kleim] v. lausua, puhua
mahtipontisesti, käydä voimakkain
sanoin *(against* jkn kimppuun)*.

declamatory [di'klæmət(ə)ri] *a.*
mahtipontinen, korkealentoinen.

declaration [dəklə'reiʃn] *s.* ilmoitus,
selitys, julistus; ~ *of war*
sodanjulistus.

declare [di'kleə] *v.* ilmoittaa, julistaa;
selittää, vakuuttaa; ilmoittaa
tullattavaksi, tullata; ~ *off* peruuttaa,
peräytyä; ~ *oneself* ilmaista aikeensa;
well, I ~! johan nyt jotakin! **-d** [-d] *a.*
tunnustautunut, vannoutunut.

declension [di'klenʃn] *s.* deklinaatio,
taivutus.

declination [dekli'neiʃn] *s.* kaltevuus;
poikkeama (fys. ym).

decline [di'klain] *v.* hylätä (tarjous
ym), kieltäytyä; laskea, vähetä,
heiketä, rappeutua; kallistua
(alaspäin), viettää; (kiel.) deklinoida;
s. laskeminen, huononeminen,
rappeutuminen; rinne; ~ *with thanks*
kieltäytyä kohteliaasti; *be on the* ~
olla laskemassa; *fall into a* ~
huonontua, heikontua; *declining
years* elämän ehtoopuoli.

declivity [di'kliviti] *s.* rinne, viettävyys.

declutch [di'klʌtʃ] *v.* irrottaa kytkin.

decoction [di'kɔkʃn] *s.* keitos, keite.

decode [di:'kəud] *v.* tulkita
(koodisanoma ym) selväkielelle.

decolleté [dei'koltei] *a.* avokaulainen.

decompos|e [di:kəm'pəuz] *v.* jakaa
alkuaineisiinsa; mädäntyä; saattaa
pilaantumaan; *-ing* mätänevä. **-ition**
[di:kɔmpə'ziʃn] *s.* mätänemis-,
hajoamistila.

decompression [di:kəm'preʃn] *s. attr.*
alipaine-.

decontamina|te [di:kən'tæmineit] *v.*
poistaa kaasu t. radioaktiivisuus;
puhdistaa saasteesta. **-tion** [-'neiʃn] *s.*
puhdistus, kaasunpoisto.

decontrol [di:kən'trəul] *v.* vapauttaa
säännöstelystä.

decor ['deikɔ:] *s.* näyttämökoristeet;
(huoneen) sisustus (värisävyt ym).

decorat|e ['dekəreit] *v.* koristaa; antaa
(jklle) kunniamerkki. **-ion** [-'reiʃn] *s.*
koristaminen, koriste; kunniamerkki;
interior ~ (kodin ym) sisustus;
Christmas ~ *s* joulukoristeet. **-ive**
['dekərətiv] *a.* koristus-, koriste-,
koristeellinen. **-or** [-ə] *s.*
(koriste)maalari; *interior* ~

sisustustaitelija.

decor|ous ['dekərəs] *a.* säädyllinen;
arvokas. **-um** [di'kɔ:rəm] *s.*
säädyllisyys, sopivuus, arvokkuus.

decoy [di'kɔi] *s.* houkutuslintu, syötti;
v. houkutella (ansaan). **~-duck**
houkutuslintu.

decrease [di:'kri:s] *v.* vähetä,
pienentyä; vähentää; *s.* ['di:kri:s]
pienentyminen, vähennys; *on the* ~
vähenemässä.

decree [di'kri:] *s.* määräys, säädös,
asetus; *v.* määrätä.

decrement ['dekrimənt] *s.* vähennys.

decrepit [di'krepit] *a.* raihnainen,
(vanhuuttaan) heikko. **-ude** [-ju:d] *s.*
raihnaisuus, vanhuudenheikkous.

decry [di'krai] *v.* halventaa.

dedica|te ['dedikeit] *v.* vihkiä (jhk,
omistaa *(to* jklle); ~ *d*
antaumuksellinen; ~ *oneself*
omistautua *(to* jhk). **-tion** [-'keiʃn] *s.*
vihkiminen; omistuskirjoitus.

deduce [di'dju:s] *v.* johtaa, päätellä
(jstk), tehdä johtopäätös.

deduct [di'dʌkt] *v.* vähentää, laskea
pois. **-ible** vähennyskelpoinen. **-ion**
[-kʃn] *s.* päätelmä, johtopäätös;
vähennys.

deed [di:d] *s.* teko, työ, urotyö;
asiakirja (lak.).

deem [di:m] *v.* pitää jnak, olla sitä
mieltä *(that* että).

deep [di:p] *a.* syvä, syvällinen,
perinpohjainen; salaperäinen; *adv.*
syvällä, -lle syvään; *s.* syvyys; *the* ~
meri; *a* ~ *one* viekas veijari; ~ *in
thought* ajatuksiin vaipu|nut
(-neena); *... were standing* 20 ~
seisoivat parissakymmenessä rivissä
(toinen toisensa) takana); *go off the* ~
end riehaantua, kiihtyä, suuttua
silmittömästi. **-en** [-n] *v.* syventää,
syvetä. **~-freeze** *v.* pakastaa; *s.*
pakastin. **~-rooted** piintynyt, syvälle
juurtunut. **~-seated** syvällä oleva.

deer [diə] *s. (pl.* = *sg.)* hirvieläin, peura
(esim. *white-tailed* ~); *fallow* ~
kuusipeura; *red* ~ saksanhirvi.

de-escalate [di:'eskəleit] *v.* supistaa,
laannuttaa.

deface [di'feis] *v.* rumentaa, pilata
(ulkonäkö).

defalcation [di:fæl'keiʃn] *s.* kavallus;

defa

120

vaillinki.

defamatory [di'fæmət(ə)ri] *a.*
häpäisevä, häväistys-.

defame [di'feim] *v.* panetella, saattaa
huonoon huutoon.

default [di'fɔ:lt] *s.* (maksun ym.)
laiminlyöminen; oikeudesta
poisjääminen; *v.* laiminlyödä maksu t.
sitoumus; jäädä tulematta oikeuteen;
in ~ of jnk puutteessa. **-er** [-ə] *s.*
(maksujen) laiminlyöjä, (sot.)
rikkomuksen tehnyt.

defeat [di'fi:t] *v.* voittaa, lyödä; tehdä
tyhjäksi; *s.* tappio, häviö. **-ist** [-ist] *a.*
& *s.* tappiomielialan vallassa oleva
(henkilö).

defecate ['defikeit] *v.* ulostaa.

defect [di'fekt] *s.* puute; vika, virhe,
vajavuus; *v.* »loikata», luopua
(puolueestaan ym). **-ion** [-kʃn] *s.*
luopumus. **-ive** [-iv] *a* puutteellinen,
epätäydellinen; virheellinen; *~ china*
vajaalaatuposliini; *mentally ~*
kehitysvammainen.

defence [di'fens] *s.* puolustus; suoja;
pl. varustukset, linnoitukset; *counsel
for the ~* puolustusasianajaja. **-less** *a.*
suojaton, puolustuskyvytön.

defend [di'fend] *v.* puolustaa; suojella
(against, from jltk). **-ant** [-ənt] *s.*
vastaaja.

defens|ible [di'fensəbl] *a.*
puolustettavissa oleva. **-ive** [-siv] *a.*
puolustava, puolustus-; *s.: be (stand,
act) on the ~* olla puolustuskannalla;
ks. *defence.*

defer 1. [di'fə:] *v.* lykätä.

defer 2. [di'fə:] *v.* taipua, mukautua *(to
jhk); buy on ~red terms*
vähittäismaksulla. **-ence** ['defr(ə)ns]
s. kunnioitus. **-ential** [defə'renʃ(ə)l] *a.*
kunnioittava.

deferment [di'fə:mənt] *s.* lykkäys.

defian|ce [di'faiəns] *s.* uhma; *bid ~ to,
set at ~* uhmata; *in ~ of* jtk uhmaten.
-t [-ənt] *a.* uhmaava, uhmaileva.

deficien|cy [di'fiʃnsi] *s.* puute,
puutteellisuus, vajavuus, vajaus; *~
diseases* puutostaudit; ks. *mental ~.* **-t**
[-nt] *a.* puutteellinen, riittämätön.

deficit ['defisit] *s.* vajaus, vaillinki.

defile 1. [di'fail] *v.* marssia ohitse; *s.*
vuorensola; kapeikko.

defile 2. [di'fail] *v.* tahrata.

defin|e [di'fain] *v.* määritellä, rajoittaa.
-ite ['definit] *a.* määrätty, tarkalleen
rajoitettu; ratkaiseva; varma,
päättäväinen; *the ~ article* määräinen
artikkeli; *~ly* varmasti, ehdottomasti.
-ition [defi'niʃn] *s.* määritys,
määritelmä, määrittely, m. sanan
tarkka merkitys; tarkkuus, terävyys.
-itive [di'finitiv] *a.* lopullinen.

defla|te [di'fleit] *v.* päästää ilma jstk,
tyhjentää; palauttaa rahan arvoa.
-tion [di'fleiʃn] *s.* deflaatio.

deflect [di'flekt] *v.* saada poikkeamaan
suunnastaan, poiketa suunnastaan.
-ion [di'flekʃn] *s.* poikkeama.

deflower [di:'flauə] *v.* raiskata.

defoli|ant [di'fəuliənt] *s.*
vesakkomyrkky. **-ate** [-eit] *v.* tuhota
lehdet.

deform [di'fɔ:m] *v.* tehdä
muodottomaksi, rumentaa. **-ed** [-d] *a.*
epämuodostunut. **-ity** [-iti] *s.*
epämuotoisuus; epämuodostuma.

defraud [di'frɔ:d] *v.* (~ *sb. of)* riistää,
riistää petoksella.

defray [di'frei] *v.* suorittaa, maksaa
(kulut).

defrost [di:'frɔst] *v.* sulattaa (jää).

deft [deft] *a.* kätevä, näppärä.

defunct [di'fʌŋ(k)t] *a.* kuollut, vainaja.

defuse [di'fju:z] *v.* tehdä (esim.
pommi) vaarattomaksi, purkaa.

defy [di'fai] *v.* uhmata; haastaa; *it
defies solution* sitä on mahdoton
ratkaista; *I ~ you to prove it* todista se,
jos osaat.

degenera|cy [di'dʒen(ə)rəsi] *s.*
degeneraatio, ks. seur. **-te** [-rit] *a.* &
s. suvustaan huonontunut (yksilö); *v.*
[-əreit] huonontua suvustaan,
rappeutua. **-tion** [-ə'reiʃn] *s.*
rappeutuminen.

degradation [degrə'deiʃn] *s.*
(virka-arvon)alennus; alennus-,
rappiotila.

degrad|e [di'greid] *v.* alentaa arvossa;
alentaa (jkn) arvoa, olla alentavaa
jklle. **-ing** *a.* alentava, halventava.

degree [di'gri:] *s.* aste; yliopistollinen
lopputukinto; (arvo)asema;
vertailuaste; *by ~s* vähitellen; *take
one's ~* suorittaa lopputukinto; *to a
certain ~* jossakin määrin;
comparative ~ komparatiivi.

dehydra|ted [di:'haidreitid] *a.* kuivattu, vedetön. **-tion** [-'reiʃn] *s.* dehydraatio.

de-icer ['di:'aisə] *s.* jäänpoistolaite t. -aine (ilm.)

deification [di:ifi'keiʃn] *s.* jumaloiminen.

deify ['di:ifai] *v.* korottaa jumalaksi, palvoa, jumaloida.

deign [dein] *v.* suvaita.

deism ['di:izm] *s.* deismi.

deity ['di:iti] *s.* jumaluus.

deject [di'dʒekt] *v.* masentaa. **-ed** [-id] *a.* masentunut, alakuloinen. **-ion** [-kʃn] *s.* masennus, alakuloisuus.

Delaware ['deləwεə] *erisn.*

delay [di'lei] *v.* viivyttää; viivytellä, hidastella; *s.* viivytys, viipyminen, hidastelu; [*the train was*] ~*ed two hours* kaksi tuntia myöhässä; *without* ~ viikastelematta, viipymättä.

delecta|ble [di'lektəbl] *a.* viehättävä. **-tion** [-'teiʃn] *s.* ilo, nautinto.

delega|te ['deligeit] *v.* lähettää valtuutettuna, valtuuttaa; *s.* [-git] valtuutettu, asiamies. **-tion** [-'geiʃn] *s.* valtuuskunta; valtuuttaminen.

delete [di:'li:t] *v.* pyyhkiä pois.

deleterious [deli'tiəriəs] *a.* vahingollinen.

deletion [di'li:ʃn] *s.* poispyyhkiminen.

Delhi ['deli] *erisn.*

deliberat|e [di'libərit] *v.* harkita, punnita, tuumia; *a.* [-rit] tarkoituksellinen, harkittu; ˅erkkainen; ~*ly* tieten tahtoen, tarkoituksella. **-ion** [-'reiʃn] *s.* harkinta; varovaisuus. **-ive** [-(ə)rətiv] *a.* neuvotteleva.

deli|cacy ['delikəsi] *s.* herkullisuus, herkku; hienotunteisuus. **-cate** [-ət] *a.* herkullinen; hieno, hento; heikko (terveys); arka(luonteinen), hienotunteinen; *s.:* ~ hienopyykki ym. **-catessen** [delikə'tesn] *s.:* ~ [*shop*] leikkeleliike, einesmyymälä. **-cious** [di'liʃəs] *a.* herkullinen; ihana, hurmaava.

delight [di'lait] *s.* ilo, ihastus, mielihyvä; *v.* ilahduttaa, ihastuttaa; ~ *in* iloita, nauttia jstk; ~*ed at* iloinen jstk, ihastunut jhk. **-ful** *a.* ihastuttava, ihana.

Delilah [di'lailə] *erisn.*

delimit [di:'limit] *v.* rajoittaa; *sharply* ~*ed* tarkasti rajattu.

delinea|te [di'linieit] *v.* hahmotella, piirtää; kuvata.

delinquen|cy [di'liŋkwənsi] *s.* laiminlyönti; rikos; *juvenile* ~ nuorisorikollisuus. **-t** [-ənt] *s.* rikoksentekijä, rikollinen.

deliri|ous [di'liriəs] *a.* houraileva; *were* ~ *with joy* olivat suunnillaan ilosta. **-um** [-əm] *s.* hourailu, (kuume)houre; ~ *tremens* [tri:menz] juoppohulluus.

deliver [di'livə] *v.* vapauttaa, päästää *(from* jstk*)*; antaa, luovuttaa *(~ up, ~ over)*; toimittaa; jakaa (posti); antaa, suunnata (isku), pitää (puhe), esittää (lasku); *be ~ed of* synnyttää; [*the doctor*] *has ~ed* [*many babies*] auttanut maailmaan; ~ *the goods* sl. pitää, mitä on luvannut. **-ance** [-rəns] *s.* pelastus, vapautus. **-y** [-ri] *s.* toimitus, hankinta; synnytys; (postin) kanto, jakelu; (puheen ym) esitys(tapa); lyönti, heitto; *special* ~ pikajakelu.

dell [del] *s.* notko.

Delphi [delfai] *erisn.* Delfoi. **d~nium** [del'finiəm] *s.* kukonkannus (kasv.).

delta ['deltə] *s.* suisto(maa).

delouse [di:'laus] *v.* puhdistaa täistä.

delude [di'lu:d] *v.* viedä harhaan, pettää.

deluge ['delju:dʒ] *s.* vedenpaisumus, tulva; *v.* tulvia, hukuttaa *(with* jhk*)*.

delu|sion [di'lu:ʒn] *s.* harha(luulo), silmänlume; harha-aistimus; *under a* ~ harhaluulon vallassa. **-sive** [-siv] *a.* pettävä, eksyttävä.

de luxe [di'luks] *a.* loisto-.

delve [delv] *v.* kaivaa.

demagogue ['deməgog] *s.* kansanvillitsijä.

demand [di'mɑ:nd] *v.* vaatia, pyytää; edellyttää; kysyä; *s.* vaatimus; kysyntä, tarve; *supply and* ~ tarjonta ja kysyntä; *on* ~ vaadittaessa; *is in great* ~ on hyvin kysytty(ä); [*tax*] ~ *note* verolippu.

demarca|te ['di:mɑ:keit] *v.* merkitä raja, rajoittaa. **-tion** [-'keiʃn] *s.* rajan merkitseminen; *line of* ~ demarkaatiolinja.

demean [di'mi:n] *v.:* ~ *oneself* käyttäytyä; *(to sth.)* alentua. **-our** [-ə]

deme   122

s. käytös.
demented [di'mentid] a. mieletön, heikkomielinen.
demerit ['di:'merit] s. vika, huono puoli, heikkous.
demesne [di'mein] s. vapaatila.
demi- ['demi] pref. puoli. **-god** puolijumala. **-john** koripullo.
demilitarized [di:'militəraizd] a. demilitarisoitu.
demise [di'maiz] v. luovuttaa; s. (kuninkaan) kuolema.
demist [di:'mist] v. kirkastaa.
demo ['deməu] lyh. (=*demonstration*) mielenosoitus.
demob [di'mɔb] v. = demobilize.
demobilization ['di:məubilai'zeiʃn] s. demobilisointi, kotiuttaminen. **-ize** [di:'məubilaiz] v. demobilisoida, palauttaa rauhankannalle.
democracy [di'mɔkrəsi] s. kansanvalta. **-rat** ['deməkræt] s. demokraatti. **-ratic** [demə'krætik] a. kansanvaltainen, demokraattinen.
demolish [di'mɔliʃ] v. repiä, hajottaa (maahan), purkaa; hävittää. **-ition** [demə'liʃn] s. hajottaminen, purkaminen; raivaus.
demon ['di:mən] s. paha henki, demoni. **-iac** [di:'məuniæk] s. pahan hengen riivaama. **-iacal** [di:mə'naiək(ə)l] a. demoninen, pirullinen. **-ic** [di:'mɔnik] a. demoninen.
demonstrable [di'demənstrəbl] a. todistettavissa oleva. **-te** [-eit] v. näyttää toteen, osoittaa; osoittaa mieltään. **-tion** [-'streiʃn] s. mielenosoitus; osoitus, (havainnollinen) esittäminen. **-tive** [di'mɔnstrɔtiv] a. mielenosoituksellinen; avoin, (esim. kiintymystä) selvästi osoittava; demonstratiivinen (pronomini). **-tor** [-eitə] s. mielenosoittaja.
demoralize [di'mɔrəlaiz] v. turmella (jkn) tavat; masentaa mieliala, heikentää kuria (sot.).
demote [di:'məut] v. alentaa (arvossa). **-tion** [-'məuʃn] s. alennus.
demur [di'mə:] v.: ~ *at* (t. *to*) vastustella, vastustaa; s. vastaväite; *without* ~ epäröimättä.
demure [di'mjuə] a. vaatimaton,

(turhan)kaino, vakava, eleetön.
demurrage [di'mʌridʒ] s. makaus-, seisontamaksu (mer.).
den [den] s. (eläimen) luola (m. *opium* ~), (paheen) pesä; (luku)soppi, boksi.
denial [di'naiəl] s. kieltäminen, kielto, epäys.
denigrate ['denigreit] v. mustata (kuv.).
denim ['denim] s. denimi, suojapukukangas, farkkukangas.
denizen ['denizn] s. asukas.
Denmark ['denmɑ:k] erisn. Tanska.
denomination [dinɔmi'neiʃn] s. nimitys; luokka, kategoria; uskonlahko, kirkkokunta. **-tor** [di'nɔmineitə] s. nimittäjä.
denote [di'nəut] v. merkitä, osoittaa, ilmaista.
dénouement [dei'nu:mɑ:(ŋ)] s. loppuratkaisu.
denounce [di'nauns] v. tuomita, arvostella ankarasti; ilmiantaa; irtisanoa.
dense [dens] a. tiheä, taaja, sakea; kovapäinen, tyhmä; *~ly populated* tiheään asuttu. **-ity** [-iti] s. tiheys, taajuus.
dent [dent] s. lommo, kuoppa; *~ed* lommoinen.
dental ['dent|l] a. hammas-; s. hammasäänne; ~ *surgeon* hammaskirurgi. **-ifrice** [-ifris] s. hammasjauhe, -tahna. **-ist** [-ist] s. hammaslääkäri. **-istry** [-istri] s. hammaslääketiede. **-ition** [den'tiʃn] s. hampaiden puhkeaminen. **-ure** [-ʃə] s. (teko)hampaat, hammasproteesi.
denude [di'nju:d] v. riisua (paljaaksi), paljastaa, riistää (~ *of*).
denunciation [dinʌnsi'eiʃn] s. ilmianto; julkinen paheksuminen, tuomitseminen.
deny [di'nai] v. kieltää; kiistää.
deodorant [di:'əudər(ə)nt] s. hajunpoistoaine, deodorantti. **-ize** [-aiz] v. poistaa (epämiellyttävä) haju.
depart [di'pɑ:t] v. lähteä; ~ *this life* kuolla; ~ *from* m. poiketa jstk; *the ~ed* vainaja(t). **-ment** s. osasto; ministeriö; departementti; ~ *store* tavaratalo. **-mental** [-'mentl] a. osasto(n)-. **-ure** [-ʃə] s. lähtö (~ *from*,

m.) poikkeaminen.

depend [di'pend] v. riippua *(on, upon* jstk), olla riippuvainen, luottaa; olla ratkaisematta; *that ~ s* riippuu asianhaaroista; *~ upon it* siitä saat olla varma. **-ability** [-ə'biliti] s. luotettavuus. **-able** [-əbl] a. luotettava. **-ant** [-ənt] s. huollettava. **-ence** [-əns] s. riippuvaisuus; luottamus. **-ency** [-ənsi] s. alusmaa. **-ent** [-ənt] a. riippuvainen; alainen, m. = *-ant; ~ clause* sivulause.

depict [di'pikt] v. kuvata.

depilatory [di'pilət(ə)ri] a. & s. ihokarvoja poistava (aine).

deple|te [di'pli:t] v. tyhjentää; *[a lake] ~ d of fish* tyhjäksi kalastettu. **-tion** [-i:ʃn] s. tyhjentäminen.

deplorable [di'plɔ:rəbl] a. valitettava.

deplore [di'plɔ:] v. valittaa.

deploy [di'plɔi] v. (sot.) levittää, levittäytyä; sijoittaa.

deponent [di'pəunənt] s. valan tehnyt todistaja.

depopula|te [di:'pɔpjulei|t] v. tehdä asumattomaksi. **-tion** [-ʃn] s. autioittaminen.

deport [di'pɔ:t] v. karkottaa maasta; *~ oneself* käyttäytyä. **-ation** [-'teiʃn] s. (maasta) karkotus. **-ment** s. käytös, esiintyminen.

depose [di'pəuz] v. panna viralta, syöstä valtaistuimelta; (valallisesti) todistaa.

deposit [di'pɔzit] s. talletus; käsiraha, vakuus; sakka, kerrostuma; v. laskea, panna; kerrostaa, saostaa; tallettaa, jättää jkn huostaan; jättää vakuudeksi. **-ion** [depə'ziʃn] s. viraltapano; (valallinen) todistus. **-or** [-ə] s. tallettaja. **-ory** [-(ə)ri] s. säilytyspaikka.

depot ['depəu] s. varikko, varasto; Am. ['di:pəu] rautatieasema, linja-autoasema.

deprav|e [di'preiv] v. turmella, pilata; *~ d* turmeltunut. **-ity** [di'præviti] s. turmeltuneisuus, turmelus.

deprecat|e ['deprikeit] v. paheksua, kehottaa välttämään. **-ion** [-'keiʃn] s. paheksuminen.

deprecia|te [di'pri:ʃieit] v. alentaa (jnk) arvoa, aleta arvossa; väheksyä. **-tion** [-'eiʃn] s. arvon aleneminen.

halventaminen. **-tory** [-ʃjət(ə)ri] a. alentava, halventava.

depredation [depri'deiʃn] s. ryöstäminen, autioittaminen.

depress [di'pres] v. painaa alas, alentaa; masentaa; *~ ed* alakuloinen, lamassa (oleva); *~ ed area* työttömyysalue; *~ ing* masentava. **-ion** [-eʃn] s. notko, syvennys; (mielen)masennus, depressio; lamakausi, talouslama; matalapaine(en alue). **-ive** [-iv] a. masentava.

depriva|l [di'praivl] s. riistäminen. **-tion** [depri'veiʃn] s. menetys; puute; riisto.

deprive [di'praiv] v. riistää *(a p. of* jkltä jtk); panna viralta (et. pappi). **-ment** s. menetys.

depth [depθ] s. syvyys; syvällisyys; *in the ~ of winter* sydäntalvella; .. *in depth* perusteellisesti; *he is out of his ~* hän ei pohjaa enää. **-charge** syvyyspommi.

deputation [depju'teiʃn] s. lähetystö.

deput|e [di'pju:t] v. valtuuttaa (edustajaksi). **-ize** ['depjutaiz] v.: *~ for* olla jkn sijaisena. **-y** ['depjuti] s. sijainen, varamies, us. attr. sijais- *(D~ Speaker* varapuhemies); valtiopäivämies.

derail [di'reil] v. suistua, suistaa raiteilta; *was ~ ed* suistui kiskoilta. **-ment** s. raiteilta suistuminen.

derange [di'rein(d)ʒ] v. panna epäjärjestykseen, hämmentää, sekoittaa; *~ d* mielenvikainen. **-ment** s. epäjärjestys, häiriö.

de|rate ['di:reit] v. vapauttaa (osittain) kunnallisverosta. **-ration** [-'ræʃn] v. vapauttaa säännöstelystä.

Derby ['da:bi, Am. 'dɔ:bi] s. derby, (ratsastus)kilpailut; paikallisottelu; Am. knalli.

derelict ['derilikt] a. isännätön, hylätty; s. (laiva)hylky, omistajaa vailla oleva esine. **-ion** ['likʃn] s. autioittaminen; laiminlyönti.

deride [di'raid] v. pilkata, ivata.

deri|sion [di'riʒn] s. pilkka, iva; *hold in ~* pitää pilkkanaan. **-sive, -sory** [di'raisiv, -səri] a. pilkallinen; naurettava, pilkka-.

deriva|tion [deri'veiʃn] s. johtaminen,

synty, alkuperä. **-tive** [di'rivətiv] s.
johdannainen, johdannaissana,
johdos.

derive [di'raiv] v. johtaa; saada (jtk);
johtua, polveutua, olla peräisin *(from
jstk)* (m. ~ *its origin from, be* ~**d**
from).

dermatolog|ist [də:mə'tɔlədʒist] s.
ihotautilääkäri. **-y** [-i] s. ihotautioppi.

deroga|te ['derəgeit] v.: ~ *from*
vähentää, rajoittaa (oikeutta ym).
-tion [-'geiʃn] s. vähentäminen,
rajoittaminen. **-tory** [di'rɔgət(ə)ri] a.
arvoa alentava, halventava,
loukkaava.

derrick ['derik] s. nosturi; *oil* ~
öljynporaustorni.

dervish ['də:viʃ] s. dervissi.

desalination [di:sæli'neiʃn] s.
suolanpoisto (merivedestä).

descant [dis'kænt] v.: ~ *upon* selostaa
laajasti; s. ['deskænt] eräänl. (korkea)
laulusäestys.

descend [di'send] v. laskeutua, astua
alas; laskea, viettää; alentua;
periytyä; ~ *upon* käydä jnk
kimppuun; *be* ~*ed from* polveutua.
-ant [-ənt] s. jälkeläinen.

descent [di'sent] s. laskeutuminen;
aleneminen; alamäki, rinne;
polveutuminen, periytyminen;
äkillinen hyökkäys; *of French* ~
syntyperältään ranskalainen.

describe [dis'kraib] v. kuvata, kuvailla;
piirtää (ympyrä ym).

descrip|tion [dis'kripʃn] s. kuvaus;
tuntomerkit; laji. **-tive** [-ptiv] a.
kuvaileva.

descry [dis'krai] v. erottaa, huomata.

desecra|te ['desikreit] v. loukata jnk
pyhyyttä, häpäistä. **-tion** [-ʃn] s.
häpäiseminen.

desegregate [di:'segrigeit] v. poistaa
rotuerottelu, yhdentää.

desert 1. ['dezət] a. autio, asumaton,
karu; s. autiomaa.

desert 2. [di'zə:t] s. ansio; *according to
his* ~*s* ansion mukaan.

desert 3. [di'zə:t] v. karata; jättää,
hylätä. **-er** [-ə] s. (sotilas)karkuri. **-ion**
[di'zə:ʃn] s. karkaaminen;
hylkääminen, hylättynä olo.

deserv|e [di'zə:v] v. ansaita. **-edly**
[-idli] adv. ansiosta, täydestä syystä.

-ing a. ansioitunut; ~ *of* jtk
ansaitseva.

desiccate ['desikeit] v. kuivata.

design [di'zain] v. hahmotella,
suunnitella, muotoilla, piirtää; aikoa,
tarkoittaa; s. luonnos, piirustus;
malli; suunnitelma; muotoilu; aie,
aikomus; juoni, hanke; ~*ed to* (t. *for*)
jhk tarkoitettu; *have* ~*s* [*upon*] punoa
juonia. **-ate** ['dezigneit] v. osoittaa,
tarkoittaa; määrätä (jhk virkaan,
tehtävään); a. [-nit] virkaan määrätty.
-ation [dezig'neiʃn] s. (virkaan)
määrääminen; nimitys, nimi. **-edly**
adv. tarkoituksellisesti, tahallaan. **-er**
[-ə] s. piirtäjä, suunnittelija,
muotoilija. **-ing** a. vehkeilevä,
juonikas.

desir|ability [dizaiərə'bility] s.
toivottavuus. **-able** [di'zaiərəbl] a.
tavoiteltava, toivottava.

desir|e [di'zaiə] v. haluta, toivoa;
pyytää; s. halu, himo; *at sb.'s* ~ jkn
toivomuksesta. **-ous** [-rəs] a. (~ *of*)
(jtk) haluava.

desist [di'zist] v. jättää sikseen, lakata
(from jstk).

desk [desk] s. pulpetti; kirjoituspöytä,
-lipasto; kassa *(pay* ~), (hotellin)
vastaanotto(tiski).

deso|late ['desəlit] a. autio, asumaton;
lohduton, murheellinen; v. ['desəleit]
autioittaa, hävittää. **-lation** [-'leiʃn] s.
hävitys; autius; yksinäisyys;
lohduttomuus.

despair [dis'peə] v. olla toivoton t.
epätoivoissaan *(of* jstk); s.
toivottomuus, epätoivo; *is the* ~ *of* on
(esim. opettajien) kauhu; *his life is*
~*ed of* hänen tilaansa pidetään
toivottomana.

despatch [dis'pætʃ] ks. dispatch.

desperado [despə'rɑ:dəu] s. (pl. ~*es*,
Am. ~*s*) häikäilemätön rikollinen,
hurjapää.

despera|te ['desp(ə)rit] a.
epätoivoinen, toivoton; hurjapäinen;
~*ly* m. hirveästi. **-tion** [despə'reiʃn] s.
epätoivo; *drive to* ~ saattaa
epätoivoon.

despicable ['despikəbl] a.
halveksittava, kurja.

despise [dis'paiz] v. halveksia.

despite [dis'pait] prep. jstk huolimatta.

despoil [dis'pɔil] v. (~ sb. of) ryöstää, riistää jklta jtk.

despond [dis'pɔnd] v. menettää rohkeutensa, olla toivoton (of jstk). **-ency** [-ɔnsi] s. alakuloisuus; epätoivo. **-ent** [-ɔnt] a. alakuloinen; epätoivoinen.

despot ['despɔt] s. itse-, hirmuvaltias, despootti. **-ic** [des'pɔtik] a. itsevaltainen, despoottinen. **-ism** [-izm] s. hirmuvalta, tyrannimaisuus.

dessert [di'zɔːt] s. jälkiruoka, hedelmät.

destination [desti'neiʃn] s. määräpaikka.

destin|e ['destin] v. määrätä (to, for jhk); it was ~ d to fail se oli tuomittu epäonnistumaan. **-y** [-i] s. kohtalo.

destitu|te ['destitjuːt] a. puutteenalainen, perin köyhä, penniltön; ~ of jtk vailla oleva. **-tion** [-'tjuːʃn] s. puutteenalaisuus, puute, hätä.

destroy [dis'trɔi] v. hävittää, tuhota, surmata. **-er** [-ɔ] s. hävittäjä (mer.).

destruc|tible [dis'trʌktɔbl] a. häviävä, hävitettävissä oleva. **-tion** [-kʃn] s. hävitys, tuho, perikato. **-tive** [-ktiv] a. tuhoava, tuhoisa, hävitys-.

desuetude [di'sju(ː)itjuːd] s.: fall into ~ jäädä pois käytännöstä.

desultory ['des(ə)lt(ə)ri] a. hajanainen, suunnitelmaton.

detach [di'tætʃ] v. irrottaa; erottaa, määrätä (sot.). **-able** [-ɔbl] a. irrotettava, irto-. **-ed** [-t] a. erillään oleva, erillinen; irrallinen; ulkopuolinen, puolueeton; riippumaton, vapaa. **-ment** s. irrottaminen, erillisyys; erillisosasto; (henkinen) riippumattomuus, objektiivisuus, välinpitämättömyys, viileys, rauha.

detail ['diːteil] s. yksityiskohta, -seikka, seikkaperäinen käsittely; v. [di'teil] esittää tarkasti, seikkaperäisesti; irrottaa, määrätä (for jhk tarkoitukseen); in ~ seikkaperäisesti. **-ed** [-d] a. yksityiskohtainen, seikkaperäinen.

detain [di'tein] v. viivyttää, pidättää (m. lak.). **-ee** [-'niː] s. pidätetty.

detect [di'tekt] v. keksiä, huomata, saada se ville. **-able** [-ɔbl] a.

havaittava. -ion [di'tekʃn] s. paljastaminen; (rikosten) selvitys. **-ive** [-iv] s. etsivä, salapoliisi; a.: ~ force etsivä poliisi. **-or** [-ɔ] s. ilmaisin.

détente [dei'tãːt] s. (pol.) jännityksen lientyminen, liennytys.

detention [di'tenʃn] s. viivyttäminen; pidättäminen, pidätys; internointi; jälki-istunto.

deter [di'tɔː] v. pelottaa, saada jättämään (jk) (from); estää.

detergent [di'tɔːdʒɔnt] a. & s. puhdistava (aine), pesuaine.

deteriora|te [di'tiɔriɔreit] v. huonontua, -taa. **-tion** [-'reiʃn] s. huonontuminen.

determina|te [di'tɔːm(i)nit] a. määrätty; varma, lopullinen. **-tion** [-'neiʃn] s. määrääminen; päätös; päättäväisyys, lujuus. **-tive** [-minɔtiv] a. määräävä.

determine [di'tɔːmin] v. määrätä; päättää; ratkaista; saada (tekemään päätöksensä); ~ d päättäväinen, luja.

deterrent [di'ter(ɔ)nt, 'det-] a. pelottava; s. pelotteluase, -keino; pelote.

detest [di'test] v. inhota, vihata. **-able** [-ɔbl] a. inhottava. **-ation** [-'teiʃn] s. inho.

dethrone [di'θrɔun] v. syöstä valtaistuimelta.

detonat|e [detɔ(u)neit] v. pamahtaa, räjähtää; räjäyttää. **-ion** [-'neiʃn] s. räjähdys. **-or** [-ɔ] s. sytytin.

detour ['diːtuɔ, 'dei-] s. kiertotie (m. tilapäinen korjaustyön aikana).

detract [di'trækt] v.: ~ from vähentää; halventaa. **-ion** [-kʃn] s. vähäksyminen. **-or** [-ɔ] s. panettelija.

detrain [diː'trein] v. purkaa (joukkoja) junasta.

detriment ['detrimɔnt] s. haitta, vahinko. **-al** [-'mentl] a. vahingollinen, haitallinen.

Detroit [dɔ'trɔit] erisn.

deuce 1. [djuːs] s. kakkonen (pelissä); (tennis) tasapeli, 40 tasan.

deuce 2. [djuːs] s. piru; what the ~! mitä hittoa! **-d** [-id] a. & adv. hiton.

Deuteronomy [djuːtɔ'rɔnɔmi] s. 5. Mooseksen kirja.

deval|uation [diːvæl]ju'eiʃn] s. devalvointi. **-ue** ['diːvælju:] v.

devalvoida, alentaa arvoa.

devasta|te ['devəsteit] v. tehdä autioksi, tuhota. **-tion** [-'teiʃn] s. tuho.

develop [di'veləp] v. kehittää (m. ~ valok.), kehittyä; laajentaa; (alkaa) rakentaa (aluetta); alkaa osoittaa (oireita, taipumusta jhk); saada (esim. tapa); ~ing country kehitysmaa; capacity to ~ kehityskykyisyys; likely to ~ kehityskykyinen. **-er** [-ə] s. aluerakentaja, »grynderi»; (valok.) kehitysneste, kehite. **-ment** s. kehittäminen, kehitys; (alue)rakentaminen, saneeraus; kehitystulos; ~ aid kehitysapu; ~ area kehitysalue.

devi|ant ['di:viənt] s. poikkeava (henkilö). **-ate** [-eit] v. poiketa; hairahtua. **-ation** [-'eiʃn] s. poikkeaminen; (kompassin) eksymä.

device [di'vais] s. laite, koje; juoni; tunnus|kuva, -lause (esim. vaakunassa); birth control ~ ehkäisyväline; she was left to her own ~s hän sai selviytyä omin päin.

devil ['devl] s. piru, paholainen; v. pariloida vahvasti maustettuna; the little ~ s! pikku peijoonit! the poor ~ raukka; [printer's] ~ oppipoika; go to the ~ mennä päin helvettiä; [work like] the ~ kuin riivattu; why the ~? miksi hitossa? between the ~ and the deep sea kahden tulen välissä. **-ish** [-iʃ] a. pirullinen. **~-may-care** huoleton, yltiöpäinen. **-ment, -ry** [-ri] s. (pirun) konstit, kujeet.

devious ['di:vjəs] a. mutkitteleva.

devise [di'vaiz] v. keksiä, suunnitella.

devoid [di'vɔid] pred. a.: ~ of jtk vailla oleva, tyhjä jstk.

devolve [di'vɔlv] v. siirtää, siirtyä (upon jklle); joutua, langeta (jkn tehtäväksi).

Devon ['devn], **-shire** [-ʃiə] erisn.

devot|e [di'vəu|t] v. pyhittää, omistaa; ~ oneself omistautua, antautua. **-ed** [-tid] a. (syvästi) kiintynyt, harras, uskollinen. **-ee** [devə(u)' i:] s.: ~ of jnk palvoja, innokas kannattaja; hurskas henkilö. **-ion** [-ʃn] s. syvä kiintymys, rakkaus (to jhk); antautuminen; antaumus; morning ~ s

aamu|hartaus, -rukous. **-ional** [-ʃnl] a. hartaus-.

devour [di'vauə] v. niellä, nielaista; ahmia; kalvaa.

devout [di'vaut] a. hurskas.

dew [dju:] s. kaste; wet with ~ kasteessa.

dewlap ['dju:læp] s. helluvainen; heltta.

dewy ['dju:i] a. kasteinen.

dext|erity [deks'teriti] s. kätevyys, taitavuus. **-(e)rous** [-trəs] a. kätevä, näppärä, taitava.

diabet|es [daiə'bi:ti:z] s. sokeritauti. **-ic** [-'betik] a. & s. sokeri autinen, diabeetikko.

diabolic(al) [daiə'bɔlik, -(ə)l] a. pirun-; pirullinen.

diadem ['daiədem] s. otsaripa, diadeemi.

diagnos|e ['daiəgnəuz] v. määrittää (tauti). **-is** [-'nəusis] s. pl. -oses [-i:z] taudinmääritys, diagnoosi.

diagonal [dai'ægənl] s. lävistäjä; a. viisto, vino; adv. vinottain, viistoon.

diagram ['daiəgræm] s. diagrammi, graafinen käyrä(stö). **-matic** [-grə'mætik] a.: ~ picture kaaviokuva.

dial ['daiəl] s. kellotaulu; osoitintaulu; (puhelimen) numerolevy; v.: ~ a number valita puhelinnumero; ~ling tone keskusmerkki; sun ~ aurinkokello.

dialect ['daiəlekt] s. murre. **-al** [-'lektl] a. murre-. **-ic** [-'lektik] s.: ~ s dialektiikka.

dialogue, Am. m. **dialog** ['daiəlɔg] s. vuoropuhelu; keskustelu.

diamet|er [dai'æmitə] s. halkaisija, läpimitta. **-rically** [daiə'metrikəli] adv. jyrkästi, täysin.

diamond ['daiəmənd] s. timantti; ruutu (korttip.); glazier's ~ lasinleikkaajan timantti.

Diana [dai'ænə] erisn.

diaper ['daiəpə] s. (vauvan) vaippa.

diaphanous [dai'æfənəs] a. läpikuultava.

diaphragm ['daiəfræm] s. pallea; (valok.) himmennin; (tekn.) välikalvo.

diarist ['daiərist] s. päiväkirjan pitäjä.

diarrh(o)ea [daiə'riə] s. ripuli.

diary ['daiəri] s. päiväkirja.

diatribe ['daiətraib] s. kiukkuinen hyökkäys, häväistyspuhe.

dibble ['dibl] s. istutuspuikko; v. istuttaa istutuspuikolla.

dibs [dibz] s. sl. kolikot, raha.

dice [dais] s. pl. (sg. *die*) arpakuutio(t); noppapeli; v. pelata noppapeliä; leikata kuutioiksi. **-y** [-i] a. vaarallinen, epävarma.

dichotomy [di'kɔtəmi] s. kaksijakoisuus.

dickens ['dikinz] s. piru, lempo.

dicker ['dikə] s. tinkiä.

dicky, dickey ['diki] s. takaistuin (kahden hengen) auton ulkopuolella; paidan etumus. **~-bird** tipu.

dictaphone ['diktəfəun] s. sanelukone.

dicta|te [dik'teit] v. sanella; määrätä, komentaa; s. ['dikteit] diktaatti, (pakko)määräys, käsky. **-tion** [-'teiʃn] s. sanelu; määräys. **-tor** [-ə] s. diktaattori; (**~-ial** [diktə'tɔ:riəl] a. diktatorinen, käskevä; ~**-ship** s. diktatuuri.

diction ['dikʃn] s. ääntäminen (Am.); esitystapa. **-ary** [-nəri] s. sanakirja.

dictum ['diktəm] s. (pl. *dicta*) painava sana, lausunto.

did [did] *imp*. ks. *do*. **-n't** [didnt] = *did not*.

didactic [di'dæktik] a. opettava, opetus-.

diddle [didl] v. puijata.

die 1. [dai] s. (pl. *dice*) arpakuutio, -noppa (tav. *one of the dice*); (pl. *dies*) leimasin, (valu)muotti.

die 2. [dai] v. kuolla, saada surmansa; kuihtua; sammua; ~ *down*, ~ *away* heiketä, hiljetä; ~ *out* kuolla sukupuuttoon; ~ *hard* olla sitkeähenkinen; ~ *in the last ditch* taistella viimeiseen asti; [*she was*] *dying to know* halusi kiihkeästi tietää; *never say* ~ älä hellitä! **~-hard** jääräpää; äärivanhoillinen.

diet 1. [daiət] s. valtiopäivät.

diet 2. [daiət] s. ruokajärjestys, -valio; v. pitää jkta ruokavaliolla; *I'm on a strict* ~ noudatan tarkkaa dieettiä; *is she still* ~*ing?* vieläkö hän on dieetillä? **-ary** [-(ə)ri] a. = *seur.*; s. (laitoksen) ruokajärjestys, ruoka. **-etic** [daii'tetik] a. ruokajärjestys-.

differ ['difə] v. erota, olla toisenlainen

(*from* kuin); olla eri mieltä; [*they*] ~ *a lot in character* poikkeavat luonteeltaan paljon toisistaan. **-ence** ['difr(ə)ns] s. ero, erotus; erilaisuus; erimielisyys, riita; *it makes no* ~ se on aivan yhdentekevää. **-ent** ['difr(ə)nt] a. erilainen (*from* kuin). **-ential** [-'renʃl] a. differentiaali-, erotus-; s.: *income* ~ s tuloerot; *wage* ~ s palkkahaitari. **-entiate** [-'renʃieit] v. erottaa, olla erotuksena; erilaistua; ~ *d* erilytynyt. **-entiation** [-renʃi'eiʃn] s. erilaistuminen, eriytyminen. **-ently** *adv*. toisin, eri tavoin (*from* kuin).

difficult ['difik(ə)lt] a. vaikea, hankala. **-y** [-i] s. vaikeus; *with* ~ vaivoin; *without* ~ helposti.

diffiden|ce ['difid(ə)ns] s. arkuus, itseluottamuksen puute. **-t** [-(ə)nt] a. arka, ujo.

diffuse [di'fju:z] v. levittää (laajalle); sekoittaa; a. [di'fju:s] hajanainen, haja-; lavea, monisanainen. **-ion** [di'fju:ʒn] s. levittäminen, leviäminen. **-ive** [-siv] a. (helposti) leviävä.

dig [dig] *dug* dug, v. kaivaa; tönäistä; sl. ymmärtää, hyväksyä; ~ *in(to)* käydä (ruoan) kimppuun; ~ *oneself in* kaivautua maahan; s. töykkäys; ~ *up (out)* kaivaa esiin; ~ *for* etsiä; a ~ *at* letkaus jklle; ~ *ging* kaivaus; ~ *gings* kultakenttä; = *digs*.

digest [di'dʒest, dai-] v. sulattaa; järjestellä, muokkailla; sulaa; s. ['daidʒest] tiivistelmä, lyhennelmä. **-ible** [-əbl] a. (helposti)sulava. **-ion** [-ʃn] s. ruoansulatus; sulattaminen. **-ive** [-iv] a. ruoansulatus-.

digit ['didʒit] s. numero, yksinumeroinen luku (0–9); sormi. **-al** [-(ə)l] a. sormi-; digitaalinen, numero-.

digitalis [didʒi'teilis] s. sormustinkukka; digitalis.

digni|fied ['dignifaid] a. arvokas. **-fy** [-fai] v. antaa arvokkuutta. **-tary** [-t(ə)ri] s. arvohenkilö. **-ty** [-ti] s. arvo(asema), arvokkuus.

digress [dai'gres] v. poiketa. **-ion** [-'greʃn] s. poikkeaminen asiasta.

digs [digz] s. pl. (puhek.) boksi.

dike, dyke [daik] s. pato, (suoja)valli, kaivanto; v. suojata vallilla; ojittaa.

dilapida|ted [di'læpideitid] *a.*
rappeutunut, ränsistynyt. **-tion**
[-'deiʃn] *s.* rappiotila, ränstyneisyys.

dilatation [dailə'teiʃn] = *dilation*

dila|te [dai'leit] *v.* laajentaa, laajeta;
puhua laajalti *(upon* jstk). **-tion**
[dai'leiʃn] *s.* laajeneminen, laajennus.

dilatory ['dilət(ə)ri] *a.* viivyttelevä,
hidas(televa).

dilemma [di'lemə] *s.* vaikea pulma.

dilettan|te [dili'tænti] *s.* (pl. **-ti** [-ti:])
harrastelija.

diligen|ce ['dilidʒ(ə)ns] *s.* ahkeruus,
uutteruus. **-t** [-nt] *a.* ahkera, uuttera.

dill [dil] *s.* tilli.

dilly-dally ['dilidæli] *v.* epäröidä,
vitkastella, aikailla.

diluent ['diljuənt] *s.* laimennusaine.

dilu|te [dai'lju:t] *v.* miedontaa,
laimentaa. **-tion** [-ʃn] *s.* laimennus.

dim [dim] *a.* hämärä, himmeä, sumea;
epäselvä; hidas(järkinen); *v.*
himmentää; sumentaa; himmentyä,
hämärtyä; sumentua; ~ *med lights*
(Am.) lähivalot.

dime [daim] *s.* Am. kymmenen sentin
hopearaha.

dimension [di'menʃn] *s.* ulottuvuus;
mitta(suhde); ~ *s* mitat, suuruus. **-al**
[-(ə)l] *a.:* *three-* ~ kolmiulotteinen.

dimin|ish [di'miniʃ] *v.* pienentää,
vähentää; pienetä, vähetä. **-ution**
[dimi'nju:ʃn] *s.* pieneneminen.
-utive [di'minjutiv] *a.*
(pienen) pieni, pikkuruinen; *s.*
diminutiivi.

dimple ['dimpl] *s.* hymykuoppa; *v.*
panna (mennä) kuopalle, olla
kuopilla.

din [din] *s.* jymy, jyske, pauhu, melu,
melske; *v.* toitottaa jkn korviin *(into a
p.'s ears),* pauhata, jyskyä.

dine [dain] *v.* syödä päivällistä; tarjota
päivällistä (jklle); ~ *out* syödä
ravintolassa. **-r** [-ə] *s.* päivällisvieras;
ravintolavaunu.

dinghy ['diŋgi] *s.* pieni vene.

dinginess ['din(d)ʒinis] *s.* likaisuus,
nuhruisuus.

dingy ['din(d)ʒi] likainen,
likaisenharmaa, nuhruinen.

dining|-car ['dainiŋkɑ:]
ravintolavaunu. **~-room** ruokasali.

dinky ['diŋki] *a.* soma.

dinner ['dinə] *s.* päivällinen;
päivälliset. ~-**jacket** smokki. ~-**party**
päivälliset. ~-**set** pöytäkalusto.

dinosaur ['dainəsɔ:] *s.* dinosaurus,
hirmulisko.

dint [dint] *s.* ks. *dent; v.* kolhia; *by* ~ *of*
jnk avulla.

diocese ['daiəsis] *s.* hiippakunta.

diorama [daiə'rɑ:mə] *s.* dioraama.

dioxide [dai'ɔksaid] *s.* dioksidi.

dip [dip] *v.* kastaa, upottaa; valaa
(kynttilöitä); kastella itsensä,
sukeltaa; vaipua; viettää, kallistua; *s.*
lyhyt uinti, kastelu; notko, kuoppa;
viettäminen; lasku (~ *in prices);*
(karjan ym) puhdistusliuos; ~ *into a
book* silmäillä; ~ *a flag* tervehtiä
lipulla (toista laivaa); ~-*ped lights*
(auton) lähivalot.

diphtheria [dif'θiəriə] *s.* kurkkumätä.

diphthong [difθɔŋ] *s.* kaksoisääntiö.

diploma [di'pləumə] *s.* diplomi,
kunniakirja. **-cy** [-si] *s.* diplomatia,
valtioviisaus; oveluus. **-t** ['dipləmæt]
s. diplomaatti. **-tic** [diplə'mætik] *a.*
diplomaattinen, valtioviisas. **-tist**
[-tist] *s.* diplomaatti; *a good* ~
valtioviisas henkilö.

dipper ['dipə] *s.* koskikara, vesilintu;
kauha; *Big D* ~ Otava.

dipsomaniac [dipsə(u)'meiniæk] *s.*
alkoholisti.

dire ['daiə] *a.* hirveä, kamala, kauhea.

direct [di'rekt, dai'rekt] *a.* suora;
suoranainen, välitön, vilpitön,
suorasukainen, selvä; *adv.* suoraan,
välittömästi; *v.* suunnata, kohdistaa;
ohjata, opastaa; johtaa; käskeä, antaa
tehtäväksi; ~ *current* tasavirta; ~ *hit*
täysosuma; ~ *speech* (kiel.) suora
esitys; ~ *tax* välitön vero. **-ion** [-kʃn]
s. suunta, taho; ohje(et); johto,
ohjaus; ~ *s for use* käyttöohje(et); *in
the* ~ *of* jhk suuntaan; ~ *finder*
suuntimislaite. **-ive** [-iv] *a.* ohjaava,
johtava; *s.* ohje, toimintaohje,
evästys. **-ly** *adv.* suoraan; heti,
viipymättä; *konj.* heti kun. **-ness**
s. suoruus. **-or** [-ə] *s.* johtaja,
johtokunnan jäsen; (filmin) ohjaaja;
board of ~ *s* johtokunta; (~ **ate** [-rit]
johtokunta; ~ **ship** johto, johtajuus).
-ory [-əri] *s.* osoitekalenteri; *telephone*
~ puhelinluettelo.

dirge [də:dʒ] s. surulaulu.

dirigible ['diridʒəbl] a. ohjattavissa oleva; s. ilmalaiva.

dirk [də:k] s. tikari.

dirt [də:t] s. lika, loka, törky; ~ cheap pilkkahintaan; ~ road maantie, soraamaton tie; fling ~ at panetella. ~-track kilpa-ajorata.

dirty ['də:ti] a. likainen; kurainen; siivoton; halpamainen; v. iata, likaantua; play a ~ trick (sl. do the ~) on sb. tehdä jklle nolo temppu.

disability [disə'biliti] s. kykenemättömyys; invaliditeetti, vamma.

disable [dis'eibl] v. tehdä kykenemättömäksi t. kelpaamattomaksi; julistaa epäpäteväksi; ~d kykenemätön; vammainen, vammautunut; ~d ex-serviceman sotainvalidi. -ment s. vammautuminen, invaliditeetti.

disabuse [disə'bju:z] v.: ~ sb. of vapauttaa jstk.

disaccord [disə'kɔ:d] s. ristiriita.

disadvantage [disəd'va:ntidʒ] s. epäedullisuus; huono puoli, haitta; be at a ~ olla epäedullisessa asemassa. -ous [disædva:n'teidʒəs] a. epäedullinen.

disaffect|ed [disə'fektid] a. nurjamielinen, tyytymätön. -ion [-kʃn] s. (poliittinen) tyytymättömyys.

disagree [disə'gri:] v. olla eri mieltä, olla ristiriidassa; [these reports] ~ eivät käy yksiin; [the climate] ~s with me ei sovi minulle. -able [disə'griəbl] a. epämiellyttävä; äreä, kärtyisä. -ment s. yhteensovittumattomuus; erimielisyys.

disallow [disə'lau] v. hylätä; evätä.

disappear [disə'piə] v. kadota, hävitä näkyvistä. -ance [-r(ə)ns] s. katoaminen.

disappoint [disə'pɔint] v. pettää (jkn) toiveet, aiheuttaa pettymys; be ~ed in at pettyä jnk suhteen; I was ~ed not to find her there petyin, kun hän ei ollut siellä. -ment s. pettymys.

disapproval [disə'pru:vl] s. paheksuminen; [he shook his head] in ~ paheksuvasti.

disapprove [disə'pru:v] v. paheksua (us. ~of), ei hyväksyä.

disarm [dis'ɑ:m] v. riisua, riistää ase(et); riisua aseensa, lopettaa varustelu; [her smile] ~ed me hellytti minut. -ament [-əmənt] s. aseistariisunta.

disarrange [disə'rein(d)ʒ] v. saattaa epäjärjestykseen.

disarray ['disə'rei] s. epäjärjestys; v. saattaa epäjärjestykseen.

disast|er [di'za:stə] s. (suuri) onnettomuus, tuho. -rous [-trəs] a. onneton, tuhoisa.

disavow ['disə'vau] v. kieltää, kieltäytyä hyväksymästä. -al [-əl] s. kieltäminen.

disband [dis'bænd] v. hajottaa, hajaantua, kotiuttaa. -ment s. hajottaminen.

dis|belief ['disbi'li:f] s. epäusko. -believe [-bi'li:v] v. olla uskomatta, epäillä (jtk).

disburden [dis'bə:dn] v. ks. unburden.

disburse [dis'bə:s] v. maksaa, suorittaa maksu.

disc, disk [disk] s. pyöreä laatta, levy; äänilevy; the sun's ~ auringon kehrä; ~ jockey (rad., TV) levypakinoitsija, »tiskijukka»; slipped ~ (nikaman) välilevytyrä.

discard [dis'ka:d] v. hylätä, heittää (kelvottomana) pois; s. pois pantu kortti (korttip.).

discern [di'sə:n] v. erottaa; huomata, nähdä; ~ing tarkkanäköinen, arvostelukykyinen. -ible [-əbl] a. havaittava. -ment s. arvostelukyky, terävä huomiokyky, tarkkanäköisyys.

discharge [dis'tʃa:dʒ] v. purkaa (kuorma ym); laukaista, ampua; suorittaa, täyttää; maksaa; päästää (sairaalasta), vapauttaa (vanki); erottaa, panna viralta; purkautua; märkiä; s. purkaminen, purkautuminen; laukaiseminen; erottaminen palveluksesta; (velvollisuuden ym) suorittaminen; vapauttaminen; märkävuoto; the river ~s into joki laskee jhk. ~-pipe laskuputki.

disciple [di'saipl] s. opetuslapsi.

disciplin|arian [disipli'neəriən] s. kurinpitäjä. -ary ['disiplinəri] a. kurinpidollinen.

discipline ['disiplin] s. kuri; oppiaine;

v. totuttaa kuriin; *well - ~ d*
kurinalainen.

disclaim [dis'kleim] *v.* luopua, kieltää.
-er [-ə] *s.* peruutus, vastalause.

disclos|e [dis'klou:z] *v.* paljastaa,
saattaa ilmi. **-ure** [-ʒə] *s.*
paljastaminen, paljastus.

dis|colour [dis'kʌlə] *v.* haalistaa, pilata
väri; haalistua, menettää värinsä.
-colo(u)ration [-'reiʃn] *s.*
haalistuminen.

discomfit [dis'kʌmfit] *v.* hämmentää,
saattaa ymmälle. **-ure** [-ʃə] *s.*
hämminki.

discomfort [dis'kʌmfət] *s.*
epämukavuus, hankaluus, vaiva.

discommode [diskə'məud] *v.* tuottaa
hankaluutta.

discom|pose [diskəm'pəuz] *v.* järkyttää
(jkn tasapainoa). **-posure** [-'pəuʒə] *s.*
hämminki, rauhattomuus.

disconcert [diskən'sə:t] *v.* saattaa
ymmälle, hämmentää; panna
sekaisin; *~ing* hämmentävä.

disconnect [diskə'nekt] *v.* erottaa,
irrottaa; katkaista (sähkövirta ym).
-ed [-id] *a.* epäyhtenäinen,
hajanainen. **-ion** [-'nekʃn] *s.*
irrottaminen; (sähk.) katkaisu.

disconsolate [dis'kɔns(ə)lit] *a.*
lohduton, epätoivoinen.

discontent [diskən'tent] *s.*
tyytymättömyys. **-ed** [-id] *a.: ~ with*
tyytymätön jhk.

discontinuance [diskən'tinjuəns] *s.*
lakkaaminen.

discontin|ue [diskən'tinju:] *v.*
lakkauttaa, lopettaa, keskeyttää;
lakata. **-uous** [-juəs] *a.* keskeytyvä,
katkonainen.

discord [disko:d] *s.* eripuraisuus,
epäsopu; epäsointu. **-ance**
[dis'ko:d(ə)ns] *s.* eripuraisuus,
ristiriita. **-ant** [dis'ko:d(ə)nt] *a.*
ristiriitainen; eripurainen;
epäsointuinen.

discotheque [diskə'tek] *s.* diskoteekki,
disko.

discount ['diskaunt] *s.* diskontto;
(vekselin) diskonttaus; alennus; *v.*
diskontata; alentaa (hintaa);
suhtautua varauksin, tinkiä (jstk
kertomuksesta ym); *cash ~*
käteisalennus; *at a ~* vähäarvoinen.

-enance [dis'kauntinəns] *v.* paheksua.

discourage [dis'kʌridʒ] *v.* lannistaa,
viedä rohkeus (jklta); koettaa estää,
saada luopumaan (*from. .-ing* jstk).
-ment *s.* lannistaminen;
mielenmasennus, alakuloisuus.

discourse [dis'kɔ:s] *s.* puhe, esitelmä,
esitys; saarna; tutkielma; *v.* puhua
laveasti (*upon* jstk).

discourte|ous [dis'kə:tjəs] *a.*
epäkohtelias. **-sy** [-isi] *s.*
epäkohteliaisuus.

discover [dis'kʌvə] *v.* löytää, keksiä,
huomata, havaita. **-y** [-ri] *s.* löytö,
keksintö.

discredit [dis'kredit] *s.* huono maine,
häpeä; *v.* ei uskoa; saattaa huonoon
huutoon, häpäistä (m. *bring ~ on*).
-able [-əbl] *a.* häpeällinen.

discreet [dis'kri:t] *a.* tahdikas,
hieno|tunteinen, -varainen.

discrepan|cy [dis'krep(ə)nsi] *s.*
poikkeavuus, ristiriita, ero.

discre|te ['diskri:t, -'-] *a.* erillinen.
-tion [dis'kreʃn] *s.* arvostelukyky;
hienotunteisuus, tahdikkuus;
toimintavapaus, ehdonvalta; *at ~*
mielin määrin; *surrender at ~*
antautua ehdoitta; *I rely on your ~*
luotan siihen, ettette puhu asiasta.

discriminat|e [dis'krimineit] *v.* erottaa;
erotella, diskriminoida. **-ing** *a.*
erottava; arvostelukykyinen. **-ion**
[-'neiʃn] *s.* arvostelukyky;
erotuskyky; erottelu; *racial ~*
rotusyrjintä.

discursive [dis'kə:siv] *a.* hajanainen.

discus ['diskəs] *s.* kiekko; *the ~ throw*
kiekonheitto.

discuss [dis'kʌs] *v.* keskustella, pohtia.
-ion [-'kʌʃn] *s.* keskustelu, pohdinta;
väittely.

disdain [dis'dein] *v.* halveksia; *s.*
ylenkatse, halveksiminen; *~ful*
halveksiva.

disease [di'zi:z] *s.* tauti. **-d** [-d] *a.*
sairas.

disembark ['disim'ba:k] *v.* nousta
maihin; purkaa laivasta. **-ation**
[disembα:'keiʃn] *s.* maihinmeno,
-astuminen.

disembody ['disim'bɔdi] *v.: -bodied*
ruumiista vapautunut, ruumiiton.

disembowel [disim'bauəl] *v.* poistaa

sisukset.

disenchant ['disin't∫ɑ:nt] v. päästää harhakuvitelmasta, avata (jkn) silmät. **-ment** s. pettymys.

disengage ['disin'geidʒ] v. irrottaa, vapauttaa; irtautua. **-d** [-d] a. vapaa, joutilas.

disentangle ['disin'tæŋgl] v. selvittää (vyyhti ym); päästää.

disfavour ['dis'feivə] s. paheksuminen; epäsuosio.

disfigure [dis'figə] v. rumentaa, turmella.

disgorge [dis'gɔ:dʒ] v. purkaa (sisästään); luopua (anastetusta).

disgrace [dis'greis] s. epäsuosio; häpeä, häpeäpilkku; v. olla häpeäksi, häpäistä; saattaa epäsuosioon. **-ful** [-f(u)l] a. häpeällinen.

disgruntled [dis'grʌntld] a. tyytymätön.

disguise [dis'gaiz] s. valepuku, naamio(itus); v. pukea valepukuun, pukea (as jksk); verhota, salata.

disgust [dis'gʌst] s. vastenmielisyys, inho; v. inhottaa, iljettää; I am ~ed minua inhottaa (with, at); ~ing vastenmielinen.

dish [di∫] s. vati, kulho; ruokalaji; v. (~ up) laittaa tarjolle (pöytään), tarjota (m. kuv.); (tav. ~ up); (puhek.) nujertaa, tuhota; ~ out jakaa; wash up the ~es tiskata astiat; ~ cloth tiskiriepu

dishabille [disə'bi:l] s.: in ~ puolipukeissa.

dis\|harmonious [disho:'məuniəs] a. epäsointuinen. **-harmony** [dis'ho:məni] s. epäsointu, epäsopu.

dishearten [dis'ho:tn] v. masentaa (jkn) mieli.

dishevelled [di'∫evld] a. tukka epäjärjestyksessä; hoitamaton.

dishonest [dis'ɔnist] a. epärehellinen, vilpillinen. **-y** [-i] s. epärehellisyys.

dishonour [dis'ɔnə] s. kunniattomuus, häpeä; v. häpäistä; jättää lunastamatta (vekseli). **-able** [-rəbl] a. häpeällinen.

dish-washer astiainpesukone.

dishy ['di∫i] a. komean näköinen.

disillusion [disi'lu:ʒn] v. haihduttaa (jkn) haaveet; they were ~ed he pettyivät. **-ment** s. pettymys.

dis\|inclination [disinkli'nei∫n] s.

haluttomuus. **-incline** ['disin'klain] v. tehdä haluttomaksi jhk; ~d haluton.

disinfect [disin'fekt] v. desinfioida, puhdistaa bakteereista. **-ant** [-ənt] a. & s. desinfioiva (aine). **-ion** [-k∫n] s. desinfektio.

disinflation [disin'flei∫n] s. palaaminen normaaliin (inflaation jälkeen).

disingenuous [disin'dʒenjuəs] a. vilpillinen.

disinherit ['disin'herit] v. tehdä perinnöttömäksi.

disintegra\|te [dis'intigreit] v. hajottaa t. hajota (alkuosiinsa); rapautua. **-tion** [disinti'grei∫n] s. hajottaminen, hajoaminen.

disinter [disin'tə:] v. kaivaa haudasta.

disinterested [dis'intristid] a. epäitsekäs, puolueeton, pyyteetön.

disjoint [dis'dʒɔint] v. irrottaa liitoksistaan, paloitella; ~ed epäyhtenäinen, hajanainen.

disk ks. *disc.*

dislike [dis'laik] s. vastenmielisyys; v. tuntea vastenmielisyyttä; I ~ him en pidä hänestä.

disloca\|te ['disləkeit] v. vääntää sijoiltaan, panna epäjärjestykseen; be ~d mennä sijoiltaan. **-tion** [dislə'kei∫n] s. sijoiltaan meno.

dislodge [dis'lɔdʒ] v. siirtää paikaltaan; karkottaa.

disloyal ['dis'lɔi(ə)l] a. uskoton; epälojaali; petollinen. **-ty** [-ti] s. uskottomuus.

dismal ['dizm(ə)l] a. synkkä; surkea, kurja.

dismantle [dis'mæntl] v. riisua (laiva ym); purkaa.

dismay [dis'mei] s. pelko; be ~ed kauhistua; in ~ kauhun vallassa.

dismember [dis'membə] v. repiä jäsen jäseneltä; paloitella, lohkoa. **-ment** s. silpominen.

dismiss [dis'mis] v. lähettää pois; erottaa palveluksesta; karkottaa (ajatus); hylätä; hajottaa. **-al** [-l] s. poislähettäminen; viraltapano, erottaminen; karkottaminen.

dismount ['dis'maunt] v. laskeutua (satulasta); heittää t. syöstä satulasta; purkaa (kone), nostaa (tykki) alustalta.

disobedien\|ce [disə'bi:djəns] s.

tottelemattomuus; *civil* ~ passiivinen
vastarinta. **-t** [-ənt] *a.* tottelematon.

disobey ['disə'bei] *v.* olla tottelematta,
ei totella.

disoblig|e ['disə'blaidʒ] *v.* olla
noudattamatta jkn toivomuksia; *I am
sorry to* ~ *you* [*but*. .] valitan, etten
voi auttaa (suostua. .). **-ing** *a.*
epäkohtelias, ynseä.

disorder [dis'ɔ:də] *s.* epäjärjestys;
sairaus, häiriö; levottomuus, meteli;
v. häiritä, saattaa epäjärjestykseen.
-ed [-d] *a.* epäjärjestyksessä oleva,
häiriintynyt. **-ly** [-li] *a.*
epäjärjestyksessä oleva; hälinöivä,
mellasteleva; järjestyksenvastainen.

disorganize [dis'ɔ:gənaiz] *v.* saattaa
hajaannustilaan t. epäjärjestykseen;
ks. *disrupt*.

disoriented [dis'ɔ:riəntid] *pp., a.* ajan
ja paikan tajun menettänyt.

disown [dis'əun] *v.* olla tunnustamatta
(omakseen), kieltää.

disparage [dis'pæridʒ] *v.* halventaa,
puhua halveksivasti jstk. **-ment** *s.*
halventaminen, väheksyminen.

dispar|ate ['dispərit] *a.*
yhteensopimaton. **-ity** [dis'pæriti] *s.*
ero, erilaisuus.

dispassionate [dis'pæʃnit] *a.* kiihkoton,
puolueeton.

dispatch [dis'pætʃ] *v.* lähettää
matkaan, panna menemään;
toimittaa; panna päiviltä, lopettaa; *s.*
(kiireellinen) lähetys; joutuisuus,
nopeus; (virallinen) ilmoitus, raportti;
with ~ nopeasti. **~-box**
asiakirjalaukku. **~-rider**
(moottoripyörä)lähetti.

dispel [dis'pel] *v.* karkottaa, hajottaa,
häivyttää mielestä.

dispensa|ble [dis'pensəbl] *a.* jota ilman
(t. vailla) voi olla. **-ry** [-(ə)ri] *s.* (esim.
sairaalan) apteekki; huoltotoimisto,
poliklinikka.

dispensation [dispen'seiʃn] *s.* jakelu;
(*divine* ~) (Jumalan) sallimus;
erivapaus.

dispens|e [dis'pens] *v.* jakaa, jaella;
valmistaa (ja jaella) lääkkeitä;
vapauttaa (*from* jstk); ~ *with* tulla
toimeen ilman jtk. **-er** [-ə] *s.*
lääkkeiden valmistaja, farmaseutti.

dispersal [dis'pə:sl] *s.* hajottaminen,

hajaantuminen.

dispers|e [dis'pə:s] *v.* hajottaa, levittää;
hajaantua. **-ion** [-ə:ʃn] *s.* hajaannus;
hajonta.

dispirit [dis'pirit] *v.* masentaa. **-ed** [-id]
a. alakuloinen.

displace [dis'pleis] *v.* siirtää; ottaa
(jkn) paikka, syrjäyttää; ~ *d persons*
siirtoväki. **-ment** *s.* paikaltaan
muuttaminen; (laivan) uppoama.

display [dis'plei] *v.* näyttää, panna
näytteille; panna esille; osoittaa,
ilmaista; *s.* näytteillepano, näyttely,
näytös; komeilu.

displeas|e [dis'pli:z] *v.:* *it* ~ *s me* se ei
miellytä minua; ~ *d* tyytymätön,
harmistunut (*at, with* jhk). **-ing** *a.*
epämieluisa, vastenmielinen. **-ure**
[dis'pleʒə] *s.* mielipaha,
tyytymättömyys.

disport [dis'pɔ:t] *v.* (vanh.): ~ *oneself*
telmiä, leikkiä.

disposable *a.* (m.) kertakäyttö-.

disposal [dis'pəuz(ə)l] *s.* järjestely;
käyttö, määräämisvalta; käsittely-
tapa, hävittäminen; *at sb.'s* ~ jkn
käytettävissä; *bomb* ~ pommi(e)n
purkaminen; *refuse* ~ jätehuolto.

dispos|e [dis'pəuz] *v.* järjestää,
järjestellä; taivuttaa, tehdä
halukkaaksi; määrätä; säätää; ~ *of*
vapaasti käyttää; päästä (suoriutua)
jstk, myydä, saada kaupaksi;
hävittää, heittää pois. **-ed** [-d] *a.*
taipuvainen, halukas (*for a walk*);
well ~ *towards* suopea jkta kohtaan.
-ition [dispə'ziʃn] *s.* järjestely;
sijoitus; määräämisvalta; mielen-,
luonteenlaatu; *of a gentle* ~
herttainen luonteeltaan; *make one's*
~ *s* valmistautua.

dispossess [dispə'zes] *v.:* ~ *sb. of* viedä,
riistää jklta jtk.

disprof ['dis'pru:f] *s.* kumoaminen;
vastatodiste.

disproportion ['disprə'pɔ:ʃn] *s.*
epäsuhde, -suhtaisuus; ~ *ed* = *seur.*
-ate [-ʃnit] *a.* epäsuhtainen,
suhteeton.

disprove [dis'pru:v] *v.* kuomota,
osoittaa vääräksi.

disputa|ble ['dispjutəbl] *a.*
kiistanalainen. **-tion** [dispju'teiʃn] *s.*
väittely.

dispute [dis'pju:t] v. väitellä; väittää (jtk) vääräksi; kiistää; taistella (voitosta); s. väittely, kiista, sanasota; *beyond* ~ kieltämättä; [*the matter*] *in* ~ kiistanalainen.

disquali|fication [diskwɔlifi'keiʃn] s. kelpaamattomuus, diskvalifiointi. **-fy** [dis'kwɔlifai] v. tehdä kelpaamattomaksi, julistaa kilpailukelvottomaksi, diskvalifioida; *-fied* esteinen; *be -fied from holding a driving licence* menettää ajokorttinsa.

disquiet [dis'kwaiǝt] s. rauhattomuus; v. tehdä rauhattomaksi; ~*ing* levottomuutta herättävä. **-ude** [-itju:d] s. levottomuus, rauhattomuus.

Disraeli [diz'reili] *erisn.*

disregard ['disri'gɑ:d] v. jättää huomioonottamatta, olla välittämättä (jstk); s. piittaamattomuus.

disrepair ['disri'peǝ] s. huono kunto.

disrepu|table [dis'repjutǝbl] a. huonomaineinen. **-te** ['disri'pju:t] s. huono maine; häpeä; *has fallen into* ~ on joutunut huonoon huutoon.

disrespect ['disris'pekt] s. epäkunnioitus; epäkohteliaisuus. **-ful** a. epäkunnioittava; epäkohtelias.

disrobe [dis'rǝub] v. riisua (et. virkapuku).

disrupt [dis'rʌpt] v. repiä rikki, hajottaa, panna sekaisin; ~ *the traffic* aiheuttaa liikennehäiriö. **-tion** [-pʃn] s. rikki repiminen; hajaannus. **-ive** [-iv] a. hajottava, repivä.

dissatis|faction ['dissætis'fækʃn] s. tyytymättömyys. **-fied** [dis'sætisfaid] a. tyytymätön.

dissect [di'sekt] v. leikellä, dissekoida; tutkia perinpohjin. **-ion** [-kʃn] s. leikkely, dissektio.

dissemble [di'sembl] v. salata (tunteensa), teeskennellä.

disseminat|e [di'semineit] v. levittää (laajalle). **-ion** [-'neiʃn] s. levittäminen.

dissension [di'senʃn] s. erimielisyys.

dissent [di'sent] v. olla eri mieltä; poiketa kirkon opista, erota kirkosta. **-er** [-ǝ] s. eriuskoinen. **-ient** [-'senʃiǝnt] a. & s. toisin ajatteleva.

dissertation [disǝ(:)'teiʃn] s. tutkielma, väitöskirja.

disservice ['dis'sǝ:vis] s. huono palvelus.

dissever [dis'sevǝ] v. rikkoa, erottaa.

dissident ['disid(ǝ)nt] a. & s. toisin ajatteleva.

dissimilar ['di'similǝ] a. erilainen. **-ity** [disimi'læriti] s. erilaisuus.

dissimula|te [di'simjuleit] v. salata; teeskennellä. **-tion** [-'leiʃn] s. teeskentely.

dissipat|e ['disipeit] v. haihduttaa; tuhlata; viettää huikentelevaa elämää. **-ed** [-id] a. huikenteleva, irstaileva. **-ion** [-'peiʃn] s. huikentelevaa (t. kevytmielinen) elämä, irstailu.

dissociate [di'sǝuʃieit] v. erottaa; ~ *oneself from* sanoutua irti jstk.

dissoluble [di'sɔljubl] a. purettavissa (oleva).

dissolu|te [di'disǝlu:t] a. moraalisesti löyhä, irstas. **-tion** [-'lu:ʃn] s. hajottaminen, hajoaminen; hajoamistila; (avioliiton ym) purkaminen; (parl.) hajaantuminen, hajoaminen.

dissolve [di'zɔlv] v. liuottaa, liueta; hajottaa, purkaa; hajaantua. **-nt** [-ǝnt] s. liuotin.

dissonan|ce [di'disǝnǝns] s. epäsointu, soraääni. **-t** [-ǝnt] a. epäsointuinen; ristiriitainen.

dissua|de [di'swei|d] v. kehottaa luopumaan *(from* jstk) t. varomaan jtk; saada luopumaan jstk. **-sion** [-ʒn] s. varoitus.

distaff ['distɑ:f] s. värttinä; rukinlapa; *on the* ~ *side* äidin puolelta.

distan|ce ['dist(ǝ)ns] s. välimatka, etäisyys; v. jättää jälkeensä; *at a* ~ matkan päässä, loitolla; *at a* ~ *of five metres* viiden metrin päässä t. päästä; *keep one's* ~ pysyä loitolla. **-t** [-(ǝ)nt] a. etäinen, kaukainen; luoksepääsemätön, viileä; ~ *ly related* kaukaista sukua (oleva).

distaste [dis'teist] s. vastenmielisyys. **-ful** a. vastenmielinen, epämiellyttävä.

distemper [dis'tempǝ] s. penikkatauti; tempera-, liimaväri; v. maalata temperaväreillä.

disten|d [dis'tend] v. laajentaa, pullistaa; pullistua. **-sion** [-nʃn] s.

laajennus, pullistuma.

distil [dis'til] v. tislata, polttaa (viinaa); puhdistaa, erottaa olennaisin osa (jstk). **-late** ['distilit] s. tisle. **-lation** [-'leiʃn] s. tislaus. **-ler** [-ə] s. (et. viskin) tislaaja. **-lery** [-əri] s. (viskin ym) tislaamo.

distinct [dis'tiŋ(k)t] a. selvästi erotettava; erillään (oleva); selvä. **-ion** [dis'tiŋ(k)ʃn] s. ero, erotus; erityispiirre, erikoislaatuisuus, hienostus; kunnianosoitus, korkea asema; _a writer of_ ~ huomattava kirjailija; _with_ ~ kunniakkaasti, (koul.) saaden kunniamaininnan. **-ive** [-iv] a. selvästi erottuva, tunnusomainen. **-ly** adv. selvästi.

distinguish [dis'tiŋgwiʃ] v. (osata) erottaa; tehdä huomatuksi, olla ominaista; ~ _oneself_ kunnostautua. **-able** [-əbl] a. erotettavissa oleva, havaittava. **-ed** [-t] huomattava, kuuluisa; erinomainen; hienostunut; arvoisa (~ _guests_).

distort [dis'tɔ:t] v. vääntää, vääristää; vääristellä. **-ion** [-ɔ:ʃn] s. vääntäminen; vääristymä.

distract [dis'trækt] v. kääntää ajatukset (huomio) pois jstk; häiritä, hämmentää; ~ _ed_ hämmentynyt, sekapäinen. **-ion** [-'trækʃn] s. ajatusten muualle suuntaava asia; hauskutus, huvi, ajanviete; hämmennys, sekapäisyys, raivo; _drive sb. to_ ~ saattaa suunniltaan.

distrain [dis'trein] v. ulosmitata (_upon_). **-t** [-t] s. ulosmittaus.

distraught [dis'trɔ:t] a. mieletön (surusta ym).

distress [dis'tres] s. tuska, kärsimys; hätä, ahdinko; uupumus; ulosotto; v. tehdä onnettomaksi, ahdistaa; uuvuttaa; _in_ ~ (m.) merihädässä; ~ _ed_ ahdingossa t. hädässä oleva, onneton, ahdistunut, huolestunut; ~ _ed area_ työttömyysalue; ~ _signal_ hätämerkki. **-ing** a. tuskallinen, huolestuttava, ahdistava.

distribut|**e** [dis'tribju(:)t] v. jakaa jaella; levittää. **-ion** [-'bju:ʃn] s. jakaminen, jako, jakelu; jakautuminen, leviäminen. **-ive** [-iv] a. jakelu-. **-or** [-ə] s. jakelija.

district ['distrikt] s. piiri, alue; seutu.

distrust [dis'trʌst] s. epäluottamus; epäluulo; v. epäillä; _I_ ~ _him_ en luota häneen. **-ful** a. epäluuloinen.

disturb [dis'tə:b] v. häiritä; sotkea; saattaa levottomaksi, järkyttää; ~ _ed_ m. häiriytynyt. **-ance** [-əns] s. häiriö, epäjärjestys; ~ _s_ m. levottomuudet, mellakointi.

dis|**union** ['dis'ju:njən] s. ero; hajaannus; eripuraisuus. **-unite** [disju(:)'nait] v. erottaa.

disuse ['dis'ju:s] s.: _fall into_ ~ joutua käytännöstä pois; ~ _d_ [-'ju:zd] käytännöstä jäänyt.

di|**syllabic** ['disi'læbik] a. kaksitavuinen. **-syllable** [di'siləbl] s. kaksitavuinen sana.

ditch [ditʃ] s. oja, kaivanto; v. ojittaa; hylätä, jättää pulaan.

dither ['diðə] v. vapista.

ditto ['ditəu] (lyh. _do._) s. (edellä) mainittu, sama; adv. samoin.

ditty ['diti] s. laulelma, laulu.

diurnal [dai'ə:nl] a. päivä(n)-, vuorokauden, päivän kestävä.

divagate ['daivəgeit] v. harhailla.

divan [di'væn, Am. 'daivæn] s. leposohva.

div|**e** [daiv] v. sukeltaa; syöksyä; s. sukeltaminen, sukellus; syöksy (ilm.); _-ing suit_ sukeltajan puku **-er** [-ə] s. sukeltaja; kuikka.

diverge [dai'və:dʒ] v. mennä eri suuntiin; poiketa, erota. **-nce** [-əns] **-ncy** [-ənsi] s. erisuuntaisuus; erilaisuus. **-nt** [-nt] a. eri suuntiin menevä; poikkeava, erilainen.

divers ['daivə(:)z] a. (vanh. & leik.) usea. **-e** [dai'və:s] a. erilainen, monenlainen. **-ify** [dai'və:sifai] v. tehdä erilaiseksi, vaihdella; _-ified_ monenlainen, vaihteleva, monipuolinen. **-ion** [dai'və:ʃn] s. poiskääntäminen, kiertotie (tietyön aikana); huvitus, hauskutus, ajanviete; harhautusliike (sot.). **-ity** [dai'və:siti]s. eri-, monenlaisuus.

divert [dai'və:t] v. kääntää toisaalle (m. huomio); huvittaa, hauskuttaa; ~ _ing_ hauska.

Dives ['daivi:z] s. rikas mies (raam.).

divest [dai'vest] v. riisua (_of_ jklta jtk).

divide [di'vaid] v. jakaa (_by_ jllak); jakaantua, hajaantua; saattaa

eripuraisiksi; äänestää; s.
vedenjakaja. ~d highway
kaksiajoratainen tie. -nd ['dividend]
s. osinko; jaettava. -r [-ə] s.: ~s
jakoharppi.

divination [divi'neiʃn] s. ennustus.

divine [di'vain] a. jumalallinen,
Jumalan; jumalainen, ihmeen ihana;
s. jumaluusoppinut; v. ennustaa,
aavistaa; ~ service jumalanpalvelus;
water~r kaivonkatsoja.

diving [daiviŋ] s. sukellus; ks. skin- ~.

divin|ing-rod taikavarpu. -ity [di'viniti]
s. jumaluus, jumalolento;
jumalallisuus; Doctor of D ~
teologian tohtori.

divi|sible [di'vizəbl] a. jaollinen. -sion
[di'viʒn] s. jakaminen, jako;
jakolasku; osasto, jaosto; divisioona;
äänestys (jossa äänestäjät jakautuvat
ryhmiin); väliseinä, raja; erimielisyys
(~ of opinion). -sor [di'vaizə] s. jakaja
(mat.).

divorc|e [di'vɔːs] s. avioero; v.: ~ sb.
ottaa ero, erota (jksta); erottaa
(kuv.). -ee [divɔ'sei] s. eronnut
henkilö.

divulge [dai'vʌldʒ] v. ilmaista
(salaisuus).

divvy ['divi] s. sl. osinko.

dixie ['diksi] s. kenttäpata; D~land
Amerikan Etelävaltiot.

dizziness [dizinis] s. huimaus.

dizzy ['dizi] a. huimausta tunteva;
pyörryttävä; v. panna pyörryksiin; I
feel~ päätäni huimaa.

do 1. [duː] did done, v. tehdä,
valmistaa, laittaa; suorittaa (tehtävä);
järjestää, siistiä (huone), kammata
(tukka); toimia, menetellä; kelvata;
riittää; tulla toimeen; menestyä,
voida; sopia; matkustaa, ajaa;
näytellä jnk osaa; katsella (jkn) paikan nähtävyyksiä; petkuttaa; a p u -
verbinä: does he want it? haluaako
hän sitä? he did not go hän ei mennyt;
don't go yet! älä vielä mene! [she plays
beautifully], doesn't she?.. eikö soita-
kin?.. eikö totta? vahvistavana:
I do want to go haluan todella mennä;
do tell me! kerro toki minulle! that will
~ se riittää; I'll make it ~ suoriudun
sillä; that will never ~, that won't ~ se
ei käy päinsä, ei sovi; how do you ~!

hauska tutustua! ~ away with tehdä
loppu jstk, lopettaa; ~ [badly, well]
by kohdella jkta (huonosti, hyvin); ~
for hoitaa jkn taloutta, (sl.) tappaa,
nujertaa; done for hukassa, mennyttä
miestä; ~ in (sl.) tappaa; ~ .. out
puhdistaa; she was done out of her
money häneltä petkutettiin rahat; ~
over korjata; ~ up korjata; panna
(kääröön), panna nutturalle; panna
napittaa; done up lopussa, »kuitti»; ~
a sum (a problem) laskea, ratkaista;
[he is] doing splendidly jaksaa
mainiosti; I could ~ with [a new car]
haluaisin, tarvitsen; ~ without tulla
toimeen ilman; I have done talking
olen lopettanut puhumisen; well done
hyvin tehty; työssä keitetty t.
paistettu; do-gooder (naiivi) idealisti;
do-it-yourself kits askarteluvälineet.

do 2. s. huijaus; kemut, pirskeet.

docil|e ['dousail] a. helposti käsiteltävä
(kasvatettava), säyseä, taipuisa;
opinhaluinen. -ity [də(u)'siliti] s.
myöntyvyys, säyseys; opinhalu.

dock 1. [dɔk] s. hierakka.

dock 2. [dɔk] v. leikata, typistää;
niukentaa; ~-tailed töpöhäntäinen.

dock 3. [dɔk] s. satama-allas, tokka,
(sulku)telakka; syytetyn aitaus
(oikeudessa), syytetyn penkki; v. tulla
telakkaan; telakoida, -itua; dry~
kuiva telakka; floating~ uiva
telakka. **-age** [-idʒ] s. telakkamaksut.
-er [-ə] s. satamatyöläinen.

docket ['dɔkit] s. nimilippu
(asiakirjoissa ym); yhteenveto; v.
varustaa nimilipulla, tehdä
(asiakirjaan) merkintä sisällyksestä.

doctor ['dɔktə] s. tohtori; lääkäri; v.
hoitaa (sairasta), tohtoroida;
sekoittaa, väärentää. **-al** [-(ə)rəl] a.
tohtorin-. **-ate** [-(ə)rit] s.
tohtorinarvo.

doctri|naire [dɔktri'nɛə] a.
teoreettinen. **-nal** [dɔk'trainl, Am.
'dɔktrinl] a. oppijärjestelmän
mukainen; oppi-.

doctrine ['dɔktrin] s. oppi;
oppijärjestelmä.

document ['dɔkjumənt] s. asiakirja;
todistuskappale; v. [-ment] todistaa,
vahvistaa (asiakirjalla); [well] ~ed
dokumentoitu. **-ary** [-'ment(ə)ri] a.

asiakirjan luonteinen; ~ *film*
dokumenttielokuva. **-ation** [-'eiʃn] s.
todistaminen.
dodder 1. ['dɔdə] s. humalavieras.
dodder 2. ['dɔdə] v. tutista. **-ing, -y** [-ri]
a. tutiseva.
dodge [dɔdʒ] v. hypähtää syrjään,
puikahtaa; väistää sivuun, välttää;
metkuilla, juonitella; s. hypähdys
syrjään; juoni, metku; laite; *tax~er*
veronkiertäjä.
dodgem ['dɔdʒəm] s. (väistämään
pyrkivä) sähköauto (huvipuistossa).
dodgy ['dɔdʒi] a. ovela; vaarallinen,
uhka-.
doe [dəu] s. kuusipeuranaaras;
naarasjänis ym.
do|er ['du:ə] s. tekijä. **-es** [dʌz] ind.
prees. 3. p. ks. do. **-esn't** ['dʌznt] =
does not. **-eth** ['du(:)iθ] = does
(vanh.).
doff [dɔf] v. riisua yltään.
dog [dɔg] s. koira; koiras (~-fox,
~-wolf); roisto; pl. ratateline
(tulisijassa); v. seurata kintereillä (m.
~ sb.'s steps); lucky ~ onnen poika;
sly ~ viekas veijari; be top ~ olla
käskijänä, olla »niskan päällä»; go to
the ~s joutua turmioon; lead sb. a ~'s
life tehdä jklle elämä
sietämättömäksi; a ~ fight (m.)
ilmataistelu; ~ paddle koiranuinti; the
~s (puhek.) vinttikoirakilpailut.
~-biscuit koiranleipä. **~-cart** kevyet
kaksipyöräiset rattaat. **~-days**
mätäkuu. **~-eared** (book)
koirankorvilla (oleva). **-ged** [-id] a.
sitkeä, itsepäinen.
doge [dəuʒ] s. doge (hist.)
doggerel ['dɔg(ə)r(ə)l] s. kalikkasäe.
dogma ['dɔgmə] s. uskonkappale,
dogmi. **-tic** [dɔg'mætik] a. dogmeja
koskeva, dogmaattinen, ylen varma,
käskevä. **-tics** [dɔg'mætiks] s.
dogmatiikka. **-tist** [-tist] s.
dogmaatikko.
dog|-rose koiranruusu. **~-violet**
aho-orvokki. **~-watch** koiranvahti
(mer.). **-wood** pensaskanukka.
doily ['dɔili] s. (pieni) alusliina.
doing ['du(:)iŋ] s. (tav. pl.) teko, toimi;
asiat; [it is all] his ~ hänen työtään;
there is nothing ~ (kaupankäynti) on
hiljaista; [Can you lend me £1?] —

Nothing ~. En voi.
doldrums ['dɔldrəmz] s. tyven vyöhyke
päiväntasaajan seuduilla;
alakuloisuus, lamakausi.
dole 1. [dəul] s. almu; the ~
työttömyysavustus; v. (tav. ~ out)
jakaa, jaella (säästeliäästi).
doleful ['dəulf(u)l] a. surkea,
surullinen.
doll [dɔl] s. nukke; tyttö, pimu,
hepsankeikka; ~'s house
nukkekaappi; ~ed up parhaissa
hepenissään.
dollar ['dɔlə] s. dollari.
dollop ['dɔləp] s. möykky.
dolly ['dɔli] s. nukke; siirtoalusta,
(esim. kamera)vaunu.
dol|orous ['dɔlərəs] s. tuskallinen,
surullinen. **-our, -or** ['dɔlə, dəu-] s.
suru, murhe.
dolphin ['dɔlfin] s. delfiini.
dolt [dəult] s. tomppeli. **-ish** [-iʃ] a.
paksupäinen, tyhmä.
domain [də'mein] s. maatila, tilus; ala,
piiri.
dome [dəum] s. kupukatto, kupoli; ~d
kaareutuva, kupera.
domesday ['du:mzdei] s.: D ~ Book
Englannin maakirja (v:lta 1086).
domestic [də'mestik] a. kodin-, koti-,
perhe-, talous-; kotoinen, kotirakas;
kotimainen; s. palvelija; ~ animals
kotieläimet; ~ help kotiapulainen; ~
policy sisäpolitiikka. **-ate** [-eit] v.
totuttaa kotielämään, kesyttää
(eläin); ~d kotona viihtyvä; kesy. **-ity**
[dəumes'tisiti] s. kotoisuus,
kotielämä, perhe-elämä.
domicil|e ['dɔmisail] s. kotipaikka; v.
asettaa asumaan; domisilioida,
kodittaa (vekseli); ~d (at, in jssk)
asuva. **-iary** [-'siljəri] a.: ~ visit
kotitarkastus; kotikäynti.
dominan|ce ['dɔminəns]s. herruus,
valta-asema. **-t** [-ənt] a. hallitseva,
vallitseva, dominantti.
domin|ate ['dɔmineit] v. hallita, kohota
(jnk) yli. **-ation** [-'neiʃn] s. herruus,
(yli)valta. **-eer** [-'niə] v. pyrkiä
hallitsemaan, tyrannisoida; ~ing
käskevä, hallitseva. **-ican**
[də'minikən] erisn. & s.
dominikaani(munkki).
dominion [də'minjən] s. yliherruus,

valta; dominio.
domino ['dɔminəu] *s.* domino(puku);
~*es*, ~*s* dominopeli.
don 1. [dɔn] *s.* yliopiston opettaja.
don 2. [dɔn] *v.* panna ylleen,
sonnustautua jhk.
dona|te [də(u)'neit] *v.* lahjoittaa. **-tion**
[-'neiʃn] *s.* lahja, lahjoitus;
(veren)luovutus.
done [dʌn] *pp.* ks. *do;* valmis; [*is the
meat*] ~ kypsä; ~ *in* uupunut,
»kuitti».
Don Juan [dɔn 'dʒu(:)ən] *erisn.*
donkey ['dɔŋki] *s.* aasi. ~**-engine** *s.*
apukone (laivassa).
donnish ['dɔniʃ] *a.* täsmällinen,
turhantarkka.
donor ['dəunə] *s.* lahjoittaja; *blood* ~
verenluovuttaja.
don't [dəunt] *lyh.* = *do not; you* ~ *say
so* eihän toki.
Don Quixote [dɔn 'kwiksəut] *erisn.*
doodle ['du:dl] *v.* piirrellä.
doom [du:m] *s.* tuomio, kohtalo, tuho;
v. (vanh.) tuomita; *the crack of* ~
tuomiopäivä. **-ed** [-d] *a.* tuomittu.
-sday tuomiopäivä; vrt. *Domesday.*
door [dɔ:] *s.* ovi; portti, sisäänkäytävä;
front ~ pääovi; *next* ~ viereisessä
talossa; *lay a th. at sb.'s* ~ sanoa jtk
jkn syyksi; *out of* ~*s* ulkosalla.
~**-keeper** ovenvartija. ~**-man**
vahtimestari. ~**-mat** kynnysmatto.
~**-nail:** *dead as a d.-n.* kuollut kuin
kivi. ~**-plate** nimilaatta. ~**-step**
(ulko)porras; kynnys. ~**-way** oviaukko,
porttikäytävä.
dope [dəup] *s.* eräänl. lakka t. rasva;
huumausaine, huume; vihje
(kilpahevosen voiton
mahdollisuuksista); *v.* antaa
huumausainetta, huumata (hevonen
ym); *doping* (urh.) huumausaineen
käyttö kilpailussa. **-(e)y** [-i] *a.* tylsä,
(kuin) huumattu.
Doric ['dɔrik] *a. & s.* doorilainen
(murre).
dorm|ancy ['dɔ:mənsi] *s.* unitila. **-ant**
[-ənt] *a.* horrostilassa oleva; uinuva;
käyttämätön. **-er** [-ə] *s.* (us. ~*-
window*) vinokaton pystyikkuna.
-itory [-itri] *s.* makuusali; Am.
(yliopp.ilas)asuntola; ~
accommodation yhteismajoitus; ~

town nukkumalähiö.
dormouse ['dɔ:maus] *s.* (pl. *-mice*)
pähkinähiiri.
Dorothy ['dɔrəθi] *erisn.*
dorsal ['dɔ:s(ə)l] *a.* selkä-.
dory ['dɔ:ri] *s.* (us. *John*~)
pietarinkala; eräänl. tasapohjainen
vene.
dosage ['dəusidʒ] *s.* annostus.
dose [dəus] *s.* annos; *v.* annostaa, antaa
lääkeannos, lääkitä; ~ *out* jaella.
doss [dɔs] *v. sl.* nukkua. **-er** [-ə] *s.*
yömajan asukki. ~**-house** yömaja.
dossier ['dɔsiei] *s.* (jtk koskevat)
asiakirjat.
dost [dʌst] *prees. sg. 2. p.* (vanh.)
dot [dɔt] *s.* pilkku, piste; *v.* pilkuttaa,
täplittää, panna (i-, j-) pilkku;
sirotella; ~ *ted line* pisteviiva.
do|tage ['dəutidʒ] *s.*
vanhuudenhöperyys; *he is in
his* ~ hän on tullut uudelleen
lapseksi. **-tard** ['dəutəd] *s.*
vanha höperö.
dote [dəut] *v.:* ~ *upon* olla
silmittömästi ihastunut jhk, palvoa
jtk; *doting* hullaantunut.
doth [dʌθ, dəθ] *prees. sg. 3. p.* (vanh.)
ks. *do.*
dotty ['dɔti] *a.* (puhek.) hassahtava,
hassahtanut.
double ['dʌbl] *a.* kaksinkertainen,
kaksois-; kaksimielinen; (kukasta)
kerrottu; *adv.* kaksin kerroin, kaksin
verroin; *s.* kaksinkertainen määrä;
kaksoisolento; kaksoiskappale;
äkkikäännös, (joen) jyrkkä polvi;
nelinpeli; *v.* kaksinkertaistaa,
kaksinkertaistua; kääntää t. taittaa
kaksinkerroin (us. ~ *up)*; tehdä
äkkikäännös (~ *back);* purjehtia
(jnk) ohitse; rientää pikamarssia; ~
dealing kaksinaamainen peli; ~ *entry*
kaksinkertainen (kirjanpito); ~ *room*
kahden hengen huone; *at the* ~
juoksumarssi(ssa)a; ~ *one's fist*
puristaa kätensä nyrkkiin; ~ [*oneself*]
up käpertyä kokoon, koukistaa
polvet. ~**-barrelled** *a.*
kaksipiippuinen. ~**-bass** kontrabasso.
~**-breasted** kaksirivinen. ~**-cross**
petkuttaa. ~**-dealer** petkuttaja,
kaksinaamainen henkilö. ~**-decker**
kaksikerroksinen bussi ym. ~**-edged**

doub 138

kaksiteräinen. ~-**faced**
kaksinaamainen. ~-**quick**
pikamarssia. ~-**talk** vilppipuhe,
kaksimielisyys.

doublet ['dʌblit] s. (miehen) tiukka
pusero, röijy (v. 1400–1600);
(sana)dubletti.

doubly ['dʌbli] adv. kaksin verroin.

doubt [daut] s. epäilys; epäröinti; v.
epäillä; olla epävarma; no ~
epäilemättä, aivan varmasti (m.
beyond ~); in ~ epävarma,
ratkaisematon; give sb. the benefit of
the ~ jättää tuomitsematta
todisteitten puuttuessa. -**ful** a.
epäilevä; epäilyttävä, kyseenalainen;
epävarma, epäröivä. -**less** adv.
epäilemättä.

douche [du:ʃ] s. suihku; huuhtelu; v.
antaa t. ottaa suihku; huuhdella.

dough [dou] s. taikina; sl. raha. -**nut**
munkkirinkilä, donitsi. -**y** [-i] a.
taikinainen.

doughty ['dauti] a. uljas.

Douglas ['dʌgləs] erisn.

dour [duə] a. kova, taipumaton.

douse, dowse [daus] v. valella vedellä;
pudota veteen; sammuttaa.

dove [dʌv] s. kyyhkynen. -**cote** s.
kyyhkyslakka. -**tail** s. sinkkaus; v.
sinkata.

Dover ['douvə] erisn.

dowager ['dauidʒə] s. (ylhäinen)
leskirouva; ~ duchess leskihertuatar.

dowdy ['daudi] a. & s. huonosti
pukeutunut (nainen);
vanhanaikainen, epäsiisti.

dowel ['dauəl] s. vaarna.

dower ['dauə] s. leskenosa
(omaisuudesta); myötäjäiset;
(luonnon) lahja; v. varustaa jllak
(with).

down 1. [daun] s. kumpuileva
kangasmaa; = dune; the D~s
Etelä-Englannin liitukiviylängöt.

down 2. [daun] s. untuva.

down 3. [daun] adv. alhaalla, alas,
alaspäin; pois pääkaupungista t.
yliopistosta; prep. alas; a. alaspäin
suunnattu; v. heittää, iskeä, pudottaa
maahan; tyhjentää; s.: up and ~
edestakaisin; ups and ~s myötä- ja
vastoinkäymiset; calm ~ tyyntyä; go
~ laskea; upota; grind ~ jauhaa

hienommaksi; knock ~ iskeä maahan;
pay ~ maksaa käteisellä; put (take,
write) ~ merkitä muistiin; be ~ on
kantaa kaunaa; be ~ and out olla
puilla paljailla; come ~ on käydä
kimppuun; is ~ with the flu on
vuoteessa flunssassa; ~ to our time
meidän päiviimme saakka; he lives ~
stream hän asuu alempana
jokivarrella; ~ town
keskikaupungilla, -lle; ~ train
Lontoosta lähtevä t. tuleva juna; ~
tools lopettaa työ, tehdä lakko.
~-**and-outs** pl. ihmishylkiöt, -rauniot.
~-**at-heel** nukkavieru. ~-**cast**
alakuloinen. -**fall** romahdus. -**grade**
alentaa arvossa. ~-**hearted**
masentunut. -**hill** s. rinne; a. viettävä;
adv. mäkeä alas. ~-**payment**
käteismaksu. -**pour** kaatosade. -**right**
suora, suoranainen, mutkaton, selvä;
adv. suoraan, suorastaan. -**stairs**
alakerroksessa, alas portaita. ~-
to-earth käytännöllinen,
realistinen. -**town**: ~ [section] ala- t.
keskikaupunki. -**trodden** poljettu.
-**ward** [-wəd] viettävä, laskeva; adv. =
seur. -**wards** [-wədz] alas(päin).

Downing Street ['dauniŋ stri:t] (kuv.)
Englannin hallitus.

downy ['dauni] a. untuvainen,
untuvanpehmeä; ylänköinen.

dowry ['dauəri] s. myötäjäiset.

dows|e [dauz] v. = douse; etsiä
taikavarvulla. [-ə] s. kaivonkatsoja.

doyen ['dɔiən] s. (diplomaattikunnan)
vanhin.

doze [douz] v. uinahtaa, torkahtaa (us.
~ off); s. torkahdus.

dozen ['dʌzn] s. tusina; ~s of times
kymmeniä kertoja; she talks nineteen
to the ~ hänen suunsa käy kuin
papupata.

drab [dræb] a. likaisenruskea; ikävä,
yksitoikkoinen; s. lutka.

drachm [dræm] s. drakma
(apteekkimitta = 3,89 g;
avoirdupois-paino dram = 1,77 g).

draft [drɑ:ft, Am. dræft] s.
suunnitelma, luonnos; asete, vekseli;
erillis-, täydennysjoukko, Am.
kutsunta; v. hahmotella, luonnostella;
valita, lähettää erilleen; Am. kutsua
(ase)palvelukseen. -**ee** [-'ti:] s. Am.

palvelukseen kutsuttu; ~ *card*
palvelukseenastumismääräys. **-sman**
[-smən] *s.* piirtäjä.

drag [dræg] *v.* laahata, raahata;
naarata; äestää; laahustaa; sujua
huonosti, olla pitkäveteinen; *s.* naara;
äes; pidäke, jarru; ~ *on* venyä, jatkua
jatkumistaan; ~ *out* venyttää
(loppumattomiin); (sl.) *in* ~ miehet
naisten vaatteissa.

draggled ks. *bedraggled.*

dragon ['dræg(ə)n] *s.* lohikäärme.
~-fly sudenkorento.

dragoon [drə'gu:n] *s.* rakuuna.

drain [drein] *v.* laskea, johtaa,
juoksuttaa (*off* pois); kuivattaa,
salaojittaa; ammentaa tyhjiin,
tyhjentää, kuluttaa loppuun; (lääk.)
dreneerata, kanavoida; valua; *s.*
viemäri; salaoja, laskuoja, -putki;
(kuv.) rasitus; (lääk.) dreeni,
laskuputki; kulaus. **-age** [-idʒ] *s.*
kuivattaminen, salaojitus;
viemäri|laitteet, -vesi. **-ing-board**
(astiain) kuivausteline. **~-pipe** *s.*
viemäriputki.

drake [dreik] *s.* urossorsa.

dram [dræm] *s.* ks. *drachm;* kulaus,
ryyppy.

drama ['drɑ:mə] *s.* näytelmä. **-tic**
[drə'mætik] *a.* draamallinen,
dramaattinen. **-tist** ['dræmətist] *s.*
näytelmäkirjailija. **-tize** ['dræmətaiz]
v. dramatisoida.

drank [dræŋk] *imp.* ks. *drink.*

drape [dreip] *v.* verhota; poimutella *s.:*
~ *s* Am. verhot. **-r** [-ə] *s.*
kangaskauppias. **-ry** [-əri] *s.*
kangastavarat; *-ries* verhot,
poimuttelu.

drastic ['dræstik] *a.* drastinen,
voimakkaasti vaikuttava.

drat [dræt] *v.:* ~ *that boy* pahuksen
poika!

draught [drɑ:ft], Am. **draft** *ks.t. s.*
veto; apaja; kulaus; annos; (laivan)
syväys; luonnos (tav. *draft);* *v.*
luonnostella; ~ *s* tammipeli; ~ *beer*
tynnyriolut. **-board** tammilauta.
-sman piirtäjä. **-smanship**
piirustustaito. **-y** [-i] *a.* vetoinen.

draw [drɔ:] *drew drawn, v.* vetää (m.
eteen, alas, esiin ym); vetää
puoleensa, houkutella; laskea

(nestettä astiasta); saada (tietoja),
herättää (huomiota); piirtää,
hahmotella, laatia; nostaa (arpa ym);
vetäytyä; hautua; *s.* veto;
vetonumero; arvonta; ratkaisematon
taistelu t. peli; ~ *a bill on* asettaa
vekseli (jkn) maksettavaksi; ~ *a
conclusion* tehdä johtopäätös; ~ *blood*
aiheuttaa verivamma; ~ *the long bow*
liioitella; ~ *back* vetäytyä taaksepäin;
~ *forth* aiheuttaa; ~ *in* lähestyä
loppuaan, lyhentyä; ~ *near* lähestyä;
~ *off* vetää, viedä pois, laskea
(viiniä); ~ *on* lähestyä; turvautua jhk,
ammentaa jstk; ~ *out* venyttää,
venyä; ~ *sb. out* saada jku lausumaan
mielipiteensä; ~ *up* laatia; asettaa t.
asettua taistelujärjestykseen,
pysähtyä; *is* ~*ing to a close* lähestyy
loppuaan; *a long* ~*n-out story*
pitkäveteinen juttu; *feel* ~ *n to* (m.)
olla taipumusta jhk; *he was not to be*
~ *n* häneltä ei saanut urkkimalla
mitään tietoja. **-back** haitta,
varjopuoli. **-bridge** laskusilta. **-ee**
[drɔ:'i:] *s.* vekselin hyväksyjä.

drawer ['drɔ:ə] *s.* (veto)laatikko;
vekselin asettaja; piirtäjä, vetäjä;
chest of ~ *s* lipasto. **-s** [drɔ:z] *s. pl.*
alushousut.

drawing *s.* piirustus. **~-pin**
piirustusnasta. **~-room** sali.

drawl [drɔ:l] *v.* puhua venytellen; *s.*
venyttelevä puhetapa.

drawn *pp.* ks. *draw;* paljastettu
(miekka); *a face* ~ *with pain* tuskan
vääristämät kasvot.

dray [drei] *s.* (lava)rattaat; ~ *man*
olutkuski.

dread [dred] *v.* pelätä; *s.* suuri pelko;
a. kauhistava. **-ful** *a.* kauhistava,
kauhea. **-nought** [-nɔːt] *s.* eräänl.
taistelulaiva.

dream [dri:m] *s.* uni, unelma, haave; *v.*
imp. & pp. ~*ed t.* ~*t* [dremt] nähdä
unta; uneksia, haaveilla. **-er** *s.*
uneksija. **-y** [-i] *a.* uneksiva, unen
kaltainen.

dreary ['driəri] *a.* synkkä, kolkko,
ikävä (run. m. *drear*).

dredge 1. [dredʒ] *s.* ruoppauskone; *v.*
ruopata. **-r** [-ə] *s.* ruoppaaja.

dredge|e 2. [dredʒ] *v.* jauhottaa,
sirotella. **-ing-box** siroterasia.

dreg 140

dreg [dreg] s.: ~ s pohjasakka (m. kuv.); to the ~ s pohjaan saakka.

drench [dren(t)ʃ] v. kastella läpimäräksi; we were ~ ed kastuimme likomäriksi.

dress [dres] v. pukea, pukeutua (m. iltapukuun); suoristaa, ojentaa (rivi); somistaa, koristaa; sitoa (haava); valmistaa, viimeistellä, muokata (nahka), hakata (kivi); kammata, järjestää, sukia, puhdistaa, leikata (viiniköynnös ym); valmistaa salaatti(kastike); s. puku, vaatetus; leninki, mekko; ~ down läksyttää; ~ up pukea t. pukeutua hienoksi (t. naamiopukuun); ~ circle ensi parvi (teatt.); ~ a coat frakki; ~ rehearsal kenraaliharjoitus; ~ shirt frakkipaita; in full ~ juhlapuvussa; evening ~ iltapuku. -er [-ə] s. pukija, valmistaja jne.; kirurgin apulainen; (ikkunan) somistaja, keittiönpöytä t. -kaappi; Am. pukeutumispöytä.

dressing s. pukeminen; ojennus; valmistaminen, muokkaaminen jne.; haavaside, sidonta; kastike, täyte (keitt.); korvike; ~ down läksytys. ~-case pieni laukku (pukeutumistarvikkeita varten). ~-gown aamutakki.

dress|maker ompelija. ~-shields kainalolaput.

dressy ['dresi] a. keikarimainen; tyylikäs, hieno.

drew [dru:] imp. ks. draw.

drib|ble ['dribl] v. tippua, tiputtaa; kuolata; pujotella (jalkap.). -let [-it] s.: in ~ s vähän kerrallaan. -s: [in] ~ and drabs = ed.

dri|ed [draid] imp. & pp. ks. dry; kuivattu. -er ['draiə] s. kuivaaja, kuivausaine.

drift [drift] s. ajelehtiminen, tuuliajo; veden t. tuulen ajama massa, lumi-, hiekkanietos; (ajatuksien) suunta; kulku; tarkoitus; v. ajelehtia; ajautua, ajaa; kasata t. kasautua nietoksiin; ~ from the land maaltapako. -er [-ə] ajoverkkoalus; vetelehtijä. ~-ice ajojää. ~-net ajoverkko.

drill [dril] v. porata, kairata; harjoittaa (sotilaita), kouluttaa, harjoitella; kylvää (riviin); s. pora, kaira; (et. ase-, marssi)harjoitus; rivikylvökone,

kylvövako.

drill(ing) s. drelli(kangas), reivas.

drily adv. kuivasti.

drink [driŋk] drank drunk, v. juoda; imeä (itseensä), nauttia täysin siemauksin jstk (tav. ~ in); s. juoma, ryyppy, väkijuomat; juopottelu; ~ to a p.'s health juoda jkn malja; be the worse for ~ olla humalassa. -able [-əbl] a. juotava. -er [-ə] s.: [hard t. heavy] ~ juoppo. -ing-bout juomakausi, -kierre. -ing-fountain s. juomalaite (koulussa ym).

drip [drip] v. tippua, tihkua; tiputtaa; s. tiputus, räystäsvuoto; ~ grind suodatinjauhatus; ~-ping wet likomärkä. ~-moulding, ~-stone vesilista. -ping paistinrasva.

drive [draiv] drove driven, v. ajaa (autoa ym; m. matkustajana), ohjata, kuljettaa; panna liikkeelle, käyttää; iskeä, lyödä (into jhk); saattaa, pakottaa jhk; ajelehtia, kiitää, (sateesta) piestä; puhkaista, kaivaa (tunneli); s. ajelu, ajo; ajotie; tarmo, puhti; rynnistys, kampanja; vietti; ~ at tähdätä, pyrkiä jhk; what is he driving at? mihin hän pyrkii? let ~ at tähdätä isku jkh; ~ sb. to despair saattaa epätoivoon; an hour's ~ tunnin ajo; I took her for a ~ vein hänet ajelulle; ~-in bank autopankki; ~-on ferry autolautta.

drivel ['drivl]v. puhua älyttömästi; s. hölynpöly.

driv|en ['drivn] pp. ks. drive; steam-~ höyrykäyttöinen; hard ~ työn rasittama. -er ['draivə] s. ajaja, kuljettaja. -ing s. (auton) ajo; ~ licence ajokortti; ~ rain sademyrsky, kaatosade; ~ test ajokoe; ~-wheel käyttöpyörä.

drizzle ['drizl] v. (sateesta) tihuttaa; s. tihkusade.

droll [drəul] a. hullunkurinen, lystikäs. -ery [-əri] s. hassutus.

dromedary ['drʌmədə)ri] s. dromedaari.

drone [drəun] s. kuhnuri (el.); laiskuri; surina; v. surista; mumista.

drool [dru:l] s. pöty; v. kuolata.

droop [dru:p] v. vaipua, painua, olla painuksissa t. riipuksissa; alkaa kuihtua, nuokkua; riutua; s.

riipuksissa olo, nuokkuminen. **-ing** *a.*
riipuksissa oleva; alakuloinen.
drop [drɔp] *s.* pisara, tippa; *pl.* tipat;
karamelli; (korva- ym) kellutin;
putoaminen, lasku; väliverho; *v.*
tippua, tiputtaa; pudota, pudottaa;
laskea; raueta, jäädä t. jättää sikseen;
jättää pois, jättää jhk; lausua
(ohimennen); hylätä (tapa ym);
vaipua maahan; tyyntyä; lakata;
poikia; *by* (t. *in*) ~*s* tipoittain; *he
~ped me a hint* hän vihjaisi minulle
ohimennen; ~ *away* jäädä, »tippua»
pois; ~ *behind* jäädä jälkeen; ~ *in*
pistäytyä tervehtimässä; ~ *off*
nukahtaa; vähetä; ~ *out* keskeyttää,
jäädä pois (jstk); ~ *through* raueta; ~
me a line! kirjoita minulle rivi tai pari;
let .. ~ antaa raueta; *ready to ~*
lopen uupunut. **~-curtain** väliverho.
~-out koulun (ym) keskeyttänyt,
yhteiskunnasta sivulle luisunut.
~-shutter pikasuljin (valok.). **-pings**
s. pl. (kynttilän) tali, (lintujen ym)
lanta.
dropsy [ˈdrɔpsi] *s.* vesipöhö.
droshky [ˈdrɔʃki] *s.* ajurinrattaat,
»vossikka».
dross [drɔs] *s.* kuona. **-y** [-i] *a.*
epäpuhdas, kuonainen.
drought [draut] *s.* (pitkäaikainen)
kuivuus.
drove 1. [drəuv] *imp.* ks. *drive.*
drove 1. [drəuv] *s.* karjalauma, lauma.
-r [-ə] *s.* karjanajaja.
drown [draun] *v.* hukkua; hukuttaa,
tulvia jnk yli, voittaa (äänellään); *be
~ed* hukkua.
drows|e [drauz] *v.* torkkua, olla
puolinukuksissa. **-y** [-i] *a.* unelias,
uninen; unettava.
drub [drʌb] *v.* piestä. **-bing** *s.*
selkäsauna.
drudg|e [drʌdʒ] *v.* raataa; *s.* raataja,
orja. **-ery** [-(ə)ri] *s.* orjatyö; raadanta.
drug [drʌg] *s.* lääkeaine; huumausaine,
huume; *v.* sekoittaa huumausaineita
(jhk); antaa jklle t. käyttää
huumausaineita; ~ *abuser (addict)*
huumeiden käyttäjä; *the ~ habit*
huumausaineiden käyttö; *a ~ on the
market* vaikeasti myytävä tavara. **-get**
[-it] *s.* lattianpeitehuopa. **-gist** [-ist] *s.*
rohdoskauppias; apteekkari. **-store**

kemikaalikauppa
(jäätelöbaareineen).
Druid [ˈdru(:)id] *s.* druidi.
drum [drʌm] *s.* rumpu; (öljy)tynnyri;
(*ear-~*) tärykalvo; *v.* rummuttaa.
-head: ~ *court martial* kenttäoikeus.
~ **major**, **~-majorette** rumpali. **-mer**
[-ə] *s.* rummunlyöjä; Am.
kauppamatkustaja. **-stick**
rumpupalikka.
drunk [drʌŋk] *pp.* ks. *drink; a.*
humaltunut, humalassa; *s.* juopunut;
get ~ juoda itsensä (t. tulla)
humalaan. **-ard** [-əd] *s.* juoppo. **-en**
[-(ə)n] *a.* humalainen; ~ *driver
(driving)* rattijuoppo(-us). **-enness** *s.*
juoppous; humala.
dry [drai] *a.* kuiva, kuivettunut; ikävä;
(puhek.) janoinen, kieltolaki- (maa
ym); *v.* kuivata, kuivettaa, kuivua,
kuivettua ~ *goods* Am. kangastavara;
~ *measure* kuivan tavaran mitta; *run
~* kuivua; ~ *up* kuivua, ehtyä; ~ *up!*
suu kiinni!
dryad [ˈdraiəd] *s.* metsänneito.
dry|-clean pestä kemiallisesti.
~-cleaning kuivapesu. **~-dock**
kuivatelakka. **-er** [-ə] *s.* kuivauslaite;
spin ~ pyykkilinko. **~-point**
radeeraus(neula). **~-rot** kuivalaho.
-shod *adv.* kuivin jaloin.
dual [ˈdju(:)əl] *a.* kaksinkertainen,
kaksois-; ks. *carriageway.* **-ity**
[dju:ˈæliti] *s.* kaksinaisuus.
dub [dʌb] *v.* lyödä ritariksi, nimittää;
jälkiäänittää (toiselle kielelle, elok.).
dubiety [dju(:)ˈbaiəti] *s.* epätietoisuus.
dubious [ˈdju:bjəs] *a.* epäilyttävä,
epäiltävä; epävarma; epäilevä.
Dublin [ˈdʌblin] *erisn.*
ducal [ˈdju:k(ə)l] *a.* herttuallinen.
ducat [ˈdʌkət] *s.* dukaatti.
duchess [ˈdʌtʃis] *s.* herttuatar.
duchy [ˈdʌtʃi] *s.* herttuakunta.
duck 1. [dʌk] *s.* sorsa, (naaras)ankka;
kullanmuru; *play ~s and drakes*
heittää voileipiä; *play ~s and drakes
with* [*one's money*] tuhlata; ~ *'s egg*
nolla pistettä (krik.); *Donald D~*
Aku Ankka.
duck 2. [dʌk] *v.* sukeltaa nopeasti;
kumartua (nopeasti), nyykäyttää
(päätään), väistää, työntää (hetkeksi)
veden alle.

duck 3. [dʌk] *s.* luja pellava t. purjekangas; ~ svalkoiset(pellava)housut.
duck|ling [ˈdʌkliŋ] *s.* ankanpoikanen.
-y [ˈdʌki] *s.* kullanmuru, tipu.
duct [dʌkt] *s.* johto; kanava, tiehyt. **-ile**
[-ail] *a.* venyvä. **-less** *a.:* ~ *glands*
umpirauhaset.
dud [dʌd] *s.* räjähtämätön ammus,
»suutari»; epäonnistunut suunnitelma
ym; katteeton (šekki); ~ *s* ryysyt.
dude [djuːd] *s.* Am. keikari.
dudgeon [ˈdʌdʒn] *s.:* *in high* ~ vihan
vimmoissaan.
due [djuː] *a.* jklle tuleva t. kuuluva
asianmukainen, oikea; maksettavaksi
langennut, erääntyvä: *s.* jklle kuuluva
(maksu ym); [*give the man*] *his* ~ se,
mitä hänelle kuuluu; ~ *s* maksut; *be* ~
to johtua, aiheutua jstk; [*it*] *was* ~ *to*
carelessness johtui
huolimattomuudesta; ~ *to* (Am.) jnk
johdosta, takia; *the train is* ~ *at 7*
junan on määrä saapua kello 7; *fall*
(*become*) ~ erääntyä; *in* ~ *course*
asianmukaisessa järjestyksessä; *in* ~
time oikeaan aikaan; aikanaan.
duel [ˈdjuː(ə)l] *s.* kaksintaistelu; *v.* olla
kaksintaistelussa. **-list** [-ist] *s.*
kaksintaistelija.
duet [djuː(ː)ˈet] *s.* duetto.
duff [dʌf] *s.* taikina; eräänl. vanukas.
duffel, duffle [ˈdʌf(ə)l] *s.:* ~ *coat*
doffelitakki.
duffer [ˈdʌ fə] *s.* pölkkypää.
dug 1. [dʌg] *s.* nisä, utare.
dug 2. [dʌg] *imp.* ks. *dig.* **-out** korsu,
maanlainen suoja.
duke [djuːk] *s.* herttua. **-dom** herttuan
arvo; = *duchy.*
dulc|et [ˈdʌlsit] *a.* suloinen,
viihdyttävä. **-imer** [-imə] *s.* symbaali.
dull [dʌl] *a.* heikkolahjainen,
hidasjärkinen; tylppä, tylsä; ikävä;
himmeä; pilvinen; kumea; heikko,
huono; *v.* tylsyttää. **-ard** [-əd] *s.*
tylsimys. **-ness** *s.* hitaus, tylsyys;
pitkäveteisyys.
duly [ˈdjuːli] *adv.* asianmukaisesti.
dumb [dʌm] *a.* mykkä; äänetön; ~
show pantomiimi; *strike* ~ mykistää.
-bell käsipaino. **-found** [-ˈfaund]
mykistää: [*he*] *was* ~ *ed* tuli
sanattomaksi ~ **-waiter** tarjoilupöytä;
Am. ruokahissi.

dummy [ˈdʌmi] *s.* sovitusnukke (*tailor's*
~), mainosnukke; lepääjä (korttip.);
esine, joka ei ole sitä miltä näyttää; *a.*
vale-, harjoitus-; [*baby's*] ~ *tutti;* ~
cartridge harjoituspatruuna.
dump [dʌmp] *v.* kaataa, pudottaa
(jysähtäen); myydä polkuhintaan; *s.*
kaatopaikka; (tilapäinen)
varastopaikka; alakuloisuus; *in the* ~ *s*
alakuloinen. **-er** [-ə] *s.* kieppiauto.
-ing *s.* polkumyynti. **-y** [-i] *a.* lyhyt ja
paksu.
dun 1. [dʌn] *a.* harmaanruskea.
dun 2. [dʌn] *s.* karhu, kiusallinen
velkoja; *v.* karhuta.
dunce [dʌns] *s.* pölkkypää, aasi.
dunderhead [ˈdʌndəhed] *s.* pölkkypää.
dune [djuːn] *s.* hiekkakinos, dyyni
dung [dʌŋ] *s.* lanta; *v.* lannoittaa. **-hill**
tunkio.
dungaress [dʌŋgəˈriːz] *s. pl.* suojapuku,
haalari(t), farkut.
dungeon [ˈdʌn(d)ʒn] *s.* (maanalainen)
vankityrmä.
dunk [dʌŋk] *v.* kastaa (leipää).
Dunkirk [dʌnˈkɔːk] *erisn.* Dunkerque.
duodenum [djuː(ː)əʊ(u)ˈdiːnəm] *s.*
pohjukaissuoli.
dupe [djuːp] *v.* petkuttaa, huiputtaa; *s.*
narri, houkkio. **-ry** [-əri] *s.* petkutus.
duplex [ˈdjuːpleks, Am. ˈduːp-] *a.*
kaksiosainen, kaksois-; ~ *apartment*
kaksikerroksinen (esim. rivitalo)
huoneisto.
dupli|cate [ˈdjuːplikit] *a.* kaksois-; *s.*
kaksoiskappale; *v.* [-ikeit] monistaa;
in ~ kahtena kappaleena. **-cator**
[-keitə] *s.* monistuskone. **-city**
[djuː(ː)ˈplisiti] *s.* petollisuus.
durability [djuərəˈbiliti] *s.* kestävyys.
durable [ˈdjuərəbl] *a.* kestävä; ~ *s*
(= ~ *consumer goods*)
kestohyödykkeet.
durence [ˈdjuər(ə)ns] *s.* (vanh.)
vankeus.
duration [djuˈ(ə)ˈreiʃn] *s.* kestäminen,
aika; *of long* ~ pitkäaikainen; *for the*
~ (sodan) ajaksi.
durbar [ˈdɔːbɑː] *s.* (Intiassa) ruhtinaan
vastaanotto.
duress(e) [djuˈ(ə)ˈres] *s.* vankeus;
pakkokeino.
Durham [ˈdʌrəm] *erisn.*
during [ˈdjuəriŋ] *prep.* aikana,

kuluessa; ~ *the day* päiväsaikaan; ~ *my absence* poissaollessani.

durst [dəːst] *imp.* ks. *dare.*

dusk [dʌsk] *s.* hämärä. **-y** [-i] *a.* hämärä, tumma.

dust [dʌst] *s.* tomu, pöly; siitepöly *s.* raha; *v.* tomuttaa, pyyhkiä pölyä; sirotella; *bite the* ~ kaatua (t. haavoittua); *kick up a* ~ nostaa meteli; *throw* ~ *in sb.'s eyes* pimittää jkn silmät. **-bin** roskapönttö. **~-bowl** tomumyrskyalue (et. Am. preeria-alueella). **~-cover,** **~-jacket** (kirjan) suojuspaperi. **-er** [-ə] *s.* pölyriepu, -huisku; sirotin. **-ing** *s.* tomuttaminen; selkäsauna. **-man** roskakuski. **-pan** *s.* rikkalapio. **-y** [-i] *a.* tomuinen.

Dutch [dʌtʃ] *a.* hollantilainen; *s.* hollantin kieli; *the* ~ hollantilaiset; ~ *treat* nyyttikestit. **-man** *s.* hollantilainen. **-woman** hollannitar.

duteous [ˈdjuːtjəs] *a.* = *dutiful.*

duti|able [ˈdjuːtjəbl] *a.* tullinalainen. **-ful** *a.* velvollisuudentuntoinen, kuuliainen.

duty [ˈdjuːti] *s.* velvollisuus; palvelus; virantoimitus, tehtävä; maksu, tulli; *stamp* ~ leimavero; *be on* ~ päivystää; olla virantoimituksessa; *off* ~ palveluksesta vapaana; *estate* ~ perintövero; *I was in* ~ *bound*..

tunsin velvollisuudekseni.. **~-free** tulliton, tullivapaa(sti).

dwarf [dwɔːf] *s.* kääpiö; *v.* estää (jkn) kasvu; tehdä kääpiömäiseksi. **-ish** [-iʃ] *a.* kääpiömäinen.

dwell [dwel] *dwelt dwelt, v.* oleskella, oleilla, asua; ~ *on,* ~ *upon* viipyä jssk, puhua jstk laveasti. **-er** [-ə] *s.* asukas. **-ing** *s.* asunto. **-ing-house** asuintalo.

dwindle [ˈdwindl] *v.* huveta, kutistua.

dye [dai] *v.* värjätä; värjäytyä; *s.* väri; (kuv.) laji; ~*d-in-the-wool* (kuv.) läpeensä aito; piintynyt. **-ing** *s.* värjäys. **-r** [-ə] *s.* värjäri. **~-stuff** väriaine. **~-works** värjäämö.

dying [ˈdaiiŋ] *a.* kuoleva, kuolin-; ~ *wish* viimeinen toivomus; *I'm* ~ *to know*.. haluaisin välttämättä tietää..

dyke [daik] *s.* pato, valli; ks. *dike.*

dynam|ic [daiˈnæmik] *a.* dynaaminen. **-ics** [-s] *s.* dynamiitti; *v.* räjäyttää dynamiitilla. **-iter** [ˈdainəmaitə] *s.* dynamiittisankari. **-o** [ˈdainəməu] *s.* dynamo (pl. ~s).

dynasty [ˈdinəsti] *s.* hallitsijasuku.

dysentery [ˈdisntri] *s.* punatauti.

dyspep|sia [disˈpepsiə] *s.* ruoansulatushäiriö. **-tic** [-tik] *a.* huonovatsainen.

dyspn(o)ea [ˈdispniə, -ˈniːə] *s.* hengenahdistus.

E

E, e [iː] e-kirjain; sävel, nuotti e.
Lyh.: **E** *east;* **Ebor.** *of York;* **E.C.**
East Central (London Postal District);
EEC *European Economic Community*
Euroopan talousyhteisö; **Ed.** *Editor;*
EFTA *European Free Trade*
Assosiation; **e. g.** *(exempli gratia)*
esim.; **E.R** *Elizabeth Regina*
kuningatar E.; **ESP** *extra-sensory*
perception; **Esq.** *Esquire* herra; **etc.** *et*
cetera ym, jne; **et seq.** ynnä seuraava;
exam. *examination;* **E. & O. E.** *errors*
and omissions excepted pidätetään
oikeus korjata virheet ja
poisjäämiset; **Exod.** *Exodus.*

each [iːtʃ] *pron.* kukin, kumpikin; ~
other toisiaan, toinen toistaan; *they*
cost a penny ~ ne maksavat pennyn
kappale; *give them one* ~ anna
kullekin yksi!

eager [ˈiːgə] *a.* innokas, innostunut;
kärkäs, halukas, hanakka;
kärsimätön; kiihkeä; ~ *to learn*
opinhaluinen. **-ness** *s.* into, innostus.

eagle [ˈiːgl] *s.* kotka. **~-eyed**
kotkansilmäinen. **-t** [-it] *s.*
kotkanpoika.

ear 1. [iə] *s.* tähkä.

ear 2. [iə] *s.* korva; *be all* ~ *s* olla
pelkkänä korvana; *a good* ~ *[for*
pitch] tarkka sävelkorva; *[play] by* ~
korvakuulon mukaan; *up to the* ~ *s in*
work kovin työn rasittama; *over head*
and ~ *s* korvia myöten (velassa).
~-ache [ˈiəreik] korvasärky. **~-drum**
tärykalvo.

earl [əːl] *s.* kreivi, jaarli. **-dom** *s.*
kreivin arvo.

earlier *komp.* aikaisempi; *adv.*
aikaisemmin, aiemmin; ennen.

early [ˈəːli] *a.* aikainen, varhainen;
adv. varhain; ~ *on* varhaisessa
vaiheessa; *an* ~ *bird* aamuvirkku; *as*

~ *as* jo; *at an* ~ *date* piakkoin; *keeps*
~ *hours* menee varhain nukkumaan.

earmark *v.* määrätä, varata jhk
tarkoitukseen. **~-mo(u)ld**
(kuulokojeen) korvaistukka. **~-muffs**
korvaläpät.

earn [əːn] *v.* ansaita; tuottaa, tuoda;
saavuttaa; ~ *ed income* ansiotulo(t).

ernest 1. [ˈəːnist] *a.* vakava, totinen; *s.*
tosi; *in* ~ tosissaan, vakavissaan.

earnest 2. [ˈəːnist] *s.* (m. ~ -*money*)
käsiraha; esimaksu.

earning [ˈəːniŋ] *s.:* ~ *s* ansiot.

ear|phone kuuloke; tav. *pl.*
kuulokkeet. **~-piece** (puhelimen)
kuuloke. **~-ring** korvarengas. **-shot**
kuulomatka.

earth [əːθ] *s.* maa, maailma; maaperä,
multa; maajohto; maakosketus;
(ketun ym) kolo, luola; *v.* kätkeä
maahan, mullata (~ *up);* (sähk.)
maadoittaa; *what on* ~ mitä ihmettä?
how on ~ kuinka kummassa; *run . . . to*
~ seurata (jälkiä) perille asti, löytää.
-en [-n] *a.* multa-, savi-. **-enware** *s.*
saviastiat, keramiikka. **-ly** *a.*
maailmallinen, maallinen; *no* ~ *use* ei
kerrassaan mitään hyötyä; *not an* ~
[chance] ei niin mitään
mahdollisuutta. **~-mover**
maansiirtokone. **-quake** maanjäristys.
-work maavalli, vallitus. **-worm**
kastemato. **-y** *a.* mullankaltainen;
karkea.

ear|trumpet kuulotorvi. **-wig** pihtihäntä
(eläint.).

ease [iːz] *s.* mukavuus, hyvä olo; rauha,
lepo; kevennys, levitys; luontevuus,
helppous; huolettomuus; *v.* lievittää,
keventää; rauhoittaa; höllentää,
löyhätä; (m. ~ *off)* lieventyä;
hellittää; *he was at [his]* ~ hän oli
luonteva, kuin kotonaan; *ill at* ~

levoton, vaivautunut, hämillään;
[*stand*] *at* ~ lepo! *with* ~ helposti.

easel ['i:zl] *s.* maalausteline.

easily ['i:zili] *adv.* helposti; [*this is*] ~
*the best*ilman muuta (ehdottomasti)
paras.

east [i:st] *s.* itä; itämaat; *a.* itäinen, itä-;
adv. itään päin; *the Far E*~ Kaukoitä;
the Middle E~ Lähi-itä (joskus)
Keski-itä; *E*~ Itä-Lontoo; ~ *of us*
itäpuolellamme: *to the* ~ *of* jstk itään,
jnk itäpuolella.

Easter ['i:stə] *s.* pääsiäinen; ~ *Day*
pääsiäispäivä.

east|**erly** ['i:stəli] *a.* itäinen; *adv.* itään,
idästä. **-ern** [-ən] *a.* itäinen;
itämainen; kreikkalaiskatolinen; *s.*
itämaalainen

East'-Indiaman *s.* Itä-Intian(kauppa)-
laiva. ~ **Indies** [-'indiz]*erisn.*Itä-Intia.

eastward(s) [-əd(z)] *adv.* itään (päin).

easy ['i:zi] *a.* helppo; mukava;
levollinen, huoleton; sävyisä; väljä;
vaivaton, luonteva; *adv.* levollisesti,
hiljaa; *s.* lyhyt pysähdys; ~ *chair*
nojatuoli; ~ *circumstances* hyvät olot;
free and ~ *manners* luonteva,
kursailematon käytös; *on* ~ *terms*
edullisin ehdoin; *take it* ~! *go* ~! älä
hätäile! **~-going** mukavuutta
rakastava, huoleton, rento.

eat [i:t] *ate eaten, v.* syödä; kuluttaa,
kalvaa, syöpyä (*into* jhk); ~ *one's
heart out*murehtia salassa; ~ *en up
with pride*pakahtumaisillaan
ylpeydestä. **-able** [-əbl] *a.* syötävä; *s.:*
~ *s*syötävä(t). **-er** [-ə] *s.: a great* ~
suursyömäri; *a poor* ~ vähäruokainen
(ihminen). **-ing-house** ruokapaikka.

eau de Cologne ['əudəkə'ləun] *s.*
kölninvesi.

eaves [i:vz] *s.* räystäs. **-drop** kuunnella
salaa. **-dropper** [-drɔpə]
salakuuntelija.

ebb [eb] *s.* luode, pakoveci;
huononeminen, rappio; *v.* laskea,
vetäytyä (rannalta); heiketä, vähetä
(m. ~ *away*); ~ *and flow* luode ja
vuoksi; *at a low* ~ huonossa tilassa.
-tide *s.* luode.

ebonite ['ebənait] *s.* eboniitti,
kovakumi.

ebony ['ebəni] *s.* eebenpuu.

ebullient [i'bʌljənt] *a.* kuohuva;

ylitsevuotava.

eccentric [ik'sentrik] *a.*
eriskummallinen; epäkeskinen; *s.*
eksentrinen, eriskummallinen
henkilö; epäkesko (mek.). **-ity**
[eksen'trisiti] *s.* eriskummallisuus,
omituinen päähänpisto.

Ecclesiastes [ikli:zi'æsti:z] *s.* Saarnaaja
(raamatun kirja).

ecclesiastic [ikli:zi'æstik] *s.* kirkonmies,
pappi. **-al** [-(ə)l] *a.* kirkollinen;
papillinen.

echelon ['eʃələn] *s.* porrastus, porras
(sot.); [*flying*] *in* ~ muodostelmassa.

echo ['ekəu] *s.* kaiku; *v.* kaikua,
kajahtaa; toistaa, matkia; ~ *-sounder*
kaikuluotain.

éclat ['eiklɑ:] *s.* loisto, loistava
menestys.

eclipse [i'klips] *s.* (taivaankappaleen)
pimennys; himmeneminen; *v.*
pimentää; saattaa varjoon.

ecolog|**ical** [ekə'lɔdʒik(ə)l] *a.*
ekologinen. **-y** [i:'kɔlədʒi] *s.* ekologia.

econom|**ic** [i:kə'nɔmik] *a.* talous-,
taloudellinen; *s.: ~ s* kansantalous,
taloustiede. **-ical** [-(ə)l] *a.*
taloudellinen, säästäväinen. **-ist**
[i(:)'kɔnəmist] *s.* taloustieteilijä; (jnk)
säästeliäs käyttäjä, säästäjä. **-ize**
[i(:)'kɔnəmaiz] *v.* käyttää säästäväisesti; olla säästäväinen, säästää.

economy [i(:)'kɔnəmi] *s.* talous;
taloudellisuus, säästäväisyys; (jnk)
säästeliäs käyttö;
tarkoituksenmukainen järjestely,
rakenne; *domestic* ~ kotitalous;
political ~ kansantalous; ~ *class* l.v.
turistiluokka; *the* ~ *of Finland*
Suomen talous(elämä).

ecsta|**sy** ['ekstəsi] *s.* haltioituminen;
hurmio(tila); ekstaasi. **-tic** [eks'tætik]
a. haltioitunut, hurmioitunut.

Ecuador ['ekwədɔ:] *erisn.*

ecumenical [i:kju'menik(ə)l] *a.*
ekumeeninen, yhteiskirkollinen.

eczema ['eksimə] *s.* ekseema,
ihottuma.

eddy ['edi] *s.* pyörre; *v.* pyöriä,
pyöriä pyrputa.

Eden ['i:dn] *erisn. & s.* Eeden,
paratiisi.

edge [edʒ] *s.* terä, (terävä) reuna;
särmä; raja, reuna, parras; kuv.

terä(vyys), kärki; v. reunustaa; hioa; tunkea; (~ *oneself into* tunkeutua (syrjittäin t. vähitellen jhk); *on* ~ ärtynyt; *set sb.'s teeth on* ~ (kuv.) vihloa, ärsyttää; *have the* ~ *on* olla jkta edullisemmassa asemassa; ~ *one's way* tunkeutua. **-ways, -wise** *adv.* syrjittäin; reunatusten; *not get a word in* ~ jäädä ilman suunvuoroa.

edg|ing s. reuna, reunus. **-y** ['edʒi] a. helposti ärtyvä.

edible ['edibl] a. syötävä.

edict ['i:dikt] s. käskykirja.

edif|ication [edifi'keiʃn] s. mielenylennys. **-ice** ['edifis] s. (komea) rakennus.

edify ['edifai] v. ylentää mieltä.

Edinburgh ['edinb(ə)rə] erisn.

edit ['edit] v. toimittaa painosta; toimittaa (sanomalehteä ym); saattaa painokuntoon; tarkistaa.

Edith ['i:diθ] erisn.

edit|ion [e'diʃn] s. painos. **-or** ['editə] s. toimittaja; julkaisija. **-orial** [edi'tɔ:riəl] a. toimituksen; s. pääkirjoitus.

educat|e ['edjuk|eit] v. kasvattaa; kouluttaa; opettaa. **-ion** [-'keiʃn] s. kasvatus; opetus; koulutus; (koulu)sivistys; *Board of E* ~ kouluhallitus; *general* ~ yleissivistys. **-ional** [-'keiʃənl] a. kasvatus-, kasvatuksellinen; opetus-. **-ionist** [-'keiʃənist] s. kasvatustieteilijä. **-ive** [-ətiv] a. kasvattava. **-or** [-eitə] s. kasvattaja.

educe [i(:)'dju:s] v. vetää esille.

Edward ['edwəd] erisn. **-ian** [ed'wɔ:diən] a. & s. Edward VII:n aikainen.

eel [i:l] s. ankerias.

eer|ie, -y ['iəri] a. kaamea, aavemainen.

efface [i'feis] v. pyyhkiä pois, poistaa; himmentää, saattaa varjoon; ~ *oneself* pysyä syrjässä.

effect [i'fekt] s. vaikutus; teho; *pl.* tavarat, omaisuus; v. saada aikaan, suorittaa; *carry into* ~ panna täytäntöön; *take* ~ astua voimaan; *in* ~ itse asiassa; *with* ~ *from* jstk (päivästä) lukien; *he spoke to the same* ~ hän tähtäsi puheessaan samaan; *I have received a cable to the* ~

that… sain sähkeen, jossa sanotaan, että…; *sound* ~s äänitehosteet. **-ive** [-iv] a. vaikuttava, tehokas, tepsivä; palveluskelpoinen; varsinainen; s.: ~ s (aktiivi)palveluskelpoiset joukot. **-ual** [-juəl] a. tehokas. **-uate** [-jueit] v. panna toimeen, toteuttaa.

effemina|cy [i'femin|əsi] s. naismaisuus. **-te** [-it] a. naismainen, velostunut.

effervesce [efə'ves] v. kuohua, porehtia, poreilla. **-nce** [-ns] s. kuohuminen. **-nt** [-nt] a. kuohuva.

effete [e'fi:t] a. loppuun kulunut.

effica|cious [efi'keiʃəs] a. tehokas (lääke ym). **-cy** ['efikəsi] s. tehokkuus.

efficien|cy [i'fiʃnsi] s. teho(kkuus); suorituskyky; (tekn.) hyötysuhde. **-t** [-nt] a. tehokas, vaikuttava; suorituskykyinen, kyvykäs, pystyvä.

effigy ['efidʒi] s. kuva; *burn a p. in* ~ polttaa jkn kuva.

efflorescence [eflɔ:'resns] s. kukkaan puhkeaminen.

efflu|ence ['efluəns] s. virtaaminen (ulos). **-ent** [-ənt] s.: *industrial* ~ s teollisuuden jätevedet.

effort ['efət] s. ponnistus, ponnistelu, yritys; *without* ~ vaivatta.

effrontery [e'frʌntəri] s. julkeus, häpeämättömyys.

effulgen|ce [e'fʌldʒns] s. loisto. **-nt** [-nt] a. säteilevä.

effu|sion [i'fju:ʒn] s. vuodatus; (lääk.) vuoto. **-sive** [i:'fju:siv] a. ylitsevuotava; ylenpalttinen.

eft [eft] s. vesilisko.

egalitarian [egəli'tɛəriən] s. tasa-arvoisuutta vaativa t. suosiva (henkilö).

egg 1. [eg] s. muna; *lay* ~ s munia; *will you have your* ~ *boiled or fried* haluatteko munanne keitettyinä tai paistettuna? **-cup** munakuppi. **-head** »intellektuelli». **-plant** munakoiso.

egg 2. [eg] v. yllyttää (tav. ~ *on*).

eglantine ['egləntain] s. villiruusu.

ego ['egou, Am. 'i:gou] s. minä. **-centric** a. itsekeskeinen. **-ism** [-izm] s. itsekkyys. **-ist** [-st] s. egoisti, itsekä ihminen. **-istic(al)** [egɒ(u)'istik, -(ə)l] a. itsekäs. **-tism** [-tizm] s. itsekeskeisyys; itserakkaus; itsekkyys;

-tist ['tist] s. itsekeskeinen ihminen; = egoist.
-tistic(al) [egə(u)'tistik, -(ə)l] a. itsekeskeinen.

egregious [i'gri:dʒəs] a. tavaton, törkeä (virhe ym).

egress ['i:gres] s. ulosmeno, uloskäynti, poistuminen.

egret [i:gret] s. jalohaikara.

Egypt ['i:dʒipt] erisn. Egypti. **-ian** [i'dʒipʃn] a. & s. egyptiläinen.

eider ['aidə] s. haahka. **-down** s. haahkanuntuva; untuvapeite.

eight [eit] lukus. kahdeksan; kahdeksikko (m. urh.). **-een** ['ei'ti:n] lukus. kahdeksantoista. **-eenth** [ei'ti:nθ] lukus. & s. kahdeksastoista. **-h** [eitθ] lukus. & s. kahdeksas (osa). **-ieth** [-iəθ] lukus. & s. kahdeksaskymmenes. **-y** [-i] lukus. kahdeksankymmentä; the -ies 80-luku.

Eire ['εərə] erisn. Eire, Irlanti.

ither ['aiðə, Am. 'i:ðə] a. & pron. jompikumpi, kumpi hyvänsä, (harv.) kumpikin; (ei) kumpikaan, (ei) myöskään; on ~ side kummallakin puolen; in ~ event kummassakin tapauksessa; adv. & konj.: ~ . .or joko. .tai; [I don't like the red dress] and I don't like the white one, — enkä pidä valkoisestakaan.

jacula|te [i'dʒækjuleit] v. huudahtaa. **-tion** [-'leiʃn] s. huudahdus; (lääk.) siemensyöksy.

ect [i(:)'dʒekt] v. heittää (ulos); häätää, karkottaa. **-ion** [-kʃn] s. ulosheittäminen; häätö; ~-seat heittoistuin.

.e [i:k] v.: ~ out lisätä, jatkaa (with llak); ~ out one's livelihood nipin apin saada toimeentulonsa, elää ituuttaa.

aborate [i'læb(ə)rit] a. huoliteltu, aidokas; v. [i'læbəreit] laatia ksityiskohtaisesti, selittää arkemmin, kehitellä.

and [i:lænd] s. hirviantilooppi.

apse [i'læps] v. kulua.

astic [i'læstik] a. joustava, kimmoisa, enyvä; s. kuminauha. **-ity** [elæs'tisiti] joustavuus, jousto.

ate [i'leit] v. täyttää ilolla t. riemulla, aisuttaa (et. pass.); she was ~d by

her success (m.) hän oli ylpeä menestyksestään. **-ion** [i'leiʃn] s. juhlamieli, ilo, riemu.

elbow ['elbəu] s. kyynärpää; mutka; taive; v. tuuppia; out at ~s nukkavieru; ~ one's way tunkeutua; ~ grease voimanponnistus, kova työ; ~ room liikkumatila.

elder 1. ['eldə] s. selja; ~-berry wine seljaviini.

eld|er 2. ['eld|ə] a. (komp. ks. old) vanhempi; s. vanhin; his ~ brother hänen vanhempi veljensä; your ~s sinua vanhemmat. **-erly** [-əli] a. vanhahko. **-est** [-ist] a. (sup. ks. old) vanhin.

Eleanor ['elinə] erisn.

elect [i'lekt] v. valita; a. (vasta)valittu (ei virkaan astunut).

election [i'lekʃn] s. valinta, valitseminen; vaalit; general ~ yleiset (valtiolliset) vaalit. **-eering** [ilekʃə'niəriŋ] s. vaalikampanja, äänten keräily.

elective [i'lektiv] a. valitseva, vaali-, valitsija-; Am. valinnainen, vapaaehtoinen.

elector [i'lektə] s. valitsijamies; (hist.) vaaliruhtinas. **-al** [-(ə)rəl] a.: ~ register vaaliluettelo. **-ate** [-(ə)rit] s. valitsijakunta, valitsijamiehet.

electri|c [i'lektrik] a. sähkö-, sähköinen; ~ blue teräksensininen; ~ chair sähkötuoli; ~ flex (t. cord) sähköjohdin, liitäntäjohto; ~ shock sähköisku; ~ torch taskulamppu. **-cal** [-k(ə)l] a. sähkö-; ~ engineering sähkötekniikka. **-cian** [ilek'triʃn] s. sähköasentaja, -mies; sähkötekniikko. **-city** [ilek'trisiti] s. sähkö. **-fication** [ilektrifi'keiʃn] s. sähköistys. **-fy** [-fai] sähköistää.

electro|cardiogram [i'lektr|ə(u)'ka:diəgræm] s. elektrokardiogrammi, sydänfilmi. **-cute** [-əkju:t] v. teloittaa sähkötuolissa; be ~d (m.) kuolla sähköiskuun. **-cution** [-ə'kju:ʃn] s. teloitus, ks. ed. **-de** [i'lektrəud] s. elektrodi.

electron [i'lektrɔn] s. elektroni (sähk.). **-ic** [-'trɔnik] a. elektroninen. **-ics** [-'trɔniks] s. elektroniikka.

electroplate [i'lektrə(u)pleit] v.

galvanoida; *s.* (galvanoitu) uushopea.

elegan|ce ['eligəns] *s.* aistikkuus. **-t**
[-ənt] *a.* hieno, aistikas, tyylikäs.

elegiac [eli'dʒaiək] *a.* eleginen, kaiho-,
surumielinen.

elegy ['elidʒi] *s.* elegia.

element ['elimənt] *s.* alkuaine;
perusaine, alkutekijä; *pl.* alkeet,
aakkoset; ainekset; *the* ~ *s*
luonnonvoimat; *in one's* ~ oikeassa
elementissään; [*there is*] *an* ~ *of truth
in it* siinä on hiven totuutta. **-al**
[eli'mentl] *a.* elementtien;
alkuvoimainen; perus-. **-ary**
[eli'ment(ə)ri] *a.* alkeis-, perus-; ~
school kansakoulu.

elephant ['elifənt] *s.* elefantti, norsu;
proved a white ~ osoittautui
tarpeettomaksi ylellisyydeksi. **-iasis**
[elifæn'taiəsis] *s.* elefanttitauti.

elevat|e ['eliveit] *v.* kohottaa,
korottaa, ylentää; ~*d* korkea, ylevä,
(puhek.) hyvällä tuulella; **-ing** mieltä
ylentävä. **-ion** [eli'veiʃn] *s.* kukkula;
korkeus (kulma) ylevyys;
korottaminen; korotuskulma; ~ *of
temperature* lämmönnousu. **-or** [-ə] *s.*
Am. hissi; kuljetin, nosturi.

eleven [i'levn] *lukus.* yksitoista; *an* ~
(urh.) joukkue; ~*ses* kello 11:n kahvi
t. tee; ~ *plus* ks. *plus*. **-th** [-θ] *lukus.*
yhdestoista; *at the* ~ *hour*
yhdennellätoista hetkellä.

elf [elf] *s.* (pl. *elves*) haltija,
keijukainen. **-in** [-in] *a.*
keijukaismainen. **-ish** [-iʃ] *a.*
keijukais(mainen); vallaton.

elicit [i'lisit] *v.* houkutella t. saada
esiin, tuoda esiin.

elide [i'laid] *v.* jättää lausumatta.

eligi|bility [elidʒə'biliti] *s.*
vaalikelpoisuus. **-ble** ['elidʒəbl] *a.*
vaalikelpoinen; tavoiteltava.

elimina|te [i'limineit] *v.* poistaa, jättää
pois; eliminoida. **-tion** [-'neiʃn] *s.*
eliminointi.

elision [i'liʒn] *s.* elisio; poisto.

elite [ei'li:t] *s.* valiojoukko,
parhaimmisto, eliitti.

elixir [i'liksə] *s.* eliksiiri; ~ *of life*
elämänneste.

Elizabeth [i'lizəbəθ] *erisn.* **-an** [-'bi:θn]:
~ *Age* Elisabetin aika.

elk [elk] *s.* hirvi.

ell [el] *s.* kyynärä (114 cm).

ellip|se [i'lips] *s.* ellipsi, soikio. **-tic(al)**
[i'liptik, -(ə)l] *a.* elliptinen.

elm [elm] *s.* jalava.

elocution [elə'kju:ʃn] *s.* suullinen
esitystaito, lausunta, kaunoluku. **-ist**
[-ist] *s.* lausuja, suullisen esityksen
taitaja.

elonga|te ['i:lɔngeit] *v.* pidentää; ~*d*
pitkänomainen. **-tion** [-'geiʃn] *s.*
pidentäminen.

elope [i'loup] *v.* karata (kotoa
rakastajan kanssa). **-ment** *s.*
karkaaminen.

eloquen|ce ['eləkw(ə)ns] *s.*
kaunopuheisuus. **-t** [-(ə)nt] *a.*
kaunopuheinen; puhuva.

else [els] *adv.* toinen, muu; muutoin;
somewhere ~ jossakin muualla; *did
you see anybody* ~ ? näitkö ketään
muuta (muita)? **-where** *adv.* muualla,
-lle.

elucida|te [i'lu:sideit] *v.* valaista;
selventää. **-tion** [-'deiʃn] *s.*
valaiseminen; selvitys.

elu|de [i'lu:|d] *v.* ovelasti välttää,
väistää; ~ *observation* jäädä
huomaamatta. **-sive** [-siv] *a.*
vältelevä, karttelevä; vaikeasti
tavoitettava, saavuttamaton. **-sory**
[-səri] *a.* pettävä.

elves [elvz] ks. *elf*.

Ely ['i:li] *erisn.*

Elysium [i'liziəm] *s.* paratiisi.

emacia|te [i'meiʃieit] *v.* laihduttaa; ~*d*
riutunut, laihtunut. **-tion** [imeisi'eiʃn]
s. laihuus.

emanate ['eməneit] *v.*: ~ *from* virrata,
haihtua, saada alkunsa (jstk).

emancipa|te [i'mænsipeit] *v.*
vapauttaa, päästää epäitsenäisyyden
tilasta. **-tion** [-'peiʃn] *s.*
vapauttaminen, vapautus.

emasculate [i'mæskjuleit] *v.* veltostaa,
heikentää; *a.* [-lit] veltostunut,
naismainen.

embalm [im'ba:m] *v.* palsamoida;
täyttää tuoksulla.

embank [im'bæŋk] *v.* padota. **-ment** *s.*
pengerrys; pato; *the E*~ (Thamesin)
rantakatu.

embargo [em'ba:gəu] *s.* (pl. ~ *es*)
embargo, sataman sulkeminen, jnk
kaupan kielto t. sulku; *v.*

takavarikoida; *lay an ~ upon*
takavarikoida.

embark [im'bɑːk] *v.* astua laivaan;
viedä laivaan, laivata; antautua,
ryhtyä (*on* jhk). **-ation** [embɑː'keiʃn]
s. laivaan nousu.

embarrass [im'bærəs] *v.* saattaa
hämille; tehdä sekavaksi; haitata,
estää; *~ed* häkeltynyt, hämillään,
(by the lack of money)
rahavaikeuksissa. **-ment** *s.*
hämmennys, tukala asema, rahapula.

embassy ['embəsi] *s.* suurlähetystö;
suurlähettiläin tehtävä.

embattled [im'bætld] *a.*
taistelujärjestyksessä oleva;
sakaraharjainen.

embed [im'bed] *v.* upottaa (*in* jhk).

embellish [im'beliʃ] *v.* kaunistaa,
koristaa. **-ment** *s.* kaunistus.

ember 1. ['embə] *s.* (tav. *pl.*) hiillos.

ember 2. ['embə] *s.*: *E~ days* yleiset
paasto- ja rukouspäivät.

embezzle [im'bezl] *v.* kavaltaa
(rahoja). **-ment** *s.* kavallus.

embitter [im'bitə] *v.* katkeroittaa; *~ed*
katkera.

emblazon [im'bleizn] *v.* koristaa
heraldisesti; julistaa, ylistää.

emblem ['embləm] *s.* vertauskuva. **-atic**
[embli'mætik] *a.* vertauskuvallinen.

embodiment [im'bɔdimənt] *s.*
ruumiillistuma.

embody [im'bɔdi] *v.* ruumiillistaa,
antaa muoto, ilmentää; sisältää; *these
machines ~ many new features* näissä
koneissa on useita uusia piirteitä.

embolden [im'bəuld(ə)n] *v.* rohkaista.

embolism ['embəlizm] *s.* veritulppa,
tulppautuminen.

emboss [im'bɔs] *v.* pakottaa (metallia).

embrace [im'breis] *v.* syleillä; sulkea
piiriinsä, käsittää; omaksua; hyväksyä
(tarjous); käyttää hyväkseen
(tilaisuutta); *s.* syleily.

embrasure [im'breiʒə] *s.* ikkuna- t.
ovisyvennys; ampuma-aukko.

embrocation [embrə(u)'keiʃn] *s.*
linimentti.

embroider [im'brɔidə] *v.* kirjoa,
kaunistella. **-y** [-ri] *s.* koruommel.

embroil [im'brɔil] *v.* tehdä sotkuiseksi;
kietoa riitaan.

embryo ['embriəu] *s.* alkio, sikiö,

(kuv.) itu, alku. **-logy** [-'ɔlədʒi] *s.*
sikiöoppi. **-nic** [-'ɔnik] *a.* alkioasteella
oleva.

emend [i(ː)'mend] *v.* korjata. **-ation**
[-'deiʃn] *s.* (tekstin) korjaus.

emerald ['emər(ə)ld] *s.* smaragdi; *~
type* l.v. nonparelli (kirjap.); *E ~ Isle*
Irlanti.

emerge [i'məːdʒ] *v.* sukeltaa esiin, tulla
näkyviin; ilmaantua, käydä ilmi. **-nce**
[-(ə)ns] *s.* esiinsukeltaminen;
ilmaantuminen. **-ncy** [-(ə)nsi] *s.*
odottamaton tapaus, vaikea tilanne,
hätätilanne; *~ brake* hätäjarru;
~ call hälytyssoitto; *~ exit*
varauloskäytävä; *~ landing*
pakkolasku; *~ ration* rautaisannos; *~
ward* päivystysosasto; *in an ~, in case
of ~* hätätilassa; *state of ~*
poikkeustila. **-nt** [-(ə)nt] *a.*: *~
countries* kehitysmaat.

emery ['eməri] *s.* smirgeli. **--paper** *s.*
smirgelipaperi.

emetic [i'metik] *s.* oksetusaine.

emigra|nt ['emigr(ə)nt] *s.* siirtolainen.
-te [-eit] *v.* muuttaa maasta. **-tion**
[-'greiʃn] *s.* maastamuutto,
siirtolaisuus.

eminen|ce ['eminəns] *s.* korkeus,
korkea arvo; suuruus, maine;
kukkula; *His E~* hänen ylhäisyytensä
(kardinaalin arvonimi). **-t** [-ənt] *a.*
korkea, ylhäinen; huomattava, etevä.
-tly *adv.* erittäin.

emir [e'miə] *s.* emiiri.

emissary ['emis(ə)ri] *s.* (salainen)
lähettiläs.

emission [i(ː)'miʃn] *s.* levittäminen,
(lämmön ym) säteily; vuodattaminen,
siemensyöksy.

emit [i'mit] *v.* lähettää (ulos), levittää,
säteillä (lämpöä ym), purkaa, syöstä;
laskea liikkeeseen.

emollient [i'mɔliənt] *a. & s.* pehmittävä
(aine, haude).

emolument [i'mɔljumənt] *s.*: *~ s*
palkkaedut, palkkiot.

emotion [i'məuʃn] *s.* mielenliikutus,
kiihtymys; tunne. **-al** [-ənl] *a.*
tunteellinen, tunne-, tunneperäinen;
~ life tunne-elämä. **-alism** [-(ə)nəlizm]
s. tunnevaltaisuus, tunneherkkyys.

emotive [i'məutiv] *a.* tunteita
herättävä, tunne-.

empathy ['empəθi] s.
tunnestautuminen, eläytyminen.

emperor ['emp(ə)rə] s. keisari.

empha|sis ['emfəsis] s. korostus;
paino(kkuus); lay (put) [special] ~ on
panna (paljon) painoa jhk, antaa
pontta jllek. -size [-saiz] v. korostaa,
tähdentää. -tic [im'fætik] a. painokas,
voimakas; ~ally pontevasti,
ponnekkaasti.

empire ['empaiə] s. imperiumi;
keisarikunta, valtakunta.

empiric [em'pirik], -al [-(ə)l] a.
kokemusperäinen.

emplacement [im'pleismənt] s. (tykin)
alusta.

employ [im'plɔi] v. käyttää; pitää
työssä, antaa työtä, työllistää; s.
palvelus. -ee [em'plɔii:, -plɔi'i:] s. jkn
palveluksessa oleva, työntekijä,
virkailija. -er [-ə] s. työnantaja. -ment
s. toimi, työ; käyttäminen; out of ~
työtön; full ~ täystyöllisyys; ~ agency
työnvälitystoimisto.

emporium [em'pɔ:riəm] s.
markkinapaikka.

empower [im'pauə] v. valtuuttaa.

empress ['empris] s. keisarinna.

emptiness ['em(p)tinis] s. tyhjyys.

empty ['em(p)ti] a. tyhjä; v. tyhjentää,
-tyä; (joesta) laskea; s.: empties tyhjät
laatikot, pullot ym.

empyrean [empi'ri(:)ən] s. (run.)
taivas.

emu ['i:mju:] s. emu (lintu).

emul|ate ['emjuleit] v. kilpailla. -ation
[-'leiʃn] s. kilpailu, kilvoittelu. -ous
[-ləs] a. kilpailunhaluinen; ~ of
kateellinen, jtk kiihkeästi haluava.

emulsion [i'mʌlʃn] s. emulsio.

enable [i'neibl] v. tehdä kykeneväksi,
mahdolliseksi jklle; valtuuttaa.

enact [i'nækt] v. säätää, määrätä;
näytellä (osaa); where .. was enacted
missä .. tapahtui. -ment s. (lain)
hyväksyminen, säädös.

enamel [i'næml] s. emali;
hammaskiille; v. emaloida.

enamour [i'næmə] v.: be ~ed of olla
rakastunut.

encamp [in'kæmp] v. leiriytyä; sijoittaa
leiriin. -ment s. leiri(paikka);
leiriytyminen.

encapsulate [in'kæpsjuleit] v.: be ~d

koteloitua.

encephalitis [ensefə'laitis] s.
aivokuume.

encase [in'keis] v. sulkea koteloon,
peittää, ympäröidä.

enchain [in'tʃein] v. panna kahleisiin.

enchant [in'tʃɑ:nt] v. lumota; hurmata;
~ing hurmaava, lumoava. -ment s.
taikavoima, lumous; tenho. -ress [-ris]
s. lumoojatar.

encircle [in'sə:kl] v. ympäröidä;
saartaa.

enclave ['enkleiv] s. erillissalue.

enclos|e [in'kləu|z] v. aidata; sulkea
sisäänsä, ympäröidä; liittää oheen; I
~ cheque oheistan šekin; ~d oheinen,
oheisena. -ure [-ʒə] s. aita(us); liite
(kirjeessä).

encompass [in'kʌmpəs] v. ympäröidä;
kuv. käsittää.

encore [ɔŋ'kɔ:] int. uudelleen! s.
takaisin kutsuminen, ylimääräinen
(numero, kappale).

encounter [in'kauntə] v. kohdata,
tavata; s. kohtaus; ottelu, kahakka.

encourage [in'kʌridʒ] v. rohkaista.
-ment s. rohkaisu.

encroach [in'krautʃ] v.: ~ upon väkisin
tunkeutua jhk, loukata (esim.
oikeutta, (esim. merestä) vallata
rannikolta maata. -ment s. (jnk)
loukkaaminen, tunkeutuminen.

encrust [in'krʌst] v. peittää kuorella (t.
jalokivillä ym).

encum|ber [in'kʌmbə] v. haitata;
rasittaa. -brance [-brəns] s. taakka.
rasitus; kiinnitys, rasite.

encyclop(a)edia [ensaiklə(u)'pi:djə] s.
tietosanakirja.

end [end] s. loppu, pää, ääri;
tarkoitusperä, päämäärä; pätkä; v.
lopettaa, päättää; loppua, päättyä; at
an ~ lopussa; in the ~ lopuksi,
lopulta; on ~ pystyssä; [for three
weeks] on ~ yhtä mittaa; to this ~ tätä
tarkoitusta varten; with this ~ in view
tämä silmämääränä, tässä
tarkoituksessa; to no ~ turhaan; bring
to an ~ lopettaa; come to an ~
päättyä, loppua; put an ~ to lopettaa,
lakkauttaa jtk; make both ~s meet
saada rahat riittämään; [it'll cost] no ~
of money valtavan paljon; ~ up in
päätyä jhk.

endanger [in'dein(d)ʒə] *v.* panna vaaralle alttiiksi, vaarantaa.

endear [in'diə] *v.* tehdä rakkaaksi; [*she*] ~*ed herself to everyone* voitti kaikkien kiintymyksen; ~*ing* herttainen, viehättävä. **-ment** *s.* hellyydenosoitus.

endeavour [in'devə] *v.* yrittää, koettaa; *s.* yritys.

endemic [en'demik] *a.* endeeminen, paikkakunnallinen; *s.* endeeminen tauti.

end|ing *s.* loppu; pääte. **-less** *a.* loputon, loppumaton.

endive ['endiv, Am. -daiv] *s.* endivia, lehtisikuri; vrt. *chicory*.

endocrin|e ['endə(u)krain] *a.*: ~ *glands* umpirauhaset. **-ologist** [-'nɔlədʒist] *s.* endokrinologi.

endorse [in'dɔ:s] *v.* kirjoittaa (jnk) selkäpuolelle, siirtää (vekseli); kuv. hyväksyä, kannattaa. **-e** [endɔ:'si:] *s.* siirron saaja. **-ment** *s.* (vekselin ym) siirto; hyväksyminen. **-r** [-ə] *s.* siirtäjä.

endow [in'dau] *v.* lahjoittaa, tehdä lahjoitus (laitokselle ym); varustaa (jllak). **-ment** *s.* lahjoitus, lahja; lahjarahasto; *natural* ~*s* luonnonlahjat.

endue [in'dju:] *v.*: ~*d with* jllak varustettu.

endurance [in'djuər(ə)ns] *s.* kestävyys; *past* ~ sietämätön(tä).

endure [in'djuə] *v.* kestää, sietää, kärsiä; olla kestävä, pysyä; *enduring* kestävä, pysyvä.

end|ways, -wise ['endweiz, -waiz] *adv.* pystyssä, pystyyn; päät vastakkain.

enema ['enimə] *s.* peräruiske, -ruisku.

enemy ['enimi] *s.* vihollinen; vihamies; *a.* vihollis-.

energetic [enə'dʒetik] *a.* tarmokas, ponteva; voimakas.

energize ['enədʒaiz] *v.* antaa energiaa.

energy ['enədʒi] *s.* tarmo(kkuus); energia (fys.).

enervate ['enə:veit] *v.* tehdä hervottomaksi, heikentää, veltostaa. **-tion** [-'veiʃn] *s.* heikontaminen; hervottomuus.

enfeeble [in'fi:bl] *v.* heikontaa.

enfilade [enfi'leid] *s.* sivustatuli.

enfold [in'fəuld] *v.* kietoa, ympäröidä; syleillä.

enforce [in'fɔ:s] *v.* väkisin saada aikaan, pakolla saattaa voimaan; pakottamalla vaatia; ~*d* väkisin saatu jne. **-ment** *s.* pakko, pakkotoimenpiteet; (lain) voimaansaattaminen (pakolla).

enfranchise [in'fræn(t)ʃaiz] *v.* antaa äänioikeus; vapauttaa.

engag|e [in'geidʒ] *v.* sitoa, sitoutua (m. ~ *oneself*); kihlata; palkata, ottaa palvelukseen; varata (paikka ym), vuokrata; vaatia (aikaa ym); kiinnittää vetää (puoleensa); aloittaa taistelu; tarttua; ~ *in* ryhtyä jhk; *be* ~*d to* olla kihloissa jkn kanssa; *are you* ~*d* [*this evening*]? onko aikasi varattu? *be* ~*d in writing* par'aikaa kirjoittaa; ~ *in writing* ryhtyä taisteluun. **-ed** [-d] *a.* varattu; kihloissa (oleva); sitoutunut, osallistuva. **-ement** *s.* sitoumus; kihlaus; taistelu, kahakka; *I have an* ~ *for tomorrow* olen sopinut tapaamisesta, olen lupautunut muualle huomenna. **-ing** *a.* miellyttävä, viehättävä.

engender [in'dʒendə] *v.* synnyttää.

engine ['en(d)ʒin] *s.* kone, moottori; veturi; *steam* ~ höyrykone; ks. *fire*-~. ~**-driver** *s.* veturinkuljettaja.

engineer [en(d)ʒi'niə] *s.* insinööri (esim. *electrical* ~, *mechanical* ~); koneenkäyttäjä; (sot.) pioneeri; Am. veturinkuljettaja; *v.* rakentaa, suunnitella, (puhek.) järjestää; keksiä; *chief* ~ ylikonemestari; yli-insinööri. **-ing** [-riŋ] *s.* insinööritaito, tekniikka; *civil* ~ tie- ja vesirakennus; *mechanical* ~ koneenrakennus; ~ *works* konepaja.

England ['iŋglənd] *erisn.* Englanti.

English ['iŋgliʃ] *a.* englantilainen; *s.* englannin kieli; *the* ~ englantilaiset; *in plain* ~ selvällä englannin kielellä, suoraan sanoen. **-man** [-mən] *s.* (pl. *-men* [-mən]) englantilainen. **-woman** [-wumən] *s.* (pl. *-women* [-wimin]) englannitar.

engorge [in'gɔ:dʒ] *v.* ahmia, täyttää; aiheuttaa verentungosta.

engraft [in'gra:ft] *v.* oksastaa; painaa syvälle (mieleen).

engrav|e [in'greiv] *v.* kaivertaa; teroittaa (muistiin). **-ing** *s.* kaiverrus;

wood ~ puupiirros.

engross [in'grəus] v. kokonaan vallata, kiinnittää (huomio ym); *be* ~*ed in* olla syventynyt jhk; ~*ing* mielenkiintoinen. **-ment** s. syventyminen.

engulf [in'gʌlf] v. nielaista.

enhance [in'hɑ:ns] v. lisätä, korottaa. **-ment** s. lisäys.

enigma [i'nigmə] s. arvoitus. **-tic** [enig'mætik] a. arvoituksellinen; (~*ally* arvoituksellisesti).

enjoin [in'dʒɔin] v. määrätä, teroittaa jkn mieleen (*on a p.*), käskeä.

enjoy [in'dʒɔi] v. nauttia, (voida) iloita, pitää (*a th.* jstk); ~ *oneself* pitää hauskaa; *he* ~*s good health* hänellä on hyvä terveys. **-able** [-əbl] a. nautittava; miellyttävä. **-ment** s. (~ *of*) jnk nauttiminen, nautinto, ilo.

enkindle [in'kindl] v. sytyttää.

enlarge [in'lɑ:dʒ] v. suurentaa, laajentaa; suurentaa; ~ *upon* puhua laajasti. **-ment** s. suurennus.

enlighten [in'laitn] v. valaista; valistaa; ~*ed* valistunut. **-ment** s. valaistus; valistus.

enlist [in'list] v. pestata; pestautua, mennä armeijaan; ~*ed men* (Am. laiv.) aliupseerit ja miehistö; ~ *sb.* [*in a cause*] hankkia jkn kannatus. **-ment** s. pestaus, pesti.

enliven [in'laivn] v. elävöittää.

enmity ['enmiti] s. vihamielisyys, vihollisuus.

ennoble [i'nəubl] v. aateloida, kuv. jalostaa.

ennui [ã:'nwi:] s. ikävystyminen, ikävä.

enorm|ity [i'nɔ:miti] s. hirvittävyys; hirmutyö. **-ous** [-məs] a. suunnaton, tavaton.

enough [i'nʌf] a. & adv. & s. kylliksi; *well* ~ melko hyvin; ~ *!* riittää! *strangely (surprisingly)* ~ kummallista kyllä; *sure* ~ [*it was there*] oli kun olikin; *I have had* ~ *of him* olen kyllästynyt häneen; *big* ~ kyllin iso; ~ *money* tarpeeksi rahaa.

enquir|e, -y ks. *inquir|e, -y.*

enrage [in'reidʒ] v. raivostuttaa; ~*d* raivostunut.

enrapture [in'ræptʃə] v. hurmata; ~*d* ihastunut.

enrich [in'ritʃ] v. rikastuttaa; tehdä (maa) hedelmälliseksi.

enrol|l, enrol [in'rəul] v. merkitä luetteloihin; merkitä jäseneksi; luetteloida; rekisteröidä; ~ *oneself* ilmoittautua jäseneksi. **-ment** s. luettelointi, rekisteröinti; (oppilas-, jäsen)määrä.

en route [ã:(n)'ru:t] adv. : ~ *to* matkalla jnnek.

en|sconce [in'skɔns] v. kätkeä; ~ *oneself* kätkeytyä. **-shrine** [in'ʃrain] v. kätkeä kuin lippaaseen, säilyttää pyhänä.

ensemble [ã:(n)'sɑ:(m)bl] s. yhteissoitto, yhtye.

ensign ['ensain] s. (arvon)merkki; lippu; Am. (meriv.) aliluutnantti.

ensilage ['ensilidʒ] s. säilörehu.

enslave [in'sleiv] v. tehdä orjaksi, orjuuttaa. **-ment** s. orjuutus, orjuus.

ensnare [in'snɛə] v. saada satimeen; kietoa pauloihinsa.

ensue [in'sju:] v. olla seurauksena, seurata (*from* jstk).

ensure [in'ʃuə] v. turvata; taata, varmistaa.

entail [in'teil] v. tehdä välttämättömäksi, tuoda mukanaan; s. sääntöperintö; *that* ~*s great expense* siihen liittyy suuria kustannuksia.

entangle [in'tæŋgl] v. tehdä sotkuiseksi; kietoa, sotkea; *get* ~*d in* sotkeutua jhk. **-ment** s. sotku, selkkaus; este; ks. *barbed wire.*

enter ['entə] v. astua, tulla, mennä jhk (sisään), ryhtyä, ruveta (jllek alalle ym); merkitä luetteloon t. kirjaan, ottaa jäseneksi, oppilaaksi ym, kirjoittautua jhk, viedä kirjaan; ~ *into details* mennä yksityiskohtiin; ~ *the Church* ryhtyä papiksi; ~ *a protest* esittää vastalause; ~ *for* ilmoittautua jhk (tutkintoon, kilpailuun ym); ~ *into* ryhtyä (keskusteluun ym), tehdä (sopimus ym); ~ *upon* astua (virkaan), ryhtyä, ottaa haltuunsa (perintö); *it never* ~*ed my head* se ei pälkähtänyt päähänikään; ~ *Macbeth* M. tulee näyttämölle.

enter|ic [en'terik] a. : ~ *fever* lavantauti. **-itis** [entə'raitis] s. suolitulehdus.

enterpris|e ['entəpraiz] s. yritys;

yritteliäisyys, yrittäjyys; *private* ~
yksityisyrittäjyys. **-ing** *a.* yritteliäs.
entertain [entə'tein] *v.* ottaa vastaan
vieraana, kestitä, pitää kutsuja;
hauskuttaa, huvittaa; ~ *sb. to dinner*
tarjota jklle päivällinen; *they* ~ *a*
great deal heillä on usein vieraita; ~
an idea ajatella, harkita; ~ [*hopes*]
elättää; **-er** [-ə] *s.* kansanhuvittaja.
-ing *a.* huvittava. **-ment** *s.* huvi,
huvitus, ilo, kestitys; ~ *tax* huvivero;
light ~ viihde.
enthral(l) [in'θrɔ:l] *v.* kahlehtia,
lumota, kiehtoa.
enthrone [in'θroun] *v.* asettaa
valtaistuimelle.
enthus|**e** [in'θju:z] *v.* (puhek.) olla
haltioissaan, innoissaan. **-iasm**
[-iæzm] *s.* innostus, into. **-iast** [-iæst] *s.*
intoilija; innokas ihailija t.
kannattaja. **-iastic** [-i'æstik] *a.*
innostunut; intoutunut, haltioitunut.
entice [in'tais] *v.* houkutella,
viekoitella. **-ment** *s.* houkutus(keino).
entire [in'taiə] *a.* kokonainen,
täydellinen, ehjä, koskematon. **-ly**
adv. kokonaan, täysin. **-ty** [-ti] *s.*
kokonaisuus; *in its* ~ kokonaan.
entitle [in'taitl] *v.* oikeuttaa; nimittää;
~*d* jonka nimi on . .
entity ['entiti] *s.* olemus, (itsenäinen)
kokonaisuus.
entomb [in'tu:m] *v.* haudata.
entomo|**logist** [entə'mɔlədʒist] *s.*
hyönteistieteilijä. **-logy** [-lədʒi] *s.*
hyönteistiede.
entourage [ɔntu'ra:ʒ] *s.* seurue.
entrails ['entreilz] *s. pl.* sisälmykset.
entrain [in'trein] *v.* lastata (joukkoja)
junaan, nousta junaan.
entrammel [in'træml] *v.* kahlehtia,
estää.
entrance 1. ['entrəns] *s.*
sisäänastuminen, tulo; (sisään)pääsy;
pääsymaksu; sisäänkäytävä, ovi.
entrance 2. [in'trɑ:ns] *v.* saattaa
hurmiotilaan t. suunniltaan (ilosta
ym).
entrant ['entrənt] *s.* (kilpailuun ym)
ilmoittautunut.
entrap [in'træp] *v.* saada satimeen;
viekoitella.
entreat [in'tri:t] *v.* pyytää hartaasti,
pyytämällä pyytää. **-y** [-i] *s.* harras

pyyntö, rukous.
entree ['ɔntrei] *s.* väliruoka.
entrench [in'tren(t)ʃ] *v.* varustaa
taisteluhaudalla; ~ *oneself* kaivautua
maahan. **-ment** *s.* vallitus.
entrepreneur [ɔntrəprə'nə:] *s.* yrittäjä.
entrust [in'trʌst] *v.* uskoa (. . *to, sb.*
with jtk jklle).
entry ['entri] *s.* sisäänkäynti, -tulo;
sisäänkäytävä; merkintä (kirjoihin);
ilmoitus, osanotto, osanottaja(t);
hakusana; ks. *bookkeeping*.
entwine [in'twain] *v.* punoa yhteen,
kietoa (jnk ympäri).
enucleate [i(:)'nju:klieit] *v.* (lääk.)
kuoria irti, poistaa.
enumera|**te** [i'nju:məreit] *v.* luetella.
-tion [-'reiʃn] *s.* luetteleminen.
enuncia|**te** [i'nʌnsieit] *v.* lausua, tuoda
esiin, julistaa; ääntää. **-tion** [-'eiʃn] *s.*
ääntäminen.
envelop [in'veləp] *v.* kääriä, verhota
jhk; ympäröidä; saarrostaa. **-e**
['enviləup] *s.* kotelo, kirjekuori,
päällys; verho.
envenom [in'venəm] *v.* myrkyttää.
envi|**able** ['enviəbl] *a.* kadehdittava.
-ous [-iəs] *a.* kateellinen; *be* ~ *of sb.'s*
success kadehtia jkn menestystä.
environ [in'vaiər(ə)n] *v.* ympäröidä.
-ment *s.* ympäristö; [*Department of*]
the E~ luonnonsuojeluministeriö.
(~**al** [-'mentl] *a.* ympäristö-). **-s**
['envir(ə)nz] *s. pl.* ympäristö.
envisage [in'vizidʒ] *v.* katsoa silmästä
silmään, katsella, tarkastella (esim.
määrätyssä valossa); kuvitella
mielessään.
envision [in'viʒn]*v.* Am. = ed.
envoy ['envɔi] *s.* lähetti(läs).
envy ['envi] *s.* kateus; kateuden kohde;
v. kadehtia.
enzyme ['enzaim] *s.* entsyymi.
eon ks. *aeon*.
epaulet(te) ['epə(u)let] *s.* olkain,
epoletti.
ephemeral [i'femərəl] *a.* päivän
kestävä, lyhytaikainen.
Ephesian [i'fi:zjən] *a. & s.* efesolainen;
~*s* Efesolaiskirje.
epic ['epik] *a.* eeppinen, kertova; *s.*
eepos.
epicure ['epikjuə] *s.* herkkusuu,
nautiskelija. **-an** [-'ri(:)ən] *a. & s.*

epikurolainen.

epi|demic [epi'demik] *a.* kulkutaudin luonteinen; *s.* kulkutauti, epidemia. **-dermis** [-'də:mis] *s.* orvaskesi. **-diascope** [-'daiəskəup] *s.* heijastuskone.

epigram ['epigræm] *s.* epigrammi, komparuno. **-matic** [epigrə'mætik] *a.* kärkevä, naseva.

epilep|sy ['epilepsi] *s.* epilepsia, kaatumatauti. **-tic** [-'leptik] *a. & s.* epileptinen; epileptikko.

epilogue ['epilɔg] *s.* loppusanat, epilogi.

Epiphany [i'pifəni] *s.* loppiainen.

episcop|al [i'piskəp(ə)l] *a.* piispallinen, piispan. **-alian** [-'peiljən] *a.* episkopaalinen. **-ate** [-it] *s.* piispan arvo, hiippakunta; piispat.

episod|e ['episəud] *s.* episodi, sivutoiminta. **-ic(al)** [epi'sɔdik, -(ə)l] *a.* episodimainen.

epistle ['i'pisl] *s.* epistola, kirje.

epitaph ['epitɑ:f] *s.* hautakirjoitus.

epithet ['epiθet] *s.* lisänimitys, epiteetti.

epitom|e [i'pitəmi] *s.* yhteenveto. **-ize** [-maiz] *v.* tehdä yhteenveto, esittää suppeassa muodossa.

epoch ['i:pɔk] *s.* käännekohta, tärkeä ajankohta t. ajanjakso; ~-*making* käänteentekevä.

Epsom ['epsəm] *erisn.; ~ salt* karvassuola.

equable ['ekwəbl] *a.* yhdenmukainen; tasainen.

equal ['i:kw(ə)l] *a.* yhtäläinen, yhtä suuri; (*to* jnk) veroinen, tasa-arvoinen; *s.* vertainen; *v.* olla yhtä suuri kuin; vetää vertoja. olla jnk veroinen; *feel ~ to* kyetä, pystyä jhk; *~ to the occasion* tilanteen tasalla; *~ mark* yhtäläisyysmerkki; *~ pay* sama palkka, samapalkkaisuus; *other things being ~* jos olosuhteet ovat muuten samat; *with ~ ease* yhtä sujuvasti. **-ity** [i:'kwɔliti] *s.* yhtäläisyys; tasa-arvoisuus; yhdenmukaisuus. **-ize** [-aiz] *v.* yhtäläistää; saattaa yhdenvertaiseksi; tasoittaa. **-ly** *adv.* yhtä; samoin; tasan.

equanimity [i:kwə'nimiti] *s.* mielentyyneys.

equa|te [i'kweit] *v.* pitää

samanarvoisena; (mat.) panna yhtäläisyysmerkki (kahden..väliin). **-tion** [-ʃn] *s.* yhtälö; tasoittaminen. **-tor** [-tə] *s.* päiväntasaaja.

equerry [i'kweri] *s.* (hovi)tallimestari.

equestrian [i'kwestriən] *a.* ratsastava; *s.* (taito)ratsastaja; ~ *statue* ratsastajapatsas.

equi|distant ['i:kwi-] *a.* yhtä kaukana oleva. **-lateral** *a.* tasasivuinen. **-librate** [-'laib-, ek'wilib-] *v.* pitää tasapainossa. **-librist** [i:'kwilibrist] *s.* tasapainotaiteilija. **-librium** [-'libriəm] *s.* tasapaino.

equine [i:'kwain] *a.* hevos-.

equinox ['i:kwinɔks] *s.* päiväntasaus (*vernal, autumnal ~*).

equip [i'kwip] *v.* varustaa; ~*ped with* jllak varustettu. **-ment** *s.* varustus, varusteet, laitteet, laite, välineistö.

equipoise ['ekwipɔiz] *s.* tasapaino.

equitable ['ekwitəbl] *a.* oikeudenmukainen; kohtuullinen.

equity ['ekwiti] *s.* oikeus, kohtuus; *pl.* kantaosakkeet.

equivalen|ce [i'kwivələns] *s.* samanarvoisuus. **-t** [-ənt] *a.* samanarvoinen, täysin vastaava; *s.* vastine; vastaava määrä, samaa merkitsevä sana.

equiv|ocal [i'kwivək(ə)l] *a.* kaksimielinen, kaksiselitteinen; epämääräinen; epäilyttävä. **-ocate** [-vəkeit] *v.* puhua kaksimielisesti.

era ['iərə] *s.* aikakausi; ajanlasku.

eradicate [i'rædiket] *v.* repiä juurineen, hävittää perinpohjin.

eras|e [i'reiz, Am. i'reis] *v.* raaputtaa pois. **-er** [-ə] *s.* pyyhekumi; *ink ~* (m) raapevesi. **-ure** [i'reiʒə] *s.* raaputettu kohta.

ere [ɛə] *prep. & adv.* (vanh.) ennen; muinoin.

erect [i'rekt] *v.* nostaa pystyyn, pystyttää; *a.* pysty, suora. **-ion** [i'rekʃn] *s.* pystyttäminen; rakennus.

ergot ['ə:gət] *s.* torajyvä.

Erin ['iərin, 'erin] *erisn.* Irlanti.

ermine ['ə:min] *s.* kärppä; kärpännahka.

ero|de [i'rəu|d] *v.* syövyttää; kuluttaa. **-sion** [-ʒn] *s.* syövytys; [*soil ~*] eroosio, tuulen ja sateen kulutustyö.

erotic [i'rɔtik] *a.* eroottinen, rakkaus-.

err [ə:] *v.* erehtyä; hairahtua.

errand ['er(ə)nd] s. tehtävä, asia; *run* [*on*] ~*s* toimittaa asioita. ~**-boy** asiapoika.

errant ['er(ə)nt] a. kuljeksiva; *knight*~ vaeltava ritari.

errat|a [e'rɑ:tə] s. *pl* (sg. *-um* [*-əm*]) painovirheitä. **-ic** [i'rætik] a. säännötön; oikullinen; epävakainen, suunnitelmaton; ~ *block* siirtolohkare.

erroneous [i'rəunjəs] a. erheellinen, väärä.

error ['erə] s. erehdys, virhe; *be in* ~ olla väärässä.

erstwhile [ə:stwail] a. muinainen.

eructation [i:rʌk'teiʃn] s. röyhtäys.

erudi|te ['eru(:)dait] a. oppinut. **-tion** [eru(:)'diʃn] s. oppi(neisuus).

erupt [i'rʌpt] v. purkautua; puhjeta. **-ion** [-pʃn] s. tulivuoren purkaus; ihottuma; (hampaiden) puhkeaminen.

erysipelas [eri'sipiləs] s. (lääk.) ruusu.

erythrocyte [i'riθrə(u)sait] s. punainen verisolu, punasolu.

escala|de [eskə'keid] s. väkirynnäkkö. **-te** ['eskəleit] v. porrastaa; laajentaa, kiihdyttää. **-tion** [-'leiʃn] s. eskalaatio, laajentaminen. **-tor** ['eskəleitə] s. liukuportaat.

escapade [eskə'peid] s. vallattomuus, syrjähyppy.

escap|e [is'keip] v. päästä pakoon, paeta; välttää, välttyä (jltk); pelastua; virrata (ulos) vuotaa; luiskahtaa; s. pako, karkaaminen; pelastus; ulosvirtaaminen, (kaasun) vuoto; *fire*~ palotikkaat; *nothing* ~*s him* mikään ei jää häneltä huomaamatta; *it* ~*s my memory* en muista sitä; (~**-valve** s. poistoventtiili). **-ist** [-ist] a. todellisuutta pakeneva.

escarpment [is'kɑ:pmənt] s. jyrkkä rinne, luiska.

eschew [is'tʃu:] v. karttaa.

escort ['eskɔ:t] s. (turva)saattue, saattojoukko; v. [is'kɔ:t, es-] saattaa.

escutcheon [is'kʌtʃn] s. vaakunakilpi.

esker ['eskə] s. harju.

Eskimo ['eskiməu] s. (pl. m. *-oes*) eskimo.

esophagus ks. *oesophagus*.

esoteric [esə(u)'terik] a. salassa pidettävä.

especial [is'peʃ(ə)l, es-] a. erityinen, vert. *special*. **-ly** adv. erikoisen, erityisen, erikoisesti, varsinkin.

Esperanto [espə'ræntəu] s. esperanto.

espionage ['espiənɑ:ʒ] s. vakoilu.

espous|al [is'pauzl] s. omaksuminen. **-e** [is'pauz] v. omaksua; (vanh.) naida.

esprit [espri:] s. henkevyys.

espy [is'pai] v. saada näkyviinsä, huomata.

esquire [is'kwaiə] s. (lyh. *Esq.*) herra; (vanh.) = *squire*.

essay ['esei] s. essee, kirjoitelma, aine; yritys, koe; v. [e'sei] koettaa. **-ist** [-ist] s. esseisti.

essence ['esns] s. olennainen osa, (sisin) olemus, ydin; esanssi, mehuste; *in* ~ sisäisesti olemukseltaan, pohjimmiltaan.

essential [i'senʃ(ə)l, e's-] a. olennainen, varsinainen; välttämätön (*to, for* jllek); s. perusedellytys, asia, pääasia; *basic* ~*s* välttämättömät tarvikkeet; ~*ly* olennaisesti, pohjimmiltaan.

establish [is'tæbliʃ] v. asettaa asemaan t. virkaan, vakiinnuttaa; perustaa, pystyttää; näyttää toteen; vahvistaa; ~ *oneself* asettua, sijoittua (jhk). **-ed** [-t] a. laillinen; vakiintunut; *E* ~ *Church* valtiokirkko. **-ment** s. vahvistaminen, perustaminen; laitos; *the E* ~ perinteinen valtakoneisto, järjestelmä.

estate [is'teit] s. maatila, (maa)omaisuus; (pesän) varat ja velat; sääty; *personal* ~ irtaimisto; *real* ~ kiinteistö; ~ *agent* kiinteistönvälittäjä; ~ *car* farmariauto; ~ *duty* perintövero.

esteem [is'ti:m] v. pitää arvossa, kunnioittaa; pitää jnak; s. arvonanto.

esthetic ks. *aesthetic*.

Est(h)onia [es'təuniə] *erisn*. Viro, Eesti. **-n** [-n] a. & s. virolainen; viron kieli.

estima|ble ['estiməbl] a. arvossapidettävä. **-te** [-meit] v. arvioida (*at* jhk hintaan): arvostella; s. [-mit] arvio; kustannusarvio; arviointi; *a rough* ~ summittainen arvio; ~*d* arvioitu. **-tion** [-'meiʃn] s. arviointi; mielipide; arvonanto, kunnioitus.

estrange [is'trein(d)ʒ] v. vieroittaa; *become* ~*d* vieraantua. **-ment** s. vieraantuminen, viileä suhde.

estuary ['estjuəri] s. (joen) suu.

et cetera [it'setrə] ynnä muut, ja niin edespäin (lyh. *etc*).

etch [etʃ] v. etsata, syövyttää. **-ing** s. etsaus.

etern|al [i'tə:n|l] a. ikuinen. **-ity** [-iti] s. ikuisuus, iankaikkisuus.

ether ['i:θə] s. eetteri. **-eal** [i(:)'θiəriəl] a. eteerinen, kevyt, ilmava. **-ealize** [i(:)'θiəriəlaiz] v. henkevöittää.

ethic|al ['eθik(ə)l] a. siveysopillinen, siveellinen. **-s** [-ks] s. pl. etiikka, siveysoppi.

Ethiopia [i:θi'əupjə] erisn. Etiopia. **-n** [-n] etiopialainen

ethn|ic(al) ['eθnik, -(ə)l] a. etninen, rotu-. **-ography** [eθ'nɔgrəfi] s. etnografia, kansatiede. **-ologist** [eθ'nɔlədʒist] s. etnologi. **-ology** [eθ'nɔlədʒi] s. etnologia.

ethology [i:'θɔlədʒi] s. etologia.

ethyl ['eθl] s. etyyli.

etiology [i:ti'ɔlədʒi] s. syyoppi, syyn selvitys.

etiqette [eti'ket] s. seurustelutavat, hyvä tapa; hovietiketti.

Eton ['i:tn] erisn. **-ian** [i(:)'təunjən] Etonin (koulun oppilas).

Etruscan [i'trʌskən] a. & s. etruski(lainen).

étude [ei'tju:d] s. etyydi.

etymolo|gical [etimə'lɔdʒik(ə)l] a. etymologinen. **-gy** [eti'mɔlədʒi] s. etymologia, sanan alkuperä.

eucalyptus [ju:kə'liptəs] s. eukalyptuspuu.

Eucharist ['ju:kərist] s. ehtoollinen.

Euclid ['ju:klid] erisn. Eukleides, (kuv.) geometria.

eugenic [ju:'dʒenik] a. rotuhygieeninen. **-s** [-s] s. rotuhygienia.

eulogize ['ju:lədʒaiz] v. ylistää.

eulogy ['ju:lədʒi] s. muistopuhe, -kirjoitus.

eunuch ['ju:nək] s. eunukki, kuohilas.

euphem|ism ['ju:fimizm] s. eufemismi, lieventävä ilmaisu. **-istic** [-'mistik] a. kaunisteleva, eufemistinen.

euphony ['ju:fəni] s. sulosointuisuus.

euphoria [ju:'fɔ:riə] s. hyvinvoinnin tunne.

Europe ['juərəp] erisn. Eurooppa. **-an** [juərə'pi(:)ən] a. & s. eurooppalainen.

euthanasia [ju:θə'neizjə] s. armokuolema.

eutrophication [ju:trəfi'keiʃn] s. (järven) rehevöityminen.

evacu|ate [i'vækjueit] v. tyhjentää, evakuoida. **-ation** [-'eiʃn] s. tyhjentäminen, evakuointi. **-ee** [-ju'i:] s. evakuoitu (henkilö).

evade [i'veid] v. väistää, välttää, vältellä; kiertää (lakia).

evaluate [i'væljueit] v. arvioida. **-tion** [-'eiʃn] s. arvionti.

evanesce [i:və'nes] v. hävitä, häipyä. **-nt** [-nt] a. nopeasti haihtuva, lyhytaikainen.

evangel|ical [i:væn'dʒelik, -(ə)l] a. evankelinen. **-ist** [i'væn(d)ʒilist] s. evankelista. **-ize** [i'væn(d)ʒilaiz] v. saarnata evankeliumia (jklle;) käännyttää kristinuskoon.

evapora|te [i'væpəreit] v. haihtua, höyrystyä; hävitä, häipyä; haihduttaa, höyrystää. **-tion** [-'reiʃn] s. haihdutus, höyrystys.

eva|sion [i'veiʒn] s. välttäminen, kierteleminen; veruke. **-sive** [-siv] a. välttelevä.

eve [i:v] aatto. **E~** erisn. Eeva.

Evelyn ['i:vlin, 'evlin] erisn.

even 1. ['i:vn] a. tasainen; sileä; vaakasuora; yhdenmukainen; tasaväkinen; parillinen; kuitti; v. tasoittaa; adv. jopa, vieläpä. **-kin:** edes; *we are* ~ olemme kuitit; *be (get)* ~ *with* maksaa samalla mitalla; *break* ~ päätyä tasapeliin, päästä omilleen; *~as a child* jo lapsena; ~ *if*, ~ *though* vaikkakin; ~ *now* [*he won't*...] nytkään; ~ *then* jo silloin, (ei) sittenkään; ~ *so* siinäkin tapauksessa, kuitenkin.

even 1. ['i:vn] s. (run.) ilta.

even-handed puolueeton, tasapuolinen.

evening ['i:vniŋ] s. ilta; *this* ~ tänä iltana; *in the* ~ illalla; ~ *dress* iltapuku.

even|ly adv. tasan; tyynesti. **-ness** s. tasaisuus. **-song** s. iltavesper.

~-tempered tasainen, tyyni. **-tide** (run.) ilta.

event [i'vent] s. tapahtuma; kilpailu, (urheilu)laji; *in the ~ of war* jos sota syttyy; *at all ~s, in any ~* joka tapauksessa. **-ful** a. vaiheikas.

eventu|al [i'ventju|əl] a. lopulta tapahtuva, lopullinen. **-ality** [-'æliti] s. mahdollisuus. **-ally** adv. lopulta, vihdoin. **-ate** [-eit] v. Am. päättyä.

ever ['evə] adv. (vanh.) aina; koskaan, milloinkaan; *~ after, ~ since* (aina) siitä lähtien; *first ~* kaikkein ensimmäinen; *for ~* ikuisesti; *England for ~* eläköön Englanti! *hardly ~* tuskin milloinkaan; *thank you ~ so much* parhaimmat kiitokseni; *be it ~ so little* olipa se kuinka pieni hyvänsä; *why ~!* miksi ihmeessä. . .! *did you ever!* oletko mokomaa kuullut! **-green** a. ikivihreä, -vihanta. **-lasting** a. iankaikkinen, ikuinen; s. ikuisuus; ikikukka. **-more** adv. alituisesti, aina.

every ['evri] a. pron. joka, jokainen; *~ now and then* silloin tällöin; *~ other* jokatoinen; *~ so often* (puhek.) silloin tällöin; *~ third day, ~ three days* joka kolmas päivä; *~ bit as good* aivan yhtä hyvä; *~ one of them* joka ainoa (heistä). **-body** s. pron. jokainen. **-day** a. jokapäiväinen, arki-. **-one** s. pron. jokainen. **-thing** s. pron. kaikki. **-where** adv. kaikkialla.

eviden|ce ['evid(ə)ns] s. todistus; todistuskappale, -aineisto; näyttö; osoitus; ilmeisyys; v. todistaa, osoittaa; *call in ~* kutsua todistajaksi; *show ~ of* osoittaa jnk merkkejä; *is* [*very much*] *in ~* on ilmeinen; [*was not*] *in ~* näkyvissä. **-t** [-(ə)nt] a. ilmeinen, selvä; silminnähtävä; (~**ly** ilmeisesti).

evil ['i:vl] a. (a. worse worst) paha, ilkeä; huono; vahingollinen; s. paha, pahuus; onnettomuus, kurjuus; synti; epäkohta; adv. pahoin, huonosti; *the E ~ One* paholainen; *return good for ~* maksaa paha hyvällä. **~-doer** pahantekijä.

evince [i'vins] v. osoittaa.

eviscerate [i'visəreit] s. poistaa sisälmykset.

evocative [i'vokətiv] a. muistoja,

tunteita herättävä.

evoke [i'vouk] v. manata, kutsua esiin; herättää.

evolution [i:və'lu:ʃn] s. kehitys; kehittely; *theory of ~* kehitys-, polveutumisoppi. **-ary** [-ʃnəri] a. kehitys-. **-ist** [-ʃənist] s. kehitysopin kannattaja.

evolve [i'vɔlv] v. kehittää, kehitellä, kehittyä; kehkeytä.

ewe [ju:] s. emälammas.

ewer ['ju(:)ə] s. (vesi)kannu.

ex- [eks] pref. entinen.

exacerbat|e [ig'zæsəbeit] v. pahentaa; ärsyttää **-ion** [-'beiʃn] s. pahentuminen.

exact [ig'zækt] a. tarkka, täsmällinen; oikea; v. vaatia. **-ing** a. vaativa. **-ion** [-kʃn] s. kiskominen; kiristys. **-itude** [-itju:d] s. täsmällisyys, tarkkuus. **-ly** adv. täsmällisesti; juuri niin, aivan; oikeastaan.

exaggera|te [ig'zædʒəreit] v. liioitella. **-tion** [-'reiʃn] s. liioittelu.

exalt [ig'zɔ:lt] v. korottaa; ylistää; *~ed* korkea, ylevä. **-ation** [-'teiʃn] s. haltioituminen, hurmio.

exam [ig'zæm] s. (puhek.) tutkinto.

examination [igzæmi'neiʃn] s. tutkimus, tarkastus; tutkinto, kuulustelu, tentti.

examine [ig'zæmin] v. tutkia, tarkastaa; kuulustella. **-e** [-'ni:] s. tutkittava. **-r** [-ə] s. tutkija, kuulustelija; tarkastaja.

example [ig'za:mpl] s. esimerkki; *set a good ~* näyttää hyvää esimerkkiä; *for ~* esimerkiksi.

exaspera|te [ig'za:sp(ə)reit] v. ärsyttää, suututtaa; *~d* suuttunut, kiukuissaan; *-ting* suututtava, ärsyttävä. **-tion** [-ə'reiʃn] s. suuttumus, katkeruus.

excavat|e ['ekskəveit] v. kovertaa; kaivaa (esiin). **-ion** [-'veiʃn] s. kaivaus. **-or** [-ə] s. kaivinkone.

exceed [ik'si:d] v. nousta (jnk) yli, ylittää, olla suurempi kuin. **-ingly** adv. tavattoman, erittäin.

excel [ik'sel] v. viedä voitto (jstk); olla etevä, mestari (in, at jssak); *~ oneself* ylittää itsensä, yltää huippusaavutukseen. **-lence** ['eks(ə)ləns] s. oivallisuus. **-lency** ['eks(ə)lənsi] s.: *His E ~* hänen

ylhäisyytensä. **-lent** ['eks(ə)lənt] *a.*
mainio, erinomainen, oivallinen.

excelsior [ek'selsiɔ:] *s.* **Am.** lastuvilla.

except [ik'sept] *v.* jättää
lukuunottamatta, sulkea pois; esittää
vastaväite *(against); prep.* (m. ~ *for*)
paitsi, lukuunottamatta; ~ *me (him)*
paitsi minun (häntä); *nobody* ~ed
(kaikki) poikkeuksetta. **-ing** *prep.*
paitsi.

exception [ik'sepʃn] *s.* poikkeus;
vastaväite; *with the* ~ *of*
lukuunottamatta; *take* ~ *to* panna
vastalause jhk. ~able *a.*
moitteenalainen. **-al** [-ʃənl] *a.*
poikkeukselli|sen, -sesti, harvinainen.

excerpt ['eksə:pt] *s.* poiminto, ote; *v.*
[ek'sə:pt] poimia, lainata jtk.

excess [ik'ses] *s.* liika(määrä);
kohtuuttomuus, liiallisuus; hurjastelu
(us. ~ *es*); ~ *fare* lisämaksu; ~
luggage liikapaino; *in* ~ *of* enemmän
kuin. **-ive** [-iv] *a.* ylenmääräinen,
yletön.

exchange [iks'tʃein(d)ʒ] *v.* vaihtaa *(for*
jhk); *s.* vaihto; (vaihto)kurssi (m. *rate*
of ~); puhelinkeskus; *bill of* ~
vekseli; *the E*~ pörssi; *Stock E*~
arvopaperipörssi; *foreign* ~ valuuttu;
foreign ~ *s* ulkomaiset kurssit; *in* ~ *for*
jnk sijaan.

exchequer [iks'tʃekə] *s.* l.v.
valtiokonttori; *Chancellor of the E*~
valtiovarainministeri.

excise 1. [ek'saiz] *s.* valmistevero,
aksiisi.

excis|e 2. [ek'saiz] *v.* (lääk.) leikata
(pois), poistaa. **-ion** [ek'siʒn] *s.*
poisleikkaaminen, poisto.

excita|bility [iksaitə'biliti] *s.*
kiihottuvuus, ärtyvyys. **-ble**
[ik'saitəbl] *a.* helposti kiihottuva.
-tion [eksi'teiʃn] *s.* kiihotus.

excite [ik'sait] *v.* kiihottaa, ärsyttää;
herättää, nostattaa; ~*d* kiihtynyt,
innostunut, jännittynyt; *exciting*
jännittävä. **-ment** *s.* kiihtymys;
jännitys.

exclaim [iks'kleim] *v.* huudahtaa; ~
against äänekkäästi vastustaa.

exclamat|ion [eksklə'meiʃn] *s.*
huudahdus; ~ *mark* huutomerkki.
-ory [eks'klæmət(ə)ri] *a.* huudahdus-.

exclu|de [iks'klu:|d] *v.* sulkea pois;

tehdä mahdottomaksi. **-sion** [-ʒn] *s.*
pois sulkeminen. **-sive** [-siv] *a.* jtk pois
sulkeva; yksinomainen, ainoa; muita
hylkivä, hieno (seurapiiri ym); ~ *of*
lukuunottamatta; ~*ly* yksinomaan.

excommunica|te [ekskə'mju:nikeit] *v.*
julistaa kirkonkiroukseen. **-tion**
[-'keiʃn] *s.* kirkonkirous,
pannaanjulistus.

excrement ['ekskrimənt] *s.* uloste(et).

excrescence [iks'kresns] *s.*
kasvannainen.

excre|te [eks'kri:t] *v.* erittää. **-tion**
[eks'kri:ʃn] *s.* erittyminen; erite.

excruciating [iks'kru:ʃieitiŋ] *a.*
kiduttava, hirvittävä.

exculpate ['ekskʌlpeit] *v.* puhdistaa
syytöksestä, julistaa syyttömäksi.

excursion [iks'kə:ʃn] *s.* huvimatka,
-retki. **-ist** [-ist] *s.* huvimatkailija.

excursive [eks'kə:siv] *a.* harhaileva,
suunnitelmaton.

excusable [iks'kju:zəbl] *a.*
puolustettavissa oleva.

excuse [iks'kju:z] *v.* puolustaa,
puolustella, antaa anteeksi;
vapauttaa, päästää jstk; *s.* [iks'kju:s]
puolustus; anteeksipyyntö; ~ *me*
suokaa anteeksi! *please* ~ *my coming*
late! anteeksi, että olen myöhässä! ~
oneself pyytää päästä jstk; *he was* ~*d*
from attendance hän sai luvan olla
poissa; *send an* ~ ilmoittaa saaneensa
esteen.

execra|ble ['eksikrəbl] *a.* inhottava. **-te**
[-kreit] *v.* inhota; kirota. **-tion**
[-'kreiʃn] *s.* kirous; inho.

executant [ig'zekjutənt] *s.* esittäjä
(esim. musiikin).

execu|te ['eksikju:t] *v.* panna toimeen,
täytäntöön; suorittaa, toimittaa;
teloittaa; esittää, soittaa. **-tion**
[-'kju:ʃn] *s.* täytäntöönpano;
suorittaminen; esitys, suoritus;
teloitus; *carry into* ~ panna
täytäntöön; (~ *er* s. pyöveli).

execut|ive [ig'zekjutiv] *a.*
täytäntöönpaneva; *s.* toimeenpaneva
elin t. valta; johtohenkilö, johtaja; ~
case asiakirjalaukku; ~ *committee*
työvaliokunta, johtokunta. **-or** [-tə] *s.*
(testamentin) toimeenpanija. **-rix**
[-triks] *s.* = ed. (nainen).

exempl|ar [ig'zempl|ə] *s.* malli. **-ary**

[-əri] *a.* mallikelpoinen, esikuvallinen; varoittava. **-ify** [-ifai] *v.* olla esimerkkinä (jstk).

exempt [ig'zem(p)t] *v.* vapauttaa *(from* jstk); *a.* vapautettu, vapaa. **-ion** [-(p)ʃn] *s.* (eri)vapautus.

exercise ['eksəsaiz] *s.* harjoitus, harjottaminen; ruumiin-, aseharjoitus, liikunta; harjoitustehtävä, -kirjoitus; *v.* harjoittaa, harjoitella; käyttää; hankkia liikuntaa, jaloitella; askarruttaa, vaivata; *take* ~ jaloitella, harrastaa liikuntaa; ~ *book* kirjoitusvihko; ~ *caution* noudattaa varovaisuutta; ~ *an influence on* olla vaikutus jkh.

exert [ig'zəːt] *v.* käyttää, ponnistaa; ~ *oneself* rasittaa itseänsä; ~ *an effect (on)* vaikuttaa. **-ion** [-əːʃn] *s.* ponnistus.

exhalation [eks(h)ə'leiʃn] *s.* huokuminen; höyry, huuru; uloshengitys.

exhale [eks'heil] *v.* huokua; haihtua, hengittää (ulos).

exhaust [ig'zɔːst] *v.* ammentaa tyhjiin, kuluttaa loppuun; tyhjentää; uuvuttaa; *s.* poistoputki; ~*ed* uupunut; ~ *fumes* pakokaasu; ~ *pipe* pakoputki. **-ion** [-ʃn] *s.* uupumus. **-ive** [-iv] *a.* tyhjentävä, perinpohjainen.

exhibit [ig'zibit] *v.* näyttää, asettaa näytteille; esittää, osoittaa; *s.* näyttelyesine, todistuskappale, näyttö. **-ion** [eksi'biʃn] *s.* näyttely; apuraha; *place on* ~ asettaa näytteille; *make an* ~ *of oneself* tehdä itsensä naurettavaksi; (~*er s.* stipendiaatti; ~*ism s.* (sairas) itsensä paljastamisen halu). **-or** [-ə] *s.* näytteillepanija.

exhilara|te [ig'ziləreit] *v.* tehdä hilpeäksi, *-ting* naurattava, ilahduttava. **-tion** [-'reiʃn] *s.* ilo(isuus), hilpeys.

exhort [ig'zɔːt] *v.* (vakavasti) kehottaa. **-ation** [egzɔː'teiʃn] *s.* kehotus.

exhume [eks'hjuːm] *v.* kaivaa (ruumis) haudasta.

exigen|cy ['eksidʒənsi, eg'zid-] *s.* pakottava tarve; ahdinko. **-t** [-(ə)nt] *a.* pakottava.

exiguous [eg'zigjuəs] *a.* niukka.

exile ['eksail, 'egz-] *s.* maanpako(laisuus); maanpakolainen; *v.* ajaa maanpakoon, karkottaa; *in* ~ maanpaossa.

exist [ig'zist] *v.* olla olemassa; ~ *on* pysyä hengissä jnk varassa. **-ence** [-(ə)ns] *s.* olemassaolo; elämä; *come into* ~ syntyä. **-ent** [-(ə)nt] *a.* olemassaoleva; vallitseva, nykyinen. **-entialism** [egzis'tenʃəlizm] *s.* eksistentialismi. **-ing** olemassa oleva.

exit ['eksit] *s.* poistuminen; ovi (ulos); (maasta) lähtö; ~ *A. A.* poistuu näyttämöltä.

exodus ['eksədəs] *s.* joukkolähtö; *the E* ~ 2. Mooseksen kirja.

ex officio [eksə'fiʃiəu] *a. & adv.* viran puolesta.

exonerate [ig'zɔnəreit] *v.* vapauttaa syytöksestä.

exorbitan|ce [ig'zɔːbit(ə)ns] *s.* kohtuuttomuus. **-t** [-(ə)nt] *a.* ylenmääräinen, kohtuuton, ylettön.

exor|cize, -ise ['eksɔːsaiz] *v.* ajaa ulos, manata pois. **-cist** [-sist] *s.* (henkien) manaaja.

exotic [eg'zɔtik] *a.* eksoottinen, vierasmaalainen.

expand [iks'pænd] *v.* laajentaa, levittää; laajeta, levitä, avautua, paisua.

expans|e [iks'pæns] *s.* laajuus, laaja ala, avaruus. **-ible** [-səbl] *a.* laajeneva, paisuva. **-ion** [-ʃn] *s.* laajeneminen, paisuminen; laajuus. **-ive** [-siv] *a.* laajeneva, laajenemis-; venyvä; laaja; avosydäminen.

expatiate [eks'peiʃieit] *v.* puhua t. kirjoittaa laveasti *(on* jstk).

expatria|te [eks'peitrieit] *v.* ajaa maanpakoon; *a.&.s.* [-iət] ulkomailla asuva; ~ *oneself* luopua kansalaisuudestaan. **-tion** [-'eiʃn] *s.* maanpako.

expect [iks'pekt] *v.* odottaa; arvella, luulla. **-ancy** [-(ə)nsi] *s.* odotus; toive; *life*-~ todennäköinen (jäljelläoleva) elinaika. **-ant** [-(ə)nt] *a.* odottava. **-ation** [ekspek'teiʃn] *s.* odotus; toive, *pl.* (perinnön) toiveet; todennäköisyys; *answer (come up to) one's* ~ [s] vastata odotuksia; ~ *of life* todennäköinen (jäljelläoleva) elinaika.

expectora|te ['eks'pektəreit] *v.* yskiä,

sylkeä. **-tion** [-'reiʃn] s. yskös.

expedien|ce, -cy [iks'pi:djəns, -ənsi] s. sopivuus; tarkoituksenmukaisuus; omanvoitonpyynti. **-t** [-ənt] a. sopiva, tarkoituksenmukainen, edullinen; s. keino, neuvo.

expedit|e ['ekspidait] v. jouduttaa, edistää; lähettää. **-ion** [-'diʃn] s. retkikunta, (tutkimus-, sota) retki; joutuisuus. **-ionary** [-'diʃən(ə)ri] a. (tutkimus)retkelle lähetetty; ~ force siirtoarmeija. **-ious** [-'diʃəs] a. joutuisa, ripeä.

expel [iks'pel] v. ajaa ulos, karkottaa; erottaa (koulusta).

expend [iks'pend] v. kuluttaa (rahaa ym). **-able** a. josta voi luopua, jnk voi uhrata. **-iture** [-itʃə] s. kustannukset, kulungit; (rahan ym) kulutus.

expens|e [iks'pens] s. meno, kulunki; pl. kustannukset, kulut, menot; at my ~ minun kustannuksellani; at the ~ of his health terveytensä kustannuksella; go to the ~ of kustantaa jtk; put sb. to great ~ aiheuttaa paljon kuluja jklle. **-ive** [-iv] a. kallis.

experience [iks'piəriəns] s. kokemus; v. kokea; by ~, from ~ kokemuksesta; ~d kokenut, taitava.

experiment [iks'perimənt] s. koe; v. [-ment] kokeilla (on, with jllak). **-al** [eksperi'mentl] a. kokeellinen koe-. **-ation** [eksperimen'teiʃn] s. kokeilu.

expert ['ekspə:t] a. asiantunteva, pätevä; s. asiantuntija. **-ise** [-'ti:z] s. asiantuntijat, asiantuntemus. **-ness** s. asiantuntemus.

expia|te ['ekspieit] v. sovittaa. **-tion** [-'eiʃn] s. sovitus; sovintouhri. **-tory** ['ekspiətəri] a. sovitus-.

expiration [ekspai(ə)'reiʃn] s. uloshengitys; päättyminen, (umpeen) kuluminen.

expir|e [iks'paiə] v. hengittää ulos; kuolla; kulua loppuun t. umpeen, päättyä, lakata olemasta voimassa. **-y** [-ri] s. päättyminen.

explain [iks'plein] v. selittää; ~ away selittää olemattomaksi; ~ oneself selittää tarkoituksensa.

explana|tion [eksplə'neiʃn] s. selitys. **-tory** [iks'plænət(ə)ri] a. selittävä.

expletive [eks'pli:tiv] a. täydentävä; s. täytesana; kirosana.

explica|ble [eks'plikəbl] a. selitettävissä oleva. **-tory** [eks'plikət(ə)ri] a. selittävä.

explicit [iks'plisit] a. selvä, täsmällinen nimenomainen, selvästi ilmaistu.

explode [iks'ploud] v. räjähtää, räjäyttää; paljastaa, osoittaa paikkansapitämättömäksi.

exploit ['eksploit] s. urotyö; v. [iks'ploit] käyttää hyödyksi; riistää. **-ation** [-'teiʃn] s. hyväksikäyttö; riistäminen, riisto.

explora|tion [eksplə'reiʃn] s. tutkiminen, tutkimus. **-tory** [iks'plɔ(:)rət(ə)ri] a. tutkimustarkoituksessa tehty.

explore [iks'plɔː] v. tutkia, tehdä tutkimusmatka. **-r** [-rə] s. tutkimusmatkailija.

explo|sion [iks'plouʒn] s. räjähdys; population ~ räjähdysmäinen väestönkasvu. **-sive** [-siv] a. räjähtävä; s. räjähdysaine (m. high ~); umpiäänne (kiel.).

exponent [eks'pounənt] s. selittäjä, tulkitsija; edustaja.

export [eks'pɔːt] v. viedä (maasta); s. ['ekspɔːt] vienti(tavara); ~s vienti. **-ation** [-'teiʃn] s. vienti. **-er** [-ə] s. maastaviejä.

expos|e [iks'pəuz] v. panna alttiiksi (to jllek), saattaa (jnk) alaiseksi, altistaa; jättää (vauva) heitteille, vaarantaa; paljastaa; valottaa (valok.); asettaa näytteille. **-ed** [-d] a. avoin, suojaton. **-ition** [ekspə'ziʃn] s. näyttely; selonteko, selitys.

expostula|te [iks'pɔstjuleit] v. : ~ with nuhdella. **-tion** [-'leiʃn] s. nuhde.

exposure [iks'pəuʒə] s. oleminen alttiina (to jllek); paljastaminen; valotus; die of ~ (tav.) paleltua kuoliaaksi; ~ meter valotusmittari.

expound [iks'paund] v. selittää, tulkita.

express [iks'pres] v. ilmaista, lausua; pusertaa ulos; a. nimenomainen; erikois-, pika-; s. pikajuna; erikois-, pikalähetti; adv. pikaisesti; ~ oneself ilmaista ajatuksensa; by ~ pikalähetyksenä. **-ible** [-əbl] a. ilmaistavissa oleva.

expression [iks'preʃn] s. ilmaiseminen; ilmaus; ilme; give ~ to ilmaista. **-less** a. ilmeetön.

expressive [iks'presiv] a. ilmekäs, puhuva; jtk ilmaiseva.

express|ly [iks'presli] adv. nimenomaan, selvästi; varta vasten. **-way** Am. moottoritie.

expropria|te [eks'prəuprieit] v. pakkolunastaa. **-tion** [-'eiʃn] s. pakkolunastus.

expulsion [iks'pʌlʃn] s. karkotus, erottaminen (koulusta).

expunge [eks'pʌn(d)ʒ] v. pyyhkiä pois, poistaa.

expurga|te [ekspə:geit] v. poistaa (loukkaavat kohdat), siivota (kirja). **-tion** [-'geiʃn] s. puhdistaminen.

exquisite ['ekskwizit, -'--] a. erinomaisen kaunis, siro, hienon-hieno; erinomaisen tarkka; pistävä.

ex-service ['eks'sə:vis] a.: ~ man (entinen) rintamamies, veteraani.

extant [eks'tænt, 'ekstənt] a. jäljellä oleva.

extempor|aneous [ekstempə'reinjəs] a. valmistamaton. **-ary** [eks'temp(ə)rəri] a. = ed. **-e** [eks'tempəri] adv. valmistautumatta; a. = ed. **-ize** [eks'tempəraiz] v. esittää, puhua valmistamatta.

extend [iks'tend] v. ojentaa; pidentää, jatkaa; laajentaa, levittää; ulottaa; suoda, osoittaa; laajeta, ulottua, levitä; ~ed order avojärjestys (sot.).

exten|sion [iks'ten ʃn] s. pidentäminen, pidennys, jatko, jatke; laajennus; laajuus, ala; avartuminen, lisärakennus; (puhelimen) liittymä, alanumero. **-sive** [-siv] a. laaja; laajakantoinen, kauas ulottuva; ~ly laajasti, laajalti.

extent [iks'tent] s. laajuus; ulottuvuus; ala, määrä; to a great ~ suuressa määrin; to a certain ~ jossakin määrin; to that ~ (m.) sikäli.

extenuat|e [eks'tenjueit] v. pienentää, vähentää; -ing circumstances lieventävät asianhaarat. **-ion** [-'eiʃn] s.: in ~ jnk puolustukseksi.

exterior [eks'tiəriə] a. ulkopuolinen, ulkonainen, ulko-; s. ulkopuoli; ulkomuoto, -näkö, asu.

extermina|te [eks'tə:mineit] v. hävittää perin pohjin t. sukupuuttoon. **-tion** [-'neiʃn] s. perin pohjin hävittäminen, tuhoaminen.

external [eks'tə:nl] a. ulkopuolinen, ulkonainen, ulko-; s. pl. ulkonaiset seikat; for ~ use ulkoisesti.

extinct [iks'tiŋ(k)t] a. sammunut; sukupuuttoon kuollut; become ~ kuolla (sukupuuttoon), sammua. **-ion** [-kʃn] s. sammuminen; sammutus; sukupuuttoon kuoleminen, loppuminen.

extinguish [iks'tiŋgwiʃ] v. sammuttaa, tukahduttaa, tehdä tyhjäksi; kuolettaa (velka). **-er** [-ə] s.: fire ~ sammutin.

extirpat|e [eksta:peit] v. poistaa juurineen; perin pohjin hävittää; leikata pois. **-ion** [-'peiʃn] s. (lääk.) poisto.

extol [iks'təul] v. ylistää.

extort [iks'tɔ:t] v. kiristää.

extortion [iks'tɔ:ʃn] s. kiristys. **-ate** [-it] a. kiristävä, kiskuri-; ~ price nylkyhinta. **-er** [-ə] s. kiristäjä, nylkyri.

extra ['ekstrə] a. ylimääräinen; erikois-; lisä-, yli-; adv. ylimääräisesti, lisää; erikoisen; s. ylimääräinen työ, maksu ym; tilapäisnäyttelijä, statisti (stage ~).

extra- pref. ulkopuolella, (jnk) ulkoinen.

extract [iks'trækt] v. vetää pois; kiristää (lupaus ym); uuttaa; poimia (kirjan kohta); ottaa (neljöjuuri); s. ['ekstrəkt] uute, ekstrakti; ote, poiminto. **-ion** [-kʃn] s. poisvetäminen poisto; syntyperä.

extra|curricular a. kurssiin t. oppimäärään kuulumaton. **-dite** [-dait] v. luovuttaa (rikollinen). **-dition** [-'diʃn] s. luovutus. **-marital** a. avioliiton ulkopuolinen. **-mural** a. kaupungin muurien (yliopiston ym) ulkopuolella, -lta oleva.

extraneous [eks'treinjəs] a. asiaankuulumaton, muu; ulkopuolinen.

extra|ordinary [iks'trɔ:dinəri] a. tavallisuudesta poikkeava, tavaton; ylimääräinen; merkillinen. **-polate** [ekst'ræpə(u) leit] v. ekstrapoloida. ~-**sensory**: -s. perception aisteista riippumaton havaitseminen. **-territorial** a. eksterritoriaali-.

extravagan|ce [iks'trævigəns] s.

tuhlaavaisuus; kohtuuttomuus,
ylellisyys. **-t** [-ənt] a. (mielettömän)
tuhlaavainen, ylellinen; liiallinen,
kohtuuton.

extrem|e [iks'tri:m] a. äärimmäinen,
äärimmäisyyksiin menevä;
äärettömän suuri; s. äärimmäisyys;
careless in the ~ äärimmäisen
huolimaton; the ~ left
äärivasemmisto. **-ist** s.
äärimmäisyysmies. **-ity** [iks'tremiti] s.
äärimmäinen hätä; äärimmäisyys;
raaja; pl. raajat; äärimmäiset keinot t.
toimenpiteet.

extricate ['ekstrikeit] v. irrottaa,
vapauttaa.

extrinsic [eks'trinsik] ulkoinen.

extrovert ['ekstrə(u)və:t] s. ulospäin
suuntautunut (ihminen).

extrude [eks'tru:d] v. työntyä ulos.

exuber|ance [ig'zju:b(ə)rəns] s.
ylenpalttinen runsaus, rehevyys. **-ant**
[-ənt] a. ylenpalttinen, ylitsevuotava;
rehevä, (esim. iloa) uhkuva,
pursuava.

exud|ate ['eksju:deit] s. tulehduserite.
-ation [-'deiʃn] s. kihoaminen. **-e**
[ig'zju:d] v. kihota, tihkua; erittää.

exult [ig'zʌlt] v. riemuita. **-ant** [-ənt] a.
riemuitseva. **-ation** [egzʌl'teiʃn] s.
riemu.

eye [ai] s. silmä, näkö; silmu, silmukka,
neulansilmä; reikä; lehtiäinen (hook
and ~); v. silmäillä, tarkastella; clap
(set) ~s on nähdä; he has an ~ for
hänelle on silmää jllek; make ~s at
keimailla jklle; see ~ to ~ with olla
aivan samaa mieltä; by the ~
silmämitalla; with an ~ to
silmälläpitäen jtk, jk silmämääränä.
-ball silmämuna; ~ to ~ silmitysten,
kasvokkain. **~-bath**
silmähaudekuppi. **-brow** kulmakarva.
~-glass monokkeli. **-lash** silmäripsi.
-let pieni reikä, paulanreikä. **-lid**
silmäluomi. **~-liner** silmänrajausväri
~-opener (hämmästyttävä) seikka
joka avaa silmät. **~-servant**
silmänpalvelija. **-shot** silmäkantama.
-sight näkö. **-sore** silmätikku. **-wash** s.
sl. humpuuki. **-witness** s.
silminnäkijä.

Eyre [ɛə] erisn.

eyrie ['aiəri] s. petolinnun pesä.

Ezekiel [i'zi:kjəl] erisn. Hesekiel.

F

F, f [ef] *s.* f-kirjain; nuotti f;
~ *sharp* fis.
Lyh.: **F.** *Fahrenheit;* **f.** *feet, foot;* **F.A.**
Football Association; **F.A.O.** *Food
and Agriculture Organization of the
United Nations;* **F.B.I.** *Federal
Bureau of Investigation* Am.
(liittovaltion) turvallisuuspoliisi; **Feb.**
February; **Fed.** *Federal, Federation;*
fig. *figure;* **Fla.** *Florida;* **F.O.** *Foreign
Office;* **FM** *frequency modulation;* **f.
o. b.** *free on board* vapaasti laivassa;
fr. *francs;* **F. R. S.** *Fellow of the Royal
Society;* **ft.** *feet, foot.*
fable [feibl] *s.* opettava; eläinsatu; taru,
tarina; *v.* kertoa satuja; ~*d* *s.*
tarunomainen.
fabric ['fæbrik] *s.* kangas, kudos;
rakenne. **-ate** [-eit] *v.* keksiä, sepittää;
väärentää. **-ation** [-'keiʃn] *s.*
sepittäminen; väärennys.
fabulous ['fæbjuləs] *a.* tarunomainen;
uskomaton, suunnaton.
facade [fə'saːd] *s.* julkisivu.
face 1. [feis] *s.* kasvot; pinta, etupuoli,
kuvapuoli, etusivu, julkisivu;
kellotaulu; hävyttömyys, »otsa»; ~ *to*
~ kasvokkain; ~ *value* nimellisarvo;
full ~ suoraan edestä; *to one's* ~
vasten silmiä; *he has the* ~ *to* hän
julkeaa; *make* ~ *s* [*at*] irvistellä; *in the*
~ *of* jnk (vaikeuden ym) edessä; jstk
huolimatta; *on the* ~ *of it* päältäpäin
katsoen; *loss of* ~ arvovallan kolaus;
»kasvojen» t. maineen menetys; *save
[one's]* ~ pelastaa »kasvonsa»; *set
one's* ~ *against* vastustaa.
face 2. [feis] *v.* olla (t. kääntyä) jhk
päin, olla (seistä t. istua) jtk
vastapäätä; olla kasvokkain, kohdata
kasvoista kasvoihin, katsoa silmästä
silmään, uhmata; päällystää, varustaa
käänteillä; *the window* ~ *s south*

ikkuna antaa etelään; ~ *it out* pitää
pintansa, ei antaa periksi; ~ *the facts*
tunnustaa tosiasiat; ~ *up to* kohdata
rohkeasti; [*the problem*] *that* ~*s us*
joka on edessämme. ~**-lift(ing)**
kasvojen nuorennusleikkaus. **-r** [-ə] *s.*
kuv. (kuin) isku kasvoihin.
facet ['fæsit] *s.* viiste, fasetti;
many-~*ed* monitahoinen.
facetious [fə'siːʃəs] *a.* leikkisä.
facial ['feiʃ(ə)l] *a.* kasvo-; *s.*
kasvojenhoito.
facil|e ['fæsail] *a.* helppo; sujuva,
luonteva; taipuisa; myöntyväinen.
-itate [fə'siliteit] *v.* helpottaa. **-ity**
[fə'siliti] *s.* helppous;
sujuvuus, luontevuus; (tav. *pl.*)
mahdollisuudet, (jhk tarvittavat)
laitteet, laitteisto.
facing ['feisiŋ] *s.* päällys(te); *pl.*
(puvun) käänteet, reunukset, kaulus.
facsimile [fæk'simili] *s.* näköispainos.
fact [fækt] *s.* tosiasia, -seikka,
todellisuus; asianlaita; *as a matter of*
~, *in point of* ~, *in* ~ itse asiassa,
oikeastaan.
facti|on ['fækʃn] *s.* (riitelevä) puolue;
nurkkakunta; puoluehenki. **-ous** [-ʃəs]
a. puoluekiihkoinen, puolue-.
factitious [fæk'tiʃəs] *a.* keinotekoinen,
teennäinen.
factor ['fæktə] *s.* tekijä, asiamies;
(Skotl.) tilanhoitaja. **-y** [-ri] *s.* tehdas,
tehdaslaitos; (~-**made**
tehdasvalmisteinen).
fact|otum [fæk'toutəm] *s.* palvelija,
»oikea käsi». **-ual** ['fæktjuəl] *a.*
tosiasiallinen, asia-.
faculty ['fæk(ə)lti] *s.* kyky; *pl.* sielun
kyvyt; tiedekunta; Am.
opettajakunta; *in possession of her
faculties* täysissä sielun- ja
ruumiinvoimissa.

fad [fæd] s. keppihevonen:
muotihullutus. **-dist** s. intoilija. **-dy**
[-i] a. oikullinen (et. ruoan suhteen).
fade [feid] v. haalistua; kuihtua,
lakastua; häipyä *(m. ~ away, ~ out);*
haalistuttaa; (rad.) ~ ... *in (out)*
vähitellen lisätä (vähentää)
kuuluvuutta; *~d* kuihtunut,
haalistunut. **-less** *a.* haalistumaton.
fading [feidiŋ] s. haalistuminen jne;
häipyminen.
f(a)eces ['fi:si:z] *s. pl.* ulosteet.
fag [fæg] v. raataa; väsyttää; s. ikävä
työ; väsymys; (koul. Engl.)
(yläluokkalaisen) »passari»; sl.
savuke; *~ged out* lopen uupunut; ~
for olla vanhemman oppilaan orjana
~-end (arvoton) jäännöspala;
savukkeen pätkä.
fag(g)ot ['fægət] s. risukimppu.
Fahrenheit ['fær(ə)nhait] *erisn.*
faience [fai'ã:(n)s] s. fajanssi.
fail [feil] v. epäonnistua, saada reput;
reputtaa; puuttua, loppua; riutua,
murtua, (äänestä) pettää, (koneesta)
pysähtyä; jäädä tapahtumatta, jättää
tekemättä; tehdä vararikko; pettää,
jättää pulaan; *s.: without~* varmasti;
I ~ to understand en ymmärrä; *he ~ed
to come* hän ei tullut. **-ing** s. heikkous;
puute; *a.* puuttuva, vähenevä; *prep.:
~ this* jos näin ei tapahdu. **-ure** [-jə] s.
epäonnistuminen; epäonnistunut
ihminen (t. asia); tekemättä
jättäminen, laiminlyönti; vararikko;
~ of crops kato; *engine ~* konevika;
heart ~ sydänhalvaus.
fain [fein] *a.* suostuvainen; *adv.: I
would ~* tahtoisin mielelläni.
faint [feint] *a.* heikko; voimaton,
raukea; epäselvä; pelokas; *s.*
pyörtymys; *v.* mennä tainnoksiin,
pyörtyä. **~-hearted** arka, pelokas.
-ing *s.: ~ fit* pyörtymiskohtaus. **-ness**
s. heikkous.
fair 1. [fɛə] *s.* markkinat; messut;
näyttely; myyjäiset; *fun ~* huvipuisto,
world's ~ maailmannäyttely.
fair 2. [fɛə] *a.* vaalea, vaaleaverinen;
oikeudenmukainen, kohtuullinen:
kohtalainen, keskinkertainen,
laatuunkäypä, melko hyvä; suotuisa,
kauniilta tuntuva; puhdas, selvä;
kaunis; *adv.* kauniisti; rehellisesti;

puhtaaksi jne; *~ and square*
rehellinen; *~ copy*
puhtaaksikirjoitettu kappale; *by ~
means or foul* hyvällä tai pahalla; *~
play* reilu peli; *the ~ sex*
naissukupuoli; *~-weather friends*
hyvän sään ystävät; *it bids ~ to* on
hyvät toiveet, että. . . ; *play ~* pelata
(nyrkkeillä ym) sääntöjen mukaan;
write out ~ kirjoittaa puhtaaksi.
-ground: *~s* tivoli; *~ people*
sirkustaiteilijat. **~-haired**
vaaleatukkainen. **-ly** *adv.* kauniisti,
rehellisesti jne; kohtalaisen, melko:
kerrassaan, kerta kaikkiaan. **-ness** s.
vaaleus; puolueettomuus jne.
~-spoken kohtelias. **-way** väylä.
fairy ['fɛəri] s. keijukainen, haltijatar;
sl. homoseksualisti; *a.* keijukais-,
ihme-; *~ cycle* lasten pyörä. **-land**
satumaa. **~-tale** satu.
faith [feiθ] *s.* usko; luottamus;
uskollisuus; kunniasana, lupaus;
Christian ~ kristinusko; *in bad ~*
vilpillisessä mielessä; *~ healer*
rukouksella parantaja. **-ful** *a.*
uskollinen; tosi. **-fully** *adv.*
uskollisesti; *Yours ~* (kirjeissä)
kunnioittavasti. **-less** *a.* uskoton,
petollinen; epäuskoinen.
fake [feik] v. (m. ~ *up)* tekaista,
väärentää; *s.* huijaus, väärennys;
tekaistu juttu, huijari; väärennetty,
vale-.
fakir ['feikiə, Am. fə'kiə] *s.* fakiiri.
falchion ['fɔ:l(t)ʃn] *s.* käyrä miekka.
falcon ['fɔ:lkən, Am. 'fæl-] *s.* haukka.
-er [-ə] *s.* haukkametsästäjä. **-ry** [-ri] *s.*
haukkametsästys.
fall [fɔ:l] *fell fallen*, *v.* pudota, kaatua:
syöksyä alas; kukistua; aleta, laskea;
langeta; joutua *(to* jklle); sattua *(on*
jhk); *s.* putoaminen; kukistuminen,
tuho; lasku; vesiputous (us. *pl.);* Am.
syksy; sademäärä *(rain ~),*
(lumen)tulo; *the F ~* *[of man]*
syntiinlankeemus; *her face fell* hänen
kasvonsa venyivät pitkiksi; *~ asleep*
nukahtaa; *~ ill* sairastua; *~ among*
joutua . . . joukkoon; *~ apart* hajota;
~ away luopua, käydä heikoksi,
riutua; *~ back* perääntyä; *~ back upon*
turvautua jhk; *~ behind* jäädä
jälkeen; *~ down* pudota; *~ for* (sl.)

ihastua jkh; ~ *in* asettua riviin; taipua sisäänpäin, mennä kuopalle; ~ *in with* (odottamatta) kohdata, suostua; ~ *into* jakautua; ~ *off* pudota, varista; vähentyä; ~ *on* käydä kimppuun; ~ *out* riitaantua; päättyä *(well* hyvin); (sot.) lähteä rivistä; ~ *short of* olla riittämätön; ~ *through* epäonnistua; ~ *to* käydä käsiksi (ruokaan); ~ *under* kuulua jhk; ~ *upon* hyökätä kimppuun.

falla|cious [fə'leiʃəs] *a.* harhaanjohtava, pettävä. **-cy** ['fæləsi] *s.* petollisuus; harha, erhe; virhepäätelmä.

fal-lal ['fæl'læl] *s.* hepenet.

fallen ['fɔ:l(ə)n] *pp.* ks. *fall.*

fallible ['fælibl] *a.* erehtyväinen; (mahdollisesti) erheellinen.

falling ['fɔ:liŋ] *a.* putoava jne; ~ *away* luopumus; ~ *off* väheneminen; huononeminen.

fall-out *s.* radioaktiivinen pöly, laskeuma.

fallow 1. ['fæləu] *a.* ruskeankeltainen. **~-deer** kuusipeura.

fallow 2. ['fæləu] *a.* kesannossa oleva; *s.* kesanto; *lie* ~ olla kesantona.

false [fɔ:ls] *a.* väärä, virheellinen; perätön; väärennetty, teko-, vale-, uskoton, petollinen, vilpillinen; ~ *hair* [*pieces*] irtotukka; *under* ~ *colours* väärällä lipulla; ~ *start* varaslähtö; *play sb.* ~ petkuttaa **-hood** *s.* valhe; valheellisuus. **-ly** *adv.* väärin, vilpillisesti: ~ *accused* aiheetta syytetty. **-ness** *s.* vääryys, valheellisuus; petollisuus, uskottomuus.

falsetto [fɔ:l'setou] *s.* falsetti.

falsies ['fɔ:lsiz] *s. pl.* rintaliivin kuppien täytteet.

falsi|fication [fɔ:lsifi'keiʃn] *s.* väärennys. **-fy** ['fɔ:lsifai] *v.* väärentää; vääristellä; osoittaa vääräksi. **-ty** ['fɔ:lsiti] *s.* vääryys, valheellisuus.

Falstaff ['fɔ:lstɑ:f] *erisn.*

falter ['fɔ:ltə] *v.* horjua: epäröidä; änkyttää, soperrella.

fame [feim] *s.* maine, kuuluisuus. **-d** [-d] *a. &. pp.* maineikas, kuuluisa.

familiar [fə'miljə] *a.* läheinen tuttu *(with* jkn kanssa): perehtynyt *(with);* hyvin tuttu *(to* jklle); tavallinen;

(liian) tuttavallinen; *s.* läheinen ystävä. **-ity** [-i'æriti] *s.* läheinen tuttavuus, tuttavallinen seurustelu; perehtyneisyys; tuttavallisuus. **-ize** [-raiz] *v.* tutustuttaa, perehdyttää; ~ *oneself* tutustua.

family ['fæmili] *s.* perhe; suku; hyvä perhe t. tunnettu suku; (kasv., eläint.) heimo; ~ *man* perheellinen mies; ~ *tree* sukupuu; *is in the ~ way* odottaa perheenlisäystä.

fam|ine ['fæmin] *s.* nälänhätä, nälkä. **-ish** ['fæmiʃ] *v.* nähdä nälkää, näännyttää nälkään; ~ *ed* nälkiintynyt.

famous ['feiməs] *a.* kuuluisa, maineikas; (vanh.) mainio.

fan 1. [fæn] *s.* viuhka; tuuletin; (viljan) pohdin, viskain; *v.* leyhytellä; lietsoa; viskata (viljaa).

fan 2. [fæn] *s.* intoilija *film* ~ »elokuvahullu»; ~ *mail* ihailijaposti.

fanatic [fə'næt|ik] *s.* intoilija, kiihkoilija; *a.* = seur. **-al** [-ikəl] *a.* kiihkoileva, fanaattinen. **-ism** [-isizm] *s.* kiihkomielisyys.

fanci|ed ['fænsiəd] *a.* kuviteltu. **-er** [-iə] *s.* tuntija; *dog-* ~ koirien ystävä. **-ful** *a.* mielikuvituksekas; mielikuvituksellinen, fantastinen; oikullinen; eriskummainen, epätodellinen.

fancy ['fænsi] *s.* mielikuvitus; kuvitelma; päähänpisto, oikku; maku, erityinen mieltymys jhk; *a.* mielikuvituksellinen, hieno, ylellisyys-, koru-; *v.* kuvitella; pitää jstk; otaksua, luulla; ~ *bread* leivonnaiset; ~ *diving* ponnahduslautahypyt; ~ *goods* koru-, ylellisyystavarat; ~ *price* satumainen, mieletön hinta; ~ *work* koruompelu; *catch the* ~ *of* miellyttää jkta; *take a* ~ *to* mieltyä jhk; ~ *oneself* luulla olevansa jtk. **~-dress** naamiaispuku; *f.-d. ball* naamiaiset. **~-free** rakastumaton.

fanfare ['fænfeə] *s.* fanfaari.

fang [fæŋ] *s.* kulma-, torahammas; myrkkyhammas.

fanlight ['fænlait] *s.* puolipyöreä ikkuna (oven yläpuolella).

fantas|tic [fæn'tæstik] *a.* mielikuvituksellinen; eriskummainen,

outo; ihana, kuin unelma. **-y**
['fæntəsi] s. mielikuvitus; mielikuva,
kuvitelma.

far [fɑ:] adv. (farther t. further, farthest
t. furthest) kaukana, kauas, etäällä,
-lle; a. etäinen, kaukainen; s.: from ~
kaukaa; as ~ as jhk saakka; as ~ as,
[in] so ~ as mikäli, sikäli kuin; so ~
toistaiseksi; thus ~ tähän saakka; ~
from kaikkea muuta kuin; go ~ päästä
t. riittää pitkälle; by ~ paljon,
verrattomasti; ~ better paljon
parempi; [by] ~ the best verrattomasti
paras; ~ and away [the best]
verrattomasti, ehdottomasti; ~ too
old aivan liian vanha; the ~ end of the
room huoneen toinen pää. **~-away,**
~-off kaukainen, etäinen.

farc|e [fɑ:s] s. ilveily; mureke (keitt.).
-ical [-k(ə)l] a. farssimainen.

fare [fɛə] s. matkalipun hinta, taksa;
ruoka; v. voida (~ ill, well); käydä;
bill of ~ ruokalista; he ~d no better
hänen ei käynyt sen paremmin. **-well**
int. hyvästi! s. & a. jäähyväis(et).

far-fetched kuv. (kaukaa) etsitty,
keinotekoinen (vertailu).

farina [fə'rainə, Am. -ri:-] s. jauho,
jauhe; Am. mannaryynit; tärkkelys.
-ceous [færi'neiʃəs] a. jauhomainen.

farm [fɑ:m] s. maatalo, -tila; farmi; v.
viljellä; vuokrata, antaa vuokralle (m.
~ out). **-er** [-ə] s. maanviljelijä;
farmari; vuokraaja; (jnk) kasvattaja.
~-hand maatyöläinen. **-house**
maalaistalo. **-ing** s. maanviljely(s); fur
~ turkistarhaus; fish ~ kalanviljely.
-stead maatalo (rakennuksineen).
-yard (maatalon) piha.

Faroe ['fɛərəu] erism.: the ~ Islands
Färsaaret. **-se** [-i:z] a. & s.
färsaarelainen.

far-reaching a. kauaskantoinen.

farrier ['færiə] s. hevosenkengittäjä.

farrow ['færəu] s. porsaspoikue; v.
porsia.

far-sighted kaukonäköinen;
pitkänäköinen.

fart [fɑ:t] (alat.) s. pieru; v. pieraista.

farth|er, -est ['fɑːðə, -ðist] komp. & sup.
ks. far; ~ east idempänä, idemmäksi.

farthing ['fɑ:ðiŋ] s. vanha engl. raha (¹/₄
pennyä); not a ~ ei pennin vertaa.

farthingale ['fɑ:ðiŋgeil] s. pönkkä- t.

tukihame.

fascina|te ['fæsineit] v. lumota,
hurmata, kiehtoa. **-tion** [-'neiʃn] s.
lumous(voima), viehätys.

fascine [fæ'si:n] s. risukimppu.

fasc|ism ['fæʃism] s. fasismi. **-ist** [-ist] s.
fasisti.

fashion ['fæʃn] s. kuosi; muoti; tapa;
hienot tavat; v. muodostaa,
muodostella; a man of ~
maailmanmies; in a ~, after a ~
tavallaan; in ~ muodissa; out of ~
vanhanaikainen; fully ~ed muotoon
neulottu; vrt. parade. **-able** [-əbl] a.
muodikas, hieno, hienoston suosima.
~-plate muotikuva.

fast 1. [fɑ:st] v. paastota; s. paasto.

fast 2. [fɑ:st] a. luja, kestävä; pysyvä
(väri), syvä (uni); nopea;
huikentelevainen, liian vapaa
(käytökseltään); adv. lujasti;
nopeasti; five minutes ~ viisi
minuuttia edellä; a ~ man elostelija;
~ friends läheiset ystävät; ~ asleep
sikeässä unessa; live ~ elää
kevytmielisesti; make ~ kiinnittää,
sulkea; stand ~ olla lujana; play ~
and loose [with] leikitellä; ~-flowing
vuolas.

fasten ['fɑ:sn] v. kiinnittää; sulkea;
mennä kiinni, tarttua; ~ upon tarttua,
takertua jhk. **-er** [-ə] s. kiinnitin,
painonappi; zip ~ vetoketju. **-ing** [-iŋ]
s. kiinnitys(laite), kiinnike, hakanen
ym.

fastidious [fæs'tidiəs] a. turhantarkka,
nirso.

fasting s. paastoaminen.

fastness ['fɑ:stnis] s. lujuus ym;
linnoitus.

fat [fæt] a. lihava, paksu; rasvainen;
ihrainen; tuottoisa, hedelmällinen; s.
rasva, ihra; the ~ of the land
yltäkylläisyys; the ~ is in the fire nyt
on piru merrassa; a ~ lot you care!
mitäpä sinä siitä välität; the ~ted calf
(raam.) syötetty vasikka.

fatal ['feit|l] a. kuolettava, kuolemaan
johtanut; kohtalokas, tuhoisa; ~
wound kuolinhaava; ~ sisters
kohtalottaret. **-ist** [-əlist] s. fatalisti.
-ity [fə'tæliti] s. kuolemantapaus;
kohtalokkuus; onnettomuus. **-ly** adv.
kuolettavasti; kohtalokkaasti; was ~

injured sai kuolemaan johtaneita vammoja.

fate [feit] s. kohtalo, osa; sallimus; kohtalotar; *he was ~ed to...* hänen kohtalonsa oli...; *ill-~ed* kovaonninen. **-ful** a. kohtalokas, ratkaiseva.

father ['fɑ:ðə] s. isä; v. panna alulle; olla jnk isä t. alkuunpanija; *~ sth. on* sanoa jotakin jkn tekemäksi. **-hood** s. isyys. **~-in-law** appi. **-land** isänmaa. **-ly** a. isällinen.

fathom ['fæðəm] s. syli (mitta); v. mitata jnk syvyys, luodata; päästä (jnk) perille, käsittää. **-less** a. pohjaton.

fatigue [fə'ti:g] s. väsymys, uupumus; v. väsyttää; *~ duty* (sot.) työpalvelu; *~ party* (sot.) työkomennuskunta.

fat|ling ['fætliŋ] s. nuori syöttöelukka, juottoporsas, -vasikka. **-ness** s. lihavuus.

fatt|en ['fætn] v. (m. *~ up*) lihottaa, syöttää, lannoittaa (maata), lihoa. **-y** ['fæti] a. rasvainen; *~ acids* rasvahapot.

fatu|ity [fə'tju(:)iti] s. älyttömyys. **-ous** ['fætjuəs] a. älytön, tylsä.

faucet ['fɔ:sit] s. (et. Am.) hana.

faugh [fɔ:] int. hyt!

fault [fɔ:lt] s. virhe, vika; (tennis) väärä syöttö; v. havaita virheelliseksi; (kallion) murtuma; *find ~ with* moittia; *whose ~ is it?* kenessä on syy? *at ~* väärillä jäljillä, ymmällä; *my memory was at ~* muistini petti. **~-finding** a. moittimishaluinen; s. moittimishalu. **-less** a. virheetön, moitteeton. **-y** [-i] a. virheellinen, puutteellinen; moitittava.

faun [fɔ:n] s. fauni.

fauna ['fɔ:nə] s. fauna, eläimistö.

faux pas ['fou'pɑ:] s. virhe, munaus.

favour, favor ['feivə] s. suosio, suosionosoitus; suopeus; suosion merkki, ruusuke ym; kirje (vanh.); v. kannattaa; suosia, olla suosiollinen; edistää, helpottaa; olla (jkn) näköinen; *~ sb. with.* suoda jklle...; *may I ask you a ~?* saisinko pyytää Teiltä palvelusta? *do me the ~ of...-ing* pyydän, että ystävällisesti; *in sb.'s ~* jkn eduksi; *be in ~ of* kannattaa jtk; *out of ~ with* jkn

epäsuosiossa; under ~ of the night yön turvin; *~ sb. with* hyväntahtoisesti suoda jklle jtk. **-able** [-rəbl] a. suosiollinen; suotuisa, edullinen. **-ed** [-d] a. suosittu; *ill-~* ruma. **-ite** [-rit] a. mieli-, lempi-; s. suosikki. **-itsm** [-ritizm] s. suosikkijärjestelmä.

fawn 1. [fɔ:n] s. kuusipeuran vasikka; vaalean keltaisenruskea (väri); a. kellertävän ruskea (m. *~-coloured*).

fawn 2. [fɔ:n] v. (koirasta) osoittaa iloaan; *~ upon* liehakoida, mielistellä.

fay [fei] s. keiju.

fealty ['fi:(ə)lti] s. vasallin uskollisuus.

fear [fiə] s. pelko; v. pelätä; *~ of God* jumalanpelko; *is in ~ of his life* pelkää henkeään; *for ~ (that)* peläten (että). **-ful** a. hirvittävä, kauhea; pelokas. **-less** a. peloton. **-some** [-səm] a. hirvittävä (tav. leik.).

feasible ['fi:zəbl] a. toteutettavissa oleva, mahdollinen; uskottava.

feast [fi:st] s. (kirkollinen) juhla; kestit, pidot; v. kestitä; juhlia; *~ one's eyes upon* nautinnokseen katsella.

feat [fi:t] s. urotyö, sankariteko; taidonnäyte.

feather ['feðə] s. höyhen, sulka; v. varustaa, peittää, sisustaa höyhenillä; *a ~ in his cap* ylpeilyn aihe; *[they are] birds of a ~* samaa maata, saman hengen lapsia; *show the white ~* osoittaa pelkuruutta; *~ oar* panna airo lappeelleen; *~ one's nest* hankkia rahaa. **~-bed** höyhenpatja. **~-brained** häälyvä, tyhjäpäinen. **-ed** a. sulitettu, höyhenpeitteinen. **-weight** höyhensarjan nyrkkeilijä. **-y** a. höyhenpeitteinen, höyhenenkevyt.

feature ['fi:tʃə] s. piirre, pl. kasvonpiirteet; luonteenomainen piirre, erikoisuus, (ohjelman) päänumero, erikoisartikkeli; v. olla luonteenomaista; esittää huomattavalla paikalla, (elok.) esittää (näyttelijä) tähtiosassa; *~ film* pitkä elokuva, pääfilmi.

febrile ['fi:brail] a. kuume-; kuumeinen.

February ['februəri] s. helmikuu.

feckless ['feklis] a. (Skotl.) voimaton, avuton.

fecund ['fi:kʌnd] a. hedelmällinen. **-ity**

[fi'kʌnditi] s. hedelmällisyys.
fed [fed] imp. & pp. ks. feed; ~ up
(with) kyllästynyt jhk.
federa|l ['fedər(ə)l] a. liitto-;
liittovaltion, Am. m. pohjoisvaltioiden; F~ Germany Saksan
liittotasavalta. **-te** ['fedəreit] v.
yhdistää t. yhdistyä (valtio)liitoksi; a.
[-rit] liitto-. **-tion** [fedə'reiʃn] s.
(valtio)liitto, liittovaltio.
fee [fi:] (lääkärin, asianjajajan ym)
palkkio, maksu; (lukukausi-,
sisäänkirjoitus)maksu; v. maksaa
palkkio.
feeble ['fi:bl] a. heikko, voimaton;
laimea. **~-minded** heikkoälyinen.
-ness s. heikkous.
feed [fi:d] fed fed, v. ruokkia, ravita,
syöttää; laiduntaa; syödä, käydä
laitumella; s. rehu; rehuannos;
syöttäminen, (koneen) syöttö; ~ on
syödä, elää jllak; ~ up lihottaa. **-back**
takaisinkytkentä, syöttö, palaute. **-er**
[-ə] s. syöjä; (lapsen) leukalappu t.
maitopullo; a large ~ suursyömäri.
-ing s. ruokkiminen; syöttö.
-ing-bottle tuttipullo.
feel [fi:l] felt felt, v. tuntea, tunnustella;
tuntua; s. tunto, tunne(lma); ~ sb.'s
pulse koetella jkn valtimoa; ~ one's
way edetä haparoiden; I ~ better voin
paremmin; I ~ cold minun on vilu; ~
[about] for haparoida, etsiä; ~ for
tuntea myötätuntoa jkta kohtaan; I
don't ~ like [going there] minua ei
haluta; do you ~ up to coming?
jaksaisitkohan tulla? **-er** [-ə] s.
tuntosarvi; (kuv.) tunnustelu; put out
~s tunnustella maaperää. **-ing** s.
tunto; tunne; mieliala; myötätunto
(~ for): a. tunteellinen,
herkkätunteinen; ill ~ katkeruus,
vihamielisyys.
feet [fi:t] pl. ks. foot.
feign [fein] v. teeskennellä, olla
olevinaan; ~ sleep olla nukkuvinaan.
-ed [-d] a. teeskennelty, vale-.
feint [feint] s. valehyökkäys, valeisku;
make a ~ of doing olla tekevinään jtk.
feldspar ['feldspa:] s. maasälpä.
felicit|ate [fi'lisiteit] v. onnitella. **-ation**
[-'teiʃn] s. onnittelu. **-ous** [-təs] a.
onnistunut; hyvin valittu. **-y** [-ti] s.
onnellisuus; onnistunut sanonta.

feline ['fi:lain] a. kissa(n)-.
fell 1. [fel] imp. ks. fall.
fell 2. a. (run.) julma, hirveä.
fell 3. s. (eläimen) turkki.
fell 4. s. ylänkö, vuorinen kangasmaa.
fell 5. v. hakata (maahan), kaataa;
kattaa (sauma).
fellow ['feləu] s. mies, poika; toveri,
kaveri; vertainen; a. -toveri; F~
akateemisen tutkinnon suorittanut
stipendiaatti; tieteellisen seuran
jäsen; my dear ~! ystävä hyvä! old ~
vanha veikko; poor ~ mies parka; ~
citizen saman maan kansalainen; ~
creature lähimmäinen; ~ soldier
aseveli; ~ worker työtoveri; [shoe]
without its ~ pariton.
fellow|-countryman [feləu-] maan-
mies. **~-feeling** yhteishenki, -tunto.
-man lähimmäinen, kanssaihminen.
-ship s. toveruus, yhteys; järjestö,
seura, veljeskunta; (Engl. yliop.)
fellow'n asema, stipendi; good ~
toverihenki.
felon ['felən] s. rikollinen; (sormi)ajos.
-ious [fi'ləunjəs] a. rikollinen. **-y** [-i] s.
(törkeä) rikos.
felt 1. [felt] s. huopa; v. vanu(tta)a;
peittää huovalla; ~ hat huopahattu.
felt 2. [felt] imp. & pp. ks. feel.
female ['fi:meil] a. naaras-,
naispuolinen, nais-; s. naaras; nainen;
~ screw mutteri.
femin|ine ['feminin] a. naisen,
naisellinen; feminiininen. **-inity**
[-'niniti] s. naisellisuus. **-ism** [-izm] s.
naisasia. **-ist** [-ist] s. naisasian
kannattaja.
femoral ['femər(ə)l] a. reisi-.
femur ['fi:mə] s. reisiluu.
fen [fen] s. räme, suo.
fenc|e [fens] s. aita, aitaus; suojus;
miekkailu; varastetun tavaran
kätköpaikka, kätkijä; v. aidata (m. ~
in, ~ round); torjua, väistää;
miekkailla; ~ with a question vältellä
kysymystä. **-ing** s. miekkailu.
fend [fend] v. torjua (tav. ~ off); ~ for
oneself huolehtia itsestään. **-er** [-ə] s.
suojus; takanristikko.
Fenian ['fi:njən] (hist.) feeniläinen
(Irlannin yhdistämistä ajavan
järjestön jäsen USA:ssa).
fennel ['fenl] s. saksankumina.

feoff ['fi:f] ks. *fief.*

ferment ['fə:ment] s. käytinaine, fermentti; hiiva; käyminen, käymistila; v. [fə(:)'ment] käydä; panna käymään; kiihdyttää, kuohuttaa. **-ation** [-'teiʃn] s. käyminen.

fern [fə:n] s. saniainen.

feroc|ious [fə'rəuʃəs] a. villi, hurja, julma. **-ity** [fə'rɔsiti] s. hurjuus, julmuus.

ferret ['ferit] s. fretti; v. metsästää fretillä; etsiä tarkoin; ~ *out* nuuskia ilmi.

Ferris wheel s. maailmanpyörä.

ferro-concrete ['ferə(u)'kɔŋkri:t] s. teräsbetoni.

ferrous ['ferəs] a. rautapitoinen, rauta-.

ferruginous [fe'ru:dʒinəs] a. rautapitoinen; ruosteenkarvainen.

ferrule ['feru:l] s. metallirengas, -hela; kenkäin.

ferry ['feri] s. lautta, -paikka, -yhteys; v. kuljettaa lautalla (t. lentokoneella); *car* ~ autolautta. **-man** [-mən] s. lautturi.

fertil|e ['fə:tail] a. hedelmällinen, viljava; kekseliäs. **-ity** [fə:'tiliti] s. hedelmällisyys. **-ization** [fə:tilai'zeiʃn] s. lannoitus; hedelmöityminen. **-ize** ['fə:tilaiz] v. lannoittaa; hedelmöittää. **-izer** ['fə:tilaizə] s. (väki)lannoite.

ferule ['feru:l] s. (kuritukseen käytetty) keppi, viivoitin.

ferv|ency ['fə:v(ə)nsi] s. = *fervour.* **-ent** [-nt] a. kuuma; palava, harras. **-id** ['fə:vid] a. palava, kiihkeä. **-our, -or** ['fə:və] s. palava into, hartaus.

festal ['festl] a. juhla-; iloinen.

fester ['festə] v. märkiä; mädättä; kalvaa, katkeroittaa; ajaa märille; s. märkähaava.

festiv|al ['festəv(ə)l, -tiv-] s. juhla, juhlat, juhliminen. **-e** ['festiv] a. juhla-, juhlava; iloinen. **-ity** [fes'tiviti] s. juhlailo; juhlallisuus, juhla (us. *pl.*).

festoon [fes'tu:n] s. (kukka- ym) köynnös; v. koristaa köynnöksillä.

fetch [fetʃ] v. noutaa, mennä noutamaan; tuottaa (hinta); aiheuttaa (esim. ~ *blood, tears*); antaa (isku); ~ *and carry* »passata». **-ing** a. viehättävä.

fête, fete [feit] s. juhla; v. juhlia (jkta).

fetid ['fetid, 'fi:t-] a. haiseva, löyhkäävä.

fetish ['fi:tiʃ, 'fet-] s. fetissi, taikaesine.

fetlock ['fetlɔk] s. (hevosen) vuohiskarvat t. kinnernivel.

fetter ['fetə] s. jalkarauta; *pl.* kahleet; v. kahlehtia.

fettle ['fetl] s. kunto; *in fine* ~ loistokunnossa.

fetus ['fi:təs] ks. *foetus.*

feud [fju:d] s. (suku)vaino, vihollisuus, riita.

feudal ['fju:dl] a. feodaali-. **-ism** [-əlizm] s. feodalismi.

fever ['fi:və] s. kuume; ~ *ed* kuumeinen, kiihtynyt. **-ish** [-riʃ] a. kuumeinen.

few [fju:] a. & s. harvat; a ~ muutamat; *every* ~ *hours* muutaman tunnin väliajoin; *are* ~ *and far between* ovat kovin harvinaisia; *quite a* ~ melkoinen määrä. **-ness** s. harvalukuisuus.

fey [fei] a. jtk aavistava, yliluonnollinen.

fez [fez] s. fetsi.

fian|cé [fi'ã:(n)sei] s. sulhanen. **-cée** [= ed.] s. morsian.

fiasco [fi'æskəu] s. fiasko, »pannukakku».

fib [fib] s. (pieni) valhe; v. valehdella.

fiber ['faibə] Am. = seur.

fibr|e ['faibə] s. syy, säie, kuitu; ~*board* kuitulevy; ~*glass* lasikuitu. **-ed** [-d] a. -syinen. **-ous** [-brəs] a. syinen, kuituinen.

fickle ['fikl] a. epävakaa, häilyväinen.

fiction ['fikʃn] s. romaanikirjallisuus; kertomus, tarina, juttu; *work of* ~ romaani; *science* ~ tieteisromaani; *fact is stranger than* ~ todellisuus on tarua ihmeellisempi.

fictitious [fik'tiʃəs] a. keksitty, kuviteltu; väärä, väärennetty, vale-.

fiddle ['fidl] s. viulu; v. soittaa viulua; hypistellä (*with* jtk), leikitellä, hääriä (us. ~ *about*); *fit as a* ~ terve ja pirteä; *play second* ~ olla toisella sijalla; ~ *away* kuluttaa hukkaan. **~-de-dee** [-di'di:] *int.* loruja! **-r** [-ə] s. viulunsoittaja. **-stick** viulunjousi; ~*s!* joutavia! höpsis!

fidelity [fai'deliti] s. uskollisuus (*to* jklle); totuudenmukaisuus; tarkkuus;

high ~ ks. *hi-fi.*

fidget ['fidʒit] s. (tav. *the* ~ s) hermostunut levottomuus t. liikehtiminen; hermostunut t. hermostuttava henkilö; v. olla levoton, liikehtiä levottomasti, hermostuksissaan hypistellä jtk *(with).* **-y** [-i] a. hermostunut, levoton.

fie [fai] *int.* hyi!

fief [fi:f] s. läänitys.

field [fi:ld] s. pelto, vainio; kenttä, taistelukenttä; kaikki pelaajat t. kilpailijat; (kuv.) ala; v. ottaa kiinni ja heittää takaisin (pallo); ~ *of action* toiminta-ala; ~ *of vision* näkökenttä; ~ *events* kenttäurheilu; ~ *marshal* sotamarsalkka; ~ *study* (t. *survey)* kenttätutkimus; *hold the* ~ pitää puoliaan. ~**-day** kenttäharjoitus. **-er** [-ə] s. (krik.) ulkopelaaja. **~-glass(es)** kenttäkiikari. **~-hospital** kenttäsairaala. **~-sports** (Engl. et.) metsästys, kalastus. **~-work** kenttävarustus.

fiend [fi:nd] s. paholainen; (jnk paheen) orja (esim. *dope-~);* intoilija. **-ish** [-iʃ] a. pirullinen.

fierce [fiəs] a. villi, raivoisa, raju, tuima, vihainen.

fiery ['faiəri] a. tulinen, palava, tuli-; hehkuva; ~ *cross* (hist.) viestikapula.

fife [faif] s. huilu; v. puhaltaa huilulla.

fif|teen ['fif'ti:n] *lukus.* viisitoista. **-teenth** [-'ti:nθ] *lukus.* viidestoista. **-th** [-θ] *lukus. & s.* viides(osa). **-tieth** [-tiəθ] *lukus.* viideskymmenes. **-ty** [-ti] *lukus.* viisikymmentä; *the fifties* 50-luku; *go* ~-~ panna puoliksi t. tasan.

fig 1. [fig] s. viikuna(puu); *I don't care a* ~ en välitä rahtuakaan.

fig 2. [fig] s.: *in full* ~ parhaissa hepenissä.

fight [fait] *fought fought,* v. taistella, otella, tapella; s. taistelu, tappelu, ottelu; taisteluhalu; *show* ~ näyttää tappelunhaluiselta; ~ *it out* selvittää tappelemalla (t. keskustelemalla); ~ *off* saada torjutuksi. **-er** [-ə] s. taistelija; (ilm.) hävittäjä.

fighting a. taisteleva, taistelu-. **~-line** s. tulilinja.

figment ['figmənt] s. juttu, keksintö.

figurative ['figjurətiv] a. kuvaannollinen, vertauskuvallinen.

figure ['figə, Am. figjə] s. numero, luku; hinta: hahmo, muoto; vartalo; kuva; kuvio; henkilö; v. kuvata; esiintyä jnak; kuvioida; ~ *of speech* kielikuva; ~ *skating* taitoluistelu; ~ *[to oneself]* arvella; ~ *out (up)* arvioida, laskea; ~ *sb. out* ymmärtää; *it* ~ *s out at £ 3* se tekee 3 puntaa; *cuts a sorry* ~ on surkean näköinen. **-d** [-d] a. kuviollinen. **-head** keulakuva.

figurine ['figjuri:n] s. pieni veistoskuva.

Fiji ['fi:dʒi:] *erisn.* Fidži-saaret.

filament ['filəmənt] s. säie, (hehku)lanka.

filbert ['filbə(:)t] s. viljelty pähkinä(pensas).

filch [filt(f)] v. näpistellä.

file 1. [fail] s. viila; v. viilata.

file 2. [fail] s. kortisto, asiakirjat, arkisto; rekisteri; (kirje- ym) kansio, mappi, asiakirjakaappi; v. järjestää kortistoon, kortistoida, arkistoida; *on* ~ kirjoissa, arkistoituna.

file 3. [fail] s. jono (sot.); v. marssia jonossa; *get into* ~ (autosta) ryhmittyä; *in single (Indian)* ~ jonossa; *in double* ~ parijonossa.

filial ['filjəl] a. lapsen, pojan, tyttären.

filibuster ['filibʌstə] s. merisissi; Am. jarruttaja (pol.).

filigree ['filigri:] s. filigraanityö.

filing ['failiŋ] s. arkistointi; ~ s vilanpuru.

Filipino [fili'pi:nəu] s. (pl. ~ s) filippiiniläinen.

fill [fil] v. täyttää; paikata (hammas); täyttyä; s.: *eat one's* ~ syödä kylläkseen; a ~ *of tobacco* piipullinen tupakkaa; ~ *an office* olla jssak virassa; ~ *in* täydentää, täyttää (lomake ym); ~ *out* pullistua, laajeta; ~ *up* täyttää, täyttyä; ~ *ed with* täynnä jtk.

fillet ['filit] s. (otsa-, hius-) nauha; lista, kaistale; (liha-, kala) filee; v. sitoa (otsa)nauhalla; leikata fileiksi.

filling s. täyte. **~-station** bensiiniasema.

fillip ['filip] s. (sormen) näpsäys; kiihoke; v. näpsäyttää.

filly ['fili] s. tammavarsa.

film [film] s. (ohut) kalvo; filmi,

elokuva; usva; kelmu; v. peittää, peittyä kalvolla; elokuvata; ~ *strip* raina. **-y** [-i] a. kalvomainen; ohut, hieno.

filter ['filtə] s. suodatin, filtteri; v. suodattaa; siivilöityä; ~ *out (through)* tihkua esiin, läpi; päästä julkisuuteen; ~-**tipped** suodatin(savuke).

filth [filθ] a. lika, saasta, törky. **-y** [-i] a. lika nen, saastainen, siivoton.

filtra|te ['filtreit] v. suodattaa; s. [-rit] suodos, filtraatti. **-tion** [-'treiʃn] s. suodatus.

fin [fin] s. evä.

final ['fainl] a. viimeinen, lopullinen, loppu-; finaalinen (kiel.); s. (kilpailun) loppuerä, loppukilpailu (us. ~s); loppututkinto (us. ~s). **-e** [fi'na:li] s. finaali, loppukohtaus. **-ist** [-əlist] s. loppuerään t. -kilpailuun päässyt kilpailija. **-ity** [fai'næliti] s. lopullisuus; lopullinen ratkaisu. **-ly** adv. lopuksi, vihdoin; lopullisesti.

financ|e [fai'næns] s. finanssioppi; pl. raha-asiat, finanssit; v. rahoittaa. **-ial** [-nʃ(ə)l] a. finanssi-, raha-; *in ~ difficulties* taloudellisissa vaikeuksissa; ~ *year* varainhoitovuosi. **-ier** [-siə, Am. finən'siə] s. rahoittaja, rahamies. **-ing** s. rahoitus.

finch [fin(t)ʃ] s. peippo.

find [faind] *found found,* v. löytää; tavata; huomata, havaita, pitää jnak; saada (selville); ~ löytö; ~ *out* saada (t. ottaa) selville, keksiä, saada ilmi; ~ *sb. guilty* julistaa jku syylliseksi; *I did not ~ it in my heart to* en hennonut; *£ 16 and all found* 16 puntaa ja vapaa ylöspito. **-er** [-ə] s. löytäjä; *(view-~)* etsin. **-ing** s. löytäminen; (valamiehistön ym) päätös; ~s tulokset, löydökset.

fine 1. [fain] s. sakko(rahat); v. sakottaa; *in ~* lyhyesti.

fine 2. [fain] a. hieno; ohut, terävä; kaunis, ihana; komea; erinomainen; adv. loistavasti, mainiosti; s. pouta; v. ohentua, ohentaa (m. ~ *down); I'm feeling ~* voin erinomaisesti; ~ *arts* taiteet; *one of these ~ days* jonakin kauniina päivänä; *he cut it rather ~* hänpä osasi saapua viime hetkessä; *these are ~ doings* (pilk.) onpa tämä

kaunista! ~-**grained** hienorakeinen. **-ly** adv. hienosti; hienoksi (leikattu ym). **-ry** [-əri] s. hienous, koristukset; mellotusuuni. **-sse** [fi'nes] s. hienovaraisuus, oveluus.

finger ['fiŋgə] s. sormi; v. hypistellä, sormeilla; *his ~s are all thumbs* hänellä on peukalo keskellä kämmentä; *put (lay) one's ~ on* osua oikeaan, osoittaa (missä vika on). ~-**board** kosketinlauta. ~-**bowl** huuhdekuppi (ruokapöydässä). **-ing** s. sormijärjestys. ~-**post** tienviitta. **-print** sormenjälki. **-stall** sormituppi. **-tip** sormenpää.

finicking ['finikiŋ] a. turhantarkka (m. *finical, finicky).*

finish ['finiʃ] v. lopettaa, päättää; viimeistellä; tehdä loppu jstk, tappaa; loppua, päättyä; s. loppu; viimeistely; silottelu; *be in at the ~* nähdä jnk ratkaiseva vaihe; ~ *up with cheese* syödä lopuksi juustoa; ~ *sb. off* (sl.) tappaa. **-ed** [-t] a. päättynyt, valmis; viimeistelty. **-ing** s. & a.: ~ *school* (tyttöjen) sisäoppilaitos; ~ *touch* viimeistely.

finite ['fainait] a. äärellinen; finiitti-.

Finland ['finlənd] erisn. Suomi.

Finn [fin] s. suomalainen. **-ish** [-iʃ] a. suomalainen; s. suomen kieli.

finny ['fini] a. evämäinen, evä-.

fiord [fjɔ:d] s. vuono.

fir [fə:] s. (jalo)kuusi; *Scotch ~* mänty.

fire ['faiə] s. tuli; valkea, takkavalkea; tulipalo; hehku; palo; v. sytyttää; ampua, laukaista; polttaa (tiiliä); innostaa; (puhek.) erottaa (toimesta); syttyä; *on ~* tulessa; *set on ~, set ~ to* sytyttää; *catch ~* syttyä; *under ~* ammunnan alaisena; ~ *away* annahan kuulua! ~ *up* tulistua. ~-**alarm** palohälytys. **-arm** tuliase. **-brand** kekäle; kiihottaja. ~-**brick** tulenkestävä tiili. ~-**brigade** palokunta. ~-**control** tulenjohto. **-damp** kaivoskaasu. **-dog** rautateline (takassa). ~-**engine** paloauto, paloruisku. ~-**escape** palotikkaat. ~-**extinguisher** sammutin. ~-**fighting** sammutustyö. **-fly** tulikärpänen. ~-**irons** takkakalusto (hiilipihdit, -hanko ym). **-man** palokuntalainen; lämmittäjä. **-place** takka. ~-**plug** paloposti. **-proof**

tulenkestävä. **-side** takka, kotiliesi.
-wood polttopuut. **-works** ilotulitus.
firing ['faiəriŋ] s. sytyttäminen jne.;
ammunta; ~ line tulilinja; ~ party
(squad) kunnialaukausosasto;
teloitusryhmä.
firkin ['fə:kin] s. nelikko, puoli
ankkuria (40 l).
firm 1. [fə:m] s. liike, toiminimi, firma.
firm 2. [fə:m] a. luja, kiinteä, vankka,
tukeva; horjumaton. **-ament** [-əmənt]
s. taivaankansi. **-ness** s. lujuus.
first [fə:st] a. ensimmäinen, ensi-;
huomattavin, etevin; adv. ensiksi;
ensimmäisen kerran; ennemmin; s.:
~ name etunimi; be on ~ name terms
olla sinuja; at ~ sight ensi näkemältä;
in the ~ place ks. place; ~ of all
kaikkein ensimmäiseksi; I shall do it
~ thing [tomorrow morning] teen sen
ensi töikseni; at ~ ensiksi, alussa;
from the ~ alusta alkaen; travel ~
matkustaa ensimmäisessä luokassa.
~-born a. & s. esikoinen. **~-class** a.
ensiluokkainen. **~-fruits** s. pl.
varhaisvihannekset ym. **~-hand** ensi
käden (tietona). **-ly** adv. ensinnäkin,
ensiksi. **~-rate** ensi luokan,
ensiluokkainen.
firth [fə:θ] s. vuono.
fiscal ['fisk(ə)l] a. finanssi-, vero-; ~
year tilivuosi.
fish [fiʃ] s. kala; v. kalastaa, onkia; a
pretty kettle of ~ kaunis soppa; ~ out
vetää esille; houkutella esiin; ~ meal
kalajauho; ~-bone ruoto; ~-breeding
kalan|viljely, -jalostus.
fisher|man ['fiʃəmən] s. kalastaja. **-y**
[-ri] s. kalastusoikeus; -ies kalavedet.
fishing ['fiʃiŋ] s. kalastus. **~-line** s.
ongensiima. **~-rod** s. ongenvapa.
~-tackle s. kalastustarvikkeet.
fish|monger ['fiʃmʌŋgə] s.
kalakauppias. **-wife** kalakauppias.
~-slice kala(ntarjoilu)veitsi. **~-pond**
kalalammikko. **-y** ['fiʃi] a.
kalamainen, kalan; samea;
epäilyttävä.
fissile ['fisail] a. halkeava.
fission ['fiʃn] s. halkeaminen; nuclear ~
ytimen halkeamisreaktio, fissio.
fissure ['fiʃə] s. halkeama; rako.
fist [fist] s. nyrkki. **-icuffs** [-ikʌfs]
nyrkkitappelu.
fistula ['fistjulə] s. avanne.

fit 1. [fit] s. (taudin) kohtaus, puuska;
by ~ s and starts puuskittain.
fit 2. [fit] a. sopiva, sovelias;
kelvollinen; hyvässä kunnossa, reipas;
v. sopia; sovittaa, soveltaa; asentaa;
tehdä kykeneväksi; varustaa (with
jllak); s.: this coat is an excellent ~
tämä takki sopii mainiosti; ~ for
service palvelus-, asekelpoinen; ~ for
work työkykyinen; [I'm] as ~ as ever I
was elämäni kunnossa; see (think) ~
pitää sopivana, parhaana; ~ in sopia
jhk, saada sopimaan; ~ on sovittaa
(pukua); ~ out varustaa; ~ up
varustaa, asentaa.
fitch ['fitʃ] s. hilleri.
fit|ful a. puuskittainen. **-fully** adv.
puuskittain, aika ajoin. **-ness** s.
sopivaisuus; kelpoisuus, ruumiillinen
kunto. **-ted** ['fitid] a. sopiva. **-ter**
['fitə] s. asentaja, (puvun) sovittaja.
-ting a. sopiva, sovelias; s. sovitus;
asennus; ~s kalusteet, laitteet,
varusteet. **-ting-out** varustaminen.
five [faiv] lukus. viisi; viitonen. **-fold** a.
& adv. viisinkertainen, -sesti. **-r** [-ə] s.
sl. viitonen (5 punnan t. dollarin
seteli). **-s** [-z] s. eräs seinäpallopeli.
fix [fiks] v. kiinnittää; saattaa
jähmeään muotoon; määrätä, sopia
(jstk); kiinnittyä, tarttua kiinni, käydä
jähmeäksi; järjestää, panna kuntoon,
majoittaa (~ up); korjata; (valok.)
kiinnittää, (tiet.) preparoida; sl.
lahjoa; s. pulma, pula; (esim.
heroiini)ruiske; sopuottelu; in a ~
pinteessä; ~ on, ~ upon päättää ottaa
jk, valita; ~ up järjestää; ~ing salt
kiinnite. **-ation** [-'seifn] s. (m. valok.)
kiinnittäminen; jähmettäminen. **-ed**
[-t] a. kiinteä; pysyväinen; ~ prices
kiinteät hinnat; ~ star kiintotähti.
-edness [-idnis] s. kiinteys. **-ity** [-iti] s.
kiinteys. **-ture** [-tʃə] s. kiinteä kalusto;
määräpäivänä pidetty kilpailut;
kantavieras; ~s kiintosisusteet, (esim.
sähkö)laitteet.
fizz [fiz] v. sähistä; poreilla; s. sähinä;
poreilu; sl. samppanja. **-le** [-l] v.
pihistä; s. pihinä; epäonnistuminen;
~ out raueta.
flabbergast ['flæbəgɑ:st] v. ällistyttää.
flabby ['flæbi] a. veltto, vetelä.
flaccid ['flæksid] a. vetelä, rento,

veltto, heikko.

flag 1. [flæg] s. lippu; v. liputtaa; antaa merkkejä lipuilla; *hoist a* ~ nostaa lippu; *lower (strike) a* ~ laskea lippu.

flag 2. [flæg] s. kurjenmiekka.

flag 3. [flæg] s. (m. ~ -*stone*) kivilaatta.

flag 4. [flæg] v. riippua rentona; kuihtua, riutua; laimentua.

flagel|lant [ˈflædʒ|ilənt] s. itsensä ruoskija. **-late** [-əleit] v. ruoskia.

flagging [ˈflægiŋ] s. laimentuminen; liputus; laattakiveys.

flagon [ˈflægən] s. (iso, pyöreä) pullo; viinikannu.

flagran|cy [ˈfleigr(ə)nsi] s. (rikoksen) räikeys. **-t** [-(ə)nt] a. huutava, räikeä.

flag|-ship lippulaiva. **-staff** lipputanko.

flail [fleil] s. varsta.

flair [ˈfleə] s. vainu, luontainen taito, vaisto(mainen kyky); tyyli, hohto.

flak [ˈflæk] s. ilmatorjuntatuli.

flake [fleik] s. hiutale; liuska, ohut kerros; v. : ~ *off* liuskoilla, kesiä.

flambeau [ˈflæmbəu] s. (pl. m. -x [-z]) soihtu.

flamboyant [flæmˈbɔiənt] a. loistava, korea; liekehtivä.

flame [fleim] s. liekki; (puhek.) heila; v. liekehtiä, leimuta, loimuta; ~ *out* leimahtaa liekkiin. ~ **-thrower** liekinheitin.

flaming a. liekehtivä; räikeä; sl. kirottu.

flamingo [fləˈmiŋgəu] s. (pl. ~ (*e*)*s*) flamingo.

Flanders [ˈflɑːndəz] *erisn.* Flanderi.

flange [flændʒ] s. laippa.

flank [flæŋk] s. sivu, kylki; sivusta; v. olla (jnk) sivulla; uhata sivustaa; hyökätä sivustaan; *in* ~ sivultapäin.

flannel [ˈflænl] s. (villa)flanelli; ~ *s* flannellihousut. **-ette** [flænˈlet] s. pumpuliflanelli.

flap [flæp] v. läimäyttää; räpytellä (siipiä); lyödä; lepattaa; s. läimäys, räpytys; liuska, kaistale, (jtk peittävä) läppä, (taskun ym) kansi; (pöydän) laskulevy; (hatun) lieri; *be in a* ~ olla jännityksessä. **-jack** s. eräänl. pannukakku; litteä puuterirasia. **-per** s. (kärpäs)lätkä, (vanh.) tytönheilakka.

flare [fleə] v. loimuta; hulmuta; s. loimu, roihu; valoraketti; ~ *up*

kuohahtaa; *a* ~ *d skirt* kellomainen hame. **-ing** a. loimuava; silmiinpistävä, räikeä.

flash [flæʃ] v. leimahtaa, välähtää; säihkyä, salamoida; leimahduttaa; singota; lennättää; s. leimahdus, välähdys, silmänräpäys; kipinä; (valok.) salamalaite; a. koreileva; ~ *of hope* toivon kipinä; ~ *of lightning* salama; ~ *bulb* salamavalolamppu; *a* ~ *in the pan* »pannukakku». ~**-back** (elok.) takautuma, takauma. **-light** vilkku(valo); salamalaite; taskulamppu. **-y** *a.* räikeä, koreileva.

flask [flɑːsk] s. taskumatti, kapeakaulainen pullo.

flat [flæt] a. litteä, laakea, tasainen, matalakorkoinen; yhdenmukainen; laimea, väljähtänyt; nimenomainen; ehdoton; alennettu (mus.); s. litteä puoli; (miekan) lape; tasanko, alava maa; huoneisto; alennusmerkki (mus.); *D* ~ des (mus.); *one of the tires went* ~ autoni (t. pyöräni) kumi puhkesi; ~ *rate* yhtenäistariffi; *fall* ~ kaatua pitkin pituuttaan, mennä myttyyn; *sing* ~ laulaa liian matalalta; ~*ly refuse* kieltäytyä jyrkästi; *the* ~ *of the hand* kämmen; *block of* ~*s* kerrostalo. **-fish** kampela. **-footed** lättäjalkainen. ~**-iron** silitysrauta. **-let** *s. : one- (two-) room* ~ yksiö, kaksio. **-ten** [-n] *v.* tehdä litteäksi, tasoittaa; tehdä laimeaksi, masentaa; käydä litteäksi, laimeaksi; ~ *out* oikaista (ilm.).

flatter [ˈflætə] v. imarrella, mairitella; ~ *oneself* kuvitella. **-er** [-rə] *s.* imartelija. **-y** [-ri] s. imartelu.

flatulen|ce [ˈflætjuləns] s. puhkuisuus, ilmavaivat, mahakaasu. **-t** [-ənt] a. ilmavaivoista kärsivä, pullistunut, tyhjä.

flaunt [flɔːnt] v. pöyhistellä; kopeilla, pöyhkeillä (jllak).

flautist [ˈflɔːtist] s. huilunsoittaja, huilisti.

flavour, flavor [ˈfleivə] s. tuoksu, maku, aromi; v. maustaa, höystää. **-ing** s. höyste, mauste.

flaw [flɔː] s. halkeama, särö; virka, virhe; v. vioittaa. **-less** *a.* virheetön.

flax [flæks] s. pellava. **-en** [-n] *a.* pellavainen, pellava-.

flay [flei] v. nylkeä.

flea [fli:] s. kirppu; *with a ~ in his ear* nolona.

fleck [flek] s. täplä, pilkku; v. tehdä täplikkääksi.

fled [fled] *imp. & pp.* ks. *flee.*

fledg|e [fledʒ] v. varustaa höyhenillä; ~*d* lentokykyinen. **-eling** [-liŋ] s. (vasta lentokykyiseksi tullut) linnunpoikanen; *a ~ blackbird* mustarastaanpoikanen.

flee [fli:] *fled fled,* v. paeta, karttaa; häipyä.

fleec|e [fli:s] s. lampaanvilla, -turkki, talja; v. nylkeä, kyniä (kuv.). **-y** [-i] a. pehmeä, villava.

fleet [fli:t] v. kiitää (ohi), häipyä; s. laivasto; a. nopea; *F~ Street* (kuv.) sanomalehdistö. **-ing** a. nopea, katoava.

Flem|**ing** [ˈflemiŋ] s. flaamilainen. **-ish** [-iʃ] a. flaamilainen; s. flaamin kieli.

flesh [fleʃ] s. liha; *lose ~* laihtua; *put on ~ lihoa; in the ~* ilmielävänä; ~ *out* a *yarn* tekaista elävä tarina. **-ly** [-li] a. lihallinen. ~**-pots** lihapadat, ylellisyys. ~**-wound** lihashaava. **-y** [i] a. lihainen, lihava.

flew [flu:] *imp.* ks. *fly.*

flex [fleks] s. sähköjohdin; v. taivuttaa. **-ibility** [-iˈbiliti] s. taipuisuus; joustavuus. **-ible** [-əbl] a. taipuisa, notkea, (kuv.) joustava; ~ *time* liukuva työaika. **-ion** [ˈflekʃn] s. taivutus.

flibbertigibbet [ˈflibətiˈdʒibit] s. tuulihattu, lörppö.

flick [flik] s. sipaisu; näpsäys; v. lyödä sipaista; ~ *knife* linkkuveitsi; *the ~s* (sl.) elokuvat.

flicker [ˈflikə] v. lepattaa; välkkyä; s. lepattava valo; (TV) välkyntä.

flier [ˈflaiə] ks. *flyer.*

flight 1. [flait] s. pako; *take* [*to*] ~ paeta; *put to ~* ajaa pakoon.

flight 2. [flait] s. lento, lentomatka; (muuttolintujen ym) parvi; (ilm.) lentue; ~ [*of stairs*] portaat, porrasvarsi; *in the first ~* kärjessä. **-y** [-i] a. häilyväinen.

flimsy [ˈflimzi] a. hatara, ohut, hauras; s. läpilyöntipaperi; ~ [*excuse*] huono.

flinch [flin(t)ʃ] v. peräytyä jstk, sävähtää; *without ~ing* silmää

räpäyttämättä.

fling [fliŋ] *flung flung,* v. singota, heittää, heitellä, (*oneself*) heittäytyä; rynnätä; s. heitto; letkaus, pistosana; ~ *out* alkaa sättiä, (hevosesta) äksyillä; *have a ~ at* yrittää jtk, letkauttaa; *have one's ~* nauttia vapaudestaan, riehua aikansa; *Highland ~* reipas skottitanssi.

flint [flint] s. piikivi. ~**-lock** piilukko(pyssy). **-y** [-i] a. piikivi-; kivikova.

flip [flip] v. näpäys; sipaisu; v. näpsäyttää; sipaista; a. ks. *flippant;* v.: ~ *up* heittää kruunua ja klaavaa.

flippan|**cy** [ˈflipənsi] s. nenäkkyys. **-t** [-ənt] a. kevyt(mielinen), epäkunnioittava, nenäkäs.

flipper [ˈflipə] s. (hylkeen ym) eväjalka, (sukeltajan) räpylä.

flirt [flə:t] v. nykäistä, heiluttaa; flirttailla, hakkailla, keimailla; s. nykäys; keimailija. **-ation** [-ˈteiʃn] s., keimailu, hakkailu. **-atious** [-ˈteiʃəs] a. keimaileva. flirttaileva.

flit [flit] v. lennellä, liihotella; muuttaa pois (salaa).

flitch [flitʃ] s. savustettu siankylki.

flitter [ˈflitə] v. lentää lepattaa.

flivver [ˈflivə] s. Am. sl. autorämä, »kärry».

float [flout] v. kellua, uida; leijailla, liehua; uittaa; laskea vesille; (vedestä) peittää alleen; panna alulle (yhtiö ym); s. koho; lautta, kelluke; (kulkueessa käyt.) vaunualusta, matalat rattaat; (m. ~ *s*) ramppivalot. **-ation** s. ks. *flotation.* **-ing** a. uiva, ajelehtiva; liikkuva; ~ *bridge* lauttasilta; ~ *capital* liikkuva pääoma; ~ *population* liikkuva väestö; ~[*rib*] vapaa; ~ *voters* puolueisiin kuulumattomat äänestäjät.

flock 1. [flɔk] s. lauma, parvi; v. kerääntyä laumoihin.

flock 2. [flɔk] s. (villa)höytäle; *pl.* flokki.

floe [flou] s. jäälautta.

flog [flɔg] v. ruoskia, piestä. **-ging** s. selkäsauna; raipparangaistus.

flood [flʌd] v. vuoksi, nousuvesi; tulva; ryöppy; v. tulvia (jnk yli), peittää veden alle; *the F~* vedenpaisumus. ~**-gate** patoluukku, sulku. ~**-light**

valaista (rakennus) valonheittimin;
~ *s* valonheitinvalaistus; *flood-lit*
juhlavalaistu. **~-lighting** (julkisivun)
valaistus. **~-tide** vuoksi.

floor [flɔ:] *s.* lattia, permanto; kerros;
v. panna lattia; iskeä lattiaan; nolata;
the first ~ ensimmäinen (t. toinen)
kerros; *take the* ~ ottaa puheenvuoro;
he was ~ed by two questions kahteen
kysymykseen hän ei osannut vastata.
-er [-rə] *s.* musertava isku, nolaus.
-ing *s.* lattianpano; lattianpeite(aine).
~-walker *s.* (tavaratalon) neuvoja,
tarkastaja.

flooz|y, -ie ['flu:zi] *s.* lutka.

flop [flɔp] *v.* pudota mätkähtää,
retkahtaa; pudottaa huolimattomasti;
s. mätkähdys; fiasko, »pannukakku»;
~ *house* Am. yömaja. **-py** [-i] *a.*
vetelä, veltto; huolimaton.

flor|a ['flɔ:rə] *s.* kasvisto. **-al** [-l] *a.*
kukka(s)-.

Florence ['flɔr(ə)ns] *erisn.* Firenze.

flor|escence [flɔ:'resns] *s.* kukinta-aika.
-iculture ['flɔ:rikʌltʃə] *s.* kukkien
viljely. **-id** ['flɔrid] *a.* runsaasti
koristeltu, korusanainen; prameileva;
punakka.

Florida ['flɔridə] *erisn.*

flor|in ['flɔr|in] *s.* engl. hopearaha, 2
sh. (nyt 10 p.) **-ist** [-ist] *s.*
kukkakauppias; ~ *'s[shop]*
kukkakauppa.

floss [flɔs] *s.* silkkijäte, (kertaamaton)
raakasilkki (m. ~ *silk);* haituva.

flotation [flə(u)'teiʃn] *s.*
(liikeyrityksen) alullepano.

flotilla [flə(u)'tilə] *s.* laivue.

flotsam ['flɔtsəm] *s.* (ajalehtiva)
hylkytavara.

flounce 1. [flauns] *s.* liehureunus;
koristaa l-reunuksella.

flounce 2. [flauns] *v.* syöksähtää,
liikkua kärsimättömästi.

flounder 1. ['flaundə] *s.* kampela.

flounder 2. ['flaundə] *v.* rämpiä;
sätkytellä; takerrella.

flour ['flauə] *s.* hieno jauho,
vehnäjauho; *v.* jauhottaa.

flourish ['flʌriʃ] *v.* kukoistaa;
menestyä; tehdä kiekuroita
(kirjoittaessa), puhua kukkaskieltä;
heiluttaa (asetta ym); *s.* kiemura,
korusana, **-lause;** (aseen, käden)

heilautus; torventoitotus, fanfaari.
-ing *a.* kukoistava.

floury ['flauəri] *a.* jauhoinen.

flout [flaut] *v.* ivata, pitää pilkkanaan
(t. halpana); *s.* iva.

flow [flou] *v.* virrata, juosta; tulvia,
vuotaa; laskeutua, riippua (väljänä);
s. virtaaminen, virta, tulva, juoksu;
aaltoilu; vuoksi.

flower ['flauə] *s.* kukka; kukoistus; *v.*
kukkia; *the* ~ *of* jnk parhaimmisto.
-ed *a.* kukallinen. **-ing** *a.* kukkiva; *s.*
kukkiminen. **~-pot** kukkaruukku. **-y**
[-ri] *a.* kukkiva; kukallinen;
korusanainen.

flowing ['flouiŋ] *a.* virtaava; aaltoileva;
sujuva.

flown [floun] *pp.* ks. *fly.*

flu [flu:] *s.* »flunssa».

flub [flʌb] *s.* kömmähdys.

fluctua|te ['flʌktjueit] *v.* vaihdella,
nousta ja laskea; häilyä. **-tion** [-'eiʃn]
s. vaihtelu, vaihteleminen,
epävakaisuus.

flue [flu:] *s.* savutorvi, hormi.

fluen|cy ['flu(:)ənsi] *s.* sujuvuus. **-t**
[-ənt] *a.* sujuva, vuolas(-puheinen);
[she] speaks ~ *French* puhuu sujuvasti
ranskaa.

fluff [flʌf] *s.* nukka, nöyhtä; untuva,
pehmeä karva; unohtaminen;
epäonnistunut yritys, möhläys; *v.* (~
out) pöyhiä, pöyhistää; ~ *a catch*
pudottaa pallo. **-y** [-i] *a.* untuvainen.

fluid ['flu:id] *a.* juokseva; häilyvä,
epävakainen; *s.* juokseva aine, neste.
-ity [flu:'iditi] *s.* juoksevuus.

fluke 1. [flu:k] *s.* ankkurinkynsi.

fluk|e 2. [flu:k] *s.* onnenosuma,
onnenpotku. **-y** [-i] *a.* onnekas.

flume [flu:m] *s.* (uitto)kouru.

flummery ['flʌməri] *s.* eräänl. kiisseli;
tyhjänpäiväinen puhe.

flummox ['flʌməks] *v.* sl. saattaa
ymmälle.

flung ['flʌŋ] *imp. & pp.* fling.

flunk [flʌŋk] *v.* reputtaa.

flunkey ['flʌŋki] *s.* lakeija.

fluor ['flu(:)ɔ:] *s.* fluori (kem.).
-escence [fluə'resns] *s.* välkehtiminen;
-escent lamp loistevalaisin. **-idate**
['fluərideit] *v.* fluoroida. **-ide**
['fluəraid] *s.* fluoridi. **-oscopy**
[fluə'rɔskəpi] *s.* läpivalaisu (lääk.).

flurry ['flʌri] s. hermostunut kiire, hälinä; tuulenpuuska; v. hermostuttaa; *flurried* hätäinen.

flush 1. [flʌʃ] v. lähteä t. ajaa lentoon.

flush 2. [flʌʃ] v. virrata, syöksyä esiin; punastua; huuhtoa (puhtaaksi), huuhdella (WC:stä) alas; saattaa punastumaan; kiihdyttää; s. virta, tulva, suihku; punastuminen; *a.* tulvillaan oleva; runsas; ~ *of victory* voitonhurma; ~ *with* jnk tasalla, jnk kanssa tasapinnassa; *he is* ~ *with money* hän on rahakas. **-ed** [-t] *a.* punastunut, hehkuva; ~ *with victory* voiton huumaama.

flush 3. [flʌʃ] s. samaa maata olevat kortit, väri.

fluster ['flʌstə] v. kiihdyttää, saattaa hämmingin valtaan; s. hämminki.

flut|e [flu:t] s. huilu; ura, uurre (pylväässä); v. soittaa huilulla (t. huilua); uurtaa. **-ing** s. uurrekoristelu. **-ist** [-ist] s. huilisti.

flutter ['flʌtə] v. lepattaa, lentää lepatella; liehua; olla levoton t. kiihdyksissä; läpättää; räpyttää; tehdä rauhattomaksi; s. lepatus; rauhattomuus, hätääntyminen; sl. vedonlyönti; ~ *ed* levoton, epävarma.

fluvial ['flu:viəl] *a.* joki-.

flux [flʌks] s. virtaaminen; vuoto; virta, tulva; kiertokulku, vaihtelu, alituinen muuttuminen; juokste.

fly 1. [flai] s. kärpänen; (kalastus)perho.

fly 2. [flai] *flew flown,* v. lentää; kiitää, rientää; liehua; lennättää, liehuttaa; s. lento(matka); yksivaljakko; teltan ovivaate; (napituksen ym) peittävä lista; *pl.* näyttämön ylinen; ~ *at* hyökätä jnk kimppuun; ~ *into a passion* vimmastua; ~ *to bits* särkyä säpäleiksi; *let* ~ [*at*] päästää (suustaan), alkaa sättiä jkta; ~ *the country* paeta maasta; ~ *past* ohilento; [*he is very*] ~ (sl.) valpas, ovela.

fly|-blow kärpäsenlika, -muna. **~-catcher** sieppo. **~-flap** kärpäslätkä.

flyer ['flaiə] s. lentäjä.

flying ['flaiiŋ] *a.* lentävä, lento-; nopea, pika-; s. lentäminen, lento; ~ *field* lentokenttä; ~ *fish* lentokala; ~ *jump* vauhdillinen hyppy; ~ *start* lentävä

lähtö.

fly|leaf s. välilehti, esilehti. **-over** ylikulkusilta. **-weight** kärpässarja(n nyrkkeilijä). **-wheel** vauhtipyörä.

foal [fəul] s. varsa; v. varsoa.

foam [fəum] s. vaahto; (m. ~ *rubber)* vaahtokumi; v. vaahdota.

fob [fɔb] *v.:* ~ *off* puijata, (on.. jku ostamaan jtk); s. kellotasku; *key* ~ avaimenperä.

focal ['fəukl] *a.* fokaali-; ~ *distance* polttoväli; ~ *point* polttopiste.

fo'c's'le ['fəuksl] s. = *forecastle.*

focus ['fəukəs] s. (pl. *foci* ['fəusai]) polttopiste, fokus; (taudin) pesäke; keskus; v. koota polttopisteeseen; tarkentaa; keskittää; *in* ~ terävä, takennettu; *out of* ~ epäselvä.

fodder ['fɔdə] s. rehu.

foe [fəu] s. (run.) vihollinen.

fog [fɔg] s. sumu; v. saattaa ymmälle. **-gy** [-i] *a.* sumuinen; hämärä, epämääräinen. **~-horn** sumutorvi.

fogy, fogey ['fəugi] s.: *old* ~ vanha hölmö.

foible ['fɔibl] s. heikkous, heikko puoli.

foil 1. [fɔil] s. metallilehti, lehtimetalli, folio; tausta; v. korostaa.

foil 2. [fɔil] v. tehdä tyhjäksi.

foil 3. [fɔil] s. floretti, harjoitusmiekka.

foist [fɔist] v. tuoda salaa; ~ *sth.* [*off*] on puijata jku ottamaan jtk.

fold 1. [fəuld] s. lammastarha, kirkon helma; v. kerätä t. sulkea tarhaan.

fold 2. [fəuld] v. taittaa, kääntää; laskostaa; kääriä; sulkea (syliin); panna ristiin; kääntyä (taittua) kokoon; s. laskos, poimu; taite; ~ *up* taittaa t. kääriä kokoon; lopettaa toimintansa.

-fold [fəuld] *suff.: ten~* kymmenkertainen, -kertaisesti.

folder ['fəuldə] s. kansio, mainoslehtinen, esite.

folding *a.* kokoonkäännettävä; ~ *bed* telttasänky; ~ *chair* telttatuoli; ~ *door*[s] kokoonkäännettävät parioivet.

foli|age ['fəuliidʒ] s. lehdet, lehdistö. **-ate** [-iit] *a.* lehtimäinen. **-o** ['fəuliəu] s. (pl. ~s) foliokoko; foliokokoinen kirja; aukeama.

folk [fəuk] s.: ~s ihmiset; sg. (vanh.) kansa; *my* ~s omaiseni; ~ *song*

kansanlaulu. **~-dance** kansantanssi.
~-dancer tanhuaja. **-lore** [-lɔ:] s.
kansanperinne, kansanrunous **-lorist**
[-lɔ:rist] s. kansanrunouden tutkija.
-sy [-si] a. kansanomainen,
vaatimaton, ystävällinen.

follicle ['fɔlikl] s. rakkula.

follow ['fɔləu] v. seurata; noudattaa;
harjoittaa (ammattia); olla (jnk)
seurauksena; *as ~ s* seuraava(t),
seuraavasti, näin; *~ up* seurata
kiinteästi t. loppuun saakka; lisätä,
täydentää (*with* jllak). **-er** [-ə] s.
kannattaja; »sulhanen». **-ing** a.
seuraava; s. kannattajat,
ystäväjoukko. **~-up** myöhempi,
toinen, jatko(hoito, -tutkimus).

folly ['fɔli] s. mielettömyys, hulluus,
hulluus.

foment [fə(u)'ment] v. hautoa; lietsoa,
kiihottaa. **-ation** [-'teiʃn] s. haude;
lietsominen.

fond [fɔnd] a. hellä, rakastava;
mieletön, turha (toivo); *be ~ of* pitää
paljon jstk. **-le** [-l] v. hyväillä, helliä.
-ness s. hellyys, rakkaus, kiintymys
(*for*).

font [fɔnt] s. kastemalja.

food [fu:d] s. ruoka; ravinto;
elintarvikkeet; *frozen ~ s* pakasteet; *~
grains* leipävilja; *~ industry*
ravintoaineteollisuus; *~ for thought*
(t. *reflection*) ajattelemisen aihe(tta).
-stuffs ravintoaineet, elintarvikkeet.

fool [fu:l] s. hullu, houkkio; narri;
kiisseli; v. hullutella; puijata, pitää
narrinaan; *play the ~* hullutella; *make
a ~ of* pitää jkta narrinaan; *a ~ 's
paradise* onnellinen tietämättömyys;
All Fools' Day aprillipäivä; *send on a
~ 's errand* juoksuttaa tyhjän takia; *~
away* kuluttaa joutaviin. **-ery** [-əri] s.
hulluttelu. **-hardy** tyhmänrohkea. **-ish**
[-iʃ] a. hupsu, hassu, järjetön,
narrimainen. **-proof** »idioottivarma»,
(erittäin) helppokäyttöinen.

foolscap [|'fu:lskæp] s. iso
kirjoituspaperi.

foot [fut] s. (pl. *feet* [fi:t]) jalka; alaosa,
-pää, -reuna, jalkopää; (vuoren)
juuri; jalkaväki; pl. pohjaiskala; v.
laskea yhteen (m. *~ up*); tanssia (m.
~ it); *on ~* jalkaisin; *keep one's feet*
pysyä jaloillaan; *put one's ~ down*

toimia päättäväisesti; *put one's ~ in it*
tehdä tökerö erehdys; *set.. on ~*
panna alulle; *~ the bill* (puhek.)
maksaa lasku. **-age** [-idʒ] s. pituus
(jaloina); Am. (elok.) kohtaus.
~-and-mouth disease suu- ja
sorkkatauti. **-ball** jalkapallo, -ilu.
-baller jalkapalloilija. **~-bridge**
porras, jalkasilta. **-fall** askelten ääni.
~-gear jalkineet. **-hills** kukkulat
vuoren juurella. **-hold** jalansija. **-ing**
s. jalansija; kanta; *obtain (gain) a ~*
saada jalansija; *on an equal ~ with*
jkn vertainen; *on a friendly ~ with*
ystävällisissä väleissä jkn kanssa; *on a
peace ~* rauhanajan kannalla.
footl|e [futl] v. hullutella; **-ing** mitätön.
foot|lights ramppivalot. **-man** lakeija,
kamaripalvelija. **-mark** jalanjälki.
-note alaviite. **-pad** (vanh.)
maantierosvo. **~-passenger**
jalankulkija. **-path** polku;
jalkakäytävä. **-print** jalanjälki. **~-race**
kilpajuoksu. **~-slogging** sl. marssi.
-sore kipeäjalkainen. **-step** askel;
jälki; *follow in sb.'s ~ s* seurata jkn
jälkiä. **-stool** jakkara. **-way** polku,
jalkakäytävä. **-wear** jalkineet. **-work**
(urh.) jalkatyö.

fop [fɔp] s. keikari. **-pery** [-əri] s.
keikarimaisuus. **-pish** [iʃ] a.
keikarimainen.

for [fɔ:, fə] prep. jnk hyväksi, puolesta,
-lle; jnk sijasta, sijaan, jtk vastaan,
-ksi, -sta; jhk katsoen, jnk suhteen;
jstk huolimatta; ilmoittaa m.
tarkoitusta, syytä, aikaa,
hintaa, suuntaa; *conj.* sillä; *as ~
me* mitä minuun tulee; *~ two years*
kaksi vuotta, (kielt.) kahteen
vuoteen; *~ all I know* mikäli tiedän;
~ all his wealth [*he is*..] kaikesta
omaisuudestaan huolimatta; *I ~ one*
minä puolestani; *~ a Finn* ollakseen
suomalainen; *tall ~ his age* pitkä
ikäisekseen; *be ~* kannattaa jtk; *I am
all ~* kannatan kovasti; *it is not ~ me
to* minun asiani ei ole; *I must say that
~ him* se on sanottava hänen
puolustuksekseen; *weep ~ joy* itkeä
ilosta; *~ fear of* jnk pelosta; *were it not
~ him* ellei häntä olisi, ilman häntä; *~
twenty pounds* 20 punnan hinnasta;
make ~ suunnata kulkunsa jnnek;

send ~ lähettää noutamaan; *phone* ~
a taxi soittaa taksi; *the train* ~ *London*
Lontooseen menevä juna; [*with a*
dog] ~ *company* seuranaan; ~ *now*
ks. *now*.

forage ['fɔridʒ] *s.* rehu; *v.* hankkia
rehua t. ravintoa, rehustaa.

foray ['fɔrei] *s.* ryöstöretki; *v.* tehdä
ryöstöretki.

forbade [fə'bæd, Am. -'beid] *imp.* ks.
forbid.

forbear 1. ['fɔ:beə] *s.:* ~ *s* esi-isät.

forbear 2. [fɔ'beə] *v.* (*-bore -borne*)
pidättyä (*from* jstk); olla
kärsivällinen. **-ance** [-rəns] *s.*
kärsivällisyys, pitkämielisyys. **-ing** *a.*
kärsivällinen.

forbid [fə'bid] *forbade forbidden*, *v.*
kieltää; *God* ~ *!* Jumala varjelkoon!
-den [-n] *pp.* ks. ed; *a.* kielletty. **-ding**
a. luotaantyöntävä, tyly.

force [fɔ:s] *s.* voima, vahvuus; valta;
(aseistettu) joukko; väkivalta, pakko;
lainvoimaisuus; *v.* pakottaa; riistää
väkipakolla; valloittaa, murtaa auki;
pinnistää, jännittää; hyötää; ~ *s* (sot.)
joukot; *Armed F~ s* puolustusvoimat;
by ~ väkipakolla; *in* ~ mieslukuisesti;
be in ~ olla voimassa; *come into* ~
tulla voimaan; ~ *back* työntää
takaisin; ~ *down* painaa alas;
~ .. *upon* pakottaa jku ottamaan jtk.
-d [-t] *a.* väkinäinen, pingotettu;
~ *landing* pakkolasku; ~ *march*
pikamarssi. **-ful** [-ful] *a.* voimakas.

forcemeat ['fɔ:smi:t] *s.* lihamureke.

forceps ['fɔ:seps] *s.* pihdit; (eläimen)
sakset.

forcible ['fɔ:səbl] *a.* pakko-; voimakas,
vakuuttava; ~ *feeding* pakkosyöttö;
forcibly pakolla, voimakkaasti.

forcing|-house *s.* kasvihuone. **~-pit** lava.

ford [fɔ:d] *s.* kahlaamo; *v.:* ~ *a river*
kahlata joen yli. **-able** [-əbl] *a.* jonka
poikki voi kahlata.

fore [fɔ:] *a.* etu-; keulanpuolinen; *s.*
keula, etuosa; *adv.:* ~ *and aft*
keulassa ja perässä; *to the* ~ esillä,
-lle; etualalla, -lle. **-arm** kyynärvarsi.
-bode [-'bəud] ennustaa. **-boding**
enne; aavistus. **-cast** [-'kɑ:st] *v.* (*imp.*
& pp. ~ t. ~*ed*) arvioida ennakolta,
ennustaa; *s.* ['--] ennuste; *weather* ~
säätiedotus. **-castle, foc's'le** ['fəuksl]

keulakansi; miehistönsuoja. **-close**
[-'kləuz] sulkea pois jstk. **-fathers**
esi-isät. **-finger** etusormi. **-front**
etuala. **-going** edellinen,
edellämainittu; *in the* ~ edellä. **-gone**
a.: ~ *conclusion* ennalta varma asia.
-ground etuala; *in the* ~ etualalla.
-hand kämmen-. **-head** ['fɔrid] otsa.

foreign ['fɔrin] *a.* ulkomaalainen,
ulkomaan; vieras (*to* jklle); *F~ Office*
ulkoministeriö. **-er** [ə] *s.*
ulkomaalainen.

fore|knowledge ['-'-] ennakkotieto.
-land niemeke. **-leg** etujalka. **-lock**
otsakihara; *take time by the* ~ ottaa
vaari ajasta. **-man** työnjohtaja;
valamiehistön puheenjohtaja. **-most**
a. etumainen, ensimmäinen; *adv.;*
first and ~ ensiksikin; *head* ~ pää
edellä. **-name** etunimi. **-noon**
aamupäivä.

forensic [fə'rensik] *a.* oikeus-.

fore|ordain ['fɔ:rɔ:'dein] määrätä
ennakolta. **-runner** [-'rʌnə]
edelläkävijä; enne. **-see** [-'si:]
aavistaa; ~ *able future* näkyvissä oleva
tulevaisuus. **-shadow** [-'ʃædəu] antaa
aavistaa. **-shorten** [-'ʃɔ:tn] lyhentää
(perspektiivisesti). **-sight**
kaukokatseisuus; harkitsevuus. **-skin**
esinahka.

forest ['fɔrist] *s.* (iso) metsä; ~ *worker*
metsätyömies, metsuri.

forestall [fɔ:'stɔ:l] *v.* ennättää (jkta)
ennen.

forest|er ['fɔristə] *s.* metsänvartija;
metsänhoitaja. **-ry** [-tri] *s.*
metsänhoito; metsätiede.

fore|taste *s.* esimaku. **-tell** [-'tel]
ennustaa. **-thought** harkinta.

forever [fər'evə] *adv.* ikuisesti.

fore|warn [-'wɔ:n] varoittaa ennakolta
-word esipuhe.

forfeit ['fɔ:fit] *v.* menettää
(rangaistuksena t. seurauksena jstk);
s. menetetty esine; pantti; *pl.*
panttileikki; *a.* menetetty. **-ure** [-ʃə] *s.*
menettäminen.

forgather [fɔ:'gæðə] *v.* kokoontua.

forgive [fə'giv] *imp.* ks. *forgive*.

forge 1. [fɔ:dʒ] *s.* paja; ahjo; *v.* takoa;
väärentää. **-r** [-ə] *s.* väärentäjä.

forge 2. [fɔ:dʒ] *v.* tunkeutua eteenpäin
(us. ~ *ahead*).

forgery ['fɔːdʒ(ə)ri] s. väärennys.

forget [fə'get] v. (-got, -gotten) unohtaa; ~ *oneself* tehdä jtk sopimatonta. **-ful** a. huonomuistinen, muistamaton. **~-me-not** lemmikki (kasv.).

forgive [fə'giv] v. (-gave, -given) antaa anteeksi; *forgiving* anteeksiantava(inen). **-ness** s. anteeksianto.

forgo [fɔː'gəu] v. (-went, -gone) olla ilman, luopua.

forgot [fə'gɔt] imp. ks. *forget*. **-ten** [-'gɔtn] pp.: *never to be* ~ unohtumaton.

fork [fɔːk] s. haarukka, hanko, äänirauta; (joen ym) haarautuma, haara; v. haarautua; nostaa, kääntää hangolla; ~ *out* (sl.) pulittaa. **-ed** [-t] a. haarainen.

forlorn [fə'lɔːn] a. hylätty, turvaton; kurja; epätoivoinen.

form [fɔːm] s. muoto, hahmo; lomake, kaava; (urh.) kunto; penkki, luokka (koulussa); muodollisuus; v. muodos|taa, -tella, -tua; järjestäytyä; *good* ~ hyvä käytöstapa; *it is bad* ~ on hyvien tapojen vastaista, tahditonta; *in* [*great*] ~, *out of* ~ hyvässä, huonossa kunnossa; *for* ~'*s sake* muodon vuoksi. **-al** [-(ə)l] a. muodollinen, kaavamainen; sovinnainen; ulkonainen; ~*ly* muodollisesti. **-alism** [-əlizm] s. formalismi; kaavamaisuus.

ormal|dehyde [fɔː'mældihaid] s., **-in** ['fɔːmalin] s. formaliini, (liuos).

orm|ality [fɔː'mæliti] s. muodollisuus, kaavamaisuus. **-at** ['fɔːmæt] s. (kirjan) muoto ja koko. **-ation** [fɔː'meiʃn] s. muodostaminen, muodostus, muodostuma; muodostelma (sot.). **-ative** [-ətiv] a. muodostava; luova, kehitys-.

ormer ['fɔːmə] a. entinen; edellinen; *the* ~ ..*the latter* edellinen .. jälkimmäinen. **-ly** adv. ennen.

ormic ['fɔːmik] a.: ~ *acid* muurahaishappo.

ormidable ['fɔːm(i)dəbl] a. pelottava, hirveä.

ormless ['fɔːmlis] a. muodoton.

ormosa [fɔː'məusə] erisn. ks. *Taiwan*.

formula ['fɔːmjulə] s. (pl. m. *-ae* [-iː]) kaava. **-ry** [-əri] s. kaavakokoelma. **-te** [-eit] v. laatia jhk sanamuotoon, formuloida. **-tion** [-'eiʃn] s. sanamuoto.

fornica|te ['fɔːnikeit] v. harjoittaa haureutta. **-tion** [-'keiʃn] s. haureus.

forrader ['fɔrədə] adv.: *I can't get any* ~ (puhek.) en pääse eteenpäin.

forsake [fə'seik] v. forsook [-'suk], forsaken ['-seikn] hylätä.

forsooth [fə'suːθ] adv. (vanh.) totta tosiaan!

forswear [fɔː'swɛə] v. (-swore, -sworn) valallisesti kieltää; luopua jstk; tehdä väärä vala (tav. ~ *oneself*); forsworn valapattuinen.

forsythia [fɔː'saiθjə] s. onnenpensas.

fort [fɔːt] s. linnake; Am. kauppa-asema.

forte [fɔːt] s. vahva puoli; s. (mus.) ['fɔːti] voimakkaasti.

forth [fɔːθ] adv. eteenpäin; esiin, näkyviin; ulos; *back and* ~ edestakaisin; *and so* ~ ja niin edespäin (jne.). **-coming** a. lähestyvä, pian ilmestyvä. **-right** a. suora (-puheinen). **-with** adv. heti, suoraa päätä.

fort|ies ['fɔːtiz] s.: *in the* ~ nelikymmenluvulla, (*is...käy*) viidettä kymmentä; *the roaring* ~ myrskyinen alue 40. ja 50. leveysasteen välissä. **-ieth** ['fɔːtiəθ] *lukus.* neljäskymmenes, -osa.

fortification [fɔːtifi'keiʃn] s. linnoittaminen; linnoitus, varustus.

fortify ['fɔːtifai] v. vahvistaa; linnoittaa, varustaa.

fortitude ['fɔːtitjuːd] s. rohkeus, (mielen)lujuus.

fortnight ['fɔːtnait] s. kaksi viikkoa. **-ly** adv. & a. joka toinen viikko (ilmestyvä).

fortress ['fɔːtris] s. linnoitus.

fortuitous [fɔː'tjuː(:)itəs] a. sattumanvarainen, satunnainen.

fortunate ['fɔːtʃnit] a. onnekas, onnellinen. **-ly** adv. onneksi.

fortune ['fɔːtʃ(ə)n] s. onni; kohtalo, osa; omaisuus, rikkaus; *make a* ~ rikastua; *tell sb. his* ~ povata. **~-hunter** onnenonkija. **~-teller** povari.

forty ['fɔ:ti] *lukus.* neljäkymmentä; ~ *winks* nokoset.

forum ['fɔ:rəm] *s.* foorumi, oikeuspaikka; näyttämö, tapahtumapaikka.

forward ['fɔ:wəd] *a.* etu-; keula-; edistynyt; varhaiskypsä; nenäkäs; ennakko-; *adv.* eteenpäin, esiin; *s.* (jalkap.) hyökkääjä; *v.* lähettää edelleen; edistää; *charges* ~ maksetaan perillä; *bring* ~ tuoda esille, siirtää (kirjanp.); *come* ~ [*as a candidate*] tarjoutua; *look* ~ *to* odottaa jtk, ennakolta iloita jstk. **-ing** *s.* huolinta; ~ *agent* huolitsija. **-ness** *s.* edistyneisyys; nenäkkyys. **-s** [-z] *adv.* eteenpäin; *backwards and* ~ edestakaisin.

fosse [fɔs] *s.* vallihauta.

fossil ['fɔsl] *a.* kivettynyt; *s.* kivettymä. **-ize** ['fɔsilaiz] *v.* kivettää, maaduttaa; kivettyä.

foster ['fɔstə] *v.* hoivata, vaalia. **~-child** kasvatuslapsi. **~-mother** kasvatusäiti.

fought [fɔ:t] *imp.* ks. *fight.*

foul [faul] *a.* likainen, saastainen, iljettävä, pahanhajuinen, pilaantunut; huono (sää ym.) epärehellinen, säännönvastainen; *v.* liata, tuhria; törmätä jhk; *s.* yhteentörmäys; väärä isku t. lyönti; *adv.* sääntöjenvastaisesti; väärin; ~ *copy* konsepti; ~ *language* karkea(ta) puhe(tta); ~ *play* epärehellinen peli; väkivalta(rikos), rikos; *fall* ~ *of* törmätä jhk, joutua hankaluuksiin jnk kanssa. **-ly** *adv.* inhottavasti jne.

found 1. [faund] *imp.* & *pp.* ks. *find.*

found 2. [faund] *v.* valaa.

found 3. [faund] *v.* perustaa; *well* ~*ed* hyvin perusteltu. **-ation** [-'deiʃn] *s.* perustaminen, perustus, perusta; alusta, pohja; säätiö; ~ *cream* puuterin (ym) alusvoide; ~ *garment* korsetti; ~ *stone* peruskivi.

founder 1. ['faundə] upota; (hevosesta) rampaantua, jäädä kiinni (suohon ym); vajota, luhistua; ajaa hevonen pilalle.

founder 2. *s.* perustaja; valaja, valuri.

foundling ['faundliŋ] *s.* löytölapsi.

foundry ['faundri] *s.* valimo.

fount [faunt] *s.* kirjasinladelma; (run.) = seur.

fountain ['fauntin] *s.* lähde; suihkukaivo; (lampun ym) säiliö; ~ *pen* täytekynä; *drinking* ~ ks. *drink.* **~-head** lähde; alkulähde.

four [fɔ:] *lukus.* neljä, nelonen; *carriage and* ~ nelivaljakko; *in* ~*s* (sot.) nelirivissä; *on all* ~*s* nelinkontin. **-fold** *a.* & *adv.* nelinkertai|nen, -sesti. **~-footed** nelijalkainen. **~-in-hand** nelivaljakko. **~-letter** *word* tuhma sana. **~-poster** pylväässänky. **~-score** kahdeksankymmentä. **~-seater** neljän hengen auto. **-some** nelinpeli. **~-square** tukeva. **-teen** neljätoista. **-teenth** *lukus.* neljästoista. **-th** *lukus.* & *s.* neljäs(osa). **-thly** *adv.* neljänneksi.

fowl [faul] *s.* (tav. *koll.*) siipikarja, kana; *v.* linnustaa. **-er** [-ə] *s.* linnustaja. **-ing-piece** lintupyssy. **~-run** kanatarha.

fox [fɔks] *s.* kettu; *v.* vaivata, hämmentää *(the problem has had me* ~*ed);* pettää. **~-brush** ketunhäntä. **-glove** sormustinkukka. **-hound** kettukoira. **~-hunt** kettujahti. **-y** [-i] *a.* kettumainen, viekas; punaisenruskea.

foyer ['fɔiei] *s.* lämpiö.

fracas ['fræka:, Am. 'freikəs] *s.* meteli.

fraction ['frækʃn] *s.* murto-osa; murtoluku. **-al** [-ʃənl] *a.* murto-.

frac|tious ['frækʃəs] *a.* riitainen, ärtyisä. **-ture** [-ktʃə] *s.* (luun) murtuma; *v.* murtaa; murtua.

fragil|e ['frædʒail, Am. -dʒəl] *a.* hauras, hento. **-ity** [frə'dʒiliti] *s.* hauraus.

fragment ['frægmənt] *s.* palanen, sirpale; katkelma. **-ary** [-əri] *a.* katkonainen, hajanainen.

fragran|ce ['freigr(ə)ns] *s.* (sulo)tuoksu. **-t** [-(ə)nt] *a.* tuoksuva.

frail [freil] *a.* hento, hauras, heikko. **-ty** [-ti] *s.* heikkous.

frame [freim] *v.* muodostaa, laatia; rakentaa; kehystää; (m. ~ *up*) laatia väärä syytös jkta vastaan; *s.* rakenne; runko; ruumiinrakenne; kehys, puitteet; puutarhalava; kuva (-ala); ~ *house* puutalo; ~ *of mind* mielentila; *is framing well* luonnistuu hyvin. **~-up** (sl.) juoni, väärä syyte. **-work** runko.

franc [fræŋk] *s.* frangi.

France [frɑːns] *erisn.* Ranska. **-s** [-is] *erisn.*

franchise ['fræn(t)ʃaiz] *s.* erioikeus; äänioikeus; toimilupa; edustussopimus.

Francis ['frɑːnsis] *erisn.* Frans; *St. ~* Franciscus Assisilainen. **-can** [fræn'siskən] *a. & s.* fransiskaani(munkki). **-co** [fr(ə)n'siskəu] *erisn.* (*San ~*).

Franco- ['fræŋkəu]: *the ~ -German war* Ranskan–Saksan sota.

frangible ['frændʒibl] *a.* särkyvä.

frank [fræŋk] *a.* vilpitön, suora, avoin; *v.* lähettää vapaakirjeenä; *~ly* rehellisesti; *~ness* vilpittömyys, suoruus.

Frank [fræŋk] *s.* frankki.

frankincense ['fræŋkinsens] *s.* suitsutus.

frantic ['fræntik] *a.* mieletön, suunniltaan oleva.

fratern|al [frə'tɜːn(ə)l] *a.* veljen-, veljellinen. **-ity** [-iti] *s.* veljeys; veljeskunta; ylioppilasyhdistys, oppilaskunta. **-ize** ['frætənaiz] *v.* veljeillä.

fratricide ['freitrisaid, 'fræt-] *s.* veljenmurha, -murhaaja.

fraud [frɔːd] *s.* petos; huijari. **-ulence** [-juləns] *s.* petollisuus. **-ulent** [-julənt] *a.* petollinen, vilpillinen.

fraught [frɔːt] *a.:* ~ *with* (jtk) täynnä, tulvillaan oleva; ~ *with danger* erittäin vaarallinen.

fray 1. [frei] *s.* riita; tappelu.

fray 2. [frei] *v.* hangata, kuluttaa; hankautua, kulua.

frazzle ['fræzl] *s.: worn to a ~* lopen uupunut, hermot riekaleina.

freak [friːk] *s.* oikku, päähänpisto; omituinen (ihminen); *v.: ~ [out]* sl. olla »pilvessä» (huumeista); ~ [*of nature*] epämuodostuma. **-ish** [-iʃ] *a.* oikullinen, omituinen.

freckle [frekl] *s.* kesakko, pisama; *v.* täplittää; tulla kesakkoiseksi; *~d* kesakkoinen.

free [friː] *a.* vapaa, riippumaton, varaamaton, esteetön; ilmainen, maksuton (m. ~ *of charge*); luonteva; (liian) vapaa, tuttavallinen; antelias; *v.* vapauttaa; ~ *and easy*

kursailematon; ~ *on board* (lyh. *f. o. b.*) vapaasti laivassa; ~ *port* vapaasatama; ~ *trade* vapaakauppa; *make sb. ~ of* [*one's library*] antaa jkn vapaasti käyttää; *make ~ with* ottaa itselleen vapauksia jnk suhteen; *set ~* vapauttaa. **-booter** merirosvo. **-born** vapaasyntyinen. **-dom** [-dəm] *s.* vapaus; (liika) vapaus, tuttavallisuus; luontevuus; ~ *of the city* kunniaporvarin arvo; ~ *of the press* painovapaus; ~ *fighter* vapaustaistelija. **-hand** *a.* käsivara-. **~-handed** antelias. **-hold** *s.* maa, johon haltijalla on täysi omistusoikeus. **~-lance** *s.* itsellinen (toimittaja ym); *v.* toimia itsellisenä. **-ly** *adv.* vapaasti; maksuttomasti; auliisti. **-mason** vapaamuurari. **-masonry** vapaamuurarius.

freesia ['friːzjə] *s.* freesia.

free|-spoken suorasukainen. **~-thinker** vapaa-ajattelija. **-way** moottoritie.

freeze [friːz] *froze* frozen, *v.* jäätyä; paleltua; pakastaa; jäädyttää; palelluttaa; *s.: wage and price ~* hinta- ja palkkasulku; *it is -ing* on pakkanen; *I am -ing* palelen kovasti; *my blood froze* jähmetyin kauhusta. **-er** [-ə] *s.* pakastin; pakastelokero. **-ing-mixture** jäädytysseos. **-ing-point** jäätymispiste.

freight [freit] *s.* (mer.) rahti; lasti; Am. rautatierahti, rahtitavara; *v.* rahdata, lastata; ~ *train* (Am.) tavarajuna. **-age** [-idʒ] *s.* rahtaus; rahti. **-er** [-ə] *s.* rahtaaja; rahtilaiva, kuljetuslentokone. **~-liner** kiitolinja-auto.

French [fren(t)ʃ] *a.* ranskalainen; *s.* ranskan kieli; *the ~* ranskalaiset; ~ *bean* leikkopapu; ~ *horn* ks. *horn;* ~ *window* ranskalainen ikkuna, lasiovi; *take ~ leave* lähteä luvatta, livistää. **-man** *s.* ranskalainen. **-woman** *s.* ranskatar.

frenzied ['frenzid] *a.* raivokas, hurja.

frenzy ['frenzi] *s.* raivo, vimma.

frequency ['friːkwənsi] *s.* taajuus, lukuisuus, (esiintymis)tiheys; frekvenssi, jaksoluku (fys.).

frequent ['friːkwənt] *a.* taaja, usein tapahtuva; lukuisa; nopea (valtimo); *v.* [fri'kwent]: ~ *a place* ahkerasti,

fres

usein käydä jssk. **-ation** [-'tei∫n] s. taaja käyminen (jssk.). **-er** [-'- -] s. *(of* jnk) kantavieras. **-ly** *adv.* usein.

fresco ['freskəu] s. (pl. ~o[e]s) fresko.

fresh [fre∫] a. raikas, raitis; tuore, veres, uusi; kokematon; reipas, virkeä; kukoistava; Am. röyhkeä; *adv.* raikkaasti; äskettäin, vasta-; ~ *wind* navakka tuuli; ~ *water* suolaton, makea vesi; ~ *from* jstk vasta tullut; *the ~ of the morning* aamun raikkaus. **-en** [-n] v. raitistaa, raikastaa, virkistää, virkistyä (m. ~ *up*); liottaa suola pois jstk. **-er** [-ə] s. = *freshman*. **-et** [-it] s. tulva (m.kuv.). **-ly** *adv.* raikkaasti jne.; vasta-. **-man** [-mən] keltanokka, »fuksi». **-ness** s. raikkaus, viileys; tuoreus; pirteys. **-water** makean veden, järvi-.

fret 1. [fret] v. vaivata, kiusata, ärsyttää; kalvaa; panna väreilemään; harmitella, olla huolissaan t. levoton; s. kärtyisyys; levottomuus; *in a ~* hermostunut; *she ~ s over trifles* hän suree turhia. **-ful** a. kärtyisä.

fret 2. [fret] s. ristikko- t. punontakoriste, v. koristaa leikkauksin. **-saw** lehtisaha.

friable ['fraiəbl] a. mureneva.

friar ['fraiə] s. (luostari)veli; *Black F~* dominikaanimunkki; *Grey F~* fransiskaanimunkki.

fricative ['frikətiv] s. rakoäänne.

friction ['frik∫n] s. kitka, hankaus. **-less** a. kitkaton.

Friday ['fraidi] s. perjantai.

fridge [fridʒ] s. = *refrigerator*.

fried [fraid] *imp. & pp.* ks. *fry*.

friend [frend] s. ystävä, ystävätär; *F~* kveekari; *make ~s with* ystävystyä jkn kanssa. **-liness** [-linis] s. ystävällisyys. **-ly** [-li] a. ystävällinen. **-ship** s. ystävyys.

frieze [fri:z] s. (rak.) friisi; eräänl. karkea villakangas.

frigate ['frigət] s. fregatti.

fright [frait] s. pelko, pelästys; (kuv.) linnunpelätti; *take ~* pelästyä; *I got a ~* säikähdin. **-en** [-n] v. pelästyttää; *~ed* pelästynyt. **-ful** a. kauhea; hirvittävä.

frigid ['fridʒid] a. kylmä; ~ *zone* kylmä vyöhyke. **-ity** [fri'dʒiditi] s. kylmyys.

frill [fril] s. röyhelö; *~s* turhat hepenet.

-ed a. röyhelöinen.

fringe [frin(d)ʒ] s. ripsu, reunus; otsatukka; v. koristaa ripsulla; reunustaa; ~ *benefits* lisäedut (palkan lisäksi); ~ *group* (esim. puolueen) ääriryhmä, -ainekset; ~ *phenomena* lieveilmiöt.

frippery ['fripəri] s. hienoudet, koreilu.

Frisian ['friziən] a. friisiläinen.

frisk [frisk] v. hypellä; suorittaa ruumiintarkastus (tunnustelemalla). **-y** [-i] a. leikkisä; vallaton.

fritter 1. ['fritə] s. eräänl. (omena- ym) paistos.

fritter 2. ['fritə] v.: ~ *away* kuluttaa t. tuhlata turhiin.

Fritz [frits] *erisn.;* a. sl. sakemanni.

frivolity [fri'voliti] s. joutavuus; kevytmielisyys. **-ous** ['frivələs] a. mitätön, joutava; kevytmielinen, pintapuolinen.

frizz [friz] v. kähertää; s. kaherretty tukka.

frizzle ['frizl] v. käristää.

frizzy ['frizi] a. kähärä, kihara.

fro [frəu] *adv.: to and* ~ edestakaisin.

frock [frok] s. (naisen) puku; (lapsen) mekko; (munkin) kaapu; ~ *coat* lievetakki.

frog [frog] s. sammakko; nyörinappi (tupsuineen ym). **-man** sammakkomies.

frolic ['frolik] s. kuje, hulluttelu; v. *(-cked)* kujeilla, ilakoida. **-some** [-səm] a. hilpeä, riehakka.

from [from] *prep.* -sta, -lta; jstk syystä; *a letter ~ him* kirje häneltä; ~ *childhood* lapsuudesta alkaen; ~ *morning till night* aamusta iltaan; ~ *1 to 2* [o'clock] yhdestä kahteen; ~ *experience* kokemuksesta, *prevent ~ .. -ing* estää jkta tekemästä jtk; *protect ~* suojata jltain; *suffer ~* kärsiä jstk, sairastaa jtk; ~ *above* ylhäältä; ~ *behind* takaa; ~ *under* alta.

frond [frond] s. (saniaisen) lehti.

front [frʌnt] s. etupuoli, -osa; julkisivu; rintama; (paidan) etumus; julkeus; a. etu-; v. olla, sijaita julkisivu jhk päin (m. ~ *on*, ~ *towards*); *in* ~ edessä, edellä; *in* ~ *of* jnk edessä; *show a bold* ~ näyttää rohkeata naamaa; ~ *door* pääovi; ~ *room* kadulle päin oleva huone. **-age** [-idʒ] s. tontin pituus

kadun suunnassa, talon edusta. **-al** [-l]
a. otsa-, rintama-; *s.* alttarivaate;
julkisivu. **-ier** [-iə] *s.* raja, rajaseutu.
-ispiece [-ispi:s] *s.* (kirjan)
otsikkokuva. **-let** [-lit] *s.* otsanauha.

frost [frɔst] *s.* pakkanen, halla, routa;
v. paelluttaa; peittää huurteella;
sokeroida, kuorruttaa; *white* ~
huurre; ~ *ed glass* himmeäksi hiottu
lasi. **-bite** paleltuma. **-bitten** hallan
vikuuttama. **-ing** *s.* kuorrutus. **-y** [-i]
a. jääkylmä, jäinen; huurteinen.

froth [frɔθ] *s.* vaahto; *v.* vaahdota;
saattaa vaahtoamaan. **-y** [-i] *a.*
vaahtoinen, vaahtoava; tyhjä,
sisällyksetön.

froward [frɔ(u)əd] *a.* uppiniskainen.

frown [fraun] *v.* rypistää otsaansa;
katsella synkästi t. vihaisesti (jkta),
paheksua jtk (~ *at, upon.*); *s.* otsan
rypistys; vihainen katse, muljautus.

frowsty [frausti] *a.* tunkkainen.

frowzy [frauzi] *a.* ummehtunut;
epäsiisti, huolimaton.

froze [frəuz] *imp.* ks. *freeze.* **-n** [frəuzn]
pp. & a. jäätynyt, jääkylmä; ~ *food*
pakasteet.

fruc|tify [frʌktifai] *v.* kantaa
hedelmää; hedelmöittää. **-tose** [-təus]
s. hedelmäsokeri.

frugal [fru:gl] *a.* säästäväinen, niukka.
-ity [fru:ˈgæliti] *s.* vaatimattomuus,
niukkuus.

fruit [fru:t] *s.* hedelmä, (koll.)
hedelmät; *pl.* sato, tuotteet. **-erer**
[-ərə] *s.* hedelmäkauppias. **-ful** *a.*
hedelmällinen, viljava; tuottoisa,
antoisa. **-ion** [fru:ˈiʃn] *s.* nauttiminen;
toteutuminen. **-less** *a.* hedelmätön;
turha.

frump [frʌmp] *s.* linnunpelätti (kuv.),
homssuinen ihminen.

frustra|te [frʌsˈtreit] *v.* tehdä tyhjäksi,
pettää. **-tion** [-ˈeiʃn] *s.*
tyhjäksitekeminen; (psyk.) turhauma,
pettymys.

fry 1. [frai] *s.* kalanpoikanen, (koll.)
pikkukalat; *salmon* ~ lohenpoikanen;
small ~ Japset, pikkuväki.

fry 2. [frai] *v.* paistaa, käristää; paistua.
-ing-pan paistinpannu; *out of the f. -p.*
into the fire ojasta allikkoon.

fuchsia [fju:ʃə] *s.* verenpisara.

fuck [fʌk] *v.* (alat.): ~ *off!* painu

hiiteen! ~ *ing* (merkityksetön)
kirosana (~ *ing nonsense, idiot*).

fuddle [fʌdl] *v.* tehdä sekapäiseksi,
päihdyttää; ryypiskellä.

fuddy-duddy [fʌdidʌdi] *s.* vanha
hölmö.

fudge [fʌdʒ] *s.* pehmeä tsinuski
(kermakaramelli); (vanh.) höpsis!

fuel [fjuəl] *s.* polttoaine; *v.* ottaa
p-ainetta, varustaa p-aineella; ~ *oil*
polttoöljy; *add* ~ *to the flames* valaa
öljyä tuleen. **-ling** *s.*
polttoainetäydennys.

fug [fʌg] *s.* sl. tunkkaisuus.

fuggy [fʌgi] *a.* tunkkainen.

fugitive [fju:dʒitiv] *a.* pakeneva;
haihtuva, lyhytaikainen, hetkellinen;
s. pakolainen; karkulainen.

fugue [fju:g] *s.* fuuga (mus.).

Fulbright [fulbrait] *erisn.*

fulcrum [fʌlkrəm] *s.* (pl. *fulcra*)
tukipiste.

fulfil [fulˈfil] (Am. m. -*fill*) *v.* saattaa
loppuun, toteuttaa, täyttää. **-ment** *s.*
toteuttaminen, toteutuminen,
täyttymys.

fulgent [fʌldʒ(ə)nt] *a.* loistava.

Fulham [fuləm] *erisn.*

full 1. [ful] *a.* täysi, täysinäinen;
täydellinen; täysilukuinen; runsas;
seikkaperäinen; täyteläinen; väljä,
runsaspoimuinen; voimakas, syvä;
adv. kokonaan, aivan; ~ *dress*
paraatipuku, juhlapuku; ~ *face*
suoraan edestä (maalattu,
valokuvattu ym); ~ *stop* piste; *at* ~
length pitkin pituuttaan; ~ *in the face*
suoraan kasvoihin; *in* ~ täydellisesti,
kokonaisuudessaan, juurta jaksain; *to
the* ~ kokonaan, täydellisesti.
~-blooded elinvoimainen;
puhdasverinen. **~-blown** täysin
puhjennut; kypsä, valmis.

full 2. [ful] *v.* vanuttaa. **-er** [-ə] *s.*
vanuttaja; ~ *'s earth* kuohusavi.

full|-face suoraan edestä. **~-fledged**
täysin kehittynyt. **~-length**
kokovartalo-.

fullness [fulnis] *s.* täysinäisyys;
täyteläisyys; runsaus; ~ *of the heart*
sydämen kyllyys; *in the* ~ *of time*
määrähetken koittaessa.

full|-time *a.* kokopäivä-. **-y** [fuli] *adv.*
täydellisesti, kokonaan;

yksityiskohtaisesti.

fulminate ['fʌlmineit] v. salamoida; räjähtää; jyristä, pauhata (against jtk vastaan).

fulness s. = fullness.

fulsome ['fulsəm] a. tympäisevä.

fumble ['fʌmbl] v. kopeloida, haparoida; käsitellä kömpelösti, toheloida, möhliä; s. möhläys.

fume [fju:m] s.: tav. ~s savu, kaasu, höyry; viha, raivo; v. savuta, höyrytä; olla kiukuissaan; tummentaa (savustamalla); in a ~ kuohuksissaan.

fumiga|te ['fju:migeit] v. savustaa, desinfioida. **-tion** [-'geiʃn] s. savustaminen.

fun [fʌn] s. leikki, pila; make ~ of pitää pilanaan; for ~, for the ~ of it, in ~ leikin vuoksi, leikillään; [it was] great ~ hyvin hauskaa; ~ fair huvipuisto.

function ['fʌŋ(k)ʃn] s. toiminta; tehtävä, toimi; (juhla)tilaisuus; (mat. ym) funktio; v. toimia. **-al** [-ʃənl] a. toiminnallinen. **-ary** [-əri] s. toimihenkilö, toimenhaltija, toimitsija.

fund [fʌnd] s. rahasto; (kuv.) suuri määrä; pl. varat; v. sijoittaa valtion arvopapereihin; the [public] ~s valtion obligaatiot; in ~s hyvissä varoissa.

fundamental [fʌndə'mentl] a. perus-; pohjimmainen; olennainen; s. perusperiaate. **-ly** adv. pohjimmiltaan.

funer|al ['fju:n(ə)r(ə)l] s. hautajaiset; a. hautajais-, hautaus-; ~ march surumarssi; ~ urn tuhkauurna. **-eal** [fju(:)'niəriəl] a. hautaus-; synkkä, murheellinen.

fung|oid ['fʌŋgɔid], **-ous** [-əs] a. sienimäinen. **-us** [-əs] s. (pl. m. -gi ['fʌndʒai, 'fʌŋgai] sieni.

funicular [fju(:)'nikjulə] a. köysi-; ~ railway köysirata.

funk [fʌŋk] s. sl. pelko; jänishousu; v. pelätä, jänistää; be in a [blue] ~ olla kovasti peloissaan.

funnel ['fʌnl] s. suppilo; savutorvi, -piippu.

funnily adv. hauskasti; omituisesti.

funny ['fʌni] a. hullunkurinen, lystikäs; omituinen. **~-bone** kyynärpään kärki, kyynärluu.

fur [fə:] s. (eläimen) turkki; turkis, turkikset; (kielen) tahma; v. koristaa turkiksilla; peittää kerrostumalla t. kattilakivellä; tehdä (kieli) tahmaiseksi; furred tahmainen.

furbelow ['fə:biləu] s. poimu-, liehureunus; ~s hepenet.

furbish ['fə:biʃ] v. kiillottaa (us. ~ up); ~ up (kuv.) kohentaa, siistiä.

fur-coat s. turkiskappa, turkki.

furious ['fjuəriəs] a. raivostunut, vimmastunut, hurja.

furl [fə:l] v. käärää t. kääriytyä kokoon; sulkea (sateenvarjo ym).

furlong ['fə:lɔŋ] s. engl. mitta (= 201 m).

furlough ['fə:ləu] s. (et.sot.) loma; v. lomauttaa.

furnace ['fə:nis] s. sulatusuuni; tulipesä, m. keskuslämmityskattila.

furni|sh ['fə:niʃ] v. varustaa (with jllk), kalustaa. **-ture** ['fə:nitʃə] s. huonekalut, kalusto, sisustus; a piece of ~ huonekalu.

furore [fjuə'rɔ:ri] s.: created a ~ herätti suurta ihastusta.

furrier ['fʌriə] s. turkkuri.

furrow ['fʌrəu] s. vako; uurre, kouru; v. kyntää; vaottaa, uurtaa; ~ed m. ryppyinen.

furry ['fə:ri] a. turkispeitteinen, tuuhea.

further ['fə:ðə] a. etäisempi; enempi, lisä-; adv. kauempana, kauemmas; edelleen; lisäksi; v. edistää, auttaa; for ~ particulars apply to lähempiä tietoja antaa; until ~ notice toistaiseksi; ~ studies lisätutkimukset, jatko-opinnot; ~ on tuonnempana. **-ance** [-r(ə)ns] s. edistäminen. **-more** [-'mɔ:] adv. lisäksi, vielä, sitä paitsi. **-most** a. etäisin.

furthest ['fə:ðist] superl. etäisin; kauimpana.

furtive ['fə:tiv] a. salainen, salavihkainen. **-ly** adv. varkain, salaa.

fury ['fjuəri] s. raivo, kiihko; rajuus; raivotar.

furze [fə:z]s. piikkiherne.

fuse [fju:z] v. sulattaa yhteen, sulauttaa toisiinsa; sulautua (yhteen), yhtyä; s. sytytin; sulake.

fuselage ['fju:zilɑ:ʒ, -lidʒ] s. (lentokoneen) runko.

fusil|ier [fju:zi'liə] *s.* muskettisoturi.
-lade [-'leid] *s.* kiväärituli, (kuv.)
ristituli.
fusion ['fju:ʒn] *s.* yhteensulautuminen,
fuusio.
fuss [fʌs] *s.* hälinä, touhu; *v.* touhuta,
hälistä turhaan; ~ *over* huolehtia
liikaa jstk; = seur.; *make a ~ about*
touhuta, tehdä suuri numero jstk; *be*
~*ed about* olla hermostunut jstk. **-er**
[-ə], **-pot** *s.* turhantouhuaja. **-y** [-i] *a.*
turhantouhukas, hermostunut.
fustian ['fʌstiən] *s.* eräänl. kangas,
parkkumi; mahtipontisuus.

fusty ['fʌsti] *a.* ummehtunut,
tunkkainen; »homehtunut».
futil|e ['fju:tail] *a.* joutava, mitätön,
turha. **-ity** [fju:'tiliti]*s.* hyödyttömyys;
joutavuus.
futur|e ['fju:tʃə] *a.* tuleva; *s.*
tulevaisuus; (kiel.) futuuri; *pl.*
termiinikauppa; ~ *tense* futuuri; *for*
the ~, *in* ~ vastedes. **-ity**
[fju(:)'tjuəriti] *s.* tuleva aika. **-ology**
[-'rɔlədʒi] *s.* futurologia.
fuzz [fʌz] *s.* nukka, untuva; sl. poliisi.
-y [-i] *a.* epäselvä, sumea; nukkainen.

G

G, g [dʒi:] *s.* g-kirjain; nuotti g; ~
sharp gis; ~ *flat* ges. Lyh.: **g.** *guinea,
gramme;* **Ga.** *Georgia;* **gal.** *gallons;*
GATT *General Agreement on Tariffs
and Trade;* **G.B.** *Great Britain;*
G.B.S. ['dʒi:bi:'es] *George Bernard
Shaw;* **G.C.E.** *General Certificate of
Education;* **Gen.** *general;* **Geo.**
George; **G.H.Q.** *General
Head-Quarters;* **G.I.** ['dʒi:'ai]
(General Issue) Am. tavallinen
sotamies; **gm.** *gramme(s);* **G.M.T.**
Greenwich mean time; **G.N.P.** *Gross
National Product;* **G.O.P.** *Grand Old
Party* republikaaninen puolue (Am.);
G.P. *General Practitioner;* **G.P.O.**
General Post Office pääpostitoimisto;
gs. *guineas.*

gab [gæb] *s.* lörpötys; *gift of the* ~ hyvä
puhelahja.

gabble ['gæbl] *v.* papattaa, sopottaa; *s.*
papatus.

gaberdine ['gæbədi:n] *s.* viitta;
gabardiini(kangas).

gable ['geibl] *s.* pääty; ~*d*-päätyinen.

Gabriel ['geibriəl] *erisn.*

gad 1. [gæd] *int.: [by]* ~ jumaliste!

gad 2. [gæd] *v.* juoksennella ympäri,
maleksia (m. ~ *about*). ~-*about*
tyhjäntoimittaja, vetelehtijä. **-fly**
paarma, saivartaja.

gadget ['gædʒit] *s.* nokkela laite,
vekotin, vehje.

Gael [geil] *s.* gaeli, skotlantilainen
keltti. **-ic** [-ik] *a.* gaelilainen; *s.* gaelin
kieli.

gaff [gæf] *s.* koukkuseiväs; kahveli
(mer.); *v.* vetää kala (vedestä)
koukkuseipäällä; *penny* ~
nurkkateatteri; *blow the* ~ päästää
salaisuus julki.

gaffe [gæf] *s.* tökeryys, kömmähdys,
munaus.

gaffer ['gæfə] *s.* vanhus, ukko.

gag [gæg] *s.* suukapula; (näyttelijän)
koominen lisäys, pila, heittovitsi; *v.*
panna suukapula (jkn) suuhun, tukkia
suu. **-sman** Am. »komiikan

tehtailija», vitsinikkari.

gaga ['gægɑ:] *a.* höppänä.

gage [geidʒ] *s.* pantti; haaste,
taisteluhansikas; *v.* panna pantiksi; =
gauge.

gaggle [gægl] *s.* (hanhi)parvi.

gai|ety ['ge(i)əti] *s.* ilo, hilpeys; *pl.*
huvitukset. **-ly** *adv.* iloisesti.

gain [gein] *v.* voittaa; ansaita; saada,
saavuttaa; saada hyötyä jstk; edistää;
s. voitto, ansio; hyöty; lisäys; ~
ground voittaa alaa; ~ *on (upon)*
päästä lähemmäksi, päästä voitolle t.
edelle; ~ *over* voittaa puolelleen. **-ful**
a. tuottava; ~*ly employed*
ansiotyössä. **-ings** *s. pl.* voitto, ansio.

Gainsborough ['geinzbrə] *erisn.*

gainsay [gein'sei] *v.* väittää vastaan.

gait [geit] *s.* käynti, astunta. **-er** [-ə] *s.*
nilkkain, säärystin.

gal [gæl] *s.* sl. = *girl.*

gala ['gɑ:lə, 'geilə] *s.* juhla.

galactic [gə'læktik] *a.* linnunradan.

Galatia [gə'leiʃjə] *erisn.: ~ns*
Galatalaiskirje.

galaxy ['gæləksi] *s.* linnunrata, (kuv.)
loistava joukko.

gale 1. [geil] *s.* myrsky; ~ *warning*
myrskyvaroitus.

gale 2. [geil] *s.* suomyrtti *(sweet-~).*

Galil|ean [gæli'li(:)ən] *a. & s.*
galilealainen. **-ee** ['gælili:] *erisn.*
Galilea. **-eo** [-'leiəu] *erisn.*

gall 1. [gɔ:l] *s.* sappi; katkeruus, viha;
sl. hävyttömyys, röyhkeys.

gall 2. [gɔ:l] *v.* hangata rikki; ärsyttää,
loukata; *s.* hankaushaava; ~*ing*
ärsyttävä.

gall 3. [gɔ:l] *s.* kasviäkämä.

gallant ['gælənt] *a.* komea; urhea;
[m. gə'lænt] ritarillinen, kohtelias
naisille; *s.* hieno mies; [m. gə'lænt]
naistenliehittelijä. **-ry** [-ri] *s.* urheus;
ritarillisuus; kohteliaisuus, liehittely.

gallbladder *s.* sappirakko.

galleon ['gæliən] *s.* kaljuuna.

gallery ['gæləri] *s.* lehteri, parveke;
(teatt.) ylin parvi; taidegalleria;

maanalainen käytävä.

galley ['gæli] s. kaleeri; (kapteenin) pursi, (laivan) keittiö. ~-**proof** s. palstavedos. ~-**slave** kaleeriorja.

Gallic ['gælik] a. gallialainen. **g** ~**ism** ['gælisizm] s. gallisisismi.

gallivant [gæli'vænt] v. juoksennella, hakkailla.

gallon ['gælən] s. gallona (engl. mitta = 4,5 l, Am. 3,8 l).

gallop ['gæləp] s. laukka; v. (-oped) laukata; panna (hevonen) laukkaamaan.

gallows ['gæləuz] s. hirsipuu; ~ humour hirtehishuumori.

gallstone sappikivi.

galumph [gə'lʌmf] v. mahtailla.

Gallup ['gæləp] erisn.: ~ poll mielipidetutkimus.

galore [gə'lɔ:] adv. runsaasti.

galosh [gə'lɒʃ] s. kalossi.

Galsworthy ['gɔ:lzwə:ði] erisn.

galvan|ic [gæl'vænik] a. galvaaninen. **-ize** [-vənaiz] v. galvanoida; (kuv.) sähköistää.

gambit ['gæmbit] s. (šakkip.) gambiitti; (kuv.) pelinavaus.

gambl|e ['gæmbl] v. pelata uhkapeliä; s. uhkapeli; ~ away menettää pelissä. **-er** [-ə] s. peluri. **-ing** s. uhkapeli.

gambol ['gæmb(ə)l] s. hyppähdys; v. hypellä.

game 1. [geim] a. rampa (jalka t. käsi).

game 2. [geim] s. peli; leikki, pila, juoni; riista; pl. m. kisat; a. urhea; valmis (for jhk); v. pelata uhkapeliä; ~ of chance uhkapeli; big ~ suurriista; play the ~ noudattaa pelin sääntöjä; none of your little ~s! ei mitään metkuja! the ~ is up peli on menetetty; make ~ of pilailla jkn kustannuksella. ~-**bag** metsästyslaukku. ~-**cock** taistelukukko. ~-**keeper** riistanvartija. ~-**laws** metsästyslait. **-ly** adv. urheasti. **-ster** s. peluri.

gaming ['geimiŋ] s. (uhka)peli.

gamma ['gæmə] s. gamma (~ rays).

gammon 1. ['gæmən] s. savustettu kinkku.

gammon 2. ['gæmən] s. humpuuki, pöty.

gamp [gæmp] s. (vanh., leik.) sateenvarjo.

gamut ['gæmət] s. asteikko.

gander ['gændə] s. uroshanhi.

Gandhi ['gændi:] erisn.

gang [gæŋ] s. joukko, joukkio, sakki, jengi; kopla, liiga; v.: ~ up liittoutua jtk vastaan (on); -**plank** laskuporras.

Ganges ['gæn(d)ʒi:z] erisn.

gangland ['gæŋlænd] s. alamaailma.

gangling ['gæŋliŋ] a. hontelo.

ganglion ['gæŋliən] s. (pl. ~s t. ganglia) hermosolmu.

gangren|e ['gæŋgri:n] s. kuolio. **-ous** [-rinəs] a. kuoliontapainen.

gangster ['gæŋstə] s. gangsteri.

gangway ['gæŋwei] s. (laivan) laskuportaat.

gannet ['gænit] s. suula (eläint.).

gantry ['gæntri] s. nosturiteline.

Ganymede ['gænimi:d] erisn.

gaol [dʒeil] s. vankila; vrt. jail. -**bird** vanki. -**er** [-ə] s. vanginvartija.

gap [gæp] s. aukko; väli, (kuv.) kuilu; ks. generation.

gape [geip] v. avata suunsa ammolleen, ammottaa; töllistellä jtk; s. töllistely; the ~s haukotus.

garage ['gæra:(d)ʒ, Am. -'rɑ:ʒ] s. autotalli, huoltoasema, korjaamo; v. ajaa t. panna talliin.

garb [gɑ:b] s. puku.

garbage ['gɑ:bidʒ] s. (ruoan)jätteet; roskakirjallisuus; ~ disposal jätehuolto.

garble [gɑ:bl] v. seuloa, typistää (mielensä mukaan).

garden ['gɑ:dn] s. puutarha; v. hoitaa puutarhaa; ~s us. puisto; lead sb. up the ~ path johtaa harhaan. -**er** [-ə] s. puutarhuri. -**ing** s. puutarhanhoito. ~-**party** puutarhajuhla.

gardenia [gɑ:'di:njə] s. gardenia.

gargantuan [gɑ:'gæntjuən] a. jättiläismäinen.

gargle ['gɑ:gl] v. kurlata; s. kurlausvesi.

gargoyle ['gɑ:gɔil] s. kattokourun nokka (irvokas ihmisen t. eläimen pää).

garish ['gɛəriʃ] a. korea, räikeä.

garland ['gɑ:lənd] s. seppele, kukkaköynnös; v. koristaa köynnöksillä.

garlic ['gɑ:lik] s. valkosipuli.

garment ['gɑ:mənt] s. vaatekappale.

garner ['gɑ:nə] s. (vilja-)aitta; v. koota

aittaan; kerätä.

garnet ['gɑ:nit] s. granaatti (kivi).

garnish ['gɑ:niʃ] v. koristaa (et. ruokaa).

garret ['gærət] s. ullakkohuone.

garrison ['gærisn] s. varuskunta; v. sijoittaa varuskunta (jhk).

garru|lity [gæ'ru:liti] s. puheliaisuus. **-lous** ['gæruləs] a. puhelias, suulas.

garter ['gɑ:tə] s. sukkanauha; the G~ sukkanauharitarikunta.

gas [gæs] s. kaasu; taistelukaasu (m. poison ~); tyhjä puhe; Am. bensiini; nukutus (ym)kaasu; v. kaasuttaa; kerskailla; step on the ~ lisätä kaasua; be ~sed saada kaasumyrkytys; ~ chamber kaasukammio; ~ station (Am.) bensiiniasema. **~-bag** (kuv.) suupaltti.

gas|-cooker kaasuliesi. **~-fitter** kaasumies.

gaseous ['geizjəs] a. kaasumainen.

gash [gæʃ] s. (ammottava) haava; v. iskeä haava jhk.

gas|-helmet kaasunaamari. **-ify** ['gæsifai] v. muuttaa kaasuksi. **~-jet** kaasuliekki.

gasket ['gæskit] s. tiiviste.

gas|-main pääkaasujohto. **~-meter** kaasumittari.

gaso|lene, -line ['gæsəli:n] s. gasoliini; (Am.) bensiini. **-meter** [gæ'sɔmitə] s. kaasukello.

gasp [gɑ:sp] v. haukkoa henkeä; huohottaa; s. raskas hengitys, huohotus; at one's last ~ henkihieverissä.

gassy ['gæsi] a. kaasu-, kaasumainen; rehentelevä.

gastr|ic ['gæstrik] a. vatsa-; ~ ulcer mahahaava. **-itis** [-'traitis] s. mahakatarri. **-onomist** [-'trɔnəmist] s. herkuttelija, gastronomi. **-onomy** [-'trɔnəmi] s. gastronomia.

gasworks s. kaasulaitos.

gat [gæt] s. (Am.) sl. revolveri.

gate [geit] s. portti; veräjä; patoluukku, sulkuportti; (urh.) yleisömäärä, tulot; ~ money pääsylipputulot. **-crasher** kuokkavieras. **~-house** portinvartijan talo. **~-post** portinpieli; between you and me and the ~ aivan meidän kesken. **-way** portti, -käytävä.

gather ['gæðə] v. kerätä, koota; korjata, poimia; rypyttää; päätellä (from jstk), saada (vaikutelma ym); kerääntyä, kokoontua; (paiseesta) kypsyä; ~ speed saada vauhtia; ~ strength voimistua. **-ing** s. väkijoukko, kokous; laskostus; märkäpaise.

gauche [gouʃ] a. kömpelö.

gaudy [gɔ:di] a. korea, pramea; s. (yliopiston) juhla (entisten kunniaksi).

gauge, (Am. m.) **gage** [geidʒ] s. normaalimitta, mitta; mittari; raideväli; mittapuu; v. mitata, vaata, arvioida.

Gaul [gɔ:l] s. gallialainen. **-ish** [-iʃ] a. gallialainen.

gaunt [gɔ:nt] a. laiha, riutunut,

gauntlet 1. ['gɔ:ntlit] s. taisteluhansikas; (urh.) suojakäsine; throw down the ~ haastaa taisteluun.

gauntlet 2. ['gɔ:ntlit] s. kujanjuoksu; run the ~ joutua ankaran arvostelun alaiseksi.

gauz|e [gɔ:z] s. harsokangas; ~ bandage harsoside; wire ~ seulaverkko. **-y** [-i] a. harsomainen.

gave [geiv] imp. ks. give.

gavel ['gævl] s. nuija, (huutokaupanpitäjän) vasara.

gawk [gɔ:k] s. tomppeli; v. tollottaa. **-y** [-i] a. kömpelö.

gawp [gɔ:p] v. tuijottaa (suu auki, ihmetellen).

gay [gei] a. iloinen, hilpeä; korea, kirjava; kevytmielinen; (puhek.) homoseksuaalinen.

gaze [geiz] v. tuijottaa, katsoa kiinteästi; s. kiinteä katse.

gazebo [gə'zi:bou] s. näköalapaikka, näkötorni.

gazelle [gə'zel] s. gaselli.

gazette [gə'zet] s. (virallinen) lehti. **-er** [gæzi'tiə] s. maantieteellinen sanakirja.

gazump [gə'zʌmp] v. korottaa jnk hinta (tarjouksen hyväksymisen ja sopimuksenteon välillä).

gear [giə] s. käyttöpyörästö, hammaspyöräkoneisto; vaihde; v. kytkeä; panna jhk vaihteeseen; ~ .. to sth. sopeuttaa jhk, sovittaa jnk mukaan; ~ up kiihdyttää vauhtia; in ~ kytkettynä; out of ~ (kuv.)

epäkunnossa, huonolla tuulella; *change* ~ vaihtaa. ~-**box** vaihdelaatikko.

gee [dʒi:] *int.* (hoputus hevoselle) hei hop! (m. ~ *up*). ~-**gee** (lastenk.) humma.

geese [gi:s] *pl.* ks. *goose.*

Geiger ['gaigə] *erisn.:* ~ *counter* geigerputki, -mittari.

gelatin|e ['dʒeləti:n] *s.* liivate. -**ous** [dʒi'lætinəs] *a.* liivatemainen.

geld [geld] *v.* kuohita. -**ing** *s.* valakka.

gem [dʒem] *s.* jalokivi.

Gemini ['dʒeminai] *s.* Kaksoset (täht.).

gen [dʒen] *s. sl.: the* ~ yleinen ilmoitus, tieto; *v.:* ~ *up* ottaa selville.

gendarme ['ʒɑ:(n)dɑ:m] *s.* santarmi.

gender ['dʒendə] *s.* suku (kiel.); (leik.) sukupuoli.

gene [dʒi:n] *s.* geeni.

genealog|ical [dʒi:ni|ə'lɔdʒik(ə)l] *a.* sukututkimus-. -**ist** [-'ælədʒist] *s.* sukututkija. -**y** [-'ælədʒi] *s.* genealogia.

general ['dʒen(ə)rəl] *a.* yleinen, yleis-; tavallinen; pää-, yli-; ylimalkainen; *s.* kenraali; *in* ~ yleensä; *in* ~ *terms* ylimalkaisesti; *in* ~ *use* yleisessä käytössä; ~ *knowledge* yleistiedot; ~ *strike* yleislakko; *secretary~* pääsihteeri; *G~ Post Office* pääpostikonttori. -**issimo** [-'lisiməu] *s.* ylipäällikkö. -**ity** [-ə'ræliti] *s.* yleisyys; ylimalkainen lausunto; *the* ~ *(of)* enemmistö. -**ization** [-ai'zeiʃn] *s.* yleistys. -**ize** [-aiz] *v.* yleistää; puhua ylimalkaisesti. -**ly** *adv.* tavallisesti, yleensä; ylimalkaisesti; ~ *speaking* yleisesti; yleisesti ottaen. ~-**purpose** *a.* monikäyttöinen. -**ship** *s.* kenraalinarvo; sotapäälliköntaito.

genera|te ['dʒenəreit] *v.* siittää, (kuv.) synnyttää, tuottaa; kehittää. -**tion** [-'reiʃn] *s.* kehittäminen; sukupolvi, suku; ~ *gap* sukupolvien välinen kuilu. -**tive** [-rətiv] *a.* siitos-; tuottava. -**tor** [-ə] *s.* generaattori.

generic [dʒi'nerik] *a.* suku-; yleinen; ~ *name* yleisnimitys.

gener|osity [dʒenə'rɔsiti] *s.* jalous; anteliaisuus. -**ous** ['dʒen(ə)rəs] *a.* jalo(mielinen); antelias, aulis; runsas.

genesis ['dʒenisis] *s.* alku; *G~* 1. Mooseksen kirja.

genetic [dʒi'netik] *a.* geneettinen. -**s** [-s] *s. pl.* perinnöllisyystiede.

Geneva [dʒi'ni:və] *erisn.; the* ~ *Convention* Genèven sopimus.

genial ['dʒi:njəl] *a.* ystävällinen, sydämellinen, iloinen; suotuisa, leuto (ilmanala). -**ity** [dʒi:ni'æliti] *s.* leutous; ystävällisyys.

genie ['dʒi:ni] *s.* (pl. ~*s* t. *genii;* henkilento.

genii ['dʒi:niai] *pl.* ks. *genius* ja ed.

genital ['dʒenitl] *a.* sukupuoli-. -**s** [-z] *pl.* sukupuolielimet.

genitive ['dʒenitiv] *s.* genetiivi.

genius ['dʒi:njəs] *s.* (pl. ~*es*) nero; nerokkuus, nerous (tav. sing.); *the* ~ *of* suojelushenki, jnk henki; (pl. *genii*) demoni, henkilento.

Geno|a ['dʒenə(u)ə] *erisn.* -**ese** [dʒenə(u)'i:z] *a. & s.* genovalainen.

genocide ['dʒenə(u)said] *s.* kansanmurha.

genre [ʒɑ:ŋr] *s.:* ~ *painting* laatukuvamaalaus.

gent [dʒent] *s.* »herrasmies»; *the* ~*s* miestenhuone.

genteel [dʒen'ti:l] *a.* (us. pilk.) hieno, ylhäinen.

gentian ['dʒenʃiən] *s.* katkero (kasv.).

gentile ['dʒentail] *a. & s.* ei-juutalainen, pakana.

gentility [dʒen'tiliti] *s.* (us. pilk.) hienous, ylhäisyys.

gentle ['dʒentl] *a.* ylhäinen, jalo(sukuinen); lempeä, lauhkea, vieno, ystävällinen, pehmeä, hiljainen; hellävarainen; *the* ~ *sex* heikompi sukupuoli. -**folk(s)** hienot ihmiset. -**man** [-mən](pl. -*men*[-mən]) herrasmies, gentlemanni, herra; *gentlemen!* hyvät herrat! ~ *'s* kamaripalvelija. -**manly** hieno, sivistynyt. -**ness** *s.* ystävällisyys, lempeys; hellävaraisuus. -**woman** (pl. -*women*) säätyläisnainen, hieno nainen.

gently ['dʒentli] *adv.* ystävällisesti, lempeästi, hiljaa, hellävaroen.

gentry ['dʒentri] *s.* säätyläiset, herrasväki.

genuflexion [dʒenju'flekʃn] *s.* polvistuminen.

genuine ['dʒenjuin] *a.* oikea, väärentämätön, aito. -**ness** *s.*

oikeaperäisyys, aitous.

genus ['dʒiːnəs] *s.* (pl. *genera*) ['dʒenərə] suku; laji.

geodesy [dʒi(ː)'ɔdisi] *s.* geodesia.

Geoffrey ['dʒefri] *erisn.*

geogra|pher [dʒi'ɔgrəfə] *s.* maantieteilijä. **-phic(al)** [dʒiə'græfik, -(ə)l] *a.* maantieteellinen. **-phy** [dʒi'ɔgrəfi] *s.* maantiede.

geolog|ical [dʒiə'lɔdʒik(ə)l] *a.* geologinen. **-ist** [dʒi'ɔlədʒist] *s.* geologi. **-y** [dʒi'ɔlədʒi] *s.* geologia.

geometry [dʒi'ɔmitri] *s.* geometria.

geo|physics [dʒiə'fiziks] *s. pl.* geofysiikka. **-politics** [-'pɔlitiks] *s. pl.* poliittinen maantiede.

Georg|e [dʒɔː'dʒ] *erisn.*: *St* ~ Pyhä Yrjö. **-ia** [-jə] *erisn.* **-ian** [-jən] *a.* Yrjöjen aikainen; *a. & s.* georgialainen.

Gerald ['dʒer(ə)ld] *erisn.*

geranium [dʒi'reinjəm] *s.* kurjenpolvi, pelargonit (kasv.).

geriatric [dʒeri'ætrik] *a.*: ~ *ward* vanhusten osasto. **-s** [-s] *s. pl.* geriatria.

germ [dʒɔːm] *s.* itu, aihe; bakteeri, taudinsiemen; ~ *warfare* bakteerisota. **-an** [-ən] *a.* täysi, oikea; *cousin* ~ täysi serkku.

German ['dʒɔːmən] *a. & s.* saksalainen; saksan kieli; ~ *measles* vihurirokko; ~ *sausage* meetvursti; ~ *silver* uushopea; ~ *text* fraktuura.

germane [dʒɔː'mein] *a.*: ~ *to* jtk koskeva, jhk liittyvä.

German|ic [dʒɔː'mænik] *a.* germaaninen. **-y** ['dʒɔːm(ə)ni] *erisn.* Saksa.

germicide ['dʒɔːmisaid] *s.* bakteereja tappava aine.

germi|nal ['dʒɔːminl] *a.* idulla oleva. **-nate** [-eit] *v.* itää. **-nation** [-'neiʃn] *s.* itäminen.

gerontology [dʒerɔn'tɔlədʒi] *s.* gerontologia.

gerrymander ['dʒerimændə] *v.* järjestellä (vaalipiireihin jako) vilpillisesti.

Gertrude ['gəːtruːd] *erisn.*

gerund ['dʒer(ə)nd] *s.* gerundi.

gestation [dʒes'teiʃn] *s.* tiineys, raskaudentila.

gesticula|te [dʒes'tikjuleit] *v.* viittoilla,

elehtiä. **-tion** [-'leiʃn] *s.* viittoilu, elehtiminen.

gesture ['dʒestʃə] *s.* (käden) liike, ele.

get [get] *got got* (vanh. & Am. *gotten*) *v.* saada, saavuttaa; hankkia (itselleen); saada kiinni; saattaa jhk tilaan t. tekemään jtk; oppia, ymmärtää; saapua, päästä jhk, tulla jksk; *pp*:n ja *a*:n yht.: ~ *hurt* loukkaantua; ~ *well* tulla terveeksi; ~ *drunk* juoda itsensä humalaan; ~ *married* mennä naimisiin; ~ *going!* ala mennä! *it's time we got going* on aika aloittaa, ryhtyä toimeen; ~ *there* (puhek.) onnistua; ~ *to know* oppia tuntemaan, tutustua; ~ *to like* ruveta pitämään jstk; ~ *wet* kastua; *I have got minulla on; what have you got to say?* mitä sinulla on sanottavaa? *you have got to obey* sinun on toteltava; ~ *a th. done* saada jk toimitetuksi; *it is* ~*ting dark* alkaa hämärtää; *I don't* ~ *you* en ymmärrä; *got it?* käsititkö? ~ *about* liikuskella, (huhusta) levitä; ~ [*an idea*] *across to* saada jku ymmärtämään; ~ *ahead* menestyä; ~ *along* tulla toimeen (*with* jkn kanssa); ~ *along with you!* mene tiehesi! älä höpise! ~ *at* päästä käsiksi jhk, saada selville jtk, tarkoittaa; lahjoa, (puhek.) tehdä pilaa, moittia; ~ *away* päästä pakoon; ~ *away with it* selviytyä; ~ *back* palata; ~ *one's own back on* kostaa; ~ *by* päästä ohi, selvitä; ~ *down to* ryhtyä toden teolla jhk; ~ *in* päästä sisään, saapua; ~ *into* nousta (esim. bussiin), mahtua jhk, joutua (jnk valtaan); *what's got into you?* mikä sinuun on mennyt? ~ *off* laskeutua, poistua (junasta ym); lähteä; selviytyä, päästä; ~ *on* edistyä, menestyä; tulla toimeen *(with* jkn kanssa); ~ *on with it!* pane toimeksi! ~ *on sb.'s nerves* käydä jkn hermoille; *how is he ~ting on?* kuinka hän voi! miten (hänen työnsä ym) sujuu? *he is ~ting on [in years]* hän alkaa tulla vanhaksi; ~ *out* päästä jstk, poistua jstk; tulla julki, saada suustaan; ~ *out!* ala painua! ~ *over* voittaa; toipua; ~ *round* taivuttaa, suostuttaa; välttää; ~ *through* selvitä jstk; ~ *up* nousta; järjestää, panna toimeen; laittaa koreaksi. **~-at-able**

[get'ætəbl] luokse päästävä.
~-together kokoontuminen. **~-up**
asu, ulkoasu.

Gethsemane [geθ'seməni] *erisn.*

gewgaw ['gju:gɔ:] *s.* halpa hely,
rihkama.

geyser ['gi:zə, Am. gaizə] *s.* kuuma
lähde; [m. Am. 'gi:zə] veden
lämmityslaite, kuumavesisäiliö.

Ghana ['gɑ:nə] *erisn.* **-ian** [gɑ:'ne(i)ən]
a. & s. ghanalainen.

ghastly ['gɑ:stli] *a.* hirvittävä, kamala;
aavemainen; *adv.* kauhean.

gherkin ['gə:kin] *s.* etikkakurkku.

ghetto ['getəu] *s.* (*pl.* ~s)
juutalaiskortteli; slummialue.

ghost [gəust] *s.* henki; aave, kummitus;
the Holy G~ Pyhä Henki; *give up the*
~ heittää henkensä; *not the ~ of a*
chance ei pienintäkään
mahdollisuutta. **-like** *a.* aavemainen.
-ly *a.* = *ed.* **~-writer**
haamukirjoittaja.

ghoul [gu:l] *s.* paha henki (joka syö
ruumiita). **-ish** [-iʃ] *a.* kaamea,
pirullinen.

giant ['dʒaiənt] *s.* jättiläinen; *a.*
jättiläis-. **-ess** [-is] *s.* jättiläisnainen.

gibber ['dʒibə] *v.* papattaa. **-ish**
['gibəriʃ] *s.* siansaksa.

gibbet ['dʒibit] *s.* hirsipuu.

gibbon ['gibən] *s.* gibboni.

gibbous ['gibəs] *a.* kupurainen, kupera.

Gibbs ['gibz] *erisn.*

gibe [dʒaib] *v.* pilkata, ivata *(at* jkta); *s.*
iva, pistosana.

giblets ['dʒiblits] *s.* (kanan ym)
sisälmykset (sydän, ym).

Gibraltar [dʒib'rɔ:ltə] *erisn.*

giddiness ['gidinis] *s.* huimaus;
ajattelemattomuus.

giddy ['gidi] *a.* huimausta tunteva;
pyörryttävä, huimaava;
ajattelematon, huikentelevainen;
I feel ~ minua huimaa.

Gideon ['gidiən] *erisn.*

Gielgud ['gilgud] *erisn.*

gift [gift] *s.* lahja; hengenlahja,
taipumus. **-ed** [-id] *a.* lahjakas; ~
[with] varustettu.

gig [gig] *s.* kiesit; laivavene.

gigantic [dʒai'gæntik] *a.* jättiläismäinen.

giggle ['gigl] *v.* tirskua, kikattaa; *s.*
kikatus.

gigolo ['ʒigələu] *s.* (*pl.* ~s)
ammattitanssittaja.

gild [gild] *v.* (*pp. m. gilt)* kullata; ks.
guild. **-ing** *s.* kultaus.

gill 1. [gil] *s.* tav. *pl.* kidukset.

gill 2. [dʒil] *s.* engl. nestemitta (¹/₄ *pint*
= 0,14 l.)

Gillespie [gi'lespi] *erisn.*

gillie ['gili] *s.* (Skotl.) kalastajan t.
metsästäjän apulainen,
palveluspoika.

gilt [gilt] *pp.* ks. *gild; a.* kullattu; *s.*
kultaus. **~-edged** kultareunainen;
g.-e. securities ensi luokan
arvopaperit.

gimcrack ['dʒimkræk] *s.* arvoton hely,
rihkama.

gimlet ['gimlit] *s.* käsipora.

gimmick ['gimik] *s.* (mainos)kikka,
niksi; (nokkela) vehje.

gin 1. [dʒin] *s.* katajanmarjaviina, gini.

gin 2. [dʒin] *s.* ansa;
puuvillanpuhdistuskone; *v.* puhdistaa
(puuvillaa); pyydystää ansaan.

ginger ['dʒin(d)ʒə] *s.* inkivääri; ~ *up*
(puhek.) piristää; ~ *beer*
inkiväärijuoma; ~ *group* (pol.)
piristysryhmä (toimintaan innostava);
~ *nut* piparpähkinä. **-bread**
piparkakku; maustekakku.

gingerly ['dʒin(d)ʒəli] *a.* varovainen;
adv. varovasti.

gingham ['giŋəm] *s.* eräänl.
puuvillakangas, gingham.

gingivitis [dʒindʒi'vaitis] *s.* ientulehdus.

ginseng ['dʒinseŋ] *s.* ginseng
(kiinalainen lääkejuuri).

gipsy, gypsy ['dʒipsi] *s.* mustalainen.

giraffe [dʒi'rɑ:f, Am. -'ræf] *s.* kirahvi.

gird 1. [gə:d] *v.* pilkata *(at).*

gird 2. [gə:d] ~*ed* — *ed* t. *girt girt, v.*
vyöttää; ympäröidä; ~ *on* sitoa
vyölleen. **-er** [-ə] *s.* kannatinpalkki.

girdle ['gə:dl] *s.* vyö, liivit; *v.* vyöttää,
ympäröidä.

girl [gə:l] *s.* tyttö; apulainen;
tyttöystävä, heila; *old* ~ tyttöseni.
-hood *s.* tyttöikä. **-ish** *a.* tyttömäinen.

giro ['dʒairəu] *s.: [national]* ~
postisiirto; *bank* ~ pankkisiirto.

girt [gə:t] *imp. & pp.* ks. *gird.*

girth [gə:θ] *s.* satulavyö; ympärysmitta.

gist [dʒist] *s.* ydin (kuv.), olennaisin osa
t. asia.

give [giv] *gave, given, v.* antaa, suoda; tuottaa, aiheuttaa, herättää; omistaa (jllek, jhk); olla, antaa jhk päin *(on to, upon); s.* kimmoisuus, peräänantaminen; ~ *and take* molemminpuoliset myönnytykset, kompromissi; *I was* ~*n to understand* minun annettiin ymmärtää; ~ *a sigh* huoata; ~ *rise to* aiheuttaa; ~ *way* antaa perään t. myöten, taipua, (liikenteestä) väistää; ~ *a cry* päästää huuto; ~ *a start* hätkähtää; ~ *away* ilmaista, paljastaa; ~ *forth* levittää, huokua, julkaista, ilmoittaa; ~ *in* antaa myöten, taipua; jättää (sisään); ~ *off* huokua, levittää; ~ *out* loppua; ilmoittaa, m. = ed.; ~ *over* loppua; ~ *up* luovuttaa, luopua jstk, jättää sikseen; ~ *oneself up to* antautua jnk valtaan. **-n** [-n] *pp. & a.* määrätty, sovittu, tietty; edellyttäen, että; ~ *to drink* viinaan menevä; ~ *a triangle ABC* tunnetaan kolmio ABC.

gizzard ['gizəd] *s.* (linnun) lihasmaha.

glacé ['glæsei, Am. -'sei] *a.* glasee-; sokeroitu.

glacial ['gleiʃəl] *a.* jää-, jäinen; *the* ~ *era* jääkausi.

glacier ['glæsjə, Am. 'gleiʃə] *s.* jäätikkö.

glad [glæd] *a.* iloinen; ilahduttava; *I am* ~ *to hear that.* . olen hauska kuulla, että; ~ *to see you!* hauska tavata (sinua)! *be (feel)* ~ *about* iloita, olla mielissään jstk; *give the* ~ *eye* iskeä silmää; ~ *rags* parhaat hepenet. **-den** [-n] *v.* ilahduttaa.

glade [gleid] *s.* metsäaukio.

gladi|ator ['glædi|eitə] *s.* gladiaattori. **-olus** [-'əuləs] *s.* miekkalilja.

glad|ly ['glædli] *adv.* iloisesti; mielihyvin. **-ness** *s.* iloisuus.

glamo|rize ['glæməraiz] *v.* luoda hohdetta jhk. **-rous** [-rəs] *a.* tenhoava.

glamour, glamor ['glæmə] *s.* lumous, romanttinen hohde.

glance [glɑ:ns] *v.* vilkaista *(at, on* jhk), katsahtaa; välkähtää; *s.* silmäys, välähdys; ~ *against,* ~ *off* sipaista jtk; ~ *over* silmäillä ylimalkaisesti, kosketella ohimennen; *take a* ~ *at* vilkaista.

gland [glænd] *s.* rauhanen. **-ers** [-əz] *s.* räkätauti. **-ular** [-julə] *a.*

rauhasmainen, rauhas-.

glar|e ['gleə] *v.* olla räikeä; pistää silmään, häikäistä; tuijottaa vihaisesti, mulkoilla *(at* jkh); *s.* räikeä valo; räikeys; mulkoilu. **-ing** [-riŋ] *a.* räikeä, häikäisevä; ~ *injustice* huutava vääryys.

Glasgow ['glɑ:sgəu, 'glæs-, 'glæz-'] *erisn.*

glass [glɑ:s] *s.* lasi; lasillinen; peili (m. *looking-*~), kiikari; ilmapuntari; tuntilasi; *pl.* silmälasit; ~ *case* lasikaappi. **~-blower** lasinpuhaltaja. **~-house** kasvihuone. **-works** lasitehdas. **-y** [-i] *a.* lasimainen; (vedestä) kirkas.

Glaswegian [glæs'wi:dʒjən] *a. & s.* glasgowlainen.

glaucoma [glɔ:'kəumə] *s.* viherkaihi.

glaz|e [gleiz] *v.* varustaa lasilla; lasittaa; kiillottaa; *s.* lasitus; kiilto; lasuuri; ~ *d tile* kaakeli. **-ier** [-jə] *s.* lasimestari.

gleam [gli:m] *s.* välkähdys, välke; pilkahdus; *v.* hohtaa; välkkyä.

glean [gli:n] *v.* poimia (tähkäpäitä); kerätä. **-er** [-ə] *s.* tähkänpoimija. **-ings** *s.:* ~ *from* poimintoja jstk.

glebe [gli:b] *s.* pappilan maa; (run.) maa, pelto.

glee [gli:] *s.* ilo; laulu kolmelle t. neljälle sooloäänelle; ~ *club* lauluseura, kuoro.

glen [glen] *s.* (kapea) laakso, notko.

glib [glib] *a.* liukas(kielinen).

glid|e [glaid] *v.* liukua, solua; *s.* liukuminen; liu'unta (mus.). **-er** [-ə] *s.* liito-, purjelentokone. **-ing** *s.* liito-, purjelento.

glimmer ['glimə] *v.* hohtaa (heikosti); tuikkia; *s.* hohde; tuike; (toivon ym) pilkahdus.

glimpse [glimps] *s.* pilkahdus, vilahdus; *catch a* ~ *of* nähdä vilahdukselta.

glint [glint] *v.* välkkyä, kimmeltää; *s.* välke.

glisten [glisn] *v.* kimallella.

glitter ['glitə] *v.* kimmallella, välkkyä; *s.* kimallus.

gloaming ['gləumiŋ] *s.* iltahämärä.

gloat [gləut] *v.:* ~ *over* ahmia silmillään jtk, tuntea vahingoniloa.

global ['gləubl] *a.* koko maapallon käsittävä, maailmanlaajuinen.

globe [gləub] *s.* pallo; maapallo, karttapallo. **~-trotter** maailmankiertäjä.

globul|ar ['glɔbjulə] *a.* pallonmuotoinen, pallo-. **-e** [-ju:l] *s.* pieni pallo, pilleri, pisara.

gloom [glu:m] *s.* synkkyys; raskasmielisyys, alakuloisuus. **-y** [-i] *a.* pimeä, synkkä; raskasmielinen, alakuloinen.

glorification [glɔ:rifi'keiʃn] *s.* ylistäminen; kirkastaminen.

glori|fy ['glɔ:ri|fai] *v.* ylistää; kirkastaa, antaa loistoa jllek. **-ous** [-əs] *a.* loistava; ihana; maineikas.

glory ['glɔ:ri] *s.* kunnia, maine; loisto, ihanuus, autuus; *v.* ylpeillä *(in jstk); to go to ~ kuolla. ~-hole* romukamari, romulaatikko.

gloss 1. [glɔs] *s.* kiilto; pintakiilto; *v.* kiillottaa; *~ over* kaunistella, peitellä.

gloss 2. [glɔs] *s.* glossa, sanan selitys; *v.* varustaa selityksillä. **-ary** [-əri] *s.* sanasto.

glossy ['glɔsi] *a.* kiiltävä, kiiltopintainen; *s.: ~ periodical* naisten (muoti- ym) lehti.

glottis ['glɔtis] *s.* äänirako (anat.).

Gloucester ['glɔstə] erisn.

glove [glʌv] *s.* hansikas; *fits like a ~* sopii kuin valettu; *be hand in ~ with* olla hyvää pataa jkn kanssa; *[handle sb.] without ~s* kovakouraisesti. **-r** [-ə] *s.* hansikkaantekijä.

glow [gləu] *v.* hehkua; *s.* hehku. **~-worm** kiiltomato.

glower ['glauə] *v.* mulkoilla *(at* jtk); *~ingly* vihaisesti.

gloxinia [glɔk'sinjə] *s.* gloksinia.

glucose ['glu:kəus] *s.* rypälesokeri.

glue [glu:] *s.* liima; *v.* liimata. **-y** [-i] *a.* liimainen, liimamainen.

glum [glʌm] *a.* synkkä, nyrpeä. **-ness** *s.* nyrpeys.

glut [glʌt] *v.* täyttää (liiaksi), ahmia *(~ oneself with);* kyllästyttää; *s.* ylitäkylläisyys, kyllästys; (liika) runsaus, liikatarjonta.

glu|ten ['glu:t|ən] *s.* gluteeni, sitkoaine. **-tinous** [-inəs] *a.* liimamainen, tahmea.

glutton ['glʌtn] *s.* ahmatti; ahma. **-ous** [-əs] *a.* ahnas. **-y** [-i] *s.* ahnaus.

glycerin(e) ['glisəri:n] *s.* glyseriini.

G-man ['dʒi:mæn] *s.* Am. sl. rikosetsivä.

gnarled [nɔ:ld] *a.* pahkainen, pahkurainen.

gnash [næʃ] *v.: ~ one's teeth* kiristellä hampaitaan.

gnat [næt] *s.* mäkärä, hyttynen; *strain at a ~* kuurnia hyttysiä.

gnaw [nɔ:] *v.* jyrsiä; jäytää.

gneiss [nais] *s.* gneissi.

gnome [nəum] *s.* menninkäinen.

gnostic ['nɔstik] *a.* gnostilainen; *s.* gnostikko.

gnu [nu:] *s.* gnu(-antilooppi).

go [gəu] *went gone, v.* mennä, lähteä, matkustaa, kulkea, käydä; sujua, onnistua; kulua; tulla jksk; antaa myöten, murtua; kuulua; riittää; mahtua; *s.* sisu, tarmo, yritys; *the story goes* kerrotaan; *be ~ing to* aikoa, olla aikeissa; *[I think] it is ~ing to rain* tulee sade; *[this] goes to show* on omiaan osoittamaan; *goes a long way towards* auttaa osaltaan paljon; *[it is true] as far as it goes* erään rajoituksin; *~ about* toimittaa; *~ at* käydä jkn kimppuun; *~ by* kulkea ohi, kulua; noudattaa jtk; matkustaa jllak, jnk (paikan) kautta; *~ down* upota, laskea, *(well with)* saavuttaa jkn suosio; *~ for* mennä noutamaan; hyökätä jkn kimppuun; *~ in for* ryhtyä jhk, ruveta harrastamaan jtk, ottaa käyttöön, käyttää; *~ off* lauета, luopua; sujua, onnistua; nukahtaa; *~ on* jatkaa, jatkua, kulua, tapahtua; *~ out* (m.) sammua; *my heart went out to her* tunsin syvää myötätuntoa häntä kohtaan; *~ over* tarkastaa; *~ through* kestää, läpikäydä; *~ through with* suorittaa loppuun, selviytyä jstk; *~ with* sopia yhteen jnk kanssa, seurustella (vakituisesti, *go steady with);* ~ *without* olla t. tulla toimeen ilman; *that goes without saying* se on itsestään selvää; *have a ~ at* yrittää jtk; *he has plenty of ~* hän on sisukas; *on the ~* menossa; *.. not bad as films ~ nowadays* nykyelokuvaksi aika hyvä.

goad [gəud] *s.* piikkisauva; kannustin; *v.* kiihottaa.

go-ahead *a.* yritteliäs; *give the g.-a.* näyttää vihreää valoa jllek.

goal [gəul] s. maali; päämäärä.
~**-keeper** maalivahti.

goat [gəut] s. vuohi; he-~ pukki; *get
sb.'s* ~ (sl.) suututtaa, ärsyttää jkta.
-**ee** [gə(u)'tiː] s. pukinparta. -**sucker**
kehrääjä(lintu).

gob [gɔb] s. pala, möykky (m. *gobbet*);
sl. suu.

gobble ['gɔbl] v. hotkia; (kalkkunasta)
kaakottaa. **-dygook** s. eräänl.
virastokieli. -**r** [-ə] s. Am.
uroskalkkuna.

go-between välittäjä.

goblet ['gɔblit] s. pikari.

goblin ['gɔblin] s. vuorenhaltija,
peikko.

go-by: *give sb. the* ~ antaa palttua, ei
olla näkevinään.

goby ['gəubi] s. tokko (eläint.).

go-cart s. lapsenrattaat.

god [gɔd] s. jumala; *thank G~* Jumalan
kiitos; *G~ willing* jos Jumala suo.
-**child** kummilapsi. **-dess** s. jumalatar.
-**father** kummi. **-fearing**
jumalaapelkäävä. ~**-forsaken**
jumalanhylkäämä. **-head** jumaluus,
jumalolento. **-less** jumalaton. **-like** a.
jumalallinen. **-ly** a. jumalinen,
hurskas. **-mother** kummi(täti).
God's-acre kirkkomaa. **-send** taivaan
lahja. **-speed:** *wish sb.* ~ toivottaa
onnea (matkalle).

go-getter s. pyrkyri.

goggle ['gɔgl] v. mulkoilla, pyörittää
silmiään; s. *pl.* suojasilmälasit.
~**-eyed** mulkosilmäinen.

going ['gəuiŋ] s. lähtö; (tien) kunto,
keli; vauhti; *I am* ~ *to* aion; *keep* ~
pitää käynnissä; *a* ~ *concern*
menestyvä liikeyritys; [*he is*] ~ *on for
50* lähes 50 vuoden ikäinen; ~*s on*
tapahtumat, (et. paheksuttava)
elämä, »peli».

goitre, goiter ['gɔitə] s. struuma.

go-kart s. mikroauto.

gold [gəuld] s. kulta; *a heart of* ~
kultainen sydän; ~ *rush* kultakuume.
~-**digger** kullankaivaja; sl.
»lompakonlaihduttaja» (nainen).
~-**dust** kultapöly. **-en** [-n] a.
kultainen; kullankeltainen; *the* ~
mean kultainen keskitie; ~ *wedding*
kultahäät. ~-**field** kultakenttä. **-finch**
tikli. **-mine** kultakaivos. **-smith**

kultaseppä.

golf [gɔlf] s. golf; v. pelata golfia.
~-**club** golfmaila, -kerho. ~-**course**,
~-**links** golfkenttä. **-er** s.
golfinpelaaja.

Golgotha ['gɔlgəθə] erisn. Golgata.

Goliath [gə'laiəθ] erisn. Goljat.

golliwog ['gɔliwɔg] s. eräänl. irvokas
nukke; mörkö.

golly ['gɔli] int. voi taivas!

golosh [gə'lɔʃ] ks. *galosh.*

Gomorrah [gə'mɔrə] erisn.

gonad ['gəunæd] s. sukupuolirauhanen.

gondo la ['gɔndələ] s. gondoli. **-lier**
[gɔndə'liə] s. gondolieeri.

gone [gɔn] pp. ks. *go;* a. mennyt,
poissa, lopussa, hävinnyt, kuollut; *in
times* ~ *by* ennen muinoin; ~ *on* (sl.)
hullaantunut jhk; *far* ~ hyvin
huonossa kunnossa. **-r** [-ə] mennyttä
kalua.

gong [gɔŋ] s. gonggongi, kumistin.

gonorrhea [gɔnə'riːə] s. tippuri.

goo [guː] s. sl. tahma;
sentimentaalisuus. **-(e)y** [-i] a.
tahmainen.

good [gud] a. *(better best)* hyvä;
ystävällinen, kiltti; hyödyllinen,
terveellinen; kelvollinen, sopiva;
kunnon; taitava; melkoinen; oikea;
pilaantumaton; (kaupp.) varma; s.
hyvä, hyöty, (jkn) paras; *pl.* tavarat;
~ *at* taitava jssk; ~ *afternoon* hyvää
päivää! ~ *morning* hyvää huomenta
(t. päivää)! ~ *day* (harv.) hyvästi! *a* ~
fellow kunnon mies, hauska mies; *G*
~ *Friday* pitkäperjantai; *a* ~ *three
miles* runsaasti 3 mailia; ~ *looks*
kauneus; *I have a* ~ *mind to* mieleni
tekee; *we had a* ~ *time* meillä oli
hauskaa; *do sb. a* ~ *turn* tehdä
ystävänpalvelus; *hold* ~ pitää
paikkansa; *make* ~ korvata, täyttää
(lupaus); onnistua; *as* ~ *as dead*
melkein kuollut; *be as* ~ *as one's word*
pitää sanansa; *is* ~ *for* (m.) pystyy
jhk, voi elää, säilyä, kestää, kykenee
maksamaan; *it is no* ~ ei kannata; *for*
~, *for* ~ *and all* lopullisesti, kerta
kaikkiaan; *we were £5 to the* ~ [tililä
oli] .. hyväksemme. ~-**bye** *int.*
hyvästi; s. jäähyväiset. ~-**fellowship**
seurallisuus, rattoisuus.
~-**for-nothing** tyhjäntoimittaja.

~-humoured hyväntuulinen. **-ish** *a.* melkoinen. **~-looking** hauskannäköinen. **-ly** [-li] *a.* kaunis, komea; melkoinen. **~-natured** hyväntahtoinen, kiltti.

goodness ['gudnis] *s.* hyvyys ~ *gracious! ~ me!* hyvänen aika! *for~' sake* herran tähden! *G ~ knows* taivas tietää.

good|s [gudz] *s. pl.* tavara(t), omaisuus; ~ *train* tavarajuna. **-tempered** hyvänluonteinen. **-will** hyvä tahto, suopeus, myötämieli. **goody** ['gudi] *s.* (et. *pl.*) makeinen; *a.* (m. ~-~) hurskasteleva.

goofy [gu:fi] *a.* hölmö, typerä.

goon [gu:n] *s.* hölmö.

goose [gu:s] *s.* (pl. *geese*) hanhi. **-berry** ['guz-] karviaismarja; *play ~* olla kolmantena pyöränä. **~-flesh** kananliha. **~-step** paraatimarssi.

gopher ['goufə] *s.* taskurotta.

Gordian ['gɔ:djən] *a.: ~ knot* Gordionin solmu.

gore 1. [gɔ:] *s.* (hyytynyt) veri, hurme, *v.* lävistää (sarvella).

gore 2. [gɔ:] *s.* kiila (vaatteessa).

gorge [gɔ:dʒ] *s.* rotko, kuilu, sola; kurkku; *v.* ahmia (m. ~ *oneself with*); ahtaa täyteen; *make one's ~ rise* inhottaa.

gorgeous ['gɔ:dʒəs] *a.* loistava, upea, komea. **-ness** *s.* loisto.

Gorgon ['gɔ:gən] *s.* gorgoni; hirviö. **-zola** [-'zəulə] *s.* juustolaji.

gorilla [gə'rilə] *s.* gorilla.

gormandize ['gɔ:məndaiz] *v.* mässäillä, herkutella. **-r** [-ə] *s.* ahmatti.

gorse [gɔ:s] *s.* piikkiherne.

gory ['gɔ:ri] *a.* hurmeinen.

gosh [gɔʃ] *int.* voi hemmetti.

goshawk ['gɔshɔ:k] *s.* kanahaukka.

gosling ['gɔslin] *s.* hanhenpoika.

gospel ['gɔsp(ə)l] *s.* evankeliumi; ~ *truth* ehdoton totuus.

gossamer ['gɔsəmə] *s.* (hämähäkin)seitti; ohut harso; *a.* harsomainen.

gossip ['gɔsip] *s.* juoru; juoruakka, kielikello; *v. (-iped)* juoruta. **-y** [-i] *a.* juoruava.

got [gɔt] *imp. & pp.* ks. *get*; ~ *up* koristeltu; *I've got . .* minulla on.

Goth [gɔθ] *s.* gootti; (kuv.) vandaali.

~-enburg ['gɔθnbə:g] *erisn.* Göteborg.

-ic [-ik] *a.* goottilainen; barbaarinen; kauhu-; *(~tales) s.* gootin kieli; gotiikka. **-land** ['gɔθlənd] *erisn.* Gotlanti.

gotten [gɔtn] ks. *get*.

gouge [gaudʒ] *s.* kourutaltta; *v.* kovertaa; ~ *out* kaivaa (silmä) kuopastaan.

gourd [guəd] *s.* kurpitsa; kalebassi.

gourmand ['guəmənd] *s.* suursyömäri.

gourmet ['guəmei] *s.* viinin t. ruokien tuntija, herkkusuu.

gout [gaut] *s.* kihti, luuvalo. **-y** [-i] *a.* luuvaloinen.

govern ['gʌv(ə)n] *v.* hallita; määrätä, ohjata, vaikuttaa; (kiel.) vaatia (jtk sijaa). **-able** [-əbl] *a.* (helposti) hallittavissa oleva. **-ess** [-is] *s.* kotiopettajatar. **-ment** *s.* hallitus; valtio(n); kuvernementti; ~ *bond* valtionobligaatio. **-mental** [-'mentl] *a.* valtion-. **-or** [-ə] *s.* maaherra, kuvernööri; johtokunnan jäsen; sl. isäukko, päällikkö; (nopeuden) säädin.

gown [gaun] *s.* (naisen) puku; viitta, virkapuku, akateeminen puku *(cap and ~)*; *night ~* yöpaita. **-sman** akateeminen kansalainen.

grab [græb] *v.* kahmaista, kouraista, tarttua; *s.* kahmaisu; koura (tekn.).

grace [greis] *s.* sulo, viehkeys; suosio(n osoitus); armo, armonaika, maksunlykkäys; pöytärukous; *v.* koristaa, kaunistaa; kunnioittaa, suoda; *say ~* lukea pöytärukous; *His G~* hänen armonsa (arkkipiispan ym puhuttelunimi); *with [a] bad ~* vastahakoisesti; *with a good ~* kernaasti; *airs and ~s* keimailu, teeskentely; *in sb.'s good ~s* jkn suosiossa; *the G~s* sulottaret. **-ful** *a.* suloinen, viehkeä. **-less** *a.* turmeltunut, häpeämätön. **~-note** (mus.) korukuvio.

gracious ['greiʃəs] *a.* suosiollinen, ystävällinen; armollinen, laupias; suloinen; *good ~! ~ me!* laupias taivas!

gradation [grə'deiʃn] *s.* asteittaisuus, asteittainen muuttuminen; *pl.* (väli) asteet, vivahdukset; äännevaihtelu.

grad|e [greid] *s.* aste, laatu, luokka;

vivahdus; Am. (koulu)luokka; arvosana, numero; (et. Am.) nousu; *v.* järjestää laadun (vaikeusasteen ym) mukaan, luokitella; sävyttää; risteyttää; parantaa (m. ~ *up);* ~ *crossing* (Am.) tasoristeys; ~ *school* (Am.) kansakoulu; *make the* ~ läpäistä, selvitä; *on the up(down)* ~ nousussa (laskussa). **-ient** [-jənt] *s.* (tien ym) kaltevuus, nousu.

gradu|al ['grædju(ə)l] *a.* asteittainen. **-ally** [-əli] *adv.* asteittain, vähitellen. **-ate** [-eit] *v.* saada akateeminen oppiarvo; jakaa asteisiin; muuttua asteittain; *s.* ['grædjuit] yliopistollisen loppututkinnon suorittanut; *-ated* (m.) asteikolla varustettu. **-ation** [-'ei∫n] *s.* yliopistollisen oppiarvon suorittaminen; lopputuktinto; Am. koulun päättäminen; ~ *ceremony* m. promootio.

graffiti [grə'fi:ti] *s. pl.* (sg. *graffito*) seinätöherrykset.

graft [grɑ:ft] *v.* oksastaa; (lääk.) siirtää; Am. harjoittaa lahjontaa; *s.* oksas; kudossiirrännäinen; sl. lahjonta.

Graham ['gre(i)əm] *erisn.; g~* (Am.) grahamjauho ym.

Grail [greil] *s.* (m. *Holy* ~) Graal(malja).

grain [grein] *s.* jyvä; vilja; graani (= 0,065 g); hitunen; juovaisuus, (puun) syy; rakeisuus, rosoisuus; purppuraväri; luonne, laatu; *v.* murentaa, tehdä rosoiseksi; juovittaa, marmoroida; *go against the* ~ olla vastenmielistä; *dyed in* ~ (pesun)kestävästi värjätty. **-ed** [-d] *a.* rakeinen, rosoinen; juovitettu.

gram [græm] ks. *gramme.*

gramma|r ['græmə] *s.* kielioppi; ~ *school* oppikoulu, Am. keskikoulu. **-rian** [grə'mɛəriən] *s.* kieliopintutkija. **-tical** [grə'mætik(ə)l] *a.* kieliopillinen.

gramme [græm] *s.* gramma.

gramophone ['græməfəun] *s.* gramofoni.

Granada [grə'nɑ:də] *erisn.*

granary ['grænəri] *s.* vilja-aitta.

grand [grænd] *a.* suur-, pää-; komea, suuri, suurenmoinen, loistava; mahtava, ylpeä; *s.* flyygeli; Am. sl. 1 000 dollaria; *G~ Duke* suurherttua, suuriruhtinas; ~ *piano* flyygeli (*baby*

~ *pieni f.*); ~ *stand* pääkatsomo. **-(d)ad** ukki. **-child** lapsenlapsi. **-daughter** pojan- t. tyttärentytär. **-father** isoisä; ~ *clock* kaappikello.

grandee [græn'di:] *s.* espanjalainen grandi.

grandeur ['græn(d)ʒə] *s.* suuruus, suurenmoisuus, komeus; ylhäisyys; ylevyys; jalous.

grandi|loquent [græn'diləkwənt] *a.* suurisanainen, mahtipontinen. **-ose** ['grændiəus] *a.* suurenmoinen, suurisuuntainen.

grand|ma ['grænmɑ:] mummi. **-mother** isoäiti. **-pa** [-pɑ:] vaari, ukki. **-parents** isovanhemmat. **-son** pojan- t. tyttärenpoika.

grange [grein(d)ʒ] *s.* maatalo.

granite ['grænit] *s.* graniitti.

gran|ny, -nie ['græni] *s.* mummi, isoäiti.

grant [grɑ:nt] *v.* suoda, antaa; myöntää; *s.* suominen jne; apuraha, määräraha; luovutus; ~ *a request* suostua pyyntöön; *~ed that* edellyttäen, että; *take sth. for* ~ *ed* pitää varmana, edellyttää jtk; *~ed!* olkoon niin!

granul|ar ['grænjulə] *a.* rakeinen. **-ate** [-eit] *v.* murentaa, rouhia; granuloida (lääk.).

granule ['grænju:l] *s.* jyvänen.

grape [greip] *s.* viinirypäle. **-fruit** greippi. **-shot** kartessi. **-vine** viiniköynnös, huhupuhe, jouru(t); [*I heard it*] *on the* ~ juorutietä.

graph [græf] *s.* diagrammi, käyrä.

graphic ['græfik] *a.* graafinen; havainnollinen, selvä. **-ally** *adv.* havainnollisesti.

graphite ['græfait] *s.* grafiitti (miner.).

graphology [græ'fɔlədʒi] *s.* grafologia.

grapnel ['græpnəl] *s.* naara (-ankkuri); entraushaka (hist.).

grappl|e ['græpl] *v.* käydä käsiksi, tarttua jhk; ~ *with* painiskella jkn kanssa; käydä tarmolla käsiksi jhk.

grasp [grɑ:sp] *v.* tarttua, käydä käsiksi jhk; pitää kiinni jstk; käsittää, tajuta; tavoitella, tarttua ahnaasti *(at* jhk); *s.* luja ote; käsityskyky; in *the* ~ of jkn vallassa; [*a problem*] *within my* ~ jonka voin ymmärtää. **-ing** *a.* ahnehtiva.

grass [grɑ:s] *s.* ruoho; nurmi(kko); sl.

marihuana, hasis; [*out*] *at* ~
laitumella; ~ **widow(er)** kesäleski.
-hopper heinäsirkka; hepokatti
(longhorned ~). **~-roots** s. tavalliset
ihmiset, kenttäväki. **-y** [-i] *a.*
ruohoinen, ruoho-.

grate 1. [greit] *s.* arina; *v.* varustaa
ristikolla.

grate 2. [greit] *v.* hieroa, raastaa;
hangata; kitistä; viiltää, vihloa; ~
upon one's nerves vihloa hermoja.

grateful *a.* kiitollinen. **-ly** *adv.*
kiitollisena, kiittäen.

grater ['greitə] *s.* raastin.

gratification [grætifi'kei∫n] *s.*
tyydyttäminen; tyydytys, ilo.

grati|fy ['grætifai] *v.* tyydyttää;
ilahduttaa; *I was -fied to hear.* .iloitsin
kuullessani. . **-fying** *a.* ilahduttava.

grating ['greitiŋ] *s.* ristikko.

gratis ['greitis] *adv.* ilmaiseksi.

gratitude ['grætitju:d] *s.* kiitollisuus.

gratui|tous [grə'tju(:)itəs] *a.* ilmainen,
maksuton. **-ty** [-i] *s.* rahalahja,
erikoispalkkio; juomaraha.

grave 1. [greiv] *a.* vakava, totinen;
tärkeä; juhlallinen.

grave 2. [greiv] *s.* hauta; *v.* kaivertaa;
painaa syvälle; ~*n image* epäjumala.

gravel ['grævl] *s.* sora; *v.* hiekoittaa;
~*led* (puhek.) ymmällä. **-ly** *a.* sora-.

graveness *s.* vakavuus.

grave|-stone hautakivi. **-yard**
hautausmaa.

graving-dock *s.* kuivatelakka.

gravita|te ['græviteit] *v.* pyrkiä
liikkumaan *(towards* jhk päin). **-tion**
[-'tei∫n] *s.* gravitaatio, vetovoima.

gravity ['græviti] *s.* vakavuus,
arvokkuus; painovoima, (maan)
vetovoima; *specific* ~ ominaispaino;
ks. *centre*.

gravy ['greivi] *s.* (paistin) kastike; sl.
(helposti ansaittu) raha, voitto; ~
~*-boat* kastikekulho.

gray [grei] *a.* Am. harmaa; ks. *grey*.
-ling [-liŋ] *s.* harjus.

graze 1. [greiz] *v.* sipaista, pyyhkäistä;
raapaista; *s.* sipaisu.

graz|e 2. [greiz] *v.* laiduntaa, olla
laitumella.

greas|e [gri:s] *s.* ihra, rasva, voide; *v.*
[gri:z] rasvata, voidella; ~ *sb.'s palm*
lahjoa. **-y** ['gri:si] *a.* rasvainen.

great [greit] *a.* suuri; tärkeä,
huomattava, erinomainen; ylevä;
ylhäinen, hieno; *s. pl.* (Oxfordin
yliop.) et. klassisen kirjallisuuden
(B.A.) loppututkinto; *that's* ~!
hienoa! *she had a* ~ *time* [*in Paris*]
hänellä oli hyvin hauskaa; G~ *Britain*
Iso-Britannia; *the G~ Powers*
suurvallat; *a* ~ *friend of mine* hyvä
ystäväni; ~ *on* innostunut,
ihastunut jhk; G~*er London*
Suur-Lontoo. **~-aunt** isän t. äidin täti.
-coat paksu päällystakki.
~-grandchild lapsenlapsen lapsi. **-ly**
adv. suuresti, paljon, hyvin;
ylevämielisesti. **-ness** *s.* suuruus,
suurenmoisuus; tärkeys; ylevyys.

grebe [gri:b] *s.* uikku.

Grecian ['gri:∫n] *a.* kreikkalainen *(a* ~
urn).

Greece [gri:s] *erisn.* Kreikka.

greed [gri:d] *s.* ahneus; (jnk) himo. **-y**
[-i] *a.* ahne, ahnas; ~ *for* jnk
himoinen.

Greek [gri:k] *a.* & *s.* kreikkalainen; *s.*
kreikan kieli; *it's* ~ *to me* se on
minulle hepreaa; [*she is*] ~ *(a* ~
woman) kreikatar; ~ [*Orthodox*]
Church ortodoksinen kirkko.

green [gri:n] *a.* vihreä, vihanta; raaka;
kypsymätön, tuore, kokematon; *s.*
vihreä väri, vihreys; nurmikko,
ruohokenttä (us. urheilu-); *pl.*
vihannekset. **-back** Am. seteli. **-ery**
[-əri] *s.* vihreys. **-gage** viherluumu.
-grocer vihanneskauppias. **-horn**
vasta-alkaja, keltanokka. **-house**
kasvihuone. **-ish** [-i∫] *a.* vihertävä.
G~**land** *erisn.* Grönlanti. **-ness** *s.*
vihreys; kypsymättömyys,
kokemattomuus. ~**-room**
(näyttelijöiden) seurusteluhuone,
seurusteluhuone. **-sward**
nurmikkoa.

Greenwich ['grinidʒ]: ~ *mean time*
(lyh. *G.M.T.)* G:n aika.

greet [gri:t] *v.* tervehtiä. **-ing** *s.*
tervehdys; ~*s telegram* onnittelu- t.
korusähke.

gregarious [gri'gɛəriəs] *a.* laumassa
elävä, lauma-; seuraa rakastava.

grenad|e [gri'neid] *s.* (käsi)kranaatti.
-ier [grenə'diə] *s.* krenatööri.

grew [gru:] *imp.* ks. *grow.*

grey [grei] a. harmaa (m. kuv.);
s. harmaa väri, harmaus;
v. harmaannuttaa, harmaantua.
~-haired harmaatukkainen.
-hound vinttikoira.
-ish a. harmahtava.
grid [grid] s. ristikko; (sähk.) hila,
johtoverkosto; = **-iron**.
gridiron ['gridaiən] s. parila, halstari.
grief [gri:f] s. suru; *come to ~*
epäonnistua, käydä huonosti.
grievance ['gri:vəns] s. jkn (mielestään)
kärsimä vääryys, valituksen t. kaunan
aihe; *air a ~* purkaa murheensa; *nurse
a ~* kantaa kaunaa.
griev|e [gri:v] v. surra *(at* jtk), surettaa;
I was ~d to hear kuulin ikäväkseni.
-ous [-əs] a. katkera; tuskallinen;
hirvittävä.
grif|fin ['grifin] s. aarni(kotka). **-fon**
[-fən] s. = ed.; koirarotu.
grill [gril] s. paahdin, grilli, parila; =
~-room; v. paahtaa, grillata,
pariloida; kiusata. **~-room** grilli
(ravintolassa).
grille [gril] s. ristikko.
grim [grim] a. kova, armoton; tuikea,
tuima; katkera, kaamea; *~ly*
ankarasti, julmasti.
grimace [gri'meis] s. irvistys, virnistys;
v. irvistää.
grim|e [graim] s. (piintynyt) lika; v.
liata, ryvettää. **-y** [-i] a. likainen,
musta.
grin [grin] v. irvistää; virnistää,
hymyillä leveästi; s. irvistys, virnistys;
~ and bear it kestää valittamatta.
grind [graind] *ground ground,* v.
jauhaa, hienontaa; hioa, teroittaa;
vääntää; sortaa, rasittaa; päntätä
(päähänsä, jkn päähän), raataa;
hienontua, hioutua; s. jauhaminen,
jauhatus; raataminen; *~ one's teeth*
kiristellä hampaita. **-er** [-ə] s.
poskihammas; teroitin. **-stone** tahko;
keep sb.'s nose to the ~ panna
raatamaan.
grip [grip] s. (luja) ote; vaikutus, valta;
kädensija, kahva; Am. matka-,
käsilaukku; v. tarttua lujasti jhk,
vallata jkn mieli; *(with* jhk) *come to
~s* joutua käsikähmään, käydä
käsiksi; *the brakes failed to ~* jarrut
eivät pitäneet; *~ ping* [*story*]

vaikuttava, järkyttävä.
gripe [graip] v. tarttua, ahdistaa; s.
puristus; *the ~s* vatsanväänteet.
grippe [grip] s. influenssa.
grisly ['grizli] a. hirvittävä, kauhea,
karmea.
grist [grist] s. jauheet, jauhettava vilja,
rouheet; *brings ~ to the mill* tuottaa
voittoa; *all is ~ that comes to his mill*
hän käyttää kaiken hyödykseen.
gristle ['grisl] s. rusto.
grit [grit] s. sora, karkea hiekka; hyvä
aines, sisu; v. kirskuttaa; kiristellä
(hampaita). **-s** [-s] s. pl. jauhamaton
kaura; karkea kaurajauho. **-ty** [-ti] s.
hiekkainen; sisukas.
grizzle [grizl] v. (lapsesta) marista,
uikuttaa.
grizzl|ed ['grizl|d] a. harmaa,
harmaatukkainen. **-y** [-i] s. (m. ~
bear) harmaakarhu.
groan [grəun] v. vaikeroida, voihkia;
natista; s. voihkina, valitus; *~s of
disapproval* nurina; *~ down* [*a
speaker*] vaientaa; *~* [*under injustice*]
huokailla; [*the table*] *~ed with food*
notkui ruokaa.
groats [grəuts] s. pl. (kaura)rouheet,
suurimot.
grocer ['grəusə] s. sekatavarakauppias;
~'s [*shop*] ruoka-, sekatavarakauppa.
-y [-ri] s.; *-ies* ruoka-, sekatavarat.
grog [grɔg] s. grogi (juoma). **-gy** [-i] a.
päihtynyt; horjuva.
groin [grɔin] s. nivustaive; holviruode;
~ed vault ristiholvi.
groom [gru:m] s. tallirenki;
kamariherra; = *bridegroom;* v. hoitaa,
ruokota (hevosta); *well-groomed*
hyvinhoidettu. **-sman** [-zmən] s.
sulhaspoika.
groove [gru:v] s. uurre, koro; rihla;
(kuv.) vanha raide, ura; v. tehdä
uurre jhk, uurtaa.
groove ['gru:vi] a. sl. hieno, loisto-,
muodinmukainen.
grope [grəup] v. hapuilla, haparoida
(for, after jtk).
gross [grəus] a. jykevä, iso, karkea;
törkeä, ruokoton; kokonais-, brutto-;
s. krossi (12 tusinaa); v. tuottaa
bruttotuloina, ansaita bruttona; *~
weight* bruttopaino; *in ~* tukussa. **-ly**
adv. karkeasti.

Grosvenor ['grəuvnə] *erisn*.

grotesque [grə(u)'tesk] *a.* groteksi, irvokas.

grotto ['grɔtəu] *s.* (pl. ~*es* t. ~*s*) luola.

grouch [grautʃ] *v.* nurista; *s.* murjotus; nyrpeä, murjottava henkilö.

ground 1. [graund] *imp. & pp.* ks. *grind*.

ground 2. [graund] *s.* maa, maaperä; pohja, perusta; syy, peruste; alue, ala, kenttä; *pl.* puistoalue; *v.* perustaa; opettaa alkeet; maattaa (sähk.); ajaa karille; (ilm.) estää (t. kieltää) nousemasta (kentällä), pakottaa laskeutumaan; *coffee~s* kahvinporo; *fishing~s* kalavedet; *hunting~s* metsästysmaat; *on what ~s?* millä perusteella; *have~s for* olla aihetta jhk; ~ crew huolto- t. kenttähenkilöstö; ~ *floor* pohjakerros; ~ *glass* (himmeäksi) hiottu lasi; ~ *rent* tontinvuokra; ~ *swell* pohjamaininki; *break* ~ raivata tietä (t. alaa); *cover* ~ kulkea, päästä eteenpäin; *covers much new* ~ käsittelee useita uusia aiheita; *hold one's* ~ pysyä kannallaan; *well~ed* hyvin perusteltu; *be well~ed in* omata hyvät pohjatiedot jssk. -**ing** *s.* pohjatiedot. -**less** *a.* perusteeton, aiheeton, perätön. -**nut** maapähkinä. -**plan** pohjapiirros.

groundsel ['graunsl] *s.* peltovilla.

groundwork perustus, pohja.

group [gru:p] *s.* ryhmä; *v.* ryhmittää, -ttyä.

grouse 1. [graus] *s.* teeri, pyy ym; *black* ~ teeri; *great* (t. *wood*) ~ metso; *red* ~ kangasriekko; *white* ~ kiiruna.

grouse 2. [graus] *v.* nurista, purnata; *s.* nurina.

grove [grəuv] *s.* lehto, metsikkö.

grovel ['grɔvl] *v.* madella, ryömiä; ~ *ing* mateleva; alhainen.

grow [grəu] *grew grown*, *v.* kasvaa; karttua, suureta, enentyä; tulla jksk; kasvattaa, viljellä; ~ *angry* suuttua; *it is* ~ *ing dark* pimenee; ~ *into* varttua, tulla jksk; ~ *out of* aiheutua, olla seurauksena jstk; *he will* ~ *out of it* hän pääsee siitä varttuessaan; ~ *on sb.* alkaa miellyttää yhä enemmän. -**er** [-ə] *s.* viljelijä.

growl [graul] *v.* murista, murahtaa,

möristä; *s.* murina.

grown [grəun] *pp.*, ks. *grow*; ~-**up** *a. & s.* aikuinen.

growth [grəuθ] *s.* kasvaminen, kasvu; sato; kasvain.

groyne [grɔin] *s.* (puinen) aallonmurtaja.

grub [grʌb] *v.* tonkia, penkoa; *sl.* syödä; *s.* toukka; *sl.* sapuska, ruoka. -**by** [-i] *a.* nuhruinen.

grudge [grʌdʒ] *v.* ei suoda, vastahakoisesti suoda; kadehtia; *s.* kauna; *have a* ~ *against, bear sb. a* ~ kantaa kaunaa jklle; *grudgingly* vastahakoisesti.

gruel ['gruəl] *s.* kauravelli. -**ling** *a.* ankara, rasittava.

gruesome ['gru:səm] *a.* kaamea, karmea.

gruff [grʌf] *a.* töykeä, karkea.

grumble ['grʌmbl] *v.* nurista, nurkua, nureksia; jyristä; *s.* nurina.

grumpy ['grʌmpi] *a.* pahantuulinen, juro.

grunt [grʌnt] *v.* röhkiä; murahtaa; ähkiä, puhkia; *s.* röhkiminen; ähkinä.

gryphon ['grifən] ks. griffin.

guano ['gwɑ:nəu] *s.* guano (lannoitusaine).

guaran|tee [gær(ə)n|'ti:] *s.* takuu, vakuus, takeet; takaaja; *v.* taata, mennä takaukseen, olla takeena jstk. -**tor** [-'tɔ:] *s.* takaaja. -**ty** ['gær(ə)nti] *s.* takaus, vakuus.

guard [gɑ:d] *v.* suojella, varjella, vartioida; varoa, olla varuillaan; *s.* vartija; vartio; junailija; suoja; suojalaite, suojus; suojelus; varuillaanolo; ~*s* kaarti; *relieve* ~ vaihtaa vartio; *stand* ~ olla vartiossa; *on one's* ~ varuillaan; [*he*] *was off* ~ ei ollut varuillaan t. valppaana. -**ed** [-id] *a.* varovainen, pidättyväinen.

guardian ['gɑ:djən] *s.* valvoja, holhooja; ~ *angel* suojelusenkeli. -**ship** *s.* holhous.

guard|room vartiotupa. -**sman** kaartilainen.

gudgeon ['gʌdʒn] *s.* syötti(kala); herkkäuskoinen narri; pultti, tappi.

guelder ['geldə] *s.*: ~ *rose* heisi(puu).

guenon [gə'nəun] *s.* marakatti (el.).

guerrilla, guerilla [gə'rilə] *s.* sissi; ~ *war* sissisota; *urban* ~ kaupunkisissi.

guess [ges] v. arvata; Am. arvella, luulla; s. arvaus; arvelu; *make (have) a ~ at* (koettaa) arvata; *at a ~* umpimähkään. **-work** arvaus.

guest [gest] s. vieras; *paying ~* (perheenjäsenenä oleva) täysihoitolainen. **-room** vierashuone. **~-worker** siirtotyöläinen.

guffaw [gʌ'fɔ:] s. naurunhohotus; v. nauraa hohottaa.

Guiana [gi'ɑ:nə] erisn.

guidance ['gaidns] s. opastus, ohjaus; neuvonta; johdatus; *child ~ clinic* kasvatusneuvola.

guide [gaid] v. opastaa, ohjata; s. opas; opastaja, opas(kirja), matkakäsikirja; *Girl G~* partiotyttö; *~d missile* ohjus. **~-line** osviitta, neuvo. **~-post** tienviitta.

guild [gild] s. kilta, ammattikunta; *G~ hall* raatihuone, kaupungintalo.

guilder ['gildə] s. guldeni.

guile [gail] s. petos, kavaluus. **-ful** a. petollinen, kavala. **-less** a. vilpitön; suora, rehellinen.

guillemot ['gilimɔt] s. (etelän)kiisla; *black ~* riskilä.

guillotine ['giləti:n] s. giljotiini; v. mestata giljotiinilla.

guilt [gilt] s. syyllisyys. **-less** a. syytön, viaton. **-y** [-i] a. syyllinen *(of* jhk); rikollinen; *~ conscience* huono omatunto; ks. *plead*.

guinea, Guinea erisn. ['gini] s. guinea (ent. engl. kultaraha = 21 sh., nyt 105 p). **~-fowl** helmikana. **~-pig** marsu.

Guinness ['ginis] s. olutlaatu.

guise [gaiz] s. muoto, hahmo, verho; *under (in) the ~ of* jnk varjolla.

guitar [gi'tɑ:] s. kitara. **-ist** [-rist] s. kitaransoittaja.

gulch [gʌltʃ] s. Am. rotko.

gulf [gʌlf] s. (meren)lahti; kuilu; *the G~ stream* Golfvirta.

gull 1. [gʌl] s. lokki.

gull 2. [gʌl] s. houkkio; v. puijata.

gullet ['gʌlit] s. ruokatorvi.

gullible ['gʌləbl] a. herkkäuskoinen.

gully ['gʌli] s. (veden uurtama) rotko, uoma, oja.

gulp [gʌlp] v. nielaista; nieleksiä, kulauttaa (kurkkuun); s. nielaisu; kulaus.

gum 1. [gʌm] s.: *~s* ikenet,

hammasliha. **-boil** ienajos.

gum 2. [gʌm] s. liima, kumi; v. sivellä t. kiinnittää liimalla; *be up a g.-tree.* olla liemessä, pinteessä. **-my** [-i] a. tahmainen.

gumption ['gʌm(p)ʃn] s. neuvokkuus, yritteliäisyys.

gun [gʌn] s. tykki; kivääri, pyssy; metsästäjä; Am. revolveri; v.: *~ sb. down* ampua (kuoliaaksi); *big ~* pomo, mahtimies; *son of a ~* (sl.) roisto. **-boat** tykkivene. **~-carriage** tykinlavetti. **~-cotton** pumpuliruuti. **-fire** tykkituli. **-man** revolverisankari. **-metal** tykkimetalli. **-nel** [-l] s. = gunwale.

gunner ['gʌnə] s. tykkimies. **-y** [-ri] s. tykistötiede; ammunta.

gunny ['gʌni] s. säkki-, juuttikangas.

gun|powder ruuti. **~-running** aseitten salakuljetus. **-shot** ampumamatka; *within ~* ampumamatkan päässä; *~ wound* ampumahaava.

gunwale ['gʌnl] s. varpekansi, reelinki, parras.

gurgle ['gə:gl] v. pulputa, solista; kurluttaa; (vauvasta) lepertää; s. pulputus; kurlutus; leperrys, jokellus.

gush [gʌʃ] v. pursuta *(out* esiin); olla ylitsepursuavan ystävällinen t. innostunut; s. pursuaminen; tunteenpurkaus. **-ing** a. (ylitse)pursuava; intoileva.

gusset [gʌsit] s. kiila, kulmavahvike.

gust [gʌst] s. (tuulen)puuska, tuulispää; purkaus.

gusto ['gʌstəu] s. nautinto; *with ~* halukkaasti, innokkaasti.

gusty [gʌsti] a. puuskainen.

gut [gʌt] s. suoli; *pl.* suolet, sisukset; suolijänne; v. poistaa sisukset; perata; *[he] has plenty of ~s* on sisukas, rohkea; *be ~ted by fire* (bussista, taloista ym) palaa niin että vain runko, seinät jää(vät). **-sy** [gʌtsi] a. sl. sisukas.

gutta-percha [gʌtə'pə:tʃə] s. guttaperkka.

gutter ['gʌtə] s. kattokouru; katuoja (m. kuv.); kouru, vako; v. (kynttilästä) valua; *the ~ press* juorulehdet. **-snipe** katupoika.

guttural ['gʌt(ə)r(ə)l] a. kurkku-; s. kurkkuäänne.

guvnor ['gʌvnə] s. sl. pomo.

guy 1. [gai] s. kaji (mer.); v. kiinnittää tukiköydellä.

guy 2. [gai] s. linnunpelätti; Am. mies kaveri, heppu; v. tehdä pilaa.

guzzle ['gʌzl] v. juoda t. syödä ahneesti; mässätä, ryypiskellä.

gym [dʒim] s. (puhek.) voimistelusali; voimistelu.

gymnas|ium [dʒim'neizjəm] s. (pl. m. -ia) voimistelusali. **-t** ['-næst] s. voimistelija. **-tic** [-'næstik] a. voimistelu-; s. harjoitus; pl. voimistelu.

gyn(a)ecolo|gy [gaini'kɔlədʒi] s. naistentautioppi. **-gist** [-st] s. gynekologi.

gyp [dʒip] v. sl. huiputtaa, huijata; s. (Cambr. yliop.) miespalvelija; give sb. ~ antaa selkään.

gypsum ['dʒipsəm] s. kipsi.

gypsy ['dʒipsi] ks. gipsy.

gyra|te [dʒai'(ə)'reit] v. kiertää, pyöriä. **-tion** [-'reiʃn] s. pyöriminen, liike. **-tory** ['-rat(ə)ri] a. kierto-.

gyroscope ['dʒaiərəskəup] s. gyroskooppi.

gyves [dʒaivz] s. kahleet (vanh.).

H

H, h [eitʃ] s. h-kirjain; *drop one's h's*
jättää ääntämättä h (sanan alussa);
H-bomb ks. *hydrogen*. Lyh.: **ha**
hectare(s); **H.E.** *His Excellency;*
H.M. *His (Her) Majesty;* **H.M.S.** *His
Majesty's Ship;* **Hon.** *Honourable,
Honorary; hire purchase, horse-power;*
H.Q. *Headquarters;* **hr(s).** *hour(s);*
H.R.H. *His (Her) Royal Highness.*
ha [ha:] *int.* haa! hah!
haberdasher [ˈhæbədæʃə] s.
lyhyttavarain kauppias; Am. miesten
asusteliike. **-y** [-ri] s.
lyhyttavara(liike).
habiliments [həˈbilimənts] s. pl. puku.
habit [ˈhæbit] s. tapa, tottumus;
(vanh.) luonto, ruumiinrakenne;
riding ~ (naisen) ratsastuspuku; *he is
in the ~ of . . -ing* hänellä on tapana:
get into bad ~s oppia huonoja tapoja.
-able [-əbl] a. asuttava. **-at** [-ət] s.
(eläimen) asuinpaikka, (kasvin)
kasvupaikka. **-ation** [-ˈteiʃn] s.
asuminen; asunto. **-ual** [həˈbitju(ə)l]
a. tavaksi tullut, tavallinen; piintynyt;
~ly tavallisesti. **-uate** [həˈbitjueit] v.
totuttaa; usein käydä jssk. **-ué**
[həˈbitjuei] s. kantavieras.
hack 1. [hæk] v. hakata (palasiksi);
köhiä, yskiä; *~ing cough* kuiva yskä,
köhä.
hack 2. [hæk] s. vuokrahevonen,
hevoskaakki; Am. taksi; (kuv.)
työjuhta; *~ work* huonosti palkattu
kirjallinen työ.
hackle [ˈhækl] s. häkilä; (kukon)
niskasulat; *pl.* niskakarvat; *v.*
häkilöidä; *make sb.'s ~s rise*
suututtaa.
hackney [ˈhækni] s. vaunu- t.
ratsuhevonen; *~ carriage*
vuokravaunut. **-ed** [-d] a.
jokapäiväinen, kulunut.

hacksaw s. metallisaha.
had [hæd] *imp. & pp.* ks. *have.*
haddock [ˈhædək] s. kolja.
Hades [ˈheidi:z] s. Haades, manala.
hadn't [ˈhædnt] = *had not.*
haemo|globin, -philia, -rrhage ks.
hemo-.
haft [ha:ft] s. varsi, kahva.
hag [hæg] s. noita-akka, akka.
Hagar [ˈheigə] *erisn.*
haggard [ˈhægəd] a. riutunut, laiha,
kuihtunut, ryppyinen.
haggis [ˈhægis] s. (lampaan
sisälmyksistä ja kaurajauhoista
valmistettu) skotlantilainen ruokalaji.
haggle [ˈhægl] v. tinkiä; kiistellä (et.
hinnasta); s. tinkiminen.
Hague [heig] *erisn.: The ~* Haag.
hail 1. [heil] *int.* terve! v. tervehtiä;
huutaa (laivalle), kutsua (auto ym);
s.: within ~ huutomatkan päässä; *~
from* olla kotoisin jstk; *be
~-fellow-well-met* olla hyvää pataa
(*with* jkn kanssa).
hail 2. [heil] s. rakeet; v. sataa rakeita.
-stone rae. **-storm** raekuuro.
hair [hεə] s. hius; hiukset, tukka;
karva, nukka; *to a ~* tarkalleen; *he
did not turn a ~* hän ei ollut
millänsäkään; *do one's ~* kammata
tukkansa; *keep your ~ on!* säilytä
malttisi! *split ~s* saivarrella, halkoa
hiuksia; *make one's ~* stand on end
pöyristyttää. **-breadth** hiuksenverta; *a
~ escape* täpärä pelastus; *have a ~
escape* välttyä jltk hiuksenhienosti.
-cloth jouhikangas. **-cut**
tukanleikkuu. **~-do** kampaus.
-dresser kampaaja; *~'s* kampaamo.
~-dryer tukankuivauslaite. **~-dye**
hiusväri. **-line** hiusraja. **-net**
hiusverkko. **-piece:** *false ~s*
hiuslisäkkeet. **-pin** hiusneula; *~ bend*

hiusneulakaarre. **~-raising** pöyristyttävä. **~'s breadth** hiuksenverta. **~-shirt** jouhipaita. **~-splitting** saivartelu. **~-style** kampaus. **~-stylist** kampaaja. **-y** [-i] *a.* karvainen.

Haiti ['heiti] *erisn.* **-an** ['heifjən] *a. & s.* haitilainen.

hake [heik] *s.* kummeliturska.

halberd ['hælbə(:)d] *s.* hilpari; pertuska.

halcyon ['hælsiən] *s.* jäälintu; ~ *days* rauhallinen, tyyni aika.

hale [heil] *a.:* ~ *and hearty* reipas, pirteä, vireä.

half [ha:f] *s.* (pl. *halves*) puoli, puolet; puolikas, puolisko; *a.* puoli-; *adv.* puoleksi; ~ *an hour* puoli tuntia; *cut in* ~ leikata kahtia; *go halves with* panna puoliksi jkn kanssa; *less by* ~ puolta vähemmän; *clever by* ~ liiankin fiksu; *not* ~ *bad* ei lainkaan hullumpi, oikein hyvä; ~ *cooked (done)* puolikypsä; ~ *measures* puolinaiset toimenpiteet; *at* ~ *past two* puoli kolmelta. **-back** (jalkap.) tukimies. **~-baked** puolikypsä; kehittymätön. **~-breed** sekarotuinen. **~-brother** velipuoli. **~-caste** *s. & a.* sekarotuinen. **~-crown** vanha puolen kruunun raha (= 2 s. 6 d.). **~-hearted** laimea, innoton. **~-mast:** *at h.-m.* puolitangossa. **~-pay:** *on h.-p.* puolella palkalla. **-penny** ['heipni] puolipenny(ä). **-seas-over** hiprakassa. **~-timbered** ristikkorakenteinen. **~-time** puoliaika. **-way** *adv.* puolitiessä. **~-witted** löyhäpäinen, vähä-älyinen.

halibut ['hælibət] *s.* ruijanpallas.

hall [ho:l] *s.* halli; sali, juhlasali; eteinen; raatihuone; suuri kartano, linna; (yliop.) ruokasali, päivällinen; *market* ~ kauppahalli.

hallelujah [hæli'lu:jə] *int.* halleluja.

hallmark *s.* hopean ja kullan leima; (kuv.) tunnusmerkki; *v.* leimata.

hallo(a) [hə'lou] *int.* hei! terve! *v.* huutaa hei, halloo.

halloo [hə'lu:] *s.* yllytyshuuto; *v.* yllyttää (koiria).

hallow ['hælou] *v.* pyhittää; *All H~s* pyhäinpäivä; *H~e'en* p-n aatto.

hallucin|**ation** [həlu:si'neiʃn] *s.*

hallusinaatio, aistiharha. **-ogenic** *a. & s.* hallusinaatioita aiheuttava (aine).

hallway Am. eteishalli

halo ['heilou] *s.* (pl. ~-*es*, ~*s*) auringon ym kehä; sädekehä.

halt 1. [ho:lt] *s.* pysähdys; pysäkki; *v.* seisahtua, pysähtyä; pysäyttää; *call a* ~ antaa pysähtymiskäsky; *come to a* ~ pysähtyä.

halt 2. [ho:lt] *v.* ontua (et. kuv.) [~ *in one's speech*] kangerrella, änkyttää; ~ [*between two opinions*] horjua. **-ingly** *adv.* kangerrellen, takeltaen.

halter ['ho:ltə] *s.* riimu; hirttonuora.

halve [ha:v] *v.* panna puoliksi. **-s** [-z] pl. ks. *half*.

halyard ['hæljəd] *s.* nostoköysi (mer.).

ham [hæm] *s.* reisi; (suolattu, savustettu) kinkku; **~-handed** kömpelö, kopelo. **-burger** [-bə:gə] hampurilainen (jauhelihapihvi + sämpylä).

hames [heimz] *s.* länget.

hamlet ['hæmlit] *s.* pieni kylä.

hammer ['hæmə] *s.* vasara, nuija; (urh.) moukari; (kiväärin) iskuri; *v.* vasaroida, takoa; *come under the* ~ joutua huutokaupalla myytäväksi; [*go at it*] ~ *and tongs* kaikin voimin; ~ **throw** moukarinheitto.

hammock ['hæmək] *s.* riippumatto.

hamper 1. ['hæmpə] *s.* eväskori.

hamper 2. ['hæmpə] *v.* estää, olla vastuksena.

Hampstead ['hæm(p)stid] *erisn.*

hamster ['hæmstə] *s.* hamsteri.

Hampton ['hæm(p)tən] *erisn.*

hamstring ['hæmstriŋ] *s.* kinnerjänne; *v.* (~*ed* t. *-strung*) katkaista (jnk) kinnerjänne; lamauttaa.

hand [hænd] *s.* käsi; (kellon) osoitin; käsiala; työmies, apumies; (korttip.) kädessä olevat kortit, pelaaja; *v.* ojentaa, antaa; jättää *(~in)*; auttaa kädestä (jhk, jstk) nousemaan; ~*s off!* näpit irti! *change* ~*s* vaihtaa omistajaa; *hold* ~*s* pidellä toisiaan kädestä; *lay (one's)* ~*s on* saada käsiinsä, löytää, käydä kimppuun; *lend (give) a* ~ auttaa; *put one's* ~ *to* ryhtyä; *try one's* ~ *at* koettaa kykyjään jssk; *wait* ~ *and foot on* palvella jkta (ylen huomaavaisesti); *at* ~ käsillä, saatavissa; *at the* ~*s of* jkn

taholta, puolelta; *by* ~ käsin; *take by
the* ~ ottaa kädestä; *in* ~ käsillä,
tekeillä; *in the* ~ *s* jkn hallussa; *take in*
~ ottaa hoitaakseen; *the situation is
well in* ~ hallitsemme tilanteen; *off* ~
suoralta kädeltä; *on* ~ käsissä,
hallussa; *on one's* ~ *s* huolehdittavana;
on one ~ .., *on the other* ~ toiselta
puolen.., toiselta puolen; *out of* ~ ei
hallittavissa; suoralta kädeltä, heti;
come to ~ saapua jklle, tulla perille;
~ *to* ~ mies miestä vastaan; *with a
heavy* ~ sortaen; ~ *down* jättää
jälkimaailmalle; *be* ~ *ed down* mennä
perintönä (esim. isältä pojalle); ~ *in*
jättää.. jhk, (asianomaiseen)
toimistoon ym; ~ *on* ojentaa
seuraavalle; ~ *over* jättää (jkn)
hoidettavaksi t. haltuun; ~ *round*
antaa kiertää. **-bag** käsilaukku. **-bell**
pöytäkello. **-bill** käsiohjelma. **-book**
käsikirja, opas. **~-brake** käsijarru.
~-cart työntökärryt. **-cuff** *s.* (tav. ~*s*)
käsiraudat; *v.* panna käsirautoihin.
-ful kourallinen; vaikeasti käsiteltävä
asia t. ihminen. **~-glass** käsipeili.

handi|cap ['hændikæp] *s.* vamma,
haitta-aste, invaliditeetti; (urh.)
tasoitus; *v.* asettaa epäedulliseen
asemaan, invalidisoida; ~*ped person*
invalidi; *mentally* ~*ped* psyykkisesti
kehitysvammainen. **-craft** [-krɑːft]
käsi|työ, -teollisuus. **-ness** *s.* kätevyys;
mukavuus. **-work** jnk (kätten) työ.

handkerchief ['hæŋkətʃif] *s.* nenäliina.

handle ['hændl] *s.* kahva, varsi, ripa,
kädensija; (kuv.) väline, veruke; *v.*
käsitellä, pidellä; kohdella; *a* ~ *to
one's name* arvonimi; *fly off the* ~
riehaantua, kimpaantua. **~bar(s)**
(polkupyörän ym) ohjaustanko.

hand|-loom kangaspuut. **~-made** käsin
tehty. **-maid** (kuv. vanh.) palvelijatar.
~-out almu; (lehdistölle annettu)
tiedote, moniste. **~-picked**
huolellisesti valittu. **~-rail** käsipuu.
~-rolled *cigarette* itsekierretty
savuke, sätkä. **-shake** kädenpuristus.

handsome ['hænsəm] *a.* kaunis,
komea; melkoinen, runsas.

hand-to-mouth: *lead a* ~ *existence* elää
kädestä suuhun.

hand|-work käsityö. **-writing** käsiala.

handy ['hændi] *a.* kätevä, taitava,

näppärä; mukava, sopiva; *may come
in* ~ saattaa osoittautua hyödylliseksi.
~-man yleismies.

hang [hæŋ] *hung hung, v.* ripustaa,
kiinnittää; verhota (lipuilla ym),
paperoida (seinät); hirttää (imp. &
pp. *hanged);* riippua, roikkua; olla
epävarma, viipyä; tulla hirtetyksi; *s.*
riippuminen; ~ *one's head* olla
häpeissään; ~ *it!* hitto soikoon; ~ *fire*
edistyä (kehittyä) hitaasti; ~ *about*
(Am. *around)* vetelehtiä joutilaana;
~ *back* vitkastella, olla haluton; ~ *by
a hair* olla hiuskarvan varassa; ~ *in
the balance* olla vaakalaudalla; ~ *on!*
odota hetkinen! ~ *on* kestää, *(to)*
riippua jssk kiinni; ~ *[up]on* (m.)
riippua jstk, tarkata; ~ *out* (sl.)
oleilla, asustaa; ~ *up* sulkea puhelin; *I
feel hung up* tunnen itseni
pettyneeksi; *get the* ~ *of* päästä perille
jstk, juonesta kiinni; *I don't care a* ~
en välitä rahtuakaan.

hangar ['hæŋgə] *s.* lentokonesuoja.

hangdog *a.: he has a* ~ *look* hän on
syyllisen näköinen.

hanger ['hæŋə] *s.* koukku, ripustin,
vaatepuu; *paper~* tapetinpanija.
~-on kuokkavieras, kyllästyttävä
seuralainen.

hang-gliding *s.* (urh.) riippuliito.

hanging ['hæŋiŋ] *s. pl.* verhot.

hang|man pyöveli. **-over** krapula. **~-up**
pakkomielle.

hank [hæŋk] *s.* vyyhti.

hanker ['hæŋkə] *v.* ikävöidä, kiihkeästi
haluta *(after* jtk).

hanky ['hæŋki] *s.* (lastenk.) nenäliina.
~-panky silmänkääntötemppu.

Hanoi [hæ'nɔi] *erisn.*

Hanover ['hænəvə] *erisn.*

Hansard ['hænzəd] *s.* raportti
parlamenttikeskusteluista.

Hanse ['hæns] *s.* Hansa-liitto. **-atic**
[hænsi'ætik] *a.* hansa-.

hansom ['hænsəm] *s.* (~ *cab)* kevyet
ajoneuvot (joissa ajajan istuin on
takana).

Hants [hænts] lyh. = *Hampshire.*

hap [hæp] *s.* (vanh.) sattuma; onni.
-hazard ['hæp'hæzəd]
sattumanvarainen; *at* ~
umpimähkään. **-less** *a.* onneton.

happen ['hæp(ə)n] *v.* tapahtua; sattua;

he ~*ed to* come hän sattui tulemaan; *as it* ~*s* sattumalta; ~ *upon* sattumalta löytää jtk. -**ing** *s.* tap htumat.

happi|ly ['hæpili] *adv.* onnellisesti; onneksi. -**ness** *s.* onni.

happy ['hæpi] *a.* onnellinen; iloinen; onnistunut, sattuva; *we shall be* ~ *to* . . mielihyvin . .; *trigger-* (t. *gun-*) ~ hanakka ampumaan. ~-**go-lucky** huoleton.

Hapsburg ['hæpsbə:g] *erisn.* Habsburg.

harangue [hə'ræŋ] *s.* (mahtipontinen) puhe; sanatulva; *v.* pitää puhe (jklle), läksyttää.

harass ['hærəs, Am. hə'ræs] *v.* rasittaa, kiusata, ahdistaa; ~*ed* kiusaantunut.

harbinger [hɑ:bin(d)ʒə] *s.* airut.

harbour, harbor ['hɑ:bə] *s.* satama; turvapaikka; *v.* majoittaa, pitää luonaan; hautoa (mielessään); ~ *dues* satamamaksut.

hard [hɑ:d] *a.* kova; vaikea, vaivalloinen, työläs; ankara, säälimätön; tarkka, tiukka; luja; *adv.* kovasti, lujasti; uutterasti, innokkaasti; tiukasti; ~ *and fast* järkkymätön, ehdoton; ~ *cash* (kova) raha, metalliraha; ~ *labour* pakkotyö; ~*lines* huono onni; ~ *liquor* väkevät (alkoholijuomat); [*learn*] *the* ~ *way* »kovassa koulussa»; ~ *by* aivan vieressä; ~ *up* rahapulassa; *try* ~ yrittää kovasti; *work* ~ tehdä työtä ahkerasti; *it is raining* ~ sataa rankasti; *he was* ~ *put to it* (*to explain* . .) hän joutui lujille (kun piti selittää). -**back** sidottu (kirja). ~-**bitten** kovapintainen, itsepäinen. -**board** kovalevy. ~-**boiled** kovaksi keitetty (m. kuv.). ~-**core** piintynyt. ~-**earned** vaivalla ansaittu.

harden ['hɑ:dn] *v.* kovettaa; karkaista, terästää; paaduttaa; kovettua; karaista; paatua. -**ed** [-d] *a.* paatunut, tunnoton.

hard|-fisted kitsas. ~-**fought** ankara, tuima. ~-**headed** käytännöllinen, asiallinen.

hardi|hood ['hɑ:dihud] *s.* pelottomuus. -**ly** *adv.* pelottomasti. -**ness** *s.* pelottomuus, sisu; kestävyys, karaistuneisuus.

hard|ly ['hɑ:dli] *adv.* tuskin; (harv.) ankarasti. -**ness** *s.* kovuus. -**ship** *s.*

vastoinkäyminen, vaikeus, kärsimys; *suffer* ~*s* kokea kovia.

hard|ware ['hɑ:dweə] rauta-, metallitavara; (tietok.) laitteisto. -**wood** *tree* lehtipuu. ~-**working** ahkera.

hardy ['hɑ:di] *a.* karaistunut, (pakkasta) kestävä; peloton, huimapäinen.

hare [heə] *s.* jänis; *first catch your* ~ älä nuolaise ennenkuin tipahtaa. -**bell** sinikello. ~-**brained** ajattelematon. -**lip** ristihuuli.

harem ['hɛərem] *s.* haaremi.

haricot ['hærikəu] *s.* : ~ *bean* leikkopapu.

hark [hɑ:k] *v.* ~ ! kuule! ~ *back to* palata (aiheeseen).

harlequin ['hɑ:likwin] *s.* ilveilijä.

harlot ['hɑ:lət] *s.* portto.

harm [hɑ:m] *s.* vahinko, paha; *v.* vahingoittaa, tehdä (jklle) pahaa; *come to* ~ kärsiä vahinkoa; *there is no* ~ *in trying* yrittäminen ei ole haitaksi; *keep out of* ~*'s way* pitää varansa. -**ful** *a.* vahingollinen. -**less** *a.* vaaraton, viaton.

harmon|ic [hɑ:'mɔnik] *a.* sopusointuinen, harmoninen. -**ica** [-ə] *s.* huuliharppu. -**ious** [hɑ:'məunjəs] *a.* sopusointuinen. -**ium** [hɑ:'məunjəm] *s.* harmoni. -**ize** [hɑ:'mənaiz] *v.* saattaa sopusointuiseksi, olla s-soinnussa; soinnuttaa. -**y** ['hɑ:m(ə)ni] *s.* sopusointu.

harness ['hɑ:nis] *s.* valjaat; tamineet, haarniska; *v.* valjastaa (m. koski, vesivoima), käyttää hyväksi; *die in* ~ kuolla työnsä ääreen.

harp [hɑ:p] *s.* harppu; *v.* soittaa harppua; ~ *on* (*the same string*) jankuttaa. -**ist** [ist] *s.* harpunsoittaja.

harpoon [hɑ:'pu:n] *s.* harppuuna; *v.* pyydystää h-lla.

harpsichord ['hɑ:psikɔ:d] *s.* klavesiini, cembalo.

harpy ['hɑ:pi] *s.* harpyija; verenimijä.

harridan ['hæridən] *s.* vanha akka.

harrier ['hæriə] *s.* jäniskoira.

Harrovian [hə'rəuvjən] *a. & s.* Harrow'n (koulun) oppilas.

harrow ['hærəu] *s.* äes, karhi; *v.* äestää; raadella, kiusata; ~*ing* tuskallinen, repivä.

harry ['hæri] v. hävittää, ryöstää, ahdistaa.

harsh [hɑːʃ] a. karkea; viiltävä, räikeä; kova, ankara.

hart [hɑːt] s. (uros)hirvi.

harum-scarum ['hɛərəm'skɛərəm] a. ajattelematon; s. hurjapää, hurja.

Harvard ['hɑːvəd] erisn.

harvest ['hɑːvist] s. elonkorjuu; sato, (kuv.) tulokset; v. korjata sato; ~ home elojuhla. **-er** [-ə] s. elonleikkaaja; leikkuukone.

has [hæz, həz, -z] prees. sg. 3. pers. ks. have.

hash [hæʃ] v. hakata hienoksi (m. ~ up); s. hakkelus; make a ~ of turmella.

hashish ['hæʃiʃ] s. hasis.

hasn't ['hæznt] = has not.

hasp [hɑːsp] s. säppi, aspi.

hassle ['hæsl] s. (Am.sl.) riita, tora.

hassock ['hæsək] s. polvityyny (kirkoissa), jalkatyyny.

haste [heist] s. kiire; v. = seur.; make ~ kiirehdi! **-en** ['heisn] v. kiiruhtaa, rientää; jouduttaa. **-ily** adv. kiireesti.

Hastings ['heistiŋz] erisn.

hasty ['heisti] a. nopea, kiireellinen; hätäinen; ajattelematon, malttamaton; kiivas, pikavihainen.

hat [hæt] s. hattu; a bad ~ lurjus; talk through one's ~ puhua puuta heinää.

hatch 1. [hætʃ] v. hautoa; hautoa mielessään; kuoriutua (munasta), kypsyä; s. hautominen; poikue.

hatch 2. [hætʃ] s. (ruuman)luukku (m. ~way), lattialuukku; tarjoiluluukku; (kaksiosaisen) oven alapuolisko.

hatchet ['hætʃit] s. kirves; bury the ~ haudata sotakirves, unohtaa vanhat vihat.

hatchway ['hætʃwei] = hatch.

hate [heit] v. vihata; s. viha; I ~ .. en voi sietää .. **-ful** a. vihattava, inhottava.

hath [hæθ] (vanh.) = has.

hatred ['heitrid] s. viha, vihamielisyys.

hatter ['hætə] s. hatuntekijä; mad as a ~ pähkähullu.

hauberk ['hɔːbəːk] s. rautapaita.

haughtiness s. ylpeys, kopeus.

haughty ['hɔːti] a. ylpeä, ylimielinen, kopea.

haul [hɔːl] v. hilata, vetää; kuljettaa;

muuttaa suuntaa (mer.); veto; apaja, saalis. **-age** [-idʒ] s. kuljetuskustannukset.

haunch [hɔːn(t)ʃ] s. lonkka, lanne; reisiliha.

haunt [hɔːnt] v. alinomaa vaivata, käydä usein (jkn luona), kummitella jssk; s. olinpaikka, pesäpaikka, tyyssija.

hautboy ['ʔəubɔi] s. oboe (mus.).

Havana [hə'vænə] erisn. Havanna; s. havannasikari.

have [hæv, həv] had had (prees. sg. 3. pers. has) apuv. olla; v. olla jklla, omistaa; saada, hankkia; nauttia, syödä, juoda; ~ to (+ inf.) täytyä, olla pakko; (pp:n kera) antaa tehdä jtk, panna jku tekemään jtk; I ~ no money minulla ei ole rahaa; he has two sisters hänellä on kaksi sisarta; she has got a good memory hänellä on hyvä muisti; I have [got] to go minun on mentävä; what have you got to say? mitä sinulla on sanottavana? have you got a cold now? oletko nyt vilustunut? what time do you have lunch? mihin aikaan syöt lounasta? will you ~ another cup? haluatko vielä kupillisen? ~ a cigarette! ota savuke! she had a new dress made hän teetti uuden puvun; I must ~ [these shoes] repaired minun täytyy korjauttaa; I won't ~ you saying such things en salli sinun sanovan sellaista; rumour has it huhu kertoo; ~ sth. on olla yllään; ~ it out with sopia riita jkn kanssa; ~ it your own way olkoon menneeksi! ~ at hyökätä jkn kimppuun; ~ sb. on petkuttaa, laskea leikkiä jkn kanssa; ~ sb. up haastaa oikeuteen; you were had sinua petkutettiin; not to be had ei saatavissa; the ~s and the ~-nots rikkaat ja köyhät.

haven ['heivn] s. satama, turvapaikka.

haven't ['hævnt] = have not.

haver ['heivə] v. puhua pötyä.

haversack ['hævəsæk] s. selkäreppu.

havoc ['hævək] s. hävitys; make ~ of, play ~ with tuhota, tehdä tuhoa jssk.

haw 1. [hɔː] s. orapihlajan marja.

haw 2. ks. hum.

Hawaii [hɑː'wa(i)iː] erisn.

haw-haw ['hɔː'hɔː] s. (naurun)hohotus.

hawk 1. [hɔːk] *s.* haukka (m. kuv.); *v.* metsästää haukalla; ~*-eyed* teräväsilmäinen.

hawk 2. [hɔːk] *v.* kakistella, rykiä.

hawk 3. [hɔːk] *v.* huutaa kaupaksi (kadulla ym); levittää (~ *gossip)*. **-er** [-ə] kulkukauppias.

hawser ['hɔːzə] *s.* touvi; köysi.

hawthorn ['hɔːθɔːn] *s.* orapihlaja.

hay [hei] *s.* heinä; *make* ~ tehdä heinää; *make* ~ *while the sun shines* takoa raudan kuumana ollessa; ~ *fever* heinänuha; *stook of* ~ = seur. **-cock** heinäsuova. **~-fork** heinähanko. **-maker** heinäntekijä. **-rick, -stack** heinäsuova.

hazard ['hæzəd] *s.* vaara, sattuma, onnenkauppa; *v.* vaarantaa, uskaltaa; *at all* ~*s* kaiken uhalla. **-ous** [-əs] *a.* vaarallinen.

haze [heiz] *s.* auer.

hazel ['heizl] *s.* pähkinänruskea. **-nut** pähkinä.

haziness *s.* utuisuus, epäselvyys.

hazy ['heizi] *a.* usvainen, utuinen; autereinen; epäselvä.

he [hiː] *pron.* hän *(mask.) a.* koiras-, uros-; ~*-goat* pukki; ~*-man* miehekäs mies.

head [hed] *s.* pää (m. kuv.); johtaja, päällikkö, päämies *(H* ~ *of State);* rehtori; yläpää, etupää; huippu, käännekohta; kärki; (pää)kohta, jakso, otsikko; nuppi, (naulan) kanta, (kirveen, vasaran) terä, (vuoteen) pääpuoli, (virran) lähde; (oluen ym) vaahto; (rahan) kuvapuoli; *v.* olla etunenässä, asettua etunenään, johtaa; varustaa otsikolla, otsikoida; *a.* ensimmäinen, pää-, yli-; *per* ~, *a* ~ henkeä kohti; *30* ~ *of cattle* 30 nautaa; *at the* ~ *of* jnk etunenässä, johdossa; *bring to a* ~ kärjistää; *come to a* ~ alkaa märkiä, kehittyä huippuunsa t. ratkaisuun; *enter into sb.'s* ~ pälkähtää päähän; *keep one's* ~ pysyä rauhallisena; *lose one's* ~ mennä päästään pyörälle, menettää harkintakykynsä, malttinsa; *take sth. into one's* ~ saada päähänsä; *talk a p.'s* ~ *off* väsyttää pitkillä puheilla; ~ *over heels* korviaan myöten, vrt. *heel;* ~ *wind* vastatuuli; ~*s or tails* kruunu vai klaava; *I cannot make* ~ *or tail of*

it siinä ei ole päätä eikä häntää; ~ *a list* olla ensimmäisenä luettelossa; ~ *for* suunnata kulkunsa jhk; *is* ~*ing for disaster* on menossa suin päin turmioon; ~ *off* pysähdyttää, käännyttää takaisin t. sivulle; ~ *first* pää edellä; ~ *on* pää edellä, (nokat) vastakkain; ~ *waiter* hovimestari. **-ache** päänsärky; sl. murhe. **-dress** päähine. **-ed** [-id] *a.* -päinen; jllak otsikolla varustettu. **-er** [-ə] *s.* sukellus, putoaminen. **-gear** päähine. **~-hunter** pääkallonmetsästäjä. **-ing** *s.* otsikko. **-land** niemi, niemeke. **~-light** (auton) etuvalo. **-line** otsikko. **-long** *a.* päätäpahkainen, äkillinen; *adv.* suin päin. **-master** rehtori. **-mistress** (koulun) johtajatar. **~-on** *adv.* nokat vastakkain; ~*-on collision* yhteenajo, törmäys. **~-phones** kuulokkeet. **-piece** kypärä; äly. **-quarters** päämaja. **-stone** hautakivi. **-strong** uppiniskainen, itsepäinen. **-way** eteneminen, vauhti; *make* ~ edistyä. **~-wind** vastatuuli. **-word** hakusana, pääsana. **-y** [-i] *a.* tuittupäinen; väkivaltainen; juovuttava.

heal [hiːl] *v.* parantaa, -tua; ~ *up* mennä umpeen. **-ing** *s.* paraneminen, -tuminen.

health [helθ] *s.* terveys; *be in good* ~ olla terveenä; ~ *centre* terveyskeskus; *your* ~*!* maljanne! **-ful** *a.* terveellinen. **-y** [-i] *a.* terve; terveellinen.

heap [hiːp] *s.* kasa, läjä; joukko; *v.* kasata, latoa, koota (us. ~ *up); ~s better* paljon parempi; ~*s of times* monen monta kertaa; *I was struck all of a* ~ minulta meni jalat alta, menin aivan hervottomaksi; ~*ed* kukkurainen.

hear [hiə] *heard heard* [hɔːd] *v.* kuulla, kuunnella; kuulustella (läksyä); saada kuulla, saada tietoja *(of, about* jstk), saada kirje *(from* jklta); ~*!* ~*!* hyvä! hyvä! *she wouldn't* ~ *of it* hän ei tahtonut kuulla puhuttavankaan siitä. **-er** [-rə] *s.* kuulija. **-ing** *s.* kuulo; kuuntelu; kuulomatka; kuulustelu; *in my* ~ minun kuulteni; *within* ~ kuulomatkan päässä; *her* ~ *is poor* hän kuulee huonosti; *hard of* ~ huonokuuloinen; ~*-aid* kuulokoje.

hearken ['hɑ:k(ə)n] v. kuunnella *(to jtk).*

hearsay ['hiəsei] s. kuulopuhe.

hearse [hə:s] s. ruumisauto.

heart [hɑ:t] s. sydän; sielu, mieli; rohkeus; ydin; *hearts* (korttip.) hertta; *after one's own ~* täysin jkn mieleinen; *learn (get) by ~* oppia ulkoa; *in my ~ of ~s* sisimmässäni; *lose ~* menettää rohkeutensa; *at ~* sisimmässäni; *I have this thing at ~* tämä asia on sydämelläni; *a change of ~* mielenmuutos; *take sth. to ~* panna kovin pahakseen; *take ~* rohkaista mielensä; *wear one's ~ on one's sleeve* olla liian avomielinen. **-ache** s. sydänsuru. **-beat** sydämenlyönti, pulssi. **-breaking** sydäntä särkevä. **-broken:** *she is ~* hänen sydämensä on murtunut. **-burn** närästys. ~ **disease** sydäntauti. **-ed** [-id] a. -sydäminen. **-en** [-n] v. rohkaista. ~**failure** sydänhalvaus. **-felt** sydämellinen, syvä.

hearth [hɑ:θ] s. liesi, takka; kotiliesi; ~ *rug* takkamatto, matto.

heart|ily ['hɑ:tili] adv. sydämen pohjasta, sydämellisesti; halukkaasti. **-iness** s. sydämellisyys; into, voima. **-less** a. sydämetön, säälimätön.

heart|-rending sydäntä vihlova. **-'s-ease** orvokki. **-sick** apea, surullinen. **-strings** sydänjuuret. **~-to-heart** avomielinen. **~-whole** jonka sydän on vapaa. **-y** ['hɑ:ti] a. vilpitön, sydämellinen, harras, lämmin; vahva, terve; runsas, tukeva (ateria).

heat [hi:t] s. kuumuus, helle; lämpö; kiivaus, kiihko; viha; (el.) kiima; (urh.) erä; v. kuumentaa, lämmittää; kuumeta; kiihottaa,-tua; *trial ~s* koe-erät; *[the bitch is]* in (on) ~ koiralla on juoksuaika; *red (white) ~* puna(valko)hehku; ~*ed* kiivas, kiihkeä; ~*edly* kiivaasti. **-er** [-ə] s. lämmityslaite.

heath [hiθ:] s. nummi, kangas; kanerva.

heathen ['hi:ðn] s. pakana; a. pakana-, pakanallinen; *the ~* (koll.) pakanat. **-dom** [-dəm] s. pakanamaailma. **-ish** [-iʃ] a. pakanallinen.

heather ['heðə] s. kanerva; ~ *bell* kanervankukka.

heating s. lämmitys; *district ~* kauko-lämpö; ~-*pad* lämpötyyny.

heat|spot kesakko. **-stroke** lämpöhalvaus. **-wave** lämpöaalto.

heave [hi:v] ~*d* – *d* (mer. m. *hove hove*) v. nostaa; heittää, hilata, hiivata; nousta, kohota, aaltoilla, paisua; olla oksentamaisillaan; s. nostaminen, kohoaminen, aaltoilu; ~ *a sigh* huokaista raskaasti; ~ *in sight* tulla näkyviin; ~ *away!* ~ *ho!* hiiop! *[the ship]* hove *to* pysähtyi.

heaven ['hevn] s. taivas; *good H~s!* laupias taivas! taivaan vallat! **-ly** [-li] a. taivaallinen; *the ~ bodies* taivaankappaleet.

heavi|ly ['hevili] adv. raskaasti, vaivalloisesti. **-ness** s. paino, raskas mieli (~ *of heart*).

heavy ['hevi] a. raskas, painava; vaikea, kova, ankara, rankka, syvä (huokaus), runsas (ateria); vaivalloinen, työläs; a ~ *[drinker]* kova; ~ *sea* korkea aallokko; *time hangs ~* aika kuluu hitaasti; *..of ~ body build* tanakkarakenteinen; *with a ~ heart* raskain sydämin; ~ *water* raskas vesi. **~-handed** kömpelö. **~-laden** huolten painama, raskautettu. **~-weight** raskaan sarjan (nyrkkeilijä ym).

Hebraic [hi(:)'breiik] a. heprealainen.

Hebrew ['hi:bru:] a. & s. heprealainen; heprean kieli, heprea; ~*s* Heprealaiskirje.

Hebrides ['hebridi:z] erisn.: *the ~* Hebridit.

heckle ['hekl] v. ahdistaa kysymyksillä.

hectare ['hektɑ:] s. hehtaari.

hectic ['hektik] a. hivuttava; kuumeinen, kiihkeä.

hector ['hektə] v. kohdella julmasti, tyrannisoida.

hedge [hedʒ] s. pensasaita, aita; (kuv.) suoja; v. aidata, ympäröidä (pensas)aidalla (m. ~ *in);* turvata itsensä (tappiolta); kierrellä; *[say yes or no,] don't ~* vastaa kiertelemättä. **-hog** siili. **-row** pensasaita.

hedonist ['hi:dənist] s. hedonisti, nautinnonhaluinen.

heed [hi:d] v. tarkata; ottaa vaarin; s. huomio; *give (pay) ~ to* ottaa vaari jstk; *take no ~ of* olla välittämättä.

-ful *a.* tarkkaavainen; *be more ~ of* ottaa enemmän huomioon. **-less** *a.* ajattelematon; huoleton.

heehaw ['hi:'hɔ:] *s.* (aasin) kiljunta; naurunhörähdys.

heel 1. [hi:l] *s.* kantapää; kanta, korko; tyvi, pää, takaosa, kannus; *sl.* roisto; *v.* panna korko, korot jhk; *head over ~s* suin päin, päistikkaa, pää kolmantena jalkana; *down at ~* kengät lintassa; *on the ~s of* jnk kintereillä; *cool* (t. *kick*) *one's ~s* odotella; *take to one's ~s* pötkiä tiehensä; *well ~ed* (sl.) rahakas; *-tap* kantalappu; lasiin jäänyt viini.

heel 2. [hi:l] *v.* kallistua (mer.).

hefty ['hefti] *a.* raskas; vankka, vahva.

hegemony [hi(:)'geməni, Am. hi'dʒem-] *s.* hegemonia, johtoasema.

heifer ['hefə] *s.* hieho.

heigh-ho ['hei'həu] *int.* hohhoi! (ilm. väsymystä, pettymystä ym.).

height [hait] *s.* korkeus; (ihmisen) pituus; korkea paikka, kukkula; jnk huippu (kuv.); *at its ~* korkeimmillaan; *six feet in ~* kuuden jalan mittainen; *in the ~ of summer* sydänkesällä. **-en** [-n] *v.* kohottaa, korottaa; lisätä, tehostaa; kohota.

heinous ['heinəs] *a.* inhottava, katala.

heir [εə] *s.* perillinen, perijä *(to* jnk, *of* jkn); *~ apparent* lähin (kruunun)perijä; *~ presumptive* todennäköinen kruununperijä (ellei lähempää synny). **-ess** [-ris] *s.* perijätär. **-loom** [-lu:m] *s.* perhekalleus, perintöesine.

held [held] *imp. & pp.* ks. **hold.**

Helen ['helin] *erisn.* Helena.

helicopter ['helikɔptə] *s.* helikopteri.

Heligoland ['heligəlænd] *erisn.* Helgolanti.

helio|centric [hi:liə(u)-] *a.* aurinkokeskinen. **-graph** [-grɑːf] *s.* heliografi. **-trope** ['heljətrəup] *s.* heliotrooppi.

heliport ['helipɔːt] *s.* helikopteriasema.

helium ['hi:ljəm] *s.* helium.

hell [hel] *s.* helvetti; *a ~ of a noise* helvetillinen melu; *raise ~* nostaa meteli; *like ~* kuin vimmattu.

he'll [hi:l] = *he will.*

Hellen|e ['heli:n] *s.* helleeni. **-ic** [he'li:nik] *a.* helleeninen. **-ism**

['helinizm] *s.* hellenismi.

hellish ['heliʃ] *a.* helvetillinen.

hello ['he'ləu, hə'ləu] *int.* hei! halloo! terve!

helm [helm] *s.* peräsin, ruori; *be at the ~* olla perässimessä; *answer the ~* totella peräsintä.

helmet ['helmit] *s.* kypärä; *[sun] ~* hellekypärä.

helmsman ['helmzmən] *s.* peränpitäjä.

helot ['helət] *s.* (kuv.) orja.

help [help] *v.* auttaa, avustaa; edistää; *s.* apu; apulainen; *~ sb. to* auttaa jkta saamaan jtk; ojentaa, tarjota jklle (pöydässä) jtk; *~ sb. out with..* auttaa (esim. takki) jkn ylle; *I could not ~ laughing* en voinut olla nauramatta; *don't be longer than you can ~* älä viivy kauemmin kuin on välttämätöntä; *~ yourself to* olkaa hyvä ottakaa; *~ sb. out* auttaa jkta (jstk pulasta); *it can't be ~ed* ei sille voi mitään; *can I be of any ~?* voinko olla avuksi? **-er** [-ə] *s.* apulainen. **-ful** *a.* avulias; hyödyllinen. **-ing** *s.* (ruoka-)annos. **-less** *a.* avuton. **-mate** [-meit], **-meet** [-mi:t] toveri, apu (tav. puoliso).

helter-skelter ['heltə'skeltə] *adv.* mullin mallin; suin päin; mukkelis makkelis; *s.* sekamelska, eräänl. liukurata (tivolissa).

helve [helv] *s.* (työkalun) varsi.

hem 1. [hem] *s.* päärme, palle; *v.* päärmätä; *~ in* (about) ympäröidä, sulkea sisäänsä.

hem 2. [mm, hm] *int.* hm! *v.* sanoa »hm», kakistella.

hemisphere ['hemisfiə] *s.* pallonpuolisko.

hemlock ['hemlɔk] *s.* katko (kasv.); katkosta valmistettu myrkky; *~ [spruce]* hemlokki (P. Am.).

hemo|globin [hi:məu'gləubin] *s.* hemoglobiini. **-philia** [-'filiə] *s.* verenvuototauti; *(~c* verenvuototautinen).

hemor|rhage ['heməridʒ] *s.* verenvuoto. **-rhoids** [-rɔidz] *s.* peräpukamat.

hemp [hemp] *s.* hamppu; = *cannabis,* ks. t. **-en** [-ən] *a.* hamppu-.

hemstitch ['hemstitʃ] *s.* reikäompelu; *v.* koristaa r-lla.

hen [hen] *s.* kana; naaraslintu; ~ *party* naistenkutsut. **-bane** hullukaali.

hence [hens] *adv.* täältä; tästä [syystä]; *five years* ~ viiden vuoden kuluttua. **-forth, -forward** *adv.* tästä lähtien.

henchman ['hen(t)ʃmən] *s.* aseenkantaja; kannattaja.

henna ['henə] *s.* henna; ~*ed* hennalla värjätty.

henpeck ['henpek] *v.*: ~*ed* tohvelin alla; ~*ed husband* tohvelisankari.

hep [hep] *a.* (sl.): ~ *to* jstk perillä, »kokenut», vrt. *hip*.

hepatitis [hepə'taitis] *s.* maksatulehdus.

her [hə:, hə] *she*-pron. objektimuoto; hänet, häntä, hänelle; *fem. poss. pron.* hänen, -nsa, -nsä; *with* ~ hänen kanssaan.

herald ['her(ə)ld] *s.* airut, sanansaattaja; *v.* ilmoittaa jnk tulo, julistaa, ennustaa. **-ic** [he'rældik] *a.* heraldinen. **-ry** [-ri] *s.* heraldiikka, vaakunatiede.

herb [hə:b] *s.* yrtti, ruohokasvi. **-aceous** [hə:'beiʃəs] *a.* ruoho-, yrtti-; ~ *border* kukkareunus puutarhassa. **-age** [-idʒ] *s.* ruohokasvit; laidunoikeus. **-al** [-(ə)l] *a.* yrtti-. **-alist** [-əlist] *s.* lääkeyrttien kasvattaja t. kauppias. **-ivorous** [hə:'bivərəs] *a.* kasvissyöjä-.

herculean [hə:kju'li:ən] *a.* valtavia voimia vaativa (~ *task*).

herd [hə:d] *s.* (karja-, eläin) lauma; -paimen; *v.* elää laumoissa, kerääntyä yhteen (us. ~ *together*); paimentaa; *the common* ~ rahvas; ~ *instinct* laumavaisto. **-sman** [-zmən] karjapaimen.

here [hiə] *adv.* täällä, tässä, tänne; tällöin, tässä kohdassa; *look* ~! kuulehan; *near* ~ tässä lähellä; ~ *you are* kas tässä, olkaa hyvä! ~ *we are* olemme perillä; ~ *goes!* nyt se alkaa! nyt aloitamme! ~*'s to..!* malja.. lle! ~ *and now* heti paikalla; ~ *and there* siellä täällä, sinne tänne; [*that's*] *neither* ~ *nor there* vailla merkitystä, asiaton. **-abouts** ['hiərəbauts] *adv.* näillä tienoin. **-after** [hiər'a:ftə] *adv.* tämän jälkeen, vastedes; *the* ~ tuleva elämä. **-by** ['hiə'bai] *adv.* tämän kautta, täten.

heredi|tary [hi'redit|(ə)ri] *a.* perintö-,

peritty, perinnöllinen. **-ty** [-i] *s.* perinnöllisyys.

Hereford ['herifəd] *erisn.*

here|sy ['herə|si] *s.* harhaoppi(suus). **-tic** [-tik] *s.* harhaoppinen, kerettiläinen. **-tical** [hi'retik(ə)l] *a.* = ed.

here|upon ['hiə-rə'pɔn] *adv.* tämän jälkeen. **-with** [-'wið] *adv.* tällä, tämän avulla.

heritage ['heritidʒ] *s.* perintö.

Hermes ['hə:mi:z] *erisn.*

hermetic [hə:'metik] *a.* ilmanpitävä, hermeettinen.

hermit ['hə:mit] *s.* erakko. **-age** [-idʒ] *s.* erakkomaja; *the* ~ Eremitaasi (-museo).

hernia ['hə:njə] *s.* tyrä (lääk.).

hero ['hiərəu] *s.* (pl. ~ *es*) sankari (m. kirjan päähenkilö), urho. **-ic** [hi'rouik] *a.* sankarillinen, sankari-, herooinen.

Herod ['herəd] *erisn.* Herodes.

heroin ['herə(u)in] *s.* heroiini.

hero|ine ['herə(u)in] *s.* sankaritar. **-ism** ['herə(u)izm] *s.* sankar(illis)uus; ~*-worship* sankarinpalvonta.

heron ['herən] *s.* haikara.

herpes ['hə:pi:z] *s.* rokahtuma; ~ *zoster* ks. *shingles*.

herring ['heriŋ] *s.* silli; *red* ~ savusilli, (kuv.) harhaanjohtava toimenpide ym. ~*-bone* (kankaan ym) kalanruotomalli; haarakäynti (suksilla mäkeä noustaessa). ~*-pond* *s.* (leik.) Atlantti.

her|s [hə:z] *pron.* (subst. muoto) hänen. **-self** [hə:'self] *pron.* itse(ä)nsä; itse.

Hert|ford ['ha:fəd] *erisn.* **-s** [ha:ts] = Hertfordshire.

he's [hi:z] = *he is, he has*.

hesita|nce, -ncy ['hezit|əns, -i] *s.* epäröinti. **-nt** [-ənt] *a.* epäröivä, epävarma; ~*ly* empien.

hesita|te ['heziteit] *v.* epäröidä, empiä, olla kahden vaiheilla. **-tion** [-'teiʃn] *s.* epäröinti, empiminen.

hetero|dox ['het(ə)rədɔks] *a.* harhaoppinen. **-doxy** [-dɔksi] *s.* harhaoppisuus. **-geneous** ['hetərə(u)'dʒi:njəs] *a.* heterogeeninen, sekakoosteinen.

hew [hju:] *v.* (pp. m. ~*n*) hakata;

veistää; ~ down kaataa (puu).

hexa|gon ['heksəgən] s. kuusikulmio.
-meter [hek'sæmitə] s. heksametri,
kuusimittasäe.

hey [hei] int. hei!

heyday ['heidei] s. kukoistus.

hi [hai] int. et. Am. hei! terve!

hiatus [hai'eitəs] s. aukko.

hiberna|te ['haibə:neit] v. olla [talvi]
horroksessa; talvehtia. **-tion** [-'neiʃn]
s. talvihorros.

Hibernian [hai'bə:njən] s. & a.
irlantilainen.

hibiscus [hi'biskəs] s. kiinanruusu.

hic|cup, -cough ['hikəp] s. nikotus; v.
nikotella.

hick [hik] s. Am. maalainen.

hickory ['hikəri] s. hikkori(puu).

hid [hid] imp. ks. hide. **-den** ['hidn] pp.
ks. hide; salainen.

hide 1. [haid] s. vuota, nahka.

hide 2. [haid] hid hid[den], v. kätkeä,
piilottaa; kätkeytyä; play ~-and-seek
olla piilosilla; in hiding piilossa.

hide|bound (kuv.) ahdasmielinen,
rajoittunut. **~-out, ~-away** s.
piilopaikka.

hideous ['hidiəs] a. inhottava, hirveä.

hiding s. selkäsauna; piilo. **~-place**
piilopaikka.

hier|archy ['haiər|ɑ:ki] s. pappisvalta,
arvoasteikko. **-oglyph** [-əglif] s.
hieroglyfi; (~-ics [-'glifiks]
h-kirjoitus).

hi-fi ['hai'fai] = high fidelity puhdas
äänentoisto.

higgle ['higl] v. tinkiä.

higgledy-piggledy ['higldi'pigldi] adv.
sikin sokin.

high [hai] a. korkea; ylhäinen; suuri;
ylevä; kova, kiivas; jnk vaikutuksen
alainen (~ on); (lihasta)
pahentumaisillaan oleva; adv.
korkealle; voimakkaasti; s. korkeus,
maksimi; ~ and dry karille (t.
syrjään) joutunut, eristetty; [search]
~ and low kaikkialta; ~ and mighty
pöyhkeä; ~ altar pääalttari; ~ colour
punakka ihonväri; ~ jump
korkeushyppy; ~ life ylhäisön elämä;
~ summer keskikesä; ~ priest
ylimmäinen pappi; ~ school
oppikoulu; the ~ seas kansainväliset
vedet; in ~ spirits iloinen; ~ tea

iltapala; a ~ old time hurjan hauskaa;
~ words kiivaat sanat; on ~ taivaissa,
korkeuksissa; the sea runs ~ merellä
käy kova aallokko; play ~ pelata
suurin panoksin; run ~ kuohua. **-ball**
Am. (viski)grogi. **-brow** älyniekka;
~s älymystö; **~-church**
korkeakirkollinen. **~-falutin**
mahtipontinen. **-flown** liioitteleva,
pöyhkeä. **~-grade** a. korkea-,
ensiluokkainen; jalo-. **~-handed**
omavaltainen; (**~-handedly**
omavaltaisesti). **-land** ylänkömaa; the
H ~s Skotlannin ylämaat. **-lander**
ylämaalainen. **-light** s. kohokohta; v.
korostaa. **-ly** adv. suuresti, ylen,
kovin; [speak] ~ [of] ylistävästi; ~
intelligent erittäin älykäs. **~-minded**
jalo, ylevämielinen. **-ness** s. korkeus;
His Royal H ~ hänen kuninkaallinen
korkeutensa. **~-octane**
korkeaoktaaninen. **~-pitched** kimeä,
korkea. **~-priced** kallis. **~-ranking**
korkea-arvoinen. **~-spirited** rohkea,
tulinen. **~-strung** hermostunut,
yliherkkä. **~-tension** a. suurjännite-.
~-water nousuvesi; h.-w. mark
korkeimman veden raja; korkein
huippu. **-way** maantie; divided ~
kaksiajoratainen tie. **-wayman**
maantierosvo.

hijack ['haidʒæk] v. kaapata
(lentokone jm). **-ing** s. (lentokoneen)
kaappaus.

hike [haik] s. jalkamatka; v. retkeillä,
reippailla; ~ up vetäistä ylös; hiking
retkeily.

hilari|ous [hi'lɛəriəs] a. hilpeä, iloinen.
-ty [hi'læriti] s. hilpeys.

Hilary ['hiləri] erisn.: ~ term
talvilukukausi.

hill [hil] s. mäki, kukkula, (pieni)
vuori; ant~ muurahaiskeko. **-billy**
Am. (us. halv.) takamaiden asukas,
vuoristolainen. **-ock** [-ək] s. mäki,
kumpu. **-side** s. rinne. **-y** [-i] a.
mäkinen.

hilt [hilt] s. (miekan) kahva.

him [him] pron. (he-pron.
objektimuoto) hänet, häntä, hänelle.
-self [-'self] pron. itse; itse(ä)nsä; he
said so ~ hän itse sanoi niin; did you
see the manager ~ tapasitko johtajan
itsensä; he is not ~ hän ei ole oma

itsensä; *by* ~ yksin(ään).

Himalayas [himə'le(i)əz] *erisn.: the* ~
Himalaja.

hind 1. [haind] *s.* saksanhirven naaras;
(vanh.) renki, moukka.

hind 2. [haind] *a.* taka-; ~ *leg*
takajalka; ~-*quarters* takapuoli,
takamukset.

hinder [hində] *v.* estää.

hind|most ['haindməust] *a.*
takimmainen. **-sight** *s.* jälkiviisaus.

hindrance ['hindrəns] *s.* este.

Hindu, -doo ['hindu:] *s.* hindu; *a.*
hindulainen. **-ism** [-izm] *s.*
hindulaisuus.

hinge [hin(d)ʒ] *s.* sarana; *v.* varustaa
saranoilla; ~ *on* (kuv.) olla jnk
varassa.

hinny ['hini] *s.* muuliaasi.

hint [hint] *s.* vihjaus, vihje, viittaus; *v.*
vihjata *(at* jhk); *drop a* ~ vihjaista;
take a ~ ottaa vihjeestä vaari.

hinterland ['hintəlænd] *s.* takamaa(t).

hip 1. [hip] *s.* kiulukka.

hip 2. [hip] *s.* lonkka, lanne; *with her
hands on her* ~ *s* kädet lanteilla.
~-**bath** istumakylpy.

hip 3. (m. **hep**) *a.* uusia virtauksia
seuraava *(s. hipster).*

hipped [hipt] *pp.: broad-* ~
leveälanteinen; [*is*] ~ *on golf* on
golfhullu (Am. sl.).

hipp|ie, -y ['hipi] *s.* hippi.

hippo ['hipəu] *s.* = ~*potamus.*

hippo|drome ['hipə|drəum] *s.*
hippodromi. **-potamus** [-'pɔtəməs] *s.*
virtahepo.

hire ['haiə] *s.* vuokra, palkka; *v.*
pestata, palkata; vuokrata; (m. ~ *out)*
antaa vuokralle; ~*d girl* palvelustyttö;
buy sth. on ~ *purchase* ostaa
osamaksulla. **-ling** [liŋ] *s.*
palkkalainen.

hirsute ['hə:sju:t, Am. -su:t] *a.*
karvainen.

his [hiz, iz] *mask. poss. pron.* hänen,
-nsa, -nsä.

hiss [his] *v.* sihistä; viheltää (jklle); *s.*
sihinä; vihellys; ~ *off* viheltää ulos.

histor|ian [his'tɔ:riən] *s.* historioitsija.
-ic [his'tɔrik] *a.* historiallinen; ~
moment h. (tärkeä) hetki. **-ical**
[his'tɔrik(ə)l] *a.* historiallinen (esim.
~ *film,* ~ *novel).*

historiography [histɔ:ri'ɔgrəfi] *s.*
historiankirjoitus.

history ['hist(ə)ri] *s.* historia; *ancient* ~
vanhan ajan historia, yleisesti
tunnettu asia; *case* ~ sairaskertomus.

histrionic [histri'ɔnik] *a.* teatteri-.
näyttelijä-.

hit [hit] *hit hit, v.* lyödä, iskeä; osua,
sattua, tavoittaa; törmätä; tavata,
keksiä sattumalta *(on, upon* jtk); *s.*
lyönti, isku; osuma; letkaus *(at* jklle);
onnistuminen, menestys; iskelmä; ~
it osua kohdalleen, oikeaan; ~ *the
mark* osua maaliin; ~ *it off* (with)
sopia yhteen; ~ *and run*
(maantiegangsterista) poistua
(onnettomuus)paikalta; *make a* ~
onnistua.

hit-and-run *driver* maantiegangsteri.

hitch [hitʃ] *v.* vetäistä, -kiskaista,
nykäistä; kiinnittää (koukulla, haalla
t. solmulla); tarttua kiinni; *s.* nykäisy;
este, vastus, pysähdys; eräänl. solmu;
half- ~ puolipolvi; *without a* ~
tasaisesti, vaikeuksitta. **-hike** *v.*
matkustaa peukalokyydillä, liftata.
-hiker liftari.

hi her ['hiðə] *adv.* (vanh.) tänne; ~
and thither sinne tänne. **-to** [-'tu:] *adv.*
tähän asti.

hive [haiv] *s.* mehiläispesä, -parvi; *v.*
sulkea m-pesään, koota varastoon,
asua lähekkäin (kuin
mehiläispesässä).

hives [haivz] *s.* nokkoskuume.

ho [həu] *int.* hei! ohoi!

hoar [hɔ:] *a.* harmaantunut; *s.* huurre,
kuura (m. ~*frost).*

hoard [hɔ:d] *s.* varasto; aarre; *v.* koota
varastoon, rohmuta, »hamstrata» (us.
~ *up).*

hoarding ['hɔ:diŋ] *s.* rohmuaminen;
(väliaikainen) aitaus (rakennuksen
ym ympärillä); ilmoitusteline.

hoarse [hɔ:s] *a.* käheä. **-ness** *s.* käheys.

hoary ['hɔ:ri] *a.* harmaantunut;
(iki)vanha.

hoax [həuks] *v.* pitää pilkkanaan,
puijata; *s.* pilanteko.

hob [hɔb] *s.* takan sivulevy; ks.
hobgoblin.

hobble ['hɔbl] *v.* ontua, nilkuttaa; *s.*
ontuminen; ~ *a horse* kytkeä hevosen
jalat. **-dehoy** [-di'hɔi] *s.* pojanjolppi.

hobby ['hɔbi] s. mieliharrastus, harraste; **hobbies** [room] askartelu(huone). **-horse** (lapsen) keppi-, keinuhevonen.

hobgoblin ['hɔbgɔblin] s. menninkäinen, mörkö.

hobnail ['hɔbnei] s. leveäkantainen naula.

hobnob ['hɔbnɔb] v. ryypiskellä yhdessä; seurustella tuttavallisesti, veljeillä.

hobo ['həubəu] s. Am. maankiertäjä.

hock [hɔk] s. reininviini; *in* ~ »kaniisa».

hockey ['hɔki] s. [ice ~] jääkiekkoilu.

hocus-pocus ['həukəs'pəukəs] s. silmänkääntötemppu.

hod [hɔd] s. laastinkantolaite.

hodge-podge ['hɔdʒpɔdʒ] ks. *hotch-potch.*

hoe [həu] s. s. kuokka; v. kuokkia, kitkeä (~ up weeds).

hog [hɔg] s. sika, karju; v. ottaa kahmimalla; *road-* ~ autohurjastelija; *go the whole* ~ tehdä jtk perin pohjin, ei jättää puolitiehen. **-back**, ~ **'s-back** harju, harjanne. **-shead** [-zhed] härkätynnyri (n. 240 l).

hoi(c)k [hɔik] v. ohjata (lentokone) äkkiä ylöspäin.

hoi polloi ['hɔi'pɔlɔi, Am. -pə'lɔi] s.: *the* ~ massat, rahvas.

hoist [hɔist] v. nostaa (lippu ym); s. nostolaite; *was* ~ *with his own petard* meni omaan ansaansa.

hoity-toity ['hɔiti'tɔiti] int. johan nyt! kaikkea vielä! a. kopea.

hokum ['həukəm] s. Am. sl. roska.

hold 1. [həuld] *held held*, v. pitää, pidellä, pitää kädessä t. hallussaan, omistaa; hoitaa (virkaa); olla jtk mieltä; sisältää, vetää; pitää jnak; pidättää, estää; kestää, olla käypä, olla voimassa, pitää paikkansa; s. ote; kiinnekohta; vaikutus; ~ *sb.'s hand* pitää jkta kädestä; ~ *one's hand* (m.) pidättyä; *he* ~ *s strange opinions* hänellä on oudot mielipiteet; ~ *back* pidättää, pidättyä, empiä, salata; ~ *by* pitää kiinni jstk; ~ *cheap* pitää vähäarvoisena; ~ *forth* puhua, »paasata», tarjota; ~ *good* pitää paikkansa; ~ *in* pitää kurissa, hillitä; ~ *off* pitää loitolla, pysyä matkan

päässä; ~ *on* pitää kiinni (*to* jstk), pysyä lujana; ~ *on!* odottakaa! ~ *out* kestää, pitää puoliaan, ojentaa, tarjota, antaa (toiveita); ~ *over* lykätä; ~ *one's own* pitää puolensa; ~ *to* = ~ *by;* ~ *sb.* *to his promise* pakottaa jku pitämään lupauksensa; ~ *up* pysähdyttää; ryöstää; ~ *up as* [*an example*] esittää; ~ *sb. up to ridicule* saattaa naurun alaiseksi; ~ *with* olla jkn puolella, hyväksyä; *a* ~ *upon (over)* vaikutus(valta) jkh; *catch (take, lay)* ~ *of* tarttua jhk; *get* ~ *of* saada käsiinsä; *let go one's* ~ hellittää otteensa. **-er** [-ə] s. haltija; pidin, imuke (*cigar-* ~). **-fast** sinkilä. **-ing** s. omistus; vuokratila, -palsta; ~ *s* m. arvopaperit; ~ *company* omistajayhtiö. **--up** ryöstö; pysähdys.

hold 2. [həuld] s. lastiruuma.

hole [həul] s. reikä, aukko; kolo, pesä, luola; kuoppa; kehno asunto; murju; pula; v. tehdä reikä jhk; lyödä (golf)pallo reikään; piileskellä; *in a* ~ pinteessä; *pick* ~ *s in* arvostella, löytää vikoja jstk. **--and-corner** salainen, vilpillinen.

holi | day ['hɔlədi, -dei] s. lupa-, juhlapäivä, loma(päivä), loma; v. lomailla; ~ *s* (lyh. sl. *hols*) loma; *bank* ~ (yleinen vapaapäivä Englannissa); ~ *-maker* lomanviettäjä. **-ness** ['həulinis] s. pyhyys.

Holland ['hɔlənd] erisn. Hollanti; *h* ~ s. hollanninpalttina; *h* ~ *s* katajanmarjaviina.

holler ['hɔlə] v. sl. huutaa, hoilata.

hollo, holloa ['hɔləu] int. halloo! hei! v. huutaa, huhuta.

hollow ['hɔləu] a. ontto; tyhjä, sisällyksetön; kuopallaan oleva (poski); kumea (ääni); s. onkalo, kolo, kuoppa; v. kovertaa, uurtaa (us. ~ *out*); adv. perinpohjin (beat sb. [*all*] ~); ~ *of the hand* kämmen. **--eyed** kuoppasilmäinen.

holly ['hɔli] s. piikkipaatsama. **-hock** [-hɔk] s. salkoruusu.

Holmes [həumz] erisn.

holm-oak ['həum'əuk] s. rautatammi.

holocaust ['hɔləkɔ:st] s. polttouhri; valtava tuho, (palo, roihu.)

holster ['həulstə] s. pistoolinkotelo.

holy ['həuli] *a.* pyhä; *H ~ Thursday* kiirastorstai, (Engl. m.) helatorstai; *~ water* vihkivesi; *H~ Week* piinaviikko; *the H~ of Holies* kaikkein pyhin.

homage ['hɔmidʒ] *s.* kunnian-, kunnioituksenosoitus; uskollisuudenvala; *pay ~ to* osoittaa kunnioitustaan jklle.

home [həum] *s.* koti; kotiseutu, -paikka; asunto; (urh.) pesä, maali; *a.* koti-; kotimainen, sisäasiain-; *adv.* kotiin, kotona; sattuvasti, kohdalleen; *v.* ks. *homing; at ~* kotona; *at ~ in* jhk perehtynyt, luonteva; *from ~* kotoa; *he left ~* hän lähti kotoa; *he went ~* hän meni kotiin; *~ economics* kotitalous; *H~ Office* sisäasiainministeriö; *~ rule* itsehallinto; *the ~ stretch* maalisuora; *~ truth* katkera totuus; *bring .. ~* perinpohjin selvittää jklle; näyttää toteen; *come ~ to* liikuttaa läheisesti jkta; *drive ~* iskeä (naula) sisään; *see sb.* ~ saattaa kotiin; *strike ~* osua asian ytimeen; [*seems to*] *have gone right ~* osuneen aivan kohdalleen. **-coming** kotiinpaluu. **-land** kotimaa. **-less** koditon. **-like** kodikas. **-ly** [-li] *a.* yksinkertainen, vaatimaton; ruma. **~-made** oma-, kotitekoinen. **-sick:** *I am ~* minulla on koti-ikävä. **-sickness** koti-ikävä. **-spun** kotikutoinen; *s.* kotikutoinen kangas. **-stead** [-sted] maatalo; Am. viljelyspalsta. **~-thrust** isku (t. sana), joka sattuu kohdalleen. **-ward** *adv.* kotiin päin (m. *~s); ~ bound* kotimatkalla (oleva). **-work** kotitehtävä(t), läksy(t).

homeopath ['həumjəpæθ] *s.* homeopaatti.

Homer ['həumə] *erisn.* Homeros.

homey ['həumi] *s.* Am. kodikas.

homicide ['hɔmisaid] *s.* tappo, henkirikos; murhaaja.

homily ['hɔmili] *s.* homilia, saarna.

homing ['həumiŋ] *a.* kotiin palaava; maalinetsivä; *~ pigeon* kirjekyyhkynen.

hominy ['hɔmini] *s.* maissipuuro, -rouheet.

homo- ['həumə(u)-] (yhd.) sama(n)-. **-geneous** [həmə'dʒi:niəs] *a.* homogeeninen, tasakoosteinen.

-nymous [hɔ'mɔniməs] *a.* samoin ääntyvä. **-sexual** *a.* homoseksuaalinen; *s.* homoseksualisti.

Honduras [hɔn'djuərəs] *erisn.*

hone [həun] *s.* kovasin; *v.* hioa.

honest ['ɔnist] *a.* rehellinen, kunniallinen; vilpitön; *earn an ~ penny* ansaita leipänsä rehellisellä tavalla. **-y** [-i] *s.* rehellisyys; *~ is the best policy* rehellisyys maan perii.

honey ['hʌni] *s.* hunaja, mesi; kullanmuru, kulta. **-comb** (hunaja)kenno, vahakakku; *v.* lävistää; *~ed* lokeroinen. **-ed** [-d] *a.* hunajainen. **-moon** *s.* kuherruskuukausi; *v.* viettää k-kuukautta. **-suckle** kuusama.

honk [hɔŋk] *s.* (villihanhen) huuto, autontorven törähdys; *v.* töräyttää.

honorary ['ɔn(ə)rəri] *a.* kunnia-; *~ secretary* palkaton sihteeri.

honours, honor ['ɔnə] *s.* kunnia; kunniallisuus; kunnianosoitus; *v.* kunnioittaa, pitää arvossa; tuottaa kunniaa; lunastaa (vekseli); *~s degree* korkeimmin arvosanoin suoritettu loppututkinto; [*birthday*] *~s* kuninkaan, kuningattaren (merkkipäivinä) suomat aatelisarvot, kunniamerkit ym; *do the ~s* [*of the table*] toimia isäntänä t. emäntänä; [*up*]*on my ~* kunniani kautta! *word of ~* kunniasana; *Your H~* Teidän Armonne. **-able** ['ɔn(ə)rəbl] *a.* kunnioitettava; kunniallinen; arvoisa, jalosukuinen (eräissä arvonimissä, lyh. *Hon.*).

hooch [hu:t] *s.* sl. (et. huono) viski.

hood [hud] *s.* huppukaulus, hilkka; (vaunun) kuomu; (Am.) (auton) konepelti; *Little Red Riding H~* punahilkka. **-lum** ['hu:dləm] *s.* Am. gangsteri, huligaani. **-oo** ['hu:du:] *s.* (paha) taika, pahanilmanlintu. **-wink** *v.* pettää, pimittää.

hoof [hu:f] *s.* (pl. m. *hooves*) kavio, sorkka; *on the ~* karjasta) elävänä.

hook [huk] *s.* haka, hakanen; koukku; sirppi; neula *(crochet ~);* *v.* kiinnittää hakasilla; saada tarttumaan koukkuun, tarttua; *~s and eyes* hakaset ja lehtiäiset; *by ~ or by crook* keinolla millä hyvänsä; [*catch*] *.. on*

~ *and line* ongella; ~ *it* (sl.) livistää.
hookah ['hukə] *s.* vesipiippu.
hooked [hukt] *a.* koukistettu;
koukuilla varustettu; huumeitten
orja; ~ *nose* kyömynenä.
hook-up *s.* (rad., TV) yhteenliittymä.
hooligan ['hu:ligən] *s.* huligaani.
hoop 1. [hu:p] *s.* vanne; (krokettipeli)
portti; *v.* vannehtia; ~*ed petticoat*
vannealushame.
hoop 2. ks. *whoop;* kirkuna. **-oe**
['hu:pu:] *s.* harjalintu.
hooray [hu'rei] *int.* hurraa.
hoot [hu:t] *v.* vastaanottaa ivahuudoin,
huutaa (us. ~ *at* jklle); törähtää; *s.*
ivahuoto, rääkynä; (huuhkajan)
huuto; (pillin) ulvonta, vihellys,
(auton) törähdys; ~ *off (out)* viheltää
ulos; *I don't care a* ~ vähät minä siitä
välitän. **-er** [-ə] *s.* höyrypilli, sireeni.
hooves pl. ks. *hoof.*
hop 1. [hɔp] *v.* hyppiä, hypellä, hypätä;
s. hyppäys, loikkaus; lentomatka; ~ *it*
(sl.) häipyä, mennä tiehensä; ~, *step
and jump* kolmiloikka (nyt *triple
jump*).
hop 2. [hɔp] *s.* humala(kasvi); (sl.)
oopiumi, huumausaine; ~*-garden*
humalisto; ~*ped up* huumausaineen
vaikutuksen alainen, -sena; ~*per*
humalannoukkija.
hope [həup] *s.* toivo, toive; *v.* toivoa
(for jtk); ~ *against* ~ toivoa kaikesta
huolimatta. **-ful** *a.* toiveikas; *young* ~
(perheen) toivo. **-less** *a.* toivoton,
epätoivoinen.
hop|-o'-my-thumb ['hɔpəmi'θʌm] *s.*
peukaloinen. **-scotch** *s.: play* ~
hypätä ruutua.
Horace ['hɔrəs] *erisn.* Horatius.
horde [hɔːd] *s.* lauma.
horizon [hə'raizn] *s.* taivaanranta;
näköpiiri. **-tal** [hɔri'zɔntl] *a.* vaakasuora; ~ *bar* rekki; ~*ly* vaakasuoraan.
hormone ['hɔːməun] *s.* hormoni.
horn [hɔːn] *s.* sarvi; torvi; tuntosarvi;
(kuun) sakara; käyrätorvi *(French* ~);
v.: ~ *in (on)* tuppautua jhk; ~ *of
plenty* runsaudensarvi; *shoe-* ~
kenkälusikka; *English* ~ *(kasv.* cor
anglais*) englannintorvi; *fog-* ~
sumusireeni; *motor* ~ auton torvi. **-ed**
[-d] *a.:* ~ *cattle* sarvikarja. **-et** [-it] *s.*
herhiläinen. **-less** *a.* sarveton, nupo.

-pipe reipas merimiestanssi.
~**-rimmed** sarvisankainen. **-y** [-i] *a.*
sarveis-, sarvimainen; känsäinen.
horoscope ['hɔrəskəup] *s.* horoskooppi.
horrendous [hɔ'rendəs] *a.* = seur.
horr|ible ['hɔrəbl] *a.* hirvittävä, hirveä;
-ibly hirveän. **-id** [-id] *a.* kauhea;
inhottava, hirveä. **-ific** [hɔ'rifik] *a.*
pöyristyttävä. **-ify** [-ifai] *v.*
pöyristyttää; *I was -ified* kauhistuin.
horror ['hɔrə] *s.* kauhistus, kauhu;
kauhunväristys, kammo; kaamea
hökötys yms.; *the* ~*s of war* sodan
kauhut; ~*-stricken, ~-struck*
kauhistunut.
hors d'oeuvre [ɔː'dəːvr] *s.* alkupalat.
horse [hɔːs] *s.* hevonen; ratsuväki;
pukki, teline; *be on one's high* ~ olla
olevinaan; *put the cart before the* ~
toimia takaperoises i. **-back:** *on* ~
ratsain: *ride on* ~ ratsastaa.
~**-chestnut** hevoskastanja. **-flesh**
hevosenliha; *a good judge of* ~ hyvä
hevostentuntija. **-flesh** *a.* kauhea.
-guards
kuninkaallinen henkivartiokaarti.
-hair jouhi. ~**-laugh** röhönauru. **-man**
ratsastaja. **-manship** ratsastustaito.
-play karkea pila. **-power**
hevosvoima. **-race** ratsastuskilpailut.
-radish piparjuuri. ~**-sense** terve
järki. **-shoe** hevosenkenkä. **-tail** korte
(kasv.). **-woman** (taitava)
ratsastajatar.
horsy ['hɔ:si] *a.* hevosrakas,
hevosurheilua harrastava.
hortatory ['hɔ:tət(ə)ri] *a.* kehottava.
horticulture ['hɔ:tikʌltʃə] *s.*
puutarhanhoito.
hosanna [hə(u)'zænə] *s.* hoosianna.
hose [həuz] *s.* (koll., kaupp.) sukat;
(ruiskun) letku, paloletku; *v.* kastella
letkulla; ~ [*down*] *a car* pestä auto
letkulla.
hosier ['həuʒə] *s.* neuletavarakauppias.
-y [-ri] *s.* trikoo-, neuletavarat.
hospice ['hɔspis] *s.* (munkkien)
vierasmaja; turva-, sairaskoti.
hospitable ['hɔspitəbl] *a.*
vieraanvarainen.
hospital ['hɔspitl] *s.* sairaala. **-ity**
[-'tæliti] *s.* vieraanvaraisuus.
host 1. [həust] *s.* suuri joukko, lauma;
sotajoukko.
host 2. [həust] *s.: the H* ~

ehtoollisleipä.

host 3. [houst] *s.* isäntä, majatalon isäntä; isäntäeläin, -kasvi.

hostage ['hostidʒ] *s.* panttivanki.

hostel ['hostl] *s.* (ylioppilas)asuntola; *youth* ~ retkeilymaja. **-ry** [-ri] *s.* (vanh.) majatalo.

hostess ['houstis] *s.* emäntä.

hostil|e ['hostail] *a.* vihamielinen. **-ity** [hɔs'tiliti] *s.* vihamielisyys; *pl.* (sot.) vihollisuudet.

hostler ['ɔslə] *s.* ks. *ostler.*

hot [hot] *a.* kuuma; tulinen, kiihkeä, intohimoinen; kirpeä; kiihkeärytminen (musiikki); ~ *air* suurisuinen puhe; ~ *dog* (kuuma) nakkisämpylä; ~ *pants* pikkupöksyt; ~ *plate* keittolevy; ~ *stuff* priima, pahuksen etevä (ihminen, esitys ym); ~ *on sb. s. tracks* aivan jkn kintereillä; ~ *ted up* lämmitetty; *things are* ~ *ting up* jännitys lisääntyy. **-bed** taimilava; (jnk) pesäpaikka. **~-blooded** kuumaverinen.

hotchpotch ['hotʃpotʃ] *s.* sekasotku.

hotel [hə(u)'tel] *s.* hotelli. **~-keeper** hotellinisäntä

hot|head tuittupää, huimapää. **~-headed** kiivas, tuittupäinen. **-house** kasvihuone; ~ *plant* ansarikasvi. **-ly** *adv.* kuumasti jne. **-ness** kuumuus. **-spur** huimapää.

hound [haund] *s.* ajokoira; *v.* ajaa (takaa).

hour ['auə] *s.* tunti; hetki; *for* ~ *s* tuntikausia; *office* ~ *s* konttoriaika; *consulting* ~ *s* vastaanottoaika; *after* ~ *s* työajan jälkeen; *at all* ~ *s* kaikkina vuorokaudenaikoina; *keep late* ~ *s* valvoa myöhään; ~ **-glass** tiimalasi. **~-hand** tuntiosoitin. **-ly** [-li] *adv.* joka tunti t. hetki; *a.* jokatuntinen.

house [haus, *pl.* 'hauziz] *s.* talo, rakennus; koti; (parlamentin) kamari, (ylä-, ala-)huone; Am. edustajainhuone; (teatt.) katsomo; kauppahuone, toiminimi; hallitsijasuku; *v.* [hauz] majoittaa, hankkia asunto (jklle); *boat*~ venevaja; *hen*~ kanala; *keep* ~ *(for)* hoitaa taloutta; *keep the* ~ pysytellä kotona; *move* ~ muuttaa (asunnosta toiseen); *bring down the* ~ saada myrskyisät suosionosoitukset

(teatterissa); ~ *party* (maakartanon) vieraat, kutsut; ~ *physician* (sairaalassa asuva) sairaalalääkäri. **~-agent** kiinteistönvälittäjä. **~-arrest** kotiaresti. **-boat** asuntolaiva. **~-bound** kotiin sidottu. **-breaker** murtovaras. **~-coat** kotiasu. **-craft** kotitalous. **-dog** vahtikoira. **-hold** ['haus(h)əuld] talous, talonväki; ~ *word* kaikkien huulilla oleva sana t. nimi; ~ *troops* (kuninkaan) henkivartiojoukot. **-holder** talonomistaja. **-keeper** taloudenhoitaja. **-keeping** taloudenhoito. **-maid** sisäkkö. **-master** koulun asuntolan valvoja(opettaja). **~-proud** kotinsa siisteydestä (ym) huolehtiva. **-top** katto. **~-training** (koiran) siisteyskasvatus. **~-warming** tupaantuliaiset. **-wife** ['hauswaif] *s.* perheenemäntä, kotirouva; ['hʌzif] käsityölaukku.

housing ['hauziŋ] *s.* asuntojen rakentaminen, asuntotuotanto; asunnot, asunto-olot; *the* ~ *question* asuntokysymys; ~ *committee* huoneenvuokralautakunta; ~ *shortage* asuntopula.

Houston ['hju:stən] *erisn.*

hove [həuv] *imp. & pp.* ks. *heave.*

hovel ['hovl, 'hʌvl] *s.* hökkeli; tönö; katos.

hover ['hovə] *v.* leijailla; maleksia (~ *about);* horjua (~ *between).* **-craft** pintaliitäjä.

how [hau] *adv.* kuinka, miten; ~ *about* . . ? mitä sanoisit(te) . . -sta? ~ *do you do?* (esiteltäessä) hyvää päivää; ~ *-d'ye-do* [-di'du:] *m.* pulma(llinen juttu); ~ *are you* kuinka voitte? ~ *is it* [*that*] mistä johtuu (m. ~ *come);* tell *her* ~ *to do it* sano hänelle miten se on tehtävä; *I don't know* ~ *to do it* en tiedä miten sen tekisin. **-ever** [-'evə] *adv.* kuinka . . tahansa; kuitenkin; *he didn't come,* ~ hän ei kuitenkaan tullut.

Howard ['hauəd] *erisn.*

howitzer ['hauitsə] *s.* haupitsi.

howl [haul] *v.* ulvoa; parkua; ~ *s.* ulvonta. **-er** [-ə] *s.* törkeä erehdys. **-ing** *a.* ulvova: valtava, törkeä; ~ *wilderness* synkkä erämaa.

howsoever ['hausəu'evə] *adv.* kuinka

.. tahansa.
hoy [hɔi] *int.* hoi! ohoi! *s.* (pieni) rannikkoalus.
hoyden ['hɔidn] *s.* rasavilli (tyttö).
hub [hʌb] *s.* (pyörän) napa; keskus.
hubbub ['hʌbʌb] *s.* hälinä.
hubby ['hʌbi] *s.* (puhek.) aviomies, »ukko».
huckaback ['hʌkəbæk] *s.* reivas.
huckleberry ['hʌklb(ə)ri] *s.* Am. mustikka.
huckster ['hʌkstə] *s.* kulkukauppias.
huddle ['hʌdl] *v.* sulloa; sulloutua yhteen, painautua toisiinsa; (talosta) kököttää; *s.* sekamelska, rykelmä; sl. salainen neuvottelu (et. *go into a* ~); ~ [*oneself*] *up* vetäytyä käppyrään.
hue 1. [hju:] *s.* värivivahdus.
hue 2. [hju:] *s.:* ~ *and cry* takaa-ajohuuto; (rikollisen) kuuluttaminen; *raise a* ~ *and cry against* (m.) paheksua kovaäänisesti.
huff [hʌf] *v.* kohdella töykeästi, vihastuttaa; *s.* vihanpuuska; *in a* ~ vihoissaan. **-y** [-i] *a.* loukkaantunut, herkkä pahastumaan; *-ily* pahantuulisesti.
hug [hʌg] *v.* sulkea syliinsä, syleillä; pitää kiinni (jstk), pysytellä lähellä; *s.* syleily; ~ *oneself on* onnitella itseään jstk.
huge [hju:dʒ] *a.* suunnaton, valtava.
hugger-mugger ['hʌgəmʌgə] *s.* salavihkaisuus; epäjärjestys, sotku; *adv.* salaa; *a.* salavihkainen.
Hugh [hju:], **-es** [hju:z] *erisn.*
Huguenot ['hju:gənət] *s.* hugenotti.
hulk [hʌlk] *s.* varastolaiva, laivahylky; roikale. **-ing** *a.* romuluinen, kömpelö.
hull 1. [hʌl] *s.* (herneen) palko; *v.* kuoria, silpiä.
hull 2. [hʌl] *s.* (laivan)runko; *v.* osua, ampua runkoon.
hullabaloo [hʌləbə'lu:] *s.* hälinä.
hullo [hʌ'ləu] *int.* halloo! hei!
hum [hʌm] *v.* surista, hyristä; hyräillä; *s.* surina; hyräily; *int.* hm! ~ *of voices* puheensorina; ~ *and haw* kangerrella, takellella; *make things* ~ panna asiat luistamaan.
human ['hju:mən] *a.* inhimillinen, ihmis-; *s.* ihminen; ~ *being* ihminen; *the* ~ *condition* ihmisenä oleminen, ihmisen osa. **-e** [hju:(:)'mein] *a.*

inhimillinen, ihmisystävällinen, humaaninen, humanistinen. **-ism** [-izm] *s.* humanismi. **-ist** [-ist] *s.* humanisti. **-itarian** [hju(:)mæni'tɛəriən] *s.* ihmisystävällinen; *s.* ihmisystävä. **-ity** [hju:'mæniti] *s.* ihmisyys; ihmiskunta; inhimillisyys, ihmisystävällisyys; *the h-ities* humanistiset tieteet. **-ize** [-aiz] *v.* inhimillistää. **-kind** [-'kaind] *s.* ihmiskunta. **-ly** *adv.* inhimillisesti, ihmisen kannalta; ~ *speaking* inhimillisesti arvostellen; *all that is* ~ *possible* kaiken, mitä ihminen voi.
humble ['hʌmbl] *a.* nöyrä; alhainen, vaatimaton, vähäpätöinen; *v.* nöyryyttää; ~ *oneself* nöyrtyä, alentua; *eat* ~ *pie* nöyryyttää itsensä.
humbug ['hʌmbʌg] *s.* humpuuki, huijaus; huijari; *int.* roskaa! *v.* petkuttaa.
humdrum ['hʌmdrʌm] *a.* yksitoikkoinen, unettava, pitkäpiimäinen; *s.* yksitoikkoisuus.
humerus ['hju:mərəs] *s.* olkaluu.
humid ['hju:mid] *a.* kostea. **-ifier** [hju:'midifaiə] *s.* ilmankostutin. **-ity** [hju(:)'miditi] *s.* kosteus.
humili|ate [hju(:)'milieit] *v.* nöyryyttää; *-ating* nöyryyttävä. **-ation** [-'eifn] *s.* nöyryytys. **-ty** [hju(:)'militi] *s.* nöyryys.
humming ['hʌmiŋ] *a.* suriseva **-bird** kolibri. ~**-top** soiva hyrrä.
hummock ['hʌmək] *s.* mäennyppylä, kumpu; kohopaikka.
humor|ist ['hju:mərist] *s.* humoristi, leikinlaskija. **-ous** ['hju:m(ə)rəs] *a.* leikkisä, humoristinen, lystikäs.
humour, humor ['hju:mə] *s.* mieliala, tuuli; huumori, leikillisyys; *v.* tehdä (jklle) mieliksi, noudattaa (oikkua ym); *not in the* ~ *for work* ei työtuulella.
hump [hʌmp] *s.* kyttyrä; kumpu; *s.* alakuloisuuden puuska; *v.* köyristää (selkä); ottaa selkäänsä, kantaa. **-back(ed)** kyttyräselkä(inen).
humph [mm, hʌmf] *int.* hm! (ilm. tyytymättömyyttä ym).
Humphr(e)y ['hʌmfri] *erisn.*
humus ['hju:məs] *s.* mullas.
Hun [hʌn] *s.* hunni, barbaari.
hunch [hʌn(t)ʃ] *s.* kyttyrä; paksu pala;

hund   218

v. köyristää, työntää esiin; *I have a ~
that* aavistan, että; *with his shoulders
~ed* selkä kyyryssä. **-back (ed)**
kyttyräselkä(inen).
hundred ['hʌndrəd] *lukus.: a ~, one ~*
sata; *one ~ and two* satakaksi; *~s of
books* satoja kirjoja. **-fold** *s. & adv.*
satakertainen, **-sesti**. **-th** [-θ] *lukus. &
s.* sadas, **-osa**. **-weight** (lyh. *cwt*)
sentneri (50,8 kg).
hung [hʌŋ] *imp. & pp.* ks. **hang**.
Hungar|ian [hʌŋ'geəriən] *a. & s.*
unkarilainen; unkarin kieli. **-y**
['hʌŋgəri] *erisn.* Unkari.
hunger ['hʌŋgə] *s.* nälkä; *v.* nähdä
nälkää; *~ for* janota, kaivata
kiihkeästi jtk; *go on a ~-strike* aloittaa
syömälakko.
hungry ['hʌŋgri] *a.* nälkäinen,
nälkiintynyt; laiha (maa); *I am ~*
minun on nälkä.
hung ks. **hang**; *~ up* pettynyt, estynyt.
hunk [hʌŋk] *s.* paksu pala.
hunker ['hʌŋkə] *s.: on one's ~s*
kyykyssä.
hunt [hʌnt] *v.* metsästää; ajaa takaa;
etsiä *(for* jtk); *s.* metsästys, ajo;
metsästys|seurue, -alue; *~ down* ajaa
väsyksiin; ottaa kiinni (rikollinen);
~ up (koettaa) saada selville. **-er**
(-ə) *s.* metsästäjä;
ajometsästyshevonen.
hunting ['hʌntiŋ] *s.* (ajo)metsästys,
(ketun)ajo. **~-ground** metsästysmaa.
huntsman *s.* jahtirenki.
hurdle [hə:dl] *s.* aita; *pl.* aitajuoksu. **-r**
[-ə] *s.* aitajuoksija. **~-race**
aitajuoksu.
hurdy-gurdy ['hə:digə:di] *s.* posetiivi.
hurl [hə:l] *v.* paiskata, singota; *s.*
heitto.
hurly-burly ['hə:libə:li] *s.* meteli,
hullunmylly.
hurr|ah [hu'rɑ:], **-ay** [hu'rei] *int. & s.*
eläköön(huuto); *v.* huutaa eläköötä.
hurricane ['hʌrikən] *s.* pyörremyrsky;
~ lamp, ~ lantern myrskylyhty.
hurried ['hʌrid] *a.* kiireellinen,
hätäinen. **-ly** *adv.* kiireesti.
hurry ['hʌri] *s.* kiire; *v.* kiirehtiä,
rientää; kiiruhtaa, jouduttaa; viedä
kiireesti; *I am in a ~* minulla on kiire;
[he won't do that again] in a ~ aivan
pian, aivan vähällä; *~ up* joudu!

hurt [hə:t] *hurt hurt, v.* loukata,
vahingoittaa; haitata, olla vahingoksi;
koskea, tehdä kipeätä; *s.* vamma,
haava; haitta; *are you ~;* oletteko
vahingoittunut? *she was ~ by their
criticism* heidän arvostelunsa loukkasi
häntä. **-ful** *a.* vahingollinen,
haitallinen.
hurtle ['hə:tl] *v.* lentää suhisten, tulla
vinkuen; singota rysähtäen.
husband ['hʌzbənd] *s.* aviomies; *v.*
hoitaa säästäväisesti, säästää. **-man**
maanviljelijä. **-ry** *s.* (hyvä)
taloudenhoito; maatalous; *animal ~*
karjanhoito.
hush [hʌʃ] *v.* vaientaa, rauhoittaa,
hyssyttää; vaieta; *s.* äänettömyys; *~
up* (m.) painaa villaisella; *~! hiljaa!
vaiti! ~ money* maksu vaitiolosta;
~~ [affair] erittäin salainen. **-aby**
[-əbai] *int.* tuuti.
husk [hʌsk] *s.* kuori, akana; *v.* kuoria.
-y [-i] *a.* karhea, käheä; vahva,
vankka; *s.* eskimokoira, rekikoira.
hussar [hu'za:] *s.* husaari.
hussy ['hʌsi, -zi] *s.* naikkonen, letukka.
hustings ['hʌstiŋz] *s.* vaalitaistelu;
vaalipuhekoroke.
hustle ['hʌsl] *v.* tuuppia, työntää,
tunkea; tungeskella; touhuta; *s.*
touhu, tungos; *~ sb. into* (. . .*-ing*)
pakottaa, panna joku kiireesti
(tekemään jtk). **-r** [-ə] *s.* huijari;
prostituoitu.
hut [hʌt] *s.* maja, mökki; parakki.
hu ch [hʌtʃ] *s.* kanikoppi; kaivosvaunu,
hiilivaunu.
hutment ['hʌtmənt] *s.* parakkileiri.
huzza [hu'za:] *int & s.* eläköön(huuto);
v. huutaa eläköötä.
hyacinth ['haiəsinθ] *s.* hyasintti.
hybrid ['haibrid] *s.* sekamuoto; *a.*
sekamuotoinen.
hydra ['haidrə] *s.* hydra, vesikäärme.
hydrangea [hai'drein(d)ʒə] *s.*
hortensia.
hydr|ant ['haidr(ə)nt] *s.* paloposti. **-ate**
[-eit] *s.* hydraatti. **-aulic** [hai'drɔ:lik]
a. hydraulinen.
hydro ['haidrəu] *s.* lyh. ks. *hydropathic*.
-carbon *s.* hiilivety. **-chloric**
['haidrə'klɔrik]; *~ acid* suolahappo.
~-electric vesivoima-. **-foil**; *~ [ship]*
kantosiipialus. **-gen** ['haidridʒ(ə)n] *s.*

vety; ~ *bomb* vetypommi; ~ *peroxide* vetysuperoksidi. **-graphy** [hai'drografi] hydrografia. **-pathic** [haidrə'pæθik] s. vesihoitolaitos. **-pathy** [hai'drɔpəθi] s. vesihoito. **-phobia** ['haidrə'fəubjə] s. vesikauhu. **-plane** ['haidrə(u)plein] s. vesitaso. **-xide** [hai'drɔksaid] s. hydroksidi.

hyena [hai(i)'i:nə] s. hyeena.

hygien|e [haidʒi:n] s. terveyssoppi, terveydenhoito. **-ic** [hai'dʒi:nik] a. hygieeninen, terveydenhoidollinen.

hymen ['haimen, -ən] s. immenkalvo.

hymn [him] s. virsi. **-al** [-nəl] a. virsi-; s. virsikirja.

hyper|- ['haipə(:)-] pref. hyper-, liika-, ylen. **-bola** [hai'pə:bələ] s. kartioleikkaus. **-bole** [-bəli] s. hyperbola, liioittelu. **-sensitive** a. yliherkkä. **-tension** s. verenpainetauti. **-trophy** [hai'pə:trɔfi] s. liikakasvu.

hyphen ['haif|n] s. yhdysmerkki; v. liittää yhdysmerkillä. **-ate** [-əneit] v. ks. ed.

hypno|sis [hip'nəusis] a. hypnoosi. **-tic** [hip'nɔtik] a. hypnoottinen. **-tism** ['hipnətizm] s. hypnotismi. **-tize** ['hipnətaiz] v. hypnotisoida.

hypochondria [haipə'kɔndriə] s. luulotauti. **-c** [-iæk] a. & s. luulotautinen.

hypo|crisy [hi'pɔkrisi] s. tekopyhyys, teeskentely. **-crite** ['hipəkrit] s. tekopyhä, ulkokultainen henkilö. **-critical** [hipə'kritik(ə)l] a. tekopyhä, ulkokultainen. **-dermic** [haipə'də:mik] a. ihonalainen; ~ *syringe* injektioruisku; s.: ~ [*injection*] pistos, injektio. **-thesis** [hai'pɔθisis] s. olettamus. **-thetic(al)** [haipə'θetik, -(ə)l] a. oletettu.

hyssop ['hisəp] s. iisoppi.

hyster|ectomy [histə'rektəmi] s. kohdunpoisto. **-ia** [his'tiəriə] s. hysteria. **-ical** [his'terik(ə)l] a. hysteerinen. **-ics** [his'teriks] s. hysteerinen kohtaus.

I

I, i [ai] s. i-kirjain.
Lyh.: **Ia.** Iowa; **ib, ibid** (ibidem) *in the same place* samassa paikassa, luvussa; **ICBM** *intercontinental ballistic missile;* **id.** (idem) sama (kuin edellä mainittu); **Id.** *Idaho;* **i.e.** (id est) *that is* se on, toisin sanoen, nimittäin; **Ill.** *Illinois;* **I.L.O.** *International Labour Organization;* **in.** *inch (es);* **Inc.** *Incorporated;* **incl.** *incuding, inclusive;* **incog.** *incognito;* **Ind.** *Indiana;* **inst.** *instant* tätä kuuta; **IOU** ['aiəu'ju:] (= *I owe you)* velkakirja; **I.Q.** *intelligence quotient;* **I.R.A.** *Irish Republican Army;* **I.T.A.** *Independent Television Authority.*

I [ai] *pers. pron.* minä.
iambic [ai'æmbik] *a.* jambi-; *s.* jambisäe.
Ian [iən] *erisn.*
ibex ['aibeks] *s.* alppikauris.
ibis ['aibis] *s.* iibis(lintu)
ice [ais] *s.* jää; jäätelö; *v.* peittää jäällä; jäätää, jäähdyttää; sokeroida, kuorruttaa; *cut no ~* jäädä tehottomaksi; *~ cube* jääkuutio; *I~ Age* jääkausi. **-berg** jäävuori. **-bound** jään saartama. **-box** Am. jääkaappi. **-breaker** jäänmurtaja. **-cap** jääkalotti. **~-cream** jäätelö. **-floe** jäälautta.
Iceland ['aislənd] *erisn.* Islanti. **-er** [-ə] *s.* islantilainen. **-ic** [ais'lændik] *a.* islantilainen; *s.* islannin kieli.
ice|-lolly jäätelöpuikko. **-pack** ahtojää; jääpussi.
icicle ['aisik] *s.* jääpuikko.
ic|ily ['aisili] *a.* jäätävän kylmästi. **-iness** *s.* jäinen kylmyys. **-ing** *s.* sokerikuorrutus; jäänmuodostus (lent.); (urh.) pitkä kiekko.
icon ['aikɔn] *s.* ikoni. **-oclast** [ai'kɔnəklæst] *s.* kuvainraastaja.
icy ['aisi] *a.* jäinen, jääkylmä, jäätävä.

Idaho ['aidəhəu] *erisn.*
idea [ai'diə] *s.* ajatus; aate, idea, käsite, (mieli)kuva; *what an ~!* mikä päähänpisto; *the ~ is to* tarkoituksena on; *I had no ~ that* ... en voinut aavistaakaan, että.
ideal [ai'diəl] *s.* ihanne; *a.* ihanteellinen, ihanne-. **-ism** [-izm] *s.* idealismi; ihanteellisuus. **-ist** [-ist] *s.* idealisti. **-istic** [-'listik] *a.* idealistinen. **-ization** [aidiəlai'zeiʃn] *s.* ihannointi. **-ize** [ai'diəlaiz] *v.* ihannoida, idealisoida.
identi|cal [ai'dentikl] *a.* identtinen, aivan sama. **-fication** [-fi'keiʃn] *s.* tunnistaminen. **-fy** [ai'dentifai] *v.* samastaa; tunnistaa; *~ oneself* todistaa henkilöllisyytensä; *~ oneself with* ruveta kannattamaan (esim. puoluetta). **-ty** [ai'dentiti] *s.* identtisyys; henkilöllisyys; *~ card* henkilöllisyystodistus; *~ disk* tuntolevy.
ideolog|ical [aidiə'lɔdʒik(ə)l] *a.* ideologinen. **-y** [aidi'ɔlədʒi] *s.* ideologia.
idiocy ['idiəsi] *s.* tylsämielisyys.
idiom ['idiəm] *s.* idiomi, (kielelle ominainen) ilmaisu. **-atic** [idiə'mætik] *a.* idiomaattinen.
idiosyncrasy [idiə'siŋkrəsi] *s.* idiosynkrasia.
idiot ['idiət] *s.* tylsämielinen; (puhek.) idiootti, pölkkypää. **-ic** [idi'ɔtik] *a.* tylsämielinen; järjetön, typerä.
idle ['aidl] *a.* laiska; toimeton, joutilas; hyödytön, turha, joutava; *v.* olla joutilaana, vetelehtiä; käydä tyhjäkäyntiä; *~ talk* joutava puhe; *~ away* kuluttaa hukkaan, hukata (aikaa). **-ness** *s.* laiskuus; toimettomuus; turhuus. **-r** [-ə] *s.* tyhjäntoimittaja.

idling tyhjä-, joutokäynti.
idly ['aidli] *adv.* joutilaana.
idol ['aidl] *s.* epäjumalankuva;
epäjumala. **-ater** [ai'dɔlətə] *s.*
epäjumalanpalvelija. **-atrous**
[ai'dɔlətrəs] *a.* epäjumalia palveleva.
-atry [ai'dɔlətri] *s.*
epäjumalanpalvelus.
idolize ['aidəlaiz] *s.* jumaloida, palvoa
epäjumalana.
idyll ['idil, 'aidil] *s.* idylli. **-ic** [i'dilik,
Am. ai'dil-] *a.* idyllinen.
if [if] *konj.* jos; -ko, -kö; *(she asked me
if..);* [*let me know*] *if* you can come
voitko tulla; ~ *only* kunpa; *as* ~
ikäänkuin.
igloo ['iglu:] *s.* (pl. ~*s*) eskimon
lumimaja.
ign|eous ['igniəs] *a.* tuli-; vulkaaninen;
-is fatuus virvatuli.
igni|te [ig'nait] *v.* sytyttää; syttyä. **-tion**
[ig'niʃn] *s.* sytytys, -laite; ~ *key*
virta-avain.
ignoble [ig'nəubl] *a.* halpamainen,
katala, alhainen.
ignomin|ious [ignə'miniəs] *a.*
häpeällinen. **-y** ['ignəmini] *s.*
(julkinen) häpeä, häpeällinen teko.
ignoramus [ignə'reiməs] *s.* oppimaton
ihminen, tolvana.
ignoran|ce ['ign(ə)r(ə)n|s] *s.*
tietämättömyys. **-t** [-t] *a.* tietämätön,
oppimaton.
ignore [ig'nɔ:] *v.* olla välittämättä,
jättää huomioon ottamatta.
ilex ['aileks] *s.* piikkipaatsama;
rautatammi.
I'll [ail] = *I will, I shall.*
ill [il] *a. (worse, worst)* sairas; huono;
adv. pahoin, huonosti; vaivoin,
tuskin; *s.* paha; haitta; *fall* ~, *be taken*
~ sairastua; *take* ... ~ panna
pahakseen; ~*s* onnettomuudet,
epäkohdat. ~**-advised** epäviisas.
~**-bred** huonosti kasvatettu,
epäkohtelias. ~**-breeding** huono
käytös, sivistymättömyys.
~**-considered** harkitsematon.
~**-defined** epämääräinen. ~**-disposed**
pahansuopa, epäsuopea.
illegal [i'li:g(ə)l] *a.* laiton. **-ity**
[ili(:)'gæliti] *s.* laittomuus.
illegib|le [i'ledʒəbl] *a.* mahdoton lukea.
-ly *adv.* niin, ettei voi lukea.

illegitim|acy [ili'dʒitiməsi] *s.*
laittomuus; avioton syntyperä. **-ate**
[-mit] *a.* laiton; avioton.
ill|fated huono-onninen. ~**-favoured**
ruma. ~**-gotten** vääryydellä hankittu.
~**-health** sairaus, huono terveys.
illiberal [i'lib(ə)rəl] *a.* kitsas;
ahdasmielinen, pikkumainen.
illicit [i'lisit] *a.* luvaton, laiton.
illimitable [i'limitəbl] *a.* rajoittamaton.
Illinois [ili'nɔi] *erisn.*
illiter|acy [i'lit(ə)rəsi] *a.*
lukutaidottomuus. **-ate** [-(ə)rit] *a. & s.*
oppimaton, lukutaidoton.
ill-mannered huonotapainen.
illness ['ilnis] *s.* sairaus.
illogical [i'lɔdʒik(ə)l] *a.* epälooginen.
ill|-starred onneton. ~**-tempered**
pahansisuinen. ~**-timed**
sopimattomaan aikaan sattuva.
~**-treat** kohdella huonosti. ~**-usage**
huono kohtelu.
illumin|ate [i'lu:min|eit] *v.* valaista;
valaista juhlavalaistuksella. **-ation**
[-'neiʃn] *s.* valaiseminen, valaistus;
juhlavalaistus; (käsikirjoituksen)
väritys. **-e** *v.* valaista, valistaa.
illu|sion [i'lu:|ʒn] *s.* aistiharhadus;
kuvitelma, harhakuva; *optical* ~
näköharha. **-sionist** *s.* silmänkääntäjä.
-sive [-siv], **-sory** [-s(ə)ri] *a.* pettävä,
petollinen.
illustr|ate ['iləstreit] *v.* valaista,
kuvittaa. **-ation** [-'treiʃn] *s.*
valaiseminen, (valaiseva) esimerkki;
kuva; ~*s* kuvitus. **-ative** [-iv] *a.:* ~ *of*
jtk valaiseva. **-ator** [-ə] *s.* kuvittaja.
-ious [i'lʌstriəs] *a.* loistava,
maineikas, kuuluisa.
ill-will *s.* pahansuopuus.
I'm [aim] = *I am.*
image ['imidʒ] *s.* kuva; kielikuva; *v.*
kuvata, kuvastaa. **-ry** [-(ə)ri] *s.* kuvat,
veistokset; kuvakieli, -rikkaus.
imagina|ble [i'mædʒ|(i)nəbl] *a.*
kuviteltavissa oleva. **-ry** [-in(ə)ri] *a.*
kuviteltu; mielikuvitus-, haave-. **-tion**
[-i'neiʃn] *s.* mielikuvitus, kuvitelma.
-tive [-(i)nətiv] *a.*
mielikuvituksellinen; ~ *power*
mielikuvitus.
imagine [i'mædʒin] *v.* kuvitella; luulla.
imbalance ['im'bæləns] *s.* tasapainon
puute, epätasapaino.

imbecil|| ['imbisi:l] *a. & s.*
vähämielinen. **-ity** [-'siliti] *s.*
vähämielisyys.

imbibe [im'baib] *v.* imeä itseensä,
juoda.

imbricate ['imbrikeit] *v.* asettaa
limittäin.

imbroglio [im'brəuliəu] *s.* sekasotku.

imbrue [im'bru:] *v.* tahrata.

imbue [im'bju:] *v.* kyllästää,
läpivärjätä; (kuv. m.) täyttää,
innoittaa.

imita|te ['imiteit] *v.* jäljitellä, matkia.
-tion [-'teiʃn] *s.* jäljittely, jäljitelmä;
~ *pearl* tekohelmi. **-tive** ['imitətiv] *a.*
jäljittelevä, jäljittely-. **-tor** [-ə] *s.*
matkija.

immaculate [i'mækjulit] *a.* tahraton,
puhdas; moitteeton.

immanen|ce ['imənəns] *s.* (Jumalan)
läsnäolo. **-t** [-ənt] *a.* sisäinen;
läsnäoleva.

immaterial [imə'tiəriəl] *a.* aineeton;
epäolennainen.

immatur|e [imə'tjuə] *a.* kypsymätön,
epäkypsä. **-ity** [-riti] *s.*
kypsymättömyys.

immeasurable [i'meʒ(ə)rəbl] *a.*
mittaamaton; ääretön.

immediacy [i'mi:djəsi] *s.* välitön
läheisyys, pikaisuus.

immediate [i'mi:djət] *a.* välitön, lähin;
heti tapahtuva, pikainen. **-ly** *adv.*
välittömästi; heti, viipymättä.

immemorial [imi'mɔ:riəl] *a.*
ikimuistoinen, ikivanha.

immens|e [i'mens] *a.* ääretön,
suunnattoman suuri, valtava; ~*ly*
äärettömän. **-ity** [-iti] *s.* äärettömyys,
suunnaton suuruus.

immer|se [i'mə:s] *v.* upottaa, kastaa
upottamalla; ~*d in thought* ajatuksiin
vaipunut. **-sion** [-ə:ʃn] *s.* upottaminen,
upotuskaste.

immigra|nt ['imigr(ə)nt] *s.*
maahanmuuttaja, siirtolainen. **-te**
[-eit] *v.* muuttaa (jhk maahan). **-tion**
[-'greiʃn] *s.* maahanmuutto.

imminen|ce ['iminəns] *s.* uhkaavuus,
uhka, läheisyys **-t** [-ənt] *a.* uhkaava,
lähellä oleva.

immitigable [i'mitigəbl] *a.* leppymätön.

immobil|e [i'məubail] *a.* liikkumaton.
-ity [imə(u)'biliti] *s.*

liikkumattomuus. **-ize** [i'məubilaiz] *v.*
immobilisoida, tehdä
liikkumattomaksi.

immodera|te [i'mɔd(ə)rit] *a.*
kohtuuton. **-tion** [-'reiʃn] *s.*
kohtuuttomuus.

immodest [i'mɔdist] *a.* säädytön;
julkea. **-y** [-i] *s.* säädyttömyys;
julkeus.

immola|te ['imə(u)leit] *v.* uhrata. **-tion**
[-'leiʃn] *s.* uhraaminen, (teuras)uhri.

immoral [i'mɔr(ə)l] *a.* moraaliton,
siveetön. **-ity** [-'ræliti] *s.* siveettömyys.

immortal [i'mɔ:tl] *a. & s.* kuolematon.
-ity [-'tæliti] *s.* kuolemattomuus. **-ize**
[-təlaiz] *v.* tehdä kuolemattomaksi,
ikuistaa.

immovable [i'mu:vəbl] *a.* liikkumaton;
järkähtämätön; kiinteä; ~*s* kiinteä
omaisuus.

immun|e [i'mju:n] *a.* immuuni, ei altis
jllek. **-ity** [-iti] *s.* immuniteetti *(to
from)*; vapaus *(from* jstk). **-ize**
['imjunaiz] *v.* immunisoida.

immure [i'mjuə] *v.* teljetä.

immutable [i'mju:təbl] *a.*
muuttumaton.

imp [imp] *s.* pikkupaholainen; vallaton
lapsi.

impact ['impækt] *s.* isku, sysäys;
törmäys, vaikutus; *v.* [im'pækt]
painaa sisään.

impair [im'pɛə] *v.* huonontaa,
heikentää. **-ment** *s.* huonontuminen,
heikkeneminen, vika.

impale [im'peil] *v.* seivästää.

impalpable [im'pælpəbl] *a.* tuskin
huomattava.

impart [im'pɑ:t] *v.* antaa, suoda;
ilmoittaa.

impartial [im'pɑ:ʃl] *a.* puolueeton. **-ity**
['impɑ:ʃi'æliti] *s.* puolueettomuus.

impassable [im'pɑ:səbl] *a.* mahdoton
kulkea, tietön.

impasse [im'pɑ:s, 'æmpɑ:s, Am.
'impæs] *s.* umpikuja.

impassioned [im'pæʃ(ə)nd] *a.*
intohimoinen, kiihkeä.

impassive [im'pæsiv] *a.* tunteeton,
välinpitämätön.

impatien|ce [im'peiʃ(ə)ns] *s.*
kärsimättömyys. **-t** [-(ə)nt] *a.*
kärsimätön; ~ *(to + inf.)* kärkäs,
innokas; (~*ly adv.* kärsimättömästi).

impeach [im'pi:tʃ] v. asettaa
kyseenalaiseksi; panna syytteeseen
(valtiorikoksesta ym). **-ment** s. syyte,
syytteeseen asettaminen.

impeccable [im'pekəbl] a. synnitön,
virheetön; *i-bly* moitteettomasti.

impecunious [impi'kju:njəs] a.
rahaton, puutteenalainen.

imped|e [im'pi:d] v. estää, ehkäistä.
-iment [im'pedimənt] s. este; (~ *in
one's speech*) puhevika.

impel [im'pel] v. ajaa, pakottaa (jhk).

impend [im'pend] v. riippua (jnk yllä);
olla tulossa, uhata; ~*ing* uhkaava.

impenetrable [im'penitrəbl] a.
läpi|tunkematon, -pääsemätön;
tutkimaton.

impeniten|ce [im'penit(ə)ns] s.
katumattomuus, paatumus. **-t** [-nt] a.
katumaton.

imperative [im'perətiv] a. käskevä;
pakottava, (ehdottoman)
välttämätön; s. imperatiivi.

imperceptible [impə'septəbl] a.
huomaamaton.

imperfect [im'pə:fikt] a.
epätäydellinen, vaillinainen,
puutteellinen; s. imperfekti. **-ion**
[-'fekʃn] s. epätäydellisyys,
puutteellisuus.

imperforate [im'pə:f(ə)rit] a. ehyt,
puhkaisematon.

imperial [im'piəriəl] a. brittiläisen
imperiumin, (mitoista) Englannin;
keisarillinen, keisarin; s. pieni
pujoparta. **-ism** [-izm] s. imperialismi.
-ist [-ist] s. imperialisti. **-istic** [-'listik]
a. imperialistinen.

imperil [im'peril] v. vaarantaa.

imperious [im'piəriəs] a. käskevä,
kopea; pakottava.

im|perishable [im'periʃəbl] a.
katoamaton. **-permanent** a.
kestämätön. **-permeable** [-'pə:miəbl]
a. läpäisemätön.

impersona|l [im'pə:sənl] a.
persoonaton, epäpersoonallinen. **-te**
[-neit] v. olennoida; näytellä, esittää
(osaa). **-tion** [-'neiʃn] s. (osan)
tulkitseminen, toisena esiintyminen.
-tor [-neitə] s. matkija.

impertinen|ce [im'pə:tinəns] s.
nenäkkyys, hävyttömyys;
asiaankuulumattomuus. **-t** [-ənt] a.

nenäkäs, hävytön; asiaankuulumaton,
sopimaton.

imperturbable [impə'tə:bəbl] a.
järkkymättömän levollinen;
järkähtämätön.

impervious [im'pə:vjəs] a.: ~ *to* jtk
läpäisemätön; ~ *to reason* kuuro
järjen äänelle.

impetu|osity [impetju'ositi] s. kiivaus.
-ous [im'petjuəs] a. kiivas, kiihkeä;
raju.

impetus ['impitəs] s. liike-,
käyttövoima; sysäys, yllyke.

impiety [im'paiəti] s. jumalattomuus;
kunnioituksen puute.

impinge [im'pin(d)ʒ] v.: ~ *[up] on*
iskeä, törmätä jhk, loukata jtk.

impious ['impiəs] a. jumalaton.

impish ['impiʃ] a. vekkulimainen.

implaca|bility [implækə'biliti] s.
leppymättömyys. **-ble** [im'plækəbl] a.
leppymätön.

implant [im'pla:nt] v. juurruttaa
(mieleen); (lääk.) istuttaa (kudosta);
s. ['--] siirrännäinen.

implement ['implimənt] s. työkalu,
väline; v. [-ment] panna täytäntöön,
toteuttaa; *agricultural* ~s
maanviljelyskalut.

implica|te ['implikeit] v. kietoa,
sotkea; ~*ed in a crime* sekaantunut
rikokseen. **-tion** [-'keiʃn] s.
sekaantuminen; (epäsuora) sisältö,
seuraamus; *by* ~ epäsuorasti.

implicit [im'plisit] a. jhk sisältyvä;
ehdoton, sokea (usko ym).

implied [im'plaid] pp. jhk sisältyvä (ei
erityisesti mainittu); *an* ~ *rebuke*
epäsuora (sanoihin kätketty) moite;
vrt. *imply.*

implore [im'plɔ:] v. hartaasti pyytää,
rukoilla.

imply [im'plai] v. sisältää, merkitä,
tarkoittaa, edellyttää; vihjata; *was he
~ing that.. ?* antoiko hän ymmärtää,
että.. ?

im|polite [impə'lait] a. epäkohtelias.
-politic [im'pɔlitik] a. epäviisas.
-ponderable [-'pɔndərəbl] a.
mahdoton punnita t. arvioida; s.: ~s
laskemattomat seikat, tekijät.

import [im'pɔ:t] v. tuoda, tuottaa
maahan; merkitä, tarkoittaa; s.
['impɔ:t] (maahan)tuonti,

tuontitavarat (us. *pl.);* merkitys, tarkoitus; tärkeys. **-ance** [-(ə)ns] *s.* tärkeys, merkitys; .. *of great ~* hyvin tärkeä. **-ant** [-(ə)nt] *a.* tärkeä, merkityksellinen. **-ation** [-'teiʃn] *s.* maahantuonti. **-er** [-ə] *s.* maahantuoja.

importunate [im'pɔ:tjunit] *a.* itsepintainen, hellittämätön, pakottava.

importun|e [im'pɔ:tju:n] *v.* pyynnöillä ahdistaa, kärttää; tungetella. **-ity** [-'tju:niti] *s.* tungettelevuus.

impos|e [im'pəuz] *v.* määrätä; ~ *oneself (one's company) on* tunkeutua, tuppautua jkn seuraan; ~ *a tax on* määrätä vero jllek; ~ *[up] on* petkuttaa, käyttää hyväkseen jtk. **-ing** *a.* mahtava, upea, valtava. **-ition** [impə'ziʃn] *s.* määrääminen; vero; rangaistustehtävä; petkutus, petos; ~ *of hands* kättenpäällepaneminen.

impossi|bility [impɔsə'biliti] *s.* mahdottomuus. **-ble** [im'pɔsəbl] *a.* mahdoton.

impost|or [im'pɔstə] *s.* petkuttaja. **-ure** [-'pɔstʃə] *s.* petkutus, petos.

impoten|ce [im'pɔt(ə)ns] *s.* voimattomuus; kykenemättömyys. **-t** [-(ə)nt] *a.* voimaton; kykenemätön, impotentti.

impound [im'paund] *v.* takavarikoida; (vanh.) teljetä aitaukseen.

impoverish [im'pɔv(ə)riʃ] *v.* köyhdyttää.

impracticable [im'præktikəbl] *a.* mahdoton toteuttaa, käytännössä mahdoton; kulkukelvoton, mahdoton kulkea.

impreca|te [im'prikeit] *v.* kirota. **-tion** [-'keiʃn] *s.* kirous.

impregnable [im'pregnəbl] *a.* valloittamaton; järkähtämätön.

impregnat|e ['impregneit] *v.* hedelmöittää; impregnoida, kyllästää; täyttää. **-ion** [-'neiʃn] *s.* hedelmöitys, kyllästäminen.

impresario [impre'saːriəu] *s.* impressaari.

impress [im'pres] *v.* painaa, leimata; juurruttaa, painaa *(on a p.* jkn mieleen); tehdä (syvä) vaikutus, tehota; pestata väkisin; *s.* ['impres] leima, merkki, jälki; *I was much ~ed*

by it se teki minuun syvän vaikutuksen; *the plan ~ed me unfavourably* suunnitelma vaikutti minusta huonolta.

impression [im'preʃn] *s.* (muuttamaton) painos; (painamalla syntynyt) jälki; vaikutus, vaikutelma, kuva; *I was under the ~ that* minulla oli se käsitys, että .. **-able** [-əbl] *a.* vaikutuksille altis. **-istic** [-ʃə'nistik] *a.* impressionistinen.

impressive [im'presiv] *a.* vaikuttava, tehoava, näyttävä.

imprint [im'print] *v.* painaa (merkki jhk); leimata; *s.* ['imprint] leima, jälki; (kustantajan) nimi ja painopaikka.

imprison [im'prizn] *v.* panna vankilaan, vangita. **-ment** *s.* vangitseminen; vankeus.

improb|ability [imprɔbə'biliti] *s.* epätodennäköisyys. **-able** [-'prɔbəbl] *a.* epätodennäköinen. **-ity** [-'prəubiti] *s.* epärehellisyys.

impromptu [im'prɔm(p)tju:] *adv. & a.* valmista|matta, -maton; *s.* improvisaatio.

improp|er [im'prɔpə] *a.* sopimaton; säädytön; väärä; ~ *fraction* epämurtoluku. **-riety** [-prə'praiəti] *s.* sopimattomuus; säädyttömyys.

improve [im'pru:v] *v.* parantaa, kohentaa; parantua, edistyä; ~ *the occasion* käyttää hyväkseen tilaisuutta; ~ *[up]on* parannella, kohentaa; *he ~s on acquaintance* hänestä saa edullisemman käsityksen kun tutustuu lähemmin; ~ *in looks* kaunistua. **-ment** *s.* parannus, paraneminen; edistys(askel).

improviden|ce [im'prɔvid(ə)ns] *s.* varomattomuus, tuhlaavaisuus. **-t** [-(ə)nt] *a.* varomaton, harkitsematon.

improvisation [imprɔvai'zeiʃn] *s.* improvisointi.

improvise ['imprəvaiz] *v.* valmistelematta sepittää t. esittää, improvisoida.

imprudent [im'pru:d(ə)nt] *a.* varomaton; epäviisas.

impuden|ce ['impjud(ə)ns] *s.* häpeämättömyys; röyhkeys. **-t** [-(ə)nt] *a.* häpeämätön, hävytön; röyhkeä, julkea.

impugn [im′pju:n] v. väittää jtk
vastaan, vastustaa, kiistää.
impulse [′impʌls] s. (alku)sysäys,
kiihoke, heräte; mielijohde; *act on* ~
toimia hetken mielijohteesta. **-sion**
[-′pʌlʃn] s. sysäys, yllyke. **-sive**
[-′pʌlsiv] a. impulsiivinen.
impunity [im′pju:niti] s.: *with* ~
rankaisematta.
impure [im′pjuə] a. epäpuhdas,
likainen. **-ity** [-riti] s. epäpuhtaus.
imputation [impju(:)′teiʃn] s. syyksi
lukeminen, syytös.
impute [im′pju:t] v.: ~ *to* lukea, sanoa
jkn syyksi.
in [in] prep. ilman. p a i k k a a: -ssa,
-ssä, -lla, -llä; ilm. m. a i k a a,
t a p a a, m i t t a a, l u k u a ym;
adv. sisään, sisällä, kotona, perillä; ~
the street kadulla ~ *London*
Lontoossa; [*I read about it*] ~ *The
Times* luin sen Timesistä; ~ *my
opinion* minun mielestäni; [*write*] ~
ink musteella; *he is blind* ~ *one eye*
hänen toinen silmänsä on sokea; ~
ten minutes kymmenen minuutin
kuluttua; ~ [*the year*] 1940 vuonna
1940; ~ *summer* kesällä; ~ *doing
this* tehdessäni (-si jne) näin; ~
haste kiireessä; ~ *English*
englannin kielellä; *one* ~ *ten* yksi
kymmenestä; 70 ~ *number*
lukumäärältään 70; *tall* ~ *stature*
kookas kasvultaan; ~ *memory of* jkn
muistoksi; ~ *order to* jotta, ks. order;
~ *reply to* vastaukseksi jhk; *the train is*
~ *juna on saapunut; the Liberals are*
~ liberaalinen puolue on vallassa; [*it
is*] *very much* »*in*» kovasti muodissa;
be in on olla selvillä jstk; *be* ~ *with sb.*
olla hyvissä väleissä jkn kanssa; ~ *so
far as* sikäli kuin; ~ *that* . . koska; *he
is* ~ *for it* hän joutuu lujille; *we are* ~
for a storm myrsky on tulossa; *ins and
outs* mutkat, yksityiskohdat.
in- (+adj.) epä-, -ton, -tön.
inability [inə′biliti] s.
kykenemättömyys.
inaccessibility [′inæksesə′biliti] s.
luoksepääsemättömyys jne. **-ble**
[inæk′sesəbl] a. luoksepääsemätön
(m. kuv.).
inaccuracy [in′ækjurəsi] s.
epätarkkuus; virheellisyys. **-te** [-it] a.

epätarkka; virheellinen.
inaction [in′ækʃn] s. toimettomuus.
-tive [-tiv] a. toimeton, joutilas,
veltto; laimea. **-tivity** [-′tiviti] s.
toimettomuus jne.
inadequacy [in′ædikwəsi] s.
riittämättömyys, puutteellisuus. **-ate**
[-wit] a. riittämätön, puutteellinen.
inadmissible [inəd′misəbl] a. mahdoton
sallia t. hyväksyä.
inadvertence [inəd′və:t(ə)ns] s.
huomaamattomuus, epähuomio. **-t**
[-(ə)nt] a. huomaamaton;
huolimaton; ~ *ly* epähuomiossa,
huomaamattaan, vahingossa.
inadvisable [inəd′vaizəbl] a. epäviisas.
inalienable [in′eiljənəbl] a.
luovuttamaton.
inane [i′nein] a. tyhjä, sisällyksetön,
mieletön.
inanimate [in′ænimit] a. eloton,
hengetön.
inanition [inə′niʃn] s. tyhjyys; (nälästä
johtuva) voimattomuus. **-ty** [in′æniti]
s. tyhjyys; typeryys.
inapplicable [in′æplikəbl] a.
(käytettäväksi) soveltumaton.
inappreciable [inə′pri:ʃəbl] a.
mitättömän pieni. **-appropriate**
[-ə′prəupriit] a. epäasianmukainen,
sopimaton.
inapt [i′næpt] a. kelpaamaton,
sopimaton, asiaankuulumaton;
taitamaton. **-itude** [-itju:d] s.
sopimattomuus.
inarticulate [ina:′tikjulit] a.
epäselvä(sti äännetty); sanaton,
mykkä; niveletön.
inartistic a. epätaiteellinen.
inasmuch [inəz′mʌtʃ] adv.: ~ *as* koska.
inattention [inə′tenʃn] s.
tarkkaamattomuus, tarkkaavaisuuden
puute. **-tive** [-tiv] a. tarkkaamaton,
huomaamaton.
inaudible [in′ɔ:dəbl] a. kuulumaton,
mahdoton kuulla.
inaugural [i′nɔ:gjur(ə)l] a.
virkaanasettajais-, avajais-; ~ *lecture*
virkaanastujaisesitelmä. **-ate** [-eit] v.
asettaa virkaan, vihkiä, avata. **-ation**
[-′reiʃn] s. vihkiminen
inauspicious [inɔ:s′piʃəs] a. onneton,
pahaenteinen.
inborn [′in′bɔ:n] a. synnynnäinen.

in|bred ['in'bred] *a.* synnynnäinen, luontainen. **-breeding** [-'bri:diŋ] *s.* sukusiitos.

incalculable [in'kælkjuləbl] *a.* mahdoton laskea, arvaamaton, lukematon.

incandescen|ce [inkæn'desns] *s.* hehkumistila. **-t** [-nt] *a.* valkohehkuinen, hehkuva; ~ *lamp* hehkulamppu.

incantation [inkæn'teiʃn] *s.* loitsu(sanat).

in|capability [inkeipə'biliti] *s.* kykenemättömyys. **-capable** [-'keipəbl] *a.* kykenemätön, kelpaamaton *(of* jhk).

incapaci|tate [inkə'pæsiteit] *v.* tehdä kykenemättömäksi t. kelpaamattomaksi *(for, from* jhk); ~*d* työkyvytön; esteellinen. **-ty** [-iti] *s.* kykenemättömyys *(for* jhk); esteellisyys.

incarcerate [in'kɑ:səreit] *v.* panna vankilaan.

incarna|te [in'kɑ:nit] *a.* lihaksi tullut, ruumiillistunut; *v.* ['inkɑ:neit] ruumiillistaa. **-tion** [-'neiʃn] *s.* lihaksi tuleminen.

incautious [in'kɔ:ʃəs] *a.* varomaton.

incendia|rism [in'sendjərizm] *s.* tuhopoltto. **-ry** [-əri] *a.* palo-; *s.* tuhopolttaja, pyromaani; kiihottaja, yllyttäjä; ~ *bomb* palopommi.

incense ['insens] *s.* suitsutus; *v.* [in'sens] suututtaa, raivostuttaa; ~*d* raivostunut.

in|centive [in'sentiv] *a.* kiihottava, kannustava; *s.* kannustin, yllyke. **-ception** [-'sepʃn] *s.* alku.

incertitude [in'sə:titju:d] *s.* epävarmuus.

incessant [in'sesnt] *a.* lakkaamaton.

incest ['insest] *s.* sukurutsaus. **-uous** [-'sestjuəs] *a.* sukurutsainen.

inch [in(t)ʃ] *s.* tuuma; *by* ~*es* tuuma tuumalta, vähitellen; *within an* ~ *of one's life* melkein hengiltä; *every* ~ kauttaaltaan.

inchoate ['inkə(u)eit] *a.* juuri alettu, epätäydellinen.

incidence ['insid(ə)ns] *s.* kohtaaminen; (taudin ym) esiintymistiheys; *angle of* ~ tulokulma; *the* ~ [*of a tax*]

jakautuminen.

incident ['insid(ə)nt] *s.* tapahtuma, tapaus (us. pol. ym, salassa pidettävä); välikohtaus; ~ *to* ks. *incidental to.* **-al** [-'dentl] *a.* satunnainen; *s.:* ~*s* satunnaiset (meno)erät; ~ *to* jhk kuuluva, liittyvä; ~ *music* näytelmämusiikki. **-ally** *adv.* sattumalta; ohimennen sanoen.

incinerat|e [in'sinəreit] *v.* polttaa tuhaksi. **-or** [-ə] *s.* jätteiden polttouuni.

incipient [in'sipiənt] *a.* alkava, alkuasteella oleva.

incis|e [in'saiz] *v.* viiltää, leikata. **-ion** [-'siʒn] *s.* viilto, leikkaus, haava. **-ive** [-siv] *a.* terävä, pureva. **-or** [-ə] *s.* etuhammas.

incite [in'sait] *v.* kiihottaa, yllyttää, kannustaa. **-ment** *s.* yllyke, kannustin.

incivility [insi'viliti] *s.* epäkohteliaisuus.

inclement [in'klemənt] *a.* ankara, kolea (sää).

inclination [inkli'neiʃn] *s.* kaltevuus(kulma); taipumus *(to* jhk), halu, mieltymys; ~ [*of the head*] nyökkäys.

incline [in'klain] *v.* taivuttaa, tehdä halukkaaksi; olla taipuvainen, halukas; kallistua, taipua; *s.* rinne; ~*d to* taipuvainen, halukas jhk; ~*d plane* kalteva pinta.

includ|e [in'klu:d] *v.* käsittää, sisältää; sisällyttää, laskea mukaan; *is this* ~*d in the price?* kuuluuko tämä hintaan? *postage* ~*d* postimaksu mukaanluettuna. **-ing** *ppr.* sisältäen, mukaan lukien.

inclu|sion [in'klu:ʒn] *s.* mukaan lukeminen. **-sive** [-siv] *a.:* ~ [*of*] sisältäen, jk mukaan luettuna; ~ *terms* (hotellissa) määrähinta (johon sisältyy kaikki); [*all-*] ~ *tour* valmismatka.

incognito [in'kɔgnitəu] *adv.* (*& a.*) tuntemattomana, salanimellä.

incoheren|ce [inkə(u)'hiər(ə)ns] *s.* yhtenäisyyden puute, hajanaisuus. **-t** [-nt] *a.* hajanainen; sekava.

incombustible [inkəm'bʌstəbl] *a.* palamaton.

incom|e ['inkəm] *s.* tulot, tulo; ~*-tax*

return veroilmoitus. **-ing** a. saapuva, virkaan astuva; ~ **tide** nousuvesi.

incommensurate [inkə'menʃ(ə)rit] a. ei verrannollinen, suhteeton.

incommod|e [inkə'məud] v. vaivata, olla vastukseksi. **-ious** [-jəs] a. epämukava, hankala.

incomparable [in'kɔmp(ə)rəbl] a. jota ei voida verrata (to, with jhk); verraton.

incompati|bility ['inkəmpætə'biliti] s. yhteen sopimattomuus. **-ble** [inkəm'pætəbl] a. yhteen sopimaton, ristiriitainen.

incompeten|ce, -cy [in'kɔmpit(ə)ns, -i] s. epäpätevyys. **-t** [-nt] a. epäpätevä; kelpaamaton.

in|complete [inkəm'pli:t] a. epätäydellinen, vaillinainen. **-comprehensible** [-kɔmpri'hensəbl] a. käsittämätön. **-conceivable** [-kən'si:vəbl] a. ei ajateltavissa oleva, uskomaton. **-conclusive** [-kən'klu:siv] a. ei vakuuttava, ei sitova.

incongru|ity [inkɔŋ'gru(:)iti] s. epäsuhta. **-ous** [-'kɔŋgruəs] a. yhteen sopimaton, jhk sopimaton.

inconsequen|ce [in'kɔnsikwəns] s. epäjohdonmukaisuus. **-t** [-ənt] a. epälooginen. **-tial** a. vähäpätöinen, merkityksetön.

inconsidera|ble [inkən'sid(ə)rəbl] a. vähäpätöinen, mitätön. **-te** [-it] a. epähieno, tahditon; ajattelematon, harkitsematon.

inconsisten|cy [inkən'sist(ə)nsi] s. yhteensoveltumattomuus, ristiriitaisuus; epäjohdonmukaisuus. **-t** [-nt] a. epäjohdonmukainen; yhteensopimaton, ristiriitainen; vaihteleva.

in|consolable [inkən'səuləbl] a. lohduton. **-conspicuous** [-kən'spikjuəs] a. huomaamaton. **-constancy** [-'kɔnst(ə)nsi] s. epävakaisuus. **-constant** [-'kɔnst(ə)nt] a. epävakainen, häilyvä, huikenteleva. **-contestable** [-kən'testəbl] a. kiistaton, eittämätön.

in|continence [in'kɔntinəns] s. kohtuuttomuus; (virtsan) pidätyskyvyttömyys. **-continent** [-'kɔntinənt] a. hillitön, kohtuuton; pidätyskyvytön. **-controvertible**

[inkɔntrə'və:təbl] a. eittämätön, kieltämätön.

inconvenien|ce [inkən'vi:njəns] s. epämukavuus, haitta; v. olla vaivaksi, haitaksi, vaivata. **-t** [-ənt] a. epämukava, hankala.

incorpora|te [in'kɔ:pəreit] v. sisällyttää, liittää kokonaisuudeksi; perustaa, rekisteröidä; liittyä. **-tion** [-'reiʃn] s. yhdistäminen, liitto.

in|correct [inkə'rekt] a. virheellinen, väärä. **-corrigible** [-'kɔridʒəbl] a. parantumaton. **-corruptible** [-kə'rʌptəbl] a. lahjomaton, katoamaton.

increas|e [in'kri:s] v. kasvaa, lisääntyä, kohota, enetä; lisätä, kartuttaa; s. ['inkri:s] lisääntyminen, lisäys, nousu; on the ~ lisääntymässä; **-ingly** yhä enemmän.

incred|ible [in'kredəbl] a. uskomaton; **-ibly** uskomattoman. **-ulity** [inkri'dju:liti] s. epäusko, vähäuskoisuus. **-ulous** [-'kredjuləs] a. epäuskoinen, epäilevä.

increment ['inkrimənt] s. kasvu, lisäys, arvonnousu (unearned ~).

incriminate [in'krimineit] v. syyttää (rikoksesta); be ~d joutua osasyyllisen asemaan.

incrustation [inkrʌs'teiʃn] s. kuori, päällystys, vrt. encrust.

incubat|e [in'kjubeit] v. hautoa. **-ion** [-'beiʃn] s. (munien) haudonta; (taudin) itäminen. **-or** [-ə] s. hautomakone; keskoskaappi.

incubus ['iŋkjubəs] s. painajainen.

inculcate ['inkʌlkeit] v. teroittaa (mieleen).

inculpate ['inkʌlpeit] v. syyttää.

incumb|ency [in'kʌmbənsi] s. kirkollinen virka. **-ent** [-ənt] s. kirkollisen viran haltija; a.: ~ on jkn velvollisuutena (oleva).

incur [in'kə:] v. hankkia itselleen, saada osakseen; ~ debts velkaantua; ~ punishment joutua rangaistavaksi.

incurable [in'kjuərəbl] a. parantumaton.

incurious [in'kjuəriəs] a. välinpitämätön.

incursion [in'kə:ʃn] s. maahanhyökkäys.

indebted [in'detid] a, velkaa, velassa;

kiitollisuudenvelassa *(to* jklle); *I am ~
to him for giving me* .. saan kiittää
häntä siitä, että hän antoi minulle ..
-ness *s.* kiitollisuudenvelka.

indec|ency [in'di:snsi] *s.* säädyttömyys.
-ent [-nt] *a.* säädytön, sopimaton,
rivo.

indecipherable [indi'saif(ə)rəbl] *a.*
mahdoton lukea t. selvittää.

indecis|ion [indi'siʒn] *s.* epäröinti. **-ive**
[-di'saisiv] *a.* ei ratkaiseva; epäröivä,
neuvoton, horjuva.

indecor|ous [in'dekərəs] *a.* sopimaton.
-um [indi'kɔ:rəm] *a.* sopimaton
käytös t. esiintyminen.

indeed [in'di:d] *adv.* todella(kin),
tosiaan; *int.* todellako? vai niin! *very
good ~* erittäin hyvä; *yes, ~* onpa
tosiaankin!

in|defatigable [indi'fætigəbl] *a.*
väsymätön. **-defensible** [-di'fensəbl]
a. mahdoton puolustaa;
anteeksiantamaton. **-definable**
[-di'fainəbl] *a.* määrittelemätön,
epämääräinen. **-definite** [-'definit] *a.*
epämääräinen; *~ article* e. artikkeli.
-delible [-'delibl] *a.* häviämätön,
lähtemätön.

indelic|acy [in'delikəsi] *s.*
tahdittomuus, epähienous. **-ate** [-it] *a.*
tahditon, epähieno.

indemni|fication [indemnifi'keiʃn] *s.*
korvaus. **-fy** [in'demnifai] *v.* turvata
tappiolta; korvata, hyvittää. **-ty**
[-'demniti] *s.* (vahingon)korvaus,
sotakorvaus.

indent [in'dent] *v.* hammastaa, tehdä
pykäläiseksi, uurtaa; (kirjap.)
sisentää (rivi); tilata (tavaraa) anoa
(for); s. ['- -] pykälä, lovi;
tavaratilaus. **-ation** [-'teiʃn] *s.*
hammastus, pykälä, lovi. **-ure** [-ʃə] *s.*
(m. *pl.*) oppisopimus; *v.* panna jhk
oppiin.

independ|ence [indi'pendəns] *s.*
riippumattomuus, itsenäisyys. **-ent**
[-ənt] *a.* riippumaton *(of* jstk),
itsenäinen; *s.* (puolueista)
riippumaton (parlamentin jäsen ym),
»villi»; *newly ~* vastaitsenäistynyt.

indescribable [indis'kraibəbl] *a.* sanoin
kuvaamaton, sanomaton.

indestructible [indis'trʌktəbl] *a.*
mahdoton hävittää.

indetermina|te [indi'tə:m(i)nit] *a.*
epämääräinen; epäröivä, horjuva.
-tion [-i'neiʃn] *s.* häilyvyys, epäröinti.

index ['indeks] *s.* (pl. *~es* t. *indices*
['indisi:z]) etusormi; osoitin;
aakkosellinen luettelo, hakemisto
(kirjan lopussa); indeksi; *v.* varustaa
aakkosellisella luettelolla t.
hakemistolla; *card ~* kortisto;
~-linked indeksiin sidottu.

India ['indjə] *erisn.* Intia; *~ paper* ohut
(raamattu- t. lentopainos)paperi.
-man Itä-Intian laiva.

Indian ['indjən] *s.* intialainen; *a.*
intialainen, intiaani-; *[Red] ~*
intiaani; *~ corn* maissi; *~ file*
hanhenmarssi; *~ ink* tussi; *~ summer*
jälkikesä. **-a** [indi'ænə] *erisn.*

india-rubber *s.* kumi.

indicat|e ['indikeit] *v.* osoittaa,
näyttää, viitata, ilmaista. **-ion**
[-'keiʃn] *s.* osoitus, ilmaus, indikaatio,
oire (joka tekee jnk hoidon
aiheelliseksi). **-ive** [in'dikativ] *a.: ~ of*
jtk osoittava, jhk viittaava; *s.*
indikatiivi. **-or** [-ə] *s.* osoitin, ilmaisin;
(autossa) suuntaviitta, vilkku.

indict [in'dait] *v.* panna syytteeseen.
-ment *s.* syyte, kanne.

Indies ['indiz] *erisn.* ks. *East, West ~*.

indifferen|ce [in'difr(ə)ns] *s.*
välinpitämättömyys; yhdentekevyys.
-t [-nt] *a.* välinpitämätön;
yhdentekevä; puolueeton;
keskinkertainen.

indigence ['indidʒ(ə)ns] *s.* köyhyys.

indigenous [in'didʒinəs] *a.*
syntyperäinen, kotimainen; *~ to* jhk
luonnostaan kuuluva.

indigent ['indidʒ(ə)nt] *a.*
puutteenalainen, köyhä.

indigesti|ble [indi'dʒestəbl] *a.* vaikeasti
sulava. **-tion** [-'dʒestʃn] *s.* huono
ruoansulatus, ruoansulatushäiriö.

indign|ant [in'dignənt] *a.* suuttunut,
närkästynyt. **-ation** [-'neiʃn] *s.*
suuttumus, närkästys, harmi. **-ity** [-iti]
s. loukkaus, nöyryytys.

indirect [indi'rekt] *a.* epäsuora,
välillinen; *~ speech* epäsuora esitys.

indiscr|eet [indis'kri:t] *a.*
harkitsematon, varomaton, epähieno.
-etion [-'kreʃn] *s.* varomattomuus,
varomaton menettely t. puhe,

tahdittomuus.

indiscriminate [indis'kriminit] *a.* umpimähkäinen, valikoimaton, mielivaltainen; ~ *ly* harkitsematta, umpimähkään, erotuksetta.

indispensable [indis'pensəbl] *a.* välttämätön, tarpeellinen.

indispos|ed [indis'pouzd] *a.* huonovointinen, pahoinvoipa; haluton, vastahakoinen. **-ition** [-pə'ziʃn] *s.* huonovointisuus; haluttomuus.

in|disputable [indis'pju:təbl] *a.* kiistämätön. **-dissoluble** [-di'sɔljubl] *a.* liukenematon; purkamaton, kestävä. **-distinct** [-dis'tiŋ(k)t] *a.* epäselvä.

indite [in'dait] *v.* sepittää.

individual [indi'vidjuəl] *a.* yksilöllinen, henkilökohtainen; yksityis-, yksittäinen; *s.* yksilö. **-ism** [-izm] *s.* individualismi. **-ity** [-'æliti] *s.* yksilöllisyys. **-ize** [-aiz] *v.* yksilöllistää. **-ly** *adv.* kukin erikseen; yksilöllisesti.

indivisible [indi'vizəbl] *a.* jaoton.

Indo|-China ['ində(u)-] *erisn.* Indo-Kiina. **~-European** *a. & s.* indoeurooppalainen.

indoctrina|te [in'dɔktrineit] *v.* iskostaa mieliin, istuttaa jtk oppia. **-tion** [-'neiʃn] *s.* opin t. aatteen iskostaminen, iskeminen jkh.

indolen|ce ['indələns] *s.* velttous, laiskuus. **-t** [-nt] *a.* veltto, laiska, saamaton.

indomitable [in'dɔmitəbl] *a.* lannistumaton.

Indonesia [ində(u)'ni:ʃə] *erisn.* Indonesia. **-n** [-n] *a. & s.* indonesialainen.

indoor ['indɔ:] *a.* sisä-, sisällä tapahtuva. **-s** [-z] *adv.* sisällä, talossa, kotona.

indorse [in'dɔ:s] ks. **endorse**.

indubitable [in'dju:bitəbl] *a.* epäilemätön, epäilyksetön, varma.

induce [in'dju:s] *v.* saada, taivuttaa (jhk); aiheuttaa, saada aikaan. **-ment** *s.* aihe, syy, vaikutin, kiihoke.

induct [in'dʌkt] *v.* asettaa virkaan. **-ion** [-'dʌkʃn] *s.* virkaanasettaminen; induktio; kutsunta (sot.); ~ *coil* induktiokela. **-ive** [-iv] *a.* induktiivinen.

indulge [in'dʌldʒ] *v.* kohdella (liian) lempeästi, hemmotella; tyydyttää (halujaan), suoda itselleen jtk; ~ *in alcohol* nauttia väkeviä. **-nce** [-(ə)ns] *s.* hemmottelu, (liika) lempeys, suopeus; (m. *self-*~) halujensa tyydyttäminen; (kirk.) ane. **-nt** [-(ə)nt] *a.* lempeä, säälivänen; myöntyväinen.

indura|te ['indjuəreit] *v.* kovettaa, koveta; paaduttaa. **-tion** [-'reiʃn] *s.* kovettuminen.

industrial [in'dʌstriəl] *a.* teollisuus-, teollinen, työ- (~ *dispute*); ~ *action* työtaistelu; ~ *estate* teollisuuskylä; ~ *relations* työmarkkinasuhteet. **-ism** [-izm] *s.* teollistuminen. **-ist** [-ist] *s.* teollisuusmies. **-ize** [-aiz] *v.* teollistaa.

industrious [in'dʌstriəs] *a.* ahkera, uuttera.

industry ['indəstri] *s.* ahkeruus, uutteruus; teollisuus; elinkeino; *film* ~ elokuva-ala.

in-dwelling *a.* sisäinen, kesto-.

inebri|ate [i'ni:briit] *a. & s.* päihtynyt; juoppo; *v.* [-ieit] päihdyttää. **-ety** [ini(:)'braiəti] *s.* juopumus.

inedible [in'edibl] *a.* syötäväksi kelpaamaton.

ineffable [in'efəbl] *a.* sanomaton.

ineffaceable [ini'feisəbl] *a.* lähtemätön.

ineffect|ive [ini'fektiv] *a.* tehoton, tulokseton; kelvoton. **-ual** [-tjuəl] *a.* tehoton, hyödytön.

inefficacy [in'efikəsi] *s.* tehottomuus.

inefficien|cy [ini'fiʃnsi] *s.* saamattomuus, tehottomuus. **-t** [-'fiʃnt] *a.* saamaton, kykenemätön; tehoton.

in|elastic *a.* joustamaton. **-elegant** *a.* epäaistikas; hienostumaton.

ineligible [in'elidʒəbl] *a.* vaalikelvoton; sopimaton, mahdoton hyväksyä.

ineluctable [ini'lʌktəbl] *a.* väistämätön.

inept [i'nept] *a.* tolkuton, typerä. **-itude** [-itju:d] *s.* typeryys, sopimattomuus, sopimaton huomautus.

inequality [ini(:)'kwɔliti] *s.* erilaisuus, erisuuruisuus, eriarvoisuus; epätasaisuus; epäsuhta.

inequitable [in'ekwitəbl] *a.* epäoikeudenmukainen.

ineradicable [ini'rædikəbl] *a.*

mahdoton hävittää, syvälle juurtunut.

inert [i'nə:t] *a.* eloton, voimaton; veltto, tylsä. **-ia** [i'nə:ʃiə] *s.* velttous, hitaus, (fys.) inertia.

inescapable [inis'keipəbl] *a.* väistämätön.

inessential [ini'senʃ(ə)l] *a.* epäolennainen, ei välttämätön.

inestimable [in'estiməbl] *a.* arvaamattoman hyvä, verraton.

inevitable [in'evitəbl] *a.* väistämätön, luonnostaan lankeava; *i-bly* väistämättömästi.

inexact [inig'zækt] *a.* epätarkka.

inexcusable [iniks'kju:zəbl] *a.* anteeksiantamaton.

inexhaustible [inig'zɔ:stəbl] *a.* tyhjentymätön, ehtymätön.

inexorable [in'eks(ə)rəbl] *a.* heltymätön.

inexpedien|cy [iniks'pi:djənsi] *s.* sopimattomuus. **-t** [-ənt] *a.* tarkoitustaan vastaamaton, sopimaton.

inexpensive [iniks'pensiv] *a.* halpa, huokea.

inexperience [iniks'piəriəns] *s.* kokemattomuus. **-d** [-t] *a.* kokematon.

inexpert [ineks'pə:t] *a.* taitamaton, harjaantumaton.

inexplicable [in'eksplikəbl] *a.* selittämätön.

inexpress|ible [iniks'presəbl] *a.* sanomaton, sanoinkuvaamaton. **-ive** [-siv] *a.* ilmeetön.

in|extricable [-'ekstrikəbl] *a.* sekava, sotkuinen, selviämätön. **-fallibility** *s.* [-fælə'biliti] erehtymättömyys. **-fallible** [-'fæləbl] *a.* erehtymätön, pettämätön.

infam|ous ['infəməs] *a.* kunniaton, häpeällinen; alhainen. **-y** ['infəmi] *s.* häpeä(llisyys); häpeällinen teko.

infancy ['infənsi] *s.* (varhais)lapsuus.

infant ['infənt] *s.* (pieni) lapsi, imeväinen; (lak.) alaikäinen; ~ *school* lastentarha. **-icide** [-'fæntisaid] *s.* lapsenmurha, -murhaaja. **-ile** [-ail] *a.* lapsen, lapsen tasolle jäänyt; ~ *paralysis* lapsihalvaus.

infantry ['infəntri] *s.* jalkaväki.

infarct ['infɑ:kt], **-ion** [-'fɑ:kʃn] *s.*: *cardiac* ~ sydäninfarkti.

infatua|te [in'fætjueit] *v.* sokaista; ~*d (with)* hullaantunut. **-tion** [-'eiʃn] *s.* hullaantuminen, lumous.

infect [in'fekt] *v.* tartuttaa, infektoida. **-ion** [-'fekʃn] *s.* tartunta; infektio(tauti). **-ious** [-'fekʃəs] *a.* tarttuva; ~ *matter* tartunta-aine.

infelicity [infe'lisiti] *s.* onnettomuus; sopimaton ilmaus; *i-ties* epäonnistuneet sanonnat.

infer [in'fə:] *v.* johtaa, päättää, päätellä (jstk). **-ence** [in'f(ə)r(ə)ns] *s.* päätelmä, johtopäätös; *by* ~ päättelemällä.

inferior [in'fiəriə] *a.* alempi, alhaisempi, huonompi *(to* jtk); *s.* arvoltaan alempi henkilö. **-ity** [-ri'ɔriti] *s.* alemmuus; ~ *complex* alemmuuskompleksi.

infern|al [in'fə:nl] *a.* helvetillinen, pirullinen; ~ *machine* helvetinkone. **-ality** [-'næliti] *s.* pirullisuus. **-o** [in'fə:nəu] *s.* helvetti.

infertil|e [in'fə:tail] *a.* hedelmätön, karu. **-ity** [-'tiliti] *s.* hedelmättömyys.

infest [in'fest] *v.* olla jssk maanvaivana; ~*ed with vermin* syöpäläisten saastuttama; *be* ~*ed with* (m.) vilistä, kuhista jtk.

infidel ['infid(ə)l] *a. & s.* vääräuskoinen, uskoton, pakana(llinen). **-ity** [-'deliti] *s.* uskottomuus; epäusko.

infiltrat|e ['infiltreit] *v.* tunkeutua, tihkua läpi; suodattaa; (kuv.) solutta(utu)a. **-ion** [-'treiʃn] *s.* suodattaminen; solutus.

infinit|e ['inf(i)nit] *a.* ääretön, rajaton, loppumaton; *the* ~ äärettömyys; ~*ly* äärettömän. **-esimal** [-'tesiməl] *a.* äärettömän pieni. **-ive** [-'finitiv] *a. & s.* infinitiivi. **-ude** [-'finitju:d] *s.* = seur. **-y** [-'finiti] *s.* äärettömyys.

infirm [in'fə:m] *a.* heikko (et. vanhuuden-), voimaton; ~ *[of purpose]* horjuva, päättämätön. **-ary** [-əri] *s.* sairaala. **-ity** [-iti] *s.* heikkous.

inflame [in'fleim] *v.* tulehduttaa; sytyttää, kiihdyttää; tulehtua; kiihtyä, tulistua.

inflamma|ble [in'flæməbl] *a.* helposti syttyvä, tulenarka. **-tion** [-flə'meiʃn] *s.* tulehdus. **-tory** [-'flæmət(ə)ri] *a.* tulehdus-; kiihottava.

inflat|e [in'fleit] v. puhaltaa ilmaa täyteen, paisuttaa; nostaa hintoja (keinotekoisesti); **-able** puhallettava. **-ed** [-id] a. pöyhkeä, mahtipontinen. **-ion** [-'fleiʃn] s. paisuttaminen; inflaatio; (~**ary** a. inflatorinen; *the* ~*ary spiral* inflaatiokierre).

inflect [in'flekt] v. taivuttaa. **-ion** [-'flekʃn] s. = **inflexion**.

aflex|ible [in'fleksəbl] a. taipumaton; järkkymätön, luja. **-ion** [-'flekʃn] s. taivutus, -muoto. **-ional** a. taivutus-.

nflict [in'flikt] v. määrätä (rangaistus); tehdä, aiheuttaa (jtk pahaa); ~ *a blow* iskeä, lyödä. **-ion** [-'flikʃn] s. (kivun, tuskan) aiheuttaminen.

aflorescence [inflo'resns] s. kukinto.

aflow ['infləu] s. sisäänvirtaus.

afluen|ce ['influəns] s. vaikutus (*on, upon* jkh); vaikutusvalta; v. vaikuttaa (jhk); *under the* ~ [*of drink*] alkoholin vaikutuksen alaisena. **-tial** [-flu'enʃ(ə)l] a. vaikutusvaltainen.

influenza [influ'enzə] s. influenssa.

aflux ['inflʌks] s. (sisään)virtaaminen, tulva, virta.

aform [in'fɔːm] v. ilmoittaa (*a p. of* jklle jtk); ~ *against* ilmiantaa; *we were* ~ *ed that* meille ilmoitettiin, että. **-al** [-l] a. vailla muodollisuuksia, epävirallinen; vapaamuotoinen; leppoisa, rento; ~ *dress* arkipuku. **-ality** [-'mæliti] s. yksinkertaisuus, epävirallisuus. **-ant** [-ənt] s. tiedonantaja, kertoja. **-ation** [infə'meiʃn] s. (lyh. *info*) ilmoitus, tieto, tiedonanto; informaatio; ilmianto. **-ative** [-ətiv] a. opettavainen. **-ed** [-d] a. asioihin perehtynyt (us. *well-*~). **-er** [-ə] s. ilmiantaja.

afra ['infrə] adv.: *see* ~ alempana (kirjassa); ~ *dig.* arvolle(en) sopimattomasti.

afraction [in'frækʃn] s. (lain) rikkominen.

afrastructure (puolustuksen ym) perusrakenne.

a|frequency s. harvinaisuus. **-frequent** [-'friːkwənt] a. harvoin tapahtuva, harvinainen, epätavallinen; ~*ly* harvoin.

afringe [in'frin(d)ʒ] v. rikkoa (lakia ym), loukata, **-ment** s. rikkominen.

infuriate [in'fjuərieit] v. raivostuttaa; ~*d* raivostunut.

infus|e [in'fjuːz] v. valaa (m. kuv.); uuttaa; hautua; kaataa kuumaa vettä (teelehtien päälle). **-ion** [-'fjuːʒn] s. valaminen, (jnk) lisääminen; haudeneste; (lääk.) infuusio.

ingen|ious [in'dʒiːnjəs] a. kekseliäs, terävä, näppärä, sukkela. **-uity** [ɛ:(n)ʒei'njuː] s. luonnollinen, naiivi nuori tyttö (teatt.). **-uity** [-i'njuː(:)iti] s. kekseliäisyys, nerokkuus.

ingenuous [in'dʒenjuəs] a. avomielinen, vilpitön; teeskentelemätön.

ingestion [in'dʒestʃ(ə)n] s. (juoman, ruoan) nauttiminen.

inglorious [in'gloːriəs] a. kunniaton, häpeällinen.

ingot ['ingət] s. (kulta- t. hopea)harkko.

ingrained ['in'greind] a. juurtunut, syöpynyt.

ingratiat|e [in'greiʃieit] v.: ~ *oneself with* päästä jkn suosioon; **-ing** mielistelevä.

ingratitude [in'grætitjuːd] s. kiittämättömyys.

ingredient [in'griːdjənt] s. aines; ~*s* ainekset.

ingress ['ingres] s. sisäänpääsy.

inhabit [in'hæbit] v. asua (jssk). **-ant** [-(ə)nt] s. asukas.

inhalation [in(h)ə'leiʃn] s. sisäänhengitys; inhalaatio.

inhale [in'heil] v. hengittää (sisään), vetää henkeensä.

inharmonious [inhɑː'məunjəs] a. epäsointuinen.

inhere [in'hiə] v.: ~ *in* olla luonnostaan, (olennaisena osana) kuulua jhk. **-nt** [-rənt] a. jhk luonnostaan luontainen.

inherit [in'herit] v. periä. **-able** [-əbl] a. perinnöllinen. **-ance** [-(ə)ns] s. perintö; perintö:

inhibit [in'hibit] v. estää, ehkäistä; ~*ed* (psyk.) estynyt. **-ion** [in(h)i'biʃn] s. ehkäisy; (psyk.) esto.

inhospitable [in'hɔspitəbl] a. epävieraanvarainen; karu, tyly.

inhuman [in'hjuːmən] a. epäinhimillinen. **-ity** [-'mæniti] s. epäinhimillisyys; julmuus.

inimical [i'nimik(ə)l] a. vihamielinen,
vahingollinen.

inimitable [i'nimitəbl] a.
jäljittelemätön; verraton.

iniquit|ous [i'nikwitəs] a.
epäoikeudenmukainen, väärä. **-y** [-iti]
s. kohtuuttomuus, vääryys; paha
teko.

initial [i'niʃl] a. alku-; s. pl.
nimikirjaimet; v. merkitä
nimikirjaimensa jhk; parafoida; ~ly
aluksi.

initiat|e [i'niʃieit] v. aloittaa, panna
alulle; ~ into tutustuttaa, perehdyttää
jhk ottaa (juhlallisesti) jäseneksi. s.
[-iit] (salaisen seuran) uusi jäsen. **-ion**
[-'eiʃn] s. alkuunpano;
perehdyttäminen, vihkiminen
(salaisin menoin). **-ive** [-ʃiətiv] s.
aloite; aloitteellisuus, aloitekyky; on
one's own ~ omasta aloitteestaan; he
took the ~ hän teki aloitteen.

inject [in'dʒekt] v. ruiskuttaa (lääkettä
ym). **-ion** [-'dʒekʃn] s. (lääke)ruiske,
injektio.

injudicious [indʒu:'diʃəs] a.
arvostelukyvytön, epäviisas.

injun [indʒən] int.: honest ~ (sl.)
kunniasanalla.

injunction [in'dʒʌŋ(k)ʃn] s. käsky,
määräys.

injur|e [indʒə] v. tehdä vääryyttä
(jklle); vahingoittaa, vammoittaa,
loukata; ~d party loukattu osapuoli,
kantaja. **-ious** [in'dʒuəriəs] a.
vahingollinen. **-y** [in(d)ʒəri] s.
vamma, vaurio; vääryys.

injustice [in'dʒʌstis] s. vääryys.

ink [iŋk] s. muste; printer's ~
painomuste; v. tahria musteeseen;
merkitä musteella; ~ed in
musteella kirjoitettu; ~-bottle, ~-pot
mustepullo; ~-stand kirjoitusteline.

inkling [iŋkliŋ] s. vihi; he got an ~ of it
hän sai vihiä siitä.

inky [iŋki] a. musteinen.

inland [inlənd] s. sisämaa; a.
sisämaan; kotimainen; ~ trade
kotimaan kauppa; ks. revenue.

in-laws [inlɔːz] s. pl. sukulaiset
avioliiton kautta.

inlay [in'lei] inlaid inlaid, v. upottaa,
koristaa upotuksin; s. upote;
(hampaan) valutäyte.

inlet [inlet] s. kapea lahdelma; aukko;
(jhk) upotettu palanen.

inmate [inmeit] s. asukas, asukki;
hoidokki.

inmost [inməust] a. sisimmäinen, sisin.

inn [in] s. majatalo; Inns of Court Engl.
neljä lakimiesseuraa, joissa
opiskellaan (barrister-tutkintoa
varten).

innards [inaːdz] s. pl. (puhek.)
sisälmykset.

innate [i'neit, 'ineit] a. synnynnäinen,
luontainen.

inner [inə] a. sisäinen, sisällinen, sisä-.
-most ks. inmost.

innings [iniŋz] s. (pl. = sg.) pelivuoro;
vallassaoloaika, vuoro.

innkeeper [inki:pə] s. majatalon
isäntä.

innocen|ce [inəsns] s. viattomuus. **-t**
[-nt] a. viaton, syytön; s. viaton
henkilö; ~s' Day viattomien lasten
päivä.

innocuous [i'nɔkjuəs] a. vaaraton,
viaton, harmiton.

innova|te [inə(u)veit] v. tehdä
uudistuksia. **-tion** [-'veiʃn] s. uudistus,
uutuus.

innuendo [inju(:)'endəu] s.
vihjaileminen, vihjailu.

innumerable [i'njuːm(ə)rəbl] a.
lukematon.

inoculat|e [i'nɔkjuleit] v. istuttaa
(tauti), rokottaa; oksastaa. **-ion**
[-'leiʃn] s. rokotus jne.

inoffensive [inə'fensiv] a. vaaraton,
viaton; kiltti, hyvänahkainen.

inoperable [in'ɔp(ə)rəbl] a. mahdoton
leikata.

inopportune [in'ɔpətjuːn] a.
(ajankohtaan) sopimaton.

inordinate [in'ɔːdnət] a. kohtuuton,
hillitön.

inorganic [inɔː'gænik] a.
epäorgaaninen.

input [input] s. jhk syötetty energia
ym; panos; syöttö, -teho.

inquest [inkwest] s. tutkimus;
[coroner's] ~ kuolemansyyn
tutkimus.

inquietude [in'kwaiitjuːd] s.
levottomuus.

inquir|e [in'kwaiə] v. kysellä,
tiedustella (for jkta) ~ into tutkia; ~

after sb. kysyä jkn vointia; *-ing* tiedonhaluinen. **-y** [-ri] *s.* kysely, tiedustelu; tutkimus; kysymys; *make inquiries* tiedustella; ~ *office* tiedonantotoimisto, neuvontatoimisto.

inquisi|tion [inkwi'zi∫n] *s.* tutkimus; *the I* ~ inkvisitio. **-tive** [-'kwizitiv] *a.* utelias, kyseliäs, tiedonhaluinen; (~**ness** *s.* uteliaisuus, tiedonhalu). **-tor** [-'kwizitə] *s.* inkvisiittori.

inroad ['inrəud] *s.* hyökkäys, ryöstöretki.

inrush *s.* syöksy, (kuv.) tulva.

insalubrious [insə'lu:briəs] *a.* epäterveellinen.

insan|e [in'sein] *a.* mielenvikainen. **-itary** [-'sænit(ə)ri] *a.* epähygieeninen. **-ity** [-'sæniti] *s.* mielenvikaisuus.

insatiable [in'sei∫iəbl] *a.* pohjaton, kyltymätön.

in|scribe [in'skraib] *v.* kirjoittaa, kaivertaa (jhk). **-scription** [-'skrip∫n] *s.* kaiverrus.

inscrutable [in'skru:təbl] *a.* tutkimaton, salaperäinen.

insect ['insekt] *s.* hyönteinen. **-icide** [-'sektisaid] *s.* hyönteismyrkky. **-ivorous** [-'tivərəs] *a.* hyönteisiä syövä.

insecur|e [insi'kjuə] *a.* epävarma. **-ity** [-riti] *s.* epävarmuus.

insemination [insemi'nei∫n] *s.: [artificial]* ~ keinosiemennys.

insens|ate [in'sens|eit] *a.* tunteeton, tunnoton, mieletön. **-ibility** [-i'biliti] *s.* tunnottomuus, tajuttomuus. **-ible** [-əbl] *a.* tunteeton, välinpitämätön; tajuton; huomaamaton. **-itive** [-itiv] *a.* tunteeton; ~ *to touch* ei kosketukselle herkkä.

inseparable [in'sep(ə)rəbl] *a.* erottamaton.

insert [in'sə:t] *v.* pistää, panna (jhk); *s.* ['- -] liite (kirjaan). **-ion** [-'sə:∫n] *s.* (sisään) pano; (väliin pantu) lisäys, lehti-ilmoitus ym, välipitsi, (kankaaseen) upotettu koriste.

inset ['inset] *s.* liite (kirjaan); upotettu kuva (t. kartta).

inshore ['in'∫ɔ:] *adv. & a.* lähellä rantaa (oleva).

inside [in'said] *s.* sisäpuoli, sisus(ta); (puhek.) vatsa; *a.* sisä-, sisäpuolella

oleva; *prep.* [- '-] sisässä; *adv.* sisässä, -llä, -lle, sisäpuolella; ~ *information* salaiset tiedot; ~ *out* nurin; ~ *of a week* vähemmässä kuin viikossa. **-r** [-ə] *s.* asioista perillä oleva.

insidious [in'sidiəs] *a.* salakavala, petollinen.

insight ['insait] *s.* oivallus; ~ *into human character* ihmisluonteen tarkka tuntemus.

insignia [in'signiə] *s. pl.* arvo-, virkamerkit.

insignifican|ce [insig'nifikəns] *s.* merkityksettömyys. **-t** [-ənt] *a.* merkityksetön, mitätön, vähäpätöinen.

insincer|e [insin'siə] *a.* vilpillinen, teeskentelevä, kiero. **-ity** [-'seriti] *s.* vilpillisyys.

insinua|te [in'sinjueit] *v.* vihjaista, vihjata; ~ *oneself into a p.'s favour* mielistellen päästä jkn suosioon; *-ting* mielistelevä. **-tion** [-'ei∫n] *s.* vihjaus; mielistely.

insipid [in'sipid] *a.* mauton; mielenkiinnoton. **-ity** [-'piditi] *s.* mauttomuus.

insist [in'sist] *v.* (itsepintaisesti) väittää, pitää kiinni (on jstk), vaatimalla vaatia, tiukata; *[but] I* ~ *[on it]* vaadin sitä ehdottomasti. **-ence** [-(ə)ns] *s.* hellittämättömyys; *at his* ~ hänen vaatimuksestaan. **-ent** [-(ə)nt] *a.* itsepäinen, hellittämätön.

insobriety [insə(u)'braiəti] *s.* juoppous.

insolen|ce [in's(ə)ləns] *s.* röyhkeys, julkeus. **-t** [-ənt] *a.* röyhkeä, julkea, hävytön.

insoluble [in'səljubl] *a.* liukenematon; mahdoton ratkaista.

insolven|cy [in'səlv(ə)nsi] *s.* maksukyvyttömyys, vararikko. **-t** [-(ə)nt] *a.* maksukyvytön.

insomnia [in'səmniə] *s.* unettomuus. **-c** [-niæk] *s.* uneton (ihminen).

insomuch [insə(u)'mʌt∫] *adv.* siinä määrin; ~ *as* sikäli kuin.

insouciance [in'su:sjəns] *s.* huolettomuus, välinpitämättömyys.

inspect [in'spekt] *v.* tarkastaa, tutkia. **-ion** [-'spek∫n] *s.* tarkastus, tarkastelu, katsastus; *for* ~ tarkastettavaksi. **-or** [-'spektə] *s.* tarkastaja.

inspiration [inspə'reiʃn] *s.*
sisäänhengitys; inspiraatio, innoitus.

inspir|e [in'spaiə] *v.* hengittää sisään;
inspiroida, innoittaa, elähdyttää;
herättää. **-it** [-'spirit] *v.* elähdyttää,
innostaa.

instability [instə'biliti] *s.* epävakaisuus.

instal|l [in'stɔ:l] *v.* asettaa, vihkiä
virkaan; asentaa. **-lation** [-stə'leiʃn] *s.*
virkaanasettajaiset; asennus. **-ment** *s.*
osamaksu; (jatkokertomuksen) osa;
~ *plan* vähittäismaksujärjestelmä;
[*we are paying*] *by monthly* ~*s*
kuukausittain.

instance ['instəns] *s.* esimerkki; tapaus;
v. mainita esimerkkinä; *at the* ~ *of*
jkn pyynnöstä; *for* ~ esimerkiksi; *in
the first* ~ ensiksi, ensinnäkin,
lähinnä; *court of first* ~ alioikeus.

instant ['instənt] *a.*
silmänräpäyksellinen, pika-; kuluva
(kuukausi); *s.* hetki, silmänräpäys; *the
13th* ~ (tav. lyh. *inst.*) tämän kuun 13.
p.; *the* ~ *that* heti kun . .; *on the* ~
heti; ~ *coffee* pikakahvi. **-aneous**
[-'teinjəs] *a.* silmänräpäyksellinen.
-ly *adv.* silmänräpäyksessä, heti.

instead [in'sted] *adv.* sen sijaan; ~ *of*
jnk sijasta, sijaan, asemesta.

instep [instep] *s.* jalkapöytä; kengän
rinta.

instigat|e ['instigeit] *v.* yllyttää,
kiihottaa. **-ion** [-'geiʃn] *s.* yllytys.

instil(l) [in'stil] *v.* tiputtaa; vähitellen
juurruttaa, istuttaa, teroittaa
(mieleen).

instinct ['instiŋ(k)t] *s.* vaisto, vietti; *a.*
[in'stiŋkt] ~ *with* jnk elähdyttämä,
täyttämä; *by* ~ vaistojensa varassa,
vaistonvaraisesti. **-ive** [-'stiŋ(k)tiv] *a.*
vaistomainen, vaistonomainen.

institu|te ['institju:t] *v.* perustaa, panna
alulle, toimeenpanna; asettaa
virkaan; *s.* (opetus- ym) laitos,
instituutti. **-tion** [-'tju:ʃn] *s.*
perustaminen, alullepaneminen;
virkaanasettaminen; tieteellinen t.
yhteiskunnallinen laitos; vakiintunut
tapa; (~**al** *care* laitoshoito; ~**alize** *v.*
laitostaa).

instruct [in'strʌkt] *v.* opettaa; antaa
tietoja, antaa ohjeita. **-ion** [-'strʌkʃn]
s. opetus; *pl.* ohjeet; (~**al:** ~ *book*
tietokirja). **-ive** [-iv] *a.* opettavainen.

-or [-ə] *s.* opettaja, neuvoja, ohjaaja.

-ress [-ris] *s.* opettajatar,
(nais)neuvoja.

instrument ['instrumənt] *s.* työkalu,
väline, koje, instrumentti;
välikappale; soittokone, soitin;
asiakirja; *v.* [-'ment] soitintaa; ~
panel kojelauta; ~*ed* (esim.
elektronisin) laitteim varustettu. **-al**
[-'mentl] *a.:* ~ *in* . . -*ing* jhk
myötävaikuttaa, jtk edistävä; ~
flying sokkolento; ~ *music*
soitinmusiikki; (~**ist** soitinmuusikko;
~**ity** [-'tæliti]: *by the* ~*ity of* jkn
avulla).

insubordina|te [insə'bɔ:dnit] *a.*
uppiniskainen, tottelematon. **-tion**
[-di'neiʃn] *s.* uppiniskaisuus.

insufferable [in'sʌf(ə)rəbl] *a.*
sietämätön.

insufficien|cy [insə'fiʃ(ə)nsi] *s.*
riittämättömyys; toiminnanvajavuus
(lääk.). **-t** [-'fiʃ(ə)nt] *a.* riittämätön,
puutteellinen.

insufflate ['insʌfleit] *v.* puhaltaa
(ilmaa) jhk.

insular ['insjulə, Am. 'insə-] *a.* saari-,
saarelais-; eristetty. **-ity** [-'læriti] *s.*
saariasema; (saaren asukkaan)
ahdasmielisyys, rajoittuneisuus (m.
insularism).

insula|te ['insjuleit] *v.* (sähk. ym)
eristää **-tion** [-'leiʃn] *s.* eristys; eriste.
-tor [-ə] *s.* eristin, eristysaine.

insulin ['insjulin] *s.* insuliini.

insult ['insʌlt] *s.* loukkaus, solvaus; *v.*
[in'sʌlt] loukata; ~*ing* loukkaava.

insuperable [in'sju:p(ə)rəbl] *a.*
ylipääsemätön, voittamaton.

insupportable [insə'pɔ:təbl] *a.*
sietämätön.

insurance [in'ʃuər(ə)ns] *s.* vakuutus; ~
policy vakuutuskirja.

insure [in'ʃuə] *v.* vakuuttaa (*against* jtk
vastaan); *the* ~*d* [*person*] vakuutuksen
ottaja.

insurgent [in'sə:dʒ(ə)nt] *a.* & *s.*
kapinallinen.

insurmountable [insə(:)'mauntəbl] *a.*
ylipääsemätön, voittamaton.

insurrection [insə'rekʃ(ə)n] *s.* kapina.
-ary [-əri] *a.* kapinallinen. **-ist** *s.*
kapinoitsija.

intact [in'tækt] *a.* koskematon,

vahingoittumaton.

intake ['inteik] s. nautittu (t. jhk otettu) määrä, (putken) imukohta.

intangible [in'tæn(d)ʒəbl] a. mahdoton koskettaa t. tuntea, käsittämätön.

integer ['intidʒə] s. kokonaisluku.

integr|al ['intigr(ə)l] a. kokonaisuuteen kuuluva, kokonainen, olennainen; s. integraali. **-ate** [-reit] v. yhdentää, tehdä kokonaiseksi, integroida; be ~d yhdentyä; ~d [school] eri roduille avoin. **-ation** [-'reiʃn] s. yhdentyminen. **-ity** [-'tegriti] s. kokonaisuus, eheys; rehellisyys, lahjomattomuus; koskemattomuus.

integument [in'tegjumənt] s. kuori, nahka, peite, kalvo.

intellect ['intəlekt] s. äly, ymmärrys. **-ual** [-'lektjuəl] a. älyllinen, älyperäinen, henkinen; s. intellektuelli, älyniekka; the ~s älymystö.

intellig|ence [in'telidʒ(ə)ns] s. äly; älykkyys; tieto, tiedot, tiedonanto; ~ department (sot. ym) tiedusteluosasto; ~ test älykkyyskoe. **-ent** [-(ə)nt] a. älykäs, intelligentti. **-entsia** [-'dʒentsiə] s. älymystö. **-ibility** [-ʒi'biliti] s. ymmärrettävyys. **-ible** [-əbl] a. ymmärrettävä.

intemper|ance [in'temp(ə)r(ə)ns] s. kohtuuttomuus, juoppous. **-ate** [-(ə)rit] a. kohtuuton, hillitön; juopotteleva.

intend [in'tend] v. aikoa; tarkoittaa. **-ed** [-id] a.; s.: my ~ (sl.) tuleva vaimoni.

intens|e [in'tens] a. voimakas, ankara, kova, tuima; kiihkeä; ~ly (m.) erittäin; syvästi. **-ify** [-ifai] v. kohottaa, lisätä, vahvistaa, voimaperäistää; lisääntyä, vahvistua. **-ity** [-iti] s. voimakkuus, ankaruus, kiihkeys. **-ive** [-iv] a. intensiivinen, voimaperäinen; ~ care unit teho-osasto.

intent [in'tent] jännittyneen tarkkaavainen (katse); hyvin halukas, innokas (on ... -ing); s. aikomus, tarkoitus; with ~ to kill surmaamisen tarkoituksessa; to all ~s and purposes itse asiassa, käytännöllisesti katsoen.

intention [in'tenʃn] s. aikomus, aie, tarkoitus. **-al** [-ʃənl] a. tahallinen. **-ed** [-ʃ(ə)nd] a.: well~ hyvää tarkoittava.

intentness s. tarkkaavaisuus, into.

inter [in'tə:] v. haudata.

inter- [intə(:)] pref. välillä, kesken; inter alia ['eiliə] muun muassa.

inter|act v. [-r'ækt] vaikuttaa toisiinsa. **-action** s. vuorovaikutus. **-breed** v. risteyttää, -ytyä. **-cede** [-'si:d] v.: ~ with a p. for puhua jklle jkn puolesta, olla välittäjänä, puoltaa.

intercept [-'sept] v. siepata (matkalla), estää (pääsemästä jhk), katkaista. **-ion** [-'sepʃn] s. sieppaaminen, estäminen. **-or** [-ə] s. torjuntahävittäjä.

intercess|ion [-'seʃn] s. välitys; esirukous. **-ory** [-'sesəri] s.: ~ prayer esirukous.

interchange v. vaihtaa (keskenään), vaihdella; s. ['- -] (keskinäinen) vaihto; vaihteleminen; (tien) eritasoliittymä. **-able** a. vaihdettava, vaihdettavissa oleva; samamerkityksinen.

inter|com ['intəkəm] lyh. s. sisäpuhelin. **-communicate** v. olla keskenään yhteydessä. **-communication** s. kanssakäyminen; viestiyhteys ~-**continental** a. mannertenvälinen. **-course** ['- -] s. seurustelu, kanssakäyminen, yhteys; [sexual ~] sukupuoliyhteys. **-current** a. välillä oleva(t). **-dependence** s. riippuvuus toisistaan. **-dict** ['intə(:)dikt] s. interdikti; v. [-'dikt] kieltää; julistaa kirkonkiroukseen. **-diction** [-'dikʃn] s. kirkonkirous.

interest ['intrəst] s. mielenkiinto, kiinnostus; harraste, harrastus; osuus, osakkuus; korko; etu, hyöty, eturyhmä, suhteet; v. kiinnostaa, herättää mielenkiintoa; take an ~ in olla kiinnostunut jstk; it is in my ~ on etujeni mukaista; [work] in the ~s of jkn parhaaksi; the landed ~ maanomistajat; the business ~s liikemaailma; in the ~[s] of truth totuuden tähden; yield (return) ~ tuottaa korkoa; [return sth.] with ~ korkoineen; he is ~ed in the rubber industry hän on osakkaana kumiteollisuudessa. **-ed** [-id] a.: ~ in jstk kiinnostunut, jtk harrastava; omia etujaan valvova, puolueellinen. **-ing** a. mielenkiintoinen, kiintoisa.

interfere [intə'fiə] v. sekaantua jhk, puuttua asiaan (m. ~ *in*); olla ristiriidassa; ~ *with* ehkäistä, häiritä; *don't* ~ *with it!* älä koske siihen! **-nce** [-rəns] s. sekaantuminen, puuttuminen jhk; ristiriita(isuus); häiriö (rad.).

interim ['intərim] a. väliaikainen; s.: *in the* ~ väliaikaisesti.

interior [in'tiəriə] a. sisä-, sisäinen; sisämaan-; s. sisäosa(t), sisus(ta); sisäkuva, interiööri; *Minister of the I~* sisä(asiain)ministeri.

interject [-'dʒekt] v. pistää väliin. **-ion** [-'dʒekʃn] s. huudahdus(sana).

inter|lace v. punoa yhteen; olla toisiinsa kietoutuneina. **-lard** v. höystää (vierailla sanoilla ym). **-leave** v. välilehdittää. **-line** v. kirjoittaa rivien väliin. **-linear** a. rivien välinen. **-lock** v. liittyä, tarttua toisiinsa; liittää toisiinsa.

interlocut|or [-'lɔkjutə] s. puhetoveri. **-ory** [-'lɔkjutəri] a. keskustelu; kaksinpuhelun luonteinen.

interloper ['intələupə] s. (toisten asioihin sekaantuva) tungettelija.

interlude ['intəlu:d] s. väliaika; välisoitto.

inter|marriage s. (seka-)avioituminen. **-marry** v. (esim. kahdesta suvusta) liittyä toisiinsa avioliiteiden kautta. **-meddle** v. sekaantua. **-mediary** [-'mi:djəri] a. välissä oleva; s. välittäjä, välikäsi. **-mediate** [-'mi:djət] a. välillä (-ssä) oleva, väli-; ~ *examination* välitutkinto; ~ *landing* välilasku.

interment [in'tə:mənt] s. hautaus.

intermezzo [intə'metsəu] s. välikohtaus, -soitto.

interminable [in'tə:m(i)nəbl] a. loputon.

inter|mingle v. sekoittaa, sekoittua (yhteen). **-mission** s. keskeytys; väliaika; *without* ~ taukoamatta. **-mittent** [-'mit(ə)nt] a. ajoittainen; ~ *fever* horkka. **-mix** v. sekoittaa, -ttua.

intern [in'tə:n] v. internoida; s. ['intə:n] (sairaalassa asuva) apulaislääkäri.

internal [in'tə:nl] a. sisä(ll)inen, sisä-; kotimaan.

international a. kansainvälinen.

internecine [-'ni:sain] s. kummallekin puolelle tuhoisa; ~ *war* hävityssota.

intern|ee [intə:'ni:] s. internoitu henkilö. **-ist** [in'tə:nist] s. sisätautilääkäri. **-ment** s. internointi.

interpellation [-pe'leiʃn] s. välikysymys.

inter|-planetary a. planeettojen välinen. **-play** s. vuorovaikutus.

interpolate [in'tə:pəleit] v. lisätä väliin, väärentää (lisäyksillä); interpoloida.

interpos|e v. asettaa väliin; välihuomautuksilla keskeyttää; tulla väliin, ryhtyä välittämään. **-ition** s. väliintulo, asiaan puuttuminen.

interpret [in'tə:prit] v. tulkita, selittää. **-ation** [-pri'teiʃn] s. tulkinta. **-er** [-ə] s. tulkki.

inter|racial a. rotujen välinen. **-relation(ship)** s. keskinäinen suhde.

interroga|te [in'terəgeit] v. kysyä, kuulustella. **-tion** [-'geiʃn] s. kyseleminen, kuulustelu; *note (mark) of* ~ kysymysmerkki. **-tive** [intə'rɔgətiv] a. kysyvä, kysymys-; s. kysymyssana. **-tory** [intə'rɔgət(ə)ri] a. kysyvä, kysymys-.

interrupt [intə'rʌpt] v. keskeyttää; katkaista, häiritä. **-ion** [-'rʌpʃn] s. keskeytys; häiriö.

intersect [-'sekt] v. leikata; leikata toisensa. **-ion** s. leikkaus(piste), risteys.

interspace ['intəspeis] s. väli.

inter|sperse [-'spə:s] v. sirotella (väliin); (kuv.) höystää. **-stice** [in'tə:stis] s. väli, rako.

inter|state a. valtioiden välinen. **-stellar** a. tähtien välinen. **-twine** v. kieto(utu)a yhteen.

interval ['intəv(ə)l] s. väliaika, tauko; välimatka; (mus.) säveleväli; *at* ~ *s* ajoittain; *at short* ~ *s* lyhyin väliajoin; *at* ~ *s of six hours* kuuden tunnin väliajoin.

interven|e [-'vi:n] v. tulla väliin, välittää, ruveta välittäjäksi, puuttua jhk; *if nothing* ~ *s* jos ei mitään (estettä) satu; *-ing* väli-. **-tion** [-'venʃn] s. väliintulo, (pol.) interventio, puuttuminen jnk valtion asioihin.

inter|view ['intəvju:] s. kohtaaminen; haastattelu, keskustelu; v.

haastatella. ~-**war** sotien väli|nen,
-set *(years* vuodet). -**weave** v. kutoa,
punoa yhteen.
intestate [in'testeit] a. testamentiton;
[he died] ~ jättämättä jälkeensä
testamenttia.
intestin|al [in'testinl] a. suoli-. -**e**
[in'testin] s. suoli, suolisto; *large
(small)* ~ paksu- (ohut)suoli.
intima|cy ['intiməsi] s. läheinen
tuttavuus, ystävyys, tuttavallisuus;
-*cies* lähentely, vapaudet. -**te** [-mit] a.
tuttavallinen, läheinen; intiimi,
yksityinen, salainen; s. läheinen
ystävä; v. [-meit] ilmoittaa; vihjaista;
~ *knowledge* perinpohjainen
tuntemus. -**tion** [-'meiʃn] s.
tiedoksianto; vihjaus, vihje.
intimida|te [in'timideit] v.
säikähdyttää, pelotella. -**tion** [-'deiʃn]
s. pelottelu.
into ['intu, 'intə] prep.: ilm. suuntaa
(illat.) jhk, jnnek; ~ *the house* taloon;
~ *that room* tuohon huoneeseen;
change ~ muuttua jksk; *translate* ~
Finnish kääntää suomen kielelle;
divide ~ *parts* jakaa osiin; *get* ~ *debt*
joutua velkaan.
intolera|ble [in'tɔl(ə)rəbl] a.
sietämätön. -**nce** [-lər(ə)ns] s.
suvaitsemattomuus. -**nt** [-lər(ə)nt] a.
suvaitsematon.
intonation [intə'neiʃn] s. äänenanto;
(kielen) sävelkulku, intonaatio.
intone [in'toun] v. lausua
(soinnukkaasti), messuta.
intoxica|nt [in'tɔksikənt] a. juovuttava;
s. juovutusjuoma; ~s väkijuomat. -**te**
[-eit] v. päihdyttää; huumata; ~*d*
päihtynyt. -**tion** [-'keiʃn] s. päihtymys;
(kuv.) hurma.
intractable [in'træktəbl] a.
uppiniskainen; vaikeasti käsiteltävä.
intramural ['intrə'mjuər(ə)l] a.
(yliopiston ym) muurien sisäpuolella
oleva t. tapahtuva.
intramuscular a.: ~ *injection* ruiske
lihakseen.
intransigent [in'trænsidʒ(ə)nt] a.
jyrkkä, myöntymätön.
intransitive [in'trænsətiv] a. & s.
intransitiivinen (verbi).
intrauterine a. kohdunsisäinen; ~
device kierukka.

intravenous a. laskimonsisäinen.
intrepid [in'trepid] a. peloton. -**ity**
[-'piditi] s. pelottomuus.
intrica|cy ['intrikəsi] s. sekavuus. -**te**
[-kət] a. sotkuinen, sekava, mutkikas,
pulmallinen.
intrigue [in'tri:g] s. vehkeily, juoni;
(salainen) rakkaussuhde; v. vehkeillä;
kiihottaa uteliaisuutta, kiinnostaa.
intrinsic [in'trinsik] a. sisäinen,
luontainen, varsinainen. -**ally** [-(ə)li]
adv. itsessään, olennaisesti.
introduc|e [intrə'dju:s] v. tuoda; viedä
sisään; esitellä, tutustuttaa; ottaa
käytäntöön, panna alulle; tehdä esitys
(parl.). -**tion** [-'dakʃn] s. johdanto;
esittely; suositus; käyttöönotto; *letter
of* ~ suosituskirje. -**tory** [-'dakt(ə)ri]
a. johdanto-, alustava.
introspec|tion [intrə'spek|ʃn] s.
introspektio. -**tive** [-tiv] a. itseään
havainnoiva.
introvert ['intrəvə:t] s. sisäänpäin
kääntynyt ihminen; v. [intrə'və:t]
kääntää sisäänpäin.
intrude [in'tru:d] v. tungetella; tupata,
tyrkyttää; ~ *oneself upon sb.*
tuppautua jkn seuraan. -**r** [-ə] s.
tungettelija, kuokkavieras.
intru|sion [in'tru:|ʒn] s. tungettelu,
tuppautuminen. -**sive** [-siv] a.
tunkeileva.
intui|tion [intju'iʃn] s. sisäinen
näkemys, intuitio. -**tive** [-'tju:itiv] a.
intuitiivinen, välittömästi tajuava.
inunda|te ['inʌndeit] v. peittää
tulvaveden alle, tulvia (yli). -**tion**
[-'deiʃn] s. tulva.
inure [i'njuə] v. karaista, totuttaa *(to
jhk.)*
invade [in'veid] v. hyökätä (maahan);
loukata. -**r** [-ə] s. maahanhyökkääjä.
invalid ['invəli:d] s. & a. raihnas, sairas
henkilö; vammainen, invalidi; a.
[in'vælid] pätemätön, mitätön; v.
[invə'li:d] vapauttaa palveluksesta
(sairauden, vamman takia). -**ate**
[in'vælideit] v. julistaa
pätemättömäksi, kumota. -**ism** ['- -] s.
raihnaisuus. -**ity** [invə'liditi] s.
pätemättömyys.
invaluable [in'væljuəbl] a. verrattoman
arvokas, arvaamattoman kallis.
invaria|ble [in'vɛəriəbl] a.

muuttumaton, pysyväinen. **-bly** *adv.* muuttumatta; poikkeuksetta, säännöllisesti, aina.

inva|sion [in'veiʒn] *s.* maahan hyökkäys; loukkaus; (kuv.) tulva. **-sive** [-siv] *a.* hyökkäävä.

in|vective [in'vektiv] *s.* herjaukset, kirosanat. **-veigh** [-'vei] *v.:* ~ *against* haukkua, sättiä, herjata jkta.

inveigle [in'vi:gl, Am. -veigl] *v.* viekoitella, houkutella.

invent [in'vent] *v.* keksiä, sepittää. **-ion** [-'venʃn] *s.* keksiminen, keksintö; kekseliäisyys *(power of ~);* sepitelmä. **-ive** [-iv] *a.* kekseliäs. **-iveness** *s.* kekseliäisyys. **-or** [-ə] *s.* keksijä. **-ory** [-əri] *s.* (kalusto-, tavara)luettelo; varasto; *make an ~ of* tehdä (kalusto-ym) luettelo, inventoida.

Inverness [invə'nes] *erisn.*

inver|se [in'və:s] *a.* päinvastainen, käännetty; ~ *ly proportional* kääntäen verrannollinen. **-sion** [-'və:ʃn] *s.* nurin kääntäminen, päinvastainen järjestys; käänteinen sanajärjestys.

invert [in'və:t] *v.* kääntää ylösalaisin t. päinvastoin; *s.* ['invə:t] homoseksualisti; ~*ed commas* lainausmerkit.

invertebrate [in'və:tibrit] *a. & s.* selkärangaton (m. kuv.).

invest [in'vest] *v.* sijoittaa (rahaa); verhota, varustaa *(with* jllak), asettaa (virkaan); piirittää. **-iture** [-itʃə] *s.* (jhk) arvoon asettaminen.

investigat|e [in'vestigeit] *v.* tutkia. **-ion** [-'geiʃn] *s.* tutkimus. **-or** [-ə] *s.* tutkija.

investiture [in'vestitʃə] *s.* virkaan asettaminen.

invest|ment [in'vest'mənt] *s.* sijoitus. **-or** [-ə] *s.* rahan sijoittaja.

inveterate [in'vet(ə)rit] *a.* piintynyt; syvälle juurtunut.

invidious [in'vidiəs] *a.* suuttumusta herättävä, loukkaava.

invigilat|e [in'vidʒileit] *v.* olla valvojana (kokeissa t. tutkinnossa). **-or** [-ə] *s.* valvoja.

invigorat|e [in'vigoreit] *v.* elähdyttää, virkistää; *-ing* virkistävä, virvoittava.

invincible [in'vinsəbl] *a.* voittamaton.

invio|la|ble [in'vaiələbl] *a.* loukkaamaton, pyhänä pidettävä. **-te** [-lit] *a.* pyhänä pidetty, koskematon,

loukkaamaton.

invisible [in'vizəbl] *a.* näkymätön.

invitation [invi'teiʃn] *s.* kutsu.

invit|e [in'vait] *v.* kutsua; kehottaa; houkutella, herättää. **-ing** *a.* houkutteleva, viehättävä.

invocation [invə(u)'keiʃn] *s.* avuksihuutaminen, rukous.

invoice ['invɔis] *s.* faktuura, tavaralasku; *v.* laskuttaa.

invoke [in'vouk] *v.* huutaa avuksi, vedota, manata (henkiä).

involuntar|y [in'vɔlənt(ə)ri] *a.* tahaton; *-ily* tahtomattaan.

involve [in'vɔlv] *v.* kietoa; sotkea, sekoittaa; sisältää, käsittää; tuoda mukanaan; ~*d* monimutkainen; ~*d in debt* velkaantunut. **-ment** *s.* (m.) osallistuminen.

invulnerable [in'vʌln(ə)rəbl] *a.* haavoittumaton.

inward ['inwəd] *a.* sisä(ll)inen, sisä-; *adv.* sisäänpäin. **-ly** *adv.* sisä(ll)isesti, sisimmässään. **-s** [-z] *adv.* sisäänpäin.

iod|ine ['aiəd|i:n] *s.* jodi. **-ize** [-aiz] *v.:* ~*d salt* jodipitoinen ruokasuola.

ion ['aiən] *s.* ioni (fys.).

Ionian [ai'ounjən] *a.* joonialainen; ~ *Sea* Joonianmeri.

Ionic [ai'ɔnik] *a.* = ed.

iota [ai'outə] *s.* kuv. hitunen.

IOU ['aiəu'ju:] *s.* velkakirja.

Iowa ['aiəwə] *erisn.*

Iran [i'rɑ:n] *erisn.* **-ian** [i'reinjən] *a. & s.* iranilainen.

Iraq [i'rɑ:k] *erisn.* Irak. **-i** [i'rɑ:ki] *a. & s.* irakilainen.

irascible [i'ræsibl] *a.* kiukkuinen, äkäinen, pikavihainen.

irate [ai'reit] *a.* vihastunut.

ire ['aiə] *s.* (run.) suuttumus.

Ireland ['aiələnd] *erisn.* Irlanti.

Irene [ai'ri:ni, ai'ri:n] *erisn.*

iridescent [iri'desnt] *a.* sateenkaaren väreissä kimalteleva.

iris ['aiəris] *a.* (silmän) kehäkalvo; kurjenmiekka.

Irish ['aiəriʃ] *a.* irlantilainen; *s.* iirin kieli; *the ~* irlantilaiset. **-man** *s.* irlantilainen. **-woman** *s.* irlannitar.

irk [ə:k] *v.* väsyttää, kiusata. **-some** [-səm] *a.* väsyttävä, kiusallinen.

iron ['aiən] *s.* rauta; silitysrauta; *a.* rautainen; raudanluja; *v.* silittää; ~*s* *(pl.)* kahleet; *steam* ~ höyryrauta; ~ *curtain* rautaesirippu; ~ *ration* rautaisannos; ~ *out* tasoittaa, poistaa; *[this]* ~ *s well* on helppo silittää. **-clad** *a.* raudoitettu; *s.* (vanh.) panssarilaiva.

ironic(al) [ai'rɔnik,-(ə)l] *a.* ivallinen, ironinen.

ironing ['aiəniŋ] *s.* silitys. ~ **-board** silityslauta.

iron|monger rautakauppias; **-mongery** rautatavarat, rautakauppa. **-sides:** *the I~* Cromwellin »rautakyljet». **-ware** rautatavara(t). **-work** rauta|työ, -osat; ~ *s* rautatehdas.

irony ['aiərəni] *s.* iva, ironia.

irradi|ate [i'reidieit] *v.* säteillä jhk, valaista, kirkastaa; antaa sädehoitoa, säteilyttää. **-ation** [-'eiʃn] *s.* säteily; sädehoito.

irrational [i'ræʃnl] *a.* järjetön, järjenvastainen, mieletön; irrationaalinen.

irreclaimable [iri'kleiməbl] *a.* peruuttamaton.

irrecognizable [i'rekəgnaizəbl] *a.* mahdoton tuntea.

irreconcilable [irekən'sailəbl] *a.* leppymätön, sovittamaton.

irrecoverable [iri'kʌv(ə)rəbl] *a.* mahdoton saada takaisin; korvaamaton.

irredeemable [iri'di:məbl] *a.* mahdoton lunastaa takaisin; peruuttamaton, toivoton.

irreducible [iri'dju:səbl] *a.* mahdoton supistaa, pienentää.

irrefutable [i'refjutəbl, iri'fju:-] *a.* kumoamaton, kieltämätön.

irregular [i'regjulə] *a.* säännötön, epäsäännöllinen, sääntöjenvastainen; epätasainen; (sot.) vakinaiseen väkeen kuulumaton; *s.:* ~ *s* vapaajoukot. **-ity** [-'læriti] *s.* epäsäännöllisyys, säännöttömyys.

irrelevan|ce [i'relivəns] *s.* asiaankuulumattomuus. **-t** *a.* [-ənt] asiaankuulumaton *(to).*

irreligious [iri'lidʒəs] *a.* uskonnoton, jumalaton.

irremediable [iri'mi:djəbl] *a.* mahdoton parantaa, auttamaton.

irremovable [iri'mu:vəbl] *a.* mahdoton siirtää t. erottaa.

irreparable [i'rep(ə)rəbl] *a.* mahdoton korjata, korvaamaton.

irreplaceable [iri'pleisəbl] *a.* korvaamaton.

irrepressible [iri'presəbl] *a.* lannistumaton, mahdoton hillitä.

irreproachable [iri'prəutʃəbl] *a.* moitteeton, nuhteeton.

irresistible [iri'zistəbl] *a.* vastustamaton.

irresolu|te [i'rezəlu:t] *a.* epäröivä, kahden vaiheilla oleva, päättämätön. **-tion** [-'lu:ʃn] *s.* epäröinti.

irrespective [iris'pektiv] *a. & adv.:* ~ *of* jstk riippumatta, jhk katsomatta, jstk välittämättä.

irresponsi|bility [irispɔnsə'biliti] *s.* edesvastuuttomuus. **-ble** [-'pɔnsəbl] *a.* (edes)vastuuton.

irretrievable [iri'tri:vəbl] *a.* mahdoton saada takaisin; korvaamaton.

irreveren|ce [i'rev(ə)r(ə)n|s] *s.* kunnioituksen puu e, ylenkatse. **-t.** [-t] *a.* ylenkatseellinen, halveksiva, epäkunnioittava.

irreversible [iri'və:səbl] *a.* peruuttamaton.

irrevocable [i'revəkəbl] *a.* peruuttamaton, kumoamaton.

irriga|te ['irigeit] *v.* kastella, huuhdella. **-tion** [-'geiʃn] *s.* (keinotekoinen) kastelu; (lääk.) huuhtelu; *[grow sth.] under* ~ keinokastelun avulla.

irrita|bility [irita'biliti] *s.* ärtyisyys. **-ble** ['iritəbl] *a.* ärtyisä, ärtyvä, helposti suuttuva. **-nt** ['irit(ə)nt] *s.* ärsyke. **-te** ['iriteit] *v.* ärsyttää, hermostuttaa. **-tion** [-'teiʃn] *s.* ärsytys; ärtymys, suuttumus.

irruption ['irʌpʃn] *s.* (maahan) hyökkäys, äkillinen tunkeutuminen.

Irving ['ə:viŋ] *erisn.*

is [iz, z] *be*-vbn *ind. prees. sg. 3. pers.* on.

Isaac ['aizək] *erisn.* Iisak.

Isaiah [ai'zaiə, Am. -'zeiə] *erisn.* Jesaja.

isinglass ['aizingla:s] *s.* kalanliima, liivate.

Islam [iz'la:m, 'izləm] *s.* muhamettilaisuus. **-ic** [iz'læmik] *a.* islamilainen. **-ite** ['izləmait] *s.* muhamettilainen.

island ['ailənd] s. saari; katu-, liikennekoroke. **-er** [-ə] s. saaren asukas.

isle [ail] s. (run.) saari. **-t** [-it] s. pieni saari.

isn't = is not.

isobar ['aisə(u)ba:] s. isobaari.

isola|te ['aisəleit] v. eristää; ~d yksittäis-, erillis-. **-tion** [-'leiʃn] s. eristäminen; eristetty asema; (~**ist** s. eristäytymispolitiikan kannattaja).

isotope ['aisə(u)təup] s. isotooppi.

Israel ['izrei(ə)l, 'izriəl] s. Israel. **-i** [iz'rei(ə)li] a. Israelin; s. israelilainen. **-ite** [-riəlait] s. israelilainen (raam.)

issue ['isju:, 'iʃu:] s. ulostulo, -virtaaminen; ulospääsy; julkaiseminen, liikkeeseen laskeminen; (lehden) numero; osakeanti, setelinanti; lapset, jälkeläiset; lopputulos, päätös; (kiista)kysymys; seuraus; v. tulla, virrata ulos, päästä t. tulla esiin; olla lähtöisin; lähettää julkisuuteen, julkaista, laskea liikkeeseen; jaella; *at ~ riidanalaisena; riidassa; the point at ~ kiistanalainen kysymys; die without ~ kuolla jättämättä rintaperillistä; join (take) ~ with* olla eri mieltä jkn kanssa. **-less** a. lapseton.

Istanbul [istæn'bu:l] erisn.

isthmus ['isməs] s. kannas.

it [it] pron. se; ~ *is fine* on kaunis ilma; ~ *is warm* on lämmintä; ~ *is raining* sataa; *make a day of ~* huvitella perusteellisesti; *catch ~* saada selkäsauna; *that's ~* (se on) oikein! *we are in for ~* nyt joudumme ikävyyksiin.

Italian [i'tæljən] a. & s. italialainen; italian kieli.

italic [i'tæli|k] s.: ~s vinokirjaimet; *print in* ~s = seur. **-ize** [-saiz] v. kursivoida.

Italy ['itəli] erisn. Italia.

itch [itʃ] s. syyhy; kutina; v. syyhyä, kutista. **-y** [-i] a. kutiseva.

item ['aitem] s. erä; (yksityinen) kohta; uutinen (~ *of news*). **-ize** ['aitəmaiz]: *an ~d bill* eritelty lasku.

iterate ['itəreit] v. toistaa.

itiner|ant [i'tin(ə)r(ə)nt, ai'tin-] a. kiertävä, kuljeksiva. **-ary** [ai'tin(ə)rəri] s. matkareitti; matkakäsikirja, -suunnitelma. **-ate** [i'tinəreit, ai'tin-] v. kiertää, matkustaa.

its [its] poss. pron. sen, -nsa.

it's [its] = it is.

itself [it'self] pron. itse; *by ~* itsekseen; itsestään; *in ~* sinänsä, itsessään; *of ~* itsestään.

Ives [aivz] erisn.

ivied ['aivid] a. muratin peittämä.

ivory ['aiv(ə)ri] s. norsunluu; norsunluuesineet, pianon kosketin; a. norsunluinen, norsunluun värinen.

ivy ['aivi] s. muratti.

J

J, j ['dʒei] s. j-kirjain. Lyh.: **Jan.**
January; **Jas.** *James* Jaakob (U.T.);
Jer. *Jeremiah;* **J.P.** *Justice of the
Peace:* **Judg.** *Judges;* **Jul.** *July;* **Jun.**
June; Junior nuorempi.

jab [dʒæb] v. töytäistä; s. töytäisy, isku;
sl. pisto, injektio.

jabber ['dʒæbə] v. lörpöttää, puhua
papattaa (m. ~ *away);* s. lavertelu,
lörpöttely.

jacaranda [dʒækə'rændə] s. jakaranda.

jack [dʒæk] s. mies, työmies, jätkä,
laivamies (tav. ~ *tar);*
(kortti)sotamies; väkivipu, »tunkki»,
talja; kohdepallo (keilapeleissä);
(keula)lippu; sl. raha; v. nostaa
väkivivulla (m. ~ *up);* ~*-in-the-box*
vieteriukko; ~*-of-all-trades*
tuhattaituri; ~*o'-lantern* virvatuli;
every man ~ joka mies.

Jack [dʒæk] erisn. Jussi; ~ *and Gill
(Jill)* Matti ja Maija, Matit ja Maijat;
before you could say J ~ *Robinson*
silmänräpäyksessä; ~ *Frost*
pakkasherra.

jackal ['dʒækɔ:l] s. sakaali; (kuv.)
kätyri.

jack|anapes ['dʒæk|əneips] s. itserakas
henkilö, nenäkäs lapsi. **-ass** [-æs]
urosaasi; pölkkypää. **-boot**
pitkävartinen saapas. **-daw** naakka.

jacket ['dʒækit] s. lyhyt takki, nuttu;
(kirjan) suojakansi, irtopäällys;
(perunan)kuori; (tekn.) vaippa; *dust
a p.'s* ~ antaa jklle selkään.

jack|-knife iso linkkuveitsi. **-pot** kaikki
panokset; *hit the* ~ korjata
suurvoitto.

Jacob ['dʒeikəb] erisn. Jaakob. **-ean**
[dʒækə'bi(:)ən] a. Jaakko I:n
aikainen. **-in** ['dʒækəbin] s. jakobiini
(Ranskassa). **-ite** ['dʒækəbait] s.
jakobiitti (Stuart-suvun kannattaja).

jade 1. [dʒeid] s. hevoskaakki;
tytönheilakka. **-d** [-id] a. lopen
väsynyt.

jade 2. [dʒeid] s. jade(kivi).

Jaffa ['dʒæfə] erisn.

jag [dʒæg] s. pykälä; v. tehdä
pykäläiseksi. **-ged** [-id], **-gy** [-i] a.
pykäläinen, rosoinen.

jaguar ['dʒægjuə:] s. jaguaari.

jail [dʒeil] s. vankila; linna (three years
in ~); be in ~ (puhek.) olla lusimassa.
-bird (leik.) vanki, »vankilakundi».
-er [-ə] s. vanginvartija.

jalopy [dʒə'lɔpi] s. Am. autorämä.

jam 1. [dʒæm] s. hillo.

jam 2. [dʒæm] v. puristaa, tunkea,
sulloa, joutua epäkuntoon t.
puristuksiin, tarttua kiinni, juuttua
(kiinni), lukkiintua; tukkia; (rad.)
häiritä (toisilla lähetyksillä); s.
puristus, (väen)tungos,
tukkeutuminen; *(traffic ~)* ruuhka,
seisaus, *(log ~)* tukkisuma; *be in a* ~
olla pinteessä; ~ *session* jazzmusiikin
improvisointitilaisuus.

Jamaica [dʒ(ə)'meikə] erisn.

jam [dʒæm] s. (oven ym) pieli.

jamboree [dʒæmbə'ri:] s. suuri
partiolaiskokous; sl. juhla, kemut.

James [dʒeimz] erisn. Jaakko, Jaakob.

Jane, Janet ['dʒænit] erisn.

jangle ['dʒæŋgl] v. rämistä, kitistä,
rämisyttää; riidellä ; räminä, melu.

janitor ['dʒænitə] s. ovenvartija,
talonmies.

January ['dʒænjuəri] s. tammikuu.

Jap [dʒæp] s. (alat.) japsi.

Japan [dʒə'pæn] erisn. Japani; s. (j ~)
(japanilainen) lakkaväri; v. lakata.
-ese [dʒæpə'ni:z] a. japanilainen; s.
(pl. = sg.) japanilainen; japanin kieli.

jar 1. [dʒa:] s. ruukku, tölkki.

jar 2. [dʒa:] v. rämistä, vihloa, olla

ristiriidassa *(against)*, järkyttää; särähtää *(on sb.'s ear)*; s. soraääni, vihlova ääni; räminä; täräys, järkytys.

jargon ['dʒɑːgən] s. siansaksa, (ammatin) erikoiskieli, mongerrus.

jarring ['dʒɑːriŋ] a. vihlova, epäsointuinen.

jasmin(e) ['dʒæsmin] s. jasmiini.

jasper ['dʒæspə] s. jaspis(kivi).

jaundice ['dʒɔːndis] s. keltatauti; kateus. **-d** [-t] a. kateellinen, ennakkoluuloinen.

jaunt [dʒɔːnt] s. huviretki; v. tehdä huviretki. **-iness** s. hilpeys jne. **-y** [-i] a. hilpeä, huoleton, itsevarma.

Java ['dʒɑːvə] erisn. Jaava. **-nese** [-'niːz] a. & s. jaavalainen.

javelin ['dʒævlin] s. (heitto)keihäs; *throwing the ~*, *~-throw* keihäänheitto.

jaw [dʒɔː] s. leuka(pieli); *pl.* kita, suu; sl. suunsoitto *(none of your ~)*, nuhdesaarna; v. sl. läksyttää; *stop ~ing at me!* lopeta suunsoittosi! **~-bone** leukaluu. **~-breaker** vaikeasti äännettävä sana.

jay [dʒei] s. närhi. **-walker** varomaton jalankulkija.

jazz [dʒæz] s. jazz(musiikki), jatsi; v. tanssia jazzia; *~ up* piristää.

jealous ['dʒeləs] a. mustasukkainen, kateellinen; arka, tarkka, jstk kiinni pitävä *(of)*; (raam.) kiivas. **-y** [-i] s. mustasukkaisuus, kateus.

Jean [dʒiːn] erisn.

jeans [dʒiːnz] s. *pl.* farmarihousut, farkut; haalarit.

jeep [dʒiːp] s. maastovaunu, jeeppi.

jeer [dʒiə] v. tehdä pilkkaa, pilkata *(at* jtk); s. pilkka, iva.

Jehovah [dʒi'houvə] erisn.

jehu ['dʒiːhjuː] s. hurja ajaja.

jejune [dʒi'dʒuːn] a. kuiva, niukka; kuiva, mielenkiinnoton.

jelly ['dʒeli] s. hyytelö; v. hyytyä, hyydyttää. **~-fish** maneetti.

jemmy ['dʒemi] s. sorkkarauta.

jenny ['dʒeni] s. *[spinning-]~* kehruukone; (liikkuva) nosturi.

jeopard|ize ['dʒepədaiz] v. vaarantaa, panna (vaaralle) alttiiksi. **-y** ['dʒepədi] s. vaara.

jeremiad [dʒeri'maiəd] s. valitusvirsi.

Jerem|iah [dʒeri'maiə] erisn. Jeremia.

-y ['dʒerimi] erisn.

Jericho ['dʒerikəu] erisn.

jerk [dʒɔːk] s. nykäys, nykäisy, nykiminen; lihaskouristus; heijaste *(knee ~)*; (urh. painonnosto) työntö; v. nykäistä, nykiä, nytkähdellä, töytäistä; *~ out* lausua töksähtäen.

jerkin ['dʒɔːkin] s. (tiukka) nahkanuttu.

jerky ['dʒɔːki] a. nytkähtelevä, nykivä.

jerry ['dʒeri] s. sl. yöastia; J~ (sl.) sakemanni. **~-built** hatarasti (ja huonoista aineista) rakennettu.

jersey ['dʒɔːzi] s. neulekangas; villatakki, jerseytakki.

Jerusalem [dʒə'ruːs(ə)ləm] erisn.

jessamine ['dʒæsəmin] = *jasmine*.

jest [dʒest] s. leikinlasku, pila; v. laskea leikkiä; *in ~* piloillaan, kurillaan. **-er** [-ə] s. hovinarri; kujeilija. **-ingly** adv. leikkisästi.

Jesuit ['dʒezjuit] s. jesuiitta.

Jesus ['dʒiːzəs] erisn. Jeesus.

jet 1. [dʒet] s. suihku, (kaasu)liekki; = *~ plane*; v. suihkuttaa, suihkuta; *~ plane* suihkulentokone; *~-propelled* suihkukäyttöinen; *~ set* hieno (super-) seurapiiri.

jet 2. [dʒet] s. gagaatti. **~-black** sysimusta.

jetsam ['dʒetsəm] s. (rannalle ajautuneet) hylkytavarat; *flotsam and ~ m.* ihmis|hylyt, -rauniot.

jettison ['dʒetisn] s. tavaran heittäminen yli laidan; v. heittää yli laidan (merihädässä), hylätä (avaruuteen).

jetty ['dʒeti] s. aallonmurtaja; laituri; a. = *jet-black*.

Jew [dʒuː] s. juutalainen. **~-baiting** juutalaisvaino.

jewel ['dʒuːəl] s. jalokivi; (kuv.) helmi v. koristaa jalokivillä. **-ler** [-ə] s. jalokivikauppias. **-lery**, **-ry** [-ri] s. jalokivet, korut.

Jew|ess ['dʒu(ː)is] s. juutalaisnainen. **-ish** [-iʃ] a. juutalainen. **-ry** ['dʒuəri] s. juutalaiset; juutalaiskortteli.

jew's-harp s. eräänl. huuliharppu.

jib [dʒib] s. viistopurje, halkaisija; v. heittää yli (laidalta toiselle); (hevosesta) vikuroida; *~ at* säikkyä jtk.

jibe [dʒaib] ks. *gibe*; Am. sl. käydä

yksiin, sopia yhteen.

jiffy ['dʒifi] *s.: in a* ~ käden
käänteessä, heti paikalla (puhek.).

jig [dʒig] *s.* vilkas tanssi, sen sävel; *v.*
tanssia »jigiä», hyppiä, hypittää.
-gered [-əd] *a.: I am* ~ *if* paha minut
periköön, jos...; ~ *up* uupunut. **-gle**
[-l] *v.* heiluttaa. **-saw** lehtisaha; ~
puzzle palapeli.

Jill [dʒil] *erisn.* ks. *Jack.*

jilt [dʒilt] *v.* pettää, hylätä; *s.*
keimailija, uskoton nainen.

Jim [dʒim] *erisn.* lyh. = *James;* ~ *Crow*
Am. (pelk.) neekeri; ~ *Crow car*
mustien vaunu.

jimjams ['dʒimdʒæmz] *s.: get the* ~
hermostusa.

jimmy ['dʒimi] *s.* Am. = *jemmy.*

jingle ['dʒiŋgl] *s.* helinä; *s.* helistä,
helistellä.

jingo ['dʒiŋgəu] *s.* (m. *-ist)*
kiihkoisänmaallinen henkilö,
sotaintoilija; *by* ~! totta vie! *jingo*
[-izm] *s.* kiihkoisänmaallisuus.

jinks [dʒiŋks] *s.: high* ~ meluisa
ilonpito.

jinx [dʒiŋks] *s.* paha taika,
pahanilmanlintu.

jitter ['dʒitə] *s.* (TV) värinä, tärinä. **-s**
[-z] *s. pl.: have the* ~ olla
hermostunut. **-y** [-ri] *a.* hermostunut.

jiu-jitsu ks. *ju-jitsu.*

jive [dʒaiv] *s.* jive-tanssi.

Joan [dʒəun] *erisn.* Johanna; ~ *of Arc*
Orleansin neitsyt.

job [dʒɔb] *s.* työ, toimi; työpaikka,
toimipaikka; asia, juttu; keinottelu; *v.*
tehdä tilapäistöitä; keinotella,
väärinkäyttää virka-asemaansa; *good
(bad)* ~ hyvä (paha) asia; *[he] made a
good* ~ *of it* teki, suoritti sen hyvin; *by
the* ~ urakalla, kappaletyönä; *odd* ~ *s*
tilapäistyöt; *on the* ~ työssä,
työpaikalla; *out of a* ~ työtön; ~
evaluation työn luokitus; ~ *lot*
summakaupalla ostettu (ostettava)
erä. **-ber** [-ə] *s.* välittäjä; urakkamies.
-bery [-əri] *s.* (virka-aseman)
väärinkäyttö, keinottelu. **-less** *a.*
työtön.

Job [dʒəub] *erisn.:* ~ *'s comforter* huono
lohduttaja; ~ *'s news* jobinposti.

Jock [dʒɔk] *erisn.* skotlantilainen
(sotilas); Am. = *athlete.*

jockey ['dʒɔki] *s.* kilpa-,
ammattiratsastaja, jokkei; *v.*
petkuttaa, juonitella; ~ *for position*
etuilla.

jocko ['dʒɔkəu] *s.* simpanssi.

jocos|e [dʒə'kəus] *a.* leikkisä. **-ity**
[dʒə(u)'kɔsiti] *s.* leikillisyys,
kujeilu.

jocular ['dʒɔkjulə] *a.* leikkisä. **-ity**
[-'læriti] *s.* leikillisyys.

jocund ['dʒɔkənd] *a.* iloinen, hilpeä.
-ity [dʒə(u)'kʌnditi] *s.* hilpeys.

jodhpurs ['dʒɔdpə:z] *s. pl.* (nilkkaan
ulottuvat) ratsastushousut.

jog [dʒɔg] *v.* tuupata, tönäistä;
virkistää (muistia); hölkytellä (us. ~
on, along), hölkätä; *s.* sysäys;
hölkytys; ~ *-ging* (kunto)hölkkä. **-gle**
[-l] *v.* täristellä, täristä; *s.* tärinä.
~ *-trot* tasainen hölkkä, (kuv.)
yksitoikkoinen elämä, vanha tahti.

Johannesburg [dʒə(u)'hænisbə:g] *erisn.*

John [dʒɔn] *erisn.* Johannes; ~ *Bull*
tyypillinen englantilainen, Englannin
kansa.

johnny ['dʒɔni] *s.* mies, kaveri.

join [dʒɔin] *v.* liittää yhteen, yhdistää;
liittyä yhteen, yhtyä; liittyä jkn
seuraan, liittyä jäseneksi; *s.*
liitoskohta; *will you* ~ *us?* tuletko
mukaamme? *would you care to* ~ *me
for lunch?* tulisitko kanssani
lounaalle? ~ *battle* ryhtyä taisteluun;
~ *forces with* liittyä (yhteen), liittyä
jkh; ~ *in* yhtyä lauluun; ~ *in [doing*
..] ottaa osaa jhk; ~ *up* mennä
armeijaan. **-er** [-ə] *s.* puuseppä. **-ery**
[-əri] *s.* puu(sepän)työ.

joint [dʒɔint] *s.* liitekohta, liitos,
sauma; nivel; reisipala, paisti; sl.
kapakka, kuppila; marihuanasavuke;
a. yhteinen, yhteis-; *v.* liittää yhteen;
 aloitella; *out of* ~ sijoiltaan, *put sb.'s
nose out of* ~ lyödä joku laudalta; ~
efforts yhteiset ponnistukset; ~ *heir*
kanssaperillinen; ~ *stock*
osakepääoma; ~ *-stock company*
osakeyhtiö. **-ed** [-id] *a.* nivelikäs. **-ly**
adv. yhteisesti, yhdessä. **-ure** [-ʃə] *s.*
leskentila.

joist [dʒɔist] *s.:* ~ *s* välipohjan palkit;
teräspalkisto (katossa).

jok|e [dʒəuk] *s.* leikinlasku, pila; *v.*
laskea leikkiä; *make a* ~ veistää vitsi;

practical ~ kepponen; *it's no* ~ siitä
on leikki kaukana; *in* ~ leikillään. **-er**
[-ə] *s.* leikinlaskija; jokeri. **-ing** *s.*
leikinlasku; ~ *apart!* leikki sikseen!

jolli|fication [dʒɔlifi'keiʃn] *s.* ilonpito.
-fy ['dʒɔlifai] *v.* pitää iloa. **-ty** ['dʒɔliti]
s. iloisuus.

jolly ['dʒɔli] *a.* iloinen, hilpeä, hauska;
iloisella tuulella, hiprakassa; *adv.*
sangen, erinomaisen; *v.:* ~ *sb. along*
pitää hyvällä tuulella, piristää jkta; *a*
~ *good fellow* kunnon mies; *you* ~
well know tiedät sangen hyvin. **-boat** *s.*
jolla.

jolt [dʒəult] *v.* täristä, täryyttää; *s.*
tärinä, tärähdys; järkytys.

Jonah ['dʒəunə] *erisn.* Joona.

Jones [dʒəunz] *erisn.: keep up with the*
~*es* olla yhtä hyvä kuin naapuri.

jonquil ['dʒɔŋkwil] *s.* keltainen narsissi.

Jordan ['dʒɔ:dn] *erisn.* Jordania; *the* ~
Jordanjoki. **-ian** [-'deinjən] *a. & s.*
jordanialainen.

Joseph ['dʒəuzif] *erisn.* Joosef.

Joshua ['dʒɔʃwə] *erisn.* Joosua.

joss|-house ['dʒɔshaus] kiinalainen
temppeli. ~**-stick** suitsutustikku.

jostle ['dʒɔsl] *v.* tuupata, tyrkätä,
töniä; tungeskella; *s.* tönäisy;
tuuppiminen.

jot [dʒɔt] *s.* piste; *v.* kirjoittaa äkkiä
muistiin, töhertää (us. ~ *down); not a*
~ ei rahtuakaan.

joule [dʒu:l] *s.* (fys.) joule.

journal ['dʒɔ:n|l] *s.* päiväkirja;
(kirjanpidossa) yhdistelykirja;
sanomalehti, aikakauskirja; *ship's* ~
lokikirja. **-ese** [dʒə:nə'li:z] *s.* (huono)
sanomalehtikieli. **-ism** [-olizm] *s.*
sanomalehti|ala, -työ; lehdistöoppi.
-ist [-olist] *s.* sanomalehtimies,
-nainen. **-istic** [-ə'listik] *a.*
sanomalehti-.

journey ['dʒə:ni] *s.* matka (et. maitse);
v. matkustaa; *go on a* ~, *make a* ~
lähteä matkalle, matkustaa. **-man**
kisälli.

joust [dʒaust] *s.* turnailu; *v.* turnailla.

Jove [dʒəuv] *erisn.* Jupiter; *by* ~! totta
totisesti!

jovial ['dʒəuvjəl] *a.* iloluontoinen,
hilpeä. **-ity** [-'viʼæliti] *s.* hilpeys.

jowl [dʒaul] *s.* leuka; poski; *cheek by* ~
vieri vieressä.

joy [dʒɔi] *s.* ilo, riemu; iloisuus; *wish a*
p. ~ toivottaa onnea jklle; *v.* (run.)
iloita (~ *in).* **-ful** *a. = joyous.* **-less** *a.*
iloton. **-ous** [-əs] *a.* riemukas, iloinen;
ilahduttava. ~**-ride** huviajo (esim.
luvatta lainatulla autolla).

jubil|ant ['dʒu:bil|ənt] *a.* riemuitseva.
-ation [-'leiʃn] *s.* riemu(itseminen).
-ee [-i:] *s.* riemujuhla, -vuosi;
50-vuotisjuhla; *Silver* ~
25-vuotisjuhla.

Jud|(a)ea [dʒu:'di(:)ə] *erisn.* Juudea.
-aic [dʒu:'deiik] *a.* juutalainen. **-aism**
['dʒu:deiizm] *s.* juutalaisuus. **-as**
['dʒu:dəs] *erisn.* (kuv.) petturi.

judge [dʒʌdʒ] *s.* tuomari; asiantuntija;
v. tuomita; ratkaista; arvostella; pitää
jnak, otaksua; *a* ~ *of wine*
viinintuntija; ~ *for yourself* ratkaise
(päättele) itse; *judging from (by)* jstk
päättellen; *Judges* Tuomarien kirja.

judgment(-ement) ['dʒʌdʒmənt] *s.*
tuomio; arvostelu, mielipide;
arvostelukyky; *pass* ~ langettaa
tuomio; *sit in* ~ istua oikeutta,
tuomita; *Day of J* ~ tuomiopäivä.
~**-seat** tuomarinistuin.

judicature ['dʒu:dikətʃə] *a.*
oikeudenkäyttö; tuomarikunta;
tuomioistuin.

judici|al [dʒu:(:)'diʃ(ə)l] *a.*
oikeudellinen, oikeus-; tuomio-,
tuomarin, tuomitseva; puolueeton; ~
murder oikeusmurha. **-ary** [-'diʃəri] *s.*
tuomarikunta. **-ous** [-'diʃəs] *a.*
järkevä, viisas, arvostelukykyinen.

Judith ['dʒu:diθ], **Judy** ['dʒu:di] *erisn.*

judo ['dʒu:dəu] *s.* judo.

jug [dʒʌg] *s.* kannu, kaadin; sl. vankila.

Juggernaut ['dʒʌgənɔ:t] *s.* (kuv.)
tuhovoima(t).

juggle ['dʒʌgl] *v.* tehdä taikatemppuja;
petkuttaa; *s.* taikatemppu; ~ *with*
facts vääristellä asiat. **-r** [-ə] *s.*
jonglööri. **-ry** [-əri] *s.*
silmänkääntötemppu, -temput.

Jugoslav ['ju:gə(u)slɑ:v] *a. & s.*
jugoslaavi, jugoslavialainen. **-ia**
[-'--] *erisn.* Jugoslavia.

jugular ['dʒʌgjulə] *a.* kaula-.

juic|e [dʒu:s] *s.* mehu; *gastric* ~
mahaneste; ~**-extractor**
mehunpuristin. **-iness** [-inis] *s.*
mehukkuus. **-y** [-i] *a.* mehukas.

ju-jitsu [dʒuː'dʒitsu:] s. jiujitsu.

jujube ['dʒuːdʒuːb] s. eräänl. pastilli, karamelli.

juke-box ['dʒuːk-] s. levyautomaatti.

julep ['dʒuːlip] s. eräänl. grogi *(mint ~).*

Juli|an ['dʒuːljən] a. juliaaninen. **-et** [-jət] *erisn.* Julia. **-us** [-jəs] *erisn.*

July [dʒu(:)'lai] s. heinäkuu.

jumble ['dʒʌmbl] v. sotkea, mättää sekaisin (us. ~ *up);* s. sekamelska. **~-sale** »kirpputori».

jumbo ['dʒʌmbou] a. iso ja kömpelö; s. jättiläis- (~ *jets).*

jump [dʒʌmp] v. hypätä, hyppiä; hypätä, loikata jnk yli; kohota äkkiä; s. hyppy, hyppäys, loikkaus; ~ *at* innokkaasti suostua (tarjoukseen ym); ~ *on (upon)* nuhdella; ~ *a claim* anastaa (toisen) valtausalue; ~ *the gun* ottaa varaslähtö; ~ *the track* suistua kiskoilta; ~ *to conclusions* hätiköiden päätellä; *high (long)* ~ korkeus-, pituushyppy. **-er** [-ə] s. neulepusero, jumpperi; hyppääjä. **-y** [-i] a. hermostunut.

junc|tion ['dʒʌŋ(k)ʃn] s. yhdistäminen; yhtymäkohta; rautatieristeys, -solmu; liitos. **-ture** [-(k)tʃə] s. (ratkaiseva) vaihe, tilanne; at *[critical]* ~ tässä kriittisessä vaiheessa.

June [dʒuːn] s. kesäkuu.

ungle ['dʒʌŋgl] s. viidakko.

junior ['dʒuːnjə] a. nuorempi; s. nuorempi t. arvoltaan alempi henkilö; Am. kolmannen vuosikurssin opiskelija (neljästä); poika.

uniper ['dʒuːnipə] s. kataja.

unk 1. [dʒʌŋk] s. romu; (mer.) suolaliha; möhkäle.

unk 2. [dʒʌŋk] s. džonkki, kiinalainen purjealus.

unket ['dʒʌŋkit] s. herajuusto t. -velli; kemut (tav. ~*ing);* v. viettää kemuja.

unkie, junky ['dʒʌŋki] s. narkomaani.

unta ['dʒʌntə] s. juntta; (espanjal.) neuvoskunta.

upiter ['dʒuːpitə] *erisn.*

uridical [dʒuə'ridik(ə)l] a. juridinen, oikeudellinen.

juris|diction [dʒuəris'dikʃn] s. oikeudenkäyttö, tuomiovalta; tuomiokunta. **-prudence** [dʒuəris'pruːdəns] s. oikeustiede.

jur|ist ['dʒuərist] s. lainoppinut. **-or** ['dʒuərə] s. valamies; palkintotuomari.

jury ['dʒuəri] s. valamiehistö; palkintolautakunta, tuomaristo. **~-box** valamiehistön aitio. **~-man** valamies. **~-mast** hätämasto.

just [dʒʌst] a. oikeudenmukainen, oikea, oikeutettu, kohtuullinen; *adv.* juuri, aivan; nipin napin, juuri ja juuri (us. *only ~);* vain (~ *a little);* ~ *a minute!* hetkinen! ~ *now* juuri nyt, juuri äsken; ~ *tell me!* kerrohan minulle! ~ *perfect* kerrassaan mainio; ~ *you wait!* odotapas vain!

justice ['dʒʌstis] s. oikeus, oikeudenmukaisuus; tuomari; *J*~ *of the Peace* rauhantuomari; *do ~ to* tehdä oikeutta, antaa ansaittu tunnustus jklle; *do ~ to the chef* syödä hyvällä ruokahalulla; *do oneself ~* osoittautua maineensa veroiseksi; *in ~* oikeutta myöten.

justi|fiable ['dʒʌstifaiəbl] a. puolustettavissa oleva, oikeutettu. **-fication** [-fi'keiʃn] s. puolustaminen, puolustus; oikeutus; vanhurskauttaminen.

justify ['dʒʌstifai] v. osoittaa oikeutetuksi, todistaa oikeaksi; puolustaa; (usk.) vanhurskauttaa. **just|ly** *adv.* oikeutta myöten, hyvällä syyllä.

jut [dʒʌt] v. pistää esiin, (us. ~ *out);* jutting ulkoneva, esiintyöntyvä.

jute [dʒuːt] s. juutti.

Jutland ['dʒʌtlənd] *erisn.* Jyllanti.

juvenil|e ['dʒuːvinail] a. nuori, nuorekas, nuoriso-; s. nuorukainen, nuori; ~ *court* nuorisotuomioistuin; ~ *delinquent* nuorisorikollinen; ~ *lead* (nuori) rakastajanosia esittävä näyttelijä. **-ity** [-'niliti] s. nuorekkuus.

juxtaposition [dʒʌkstəpə'ziʃn] s. rinnakkain asettaminen.

K

K, k [kei] s. k-kirjain. Lyh.: **K.** *King,
Knight;* **Kan.** *Kansas;* **K.C.** *King's
Counsel;* **kg.** *kilogramme;* **km.**
kilometre; **KGB** [Neuvostoliiton
valtiollinen poliisi]; **K.O.** ['keiəu]
knock-out; **Kt.** *Knight;* **Ky.** *Kentucky;*
kw. *kilowatt.*

Kaffir ['kæfə] s. kafferi.

kale, kail [keil] s. lehtikaali.

kaleidoscop|e [kə'laidəskəup] s.
kaleidoskooppi, kuvakiikari. **-ic**
[-'skɔpik] a. aina vaihteleva, kirjava.

kangaroo [kæŋgə'ru:] s. kenguru.

Kansas ['kænsəs] *erisn.*

kaolin ['ke(i)əlin] s. posliinisavi,
kaoliini.

kapok ['keipɔk] s. kapokki.

Karachi [kə'ra:tʃi] *erisn.*

karat ks. *carat.*

kart [ka:t] s. mikroauto.

Kashmir [kæʃ'miə] *erisn.*

Kate [keit] *erisn.*

kayak ['kaiæk] s. kajakki.

kedge ['kedʒ] v. varpata; s.
varppiankkuri.

keel [ki:l] s. köli, emäpuu; v. kallistaa
kumoon; ~ *over* pyörtyä, kaatua
kumoon. **-son** sikopalkki (mer.).

keen [ki:n] a. terävä; kova, ankara,
pureva; tarkka; v. valittaa; ~ *on*
innokas   kärkäs; .. *is not very* ~ *on*
ei paljon välitä -sta; **-ness** s. terävyys;
innokkuus. **--witted** terävä-älyinen.

keep [ki:p] *kept kept,* v. pitää; täyttää
(lupaus); suojella; pitää kunnossa t.
hallussa, säilyttää; pitää kaupan,
ylläpitää, elättää; pidättää, viivyttää;
estää *(from),* salata *(from* jklta);
pysyä, pysytellä (jnak, jssk); säilyä; s.
elatus; linna, linnoitus; ~ *doing sth.*
jatkuvasti tehdä jtk; *she kept laughing*
hän nauroi nauramistaan; ~ *talking*
puhua lakkaamatta; ~ *going* pitää

käynnissä; ~ *sb. waiting* antaa jkn
odottaa; ~ [*on*] *writing* jatkaa
kirjoittamista; ~ *one's room* pysyä
huoneessaan; ~ *house for* hoitaa jkn
taloutta; ~ *time* (kellosta) käydä
oikein, pysyä tahdissa; ~ *at it* ahertaa;
~ *away* pysytellä poissa, pitää
loitolla; ~ *back* jäädä jälkeen,
pidättää, ehkäistä, jättää kertomatta;
~ *sth. by one* pitää mukanaan; ~ *from*
pidättää jstk, salata jklta; ~ *in with*
pysyä hyvissä väleissä jkn kanssa; ~
off pysyä erossa (jstk); ~ *on* jatkaa; ~
on doing jatkuvasti t. lakkaamatta
tehdä jtk; ~ *on at a p.* alinomaa
vaivata, jankuttaa; ~ *out of* pysyä
loitolla jstk; ~ *to* pitää kiinni jstk,
pysyä jssk, olla uskollinen jllek; ~
sth. to oneself pitää omana tietonaan;
~ *to oneself* olla omissa oloissaan,
eristäytyä; ~ *under* pitää kurissa; ~
up pitää korkealla, pitää kunnossa;
pitää yllä, vireillä; jatkaa
hellittämättä; ~ *up with* pysyä jkn
tasalla; ylläpitää samaa elintasoa kuin
(naapuri *the Joneses*); *for* ~ *s*
ainiaaksi. **-er** [-ə] s. vartija;
riistanvartija; *inn* ~ majatalonisäntä;
goal-~ maalivahti. **-ing** s. säilö,
huolenpito; sopusointu; *in safe* ~
varmassa tallessa; *in* ~ *with*
sopusoinnussa jnk kanssa; *be out of* ~
[*with*] olla ristiriidassa, sopia huonosti
yhteen jnk kanssa. **-sake** [-seik]
muistoesine.

keg [keg] s. pieni tynnyri, lekkeri.

kelpie ['kelpi] s. (pahansuopa)
vedenhaltija.

Kelt ks. *Celt.*

ken [ken] s.: *is beyond my* ~ on
tietopiirin ulkopuolella, käy yli
ymmärrykseni.

kennel ['kenl] s. koirankoppi;

koiratarha.

Kensington ['kenziŋtən] *erisn.*

Kent [kent] *erisn.* **-ish** [-iʃ] *a.* kentiläinen.

Kentucky [ken'tʌki] *erisn.*

Kenya ['kenjə] *erisn.*

kept [kept] *imp. & pp.* ks. *keep.*

kerb [kə:b] *s.* (katukäytävän) reunakiveys. **-stone** reunakivi.

kerchief ['kə:tʃif] *s.* huivi, pääliina.

kernel ['kə:nl] *s.* (pähkinän ym) sydän, ydin; jyvä.

kerosene ['kerəsi:n] *s.* palööljy.

kestrel ['kestr(ə)l] *s.* tuulihaukka.

Keswick ['kezik] *erisn.*

ketchup ['ketʃəp] *s.* (kirpeä) kastike.

kettle ['ketl] *s.* vesipannu; *quite another ~ of fish* aivan eri juttu. **~-drum** patarumpu.

Kew [kju:] *erisn.*

key [ki:] *s.* avain; ratkaisu, selitys; sävellaji, äänilaji; kosketin, näppäin; läppä; kiila; *v.* kiilata; virittää; *~ money* kynnysraha; *~ position* avainasema; *~ signature* nuottiavain; *~ed up* jännittynyt. **-board** koskettimisto. **-hole** avaimenreikä. **-note** perussävel; pääajatus. **-stone** (holvin) päätekivi; (kuv.) keskeinen seikka.

Keynes [keinz] *erisn.*

khaki ['kɑ:ki] *a.* ruskeankellertävä; *s.* khakikangas.

khan [kɑ:n] *s.* kaani.

kibbutz [ki'bu:ts] *s.* (pl. *-zim*) *s.* kibutsi.

kick [kik] *v.* potkaista, potkia; *s.* potku, potkaisu; (ponnahdus)voima, ponsi; jännitys, -piristys; (jalkapallon) potk(ais)ija; *~ against* panna vastaan; *~ out* ajaa pois; *~ up a row (a fuss)* ruveta rähjäämään; **~-off** alkupotku.

kickshaw ['kikʃɔ:] *s.* herkkupala; arvoton hely.

kid 1. [kid] *s.* vohla, kili; vohlannahka; lapsi; tenava, muksu; *~ gloves* silohansikkaat. **-dy** [-i] *s.* lapsi.

kid 2. *v.* kiusoitella, laskea leikkiä, narrata, pelleillä; *you are ~ding me!* vedät minua nenästä!

kidnap ['kidnæp] *v.* siepata, ryöstää. **-ping** *s.* (lapsen ym) ryöstö, sieppaus, kidnappaus.

kidney ['kidni] *s.* munuainen; luonnonlaatu; *~ bean* turkinpapu; *~ machine* munuaiskone.

Kilimanjaro [kilimən'dʒɑ:rəu] *erisn.*

kill [kil] *v.* tappaa, surmata; tehdä musertava vaikutus; *s.* tappo, saalis. **-ing** *a.* musertava; vastustamaton, viehättävä; *he is too ~* hän on kerrassaan sukkela. **-joy** ilonpilaaja.

kiln [kiln] *s.* (tiili-, kuivaus)uuni.

kilo|gram(me) ['kilə(u)|græm] *s.* kilogramma. **-metre, -meter** [-mi:tə] *s.* kilometri.

kilt [kilt] *s.* (skotlantilaisen miehen) lyhyt laskoshame, kiltti. **-ed** kilttiä käyttävä.

kimono [ki'məunəu] *s.* kimono.

kin [kin] *s.* suku(laisus), heimo; *a.* sukua *(to* jklle); *next of ~* lähiomaiset.

kind [kaind] *s.* laji, laatu; *a.* ystävällinen, hyväntahtoinen, kiltti; *nothing of the ~* ei sinne päinkään! *I ~ of expected it* jotenkin sitä aavistinkin; .. *of a ~* jonkinlainen (m. huononpuoleinen); *with ~ regards* sydämellisin terveisin; *in ~* luonnossa; *payment in ~* luontoisedut; *repay .. in ~* maksaa samalla mitalla.

kindergarten ['kindəgɑ:tn] *s.* lastentarha.

kind-hearted hyväsydäminen.

kindl|e ['kindl] *v.* sytyttää; syttyä, leimahtaa liekkiin. **-ing** *s.* sytykkeet.

kindliness ['kaindlinis] *s.* ystävällisyys.

kind|ly ['kaindli] *a.* ystävällinen; leuto; *adv.* ystävällisesti. **-ness** *s.* ystävällisyys, hyvyys; ystävällinen teko, palvelus.

kindred ['kindrid] *s.* sukulaisuus; sukulaiset; *a.* sukulainen, sukua oleva; *~ spirit* hengenheimolainen.

kine [kain] *s. pl.* (vanh.) = *cows.*

king [kiŋ] *s.* kuningas; *Kings* Kuningasten kirjat (raam.). **-cup** *s.* leinikki. **-dom** *s.* kuningaskunta; valtakunta; *animal ~* eläinkunta. **-fisher** kuningaskalastaja. **-ly** [-li] *a.* kuninkaallinen. **-ship** *s.* kuninkuus.

kink [kiŋk] *s.* (köyden) sykkyrä, mutka; *v.* kiertyä. **-y** [-i] *a.* mutkainen, m. kieroutunut.

kin|sfolk ['kinzfəuk] *s.* sukulaiset. **-ship** ['kinʃip] *s.* sukulaisuus. **-sman,**

-swoman sukulainen.

kiosk [ki'ɔsk] s. myyntikoju.

kip [kip] v.: ~ down mennä
nukkumaan.

kipper ['kipə] s. savusilli; v. kuivata
(savussa t. ilmassa).

kirk [kə:k] s. (skotl.) = church.

kiss [kis] s. suudelma; v. suudella; the
~ of life suusta suuhun -menetelmä;
~ the dust joutua häviölle, saada
surmansa; ~ the rod nöyrästi alistua.
-er [-ə] s. sl. suu, »kuono».

kit [kit] s. sotilaan varusteet;
urheiluvarusteet; välineet, pakkaus;
= kitten. ~-bag (sotilaan) varussäkki;
matkareppu.

kitchen ['kitʃin, -(ə)n] s. keittiö; ~
garden kasvitarha. -ette [-'net] s.
keittokomero.

kite [kait] s. leija; haarahaukka;
kiskuri, huijari; fly a ~ tunnustella
mielipiteitä.

kith [kiθ] s.: ~ and kin ystävät ja
sukulaiset.

kitten ['kitn] s. kissanpoikanen; v.
saada poikasia. -ish [-iʃ] a.
kissanpoikamainen.

kitty ['kiti] s.: in the ~ koossa,
kerättynä.

kleptomaniac [kleptə(u)'meiniæk] s.
kleptomaani.

knack [næk] s. taito, näppäryys;
temppu; have the ~ of osata konsti.
-er [-ə] s. (vanhojen talojen ym)
romuttaja; hevosten teurastaja.

knapsack ['næpsæk] s. selkäreppu.

knav|e [neiv] s. lurjus, roisto;
(korttipelissä) sotamies. -ery [-əri] s.
konnantyö. -ish [-iʃ] a. konnamainen.

knead [ni:d] v. sotkea, vaivata
(taikinaa).

knee [ni:] s. polvi; on one's ~s
polvillaan. ~-breeches polvihousut.
-cap polvilumpio. ~-deep polviin
saakka (ulottuva).

kneel [ni:l] knelt knelt, v.: ~ [down]
polvistua.

knell [nel] s. kellonsoitto; kuolinkellot.

knelt [nelt] imp. & pp. ks. kneel.

knew [nju:] imp. ks. know.

knicker|bockers ['nikəbɔkəz] s. väljät
polvihousut. -s [-'nikəz] s. (vanh.)
naisten (alus)housut.

knick-knack ['niknæk] s. koriste-esine;

~s korut, koristeet, hepenet.

knife [naif] s. (pl. knives) veitsi; v.
iskeä veitsellä, puukottaa; get one's ~
into käydä jkn kimppuun. ~-grinder
veitsenteroittaja. ~-rest veitsiteline.

knight [nait] s. ritari; aatelismies
(jonka arvonimi Sir ei ole
perinnöllinen); (šakkipelissä)
hevonen; v. lyödä ritariksi; korottaa
knight-arvoon; K ~ Commander
(ritarikunnan) komentaja. ~-errant
vaeltava ritari. -hood s. ritarius,
ritarinarvo. -ly [-li] a. ritarillinen,
ritarin.

knit [nit] ~ted ~ted t. knit knit, v.
neuloa, kutoa (sukkaa ym); liittää
yhteen, yhdistää; with ~ted brows otsa
rypyssä; a well-~ frame hyvä
ruumiinrakenne. -ting s. neulominen;
neuletyö; (~-machine neulomakone;
~-needle sukka(ym) puikko). -wear
neulevaatteet.

knives [naivz] pl. ks. knife.

knob [nɔb] s. nuppi, oven kädensija;
pahka; palanen (hiiltä ym). -bly [-bli]
a. kyhmyinen. -kerrie [-keri]
(afrikkal.) nuppipäinen ase. -stick
nuppipäinen keppi.

knock [nɔk] v. lyödä, iskeä, kolauttaa;
kolkuttaa (at jhk); hämmästyttää;
Am. moittia t. arvostella ankarasti; s.
kolkutus; ~ about lyödä,
pahoinpidellä; harhailla, kierrellä,
viettää epäsäännöllistä elämää; ~
back (sl.) juoda; ~ down iskeä
maahan; alentaa hintoja
(huutokaupassa); ~ off lopettaa
(työ), vähentää (hinnasta); ~ on the
head (m.) tehdä loppu jstk; ~ out
tyrmätä; tuhota; ~ under alistua; ~
over kaataa kumoon; ~ up järjestää,
tekaista kädenkäänteessä; lopen
väsyttää. ~-about clothes työvaatteet.
~-down musertava; jk.-d. price alin
hinta. -er [-ə] s. (oven)kolkutin.
~-out tyrmäys(isku); sl. täysosuma;
k.-o. pills huumauspillerit.

knoll [nəul] s. kumpu.

knot [nɔt] s. solmu; nauharuusuke,
solmuke; (hius)sykerö; (mer.)
solmuväli; nystermä, pahka,
oksankohta (puussa); pulma, vaikeus;
v. solmia, tehdä solmu(ja); mennä
solmuun; running ~ juoksusolmu.

-ted [-id] *a.* solmuinen, oksainen. **-ty** [-i] *a.* oksainen; pulmallinen, vaikea, visainen.

knout [naut] *s.* solmuruoska.

know [nəu] *knew known, v.* tietää, tuntea, osata; *s.: in the ~* asiasta tietoinen; *~ about (of)* tietää, olla tietoinen jstk; *not that I ~* ei minun tietääkseni; *~ what's what, ~ the ropes* olla perillä asioista; *get to ~* oppia tuntemaan; *he ~s how to play chess* hän osaa pelata šakkia. **~-how** asiantuntemus ja taito, taitotieto. **-ing** *a.* viekas; viisas. **-ingly** *adv.* tietoisesti, tahallisesti.

knowledge ['nɔlidʒ] *s.* tieto; tiedot; *~ of* jnk tuntemus, taito; *not to my ~* ei minun tietääkseni; *to the best of my ~* mikäli tiedän. **-able** [-əbl] *a.* tiedokas, tietävä.

known [nəun] *pp. & a.* tunnettu, tuttu; *he is ~ by* hänet tunnetaan (jstk); *make ~* ilmoittaa, julkistaa.

Knox [nɔks] *erisn.*

knuckle ['nʌkl] *s.* rysty; (keitt.) potka; *v.: ~ under* antaa myöten, alistua; *~ down* antaa periksi, *(.. to work)*

käydä käsiksi työhön. **~-duster** nyrkkirauta.

koala [kəu'ɑ:lə] *s.* pussikarhu.

kodak ['kəudæk] *s.* kodak-käsikamera.

Koh-i-noor ['kɔ(u)inuə] *s.* Koh-i-noor timantti (brittil. kruununkalleus).

kohlrabi ['kəul'rɑ:bi] *s.* kyssäkaali.

Koran [kɔ'rɑ:n] *s.: the ~* Koraani.

Korea [kɔ'riə] *erisn.* **-n** [-n] *a. & s.* korealainen.

kosher ['kəuʃə] *a. & s.* (juutalaisen uskonnon mukaan) puhdas (ruoka t. ravitsemusliike).

kowtow ['kau'tau] *v.* kumarrella.

kraal [krɑ:l] *s.* eteläafrikkal. (aidattu) kylä, karja-aitaus.

Kremlin ['kremlin] *s.: the ~* Kreml.

kudos ['kju:dɔs] *s.* (puhek.) maine, kunnia.

kudu ['ku:du:] *s.* kudu(antilooppi).

Ku-Klux-Klan ['kju: klʌks 'klæn] *s.* amerikkal. salaseura.

Kurd [kɔ:d] *s.* kurdi. **-ish** [-iʃ] *a.* kurdilainen.

Kuwait [ku'weit] *erisn.* **-i** [-i] *a.* kuwaitilainen.

L

L, l [el] *s.* l-kirjain. Lyh.: £ (= libra)
pound sterling punta; **La.** *Louisiana;*
Lab. *Labrador; Labour;* **lat.** *latitude;*
lb. (=libra) *pound* naula; **l. c.** *lower
case; loc. cit.;* **L. C. C.** *London
County Council;* **Ld** *Lord;* **L. C. M.**
Least Common Multiple; **Lib.** *Liberal;*
Lieut. *Lieutenant* luutnantti; **LL. B.**
Bachelor of Laws l.v. oikeustieteen
kandidaatti; **loc. cit.** (= loco citato)
yllä mainitussa paikassa; **long.**
longitude; **LP** *long-playing;* **LPG**
liquefied petroleum gas; **LSD** *lysergic
acid diethylamide* (aistiharhoja
synnyttävä) huume; **Lt.** *Lieutenant;*
Lt.-Gen. *Lieutenant-General;* **Ltd.**
limited.

lab [læb] (lyh.) = *laboratory.*

label ['leibl] *s.* nimi-, osoitelippu;
etiketti; *v.* varustaa nimi-,
osoitelipulla; (kuv.) luokitella (jhk
ryhmään).

labial ['leibiəl] *a.* huuli-; *s.* huuliäänne.

labor|atory [lə'bɔrət(ə)ri, Am.
'læb(ə)rət(ə)ri] *s.* laboratorio. **-ious**
[lə'bɔːriəs] *a.* suuritöinen,
vaivalloinen, työläs, raskas (tyyli);
työteliäs.

labour, labor ['leibə] *s.* työ; raadanta,
ponnistus; työvoima; työläiset;
synnytyspoltot; *(L~)* työväenpuolue;
v. tehdä työtä, ponnistaa; käydä,
edetä vaivalloisesti; huolitella
(liiaksi); *hard ~* pakkotyö; *~ dispute*
työselkkaus; *~ force* työvoima; *L~
Party* työväenpuolue; *~ pains*
synnytyspoltot; *~ relations*
työelämänsuhteet; *I will not ~ the
point* en käsittele tätä kohtaa kovin
pitkään; [*he*] *is ~ing under a false
impression* on harhakäsityksen
vallassa; *~-saving appliances*
työtäsäästävät laitteet, koneet.

-ed [-d] *a.* ei luonteva, väkinäinen;
vaivalloinen *(~ breathing).* **-er** [-rə]
s. työläinen, työmies. **~-intensive**
työvoimavaltainen.

Labrador ['læbrədɔ:] *erisn.*

laburnum [lə'bə:nəm] *s.* kultasade
(kasv.).

labyrinth ['læbərinθ] *s.* labyrintti,
sokkelo. **-ine** [læbə'rinθain] *a.*
sokkeloinen.

lac [læk] *s.* kumilakka.

lace [leis] *s.* nauha; paula; pitsi; (kulta-,
hopea) punos; *v.* nyörittää,
pauloittaa (m. *~ up);* koristaa
nauhuksin; »terästää» väkijuomalla;
~ into piestä jkta; *~d* nyöri-, nauha-;
~-pillow nypläystyyny.

lacerate ['læsəreit] *v.* repiä, raadella.

lachrym|al ['lækrim|əl] *a.* kyynel-. **-ose**
[-əus] *a.* kyynelehtivä, itkeskelevä.

lacing *s.* nyöritys, punos; ks. *lace.*

lack [læk] *s.:* ~ *of* jnk puute; *v.* olla jtk
vailla, jnk puutteessa; *he ~ s character*
häneltä puuttuu luonnetta; *I ~ words
with which to express* en voi sanoin
ilmaista; *be ~ing* puuttua; *he is not
~ing in courage* häneltä ei puutu
rohkeutta.

lackadaisical [lækə'deizik(ə)l] *a.*
raukea, tunteileva.

lackey ['læki] *s.* lakeija; *v.* palvella;
hännystellä.

lack-lustre *a.* kiilloton, hohdoton.

laconic [lə'kɔnik] *a.* lakoninen,
harvasanainen.

lacquer ['lækə] *s.* lakka(väri); *v.* lakata.

lact|ation [læk'teiʃn] *s.* maidoneritys;
imettäminen. **-ic** ['læktik] *a.:* ~ *acid*
maitohappo.

lacuna [lə'kju:nə] *s.* (pl. *~s, ~ē*)
aukko.

lad [læd] *s.* poika, nuorukainen.

ladder ['lædə] *s.* tikapuut, tikkaat;

silmäpako (sukassa); *v.*: [*stockings*] *that won't* ~ joista silmät eivät juokse. **~proof** ks. ed.

laddie ['lædi] *s.* (pieni) poika.

lad|e [leid] *laded laden, v.* lastata, kuormata; ~*n with sorrow* surun painama. **-ing** *s.* lastaus; *bill of* ~ konossementti.

la-di-da ['lɑ:di'dɑ:] *a.* (teennäisen) hieno.

ladies ['leidiz] *pl.* ks. *lady*; *sg.*: *a* ~ naistenhuone.

ladle ['leidl] *s.* kauha; *v.* ammentaa (kauhalla).

lady ['leidi] *s.* (sivistynyt t. hieno) nainen; *L*~ lady, aatelisnainen; *attr.* nais-; *the* ~ *of the house* talon emäntä; *Our L* ~ Neitsyt Maria; *L*~ *Day* Marian ilmestyspäivä; *ladies and gentlemen!* hyvät naiset ja herrat; **-bird,** ~**-bug** leppäkerttu. ~**-killer** naistenhurmaaja. **-like** sivistyneelle naiselle sopiva, hienosti käyttäytyvä. **-ship** *your L*~ Teidän armonne.

lag 1. [læg] *v.* vitkastella; *s.* jäljessä olo, viivytys, myöhästyminen *(time* ~*)*; sl. *(old* ~*)* vanha »vankilakundi»; ~ *behind* jäädä jälkeen.

lag 2. *v.* lämpöeristää.

lager ['lɑ:gə] *s.* l.v. pilsneri.

laggard ['lægəd] *s.* vitkastelija, nahjus.

lagoon [lə'gu:n] *s.* laguuni.

laid [leid] *imp. & pp.* ks. *lay*; ~ *up* vuoteenomana.

lain [lein] *pp.* ks. *lie 2.*

lair [lɛə] *s.* (eläimen) pesä.

laird [lɛəd] *s.* (Skotl.) kartanonomistaja.

laity ['leiiti] *s.*: *the* ~ maallikot.

lake 1. [leik] *s.* järvi; *L*~ *poets* järvikoulun runoilijat; *L*~ *District* järviseutu.

lake 2. [leik] *s.* (punainen) lakkaväri.

lam [læm] *v.* piestä.

lama ['lɑ:mə] *s.* lama, budhalainen munkki. **-sery** [-səri] *s.* lamalaisluostari.

lamb [læm] *s.* karitsa; *v.* vuonia.

lambast, -e [læm'beist] *v.* sl. piestä; sättiä; *got* ~*d* sai kyllä kunniansa.

lambent ['læmbənt] *a.* (liekistä) nuoleksiva; tuikkiva, (lempeästi) säkenöivä (äly).

lamb|kin [læmkin] *s.* pieni karitsa.

-like lammasmainen.

lame [leim] *a.* ontuva, rampa; epätyydyttävä, vaillinainen; *v.* rampauttaa, (kuv.) lamaannuttaa; ~ *duck* siipirikko; ~*ly* heikosti.

lament [lə'ment] *s.* vaikeroida, valittaa; surra; *s.* vali us. **-able** ['læməntəbl] *a.* valitettava, surkea. **-ation** [læmen'teiʃn] *s.* valitus(virsi); *L*~*s* Valitusvirret (raam.).

lamin|a ['læmin|ə] *s.* (pl. *-ae* [-i:]) liuska, suomu, ohut levy. **-ar** [-ə] *a.* liuska-, liuskainen. **-ate** [-eit] *v.* valssata, takoa levyiksi; peittää metallilevyillä; ~*d* kerros-, levy-.

lamp [læmp] *s.* lamppu; lyhty. **-black** nokimusta (väri). **-light** lampunvalo. ~**-post** lyhtypylväs. **-shade** lampunvarjostin.

lampoon [læm'pu:n] *s.* häväistyskirjoitus; *v.* (pilkkakirjoituksin) herjata. **-ist** [-ist] *s.* pilkkakirjoitusten tekijä.

lamprey ['læmpri] *s.* nahkiainen.

lance [lɑ:ns] *s.* keihäs, peitsi; *v.* puhkaista lansetilla; ~*-corporal* korpraali. **-let** [-lit] *s.* suikulainen. **-r** [-ə] *s.* keihäsmies; *pl.* lansieeri (tanssi). **-t** [-it] *s.* (lääk.) lansetti; ~ *window* suippokaari-ikkuna.

land [lænd] *s.* maa, maaperä; maa, valtakunta; maaomaisuus; *v.* nousta maihin, laskea maihin, (lentok.) laskeutua; vetää maihin, pyydystää (kaloja); saattaa, joutua jhk, päätyä jhk; ~*s* tilukset, maat; *by* ~ maitse; *on* [*dry*] *land* kuivalla maalla, maissa; [*find out*] *how the* ~ *lies* millä kannalla asiat ovat; ~ *oneself in difficulties* joutua vaikeuksiin; [*he*] ~*ed me one in the eye* iski minua silmään. ~**-agent** tilanhoitaja; kiinteistönvälittäjä. **-ed** [-id] *a.* maata omistava, maa-; ~ *property* maaomaisuus. **-fall** maantuntu (merimatkan jälkeen). **-holder** maanvuokraaja. **-ing** *s.* maihinnousu, (ilm.) lasku; porrastasanne; ~ *gear* laskuteline; ~*-net* kalahaavi; ~*-stage* laituri. **-lady** vuokraemäntä. **-less** tilaton. ~**-locked** maan ympäröimä. **-lord** (vuokra)isäntä. ~**-lubber** [-lʌbə] »maakrapu». **-mark** ['læn(d)mɑ:k] maamerkki; (kuv.) virstanpylväs. **-owner** maanomistaja. **-scape**

['lændskeip] maisema. **-slide**
['læn(d)slaid] maanvieremä; *a
Democratic* ~ äänivyöry
demokraattien hyväksi. **-slip**
[læn(d)slip] maanvieremä. **-sman**
»maakrapu». **-ward** *a.*
maanpuoleinen, maa-; *adv.* = seur.
-wards maihin, (rantaan) päin.

lane [lein] *s.* kuja, kujanne, (ajo)kaista
(urh.) rata; (valtamerilaivan) reitti;
get into ~ ryhmittyä; *keep in* ~ pysyä
kaistalla.

language ['læŋgwidʒ] *s.* kieli; *bad* ~
kiroukset, säädytön puhe.

langu|id ['læŋg|wid] *a.* veltto,
voimaton, raukea; laimea. **-ish** [-wiʃ]
v. käydä raukeaksi, veltostua; riutua;
kaivata, ikävöidä *(for* jtk). **-or** [-ə] *s.*
voimattomuus, velttous, raukeus,
tylsyys; kaiho (us. *pl.).* **-orous** [-ərəs]
a. raukea, haluton.

lank [læŋk] *a.* suorana riippuva
(tukka); hoikka, pitkä ja laiha.
-y [-i] *a.* hontelo.

lanolin ['lænəli:n] *s.* lanoliini.

lantern ['læntən] *s.* lyhty; *magic* ~
taikalyhty.

lanyard ['lænjəd] *s.* taljaköysi.

Laos [laus] *erisn.* **Laotian** ['lauʃn] *s. &
a.* laosilainen.

lap 1. [læp] *v.* latkia; loiskia; *s.*
loiskina.

lap 2. [læp] *s.* helma, syli; kierros
(kilpailussa); *v.* kietoa, kääriä; *in
Fortune's* ~ onnettaren huomassa;
~*ped in luxury* ylellisyyden
ympäröimä(nä); ~ *over* peittää
osaksi, ulottua yli. **~dog** sylikoira.

lapel [lə'pel] *s.* käänne (takissa),
rinnuslieve.

lapidary ['læpidəri] *a.* kiveen
kaiverrettu, kivi-; ytimekäs; *s.*
jalokivien hioja.

lapis-lazuli [læpis'læzjulai] *s.*
lasuurikivi.

Lapland ['læplænd] *erisn.* Lappi. **-er**
[-ə] *s.* lappalainen.

Lapp [læp] *s. & a.* lappalainen,
saamelainen; lapinkieli(nen). **-ish** [-iʃ]
s. lappalainen; *s.* lapin kieli.

lapse [læps] *s.* (huomaamattomuus)-
virhe, erehdys; hairahdus; luopumus;
(ajan) kuluminen; *v.* luisua, vaipua
(into) jhk; luopua (uskosta),

hairahtua; raueta.

lapwing ['læpwiŋ] *s.* töyhtöhyyppä.

larboard ['lɑ:bəd] *s.* (mer.) paapuuri.

larceny ['lɑ:sni] *s.* varkaus; *petty* ~
näpistely.

larch [lɑ:tʃ] *s.* lehtikuusi.

lard [lɑ:d] *s.* sianihra, laardi; *v.*
silavoida; (kuv.) höystää. **-er** [-ə] *s.*
ruokakomero.

large [lɑ:dʒ] *a.* suuri, iso; laaja, avara;
runsas; suuripiirteinen; *s.: at* ~
vapaalla jalalla, vapaana; yleensä;
kokonaisuudessaan; *by and* ~
yleensä. **-ly** *adv.* suureksi osaksi;
avokätisesti. ~**-scale** laaja, suur-.
-ss(e) [lɑ:'dʒes] *s.* (vanh.)
anteliaisuus.

largish ['lɑ:dʒiʃ] *a.* suurehko.

lark 1. [lɑ:k] *s.* leivonen.

lark 2. [lɑ:k] *s.* kepponen, kuje; *v.*
hullutella, pelleillä (m. ~ *about);
what a* ~! miten sukkelaa!

larkspur ['lɑ:kspə:] *s.* kukonkannus
(kasv.).

larv|a ['lɑ:və] *s.* (pl. *-ae* [-i:]) *s.* toukka.
-al [-(ə)l] *a.* toukka-.

laryn|geal [lærin'dʒi(:)əl] *a.*
kurkunpään-. **-gitis** [-'dʒaitis] *s.*
kurkunpääntulehdus.

larynx ['læriŋks] *s.* kurkunpää.

lascivious [lə'siviəs] *a.* irstas,
hekumallinen.

laser ['leizə] *s.* laser(säde) (~ *beam).*

lash [læʃ] *v.* sivaltaa, ruoskia, huitoa,
huitaista, potkaista (tav. ~ *out);*
(kuv.) suomia; sitoa, köyttää; *s.*
piiskan siima; sivallus, ruoskiminen;
(silmä)ripsi; ~ *out at* (t. *against)* (m.)
puhjeta solvauksiin, purkaa sisuaan.
-ing *s.* ruoskiminen; sidenuora; ~*s of*
runsas määrä.

lass [læs] *s.* tyttö. **-ie** [-i] *s.* = *ed.*

lassitude ['læsitju:d] *s.* väsymys,
raukeus.

lasso ['læsəu] *s.* (pl. ~*s,* ~*es*) suopunki,
lasso; *v.* pyydystää lassolla.

last 1. [lɑ:st] *s.* lesti; *stick to one's* ~
pysyä lestissään.

last 2. [lɑ:st] *a.* viimeinen; viime;
vihoviimeinen; *adv.* viimeiseksi,
viimeksi, viimeisenä; *s.* viime (kirje,
vitsi ym); ~ *night* eilen illalla; ~ *but
one* viimeisen edellinen; *at* ~ viimein,
lopuksi; *at long* ~ vihdoin viimein; *to*

the ~ loppuun saakka; *the* ~ *two*
[*guests*] kaksi viimeistä; *the* ~ *thing in*
[*gloves*] viimeinen uutuus . . -alalla.
when I ~ *saw her* kun viimeksi tapasin
hänet.

last 3. [lɑ:st] *a.* kestää, jatkua; säilyä.
-ing *a.* kestävä, pysyvä.

lastly *adv.* lopuksi.

latch [lætʃ] *s.* säppi, amerikkalainen
lukko. **-key** ulko-oven avain; ~ *child*
avainlapsi.

late [leit] *a.* (~ *r* ~ *st* t. *latter last*)
myöhäinen; myöhästynyt; vainaja;
entinen; *adv.* myöhään; *the* ~ *John
Smith* J. S.-vainaja; *the* ~ *Prime
Minister* entinen pääministeri; *be* ~ *for*
myöhästyä jstk; *of* ~ *years* viime
vuosina; *of* ~ = seur. **-ly** *adv.* viime
aikoina, äskettäin.

laten|cy [ˈleit(ə)nsi] *s.* (taudin)
piilevyys. **-t** [-nt] *a.* piilevä, latentti.

later [ˈleitə] *komp.* ks. *late*; ~ *on*
myöhemmin; *not* ~ *than* viimeistään.

lateral [ˈlæt(ə)rəl] *a.* sivu-.

latest [ˈleitist] *sup.* ks. *late*; *at the* ~
viimeistään.

latex [ˈleiteks] *s.* kumimaito; lateksi
(kem.).

lath [lɑ:θ] (pl. *la:ðz*) *s.* säle, lista, rima.

lathe [leið] *s.* sorvi(penkki).

lather [ˈlɑ:ðə, Am. læðə] *s.*
saippuavaahto, vaahto; *v.* vaahdota;
saippuoida vaahtoiseksi; löylyttää.

Latin [ˈlætin] *a.* latinalainen,
latinankielinen, romaaninen; *s.*
latina(n kieli). **-ist** [-ist] *s.* latinisti.

latish [ˈleitiʃ] *a.* myöhähkö.

latitud|e [ˈlætitju:d] *s.* leveysaste;
(toiminta- ym) vapaus. **-inarian**
[-iˈnɛəriən] *s.* vapaamielinen,
suvaitseva henkilö.

latrine [ləˈtri:n] *s.* käymälä.

latter [ˈlætə] *a.* ks. *late*; jälkimmäinen;
viimeksimainittu; *the former* . . *the* ~
edellinen . . jälkimmäinen. **~-day** *a.*
uudenaikainen; *L.-d. Saints*
mormonit. **-ly** *adv.* äskettäin, viime
aikoina.

lattice [ˈlætis] *s.* ristikko. **-d** [-t] *a.*
ristikolla varustettu.

Latvia [ˈlætviə] *erisn.* **-n** [-n] *a.* & *s.*
latvialainen.

laud [lɔ:d] *v.* (run.) ylistää. **-able** [-əbl]
a. kiitettävä. **-anum** [ˈlɔ:dnəm] *s.*

oopiumiliuos. **-ation** [-ˈdeiʃn] *s.*
ylistys. **-atory** [-ət(ə)ri] *a.* ylistelevä.

laugh [lɑ:f] *v.* nauraa *(at* jllek, jtk); *s.*
nauru, naurahdus; ~ *down* vaientaa
naurulla; ~ *off* kuitata naurulla; *it is
no* ~*ing matter* se ei ole naurun asia; *I
had a good* ~ nauroin makeasti; *have
the* ~ *of* kääntää pilkka naurajaan.
-able [-əbl] *a.* naurettava. **-ing-gas**
ilokaasu. **-ing-stock** *s.* pilan kohde.
-ter [ˈlɑ:ftə] *s.* nauru; *lit of* ~
naurunpuuska.

Laughton [ˈlɔ:tn] *erisn.*

launch [lɔ:n(t)ʃ] *v.* sinkauttaa, singota,
ampua, laukaista (avaruuteen); panna
alulle, aloittaa (hyökkäys, uusi liike
ym); laskea teloilta, s. vesillelasku;
(iso) moottorivene; isovene; ~ *out
in*[*to*] heittäytyä, syöksyä jhk, alkaa
(solvata); ~ *out* (m.) elää leveästi,
laajentaa (liikettään). **-ing** *s.*
vesillelasku; (raketin ym)
ampuminen; ~*pad* (ohjuksen)
lähtöalusta.

laund|er [ˈlɔ:nd|ə] *v.* pestä (ja silittää);
will this ~ *well?* onko tätä helppo
pestä? **-erette** [-əˈret] *s.* itsepalvelu-
pesula. **-ress** [-ris] *s.* pesijä. **-ry** [-ri] *s.*
pesulaitos, pesula; pyykki(vaatteet).

laureate [ˈlɔ:riit] *a.* laakerein
seppelöity; *poet* ~ hovirunoilija.

laurel [ˈlɔr(ə)l] *s.* laakeripuu; *pl.*
laakeriseppele, laakerit. **-led** [-d] *a.*
laakerein seppelöity.

lav [læv] *lyh.* = *lavatory.*

lava [ˈlɑ:və] *s.* laava.

lavatory [ˈlævət(ə)ri] *s.* pesuhuone,
mukavuuslaitos, WC.

lave [leiv] *v.* (run.) pestä, huuhtoa.

lavender [ˈlævində] *s.* laventeli;
laventelinsininen.

lavish [ˈlæviʃ] *a.* tuhlaavainen;
ylenmääräinen; *v.* tuhlata; ~*ly*
tuhlaten.

law [lɔ:] *s.* laki; sääntö: oikeus,
oikeudenkäyttö, oikeustiede; *read* ~
opiskella oikeustiedettä; *go to* ~ *with*
nostaa kanne jkta vastaan; *lay down
the* ~ määrätä, esiintyä käskijänä;
make ~*s* säätää lakeja. **~-abiding**
lainkuuliainen. **~-court** oikeus. **-ful** *a.*
laillinen. **-less** *a.* laiton; lakia
tottelematon.

lawn 1. [lɔ:n] *s.* hieno aivina, palttina.

lawn 2. [lɔːn] *s.* ruohokenttä. ~**-mower** ruohonleikkuukone. ~**-tennis** tennis.

Lawrence [ˈlɔr(ə)ns] *erisn.*

law|suit [ˈlɔːsjuːt] *s.* oikeusjuttu. **-yer** [ˈlɔːjə] *s.* asianajaja, lakimies.

lax [læks] *a.* leväperäinen, höllä, löyhä. **-ative** [-ətiv] *s.* ulostusaine. **-ity** [-iti] *s.* leväperäisyys.

lay 1. [lei] *s.* laulu, balladi.

lay 2. [lei] *s.* maallikko-; ~ *preacher* maallikkosaarnaaja.

lay 3. [lei] *imp.* ks. *lie 2.*

lay 4. [lei] *laid laid, v.* asettaa, panna, laskea, sijoittaa; kattaa (pöytä), lyödä (vetoa), kaataa lakoon (vilja); munia; hiljentää, saada asettumaan *(~ the storm);* sitoa (pölyä); karkottaa (henki); suunnata (tykki); laatia (suunnitelma); esittää; *s.* asema; ~ *bare* paljastaa; ~ *by the heels* pidättää, vangita; ~ *hands on* ks. *hand;* ~ *hold of* anastaa, ottaa haltuunsa; ~ *low* kaataa maahan; ~ *oneself open to* asettua alttiiksi jllek; ~ *waste* hävittää; ~ *about one* huitoa ympärilleen; ~ *aside* panna syrjään, säästöön, luopua jstk; ~ *by =* ~ *aside;* ~ *down* laskea (maahan), määrätä, uhrata (henkensä), tehdä (suunnitelma); ~ *off* pakkolomauttaa; Am. lakata, lopettaa; ~ *on* panna jnk päälle, määrätä (veroa), iskeä; sivellä; ~ *on water (electricity) to a house* asentaa taloon vesijohtoputket (sähköjohdot); ~ *it on thick* liioitellen kehua, imarrella; ~ *out* levittää (näytteille), pukea (ruumis), kuluttaa (rahaa), suunnitella (puutarha ym); ~ *up* varastoida, tallettaa; panna (laiva) teloille; *laid up* vuoteen omana; *the ~ of the land* asiaintila. **-about** hulttio, tyhjäntoimittaja. ~**-by** levennys (autotiellä). **-er** [-ə] *s.* kerros; vedonlyöjä; (kanasta) munija; taivukas; *v.* lisätä taivukkaista.

layette [leiˈet] *s.* vauvan varusteet.

lay|-figure [ˈleiˈfigə] malli-, nivelnukke. **-man** [-mən] maallikko. ~**-out** [-ˈaut] suunnitelma; sommittelu, (tekstin) asettelu; pohjapiirros.

Lazarus [ˈlæz(ə)rəs] *erisn.* Lasarus.

laz|e [leiz] *v.* laiskotella. **-iness** [-inis] *s.* laiskuus.

lazy [ˈleizi] *a.* laiska; joutilas. ~**-bones** laiskuri.

lea [liː] *s.* (run.) niitty.

leach [liːtʃ] *v.* uuttaa, liuottaa.

lead 1. [led] *s.* lyijy; luoti (mer.); välike (kirjap.); *pl.* lyijykatto; *v.* peittää, lisätä painoa (lyijyllä); ~ *pencil* lyijykynä; *black* ~ lyijykivi, grafiitti; *white* ~ lyijyvalkoinen; *swing the* ~ (sl.) pinnata.

lead 2. [liːd] *led led, v.* johtaa; viedä *(to* jhk); olla ensimmäisenä, johdossa, jnk etunenässä; taluttaa; (korttip.) aloittaa; *s.* johto (m. johtolanka), ohjaus, johtoasema; (korttip.) alkamisvuoro; talutushihna; sähköjohto; (teatt.) pääosa(n esittäjä); ~ *sb. to believe* saada jku uskomaan; ~ *[a life]* viettää; ~ *sb. a dog's life* kiusata, tehdä jkn elämä katkeraksi; ~ *the way* kulkea etunenässä; ~ *off* aloittaa; ~ *on* houkutella (jatkamaan); ~ *up to* olla alkuna jhk, vähitellen johtaa jhk; *follow the* ~ seurata esimerkkiä; *take the* ~ mennä johtoon; ~*-in* antennijohto.

leaden [ˈledn] *a.* lyijyinen; raskas; ~ *coffin* lyijyarkku.

leader [ˈliːdə] *s.* johtaja; pääkirjoitus; etumainen hevonen. **-ette** [-ˈret] *s.* lyhyt pääkirjoitus. **-ship** *s.* johto, johtajuus.

leading [ˈliːdiŋ] *a.* johtava; pää-, huomattavin; ~ *article* pääkirjoitus; ~ *lady* naispääosan esittäjä; ~ *question* johdatteleva kysymys. ~**-rein** ohjas. ~**-string** *in* ~ *strings* (kuv.). talutusnuorassa.

leaf [liːf] *s.* (pl. *leaves*) lehti; pöytälevy, ikkunaluukku, oven puolisko; (ohut) metallilevy; *v.:* ~ *through a book* selailla kirjaa; *come into* ~ puhjeta lehteen; *turn over a new* ~ aloittaa uusi elämä. **-age** [-idʒ] *s.* lehvät. **-less** *a.* lehdetön. **-let** *s.* pieni lehti; lentolehtinen, esite. **-y** [-i] *a.* lehtevä.

league 1. [liːg] *s.* (matkan) mitta, n. 3 mailia.

league 2. [liːg] *s.* liitto; (urh.) liiga; *v.* yhdistää, yhtyä liitoksi, liittoutua; *the L~ of Nations* Kansainliitto; *the Arab*

L~ arabiliitto.

Leah [liə] *erisn.* Leea.

leak [li:k] *s.* vuoto; *v.* vuotaa; *spring a* ~ saada vuoto; ~ *out* tulla tietoon, joutua ilmi. **-age** [-idʒ] *s.* vuotanut määrä, vuoto (m. kuv.). **-y** [-i] *a.* vuotava.

lean 1. [li:n] *a.* laiha; *s.* lihan rasvaton osa, laiha liha; ~ *years* puutteen ajat.

lean 2. [li:n] leant leant t. ~*ed* ~*ed, v.* nojata, nojautua; turvata *(upon* jhk); olla taipuvainen, kallistua *(towards* jhk); asettaa nojalleen. **-ed** [li:nd] *imp. & pp.* **-ing** *s.* taipuvuus *(to* jhk).

leanness *s.* laihuus.

leant [lent] *imp. & pp.* ks. **lean.**

lean-to *s.* katos, vaja.

leap [li:p] leapt leapt (~*ed*~*ed) v.* hypätä, hypähtää; *s.* hyppy; *by* ~*s and bounds* jättiläisaskelin. **-ed** [lept, li:pt] *imp. & pp.* **-frog** *s.: pay* ~ hypätä pukkia. **-t** [lept] *imp. & pp.* ks. **leap.** ~**-year** [li:pjɔ:] karkausvuosi.

learn [lə:n] learnt learnt t. ~*ed*~*ed, v.* oppia, opetella; saada tietää, kuulla. **-ed** [-t] *imp. & pp.; a.* [-id] oppinut. **-er** [-ə] *s.* aloittelija, harjoittelija. **-ing** *s.* oppi, oppineisuus. **-t** [lə:nt] *imp. & pp.* ks. **learn.**

lease [li:s] *s.* vuokraaminen; vuokra-aika, -sopimus; *v.* antaa t. ottaa vuokralle; *on* ~ vuokralla, -lle; *gave him a new* ~ *of life* muutti hänen elämänsä. **-hold** vuokratila.

leash [li:ʃ] *s.* talutushihna; *v.* kytkeä talutushihnaan; *hold in* ~ pitää aisoissa; *strain at the* ~ pyrkiä vapautumaan.

least [li:st] *sup.* ks. **little;** *a.* vähin, vähäisin, pienin; *adv.* vähiten; *at* ~ ainakin; *not in the* ~ ei vähintäkään; *to say the* ~ *[of it]* liioittelematta.

leather ['leðə] *s.* nahka; hihna; *v.* peittää nahalla; antaa remmiä. **-ette** ['-'ret] *s.* nahkajäljitelmä. **-ing** *s.* selkäsauna. **-y** [-i] *a.* nahkamainen, sitkeä.

leave 1. [li:v] *s.* lupa; loma, virkavapaus (m. ~ *of absence);* jäähyväiset; *by your* ~ luvallanne; *on* ~ lomalla; *take* ~ *of* jättää jäähyväiset jklle; *take* ~ *of one's senses* menettää järkensä.

leave 2. [li:v] *left left, v.* jättää; lähteä

jstk; hylätä; jättää jälkeensä; testamentata; *she has left for London* hän on lähtenyt Lontooseen; *[the car] left the road* suistui tieltä; ~ *it at that* jättää asia sikseen; ~ *alone* jättää rauhaan, olla sekaantumatta jhk; ~ *behind* jättää jälkeensä; sivuuttaa; ~ *by will* testamentata; ~ *for* lähteä jnnek; ~ *off* lakata käyttämästä, luopua tavasta; *[he] left off smoking* lopetti tupakoimisen; ~ *out* jättää pois; ~ *a matter over* jättää toistaiseksi.

leaven ['levn] *s.* hapatus; *v.* hapattaa.

leaves [li:vz] *pl.* ks. **leaf.**

leavings ['li:viŋs] *s. pl.* jätteet, tähteet.

Leban|**ese** [lebə'ni:z] *s. & a.* libanonilainen. **-on** ['lebənən] *erisn.* Libanon.

lecher|**ous** ['letʃ(ə)rəs] *a.* irstas. **-y** ['letʃəri] *s.* irstailu, elostelu.

lectern ['lektə(:)n] *s.* (tekstin)lukupulpetti.

lecture ['lektʃə] *s.* luento; nuhdesaarna; *v.* luennoida; läksyttää; *deliver (give) a* ~ pitää luento; *read sb. a* ~ läksyttää jkta. **-r** [-rə] *s.* luennoitsija, yliopiston lehtori.

led [led] *imp. & pp.* ks. **lead.**

ledge [ledʒ] *s.* (seinästä) ulkoneva lista, reunus, (kallioseinämän) ulkonema, uloke (m. vedenalainen). **-r** ['ledʒə] *s.* pääkirja; iso laakea kivi; poikkipalkki.

lee [li:] *s.* tuulensuoja, suojanpuoli; ~ *shore* suojanpuolella oleva ranta.

leech [li:tʃ] *s.* iilimato; (kuv.) verenimijä.

leek [li:k] *s.* purjosipuli.

leer [liə] *s.* vilkuileminen; *v.* vilkuilla, virnailla.

lees [li:z] *s. pl.* pohjasakka.

lee|**ward** ['li:wəd, mer. lu(:)əd] *a. & adv.* tuulen alla (oleva), suojanpuolella, -lle; *to* ~ suojanpuolelle. **-way** ['li:wei] *s.* (mer.) sorto; *make up* ~ korvata menetetty aika, päästä tasoihin töissänsä.

left 1. [left] *imp. & pp.* ks. **leave;** *be* ~ (m.) olla jäljellä.

left 2. [left] *a.* vasen; *s.* vasen puoli; *adv.* vasemmalla, -lle; *the L*~ vasemmisto; *on my* ~ vasemmalla puolellani; *to the* ~ vasemmalle; *turn* ~ kääntykää vasemmalle. **~-hand** *a.* vasemmanpuoleinen. **~-handed** *a.* vasenkätinen; kömpelö; *l.-h. compliment* kyseenalainen kohteliaisuus. **~-luggage** *l-l. office* tavarasäilö. **~-over** *s.:* ~-*overs* tähteet. **~-wing** vasemmistolainen, vasemmisto-, vasemman siiven.

leg [leg] *s.* sääri, jalka; reisi(liha); housunlahje; (sukan ym) varsi; matkaosuus, taipale; petkuttaja; *v.:* ~ *it* pötkiä tiehensä; *give sb. a* ~ *up* auttaa jkta hevosen selkään; *keep one's* ~*s* pysyä pystyssä; *pull sb.'s* ~ puhua jklle perättömiä, huiputtaa jkta; *shake a* ~ tanssia; *take to one's* ~*s* lähteä käpälämäkeen; *on one's last* ~ viimeisillään; *has not a* ~ *to stand on* ei ole millä puolustautua.

legacy ['legəsi] *s.* testamenttilahjoitus, perintö.

legal ['li:g(ə)l] *a.* laillinen, lainmukainen; oikeus-. **-ity** [li:ˈgæliti] *s.* laillisuus. **-ize** [ˈli:gəlaiz] *v.* laillistaa.

lega|te ['legit] *s.* paavin lähettiläs. **-tee** [legəˈti:] *s.* testamenttilahjoituksen saaja. **-tion** [liˈgeiʃn] *s.* lähetystö.

legend ['ledʒ(ə)nd] *s.* (pyhimys) taru, legenda; (kuvan) selitykset, kuvateksti. **-ary** [-(ə)ri] *a.* tarunomainen.

legerdemain ['ledʒədəˈmein] *s.* silmänkääntötemput.

legging ['legiŋ] *s.:* ~*s* säärykset.

legi|bility [ledʒiˈbiliti] *s.* luettavuus. **-ble** [ˈledʒəbl] *a.* helposti luettava, selvä.

legion ['li:dʒn] *s.* legioona; leegio; *foreign* ~ muukalaislegioona. **-ary** [-əri] *s.* legioonasotilas.

legislat|e [ˈledʒisleit] *v.* säätää lakeja. **-ion** [-ˈleiʃn] *s.* lainsäädäntö. **-ive** [-lətiv] *a.* lakia säätävä. **-or** [-ə] *s.* lainsäätäjä. **-ure** [-ʃə] *s.* lakia säätävä elin.

legitima|cy [liˈdʒitimləsi] *s.* laillisuus; aviollinen syntyperä. **-te** [-it] *a.* laillinen; oikeutettu; avioliitossa syntynyt, *v.* [-eit] laillistaa, julistaa lailliseksi. **-tion** [-ˈmeiʃn] *s.* laillistus. **-tize** [-ətaiz] *v.* laillistaa.

leg-pulling *s.* petkutus.

leguminous [leˈgju:minəs] *a.:* ~ *plant* palkokasvi.

Leicester ['lestə], **Leigh** [li:], **Leighton** ['leitn] *erisn.*

leisure ['leʒə] *s.* joutoaika, vapaa-aika (m. ~ *time*); *at* ~ jouten, vapaana; *at one's* ~ kun on (sopivaa) aikaa, sopivassa tilaisuudessa. **-d** [-d] *a.:* ~ *class[es]* joutilas (ylä)luokka. **-ly** [-li] *a.* verkkainen, hidas.

lemming ['lemiŋ] *s.* sopuli.

lemon ['lemən] *s.* sitruuna, -puu; sitruunankeltainen (väri); ~ *squash* sitruunajuoma; ~-*squeezer* sitruunanpuristin. **-ade** [-ˈneid] *s.* limonaati.

lemur ['li:mə] *s.* puoliapina; maki.

lend [lend] *lent lent, v.* lainata, antaa lainaksi; antaa; ~ *an ear* kuunnella; ~ *a [helping] hand* auttaa; ~ *oneself to* antautua jhk; ~*s itself to* sopii, on omiaan jhk. **-ing-library** *s.* lainakirjasto.

length [leŋθ] *s.* pituus; välimatka; veneen-, hevosmitta; (kangas)kappale, pala; *a journey of some* ~ verraten pitkä matka; *two feet in* ~ kahden jalan pituinen; *at* ~ laajasti, yksityiskohtaisesti (us. *at great* ~); vihdoin; *at full* ~ pitkin pituuttaan; *go the* ~ *of (. .-ing)* mennä niin pitkälle, että; *go all* ~*s* olla valmis mihin tahansa. **-en** [-(ə)n] *v.* pidentää, pidetä. **-wise** *adv.* pitkittäin. **-y** [-i] *a.* pitkä, pitkällinen, pitkäveteinen.

leni|ence, -ency ['li:njəns, -i] *s.* lempeys. **-ent** [-ənt] *s.* lempeys, armeliaisuus.

lens [lenz] *s.* linssi, mykiö.

lent [lent] *imp. & pp.* ks. **lend**.

Lent [lent] *s.* paastonaika; ~ *term* kevätlukukausi.

lentil ['lentil] *s.* virvilä.

Leonard ['lenəd] *erisn.*

leonine ['li(:)ənain] *s.* leijonamainen.

leopard ['lepəd] *s.* leopardi, pantteri. **-ess** [-is] *s.* naarasleopardi.

leotard ['li:əta:d] *s.* Am. trikoot.

leper ['lepə] *s.* spitaalitautinen.

lepr|osy ['leprəsi] *s.* le- ra. **-ous** [-əs] *a.* spitaalinen.

lese-majesty ['li:zˈmædʒisti] *s.* majesteettirikos.

lesion ['li:ʒn] *s.* vamma, vika.

less [les] *komp. ks. little; a.* vähäisempi, pienempi; *pron. & adv.* vähemmän; *prep.* miinus, vähennettynä jllak; *of ~ importance* vähemmän tärkeä; *in ~ than no time* tuossa tuokiossa; *much ~* vielä vähemmän, saati; *none the ~* yhtäkaikki, kuitenkin; *the ~* sitä vähemmän; mitä vähemmän.

lessee [le'si:] *s.* vuokralainen.

lessen ['lesn] *v.* vähentää, pienentää, vähetä, pienentyä, aleta.

lesser ['lesə] *a.* vähempi, pienempi.

lesson ['lesn] *s.* läksy, tehtävä; (oppi)tunti; opetus, ojennus; (saarna)teksti; *read sb.* a ~ ojentaa jkta.

lessor [le'sɔ:] *s.* vuokraaja, vuokranantaja.

lest [lest] *konj.* ettei, jottei, että.

let 1. [let] *let let, v.* antaa, sallia; päästää; vuokrata, antaa vuokralle; *let's start at once!* alkakaamme heti! *don't let's start yet!* älkäämme vielä alkako! *to be ~* vuokrattavana; *~ fly at* laukaista, purkaa vihaansa jkh; *~ go* päästää irti, hellittää; *~ oneself go* innostua liikaa; *~ blood* iskeä suonta; *~ alone* jättää rauhaan; saati sitten; *~ down* laskea alas; *~ sb. down* tuottaa jklle pettymys; *~ in* päästää sisälle; *~ oneself in for* hankkia itselleen (harmia ym); *~ into* päästää jhk, (into a secret)* ilmaista, uskoa jklle; *~ off* laskea pois, laukaista (m. kuv.); päästää (vähemmällä rangaistuksella), antaa anteeksi; *~ on* kieliä; *~ out* päästää ulos, väljentää; päästää (salaisuus) julki; vuokrata pois; *~ it be done at once!* tehtäköön se heti! *let ABC be .. otaksutaan, että ABC on .. ~-down* pettymys; *~-up* tauko.

let 2. [let] *s.* verkkosyöttö (tennis); *without ~ or hindrance* esteittä.

lethal ['li:θl] *a.* kuolettava.

lethargic [le'θɑ:dʒik] *a.* horros-. **-y** ['leθədʒi] *s.* horros, letargia.

Lethe ['li:θi(:)] *erisn.* Lethe, unohduksen virta.

Lett [let] *s.* latvialainen.

letter ['letə] *s.* kirjain; kirje; *pl.* kaunokirjallisuus, oppi; *a man of ~s* kirjailija; *to the ~* kirjaimellisesti,

sanasta sanaan; *~ to the editor* yleisönosasto (sanomalehdessä). **~-box** postilaatikko. **-ed** [-d] *a.* paljon lukenut **~-head** (esim. firman) nimi ja osoite (paperin yläreunassa). **-ing** *s.* kirjaimet, kirjaintyyli; tekstaus. **-press** (kuvitetun kirjan) teksti, kohopaino. **~-weight** kirjepainin.

lettuce ['letis] *s.* lehtisalaatti.

leuk|emia [lju:'ki:mjə] *s.* leukemia. **-ocyte** ['lju:kəsait] *s.* valkoinen verisolu, valkosolu.

levant [li'vænt] *v.* paeta maksamatta velkojaan.

levee ['levi] *s.* (kuninkaan ym) aamuvastaanotto; rantavalli.

level ['levl] *s.* vesivaaka; tasopinta, taso; tasainen maa, tasanko; *a.* vaakasuora; tasapäinen (lusikka), tasainen, tasaväkinen; samalla tasolla oleva; *v.* tasoittaa (m. *~ off)*; poistaa eroavuudet, tehdä tasaiseksi; tehdä yhdenvertaiseksi; suunnata, kohdistaa; *above sea ~* merenpinnan yläpuolella; *on a ~ with* samalla tasolla kuin, yhdenvertainen; *on the ~* (puhek.) rehellinen; *~ crossing* (rautatien) taso|risteys, -ylikäytävä; *do one's ~ best* tehdä parhaansa; *~ with the ground* hajottaa maan tasalle. **~-headed** maltillinen. **-ness** *s.* tasaisuus.

lever ['li:v|ə] *s.* vipu, -varsi; *v.* nostaa, siirtää vivulla. **-age** [-(ə)ridʒ] *s.* vipu-, nostovoima; (kuv.) apukeino. **-et** ['levərit] *s.* jäniksenpoika.

Levi ['li:vai] *erisn.* Leevi.

leviathan [li'vaiəθ(ə)n] *s.* merihirviö; (kuv.) jättiläinen.

levitation [levi'teiʃn] *s.* kohoaminen ilmaan (spiritistisenä ilmiönä).

Levit|e ['li:vait] *s.* leviitta. **-icus** [li'vitikəs] *s.* 3. Mooseksen kirja.

levity ['leviti] *s.* keveys, kevytmielisyys, huikentelevaisuus.

levy ['levi] *v.* kantaa (veroa), ottaa (sotaväkeä); *s.* veronkanto, sotaväenotto.

lewd [lu:d] *a.* irstas, rivo.

Lewis ['lu(:)is] *erisn.*

lexicographer [leksi'kɔgrəfə] *s.* sanakirjan tekijä.

Lhasa ['læsə] *erisn.*

liability [laiə'biliti] *s.*

vastuuvelvollisuus, sitoumus; ~ *for accidents* tapaturma-alttius; *l-ties* (pl.) velat, vastattavat.

liable ['laiəbl] *a.* altis; ~ *for* vastuunalainen, vastuussa jstk; ~ *to catch cold* altis kylmettymiselle; ~ *to a fine* sakon alainen; ~ *to make mistakes* erehdyksiin taipuvainen, erehtyväinen.

liaison [li'eizn, Am. 'liəzɔn] *s.* yhteys; rakkaussuhde; ~ *officer* yhdysupseeri; ~ *interpretation* neuvottelutulkinta.

liar ['laiə] *s.* valehtelija.

lib [lib]: *Women's L* ~ naisten vapautusliike.

libation [lai'beiʃn] *s.* juomauhri; juomingit.

libel ['laib(ə)l] *s.* herjauskirjoitus, kunnianloukkaus; *v.* herjata, häväistä. **-lous** [-əs] *a.* herjaava, kunniaa loukkaava.

liber|al ['lib(ə)rəl] *a.* antelias, jalomielinen, aulis, runsas; vapaa, vapaamielinen; ennakkoluuloton; *s.* (*L* ~) liberaali, vapaamielinen. **-alism** [-lizm] *s.* liberalismi, vapaamielisyys. **-ality** [libə'ræliti] *s.* anteliaisuus, aulius, ennakkoluulottomuus jne. **-ate** ['libəreit] *v.* vapauttaa. **-ation** [-'reiʃn] *s.* vapauttaminen.

Liberia [lai'biəriə] *erisn.*

libertine ['libəti:n] *s.* elostelija.

liberty ['libəti] *s.* vapaus; (etu)oikeus; ~ *of action* toimintavapaus; *take the* ~ *of doing* . . rohjeta tehdä jtk; *at* ~ vapaa, esteetön, joutilas; *liberties* erivapaudet.

libidinous [li'bidinəs] *a.* himokas.

libido [li'bi:dəu] *s.* sukupuolivietti, viettienergia.

librar|ian [lai'breəriən] *s.* kirjastonhoitaja. **-y** ['laibrəri] *s.* kirjasto.

Libya ['libiə] *erisn.* Libya. **-n** [-n] *a.* & *s.* libyalainen.

lice [lais] *pl.* ks. *louse.*

licence ['lais(ə)ns] *s.* erikoislupa, lupakirja, lisenssi; (liika) vapaus, vallattomuus, kurittomuus; *driving* ~ ajokortti; *poetic* ~ runoilijan vapaus.

licens|e ['lais(ə)ns] *v.* myöntää lupa, oikeuttaa, valtuuttaa. **-ed** [-t] *a.* lailliset oikeudet omaava; ~ *premises* anniskelupaikka. **-ee** [-'si:] *s.*

lupakirjan haltija.

licen|tiate [lai'senʃiit] *s.* lisensiaatti (*in* jnk). **-tious** [-ʃəs] *a.* hillitön, vallaton, irstaileva.

lichen ['laikən] *s.* jäkälä.

lick [lik] *v.* nuolla; latkia (~ *up*); piestä; voittaa, päihittää; *s.* nuoleminen; sivallus; ~ *into shape* muokata, siistiä, opettaa tapoja. ~ *the dust* kaatua, tulla voitetuksi; ~ *sb.'s boots* hännystellä jkta. **-ing** *s.* selkäsauna.

licorice ['likəris] = *liquorice.*

lid [lid] *s.* kansi; [*eye*] ~ silmäluomi.

lie 1. [lai] valhe; *v.* valehdella; *tell* ~ *s* valehdella; *he is lying* hän valehtelee; *white* ~ viaton valhe, hätävalhe; *give the* ~ *to* osoittaa vääräksi; ~ *detector* valheenpaljastuskoje.

lie 2. [lai] *lay lain,* ppr. *lying, v.* maata, olla pitkällään; sijaita, olla; levätä; *s.* asema; ~ *down* paneutua maata; ~ *open to* olla alttiina jllek; *as far as in me lies* mikäli minusta riippuu; *take sth. lying down* alistua jhk mukisematta; *the* ~ *of the land* asiaintila. **~-abed** unikeko.

lief [li:f] *adv.* (vanh.) kernaasti.

liege [li:dʒ] *a.* feodaali-; *s.* läänitysherra (m. ~ *lord);* vasalli. **-man** vasalli.

lien ['li:ən] *s.* pidätysoikeus (lak.).

lieu [lju:] *s.:* *in* ~ *of* jnk asemesta.

lieutenancy [lef'tenəsi] *s.* luutnantin arvo.

lieutenant [lef'tenənt, Am. lu:'ten-] *s.* luutnantti; sijainen; käskynhaltija; *second* ~ aliluutnantti, vänrikki. **~-general** kenraaliluutnantti.

life [laif] *s.* (pl. *lives*) elämä; henki; elämänkulku, elinaika, elämäkerta; eloisuus, vilkkaus; *early* ~ nuoruus; *see* ~ nähdä maailmaa; *as large as* ~ luonnollisessa koossa, (kuv.) ilmielävänä; *for* ~ elinajaksi, elinkautis-; *for one's* ~, *for dear* ~ henkensä edestä; *for the* ~ *of me I could not* . . en kuolemaksenikaan voinut.; *from* ~ luonnon (elävän mallin) mukaan; *in real* ~ todellisuudessa; *portray to the* ~ kuvata luonnonmukaisesti; *bring to* ~ palauttaa henkiin; ~ *sentence* elinkautinen tuomio; ~ *story* elämäkerta; *kiss of ~* ks. *kiss.* **-belt** pelastusvyö. **-blood** sydänveri. **-boat** pelastusvene. **~-buoy** pelastusrengas. **~-giving** elähdyttävä. **~-guard** henkivartija; vahti, hengenpelastaja (uimarannalla); *L ~ Guards* henkikaarti. **~-jacket** pelastusliivi. **-less** *a.* hengetön, laimea. **-like** *a.* ilmielävä, luonnonmukainen. **~-line** pelastusköysi, turvaköysi. **-long** elinkautinen, elinikäinen. **~-preserver** patukka. **~-size** luonnollista kokoa oleva. **-time** elinaika, ihmisikä; *the chance of a ~* elämäri (-si, -nsä) tilaisuus. **~-work** elämäntyö.

lift [lift] *v.* nostaa, kohottaa; poistaa, kumota; kohota, (sumusta ym) hälvetä, häipyä; sl. varastaa; *s.* nostaminen; hissi, nostolaite; peukalokyyti; *~ potatoes* nostaa perunoita; *~ up one's voice* korottaa äänensä; *give sb. a ~* ottaa kyytiin; *air ~* ilmasilta; *ski ~* hiihtohissi. **~-boy** hissipoika.

liga|ment ['ligəmənt] *s.* nivelside. **-ture** ['ligətʃə] *s.* suonen sitominen; (mus.) sidonta.

light 1. [lait] *s.* valo, päivänvalo, valkeus; kynttilä, lamppu, lyhty, majakka, tulitikku; tuli, valaistus; valistus, ymmärrys; *pl.* ks. *lights; a.* valoisa; vaalea; *v. (lit* litt. *~ed ~ed)* sytyttää, valaista, syttyä (m. *~ up);* *shining ~s* nerot; *according to one's ~s* ymmärryksensä mukaan; *in the ~ of* jnk valossa; *see the ~* syntyä; tulla julkiseksi, oivaltaa totuus, (usk.) kokea kääntymys; *throw (shed) ~ upon* valaista; *~ up* kirkastua; sytyttää piippu ym; *bring to ~* saattaa päivänvaloon; *come to ~* tulla ilmi; *~ year* valovuosi.

light 2. [lait] *a.* kevyt, keveä; vähäinen, lievä (rangaistus), vieno (tuuli), mieto (viini), kuohkea (maa); huoleton, kevytmielinen, pintapuolinen; *adv.* kevyesti; *v.* laskeutua; *~ music* viihdemusiikki; *~ [reading]* ajanviete-; *~ sleep* herkkä uni; *make ~ of* vähäksyä; *with a ~ heart* keveällä mielellä; *[travel] ~* vähin matkatavaroin; *~ come, ~ go* mikä laulaen tulee, se viheltäen menee; *~*

on, upon sattua löytämään. **~-armed** kevytaseinen.

lighten ['laitn] *v.* valaista; kirkastua; salamoida; keventää, huojentaa; keventyä.

lighter 1. ['laitə] *s.* sytytin.

lighter 2. ['laitə] *s.* lotja, proomu.

light|-fingered *a.* näpistelevä. **~-headed** ajattelematon. **~-hearted** huoleton, hilpeä.

lighthouse *s.* majakka.

lighting *s.* valaistus.

light-minded *a.* kevytmielinen.

lightness *s.* keveys.

lightning ['laitniŋ] *s.* salama; *flash of ~* salaman leimahdus; *like ~* salamannopeasti. **~-conductor, ~-rod** ukkosenjohdatin.

lights [laits] *s. pl.* (eläimen) keuhkot (ravintona).

lightship *s.* majakkalaiva.

lightsome [-səm] *a.* kepeä, siro; eloisa, hilpeä.

lightweight *a. & s.* kevyen sarjan (nyrkkeilijä).

lign|eous ['lign|iəs] *a.* puu-, puunkaltainen. **-ite** [-ait] *s.* ruskohiili.

likable ['laikəbl] *s.* miellyttävä, rakastettava.

like 1. [laik] *a.* kaltainen, näköinen; sellainen kuin, sama(nlainen); *adv., prep.* niinkuin, kuten; *s.* sama, vertainen; *~ this* tällä tapaa, näin; *don't talk ~ that* älä puhu tuollaista a; *what is he ~* millainen hän on? *people ~ that* sellaiset ihmiset; *I feel ~ going* minua haluttaa mennä; *look ~* olla jkn näköinen; [*it*] *looks ~ gold* näyttää kullalta; *he looks ~ winning* hän näyttää voittavan; [*it is*] *just ~ him* aivan hänen tapaistaan; *something ~ .. suunnilleen ..; ~ anything (~ hell)* hirveästi; *there is nothing ~ walking* ei ole mitään kävelyn veroista; *music, .. and the ~* ja muut sen tapaiset (taiteet); *did you ever hear the ~?* oletko kuullut moista? *~s and dislikes* sympatiat ja antipatiat.

like 2. [laik] *v.* pitää jstk, olla mieltynyt; haluta kernaasti; *do you ~ fish?* pidätkö kalasta; *how do you ~ this [one]?* mitä pidät tästä? *I didn't ~ to disturb him* en halunnut häiritä häntä; *if you ~* jos haluat(te); *~ sth.*

better pitää enemmän jstk; *I should ~ to go* haluaisin mennä, menisin mielelläni. **-able** = *likable*.

like|lihood ['laiklihud] *s.* todennäköisyys; *in all ~* varsin todennäköisesti. **-ly** [-li] *a.* uskottava, todennäköinen; lupaavannäköinen, sopiva; *adv.: very ~, most ~, as ~ as not* varsin todennäköisesti; *he is not ~ to come* hän tuskin tulee. **-n** [-(ə)n] *v.* verrata *(to* jhk). **-ness** *s.* yhdennäköisyys; muoto, hahmo; muotokuva; . . *is a good ~* (kuva) on hyvin näköinen. **-wise** *adv.* samoin.

liking ['laikiŋ] *s.* mieltymys; *have a ~ for* pitää jstk; *to one's ~* jklle mieleen, mieleinen.

lilac ['lailək] *s.* syreeni(pensas); vaalean sinipunerva, lila(n värinen).

lilt [lilt] *s.* iloinen ja rytmillinen laulu.

lily ['lili] *s.* lilja; *~ of the valley* kielo. **~-livered** pelkurimainen.

Lima ['li:mə] *erisn.*

limb [lim] *s.* raaja; (ruumiin) jäsen; (puun) oksa; *artificial ~* proteesi; *escaped with life and ~* selvisi vammoitta. **-ed:** *long-~* pitkäraajainen.

limber 1. ['limbə] *a.* taipuisa, notkea; *v.: ~ [oneself] up* verrytellä.

limber 2. ['limbə] *s.* tykinlavetin (irrotettava) etuosa.

limbo ['limbəu] *s.* (pl. *~s)* helvetin esikartano; (kuv.) roskis; sl. panttilainaamo; *is in ~* on jäänyt syrjään, hylätyksi, on vaipunut unohduksiin.

lime 1. [laim] *s.* kalkki; lintuliima *(bird-~); v.* kalkita; pyydystää lintuliimalla; *quick ~* sammuttamaton kalkki; *slaked ~* sammutettu kalkki.

lime 2. [laim] *s.* lehmus; limetti (Citrus); sitruunamehu.

lime|kiln kalkkiuuni. **-light** parrasvalot, (kuv.) julkisuuden valokeila.

limerick ['limərik] *s.* viisisäkeinen tilapäisruno.

limestone *s.* kalkkikivi.

limit ['limit] *s.* raja; raja-arvo t. -hinta, *v.* rajoittaa; *set a ~ to* rajoittaa; *within ~s* kohtuuden rajoissa; *that's the ~!* se on jo huippu! **-ation** [-'teiʃn] *s.* rajoitus. **-ed** [-id] *a.* rajoitettu; niukka; *~ [liability] company* yhtiö,

jossa on rajoitettu vastuuvelvollisuus. **-less** *a.* rajaton.

limousine ['liməzi:n] *s.* umpiauto; (matala) pienoisbussi (et. lentokentällä).

limp 1. [limp] *v.* ontua, nilkuttaa; *s.* nilkutus.

limp 2. [limp] *a.* pehmeä; veltto, hervoton; nidottu.

limpet ['limpit] *s.* maljakotilo, (kuv.) iilimato.

limpid ['limpid] *a.* kirkas, läpikuultava. **-ity** [-'piditi] *s.* läpikuultavuus.

linage ['lainidʒ] *s.* rivimäärä.

linchpin ['lintʃpin] *s.* sokkanaula.

Lincoln ['liŋkən] *erisn.*

linden ['lindən] *s.* lehmus.

line 1. [lain] *s.* nuora, köysi, siima; (puhelin- ym) johto; viiva, linja, uurre; rivi, jono, säe; (laiva)reitti, linja, rata, suunta, (ajoraʤan) kaista; suku; (toimi)ala, tavaralaji; *pl.* m. vuorosanat, suuntaviivat, periaatteet, (vihkimä)todistus; *the ~* (m.) päiväntasaaja; *hard ~s!* olipa huono onni! *~ engaged* (Am. *~ busy)* varattu! *bring sth. into ~* saattaa sopusointuun; *come (fall) into ~* mukautua; *drop me a ~!* kirjoita minulle muutama sana! *get into ~* ryhmittyä (ajoradalle, kaistalle); *take a strong ~* ottaa luja asenne; *on the ~s laid down by* jkn viitoittamaa tietä; *on the same ~s* samaan tapaan; *one must draw the ~ somewhere* kaikella on rajansa; *it is not in my ~* se ei kuulu minun alaani; *ship of the ~,* *~-of-battle ship* linjalaiva.

line 2. [lain] *v.* viivoittaa; uurtaa; reunustaa, asettaa riviin (m. *~ up);* sisustaa, vuorata; täyttää (taskut); *~ up* asettua riviin; *a road ~d with trees* puitten reunustama tie; *~ one's pockets* kääriä rahaa.

line|age ['lini|idʒ] *s.* sukuperä. **-al** [-əl] *a.* suoraan alenevassa t. ylenevässä polvessa. **-aments** [-əmənts] *s. pl.* (kasvon)piirteet. **-ar** [-ə] *a.* viiva-; *~ measure* pituusmitta. **-man** puhelinlinjamies.

linen ['linin] *a.* liinainen; *s.* pellava; liinavaatteet. **~-draper** kangaskauppias.

liner ['lainə] *s.* vuorolaiva,

valtamerialus; vuorokone.

linesman ['lainzmən] s. linjatuomari.

line-up s. järjestäytyminen; (urh.) kokoonpano; epäillyn tunnistamistilaisuus.

linger ['liŋgə] v. viipyä, vitkastella, viivytellä; (taudista) pitkittyä; (~ on) elää kituuttaa.

lingerie ['lɛ̃:ɲəri:] s. naisten alusvaatteet.

lingering a. vitkasteleva; pitkällinen.

lingo ['liŋgəu] s. (pl. ~ es) siansaksa, mongerrus.

lingual ['liŋgw(ə)l] s. kieli-, kielen. **-ist** ['liŋgwist] s. kielimies, kielitaitoinen henkilö; kielitieteilijä. **-istic** [-'wistik] a. kielitieteellinen, kielellinen.

liniment ['linimənt] s. linimentti.

lining ['lainiŋ] s. sisusta, vuori, vuoraus.

link [liŋk] s. rengas, silmukka, nivel; yhdistää; ~ s kalvosinnapit; v. yhdistää, liittää yhteen; yhtyä. **-boy** s. soihdunkantaja.

links [liŋks] s. pl. (us. a links) golf-kenttä; ruohoa kasvava.

linnet ['linit] s. hemppo.

lino ['lainəu] s. (lyh.) linoleumi. **-leum** [li'nəuljəm] s. korkkimatto. **-type** ['lainə(u)-] s. linotyyppi.

linseed ['linsi:d] s. pellavansiemen; ~ oil liinaöljy.

linsey-woolsey ['linzi'wulzi] s. karkea puolivillakangas.

lint [lint] s. liinanöyhtä.

lintel ['lintl] s. (oven ym) päällyslauta, kamana.

lion ['laiən] s. leijona; merkkihenkilö; the ~ 's share suurin (t. paras) osa. **-ess** [-is] s. naarasleijona. **~-hearted** uljas. **~-hunter** kuuluisuuksien metsästäjä. **-ize** [-aiz] v. juhlia (sankarina).

lip [lip] s. huuli; reuna, parras, (astian nokka); (sl.) hävyttömyys; lower (upper) ~ ala-, ylähuuli; hang on a p. 's ~ s hartaasti kuunnella jkta. **~-reading** huulioluku, huuliltaluku. **~-service** (pelkät) kauniit sanat, tyhjät lupaukset. **-stick** huuli|puikko, -puna.

lique|fy ['likwifai] v. sulattaa, nesteyttää; sulaa; -fied petroleum gas nestekaasu (LPG).

liqueur [li'kjuə] s. likööri.

liquid ['likwid] a. nestemäinen, juokseva, sula; selkeä, kirkas; s. neste. helposti muuttuva; helposti rahaksi vaihdettava. **-ate** [-eit] s. suorittaa (maksu); maksaa velkansa; »likvidoida», panna päiviltä. **-ation** [-'deiʃn] s. suoritus, konkurssiselvitys; go into ~ tehdä vararikko. **-ator** [-eitə] s. selvitysmies. **-iser** [-aizə] s. tehosekoitin.

liquor ['likə] s. väkijuoma; the worse for ~ humalassa.

liquorice ['likəris] s. lakritsi.

Lisbon ['lizbən] erisn. Lissabon.

lisp [lisp] v. sammaltaa; s. sammallus.

lissom(e) ['lisəm] a. notkea, ketterä.

list 1. [list] s. luettelo, lista; reunus, hulpio; pl. turnajaispaikka; v. luetteloida; enter the ~ s (against) ryhtyä taisteluun t. kilpasille.

list 2. v. kallistua; s. (laivan) kallistuma.

list 3. v. (vanh.) haluttaa (the wind bloweth where it listeth).

listen ['lisn] v. kuunnella; ~ to kuunnella jtk, jkta, m. noudattaa neuvoa ~ in (to) kuunnella (radiota), (m. ~ in on) k. salaa radiolähetystä. **-er** [-ə] s. kuuntelija (m. radio-).

listless ['listlis] a. haluton, raukea.

lit [lit] imp. & pp. ks. light.

litany ['litəni] s. litania, rukous.

liter ['li:tə] s. Am. litra.

liter|acy ['lit(ə)rəsi] s. luku- ja kirjoitustaito. **-al** [-r(ə)l] a. kirjaimellinen, sananmukainen; kirjain-; ~ translation sanatarkka käännös. **-ally** [-rəli] adv. kirjaimellisesti, sananmukaisesti. **-ary** [-rəri] a. kirjallinen; ~ critic kirjallisuusarvostelija. **-ate** [-tərit] a. & s. luku- ja kirjoitustaitoinen. **-ature** ['lit(ə)ritʃə] s. kirjallisuus.

lithe [laið] a. taipuisa, notkea.

lithograph ['liθəgrɑ:f, et. Am. -græf] s. kivipainos. **-y** [li'θɔgrəfi] s. kivipaino.

Lithuania [liθju(:)'einjə] erisn. Liettua. **-n** [-n] a. & s. liettualainen; liettuan kieli.

litig|ant ['litigənt] s. asianosainen. **-ate** [-geit] v. käräjöidä. **-ation** [-'geiʃn] s.

käräjöinti, riita-asia. **-ious** [li'tidʒəs]
a. riidanhaluinen, oikeudenkäynti-.

litmus ['litməs] *s.* lakmus; ~ *paper*
lakmuspaperi.

litre ['li:tə] *s.* litra.

litter ['litə] *s.* roskat; epäjärjestys,
sotku; pahnat; poikue; paarit; *v.*
sotkea, roskata (~ *sth. up with . .*);
levittää pahnoja; poikia; ~*-bin*,
roskapönttö; ~*-lout* »roskaaja»,
roskien heittelijä.

little ['litl] *a.* (komp. *less least* t. *smaller
smallest*) pieni, pikku; vähäinen,
mitätön; pikkumainen; *s.* vähäinen
määrä; *adv.* vähän, hiukkasen, ei
juuri ollenkaan; ~ *one* pienokainen; *a*
~ vähän, hiukan, jonkin verran; *a* ~
thing pikkuasia; ~ *by* ~ vähitellen;
not a ~ melkoisesti; ~ *better than*
tuskin parempi kuin; *he* ~ *knew that*
hän tuskin aavisti, että. ~**-go**
valmistava tutkinto (Cambr.).

littoral ['litər(ə)l] *a.* rannikko-.

liturgy ['litə(:)dʒi] *s.* liturgia.

livable ['livəbl] *a.* siedettävä,
asuttavaksi kelpaava.

live [liv] *v.* elää, olla elossa; asua;
viettää (elämää); *a.* [laiv] elävä;
hehkuva, palava; ladattu, (sähk.)
jännitteinen; eloisa, tarmokas; *adv.*
[laiv] suorana lähetyksenä; ~ *on one's
salary* elää palkallaan, *on fruit*
hedelmillä; ~ *to see* kokea; ~ *up to*
elää jnk mukaan; ~ *out the night* elää
yli yön; ~ *down* voit aa (suru ym); *a*
~ *broadcast* suora lähetys; *a* ~ *wire*
(kuv.) tarmonpesä (elämää ja tarmoa
uhkuva).

live|lihood ['laivlihud] *s.* toimeentulo,
elatus. **-liness** *s.* vilkkaus. **-long**
['livləŋ, Am. 'laiv-]: *the* ~ *day* koko
pitkän päivän.

lively ['laivli] *a.* eloisa, vilkas; pirteä;
elävä, havainnollinen; kiihkeä,
voimakas; (leik.) jännittävä,
vaarallinen *(make things* ~ *for)*.

liven ['laivn] *v.*: ~ *up* vilkastuttaa.

liver ['livə] *s.* maksa. **-ish** [-riʃ] *a.*
maksatautinen, (kuv.) äreä.

liveried ['livərid] *a.* livreepukuinen.

Liver|pool ['livəpu:l] *erisn.* **-pudlian**
[-'pʌdliən] *a. & s.* liverpoolilainen.

liverwort [-wə:t] *s.* maksasammal.

livery ['livəri] *s.* livree, lakeijan puku;

~ *company* eräitten Lontoon
ammattikuntien nimitys; ~ *stable*
vuokratalli. **-man**
ammattikuntalainen, vuokratallin
hoitaja.

lives [laivz] *s. pl.* ks. *life.*

livestock ['laivstɔk] *s.* karja; *l.-s.
rearing* karjanhoito.

livid ['livid] *a.* lyijynharmaa,
kalmankalpea.

living ['liviŋ] *a.* elävä, nykyään elävä;
elinvoimainen; ilmielävä; *s.* elatus,
toimeentulo; pastoraatti; *the* ~
elossaolevat; ~ *standard* elintaso;
within ~ *memory* miesmuistiin; ~
wage toimeentuloon riittävä palkka.
~**-room** olohuone. ~**-space** elintila.

Livingstone ['liviŋstən] *erisn.*

lizard ['lizəd] *s.* sisilisko.

llama ['lɑ:mə] *s.* laama(eläin).

Llewellyn [lu:'elin] *erisn.*

lo [ləu] *interj.* katso!

load [ləud] *s.* lasti, taakka, kuorma;
kuormitus; *v.* kuormata, lastata;
sälyttää, kuormittaa; ladata;
väärentää (painoa lisäämällä); ~*ed
table* notkuva pöytä; ~*ed question*
johdatteleva kysymys. **-er** [-ə] *s.*
kuormauslaite. **-ing** *s.* lastaus,
kuormaus; lataus. ~**-line** lastiviiva.
-stone ks. *lode-.*

loaf 1. [ləuf] *s.* (pl. *loaves)* leipä,
kakku; sokerikeko; *meat* ~
lihamureke »limppu»; ~ *sugar*
kekosokeri; *use one's* ~ (sl.) käyttää
päänuppiaan.

loaf 2. [ləuf] *v.* maleksia, vetelehtiä. **-er**
[-ə] *s.* tyhjäntoimittaja.

loam [ləum] *s.* hiekansekainen savi,
(viljava) savimaa. **-y** [-i] *a.* savinen,
savipitoinen.

loan [ləun] *s.* laina; *v.* (et. Am.) antaa
lainaksi; *ask for the* ~ *of* pyytää
lainaksi; *raise a* ~ ottaa laina; *on* ~ *to*
lainassa jklla. **-word** lainasana.

loath [ləuθ] *a.* haluton, vastahakoinen;
be ~ *to* vastahakoisesti tehdä jtk;
nothing ~ varsin halukas. **-e** [ləuð] *v.*
inhota. **-ing** ['ləuðiŋ] *s.* inho. **-some**
['ləuðsəm] *a.* inhottava.

loaves [ləuvz] *pl.* ks. *loaf.*

lob [lɔb] *v.* (tennis) lyödä (pallo)
korkealle; *s.* koholyönti.

lobby ['lɔbi] *s.* eteinen, eteishalli,

lämpiö; keskusteluhuone t. käytävä; painostusryhmä; *v.* painostaa edustajia, harjoittaa käytäväpolitiikkaa. **-ist** [-ist] *s.* lobbyisti (joka yrittää painostaa edustajia).

lobe [ləub] *s.* lohko, liuska; ~ *of the ear* korvannipukka.

lobster ['lɔbstə] *s.* hummeri.

lobule ['lɔbju:l] *s.* liuska.

local ['ləuk(ə)l] *a.* paikallinen, paikallis-; ~ kapakka; ~ *colour* paikallisväri; ~ *government* kunnallishallinto; ~ *time* paikallista aikaa. **-ism** [-izm] *s.* rajoittuneisuus, nurkkapatriotismi; paikallinen kieliomituisuus. **-ity** [lə(u)'kæliti] *s.* paikkakunta; *bump (sense) of* ~ paikallisvaisto. **-ize** [-aiz] *v.* paikallistaa, rajoittaa jhk paikkaan. **-ly** *adv.* paikallisesti, jllak paikkakunnalla.

loca|te [lə(u)'keit] *v.* sijoittaa, paikantaa; *be ~d in* sijaita jssak. **-tion** [-'keiʃn] *s.* asema, paikka, sijainti; et. Et. Afr. (mustien) asutusalue; *on ~* luonnossa, studion ulkopuolella.

loch [lɔk] *s.* (Skotl.) järvi.

lock 1. [lɔk] *s.* kutri, kihara.

lock 2. [lɔk] *s.* lukko (m. kiväärin), lukkolaite; (kanavan) sulku; sulkeminen, kiinnitarttuminen, lukko, sidonta (urh.); *v.* lukita, sulkea, teljetä (us. ~ *in*, ~ *out*); mennä lukkoon, olla lukittavissa; tarttua lujasti kiinni; *under ~ and key* lukkojen ja telkien takana; ~, *stock & barrel* kaikki tyynni; ~ *into one's arms* sulkea syliinsä; ~ *away* panna lukon taakse; ~ *up* lukita (talon ovet), teljetä (vankilaan ym). **-er** [-ə] *s.* pieni kaappi, lokero; arkku. **-et** [-it] *s.* medaljonki. **~-gate** sulkuportti. **-jaw** jäykkäkouristus. **~-keeper** sulkuvahti. **-out** *s.* työnsulku. **-smith** lukkoseppä. **~-up** putka, vankila.

locomo|tion [ləukə'məuʃn] *s.* paikaltaan liikkuminen; liikkumiskyky; *means of* ~ kulkuväline. **-tive** ['ləukəməutiv] *a.* liikkumis-, liike-; *s.* veturi.

locum-tenens ['ləukəm'ti:nenz] *s.* sijainen.

locust ['ləukəst] *s.* heinäsirkka; ~ *tree* johanneksenleipäpuu.

lode [ləud] *s.* malmisuoni. **-star** pohjantähti, (kuv.) johtotähti. **-stone** magneetti(rauta).

lodg|e [lɔdʒ] *s.* (portinvartijan) maja, mökki; (vapaamuurari)loosi; *v.* majoittaa, sijoittaa, ottaa asumaan luokseen; majailla, asua (tilapäisesti); tallettaa; jäädä, tarttua jhk; ~ *a complaint* esittää, tehdä valitus; ~ *in the mind* jäädä mieleen. **-(e)ment** *s.* asema, jalansija; kasaantuminen. **-er** [-ə] *s.* vuokralainen, asukki. **-ing** *s.* asunto; *pl.* vuokrahuoneet; *board and* ~ täysihoito; *live in* ~ *s* asua vuokralaisena (kalustetuissa huoneissa); ~ *house* matkustajakoti.

loft [lɔft] *s.* ullakko; parveke (kirkossa ym). **-iness** [-inis] *s.* ylevyys. **-y** [-i] *a.* korkea; ylevä, jalo; ylhäinen, ylpeä.

log [lɔg] *s.* tukki, pölkky; (mer.) loki; (m. ~*book*) lokikirja; *v.* kaataa tukkipuita; ~*cabin* hirsimaja.

loganberry ['ləugənb(ə)ri] *s.* musta vadelma.

logarithm ['lɔgəriθm, -riðm] *s.* logaritmi.

loggerhead ['lɔgəhed] *s.: at* ~ *s with* tukkanuottasilla jkn kanssa.

logging ['lɔgiŋ] *s.* metsänhakkuu.

logic ['lɔdʒik] *s.* logiikka; loogisuus. **-al** [-(ə)l] *a.* looginen. **-ian** [lə(u)'dʒiʃn] *s.* loogikko.

logistics [lə(u)'dʒistiks] *s.* huolto (sot.)

log-rolling *s.* (pol.) lehmä|kauppa, -kaupat.

loin [lɔin] *s. pl.* kupeet; *sg.* munuaispaisti; *gird up one's* ~ *s* vyöttää kupeensa. **~-cloth** lannevaate.

loiter ['lɔitə] *v.* vetelehtiä, kuljeksia joutilaana; ~ *away one's time* tuhlata aikaansa. **-er** [-rə] *s.* tyhjäntoimittaja.

loll [lɔl] *v.* loikoilla, kellehtiä, lojua, nojailla (~ *about;*) roikkua.

lollipop ['lɔlipɔp] *s.* tikkukaramelli; ~*s* namuset.

lolly ['lɔli] *s.* tikkukaramelli; (sl.) raha; *icecream* ~ jäätelötikku.

London ['lʌndən] *erisn.* Lontoo. **-er** [-ə] *s.* lontoolainen.

lone [ləun] *a.* (run.) yksinäinen; *play a* ~ *hand* toimia yksin. **-liness** [-linis] *s.* yksinäisyys. **-ly** [-li] *a.* yksinäinen;

syrjäinen. **-r** [-ə] s. yksinäinen susi (m. *lone wolf*). **-some** [-səm] a. = ed.; autio.

long 1. [loŋ] v. ikävöidä; kaivata (*for* jtk); ~*ed* -*for* kaivattu.

long 2. [loŋ] a. pitkä, pitkäaikainen; pitkällinen; adv. kauan; ~ *dozen* kolmetoista; ~ *jump* pituushyppy; ~ *measure* pituusmitta; *in the* ~ *run* ajan pitkään; *of* ~ *standing* pitkäaikainen; *all day* ~ kaiken päivää; ~ *ago*, ~ *since* aikoja sitten; *as* ~ *as* niin kauan kuin, jos vain; *no* ~*er* ei kauempaa, ei enää; *don't be* ~! älä viivy kauan! *he was* ~ *in coming* hän viipyi kauan; *before* ~ ennen pitkää; *the* ~ *and the short of it is* sanalla sanoen; *so* ~! näkemiin! **~-bow** s. käsijousi; *draw the l.-b.* liioitella. **~-distance** a. kauko-; (urh.) pitkänmatkan.
~-drawn-out pitkäveteinen. **-er** [-gə] a. pitempi; kauemmin; *I can't wait any* ~ en voi enää odottaa.

longev|al [lɔn'dʒi:v(ə)l] a. pitkäikäinen. **-ity** [-'dʒeviti] s. pitkäikäisyys, korkea ikä.

longhand s. tavallinen kirjoitus (vastak. pikakirjoitus *shorthand*).

longing ['lɔŋiŋ] s. kaipaus, halu.

long|ish ['lɔŋiʃ] a. pitkähkö; pitkulainen. **-itude** ['lɔn(d)ʒitju:d] s. pituusaste. **-itudinal** [lɔn(d)ʒi'tju:dinl] a. pitkittäis-, pituus-.

long-|lived [-livd] pitkäikäinen, kestävä. **~-range** kaukaskantoinen, pitkän tähtäimen. **-shoreman** satamatyöläinen. **~-sighted** pitkä-, kaukonäköinen. **~-standing** kauan kestänyt, vanha. **~-suffering** pitkämielinen; s. pitkämielisyys.
~-term pitkäaikainen, pitkän tähtäimen; myöhäis-. **~-winded** [-'windid] pitkäveteinen.

loo [lu:] s. (puhek.) vessa.

loofah ['lu:fə] s. saunasieni, pesusieni.

look [luk] v. katsoa, katsella; etsiä (*for* jtk); näyttää jltk; olla, antaa jhk päin; s. katse, silmäys; ilme, näkö; pl. ulkomuoto, ulkonäkö; *good* ~ s kaunis ulkomuoto, kauneus; ~ *here!* kuulehan! kuulkaahan! ~ *about* silmällä ympärilleen, katsella ympäristöä, (~ *about one for*) etsiä; ~ *after* hoitaa, huolehtia jstk; ~ *alive!*

pidä kiirettä! joutukaa! ~ *at* katsella, katsoa jtk, jkta; *would you please* ~ *at this?* olkaa hyvä ja vilkaiskaa tätä! *to* ~ *at him* ulkonäöstä päätellen; ~ *down* [*up*]*on* halveksia; ~ *for* hakea, etsiä; odottaa; *be* ~*ing for* etsiskellä; ~ *forward to* odottaa, iloita ennakolta; ~ *in* käväistä; ~ *into* tutkia, ottaa selkoa; ~ *on* olla katsojana, katsella, pitää jnak (*as*); ~ *out* katsella ulos; olla varuillaan; ~ *over*, ~ *through* tarkastaa, käydä läpi; ~ *to* pitää huolta jstk, hoitaa, odottaa (*sb. for* jklta jtk); ~ *up sb.* pistäytyä jkta katsomassa, (. . *a word*) hakea (sanakirjasta), parantua, (hinnoista) nousta; ~ *up to* kunnioittaa; *it* ~ *s like rain* näyttää tulevan sade; *he does not* ~ *his age* hän ei näytä niin vanhalta kuin hän on; *give a* ~ luoda silmäys; *have a* ~ *at* vilkaista; *let me have a* ~! annahan kun katson! *I can see it by your* ~ s näen sen päältänne. **-ed** [-t] *pp.* : ~-*for* odotettu; *be well* ~ *upon* nauttia arvonantoa. **-er-on** ['lukə'rɔn] katselija. **~-in** s. (voiton)mahdollisuus. **-ing-glass** peili.

look-out s. tähystyspaikka; tähystelijä; toiveet, mahdollisuudet.

loom 1. [lu:m] s. kangaspuut, kutomakone.

loom 2. [lu:m] v. kangastaa, häämöttää; kohota (esille); ~ *large* näyttää valtavalta t. uhkaavalta.

loon 1. [lu:n] s. kuikka.

loon 2. [lu:n] s. tolvana.

loony ['lu:ni] s. sl. mielipuoli.

loop [lu:p] s. silmukka, mutka, polveke; raksi; v. tehdä silmukka; kiinnittää silmukalla; ~ *the loop* (ilm.) tehdä surmansilmukka. **-hole**, tähystyssaukko, ampuma-aukko; (kuv.) veruke, porsaanreikä.

loose [lu:s] a. irtonainen, vapaa; irrallaan oleva, löyhä, höllä; väljä; kuohkea; epätarkka; huolimaton; siveetön, kevytmielinen; v. päästää irti; ~ *tongue* lörpöttelevä kieli; *at a* ~ *end* toimeton, työtön; *on the* ~ lystäilemässä, huonoilla teillä; vapaalla jalalla; *break* ~ tempautua irti, karata; *come* (*work*) ~ irtautua, lähteä irti, löystyä; *let* ~ päästää irti, valloilleen; ~ [*a p.'s*] *tongue* saada

kielenkannat irtoamaan. ~-**fitting** *a.*
väljä. -**ly** *adv.* vapaasti, löyhästi;
irrallaan jne. -**n** ['luːsn] *v.* irrottaa,
hellittää, päästää irti; löyhentää;
irtaantua; höltyä; kirvoittaa (jkn
kieli). -**ness** *s.* löyhyys jne.;
kevytmielisyys.

loot [luːt] *v.* ryöstää; *s.* (sota)saalis.
lop 1. [lɔp] *s.* hakata pois, katkoa (us.
~ *off*), karsia.
lop 2. [lɔp] *v.* roikkua. ~-**eared**
luppakorva-.
lope [ləup] *v.:* ~ *along* loikata.
lop-sided *a.* vino, toiselle puolelle
kallistuva.
loquac|ious [lə(u)'kweiʃəs] *a.* puhelias,
lörpöttelevä. -**ity** [lə(u)'kwæsiti] *s.*
puheliaisuus.
lord [lɔːd] *s.* herra, valtias, isäntä;
lordi; *v.:* ~ *it* [*over*] (herrana) hallita,
vallita; *the L*~ Herra, Jumala; *Our
L*~ Herramme ja Vapahtajamme; *the
L*~*'s Prayer* Isä meidän rukous; *the
House of L*~*s* parlamentin ylähuone;
L~ *Mayor* Lontoon Cityn
ylipormestari; *L*~ *Mayor's Show* ed:n
virkaanasettajaiskulkue; *live like a* ~
herrastella. -**ly** [-li] *a.* ylhäinen,
kopea; ylväs, komea. -**ship** *s.* lordin
arvo; *his L*~ hänen ylhäisyytensä.
lore [lɔː] *s.* oppi, tietämys.
lorgnette [lɔː'njet] *s.* lornjetti.
lorn [lɔːn] *a.* (run.) hylätty.
Lorraine [lɔ'rein] *erisn.* Lothringen.
lorry ['lɔri] *s.* kuorma-auto.
Los Angeles [lɔs'æn(d)ʒiliːz] *erisn.*
los|e [luːz] *lost lost, v.* kadottaa,
menettää; hukata; joutua tappiolle,
hävitä; (kellosta) jätättää; ~ *one's
head* joutua päästään pyörälle; ~
one's way eksyä; ~ *oneself* = ed., in
sth. vrt. *lost.* -**er** [-ə] *s.: he is a bad* ~
hän suuttuu häviöstä; *come off a* ~
joutua alakynteen. -**ing** *a.: a* ~ *game*
tappioon päättyvä peli.
loss [lɔs, lɔːs] *s.* tappio, menetys, häviö;
~ *of blood* verenhukka; *without* ~ *of
time* viipymättä; *be at a* ~ olla
ymmällään; *I am at a* ~ *to know* en
tiedä miten keksisin; [*he was*] *at a* ~
for a word ei löytänyt oikeata sanaa.
lost [lɔst] *pp. & a.* ks. *lose;* kadonnut,
hävinnyt, eksynyt, hukkaan joutunut,
kadotettu; hukka-, turha; *be* ~

hukkua, eksyä, joutua turmioon,
haaksirikkoutua; ~ *in thought*
ajatuksiin vaipunut; ~ *to* kokonaan
vailla, kykenemätön tuntemaan
(sääliä ym); *be* ~ *on* ei tehota jkh;
give sth up for ~ pitää menetettynä.
lot [lɔt] *s.* arpa, osa, kohtalo; osuus,
erä; palsta, tontti; joukko; *v.:* ~ *out*
jakaa osiin; *a* ~ *of*, ~ *s of* paljon; *the*
~ koko määrä; *bad* ~ kelvoton
olento, heittiö; *cast (draw)* ~ *s* heittää
arpaa; *cast (throw) in one's* ~ *with*
jakaa hyvät ja pahat jkn kanssa; *by* ~
arvalla; *fall to one's* ~ joutua jkn
osaksi.
loth [ləuθ] ks. *loath.*
lotion ['ləuʃn] *s.* (lääke)liuos,
kasvovesi, hiusvesi.
lottery ['lɔtəri] *s.* arpajaiset; onnenpeli;
~ *ticket* arpa(lippu).
lotus ['ləutəs] *s.* lootuskukka.
loud [laud] *a.* äänekäs, kova, meluisa;
räikeä (väri); *adv.* äänekkäästi,
ääneen; *don't talk so* ~ älä puhu niin
äänekkäästi; *speak* ~*er!* puhu(kaa)
kovemmin! -**ly** *adv.* kovaa, kovasti,
räikeästi. -**ness** *s.* äänekkyys.
~-**speaker** kaiutin (m. ~-*hailer*).
Louisiana [lu(ː)iːzi'ænə] *erisn.*
lounge [laun(d)ʒ] *v.* vetelehtiä,
loikoilla, laiskotella; *s.* halli, (hotellin
ym) olohuone; ~ [*chair*] lepotuoli,
laiskanlinna; ~ *suit* arkipuku;
~-*lizard* gigolo.
lour, lower [lauə] *v.* näyttää uhkaavalta
t. synkältä; *at* rypistää kulmiaan,
katsoa vihaisesti jkta.
lous|e [laus] *s.* (pl. *lice*) täi. -**y** ['lauzi]
a. täinen; saastainen, kurja; [*he is*] ~
with money (sl.) . . -llä on rahaa kuin
roskaa.
lout [laut] *s.* moukka, tolvana. -**ish** [-iʃ]
a. moukkamainen, moukkamainen.
lovable ['lʌvəbl] *a.* rakastettava.
love [lʌv] *s.* rakkaus, lempi; rakastettu,
lemmitty, kulta; (tenniksessä) nolla;
v. rakastaa, lempiä, pitää paljon jstk;
(~ *to*) hyvin mielellään tehdä jtk; *in*
~ *with* rakastunut jkh; *fall in* ~
[*with*] rakastua; *give (send) one's* ~
to lähettää terveisensä; *my* ~ *to* . .
sydämelliset terveiset . . -lle; *make* ~
rakastella; *not for* ~ *or money* ei
mistään hinnasta; *there is no* ~ *lost*

between them he eivät siedä toisiaan; *what a ~ of a dog!* miten herttainen koira! **~affair** rakkausjuttu. **~bird** ruusupapukaija. **-d** [-d] *a.: our ~ ones* läheisimpämme. **-liness** *s.* ihanuus, kauneus. **-ly** [-li] *a.* kaunis, ihana, viehättävä, suloinen. **~-making** rakastelu. **~-match** rakkausavioliitto. **-r** [-ə] *s.* rakastaja; *the ~s* rakastavaiset. **-sick** lemmensairas, kaihoisa. **~-story** rakkausromaani.

loving ['lʌviŋ] *a.* rakastava, hellä. **~-kindness** hellyys, rakkaus, armo.

low 1. [ləu] *s.* (lehmän) ammuminen; *v.* ammua.

low 2. [ləu] *a.* matala, alhainen, alava; heikko, hiljainen; halpa (hinta); niukka; alakuloinen; halpamainen; *adv.* matalalla, -lle, syvään; matalalla t. hiljaisella äänellä; *s.* matalapaine, alin kohta t. hinta; *~ condition* alakunto(isuus); *~ spirits* alakuloisuus; *~ tide* laskuvesi; *bring ~* nöyryyttää; *lay ~* kaataa maahan, voittaa; *lie ~* maata maassa, pysytellä piilossa t. hiljaa; *run ~* olla ehtymäisillään. **~-born** alhaissyntyinen. **~-bred** sivistymätön. **-brow** yksinkertainen sielu, epä-älyllinen ihminen (vastak. *highbrow*).

low-down: *give sb. the l.-d. on* (sl.) kertoa jklle totuus jstk, antaa yksityistä laatua olevia tietoja.

Lowell ['lə(u)əl] *erisn.*

lower 1. ['ləuə] *a. & adv.* alempi, alempana (oleva), ala~; *v.* alentaa, laskea alas; vähentää, halventaa; aleta, vähetä; *[in the] ~ case* pienillä kirjaimilla; *~ oneself* alentua. **-most** *a.* alin.

lower 2. ['lauə] ks. *lour*.

lowland *s.* alamaa; *the L~s* Skotlannin alamaat.

low|liness ['ləulinis] *s.* nöyryys. **-ly** ['ləuli] *a.* nöyrä, vaatimaton. **~-lying** alava. **~-necked** avokaulainen. **-ness** *s.* alavuus; alhainen asema, alhaisuus; halpamaisuus. **~-pitched** (mus.) matala. **-spirited** alakuloinen.

loyal ['lɔi(ə)l] *a.* uskollinen; lojaali, (lain)kuuliainen. **-ist** [-ist] *s.* hallituksen kannattaja. **-ty** [-ti] *s.* uskollisuus, lojaalius.

lozenge ['lɔzin(d)ʒ] *s.* vinoneliö;

pastilli, tabletti.

lubber ['lʌbə] *s.* tolvana, moukka. **-ly** [-li] *a.* kömpelö.

lubric|ant ['lu:brikənt] *s.* voiteluöljy. **-ate** [-keit] *v.* voidella. **-ation** [-'keiʃn] *s.* voitelu. **-ator** [-eitə] *s.* voitelulaite. **-ity** [lju:'brisiti] *s.* liukkaus; irstaus.

lucent ['lu:snt] *a.* loistava.

lucerne [lu:'sə:n] *s.* (kasv.) sinimailanen.

lucid ['lu:sid] *a.* kirkas; selvä, -järkinen. **-ity** [lu:'siditi] *s.* kirkkaus; selkeys.

Lucifer ['lu:sifə] *s.* kointähti; saatana.

luck [lʌk] *s.* (onnellinen) sattuma, onni; *good ~!* onneksi olkoon! *bad ~* huono onni; *worse ~* sitä pahempi; *he is down on his ~* hänellä on huono onni. **-ily** [-ili] *adv.* onneksi. **-less** *a.* onneton, kovaonninen. **-y** [-i] *a.* onnekas; *a ~ chance* onnellinen sattuma.

lucrative ['lu:krətiv] *a.* tuottava, kannattava.

lucre ['lu:kə] *s.* (halv.) hyöty, raha, mammona.

ludicrous ['lu:dikrəs] *a.* naurettava, hullunkurinen.

luff [lʌf] *v.* (mer.) luovia.

lug [lʌg] *v.* raahata, vetää; *s.* tempaisu. **-gage** ['lʌgidʒ] *s.* matkatavarat; *~-rack* matkatavarahylly. **-ger** ['lʌgə] *s.* (mer.) loggertti.

lugubrious [l(j)u:'gju:briəs] *a.* surullinen, synkkä, suru-.

Luke [lu:k] *erisn.* Luukas.

lukewarm ['lu:kwɔ:m] *a.* haalea; laimea.

lull [lʌl] *v.* tuuditella nukuksiin; tyynnyttää; lievittää; (myrskytä) tyyntyä; *s.* tyven; (myrskyn, kivun) taukoaminen. **-aby** [-əbai] *s.* kehtolaulu.

lumbago [lʌm'beigəu] *s.* noidannuoli.

lumbar ['lʌmgə] *a.* lanne-, lumbaali-.

lumber ['lʌmbə] *s.* roju, romu; (et. Am.) puutavara, hirret, lankut; *v.* täyttää romulla, säilyttää; liikkua kömpelösti, kolistella; *~ industry* metsäteollisuus. **-ing** *a.* kömpelö, raskas; *s.* metsänhakkuu, metsätyöt. **-jack, -man** metsätyömies, metsuri. **~-room** romuhuone.

lumin|ary ['lu:minəri] *s.* valaiseva

taivaankappale; (kuv.) »tähti», nero.
-osity [-'nɔsiti] s. valovoima,
kirkkaus. **-ous** [-əs] a. valoisa,
loistava, valaiseva; selvä; ~ *badge*
heijastin.

lump [lʌmp] s. möykky, kokkare, kasa;
(sokeri)pala; kuhmu, pahkura;
köntys; v. kasata yhteen, käsitellä
summittaisesti, mitata kaikki samalla
mitalla (us. ~ *together*); kasautua; ~
sugar palasokeri; ~ *sum*
kokonaissumma, »könttäsumma»; a
~ *in one's throat* pala kurkussa; *in the*
~ summakaupalla; ~ *along* kävellä
raskaasti. **-ish** [-iʃ] a. tanakka;
kömpelö. **-y** [-i] a. möykkyinen,
pahkurainen.

lunacy ['lu:nəsi] s. mielenvikaisuus.

lunar ['lu:nə] a. kuu-, kuun; ~ *month*
kuunkierto (n. 29 1/2 vrk).

lunatic ['lu:nətik] a. & s.
mielenvikainen; ~ *fringe*
äärimmäisyysainekset.

lunch [lʌntʃ] s. lounas; v. lounastaa.
-eon [-n] s. lounas, lounaskutsut.

lung [lʌŋ] s. keuhko.

lunge [lʌndʒ] s. (miekan) pisto, isku;
hyökkäys; v. iskeä, syöksyä.

lupin(e) ['lu:pin] s. lupiini.

lurch 1. [lə:ʃ] s. horjuminen, (laivan)
kallistuminen; v. horjua, horjahdella,
kallistua.

lurch 2. [lə:tʃ] s.: *leave in the* ~ jättää
pulaan, oman onnensa nojaan.

lure [ljuə] s. houkutin, syötti; v.
houkutella, vietoitella.

lurid ['luərid] a. hehkuva; karmaiseva,
kaamea.

lurk [lə:k] v. olla väijyksissä, väijyä,
piilotella. **-ing-place** s. piilopaikka.

luscious ['lʌʃəs] a. herkullinen,
mehevä; uhkea; äitelä.

lush [lʌʃ] a. rehevä, mehevä; s. Am. sl.
juoppo.

lust [lʌst] s. himo, halu; v. himoita
(after, for). **-ful** a. himokas,

hekumallinen. **-ily** *adv.* voimakkaasti,
reippaasti.

lustr|e, luster ['lʌstə] s. loisto, kiilto,
hohde; kristallikruunu. **-ous** ['lʌstrəs]
a. kiistävä, loistava.

lusty ['lʌsti] a. voimakas, terve, reipas,
elinvoimainen.

lute [lu:t, lju:t] s. luuttu.

Lutheran ['lu:θ(ə)r(ə)n] a. & s.
luterilainen.

lutist ['lu:tist] s. luutunsoittaja.

Luxemburg ['lʌks(ə)mbə:g] erisn.

luxuri|ance [lʌg'zuəriəns] s. reheyys;
yltäkylläisyys. **-ant** [-iənt] a.
rehottava, rehevä. **-ate** [-ieit] v.
rehottaa; elää ylellisesti, hekumoida
(in jssk). **-ous** [-iəs] a. ylellinen, upea;
ylellisyyttä rakastava,
nautinnonhimoinen.

luxury ['lʌkʃ(ə)ri, -uri] s. ylellisyys,
loisto; *pl.* ylellisyystavarat; a ~ *hotel*
loistoluokan hotelli.

lyceum [lai'siəm] s. luentosali;
kirjallinen seura ym.

Lydia ['lidiə] erisn.

lye [lai] s. lipeä.

lying 1. ['laiiŋ] ks. *lie 1;* s.
valehteleminen.

lying 2. ks. *lie 2;* ~ *-in* (vanh.)
lapsivuode.

Lyly ['lili] erisn.

lymph [limf] s. imuneste, lymfa; ~
node (gland) imusolmuke. **-atic**
[-'fætik] a. imu-; veltto; s. imusuoni.

lynch [lin(t)ʃ] v. lynkata; ~ *ing*
lynkkaus.

lynx [liŋks] s. ilves. **~-eyed**
teräväsilmäinen.

Lyons ['laiənz] erisn.

lyre ['laiə] s. lyyra (mus.).

lyric ['lirik] a. lyyrinen; s. lyyrinen
runo; *pl.* lyriikka, laulurunous, laulun
sanat, sanoitus. **-al** [-(ə)l] a. lyyrinen.
-ist ['lirisist] s. lyyrikko.

lysol ['laisɔl] s. lysoli.

M

M, m. [em] s. m- kirjain. Lyh.: **M.**
Majesty, Master, Member; Monsieur;
m. *metre, mile, minute* ym; **'m** = *am;*
M. A. *Master of Arts; Military
Academy;* **Maj.** *Major;* **Mar.** *March;*
Mass. *Massachusetts;* **Matt.** *Matthew;*
M.B.E. *Member of (the Order of) the
British Empire;* **M.C.** *Master of
Ceremonies, Member of Congress;*
M.D. *Doctor of Medicine;* **Md.**
Maryland; **Me.** *Maine;* **mg.**
milligram(me); **Mich.** *Michigan;*
Minn. *Minnesota;* **Mirv** (lyh.) *multiple
independently-targeted re-entry vehicle*
monikärkiohjus; **Miss.** *Mississippi;*
MLF *multilateral force;* **M.O.** *Medical
Officer; money order;* **Mo.** *Missouri;*
mod cons *modern conveniences;*
Mont. *Montana;* **M.P.** *Member of
Parliament;* **m.p.h.** *miles per hour;*
Mr, Mrs, Ms ks. sanak.; **MS.**
manuscript; **M.Sc.** *Master of Science* l.
v. luonnont. maisteri; **M/S** *motor ship;*
Mt *Mount.*
ma [ma:] lyh. = *mamma.*
ma'am [mæm] lyh. (= *madam)* rouva!
(esim. emännälle t. asiakkaalle).
Mac [mæk] *pref.* (jkn) poika (skotl.
nimissä).
mac lyh. = *mackintosh.*
macabre [mə'ka:bə] *a.* kaamea.
macadam [mə'kædəm] s. sepeli. **-ize**
[-aiz] *v.* päällystää sepelikivillä.
maca|roni [mækə'rəuni] s.
makaroni(t). **-roon** [-'ru:n] s.
mantelileivos.
Macbeth [mək'beθ] *erisn.*
mace 1. [meis] s. nuija; virkasauva.
mace 2. [meis] s. muskottikukka.
Macedonia [mæsi'dəunjə] *erisn.*
macerate [ˈmæsəreit] *v.* liottaa.
Mach [ma:k]: ~ *two* kaksi kertaa ääntä
nopeammin.

machete [mə'tʃeiti] s. (Et. Am.) pitkä
veitsi.
machiavellian [mækiə'veljən] *a.*
tunnoton, häikäilemätön.
machination [mæki'neiʃn] s. vehkeily,
salajuoni.
machine [mə'ʃi:n] s. kone; polkupyörä,
auto ym; (puolue- ym) koneisto; *v.*
ommella (painaa ym) koneella;
koneistaa, työstää. **~-gun**
konekivääri; *v.* ampua konekiväärillä;
light m.-*g.* pikakivääri. **~-made**
koneella tehty, kone-. **-ry** [-əri] s.
koneet, koneisto. **~-shop** konepaja.
~-tool työstökone.
machinist [mə'ʃi:nist] s.
koneenrakentaja; koneen|hoitaja,
-käyttäjä; koneellaompelija.
Mac|Intyre ['mækintaiə], **-kay**
[mə'kai], **-kenzie** [mə'kenzi] *erisn.*
mackerel ['mækrl] s. makrilli; ~ *sky*
hattarainen (juovikas) taivas.
mackintosh ['mækintɔʃ] s. sadetakki.
Mac|lean [mə'klein], **-leod** [-'klaud],
-millan [mək'milən], **-pherson**
[mək'fə:sn] *erisn.*
macro|cosm ['mækrəkɔzm] s.
maailmankaikkeus. **-scopic** [-'skɔpik]
a. paljain silmin näkyvä.
macul|a ['mækjulə] s. (pl. *-ae)* pilkku,
täplä.
mad [mæd] *a.* hullu, mieletön, raivoisa;
hullaantunut *(on, about)* jhk;
raivostunut, suuttunut *(with* jklle);
like ~ kuin hassu; *drive* ~ saattaa
suunniltaan; *go* ~ tulla hulluksi; ~ *as
a hatter (a March hare)* pähkähullu.
Madagascar [mædə'gæskə] *erisn.*
Madam ['mædəm] s. arvoisa rouva,
neiti! *(Dear M~).*
Madame ['mædəm] s. rouva.
madcap ['mædkæp] s. huimapää,
kaistapää.

madden ['mædn] v. tehdä hulluksi, saada raivostumaan. **-ing** a. raivostuttava, hermostuttava.

madder ['mædə] s. värimatara

made [meid] imp. & pp. ks. make; ~ up of jstk koostuva, kokoonpantu; ~ out on bearer omistajan nimeen asetettu; a ~ man menestynyt mies. **~-up** a. teko-; ehostettu, »meikattu»; a ~-up story tekaistu juttu.

Madeira [mə'diərə] erisn.

mad|house hullujenhuone. **-man** mielipuoli. **-ness** mielipuolisuus, hulluus, raivo.

madonna [mə'dɔnə] s. madonna(nkuva).

Madrid [mə'drid] erisn.

madrigal ['mædrigl] s. madrigaali.

maelstrom ['meilstrəum] s. pyörre, kurimus.

maenad ['mi:næd] s. raivotar.

maestro [mɑ:'estrəu] s. mestari.

Mafia ['mæfiə, Am. mɑ:-] s. mafia.

magazine [mægə'zi:n] s. aikakaus|kirja, -lehti; patruunalipas; (ammus)varasto.

Magdalen ['mægdəlin] erisn.; ~ ['mɔ:dlin] College.

maggot ['mægət] s. mato, toukka. **-y** [-i] a. matoinen.

Magi ['meidʒai] s. pl. itämaiden tietäjät.

magic ['mædʒik] s. taikavoima; noituus, magia; (attr.) taika-. **-al** [-(ə)l] a. maaginen, taika-, lumous-. **-ian** [mə'dʒiʃn] s. noita, taikuri, velho.

magist|erial [mædʒis'triəriəl] a. esivallan, määräävä, käskevä. **-rate** ['mædʒistrit] s. rauhan- t. poliisituomari (police ~).

magn|animity [mægnə'nimiti] s. ylevämielisyys. **-animous** [-'næniməs] a. jalo-, ylevämielinen.

magnate ['mægneit] s. magnaatti, pohatta.

magnesi|a [mæg'ni:ʃə] s. magneesia. **-um** [-'ni:zjəm] s. magnesium.

magnet ['mægnit] s. magneetti. **-ic** [mæg'netik] a. magneettinen; voimakkaasti puoleensavetävä; ~ tape ääninauha. **-ism** [-izm] s. magnetismi, vetovoima. **-ize** [-aiz] v. tehdä magneettiseksi; vetää voimakkaasti puoleensa. **-o**

[mæg'ni:təu] s. (pl. ~s) magneetto.

magnif|ication [mægnifi'keiʃn] s. suurennus. **-icence** [-'nifisns] s. suurenmoisuus, loisto, komeus. **-icent** [-'nifisnt] a. komea, upea, loistava, suurenmoinen.

magnify ['mægnifai] v. suurentaa; suurennella; ~ing glass suurennuslasi.

magniloq|uence [mæg'niləkwəns] s. suurisanaisuus. **-ent** [-ənt] a. suurisanainen, kerskaileva.

magnitude ['mægnitju:d] s. suuruus(luokka), tärkeys.

magnolia [mæg'nəuljə] s. magnolia.

magpie ['mægpai] s. harakka.

Mahara|ja(h) [mɑ:(h)ə'rɑ:dʒə] s. maharadža. **-nee** [-'ru:ni.] s. maharadžan puoliso.

Mahatma [mə'hætmə] s. mahatma.

mahogany [mə'hɔgəni] s. mahonki(puu).

Mahomet [mə'hɔmit] = Mohammed.

mahout [mə'haut] s. norsunajaja.

maid [meid] s. neito, impi; palvelustyttö, kotiapulainen (m. ~-servant); ~ of honour hovineiti, (Am.) morsiusneito.

maiden ['meidn] s. neito; a. neitseellinen; naimaton, ensi-, esikois-; ~ aunt naimaton täti; ~ name tyttönimi; ~ speech, ~ voyage neitsytpuhe, -matka. **-hair** hiussaniainen. **-hood** s. neitsyys. **-ly** s. neitseellinen, ujo, sievä.

mail 1. [meil] s. (rengas)panssari; coat of ~ panssaripaita. **-ed** [-d] a. panssaroitu; the ~ fist asevoima.

mail 2. [meil] s. posti; t. lähettää postissa, postittaa. **-box** Am. postilaatikko. **-coach** postivaunut. **~-order** business postimyyntiliike. **~-train** postijuna.

maim [meim] v. tehdä raajarikoksi, ruhjoa; ~ed rampa, rujoutunut; be ~ed rampautua.

main [mein] a. pää-, pääasiallisin, tärkein, olennaisin; s. pääputki, -johto (us. the ~s); meri, ulappa (run.); ~ body päävoimat; the ~ chance mahdollisuus ansaita rahaa; ~ line päärata; by ~ force äärimmäisin ponnistuksin; in the ~ pääasiassa; with might and ~ väellä ja voimalla;

Main 270

~ *s voltage* verkkojännite. **-land**
[-lənd] manner, mantere. **-ly** *adv.*
pääasiallisesti. **-sail** isopurje. **-spring**
päävaikutin. **-stay** suurharus (mer.);
päätuki, tuki ja turva.

Maine [mein] *erisn.*

main|tain [mein'tein] *v.* ylläpitää, pitää
yllä; pitää kunnossa; elättää; väittää,
puolustaa (kantaansa); ~ *one's
position* säilyttää asemansa. **-tenance**
['meintinəns] *s.* ylläpito; elatus;
huolto; ~ *crew* huoltohenkilöstö.

maisonnette [mezə'net] *s.* pieni
huoneisto t. talo.

maize [meiz] *s.* maissi.

majes|tic [mə'dʒestik] *a.*
majesteettinen. **-ty** ['mædʒisti] *s.*
majesteetti; mahtavuus, ylevyys; *Her
M~* hänen majesteettinsa.

majolica [mə'dʒɔlikə] *s.* majolika.

major ['meidʒə] *a.* suurehko, suuri,
pää-; *s.* majuri; täysi-ikäinen; (mus.)
duuri; Am. pääaine; *v.* opiskella
pääaineenaan; *C~* C duuri. **-domo**
[-'dəuməu] *s.* hovimestari. **~-general**
kenraalimajuri. **-ity** [mə'dʒɔriti] *s.*
enemmistö; täysi-ikäisyys.

Majorca [mə'dʒɔːkə] *erisn.* Mallorca.

make [meik] *made* made, *v.* tehdä,
valmistaa, laatia, laittaa, keittää;
hankkia, ansaita rahaa *(by* jllak);
saavuttaa tulos; arvioida; suorittaa
(matka); laskea (satamaan); nimittää,
tehdä jksk; saada jku tekemään jtk;
lähteä, matkata, suunnata matkansa
(for, towards jhk); *s.* teko, rakenne;
valmiste, tuote; kuosi, laatu,
(tavara)merkki; ~ *believe*
teeskennellä, uskotella; ~ *do* [*with*]
tulla toimeen jllak, tyytyä jhk; ~
money ansaita rahaa, rikastua; ~ *a
speech* pitää puhe; ~ *war upon* sotia
jtk vastaan; *she will* ~ *a good wife*
hänestä tulee hyvä puoliso; ~ *it*
onnistua aikeissaan; ~ *it 20!* annetaan
olla 20, sanotaan 20! ~ *as if* olla
olevinaan; ~ *away* pötkiä pakoon; ~
away with hävittää, tuhlata; tappaa; ~
for suunnata kulkunsa jtk kohti,
hyökätä, sännätä jnnek; edistää,
myötävaikuttaa jhk; ~ *of* selittää,
käsittää; *what do you* ~ *of it?* miten
sen selität? ~ *little of* välittää vähät
jstk; ~ *much of* pitää tärkeänä, helliä;

~ *off* laittautua tiehensä; ~ *off with*
varastaa, siepata; ~ *out* ymmärtää,
saada selville; erottaa, huomata;
kirjoittaa (lasku, šekki); esittää
(jnak), sanoa olevan(sa) jtk; ~ *out of*
valmistaa jstk; ~ *over* korjata,
muuttaa; luovuttaa *(to* jklle); ~ *up*
näyttää, korvata; keksiä, sepittää;
panna kokoon, valmistaa, kääriä
(kokoon); sopia (riita); naamioida,
sminkata; meikata; siivota (huone),
sijata (vuode); taittaa (kirjap.);
suunnitella (painoasu ym); ~ *up for*
hyvittää; ~ *up to sb.* pyrkiä jkn
suosioon; ~ *up one's mind* päättää; *on
the* ~ (sl.) rahaa tavoittelemassa.
~-believe teeskentely, uskottelu. **-r**
[-ə] *s.* valmistaja; *our M~* Luoja.
-shift hätävara. **~-up** naamioitus,
ehostus »meikkaus», meikki;
rakenne, luonne, kokoonpano; taitto
(kirjap.). **~-weight** täyte, painon lisä.

making ['meikiŋ] *s.* valmistaminen; *pl.*
ainekset; ansiot, voitto; *my own* ~
omaa tekoani; *be the* ~ *of* taata jkn
menestys; *he has in him the* ~ *s of a
great man* hänessä on suurmiehen
ainesta.

mal- [mæl-] *pref.* huonosti-, epä-.

malacca [mə'lækə] *s.: ~* [*cane*]
kävelykeppi.

maladjust|ed *a.* huonosti sopeutunut,
sopeutumaton. **-ment** *s.*
sopeutumattomuus.

maladministration *s.* huono hoito t.
hallinto.

maladroit ['mælə'drɔit] *a.* kömpelö.

malady ['mælədi] *s.* tauti.

malaise [mæ'leiz] *s.* (epämääräinen)
pahoinvointi, pahan olon tuntu.

malaria [mə'lɛəriə] *s.* malaria.

Malay [mə'lei] *a. & s.* malaiji(lainen);
malaijin kieli. **-sia** [-zjə] *erisn.*
Malesia.

Malcolm ['mælkəm] *erisn.*

malcontent ['mælkəntent] *s.*
tyytymätön.

male [meil] *a.* uros-, koiras-,
miespuolinen; *s.* mies; ~ *child*
poikalapsi; ~ *choir* mieskuoro; ~
flower hedekukka ~ [*screw*]
ulkokierteinen.

male|diction [mæli'dikʃn] *s.* kirous.
-factor ['mælifæktə] *s.* pahantekijä.

-ficent [mə'lefisnt] a. vahingollinen.
-volence [mə'levələns] s.
pahansuopuus. **-volent** [mə'levələnt]
a. pahansuopa, ilkeä.

malform|ation ['mælfɔː'meiʃn] s.
epämuodostuma. **-ed** [-'fɔːmd] a.
epämuodostunut.

malic|e ['mælis] s. pahanilkisyys,
ilkeys; vahingoittamisaikomus; *bear*
~ *kantaa kaunaa.* **-ious** [mə'liʃəs] a.
ilkeä, pahansuopa, vahingoniloinen.

malign [mə'lain] a. paha,
vahingollinen; v. parjata. **-ancy**
[mə'lignənsi] s. pahanlaatuisuus. **-ant**
[mə'lignənt] a. ilkeä, kiukkuinen;
(taudeista) pahanlaatuinen. **-ity**
[mə'ligniti] s. pahuus, ilkeys;
pahanlaatuisuus.

malinger [mə'lingə] v. tekeytyä
sairaaksi, pinnata.

Mall [mæl]: *the* ~ katu St. Jamesin
puistossa.

mallard ['mæləd] s. sinisorsa.

malleable ['mæliəbl] a. takokelpoinen;
taipuisa; ~ *iron* takorauta.

mallet ['mælit] s. (puu)nuija.

mallow ['mæləu] s. malva (kasv.).

mal|nutrition ['mælnju(ː)'triʃn] s.
vajaaravitsemus. **-occlusion** s.
purentavirhe. **-odorous** [mæ'ləudərəs]
a. pahanhajuinen. **-practice**
[-'præktis] s. väärä menettely,
virka-aseman väärinkäyttö.

malt [mɔːlt] s. mallas; v. imeltää, -tyä.

Malt|a ['mɔːltə] erisn. **-ese** [-'tiːz] a. &
s. maltalainen.

Malthusian [mæl'θjuːzjən] a. & s.
Mathusin teorian (kannattaja).

maltreat [mæl'triːt] v. pidellä pahoin.
-ment s. pahoinpitely.

malversation [mælvə'seiʃn] s. kavallus.

mamba ['mæmbə] s. mamba (käärme).

mamma [mə'maː] s. äiti.

mammal ['mæm(ə)l] s. nisäkäs. **-ian**
[mæ'meiljən] a. nisäkäs-.

mammon ['mæmən] s. mammona.

mammoth ['mæməθ] s. mammutti; a.
jättiläiskokoinen.

mammy ['mæmi] s. (lastenk.) äiti;
(neekeri)lastenhoitaja.

man [mæn] s. (pl. *men*) mies; ihminen
(m. ihmiset, ihmiskunta) et. *pl.*
miehet, miehistö, työmiehet; (šakkip.
ym) nappula; sotamies; v. miehittää;

Man is mortal ihminen on
kuolevainen; *all men must die*
kaikkien ihmisten täytyy kuolla; ~ *by*
~ mies mieheltä; *to a* ~ yhtenä
miehenä; *I'm your* ~ hyväksyn
tarjouksenne; ~ *oneself* rohkaista
itsensä; *the old* ~ (m.) isäukko.

manacle ['mænəkl] s. *pl.* käsiraudat; v.
panna käsirautoihin.

manage ['mænidʒ] v. käsitellä; hoitaa,
johtaa; pitää kurissa; suoriutua (jstk),
onnistua (tekemään); jaksaa (syödä);
[she] ~ *d to control her temper* kykeni
säilyttämään malttinsa; *I think I can*
~ *that* luulen voivani sen tehdä.
-ability [-ə'biliti] s. mukautuvuus.
-able [-əbl] a. helppo käsitellä;
mukautuva. **-ment** s. käsittely; hoito,
hallinto, (liikkeen) johto; viisas
menettely. **-r** [-ə] s. (liikkeen) johtaja,
isännöitsijä; taloudenhoitaja, emäntä
(tav. *good, bad* ~). **-ress** [-əris] s.
johtajatar. **-rial** [mænə'dʒiəriəl] a.
johto-, liikkeenjohdollinen.

managing ['mænidʒiŋ] a. hallitseva,
johtava, kiskeva; ~ *director*
toimitusjohtaja; ~ *committee*
johtokunta.

Manchester ['mæntʃistə] erisn.

Manchu [mæn'tʃuː] a. & s.
mantšulainen; mantšun kieli. **-ria**
[-'tʃuəriə] erisn. Mantšuria.

Mancunian [mæn'kjuːnən] a. & s.
manchesterilainen.

mandarin ['mændərin] s. mandariini
(kiina); ~ [*orange*] mandariini
(hedelmä).

mandat|e ['mændeit] s.
mandaatti(alue); valtuus. **-ory**
['mændət(ə)ri] a. käsky-, pakollinen;
s. (m. *-ary*) mandaattialueen
holhoojavaltio.

mandible ['mændibl] s. alaleuka,
alaleuanluu.

mandolin ['mændəlin] s. mandoliini.

mandrake ['mændreik] s. alruuna.

mane [mein] s. (hevosen ym) harja.

man-eater ihmissyöjä(tiikeri, -hai)

maneuver (Am.) ks. *manoeuvre*.

manful ['mænf(u)l] a. miehekäs,
urhoollinen; ~*ly* urheasti.

manganese [mæŋgə'niːz] s. mangaani.

mange [mein(d)ʒ] s. syyhy.

mangel-wurzel ['mæŋgl'wəːzl] s.

mangoldi.
manger ['mein(d)ʒə] s. purtilo, seimi.
mangle 1. ['mæŋgl] s. mankeli; v.
mankeloida.
mangle 2. ['mæŋgl] s. silpoa, runnella.
mang|o ['mæŋ|gəu] s. (pl. m. -oes)
mangopuu, -hedelmä. **-rove** [-grəuv]
s. mangrovepuu.
mangy ['mein(d)ʒi] a. syyhyinen.
man-handle v. pidellä pahasti.
Manhattan [mæn'hæt(ə)n] erisn.
manhole s. miesluukku (tekn.).
manhood ['mænhud] s. miehuus,
miehuullisuus; miespuolinen väestö;
reach ~ ehtiä miehuusikään.
mania ['meinjə] s. mania, kiihko,
vimma. **-c** [-iæk] a. = seur.; s.
raivohullu. **-cal** [mə'naiək(ə)l] a.
hullu, raivoisa.
manic ['mænik] a. maaninen.
manicur|e ['mænikjuə] s. käsienhoito.
-ist [-rist] s. manikyristi.
manifest ['mænifest] a. ilmeinen, selvä,
silminnähtävä; v. tuoda julki, selvästi
osoittaa, ilmaista; (refl. t. pass.)
ilmetä, näkyä; s. (laivan) lastiluettelo.
-ation [-'teiʃn] s. ilmeneminen;
osoitus, ilmaus. **-o** [-'festəu] s. (pl. ~s,
Am. ~es) julistus, manifesti.
manifold ['mænifəuld] a. moninainen,
monenlainen; v. monistaa.
manikin ['mænikin] s. kääpiö;
mallinukke.
Manil(l)a [mə'nilə] erisn.
manipulat|e [mə'nipjuleit] v. käsitellä,
pidellä; taitavasti käsitellä (m. omaksi
edukseen). **-ion** [-'leiʃn] s. käsittely.
mankind [mæn'kaind] s. ihmiskunta,
ihmissuku; ['mænkaind] miehet,
miesväki.
man|like a. miesmäinen. **-ly** [-li]
miehekäs. ~**-made** a. teko- (m.-m.
moon).
manna ['mænə] s. manna (raam.).
mannequin ['mænikin] s. mallinukke,
sovitusnukke.
manner ['mænə] s. tapa; käytös; tyyli;
maneeri; laji; pl. tavat, käytös,
esiintymistapa; in this ~ tällä tavoin;
all~ of kaikenlaisia; in a ~ of
speaking niin sanoakseni; [good] ~s
hyvät tavat, hieno käytös; to the ~
born luonnostaan jhk sopiva, jhk
syntynyt. **-ed** [-d] a. teennäinen;

well-~ hyvätapainen; ill-~
epäkohtelias. **-ism** [-rizm] s. maneeri,
totunnaistapa. **-ly** a.
hienokäytöksinen, kohtelias.
mannish ['mæniʃ] a. miesmäinen,
epänaisellinen.
manoeuvre [mə'nu:və] s. manööveri,
(aluksen ym) liike; ovela
menettelytapa, juoni; pl.
sotaharjoitus; v. (sot.) liikehtiä,
manövroida; ohjata; menetellä
ovelasti, käsitellä taitavasti.
man-of-war s. sotalaiva.
manometer [mə'nɔmitə] s. manometri,
painemittari.
manor ['mænə] s. kantatila,
herraskartano (m. ~ -house).
man-power miesvahvuus; työvoima.
mansard ['mænsa:d] s.: ~ roof
taitekatto.
manse [mæns] s. (et. Skotl.) pappila.
mansion ['mænʃn] s. (komea)
asuinrakennus; the M~ House Lord
Mayorin virka-asunto; ~s (komea)
kerrostalo.
manslaughter ['mænslɔ:tə] s. tappo
(voluntary ~), kuolemantuottamus
(involuntary ~).
mantelpiece ['mæntlpi:s] s. takan
reunus.
mantilla [mæn'tilə] s. mantilja.
mantis ['mæntis] s. rukoilijasirkka.
mantle ['mæntl] s. vaippa, viitta;
verho; (tekn.) päällys, hehkusukka;
v. verhota, peittää; nousta
(kasvoihin).
manual ['mænjuəl] a. käsi-; s.
käsikirja; (urkujen) manuaali; ~ work
ruumiillinen työ; ~ alphabet sormi-
aakkoset; ~ training veisto, käsityö.
manufac|ture [mænju'fæktʃə] s.
valmistus; (tehdas)valmiste;
teollisuus(haara); v. valmistaa. **-urer**
[-'fæktʃ(ə)rə] s. tehtailija. **-uring**
[-'fæktʃ(ə)riŋ] s. valmistus; ~ town
tehdaskaupunki.
manure [mə'njuə] s. lanta; v.
lannoittaa.
manuscript ['mænjuskript] s.
käsikirjoitus; in ~
käsikirjoitusasteella.
Manx [mæŋks] a. Man-saaren; s.
Man-saaren kieli. **-man** s. Man-saaren
asukas.

many ['meni] a. *(more most)* moni, monta, usea(t); s. joukko, paljous; ~ a . . moni, usea; *one too* ~ yksi liikaa; *a great* ~ suuri joukko; *a good* ~ sangen monta. **~-sided** monipuolinen.

Maoism ['mauizm] s. maolaisuus.

Maori ['mauri] s. maori (Uuden Seelannin alkuasukas).

map [mæp] s. kartta; v. kartoittaa; ~ *out* suunnitella; ~*ping* kartanpiirustus.

maple ['meipl] s. vaahtera.

mar [ma:] v. vahingoittaa, turmella; *make or* ~ joko parantaa tai pilaa.

marabou ['mærəbu:] s. marabuhaikara.

marathon ['mærəθ(ə)n] s. maratonjuoksu; *attr.* kestävyys .

maraud [məˈrɔ:d] v. rosvoilla, ryöstellä. **-er** [-ə] s. rosvo.

marble ['ma:bl] s. marmori; pieni (kivinen ym) pelikuula; *pl.* kuulapeli, kokoelma marmoriveistoksia; a. marmorinen; v. marmoroida; ~*d* marmoroitu.

March [ma:tʃ] s. maaliskuu.

march [ma:tʃ] v. marssia, marssittaa; s. marssi; kulku, edistyminen; ~*[es]* rajamaa; *dead* ~ surumarssi; ~ *past* ohimarssi; ~*ing orders* lähtökäsky.

marchioness ['ma:ʃ(ə)nis] s. markiisitar.

mare [mɛə] s. tamma; ~*'s nest* tyhjä haave.

margarine ['ma:gərin, 'ma:dʒə-] s. margariini.

marge [ma:dʒ] s. (lyh.) = ed.

margin ['ma:dʒin] s. reuna, laita, parras; marginaali (m. liik.); ylijäämä, (tinkimis- t. peli)vara, liikkumavara; voitto; [*won*] *by a narrow* ~ niukasti, täpärästi. **-al** [-l] a. reuna-, raja-, ääreinen, minimi-; ~ *note* reunahuomautus.

margrave ['ma:greiv] s. rajakreivi.

marguerite [ma:gəˈri:t] s. päivänkakkara.

Maria [məˈraiə] *erisn.: Black* ~ Musta Maija (auto).

marigold ['mærigould] s. kehäkukka.

mari juana, -huana [mæri(h)'wa:nə] s. marihuana.

marine [məˈri:n] a. meri-, meren; s. laivasto *(merchant* ~ kauppalaivasto);

merisotilas; *Royal* ~*s* (Engl.) merijalkaväki; *tell that to the* ~*s* uskottele sitä muille. **-r** ['mærinə] s. merenkulkija, merimies.

marital ['mæritl] a. aviomiehen, avio-; ~ *status* siviilisääty.

maritime ['mæritaim] a. meri-, (meren)rannikko-, merenkulku-; ~ *power* merivalta.

marjoram ['ma:dʒ(ə)rəm] s. meirami.

Mark [ma:k] *erisn.* Markus.

mark 1. [ma:k] s. markka.

mark 2. [ma:k] s. merkki; tunnus; (tavara)leima; jälki, arpi; todistus jstk; maalitaulu, pilkka, tavoite; (täysi) mitta; arvosana, piste; (urh.) lähtöviiva; v. merkitä, leimata, **nimiluida;** painaa leima, **jättää jälvi** jhk; olla (jnk) merkkinä; panna merkille, huomata; arvostella (koe ym); *hit the* ~ osata maaliin; *make one's* ~ kunnostautua; *miss the* ~ osua harhaan, epäonnistua; *below the* ~ ala-arvoinen; *that is up to the* ~ se täyttää mitan; *I don't feel up to the* ~ en tunne olevani hyvässä kunnossa; *beside (wide) of the* ~ asiaton; *men of* ~ merkkimiehet; ~ *time* polkea tahtia, kävellä (marssia) paikallaan, (kuv.) polkea paikallaan; ~ *off* merkitä, viitoittaa; ~ *out* viitoittaa; osoittaa joukosta, valita; ~ *up (down)* hinnoittaa kalliimmaksi (halvemmaksi); ~ *my words!* sano minun sanoneen! **-ed** [-t] *pp. & a.* merkitty; ilmeinen, selvä; huomattava. **-edly** [-idli] *adv.* selvästi, ilmeisesti. **-er** [-ə] s. merkitsijä, markööri; kirjanmerkki.

market ['ma:kit] s. tori; markkinat, kauppahalli (m. ~ *hall);* menekki, kauppa; v. tuoda markkinoille, markkinoida; *in (on) the* ~ markkinoilla; *put on the* ~ laskea kauppaan; *find a* ~ mennä kaupaksi; ~ *garden* kauppapuutarha; ~ *research* markkinatutkimus. **-able** [-əbl] a. kaupaksi menevä, kysytty. **~-gardener** kauppapuutarhuri. **-ing** s. markkinointi. **~-place**, **~-square** kauppatori. **~-stall** myyntikoju. **~-town** markkinakaupunki, kauppala.

marking ['ma:kiŋ] s. merkintä, merkki;

(kokeen ym) arvostelu; (kirjava) kuvitus (täplät ym). ~**-ink** merkintämuste. ~**-iron** polttorauta.

marksman [ˈmɑːksmən] s. tarkka-ampuja. **-ship** s. ampumataito.

mark-up s. hinnankorotus.

marl [mɑːl] s. merkeli.

Marlborough [ˈmɔːlb(ə)rə, ˈmɑːl-] erisn.

Marlowe [ˈmɑːləu] erisn.

marmalade [ˈmɑːməleid] s. appelsiini/hillo, -marmelaati.

marmoset [ˈmɑːməzet] s. kynsi-apina; silkkiapina, marmoseti.

marmot [ˈmɑːmət] s. murmeli.

maroon 1. [məˈruːn] a. ruskeanpunainen, kastanjanruskea.

maroon 2. [məˈruːn] s. (Länsi-Intian) karkulaisneekeri; v. jättää asumattomalle saarelle.

marque [mɑːk] s.: letter of ~ kaapparikirja.

marquee [mɑːˈkiː] s. iso teltta.

marquess [ˈmɑːkwis] s. markiisi.

marquetry [ˈmɑːkitri] s. upotustyö (huonekaluissa).

marquis [ˈmɑːkwis] s. markiisi. **-e** [mɑːˈkiːz] s. (ei Engl.) markiisitar.

marriage [ˈmæridʒ] s. avioliitto, naiminen; häät; ~ portion myötäjäiset; ~ settlement avioehto; give in ~ naittaa (tytär); ask in ~ kosia; take in ~ naida. **-able** [-əbl] a. naimaikäinen.

married [ˈmærid] a. naimisissa (oleva), avioliitto-; ~ life avioelämä; get ~ to mennä naimisiin jkn kanssa.

marrow [ˈmærəu] s. ydin; vegetable ~ kurpitsa; to the ~ luita ja ytimiä myöten; ~ bone ydinluu. **-bones** polvet. ~**-fat** silpoydinherne. **-y** [-i] a. ytimekäs.

marry [ˈmæri] v. naittaa, vihkiä; naida; mennä naimisiin; ~ sb. off naittaa.

Mars [mɑːz] erisn.

Marseilles [mɑːˈseilz] erisn. Marseille.

marsh [mɑːʃ] s. suo, räme; ~ gas suokaasu; ~-mallow salkoruusu; eräänl. makeinen; ~ marigold rentukka; ~ tea suopursu.

marshal [ˈmɑːʃ(ə)l] s. (sota)marsalkka, juhlamenojen ohjaaja; poliisipäällikkö; v. järjestää; johdattaa, ohjata.

marshy [ˈmɑːʃi] a. rämeinen.

marsupial [mɑːˈsjuːpiəl] s. pussieläin.

mart [mɑːt] s. markkinapaikka.

marten [ˈmɑːtin] s. näätä.

Martha [ˈmɑːθə] erisn. Martta.

martial [ˈmɑːʃ(ə)l] a. sotainen, sotaisa, sota-; ~ law sotalaki; court ~ sotaoikeus.

Martian [ˈmɑːʃjən] a. Marsin, marsilainen; s. marsilainen.

martin [ˈmɑːtin] s. räystäspääsky.

martinet [mɑːtiˈnet] s. ankara kurinpitäjä.

martingale [ˈmɑːtingeil] s. rintahihna.

Martinmas [ˈmɑːtinməs] s. Martinpäivä (marrask. 11 p.).

martyr [ˈmɑːtə] s. marttyyri; (~ to jkn) uhri; v. tehdä marttyyriksi, kiduttaa. **-dom** [-dəm] s. marttyyrius, marttyyrikuolema.

marvel [ˈmɑːv(ə)l] s. ihme; v. ihmetellä (at jtk); a ~ of jnk perikuva. **-lous** [-əs] a. ihmeellinen.

Marx|ian, -ist [mɑːks|jən, -ist] a. & s. marxilainen.

Mary [ˈmɛəri] erisn. Maria; the Virgin [~] Neitsyt Maria.

marzipan [mɑːziˈpæn] s. marsipaani.

mascara [mæsˈkɑːrə] s. ripsiväri.

mascot [ˈmæskət] s. maskotti.

masculin|e [ˈmɑːskjulin, ˈmæs-] a. miespuolinen, miehekäs; maskuliininen; miesmäinen. **-ity** [mæskjuˈliniti] s. miehekkyys ym.

mash [mæʃ] s. mäski; ape, sose, sekoitus; v. survoa; ~ed potatoes perunasose.

mashie [ˈmæʃi] s. eräänl. golfmaila.

mask [mɑːsk] s. naamio, naamari; naamioitu henkilö v. naamioida; peittää, salata; death ~ kuolinnaamio; gas~ kaasunaamari; ~ed ball naamiaiset.

masochist [ˈmæsəkist] s. masokisti.

mason [ˈmeisn] s. muurari; vapaamuurari (m. free~). **-ic** [məˈsɔnik] a. vapaamuurari-. **-ry** [-ri] s. muuraus(työ), kivityö.

masque [mɑːsk] s. naamionäytelmä. **-rade** [mæskəˈreid] s. naamiohuvit; v. esiintyä valepuvussa (as jnak).

mass 1. [mæs] s. messu; High~ juhlamessu; Low~ hiljainen messu.

mass 2. [mæs] s. ainemäärä, massa;

joukko, paljous, rykelmä; ~es of
joukoittain; *the* ~es rahvas; *in the* ~
kokonaisuutena; ~ *meeting*
joukkokokous; ~ *production*
massatuotanto; ~ *together* koota
yhteen, kokoontua, kasautua; vrt.
media.

Massachusetts [mæsə't∫u:səts] *erisn.*

massacre ['mæsəkə] *s.* joukkosurma,
verilöyly; *v.* surmata joukoittain,
teurastaa.

mass|age ['mæsɑ:3] *s.* hieronta; *v.*
hieroa. **-eur** [mæ'sə:], **-euse** [mæ'sə:z]
s. hieroja.

massive ['mæsiv] *a.* jykevä, raskas,
valtava.

massy ['mæsi] *a.* jykevä.

mast 1. [mɑ:st] *s.* tammen- t.
pyökinterhot (sianruokana).

mast 2. [mɑ:st] *s.* masto; salko; *before
the* ~ tavallisena matruusina;
two-master kaksimastoinen alus.

master ['mɑ:stə] *s.* mestari; herra,
isäntä, esimies, opettaja;
(kauppalaivan) kapteeni; nuoriherra;
(m. ~ *of hounds*) ajometsästyksen
johtaja; *v.* olla perehtynyt jhk,
hallita; hillitä; *a.* mestari(llinen);
pää-; *head* ~ rehtori; *music*~
musiikinopettaja; ~ *mason*
muurarimestari; *M*~ *of Arts* (l.v.)
filosofian maisteri; *be one's own* ~
olla oma herransa. ~**-builder**
rakennusmestari. **-ful** *a.* käskevä,
hallitseva. ~**-key** yleisavain. **-ly** [-li] *a.*
mestarillinen, taitava. ~**-mind** *s.* (jnk)
sielu; *v.* olla jnk sieluna. **-piece**
mestariteos. **-ship** opettajanvirka,
mestarin-, kapteenin ym arvo;
hallinta. ~**-stroke** *s.* mestari, taitava
veto. **-y** [-ri] *s.* mestaruus, täydellinen
hallinta; herruus, ylivalta.

mast-head mastonhuippu.

mastic ['mæstik] *s.* mastiksi, kiviliima.

masticate ['mæstikeit] *v.* pureskella.

mastiff ['mæstif] *s.* mastiffi (koira).

mastoid ['mæstɔid] *a.* & *s.*: [*process*]
kartiolisäke (anat.).

masturbation [mæstə'beiʃn] *s.*
itsetyydytys.

mat 1. [mæt] *s.* karkea matto,
kynnysmatto *(door-*~*)*; alusliina,
tabletti; *v.* tehdä takkuiseksi, mennä
takkuun; *beer* ~ olutlasin alusta.

mat(t) 2. *a.* kiilloton, himmeä.

matador ['mætədɔ:] *s.* matadori.

match 1. [mætʃ] *s.* tulitikku.

match 2. [mætʃ] *s.* vertainen,
tasaveroinen; ottelu, kilpailu;
avioliitto, naimiskauppa; *v.* olla jnk
vertainen, vetää vertoja; sopia
yhteen, sopia jhk; sovittaa yhteen;
naittaa; *he is up against more than his*
~ hän on tavannut etevämpänsä; *find
(meet) one's* ~ tavata vertaisensa
vastustaja; [*he is*] *a good* ~ hyvä
naimiskauppa; ~ *one's strength
against* ryhtyä kilpasille jkn kanssa;
they are well ~*ed* he sopivat hyvin
yhteen, he ovat toistensa veroiset
vastustajat; *a hat to* ~ (väritään jhk)
supiva hattu. ~**-box** tulitikkurasia.
-less *a.* verraton. **-lock** piilukko.
-maker naimiskauppojen järjestäjä.
-wood: *smashed to* ~ pirstaleina.

mate 1. [meit] *s.* (šakkip.) matti; *v.*
tehdä matiksi.

mate 2. [meit] *s.* toveri, kaveri;
puoliso; (linnun) pari; perämies;
apulainen (esim. *cook's* ~); *v.*
yhdistää; naittaa, mennä naimisiin;
(eläimistä) pariutua, paritella.

mater ['meitə] *s.* (koul.) äiti; *Alma M*~
['mɑ:tə] yliopisto.

material [mə'tiəriəl] *a.* aineellinen,
ruumiillinen; olennainen; tärkeä; *s.*
aine, aines, aineisto; kangas; *pl.*
tarvikkeet; *writing* ~*s*
kirjoitustarvikkeet. **-ism** [-izm] *s.*
materialismi. **-ist** [-ist] *s.* materialisti.
-istic [-'listik] *a.* materialistinen. **-ize**
[-aiz] *v.* toteutua; muuttaa aineeksi,
aineellistua, ruumiillistua. **-ly** *adv.*
aineellisesti, olennaisesti,
huomattavasti.

matern|al [mə'tə:nl] *a.* äidillinen;
äidin(puoleinen); ~ *uncle* eno. **-ity**
[-iti] *s.* äitiys; ~ *benefit* äitiysavustus;
~ *hospital* synnytyslaitos; ~ *nurse*
kätilö.

matey ['meiti] *a.* tuttavallinen.

mathemat|ical [mæθi'mætik(ə)l] *a.*
matemaattinen. **-ician** [-mə'tiʃn] *s.*
matemaatikko. **-ics** [-iks] *s.*
matematiikka (lyh. koul. *maths,* Am.
math).

matin ['mætin] *s.:* ~*s* aamuhartaus. **-ée**
[-ei] *s.* matinea, päivänäytäntö.

mating s.: ~ season pariutumisaika.

matric [mə'trik] lyh. = matriculation.

matricide ['meitrisaid] s. äidinmurha, -murhaaja.

matriculat|e [mə'trikjuleit] v. merkitä yliopiston kirjoihin, päästä (ylioppilaaksi) yliopistoon. **-ion** [-'leiʃn] s. yliopiston kirjoihin kirjoittautuminen; ~ examination yliopiston pääsytutkinto, l.v. ylioppilastutkinto.

matrimon|ial [mætri'məunjəl] a. avio-. **-y** ['mætriməni] s. avioliitto, aviosäätty.

matrix ['meitriks] s. (pl. m. -ices [-isi:z] valumuotti, matriisi; kynsimarto.

matron ['meitr(ə)n] s. (arvokas) rouva, keski-ikäinen nainen; (laitoksen) johtajatar t. ylihoitaja, (koulun ym) emäntä. **-ly** [-li] a. rouvamainen, arvokas.

matter ['mætə] s. aine, materia; asia, kysymys; (puheen ym) aihe; märkä (lääk.); v. olla tärkeä, merkityksellinen; märkiä; postal ~ posti(lähetys); printed ~ painotuote; no ~! ei sillä väliä; no ~ who .. yhdentekevää kuka ..; as ~s stand asiain näin ollen; a ~ of six miles suunnilleen kuusi mailia; a ~ of taste makuasia; a ~ of time ajan kysymys; as a ~ of fact oikeastaan, itse asiassa; what is the ~? mikä nyt on? what is the ~ with him? mikä häntä vaivaa? there is something the ~ jotakin on hullusti; settle ~s sopia asia; for that ~ muuten; it does not ~ ei merkitse mitään; it does not ~ to me minulle on yhdentekevää. **~-of-fact** a. asiallinen, kuiva.

Matthew ['mæθju:] erisn. Matteus; Matti.

matting ['mætiŋ] s. mattoainekset, (niini- ym) matto; coconut ~ kookosmatto.

mattock ['mætək] s. hakku, kuokka.

mattress ['mætris] s. patja.

maturate ['mætjureit] v. (paiseesta) kypsyä, märkiä.

matur|e [mə'tjuə] a. kypsyä; täysin kehittynyt; erääntynyt; v. kypsyä, kypsyttää; erääntyä; after ~ deliberation huolellisesti harkittuani. **-ity** [-riti] s. kypsyys, kypsyneisyys;

erääntymisaika.

matutinal [mætju(:)'tainl] a. aamu-.

Maud [mɔ:d] erisn.

maudlin ['mɔ:dlin] a. herkkäitkuinen, (juopumuksesta) liikuttunut.

Maugham [mɔ:m] erisn.

maul [mɔ:l] v. pidellä pahoin.

maunder ['mɔ:ndə] v. puhua tolkuttomasti, sopottaa.

Maundy ['mɔ:ndi] s.: ~ Thursday kiirastorstai.

mausoleum [mɔ:sə'li(:)əm] s. mausoleumi, hautarakennus.

mauve [mɔ:v] s. & a. malvanväri(nen).

maverick ['mævrik] s. (omistajan leimalla) merkitsemätön vasikka; omapäinen yksilö, (pol.) villi.

mavis ['meivis] s. laulurastas.

maw [mɔ:] s. maha; (kuv.) kita.

mawkish ['mɔ:kiʃ] a. tympeä, äitelä; tunteileva.

maxill|a [mæk'silə] s. (pl. -æ [-i:] yläleuanluu. **-ary** [-ri] a.: ~ sinus poskiontelo.

maxim ['mæksim] s. perusohje, sääntö. **-um** [-ə] s. (pl. -ima) enimmäismäärä, maksimi; enimmäis-; ~ speed suurin sallittu vauhti.

may [mei] apuv. (imp. might) voi, saattaa; saa(da), on lupa; it ~ be true se saattaa olla totta; ~ be kenties; however that ~ be olipa asia miten tahansa; ~ I come in? — Yes, you~! Saanko tulla sisälle? — Saat kyllä! ~ he live long! eläköön hän kauan! that ~ or ~ not be true se ehkä on tai ehkä ei ole totta; you might do me a favour voisit(kohan) tehdä minulle palveluksen. **-be** [-bi] adv. kenties.

May [mei] toukokuu; m~ orapihlajankukka; M~ Day vapunpäivä; ~fly päivänkorento; ~ing vapunvietto; ~ queen vappukuningatar.

mayhem ['meihem] s. hävitys, sekasorto.

mayonnaise [meiə'neiz] s. majoneesi(kastike).

mayor [mɛə] s. pormestari. **-aity** [-rəlti] s. pormestarin virka. **-ess** [-ris] s. pormestarinrouva.

maze [meiz] s. sokkelo, labyrintti; hämminki; in a ~ hämmentynyt.

mazurka [mə'zə:kə] s. masurkka.

Mc = *Mac.* -**Cormick** [mə'kɔ:mik],
-**Gregor** [mə'gregə] -**Lean** [mə'klein],
-**luhan** [mə'klu:ən] *erisn.*

me [mi:, mi] *pron.* (obj. muoto) minua,
minut, minulle; *it's* ~ (puhek.) minä
täällä; *with* ~ kanssani, mukanani.

mead [mi:d] *s.* sima; = seur.

meadow ['medəu] *s.* niitty. -**sweet** *s.*
mesiangervo.

meagre, meager ['mi:gə] *a.* laiha,
niukka.

meal 1. [mi:l] *s.* ateria.

meal 2. [mi:l] *s.* jauhot (et. karkeat).
-**ies** [-iz] *s.* (Et.-Afr.) maissi.

mealtime *s.* ruoka-aika.

mealy ['mi:li] *a.* jauhoinen,
jauhomainen. -**mouthed**
(teeskentelevän) kaunissanainen.

mean 1. [mi:n] *a.* alhainen, huono,
kehno; halpamainen; kitsas, saita.

mean 2. [mi:n] *meant meant, v.*
tarkoittaa; merkitä; aikoa; *he* ~ *s*
business hän tarkoittaa täyttä totta, on
tosissaan; [*it*] ~ *s a lot to me* merkitsee
minulle paljon; *is this meant for me?*
onko tämä (tarkoitettu) minulle?
onko se minua varten?

mean 3. [mi:n] *a.* keski-,
keskimääräinen; *s.* keskiarvo,
keskiverto; *the golden* ~ kultainen
keskitie; vrt. **means.**

meander [mi'ændə] *v.* mutkitella,
(kuv.) harhailla.

meaning ['mi:niŋ] *s.* merkitys; *a.*
merkitsevä, puhuva. -**ful** mielekäs,
paljon merkitsevä. -**less** *a.* mitään
merkitsemätön.

meanness ['mi:nnis] *s.* halpamaisuus;
saituus; kehnous.

means [mi:nz] *s.* (pl. t. sg.) keino,
väline(et), välikappale, tapa; varat,
omaisuus; *a man of* ~ varakas mies;
beyond one's ~ yli varojensa; *by* ~ *of*
jnk avulla; *by all* ~ kaikin mokomin;
by no ~, *not by any* ~ ei suinkaan; ~
test tarvehankinta.

meant [ment] *imp. & pp.* ks. **mean.**

mean|time *s. & adv.: [in the]* ~ sillä
välin. -**while** *adv.* = ed.

measl|es ['mi:zlz] *s.* tuhkarokko. -**y** [-li]
a. (puhek.) mitätön.

measurable ['meʒ(ə)rəbl] *a.*
mitattavissa oleva.

measure ['meʒə] *s.* mitta,

mittayksikkö; määrä, suuruus,
laajuus, kohtuus, raja; toimenpide;
runomitta, poljento, tahti; *v.* mitata,
olla jnk mittainen, ottaa jksta mittaa
(~ *sb for a coat*); arvioida, mittailla;
liquid ~ nestemitta; *tape* ~
mittanauha; *take* ~ *s* ryhtyä toimiin,
toimenpiteisiin; *beyond* ~ ylen
määrin; *in some* ~ jossakin määrin; *in*
large ~ suuressa määrin; *made to* ~
mitan mukaan tehty; *get (take) the* ~
(kuv.) ottaa mittaa jksta; *the room* ~ *s*
4 by 5 metres huone on 4 metriä leveä
ja 5 metriä pitkä; ~ *out* jakaa, mitata
(jklle); ~ *up to* (kuv.) olla jnk
mittainen; ~ *one's strength with*
mitellä voimiaan; *the greatest common*
~ suurin yhteinen tekijä. -**d** [-d] *a.*
mitattu, tasainen, punnittu; *in* ~
terms harkituin sanoin. -**ment** *s.*
mittaus; ~ *s* mitat.

meat [mi:t] *s.* liha (ruokana); *tinned*
(canned) ~ lihasäilykkeet. ~-**offering**
ruokauhri. ~-**pie** lihapasteija. -**y** [-i]
a. lihakas.

meatus [mi'eitəs] *s.* käytävä (anat.).

mechan|ic [mi'kænik] *s.* mekaanikko.
-**ical** [-(ə)l] *a.* koneellinen, kone-,
mekaaninen; konemainen; ~
engineering koneenrakennus; ~-*ly*
operated konekäyttöinen. -**ics** [-s] *s.*
pl. mekaniikka, koneoppi. -**ism**
['mekənizm] *s.* koneisto. -**ization**
[mekənai'zeiʃn] *s.* koneistaminen. -**ize**
['mekənaiz] *v.* koneistaa; ~ *d unit*
moottoroitu yksikkö.

medal ['medl] *s.* mitali, muistomitali;
the reverse of the ~ mitalin toinen
puoli. -**lion** [mi'dæljən] *s.* iso mitali.
-**list** *s.* mitalin saaja.

meddle ['medl] *v.:* ~ *in, with*
sekaantua jhk; sotkeutua toisten
asioihin. -**some** [-səm] *a.*
turhantouhukas.

media ['mi:djə] *pl.* ks. **medium;** *mass* ~
[*of communication*] joukkoviestimet.

mediaeval ks. **medieval.**

medi|al ['mi:djəl] *a.* keski-. -**an** [-ən] *s.*
mediaani, keskijana.

mediat|e ['mi:dieit] *v.* välittää, toimia
välittäjänä. -**ion** [mi:di'eiʃn] *s.* välitys.
-**or** [-ə] *s.* välittäjä, sovittelija.

medic ['medik] *s.* sl. lääketieteen
opiskelija, lääketieteellinen. -**al** [-kl]

a. lääkäri(n)-; ~ *man* lääkäri; *M* ~ *Officer (of Health)* alue-, kunnanlääkäri; ~ *treatment* lääkärinhoito. **-ament** [me'dikəmənt] *s.* rohto, lääke. **-ate** [-eit] *v.* kyllästää lääkeaineella. **-ation** [-'keiʃn] *s.* lääkehoito. **-inal** [me'disinl] *a.* lääke-.

medicine ['medsin] *s.* lääke; lääketiede. ~-*man* poppamies.

medico-legal ['medikəu-] *a.* oikeuslääketieteellinen.

medieval [medi'i:v(ə)l] *a.* keskiaikainen, keskiajan.

mediocr|e ['mi:diəukə] *a.* keskinkertainen, huononpuoleinen. **-ity** [mi:di'ɔkriti] *s.* keskinkertaisuus, keskinkertainen ihminen.

medit|ate ['medi|teit] *v.* miettiä, mietiskellä *(on, upon);* harkita, aikoa. **-ation** [-'teiʃn] *s.* mietiskely. **-ative** [-tətiv] *a.* mietiskelevä.

Mediterranean [meditə'reinjən] *a. & s.: the* ~ Välimeri.

medium ['mi:diəm] *s.* (pl. *media* t. ~*s*) väline, välikappale, meedio; väliaine, elatusaine; keskilaatu, -tie; *a.* keskinkertainen, keskikokoinen, keski-; *through the* ~ *of* jnk avulla, välityksellä; ~ *of exchange* maksu-väline; ~*sized* keskikokoinen; ~ *waves* keskipitkät aallot; *a happy* ~ kultainen keskitie; vrt. *media.*

medley ['medli] *s.* sekasotku, sekoitus.

medulla [me'dʌlə] *a.* ydin (anat.).

meed [mi:d] *s.* (run.) palkinto.

meek [mi:k] *a.* sävyisä, nöyrä, lempeä, alistuva.

meerschaum ['miəʃəm] *s.* merenvaha, -piippu.

meet 1. [mi:t] *met met, v.* kohdata, tavata (m. toisensa); tulla t. mennä (jkta) vastaan; täyttää (toivomus), tyydyttää (tarve), vastata (vaatimuksia), maksaa (lasku); torjua (vastaväite); kokea, saada osakseen; sattua yhteen, yhtyä; kokoontua; *s.* (ketunajajien) kokoontuminen, kokoontumispaikka; Am. kilpailu(t); ~ *a p. halfway* käydä puolitiehen vastaan; ~ *the case* olla riittävä; ~ *with* kokea; joutua jhk; ~ *with an accident* joutua onnettomuuden uhriksi.

meet 2. [mi:t] *a.* (vanh.) sopiva.

meeting *s.* kokous; tapaaminen; kilpailut. **~-house** (kveekarien) rukoushuone. **~-place** kokouspaikka.

megalomania ['megələ(u)'meinjə] *s.* suuruudenhulluus. **-c** [-niæk] *s.* suuruudenhullu.

megaphone ['megəfəun] *s.* megafoni, huutotorvi.

melanchol|ia [melən'kəuljə] *s.* (lääk.) raskas-, synkkämielisyys. **-ic** [-'kɔlik] *a.* synkkä-, raskasmielinen, alakuloinen. **-y** ['melənkəli] *s.* surumielisyys, alakuloisuus; *a.* surumielinen, alakuloinen, murheellinen.

mélange [mei'lɑ:(n)ʒ] *s.* sekoitus.

Melbourne ['melbən] *erisn.*

mêlée ['melei] *s.* kahakka, tuoksina.

meliorate ['mi:liəreit] *v.* parantaa.

mellifluous [me'lifluəs] *a.* hunajainen, sulosointuinen.

mellow ['meləu] *a.* kypsä, mehukas; täyteläinen, pehmeä; möyheä, kuohkea; hillitty, lempeä; (puhek.) iloisella tuulella, hiprakassa; *v.* kypsyttää; kypsyä, pehmetä.

melod|ic [mi'lɔdik] *a.* melodinen. **-ious** [mi'ləudjəs] *a.* sointuva, soinnukas.

melodramatic [melədrə'mætik] *a.* melodramaattinen.

melody ['melədi] *s.* sävel(mä), melodia.

melon ['melən] *s.* meloni.

melt [melt] *v.* (pp. *a.* metallista *molten)* sulattaa; saada heltymään, hellyttää; sulaa; heltyä; ~ *away* hajota, hälvetä; ~ *down* sulattaa metallia; ~*ed butter* voisula; *molten metal* sula metalli. **-ing-point** sulamispiste. **-ing-pot** sulatusastia, (kuv.) valinkauha.

member ['membə] *s.* jäsen; (vanh.) ruumiinosa; *M~ of Parliament* parlamentin jäsen. **-ship** *s.* jäsenyys; jäsenmäärä; ~ *card* jäsenkortti.

membran|e ['memb|rein] *s.* kalvo (anat. ym). **-ous** [-rənəs] *a.* kalvoinen.

memento [mə'mentəu] *s.* (pl. ~*s,* ~*es*) muisto.

memo ['meməu] *s.* lyh. = *memorandum.*

memoir ['memwɑ:] *s.: ~ s* muistelmat.

memor|able ['mem(ə)rəbl] *a.* (iki)muistettava, mieleen painuva. **-andum** [-'rændəm] *s.* muistio, muistiinpano(t). **-ial** [ˈmiˈmɔːriəl] a. muisto-; s. muistomerkki; pl. muistiinpanot, kronikka; anomus; M~ Day kaatuneiden muistopäivä. **-ize** [ˈmeməraiz] v. painaa muistiinsa, oppia ulkoa.

memory [ˈmeməri] s. muisti; muisto; muistuma; [I have] a bad ~ for names ..lla on huono nimimuisti; in ~ of jkn muistoksi; within living ~ miesmuistiin.

men [men] s. pl. (ks. man) ihmiset, miehet.

menace [ˈmenəs] s. uhka; v. uhata; menacing uhkaava.

menage [meˈnɑːʒ] s. talous.

menagerie [miˈnædʒəri] s. eläintarha, -näyttely.

mend [mend] v. korjata paikata, parsia; parantaa; parantua, toipua; s. paikka, parsima; ~ the fire kohentaa tulta; ~ one's pace jouduttaa askeleitaan; ~ one's ways parantaa tapansa; on the ~ paranemaan päin; invisible ~ing taideparsinta.

mendac|ious [menˈdeiʃəs] a. valheellinen. **-ity** [-ˈdæsiti] s. valheellisuus.

mendicant [ˈmendikənt] s. kerjäläinen; kerjäläismunkki.

menfolk [ˈmenfəuk] s. (puhek.) miesväki.

menial [ˈmiːnjəl] a. palvelus-, halpa; s. palkollinen.

meningitis [meninˈdʒaitis] s. aivokalvontulehdus.

menopause [ˈmenəpɔːz] s. vaihdevuodet, menopaussi.

menses [ˈmensiːz] s. pl. kuukautiset.

menstru|al [ˈmenstruəl] s.: ~ cycle kuukautiskierto. **-ation** [-eiʃn] s. = menses.

mensuration [mensjuˈreiʃn] s. mittaus.

mental [ˈmentl] a. mielen, sielun; hengen, henkinen, älyllinen, sielullinen; mielisairas; ~ arithmetic päässälasku; ~ deficiency kehitysvammaisuus; ~ home, ~ hospital mielisairaala. **-ity** [menˈtæliti] s. mielenlaatu, mentaliteetti. **-ly** adv. henkisesti; ajatuksissa, itsekseen; ~ defective (subnormal t. retarded) kehitysvammainen.

menthol [ˈmenθɔl] s. mentoli.

mention [ˈmenʃn] v. mainita; s. maininta; don't ~ it! ei kestä kiittää! not to ~ .. (jstk) puhumattakaan; honourable ~ kunniamaininta.

mentor [ˈmentɔː] s. ohjaaja, neuvonantaja, mentori.

menu [ˈmenjuː] s. ruokalista.

Mephistopheles [mefisˈtɔfiliːz] erisn.

mercantile [ˈmɔːk(ə)ntail] s. kauppa-.

mercenary [ˈmɔːsin(ə)ri] a. palkka-; omanvoitonpyyntöinen, rahanahne; s. palkkasoturi.

mercer [ˈmɔːsə] s. silkki-, kangaskauppias.

merchandise [ˈmɔːtʃ(ə)ndaiz] s. kauppatavarat.

merchant [ˈmɔːtʃ(ə)nt] s. (tukku)kauppias; ship kauppa-alus; ~ service kauppalaivasto. **-man** kauppa-alus.

merci|ful [ˈmɔːsifl] a. armelias, sääliväinen; ~ly m. onnellisen, onneksi. **-less** a. armoton, säälimätön.

mercurial [mɔːˈkjuəriəl] a. elohopea-, vilkas, eloisa.

mercury [ˈmɔːkjuri] s. elohopea; M~ Merkurius.

mercy [ˈmɔːsi] s. armeliaisuus; sääli, armo; onni, siunaus; it is a ~ on siunattu asia; have ~ upon armahtaa jkta; at the ~ of jkn armoilla; sister of ~ laupeudensisar; ~ killing armomurha.

mere [miə] a. pelkkä, paljas; ~ folly sulaa hulluutta; a ~ child vain lapsi. **-ly** adv. pelkästään, ainoastaan.

meretricious [meriˈtriʃəs] a. epäaito, koreileva.

merge [mɔːdʒ] v. sulautua, yhtyä jhk; sulattaa, liittää yhteen, fuusioi|da, -tua. **-r** [-ə] s. yhtyminen, fuusio.

merid|ian [məˈridiən] a. & s. meridiaani(-); huippukohta. **-ional** [-l] a. eteläinen, eteläranskalainen.

meringue [məˈræŋ] s. marenki.

merino [məˈriːnəu] s. (pl. ~s) merinolammas; merinolanka, -kangas.

merit [ˈmerit] s. ansio, arvo; v. ansaita; a man of ~ ansioitunut mies; [judge a case] on its own ~s objektiivisesti, yksilöllisesti; make a ~ of lukea ansiokseen; [well-] ~ed hyvin ansaittu. **-orious** [-ˈtɔːriəs] a. ansiokas.

merlin ['mə:lin] s. ampuhaukka.
mer|maid ['mə:meid] s. merenneito.
-man [-mən] merenhaltija.
merri|ly adv. ks. **merry**. **-ment** s.
hilpeys, iloisuus.
merry ['meri] a. iloinen, hilpeä,
hauska, hupaisa; make ~ huvitella,
pitää hauskaa. **~-go-round** karuselli.
~-making huvitus, ilonpito.
mesh [meʃ] s. (verkon) silmukka; pl.
verkko, ansa; v. pyydystää verkkoon.
-work verkko.
mesmerize ['mezməraiz] v.
hypnotisoida.
Mesopotamia [mesəpə'teimjə] erisn.
mess [mes] s. sekasotku, sotku; (mer.)
messi; v. sotkea, liata; ruokailla
yhdessä; make a ~ of pilata; ~ about
vetelehtiä; [they] cleaned up the ~
siivosivat jäljet; a ~-up sotku.
mess|age ['mesidʒ] s. sanoma, viesti,
ilmoitus; go on a ~ mennä asialle.
-enger ['mesindʒə] s. sanansaattaja,
lähetti.
Messiah [mi'saiə] s. Messias.
messmate s. messitoveri.
mess-room s. messi.
Messrs. ['mesəz] s. (lyh. = Messieurs)
herrat (toiminimen yhteydessä).
messy ['mesi] a. sotkuinen.
met [met] imp. & pp. ks. **meet**.
metabolism [me'tæbəlizm] s. (ruumiin)
aineenvaihdunta.
metal ['metl] s. metalli; pl.
rautatiekiskot; gun ~ pronssi; ~led
road sepelipäällysteinen tie. **-lic**
[mi'tælik] a. metalli-; metallinen.
-lurgy [me'tælədʒi] s. metallurgia.
metamorphosis [metə'mɔ:fəsis] s. (pl.
-oses [-əsi:z]) muodonvaihdos,
metamorfoosi.
metaphor ['metəfə] s. kielikuva,
metafora. **-ical** [-'fɔrik(ə)l] a.
vertauskuvallinen.
metaphysic|al [metə'fizik(ə)l] a.
metafyysillinen. **-s** [-'fiziks] s. pl.
metafysiikka.
metastas|is [mə'tæstəsis] s. (pl. -es)
haara-, etäispesäke (lääk.).
mete [mi:t] v.: ~ out jakaa, jaella.
meteor ['mi:tjə] s. meteori. **-ic**
[mi:ti'ɔrik] a. meteorin kaltainen. **-ite**
[-rait] s. meteoriitti. **-ological**
[-rə'lɔdʒik(ə)l] a. ilmatieteellinen.

-ologist [-'rɔlədʒist] s. meteorologi.
-ology [-'rɔlədʒi] s. meteorologia,
ilmatiede.
meter ['mi:tə] s. mittari; Am. metri; ~
maid lappuliisa.
methinks [mi'θiŋks] v. minusta näyttää
(vanh.).
method ['meθəd] s. menetelmä,
menettelytapa, metodi; järjestys,
säännöllisyys. **-ical** [me'θɔdik(ə)l] a.
metodinen, metodin mukainen,
menetelmällinen. **-ist** [-ist] s.: M~
metodisti. **-ology** [-'dɔlədʒi] s.
metodiikka.
meths lyh. = methylated spirit l.v.
liekkiviina; ~ drinker asunnoton
alkoholisti, puliukko.
Methuen ['meθjuin] erisn.
Methuselah [mi'θju:zələ] erisn.
methyl ['meθil] s. metyyli (kem.). **-ate**
[-eit] v.: ~d spirit talousprii.
meticulous [mi'tikjuləs] a. erittäin
tarkka; pikkutarkka.
metr|e, meter ['mi:tə] s. metri;
runomitta. **-ic** ['metrik] a. metri-; ~
system metrijärjestelmä; go ~ siirtyä
m-järjestelmään. **-ication**
m-järjestelmään siirtyminen. **-ical**
['metrik(ə)l] a. metrinen;
runomittainen.
metro|polis [mi'trɔpəlis] s. (suuri)
pääkaupunki. **-politan**
[metrə'pɔlit(ə)n] a. suurkaupungin; s.
arkkipiispa, metropoliitta.
mettle ['metl] s. luonnonlaatu;
rohkeus, into; put . . on his ~
innostaa tekemään parastaan. **-some**
[-səm] a. rohkea, tulinen.
mew 1. [mju:] s. kalalokki.
mew 2. [mju:] v. (us. ~ up) teljettly
sisään; s. häkki; ~s rivi
tallirakennuksia, tallikuja.
mew 3. [mju:] v. naukua.
mewl [mju:l] v. parkua, inistä.
Mexic|an ['meksik|ən] a. & s.
meksikolainen. **-o** [-əu] erisn.
mezz|anine ['mezəni:n] s. puolikerros.
-o-soprano ['medzə(u)-] s.
mezzosopraano.
Miami [mai'æmi] erisn.
miaow [mi'au] v. naukua.
miasma [mi'æzmə] s. myrkyllinen
höyry.
mica ['maikə] s. kiille.

Micah ['maikə] *erisn.* Miika.

mice [mais] *s. pl.* ks. *mouse.*

Michael ['maikl] *erisn.* Mikael.

Michaelmas ['miklməs] *s.*
mikkelinpäivä (syysk. 29. p.); ~ *daisy*
syysasteri.

Michigan ['miʃigən] *erisn.*

mickey ['miki] *s.: take the* ~ [*out of sb.*]
tehdä naurettavaksi, pilkata.

microbe ['maikrəub] *s.* mikrobi.

micro|cosm ['maikrə(u)kɔzm] *s.*
mikrokosmos. **-film** mikrofilmata.
-meter [mai'krɔmitə] mikrometri.
~-organism mikrobi.

micro|phone ['maikrəfəun] *s.*
mikrofoni. **-scope** [-skəup] *s.*
mikroskooppi. **-scopic** [-'skɔpik] *a.*
mikroskooppinen, pienen pieni.

mid [mid] *a.* keski-, väli-; *in* ~*-Atlantic*
keskellä Atlanttia; *in* ~ *air* taivaan ja
maan välillä; *from* ~*-June* kesäkuun
puolivälistä. **-day** keskipäivä.

midden ['midn] *s.* tunkio.

middle ['midl] *a.* keski-, väli-; *s.*
keskikohta, -osa, keskus; ~ *age*
keski-ikä; *the M~ Ages* keskiaika; ~
distance (kuvan) keskiala; *the M~*
East Lähi-itä, (joskus) Keski-itä;
~*-weight* keskisarjan (nyrkkeilijä); *in*
the ~ *of* jnk keskellä. **~-aged**
keski-ikäinen. **~-class** keskiluokan.
-man välittäjä.

middling ['midliŋ] *a.* keskinkertainen,
mukiinmenevä; *adv.* kohtalaisen.

midge [midʒ] *s.* (survias)sääski. **-t** [-it]
s. kääpiö.

mid|land *a.* sisämaan; *the M~s*
Keski-Englanti. **-night** keskiyö. **-riff**
[-rif] *s.* pallea. **-stream** *s.: in* ~
keskellä virtaa. **-shipman** merikadetti.

midst [midst] *s.* keskus; *in the* ~ *of*
keskellä, joukossa.

mid|summer juhannus. **-way:** ~
[*between*] puolivälissä.

Mid-west *erisn.* Am. keskilänsi.

midwife ['midwaif] *s.* (pl. *midwives*)
kätilö. **-ry** [-wif(ə)ri] *s.*
kätilönammatti.

midwinter *s.* sydäntalvi.

mien [mi:n] *s.* katsanto, näkö.

miff [mif] *s.: in a* ~ myrtynyt; ~*ed*
loukkaantunut, myrtynyt.

might 1. [mait] *v.* ks. *may.*

might 2. [mait] *s.* mahti, voima; *by* ~

and main kaikin voimin. **-ily** *adv.*
voimakkaasti; suuresti, ylen,
valtavan. **-y** [-i] *a.* mahtava,
voimakas; suuri, valtava; *adv.*
(puhek.) valtavan; *high and* ~ ks.
high.

mignonette [minjə'net] *s.* reseda.

migraine [mi:'grein] *s.* migreeni.

migr|ant ['maigr(ə)nt] *a. & s.*
muuttolintu. **-ate** [-'greit] *v.* muuttaa,
siirtyä. **-ation** [-'greiʃn] *s.* siirtyminen,
muutto, vaellus; ~ *to towns*
muuttoliike kaupunkiin, maaltapako.
-atory [-ət(ə)ri] *a.* muutto-, vaeltava.

mikado [mi'ka:dəu] *s.* mikado.

mike [maik] *s. sl.* = *microphone.*

milage ['mailidʒ] ks. *mileage.*

Milan [mi'læn] *erisn.* Milano. **-ese**
['miləni:z] *a. & s.* milanolainen.

milch [miltʃ] *a.: ~ cow* lypsylehmä (m.
kuv.).

mild [maild] *a.* lempeä, vieno; lievä;
lauhkea, leuto; mieto; *to put it* ~*ly*
lievästi sanoen.

mildew ['mildju:] *s.* härmä, home,
(viljan) ruoste. **-y** [-i] *a.* härmäinen.

mile [mail] *s.* maili,
englanninpeninkulma (= 1609 m);
nautical ~ meripeninkulma (= 1853
m). **-age** [-idʒ] *s.* mailimäärä, maksu
maililta. **-ometer** [-'ɔmitə] *s.*
matkamittari. **-stone** *s.*
peninkulmapatsas; (kuv.)
virstanpylväs.

milit|ant ['milit(ə)nt] *a.* taisteleva,
sotiva; *s. l.v.* taisteleva radikaali.
-arism [-ərizm] *s.* militarismi,
sotilasvalta. **-ary** [-(ə)ri] *a.* sotilas-,
sotilaallinen, sota-; ~ *forces*
sotavoimat; *compulsory* ~ *service*
asevelvollisuus; *the* ~ sotaväki. **-ate**
[-eit] *v.: ~ against* toimia jtk vastaan.
-ia [mi'liʃə] *s.* miliisi, nostoväki
(~**man** miliisimies).

milk [milk] *s.* maito; *v.* lypsää. **-er** [-ə]
s. lypsäjä, lypsykone (m.
-ing-machine). **-maid** maitotyttö,
karjakko. **-man** maitokauppias. **-sop**
maitonaama, mammanpoika. **-y** [-i] *a.*
maitoinen, maitomainen,
maidonvalkoinen; *the M~ Way*
linnunrata.

mill [mil] *s.* mylly; tehdas; kutomo,
kehräämö; *(saw* ~) saha(laitos); *v.*

jauhaa, rouhia; vanuttaa; pyältää (rahan reuna); *be ~ing about (around)* parveilla, tungeksia. **-board** paksu pahvi.

millenni|al [mi'leniəl] *a.* tuhatvuotinen. **-um** [-iəm] *s.* tuhatvuotinen valtakunta; vuosituhat.

millepede ['milipi:d] *s.* kaksoisjalkainen (tuhatjalkainen).

miller ['milə] *s.* mylläri.

millet ['milit] *s.* hirssi.

mill-hand tehdastyöläinen.

milliard ['miljɑ:d] *s.* miljardi; Am. sata miljoonaa.

milligram(me) ['miligræm] *s.* milligramma. **-metre**, Am. **-meter** millimetri.

milliner ['milinə] *s.* modisti; *~'s* muotiliike, (naisten) hattukauppa. **-y** [-ri] *s.* muotitavarat, naisten hatut ym.

million ['miljən] *s.* miljoona. **-aire** [-'nɛə] *s.* miljoonamies; *~ city* miljoonakaupunki.

mill|-pond myllyallas; *like a m.p.* aivan tyven. **-race** myllyn kouru. **-stone** myllynkivi. **-wheel** myllyn ratas.

milt [milt] *s.* maiti.

Milton ['milt(ə)n], **Milwaukee** [mil'wɔ:ki(:)] *erisn.*

mime [maim] *s.* miiminen näytelmä, pantomiimi; pantomiimia; *v.* esittää pantomiimia; matkia. **-ograph** ['mimiəgrɑ:f] *s.* eräänl. monistuskoje; *v.* monistaa.

mimic ['mimik] *a.* matkiva, jäljittelevä; *s.* matkija; *v.* (*-cked*) matkia, jäljitellä; *~ colouring* suojaväri. **-ry** [-ri] *s.* jäljittely(taito); suojeleva yhdennäköisyys (*protective ~*).

mimosa [mi'məuzə] *s.* mimoosa.

minaret ['minəret] *s.* minareetti.

mince [mins] *v.* hakata hienoksi, pienentää; kaunistella, hienostella; sipsutella; *s.* lihahakkelus; *~d meat* jauheliha; *does not ~ matters (words)* ei seulo sanojansa, ei kaunistele; *~ pie* l.v. hedelmätorttu, ks. seur. **-meat** hedelmätäyte (*ks.* rusinoita, omenaa, mausteita ym). **-r** [-ə] *s.* lihamylly.

mincing *a.* teeskentelevä, sipsuttelevä jne. **-machine** *v.* lihamylly.

mind [maind] *s.* mieli, sielu, henki, järki; mielenlaatu, mielentila (*state of*

~), ajatus; halu; *v.* huolehtia, pitää huolta, hoitaa, varoa; välittää, pitää väliä; *not in one's right ~*, *out of one's ~* järjiltään; *change one's ~* muuttaa mielensä; *he had a good ~ to* hänen teki kovasti mieli; *she has something on her ~* jokin painaa hänen mieltään; *know one's own ~* tietää mitä tahtoo; *make up one's ~* päättää; *set one's ~ on* haluta ehdottomasti; *speak one's ~* sanoa suorat sanat; *in two ~s* kahden vaiheilla; *beat (keep) in ~* pitää mielessään; *call to ~* palauttaa mieleen, muistaa; *put sb. in ~ of* muistuttaa jkta; *be of one ~* olla samaa mieltä; *to my ~* mielestäni; *mieleni mukainen; ~ you!* ota huomioon, huomaa se! *~ the dog* varokaa koiraa; *~ you come early* muista tulla aikaisin; *don't ~ me* älä välitä minusta; *if you don't ~* teillä ole mitään sitä vastaan; *I don't ~ going ..* menen mielelläni; *I don't ~ if I do (kiitos)* mielihyvin; *do you ~ my smoking?* sallitteko, että poltan? *would you ~ opening the window!* olisitteko hyvä ja avaisitte ikkunan! *never ~* älä välitä! **-ed** [-id] *a.* halukas, jllak tuulella; (yhd.) -mielinen, (jstk) kiinnostunut (*air-minded*). **-er** [-ə] *s.*: *baby-~* vauvan (päivä)hoitaja. **-ful** *a.*: *~ of* jstk huolehtiva. **-less** *a.* älytön; *~ of (danger) ..* piittaamaton.

mine 1. [main] *poss. pron.* (subst. muoto) minun; *a friend of ~* eräs ystäväni.

mine 2. [main] *s.* kaivos; (kuv.) lähde, kultakaivos; miina; *v.* harjoittaa kaivostoimintaa, louhia (malmia ym); kaivaa (kaivantoja ym) jnk alle; miinoittaa; (kuv.) *= undermine; lay ~s* laskea miinoja. **-detector** miinaharava. **-field** miinakenttä. **-layer** miinanlaskija. **-r** [-ə] *s.* kaivosmies; miinoittaja.

mineral ['min(ə)r(ə)l] *s.* kivennäinen, mineraali; *a.* kivennäis-; *~ water* kivennäisvesi; *the ~ kingdom* kivikunta. **-ogy** [minə'rælədʒi] *s.* kivennäistiede, mineralogia.

mine-sweeper miinanraivaaja.

mingle ['miŋgl] *v.* sekoittaa; sekoittua, liittyä jhk (*with*).

mingy ['mindʒi] *a.* saita.

mini ['mini] *pref.* pienois-; ~ *skirt* minihame.

miniature ['minjotʃə] *s.* pienoiskuva, miniatyyri; *a.* pienois-; *in* ~ pienoiskoossa.

minim ['minim] *s.* puolinuotti; nestemitta. **-al** [-(ə)l] *a.* häviävän pieni, minimaalinen. **-ize** [-aiz] *v.* saattaa mahdollisimman pieneksi, minimoida; vähätellä. **-um** [-əm] *s.* (pl. *-ima*) vähimmäismäärä, minimi; *a.* vähimmäis-.

mining ['mainiŋ] *s.* kaivostyö, -teollisuus; miinoitus; *the* ~ *industry* kaivosteollisuus; *open-cast* ~ avolouhinta; vrt. *quarry*.

minion ['minjən] *s.* suosikki, kätyri; kolonelli (kirjasinlaji); ~ *of the law* poliisi.

minist|er ['ministə] *s.* ministeri; lähettiläs; pappi; (~ *of, to)* palvelija, välikappale; *v.: ~ to* palvella, huolehtia, täyttää (tarve); *Prime M*~ pääministeri. **-erial** [-'tiəriəl] *a.* ministeri(n)-, hallituksen, papin-. **-ration** [-'treiʃn] *s.* palvelus, apu; (papin) virantoimitus. **-ry** ['ministri] *s.* ministeriö; ministeristö; papinvirka, ministerinvirka, ministerikausi.

miniver ['minivə] *s.* kärpännahka.

mink [miŋk] *s.* minkki, minkinnahka.

Minne|apolis [mini'æpəlis], **-sota** [-'səutə] *erisn.*

minnow ['minəu] *s.* mutu (kala).

minor ['mainə] *a.* vähäinen, pieni; (mus.) molli-; *s.* alaikäinen; molli (m. ~ *key);* Am. sivuaine; ~ *in* opiskella jtk sivuaineena; *Asia M*~ Vähä-Aasia; *of* ~ *importance* vähemmän tärkeä, melko vähäpätöinen. **-ity** [mai'nɔriti] *s.* vähemmistö; alaikäisyys; ~*report* eriävä mielipide.

minster ['minstə] *s.* luostari- t. tuomiokirkko.

minstre ['minstr(ə)l] *s.* kuljeksiva laulaja, trubaduuri; neekeriksi naamioitunut laulaja. **-sy** [-si] l.v. trubaduurilaulu, -runous.

mint 1. [mint] *s.* minttu (kasv.).

mint 2. [mint] *s.* rahapaja; *v.* lyödä rahaa; *in* ~ *condition* uudenveroinen.

minuet [minju'et] *s.* menuetti.

minus ['mainəs] *prep.* miinus (mat.);

vailla jtk; *a.* negatiivinen. **-cule** ['minəskju:l] *a.* hyvin pieni.

minute 1. [mai'nju:t] *a.* pienen pieni, vähäinen; yksityiskohtainen, tarkka.

minute 2. ['minit] *s.* minuutti; hetki; muistiinpano, lyhyt kirjelmä; *pl.* pöytäkirja; *v.* merkitä pöytäkirjaan t. muistioon; *at ten* ~ *s to five* 10 minuuttia vailla viisi; *just a* ~! odota hetkinen! *the* ~ *[that]* heti kun. ~**-book** pöytäkirja. ~**-hand** minuuttiosoitin.

minutely [mai'nju:tli] *adv.* yksityiskohtaisesti, tarkasti.

minutiae [mai'nju:ʃii:] *s. pl.* pikkuseikat, yksityiskohdat.

minx [miŋks] *s.* veitikka, (tytön)heilakka.

miracle ['mirəkl] *s.* ihme, -työ; ~*play* miraakkelinäytelmä. **-ulous** [mi'rækjuləs] *s.* ihmeellinen, ihme-.

mirage ['mira:ʒ] *s.* kangastus.

mire ['maiə] *s.* lieju, muta; räme; *v.* liata, tahrata.

mirror ['mirə] *s.* peili, kuvastin; *v.* kuvastaa; *driving* ~ peruutuspeili.

mirth [mə:θ] *s.* hilpeys, ilo. **-ful** *a.* hilpeä. **-less** *a.* iloton.

miry ['maiəri] *a.* liejuinen.

mis- [mis-] *pref.* epä-, harhaan, väärin. **-adventure** onnettomuus. **-alliance** epäsäätyinen avioliitto.

misanthrop|e ['miz(ə)nθrəup], **-ist** [mi'zænθrəpist] *s.* ihmisvihaaja. **-y** [mi'zænθrəpi] *s.* ihmisviha.

mis|application virheellinen käyttö. **-apply** käyttää väärin.

misapprehen|d ymmärtää väärin. **-sion** väärinkäsitys.

misappropria|te anastaa, kavaltaa. **-tion** väärinkäyttö, kavallus.

misbehav|e käyttäytyä huonosti. **-iour** huono käytös.

misbeliever vääräuskoinen.

miscalcula|te arvioida väärin. **-tion** väärä arviointi.

mis|carriage *s.* epäonnistuminen; keskenmeno; (kirjeen) hukkaanjoutuminen. **-carry** *v.* epäonnistua, raueta tyhjiin; joutua kadoksiin; *she -carried* hänellä oli keskenmeno. **-cast** *v.* antaa (jklle) sopimaton osa (teatt.)

miscegenation [misidʒi'neiʃn] *s.*

rotujen sekoitus.

miscellan|eous [misi'leinjəs] *a.* sekalainen, monenlainen. **-y** [mi'seləni] *s.* sekoitus, kokoelma (sekalaisia kirjoitelmia.)

mischance *s.* epäonni, onnettomuus.

mischief ['mistʃif] *s.* paha, vahinko; ilkivalta; vallattomuus, kuje; vekkuli, ilkimys, kelmi; *make ~ (between) ~* aiheuttaa epäsopua; *he means ~* hänellä on paha mielessä; *get into ~* joutua ikävyyksiin; *be up to ~* hautoa jtk kujetta. **~-maker** ilkityön tekijä; kujeilija.

mischievous ['mistʃivəs] *a.* vahingollinen, vallaton, kujeileva, ilkamoiva, ilkikurinen.

mis|conceive *v.* käsittää väärin. **-conception** *s.* väärinkäsitys.

misconduct ['-'kɔndəkt] *s.* huono käytös; rikkomus, aviorikos; *v.* ['-kən'dʌkt] *v.* johtaa, hoitaa huonosti; *~ oneself* käyttäytyä huonosti.

mis|construction *s.* väärä tulkinta. **-construe** *v.* tulkita väärin.

miscreant ['miskriənt] *s.* roisto, konna.

mis|deal *v.* jakaa väärin (korttipelissä). **-deed** *s.* ilkityö. **-demeanour** *s.* rikkomus. **-direct** *v.* ohjata väärään suuntaan, johtaa harhaan, käyttää väärin, osoittaa (kirje) väärin. **-doing** *s.* paha teko, rikkomus.

mis-en-scène ['mi:zã:(n)'sein] *s.* lavastus.

miser ['maizə] *s.* saituri.

miserable ['miz(ə)rəbl] *a.* onneton, kurja, surkea, viheliäinen.

miserliness *s.* saituus.

miserly ['maizəli] *a.* saita.

misery ['miz(ə)ri] *s.* surkeus, kurjuus, hätä, onnettomuus.

mis|fire *v.* ei laueta, pettää. **-fi** *s.* huonosti sopiva puku ym; sopimaton (t. sopeutumaton) henkilö. **-fortune** *s.* huono onni, onnettomuus. **-give** *v.*: *his heart misgave him* hänellä oli epäilyksiä, hän aavisti pahaa. **-giving** *s.* epäilys, paha aavistus.

misgovern *v.* hallita huonosti. **-ment** *s.* huono hallinto, hoito.

mis|guided *a.* harhaan johdettu; *~conduct* huono käytös. **-hap** *s.* onnettomuus. **-hear** *v.* kuulla väärin.

mishmash ['miʃmæʃ] *s.* sotku.

mis|inform *v.* antaa vääriä tietoja. **-interpret** *v.* tulkita väärin. **-judge** *v.* arvostella väärin, erehtyä jstk. **-lay** *v.* hukata. **-lead** *v.* johtaa harhaan; *~ing* erehdyttävä.

mismanage *v.* hoitaa huonosti. **-ment** *s.* huono hoito.

misnomer ['mis'nəumə] *s.* väärä nimitys.

misogynist [mai'sɔdʒinist, mi-] *s.* naistenvihaaja.

mis|place *v.* panna väärään paikkaan; *~d* (m) väärään henkilöön kohdistettu. **-print** *s.* painovirhe. **-pronounce** *v.* ääntää väärin. **-quote** *v.* lainata t. mainita virheellisesti. **-read** *v.* lukea t. ymmärtää väärin. **-represent** *v.* esittää väärin t. väärässä valossa. **-representation** *s.* vääristely, väärien tietojen antaminen. **-rule** *s.* huono hallinto.

miss 1. [mis] *v.* osua harhaan, ei osua jhk; ei tavoittaa, ei ymmärtää, ei nähdä t. kuulla; menettää, jäädä ilman; laiminlyödä, jättää pois t. väliin (*~ out*); kaivata; s. harhaisku, -lyönti, laukaus ym; *~ the train* myöhästyä junasta; *~ one's mark* epäonnistua; *~out* jättää pois; [*he*] *~ed his footing* luiskahti, horjahti; *you can't ~ the house* et voi olla löytämättä taloa; *give sth. a ~* luopua jstk, olla ottamatta, jättää menemättä jnnk.

Miss 2. [mis] *s.* neiti.

missal ['mis(ə)l] *s.* katol. rukouskirja.

misshapen [mis'ʃeipn] *a.* epämuotoinen.

missile ['misail] *s.* heittoase; ohjus; *~ base* ohjustukikohta; ks. *anti-.*

missing ['misiŋ] *a.* puuttuva; kadonnut; *be ~* puuttua, olla kadoksissa; [*a book*] *with two pages ~* josta puuttuu kaksi sivua; *the ~* (sot.) kadonneet.

mission ['miʃn] *s.* lähetys, -työ, -asema; lähetystö; tehtävä, asia; *sense of ~* kutsumustietoisuus; *the Apollo ~* A.-lento. **-ary** [ɔri] *a.* lähetys-; *s.* lähetyssaarnaaja.

missis ['misis], **missus** ['misəs] *s.* (puhek.) rouva; eukko.

Mississippi [misi'sipi] *erisn.*

missive ['misiv] *s.* kirjelmä.

Missouri [mi'zuəri] *erisn.*

mis|spell *v.* tavata t. kirjoittaa väärin. **-spent** *pp. & a.* huonosti käytetty, hukkaan kulunut. **-state** *v.* esittää väärin.

mist [mist] *s.* usva, sumu, utu; *Scotch~* vihmasade; *v.* sumentaa; sumentua (~ *over*).

mistak|e [mis'teik] *s.* erehdys, virhe; *v.* (*-took, -taken*) ymmärtää väärin, erehtyä; *make a ~* erehtyä; *and no ~* se on varma; *by ~* erehdyksessä; ~ *sb. for* pitää jkta jnak, luulla toiseksi; *there is no mistaking it* siitä ei voi erehtyä. **-en** [-(ə)n] *a.* virheellinen, väärä; harhaan osunut; *be ~* erehtyä; *if I am not ~* ellen erehdy. **-enly** *adv.* erheellisesti.

mister ['mistə] *s.* herra (kirjoitettuna *Mr).*

mistime *v.* tehdä t. sanoa sopimattomaan aikaan; ~*d* sopimaton.

mistletoe ['misltəu] *s.* misteli.

mistress ['mistris] *s.* (talon) emäntä, valtijatar; (sukunimen edessä lyh. *Mrs)* rouva (äänt. 'misiz*)* rakastajatar; opettajatar; *is ~ of the situation* hallitsee tilanteen.

mistrust *v.* ei luottaa, epäillä; *s.* epäluottamus. **-ful** *a.* epäilevä.

misty ['misti] *a.* usvainen, sumuinen, epäselvä.

misunderstand *v.* käsittää väärin. **-ing** *s.* väärinkäsitys.

misuse [mis'ju:z] *v.* käyttää väärin, pidellä pahoin; *s.* ['misju:s] väärinkäyttö.

mite [mait] *s.* ropo; hitunen; pienokainen; (eläint.) punkki.

mitigat|e ['mitigeit] *v.* lieventää, huojentaa; *-ing* lieventävä.

mitre, miter ['maitə] *s.* (piispan) hiippa.

mitt [mit] *s.* = seur.; (urh.) räpylä. baseballhansikas.

mitten ['mitn] *s.* lapanen; puolihansikas; *get the ~* saada rukkaset.

mix [miks] *v.* sekoittaa, -ttua; sekaantua; yhdistää, -tyä; seurustella; *s.* seos, sekoitus; ~ *in society* ottaa osaa seuraelämään; *get ~ed up in* sekaantua jhk. **-ed** [-t] *a.* sekoitettu,

seka-; ~ *doubles* sekanelinpeli (tennis); ~ *school* yhteiskoulu; *with ~ feelings* sekavin tuntein; *a ~ company* (seura jossa on) miehiä sekä naisia; ~ *marriage* seka-avioliitto; ~ *up* m. hämmentynyt, neuvoton. **-er** [-ə] *s.* sekoitin, (puhek.) sekoittaja (m. ~ *tap),* vatkain; *[school] ~* ruoanvalmistuskone, yleiskone; *a good ~* (hyvä) seuraihminen. **-ture** [-tʃə] *s.* sekoitus, seos; lääkeseos. **~-up** *s.* sekasotku.

mizzen, mizen ['mizn] *s.* mesaanipurje; ~*[mast]* mesaanimasto.

mnemonics [ni(:)'mɔniks] *s. pl.* muistitaito.

mo [məu] *lyh.* hetkinen.

moan [məun] *v.* valittaa, voihkia; *s.* valitus, voihkina.

moat [məut] *s.* vallihauta.

mob [mɔb] *s.* roskaväki, meluava väkijoukko; *v.* ahdistaa, tungeksia jkn ympärillä; ~ *law* nyrkkivalta.

mobil|e ['məubail] *a.* liikkuva; eloisa; ~ *unit* kevyt osasto. **-ity** [mə(u)'biliti] *s.* liikkuvuus. **-ization** [məubilai'zeiʃn] *s.* liikekannallepano. **-ize** ['məubilaiz] *v.* asettaa liikekannalle, mobilisoida.

mobster ['mɔbstə] *s.* gangsteri.

moccasin ['mɔkəsin] *s.* mokkasiini.

mocha ['məukə] *s.* mokka(kahvi).

mock [mɔk] *v.* pilkata, ivata (m. ~ *at);* tehdä tyhjäksi, pettää; uhmata; *a.* teko-, vale-; ~*modesty* teeskennelty vaatimattomuus; ~ *turtle* [*soup*] mukailtu kilpikonnakeitto. **-ery** [-əri] *s.* pilkka, iva; jnk irvikuva. **-ing** *s.* pilkka; *a.* ilkkuva; (~*bird* matkijalintu; **~-ly** *adv.* ivaten). **~-up** *s.* (koneen) malli.

modal ['məudl] *a.* modaali-.

mode [məud] *s.* tapa, muoto; (kiel.) tapaluokka; (mus.) sävellaji.

model ['mɔdl] *s.* malli (m. taiteilijan); valokuvamalli; pienoismalli; esikuva; mannekiini; *attr.* esikuvallinen, malli-; *v.:* ~ *after,* [*up*]*on* muovata, muodostaa, laatia jnk mukaan; *[fashion]* ~ mannekiini; ~ *aircraft* lennokki; *a ~ wife* ihannevaimo; *on the ~ of* jnk mallin mukaan. **-ling** *s.* muovailu.

moderat|e ['mɔd(ə)rit] *a.* maltillinen,

kohtuullinen; keskinkertainen; s. maltillinen; v. [-eit] hillintä, lieventää; tyyntyä, asettua; ~ -price kohtuuhintainen; ~ly large kohtalaisen suuri. -ion [mɔudə'reiʃn] s. kohtuullisuus, maltillisuus; pl. (tav. lyh. Mods) alkututkinto B.A.-oppiarvoa varten Oxfordissa; in ~ kohtuullisesti. -or ['mɔdəreitə] s. (kirkon) esimies; (yliop. alkututkinnon) kuulustelija; (fys.) hidastin.

modern ['mɔdən] a. nykyaikainen, nykyajan-; uudenaikainen; uuden ajan; ~ languages uudet kielet. -ism [-izm] s. modernismi. -ity [mɔ'dəːniti] s. uudenaikaisuus. -ize [-aiz] v. ajanmukaistaa, nykyaikaistaa.

modest ['mɔdist] a. vaatimaton; säädyllinen; kohtuullinen. -y [-i] s. vaatimattomuus.

modi|cum ['mɔdikəm] s. pieni määrä. -fication [mɔdifi'keiʃn] s. muutos, muunnos, modifikaatio; lievennys; (kiel.) määräys. -fy ['mɔdifai] v. muuttaa, muuntaa, muodostella; lieventää; (kiel.) määrätä.

mod|ish ['mɔudiʃ] s. muodinmukainen. -iste [mɔu'diːst] s. modisti.

modulat|e ['mɔdjuleit, Am. -dʒu-] v. moduloida, vaihtaa sävellajia (~ from t. to). -ion [-'leiʃn] s. moduloiminen.

module ['mɔdjuːl] s.: lunar ~ kuumoduuli, laskeutumisalus; service ~ huolto-osa.

Mogul [mɔ(u)'gʌl] s. moguli.

mohair ['mɔuheə] s. mohairlanka, -kangas.

Mohammed [mɔ(u)'hæmed] erisn. Muhammed. -an -[id(ə)n] a. & s. muhamettilainen.

moiety ['mɔiəti] s. puolikas, osa.

moil [mɔil] v.: toil and ~ raataa.

moist [mɔist] s. kostea. -en ['mɔisn] v. kostuttaa; tulla kosteaksi. -ure [-ʃə] s. kosteus.

moke [mɔuk] s. sl. aasi.

molar ['mɔulə] s. poskihammas.

molasses [mɔ'læsiz] s. (tumma) siirappi, melassi.

mold, -er, -ing ks. mould ym.

mole 1. [mɔul] s. syntymämerkki.

mole 2. [mɔul] s. aallonmurtaja; laiturinvarsi.

mole 3. [mɔul] s. maamyyrä.

molecul|ar [mɔ(u)'lekjulə] a. molekyyli-. -e ['mɔlikjuːl] s. molekyyli.

mole|hill myyränkeko; make a mountain out of a ~ tehdä kärpäsestä härkänen. -skin myyrännahka; molski(kangas).

molest [mɔ(u)'lest] v. vaivata, kiusata, hätyyttää, hätyytellä. -ation [-'teiʃn] s. hätyyttäminen; kiusa, häirintä.

moll [mɔl] s. gangsterin tyttöystävä, lutka.

mollify ['mɔlifai] v. lievittää, lepyttää, rauhoittaa.

mollusc ['mɔləsk] s. nilviäinen.

mollycoddle ['mɔlikɔdl] s. mammanpoika, arkajalka; v. lellitellä.

molten ['mɔult(ə)n] pp. (vanh.) ks. melt; sula, sulatettu.

moment ['mɔumənt] s. hetki, tuokio, silmänräpäys; tärkeys, merkitys; spare ~s joutohetket; the ~ [that] heti kun; at the ~ tällä hetkellä; at any ~ millä hetkellä hyvänsä; in a ~ tuossa tuokiossa, heti; not for a ~ ei hetkeäkään; affairs of great ~ tärkeät asiat. -arily [-ɔrili] adv. hetkellisesti. -ary [-ɔri] a. hetkellinen, lyhytaikainen. -ous [mɔ(u)'mentəs] a. tärkeä, merkityksellinen; kohtalokas. -um [mɔ(u)'mentəm] s. vauhti; liikevoima, impulssi.

monarch ['mɔnək] s. hallitsija, monarkki. -ic(al) [mɔ'nɑːkik(ə)l] a. monarkkinen. -ist [-ist] s. monarkisti. -y [-i] s. monarkia: absolute ~ rajaton yksinvalta.

monast|ery ['mɔnəstri] s. munkkiluostari. -ic [mɔ'næstik] a. munkki-, luostari-. -icism [mɔ'næstisizm] s. munkkilaitos.

Monday ['mʌndi] s. maanantai; on ~ maanantaina.

monetary ['mʌnit(ə)ri] a. raha(n)-; ~ reform rahanuudistus; ~ unit rahayksikkö.

money ['mʌni] s. raha; ~ order maksuosoitus; ready ~ käteinen raha; make ~ ansaita rahaa, hankkia; get one's ~ 's worth hyötyä koko rahan edestä. ~ -box säästölipas. -ed [-d] a. rahakas; the ~ interest rahamaailma,

moot

pääomapiirit. ~ **-lender** koronkiskuri.
~ **-market** rahamarkkinat.

monger ['mʌŋgə] s. -kauppias (esim.
fish ~); -lietsoja.

Mongol ['mɔŋgɔl] s. mongoli, attr.
mongoloidi; a. mongolialainen. **-ian**
[-'gəuljən] a. mongolialainen; s.
mongolian kieli. **-oid** [-gəlɔid] s.
mongoloidi.

mongoose ['mɔŋgu:s] s. mungo.

mongrel ['mʌŋgr(ə)l] a. & s.
sekarotuinen (eläin); rakki.

monitor ['mɔnitə] s. järjestäjä (koul.);
(rad.) tarkkain, monitori;
panssaritykkiveneь; v. (rad. TV)
tarkkailla.

monk [mʌŋk] s. munkki.

monkey ['mʌŋki] s. apina, (kuv.)
marakatti; v. kujeilla; ~ about with
hypistellä; ~ business (t. tricks)
koirankujeet; has a ~ on his back (sl.)
.. käyttää huumeita; get one's ~ up
kimpaantua. ~ **-nut** maapähkinä. ~
-wrench vaihtoavain, jakoavain.

monocle ['mɔnɔkl] s. monokkeli.

mono|gamy [mə'nɔgəmi] s.
yksiavioisuus. **-gram** ['mɔnəgræm] s.
monogrammi. **-graph** ['mɔnəgra:f] s.
erikoistutkimus, monografia. **-lith**
['mɔnəliθ] s. yhdestä kivilohkareesta
tehty patsas. **-logue** ['mɔnəlɔg] s.
yksinpuhelu. **-mania** [mɔnə'meinjə] s.
monomania. **-plane** ['mɔnəplein] s.
yksitaso.

monopol|ize [mə'nɔpəlaiz] v. ottaa
yksinoikeudekseen. **-y** [-i] s.
yksinoikeus, monopoli.

monorail ['mɔnə(u)reil] s.
yksikiskoinen (rata).

mono|syllabic ['mɔnəsi'læbik] a.
yksitavuinen. **-syllable** ['-siləbl] s.
yksitavuinen sana.

monotheism ['mɔnəθi:izm] s.
yksijumalaisuus.

mono|tone ['mɔnətəun] s.
yksitoikkoinen sävel ym. **-tonous**
[mə'nɔtnəs] a. yksitoikkoinen. **-tony**
[mə'nɔtəni] s. yksitoikkoisuus. **-xide**
[mɔ'nɔksaid] s.: carbon ~
hiilimonoksidi; häkä.

Monroe [mən'rəu] erisn.

monsoon [mɔn'su:n] s. monsuuni;
sadekausi.

monster ['mɔnstə] s. hirviö; epäsikiö;

attr. suunnattoman iso; a ~ of cruelty
luonnottoman julma (ihminen).

monstr|osity [mɔns'trɔsiti] s.
luonnottomuus; epäsikiö. **-ous**
['mɔnstrəs] a. luonnoton,
epämuotoinen; suunnaton (puhek.)
pöyristyttävä, hirveä.

montage [mɔn'ta:ʒ] s. (elok.) leikkaus.

Montague ['mɔntəgju:] erisn.

Montana [mɔn'tænə] erisn.

Monte|negro [mɔnti'ni:grəu]. **-video**
[-vi'de(i)əu] erisn.

Montgomery [mɔn(t)'gʌm(ə)ri] erisn.

month [mʌnθ] s. kuukausi; this day ~
kuukauden kuluttua. **-ly** a.
kuukautinen, kuukausi-; s.
kuukausijulkaisu; adv. kuukausittain.

Montreal [mɔntri'ɔ:l] erisn.

monument ['mɔnjumənt] s.
muisto|patsas, -merkki. **-al** [-'mentl]
a. muisto-; valtava,
monumentaalinen.

moo [mu:] v. ammus.

mooch [mu:tʃ] v. vetelehtiä.

mood 1. [mu:d] s. tapamuoto (kiel.).

mood 2. [mu:d] s. mieli, mieliala; in a
cheerful ~ hilpeällä tuulella; in the ~
for work työtuulella; when the ~ takes
me kun olen sillä tuulella. **-iness** [-inis]
s. äreys, paha tuuli. **-y** [-i] a.
oikullinen; pahantuulinen, äreä,
synkkä.

moon [mu:n] s. kuu; v.: ~ about elää
yläilmoissa; once in a blue ~
aniharvoin. **-beam** kuunsäde. **-calf**
hölmö. **-light** kuunvalo, kuutamo. **-lit**
kuutamo-. **-shine** s. pontikka,
salakuljetettu alkoholi; puhdas puhe.
-shiner (alkoholin) salapolttaja t.
-kuljettaja. **-struck** s. mielipuoli. **-y**
[-i] a. uneksiva, haaveksiva.

moor 1. [muə] s. nummi; ~-cock
kangasriekko (koiras); ~-hen
liejukana.

moor 2. [muə] v. kiinnittää (laiva).

Moor [muə] s. mauri.

moorings s. pl. kiinnitysköydet,
-ketjut; kiinnityspaikka.

Moorish ['muəriʃ] a. maurilainen.

moorland s. kangasmaa.

moose [mu:s] s. (pl. sama)
(pohjoisamer.) hirvi.

moot [mu:t] a.: ~ point kiistanalainen
kohta; v. pohtia, ottaa keskustelun

alaiseksi.

mop [mɔp] s. köysi-, riepuluuta,
moppi; ~ *(of hair)* kuontalo; v.
pyyhkiä; ~ *one's brow* pyyhkiä hikeä
otsaltaan; ~ *up* pyyhkiä (kuivaksi),
puhdistaa (vihollisista), (puhek.)
kaataa kurkkuunsa; *he will ~ the floor
with you* hän tyrmää sinut, panee
pataluhaksi (esim. väittelyssä).

mop|e [məup] v. olla alakuloinen,
murjottaa; *the ~s* masennus,
murjotus. **-ish** [-iʃ] a. alakuloinen.

moped ['məuped] s. mopedi, mopo.

moraine [mɔ'rein] s. moreeni.

moral ['mɔr(ə)l] s. siveellinen,
moraalinen; s. moraali, opetus; *pl.*
moraali, siveellisyys; ~ *philosophy*
etiikka. **-e** [mɔ'rɑ:l] s. (sotajoukon)
moraali, taistelumieli. **-ist** [-ist] s.
siveyssaarnaaja. **-ity** [mə'ræliti] s.
siveyssoppi, etiikka, moraali; ~ *[play]*
moraliteetti (keskiaik. näytelmä). **-ize**
[-aiz] v. moralisoida, saarnata
moraalia. **-ly** adv. siveellisesti; *it is ~
impossible* se on käytännöllisesti
katsoen mahdotonta.

morass [mɔ'ræs] s. suo, räme.

moratorium [mɔrə'tɔ:riəm] s. (sovittu)
velkojen maksun lykkäys.

Moravia [mə'reivjə] erisn. Määri. **-n**
[-n] a. & s. määriläinen.

Moray ['mʌri] erisn.

morbid ['mɔ:bid] a. sairas,
patologinen; sairaalloinen. **-ity**
[mɔ:'biditi] s. sairaalloisuus,
morbiditeetti.

mordant ['mɔ:d(ə)nt] a. pureva (m.
kuv.), syövyttävä.

more [mɔ:, mɔə] a. & adv. enemmän,
enempi, useampia; vielä lisää; *some ~
butter* vähän lisää voita; ~ *and ~* yhä
enemmän; ~ *or less* enemmän tai
vähemmän, jotakuinkin; *never ~* ei
milloinkaan enää; *no ~* ei enää, ei
enempää; *once ~* vielä kerran; *[all]
the ~* sitä enemmän; *the ~ so as*
etenkin koska; ~ *beautiful* kauniimpi;
~ *easily* helpommin; *have you any ~
paper?* onko sinulla vielä paperia?
would you like some (a little) ~ soup?
haluaisitko vähän keittoa lisää? *may I
have one ~?* saisinko vielä yhden?

moreover [mɔ:'rəuvə] adv. sitäpaitsi,
lisäksi.

morganatic [mɔ:gə'nætik] a.
morganaattinen.

morgue [mɔ:g] s. ruumishuone.

moribund ['mɔribənd] a. kuoleva,
kuolemaisillaan (oleva).

Mormon ['mɔ:mən] s. mormoni.

morn [mɔ:n] s. (sun.) aamu.

morning ['mɔ:niŋ] s. aamu; aamupäivä;
good ~ hyvää huomenta! hyvää
päivää! *in the ~* aamulla; *one ~*
eräänä aamuna; *this ~* tänä aamuna;
~ *coat* saketti; ~ *-glory* päivänsini
(kasv.); *the ~ star* kointähti, Venus.

Morocc|an [mə'rɔk|ən] a. & s.
marokkolainen. **-o** [-əu] erisn.
Marokko; m~ sahviaani.

moron ['mɔ:rɔn] s. heikkolahjainen,
debiili.

morose [mə'rəus] a. kärtyisä, äreä.
-ness s. äreys, jurous.

Morpheus ['mɔ:fju:s] erisn. unen
jumala.

morphine ['mɔ:fi:n] s. morfiini (m.
morphia [-jə]).

morphology [mɔ:'fɔlədʒi] s.
muoto-oppi.

morris ['mɔris] s.: ~ *dance* engl.
kansantanhu.

morrow ['mɔrəu] s. seuraava päivä,
huomispäivä.

Morse [mɔ:s] erisn.: *the ~ code*
morseaakkoset.

morsel ['mɔ:sl] s. palanen, suupala.

mortal ['mɔ:tl] a. kuolevainen;
kuolettava, kuolin-; maallinen,
katoava; sl. kauhea, kuolettavan
ikävä ym; s. kuolevainen (ihminen);
~ *enemy* verivihollinen; ~ *fear*
hengenhätä; ~ *remains* maalliset
jäännökset; ~ *sin* kuolemansynti. **-ity**
[mɔ:'tæliti] s. kuolleisuus,
kuolevaisuus. **-ly** adv. kuolettavasti;
sydänjuuriaan myöten (~ *offended*).

mortar 1. ['mɔ:tə] s. huhmar;
kranaatinheitin, (hist.) mörssäri.

mortar 2. ['mɔ:tə] s. muurilaasti; v.
rapata. **-board** (Engl. akateemisen
viitan kanssa käytetty) nelikulmainen
lakki.

mortgag|e ['mɔ:gidʒ] s. (lak.) kiinnitys;
kiinnitetty velkakirja; v. kiinnittää;
raise a ~ ottaa kiinnitys. **-ee** [-'dʒi:] s.
kiinnityksenhaltija.

mortician [mɔ:'tiʃn] s.

hautajaisurakoitsija (Am.).
mortification [mɔ:tifi'keiʃn] s. nöyryytys, syvä pettymys; (lääk.) kuolio.
mortify ['mɔ:tifai] v. kiduttaa (lihaansa); nöyryyttää, loukata; kuoleutua; ~ ing nöyryyttävä, loukkaava.
mort|ise, -ice ['mɔ:tis] s. tapinreikä, liitos.
mortuary ['mɔ:tjuəri] s. ruumishuone; a. hautaus-.
mosaic [məu'zeiik] s. & a. mosaiikki(-).
Mosaic [məu'zeiik] a. Mooseksen.
Moscow ['mɔskəu] erisn. Moskova.
Moselle [mə'zel] erisn. & s. Mosel(viini).
Moses ['məuziz] erisn. Mooses.
Moslem ['mɔzləm] a. & s. muhamettilainen.
mosque [mɔsk] s. moskeija.
mosquito [mɔs'ki:təu] s. (pl. ~es) moskiitto, sääski. ~ -net hyttysverkko.
moss [mɔs] s. sammal. ~ -grown sammalpeitteinen. -y [-i] a. sammaleinen.
most [məust] a. enimmät, useimmat; suurin, enin; adv. eniten; erittäin; the ~ beautiful kaunein; ~ of all kaikkein eniten; ~ of them useimmat heistä; at [the] ~, at the very ~ enintään; for the ~ part suurimmaksi osaksi, enimmäkseen; for ~ of the summer suurimman osan kesästä; make the ~ of ottaa kaikki irti jstk; ~ certainly aivan varmaan; a ~ delightful evening erittäin hauska ilta. -ly adv. enimmäkseen, useimmiten.
mote [məut] s. tomuhiukkanen; rikka (toisen silmässä).
motel [məu'tel] s. motelli.
moth [mɔθ] s. yöperhonen; (pl. = sg.) koi. ~-eaten koinsyömä.
mother ['mʌðə] s. äiti, emo; v. hoivata äidin tavoin; ~ country emämaa, kotimaa; ~ tongue äidinkieli; ~ wit luontainen äly; ~ superior luostarin johtajatar; M ~ 's Day äitienpäivä. -craft äitiysneuvonta, lastenhoito. -hood äitiys. ~-in-law anoppi. -less äiditön. -ly [-li] a. äidillinen, äidin. ~-of-pearl helmiäinen.
nothy ['mɔθi] a. koinsyömä.

motif [mə(u)'ti:f] s. (taideteoksen) aihe, mm. mus.
motion ['məuʃn] s. liike; liikunta; käynti; esitys, ehdotus (parlamentissa ym) v. antaa merkki, viitata; the ~ was adopted (carried) ehdotus hyväksyttiin; in ~ liikkeessä; set in ~ panna käyntiin; he made a ~ with his hand hän viittasi kädellään; ~ picture elokuva; time and ~ studies työntutkimukset. -less liikkumaton.
motivat|e ['məutiveit] v. perustella; motivoida. -ation [-'veiʃn] s. perustelu; motivaatio.
motive ['məutiv] a. liike-; s. vaikutin, peruste, motiivi; ~ power käyttövoima.
motley ['mɔtli] a. kirjava; s. narrinpuku.
motor ['məutə] s. moottori; liikehermo (m. ~ nerve), liikkeelle paneva voima; auto; v. ajaa autolla, autoilla, viedä (jku jnnek) autossa; ~ bicycle moottoripyörä; ~ lorry, ~ truck kuorma-auto; ~ trouble moottorivika. ~-bike (puhek.) moottoripyörä. ~-car auto. -ing s. autoilu. -ist s. autoilija. -ize [-raiz]: ~d troops moottoroidut joukot. -man (esim. raitiovaunun) kuljettaja. -way moottoritie.
mottle ['mɔtl] v. täplittää; ~d täpläkäs, kirjava.
motto ['mɔtəu] s. (pl. m. ~es) tunnus, -lause.
mould 1. [məuld] s. (ruoka)-multa.
mould 2. [məuld] s. home, homesieni; v. homehtua.
mould 3. [məuld] s. muotti; vuoka; (vuoka)hyytelö, vanukas; muoto, rakenne; v. valaa (jhk) muottiin, muovata, muovailla.
moulder ['məuldə] v. lahota, maatua, kuihtua.
moulding ['məuldiŋ] s. lista, reunus.
mouldy ['məuldi] a. homeinen, homehtunut (m. kuv.).
moult [məult] v. olla sulkasadossa; luoda karvansa; -ing s. sulkasato.
mound [maund] s. kumpu, valitus.
mount 1. [maunt] s. vuori (lyh. Mt); the Sermon on the M~ vuorisaarna.
mount 2. [maunt] v. nousta, kiivetä (vuorelle ym); asentaa, pystyttää,

kiinnittää alustalle, kehystää, istuttaa (jalokivi jhk); asettaa näyttämölle; varustaa ratsuilla; nousta, kohota (m. ~ *up*); *s.* alusta, pahvi|lasta, -kehys; objektiivilasi, aluslasi; ratsu; ~ *an attack* ryhtyä hyökkäykseen; ~ *guard* asettaa vartioon, olla vartiossa; ~ *a horse* nousta hevosen selkään; ~ *ed troops* ratsuväki.

mountain ['mauntin] *s.* vuori; (kuv.) röykkiö; ~ *ash* pihlaja. **-eer** [-'niə] *s.* vuoristolainen, vuorikiipeilijä: *v.* harjoittaa vuorikiipeilyä. **-eering** *s.* vuorikiipeily. **-ous** [-əs] *a.* vuorinen.

mountebank ['mauntibæŋk] *s.* puoskari, huijari.

mount|ed ['mauntid] *a. & pp.* ks. *mount;* ratsastava, ratsu-. **-ing** *s.* asentaminen, kehys, kiinnitys; alusta.

mourn [mɔ:n] *v.* surra *(for* jtk). **-er** [-ə] *s.* sureva. **-ful** *a.* valittava, surullinen, murheellinen, suru-. **-ing** *a.* suru-; *s.* suru; surupuku; *in* ~ surupuvussa: *go into* ~ pukeutua surupukuun.

mouse [maus] *s.* (pl. *mice* [mais]) hiiri; *v.* [mauz] pyydystää hiiriä; ~ *typhus* hiirilavantauti. **-trap** hiirenloukku.

mousse [mu:s] *s.* kermahyytelö t. -jäätelö.

moustache [məs'ta:ʃ, Am. 'mʌstæʃ] *s.* viikset.

mousy ['mauzi] *a.* hiirenkarvainen; arka, ujo.

mouth [mauθ] *s.* (pl. äänt. mauðz) suu; aukko; sisään (ulos-)käytävä; *v.* [mauð] puhua liioitellun selvästi (leukoja liikutellen); ottaa suuhunsa; *by* ~ suun kautta; *by word of* ~ suullisesti; *give* ~ ruveta haukkumaan; *down in the* ~ alla päin; *have one's heart in one's* ~ olla sydän kurkussa. **-ful** *s.* suuntäysi. **--organ** huuliharppu. **-piece** suukappale; puhetorvi. **~-to-mouth** ks. *resuscitation.*

movable ['mu:vəbl] *a.* liikkuva, siirrettävä. **-s** [-z] *s. pl.* irtain omaisuus.

move [mu:v] *v.* liikuttaa (m. kuv.); siirtää, panna liikkeelle; saada tekemään, herättää (tunteita); esittää, tehdä ehdotus (parl. ym); liikkua, olla liikkeessä, siirtyä, muuttaa; *s.* siirto, veto, toimenpide; ~ *heaven and earth* mullistaa maat ja

taivaat; ~ *house* muuttaa: ~ *in* muuttaa; (taloon); ~ *out* muuttaa pois; ~ *on* kulkea eteenpäin; *a masterly* ~ mestaritemppu; *a wrong* ~ väärä siirto, erehdys; *on the* ~ liikkeellä; *get a* ~ *on!* (sl.) pidä kiirettä! *make a* ~ ryhtyä toimenpiteisiin. **-ment** *s.* liike, liikunta; koneen liikkuva osa, koneisto; (sävellyksen) osa; aikamitta, suolen toiminta; tempo. **-r** [-ə] *s.* ehdotuksen tekijä.

movie ['mu:vi] *s.* elokuva; *the* ~ *s* elokuvat.

moving *a.* liikkuva; liikuttava; ~ *picture* elokuva; ~ *staircase* liukuportaat.

mow 1. [mau] *s.* heinäsuova, ruko.

mow 2. [mau] *v.* (pp. *mown)* niittää, leikata. **-er** [-ə] *s.* niittomies, niitto- t. ruohonleikkuukone. **-ing** *s.:* ~*-machine* niittokone.

Mozambique [mouzəm'bi:k] *erisn.* Mosambik.

Mr ['mistə] lyh. *(mis er)* herra.

Mrs ['misiz] lyh. *(mistress)* rouva.

Ms rouva tai neiti.

much [mʌtʃ] *s. & adv.* (more, most) paljon, hyvin; suunnilleen, melkein; *how ~ is. .?* paljonko maksaa . .? ~ *better* paljon parempi; *so ~ the better* sitä parempi; ~ *the best* verrattomasti paras; ~ *the same* melkein sama; ~ *as usual* suunnilleen tavalliseen tapaan; ~ *as I disliked the idea* vaikka ajatus oli minulle vastenmielinen; *as* ~ *again* saman verran lisää; *ten times as* ~ kymmenen kertaa niin paljon; *make* ~ *of* pitää tärkeänä, liioitella; ymmärtää, saada paljon irti jstk; *I thought as* ~ sitäpä minä ajattelinkin; *not* ~ *of a linguist* ei erityisen etevä kielissä; *he is too* ~ *for me* en vedä hänelle vertoja; *that* ~ tuon verran. **-ness** *s.: much of a* ~ melkein samanlaisia.

mucilage ['mju:silidʒ] *s.* kasvilima; liimaliuos.

muck [mʌk] *s.* sonta, loka, lika, törky; *v.* liata (m. ~ *up*); ~ *about* vetelehtiä, lorvailla; *make a* ~ *of* tuhria, turmella; ~*-raker* »tunkiontonkija». **-y** [-i] *a.* sontainen, likainen.

muc|ous ['mju:kəs] *a.* limainen; ~

membrane limakalvo. **-us** ['mju:kəs]
s. lima.

mud [mʌd] *s.* lieju, muta, loka; *fling* ~
at mustata jkta.

muddle ['mʌdl] *v.* sotkea, tehdä
sekavaksi: *s.* sotku; epäselvyys; *in a* ~
sekaisin; *make a* ~ *of* turmella,
sotkea; ~ *through* jotenkuten
suoriutua. ~**-headed** sekava.

muddy ['mʌdi] *a.* liejuinen, lokainen;
sekava; *v.* liata, samentaa.

mud|bath savikylpy. ~**-flat** mutaranta.
-guard lokasuojus. **-lark** katupoika.
~**-slinging** panettelu, mustaaminen.

muezzin [mu(:)'ezin] *s.* rukoushetkiin
kutsuja.

muff 1. [mʌf] *s.* käsipuuhka, muhvi; *ear*
~*s* korvaläpät.

muff 2. [mʌf] *s. v.* epäonnistua, pilata;
s. mämmikoura; ~ *a ball* pudottaa
pallo.

muffin ['mʌfin] *s.* teekakku.

muffle ['mʌfl] *v.* kääriä, kietoa;
vaimentaa ; ~*d* tukahdutettu. **-r** [-ə] *s.*
lämmin kaulahuivi; äänenvaimennin.

mufti ['mʌfti] *s.* siviilivaatteet (tav. *in*
~); mufti.

mug [mʌg] *s.* muki, tuoppi; sl. naama;
tomppeli; kirjatoukka; *v.* mukiloida,
pahoinpidellä, hakata; ~ *up* ahertaa
(tutkintoa varten).

mugg|er ['mʌgə] *s.* katuroisto. **-ing**
s. pahoinpitely, mukilointi.

mug|gy ['mʌgi] *a.* (ilmasta) kostea,
painostava. **-wump** [-wʌmp] *s.* Am.
pomo.

mulatto [mju(:)'lætəu, Am. mə'l-] *s.*
(pl. ~*s*, ~*es*) mulatti.

mulberry ['mʌlb(ə)ri] *s.* silkkiäispuun
marja, silkkiäispuu.

mulch [mʌltʃ] *s.* olkipeite.

mule [mju:l] *s.* muuli, (kuv.) jääräpää.
-teer [-i'tiə] *s.* muulinajaja.

mulish ['mju:liʃ] *a.* härkäpäinen.

mull 1. [mʌl] *v.* kuumentaa ja höystää
(viiniä ym); ~*ed claret* l.v. glögi.

mull 2. [mʌl] *s.* hieno musliini.

mullet ['mʌlit] *s.: red* ~ mullo (kala).

mullion ['mʌliən] *s.* (ikkunainvälinen)
kapea pystypiena. **-ed** [-d] *a.*
moniosainen (~ *window*).

multi- ['mʌlti] *pref.* moni-. **-coloured**
monivärinen, kirjava. **-farious**
[-'feəriəs] moninainen. **-form**

monenmuotoinen. -lateral monen
(valtion) välinen, multilateraalinen.
~**-lingual** monikielinen. ~**-millionaire**
monimiljoonikko.

multipl|e ['mʌltipl] *s.* moninkertainen,
moninainen, moni-, *s.* (mat.)
kerrannainen; ~ *shop* ks. chain-store;
least common ~ pienin yhteinen
jaettava. **-ication** [-i'keiʃn] *s.*
kertolasku; lisääntyminen; ~ *table*
kertomataulu. **-icity** [-'plisiti] *s.*
moninaisuus, paljous.

multiply ['mʌltiplai] *v.* kertoa (mat.),
moninkertaistaa, -tua; lisätä;
lisääntyä.

multitud|e ['mʌltitju:d] *s.*
(kansan)joukko, paljous; *the* ~
rahvas. **-inous** [-'tju:dinəs] *a.* lukuisa.

mum 1. [mʌm] *int.* vaiti! *a.* äänetön; *v.*
näytellä elenäytelmässä (tav. *go
mumming*); *mum's the word* ei
hiiskahdutakaan! *keep* ~ *about* olla
hiiskumatta jstk.

mum 2. [mʌm] *s.* = *mummy.*

mumble ['mʌmbl] *v.* mutista, mumista;
s. mumina.

mumbo-jumbo ['mʌmbəu 'dʒʌmbəu] *s.*
tyhjä rituaali, siansaksa.

mumm|er ['mʌmə] *s.*
pantomiiminäyttelijä. **-ery** [-ri] *s.*
pantomiimi.

mummify ['mʌmifai] *v.* muumioida;
muumioitua, kuivettua.

mummy 1. ['mʌmi] *s.* muumio.

mummy 2. ['mʌmi] *s.* = *mamma.*

mumps [mʌmps] *s. pl.* sikotauti.

munch [mʌn(t)ʃ] *v.* rouskutella, syödä
mutustaa.

mundane ['mʌndein] *a.* maailmallinen,
maallinen, maailman-.

Munich [mju:nik] *erisn. München.*

municipal [mju(:)'nisip(ə)l] *a.*
kunnallis-, kunnan, kaupungin. **-ify**
[-'pæliti] *s.* kunta; kaupunginhallitus,
kunnanhallitus.

municen|ce [mju:'nifisns] *s.*
antieliaisuus. **-t** [-nt] *a.* antelias.

muniment ['mju:nimənt] *s.* (tav. *pl.*)
asiakirja; ~ *room* arkisto.

munition [mju:'niʃn] *s.* (tav. *pl.*)
sotatarvikkeet, ammukset; *v.*
varustaa sotatarvikkeilla.

mural ['mjuər(ə)l] *a.* seinä-, muuri-; ~
painting seinämaalaus.

murder ['mɔ:də] s. murha; v. murhata; pilata, pidellä pahoin (kieltä, musiikkia); ~ will out rikos tulee aina ilmi. **-er** [-rə] s. murhaaja. **-ess** [-ris] s. murhaajatar. **-ous** ['mɔ:d(ə)rəs] a. murhaava.

murky ['mɔ:ki] a. pimeä, synkeä.

murmur ['mɔ:mə] s. suhina, solina, surina; mutina, nurina; (sydämen) sivuääni; v. suhista, solista, surista; mutista, mumista, nurista, napista; ~ of voices puheensorina.

murphy ['mɔ:fi] s. sl. peruna.

murrain ['mʌrein] s. karjarutto, suu- ja sorkkatauti.

Murray ['mʌri] erisn.

muscatel [mʌskə'tel] s. muskatelliviini, -rypäle.

muscle ['mʌsl] s. lihas, lihakset; lihasvoima.

Muscovite ['mʌskəvait] s. moskovalainen.

muscular ['mʌskjulə] a. lihas-; jäntevä, voimakas, lihaksikas. **-ity** [-'læriti] s. jäntevyys.

muse 1. [mju:z] v. miettiä, mietiskellä (on, upon).

muse 2. [mju:z] s. runotar, muusa.

museum [mju:'ziəm] s. museo.

mush [mʌʃ] s. pehmeä massa, sose; Am. maissipuuro, tunteellinen höpötys.

mushroom ['mʌʃrum] s. (herkku)sieni; (attr.) sienimäinen, äkillinen; v. kasvaa äkkiä, kuin sieniä sateella; go ~ing sienestää.

mushy ['mʌʃi] a. tunteileva.

music ['mju:zik] s. musiikki, säveltaide; nuotit; ~ master (mistress) soitonopettaja; ~ paper nuottipaperi; ~ stand nuottiteline; ~-stool pianotuoli; face the ~ vastata seurauksista; set [a poem] to ~ säveltää. **-al** [-(ə)l] a. musikaalinen, musiikki, musiikin; s. musikaali; ~ box soittorasia; ~ chairs Jerusalemin suutari (leikki); ~ comedy musikaali.

music-hall varieteeteatteri.

musician [mju:(:)'ziʃn] s. soittotaiteilija, muusikko; säveltäjä.

musk [mʌsk] s. myski; ~-rat piisami.

musket ['mʌskit] s. musketti(kivääri). **-eer** [-'tiə] s. musketti soturi. **-ry** [-ri] s. ampumakoulutus; kivääriammunta.

Muslim ['mʌzlim] s. = Moslem.

muslin ['mʌzlin] s. musliini.

musquash ['mʌskwɔʃ] s. piisami, piisaminnahka.

muss [mʌs] s. sekasorto, sotku; v. (~ up) sotkea.

mussel [mʌsl] s. simpukka.

Mussulman ['mʌslmən] s. & a. (pl. ~s) muhamettilainen.

must 1. [mʌst] s. viininmehu, käymätön rypälemehu; a. raivo (esim. urosnorsusta).

must 2. [mʌst] apuv. täytyy (ks. kieliopp.); I ~ minun täytyy; you ~ not et saa; he ~ be very rich hän on varmaan hyvin rikas; [that novel] is a ~ for you sinun on ehdottomasti luettava . .

mustache ks. moustache.

mustachio [məs'ta:ʃiəu] s. (pitkät) viikset.

mustang ['mʌstæŋ] s. villi preeriahevonen.

mustard ['mʌstəd] s. sinappi; grain of ~ seed sinapinsiemen (raam.); ~ gas sinappikaasu. ~ -pot sinappiastia, -tölkki.

muster ['mʌstə] s. (sotajoukon) katselmus, tarkastus; kokous; v. tarkastaa (joukkoa); koota; (~ up all one's courage); pass ~ kelvata. ~ -roll miehistöluettelo.

mustn't ['mʌsnt] = must not.

musty ['mʌsti] a. homeinen, ummehtunut; vanhentunut.

muta|bility [mju:tə'biliti] s. muuttuvuus. **-ble** ['mju:təbl] a. muuttuva, epävakainen. **-tion** [-'teiʃn] s. muutos, mutaatio; [vowel] ~ ääntiönmukaus.

mute [mju:t] a. mykkä; äänetön, sanaton; s. mykkä; (teatt.) statisti; (viulun) vaimennin; v. asettaa jhk sordiini (mus.); the b is ~ b-kirjain ei äänny.

mutila|te ['mju:tileit] v. silpoa; typistää, runnella. **-tion** [-'leiʃn] s. silpominen.

mutin|eer [mju:ti'niə] s. kapinoitsija. **-ous** ['mju:tinəs] a. kapinallinen. **-y** ['mju:tini] s. kapina; v. kapinoida.

mutt [mʌt] s. sl. tollo, tomppeli.

mutter ['mʌtə] v. mutista, mumista; s. mutina, mumina; soperrus.

mutton ['mʌtn] s. lampaanliha; *leg of ~* lampaanpaisti.

mutual ['mju:tjuəl] *a.* molemminpuolinen, keskinäinen; *~ friend* yhteinen ystävä. **-ity** [-'æliti] *s.* molemminpuolisuus.

muzzle ['mʌzl] *s.* kuono, turpa; kuonokoppa; (tykin) suu; *v.* panna (koiralle ym) kuonokoppa; (kuv.) tukkia jnk suu; *~ velocity* (ammuksen) alkunopeus. **~-loader** suustaladattava tykki.

muzzy ['mʌzi] *a.* sekapäinen, tylsä.

my [mai] *poss.pron.* minun; *~ book* kirjani.

mycology [mai'kɔlədʒi] *s.* sienitiede.

myna(h) ['mainə] *s.* laulukottarainen.

myo|cardium [maiəu'ka:djəm] *s.* sydänlihas. **-ma** [mai'əumə] *s.* lihaskasvain.

myop|ia [mai'əupjə] *s.* likinäköisyys. **-ic** [mai'ɔpik] *a.* likinäköinen.

myriad ['miriəd] *s.* myriadi, lukematon joukko.

myrmidon ['mə:midən] *s.* käskyläinen, palkkalainen.

myrrh [mə:] *s.* mirhami, myrha.

myrtle ['mə:tl] *s.* myrtti.

myself [mai'self] *refl.pron.* (m. vahvistavana) itse; *I have hurt ~* olen loukannut itseni; *I saw it ~* näin sen itse; *I am not ~* en ole oma itseni; *[all] by ~* yksin(äni); ilman apua.

mysterious [mis'tiəriəs] *a.* salaperäinen. **-ness** *s.* salaperäisyys.

mystery ['mist(ə)ri] *s.* mysteeri(o), salaperäisyys; mysteerinäytelmä *(~ play); an unsolved ~* ratkaisematon arvoitus; *lost in ~* salaperäisyyden verhoama.

mystic ['mistik] *a.* mystinen, salaperäinen; *s.* mystikko. **-al** [-(ə)l] *a.* = ed. **-ism** ['mistisizm] *s.* mystiikka.

mysti|fication [mistifi'keiʃn] *s.* salaperäinen t. hämärä juttu, salakähmäisyys. **-fy** ['mistifai] *v.* saattaa ymmälle, hämmentää; *I was -fied* olin aivan ymmälläni. **-que** [mis'ti:k] *s.* salaperäinen viehätys; mystiikka.

myth [miθ] *s.* taru, myytti. **-ic** [-ik] *a.* = seur. **-ical** [-ik(ə)l] *a.* myyttinen, taru-; kuviteltu. **-ological** [miθə'lɔdʒik(ə)l] *a.* mytologinen. **-ology** [mi'θɔlədʒi] *s.* mytologia, jumalaistarusto.

N

N, n [en] *s.* n-kirjain.

Lyh.: **N.** *North;* **n.** *neuter, noon, noun;*
NASA *National Aeronautics and
Space Administration;* **NATO**
['neitəu] *North Atlantic Treaty
Organization;* **N.B.** (= *nota bene*)
note carefully huomaa tarkoin;
N.C.O. *non-commissioned officer*
aliupseeri; **N.E.** *North-east;* **Neb.**
Nebraska; **Nev.** *Nevada;* **N.H.S.**
National Health Service; **No., Nos**
number(s) numero(t); **non-U**
rahvaanomaista kieltä; **Nov.**
November; **nr** *near;* **NSPCC** *National
Society for the Provention of Cruelty to
Children;* **N.S.W.** *New South Wales;*
N.T. *New Testament;* **Num.** *Numbers*
4. Mooseksen kirja; **N.W.** *North-west;*
N.Y. *New York;* **N.Z.** *New Zealand.*

nab [næb] *v.* saada kiinni, napata.
nabob ['neibɔb] *s.* (intial.) pohatta.
nacre ['neikə] *s.* helmiäinen.
nadir ['neidiə] *s.* nadiiri; alin kohta,
aallonpohja (kuv.).
nag 1. [næg] *s.* pieni hevonen.
nag 2. [næg] *v.* nalkuttaa.
naiad ['naiæd] *s.* (pl. ~s t. ~es [-i:z])
vedenneito.
nail [neil] *s.* kynsi; naula; *v.* naulata;
naulita; saada kiinni, pysähdyttää;
pay on the ~ maksaa heti, viipymättä;
hard as ~s loistokunnossa,
säälimätön; *hit the ~ on the head* osua
naulan kantaan; *~ one's colours to the
mast* pysyä sitkeästi päätöksessään; *~
sb. down to* pakottaa ilmaisemaan
aikeensa. ~**-brush** kynsiharja. ~**-file**
kynsiviila. ~**-varnish** kynsilakka.
naïve, naive [nɑ:'i:v, nai'i:v] *a.* naiivi,
(lapsellisen) yksinkertainen, lapsekas.
-té, -ty [nɑ:'i:vtei, -ti] *s.* naiivius;
välittömyys.
naked ['neikid] *a.* alaston, paljas,

paljastettu; *the ~ truth* alaston totuus;
with the ~ eye paljaalla silmällä. **-ness**
s. alastomuus.
namby-pamby ['næmbi'pæmbi] *a.*
äitelä, tunteileva; *s.* (lapsekas)
tunteilu.
name [neim] *s.* nimi; maine; *v.* nimittää
(after jkn mukaan); nimetä, sanoa,
mainita; *family ~* sukunimi; *know by
~* tuntea nimeltä; *in ~* nimellisesti; [*a
man*] *of the ~ of* Smith
Smith-niminen; *they ~d him John* he
panivat hänelle nimeksi John; *give
one's ~* mainita nimensä; *call a p. ~s*
haukkua jkta. **-less** *a.* nimetön. **-ly**
adv. nimittäin (lyh. *viz.*). **-sake** [-seik]
kaima.
nancy ['nænsi] *s.* naismainen mies.
nankeen [næŋ'ki:n] nankiini.
Nanking [næn'kin] *erisn.*
nanny ['næni] *s.* lastenhoitaja.
nanny-goat vuohi.
nap 1. [næp] *s.* nokkaunet; *v.*
torkahtaa; *catch sb. ~ping* yllättää
jku.
nap 2. [næp] *s.* nukka.
napalm ['neipɑ:m] *s.* (sot.) napalm
(palopommeihin käyt. seos).
nape [neip] *s.: ~ of the neck* niska.
napery ['neipəri] *s.* pöytäliinat,
lautasliinat (vanh.).
naphtha ['næfθə] *s.* nafta, vuoriöljy.
-lene [-li:n] *s.* naftaliini.
napkin ['næpkin] *s.* lautasliina;
(vauvan) vaippa.
Naples ['neiplz] *erisn.* Napoli.
nappy ['næpi] *s.* (vauvan) vaippa.
narcissus [nɑ:'sisəs] *s.* (pl. m. *-ssi* [-sai])
narsissi.
narcotic [nɑ:'kɔtik] *a.* narkoottinen; *s.*
narkoottinen aine, huumausaine.
nard [nɑ:d] *s.* nardus (voide).
nark [nɑ:k] *s.* ilmiantaja, vakoilija; *v.:*

~**ed** loukattu.

narra|te ['næ'reit] v. kertoa. **-tion** [næ'reiʃn] s. kertomus. **-tive** ['nærətiv] a. kertova, kertoma-; s. kertomus. **-tor** [-ə] s. kertoja.

narrow ['nærəu] a. ahdas, kapea; ahdasmielinen; niukka, pieni, rajoittunut; tarkka; v. tehdä ahtaammaksi, kaventaa; rajoittaa, supistaa; käydä ahtaammaksi, kaventua, supistua; s. (tav. *pl.*) ahdas väylä, salmi; ~ *circumstances* ahtaat olot; *have a* ~ *escape* töin tuskin päästä pakoon; *the* ~ *way* kaita tie (raam.). **-ly** adv. töin tuskin, täpärästi; tarkasti. **~-gauge** [-geidʒ] kapearaiteinen. **~-minded** ahdasmielinen.

narwhal ['nɑ:w(ə)l] s. sarvivalas.

nasal ['neiz(ə)l] a. nasaalinen, nenä-; s. nenä-äänne.

nascent ['næsnt] a. syntyvä.

nastiness ['nɑ:stinis] s. likaisuus, siivottomuus; ks. *nasty.*

nasturtium [nəs'tə:ʃəm] s. krassi.

nasty ['nɑ:sti] a. likainen, siivoton, ruokoton, inhottava, ilkeä, paha; epämiellyttävä.

Natal [nə'tæl] *erisn.*

natal ['neitl] a. syntymä-.

natation [nei'teiʃn] s. uinti.

nation [neiʃn] s. kansa, -kunta; ~-*wide* valtakunnallinen.

national ['næʃ|nəl] a. kansallinen, kansallis-, kansan-; s. kansalainen; ~ *anthem* kansallislaulu; ~ *debt* valtionvelka; ~ *income* kansantulo; ~ *service* (yleinen) asevelvollisuus. **-ism** [-nəlizm] s. kansallismielisyys, -kiihko. **-ist** [-nəlist] s. kansallismielinen, -kiihkoinen. **-istic** [-nə'listik] a. nationalistinen, kiihkokansallinen. **-ity** [næʃə'næliti] s. kansallisuus. **-ize** [-nəlaiz] v. kansallistaa, sosialisoida; antaa (jklle) kansalaisoikeudet.

nationhood s.: *reach* ~ itsenäistyä.

nativ|e ['neitiv] a. synnynnäinen, luontainen; syntymä-, synnyin-; syntyperäinen; kotimainen; s. alkuasukas, syntyperäinen kansalainen; ~ *country* synnyinmaa; ~ *language* äidinkieli; *a* ~ *of Scotland* syntyperäinen skotlantilainen; *go* ~

omaksua paikallisten asukkaiden elämäntavat. **-ity** [nə'tiviti] s. syntymä (et. Kristuksen).

NATO, Nato ['neitəu] s. Atlantin liitto, ks. lyh.

natter ['nætə] v. lörpöttää; narista, nurista.

natty ['næti] a. soma, siisti.

natural ['nætʃrəl] a. luonnollinen, luonnon-; luonnonmukainen; luonteva, teeskentelemätön; s. tasoitusmerkki; heikkolahjainen, tylsämielinen; ~ *child* avioton lapsi; ~ *gas* luonnonkaasu, maakaasu; ~ *note* tasoitettu nuotti. **-ist** [-ist] s. luonnontieteilijä. **-ize** [-aiz] v. antaa (jklle) kansalaisoikeudet; kotiuttaa (kasvi, sana ym). **-ly** adv. luonnollisesti, luontevasti; tietysti; luonnostaan.

nature ['neitʃə] s. luonto; laatu, luonne; *by* ~ luonnostaan; *good* ~ hyväluonteisuus; *in the* ~ *of* jnk luonteinen; *things of this* ~ tällaiset asiat.

naught [nɔ:t] s. nolla (tav. *nought*); ei mitään; *come to* ~ raueta tyhjiin, mennä myttyyn. **-y** [-i] s. paha, tuhma, hieman sopimaton.

nause|a ['nɔ:sjə] s. pahoinvointi. **-ate** [-ieit] v. kuvottaa. **-ous** [-s] a. inhottava, kuvottava.

nautical ['nɔ:tik(ə)l] a. merenkulku-, meri-; ~ *mile* ks. *mile.*

naval ['neivl] a. laivasto-, meri-; ~ *base* laivastotukikohta.

nave [neiv] s. (kirkon) keskilaiva.

navel ['neivl] s. napa (anat.).

navig|able ['nævigəbl] a. purjehduskelpoinen. **-ate** [-eit] v. purjehtia, ohjata. **-ation** [-'geiʃn] s. merenkulku; purjehdus, ohjaus. **-ator** [-eitə] s. merenkulkija.

navvy ['nævi] s. kanava-, ratatyömies.

navy ['neivi] s. merivoimat; laivasto; ~ *blue* tumman sininen.

nay [nei] adv. ei (vanh.); jopa; s. ei-ääni.

Nazar|ene [næzə'ri:n] s. nasarealainen. **-eth** ['næz(ə)riθ] *erisn.* Nasaret.

Nazi ['nɑ:tsi] s. & a. natsi(lainen). **-sm** [-zm] s. kansallissosialismi, natsilaisuus.

neap [ni:p] s. (tav. ~-*tide*) matalimman

vuoksen aika.

Neapolitan [niə'pɔlitn] *a. & s.*
napolilainen.

near [niə] *a.* lähellä oleva, läheinen,
lähi-; kitsas, täpärä;
vasemmanpuoleinen; *adv. & prep.*
lähellä, -lle; tarkasti; lähes; *v.*
lähestyä: *~ at hand* käsillä, aivan
lähellä, -lle; *by* lähellä; *it was a ~ miss*
(t. *thing*) olipa täpärällä; täpärä
paikka; *I was ~ to tears* olin itkuun
purskahtamaisillani; . . *is ~ing
completion* on valmistumaisillaan. **-ly**
adv. lähes, melkein; läheisesti;
tarkoin; *not ~* ei lähimainkaan. **-ness**
s. läheisyys. **~-sighted** likinäköinen.

neat 1. [ni:t] *s. (pl. = sg.)* nauta,
-karja.

neat 2. [ni:t] *a.* soma, siro; siisti,
huoliteltu; taitava, taidokas,
huolellinen; sekoittamaton. **-ness**
siisteys.

Nebraska [ni'bræskə] *erisn.*

nebul|a ['nebjulə] *s. (pl. -ae* [-i:])
tähtisumu. **-ous** [-əs] *a.* utuinen,
pilvimäinen.

necessar|y ['nesis(ə)ri] *a.* välttämätön;
s.: the -ies [*of life*]
välttämättömyystarvikkeet; *-ily*
välttämättä, pakosta, ilman muuta.

necessi|tate [ni'sesiteit] *v.* tehdä
välttämättömäksi, vaatia, edellyttää.
-tous [-itəs] *a.* puutteenalainen,
köyhä. **-ty** [-s(i)ti] *s.* välttämättömyys,
pakko; välttämätön tarve; puute,
köyhyys; *the -ties of life* perustarpeet;
of ~ välttämättä; *~ knows no law*
hätä ei lue lakia.

neck [nek] *s.* kaula (ja niska); (pullon)
kaula; kapea kannas (*~ of land*); *v.*
halailla, rakastella; vrt. *nape;* *~ and
crop* päätä pahkaa; *~ and ~* rinta
rinnan; *~ or nothing* maksoi mitä
maksoi. **-band** kauluri. **-lace** [-lis]
kaulanauha, -koru. **-let** kaulakoriste;
kauluri. **-line** pääntie. **-tie** solmio.
-wear solmiot, kaulukset.

necro|mancer ['nekrə(u)mænsə] *s.*
manaaja, ks. seur. **-mancy** [-mænsi] *s.*
henkien manaaminen. **-polis**
[-'rɔpəlis] *s.* (iso) hautausmaa. **-psy**
[-psi] *s.* ruumiinavaus. **-sis** [ne'krəusis]
s. kuolio, nekroosi.

nectar ['nektə] *s.* nektari (jumalten

juoma); mesi. **-ine** ['nekt(ə)rin] *s.*
nektariinipersikka.

née [nei] *a.* omaa sukua.

need [ni:d] *s.* tarve; hätä, puute; *v.*
tarvita, olla tarpeen; *he ~ not know*
hänen ei tarvitse tietää; *we did not ~*
to hurry meidän ei tarvinnut kiiruhtaa;
if ~ be jos tarve vaatii; *a friend in ~ is
a friend indeed* hädässä ystävä
tunnetaan. **-ful** *a.* tarpeellinen; *s.*
(tarvittavat) rahat. **-iness** *s.* puute.

needle ['ni:dl] *s.* silmäneula, neula;
neulanen; (sukka)puikko;
(kompassin) neula, osoitin, (ruiskun)
piikki; kaiverrin.

needless ['ni:dlis] *a.* tarpeeton, turha.

needle|woman käsityöihminen. **-work**
ompelus, käsityö.

needn't ['ni:dnt] = *need not.*

need|s [ni:dz] *adv.* välttämättä; *must ~*
täytyy välttämättä (tav. pilk.). **-y**
['ni:di] *a.* puutteenalainen, köyhä.

ne'er-do-well ['nɛədu(:)wel] *s.* hulttio.

nefarious [ni'fɛəriəs] *a.* katala,
rikollinen.

nega|te [ni'geit] *v.* kieltää, mitätöidä.
-tion [-'geiʃn] *s.* kieltäminen, kielto.
-tive ['negativ] *a.* kieltävä, kielteinen,
kielto-; *s.* kieltävä lause, vastaus;
kieltosana; negatiivi (valok.); *v.*
osoittaa vääräksi kieltää, tehdä
tyhjäksi: *answer in the ~* vastata
kieltävästi.

neglect [ni'glekt] *v.* laiminlyödä, jättää
hoitamatta t. tekemättä; *s.*
laiminlyönti; leväperäisyys; *in a state
of ~* hoitamaton, huonosti hoidettu.
-ful *a.* huolimaton, leväperäinen.

négli|gé, -gee ['negliʒei] *s.* (väljä)
kotipuku.

neglig|ence ['neglidʒ(ə)ns] *s.*
huolimattomuus, huono hoito,
laiminlyönti. **-ent** [-ʒ(ə)nt] *s.*
huolimaton, välinpitämätön,
leväperäinen. **-ible** [-əbl] *a.*
vähäpätöinen, mitätön.

negoti|able [ni'gəuʃiəbl] siirrettävä,
siirtokelpoinen. **-ate** [-eit] *v.*
neuvotella, saada aikaan; siirtää
(šekki); suoriutua, päästä jnk yli.
-ation [-'eiʃn] *s.* neuvottelu. **-ator**
[-eitə] *s.* neuvottelija.

negress [ni:gris] *s.* neekerinainen.

Negro ['ni:grəu] *s.* (pl *~es*) neekeri.

-id ['-ɔid] *a.* neekerinsukuinen, neekerin-.

Negus ['ni:ɡəs] *s.* (Etiopian) negus.

Nehemiah [ni:i'maiə] *erisn.* Nehemia.

Nehru ['nɛəru:] *erisn.*

neigh [nei] *s.* hirnua; *s.* hirnunta.

neighbour, neighbor ['neibə] *s.* naapuri; lähimmäinen; ~*ing* naapuri-, lähi-. **-hood** *s.* lähistö, ympäristö, lähiseutu; paikka, seutu, tienoo; läheisyys; *in the* ~ *of* .. (m.) noin .. **-ing** *a.* naapuri-, **-liness** *s.* naapurisopu. **-ly** [-li] *a.* naapuri(n)-: ystävällinen, seurallinen.

Neil, Neill [ni:l] *erisn.*

neither ['naiðə, Am. 'ni:ðə] *pron.* ei kumpikaan; *konj.* ei .. -kään; ~ .. *nor* ei .. eikä; *I like* ~ *of them* en pidä kummastakaan; [*if you don't go*], ~ *will I* en minäkään (mene).

nemesis ['nemisis] *s.* (taivaallinen) kosto, rangaistus.

neo- ['ni:ə(u)-] *pref.* uusi-, uus-. ~**colonialism** uuskolonialismi.

neon ['ni:ɔn] *s.:* ~ *light* valomainos.

neo|phyte ['ni:əufait] *s.* vastakääntynyt; noviisi. **-plasm** [-plæzm] *s.* kasvain.

Nepal [ni'pɔ:l] *erisn.* **-ese** [nepə'li:z] *a. & s.* nepalilainen.

nephew ['nevju:, Am. 'nef-] *s.* veljen- t. sisarenpoika.

nephritis [ne'fraitis] *s.* munuaistulehdus.

nepotism ['nepətizm] *s.* sukulaisten suosinta.

Neptune ['neptju:n] *erisn.* Neptunus.

Nereid ['niɔriid] *s.* merenneito.

Nero ['niɔrɔu] *erisn.*

nerv|e [nɔ:v] *s.* hermo; (lehden) suoni; voima, lujuus, sisu, uskallus; *v.* vahvistaa; rohkaista; *war of* ~*s* hermosota; [*the noise*] *gets on my* ~*s* käy hermoilleni; [*she*] *is suffering from* ~*s* on huonohermoinen; *he had the* ~ *to suggest* hänellä oli otsaa ehdottaa; *lose one's* ~ menettää rohkeutensa; *what a* ~*!* kuinka röyhkeätä! ~ *oneself* jännittää voimansa; (~*less a.* voimaton; ~**racking** hermoja vihlova).

-ous [-əs] *a.* hermo-; hermostunut, herkkähermoinen; ~ *energy* hermoenergia; ~ *strain* hermopaine; ~ *system* hermosto. **-ousness** *s.*

herkkähermoisuus. **-y** [-i] *s.* hermostunut; röyhkeä (sl.).

nescience ['nesiəns] *s.* tietämättömyys.

nest [nest] *s.* pesä; *v.* pesiä; *a* ~ *of tables* sarjapöytä; *machine-gun* ~ konekivääripesäke; *go* ~*ing* etsiä linnunpesiä. ~**egg** pesämuna. **-le** ['nesl] *v.* asettua t. levätä mukavasti, painautua hellästi (*against* jtk vastaan); pidellä hellästi (sylissään). **-ling** ['nes(t)liŋ] *s.* linnunpoika.

net 1. [net] *a.* netto-, puhdas; *v.* saada puhdasta voittoa, netota; ~ *prise* nettohinta.

net 2. [net] *s.* verkko; ansa; harsokangas; *v.* pyydystää verkkoon, kietoa pauloihinsa; suojata verkolla; laskea verkot (jokeen); ~[*ball*] (tennis) verkkopallo. ~**-ball** eräänl. koripallo.

nether ['neðə] *a.* alempi-, ala-.

Netherlands ['neðələndz]: *the* ~ Alankomaat.

nethermost *a.* alin.

netting *s.* verkko.

nettle ['netl] *s.* nokkonen; *v.* polttaa nokkosiin, ärsyttää; ~*d* kiukustunut. ~**rash** *s.* nokkosihottuma.

network verkko, verkosto; (rad.) verkkoryhmä.

neur|al ['njuərəl] *a.* hermo-. **-algia** [-'rældʒə] *s.* hermosärky. **-asthenia** [-æs'θi:njə] *s.* heikkohermoisuus. **-itis** [-'raitis] *s.* hermotulehdus. **-ologist** [-'rɔlədʒist] *s.* neurologi. **-ology** [-'rɔlədʒi] *s.* hermotautioppi. **-osis** [-'rɔusis] *s.* (pl. *-oses* [-si:z]) *s.* neuroosi. **-otic** [-'rɔtik] *a.* neuroottinen *s.* neurootikko.

neut|er ['nju:t|ə] *a.* neutrisukuinen sana, sukupuoleton eläin; ~*ed* kastroitu. **-ral** [-r(ə)l] *a.* puolueeton, neutraali; epämääräinen, keskivälillä oleva; (kem.) neutraali: *s.* puolueeton valtio t. henkilö; *in* ~ *gear* (auto) vapaalla. **-rality** [-'ræliti] *s.* puolueettomuus; *armed* ~ aseellinen p. **-ralize** [-rəlaiz] *v.* neutraloida. **-ron** ['nju:trɔn] *s.* neutroni.

Nevada [ne'va:də] *erisn.*

never ['nevə] *adv.* ei koskaan, ei milloinkaan, ei lainkaan; [*he*] *answered* ~ *a word* ei vastannut sanaakaan; ~ *once* ei kertaakaan;

well, I ~ ! onko mokomaa kuultu! (sl.)
buy sth. on the ~-~ vähittäismaksulla.
~-**failing** pettämätön, ehtymätön.
-**more** adv. ei milloinkaan enää.
-**theless** [-θ(ə)'les] adv. siitä
huolimatta, sittenkin.

new [nju:] a. uusi; nyky-; tuore;
tottumaton, outo; uudenaikainen; ~
to the work kokematon työssä; ~ from
jstk vasta tullut; ~ Year's Day
uudenvuodenpäivä; ~ Deal (Am.) v.
1932 uudistusohjelma. ~-**born**
vastasyntynyt.

Newcastle ['nju:kɑ:sl] erisn.; carry
coals to ~ mennä merta edemmäksi
kalaan.

newcomer s. uusi tulokas.

newel ['nju:əl, Am. nu:l] s.
kierreportaiden (keskus)pylväs.

new-fangled uusi, uudenaikainen.

Newfoundland ['nju:f(ə)nd'lænd]
erisn.: ~ [dog] [nju(:)'faundlənd]
newfoundlandinkoira.

newish ['nju:iʃ] a. uudehko.

new|ly adv. äskettäin, vasta-;
uudestaan; the ~-weds vastanaineet.
-**ness** s. uutuus.

New Orleans [nju:'ɔ:liənz] erisn.

news [nju:z, Am. nu:z] s. (käyt. sg:na)
uutinen, uutiset; a piece of ~ uutinen;
the latest ~ viimeiset uutiset; what['s
the] ~? mitä uutta? Here's the ~!
uutiset (rad. ym). -**agent**
lehdenmyyjä. -**boy** s. lehdenmyyjä.
-**cast** (rad. & TV) uutislähetys.
-**caster** uutisten lukija. -**letter**
kiertokirje, tiedotus(lehti). -**monger**
juorukello, juorutäti. -**paper** ['nju:s-]
sanomalehti. -**print** s.
sanomalehtipaperi (paperilaatuna).
-**reel** uutiskatsaus (elok.). -**stand**
sanomalehtikoju. -**vendor**
lehdenmyyjä. -**y** ['nju:zi] a. (puhek.)
täynnä uutisia (oleva).

newt [nju:t] s. vesilisko.

Newton ['nju:tn] erisn. -**ian**
[nju(:)'təunjən] a. Newtonin.

New Year uusi vuosi; wish sb. a happy
N~ Y~ toivottaa hyvää uutta vuotta;
N~ Y~'s Eve uudenvuodenaatto.

New York ['nju:'jɔ:k], **New Zealand**
[nju:'zi:lənd] erisn. Uusi Seelanti;
New ~er uusseelantilainen.

next [nekst] a. lähin, lähinnä oleva t.

seuraava; ensi, seuraava; adv.
lähinnä, tämän t. sen jälkeen, sitten;
seuraavan kerran, seuraavaksi; ~ best
lähinnä paras; ~ door viereisessä
talossa; ~ door to melkeinpä; ~ week
ensi viikolla; ~ year ensi vuonna; ~ to
lähinnä (jtk; jkn) vieressä; melkein;
what ~! se vielä puuttui! the ~ day
seuraavana päivänä.

nexus ['neksəs] s. yhdysside.

Niagara [nai'ægərə] erisn.

nib [nib] s. teräskynä, kynänterä;
kärki.

nibble [nibl] v. nakertaa; (kalasta)
nykiä; näykkiä (m. kuv. ~ at), nälviä;
s. puraisu; nykäisy, nykäys.

niblick ['niblik] s. eräänl. (raskas)
golfmaila.

Nicaragua [nikə'rægjuə] erisn.

nice [nais] a. miellyttävä, herttainen,
hauska, mukava, viehättävä,
ystävällinen; soma, kaunis; tarkka,
turhantarkka; nirso;
arka(luonteinen), hankala;
(hienon)hieno; a ~ mess kaunis
sotku. ~-**looking** hauskan näköinen.
-**ly** adv. miellyttävästi; hyvin,
erinomaisesti (suits me ~). -**ty** [-iti] s.
tarkkuus; nirsous, hienous;
arkaluonteisuus; hiuksenhieno ero; to
a ~ aivan tarkalleen (oikein); n-ties
yksityiskohdat, pikkuasiat.

niche [nitʃ] s. seinäkomero, syvennys.

Nicholas ['nikələs] erisn. Nikolai.

nick [nik] s. uurros, lovi, rasti; v. tehdä
lovi; sl. vankila; in the ~ (m.) kiven
sisällä; in the ~ of time
yhdennellätoista hetkellä; old N~
paholainen, »vanha kehno».

nickel ['nikl] s. nikkeli; 5 sentin raha;
v. nikkelöidä; ~ silver uushopea.

nickname ['nikneim] s. lisä-,
lempinimi; v. antaa lisänimi.

Nicodemus [nikə'di:məs] erisn.

Nicosia [nikə(u)'si(:)ə] erisn.

nicotine ['nikəti:n] s. nikotiini.

niece [ni:s] s. veljen- t. sisarentytär.

nifty ['nifti] a. hieno, tyylikäs; sukkela.

Nigel ['naidʒ(ə)l], **Nigeria** [nai'dʒiəriə]
erisn.

niggard ['nigəd] s. kitupiikki. -**liness** s.
kitsaus. -**ly** a. kitsas, saita; niukka.

nigger ['nigə] s. (halv.) nekru.

niggle ['nigl] v. olla turhantarkka,

saivarrella.

nigh [nai] *adv. & prep.* (run. & vanh.) lähellä.

night [nait] *s.* yö; *at* ~ yöllä, illalla; *by* ~, *in the* ~ yöllä; *all* ~ koko yön; *stay over* ~ jäädä yöksi; *last* ~ viime yönä, eilen illalla; *make a* ~ *of it* juhlia yö läpeensä. **-cap** yömyssy. **-club** yökerho. **-dress, -gown** yöpuku, -paita. **-fall** iltahämärä. **-ie** [-i] *s.* yöpaita. **-ingale** *s.* satakieli. **-jar** kehrääjä (lintu). **-ly** *a.* öinen, jokaöinen, yö-; *adv.* joka yö. **~-line** pitkäsiima. **-mare** painajainen. **~-school** iltakoulu. **-shade** koiso (kasv.).

nihil|**ism** [ˈnailizm] *s.* nihilismi. **-ist** [-ist] *s.* nihilisti.

nil [nil] *s.* nolla, ei mitään.

Nile [nail] *erisn.: the* ~ Niili.

nimble [ˈnimbl] *a.* ketterä, nopea; sukkela.

nimbus [ˈnimbəs] *s.* (pl. ~*es* t. *nimbi* [-bai]) sädekehä; sadepilvi.

nincompoop [ˈninkəmpu:p] *s.* hölmö, tomppeli.

nine [nain] *lukus.* yhdeksän; yhdeksikkö, yhdeksäinen. **-fold** *a. & adv.* yhdeksänkertai|nen, -sesti. **-pins** [-pinz] *s. pl.* keilapeli. **-teen** [-ˈti:n] *lukus.* yhdeksäntoista; *talks ~ to the dozen* hänen suunsa käy kuin papupata. **-teenth** [-ˈti:nθ] *lukus.* yhdeksästoista. **-tieth** [-ˈtiiθ] *lukus.* yhdeksäskymmenes. **-ty** [-ti] *lukus.* yhdeksänkymmentä; *the nineties* 90-luku.

Nineveh [ˈninivi] *erisn.* Ninive.

ninny [ˈnini] *s.* hölmö, tomppeli.

ninth [nainθ] *lukus. & s.* yhdeksäs(osa).

Niobe [ˈnaiəbi] *erisn.*

nip [nip] *v.* nipistää, puraista; (pakkasesta) purra, tuhota; pinkaista (~ *along*); *s.* pakkanen, (pakkasen) tuntu; ryyppy, kulaus; ~ *in the bud* tukahduttaa alkuunsa; ~ *off* nipistää poikki. **-per** [-ə] *s.* (puhek.) (pojan)vesseli; [*a pair of*] ~ *s* pihdit, (ravun) sakset. **-ping** *a.* pureva.

nipple [ˈnipl] *s.* nänni; (tuttipullon) tutti.

nippy [ˈnipi] *a.* nopea, nopsa; pureva (pakkanen); *look* ~ *!* kiiruhda!

nisi [ˈnaisai] *lat. konj.: decree* ~ (toistaiseksi voimassaoleva) avio- t. asumuseropäätös.

Nissen *hut* aaltopeltiparakki.

nit [nit] *s.* saivar, (täin)muna.

nitr|**ate** [ˈnait|reit] *s.* nitraatti. **-e** (Am. *niter*) *s.* kalisalpietari. **-ic** [-rik] *a.:* ~ *acid* typpihappo. **-ogen** [-ridʒən] *s.* typpi. **-ous** [-rəs] *a.:* ~ *oxide* ilokaasu.

nitwit [nitwit] *s.* tollo, pölkkypää.

nixie [ˈniksi] *s.* vedenneito.

no [nəu] *adv.* ei; *pron.* ei mikään, ei kukaan; *s.* (pl. ~*es*) ei(ääni); *the* ~ *es have it* enemmistö on asiaa vastaan; ~ *one* ei kukaan; *there is* ~ *denying* [*it*] ei voida kieltää; *things are* ~ *better* asiat eivät ole sen paremmalla kannalla; ~ *end of* vaikka millä mitalla; *it's* ~ *go* (puhek.) se on mahdotonta, ei onnistu; *in* ~ *time* [*at all*] tuossa tuokiossa.

no., nos. [nʌmbə, -z] *lyh.* n:o, numerot.

Noah [ˈnə(u)ə] *erisn.* Nooa.

nob [nob] *s. sl.* kallo, pää; tärkeä t. ylhäinen henkilö.

nobble [ˈnobl] *v.* (vahingoittamalla t. huumaamalla) estää kilpa-ajohevosen voitto; puijaamalla hankkia.

nobby [ˈnobi] *a.* hieno (sl.).

Nobel [nəuˈbel] *erisn.; ~ Prize-winner* Nobelin palkinnon saaja.

nobility [nə(u)ˈbiliti] *s.* jalous, ylevyys; (ylempi) aatelisto; aatteluus.

noble [ˈnəubl] *a.* ylhäinen, aatelinen; jalo, ylevä; komea, uljas; *s.* aatelinen, aatelismies. **-man** aatelismies. **~-minded** ylevämielinen. **-woman** aatelisnainen.

nobly [ˈnəubli] *adv.* jalosti, ylevästi, uljaasti.

nobody [ˈnəub(ə)di] *pron.* ei kukaan; *s.* vähäpätöinen (t. mitäänsanomaton) ihminen, nolla.

nocturn|**al** [nɔkˈtə:nl] *a.* yöllinen, yö-. **-e** [ˈnɔktə:n] *s.* nokturni.

nod [nɔd] *s.* nyökäyttää päätänsä, nyökätä; nuokkua; torkahtaa; *s.* (pään)nyökkäys; ~ *approval* nyökätä hyväksyvästi; *a ~ding acquaintance* hyvänpäiväntuttu; *on the* ~ (sl.) luotolla.

nodal [ˈnəudl] *a.: ~ point* solmukohta.

noddle [ˈnɔdl] *s.* päänuppi (leik.).

nod|**e** [nəud] *s.* kyhmy, oksanpaikka;

pahkura, nystyrä. **-ular** ['nɔdjulə] *a.*
kyhmyinen, nystyrämäinen. **-ule**
['nɔdju:l] *s.* kyhmy, nystermä.
noggin ['nɔgin] *s.* = *1/4 pint.*
no-go: ~ *area* kielletty alue.
noise [nɔiz] *s.* (kova) ääni, melu,
kolina, hälinä; kohina; *v.:* ~ *abroad*
toitottaa maailmalle; *it was* ~*d*
abroad huhuttiin; *make a* ~ meluta
(*..in the world* herättää huomiota); *a*
big ~ pomo, mahtitekijä. **-less** *a.*
äänetön.
noisi|ly *adv.* meluavasti. **-ness** *s.*
äänekkyys, meluisuus.
noisome ['nɔisəm] *a.* inhottava,
pahanhajuinen.
noisy ['nɔizi] *a.* äänekäs, meluava,
meluisa; kirkuva, räikeä.
nomad ['nɔməd, 'nɔumæd] *s.*
paimentolainen. **-ic** [nɔ(u)'mædik] *a.*
paimentolais-.
no-man's-land *s.* ei kenenkään maa.
nom de plume ['nɔmdə'plu:m] *s.*
kirjailijanimi.
nomenclature ['nɔ(u)menkleitʃə] *s.*
nimistö, oppisanasto.
nomin|al ['nɔminl] *a.* nimellinen,
nimellis-, nimi-; ~*ly* nimellisesti. **-ate**
v. nimetä, panna ehdolle; nimittää.
-ation [-'neiʃn] *s.* nimeäminen,
ehdollepano; nimitys(oikeus). **-ative**
['nɔm(i)nətiv] *a. & s.* nominatiivi(-).
-ee [nɔmi'ni:] *s.* ehdollepantu.
non- [nɔn-] *pref.* ei-, epä-, -ton, -tön.
nonagenarian [nɔunədʒi'neəriən] *s.*
yhdeksänkymmenvuotias.
non|-aggression *s.:* ~ *pact*
hyökkäämättömyyssopimus.
~**-aligned** *a.* sitoutumaton.
~**-appearance,** ~**-attendance** *s.*
poisjääminen (oikeudesta, koulusta).
~**-biodegradable** *a.* luonnon kiertoon
palautumaton.
nonce [nɔns] *s.: for the* ~ tällä hetkellä,
tilapäisesti.
nonchalan|ce ['nɔnʃ(ə)ləns] *s.*
välinpitämättömyys. **-t** [-ənt] *a.*
välinpitämätön, huoleton.
non-combatant *a. & s.* ei taisteleva,
taisteluun osallistumaton.
non-commissioned *a.:* ~ *officer*
aliupseeri (lyh. *N.C.O.*).
non|-committal *a.* pidättyväinen,
varovainen. **-conformist** [-kən'fɔ:mist]

s. nonkonformisti, vapaakirkollinen.
-conformity *s.* nonkonformismi; (~
to) (yhteen)sopeutumattomuus.
~**-delivery** *s.: in case of* ~ jos (kirje
ym) ei saavu määräpaikkaan.
-descript ['nɔndiskript] *a.*
epämääräinen.
none [nʌn] *pron.* ei kukaan, ei mikään;
adv. ei yhtään; ~ *of that!* lakkaa jo!
it's ~ *of your business* se ei kuulu
sinuun; ~ *the less* sittenkin, siitä
huolimatta; ~ *too good* aika huono; *he*
was ~ *the worse for his fall* hän ei
loukkaantunut kaatuessaan.
non|entity [nɔ'nentiti] *s.*
olemattomuus, olematon asia;
(henkilöstä) nolla. ~**-essential** *a. & s.*
epäolennainen (asia t. tarvike).
~**-existent** *a.* olematon.
~**-intervention** *s.* puuttumattomuus.
~**-payment** *s.* maksun
laiminlyöminen.
nonpareil ['nɔnpəreil, Am. -pə'rel] *s.*
nonparelli (kirjap.); verraton
(henkilö t. asia).
nonplus ['nɔn'plʌs] *v.* saattaa ymmälle;
be ~*sed* olla sanattomana, nolona.
non|-proliferation *s.:* ~ *treaty*
ydinsulkusopimus. ~**-resident** *s.*
vieraspaikkakuntalainen.
nonsens|e ['nɔns(ə)ns] *s.* mieletön
puhe, hölynpöly, pöty; *int.* loruja!
-ical ['sensik(ə)l] *a.* mieletön,
tolkuton.
non|-smoker *s.* tupakoimaton;
tupakoimattomien vaunu(osasto).
~**-stop** *a. & s.* ilman välilaskua;
tauoton; ~ *train* pikajuna. ~**-union** *s.*
järjestäytymätön (työläinen).
~**-violent** väkivallaton. ~**-white**
värillinen, tummaihoinen, musta.
~**-woven:** ~ *fabric* kuitukangas.
noodle ['nu:dl] *s.* hölmö; tav. *pl.*
nuudelit, lankamakaronit.
nook [nuk] *s.* soppi, kolkka, nurkka.
noon [nu:n] *s.* puolipäivä, keskipäivä;
at ~ puolenpäivän aikaan. **-day, -tide**
= ed.
noose [nu:s] *s.* vetosolmu, *v.* pyydystää
ansaan (lassolla ym).
nope [nəup] *s.* (sl.) *int.* ei; ei käy.
nor [nɔ:] *konj.* eikä, ei myöskään;
neither... ~ ei... eikä.
Nordic ['nɔ:dik] *a. & s.*

pohjoismaalainen.
Norfolk ['nɔ:fək] *erisn.*
norm [nɔ:m] *s.* normi, sääntö. **-al** [-(ə)l]
a. normaali, säännönmukainen. **-ality**
[nɔ:'mæliti] *s.* säännönmukaisuus,
normaalisuus. **-alize** [-əlaiz] *v.*
normaalistaa. **-ally** *adv.* normaalisti,
normaalioloissa, tavallisesti.
Norman ['nɔ:mən] *s. & a.*
normanni(lainen); *the ~ Conquest*
Englannin normannivalloitus (v.
1066).
Norse [nɔ:s] *a.*, **-man** *s.*
muinaisskandinaavi(nen) t.
norjalainen; (muinais)norja.
north [nɔ:θ] *s.* pohjoinen; *a.*
pohjoinen, pohjois-; *adv.* pohjoiseen,
-essa; [*to the*] *~ of* pohjoiseen jstk; *the
N~ Sea* Pohjanmeri.
Northampton [nɔ:'θæm(p)tən] *erisn.*
north|-east *s. & a.* koillinen, koillis-
~**-easter** koillistuuli, -myrsky.
~**-easterly** *a.* koillis-; *adv.* koilliseen,
-sesta. ~**-eastern** koillinen.
northerly ['nɔ:ðəli] *a.* pohjois-; *adv.*
pohjoiseen, -sesta.
northern ['nɔ:ð(ə)n] *a.* pohjoinen,
pohjois-; *~ lights* revontulet. **-er** [-ə]
s. Am. pohjoisvaltioiden asukas.
-most *a.* pohjoisin.
Northumberland [nɔ:'θʌmbələnd]
erisn.
north|ward *a.* pohjoinen; *adv.*
pohjoiseen (m. *~s*). **-west** *s.* luode; *a.*
luoteis-. **-wester** luoteistuuli, -myrsky.
-westerly *a.* luoteis-; *adv.* luoteiseen,
-sesta. **-western** luoteinen, luoteis-.
Norway ['nɔ:wei] *erisn.* Norja.
Norwegian [nɔ:'wi:dʒn] *a. & s.*
norjalainen, norjan kieli.
Norwich ['nɔridʒ, Am. 'nɔ:witʃ] *erisn.*
nose [nəuz] *s.* nenä; nokka, torvi;
vainu; *v.* haistaa, vainuta, nuuskia,
urkkia (*~ after, for*); *~ sth. out*
urkkia, keksiä; *lead by the ~* vetää
nenästä, pitää narrinaan; *pay through
the ~* maksaa kohtuuttomasti; *poke
(thrust) one's ~ into* pistää nenänsä
jhk; *thumb one's ~ at* näyttää pitkää
nenää; *turn up one's ~ at* nyrpistää
nenäänsä jllek. ~**-bag** rehupussi.
-bleed verenvuoto nenästä. ~**-dive** *s.*
pystysyöksy (ilm.) *v.* syöksyä. **-gay**
[-gei] *s.* kukkavihko. **-y, nosy** [-i] *a. &*

s. (sl.) utelias (henkilö).
nosh [nɔʃ] *s.* (sl.) ruoka; *~ -up* hyvä
ateria.
nostalgia [nɔs'tældʒə] *s.* koti-ikävä;
kaiho, menneiden aikojen kaipuu.
nostril ['nɔstril] *s.* sierain.
nostrum ['nɔstrəm] *s.* puoskarin lääke,
patenttilääke (m. kuv.).
nosy ks. *nosey.*
not [nɔt] *adv.* ei; *~ at all* ei lainkaan; ei
kestä kiittää; kaikin mokomin; *~ to
say.* . etten sanoisi. .; *~ that I know
of* ei minun tietääkseni.
nota bene ['nəutə'benei] (tav. lyh. *N.
B.*) huomaa, huom.
notability [nəutə'biliti]
s. merkittävyys;
merkkihenkilö.
notab|le ['nəutəbl] *a.* merkittävä,
huomattava; silmiinpistävä; *s.*
merkkihenkilö. **-ly** *adv.*
huomattavasti, varsinkin.
notary ['nəutəri] *s.* notaari; *~ public*
julkinen notaari.
notation [nə(u)'teiʃn] *s.*
merkitsemistapa, merkkijärjestelmä.
notch [nɔtʃ] *s.* pykälä, lovi, uurros;
ahdas sola (Am.); *v.* tehdä lovi,
uurtaa; *~ up* saada, merkata (tulos).
note [nəut] *s.* muistiinpano, merkintä
konsepti; (lyhyt) kirje; huomautus,
selitys; huomio; seteli, velkakirja;
sävel, nuotti, sävy; merkki; tärkeys,
merkittävyys; nootti (pol.); *v.* merkitä
muistiin; panna merkille, huomata;
(us. *~ down*); *~ of exclamation*
huutomerkki; *~ of hand* velkakirja;
bank-~ seteli; . . *of note* huomattava;
compare ~s vaihtaa mielipiteitä,
vertailla huomioitaan; *make a ~ of*
merkitä muistiin; *take ~ of* panna
merkille; *take ~s* tehdä
muistiinpanoja; *is ~d for* on kuuluisa
jstk. **-book** muistikirja. **-case**
lompakko. **-d** [-id] *a.* kuuluisa,
tunnettu, merkittävä. ~**-paper**
kirjepaperi. **-worthy** huomattava.
nothing ['nʌθiŋ] *pron.* ei mikään, ei
mitään; *s.* tyhjä, nolla, vähäpätöinen
asia; *adv.* ei lainkaan, ei ensinkään;
for ~ ilmaiseksi; [*it*] *went for ~* meni
hukkaan; *it is good for ~* se ei kelpaa
mihinkään; *come to ~* mennä
myttyyn, [*I can*] *make ~ of* en voi

ymmärtää: *to say* ~ *of* jstk puhumattakaan; ~ *doing* ei tule mitään, ei voi auttaa; *is* ~ *like* [*so good as*] ei ole läheskään; *there is* ~ *for it but to*.. ei auta muu kuin .. **-ness** s. tyhjyys, olemattomuus.

notice ['noutis] s. huomio; tiedonanto, tiedotus; ilmoitus; kuulutus; varoitus, irtisanominen; maininta, arviointi (lehdessä); v. huomata, panna merkille, ottaa huomioon; mainita; *bring to sb.'s* ~ ilmoittaa jklle, saattaa jkn tietoon; *give* ~ sanoa t. sanoutua irti; *take* ~ *of* panna merkille, kiinnittää huomiota; *at short* ~ lyhyessä ajassa; *at a moment's* ~ viipymättä; *at a month's* ~ kuukauden irtisanomisajalla; *good* ~ *s* hyvä arvostelu. **-able** [-əbl] a. huomattava, havaittava. **~-board** ilmoitustaulu.

notifi|able [nəuti|'faiəbl] a. (viranomaisille ym) ilmoitettava. **-cation** [-fi'keiʃn] s. ilmoitus.

notify ['noutifai] v. ilmoittaa.

notion ['nouʃn] s. käsitys, ajatus; ~ *s* (Am.) pikkutavarat, (pienet) lahjaesineet.

notori|ety [nəutə'raiəti] s. kuuluisuus (et. pah. merk.). **-ous** [nə(u)'tɔːriəs] a. tunnettu (et. pah. merk.), huonossa huudossa oleva.

Nottingham ['nɔtiŋəm] *erisn.*

notwithstanding [nɔtwið'stændiŋ] *prep.* jstk huolimatta; *adv.* siitä huolimatta, kuitenkin.

nougat ['nuːgɑː] s. nugaa.

nought [nɔːt] s. nolla; ei mitään; *set sb. at* ~ halveksia; *it came to* ~ se meni myttyyn, asia raukesi.

noun [naun] s. substantiivi.

nourish ['nʌriʃ] v. ravita, ruokkia; elättää; pitää vireillä; ~*ing* ravitseva. **-ment** s. ravinto.

novel ['nɔvl] a. uusi, outo, ennen näkemätön; s. romaani. **-ette** [nɔvə'let] s. pienoisromaani. **-ist** ['nɔvəlist] s. romaanikirjailija. **-la** [nəu'velə] s. = novelette. **-ty** [-ti] s. uutuus; ~ *shop* lahjaesinekauppa.

November [nə(u)'vembə] s. marraskuu.

novic|e ['nɔvis] s. noviisi; aloittelija, vasta-alkaja. **-iate** [nə(u)'viʃiət] s.

noviisiaika, (et. munkin, nunnan) koeaika (m. *novitiate*).

now [nau] *adv.* nyt; *konj.* nyt kun; (selityksenä, varoituksena) no niin, kas noin; [*do it*] ~ nyt heti; ~ ..., ~ milloin…milloin; ~ *and again*, ~ *and then* silloin tällöin; ~ *that*.. nyt kun..; ~ *then!* no niin! kas niin! *by* ~ tähän mennessä; *he ought to be here by* ~ hänen pitäisi jo olla täällä; *for* ~ tällä kertaa, toistaiseksi; *just* ~ (m.) juuri äsken; *till* ~, *up to* ~ tähän saakka. **-adays** [-ədeiz] *adv.* nykyään.

no|where *adv.* ei missään. **-wise** *adv.* ei millään tavalla.

noxious ['nɔkʃəs] a. vahingollinen, epäterveellinen, myrkky-.

nozzle ['nɔzl] s. suukappale, suutin.

nuance [nju(ː)ɑːns] s. vivahdus, vivahde.

nub [nʌb] s. pieni (hiili)palanen; (puhek.) (jutun) kärki, ydin.

nubile ['njuːbail] a. naimaikäinen.

nucle|ar ['njuːkliə, Am. 'nuː] a.: ~ *physics* ydinfysiikka; ~ *power station* atomivoimala; ~*-powered* atomikäyttöinen; ~ *test* ydinasekoe. **-ic** [-'kliːik] a.: ~ *acid* nukleiinihappo.

nucleus ['njuːkliəs] s. (pl. *-ei* [-iai]) ydin; (solun) tuma.

nude [njuːd] a. alaston, paljas; s. alaston (malli, ruumis, kuva); *in the* ~ alastomana, alasti.

nudge [nʌdʒ] v. tyrkätä (kyynärpäällä), tönäistä; s. tönäisy.

nudi|st [-ist] s. nudisti. **-ty** [-iti] s. alastomuus.

nugatory ['njuːgət(ə)ri] a. mitätön.

nugget ['nʌgit] s. kultakimpale.

nuisance ['njuːsns] s. vastus, mieliharmi, kiusan(kappale); *what a* ~! kuinka harmillista! *commit no* ~ siivottomuus kielletty!

null [nʌl] *pred.* a. pätemätön, mitätön (tav. ~ *and void*). **-ify** [-ifai] v. mitätöittää, mitätöidä. **-ity** [-iti] s. mitättömyys.

numb [nʌm] a. puutunut, turta, (~ *with cold*) kohmettunut; v. puuduttaa, turruttaa.

number ['nʌmbə] s. numero, luku (m.kiel.); lukumäärä, määrä, joukko; *pl.* runo; v. laskea, lukea; numeroida;

olla lukumäärältään; lukea jhk joukkoon (~ *among*); be ~ed among kuulua jhk joukkoon; *they ~ed twenty* heitä oli kaksitoista; *a* ~ *of* muutamia, useita; *a large* ~ *of* suuri määrä, suuri joukko; *exceed sth. in* ~ [s] olla suurempi kuin; *times without* ~ lukemattomia kertoja: *take care of* ~ *one* katsoa omaa etuansa; *Numbers* 4. Mooseksen kirja. **-less** *a.* lukematon.

numbness ['nʌmnis] *s.* puutuneisuus, turtumus.

numer|al ['nju:m(ə)rəl] *a.* luku-; *s.* luku, numero; lukusana. **-ation** [-'reiʃn] *s.* laskeminen, numerointi. **-ator** [-eitə] *s.* osoittaja (mat.). **-ical** [nju:'merik(ə)l] *a.* luku-, numero-, lukumääräinen (~ *strength*). **-ous** [-əs] *a.* lukuisa(t).

numis|matics [nju:miz'mætiks] *s.* rahatiede. **-matist** [-'miz-] *s.* rahojen ja mitalien keräilijä, numismaatikko.

numskull ['nʌmskʌl] *s.* pölkkypää.

nun [nʌn] *s.* nunna.

nuncio ['nʌnʃiou] *s.* nuntius.

nunnery ['nʌnəri] *s.* nunnaluostari.

nuptial ['nʌpʃ(ə)l] *a.* hää-, avio-; *s.* (tav. *pl.*) häät.

Nuremberg ['njuərəmbə:g] *erisn.* Nürnberg.

nurs|e [nə:s] *s.* lapsenhoitaja, sairaanhoitaja; imettäjä (tav. *wet~*); *v.* hoitaa (sairaita); imettää; hoivata; helliä; hautoa mielessään; *-ing staff* hoitohenkilökunta: ~ *feelings of revenge* hautoa kostoa. **-(e)ling** *s.* sylilapsi, hoidokki.

nursery ['nə:sri] *s.* lastenhuone; taimisto, taimitarha; [*day*] ~ seimi, päiväkoti; ~ *rhymes* lastenlorut. **-man** *s.* kauppapuutarhuri.

nursing *s.* sairaanhoito, hoito; ~ *bottle* tuttipullo; ~ *home* (yksityis)sairaala, sairaskoti.

nurture ['nə:tʃə] *s.* hoito, kasvatus; *v.* kasvattaa.

nut [nʌt] *s.* pähkinä; mutteri; pää (sl.); (vanh.) keikari; *a hard* ~ *to crack* kova pähkinä purtavaksi: *be ~s about (over)* olla hullaantunut jhk; *go ~s* mennä päästään vialle; *go ~ting* poimia pähkinöitä; *off one's* ~ päästään vialla. **~-crackers** pähkinäsakset.

nutmeg ['nʌtmeg] *s.* muskotti(pähkinä).

nutria ['nju:triə] *s.* rämemajava; nutria (turkis).

nutri|ent ['nju:triənt] *a.* ravitseva; *s.* ravintoaine. **-ment** *s.* ravinto. **-tion** [-'riʃn] *s.* ravitsemus, ravinto: (~-**al** *a.* ravitsemus-.) **-tious** [-'riʃəs] *a.* ravitseva. **-tive** [-tiv] *a.* ravitseva, ravinto-.

nutshell *s.* pähkinänkuori: *in a* ~ pähkinänkuoressa, suppeasti ilmaistuna.

nutty ['nʌti] *a.* pähkinänmakuinen; hassahtava (sl.).

nuzzle ['nʌzl] *v.* hieroa kuonoa, painautua (jtk vastaan).

nylon ['nailən] *s.* nailon; ~*s* nailonsukat.

nymph [nimf] *s.* nymfi; kaunokainen.

O

O, o [əu] *s.* o-kirjain; nolla.
Lyh.: **O.** *Ohio;* **OAS** *Organization of American States;* **OAU** *Organization of African Unity;* **OBE** [*Officer of the*] *Order of the British Empire;* **Oct.** *October;* **oct.** *octavo;* **OECD** *Organization for Economic Co-operation and Development;* **O.E.D.** *Oxford English Dictionary;* **O.E.E.C.** *Organisation for European Economic Co-operation;* **O.H.M.S.** *On His (Her) Majesty's Service;* **O.K.** ['əu 'kei] *all correct* (ihan) hyvä, oikein kunnossa, vrt. sanak.; **Okla.** *Oklahoma;* **O-level** *(Ordinary)* tutkinto Englannissa; **Ont.** *Ontario;* **op. cit.** *(opere citato) in the work quoted* edellämainitussa teoksessa; **Ore(g).** *Oregon;* **O.T.** *Old Testament;* **Oxon.** *(of) Oxford;* **oz.** *ounce(s).*
o [əu] *int.* oi! voi! (tav. *oh*).
o' [ə] = *of.*
O' [ə(u)] *pref.* (irlant. nimissä, esim. *O'Connor)* jälkeläinen.
oaf [əuf] *s.* idiootti, hölmö. **-ish** [-iʃ] *a.* moukkamainen.
oak [əuk] *s.* tammi. **~-apple** *s.* väriomena. **-en** [-n] *a.* tamminen.
oakum ['əukəm] *s.* tappura.
oar [ɔ:, ɔə] *s.* airo; soutaja; *put in one's ~* sekaantua jhk; *pull a good ~* soutaa hyvin. **-lock** hankain. **-sman** ['ɔ:zmən] soutaja.
oasis [ə(u)'eisis] *s.* (pl. *oases* [-si:z]) keidas.
oat [əut] *s.* kaura; *sow one's wild ~s* hurjastella (nuorena). **-cake** kauraleipä, -kakku. **-meal** kaurajauhot, -ryynit, -puuro.
oath [əuθ, pl. əuðz] *s.* vala; kirous; *take an~* vannoa vala; *on ~* valallisesti; *put sb. on his ~* ottaa jklta vala.

Obadiah [əubə'daiə] *erisn.*
obdur|acy ['ɔbdjurəsi] *s.* paatumus, kovuus. **-ate** [-it] *a.* itsepintainen, kova, taipumaton; paatunut.
obedi|ence [ə'bi:djəns] *s.* tottelevaisuus. **-ent** [-ənt] *a.* tottelevainen, kuuliainen.
obeisance [ə(u)'beis(ə)ns] *s.* (nöyrä) kumarrus; kunnioitus; *do ~ to* tervehtiä kunnioittavasti (kuin alamainen).
obelisk ['ɔbilisk] *s.* obeliski.
obes|e [ə(u)'bi:s] *a.* liikalihava. **-ity** [-iti] *s.* liikalihavuus.
obey [ə'bei] *v.* totella, noudattaa.
obfuscate ['ɔbfʌskeit] *v.* pimentää, sumentaa, hämmentää.
obituary [ə'bitjuəri] *s.* muistosanat; *a.* kuolin- (*~ notice*).
object ['ɔbdʒikt] *s.* kappale, esine, kohde; objekti (kiel.); tarkoitus, päämäärä; (naurettava, outo) ilmestys, olento; *v.* [əb'dʒekt] väittää *(to, against* jtk vastaan), vastustaa, paheksua; *if you don't ~* ellei teillä ole mitään sitä vastaan; *salary no ~* palkka ei pääasia; *with the ~ of earning fame* saavuttaakseen mainetta. **~-glass** objektiivi (fys.).
objection [əb'dʒekʃn] *s.* muistuttaminen, huomautus, va taväite; *I have no ~* minulla ei ole mitään sitä vastaan; *raise an ~* esittää vastaväite; *take ~ to* paheksua; *open to ~* = seur. **-able** [-əbl] *a.* moitittava; vastenmielinen, epämieluinen.
object|ive [əb'dʒektiv] *a.* objektiivinen, puolueeton, ulkokohtainen; objekti-; *s.* objektiivi; (sot. ym) kohde, tavoite; tarkoitus(perä). **-ivity** [-'tiviti] *s.* objektiivisuus.
objectless tarkoitukseton.

object-lesson s. havainto|-opetus, -esimerkki.

objector [əb'dʒektə] s. vastustaja (ks. *conscientious ~*).

oblation [ə(u)'bleiʃn] s. uhri.

obliga|te ['obligeit] v.: *I felt ~d to help* tunsin velvollisuudekseni auttaa. **-tion** [-'geiʃn] s. velvoitus, velvollisuus; kiitollisuudenvelka; *be under an ~ to* olla kiitollisuudenvelassa jklle. **-tory** ['obligət(ə)ri] a. pakollinen.

oblig|e [ə'blaidʒ] v. velvoittaa; tehdä (jklle) palvelus; *I was ~d to...* minun oli pakko; *I am ~d to you for it* olen kiitollinen sinulle siitä; *please ~ me by...* tahtoisitteko hyväntahtoisesti...? *can you ~ me with...?* voitko lainata minulle...? **-ing** a. ystävällinen, avulias.

oblique [ə'bli:k] a. vino, viisto; epäsuora.

obliterate [ə'blitəreit] v. pyyhkiä pois; (tyystin) hävittää, haihduttaa (muistista). **-tion** [-'reiʃn] s. poispyyhkiminen; (tyystin) hävittäminen.

obliv|ion [ə'bliviən] s. unohdus. **-ious** [-iəs] a. muistamaton; *be ~ of* unohtaa.

oblong ['obloŋ] a. pitkulainen, pitkänomainen; s. suorakaide.

obloquy ['obləkwi] s. panettelu, huono maine.

obnoxious [əb'nokʃəs] a. vastenmielinen, inhottava.

obo|e ['əubəu] s. oboe (mus.). **-ist** ['əubə(u)ist] s. oboisti.

O'Brien [ə(u)'braiən] erisn.

obscen|e [əb'si:n] a. ruokoton, säädytön, rivo. **-ity** [əb'seniti] s. säädyttömyys; rivous.

obscur|e [əb'skjuə] a. hämärä, himmeä, epäselvä; tuntematon, mitätön, huomaamaton; v. pimentää, peittää (näkyvistä); tehdä hämäräksi; saattaa varjoon. **-ity** [-riti] s. hämäryys jne.; huomaamaton asema.

obsequies ['obsikwiz] s. pl. hautajaiset.

obsequious [əb'si:kwiəs] a. liehakoiva, matelava.

observa|ble [əb'zə:v|əbl] a. havaittava. **-nce** [-(ə)ns] s. *(~ of)* jnk noudattaminen; (uskonnolliset) menot. **-nt** [-(ə)nt] a. tarkkaavainen;

jtk noudattava. **-tion** [obzə(:)'veiʃn] s. tarkkailu; huomio, havainto; huomautus; huomiokyky; *~ post* tähystyspaikka; *keep under ~* tarkkailla. **-tory** [-ətri] s. observatorio.

observe [əb'zə:v] v. noudattaa, ottaa vaarin, viettää (juhlaa); huomata, havaita, tarkata, tehdä havaintoja; huomauttaa. **-r** [-ə] s. huomioit(si)ja, havainnoitsija, tarkkailija; tähystäjä.

obsess [əb'ses] v. ahdistaa, riivata; *he was ~d [by an idea]...* vaivasi häntä pakkomielteen tavoin. **-ion** [əb'seʃn] s. pakkomielle. päähänpiintymä. **-ive** [-iv] a. pakkomielteen tapainen, (päähän) piintynyt.

obsol|escent [obsə'lesnt] a. käytännöstä jäävä, vanhahtava. **-ete** ['obsəli:t] a. vanhentunut, käytöstä jäänyt.

obstacle ['obstəkl] s. este; *~ race* estejuoksu.

obstetric, ~al [ob'stetrik] a. synnytys-. **-ician** [-'triʃn] s. synnytyslääkäri. **-s** [-s] s. synnytysoppi.

obstin|acy ['obstinəsi] s. uppiniskaisuus. **-ate** [-nit] a. uppiniskainen, itsepintainen.

obstreperous [əb'strep(ə)rəs] a. meluava, kuriton.

obstruct [əb'strʌkt] v. tukkia, sulkea; estää, pidättää, olla tiellä; jarruttaa. **-ion** [əb'strʌkʃn] s. tukkiminen; este; tukkeutuma (lääk.); *policy of ~* jarrutuspolitiikka; *(~ism* jarrutuspolitiikka). **-ive** [-iv] a. estävä, tukkiva.

obtain [əb'tein] v. saada, saavuttaa, hankkia; olla käytössä, voimassa t. vallalla. **-able** [-əbl] a. saatavissa oleva.

obtru|de [əb'tru:|d] v. tyrkyttää, pakottaa ottamaan; *~ oneself upon* tunkeutua jnk seuraan. **-sive** [-siv] a. tunkeileva.

obtuse [əb'tju:s] a. tylppä, tylsä; typerä, hidas.

obverse ['obvə:s] s. (rahan ym) kuvapuoli, etupuoli.

obviate ['obvieit] v. torjua, estää, saada ehkäistyksi.

obvious ['obviəs] a. ilmeinen, (itsestään) selvä; silminnähtävä.

-ly *adv.* aivan ilmeisesti.
ocarina [ɔkə'ri:nə] *s.* okariina.
occasion [ə'keiʒn] *s.* tilaisuus; aihe,
syy; tarve; välitön syy; *v.* aiheuttaa;
on ~ silloin tällöin; *on several* ~s
useita kertoja; *on this* [*festive*] ~ tässä
(juhla)tilaisuudessa; *give* ~ *to*
aiheuttaa; *rise to the* ~ olla tilanteen
tasalla. **-al** [-(ə)l] *a.* tilapäinen,
satunnainen; tilapäis-. **-ally** *adv.*
silloin tällöin, joskus.
Occident ['ɔksid(ə)nt] *s.: the* ~
länsimaat. **-al** [-'dentl] *a.* länsimainen.
occiput ['ɔksipʌt] *s.* takaraivo.
occlude [ɔ'klu:d] *v.* tukkia. **-sion** [-ʒn]
s. tukkeuma; purenta (hammasl.).
occult [ɔ'kʌlt] *a.* salainen, sala-. **-ism**
['ɔk(ə)ltizm] *s.* salatiede. **-ist**
['ɔk(ə)ltist] *s.* salatieteiden
harjoittaja.
occupa|nt ['ɔkjupənt] *s.* haltija,
omistaja. **-tion** [-'peiʃn] *s.* haltuun-
otto, valtaus, miehitys (sot.);
ammatti; toimi, tehtävä; ~ *troops*
miehitysjoukot; *by* ~ ammatiltaan.
-tional [ɔkju'peiʃənl] *a.: ~ diseases*
ammattitaudit; ~ *risks* ammatin
aiheuttamat vaarat; ~ *therapy*
toimintaterapia.
occupy [ɔkjupai] *v.* asua, olla jssk;
täyttää (tila, ajatukset), askarruttaa;
ottaa haltuunsa, vallata, miehittää;
hoitaa (virkaa); *the seat is occupied*
paikka on varattu; *be occupied in* olla
jssk työssä, puuhata (m. ~ *oneself
with*).
occur [ə'kə:] *v.* esiintyä, sattua,
tapahtua; ~ *to* juolahtaa jkn mieleen;
it ~ *red to me that* tulin ajatelleeksi,
että. **-rence** [ə'kʌr(ə)ns] *s.*
esiintyminen; tapahtuma, tapaus.
ocean ['ouʃn] *s.* valtameri. **-ography**
[ouʃjə'nɔgrəfi] *s.* valtamerentutkimus.
ocelot ['ousilɔt] *s.* otselotti.
ochre ['ouka] *s.* okra, vaalean
ruskeankeltainen.
o'clock [ə'klɔk] ks. *clock.*
oct|agon ['ɔktəgən] *s.*
kahdeksankulmio. **-ane** ['ɔktein] *s.*
oktaani. **-ave** ['ɔktiv] *s.* oktaavi
(mus.). **-avo** [ɔk'teivəu] *s.* (kirjan)
oktaavokoko.
October [ɔk'təubə] *s.* lokakuu.
octogenarian ['ɔktə(u)dʒi'nɛəriən] *a.*

kahdeksankymmenvuotias.
octo|pus ['ɔktəpəs] *s.* mustekala,
meritursas. **-roon** [-'ru:n] *s.*
kvarteronin ja valkoihoisen lapsi.
ocul|ar ['ɔkjulə] *a.* silmä-,
silminnäkijän. **-ist** [-ist] *s.*
silmälääkäri.
odalisque ['oudəlisk] *s.* odaliski.
odd [ɔd] *a.* epätasainen, pariton;
paripuoli, ylimääräinen; tilapäinen,
eriskummallinen, outo, omituinen; *s.*
ks. *odds; three pounds* ~ runkoe
puntaa ja risat; *twenty* ~ *years*
kolmattakymmentä vuotta; *an* ~
fellow eriskummallinen olento; ~ *jobs*
tilapäistyöt; *at* ~ *moments*
joutohetkinä; *the* ~ *money* loput
rahat; ~ *man out* pelistä pudonnut,
(kuv.) »outo lintu». **-ity** [-iti] *s.*
kummallisuus, omituisuus; omituinen
olento, kapine. **-ly** *adv.* oudosti; ~
enough ihme kyllä. **-ments** *s.*
jäännöspalat, sekalaiset tavarat. **-s**
[-z] *s. pl.* (käyt. m. *sg*:na) erotus,
erilaisuus; etu, voitonpuoli; (urh.)
tasoitus; ~ *and ends* jäännöspalat,
pikkutavarat, kama; *at* ~ huonoissa
väleissä; *by long* ~ ylivoimaisesti; *the*
~ *are in our favour* meillä on
suuremmat voitonmahdollisuudet;
[*fight*] *against heavy* ~ valtavaa
ylivoimaa vastaan; *the* ~ *are that* on
hyvin luultavaa että; *give (receive)* ~
(urh.) antaa (saada) tasoitusta; *lay* ~
of 3 to 1 lyödä vetoa kolme yhtä
vastaan.
ode [əud] *s.* oodi.
odi|ous ['oudjəs] *a.* vastenmielinen,
inhottava. **-um** [-jəm] *s.*
inho(ttavuus), vastenmielisyys.
odorous ['oudərəs] *a.* tuoksuva.
odour, Am. m. **odor** ['oudə] *s.* tuoksu,
haju, lemu. **-less** *a.* hajuton.
Odyssey ['ɔdisi] *s.* odysseia,
` seikkailuretki.
(o)edema [i(:)'di:mə] *s.* turvotus
(lääk.).
Oedipus ['i:dipəs] *erisn.* Oidipus.
(o)esophagus [i:'sɔfəgəs] *s.* ruokatorvi.
(o)estrogen ['i:strədʒən] *s.*
estrogeeni.
of [ɔv, əv] *prep.* ilmaisee omistajaa,
alkuperää ym; vastaa suomen
genetiiviä; liittyy lukuisiin verbeihin

ja adjektiiveihin; *(think, speak ~, guilty ~); the children ~ the family* perheen lapset; *a house ~ stone* kivitalo; *die ~ hunger* kuolla nälkään; *the works ~ Shakespeare* S:n teokset; *the fear ~ God* jumalanpelko; *a man ~ honour* kunnian mies; *the city ~ Rome* Rooman kaupunki; *all ~ us* me kaikki; *[a girl] ~ ten* kymmenen vuoden ikäinen; *south ~ jnk* eteläpuolella; *~ necessity* pakosta.

off [ɔ:f, ɔf] *adv.* pois, poissa; lopussa, poikki, peruutettu; *prep.* -sta, -stä pois jstk; *(take ~);* irti *(cut ~);* loitolla, jnk matkan päässä; edustalla, ulkopuolella; *a.* etäisempi; oikeanpuoleinen; *~ and on* aika ajoin, silloin tällöin; *an ~ chance* vähäinen mahdollisuus; *~ colour* huonossa kunnossa; *~ duty* vapaa virantoimituksesta; *~ season* hiljainen kausi; *~ shore* vähän matkan päässä rannasta; *is ~ smoking* on tupakkalakossa; *~ the map* poissa pelistä; *be ~* lähteä pois, tiehensä; *be ~ with you!* tiehesi siitä! *I'm ~* nyt lähden; *far ~* kaukana; *I'll take a day ~* pidän päivän vapaata; *an hour ~* tunnin vapaa-aika; *be well ~* olla hyvissä varoissa; *cut ~* katkaista; *declare ~* peruuttaa; *[the engagement] is ~* on purettu; *fall ~ the horse* pudota hevosen selästä; *finish ~* viimeistellä; *take ~* riisua; sulkea, sammuttaa; *[the meat is] a bit ~* hieman pahentunutta; *[just] ~ Piccadilly* aivan P:n lähistöllä; *a street ~ the Strand* S:lta poikkeava sivukatu.

offal [ˈɔf(ə)l] *s.* tähteet, roska, (teurastus)jätteet, sisälmykset.

offence [əˈfens] *s.* rikkomus, rike; loukkaus; *no ~ [meant]!* ei millään pahalla! älä suutu! en tarkoittanut mitään pahaa; *give ~* herättää pahennusta, loukata; *take ~* loukkaantua, panna pahakseen; *weapons of ~* hyökkäysaseet.

offend [əˈfend] *s.* loukata; uututtaa; rikkoa *(against jkt vastaan); be ~ed* loukkaantua. **-er** [-ə] *s.* rikoksentekijä.

offensive [əˈfensiv] *a.* hyökkäys-; loukkaava; vastenmielinen,

inhottava; *s.* hyökkäys; *~ weapons* hyökkäysaseet.

offer [ˈɔfə] *v.* tarjota, t. rjoutua, uhrata (m. *~ up);* esittää; yrittää; *s.* tarjous; *~ for sale* tarjota kaupaksi; *~ resistance* tehdä vastarintaa; *as occasion ~ s* tilaisuuden ilmaantuessa; *on ~* tarjolla, kaupan. **-ing** [ˈɔf(ə)riŋ] *s.* uhri. **-tory** [-t(ə)ri] *s.* uhrilahja.

off-hand [ˈɔ:fˈhænd] *adv.* valmistamatta, suoralta kädeltä; *a.* harkitsematon; siekailematon. **-ed** [-id] *a.* ks. ed.

office [ˈɔfis] *s.* virka; toimi, tehtävä; palvelus; toimisto, konttori; *pl.* talousrakennukset, keittiön puoli; *O~-ministeriö (Foreign ~, War ~); ~ hours* virka-aika; *by virtue of one's ~* viran puolesta; *be in ~* olla virassa; olla hallituksessa; *hold an ~* olla jssk virassa; *by the good ~ s of jkn* suosiollisella avulla. **~-block** toimistotalo. **~-boy** asiapoika.

officer [ˈɔfisə] *s.* virkamies, virkailija; upseeri; poliisikonstaapeli; *~s* (m.) päällystö.

official [əˈfiʃ(ə)l] *a.* virallinen, virka-; *s.* virkamies, virkailija. **-dom** [-dəm], **-ism** [-əlizm] *s.* virkavalta(isuus). **-ese** [əfiʃəˈliːz] *s.* (kankea) virastokieli.

offic|iate [əˈfiʃieit] *v.* toimittaa jumalanpalvelus, m. esim. vihkiminen; toimia jnak. **-ious** [-ʃəs] *a.* tungetteleva, turhantouhuisa, virkaintoinen.

off|ing [ˈɔfiŋ] *s.* ulappa; *in the ~* näkyvissä, tulossa. **-ish** [-iʃ] *a.* jäykkä, pidättyväinen.

off|-licence alkoholin myyntioikeus. **~-print** eripainos. **~-putting** hämmentävä. **~-scourings** hylkytavara, hylkiöt. **-set** *v.* korvata; *s.* vastapaino, vastike; offset-painanta; = seur. **-shoot** (juuri)vesa, verso. **~-shore** *~ islands* rannikkosaaret; *~ technology* meritekniikka. **-side** paitsio (urh.). **-spring** jälkeläinen, -set.

oft [ɔ:ft] *adv.* (run. ym) usein.

often [ˈɔ(:)fn] *adv.* usein, useasti; *it ~ rains here in April* täällä sataa usein huhtikuussa; *more ~ than not* useimmiten.

ogive [ˈoudʒaiv] *s.* suippokaari.

ogle ['əugl] v. katsoa rakastuneesti, »tuijottaa».

ogr|e ['əugjə] s. jättiläinen, ihmissyöjä **-ess** [-ris] s. syöjätär. **-ish** [-riʃ] a. hirvittävä.

oh [əu] int. oi! voi! ai!

Ohio [ə(u)'haiə(u)] erisn.

oil [ɔil] s. öljy; nafta; ~ s öljyvärit; v. öljytä, voidella öljyllä; strike ~ löytää öljylähde; ~ ed silk vahatafti. **~-cake** öljy-, rehukakku. **-cloth** vahakangas. **~-colours** öljyvärit. **~-field** öljykenttä. **~-rig** öljynporaus|torni, -lautta. **-skin** öljykangas; ~ s öljyvaatteet. **~-slick** öljylautta. **~-well** öljylähde. **-y** [-i] a. öljyinen, öljy-; rasvainen; liukas; liehakoitseva.

ointment ['ɔintmənt] s. voide.

OK ['əukei] vrt. seur. ja lyh.

okay ['əu'kei] (vrt. ed. ja lyh.) hyvä (on); v. hyväksyä.

Oklahoma [əuklə'həumə] erisn.

old [əuld] a. (komp. ~ er, ~ est ja elder, eldest) vanha, iäkäs; vanhanaikainen; (vanha ja) kokenut; three years ~ kolmen vuoden ikäinen; ~ age vanhuus; an ~ hand at vanha tekijä jssk; ~ maid ikäneito; the ~ man isäukko, ukko (aviomies); ~ fellow, ~ thing veikkoseni; ~ boy entinen oppilas; of ~ ennen muinoin. **-en** [-n] a.: in ~ times entisinä aikoina. **~-fashioned** vanhanaikainen. **-ish** [-iʃ] a. vanhahko. **~-timer** (kuv.) veteraani. **~-world** a. entisajan.

oleaginous [əuli'ædʒinəs] a. öljymäinen.

oleander [əuli'ændə] s. oleanteri.

oleograph ['əuliə(u)graː:f] s. öljypainos.

olfactory [əl'fæktəri] a. haju-.

oligarchy ['ɔligɑ:ki] s. harvainvalta.

olive ['ɔliv] s. öljypuu; oliivi; a. oliivinvärinen; ~ branch (kuv.) rauhanpalmu.

Olymp|ian [ɔ'limpiən] a. & s. olympolainen. **-ic** [-ik] a.: ~ games olympiakisat (m. the ~ s).

Omaha ['əuməhɑ:] erisn.

omelet(te) ['ɔmlit] s. munakas.

omen ['əumen] s. enne; v. ennustaa.

ominous ['ɔminəs] a. enteellinen, huonoenteinen.

omission [ə(u)'miʃn] s. poisjättäminen.

---

huomaamattomuus, laiminlyönti.

omit [ə(u)'mit] v. jättää pois, jättää tekemättä t. mainitsematta; laiminlyödä.

omnibus ['ɔmnibəs] s. linja-auto (tav. lyh. bus); ~ [volume] kokoomateos.

omni|potence [ɔm'ni|pɔt(ə)ns] s. kaikkivaltius. **-potent** [-pɔt(ə)nt] a. kaikkivaltias. **-present** [ɔmni'prez(ə)nt] a. kaikkialla läsnäoleva. **-science** [-siəns] s. kaikkitietävyys. **-scient** [-siənt] a. kaikkitietävä. **-vorous** [-v(ə)rəs] a. kaikkiruokainen.

on [ɔn] prep. ilm. paikkaa; jnk päällä, -lle, pinnalla, -lle; -lla, -llä, -lle, -ssa, -ssä; varrella; ilm. m. kohdetta, aikaa, tilaa ym; adv. yllä, ylle; edelleen, eteenpäin; ~ the Thames T:n varrella; march ~ the [enemy's] capital marssia pääkaupunkia kohti; shut one's door ~ sulkea ovensa jklta; write ~ . . . . kirjoittaa jstk aiheesta; a lecture ~ Japan J-ia käsittelevä esitelmä; ~ Tuesday tiistaina; ~ Sundays sunnuntaisin; ~ the 1st of April huhtikuun ensimmäisenä; ~ my arrival heti saavuttuani; ~ his advice hänen neuvostaan; live ~ elää jstk; ~ fire tulessa; blow ~ blow iskua toisensa jälkeen; be ~ olla käynnissä, (teatterin) ohjelmana ym; [the lights are] ~ palavat; he left the tap ~ jätti vesihanan auki; have ~ olla yllä; from that day ~ siitä päivästä eteenpäin; even ten years ~ vielä 10 vuoden perästä; ~ and off aika ajoittain, silloin tällöin; ~ and ~ keskeytymättä; ~ to johonkin, jnk päälle, (puhek.) jyvällä jksta, jtk; [he leapt] ~ to his horse hevosensa selkään; what's ~ [this afternoon]? mitä ohjelmaa on . . .?

once [wʌns] adv. kerran; aikoinaan, ennen; konj. niin pian kuin, kun vain; ~ more, ~ again kerran vielä; ~ (and) for all kerta kaikkiaan, lopullisesti, tämän ainoan kerran; in a while, ~ and again silloin tällöin, aika ajoin; ~ or twice kerran tai pari; ~ a day kerran päivässä; ~ upon a time there was . . . olipa kerran . . .; at ~ heti; yhdellä kertaa, samalla; all at ~ yhtäkkiä; for ~ tällä kertaa,

kerrankin; *this* ~ tämän ainoan
kerran.
oncoming *a.* lähestyvä.
one [wʌn] *lukus.* yksi; *pron.* jonkin,
joku, eräs; ainoa; toinen (kahdesta);
us. epämääräisenä subjektina (~
never can tell ei voi koskaan tietää);
that's not the ~ I mean tuo ei ole se,
jota tarkoitan; [*yours may be the right
answer] and mine the wrong* ~ ja
minun väärä; ~ *day* eräänä päivänä;
~ *and all* jokainen, kaikki; ~ *after
another* toinen toisensa jälkeen; ~
another toisiaan; ~ . . . *the other*
toinen . . . toinen; ~ *at a time* yksi
kerrallaan; ~ *by* ~ yksitellen; *the last
but* ~ viimeisen edellinen; *at* ~ yhtä
mieltä, sovussa; *it is all* ~ *to me* se on
minulle yhdentekevää; *I for* ~ minä
puolestani; *for* ~ *thing* ensinnäkin; *be
~ up* (*on sb.*) olla jkta hieman edellä
t. parempi (*s. one-upmanship*). ~
-eyed silmäpuoli. **-ness** *s.* ykseys.
O'Neill [ə(u)'ni:l] *erisn.*
onerous ['ɔnərəs] *a.* rasittava, raskas.
one|self [wʌn'self] *pron.* itse;
itse(änsä); *be* ~ olla oma itsensä;
defend ~ puolustautua; [*one should't
live*] *for* ~ *alone* vain itsel neen.
~-sided yksipuolinen. **~-time**
entinen. **~-track** yksiraiteinen; (kuv.)
rajoitettu. **~-way** yksisuuntainen
(liikenne).
onion ['ʌnjən] *s.* sipuli.
onlooker ['ɔnlukə] *s.* katselija.
only ['əunli] *a.* ainoa; *adv.* ainoastaan,
vain; *vasta;* *konj.* mutta; *if* ~ kunpa!
kunhan vain; ~ *yesterday* vasta eilen;
~ *too glad* erittäin iloinen.
onomatopoeic [ɔnəmətə'pi:ik] *a.*
(luonnon) ääntä jäljittelevä.
on|rush ['ɔnrʌʃ] *s.* rynnistys, tulva. **-set**
[-set] *s.* hyökkäys; alku. **-slaught**
[-slɔ:t] *s.* ankara hyökkäys.
Ontario [ɔn'teəriəu] *erisn.*
onto ['ɔntu, 'ɔntə] *prep.* johonkin, jnk
päälle (= *on to*).
onus ['əunəs] *s.* velvollisuus, vastuu.
onward ['ɔnwəd] *a.* etenevä; *adv.* (m.
~ *s*) eteenpäin.
onyx ['ɔniks] *s.* onyks (kivi).
oodles ['u:dlz] *s. pl.:* ~ *of* massoittain.
oof [u:f] *s.* sl. raha(t).
oomph [u:mf] *s.* puhti; hemaisevuus,

seksikkyys.
ooz|e [u:z] *s.* lieju, muta; *v.* tihkua,
vuotaa (*away* kuiviin). **-y** [-i] *a.*
liejuinen.
opacity [ə(u)'pæsiti] *s.*
läpikuultamattomuus; samennus.
opal ['əup(ə)l] *s.* opaali (miner.).
-escent [-'lesnt] *a.* opaalinhohtoinen,
läikehtivä.
opaque [ə(u)'peik] *a.* läpikuultamaton;
samea.
open ['əupn] *a.* avonainen, avoin;
avoinna, auki, aukinainen; aukea;
vapaa, esteetön, suojaton;
vastaanottavainen, altis, alttiina (*to
jllek*); ratkaisematon; vilpitön; *v.*
avata; aloittaa; avautua, aueta; alkaa;
in the ~ *air* ulkoilmassa, taivasalla; *an*
~ *city* avoin kaupunki; *with* ~ *hands*
avoimin käsin; *an* ~ *question*
ratkaisematon kysymys; ~ *winter*
leuto talvi; ~ *spaces* puistikot,
puistot; ~ *to doubt, to question*
epäilyksen-, kyseenalainen; *come into
the* ~ paljastaa (aikeensa ym); *lay* ~
paljastaa, vrt. *lay;* ~ *out* avata,
avautua; ~ *up* avata, raivata; *the
window* ~ *s on to . . .* ikkunasta on
näköala (jhk). ~ **-air** ulkoilma-.
~ **-cast** avo- (*o.-c. mine*). **-er** [-ə] *s.:*
tin- ~ säilykerasian avaaja. **-eyed**
avoimin silmin; valpas. ~ **-handed**
avokätinen, antelias. ~ **-hearted**
avomielinen, sydämellinen. **-ing** *s.*
aukko; avajaiset; tilaisuus,
mahdollisuus; avaus. **-ly** *adv.*
avoimesti, suoraan. ~ **-minded**
ennakkoluuloton, avoin. **-ness**
avonaisuus; avoimuus. ~ **-work**
reikäommel.
opera ['ɔpərə] *s.* ooppera.
operable ['ɔp(ə)rəbl] *a.*
leikkauskelpoinen.
opera-glass(es) teatterikiikari. ~ **-hat**
(kokoon painettava) silinteri.
operate ['ɔpəreit] *v.* olla käynnissä,
toimia, vaikuttaa; leikata (lääk.);
käyttää (konetta); suorittaa
sotatoimia; ~ *on* leikata jku;
operating theatre leikkaussali.
operatic [ɔpə'rætik] *a.* ooppera-.
operat|ion [ɔpə'reiʃn] *s.* toiminta;
leikkaus (lääk.); sotatoimi, operaatio;
liiketoimi; *be in* ~ toimia; *in full* ~

täydessä käynnissä; (~-al [-ənl] a. käyttö; käyttövalmis). -ive ['ɔp(ə)rətiv] a. toimiva, vaikuttava, tehokas; käytännöllinen; leikkaus-; s. (tehdas)työläinen; *become* ~ astua voimaan. -or [-ə] s. koneenhoitaja; kirurgi; *telephone* ~ puhelinvälittäjä; *wireless* ~ radiosähköttäjä.

operetta [ɔpə'retə] s. operetti.

ophthalmologist [ɔfθæl'mɔlədʒist] s. silmälääkäri.

opiate ['əupiət] s. oopiumipitoinen aine, nukutusaine.

opine [ə(u)'pain] v.: ~ *that* olla sitä mieltä (että).

opinion [ə'pinjən] s. mielipide; käsitys; lausunto; *public* ~ julkinen mielipide; *in my* ~ minun mielestäni; *be of the* ~ *that* olla sitä mieltä, että; ~ *poll* mielipidetutkimus. **-ated** [-eitid] a. omapäinen.

opium ['əupjəm] s. oopiumi.

opossum [ə'pɔsəm] s. amerikkal. pussirotta (m. *possum*).

opponent [ə'pəunənt] s. vastustaja, vastaväittäjä.

opportun|e [ə'pɔtjuːn] a. sopiva, otollinen. **-ism** [-izm] s. opportunismi (pol.). **-ity** [ɔpə'tjuːniti] s. (sopiva) tilaisuus; pl. m. mahdollisuudet; *take (avail oneself of) the* ~ käyttää tilaisuutta hyväkseen.

oppose [ə'pəuz] v. asettaa vastaan, jnk vastakohdaksi; vastustaa; *be* ~d *to* olla jtk vastaan, vastustaa.

opposi|te ['ɔpəzit] a. vastakkainen, päinvastainen; vastapäätä (oleva); s. vastakohta; ~ *number* (vastaavassa asemassa oleva) virkaveli, kollega. **-tion** [ɔpə'ziʃn] s. vastakkaisuus, vastakkainen asema; vastustus, vastarinta; (pol.) oppositio(puolue).

oppress [ə'pres] v. sortaa; painaa (maahan), ahdistaa. **-ion** [ə'preʃn] s. sorto; paine, rasitus, ahdistus, masennus. **-ive** [-iv] a. painostava; tyrannimainen, sorto-. **-or** [-ə] s. sortaja.

opprobri|ous [ə'prəubri|əs] a. herjaava, häväistys-; häpeällinen. **-um** [-əm] s. häpeä, häväistys.

opt [ɔpt] v.: ~ *for* valita jtk; ~ *out* (puhek.) kieltäytyä.

optic ['ɔptik] a. optinen; näkö; ~ *nerve*

näköhermo. **-al** [-(ə)l] a. optinen; ~ *illusion* näköharha. **-ian** [ɔp'tiʃn] a. optikko. **-s** [-s] s. pl. optiikka, valo-oppi.

optim|ism ['ɔptimizm] s. optimismi. **-ist** [-ist] s. optimisti. **-istic** [-'mistik] a. optimistinen. **-um** [-əm] a. & s. paras, suotuisin (m. *optimal*).

option ['ɔpʃn] s. vapaus valita, valinnanvara; etuosto- (t.) myynti)oikeus; *I had no* ~ minulla ei ollut valinnan varaa; *local* ~ kunnallinen itsemääräämisoikeus. **-al** [-l] a. valinnainen, vapaaehtoinen.

opul|ence ['ɔpjuləns] s. rikkaus, äveriäisuus. **-ent** [-ənt] a. rikas, äveriäs; runsas, upea.

or [ɔː] *konj.* tai; eli; vai; ~ *else* tai muuten; *twenty* ~ *so* parikymmentä.

orac|le ['ɔrəkl] s. oraakkeli; viisas vastaus. **-ular** [ɔ'rækjulə] a. oraakkelimainen; salaperäinen, hämärä.

oral ['ɔːr(ə)l] a. suu(n)-; suullinen. **-ly** ['ɔːrəli] a. suullisesti; suun kautta.

Orange ['ɔrin(d)ʒ] *erisn.* Orania; ~ *Free State* Oranjen vapaavaltio. **-man** (Pohj. Irl.) protestanttisen salaseuran jäsen.

orange ['ɔrin(d)ʒ] s. & a. appelsiini, -puu; oranssinvärinen, ~-*blossom* oranssinkukka. **-ade** [-'eid] s. appelsiinijuoma, -limonaati.

orang-outang [ɔ'ræŋuˈtæŋ] s. oranki (m. -*utan*, -*outan*).

ora|te [ɔː'reit] v. paasata, saarnata (leik.). **-tion** [ɔː'reiʃn] s. (juhlallinen) puhe; (suora, epäsuora) esitys.

orator ['ɔrətə] s. (kauno)puhuja. **-ical** [ɔrə'tɔrik(ə)l] a. puhetaidollinen. **-io** [ɔrə'tɔːriəu] a. oratorio (mus.). **-y** [-(ə)ri] s. puhetaito, kaunopuheisuus.

orb [ɔːb] s. pallo; taivaankappale; valtakunnanomena; ~-*ed* pyöreä. **-it** [-it] s. rata (avaruudessa); kierros; silmäkuoppa; v. kiertää rataansa; *in* ~ radallaan; *go into* ~ asettua radalleen (avaruudessa).

orchard ['ɔːtʃəd] s. hedelmätarha.

orchestra ['ɔːkistrə] s. orkesteri; orkesterisyvennys (m. ~ *pit*). **-al** [ɔː'kestr(ə)l] a. orkesteri-. **-ate** [-eit] v. sovittaa orkesterille. **-ation** [-'treiʃn] a. orkesterointi.

orchid ['ɔ:kid] *s.* orkidea, kämmekkä.
ordain [ɔ:'dein] *v.* vihkiä papiksi;
säätää.
ordeal [ɔ:'di:l] *s.* tulikoe, koetus.
order ['ɔ:də] *s.* järjestys;
päiväjärjestys; käsky, määräys; tilaus,
(maksu)osoitus; (suuruus)luokka,
aste; ritarikunta, veljeskunta; ritari-,
kunniamerkki; (kasv. ym) lahko; *v.*
käskeä, määrätä, antaa käsky; tilata;
~ *of battle* taisteluryhmitys; ~ *of the
day* päiväkäsky; *by* ~ *of* jnk
määräysten mukaisesti; *in* ~
kunnossa, järjestyksessä; *[is] in* ~
(m.) paikallaan; *in* ~ *that* jotta; *in* ~
to learn oppiakseen, -eni, -esi jne.,
oppimaan; *in* ~ *of size*
suuruusjärjestyksessä; *on* ~
tilattu(na), tilauksessa; *on the* ~*s of*
jnk käskystä; *out of* ~ epäkunnossa;
keep ~ pitää yllä järjestystä; *made to*
~ tilauksesta tehty; *money* ~
postiosoitus; *holy* ~*s* hengellinen
sääty; *he took holy* ~*s* hänet vihittiin
papiksi; ~ *sb. about* komennella jkta.
-liness [(hyvä) järjestys,
säännöllisyys.
orderly ['ɔ:dəli] *a.* järjestyksessä oleva,
siisti, järjestystä rakastava,
säntillinen; *s.* lähetti (sot.); ~ *officer*
päivystävä upseeri; *medical* ~
lääkintämies.
ordinal ['ɔ:dinl] *a. & s.* järjestys(luku).
ordinance ['ɔ:dinəns] *s.* määräys,
sääntö, säännös.
ordin|ary ['ɔ:dinri] *a.* tavallinen;
jokapäiväinen, arki-; vakinainen; *out
of the* ~ epätavallinen, tavallisuudesta
poikkeava(a); *physician in* ~ *to the
King* kuninkaan henkilääkäri; ~
seaman puolimatruusi; *-arily*
tavallisesti. **-ation** [-'neiʃn] *s.*
papiksivihkiminen.
ordnance ['ɔ:dnəns] *s.* tykistö; [*Army*]
O~ *Deparment* taisteluvälineosasto;
O~ *Survey map* topografikartta.
ordure [ɔ:'djuə] *s.* lanta.
ore [ɔ:] *s.* malmi.
oregano [ə'regənəu] *s.* oregano
(mauste).
Oregon ['ɔrigən] *erisn.*
organ ['ɔ:gən] *s.* urut; elin;
äänenkannattaja; väline; *mouth* ~
huuliharppu; *barrel* ~ posetiivi.

~**-blower** urkujenpolkija. ~**-grinder**
posetiivinsoittaja.
organ|die, -y ['ɔ:gəndi] *s.* organdi.
organ|ic [ɔ:'gænik] *a.* elimellinen;
orgaaninen. **-ism** ['ɔ:gənizm] *s.*
elimistö, organismi. **-ist** ['ɔ:gənist] *s.*
urkuri. **-ization** [ɔ:gənai'zeiʃn, Am.
-ni'z-] *s.* järjestely, organisointi;
järjestö; organisaatio. **-ize**
['ɔ:gənaiz] *v.* järjestää,
org| nisoida; järjestäytyä.
organ-**loft** urkulehteri. ~**-stop**
urkurekisteri.
orgy ['ɔ:dʒi] *s.* juomingit, orgiat.
oriel ['ɔ:riəl] *s.* ulokeikkuna.
orient ['ɔ:riənt] *s.: the* O~ itämaat; *v.*
['ɔ:rient] ks. *orientate*. **-al** [ɔ:ri'entl] *a.*
itämainen; *s.* itämaalainen. **-alist**
[ɔ:ri'entəlist] *s.* itämaiden kielten ja
kirjallisuuden tutkija. **-ate** ['ɔ:rienteit]
v. määrätä jnk asema; ~ *oneself*
orientoitua, suunnistautua; ~*d
towards* jhk päin suuntautunut,
asennoitunut. **-ation** [ɔ:rien'teiʃn] *s.*
orientoiminen, suunnistautuminen.
-eering [-'tiəriŋ] *s.* (urh.) suunnistus.
orifice ['ɔrifis] *s.* aukko, suu.
origin ['ɔridʒin] *s.* alkuperä; alkulähde,
alku, synty. **-al** [ə'ridʒənl] *a.*
alkuperäinen; omaperäinen,
omintakeinen; *s.* alkuperäisteos t.
-kappale, alkuteksti, omalaatuinen
ihminen, tyyppi, originaali; ~ *sin*
perisynti; *in the* ~ alkukielellä. **-ality**
[əridʒi'næliti] *s.* alkuperäisyys;
omintakeisuus; omalaatuisuus. **-ally**
[ə'ridʒnəli] *adv.* alkuaan, aluksi;
omintakeisesti.
origina|te [ə'ridʒineit] *v.* saada
alkunsa, olla peräisin t. lähtöisin (*in,
from* jstk); panna alulle, alkaa. **-tor**
[-ə] *s.* alkuunpanija.
oriole ['ɔ:riəul] *s.* kuhankeittäjä
(eläint.).
Orion [ə'raiən] *erisn.*
orlop ['ɔ:lɔp] *s.* ruumakansi.
ormolu ['ɔ:məlu:] *s.* kultapronssi (ym).
ornament ['ɔ:nəmənt] *s.* koriste,
koristus; *v.* [-ment] koristaa,
koristella. **-al** [-'mentl] *a.*
koristeellinen, koriste-, koru-. **-ation**
[-men'teiʃn] *s.* koristelu.
ornate [ɔ:'neit] *a.* koristeltu, koru-; ~
language (m.) kukkaskieli.

ornitho|logist [ɔ:ni'θɔlədʒist] s. ornitologi. **-logy** [-lədʒi] s. lintutiede, ornitologia.

orphan ['ɔ:f(ə)n] a. & s. orpo; v. : be ~ed jäädä orvoksi. **-age** [-idʒ] s. orpokoti.

Orpheus ['ɔ:fju:s] erisn. Orfeus.

orris ['ɔris] s. : ~-root orvokinjuuri.

orthodox ['ɔ:θədɔks] a. oikeaoppinen; the O~ Church ortodoksinen kirkko. **-y** [-i] s. oikeaoppisuus.

ortho|graphic [ɔ:θə'græfik] a. oikeinkirjoitus-. **-graphy** [ɔ:'θɔgrəfi] s. oikeinkirjoitus. **-p(a)edic** [ɔ:θə(u)'pi:dik] a. ortopedinen.

oscilla|te ['ɔsileit] v. heilahdella; värähdellä. **-tion** [-'leiʃn] s. heilahdus; värähtely.

osier ['əuʒə] s. koripaju.

osprey ['ɔspri] s. (kala)sääksi, kalasääski.

oss|eous ['ɔsiəs] a. luu-. **-ification** [ɔsifi'keiʃn] s. luutuminen. **-ify** ['ɔsifai] v. luutua, luuduttaa; kovettua, piintyä.

ostensib|le [ɔs'tensəbl] a. näennäinen; -ly näön vuoksi.

ostenta|tion [ɔsten'teiʃn] s. pröystäily. **-tious** [-ʃəs] a. komeileva, pöyhkeilevä.

osteopath ['ɔstiəpæθ] s. osteopaatti.

ostler ['ɔslə] s. tallirenki.

ostrac|ism ['ɔstrəsizm] a. sulkeminen seurapiiristä. **-ize** [-saiz] v. sulkea seurapiiristä (yhteiskunnasta); (vanh.) karkottaa maasta.

ostrich ['ɔstritʃ] s. strutsi.

Othello [ɔ(u)'θeləu] erisn.

other ['ʌðə] pron. toinen, muu; s. toinen; (the) ~s toiset, muut; ~ people toiset ihmiset; [please,] let me see some ~s näyttäkää minulle joitakin muita; the ~ day tässä eräänä päivänä, äskettäin; every ~ joka toinen; someone or ~ joku; some time or ~ vielä joskus; one...the ~ toinen...toinen; on the ~ hand toisaalta; on the ~ side of jnk toisella puolella; the ~ way about aivan päinvastoin; among ~s muitten muassa, mm. **-wise** adv. toisin; muussa suhteessa, muutoin; the merits or ~ edut tai haitat.

otiose ['əuʃiəus] a. tarpeeton,

toimeton.

otitis [ə(u)'taitis] s. (keski)korvantulehdus.

otologist [ə(u)'tɔlədʒist] s. korvalääkäri.

Ottawa ['ɔtəwə] erisn.

otter ['ɔtə] s. saukko.

Ottoman ['ɔtəmən] s. & a. turkkilainen; o~ leposohva.

ought [ɔ:t] apuv. pitäisi; I ~ to go minun pitäisi mennä; he oughtn't hänen ei pitäisi, hän ei saisi...; vrt. aught.

ounce [auns] s. unssi.

our ['auə] pron. meidän, -mme. **-s** [-z] pron. (subst. muoto) meidän; a friend of ~ eräs ystävämme. **-selves** ['-'selvz] pron. (me) itse; itsemme, itseämme; [we want to see it] for ~ omin silmin; all by ~ yksinämme, keskenämme.

oust [aust] v. karkottaa, syrjäyttää; ~ sb. of riistää jklta jtk.

out [aut] adv. ulkona, ulos; poissa, pois; julkisuudessa; ilmi; puhjennut, ilmestynyt; lakossa; poissa muodista; lopussa, loppuun; sammunut; prep.: ~ of ulos, esiin jstk; ulkopuolella; poissa jstk; -sta, -stä; a. ulko-; interj. ulos! s.: the ins and ~s mutkat, yksityiskohdat; ~ there siellä ulkona: ~ and about jalkeilla; ~ and away verrattomasti; ~ and out läpeensä; be ~ m. erehtyä; the estimate was ~ by.. arviossa oli ..n erehdys; [one] ~ of ten yksi kymmenestä; ~ of doors ulkosalla; ~ of pity säälistä; ~ of work työtön; we are ~ of sugar sokerimme on loppunut; be ~ for sth. haluta, tavoitella; be ~ to aikoa, pyrkiä; cut it ~ lopeta jo! ~ with it! suu puhtaaksi! have it ~ with selvittää asiansa jkn kanssa; hear sb. ~ kuunnella loppuun saakka; put ~ sammuttaa; be put ~ (by) häiriintyä, joutua pois tolaltaan (jnk johdosta); her Sunday ~ hänen vapaasunnuntainsa; now it is ~ nyt se on sanottu; [you are] not far ~ melkein oikeahan; tired ~ lopen uupunut.

out- pref. verbiin liitettynä ilm. us. toiminnan ylittämistä. (Verbeissä ensi tavu painoton, muuten painollinen.) **~-and-out** täydellinen, kertakaikkinen. **-back** (austr.)

asumaton sydänmaa, takamaat.
-balance painaa enemmän kuin. **-bid**
tarjota enemmän kuin. **-board** perä-.
-break syttyminen,
puhkeaminen. **-building**
ulkorakennus. **-burst** purkaus,
puuska. **-cast** *a.* hylätty; *s.* hylkiö.
-caste *s.* kastiton. **-class** voittaa
yliviomaisesti. **-come** tulos, seuraus.
-crop *s.* (kallion, malmin) paljastuma.
-cry huuto, hälinä. **-dated**
vanhanaikainen, vanhentunut.
-distance jättää (kilpailussa)
taakseen. **-do** voittaa, viedä voitto
jksta, ylittää. **-door** *a.* ulkoilma-;
avo-. **-doors** *adv.* ulkona,
ulkoilۇ assa, ulos.

outer ['autə] *a.* ulompi, ulko-; ~ *space*
ulkoavaruus. **-most** *a.* ulommainen,
uloin.

out|**face** *v.* saattaa hämilleen; uhmata.
-fall (joen) suu. **-fit** varusteet, puvut;
Am. ryhmä, joukkue; *bride's* ~
kapiot. **-fitter** *s.*: *gentlemen's* ~
miesten pukimo. **-flank** saartaa (sot.);
~ *movement* saartoliike. **-flow** *s.*
virta, (kuv.) tulva. **-going** *a.* lähtevä;
~*s* menot. **-grow** kasvaa jtk
suuremmaksi; ~ *a habit* päästä jstk
tavasta; *she has* ~*n this dress* tämä
puku on käynyt hänelle liian pieneksi.
-growth kasvannainen. **-herod** *v.*
voittaa julmuudessa. **-house**
ulkorakennus. **-ing** *s.* (huvi)retki.
-landish ulkomainen, vieras, outo.
-last kestää kauemmin kuin. **-law** *s.*
henkipatto; *v.* julistaa
lainsuojattomaksi. **-lawry**
lainsuojattomuus. **-lay** kustannukset.
-let ulospääsy; suu, laskukohta;
(kuv.) purkautumistie. **-line** *s.*
ääriviiva(t); luonnos; pääpiirteet,
yleiskatsaus; *v.* hahmotella. **-live** elää
kauemmin kuin. **-look** näköala,
näkymä; tulevaisuudennäkymä(t);
asenne, ajattelutapa; *further* ~
(säännuste) odotettavissa; *outlook on
life* elämänkatsomus. **-lying** syrjäinen.
-manoeuvre, Am. *-maneuver* toimia
taitavammin, olla ovelampi kuin.
-match voittaa. **-moded**
vanhanaikainen. **-number** olla (jtk)
lukuisampi. ~-**of-date** vanhentunut.
~-**of-door** *ks. outdoor.* ~-**of-the-way**

syrjäinen. ~-**patient** avohoito-,
poliklinikkapotilas. **-post** etuvartio.
-pouring vuodatus. **-put** *s.* tuotanto,
tuotos; teho; (ATK) tulostus.
outrage ['autreidʒ] *s.* väkivalta(isuus);
törkeä loukkaus, rikos (esim.
ihmisyyttä vastaan); *v.* tehdä
väkivaltaa, törkeästi loukata; *bomb* ~
pommiattentaatti. **-outs** [aut'reidʒəs]
a. törkeä, loukkaava, häpeällinen.
outre ['u:trei] *a.* säädytön.
out|**rider** esiratsastaja. **-rigger**
pönkkäpuomi (mer.). **-right** *adv.*
suoraan, avoimesti; suoraa päätä, heti
paikalla; kerta kaikkiaan,
kauttaaltaan, kokonaan; *a.* ['- -]
täydellinen; (aivan) selvä. **-rival**
syrjäyttää. **-run** voittaa (nopeudessa),
ylittää. **-set** alku; *at the* ~ alussa.
-shine himmentää loistollaan.
outside ['aut'said] *s.* ulkopuoli, -kuori,
pinta; *a.* ulkopuolinen, ulkonainen,
ulko-; *adv.* ulkopuolella, -lle, ulkona,
ulos; *at the* [*very*] ~ enintään; ~ *of* jnk
ulkopuolella; (puhek., et. Am.)
lukuunottamatta, paitsi; ~ *broadcast*
ulkolähetys (TV, rad.); *an* ~ *estimate*
korkein mahdollinen arvio. **-r** [-ə] *s.*
sivullinen, ulkopuolinen.
out|**size** *a.* normaalia isompi (koko).
-skirts *s. pl.* (kaupungin) liepeet,
laitaosat; *on the* ~ [*of the town*]
laidoilla. **-smart** voittaa viekkaudessa.
-spoken suorasukainen. **-spread**
levitetty. **-standing** *a.* huomattava;
silmiinpistävä; maksamaton. **-stay** *v.*:
~ *one's welcome* viipyä (vierailulla)
liian kauan. **-stretched** ojennettu;
pitkällään; *with arms* ~ käsivarret
ojossa. **-strip** voittaa, ylittää,
sivuuttaa. **-vote** *v.*: . . . *was*
~*d*. . . äänestettiin kumoon.
outward ['autwəd] *a.* ulko-, ulkoinen,
ulkonainen; *adv.* ulospäin; ~-*bound*
matkalla vieraan maan satamaan. **-ly**
adv. ulkonaisesti. **-s** [-z] *adv.*
ulos(päin).
out|**wear** kestää kauemmin kuin.
-weigh painaa vaa'assa enemmän
kuin. **-wit** olla (toista) ovelampi.
-work *s.* ulkovarustus. **-worn** (kuv.)
kulunut.
ouzel ['u:zl] mustarastas.
ova ['əuvə] *s. pl. ks. ovum.* **-l** [-(ə)l]

a. soikea; *s.* soikio. **-ry** [-əri] *s.*
munasarja.

ovation [ə(u)'veiʃn] *s.* myrskyisä
suosionosoitus.

oven ['ʌvn] *s.* (leivin)uuni; ~*proof dish*
tulenkestävä vuoka.

over ['əuvə] *prep. & adv.* yläpuolella,
-lle; päällä, -lle; yli; *adv.* m. läpi;
uudelleen, jäljellä; ohi, lopussa;
(adj:n ed.) ylen, kovin; ~ *and above*
lisäksi; ~ *again* vielä kerran,
uudelleen; ~ *and* ~ *again* kerran
toisensa jälkeen; ~ *against* jtk
vastassa, vastakohtana; ~ *much*
liiaksi; ~ *there* tuolla; ~ *a cup of tea*
teekupposen ääressä; *knock* ~ iskeä
kumoon; *show sb.* ~ *the house* näyttää
jklle talonsa; *think it* ~ miettiä asiaa;
turn ~ kääntää, kääntyä toiselle
kyljelleen; *all* ~ kauttaaltaan,
ylt'yleensä; *all* ~ *Europe* kaikkialla
Euroopassa; *it's all* ~ *with him* hän on
mennyttä; [*that's*] *Smith all* ~ aivan
Smithin kaltaista; *what remains* ~
ylijäämä, tähteet; *Over! Over to you!*
(rad.) kuuntelen!

over- [əuvə] *pref.* yli-, liika. (Paino
jälkimmäisellä osalla, milloin ei ole
toisin merkitty.) **-act** liioitella (osassa
ym). **-all** ['əuvɔːl] *a.* kokonais-,
yleinen; *s.* työtakki; ~*s* suojapuku,
haalarit. **-awe** masentaa, pelottaa; ~*d*
pelon lamauttama. **-balance** menettää
tasapainonsa, horjahtaa; kaataa; olla
jtk suurempi. **-bear** musertaa, voittaa.
-bearing *a.* käskevä, mahtava,
määräilevä. **-bid** tarjota liian paljon
(t. enemmän kuin). **-blown** (kukasta)
liiaksi auennut, lakastumaisillaan.
-board ['əuvəbɔːd] *adv.* yli laidan.
-burden *v.* rasittaa liikaa. **-cast** *a.*
pilvessä. **-charge** *v.* ylikuormittaa;
vaatia liian suuri hinta; *s.* ['- -]
ylihinta. **-cloud** peittää pilveen. **-coat**
['əuvəkəut] päällystakki. **-come** *v.*
voittaa; ... *was* ~ *by weariness*
(hänet) valtasi väsymys. **-crowd** *v.:*
~*ed* tungokseen asti täynnä,
täpötäysi; ~*ing* liikakansoitus,
tilanahtaus. **-do** liioitella; ~*done* liiaksi
keitetty t. paistunut; ~ *it* mennä
liiallisuuksiin, rasittaa itseään liikaa.
-dose ['əuvə'dəus] *s.* liika-annos(tus).
-draft ['əuvədrɑːft] *s.* pankkitilin

ylitys. **-draw** *v.:* ~ *one's account*
ylittää tilinsä. **-dress** pukeutua liian
koreilevasti. **-due** *a.* myöhästynyt,
myöhässä; erääntynyt. **-eat** syödä
liikaa. ~**-estimate** yliarvioida.
~**-exertion** liikarasitus. ~**-exposure**
liikavalotus (valok.). **-flow** *v.* tulvia
(jnk) yli; olla tulvillaan, uhkua
(*with* jtk); *s.* ['- -] tulva; liika
(väestö). **-flowing** *a.* ylitsevuotava.
-grown *a.* (jnk) peittämä; liian pitkä
ikäisekseen. **-hand** ['- -] *a.* yli olan
(löyty). **-hang** riippua, ulottua yli;
uhata; ~*ing* alava. **-haul** *v.*
tarkastaa perin pohjin, läpikäydä; *s.*
['- -] tutkimus. **-head** ['əuvə'hed] *adv.*
pään yläpuolella, taivaalla; ilma-; ~
[*costs*] yleiskustannukset. **-hear** sattua
kuulemaan. **-indulge** käyttää (*in* jtk)
liikaa; hemmotella liikaa. **-joyed** *a.*
suunniltaan ilosta (oleva). **-land** ['- -]
adv. maitse. **-lap** *v.* peittää osittain,
sattua (osaksi) yhteen, mennä ristiin;
~*ping* limittäin oleva. **-leaf** *adv.*
seuraavalla sivulla. **-load**
ylikuormittaa; *s.* ['- -] ylikuormitus.

overlook *v.* ei huomata; antaa
anteeksi, olla välittämättä; pitää
silmällä; *his window* ~*s the garden*
hänen ikkunastaan on näköala
puutarhaan; *I* ~*ed it* se jäi minulta
huomaamatta.

over|lord ['- -] *s.* valtaherra. **-ly**
['əuvəli] *adv.* (Am. & Skotl.) liiaksi.
-mastering *a.* ylivoimainen, hillitön.
-much ['- -] *adv.* (aivan) liikaa. **-night**
adv. yli yön, yhdessä yössä. **-pass**
ylikulkusilta. **-pay** maksaa liikaa jklle.
-power saada valtaansa, vallata;
voittaa, kukistaa; ~*ing* musertava,
valtava. **-production** liikatuotanto.
-rate yliarvioida. **-reach** *v.* puijata; ~
oneself karkottaa liian korkealle t.
kauas. **-ride** valittaa vähät jstk;
kumota. **-riding** ensiarvoinen,
kaikkivoittava. **-rule** kumota. **-run**
levitä, tulvia jnk yli, olla jnk
vitsauksena; ylittää (aika). **-sea(s)**
['- -] *a.* merentakainen; *adv.* meren
takana. **-seer** ['əuvəsiːə] työnjohtaja,
valvoja. **-shadow** varjostaa, saattaa
varjoon. **-shoe** ['əuvəʃuː]
päällyskenkä, kalossi. **-shoot** *v.:* ~ *the
mark* (kuv.) ampua yli. **-sight**

['ouvəsait] s. (tarkkaamattomuudesta johtunut) erehdys, huolimattomuus; valvonta, silmälläpito *(under the ~ of)*. **-sleep** nukkua liian kauan. **-spill** liikaväestö. **-state** liioitella. **-statement** s. ylisanat, ylisanojen käyttö. **-stay** v.: ~ *one's time* viipyä yli ajan. **-step** ylittää. **-stock** hankkia liian suuri varasto. **-strain** ['- '-] v. rasittaa liikaa; s. liikarasitus.

overt ['əuvə:t] a. avoin, julkinen.

over|take tavoittaa, (autosta) ohittaa; yllättää. **-tax** ['- '-] rasittaa liikaa; verottaa liikaa. **-throw** v. kaataa (kumoon), kukistaa, tehdä loppu jstk; s. ['- -] kukistuminen, tuho. **-time** a. ylityö; ~ *work* ~ tehdä ylitöitä.

overture ['əuvətjuə] s. (us. *pl.*) tunnustelu(t); (mus.) alkusoitto; *peace* ~ s rauhantunnustelut.

over|turn kaataa kumoon; kaatua, mennä kumoon. **-value** yliarvioida. **-weening** a. omahyväinen, ylimielinen. **-weight** ['- '-] liikapaino. **-whelm** v. hukuttaa alleen; vallata kokonaan, musertaa; ~ *ed by grief* menehtymäisillään suruun; ~ *ing* valtava, musertava. **-work** ['- '-] v. teettää t. tehdä liikaa työtä; s. liikarasitus. **-wrought** ['-'rɔ:t] a. liiaksi rasittunut t. kiihottunut, pingottunut.

Ovid ['ɔvid] *erisn*. Ovidius.

ov|iduct ['əuv|idʌkt] s. munanjohdin. **-oid** [-ɔid] a. munanmuotoinen. **-um** [-əm] s. (pl. *ova)* muna.

owe [əu] v. olla velkaa; olla kiitollisuuden velassa, saada kiittää *(sb, sth.* jkta jstk).

Owen ['ə(u)in] *erisn*.

owing ['əuiŋ] a. velkana oleva, maksamatta (oleva); ~ *to* jnk johdosta, vuoksi, takia.

owl [aul] s. pöllö. **-ish** [-iʃ] a. juhlallisen näköinen.

own [əun] a. oma; v. omistaa; tunnustaa omakseen; tunnustaa, myöntää; *he has a house of his* ~ hänellä on oma talo; *hold one's* ~ pitää puoliaan; *come into one's* ~ saada (ansaitsemansa) tunnustus; *get one's* ~ *back* maksaa samalla mitalla; *on one's* ~ omin päin, omin avuin (t. neuvoin), yksin, itse; *be on one's* ~ olla riippumaton; [*may I have it] for my very* ~ ikiomakseni; ~ *up to* tunnustaa. **-er** [-ə] s. omistaja. **-ership** s. omistus, omistusoikeus.

ox [ɔks] s. (pl. *oxen)* härkä; ~*-cart* härkävankkurit; *-eye daisy* päivänkakkara.

Oxbridge ['ɔksbridʒ] s. Oxford ja Cambridge (vastak. *Redbrick* uudet yliopistot); a. Oxfordin ja Cambridgen, (yläluokan) älymystön.

Oxford ['ɔksfəd] s.: ~ *blue* tummansininen.

oxid|e ['ɔksaid] s. oksidi (kem.) **-ize** ['ɔksidaiz] v. hapettaa, -ttua.

Oxonian [ɔk'səunjən] a. oxfordilainen; Oxfordin yliopiston (opiskelija).

oxygen ['ɔksidʒ(ə)n] s. happi (kem.); ~ *apparatus* happilaite. **-ate** [-eit] v. hapettaa.

oyster ['ɔistə] s. osteri. ~*-bed* osterisärkkä.

ozone ['əuzəun] s. otsoni (kem.).

P

P, p [piː] *s.* p-kirjain; *mind one's P's and Q's* olla varovainen, varoa sanojansa. Lyh.: **p.** *page;* **p.a.** *per annum* vuodessa; **Pa.** *Pennsylvania* **P.A.Y.E.** *pay as you earn* veron ennakkopidätys; **P.C.** *postcard; Police Constable, Privy Councillor;* **pd** *paid* maksettu; **Ph. D.** *Doctor of Philosophy;* **Phil.** *Philippians* Filippiläiskirje; **pl.** *plural;* **P.M.** *Prime Minister;* **p.m.** (= post meridiem) *after noon* j.p.p.; **P.M.G.** *Postmaster General;* **P.O.** *Postal Order, Post Office, Personnel Officer;* **P.O.W.** *prisoner of war;* **p.p.** = per procurationem, *representing;* **pp.** *pages;* **pro tem.** (= pro tempore) väliaikainen; **Prov.** *Proverbs;* **prox.** (= proximo) *of next month;* **P.S.** *postscript;* **pt.** *pint;* **Pte** *Private* sotamies; **P.T.O.** *please turn over* käännä.

pa [paː] *s.* (puhek.) isä, pappa, isi.

pace [peis] *s.* askel; käynti, astunta; tahti, nopeus; *v.* astua, astella; mitata askelin, käydä tasakäyntiä; (m. ~*out,* ~ *off);* määrätä tahti; *at a quick* ~ hyvää vauhtia; *keep* ~ *with* pysyä jnk rinnnalla; *go the* ~ huvitella, hummata; *put sb. through his* ~*s* tutkia jnk taitoa; *set the* ~ määrätä vauhti; *shows his* ~*s* näyttää taitoaan. **-maker** vetäjä, vauhdinpitäjä (urh.); (lääk.) tahdistin.

pachyderm ['pækidəːm] *s.* paksunahkainen eläin.

pacific [pə'sifik] *a.* rauhaa rakastava, rauhallinen; *the P* ~ [*Ocean*] Tyyni meri, Iso valtameri. **-ation** [pæsifi'keiʃn] *s.* rauhan palauttaminen, rauhoittaminen.

paci|fier ['pæsi|faiə] *s.* Am. tutti. **-fist** [-fist] *s.* pasifisti, rauhanaatteen kannattaja. **-fy** [-fai] *v.* rauhoittaa;

palauttaa rauha (maahan).

pack [pæk] *s.* mytty, pakkaus, Am. (esim. savuke)paketti, rasia; pinkka, pakka; lauma, parvi, joukko, kopla; (koira-)ajue; ahtojää; (kylmät) kääreet; *v.* pakata; sulloa (täyteen); panna kosteaan kääreeseen; säilöä tölkkeihin; tilkitä; tamponoida; ~ *it in!* (sl.) lopeta! ~ *sb. off* lähettää matkaan; ~ *up* pakata tavaransa, (puhek.) lopettaa työ, sl. (koneesta) pysähtyä; ~ *it in* (sl.) lopeta jo! *send sb.* ~*ing* ajaa tiehensä. **-age** [-idʒ] *s.* pakkaus; käärö, paketti; *v.* pakata, kääriä paperiin; ~ *deal* paketti-ratkaisu; ~ *tour* valmismatka. **-ed** [-t] *a.* täpötäysi; ~ *lunch* eväspaketti.

packet ['pækit] *s.* (pieni) käärö, paketti, nippu, rasia; = seur. ~**-boat** postilaiva.

pack|-horse kuormahevonen. ~**-ice** ahtojää. **-ing** *s.* pakkaus (aine); tölkitys; (haavan) tamponointi; tiiviste; ~ *case* pakkilaatikko. **-thread** purjelanka.

pact [pækt] *s.* sopimus.

pad [pæd] *s.* pehmuste, täyte, toppaus; tyyny, säärisuojus (urh.); lehtiö; polkukäsnä; värityyny; *v.* pehmustaa, täyttää (vanulla); astella, tallustaa; *launching* ~ (raketin) lähtöalusta. **-ding** *s.* pehmuste, (vanu)täyte, toppaus; palstantäyte.

paddle ['pædl] *s.* mela; siipi; *v.* meloa; kahlata, polskutella. ~**-wheel** siipiratas.

paddock ['pædək] *s.* hevoshaka, aitaus.

Paddy ['pædi] *s.* irlantilainen; *p* ~ kiukunpuuska; *p* ~ *field* riisipelto.

padlock ['pædlɔk] *s.* munalukko; *v.* sulkea munalukolla.

p(a)ediatrics ks. *pediatrics.*

paean ['pi:ən] *s.* ylistyslaulu.

pagan ['peigən] *a.* pakanallinen, pakana-; *s.* pakana. **-ism** [-izm] *s.* pakanuus.

page 1. [peidʒ] *s.: ~* [*boy*] hotellipoika; hovipoika, paaši; (pieni) sulhaspoika.

page 2. [peidʒ] *s.* sivu; *v.* numeroida (kirjan) sivut.

pageant ['pædʒ(ə)nt] *s.* historiallinen kulkue t. näytelmä; loistava näytelmä. **-ry** [-ri] *s.* komeus, loisto.

pagination [pædʒi'neiʃn] *s.* sivujen numerointi.

pagoda [pə'gəudə] *s.* pagodi.

paid [peid] *imp. & pp.* ks. *pay*.

pain [pein] *s.* tuska, kipu, kärsimys; *pl.* vaiva(nnäkö); *v.* tuottaa tuskaa; kiusata, vaivata; *she is in great ~* hänellä on kovat tuskat; *it gives me ~* minua surettaa; *take ~s* nähdä vaivaa; *be at ~s to* yrittää kovasti; *for his ~* vaivannäkönsä palkaksi; *on* (*under*) *~ of death* kuolemanrangaistuksen uhalla. **-ed** [-d] *a.* kiusaantunut. **-ful** *a.* tuskallinen; piinallinen. **~-killer** särkylääke. **-less** *a.* kivuton, tuskaton. **painstaking** *a.* (erittäin) huolellinen, tunnontarkka, tunnollinen.

paint [peint] *s.* maali; *v.* maalata; m. meikata, sminkata; sivellä (*with iodine*); (kuv.) kuvailla; *~s* (pl.) värit, värilaatikko; *~ sth. green* maalata vihreäksi; *~ the town red* juhlia, hurjastella. **~-brush** pensseli. **-er** [-ə] *s.* maalari, taidemaalari; kiinnitysköysi. **-ing** *s.* maalaus.

pair [peə] *s.* pari; *v.* yhdistää pariksi, muodostaa pari; *a ~ of boots* saapaspari: *a ~ of scissors* (*tongs*) sakset, pihdit; *carriage and ~* parivaljakko; *~ off* järjestää, järjestyä pareittain.

pajamas = *pyjamas*.

Pakistan [pɑ:kis'tɑ:n] *erisn.* **-i** [-i] *a. & s.* pakistanilainen.

pal [pæl] *s.* kaveri, toveri; *v.: ~ up with* ystävystyä.

palace ['pælis] *s.* palatsi, linna.

palan|quin, -keen [pælən'ki:n] *s.* kantotuoli.

palat|able ['pælətəbl] *a.* maukas. **-al** [-l] *a.* laki(äänne).

palate ['pælit] *s.* kitalaki; (kuv.) maku; ks. *cleft*.

palatial [pə'leiʃ(ə)l] *a.* palatsimainen, loistava, upea.

palatinate [pə'lætinit] *s.: the* [*Rhine*] *P ~* Pfalz.

palaver [pə'lɑ:və] *s.* palaveri, neuvottelu, lavertelu; *v.* jaaritella.

pale 1. [peil] *a.* kalpea; vaalea; *v.* kalveta; *~-face* valkonaama.

pale 2. [peil] *s.* paalu, seiväs; (kuv.) raja; *is beyond the ~* ei sovi säädylliseen seuraan.

paleontolo|gist ['pælion'tɔlədʒist, Am. 'peil-] *s.* paleontologi. **-gy** [-lədʒi] *s.* paleontologia.

Palestin|e ['pælistain] *erisn.* Palestiina. **-ian** [-'tinjən] *a. & s.* palestiinalainen.

palette ['pælit] *s.* paletti.

palfrey ['pɔ:lfri] *s.* pieni (naisen) ratsu (run.).

paling ['peiliŋ] *s.* paaluaita.

palisade [pæli'seid] *s.* paaluvarustus.

pall 1. [pɔ:l] *s.* paarivaate; *~-bearer* kantaja (hautajaisissa).

pall 2. [pɔ:l] *v.* käydä kyllästyttäväksi; *~ upon* tympäistä.

pallet ['pælit] *s.* olkivuode; kuormalava.

pallia|te ['pælieit] *v.* lievittää; lieventää. **-tion** [-'eiʃn] *s.* lievitys, lievennys. **-tive** [-iativ] *s.* lievike.

pallid ['pælid] *a.* kalpea, väritön.

Pall Mall ['pæl'mæl, 'pel'mel] *erisn.* katu Lontoossa.

pallor ['pælə] *s.* kalpeus.

palm 1. [pɑ:m] *s.* kämmen; *v.* piilottaa kämmeneensä; *~ sth. off upon* puijata jku ottamaan jtk; *oil sb.'s ~* lahjoa.

palm 2. [pɑ:m] *s.* palmu; voitonpalmu; *bear* (*carry off*) *the ~* voittaa; *yield the ~ to* tunnustaa jku voittajakseen; *P~ Sunday* palmusunnuntai. **-er** [-ə] *s.* pyhiinvaeltaja.

palmist ['pɑ:mist] *s.* kädestäennustaja. **-ry** [-ri] *s.* kädestäennustaminen.

palmy ['pɑ:mi] *a.* kukoistava, menestyksekäs.

palpable ['pælpəbl] *a.* kouraantuntuva, ilmeinen; käsin tunnettav|a, -issa; *-bly* selvästi. **-te** ['pælpeit] *v.* tunnustella, palpoida (lääk.).

palpitat|e ['pælpiteit] *v.* tykyttää. **-ion** [-'teiʃn] *s.* sydämentykytys.

palsy ['pɔ:lzi] *s.* halvaantuminen, halvaus; *palsied* halvaantunut.

palter ['pɔ:ltə] v. kieroilla.

paltry ['pɔ:ltri] a. vähäpätöinen, mitätön, surkea.

pamper ['pæmpə] v. hemmotella; ~*ed* hemmoteltu.

pamphlet ['pæmflit] s. (ajankohtainen) kirjoitelma, pamfletti. **-eer** [-'tiə] s. poliittinen kynäilijä.

pan [pæn] s. pannu; laakea kasari; allas; vaakakuppi; (WC) pönttö; v. huuhtoa (laakeassa astiassa); (elok.) panoroida; ~ [*for gold*] huuhtoa kultaa; ~ *out well* onnistua.

Pan [pæn] *erisn.*

pan- [pæn] *pref.* kaikki-, yleis-. **-acea** [-ə'siə] s. yleislääke.

panache [pæ'na:ʃ] s. komeilu.

Panama [pænə'mɑ:] *erisn.*

pancake s. pannukakku; ohukainen; ~ *landing* (ilm.) sakkalasku.

pancre|as ['pæŋkri|əs] s. haima (anat.) **-atic** [-'ætik] a. haima-.

panda ['pændə] s. panda; P~ *car* poliisiauto.

pandemonium [pændi'məunjəm] s. sekasorto.

pander ['pændə] s. parittaja; v. olla apurina t. parittajana; ~ *to* kiihottaa, vedota (vaistoihin).

pane [pein] s. (lasi-, ikkuna)ruutu.

panegyric [pæni'dʒirik] s. ylistyspuhe, -kirjoitus.

panel ['pænl] s. paneeli, laudoitus; levy, ruutu; kaistale (puvussa); pitkä ja kapea kuva; kojetaulu; korokekeskustelun (ym) osanottaja, asiantuntijaryhmä; (Engl.) sairausvakuutuslääkärien luettelo; v. paneloida; ~ *discussion* korokekeskustelu; ~ *doctor* sairauskassan lääkäri; ~ *led walls* paneloidut seinät. **-ling** s. paneeli.

pang [pæŋ] s. äkillinen kipu, pistos; tuska.

panic ['pænik] s. pakokauhu, paniikki; v. (-*cked*) joutua kauhun valtaan. **-ky** [-i] a. pakokauhuinen. ~**-stricken** kauhun vallassa oleva.

pannier ['pæniə] s.: ~ *s* (esim. aasin) tavarakorit, moottoripyörän (takana käyt.) laukkupari.

panoply ['pænəpli] s. täysi sota-asu (m. kuv.), sotisopa.

panorama [pænə'rɑ:mə] s. panoraama;

laaja näköala. **-ic** [pænə'ræmik] a.: ~ *car* näköalavaunu.

pansy ['pænzi] s. orvokki; naismainen nuorukainen.

pant [pænt] v. läähättää; huohottaa; s. huohotus; ~ *for* kaihota, kiihkeästi haluta; ~ *for breath* haukkoa henkeä.

pantaloon [pæntə'lu:n] s. narri; ~*s* (leik.) = *pants*.

pantechnicon [pæn'teknikən] s. muuttovaunu(t).

pantheism ['pænθi(:)izm] s. panteismi.

pantheon [pæn'θi:ɔn] s. pantheon.

panther ['pænθə] s. pantteri.

panti|es ['pænti z] s. (naisten ja lasten) pikkupöksyt, -housut.

pantile ['pæntail] s. kattotiili.

pantomime ['pæntəmaim] s. elenäytelmä, pantomiimi.

pantry ['pæntri] s. ruokasäiliö.

pants [pænts] s. pl. housut; *hot* ~ (1971-2) mikrohousut.

pap [pæp] s. velli, pöperö, sose.

papa [pə'pɑ:] s. isä, pappa.

pap|acy ['peip|əsi] s. paavinvalta, paavius. **-al** [-(ə)l] a. paavin-, paavillinen.

pap|aw [pə'pɔ:], **-aya** [pə'pɑ:jə] s. papaijapuu.

paper ['peipə] s. paperi; sanomalehti; esitelmä tutkielma, kirjoitus; tutkintokysymykset; seinäpaperi; *pl.* asiakirjat, paperit; v. tapetoida, paperoida; *read a* ~ *on* pitää esitelmä jstk; *send in one's* ~ *s* lähettää eronpyyntö; *on* ~ teoriassa. **-back** paperikantinen (kirja), taskukirja. ~**-clip** liitin. ~**-hanger** tapetoija. ~**-knife** paperiveitsi. ~**-mill** paperitehdas. ~**-weight** paperipaino. ~**-work** paperisota.

papis|t ['peipist] s. (halv.) katolilainen. **-ical** [pə'pistikl] a. paavillinen.

paprika ['pæprikə, Am. pə'pri:kə] s. paprika.

papyrus [pə'paiə|rəs] s. (pl. *papyri* [-rai]) papyrus.

par [pɑ:] s. tasa-arvo, pari(kurssi); *on a* ~ *with* tasa-arvoinen; *at* ~ nimelliskurssia vastaavassa arvossa; *I'm not feeling quite up to* ~ en ole täysin kunnossa.

parab|le ['pærəbl] s. vertaus. **-ola** [pə'ræbələ] s. paraabeli. **-olical**

[pærə'bolik(ə)l] *a.* vertauksellinen.
parachut|e ['pærəʃuːt] *s.* laskuvarjo; *v.*
hypätä l-lla. **-ist** [-ist] *s.*
laskuvarjohyppääjä.

parade [pə'reid] *s.* komeilu; paraati;
paraatikenttä, kävelypaikka; *v.*
näytellä (jtk), komeilla (jllak);
marssia, marssittaa paraatissa; kävellä
edestakaisin; *make a ~ of* komeilla
jllak; *fashion ~* muotinäytös.
~-ground paraatikenttä.

paradigm ['pærədaim] *s.* muotosarja;
esimerkki.

paradise ['pærədais] *s.* paratiisi; *bird of
~* paratiisilintu.

paradox ['pærədɔks] *s.* paradoksi. **-ical**
[-'dɔksik(ə)l] *a.* paradoksinen.

paraffin ['pærəfin] *s.* parafiini; (*~
wax*), paloöljy, petroli (*~ oil,* Am.
kerosene); liquid *~* p-öljy; *~ lamp*
öljylamppu.

paragon ['pærəgən] *s.* esikuva.

paragraph ['pærəgrɑːf] *s.* kappale;
lyhyt (sanomalehti)kirjoitus, uutinen.

Paragway ['pærəgwai] *erisn.*

parakeet ['pærəkiːt] *s.*
(pitkäpyrstöinen) papukaija.

parallel ['pærəlel] *a.* yhdensuuntainen,
rinnakkainen: *s.* yhdensuuntaisviiva,
rinnakkais|ilmiö, -tapaus; leveyspiiri;
v. olla yhdensuuntainen, olla
rinnastettavissa jhk; *without a ~*
vertaa vailla; *~ bars* nojapuut; *draw a
~ between* verrata toisiinsa. **-ism**
[-izm] *s.* yhdensuuntaisuus,
rinnakkaisuus. **-ogram** [-'leləgræm] *s.*
suunnikas.

paral|yse ['pærəlaiz] *v.* halvata;
lamauttaa. **-ysis** [pə'rælisis] *s.* halvaus.
-ytic [pærə'litik] *a. & s.* halvaantunut.

paramilitary *a.* puolisotilaallinen.

paramount ['pærəmaunt] *a.* ylin,
korkein; erittäin suuri.

paramour ['pærəmuə] *s.* rakastaja, -tar.

paranoic, -iac [pærə'nəuik, -nɔiæk] *a.
& s.* vainoharhainen.

parapet ['pærəpit] *s.* kaide;
rintavarustus (sot.).

paraphernalia [pærəfə'neiljə] *s.*
varusteet, tarvikkeet, pikkutavarat.

paraphrase ['pærəfreiz] *s.* parafraasi,
mukaelma; *v.* lausua toisin sanoin.

parasit|e ['pærəsait] *s.* loinen, loiseläin,
-kasvi. **-ic** [pærə'sitik] *a.* lois-.

parasol ['pærəsɔl] *s.* päivänvarjo.

paratroop|s ['pærətruːps] *s.* laskuvarjo-
joukot; *-er* laskuvarjolääkäri.

paratyphoid ['pærə'taifɔid] *s.*
paratyfus.

parboil ['pɑːbɔil] *v.* kiehauttaa.

parcel ['pɑːsl] *s.* käärö, paketti; erä
(kauppa); *v.* jakaa osiin (tav. *~ out*);
~ of land maapalsta; *part and ~ of*
jnk olennainen osa; *by ~ post*
postipakettina; *~ sth. up* paketoida.

parch [pɑːtʃ] *v.* paahtaa, polttaa;
paahtua, kärventyä; *~ed with thirst*
janoon näännytämäisillään.

parchment ['pɑːtʃmənt] *s.* pergamentti.

pard [pɑːd] *s.* sl. kaveri.

pardon ['pɑːdn] *s.* anteeksianto;
armahdus; synninpäästö; *v.* antaa
anteeksi; armahtaa; *I beg your ~*
suokaa anteeksi! (kysymyksenä) mitä
sanoitte? kuinka? **-able** [-əbl] *a.*
anteeksiannettava. **-er** [-ə] *s.*
anekauppias.

pare [pɛə] *v.* leikata (kynsiä ym);
kuoria; *~ down* [*expenses*] vähentää.

parent ['pɛər(ə)nt] *s.* äiti, isä, toinen
vanhemmista; *one-~ family*
yksinhuoltajaperhe; *~s* vanhemmat.
-age [-dʒ] *s.* syntyperä (m. *~ hood*). **-al**
[pə'rentl] *a.* isän-, äidin-,
vanhempien.

parenthe|sis [pə'renθisis] *s.* (pl. *-ses*
[-siːz]) välilause; sulkumerkki, sulkeet
(tav. *pl*). **-tic(al)** [pær(ə)n'θetik, -(ə)l]
a. väliinliitetty, parenteettinen.

pariah ['pæriə] *s.* paria.

paring ['pɛəriŋ] *s.*: *~s* lastut, kuoret,
(poisleikatut) kynnenreunat.

Paris ['pæris] *erisn.* Pariisi.

parish ['pæriʃ] *s.* seurakunta; pitäjä; *~
register* kirkonkirjat. **-ioner** [pə'riʃənə]
s. seurakuntalainen.

Parisian [pə'rizjən] *a. & s.*
pariisilainen.

parity ['pæriti] *s.* tasa-arvoisuus,
yhtäläisyys, pariteetti.

park [pɑːk] *s.* puisto, luonnonpuisto
(*national ~*); paikoitusalue (*car ~*);
tykkivarikko; *v.* pysäköidä; *~ing
meter* pysäköintimittari; *~ing lot*
paikoitusalue; *~ place* pysäköimis-
paikka. **-y** [-i] *a.* sl. kolea, kylmä.

parl|ance ['pɑːl|əns] *s.*: *in common ~*
tavallisessa puheessa. **-ey** [-i] *s.*

neuvottelu; v. neuvotella, hieroa sovintoa.

parliament ['pɑ:ləmənt] s. parlamentti. **-arian** [-men'tɛəriən] s. parlamentaarikko. **-ary** [-'ment(ə)ri] a. parlamentin.

parlour, parlor ['pɑ:lə] s. sali (vanh.), olohuone; *hairdersser's* ~ (Am.) kampaamo; ~ *game* seuraleikki. ~-**car** salonkivaunu. ~-**maid** sisäkkö (ei Am.).

parlous [pɑ:ləs] a. vaarallinen.

parochial [pə'rəukjəl] a. pitäjän, seurakunnan; ahdasmielinen, rajoittunut.

parody ['pærədi] s. parodia, ivamukailu; v. parodioida.

parole [pə'rəul] s. kunniasana; tunnussana; v. vapauttaa ehdonalaisesti; *out on* ~ l.v. ehdonalaisessa vapaudessa.

paro|tid [pə'rə|tid] a.: ~ *gland* korvasylkirauhanen. **-titis** [-'taitis] s. sikotauti.

paroxysm ['pærəksizm] s. puuska, kohtaus.

parquet ['pɑ:kei] s. parketti(lattia).

parr [pɑ:] s. nuori lohi.

parricide ['pærisaid] s. isänmurhaaja, isän (t. lähteisen sukulaisen) murha.

parrot ['pærət] s. papukaija.

parry ['pæri] v. väistää, torjua.

parse [pɑ:z] v. (kiel.) jäsentää (lause).

parsimo|nious [pɑ:si'məunjəs] a. säästäväinen, kitsas. **-ny** ['pɑ:siməni] s. kitsaus.

parsley ['pɑ:sli] s. persilja.

parsnip ['pɑ:snip] s. palsternakka.

parson [pɑ:sn] s. pastori, kirkkoherra. **-age** [idʒ] s. pappila.

part [pɑ:t] s. osa; osuus, tehtävä, asia; ääni (mus.); *pl.* seutu, tienoo; v. jakaa, erottaa; jakautua; erota *(from);* panna t. mennä jakaukselle; *adv.* osaksi; *principal* ~ *s* (verbin) teemamuodot; ~ *s of speech* sanaluokat; *in these* ~ *s* näillä tienoin; *for my* ~ omasta puolestani; *for the most* ~ suurimmaksi osaksi; *in* ~ osittain; *on his* ~ hänen taholtaan; *take* ~ *in* ottaa osaa jhk; *take in ill* ~ pahastua; ~ *with* luopua jstk; ~ *company* erota; ~-*owner* osakas; ~-*payment* osamaksu.

partake [pɑ:'teik] v. (-*took -taken)* ottaa osaa, osallistua jhk, olla mukana jssk; *it* ~ *s of* on jnk luonteinen, vivahtaa jhk.

partial ['pɑ:ʃ(ə)l] a. osittainen, osa-; puolueellinen; ~ *to* mieltynyt jhk. **-ity** [pɑ:ʃi'æliti] s. puolueellisuus; erikoinen mieltymys *(to, for* jhk). **-ly** *adv.* osittain; puolueellisesti.

particip|ant [pɑ:'tisipənt] s. osallinen, osanottaja. **-ate** [-eit] v. ottaa osaa, osallistua *(in* jhk). **-ation** [-'peiʃn] s. osanotto, osallistuminen.

particip|ial [pɑ:ti'sipiəl] a. partisiippi-. **-le** ['pɑ:tisipl] s. partisiippi; *present (past)* ~ partisiipin preesens, perfekti.

particle ['pɑ:tikl] s. hitunen, hiukkanen; (kiel.) partikkeli.

particolo(u)red ['pɑ:tikʌləd] a. kirjava.

particular [pə'tikjulə] a. erityinen, erikoinen; määrätty, tietty; yksityiskohtainen, tarkka; turhantarkka, nirso; *s.* yksityiskohta; *pl.* tarkemmat tiedot; *in* ~ erikoisesti, nimenomaan; *full* ~ *s* tarkat tiedot; *for* ~ *s apply to...* tarkempia tietoja antaa...; *that* ~ *hat* juuri tuo hattu. **-ity** [-'læriti] s. seikkaperäisyys, yksityiskohtaisuus, (pikku)tarkkuus. **-ize** [-raiz] v. mainita yksitellen; kertoa yksityiskohtaisesti, olla seikkaperäinen. **-ly** *adv.* erityisesti, erikoisen; varsinkin, erittäinkin.

parting ['pɑ:tiŋ] a. jäähyväis-. ero-; *s.* eroaminen, ero; jakaus; ~ *of ways* tienhaara.

partisan (-zan) ['pɑ:ti'zæn] s. puolue|mies, -pukari; partisaani, sissi. **-ship** s. puoluehenki.

partition [pɑ:'tiʃn] s. jakaminen, jako; väliseinä; lokero; v. jakaa; osittaa; ~ *off* jakaa (väliseinällä).

partly ['pɑ:tli] *adv.* osaksi, osittain.

partner ['pɑ:tnə] s. osakas, yhtiötoveri; kumppani; (tanssi-, peli)kumppani, partneri; puoliso. **-ship** s. yhtiötoveruus; kumppanuus.

partridge ['pɑ:tridʒ] s. peltopyy.

part-|song, -singing moniääninen laulu. **-time** osapäivä(työ *work).* ~ **-timer** osapäivätyöntekijä.

parturition [pɑ:tju(ə)'riʃn] s. synnytys.

party [pɑ:ti] s. puolue; joukko, ryhmä

(m. sot.); seura, seurue; kutsut; asianosainen, osapuoli; (puhek.) henkilö; *a ~ to* osallinen jhk; *be one of the ~* olla mukana jssk; *give (throw) a ~* pitää kutsut; ~ *game* seuraleikki; ~ *line* puolueen politiikka; m. yhteinen puhelinjohto; ~ *spirit* puoluehenki; *~-wall* (rakennusten ym välinen) yhteinen muuri.

paschal ['pɑːsk(ə)l] *a.* pääsiäis-.

pasha ['pɑːʃə] *s.* pašša.

pass 1. [pɑːs] *v.* kulkea, mennä (jnk) ohi, läpi, poikki; siirtyä; kulua, mennä; mennä ohi, kadota, lakata; muuttua; tapahtua, sattua; tulla hyväksytyksi, läpäistä, suoriutua jstk; olla käypä, käydä täydestä; *(~ for)* käydä jstk; jäädä huomioon ottamatta; (korttipelissä) passata; antaa mennä, viedä; hyväksyä; kiertää (kädestä käteen); panna kiertämään, ojentaa; ylittää, voittaa; viettää, kuluttaa; lausua, langettaa; ~ *away* loppua, kuolla; ~ *by* kulkea, mennä ohitse; jättää huomioonottamatta, sivuuttaa; ~ *for* käydä jstk; ~ *off* hävitä, mennä ohi; käydä, päättyä *(well* hyvin); sanoa olevan *(as, for* jtk); ~ *oneself off as…* sanoa olevansa…; ~ *on* jatkaa matkaa, lähettää edelleen, ojentaa seuraavalle; ~ *out* menettää tajuntansa, »sammua»; ~ *over* jättää huomaamatta, syrjäyttää; ~ *through* käydä läpi, kokea; ~ *the time of day* vaihtaa pari sanaa (jnk kanssa); ~ *up* päästää käsistään; hylätä; *bring to ~* saada aikaan; *come to ~* tapahtua; *let it ~* jätä se silleen; *make a ~ (make passes) at* (sl.) lähennellä.

pass 2. [pɑːs] *s.* hyväksyminen (arvosanalla välttävä); passi, lupalippu; vapaalippu; (vaikea) tilanne, asema; isku; sola, väylä; *things have come to such a ~* on jouduttu siihen, että. **-able** [-əbl] *s.* kulkukelpoinen; mukiinmenevä, kohtalainen; välttävä.

passage ['pæsidʒ] *s.* läpikulku, kauttakulku, kulku, (meri)matka; käytävä; väylä; (kirjan) kohta, kappale; tiehyt, tie; *pl.* sananvaihto; *bird of ~* muuttolintu; *force a ~ through* tunkeutua läpi; ~ *of arms*

miekanmittely; ~ *[of a bill]* hyväksyminen; ~ *money* (laiva)lipun hinta; *-way* käytävä.

pass-book vastakirja.

passée ['pɑːsei] *a.* kuihtunut.

passenger ['pæs(i)n(d)ʒə] *s.* matkustaja; (ryhmän) toimeton jäsen.

passer-by ['pɑːsə bai] *s.* ohikulkija; vastaantulija.

passing ['pɑːsiŋ] *a.* ohimenevä, lyhytaikainen; *s.* ohimeno, lähtö (m. kuolema); *in ~* ohimennen.

passion ['pæʃn] *s.* intohimo, voimakas tunne; vimma, raivo, suuri mieltymys *(for* jhk); *fly into a ~* vimmastua; *the P ~* Kristuksen kärsimys; *P~ Week* piinaviikko; *P~ play* kärsimysnäytelmä. **-ate** ['pæʃənit] *a.* intohimoinen, kiihkeä, tulinen.

passiv|e ['pæsiv] *a.* passiivinen (m. kiel.); *s.:* ~ *[voice]* passiivi. **-ity** [pæ'siviti] *s.* passiivisuus.

pass-key ['pɑːskiː] *s.* yleisavain.

Passover ['pɑːsəuvə] *s.* juutalaisten pääsiäinen.

pass|port ['pɑːspɔːt] passi. **-word** tunnussana.

past [pɑːst] *a.* viime; mennyt; *s.* menneisyys, entisyys, mennyt aika; *prep.* (jnk) ohi, yli; (jnk) ulkopuolelle; *adv.* ohi, ohitse; ~ *tense* mennyt aika, imperfekti; *five minutes ~ ten* viisi minuuttia yli kymmenen; *half ~ six* puoli seitsemän; ~ *endurance* sietämätön(tä); ~ *recovery* parantumaton; *I wouldn't put it ~ him to…* enpä ihmettelisi jos hän…

paste [peist] *s.* taikina; tahna; liisteri; *v.* liisteröidä; ~ *up (in),* ~ *…over with* liimata jhk, jnk päälle. **-board** pahvi.

pastel ['pæstl, Am. pæ'stel] *s.* pastelli, väriliitu(maalaus).

pastern ['pæstən] *s.* (hevosen) vuohinen.

pasteurize ['pæstəraiz] *v.* pastöroida.

pastiche [pæs'tiːʃ] *s.* pastissi, jäljitelmä.

pastille ['pæstil, Am. pæs'tiːl] *s.* pastilli.

pastime [pɑːstaim] *s.* ajanviete, huvi, virkistys; *as a ~* ajankuluksi.

pastmaster *s.* mestari (jssk).

pastor ['pɑːstə] *s.* pappi, pastori, sielunpaimen. **-al** [-(ə)r(ə)l] *a.* paimen-, maalais-; *s.* pastoraali,

paimenruno; ~ [*letter*] paimenkirje; ~
care sielunhoito. **-ate** [-orit] *s.*
seurakuntapapin virka, pastorit.

pastry ['peistri] *s.* murotaikina, tortut,
leivonnaiset. ~~**-cook** sokerileipuri.

pasturage ['pɑːstjuridʒ] *s.* laidun;
laiduntaminen.

pasture ['pɑːstʃə] *s.* laidun; *v.* olla
laitumella, laiduntaa.

pasty 1. ['pæsti, 'pɑːsti] *s.* piirakka,
pasteija.

pasty 2. ['peisti] *a.* taikinamainen,
tahnamainen; ~ [*-faced*] kalpea (ja
lihava).

pat [pæt] *v.* taputtaa; *s.* taputus;
(voi)nokare; *adv.* sopivasti,
parahiksi; aivan valmiina; *stand* ~
pysyä kannallaan.

Pat [pæt] *erisn.; s.* irlantilainen.

patch [pætʃ] *s.* paikka, tilkku; lappu;
laastari, kauneuspilkku, läiskä,
laikku; maatilkku; *v.* paikata; ~ *up*
korjata hätiköiden, kyhätä kokoon,
sopia (riita); *is not a* ~ *on* ei ole
mitään jnk rinnalla. ~~**-work** tilkkutyö.
-y [-i] *a.* paikattu, läiskäinen,
epähtenäinen, epätasainen.

pate [peit] *s.* pää, kallo (leik.);
curly--d kiharapäinen.

paten ['pæt(ə)n] *s.* öylättilautanen.

patent [peitnt] *a.* ilmeinen, avoin,
julkinen, patentti-; [m. 'pæt-]
patentti, oikeus; *v.* hakea patentti
jllek; ~ *leather* [pei-] kiiltonahka;
letters ~ [pæt-] lupakirja; *P*~ *Office*
[pæt-] patenttitoimisto; ~*ed*
patentoitu. **-ee** [peit(ə)n'tiː] *s.*
patentinhaltija.

pater ['peitə] *s.* isäukko.

patern|al [pə'tɔːn|l] *a.* isän,
isänpuoleinen; isällinen; ~
grandmother isän äiti. **-ity** [-iti] *s.*
isyys.

path [pɑːθ] *s.* [pl. -ðz] polku; (urh.)
rata; (kuv.) tie.

pathetic [pə'θetik] *a.* liikuttava,
surkea.

pathless *a.* tietön.

patho|logical [pæθə'lɔdʒik(ə)l] *a.*
patologinen. **-logy** [pə'θɔlədʒi] *s.*
tautioppi, patologia.

pathos ['peiθɔs] *s.* liikuttavuus, sääliä
herättävä asia ym.

pathway ['pɑːθwei] *s.* polku.

patien|ce ['peiʃns] *s.* kärsivällisyys;
pasianssi. **-t** [-nt] *a.* kärsivällinen; *s.*
potilas.

patina ['pætinə] *s.* patina (kuv.).

patio ['pɑːtiou] *s.* (sisä)piha.

patriarch ['peitriɑːk] *s.* patriarkka. **-al**
[-'ɑːk(ə)l] *a.* patriarkallinen.

Patricia [pə'triʃə] *erisn.*

patrician [pə'triʃ(ə)n] *s.* patriisi, ylimys;
a. patriisi-.

patricide ['pætrisaid] *s.*
isänmurha(aja).

patrimony ['pætriməni] *s.* isänperintö.

patriot ['peitriət, Am. pæt-] *s.*
isänmaanystävä. **-ic** [pætri'ɔtik] *a.*
isänmaallinen. **-ism** [-izm] *s.*
isänmaanrakkaus, isänmaallisuus.

patrol [pə'troul] *s.* (kulku)vartio;
partio, -retki; *v.* olla kulkuvartiossa,
partioida.

patron ['peitr(ə)n] *s.* suojelija,
(taiteen)suosija; ~ *saint*
suojeluspyhimys. **-age** ['pætrənidʒ] *s.*
suojelus. **-ize** ['pætrənaiz] *v.* suojella,
avustaa, tukea; kohdella suojelevasti
t. holhoavasti; *-izing* holhoava.

patronymic [pætrə'nimik] *s.* sukunimi
(isän nimestä muodostettu).

patten ['pætn] *s.* puukenkä.

patter 1. ['pætə] *s.* (myyjien ym)
erikoiskieli, papatus; *v.* (puhua)
papattaa, lasketella.

patter 2. ['pætə] *v.* rapista, ropista; *s.*
ropina.

pattern ['pætən] *s.* malli, kaava;
esikuva; näyte; kuvioitus; *v.* valmistaa
(jnk mukaan (*upon, after*)); kuvioida;
~*ed* kuvioitu, kuviollinen.

patty ['pæti] *s.* pasteija.

paucity ['pɔːsiti] *s.* harvalukuisuus.

Paul [pɔːl] *erisn.* Paavali (*St.* ~). **-ine**
[-ain] *a.* Paavalin.

paunch [pɔːn(t)ʃ] *s.* pullea vatsa,
möhömaha.

pauper ['pɔːpə] *s.* kunnan avustusta
nauttiva köyhä. **-ism** [-rizm] *s.*
köyhyys. **ize** [-raiz] *v.* saattaa
puutteeseen.

pause [pɔːz] *s.* tauko, pysähdys,
keskeytys; *v.* pitää tauko, pysähtyä;
jäädä miettimään.

pave [peiv] *v.* kivetä; kestopäällystää;
~ *the way* tasoittaa tie. **-ment** *s.*
katukiveys; jalkakäytävä.

pavilion [pə'viljən] s. (katsoja-, näyttely) pavilonki, iso teltta.

paving ['peiviŋ] s. kiveys.

paw [pɔː] s. käpälä, tassu (m. leik. kädestä); v. kuopia maata; kopeloida, pidellä kompelösti; *I don't like being ~ed about* en pidä lääppimisestä.

pawky ['pɔːki] a. (Skotl.) ovela.

pawn 1. [pɔːn] s. (šakki) sotamies, šakkinappula.

pawn 2. [pɔːn] s. pantti, vakuus; v. pantata. **-broker** panttilainaaja. **-shop** panttilainakonttori.

pay [pei] *paid paid*, v. maksaa (*sb. for sth.* jklle jstk); palkita, korvata, kannattaa; s. palkka, maksu; *~ attention to* kiinnittää huomiota jhk; *~ a visit to* käydä vierailulla jkn luona; *~ one's way* maksaa kustannukset itse, maksaa omasta puolestaan; *it does not ~* se ei kannata; *~ out (away)* höllentää (köyttä); *~ sb. out* maksaa, kostaa jklle; *~ down* maksaa käteisellä; *~ sb. off* antaa lopputili; *~ up* suorittaa loppuun; *in sb.'s ~* jkn palveluksessa; *well-paid* hyvin palkattu. **-able** ['pe(i)əbl] a. maksettava (*to* jklle). **~-as-you-earn** (= *P.A.Y.E.*) veron ennakkopidätys. **~-day** palkkapäivä. **~-desk** kassa. **-ee** [pe(i)'iː] s. maksunsaaja. **-ing** a. kannattava; vrt. *guest.* **~-load** hyötykuorma. **-master** talousupseeri. **-ment** s. maksu, suoritus; *in ~ of* (esim. laskun) suoritukseksi; *stop ~* lakkauttaa maksunsa; *~ received* kuitataan. **~-off** (kuv.) tilinteon hetki; huipentuma. **-ola** [-'əulə] s. (salainen) lahjus. **~-packet** tilipussi. **~-roll,** **~-sheet** palkkalista.

pea [piː] s. herne; *as like as two ~s* kuin kaksi marjaa.

peace [piːs] s. rauha; (laillinen) järjestys; sovinto; *make ~* solmia rauha; *at ~* rauhan tilassa; *~ of mind* mielenrauha. **-able** [-əbl] a. sopuisa, rauhaa rakastava. **-ful** a. rauhallinen, hiljainen. **-maker** rauhantekijä. **~-offering** sovintouhri. **~-keeping** rauhanturva-.

peach 1. [piːtʃ] s. persikka; »loistokappale», kaunotar.

peach 2. [piːtʃ] v. (sl.) *~ upon*

ilmiantaa, kannella.

pea|cock [piːkɔk] riikinkukko. **-hen** riikinkukon naaras. **~-jacket** merimiehen nuttu.

peak 1. [piːk] s. huippu, vuoren huippu; (lakin) lippa; (kuv.) huippu(kohta); *~ price* huippuhinta; *~ hours of traffic* ruuhka-aika; *during off-~ periods* hiljaisena (pienen kulutuksen) aikana.

peak 2. [piːk] v. (tav. *~ and pine*) riutua, kuihtua.

peaked [piːkt] a. suippo; laiha, riutunut; *~ cap* lippalakki.

peal [piːl] s. kellojensoitto; jyrähdys, (naurun)remahdus, helinä; v. soida; raikua, jyristä; *~s of laughter* raikua nauru; *~ of thunder* ukkosenjyrähdys.

peanut ['piːnʌt] s. maapähkinä.

pear [pɛə] s. päärynä(puu).

pearl [pɔːl] s. helmi; v. helmeillä; *~ button* helmiäisnappi. **~-barley** helmisuurimot. **~-oyster** helmisimpukka. **-y** [-i] a. helmimäinen, hohtava; *p-ies (costermonge*rin) helmiäisnapein koristettu puku; (leik.) hampaat.

peasant ['peznt] s. talonpoika, maalainen. **-ry** [-ri] s. maalaisväestö.

pease [piːz] s.: *~ pudding* hernemuhennos.

pea-soup [piː'suːp] s. hernekeitto. **-er** [-ə] herneolkasumu.

peat [piːt] s. turve; *~ moss* rahkasuo.

pebbl|e ['pebl] s. (pyöreähkö) pikkukivi. **-y** [-i] a. sorainen, kivinen; *~ beach* somerikko (-ranta).

pecan [pi'kæn] s. pekanpähkinä.

pecc|able ['pekəbl] a. synnillinen, syntiin taipuvainen. **-adillo** [-ə'diləu] s. (pl. *~es*) pikkusynti, rike.

peck 1. [pek] s. tilavuusmitta = n. 9 l; *a ~ of* melkoisesti, aika läjä.

peck 2. [pek] v. nokkia (*at* jtk); hakata nokalla (reikä); antaa (nopea) suukko; *~ at one's food* syödä nirsoillen, näykkiä. **-er** [-ə] s.: *keep one's ~ up* pysyä rohkeana. **-ish** [-iʃ] a. nälkäinen.

pectoral ['pektər(ə)l] a. rinta-.

peculat|e ['pekjuleit] v. kavaltaa. **-ion** [-'leiʃn] s. kavallus.

peculiar [pi'kjuːliə] a. ominainen,

luonteenomainen *(to);* erityinen;
omituinen, (eris)kummallinen. **-ity**
[-li'æriti] *s.* erikoisuus, omituisuus. **-ly**
adv. erityinen, erikoisesti, erikoisen;
omituisesti.

pecuniary [pi'kju:njəri] *a.* rahallinen,
raha-.

peda|gogic(al) [pedə'gɔdʒik, -(ə)l] *a.*
kasvatusopillinen. **-gogue** ['pedəgɔg]
s. opettaja. **-gogy** ['pedəgɔdʒi] *s.*
kasvatusoppi.

pedal ['pedl] *s.* poljin, pedaali; *v.*
polkea, ajaa pyörällä.

pedant ['ped(ə)nt] *s.* pedantti,
(turhantarkka) saivartelija. **-ic**
[pi'dæntik] *s.* pikkutarkka. **-ry** [-ri] *s.*
pedanttisuus.

peddle ['pedl] *v.* harjoittaa
kulkukauppaa; puuhata joutavia;
kaupustella; levitellä (juoruja). **-r** [-ə]
= *pedlar.*

pedestal ['pedistl] *s.* jalusta.

pedestrian [pi'destriən] *s.* jalankulkija;
a jalka-; ~ *crossing* suojatie.

pediatri|cian [pi:diə'triʃn] *s.*
lastenlääkäri. **-cs** [pi:di'ætriks] *s.*
lastentautioppi.

pedicle ['pedikl] *s.* varsi.

pedicure ['pedikjuə] *s.* jalkojenhoito.

pedigree ['pedigri:] *s.* suku|puu, -taulu;
~ *cattle* kantakirjakarja.

pediment ['pedimənt] *s.* päätykolmio.

pedlar ['pedlə] *s.* kulkukauppias,
kaupustelija.

pedometer [pi'dɔmitə] *s.* askelmittari.

pee [pi:] *v.* pissiä.

peek [pi:k] *v.* tirkistää; *s.*
(salavihkainen) kurkistus.

peel [pi:l] *s.* kuoria; *v.* kuoria,
kuoriutua; (us. ~ *off)* kesiä, hilseillä,
liuskoilla; riisuutua (sl.); ~*ings*
kuoret (perunain ym).

peep 1. [pi:p] *v.* tirkistää, pistää esiin;
s. tirkistys; ~ *out* (esim. kuu)
kurkistaa; ~ *of day* aamun sarastus; ~
ing Tom tirkistelijä.

peep 2. [pi:p] *v.* piipittää; *s.* piipitys,
vikinä.

peep|er sl. silmä. **~-hole** tirkistysreikä.

peer 1. [piə] *v.* katsoa tarkasti t.
silmiään siristellen.

peer 2. [piə] *s.* vertainen; pääri; ~*s of
the realm* valtakunnan päärit
(ylähuoneen jäsenet). **-age** [-ridʒ] *s.*

päärinarvo, päärit; aateliskalenteri.
-ess [-ris] *s.* päärität. **-less** *a.* verraton,
vertaa vailla (oleva).

peeved [pi:vd] *a.* ärtynyt.

peevish ['pi:viʃ] *a.* ärtyisä, äreä,
oikullinen.

peewit ['pi:wit] ks. *pewit.*

peg [peg] *s.* tappi, vaarna,
(vaate)naula, pyykkipoika; (teltta-)
puikko; (konjakki- t. viski)grogi;
(viulun) tappi; (kuv.) tekosyy; *v.*
kiinnittää naulalla, vaarnalla (us. ~
down); vakauttaa (hinnat, palkat); ~
away ahertaa; ~ *sb. down* pakottaa
pysymään asiassa t. ohjelmassa; ~ *out*
merkitä raja, pyykittää (t, (puhek.)
heittää henkensä; *take sb. down a* ~
or two nolata, nöyryyttää.

pejorative ['pi:dʒ(ə)rətiv] *a. & s.*
halventava, pejoratiivinen (sana).

peke [pi:k] *s.* lyh. = seur.

Pekinese [pi:ki'ni:z] *s.*
kiinanpalatsikoira.

Peking [pi:'kiŋ] *erisn.*

pelf [pelf] *s.* (halv.) raha.

pelican ['pelikən] *s.* pelikaani.

pellet ['pelit] *s.* (paperi- ym) pallo,
pieni kuula, pilleri.

pellicle ['pelikl] *s.* ohut kalvo.

pell-mell ['pel'mel] *adv.* suin päin,
mullin mallin.

pellucid [pe'lu:sid] *a.* läpikuultava,
kirkas; selkeä.

pelt 1. [pelt] *v.* heitellä, pommittaa
(jllak); ~*ing rain* rankkasade; *at full*
~ täyttä vauhtia.

pelt 2. [pelt] *s.* (lampaan ym) turkki,
vuota.

pelvis ['pelvis] *s.* (pl. *pelves* [-i:z])
lantio (anat.).

pemmican ['pemik(ə)n] *s.* kuivattu
liha, pemmikaani.

pen 1. [pen] *s.* kynä; *v.* kirjoittaa;
fountain ~ täytekynä; ~ *friend,* ~ *pal*
kirjeenvaihtotoveri.

pen 2. [pen] *s.* karsina, tarha, aitaus; *v.*
(tav. ~ *in,* ~ *up)* sulkea (tarhaan);
play ~ leikkikehä.`

penal ['pi:nl] *a.* rikos-, rangaistus-; ~
code rikoslaki; ~ *colony*
rangaistussiirtola; ~ *servitude*
pakkotyö. **-ize** ['pi:nəlaiz] *v.* saattaa
rangaistuksen alaiseksi; määrätä
(urheilijalle) rangaistus. **-ty** ['penlti] *s.*

rangaistus; sakko; (urh. m.) tasoitus; ~ *kick* rangaistuspotku; *pay the* ~ kestää seuraukset, maksaa jstk; *under* ~ *of £5* viiden punnan sakon uhalla.

penance ['penəns] *s.* katumus (harjoitus); *do* ~ *for* sovittaa jtk.

penchant ['pa:ŋ'ʃa:ŋ] *a.* mieltymys (*for*).

pencil ['pensl] *s.* (lyijy)kynä; värikynä; *v.* kirjoittaa, piirtää lyijykynällä; ~*led eyebrows* kauniit, hienon muotoiset kulmakarvat. ~-**case** kynärasia.

pend|ant ['pendənt] *s.* riipus, kaulakoru; (vasta)pari. -**ent** [= ed.] *a.* riippuva; ratkaisematon. -**ing** *a.* ratkaisematon; *prep.* kuluessa, kestäessä; ~ *his return* hänen paluutaan odotellessa; *patent* ~ patenttia haetaan; *leave sth.* ~ jättää (asia) lepäämään.

pendul|ous ['pendjul|əs] *a.* riippuva, heiluva. -**um** [-əm] *s.* heiluri.

Penelope [pi'neləpi] *erisn.*

penetra|ble ['penitrəbl] *a.* läpäistävissä oleva. -**te** [-eit] *v.* tunkeutua (jnk) läpi; päästä perille, käsittää; ~*ting* tarkkasilmäinen, läpitunkeva, terävä. -**tion** [-'treiʃn] *s.* tunkeutuminen jhk (*peaceful* ~); terävyys, terävä-älyisyys. -**tive** [-ətiv] *a.* läpitunkeva.

penguin ['peŋgwin] *s.* pingviini.

penholder ['penhəuldə] *s.* kynänvarsi.

penicillin [peni'silin] *s.* penisilliini.

peninsula [pi'ninsjul|ə] *s.* niemimaa. -**r** [-ə] *a.* niemimäinen, niemimaa-.

penis ['pi:nis] *s.* siitin.

peniten|ce ['penit(ə)ns] *s.* katumus. -**t** [-nt] *a.* katuva; *s.* parannuksentekijä. -**tial** [-'tenʃ(ə)l] *a.* katumus-. -**tiary** [-'tenʃəri] *s.* työlaitos; kuritushuone, Am. vankila.

pen|knife kynäveitsi. -**man** kynänkäyttäjä; (~ *ship* kaunokirjoitus(taito)). ~-**name** kirjailijanimi.

pennant ['penənt] *s.* viiri.

penniless ['penilis] *a.* pennitön.

pennon ['penən] *s.* lippu, viiri.

Pennsylvania [pensil'veinjə] *erisn.*

penny ['peni] *s.* (pl. *pence*-[pens], *pennies*) penny (= 1/100 puntaa); *turn an honest* ~ ansaita hieman

ylimääräistä rahaa; [*it will*] *cost a pretty* ~ maksaa sievoisen summan; *spend a* ~ käydä WC:ssä. ~-**wise** saita (pikkuasioissa). -**worth** ['peniwə:θ, 'penəθ] *a* ~ *of* pennyllä jtk.

pension ['penʃn] *s.* eläke; ['pa:ŋsiɔ:ŋ] täysihoitola; *v.* antaa eläke; *panna eläkkeelle* (m. ~ *off*). -**able** [-əbl] *a.* eläkkeeseen oikeutettu. -**er** [-ə] *s.* eläkeläinen.

pensive ['pensiv] *a.* miettiväinen, ajatuksiin vaipunut.

pent [pent] *a.:* ~-*up* tukahdutettu.

penta|gon ['pentə|gən] *s.* viisikulmio; *the P*~ Yhdysvaltain sotaministeriö (viisikulmainen rakennus). -**teuch** [-tju:k] *s.: the* ~ viisi Mooseksen kirjaa. -**thlon** [pen'tæθlɔn] *s.* viisiottelu (urh.).

Pentecost ['pentikɔst] *s.* (juutalaisten) helluntai.

penthouse ['penthaus] *s.* katos, vaja; katolle rakennettu huoneisto, kattoasunto.

penultimate [pi'nʌltimit] *a. & s.* viimeisen edellinen.

penu|rious [pi'njuəriəs] *a.* puutteenalainen; saita. -**ry** ['penjuri] *s.* köyhyys.

peon ['pi:ən] *s.* peoni, köyhä päivätyöläinen (Keski- & Et. Am.).

peony ['piəni] *s.* pioni (kasv.).

people [pi:pl] *s.* ihmiset, väki; kansa (pl. ~*s*); *v.* kansoittaa, asuttaa; *some* ~ jotkut ihmiset; *several* ~ *were hurt* useita henkilöitä loukkaantui; *crowded with* ~ täynnä ihmisiä; *my* ~ kotiväkeni, perheeni; *the* ~ (m.) kansa, rahvas; ~ *say* sanotaan; *country* ~ maalaiset; *thickly* ~*d* tiheään asuttu.

pep [pep] *s.* sisu, puhti; *v.:* ~ *up* antaa puhtia; ~ *pill* piristys-, huumepilleri; ~ *talk* innostava, ryhdistävä puhe.

pepper ['pepə] *s.* pippuri; *v.* pippuroida; ampua, pommittaa (kuv.). ~-**and-salt** mustan ja valkean (t. harmaan) kirjava (kangas). ~-**castor** pippuritölkki. -**corn** pippurimarja. -**mint** piparminttu. -**y** [-ri] *a.* pippurinen; tuittupäinen, kiivas.

peptic ['peptik]: ~ *ulcer* mahahaava.

per [pə:] *prep.* kautta, -ssa, -lla,

-llä; ~ *annum* vuodessa; ~ *cent* prosentti(a); ~ *head* hengeltä; ~ *post* postitse; ~ *se* sinänsä.

peradventure [p(ə)rəd'ventʃə] *adv.* mahdollisesti (vanh.).

perambulat|e [pə'ræmbjuleit] *v.* kulkea edestakaisin t. jnk läpi. **-or** [-ə] *s.* lapsenvaunut (lyh. *pram*).

perceive [pə'si:v] *v.* tajuta, oivaltaa; havaita, huomata.

percentage [pə'sentidʒ] *s.* prosentti, -määrä; ~ *point* prosenttiyksikkö.

percep|tible [pə'sep|təbl] *a.* havaittava; *p-ibly* havaittavasti, silminnähtävän. **-tion** [-ʃn] *s.* havainto, oivallus; havaintokyky, käsityskyky; *sense* ~ aistimus. **-tive** [-tiv] *a.* havainto-; tarkkanäköinen, terävä.

perch 1. [pə:tʃ] *s.* ahven.

perch 2. [pə:tʃ] *s.* orsi; (kuv.) korkea asema; mitta (= 5,5 yardia); *v.* istua orre|lle -lla, asettua jhk; ~ *ed on stools* korkeilla (esim. baari)tuoleilla istuen.

perchance [pə'tʃa:ns] *adv.* (vanh.) sattumalta, ehkä.

percipient [pə'sipiənt] *a.* (kuv.) tarkkanäköinen.

percolat|e [pə'kəleit] *v.* tihkua läpi, siivilöidä, suodattaa. **-or** [-ə] *s.* aromikeitin.

percussion [pə'kʌʃn] *s.* isku, lyönti; koputus (lääk.); ~ *cap* nallihattu; ~ *instruments* lyömäsoittimet.

perdition [pə:'diʃn] *s.* tuomio, perikato; kadotus.

peregrin|ation [perigri'neiʃn] *s.* vaellus. **-e** ['perigrin] *s.:* ~ [*falcon*] muuttohaukka.

peremptory [pə'rem(p)t(ə)ri, 'perəm-] *a.* ehdoton, jyrkkä.

perennial [pə'renjəl] *a.* & *s.* monivuotinen (kasvi); ~ *youth* ikinuoruus.

perfect ['pə:fikt] *a.* täydellinen; virheetön, moitteeton, täysin oppinut; *v.* [pə'fekt] täydellistää, kehittää täydelliseksi, hankkia täydellinen taito; *s.: present* ~ perfekti; *past* ~ pluskvamperfekti. **-ion** [pə'fekʃn] *s.* täydellisyys; *to* ~ erinomaisesti, mestarillisesti. **-ly** *adv.* täydellisesti, erinomaisesti; erinomaisen, aivan.

perfid|ious [pə(:)'fidiəs] *a.* petollinen,

kavala. **-y** ['pə:fidi] *s.* petollisuus, petos.

perfora|te ['pə:fəreit] *v.* lävistää, puhkaista; ~ *d ulcer* puhjennut mahahaava. **-tion** [-'reiʃn] *s.* lävistäminen; reikä, -rivit, rei'itys. **-tor** [-ə] *s.* rei'ityskone.

perforce [pə'fɔ:s] *adv.* pakosta, välttämättä.

perform [pə'fɔ:m] *v.* toimittaa, suorittaa, tehdä; esittää (esim. laulaa, soittaa, näytellä); tehdä temppuja; esiintyä. **-ance** [-əns] *s.* suoritus(kyky); esitys, näytös. **-er** [-ə] *s.* esiintyjä, esittäjä. **-ing** (eläimistä) opetettu, sirkus-.

perfume ['pə:fju:m] *s.* tuoksu; hajuvesi; *v.* [pə'fju:m] parfymoida, hajustaa, pirskottaa hajuvettä.

perfunctory [pə'fʌŋ(k)t(ə)ri] *a.* huolimaton, pintapuolinen, välinpitämätön, vain muodon vuoksi tapahtuva.

pergola ['pə:gələ] *s.* lehti|kuja, -maja.

perhaps [pə'hæps, præps] *adv.* ehkä, kenties.

peril ['peril] *s.* vaara; *in* ~ *of one's life* hengenvaarassa. **-ous** [-əs] *a.* vaarallinen.

perimeter [pə'rimitə] *s.* kehä.

period ['piəri|əd] *s.* (ajan)jakso, (aika)kausi; (opetus)tunti; lausejakso, lause; piste; tauko; tyyli-(huonekalu ym); kuukautiset. **-ic** [piəri'ɔdik] *a.* jaksoittainen, ajoittainen. **-ical** [-'ɔdik(ə)l] *a.* = ed.: määräajoin ilmestyvä; *s.* aikakauslehti; ~ *ly* määräajoin; aika ajoin. **-icity** [-ə'disiti] *s.* jaksollisuus.

peri|patetic [peripə|'tetik] *a.* kiertävä. **-pheral** [pə'rifərl] *a.* periferinen, ääreis-, ulko-. **-phery** [pə'rifəri] *s.* kehä. **-pharastic** [peri'fræstik] *a.* kiertäen esittävä. **-scope** ['periskəup] *s.* periskooppi.

perish ['periʃ] *v.* menehtyä, tuhoutua, kuolla; mennä pilalle; turmella; *I was* ~*ed with cold* olin jäätyä, palelin kuin koira. **-able** [-əbl] *a.* katoava; helposti pilaantuva; ~ *s* pl. helposti pilaantuvat (ruoka)tavarat. **-ing** *a.* hirveä, kamala.

periton|eum [peritə'ni:əm] *s.* vatsakalvo. **-itis** [-'naitis] *s.*

vatsakalvontulehdus.
periwig ['periwig] s. tekotukka.
periwinkle ['periwinkl] s. talvikki; ~ *shell* rantakotilo.
perjur|e ['pə:dʒ|ə] v.: ~ *oneself* vannoa väärin; -*ed* valapattoinen. **-er** [-(ə)rə] s. valapatto. **-y** [-(ə)ri] s. väärä vala.
perk [pə:k] **1.** v. (tav. ~ *up)* rohkaistua, piristyä; virkistää; **2.** (kahvista) pulputa, keittää (aromikeittimessä). **-s** [-s] s. (lyh. = *perquisites)* lisäedut. **-y** [-i] a. pirteä, riuska; kopea, nenäkäs.
perm [pə:m] s. (lyh.) permanentti.
permanen|ce ['pə:mənəns] s. pysyvyys. **-cy** [-si] = ed.; vakinainen toimi.
permanent ['pə:mənənt] a. pysyvä, kestävä; vakinainen; ~ *way* (rautatie)rata; *~ed* kestolaineet; ~ *way* (rautatie)rata.
permea|ble ['pə:mjəbl] a. läpäisevä. **-te** [-ieit] v. tunkeutua (jhk t. jnk läpi).
permis|sible [pə'misəbl] a. sallittu, luvallinen. **-sion** [-'miʃn] s. lupa. **-sive** [-misiv] a. suvaitsevainen, salliva; *(~ness* sallivuus).
permit [pə'mit] v. sallia; s. ['pə:mit] lupa, -kirja; *smoking not ~ted* tupakointi kielletty; *weather ~ting* jos sää sallii.
permutation [pə:mju(:)'teiʃn] s. muutos; vaihtelu.
pernicious [pə'niʃəs] a. turmiollinen, tuhoisa; pahanlaatuinen (~ *anemia).*
pernickety [pə'nikiti] a. turhantarkka, pikkutarkka.
peroration [perə'reiʃn] s. puheen (loppu)yhteenveto.
peroxide [pə'rɔksaid] s.: ~ [*of hydrogen]* vetysuperoksidi; ~ *hair* valkaistu tukka.
perpendicular [pə:p(ə)n'dikjulə] a. & s. kohtisuora (viiva); luotiviiva. **-ly** adv. kohtisuoraan.
perpetra|te ['pə:pitreit] v. tehdä (rikos ym). **-tion** [-'treiʃn] s. syyllistyminen jhk. **-tor** [-ə] s. (rikoksen ym) tekijä, syyllinen.
perpetu|al [pə'petjuəl] a. ikuinen; alituinen; lakkaamaton, yhtämittainen; ~ *motion [machine]* ikiliikkuja. **-ate** [-eit] v. ikuistaa; säilyttää. **-ity** [pə:pi'tju(:)iti] s. pysyvyys, ikuisuus; elinkorko; *in* ~ ikuisiksi ajoiksi.

perplex [pə'pleks] v. saattaa ymmälle, hämmentää; *~ed* ymmällään oleva, hämmentynyt. **-ity** [-iti] s. hämmennys, neuvottomuus, pulmallisuus; pulmallinen tilanne.
perquisite ['pə:kwizit] s. (us. *pl.)* lisäetu (palkan lisäksi), etuoikeus.
persecu|te ['pə:sikju:t] v. vainota, ajaa takaa; hätyyttää. **-tion** [-'kju:ʃn] s. vaino; ~ *mania* vainohulluus.
persever|ance [pə:si'viər(ə)ns] s. hellittämättömyys, sitkeys, kestävyys. **-e** [-'viə] v. pysyä lujana; itsepintaisesti jatkaa *(in,* with jtk). **-ing** a. hellittämätön, sitkeä, sinnikäs.
Persia ['pə:ʃə] *erisn.* **-n** ['pə:ʃn] a. & s. persialainen; persian kieli.
persiflage ['pə:sifla:ʒ] s. pilanteko.
persimmon [pə:'simən] s. persimoni.
persist [pə'sist] v. pysyä järkähtämättömänä, ei hellittää, pitää kiinni *(in* jstk); edelleen jatkua, pysyä elossa. **-ence** [-(ə)ns] s. itsepintaisuus, hellittämättömyys (m. *-ency);* jatkuminen. **-ent** [-(ə)nt] a. itsepintainen, hellittämätön; lakkaamaton, jatkuva.
person ['pə:sn] s. henkilö; persoona (kiel.); ulkomuoto, olemus; *in* ~ henkilökohtaisesti. **-a** [pə:'səunə] s.: ~ *non grata* ['grɑ:tə] ei-toivottu henkilö. **-able** [-əbl] a. hauskannäköinen. **-age** [-idʒ] s. (huomattava) henkilö. **-al** [-l] a. oma-, henkilökohtainen; persoona- (kiel.); *don't be too* ~ älä mene henkilökohtaisuuksiin; ~ *property (estate)* irtain omaisuus. **-ality** [pə:sə'næliti] s. persoonallisuus; henkilöys, henkilö; *-alities* henkilökohtaisuudet. **-ally** [-əli] adv. henkilökohtaisesti; ~ *I[think]* minä puolestani. **-ate** ['pə:səneit] v. esittää jkta, esiintyä jkna. **-ification** [pə:sɔnifi'keiʃn] s. henkilöitymä, ruumiillistuma. **-ify** [pə:'sɔnifai] v. olennoida, personoida. **-nel** [pə:sə'nel] s. henkilökunta.
perspective [pə'spektiv] s. & a. perspektiivi(nen); laaja näköala; *[put. .] in* ~ oikeaan perspektiiviin; *see things in* ~ nähdä asiain oikeat suhteet.
perspex ['pə:speks] s. pleksilasi.
perspica|cious [pə:spi'keiʃəs] a.

tarkkanäköinen, terävä-älyinen. **-city** [-'kæsiti] s. tarkkanäköisyys, terävyys.

perspic|uity [pə:spi'kju(:)iti] s. selvyys. **-uous** [pə'spikjuəs] a. selvä, havainnollinen.

perspiration [pə:spə'reiʃn] s. hikoilu; hiki.

perspire [pəs'paiə] v. hikoilla.

persua|de [pə'swei|d] v. saada vakuuttuneeksi; taivuttaa, suostuttaa, suostutella. **-sion** [-ʒn] s. vakuuttelu; suostuttelukyky; vakaumus; uskomus, uskontokunta; (leik.) laji, luokka. **-sive** [-siv] a. suostutteleva; vakuuttava; (~ **ness** s. suostuttelukyky).

pert [pə:t] s. nenäkäs.

pertain [pə'tein] v.: ~ **to** kuulua, liittyä jhk, koskea jtk.

pertina|cious [pə:ti'neiʃəs] a. itsepintainen; hellittämätön. **-city** [-'næsiti] s. itsepintaisuus.

pertinen|ce, -cy ['pə:tinəns, -i] s. sattuvuus, sopivuus. **-t** [-ənt] a. sattuva, asiaankuuluva; (to jhk) kuuluva; ~ **ly** m. asiallisesti.

pertness [pə:tnis] s. nenäkkyys.

perturb [pə'tə:b] v. hämmentää; herättää levottomuutta, kuohuttaa; ~ **ed** levoton, huolestunut. **-ation** [-'beiʃn] s. hämminki, sekasorto.

Peru [pə'ru:] erisn.

perus|al [pə'ru:z(ə)l] s. lukeminen, tarkastelu. **-e** [pə'ru:z] v. lukea (tarkkaavasti); tutkia.

Peruvian [pə'ru:vjən] a. & s. perulainen; ~ **bark** kiinankuori.

perva|de [pə:'vei|d] v. tunkeutua (kaikkialle), täyttää kokonaan. **-sive** [-siv] a. kaikkialle tunkeutuva, leviävä.

perver|se [pə'və:s] a. turmeltunut, paha(ntapainen), väärä; harhaviettinen. **-sion** [pə'və:ʃn] s. turmeleminen; kieroutuminen, vääristely. **-sity** [-iti] s. luonnottomuus; pahantapaisuus.

pervert [pə'və:t] v. tehdä kieroksi, vääristellä; johtaa harhateille, turmella; s. ['pə:və:t] luopio; kieroutunut ihminen.

pervious ['pə:vjəs] a.: ~ **to** jtk läpäisevä; altis jllk.

pesky ['peski] a. (puhek.) harmillinen.

pessary ['pesəri] s. pessaari.

pessim|ism ['pesimizm] s. pessimismi. **-ist** [-ist] s. pessimisti; (~**ic** pessimistinen; ~**ically** pessimistisesti).

pest [pest] s. maanvaiva, vitsaus; tuho|hyönteinen, -eläin.

pester ['pestə] v. kiusata, ahdistaa.

pesti|cide ['pestisaid] s. tuholaismyrkky. **-ferous** [-'tif(ə)rəs] a. turmiollinen, tuhoisa.

pestilen|ce ['pestiləns] s. rutto. **-t** [-ənt] a. turmiollinen, tuhoisa. **-tial** [-'lenʃ(ə)l] a. turmiollinen; (puhek.) sietämätön.

pestle ['pesl] s. (huhmaren) survin.

pet 1. [pet] s. lemmikki, -eläin; (attrib.) lempi-, mieli-; v. hyväillä, rakastella; ~**ting and necking** halailu, rakastelu; ~ **name** lempinimi; one's ~ **aversion** se mitä eniten inhoaa.

pet 2. [pet] s. pahantuulen puuska; in a ~ pahalla tuulella.

petal ['petl] s. terälehti.

petard [pe'ta:d] s. (vanh.) miina; ks. **hoist.**

Peter ['pi:tə] erisn. Pietari.

peter ['pi:tə] v.: ~ **out** ehtyä, kuivua (kokoon), tyrehtyä.

petite [pə'ti:t] a. siro, pieni.

petition [pə'tiʃn] s. anomus; v. anoa (for jtk). **-er** [-ə] s. anoja; kantaja (avioerojutussa).

petrel ['petr(ə)l] s.: stormy ~ myrskypääsky.

petri|faction [petri'fækʃn] s. kivettymä. **-fy** ['petrifai] v. kivettää, muuttaa kiveksi; kivettyä; was -fied jähmettyi kauhusta.

petrol ['petr(ə)l, -ɔl] s. (moottori)bensiini. **-eum** [pi'trəuljəm] s. kivi-, vuoriöljy.

petticoat ['petikout] s. alushame; ~ **dress** liivihame.

pettifogg|er ['petifɔgə] s. (huonomaineinen) asianajaja. **-ing** a. kieroileva, pikkumainen.

pettiness s. mitättömyys.

pettish ['petiʃ] a. ärtyisä, oikullinen, pahantuulinen.

petty ['peti] a. pieni, pikku-; vähäpätöinen, mitätön, pikkumainen; ~ **officer** aliupseeri (laivastossa); ~

farmer pienviljelijä.

petul|ance ['petjuləns] *s.* kärtyisyys.
-ant [-ənt] *a.* tuittupäinen, ärtyisä.

petunia [pi'tju:njə] *s.* petunia.

pew [pju:] *s.* kirkonpenkki.

pewit ['pi:wit] *s.* töyhtöhyyppä.

pewter ['pju:tə] *s.* tina(seos),
tina-astiat.

phaeton ['feitn] *s.* (avoimet)
nelipyöräiset vaunut.

phalan|x ['fælæŋks] *s.* (pl. m. **-ges**
[-ndʒi:z]) falangi, taistelurintama;
(sormi- t. varvas)jäsen.

phantasm ['fæntæzm] *s.* haave-,
unikuva; houre, aave. **-agoria**
[-ə'gɔ:riə] *s.* harhakuvien sarja.

phantasy ks. *fantasy*.

phantom ['fæntəm] *s.* aave, haamu;
harhakuva.

Pharaoh ['fɛərəu] *s.* faarao.

pharis|aic [færi'seiik] *a.* farisealainen,
tekopyhä. **-ee** ['færisi:] *s.*
farisealainen.

pharma|ceutical [fɑ:mə'sju:tik(ə)l] *s.*
farmaseuttinen. **-cist** [-sist] *s.*
apteekkari, rohdoskauppias. **-cy** [-si]
s. farmasia; apteekki, rohdoskauppa.

pharyn|geal [færin'dʒi:əl] *a.* nielu-. **-x**
['færiŋks] *s.* nielu.

phase [feiz] *s.* vaihe, kausi; jakso; *v.*
sovittaa vaiheittain; ~ *in* ottaa
käyttöön (~ *out* lopettaa) vähitellen.

pheasant ['feznt] *s.* fasaani.

phenol ['fi:nɔl] *s.* fenoli.

phenomen|al [fi'nɔmin(ə)l] *a.*
ilmiömäinen. **-on** [-ən] *s.* (pl. **-ena**)
ilmiö.

phial ['faiəl] *s.* pieni lasipullo.

Philadelphia [filə'delfjə] *erisn.*

philander [fi'lændə] *v.* hakkailla. **-er**
[-rə] *s.* (naisten) liehittelijä,
naistenmetsästäjä.

philanthrop|ic [filən'θrɔpik] *a.*
ihmisystävällinen. **-ist** [fi'lænθrəpist]
s. ihmisystävä. **-y** [fi'lænθrəpi] *s.*
ihmisystävällisyys, filantropia.

philatel|ist [fi'lætəlist] *s.*
postimerkkien keräilijä. **-y** [i] *s.*
filatelia, postimerkkeily.

Philip ['filip] *erisn.* Filip. **-pi** [fi'lipai]
erisn. **-pians** [fi'lipiənz] *s.*
Filippiläiskirje.

Philippine ['filipi:n] *erisn.: the ~
Islands, the ~ s* Filippiinit.

Philistine ['filistain] *s.* filistealainen;
poroporvari.

philolog|ical [filə'lɔdʒik(ə)l] *a.*
filologinen. **-ist** [fi'lɔlədʒist] *s.* filologi,
kielentutkija. **-y** [fi'lɔlədʒi] *s.*
kielitiede, filologia.

philosoph|er [fi'lɔsəf|ə] *s.* filosofi; ~ *s'
stone* viisasten kivi. **-ic(al)** [filə'sɔfik,
-(ə)l] *a.* filosofinen. **-ize** [-aiz] *v.*
filosofoida. **-y** [-i] *s.* filosofia.

philtre ['filtə] *s.* lemmenjuoma.

phiz [fiz] *s.* naama (puhek.).

phlegm [flem] *s.* lima, yskös, -kset,
flegmaattisuus. **-atic** [fleg'mætik] *a.*
flegmaattinen, hidasluonteinen.

phlox [flɔks] *s.* leimukukka.

phobia ['foubiə] *s.* kammo, fobia.

Phoenicia [fi'niʃiə] *erisn.* Foinikia. **-n**
[-n] foinikialainen.

phoenix ['fi:niks] *s.* feenikslintu.

phone [foun] (lyh.) *s.* puhelin; *v.*
soittaa puhelimella; *picture ~*
näköpuhelin.

phonetic [fə(u)'netik] *a.* foneettinen.
-ian [founi'tiʃn] *s.* foneetikko. **-s** [-s] *s.*
fonetiikka.

phoney ['founi] *a.* sl. teko-, epäaito; ~
war hämäräsota.

phonograph ['founəgræf] *s.* Am.
gramofoni.

phony ks. *phoney; s.* petkuttaja.

phosphate ['fɔsfeit] *s.* fosfaatti.

phosphor|escence ['fɔsfə'resns] *s.*
fosforihohde. **-ous** ['fɔsf(ə)rəs] *a.*
fosfori-. **-us** ['fɔsf(ə)rəs] *s.* fosfori.

photo ['fəutəu] *s.* (pl. ~s) valokuva.
-composition valoladonta. **-copy** *s. &
v.* valokopio, -ida. ~ **-finish camera**
maalikamera. **-genic** [fəutə'dʒi:nik]
valokuvauksellinen.

photograph ['fəutəgrɑ:f, Am. -græf] *s.*
valokuva; *v.* valokuvata; *she ~ s well*
hän onnistuu valokuvassa. **-er**
[f(ə)'tɔgrəfə] *s.* valokuvaaja. **-ic**
[-'græfik] *a.* valokuvaus-. **-y**
[f(ə)'tɔgrəfi] *s.* valokuvaus.

photo|micrograph *s.* mikrovalokuva.
-stat [-stæt] *s.* valokopio.

phrase [freiz] *s.* lauseparsi,
sanonta(tapa), ilmaisu; *v.* ilmaista.
-ology [-i'ɔlədʒi] *s.* fraseologia.

phren|etic [fri'netik] *a.* hurja, raivoisa.
-ology [-'nɔlədʒi] *s.* frenologia.

phthisis ['θaisis] *s.* keuhkotauti.

phut [fʌt]: *go* ~ raueta, mennä myttyyn.

physic ['fizik] *s.* lääke; (vanh.) lääketiede; *v.* (~*ked*, ~*king*) lääkitä. **-al** [-(ə)l] *a.* fyysinen; ruumiillinen; fysikaalinen; ~ *education* liikuntakasvatus; ~*exercise* liikunta; ~ *training* voimistelu. **-ian** [fi'ziʃn] *s.* lääkäri. **-ist** ['fizisist] *s.* fyysikko. **-s** ['fiziks] *s.* fysiikka.

physiolog|**ical** [fiziə'lɔdʒik(ə)l] *a.* fysiologinen. **-ist** [-'ɔlədʒist] *s.* fysiologi. **-y** [-'ɔlədʒi] *s.* fysiologia.

physiotherapy ['fiziə(u)-] *s.* fysikaalinen hoito.

physique [fi'zi:k] *s.* ruumiinrakenne.

pianist ['piənist] *s.* pianisti, pianonsoittaja.

piano [pi'ænəu] *s.* (pl. ~*s*) piano; *upright* ~ pianiino; *grand* ~ flyygeli; *sottage* ~ pieni pianiino.

pibroch ['pi:brɔk] *s.* säkkipillisävelmä, -sävellys.

picaresque [pikə'resk] *a.* veijari-.

Piccadilly [pikə'dili] *erisn.*

piccolo ['pikələu] *s.* pikkolohuilu.

pick [pik] *s.* hakku; (jnk) paras osa, valio; *v.* poimia, noukkia; nyppiä, nokkia; nyhtää; perata, puhdistaa, kaivella; valikoida; syödä nirsoillen (~ *at*); tiirikoida; (us. ~ *up*) iskeä; *a tooth* ~ hammastikku; ~ *a p.'s pocket* varastaa jkn taskusta: ~ *a quarrel* haastaa riitaa; ~ *one's way* kulkea varovaisesti; ~ *to pieces* repostella, antaa murhaava arvostelu; ~ *at* näykkiä; ~ *off* napsia, ampua alas; ~ *on sb.* valita (tekemään jtk vastenmielistä); ~ *out* valita; saada selville, erottaa; ~ *over* tarkastaa yksitellen, valikoida; ~ *up* kuokkia, poimia, nostaa (maasta); saada (käsiinsä); oppia; noutaa, ottaa mukaan (matkustajia); löytää (sattumalta); saada takaisin (voimansa), toipua; ~ *up speed* lisätä nopeutta; ~ *up* (m.) tutustua, iskeä (~ *up a girl*) (m. ~*up with*). **-aback** [-əbæk] *adv.* (jkn) selässä t. hartioilla. **-axe** hakku. **-ed** [-t] *a.* valikoitu, valio-.

pickerel ['pikər(ə)l] *s.* nuori hauki.

picket ['pikit] *s.* seiväs, paalu; (sot.) järjestyspartio, vartiomies;

lakkovahti, -vahdit; *v.* kiinnittää paaluun; asettaa vartio(on), olla (lakko)vahtina.

picking ['pikin] *s.:* ~*s* saalis.

pickle ['pikl] *s.* suolavesi, etikkaliemi; vallaton lapsi, vintiö; *pl.* pikkelsi, sekavihannessalaatti; *v.* säilöä (etikkaliemeen); *in a [sad]* ~ pahassa pulassa; ~*d* (sl.) kännissä.

pick-me-up piristysryyppy.

pick|**pocket** taskuvaras. ~ **-up** (levysoittimen) äänivarsi; pakettiauto; tilapäistuttava, (isketty) heila; kiihtyvyys.

picnic ['piknik] *s.* huviretki; *v.* (imp. & pp. ~*ked*) olla huviretkellä. **-ker** [-ə] *s.* retkeilijä.

pictorial [pik'tɔ:riəl] *a.* kuva-, kuvitettu; *s.* kuvalehti.

picture ['piktʃə] *s.* kuva, muotokuva; taulu; kuvaus; *pl.: the* ~*s* elokuvat; *v.* kuvata, kuvailla; kuvitella (*to oneself* mielessään); ~ *hat* leveälierinen (naisen) hattu; ~ *postcard* kuvapostikortti; *(she) looks the* ~ *of health* on kuin itse terveys. ~ **-card** kuvakortti (korttip.). ~ **-gallery** taidemuseo. **-sque** [piktʃə'resk] *a.* maalauksellinen.

piddle ['pidl] *v.* (lastenk.) pissiä.

piddling ['pidlin] *a.* mitätön.

pidgin ['pidʒin] *s.* sekakieli; *P~ English* pidginenglanti.

pie [pai] *s.* piiras; *[have] a finger in the* ~ sormet pelissä; ~*-crust* piirakankuori. **-bald** [-bɔ:ld] *a.* laikullinen, kirjava.

piece [pi:s] *s.* palanen, pala, kappale (m. teatteri-); pelinappula; raha; tykki, kivääri; (kangas) pituus; esine; *v.* yhdistää; paikata; (~ *together*) panna kokoon; *a* ~ *of advice* neuvo; *a* ~ *of news* uutinen; *give sb. a* ~ *of one's mind* sanoa jklle suorat sanat; *pay by the* ~ maksaa kappalepalkkaa; *[all] of a* ~ samaa maata; *in* ~*s* sirpaleina; *go to* ~*s* mennä säpäleiksi, menettää hermonsa; *take to* ~*s* hajottaa osiinsa. **-meal** *adv.* pala palalta, vähän kerrallaan. ~**-work** urakkatyö.

pied [paid] *a.* kirjava, laikullinen.

pier [piə] *s.* aallonmurtaja, iso (satama)laituri; ~*-glass* korkea (kokovartalo)peili.

pierc|e ['piəs] v. tunkeutua (jhk), tunkeutua (jnk) lävitse, lävistää, puhkaista. **-ing** a. läpitunkeva, ı ureva.

pietism ['paiətizm] s. pietismi.

piety ['paiəti] s. hurskaus.

piffl|e ['pifl] s. (puhek.) hölynpöly, pöty; **-ing** turhanaikainen.

pig [pig] s. sika, porsas; harkko; ks. *poke.*

pigeon ['pidʒin, -ən] s. kyyhkynen. **-hole** s. lokero; v. panna lokeroon, panna sivuun, lykätä asia toistaiseksi.

pigg|ery ['pigəri] s. sikala. **-ish** [-iʃ] a. siivoton. **-yback:** ride ~ leikkiä »reppuselässä».

pig|-headed itsepäinen. **~-iron** harkkorauta.

pigment ['pigmənt] s. väriaine.

pigmy ['pigmi] ks. *pygmy.*

pig|sty sikolätti. **-tail** (sian)saparo; rullatupakka. **-wash** sianruoka.

pike [paik] s. keihäs; hauki; m. *turnpike.* **-man** tulliportin vartija. **-staff** keihäänvarsi.

pilaster [pi'læstə] s. pilasteri.

Pilate ['pailət] erisn. Pilatus.

pilchard ['piltʃəd] s. sardiini.

pile 1. [pail] s. pino, kasa; iso rakennus(ryhmä); v. kasata, pinota, latoa; *funeral* ~ polttorovio; *nuclear* ~ ydinmiilu; ~ *of arms* kiväärikeko; *make one's* ~ rikastua; ~ *it on* liioitella, panna omiaan; ~ *on the agony* kuvailla piinallisen yksityiskohtaisesti.

pile 2. [pail] s. paalu.

pile 3. [pail] s. karvat, nukka.

pile 4. [pail] s.: ~ s peräpukamat.

pile|-driver paalujuntta. **~-dwelling** paalurakennus.

pilfer ['pilfə] v. näpistellä. **-age** [-ridʒ] s. näpistely.

pilgrim ['pilgrim] s. pyhiinvaeltaja. **-age** [-idʒ] s. pyhiinvaellusmatka.

pill [pil] s. pilleri; *the* ~ ehkäisypilleri.

pillage ['pilidʒ] s. ryöstäminen; ryöstösaalis; v. ryöstää.

pillar ['pilə] s. pilari, pylväs, patsas; tukipylväs. **~-box** Engl. postilaatikko.

pill-box s. pillerirasia; (sot.) tulikorsu, -pesäke.

pillion ['piljən] s. (naisen) satulatyyny; *ride* ~ istua moottoripyörän takana.

pillory ['piləri] s. kaakinpuu, häpeäpaalu; v. panna kaakinpuuhun, häpäistä.

pillow ['pilou] s. päänalunen, pielus. **~-case**, **~-slip** tyynyliina.

pilot ['pailət] s. luotsi; (lentokoneen) ohjaaja; v. luotsata, ohjata; ~ *study* esitutkimus. **-age** [-idʒ] s. luotsaus; luotsimaksu.

pimento [pi'mentou] s. jamaikanpippuri.

pimp [pimp] s. parittaja.

pimpernel ['pimpənel] s. puna-alpi; *the Scarlet P~* Punainen neilikka.

pimpl|e ['pimpl] s. näppylä, finni. **-ed** [-d], **-y** [-i] a. näppyinen.

pin [pin] s. (nuppi)neula; tappi, nasta, pultti; (viulun) tappi; *pl.* koivet; v. kiinnittää (neulalla ym); naulata, (kuv.) naulita, estää liikkumasta (m. ~ *down*); *hair*~ hiusneula; *rolling* ~ kaulin; *tie* ~ solmioneula; *I don't care a* ~ en välitä vähääkään; *[I have]* ~ *s and needles in my foot* (jalkojani) pistelee; ~ *one's faith on* panna toivonsa (jhk); ~ *down* (kuv.) panna seinää vastaan, (. . to a promise) pakottaa pitämään lupaus.

pinafore ['pinəfɔː] s. esiliina.

pinball s. l. v. fortunapeli.

pincers ['pinsəz] s. pl. hohtimet; (äyriäisen) sakset; *pincer movement* pihtiliike.

pinch [pin(t)ʃ] v. nipistää; puristaa; pitää ahtaalla, kiristää; säästää, kituuttaa; (sl.) kähveltää; »napata» kiinni; s. nipistys; hyppysellinen; puristus; pula, ahdinko; *at a* ~ hätätilassa, jos lujalle ottaa; *get* ~ *ed* joutua kiinni. **-ed** [-t] a. kireä.

pine 1. [pain] v. riutua; kaihota. ikävöidä (for).

pine 2. [pain] s. mänty, honka. **-al** [-iəl] a.: ~ *gland* käpyrauhanen. **-apple** ananas. **~-cone** männynkäpy.

ping [piŋ] s. räsähdys. **~-pong** s. pingis.

pinion ['pinjən] s. siivenkärki, siipi; pieni hammaspyörä; v. leikata (linnun) siivenkärki; sitoa käsivarret kylkiin.

pink 1. [piŋk] s. neilikka; vaaleanpunainen väri, ruusunpuna;

(jnk) huippu; *a.* vaaleanpunainen; ~
[*coat*] ketunajajan punainen takki; *the*
~ *of perfection* itse täydellisyys; *in the*
~ loistokunnossa.

pink 2. [piŋk] *v.* rei'ittää, lävistää.

pin-money *s.* taskuraha.

pinnace ['pinis] *s.* (sotalaivan)
laivavene.

pinnacle ['pinəkl] *s.* torninhuippu,
pikkutorni; (kuv.) huippu.

pinny *s.* (lastenk.) essu (*pinafore*).

pin|point *v.* määrittää tarkka sijainti; *s.*
neulankärki; ~ *bombing*
tarkkuuspommitus. **~-prick**
neulanpisto (kuv.). **~-up**
kansikuvatyttö.

pint [paint] *s.* »paintti», tuoppi,
(nestemitta = 0,57 l).

pioneer [paiə'niə] *s.* tienraivaaja,
uranuurtaja; pioneeri; *v.* olla
tienraivaajana.

pious ['paiəs] *a.* hurskas; (vanh.)
vanhempia kunnioittava.

pip 1. [pip] *s.* (appelsiinin ym) siemen.

pip 2. [pip] *s.* (pelikortin ym) silmä;
(upseerin) tähti; (rad. ym)
äänimerkki (piip); piipitys; *v.* ampua;
have the ~ olla masentunut.

pipe [paip] *s.* putki, johto; piippu,
ruokopilli, huilu; *pl.* säkkipilli; *v.*
soittaa ruokopillillä ym; kutsua
vihellettämällä; piipittää; varustaa
putkilla; ~ *cream on sth.* pursottaa
kermaa jhk; ~*d water* vesijohto; ~
down ole hiljaa, lakkaa jo; ~*-dream*
haave. **-line** johto; *in the* ~ tulossa. **-r**
[-ə] *s.: pay the* ~ maksaa viulut
(kuv.). **~-rack** piipputeline.

pipette [pi'pet] *s.* pipetti.

piping *a.* piipittävä jne; *s.* piipitys;
tere(sauma, -reuna); putket, putkisto;
sokerikuorrute, pursotettu
kermavaahto ym; ~ *hot* kihisevän
kuuma; *the* ~ *times of peace* hilpeä
rauhan aika.

piqu|ancy ['pi:kənsi] *s.* kirpeys. **-ant**
[-ənt] *a.* kiihottava, piristävä, kirpeä.

pique [pi:k] *v.* loukata; *s.* harmi,
loukattu ylpeys; ~ *oneself* [*up*]*on*
ylpeillä jstk; ~*d* [*at*] harmissaan,
loukkaantunut.

piqué [pi:kei] *s.* pikee(kangas).

piquet [pi'ket] *s.* piketti (korttipeli).

piracy ['paiərəsi] *s.* merirosvous;

salapainatus.

pirat|e ['paiərit] *s.* merirosvo, -laiva; *v.*
rosvota; painaa luvatta. **-ical**
[pai'rætik(ə)l] *a.* merirosvo-.

pisciculture ['pisikʌltʃə] *s.* kalanviljely.

pish [piʃ] *int.* pyh! mitä vielä!

piss [pis] *v.* (alat.) kusta.

pistil ['pistil] *s.* emi (kasv.).

pistol ['pistl] *s.* pistooli. **~-shot**
pistoolinlaukaus.

piston ['pistən] *s.* mäntä. **~-rod**
männän varsi.

pit [pit] *s.* kuoppa; kaivos; onkalo,
kuilu; takapermanto,
orkesterisyvennys; (rokon) arpi;
(autok.) varikko; Am. (esim.
luumun) kivi; *v.* tehdä kuoppia jhk,
tehdä arpiseksi; panna tappelemaan,
ärsyttää; Am. poistaa kivi, kivet
(hedelmästä); *the* [*bottomless*] ~
helvetti; ~ *of the stomach* sydänala;
cock ~ kukkotaisteluareena; ~ *one's
strength against* ryhtyä taisteluun.

pit-a-pat ['pitəpæt] *adv.: go* ~
(sydämestä) läpättää, (jaloista)
kapsta, kopista.

pitch 1. [pitʃ] *s.* piki; *v.* pietä; ~*-dark*
pilkkopimeä.

pitch 2. [pitʃ] *v.* pystyttää (telttä ym);
heittää, paiskata, singota; (laivasta)
kiikkua (vasten aallokkoa); virittää,
asettaa (jllk korkeudelle); leiriytyä;
pudota, syöksyä (*into* jnk kimppuun);
s. korkeus, huippu; aste;
sävelkorkeus (*high*- ~*ed* korkea, *low*-
~*ed* matala); ~*ed battle* suunniteltu
taistelu (joukot rintamaan
ryhmitettynä); ~ *hay* hangota heinää;
~ *in* (puhek.) panna toimeksi; ryhtyä
tarmolla työhön; ~ *into* hyökätä jnk
kimppuun, käydä käsiksi (työhön); ~
out heittää ulos; [*they*] *were* ~*ed out of
the car* sinkoutuivat autosta; ~ *upon*
sattua löytämään.

pitch-blende *s.* pikivälke.

pitch|er ['pitʃə] *s.* kannu; syöttäjä
(baseball). **-fork** heinähanko; *v.*
nostaa hangolla. **-y** [-i] *a.* pikinen;
pikimusta.

piteous ['pitiəs] *a.* säälittävä, surkea,
kurja.

pitfall ['pitfɔ:l] *s.* salakuoppa, (kuv.)
ansa, (piilevä) vaara.

pithead kaivosaukko.

pith [piθ] s. ydin; (ydin)mehu, voima; (sitruunan ym valkoinen) sisäkuori. **-y** [-i] a. ytimekäs; tarmokas.

piti|able ['pitiəbl] a. säälittävä, surkea. **-ful** a. = ed.; sääliväinen. **-less** a. säälimätön.

pitman ['pitmən] s. kaivostyöläinen.

pittance ['pit(ə)ns] s. huono palkkio, nälkäpalkka.

pitted ['pitid] pp., a. kuoppainen; ~ with smallpox rokonarpinen.

pituitary [pi'tju(:)it(ə)ri] a & s.: ~ [gland] aivolisäke.

pity ['piti] s. sääli; v. sääliä, surkutella; what a ~! mikä vahinko! out of ~ säälistä; have (take) ~ on sääliä jkta.

pivot ['pivət] s. tappi; nasta, keskus; v. asettaa, pyöriä (tapin ym) varassa. **-al** [-l] a. keskeinen, tärkeä.

pixy, pixie ['piksi] s. keijukainen.

placable ['plækəbl, 'plei-] a. sovinnollinen, lempeä.

placard ['plækɑːd] s. (mainos)juliste; v. kiinnittää, juliste(ita), mainostaa.

placate [plə'keit] v. lepyttää.

place [pleis] s. paikka; paikkakunta; talo, koti; toimi(paikka); sija; asema; v. asettaa, sijoittaa; in ~ (oikealla) paikallaan; in ~ of jnk sijasta, asemesta; in ~ s paikoitellen; in the first ~ ensiksi, ensinnäkin; out of ~ asiaankuulumaton, sopimaton; give ~ väistyä; go ~ s (puhek.) menestyä; take ~ tapahtua; [come] to my ~ minun kotiini; ~ an order with antaa jklle tilaus.

placebo [plə'siːbəu] s. rauhoittava näennäislääke.

placid ['plæsid] a. tyyni, levollinen. **-ity** [plæ'siditi] s. tyyneys.

placket ['plækit] s. hameen (sivu)halkio, tasku.

plagiar|ism ['pleidʒiərizm] s. plagiointi, plagiaatti. **-ize** [-aiz] v. plagioida, »varastaa».

plagu|e [pleig] s. maanvaiva, vitsaus; (paise)rutto; v. ahdistaa, kiusata. **~-spot** ruttopesä. **-y** [-i] a. sietämätön.

plaice [pleis] s. punakampela.

plaid [plæd] s. (skotl.) ruudukas villa|vaippa, -huopa.

plain [plein] a. selvä, ilmeinen; yksinkertainen; kaunistelematon,

koruton; suora, -sukainen; yksivärinen; ruma; tasainen; s. tasanko; ~ clothes siviilipuku; ~ cooking, ~ food kotiruoka; ~ dealing reiluus, vilpittömyys; ~ speaking suorat sanat. **~-clothes man** siviilipukuinen (sala)poliisi. **-ly** adv. selvästi jne. **-ness** s. selvyys jne. **~-spoken** suorasukainen.

plaint [pleint] s. kanne. **-iff** [-if] s. kantaja (lak.). **-ive** [-iv] a. valittava.

plait [plæt] s. palmikko; v. palmikoida; in a ~ palmikolla.

plan [plæn] s. suunnitelma, luonnos; pohjapiirros, asemakaava; v. laatia suunnitelma, suunnitella; according to ~ suunnitelmien mukaisesti; ~ned economy suunnitelmatalous.

plane 1. s. plataani (m. ~-tree).

plane 2. [plein] s. taso, pinta; höylä; v. tasoittaa, höylätä.

plane 3. [plein] s. lyh. = aeroplane.

planet ['plænit] s. kiertotähti, planeetta (täht.). **-arium** [-'teəriəm] s. planetaario. **-ary** [-(ə)ri] a. planeetan-.

plangent ['plæn(d)ʒənt] a. raikuva, kumiseva.

plank [plæŋk] s. lankku, lauta; pl. puolueohjelman pääkohdat; v. laudoittaa; ~-bed lavitsa; ~ down lyödä pöytään (rahat). **-ton** [-tən] s. keijusto.

planning s. suunnittelu; town ~ kaupunkisuunnittelu.

plant [plɑːnt] s. kasvi, taimi; (teollisuus)laitos, tehdas; (sl.) petkutus; v. istuttaa, asettaa, sijoittaa; perustaa, juuruttaa; kätkeä (varastettua tavaraa); ~ oneself . . asettua jhk; power ~ voimalaitos.

Plantagenet [plæn'tædʒ(i)nit] erisn.

plantain ['plæntin] s. (piha)ratamo; pisanki, banaanilaji.

plant|ation [plæn'teiʃn] s. istutus, (tee-, kahvi- ym) viljelys. suurviljelmä, plantaasi. **-er** ['plɑːntə] s. viljelijä, plantaasinomistaja.

plaque [plɑːk] s. muistolevyke, muistolaatta, plaketti.

plash [plæʃ] s. loiske; v. loiskia, roiskahtaa.

plasm ['plæz(ə)m] s. protoplasma. **-a** ['plæzmə] s. verineste, -plasma.

plaster [plɑːstə] *s.* laastari; kipsilaasti;
v. laastaroida; rapata, kalkita;
liisteröidä; töhriä; *in* ~ kipsissä
(lääk.); ~ *of Paris* valukipsi. **-er** [-rə]
s. kipsityöläinen.

plastic [ˈplæsti|k] *a.* plastinen,
muovautuva; veistoksellinen;
taipuisa; *s.* muovi; ~ *surgery*
muovauskirurgia. **-ine** [-siːn] *s.*
muovailuvaha. **-ity** [-ˈtisiti] *s.*
plastisuus jne.

plate [pleit] *s.* lautanen, vati; levy,
laatta; nimi|laatta, -kilpi; kuvalaatta;
(vaski- ym) piirros; valokuvauslevy;
liitekuva; (hopea- ym) pöytäkalusto;
kate; palkintopokaali (urh.);
(hammasl.) (kita)levy, proteesi; *v.*
päällystää metallilevyllä, panssaroida;
silata, hopeoida, kullata; ~ *glass*
peililasi; *home* ~ kotipesä (urh.);
number ~ (auton) rekisterikilpi.

plateau [ˈplætəu] *s.* ylätasanko.

plateful *s.* lautasellinen.

plate-rack kuivausteline.

platform [ˈplætfɔːm] *s.* koroke, lava;
asemasilta, laituri; puolueohjelma.

platinum [ˈplætinəm] *s.* platina.

platitud|e [ˈplætitjuːd] *s.* lattea
huomautus; mauttomuus. **-inous**
[-ˈtjuːdinəs] *a.* lattea, kulunut.

Plato [ˈpleitəu] *erisn.* Platon. **p-nic**
[pləˈtɔnik] *a.* platoninen.

platoon [pləˈtuːn] *s.* joukkue.

platter [ˈplætə] *s.* tarjoiluvati.

platypus [ˈplætipəs] *s.* nokkaeläin.

plaudits [ˈplɔːdits] *s.* kättentaputukset,
suosionosoitukset.

plaus|libility [plɔːzəˈbiliti] *s.*
uskottavuus. **-ible** [ˈplɔːzəbl] *a.*
todennäköinen, uskottava; näyttävä,
vakuuttava(lta tuntuva).

play [plei] *v.* leikkiä, leikitellä;
ilakoida, kujeilla; pelata; soittaa;
näytellä; (hymystä ym) väreillä,
väikkyä; olla toiminnassa, toimia;
suuntautua, suunnata; siirtää; *s.*
leikki, kisailu; liike, vilske, peli;
näytelmä, teatterinäytäntö; välys,
liikkumavara; ~ *fair*, ~ *the game*
pelata rehellistä peliä; ~ *sb. false*
pettää; ~ *at keeping shop* eikkiä
kauppaa; ~ *war-game* leikkiä sotaa;
~ *into the hands of* pelata jnk toisen
pussiin; ~ *sb. off against* [*another*]

yllyttää (omaksi edukseen) jkta
(toista vastaan); ~ *on* [*sb.'s feelings*]
käyttää hyväkseen; *the guns* ~*ed on
the fort* tykit tulittivat linnaketta; ~*ed
out* poissa pelistä, uupunut; ~*up*
ponnistaa voimansa (pelissä); ~
mainostaa, yllyttää; ~ *up to* (näytellä
niin että) auttaa (vastanäyttelijää),
mielistellä; ~ *of colours* värien
vivahtelu; ~ *of features*
kasvojenilmeet; *be at* ~ leikkiä; *bring
into* ~ panna liikkeelle; *come into* ~
alkaa toimia t. vaikuttaa; *give full* ~ *to*
päästää valloilleen; *a* ~ *on words*
sanaleikki. **~-back** nauhurin
toistolaite. **-bill** teatteri-ilmoitus,
-juliste. **-boy** rattopoika. **-er** [-ə] *s.*
pelaaja (et. ammatti-); näyttelijä.
-fellow leikkitoveri. **-ful** *a.* leikillinen,
leikkimielinen. **-goer**
teatterissakävijä. **-ground**
leikkikenttä. **-house** teatteri. **-ing** *s.*
(~*-cards* pelikortit; ~ *field*
urheilukenttä.) **-mate** leikkitoveri.
~-off uusintaottelu, loppusarja.
~-pen leikkikehä. **~-suit** leikkipuku.
-thing leikkikalu, lelu. **-time** leikin
aika. **-wright** näytelmäkirjailija.

plea [pliː] *s.* (vastaajan) puolustus; ~
for mercy armonanomus; *on the* ~ *of
ill health* vedoten sairauteen.

plead [pliːd] *v.* puhua (asianajajana)
oikeudessa, ajaa (jkn asiaa); esittää
puolustukseksi, vedota jhk; pyytää,
anoa; ~ *guilty* tunnustaa
syyllisyytensä; ~ *not guilty* kieltää
syyllisyytensä. **-ing** *s.* ks. yllä; (~*s*)
puolustusasianajajan ja syyttäjän
lausunnot; *a.* anova, rukoileva.

pleasant [ˈpleznt] *a.* miellyttävä,
hauska; [*have a*] ~ *journey!* onnea
matkalle! **-ry** [-ri] *s.* leikinlasku,
leikki, pila.

pleas|e [pliːz] *v.* miellyttää, olla jkn
mieleen, tehdä (jklle) mieliksi;
ilahduttaa; suvaita; haluta; *come in,* ~
ole hyvä ja käy sisälle; *this way,* ~
tätä tietä, olkaa hyvät (m. esim. *ring
the bell,* ~ ; *two coffees,* ~); *yes,* ~
kyllä, kiitos; ~ *yourself* tee niinkuin
haluat; *as you* ~ kuten haluat(te); ~
God jos Jumala suo. **-ed** [-d] *a.*
tyytyväinen, iloinen. **-ing** *a.*
miellyttävä, mieluinen.

pleasurable ['pleʒ(ə)rəbl] *a.* mieluisa, hauska.

pleasure ['pleʒə] *s.* mielihyvä, ilo; huvi, nautinto; halu, tahto, mieli; *take ~ in* [..*-ing*] tehdä jtk mielellään, nauttia jstk; *may I have the ~ of*..suotteko minulle.., saanko luvan? *with ~* mielelläni, mielellään; *at your ~* milloin haluat. **~-ground** huvipuisto.

pleat [pli:t] *s.* laskos; *v.* laskostaa; *~ed* m. pliseerattu.

pleb|eian [pli'bi(:)ən] *a.* alhaissyntyinen, rahvaanomainen; *s.* plebeji. **-iscite** ['plebisit, Am. -sait] *s.* kansanäänestys.

pledge [pledʒ] *s.* pantti, vakuus; juhlallinen lupaus; (jkn) malja; *v.* antaa pantiksi; sitoutua maksamaan; juoda jkn malja; *~ oneself* sitoutua; *~ one's word* antaa (kunnia)sanansa; *take the ~* tehdä raittiuslupaus.

plenary ['pli:nəri] *a.* rajaton; *~ session* täysistunto.

pleni|potentiary ['plenipə'tenʃ(ə)ri] *a. & s.* täysivaltainen (lähettiläs). **-tude** ['plenitju:d] *s.* runsaus.

plent|eous ['plentjəs] *a.* (run.) = seur. **-iful** ['plentif(u)l] *a.* runsas, yltäkylläinen.

plenty ['plenti] *s.* runsaus, yltäkylläisyys; (puhek.) aivan; *~ of* runsaasti, paljon; *in ~* runsaasti; *~ big enough* ihan tarpeeksi iso.

plethora ['pleθərə] *s.* runsaus, (lääk.) liikaverisyys.

pleurisy [pluərisi] *s.* keuhkopussintulehdus.

plexus ['pleksəs] *s.* punos, verkosto.

pli|able ['plaiəbl] *a.* notkea; taipuisa, myöntyväinen. **-ancy** [-ənsi] *s.* taipuisuus. **-ant** [ənt] *a.* = pliable.

pliers ['plaiəz] *s. pl.* (taivutus) pihdit.

plight 1. [plait] *s.* ahdinko; *in a sad ~* surkeassa tilassa.

plight 2. [plait] *v.* antaa (sanansa); *~ed* (vanh.) kihlautunut.

Plimsoll ['plimz(ə)l] *s.:* *~ line* lastiviiva; *p~s* kumitossut.

plinth [plinθ] *s.* (pylvään) aluslaatta.

plod [plɔd] *v.:* *~ [along]* kulkea raskain askelin, laahustaa; uurastaa, ahertaa (us. *~ [away] at*). **-der** [-ə] *s.* työjuhta, raataja.

plonk 1. [plɔŋk] *v.* pudottaa.

plonk 2. *s.* (sl.) viina(kset).

plop [plɔp] *s.* molskahdus; *v.* pudota molskahtaen, plumpsahtaa.

plot [plɔt] *s.* maatilkku, palsta; juoni; sala|juoni, -liitto; *v.* vehkeillä, punoa salajuonia; suunnitella, piirtää (kartta, käyrä), esittää graafisesti. **-ter** [-ə] *s.* vehkeilijä.

plough [plau] *s.* aura; sl. reput; *v.* kyntää; uurtaa; sl. reputtaa; *the P~* Otava; *~ back [profits into the firm]* sijoittaa (voitot) uudelleen (yritykseen); *~ through* raivata tiensä, kahlata jnk läpi. **-man** kyntäjä. **-share** auranterä.

plover ['plʌvə] *s.* kurmitsa.

plow [plau] *s.* Am. = *plough*.

ploy [plɔi] *s.* metku, homma.

pluck [plʌk] *v.* kyniä; poimia; nykiä, nyhtäistä, nyppiä (*~ at*); (sl.) reputtaa; (sl.) petkuttaa; *s.* rohkeus, sisu; *~ [a guitar]* näppäillä *~ up courage* rohkaista mielensä. **-y** [-i] *a.* rohkea, sisukas.

plug [plʌg] *s.* tulppa, tappi; pistotulppa, pistoke (sähk.); mainos; tupakkalevy; *v.* tukkia tulpalla; (sl.) ampua, iskeä nyrkillä; toitottaa, mainostaa, esim. laulattaa laulattamistaan (tehdäkseen tunnetuksi); *~ [away at]* ahertaa jnk ääressä; *~ in* kytkeä (pistorasiaan).

plum [plʌm] *s.* luumu; (kuv.) makupala (esim. hieno virka); *~ cake* rusinakakku; *~ duff* rusinavanukas; *~ pudding* englantilainen jouluvanukas.

plumage ['plu:midʒ] *s.* höyhenpeite, höyhenet.

plumb [plʌm] *s.* lyijyluoti, mittaluoti; *a.* luoti-, pystysuora; täydellinen; *adv.* luoti-, pystysuorassa, -aan; suoraan; *v.* luodata; tutkia, päästä selville; *out of ~* vinossa; *~ [crazy]* aivan, pähkä-. **-ago** [plʌm'beigəu] *s.* grafiitti; lyijykukka. **-er** ['plʌm] *s.* putkityöläinen. **-ing** ['plʌmiŋ] *s.* putkityö(t), putkisto. **~-line** luotinuora.

plume [plu:m] *s.* sulka, -töyhtö; *v.* (linnusta) siistiä (höyhenet); *~ oneself on* pöyhistellä, ylpeillä jllak; *in borrowed ~s* lainahöyhenissä.

plummet ['plʌmit] *s.* mittaluoti,

luotain; lyijypaino; *v.* romahtaa.

plump 1. [plʌmp] *a.* pullea, pyylevä; *v.* lihottaa, lihoa, paisua, pulskistua (m. ~ *up,* ~ *out*).

plump 2. [plʌmp] *v.* pudottaa, pudota mätkähtäen; *adv.* mätkähtäen; mäiskis; päin naamaa; *a.* suora, ehdoton; ~ *for* äänestää (vain yhtä), antaa jakamaton kannatus. **-ness** *s.* pulleus

plunder ['plʌndə] *v.* ryöstää, rosvota; *s.* ryöstö; (ryöstö)saalis.

plunge [plʌn(d)ʒ] *v.* upottaa, syöstä; saattaa (jhk tilaan); syöksyä, sukeltaa; (laivasta) puskea; (sl.) pelata uhkapeliä; *s.* sukellus, syöksy; ~ *d in darkness* pilkkopimeä; ~ *d in thought* syvissä mietteissä; *take the* ~ ottaa ratkaiseva askel. **-r** [ə] *s.* mäntä.

plunk [plʌŋk] ks. *plonk 1.*

pluperfect ['plu:'pə:fikt] *s.:* ~ [*tense*] pluskvamperfekti.

plural ['pluər(ə)l] *a.* monikollinen; *s.* monikko. **-ity** [-'ræliti] *s.* paljous; enemmistö.

plus [plʌs] *prep.* ynnä, plus; *a.* plus-, positiivinen; *s.* plusmerkki; *the 11*~ (t. *eleven +*) [*examination*] keskikoulun pääsytutkinto. **-fours** [plʌs'fɔ:z] *s. pl.* pussihousut.

plush [plʌ∫] *s.* nukkakangas, plyysi; *a.* (sl.) ylellinen, hieno (m. *-y*).

pluto|cracy [plu:'tɔkrəsi] *s.* plutokratia, rahavalta. **-crat** ['plu:təkræt] *s.* raharuhtinas; (~ **ic** [-'krætik] *a.* plutokraattinen).

ply 1. [plai] *s.* säie; paksuus, kerros, laskos; *three*~ kolmisäikeinen, -nkertainen.

ply 2. [plai] *v.* käyttää (ahkerasti t. kaikin voimin), harjoittaa (ammattia ym); liikennöidä (us. *between*); ~ *sb. with* tyrkyttää jklle jtk, ahdistaa (kysymyksillä); ~ *one's needle* ommella ahkerasti.

Plymouth ['pliməθ] *erisn.*

plywood ['plaiwud] *s.* vaneri.

pneum|atic [nju(:)'mætik] *a.* ilma-; ~ *post* putkiposti. **-onia** [-'məunjə] *s.* keuhkokuume.

poach 1. [pəut∫] *v.* keittää muna kuorretta; ~ *ed egg* hyydytetty muna.

poach 2. *v.* harjoittaa salametsästystä t. -kalastusta, tunkeutua luvatta (on

jhk). **-er** [-ə] *s.* salametsästäjä. **-ing** *s.* salametsästys.

pock [pɔk] *s.* rokko, rokonarpi.

pocket ['pɔkit] *s.* tasku; (kuv.) kukkaro, pussi; (kuv.) pesäke; *v.* pistää taskuunsa, tienata; pitää hyvänään, niellä (loukkaus); *a.* tasku-(kokoinen); *I am £2 in (out of)* ~ tienasin (menetin) 2 puntaa. **~-book** lompakko. **~-money** taskurahat.

pockmarked *a.* rokonarpinen.

pod [pɔd] *s.* palko; *v.* muodostaa palkoja; silpoa. **-ded** [-id] *a.* palko-.

podgy ['pɔdʒi] *a.* lyhyt ja paksu, tukeva, pullea.

Poe [pəu] *erisn.*

poem ['pəuim] *s.* runo.

poet ['pəuit] *s.* runoilija. **-ess** [-is] *s.* (nais)runoilija. **-ic** [pə(u)'etik] *a.* runollinen, runo-; runomuotoinen (tav. *-ical*). **-ry** ['pəuitri] *s.* runous; runollisuus; runot; *a piece of* ~ runo.

po-faced ['pəufeist] *a.* tyhmän juhlallinen.

pogrom ['pɔgrəm] *s.* (juutalais)vaino.

poign|ancy ['pɔinənsi] *s.* kipeys, tuskallisuus. **-ant** [-ənt] *a.* kirvelevä, tuskallinen, kipeä, syvä.

poinsettia [pɔin'setjə] *s.* joulutähti (kasv.).

point [pɔint] *s.* piste, kohta; ajankohta; (desimaali)pilkku, (kompassin)piiru, aste; yksityiskohta; (hyvä t. huono) puoli; (asian) ydin, ydinkohta, tärkein kohta, kärki, vitsi, (itse) asia, tarkoitus; tunnus, ominaisuus; (neulan ym) kärki; niemi; syövytysneula, kaiverrin; asia, seikka, kysymys (~ *of conscience); pl.* vaihde (rautat.); *v.* terävöittää; antaa kärkeä t. pontta; osoittaa (sormella) (*at, to*), viitata; suunnata, tähdätä) huomauttaa (tav. ~ *out);* olla suunnattuna; (koirasta) seisoa (lintua ym); *a* ~ *of honour* kunnia-asia; ~ *of view* näkö|kohta, -kanta; *in* ~ *of fact* itse asiassa; .. *in* ~ kysymyksessä oleva; *a case in* ~ valaiseva esimerkki; *full* ~ piste; *strong* ~ vahva puoli; *to the* ~ asiallinen, sattuva; .. *is beside the* ~ on epäolennaista, ei kuulu asiaan; *on the* ~ *of falling* putomaisillaan; *at the* ~ *of* *death* viimeisillään; *at the ~ of the sword* väkivallan edessä; *up to a ~* tiettyyn määrään, rajaan asti: *come to the ~* tulla itse asiaan; *when it came to the ~* toden tullen; *make* (t. *raise*) *a ~* esittää näkökohta(naan); *make a ~ of* pitää tärkeänä, välttämättömänä; *makes the ~ that* tuo esille sen seikan, että; [*he*] *made three* ~s esitti kolme väitettä; *my ~ is* tarkoitan (että); *win on ~s* voittaa pisteillä; *I don't see the ~ of the story* en tajua jutun ydintä, kärkeä; *there is no ~ in. . .ing* ei kannata; *he mistook my ~* hän käsitti väärin tarkoitukseni; *carry one's ~* päästä tarkoituksensa perille.

~-**blank** *a.* suorasuuntaus-; jyrkkä; *adv.* suoralta kädeltä, muitta mutkitta; *at p.-b. range* lähietäisyydeltä. ~-**duty** *s.: constable on p.-d.* liikennepoliisi. -**ed** [-id] *a.* terävä; pisteliäs, purevan ivallinen; tarkoituksellinen; ~ *arch* suippokaari. -**edly** *adv.* ks. ed.; nimenomaan, korostetusti. -**er** [-ə] *s.* osoitin; karttakeppi; pointteri (koira). ~-**lace** ommeltu pitsi. -**less** *a.* (kuv.) tarkoitukseton, aiheeton. -**sman** *s.* vaihdemies (rautat.).

poise [poiz] *v.* pitää tasapainossa, pitää jssk asennossa; riippua ilmassa; *s.* (et. henkinen) tasapaino; ryhti, (pään) asento.

poison ['poizn] *s.* myrkky; *v.* myrkyttää; ~*ed* myrkytetty. ~-**gas** myrkkykaasu. -**ing** *s.* myrkytys. -**ous** [-əs] *a.* myrkyllinen.

poke [pouk] *v.* sysätä, tuupata, tönäistä; pistää; kohentaa (tulta); *s.* töykkäys; (bahyttihatun) esiinpistävä lieri; ~ *about* etsiä, penkoa, haparoida; ~ *fun at* tehdä pilaa jksta) ~ *into* [*another's affairs*] pistää nenänsä; *buy a pig in a ~* ostaa sika säkissä. ~-**bonnet** bahyttihattu.

poker ['poukə] *s.* hiilihanko; pokeri(peli). ~-**face** pokerinaama. ~-**work** polttokaiverrus.

poky ['pouki] *a.* pieni, ahdas, Am. ikävä.

Poland ['pouland] *erisn.*

polar ['poulə] *a.* napaseudun, napa-; polaarinen (sähk.); ~ *bear* jääkarhu; ~ *circle* napapiiri.

pole 1. [poul] *s.* napa; *North P~* pohjoisnapa.

pole 2. [poul] *s.* pylväs, seiväs, tanko; riuku, salko; pituusmitta (5,5 yards); *v.* sauvoa; ~ *vault* seiväshyppy; *up the ~* pulassa.

Pole [poul] *s.* puolalainen.

pole|-**axe** ['poulæks] tappara, teurastajan kirves. -**cat** hilleri (eläin.).

polemic [pə'lemik] *a.* poleeminen; *s.* polemiikki, kiista(kirjoitus). (m. ~*s*); poleemikko.

pole-star *s.* pohjantähti.

police [pə'li:s] *s.* poliisi(laitos) *(the ~);* ~ *constable* poliisi(mies); *v.* valvoa järjestystä jssk. -**man** poliisi(konstaapeli). -**woman** naispoliisi.

policy 1. ['polisi] *s.* politiikka, valtioviisaus; menettelytapa, ohjelma, toimintaperiaate; *it was good ~* [*to*] oli viisasta, hyvin harkittua; *long-range ~* pitkän tähtäyksen ohjelma.

policy 2. ['polisi] *s.* vakuutuskirja; ~ -*holder* vakuutettu.

polio ['pouli|əu] *s.* = seur. -**myelitis** [-ə(u)maiə'laitis] *s.* lapsihalvaus, polio.

polish ['polif] *v.* kiillottaa; hioa; viimeistellä, sivistää; kiillottua; *s.* kiilto; kiillotusaine, kiilloke; ~ *off* lopettaa nopeasti; ~*ed manners* hienostuneet tavat; *shoe ~* kenkävoide.

Polish ['poulif] *a. & s.* puolalainen; *s.* puolan kieli.

polite [pə'lait] *a.* kohtelias; hieno, sivistynyt; *in ~ society* sivistyneessä seurassa. -**ness** *s.* kohteliaisuus.

politic ['politik] *a.* viisas, harkittu; harkitseva, varovainen; *the body ~* valtio. -**al** [pə'litik(ə)l] *a.* poliittinen, valtiollinen; ~ *economy* kansantaloustiede; ~ *science* valtiotiede. -**ian** [poli'tiʃn] *s.* poliitikko. -**s** [-s] *s. pl.* politiikka; valtiotaito.

polity ['politi] *s.* valtiomuoto.

polka ['polkə] *s.* polkka; ~-*dot* [*scarf*] isopilkullinen.

poll [poul] *s.* vaaliluettelo; äänestys; ääntenlaskenta; äänestyspaikka (m.

-ing place); v. latvoa (puu), katkaista (sarvet); laskea äänet; äänestää; saada (äänimäärä); tutkia (yleisön) mielipiteitä; *public opinion ~* mielipidetutkimus; *go to the ~ s* mennä äänestämään; *the ~ was high* äänestysprosentti oli korkea; *~ beast* nutipää.

Poll [pɔl] s. (*p~*) papukaija.

pollard ['pɔləd] s. nutipää; latvottu puu; v. latvoa.

poll|en ['pɔlin] s. siitepöly. **-inate** [-eit] v. pölyttää. **-ination** [-'neiʃn] s. pölytys.

poll|ing-booth äänestyskoppi. **-ing-place** vaalihuoneisto. **-ster** ['pəulstə] mielipiteiden tutkija. **~-tax** henkiraha.

pollu|tant [pə'lu:tənt] s. saate; saastuttaja. **-te** [pə'lu:t] v. saastuttaa; pilata, liata; häväistä. **-tion** [-ʃn] s. saastuminen, saastuneisuus (esim. *air ~*).

polo ['pəuləu] s. poolopeli; *water ~* vesipallo; *~-neck* poolokauluksinen.

polonaise [pɔlə'neiz] s. poloneesi.

poltroon [pɔl'tru:n] s. pelkuri. **-ery** [əri] s. raukkamaisuus.

poly- ['pɔli-] pref. moni-. **-gamous** [pɔ'ligəməs] a. moniavioinen. **-gamy** [pɔ'ligəmi] s. moniavioisuus. **-glot** [-glɔt] a. & s. monikielinen (henkilö). **-gon** [-gən] s. monikulmio. **P~nesian** [-'niz:jən] a. polyneesialainen.

poly|syllabic [pɔli|si'læbik] a. monitavuinen. **-syllable** [-siləbl] s. monitavuinen sana. **-theism** [-θi:izm] s. monijumalaisuus.

pomade [pə'mɑ:d] s. pomada.

pomegranate ['pɔmgrænit] s. granaattiomena.

pomelo ['pɔmiləu] s. greippi; pummelo.

Pomerania [pɔmə'reinjə] erisn. Pommeri. **-n** [-n] pommerilainen; pommerinpystykorva.

pommel ['pɔml] s. satulan nuppi; v. mukiloida.

pomp [pɔmp] s. loisto, upeus.

Pompeii ['pɔm'pi:ai] erisn. Pompeji.

pompon [pɔmpɔn] s. pumpula, tupsu.

pomp|osity [pɔm'pɔsiti] s. mahtipontisuus. **-ous** ['pɔmpəs] a.

pöyhistelevä; mahtipontinen.

pond [pɔnd] s. lammikko.

ponder ['pɔndə] v. punnita, harkita, miettiä (m. *~ over*). **-able** [-rəbl] a. punnittavissa oleva; *~s* huomionarvoiset seikat ym. **-ous** ['pɔnd(ə)rəs] a. raskas, kömpelö; ikävä.

pongee [pɔn'dʒi:] s. pehmeä, paksu (raaka)silkki.

poniard ['pɔnjəd] s. tikari.

ponti|ff ['pɔntif] s. paavi; ylimmäinen pappi. **-fical** [-'tifik(ə)l] a. paavillinen; *~s* piispan ym messupuku. **-ficate** [-'tifikət] s. paavius.

pontoon [pɔn'tu:n] s. ponttoni, kelluke.

pony ['pəuni] s. pieni hevonen, poni; *~-tail* poninhäntä (kampaus); *~-trekking* (pitkä) ratsastusretki.

poodle ['pu:dl] s. villakoira.

pooh [pu:] int. pyh! **~-pooh** [pu:'pu:] v. nyrpistää nenäänsä jllek, vähätellä.

pool 1. [pu:l] s. lätäkkö, lammikko; uima-allas; suvanto.

pool 2. [pu:l] s. (yhteis)panos, potti; eräänl. biljardipeli; (liik.) rengas; v. panna yhteiseen rahastoon, lyödä yhteen; *football ~s* jalkapalloveikkaus; *do the ~s* veikata; *~ coupon* veikkauskuponki.

poop [pu:p] s. perä, peräkansi.

poor [puə] a. köyhä; niukka; kehno, huono, karu, laiha (maa); parka, raukka; *~ thing* lapsiparka! *ihmisparka! the ~* köyhät; *the ~ white* köyhtyneet valkoiset; *~ in minerals* vähämineraalinen. **~-box** s. kolehtilipas. **~-law** köyhäinhoitolaki. **-ly** adv. niukasti, kehnosti; a. huonovointinen, huonossa kunnossa; *~ off* huonoissa varoissa.

pop [pɔp] s. pamaus; limonaati ym; v. pamahtaa; laukaista; tulla tupsahtaa, livahtaa, pistää nopeasti; (sl.) pantata, viedä kaniin: adv. pamahtaen; *~ in* pistäytyä, piipahtaa jssk; *~ off* (sl.) kuolla kupsahtaa; *~ out* pulpahtaa esiin, pullistua ulos; *~ the question* kosia; *in ~* pantissa, kanissa; *~-eyed* silmät selällään. **~-corn** paahdettu maissi.

Pop [pɔp] s. (sl.) isäukko; *pop* (lyh.) *= popular; ~* [*concert*] viihde-; *~ tune* iskelmä.

pope [pəup] s. paavi. **-ry** [-əri] s. paavilaisuus.

pop-gun s. ilmakivääri.

popinjay ['pɔpindʒei] s. itserakas narri, keikari.

popish ['pəupiʃ] a. paavillinen.

poplar ['pɔplə] s. poppeli; *trembling* ~ haapa.

poplin ['pɔplin] s. popliini(kangas).

poppet ['pɔpit] s. kullanmuru.

poppy ['pɔpi] s. unikko; ~*cock* hölynpöly.

pop-shop s. panttikonttori, kani.

populace ['pɔpjuləs] s. rahvas, massat, kansa.

popular ['pɔpjulə] a. kansan-; kansantajuinen, kansanomainen; suosittu; (hinnasta) halpa; ~ *front* kansanrintama. **-ity** [-'læriti] s. kansansuosio, yleinen hyväksyntä. **-ize** [-raiz] v. tehdä suosituksi; esittää yleistajuisessa muodossa, popularisoida. **-ly** adv. kansan keskuudessa; yleistajuisesti.

popul|ate ['pɔpjuleit] v. kansoittaa, asuttaa; *densely (thickly)* ~d taajaan asuttu. **-ation** [-'leiʃn] s. väestö, asukkaat; väkiluku; asutus; (tiet.) populaatio, kanta. **-ous** [-əs] a. taajaväkinen.

porcelain ['pɔ:slin] s. posliini.

porch [pɔ:tʃ] s. kuisti, Am. vilpola, veranta.

porcupine ['pɔ:kjupain] s. piikkisika.

pore 1. [pɔ:] s. (iho)huokonen.

pore 2. [pɔ:] v.: ~ *over (upon)* miettiä, pohtia jtk; ~ *over books* istua nenä kirjassa.

pork [pɔ:k] sianliha. ~**-butcher** s. leikkeleliike. **-er** [-ə] s. syöttösika.

porn [pɔ:n] puhek. (lyh.) porno.

pornograph|ic [pɔ:nə'græfik] a. pornografinen. **-y** [-'nɔgrəfi] s. pornografia.

por|osity [pɔ:'rɔsiti] s. huokoisuus. **-ous** [pɔ:'rəs] a. huokoinen.

porphyry ['pɔ:firi] s. porfyyri.

porpoise ['pɔ:pəs] s. pyöriäinen (eläint.).

porri|dge ['pɔri|dʒ] s. puuro. **-nger** [-n(d)ʒə] s. (pieni) kulho, kuppi.

port 1. [pɔ:t] s. satamakaupunki, satama (m. kuv.).

port 2. [pɔ:t] s. portviini.

port 3. [pɔ:t] ks. *port-hole*.

port 4. [pɔ:t] s. (laivan) vasen sivu, paapuuri; v. kääntää paapuuriin.

port 5. [pɔ:t] s. (vanh.) ryhti. **-able** [-əbl] a. kannettava; ~ *radio [set]* matkaradio. **-age** [-idʒ] s. kuljetus, -maksu; veneiden ym kuljetus maitse (esim. joen kulkukelvottoman osan ohi), v. kuljettaa (veneitä) maitse.

port|al ['pɔ:tl] s. (komea) portti. **-cullis** [pɔ:t'kʌlis] s. laskuristikko.

porten|d [pɔ:'tend] v. ennustaa. **-t** ['pɔ:tent] s. enne, merkki; ihme(olento). **-tous** [pɔ:'tentəs] a. pahaenteinen; ihmeellinen, tavaton.

porter 1. ['pɔ:tə] s. ovenvartija, (hotellin) portieeri; kantaja.

porter 2. ['pɔ:tə] s. portteri (olut).

porterage [-ridʒ] s. kuljetus; kantopalkka.

portfolio [pɔ:t'fouljəu] s. (pl. ~*s*) salkku; [*minister*] *without* ~ salkuton.

porthole s. (hytin ym.) ikkuna; (ampuma-)aukko.

portico ['pɔ:tikəu] s. (pl. ~[*e*]*s*) pylväikkö, pylväshalli.

portion ['pɔ:ʃn] s. osa; osuus, annos; perintöosa; myötäjäiset; kohtalo; v. jakaa (us. ~ *out*).

portliness s. muhkeus; ks. seur.

portly ['pɔ:tli] a. muhkea, pyylevä.

portmanteau [pɔ:t'mæntəu] s. (pl. ~*s*, ~*x* [-z]) (kaksiosainen) matkalaukku; ~ *word* yhdistesana.

portrait ['pɔ:trit] s. muotokuva, kuva; kuvaus. **-ure** [-ʃə] s. muotokuvamaalaus.

portray [pɔ:'trei] v. maalata, piirtää (jkn) kuva; kuvata, kuvailla; esittää (jkn osaa). **-al** [-'(i)əl] s. (muoto)kuva, kuvaus.

Portsmouth ['pɔ:tsməθ] erisn.

Portug|al ['pɔ:tjug(ə)l] erisn. Portugali. **-uese** [-'gi:z] a. & s. portugalilainen; portugalin kieli.

pose [pəuz] v. asettaa (kysymys ym), esittää; asettaa jhk asentoon; olla (taiteilijan) mallina, poseerata; sanoa olevansa, esiintyä (*as* jnak); s. asento, asenne; [*this*] ~*s many problems for* aiheuttaa . . . -lle paljon ongelmia. **-r** [-ə] s. hämmennyttävä kysymys. **-ure** ['-zə:] s. vaikutuksen tavoittelija.

posh [pɔʃ] a. (puhek.) hieno, upea.

posi|tion [pə'ziʃn] s. asema; asento; tila, paikka; virka; kanta; in ~ oikealla paikallaan, (sot.) asemissa; [I regret I am not] in a ~ to help etten voi auttaa. **-tive** ['pɔz(i)tiv] a. nimenomainen, selvä, jyrkkä, ehdoton; (ehdottoman) varma; positiivinen (mat. ym), myönteinen; todellinen, täydellinen, oikea; s. positiivi (kiel. ym); ~ly ehdottomasti, aivan varmasti.

posse ['pɔsi] s. et. Am. (poliisi)joukko, järjestysjoukko.

possess [pə'zes] v. omistaa, vallata, hallita, pitää vallassaan; riivata; ~ oneself of (vanh.) ottaa valtaansa; what ~ed you to do that? mikä sai sinut tekemään sellaista? **-ed** [-t] a. mieletön, hullu; be ~ of omistaa; ~ by jnk riivaama. **-ion** [pə'zeʃn] s. omistaminen, omistus; pl. omaisuus, alusmaat; in my ~ hallussani; be in ~ of omistaa; take ~ of ottaa haltuunsa. **-ive** [-iv] a. omistus, possessiivi-; omistushaluinen; s. possessiivi(pronomini). **-or** [-ə] s. omistaja.

posset ['pɔsit] s. olutjuusto.

possi|bility [pɔsə'biliti] s. mahdollisuus. **-ble** ['pɔsəbl] a. mahdollinen; if ~ mikäli mahdollista. **-bly** adv. mahdollisesti, ehkä; I cannot ~ en mitenkään voi.

possum ['pɔsəm] s.: play ~ olla nukkuvinaan, tekeytyä kuolleeksi.

post 1. [pəust] s. pylväs; (oven- ym) pieli; v. kiinnittää (ilmoitustaululle), ilmoittaa (julisteessa ym); winning ~ maali.

post 2. [pəust] s. postiasema, vartiopaikka (sot.); toimi, virka; postikyyti; kauppa-asema; v. panna postiin, postittaa; asettaa jhk, sijoittaa; viedä kirjaan (kirjanp.); kiiruhtaa; by ~ postitse; by return of ~ paluupostissa; will you take [the letters] to the ~ veistkö postiin; keep sb. ~ed pitää ajan tasalla. **-age** [-idʒ] s. postimaksu; ~ stamp postimerkki. **-al** [-əl] a. posti-; ~ order postiosoitus. **-card** postikortti. ~**-chaise** postivaunut.

post- ['pəust-] pref. jälki-, myöhäis-.

-date v. päivätä (todellista päivämäärää) myöhemmäksi.

poster ['pəustə] s. (mainos)juliste.

post|erior [pɔs'tiəriə] a. myöhempi; taka-; s. takapuoli, takamukset. **-erity** [pɔs'teriti] s. jälkeläiset; jälkimaailma.

postern ['pɔstə:n] s. takaovi, sivuovi; salaovi.

post|code postinumero. **-exchange** s. (lyh. PX) sot. kanttiini. **-free** adv. postimaksutta. **-graduate** a.: ~ studies jatko-opinnot (perus)tutkinnon jälkeen. ~**-haste** adv. kiireen kaupalla.

posthumous ['pɔstjuməs] a. isän kuoleman jälkeen syntynyt; jälkeenjäänyt.

postilion [pɔs'tiljən] s. esiratsastaja.

post|man s. postinkantaja. **-mark** s. postileima. **-master** postinhoitaja (m. -mistress); P~ General postilaitoksen pääjohtaja.

post-mortem ['pəus(t)'mɔ:təm] s. ruumiinavaus.

post|-office s. postitoimisto; postilaitos; p.-o. box postilokero. **-operative** a. leikkauksenjälkeinen. ~**-paid** a. postimaksu maksettu, frankeerattu.

postpone [pəus(t)'pəun] v. siirtää tuonnemmaksi, lykätä. **-ment** s. lykkäys.

postcript ['pəusskript] s. jälkikirjoitus.

postulate ['pɔstjuleit] v. edellyttää, vaatia, panna ehdoksi, pitää selviönä; s. [-lit] postulaatti, edellytys.

posture ['pɔstʃə] s. asento; v. asettua (teennäiseen) asentoon, poseerata.

post-war ['pəust'wɔ:] a. sodanjälkeinen.

posy ['pəuzi] s. kukkakimppu.

pot [pɔt] s. saviastia, ruukku; kannu, pannu, pata; purkki; (urh.) pokaali; sl. marihuana ym; v. panna säilöön ruukkuun, säilöä; istuttaa ruukkuihin; ampua, ks. shot; a ~ of tea kannullinen teetä; a ~ of money suuret rahat; a big ~ iso pomo; [chamber] ~ yöastia; go to ~ mennä myttyyn, sortua; keep the ~ boiling hankkia pataan pantavaa.

potable ['pəutəbl] a. juotava.

pota|sh ['pɔtæʃ] s. potaska. **-ssium**

[pə'tæsjəm] s. kalium.

potation [pə(u)'teiʃn] s. juominen, ryyppy.

potato [pə'teitəu̯] s. (pl. ~es) peruna.

pot|-bellied pulleavatsainen. **~ -boiler** (et. kirjallinen) leipätyö.

potency ['pəut(ə)nsi] s. voima, teho; mahdollisuus.

potent ['pəut(ə)nt] a. voimakas, tehokas, mahtava. **-ate** [-eit] s. mahtimies. **-ial** [pətən(t)(ə)l] a. mahdollinen; s. potentiaali- **-iality** [pətenʃi'æliti] s. mahdollisuus.

pother ['pɔðə] s. hälinä, touhu.

pot|-herb s. **~-hole** hiidenkirnu, luola; (tien) kuoppa. **~-holer** luolantutkija. **~-hook** patakoukku; koukero.

potion ['pəuʃn] s. (lääke-, myrkky-)juoma.

pot-luck s.: *take p.-l.* syödä mitä talossa on suuhunpantavaa.

Potomac [pə'təumæk] *erisn.*

pot-plant ruukkukasvi (m. *potted plant).*

potpourri [pəu'puri] s. (mus.) potpuri, sekoitus.

pot|sherd ruukunsirpale. **-shot** läheltä ammuttu laukaus.

potter 1. ['pɔtə] v. puuhata yhtä ja toista, puuhailla; ~ *away* vetelehtiä, kuluttaa turhaan.

potter 2. ['pɔtə] s. savenvalaja; ~'s *wheel* savenvalajan pyörä. **-y** [-ri] s. saviastiat, keramiikka.

potty ['pɔti] a. sl. mitätön; hassahtanut; hullaantunut *(about* jhk).

pouch [pautʃ] s. pussi, (tupakka)massi, (patruuna)laukku; (anat.) pussi, tasku; (vanh.) kukkaro; v. panna pussiin.

pouf(fe) [pu:f] s. lattiatyyny.

poulterer ['pəult(ə)rə] s. lintukauppias.

poultice ['pəultis] s. haude.

poultry ['pəultri] s. siipikarja; ~ *farm* kanala.

pounce [pauns] v.: ~ *upon* syöksyä (alas) jnk kimppuun, iskeä (kyntensä) jhk; (kuv.) tarttua hanakasti jhk; s. syöksy.

pound 1. [paund] v. survoa rikki; lyödä, mukiloida, jyskyttää, takoa, hakata, paukuttaa; ~ *along* tallustaa.

pound 2. [paund] s. tarha, aitaus.

pound 3. [paund] s. naula (= 454 g);

punta (m. ~ *sterling); a ~ note* punnan seteli. **-age** [-idʒ] s. maksu t. palkkio punnalta. **-er** [-ə] s. (yhd.): *a twenty-~* 20 naulan painoinen (kala).

pour [pɔ:] v. kaataa, valaa; vuodattaa; vuotaa; virrata vuolaana, syöksyä kohisten; s.: *down~* kaatosade; ~ *out* kaataa (teetä ym), (kuv.) vuodattaa; *the rain ~ed down* satoi kaatamalla; *it never rains but it ~s* vahinko tulee harvoin yksinään.

pout [paut] v. työntää huulensa pitkälle, nyrpistää huulet; olla nyrpeä; s. nyrpistys, nyrpeä ilme. **-er** [-ə] s. kupukyyhkynen.

poverty ['pɔvəti] s. köyhyys; ~ *of* jnk puute. **~-stricken** puutteenalainen.

powder ['paudə] s. jauhe, pulveri; ihojauhe; puuteri; ruuti; v. hienontaa jauheeksi; puuteroida; sirotella *(with* jtk); ~ *room* naistenhuone; ~*ed sugar* pölysokeri. **~-puff** puuterihuisku. **-y** [-ri] a. jauhomainen.

Powell ['pəuəl, 'pau-] *erisn.*

power ['pauə] s. voima, kyky; valta, mahti; valtuus; potenssi (mat.); (puhek.) paljon, kosolti *(a ~ of good); the Great P~s* suurvallat; [*the party] in ~* vallassa oleva; *water ~* vesivoima; *electric ~* sähkö\voima, -energia; ~ *plant,* ~ *station* voimalaitos, voimala; [*he did] everything in his ~* kaiken voitavansa; [*it was not] within his ~* hänen vallassaan; *the ~s that be* (leik.) vallanpitäjät. **~-current** vahvavirta. **-ed** [-d] a.: *diesel-~* dieselkäyttöinen. **-ful** a. voimakas, väkevä, mahtava. **-less** a. voimaton; kykenemätön. **~-line** voimajohto. **~-loom** kutomakone.

pow-wow ['pau'wau̯] s. (leik.) neuvottelu; v. neuvotella.

pox [pɔks] s. rokko.

practicable ['præktikəbl] a. mahdollinen (toteuttaa), käyttökelpoinen; kulkukelpoinen.

practical ['præktik(ə)l] a. käytännöllinen, käyttökelpoinen; tosiasiallinen. **-ity** [-'kæliti] s. käytännöllisyys. **-ly** *adv.* käytännöllisesti (katsoen), käytännössä, itse asiassa, melkeinpä.

practice ['præktis] s. käytäntö;

harjoitus, harjoittelu; harjaannus;
tottumus, tapa; (lääkärin ym)
praktiikka, asiakaspiiri; *pl.* (vanh.)
metkut, juonet; *v.* Am. = *practise; in*
~ käytännössä; *put into* ~ panna
toimeen, toteuttaa käytännössä; *out
of* ~ taitamaton (harjoituksen
puutteessa).

practis|e ['præktis] *v.* harjoitella;
toteuttaa käytännössä, harjoittaa
(ammattia), toimia (jnak). **-ed** [-t] *a.*
harjaantunut, taitava.

practitioner [præk'tiʃnə] *s.: general* ~
yleislääkäri.

pragma|tic [præg'mætik] *a.*
pragmaattinen; käytännöllinen;
asiantunteva, kokenut, asiallinen;
itsevarma.

Prague [prɑːg] *erisn.* Praha.

prairie ['prɛəri] *s.* preeria.

praise [preiz] *v.* kiittää, kehua; ylistää;
s. ylistys, kiitos. **-worthy** *a.* kiitettävä.

pram [præm] *s.* (lyh.) lastenvaunut, ks.
perambulator.

prance [prɑːns] *v.* (hevosesta)
hypähdellä; pöyhistellä, keikailla (m.
~ *about);* *s.* hypähdys, pyörähdys.

prank [præŋk] *v.* koristella (tav. ~ *out);*
s. kuje(ilu); *play* ~ s tehdä kujeita,
»pelleillä». **-ish** [-ʃ] *a.* ilveilevä,
kujeileva.

prat [præt] *s.* (sl.) pylly. **-fall** [-] *s.* munaus.

prate [preit] *v.* jaaritella, laverrella; *s.*
lavertelu.

prattle ['prætl] *v.* lörpötellä; (lapsesta)
leperrellä; *s.* lepertely; rupattelu.

prawn [prɔːn] *s.* katkarapu.

pray [prei] *v.* rukoilla; pyytää hartaasti.
-er ['prɛə] *s.* rukous; *pl.* m.
hartaushetki; ['preiə] rukoilija; *the
Lord's* ~ Isä meidän rukous; *say one's*
~ s lukea rukouksensa; (~**-book** *s.*
rukouskirja, kirkkokäsikirja; *(Book
of Common P~)*).

pre- [priː-] *pref.* ennakko-, etu-, esi-.

preach [priːtʃ] *v.* saarnata; julistaa. **-er**
[-ə] *s.* saarnaaja.

preamble [priː'æmbl] *s.* johdanto.

prearrange *v.* järjestää ennakolta.

prebendary ['preb(ə)nd(ə)ri] *s.* (l. v.)
kaniikki.

precarious [pri'kɛəriəs] *a.* epävarma,
vaaranalainen, horjuva, arveluttava.

precaution [pri'kɔːʃn] *s.* varokeino,

varovaisuus (toimenpide). **-ary** [-əri]
a. varovaisuus-, varo-.

preced|e [pri(ː)'siːd] *v.* käydä edellä,
edeltää; olla (jnk) edellä (arvossa),
olla (jtk) aikaisempi. **-ence** [-(ə)ns] *s.*
aikaisemmuus; etusija; *order of* ~
arvojärjestys. **-ent** ['presid(ə)nt] *s.*
ennakkotapaus, -päätös. **-ing** *a.* jtk
edeltävä, edellinen.

pre|centor [pri(ː)'sentə] *s.* kanttori.
-cept ['priːsept] *s.* ohje; määräys.
-ceptor [pri'septə] *s.* opettaja.

precinct ['priːsiŋ(k)t] *s.* alue, Am. piiri;
pl. ympäristö.

precious ['preʃəs] *a.* kallis,
kallisarvoinen; (puhek.) aikamoinen;
adv. perin; ~ *stone* jalokivi.

precipice ['presipis] *s.* jyrkänne.

precipit|ant [pri'sipit(ə)nt] *s.* saostin
(kem.). **-ate** [-eit] *v.* syöstä alas,
suistaa maahan; jouduttaa; saostaa
(kem.); *a.* [-it] hätiköity, äkillinen; *s.*
[-it] saoste, m. sade, lumi. **-ation**
[-'teiʃn] *s.* kova kiire; sade(määrä),
sadanta; lumentulo; saostaminen,
tiivistyminen. **-ous** [-əs] *a.* äkkijyrkkä.

précis ['preisiː; Am. prei'siː] *s.* (*pl.*
sama [-siːz]) yhteenveto.

precise [pri'sais] *a.* tarkka;
täsmällinen, säntillinen;
turhantarkka. **-ly** *adv.* tarkasti,
tarkkaan; juuri; aivan niin.

precision [pri'siʒn] *s.* tarkkuus.

preclude [pri'kluːd] *v.* estää, ehkäistä,
sulkea pois.

pre|cocious [pri'kəuʃəs] *a.*
varhaiskypsä. **-cocity** [-'kɔsiti] *s.*
varhaiskypsyys.

precon|ceive ['priːkən'siːv] *v.* omaksua
ennakolta; ~*ed opinion* ks. seur.
-ception [-'sepʃn] *s.*
ennakkomielipide. **-certed** [-'səːtid] *a.*
ennalta sovittu. **-dition** [-'diʃn] *s.*
ehto, edellytys.

precursor [priː'kəːsə] *s.* edelläkävijä;
enne, airut. **-y** [-ri] *a.* edeltävä.

predate [priː'deit] *v.* päivätä
aikaisemmaksi, olla jtk aikaisempi.

predator ['predətə] *s.* petoeläin. **-y** [-ri]
a. rosvo-, peto-.

predecessor ['priːdisesə] *s.* edeltäjä.

predestin|ation [pri(ː)desti'neiʃn] *s.*
ennaltamääräys. **-ed** [-'destind] *a.*
ennakolta määrätty.

predetermine ['pri:di'tə:min] v. ennakolta määrätä t. päättää.

predicament [pri'dikəmənt] s. pulmallinen tilanne.

predicate ['predikeit] v. väittää; s. [-kit] predikaatti; a. predikatiivinen (substantiivi ym).

predict [pri'dikt] v. ennustaa. **-ion** [-'dikʃn] s. ennustus.

predilection [pri:di'lekʃn] s. erityinen mieltymys (for jhk).

predispos|e ['pri:dis'pəuz] s. tehdä vastaanottavaiseksi t. alttiiksi; ~d to altis jllek. **-ition** [-spə'ziʃn] s. taipumus, alttius (to jhk).

predomin|ance [pri'dominəns] s. ylivalta, voitolla oleminen; male ~ miesvaltaisuus. **-ant** [-ənt] a. vallitseva. (~ly valtaosaltaan, pääasiassa). **-ate** [-eit] v. vallita, olla vallalla, olla vallitsevana, olla enemmistönä.

pre-eminen|ce [pri(:)'eminəns] s. etevämmyys, paremmuus. **-t** [-ənt] a. (mitä) etevin, erinomainen; (~ly adv. erityisesti, mitä suurimmassa määrin).

pre-empt [pri(:)'em(p)t] v. hankkia etukäteen t. ennakolta. **-ion** [-ʃn] s. ennakko-osto(-oikeus).

preen [pri:n] v. siistiä (sulkansa); ~ oneself siistiytyä, (on) ylpeillä jllak.

pre-exist ['pri:ig'zist] v. olla olemassa ennen jtk muuta. **-ent** [-(ə)nt] a. aikaisempi.

prefab ['pri:'fæb] s. elementtitalo. **-ricate** [-rikeit] v. valmistaa (standardiosia) etukäteen; ~d unit (rakennus)elementti.

pre|face ['prefis] s. esipuhe, alkulause; v. varustaa esipuheella, aloittaa. **-fatory** [-fət(ə)ri] a. alustava, alku-; ~ note lyhyt alkulause.

prefect ['pri:fekt] s. prefekti, (joskus) maaherra; (koulussa) valvojaoppilas.

prefer [pri'fə:] v. pitää enemmän, pitää parempana (to jtk); haluta kernaammin; esittää; korottaa, ylentää; I ~ working to doing nothing teen mieluummin työtä kuin olen laiskana. **-able** ['pref(ə)rəbl] a. parempi (to kuin). **-ably** adv. mieluummin. **-ence** ['pref(ə)r(ə)ns] s. etusija; mieltymys; suosituimmuus; have a ~ for pitää enemmän jstak; in ~

to mieluummin kuin. **-ential** [prefə'renʃ(ə)l] a. etuoikeus-, preferenssi-. **-ment** s. (virka)ylennys. **-red** [pri'fə:d] a.: ~ stock etuoikeutetut osakkeet.

prefix ['pri:fiks] s. esiliite, liite (nimen edessä), titteli; v. [pri:'fiks] liittää eteen.

pregn|ancy ['pregnənsi] s. raskaus; (kuv.) merkityksellisyys, painavuus, sisällökkyys. **-ant** [-ənt] a. raskaana oleva, (eläin) tiine; (kuv.) merkittävä, paljon puhuva, tärkeä; ~ with täynnä jtk.

prehensile [pri'hensail] a. tarttuma-.

prehistoric, -al ['pri:(h)is'tɔrik, -l] a. esihistoriallinen.

prejudge v. ennakolta tuomita, ratkaista.

prejudic|e ['predʒudis] s. ennakkoluulo; haitta (lak.); v. tehdä ennakkoluuloiseksi; vahingoittaa; ~ sb. in favour of tehdä jllek suopeaksi, ..sb. against saattaa viero(ksu)maan, vahingoittaa, without ~ [to] tuottamatta haittaa. **-ed** [-t] a. puolueellinen, ennakkoluuloinen. **-ial** [-'dij(ə)l] a. haitallinen, vahingoittava.

prela|cy ['preləsi] s. prelaatinarvo, prelaatit. **-te** ['prelit] s. prelaatti.

preliminar|y [pri'lim(i)nəri] a. valmistava, alustava; s. pl.: -ies esivalmistelut, alustavat keskustelut.

prelude ['prelju:d] a. alkusoitto; johdanto, alku (to jhk).

prematur|e [premə'tjuə] a. ennenaikainen; harkitsematon; ~ baby keskonen; ~ birth ennenaikainen synnytys. **-ely** adv. ennen aikojaan. **-ity** [-riti] s. ennenaikaisuus.

premeditat|e [pri(:)'mediteit] v. (ennakolta) harkita. **-ed** [-id] a. harkittu. **-ion** [-'teiʃn] s. ennakkoharkinta; tahallisuus.

premier ['premjə] s. pääministeri. **-ship** s. pääministerin virka.

premise ['premis] s. peruste, premissi (m. premiss); pl. kiinteistö(n alue); business ~s liikehuoneisto; on the ~s itse paikalla; licensed ~s anniskelupaikka.

premium ['pri:mjəm] s. palkinto;

vakuutusmaksu; palkkio, oppirahat;
välityspalkkio; *at a* ~ (kuv.)
korkeassa kurssissa; *put a* ~ *on* olla
houkutuksena jhk, tehdä jk
edulliseksi; *P*~ **bond**
palkinto-obligaatio.

premoni|tion [pri:mə'niʃn] *s.*
ennakkoaavistus. **-tory**
[pri'mɔnit(ə)ri] *a.* varoittava, jtk
ennakoiva (~ *of*).

prenatal ['pri:'neitl] *a.:* ~ *care*
äitiyshuolto.

pre|occupation [pri(:)ɔkju'peiʃn] *s.*
ajatusten keskittäminen (täysin) jhk;
his greatest ~ *was.*. häntä askarrutti
eniten.. **-occupy** [-'ɔkjupai] *v.*
askarruttaa jkn mieltä, kokonaan
vallata jkn ajatukset; *-occupied* (m.)
ajatuksiin vaipunut. **-ordain** [-ɔː'dein]
v. ennakolta määrätä.

prep [prep] *s.* (koul.) tehtävien
valmistus, kotitehtävät; valmistava
koulu (~ *school*).

pre|packaged, -packed *pp.* (valmiiksi)
pakattu.

prepaid ['- '-] *pp.* etukäteen maksettu.

prepara|tion [prepə'reiʃn] *s.*
valmistaminen, valmistelu; valmiste;
pl. valmistelut; *in* ~ valmisteilla;
without ~ valmistamatta. **-tory**
[pri'pærət(ə)ri] *a.* valmistava,
alustava; ~ *to* ennen jtk; ~ *school*
valmistava koulu.

prepare [pri'pεə] *v.* valmistaa, -autua;
varustautua; valmentaa, -autua; ~ *d*
valmis. **-dness** [-ridnis] *s.* valmius.

prepay ['pri:(')'pei] *v.* maksaa
ennakolta. **-ment** *s.* ennakkomaksu.

prepondera|nce [pri'pɔnd(ə)r(ə)ns] *s.*
voittopuolisuus, ylivoima(isuus);
suurempi merkitys. **-nt** [-rənt] *a.*
vallitseva, voitolla oleva, ratkaiseva.
-te [-reit] *v.* olla painavampi (kuin),
olla voiton puolella, olla
merkitsevämpi (m. ~ *over*).

preposition [prepə'ziʃn] *s.* prepositio.

prepossess [pri:pə'zes] *v.* ennakolta
tehdä suopeaksi (*towards*), tehdä
edullinen vaikutus. **-ing** *a.* puoleensa
vetävä, miellyttävä.

preposterous [pri'pɔst(ə)rəs] *a.*
järjetön, mahdoton, nurinkurinen;
naurettava.

prerecorded *pp.* nauhoitettu.

prerequisite ['pri:'rekwizit] *s.*
välttämätön edellytys, ehto.

prerogative [pri'rɔɡətiv] *s.* etuus,
etuoikeus.

presage ['presidʒ] *s.* enne, aavistus; *v.*
[pri'seidʒ] ennustaa, tietää jtk.

presbyter ['prezbitə] *s.* (seurakunnan)
vanhin. **-ian** [prezbi'tiəriən] *a. & s.*
presbyteeri(nen).

prescien|ce ['preʃiən]s, 'pri:ʃ-, 'pres-] *s.*
ennakkotietämys. **-t** [-t] *a.* ennakolta
tietävä.

prescribe [pri'skraib] *v.* määrätä
(hoitotapa t. lääke); ~ *d time*
määräaika.

prescript ['pri:skript] *s.* määräys. **-ion**
[pris'kripʃn] *s.* määräys; resepti, ohje.

presence ['prezns] *s.* läsnäolo,
ulkonainen olemus ja ryhti; ~ *of mind*
mielenmaltti; *in the* ~ *of* jkn
läsnäollessa; *the* ~ *of arsenic was
suspected* siinä epäiltiin olevan
arsenikkia.

present 1. ['preznt] *a.* läsnäoleva;
nykyinen; käsillä (t. kyseessä) oleva,
tämä; *s.: the* ~ nykyaika, nykypäivä;
preesens (m. ~ *tense*); *those* ~
läsnäolevat; *be* ~ *at* olla läsnä jssk; *at*
~ nykyään; tällä hetkellä; *for the* ~
toistaiseksi; tällä hetkellä; *the* ~ *writer*
tämän kirjoittaja.

present 2. ['preznt] *s.* lahja; *v.*
[pri'zent] esittää, esiintuoda, lausua;
näyttää, osoittaa; tarjota, ojentaa;
lahjoittaa; (TV) juontaa; *make sb. a*
~ *of* antaa jklle lahjaksi; ~ *sb. with*
lahjoittaa jklle jtk; ~ *oneself*
näyttäytyä, saapua jnnek; ~ *itself*
ilmaantua, tarjoutua; ~ *arms!* eteen,
vie! **-able** [pri'zentəbl] *a.*
esiintymis|kuntoinen. -kelpoinen.
-ation [prezen'teiʃn] *s.* esittäminen,
esittely, esitys, näyttäminen jne.;
lahjoittaminen; ~ *copy* lahjakappale.
~**-day** *a.* nykyajan, nyky-. **-er** ['--'--] *s.*
(TV) juontaja.

presentiment [pri'zentimənt] *s.*
ennakkoaavistus.

presently ['prezntli] *adv.* pian, hetken
perästä; Am. tällä hetkellä.

preserv|ation [prezə(:)'veiʃn] *s.*
suojeleminen, suojelu; säilöntä; *in a
good state of* ~ hyvässä kunnossa.
-ative [pri'zə:vətiv] *s.* säilyte,

säilöntäaine.

preserve [pri'zə:v] v. suojella, varjella; säilyttää; säilöä, hillota; rauhoittaa (riista); s. säilyke, hillo (us. pl.); (riistan) rauhoitusalue (game ~).

preside [pri'zaid] v. olla (toimia) puheenjohtajana, johtaa. **-ncy** ['prezid(ə)nsi] s. presidentin virka, presidenttikausi.

president ['prezid(ə)nt] s. presidentti, puheenjohtaja, esimies, m. rehtori. **-ial** [-'denʃ(ə)l] a. presidentti-; ~ election presidentinvaali.

press [pres] v. painaa, pusertaa; silittää, prässätä; tunkea; ahdistaa; painostaa, pakottaa; (hist.) värvätä, pestata; tyrkyttää; vaatimalla vaatia, pyytämällä pyytää, tiukata (sb. for jklta jtk); kiirehtiä; tunkeutua; rientää (on, forward eteenpäin); olla kiireellinen; s. paino, puristus; tungos, ahdinko, kiire(ellisyys); puserrin, painin; sanomalehdistö; kirjapaino; painokone; paine, ruuhka; kaappi; ~ the button painaa nappia; ~ heavily on olla jklle raskaana painona; ~ sth. upon tyrkyttää jklle; time ~es aika rientää; I am ~ed for money olen rahapulassa; hard ~ed ahtaalla; ready for the ~ painoon valmis; in the ~ painossa; have a good ~ saada hyvät arvostelut; ~ conference lehdistötilaisuus; P~ Council julkisen sanan neuvosto.

press-agent (mainos)agentti. **~-button war** atomisota. **~-cutting** sanomalehtileike. **~-gallery** lehdistöparvee.

pressing ['presiŋ] a. pakottava, kiireellinen; hellittämätön, itsepintainen. **-ure** ['preʃə] s. paine; paino; ahdinko, hätä; painostus; atmospheric ~ ilmanpaine; bring ~ to bear upon, put ~ upon painostaa; ~ cooker painekeitin; ~ group painostusryhmä. **-urized** [-raizd]: ~ suit painepuku.

presti|ge [pres'ti:ʒ] s. arvovalta, maine. **-gious** [-'tidʒəs] a. arvossapidetty, arvovaltainen.

presuma|ble [pri'zju:məbl] a. luultava; **-bly** todennäköisesti, luultavasti.

presum|e [pri'zju:m, Am. -'zu:m] v.

olettaa, edellyttää; rohjeta, uskaltaa, ottaa vapaus; ~ upon [sb.'s kindness] käyttää väärin, käyttää hyväkseen. **-ing** a. liian rohkea, julkea.

presumpt|ion [pri'zʌm(p)/ʃn] s. olettamus, otaksuma; julkeus. **-ive** [-tiv] a. oletettu, otaksuttu, todennäköinen; vert. heir. **-uous** [-tjuəs] a. röyhkeä, julkea.

presuppos|e [pri:sə'pəuz] v. edellyttää; otaksua. **-ition** [-sʌpə'ziʃn] s. otaksuma; edellytys.

pretence [pri'tens] s. veruke, tekosyy; teeskentely; under the ~ of jnk varjolla; false ~s epärehelliset keinot.

pretend [pri'tend] v. uskotella; olla olevinaan (jtk), teeskennellä; ~ to be ill teeskdytä sairaaksi; ~ to the throne tavoitella kruunua. **-ed** [-id] a. teeskennelty. **-er** [-ə] s. kruunun tavoittelija; the Old (Young) P~ Jaakko II:n poika (pojanpoika).

pretense (Am.) ks. pretence.

preten|sion [pri'tenʃn] s. vaatimus; vaateliaisuus, luulot (itsestään); [he] makes no ~s to ei väitä olevansa t. omistavansa. **-tious** [-ʃəs] a. vaatelias, suurilluuloinen, suurellinen.

preterite ['pret(ə)rit] s. menneen ajan muoto, imperfekti.

preternatural ['pri:tə-] a. yliluonnollinen.

pretext ['pri:tekst] s. tekosyy, veruke; on (under) the ~ of . . .ing sillä tekosyyllä, että . ., koska muka . .

Pretoria [pri'tɔ:riə] erisn.

prettily adv. sievästi jne.

pretty ['priti] a. sievä, soma, kaunis; (ivall.) hieno, siisti; adv. jotensakin, aika, melko; ~ much [the same] melkein; a ~ penny sievoinen summa.

prevail [pri'veil] v. olla voitolla, päästä voitolle, voittaa (m. ~ over); vallita, olla yleinen; ~ upon taivuttaa, saada jku (tekemään jtk); ~ing vallitseva.

preval|ence ['prevələns] s. yleisyys. **-ent** [-ənt] a. vallalla oleva, vallitseva, yleinen.

prevarica|te [pri'værikeit] v. kieroilla, luikerrella. **-tion** [-'keiʃn] s. kiemurtelu, kieroilu.

prevent [pri'vent] v. estää, ehkäistä, torjua; [my cold] ~s me from going out (t. my going out) estää minua

menemästä ulos. **-able** [-əbl] a.
estettävissä oleva. **-ion** [-'venʃn] s.
ehkäisy; ~ of cruelty to animals
eläinsuojelu. **-ive** [-iv] a. estävä,
ehkäisevä; P~ Service merivartiosto;
under ~ detention turvasäilössä.

preview s. ennakkonäytös, -näytäntö.

previous ['pri:vjəs] a. edellinen,
aikaisempi; ennenaikainen, hätäinen;
~ to ennen jtk. **-ly** adv. aikaisemmin.

pre-war ['pri:'wɔ:] a. sodanedellinen;
~ conditions ennen sotaa vallinneet
olot.

prey [prei] s. saalis; v.: ~ [up] on
pyydystää; ryöstää, kalvaa, ahdistaa;
beast of ~ petoeläin; fall a ~ to joutua
jnk uhriksi; be a ~ to [fears] olla
(pelkojen) ahdistama.

price [prais] s. hinta; v. määrätä hinta,
hinnoitella; at any ~ mihin hintaan
tahansa; at that ~ sillä hinnalla;
what's the ~ of?.. mitä ..maksaa?
what ~ [your principles] now? minkä
arvoisia ovat nyt..? ~ s are going up
hinnat nousevat; put a ~ on sb.'s head
luvata palkkio jkn kiinniottamisesta.
~-control hintasäännöstely; p.-
controlled h-n alainen. **-less** a.
arvaamattoman kallis; verraton.
-y [-i] a. sl. kallis, tyyris.

prick [prik] v. pistää; lävistää; merkitä
pistein (us. ~ out); pistellä; (vanh.)
ratsastaa lujaa; s. oas, piikki, pisto;
(alat.) kikkeli; ~ out istuttaa (taimia);
~ up one's ears höristää korviaan; ~ s
of conscience omantunnonvaivat;
[kick] against the ~s tutkainta
vastaan; a stupid ~ ääliö. **-er** [-ə] s.
lävistin, naskali. **-le** [-l] s. oas, piikki;
v. pistää, pistellä. **-ly** [-li] a. okainen,
piikkinen; ärtyisä; ~ heat
ihojäkälä(tauti).

pride [praid] s. ylpeys; ylimielisyys;
kukoistus; v.: ~ oneself upon ylpeillä
jstk; proper ~ omanarvontunto; take
[a] ~ in ylpeillä jstk; a ~ of [lions]
lauma.

priest [pri:st] s. pappi (et. katol.); high
(t. chief) ~ ylipappi. **-ess** [-is] s.
papitar. **-hood** s. pappeus; papisto. **-ly**
a. papillinen, pappis-.

prig [prig] s. omahyväinen narri,
saivartelija, turhantärkeä ihminen.
-gish [-iʃ] a. omahyväinen; (~ness s.

omahyväisyys).

prim [prim] a. sievistelevä,
kainosteleva, sovinnainen; v.
suipistaa (suutaan ym).

prim|acy ['praim|əsi] s. ensimmäinen
sija; arkkipiispan arvo. **-arily** [-(ə)rili,
Am. -'meərili] adv. ensisijassa,
etupäässä. **-ary** [-əri] a. alku-,
alkuperäinen, alkeis-, perus-;
pääasiallinen, pää-; s. pl. primaries
esivaalit; ~ colours perusvärit; ~
education alkeisopetus,
peruskoulutus; of ~ importance
ensisijaisen tärkeä. **-ate** [-it] s.
arkkipiispa, priimas; ~ s [prai'meitiz]
kädelliset [nisäkkäät].

prim|e [praim] a. ensi(mmäinen),
alku-, paras, pääasiallinen, tärkein;
ensiluokkainen; s. (jnk) ensimmäinen
osa, alku, (~ of the year) kevät, (jnk)
paras osa, kukoistus; v. pohjustaa
(maalilla ym); varustaa
sytytyspanoksella; valmentaa, sulloa
täyteen (tietoja); ~ cost oma hinta;
P~ Minister pääministeri; ~ mover
alkuunpanija; ~ number jaoton luku;
the ~ of life elämän kevät; past his ~
ei enää parhaassa iässään. **-er** [-ə] s.
alkeiskirja. **-eval** [-'i:v(ə)l] a.
muinainen, alku-; ~ forest
aarniometsä. **-ing** s. sytytin;
pohjaväri.

primitive ['primitiv] a. alku|peräinen,
-kantainen, alku-; kanta-, juuri-.

primo|geniture [praimə(u)'dʒenitʃə] s.
esikoisuus, esikoisoikeus. **-rdial**
[-'mɔ:djəl] a. alku-.

primrose ['primrəuz] s. esikko, (attr.)
kukkas-; ~ path lavea tie.

primula ['primjulə] s. esikko, primula.

primus ['praiməs] s. priimuskeitin.

prince [prins] s. prinssi, ruhtinas. **-ly** a.
ruhtinaallinen. **-ss** [prin'ses] s.
prinsessa, ruhtinatar; ~ royal Engl.
kuninkaan vanhin tytär.

principal ['prinsəp(ə)l] a.
pääasiallinen, pää-; tärkein; s.
esimies, johtaja, rehtori;
toimeksiantaja; (lainan ym) pääoma;
~ parts (verbin) teemamuodot. **-ity**
[-i'pæliti] s. ruhtinaskunta (esim. the
P~ of Monaco); the P~ Wales. **-ly**
adv. etupäässä.

principle ['prinsəpl] s. periaate;

prinsiippi, alkuperuste; *in* ~ periaatteessa; *on* ~ periaatteesta, periaatteellisista syistä. **-d** [-d] *a.: low*-~ periaatteeton.

prink [priŋk] *v.:* ~ *oneself up* laittautua koreaksi, pynttäytyä, pyntätä.

print [print] *s.* painoteksti; paino, painatus; (valok.) kopio; vedos; (vaski)piirros; painettu kangas; (yhdyssanoissa) merkki, jälki; *v.* painaa, painattaa, julkaista painosta; tekstata painokirjaimin; kopioida (valok.); *in small* ~ pientä tekstiä; *is in* ~ on ilmestynyt painosta; *out of* ~ loppuunmyyty; *news* ~ sanomalehtipaperi; ~*ed matter* painotuote. **-er** [-ə] *s.* kirjanpainaja; ~*'s error* painovirhe; ~*'s ink* painomuste.

printing *a.* paino-; *s.* painaminen; painos; kirjapainotaito. **~-press** painokone; kirjapaino.

prior ['praiə] *a.* aikaisempi, varhaisempi; ~ *to* ennen; *s.* priori. **-ess** [-ris] *s.* prioritar. **-ity** [prai'ɔrəti] *s.* aiemmuus; etuoikeus, etusija; *according to* ~ tärkeysjärjestyksessä; ~ *call* pikapuhelu. **-y** [-ri] *s.* luostari.

prise ks. *prize 3.*

prism ['prizm] *s.* prisma, särmiö. **-atic** [priz'mætik] *a.* prisma(n)-.

prison ['prizn] *s.* vankila; vankeus. **-er** [-ə] *s.* vanki; ~ [*of war*] sotavanki; ~ *at the bar* syytetty; *take sb.* ~ ottaa vangiksi, vangita.

prissy ['prisi] *a.* turhantarkka, sievistelevä.

pristine ['pristain] *a.* muinainen; alkuperäinen.

privacy ['privəsi, Am. 'prai-] *s.* oma rauha, yksityiselämä, eristäytyminen; *disturb sb.'s* ~ häiritä jkn rauhaa; *in strict* ~ aivan salaa, hiljaisuudessa.

privat|e ['praivit] *a.* yksityis-, yksityinen; salainen, luottamuksellinen; henkilökohtainen; *s.* tavallinen sotamies (m. ~ *soldier); keep* ~ pitää salassa; *in* ~ yksityisesti, kahden kesken; *in one's* ~ *capacity* yksityishenkilönä; ~ *eye* (sl.) salapoliisi; ~ *life* yksityiselämä. **-eer** [praivə'tiə] *s.* kaapparilaiva. **-ely** *adv.* yksityisesti, salaa.

privation [prai'veiʃn] *s.* puute,

kieltäymys, puutteenalaisuus.

privet ['privit] *s.* aitalikusteri.

privilege ['privilidʒ] *s.* etuoikeus, erioikeus; *v.* myöntää etuoikeus; ~*d* etuoikeutettu; *the under-*~ vähäväkiset.

privy ['privi] *s.* ulkohuone, käymälä; ~ *to* tietoinen jstk, osallinen jhk; *P~ Council* Valtakunnanneuvosto.

prize 1. [praiz] *s.* palkinto; (arpajais)voitto; (kuv.) etu, voitto; *(attr.)* palkinnon saanut, palkittu; *v.* arvioida, pitää suuressa arvossa; ~ *poem* palkittu runo.

prize 2. [praiz] *s.* kaapattu, vallattu alus; ~ *money* saalisraha.

prize 3. [praiz] *v.:* ~ *open,* ~ *up* vääntää auki (kangella).

prize|-fight nyrkkeilyottelu. **~-fighter** ammattinyrkkeilijä. **-man** *s.* palkinnonsaaja.

pro 1. [prou] *pref.* puoltava; *s.* puoltaja, kannattaja; ~ *and con* puolesta ja vastaan; ~*s and cons* valo- ja varjopuolet; ~*-Arab* arabiystävällinen; ~ *forma* muodon vuoksi.

pro 2. [prou] *lyh.* = *professional.*

proba|bility [prɔbə'biliti] *s.* todennäköisyys; *in all* ~ todennäköisesti. **-ble** ['prɔb(ə)bl] *a.* todennäköinen, luultava. **-bly** *adv.* luultavasti.

probate ['proubit] *s.* jälkisäädöksen vahvistus.

probation [prə'beiʃn] *s.* koe; koeaika; ehdonalainen tuomio; ~ *officer* (nuoren rikoksentekijän) valvoja. **-ary** [-əri] *a.* koe-. **-er** [-ə] *s.* kokelas, (sairaanhoito)oppilas; ehdonalaisen tuomion saanut.

probe [proub] *s.* koetin(puikko), sondi (lääk.); *v.* sondeerata; tutkia perusteellisesti, penkoa (esim. skandaalia).

probity ['proubiti] . rehellisyys.

problem ['prɔbləm] *s.* probleema, tehtävä (mat.); ongelma. **-atic(al)** [prɔbli'mætik, -l] *a.* ongelmallinen, pulmallinen; epävarma.

proboscis [prə'bɔsis] *s.* kärsä.

procedure [prə'si:dʒə] *s.* menettelytapa; *legal* ~ oikeudenkäyntijärjestys.

proceed [prə'si:d] v. edetä, kulkea, jatkaa (matkaa), siirtyä, ryhtyä (to jhk); menetellä; nostaa syyte (against jkta vastaan); jatkua, kestää; aiheutua, olla peräisin. **-ing** s. menettely(tapa), toimenpide; ~s (tieteellisen seuran ym) asiakirjat; legal ~ s oikeudenkäynti; take ~ s against nostaa syyte jkta vastaan. **-s** ['prəusi:dz] s. pl. voitto, tuotto.

process ['prəuses, Am. 'prɔs-] s. prosessi, toiminta, tapahtuma, (valmistus)menetelmä; haaste; v. käsitellä; [prə'ses] kulkea (saattueessa). in ~ of construction rakenteilla; in ~ of time ajan mittaan. **-ing** s. käsittely, jalostus. **-ion** [prə'seʃn] s. juhlakulkue, saattue.

pro|claim [prə'kleim] v. julistaa; kuuluttaa; he was ~ ed king hänet huudettiin kuninkaaksi; ~ [a meeting] julistaa laittomaksi. **-clamation** [prɔklə'meiʃn] s. julistus.

proclivity [prə'kliviti] s. taipumus (to, towards jhk).

procrastina|te [prəu'kræstineit] v. viivytellä, vitkastella; lykätä. **-tion** [-'neiʃn] s. viivyttely.

procrea|te ['prəukrieit] v. siittää, synnyttää. **-tion** [-'eiʃn] s. sikiäminen.

proctor ['prɔktə] s. proktori (järjestyksen valvoja); edustaja (m. kruunun e. avioerojutuissa).

procura|tion [prɔkju(ə)'reiʃn] s. hankkiminen; valtuutus, prokuura. **-tor** ['prɔkju(ə)reitə] s. maaherra; asiamies, valtuutettu.

procure [prə'kjuə] v. hankkia, toimittaa (for jklle). **-r** [-rə], **-ss** [-ris] s. parittaja.

prod [prɔd] v. tyrkätä (kepillä ym); (kuv.) yllyttää; s. töykkäys, survaisu.

prodigal ['prɔdig(ə)l] a. tuhlaavainen; the ~ son tuhlaajapoika. **-ity** [-'gæliti] s. tuhlaavaisuus.

prodigious [prə'didʒəs] a. eriskummainen; suunnaton.

prodigy ['prɔdidʒi] s. ihme; ihmeolento; infant ~ ihmelapsi.

produce [prə'dju:s] v. esittää, tuottaa, valmistaa; aiheuttaa, saada aikaan, synnyttää; näyttää, kaivaa esille; ohjata (näytelmä); s. ['prɔdju:s] tuote, sato; farm ~

maataloustuotteet. **-r** [-ə] s. tuottaja, valmistaja; (ohjelman) toimittaja; ~ gas generaattorikaasu.

product ['prɔdəkt] s. tuote; tulos, hedelmä (kuv.); tulo (mat.). **-ion** [prə'dʌkʃn] s. tuotanto; tuote (m. kuv.) teos; esitys, esittäminen jne. **-ive** [prə'dʌktiv] a. tuottoisa, tuottelias; antoisa. **-iveness, -ivity** [prɔdʌk'tiviti] s. tuottavuus, tuotteliaisuus, tuotantokyky.

profan|e [prə'fein] a. epäpyhä; maallinen; jumalaton, pakanallinen; pyhyyttä loukkaava, häpäisevä; v. häväistä, rienata. **-ity** [prə'fæniti] s. rienaava puhe, rienaukset (-ities).

profess [prə'fes] v. vakuuttaa, väittää, selittää (olevansa, tuntevansa jtk); julkisesti tunnustaa (oppia); harjoittaa (ammattia), olla (jnk aineen) professori. **-ed** [-t] a. julkinen, tunnustava, itseään jksk sanova. **-edly** [-idli] adv. julkisesti, omien sanojensa mukaan, muka.

profession [prə'feʃn] s. ammatti (et. akateeminen); ammattikunta; vakuutus; tunnustus; by ~ ammatiltaan; make ~ s of friendship vakuuttaa ystävyyttään; the medical ~ lääkärikunta. **-al** [-l] a. ammattimainen, ammatti-; s. ammattilainen (m. urh., lyh. pro); (~-ism ammattilaisuus).

professor [prə'fesə] s. professori. **-ship** s. professorinvirka.

proffer ['prɔfə] v. tarjota.

proficien|cy [prə'fiʃnsi] s. (hyvä) taito, etevyys. **-t** [-nt] a. taitava, etevä (in, at jssk).

profile ['prəufail] s. sivukuva, profiili.

profit ['prɔfit] s. hyöty, voitto; v. hyötyä (by jstk); hyödyttää; make a ~ saada voittoa; [sell sth.] at a ~ voitolla; [do sth.] for ~ voiton toivossa, ansiomielessä; ~ and loss account tulostili. **-able** [-əbl] a. edullinen, tuottoisa, kannattava. **-ably** adv. edullisesti, voitolla. **~-sharing** voitonjakojärjestelmä.

profiteer [prɔfi'tiə] v. keinotella (käyttäen hyväkseen pula- t. esim. sota-aikaa); s. (sota-ajan) keinottelija. **-ing** [-rin] s. keinottelu.

proflig|acy ['prɔfligəsi] s. paheellinen

elämä, moraalittomuus. **-ate** [-git] *a.*
irstas, hurjasteleva; tuhlaavainen; *s.*
irstailija; tuhlari.

pro|found [prə'faund] *a.* syvä;
syvällinen; syvämielinen;
perinpohjainen. **-fundity** [-'fʌnditi] *s.*
syvyys, syvällisyys.

profu|se [prə'fju:s] *a.* hyvin runsas,
ylenpalttinen; antelias, tuhlaileva;
~ *ly* runsain mitoin. **-sion** [-'fju:ʒn] *s.*
tuhlaavaisuus, runsaus ylenpalttisuus;
in ~ runsaasti.

progen|itor [prɔ(u)'dʒenitə] *s.*
kantaisä. **-y** ['prɔdʒini] *s.* jälkeläiset.

prognos|is [prɔg'nəusis] *s.* ennuste,
prognoosi. **-tic** [-'nɔstik] *a.* ennustava
(of jtk).

programme ['prougræm] *s.* ohjelma
(m. *program,* et. Am.); *v.*
ohjelmoida.

progress ['prougres, Am. prɔg-] *s.*
eteneminen, kulku; edistyminen,
edistys, kehitys; (vanh.) virallinen
matka; *v.* [prə'gres, prɔ(u)-] edetä,
jatkaa; edistyä; *make* ~ edistyä, m.
toipua; *in* ~ käynnissä, meneillään.
-ion [prə'greʃn] *s.* eteneminen; sarja
(mat.). **-ive** [prə'gresiv] *a.* etenevä,
edistyvä; (asteittain) kasvava t.
paheneva; progressiivinen; *s. & a.*
edistysmielinen, edistyksellinen,
uudistusmielinen.

prohibit [prə'hibit] *v.* kieltää; estää.
-ion [prɔ(u)i'biʃn] *s.* kielto; kieltolaki;
(~**ist** *s.* kieltolain kannattaja). **-ive**
[-iv] *a.* (esim. ostohalua) estävä;
huimaava (hinta). **-ory** [-əri] *a.*
ehkäisevä; huikea.

project ['prɔdʒekt] *s.* projekti,
suunnitelma; *v.* [prə'dʒekt]
suunnitella, tehdä ehdotus; heijastaa,
projisioida (m. lääk.); singota;
työntyä, pistää esiin. **-ile**
[prə'dʒektail, Am. -ktl] *s.* ammus; *a.*
heitto-. **-ing** *a.* ulkoneva. **-ion**
[prə'dʒekʃn] *s.* heittäminen;
ulkonema; projektio. **-or** [prə'dʒektə]
s. kuvanheitin, projektori.

prolapse ['proulæps] *s.*
esiinluiskahtaminen.

prole [proul] *s.* (puhek.) proletaari.

proletar|ian [proule'teəriən] *a.*
köyhälistö-; *s.* proletaari. **-iat** [-iət] *s.*
köyhälistö, nyk. palkkatyöväki.

prolifera|te [prə'lifəreit, Am. prəu-] *v.*
lisääntyä (nopeasti). **-tion** [-'reiʃn] *s.:*
nuclear non-~ *treaty*
ydinsulkusopimus.

pro|lific [prə'lifik] *a.* tuottelias,
hedelmällinen. **-lix** ['prəuliks, Am.
prəu'liks] *a.* pitkäveteinen,
monisanainen. **-logue** ['prɔulɔg] *s.*
esinäytös, prologi.

prolong [prə'lɔŋ] *v.* pidentää, pitkittää;
jatkaa; ~*ed* pitkällinen,
pitkä(aikainen). **-ation** [prɔulɔŋ'geiʃn]
s. pidennys; jatke, jatkos.

prom [prɔm] *s.* (lyh.) = *promenade
concert* kävelykonsertti; (koul.)
tanssiaiset.

promenade [prɔn i'nɑːd, Am. -neid] *s.*
kävely; kävelykatu; (teatt.) lämpiö; *v.*
kävellä, kävelyttää.

prominen|ce ['prɔminəns] *s.* ulkonema,
kohoama; huomattava asema; *give* ~
to asettua etualalle. **-t** [-ənt] *a.*
ulkoneva, huomiotaherättävä,
silmäänpistävä; huomattava, etevä,
tärkeä; *figure* ~ *ly in* olla
huomattavalla sijalla.

promiscu|ity [prɔmis'kju(:)iti] *s.*
promiskuiteetti, vapaat
sukupuolisuhteet; sekamelska. **-ous**
[prə'miskjuəs] *a.* sekava, sekalainen;
valikoimaton, tilapäinen; (~*ly adv.*
ilman erotusta, valikoimatta).

promis|e ['prɔmis] *s.* lupaus; *v.* luvata;
antaa toiveita jstk, näyttää
lupaavalta; *. . of great* ~ varsin
lupaava; *there was every* ~ *of* kaikki
näytti lupaavan; *the P~d Land*
Luvattu maa. **-ing** *a.* lupaava.
-sory [-əri] *a.: * ~ *note* velkakirja,
sitoumus.

promontory ['prɔməntri] *s.* (kallio-)
niemeke, niemi.

promo|te [prə'məu|t] *v.* ylentää;
edistää; panna alulle, perustaa; tehdä
(laki)esitys; Am. siirtää (seuraavalle)
luokalle. **-ter** [-tə] *s.* alkuunpanija.
-tion [-ʃn] *s.* korotus, (virka)ylennys;
edistäminen.

prompt [prɔm(p)t] *a.* nopea, ripeä, heti
valmis; pikainen; täsmällinen; *v.*
saada (tekemään jtk), yllyttää,
kuiskata (teatt.); *for* ~ *cash* heti
käteiselllä; *give sb.* ~ *s* kuiskata
(näyttelijälle). ~ **-box** kuiskaajan

koppi. **-er** [-ə] s. kuiskaaja (teatt.).
-ing s.: ~ s [of conscience] kehotukset.
-itude [-itju:d] s. ripeys, valmius. **-ly**
adv. heti (paikalla).
promulgate ['prɒmlgeit] v. julistaa,
kuuluttaa; levittää.
prone [prəun] a. vatsallaan (maassa)
makaava; ~ to altis, taipuvainen jhk.
prong [prɒŋ] s. (haarukan ym) piikki;
haara.
pro|nominal [prə'nɒminl] a.
pronomini-. **-noun** ['prəunaun] s.
pronomini.
pronounc|e [prə'nauns] v. ääntää;
lausua (mielipiteensä), julistaa; ~
judgment langettaa tuomio; -ing
dictionary ääntämissananakirja. **-ed**
[-t] a. selvä, ilmeinen, jyrkkä. **-ment**
s. (julki)lausuma.
pronto ['prɒntəu] adv. sl. heti.
pronunciation [prənʌnsi'eiʃn] s.
ääntäminen, ääntämys.
proof [pru:f] s. todistus, todiste;
koe(tus); (alkoholijuoman)
väkevyysaste; korjausvedos; a.
kestävä, läpäisemätön, jtk pitävä; v.
tehdä vedenpitäväksi; bomb-~
pomminkestävä; sound-~
ääneristetty; put to the ~ panna
koetukselle; ~ against temptation
kiusauksen kestävä, voittava.
~-reader oikaisulukija. **~-sheet**
korjausvedos.
prop [prɒp] s. tuki; tukipylväs (~ and
stay); v. tukea, kannattaa, pönkittää
(m. ~ up); pit ~ kaivospölkky.
propagand|a [prɒpə'gændə] s.
propaganda. **-ist** [-dist] s. p:n
levittäjä.
propaga|te ['prɒpəgeit] v. lisätä,
levittää; lisääntyä. **-tion** [-'geiʃn] s.
lisääntyminen; levittäminen.
propel [prə'pel] v. työntää, ajaa,
kuljettaa eteenpäin; jet-~ed
suihkukäyttöinen. **-ler** [-ə] s. potkuri.
propensity [prə'pensiti] s. taipumus,
alttius (to jhk).
proper ['prɒpə] a. sopiva, oikea,
asianmukainen; sovelias, säädyllinen;
varsinainen; (~ to) jllk ominainen,
tyypillinen; (puhek.) aikamoinen,
todellinen; ~ noun (name) erisnimi;
deem (think) it ~ pitää sopivana; in
the ~ sense of the word sanan

varsinaisessa merkityksessä. **-ly** adv.
oikein; sopivasti, säädyllisesti;
kunnollisesti, kunnolla; ~ speaking
oikeastaan. **-ty** [-ti] s. omaisuus;
ominaisuus; maatila; kiinteistö;
personal ~ irtaimisto; -ties (lyh. props)
näyttämötarvikkeet.
prophe|cy ['prɒfisi] s. ennustus. **-sy**
[-sai] v. ennustaa.
prophet ['prɒfit] s. profeetta,
ennustaja. **-ess** [-is] s. naisprofeetta.
-ic [prə'fetik] a. profeetan, (~ of jtk)
ennustava.
prophyl|actic [prɒfi'læktik] a. & s.
ehkäisevä (hoito, lääke). **-axis**
[-'læksis] s. ennakkotorjunta.
propinquity [prə'piŋkwəti] s. läheisyys
(m. kuv.); samankaltaisuus.
propiti|ate [prə'piʃieit] v. lepyttää,
tehdä suosiolliseksi. **-ation** [-'eiʃn] s.
lepyttäminen. **-atory** [-ət(ə)ri] a.
lepyttävä. **-ous** [prə'piʃəs] a.
suosiollinen, suotuisa.
proportion [prə'pɔ:ʃn] s. suhde;
(suhteellinen) määrä, osa, osuus; pl.
mittasuhteet, mitat, koko; v.: ~ to
suhteuttaa jhk, muodostaa
sopusuhtaisesti; in ~ [to] suhteessa
jhk, jnk mukaan, vastaavasti; out of ~
suhteeton, suhdaton; well-~ed
sopusuhtainen. **-al** [-ənl] a.
suhteellinen; verrannollinen; ~
representation suhteellinen vaalitapa.
-ate [-nit] a. oikeassa suhteessa oleva,
suhteellinen.
proposal [prə'pəuz(ə)l] s. ehdotus,
suunnitelma; naimatarjous, kosinta.
propos|e [prə'pəuz] v. esittää,
ehdottaa; aikoa; kosia. **-ition**
[prɒpə'ziʃn] s. ehdotus, esitys; väite,
väittämä (mat.); (puhek.) tehtävä,
»urakka»; a tough ~ kova pähkinä
purtavaksi.
propound [prə'paund] v. esittää.
propriet|ary [prə'praiətəri, Am. -teri]
a. omistus-; patentoitu (~ medicine);
~ rights omistusoikeus. **-or** [-tə] s.
omistaja; landed ~ tilanomistaja.
-ress [-tris] s. omistaja (nainen).
propriety [prə'praiəti] s. säädyllisyys,
hyvät tavat; sopivuus,
asianmukaisuus.
propul|sion [prə'pʌlʃn] s. työntövoima,
työntö; jet ~ suihkuvoima. **-sive** [-siv]

a. työntö-, käyttö-.
prorogue [prə'rəug] *v.* keskeyttää.
prosaic [prə(u)'zeiik] *a.* proosallinen.
pro|scribe [prə'skraib] *v.* (vanh.)
julistaa lainsuojattomaksi; leimata,
tuomita (vaarallliseksi). **-scription**
[-'krip∫n] *s.* (vanh.) lainsuojattomuus.
prose [prəuz] *s.* proosa; *in* ~
suorasanaisesti.
prosecu|te ['prɔsikju:t] *v.* haastaa
oikeuteen, asettaa syytteeseen; ~ *[a
trade]* harjoittaa. **-tion** [-'kju:∫n] *s.* jnk
harjoittaminen, jatkaminen; syyte,
kanne; syyttäjä(puoli). **-tor** [-ə] *s.*
kantaja; *Public P~* virallinen syyttäjä.
prosely|te ['prɔsi|lait] *s.*
käännynnäinen. **-tize** [-litaiz] *v.*
käännyttää.
prosody ['prɔsədi] *s.* runo-oppi.
prospect ['prɔspekt] *s.* näköala,
näkymä; *pl.* tulevaisuuden toiveet,
mahdollisuudet; *v.* [prɔs'pekt]: ~ *for*
etsiä (mineraaleja, malmeja),
prospektata; *in* ~ näkyvissä.
prospect|ive [prɔs'pekt|iv] *a.* tuleva.
-or [-ə, Am. 'prɔs-] *s.* (öljyn-, malmin)
etsijä, prospektori. **-us** [-əs] *s.*
esittelyvihkonen, esite.
prosper ['prɔs|pə] *v.* onnistua,
menestyä, kukoistaa; olla
suosiollinen, siunata. **-ity** [-'periti] *s.*
onni, menestys, kukoistus;
hyvinvointi vauraus. **-ous** [-p(ə)rəs] *a.*
menestyksellinen, hyvinvoipa,
vauras, onnekas, suotuisa.
prostate ['prɔsteit] *s.* eturauhanen.
prosthe|sis ['prɔs|θisis] *s.* proteesi. **-tic**
['θetik] *a.* proteesi-.
prostitu|te ['prɔstitju:t] *s.* prostituoitu;
v. prostituoida. **-tion** [-'tju:∫n] *s.*
prostituutio; väärinkäyttö *(of* jnk).
prostra|te ['prɔstreit] *a.* pitkällään
oleva, maassa makaava, maahan
lyöty; *v.* [prɔs'treit] syöstä maahan,
kaataa; uuvuttaa; ~ *oneself* heittäytyä
maahan. **-tion** [prɔs'trei∫n] *s.* maahan
lyöminen; uupumus.
prosy ['prəuzi] *s.* pitkäveteinen, ikävä.
protagonist [prə(u)'tægənist] *s.*
päähenkilö; esitaistelija.
protean ['prə(u)tiən] *s.* muotoaan
muuttava.
protect [prə'tekt] *v.* suojella, suojata,
varjella. **-ion** [-'tek∫n] *s.* suojelus;

suoja, turva. **-ionist** [-'tek∫ənist] *s.*
suojelutullien puoltaja. **-ive** [-iv] *a.*
suojelu-, suoja-; ~ *tariff* suojelutulli.
-or [-ə] *s.* suojelija; suojain, suojus,
suojalaite; valtionhoitaja. **-orate**
[-ərit] *s.* protektoraatti.
protegé ['prəuteʒei] *s.* (fem. *-gée)*
suojatti.
protein ['prəuti:n] *s.* valkuaisaine,
proteiini.
protest [prə'test] *v.* vakuuttaa; esittää
vastalause, vastustaa; *[~ against]* *s.*
['prəutest] vastalause; (vekselin)
protesti. *lodge (make) a* ~ esittää
vastalauseensa. **-ant** ['prɔtist(ə)nt] *s.*
& a. protestantti(nen). **-ation**
[prəutes'tei∫n] *s.* vakuutus;
vastalause.
protocol ['prəutəkɔl] *s.*
sopimusluonnos, protokolla. **-n**
['prəutɔn] *s.* protoni. **-plasm** [-plæzm]
s. protoplasma, alkulima. **-type** [-taip]
s. prototyyppi, alkumuoto.
protract [prə'trækt] *v.* venyttää (aikaa),
pitkittää. **-ed** [-id] *a.* pitkällinen. **-ion**
[-'træk∫n] *s.* pitkittäminen. **-or** [-ə] *s.*
astelevy (geom.).
protru|de [prə'tru:d] *v.* työntää, pistää,
työntyä esiin; *-ding* esiin pullistuva,
ulkoneva. **-sion** [-'tru:ʒn] *s.* esiin
pullistuminen, ulkonema.
protuberan|ce [prə'tju:b(ə)rəns] *s.*
pullistuma; kyhmy, ulkonema. **-t**
[-ənt] *a.* ulkoneva, esiinpullistuva.
proud [praud] *a.* ylpeä; ylväs, uljas; *be*
~ *of* ylpeillä jstk; *do sb.* ~ kestitä
ruhtinaallisesti; ~ *flesh* liikaliha.
prove [pru:v] *v.* todistaa, näyttää
toteen; osoittautua (jksk); *all ~d in*
vain kaikki oli turhaa; ~ *oneself*
täyttää odotukset. **-n** [-(ə)n] *a.*
todistettu.
provenance ['prɔvinəns] *a.* alkuperä.
provender ['prɔvində] *s.* rehu; (leik.)
ruoka, sapuska.
proverb ['prɔvə(:)b] *s.* sananlasku;
Book of P~s (raam.) Sananlaskut.
-ial [prə'və:biəl] *a.* sananparren
tapainen; yleisesti tunnettu, maan
kuulu. **-ially** *adv.* sananlaskun
tapaan; tunnetusti.
provide [prə'vaid] *v.* hankkia,
varustaa, varata; huolehtia, pitää
huolta, elättää *(for* jkta); ryhtyä

toimenpiteisiin t. varokeinoihin
against jnk varalta); määrätä. **-d** [-id]
konj.: ~ [*that*] sillä ehdolla,
edellyttäen että.

provid|ence [ˈprɒvid(ə)ns] *s.*
huolenpito (tulevaisuudesta),
säästäväisyys; *P~* sallimus,
kaitselmus. **-ent** [-(ə)nt] *a.* huolehtiva,
tarkka, säästäväinen. **-ential**
[-ˈdenʃ(ə)l] *a.* kaitselmuksen antama,
ihmeellinen. **-ing** [prəˈvaidiŋ] *konj.*
edellyttäen että, kunhan vain.

province [ˈprɒvins] *s.* maakunta, lääni;
(toimi)ala, alue; *the* ~ *s* maaseutu.

provincial [prəˈvinʃ(ə)l] *a.* maakunta-;
maaseutu-, maalais-; ahdasmielinen;
s. maalainen. **-ism** [-izm] *s.*
murteellisuus.

provision [prəˈviʒn] *s.* huolenpito,
ennaltavaraaminen; varokeino; (lak.)
määräys; *pl.* elintarvikkeet; *v.*
muonittaa; *make* ~ *for* pitää huolta,
huolehtia jstk; varautua jhk. **-al** [-l] *a.*
väliaikainen.

proviso [prəˈvaizəu] *s.* (pl. ~ *es*) ehto,
varaus.

provoca|tion [prɒvəˈkeiʃn] *s.* yllytys,
ärsyttäminen; provokaatio; *without* ~
aiheettomasti. **-tive** [prəˈvɒkətiv] *a.*
provosoiva, ärsyttävä; ~ *of* jtk
aiheuttava, herättävä.

provok|e [prəˈvəuk] *v.* ärsyttää,
suututtaa, yllyttää; aiheuttaa,
synnyttää, provosoida. **-ing** *a.*
ärsyttävä, harmillinen.

provost [ˈprɒvəst, Am. ˈprəu-] *s.*
(collegen) rehtori; (Skotl.)
pormestari; ~ *marshal* [prəˈvəu-]
sotatuomari.

prow [prau] *s.* keula, kokka.

prowess [ˈprauis] *s.* miehuullisuus;
taitavuus.

prowl [praul] *v.* hiiviskellä, vaania
saalista; ~ *car* partioauto. **-er** *s.*
saalistaja; = ed.

proxim|al [ˈprɒksim(ə)l] *a.* lähin,
tyvenpuoleinen. **-ity** [prɒkˈsimiti] *s.*
läheisyys; ~ *of blood* lähisukulaisuus.
-o [ˈprɒksiməu] *adv.:* (vanh.) on the
10th ~ (lyh. *prox.)* tulevan kuun
10. p:nä.

proxy [ˈprɒksi] *s.* valtuutettu edustaja;
valtakirja; [*vote*] *by* ~ valtakirjalla.

prude [pru:d] *s.* turhankaino, tekosiveä

nainen.

pruden|ce [ˈpru:d(ə)ns] *s.*
harkitsevuus, varovaisuus. **-t** [-nt] *a.*
harkitseva, järkevä, varovainen. **-tial**
[pru:(ˈ)denʃ(ə)l] *a.* varovaisuus-.

prud|ery [ˈpru:dəri] *s.* (liika)
häveliäisyys. **-ish** [-iʃ] *a.* turhankaino,
tekosiveä.

prune 1. [pru:n] *s.* kuivattu luumu.

prun|e 2. [pru:n] *v.* leikata, karsia,
oksia. **-ing-hook, -ing-knife**
puutarhaveitsi.

prurient [ˈpruəriənt] *a.* himokas.

Prussia [ˈprʌʃə] *erisn.* Preussi. **-n** [-n] *a.
& s.* preussilainen.

prussic [ˈprʌsik] *a.:* ~ *acid* sinihappo.

pry [prai] *v.* nuuskia, urkkia; ~ *open*
vääntää auki. **-ing** *a.* urkkiva,
nuuskiva, utelias.

psalm [sɑ:m] *s.* psalmi. **-ist** *s.*
psalminkirjoittaja.

psalter [ˈsɔ:ltə] *s.* psalttari.

pseudo- [sjuˈdəu-] *pref.* vale-,
näennäis-. **-nym** [-dɒnim] *s.* salanimi.

psych|e [ˈsaiki(:)] *s.* psyyke, sielu.
-edelic [saikiˈdelik] *a.* psykedeelinen.
-iatrist [saiˈkaiətrist] *s.* psykiatri.
-iatry [saiˈkaiətri] *s.* mielitautioppi,
psykiatria. **-ic** [ˈsaikik] *s.* meedio; *a.*
ks. seur. **-ical** [ˈsaikik(ə)l] *a.*
sielullinen, psyykkinen.

psychoanal|yse [saikə(u)ænəlˈaiz] *v.*
psykoanalysoida. **-ysis** [-əˈnæləsis] *s.*
psykoanalyysi. **-yst** [-ist] *s.*
psykoanalyytikko.

psycholog|ical [saikəˈlɒdʒik(ə)l] *a.*
sielutieteellinen, psykologinen; ~
moment oikea, otollinen hetki. **-ist**
[saiˈkɒlədʒist] *s.* psykologi. **-y**
[saiˈkɒlədʒi] psykologia.

psycho|pathic [saikə(u)ˈpæθik] *a.*
luonnevikainen. **-sis** [saiˈkəusis] *s.*
psykoosi. **-therapy** [ˈ- -ˈθerəpi] *s.*
psykoterapia.

ptarmigan [ˈtɑ:migən] *s.* kiiruna,
riekko.

ptomaine [ˈtəumein] *s.* ruumismyrkky.

pub [pʌb] *s.* »pubi», krouvi, kapakka.

puberty [ˈpju:bəti] *s.* murrosikä,
puberteetti.

public [ˈpʌblik] *a.* yleinen, julkinen;
yleisesti tunnettu; valtion, kansan; *s.*
yleisö; ~ *-address system* kaiutin-
laitteet (julkisissa paikoissa);

~ *assistance* huoltoapu; ~ *authority home* vanhainkoti; ~ *house* kapakka; ~ *life* julkinen (valtiollinen) elämä; ~ *school* engl. sisäoppilaitos (Eton, Harrow ym); (Am.) kansakoulu; ~ *relations officer* suhdetoiminta-virkailija, tiedotussihteeri; ~ *spirit* kansalaismieli; ~ *utilities* ks. t.; *go* ~ siirtyä pörssiin; *make* ~ julkaista, julkistaa; *in* ~ julkisesti; *the general* ~ suuri yleisö. **-an** [-ən] s. kapakoitsija; publikaani. **-ation** [-'keiʃn] s. julkaiseminen, kuuluttaminen; julkaisu.**-ist** ['pʌblisist] s. (poliittinen) kynäilijä, sanomalehtimies. **-ity** [pʌb'lisiti] s. julkisuus; mainostus, mainonta; ~ *agent* PR-mies (-nainen), tiedotussihteeri. **-ize** ['pʌblisaiz] v. mainostaa. ~**-spirited** a. yhteistä hyvää harrastava, yhteiskunnallisesti ajatteleva.

publish ['pʌbliʃ] v. julkaista; kuuluttaa; kustantaa. **-er** [-ə] s. kustantaja. **-ing** s. kustannustoiminta; ~ *house* kustannusliike.

puce [pju:s] a. punaisenruskea.

puck [pʌk] s. menninkäinen; (jää)kiekko; ~*ish* veitikkamainen.

pucker ['pʌkə] v.: ~ [*up*] rypistää, poimuttaa, kurtistaa; rypistyä; s. ryppy, poimu.

pudding ['pudiŋ] s. vanukas; *black* ~ verivanukas, palttu.

puddle ['pʌdl] s. lätäkkö, rapakko; saviseos; v. mellottaa, putlata; ~ *up* rapata umpeen.

pudgy ['pʌdʒi] a. lyhyt ja paksu, lylleröinen.

puer|**ile** ['pjuərail] a. lapsellinen, lapsekas. **-ility** [-'riliti] s. lapsellisuus. **-peral** [pju(:)'ə:pərl] a.: ~ *fever* lapsivuodekuume.

Puerto Rico ['pwə:tə(u) 'ri:kəu] *erisn.* (*s. & a. P. Rican*).

puff [pʌf] s. henkäys, tuulahdus; puuska, tuprahdus, pöllähdys; (ihojauhe)huisku; kohokas (keitt.); »puhvi», mainostus; v. puhaltaa, puhista, puuskuttaa, läähättää; (~ *out*) tupruttaa; tupruta; paisua; kehua, mainostaa; ~ [*away*] *at* tuprutella; ~*ed* hengästynyt; ~*ed up* [*with pride*] ylpeä, pöyhistelevä. ~**-ball** tuhkelo, kuukunen. **-in**

['pʌfin] s. lunni (eläint.). ~**-paste** kohotaikina. **-y** [-i] a. paisunut, pöhöttynyt; hengästynyt.

pug [pʌg] s. mopsi; ~**-nose** nykerönenä.

pugil|**ism** ['pju:dʒilizm] s. nyrkkeily. **-ist** [-ist] s. nyrkkeilijä.

pugnac|**ious** [pʌg'neiʃəs] a. taistelunhaluinen. **-ity** [pʌg'næsiti] s. taistelun-, riidanhalu.

puke [pju:k] v. oksentaa.

pule [pju:l] v. vikistä.

pulchritude ['pʌlkritju:d] s. kaunis ulkonäkö.

pull [pul] v. vetää, kiskoa, tempoa, kiskaista; soutaa; s. vetäisy, veto, tempaus; siemaus; kulaus; henkisavu; soutu(matka); ripa; veto(voima), vaikutusvalta; ~ *a face* virnistellä; ~ *a fast one* yllättää; ~ *a p.'s leg* pettää jkta; ~ *down* hajottaa, purkaa; heikontaa, masentaa; ~ *in* (junasta) saapua asemalle; ~ *off* voittaa (palkinto); ~ *out* lähteä vesille; ~ *round* toipua; ~ *through* toipua, auttaa selviämään, suoriutua; ~ *oneself together* koota voimansa; ~ *together* vetää yhtä köyttä; ~ *up* kiskoa (juurineen), pysähdyttää (hevonen, auto), pysähtyä; ~*-up* levähdyspaikka; *a* ~ *at a bottle* kulaus.

pullet ['pulit] s. nuori kana.

pulley ['puli] s. väkipyörä.

pull-over ['puləuvə] s. pujopaita, villapaita.

pulmonary ['pʌlmənəri] a. keuhko:.

pulp [pʌlp] s. (hedelmän) sisus, (hammas) ydin; massa, sohjo, möhjö; v. hienontaa massaksi, möyhentää; *mechanical* ~ puuhioke; ~ *magazine* halpa roskalehti.

pulpit ['pulpit] s. saarnatuoli.

pulpy ['pʌlpi] a. mehevä, möyheä.

pulsa|**te** [pʌl'seit] v. tykyttää, sykkiä. **-tion** [-'seiʃn] s. tykytys; lyönti.

pulse 1. [pʌls] s. pulssi; syke, sykintä; tykytys; v. sykkiä; ~*d* värähdys-; *feel sb.'s* ~ tunnustella jkn valtimoa.

pulse 2. [pʌls] s. palkohedelmät.

pulverize ['pʌlvəraiz] v. survoa ti. jauhaa hienoksi, tehdä silppua (nuuskaa) jstk; hajota tomuksi.

puma ['pju:mə] s. puuma.

pumice ['pʌmis] s. hohkakivi (m. ~-*stone*).

pummel ['pʌml] v. iskeä nyrkillä.

pump 1. [pʌmp] s. pumppu; v. pumputa; urkkia tietoja (jklta).

pump 2. [pʌmp] s. avokenkä.

pumpkin ['pʌm(p)kin] s. kurpitsa.

pump-room s. kaivohuone.

pun [pʌn] s. sanaleikki, sutkaus; v. keksiä sanaleikkejä.

Punch 1. [pʌn(t)ʃ] s. ilveilijä; ~ *and Judy show* nukketeatteri.

punch 2. [pʌn(t)ʃ] s. meisti; naskali; nyrkinisku, täräyttää, pistää reik(i)ä, lävistää, meistää; ~[*ed*] *card* reikäkortti; *pull one's* ~ *es* antaa (tahallaan) tehottomia iskuja; ~-*up* katu- t. nyrkkitappelu (Am. ~-*out*)

punch 3. [pʌn(t)ʃ] s. hehkuviini, glögi.

punctilious [pʌŋ(k)'tiliəs] a. pikkutarkka, muodollinen.

punctual ['pʌŋ(k)tjuəl] a. täsmällinen. **-ity** [-tju'æliti] s. täsmällisyys.

punctuate ['pʌŋ(k)tjueit] v. varustaa välimerkein; keskeyttää. **-ion** [-'eiʃn] s. välimerkkien käyttö.

puncture ['pʌŋktʃə] s. puhkaisu; rengasrikko; (lääk.) punktio; v. pistää, puhkaista; mennä puhki.

pundit ['pʌndit] s. oppinut (hindulainen); asiantuntija.

pung|ency ['pʌndʒ(ə)nsi] s. purevuus, kirpeys, kitkeryys. **-ent** [-(ə)nt] a. pistävä, terävä, kirpeä; pureva, kärkevä.

punish ['pʌniʃ] v. rangaista, kurittaa; pidellä pahoin; (puhek.) verottaa (esim. viinipulloa), tehdä puhdasta jäljeä jstk. **-able** [-əbl] a. rangaistava. **-ment** s. rangaistus.

punitive ['pju:nitiv] a. rangaistus-.

Punjab [pʌn'dʒɑ:b] erisn.

punk [pʌŋk] s. taula (Am.); arvoton roska, pöty; *attr.* sl. mätä, kelvoton.

punnet ['pʌnit] s. (marja)rasia, (muovi)tuokkonen.

punster ['pʌnstə] s. sanaleikkien laatija, vitsailija.

punt 1. [pʌnt] s. laakeapohjainen vene, ruuhi; v. sauvoa (venettä).

punt 2. [pʌnt] v. potkaista (palloa) lennosta; lyödä vetoa (hevosesta). **-er** [-ə] s. vedonlyöjä, ks. ed.

puny ['pju:ni] a. heiveröinen; pieni;

vähäinen.

pup [pʌp] s. pentu, penikka; -poikanen; *sell a man a* ~ petkuttaa.

pupa ['pju:|pə] s. (pl. *-ae*[-i:]) (hyönteis)kotelo. **-te** [-peit] v. koteloitua.

pupil ['pju:pl] s. oppilas; (anat.) silmäterä.

puppet ['pʌpit] s. sätkynukke, marionetti; ~ [*government*] nukke-; *glove* ~ käsinukke. **~-show** s. nukketeatteri.

puppy ['pʌpi] s. pentu, penikka; nulikka, vintiö.

purblind ['pə:blaind] a. heikkonäköinen, puolisokea; hidas.

purchase ['pə:tʃəs] v. ostaa, hankkia; s. osto, hankinta; ostos; luja ote; *purchasing power* ostovoima; ~ *tax* liikevaihtovero. **~-money** ostohinta.

pure ['pjuə] a. puhdas; tahraton; sekoittamaton; oikea, aito; pelkkä, silkka. **-ly** adv. pelkästään, yksinomaan.

purgation [pə:'geiʃn] s. puhdistus; vatsan tyhjennys.

purgat|ive ['pə:gətiv] a. ulostava; s. ulostuslääke. **-ory** [-t(ə)ri] s. kiirastuli.

purge [pə:dʒ] v. puhdistaa, pestä puhtaaksi; tyhjentää vatsa; s. ulostuslääke; puhdistus (et.pol.).

puri|fication [pjuərifi'keiʃn] s. puhdistaminen, puhdistus. **-fy** ['pjuərifai] v. puhdistaa.

pur|ism ['pjuərizm] s. purismi, puhdaskielisyys. **-ist** [-ist] s. kielenpuhdistaja.

puritan ['pjuərit(ə)n] s.: P~ puritaani; a. ks. seur. **-ic(al)** [-'tænik, -(ə)l] a. puritaaninen.

purity ['pjuəriti] s. puhtaus.

purl 1. [pə:l] v. solista; s. solina.

purl 2. [pə:l] s. nurja (neulonta); ~ *and plain* nurin ja oikein; v. neuloa nurjaa.

purlieu ['pə:lju:] s.: ~ s ympäristö, (kaupungin) laitamat.

purloin [pə:'lɔin] v. varastaa.

purple ['pə:pl] s. purppura(väri); a. purppuranpunainen, -värinen, punasinervä; v. purppuroida; *born in the* ~ kuninkaallista sukua.

purport ['pə:pət] s. tarkoitus, sisältö; [Am. pə:'pɔ:t] tarkoittaa; pyrkiä, olemaan, haluta olla.

purpose ['pə:pəs] s. tarkoitus, päämäärä; aikomus; v. aikoa, tarkoittaa; set ~ vakaa aikomus; *answer (serve) the* ~ vastata tarkoitusta; *for the* ~ *of visiting*.. vieraillakseen jssk (jkn luona); *on* ~ ehdoin tahdoin, tahallaan; *to the* ~ tarkoituksenmukainen, asianmukainen; *to no* ~ hyödyttömästi, turhaan; *it would serve no* ~ se olisi tarkoituksetonta; *achieve one's* ~ saavuttaa päämääränsä; *a* ~ [*novel*] tendenssi-. **-ful** *a.* määrätietoinen; merkityksellinen. **-ly** *adv.* tahallaan, ehdoin tahdoin; nimenomaan.

purr [pə:] v. (kissasta) kehrätä, s. kehrääminen, hyrinä.

purse [pə:s] s. kukkaro; rahat, kassa; palkinto, rahalahja; v. (us. ~ up) nyrpistää, suipistaa; *tighten the* ~ *strings* supistaa menoja. **~-proud** rahoistaan ylpeä. **-r** [-ə] s. (laivan) purseri.

pursu|ance [pə'sju(:)əns] s.: *in* ~ *of* jnk mukaisesti, jtk noudattaen. **-ant** [-ənt] *a.: ~ to* jnk mukaisesti.

pursu|e [pə'sju:] v. ajaa takaa, ahdistaa; tavoitella; jatkaa; noudattaa, seurata; harjoittaa (ammattia ym); ~ *a course* noudattaa jtk linjaa; *he was ~ d by misfortune* häntä vainosi epäonni. **-it** [pə'sju:t] s. (takaa)ajo; tavoittelu, pyrkimys; toiminta, harrastus; *the ~ of knowledge* tiedon etsintä; *literary ~ s* kirjalliset harrastukset.

purulent ['pjuərulənt] *a.* märkivä.

purvey [pə:vei] v. hankkia (muonaa). **-or** [-ə] s. hankkisija; muonames ari; *~ [s] to the King* hovihankkija.

pus [pʌs] s. (lääk.) märkä.

push [puʃ] v. työntää, sysätä; töytäistä; painaa (nappia); tunke(utu)a; yllyttää, painostaa; mainostaa, auttaa eteenpäin; s. töytäisy, sysäys; ponnistus; (häikäilemätön) yritteliäisyys; hyökkäys (sot.); *~ along* (puhek.) lähteä; *~ sb. around* komennella, hätistää; *~ off* työntää (vene) vesille; lähteä ä, »häipyä»; häipyä; *~ on* jatkaa matkaa; *~ over* työntää kumoon; *~ sth. through*

ajaa.. läpi; *be ~ ed for money* olla rahapulassa. **~-bike** polkupyörä. **~-button** painonappi, sähkönappula. **~-cart** työntökärryt. **~-chair** lastenrattaat. **-er** [-ə] s. kiipijä; huumekauppias. **-ing** *a.* tarmokas (m. häikäilemätön). **~-over** helppo tehtävä.

pusillanimous [pju:si'læniməs] *a.* raukkamainen, arka.

puss [pus] s. kissa, mirri. **-y** [-i] s. mirri (m. *~-cat*); (~ **foot** v. hiiviskellä).

pustule ['pʌstju:l, Am. -tʃu:l] s. näppylä.

put 1. [put] *put put*, v. panna, pistää, laittaa; sijoittaa; saattaa (jhk tilaan); arvioida; esittää; ilmaista, lausua, sanoa; ~ *an end to* lopettaa; ~ *the shot* työntää kuulaa; ~ *about* kääntää (laiva); levittää; vaivata; *be much ~ about* olla hyvin huolestunut; ~ *across* saada onnistumaan, saada (jku) ymmärtämään; ~ *away* panna pois, panna sivuun, heittää menemään, luopua, panna telkien taas (esim. mielisairaalaan), lopettaa (eläin); pistellä poskeensa; lähteä (rannasta); ~ *back* palata (satamaan), panna paikoilleen, siirtää taaksepäin, viivästyttää; ~ *by* panna syrjään, säästöön; ~ *down* merkitä muistiin; kukistaa, nolata; arvioida (*at* jksk), pitää (*as, for* jnak), lukea jnk syyksi (*to*); ~ *forth* työntää (esille), versoa; esittää; ponnistaa; ~ *forward* esittää, ehdottaa; ~ *in* poiketa satamaan; esittää, pistää väliin (sanoja); ~ *in an appearance* näyttäytyä; ~ *in for* hakea (virkaa ym); ~ *into Finnish* kääntää suomen kielelle; ~ *into words* ilmaista sanoin; ~ *off* lykätä; torjua, saada luopumaan jstk; lähteä (merelle); *he was ~ off his food by...* vei häneltä ruokahalun; *I am not to be ~ off minusta ei pääse*; ~ *on* pukea ylleen; panna liikkeelle t. näyttämölle, esittää (ohjelma), avata (radio); (puhek.) puijata, petkuttaa; ~ *on flesh (weight)* lihoa; ~ *it on* liioitella; ~ *out* pujaa ulos; sammuttaa; nyrjähdyttää, saattaa ymmälle, ärsyttää, harmittaa; lainata (korkoa vastaan); lähettää (radiossa); lähteä (merelle); ~ *it over on* (puhek.) uskotella; ~ *sth. over to* saada

uskotella; ~ *sth. over to* saada
ymmärtämään; ~ *through* saattaa
päätökseen; yhdistää *(to* jkn
puhelinnumeroon); *hard* ~ *to it*
pahassa pulassa; ~ *up* pystyttää;
esittää, asettaa ehdokkaaksi, tarjota;
majoittaa; panna pakettiin; ~ *up at*
majoittua jhk; ~ *sb. up to* perehdyttää
jhk, yllyttää jhk; ~ *up a [good] fight*
pitää hyvin puoliaan; ~ *up with*
alistua jhk, sietää; ~ *upon* petkuttaa;
[it's all] ~ *on* teeskentelyä.
put 2. ks. **putt.**
putre|faction [pju:tri'fækʃn] *s.*
mädäntyminen. **-fy** ['pju:trifai] *v.*
mädäntyä; mädättää. **-scent**
[pju:'tresnt] *a.* mätänevä.
putrid [pju:trid] *a.* mädäntynyt,
pilaantunut, (sl.) mätä, inhottava. **-ity**
[-'triditi] *s.* mädännys.
putt [pʌt] *v.* putata (golf)pelissä. **-ees**
['pʌtiz] *s. pl.* (hihna)säärystimet. **-ing:**
~ *green* viheriö (golf-kentällä).
putty ['pʌti] *s.* kitti; *v.* kitata.
put-up *a.* salaa valmistettu; *s.* ~ *job*
petkutus.

puzzl|e ['pʌzl] *v.* saattaa ymmälle,
tuottaa päänvaivaa; vaivata päätänsä
*(over j*llak); *s.* pulma, pulmallinen
asia; arvoitus; ~ *out* selvittää;
crossword ~ ristisanatehtävä,
sanaristikko. **-ing** *a.* arvoituksellinen,
käsittämätön; hämmentävä.
Pygmalion [pig'meiljən] *erisn.*
pygmy ['pigmi] *s.* kääpiö.
pyjamas [pə'dʒɑ:məz] *s.* yöpuku,
pyjama.
pylon ['pailən] *s.* korkea (voimajohto-
ym) pylväs, (lentokentän) valomasto;
pyloni.
pyramid ['pirəmid] *s.* pyramidi.
pyre ['paiə] *s.* (hauta)rovio.
Pyrenees [pirə'ni:z] *s.: the* ~
Pyreneiden vuoret.
pyrites [pai'raiti:z] *s.* kiisu (miner.).
pyrotechnic [pairə(u)'teknik] *a.*
ilotulitus-; ~ *display* ilotulitus. **-s** [-s]
s. pl. ilotulitus(tekniikka).
Pythagoras [pai'θægəræs] *erisn.*
python ['paiθ(ə)n] *s.* pytonkäärme,
jättiläiskäärme.

Q

Q; q [kju:] s. q-kirjain.
Lyh.: **Q.C.** *Queen's Counsel;* **Q.E.D.**
(quod erat demonstrandum) *which
was to be proved* mikä oli todistettava;
Q.M.G. *Quartermaster General;* **qr.**
quarter(s); **qt** *quart(s);* **q.t.** *on the
[strict] q.t.:* kaikessa hiljaisuudessa;
Que. *Quebec;* **q.v.** (quod vide) *which
see* katso tätä.
qua [kwei] *konj.* jnk asemassa.
quack [kwæk] s. (ankan) kaakatus;
puoskari (m. ~ *doctor);* v. kaakattaa;
puoskaroida. **-ery** [-əri] s.
puoskarointi.
quad [kwɔd] lyh. = *quadrangle;* ~ *s* =
quadruplets. **-rangle** ['kwɔdrængl] s.
nelikulmio; (collegen) piha. **-rangular**
[-'drængjulə] a. nelikulmainen. **-rant**
[-r(ə)nt] s. kvadrantti. **-rilateral**
[-ri'læt(ə)r(ə)l] a. nelisivuinen. **-rille**
[kwɔ'dril] s. katrilli. **-roon** ['dru:n] s.
kvarteroni.
quadru|ped ['kwɔdru|ped] s. & a.
nelijalkainen. **-ple** [-pl] a. & s.
nelinkertainen (määrä); v.
nelinkertaistaa, -tua. **-plet** [-plit] s.:
~ *s* neloset.
quaff [kwɔf, Am. kwæf] v. ryypätä
(hitaasti); s. pitkä siemaus.
quagmire ['kwægmaiə] s. suo.
quail 1. [kweil] s. viiriäinen.
quail 2. [kweil] v. menettää
rohkeutensa, vavahtaa, sävähtää.
quaint [kweint] a. (viehättävästi)
vanhanaikainen, (erikoisuutensa
takia) viehättävä, erikoinen. **-ness** s.
erikoisuus.
quak|e [kweik] v. järistä, huojua;
väristä (vilusta ym) tutista; s. vapina,
(maan)järistys; *Q~r* kveekari.
quali|fication [kwɔlifi'keif(n] s.
rajoitus, varaus; (tarpeellinen)
edellytys; pätevyys; *has she the*

necessary ~ s täyttääkö hän
pätevyysehdot? *with certain ~ s* eräin
varauksin. **-fied** ['kwɔlifaid] a. pätevä
(for jhk), tutkinnon suorittanut;
varauksellinen. **-fier** ['kwɔlifaiə] s.
määre, määräys. **-fy** ['kwɔlifai] v.
määrittää (kiel.); pätevöittää, antaa
pätevyys; suorittaa tutkinto, hankkia
pätevyys, pätevöityä, suoriutua (jhk
for; esim. urh. jatkoon); ~ *ing contest*
karsintakilpailu.
qualitative ['kwɔlitətiv] a. laatu-.
quality ['kwɔliti] s. laatu, hyvä laatu;
ominaisuus.
qualm [kwɑ:m, kwɔ:m] s. tunnonvaiva,
epäily; äkillinen pahoinvointi,
kuvotus; *he felt no ~ s about.* . häntä ei
arveluttanut. .
quandary ['kwɔndəri] s. pula; *be in a ~
about* epäröidä, olla pulassa jnk
suhteen.
quantitative ['kwɔntitətiv] a. määrää
koskeva; kvantitatiivinen.
quantity ['kwɔntiti] s. määrä, paljous;
suure (mat.); *in great q-ties* runsain
määrin.
quantum ['kwɔntəm] s. määrä; kvantti
(fys.).
quarantine ['kwɔr(ə)nti:n] s.
karanteeni; v. panna karanteeniin.
quarrel ['kwɔr(ə)l] s. riita, kiista,
erimielisyys; v. riidellä, riitaantua;
valittaa; *pick a ~ with* haastaa riitaa
jkn kanssa; ~ *with one's bread and
butter* jättää leipätyönsä. **-ling** s.
riitely, epäsopu. **-some** a. riitaisa.
quarry 1. ['kwɔri] s. saalis, riista.
quarry 2. ['kwɔri] s. louhos; v. louhia;
penkoa (esiin).
quart [kwɔ:t] s. neljännes|gallonaa
(Engl. 1,1 l, Am. 0,9 l)
quarter ['kwɔ:tə] s. neljäsosa,
neljännes; »nelikko» (8 *bushels* = n.

290 l); painomitta (12,7 kg);
neljännesdollari, 25 senttiä;
neljännesvuosi, vuosineljännes;
ilmansuunta, suunta, puoli, taho;
kaupunginosa; (sot.) armahdus,
armo; *pl.* asunto, (puhek.) kortteeri;
v. jakaa neljään osaan; majoittaa,
sijoittaa; *a ~ of an hour*
neljännestunti; [*at*] *a ~ to six*
neljännestä vailla kuusi; *at close ~ s*
läheltä; *from all ~ s* joka taholta; *take
up one's ~ s* majoittua (jhk); *cry ~*
pyytää armoa; *hind~ s* (eläimen)
takapuoli. **~-day**
neljännes(maksu)päivä. **~-deck**
puolikansi. **-ly** *a.* joka neljännesvuosi
tapahtuva t. ilmestyvä; *s.* neljästi
vuodessa ilmestyvä julkaisu. **-master**
majoitusmestari (lyh. *Q.M.*);
aliperämies; *Q~ General*
päämajoitusmestari. **-n** [-n] *s.* neljän
naulan leipä, neljännestuoppi *(pint).*
~ -sessions (neljännesvuosittain
pidetyt) käräjät.
quartet(te) [kwɔː'tet] *s.* kvartetti,
kvartetto.
quarto [kwɔː'təu] *s.* nelitaite,
neljänneskoko.
quartz [kwɔːts] *s.* kvartsi.
quasar ['kweisɑ] *s.* kvasaari (täht.).
quash [kwɔʃ] *v.* kumota, mitätöintää.
quasi(-) ['kweisɑi] *pref.* näennäis-;
~-official puolivirallinen.
quassia ['kwɔʃə] *s.* kvassia.
quaternary [kwə'tɜːnəri] *a.* kvartääri-
(geol.).
quatrain ['kwɔtrein] *s.* nelisäkeinen
runo, nelisäe.
quaver ['kweivə] *v.* väristä, väräjöidä;
s. värinä; kahdeksasosanuotti.
quay [kiː] *s.* satamalaituri. **-age** [-idʒ] *s.*
laiturimaksu.
queasiness *s.* pahoinvointi, kuvotus.
queasy ['kwiːzi] *a.* kuvottava; huono
(vatsa); yliherkkä.
Quebec [kwi'bek] *erisn.*
queen [kwiːn] *s.* kuningatar; rouva
(korttip.); *Q~ Dowager*
leskikuningatar; *Q~ Mother*
kuningataräiti. **-ly** *a.* majesteettinen,
kuningatarmainen.
queer [kwiə] *a.* omituinen, outo,
kummallinen; epäiltyttävä;
huonovointinen; *sl.*

homoseksuaalinen; *s.*
homoseksualisti; *v.* pilata (jkn
mahdollisuudet, m. *~ sb.'s pitch*); *feel
very ~* voida huonosti; *in Q ~ street*
rahavaikeuksissa. **-ness** *s.* omituisuus.
quell [kwel] *v.* kukistaa, tukahduttaa.
quench [kwen(t)ʃ] *v.* sammuttaa
(jano); tukahduttaa, hillitä.
querulous ['kwerʊləs] *a.* valittava,
ruikuttava.
query ['kwiəri] *s.* kysymys,
kysymysmerkki; *v.* kysellä, kysyä;
epäillä, varustaa kysymysmerkillä.
quest [kwest] *s.* etsintä; *v.* etsiä; *in ~ of*
etsimässä jtk.
question ['kwestʃn] *s.* kysymys;
(puheenaoleva) asia; epäilys; *v.*
kuulustella; asettaa kyseenalaiseksi,
epäillä; *ask sb. a ~* kysyä jklta, tehdä
kysymys jklle; ks. *beg; call in ~*
asettaa kyseenalaiseksi; *that is out of
the ~* siitä ei voi olla puhettakaan; *se
ei tule kysymykseenkään; when it is a
~ of* . . *kun* . . *on* kyseessä; *the person in*
puheena oleva henkilö. **-able** [-əbl] *a.*
kyseenalainen, epävarma;
epäilyttävä. **~-mark** kysymysmerkki.
~-master *l.v.* tietokilpailun juontaja.
-naire [-tʃə'nɛə] *s.* kyselykaavake.
queue [kjuː] *s.* jono; niskapalmikko; *v.*
jonottaa (us. *~ up*); *jump the ~*
etuilla.
quibble ['kwibl] *s.* sanaleikki;
saivartelu; *v.* saivarrella, halkoa
hiuksia.
quick [kwik] *a.* nopea, pikainen,
vikkelä; nokkela, terävä (äly ym);
äkkipikainen; *adv.* nopeasti,
vikkelään; *s.: the ~* elävä liha; *be ~!*
joudu! *~ temper* äkkipikaisuus; *~ wits*
sanavalmius; *cut to the ~* loukata
syvästi; *the ~ and the dead* (raam.
ym) elävät ja kuolleet. **-en** [-(ə)n] *v.*
vilkastuttaa, elvyttää; jouduttaa;
saada eloa, elpyä; vilkastua. **~-firing**
pika-. **~-freeze** pakastaa. **-lime**
sammuttamaton kalkki. **-ly** *adv.*
nopeasti. **-ness** *s.* ripeys, joutuisuus,
nopeus. **-sand** juoksuhiekka. **-set:** *~
hedge* pensasaita (tav. orapihlaja-).
~-silver elohopea. **~-tempered**
äkkipikainen. **~-witted** sukkela,
nopeaälyinen.
quid 1. [kwid] *s.* (pl. *quid*) punta (sl.)

quid 2. [kwid] s. tupakkamälli.

quiesc|ence [kwai'es|ns] s. lepo, lepotila; toimettomuus. **-ent** [-nt] a. liikkumaton, levossa oleva, uinaileva.

quiet ['kwaiət] a. hiljainen, tyyni, rauhallinen; vaitelias, äänetön; s. lepo, rauha; hiljaisuus; v. hiljentää, tyynnyttää, rauhoittaa; rauhoittua, tyyntyä (tav. ~ *down*); *be ~! hiljaa! keep sth.* ~ pitää salassa; *on the ~* salaa. **-en** [-n] v. rauhoittaa, tyynnyttää; hiljetä (~*down*). **-ly** adv. hiljaa, rauhallisesti. **-ude** ['kwaiətju:d] s. rauha(llisuus) jne. **-us** [kwai'i:təs] s. (vanh.) armonisku, kuolema.

quill [kwil] s. siipisulka, sulkakynä; (siilin) piikki; v. röyheltää. ~**-driver** kynäniekka.

quilt [kwilt] s. (tikattu) vuodepeite; v. sisustaa vanulla, tikata (peite). **-ing** s. tikkaus.

quince [kwins] s. kvitteni.

quinine [kwi'ni:n, Am. 'kwainain] s. kiniini.

quinquagenarian [kwiŋkwədʒi'neəriən] s. viisikymmenvuotias.

quins [kwinz] lyh. = *quintuplets.*

quinsy ['kwinzi] s. kurkkupaise.

quintal ['kwintl] s. sentneri (100 kg).

quintessence [kwin'tesns] s. (jnk) olennainen osa; perikuva.

quintuplet ['kwintjuplit] s.: ~ s viitoset (lyh. *quins*).

quip [kwip] s. pistosana, sutkaus.

quire ['kwaiə] s. kirja (24 arkkia).

quirk [kwə:k] s. letkaus, sutkaus; oikku; koukero.

quit [kwit] v. jättää, luovuttaa, luopua jstk; hylätä; lakata jstk; lähteä pois, matkustaa, muuttaa; a. jstk vapaa, kuitti; *get ~ of* päästä jstk; *we are ~ s*

olemme kuitit; *double or ~* tupla tai kuitti, ota tai jätä.

quite [kwait] adv. aivan, kokonaan, täydellisesti; täysin, oikein, todella; melkoisen, varsin; ~ *a beauty* oikea kaunotar; ~ [*so*] aivan niin, juuri niin; *it is ~ the thing* on viimeistä muotia.

quit|s [kwits] a.: *be ~ with* olla kuitti jksta; *call it ~* »panna pillit pussiin»; *cry ~* selvittää välinsä. **-tance** [-(ə)ns] s. (vanh.) vapautus; maksukorvaus. **-ter** s. luopuja.

quiver 1. ['kwivə] s. (nuoli)viini.

quiver 2. ['kwivə] v. vavista, väristä; s. vapina; värähdys.

quixotic [kwik'sɔtik] a. romanttisen ihanteellinen, epäkäytännöllinen.

quiz [kwiz] s. tietokilpailu, visailu; (vanh.) ilkamoiva katse; v. kysellä; (vanh.) kiusoitella; ~*-master* juontaja. **-zical** [-ik(ə)l] a. koominen, ilkikurinen.

quod [kwɔd] s. sl. vankila.

quoin [kɔin] s. kulma(kivi); kiila.

quoit [kɔit] s. heittorengas, *pl.* heittorengaspeli.

quondam ['kwɔndæm] a. entinen.

quorum ['kwɔ:rəm] s. päätösvaltainen jäsenluku.

quot|a ['kwoutə] s. (suhteellinen) osuus, määräosuus; kiintiö. **-ation** [kwə(u)'teiʃn] s. lainaus, sitaatti; hintailmoitus, noteeraus; ~ *marks* lainausmerkit.

quote [kwəut] v. lainata, siteerata; (tav. ~ *at*) ilmoittaa hinta t. kurssi; *the ~ s are his* lainausmerkit hänen.

quoth [kwəuθ] v. (vanh.): ~ *I* sanoin; ~ *he* hän sanoi.

quotidian [kwɔ'tidiən] a. päivittäinen.

quotient ['kwəuʃnt] s. (mat.) osamäärä (*intelligence ~*).

R

R, r [a:] *s.* r-kirjain; *the three R's =
reading, (w)riting, (a)rithmetic* (kuv.)
opin alkeet.
Lyh.: **R.** *Regina* [ri'dʒaɪnə] kuningatar;
Rex kuningas; **R.A.** *Royal Academy,
Royal Artillery;* **R.A.C.** *Royal
Automobile Club;* **R.A.F.** ['ɑːrei'ef]
Royal Air Force; **R.C.** *Roman
Catholic, Red Cross;* **rd.** *road;*
R.C.S. *Royal College of Surgeons;*
R.D. *refer to drawer* katteeton; **R.E.**
Royal Engineers; **recd.** *received;* **ref.**
reference; **Regt.** *regiment;* **Rev.**
Reverend; Revelation; **R.I.** *Rhode
Island;* **R.I.P.** *may he (she) rest in
peace;* **R.L.S.** *Robert Louis Stevenson;*
R.N. *Royal Navy;* **Rom.** *Romans*
Roomalaiskirje; **R.S.P.C.A.** *Royal
Society for the Prevention of Cruelty to
Animals* kuninkaallinen
eläinsuojeluyhdistys; **R.S.V.P.** *please
reply;* **Rt Hon.** *Right Honourable;* **Rt
Rev.** *Right Reverend;* **R.V.** *Revised
Version.*
rabbi['ræbai] *s.* rabbi; rabbiini.
rabbit ['ræbit] *s.* kani, kaniini; *v.*
pyydystää kaniineja. **~-hutch**
kaninkoppi. **~-warren** kaniinitarha.
rabble ['ræbl] *s.* roskaväki.
rabid ['ræbid] *a.* raivoisa, hurja. **-ity**
[ræbiditi] *s.* raivo, vimma.
rabies ['reibiːz] *s.* raivotauti,
vesikauhu.
raccoon [rə'kuːn] *s.* pesukarhu.
race 1. [reis] *s.* rotu, suku; ~ *riot*
rotumellakka.
race 2. [reis] *s.* (kilpa-)ajot (esim. rata-,
maasto-); (ratsastus- soutu)kilpailut;
kilpailu; elämäntaival; virta,
(myllyn)kouru; *v.* juosta, kiitää;
kilpailla; juosta, ajaa, ratsastaa kilpaa
(*sb.* jkn kanssa); kasvattaa
kilpahevosia; *boat* ~ soutukilpailut;

motor ~ autokilpailut; *the* ~*s*
ratsastuskilpailut; *the racing world*
hevosurheilun (autokilpailujen)
harrastajat; *run a* ~ juosta kilpaa; *his*
~ *is* run hänen maallinen vaelluksensa
on päättynyt. **~-card** kilpailuohjelma.
~-course kilparata. **~-horse**
kilpahevonen. **~-meeting**
ratsastuskilpailut.
raceme [rə'siːm] *s.* terttu.
racer ['reisə] *s.* kilpahevonen, -auto,
pikamoottori.
Rachel ['reitʃ(ə)l] *erisn.* Raakel.
racial ['reiʃ(ə)l] *a.* rotu-. **-ism** [-əlizm] *s.*
rotukiihkoilu. **-ist** *s.* rotukiihkoilija.
raciness ['reisinis] *s.* eloisuus, väkevä
maku t. tuoksu.
racing ['reisiŋ] *s. attr.* kilpa-; ~*car*
kilpa-auto; *a* ~ *man* hevosurheilun t.
kilpa-ajojen harrastaja.
racis|m ['reis|izm] *s.* rotuviha, rasismi.
-t [-ist] *s.* rotukiihkoilija.
rack 1. [ræk] *s.* ristikko, häkki; (uunin
ym) ritilä; teline, hylly;
vaatenaulakko; piinapenkki; *v.*
kiduttaa; raastaa, kiusata, vaivata;
~-railway hammasrata; ~ *one's brains*
vaivata päätänsä; *a* ~*ing headache*
hirveä päänsärky.
rack 2. [ræk] *s.* tuulen ajamat pilvet; *go
to* ~ *and* ruin joutua perikatoon.
racket 1. ['rækit] *s.* (tennis)maila; *pl.*
eräänl. pallopeli.
racket 2. ['rækit] *s.* meteli, hälinä;
kiristys, (rikos)keikka, *v.* viettää
iloista elämää, reuhata (us. ~ *about);
stand the* ~ vastata seurauksista. **-eer**
[ræki'tiə] *s.* gangsteri **-eering** *s.*
(järjestetty) rahankiristys.
racoon ks. *raccoon.*
racquet ['rækit] *s.* ks. *racket 1.*
racy ['reisi] *a.* eb isa, pirteä,
voimakas; mehevä (tyyli);

piristävä (m. uskallettu).

radar ['reidə, 'reidɑ:] s. tutka.

radial ['reidjəl] a. säde-, säteittäinen; värttinäluu-.

radia|nce ['reid|jəns] s. säteily, hohde. **-nt** [-jənt] a. säteilevä. **-te** [-ieit] v. säteillä, sädehtiä. a. [-iət] sädemäinen. **-tion** [-i'eiʃn] s. säteily; sädehoito. **-tor** [-ieitə] s. lämpöpatteri; (auton) jäähdytin.

radical ['rædik(ə)l] a. radikaali, jyrkkä; perusteellinen, perinpohjainen; juuri-; s. radikaali (m. kem.); (sanan) juuri. **-ism** [-izm] s. jyrkkyys, äärimmäisyyskanta. **-ly** adv. täysin, perin pohjin.

radio ['reidiəu] s. radio; v. (~ed) lähettää radiosanoma, radioida; by ~ radioteitse, radion avulla; on the ~ radiossa. **-active** radioaktiivinen. **-graph** [-grɑ:f] v. & s. (ottaa) röntgenkuva. **-location** tutka. **-logist** [reidi'ɔlədʒist] röntgenologi. **-therapy** s. sädehoito.

radish ['rædiʃ] s. retiisi.

radium ['reidiəm] s. radium.

radius ['reidjəs] s. (pl. *radii* [-iai]) säde (geom.); värttinäluu.

radix ['reidiks] s. pl. *ices* [-isi:z] juuri; kantaluku.

raffia ['ræfiə] s. raffiniini.

raffish ['ræfiʃ] a. elosteleva.

raffle ['ræfl] s. arpajaiset, arvonta; v. arpoa.

raft [rɑ:ft] s. lautta; tukkilautta; v. lautata. **-er** [-ə] s. kattoparru, lauttamies.

rag 1. [ræg] s. repale, riekale, riepu, rätti; ~ s lumput, ryysyt; *red* ~ punainen vaate; ~ *bag* tilkkupussi; ~ *paper* lumppupaperi. **~-and-bone man** lumppukauppias.

rag 2. [ræg] v. kiusoitella, härnätä; metelöidä; s. meteli, metakka; (ylioppilaiden) hulina.

ragamuffin ['rægəmʌfin] s. resupekka, ryysyläinen.

rage [reidʒ] s. raivo, vimma; kiihko, villitys; v. raivota, olla raivoissaan; riehua; *is* [*all*] *the* ~ on viimeistä muotia; *fly into a* ~ raivostua.

rag|ged ['rægid] a. rosoinen, epätasainen; takkuinen; repaleinen, ryysyinen.

rag|tag ['rægtæg] s.: ~ *and bobtail* roskaväki. **-time** s. synkopoitu (neekeri) sävelmä; *attr.* koominen.

raid [reid] s. hyökkäys; ryöstöretki; ylläkköetsintä, ratsia; v. tehdä ryöstöretki jhk, toimeenpanna ratsia; *air* ~ ilmahyökkäys. **-er** [-ə] s. kaapparilaiva, pommikone.

rail 1. [reil] s. kaide, suojakaide, tanko; reelinki, parras; (rata-) kisko; v. aidata (us. ~ *in*, ~ *off*); *by* ~ rautateitse; ~ s raiteet, kiskot; *off the* ~ s raiteilta suistunut; epäjärjestyksessä; poissa tolaltaan; ~ *car* kiskobussi.

rail 2. [reil] v. (katkerasti) moittia, sättiä, haukkua (*at*, *against*).

railhead s. radanpäätekohta.

railing ['reiliŋ] s.: ~ s kaiteet.

raillery ['reiləri] s. kiusoittelu, pilailu, naljailu.

rail|road ['reilrəud] s. Am. rautatie. **-way** [-wei] s. rautatie; ~ *carriage* rautatievaunu.

raiment ['reimənt] s. puku, asu.

rain [rein] s. sade; v. sataa, vuodattaa; *the* ~ s sadekausi; ~ *or shine* satoi tai paistoi; *it is* ~*ing cats and dogs* sataa kuin saavista kaataen. **-bow** [-bəu] sateenkaari; ~ *trout* kirjolohi. **-fall** sademäärä. **~-gauge** [-geidʒ] sademittari. **-proof** sateenpitävä. **-y** [-i] a. sateinen, sade-; *a* ~ *day* (kuv.) paha päivä.

raise [reiz] v. kohottaa, nostaa; pystyttää, rakentaa; korottaa; kasvattaa, viljellä; loihtia esiin; herättää, aiheuttaa, synnyttää; esittää; hankkia (laina ym); pestata; s. nousu, korotus, Am. palkankorotus; ~ *the blockade (the siege)* lopettaa saarto (piiritys); ~ *money* hankkia rahaa. **-d** [-d] a. koho-. **-r** [-ə] s. -kasvattaja.

raisin ['reizn] s. rusina.

rajah ['rɑ:dʒə] s. intial. ruhtinas.

rake 1. [reik] s. harava; v. haravoida, harata, kaapia; kerätä (kokoon); tutkia tarkoin, nuuskia; ampua pitkittäin, pyyhkäistä; ~ *out* [*a fire*] kohentaa; ~ *up* kaivaa esille. **~-off** (laiton) palkkio, osuus.

rake 2. [reik] s. elostelija.

rake 3. [reik] s. kallistuma; v. kallistua

taaksepäin, viettää.

rakish ['reikiʃ] a. elosteleva; railakas, rempseä.

Raleigh ['rɔːli, 'ræli] erisn.

rally 1. ['ræli] v. koota, kerätä uudelleen; koota (voimansa); kokoontua; järjestäytyä uudestaan; saada uusia voimia, toipua; s. kokoontuminen, uudelleen järjestäytyminen; toipuminen; (joukko)kokous; ralli, kilpailu.

rally 2. ['ræli] v. kiusoitella.

Ralph [reif, rælf] erisn.

ram [ræm] s. muurinmurtaja; (laivan) puskuri; (juntan) survin; puristusmäntä; v. iskeä, työntää; ahtaa, tunkea, juntata; puskea, törmätä jhk.

rambl|e ['ræmbl] v. kuljeskella, vaeltaa, retkeillä; harhailla; rönsyillä; puhua hajanaisesti; s. kävely, retki. **-er** [-ə] s. vaeltaja; köynnösruusu. **-ing** a. harhaileva; laaja ja säännötön; hajanainen.

Rameses ['ræmisiːz] erisn.

rami|fication [ræmifi'keiʃn] s. haaraantuma. **-fy** ['ræmifai] v. haaraantua.

ramp [ræmp] v. riehua; kohota, viettää; nousta (takajaloille); huijata; s. nousutie, ramppi, ajoluiska; huijaus. **-age** [ræm'peidʒ] v. riehua, raivota; be on the ~ riehua kuin mieletön. **-ant** [-ənt] a. hillitön; rehottava; be ~ rehottaa, olla valloillaan; lion ~ takajaloilleen noussut leijona.

rampart ['ræmpɑːt] s. valli, varustus.

ramrod ['ræmrɔd] s.latasin.

ramshackle ['ræmʃækl] a. huojuva, rappeutunut.

ran [ræn] imp. ks. run.

ranch [ræn(t)ʃ] s.karjafarmi. **-er** [-ə] s. karjafarmari.

rancid ['rænsid] a. eltaantunut. **-ity** [-'siditi] s. eltaantuneisuus.

rancorous ['ræŋkərəs] a. kiukkuinen, katkera.

rancour ['ræŋkə] s. kauna, piintynyt viha; kiivaus.

rand [rænd] Et. Afrikan rahayksikkö.

random ['rændəm] s.: at ~ umpimähkään; a. umpimähkäinen; ~ sample otos.

randy ['rændi] a. villi, raisu; rietas.

rang [ræŋ] imp. ks. ring.

range [rein(d)ʒ] s. rivi, jono (esim. vuori-); alue, ala; (vaikutus)piiri; kantomatka, toimintasäde, ulottuvuus, vaihteluväli; ampumarata; hella, liesi; v. asettaa riviin, järjestää; sovittaa, luokittaa; vaeltaa, kulkea, tarpoa, samoilla (us. through, along), (kuv.) harhailla; ulottua, vaihdella jstk jhk (between; from . . to); kuulua (jhk luokkaan); ~ of mountains vuorijono; ~ of vision näköpiiri; within ~ kantomatkan päässä; ~ [the seas] purjehtia; ~ with olla samassa tasossa kuin, kuulua jhk. **~-finder** etäisyysmittari.

ranger ['rein(d)ʒə] s. metsänvartija; ratsujääkäri; tarpoja.

Rangoon [ræŋ'guːn] erisn.

rank 1. [ræŋk] s. rivi, jono; pirssi; arvo; virka-arvo, arvoaste, sääty; v. järjestää riviin; lukea jhk, luokittaa; kuulua jhk (luokkaan), olla arvoltaan jk; ~ and file rivimiehet, miehistö; ~ above (next to) olla arvoltaan jkta ylempi (jkta lähinnä).

rank 2. [ræŋk] a. (liian) rehevä; pahanhajuinen, eltaantunut; inhottava, ilkeä, törkeä; ~ with [thistles] jnk vallassa.

ranker ['ræŋkə] s.rivimies; upseeri.

rankle ['ræŋkl] v. kalvaa, katkeroittaa.

ransack ['rænsæk] s. tutkia tarkoin; ryöstää.

ransom ['rænsəm] s. lunnaat; v. lunastaa vapaaksi; hold . . to ~ säilyttää panttivankina (kunnes lunnaat on maksettu).

rant [rænt] v. kerskua, pöyhkeillä; pauhata; s. pöyhkeilevää puhe, sanatulva. **-ing** a. mahtipontinen.

rap [ræp] s. lyönti, sivallus; koputus; kolkutus; v. läpsäyttää, koputtaa; ~ out sanoa kivahtaa, lasketella; I don't care a ~ en välitä vähääkään.

rapac|ious [rə'peiʃəs] s. saaliinhimoinen, peto-. **-ity** [rə'pæsiti] s. saaliinhimo.

rape 1. [reip] v. ryöstää; raiskata; s. raiskaus.

rape 2. [reip] s.l.v. lanttu ,rapsi.

Raphael ['ræfe(i)əl] erisn.

rapid ['ræpid] a. nopea, pikainen;

rave

vuolas; *s.* koski (tav. *pl.*). **-ity**
[rə'piditi] *s.* nopeus.

rapier ['reipiə] *s.* pistomiekka.

rapine ['ræpin] *s.* ryöstö.

rapport [ræ'pɔ:] *s.* läheinen suhde,
sopusointu.

rapscallion [ræp'skæljən] *s.* roisto,
konna.

rapt [ræpt] *a.* hurmaantunut,
haltioitunut.

raptur|e ['ræptʃ|ə] *a.* ihastus, hurmaus;
go into ~*s* joutua haltioihinsa. **-ous**
[-(ə)rəs] *a.* haltioitunut,
hurmaantunut.

rare [reə] *a.* ohut; harvinainen;
harvinaisen hyvä, verraton; Am.
puolikypsä (liha); *at* ~ *intervals, on* ~
occasions perin harvoin. **-faction**
[reəri'fækʃn] *s.* ohentuminen. **-fy**
['reərifai] *v.* ohentaa, -tua. **-ly** *adv.*
harvoin.

rarity ['reəriti] *s.* ohuus; harvinaisuus;
harvinainen esine, kalleus.

rascal ['ra:sk(ə)l] *s.* roisto, lurjus,
veijari. **-ly** [-əli] *a.* roistomainen.

rase [reiz] *ks. raze.*

rash 1. [ræʃ] *s.* ihottuma.

rash 2. [ræʃ] *a.* äkkipikainen,
huimapäinen, harkitsematon.

rasher ['ræʃə] *s.* ohut (pekoni- ym)
viipale.

rasp [rɑ:sp] *s.* jämssi, raspi, karkea
viila; *v.* raastaa; ärsyttää; rahista;
~ *ing* kirskuva, rahiseva: ~ *[away] on*
a violin vinguttaa viulua.

raspberry ['rɑ:zb(ə)ri] *s.* vadelma,
-pensas; sl. halveksiva tuhahdus,
(suun) mäiskähdys.

rat [ræt] *s.* rotta; luopio; *v.* pyydystää
rottia; pettää puolueensa; *smell a* ~
aavistaa pahaa; ~ *race*
(häikäilemätön) elintasokilpailu.

ratable ['reitəbl] *a.* verotettava,
arvioitavissa oleva.

ratan [rə'tæn] *ks. rattan.*

ratchet ['rætʃit] *s.* pidätyshaka, säppi,
-pyörä.

rate 1. [reit] *v.* torua, läksyttää.

rate 2. [reit] *s.* määrä, aste (suhteessa
jhk); hinta; noteeraus, kurssi; tariffi,
taksa; vauhti, nopeus; kunnallisvero,
maksu; luokka; *v.* arvioida (*at* jhk
hintaan); lukea (jhk kuuluvaksi),
pitää jnak; verottaa; kuulua jhk

(arvo)luokkaan; arvostaa; *birth* ~
syntyvyys; *pulse* ~; *of exchange*
kurssi; ~ *of interest* korkokanta;
first:~ erinomainen; *at a cheap* ~
halvalla; *at any* ~ joka tapauksessa;
at the ~ *of 6 miles an hour* 6 mailin
tuntinopeudella. **-payer**
veronmaksaja.

rather ['rɑ:ðə] *adv.* mieluummin;
ennemminkin; jokseenkin, melko,
aika; melkein; (puhek.) ilman muuta!
kyllä vain! *I'd* ~ *[go]* mieluummin
menisin, haluaisin mieluummin; *I'd* ~
[she didn't know] soisinpa, ettei; *I* ~
think luulenpa, että; *I* ~ *like him*
pidän hänestä varsin paljon; ~ *a lot*
[to pay] melkoinen hinta; ~ *too much*
koko joukon (t. aika lailla) liikaa.

rati|fication [rætifi'keiʃn] *s.* vahvistus.
-fy ['rætifai] *v.* vahvistaa, ratifioida.

rating 1. ['reitiŋ] *s.* nuhteet, läksytys.

rating 2. ['reitiŋ] *s.* arviointi; luokitus,
luokka; ~ *s* (sotalaivan) alipäällystö ja
matruusit

ratio ['reiʃiəu] *s.* (pl. ~ *s*) suhde.

ration ['ræʃn] *s.* (elintarvike)-annos; *v.*
säännöstellä; annostella; ~ *card*
elintarvikekortti; ~ *ing* säännöstely.

rational ['ræʃənl] *a.* järkiperäinen;
järkevä, järjellinen; järjenmukainen.
-e [ræʃə'nɑ:l(i)] *s.* järjellinen perusta.
-ize ['ræʃnəlaiz] *v.* rationalisoida,
järkeistää. **-ly** ['ræʃnəli] *adv.*
järjellisesti jne.

rat(t)an [ræ'tæn] *s.* rottinki.

ratter ['rætə] *s.* rottakoira.

rattle ['rætl] *v.* kalista; kalistaa,
rämistää; pälpättää; lasketella
nopeasti (runoa ym); (puhek.)
järkyttää, hermostuttaa; *s.* kalina,
helinä, räminä; helistin, räikkä;
papatus; ~ *[of bottles]* kolina; ~ *[of*
hail] ropina. ~**-brained**
hupakkomainen, lörppö. **-snake**
kalkkarokäärme. **-trap** *s. & a.* rämä.

rattling ['rætliŋ] *a.* kaliseva; sl. huima,
tavaton, aikamoinen; *adv.* hurjan.

raucous ['rɔ:kəs] *a.* käheä, karhea.

ravage ['rævidʒ] *v.* tuhota, hävittää,
ryöstää; *s.* (tav. *pl.*) tuho, hävitys.

rave [reiv] *v.* hourailla; riehua; ~ *about*
olla haltioissaan jstk.

ravel ['ræv(ə)l] *v.* purkaa; purkautua;
sotkea; ~ *out* selvittää.

raven 1. ['reivn] s. korppi.

raven 2. ['rævn] v. vaania saalista; ~ing saaliinhimoinen. **-ous** ['rævinəs] a. saaliinhimoinen; ahnas; ~ appetite valtava ruokahalu.

ravine [rə'vi:n] s. rotko, kuilu.

raving ['reiviŋ] a. houraileva; ~ mad pähkähullu; s.: ~ s houreet.

ravish ['ræviʃ] v. hurmata, lumota; (vanh.) raiskata; ~ing hurmaava. **-ment** s. hurmio, ihastus.

raw [rɔ:] a. raaka, kypsymätön; harjaantumaton, kokematon; verestävä, avoin, kylmä, raaka (ilma); s. veresliha; touch . . on the ~ koskea arkaan kohtaan; ~ [hide] parkitsematon; ~ materials raaka-aineet; ~ recruit alokas; he got a ~ deal häntä kohdeltiin epäoikeudenmukaisesti. ~**-boned** luiseva.

ray 1. [rei] s. rausku.

ray 2. [rei] s. (auringon-, valon) säde; X~s röntgensäteet; a ~ of hope toivonpilkahdus.

rayon ['reiɔn] s. raion.

raze, rase [reiz] v. hävittää (maan tasalle), tuhota (tav. ~ to the ground)

razor ['reizə] s. partaveitsi; safety ~ parranajokone. ~**-edge** s. veitsen terä, kriitillinen tilanne.

razzle (-dazzle) ['ræzl] s. hulina, hummailu.

re [ri:] prep. mitä tulee jhk, jtk koskien.

re- [ri:] pref. jälleen, uudelleen, takaisin.

reach [ri:tʃ] v. ojentaa; ulottua; saavuttaa, tavoittaa; saapua; päästä jhk; s. ojentaminen, ulottuma, kantomatka; (joen) suora juoksu; ~ [out] for kurkottaa jtk ottaakseen; can you ~ .. ulotutko? [his voice] didn't ~ to the back of the hall ei kantanut salin takaosaan; out of ~ saavuttamaton; within [easy] ~ lähellä, käden ulottuvilla; ~-me-downs valmiina ostetut vaatteet.

react [ri(:)æk|t] v. reagoida (to jhk); ~ against reagoida jtk vastaan, vastustaa; ~ [up] on vaikuttaa, kohdistua takaisin jhk. **-ion** [-ʃn] s. vastavaikutus, reaktio; taantumus; (~ ary a. & s. taantumuksellinen). **-or** [-tə] s. reaktori (nuclear~).

read [ri:d] read read [red] v. lukea; opiskella; tulkita, selittää; olla luettavissa, kuulua; a. [red]: well~ paljon lukenut; ~ a paper pitää esitelmä; ~ sb. a lesson antaa läksytys jklle; ~ over lukea läpi; ~ up opiskella, perehtyä jhk; this play ~ s better than it acts luettuna tämä näytelmä on parempi kuin näyttämöllä. **-able** [-əbl] a. lukemisen arvoinen. **-er** [-ə] s. lukija; oikolukija; luennoitsija, l.v. dosentti; lukukirja. (~**ship** l.v. dosentintoimi; lukijakunta).

readi|ly ['redili] adv. mielellään, kernaasti, helposti. **-ness** s. valmius, alttius; nopeus, helppous; ~ of resource neuvokkuus; ~ of wit sukkeluus, sanavalmius; in ~ valmiina.

reading ['ri:diŋ] s. lukeneisuus; lukeminen, (sisä)luku; luentatilaisuus; tulkinta; lukema; käsittely (parl.); a. lukeva, luku-. ~**-room** s. lukusali.

readjust [ri:ə'dʒʌst] v. asettaa jälleen kuntoon, tarkistaa; ~ oneself sopeutua.

ready ['redi] a. valmis, aulis, altis, halukas; ripeä; helppo, mukava, nokkela; s. (sl.) the ~ käteinen (raha); ~ at hand lähellä, käsillä, saatavissa; ~ consent aulis suostumus; ~ money käteinen; a ~ pen sujuva kynä; ~ reckoner tulostaulukko; ~ wit sanavalmius; get ~ valmistaa, -autua; ~ cooked valmiiksi keitettynä, paistettuna. ~**-made** valmis; a r.-m. coat valmiina ostettu takki.

reafforestation [ri:əfɔris'teiʃn] s. metsänistutus.

reagent [ri(:)'eidʒnt] s. reagenssi.

real ['riəl] a. todellinen, tosiasiallinen; oikea, aito; kiinteä (lak.); ~ estate kiinteistö; ~ life todellisuus. **-ism** [-izm] s. realismi. **-ist** [-ist] s. realisti. **-istic** [riə'listik] a. realistinen. **-ity** [ri(:)'æliti] s. todellisuus; in ~ todellisuudessa; -ities tosiasiat. **-ization** [-ai'zeiʃn] s. toteuttaminen, toteutuminen. **-ize** [-aiz] v. toteuttaa, panna täytäntöön; käsittää, oivaltaa; muuttaa rahaksi; tuottaa (hinta); hankkia, ansaita (rahaa). **-ly** [-i] adv.

todella(kin), tosiaan; todellako? niinkö?

realm [relm] s. valtakunta.

realtor ['riəltɔ] s. kiinteistönvälittäjä.

realty ['riəlti] s. kiinteistö.

ream [ri:m] s. riisi (paperia).

reanimate ['ri(:)'ænimeit] v. herättää uudelleen henkiin, elvyttää.

reap [ri:p] v. leikata, korjata (viljaa). **-er** [-ə] s. elonkorjaaja; = seur. **-ing-machine** leikkuukone.

reappear ['ri:ə'piə] s. jälleen ilmestyä (näkyviin).

rear 1. [riə] v. kohottaa, pystyttää; kasvattaa; viljellä; (hevosesta) karahtaa pystyyn.

rear 2. [riə] s. takaosa; selusta, selkäpuoli; jälkijoukko; attr. taka-; attack (take) in the ~ hyökätä selustaan; bring up the ~ olla, tulla viimeisenä; at the ~ of jnk takana; ~most takimmainen. **~-admiral** kontra-amiraali. **~-guard** jälkijoukko.

rearm ['ri:'ɑ:m] s. aseistaa, varustautua uudelleen. **-ament** s. varustautuminen (uudelleen), varustelu.

rearrange ['ri:ə'rein(d)ʒ] v. järjestää uudelleen.

rearview: ~ mirror auton taustapeili.

rearward [-wəd] a. takimmainen; adv. (m. ~s) taaksepäin.

reason ['ri:zn] s. järki, syy, aihe, peruste; v. käyttää järkeään, ajatella järkevästi; puhua järkeä (with jklle); päätellä; pohtia, väitellä; järkisyillä taivuttaa (jhk, jstk luopumaan); by ~ of jnk johdosta; without ~ ilman syytä, aiheettomasti; [he will do] anything within ~ kaikkea mitä kohtuudella voi vaatia; it stands to ~ [that] on itsestään selvää; ~ out tehdä itselleen selväksi. **-able** [-əbl] a. järkevä; kohtuullinen. **-ableness** s. järkevyys; kohtuullisuus. **-ably** adv. (m.) kohtuudella; kohtalaisen, melko. **-ed** pp., a. harkittu, perusteltu. **-ing** s. todistelu, perustelu; pohdinta, pohdiskelu, ajatuksenjuoksu.

reassur|e [ri:ə'ʃuə] v. uudelleen saada vakuuttuneeksi, saada rauhoittumaan; re-assure jälleenvakuuttaa. **-ing** a. vakuuttava, rauhoittava.

rebate ['ri:beit] s. alennus.

rebel ['rebl] s. kapinoitsija, kapinallinen; v. [ri'bel] kapinoida, nousta kapinaan. **-lion** [ri'beljən] s. kapina. **lious** [ri'beljəs] a. kapinallinen.

rebirth ['ri:'bə:θ] s. uudestisyntyminen; elpyminen.

rebound [ri'baund] v. ponnahtaa takaisin, kimmahtaa takaisin, pompata; s. takaisinkimmahdus.

rebuff [ri'bʌf] v. torjua, työntää luotaan; s. nolaus, töykeä vastaus.

rebuild ['ri:'bild] v. rakentaa uudelleen.

rebuke [ri'bju:k] v. nuhdella ankarasti; s. nuhde, moite.

rebus ['ri:bəs] s. kuva-arvoitus.

rebut [ri'bʌt] v. kumota, todistaa vääräksi, torjua. **-tal** [-l] s. kumoaminen.

recalcitrant [ri'kælsitr(ə)nt] a. uppiniskainen, niskoitteleva.

recall [ri'kɔ:l] v. kutsua takaisin; palauttaa mieleen, muistaa; peruuttaa, kumota; s. takaisinkutsu, kotiin kutsuminen; past ~ peruuttamaton.

recant [ri'kænt] v. luopua (kannastaan), peruuttaa.

recap [ri'kæp] v. pinnoittaa (rengas); vrt. seur.

recapitulate [ri:kə'pitjuleit] v. toistaa lyhyesti, kerrata pääkohdittain (lyh. recap).

re|capture ['ri:'kæptʃə] v. vallata takaisin. **-cast** [-kɑ:st] v. valaa uudestaan, muokata uudelleen; muuttaa (näytelmän) osajakoa.

recce ['reki] s. (sot.) sl. tiedustelutehtävä.

recede [ri'si:d] v. vetäytyä takaisin, (kuv.) väistyä, viettää alaspäin; (hinnasta) laskea.

receipt [ri'si:t] s. vastaanottaminen; kuitti; (tav. pl.) maksut, tulot; v. merkitä kuitatuksi, kuitata; I am in ~ of your letter (vanh.) olen saanut kirjeenne; on ~ of saatua(ni).

receiv|e [ri'si:v] v. ottaa vastaan, vastaanottaa; saada (osakseen), kokea; kätkeä (varastettua tavaraa); ottaa vastaan vieraita; payment ~d

maksettu. **-er** [-ə] s. vastaanottaja;
(radio)vastaanotin; varastetun
tavaran kätkijä. **-ing** *a. & s.: ~ set*
radiovastaanotin.

recent ['ri:snt] *a.* tuore, veres, uusi;
äskeinen, vasta tapahtunut; *in ~ years*
viime vuosina; *of ~ occurrence*
äskettäin tapahtunut. **-ly** *adv.*
äskettäin.

recep|tacle [ri'septəkl] *s.* säiliö, astia.
-tion [ri'sepʃn] *s.* vastaanottaminen,
-otto; (~**ist** *s.* vastaanottoapulainen,
portieeri). **-tive** [-iv] *a.*
vastaanottavainen, altis, herkkä.
-tivity [-'tiviti] *s.* herkkyys, alttius.

recess [ri'ses, Am. 'ri:ses] *s.* väliaika,
loma (et. parlamentin); sopukka,
kätkö; komero, syvennys. **-ion**
[-'seʃn] *s.* väistyminen, poistuminen;
suhdanteentauma, lyhyt lama. **-ional**
[-'seʃənl] *a. & s.: ~ [hymn]*
loppuvirsi. **-ive** [-iv] *a.* väistyvä.

recidivist [ri'sidivist] *s.* rikoksen uusija.

recip|e ['resipi] *s.* (ruoka)resepti, ohje.
-ient [ri'sipiənt] *s.* vastaanottaja.

reciproc|al [ri'siprək(ə)l] *a.*
molemminpuolinen, vastavuoroinen,
keskinäinen. **-ate** [-eit] *v.* vastata
(tunteeseen ym), antaa t. osoittaa
vuorostaan; liikkua edestakaisin. **-ity**
[resi'prositi] *s.* molemminpuolisuus,
vastavuoroisuus.

recita|l [ri'saitl] *s.* selonteko; lausunta-,
musiikkiesitys, konsertti. **-tion**
[resi'teiʃn] *s.* lausunta, -esitys.

recite [ri'sait] *v.* lukea ääneen, lausua;
luetella, kertoa.

reckless ['reklis] *a.* huoleton;
piittaamaton, uhkarohkea,
huimapäinen; vastuuton.

reckon ['rek(ə)n] *v.* laskea, lukea,
ottaa lukuun, huomioon *(with)*; pitää
(as jnak); tehdä tiliä *(with* jkn
kanssa); ~ *upon* luottaa jhk; *I ~*
arvelen, luulen; ~ *without one's host*
erehtyä laskuissaan. **-er** [-ə] *s.:* ks.
ready ~. **-ing** *s.* laskeminen, lasku; *the
day of ~* tilinteon päivä; *be out in
one's ~* erehtyä laskuissaan.

re|claim [ri'kleim] *v.* voittaa takaisin,
voittaa (maata) viljelykselle, parantaa
(maata); käännyttää parannukseen *(a
~ed drunkard);* vaatia takaisin.
-clamation [-klə'meiʃn] *s.* takaisin

voittaminen, (suon) kuivatus,
parannus.

recline [ri'klain] *v.* nojata jhk;
paneutua pitkälleen, levätä.

recluse [ri'klu:s] *s.* erakko.

recogn|ition [rekəg'niʃn] *s.*
tunteminen; tunnustus. **-izable**
['rekəgnaizəbl] *a.* tunnettava. **-ize**
['rekəgnaiz] *v.* tuntea (jku jksk),
tunnistaa; tunnustaa, myöntää,
tajuta; tiedostaa (psyk.).

recoil [ri'koil] *v.* kavahtaa, ponnahtaa
t. kohdistua takaisin; (aseesta)
potkaista; *s.* kimmahdus; potkaisu.

recollect [rekə'lekt] *v.* palauttaa
mieleen, muistaa; ~ *oneself* malttaa
mielensä. **-ion** [-kʃn] *s.* mieleen
palauttaminen; muisto; *to the best of
my ~* mikäli muistan.

recommence ['ri:kə'mens] *v.* aloittaa
uudestaan.

recommend [rekə'mend] *v.* suositella,
puoltaa; jättää, uskoa (jkn haltuun);
kehottaa. **-ation** [-'deiʃn] *s.* suositus,
suosittelu; ehdotus, neuvo.

recompense ['rekəmpens] *v.* palkita;
hyvittää, korvata; *s.* palkinto,
hyvitys.

reconcil|e ['rekənsail] *v.* sovittaa;
saattaa sopusointuun; ~ *oneself to*
sopeutua, alistua jhk. **-iation**
[-sili'eiʃn] *s.* sovinto, sovittelu.

recondite [ri'kəndait, 'rekən-] *a.*
hämärä, salattu; vaikeatajuinen.

recondition [ri:kən'diʃn] *v.* panna
kuntoon, korjata.

recon|naissance [ri'kɔnis(ə)ns] *s.*
tiedustelu (sot.); ~ *in force*
väkivaltainen tiedustelu. **-noitre**
[rekə'nɔitə] *v.* tiedustella (sot.).

re|consider ['ri:kən'sidə] *v.* ottaa
uudelleen harkittavaksi, harkita
(tarkemmin). **-construct** [-kəns'trʌkt]
v. rakentaa uudelleen; rekonstruoida.

record [ri'kɔ:d] *v.* merkitä
pöytäkirjaan, luetteloon; kirjoittaa,
merkitä muistiin; kertoa, esittää
(kirjallisesti); nauhoittaa, äänittää,
levyttää, tallentaa (koje) rekisteröidä;
s. ['rekɔ:d] muistiinmerkitty tieto;
asiakirja; pöytäkirja; merkintä;
aikakirja; ennätys; äänilevy; maine,
entisyys; *pl.* arkisto; *R ~ Office*
valtion arkisto; ~ *card* (arkisto)kortti;

~ *changer* levynvaihtaja; ~ *player* levysoitin; *case* ~ sairaskertomus; *bear* ~ *to* todistaa; *off the* ~ pöytäkirjan ulkopuolella; *on* ~ tunnettu, aikakirjoissa mainittu; *break (beat) the* ~ lyödä ennätys; ~*ed times* historiallinen aika; ... *with a good* ~ hyvämaineinen. **-er** [-ə] *s.* kaupungintuomari; merkitsemislaite; nokkahuilu; *tape* ~ nauhuri. **-ing** *s.* äänite, äänitys.

recount [ri:'kaunt] *v.* kertoa, selostaa (perusteellisesti); *re-count* ['ri:-] laskea uudelleen.

recoup [ri'ku:p] *v.* korvata, hyvittää.

recourse [ri'kɔ:s] *s.: have* ~ *to* turvautua jhk.

recover [ri'kʌvə] *v.* saada takaisin, voittaa takaisin; toipua, tointua; ~ *damages* saada vahingonkorvausta; ~ *consciousness* palata tajuihinsa; *re-cover* ['ri:-] peittää, verhota uudelleen. **-y** [-ri] *s.* takaisin saaminen; paraneminen, toipuminen; *beyond (past)* ~ parantumaton, auttamaton.

recreant ['rekriənt] *a.* raukkamainen, petollinen; *s.* petturi.

recreate ['ri:kri'eit] *v.* luoda uudestaan. **-tion** [rekri'eiʃn] *s.* virkistys, huvi(tus); ~ *ground* leikki-, urheilukenttä.

recrimination [rikrimi'neiʃn] *s.* vastasyytös.

recrudescence [ri:kru:'desns] *s.* uudelleen puhkeaminen.

recruit [ri'kru:t] *s.* alokas; *v.* värvätä, hankkia (lisäväkeä); saattaa ennalleen, palauttaa, voimistua. **-ment** *s.* värväys.

rectangle ['rektæŋgl] *s.* suorakulmio. **-ular** [-'tæŋgjulə] *a.* suorakulmainen.

rectifiable ['rektifaiəbl] *a.* oikaistavissa oleva. **-cation** [-fi'keiʃn] *s.* oikaiseminen.

rectify ['rektifai] *v.* oikaista, korjata; puhdistaa (kem.) **-linear** [-'liniə] *a.* suoraviivainen. **-tude**[-tju:d] *s.* rehellisyys, rehtiys.

rector ['rektə] *s.* kirkkoherra. **-y** [-ri] *s.* pappila.

rectum ['rektəm] *s.* peräsuoli.

recumbent [ri'kʌmbənt] *a.* nojaava, lepäävä.

recuperate [ri'kju:p(ə)reit] *v.* toipua, parantua.

recur [ri'kə:] *v.* palata; esiintyä jälleen, uusiutua, toistua. **-rence** [ri'kʌr(ə)ns] *s.* palaaminen, uusiutuminen. **-rent** [ri'kʌr(ə)nt] *a.* (säännöllisesti) uusiutuva.

re-cycle *v.* käsitellä (jätteitä) kiertokäyttöä varten; ~ *d paper* kiertokäyttöpaperi; *recycling* kiertokäyttö.

red [red] *a.* punainen; *s.* puna(väri); ~ *deal* mäntypuu; ~ *Indian* intiaani; ~ *lead* mönjä; ~ *tape* byrokratia, virkavalta(isuus); *be in the* ~ olla velkaantunut; *see* ~ raivostua; *turn* ~ tulla punaiseksi, punastua; *paint the town* ~ (sl.) riehua, hurjistella. **-breast** punarintasatakieli. **-brick**: ~ *universities* Englannin uudet (punatiili)yliopistot. **-coat** punatakki (brittil. sotilas).

redden ['redn] *v.* värjätä punaiseksi, punata; tulla punaiseksi, punastua. **-ish** [-iʃ] *a.* punertava.

redecorate [ri:'dekəreit] *v.* kunnostaa (esim. huoneisto).

redeem [ri'di:m] *v.* ostaa, voittaa takaisin; lunastaa (vapaaksi); vapahtaa; ~ *one's word* täyttää lupauksensa. **-er** [-ə] *s.* lunastaja (*R*~).

redemption [ri'dem(p)/ʃn] *s.* takaisinosto, lunastaminen; lunastus; vapauttaminen. **-ive** [-tiv] *a.* lunastus-.

re-deployment *s.* uudelleenjärjestely, siirto **-development** *s.* (esim. alueen) saneeraus.

red-handed *a.: catch sb. r.-h.* tavata verekseltään, itse teossa. **-hot** hehkuvan punainen. **-letter**: *r.-l. day* juhla-, merkkipäivä.

redo [ri:du:] *v.: have sth.* ~ *ne* maalauttaa, kunnostaa.

redolent ['redə(u)lənt] *a.:* ~ *of* jltk tuoksuva, jtk muistuttava.

redouble [ri'dʌbl] *v.* lisätä; voimistua.

redoubt [ri'daut] *s.* (sot.) redutti. **-able** [-əbl] *a.* pelottava.

redound [ri'daund] *v.:* ~ *to* koitua, olla (jklle kunniaksi); ~ *upon* kohdistua (takaisin) jkh.

redress [ri'dres] *v.* korjata, parantaa;

hyvittää; s. hyvitys; korjaaminen; ~
the balance palauttaa tasapaino;
re-dress ['ri:-] pukea uudelleen.
redskin s. intiaani, punanahka.
red-tapism s. virkavalta(isuus).
reduce [ri'dju:s] v. alentaa, vähentää,
supistaa, pienentää, heikentää;
saattaa jhk tilaan, muuttaa (to jksk),
muuntaa; pelkistää; laihduttaa,
laihtua; ~ to despair saattaa
epätoivoon; ~ to [a] pulp hienontaa
möyhyksi, survoa puuroksi; ~ to the
ranks alentaa rivimieheksi; at ~ d
prices alennetuin hinnoin; in ~ d
circumstances puutteessa.
reduction [ri'dʌkʃn] s. (hintojen)
alennus, vähennys, väheneminen:
pienennetty kuva, kartta ym.
redund|ancy [ri'dʌndənsi] s.
ylenpalttisuus; liikasanaisuus;
työvoiman vapautuminen,
vajaatyöllisyys; ~ payment eroraha.
-ant [-ənt] a. ylenpalttinen,
liikanainen; liikasanainen; make ~
tehdä tarpeettomaksi.
reduplicate [ri'dju:plikeit] v.
kaksinkertaistaa, kahdentaa.
red|wing punakylkirastas. **-wood**
punapuu
re-echo ['ri(:)'ekəu] v. kaikua;
kajahduttaa, toistaa.
reed [ri:d] s. ruoko (mus.) suuhineen
ruokolehti; ruokopilli; pirta; the ~ s
ruokolehtisoittimet ~ **-mace**
osmankäämi (kasv.).
re-edit ['ri:'edit] v. toimittaa uudestaan.
reedy ['ri:di] a. kaislikkoinen;
ruokomainen; säröinen (ääni).
reef [ri:f] s. reivi (purjeessa);
(kallio)riutta, särkkä; v. reivata. **-er**
[-ə] s. (paksu) nuttu, merimiestakki;
Am. sl. marihuanasavuke.
reek [ri:k] s. haju, savu; v. haista,
savuta, höyrytä. **-ie** erisn.; Auld R~
(leik.) Edinburg.
reel [ri:l] s. kela, rulla, puola (~ of
cotton); filmirulla; vilkas
(skottilais)tanhu; hoipertelu; v.
kelata; pyöriä horjua, hoiperrella;
news ~ uutiskatsaus; off the ~ yhteen
menoon; ~ off (kuv.) lasketella.
re-elect ['ri:i'lekt] v. valita uudelleen.
-ion [-kʃn] s. uudelleen valitseminen.
re-|embark ['ri:im'ba:k] v. viedä t.

astua jälleen laivaan. **-enter** [-'entə] v.
tulla uudelleen sisälle (jnnek), viedä
uudelleen kirjoihin. **-entry** s. paluu.
-establish [-is'tæbliʃ] v. vakiinnuttaa
uudelleen.
reeve [ri:v] s. vouti.
refectory [ri'fekt(ə)ri] s. (luostarin)
ruokasali.
refer [ri'fə:] v. neuvoa, lähettää, ohjata
(jnnek, jkn luo), alistaa, jättää (jnk
ratkaistavaksi); viitata jhk, tarkoittaa;
vedota jhk, kääntyä jkn puoleen,
katsoa, etsiä (tietoja) jstk; mainita,
katsoa (jnk) johtuvan (to jstk), pitää
seurauksena jstk; don't ~ to this again
älä toiste puhu tästä; we ~ red him
to… kehotimme häntä
kääntymään…n puoleen; ~ ring to
viitaten jhk. **-ee** [refə'ri:] s.
riidanratkaisija; (kehä-, ero)tuomari.
-ence ['refr(ə)ns] s. viittaus, viite;
maininta, suositus, pl. todistus; ~ s
(m.) lähdekirjallisuus; book of ~
hakuteos; have ~ to koskea jtk; with
~ to mitä jhk tulee, koskien jtk.
-endum [refə'rendəm] s.
kansanäänestys.
refill [ri:'fil] v. täyttää uudelleen; s.
['ri:fil] (esim. kynän) mustesäiliö,
varaparisto ym.
refine [ri'fain] v. puhdistaa; jalostaa;
puhdistua, hienostua, jalostua; ~
upon parannella (pikkutarkasti). **-d**
[-d] a. hienostunut; puhdistettu.
-ment s. puhdistus; hienostuneisuus,
hienous. **-ry** [-əri] s. puhdistamo,
jalostuslaitos; sugar ~ sokeritehdas.
refit ['ri:'fit] v. kunnostaa; s.
kunnostaminen.
reflect [ri'flekt] v. heijastaa, kuvastaa;
tuottaa (kunniaa, häpeää) (on, upon
jklle); heijastua, kuvastua; tuumia,
miettiä; ~ [up] on tuottaa häpeää
jklle, saattaa epäedulliseen valoon.
-ion [-kʃn] s. heijastus, peilikuva,
varjo; mietiskely; miete; huomautus,
moite. **-ive** [-iv] a. mietiskelevä. **-or**
[-ə] s. heijastin.
reflex ['ri:fleks] s. heijastus; heijaste,
refleksi (m. ~ action). **-ion** [ri'flekʃn]
s. = reflection. **-ive** [ri'fleksiv] a. & s.
refleksiivi-
reflux ['ri:flʌks] s. takaisinvirtaaminen;
luode, pakovesi.

reform [ri'fɔ:m] v. uudistaa, parantaa; parantua, tehdä parannus; s. uudistus, parannus, reformi; R~ Bill engl. vaalilain uudistus; re-form ['ri:-] muodostaa, -tua uudelleen. **-ation** [refə'meiʃn] s. parannus; the R~ uskon uhdistus; re-formation ['ri:fɔ'meiʃn] uudelleenjärjestely. **-tory** [-ət(ə)ri] a. uudistus-; s. (vanh.) kasvatuslaitos, ks. approved school. **-ed** [-d] a. parannettu: reformoitu; parannuksen tehnyt. **-er** [-ə] s. uskonpuhdistaja; uudistaja.

refract [ri'frækt] v. taittaa (säteitä). **-ion** [-kʃn] s. taittuminen. **-ive** [-iv] a. ~ defect taittovirhe. **-ory** [-(ə)ri] a. vastahakoinen, niskoitteleva, itsepäinen; vaikeasti käsiteltävä.

refrain 1. [ri'frein] s. kertosäe, kertauma.

refrain 2. [ri'frein] v. pidättyä (from jstk).

refresh [ri'freʃ] v. virkistää, virvoittaa, vahvistaa, elähdyttää. **-er** [-ə] s. lisäpalkkio (asianajajalle); virvoitusjuoma; ~ course kertauskurssi. **-ment** s. virkistys, virvoitus; pl. virvokkeet; ~ room ravintola, kahvila, baari.

refrigera|te [ri'fridʒəreit] v. jäähdyttää; pakastaa. **-tion** [-'reiʃn] s. jäähdytys; under ~ kylmäsäiliössä. **-tor** [-ə] s. jääkaappi, jäähdyttämö.

refuel [ri:'fju:əl] v. ottaa (lisää) polttoainetta, tankata. **-ling** s. tankkaus.

refug|e ['refju:dʒ] s. pakopaikka, turva(paikka): take~ in turvautua; street-~ suojakoroke. **-ee** [refju:(:)'dʒi:] s. pakolainen.

refulgent [ri'fʌldʒ(ə)nt] v. loistava, hohtava.

refund [ri'fʌnd] v. maksaa takaisin, korvata; s. ['--]: tax~ veronpalautus.

refurbish [ri:'fɔ:biʃ] v. kiillottaa (uudelleen), kohentaa.

refusal [ri'fju:zl] s. kielto, epäys, kieltäytyminen.

refuse [ri'fju:z] v. kieltää, evätä; kieltäy yä, olla suostumatta; hylätä, antaa rukkaset; (hevosesta) kieltäytyä hyppäämästä (esteen yli); s. ['refju:s] jätteet, hylkytavara; ~ disposal jätteiden käsittely t. hävittäminen, jätehuolto.

refut|able ['refjutəbl] a. kumottavissa oleva. **-ation** [refju(:)'teiʃn] s. kumoaminen.

refute [ri'fju:t] v. kumota, osoittaa vääräksi.

regain [ri'gein] v. saada takaisin, saavuttaa jälleen.

regal ['ri:g(ə)l] a. kuninkaallinen. **-e** [ri'geil] v. kestitä; ilahduttaa; ~ [oneself] on herkutella jllak. **-ia** [ri'geiljə] s. pl. kuninkaalliset arvonmerkit; kruununkalleudet.

regard [ri'ga:d] v. katsella; katsoa jksk, pitää jnak (as); ottaa huomioon; koskea; s. huomio(on otto); kunnioitus, arvonanto; pl. terveiset; as ~ s mitä jhk tulee; kind ~ s sydämelliset terveiset; have a great ~ for kunnioittaa jkta; ~ must be had to on otettava huomioon; in (with) ~ to jnk suhteen, jstk (asiasta); in this ~ tässä suhteessa. **-ful** a. huomaavainen, (of jtk) huomioonottava. **-ing** prep. jtk koskien, mitä jhk tulee. **-less** a. & adv.: ~ of jstk välittämättä, huolimatta.

regatta [ri'gætə] s. (purjehdus)kilpailut.

regency ['ri:dʒnsi] s. sijais-, holhoojahallitus.

regenera|te [ri'dʒenəreit] v. synnyttää uudestaan, uudistaa, -tua; a. [-ərit] uudestisyntynyt. **-tion** [-'reiʃn] s. uudestisyntyminen.

regent ['ri:dʒnt] s. (sijais)hallitsija, valtionhoitaja.

regicide ['redʒisaid] s. kuninkaan murhaaja, -murha.

regim|e [rei'ʒi:m] s. hallitusjärjestelmä; (poliittinen) järjestelmä. **-en** ['redʒimen] s. ruokavalio, hoitojärjestelmä. **-ent** ['redʒ(i)mənt] s. rykmentti; v. [-ment] järjestää (rykmentiksi, pitää kovassa kurissa. **-ental** [redʒi'mentl] a. rykmentin; s.: ~ s (pl.)sotilaspuku. **-entation** [-men'teiʃn] s. kurinalaisuus.

region ['ri:dʒn] s. seutu, tienoo, alue; ala. **-al** ['ri:dʒən] a. alueellinen; ~ costume kansallispuku.

register ['redʒistə] s. luettelo, rekisteri: nimikirja, (luokan) päiväkirja;

säätölaite, (uunin) pelti; ääniala; v.
merkitä luetteloon t. kirjoihin,
rekisteröidä; kirjata; osoittaa;
ilmoittautua, kirjoittautua; ~ office
ks. registry; ~ed letter kirjattu kirje;
~ed nurse laillistettu sairaanhoitaja.

registr|ar [redʒis'tra:] s. kirjaaja. **-ation**
['-'treiʃn] s. rekisteröinti, kirjaaminen;
ilmoittautuminen.

registry ['redʒistri] s. rekisteritoimisto,
arkisto; paikanvälitystoimisto; was
married at a ~office vihittiin
siviiliavioliittoon.

regress [ri'gres] v. palautua. **-ion**
[ri'greʃn] s. palautuminen,
taantuminen.

regret [ri'gret] v. olla pahoillaan,
murehtia, pahoitella, katua; s. suru,
mielipaha, ikävä; pahoittelu; I ~ to
say valitettavasti. **-ful** a.
murheellinen, pahoitteleva. **-table**
[-əbl] a. valitettava.

regular ['regjulə] a. säännöllinen;
säännönmukainen, laillinen;
täsmällinen; vakinainen, varsinainen;
(puhek.) oikea, todellinen; s. (sot.)
vakinainen väki; kanta-asiakas; ~ size
(Am.) tavallista kokoa. **-ity** [-'læriti]
s. säännöllisyys; täsmällisyys. **-ize**
[-raiz] v. tehdä säännönmukaiseksi,
laillistaa. **-ly** adv. säännöllisesti.

regula|te ['regjuleit] v. järjestää,
säätää; ohjata. **-tion** [-'leiʃn] s.
sääntely; määräys; pl. säännöt,
ohjesääntö; a. säädetty, ohjesäännön
mukainen. **-tor** [-ə] s. säädin (tekn.).

regurgitate [ri'gə:dʒiteit] v. virrata,
syöksyä takaisin.

rehabilita|te [ri:ə'biliteit] v. saattaa
entiseen arvoonsa, palauttaa jkn
kunnia; kuntouttaa; kunnostaa. **-tion**
[-'teiʃn] s. rehabilitaatio, hyvitys;
kuntotus; ~ centre kuntoutuslaitos.

rehash [ri:'hæʃ] v. panna uuteen
järjestykseen, uusia; s. uudestaan
»lämmitetty» materiaali.

rehears|al [ri'hə:sl] s. harjoitus; dress ~
pääharjoitus. **-e** [ri'hə:s] v. harjoitella
(teatt. ym); kerrata.

rehouse ['ri:'hauz] v. hankkia uusi
asunto jklle.

reign [rein] v. hallita; vallita; s. hallitus,
valta; hallitusaika.

reimburse [ri:im'bəs] v. maksaa,

suorittaa takaisin; korvata. **-ment** s.
takaisinmaksu.

rein [rein] s. ohjas (tav. pl.); v.: ~ in
hillitä; draw ~ pysähdyttää hevonen;
give ~ to päästää valloilleen; hold
the ~s pidellä ohjaksia.

reincarnation [ri:inka:'neiʃn] s. uusi
lihaksi tuleminen.

reindeer ['reindiə] s. poro.

reinforce [ri:in'fɔ:s] v. vahvistaa; ~d
concrete teräsbetoni. **-ment** s.
vahvistus, vahvennus; s.
täydennysjoukot.

re|instate ['ri:in'steit] v. asettaa jälleen
(oikeuksiinsa ym). **-insure** [-in'ʃuə] v.
jälleenvakuuttaa.

reissue ['ri:'isju:] s. (korjaamaton) uusi
painos; v. julkaista uudelleen.

reitera|te [ri:'itəreit] v. toistaa (yhä
uudelleen). **-tion** [-'reiʃn] s.
toistaminen.

reject [ri'dʒekt] v. hylätä, torjua, ei
hyväksyä; antaa yären; s. [ri:dʒekt];
~s hylkytavarat. **-ion** [-dʒekʃn] s.
hylkääminen.

rejoic|e [ri'dʒɔis] v. iloita, riemuita (in,
at jstk); ilahduttaa. **-ings** s. pl. ilo,
riemu, juhla.

rejoin [ri'dʒɔin] v. vastata; ['ri:dʒɔin]
liittyä jälleen jkn seuraan, palata jhk.
-der [-də] s. vastaus; vastine.

rejuvena|te [ri'dʒu:vineit] v.
nuorentaa, -tua. **-tion** [-'neiʃn] s.
nuortuminen; nuorennus.

rekindle [ri:'kindl] v. sytyttää
uudestaan, elpyä.

relapse [ri'læps] v. langeta, sortua
jälleen jhk; s. (taudin) uusiutuminen.

relate [ri'leit] v. kertoa; asettaa
yhteyteen; ~ to tarkoittaa, koskea
jtk; olla yhteydessä jnk kanssa; ~d to
jklle sukua oleva, jhk liittyvä.

relation [ri'leiʃn] s. suhde; sukulainen;
in ~ to jnk (asian) suhteen, jhk
nähden; public ~s yleisösuhteet. **-ship**
s. yhteys, suhde; sukulaisuus.

relativ|e ['relətiv] a. suhteellinen, jtk
koskeva (~ to); keskinäinen;
relatiivinen; s. sukulainen;
relatiivipronomini; my ~s
sukulaiseni. **-ely** adv. suhteellisen. **-ity**
[-'tiviti] s. suhteellisuus.

relax [ri'læks] v. höllentää, hellittää;
veltostaa; lieventää; rentouttaa;

höltyä; herpautua; rentoutua;
laimeta. **-ation** [ri:læk'seifn] s.
virkistys; rentou|tuminen, -ttaminen,
laukeaminen.

relay [ri'lei] s. vaihtohevoset, uudet
miehet (toisten sijaan); (rad.) rele,
releoitu ohjelma; v. releoida; ~ race
['ri:lei] viestinjouksu; work in (by) ~s
tehdä vuorotyötä; re-lay ['ri:-] laskea
jälleen (kaapeli ym), uusia.

release [ri'li:s] v. päästää irti,
vapauttaa; irrottaa; luopua jstk; antaa
lupa julkaista (uutinen) t. esittää
(elokuva), julkistaa; s. irrottaminen;
vapauttaminen, vapautus;
irrotuslaite; julkistaminen, (filmin)
esittämislupa.

relegate ['religeit] v. karkottaa; siirtää
(jkn ratkaistavaksi ym); be ~d pudota
alempaan sarjaan t. sarjasta.

relent [ri'lent] v. antaa myöten, heltyä.
-less a. säälimätön.

relevan|ce, -cy ['relivəns, -i] s.
asiallisuus, asianmukaisuus. **-nt** [-ənt]
a. asiaan kuuluva, liittyvä, relevantti
(to); asiallinen.

relia|bility [rilaiə'biliti] s. luotettavuus.
-ble [ri'laiəbl] a. luotettava. **-nce**
[ri'laiəns] s. luottamus; place ~ (on,
in) luottaa jkh. **-nt** [ri'laiənt]
luottavainen.

relic ['relik] s. pyhäi|njäännös, jäänne;
muisto; ~s (m.) jäännökset.

relief [ri'li:f] s. helpotus, huojennus;
apu, avustus, huolto; vapautus;
vartionvaihto; koho-, korkokuva; ~
map korkokartta; on ~ huollon
varassa; stand out in ~ (selvästi)
erottua jstk.

relieve [ri'li:v] v. helpottaa, huojentaa,
lieventää, keventää; auttaa, tulla
avuksi, vapauttaa; vaihtaa (vahti)
(leik.) varastaa; kohottaa (näkyviin),
antaa vaihtelua; ~ oneself käydä
tarpeillaan.

reli|gion [ri'lidʒn] s. uskonto. **-gious**
[-ʒəs] a. uskonnon; uskonnollinen,
hurskas; tunnollinen; ~ house
luostari.

relinquish [ri'liŋkwiʃ] v. jättää; luopua
jstk.

reliquary ['relikwəri] s.
pyhäinjäännöslipas.

relish ['reliʃ] s. (miellyttävä) maku,

höyste; viehätys; v. pitää jstk, nauttia
jstk; maistua jltk, vivahtaa jhk; with
~ mieltymyksellä.

reluctan|ce [ri'lʌktəns] s.
vastahakoisuus, vastenmielisyys. **-t**
[-ənt] a. vastahakoinen, haluton.

rely [ri'lai] v.: ~ [up] on luottaa jhk,
jkh; you may ~ upon my coming voit
luottaa siihen, että tulen.

remain [ri'mein] v. jäädä; pysyä, olla
edelleen; olla jäljellä; s.: ~s (pl.)
jäännökset, tähteet; maalliset
jäännökset, tomu; I ~ yours faithfully
kunnioittaen; that ~s to be seen
saammepa nähdä. **-der** [-də] s.
jäännös, ylijäämä. **-ing** a. jäljellä
oleva.

remand [ri'mɑ:nd] v. palauttaa
(vankilaan); ~ home l.v. koulukoti.

remark [ri'mɑ:k] v. huomata;
huomauttaa (on jstk); s. huomautus,
muistutus; worthy of ~
huomionarvoinen. **-able** [-əbl] a.
huomattava, merkittävä. **-ably** adv.:
~ good harvinaisen hyvä.

remarry ['ri:'mæri] v. mennä uusiin
naimisiin (jkn kanssa).

remedi|able [ri'mi:dʒəbl] a.
parannettavissa oleva. **-al** [-jəl] a.
parantava; ~ gymnast
lääkintävoimistelija; ~ course(s)
tukiopetus.

remedy ['remidi] s. parannuskeino,
lääke; apu(keino); v. auttaa, korjata

rememb|er [ri'membə] v. muistaa; I
~ed to post [the letter] muistin
postittaa; I ~ posting muistan
panneeni (kirjeen) postiin; . . .? —
Not that I ~ muistaakseni en (ole);
please ~ me (to) sanohan terveisiä
(-lle). **-rance** [-r(ə)ns] s. muisto;
muistolahja; ~s Day kaatuneitten
muistopäivä.

remind [ri'maind] v. muistuttaa. **-er** [-ə]
s. muistutus.

reminisce [remi'nis] v. muistella. **-nce**
[-ns] s. muistuma, muisto, muistelma.
-nt [-nt] a. muistelava; ~ of jtk
muistuttava.

remiss [ri'mis] a. (~ in) jstk
huolimaton, välinpitämätön, veltto.
-ion [ri'miʃn] s. anteeksiantamus;
lievennys, vähennys.

remit [ri'mit] v. antaa anteeksi,

peruuttaa (vero ym); lieventää, vähentää; lykätä, alistaa; lähettää (rahaa); heiketä. **-tance** [-(ə)ns] s. rahalähetys. **-ent** [-ənt] a. jaksottainen, vaihteleva.

remnant ['remnənt] s. jäännös; jäännöspala; ~ s tähteet.

remonstr|ance [ri'mɒnstr(ə)ns] s. vastaväite. **-ate** [-eit] v. välttää vastaan, panna vastalause; nuhdella (with jkta).

remorse [ri'mɔːs] s. tunnonvaivat, katumus. **-ful** a. katuva. **-less** a. armoton, säälimätön.

remote [ri'məut] a. kaukainen, etäinen; syrjäinen; ~ control kauko-ohjaus; not the ~ st idea ei aavistustakaan; ~ly related kaukaista sukua. **-ness** s. kaukaisuus.

remount [riː'maunt] v. jälleen nousta (hevosen selkään, tikapuille); hankkia uusia hevosia; kehystää uudelleen; s. uusi hevonen; vrt. **mount.**

remov|able [ri'muːvəbl] a. siirrettävä, irrotettava. **-al** [(ə)l] s. siirtäminen, muutto; viraltapano; poistaminen; ~ van muuttovaunu.

remove [ri'muːv] v. ottaa pois, poistaa; siirtää, muuttaa; erottaa, panna viralta; siirtyä pois, muuttaa; s. siirto ylemmälle luokalle; aste, askel; get one's ~ päästä luokalta. **-d** [-d] a. kaukainen, etäinen; first cousin once ~ serkun lapsi. **-r** [-ə] s. muuttofirma; [stain] ~ poistoaine.

remunera|te [ri'mjuːn|əreit] v. palkita, hyvittää, korvata. **-tion** [-ə'reiʃn] s. hyvitys, korvaus. **-tive** [-(ə)rətiv] a. kannattava, tuottoisa.

renaissance [rə'neis(ə)ns] s. renessanssi.

renal ['riːn] a. munuais-.

rename ['riː'neim] v. antaa jklle uusi nimi.

renescence [ri'næsns] s. elpyminen.

rend [rend] rent rent, v. repiä, raastaa.

render ['rendə] v. antaa; jättää, luovuttaa (us. ~ up); osoittaa, tehdä; esittää, tulkita, ilmaista; kääntää (jllek kielelle); tehdä jksk; rapata; ~ good for evil maksaa paha hyvällä; ~ a service tehdä palvelus. **-ing** s. tulkinta, esitys, käännös.

rendezvous ['rɒndivuː] s. (sovittu) kohtaus, kohtauspaikka; v. kohdata.

rendition [ren'diʃn] s. esitys, tulkinta.

renegade ['renideid] s. luopio.

renege [ri'niːg] v. (kortti.) ei tunnustaa väriä; ~ on pettää sanansa.

renew [ri'njuː] v. uudistaa, uusia; elvyttää; toistaa. **-al** [-l] s. uusiminen, uusinta.

rennet ['renit] s. juoksutin.

renounce [ri'nauns] v. luopua jstk; hylätä, kieltäytyä tunnustamasta.

renovate ['renəveit] v. uudistaa, kunnostaa, korjata.

renown [ri'naun] s. kuuluisuus, maine; ~ed maineikas.

rent 1. [rent] s. halkeama, repeämä; v. imp. & pp. ks. rend.

rent 2. [rent] s. vuokra; v. vuokrata; antaa arennille. **-al** [-l] s. vuokra, arenti; a. vuokra-.

renunciation [rinʌnsi'eiʃn] s. luopuminen; kieltäymys.

reopen [ri'əupn] v. avata t. avautua uudelleen.

reorganize ['riː'ɔːgənaiz] v. järjestää uudelleen.

rep [rep] s. ripsi; sl. lyh. ks. repertory.

repair 1. [ri'peə] v.: ~ to lähteä jnnek.

repair 2. [ri'peə] v. korjata, panna kuntoon; parantaa, korvata (vahinko); hyvittää; s. korjaus, kunnostaminen (m. pl.); kunnossapito, kunto; during ~ s korjaustöiden aikana; in good ~ hyvässä kunnossa; out of ~ epäkunnossa.

repara|ble ['rep(ə)rəbl] a. korvattavissa oleva. **-tion** [-ə'reiʃn] s. korvaus, hyvitys; sotakorvaus; ~ s sotakorvaukset.

repartee [repa:'tiː] s. sukkela vastaus; he is good at ~ hän ei jää vastausta vaille, on sanavalmis.

repast [ri'pɑːst] s. ateria.

repatriate [riː'pætrieit] v. palauttaa kotimaahan.

repay [riː'pei] v. maksaa takaisin; korvata, palkita. **-able:** the loan is ~ over 10 years lainan maksuaika on 10 vuotta. **-ment** s. takaisinmaksu.

repeal [ri'piːl] v. peruuttaa, kumota; s. peruutus, kumoaminen.

repeat [ri'pi:t] v. toistaa; uudistaa; toistua; s. (rad.) uusinta; uusintatilaus; kertausmerkki(mus.). **-edly** [-idli] adv. yhä uudelleen, toistuvasti.

repel [ri'pel] v.työntää takaisin, torjua; olla (jklle) vastenmielinen. **-lent** [-ənt] a. luotaan työntävä, vastenmielinen, epämiellyttävä; mosquito ~ hyttyskarkote; water-~ vettä hylkivä.

repent [ri'pent] v. katua (m. ~ of); (usk.m.) tehdä parannus. **-ance** [-əns] s. katumus; parannus. **-ant** [-ənt] a. katuvainen.

repercussion [ri:pə:'kʌʃn] s. takaisin kimmahdus, kaiku, kajahdus; kauaskantoinen seuraus.

repert|oire ['repət|wa:] s. ohjelmisto. **-ory** [-(ə)ri] s. = ed.; (kuv.) aarteisto; ~ theatre teatteri, jossa ohjelmat vaihtuvat (mutta näyttelijäkunta, r. company pysyy samana).

repeti|tion [repi'tiʃn] s. toistaminen, toisto, kertaaminen; ulkoläksy. **-tive** [ri'petitiv] a. kertautuva.

repine [ri'pain] v. nurista (jtk vastaan), nurkua.

replace [ri'pleis] v. asettaa takaisin; astua jkn sijaan, täyttää jkn paikka, korvata. **-ment** s. korvaaminen; sijainen; varaosa, m. proteesi.

replenish [ri'pleniʃ] v. täyttää, täydentää.

reple|te [ri'pli:t] a. täynnä (with jtk), täpötäynnä. **-tion** [-ʃn] s. täyteys; to ~ kyllästymiseen asti.

replica ['replikə] s. kaksoiskappale, taitelijan oma kopio.

reply [ri'plai] v. vastata; s. vastaus; in ~ to vastauksesi jhk.

report [ri'pɔ:t] v. ilmoittaa, tehdä ilmoitus; kertoa; selostaa, raportoida; ilmoittautua; toimia uutisten hankkijana; s. kertomus, selonteko; lausunto, selostus, raportti; reportaasi; huhu; maine; (koulu)todistus; pamaus, laukaus; ~ed speech epäsuora esitys; of good ~ hyvämaineinen; ~ has it huhu kertoo. **-age** [ri'pɔ:tidʒ] s. reportterin työ. **-er** [-ə] s. uutistenhankkija, reportteri, selostaja. **-ing** s. reportaasi, selostus.

repose 1. [ri'pəuz] v. panna (one's trust luottamuksensa), in jhk.

repos|e 2. [ri'pəuz] v. levätä, lepuuttaa; s. lepo; tyyneys, rauha. **-itory** [ri'pozit(ə)ri] s. säilytys-, talletuspaikka; aarreaitta, varasto.

reprehend|d [repri'hend] v. nuhdella. **-sible** [-'hensəbl] a. moitittava, tuomittava.

represent [repri'zent] v. esittää, kuvata; edustaa; väittää, sanoa (jnk olevan); näytellä. **-ation** [-'teiʃn] s. esitys, kuvaus; edustus; ~s vetoomukset, vastaväitteet. **-ative** [-ətiv] a.: ~ of jtk kuvaava, edustava, tyypillinen; s. edustaja, asiamies; House of R~s (Am.) edustajainhuone.

repress [ri'pres] s. tukahduttaa, (psyk.) torjua; kukistaa. **-ion** [-'preʃn] s. tukahduttaminen, torjunta. **-ive** [-iv] a. tukahduttava.

reprieve [ri'pri:v] v. lykätä (kuolemantuomion toimeenpano); suoda huojennusta, lievittää, s. lykkäys, armonaika.

reprimand ['reprimɑ:nd] v. (ankarasti) nuhdella; s. nuhteet, nuhtelu.

reprint ['ri:'print] v. painaa uudelleen; s. (tav. korjaamaton) uusi painos; eripainos.

reprisal [ri'praiz(ə)l] s. kostotoimenpide, repressaali.

reproach [ri'proutʃ] v. moittia, soimata; s. moite; soimaus; häpeäpilkku; beyond ~ nuhteeton. **-ful** a. moittiva.

reprobate ['reprəbeit] a. & s. kadotukseen tuomittu, turmeltunut, moraaliton; v. paheksua (ankarasti), tuomita.

repro|duce [ri:prə'dju:s] v. tuottaa uudelleen; lisätä (sukuaan), lisääntyä; toisintaa, toistaa; jäljentää, kopioida; ~ one's kind lisätä sukuansa. **-duction** [-'dʌkʃn] s. suvun lisääminen, jatkaminen; lisääntyminen; jäljennös; sound ~ äänentoisto.

reprography [ri'prɔgrəfi] s. monistus.

reproof [ri'pru:f] s. moite, nuhde.

reprove [ri'pru:v] v. moittia; nuhdella, ojentaa.

reptile ['reptail] s. matelija.

republic [ri'pʌblik] s. tasavalta. **-an** [-ən] s. tasavaltalainen, (R~) republikaani.

repudia|te [ri'pju:dieit] v. hylätä, kieltää, kieltäytyä tunnustamasta t. maksamasta. **-tion** [-'eiʃn] s. hylkääminen.

repugnan|ce [ri'pʌgnəns] s. vastenmielisyys. **-t** [-ənt] a. vastenmielinen, inhottava.

repul|se [ri'pʌls] v. lyödä takaisin, torjua, hylätä (tarjous ym); s. torjuminen. **-sion** [-'pʌlʃn] s. repulsio (fys.); vastenmielisyys. **-sive** [-iv] a. vastenmielinen, inhottava.

reputa|ble ['repjutəbl] a. hyvämaineinen, arvossapidetty. **-tion** [-'teiʃn] s. maine; *have a ~ for* olla tunnettu jstk.

repute [ri'pju:t] s. maine, arvo; v.: *is ~d to be* (hänen) sanotaan olevan, häntä pidetään jnak; *~d* oletettu; *well ~d* hyvämaineinen; *by ~* kuulopuheelta; *~dly* otaksuttavasti.

request [ri'kwest] s. pyyntö; kysyntä; v. pyytää, kehottaa; *in great ~* hyvin kysytty; *by* (t. *on*) *~* pyynnöstä; *at the ~ of* jkn pyynnöstä.

requiem ['rekwiem] s. sielumessu.

require [ri'kwaiə] v. vaatia, käskeä; tarvita, olla tarpeen; *if ~d* tarvittaessa. **-ment** s. vaatimus, tarve; *pl.* vaatimukset; edellytykset.

requisi|te ['rekwizit] a. tarpeellinen, tarvittava, välttämätön; s. *pl.* tarvikkeet, varusteet. **-tion** ['ziʃn] s. pakko-otto; v. (sot.) määrätä luovutettavaksi; [*the bus*] *was in constant ~* tarvittiin alinomaa.

requit|al [ri'kwait] s. korvaus, palkka, kosto. **-e** [ri'kwait] v. korvata, maksaa (takaisin).

reredos ['riədɔs] s. alttariseinä.

rescind [ri'sind] v. kumota.

rescue ['reskju:] v. pelastaa, vapauttaa; s. pelastaminen, apu; hengenpelastus; *came to the ~* tuli apuun.

research [ri'sə:tʃ] s. (tarkka) etsintä; tieteellinen tutkimus; v. tehdä tutkimustyötä, tutkia. **-er** [-ə] s. tutkija.

resect [ri'sekt] v. (pois).

reseda ['residə, ri'si:də] s. (tuoksu)reseda.

resemblance [ri'zembləns] s. yhdennäköisyys, samankaltaisuus;

bear a ~ to = seur.

resemble [ri'zembl] v. muistuttaa, olla jkn näköinen.

resent [ri'zent] v. olla harmissaan, loukkaantunut jstk, panna jtk pahakseen. **-ful** a. harmistunut. **-ment** s. mielipaha, harmi; katkera mieli, kauna, kaunaisuus.

reservation [rezə'veiʃn] s. varaus (m. paikka-); (intiaani)reservaatti; *with ~s* eräin varauksin; *mental ~* salainen varaus.

reserv|e [ri'zə:v] v. varata, pidättää; tilata (huone ym.); s. vara, varasto; vararahasto, varanto; reservi, *pl.* varajoukot; pidättyväisyys, varovaisuus; reservaatti, jhk varattu maa-alue; *in ~* varalla; *without ~* varauksetta; ilman hintarajoituksia; *~ price* alin hinta; *central ~* (moottoritien) keskikaista; *nature ~* luonnonsuojelualue. **-ed** [-d] a. varattu; varautunut, pidättyväinen. **-ist** [-ist] s. reserviläinen. **-oir** ['rezəvwɑ:] s. vesisäiliö, säiliö, allas; (kuv.) varasto.

resettlement s. (uudelleen)asuttaminen.

reshape v muovata uudestaan.

reshuffle s. uudelleen|ryhmitys, -järjestely.

resid|e [ri'zaid] v. asua (*at, in* jssk), oleskella; m. kuulua (*in jklle*). **-ence** ['rezid(ə)ns] s. oleskelu; asuinpaikka (*place of ~*), (komea) virka-asunto; *take up one's ~* asettua asumaan; *hall of ~* ylioppilasasuntola. **-ent** ['rezid(ə)nt] a. jssk asuva; s. vakinainen asukas; hallituksen edustaja (esim. protektoraatissa); apulaislääkäri. **-ential** [rezi'den ʃ(ə)l] a. asunto-; *~ waste* asumisjätteet.

resid|ual [ri'zidjuəl] a. jäljellä oleva, jäännös-, jäämä-. **-ue** ['rezidju:] s. jäännös, ylijäämä; puhdas jäämistö. **-uum** [-juəm] s. (esim. palamis)jäte, tuote.

resign [ri'zain] v. luopua jstk. luovuttaa; erota; *~ oneself to* alistua jhk. **-ation** [rezig'neiʃn] s. (virasta) eroaminen, luopuminen; erohakemus; (kohtaloonsa) alistuminen. **-ed** [-d] a. alistuva, kohtaloonsa tyytynyt, nöyrä.

resili|ence [ri'ziliəns] s. kimmoisuus, joustavuus. **-ent** [-ənt] a. kimmoisa, joustava.

resin ['rezin] s. hartsi, pihka. **-ous** [-əs] a. hartsimainen.

resist [ri'zist] v. vastustaa, tehdä vastarintaa, torjua. **-ance** [-əns] s. vastarinta, vastustus, -kyky; *the R~* vastarintaliike; ~ *coil* vastuskela (sähk.). **-ant** [-ənt] a. vastustuskykyinen. **-er** [-ə]: *draft ~* aseistakieltäytyjä. **-less** a. vastustamaton.

resole ['ri:saul] v. pohjata.

resolu|te ['rezəlu:t] a. päättäväinen, varma, jyrkkä. **-tion** [-'lu:ʃn] s. päättäväisyys, lujuus; päätös; päätöslause(lma), ponsi; hajottaminen; ratkaisu, selvitys; (lääk.) (tulehduksen) sulaminen.

resolve [ri'zɔlv] v. päättää; ratkaista, selvittää; hajottaa, hajota; s. päätös; päättäväisyys; *the matter ~s itself into this* asia on (yksinkertaisesti) tämä.

reson|ance ['reznəns] s. resonanssi, kaje. **-ant** [-ənt] a. kaikuva, kajahteleva, soinnukas.

resort [ri'zɔ:t] v.: ~ *to* turvautua jhk, ryhtyä käyttämään jtk; (ahkerasti) käydä jssk; s. turvautuminen jhk, (apu)keino; oleskelupaikka; *health ~* hoitola, parantola; *holiday ~* lomanviettopaikka; *in the last ~* viime kädessä, viimeisenä keinona.

resound [ri'zaund] v. kajahtaa, kaikua; raikua; kajauttaa.

resource [ri'sɔ:s] s. (apu)neuvo, keino; neuvokkuus; *pl.* varat, voimavarat; *natural ~s* luonnonvarat; *leave to their own ~s* jättää oman onnensa nojaan. **-ful** a. neuvokas.

respect [ris'pekt] v. kunnioittaa, pitää arvossa; ottaa huomioon; s. kunnioitus, arvonanto; huomio(on ottaminen), *pl.* kunnioittavat terveiset; *pay one's ~s [to]* käydä tervehdyskäynnillä; *in ~ of, with ~ to* jhk nähden, jnk suhteen; *in every ~* joka suhteessa; *without ~ to persons* henkilöön katsomatta. **-ability** [-ə'biliti] s. kunnioitettavuus, arvossapidetty asema. **-able** [-əbl] a. kunnioitettava, arvossapidetty; säädyllinen, kunniallinen; joltinen.

-ful a. kunnioittava. **-ing** *prep.* mitä jhk tulee. **-ive** [-iv] a. eri; kullekin kuuluva, kunkin erikseen; [*we went*] *to our ~ rooms* kukin omaan huoneeseensa. **-ively** *adv.* kukin erikseen, vastaavasti, mainitussa järjestyksessä.

respira|tion [respə'reiʃn] s. hengitys. **-tor** ['respəreitə] s. hengityslaite; m. kaasunaamari. **-tory** ['respiratri] a. hengitys-; ~ *organs* hengityselimet.

respire [ris'paiə] v. hengittää; hengähtää.

respite ['respait, Am. 'respit] s. hengähdystauko; lykkäys; v. antaa lykkäystä; suoda helpotusta.

resplend|ence [ris'plendəns] s. loisto, hohde. **-ent** [-ənt] a. loistava, hohtava.

respond [ris'pɔnd] v. vastata, laulaa vastaus (kirkossa); reagoida, ottaa kantaa; ~ *to* (m.) olla herkkä jllek. (kuv.) totella jtk. **-ent** [-ənt] s. vastaaja (lak.).

respons|e [ris'pɔn|s] s. vastaus, (seurakunnan) vastalaulu; vastakaiku; reaktio. **-ibility** [rispɔnsə'biliti] s. vastuu, vastuunalaisuus; tehtävä, velvollisuus; vastuukykyisyys. **-ible** [-səbl] v. vastuunalainen, vastuussa (*for* jstk); vastuullinen; luotettava. **-ive** [-siv] a. vastaus-; herkkä, altis, myötämielinen; *struck ~ chords* herätti vastakaikua.

rest 1. [rest] v. jäädä; s. jäännös; *the ~* loput, muut; *for the ~* muutoin; *you may ~ assured* voitte olla varma; *it ~s with him* hänen asiansa on.

rest 2. [rest] s. lepo, rauha; lepopaikka, (merimies)koti; tauko; tuki, noja; haudan lepo; v. levätä; lepuuttaa, antaa levätä; nojata, nojautua, olla jnk varassa t. kiinnitetty jhk, luottaa, viipyä (*on* jssk); *at ~* levollinen, levossa, kuollut; *set sb's mind at ~* rauhoittaa, tyynnyttää; *day of ~* lepopäivä; *the matter cannot ~ here* asia ei saa jäädä sikseen. **~-cure** lepohoito.

restaurant ['restrɔ:ŋ, Am. -tərənt] s. ravintola.

rest|ful ['restf(u)l] a. rauhallinen. **-ing-place** s. lepopaikka.

restitution [resti'tju:ʃn] *s.* palauttaminen ennalleen; korvaus, hyvitys.

restive ['restiv] *a.* vikuri, äksy; vaikea käsitellä, hankala.

restless *a.* levoton, rauhaton.

restorat|ion [restɔ'reiʃn] *s.* entiselleen saattaminen; palauttaminen (oikeuksiin, valtaan); restauraatio; entistäminen. **-ive** [ris'tɔ:rətiv] *a. & s.* vahvistava (lääke).

restore [ris'tɔ:] *v.* palauttaa (entiselleen), asettaa jälleen (virkaan ym); antaa takaisin; korjata, entistää, restauroida; parantaa; *be ~d* toipua; *I feel completely ~d* olen täysin entiselläni.

restrain [ris'trein] *v.* pidättää, estää, hillitä, tukahduttaa; teljetä jhk, rajoittaa jkn vapautta. **-edly** [-idli] *s.* pidäke, pidättyvyys; rajoitus, hillike, pakko; *without ~* esteettä, vapaasti; *put under ~* pidättää.

restrict [ris'trikt] *v.* rajoittaa; *~ed* rajoitettu. **-ion** [-kʃn] *s.* rajoitus. **-ive** [-iv] *a.* rajoittava.

result [ri'zʌlt] *v.* olla seurauksena t. tuloksena, aiheutua (from jstk); *~ in* viedä, johtaa jhk; *s.* tulos, seuraus; *the ~ing* (siitä) seuraava, seurauksena ollut.

resum|e [ri'zju:m] *v.* ottaa takaisin, ryhtyä jälleen jhk; jatkaa (puhetta); *~ one's seat* istuutua uudelleen. **-ption** [ri'zʌm(p)ʃn] *s.* takaisin ottaminen, ryhtyminen jälleen (jhk), jatkaminen.

résumé ['rezju(:)mei] *s.* yhteenveto.

resurface ['ri:'sɔ:fis] *v.* päällystää (tie) uudelleen; (vedenalaisesta) palata pinnalle.

resurgence [ri'sɔ:dʒ(ə)ns] *s.* elpyminen.

resurrec|t [rezə'rekt] *v.* elvyttää; kaivaa maasta; herättää kuolleista. **-tion** [-'rekʃn] *s.* ylösnousemus; elpyminen.

resuscita|te [ri'sʌsiteit] *v.* elvyttää; herätä henkiin. **-tion** [-'teiʃn] *s.* henkiinherättäminen; *mouth-to-mouth ~* suusta suuhun -menetelmä.

retail ['ri:teil] *s.* vähittäismyynti; *v.* [m. -'-] myydä vähittäin; levitellä (huhuja ym); *sell [by] ~* myydä vähittäin. **-er** [ri:'teilə] *s.* väittäiskauppias.

retain [ri'tein] *v.* pidättää, pitää

(sisällään), säilyttää; muistaa; *~ing fee* etumaksu (asianajajalle). **-er** [-ə] *s.* ennakkomaksu; *pl.* seurue.

retalia|te [ri'tælieit] *v.* maksaa takaisin (t. samalla mitalla), kostaa. **-tion** [-'eiʃn] *s.* kosto.

retard [ri'tɑ:d] *v.* viivyttää, hidastaa, pidättää; *mentally ~-ed* kehitysvammainen. **-ation** [-'deiʃn] *s.* hidastaminen jne; *mental ~* kehitysvammaisuus.

retch [retʃ] *v.* röyhtäistä.

retell ['ri:'tel] *v.* kertoa uudelleen, mukailla.

reten|tion [ri'tenʃn] *s.* pidättäminen, säilyttäminen (muistissa), jääminen; (lääk.) umpi. **-tive** [-'tentiv] *a.* pidättävä; pettämätön (muisti).

retic|ence ['retisns] *s.* vaiteliaisuus; pidättyvyys. **-ent** [-nt] *v.* vaitelias, pidättyvä.

reti|culate [ri'tikjulit] *a.* verkkomainen, verkko-. **-cule** ['retikju:l] *s.* (pieni) käsilaukku. **-na** ['retinə] *s.* verkkokalvo.

retinue ['retinju:] *s.* seurue, saattue.

retir|e [ri'taiə] *v.* vetäytyä pois t. syrjään; erota (virasta); perääntyä; mennä levolle; antaa peräänntymiskäsky; erottaa (sot.); *~ on a pension* asettua eläkkeelle; *she ~d into herself* sulkeutui kuoreensa. **-ed** [-d] *a.* syrjäinen, yksinäinen; virasta eronnut, eläkkeellä oleva; *on the ~ list* (upseerista) eläkkeellä; *~pay* eläke. **-ement** *s.* vetäytyminen syrjään; yksinäisyys, eristyneisyys; ero (virasta), eläkkeelle asettuminen, eläkevuodet. **-ing** *a.* vaatimaton, syrjässä pysyvä; eläke-.

retort 1. [ri'tɔ:t] *v.* vastata kärkevästi; maksaa takaisin t. samalla mitalla; *s.* terävä t. kärkevä vastaus.

retort 2. [ri'tɔ:t] *s.* tislausastia.

retouch [ri:'tʌtʃ] *v.* parannella, retusoida.

retrace [ri'treis] *v.:* palauttaa muistiin, *(~ one's steps)* palata samaa tietä.

retract [ri'trækt] *v.* vetää takaisin t. sisään; peruuttaa (sanansa). **-able** [-əbl] *a.* jonka voi peruuttaa; = seur. **-ile** [-ail] *a.* sisään vedettävä.

retrain ['ri:'trein] *v.* kouluttaa uudestaan.

retread ['ri:'tred] v.: ~ [a tyre] panna (renkaaseen) uusi kulutuspinta.

retreat [ri'tri:t] v. perääntyä, peräytyä, vetäytyä takaisin; s. perääntyminen; perääntymismerkki; yksinäisyyteen vetäytyminen; pako-, lepopaikka; hiljentymiskokous; iltasoitto; *beat a* [*hasty*] ~ luopua (yrityksestä); *sound the* ~ antaa perääntymismerkki.

retrench [ri'tren(t)ʃ] v. supistaa; karsia; vähentää menojaan. **-ment** s. menojen supistaminen.

retribution [retri'bju:ʃn] s. kosto, palkka, rangaistus.

retriev|able [ri'tri:vəbl] a. mahdollinen saada takaisin; korvattavissa oleva. **-al** [-əl] s. takaisin saaminen; korjaaminen; *lost beyond* ~ auttamattomasti menetetty.

retrieve [ri'tri:v] v. saada t. voittaa takaisin; noutaa (riista); korjata, hyvittää, pelastaa. **-r** [-ə] s. noutaja(koira).

retroactive a. taannehtiva.

retrogr|ade ['retrə|greid] a. taaksepäin kulkeva; huononeva, taantuva; v. kulkea taaksepäin. **-ession** [-'greʃn] s. taaksepäin meneminen, taantuminen. **-essive** [-'gresiv] a. taantuva, taantumuksellinen.

retrospect ['retrəspekt] s. silmäys taaksepäin; *in* ~ muistellessa. **-ive** [- -'- -] a. taaksepäin katsova, takautuva; ~ *view* katsaus taaksepäin.

return [ri'tə:n] v. palata, tulla takaisin; palauttaa, lähettää takaisin, maksaa takaisin, vastata jhk, ilmoittaa (virallisesti), julistaa; tuottaa; valita parlamenttiin; s. paluu, paluumatka; palautus, palauttaminen; palkitseminen; ilmoitus; tiedot, tulokset (~s); voitto; vaali; ~ *a call* käydä vastavierailulla; ~ *thanks* lausua kiitokset, lukea ruokarukous; *on my* ~ palatessani; ~ *of an illness* taudin uusiutuminen; ~ *service* vastapalvelus; *census* ~s henkikirjat, *income-tax* ~ veroilmoitus; *many happy* ~s toivotan onnea (syntymäpäivän johdosta); ~s *of population* väestötilasto; *by* ~ paluupostissa; *in* ~ jnk sijaan, palkaksi, kiitokseksi jstk;

vastaukseksi.

reunification ['ri:ju:nifi'keiʃn] s. (jälleen) yhdistäminen.

reunion ['ri:'ju:njən] s. jälleenyhdistäminen; kokoontuminen, kokous;*a family* ~ sukukokous.

rev [rev] v.: ~ *up* lisätä nopeutta, kiihdyttää moottoria.

revalue [ri:'vælju:] v. arvioida uudelleen; revalvoida.

reveal [ri'vi:l] v. ilmaista; paljastaa; ~*ed itself* tuli ilmi, paljastui.

reveille [ri'væli, Am. 'revəli] s. aamusoitto.

revel ['revl] v. juhlia, remuta, hurjistella; ~ *in* hekumoida, nauttia jstk; s. (us. *pl.*) kemut, juhlat.

revelation [revi'leiʃn] s. paljastaminen; (yllättävä) tieto, paljastus; (jumalallinen) ilmoitus; *the R*~ (m. *R*~s) ilmestyskirja.

revel|ler ['revl|ə] s. juhlija, juomaveikko. **-ry** [-ri] s. meluisa juhliminen, juomingit.

revenge [ri'ven(d)ʒ] v. kostaa; s. kosto, kostonhalu; hyvitys; (pelissä) revanssi; ~ *oneself, be* ~d [*upon*] kostaa jklle. **-ful** a. kostonhimoinen.

revenue ['revinju:] s. tulot (et. valtion); *Inland* ~ valtion vero-, aksiisi- ym tulot.

reverbera|te [ri'və:b(ə)reit] v. kaikua, kajahtaa; heijastaa, -tua. **-tion** [-'reiʃn] s. kajahdus, kajahtelu; *pl.* heijastumat, jälkivaikutukset.

revere [ri'viə] v. kunnioittaa.

reveren|ce ['rev(ə)r(ə)ns] s. kunnioitus; (vanh.) syvä kumarrus; v. kunnioittaa. **-d** [-(ə)nd] a. kunnioitettava, kunnianarvoinen; s. pastori (tav. *Rev.*). **-t** [-(ə)nt], **-tial** [-'renʃl] a. kunnioittava.

reverie ['revəri] s. haaveilu; *lost in* ~ unelmiin vaipunut.

revers [ri'viə] s. (takin) käänne.

reversal [ri'və:sl] s. kääntäminen päinvastaiseksi, kumoaminen; mullistava muutos.

rever|se [ri'və:s] a. päinvastainen, vastakkainen, käänteinen, kääntö-; s. vastakohta; taka-, kääntöpuoli; epäonni, vastoinkäyminen; v. kääntää nurin, ylösalaisin, toisin päin;

peräyttää, muuttaa kokonaan, mullistaa; kumota, peruuttaa; kääntyä päinvastaiseksi; *put.. in ~* peruuttaa, peräyttää (auto); *~ gear* peruutusvaihde; *rather the ~* pikemminkin päinvastoin. **-sible** [-əbl] *a.* käännettävissä oleva, kääntö-. **-sion** [ri'və:ʃn] *s.* pala|uttaminen, -utuminen; *~ to type* atavismi.

revert [ri'və:t] *v.* palata; joutua takaisin, palautua.

revetment [ri'vetmənt] *s.* betonipäällystys.

review [ri'vju:] *v.* tarkastella, selostaa; luoda silmäys taaksepäin; arvostella (kirjaa); (sot.) tarkastaa; (koul.) kertaus; *s.* (uudelleen) tarkastelu, tarkastus; katselmus (sot.); arvostelu, selonteko; aikakauslehti; *come under ~* joutua tarkastettavaksi. **-er** [-ə] *s.* arvostelija

revile [ri'vail] *v.* herjata, solvata, pilkata. **-ment** *s.* herjaus.

revi|se [ri'vaiz] *v.* tarkistaa, korjata; *s.* tarkistusvedos; *R~d Version* tarkistettu raamatunkäännös (1885). **-sion** [-'viʒn] *s.* tarkistus, tarkistettu laitos.

revisit ['ri:'vizit] *v.* käydä uudelleen jssk.

revival [ri'vaiv|l] *s.* elvyttäminen; elpyminen, henkiin herääminen; herätys(liike); uusintaesitys (teatt.); *the R~ of Learning* renessanssi. **-ist** [-əlist] *s.* herätyssaarnaaja.

revive [ri'vaiv] *v.* elpyä, virota, tulla tajuihinsa; vilkastua; elvyttää, herättää henkiin; *~ a play* ottaa kappale uudelleen ohjelmistoon.

revoca|ble ['revəkəbl] *a.* peruutettavissa oleva. **-tion** [-'keiʃn] *s.* kumoaminen.

revoke [ri'vəuk] *v.* peruuttaa, kumota; olla tunnustamatta maata (korttip.).

revolt [ri'vəult] *v.* nousta kapinaan; joutua kuohuksiin, inhottaa; *s.* kapina; *~ from* luopua. **-ing** *a.* kuohuttava, inhottava; *~ly* inhottavan.

revolution [revə'lu:ʃn] *s.* kierros; vallankumous; *the Industrial R~* teollisuuden läpimurto. **-ary** [-əri] *a. & s.* (vallan)kumouksellinen. **-ize**

[-aiz] *v.* mullistaa.

revolv|e [ri'vɔlv] *v.* kiertää (jnk ympäri); panna kiertämään; hautoa mielessään, punnita. **-er** [-ə] *s.* revolveri. **-ing** *a.* kierto-; *~ stage* pyörönäyttämö

revue [ri'vju:] *s.* revyy.

revulsion [ri'vʌlʃn] *s.* äkillinen muutos, käänne; inho.

reward [ri'wɔ:d] *s.* palkinto, palkka; löytöpalkkio; *v.* palkita; *~ing* antoisa.

Reynard ['renəd] *erisn.*

Reynolds ['renldz] *erisn.* Repolainen.

rhapsody ['ræpsədi] *s.* rapsodia; sanatulva, vuodatus.

Rhenish ['reniʃ] *s.* reininviini.

rhetoric ['retərik] *s.* puhetaito, kaunopuheisuus. **-al** [ri'tɔrik(ə)l] *a.* korusanainen; retorinen. **-ian** [-'riʃn] *s.* kaunopuhuja.

rheumat|ic [ru(:)'mætik] *a. & s.* reumaattinen (henkilö). **-ism** ['ru:mətizm] *s.* reumatismi. **-oid** ['ru:mətɔid] *a.: ~ arthritis* nivelreuma.

Rhine [rain] *erisn.: the ~* Rein.

rhino ['rainou] *s.* (lyh.) = seur. **-ceros** [rai'nɔs(ə)rəs] *s.* sarvikuono. **-logy** [-'nɔlədʒi] *s.* nenätautioppi.

rhizome ['raizəum] *s.* juurakko.

Rhodes [rəudz] *erisn.* Rhodos; *~ scholar* Cecil Rhodes-stipendiaatti. **-ia** [rə(u)'di:zjə] *erisn.*

rhododendron [rəudə'dendr(ə)n] *s.* alppiruusu.

rhomb [rɔm] *s.* vinoneliö. **-us** [-əs] *s.* vinoneliö.

rhubarb ['ru:bɑ:b] *s.* raparperi.

rhumb [rʌm] *s.* kompassipiiru.

rhyme [raim] *s.* loppusointu; loppusointuinen runo; *v.* riimitellä; muodostaa loppusointu, rimmata. **-ster** [-stə] *s.* riiminikkari.

rhythm ['riðm] *s.* rytmi, poljento. **-ic(al)** [-ik, -ik(ə)l] *a.* rytmillinen, rytmikäs.

rib [rib] *s.* kylkiluu; kylkipala; (lehden) suoni; (veneen) kaari, (sateenvarjon) ruode; kohojuova (kankaassa); *v.* Am. (sl.) kiusata, härnätä; vrt. *ribbed*.

ribald ['rib(ə)ld] *a.* ruokoton, rivo. **-ry** [-ri] *s.* rivous.

ribbed ['ribd] *a.* kohojuovainen, ruode-, vako-.

ribbon ['ribən] *s.* nauha; ritarikunnan

nauha; suikale; *pl.* ohjakset; *typewriter*
~ värinauha.
rice [rais] *s.* riisi, -suurimot.
rich [ritʃ] *a.* rikas; runsas;
hedelmällinen, tuottoisa;
kallisarvoinen, loistava, uhkea;
voimakas, syvä (väri), täyttävä,
rasvainen (ruoka); mehevä,
täyteläinen; ~ *in* jossa on runsaasti.
rich|es ['ritʃiz] *s. pl.* rikkaus,
rikkaudet. **-ly** *adv.* upeasti ym;
runsaasti, runsain määrin.
Richmond ['ritʃmənd] *erisn.*
richness *s.* rikkaus, runsaus, loisto,
hedelmällisyys jne.
rick [rik] *s.* suova, haasia; *v.* panna
suovalle.
ricket|s ['rikits] *s.* riisitauti. **-y** [-iti] *a.*
vaappuva, huojuva.
rickshaw ['rikʃɔ:] *s.* rikša.
ricochet ['rikəʃet] *s.* kimmahdus,
kimmoke (sot.); *v.* kimmota,
kimmahtaa.
rid [rid] *rid rid, v.* vapauttaa, päästää
(of jstk); *get* ~ *of* päästä jstk. **-dance**
[-əns] *s.* vapautus; pääseminen; *a*
good ~ *!* hyvä että pääsit siitä t.
hänestä.
ridden ['ridn] *pp.* ks. *ride.*
riddle 1. ['ridl] *s.* arvoitus; *v.* selittää
(arvoitus).
riddle 2. ['ridl] *s.* (karkea) seula; *v.*
seuloa; ampua seulaksi; tehdä
tyhjäksi; ~*d with* täynnä (reikiä).
ride [raid] *rode ridden, v.* ratsastaa,
ajaa, ajella; istua hajareisin; keinua,
keinutella, leijailla; antaa ratsastaa;
pitää vallassaan, ahdistaa; *s.*
ratsastusretki, ajelu; ratsastustie; ~ *at*
anchor olla ankkurissa; ~ *down*
ratsastaa kumoon, tavoittaa; ~ *out a*
gale (laivasta) kestää myrsky; *ridden*
by fears pelon vallassa; *go for a* ~
lähteä ratsastamaan t. ajelulle; *take*
sb. for a ~ (puhek.) huijata,
petkuttaa. **-r** [-ə] *s.* ratsastaja;
(asiakirjan) liite.
ridge [ridʒ] *s.* (katon) harja, (vuoren)
harjanne; harju; terävä reuna; ~ *pole*
kurkihirsi, (teltan) kattoriuku.
ridicul|e ['ridikju:l] *s.* pilkka; *v.*
pilkata, pitää pilkkanaan (m. *hold up*
to ~). **-ous** ['ridikjuləs] *a.* naurettava.
riding 1. ['raidiŋ] *s.* ratsastus.

~**-breeches** ratsastushousut. ~**-habit**
(naisen) ratsastuspuku.
riding 2. ['raidiŋ] *s.* (Yorkshire)
hallintopiiri.
rife [raif] *a.* yleinen, laajalle levinnyt;
~ *with* täynnä jtk.
riffle ['rifl] *v.* sekoittaa (kortit)
selaamalla, selata (~ *through sth.*).
riff-raff ['rifræf] *s.* roskaväki.
rifle ['raifl] *v.* riistää, ryöstää puti
puhtaaksi; rihlata; *s.* kivääri. **-man**
(tarkka-)ampuja. **-range**
ampumarata; kiväärin kantomatka.
rift [rift] *s.* rako, halkeama, repeämä,
särö; valtimo.
rig 1. [rig] *v.* takiloida, köysittää; *s.*
takila, köysistö; poratorni; kamppeet,
(korea) asu (tav. ~*-out*); ~ *ged-up*
pyntätty; *oil* ~ öljynporauslautta.
rig 2. [rig] *s.* huijaus, keplottelu; *v.*
huijata; ~*ged election* vaalipetos.
rigg|er ['rigə] *s.* (lento)mekaanikko.
-ing *s.* takila; keplottelu, juoni *(price*
~).
right [rait] *a.* oikea, todellinen;
asianmukainen; oikeanpuolinen;
suora; *adv.* suoraan, -ssa; oikein,
sopivasti; aivan, tarkoin, (~ *to)* jhk
saakka; oikealle; *s.* oikeus; oikea
puoli; oikeisto; *v.* oikaista, suoristaa,
-tua; hankkia oikeutta; *you were quite*
~ *to* teit aivan oikein kun; *that's* ~
pitää paikkansa; ~ *you are! ~ oh!* olet
oikeassa! *[all]* ~ *!* hyvä on! *is all* ~ on
kunnossa, terve; *be [in the]* ~ olla
oikeassa; *get sth.* ~ selvittää; *come* ~
selvitä; *put (set)* ~ oikaista, korjata,
ohjata oikeaan; panna kuntoon,
järjestää; *put [a watch]* ~ asettaa
kohdalleen; ~ *away (off)* suoraa
päätä, viipymättä; ~ *of way*
etuajo-oikeus, läpikulkuoikeus; *yield*
~ *of way* antaa tietä, väistää; ~ *on*
suoraan eteenpäin; ~ *to the bottom*
pohjaan saakka; *not quite* ~ *in the*
head vähän päästään vialla; *by* ~ *[s]*
oikeuden mukaan *by* ~ *of* tyh
nojalla; *in one's own* ~ syntyperän
nojalla; omasta takaa; *on my* ~
[hand] oikealla puolellani; *[to the]* ~
oikealle. ~**-about:** *r.-a. face*
täyskäännös. ~**-angled**
suorakulmainen. **-eous** [-ʃəs] *a.*
oikeamielinen, vanhurskas;

oikeudenmukainen. **-ful** a.
oikeudenmukainen, laillinen. **~-hand**
a. oikeanpuoleinen; r.-h. man jkn
oikea käsi. **~-handed** oikeakätinen.
-ly adv. oikein, hyvällä syyllä,
oikeutetusti. **~-minded**
oikeamielinen.

rigid ['ridʒid] a. jäykkä, kankea;
ankara, vaikea. **-ity** [ri'dʒiditi] s.
jäykkyys; ankaruus.

rigmarole ['rigm(ə)rəul] s. loru.

rigorous ['rig(ə)rəs] a. ankara, tiukka.

rigour, rigor ['rigə] s. ankaruus,
kovuus.

rile [rail] v. suututtaa, ärsyttää.

rill [ril] s. puro.

rim [rim] s. reuna; (pyörän) vanne;
gold ~ med kultasankaiset; red-~ med
punareunaiset (silmät).

rime 1. [raim] s. = rhyme.

rime 2. [raim] s. huurre, kuura; ~d
with frost huurteinen.

rind [raind] s. kuori; kaarna.

riderpest ['rindəpest] s. karjarutto.

ring 1. [riŋ] rang rung, v. soida, helistä,
kaikua; soittaa; julistaa maailmalle;
kuulostaa, kajahtaa; s. soitto,
kellonsoitto; helinä, kilinä; ~ the bell
for the nurse soittaa hoitajaa; it rang a
bell toi mieleen muiston; ~ off
lopettaa puhelu; ~ up soittaa (jklle
puhelimella); there is a ~ at the door
ovikello soi; give me a ~! soita(han)
minulle!

ring 2. [riŋ] s. sormus, rengas; kehä;
piiri; (nyrkkeily)kehä (prize-~);
aitaus (liik.) rengas(tuma); the ~ m.
vedonlyöjät; v. ympäröidä, saartaa
(~ in); rengastaa. **-ed** [-d] a. renkailla
varustettu, sormuksin koristettu.
~-finger nimetön sormi. **-ing** a.
kaikuva, raikuva; s. helinä. **~-leader**
johtaja, yllyttäjä. **-let** s. kihara, kutri.
~-master sirkuksen johtaja. **-worm**
savipuoli (lääk.).

rink [riŋk] s. luistinrata.

rinse [rins] v. huuhtoa; s. huuhtelu.

Rio ['ri:əu] **Rio de Janeiro**
[-dədʒə'niərou] erisn.

riot ['raiət] s. mellakka, meteli, kahina;
järjestyshäiriö; v. mellakoida;
mellastaa, hurjistella; a ~ of colour
värien yltäkylläisyys, väriloisto; run ~
riehaantua; rehottaa. **-er** [-ə] s.

mellakoitsija. **-ing** s. mellakointi. **-ous**
[-əs] a. levoton, mellakoiva.

rip [rip] v. repiä, reväistä; ratkoa;
viiltää, leikata auki; revetä; s.
repeämä; (puhek.) elostelija (an old
~); ~-cord laukaisunaru; let things ~
on

ripe [raip] a. kypsä, kypsynyt; valmis
(~ for). **-n** [-n] v. kypsyä; kypsyttää.
-ness s. kypsyys.

riposte [ri'poust] s. vastapisto.

ripping a. hieno, loisto-.

ripple ['ripl] s. väre(ily), solina,
liplatus; v. väreillä, solista; saada
väreilemään.

rise [raiz] rose risen, v. nousta, kohota,
yletä; menestyä; saada alkunsa,
syntyä, ilmaantua; lopettaa istunto; s.
nousu; ylämäki, kukkula, töyräs;
palkankorotus; synty, alku(perä),
(alku)lähde; ~ against nousta
kapinaan; rose to the occasion nousi
tilanteen tasalle; the fish ~s kala syö;
give ~ to aiheuttaa jtk. **-n** ['rizn] pp.
noussut jne.; ylösnoussut. **-r** [-ə] s.:
early ~ aamunvirkku.

risible ['rizibl] s. naurunalainen,
nauru-.

rising ['raizŋ] a. nouseva, kohoava;
menestyvä; s. kansannousu; ~
generation nouseva polvi; ~ ground
nousu; he is ~ [twelve] lähes
(12-vuotias).

risk [risk] s. vaara, riski; v. vaarantaa,
uskaltaa; the ~ of antautua jhk
vaaraan; at the ~ of his life henkensä
kaupalla; at owner's ~ omistajan
vastuulla. **-y** [-i] a. vaarallinen.

rite [rait] s.: ~ s
(jumalanpalvelus)menot.

ritual ['ritjuəl] s. kirkkokäsikirja;
jumalanpalvelusmenot.

rival ['raivl] s. kilpailija, attr.
kilpaileva; v. kilpailla, vetää vertoja
(jllek); without a ~ vertaa(nsa) vailla.
-ry [-ri] s. kilpailu.

rive [raiv] v. (rive, rived, riven)
repäistä; haljeta.

river ['rivə] s. joki; ~ s [of blood] virrat.
~-basin jokialue. **~-bed** joenuoma.
-side jokivarsi.

rivet ['rivit] s. niitti; v. niitata; naulita,
kiinnittää (katseensa); herättää
(suurta kiinnostusta), pysähdyttää.

rivulet ['rivjulit] s. puro.

roach [rəutʃ] s. särki.

road [rəud] s. tie; katu; pl. reti; ~ accident liikenneturma; ~ sign; liikennemerkki; ~ safety liikenneturvallisuus; ~ transport maantiekuljetus; the rule of the ~ liikennejärjestys; on the ~ matkalla; get out of the ~! pois tieltä! ~-**hog** autohurjastelija. ~-**house** tienvarren ravintola. ~-**metal** sepeli. ~-**sense** liikennekulttuuri. -**side** tiepuoli. -**stead** reti. -**ster** [-stə] s. (vanh.) pieni avoauto. -**way** ajotie.

roam [rəum] v. kuljeskella, harhailla.

roan [rəun] a. ruskeanharmaa; s. kimo.

roar [rɔː] v. karjua, mylviä, ulvoa, ärjyä; pauhata, kohista; ~ karjunta, ulvonta; pauhu, kohina; ~ of applause suosionmyrsky; ~s of laughter naurunremahdukset. -**ing** a. ulvova, meluava; myrskyinen; ~ trade suunnaton menekki.

roast [rəust] v. paahtaa; paistaa; paistua; s. paisti; a. paistettu, paahdettu. -**er** [-ə] s. paahdin.

rob [rɔb] v. ryöstää, riistää; he was ~bed of his money häneltä ryöstettiin rahat. -**ber** [-ə] s. rosvo, ryöväri. -**bery** [-əri] s. rosvous, ryöstö.

robe [rəub] s. viitta, kaapu; puku, -asu (us. pl.) (naisen) iltapuku; aamutakki, kylpyviitta (bath~). v. pukea (in, jhk).

robin ['rɔbin] s.: ~ redbreast punarintasatakieli; R~ Goodfellow tonttu.

robot ['rəubɔt] s. robotti.

robust [rə(u)'bʌst] s. roteva, vahva, vankka.

rock 1. [rɔk] s. kallio, kivi(laji), vuorilaji; paasi, luoto, kari; kova karamelli; the R~ Gibraltar; ~-bottom alin mahdollinen (hinta); ~ salt karkea suola; on the ~s puilla paljailla; Am. jäiden kanssa.

rock 2. [rɔk] v. keinutella, heiluttaa, tuudittaa; keinua, heilua, huojua. -**er** [-ə] s. (keinutuolin ym) jalas; pärinäpoika (Mods and Rockers); off his ~ tärähtänyt.

rockery ['rɔkəri] s. kivikko(istutus).

rocket ['rɔkit] s. raketti, ohjus; v. kohota äkkiä. -**ry** [-ri] s. rakettioppi.

rock|-garden kivikkopuutarha. ~-**oil** vuoriöljy.

rocking|-chair keinutuoli. ~-**horse** kiikkuhevonen.

rocky ['rɔki] a. kallioinen; kova kuin kallio; kivikkoinen; huojuva; the R~ Mountains (m. the Rockies) Kalliovuoret.

rococo [rə'kəukəu] s. rokokootyyli(nen).

rod [rɔd] s. vitsa; tanko, keppi; varsi, sauva; ongenvapa; virkasauva; pituusmitta (5,03 m.)

rode [rəud] imp. ks. ride.

rodent ['rəud(ə)nt] s. jyrsijä.

rodeo [rəu'deiəu, Am. 'rəudiəu] s. cowboynäytös t. kilpailut.

roe 1. [rəu] s. metsäkauris.

roe 2. [rəu] s. mäti; soft ~ maiti.

roentgen ['rɔntʃən, Am. 'rentg-] s.: ~ film röntgenkuva. -**ogram** [-'genəgræm] s. = ed.

rogation [rə(u)'geiʃn] s.: ~s rukoukset; ~ days kolme rukouspäivää (helatorstain edellä).

Roger ['rɔdʒə] s.: Sir ~ de Coverley engl. maalaistanssi; the Jolly R~ merirosvolippu.

rogu|e [rəug] s. kelmi, rosto; veitikka, veijari; (elefantista) erakko, raivo. -**ery** [-əri] s. konnantyö; kuje(et). -**ish** [-iʃ] a. roistomainen; veitikkamainen.

roil [rɔil] v. sekoittaa; ärsyttää.

roisterer ['rɔistərə] s. räyhääjä.

role, rôle [rəul] s. osa, rooli.

roll [rəul] s. käärö; rulla, tela; luettelo; (kangas)pakka; sämpylä; kääryle; keinunta, jyrinä, pärinä; kääretorttu; v. vierittää, kierittää; kiertää, kääriä, kaulia, jyrätä, valssata; vieriä, kieriä, pyöriä, vyöryä; piehtaroida; keinua; jyristä, päristä; ääntää täryäänteenä (~ one's r's); ~ of honour kaatuneiden luettelo; call the ~ pitää nimenhuuto; ~ out kaulia, kaaviloida; ~ up kääriä kokoon, kääriytyä. ~-**call** nimenhuuto.

roller ['rəulə] s. rulla, valssi, tela, kaulin, jyrä; papiljotti; maininki, hyökyaalto; ~ blind kierrekaihdin; ~ towel telapyyhe. ~-**skates** rullaluistimet.

rollick ['rɔlik] v. mellastaa. -**ing** a. hilpeä, riehakas.

rolling *a. & s.* ks. *roll.* ~**-mill**
valssilaitos. ~**-pin** kaulin. ~**-stock**
liikkuva kalusto (rautat.).
roll|**-on** *a.* kieppo- ~**-top** [*desk*]
liukukantinen.
roly-poly ['rəulipəuli] *s.* eräänl.
kääretorttu.
Roman ['rəumən] *a. & s.* roomalainen;
roomalaiskatolinen; [*Epistle to the*] ~*s*
Roomalaiskirje.
romance [rə'mæns] *s.* romanttinen
kertomus, seikkailuromaani;
romanssi; romantiikka; *R*~
romaaninen (kieli); *v.* sepittää
romaaneja; ks. *romanticize.*
Romanesque [rəumə'nesk] *a. & s.*
romaaninen (tyyli.)
Roman|**ic** [rə(u)'mænik] *a.*
romaaninen.
romantic [rə'mænti|k] *a.* romanttinen,
haaveellinen; *s.* romantikko. ~**-ism**
[-sizm] *s.* romantiikka. ~**-ist** [-sist] *s.*
romantikko. ~**-ize** [-saiz] *v.*
romantisoida.
Romany ['rɔməni] *s.* mustalainen,
romaani; mustalaisten kieli.
Rome [rəum] *erisn.* Rooma.
Romeo ['rəumiəu] *erisn.*
romp [rɔmp] *v.* telmiä, mellastaa; *s.*
rasavilli; mekastus. ~**-er(s)** [-ə(z)] *s.*
lasten leikkipuku, potkuhousut. ~**-ish**
[-iʃ] *a.* riehakas, vallaton.
rondavel ['rɔndəvel] *s.* (Afr.) pyöreä
maja.
rood [n :d] *s.* risti, ristinpuu;
pinnanmitta (= ¼ *acre*).
roof [ru:f] *s.* katto; katos; *v.* kattaa.
~**-ing** *s.* kattaminen; kattoainekset.
~**-rack** auton tavarateline (katolla).
~**-tree** kurkihirsi.
rook 1. [ruk] *s.* (šakkip.) torni.
rook 2. [ruk] *s.* naakka; korttihuijari;
v. petkuttaa pelissä. ~**-ery** [-əri] *s.*
naakkayhdyskunta. ~**-ie** [-i] *s.* (sot.sl.)
monni.
room [ru:m, rum] *s.* huone; tila, sija; *v.*
asua; *there is* ~ *for improvement* on
parantamisen varaa; *make* ~ *for*
väistyä jkn tieltä. ~**-y** [-i] *a.* avara,
tilava.
Roosevelt ['rouzəvelt] *erisn.*
roost [ru:st] *s.* orsi; *v.* istua orrella, olla
yöpuulla; *go to* ~ mennä yöpuulle;
rules the ~ on kukkona tunkiolla. ~**-er**

[-ə] *s.* kukko.
root [ru:t] *s.* juuri; (tav. *pl.*) juurikas;
alku, (perus)syy; (kiel.) kanta; *v.*
juurruttaa; juurtua; tonkia, penkoa
(m. ~ *about);* ~*s* juurekset; *square* ~
neliöjuuri; ~ *and branch* perinjuurin;
pull up by the ~*s* hävittää perinjuurin;
take ~ juurtua; ~ *out* hävittää
juurineen; *fear* ~*ed him to the spot*
pelko naulitsi hänet siihen paikkaan;
~ *crops* juurekset. **-ed** [-id] *a.*
juurtunut, piintynyt. **-le** [-l] *v.* tonkia.
-less *a.* juureton.
rope [rəup] *s.* köysi, nuora; *v.* sitoa
kiinni nuoralla, köyttää; ~ *off* sulkea
(alue) nuoralla; ~ *sb. in* saada jku
mukaan t. kiedotuksi jhk; ~ *of pearls*
helminauha; [*give sb.*] *plenty of* ~
vapaat kädet; *he knows the* ~*s* on
perillä asioista. ~**-ladder**
köysitikkaat. ~**-dancer,** ~**-walker**
nuorallatanssija.
ropy ['rəupi] *a.* sitkeä.
rorqual ['rɔ:kwəl] *s.* uurteisvalas.
rosary ['rəuzəri] *s.* rukousnauha;
ruusutarha.
rose 1. [rəuz] *imp.* ks. *rise.*
rose 2. [rəuz] *s.* ruusu; ruusuke;
(ruiskukannun) siivilä; ruusunpuna;
a. ruusunpunainen; *under the* ~
salassa. **-ate** ['rəuziit] *a.*
ruusunpunainen. **-bud** ruusunnuppu.
~**-coloured** ruusunpunainen. **-mary**
[-m(ə)ri] *s.* rosmariini.
rosette [rə(u)'zet] *s.* ruusuke.
rosin ['rɔzin] *s.* (jousi)hartsi; *v.*
hartsata.
roster ['rɔstə] *s.* nimilista, (palvelu-,
työ)lista.
rostrum ['rɔstrəm] *s.* puhujalava.
rosy ['rəuzi] *a.* ruusuinen,
ruusunpunainen.
rot [rɔt] *v.* mädätä, lahota; mädättää;
puhua roskaa; *s.* (puun) laho; moska;
[*tommy*] ~*!* joutavia! pötyä!
rota ['rəutə] *s.* ks. *roster;* työvuorot.
Rotarian [rəu'teəriən] *s.* rotari.
rota|**ry** ['rəut|əri] *a.* pyörivä. **-te** [-'teit]
v. kiertää, pyöriä; pyörittää, panna
kiertämään. ~**-tion** [-'teiʃn] *s.*
kiertäminen, pyöriminen; kiertoliike,
kierros; ~ *of crops* vuoroviljely. **-tory**
[-ət(ə)ri] *a.* = *rotary.*
rote [rəut] *s.: by* ~ ulkoläksynä, ulkoa.

rotisserie [rəu'tisəri] s. varraspaahdin.
rotor ['rəutə] s. roottori.
rotten ['rɔtn] a. mädännyt, mätä, laho;
pilaantunut; rappeutunut;
turmeltunut; sl. mätä, kelvoton,
kurja; ~ **Row** ks. **Row. -ness** s.
mädännäisyys, turmeltuneisuus.
rotter ['rɔtə] s. renttu, roisto.
rotund [rə(u)'tʌnd] a. pyöreä; pullea.
-ity [-iti] s. pyöreys, pulleus.
rouble ['ru:bl] s. rupla.
roué ['ru:ei] s. irstailija.
rouge [ru:ʒ] s. poskipuna; v. punata.
rough [rʌf] a. epätasainen, rosoinen;
mäkinen; pörröinen, takkuinen;
karhea, karkea, hiomaton,
muokkaamaton; myrskyinen, raju;
kovakourainen, töykeä, karski,
ankara, kova; huonokäytöksinen,
sivistymätön; summittainen; s.
huligaani, kovanaama; v. tehdä
rosoiseksi, karkeaksi jne; muokata
karkeasti; adv. karkeasti, töykeästi;
~ copy konsepti; ~ draft luonnos; a ~
estimate karkea, summittainen arvio;
~ passage myrskyinen merimatka;
~ through ~ and smooth myötä- ja
vastoinkäymisessä; have a ~ time
kokea kovaa; in the ~ puolivalmiina;
~ it elää epämukavissa oloissa. **-age**
[-idʒ] s. karkea ravinto. ~**-and-ready**
karkeahko, mukiinmenevä.
~**-and-tumble** tappelunnujakka. **-cast**
s. karkea luonnos; rappaus; v.
luonnostaa; rapata. ~**-dry**
silittämätön. **-en** [-n] v. tehdä t. tulla
karkeaksi, epätasaiseksi ym. ~**-hew**
hakata karkeaksi. ~**-house** Am.
mellastelu. **-ly** adv. karkeasti, tylysti
jne.; kovakouraisesti; ~[speaking]
suunnilleen, arviolta. **-neck** sl.
tappelupukari, huligaani. **-ness** s.
rosoisuus, karkeus jne. ~**-rider**
hevosenkesyttäjä. **-shod** ride ~ over
kohdella häikäilemättömästi.
roulette [ru(:)'let] s. rulettipeli.
Roumania [ru(:)'meinjə] erisn. ks.
Rumania.
round [raund] a. pyöreä; runsas,
melkoinen; aimo, kelpo; ripeä; s.
piiri, kierros, kierto(kulku);
tarkastuskierros; sarja, vuoro, erä;
piiritanssi, panos, laukaus(sarja);
adv. ympäri, ympärillä; takaisin; prep.

ympäri; v. pyöristää, -tyä; ympäröidä;
kiertää, purjehtia jnk ympäri;
kääntyä ympäri; ~ about (m.) noin; ~
game seuraleikki (piirissä); a good ~
sum sievoinen summa; ~-the-clock
ympärivuorokautinen; ~ trip (tour)
rengas-, kiertomatka; ~ of beef
reisipala; in ~ numbers pyörein
luvuin; all the year ~ ympäri vuoden;
ask sb. ~ pyytää jkta käymään
talossa; look ~ katsella ympärilleen t.
taakseen; have we enough to go~?
riittääkö koko seurueelle? hand ~
jaella; show sb. ~ olla jkn oppaana; ~
off pyöristää; ~ out pyöristyä; ~ up
ajaa kokoon (karja), saartaa. **-about**
a. epäsuora, kiertävä; s.
liikenneympyrä; karuselli; ~ way
kiertotie; in a ~ way epäsuorasti. **-ers**
[-əz] s. eräänl. pallopeli. **-head** (hist.)
keropää. **-ish** a. pyöreähkö. **-ly** adv.
peittelemättä; voimakkaasti,
perusteellisesti. ~**-up** s. (karjan)
koolleajaminen; ratsia.
rouse [rauz] v. herättää; kiihottaa,
innostaa; ajaa esiin; herätä (tav. ~
up).
roustabout ['raustəbaut] s. (sirkuksen
ym) apumies.
rout 1. [raut] s. hurja pako; (vanh.)
suuret kutsut; v. lyödä perin pohjin,
ajaa pakosalle (m. put to ~).
rout 2. [raut] v. tonkia, myllertää,
kaivaa esiin, nuuskia; ~ sb. out of bed
ajaa jku vuoteesta.
route [ru:t] s. tie, reitti; en ~ ['ɔ:ŋru:t]
to (t. for) matkalla jnnek; [raut]
marssikäsky (raut.).
routine [ru:'ti:n] s. (jokapäiväiset)
tehtävät, rutiini.
rove [rəuv] v. harhailla, kuljeskella. **-r**
[-ə] s. vaeltaja; (vanh.) merirosvo.
row 1. [rəu] s. rivi; in the front ~
ensimmäisessä tuolirivissä; the R~
Hyde Parkin ratsastuspolku (m.
Rotten R~).
row 2. [rəu] v. soutaa; s. soutumatka,
veneretki; shall I ~ you across?
soudanko sinut toiselle puolelle?
row 3. [rau] s. melu, meteli; riita; v.
riidellä (with); get into a ~ saada
haukkumisia; make (kick up) a ~
alkaa rähjätä, aloittaa riita.
rowan ['rauən, 'rəu-] s. pihlaja,

pihlajanmarja (m. ~-berry).
rowdy ['raudi] s. tappelupukari,
räyhääjä; a. mellastava; ~ scenes
hulinointi(a). -**ism** [-izm] s.
huliganismi.
rowel ['rauəl] s. kannuksen pyörä.
row|er ['rə(u)ə] soutaja. -**ingboat**
soutuvene. -**lock** ['rɔlək, 'rʌlək]
hanka(in).
royal ['rɔi(ə)l] a. kuninkaallinen,
kuninkaan-; loistava, komea; the R~
Academy Engl. kuninkaallinen
taideakatemia; R~ Air Force
kuninkaalliset ilmavoimat; the R~
Society Englannin tiedeakatemia. -**ist**
[-ist] s. kuningasmielinen. -**ty** [-ti] s.
kuninkaallinen henkilö, (koll.)
kuninkaallliset; -ties tekijänpalkkiot.
rub [rʌb] v. hieroa, hangata;
hankautua; s. hieronta, hankaus;
este, loukkaus, hankaluus; ~ sth. dry
(clean) hangata kuivaksi, puhtaaksi;
~ along selvitä jotenkuten; ~ down
hieroa, hangata (lujaa), ruokota
(hevonen); ~ off (out) hangata pois,
puhdistaa, hankautua, kulua; ~ sb.
out Am.(sl.) nitistää, tappaa. ~ up
kiillottaa, uudistaa, elvyttää; there's
the ~ siitä juuri kenkä puristaa; you
needn' ~ it in älä viitsi sitä aina
alleviivata t. jankuttaa.
rubber 1. ['rʌbə] s. kumi; raapekumi;
hankaaja, hieroja; ~s kalossit,
päällyskengät.
rubber 2. ['rʌbə] s. robbertti
(korttipelissä).
rubberneck ['rʌbənek] Am. s. utelias
turisti, nähtävyyksien katselija.
rubbish ['rʌbiʃ] s. roskat, rikat, roska,
törky; ~! lorua! pötyä! höpsis!
rubble ['rʌbl] s. kivi-, tiilimurska.
rubicund ['ru:bikənd] a. punakka.
rubric ['ru:brik] s. otsikko.
ruby ['ru:bi] s. rubiini;
rubiininväri(nen).
ruche [ru:ʃ] s. (pitsi)röyhelö.
ruck 1. [rʌk] s.: the ~ suuri massa.
ruck 2. [rʌk] s. ryppy; v. rypistyä, -tää.
rucksack ['ruksæk] s. selkäreppu.
ructions ['rʌkʃnz] s. meteli.
rudder ['rʌdə] s. peräsin.
ruddiness s. punakkuus.
ruddy ['rʌdi] a. punertava.
rude [ru:d] a. töykeä, epäkohtelias,

tyly, karkea, raaka; sopimaton,
hiomaton; alkeellinen,
karkeatekoinen; raju, väkivaltainen;
vankka (terveys) be ~ to loukata jkta.
-**ness** s. karkeus, epäkohteliaisuus.
rudiment ['ru:dimənt] s. jäte,
surkastuma, pl. alkeet. -**ary** [-'mentri]
Rudyard ['rʌdjəd] erisn.
rue [ru:] v. katua; s. ruutapensas. -**ful**
a. murheellinen, katuva.
ruff [rʌf] s. (linnun)töyhtökaulus;
kaularöyhelö; suokukko; kiiski;
(korttip.) v. ottaa valtilla.
ruffian ['rʌfjən] s. rähinöitsijä. -**ly** a.
huligaani, huligaanimainen,
räyhäävä.
ruffle ['rʌfl] v. panna väreilemään,
pöyhistää, pörröttää (m. ~ up); tehdä
levottomaksi, hermostuttaa; s.
röyhelö, poimutus; väreily; is easily
~d kiihtyy, hermostuu helposti.
rug [rʌg] s. (matka)huopa, matto,
ryijy.
Rugby ['rʌgbi] erisn.; s. = ~ football
rugby(peli).
rugged ['rʌgid] a. epätasainen,
rosoinen, karkea, uurteinen,
kallioinen; karski, karu; ~ features
säännöttömät piirteet.
rugger ['rʌgə] s. = Rugby football.
ruin ['ru:in] s. sortuminen, tuho,
perikato; raunio (us. pl.); v. tuhota,
saattaa perikatoon t. turmioon; in ~s
raunioitunut; it will be the ~ of koituu
jkn turmioksi. -**ous** [-əs] a. tuhoisa,
häviöön saattava; raunio-.
rul|e [ru:l] s. sääntö, ohje; (yleinen)
tapa; määräys; (tuomioistuimen)
päätös; hallitusvalta; mittapuu,
viivoitin; v. vallita, hallita, hillitä;
ratkaista; viivoittaa; ~s säännöt; as a
~ yleensä; by ~ säännönmukaisesti;
make it a ~ ottaa tavaksi, pitää
tapanaan; work to ~ (työläisistä)
jarruttaa; ~ out sulkea pois; be ~d by
olla jnk vallassa; prices ~d high
hintataso oli korkea. -**er** [-ə] s.
hallitsija; viivoitin. -**ing** a. vallitseva,
hallitseva; s. (oikeuden) päätös.
rum 1. [rʌm] s. rommi; ~-runner
alkoholin salakuljettaja.
rum 2. [rʌm] a. sl. eriskummainen (m.
~my).
Rumania [ru(:)'meinjə] erisn.

Romania. **-n** [-n] *a. & s.* romanialainen.

rumble ['rʌmbl] *v.* jyristä, jyristellä; (vatsasta) kurista; *s.* jyrinä; kurina; (auton) takaistuin.

rumbustious [rʌm'bʌstʃəs] *a.* meluava, raju.

rumina|nt ['ru:minənt] *s.* märehtijä. **-te** [-eit] *v.* märehtiä; (kuv.) miettiä, hautoa. **-tive** [-ətiv] *a.* mietiskelevä.

rummage ['rʌmidʒ] *v.* etsiä tarkoin, penkoa, nuuskia; *s.* etsintä; kama; ~ *sale* l.v. kirpputori.

rummy ['rʌmi] *a.* = *rum* 2.

rumour, rumor ['ru:mə] *s.* huhu; *v.* levittää huhua, kertoa; *it is ~ed* huhutaan.

rump [rʌmp] *s.* (eläimen) takapuoli. **-steak** *s.* reisipaisti.

rumple ['rʌmpl] *v.* rypistää.

rumpus ['rʌmpəs] *s.* meteli, hälinä.

run 1 [rʌn] *ran run, v.* juosta, kiiruhtaa, paeta; käydä, kulkea; kulua; purjehtia; olla käynnissä; olla ohjelmistossa; olla voimassa; jatkua, ulottua, levitä; virrata, vuotaa; ottaa osaa kilpailuun, asettua ehdokkaaksi *(for)*; asettaa (ehdokas); pitää (autoa); sulaa; märkiä; (musteesta) läpäistä; tulla jksk; pistää, työntää (jhk, jnk läpi); panna käyntiin, pitää käynnissä; kuljettaa, ohjata; johtaa, hoitaa (liikettä, konetta); sulattaa, valaa; harsia; ~ *the blockade* murtaa saarto; ~ *for it* lähteä käpälämäkeen; *the letter ~s as follows* kirje kuuluu seuraavasti; *this verse ~s smoothly* tämä säe on luonteva; *it ~s in the family* kulkee perintönä; ~*cold* (verestä) hyytyä; ~ *dry* ehtyä, kuivua; ~ *high* nousta, kuohua, olla valloillaan; ~ *wild* olla villiintynyt; ~ *a p. close* olla jkn kintereillä, melkein jkn veroinen; ~ *across* kohdata odottamatta; ~ *away* paeta, karata; ~ *down* (kellosta ym) pysähtyä, kulua loppuun; ajaa jku kumoon, törmätä jhk; saada kiinni; halventaa, puhua pahaa; *be* ~ *down* olla rasittunut, huonossa kunnossa; ~ *for* asettua ehdokkaaksi; ~ *in* panna putkaan; ~ *into debt* velkaantua; *the book has* ~ *into several editions* kirjasta on ilmestynyt useita painoksia; ~ *off*

laskea pois, tyhjentää; ottaa (kopioita); ratkaista; ~ *on* jatkaa, -ua; soittaa suutansa; ~ *out* loppua, päättyä; *I have* ~ *out of sugar* sokerini on lopussa; ~ *over* vuotaa yli, ajaa yli; nopeasti kerrata, silmäillä; ~ *through* lävistää; tuhlata; nopeasti tarkastaa, läpikäydä; ~ *to* nousta jhk; olla varaa jhk; kehittyä, tulla jksk; ~ *up* nopeasti kartuttaa, karttua, rakentaa, ommella (hätäisesti), *(against)* kohdata; ~ *up a bill* ostaa tiliin.

run 2. *s.* juoksu, kulku; (lyhyt) matka, retki, ajo, ajelu; kulku, käynti; suunta; vilkas kysyntä, ryntäys *(on a bank* pankkiin); jakso, kausi; (mus.) juoksutus; Am. silmäpako (sukassa); *at a* ~ juosten; *on a* ~ juoksussa; *the common* ~ *of men* tavalliset ihmiset; *in the long* ~ aikaa myöten; *sheep-~ lammaslaidun; [the play]* had a ~ *of six months* näyteltiin puoli vuotta.

run|about *s.* pieni auto. **-away** *s.* karkuri, pakolainen, pillastunut hevonen; *a.* karannut, pillastunut. **~-down** *a.* rasittunut; *s.* yhteenveto.

rune [ru:n] *s.* (tav. *pl.*) riimukirjoitus, -kirjain.

rung 1. [rʌŋ] *s.* (tikapuun) puola.

rung 2. [rʌŋ] *pp.* ks. *ring.*

runnel ['rʌnl] *s.* puro; katuoja.

runner ['rʌnə] *s.* juoksija, kilpailija; köynnöspapu, rönsy; (reen) jalas; (liuku)rengas; kaitaliina, kapea matto. **~-up** toiseksi tullut (urh.).

running *a.* juokseva, jatkuva, keskeytymätön; peräkkäin(en); *s.* juoksu, kilpailun kulku; ~ *fight* peräytymistaistelu; ~ *hand* sujuva käsiala; ~ *jump* vauhdillinen hyppy; ~ *knot* juoksusolmu; ~ *sore* märkähaava; *three days* ~ kolme päivää perätysten; *he is in (out of) the* ~ hänellä on hyvät (huonot) voitonmahdollisuudet. **~-board** *s.* astinlauta.

run-of-the-mill *a.* tavallinen, keskinkertainen.

runt [rʌnt] *s.* kitukasvuinen (pentu ym); käppänä.

runway ['rʌnwei] *s.* kiitorata.

rupture ['rʌptʃə] *s.* murtuminen, katkeaminen, välien rikkoutuminen; repeämä (lääk.); *v.* ratketa, revetä.

rural ['ruər(ə)l] a. maalais-, maaseudun-; ~ areas maaseutu.

ruse [ru:z] s. metku, (sota)juoni.

rush 1. [rʌʃ] s. kaisla.

rush 2. [rʌʃ] v. rynnätä, syöksyä, hyökätä (at jkn kimppuun); syöksähtää, virrata; hoputtaa, (liiaksi) kiirehtiä; s. ryntäys, rynnäkkö; kiire; don't ~ to conclusions! älä tee hätäisiä johtopäätöksiä! ~ hours ruuhka-aika.

rusk [rʌsk] s. korppu.

russet ['rʌsit] a. & s. punaisenruskea(väri); eräs omenalaji.

Russia ['rʌʃə] erisn. Venäjä. **-n** [-(ə)n] a. & s. venäläinen; s. venäjä, venäjän kieli; a Russian [woman] venakko. **r-nize** [-naiz] v. venäläistää.

rust [rʌst] s. ruoste (m. kasvi-); v. ruostua, ruostuttaa; ~less ruostumaton.

rustic ['rʌstik] a. maalais-, talonpoikais-; koruton; moukkamainen; s. maalainen; moukka. **-ate** [-eit] v. maalaistua; karkottaa (opiskelija) määräajaksi. **-ity** [rʌs'tisiti] s. maalaisuus.

rustle [rʌsl] v. kahista, kahisuttaa; varastaa karjaa; s. kahina; rapina; ~ up hankkia. **-r** [-ə] s. karjavaras.

rusty ['rʌsti] a. ruosteinen, ruostunut, ruosteenkarvainen; vanhentunut; ränsistynyt; äreä.

rut 1. [rʌt] s. pyöränjälki; ura; vanha totuttu tapa.

rut 2. [rʌt] s. kiima-aika; v. olla kiimainen.

rutabaga [ru:tə'beigə] s. lanttu.

Ruth [ru:θ] erisn. Ruut.

Rutherford ['rʌðəfəd] erisn.

ruthless ['ru:θlis] a. säälimätön, julma.

rutt|ed ['rʌtid] -**y** ['rʌti] a. pyöränjälkiä täynnä oleva.

rye [rai] s. ruis; (ruis)viski.

S

S,s [es] *s.*-kirjain. Lyh.: **S.** *Saint, South;* **s.** *second*[*s*]*, shilling*[*s*]*;* **S. A.** *Salvation Army, South Africa;* **Sat.** *Saturday;* **S. C.** *South Carolina;* **S. Dak.** *South Dakota;* **S. E.** *south-east;* **SEATO** *South-East Asia Treaty Organization* Kaakkois-Aasian sopimusjärjestö *;***Sec.** *secretary;* **sec.** *second;* **Sen., Senr** *senior;* **Sept.** *September;* **seq., seqq.** (et. *sequentes*) ynnä seuraava(t); **Sergt** *sergeant;* **sh.** *shilling(s);* **SNP** *Scottish National Party;* **S.O.S.** ks. sanak.; **S.P.C.A.** *Society for the Prevention of Cruelty to Animals;* **Sr.** *senior;* **sq.** *square;* **s.s.** *steamship;* **St.** *Saint* [sən(t), sin(t), sn(t)]*; street;* **st.** *stone* (painomitta); **Sun.** *Sunday;* **Supt** *superintendent;* **S.W.** *south-west.*

Sabbath ['sæbəθ] *s.* sapatti, lepopäivä; *s-tical* [sə'bætik] sapatti-.

sable ['seibl] *s.* soopeli, soopelinnahka; *a.* musta, synkkä.

sabot ['sæbəu] *s.* puukenkä.

sabotage ['sæbətɑ:ʒ] *s.* sabotaasi; *v.* sabotoida. **-eur** [-tɔ:] *s.* sabotööri.

sabre ['seibə] *s.* sapeli.

sac [sæk] *s.* pussi (anat.).

saccharin ['sækərin] *s.* sakariini. **-e** [-rain] *a.* imelä, sokerinen.

sacerdotal [sæsə'dəutl] *a.* papillinen.

sachet ['sæʃei] *s.* hajustepussi.

sack 1. [sæk] *s.* säkki; *v.* panna säkkiin; (puhek.) antaa potkut; *get (give) the* ~ saada (antaa) potkut.

sack 2. *v.* ryöstää (vallattu kaupunki ym); *s.* ryöstäminen.

sack 3. *s.* sekti.

sack|cloth säkkikangas; *in* ~ *and ashes* säkissä ja tuhassa. **~-race** säkkijuoksu.

sacral ['seikr(ə)l] *a.* ristiluun-.

sacrament ['sækrəmənt] *s.* sakramentti; *administer the* ~ jakaa Herran ehtoollista.

sacred ['seikrid] *a.* pyhitetty, pyhä; kirkollinen, hengellinen; ~ *music* kirkkomusiikki; ~ *to the memory of* jkn muistolle pyhitetty. **-ness** *s.* pyhyys.

sacrifice ['sækrifais] *v.* uhrata; *s.* uhri; uhraus, kieltäymys; *at a* ~ alihintaan. **-cial** [sækri'fiʃ(ə)l] *a.* uhri-.

sacrilege ['sækrilidʒ] *s.* pyhyyden loukkaus. **-ious** [-'li:dʒəs] *a.* pyhää häpäisevä.

sacrist|an ['sækrist|ən] *s.* suntio. **-y** [-i] *s.* sakaristo.

sacrosanct ['sækro(u)sæŋ(k)t] *a.* pyhä ja loukkaamaton.

sad [sæd] *a.* murheellinen, alakuloinen, surullinen; valitettava, surkea, kurja; taikinainen. **-den** [-n] *v.* tehdä murheelliseksi, tulla alakuloiseksi.

saddle ['sædl] *s.* satula; *v.* satuloida; sälyttää, rasittaa; *he was* ~*d with* hänellä oli taakkana. **-backed** *a.* notkoselkä. **-bag** satulalaukku. **-r** [-ə] *s.* satulaseppä. **-ry** [-əri] *s.* satulavarusteet.

sadis|m ['seidizm] *s.* sadismi. **-t** ['seidist] *s.* sadisti. **-tic** [sə'distik] *a.* sadistinen.

sad|ly *adv.* synkästi, surullisesti; kipeästi. **-ness** *s.* surullisuus.

safari [sə'fɑ:ri] *s.* metsästysretki, safari.

safe [seif] *a.* turvallinen, turvassa oleva; varma; vahingoittumaton, eheä, luotettava; vaaraton; *s.* kassakaappi; kylmä kaappi (tav. *meat* ~*);* ~ *and sound* vahingoittumattomana; *at a* ~ *distance* sopivan välimatkan päässä; *to be on the* ~ *side* varmuuden vuoksi.

~-**conduct** turvakirja, kulkulupa.
~-**deposit:** *s.-d. box* tallelokero.
~-**guard** *s.* suoja; *v.* suojella, turvata.
~-**keeping** *s.* säilö, huosta. **-ly** *adv.*
turvallisesti, onnellisesti; huoleti.
safety ['seifti] *s.* turvallisuus, varmuus;
~ *razor* parranajokone; *in* ~ turvassa;
play for ~ olla varovainen. ~-**catch**
varmuuslukko. ~-**curtain** paloverho.
~-**glass** särkymätön lasi. ~-**pin**
hakaneula ~-**valve** *s.* varaventtiili.
saffron ['sæfrən] *s.* sahrami; *a.*
sahraminkeltainen.
sag [sæg] *v.* painua, laskeutua; notkua;
laskea; *s.* painuminen.
saga ['sɑ:gə] *v.* sankaritaru.
sagac|ious [sə'geiʃəs] *a.* älykäs, viisas.
-ity [sə'gæsiti] *s.* terävä-älyisyys.
sage 1. [seidʒ] *a.* salvia (kasv.). **-brush**
marunapensas.
sage 2. [seidʒ] *a.* viisas; *s.* viisas,
filosofi.
sago ['seigəu] *s.* saagosuurimot.
Sahara [sə'hɑ:rə] *erisn.: the* ~ Saharan
erämaa.
sahib ['sɑ:(h)ib] *s.* eurooppalaisen
arvonimi Intiassa, herra.
said [sed] *imp. & pp. ks. say; the* ~
mainittu, puheenaoleva.
Saigon [sai'gɔn] *erisn.*
sail [seil] *s.* purje; purjehdus;
purjealus; (myllyn) siipi; *v.* purjehtia;
lähteä matkalle; liidellä; ohjata
(laivaa); *in full* ~, *under* ~ täysin
purjein; *make* ~ lisätä purjeita; *set* ~
nostaa purjeet; *take in* ~ vähentää
purjeita. ~-**cloth** purjekangas.
sailing *s.* purjehtiminen, purjehdus; ~*s*
laivojen lähtöajat; *plain* ~
yksinkertainen tehtävä. ~-**boat**
purjevene. ~-**ship** purjealus.
sail|or ['seilə] *s.* merimies; *be a bad* ~
olla altis meritaudille. **-plane**
purjelentokone.
sainfoin ['seinfɔin] *s.* esparsetti
(rehukasvi).
saint [seint, lyh. *St* sənt, sin(t), sn(t)]
s. pyhimys; pyhä; *St Paul* apostoli
Paavali. **-ed** [-id] *a.* pyhä,
pyhimykseksi julistettu. **-ly** *a.*
pyhimyksen kaltainen, pyhä, hurskas.
-liness *s.* pyhimyksen kaltaisuus.
saith [seθ] (vanh.) = *says.*
sake [seik] *s.: for my* ~ minun tähteni;

for the ~ *of peace* rauhan vuoksi.
salaam [sə'lɑ:m] *s.* (itämainen)
tervehdys; *v.* tervehtiä.
salable ['seiləbl] *a.* kaupaksi menevä.
salacious ['sə'leiʃəs] *a.* rivo.
salad ['sæləd] *s.* salaatti. ~-**dressing**
salaattikastike.
salamander [sælə'mændə] *s.*
salamanteri.
sal-ammoniac [sælə'məuniæk] *s.*
salmiakki.
salaried ['sælərid] *a.* palkkaa nauttiva;
~ *staff* toimihenkilöt.
salary ['sæləri] *s.* (kuukausi)palkka.
sale [seil] *s.* myynti; menekki;
alennusmyynti, loppuunmyynti;
huutokauppa; *for* ~ myytävänä; *on* ~
kaupan; ~*s promotion* myynnin
edistäminen; ~*s tax* (Am.)
liikevaihtovero; ~ *of work* myyjäiset.
-able ['seiləbl] = *salable.*
sales|man *s.* myyjä, kauppa-apulainen;
(~**ship** *s.* myyntitaito). **-woman** *s.*
myyjätär.
salicylic [sæli'silik] *a.:* ~ *acid*
salisyylihappo.
salient ['seiljənt] *a.* esiinpistävä,
ulkoneva; silmiinpistävä,
huomattava; *s.* rintaman niemeke,
kieleke.
saline ['seiloin] *s.* suolaliuos; *a.*
suolapitoinen, suola-.
Salisbury ['sɔ:lzb(ə)ri] *erisn.*
saliva [sə'laivə] *s.* sylki. **-ry** ['sælivəri] *s.*
sylki-.
sallow 1. ['sæləu] *s.* paju.
sallow 2. ['sæləu] *a.* keltaisenkalvakka,
kalpea.
sally ['sæli] *s.* (ulos)hyökkäys; sutkaus;
v. tehdä hyökkäys; ~ *forth (out)*
lähteä matkaan (retkelle ym).
Salk [sɔ:(l)k] *erisn.*
salmon ['sæmən] *s.* lohi.
Salome [sə'ləumi] *erisn.*
Salonika [ə'lɔnikə] *erisn.* Salonki.
saloon [sə'lu:n] *s.* salonki, sali (esim.
laivassa); baari, kapakka; *billiard* ~
biljardisali; *shaving* ~ parturinliike.
salsify ['sælsifi] *s.* pukinparta (kasv.);
black ~ mustajuuri.
salt [sɔ:lt] *s.* suola; *a.* suola-, suolainen,
suolattu; kirpeä; *v.* suolata, panna
suolaan; *old* ~ merikarhu; *smelling*
~*s* hajusuola; *take [a story] with a*

grain of ~ uskoa varauksin; *worth his* ~ palkkansa arvoinen. ~**-cellar** suola-astia.

salt|petre ['sɔːltpiːtə] *s.* salpietari. **-y** [-i] *a.* suolainen.

salubri|ous [səˈluːbriəs] *a.* terveellinen. **-ty** [-ti] *s.* terveellisyys.

saluta|ry ['sæljutə)ri] *a.* terveellinen; hyödyllinen. **-tion** [-juː)ˈteiʃn] *s.* tervehdys.

salute [səˈluːt] *s.* tervehdys; kunnianteko, kunnialaukaus; *v.* tervehtiä; tehdä kunniaa, ampua kunnialaukauksia; *take the* ~ tarkastaa paraati.

salvage ['sælvidʒ] *s.* (meri)pelastus; pelastettu tavara; pelastuspalkkio; *v.* pelastaa (haaksirikosta, tulipalosta).

salvation [sælˈveiʃn] *s.* (sielun) pelastus; *S~ Army* Pelastusarmeija. **-ist** [-ist] *s.* pelastusarmeijalainen.

salve [sɑːv, sælv] *s.* voide, salva; *v.* voidella, lievittää; [sælv] pelastaa, ks. *salvage*.

salv|er ['sælvə] *s.* tarjotin. **-o** [-əu] *s.* (pl. ~*s*, ~*es*) yhteislaukaus; suosionmyrsky.

Sam [sæm] *erisn.:* Uncle ~ Setä Samuli (= Yhdysvallat); ~ *Browne belt* upseerinvyö.

Samari|a [səˈmeəriə] *erisn.* **-tan** [səˈmæritən] *a. & s.* samarialainen.

same [seim] *a.* sama; samanlainen; *one and the* ~ sama; *at the* ~ *time* samalla (kertaa), samanaikaisesti; kuitenkin; *all (just) the* ~ sittenkin, siitä huolimatta; *it is all the* ~ *to me* se on minusta samantekevää, ei sillä ole väliä; *much the* ~ jotensakin sama; *the very* ~ juuri sama; *the* ~ *to you!* samoin! **-ness** *s.* samankaltaisuus; yksitoikkoisuus.

Samoa [səˈmə(u)ə] *erisn.*

Samoyed [sæmɔiˈed] *s.* samojedi; ~ [*dog*] [sæˈmɔied] samojedinpystykorva.

sample [sɑːmpl] *s.* näyte, malli; tavaranäyte, näytepalanen; *v.* ottaa näyte; maistaa, kokeilla; *up to* ~ näytteen mukainen, vaadittua kokoa ym.; [*random*] ~ otos, otanta. **-r** [-ə] *s.* nimikoimisliina.

Samson ['sæmsn] *erisn.* Simson.

Samuel ['sæmju(ə)l] *erisn.*

sanatorium [sænəˈtɔːriəm] *s.* (pl. m. -*ia*) parantola.

sancti|fication [sæŋ(k)tifiˈkeiʃn] *s.* pyhittäminen, pyhitys. **-fy** ['sæŋktifai] *v.* pyhittää. **-monious** [-ˈməunjəs] *a.* tekopyhä.

sanction ['sæŋ(k)ʃn] *s.* vahvistaminen, hyväksyminen; pakote; *v.* vahvistaa, hyväksyä.

sanct|ity ['sæŋ(k)titi] *s.* pyhyys, loukkaamattomuus. **-uary** [-tjuəri] *s.* pyhäkkö; turvapaikka; *bird* ~ lintujen suojelualue; *take* ~ etsiä suojaa. **-um** [-təm] *s.* pyhäkkö.

sand [sænd] *s.* hiekka; *pl.* hiekkaranta, -särkkä, -aavikko; *v.* hiekoittaa; sekoittaa hiekkaa jhk.

sandal ['sændl] *s.* sandaali, sannikas. **-wood** santelipuu.

sandbag *s.* hiekkasäkki; *v.* suojata hiekkasäkeillä.

sand|man ['sæn(d)-] *s.* nukkumatti. **-piper** *s.. green* ~ metsäviklo. ~**-pit** (lasten) hiekkalaatikko. **-stone** hiekkakivi.

sandwich ['sænwidʒ, -witʃ] *s.* (kaksinkertainen) voileipä; *v.* pistää, likistää jnk väliin. ~**-man** mainosjulisteiden kantaja.

sandy ['sændi] *a.* hiekkainen, hiekka-; hiekanvärinen.

Sandy ['sændi] *s.* (leik.) skotti. **-s** [sændz] *erisn.*

sane [sein] *a.* täysijärkinen, tervejärkinen, viisas; järkevä.

sang [sæŋ] *imp.* ks. *sing.*

sanguin|ary ['sæŋgwinəri] *a.* verinen, verenhimoinen. **-e** ['sæŋgwin] *a.* sangviininen, toiveikas; verevä.

sanit|ary ['sænit(ə)ri] *a.* terveys-, saniteetti-, terveydenhoidollinen; hygieeninen; ~ *towel (napkin)* terveysside. **-ation** ['teiʃn] *s.* terveydenhoito; et. viemärilaitteet, viemäröinti. **-y** ['sæniti] *s.* täysi-, tervejärkisyys.

sank [sæŋk] *imp.* ks. *sink.*

Santa Claus ['sæntəˈklɔːz] *s.* joulupukki.

sap 1. [sæp] *s.* mehu, mahla; elinvoima; sl. tomppeli; *v.* juoksuttaa mahla; kuluttaa loppuun (voimat).

sap 2. [sæp] *s.* juoksukaivanto, taisteluhauta; *v.* kaivaa taisteluhautoja; kaivaa perustukset (jnk alta), heikentää.

sapien|ce ['seipiəns] *s.* viisaus. **-t** [-ənt] *a.* viisasteleva, rikkiviisas.

sap|less ['sæplis] *a.* mehuton, kuiva. **-ling** [-liŋ] *s.* nuori puu, puun taimi; nuorukainen.

sapper [sæpə] *s.* pioneeri.

sapphire ['sæfaiə] *s.* safiiri.

sappy ['sæpi] *a.* mehukas, nuori ja elinvoimainen.

Sarah ['sɛərə] *erisn.* Saara.

sarcas|m ['sɑːkæzm] *s.* pureva iva, pistosana. **-tic** [sɑːˈkæstik] *a.* (purevan) ivallinen.

sarcoma [sɑːˈkoumə] *s.* sarkooma.

sarcophagus [sɑːˈkɔfəgəs] *s.* pl. *-gi* [-gai] sarkofagi.

sardine [sɑːˈdiːn] *s.* sardiini.

Sardinia [sɑːˈdinjə] *erisn.* **-n** [-n] *a. & s.* sardinialainen.

sardonic [sɑːˈdɔnik] *a.* katkeran ivallinen, sardoninen.

sartorial [sɑːˈtɔːriəl] *a.* räätälin-.

sash 1. [sæʃ] *v.* (leveä) vyö; olkavyö.

sash 2. [sæʃ] *s.*: ~ *window* liukuikkuna.

Sassenach ['sæsənæk] *s.* (Skotl. Irl.) englantilainen.

sat [sæt] *imp. & pp.* ks. *sit.*

Satan ['seitn] *s.* saatana.

satanic [səˈtænik] *a.* saatanallinen, pirullinen.

satchel ['sætʃ(ə)l] *s.* (koulu)laukku.

sate [seit] *v.* tyydyttää, täyttää; ~*d* kyllänen.

sateen [sæˈtiːn] *a.* puuvillasatiini.

satellite ['sætəlait] *s.* satelliitti, kiertolainen, tekokuu; satelliittivaltio, seurailija.

satiate ['seiʃieit] *v.* tyydyttää; ~*d* kyllänen; kyllääntynyt.

satiety [səˈtaiəti] *s.* kylläisyys, kyllästymys.

satin ['sætin] *s.* atlassilkki, satiini; silkinsileä; *v.* satinoida.

satir|e ['sætaiə] *s.* satiiri. **-ical** [səˈtirik(ə)l] *a.* satiirinen, pilkallinen. **-ist** ['sætərist] *s.* satiirikko. **-ize** ['sætəraiz] *v.* pilkata.

satis|faction [sætisˈfækʃn] *s.* tyydytys; mielihyvä, ilo; hyvitys; korvaus; *demand* ~ vaatia hyvitystä; *give* ~ tyydyttää, olla mieliksi. **-factory** [-ˈfækt(ə)ri] *a.* tyydyttävä, riittävä.

-fied ['sætisfaid] *a.* tyytyväinen; kyllänen, ravittu; vakuuttunut; *I am* ~ *that* olen vakuuttunut siitä, että. . **-fy** ['sætisfai] *v.* tyydyttää; olla jklle mieleen, täyttää, vastata (jtk); hyvittää; saada vakuuttuneeksi; ~ *oneself* [*of, that*] vakuuttautua, saada varmuus jstk.

satura|te ['sætʃəreit] *v.* kyllästää. **-tion** [-ˈreiʃn] *s.* kyllästäminen, kyllästys.

Saturday ['sætədi] *s.* lauantai.

Saturn ['sætən] *erisn.* Saturnus. **-alian** [-ˈneiliən] *a.* hillitön, remuava. **-ine** [-ain] *a.* hidas, raskas(mielinen), synkkä.

satyr ['sætə] *s.* satyyri.

sauce [sɔːs] *s.* kastike; (puhek.) nenäkkyys; *v.* (puhek.) olla röyhkeä jklle. ~**-boat** kastikemalja. **-pan** [-pən] kasari. **-r** [-ə] *s.* teevati; *flying* ~ lentävä lautanen.

sauciness *s.* nenäkkyys.

saucy ['sɔːsi] *a.* nenäkäs, hävytön; sl. tyylikäs.

Saul [sɔːl] *erisn.* Saul.

saunter ['sɔːntə] *v.* maleksia, kuljeskella; *s.* kävelyretki.

saurian ['sɔːriən] *s.*: ~*s* liskot.

sausage ['sɔsidʒ] *s.* makkara; ~ *roll* makkarapasteija.

savage ['sævidʒ] *a.* villi, sivistymätön, raakalais-; vihainen, raivostunut; *s.* villi-ihminen, raakalainen (m. kuv.); *v.* (hevosesta ym): tallata, polkea, purra. **-ry** [-ri] *s.* luonnonvarainen t. villi tila; raakuus, julmuus.

savanna(h) [səˈvænə] *s.* ruohoaavikko.

savant ['sævənt] *s.* oppinut.

save [seiv] *v.* pelastaa, vapahtaa; säästää; (vanh.) varjella; *prep.* lukuunottamatta, paitsi; ~ *one's breath* pysyä vaiti; ~ *up* panna säästöön.

Savile ['sævil] *erisn.*: ~ *Row* hienojen räätälien katu Lontoossa.

saving ['seiviŋ] *a.* pelastava, sovittava; säästävä; säästö-; *s.* säästäminen; *pl.* säästöt; *prep.* lukuunottamatta; ~ *clause* varaus. **-ly** *adv.* säästäväisesti. **-s-bank** säästöpankki.

saviour ['seiviə] *s.*: *the S*~ Vapahtaja.

savory ['seivəri] *s.* kynteli.

savour ['seivə] *s.* maku; tuntu; vivahdus; *v.*: ~ *of* maistua jltk;

haiskahtaa jllek, vivahtaa jhk. **-y** [-ri] Am.**savory** a. maukas; s.(suolainen ym) alkupala, suolapala (us. aterian päätteeksi).

savoy [sə'vɔi] s. savoijinkaali; S~ Savoiji.

savvy ['sævi] v. sl. hoksata; s. äly, ymmärrys.

saw 1. [sɔ:] imp. ks. see.

saw 2. [sɔ:] s. sananparsi.

saw 3. [sɔ:] s. saha; v. (pp. sawn, Am. ~ed) sahata, huitoa; ~ away at vinguttaa (viulua). **-dust** sahajauhot. **-mill** saha(laitos) **-yer** ['sɔ:jə] s. sahaaja.

saxifrage ['sæksifridʒ] s. kivirikko.

Saxon ['sæksən] a. & s. (anglo)saksilainen. **-y** [-i] erisn. Saksi.

saxophon|e ['sæksəfəun] s. saksofoni. **-ist** [sæk'sofənist] s. saksofoninsoittaja.

say [sei] v. said said; (sg. 3 pers. says [sez]) sanoa; lausua, lukea; väittää; s. sanottava; sananvalta; [let us] ~ .. sanokaamme esimerkiksi; I ~! kuulehan; they ~, it is said sanotaan; that is to ~ toisin sanoen; you don't ~! mitä sanoittekaan! to ~ nothing of puhumattakaan; nothing to ~ for himself ei mitään sanottavaa puolustuksekseen; ~ over toistaa; he had no ~ in the matter hänellä ei ollut mitään sananvaltaa asiassa. **-ing** s. sanonta; sanan-, puheenparsi; it goes without ~ on itsestään selvää.

scab [skæb] s. (haavan) rupi; syyhy, kapi; lakonrikkuri.

scabbard ['skæbəd] s. miekan tuppi.

scabby ['skæbi] a. rupinen; syyhyinen.

scabi|es ['skeibiiːz] s. syyhy. **-ous** [-əs] a. syyhyinen.

scabrous ['skeibrəs] a. rosoinen, karkea; säädyllisyyttä loukkaava, rivo.

scaffold ['skæf(ə)ld] s. rakennustelineet; mestauslava. **-ing** s. telineet; tubular ~ putkitelineet.

scald [skɔ:ld] v. polttaa (kuumalla vedellä, höyryllä); huuhtoa kiehuvalla vedellä; kuumentaa (maito); s. palohaava; ~ing tears katkerat kyynelet; ~ed [almonds] kaltatut.

scale 1. [skeil] s. vaakakuppi; [pair of] ~s vaaka; turn (tip) the ~s ratkaista.

scale 2. [skeil] s. mittakaava, asteikko; skaala (mus.); v. kiivetä, kavuta (tikkailla); kaavoittaa; ~ model pienoismalli; on a large ~ suuressa mittakaavassa; ~ up (down) korottaa, alentaa (asteittain).

scale 3. [skeil] s. suomu(s); hilse; suojuslehti; kattilakivi; v. suomustaa; kuoria, puhdistaa; kesiä, hilseillä (~ off). **-d** [-d] a. suomuinen.

scaling|-down s. vähentäminen. **~-up** korotus, tehostaminen.

scallop ['skɔləp] s. kampasimpukka; simpukankuori (m. ~-shell); pl. pykäläreunus; v. gratinoida (keitt.); koristaa pykäläreunuksella.

scallywag ['skæliwæg] s. hulttio, heittiö (us. leik.).

scalp [skælp] s. päänahka; v. nylkeä jklta päänahka. **-el** [-(ə)l] s. leikkausveitsi (lääk.).

scaly ['skeili] a. suomuinen.

scamp [skæmp] s. lurjus, hulttio; v. hutiloida. **-er** [-ə] v. juosta, pinkaista, pötkiä pakoon, luikkia (~ off); s. juoksu, porhallus.

scan [skæn] v. tarkoin tutkia; skandeerata (runoa); s. (TV) ositus.

scandal ['skændl] s. pahennus, häpeä; häväistys, -juttu; panettelu. **-ize** [-aiz] v. herättää pahennusta, loukata; be ~d at pahentua jstk. **~-monger** juorutäti, juorukello. **-ous** [-əs] a. pahennusta herättävä, häpeällinen; herjaus-.

Scandinavia [skændi'neivjə] erisn. Skandinavia. **-n** [-n] s. & a. skandinaavi, -nen.

scant [skænt] a. niukka. **-ily** adv. niukasti. **-iness** s. niukkuus; puute. **-ling** [-liŋ] s. soiro. **-ty** [-ti] a. niukka, riittämätön; säästeliäs, karu.

scape [skeip] s. vana.

scape|goat ['skeipgəut] syntipukki. **-grace** hulivili.

scar [skɑ:] s. arpi; kalliojyrkänne; v. arpeutua; ~red arpinen; war~red sodan runtelema.

scarab ['skærəb] s. skarabee.

Scarborough ['skɑːbrə] erisn.

scarc|e ['skɛəs] a. niukka, riittämätön; harvinainen; food is ~ ruoasta on puute; make oneself ~ laittautua tiehensä, häipyä. **-ely** adv. tuskin. **-ity**

[-iti] s. niukkuus, vähyys, (jnk) puute.

scare [skeə] v. pelästyttää; s. säikähdys; paniikki. **-crow** [-krəu] linnunpelätin. **-monger** kauhujuttujen kertoja.

scarf 1. [skɑ:f] s. (pl. -ves, -fs) kaulaliina, huivi.

scarf 2. [skɑ:f] s. jatko, liitos; v. jatkaa (limitysten).

scarify ['skɛərifai] v. leikellä, naarmuttaa (ihoa); arvostella purevasti; karhita.

scarlet [skɑ:lit] a. & s. helakanpunainen; ~ fever tulirokko; ~ runner ruusupapu.

scarp [skɑ:p] s. jyrkkä rinne.

scarred [skɑ:d] a. arpinen.

scathe [skeið] s. & v.: scathing musertava, murhaava; pureva. **-less** a. vahingoittumaton.

scatter ['skætə] v. sirotella, sirottaa; hajottaa; tehdä tyhjäksi; tuhlata; hajaantua; ~ed hajallaan, erillään, harvassa oleva. **~-brain(ed)** hupakko.

scavenge ['skævindʒ] v. puhdistaa (katu). **-r** [-ə] s. haaskaeläin; kadun|lakaisija, -puhdistuskone.

scenario [si'nɑ:riəu] s. (elokuvan) käsikirjoitus.

scene [si:n] s. tapahtumapaikka, näyttämö; kohtaus, kuvaelma; näkymä; pl. näyttämökoristeet, kulissit; the ~ closes esirippu laskee; the ~ is laid in tapahtumapaikkana on; change of ~ ympäristön vaihdos; behind the ~s kulissien takana; make a ~ panna toimeen kohtaus. **-ry** [-əri] s. näyttämökoristeet; maisema, luonto. **~-shifter** kulissimies.

scenic ['si:nik] a. näyttämöllinen, näyttämö-, teatteri-.

scent [sent] v. haistaa, vainuta; aavistaa; levittää tuoksua, hajua jhk; s. haju, tuoksu; hajuvesi; vainu; (otuksen) jäljet; on the ~ jäljillä; put off the ~ eksyttää. **~-bottle** hajuvesipullo. **-ed** [-id] a. parfymoitu, tuoksuva; keen~ tarkkavainuinen. **-less** a. hajuton.

sceptic ['skeptik] s. epäilijä, skeptikko. **-al** [-əl] a. epäilevä, skeptinen. **-ism** ['skeptisizm] s. skeptisyys.

sceptre, -ter ['septə] s. valtikka.

schedule ['ʃedju:l, Am. 'skedʒl] s. luettelo; taulukko, aikataulu; v.

merkitä luetteloon, taulukkoon; on ~ aikataulun mukaisesti, täsmälleen määräaikana.

schematic [ski'mætik] a. kaava-, kaavio-.

schem|e [ski:m] s. kaava; järjestelmä; suunnitelma; ehdotus, luonnos; juoni, vehkeily; v. laatia suunnitelma; juonitella, vehkeillä. **-er** [-ə] s. juonittelija, vehkeilijä. **-ing** a. juonitteleva.

Schenectady [ski'nektədi] erisn.

schism ['sizm] s. skisma, uskonriita; hajaannus. **-atic** [siz'mætik] a. hajaannusta lietsova.

schist [ʃist] s. liuske.

schizophrenia [skitsə(u)'fri:njə] s. jakomielitauti.

scholar ['skɔlə] s. oppinut, tiedemies; stipendiaatti; (vanh.) koululainen; (puhek.) lukumies; a Latin ~ Latinan tutkija. **-ly** a. oppinut; tieteellisen perinpohjainen. **-ship** s. stipendi; oppineisuus.

scholastic [skə'læsti|k] a. koulu-, opetus-; turhantarkka; skolastinen. **-ism** [-sizm] s. skolastiikka.

school 1. [sku:l] s. (kala)parvi.

school 2. [sku:l] s. koulu, opisto; koulukunta; tiedekunta; ~ s m. tutkinto; v. opettaa, harjoittaa; pitää kurissa; kouluttaa; at ~ koulussa; go to ~ käydä koulua. **-boy**, **-girl** koulupoika, -tyttö. **~-days** koulu-uleika. **-fellow**, **-mate** koulutoveri. **-ing** s. koulutus, kouluopetus. **~-ma'am**, **-marm** [mɑ:m] s. (leik.) opettajatar. **-master** (koulun)opettaja. **-mistress** naisopettaja. **-teacher** (kansa)koulunopettaja.

schooner ['sku:nə] s. kuunari.

sciatic [sai'ætik] a.: ~ nerve lonkkahermo. **-a** [-ə] s. iskias.

scien|ce ['saiən|s] s. tiede; [natural] ~ luonnontiede; tieto, teoria; ~ fiction tieteisromaani. **-tific** [-'tifik] a. tieteellinen; tiede-. **-tist** [-tist] s. tiedemies; luonnontieteilijä.

Scilly ['sili] erisn.

scimitar ['simitə] s. käyräsapeli.

scintillate ['sintileit] v. säkenöidä, välkkyä, tuikkia.

scion ['saiən] s. vesa, pistokas; jälkeläinen.

scissors ['sizəz] s. pl. sakset (m. a pair of ~).

sclerosis [sklə'rəusis] s. skleroosi (lääk.).

scoff [skɔf] v.: ~ at pilkata, pitää jkta pilkkanaan; s. pilkka. **-er** [-ə] pilkkaaja. **-ingly** adv. pilkallisesti.

scold [skəuld] v. torua, nuhdella, pauhata; s. äkäpussi. **-ing** s. torumiset, läksytys.

scollop ['skɔləp] = scallop.

sconce [skɔns] s. lampetti.

scone [skɔn, skəun] s. eräänl. teeleipä.

Scone [sku:n] erisn.

scoop [sku:p] s. kauha, äyskäri; (jauho)lapio; (hyvä) kaappaus, jymyuutinen; v. ammentaa, tyhjentää; (sl.) korjata voitto, kahmaista, kaapata (uutinen).

scoot [sku:t] v. juosta, luikkia tiehensä. **-er** [-ə] s. potkulauta; (motor) ~) skooteri.

scope [skəup] s. ulottuvuus, ala, alue, puitteet; liikkumatila, -vara, toiminta-ala; . . of wide ~ laajakantoinen; is beyond the ~ of a child ylittää lapsen mahdollisuudet.

scorbutic [skɔ:'bju:tik] a. keripukkia sairastava.

scorch [skɔ:tʃ] v. kärventää, polttaa; kärventyä; ajaa hurjaa vauhtia; ~ed earth policy poltetun maan taktiikka. **-er** [-ə] s. polttavan kuuma päivä; vauhtihirmu.

score [skɔ:] s. lovi, uurre; pistemäärä, m. maali (jalkap.); laskun erä; kaksikymmentä, tiu; lasku, tili, velka; partituuri; v. uurtaa, piirtää; merkitä viivalla, alleviivata (~ under); merkitä tileihin; merkitä pisteet, saada pisteitä, tehdä maali; what is the ~? mikä on pistetilanne? on that ~ sen asian suhteen; on the ~ of jstk syystä; on a new ~ uudestaan; a long ~ pitkä velkaluettelo; three ~ and ten 70 vuotta; ~s of joukoittain; pay off old ~s maksaa vanhoja kalaveloja; ~ a success saavuttaa menestys; ~ off nolata; ~ out pyyhkiä pois. **-r** [-ə] s. (pisteiden) merkitsijä, markööri; maalin tekijä.

scoria ['skɔ:riə] s. (pl. -iae [-ii:]) kuona.

scorn [skɔ:n] s. ylenkatse, v. halveksia, ylenkatsoa; pilkata; laugh . . to ~ pitää

pilkkanaan. **-ful** a. halveksiva, ylenkatseellinen; pilkallinen.

scorpion ['skɔ:pjən] s. skorpioni.

Scot [skɔt] s. skotlantilainen, skotti.

scotch [skɔtʃ] v. (vanh.) tehdä vaarattomaksi, haavoittaa.

Scotch [skɔtʃ] a. skotlantilainen; s. Skotlannin murre; (skotlantilainen) viski; the ~ skotlantilaiset. **-man** skotlantilainen. **-woman** skotlannitar.

scot-free [skɔtfri:] a. rankaisematon, vahingoittumaton; go ~ päästä rankaisematta.

Scotland [skɔtlənd] erisn. Skotlanti; ~ Yard Lontoon poliisin päämaja.

Scots [skɔts] s. skotit; skotlannin murre; a. skotlantilainen.

-man ks. Scotsman.

Scott|icism ['skɔtisizm] s. skotlantilainen sana t. puheenparsi.

-ish ['skɔtiʃ] a. & s. = Scotch.

scoundrel ['skaundr(ə)l] s. konna, roisto. **-ly** a. roistomainen.

scour 1. ['skauə] v. puhdistaa, kiillottaa, hangata; huuhtoa puhtaaksi; s. hankaaminen, puhdistus; ~er patasuti.

scour 2. ['skauə] v. etsiä (kaikkialta); ~ the woods tutkia metsä läpikotaisin.

scourge [skə:dʒ] s. vitsaus, rangaistus; (vanh.) ruoska; v. kurittaa, rangaista.

scout 1. [skaut] s. tiedustelija, tiedustelukone (t. -laiva); liikenteen valvoja; miespalvelija (Oxf.); v. tiedustella; [boy] ~ partiopoika; girl ~ (Am.) partiotyttö (Engl. girl guide).

scout 2. [skaut] v. hylätä, torjua (halveksivasti).

scout|ing s. tiedustelu; partiotoiminta. **-master** partiojohtaja.

scow [skau] s. lotja.

scowl [skaul] v. rypistää kulmiaan, katsoa tuimasti (at, on jkh); s. murjotus, tuima t. synkkä katse.

scrabble ['skræbl] v. töhertää, raapustaa.

scrag [skræg] s. laiha, hintelä olento; sl. kaula. **-gy** [-i] a. ruipelo, luiseva.

scramble ['skræmbl] v. kavuta, kiivetä; ryömiä; (~ for) tavoitella jtk, tapella jstk; s. kapuaminen; tavoittelu, kilparyntäys, tappelu (for jstk);

~ *d eggs* munakokkeli. **-r** [ə] *s.* puheensekoitin.

scrap [skræp] *s.* pala, hitunen; lehtileikelmä; *attr.* jäte-; romu, hylkytavara; *pl.* lehtileikkeet, (valo-, kiilto)kuvat ym; tähteet; *v.* hylätä kelvottomana, romuttaa; tapella; ~ *iron* rautaromu. ~**-book** leikekirja.

scrap|**e** [skreip] *v.* raapia, hangata; kaapia, raapaista (jalkaa); kitkuttaa (viulua); kirskua; *s.* raapiminen; ~ [*up*] *an acquaintance* hieroa tuttavuutta; ~ *through* läpäistä töin tuskin; ~ *together* haalia kokoon; *get into a* ~ joutua pinteeseen. **-er** [-ə] *s.* kaavinrauta. **-ing:** ~*s* raappeet.

scrappy [ˈskræpi] *a.* epäyhtenäinen, kokoonhaalittu.

scratch [skrætʃ] *v.* kynsiä, raapia, naarmuttaa; repiä; ~ naarmu, piirto; raaputus; lähtöviiva, nolla pistettä (urh.); *a.* kokoonhaalittu, sekalainen, tilapäinen; ~ *along* alkaa kituuttaa; *was not up to* ~ petti odotukset; *start from* ~ lähteä (kilpailuun) ilman tasoitusta, alkaa tyhjästä; ~ [*race*] ilman tasoitusta. **-y** [-i] *a.* raapiva; huolimattomasti tehty, kokoonkyhätty.

scrawl [skrɔːl] *v.* raapustaa; *s.* harakanvarpaat, töherrys.

scrawny [ˈskrɔːni] *a.* laiha, ruipelo.

scream [skriːm] *v.* kirkua, huutaa; *s.* kirkaisu, parkaisu; äärimmäisen hullunkurinen olento t. asia. **-er** [-ə] *s.* hullunkurinen juttu. **-ing** *a.* kirkuva; hullunkurinen, verraton.

screech [skriːtʃ] *v.* huutaa, kirkua kiljua. ~**-owl** (Am.) sieppopöllö.

screen [skriːn] *s.* varjostin; suojus, irtoseinä, suojaverkko; valkokangas; kuvapinta, -ruutu; karkea seula; *v.* suojella; peittää, peitellä; sovittaa valkokankaalle; elokuvata; seuloa; tutkia, ottaa selville (jkn menneisyys ym); *smoke* ~ savuverho; ~ *play* filmatisointi; ~ *off* erottaa väliseinällä. **-ing** *s.* (joukkuepeleissä) miesvartiointi.

screw [skruː] *s.* ruuvi; potkuri; tötterö; saituri; sl. palkka; koni; *v.* ruuvata, kiertää; kiinnittää ruuvilla; kiristää (*out of* jklta); ahdistaa; olla sukupuoliyhteydessä jkn kanssa; ~ *up*

kiertää kiinni; ~ *up one's courage* rohkaista mielensä; ~ *thread* ruuvinkierteet. **-ed** [-d] *a.* sl. hutikassa, kännissä. ~**-driver** ruuvitaltta. ~**-topped** kierrekantinen.

scribble [ˈskribl] *v.* töhertää, raapustaa, kyhätä kokoon; *s.* töherrys. **-r** [-ə] *s.* tuhertaja, (mitätön) kynäilijä.

scribe [skraib] *v.* kirjuri; kirjanoppinut.

scrimmage [ˈskrimidʒ] *s.* yhteenotto; kahakka (m. jalkap.).

scrimp [skrimp] *v.* = *skimp.*

scrip [skrip] *s.* väliaikainen osakekirja; (vanh.) laukku.

script [skript] *s.* (elokuva-, TV-) käsikirjoitus; kirjoituskirjake; ~ *girl* kuvaussihteeri. **-ural** [-ʃ(ə)r(ə)l] *a.* raamatun-. **-ure** [-ʃə] *s.:* *S*~[*s*] Pyhä kirja, raamattu.

scrofula [ˈskrɔfjulə] *s.* risatauti.

scroll [skroul] *s.* (pergamentti)käärö; kierukka(koriste). **-ed** [-d] *a.* kierukoilla koristettu.

scrounge [ˈskraundʒ] *v.* anastaa, kähveltää.

scrub 1. [skrʌb] *v.* hangata, pestä (harjalla ja saippualla); *s.* kuuraus.

scrub 2. [skrʌb] *s.* (kitukasvuisten puitten muodostama) pensaikko; ~**-pine** kääpiömänty. **-by** [-bi] *a.* kitukasvuinen, vaivais-.

scruff [skrʌf] *s.:* ~ *of the neck* niska(villat). **-y** [-i] *a.* nuhruinen.

scrummage [ˈskrʌmidʒ] *s.* ks. *scrimmage.*

scrumptious [ˈskrʌm(p)ʃəs] *a.* (puhek.) herkullinen.

scruple [ˈskruːpl] *s.* painomitta (1,29 g); (omantunnon) epäilys, empiminen; *v.* empiä, häikäillä; *have* ~*s about* arkailla (tehdä jtk); *a man of no* ~*s* häikäilemätön mies.

scrupul|**osity** [skruːpjuˈlɔsiti] *s.* tunnollisuus. **-ous** [ˈskruːpjuləs] *a.* tunnontarkka, tunnollinen; (pikku)tarkka.

scrutin|**ize** [ˈskruːtinaiz] *v.* tarkoin tutkia, tarkastella. **-y** [-ni] *s.* tarkka tutkimus, tarkistus.

scuba [ˈskuːbə] *s.* (urheilu)sukeltajan paineilmalaitteet.

scud [skʌd] *v.* kiittää, pyyhkäistä (ohi, yli).

scuff [skʌf] v. laahata.

scuffle ['skʌfl] s. tappelu, meteli; v. tapella, olla käsikähmässä; ~s metelöinti.

scull [skʌl] s. airo, mela; v. meloa, soutaa.

scullery ['skʌləri] s. astiainpesuhuone.

sculp|tor ['skʌlptə] s. kuvanveistäjä. **-tress** [-tris] s. (nais)kuvanveistäjä. **-tural** [-tʃər[ə]l] s. kuvanveisto-. **-ture** [-tʃə] s. kuvanveisto(taide); veistos; v. veistää, muovata.

scum [skʌm] s. kuohu, vaahto; kuona; roskaväki; v. kuoria vaahtoa.

scupper ['skʌpə] s. (mer.) valumisreikä; v. upottaa; sl. tuhota.

scurf [skə:f] s. hilse. **-y** [-i] a. rupinen, hilseilevä.

scurril|ity [skə'riliti] s. törkeys. **-ous** ['skʌriləs] a. karkea, törkeä, rivo.

scurry [skʌri] v. juosta, kipittää; s. hoppu, hätäily, ryntäys.

scurvy ['skə:vi] s. keripukki; a. alhainen, ilkeä, katala.

scutcheon ['skʌtʃən] s. = escutcheon.

scuttle 1. ['skʌtl] s.: [coal-] ~ hiilisanko.

scuttle 2. ['skʌtl] s. luukku; v. upottaa (avaamalla laivan venttiilit tms.).

scuttle 3. ['skʌtl] v. luikkia, pötkiä pakoon.

scythe [saið] s. viikate.

sea [si:] s. meri; (hyöky)aalto, aallokko, merenkäynti; at ~ merellä, (kuv.) ymmällä, neuvoton; by ~ meritse; heavy ~ ankara merenkäynti; the high ~s aava meri; go to ~ lähteä merille, ruveta merimieheksi; put [out] to ~ lähteä vesille; ~ front ranta; S~ Lord amiraliteetin jäsen. **-board** merenrannikko. **~-calf** hylje. **~-dog** hylje; vanha merikarhu. **-faring** a. purjehtiva; s. merenkulku. **~-front** merenranta. **~-going** valtameri-. **~-gull** lokki. **~-horse** merihevonen (kala). **~-legs:** get one's s.-l. saada meritottumusta. **~-lion** merileijona.

seal 1. [si:l] s. hylje.

seal 2. [si:l] s. sinetti; leima; leimasin; vahvistus; v. varustaa sinetillä, leimata; vahvistaa, sinetöidä; sulkea (~ up), tiivistää; his fate is ~ed hänen

kohtalonsa on ratkaistu, sinetöity.

sealer ['si:lə] s. hylkeenpyytäjä; hylkeenpyyntialus.

sealing ['si:liŋ] s. sinetöinti. **~-wax** sinettilakka.

sealskin s. hylkeennahka.

seam [si:m] s. sauma; liitos, juotos; pitkä arpi; (geol.) juonne; v. ommella sauma, yhdistää saumalla; saumata.

seaman ['si:mən] s. merimies; ordinary ~ puolimatruusi. **-like** a. hyvän merimiehen (kaltainen). **-ship** s. purjehdustaito.

seam|stress ['semstris] s. ompelija. **-y** ['si:mi] a. ~ side nurja puoli; the ~ side of life elämän ankeus.

Sean [ʃɔ:n] erisn.

seance ['seiɑ:(ŋ)s] s. istunto.

sea|-piece merimaisema (maalaus). **-plane** vesitaso. **-port** satama(kaupunki). **~-power** merivalta.

sear [siə] v. polttaa, kärventää; paahduttaa, kovettaa.

search [sə:tʃ] v. etsiä, hakea tarkoin; tutkia, tarkastaa; s. etsintä, tutkiminen, tarkastus; ~ a house toimittaa kotietsintä; ~ out hakea käsiinsä, saada selville; ~ one's memory kaivella muistiaan; be in ~ of etsiä jtk; personal ~ ruumiintarkastus. **-ing** a. tutkiva, läpitunkeva; perinpohjainen. **-light** valonheitin.

sea|scape merimaisema. **-shore** merenranta. **-sick** merisairas. **-sickness** meritauti. **-side** merenrannikko; at the ~ rannikolla.

season ['si:zn] s. vuodenaika; kausi; sopiva aika; sesonki, huvi-, kylpykausi; v. kypsyttää, kuivata (puutavaraa); totuttaa; höystää, maustaa; kypsyä; in ~ oikeaan aikaan, ajallansa; strawberries are in ~ on mansikka-aika; out of ~ sopimattomaan aikaan; ~ed kypsä, kuiva; ~ ticket kausilippu. **-able** [-əbl] a. (vuodenaikaan)sopiva, oikeaan aikaan saatu. **-al** ['si:zənl] a. vuodenajan mukainen, kausiluonteinen. **-ing** s. höyste, mauste.

seat [si:t] s. istuin, istumapaikka; pesäpaikka, tyyssija, sijainti; (teatt.)

paikka; edustajanpaikka (parl.);
takapuoli; *v.* asettaa istumaan, antaa
istua; osoittaa istumapaikka; sijoittaa;
varustaa istuimilla; *country* ~
kartano; ~ *of learning* opinahjo; *have
a good* ~ istua hyvin satulassa; *take a*
~ istuutua; **-ed** [-id] *a.: be* ~ istua;
deep-~ syvälle juurtunut. **~-belt**
turvavyö, varmuusvyö. **-er** [-ə] *s.:
two-*~ kahden hengen auto ym.
Seattle [si'ætl] *erisn.*
sea|-urchin merisiili. **~-wall** rantapato.
-weed merilevä. **-worthy**
merikelpoinen.
sebaceous [si'beiʃəs] *a.* tali-.
sece|de [si'si:d] *v.* erota, luopua. **-ssion**
[-'seʃn] *s.* eroaminen, luopuminen.
seclu|de [si'klu:d] *v.* sulkea pois,
erottaa; ~ *d* erillään oleva, syrjäinen,
yksinäinen; ~ *d life* erakoelämä.
-sion [-'klu:ʒn] *s.* poissulkeminen;
eristyneisyys, yksinäisyys.
second [*'sek*(ə)nd] *a.* toinen, seuraava;
s. toinen (järjestyksessä), lähin mies;
todistaja (kaksintaistelussa); sekunti;
pl. toisen luokan (t. sekunta)tavara;
v. kannattaa, puoltaa, avustaa;
[si'kɔnd] komentaa toisiin tehtäviin
(sot.); *every* ~ joka toinen; ~ *best*
lähinnä paras; ~ *in command*
(päällikön) lähin mies; ~ *nature*
»toinen luonto»; ~ *sight*
selvänäköisyys; *on* ~ *thoughts* asiaa
harkittuaan (-ani); *be* ~ *to none* vetää
vertoja kenelle tahansa. **-ary** [-(ə)ri]
a. toisarvoinen; toisen luokan; sivu-,
lisä-; toinen; ~ *education*
oppikouluopetus; ~ *school*
oppikoulu. **-er** [-ə] *s.* kannattaja.
~-hand toisen käden; käytetty,
vanha, antikvaarinen; *buy s-h.* ostaa
käytettynä t. antikvariaatista. **-ly** *adv.*
toiseksi. **~-rate** toisen luokan.
secrecy [*'si:krisi*] *s.* salaperäisyys;
vaitiolo, vaiteliaisuus; *in* ~ salassa;
bound to ~ vaitiolovelvollinen.
secret [*'si:krit*] *a.* salainen, sala-; *s.*
salaisuus; ~ *service* salainen
tiedustelupalvelu; *in* ~ salassa; *an open*
~ julkinen salaisuus; *keep.* . ~ pitää
salassa. **-arial** [sekrə'tɛəriəl] *a.*
sihteerin-. **-ariat** [sekrə'tɛəriət] *s.*
sihteeristö. **-ary** [*'sekrətri*] *s.* sihteeri;
S~ of State ministeri; (Am.)

Yhdysvaltain ulkoministeri; *Foreign
S~*, *Home S~* ulkoasiain-,
sisäasiainministeri; ~ *-general*
pääsihteeri.
secre|te [si'kri:t] *v.* erittää; kätkeä.
-tion [si'kri:ʃn] *s.* eritys; erite. **-tive**
[*'si:kritiv*] *a.* sala|peräinen,
-myhkäinen. **-tory** [-əri] *a.* eritys-.
secretly *adv.* salassa, salaa.
sect [sekt] *s.* (uskon)lahko. **-arian**
[-'tɛəriən] *s.* lahkolainen; (~**ism** *s.*
lahkolaisuus).
section [*'sekʃn*] *s.* leikkaus;
poikkileikkaus; osa, kappale; osasto,
jaosto, luokka; (hedelmän) lohko;
pykälä; kaupunginosa; *v.* leikata
poikki; *microscopic* ~
mikroskooppinen valmiste; ~ *mark*
pykälänmerkki. **-al** [-ənl] *a.* osaston,
piiri-, paikallis-; (osista) koottava.
sector [*'sektə*] *s.* sektori, lohko.
secular [*'sekjulə*] *a.* maailma|llinen,
-nmielinen, maallinen, ajallinen. **-ism**
[-rizm] *s.* maallmallisuus. **-ize** [-raiz]
v. maallistaa.
secur|e [si'kjuə] *a.* turvallinen,
turvattu, varma; tallessa oleva,
suojattu; lujasti kiinni, tukeva; *v.*
varmistaa, lujittaa; sulkea lukkojen
taakse, kiinnittää (lujasti); turvata,
taata; hankkia itselleen, onnistua
saamaan, saada. **-ity** [-riti] *s.*
turvallisuus, varmuus; vakuus, takuu,
takaaja; (tav. *pl.*) arvopaperit; *S~
Council* turvallisuusneuvosto.
sedan [si'dæn] *s.* iso umpiauto; ~
[*chair*] kantotuoli.
sed|ate [si'deit] *a.* tyyni, levollinen,
hillitty. **-ative** [*'sedətiv*] *s.* rauhoittava
lääke. **-entary** [*'sednt(ə)ri*] *a.*
paikallaan istuva, istuma-.
sedge [sedʒ] *s.* sara-, -heinä.
sediment [*'sedimənt*] *s.* sakka. **-ary**
[*'mentəri*] *a.* kerrostunut. **-ation**
[-men'teiʃn] *s.: ~ rate* (veren)
laskeutumisarvo »senkka».
sedi|tion [se'diʃn] *s.* kapinahenki,
kapinanlietsonta. **-tious** [-ʃəs] *a.*
kapinallinen.
seduc|e [si'dju:s] *v.* houkutella;
vietellä. **-er** [-ə] *s.* viettelijä. **-tion**
[si'dʌkʃn] *s.* vietteleminen, *pl.*
viettelykset. **-tive** [si'dʌktiv] *a.*
houkutteleva.

sedulous ['sedjuləs] *a.* uuttera.

see 1. [si:] *s.* piispanistuin, hiippakunta; *the Holy S~* paavinistuin, pyhä istuin.

see 2. [si:] *saw seen*, *v.* nähdä; huomata; havaita; ymmärtää, käsittää; kokea, olla (jnk) todistajana; käydä jkn luona, ottaa vastaan (vieras), tavata; pitää huolta, huolehtia; katsoa, ottaa selvä; *I ~* ymmärrän, aivan niin; *.. you ~* näetkös; *as far as I can ~* ymmärtääkseni; *I do not ~ my way* en tiedä mitä tehdä; *~ page 15* ks. siv. 15; *~ sb. home* saattaa kotiin; *go to ~ a p.* mennä jkta tervehtimään; *he ~s nobody* hän ei seurustele kenenkään kanssa; *~ into* tutkia; *~ a p. off* saattaa (asemalle ym); *~ out* katsoa jtk loppuun asti, saattaa ulos; *~ over* käydä katsomassa, tarkastaa; *~ through* auttaa jkta selviytymään, hoitaa (asia) loppuun; *~ to* huolehtia, hoitaa, valvoa; *~ to it that* pidä huolta että; *he ~s (is seeing) things* hänellä on näköharhoja; *let me ~* annahan kun mietin.

seed [si:d] *s.* (pl. *~ s.* t. sama) siemen; kylvö(siemen), *v.* siementyä; kylvää; poistaa siemenet jstk; (et. tennis) erotella parhaat pelaajat huonommista; *run to ~* kuihtua, käydä nukkavieruksi. **~-cake** kuminakakku. **~-corn** siemenvilja. **-ed** [-id] *a.* siemenetön; ks. *seed* (tennis). **~-leaf** sirkkalehti. **-less** *a.* siemenetön. **-ling** [-liŋ] *s.* taimi. **~-potatoes** siemenperunat. **-sman** *s.* siemenkauppias. **-y** [-i] *a.* kulunut, nukkavieru, rapistunut; (puhek.) masentunut, huonovointinen.

seeing ['si:iŋ] *konj.*: *~ [that]* koska, ottaen huomioon että.

seek [si:k] *sought sought*, *v.* hakea, etsiä; tavoitella; pyytää; koettaa; *~ out* etsiä käsiinsä; *sought-after* haluttu.

seem [si:m] *v.* näyttää, tuntua; *so it ~s* siltä näyttää; *it ~s to me [that]* nähdäkseni.., minusta näyttää, tuntuu (siltä että). **-ing** *a.* näennäinen. **-ingly** *adv.* näennäisesti. **-ly** *a.* sopiva, säädyllinen.

seen [si:n] *pp.* ks. *see*.

seep [si:p] *v.* tihkua.

seer ['si(:)ə] *s.* tietäjä, ennustaja.

seesaw ['si:sɔ:] *s.* keinunta; keinulauta; *attr.* keinuva; *v.* keinua, kiikkua.

seethe [si:ð] *v.* kuohua, kiehua.

segment ['segmənt] *s.* lohko; segmentti, leike; (anat.) jaoke.

segrega|te ['segrigeit] *v.* erottaa, eristää; eristäytyä. **-tion** [-'geiʃn] *s.* erottaminen, erottelu.

seine [sein] *s.* nuotta.

seis|mic ['saizmik] *a.* maanjäristys-. **-mograph** [-məgrɑːf] *s.* seismografi.

seiz|e [si:z] *v.* tarttua, ottaa kiinni, siepata; vallata, ottaa saaliiksi; takavarikoida; (tekn.) takertua, juuttua (*~ up*); *be ~d with* joutua jnk valtaan; *~ [upon] a chance* ottaa tilaisuudesta vaarin. **-ure** ['si:ʒə] *s.* anastaminen, valtaus; takavarikointi; kohtaus.

seldom ['seldəm] *adv.* harvoin.

select [si'lekt] *a.* valikoitu; mainio, valio-, ensiluokkainen; *v.* valikoida, valita; *S~ committee* valiokunta. **-ion** [-kʃn] *s.* valinta; valikoima. **-ive** [-iv] *a.* selektiivinen. **-ivity** [-'tiviti] *s.* valikoivuus, selektiivisyys.

self [self] *s.* (pl. *selves*) minä, (oma) itse; *pron.* ks. *my~* jne. **~-assertion** itsevarmuus, itsetehostus. **~-centred** [-'sentəd] itsekeskeinen. **~-command** itsehillintä. **~-confident** itsevarma. **~-conscious** itsetajuinen (psyk.); vaivaantunut, hämillinen. **~-contained** *a.* erillinen, riippumaton; umpimielinen. **~-control** itsehillintä. **~-defence** itsepuolustus. **~-denial** itsensä kieltäminen. **~-determination** itsemääräämisoikeus. **~-educated** itseoppinut. **~-effacing** syrjään vetäytyvä. **~-employed** itsenäinen yrittäjä. **~-evident** *a.* itsestään selvä, (aivan) ilmeinen. **~-explanatory** itsestään selvä. **~-government** itsehallinto. **~-help** oma apu. **~-immolation** *by fire* polttoitsemurha. **~-important** omahyväinen. **~-indulgent** nautinnonhaluinen, mukavuutta rakastava. **~-inflicted** itse(nsä) aiheuttama.

selfish ['selfiʃ] *a.* itsekäs. **-ness** *s.* itsekkyys.

selfless *a.* epäitsekäs.
self|-locking automaattisesti
sulkeutuva. **~-made:** *he is a s.-m.
man* hän on itse luonut asemansa.
~-possessed hillitty, rauhallinen.
~-possession itsehillintä, maltti.
~-preservation itsesäilytys.
~-realization itsensä toteuttaminen.
~-reliance itseluottamus. **~-respect**
itsekunnioitus. **~-restraint**
itsehillintä. **~-righteous**
omahyväinen. **~-sacrifice** *s.*
uhrautuvaisuus. **~-same:** *the* ~ aivan
sama. **~-satisfied** omahyväinen.
~-seeking itsekäs. **~-service**
itsepalvelu-. **~-starter**
(automaatti)käynnistin. **~-sufficiency**
omavaraisuus; itserakkaus.
~-supporting riippumaton, itsensä
elättävä; omavarainen. **~-taught**
itseoppinut. **~-willed** itsepäinen.
sell [sel] *sold sold, v.* myydä (m. kuv.);
mennä kaupaksi; (tav. pass.)
petkuttaa; *s.* (puhek.) pettymys *(what
a ~!); it ~s well* sillä on hyvä
menekki; ~ *off,* ~ *out* myydä loppuun
(varasto); ~ *out* (m.) myydä
osuutensa, osakkeensa; ~ *up* myydä
(jkn omaisuus) pakkohuutokaupalla;
[I've] been sold. . on petkutettu; *be
sold on* olla ihastunut jhk; **-er** [-ə] *s.*
myyjä; *best ~* menekkikirja **~-out**
petos.
selvage ['selvidʒ] *s.* hulpio.
selves [selvz] *pl.* ks. self.
semantics [si'mæntiks] *s.*
merkitysoppi.
semaphore ['seməfɔ:] *s.* semafori.
semblance ['sembləns] *s.* ulkonäkö;
hahmo, muoto.
semen ['si:men] *s.* siemenneste.
semester [si'mestə] *s.* et. Am.
lukukausi.
semi- ['semi-] *pref.* puoli-. **-breve**
[-bri:v] *s.* kokonuotti. **-circular** *a.*
puoliympyrän muotoinen. **-colon** *s.*
puolipiste. **~-detached** *a.* puoleksi
erillinen. **-final** *s.* välierä.
~-manufactured goods
puolivalmisteet.
seminal ['seminl] *a.* siemen-;
herätteitä antava.
seminar ['semi|na:] *s.* seminaari
(yliop.) **-y** [-nəri] *s.* katol.

pappisseminaari.
Semit|e ['semait, 'si:m-] *s.*
seemiläinen. **-ic** [si'mitik] *a.* = ed.
semolina [semə'li:nə] *s.*
mannasuurimot.
sempstress ks. *seamstress.*
senat|e ['senit] *s.* senaatti. **-or** ['senətə]
s. senaattori.
send [send] *sent sent, v.* lähettää;
lennättää, panna (tekemään jtk);
(vanh.) suoda; ~ *flying* ajaa
pakosalle, lennättää menemään; ~
mad (crazy) tehdä hulluksi; ~ *down*
erottaa määräajaksi; ~ *for* lähettää
noutamaan; ~ *forth* levittää, kasvaa
(oksia); ~ *in* jättää (anomus ym); ~
off lähettää; ~ *on* lähettää edelleen;
~ . . . *up* (sl.) tehdä naurunalaiseksi,
pilkata. **-er** [-ə] *s.* lähettäjä.
Senegal [seni'gɔ:l] *erisn.*
senescent [se'nesnt] *a.* vanheneva.
senil|e ['si:nail] *a.* vanhuuden, -heikko,
höperö. **-ity** [si'niliti] *s.*
vanhuudenheikkous.
senior ['si:njə] *a.* vanhempi; *a.* (jkta)
vanhempi henkilö, vanhin; ~ [*man*]
vanhempi opiskelija; ~ *partner*
liikkeen johtaja; *he is 2 years my* ~
hän on kaksi vuotta minua vanhempi.
-ity [si:ni'ɔriti] *s.* vanhemmuus;
(suurempi) virkaikä.
sensation [sen'sei∫n] *s.* aisti, aistimus,
tunne; sensaatio, kohu; *create a* ~
herättää valtavaa huomiota. **-al** [-ənl]
a. suurta huomiota herättävä,
sensaatiomainen, kohu-, jymy-.
sense [sens] *s.* aisti; taju, tunto,
vaikutelma; järki, ymmärrys;
merkitys; mielipide; *v.* aistia, aistimin
havaita; vaistota, tajuta; *the five ~s*
viisi aistia; ~ *of beauty* kauneudentaju
~ *of duty* velvollisuudentunto;
common ~ terve järki; *good* ~ hyvä
ymmärrys t. arvostelukyky *in a* ~
eräässä mielessä; *make* ~ olla
järkevää, mielekästä; *it doesn't make*
~ siinä ei ole mitään tolkkua; *come to
one's ~s* tulla järkiinsä; *have you
taken leave of your ~s?* oletko
järjiltäsi! **-less** *a.* tajuton, järjetön,
mieletön.
sensibility [sensi'biliti] *s.* herkkyys,
herkkä tunto, herkkätunteisuus (us.
pl.)

sensible ['sensəbl] a. järkevä, ymmärtäväinen; tietoinen (of jstk); aistimin havaittava. **-ness** s. järkevyys.

sensitiv|e ['sensitiv] a. herkkä (to jllek), arka (about jstk), vastaanottavainen; herkkätuntoinen, -tunteinen; valonherkkä (filmi); ~ to criticism arka arvostelulle. **-eness, -ivity** [-'tiviti] s. herkkyys.

sens|itize ['sensitaiz] v. tehdä (valon)herkäksi. **-ory** ['sensəri] a. aistin-, tunto-; aistinelinten; ~ disturbance m. aistivamma.

sensual ['senʃuəl, sensjuəl] a. aistillinen. **-ism** [-izm], **-ity** [-'æliti] s. aistillisuus.

sensuous ['sensjuəs] a. aisteihin vaikuttava, aisti-; aisti-iloinen.

sent [sent] imp. & pp. ks. send.

senten|ce ['sentəns] s. lause; tuomio; v. tuomita; pass ~ langettaa tuomio. **-tious** [sen'tenʃəs] a. mietelauseita sisältävä, saarnaava.

sentient ['senʃnt] a. tunteva.

sentiment ['sentimənt] s. tunne; tunteellisuus; mielipide. **-al** [-'mentl] a. tunne-; (liika)tunteellinen, tunteileva. **-ality** [-men'tæliti] s. (liika)tunteellisuus, sentimentaalisuus.

sentinel ['sentinl] s. vartiomies.

sentry ['sentri] s. vartiomies; on ~-go vartiossa. ~-**box** vahtikoju.

sepal ['sepəl] s. verholehti.

separable ['sep(ə)rəbl] a. erotettavissa oleva.

separa|te ['sepəreit] s. erottaa; irrottaa; jakaa; erota, lähteä irti: separoida (maito); a. ['seprit] erillään oleva, erillinen; **-tely** adv. erikseen. **-tion** [-'reiʃn] s. erottaminen, eroaminen, ero; asumusero. **-tism** ['sep(ə)rətizm] s. eristäytymispyrkimys. **-tor** [-ə] s. separaattori.

sepia ['si:pjə] s. seepia(väri).

sepoy ['si:pɔi] s. hindusotilas.

sepsis ['sepsis] s. verenmyrkytys.

September [sep'tembə] s. syyskuu.

septic ['septik] a. septinen (lääk.).

septuagenarian [septjuədʒi'neəriən] a. seitsenkymmenvuotias.

sepulchral [si'pʌlkr(ə)l] a. hauta-, hautajais-, haudankolea.

sepul|chre, -cher ['sep(ə)l|kə] s. hauta(kammio). **-ture** [-tʃə] s. hautaus.

se|quel ['si:kw(ə)l] s. jatko, seuraus; in the ~ sittemmin. **-quela** [si'kwi:lə] s. (pl. ~ e [-i:]) jälkitauti. **-quence** ['si:kwəns] s. jakso, sarja; järjestys, peräkkäisyys.

sequest|er [si'kwest|ə] v. erottaa, eristää; takavarikoida; ~ oneself from the world vetäytyä erilleen maailmasta; ~ed syrjäinen, yksinäinen. **-rate** [-reit] v. takavarikoida. **-ration** [-'reiʃn] s. takavarikointi.

sequin ['si:kwin] s. sekiini (raha); paljetti.

sequoia [si'kwɔiə] s. mammuttipetäjä.

seraph ['serəf] s. serafi.

Serb [sə:b] s. serbi(alainen). **-ia** [-jə] erisn. **-ian** [-jən] a. & s. serbialainen, serbian kieli.

sere [siə] a. kuivettunut.

serenade [seri'neid] s. serenadi; v. laulaa (soittaa) s. jklle.

seren|e [si'ri:n] a. seesteinen, tyyni ja kirkas, selkeä, rauhallinen. **-ity** [si'reniti] s. seesteisyys, tyyneys, rauha.

serf [sə:f] s. maaorja. **-dom** s. maaorjuus.

serge [sə:dʒ] s. sarssi (kangas).

sergeant ['sɑ:dʒənt] s. kersantti, ylikonstaapeli; master ~ ylivääpeli.

serial ['siəriəl] a. sarja-; s. jatkokertomus, sarjafilmi. **-ize** [-aiz] v. julkaista, t. esittää (sarjan) osina. **-ly** adv. jaksoittain, jatkokertomuksena.

series ['siəri:z] s. (pl. = sg.) sarja, jakso.

series ['siəriəs] a. vakava, totinen; merkittävä; arveluttava. **-ly** adv. vakavasti; ~ speaking v. puhuen. **-ness** s. vakavuus.

serjeant ['sɑ:dʒ(ə)nt] s.: S~ -at Armes järjestyksenvalvoja.

sermon ['sə:mən] s. saarna; nuhdesaarna. **-ize** [-aiz] v. saarnata.

serous ['siərəs] a. (veri)herainen.

serpent ['sə:p(ə)nt] s. käärme. **-ine** [-ain] a. kiemurteleva.

serrated [se'reitid] a. sahalaitainen.

serried ['serid] a. tiheä, tiivis.

serum ['siərəm] *s.* (veri)hera, seerumi.

servant ['sə:v(ə)nt] *s.* palvelija; *public* ~ valtion virkamies.

serve [sə:v] *v.* palvella, olla (sota)palveluksessa; vastata jtk, sopia, hyödyttää, kelvata, riittää; tarjoilla, jaella (ruokaa); toimia, olla (*as* jnak), toimittaa (haaste); syöttää (tennis); syöttö (tennis); ~ *one's time* kärsiä rangaistuksensa; ~ *on a committee* olla komitean jäsenenä; ~*s to show it* osoittaa (että); *that* ~ *s him right* se on hänelle parahiksi; *that will* ~ *as a warning* se on varoitukseksi; *the wind* ~*d us* tuuli oli suotuisa; *dinner is* ~*d* päivällinen on katettu; ~ *out* jakaa. **-r** ['sə:və] *s.* tarjoilija; [*salad*] ~*s* lusikat.

service ['sə:vis] *s.* palvelus, palvelu, palvelut; ase-, sotapalvelus; virantoimitus, virka; jumalanpalvelus; tarjoilu; pöytäkalusto, astiasto; (laiva- ym) vuoro, kulkuvuorot; puolustushaara; (sot.) syöttö (tennis); *v.* huoltaa; *branch* (t. *arm*) *of* ~ aselaji; *civil* ~ siviilihallinto; *public* ~ *s* yleiset (et. teknilliset) laitokset; *social* ~ *s* sosiaalihuolto, -palvelut; *youth* ~ nuorisotyö; *at your* ~ käytettävissänne; *on* ~ virantoimituksessa; *be of* ~ *to* olla hyödyksi, avuksi jklle; *a good* ~ *of trains* hyvät junayhteydet; *fit for* ~ asekuntoinen; ~ *aircraft* sotilaslentokone; ~ *entrance* keittiönovi; ~ *flat* huoneisto palvelutalossa; ~ *industries* palveluelinkeinot. **-able** [-əbl] *a.* käyttökelpoinen, kestävä. **-man** rintamamies. ~**-pipe** talonjohto (vesi- t. kaasu-). ~**-station** huoltoasema, huoltamo.

serviette [sə:vi'et] *s.* lautasliina.

servil|e ['sə:vail] *a.* orjamainen, orjallinen, nöyristelevä. **-ity** [sə:'viliti] *s.* orjamaisuus.

servitude ['sə:vitju:d] *s.* orjuus.

sesame ['sesəmi] *s.* seesam(i).

session ['seʃn] *s.* istunto; lukukausi; *pl.* käräjät; *is in* ~ istuu.

set 1. [set] *set set, v.* panna, asettaa, sijoittaa: asettaa sijoilleen; sovittaa, säännellä, panna kuntoon, määrätä;

kehystää, koristaa (jalokivillä ym); istuttaa; saattaa kovettumaan, hyydyttää, kiinnittää; teroittaa; panna tekemään jtk; lujittaa, vakiintua; kovettua, hyytyä, jäykistyä; tehdä hedelmää; (auringosta ym) laskea, mennä mailleen; *pp.* paikoilleen asetettu: määrätty, varma, säädetty; jähmettynyt, jäykkä, kiinteä, liikkumaton, tuijottava; järkkymätön; vakiintunut, muodollinen; ~ *sb. an example* olla esimerkkinä jklle; ~ *going* panna liikkeelle; ~ *one's heart on* ottaa sydämenasiakseen; ~ *the pace* määrätä vauhti; ~ *the questions* [*for an examination*] laatia tutkintokysymykset; ~ *the table* kattaa; ~ *one's teeth* purra yhteen hampaansa; ~ *a trap* virittää ansa; ~ *to music* sävseltää; ~ *type* latoa (kirjap.); ~ *about* ryhtyä jhk; ~ *against* verrata jhk, yllyttää jtk vastaan; ~ *apart* panna erilleen, talteen; ~ *aside* panna syrjään, jättää huomioonottamatta, (lak.) hylätä; ~ *at ease* rauhoittaa; ~ *at nothing* halveksia; ~ *back* ehkäistä, siirtää taaksepäin; ~ *down* kirjoittaa muistiin; lukea jnk syyksi, ansioksi, pitää jnak; ~ *forth* esittää, kuvata; lähteä liikkeelle; ~ *forward* siirtää eteenpäin, esittää; ~ *in* alkaa; ~ *off* lähteä: tehostaa (jkn vaikutusta), saada jku (puhumaan jstk); räjäyttää, laukaista; ~ *on* kiihottaa, usuttaa; hyökätä kimppuun; ~ *out* lähteä, ryhtyä; suunnitella, asettaa esille; ~ *to* ryhtyä jhk; ~ *up* pystyttää; perustaa (liike), auttaa perustamaan (liike); päästää (huuto ym); latoa (kirjap.); ~ *oneself up as* olla olevinaan jtk; *be well* ~ *up* olla hyvin varustettu: *well* ~ *up* [*figure*] ryhdikäs; ~ *upon* hyökätä kimppuun; *a* ~ *phrase* vakiintunut puhetapa; *be* ~ *against* pontevasti vastustaa; ~ *books* kurssikirjat; *at the* ~ *time* määräaikaan; *he is* ~ [*up*] *on* hän on varmasti päättänyt, hän haluaa sydämestään; *have one's hair* ~ kampauttaa tukkansa.

set 2. [set] *s.* kokoelma, astiasto, kalusto, (vaatekerrasto); kerta, sarja, jakso, ryhmä, joukko, seurue, nurkkakunta, (seura)piiri; lavastus, lavasteet; kuvauspaikka; istukas, vesa; (tuulen ym) suunta; suuntaus; (tennis) erä; asento; *a toilet ~* toalettivälineet; *the smart ~* ks. *smart; ~ theory* joukko-oppi; *~ of teeth* tekohampaat; *condiment ~* mausteikko; *radio ~* radiovastaanotin; *make a dead ~ at* hyökätä (voimakkaasti) jtk vastaan.

set-back takaisku. **~-down** nolaus. **-piece** huolella valmistettu esitys; eräänl. lavaste. **-square** kulmaviivoitin.

sett [set] *s.* katukivi.

settee [se'ti:] *s.* (pieni) sohva.

setter ['setə] *s.* setteri.

setting *a.* laskeva; *s.* asettaminen; sovitus, musiikki; (jalokiven) kehys, puitteet; näyttämöllepano; ympäristö; kovettuminen, hyytyminen; *~ lotion* kampausneste. **~-in** alku.

settle 1. ['setl] *s.* puusohva.

settl|e 2. ['setl] *v.* asettaa, sijoittaa (pysyvästi), kiinnittää; vakiinnuttaa; määrätä; päättää; järjestää; sovittaa (riita), suorittaa (maksu), tilittää; asuttaa; rauhoittaa, selvittää (neste); asettua (vakituisesti); asettua asumaan, (*~ down*) asettua aloilleen, vakiintua; päättyä; laskeutua; (nes eestä) selvitä; *that's ~d* asia on päätetty; [*that*] *~s the matter* ratkaisee asian; *~ to work* keskittyä, ryhtyä työhön; *~ down to married life* avioitua. **-ed** [-d] *a.* määrätty, päätetty, sovittu; maksettu; vakiintunut, vakava; pysyvästi asuva; *~ weather* pysyvästi kaunis sää. **-ement** *s.* määrääminen; suoritus; sopimus; (uudis)asutus, siirtokunta; jklle määrätty rahasumma, eläke, elinkorko ym; setlementti, yhteiskunnallinen työkeskus. **-er** [-ə] *s.* siirtolainen; uudisasukas. **-ing** *s.* ratkaiseminen; selvitys.

set|-to ['set'tu:] tappelu, sanakiista. **~-up** järjestely, organisaatio.

seven ['sevn] *lukus.* seitsemän; *s.* seitsikko. **-fold** *a.* seitsenkertainen; *adv.* s-kertaisesti. **-teen** [-'ti:n] *lukus.* seitsemäntoista. **-th** [-θ] *lukus.*

seitsemäs, -osa. **-tieth** [-tiəθ] *lukus.* seitsemäskymmenes. **-ty** [-ti] *lukus.* seitsemänkymmentä.

sever ['sevə] *v.* erottaa, katkaista; erota.

several ['sevr(ə)l] *a.* erillinen, erityinen, eri; *pron.* useat, monet. **-ly** *adv.* (kukin) erikseen.

severance ['sevər(ə)ns] *s.* erottaminen; *~ pay* eroraha.

sever|e [si'viə] *a.* ankara, kova; raaka; karu (tyyli ym); *~ly* ankarasti, pahasti (haavoittunut ym). **-ity** [si'veriti] *s.* ankaruus.

sew [səu] *v.* (pp. *sewn, sewed*) ommella; nitoa (kirja); *~ on* ommella jhk (nappi); *~ up* ommella yhteen t. umpeen.

sewage ['sju:idʒ] *s.* viemärivesi; *~ worker* puhtaanapitotyömies, roskakuski.

sewer ['sjuə] *s.* viemäri. **-age** [-ridʒ] *s.* viemäröinti.

sewing ['səu(i)iŋ] *s.* ompelu(työ); *~-machine* ompelukone.

sewn [səun] *pp.* ks. *sew.*

sex [seks] *s.* sukupuoli; seksi; *~ appeal* sukupuolinen viehätysvoima. **-y** [-i] *a.* seksikäs.

sexagenarian [seksədʒi'nɛəriən] *s.* kuusikymmenvuotias.

sexless ['sekslis] *a.* suvuton.

sext|ant ['sekst(ə)nt] *s.* sekstantti. **-et (te)** [-'tet] *s.* sekstetti.

sexton ['sekstən] *s.* suntio.

sexual ['sekʃuəl] *a.* sukupuoli-; *~drive* sukupuolivietti. **-ity** [-'æliti] *s.* sukupuolisuus.

shabby ['ʃæbi] *a.* nukkavieru; kehno, kurja.

shack [ʃæk] *s.* hökkeli, röttelö; *~ up with, ~ together* asua jkn kanssa.

shackle ['ʃækl] *s.* *~s* käsiraudat, kahleet; *v.* kahlita.

shad [ʃæd] *s.* pilkkusilli.

shade [ʃeid] *s.* varjo, siimes; varjostin; (väri) vivahdus; hiven, hivenen verta; *v.* varjostaa, himmentää; *~ off* sulautua (*into* jksk); *be thrown into the ~ (by)* jäädä jkn varjoon.

shadow ['ʃædəu] *s.* varjo; unikuva, aavistus; *v.* varjostaa (m. kuv.); *a ~ cabinet* varjohallitus; *~s under the eyes* mustat silmänaluset; *without a ~*

of doubt ilman pienintäkään epäilystä.
-y [-ə(u)i] a. varjoisa; hämärä.
shady ['ʃeidi] a. varjoisa; epäilyttävä, hämäräperäinen.
shaft [ʃɑːft] s. varsi; nuoli; aisa; akseli, runko; kaivos-, hissikuilu; pylväs, pylvään varsi.
shag [ʃæg] s. eräänl. karkea tupakka. **-gy** [-i] a. takkuinen, pörröinen; tuuhea.
shagreen [ʃægˈriːn] s. šagriininahka.
shah [ʃɑː] s. šaahi.
shake [ʃeik] shook shaken, v. pudistaa, ravistaa, ravistella; järkyttää, horjuttaa; heikontaa; vapista, täristä, väristä; s. puhdistus, ravistus; tärinä, värinä; järkytys; ~ hands with puristaa jkn kättä; ~ in one's shoes tutista pelosta; ~ up ravistaa (hereille), pöyhiä; in two ~s käden käänteessä; is no great ~ (sl.) ei ole paljon mistään kotoisin; milk ~ maitopirtelö. **-down** tilapäinen vuode. **-r** [-ə] s. sekoitin.
Shakespeare ['ʃeikspiə] erisn. **-an** [-ˈpiəriən] a. & s. Shakespearen (tutkija).
shaky ['ʃeiki] a. vapiseva, tärisevä; horjuva; hatara; epävarma.
shale [ʃeil] s. savi, -kivi.
shall [ʃæl] apuv. (imp. should) käytetään futuuria muod.; ilmaisee pakkoa, ehtoa, epävarmuutta ym; ~ I open the window? avaanko ikkunan? he says he won't go, but I say he ~ hän sanoo, ettei hän mene, mutta minä sanon, että hänen täytyy.
shallot [ʃəˈlɔt] s. šalottesipuli.
shallow ['ʃæləu] a. matala, laakea; pintapuolinen, pinnallinen; s. kari, matalikko; v. madaltua.
shalt [ʃælt] v. (vanh.) 2. pers. prees. ks. shall; thou ~ not. . sinun ei pidä . .
sham [ʃæm] v. teeskennellä, olla olevinaan; s. petkutus, teeskentely, väärennys, jäljennös; huijari; a. väärä, jäljitelty; teko-, vale-; ~ illness tekeytyä sairaaksi.
shamateur ['ʃæmətə:] s. sala-ammattilainen. **-ism** sala-ammattilaisuus.
shamble ['ʃæmbl] v. laahustaa.
shambles ['ʃæmblz] s. teurastuspaikka, verilöyly; sekasorto.

shame [ʃeim] s. häpeä, häpy; v. saattaa häpeään, tuottaa häpeää jklle, häväistä; for ~! hyi, häpeä! (m. ~ on you!); put to ~ saattaa häpeään; what a ~! mikä vahinko! **-faced** a. ujo, arka, häpeilevä. **-ful** a. häpeällinen. **-less** a. häpeämätön, julkea.
shammy ['ʃæmi] s. säämiskä.
shampoo [ʃæmˈpuː] s. tukanpesu, sampoo; ~ and set pesu ja kampaus.
shamrock ['ʃæmrɔk] s. apilanlehti (Irlannin kansallinen tunnus).
Shanghai [ʃæŋˈhai] erisn.; s~ (juottaa humalaan ja) viedä laivaan merimieheksi.
shandy ['ʃændi] s. (m. ~ gaff) oluen ja (inkivääri)limonadin sekoitus.
shank [ʃæŋk] s. sääri; varsi; on S~'s mare jalkapatikassa.
shan't ['ʃɑːnt] lyh. = shall not.
shantung [ʃænˈtʌŋ] s. raakasilkki.
shanty ['ʃænti] s. koju, hökkeli, röttelö; ~-**town** hökkelikylä.
shape [ʃeip] s. muoto, hahmo; kunto, järjestys; kaava, malli, muotti; hyytelö (muotissa); v. muovata, muodostaa; muodostua, muotoutua; take ~ hahmottua. **-less** a. muodoton, muotopuoli. **-ly** a. sopusuhtainen, kaunismuotoinen.
shard [ʃɑːd] s. siru.
share [ʃɛə] s. osa, osuus; osake; auranterä, v. jakaa; olla osallisena, olla mukana (in jssk); go ~s jakaa tasan, tasata. **-holder** osakas.
shark [ʃɑːk] s. hai; huijari.
sharp [ʃɑːp] a. terävä; selväpiirteinen, jyrkkä; kirpeä; kimeä, pistävä, pureva; tarkka; nopea, ripeä; älykäs, sukkela; ovela, viekas; adv. terävästi jne.; täsmälleen; s. (mus.) risti, ylennetty nuotti; (puhek.) = sharper; ~ is the word! joudu! look ~! pidä kiirettä! ~ practice metku, huijaus; at 7,30 ~ täsmälleen puoli kahdeksalta; C~ cis. **-en** [-n] v. teroittaa, hioa; tehdä kirpeämmäksi; käydä terävämmäksi. **-ener** [-nə] s. teroitin. **-er** [-ə] s.: [card-]~ (kortti)huijari. **-ness** s. terävyys jne. **-set** a. nälkäinen, nälkiintynyt. **-shooter** tarkka-ampuja. ~-**sighted** tarkkanäköinen. ~-**witted** teräväpäinen.

shatter [´ʃætə] v. pirstoa, murskata; järkyttää; tuhota; mennä pirstaleiksi, särkyä; ~ed health murtunut terveys; nerve~ ing hermoja vihlova.

shave [ʃeiv] v. ajaa (partansa); leikata, vuolla; hipaista; s. parranajo, hipaisu; ~ past viistää ohi; have a ~ ajaa, ajattaa partansa; by a close (narrow) ~ hädin tuskin, täpärästi. -n pp., a.: well-~ sileäksi ajeltu. -r [-ə] s.: [dry-] ~ parranajokone.

Shavian [´ʃeivjən] a. & s. G. B. Shawn (ihailija).

shaving [´ʃeiviŋ] s. parranajo; pl. lastut. ~-brush partasuti. ~-cream partavaahdoke.

Shaw [ʃɔ:] erisn.

shawl [ʃɔ:l] s. hartiahuivi.

she [ʃi:, ʃi] pron. hän (fem.; m. aluksesta, maasta); a. naaras-; ~-cat naaraskissa.

sheaf [ʃi:f] s. (pl. sheaves) lyhde; nippu.

shear [ʃiə] v. (pp. m. shorn) keritä (lampaita ym); riistää (of jtk) s.: ~s isot sakset, keritsimet.

sheath [ʃi:θ, pl. -ðz] s. tuppi (m. anat.); suojus. -e [ʃi:ð] v. panna tuppeen.

sheaves [ʃi:vz] pl. ks. sheaf.

Sheba [´ʃi:bə] erisn. Saba.

shed 1. [ʃed] s. vaja, katos; (karja)suoja.

shed 2. [ʃed] shed shed, v. vuodattaa, valaa; levittää, luoda (valoa, nahkansa); varistaa, pudottaa; vähentää (vaatteita), luopua (aatteista).

sheen [ʃi:n] s. loisto, kiilto. -y [-i] a. kiiltävä.

sheep [ʃi:p] s. (pl. = sg.) lammas; make ~ s eyes at luoda lemmekkäitä silmäyksiä jkh. ~-dip lampaiden desinfioimiseen, -allas. ~-farming lampaanhoito. ~-fold lammastarha. -ish [-iʃ] a. ujo, hämillinen; lammasmainen. ~-run lammaslaidun. ~-shearing keritsemisaika. ~-skin lammastalja; pergamentti; Am. diplomi.

sheer 1. [ʃiə] a. puhdas, silkka, pelkkä; kohtisuora, äkkijyrkkä; adv. (kohti)suoraan.

sheer 2. [ʃiə] v. mutkailla, poiketa suunnasta; ~ off lähteä tiehensä,

(from) paeta jkta.

sheet [ʃi:t] s. lakana; (ohut) levy, laatta, folio; (paperi)arkki; jalus (mer.); ~ of flame tulimeri; ~ anchor vara-ankkuri; ~ copper kuparilevy; ~ iron (ohut)teräslevy ~ lightning pintasalama, elosalama. -ing s. lakanakangas.

Sheffield [´ʃefi:ld] erisn.

sheik(h), [ʃeik] s. šeikki.

Sheila [´ʃi:lə] erisn.

shekel [´ʃekl] s.: ~ s (sl.) raha, kolikot.

shelf [ʃelf] a. (pl. shelves) hyllly; kallionkieleke; riutta; on the ~ »hyllyllä».

shell [ʃel] s. kuori, äyriäinen, simpuk|ka, -ankuori; kranaatti; tykinammus; (rakennuksen) runko; v. kuoria, silpiä; tulittaa (tykeillä); ampua; ~ splinter (fragment) kranaatinsirpale. -ac [ʃə´læk] s. kumilakka. ~-fish kuoriaiseläin, simpukka. ~-shock »kranaattikauhu», sotaneuroosi.

shelter [ʃeltə] s. suoja, turva; turvapaikka; suojanpuoli; katos; väestönsuoja (air-raid ~); v. suojata, suojella; pitää luonaan, ottaa suojiinsa; etsiä suojaa; take ~ suojautua. -ed [-d] a. suojattu, suojainen.

shelve [ʃelv] v. asettaa hyllylle, varustaa hyllyillä; panna syrjään, lykätä; v. viettää, olla kalteva. -s pl. ks. shelf.

shenandigan(s) [ʃi´nændigæn] s. metku(t).

shepherd [´ʃepəd] s. paimen; v. paimentaa; ~ 's purse lutukka (kasv.). -ess [-is] s. paimentyttö.

sherbet [´ʃə:bət] s. sorbetti, mehujäätelö.

sherd [ʃə:d] = shard.

sheriff [´ʃerif] s. (kreivikunnan) šeriffi; Am. šeriffi, poliisimestari.

sherry [´ʃeri] s. šerry.

she's [ʃi:z] lyh. = she is, she has.

Shetland [´ʃetlənd] erisn.: the ~ s Shetlannin saaret.

shew [ʃəu] v. (vanh.) = show. -bread s näkyleipä (raam.).

shibboleth [´ʃibəleθ] s. puolueen iskulause.

shield [ʃi:ld] s. kilpi; suoja, turva;

suojain, suojustin, suojus, suojalevy; *v.* suojata, suojella.

shift [ʃift] *v.* muuttaa, vaihtaa, siirtää; muuttua, vaihtua, siirtyä; kääntyä; suoriutua; *s.* muutos, vaihto; keino, neuvo; juoni, temppu; (työ)vuoro; ~ *one's ground* muuttaa kantaansa; ~ *for oneself* suoriutua omin neuvoin; ~ *off* [a burden] siirtää, vierittää (toisen niskoille); *the scene* ~ *s* näyttämö vaihtuu; *make* ~ suoriutua, tulla toimeen jotenkuten; *work in* ~ *s* tehdä vuorotyötä; *in three* ~ *s* tehdä kolmessa vuorossa. **-less** *a.* neuvoton, avuton. **-y** [-i] *a.* viekas, ovela.

shilling [ʃiliŋ] *s.* šillinki.

shilly-shally [ʃiliʃæli] *s.* (~*ing*) epäröinti; *v.* epäröidä, olla kahden vaiheilla, soutaa ja huovata.

shimmer [ʃimə] *v.* hohtaa, kimmeltää; *s.* välke.

shin [ʃin] *s.* sääriluu; *v.: ~ up* kavuta jhk; ~ *-guard* säärensuojus.

shindy [ʃindi] *s.* meteli.

shine [ʃain] *shone shone, v.* loistaa, paistaa; kiiltää, hohtaa; (puhek.; pp. *shined*) kiillottaa; *s.* loisto, kiilto; päivänpaiste; (sl.) meteli; ~ *at* olla etevä jssk; *rain or* ~ satoipa tai paistoi.

shingle 1. [ʃiŋgl] *s.* kattopäre, paanu; mainoskilpi; lyhyt leikkotukka; *v.* kattaa paanuilla; leikata lyhyeksi, šinglata.

shingle 2. [ʃiŋgl] *s.* somerikko, rantasora.

shingles [ʃiŋglz] *s.* vyöruusu.

shiny [ʃaini] *a.* kiiltävä, kirkas; kiiltäväksi kulunut.

ship [ʃip] *s.* laiva; *v.* laivata; ottaa, lastata laivaan; pestata laivaan, pestautua; astua laivaan; ~ *'s company* laivan miehistö; ~ *water* saada laine laivaan; ~ *off* lähettää. **-board:** *on* ~ laivassa. **~-broker** meklari. **-load** laivanlasti(llinen). **-mate** laivakumppani. **-ment** *s.* laivaus. **-owner** laivanvarustaja. **-per** [-ə] *s.* laivaaja. **-ping** *s.* (jnk maan) laivat, tonnisto; laivaliikenne; ~ *agent* laivausasiamies. **-shape** *adv.* hyvässä järjestyksessä. **~-way** (laivan) rakennusalusta. **-wreck** [ʃiprek] *s.* haaksirikko; *v.* tuhota; *be*

~ *ed* tehdä haaksirikko. **-wright** [-rait] laivanrakentaja. **-yard** laivanveistämö.

shire [ʃaiə] *s.* kreivikunta, tav. suffiksina nimissä: *-shire* [-ʃiə, -ʃə].

shirk [ʃə:k] *v.* vältellä, kaihtaa, pakoilla, »pinnata». **-er** [-ə] »pinnari».

shir(r) [ʃə:] *v.* rypyttää.

shirt [ʃə:t] *s.* (miehen) paita; paitapusero; *keep your* ~ *on* älähän kiihdy; *in his* ~ *-sleeves* paitahihasillaan. **~-front** paidanrinnus. **-ing** *s.* paitakangas.

shit [ʃit] *s.* (alat.) paska; sl. hasis.

shiver 1. [ʃivə] *s.* pirstale, siru; *v.* pirstoa, pirstoutua.

shiver 2. [ʃivə] *v.* väristä, vapista; *s.* väristys, puistatus; *gives me the* ~ *s* karmii selkäpiitäni.

shoal 1. [ʃəul] *s.* kalaparvi; liuta, lauma.

shoal 2. [ʃəul] *s.* matalikko; *pl.* (kuv.) karikot.

shock 1. [ʃɔk] *s.* kuhilas.

shock 2. [ʃɔk] *s.* kuontalo.

shock 3. [ʃɔk] *s.* isku, kolaus, tärskäys; järkytys; (lääk.) šokki; *v.* järkyttää, kauhistuttaa; šokeerata; *electric* ~ sähköisku, -šokki; ~ *absorber* iskunvaimennin; ~ *troops* iskujoukot; *be* ~ *ed at* järkyttyä. **-er** [-ə] *s.* kauhuromaani. **-ing** *a.* pöyristyttävä, pahennusta herättävä, järkyttävä; (puhek.) hirveän huono, kehno; (~*ly* pöyristyttävän, hirveän).

shod [ʃɔd] *imp.* & *pp.* ks. shoe.

shoddy [ʃɔdi] *s.* lumppukangas; *a.* kehno.

shoe [ʃu:] *s.* kenkä (et. puoli-); hevosenkenkä; jarrukenkä; *v.* (shod, shod) kengittää; raudoittaa; ~ *trees* lestit. **-black** kengänkiillottaja. **-horn** kenkälasta. **~-lace** kengännauha. **-maker** suutari. **-shine** Am. kengänkiillotus.

shone [ʃɔn, Am. ʃəun] *imp.* & *pp.* ks. shine.

shoo [ʃu:] *v.* (~*ed*) hätistää; *int.* huis! pois!

shook [ʃuk] *imp.* ks. shake.

shoot [ʃu:t] *shot shot, v.* ampua; metsästää; heittää; syöksyä, kiitää; viilettää (ohi ym); versoa, työntää, kasvaa (versoja); työntyä, pistää

esiin; vihloa; näpätä (kuva), kuvata;
s. vesa; kouru, liukurata;
metsästysseurue; ~ a glance at luoda
silmäys jhk; ~ a rapid laskea koskea;
~ forth työntyä esiin, puhjeta; ~ off
pinkaista (tiehensä, matkaan),
laukaista; ~ up kasvaa (nopeasti)
pituutta, nousta huimasti; ~ing pain
viiltävä kipu; ~ing star tähdenlento.
shooting ['ʃuːtiŋ] s. ammunta;
metsästys; metsästysoikeus, alue.
~-**box** metsästysmaja. ~-**gallery**
ampumarata.

shop [ʃɔp] s. kauppa, myymälä;
työpaja, verstas; v. käydä ostoksilla
(go ~ping); closed ~ tehdas, joka
käyttää vain järjestäytynyttä työväkeä
(vastak. open ~); talk ~ puhua
ammattiasioista; ~ assistant
liikeapulainen, shop on sb. ilmiantaa.
-**keeper** kauppias. -**lifter**
myymälävaras. -**ping** s. ostokset; go ~
tehdä ostoksia; ~ bag ostoslaukku; ~
centre ostoskeskus. -**py** [-i] a.
kauppa-, ammatti-. ~-**steward**
(pää)luottamusmies. -**walker**
(tavaratalon) opas.

shore 1. (vanh.) imp. ks. shear.
shore 2. [ʃɔː] s. tuki, pönkkä; v.: ~ sth.
up pönkittää.
shore 3. [ʃɔː] s. ranta on ~ maissa; on
the ~ rannalla.

shorn [ʃɔːn] pp. ks. shear.

short [ʃɔːt] a. lyhyt, -aikainen; vajaa;
riittämätön, niukka; töykeä,
lyhytsanainen; murea, kuohkea;
sekoittamaton, väkevä (juoma); adv.
lyhyesti, äkkiä; s. pl. šortsit, lyhyet
housut; ~ measure vajaa mitta; ~
sight lyhytnäköisyys; ~ story novelli;
~ temper kärsimättömyys; . . is ~ for
on lyhennys nimestä . . ; ~ of breath
hengästynyt; be ~ of olla jtk vailla; be
~ with olla töykeä jklle; anything ~ of
kaikkea muuta paitsi; come (fall) ~ of
pettää (odotukset), olla riittämätön;
cut ~ katkaista äkkiä; make ~ work of
tehdä pikainen loppu jstk; pull up ~
seisahtua äkkiä; run ~ olla
loppumassa; stop ~ pysähtyä äkkiä;
he stops ~ of nothing hän ei häikäile
mitään; for ~ lyhyesti; in ~ lyhyesti,
sanalla sanoen. -**age** ['ʃɔːtidʒ] s.
puute, niukkuus. -**bread** muroleivos.

~-**circuit** oikosulku. -**coming** puute,
vajavaisuus. ~-**cut** oikotie. ~-**dated**
lyhytaikainen. -**en** ['ʃɔːtn] v. lyhentää;
vähentää; lyhetä, vähetä. -**ening** s.
(leipomiseen käyt.) rasva. -**fall**
vajaus. -**hand** pikakirjoitus.
~-**handed** vailla riittävää miehistöä,
työvoimaa. ~-**lived** lyhytaikainen. -**ly**
adv. lyhyesti; pian, piakkoin; ~ before
vähän ennen. -**ness** s. lyhyys ym.
~-**sighted** lyhytnäköinen.
~-**tempered** äkkipikainen. ~-**term**
lyhytaikainen, lyhyen tähtäimen;
varhais-. ~-**winded** helposti
hengästyvä.

shot 1. [ʃɔt] imp. & pp. ks. shoot; a.
vivahteleva, läikehtivä.
shot 2. [ʃɔt] s. laukaus, m. heitto,
yritys, arvaus; tykinkuula; ammus;
ampuja; (urh.) kuula; lääkeruiske;
kuva; haulit; like a ~ kuin
ammuttuna; off like a ~ nuolen
nopeudella; have a ~ at yrittää; put
the ~ työntää kuulaa; not by a long ~
ei likimainkaan. ~-**gun** haulikko.
~-**put** kuulantyöntö.

should [ʃud, ʃəd] v. imp. & kondit. ks.
shall; you ~ not . . sinun ei pitäisi . . ; if
he ~ come jos hän sattuisi tulemaan.

shoulder ['ʃəuldə] s. hartia, olkapää;
ulkonema; v. nostaa olkapäälle; ottaa
kantaakseen; ~ of mutton
lampaanlapa; head and ~s above
päätään pitempi (kuv.); give the cold
~ to kohdella kylmästi; put one's ~ to
the wheel puskea (töitä); rub ~s with
veljeillä; ~ arms! kiväärit olalle!
-**blade** lapaluu. ~-**strap** olkain.

shout [ʃaut] v. huutaa (at jklle); s.
huuto; ~ sb. down.

shove [ʃʌv] v. työntää, sysätä; s. sysäys,
tyrkkäys.

shovel ['ʃʌvl] s. lapio; v. lapioida,
luoda (lunta).

show [ʃəu] showed shown, v. näyttää,
osoittaa; asettaa näytteille; näkyä,
näyttäytyä; tulla näkyviin, ilmestyä; s.
näytelmä, näytäntö, esitys, revyy,
juhlakulkue ym; näyttely;
(ulko)näkö; komeus, loisto; sl. asia,
höskä, (koko) hoito; ~ oneself . .
(itself) osoittautua, ilmetä; ~ off
komeilla, ylvästellä jllak; ~ sb. over
the house näyttää jklle taloa; ~ up

paljastaa; näyttäytyä, näkyä selvästi; ~ sb. up for what he is paljastaa jkn todellinen luonne; flower~ kukkanäyttely; by ~ of hands käsiä nostamalla; be on ~ olla näytteillä; not even a ~ of [resistance] ei edes näön vuoksi; who is running this ~? kuka tässä määrää? ~-case lasikko. ~-down välienselvittely; force a s.-d. pakottaa paljastamaan korttinsa. ~-girl revyytyttö.

shower ['ʃauə] s. sadekuuro; ryöppy, suihku; v. virrata ryöppynä, tulvia; antaa ylenmäärin, syytää. ~-**bath** suihku. -**y** [-ri] a. kuuroinen.

show|iness ['ʃə(u)inis] s. komeilu, loisto. -**ing** a. vaikutus, esitys. -**man** s. (revyyteatterin ym) johtaja, show-mies; (~ship esiintymiskyky). -**piece** näyttelyesine, (kuv.) mallikappale. ~-**room** näyttelysali. ~-**up** paljastus. ~-**window** näyteikkuna. -**y** ['ʃə(u)i] a. korea, pramea.

shrank [ʃræŋk] imp. ks. shrink.

shrapnel ['ʃræpnl] s. srapnelli.

shred [ʃred] v. leikata suikaleiksi, repiä rikki; not a ~ of truth ei totuuden hiventäkään.

shrew [ʃru:] s. äkäpussi; (eläint.)

shrewd [ʃru:d] a. terävä, älykäs, viisas.

shrewish ['ʃru:iʃ] a. toraisa.

shriek [ʃri:k] v. huutaa, kirkua; s. kirkaisu.

shrift [ʃrift] s.: [get] short ~ lyhyt armonaika.

shrike [ʃraik] s. lepinkäinen.

shrill [ʃril] a. kimeä, kimakka.

shrimp [ʃrimp] s. katkarapu; pikkuinen olento, käppänä.

shrine [ʃrain] s. pyhäinjäännöslipas; alttari, pyhäkkö.

shrink [ʃriŋk] v. (shrank shrunk, adj:na shrunken) kutistua, vanua; kutistaa; kavahtaa (jtk), vetäytyä pois, kaihtaa (us. ~ back from, ~ [away] from). -**age** [-idʒ] s. kutistuminen; allowance for ~ kutistumavara. -**er** [-ə] s.: head~ (sl.) psykiatri. -**ing** a. (m.) arka, epäröivä.

shrive [ʃraiv] shrove shriven, v. (vanh.) ripittää.

shrivel ['ʃrivl] v. kurtistaa; mennä

kurttuun, rypistyä. -**led** [-d] a. kurttuinen, kuivettunut.

shroud [ʃraud] s. käärinliinat; verho; v. kietoa käärinliinaan, verhota.

shrove [ʃrəuv] imp. ks. shrive.

Shrove [ʃrəuv]: ~ Tuesday laskiaistiistai.

shrub [ʃrʌb] s. pensas. -**bery** [-əri] s. pensaikko.

shrug [ʃrʌg] v. kohauttaa (olkapäitään); s. olankohautus.

shrunk(en) [ʃrʌŋk, -n] pp. ks. kutistunut.

shudder ['ʃʌdə] v. väristä, vapista; s. väristys, puistatus.

shuffle ['ʃʌfl] v. laahustaa; sekoittaa (kortteja); sysätä; kierrellä ja kaarrella; s. laahaaminen; (jalan) raapaisu; sekoittaminen; veruke, metku; ~ off karistaa harteiltaan (esim. vastuu); ~ through [one's work] tehdä hätäisesti; [re]~ [of the Cabinet] uudelleenjärjestely; ~-**board** eräänl. ruutupeli.

shun [ʃʌn] v. karttaa, kaihtaa.

shunt [ʃʌnt] v. vaihtaa sivuraiteelle; (kuv.) kääntää muille raiteille; s. vaihto sivuraiteelle; sivuvirtapiiri, sivukytkentä (sähk., rad.).

shut [ʃʌt] shut shut, v. sulkea, panna kiinni; sulkeutua, mennä kiinni; ~ one's eyes to ei olla näkevinään; ~ down lopettaa työt; ~ in sulkea sisään; ~ off [from] sulkea jstk, eristää; ~ out sulkea ovi jklta; ~ up sulkea, teljetä lukkojen taakse, (puhek.) tukkia (suu); ~ up! suu kiinni! the window ~s easily ikkuna on helppo sulkea. ~-**down** työnseisaus. -**ter** [-ə] s. ikkunaluukku; (valok.) suljin.

shuttle ['ʃʌtl] s. sukkula. -**cock** sulkapallo.

shy 1. [ʃai] arka, ujo, (~ of) jtk kaihtava; vauhko; v. säikkyä (at jtk); fight ~ of pysyä loitolla jstk.

shy 2. [ʃai] v. heittää, viskata; s. heitto; have a ~ at (m.) yrittää.

Shylock ['ʃailɔk] erisn.

shyster ['ʃaistə] s. Am. keinoja kaihtamaton lakimies.

Siam ['saiæm] erisn. Siam, Thaimaa. -**ese** ['saiə'mi:z] a. & s. siamilainen; siamin kieli.

Siberia ['sai'biəriə] *erisn.* Siperia. **-n** [-n] *a. & s.* siperialainen.

sibilant ['sibilənt] *s.* suhuäänne.

siblings ['siblinz] *s.* sisarukset.

sibyl ['sibil] *s.* ennustajanainen.

Sicil|ian [si'siljən] *a. & s.* sisilialainen. **-y** ['sisili] *erisn.* Sisilia.

sick 1. [sik] *a.* pahoinvoipa; sairas; ~ *of* kyllästynyt, tympääntynyt jhk; ~ *at heart* tuskainen, epätoivoinen; *feel* ~ olla pahoinvoipa. **~-bay** (laivan) sairaala. **-en** ['sikn] *v.* sairastua; inhottaa, iljettää, tympäistä; ~*ing* inhottava, ällöttävä. **~-fund** sairaskassa.

sick 2. *v.* usuttaa (*on* jkn kimppuun); ~ *him!* käy kiinni!

sickle ['sikl] *s.* sirppi.

sick|-leave sairasloma. **~-list** sairasluettelo. **-ly** ['sikli] *a.* sairaalloinen. **-ness** *s.* sairaus; pahoinvointi.

side [said] *s.* sivu, syrjä, reuna; kylki; puoli, suunta; (vuoren)rinne; puolue; *a.* sivu-, syrjä-; *v.:* ~ *with* asettua jkn puolelle, pitää jkn puolta; ~ *issue* sivuseikka; *change* ~ s siirtyä toiselle puolelle, vaihtaa puolta; *take* ~ s *with* ruveta jkn puolelle; ~ *by* ~ rinnatusten, vierekkäin; *at my* ~ vieressäni, viereeni; *by the* ~ *of* jkn rinnalla, viere sä; *on both* ~ s molemmin puolin; *on the* ~ sivuansiona; *on the small* ~ pienenpuoleinen; *put on* ~ olla olevinaan. **-board** *s.* tarjoilupöytä, astiakaappi. **~-car** sivuvaunu. **~-burns** pulisongit. **~-effect** sivuvaikutus. **~-light** välähdys; lisävalaistus. **~-line:** *as a s.-l.* sivuansiona. **-long** *a.* sivu-, syrjä-; *adv.* syrjästä.

sidereal [sai'diəriəl] *a.* tähti-.

side|-saddle *s.* naistensatula. **~-slip** *s.* (auto) sivuluisu. **~-splitting** *a.* ratki riemukas. **-step** väistää. **~-track** sivuraide, syrjätie; *v.* johtaa syrjään; lykätä (ehdotuksen) käsittely. **~-walk** jalkakäytävä (Am.). **-ways** sivulle, syrjittäin; syrjä-.

siding ['saidiŋ] *s.* pistoraide.

sidle ['saidl] *v.* kulkea, lähestyä sivuittain t. varovasti.

siege [si:dʒ] *s.* piiritys; *lay* ~ *to*

piirittää; *raise the* ~ lopettaa piiritys.

sieve [siv] *s.* seula, sihti.

sift [sift] *v.* seuloa; erottaa; tutkia, pohtia. **-er** [-ə] *s.* (pieni) siivilä.

sigh [sai] *v.* huoata, huokailla; ikävöidä; (tuulesta) humista; *s.* huokaus.

sight [sait] *s.* näkö(kyky, -aisti); näkeminen, katseleminen; näky, nähtävyys; näköpiiri; näkökanta; (pyssyn) tähtäin, jyvä; (puhek.) melkoisesti, paljon; *v.* saada näkyviinsä, päästä (maan ym) näkyviin; *at the* ~ *of.* . nähdessään (-säni jne); *catch* ~ *of* saada näkyviinsä; *lose* ~ *of* kadottaa näkyvistä; *see the* ~ s katsella (seudun) nähtävyyksiä; *at (on)* ~ esitettäessä (kaupp.), paikalla (jtk, jkn nähdessään); *play music at* ~ soittaa suoraan nuoteista; *at first* ~ ensi näkemältä; *know by* ~ tuntea ulkonäöltä; *in* ~ näkyvissä; *in the* ~ *of* jkn nähden; *out of* ~ (poissa) näkyvistä; *within* ~ näkyvissä. **-ed** *a.* näkevä *(the* ~); *weak-* ~ heikkonäköinen. **-less** *a.* sokea. **-ly** *a.* miellyttävä. **-seeing** *s: go* ~ katsella nähtävyyksiä. **-seer** *s.* nähtävyyksien katselija.

sign [sain] *s.* merkki; tunnus; enne; oire; kyltti, (nimi)kilpi; *v.* allekirjoittaa, kirjoittaa nimensä jhk; merkitä; antaa merkki, viitata; *at a* ~ *from* saatuaan jklta merkin; ~ *away* (kirjallisesti) luovuttaa; ~ *on* tehdä sopimus, pestautua (laivaan).

signal ['signl] *s.* merkki; signaali; (rautat.) opas in; *a.* erinomainen, etevä, huomattava; *v.* ilmoittaa merkillä, antaa merkki, välittää viesti; *S* ~ *Corps* viestijoukot. **~-box** asetinlaite. **-ize** [-əlaiz] *v.* tehdä huomattavaksi, antaa loistoa. **-ler** [-ələ] *s.* merkinantolaite; = seur. **-man** *s.* viestittäjä.

signa|tory ['signət(ə)ri] *s.* allekirjoittaja; ~ *power* allekirjoittajavaltio. **-ture** [-itʃə] *s.* allekirjoitus, nimikirjoitus; ~ *tune* (TV-ohjelman) tunnus; *key* ~ (mus.) etumerkintö.

signboard *s.* kyltti, kilpi.

signet ['signit] *s.* sinetti.

signific|ance ['sig'nifikəns] s. merkitys, tärkeys. **-ant** [-ənt] a. merkittävä, tärkeä. **-ative** [-ətiv] a.: ~ *of* jtk merkitsevä.

signify ['signifai] v. osoittaa, merkitä.

sign-post tienviitta.

silage ['sailidʒ] s. säilörehu.

silence ['sailəns] s. äänettömyys, vaitiolo; hiljaisuus; v. saattaa vaikenemaan, vaientaa; ~ *!* vaiti! hiljaa! *dead* ~ kuolonhiljaisuus; *in* ~ ääneti; *pass over in* ~ sivuuttaa vaieten. **-r** [-ə] s. äänenvaimennin.

silent ['sailənt] a. äänetön, hiljainen; harvapuheinen, vaitelias; mykkä; *be* ~ vaieta. **-ly** adv. hiljaa, hiljaisuudessa.

silhouette [silu(:)'et] s. siluetti.

sili|cate ['sili|kit] s. silikaatti. **-cosis** [-'kousis] s. kivikeuhko (lääk.).

silk [silk] s. silkki, silkkilanka, **-kangas;** *pl.* silkkitavarat; *attr.* silkkinen, silkki-; ~ *hat* silinteri. **-en** [-n] a. silkkinen, silkinhieno. **-worm** silkkiäistoukka. **-y** [-i] a. silkinhieno, -pehmeä.

sill [sil] s. ikkunalauta; kynnys.

silliness s. typeryys, tyhmyys.

silly ['sili] a. yksinkertainen, typerä, ajattelematon, ymmärtämätön, hassu; s. hupsu; *don't be* ~ *!* höpsis!

silo ['sailou] s. siilo.

silt [silt] s. hiesu; liete; v. liettää, liettyä.

silver ['silvə] s. hopea; hopearaha(t), -astiat, hopeat; a. hopeinen, hopea-, hopeankirkas, -heleä; v. hopeoida; ~ *plate* hopea-astiat, pöytähopeat; ~-*plated* hopeoitu; *every cloud has a* ~ *lining* ei niin pahaa, ettei jotakin hyvää; *was born with a* ~ *spoon in his mouth* syntyi rikkauteen. **-y** [-(ə)ri] a. hopea-, hopeanhohtava, -heleä.

Simeon ['simiən] erisn.

similar ['similə] a. samanlainen, (~ *to*) jnk kaltainen. **-ity** [-'læriti] s. samanlaisuus, yhtäläisyys. **-ly** adv. samalla tavoin, samoin.

simil|e ['simili] s. vertaus. **-itude** [si'militju:d] s. kaltaisuus, hahmo; vertaus.

simmer ['simə] v. (antaa) hiljalleen kiehua, porista.

Simon ['saimən] erisn.

simoom [si'mu:m] s. samumtuuli.

simper ['simpə] v. hymyillä typerästi t. teennäisesti; typerä hymy.

simple ['simpl] a. yksinkertainen; koruton, vaatimaton; vilpitön, suora; typerä, herkkäuskoinen; selvä; pelkkä; s. lääkekasvi. ~-**hearted** yksinkertainen, vilpitön. ~-**minded** luottavainen, teeskentelemätön; heikkoälyinen. **-ton** [-t(ə)n] s. tolvana, hölmö.

simpl|icity [sim'plisiti] s. yksinkertaisuus; luonnollisuus, koruttomuus; vilpittömyys; typeryys. **-ification** [simplifi'keiʃn] s. yksinkertaistaminen. **-ify** ['simplifai] v. yksinkertaistaa. **-y** ['simpli] adv. yksinkertaisesti jne; ainoastaan, vain; kerta kaikkiaan, suorastaan.

simula|te ['simjuleit] v. teeskennellä, tekeytyä (jksk). **-tion** [-'leiʃn] s. teeskentely.

simultan|eity [simltə'niəti] s. samanaikaisuus. **-eous** [-'teinjəs] a. samanaikainen; simultaani-; (~**ly** adv. yhtä aikaa).

sin [sin] s. synti; v. tehdä syntiä, rikkoa.

Sinai ['sainiai] erisn.

since [sins] prep. jstk asti, alkaen; konj. sen jälkeen kun, sitten kun; koska; adv. sen jälkeen, sittemmin; *ever* ~ aina siitä alkaen; ~ *then* siitä asti, siitä saakka.

sincer|e [sin'siə] a. vilpitön, suora, rehellinen; ~*ly yours* l.v. parhain terveisin. **-ity** [sin'seriti] s. vilpittömyys.

sine [sain] s. (mat.) sini.

sinecure ['sainikjuə] s. nimivirka, laiskanvirka.

sinew ['sinju:] s. jänne, *pl.* voima. **-y** [-i] a. jäntevä, voimakas.

sinful ['sinf(u)l] a. syntinen.

sing [siŋ] *sang sung*, v. laulaa, m. sihistä, humista; ~ *out* huutaa; ~ *up!* laulakaa kovemmin; ~ *sb's praises* ylistää.

Singapore [siŋgə'pɔ:] erisn.

singe [sin(d)ʒ] v. kärventää.

singer ['siŋə] s. laulaja, -tar.

Sin(g)halese [siŋhə'li:z] a. & s. singalilainen (Sri Lankan asukas); singalin kieli.

singing ['siŋiŋ] *s.* laulu. **~-master** laulunopettaja.

single ['siŋgl] *a.* ainoa; yksinkertainen, yhden hengen; yksittäinen, yksittäis-; naimaton; *s.* kaksinpeli; *v.:* ~ *out* valita, valikoida (jstk); ~ *combat* kaksinkamppailu; ~ *file* jono, hanhenmarssi; ~ *life* naimattomuus; ~ *room* yhden hengen huone; *every* ~ [*one*] joka ikinen; *remain* ~ jäädä naimattomaksi. **~-breasted** yksirivinen. **~-entry** yksinkertainen (kirjanp.). **~-handed** *a. & adv.* yksinään, ilman apua. **~-hearted,** **~-minded** uskollinen, vilpitön; määrätietoinen. **-ness** *s.* naimattomuus, yksinäisyys; ~ *of purpose* määrätietoisuus. **-ton** [-tn] *s.* ainoa kortti (jtk maata). **~-track** yksiraiteinen.

singlet ['siŋglit] *s.* ihokas.

singly ['siŋgli] *adv.* yksitellen, kukin erikseen; yksinään.

singsong ['siŋsɔŋ] *s.* yhteislauluhetki; *in a* ~ *manner* yksitoikkoisesti (nousten ja laskien), rallattaen.

singular ['siŋgjulə] *a.* tavaton, harvinainen, merkillinen, erinomainen; omituinen; *s.* yksikkö. **-ity** [-'læriti] *s.* erikoisuus, omituisuus. **-ly** *adv.* erityisesti, merkillisen, erittäin.

sinister ['sinistə] *a.* pahaa ennustava, pahaenteinen, paha, synkkä; vasen (her.).

sink [siŋk] *v.* (*sank sunk,* adj:na *sunken*) upota; vajota, vaipua; painua, laskeutua; laskea, aleta, vähetä; sortua, upottaa (laiva); kaivaa (kaivo ym); vähentää, alentaa; kuolettaa (velka); kiinnittää (rahaa jhk); unohtaa, jättää sikseen; *s.* viemäri(allas), astiainpesuallas; ~ *in* painua mieleen; *he is* ~*ing fast* hänen loppunsa lähenee nopeasti; *a* ~ *of iniquity* paheen pesä. **-er** [-ə] *s.* paino. **-ing** *s.* lamauttaminen jne.

sin|less ['sinlis] *a.* synnitön. **-ner** ['sinə] *s.* syntinen.

Sino- ['sainəu] *a.* Kiinan-.

sinu|osity [sinju'ɔsiti] *s.* mutkaisuus, (joen) polveke. **-ous** ['sinjuəs] *a.* mutkainen, polveileva.

sinus ['sainəs] *s.* (nenän) sivuontelo.

-itis [-'saitis] *s.* sivuontelontulehdus.

Sion ['saiən] *erisn.*

Sioux [su:, *pl.* su:z] *s.* sioux-intiaani.

sip [sip] *v.* maistella; *s.* pieni kulaus.

siphon ['saif(ə)n] *s.* sifoni; *v.* juoksuttaa; ~ *off* johtaa muualle.

Sir [sə:, sə] *s.* (hyvä) herra! *baronetin* ja *knightin* arvonimi (ristimänimen edessä; *Dear S*~ arvoisa herra (t. johtaja ym).

sire ['saiə] *s.* isä (run. e eläimistä).

siren ['saiərin] *s.* seireeni; (sumu- ym) sireeni.

sirloin ['sə:lɔin] *s.* paisti.

sisal ['sais(ə)l] *s.* sisalhamppu.

siskin ['siskin] *s.* vihervarpunen.

sissy ['sisi] *s.* ks. *cissy.*

sister ['sistə] *s.* sisar; ~ *of charity* laupeudensisar; *brothers and* ~*s* sisarukset; ~ *nation* veljeskansa. **-hood** *s.* sisarkunta. **~-in-law** käly. **-ly** [-li] *a.* sisarellinen, sisaren.

Sistine ['sistain] *a.* Sikstuksen.

sit [sit] *sat sat, v.* istua; pitää kokousta; hautoa; olla, sijaita; ~ *heavy on* painaa, masentaa; ~ *down* istuutua; ~ *for an examination* mennä tenttiin, olla tentissä; ~ *for one's picture* istua mallina; ~ *in* osoittaa mieltään (valtaamalla jk rakennus ym); ~ *on* olla jäsenenä jssk, (puhek.) nolata, nujertaa; ~ *out* jäädä istumaan tanssin ajaksi, viipyä loppuun saakka; ~ *up* nousta istumaan, ~ *up late* valvoa myöhään; ~-*down strike* istumalakko. **-com:** [*a TV*] ~ tilannekomedia.

site [sait] *s.* paikka, sijainti; rakennuspaikka, tontti; ~ *plan* asemapiirros.

sitt|er ['sitə] *s.* (maalarin) malli; hautova lintu; helppo saalis t. tehtävä; ks. *baby-*~. **-ing** *s.* istunto; *at one* ~ yhteen menoon. **-ing-room** olohuone.

situat|ed ['sitjueitid] *a.* sijaitseva, jssk asemassa oleva; *be* ~ sijaita. **-ion** [-'ei∫n] *s.* asema; tila(nne), olosuhteet; palveluspaikka, toimi.

six [siks] *lukus.* kuusi; *s.* kuutonen; *at* ~*es and sevens* sikin sokin. **-fold** *a.* kuusinkertainen. **-pence** kuuden pennyn raha. **-penny** *a.* kuuden pennyn; ~ *bit (piece)* = ed. **-teen** *lukus. & s.* [-'ti:n] kuusitoista. **-teenth**

kuudestoista. **-th** [-θ] *lukus. & s.*
kuudes, -osa. **-tieth** [-tiiθ] *lukus. & s.*
kuudeskymmenes. **-ty** [-ti] *lukus.*
kuusikymmentä.
sizable [saizəbl] *a.* isonlainen,
suurehko, melkoinen.
size 1. [saiz] *s.* koko, suuruus;
(käsineiden ym) numero; *v.* järjestää
koon mukaan; ~ *up* arvioida,
mittailla, arvostella; *of a* ~
samankokoisia; *full (life)* ~
luonnollinen koko; *medium-*~
keskikokoinen.
size 2. [saiz] *s.* liimavesi, liisteri; *v.*
liisteröidä.
sizeable ks. *sizable.*
sizzle ['sizl] *v.* käristä, pihistä; *s.*
pihinä.
skat|e [skeit] *s.* luistin; (eläint.)
rausku; *v.* luistella; (~*board*
rullalauta). **-ing** *s.* luistelu; ~*-rink*
luistinrata.
skedaddle [ski'dædl] *v.* luikkia
tiehensä, livistää.
skein [skein] *s.* pasma, kaarto, vyyhti.
skeleton ['skelitn] *s.* luuranko; luusto;
runko, kehä, kehikko; luonnos; ~ *key*
tiirikka; ~ *in the cupboard* (ikävä)
perhesalaisuus.
skeptic ks. *sceptic.*
skerr|y ['skeri] *s.* luoto; -*ies*
saaristo.
sketch [sketʃ] *s.* luonnos, ääripiirros;
lyhyt näytelmä, sketsi, tuokiokuva; *v.*
tehdä luonnos, luonnostella. ~*-book*
luonnoskirja. **-y** [-i] *a.*
luonnosmainen.
skew [skju:] *a.* vino, viisto.
skewer ['skjuə] *s.* paistinvarras.
ski [ski:] *s.* (pl. *ski, skis*) suksi; *v.*
(ski'd) hiihtää.
skid [skid] *s.* jarru(kenkä);
luisuminen, (sivu)luisto t. -luisu,
non~ luisumaton; *S*~ *Row* Am.
kodittomien slummialue.
skiff [skif] *s.* kevyt vene.
ski|er [ski:ə, ʃi:ə] *s.* hiihtäjä. **-ing** *s.*
hiihto. ~*-jump* mäkihyppy. ~*-lift*
hiihtohissi.
skilful, Am. **skill-** *a.* taitava.
skill [skil] *s.* taitavuus, taito. **-ed** [-d] *a.*
taitava, pystyvä; ammattitaitoinen,
ammattitaitoa vaativa; ~ *workman*
ammattimies.

skillet ['skilit] *s.* paistinpannu; (Engl.)
pitkävartinen, jalallinen kasari.
skim [skim] *v.* kuoria, kermoa; lukea
nopeasti lävitse, silmäillä; keveysti
koskettaa, pyyhkäistä, liukua yli; ~
milk kuorittu maito. **-mer** [-ə] *s.*
kuorimiskauha.
skimp [skimp] *v.* säästää, kitsastella. **-y**
[-i] *a.* niukka, kitsas.
skin [skin] *s.* iho, nahka; vuota; kuori,
kalvo; *v.* nylkeä, kuoria; huiputtaa; ~
and bone luuta ja nahkaa; ~ *off* riisua
yltään (kääntämällä nurin); ~ *over*
(haavasta) parantua; *by the* ~ *of one's
teeth* hädin tuskin; *get under one's* ~
kaivella (mieltä), kismittää; *keep
one's eyes* ~*ned* olla silmä kovana.
~*-deep* pinnallinen. ~*-diving*
urheilusukellus. ~*-flint* kitupiikki.
~*-game* huijaus. ~*-grafting*
ihonsiirto. **-ny** [-ni] *a.* luuta ja nahkaa.
skip [skip] *v.* hyppiä, hypellä, hypätä
yli, jättää mainitsematta t. lukematta,
sivuuttaa (m. ~ *over)*; *s.* hyppäys;
mainitsematta jättäminen.
skipper ['skipə] *s.* kapteeni, kippari.
skipping-rope *s.* hyppynuora.
skirmish ['skə:miʃ] *s.* kahakka, ottelu;
v. kahakoida.
skirt [skə:t] *s.* hame; (us. *pl.*) reuna,
liepeet; *v.* reunustaa, sivuta; (~
along) kulkea jtk pitkin. **-ing-board** *s.*
jalkalista.
skit [skit] *s.* pila, hupailu. **-tish** [-iʃ] *a.*
arka, vauhko; kujeileva, keimaileva,
huikenteleva.
skittle ['skitl] *s.* keila; ~*s* keilapeli; *beer
and* ~*s* huvitukset.
skive ['skaiv] *v.* ohentaa (nahkaa); sl.
pinnata.
skivvy ['skivi] *s.* piikatyttö.
skua ['skju:ə] *s.* kihu.
skulk [skʌlk] *v.* pysytellä piilossa,
piileskellä, hiipiä; ~ *away* luikkia
tiehensä.
skull [skʌl] *s.* kallo. ~*-cap* patalakki,
kalotti.
skunk [skʌŋk] *s.* haisunäätä; roisto.
sky [skai] *s.* taivas; *in the* ~ taivaalla; *to
the skies* maasta taivaaseen. ~*-blue*
taivaansininen. **-jack** *s.* ks. *highjack.*
-lark *s.* kiuru, leivo; *v.* kujeilla. **-light**
kattoikkuna. ~*-line* (kaupungin)
siluetti. ~*-rocket* kohota huimaavasti

-scraper pilvenpiirtäjä. **-ward(s)** adv. taivasta kohti. **~-writing** (lentokoneen) savukirjoitus.

slab [slæb] s. laatta, levy; pintalauta.

slack [slæk] a. löysä, hölllä, veltto, vetelä; hidas; laimea; s. hiilimurska; pl. väljät housut; v. olla vetelä, veltto; höllentää; grow ~ höltyä; have a ~ rentoutua; ~ up hiljentää vauhtia. **-en** [-n] v. höltyä, löyhtyä; käydä veltoksi; laimentua, heikontua, hidastua; hellittää; vähentää, hiljentää. **-er** [-ə] s. pinnari, vetelys.

slag [slæg] s. kuona; basic ~ tuomaskuona.

slain [slein] pp. ks. slay.

slake [sleik] v. sammuttaa (jano, kalkkia).

slalom ['slɑːləm] s. pujottelu.

slam [slæm] v. paiskata (kiinni); paukahtaa (kiinni); s. paukahdus; slammi (korttip.).

slander ['slɑːndə, Am. 'slæn-] v. panettelu; v. panetella, parjata. **-ous** [-(ə)rəs] a. panetteleva, loukkaava.

slang [slæŋ] s. slangi; schoolboy ~ koululaisslangi. **-y** [-i] a. slangimainen.

slant [slɑːnt] v. olla kallellaan, viettää; tehdä viistoksi, viettäväksi; esittää väärässä valossa; s. vieru, rinne kaltevuus; Am. näkökohta, näkymä, mielipide; on the ~ vinossa. **-ing** a. vino, viisto, kalteva.

slap [slæp] v. läjäyttää, läjäyttää, mätkäyttää; s. läimäys; adv. päistikkaa, suoraa päätä. **~-bang** suin päin. **-dash** a. hutiloitu, huolimaton; adv. umpimähkään. **-happy** a. raju, kiihkeä, huoleton. **-stick** s.: ~ comedy remuava näytelmä. **~-up** hieno, ensiluokkainen.

slash [slæʃ] v. viiltää auki; huitoa ympärilleen, läimäyttää; antaa murskaava arvostelu; s. isku, viillos, viiltohaava; ~ing ankara, murskaava.

slat [slæt] s. poikkipiena, rima; slatted säle-.

slate [sleit] s. liuskakivi; liuskelaatta; kivitaulu; v. peittää t. kattaa liuskelaatoilla; ankarasti arvostella (give a good slating to); ~ pencil kivikynä, rihveli; a clean ~ puhtaat paperit. **~-coloured** siniharmaa.

slattern ['slætən] s. homssu. **-ly** adv. sottainen, homssuinen.

slaty ['sleiti] a. liuskeinen.

slaughter ['slɔːtə] s. teurastus; verilöyly; v. teurastaa. **~-house** teurastamo.

Slav [slɑːv] s. & a. slaavi(lainen).

slave [sleiv] s. orja; v. raataa. **~-driver** orjapiiskuri. **~-trade** orjakauppa.

slaver 1. ['sleivə] s. orja|laiva, -kauppias.

slaver 2. ['slævə] v. kuolata; s. kuola; karkea imartelu.

slavery ['sleivəri] s. orjuus.

slavey ['sleivi] s. piika.

Slavic ['slævik] a. slaavilainen.

slavish ['sleiviʃ] a. orjamainen, orjallinen.

Slavonic [slə'vonik] = Slavic.

slay [slei] slew slain, v. lyödä kuoliaaksi, tappaa, surmata.

sleazy ['sliːzi] a. likainen, siivoton.

sled [sled] s. kelkka, reki.

sledge 1. [sledʒ] s. reki, kelkka; ajaa reellä t. kelkalla; laskea mäkeä.

sledge 2. [sledʒ] s.: ~[-hammer] moukari.

sleek [sliːk] s. sileä, kiiltävä (ja pehmeä), liukas, mielistelevä; v. silittää, (antaa) liukua.

sleep [sliːp] slept slept, v. nukkua; viettää yö (jssk); torkkua; antaa yösija; s. uni; ~ with maata jkn kanssa; ~ away nukkumalla kuluttaa; ~ off nukkumalla parantaa; want of ~ unettomuus; get to ~ päästä uneen, saada unta; go to ~ vaipua uneen; nukahtaa; put to ~ nukuttaa. **-er** [-ə] s. nukkuja; ratapölkky; makuuvaunu.

sleeping ['sliːpiŋ] a. nukkuva; s. uni, nukkuminen; the S~ Beauty Prinsessa Ruususen. **~-bag** makuupussi. **~-car** makuuvaunu. **~-draught** [-drɑːft] unijuoma, -lääke. **-er** [-ə] s. nukkuja. **~-pill** unitabletti. **~-sickness** unitauti.

sleep|less ['sliːplis] a. uneton. **-lessness** s. unettomuus. **~-walker** unissakävijä. **-y** [-i] a. uninen, unelias; (~-head unikeko).

sleet [sliːt] s. lumi|räntä, -sohju; v. sataa räntää.

sleeve [sliːv] s. hiha; (äänilevyn) kotelo; laugh up one's ~ nauraa salavihkaa; have sth. up one's ~ pitää jtk varalla, takataskussa. **-less** *a.* hihaton.

sleigh [slei] *s.* reki; *v.* ajaa reellä; ~ *bell* kulkunen. **-ing** *s.* reellä ajaminen, rekikeli.

sleight [slait] *s.:* ~ *-of-hand* silmän-kääntötemppu; (sormi)näppäryys.

slender ['slendə] *a.* solakka, hoikka; vähäinen, heikko, niukka.

slept [slept] *imp. & pp.* ks. *sleep.*

sleuth [slu:θ] *s.:* ~ [*-hound*] verikoira; salapoliisi.

slew [slu:] *imp. & pp.* ks. *slay.*

slice [slais] *s.* viipale, palanen; kala-, kakkulapio; *v.* leikata viipaleiksi; ~ *a ball* lyödä viistoon.

slick [slik] *a.* kiiltävä, sileä, liukas; mielistelevä; ovela; nokkela; *adv.* suoraan; ovelasti, etevästi. **-er** [-ə] *s.* eräänl. sadetakki; huiputtaja.

slid [slid] *imp. & pp.* ks. *slide.*

slide [slaid] *slid slid, v.* liukua, luistaa, luisua; luiskahtaa, pujahtaa; sujauttaa; *s.* liukuminen; liukurata, kelkkamäki; maanvieremä; luisti; kuultokuva, diapositiivi, mikroskooppinen valmiste; *hair* ~ hiussolki; *let things* ~ antaa mennä. **~-fastener** vetoketju. **~-rule** laskutikku.

sliding ['slaidiŋ] *a.* liukuva, työntö-; ~ *door* liukuovi; ~ *scale* liukuva (palkka-)asteikko.

slight [slait] *a.* hento, hoikka, heikko; vähäinen, vähäpätöinen, lievä; *v.* väheksyä, kohdella epäkunnioittavasti; *s.* loukkaus. **-ingly** *adv.* halveksien. **-ly** *adv.* lievästi; hiukan, jossakin määrin.

slim [slim] *a.* solakka, hoikka; ovela; riittämätön, huono; *v.* laihduttaa. **-ming** *s.* laihdutus.

slim|e [slaim] *s.* muta, lieju; lima. **-y** [-i] *a.* mutainen, limainen; mielistelevä.

sling [sliŋ] *s.* linko; kantoside, kanto|hihna, -remmi; kantoside; *v.* *(slung slung)* lingota, heittää, sinkauttaa, nostaa (raksilla ym); ~ *mud at* mustata.

slink [sliŋk] *slunk slunk, v.* livahtaa, hiipiä.

slip [slip] *v.* liukua, luistaa; luiskahtaa, kompastua, tehdä erehdys; päästä

(kädestä ym), lipsahtaa; pujahtaa, hiipiä; laskea käsistään t. irti; sujauttaa, pistää jhk; (~ *on*) vetäistä ylleen; (~ *off*) heittää yltään, riisua; *s.* luiskahdus, kompastus; erehdys, lipsahdus; liuska, suikale; alushame, (pieluksen) päällinen; pistokas; telapohja, telat; *a mistake has* ~*ped in* tähän on päässyt pujahtamaan virhe; *let.* . ~ tulla sanoneeksi, päästää käsistään, päästää irti; ~ *a stitch* nostaa, jättää neulomatta (silmä); ~ *up* (sl.) erehtyä; *a* ~ *of a boy* hintelä poika; *a* ~ *of the pen* kirjoitusvirhe; *give (sb.) the* ~ päästä livahtamaan (jkn käsistä); *a gym-*~ voimistelupuku. **~-knot** juoksusolmu. **-over** pujoliivi. **-ped** *disc* selkärangan tyrä. **-per** [-ə] *s.* tohveli, kevyt avokenkä. **-pery** [-əri] *a.* liukas. **-py** [-i] *a.* = ed.; *look* ~ ! pidä kiirettä! **-shod** huolimaton. **~-up** lipsahdus. **-way** *s.* telapohja.

slit [slit] *slit slit, v.* leikata, viiltää auki; halkaista; revetä; *s.* viillos, rako, lovi, repeämä, luukku.

slither ['sliðə] *v.* luisua, luiskahtaa, liukua. **-y** [-i] *a.* liukas.

sliver ['slivə] *s.* säle, lastu.

slobber ['slɔbə] *v.* kuolata; *s.* kuola; tunteileva, joutava puhe.

sloe [sləu] *s.* oratuomi.

slog [slɔg] *v.* iskeä kovasti, jysäyttää; ~ *along* laahustaa; ~ *away* ahertaa, uurastaa.

slogan ['sləugən] *s.* iskulause.

sloop [slu:p] *s.* pursi, sluuppi.

slop [slɔp] *v.* läikyttää, tuhria; läikkyä maahan (m. ~ *over);* ~ *s* likavesi, astiainpesuvesi; liemiruoka, velli; valmiit vaatteet, väljät housut. **~-basin** (teeastiaston) huuhdekuppi.

slop|e [sləup] *s.* kaltevuus, viettävyys; rinne; *v.* viettää, kallistua; tehdä kaltevaksi; ~ *off* livistää. **-ing** *a.* viettävä, kalteva.

sloppy ['slɔpi] *a.* kurainen, lokainen; (ruoasta) latkuinen; hutiloiva, huolimaton; tunteileva.

slosh [slɔʃ] *s.* sohju; lotina *v.* sl. iskeä, läimäyttää; ~ *about* rämpiä.

slot [slɔt] *s.* rako, (kapea) aukko; *v.* sijoittaa, sovittaa *(into, together).* **~-machine** automaatti.

sloth [sləuθ] s. hitaus, laiskuus; laiskiainen. **-ful** a. laiska.

slouch [slautʃ] s. ryhditön käynti t. asento; v. kävellä veltosti, laahustaa; ~ about vetelehtiä; ~-hat lerppalierinen hattu. **-ing** a. lerpallaan oleva; ryhditön.

slough 1. [slau] s. räme, suo.

slough 2. [slʌf] s. (käärmeen) nahka; kuollut kudos, rupi; v. luoda nahkansa, (m. ~ off) päästä, luopua (esim. tavasta).

Slouvak ['slouvæk] s. & a. slovakki, slovakialainen. **-ai** [slə(u)'vækiə] erisn.

sloven ['slʌvn] s. homssu; hutilus. **-ly** a. huolimaton, epäsiisti.

Slovene [sləu'viːn] s. sloveeni.

slow [sləu] a. hidas, verkkainen; hidasjärkinen; yksitoikkoinen, ikävä; haluton; (kellosta) jäljessä; adv. hitaasti; v. ~ down (up) hiljentää vauhtia; the clock is five minutes ~ kello on 5 minuuttia jäljessä. **-coach** kuhnus. ~**-motion** hidastettu. ~**-witted** hidasjärkinen.

sludge [slʌdʒ] s. lieju, muta; lumisohju; lietteet.

slug [slʌg] s. etana; luoti; kirjasinrivi; v. Am. (puhek.) lyödä kumauttaa; ~**-abed** unikeko. **-gard** [-əd] s. laiskuri, kuhnus. **-gish** [-iʃ] a. hidas, laiska, saamaton; (~ness hitaus, velttous).

sluice [sluːs] s. sulku, patoluukku; (m. ~ way) huuhdontakouru; v. huuhtoa; virrata; ~ off laskea sulusta. ~**-gate** sulkuportti.

slum [slʌm] s.: the ~s slummi, köyhälistökortteli; v.: go ~ming tehdä suunnityötä.

slumber ['slʌmbə] s. uinahdus, uni; v. uinailla. **-ous** [-rəs] a. unelias.

slump [slʌmp] s. (äkillinen) hintojen lasku, lama; v. retkahtaa, lyyhistyä, (hinnoista) romahtaa.

slung [slʌŋ] imp. & pp. ks. sling.

slunk [slʌŋk] imp. & pp. ks. slink.

slur [sləː] v. puhua, ääntää epäselvästi; (us. ~ over) sivuuttaa vähällä, liukua jnk yli; s. (häpeä) tahra; (mus.) legatokaari.

slurp [sləːp] v. hörppiä.

slurry ['slʌri] s. vetelä savi, muta.

slush [slʌʃ] s. lumisohju; lieju; tunteilu. **-y** [-i] a. sohjoinen, loskainen.

slut [slʌt] s. letukka, »lumppu». **-tish** [-iʃ] a. epäsiisti, homssainen.

sly [slai] a. ovela, viekas; veitikkamainen; on the ~ salaa. **-boots** veijari. **-ly** adv. viekkaasti, ovelasti.

smack 1. [smæk] s. (sivu)maku, (jnk) vivahdus; v.: ~ of maistua, vivahtaa jhk.

smack 2. [smæk] s. kalastusalus.

smack 3. [smæk] s. läimäys, läjäys; muisku; v. läimäyttää, läjäyttää; maiskauttaa, muiskauttaa; adv. suoraa päätä. **-ing** s. selkäsauna.

small [smɔːl] a. pieni, vähäinen; mitätön; kapea, ohut, heikko, hieno; pikkumainen; ~ of the back ristiselkä; ~ beer mieto olut; vähäpätöiset asiat; ~ change vaihtorahat, pikkurahat; ~ talk kevyt keskustelu, rupattelu; feel ~ tuntea itsensä noloksi; look ~ näyttää nololta; in a ~ way pienessä mittakaavassa, vaatimattomasti; the still ~ voice omantunnon ääni. ~**-holder**, ~**-holding** s. pien(viljelijä, -tila. ~**-minded** pikkumainen. **-ness** s. pienuus, mitättömyys. **-pox** isorokko.

smarmy ['smaːmi] a. (puhek.) imarteleva.

smart [smaːt] a. hieno, siisti, muodikas, tyylikäs; sukkela, neuvokas, nokkela, taitava, älykäs; nopea; ankara, kova; v. koskea kipeästi, kirvellä; tuntea tuskaa; s. (m. ~ing pain) kirvelevä kipu; ~ aleck neropatti; ~ set (hienot) piirit, seurapiiri-ihmiset; ~ for kärsiä, maksaa jstk. **-en** [-n] v.: ~ [up] somistaa, siistiytyä. **-ness** s. sukkeluus, nokkeluus, oveluus; hienous, tyylikkyys.

smash [smæʃ] v. murskata, rikkoa, särkeä; iskeä, paiskata; tehdä vararikko; törmätä, rysähtää (into jhk.) s. murskautuminen; (m. ~-up) yhteentörmäys; kolari; romahdus; (tennis) iskulyönti; go ~ romahtaa; ~-and-grab raid ikkunamurto. **-er** [-ə] murskaava isku. **-ing** a. jymäyttävä, tyrmäävä.

smattering ['smæt(ə)riŋ] s. vähäinen tuntemus, jonkinlaiset tiedot (of jstk).

smear [smiə] v. voidella; töhriä, tahr|ata, -aantua; s. (rasva)tahra; sivellinvalmiste (lääk.).

smell [smel] smelt smelt, v. haistaa, tuntea hajua; haista, tuoksua; s. haju, tuoksu; ~ out saada, vihiä jstk. **-ing-salts** hajusuola. **-y** [-i] a. pahanhajuinen.

smelt 1. [smelt] imp. & pp. ks. smell.

smelt 2. [smelt] v. sulattaa (malmeja); ~ing works sulatto.

smelt 3. [smelt] s. kuore.

smile [smail] v. hymyillä (at jllek, jklle); s. hymy; ~ upon (m.) suosia; be all ~s olla pelkkänä hymynä.

smirch [smə:tʃ] v. tahrata; s. (kuv.) tahra.

smirk [smə:k] s. (typerä) hymy; v. hymyillä (itserakkaasti).

smite [smait] smote smitten, v. lyödä, iskeä; kurittaa, tuhota; kohdata, osua; smitten with jnk valtaama; smitten with sb. ihastunut jkh.

smith [smiθ] s. seppä. **-ereens** ['smiðə'ri:nz] s. säpäleet; to ~ säpäleiksi, pirstoiksi. **-y** ['smiði] s. paja.

smitten ['smitn] pp. ks. smite.

smock [smɔk] s. työpusero (m. ~-frock); suojapuku; v. koristaa rypytyksin. **-ing** s. poimukoristelu.

smog [smɔg] smog, savusumu.

smoke [smouk] s. savu; v. savuta, höyrytä; tupakoida, polttaa; savuttaa, savustaa; have a ~ panna tupakaksi; end in ~ raueta tyhjiin; ~ out savustaa (esiin). **~-bomb** savupommi. **~-dried** savustettu. **~-screen** savuverho. **~-stack** savupiippu.

smoker ['smoukə] s. tupakoitsija; tupakkavaunu.

smoking ['smoukiŋ] s. tupakoiminen jne. **~-jacket** tupakkatakki.

smoky ['smouki] a. savuava, savuinen, savuttunut.

smooth [smu:ð] a. sileä, tasainen; pehmeä; tyven, tasaisesti virtaava; helppo, esteetön, sujuva, hiottu; imarteleva; v. silittää, tasoittaa; silitellä; tasoittua, tyyntyä (~down); s. silitys; ~ away poistaa, raivata tieltä (vaikeuksia); ~ over (m.)

peittää villaisella. **~-faced** parraton, nuoren näköinen, (kuv.) teeskentelevän ystävällinen, mielistelevä. **-ly** adv. tasaisesti; sujuvasti, hyvin. **-ness** s. sileys, siloisuus, sujuvuus. **~-spoken** (teeskentelevän) kohtelias.

smote [smout] imp. ks. smite.

smother ['smʌðə] v. tukehduttaa; tukahduttaa, vaientaa; kasata (jnk) päälle.

smoulder ['smouldə] v. kyteä, savuta, hiipua; s. hiipuminen.

smudge [smʌdʒ] s. tahra; v. tahrata, tuhria.

smug ['smʌg] a. omahyväinen.

smuggle ['smʌgl] v. salakuljettaa. **-er** [-ə] s. salakuljettaja. **-ing** s. salakuljetus.

smut [smʌt] s. (noki-, lika)tahra; (viljan) noki; ruokoton puhe; v. noeta, tahrata. **-ty** [-i] a. likainen, ruokoton.

snack [snæk] s. välipala, eväs. **~-bar** pikabaari.

snaffle ['snæfl] s. nivelkuolaimet; v. sl. kähveltää.

snag [snæg] s. (oksan) tynkä; uppotukki; hankaluus, vastus, pulma.

snail [sneil] s. etana.

snake [sneik] s. käärme. **~-charmer** käärmeenlumooja. **-y** [-i] a. käärmemäinen.

snap [snæp] v. näykätä, siepata; katkaista, naksauttaa; napsauttaa; näpsäyttää, näpätä (kuva); pamauttaa; taittua, katketa; tiuskaista, kivahtaa; s. näykkäys, haukkaisu, naksautus, naksaus; jousilukko, painonappi, neppari (m. ~-fastener); tuokiokuva; (puhek.) vauhti; piparkakku; attr. yllätys-; adv. naksahtaen; ~ at näykätä, puraista; tiuskaista jklle (m. sb.'s head off); ~ into it! joudu! ~ one's fingers at (kuv.) viitata kintaalla; ~ up siepata; a cold ~ (lyhyt) pakkaskausi. **~-dragon** leijonankita. **-ish** [-iʃ] a. ärtyisä, vihainen. **-py** [-i] a. vikkelä; make it ~ joudu! **~-shot** tuokiokuva, valokuva.

snare [snɛə] s. ansa, paula; v. pyydystää ansaan.

snarl [snɑ:l] v. murista, äristä; (seka)sotku; s. murahdus, murina.

snatch [snætʃ] v. siepata, temmata; (~ at) tavoitella, tarttua jhk; s. tempaus, sieppaus; pätkä, palanen; a ~ of sleep torkahdus; in ~es pätkittäin.

sneak [sni:k] v. hiipiä, hiiviskellä; (koul.) kannella; (koul.) pihistää s. (halpamainen) raukka; kielijä. **-ers** s. pl. kumitossut. **-ing** a. salainen. **-y** [-i] a. luihu.

sneer [sniə] s. ivahymy, halveksiva katse, pistosana; v. hymyillä ivallisesti, virnuilla.

sneeze [sni:z] v. aivastaa; s. aivastus.

snicker ['snikə] v. hihittää; s. hihitys, tirskunta, tirskahdus.

sniff [snif] v. nuuskia, (koira) nuuhkia; niiskuttaa; (~ at) haistella, tuhahtaa, halveksivasti jllek, halveksia; s. haisteleminen; tuhahdus. **-le** [-l] v. ks. snuffle. **-y** [-i] a. halveksiva; pahalta haiskahtava.

snigger ['snigə] ks. snicker.

snip [snip] v. leikata, leikellä (saksilla); s. leikkaaminen; leikattu palanen, hitunen, pala.

snipe [snaip] s. kurppa; v. metsästää kurppia; ampua piilopaikasta. **-r** [-ə] s. sala-ampuja.

snippet [' nipit] s. palanen, suikale; pl. (esim. uutis)palat. **-y** [-i] a. katkelmallinen.

snivel ['snivl] v. (itkeä) vetistellä, (nenästä) vuotaa; s. vetistely, ruikutus. **-ler** [-ə] s. räkänenä; tillittäjä.

snob [snɔb] s. hienostelija. **-bery** [-əri] s. hienostelu. **-bish** [-iʃ] a. hienosteleva; keikaileva.

snook [snu:k] s.: cock a ~ näyttää pitkää nenää. **-er** ['snukə] s. eräänl. biljardipöydällä pelattava peli.

snoop [snu:p] v.: ~ into nuuskia, urkkia.

snooty ['snu:ti] a. (puhek.) koppava, ollakseen.

snooze [snu:z] s. torkahdus; v. torkahtaa, ottaa nokkaunet.

snore [snɔ:] v. kuorsata; s. kuorsaus.

snort [snɔ:t] v. korskua, pärskyä; puhista; s. korskunta.

snot [snɔt] s. (alat.) räkä. **-ty** [-i] a. räkäinen; s. (sl.) meriupseerikokelas; ~-nosed koppava.

snout [snaut] s. kärsä, kuono; nokka.

snow [snəu] s. lumi, lumentulo; sl. heroiini, kokaiini; v. sataa lunta; ~ed up lumen saartama; be ~ed under with olla jhk hukkumaisillaan. **-ball** s. lumipallo; v. kasvaa kasvamistaan. **~-boots** päällyskengät. **~-bound** lumen saartama. **~-capped** lumipeitteinen.

Snowdonia [snəu'dəunjə] erisn.

snow-drift kinos, nietos. **-drop** lumikello. **-fall** lumisade, lumentulo. **~-line** lumiraja. **~-man** lumiukko. **-mobile** moottorikelkka. **~-plough** lumiaura. **~-storm** lumimyrsky, pyry. **-y** [-i] a. luminen, lumivalkoinen.

snub [snʌb] v. kohdella töykeästi, nolata; v. nolaus; a. tylppä; I was ~bed sain nenälleni. **~-nosed** nykerönenäinen.

snuff 1. [snʌf] s. (kynttilän) karsi; v. niistää (kynttilä); ~ out sammuttaa; (puhek.) kuolla.

snuff 2. [snʌf] s. nuuska; v. = sniff; take ~ nuuskata. **~-box** nuuskarasia.

snuffers [snʌfəz] s. pl. kynttiläsakset.

snuffle ['snʌfl] v. puhista, puhua nenäänsä, tuhista, honottaa; s. puhina, honotus.

snug [snʌg] a. suojaisa, hyvin peitetty, mukava, turvallinen, viihtyisä. **-gle** [-l] v. painautua (up to) jkta lähelle, asettua mukavaan asentoon; painaa (syliinsä).

so [səu] adv. niin, siten; konj. joten, niinpä, siis; is that ~? niinkö? I hope ~ toivon niin; (He is late.) — So he is. — Niin on; so what? ja entä sitten? I told you ~ sanoinhan sen; you don't say ~ eihän toki; if ~ siinä tapauksessa; ~ far toistaiseksi; ~ far as mikäli; [I was wrong, but] ~ were you niin olit sinäkin; and ~ forth (on) jne; ~ long! näkemiin! ~ as to learn oppiakseen; ~ that jotta, niin että; not ~ much as ei edes...; a mile or ~ noin mailin verran; so-so jotenkuten, mukiinmenevä(sti); so-and-so se ja se; ~-called niin sanottu.

soak [səuk] v. liottaa; kastella läpimäräksi; imeä itseensä; liota; imeytyä (in jhk); ryyppätä; be ~ed through olla läpimärkä. **-er** [-ə] s. juoppo; saderyöppy.

soap [səup] s. saippua; v. saippuoida;

soft ~ suopa, (kuv.) imartelu; ~ *opera*
hempeä radio- t. TV-sarja. **~-box
orator** katupuhuja. **~-suds**
saippuavaahto. **-y** [-i] *a.* saippuainen,
mielistelevä.

soar [sɔ:] *v.* leijailla, liidellä, kohota
korkealle; ~*ing* purjelento.

sob [sɔb] *v.* nyyhkyttää; *s.* nyyhkytys.
~-stuff nyyhkyfilmi, -kirja ym.

sober [ˈsəubə] *a.* raitis; selvä; järkevä,
maltillinen; tyyni, vakava(mielinen,
hillitty; *v.* saada selviämään;
vakavoittaa, saattaa t. tulla järkiinsä;
be ~ olla selvänä t. selvin päin; ~ *up*
selvitä humalasta; ~*ing* vakavoittava.
~-sides tosikko.

sobriety [sə(u)ˈbraiəti] *s.* raittius;
selvänä olo; kohtuullisuus, maltti,
pidättyväisyys.

sobriquet [ˈsəubrikei] *s.* liikanimi.

soccer [ˈsɔkə] *s.* (puhek.)
jalkapallo(peli); ks. *association.*

socia|bility [səufəˈbiliti] *s.* seurallisuus.
-ble [ˈsəufəbl] *a.* seuraa rakastava,
seurallinen, seuranhaluinen.

social [ˈsəuf(ə)l] *a.* yhteiskunnallinen,
sosiaalinen, yhteiskunta-; seura-,
seuraelämän; *s.* iltama, illanvietto; ~
functions, ~ *life* seuraelämä; ~
intercourse kanssakäyminen; ~ *order*
yhteiskuntajärjestys; ~ *security*
sosiaaliturva; ~ *worker*
huoltotyöntekijä. **-ism** [-izm]
sosialismi. **-ist** [-ist] *s.* sosialisti. **-istic**
[səufəˈlistik] *a.* sosialistinen. **-ite** [-ait]
s. seurapiiri-ihminen. **-ize** [-aiz] *v.*
sosialisoida.

soci|ety [səˈsaiəti] *s.* yhteiskunta;
yhdistys; seura; seuraelämä;
seurapiirit, hienosto. **-ology**
[sausiˈɔlədʒi] *s.* sosiologia.

sock 1. [sɔk] *s.* (miehen) sukka,
puolisukka; irtopohja; *pull up one's* ~
näyttää mihin pystyy.

sock 2. [sɔk] *v.* iskeä; *give sb.* ~*s*
löylyttää.

socket [ˈsɔkit] *s.* ontelo, (silmä-,
nivel)kuoppa; (lampun) pidin; [*wall*]
~ pistorasia.

Socrates [ˈsɔkrəti:z] *erisn.*

sod [sɔd] *s.* turve, nurmi.

soda [ˈsəudə] *s.* sooda(vesi)

sodden [ˈsɔdn] *a.* liotettu, likomärkä;
taikinainen, (juomisesta) tylsä.

sodium [ˈsəudjəm] *s.* natrium.

Sodom [ˈsɔdəm] *erisn.* Sodoma.

soever [sə(u)ˈevə] *suff.* hyvänsä,
tahansa (esim. *what~*).

sofa [ˈsəufə] *s.* sohva.

Sofia [ˈsəufjə] *erisn.* (kaupunki).

soft [sɔft] *a.* pehmeä, vieno, mieto;
hillitty; hiljainen, matala; lempeä;
hellä; heikko, veltto, typerä; ~ *drink*
alkoholiton juoma; ~ *goods* tekstiilit;
~ *job (thing)* helppo, hyvin maksettu
työ; *have a* ~ *spot for* pitää paljon
jksta; *be* ~ *about* olla hassuna jkh. **-en**
[ˈsɔfn] *v.* pehmittää, pehmentää,
tehdä notkeaksi; lieventää; hellyttää;
veltostaa, heikontaa; pehmetä,
leppyä. **~-headed** typerä. **~-hearted**
helläsydäminen. **-land** tehdä pehmeä
lasku. **-ly** *adv.* pehmeästi jne, hiljaa.
-ness *s.* pehmeys. **~-pedal** vaimentaa.
~-spoken pehmeä-ääninen,
ystävällinen. **-ware** (tietok.)
ohjelmisto. **-wood** kuusi- t.
mäntypuu.

soggy [ˈsɔgi] *a.* likomärkä, vetinen,
vesiperäinen.

Soho [ˈsəuhəu] *erisn.*

soil 1. [sɔil] *s.* maa, maaperä.

soil 2. [sɔil] *v.* liata, tahrata; likaantua;
s. tahra. **~-pipe** laskuputki.

sojourn [ˈsɔdʒɔ:n] *v.* oleskella, viipyä;
s. oleskelu; ~ *permit* o.lupa.

solace [ˈsɔləs] *s.* lohdutus, lohtu, *v.*
lohduttaa.

solar [ˈsəulə] *a.* aurinko-; ~*system*
aurinkokunta.

sold [səuld] *imp. & pp.* ks. *sell; be* ~ *on*
olla mielistynyt jhk.

solder [ˈsɔldə Am. ˈsɔdə] *s.* juote; *v.*
juottaa. **-ing-iron** juotin.

soldier [ˈsəuldʒə] *s.* sotilas, sotamies;
v. palvella sotamiehenä *common* ~
tavallinen sotamies. **-ly** *a.* sotaväki,
sotilaat.

sole 1. [səul] *s.* jalkapohja, antura,
(kengän)pohja; meriantura (eläint.);
v. pohjata.

sole 2. [səul] *a.* ainoa, yksinomainen.
-ly [-li] *adv.* ainoastaan,
yksinomaan.

solecism [ˈsɔlisizm] *s.* kielivirhe;
sopimaton käytös.

solemn [ˈsɔləm] *a.* juhlallinen, juhla-;
vakava. **-ity** [səˈlemniti] *s.*

juhlallisuus. **-ize** [-naiz] *v.* viettää juhlallisesti, juhlia; juhlistaa.

solicit [sə'lisit] *v.* (kiihkeästi) pyytää, anoa; ahdistaa pyynnöillään; (katutytöstä) pyydystellä. **-ation** [-'teiʃn] *s.* harras pyyntö, pyytely. **-or** [-ə] *s.* asianajaja. **-ous** [-əs] *a.* innokas, halukas; huolestunut. **-ude** [-ju:d] *s.* huoli, huolestuneisuus.

solid ['sɔlid] *a.* kiinteä, jähmeä; tiivis; kauttaaltaan samaa ainetta, täysipitoinen; tukeva, uja, vankka; luotettava, varma; vakavarainen; *s.* kiinteä aine t. ravinto, jähmeä aine. **-arity** [-'dæriti] *s.* yhteistunto, yhteenkuuluvaisuuden tunne. **-ify** [sə'lidifai] *v.* tehdä lujaksi, kiinteäksi, jähmettää, -ttyä. **-ity** [sə'liditi] *s.* kiinteys; lujuus; luotettavuus, vakavaraisuus.

solilo|quize [sə'liləkwaiz] *v.* puhua itsekseen. **-quy** [-kwi] *s.* yksinpuhelu.

solitaire [sɔli'tɛə] *s.* yksinäinen jalokivi (korussa); pasianssi.

soli|tary ['sɔlit(ə)ri] *a.* yksinäinen; ainoa; ~ *confinement* yksinäisselli. **-tude** [-ju:d] *s.* yksinäisyys, yksinäinen elämä; autio paikka.

solo ['səul|əu] *s.* (pl. ~s) soolo, -osa, -kappale; ~ *flight* yksinlento. **-ist** [-ə(u)ist] *s.* solisti.

Solomon ['sɔləmən] *erisn.* Salomo.

solstice ['sɔlstis] *s.* päivänseisaus.

sol|ubility [sɔlju'biliti] *s.* liukenevuus. **-uble** ['sɔljubl] *a.* liukeneva; ratkaistavissa oleva. **-ution** [sə'lu:ʃn] *s.* liuos; ratkaisu, vastaus. **-vable** ['sɔlvəbl] *a.* ratkaistavissa oleva.

solve [sɔlv] *v.* ratkaista, selvittää. **-ncy** [-(ə)nsi] *s.* maksukyky. **-nt** [-(ə)nt] *a.* maksukykyinen; *s.* liuotin.

Somali [sə(u)'ma:li] *s. & a.* somalialainen, somali(t).

sombre, somber ['sɔmbə] *a.* tumma, synkkä.

some [sʌm] *pron.* joku, jokin; eräs; muutamat, jotkut; vähän, hiukan; noin; ~ *day* [*or other*] jonakin päivänä; ~ *more* [sə'mɔ:] vähän lisää; ~ *time* jonkin aikaa, joskus (tulevaisuudessa); ~ *woman!* aikamoinen nainen! **-body** [-bɔdi] *pron.* joku; tärkeä henkilö. **-how** *adv.* jollakin tapaa, tavalla tai toisella.

-one *pron.* joku.

somersault ['sʌməsɔ:lt] *s.* kuperkeikka.

Somerset ['sʌməsit] *erisn.*

some|thing ['sʌmθiŋ] *pron.* jotakin; *adv.:* ~ *like* suunnilleen noin; .. *or* ~ tai jtk sen tapaista; *he is* ~ *of a carpenter* hänessä on puusepän vikaa; ~ *of a hero* eräänlainen sankari. **-time** *a.* entinen (subst. ed.); *vrt. some time.* **-times** *adv.* välistä, toisinaan, joskus. **-what** *adv.* jonkin verran, hiukan, vähän. **-where** *adv.* jossain, jonnekin; ~ *else* muualla.

somnambul|ism [sɔm'næmbjulizm] *s.* unissakäynti. **-ist** [-ist] *s.* unissakävijä.

somnol|ence ['sɔmnələns] *s.* uneliaisuus. **-ent** [-nt] *a.* unelias.

son [sʌn] *s.* poika; ~ *-in-law* vävy; *S~ of Man* Ihmisen Poika.

sonata [sə'na:tə] *s.* sonaatti.

song [sɔŋ] *s.* laulu; *the S~ of S~s* Korkea veisu; *for a* ~ pilkkahinnasta. **~-bird** laululintu. **~-hit** iskelmä. **~-ster** [-stə] *s.* laulaja; = ~ *-bird.*

sonnet ['sɔnit] *s.* sonetti. **-eer** [sɔni'tiə] *s.* sonettirunoilija.

sonny ['sʌni] *s.* poju.

sonor|ity [sə'nɔriti] *s.* soinnukkuus. **-ous** [-'nɔ:rəs] *a.* soinnikas; mahtava (ääni).

soon [su:n] *adv.* pian; ~ *after* kohta sen jälkeen (kun); *as* ~ *as* heti kun; [*just*] *as* ~ yhtä kernaasti. **-er** [-ə] *komp.* ennemmin; kernaammin; ~ *or later* ennemmin tai myöhemmin; *no* ~ [*had he*] .. *than* tuskin .. kun; *the* ~ *the better* mitä pikemmin sen parempi; *I'd* (*I would*) ~ haluaisin mieluummin.

soot [sut, su:t] *s.* noki; *v.* noeta.

sooth|e [su:ð] *v.* rauhoittaa, tyynnyttää; lievittää; **-ing** lievittävä; **-ingly** tyynnyttävästi.

soothsayer ['su:θseiə] *s.* ennustaja.

sooty ['su:ti] *a.* nokinen.

sop [sɔp] *s.* (kastettu) leipäpala; makupala (lepyttämiseksi); *v.* kastaa; **~-ping** [*wet*] likomärkä.

Sohpia [sə'faiə] *erisn.* Sofia.

sophist ['sɔfist] *s.* sofisti. **-ic(al)** [sə'fistik, -(ə)l] *a.* sofistinen; viisasteleva. **-icated** [sə'fistikeitid]

maailmaa kokenut, hieno,
hienostunut, sofistikoitu, hyvin
uudenaikainen, pitkälle kehitetty,
taidokas, konstikas, mutkikas.
-ication [-'keiʃn] s. hienous ym. **-ry**
[-ri] s. viisastelu.

Sophocles ['sɔfəkli:z] erisn.

sophomore ['sɔfəmɔ:] s. toisen vuoden
opiskelija (Am.).

soporific [səupə'rifik] a. & s.
uni(lääke).

soppy ['sɔpi] a. likomärkä.

soprano [sə'prɑ:nəu] s. sopraano.

sorcer|er ['sɔ:s(ə)rə] s. noita. **-ess** [-is]
s. noita. **-y** [-i] s. noituus.

sordid ['sɔ:did] a. likainen, kurja;
alhainen, halpamainen.

sore [sɔ:] a. kipeä, arka, hellä,
tulehtunut; vihainen, ärtynyt,
pahoillaan; tuskallinen, vaikea; s.
kipeä kohta, (märkä)haava; in ~ need
huutavassa puutteessa; ~ point arka
kohta; a ~ throat kaulakipu; old ~s
vanhat haavat. **- ly** adv. tuskallisesti,
ankarasti; kovasti.

sorority [sə'rɔriti] s. naisylioppilaiden
yhdistys, naisten kerho (Am.)

sorrel 1. ['sɔr(ə)l] s. suolaheinä.

sorrel 2. ['sɔr(ə)l] a. punaruskea; s.
raudikko.

sorrow ['sɔrəu] s. suru, murhe; v. surra,
murehtia. **-ful** ['sɔrəf(u)l] a.
surullinen, murheellinen.

sorry ['sɔri] a. pahoillaan oleva;
surkea, kurja; [I am so] ~ ! (pyydän)
anteeksi! I am ~ for him säälin häntä;
I am ~ to say valitettavasti minun
täytyy sanoa.

sort [sɔ:t] s. laji, laatu; v. lajitella,
järjestää, luokitella, (~ out)
valikoida; a ~ of,. . of a ~, . . of ~s
jonkinlainen; all ~s of kaikenlaiset;
nothing of the ~ ei sinne päinkään; ~
of niin sanoakseni, tavallaan; [he is] a
good ~ kelpo mies; out of ~s
huonossa kunnossa, huonolla
tuulella; ~ out panna järjestykseen,
selvittää; [it] ~s ill with sopii huonosti
jhk.

sortie ['sɔ:ti] s. (ulos)hyökkäys.

SOS ['esəu'es] s. hätämerkki.

sot [sɔt] s. juoppolalli. **-tish** [-iʃ] a.
(juomisesta) tylsistynyt.

sough [sau] s. humina, suhina; v.

suhista, vinkua.

sought [sɔ:t] imp. & pp. ks. seek.
~-after haluttu, kysytty.

soul [səul] s. sielu; poor ~ ihmisparka;
not a ~ ei ristinsielua; he is the ~ of
honour hän on itse rehellisyys; upon
my ~ ! kunniani kautta! **-ful** a.
sielukas, tunteikas. **-less** a.
sieluton, tunteeton. **~-mate**
hengenheimolainen. **~-stirring**
järkyttävä.

sound 1. [saund] s. salmi; (kalan)
uimarakko.

sound 2. [saund] a. terve;
vahingoittumaton, turmeltumaton,
pilaantumaton, hyvin säilynyt; hyvin
perusteltu, oikea, luja, kestävä,
luotettava, perinpohjainen; syvä
(uni); adv.: ~ asleep syvässä unessa.

sound 3. [saund] v. luodata (syvyys),
tutkia, tunnustella (jnk mielipidettä);
s. koetinpuikko; ~ings (veden)
syvyys.

sound 4. [saund] s. ääni; äänne, sointu;
v. kuulostaa; kuulua, aiheuttaa ääni
(soittaa, toitottaa, puhaltaa, antaa
merkki ym); ääntyä; it ~s all right se
kuulostaa oikealta; ~ the alarm antaa
hälytysmerkki; ~ barrier äänivalli; ~
broadcasting ääniradio. **~-box**
äänirasia. **-ing-board** kaikupohja.

sounding-lead v. mittaluoti.

sound|less a. äänetön. **-ness** s. terveys,
virheettömyys; luotettavuus,
pätevyys. **~-proof** äänieristetty.
~-track ääniraita (elok.). **~-wave**
ääniaalto.

soup [su:p] s. liemi, keitto; in the ~
»liemessä». **~-kitchen** ruoanjakelu.
~-plate syvä lautanen. **-spoon**
ruokalusikka.

sour ['sauə] a. hapan; äreä, nyrpeä; v.
hapattaa, katkeroittaa; hapantua; ~
grapes happamia, sanoi kettu!

source [sɔ:s] s. lähde, alkulähde;
deduct. . at ~ pidättää ennakolta.

sourness s. happamuus jne.

souse [sauz] v. kaataa (jnk päälle);
suolata, säilöä (etikkaliemessä); ~d
(sl.) kännissä.

south [sauθ] s. etelä; a. eteläinen,
etelä-; adv. etelässä, etelään; ~ of
jstk etelään, jnk eteläpuolella; S~
Africa Etelä-Afrikka.

Southampton [sau'θæm(p)tən] *erisn.*

south|-east *s. & a.* kaakko, -inen.
~**-easter** *s.* kaakkoistuuli. ~**-easterly**,
-eastern *a.* kaakkoinen. **-erly** ['saðəli]
a. eteläinen.

southern ['saðən] *a.* eteläinen; ~
Africa eteläinen A. **-er** [-ə] *s.*
(P.-Am.) etelävaltiolainen.

Southey ['sauði, saði] *erisn.*

southward ['sauðwəd] *a.* eteläinen;
adv. (m. ~*s*) etelään päin.

south|-west [mer. sau'west] *s.* lounas;
a. lounainen. ~**-wester** [sau'westə]
lounaistuuli. ~**-westerly** lounainen,
lounais-. ~**-western** lounainen.

souvenir ['su:v(ə)niə] *s.* muisto(esine),
matkamuisto.

sou'wester [sau'westə] *s.*
öljykangaslakki.

sovereign ['sɔv|rin] *a.* korkein, ylin,
ylhäinen; itsenäinen, riippumaton;
yksinvaltias; pettämätön (lääke); *s.*
hallitsija, yksinvaltias; punnan
kultaraha. **-ty** [-r(ə)nti] *s.* ylin valta,
yliherruus; riippumattomuus;
yksinvaltius.

Soviet ['səuviet] *s.* Neuvostoliiton,
neuvostoliittolainen; ~ *Russia*
Neuvosto-Venäjä.

sow 1. [sau] *s.* emäsika.

sow 2. [səu] *v.* (pp. -n t. -ed) kylvää,
sirotella. **-er** [-ə] *s.* kylväjä. **-ing** *s.*
kylvö.

soy [sɔi] *s.* ~[-*bean*] soijapapu.

sozzled ['sɔzld] *a.*
sika-(tukki)humalassa.

spa [spɑ:] *s.* kivennäislähde,
terveyskylpylä.

space [speis] *s.* avaruus; tila; ala,
välimatka, etäisyys; väli; aika(väli);
välike; *v.* asettaa, jättää tilaa (rivien
ym) väliin; ~ [*out*] harventaa; *living*
~ elintila; *open* ~s aukiot; ~ *age*
avaruusaika; ~ *suit* avaruuspuku;
spacing rivien väli, välike. ~**-bar**
välikenäppäin. ~**-craft** avaruusalu|s,
-kset. ~**-flight** avaruuslento. ~**-probe**
avaruusluotain.

spacious ['speiʃəs] *a.* tilava, avara.

spade [speid] *s.* lapio; pata (korttip.);
call a ~ *a* ~ nimittää asioita niiden
oikealla nimellä.

Spain [spein] *erisn.* Espanja.

span 1. [spæn] *s.* jänneväli; vaaksa;

siltakaari; siipiväli; (elin)aika;
valjakko; *v.* ulottua jnk yli, poikki;
käsittää, mitata; *a short* ~ [*of time*]
lyhyt hetki.

span 2. [spæn] *imp.* ks. *spin.*

spangle ['spæŋgl] *s.* hely, paljetti; ~*d*
helyinen, kimalteleva.

Spaniard ['spænjəd] *s.* espanjalainen.

spaniel ['spænjəl] *s.* spanieli.

Spanish ['spæniʃ] *a.* espanjalainen; *s.*
espanjan kieli.

spank [spæŋk] *v.* läimäyttää, antaa
selkäsauna; *s.* läimäys. **-ing** *a.* mainio,
aimo; *s.* selkäsauna.

spanner ['spænə] *s.* ruuviavain;
adjustable ~ jakoavain.

spar 1. [spɑ:] *s.* sälpä (miner.).

spar 2. [spɑ:] *s.* parru; riuku.

spar 3. [spɑ:] *v.* huitoa nyrkeillään,
nyrkkeillä; kinata; *s.* nyrkkisillä olo;
sanasota; ~*-ring partner*
harjoitusvastustaja (nyrkk.).

spar|e [spɛə] *v.* säästää; tulla toimeen
ilman, suoda; armahtaa; *a.* niukka;
ylimääräinen, käyttämätön, jouto-,
vapaa, vara-; hintelä, salskea (*tall and*
~); *s.* varaosa; *to* ~ liikaa,
liikenemään; *enough and to* ~
enemmän kuin kylliksi, liiaksikin; ~
part varaosa; ~ *room* vierashuone; ~
rib (sian) kylkiliha; ~ *time* joutoaika;
if we are ~*d* jos meille elonpäiviä
suodaan; ~ *the rod and spoil the child*
ei lapsi kuritta kasva. **-ely** *adv.*
säästeliäästi, niukalti; ~ *built*
varreltaan hoikka. **-ing** *a.* säästeliäs,
niukka, kitsas; vähäinen; -*ly*
säästeliäästi.

spark [spɑ:k] *s.* kipinä; ilonpitäjä,
keikari; *v.* räiskyä, kipinöidä.
-ing-plug ~ säkenöidä, säihkyä;
välkkyä, kimallella; helmeillä,
poreilla; *s.* kimmellys, välke.

sparrow ['spærəu] *s.* varpunen.

sparse [spɑ:s] *a.* harva, hajallaan
oleva; niukka; ~-*ly populated* harvaan
asuttu.

Sparta ['spɑ:tə] *erisn.* **-n** [-(ə)n] *s. & a.*
spartalainen.

spasm [spæzm] *s.* äkillinen
lihaskouristus. **-odic** [-'mɔdik] *a.*
kouristuksenomainen.

spastic ['spæstik] *s.* spastikko.

spat 1. [spæt] *imp. & pp.* ks. *spit.*

spat 2. [spæt] *s.: ~ s* (pl.) lyhyet (miesten) säärystimet.

spate [speit] *s.* tulva, kuohut.

spatial ['speiʃ(ə)l] *a.* avaruus-, tila-.

spatter ['spætə] *v.* roiskuttaa (likaa ym); ropista; *s.* pärske, roiske.

spatula ['spætjulə] *s.* lastain, spaatteli.

spavin ['spævin] *s.* patti.

spawn [spɔ:n] *s.* mäti; (halv.) sikiöt; *v.* kutea, laskea mätiä; ~*ing-bed* kutupaikka.

speak [spi:k] *spoke spoken, v.* puhua, keskustella; pitää puhe; sanoa, lausua; puhutella; ~ *for* puhua jkn puolesta; *it ~s well for him* se todistaa hänestä hyvää; *not to* ~ *of* puhumattakaan; ~ *one's mind* puhua suunsa puhtaaksi; ~ *out* = ed., m. = ~ *up;* ~ *up* korottaa äänensä, puhua selvästi ~*-easy* salakapakka. **-er** [-ə] *s.* puhuja; puhemies.

speaking *a.* puhuva, puhe-; ilmeikäs; ~ *acquaintance* hyvän päivän tuttu; *not on* ~ *terms* with huonoissa väleissä jkn kanssa; *French-~ city* ranskankielinen kaupunki. ~*-tube* puheputki.

spear [spiə] *s.* keihäs, peitsi; *v.* keihästää, lävistää; ~ *side* miehen puoli. **-head** kärkijoukko.

spec [spek] *s.* (lyh.) keinottelu; *on ~* keinottelumielessä; ks. ~*s.*

special ['speʃ(ə)l] *a.* erityinen, erikoinen, erikois-; ylimääräinen, poikkeus-; *s.* ylimääräinen juna ym; ~ *delivery* pikajakelu; ~ *edition* lisälehti; ~ *effects* trikkikuvaus. **-ist** [-əlist] *s.* erikoistuntija, spesialisti. **-ity** [speʃi'æliti] *s.* erikoisuus; erikoisala. **-ize** [-əlaiz] *v.* erikoistua. **-ly** *adv.* erityisesti; varta vasten, nimenomaan. **-ty** [-ti] *s.* erikoisala.

specie ['spi:ʃi:] *s.* metalliraha. **-s** [-i:z] *s.* (*pl.* = *sg.*) laji.

specific [spi'sifik] *a.* ominainen, erityinen, spesifinen; nimenomainen; ~ *gravity* ominaispaino. **-ation** [spes(i)fi'keiʃn] *s.* erittely; ~*s for* eritelty kustannusarvio, eritelmä.

speci|fy ['spesi|fai] *v.* eritellä, luetella yksityiskohtaisesti; *-fied* m. yksilöidy. **-men** [-mən] *s.* näyte(kappale).

specious ['spi:ʃəs] *a.* kauniin näköinen, ulkokiiltoinen, näennäinen.

speck [spek] *s.* pieni pilkku, täplä, tahra; *v.* pilkuttaa. **-le** [-l] *s.* pieni täplä, pilkku; *v.* täplittää; ~*d* täplikäs, kirjava.

specs [speks] *s. pl.* silmälasit.

spectacle ['spektəkl] *s.* näytös, näky, näytelmä; *pl.* silmälasit; *make a ~ of oneself* tehdä itsensä naurettavaksi. **-d** [-d] *a.* silmälasipäinen.

specta|cular [spek'tækjulə] *a.* komea, valtava, huomiota herättävä. **-tor** [spek'teitə] *s.* katselija.

spectr|al ['spektr(ə)l] *a.* aavemainen, aave-; spektraali- (fys.). **-e** ['spektə] *s.* aave, kummitus. **-um** [-rəm] *s.* (*pl. -a*) *s.* kirjo, spektri.

specula|te ['spekjul|eit] *v.* miettiä, pohtia, tehdä uhkarohkeita kauppoja, keinotella. **-tion** [-'leiʃn] *s.* pohdiskelu, pohdinta; keinottelu. **-tive** [-ətiv] *a.* spekulatiivinen, mietiskelevä, teoreettinen; keinotteleva. **-or** [-eitə] *s.* keinottelija.

sped [sped] *imp. & pp.* ks. *speed.*

speech [spi:tʃ] *s.* puhekyky; puhe; *deliver (make) a ~* pitää puhe (*on* jstk); *part of ~* sanaluokka; ~ *disorder* puhevika. ~*-day* (koulun) lopettajaiset. **-ify** [-ifai] *v.* pitää (huonoja) puheita. **-less** *a.* sanaton, mykkä.

speed [spi:d] *sped sped, t. ~ed, ~ed, v.* kiiruhtaa, rientää; ajaa liian nopeasti, ylittää sallittu nopeus; (vanh.) suoda menestystä; *s.* nopeus, vauhti; sl. amfetamiini; ~ *up (~ed)* lisätä nopeutta; *at full* ~ täyttä vauhtia. ~*-boat* pikamoottori. **-iness** *s.* joutuisuus. **-ing** ylinopeus. ~*-limit* nopeusraja. **-ometer** [spi'dɔmitə] *s.* nopeusmittari. ~*-way* kilpa-ajorata. **-well** *s.* tädyke (kasv.). **-y** [-i] *a.* nopea, joutuisa, ripeä, pikainen.

speleology [speli'ɔlədʒi] *s.* luolantutkimus.

spell 1. [spel] *s.* rupeama, (lyhyt) ajanjakso, kausi, tovi; (työ)vuoro.

spell 2. [spel] *s.* loitsu, lumous; *v.* (m. *spelt spelt*) tavata, kirjoittaa (oikeinkirjoitusta); muodostaa (sana); merkitä, tietää; *under a ~* lumoissa; ~ *out* tavata kokoon, sanoa selvin sanoin; ~*-bound* lumottu. **-ing**

s. kirjoitustapa, oikeinkirjoitus, tavaaminen; ~*-bee* oikeinkirjoituskilpailu; ~*-book* aapiskirja.

spelt [spelt] *imp.* ks. *spell*.

spencer ['spensə] *s*. (hist.) jakku.

spend [spend] *spent spent, v*. kuluttaa, käyttää; viettää (aika); tuhlata; uuvuttaa. **-thrift** *s*. tuhlaaja.

spent [spent] *imp. & pp.* ks. *spend;* uupunut; käytetty.

sperm [spə:m] *s*. siemenneste; ~ *whale* kaskelotti. **-aceti** [-ə'seti] *s*. valaanrasva, valaanpäävaha.

spew [spju:] *v*. oksentaa.

spher|e [sfiə] *s*. pallo; ala, piiri; sfääri, taivas, taivaankappale. **-ical** ['sferik(ə)l] *a*. pallomainen, -nmuotoinen.

sphinx [sfiŋks] *s*. sfinksi.

spice [spais] *s*. mauste, mausteet; (kuv.) höyste; *v*. maustaa, höystää.

spick and span ['spikən'spæn] *a*. uuden uutukainen, kiiltävä.

spicy ['spaisi] *a*. maustettu, höystetty, hiukan sopimaton.

spider ['spaidə] *s*. hämähäkki; ~ ['s] *web* hämähäkin verkko, seitti. **-y** [-ri] *a*. hyvin ohut.

spied *imp. & pp.* ks. *spy*.

spigot ['spigət] tulppa, tappi.

spike [spaik] *s*. piikki, naula, hokki; tähkä; *v*. varustaa piikeillä, naulata (umpeen); ~ *heels* piikkikorot. **-nard** [-nɑ:d] *s*. nardus, -öljy.

spiky ['spaiki] *a*. terävä, piikkinen.

spill 1. [spil] (m.) *spilt spilt, v*. kaataa, valaa, vuodattaa, läikyttää; pudottaa selästä; valua, läikkyä maahan; *s*. putoaminen. **-over** liika-. **-way** tulva-aukko.

spill 2. [spil] *s*. sytytyslastu, -liuska.

spilt [spilt] *imp. & pp.* ks. *spill*.

spin [spin] *v*. (imp. *spun*, vanh. *span*, pp. *spun*) kehrätä, punoa; pyörittää; pyöriä, kieriä; *s*. pyöriminen, syöksykierre (ilm.); lyhyt ajelu; souturetki ym; ~ *a yarn* kertoa merimiesjuttuja, tarinoida; ~ *out* venyttää, pitkittää; ~ *round* pyörähtää ympäri. **-dryer** pyykin kuivauslinko.

spinach ['spinidʒ] *s*. pinaatti.

spinal ['spainl] *a*. selkäranka-; ~ *column* selkäranka; ~ *cord* selkäydin.

spindle ['spindl] *s*. värttinä; kara, pystyakseli; varpa. **-legged**, **-shanked** hoikkasäärinen. **-shanks** *s*. koipeliini. **-shaped** *a*. sukkulamainen.

spindly ['spindli] *a*. ohut, hoikka.

spindrift ['spindrift] *s*. pärske.

spine [spain] *s*. selkäranka; harja(nne); piikki; ~*-chilling* selkäpiitä karmiva. **-less** *a*. selkärangaton, ryhditön.

spinner ['spinə] *s*. kehrääjä.

spinney ['spini] *s*. tiheikkö.

spinning ['spiniŋ] *s*. kehrääminen, kehruu. ~*-jenny*, ~*-machine* kehruukone. ~*-wheel* rukki.

spinster ['spinstə] *s*. naimaton nainen, ikäneito.

spiny ['spaini] *a*. okainen, piikkinen.

spiraea [spai'riə] *s*. angervo.

spiral ['spaiər(ə)l] *a*. kierukkainen, kierre-; *s*. kierukka, spiraali.

spire ['spaiə] *s*. (tornin ym) huippu.

spirit ['spirit] *s*. henki; henkiolento, aave; rohkeus, into, tulinen mieli; eloisuus; luonne, sisäinen olemus, *pl*. mieliala; (m. *pl*.) alkoholi, väkijuomat; *v.*: ~ *away, off* loihtia pois; ~ *up* elähdyttää, rohkaista; *the Holy S~* Pyhä Henki; *evil* ~ paha henki; *in high* ~ *s* hilpeä, hyvällä tuulella; *low* ~ *s* alakuloisuus, huono tuuli. **-ed** [-id] *a*. rohkea, tulinen, eloisa; henkevä. **-less** *a*. hengetön, alakuloinen, arka, tarmoton, eloton. ~*-level* vesivaaka.

spiritual ['spiritjuəl] *a*. henki-; hengellinen; *s*. hengellinen laulu. **-ism** *s*. spiritualismi, spiritismi. **-ist** *s*. spiritisti. **-ity** [-'æliti] *s*. henkisyys. **-ize** *v*. henkevöittää, henkistää.

spirituous ['spiritjuəs] *a*. alkoholipitoinen.

spirt [spə:t] ks. *spurt*.

spit 1. [spit] *s*. paistinvarras, kieleke; *v*. panna vartaaseen; lävistää.

spit 2. [spit] *spat spat, v*. sylkeä; (kissata) sähistä; sataa tihuuttaa; *s*. sylki; *is the* ~ *of* on ilmetty (isänsä ym). **-fire** kiukkupussi, tuittupää.

spite [spait] *s*. pahanilkisyys; kauna; *v*. loukata, suututtaa; *in* ~ *of* jstk

huolimatta; *out of* ~ pahuuttaan; *have
a* ~ *against* kantaa kaunaa jtk
vastaan. **-ful** *a.* ilkeä, pahansuopa.

spitt|le ['spitl] *s.* sylki. **-oon** [spi'tu:n]
s. sylkiastia.

spitz [spits] *s.* pystykorva. **S-bergen**
[-bə:gən] *erisn.* Huippuvuoret.

spiv [spiv] *s.* työnkarttaja.

splash [splæʃ] *v.* räiskyttää; roiskua,
loiskia; julkaista etusivulla t. suurin
otsikoin; *s.* roiske, loiske; läiskä,
tahra; *make a* ~ herättää huomiota.
~**-board** kurasuojus. ~**-down** lasku
(mereen).

splay [splei] *v.* viistää (ikkunan ym)
pieli. ~**-foot** lättäjalka.

spleen [spli:n] *s.* perna;
raskasmielisyys, huono tuuli;
ärtyisyys; *vent one's* ~ *on* purkaa
sisuaan jhk.

splend|id ['splendid] *a.* loistava,
komea, upea, suurenmoinen; mainio.
-our, -or [-ə] *s.* loiste; loisto, komeus.

splenetic [spli'netik] *a.* ärtyisä,
kiukkuinen.

splice [splais] *v.* pujoa, pleissata; liittää
yhteen (m. avioliittoon); *s.* pujos.

splint [splint] *s.* säle; lasta. **-er** [-ə] *s.*
lastu; säle, sirpale, siru; *v.* pirstoa,
lohkaista; pirstoutua, lohjeta.

split [split] *split split*, *v.* halkaista,
lohkaista, pirstoa; jakaa; haljeta,
pirstoutua; hajautua; joutua
epäsopuun, olla eri mieltä; *s.*
halkeama, rako; hajaannus, epäsopu;
puolipullo; *a.* halkaistu, jakautunut;
~ *on* (koul.) kieliä, ilmiantaa; ~ *hairs*
saivarrella; ~ *one's sides* [*with
laughter*] nauraa haljetakseen; ~ *the
difference* panna riita tasan; ~ *up*
jakautua; *a* ~*ting headache* ankara
päänsärky; *a* ~ *second* sekunnin
murto-osa.

splotch [splɔtʃ] *s.* läiskä.

splurge ['splə:dʒ] *s.* mahtailu,
paisutettu kuvaus.

splutter ['splʌtə] *v.* purskua, pärskyä,
puhua (kiihtyneenä) epäselvästi,
solkata; *s.* ks. *sputter.*

spoil [spɔil] *s.* (ryöstö)saalis,
sotasaalis; *pl.* (voittavan puolueen
haltuun joutuvat) valtion virat, voitot;
v. (*spoilt spoilt* t. ~*ed* ~*ed*) tuhota,
turmella, pilata; hemmotella;

pilaantua; ~*ing for a fight*
tappelunhaluinen. ~**-sport**
ilonpilaaja.

spoke 1. [spəuk] *s.* (pyörän) puola,
jarru(kenkä); *put a* ~ *in sb.'s wheel*
panna esteitä jkn tielle.

spoke 2. [spəuk] *imp.* ks. *speak.* **-n** [-n]
pp. ks. *speak*; puhuttu, suullinen; ~
English englantilainen puhekieli.
-sman *s.* edustaja.

spoliation [spəuli'eiʃn] *s.* ryöstäminen;
(asiakirjan) turmeleminen.

sponge [spʌn(d)ʒ] *s.* sieni(eläin);
pesusieni; *v.* sienellä pyyhkäistä t.
puhdistaa; ~ [*on*] elää jkn
kustannuksella, elää loisena; *throw up
the* ~ luopua (kilpailusta). ~**-cake**
sokerikakku. **-r** [-ə] *s.* (kuv.) loinen;
pummi.

spongy ['spʌn(d)ʒi] *a.* sienimäinen,
huokoinen, kuohkea.

sponsor ['spɔnsə] *s.* kummi; takaaja; *v.*
taata, tukea; kustantaa (esim.
TV-ohjelma).

spontan|eity [spɔntə'ni:əti] *s.*
vapaaehtoisuus, välittömyys. **-eous**
[spɔn'teinjəs] *a.* tahaton, itsestään
syntyvä, spontaaninen; ~ *combustion*
itsesytytys; (~**ly** *adv.* spontaanisesti,
itsestään).

spoof [spu:f] *s.* sl. huijaus; *v.* puijata.

spook [spu:k] *s.* aave, kummitus. **-y** [-i]
a. aavemainen.

spool [spu:l] *s.* puola, rulla, kela; *v.*
puolata, kelata.

spoon [spu:n] *s.* lusikka; eräänl.
golfmaila; sl. rakastunut houkkio; *v.*
ottaa lusikalla; sl. lemmiskellä. ~**-fed**
a. keinotekoisesti ylläpidetty. **-ful** *s.*
lusikallinen. **-y** [-i] *s.* houkkio; *a.*
lemmekäs.

spoor [spuə] *s.* (eläimen) jälki.

sporadic [spə'rædik] *a.* erillisenä,
satunnaisena ilmenevä.

spore [spɔ:] *s.* itiö.

sporran ['spɔr(ə)n] *s.* (skotl. pukuun
kuuluva) turkiskukkaro.

sport [spɔ:t] *s.* urheilu; leikinlasku,
kujeilu, huvi; *pl.* m. kisat, kilpailut; *v.*
leikkiä, kisailla; kantaa ylpeänä; *a*
[*good*] ~ reilu kaveri; *athletic* ~*s*
yleisurheilu; *in* ~ leikillä, huvin
vuoksi; *make* ~ *of* pitää pilanaan; *the*
~ *of Fortune* kohtalon leikkikalu. **-ing**

a. urheilu-, urheilua harrastava; reilu, rehti; ~ *chance* hyvin pieni mahdollisuus. **-ive** [-iv] *a.* leikillinen, kujeileva. **-sman** *s.* urheilija; reilu mies; (~**like** *a.* urheilijamainen; reilu, rehellinen; ~**ship** *s.* reilu urheiluhenki).

spot [spɔt] *s.* pilkku, täplä; tahra; näppylä, finni; paikka, kohta; vähäinen (määrä); *v.* pilkuttaa; tahrata; huomata, tuntea (jksk); havainnoida; ~ *cash* käteisellä; ~ *check* pistokoe; ~ *price* käteishinta; *a* ~ *of work* hiukan työtä; *in a* ~ pulassa; vaarassa; *on the* ~ paikalla, heti paikalla; *be on the* ~ olla saapuvilla; *put sb. on the* ~ (gangsterista) kolkata, nitistää. **-less** *a.* tahraton, puhdas. **-light** valokeila, valonheitin. **-ted** [-id] *a.* laikullinen, pilkukas; ~ *fever* aivokalvontulehdus. **-ter** [-ə] *s.* (tykistön) tähystäjä. **-ty** [-i] *a.* pilkullinen, täplikäs, kirjava.

spouse [spauz] *s.* puoliso.

spout [spaut] *s.* (astian) nokka, torvi; kouru, syöksytorvi; suihku; *v.* ruiskuttaa; suihkuta, ryöpytä; lausua mahtipontisesti.

sprain [sprein] *v.* nyrjäyttää, niukahtaa; *s.* nyrjähdys.

sprang [spræŋ] *imp.* ks. **spring.**

sprat [spræt] *s.* kilohaili.

sprawl [sprɔ:l] *v.* loikoa (jäsenet levällään), lojua; ojennella; haarautua eri tahoille, suikertaa; ~ *ing hand* epätasainen käsiala.

spray [sprei] *s.* pieni oksa, lehvä (jossa kukkia, marjoja; m. koriste); roiske, hyrsky, suihku; suihkutin (m. *-er*); *v.* ruiskuttaa, suihkuttaa; *hair* ~ hiuslakka, -kiinnite. ~**-gun** (maalausym) ruisku.

spread [spred] *spread spread, v.* levittää; hajottaa; ojentaa; kehittää auki, avata; levitä; hajaantua, ulottua; *s.* leviäminen; laajuus, ulottuvaisuus; (puhek.) kestit; (voileipä)tahna; *wing* ~ siipienväli; *bed*~ vuodepeite; ~ *the table* kattaa pöytä; ~ *oneself* levennellä (m. kuv.); *with . .* ~ *out over* jaettuna, siroteltuna.

spree [spri:] *s.* riehakka ilonpito; *go on the* ~ mennä juhlimaan.

sprig [sprig] *s.* pieni oksa, lehvä; nuorukainen, vesa; ~ *ged muslin* kukikas musliini.

sprightly ['spraitli] *a.* vilkas, eloisa.

spring [spriŋ] *sprang sprung, v.* hypätä, ponnahtaa, hypähtää, rynnätä, syöksähtää, saada alkunsa, syntyä puhjeta, pulpahtaa esiin; polveutua; (yllättäen) esittää, pamauttaa; räjäyttää, laukaista; räjähtää; *s.* kevät; hyppäys, ponnahdus; joustavuus, kimmoisuus; jousi, joustin; lähde, alkulähde; ~ *a leak* saada vuoto; ~ *a mine* räjäyttää miina; ~ *up* saada alkunsa, syntyä, ilmaantua; ~ *a surprise on* yllättää; *bed (mattress)* jousipatja; ~ *tide* tulvavuoksen aika. ~**-board** ponnistuslauta. **-bok** hyppyantilooppi. ~**-cleaning** kevätsiivous. **-time** kevät(aika). **-y** [-i] *a.* joustava.

sprinkl|e ['spriŋkl] *v.* suihkuttaa, pirskottaa; sirotella. **-er** *s.* suihkutin, sammutuslaite. **-ing** *s.* roiske; hitunen, pieni määrä.

sprint [sprint] *s.* pikajuoksu. **-er** [-ə] *s.* pikajuoksija, sprintteri.

sprite [sprait] *s.* henkiolento, keijukainen.

sprocket ['sprɔkit] *s.: ~ wheel* ketjupyörä.

sprout [spraut] *v.* versoa, orastaa; *s.* oras, verso; [*Brussels*] ~ *s* ruusukaali.

spruce 1. [spru:s] *a.* huoliteltu, hieno; *v.: ~ oneself up* laittautua hienoksi, kohentaa asuaan, somistautua.

spruce 2. [spru:s] *s.* kuusi.

sprung [sprʌŋ] *pp.* ks. **spring.**

spry [sprai] *a.* virkeä, vireä.

spud [spʌd] *s.* pieni lapio; sl. peruna.

spume [spju:m] *s.* vaahto, kuohu; *v.* vaahdota.

spun [spʌn] *pp.* ks. **spin.**

spunk [spʌŋk] *s.* tulisuus, rohkeus; sisu. **-y** [-i] *a.* sisukas.

spur [spə:] *s.* kannus; kannustin, kiihoke; vuoren haara; *v.* kannustaa; yllyttää; (run.) ratsastaa täyttä laukkaa; *put (set)* ~ *s to* kannustaa; *on the* ~ *of the moment* hetken mielijohteesta.

spurious ['spjuəriəs] *a.* väärä, väärennetty; vale-, teko-.

spurn [spə:n] v. torjua luotaan; hylätä (halveksien).

spurt [spə:t] v. ponnistaa rajusti voimiaan, kiriä; (m. *spirt*) ruiskauttaa, ruiskahtaa, ruiskuta, purskua; s. pinnistys, (loppu)kiri; suihku, ruiskaus.

sputter ['spʌtə] v. käristä; pärskyttää, pärskyä; puhua sopottaa; s. räiske; epäselvä puhe.

sputum ['spju:təm] s. yskös, yskökset (lääk.).

spy [spai] s. vakoilija, urkkija; v. vakoilla (*on* jkta); huomata, keksiä; ~ *out* nuuskia tietoonsa. **-ing** s. vakoilu. ~-**glass** kaukoputki.

squabble ['skwɔbl] v. kinata; s. kina, tora.

squab [skwɔb] s. kyyhkynen.

squad [skwɔd] s. ryhmä, joukkue. **-ron** [-r(ə)n] s. ratsuväenosasto, eskadroona; laivue (ilm., mer.).

squalid ['skwɔlid] a. likainen, kurja. **-ity** [-'liditi] s. likaisuus.

squall [skwɔ:l] v. kirkua; s. kirkuna; vihuri, (sade)puuska. **-y** [-i] a. puuskainen.

squalor ['skwɔlə] s. likaisuus, kurjuus, siivottomuus, saasta.

squander ['skwɔndə] v. tuhlata.

square [skweə] s. neliö (m. mat.), nelikulmio; ruutu, ruudukko, levy; aukio; kulma|mitta, -viivoitin; a. neliönmuotoinen, neliö; nelikulmainen, -sivuinen; suorakulmainen; tanakka, vanttera; kunnossa, järjestyksessä oleva; tasoitettu (tili); perusteellinen; rehellinen, suora; sovinnainen; v. tehdä neliönmuotoiseksi, nelikulmaiseksi; järjestää neliön muotoon; korottaa toiseen potenssiin (mat.); sovittaa (yhteen); tasoittaa, selvittää (tilit); sopia yhteen, olla yhtäpitävä; lahjoa; *adv.* suorassa (kulmassa), suoraan; ~ *deal* rehellinen kauppa; ~ *meal* tukeva ateria; ~ *measure* pinnanmitta; ~ *refusal* jyrkkä kielto; ~ *root* neliöjuuri; *get* ~ *with* päästä tasoihin jkn kanssa; *on the* ~ rehellisesti; ~ *accounts with* selvittää tilit, välit; ~ *one's shoulders* ryhdistäytyä; ~ *up* selvittää; ~ *up to* kohdata lujana.

~-**built** leveäharteinen, tanakka. **-ly** *adv.* rehellisesti, suoraan. **-ness** s. neliömäisyys; rehellisyys. **-toes** s. (turhantarkka) pedantti.

squash [skwɔʃ] v. musertaa, litistää; ahtaa, ahtautua jhk, tunkeutua; nolata, vaientaa; s. tungos; eräänl. kurpitsa; seinäpallo(peli); ~ *hat* pehmeä huopahattu; *lemon-* ~ sitruunajuoma. **-y** [-i] a. pehmeä, vetelä.

squat [skwɔt] v. istua kyykkyasennossa, kyykkiä, kököttää; kyyristyä; asettua (luvatta) jhk asumaan; a. lyhyt ja paksu, vanttera. **-ter** [-ə] s. uudisasukas, ks. ed.; lammasfarmari.

squaw [skwɔ:] s. intiaanivaimo.

squawk [skwɔ:k] v. rääkäistä, rääkyä; s. rääkäisy.

squeak [skwi:k] v. vikinä; v. vinkua, vikistä, kitistä; (kengästä) narista; sl. ilmiantaa; *a narrow* ~ täpärä pelastus. **-y** [-i] a. vikisevä, vinkuva.

squeal [skwi:l] v. kimeä huuto, kiljahdus; v. kiljua, kirkua; ilmiantaa. **-er** [-ə] s. ilmiantaja.

squeamish ['skwi:miʃ] a. huonovatsainen, nirso; turhantarkka; arkatuntoinen.

squeeze [skwi:z] v. pusertaa, puristaa; kiskoa, kiristää (rahaa); sulloa, tunkea, -eutua; s. puristus, puserrus, likistys; *it was a* [*tight*] ~ oli täpärällä.

squelch [skwel(t)ʃ] v. rämpiä, lotista.

squib [skwib] s. sähikäinen; pilkkakirjoitus.

squid [skwid] s. pieni mustekala, kalmari.

squint [skwint] v. katsoa kieroon, karsastaa; s. karsastus. ~-**eyed** kierosilmäinen.

squire ['skwaiə] s. tilanomistaja, kartanonherra; aseenkantaja; knaappi; (naisen) ritari; Am. rauhantuomari; v. olla kavaljeerina, saattaa.

squirm [skwə:m] v. kiemurrella, vääntelehtiä; olla vaivautunut, hämmentynyt.

squirrel ['skwir(ə)l] s. orava.

squirt [skwə:t] v. ruiskuttaa; suihkuta; s. suihku; pieni ruisku.

St [sən(t), sin(t), sn(t)] lyh. = *Saint; St Bernard* bernhardilaiskoira; *St Paul's*

Paavalin katedraali Lontoossa; *St Peter's* Pietarinkirkko Roomassa.

stab [stæb] *s.* isku, pisto, pistos; sl. yritys; *v.* pistää, iskeä, lävistää, puukottaa.

stabil|ity [stə'biliti] *s.* vakavuus, lujuus. **-ize** ['steibilaiz] *v.* vakaannuttaa, vakauttaa; *-izing* tasapainottava.

stable 1. ['steibl] *a.* vankka, vakava, vakaa, kestävä; vakinainen; vakaantunut.

stable 2. ['steibl] *s.* talli, (jnk tallin) kilpa-ajohevoset; *v.* panna talliin. **-man** tallirenki.

stack [stæk] *s.* auma, suova; kasa, pino; savutorvi(ryhmä); *v.* aumata, kasata, pinota; Am. jakaa pelikortit väärin.

stadium ['steidjəm] *s.* stadion.

staff [sta:f] *s.* sauva, keppi, salko; esikunta; henkilökunta, henkilöstö; (pl. *staves*) nuottiviivasto; ~ *college* sotakorkeakoulu; ~ *officer* yleisesikuntaupseeri; ~ *room* opettajainhuone; *teaching* ~ opettajakunta.

stag [stæg] *s.* uroshirvi; osakekeinottelija; ~ *party* herrakutsut. **~-beetle** tamminkainen (eläint.).

stage [steidʒ] *s.* lava, koroke; näyttämö, teatteri; tapahtumapaikka; (kehitys)aste, vaihe; postiasema, kyytiväli, etappi; *v.* asettaa näyttämölle, lavastaa, järjestää; *landing* ~ laituri; *by easy* ~ *s* lyhyin päivämatkoin, mukavasti; *go on the* ~ ruveta näyttelijäksi; ~ *directions* näyttämöohjeet; ~ *fright* ramppikuume; ~ *manager* näyttämömestari; ~ *whisper* teatterikuiskaus. **~-coach** postivaunut. **-r** [-ə] *s.: old* ~ kokenut tekijä. **~-struck** *a.* teatterikärpäsen purema.

stagger ['stægə] *v.* horjua, hoiperrella; saattaa horjumaan; saattaa (aivan) ymmälle; porrastaa; *s.* horjuminen; *the* ~ *s* (karjan) huimaustauti; *I was* ~ *ed to hear* tyrmistyin kuullessani; ~ *ed with admiration* ihailusta suunniltaan.

staging ['steidʒiŋ] *s.* näyttämöllepano, lavastus.

stagna|nt ['stægnənt] *a.* seisova (vesi); lamaantunut, laimea. **-te** [-'neit] *v.* seisoa paikallaan; lamaantua. **-tion** [-'neiʃn] *s.* seisahtuminen, pysähdystila.

stagy ['steidʒi] *a.* teatraalinen.

staid [steid] *a.* vakava, maltillinen.

stain [stein] *v.* tahrata; värittää, värjätä; petsata; tahraantua, värjääntyä; *s.* tahra; häpeätahra; väriaine, värjäys (tiet.); ~ *ed glass* lasimaalaus. **-less** *a.* tahraton; ~ *steel* ruostumaton teräs.

stair [stɛə] *s.* porras, *pl.* portaat. **-case** portaat, portaikko. **~-rod** mattotanko. **-way** = *-case*.

stake [steik] *s.* seiväs, paalu; polttorovio; (peli)panos, osuus; vedonlyönti; *pl.* (raha)palkinto; *v.* tukea seipäillä; merkitä paaluilla; panna peliin, panna alttiiksi, uskaltaa (*on* jnk varaan); *be at* ~ olla kysymyksessä; *perish at the* ~ kuolla roviolla; *pull up* ~ *s* (puhek.) muuttaa; ~ *off (out)* viitoittaa (paaluilla).

stala|ctite ['stælə|ktait] *s.* (riippuva) tippukivi. **-gmite** [-gmait] *s.* tippukivipylväs.

stale [steil] *a.* vanha, väljähtänyt, ummehtunut, nuutunut; kulunut; *v.* nuutua, väljähtyä. **-mate** [-meit] *s.* pattiasema (šakkip.); umpikuja; *v.* saattaa umpikujaan. **-ness** *s.* ummehtuneisuus; kuluneisuus.

stalk 1. [stɔ:k] *s.* korsi, varsi; *[chimney-]~* (tehtaan) piippu.

stalk 2. [stɔ:k] *v.* hiipimällä lähestyä (riistaa); astella ylväästi, korskeasti; *s.* ylväs käynti; *deer* ~ *ing* hirvenpyynti. **-ing-horse** tekosyy, veruke.

stall [stɔ:l] *s.* pilttuu; kauppakoju, myymäpöytä; etupermantopaikka (teatt.); kuori-istuin; tuppi; kuolio (ilm.); *v.* panna talliin, pitää pilttuussa; seisahtua; (lentokoneesta) joutua kuolioon, sakata; verukkeilla viivyttää, puolustautua taitavasti, (~ *off*) torjua, väistellä; *orchestra* ~ *s* etupermanto. **~-fed** lihotettu, sisällä ruokittu. **-ion** ['stæljən] *s.* ori.

stalwart ['stɔ:lwət] *a.* roteva, urhea, luja; *s.: party* ~ *s* puolueen tukipylväät.

stamen ['steimen] *s.* hede.

stamina ['stæminə] s. vastustuskyky, kestävyys.

stammer ['stæmə] v. änkyttää; s. änkytys.

stamp [stæmp] v. polkea, tömistää; survoa; leimata, painaa leima; lyödä rahaa; varustaa postimerkillä; s. leimasin, leima; karttamerkki; postimerkki (m. *postage*-~); laatu, laji; ~ *out* tukahduttaa; . . *is* ~*ed in my mind (on my mind)* on painunut mieleeni. **~-collector** postimerkkien keräilijä. **~-duty** leimavero.

stampede [stæm'pi:d] s. hurja pako, pakokauhu; v. lähteä hurjaan pakoon.

stance [stæns] s. (lyönti)asento (urh.); asenne.

stanch [stɑ:n(t)ʃ] v. pysähdyttää, tyrehdyttää; *a*. ks. **staunch**. **-ion** ['stɑ:nʃn] s. tuki, pylväs.

stand [stænd] *stood stood*, v. seisoa, olla pystyssä; nousta (~ *up*); seisahtua, olla pysähdyksissä; astua, asettua; olla, sijaita, olla jssk tilanteessa; pysyä pystyssä, jatkua, pysyä voimassa; suunnata kulku jhk (mer.); asettaa pystyyn; pitää puolensa; kestää, kärsiä, sietää; maksaa jkn puolesta; s. seisahdus; vastarinta; asema, paikka; asenne, kanta; taksiasema; lava, (katsoja)parveke; myyntikoju; alusta, jalusta, teline; Am. todistajan aitio; *as matters* ~ nykytilanteessa; ~*s convicted of* on tuomittu syylliseksi jhk; *I* ~ *corrected* myönnän olleeni väärässä; ~ *one's ground* pitää puoliaan; *I cannot* ~ *that fellow* en voi sietää tuota miestä; ~ *the test* kestää koetus; *he stood us drinks* hän tarjosi meille ryypyt; ~ *about (around)* seisoskella; ~ *aside!* ~ *clear!* pysykää loitolla! ~ *by* seisoa vieressä, katselijana; olla jkn puolella, tukea, pysyä uskollisena jllek; ~ *for* edustaa, merkitä; ajaa (jtk asiaa); olla ehdokkaana (parlamenttiin ym); ~ *off* pysyä loitolla; tilapäisesti erottaa; ~ *on* pitää tärkeänä (esim. ~ *on ceremony* kursailla); ~ *out* pistää esiin, erottautua, olla silmiinpistävä, pitää puoliaan; ~ *over* jäädä toistaiseksi; ~ *to* pitää kiinni jstk, pysyä (sanassaan);

asettua vartiopaikalleen; *he* ~*s to win* hän melko varmasti voittaa; ~ *up* nousta (seisomaan); ~ *up for* puolustaa; ~ *up to* nousta vastustamaan, uhmata; ~ *well with* olla hyvissä väleissä jkn kanssa; *bring to a* ~ seisahduttaa; *come to a* ~ seisahtua; *make a* ~ asettua vastarintaan; *make a public* ~ julkisesti ottaa kanta(a); *take one's* ~ asettua paikalleen, valita kantansa.

standard ['stændəd] s. lippu; (raha-, mitta)yksikkö; normaalimitta; perustyyppi, malli, normi, taso; mittapuu; (metallin) -pitoisuus; (raha)kanta; runko; kannatin, pylväs; *a*. standardi-, vakio-, normaali-, malli-; klassi(lli)nen; mallikelpoinen; ~ *of living* elintaso; *gold* ~ kultakanta; *be up to* ~ vastata vaatimuksia; *of high* ~ korkeatasoinen, tasokas; *below* ~ ala/mittainen, -arvoinen; ~ *lamp* jalkalamppu; ~ *rose* runkoruusu; ~ *English* englannin yleiskieli, kirjakieli; ~ *work* merkkiteos. **~-bearer** lipunkantaja. **-ize** [-aiz] s. standardoida.

stand|-by s. apu, tuki. **-ee** [stæn'di:] s. seisomapaikalla oleva. **-in** s. sijainen.

standing ['stændiŋ] *a*. seisova; pysyvä, vakinainen; s. kesto, aika; asema, arvo; ~ *army* vakinainen armeija; ~ *corn* kasvava vilja; ~ *joke* aina toistuva pila; ~ *jump* vauhditon hyppy; . . *of long* ~ pitkäaikainen; . . *of many years'* ~ monivuotinen; . . *of high* ~ korkeassa asemassa oleva. **~-room** seisomatila, -paikka.

stand|-offish *a*. pidättyväinen, torjuva. **-point** ['stæn(d)-] s. näkökanta. **-still** s. seisahtuminen; *be at a* ~ olla seisahduksissa; *come to a* ~ pysähtyä. **~-up** *a*.: ~ *collar* pystykaulus; ~ *fight* kunnon taistelu; ~ *buffet* seisova pöytä.

stank [stæŋk] *imp*. ks. **stink**.

stanza ['stænzə] s. säkeistö.

staple ['steipl] s. (paikan) päätuote; pääaines, pääsisältö; kuitu; (nitoma)sinkilä; *a*. pääasiallinen, pää-; tapuli-; v. nitoa; ~ [*food*] tärkein, pää-. **-r** [-ə] s. nitomakoje.

star [stɑ:] s. tähti (m. elok., urh.); v. koristaa tähdillä; näytellä pääosaa, antaa tähtiosa jklle; S~s and Stripes Yhdysvaltain tähtilippu.

starboard ['stɑ:bəd] s. (aluksen) oikea puoli, tyyrpuuri.

starch [stɑ:tʃ] s. tärkkelys, tärkki; jäykkyys; v. kovettaa, tärkätä. **-y** [-i] a. tärkkelyspitoinen; kankea.

star|dom ['stɑ:dɔm] s. tähdet, tähden asema (elok.) **-fish** meritähti.

star|e [stɛə] v. tuijottaa; töllistellä; s. tuijotus; ~ sb. down tuijottamalla saattaa hämille. **-ing** a. tuijottava; liian silmiinpistävä, räikeä.

stark [stɑ:k] a. kankea, jäykistynyt; täydellinen, pelkkä; adv. ~ [staring] mad silmittömän; ~ naked ilkialaston.

star|light, -lit a. tähtikirjas.

starling ['stɑ:liŋ] s. kottarainen.

starry ['stɑ:ri] a. tähtiä täynnä (oleva); tähtikirkas; tähti-.

star-spangled: S.-S. Banner = Stars and Stripes.

start [stɑ:t] v. lähteä (matkaan, liikkeelle); aloittaa, alkaa, ryhtyä; panna käyntiin, käynnistää, auttaa alkuun; saada (tekemään jtk); antaa lähtömerkki; säpsähtää, hätkähtää; syöksyä; kavahtaa (pystyyn); irrottaa, irtaantua, höltetä; s. lähtö, startti; alku; etumatka; hätkähdys; lähtöviiva; ~ out lähteä matkaan, ryhtyä jhk; ~ up kavahtaa pystyyn, käynnistää; to ~ with aluksi; by fits and ~s puuskittain; get the ~ of päästä jkn edelle; give a ~ hätkähtää. **-er** [-ə] s. lähtijä, kilpailija; lähettäjä; käynnistin. **-ing-point** (kuv.) lähtökohta.

startl|e [stɑ:tl] v. hätkähdyttää, säikähdyttää, hämmästyttää; be ~d hätkähtää, pelästyä. **-ing** a. hätkähdyttävä, yllättävä.

starvation [stɑ:'veiʃn] s. nälkään nääntyminen t. nääntnytys; nälkä; ~ wages nälkäpalkka.

starve [stɑ:v] v. nääntyä nälkään, nähdä nälkää; nääntnyttää nälkään; pitää nälässä; ~ to death kuolla nälkään; starving for jnk nälkäinen. **-ling** [-liŋ] s. nälkiintynyt olento.

state [steit] s. tila, asema, kunto; arvo; komeus, loisto; valtio, Am. osavaltio;

a. juhla-; valtio(n)-, osavaltion; valtiollinen; v. esittää, ilmoittaa, sanoa, selittää, kertoa; määrätä; ~ of mind mielentila; in [quite] a ~ aivan kiihdyksissään; in ~ juhlallisesti, juhlamenoin; lie in ~ (arkusta) olla kunniakorokkeella; the S~s Yhdysvallat; S~ Department (Am.) ulkoministeriö. **-craft** valtiotaito. **-hood** s. (itsenäisen) valtion asema. **-liness** s. komeus, upeus. **-ly** [-li] a. komea, upea; ylväs, arvokas. **-ment** s. väite, selonteko, ilmoitus, lausuma; ~ of accounts tiliote. **-room** (ensi luokan) hytti. **-smanship** s. valtiotaito.

static ['stætik] a. staattinen, lepo-. **-s** [-s] s. statiikka; ilmastohäiriöt (rad.).

station ['steiʃn] s. asema, (määrätty) paikka; rautatieasema, pysäkki; sotilas-, laivastoasema; (yhteiskunnallinen) asema, sääty; v. määrätä jhk asemapaikkaan, sijoittaa; ~ oneself asettua. **-ary** [-əri] a. paikallaan pysyvä, kiinteä, muuttumaton. **-er** [-ə] s. paperikauppias. **-ery** [-əri] s. kirjoitustarvikkeet, paperitavarat. **~-wagon** farmariauto.

statis|tical [stə'tis|tik(ə)l] a. tilastollinen. **-tician** [-'tiʃn] s. tilastotieteilijä. **-tics** [-tiks] s. tilasto, -tiede.

statuary ['stætjuəri] s. kuvanveistotaide, -veistokset.

statue ['stætju:] s. kuvapatsas, veistos. **-sque** [-ju'esk] a. veistoksellinen. **-tte** [-ju'et] s. pienoisveistos.

stature ['stætʃə] s. (ruumiin)koko, varsi; short of ~ lyhytkasvuinen, varreltaan lyhyt.

status ['steitəs] s. asema, tila, (yhteiskunnallinen) arvostus; ~ symbol statussymboli.

statut|e ['stætju:t] s. asetus, laki; ohjesääntö. **-ory** [-tjutəri] a. lakisäeteinen.

staunch [stɔ:n(t)ʃ] a. luja, järkkymätön; luotettava, uskollinen; v. tyrehdyttää.

stave [steiv] s. (esim. tynnyrin) laidas, laitalauta; ~s nuottiviivasto; v. (imp. & pp. ~d t. stove); ~ in iskeä reikä, puhkaista; ~ off torjua, viivyttää.

stay [stei] *v.* jäädä, viipyä; oleskella, asua (tilapäisesti); pysyä, pysytellä; pitää puoliansa, kestää (kilpailussa); pysähdyttää, ehkäistä; lykätä; tukea; *s.* viipyminen, oleskelu, olo; kestävyys; tuki; harus (mer.); (lak.) lykkäys; ~*s* korsetti; ~ *where you are* pysy paikallasi; ~ *away* jäädä pois, pysyä poissa; ~ *for* jäädä (odottamaan jtk); ~ *on* jäädä edelleen; ~ *one's hand* hillitä itsensä; ~ *put* pysyä paikallaan; ~ *up* valvoa; *it has come to* ~ se on jäänyt käytäntöön, tullut pysyväiseksi. ~**-at-home** *a.* kotona viihtyvä; *s.* kotikissa. **-ing-power** kestävyys.

stead [sted] *s.: in my* ~ minun sijastani; *stand sb. in good* ~ olla jklle suureksi hyödyksi. **-fast** [-fɑ:st] *a.* vakava, luja, järkkymätön; kestävä. **-iness** *s.* vakavuus, lujuus. **-y** [-i] *a.* vakava, tukeva, tasainen, säännöllinen; luja, luotettava; vakaantunut; *v.* tehdä t. tulla vakavaksi, vakaantua; ~ *!* älkää hätäilkö; rauhallisesti!

steak [steik] *s.* pihvi; kalafilee.

steal [sti:l] *stole, stolen, v.* varastaa; hiipiä varkain t. salavihkaa; ~ *away* hiipiä, puikahtaa pois; ~ *a glance at* vilkaista salavihkaa jhk; ~ *a march on* ennättää jkn edelle. **-ing** *s.* varastaminen, varkaus.

stealth [stelθ] *s.: by* ~ salaa, salavihkaa. **-ily** *adv.* = ed. **-y** [-i] *a.* salainen, salavihkainen, hiipivä.

steam [sti:m] *s.* höyry; huuru, *v.* höyrytä; höyryttää; keittää höyryssä; ~ *off* lähteä höyryten; *get up* ~ (kuv.) terästää tarmoaan; *let off* ~ purkaa tunteitaan; ~*ing hot* höyryävän kuuma. ~**-engine** höyrykone. **-er** [-ə] *s.* höyrylaiva; höyrykeitin. ~**-roller** höyryjyrä. **-ship** höyrylaiva. **-y** [-i] *a.* höyryävä, höyry-; huuruinen.

stearin [ˈsti:ərin] *s.* steariini.

steed [sti:d] *s.* (sota)ratsu.

steel [sti:l] *s.* teräs; (run.) miekka; *v.* terästää, karaista; *cold* ~ teräaseet (vastak. ampuma-aseet); ~ *works* terästehdas. ~**-clad** panssaroitu. **-y** [-i] *a.* teräs-, teräksinen. **-yard** puntari.

steep 1. [sti:p] *a.* (äkki)jyrkkä; *s.* jyrkänne.

steep 2. [sti:p] *v.* upottaa, liottaa; kyllästää; ~*ed in* jhk vajonnut, syvästi perehtynyt *(in his subject).* **-en** [-n] *v.* jyrkentää, -tyä.

steeple [ˈsti:pl] *s.* kirkontorni. **-chase** esteratsastus, -juoksu. **-d** [-d] *a.* tornilla varustettu. **-jack** torninrakentaja.

steer 1. [stiə] *s.* nuori härkä.

steer 2. [stiə] *v.* ohjata, pitää perää; ~ *clear of* välttää. **-age** [-ridʒ] *s.* välikansi; ~*-way* (aluksen ohjaukseen tarvittava) pienin nopeus. **-ing-gear** ohjauslaite. **-ing-wheel** ohjauspyörä. **-sman** *s.* peränpitäjä.

stellar [ˈstelə] *a.* tähti-, tähtimäinen.

stem [stem] *s.* runko, varsi, (lasin) jalka; (sanan) vartalo, kanta; (aluksen) keula(vannas); *v.* ehkäistä, hillitä; padota; ~ *from* juontaa alkunsa jstk.

stench [sten(t)ʃ] *s.* haju, löyhkä.

stencil [ˈstensl] *s.* malline, šabloni, luotta; ~ *paper* luottapaperi, monistusvahapaperi.

stenograph er [steˈnɔgrəf|ə] *s.* pikakirjoittaja. **-y** [-i] *s.* pikakirjoitus.

stentorian [stenˈtɔ:riən] *a.* jylisevä, ukkosen kaltainen.

step 1. [step] *s.* askel; toimenpide; astunta, käynti; (jalan)jälki; porras, askelma; sävelaskel; (tikapuitten) puola; astuin; ylennys (virassa) *pl.* (ulko)portaat, tikkaat; *v.* astua; käydä, kulkea; mitata askelin (~ *off);* tanssia; *[pair of]* ~*s* tikkaat; *door* ~ kynnys; *keep* ~ *with* pysyä jkn tasalla; *take* ~ *s* [*to*] ryhtyä toimiin, toimenpiteisiin; ~ *by* ~ askel askeleelta, asteittain; *out of* ~ epätahdissa; ~ *in* astua sisään, käydä käsiksi asiaan, sekaantua jhk; ~ *on it!* joudu! ~ *out* lähteä juhlimaan; ~ *up* [*the scale*] lisätä.

step- [step-] *pref.* -puoli. **-child** lapsipuoli. **-daughter** tytärpuoli.

Stephen [ˈsti:vn] *erisn.* Tapani.

step-ladder tikapuut, tikkaat.

steppe [step] *s.* aro.

stepping-stone *s.* (kuv.) astinlauta.

step|sister, -son *s.* sisar-, poikapuoli.

stereo [ˈstiəri|əu] *s.: ~ disk* stereolevy. **-phonic** [-əˈfɔnik] *a.* stereofoninen. **-phony** [-ˈɔfəni] *s.* stereofoninen

äänentoisto. **-scope** [-əskəup] s.
stereoskooppi. **-type** [-ətaip] s.
stereotypialaatta (kirjap.); v.
kaavoittaa; ~d kaavamainen,
kaavoittunut.

steril|e ['sterail] a. hedelmätön, karu;
steriili. **-ity** [ste'riliti] s.
hedelmättömyys. **-ize** ['sterilaiz] v.
steriloida.

sterling ['stə:lin] a. täysipitoinen; aito;
pound ~ sterlinkipunta; ~ area
puntablokki.

stern 1. [stə:n] a. ankara, kova, tuima.

stern 2. [stə:n] s. (laivan) perä; down by
the ~ perälastissa.

sternum ['stə:nəm] s. rintalasta.

stertorous ['stə:tərəs] a. koriseva.

stethoscope ['steθəskəup] s. kuulotorvi
(lääk.).

stevedore ['sti:vidɔ:] s. ahtaaja.

stew [stju:] v. keittää muhennokseksi,
muhentaa; kiehua hiljalleen, porista;
ahertaa, raataa (kouluk.); s.
muhennos; in a ~ suunniltaan
(levottomuudesta).

steward ['stjuəd] s. tilanhoitaja;
taloudenhoitaja; (laivan,
lentokoneen) stuertti, tarjoilija;
(juhlien) ylivalvoja, marsalkka,
intendentti; Lord High S~ of England
Englannin lordiylimarsalkka; shop ~
ks. t. **-ess** [-is] s. (laivan) siivooja,
lentoemäntä. **-ship** s. taloudenhoito,
tilanhoito.

Stewart [stjuət] erisn.

stick 1. [stik] s. tikku, (pieni) oksa,
risu; (kävely)keppi, sauva, puikko,
tanko.

stick 2. [stik] stuck stuck, v. pistää;
lävistää; kiinnittää, liimata,
liisteröidä; sietää; takertua, tarttua
kiinni, tahmautua, juuttua; jäädä,
olla, riippua kiinni (jssk); pysyä
uskollisena (jllek); takertua,
hämmentyä puheessaan; epäröidä,
arastella (at jtk); he ~s at nothing hän
ei arastele, häikäile mitään; ~ around
pysyä lähettyvillä; ~ by pysyä
uskollisena; ~ out pistää esiin,
törröttää; ~ it out kestää loppuun asti;
~ out for vaatia; ~ to pitää kiinni jstk;
~ up (sl.) ryöstää; ~ up for puolustaa
jtk; ~ it! älä hellitä! [out] in the ~s
(Am.) Jumalan selän takana; a stuck

pig pistetty sika; get stuck in the mud
juuttua liejuun. **-er** [-ə] s.
itsepintainen henkilö, uurastaja;
tarralipuke, liimattu (hinta-
ym)lappu. **-iness** s. tahmeus.
-ing-plaster kiinnelaastari.
~-**in-the-mud** patavanhoillinen.

stickle|back ['stikl|bæk] s. rautakala. **-r**
[-ə] s.: ~ for jnk itsepintainen
puoltaja.

stick-up s. (sl.) ryöstö.

sticky ['stiki] a. tahmea, sitkeä,
mutainen; vastahakoinen, hankala;
[he] came to a ~ end sai hurjan lopun,
(sl.) kuoli kuin koira.

stiff [stif] a. kankea, jäykkä;
taipumaton; sitkeä; vaikea, tiukka,
ankara (työ), kova, navakka (tuuli);
korkea (hinta); s. (sl.) ruumis; keep a
~ upper lip pysyä lujana; scare sb. ~
pelästyttää puolikuoliaaksi. **-en** [-n] v.
jäykistää; jäykistyä, kangistua;
(tuulesta) kiihtyä, (hinnasta) nousta.
-ening s. jäykiste. ~-**necked**
jäykkäniskainen, itsepintainen. **-ness**
s. kankeus, jäykkyys jne.

stifle ['staifl] v. tukehduttaa;
tukahduttaa; tukehtua; stifling
tukahduttava.

stigma ['stigmə] s. häpeämerkki; (pl.
-ta) stigma (usk.). **-tize** [-taiz] v.
merkitä, leimata (as jksk);
stigmatisoida.

stile [stail] s. jalkaporras.

stiletto [sti'letəu] s. (pl. ~[e]s) stiletti;
~ heels piikkikorot.

still 1. [stil] a. hiljainen, tyyni;
liikkumaton; äänetön; adv. vielä,
yhä; kuitenkin; v. hiljentää,
tyynnyttää, vaientaa; s. liikkumaton
kuva, yksittäiskuva; ~-life (pl. -lifes)
asetelma (maal.).

still 2. [stil] s. tislauslaite; viinapannu.

still-born kuolleena syntynyt.

stillness s. hiljaisuus, rauha.

stilt [stilt] s.: ~s puujalat. **-ed** [-id] a.
väkinäinen, kankean muodollinen.

stimul|ant ['stimjulənt] s. kiihotusaine,
piristysaine. **-ate** [-eit] v. kiihottaa,
virkistää, piristää, stimuloida. **-ation**
[-'leiʃn] s. stimulaatio, piristys,
stimulanssi. **-us** [-əs] s. (pl. -i [-ai])
kiihoke, ärsyke; yllyke, virike;
kannustin.

sting [stiŋ] *stung stung, v.* pistää; polttaa, kirvellä, haavoittaa, loukata; varastaa, puijata; *s.* pistin, piikki; pisto(s); ota; *he was stung for* [£ 5] häneltä puijattiin.

sting|iness ['stin(d)ʒ|inis] *s.* saituus. **-y** [-i] *a.* saita, kitsas; niukka.

stink [stiŋk] *v.* (imp. *stank* t. *stunk*, pp. *stunk*) löyhkätä, haista; *s.* löyhkä; ~*ing* löyhkäävä; ilkeä, inhottava.

stint [stint] *v.* rajoittaa, supistaa; kitsastella; *s.* tehtävä; *one's daily* ~ päivittäinen urakka, tehtävä; *without* ~ kitsastelematta, säästämättä vaivojaan; [*she*] ~*ed herself of* ei suonut itselleen.

stipend ['staipend] *s.* (vakinainen) palkka. **-iary** [-'pendʒəri] *a.* palkkaa nauttiva.

stipple ['stipl] *v.* pilkuttaa, pisteittää (maal.)

stipula|te ['stipjuleit] *v.* panna (sopimuksen) ehdoksi, sisällyttää sopimukseen. **-tion** [-'leiʃn] *s.* välipuhe, sopimus, ehto.

stir [stə:] *v.* panna liikkeelle, liikuttaa; kohentaa, hämmentää; kiihottaa, saattaa kuohuksiin; liikkua, liikahtaa, olla liikkeessä; olla jalkeilla, nousta (aamulla); *s.* liike, liikahdus; häly, hälinä; (sl.) vankila; ~ *up* sekoittaa, herättää, yllyttää; *make a* ~ herättää huomiota. **-ring** *a.* mieltä liikuttava, jännittävä, innostava; toimelias.

stirrup ['stirəp] *s.* jalustin.

stitch [stitʃ] *s.* pisto; silmä, silmukka; ommel; pistos, kipu; *v.* ommella; nitoa.

stoat [stəut] *s.* kärppä.

stock [stɔk] *s.* runko, pölkky; kanta; suku; (kiväärin) tukki; varsi; varasto; karja, -kanta; (tav. *pl.*) arvopaperit, osakkeet; leukoija; liha-, perusliemi; kova kaulus; *pl.* jalkapuu; *pl.* telapohja; *a.* varasto-; vakio-, tavallinen; *v.* panna varastoon, varustaa; varastoida, pitää varastossa; *Government* ~[*s*] valtion obligaatiot; *S* ~ *Exchange* arvopaperipörssi; ~ *in hand* varat; *take* ~ inventoida; *take* ~ *of* mittailla, arvioida; *in* ~ varastossa; *of good* ~ hyvää rotua; *on the* ~*s* (laivasta) rakenteilla; ~ *answers* (*questions*) vakiovastaukset,

-kysymykset; ~ *joke* vanha vitsi; ~ *size* vakiokoko.

stockade [stɔ'keid] *s.* paalutus, paaluvarustus.

stock|-book *s.* varastokirja; ~**-broker** osakevälittäjä. ~**-farmer** karjankasvattaja. **-fish** kapakala. **-holder** osakkeenomistaja.

stockinet [stɔki'net] *s.* neulekangas.

stocking ['stɔkiŋ] *s.* (pitkävartinen) sukka.

stock|-in-trade *s.* varasto; (kuv.) jhk luonnostaan kuuluvat tarvikkeet vakio|varusteet, -välineet. **-ist** [-ist] *s.* tukkumyyjä. ~**-jobber** osakekeinottelija. **-pile** *v.* varastoida. ~**-raising** karjankasvatus, -jalostus. ~**-still** *adv.* hievahtamatta. ~**-taking** inventointi. **-y** *a.* vanttera, tanakka.

stodgy ['stɔdʒi] *a.* raskas, vaikeasti sulava; yksitoistinen, ikävä.

stogy ['stəugi] *s.* Am. halpa sikari.

stoic ['stəuik] *s. & a.* stoalainen. **-al** [-(ə)l] *a.* stoalainen, lujaluonteinen. **-ism** [-isizm] *s.* stoalaisuus.

stoke [stəuk] *v.* lämmittää. **-hold, -hole** (laivan) kattilahuone. **-r** [-ə] *s.* lämmittäjä.

stole 1. [stəul] *s.* pitkä, kapea puuhka; stoola (m. kirk.)

stole 2. [stəul] *imp. ks. steal.* **-n** [-(ə)n] *pp.*

stolid ['stɔlid] *a.* hidas, tylsä. **-ity** [-'liditi] *s.* hitaus.

stomach ['stʌmək] *s.* maha, -laukku; vatsa; (ruoka)halu; *v.* voida syödä (jtk); (kuv.) niellä, sulattaa; *have no* ~ *for* olla halun jhk.

stomp [stɔmp] *v.:* ~ *away* tallustaa.

stone [stəun] *s.* kivi, (hedelmän) siemen; painomitta (14 naulaa); (sappi- ym) kivi; *v.* kivittää; poistaa siemenet jstk; *S*~ *Age* kivikausi; ~*d* humalassa, umpikännissä. **-crop** maksaruoho. ~**-deaf** umpikuuro. ~**-mason** kivenhakkaaja. ~'**s throw** kivenheitto. ~**-walling** jarrutus (pol.). **-ware** keramiikka.

stoniness *s.* kivisyys; kovuus.

stony ['stəuni] *a.* kivinen, kivi-, kivenkova; tunteeton, kylmä; ~ *broke* (sl.) puilla paljailla.

stood [stud] *imp. ks. stand.*

stooge [stu:dʒ] *s.* hanttimies,

hantlankari; narri; *v.* olla jkn
hantlankarina.

stook [stuk] *s.* kuhilas, suova.

stool [stu:l] *s.* jakkara, rahi; ~s ulostus.

stoop [stu:p] *v.* kumartua, käydä
kumarassa, olla kumaraselkäinen;
nöyrtyä, alentua; taivuttaa, kallistaa;
s. kumara asento, kumaraselkäisyys;
Am. kuisti (Et. Afr. *stoep*).

stop [stɔp] *v.* tukkia, sulkea; täyttää
(hammas); pysähdyttää, seisahduttaa;
lopettaa, lakkauttaa; pidättää, estää;
pysähtyä, lakata, keskeyttää, viipyä,
(puhek.) asua (tilapäisesti);
himmentää (valok.); *s.* pysähdys,
seisahdus; pysäkki; lakkaaminen,
loppu; keskeytys, este; välimerkki
(full ~ piste); rekisteri (mus.);
(valok.) himmennin; [*he*] ~*ped to
smoke* hän pysähtyi tupakalle; *he*
~*ped smoking* lopetti tupakanpolton;
~ *dead (short)* seisahtua äkkiä; ~
payment lakkauttaa maksut; ~ *over at*
(matkalla) pysähtyä (jnnek); *come to
a* ~ pysähtyä; *put a* ~ *to* tehdä loppu
jstk. ~**-cock** sulkuhana. **-gap**
hätävara, korvike. ~**-over** pysähdys
(matkalla). **-page** [-idʒ] *s.* sulkeminen,
tukkiminen; pysähdys, seisahdus,
keskeytys. **-per** [-ə] *s.* tulppa; *v.* panna
tulppa jhk.

stopping *s.* (hampaan) täyte. ~**-place**
pysäkki.

stop-press painatuksen aikana
saapuneet uutiset.

stop-watch *s.* sekuntikello.

storage ['stɔ:ridʒ] *s.* varastointi;
varastotila; varaston vuokra; ~
battery akku; *in cold* ~
jäähdyttämössä.

store [stɔ:] *s.* varasto; joukko, paljous;
myymälä, kauppa, (et. Am.); ~s
tavaratalo, suurmyymälä;
ampumatarvikkeet, muonavarat ym;
v. koota varastoon (us. ~ *up*),
varastoida, varustaa; panna säilöön;
set [great] ~ *by* pitää suuressa arvossa;
in ~ varastossa, varalla; *is in* ~ *for*
odottaa.., on (jklla) edessään.
~**-house** varastohuone; (kuv.)
aarreaitta. ~**-keeper** varastonhoitaja;
kauppias. ~**-room** varastohuone,
ruokasäiliö.

storey, Am. **story** ['stɔ:ri] *s.* kerros; *a*

little wrong in the upper ~ vähän
löylynlyömä. **-ed** [-d] *a.*
-kerroksinen.

storied ['stɔ:rid] *a.* tarunomainen;
-storied -kerroksinen.

storing ['stɔ:riŋ] *s.* varastoiminen.

stork [stɔ:k] *s.* kattohaikara.

storm [stɔ:m] *s.* ankara myrsky,
rajuilma; rynnäkkö; *v.* vallata
väkirynnäköllä, rynnätä (jnnek);
raivota, pauhata (*at* jklle); myrskytä;
take by ~ (kuv.) valloittaa
täydellisesti. **-ing** *s.* rynnäkkö; ~
party hyökkäysosasto. ~**-tossed**
myrskyn heittelemä, vellova (*sea*
meri). **-y** [-i] *a.* myrskyinen,
myrskyisä; raju.

story 1. ['stɔ:ri] *s.* kertomus, tarina,
satu; juttu, juoni; *short* ~ novelli; *as
the* ~ *goes* kuten kerrotaan; *tell stories*
panna omiaan. ~**-book** satukirja.

story 2. ['stɔ:ri] ks. *storey.*

stout [staut] *a.* tukeva, vahva, luja;
peloton, urhea, päättäväinen;
pyylevä, lihava(hko); *s.* portteri,
vahva olut. ~**-hearted** rohkea. **-ness**
s. tukevuus; lihavuus.

stove 1. [stəuv] *imp. & pp.* ks. *stave.*

stove 2. [stəuv] *s.* uuni, kamiina; liesi;
~**-pipe** *hat* silinteri.

stow [stəu] *v.* ahtaa, sulloa. **-away**
['stə(u)əwei] *s.* salamatkustaja,
»jänis».

Strachey ['streitʃi] *erisn.*

straddle ['strædl] *v.* seisoa t. istua
hajasäärin; (kuv.) ei ottaa kantaa,
pysyä puolueettomana; (sot.)
haarukoida; *s.* hajasäärin seisominen.

straggl|e ['strægl] *v.* jäädä jälkeen; olla
hajallaan; levitä epäsäännöllisesti,
versoa joka taholle. **-er** [-ə] *s.* rivistä
poisjäänyt, jälkeenjäänyt. **-ing** *a.*
harhaileva; joka tahoile työntyvä t.
haarautuva; rönsyilevä.

straight [streit] *a.* suora; rehellinen,
vilpitön; peittelemätön, selvä;
sekoittamaton; *s.* suora linja; *adv.*
suoraan, suorassa, suoraa päätä; *keep
a* ~ *face* olla nauramatta; *keep* [*sb.*] ~
pysyä (pitää jku) poissa rikoksen
tieltä; *put things* ~ panna kuntoon; ~
away (off) heti paikalla, viipymättä; ~
out suoralta kädeltä. **-en** [-n] *v.*
suoristaa, oikaista; suoristua, oieta;

järjestää. **-forward** a. suora, vilpitön.
-way adv. heti.

strain [strein] v. jännittää, pingottaa;
pinnistää; rasittaa; venähdyttää;
siivilöidä; siiviöityä; s. ponnistus,
pingotus, rasitus; venähdys; pl.
sävelet; suku, (esim. hyönteis)kanta;
(ominais)piirre, sävy; ~ a point
tulkita liian vapaasti (esim. jkn eduksi
in a p.'s favour); ~ at riuhtoa, kiskoa;
in a lofty ~ korkealentoisin sanoin; in
the same ~ samaan tyyliin, sävyyn.
-ed [-d] a. jännitetty, pingotettu;
väkinäinen; ~ relations kireät välit.
-er [-ə] s. siivilä.

strait [streit] a. (vanh.) ahdas; s. pl.
ahdinko, pula; salmi (us. pl.); ~
jacket pakkopaita; the S~s of Dover
Calais'n salmi. **-en** [-n] v. kiristää;
in ~ed circumstances niukoissa
varoissa. **-laced** a. ahdasmielinen,
ankara.

strand 1. [strænd] s. (run.) ranta; v.
ajaa, ajautua rantaan; ~-ed hädässä,
avuttomana.

strand 2. [strænd] s. säie.

strange [strein(d)ʒ] a. vieras, outo,
tuntematon; merkillinen, omituinen,
tottumaton; ~ to say kumma kyllä.
-ness s. vieraus; omituisuus. **-r** [-ə] s.
vieras, muukalainen.

strangle ['stræŋgl] v. kuristaa,
tukehduttaa. **~-hold** kuristusote.

strangulation [stræŋgju'leiʃn] s.
kuristus; kuroutuma.

strap [stræp] s. hihna, remmi; raksi;
hiomahihna (m. strop); v. kiinnittää
hihnalla; hioa (m. strop); kiinnittää
laastarilla; antaa remmiä; shoulder ~
olkain; ~-hanger seisoja (bussissa).
-ping a. roteva, iso.

strata ['strɑːtə] ks. stratum.

stratagem ['strætidʒəm] s. (sota)juoni.

strateg|ic, -al [strə'tiːdʒik, -(ə)l] a.
sotataidollinen, strateginen. **-ist**
['strætidʒist] s. strateegikko. **-y**
['strætidʒi] s. strategia,
sodanjohtotaito.

Stratford ['strætfəd] erisn.

stratify ['strætifai] v. kerrostaa, -tua.

stratosphere ['strætə(u)sfiə] s.
stratosfääri.

stratum ['strɑːtəm] s. (pl. strata)
kerrostuma; (yhteiskunta)kerros.

straw [strɔː] s. oljet; (olki)pilli; hiukka;
[drinking] ~ imupilli; the last ~
viimeinen pisara (maljassa); I don't
care a ~ en välitä rahtuakaan; catch
(clutch) at a ~ tarttua oljenkorteen; a
man of ~ bulvaani, olkinukke. **-berry**
[-b(ə)ri] mansikka; (~ mark
punertava syntymämerkki).

stray [strei] v. harhailla, kuljeskella;
poiketa (oikealta tieltä); joutua
harhaan, hairahtua; s. eksynyt
(eläin), koditon (lapsi); pl.
radiohäiriöt; a. eksyksiin joutunut;
satunnainen, haja-; ~ bullet
harhaluoti; ~ dog kulkukoira.

streak [striːk] s. viiru, juova;
(luonteen) piirre, vivahde; hiven; v.
raidoittaa, juovittaa; viuhahtaa; ~ off
pyyhältää. **-y** [-i] a. juovikas,
raitainen.

stream [striːm] s. puro, joki; (kuv.)
virta(us); (oppilaista) tasoryhmä; v.
virrata, tulvia, vuotaa; up ~, down ~
vasta-, myötävirtaan; ~-lined
virtaviivainen. **-er** [-ə] s. viiri;
serpentiini; (revontulen) säde. **-let**
[-lit] s. puro.

street [striːt] s. katu; ~ arab
katupoika; in the ~ kadulla; the man
in the ~ kadun mies. **~-car**
raitiovaunu (Am.) **~-walker**
katutyttö.

strength [streŋθ] s. voima, välkevyys,
lujuus; miesluku, vahvuus (sot.); ~ of
mind mielenlujuus; on the ~ of jnk
nojalla, perusteella. **-en** [-n] v.
vahvistaa, lujittaa; voimistua,
vahvistua.

strenuous ['strenjuəs] a. uuttera,
uupumaton; ponnistuksia kysyvä,
rasittava

strepto|coccus ['streptə(u)|'kɔkəs] s.
(pl. -cocci [-'kɔkai] streptokokki.
-mycin [-'maisin] s. streptomysiini.

stress [stres] s. paino; (henkinen)
paine, stressi; korko, paino (kiel.); v.
painottaa, korostaa; lay ~ on
tähdentää; in times of ~ raskaina
aikoina.

stretch [stretʃ] v. venyttää, venytellä;
levittää; ponnistaa, antaa ponnistusta
vaativia tehtäviä; (~ out) ojentaa,
kurkottaa; liioitella; ulottua; levitä;
venyä; s. pingotus; venytys; laajuus,

ala, väli, matka; ~ *the law* venyttää lakia (jkn eduksi); ~ *the truth* vääristellä totuutta (liioitellen); ~ *a point* tehdä myönnytyksiä; ~ *one's legs* verrytellä koipiaan; ~ *oneself out* loikoa pitkin pituuttaan; *at a* ~ yhtä päätä. **-er** [-ə] s. paarit; venytyskoje; ~*-bearer* sairaan-, paarinkantaja.

strew [stru:] v. (pp. m. ~n) sirotella, ripotella; peittää *(with* jllak).

striated [strai'eitid] a. juovikas.

stricken ['strikn] *pp. & a.* ks. *strike*; jnk kohtaama; ~ *in years* iäkäs.

strict [strikt] a. tarkka, tiukka, ankara; ehdoton; *the* ~ *sense of the word* sanan ahdas merkitys; ~*ly speaking* tarkasti katsoen, sanoen. **-ness** s. ankaruus. **-ure** [-ʃ-ə] s. (tav. *pl.*) ankara arvostelu, moitteet; (lääk.) ahtauma, kurouma.

stride [straid] *strode stridden,* v. astua pitkin askelin, harpata, harppoa; s. pitkä askel, harppaus; *pl.* edistys(askelet); *make great* ~*s* edistyä nopeasti; *take..in one's* ~ suoriutua jstk helposti.

strident ['straidnt] a. korviasärkevä, vihlova.

strife [straif] s. epäsopu, kiista, taistelu.

strike [straik] v. *(struck, struck,* vanh. pp. *stricken)* lyödä, iskeä, sattua, osua jhk, kohdata; törmätä jhk; vaikuttaa jkh (voimakkaasti), herättää huomiota; juolahtaa mieleen, tuntua, näyttää jksta *(as* jltk); löytää; laskea (purje), purkaa (teltta), päättää (kauppa); pyyhkäistä tasaiseksi (mitta); ajaa karille, törmätä jhk, karahtaa (kallioon); laskea lippu, antautua; lähteä, suunnata kulkunsa *(towards* jnnek); juurtua; ryhtyä lakkoon, lakkoilla; s. lakko; *general* ~ yleislakko; *on* ~ lakossa; *come out on* ~, *call a* ~ ryhtyä lakkoon; ~ *an attitude* asettua teennäiseen asentoon; ~ *dumb* mykistää; ~ *home* osua naulan kantaan, kohdalleen; ~ *a light* sytyttää tulitikku; ~ *oil* löytää öljysuoni; ~ *root* juurtua; ~ *work* lopettaa työ; ~ *at* suunnata isku jhk; ~ *down* iskeä maahan; ~ *in* keskeyttää jkn puhe, syöksyä sisälle; ~ *off* hakata poikki; pyyhkiä pois; ottaa (painos); ~ *out* pyyhkiä pois;

lyödä tarmokkaasti; lähteä liikkeelle, lähteä uimaan; ~ *up* virittää (laulu), tehdä (tuttavuus); *[an idea]* struck me juolahti mieleeni. ~*-breaker* rikkuri. ~**-pay** lakkoavustus. **-r** [-ə] lakkolainen.

striking ['straikiŋ] a. huomiota herättävä, silmäänpistävä; lyövä, isku-; ~*ly* huomiotaherättävän.

string [striŋ] s. nyöri, naru, nuora; kieli, jänne; rivi, jono, ketju, sarja; ~*s* jouset (mus.); v. *(strung strung)* varustaa kielillä, nyörillä ym; pujottaa, ripustaa rihmaan; jännittää, pingottaa (tav. ~ *up); pull* ~*s* käyttää suhteitaan t. vaikutusvaltaansa; *no* ~*s attached* ilman ehtoja; *high[ly]* strung hermoherkkä; ~ *band* jousiorkesteri. **-ed** [-d] a. kieli-.

string|ency ['strin(d)ʒ(ə)nsi] s. jyrkkyys, ankaruus. **-ent** [-(-ə)nt] a. ankara, tiukka; kireä.

stringy ['strini] a. kuituinen; sitkeä.

strip [strip] v. repiä pois; kuoria; riisua; ryöstää paljaaksi; riisuutua; s. kaistale, liuska; ~ *sb. of* riistää, ryöstää jklta jtk; ~ *cartoon, comic* ~ sarjakuva; ~*-tease* riisuutumistanssi; *landing-*~ (pieni) laskeutumiskenttä.

strip|e [straip] s. juova, raita; (sot.) nauha; (vanh.) raipanisku. **-ed** [-t] a. raitainen. **-ling** ['striplin] s. nuorukainen, huiskale.

striv|e [straiv] *strove striven,* v. pyrkiä, ponnistella; taistella, kilpailla. **-ing** s. ponnistelu; kilvoitus.

strode [stroud] *imp.* ks. *stride.*

stroke [strouk] s. lyönti, veto, vetäisy, isku; halvaus; (kynän)veto, piirto; peräairon soutaja; sively; v. sivellä, silittää; olla peräairon soutajana; *a good* ~ *of business* hyvä kauppa; *a* ~ *of genius* neronleimaus; *a* ~ *of luck* onnenpotkaus; *on the* ~ *[of]* lyönnilleen, täsmälleen.

stroll [stroul] v. kuljeskella, vaeltaa; s. kävely. **-er** [-ə] s. kävelijä.

strong [stroŋ] a. vahva, voimakas, väkevä; luja; mieslukuinen; ~ *point* tuliasema (sot.); *my* ~ *point* vahva puoleni; *still going* ~ hyvissä voimissa; *go it rather* ~ liioitella. ~**-box** kassakaappi. **-hold** linnoitus. **-ly** *adv.* voimakkaasti, kovasti.

~**-minded** lujaluonteinen. ~**-room** kassaholvi.

strontium ['strɔntiəm, Am. -nʃiəm] s. strontium.

strop [strɔp] s. hiaisin; raksi (mer.); v. hioa (partaveitsi).

strove [strəuv] imp. ks. strive.

struck [strʌk] imp. & pp. ks. strike.

struc|tural ['strʌktʃ(ə)r(ə)l] a. rakenteellinen. **-ture** [-tʃə] s. rakenne, kokoonpano; rakennus.

struggle ['strʌgl] v. ponnistella, kamppailla, taistella; sätkytellä; s. ponnistelu, ponnistus; kamppailu, taistelu; the ~ for existence olemassaolon taistelu.

strum [strʌm] v. rimputtaa; s. rimputus.

strumpet ['strʌmpit] s. lutka.

strung [strʌŋ] imp. & pp. ks. string; ~ up jännittynyt.

strut [strʌt] v. astua ylväästi, kukkoilla; s. (kukon)tepastelu; (vino) tuki, pönkkä.

strychnine ['strikni:n] s. strykniini.

Stuart [stjuət] erisn.

stub [stʌb] s. kanto; pätkä; (šekin) kanta; v.: ~ one's toe kolhaista varpaansa jhk; ~ out sammuttaa, tumpata (savuke).

stubbl|e ['stʌbl] s. sänki. **-y** [-i] a. sänkinen.

stubborn ['stʌbən] a. itse|päinen, -pintainen, uppiniskainen, taipumaton. **-ness** s. itsepäisyys jne.

stubby ['stʌbi] a. lyhyt ja paksu.

stucco ['stʌkəu] s. stukki (työ); v. (~ed) koristaa s:llä.

stuck [stʌk] imp. & pp. ks. stick; be ~ tarttua, juuttua kiinni, olla kiikissä. ~-up a. itserakas, pöyhkeä, ylpeä.

stud 1. [stʌd] s.: ~ farm hevossiittola. ~**-book** kantakirja.

stud 2. [stʌd] s. (paidan- ym) nappi, irtonappi; (koriste)naula, nasta; v. nastoittaa, koristaa, peittää (with jllak); press ~ painonappi, neppi; ~ded with täynnä jtk, jnk peittämä.

student ['stju:d(ə)nt] s. opiskelija, tutkija(tyyppi), lukupää; ylioppilas; medical ~ lääketieteen opiskelija.

stud-horse siitosori.

studied ['stʌdid] a. harkittu, tahallinen.

studi|o ['stju:d|iəu] s. studio, ateljee; esittämö (rad.). **-ous** [-jəs] a. ahkera, opinhaluinen; huolellinen, harkittu; innokas, halukas; (~ness s. harrastus, into.)

study ['stʌdi] s. tutkimus, opiskelu, opinnot; opintoaine; tutkielma, harjoitelma, harjoitus (mus.); luku-, työhuone; pyrkimys; v. tutkia, opiskella, harjoittaa opintoja; pitää silmämääränään, harrastaa, pyrkiä; in a brown ~ syvissä mietteissä; ~ circle opintokerho.

stuff [stʌf] s. aine; aines, ainekset; tavara; asia(t); (villa)kangas; v. täyttää; ahtaa täyteen; pehmustaa; syöttää valheita; ~ and nonsense! hölynpölyä! roskaa! doctor's ~ lääkkeet; garden (t. green) ~ puutarhatuotteet; ~ed m. murekkeella täytetty; ~ed shirt turhantärkeä henkilö. **-iness** s. ummehtuneisuus. **-ing** s. täyte, pehmuste; mureke. **-y** [-i] a. ummehtunut, raskas, tunkkainen; ikävä, »kuiva», ahdasmielinen.

stultify ['stʌltifai] v. tehdä naurettavaksi; tehdä tyhjäksi.

stumbl|e ['stʌmbl] v. kompastua; kangerrella (puheessa); s. kompastus; hairahdus; ~ along hoippua, kompuroida; ~ upon äkkiarvaamatta kohdata. **-ing-block** kompastuskivi.

stump [stʌmp] s. kanto; pätkä; tynkä; pl. (puhek.) jalat; v. kompuroida (~ along;) saattaa ymmälle, panna pussiin (kysymyksillä); (~ a district) kiertää pitämässä (poliittisia) puheita; stir your ~s! ala liikkua! be ~ed tulla sanattomaksi; ~ up maksaa, pulittaa. **-y** [-i] a. lyhyenläntä.

stun [stʌn] v. (iskulla) huumata, iskeä pökerryksiin; typerryttää; ~ned pökertynyt; ~ning (puhek.) hemaiseva, tyrmäävä.

stung [stʌŋ] imp. & pp. ks. sting.

stunk [stʌŋk] pp. ks. stink.

stunt 1. [stʌnt] v. ehkäistä (kasvu); ~ed surkastunut, kitukasvuinen.

stunt 2. [stʌnt] s. taidonnäyte, loistonumero; (publicity ~) mainostemppu; ~ flying taitolento. ~**-man** (vaarallisten osien) sijaisnäyttelijä.

stupe|faction [stju:piˈfækʃn] s. ällistys, tyrmistys. **-fy** [ˈstju:pifai] v. huumata, turruttaa; ällistyttää. **-ndous** [stju(:)ˈpendəs] a. hämmästyttävä; suunnaton.

stupid [ˈstju:pid] a. tylsä, typerä, tyhmä. **-ity** [stju(:)ˈpiditi] s. typeryys, tylsyys.

stupor [ˈstju:pə] s. horros; huumaustila; tylsyys.

sturdy [ˈstə:di] a. vahva, vankka, luja, tukeva, tanakka.

sturgeon [ˈstə:dʒ(ə)n] s. sampi.

stutter [ˈstʌtə] v. änkyttää; s. änkytys.

sty 1. [stai] s. sikolätti.

sty, stye 2. [stai] s. näärännäppy.

styl|e [stail] s. tyyli, tyylikkyys, kuosi, malli; arvonimi; ajanlasku; piirustuspuikko, kaiverrin; v. nimittää; muotoilla; it is bad ~ osoittaa huonoa aistia, on mautonta; in ~ komeasti. **-ish** [-iʃ] a. tyylikäs, aistikas, muodinmukainen. **-ist** [-ist] s. tyyliniekka, stilisti. **-istic** [ˈlistik] a. tyyli. **-ize** [-aiz] v. tyylitellä. **-us** [-əs] s. (levysoittimen) neula.

stymie [ˈstaimi] s. hankala tilanne (golfpelissä); v. estää.

Styria [ˈstiriə] erisn. Steiermark.

suav|e [swɑːv] a. rakastettava, miellyttävä; ~ manners sulava käytös. **-ity** [ˈswæviti] s. rakastettavuus.

sub- [ˈsʌb-, səb-] pref. ala-, ali.

sub|altern [ˈsʌbltən] s. yliupseeri. **-conscious** a. alitajuinen; the ~ alitajunta. **-continent** s. subkontinentti; the Indian ~ Etu-Intia. **-culture** alakulttuuri. **-cutaneous** a. ihonalainen. **-divide** v. jakaa alaosastoihin. **-division** s. alaosasto.

subdue [səbˈdju:] v. kukistaa, nujertaa; voittaa; hillitä; ~d hillitty, hiljainen, (valo) himmennetty.

sub|editor s. toimitussihteeri. **-group** a. alaryhmä. **-head(ing)** s. alaotsikko.

subject 1. [ˈsʌbdʒikt] a.: ~ to jkn vallan alainen, jstk riippuvainen; jllek altis; adv.: ~ to edellyttäen että; s. alamainen, kansalainen; subjekti (kiel.); aine, aihe, kohde, teema; henkilö; ~ to certain restrictions eräin rajoituksin; [the plan] is made ~ to

your approval edellyttää hyväksymystänne; change the ~ muuttaa puheenaihetta; [while we are] on the ~ of puhuessamme . . -sta; ~ matter aihe, sisällys, sisältö.

subject 2. [səbˈdʒekt] v.: ~ [to] alistaa valtaansa, kukistaa. **-ion** [-ˈdʒekʃn] s. alistaminen; alamaisuus; vallanalaisuus. **-ive** [-iv] a. subjektiivinen, omakohtainen. **-ivity** [-ˈtiviti] s. subjektiivisuus, omakohtaisuus.

subjoin [ˈsʌbˈdʒɔin] v. liittää.

subjuga|te [ˈsʌbʒugeit] v. alistaa, kukistaa. **-tion** [-ˈgeiʃn] s. kukistaminen.

subjunctive [səbˈdʒʌŋ(k)tiv] s. konjunktiivi.

sublet [ˈsʌbˈlet] v. vuokrata alivuokralaiselle.

sub-lieutenant [ˈsʌblefˈtenənt] aliluutnantti.

sublimat|e [ˈsʌblimeit] v. sublimoida, härmistää; ylevöityä. **-ion** [-ˈmeiʃn] s. sublimaatio, sublimointi.

sublim|e [səˈblaim] a. ylevä, ylhäinen; hämmästyttävä. **-ity** [səˈblimiti] s. alitajuinen.

sub|-machine: ~ gun konepistooli. **-marine** [ˈsʌbməriːn] a. vedenalainen; s. sukellusvene.

sub|merge [səbˈmə:dʒ] v. upottaa, peittää, tulvia jnk yli; (laivasta) sukeltaa; vajota; ~d rock vedenalainen kari; the ~ tenth (vanh.) köyhin väestö. **-mergence** [-(ə)ns] s. uppoaminen; sukelluksissa olo. **-mersion** [-ˈmə:ʃn] s. upottaminen, uppoaminen.

submis|sion [səbˈmiʃn] s. alistaminen; alistuminen; nöyryys; tarkastettavaksi jättäminen. **-sive** [-ˈmisiv] a. alistuva, nöyrä; (~ness nöyryys).

submit [səbˈmit] v. alistua, suostua, mukautua (to jhk); alistaa, jättää (tarkastettavaksi ym); huomauttaa (kunnioittavasti).

subnormal [-ˈ-] a. normaalia alempi; mentally ~ kehitysvammainen.

subordina|te [səbˈɔːdnit] a. alempi, -arvoinen; alisteinen (lause); s. (jkn) alainen; v. [-ineit] saattaa jkn alaiseksi. **-tion** [-iˈneiʃn] s. alempi (virka-) asema, alistussuhde.

suborn [sʌ'bɔ:n] *v.* lahjoa, houkutella (väärään valaan).

subpoena [səb'pi:nə] *s.* haaste; *v. (imp. & pp. ~ed)* haastaa oikeuteen.

sub|scribe [səb'skraib] *v.* sitoutua maksamaan, merkitä puolestaan (jk summa) avustaa; tilata; yhtyä *(to* jhk), hyväksyä; ~ *to* tilata. **-r** [-ə] *s.* tilaaja; avustaja; allekirjoittaja. **-scription** [səb'skripʃn] *s.* tilaus; merkitty summa, avustus(määrä); maksu; allekirjoitus; *by public ~* julkisella keräyksellä.

subsequent ['sʌbsikwənt] *a.* seuraava, myöhempi; ~ *to* (jnk) jälkeen. **-ly** *adv.* jäljestäpäin, myöhemmin.

subserv|e [səb'sə:v] *v.* edistää. **-ience** [-jəns] *s.* nöyristely. **-ient** [-jənt] *a.* nöyristelevä; ~ *to* jtk edistävä.

subside [səb'said] *v.* vaipua, painua, laskea; asettua, tyyntyä. **-nce** [səb'said(ə)ns, 'sʌbsid-] *s.* laske(utu)minen; asettuminen, tyyntyminen.

subsid|iary [səb'sidjəri] *a.* auttava, apu-, lisä-; ~ *company* tytäryhtiö. **-ize** ['sʌbsidaiz] *v.* tukea, avustaa. **-y** ['sʌbsidi] *s.* avustus, (valtion)apu; *[food]* ~ tukipalkkio.

subsist [səb'sist] *v.* olla olemassa, pysyä pystyssä, saada elatuksensa, elää *(on* jstk). **-ence** [-(ə)ns] *s.* ylläpito, elatus; ~ *economy* luontoistalous; ~ *level* minimitoimeentulo.

subsoil ['sʌbsɔil] *s.* jankko, pohja; ~ *water* pohjavesi.

substance ['sʌbst(ə)ns] *s.* aine; aines; pääsisällys, ydin; se mikä on olennaista, todellisuus, olemus; painavuus; omaisuus; (filos.) substanssi; *in ~* pääasiassa; *[a man] of ~* varakas.

substandard [-'--] *a.* heikkotasoinen; (sivistyneeseen) yleiskieleen kuulumaton.

substantial [səb'stænʃ(ə)l] *a.* huomattava, melkoinen; luja; vankka, tukeva (ateria); painava, todellinen; olennainen, pääasiallinen; varakas, **-ly** *adv.* suurin piirtein, pääkohdittain.

substan|tiate [səb'stænʃieit] *v.* näyttää toteen; esittää pätevät syyt jhk;

vahvistaa. **-tive** ['sʌbst(ə)ntiv] *s.* substantiivi, nimisana.

substi|tute ['sʌbstitju:t] *v. : ~ [for]* asettaa (jnk) tilalle; *s.* sijainen, varamies; korvike. **-tion** [-'tju:ʃn] *s.* korvaaminen.

substratum ['sʌbstrɑ:təm] *s.* pohja, perusta.

subsume [səb'sju:m] *v.* sisällyttää, lukea *(under* jhk).

subtenant [-'--] *s.* alivuokralainen.

subterfuge ['sʌbtəfju:dʒ] *s.* veruke.

subterranean [sʌbtə'reinjən] *a.* maanalainen.

subtitle *s.* alaotsikko; ~*s* (elok.) teksti(tys); ~*d film* tekstillä varustettu filmi.

subtle [sʌtl] *a.* hienon hieno, herkkä; terävä; vaikeasti selitettävissä (oleva), aavistuksellinen; sukkela, ovela **-ty** [-ti] *s.* hienous, herkkyys; terävyys; hiuksenhieno ero, saivartelu.

subtopia [sʌb'təupjə] *s.* l.v. kaupungistunut maaseutu, esikaupunki.

subtract [səb'trækt] *v.* vähentää. **-ion** [-'trækʃn] *s.* vähentäminen; vähennyslasku.

subtropical ['sʌb'trɔpik(ə)l] *a.* subtrooppinen.

suburb ['sʌbə:b] *s.* esikaupunki. **-an** [sə'bə:bn] *a. & s.* esikaupungin, -kaupunkilainen. **-ia** [sə'bə:biə] *s.* (us. halv.) esikaupunkilais|elämä, -mentaliteetti.

subvention [səb'venʃn] *s.* subventio, tukipalkkio.

subversive [səb'və:siv] *a.* kumouksellinen, mullistava.

subvert [sʌb'və:t] *v.* kumota, mullistaa.

subway ['sʌbwei] *s.* (jalankulku-) tunneli; maanalainen rautatie (et. Am.).

succeed [sək'si:d] *v.* onnistua *(in . . -ing);* seurata (jkta); ~ *to the throne* nousta valtaistuimelle.

success [s(ə)k'ses] *s.* menestys, onni; *be a ~* onnistua, menestyä; *meet with ~* menestyä. **-ful** *a.* menestyksellinen, menestyksekäs; (~**ly** menestyksellisesti). **-ion** [-'seʃn] *s.* peräkkäin seuraaminen; sarja, jono; vallanperimys(järjestys); *in ~* peräkkäin;

~ **duty** perintövero. **-ive** [-iv] *a.*
välittömästi seuraava, peräkkäinen;
for three ~ days kolme päivää
peräkkäin. **-ively** *adv.* peräkkäin.
-or [-ə] *s.* seuraaja; vallanperijä.

succinct [sək'siŋ(k)t] *a.*
lyhyt(sanainen), suppea.

succour, -cor ['sʌkə] *s.* apu; *v.* tulla
avuksi, auttaa.

succulen|ce ['sʌkjuləns] *s.* mehevyys.
-t [-ənt] *a.* mehevä; ~ *plant*
mehikasvi.

succumb [sə'kʌm] *v.:* ~ *to* antaa
myöten, taipua; kuolla, menehtyä
jhk.

such [sʌtʃ] *pron. & a.* sellainen,
moinen; ~ *a man* sellainen mies; *at ~
a moment* sellaisella hetkellä; ~ *as*
sellainen, (sellaiset) kuin; kuten
esimerkiksi; ~ *being the case* (asian)
niin ollen; *no ~ thing* ei
sinnepäinkään, ei suinkaan; *as ~*
sinänsä, sellaisenaan.

suck [sʌk] *v.* imeä; imeskellä; *s.*
imeminen; ~ *in*, ~ *up* imeä itseensä;
~ *[down] into* (pyörteestä) niellä; ~
up to mielistellä; *give* ~ imettää. **-er**
[-ə] *s.* juurivesa; imuri, imuputki;
tikkukaramelli; (sl.) hyväuskoinen
narri. **-le** [-l] *v.* imettää. **-ling** [-liŋ] *s.*
rintalapsi; maitovasikka; *babes and
~s* lapset ja imeväiset.

suction ['sʌkʃn] *s.* imeminen, imu.
~-pipe imuputki.

Sudan [su(:)'dæn] *erisn.* **-ese** [-də'ni:z]
a. & s. sudanilainen.

sudden ['sʌdn] *a.* äkillinen,
odottamaton, äkkinäinen; *all of a ~*
äkkiä. **-ly** *adv.* äkkiä. **-ness** *s.*
äkillisyys.

suds [sʌdz] *s. pl.* saippuavesi, -vaahto
(tav. *soap-~*).

sue [sju:] *v.* haastaa oikeuteen; hakea
oikeustietä; pyytää, hakea (*for* jtk).

suède [sweid] *s.* mokkanahka.

suet [sjuit] *s.* (naudan t. lampaan)
munuaisrasva.

Suez ['su(:)iz] *erisn.*

suffer ['sʌf|ə] *v.* kärsiä (tuskaa, tappio
ym), kokea (muutos); kärsiä
vahinkoa; kestää, sietää; suvaita,
sallia; *he is ~ing from* häntä vaivaa,
hän sairastaa t. potee jtk; *he will have
to ~ for it* hän saa sen maksaa. **-able**

[-(ə)rəbl] *a.* siedettävä. **-ance**
[-(ə)rəns] *s.: on ~* armosta. **-ing**
[-(ə)riŋ] *s.* kärsimys.

suffice [sə'fais] *v.* riittää, olla kylliksi;
tyydyttää; ~ *it to say* riittäköön, kun
sanon.

sufficien|cy [s(ə)'fiʃ(ə)nsi] *s.* riittävyys,
riittävä määrä; riittävä toimeentulo. **-t**
[-(ə)nt] *a.* riittävä; *be ~ [for]* riittää;
(~**ly** *adv.* kyllin, tarpeeksi).

suffix ['sʌfiks] *s.* loppuliite, suffiksi; *v.*
[m. sʌ'fiks] liittää.

suffocat|e ['sʌfəkeit] *v.* tukehduttaa;
tukehtua, läkähtyä; *-ing*
tukahduttava. **-ion** [-'keiʃn] *s.*
tukehtuminen.

Suffolk ['sʌfək] *erisn.*

suffrag|e ['sʌfridʒ] *s.* ääni, äänioikeus;
hyväksymys; *woman ~* naisten
äänioikeus. **-ette** [sʌfrə'dʒet] *s.*
sufragetti. **-ist** [-ist] *s.* naisten
äänioikeuden esitaistelija.

suffu|se [sə'fju:z] *v.* valaa, peittää; ~*d
with tears* kyyneleitä tulvillaan. **-sion**
[sə'fju:ʒn] *s.* valaminen, peittäminen;
hohde, puna.

sugar ['ʃugə] *s.* sokeri; *v.* sokeroida; ~
beet sokerijuurikas; ~*-coating*
sokerointi. **~-basin** sokeriastia.
~-cane sokeriruoko. **-loaf**
sokerikeko. **~-refinery** sokeritehdas.
~-tongs sokeripihdit. **-y** [-ri] *a.*
sokerinen, hunajanmakea; äitelä.

suggest [sə'dʒest] *v.* johdattaa mieleen;
ehdottaa, esittää; ~*s itself* johtuu
mieleen. **-ion** [-ʃn] *s.* ehdotus, esitys,
vihje; suggestio. **-ive** [-iv] *a.* (~ *of*) jtk
mieleenjohdattava; herätteitä antava,
suggestiivinen, puhuva; vihjaileva,
kaksimielinen.

suicid|al [sjui'saidl] *a.* itsemurha-. **-e**
['sjuisaid] *s.* itsemurha; itsemurhaaja.

suit [sju:t] *s.* (miehen) puku; (naisen)
kävelypuku, jakkupuku; anomus,
(vanh.) kosinta; oikeusjuttu; väri,
maa (korttip.); *v.* sopia, soveltua;
pukea, olla jklle sopiva; miellyttää;
olla sopusoinnussa (*with* jnk kanssa);
sovittaa, sopeuttaa; *bring a ~
[against]* nostaa syyte; ~ *of armour*
haarniska; *dress ~* frakki; *[two-t.
three-] piece* ~ yhdistelmäasu; *follow
~* tunnustaa maata, seurata
esimerkkiä;

~ *oneself* tehdä mielensä mukaan.
-ability [-ə'biliti] *s.* sopivaisuus. **-able**
[-əbl] *a.* sopiva, soveltuva. ~-**case** *s.*
matkalaukku.

suite [swi:t] *s.* seurue; kalusto,
huoneisto; (orkesteri)sarja; ~ *of
rooms* huoneisto.

suit|ed ['sju:tid] *a.* sopiva, omiaan (*to,
for* jhk). **-ing** *s.* pukukangas. **-or** [-ə] *s.*
kosija; kantaja (lak.).

sulf- ks. *sulph-*.

sulk [sʌlk] *v.* olla pahalla tuulella,
murjottaa; *be in the* ~ *s* = ed. **-iness** *s.*
murjotus. **-y** [-i] *a.* pahantuulinen; *s.*
ravirattaat.

sullen ['sʌlən] *a.* nyreä, juro,
murjottava; synkkä. **-ness** *s.* nyrpeys,
jurous.

sully ['sʌli] *v.* liata, tahrata.

sulph|ate ['sʌlfeit] *s.* sulfaatti. **-ite**
[-fait] *s.* sulfiitti. **-onamide**
[sal'fɔnəmaid] *s.: ~ drugs*
sulfalääkkeet.

sulphur ['sʌlfə] *s.* rikki (kem.). **-etted**
['sʌlfjuretid] *a.: ~ hydrogen*
rikkivety. **-eous** [sʌl'fjuəriəs] *a.* rikki-.
-ic [sʌl'fjuərik] *a.: ~ acid*
rikkihappo.

sultan [sʌlt(ə)n] *s.* sulttaani. **-a**
[sʌl'tɑ:nə] *s.* sulttaanitar; eräänl.
rusina.

sultry ['sʌltri] *a.* helteinen, painostava,
hiostava.

sum [sʌm] *s.* summa, rahamäärä;
laskuesimerkki; *v.: ~ up* laskea
yhteen; esittää pääkohdittain; *to ~
up, in* ~ yhteenvetona, lyhyesti
sanoen; *do ~ s* suorittaa laskutehtäviä;
~ *total* kokonaissumma,
loppusumma; ~ *ming-up* yhteenveto.

Sumatra [su(:)'mɑ:trə] *erisn.*

summarize ['sʌməraiz] *v.* tehdä
yhteenveto jstk.

summary ['sʌməri] *a.* suppea,
pääkohdittainen; ylimalkainen, äkkiä
tehty; *s.* lyhennelmä, yhteenveto; *in a
~ fashion* ylimalkaisesti.

summer ['sʌmə] *s.* kesä; *v.* viettää
kesää; ~ *lightning* elosalama(t); ~
school (yliopiston) kesäkurssit,
kesäyliopisto; ~ *time* kesäaika.
~-**house** huvimaja. **-y** [-ri] *a.*
kesäinen.

summit ['sʌmit] *s.* huippu,

huippukohta; ~ [*conference*]
huipputason kokous.

summon ['sʌmən] *v.* kutsua, kutsuttaa
luokseen; kutsua koolle; haastaa
oikeuteen; koota (esim. tarmonsa); ~
up one's courage rohkaista mielensä.
-s [-z] *s.* (pl. ~ *es*) kehotus, käsky;
haaste; *serve a ~ on* haastaa
oikeuteen.

sump [sʌmp] *s.* likakaivo, öljypohja.

sumptu|ary ['sʌm(p)tju|əri] *a.*
ylellisyyttä rajoittava. **-ous** [-əs] *a.*
kallis(arvoinen), upea, loistelias.
-ousness *s.* upeus.

sun [sʌn] *s.* aurinko; *v.: ~* [*oneself*]
paistattaa päivää; ~ *lamp*
alppiaurinkolamppu; ~ *tan* rusketus.
~-**bath** auringonkylpy. **-beam**
auringonsäde. **-blind** sälekaihdin,
ulkokaihdin. **-burn** päivetys. **-burnt**
päivettynyt.

sundae ['sʌndei] *s.* (hedelmä-,
pähkinä)jäätelö.

Sunday ['sʌndi] *s.* sunnuntai; *on* ~ *s*
sunnuntaisin; ~ *best* pyhävaatteet; ~
school pyhäkoulu.

sunder ['sʌndə] *v.* erottaa, särkeä
(kuv.).

sun|-dial aurinkokello. **-down**
auringonlasku. **-downer** iltadrinkki;
(Austr.) kulkuri. ~-**dried** auringossa
kuivattu.

sundry ['sʌndri] *a.* erilaiset,
kaikenlaiset, useat; *all and* ~
itsekukin, joka ainoa; *s.: sundries*
sekalaiset kulut t. tavarat.

sunflower auringonkukka.

sung [sʌŋ] *pp.* ks. *sing*.

sun|-glasses aurinkolasit. ~-**helmet**
hellekypärä.

sunk [sʌŋk] *pp.* ks. *sink*; uponnut,
upotettu. **-en** [-n] *a.: ~ cheeks*
kuopallaan olevat posket; ~ *rock*
vedenalainen kari.

sun|less *a.* auringoton. **-light**
auringonvalo. **-lit** *a.* päivänpaisteinen.
-ny ['sʌni] *a.* aurinkoinen,
päivänpaisteinen; säteilevä. **-rise**
auringonnousu. **-set** auringonlasku.
-shade päivänvarjo, markiisi. **-shine**
auringonpaiste. ~-**spot**
auringonpilkku. **-stroke**
auringonpisto. ~-**up**
auringonnousu.

sup [sʌp] v. illastaa; ottaa siemaus; s. siemaus, kulaus.

super ['sju:pə] s. = supernumerary; a. suur-, loisto-, upea.

super- ['sju:pə] pref. ~-powers supervallat. **-able** [sju:p(ə)rəbl] a. voitettavissa oleva. **-abundant** a. yltäkylläinen. **-annuated** [-'rænjueitid] a. yli-ikäinen, aikansa palvellut, eläkkeelle pantu.

superb [sju(:)'pə:b] a. komea, suurenmoinen; erinomainen.

super|cargo ['sju:pə|ka:gəu] lastiperämies. **-charger** (tekn.) ahdin. **-cilious** [-'siliəs] ylimielinen, ylpeä. **-ego** [-'ri:gəu] s. yliminä. **-erogatory** [-re'rɔgət(ə)ri] ym. ylimääräinen. **-ficial** [-'fiʃ(ə)l] pinnallinen; pintapuolinen; pinta-. **-ficiality** [-fiʃi'æliti] pintapuolisuus.

superfine a. hienon hieno.

superflu|ity [sju:pə'flu(:)iti] s. liikanaisuus. **-ous** [sju(:)'pə:fluəs] a. liikanainen, tarpeeton.

super|heat tulistaa (höyryä). **-human** yli-inhimillinen. **-impose** asettaa päälle.

superintend [sju(:)prin'tend] valvoa. **-ence** [-əns] (yli)valvonta, johto. **-ent** [-ənt] (yli)valvoja; tarkastaja.

superior [sju(:)'piəriə] a. ylempi; yli; korkeampi (arvoltaan); parempi, etevämpi (to kuin); erittäin hyvä, etevä; ylimielinen; s. (jkta) ylempi, korkeampi; esimies; [Father, Mother] S~ luostarinjohtaja, -tar; ~ numbers ylivoima; be ~ to sb. voittaa jku jssk. **-ity** [-i'ɔriti] s. etevämmyys, paremmuus; korkeampi arvo.

superlative [sju(:)'pə:lətiv] a. superlatiivinen; s. superlatiivi, yliaste. **-ly** adv. ylenpalttisen.

super|man yli-ihminen. **-market** (iso) valintamyymälä, suurmyymälä. **-natural** yliluonnollinen. **-normal** normaalin ylittävä. **-numerary** [-'nju:m(ə)rəri] a. liika-, ylimääräinen; s. ylimääräinen (henkilö); statisti. **-scription** [-'skripʃn] päällekirjoitus. **-sede** [-'si:d] syrjäyttää; astua (jkn) sijaan, korvata. **-session** syrjäyttäminen. **-sonic** [-'sɔnik] ääntä nopeampi, yliääni-.

superstit|ion [sju(:)pə'stiʃn] s. taikausko. **-ous** [-'stiʃəs] a. taikauskoinen.

super|structure ylärakenne; kansirakenteet. **-tax** lisävero. **-vene** [-'vi:n] tulla, tapahtua jkn lisäksi. **-vise** ['sju:pəvaiz] valvoa, pitää silmällä, johtaa, ohjata. **-vision** [-'viʒn] (ylin) valvonta. **-visor** [-vaizə] valvoja, tarkastaja, (työn)johtaja; (~y a. valvonta-), esimies-.

supine ['sju:pain] a. (selällään) makaava; veltto.

supper ['sʌpə] s. illallinen; the Lord's ~ Herran ehtoollinen; have ~ illastaa.

supplant [sə'pla:nt] v. tunkea syrjään, syrjäyttää.

supple ['sʌpl] a. taipuisa, notkea; pehmeä; myöntyvä, nöyrä.

supplement ['sʌplimənt] s. lisäys, liite; täydennys(osa); v. [sʌpli'ment] täydentää, liittää. **-ary** [sʌpli'ment(ə)ri] a. liite-, täyte-, täydennys-. **-ation** [-men'teiʃn] s. täydennys.

suppleness s. notkeus jne.

suppliant ['sʌpliənt] a. rukoileva, anova; s. (armon) anoja.

supplica|te ['sʌplikeit] v. rukoilla, anoa. **-tion** [-'keiʃn] s. (nöyrä) rukous.

supplier [sə'plaiə] s. hankkija.

supply 1. [sə'plai] v. varustaa, hankkia, toimittaa; täyttää (tarve), korvata (menestys), m. olla jkn sijaisena; s. hankinta; varasto; tarjonta; sijais-; supplies tarvikkeet, varasto(t), muonavarat, m. määrärahat; ~ column huoltokolonna (sot.); ~ ship varastolaiva; water ~ vesihuolto, veden saanti.

supply 2. ['sʌpli] adv. notkeasti, pehmeästi.

support [sə'pɔ:t] v. kannattaa, tukea; pitää yllä t. voimassa; elättää, ylläpitää, huoltaa; puolustaa, vahvistaa; kestää, sietää; s. kannatus; tuki, kannatin; ylläpito, elatus; speak in ~ of puhua jkn puolesta; a ~ing actress sivuosan esittäjä; price ~s tukipalkkiot. **-able** [-əbl] a. siedettävä. **-er** [-ə] s. kannattaja, puoluelainen; tukija.

suppos|e [sə'pəuz] v. otaksua, olettaa;

edellyttää; arvella, luulla; ~ *it were
true* entä jos se olisi totta; *I ~ I must*
minun kai täytyy; *I ~ so* luultavasti,
kyllä kai; ~ *we go* ehkäpä lähdemme;
everybody is ~ d to jokaisen
edellytetään... **-ed** [-d] *a.* otaksuttu,
kuviteltu. **-edly** [-idli] *adv.*
otaksuttavasti. **-ing** edellytettäen että.
-ition [sʌpəˈziʃn] *s.* otaksuma, luulo,
arvelu. **-itory** [səˈpozit(ə)ri] *s.*
peräpuikko (lääk.).

suppress [səˈpres] *v.* tukahduttaa,
torjua; pidättää, hillitä; lakkauttaa;
salata, vaieta (jstk). **-ion** [səˈpreʃn] *s.*
tukahduttaminen, torjunta;
salaaminen; lakkauttaminen,
sorto(toimenpiteet).

suppura|te [ˈsʌpju(ə)reit] *v.* märkiä.
-tion [-ˈreiʃn] *s.* märkiminen.

supranational [ˈsjuːprəˈnæʃnəl] *a.*
ylikansallinen.

supremacy [sjuˈpreməsi, səˈprem-] *s.*
yliherruus, ylivalta, valta-asema.

supreme [sjuː(ˈ)ˈpriːm, səˈpriːm] *a.*
ylin, korkein; mitä suurin,
äärimmäinen; *the S~ Being* Korkein.
-ly *adv.* äärettömän.

sur|charge [səːˈtʃɑːdʒ] *v.* ylikuormittaa;
veloittaa lisämaksua; *s.* [ˈsəː-]
ylikuormitus; lisämaksu; *import ~*
tuontivero.

sure [ʃuə] *a.* varma, vakuuttunut;
luotettava, taattu; *adv.* Am. totta kai;
~ *enough* (aivan) varmasti, tosiaan;
for ~ varmasti; *to be ~!* tietysti, totta
kai! (m.) tosin; *he is ~ to win* hän
varmasti voittaa; *I'm ~ I don't know*
en tosiaankaan tiedä; *make ~*
hankkia varmuus, varmistautua,
vakuuttautua. **-ly** *adv.* varmasti;
tosiaan; totta kai; ~ *you did not
believe it?* et kai sinä uskonut sitä? **-ty**
[-riti] *s.* varmuus; takaaja; *stand ~ for*
olla jkn takaajana.

surf [səːf] *s.* (ranta)tyrskyt. ~**-board**
lainelauta.

surface [ˈsəːfis] *s.* pinta; ulkopuoli,
-kuori; *attr.* pinnallinen; *v.* päällystää,
(kuv. ym) nousta pintaan, tulla
tietoisuuteen; ~ *mail* laivaposti,
maanteitse kuljetettava posti; ~*d*
päällystetty.

surfeit [ˈsəːfit] *s.* ylensyöminen;
kyllästymys; *v.* ahtaa täyteen, täyttää

(liiaksi), tympeyttää; (refl.) ahmia
itseensä.

surf|ing, -riding *s.* tyrskyratsastus,
lainelautailu.

surge [səːdʒ] *v.* aaltoilla, kuohua; *s.*
aaltoilu, kuohahdus.

surg|eon [ˈsəːdʒən] *s.* kirurgi; (sotilas-,
laiva)lääkäri. **-ery** [-(ə)ri] *s.* kirurgia;
vastaanottohuone. **-ical** [-ik(ə)l] *a.*
kirurginen.

surliness [ˈsəːlinis] *s.* äreys jne.

surly [ˈsəːli] *a.* äreä, nyreä, tyly, juro.

surmise [ˈsəːmaiz] *s.* otaksuma, arvelu;
v. [səːˈmaiz] otaksua, arvella,
aavistaa, arvata.

surmount [səˈmaunt] *v.* kohota, nousta
yli, yläpuolelle; voittaa; ~*ed with* jnk
peittämä. **-able** [-əbl] *a.* voitettavissa
oleva.

surname [ˈsəːneim] *s.* sukunimi;
lisänimi.

surpass [səːˈpɑːs] *v.* ylittää, olla
etevämpi, parempi; ~*ing* verraton,
erinomainen.

surplice [ˈsəːplis] *s.* messupaita.

surplus [ˈsəːpləs] *s.* ylijäämä; *attr.*
liika-.

surpris|e [səˈpraiz] *s.* yllätys;
hämmästys; *v.* yllättää;
hämmästyttää; *in ~* hämmästyneenä;
to my ~ hämmästyksekseni; *take by ~*
yllättää; vallata äkkirynnäköllä; *I am
~d at you* tätä en olisi sinusta
uskonut; *I should not be ~d if* enpä
ihmettelisi jos. **-ing** *a.* yllättävä,
hämmästyttävä. **-ingly** *adv.*
ihmeteltävän, hämmästyttävän; ihme
kyllä (~ *enough*).

surrealism [səˈriəlizm] *s.* surrealismi.

surrender [səˈrendə] *v.* luovuttaa,
luopua (jstk); antautua; *s.* luovutus;
antautuminen; ~ *oneself to* antautua,
heittäytyä (jnk) valtaan, langeta jhk.

surreptitious [sʌrəpˈtiʃəs] *a.* salainen,
luvaton.

Surrey [ˈsʌri] *erisn.*

surrogate [ˈsʌrəgit] *s.* (piispan)
sijainen.

surround [səˈraund] *v.* ympäröidä;
saartaa. **-ings** *s. pl.* ympäristö.

surtax [ˈsəːtæks] *s.* lisävero.

surveillance [səːˈveiləns] *s.* valvonta.

survey [səːˈvei] *v.* silmäillä, katsella,
antaa t. esittää yleiskatsaus;

tarkastaa; mitata, kartoittaa; *s.*
['sə:vei] yleissilmäys, (yleis)katsaus;
tarkastus; (maan)mittaus, kartoitus;
asemakartta. **-or** [sə(:)'ve(i)ə] *s.*
maanmittari; tarkastaja.

survival [sə'vaivl] *s.* eloonjääminen;
jäännös, jäänne; ~ *[time]* jäljellä
oleva elinaika.

surviv|e [sə'vaiv] *v.* jäädä eloon jkn
jälkeen, elää kauemmin kuin; jäädä
henkiin, säilyä hengissä. **-or** [-ə] *s.*
eloonjäänyt.

suscept|ibility [səsepti'biliti] *s.*
vastaanottavuus; alttius, herkkyys;
s-ities tunteet. **-ible** [sə'septəbl] *a.*
vastaanottava, altis (*to* esim. taudille);
herkkä; *is it ~ of proof* voidaanko se
todistaa; *[testimony]* ~ *of error* jossa
erehdys on mahdollinen.

suspect [səs'pekt] *v.* epäillä; arvella; *a.*
& s. ['sʌspekt] epäilyksenalainen;
epäilty.

suspend [səs'pend] *v.* ripustaa;
keskeyttää; lakkauttaa; lykätä (t.
tehdä ehdonalaiseksi); pidättää
virantoimituksesta, erottaa, ottaa
ajokortti pois (määräajaksi); *be ~ed*
riippua; ~ *ed animation* valekuolema.
-ers [-əz] *s. pl.* sukkanauhat; Am.
housunkannattimet.

suspen|se [səs'pens] *s.* epävarmuus,
epätietoisuus; jännitys, (tuskallinen)
odotus. **-sion** [-'penʃn] *s.*
ripustaminen, riippuminen;
lakkautus, keskeyttäminen, lykkäys;
pidättäminen virantoimituksesta;
suspensio; ~ *bridge* riippusilta.

suspicion [səs'piʃn] *s.* epäluulo,
epäily(s); arvelu, aavistus; *under ~ of*
epäiltynä jstk.

suspicious [səs'piʃəs] *a.* epäluuloinen;
epäilyttävä; arveluttava; *be ~ of*
epäillä jkta. **-ness** *s.* epäluuloisuus;
epäilyttävyys.

sustain [səs'tein] *v.* kannattaa, tukea;
pitää yllä; pitkittää (nuottia);
ylläpitää, elättää; kestää; saada
(vamma), kärsiä (menetys);
hyväksyä, vahvistaa; esittää (osaa)
hyvin. **-ed** [-d] *a.* jatkuva, pitkittynyt,
pitkäjänteinen; *a ~ effort* sitkeä
ponnistus.

sustenance ['sʌstinəns] *s.* elatus,
ravinto.

sutler ['sʌtlə] *s.* (vanh.) kanttiinin
pitäjä.

suture ['sju:tʃə] *s.* sutuura (anat.);
ommel (lääk.); *v.* ommella.

suzerain ['su:zərein] *s.* yliherra. **-ty** [-ti]
s. yliherruus.

svelte [svelt] *a.* hoikka.

swab [swɔb] *s.* köysiluuta; (vanu- t.
sideharso)tukko; *v.* puhdistaa
köysiluudalla; ~ *[up]* pyyhkiä
(sideharsotukolla ym).

swaddl|e ['swɔdl] *v.* kapaloida. **-ing:** ~
clothes kapalovaatteet.

swag [swæg] *s.* sl. saalis, varastettu
tavara.

swagger ['swægə] *v.* rehvastella; *s.*
rehvasteleva käynti, rehvastelu.

swain [swein] *s.* (maalais)nuorukainen,
ihailija, kosija.

swallow 1. ['swɔləu] *v.* niellä, nielaista;
(kuv.) arvelematta uskoa, pitää
hyvänään, sulattaa (loukkaus); *s.*
kulaus, siemaus.

swallow 2. ['swɔləu] *s.* pääskynen. **-tail**
hännystakki.

swam [swæm] *imp.* ks. **swim.**

swamp [swɔmp] *s.* suo, räme; *v.* tulvia
jnk yli, täyttää vedellä; vallata,
hukuttaa, jhk; *I am~ed with* work
olen hukkua työhön. **-y** [-i] *a.*
rämeinen.

swan [swɔn] *s.* joutsen; ~ *'s down*
joutsenenuntuva; ~ *-upping*
joutsenten merkitseminen; ~ *nery*
joutsentarha.

swank [swæŋk] *s.* pöyhkeily, prameilu;
v. prameilla, mahtailla. **-y** [-i] *a.* sl.
komeileva.

Swansea ['swɔnzi] *erisn.*

swap [swɔp] ks. **swop.**

sward [swɔ:d] *s.* nurmikko.

swarm 1. [swɔ:m] *s.* parvi; lauma;
ihmisvilinä; *v.* parveilla; ~ *with* vilistä
jtk.

swarm 2. [swɔ:m] *v.:* ~ *[up]* kiivetä,
kavuta.

swarthy ['swɔ:ði] *a.* tummaverinen.

swash [swɔʃ] *v.* loiskia. **-buckler** *s.*
sapelinkalistaja, rehentelijä.

swastika ['swɔstikə] *s.* hakaristi.

swat [swɔt] *v.* lyödä (läimäyttää); ~ *ter*
kärpäslätkä.

swath [swɔ:θ] *s.* heinäluoko,
viikatteenjälki.

swathe [sweiθ] *v.* kääriä.

sway [swei] *v.* huojua, horjua; heiluttaa, keinuttaa; kallistaa; ohjata, vaikuttaa (*a p.* jkh); hallita, vallita; *s.* heiluminen; (yli)valta, herruus; *hold ~ over* hallita. **~-backed** notkoselkäinen.

swear [swɛə] *swore* sworn, *v.* vannoa; vannottaa; kiroilla; *s.* kirous; *~ at* kiroilla, sadatella jkta; *~ by* m. sokeasti uskoa jhk; *~ in* vannottaa jklla virkavala; *~ to* vannoa (jnk olevan totta); *~ sb. to secrecy* vannottaa vaikenemaan. **~-word** kirosana.

sweat [swet] *s.* hiki; hikoilu; raadanta; *v.* (imp. & pp. *sweat* t. *-ed*) hikoilla, hiota; saattaa hikoilemaan; raataa; hiostaa (työläisiä), pitää nälkäpalkalla; *cold ~* tuskanhiki; *by the ~ of one's brow* otsansa hiessä; *all of a ~*, *in a* [*cold*] *~* hiestä märkänä, m. kauhun vallassa. **-er** [-ə] *s.* neulepusero. **-ing** *s.* riisto. **-y** [-i] *a.* hikinen.

swede [swi:d] *s.* lanttu; *S~* ruotsalainen.

Sweden ['swi:dn] *erisn.* Ruotsi.

Swedish ['swi:diʃ] *a. & s.* ruotsalainen; *s.* ruotsi, ruotsin kieli.

sweep [swi:p] *swept* swept, *v.* lakaista; pyyhkäistä; nuohota; raivata (miinoja); kulkea nopeasti, kiitää (ohi, yli), liukua jnk yli; astua arvokkaasti, kaartua, laskeutua; *s.* lakaisu, pyyhkäisy; kaarros, mutka, kaartuva tie; ulottuvaisuus, laaja näkymä, ala, piiri, (silmän)kantama; nuohooja; m. *= ~-stake*; *~ away* viedä mukanaan; lakaista pois, hävittää; *~ down* syöksyä jnk kimppuun; *~ up* lakaista kokoon; *~ all before one* saada valtava menestys; *~ of a net* apaja; *~ of an oar* aironveto; *make a clean ~ of* tehdä puhdasta jälkeä. **-er** [-ə] *s.* lakaisija, kadunlakaisukone; *mine~* miinanraivaaja. **-ing** *a.* kaartuva; yleistävä, täydellinen, laaja(kantoinen); *s.* : *~s* rikat, roskat. **~-stake(s)** *s.* eräänl. vedonlyönti ratsastuskilpailuissa (jossa potti jaetaan arpomalla (esim. kolmelle).

sweet [swi:t] *a.* makea; tuoksuva; sointuva; suloinen, herttainen; tuore, raitis; kallis, armas; *s.* karamelli, makea jälkiruoka, *pl.* makeiset; *pl.* ilot, nautinnot; *sg.* armas, kulta; *~ pea* hajuherne; *~ potato* bataatti; *~ water* makea, suolaton vesi; *has a ~ tooth* pitää makeisista; *be ~ on* olla rakastunut jkh. **-bread** kateenkorva. **-brier** orjanruusu. **-en** [-n] *v.* tehdä t. tulla makeaksi, makeuttaa; sulostuttaa; lieventää; puhdistaa. **-ening** *s.* makeuttamisaine. **-heart** kulta, rakastettu. **-ie** [-i] = ed. **-ish** [-iʃ] *a.* makeahko. **-meat** karamelli, *pl.* makeiset. **-ness** *s.* makeus; suloisuus, miellyttävyys jne. **~-scented** hyvänhajuinen. **~-tempered** hyvä-, lempeäluontoinen. **~-william** harjaneilikka.

swell [swel] *v.* (pp. *swollen*) paisua, pullistua; ajettua, turvota; kuohua; kohota; kasvaa, laajeta; paisuttaa, laajentaa; suurentaa, lisätä; *s.* paisuminen; pullistuma; lisääntyminen, nousu, (äänen) voima; (maan) kohoaminen, aaltoilu; mainingit; keikari, tyylikäs nainen; mestari (*at* jssk); *a.* tyylikäs, hieno; *have a ~ed head* olla itserakas; *what a ~ you are looking* kuinka hieno olet. **-ing** *s.* paisuminen; ajettuma, turpoama, turvotus, kuhmu; kohoilu.

swelter ['sweltə] *v.* nääntyä kuumuuteen. **-ing** *a.* tukahduttava, näännyttävä(n kuuma).

swept [swept] *imp. & pp.* ks. *sweep*; *be ~ off one's feet* haltioitua.

swerve [swə:v] *v.* poiketa (suunnasta), (äkkiä) kääntyä, väistää; horjua; saada poikkeamaan, kum_jtn; *s.* heilahdus, äkkikäännös, koukkaus; kierteinen liike t. pallo.

swift [swift] *a.* nopea, ripeä, pikainen; vuolas; *s.* tervapääsky. **-ness** *s.* nopeus jne.

swig [swig] *v.* juoda (pitkin kulauksin); *s.* siemaus.

swill [swil] *v.* huuhtoa (us. *~ out*); juoda (ahnaasti); *s.* huuhtelu; sianruoka, likavesi.

swim [swim] *swam* swum, *v.* uida, kellua, leijua; tulvia, olla tulvillaan (jtk); uida jnk yli; uittaa; *s.* uinti; *my* *head* ~*s* minua huimaa; *have a* ~ käydä uimassa; *go for a* ~, *go* ~*ming* mennä uimaan; *be in the* ~ liikkua piireissä, olla mukana; ~*-suit* uimapuku. **-mer** [-ə] *s.* uimari.

swimming ['swimiŋ] *s.* uinti; *a.* uiva, uima-; (kynneliä) tulvillaan. ~*-bath* uima-allas, -halli. ~*-bladder* uimarakko. **-ly** *adv.* sujuvasti, vaivattomasti. ~*-pool* uima-allas (tav. ulkona).

swindle ['swindl] *v.* petkuttaa, huijata; *s.* petkutus, huijaus. **-r** [-ə] *s.* huijari, keinottelija.

swine [swain] *s.* (*pl.* = *sg.*) sika.

swing [swiŋ] *swung swung, v.* heilua, keinua, kiikkua; heilahtaa, heiluttaa, keinuttaa, kiikuttaa; kääntyä; pyörittää, pyörähdyttää, m. kääntää jkn mieli; saada jtk onnistumaan; *s.* heiluminen, heilahdus; keinu; liikkumavara; vauhti, poljento; ~ [*for sth.*] joutua hirteen; ~ *round* pyörähtää ympäri; ~ *to* lennähtää kiinni; *go with a* ~ sujua hyvin; *in full* ~ täydessä vauhdissa. ~*-bridge* kääntösilta. **-ing** *a.* heilahteleva, kääntö-; iloinen, huvitteleva, poljennollinen.

swingeing [swin(d)ʒiŋ] *a.* (puhek.) valtava, suunnaton.

swingle ['swiŋgl] *s.* lihta. ~*-tree* viippa.

swinish ['swainiʃ] *a.* sikamainen, siivoton.

swipe [swaip] *v.* iskeä lujaa; »pihistää»; *s.* luja isku.

swirl [swə:l] *s.* pyörre; *v.* kieppua, tuprutа.

swish [swiʃ] *v.* sivaltaa; *s.* viuhahdus, kahina; *a.* (puhek.) hieno.

Swiss [swis] *a.* & *s.* sveitsiläinen; ~ *roll* kääretorttu; ~ *woman* sveitsitär.

switch [switʃ] *s.* vitsa, vapa; vaihde (rautat.), katkaisija (sähk.); irtopalmikko; *v.* piestä, huiskia, vaihtaa (rautat.), kytkeä, kääntää (toisaalle); ~ *off* katkaista (virta, yhteys); ~ *on* avata (radio ym), käynnistää, sytyttää; ~ *off the light* sammuttaa valo. **-back** vuoristorata (huvipuistossa). ~*-board* kytkentaulu; keskus|pöytä, -taulu.

Switzerland ['swits(ə)lənd] *erisn.* Sveitsi.

swivel ['swivl] *s.* (käántö)tappi; leikari; *v.* kääntyä (tapin varassa); ~ *chair* kääntötuoli.

swollen ['swəul(ə)n] *pp.* ks. *swell*.

swoon [swu:n] *v.* pyörtyä, mennä tainnoksiin; *s.* pyörtymys.

swoop [swu:p] *v.*: ~ [*down upon*] syöksyä, syöksähtää, iskeä jnk kimppuun; *s.* syöksähdys.

swop, swap [swɔp] *v.* (puhek.) vaihtaa.

sword [sɔ:d] *s.* miekka, kalpa; *cross (measure)* ~*s* mitellä miekkojaan; *put to the* ~ surmata. ~*-belt* miekankannike. ~*-cut* miekanhaava. **-fish** miekkakala. **-play** miekkailu. **-sman** [sɔ:dzmən] miekkailija.

swore [swɔ:] *imp.* ks. *swear*.

sworn [swɔ:n] *pp.* ks. *swear*; valallinen, vannonut, vannoutunut.

swot [swɔt] *v.* päntätä päähänsä, ahertaa; *s.* kirjatoukka.

swum [swʌm] *pp.* ks. *swim*.

swung [swʌŋ] *imp.* & *pp.* ks. *swing*.

sybarite ['sibərait] *s.* nautiskelija.

sycamore ['sikəmɔ:] *s.* sykomori, (metsä)viikunapuu; plataani(laji), vuoristovaahtera.

sycophant ['sikəfənt] *s.* liehakoitsija.

Sydney ['sidni] *erisn.*

syllab|ic [si'læbik] *a.* tavu-. **-le** ['siləbl] *s.* tavu; *not a* ~! *ei* sanaakaan! **-us** ['siləbəs] (*pl.* *-i* [-ai], ~*es*) *s.* opinto-ohjelma, -suunnitelma.

syllogism ['silədʒizm] *s.* päätelmä.

sylph [silf] *s.* ilmanhenki; keijukainen.

sylvan ['silvən] *a.* metsä(n)-.

symbol ['simb(ə)l] *s.* vertauskuva, symboli; merkki, tunnus. **-ic(al)** [-'bɔlik, -(ə)l] *a.* vertauskuvallinen. **-ize** [-aiz] *v.* symboloida, ilmasta vertauskuvin.

symmetr|ical [si'metrik(ə)l] *a.* tasasuhtainen, symmetrinen. **-y** ['simitri] *s.* tasasuhtaisuus.

sympath|etic [simpə'θetik] *a.* myötä|mielinen, -tuntoinen, osaaottava. **-ize** ['simpəθaiz] *v.* suhtautua myötämielisesti (*with* jhk), ilmaista myötätunto(nsa), ottaa osaa jhk; ~*r* kannattaja. **-y** ['simpəθi] *s.* myötätunto, osanotto, vastakaiku.

sym|phony ['simfəni] *s.* sinfonia. **-posium** [-'pəuzjəm] *s.* (*pl.* *-ia*) (tieteellinen) kongressi, symposiumi; yhteisjulkaisu.

symptom [ˈsim(p)təm] *s.* oire. **-atic** [-ˈmætik] *a.* oireellinen.

synagogue [ˈsinəgɔg] *s.* synagoga.

synchron|ism [ˈsiŋkrənizm] *s.* samanaikaisuus. **-ize** [-aiz] *v.* synkronoida; olla samanaikainen kuin. **-ous** [-əs] *a.* samanaikainen.

syncop|ate [ˈsiŋkəpeit] *v.* synkopoida. **-ation** [-ˈpeiʃn] synkooppi (mus.). **-e** [ˈsiŋkəpi] *s.* tajuttomuudentila.

syndicate [ˈsindikit] *s.* syndikaatti; *v.* [-keit] julkaista syndikaatin kautta.

syndrome [ˈsindrəum] *s.* oireyhtymä.

Synge [siŋ] *erisn.*

synod [ˈsinəd] *s.* kirkolliskokous.

synonym [ˈsinənim] *s.* synonyymi. **-ous** [siˈnɔniməs] *a.* samanmerkityksinen.

synop|sis [siˈnɔpsis] *s.* (pl. *-ses*) yhteenveto. **-tic** [siˈnɔptik] *a.* yleiskatsauksellinen.

syntactic [sinˈtæktik] *a.* lauseopillinen.

syntax [ˈsintæks] *s.* lauseoppi.

synthe|sis [ˈsinθisis] *s.* (pl. *-ses* [-siːz]) synteesi, yhdistäminen. **-size** [-saiz] *v.* syntetoida. **-tic** [-ˈθetik] *a.* synteettinen.

syntonic [sinˈtɔnik] *a.* viritys-.

syphil|is [ˈsifilis] *s.* kuppatauti. **-itic** [-ˈlitik] *a.* kuppatautinen.

syphon ks. *siphon.*

Syracuse [ˈsaiərəkjuːz] *erisn.* Syrakusa; Am. [ˈsirəkjuːs].

Syria [ˈsiriə] *erisn.* Syyria. **-n** [-n] *a. & s.* syyrialainen.

syringe [ˈsirin(d)ʒ] *s.* (lääke- ym) ruisku; *v.* ruiskuttaa.

syrup [ˈsirəp] *s.* siirappi. **-y** [-i] *a.* siirappimainen.

system [ˈsistəm] *s.* järjestelmä, systeemi; elimistö; *nervous* ~ hermosto; *railway* ~ rautatieverkko. **-atic** [-ˈmætik] *a.* järjestelmällinen. **-atize** [-ətaiz] *v.* laatia järjestelmäksi, systemoida.

T

T, t [ti:] s. t-kirjain; *to a T* täsmälleen, pilkulleen; *T-square* kulmaviivoitin; *cross the Ts* olla pikkutarkka.
Lyh.: **T.B.** *tuberculosis;* **Tenn.** *Tennessee;* **Tex.** *Texas;* **T.F.** *Territorial Force;* **Thess.** *Thessalonians;* **Thurs.** *Thursday* **T.N.T** ['ti:en'ti:] *trinitrotoluene;* **T.O.** *turn over;* **Treas.** *Treasurer;* **T.T.** *teetotaller;* **T.U.** *trade union;* **T.U.C.** *Trades Union Congress;* **Tu., Tues.** *Tuesday;* **TV** ['ti:'vi:] *television.*

tab [tæb] s. (veto)liuska, kaistale, nipukka; raksi; *keep ~ s* (t. *a ~*) on pitää kirjaa jstk.

tabard ['tæbəd] s. (ritarin) asetakki t. lyhyt viitta.

tabby ['tæbi] s. läikesilkki; *~ [-cat]* juovikas kissa.

tabernacle ['tæbə(:)nækl] s.; *the T~* liitonmaja; kirkkoteltta; *Feast of T~ s* lehtimajanjuhla.

table ['teibl] s. pöytä; taulu, laatta; taulukko; ks. *~-land;* v. lykätä, siirtää; esittää, panna asialistalle; *at ~* ruokapöydässä; *keep a good ~* tarjota hyvää ruokaa; *turn the ~ s on* maksaa samalla mitalla jklle; *~ of contents* sisällysluettelo.

tableau ['tæbləu] s. (pl. *~ x [-z]*) kuvaelma.

table|-cloth (pl. *-ths [-klɔθs]*) pöytäliina. **~-land** tasanko, laakio. **-spoon** ruokalusikka.

tablet ['tæblit] s. levy, laatta (esim. kirjoitus-), muistotaulu; tabletti; (saippua)pala.

table|-talk pöytäkeskustelu. **-ware** pöytäkalusto.

tabloid ['tæblɔid] s. pienikokoinen (us. kohu-)uutislehti.

taboo [tə'bu:] s. tabu; v. tehdä tabuksi, kieltää mainitsemasta; *the subject is*

~ ed siitä asiasta ei puhuta.

tabouret ['tæbərit] s. jakkara.

tabul|ar ['tæbjulə] a. taulukko-, taulukon tapaan laadittu. **-ate** [-eit] v. laatia taulukko (jstk), taulukoida.

tacit ['tæsit] a. äänetön, sanaton. **-urn** [-ə:n] a. vaitelias, harvapuheinen. **-urnity** ['-tə:niti] s. vaiteliaisuus.

tack [tæk] s. nupi, mattonaula, nasta; harsimapisto, *pl.* harsinta; halssi, luovi (mer.); suunta; v. kiinnittää nauloilla; harsia; liittää; (mer.) luovia; *hard ~* laivakorppu.

tackle ['tækl] s. välineet, vehkeet; takila (mer.); talja; v. iskeä kiinni, käydä käsiksi jhk, käydä jkn kimppuun.

tacky ['tæki] a. tahmea.

tact [tækt] s. tahdikkuus. **-ful** a. tahdikas, hienotunteinen.

tacti|cal ['tæktik(ə)l] a. taktinen. **-cian** [tæk'tiʃn] s. taktikko; taktikoitsija. **-cs** ['tæktiks] s. taktiikka; taktikointi.

tactile ['tæktail] a. kosketus-, tunto-.

tactless ['tæktlis] a. tahditon, epähieno.

tadpole ['tædpəul] s. sammakonpoikanen.

taffeta ['tæfitə] s. tafti(kangas).

taffrail ['tæfreil] s. peräparras.

tag [tæg] s. hintalippu, osoitelippu; (kengännauhan) kovike, loppupää; kertosäe; kulunut lauseparsi; hippaleikki; v. kiinnittää jhk *(to, on to)*, seurata kintereillä *(along after)*; varustaa osoitelipulla; *play ~* olla hippasilla; *question ~* loppuun liitetty kysymys *(isn't it?)*.

Tahiti [tɑ:'hi:ti] erisn.

tail [teil] s. häntä, pyrstö; taka-, selkäpuoli, loppupää; laahus, lieve; *pl.* = *~ coat;* v. seurata jkn jälkiä (itsepintaisesti); *~ away (off)* jäädä

jälkeen, vähetä, huveta; *heads or* ~s
kruunu vai klaava; *turn* ~ lähteä
käpälämäkeen. ~**-board** perälauta.
~**-coat** hännystakki. ~**-light** perä-,
takavalo. ~**-spin** syöksykierre.

tailor ['teilə] *s.* räätäli; *v.* harjoittaa
vaatturinammattia; valmistaa,
muovata, sovittaa (*to* jnk
mukaiseksi); ~*ed* räätälin tekemä.
-ing *s.* vaatturintyö. ~**-made** et. naisen
kävelypuku.

taint [teint] *s.* (häpeä)tahra, saastunut,
tartunta; jnk merkki, leima; *v.*
saastuttaa, pilata; pilaantua.

Taiwan [tai'wɑn, -'wɑ:n] *erisn.* **-ese**
[-'ni:z] *a. & s.* taiwanilainen.

take [teik] *took taken, v.* ottaa; tarttua;
ottaa haltuunsa, vallata, valloittaa;
ottaa kiinni, vangita; nauttia
(ravintoa); vuokrata (huone), tilata,
ostaa (lippu); viedä, kantaa (pois),
kuljettaa; ottaa vastaan, omaksua;
käsittää, tajuta; pitää jnak;
suhtautua; kokea, tuntea; suorittaa,
tehdä; käyttää, kuluttaa, vaatia;
tehota, tulla suosituksi; kestää;
matkustaa jllak, paeta jhk; *s.* saalis,
kertynyt kassa; ~ *a class* opettaa
luokkaa; ~ [*a*] *cold* vilustua; ~ *a
fence* hypätä aidan yli; ~ *notes*
tehdä muistiinpanoja; ~ *an oath*
vannoa vala; ~ *place* tapahtua;
~ *the consequences* tyytyä
seurauksiin; ~ [*it*] *ill* pahastua
jstk; *be* ~ *n ill* sairastua; *I* ~ *it that*
arvelen, otaksun, että; ~ *after*
muistuttaa jkta; ~ *along* ottaa
mukaansa; ~ *back* ottaa takaisin,
peruuttaa; ~ *down* m. merkitä
muistiin; nolata, nöyryyttää; ~ *in*
ottaa luokseen, tilata (lehteä); viedä
pöytään; tajuta; petkuttaa, puijata;
pienentää (vaatteita); ~ *for* luulla
jksk, pitää jnak; *what do you* ~ *me for*
miksi minua luulette? ~ *off* ottaa
pois, riisua; vähentää (hinnasta);
matkia, jäljitellä; hypätä, ponnistaa;
(lentokoneesta) nousta ilmaan; ~
oneself off laittautua tiehensä; ~ *on*
ottaa tehtäkseen, omaksua, ottaa
(esim. palvelukseen, vastustajakseen
ym); kiihtyä, tulla muotiin; ~ *out*
viedä ulos, ottaa pois, hankkia
(patentti ym); ~ *it out on* purkaa

kiukkunsa jkh; ~ *over* ottaa
haltuunsa; ryhtyä, joutua (jnk)
johtoon; ~ *to* mieltyä jhk (m. ~
kindly to), ruveta harrastamaan jtk; ~
to drink ratketa juomaan; ~ *up* imeä
itseensä; viedä (aikaa, tilaa); ryhtyä
jhk; jatkaa; keskeyttää (moittien),
oikaista; ~ *up* (*with*) ruveta
suhteisiin; ~ *it upon oneself* ottaa
asiakseen. ~**-down** nolaus. ~**-in**
huijaus. ~**-home pay** käteen jäävä
palkka. ~**-n** [-(ə)n] *pp.* (m.) varattu; ~
with ihastunut jhk; *was* ~ *ill* sairastui.
~**-off** irvikuva; ponnistus-,
starttipaikka, (lentokoneen) lähtö.
~**-over** valtaanpääsy, vallananastus; *t.
-o. bid* ostotarjous.

taking ['teikiŋ] *a.* miellyttävä,
houkutteleva; *s.:* ~s tulot, kassa.

talc [tælk] *s.* talkki (m. *talcum*).

tale [teil] *s.* kertomus, tarina; *fairy* ~
satu; *tell* ~s [*out of school*] kieliä.
-bearer *s.* kantelija. **-bearing** *s.*
kieliminen.

talent ['tælənt] *s.* kyky,
luonnonlahja(t), taipumus; leiviskä
(raam.). **-ed** [-id] *a.* lahjakas.

talisman ['tælizmən] *s.* taikakalu.

talk [tɔ:k] *v.* puhua, puhella,
keskustella, m. juoruta; *s.* puhelu,
keskustelu; jutteluhetki; neuvottelu;
pakina (m. esim. radio)esitelmä;
puheenaihe, juoru; ~ *at* pistellä jkta;
~ *away* puhua papattaa, puhua
puhumistaan; ~ *big* kerskua; ~ *down
to* puhua (kuin) ylemmältä tasolta; ~
over keskustella, neuvotella; taivuttaa
jku jhk (m. ~ *round*); [*it is*] *the* ~ *of
the town* yleisenä puheenaiheena.
-ative [-ətiv] *a.* puhelias, suulas. **-ie**
[-i] *s.* äänielokuva. **-ing-to** *s.* läksytys.

tall [tɔ:l] *a.* pitkä, kookas; korkea; sl.
liiallinen, uskomaton. **-boy** korkea
lipasto.

tallow ['tæləu] *s.* tali.

tally ['tæli] *s.* pykäläpuu; tili;
vastakirja; nimilippu; *v.* olla
yhdenmukainen, olla yhtäpitävä,
käydä yksiin (*with* jnk kanssa).

talon ['tælən] *s.* (petolinnun) kynsi;
emälippu, talonki.

tamarisk ['tæmərisk] *s.* tamariski(puu).

tambourine [tæmbə'ri:n] *s.* tamburiini
(mus.).

tare

tame [teim] *a.* kesy; sävyisä; laimea, ponneton, mielenkiinnoton; *v.* kesyttää; kukistaa.

Tammany ['tæməni] *erisn.:* ~ *Hall* (häikäilemätön) poliittinen järjestö New Yorkissa.

tam-o'-shanter ['tæmə'ʃæntə] *s.* pyöreä skotlantilainen lakki.

tamp [tæmp] *s.* tukkia, sulloa, painella (us. ~ *down*).

tamper ['tæmpə] *v.:* ~ *with* peukaloida (omavaltaisesti), kopeloida; sekaantua jhk; lahjoa.

tampon ['tæmpən] *s.* tamponi, tukko; *v.* tamponoida.

tan [tæn] *s.* nahkurinparkki; keltaisenruskea väri; rusketus; *a.* nahanruskea; *v.* parkita; päivettyä; ~*ned* päivettynyt; ~ *sb.'s hide* löylyttää.

tandem ['tændəm] *s.:* ~ *bicycle* tandempyörä; [*drive*] ~ peräkkäin.

tang [tæŋ] *s.* (jllek ominainen) haju, lemu, tuoksu (*the* ~ *of the sea air);* (villan ym) ruoti; helähdys.

tangent [tæn(d)ʒ(ə)nt] *s.* sivuaja, tangentti; *fly (go) off at a* ~ poiketa äkkiä suunnastaan (uudelle raiteelle). **-ial** *a.* [-'dʒenʃəl] jtk sivuava, hipaiseva, sekundäärinen.

tangerine [tæn(d)ʒə'ri:n] *s.* mandariini.

tangible ['tæn(d)ʒəbl] *a.* käsin kosketeltava; kouraantuntuva.

Tangier [tæn'dʒiə] *erisn.* Tanger.

tangl|e ['tæŋgl] *s.* takku, sekasotku, sotkuinen vyyhti; *v.* sotkea, sekoittaa, kietoa; sotkeutua; *in a* ~ sekaisin, ylösalaisin. **-ed** [-d] *a.* sotkuinen, sekava, takkuinen.

tango ['tæŋgəu] *s.* tango.

tank ['tæŋk] *s.* (suuri) säiliö; panssarivaunu; *get* ~*ed up* (sl.) juoda päänsä täyteen. **-age** [-idʒ] *s.* säiliön tilavuus.

tankard ['tæŋkəd] *s.* kolpakko.

tanker ['tæŋkə] *s.* säiliöalus, tankkeri.

tann|er ['tænə] *s.* nahkuri; (sl.) kuuden pennyn raha (nyt 2 1/2 p). **-ery** [-əri] *s.* nahkurinverstas. **-ic** [-ik] *a.:* ~ *acid* parkkihappo. **-in** [-in] *s.* = ed. **-ing** *s.* selkäsauna.

tannoy ['tænɔi] *s.* (tavaratalon ym) kaiutin, ulkokaiutin.

Tanzania [tænzə'niə] *erisn.*

tansy [tænzi] *s.* pietaryrtti.

tantaliz|e ['tæntəlaiz] *v.* kiusata, härnätä. **-ing** *a.* tuskallinen, sietämätön.

tantamount ['tæntəmaunt] *a.* samanarvoinen; *is* ~ *to* merkitsee samaa kuin.

tantrum ['tæntrəm] *s.* pahantuulen puuska.

tap 1. [tæp] *v.* kopauttaa, naputtaa; *s.* naputus; ~*s* iltasoitto; ~*-dancing* steppaus.

tap 2. [tæp] *s.* tappi, tulppa; hana; (juoman) laatu; *v.* laskea, juoksuttaa; urkkia (tietoja); *on* ~ valmiina laskettavaksi; runsaasti saatavissa; *turn the* ~ *on (off)* avata (sulkea) hana; ~ [*a telephone*] kuunnella salaa.

tape [teip] *s.* kapea nauha; reunanauha; mittanauha; maalinauha; tarra-, liimanauha, teippi, sähkenauha; (nauhurin) ääninauha; *v.* sitoa nauhalla, kiinnittää teipillä; nauhoittaa; *adhesive* ~ laastarinauha. **-line** = seur. **~-measure** mittanauha. **~-recorder** nauhoitin, nauhuri, magnetofoni.

taper ['teipə] *v.* ohut vahakynttilä; *a.* suippeneva; *v.* suipentua, suipentaa (*m.* ~ *off*).

tapestry ['tæpistri] *s.* (kudottu) seinävaate, gobeliini.

tapeworm ['teipwə:m] *s.* heisimato; *broad* ~ lapamato.

tapioca [tæpi'əukə] *s.* tapiokasuurimot.

tapir ['teipə] *s.* tapiiri (eläint.).

tap|**-room** ['tæprum] *s.* baari, tarjoiluhuone. **~-water** vesijohto-vesi.

tapster ['tæpstə] *s.* viinuri.

tar [ta:] *s.* terva; (puhek.) merimies (*m. Jack T~);* *v.* tervata; ~*red* tervattu, asfaltoitu.

tarantula [tə'ræntjulə] *s.* juoksijahämähäkki.

tardiness *s.* hitaus.

tardy ['ta:di] *a.* hidas, myöhäinen; vastahakoinen.

tare 1. [teə] *s.* (us. *pl.*) rehuvirna; *pl.* luste (raam.).

tare 2. [teə] *s.* taara (kaupp.).

target ['tɑ:git] *s.* maalitaulu; tavoite; *v.* suunnata.

tariff ['tærif] *s.* (tulli)tariffi, taksa; tulli; hintaluettelo.

tarmac ['tɑ:mæk] *s.* kestopäällyste, asfaltti; lentokentän kiitoradat.

tarn [tɑ:n] *s.* vuorilampi.

tarnish ['tɑ:niʃ] *s.* himmentää; mustata, tahrata; himmentyä; (metallista) mustua; *s.* himmeys; tahra.

tarpaulin [tɑ:'pɔ:lin] *s.* tervavaate, presenninki, »pressu».

tarry 1. ['tɑ:ri] *a.* tervainen.

tarry 2. ['tæri] *v.* viipyä, vitkastella; odottaa.

tart 1. [tɑ:t] *a.* hapan, kirpeä; terävä, pureva.

tart 2. [tɑ:t] *s.* hedelmätorttu; sl. katutyttö, henttu.

tartan ['tɑ:tn] *s.* (Skotl.) tartaani(malli), (skotti)ruudutus.

tartar ['tɑ:tə] *s.* viinikivi; hammaskivi; *cream of* ~ puhdistettu viinikivi. **-ic** [tɑ:'tærik] *a.:* ~ *acid* viinihappo.

Tartar ['tɑ:tə] *s.* tataari; *catch a* ~ tavata voittajansa.

tartlet ['tɑ:tlit] *s.* pieni torttu.

tart|ly *adv.* terävästi jne. **-ness** *s.* kirpeys; purevuus.

task [tɑ:sk] *s.* tehtävä, työ; kotitehtävä; *v.* rasittaa, koetella (voimia); *set sb. a* ~ antaa tehtäväksi; *take to* ~ vaatia tilille; ~*-force* taisteluryhmä, erikoisosasto. **-master** isäntä, (vaativa) työnjohtaja.

Tasmania [tæz'meinjə] *erisn.*

tassel ['tæsl] *s.* tupsu. **-led** [-d] *a.* tupsukoristeinen.

taste [teist] *v.* maistaa, maistella; kokea, saada maistaa jtk; maistua; *s.* makuaisti; maku; hyvä maku, aisti; mieltymys; ~*s differ* on monenlaista makua; *a matter of* ~ makuasia; *it would be bad* ~ *to* osoittaisi huonoa makua; *not to my* ~ ei minun mieleeni. **-ful** *a.* aistikas. **-less** *a.* mauton, epäaistikas.

tasty ['teisti] *a.* maukas.

tat [tæt] *v.* tehdä sukkulapitsiä; ks. *tit.*

ta-ta [tæ'tɑ:] *int.* (lastenk.) hyvästi! hei hei!

Tate [teit] *erisn.* (~ *Gallery*).

tatter ['tætə] *s.:* ~*s* ryysyt. **-demalion** [-də'meiljən] *a.* ryysyinen, repaleinen.

tattle ['tætl] *v.* laverrella, juoruilla; *s.* juoruilu, suunsoitto.

tattoo 1. [tə'tu:] *s.* iltasoitto; *the devil's* ~ (hermostunut) sormilla rummuttaminen.

tattoo 2. [tə'tu:] *v.* (~*ed*) tatuoida; *s.* tatuointi.

tatty ['tæti] *a.* siivoton, halpa.

taught [tɔ:] *imp. & pp.* ks. *teach.*

taunt [tɔ:nt] *s.* pilkka, iva, pistosana; *v.* pilkata, ivata. **-ingly** *adv.* pilkaten, ivaten.

taut [tɔ:t] *a.* tiukka, kireä.

tautology [tɔ:'tɔlədʒi] *s.* tautologia, toisto.

tavern ['tævən] *s.* kapakka. **~-keeper** *s.* kapakoitsija.

tawdriness *s.* koreus, räikeys.

tawdry ['tɔ:dri] *a.* koreileva, räikeä.

tawny ['tɔ:ni] *a.* ruskeankeltainen.

tax [tæks] *v.* verottaa; arvioida; rasittaa, panna koetukselle; syyttää (*with* jstk); *s.* vero (et. valtion); taakka, rasitus; ~ *dodging*, ~ *evasion* verojen kiertäminen; ~ *refund* veronpalautus; ~ *return* veroilmoitus; *after* ~*es* veronpidätyksen jälkeen; *vrt. income.* **-able** [-əbl] *a.* veronalainen. **-ation** [-'seiʃn] *s.* verotus. **~-deductible** (verotuksessa) vähennyskelpoinen. **-ing** *a.* rasittava. **~-free** verovapaa, veroton.

taxi ['tæksi] *s.* vuokra-auto, taksi; *v.* (~*ed*) ajaa maassa, rullata (ilm.). **~-man** vuokra-autoilija. **-meter** taksimetri. **~-rank**, **~-stand** taksiasema, »pirssi».

tax|man verottaja. **-payer** veronmaksaja.

tea [ti:] *s.* tee(lehdet, -ateria); *afternoon* ~ iltapäivätee; *high* ~ teeillallinen; ~ *wagon* tarjoilupöytä; *. . [is] not my cup of* ~ ei ole minun makuuni. **~-bag** teepussi. **~-ball** teekuula. **~-caddy** teerasia.

teach [ti:tʃ] *taught* taught, *v.* opettaa; olla opettajana. **-able** [-əbl] *a.* oppivainen. **-er** [-ə] *s.* opettaja. **~-in** yleiskeskustelu. **-ing** *s.* opetus.

tea|cup teekuppi; *a storm in a* ~ myrsky vesilasissa. **-house** teehuone.

teak [ti:k] s. tiikki (puu).

teal [ti:l] s. tavi.

team [ti:m] s. valjakko; joukkue (urh.), työryhmä; ~ *spirit* yhteishenki. **-ster** [-stə] s. kuorma-auton kuljettaja. **~-work** (ryhmän) yhteistyö, tiimityö.

tea|-party s. teekutsut. **~-pot** teekannu.

tear 1. [tiə] s. kyynel; pisara; *in* ~ *s* itkien; *choking with* ~ *s* itku kurkussa.

tear 2. [teə] *tore torn, v.* repiä, reväistä; raadella; revetä, repeytyä; syöksähtää, syöksyä; s. repeämä; ~ *oneself away* riistäytyä irti; ~ *up* kiskoa (irti, maasta), repiä rikki; *vrt.* **wear**.

tear|ful [ˈtiəf(u)l] a. kyyneleinen. **-less** a. kyyneletön.

tearing [ˈteəriŋ] a. kiihkeä, raju.

tearoom l.v. kahvila.

tease [ti:z] v. ärsyttää, kiusoitella, härnätä; tupeerata; s. kiusanhenki. **-l** [-l] s. karstaohdake. **-r** [-ə] s. kiusanhenki; pulmallinen kysymys t. tehtävä.

tea|-service, **~-set**, **~-things** teeastiasto. **-spoon** teelusikka; ~ *ful* teelusikallinen. **~-urn** s. (iso) teekeitin.

teat [ti:t] s. nänni.

tec [tek] s. sl. = *detective*.

technic [ˈteknik] s. ks. *technique*. **-al** [-(ə)l] a. teknillinen, tekninen; ammatti-. **-ality** [-ˈkæliti] s.: *t-ities* teknilliset yksityiskohdat. **-ian** [-ˈniʃn] s. teknikko.

techn|ics [ˈtekn|iks] s. pl. tekniikka. **-ique** [tekˈniːk] s. (teknillinen) taito, tekniikka. **-ological** [-əˈlɔdʒikə)l] tekninen. **-ology** [tekˈnɔlədʒi] s. teknologia, tekniikka.

teddy [ˈtedi] s.: ~ *-boy* lättähattu (1950–60).

Te Deum [ti:ˈdi(:)əm] s. ylistysvirsi.

tedious [ˈti:djəs] a. ikävä, pitkästyttävä. **-ness** s. pitkäveteisyys.

tedium [ˈti:djəm] s. yksitoikkoisuus, ikävyys.

tee [ti:] s. (golf) tiiauspaikka.

teem [ti:m] v.: ~ *with* vilistä, kihistä, kuhista. **-ing** s. ~ *with* jtk täynnä, vilisevä.

teen|s [ti:nz] s. pl. ikävuodet 13–19.

~**-ager** s. 13–19-vuotias, l.v. teini-ikäinen.

teeny [ˈti:ni] a. (lastenk.) = *tiny*.

teeter [ˈti:tə] v. keinua, häilyä.

teeth [ti:θ] s. pl. ks. *tooth; in the* ~ *of* jnk uhalla, jstk välittämättä; *by the skin of one's* ~ täpärästi, niukin naukin; *cast sth. in sb.'s* ~ sanoa vasten naamaa. **-e** [ti:ð] v. saada (maito)hampaita. **-ing** [ti:ðiŋ] s. hampaiden puhkeaminen.

teetotal [ti:ˈtəutl] a. raittius-. **-ler** [-ə] s. absolutisti, ehdottoman raittiuden kannattaja.

tegument [ˈtegjumənt] s. peite, kalvo, kuori.

Teheran [tiəˈrɑ:n] *erisn.*

tele|cast [ˈteli|kɑ:st] s. televisiolähetys. **-communications** s. tietoliikenne. **-gram** [-græm] s. sähke.

telegraph [ˈteligrɑ:f] v. lennätin; v. sähköttää. **-ic** [teliˈgræfik] a. lennätin-; ~ *address* sähkeosoite. **-ist** [tiˈlegrəfist] s. sähköttäjä. **-y** [tiˈlegrəfi] s. sähkötys.

telepath|ic [teliˈpæθik] a. telepaattinen. **-y** [tiˈlepəθi] s. telepatia, ajatuksensiirto.

telephon|e [ˈtelifəun] s. puhelin; v. soittaa (puhelimella); *by* ~ puhelimitse; *desk* ~ pöytäpuhelin; *you are wanted on the* ~ sinua kysytään puhelimessa. **-ic** [-ˈfɔnik] a. puhelin-. **-y** [tiˈlefəni] s. puhelintekniikka.

tele|photo s. lennätinkuva; ~ *lens* teleobjektiivi. **-printer** s. kaukokirjoitin. **-scope** s. kaukoputki; v. työntää kokoon. **-viewer** s. television katselija. **-vise** [ˈtelivaiz] v. televisioida. **-vision** s. [ˈteliviʒn] televisio; ~ *broadcast* t-lähetys; ~ *set* televisio(vastaanotin); ~ *screen* kuvaruutu.

tell [tel] *told told, v.* kertoa, sanoa; puhua; ilmaista, ilmoittaa; käskeä, kehottaa, pyytää; tuntea (jstk), erottaa; laskea, lukea, vaikuttaa; (~ *on*) käydä jkn voimille; *who can* ~ ken tietää; ~ *apart* erottaa; ~ *fortunes* ennustaa; ~ *a lie* valehdella; ~ *tales* kieliä; ~ *off* määrätä *(for* jhk); ~ *sb. off* torua; ~ *over* laskea; ~ *on sb.* kannella. **-ing** a. tehokas; painava (väite). **-tale** *a.* kielivä, paljonpuhuva.

telly ['teli] *s.* (puhek.) televisio.

temerity [ti'meriti] *s.* uhkarohkeus.

temper ['tempə] *s.* luonto, luonteenlaatu; (hyvä, huono) tuuli, mielentila; kiivaus, kiukku; karkaisu; *v.* sekoittaa (savea), karkaista (metallia), (teräksestä) päästää; lieventää, lauhduttaa; *get into a ~* suuttua, kiivastua; *lose one's ~* menettää malttinsa; *out of ~* huonolla tuulella.

temperament ['temp(ə)rəmənt] temperamentti. **-al** [-'mentl] *a.* luontainen; temperamentikas, oikukas.

tempera|nce ['temp(ə)r(ə)ns] *s.* kohtuullisuus; *~ hotel* raittiushotelli. **-te** [-rit] *a.* kohtuullinen; maltillinen; leuto, lauhkea. **-ture** ['tempritʃə] *s.* lämpömäärä; lämmönnousu; *take sb.'s ~* mitata kuume.

tempest ['tempist] *s.* myrsky, rajuilma. **-ous** [tem'pestjuəs] *a.* myrskyinen, raju.

Templar ['templə] *s.: [Knight] ~* temppeliherra.

temple 1. ['templ] *s.* temppeli; *[Inner, Middle] T~* lakimieskollegioita Lontoossa.

temple 2. ['templ] *s.* ohimo; kankaan pingotin.

tempo ['tempəu] *s.* aikamitta (mus.), nopeus, tahti.

tempor|al ['temp(ə)r(ə)l] *a.* ajallinen, maallinen; aikaa osoittava, temporaali-; ohimo- (anat.). **-ary** [-rəri] *a.* väliaikainen; tilapäinen, satunnainen. **-ize** [-aiz] *v.* pitkittää asiaa, viivytellä.

tempt [tem(p)t] *v.* houkutella, viekoitella; kiusata, panna koetukselle; uhmailla; *I am ~ed to . .* minulla on hyvä halu . . **-ation** [-'teiʃn] *s.* kiusaus, viettelys. **-er** [-ə] *s.* kiusaaja. **-ing** *a.* houkutteleva. **-ress** [-ris] *s.* viettelijätär.

ten [ten] *lukus.* kymmenen; *s.* kymppi; *the upper ~* yhteiskunnan kerma; *at ~* kello kymmenen.

tenable ['tenəbl] *a.* kestävä, luja; paikkansa pitävä, voimassa oleva.

tenac|ious [ti'neiʃəs] *a.* luja; tahmea; sitkeä; itsepintainen, hellittämätön,

hyvä (muisti). **-ity** [ti'næsiti] *s.* sitkeys, itsepintaisuus.

tenancy ['tenənsi] *s.* arenti; vuokra-aika.

tenant ['tenənt] *s.* (tilan)vuokraaja; vuokralainen; asukas; *v.* asua vuokralla; *~ farmer* vuokratilallinen. **-ry** [-ri] *s.* (tilan) vuokraajat.

tench [tenʃ] *s.* suutari (kala).

tend 1. [tend] *s.* hoitaa, hoivata; vartioida, paimentaa.

tend 2. [tend] *v.* suuntautua, kulkea (jhk päin); pyrkiä, tarkoittaa, tähdätä; olla taipuvainen (jhk); osaltaan vaikuttaa. **-ency** [-ənsi] *s.* taipumus, pyrkimys, tendenssi, suunta. **-entious** [-'denʃəs] *a.* tendenssimäinen.

tender 1. ['tendə] *s.* hoitaja; apulaiva; hiilivaunu, tenderi.

tender 2. ['tendə] *v.* tarjota, esittää (anomus); tehdä tarjous; *s.* (hankinta)tarjous; *legal ~* laillinen maksuväline.

tender 3. ['tendə] *a.* hauras, murea; hento, arka, herkkä, hellä; *in ~ years* lapsuudessa; *a ~ subject* arkaluonteinen asia. **-foot** uusi tulokas; (partio)alokas. **~-hearted** helläsydäminen. **-ize** [-raiz] *v.* pehmentää. **-loin** *s.* sisäfilee. **-ly** *adv.* hellästi. **-ness** *s.* hentous, herkkyys; hellyys.

tendon ['tendən] *s.* jänne.

tendril ['tendril] *s.* kärhi (kasv.).

tenement ['tenəmənt] *s.* (halpa) vuokratalo. **~-house** vuokrakasarmi.

Tenerife [tenə'ri:f] *erisn.*

tenet ['ti:net] *s.* periaate, oppi.

ten|fold ['tenfəuld] *a. & adv.* kymmenkertainen, -sesti. **-ner** ['tenə] *s.* kympin seteli.

Tennessee [tenə'si:] *erisn.*

tennis ['tenis] *s.* tennis. **~-court** tenniskenttä.

Tennyson ['tenisn] *erisn.*

tenon ['tenən] *s.* tappi; *v.* liittää (tapilla).

tenor ['tenə] *s.* (elämän) juoksu, kulku; sisällys, perusajatus; tenori (mus.).

tense 1. [tens] *s.* aikaluokka.

tens|e 2. [tens] *a.* jännittynyt, kireä, pingottunut; *v.* jännittää. **-eness** *s.*

kireys **-ile** [-ail] *a.* veto-, venyvä; ~ *strength* vetolujuus. **-ion** ['tenʃn] *s.* jännitys, pingotus; jännite (sähk.); *high* ~ suurjännite; *low* ~ pienjännite.

tent [tent] *s.* teltta; ~ *peg* t-vaarna.

tent|acle ['tentəkl] *s.* tuntosarvi, lonkero. **-ative** [-ətiv] *a.* kokeileva, kokeilu-; alustava; (~**ly** kokeeksi, kokeilumielessä).

tenter ['tentə] *s.* pingotuskehys. **-hooks** : *on* ~ kuin tulisilla hiilillä.

tenth [tenθ] *lukus.* kymmenes; *s.* kymmenesosa; kymmenys.

tenu|ity [te'nju(:)iti] *s.* ohuus; hienous. **-ous** ['tenjuəs] *a.* ohut, hieno, hatara.

tenure ['tenjuə] *s.* omistus, omistus|ehdot, -oikeus; ~ *of office* toimiaika.

tepee ['ti:pi:] *s.* intiaanitelltta.

tepid ['tepid] *a.* haalea. **-ity** [te'piditi] *s.* haaleus.

tercentenary [tə:sen'ti:nəri] *a. & s.* kolmisatavuotis(päivä, -juhla).

tergiversate ['tə:dʒivəseit] *v.* kääntää kelkkansa; horjua.

term [tə:m] *s.* määräaika, aika; lukukausi; käräjäkausi; oppi-, ammattisana, termi; sanamuoto, sanat; *pl.* ehdot, sopimus; suhde, välit; *v.* nimittää; *during his* ~ *of office as President* hänen presidenttikautenaan; *what are your* ~*s* mitkä ovat ehtonne? paljonko vaaditte? *come to* ~*s* sopia; *on good (bad)* ~*s with* hyvissä (huonoissa) väleissä jkn kanssa; *on* ~*s of intimacy* tuttavallisissa suhteissa; *in* ~*s of praise* kiittävin sanoin; *in* ~*s of money* rahamääräisesti; ~*s of trade* (ulkomaankaupan) vaihtosuhteet.

termagant ['tə:məgənt] *s.* syöjätär, äkäpussi.

termin|al ['tə:minl] *a.* loppu-, pääte-; *s.* loppu, pää; pääteasema. **-ate** [-eit] *v.* lopettaa, päättää: loppua, päättyä (*in* jhk). **-ation** [-'neiʃn] *s.* päättyminen, loppu; pääte. **-ology** [-'nɔləʒi] *s.* oppi-, ammattisanasto. **-us** [-əs] *s.* (pl. *-i* [-ai] pääteasema, -piste.

termite ['tə:mait] *s.* termiitti.

tern [tə:n] *s.* tiira (eläint.).

terrace ['terəs] *s.* penger, terassi; *v.*

pengertää. **-d** [-d] *a.* pengerretty; ~ *house* rivitalo.

terrain [tə'rein] *s.* maasto.

terrapin ['terəpin] *s.* suokilpikonna.

terrestrial [ti'restriəl] *a.* maallinen, maa-, maan; *s.* maan asukas.

terrib|le ['terəbl] *a.* hirmuinen, hirveä, kauhea. **-ly** *adv.* hirveän, kauhean, hirveästi jne.

terrier ['teriə] *s.* terrieri.

terri|fic [tə'rifik] *a.* hirveä; hurja; valtava, suunnaton, hurjan hieno. (~**ally** *adv.* hirvittävä|n, -sti). **-fy** ['terifai] *v.* kauhistuttaa, pelottaa.

territor|ial [teri'tɔ:riəl] *a.* alueellinen, alue-; *s.* territoriaaliarmeijan sotilas; ~ *waters* aluevedet. **-y** ['terit(ə)ri] *s.* alue; territorio (Am.).

terror ['terə] *s.* kauhu, pelko, kammo; *be in* ~ *of* pelätä; *reign of* ~ hirmu|valta, -hallitus; *a [holy]* ~ pelottava ihminen; kauhukakara. **-ism** [-rism] *s.* terrorismi. **-ist** [-rist] *s.* terroristi. **-ize** [-raiz] *v.* pitää kauhun vallassa, terrorisoida.

terry ['teri] *s.* ~ *cloth* frotee.

terse [tə:s] *a.* suppea, lyhyt, niukkasanainen; asiallinen, täsmällinen.

tertiary ['tə:ʃəri] *a.* tertiääri-.

tesselated ['tesileitid] *a.* ruudukas, mosaiikki-.

test [test] *s.* koe, koetus; testi; tutkimus, tarkastus, mittaus; reagenssi; *v.* koetella; testata; *written* ~ koekirjoitus; ~ *case* ennakkotapaus; ~ *match* (krik.) maaottelu; ~ *pilot* koelentäjä; *put to the* ~ panna koetukselle; *stand the* ~ kestää koetus.

testament ['testəmənt] *s.* testamentti, jälkisäädös.

testat|e ['testit] *a.* testamentin tehnyt. **-or** [tes'teitə] *s.* testamentintekijä. **-rix** [tes'teitriks] *s.* = ed. (nainen).

testicle ['testikl] *s.* kives.

testi|fy ['testifai] *v.* todistaa; valalla vahvistaa, vakuuttaa. **-monial** [-'məunjəl] *s.* (kirjallinen) todistus, suositus; (us. yhteinen) muistolahja. **-mony** [-məni] *s.* todistus; *bear* ~ *to* todistaa; *in* ~ *of* todistukseksi.

testiness ['testinis] *s.* ärtyisyys.

test-tube ['testju:b] *s.* koeputki.

testy ['testi] *a.* ärtyisä, kärsimätön.

tetanus ['tetanas] *s.* jäykkäkouristus.

tetchy ['tetʃi] *a.* helposti ärtyvä, kärtyisä.

tether ['teðə] *s.* lieka; *v.* panna liekaan, kytkeä; *at the end of one's* ~ katkeamispisteessä.

tetragon ['tetrəgən] *s.* nelikulmio.

tetter ['tetə] *s.* savipuoli.

Teuton ['tju:tn] *s.* teutoni, germaani, saksalainen. **-ic** [-'tɔnik] *a.* saksalainen.

Tex|an ['teks|n] *a. & s.* texasilainen. **-as** [-əs] *erisn.*

text [tekst] *s.* teksti; raamatunlause; puheen aihe; ~ *hand* tekstaus. **-book** oppikirja. **-ile** [-ail] *a.* kutoma-, kudottu; *s.:* ~ *s* tekstiilit. **-ual** [-juəl] *a.* tekstin-; tekstin mukainen. **-ure** [-ʃə] *s.* kudos, kudonta; rakenne, laatu.

Thackeray ['θækəri] *erisn.*

Thai [tɑi] *a. & s.* thaimaalainen. **-land** [-lənd] *erisn.* Thaimaa.

Thames [temz] *erisn.: [he] isn't the sort that will set the* ~ *on fire* ei ole ruudinkeksijä.

than [ðæn, ðən, ðn] *konj.* kuin.

thank [θæŋk] *v.* kiittää; *s.:* ~ *s* kiitoksia, kiitokset; ~ *you [very much]* paljon kiitoksia; ~ *God* Jumalan kiitos; ~ *s to* (jkn, jnk) ansiosta. **-ful** *a.* kiitollinen. **-less** *a.* kiittämätön, epäkiitollinen. ~**-offering** kiitosuhri. **-sgiving** kiitosrukous, kiitos; *T*~ *day* yleinen kiitospäivä.

that [ðæt] *pron.* (pl. *those*) tuo, se; [tav. ðət, ðt] joka, mikä; *konj.* [ðət] että, jotta, niin että; kun; niin; (jää usein suomessa vastineetta); ~ *very night* juuri sinä yönä, jo samana iltana (yönä); ~ *being so (the case)* niin ollen; *is* ~ *you?* sinäkö siellä? *what is* ~ *to me?* mitä se minua liikuttaa; ~ *is* (lyh. *i.e.*) nimittäin; *make haste, that's a good boy* pidä kiirettä, niin olet kiltti; ~ *s all [there is to it]* siinä kaikki; ~ *'s it* no niin; ~ *'s right* aivan oikein; ~ *'s* ~ *!* se siitä! ~ *s why* sen tähden; *for his sake and* ~ *of his family* hänen ja hänen perheensä tähden; *not so silly as all* ~ ei nyt sentään niin tyhmä, ... *at* ~ päälle päätteeksi; *for all* ~ siitä huolimatta; *what of* ~ *?* entä sitten?

the man [that] we saw mies, jonka näimme; *all* ~, *anything* ~, *everything* ~ kaikki mikä; *not* ~ *I have any objection* minulla ei oikeastaan ole mitään sitä vastaan; *now* ~ nyt kun; ~ *much* niin paljon; *fool* ~ *you are!* senkin pöllö! *O[h]* ~ *!* kunpa!

thatch [θætʃ] *s.* katto-oljet; *v.* kattaa oljilla; ~ *ed roof* olkikatto.

thaw [θɔ:] *v.* sulaa, sulattaa; (säästä) olla leuto; *s.* suojasää.

the [ðə, ði(:)] *määr. art. & pron.* se; sellainen; *adv.* sitä (komp. ed.); ~ . . ~ kuta . . sitä; ~ *idea!* mikä ajatus; *so much* ~ *better* sitä parempi.

theatre ['θiətə] *s.* teatteri; luento-, leikkaussali *(operating* ~*)* näyttämö, tapahtumapaikka; ~ *of war* sotanäyttämö; ~*-goer* teatterissakävijä. **-ical** [θi'ætrik(ə)l] *a.* teatteri-, näyttämö-; teatraalinen, teeskennelty; *s.:* ~ *s* (us. amatööri)näytäntö, -näytännöt.

thee [ði:] (vanh.) objektimuoto, ks. *thou;* sinut, sinua jne.

theft [θeft] *s.* varkaus.

their [ðɛə] *poss. pron.* heidän, niiden, -nsa, -nsä. **-s** [-z] *poss. pron.* ks. ed. (itsenäinen muoto).

theism ['θi:izm] *s.* teismi.

them [ðem, ðəm, ðm] *pron.* objektimuoto, ks. *they:* heidät, heitä, niitä, ne jne. **-selves** [-'selvz] *pers. & refl. pron.* (he) itse; itsensä, itseänsä; *they hurt* ~ he loukkaantuivat.

theme [θi:m] *s.* aine, aihe; kirjoitustehtävä: teema (mus.); ~ *song* tunnussävel.

then [ðen] *adv.* silloin; sitten, sen jälkeen; niin muodoin, siis; *a.* silloinen; *now and* ~ silloin tällöin; ~ *and there* heti paikalla; *before* ~ ennen sitä; *but* ~ mutta toiselta puolen; *by* ~ siihen mennessä; *now* ~ no niin; *till* ~ siihen asti; *what* ~ *?* entä sitten?

thence [ðens] *adv.* sieltä, siksi. **-forth, -forward** *adv.* siitä lähtien.

theocracy [θi'ɔkrəsi] *s.* teokratia.

Theodore ['θiədɔ:] *erisn.*

theolog|ian [θiə'ləudʒiən] *s.* teologi. **-ical** [-'lɔdʒik(ə)l] *a.* teologinen. **-y** [θi'ɔlədʒi] *s.* jumaluusoppi, teologia.

theorem ['θiərəm] s. väittämä.

theoretic(al) [θiə'retik, -(ə)l] a. teoreettinen, tietopuolinen.

theor|ist ['θiərist] s. teoreetikko. **-ize** [-aiz] v. esittää teorioja. **-y** ['θiəri] s. teoria.

theosoph|ic(al) [θiə'sɔfik, -(ə)l] a. teosofinen. **-ist** [θi'ɔsəfist] s. teosofi. **-y** [θi'ɔsəfi] s. teosofia.

therap|eutic(al) [θerə'pju:tik, -(ə)l] a. terapeuttinen. **-ist** ['θerəpist] s. terapeutti. **-y** ['θerəpi] s. hoito, terapia.

there [ðɛə] adv. siellä, siinä, sinne; tuolla, tuossa, tuonne; siinä kohdin; interj. kas niin! ~ is, ~ are on; ~ is someone at the door ovella on joku; ~ were four people in the room huoneessa oli neljä henkeä; ~ was no one ~ siellä ei ollut ketään; ~ is thought to be arvellaan olevan; ~, don't cry! kas niin, älä itke! ~ and back edestakaisin, meno ja paluu; ~ and then siinä samassa; ~ you are kas tuossa, m. ole hyvä! not all ~ vähän päästään vialla; from ~ sieltä, tuolta; get ~ päästä perille, m. onnistua; out ~ tuolla ulkona; while ~ siellä ollessa; ~ is no knowing on mahdotonta tietää; ~ is no denying [the fact] ei kannata kieltää. **-abouts** [-rəbauts] adv. niillä seuduin; niillä main, suunnilleen. **-after** [-'--] adv. sen jälkeen. **-by** [-'-'] adv. siten, sen kautta, sillä tavalla; ~ hangs a tale siihen liittyy tarina. **-fore** adv. sen vuoksi, sen tähden, siksi. **-'s** [ðɛəz] = there is, there has. **-upon** ['--'-] adv. sen jälkeen.

therm [θə:m] s. lämpöyksikkö. **-al** [-(ə)l] a. lämpö-; s. termiikki; ~ springs kuumat lähteet.

thermo|dynamics ['θə:m|ə(u)-] s. termodynamiikka. **-meter** [θə:'mɔmitə] s. lämpömittari; clinical ~ kuumemittari. **-s** [-əs] s. termospullo. **-stat** s. termostaatti, lämmönsäädin.

thesaur|us [θi(:)'sɔ:rəs] s. (pl. -i [-ai]) aarreaitta; sanakirja.

these [ði:z] pron. (ks. this) nämä; ~ days nykyään; one of ~ [fine] days jonakin kauniina päivänä.

thesis ['θi:sis] s. (pl. theses [-si:z])

väitöskirja; teesi, väittämä.

Thessalonian [θesə'ləunjən] a. & s.: ~s Tessalonikalaiskirje.

thews [θju:z] s. pl. jänteet, lihakset; voima.

they [ðei] pers. pron. he, ne; ~ say sanotaan että . . . **-'d** = they had, they would. **-'re** ['ðeiə, ðɛə] = they are. **-'ve** = they have.

thick [θik] a. paksu; tiheä, taaja; sakea, samea; käheä; epäselvä; tuttavallinen; ~ soup suurustettu keitto; ~ with täpötäynnä, jnk paksulti peittämä; a bit ~! liian paksua, liikaa, vaikea sulattaa; [they are] very ~ (t. as ~ as thieves) he ovat henkiystäviä; ~ and fast tuhkatiheään; lay it on ~ imarrella ylen määrin; through ~ and thin kaikissa vaiheissa; in the ~ of it jnk tuoksinassa; puristuksessa. **-en** [-n] v. tehdä paksuksi, sakeaksi; suurustaa, lisätä; paksuta, käydä sakeaksi; taajeta; käydä mutkalliseksi. **-et** ['θikit] s. tiheikkö. **~-headed** paksupäinen. **-ly** adv. paksusti, tiheästi; ~ populated tiheään asuttu. **-ness** s. paksuus; tiiviys, vahvuus jne. **~-set** tanakka; tiheään istutettu, taaja. **~-skinned** paksunahkainen.

thief [θi:f] s. (pl. thieves) varas.

thiev|e [θi:v] v. varastaa. **-ery** [-əri] ks. thief. **-ish** [-iʃ] a. varasteleva.

thigh [θai] s. reisi. **~-bone** s. reisiluu.

thimble ['θimbl] s. sormustin.

thin [θin] a. ohut, hieno; laiha; mieto, heikko; harva, -lukuinen; läpinäkyvä, hatara; v. ohentaa, tehdä ohueksi; harventaa; ohentua, harveta, hälvetä; [have] a ~ time kurjat, ikävät oltavat; ~ ly populated harvaan asuttu.

thine [ðain] poss. pron. (vanh.) sinun.

thing [θiŋ] s. esine, kappale; asia, seikka; olento, olio; pl. tavarat, kapineet, vehkeet, päällysvaatteet ym; poor [little] ~ pikku raukka; it's not at all the ~ se ei ole lainkaan sopivaa, asianmukaista; quite the ~ korkeinta muotia; I don't feel quite the ~ en ole oikein hyvässä kunnossa; as ~s go näissä oloissa; for one ~ ensiksikin; [the] first ~ kaikkein ensimmäiseksi, ensi työkseni; the latest ~ in hats viimeinen

hattu-uutuus; *it will only make* ~ *s*
worse se vain pahentaa tilannetta;
[*well.*] *of all* ~ *s!* onko mokomaa
kuultu!

thingummy [ˈθiŋ(ə)mi] *s.* (leik.)
se ja se (unohtuneen nimen
asemesta).

think [θiŋk] *thought thought, v.* ajatella
(about, of jtk), miettiä; arvella, luulla;
kuvitella; pitää jnak; *I* ~ *not* tuskin,
enpä luule; *to* ~ *that* kuvitella että; *I*
should ~ *so* saattaisi luulla, että; *I*
can't ~ *[how]* en voi käsittää; *I can't*
~ *of his name* en saa päähäni (en
muista) hänen nimeään; *I thought as*
much sitähän arvelinkin; *I thought I*
heard olin kuulevinani; ~ *little of*
pitää vähäarvoisena; *I* ~ *nothing of it*
en pidä sitä minään; ~ *fit* katsoa
sopivaksi; ~ *out* suunnitella; ~ *it over*
miettiä tarkasti, harkita; *. . , don't you*
~ *?* eikö sinustakin (teistäkin)? **-er** [-ə]
s. ajattelija. **-ing** *a.* ajatteleva,
järkevä; *s.* ajatteleminen, ajattelu;
way of ~ ajatustapa, mielipide; *to my*
~ käsitykseni mukaan. ~**-tank**
aivoriihi.

thinn|ess [ˈθin|nis] *s.* ohuus;
harvuus; laihuus. **-ish** [-iʃ] *a.*
ohuehko.

third [θəːd] kolmas; *s.* kolmasosa,
kolmannes; terssi (mus.). **-ly** *adv.*
kolmanneksi. ~**-rate** *a.* kolmannen
luokan.

thirst [θəːst] *s.* jano; halu, himo; *v.; ~*
[for, after] haluta, janota jtk; (vanh.)
olla janoinen. **-y** [i] *a.* janoinen; *I am*
~ minun on jano.

thirteen [ˈθəːtiːn] *lukus.* kolmetoista.
-th [-θ] *s.* kolmastoista.

thirtieth [ˈθəːtiiθ] kolmaskymmenes.

thirty [ˈθəːti] kolmekymmentä.

this [ðis] *pron.* (pl. *these*) tämä; nyt
kuluva; ~ *day week* tästä päivästä
viikon kuluttua; ~ *morning* tänä
aamuna; ~ *year* tänä vuonna; ~ *and*
that sitä ja tätä; *by* ~ *time* tähän
mennessä; *like* ~ näin; ~ *much* näin
paljon; ~ *is to inform you that. .* täten
ilmoitamme, että.

thistle [ˈθisl] *s.* ohdake.

thither [ˈðiðə] *adv.* (vanh.) sinne; ks.
hither.

tho' [ðəu] *lyh.* = *though*

thole [θəul] *s.* hankain (m. *~-pin*).

Thom|as [ˈtɔməs] *erisn.* Tuomas. **-pson**
[ˈtɔm(p)sn] *erisn.*

thong [θɔŋ] *s.* nahkahihna,
piiskansiima.

thora|cic [θɔːˈræsik] *a.* rinta-. **-x**
[ˈθɔːræks] *s.* rinta(kehä).

thorn [θɔːn] *s.* piikki, oka; orapihlaja; *a*
~ *in one's flesh* jkn silmätikkuna; *on*
~*s* kuin kuumilla kivillä. **-y** [-i] *a.*
okainen, piikkinen; ohdakkeinen.

thorough [ˈθʌrə] *a.* perinpohjainen,
perusteellinen, täydellinen; *have a* ~
knowledge of tuntea perin pohjin.
-bred *a.* täysiverinen,
puhdasrotuinen; *s.* rotueläin. **-fare** *s.*
liikeväylä, valtatie; *No* ~ *!* läpikulku
kielletty! ~**-going** perinpohjainen,
täydellinen. **-ly** *adv.* perin pohjin,
kauttaaltaan; kokonaan, täydellisesti,
läpeensä. ~**-paced** täydellinen,
piintynyt.

those [ðəuz] *pron. pl.* (ks. *that*) nuo, ne;
~ *absent* poissaolevat; ~ *around him*
ympärillä olevat, hänen
ympäristönsä; ~ *who* ne, jotka.

thou [ðau] *pron.* (vanh. & run.) sinä.

though [ðəu] *konj.* vaikka(kin), tosin,
jos kohta, joskin; *adv.* kuitenkin, (ei)
kuitenkaan; [*he said he would come;*]
he didn't, ~ mutta ei tullutkaan; *as* ~
ikäänkuin.

thought [θɔːt] *s.* ajatus, miete, ajattelu,
ajatteleminen, harkinta; aikomus,
aikeet; *v. imp. & pp.* ks. *think; at the*
~ *of* jtk ajatellessani; *is in my* ~*s* on
mielessäni; *on second* ~*s* asiaa
harkittuani. **-ful** *a.* miettivä,
ajatteleva; huomaavainen,
hienotunteinen. **-fulness** *s.*
mietteliäisyys; huolenpito. **-less** *a.*
ajattelematon, huomaamaton.
-lessness *s.* ajattelemattomuus.

thousand [ˈθauz(ə)nd] *lukus.* tuhat; ~ *s*
of tuhansittain, tuhansia. **-fold** *a.*
tuhatkertainen. **-th** [-θ] *lukus. & s.*
tuhannes, -osa.

thraldom [ˈθrɔːldəm] *s.* orjuus.

thrall [θrɔːl] *s.* orja; orjuus.

thrash [θræʃ] *v.* puida (tav. *thresh*);
piestä, löylyttää; ~ *out* selvittää. **-ing**
s. selkäsauna.

thread [θred] *s.* rihma, lanka; kuitu,
säie; (kertomuksen) juoni; yhteys;

(ruuvin) kierre; *v.* pujottaa lanka (neulaan), pujottaa (helmiä) nauhaan; *hang by a* ~ olla hiuskarvan varassa; ~ *one's way through* tunkeutua jnk läpi, pujottautua; ~ *a film* pujottaa filmi (projektoriin), [*black hair*] ~ *ed with silver* jossa on hopeajuovia. **-bare** *a.* nukkavieru, kulunut.

threat [θret] *s.* uhka, uhkaus. **-en** [-n] *v.* uhata, uhkailla; näyttää uhkaavalta; ~ *ing* uhkaava.

three [θri:] *lukus.* kolme; *s.* kolmonen. **~-cornered** kolmikulmainen; *t.-c. hat* kolmikolkkahattu. **~-decker** kolmikerroksinen (voileipä ym.). **~-dimensional** kolmiulotteinen. **-fold** kolminkertai|nen, -sesti. **~-master** kolmimastolaiva. **-pence** ['θrep(ə)ns] kolme pennyä, kolmen pennyn raha. **-penny** ['θrepəni, θri-] kolmen pennyn. **~-ply** *a. & s.* kolmiviilu (vaneri); kolmisäikeinen. **-score** [-'sko:] kuusikymmentä; ~ *and ten* seitsemänkymmentä (vuotta).

thresh [θreʃ] *v.* puida. **-ing** *s.* puinti. **-ing-floor** *s.* riihi, puimalattia.

threshold ['θreʃ(h)əuld] *s.* kynnys.

threw [θru:] *imp.* ks. *throw.*

thrice [θrais] *adv.* (harv.) kolmesti.

thrift [θrift] *s.* säästäväisyys, taloudellisuus; ruohoneilikka. **-less** *a.* tuhlaileva. **-y** [-i] *a.* säästäväinen, taloudellinen: Am. hyvin toimeentuleva.

thrill [θril] *v.* sävähdyttää, vavahduttaa, sykähdyttää, ihastuttaa; sävähtää, vavahtaa, väristä; *s.* väristys, värinä; *the* ~ *of a lifetime* elämän jännittävin kokemus. **-er** [-ə] *s.* jännitysromaani, jännäri. **-ing** *a.* jännittävä, hurmaava.

thriv|e [θraiv] *throve thriven, v.* menestyä, kukoistaa, (kasvista) viihtyä.

thro' [θru:] = *through.*

throat [θrəut] *s.* kaulan etuosa; kurkku, nielu; kapea aukko; *a sore* ~ kaulakipu; *don't thrust.. down my* ~ älä yritä tyrkyttää minulle..

throb [θrɔb] *v.* tykyttää, sykkiä, jyskyttää; *s.* tykytys, sykintä, jyske; *my head* ~ *bed* päässäni takoi ja jyskytti.

throe [θrəu] *s.:* ~ *s* tuska(t), vaiva(t), et. synnytystuskat.

thromb|osis [θrɔm'bəusis] *s.* tromboosi, verisuonitukos. **-us** ['θrɔmbəs] *s.* (pl. *-i* [-ai] veritukko, veritulppa.

throne [θrəun] *s.* valtaistuin; *come to the* ~ nousta valtaistuimelle.

throng [θrɔŋ] *s.* (väen)tungos, joukko; hyörinä; *v.* tungeksia, tulla laumoittain, täyttää ahdinkoon asti.

throstle ['θrɔsl] *s.* laulurastas.

throttle ['θrɔtl] *v.* kuristaa, tukahduttaa; *s.* (m. *~-valve*) kuristusläppä; ~ *down* vähentää kaasua.

through [θru:] *prep.* läpi, lävitse; jnk kautta, avulla, välityksellä; jstk syystä; *adv.* läpi; alusta loppuun, läpeensä; *a.* läpikulkeva, kauttakulku-; ~ *and* ~ kauttaaltaan, läpeensä; *all* ~ koko ajan; *wet* ~ läpimärkä; ~ *no fault of his own* ilman omaa syytään; *fall* ~ epäonnistua; *get* ~ *to* päästä puhelinyhteyteen jkn kanssa; *go* ~ läpikäydä, kestää, (*with*) suorittaa loppuun; *are you* ~ *with it?* oletko valmis? *I am* ~ *with him* olen saanut hänestä kylläkseni; ~ *traffic* kauttakulkuliikenne; ~ *train* kauko-, pikajuna. **-out** [θru(:)'aut] *adv.* kauttaaltaan; alusta loppuun; kaikkialla; koko matkan, koko ajan; *prep.:* ~ *Europe* kaikkialla Euroopassa; ~ *the year* koko vuoden.

throve [θrəuv] *imp.* ks. *thrive.*

throw [θrəu] *threw thrown, v.* heittää; lennättää, paiskata (maahan), luoda (katse); heittää satulasta; syöstä, saattaa jhk; heittää arpaa (noppakuutiolla); punoa (silkkiä), rakentaa (silta), muovata (savea), luoda (nahkansa), poikia; *s.* heitto; heittomatka; ~ *light on* valaista (asiaa); ~ *away* heittää pois, tuhlata; ~ *back to* muistuttaa (esivanhemmista); ~ *down* heittää kumoon; ~ *in* tokaista väliin, antaa kaupanpäällisiksi; ~ *in one's hand* luopua (yrityksestä); ~ *off* heittää yltään, riisua; päästä (taudista); pudistaa hihastaan (runoja ym); ~ *on* heittää ylleen; ~ *oneself on* etsiä tukea t. turvaa jklta, heittäytyä jkn

huollettavaksi: ~ *out* hylätä
(lakiehdotus); rakentaa (siipi jhk);
katkaista (tekn.); hämmennyttää,
saattaa tolaltaan; ~ *over* hylätä,
rikkoa välinsä jkn kanssa; ~ *up* antaa
ylen; luopua jstk; ~ *up the cards*
vetäytyä pelistä; *at the first* ~ ensi
heitolla. **~-back** *(to)* atavistinen piirre
ym. **-n** ['θrəʊn] *pp.*

thru [θru:] Am. = *through.*

thrum [θrʌm] *v.* rämpyttää, paukuttaa.

thrush 1. [θrʌʃ] *s.* rastas.

thrush 2. [θrʌʃ] *s.* sammastauti:
sädemätä (hevosissa).

thrust [θrʌst] *thrust thrust, v.* työntää,
tunkea, iskeä, pistää: pistää nenänsä
jhk, tuppautua; *s.* työntö, isku, pisto:
hyökkäys, isku (sot.); ~ *upon*
tyrkyttää; ~ *oneself* [*up*]*on*
tunkeutua, tuppautua jkn seuraan.

thud [θʌd] *s.* tömähdys, jysähdys; *v.*
jymähtää, tömähtää.

thug [θʌg] *s.* (intial.) kuristaja; rosvo,
roisto, murhamies.

thumb [θʌm] *s.* peukalo; *v.* peukaloida,
hypistellä, liata; *under the* ~ *of* jkn
vallassa, vaikutuksen alaisena; *by rule
of* ~ sormituntumalla; ~ *a lift* pyytää
peukalokyytiä; *a* ~*ed ride*
peukalokyyti. **~-index**
sormihakemisto. **~-nail** *s.: t.-n. sketch*
pienoisluonnos. **~-screw** *s.*
peukaloruuvi. **-tack** Am.
piirustusnasta.

thump [θʌmp] *s.* tömähdys, kova isku;
v. jyskyttää, takoa; mukiloida;
jysähtää. **-er** [-ə] *s.* roikale, emävalhe.
-ing *a.* suunnaton, hillitön.

thunder ['θʌndə] *s.* ukkonen,
(ukkosen) jyrinä; pauhu; *v.* jylistä,
jyristä; *it is* ~*ing* ukkonen jyrisee; ~
against pauhata jtk vastaan; ~ *out*
ärjyä; *a clap (peal) of* ~
ukkosenjyrähdys. **-bolt** ukonnuoli;
like a ~ kuin salama kirkkaalta
taivaalta. **-clap** ukkosenjyrähdys. **-ing**
a. suunnaton, hillitön (raivo). **-ous**
['θʌnd(ə)rəs] *a.* ukkosenkaltainen,
uhkaava. **~-storm** ukonilma. **-struck**
ukkosen iskemä; tyrmistynyt. **-y** [-i] *a.*
painostava; ukkos-.

Thursday ['θɜ:zdi] *s.* torstai.

thus [ðʌs] *adv.* siten, sillä tavalla; täten,
niin: siis, niin ollen; ~ *far* näin

pitkälle, siihen asti.

thwack [θwæk] *v.* lyödä, läimäyttää.

thwart [θwɔ:t] *v.* tehdä tyhjäksi,
ehkäistä: *s.* tuhto; *be* ~*ed in* pettyä
jssk.

thy [ðai] *pron.* (vanh.) sinun. **-self**
[-'self] *pron.* (sinä) itse, itsesi, itseäsi.

thyme [taim] *s.* ajuruoho, timjami.

thyroid ['θairɔid] *a.: ~ gland*
kilpirauhanen. **-ectomy** [-'dektəmi] *s.*
struumaleikkaus.

tiara [ti'ɑ:rə] *s.* otsaripa; paavin
kruunu.

Tiber ['taibə] *the* ~ Tiberjoki. **-ius**
[-'biəriəs] *erisn.*

Tibet [ti'bet] *erisn.* Tiibet. **-an** [-(ə)n] *a.
& s.* tiibetiläinen.

tibia ['tibiə] *s.* sääriluu.

tic [tik] *s.* (hermostunut) nykiminen,
hermoväre.

tick 1. [tik] *s.* tikitys, raksutus; rasti,
kruksi; *v.* tikittää; (puhek.) toimia,
käydä; ~ *off* merkitä, kruksata; ~ *sb.
off* nuhdella; ~ *over* käydä
tyhjäkäyntiä; *keep . . ~ing over* pitää
toiminnassa; *in two* ~*s* hetkessä.

tick 2. [tik] *s.* punkki.

tick 3. [tik] *s.* patjanpäällys.

tick 4. [tik] *s.* (puhek.) luotto; *on* ~
velaksi, tilille.

ticker ['tikə] *s.* (puhek.) kello; **~-tape**
sähkenauha, serpentiini.

ticket ['tikit] *s.* lippu, pääsylippu;
arpalippu, hintalippu, lupalippu;
ilmoituskortti; Am. ehdokasluettelo;
v. varustaa hinta-, nimilipulla; *single*
(Am. *one-way*) ~ menolippu; *return*
~ meno-paluulippu; *out* [*of prison*] *on*
~ *of leave* ehdonalaisessa vapaudessa;
that's just the ~ sillä lailla! niin sitä
pitää! **~-office** lippumyymälä.

ticking *s.* patjakangas.

tickl|e ['tikl] *v.* kutittaa, kutkuttaa:
hivellä, mairitella; kutista; huvittaa,
ihastuttaa; *he was* ~*d to death (at) . .*
huvitti häntä suunnattomasti, hän
ihastui ikihyväksi . . sta. **-ish** [-iʃ] *a.*
kutiava; pulmallinen, arkaluontoinen.

tidal ['taidl] *a.* vuorovesi-; ~ *wave*
tulva-aalto.

tiddlywinks ['tidliwiŋks] *s.* kirppupeli.

tide [taid] *s.* vuorovesi, luode
ja vuoksi: virta, tulva;
(tapahtumien) kulku,

käännekohta; (vanh.) aika (esim. *Easter~); at low ~* laskuveden aikana; *the ~ is in* on nousuveden aika; *swim with the ~* kulkea virran mukana; *turn of the ~* käänne; *~ over* suoriutua jstk; *~ sb. over* auttaa suoriutumaan: *will £ 5 ~ you over?* riittääkö viisi puntaa ensi hätään? **~-way** vuoroveden väylä.

tidiness *s.* siisteys.

tidings ['taidiŋz] *s. pl.* sanoma, viesti.

tidy ['taidi] *a.* siisti; hyvässä järjestyksessä oleva, järjestystä rakastava; sievoinen, melkoinen; *s.* pieni rasia, säiliö, kori; *v.* siivota, siistiä, järjestää (us. *~ up); ~ oneself* [*up*] siistiytyä.

tie [tai] *v.* (ppr. *tying*) sitoa, solmia, kiinnittää; ehkäistä, sitoa (määräyksin); pelata tasapeli (*with* jkta vastaan); *s.* solmio; side, yhdysside, kahle; sidepalkki, Am, ratapölkky; sidekaari (mus.); tasapeli; *black ~* smokki; *white ~* frakki; *family ~ s* perhesiteet; *~ down* sitoa; kahlehtia; *~ oneself down to* sitoutua noudattamaan; *~ up* sitoa (kiinni); kytkeä; kiinnittää (omaisuus); *~ with* m. liittyä. **~-beam** sidepalkki.

tier [tiə] *s.* rivi; *~ s of seats* porrasmaisesti kohoavat penkkirivit.

tiff [tif] *s.* kinastelu, kina; *v.* kinastella.

tiffin ['tifin] *s.* lounas.

tiger ['taigə] *s.* tiikeri; Am. jaguaari, puuma ym.

tight [tait] *a.* tiivis; luja, kiinteä, tiukka, ahdas; kireä, pingotettu; (puhek.) kitsas, saita; sl. päissään; *adv.* tiukasti, lujasti; *s.: ~ s* sukkahousut, trikoot; *in a ~ corner* (*spot*) pinteessä; *money is ~* raha on tiukassa; *air~, water~* ilman-, vedenpitävä; *sit ~* pitää puoliaan, pysyä lujana. **-en** [-n] *v.* kiristää, tiukentaa; tiukentua, kiristyä. **~-fisted** saita. **~-lipped** salamyhkäinen, puhumaton. **-rope** *s.: ~ performer* nuorallatanssija.

tigress ['taigris] *s.* naarastiikeri.

tike [taik] ks. *tyke.*

tile [tail] *s.* (katto)tiili; kaakeli, laatta; *v.* peittää, kattaa tiilillä; [*out*] *on the ~ s* hummaamassa; *has a ~ loose* on

hieman hassahtanut.

till 1. [til] *prep.* jhk asti, saakka; *konj.* kunnes; *not ~ then* vasta silloin; *not ~* m. ei ennen kuin; *~ tomorrow* huomiseen.

till 2. [til] *s.* kassalaatikko.

till 3. [til] *v.* viljellä, muokata. **-age** [-idʒ] *s.* maan viljely; viljelysmaa. **-er 1.** [-ə] *s.* viljelijä.

tiller 2. ['tilə] *s.* ruorinkampi.

tilt [tilt] *s.* kallistuma; turnajaiset; *v.* kallistua, -taa; taittaa peistä; syöksyä, hyökätä: *run full ~ against* syöksyä suin päin jtk vastaan; *~ over* kiepahtaa. **~-yard** *s.* turnauskenttä.

tilth [tilθ] *s.* (maan) viljely, muokkaus.

timber ['timbə] *s.* hirret, rakennuspuut, puutavara; hirsi; hirsimetsä: *~ line* puuraja; *in the ~ trade* puutavara-alalla. **-ed** [-d] hirsi-; metsää kasvava. **~-yard** lautatarha.

timbre [tæbr] *s.* (äänen) väri.

time [taim] *s.* aika; aikakausi; määräaika; tilaisuus; tahti (mus.); kerta; *v.* ajoittaa; määrätä, valita, (urh.) ottaa aika; *what ~ is it?* mitä kello on? [*at*] *any ~* milloin tahansa; [*at*] *what ~?* mihin aikaan? *~ and again* kerran toisensa jälkeen; *from ~ out of mind* ammoisista ajoista; *another ~* toiste; *next ~* ensi kerralla; *beat ~* lyödä tahtia; *is doing ~* on kärsimässä rangaistusaikaansa; *have a good ~ - (the ~ of one's life)* pitää hauskaa (äärettömän hauskaa); *lose ~* (kellosta) jätättää; *pass the ~ of day with* ks. *pass; take your ~!* älä hätäile! *all the ~* koko ajan; *at a ~* yhdellä kertaa, kerrallaan; *at one ~* kerran (aikaisemmin); *at the ~* silloin; *at ~ s* silloin tällöin, joskus; *at the same ~* samalla, kuitenkin; *at my ~ of life* minun iässäni; *behind one's ~* ajastaan jäljessä; *by that ~* siihen mennessä; *for a ~* jonkin aikaa; *for the ~ being* tällä haavaa, nykyään, toistaiseksi; *from ~ to ~* aika ajoin, välistä; *in ~* ajoissa; *in* [*the course of*] *~* aikaa myöten; *in good ~* hyvissä ajoin; sopivaan aikaan; *in no ~* tuossa tuokiossa, silmänräpäyksessä; *many ~ s* monta kertaa; *on ~* määräaikana, täsmälleen; *three ~ s as much* kolme kertaa enemmän; *~* [*and motion*]

studies työntutkimukset; *well-~ d*
ajankohtaan sopiva; *ill-~ d*
sopimaton. **~-bargain**
termiinikauppa. **~-bomb** aikapommi.
~-card kellokortti. **~-fuse**
aikasytytin. **~-honoured** vanha ja
kunnianarvoisa. **~-keeper** kello.
~-lag s. aikaväli, viive. **-less** *a.*
ajaton, loputon. **-liness** *s.* sopivuus.
-ly *a.* oikeaan aikaan tapahtuva,
sopiva. **-piece** (pöytä)kello. **-r** [-ə] *s.*
ajannottaja (urh.), ajan(otto-,
-säätölaite. **-server** *s.* pyrkyri, kiipijä.
~-signal aikamerkki. **-table** aikataulu,
lukujärjestys.

timid ['timid] *a.* arka, pelokas, ujo. **-ity**
[ti'miditi] *s.* arkuus jne. **-ly** *adv.* arasti.

timing *s.* ajanmäärääminen, -otto;
ajoitus.

timorous ['timərəs] *a.* arka, pelokas.

timothy ['timəθi] *s.: ~* [*grass*] timotei.

timpani ['timpəni] *s.* patarummut.

tin [tin] *s.* tina; läkkipelti; säilykerasia,
tölkki; vuoka; sl. raha; *v.* tinata;
tölkittää, säilöä; *~ god* savijalkainen
jumala. **~-hat** (sl.) kypärä.

tincture ['tiŋ(k)tʃə] *s.* tinktuura; sävy;
vivahde.

tinder ['tində] *s.* taula. **~-box** tulukset.

tine [tain] *s.* haara, piikki.

tinfoil ['tinfɔil] *s.* (ohut) tinapaperi,
lehtitina.

tinge [tin(d)ʒ] *v.* värittää, sävyttää; *s.*
vivahdus, sivumaku.

tingle ['tingl] *v.* pistellä, kihelmöidä;
olla jännittyneen odotuksen vallassa
(*~ with excitement*); *s.* kihelmöinti.

tinker ['tiŋkə] *s.* kattilanpaikkaaja,
peltiseppä; *v.* yrittää (kömpelösti)
korjata, peukaloida, m. puuhata (*~
away at*).

tinkle ['tiŋkl] *v.* helistä, kilistä,
kilistellä; *s.* helinä, kilinä.

tin|man peltiseppä. **-ned** [tind] *a.*
tinattu; *~ goods* säilykkeet; *~ fruit*
säilykehedelmät. **~-opener**
säilyketölkin avaaja. **~-plate** *s.*
läkkipelti; *v.* tinata.

tinsel ['tins(ə)l] *s.* kulta- t.
hopeapaperi, korurihkama.

tinsmith peltiseppä.

tint [tint] *s.* värisävy, väri; *v.* värjätä,
värittää.

tintinnabulation [tintinæbju'leiʃn] *s.*

helinä, kilinä.

tiny ['taini] *a.* pienen pieni, vähäinen,
hento(inen).

tip 1. [tip] *s.* kärki, pää, nipukka; hela,
(kepin) kenkäin; *v.* varustaa kärjellä,
helalla ym; *the word was on the ~ of
my tongue* sana pyöri kielelläni.

tip 2. [tip] *s.* juomaraha; vihje; kevyt
lyönti; kaatopaikka; *v.* kevyesti
lyödä, koskettaa; keikauttaa, kaataa
(kumoon), kaataa, tyhjentää
(jätteitä); antaa juomarahaa; antaa
vihje (kilpailevien
mahdollisuuksista); kaatua, keikahtaa
(m. *~ over*); kallistua; *~ sb. the wink*
antaa (jklle salaa) merkki; *~ the scale*
kallistaa vaakakuppi *(for* t. *against)*;
~ the winner veikata jku voittajaksi;
~ off antaa varoittava vihje.

tippet ['tipit] *s.* (turkis)kauluri.

tipping *s.* jätteiden kaataminen t.
kaatopaikalle kuljetus, vrt. *tip.*

tipple ['tipl] *v.* ryyppiskellä; *s.* ryyppy.
-er [-ə] *s.* ryyppiskelijä.

tipster ['tipstə] *s.* vihjeiden myyjä.

tipsy ['tipsi] *a.* hieman päihtynyt,
hiprakassa.

tip|-tilted: *t.-t. nose* pystynenä. **-toe**
adv.: on ~ varpaisillaan; *v.* kulkea
varpaisillaan. **-top** ensiluokan, loisto-.
~-up: *lorry* kippiauto; **~-seat**
saranaistuin.

tirade [tai'reid] *s.* sanatulva.

tire 1. ['taiə] *s.* (pyörän) kumirengas
(Engl. *tyre*).

tire 2. ['taiə] *v.* väsyttää, uuvuttaa;
väsyä, kyllästyä *(of* jhk). **-d** [-d] *a.*
väsynyt, uupunut; *~ out* lopen
uupunut; *~ of life* elämään
kyllästynyt; (**~ness** *s.* väsymys). **-less**
a. väsymätön. **-some** [-səm] *a.* ikävä,
ikävystyttävä.

tiro, tyro ['taiərəu] *s.* (pl. *~s*)
vasta-alkaja.

'tis [tiz] *= it is.*

tissue ['tisju:] *s.* kudos, kangas;
(pehmeä) paperi *(face ~, toilet ~);* ~
paper silkkipaperi.

tit 1. [tit] *s.* tiainen.

tit 2. [tit] *s.: ~ for tat* verta verrasta;
give ~ for tat maksaa samalla mitalla.

Titan ['taitn] *s.* titaani, jättiläinen. **t~ic**
[tai'tænik] *a.* jättiläis-, titaaninen.

titbit ['titbit] *s.* makupala.

tithe [taið] *s.* (us. *pl.*) kymmenysvero, kymmenykset.

titilla|te ['titileit] *v.* kutkuttaa, kiihottaa. **-tion** [-'leiʃn] *s.* kutkutus, hively.

titivate ['titiveit] *v.* (puhek.) pyntätä; laittautua hienoksi.

titlark ['titlɑ:k] *s.* kirvinen (eläint.).

title ['taitl] *s.* (kirjan) nimi; päällekirjoitus, otsikko; arvonimi; oikeusvaatimus, oikeus; saantokirja (m. ~ *deed*); ~ *page* nimilehti; ~ *role (part)* nimiosa. **-d** [-d] *a.* aatelinen.

titmouse ['titmaus] *s.* (pl. *-mice*) tiainen.

titr|ate ['taitreit] *v.* (kem.) titrata. **-e** ['taitə] *s.* titteri.

titter ['titə] *v.* hihittää, tirskua; *s.* hihitys, tirskunta.

tittle ['titl] *s.: not one jot or* ~ ei hitustakaan. **~-tattle** *s.* lavertelu, juoruilu; *v.* laverrella.

titular ['titjulə] *a.* nimi-, nimellinen; ~ *saint* nimikkopyhimys.

Titus ['taitəs] *erisn.*

to [tu:, tu, tə] *prep.* (ilm. suuntaa, aikaa, suhdetta ym); ~ *school* kouluun; ~ *London* Lontooseen; ~ *the station* asemalle; *who did you give it* ~? kenelle sen annoit; *adv.* kiinni, paikoillaan, -lleen; [*I am ready*] ~ *help* auttamaan; [*he wants*] *me* ~ *go* minun menevän; [*she is too young*]~ *marry* mennäkseen naimisiin; *ten* ~ *one* [*he will not come*] kymmenen yhtä vastaan (ettei . .); ~ *a hair* täsmälleen; *what is that* ~ *me?* mitä se minua liikuttaa? ~ *death* kuoliaaksi; *it seemed to me* minusta näytti; *here's* ~ *you!* maljanne! *a quarter* ~ *ten* neljännestä vailla kymmenen; *sings* ~ *a guitar* laulaa kitaran säestyksellä; ~ *my knowledge* minun tietääkseni; *you were a fool* ~ *believe him* olit hullu kun uskoit häntä; ~ *and fro* edestakaisin; *come* ~ virota; *a room* ~ *himself* oma huone.

toad [təud] *s.* rupisammakko. **-stool** *s.* (myrkky)sieni. **-y** [-i] *s.* liehakoitsija; *v.* liehakoida, hännystellä.

toast [təust] *v.* paahtaa (leipää ym); lämmittää, lämmitellä; juoda, esittää jkn malja; *s.* paahtoleipä; jkn malja; *give (propose) a* ~ esittää jkn malja.

-er [-ə] *s.* leivän paahdin. **~-master** *s.* juhlamarsalkka (päivällisillä).

tobacco [tə'bækǀəu] *s.* tupakka. **-nist** [-ənist] *s.* tupakkakauppias.

toboggan [tə'bɔgən] *s.* ohjaskelkka; *v.* laskea mäkeä.

Toc H ['tɔk eitʃ] (1. maailmansodan) veteraanien yhdistys.

tocsin ['tɔksin] *s.* hätäkello, varoitusmerkki.

today [tə'dei] *adv.* tänään; *s.* tämä päivä, nykypäivä; ~'s *päivän* (lehti ym).

toddle ['tɔdl] *v.* taapertaa, lyllertää. **-r** [-ə] *s.* pallero.

toddy ['tɔdi] *s.* toti.

to-do [tə'du:] *s.* touhu, hälinä.

toe [təu] *s.* varvas; *v.* varustaa kärjellä; ~ *the line* alistua kuriin. **~-cap** (kengän) kärkilappu. **~-nail** varpaankynsi.

toff [tɔf] *s.* hieno herra, keikari.

toffee ['tɔfi] *s.* toffee(karamelli).

tog [tɔg] *s.:* ~ *s* (puhek.) vaatteet; ~ *oneself out* laittautua hienoksi.

together [tə'geðə] *adv.* yhdessä, yhteen; samaan aikaan, samalla kertaa; yhteen menoon; *call* ~ kutsua kokoon; *get* ~ kokoontua.

toggle ['tɔgl] *s.* nappula.

toil [tɔil] *s.* vaivalloinen työ, raadanta, aherrus; *v.* raataa, ahertaa, hääriä; ~ *along* ponnistella vaivalloisesti eteenpäin.

toilet ['tɔilit] *s.* pukeutuminen; WC, käymälä; ~ *articles* toalettivälineet; *is* ~ *-trained* (lapsesta) on oppinut siistiksi. **~-paper** WC-paperi.

toils [tɔilz] *s.* verkko, ansa.

toilsome ['tɔilsəm] *a.* vaivalloinen, työläs.

token ['təukn] *s.* merkki, osoitus; muisto; rahamerkki; lahjakortti; *in* ~ *of* merkiksi jstk; [*then*] *by the same* ~ niin ollen; ~ *payment* symbolinen maksu; ~ *resistance* (vain) nimellinen vastarinta.

Tokyo ['təukjəu] *erisn.* Tokio.

told [təuld] *imp. & pp.* ks. *tell; all* ~ yhteensä; *I* ~ *you so* sanoinhan sen.

tolera|ble ['tɔl(ə)rəbl] *a.* siedettävä, kohtalainen, mukiinmenevä. **-bly** [-əbli] *adv.* melko, kohtalaisen. **-nce** [-(ə)ns] *s.* suvaitsevaisuus; sietokyky.

-nt [-(ə)nt] *a.* suvaitsevainen. **-te** [-eit] *v.* suvaita, sietää; kestää. **-tion** [-'rei∫n] *s.* suvaitsevaisuus.

toll 1. [təul] *v.* soida, kumahtaa; soittaa (kuolinkelloja); *s.* kellojensoitto.

toll 2. [təul] *s.* satama-, tievero, silta-, satamamaksu; jauhatusvero; *take ~ of* verottaa (kuv.); *~ on the roads* tiet. liikenneturmien uhrit; *~ call* kaukopuhelu. **~-bar** tullinpuomi.

Tom [tɔm] *erisn.: s. any ~*, *Dick and Harry* kuka hyvänsä.

tomahawk ['tɔməhɔ:k] *s.* intiaanien sotakirves.

tomato [tə'mɑːtəu] *s.* (pl. *~es*) tomaatti.

tomb [tu:m] *s.* hauta; hauta|holvi, -patsas. **-stone** hautakivi.

tom|boy ['tɔmbɔi] *s.* rasavilli (tyttö). **-cat** kollikissa.

tome [təum] *s.* (iso) kirja; teoksen osa.

tomfool ['tɔm'fu:l] *s.* narri. **-ery** [-əri] *s.* hupsuttelu.

tommy ['tɔmi] *s.* brittiläinen sotamies (m. *T~ Atkins*); *~ rot* pöty. **~-gun** konepistooli.

tomorrow [tə'mɔrou] *adv.* huomenna; *s.* huomispäivä; *the day after ~* ylihuomenna.

ton [tʌn] *s.* tonni (Engl. = 1016 kg, Am. 907 kg); rekisteritonni; *the ~* (sl.) 100 mailia tunnissa.

tonal ['təunl] *a.* tonaalinen. **-ity** [tə(u)'næliti] *s.* tonaalisuus.

tone [təun] *s.* ääni, äänensävy; ääniaskel, (koko)sävel; luonne, leima, sävy, henki; värisävy; *v.* soinnuttaa yhteen, virittää; olla sopusoinnussa *(with)*; *darker in ~* tummempi sävyltään; *muscular ~* jänteys; *~ down* lieventää, tasoittaa, vaimentaa (värisävyä), lieventyä; *~ up* vahvistaa. **-less** *a.* soinnuton.

tongs [tɔŋz] *s. pl.* [*a pair of*] *~* pihdit; *fire ~* hiilipihdit.

tongue [tʌŋ] *s.* kieli; kieleke; (laudan) ruode; (kengän) iltti; *confusion of ~s* kieltensekoitus; *gift of ~s* kielillä puhumisen lahja; *mother ~* äidinkieli; *ready ~* kerkeä kieli; *find one's ~* saada puhelahjansa takaisin; *had lost his ~* ei saanut sanaakaan suustaan; *give ~* haukkua, huutaa; *hold one's ~* pitää suunsa kiinni. **~-tied** mykkä,

sanaton. **~-twister** hokema (jossa kieli menee solmuun).

tonic ['tɔnik] *a.* vahvistava; sävel-; *s.* vahvistava lääke; perussävel.

tonight [tə'nait] *adv.* tänä iltana (yönä).

tonnage ['tʌnidʒ] *s.* (laivan) vetoisuus, tonniluku; tonnisto; tonnimaksu.

tonsil ['tɔnsl] *s.* (suussa) kitarisa, risa. **-lectomy** [-'ektəmi] *s.* kitarisan poisto. **-litis** [tɔnsi'laitis] *s.* kitarisan tulehdus.

tonsure ['tɔn∫ə] *s.* tonsuuri.

too [tu:] *adv.* liian, liiaksi; myöskin; sen lisäksi, sitä paitsi; *I was only ~ glad to go* menin kovin mielelläni; *won't you come, ~?* ettekö tekin tule? *all ~ soon* aivan liian pian; *one ~ many* yksi liikaa.

took [tuk] *imp.* ks. *take*.

tool [tu:l] *s.* työkalu, väline; välikappale; *v.* koristella (kirjan kansia); sl. ajaa (taitavasti), ajella; *~ up* varustaa työkoneilla.

toot [tu:t] *v.* töräyttää, toitottaa, törähtää; *s.* törähdys.

tooth [tu:θ] *s.* (pl. *teeth*) hammas, (kamman) piikki; *v.* varustaa hampailla, hammastaa; [*fight*] *~ and nail* kynsin hampain; vrt. *teeth.* **-ache** hammassärky. **-brush** hammasharja. **~-comb** tiheä kampa. **-less** *a.* hampaaton. **~-paste** hammastahna. **-pick** hammastikku. **~-powder** hammasjauhe. **-some** [-səm] *a.* herkullinen.

tootle ['tu:tl] *v.* töräy|ttää, -tellä.

top 1. [tɔp] *s.* hyrrä; [*sleep*] *like a ~* kuin tukki.

top 2. [tɔp] *s.* huippu, latva, kärki; jnk yläosa, -pää, -reuna; (pöydän) levy, kansi, päälaki, laki; kuomu, (auton) katto; korkein määrä, huippukohta; (kasvin) naatti, kaalin pää; märssy (mer.); *a.* ylin, päällimmäinen; etevin, ensimmäinen, huippu-; *v.* kohota jnk yli, voittaa, ylittää; latvoa, katkaista latva; olla ensimmäisenä jssk; saavuttaa (mäen) huippu; [*it was*] *~s!* hienoa! huippuluokkaa! *at the ~* ylinnä; *at the ~ of one's speed, at ~ speed* täyttä vauhtia; *at the ~ of one's voice* täyttä kurkkua; *on ~, on the ~ of* (jnk) päällä, päälle, jnk lisäksi; *from* ~ *to toe* kiireestä kantapäähän; *blow one's* ~ räjähtää, menettää malttinsa; *come out* ~ olla luokan priimus; ~ *dog* voittaja; ~ *secret* erittäin salainen; ~ *and tail* perata (marjoja).

topaz ['taupæz] *s.* topaasi.

top|-boots kaulussaappaat. **-coat** päällystakki.

topee, topi ['taupi] *s.* hellekypärä.

toper ['taupə] *s.* juoppo, ryyppymies.

topgallant *s.: ~ sail* prammipurje.

top|-hat silinteri. **~-heavy** *a.* liian painava yläpäästä. **~-hole** *a.* ensiluokkainen.

topic ['tapik] *s.* (keskustelun ym) aihe. **-al** [-(ə)l] *a.* ajankohtainen; paikallinen.

top|knot nauharuusuke; töyhtö. **-less** *a.* yläosaton. **~-level** *a.* korkean tason. **-mast** märssytanko. **-most** *a.* ylin, korkein. **~-notch** *a.* = *topping.*

topograph|er [tə'pɔgrəf|ə] *s.* topografi. **-y** [-i] *s.* topografia.

topp|er ['tɔpə] *s.* silinterihattu. **-ing** *a.* loisto-.

topple ['tɔpl] *v.* huojua; kaatua, keikahtaa kumoon (tav. ~ *over, down);* kaataa, syöstä.

topsy-turvy ['tɔpsi'tə:vi] *adv.* ylösalaisin, mullin mallin.

toque [tauk] *s.* pieni (naisen) päähine, eräänl. baskeri.

torch [tɔ:tʃ] *s.* soihtu (m. kuv.); *electric* ~ taskulamppu; ~ *song* nyyhkyiskelmä. **-light:** ~ *procession* soihtukulkue.

tore [tɔ:] *imp.* ks. *tear.*

toreador ['tɔriədɔ:] *s.* toreadori.

torero [tɔ'riərəu] *s.* härkätaistelija, torero.

torment ['tɔ:mənt] *s.* piina, tuska, kidutus; *v.* [tɔ:'ment] kiduttaa, ahdistaa. **-or** [tɔ:'mentə] *s.* kiusanhenki.

torn [tɔ:n] *pp.* ks. *tear; a.* repeytynyt, risainen; ~ *[by war]* raastama.

tornado [tɔ:'neidəu] *s.* (pl. ~*es*) pyörremyrsky.

Toronto [tə'rɔntəu] *erisn.*

torpedo [tɔ:'pi:dəu] *s.* (pl. ~*es*) torpedo; sähkörausku (eläint.); *v.* torpedoida. **~-boat** torpedovene.

torpid ['tɔ:pid] *a.* turtunut, tylsä,

hidas; horrostilassa. **-ity** [tɔ:'piditi] *s.* turtumus, horros.

torpor ['tɔ:pə] *s.* horrostila; velttous, tylsyys.

torque [tɔ:k] *s.* vääntövoima.

torrent ['tɔr(ə)nt] *s.* virta, tulva; ryöppy; *it rained in* ~ *s* satoi kaatamalla. **-ial** [tɔ'renʃ(ə)l] *a.* rankka, kaato-.

torrid ['tɔrid] *a.* auringon polttama, polttavan kuuma; ~ *zone* kuuma vyöhyke.

torsion ['tɔ:ʃn] *s.* vääntyminen, kiertyminen.

tort [tɔ:t] *s.* (siviilioikeudellinen) rikkomus.

tortoise ['tɔ:təs] *s.* kilpikonna. **-shell** *s.* kilpikonnanluu.

tortuous ['tɔ:tjuəs] *a.* kiemurteleva; kiertelevä, mutkitteleva.

torture ['tɔ:tʃə] *s.* kidutus, piina; *v.* kiduttaa, rääkätä.

Tory ['tɔ:ri] *s.* konservatiivisen puolueen jäsen t. parlamentti-edustaja. **-ism** *s.* tory-politiikka.

tosh [tɔʃ] *s.* sl. roska, pöty.

toss [tɔs] *v.* heittää, viskata; paiskata, keikauttaa, heilauttaa, heitellä; heittelehtiä; keinua, keikkua; aaltoilla; *s.* heitto, viskaus, (pään)keikaus; ~ *one's head* nakella niskojaan; ~ *off* kulauttaa kurkkuunsa, panna t. paiskata paperille; *let's* ~ *[up]* heittäkäämme kruunua ja klaavaa. **~-up** *s.* arvanheitto; *it is a t.-u. [whether]* on sattuman varassa.

tot 1. [tɔt] *s.* pallero, lapsi; kulaus.

tot 2. [tɔt] *s.* yhteenlasku; *v.: ~ up* laskea yhteen, olla yhteensä.

total ['təutl] *a.* kokonainen, täydellinen; *s.* kokonaismäärä, koko summa; *v.* tehdä yhteensä, nousta jhk summaan; laskea yhteen (m. ~ *up); it* ~ *led £ 10* loppusumma oli 10 puntaa. **-itarian** [təutæli'teəriən] *a.* totalitaarinen. **-ity** [tə(u)'tæliti] *s.* kokonaisuus. **-izator** ['təutəlaizeitə] *s.* totalisaattori. **-ly** *adv.* kokonaan, täydellisesti.

tote [təut] *v.* kuljettaa, kantaa; ~ *bag* kantolaukku; = *totalizator.*

totem ['təutəm] *s.* toteemi.

Tottenham ['tɔtnəm] *erisn.*

totter ['tɔtə] v. horjua, hoippua; huojua; [the empire] is ~ing to its fall on romahtamaisillaan.

toucan ['tu:kən] s. tukaani.

touch [tʌtʃ] v. koskea, koskettaa, kosketella; kajota, hipaista; vikuuttaa; ulottua jhk; näpätä (kieliä); liikuttaa (jkta, jkn sydäntä); lainata (rahaa); käydä (satamassa); olla rajakkain; s. kosketus; tunto; siveltimenkäyttö; vetäisy, piirto, tyyli; vivahdus, häive; lievä (taudin)kohtaus; ~ at käydä, poiketa (satamassa); ~ down laskeutua maahan; ~ sb. for (sl.) pyytää lainaksi, vipata jklta; nothing can ~ it ei mikään vedä sille vertoja; ~ off laukaista, räjäyttää; saada aikaan; ~ on (upon) kosketella (jtk asiaa); ~ up korjailla, parannella, verestää (muistia); finishing ~es viimeistely; in ~ with kosketuksessa jkh; get into ~ with asettua (jkn kanssa) yhteyteen; we lost ~ kadotimme toisemme näkyvistä; put to the ~ koetella; is soft to the ~ tuntuu pehmeältä; a near ~ täpärä pelastus. **~-and-go** hiuskarvan varassa. **-ed** [-t] a. liikuttunut; hieman tärähtänyt. **~-hole** sankkireikä. **-iness** s. ärtyisyys. **-ing** a. liikuttava; prep. mitä (jhk) tulee. **-stone** koetinkivi. **-wood** taula. **-y** [i] a. herkkä pahastumaan.

tough [tʌf] a. sitkeä; itsepintainen, taipumaton, sisukas; vahva; vaikea, työläs, raaka, roistomainen; vaativa, ankara (koulu); s. huligaani; a ~ fight kiivas tappelu; ~ guy kovanaama; a ~ problem kiperä ongelma. **-en** [-n] v. tehdä sitkeäksi, sitkistyä. **-ness** s. sitkeys tm.

tour [tuə] s. matka, kiertomatka; v. matkustaa, matkustella; olla kiertomatkalla; on ~ kiertueella; ~ing company kiertue. **-ism** [-rizm] s. matkailu, turismi. **-ist** [-rist] s. matkailija; ~ office matka(ilu)toimisto.

tourn|ament ['tuənəmənt] s. turnajaiset, kilpailut. **-ey** ['tuəni] s. turnajaiset. **-iquet** ['tuənikei] s. suonenpuristin (lääk.).

tousle [tauzl] v. saattaa epäjärjestykseen, pörröttää.

tout [taut] v. pyydystellä (asiakkaita); urkkia tietoja (kilpahevosista); s. asiakkaitten pyydystelijä; kilpa-ajovakooja.

tow 1. [təu] s. rohtimet.

tow 2. [təu] v. hinata; laahata perässään; s.: have in ~ hinata; take in ~ ottaa hinattavakseen.

toward [tə'wɔ:d] prep. = seur.; adj. ['tə(u)əd] käsillä, tulossa.

toward(s) [tə'wɔ:dz, tɔ:dz] prep. jtk kohti, jhk päin; jkta kohtaan, jnk suhteen; varten, jnk varalle, hyväksi; lähes, tienoilla; do something ~ bringing it about tehdä jtk sen aikaansaamiseksi; ~ the end of jnk loppupuolella; ~ evening illansuussa.

towel ['tau(ə)l] s. pyyhe; throw in the ~ tunnustaa hävinneensä. **~-horse, ~-rack** pyyheteline. **~-rail** pyyhetanko. **-ling** s. pyyhekangas.

tower ['tauə] s. torni; v.: ~ [above] kohota korkealle (jnk yli); liidellä korkealla; a ~ of strength tukipylväs. **-ing** a. pilviä hipova; kiihkeä, raju.

towing ['tə(u)iŋ] s. hinaus.

town [taun] s. kaupunki; go to ~ mennä (lähimpään) kaupunkiin, Lontooseen; man about ~ seurapiirileijona; ~ and gown (Oxf. & Cambr.) kaupunkilaiset ja ylioppilaat; ~ clerk kaupunginsihteeri; ~ council kaupunginvaltuusto; ~ hall kaupungintalo, raatihuone. **-ee** [-'ni:] s. (yliopp. sl.) kaupunkilainen. **-sfolk, -speople** s. kaupunkilaiset.

township s. (piiri)kunta, kaupunki(kunta); (Afr.) mustien esikaupunki.

tox|(a)emia [tɔk'si:miə] s. toksemia, myrkkyverisyys. **-ic** ['tɔksik] a. myrkyllinen. **-in** ['tɔksin] s. toksiini.

toy [tɔi] s. leikkikalu, lelu; v. leikitellä; ~ soldier tinasotilas.

trace 1. [treis] s. vetohihna; kick over the ~s karata aisoista.

trace 2. [treis] s. jälki; merkki; v. seurata jälkiä, päästä jäljille; piirtää ääriviivat, hahmotella, kalkioida; ~ sth. back to johtaa, seurata; on the ~s of jnk jäljillä; a ~ of hivenen verran, hitunen; ~ elements hivenaineet. **-able** [-əbl] a. jonka jälkiä voi seurata.

-r [-ə] *s.:* ~ *bullet* valojuova-ammus.
-ry [-əri] *s.* koristelu, ruususto.
trach|**ea** [trə'kiə] *s.* henkitorvi. **-oma**
[-'kəumə] *s.* trakooma.
tracing ['treisiŋ] *s.* kalkiointi.
track [træk] *s.* jälki, jäljet; rata (m.
urh.); ura, tie, polku, raide; *v.*
seurata (jkn) jälkiä, jäljittää; *on the ~
of* jkn jäljillä; *keep ~ of* pysyä
(asioiden tasalla); *leave the ~* suistua
kiskoilta; *lose ~ of* kadottaa yhteys
jkh; ~ *and field* [*events*] yleisurheilu;
~ *suit* verryttelypuku; *make ~ s* (sl.)
livistää; *made ~ s for* säntäsi jnnek; ~
down saada kiinni (jälkiä seuraten);
~ *er dog* vainukoira. **-less** *a.* tietön.
tract 1. [trækt] *s.* seutu, tienoo;
elimistö, elimet.
tract 2. [trækt] *s.* (usk.) lentolehtinen,
traktaatti.
tract|**ability** [træktə'biliti] *s.* sopuisuus.
-able ['træktəbl] *a.* sopuisa, sävyisä.
traction ['trækʃn] *s.* vetäminen, veto;
~ *engine* lokomobiili.
tractor ['træktə] *s.* traktori.
trade [treid] *s.* kauppa, kaupankäynti,
tavaranvaihto; liike-elämä; ammatti,
elinkeino, käsityö; ammattikunta; *v.*
käydä kauppaa, myydä (*in* jtk);
vaihtaa (*for* jhk); ~ *in* [*a car*] antaa ..
osamaksuna (uudesta); ~ [*up*]*on*
käyttää hyväkseen jtk; ~ *mark*
tavaramerkki; ~ [*s*] *union*
ammattiyhdistys t. -liitto; *Board of
T~* kauppaministeriö. **-r** [-ə] *s.*
kauppias; kauppalaiva. **-sman** *s.*
kauppias. **-speople** *pl.* kauppiaat.
~-unionist ammattiyhdistyksen t.
-liiton jäsen. **~-wind** pasaatituuli.
trading ['treidiŋ] *s.* kauppa-.
tradition [trə'diʃn] *s.* perimätieto;
perinnäistapa, perinne, traditio. **-al**
[-l] *a.* perinteellinen.
traduce [trə'dju:s] *v.* panetella,
parjata. **-r** [-ə] *s.* panettelija.
Trafalgar [trə'fælgə] *erisn.*
traffic ['træfik] *s.* kauppa,
kaupankäynti (et. luvaton); liikenne;
v. (*-cked*) käydä kauppaa (*in* jllak).
~-jam liikenneruuhka. **-king** *s.*
kaupankäynti. **~-light** liikennevalo.
trag|**edian** [trə'dʒi:diən] *s.*
murhenäytelmän näyttelijä t.
kirjoittaja. **-edy** ['trædʒidi] *s.*

murhenäytelmä. **-ic** [trædʒik] *a.*
traaginen, surullinen. **-icomic** *a.*
surkuhupaisa.
trail [treil] *v.* vetää, laahata perässään;
laahata, viistää maata; laahustaa;
seurata jälkiä; suikertaa; *s.* jälki,
juova, (tähden) pyrstö; polku; *on his
~* hänen jäljillään; ~ *arms!* kivääri
käteen! **-er** [-ə] *s.* lonkerokasvi;
perävaunu, asuntovaunu;
mainospalat (tulevasta elokuvasta).
train [trein] *v.* harjoittaa,
harjaannuttaa, opettaa, totuttaa;
valmentaa, kouluttaa; harjoitella,
valmentautua; suunnata (*on* jhk); *s.*
juna; laahustin; pyrstö; seurue,
saattue; jono; sarja; ~ *of thought*
ajatusketju; *express* (*fast*) ~ pikajuna;
corridor ~ käytäväjuna; *by ~* junassa,
rautateitse; *bring in its ~* tuoda
mukanaan. **~-bearer**
laahuksenkantaja. **~-driver**
junankuljettaja. **-ed** [-d] *a.* opetettu,
harjaantunut, koulutettu. **-ee** [-'ni:] *s.*
oppilas, harjoittelija. **-er** [-ə] *s.*
valmentaja, (eläinten) kouluttaja.
training ['treiniŋ] *s.* koulutus;
valmennus. **~-college**
opettajaseminaari. **~-ship** koululaiva.
train-oil ['treinɔil] *s.* valaanrasva.
traipse ks. *trapes.*
trait [treit] *s.* (luonteen)piirre.
trait|**or** ['treitlə] *s.* kavaltaja, petturi.
-orous [-(ə)rəs] *a.* petollinen, kavala.
-ress [-tris] *s.* kavaltaja (nainen).
trajectory [trə'dʒəkt(ə)ri] *s.* (tähden,
ammuksen) rata.
tram [træm] *s.* raitiovaunu (m. *-car*).
~-line raitiotie, -linja.
trammel ['træm(ə)l] *s. pl.* kahleet; *v.*
kahlehtia, estää, vaikeuttaa kulkua.
tramp [træmp] *v.* astua raskaasti,
(puhek.) tallustaa; taivaltaa, kulkea
jalan; viettää kulkurin elämää; *s.*
askelten ääni, töminä; jalkamatka;
maankiertäjä, kulkuri; [*ocean*] ~
hakurahtilaiva. **-le** [-l] *v.* polkea,
tallata; *s.* tömistys; ~ *on* tallata
jalkoihinsa, polkea.
tramway ['træmwei] *s.* raitiotie.
trance [trɑ:ns] *s.* transsi, unitila;
haltiotila.
tranquil ['træŋkwil] *a.* tyyni. **-lity**
[-'kwiliti] *s.* tyyneys, rauha. **-lize**

[-aiz] v. tyynnyttää; (~r rauhoite, rauhoittava lääke).

trans- pref. poikki, yli.

transact [træn'zækt] v. toimittaa, hoitaa; ~ business with olla liikeasioissa jkn kanssa. **-ion** [-'zækʃn] s. toimittaminen, hoito; liike|toimi, -asia; pl. (seuran) julkaisut.

transatlantic a. Atlantin takainen, Atlantin [ylittävä]; ~ liner Atlantin vuorolaiva.

transcend [træn'send] v. ylittää; voittaa. **-ence** [-əns] s. etevämmyys. **-ent** [-ənt] a. erinomainen, ylivoimainen. **-ental** [-'dentl] a. ylimaallinen, tuonpuoleinen, transsendenttinen (meditation mietiskely).

transcribe [træns'kraib] v. jäljentää, siirtää (esim. pikakirjoituksesta tavalliseen).

transcript ['trænskript] s. jäljennös. **-ion** [-'kripʃn] s. jäljentäminen; siirtokirjoitus; nauhoitelähetys (rad.); phonetic ~ tarkekirjoitus.

transept ['trænsept] s. (kirkon) poikkilaiva.

transfer [træns'fə:] v. siirtää (m. lak.); siirtyä, vaihtaa (junaa ym); s. ['trænsfə] siirto; siirtolippu; siirtokirja (lak.) **-able** [-'fə:rəbl] a. siirrettävä. **-ence** ['trænsf(ə)r(ə)ns] s. siirtäminen, siirto; (psyk.) tunteensiirto.

trans|figuration [trænsfigju'reiʃn] s. muodonmuutos; Kristuksen kirkastus. **-figure** [-'figə] v. muuttaa (jnk) muoto; kirkastaa. **-fix** [-'fiks] v. lävistää; lamauttaa; ~ed m. kuin paikoilleen naulittuna.

transform [træns'fɔ:m] v. muuttaa, muuntaa. **-ation** s. muodonmuutos, muuttuminen; muuntaminen. **-er** [-ə] s. muuntaja (tekn.).

transfu|se [træns'fju:z] v. kaataa, valaa; siirtää (verta). **-sion** [-'fju:ʒn] s. verensiirto; [blood] ~ service veripalvelu.

transgress [træns'gres] v. rikkoa (lakia ym). **-ion** [-'greʃn] s. rikkomus, synti. **-or** [-ə] s. (lain)rikkoja; syntinen.

transient ['trænziənt] a. hetkellinen, ohimenevä, lyhytaikainen.

transistor [træn'zistə] s. transistori.

transit ['trænsit] s. kauttakulku; in ~ matkalla. **-ion** [-'ziʒn] s. siirtyminen, muutos; ~ period siirtymäkausi. **-ional** [-'ziʒnl] a. siirtymä-. **-ive** ['trænsətiv] a. transitiivinen. **-ory** [-tri, Am. -təri] a. ohimenevä, haihtuva, lyhytaikainen.

trans|late [trænz'leit] v. kääntää (kielestä toiseen); siirtää, muuttaa jksk; tulkita; [please] ~ this into Finnish suomenna tämä; [she ~d] it into English käänsi sen englanniksi; [has been] ~d into many languages käännetty monelle kielelle. **-lation** [-'leiʃn] s. käännös. **-lator** [-ə] s. kielenkääntäjä.

translucent [trænz'lu:snt] a. läpikuultava.

transmigration [trænzmai'greiʃn] s.: ~ [of souls] sielunvaellus.

trans|missible [trænz'misəbl] a. siirrettävissä oleva (esim. tarttuva t. perinnöllinen). **-mission** [-'miʃn] s. lähettäminen, siirto, luovuttaminen; (radio)lähetys; periytyminen; tarttuminen; (lämmön ym) johtaminen: voimansiirto; data ~ tietojen välitys.

transmit [trænz'mit] v. lähettää (m. rad.), välittää, kuljettaa edelleen, viestittää; siirtää; jättää perinnöksi; päästää läpi (valoa), johtaa; tartuttaa (tauti); be ~ted tarttua. **-tal slip** lähetelippu. **-ter** [-ə] s. lähetin (rad.).

transmutation [trænzmju(:)'teiʃn] s. muuttuminen, muutos.

transmute [trænz'mju:t] v. muuttaa, muuntaa.

transom ['trænsəm] s. (ikkunan ym) kamana, (oven yläpuolella oleva) ikkuna; poikkipuu.

transpar|ency [træns'pɛər(ə)nsi] s. läpikuultavuus; kiiltokuva, diakuva; **-ent** [-(ə)nt] a. läpinäkyvä.

transpire [træns'paiə] v. tulla ilmi t. tietoon; tapahtua; huokua, hiota.

transplant [træns'plɑ:nt] v. istuttaa uudelleen, siirtää (m. lääk.); s. ['--] siirrännäinen. **-ation** [-'teiʃn] s. uudelleen istutus; (kudoksen, elimen)siirto.

transport [træns'pɔ:t, tra:n-] v. kuljettaa; lähettää rangaistussiirtolaan; s. ['trænspɔ:t, 'tra:n-] kuljetus;

siirto: kuljetusalus t. -lentokone;
kiihko, puuska; ~ *ed with joy*
suunniltaan ilosta; *public* ~ julkiset
kulkuneuvot; [*lost*] *in* ~ matkalla; *in*
~ s [*of joy*] riemuissaan; ~ *column*
huoltokolonna. **-ation** [-'teiʃn] *s.*
kuljettaminen, kuljetus.

transpos|e [træns'pəuz] *v.* muuttaa,
siirtää (toiseen paikkaan t.
järjestykseen); transponoida, siirtää
(sävellajista toiseen). **-ition** [-pə'ziʃn]
s. siirto; transponointi.

transship *v.* siirtää laivasta toiseen.

Transvaal ['trænzvɑːl] *erisn.*

transverse ['trænzvəːs] *s.* poikittainen,
poikki-. **-ly** *adv.* poikittain.

trap [træp] *s.* ansa, loukku; kiesit;
(viemärin) vesilukko; sl. suu; =
~ *-door*; *v.* pyydystää satimeen;
asettaa ansoja; *set (lay) a* ~ *for*
virittää ansa jklle; *be* ~ *ped in* jäädä
loukkuun. **~-door** *s.* laskuovi, katto-,
lattialuukku.

trapse, traipse [treips] *v.* talsia,
tallustaa.

trapez|e [trə'piːz] *s.* trapetsi;
kiikkurekki. **-ium** [-jəm] *s.*
puolisuunnikas, Am. epäkäs.

trap|per ['træp|ə] *s.* turkismetsästäjä,
ansastaja. **-pings** [-iŋz] *s.* (virka-asuun
kuuluvat) tamineet, koristukset. **-s**
[-s] *s. pl.* (puhek.) kamppeet,
vehkeet.

trash [træʃ] *s.* jätteet, törky, roju,
roska, roina; roskaväki; *white* ~
(Am.) köyhät valkoiset. **-y** [-i] *a.*
arvoton, roska-.

trauma ['trɔːmə] *s.* vamma.

travail ['træveil] *s.* (vanh.)
synnytystuskat; vaiva, ponnistus.

travel ['trævl] *v.* matkustaa, -tella;
kulkea, edetä; tehdä matka; olla
kauppamatkustajana; *s.* matkustus,
matkustaminen; ~ *s* matkat, m.
matkakuvaus; ~ *office*
matkatoimisto. **-led** [-d] *a.* paljon
matkustanut. **-ler** [-ə] *s.* matkustaja;
kauppamatkustaja (m. *commercial*
~). **-ling** *a.* matkustava, matka-; *s.*
matkustus, matkat; ~ *expenses*
matkakulut; ~ *salesman*
kauppamatkustaja. **-ogue** ['trævələg]
s. matka|kuvaus, -filmi.

traverse ['trævə(ː)s] *v.* kulkea jnk yli,

poikki; matkustaa jnk poikki, halki;
virrata jnk halki, läpi; *s.*
(vuorenseinämää) pitkin poikin vievä
tie; poikkivalli.

travesty ['trævisti] *s.* travestia, irvikuva; *v.* ivaillen mukailla.

trawl [trɔːl] *s.* laahusnuotta; *v.* kalastaa
laahusnuotalla. **-e** [-ə] *s.* troolari:
troolikalastaja.

tray [trei] *s.* tarjotin: alusta.

treacher|ous ['tretʃ(ə)rəs] *a.*
petollinen, salakavala. **-y** [-ri] *s.*
petos, petollisuus.

treac|le ['triːkl] *s.* siirappi, melassi. **-y**
[-i] *a.* siirappimainen.

tread [tred] *trod trodden, v.* astua,
astella, kulkea; polkea; *s.* astunta,
käynti, askel; askelma; kulutuspinta;
~ *on air* olla haltioissaan; ~ *the*
boards toimia näyttelijänä. **-le** [-l] *s.*
poljin; *v.* polkea. **-mill** polkumylly;
yksitoikkoinen raadanta.

treason ['triːzn] *s.* maanpetos,
valtiopetos. **-able** [-əbl] *a.*
maanpetoksellinen.

treasure ['treʒə] *s.* aarre; kalleus; *v.*
pitää suuressa arvossa; säilyttää
(muistissa), koota (tav. ~ *up*). **-r** [-rə]
s. rahastonhoitaja; talousjohtaja.
~-trove aarrelöytö.

treasury ['treʒ(ə)ri] *s.* aarreaitta;
(valtion) rahasto; *the T* ~ l.v.
valtiovarainministeriö; *First Lord of*
the T ~ l.v. valtiovarainministeri; *T* ~
Bench hallituksen penkki
(alahuoneessa).

treat [triːt] *v.* kohdella; käsitellä;
hoitaa (lääk.); kestitä, tarjota (*to* jtk);
s. (erikoinen) ilo, nautinto; kestit,
pidot; ~ *of* koskettela, käsitellä jtk; ~
with neuvotella jkn kanssa; *stand* ~
maksaa kestitys; *this is my* ~ minä
maksan; *what a* ~ *it is* [*to*] kuinka
hauskaa on; *a school* ~ kouluretki.
-ise [-iz] *s.* tutkielma. **-ment** *s.*
kohtelu; käsittely; hoito, hoitotapa. **-y**
[-i] *s.* (valtioiden välinen) sopimus;
peace ~ rauhansopimus.

treb|le ['trebl] *a.* kolminkertainen:
diskantti- (mus.); *s.* sopraano,
diskantti; *v.* kolminkertaistaa, -tua.
-ly *adv.* kolminkertaisesti.

tree [triː] *s.* puu; [*boot-*] ~ kenkälesti;
v. ajaa puuhun; *Christmas* ~

joulukuu; *family* ~ sukupuu; *up a* ~ pulassa, kiikissä. **-less** *a.* puuton.

trefoil ['trefɔil] *s.* apila; apilanlehti, kolmilehtikoriste.

trek [trek] *v.* (Et. Afr.) matkustaa härkävankkureilla; *s.* (pitkä, vaivalloinen) retki; *on the* ~ matkalla, taipaleella.

trellis ['trelis] *s.* säleikkö, säleristikko. **-ed** [-t] *a.* säleiköllä varustettu.

trembl|e ['trembl] *v.* vapista, väristä; olla huolissaan t. levoton (*with* jstk, *for* jksta); *s.* vavistus, väristys; *be all of a* ~ väristä kuin haavanlehti. **-ing** *a.* vapiseva.

tremendous [tri'mendəs] *a.* valtava, suunnaton; ~*ly* suunnattoman.

tremor ['tremə] *s.* vavistus, väristys; värinä, väräjäminen; *earth* ~ maan tärähtely.

tremulous ['tremjuləs] *a.* vapiseva, värisevä; arka, pelokas.

trench [tren(t)ʃ] *s.* kaivanto; ampumahauta; *v.* ampumahautoja; ~ *warfare* asemasota. **-ant** [-(ə)nt] *a.* terävä, pureva. **~-coat** sadetakki. **-er** [-ə] *s.* leikkuulauta, leipälauta; *a poor* ~*man* pieniruokainen.

trend [trend] *v.* kääntyä, kallistua (jhk päin); *s.* suunta(us), kehitys, tendenssi.

trephine [tri'fi:n, Am. -fain] *v.* trepanoida.

trepidation [trepi'deiʃn] *s.* (tuskainen) levottomuus, hämmennys, hätäily; väriseminen.

trespass ['trespəs] *v.:* ~ [*up*] *on* luvatta mennä jkn alueelle, tunkeutua jhk, loukata jkn oikeuksia, väärinkäyttää; (~ *against* rikkoa jtk vastaan; *s.* tunkeutuminen toisen alueelle, vahingonteko; synti, rikkomus; ~*ers will be prosecuted* pääsy sakon uhalla kielletty (m. *no* ~*ing!*).

tress [tres] *s.* suortuva; *pl.* kutrit.

trestle ['tresl] *s.* pukki; ~*-bridge* pukkisilta.

tri- [trai-] *pref.* kolme-, kolmi-.

triad ['traiæd] *s.* kolmikko, kolmisoire.

trial ['trai(ə)l] *s.* koetus, koe, kokeilu; koettelemus; oikeudenkäynti, tutkimus; koe|matka, -ajo; ~*s* (urh.) karsinnat; ~ *trip* koematka; *give sb.*

(*sth.*) *a* ~ antaa jkn koettaa, kokeilla jllak; *on* ~ kokeeksi; *on* ~ *for murder* syytteessä murhasta; *be brought (put) to* ~ joutua oikeuteen.

triang|le ['traiæŋgl] *s.* kolmio, kolmikulmio; triangeli (mus.). **-ular** [-'æŋgjulə] *a.* kolmikulmainen.

tribal ['traibl] *a.* heimo-. **-ism** *s.* heimokulttuuri.

tribe [traib] *s.* heimo; lauma. **-sman** *s.* heimolainen, heimon jäsen.

tribulation [tribju'leiʃn] *s.* ahdistus, kärsimys.

tribunal [tri'bju:nl] *s.* tuomioistuin; *rent* ~ vuokralautakunta.

tribune ['tribju:n] *s.* kansantribuuni; kansanjohtaja; puhujalava, koroke.

tributary ['tribjut(ə)ri] *a.* verovelvollinen; sivu-; *s.* sivujoki; verovelvollinen (valtio, kansa ym).

tribute ['tribju:t] *s.* vero; kunnioituksenosoitus, juhlinta; *pay* [*a*] ~ *to* kunnioittaa (jkn muistoa); *floral* ~*s* kukkatervehdykset.

trice [trais] *s.: in a* ~ käden käänteessä, tuossa tuokiossa; *v.:* ~ *up* hinata, nostaa.

trick [trik] *s.* kepponen, metku, juoni, niksi, temppu, (valok. ym) trikki, taitotemppu; omituisuus, tapa; tikki (korttip.); *v.* petkuttaa, narrata jkta; *play a* ~ *on* tehdä jklle kepponen; *do the* ~ tepsiä; *a dirty* ~ nolo (ruma) temppu; *he is up to* ~*s* hänellä on koiruus mielessä; ~ *out (up)* koristella. **-ery** [-əri] *s.* temput, metkut, petkutus.

trickle ['trikl] *v.* valua hitaasti, tihkua; ~ *out* m. tulla ilmi.

trick|ster ['trikstə] *s.* huijari. **-sy** [-si] *a.* vallaton, kujeileva. **-y** [-i] *a.* juonikas, taitoa kysyvä, kiperä.

tri|colo(u)r ['trikələ] *s.* trikolori (lippu). **-cycle** ['traisikl] *s.* kolmipyörä. **-dent** ['traid(ə)nt] *s.* kolmikärki. **-dimensional** ['traidi'menʃənl] *a.* kolmiulotteinen.

triennial [trai'enjəl] *a.* kolmivuotis-, kolmivuotinen.

trifl|e ['traifl] *s.* joutava, tyhjänpäiväinen asia, mitättömyys; pieni summa rahaa; eräänl. (kermavaahto) kakku; *v.* leikitellä, kujeilla; kuluttaa turhaan (tav. ~

away); *a* ~ . . hiukan; *he is not to be*
~*d with* hänen kanssaan ei ole
leikkimistä; ~ *with one's food* syödä
nirsoillen. **-ing** *a.* mitätön, joutava; *is
no* ~ *matter* ei ole leikin asia.

trig [trig] *a.* sievä, sorea; *v.* koristaa,
pyntätä (us. ~ *out*).

trigger ['trigə] *s.* liipaisin; *v.: ~ off*
panna alkuun; ~*-happy*
liipaisinherkkä.

trigonometry [trigə'nɔmitri] *s.*
trigonometria.

trilateral [trai'læt(ə)r(ə)l] *a.*
kolmisivuinen.

trilby ['trilbi] *s.: ~* [*hat*] (miesten)
pehmeä huopahattu.

trill [tril] *s.* liverrys; trilli; *v.* livertää,
liverrellä; ~*ed* tremuloitu.

trillion ['triljən] *s.* triljoona; Am. =
biljoona.

trilogy ['triləʒi] *s.* trilogia.

trim [trim] *a.* hyvin hoidettu; siisti,
sorea; hyvässä kunnossa oleva; *v.*
siistiä, somistaa; koristaa; leikata,
tasoittaa (m. lastin paino); puhdistaa;
trimmata (purjeet); (kuv.) luovia,
horjua; *s.* asu, kunto; *in good* ~
hyvässä kunnossa; *in fighting* ~
taisteluvalmis. **-mer** [-ɔ] *s.* (hattujen
ym) somistaja; tuuliviiri (joka horjuu
kahden puolueen välillä). **-ming** *s.*
(tukan) tasoitus, trimmaus, koristeet.

trinitrotoluene [trai'naitrə(u)'tɔljui:n]
s. trotyyli.

trinity ['triniti] *s.* kolminaisuus; *T~
term* kevätlukukausi.

trinket ['trinkit] *s.* koriste, hely.

trio ['tri(:)əu] *s.* (pl. ~*s*) trio.

trip [trip] *v.* sipsuttaa, kulkea kevein
askelin; kompastua, astua harhaan;
erehtyä, hairahtua; kampata (tav. ~
up); laukaista (säppi); *s.* matka, retki,
huviretki; kompastus; erehdys;
sipsutus; *catch sb.* ~*ping* yllättää
virheestä.

tripartite ['trai'pɔ:tait] *a.*
kolmiosainen; ~ *pact* kolmen vallan
sopimus.

tripe [traip] *s.* sisälmykset, (naudan)
vatsa (ruokana); sl. roska, sotku.

triple ['tripl] *a.* kolminkertainen,
kolmi-; *v.* kolminkertaistua; *T~
Alliance* kolmiliitto. **-et** [-it] *s.*
kolmikko; ~*s* kolmoset. **-ex** [-eks] *a.*

kolminkertainen: särkymätön (lasi).
-icate [-ikit] *s.* kolmoiskappale.

tripod ['traipɔd] *s.* kolmijalka.

Tripoli ['tripəli] *erisn.* Tripolis.

tripos ['traipɔs] *s.* erikoistutkinto
(Cambr.).

tripp|er ['tripə] *s.* huvimatkailija,
retkeilijä. **-ingly** *adv.* sipsuttaen,
keveästi.

triptych ['triptik] *s.* triptyykki,
kolmiosainen alttaritaulaus.

trisyllabic ['traisi'læbik] *a.*
kolmitavuinen.

trite [trait] *a.* kulunut, arkipäiväinen.

triumph ['traiəmf] *s.* riemusaatto,
voittokulkue; loistava voitto;
voitonriemu; *v.: ~ over* saavuttaa
(loistava) voitto jksta; riemuita jstk.
-al [trai'ʌmf(ə)l] *a.* voitto-, riemu-; ~
arch voittokaari. **-ant** [trai'ʌmfənt] *a.*
voittoisa, voitokas; voitonriemuinen.

triumvirate [trai'ʌmvirit] *s.*
triumviraatti.

triune ['traiju:n] *a.* kolmiyhteinen.

trivet ['trivit] *s.* kolmijalka (padan
alusta); *right as a* ~ hyvässä
kunnossa.

trivial ['triviəl] *a.* merkityksetön,
mitätön, joutava; tyhjänpäiväinen,
pintapuolinen. **-ity** [-'æliti] *a.* mitätön
asia, mitättömyys.

trochee ['trəuki:] *s.* trokee.

trod, -den [trɔd, -n] *imp. & pp.* ks.
tread.

Trojan ['trəudʒ(ə)n] *a. & s.*
troijalainen; *work like a* ~ puskea
töitä.

troll 1. [trəul] *v.* rallattaa; laulaa
kaanonia; kalastaa uistimella; ~*ing
spoon* uistin.

troll 2. [trəul] *s.* peikko.

trolley ['trɔli] *s.* resiina (raut.);
käsirattaat; kosketus-,
virranottokiekko; Am. raitiovaunu;
[*tea*] ~ tarjoilupöytä; ~ *bus*
johdinauto.

trollop ['trɔləp] *s.* lutka.

trombone [trɔm'bəun] *s.*
(veto)pasuuna.

troop [tru:p] *s.* joukko, parvi;
eskadroona; *pl.* joukot, sotaväki; *v.*
kokoontua, kerääntyä; marssia,
kulkea, lähteä (rivissä); ~*ing the
colours* lippuparaati. ~**-carrier**

joukkojenkuljetuskone. **-er** [-ə] s.
ratsumies; ratsuhevonen;
kuljetuslaiva (m. *troopship*).

trope [trəup] s. kielikuva.

trophy ['trəufi] s. voitonmerkki,
palkinto.

tropic ['trɔpik] s. kääntöpiiri; *pl.*
tropiikki. **-al** [-(ə)l] *a.* trooppinen.

trot [trɔt] *v.* ravata, ajaa ravia, juosta
hölkyttää; panna ravaamaan; *s.* ravi,
hölkytys; ~ *out* tuoda näytteille,
pyrkiä loistamaan (jllak).

troth [trəuθ] s. (vanh.) uskollisuus;
plight one's ~ kihlautua.

trotter ['trɔtə] s. ravuri; sorkat.

troubadour ['tru:bəduə] s. trubaduuri.

trouble ['trʌbl] s. huoli, harmi,
häiriö(t), ikävyydet,
vastoinkäyminen, levottomuus
vaivannäkö, vaiva; tauti; *v.* tehdä
levottomaksi, huolestuttaa, häiritä,
vaivata; vaivautua, olla levoton (m. ~
oneself); samentaa; *in* ~ vaikeuksissa,
hädässä; *give* ~ tuottaa vaivaa,
huolta; *have* ~ *with* joutua
hankaluuksiin jkn kanssa; *ask (look)
for* ~ etsimällä etsiä ikävyyksiä, olla
varomaton; *get into* ~ joutua
ikävyyksiin; *take* ~ nähdä vaivaa;
they are so little ~ heistä on niin vähän
vaivaa; *may I* ~ *you for* olkaa hyvä
antakaa minulle; ~ *about* (m.)
välittää. **-d** [-d] *a.* levoton,
huolestunut; kuohuva; ~ *area*
levottomuusalue; ~ *waters* samea
vesi; ~ *with* jnk vaivaama. **-shooter** s.
(taitava) sovittelija. **-some** *a.*
harmillinen, kiusallinen.

troublous ['trʌbləs] *a.* levoton,
rauhaton.

trough [trɔf] s. kaukalo; (~ *of the sea*)
aallonpohja.

trounce [trauns] s. löylyttää, pidellä
pahoin.

troupe [tru:p] s. näyttelijäseurue.

trousers ['trauzəz] s. *pl.* housut (m. *a
pair of* ~).

trosseau ['tru:səu] s. kapiot.

trout [traut] s. taimen, purolohi.

trowel ['trau(ə)l] s. muurauslasta; pieni
puutarhalapio.

troy [trɔi] s. : ~ [*weight*] troypaino. **T~**
erisn. Troija.

tru|ancy ['tru(:)ənsi] s. pinnaaminen,

laiminlyönti. **-ant** [-ənt] *a.*
laiskotteleva, velvollisuutensa
laiminlyövä; *s.* pinnari, lintsari; *play*
~ jäädä luvatta pois koulusta,
lintsata.

truce [tru:s] s. aselepo.

truck 1. [trʌk] *v.* vaihtaa (*for* jhk); ~
system palkan suorittaminen
tavarana; *we have no* ~ *with* emme
ole missään tekemisissä (jkn) kanssa;
~ *farm* kauppapuutarha; *garden* ~
vihannekset.

truck 2. [trʌk] s. (et. Am.)
kuorma-auto; telavaunu,
työntörattaat; avoin tavaravaunu; *v.*
kuljettaa kuorma-autossa; kärrätä.

truckle ['trʌkl] *v. : ~ to* nöyristellä,
kumarrella; ~*-bed* pyörillä liikkuva
sänky.

trucul|ence ['trʌkjuləns] s. hurjuus,
julmuus. **-ent** [-ənt] *a.* hurja, julma,
raaka.

trudge [trʌdʒ] *v.* tallustella, laahustaa,
talsia; *s.* (vaivalloinen) kulku,
tallustus.

true [tru:] *a.* tosi, todenperäinen;
todellinen, oikea, aito; uskollinen,
vilpitön; tarkka, (tyypin) mukainen;
puhdas (sävel); *adv.* tarkkaan,
suora|an, -ssa; *come* ~ toteutua; *out
of* ~ kiero; ~, . . [*but*] tosin; ~ *to the
letter* kirjaimellisesti tosi; ~ *to life*
todenmukainen; *be* ~ *to one's word*
olla sanansa mittainen. ~*-blue*
ehdottoman luotettava
(konservatiivi).

truffle ['trʌfl] s. multasieni.

truism ['tru(:)izm] s. selviö.

truly ['tru:li] *adv.* todellakin, tosiaan;
vilpittömästi; uskollisesti;
täsmällisesti; totisesti; *Yours* ~
(kirjeessä) kunnioittavasti.

trump [trʌmp] s. valtti; kunnon mies; *v.*
ottaa valttikortilla, lyödä valtti
pöytään; *the last* ~ tuomiopäivän
pasuuna; *turn up* ~ *s* osoittautua
yllättävän hyväksi, onnistua; ~ *up*
keksiä, sepittää; ~*ed-up* tekaistu.

trumpery ['trʌmp(ə)ri] *a.* kiiltokorea;
arvoton; *s.* (koru)rihkama, tyhjä
puhe.

trumpet ['trʌmpit] s. torvi;
torventörähdys; *v.* toitottaa; *blow
one's own* ~ leuhkia, kehua itseään.

~**-call** torventoitotus. **-er** [-ə] s. torvensoittaja.

truncate ['trʌŋkeit] v. typistää, katkaista.

truncheon ['trʌnʃn] s. patukka.

trundle ['trʌndl] v. kierittää, työntää (vaunuja); vieriä; pyöriä; s. pieni pyörä.

trunk [trʌŋk] s. (puun) runko; vartalo; (elefantin) kärsä; matka-arkku; jnk pääosa; (auton) tavaratila (Am.); pl. lyhyet (urheilu)housut; ~*call* kaukopuhelu; ~ *road* valtatie. **~-line** päärata.

trunnion ['trʌnjən] s. kara, tappi.

truss [trʌs] s. (heinä-, olki) kimppu; huiskilo; (katon ym) tukiansas; kohjuvyö; v. sitoa kimpuksi; tukea, vahvistaa; sitoa (lintu).

trust [trʌst] s. luottamus, usko; luotto: vastuu, holhous, jkn huostaan uskottu omaisuus; trusti (kaupp.); säätiö; v. luottaa, uskoa, panna luottamuksensa jhk; hartaasti toivoa, olla varma, uskoa; (jtk jklle t. jkn haltuun); antaa luottoa; *I ~ it will be all right* luotan siihen että asia järjestyy; *put ~ in, ~ in (t. to)* luottaa jhk; *hold sth. in ~ for* hoitaa jkn omaisuutta; *on ~* hyvässä uskossa; velaksi; *position of ~* luottamustoimi. **-ed** [-id] a. luotettava, uskottu. **-ee** [-'ti:] s. uskottu mies; luottamusmies. ~s m. johtokunta, hallitus. **-eeship** s. YK:n holhousalueen valvonta. **-ful, -ing** a. luottavainen. **-worthy** a. luotettava. **-y** [-i] a. uskollinen, kelpo; s. luottovanki.

truth [tru:θ, *pl.* -ðz] s. totuus; totuudenmukaisuus; *to tell the ~* totta puhuakseni; *in ~* tosiaan. **-ful** a. tosi, totuudenmukainen; totuudellinen.

try [trai] v. koettaa, yrittää; koetella, panna koetukselle; tutkia, kuulustella; käsitellä (asiaa); kysyä (voimia), rasittaa; s. koetus, yritys; *tried* koeteltu; *he is to be tried for murder* hän on syytettynä murhasta; ~ *one's hand at* koettaa kykyjään jssk; ~ *on* sovittaa ylleen (pukua); ~ *out* kokeilla; *have a ~ [at]* yrittää jtk. **-ing** a. voimia kysyvä, rasittava; kärsivällisyyttä koetteleva, hermostuttava. ~**- out** (urh.)

karsinta.

tryst [trist] s. (vanh.) sovittu kohtaus(paikka); *break ~* jäädä saapumatta sovittuun kohtaukseen.

Tsar [zɑ:] s. ks. *Czar.*

tsetse ['tsetsi] s. tsetsekärpänen.

tub [tʌb] s. saavi, pesusoikko, pytty, sammio; (puhek.) kylpy; *(bath ~)* kylpyamme; (hidas) laiva, »purkki»; v. kylvettää; ~*-thumper* katupuhuja.

tuba ['tju:bə] s. tuuba (mus.).

tubby ['tʌbi] a. pullea.

tube [tju:b] s. putki, tuubi, purso, putkilo; letku; kanava, tiehyt; maanalainen, metro *(the T~);* Am. radioputki.

tuber ['tju:b|ə] s. juurimukula. **-cle** [-ə:kl] s. nystyrä, tuberkkeli.

tubercul|ar, -ous [tju(:)'bə:kjulə, -ləs] s. tuberkuloottinen. **-osis** [-'ləusis] s. tuberkuloosi.

tubing [tju:biŋ] s. putki, putket, letkut; putkiainekset.

tubular ['tju:bjulə] a. putkimainen, putki-.

tuck [tʌk] s. laskos; sl. leivokset, namuset; v. laskostaa, poimuttaa; työntää, pistää, kääntää, kääriä *(up* ylös); ~ *in, into* pistää poskeensa (ruokaa); ~ *sb. up (in bed)* huolellisesti peitellä vuoteeseen. **-er** [-ə] s. röyhelö; *best bib and ~* pyhäpuku.

tuckshop s. makeiskauppa.

Tudor ['tju:də] *erisn.*

Tuesday ['tju:zdi, -dei] s. tiistai.

tuft [tʌft] s. töyhtö, tupsu, (heinä)tukko, mätäs. **-ed** [-id] a. töyhdöin koristettu, tuuhea. ~**-hunter** (ylhäisten) hännystelijä.

tug [tʌg] v. vetää, kiskoa; riuhtoa; hinata; raahata; s. vetäisy, tempaus; voimainponnistus; hinaaja (m. *-boat).* ~**-of-war** köydenveto.

tuition [tju(:)'iʃn] s. opetus.

tulip ['tju:lip] s. tulppaani.

tulle [tju:l] s. tylli.

tumble ['tʌmbl] v. kellahtaa (kumoon); pudota; romahtaa, luhistua; syöksyä, rynnätä, heittäytyä; piehtaroida, heittää kuperkeikkaa; heittelehtiä (aalloista) vyöryä; heittää mullin mallin, panna sekaisin; kaataa kumoon; s. kaatuminen,

kuperkeikka; epäjärjestys; ~ *to* (sl.)
tajuta, äkätä. **-down** *a.* rappeutunut.
-r [-ə] (jalaton) juomalasi.

tumbrel, -il [ˈtʌmbr(ə)l, -il] *s.*
lantakärryt; ammusrattaat.

tumid [ˈtjuːmid] *a.* ajettunut; mahtipontinen. **-ity** [-ˈmiditi] *s.* pöhötys.

tummy [ˈtʌmi] *s.* (lastenk.) vatsa.

tumour, tumor [ˈtjuːmə] *s.* kasvain,
tuumori (lääk.).

tumult [ˈtjuːmʌlt] *s.* mellakka, meteli;
melske, temmellys, (tunteiden)
kuohu, myllerrys; sekasorto. **-uous**
[-ˈmʌltjuəs] *a.* raju, myrskyisä.

tumul|us [ˈtjuːmjuləs] *s.* (pl. *-i* [-ai])
hautakumpu.

tun [tʌn] *s.* iso viinitynnyri.

tune [tjuːn] *s.* sävel(mä), laulu; viritys;
vire; *v.* virittää; soveltaa *(to* jhk), olla
sopusoinnussa *(with* jnk kanssa); *in ~*
puhtaasti; *in ~ with* sopusoinnussa;
out of ~ epävireessä; *sing out of ~*
laulaa väärin; *change one's ~* muuttaa
asennettaan; ~ *in to* virittää (radio)
(oikealle aaltopituudelle); ~ *up*
virittää, trimmata (moottori). **-ful** *a.*
sointuva. **-less** *a.* epäsointuinen. **-r** [-ə]
s.: piano-~ pianonvirittäjä.

tungsten [ˈtʌŋstən] *s.* volframi.

tunic [ˈtjuːnik] *s.* tunika; pitkä pusero;
(ase)takki.

tuning [ˈtjuːniŋ] *s.* viritys. **~-fork**
äänirauta.

Tunisia [tjuˈ(ː)niziə] *erisn.* **-n** [-n] *a.&*
s. tunisialainen.

tunnel [ˈtʌnl] *s.* tunneli, maanalainen
käytävä: *v.* rakentaa tunneli (jnk
läpi).

tunny [ˈtʌni] *s.* tonnikala.

tuppence [ˈtʌpəns] *s.* = *twopence*

turban [ˈtəːbən] *s.* turbaani; ~*ed*
turbaanipäinen.

turbid [ˈtəːbid] *a.* samea. **-ity** [təːˈbiditi]
s. sameus; (lääk.) samennus.

turbine [ˈtəːbin] *s.* turbiini.

turbot [ˈtəːbət] *s.* kampela.

turbul|ence [ˈtəːbjuləns] *s.*
levottomuus, kuohunta, melske. **-ent**
[-ənt] *a.* melskeinen, myrskyisä,
hurja.

tureen [tjuˈriːn] *s.* liemikulho.

turf [təːf] *s.* turve; *v.* peittää turpeilla;
the ~ kilpa-ajot, hevosurheilu.

turgid [ˈtəːdʒid] *a.* pöhöttynyt;

mahtipontinen, monisanainen. **-ity**
[-ˈdʒiditi] *s.* pöhöttyneisyys;
mahtipontisuus.

Turk [təːk] *s.* turkkilainen; rasavilli.
-estan [-isˈtaːn] *erisn.*

Turkey [ˈtəːki] *erisn.* Turkki; ~ *carpet*
itämainen matto.

turkey [ˈtəːki] *s.* kalkkuna; *talk* ~ Am.
sanoa suorat sanat. **~-cock**
kalkkunakukko.

Turkish [ˈtəːkiʃ] *a.* turkkilainen; *s.*
turkki, turkin kieli; ~ *towel*
froteepyyhe.

turmeric [ˈtəːmərik] *s.* kurkuma.

turmoil [ˈtəːmɔil] *s.* levottomuus,
sekasorto, melske.

turn [təːn] *v.* kääntää, vääntää, kiertää,
pyörittää, suunnata, kohdistaa;
kääntää nurin, muuttaa, tehdä jksk;
kääntää (jhk kieleen); sorvata;
pyöriä, kääntyä; poiketa; suuntautua;
muuttua, tulla jksk; hapantua,
hapattua; *s.* kääntäminen, käännös;
kierros; mutka; muutos, käänne,
-kohta; kerta, vuoro; lyhyt kävely t.
retki; *(a good ~)* palvelus; pelästys,
»kolaus»; mielenlaatu, taipumus;
(lauseen ym) käänne, muoto; ~ *one's*
coat muuttaa mielipidettä, luopua; ~
sb.'s head nousta jklle päähän; ~ *an*
honest penny ansaita (rahaa); ~ *inside*
out kääntää nurin; ~ *to account*
käyttää hyväkseen; *not* ~ *a hair* ei olla
millänsäkään; *he has* ~*ed 50* hän on
täyttänyt 50 vuotta; ~ *about* kääntyä
ympäri; ~ *away* kääntyä pois,
käännyttää ovelta; ~ *back* kääntyä
takaisin; ~ *down* kiertää pienemmälle
(liekki); hylätä (tarjous); ~ *in*
(puhek.) mennä maata, *(sth.)*
palauttaa; ~ *off* kiertää kiinni, sulkea
(hana); kääntyä, poiketa (jllek tielle);
~ *on* avata (hana); sytyttää; riippua
jstk; käydä (äkkiä) kimppuun; ~ *out*
ajaa ulos, karkottaa; tyhjentää,
penkoa, siivota; tuottaa, valmistaa;
lähteä (talosta); osoittautua; päättyä;
~ *out a failure* epäonnistua; *if all* ~*s*
out well jos kaikki käy hyvin; ~ *over*
kääntää (kylkeä), kääntyä ylösalaisin
kaataa; mennä kumoon; kääntää
(lehteä), selailla; pohtia (mielessään)
siirtää, luovuttaa; *please* ~ *over!* (lyh
P.T.O.)käännä! ~ *round* kääntyä

ympäri t. jhk päin, kääntyä kulmasta *(round the corner)*; ~ *to* kääntyä jkn puoleen; ryhtyä jhk; ~ *up* kääntää ylös, pystyyn, kääntyä ylöspäin; tulla, ilmestyä, ilmaantua; ~ *upon* riippua jstk; käydä (odottamatta) kimppuun; *his stomach ~ed* häntä kuvotti; *well~ed out* hyvin pukeutunut; *right (left) about ~!* täyskäännös oikeaan (vasempaan)! *in ~* vuorostaan, vuorotellen; *by ~s* vuorotellen; *done to a ~* parahiksi paistettu ym; *take ~s* vuorotella; *take a ~ at the wheel* vuorostaan ajaa; *at every ~* joka käänteessä, joka askeleella, alituisesti; *has a practical ~ of mind* on käytännöllinen; ~ *of the year* vuodenvaihde; *what a ~ it gave me!* kuinka pelästyinkään! **-coat** »tuuliviiri», luopio. **~-down** kääntö-(kaulus). **-er** [-ə] s. sorvari. **-ing** s. käännös, käänne; kadunkulma; *~-point* käännekohta.

turnip ['tə:nip] s. nauris.

turnkey s. vanginvartija.

turn|-out s. väenpaljous, osanotto jhk; (tehtaan) tuotanto; varusteet. **-over** s. liikevaihto; (työntekijöiden ym) vaihtuvuus, vaihtumisnopeus; *annual ~* vuosivaihto. **-pike** tullipuomi, (maksullinen) moottoritie. **-stile** kääntö-, ristiportti. **~-table** kääntölava (rautat.), (levysoittimen) levylautanen.

turpentine ['tə:p(ə)ntain] s. tärpätti.

turpitude ['tə:pitju:d] s. kataluus, halpamaisuus.

turquoise ['tə:kwɔiz] s. turkoosi.

turret ['tʌrit] s. (pieni) torni; panssari-, tykkitorni.

turtle [tə:tl] s. merikilpikonna; ~ [*soup*] kilpikonnanliemi; *turn ~* mennä kumoon, kaatua (mer.). **~-dove** tunturikyyhkynen.

Tuscany ['tʌskəni] *erisn.* Toskana.

tusk [tʌsk] s. (norsun ym) syöksyhammas.

Tussaud's ['tju:səuz] s.: *Madame ~* vahakabinetti Lontoossa.

tussle ['tʌsl] s. käsikähmä, tappelu; *v.* tapella.

tussock ['tʌsək] s. ruohomätäs.

tussore ['tʌsɔ:] s. eräänl. karkea (raaka)silkki.

tut [tʌt] *int.: ~! ~! ~!* ole vaiti! pyh!

tutel|age ['tju:tilidʒ] s. holhous. **-ary** [-əri] *a.* suojelus-.

tutor ['tju:tə] s. yksityis-, kotiopettaja; opintojen ohjaaja; holhooja; *v.* opettaa (yksityisesti); ohjata jkn opintoja (yliopistossa); hillittä. **-ial** [tju(:)'tɔ:riəl] s. ohjaustunti.

tutu ['tu:tu:] s. balettihame.

tuxedo [tʌk'si:dou] s. (pl. ~s) Am. smokki.

TV ['ti:'vi:] s. ks. *television*.

twaddle ['twɔdl] *v.* höpöttää; s. pötypuhe, palturi.

twain [twein] (vanh.) kaksi; *in ~* kahtia.

twang [twæŋ] s. helähdys; nenä-ääni; *v.* näppäillä; puhua nenäänsä, honottaa.

tweak [twi:k] *v.* nipistää; vääntää; s. nipistys.

twee [twi:] s. (puhek.) söpö.

tweed [twi:d] s. tweed (kangas).

tweeny ['twi:ni] s. palvelus-, aputyttö.

tweet [twi:t] *v.* piipittää.

tweeze [twi:z] *v.: ~ out* nyhtää. **-rs** [-əz] s. *pl.* atulat, pinsetit, pinsetit.

twelfth [twelfθ] *a.* kahdestoista; *T~-night* loppiaisaatto.

twelve [twelv] *lukus.* kaksitoista. **-month** s. vuosi.

twentieth ['twentiiθ] *lukus. & s.* kahdeskymmenes, -osa.

twenty ['twenti] *lukus.* kaksikymmentä; *s.: in the twenties* kaksikymmenluvulla.

twice [twais] *adv.* kahdesti, kaksi kertaa.

twiddle ['twidl] *v.* pyöritellä (peukaloitaan); ~ *with* hypistellä; ~ *one's thumbs* m. olla laiskana.

twig 1. [twig] s. (hento) oksa, varpu; taikavarpu.

twig 2. [twig] *v.* (puhek.) äkätä, hoksata.

twilight ['twailait] s. (ilta-, aamu-)hämärä; ~ *of the gods* Ragnarök.

twill [twil] s. toimikas.

twin [twin] s. kaksonen; kaksoisveli, -sisar; jnk pari; *a.* kaksois-, pari-.

twine [twain] *v.* punoa, kiertää; kietoa; kietoutua; kiemurrella; s. (kerrattu) lanka, nyöri; kiemura.

twinge [twin(d)ʒ] *s.* (äkillinen) vihlova kipu, vihlaisu; ~ [*of conscience*] pistos.

twinkl|e ['twiŋkl] *v.* tuikkia, kimmeltää, välkkyä; *s.* tuike, välke; (silmän) pilke, pilkahtelu. **-ing** *s.: in the ~ of an eye* silmänräpäyksessä.

twirl [twəːl] *v.* pyörittää, kiertää; pyöriä; *s.* pyörähdys; kiekura.

twist [twist] *v.* kiertää, punoa; vääntää; väännellä, vääristellä; vääntyä, kiertyä; mutkitella; *s.* kiertäminen, vääntö; mutka; punontalanka, kierrelanka, punos; (luonteen) omituisuus, kierous; ~ *one's ankle* nyrjäyttää nilkkansa; ~ *off* vääntää poikki. **-er** [-ə] *s.* kierrepallo; kiero ihminen; pulmallinen tehtävä, kova pähkinä.

twit [twit] *v.* pistellä, kiusoitella.

twitch [twitʃ] *v.* nykäistä, tempaista; nytkähdellä, nykiä; *s.* nykäys; nytkähdys, värähdys.

twitter ['twitə] *v.* visertää; *s.* viserrys; *in a* ~ kiihdyksissä, hermostunut. **-y** [-ri] *a.* hermostunut.

two [tuː] *lukus.* kaksi; molemmat; *s.* kakkonen; *in* ~ kahtia; ~ *and* ~ parittain; *put* ~ *and* ~ *together* tehdä johtopäätöksiä; *one or* ~ pari; *in a day or* ~ parissa päivässä, parin päivän kuluttua. **~-decker** kaksikerroksinen bussi. **~-edged** kaksiteräinen. **-fold** *a. & adv.* kaksinkertainen, -sesti. **-pence** ['tʌpəns] kaksi pennyä. **-penny** ['tʌpni] kahden pennyn. **~-piece** kaksiosainen. **~-ply** kaksisäikeinen. **~-seater** kahden hengen auto. **~-timing** *a.* petollinen. **~-way** kaksisuuntainen (liikenne).

tycoon [tai'kuːn] *s.* (teollisuus)pomo, pohatta, rahamies.

tyke [taik] *s.* rakki.

tympan|ic [tim'pænik] *a.:* ~ *membrane* tärykalvo. **-um** ['timpənəm] *s.* täryontelo; päätykolmio.

Tyne [tain] *erisn.*

type [taip] *s.* tyyppi, perikuva, perusmuoto; kirjasin, kirjake; *v.* kirjoittaa koneella; *in* ~ ladottu(na). **-cast** *v.* antaa näyttelijälle (hänen tyypilleen) sopiva rooli. **~-script:** *in* ~ koneellakirjoitettu(na). **~-setter** latoja. **~-setting machine** latomakone. **-script:** *in* ~ koneella-kirjoitettu(na). **~-write** kirjoittaa koneella. **-writer** kirjoituskone.

typhoid ['taifɔid] *s. & a.:* ~ [*fever*] lavantauti.

typhoon [tai'fuːn] *s.* hirmumyrsky, taifuuni.

typhus ['taifəs] *s.* pilkkukuume.

typi|cal ['tipik(ə)l] *a.* tyypillinen, luonteenomainen. **-fy** [-fai] *v.* olla tyypillinen, olla esimerkkinä jstk.

typ|ing ['taipiŋ] *s.* konekirjoitus. **-ist** [-ist] *s.* konekirjoittaja.

typograph|er [tai'pɔgrəf|ə] *s.* kirjaltaja. **-ic(al)** [-'græfik, -(ə)l] *a.* kirjapainon-, paino-; ~ *error* painovirhe. **-y** [-i] *s.* kirjapainotaito.

tyrann|ical [ti'rænik(ə)l] *a.* tyrannimainen, itsevaltainen. **-ize** ['tirənaiz] *v.:* ~ [*over*] sortaa, tyrannisoida. **-ous** ['tirənəs] *a.* = *-ical*. **-y** ['tirəni] *s.* tyrannia.

tyrant ['taiər(ə)nt] *s.* tyranni.

tyre [taiə] *s.* (pyörän) kumirengas.

tyro ['taiərəu] *s.* vasta-alkaja.

Tyrol ['tir(ə)l] *erisn.* Tiroli. **-ese** [tirə'liːz] *a. & s.* tirolilainen.

U

U, u [ju:] *s.* u-kirjain; *U-boat* saksalainen sukellusvene. Lyh.: **UDA** *Ulster Defence Association;* **UDI** *Unilateral Declaration of Independence;* **UFO** ['ju:fəu] *unidentified flying object;* **UHF** *ultra high frequency;* **U.K.** *United Kingdom (of Great Britain and Northern Ireland);* **ult.** (ultimo) *last month* viime kuuta; **U.N.** *United Nations* Y.K.; **UNESCO** [ju(:)'neskəu] *United Nations Educational, Scientific and Cultural Organization;* **UNICEF** *United Nations Children's Emergency Fund;* **UNO** ['ju:nəu] *United Nations Organization;* **UNRRA** *United Nations Relief and Rehabilitation Association;* **U.S., U.S.A.** *United States (of America);* **U.S.S.R.** *Union of Soviet Socialist Republics;* **Ut.** *Utah.*

ubiquit|ous [ju:'bikwitəs] *a.* kaikkialla läsnäoleva. **-y** [-ti] *s.* läsnäolo kaikkialla.

udder ['ʌdə] *s.* utare.

Uganda [ju:'gændə] *erisn.*

ugh [əg, ə, ə:] *int.* huh! hyi!

ugli|fy ['ʌglifai] *v.* rumentaa. **-ness** *s.* rumuus.

ugly ['ʌgli] *a.* ruma, vastenmielinen, inhottava; paha, ilkeä.

ukase [ju:'keiz] *s.* ukaasi.

Ukraine [ju(:)'krein] *erisn; the ~* Ukraina.

ukulele [ju:kə'leili] *s.* havajilainen kitara, ukulele.

ulcer ['ʌlsə] *s.* haava; mätäpaise; [*gastric*] *~* mahahaava. **-ate** [-reit] *v.* märkiä. **-ation** [-'reiʃn] haavauma. **-ous** ['ʌls(ə)rəs] *a.* märkäinen.

Ulster ['ʌlstə] *erisn.* (us. = Pohjois-Irlanti); *u~* ulsteri.

ulterior [ʌl'tiəriə] *a.* toisella puolen sijaitseva, etäisempi, pohjalla oleva, taka-, salattu.

ultim|ate ['ʌltimit] *a.* viimeinen, lopullinen; perus-; (*~ly adv.* lopuksi, lopulta). **-atum** [ʌlti'meitəm] *s.* (pl. m. *-ata* [-eitə] uhkavaatimus. **-o** [-əu] *adv.* viime kuun (lyh. *ult.*).

ultra ['ʌltrə] *a.* ääri-, äärimmäis-. **-conservative** *a.* pata-, rutivanhoillinen. **-marine** *s.* merensininen. **-violet** *a.* ultravioletti.

ululate ['ju:ljuleit] *v.* ulista.

Ulysses [ju(:)'lisi:z] *erisn.* Odysseus.

umber ['ʌmbə] *s. & a.* umbranväri.

umbilical [ʌmbi'laik(ə)l] *a.: ~ cord* napanuora.

umbrage ['ʌmbridʒ] *s.* siimes; pahennus; *take ~* pahastua, loukkaantua.

umbrella [ʌm'brelə] *s.* sateenvarjo.

umpire ['ʌmpaiə] *s.* erotuomari; riidanratkaisija; *v.* olla erotuomarina.

umpteen ['ʌm(p)ti:n] *a.* sl.; *for the ~th time* sen(kin) seitsemän kertaa, lukemattomia kertoja.

un- [ʌn-] *pref.* epä-, -ton, -tön.

un|abashed häkeltymätön, ujostelematon. **-abated** vähentymätön, heikentymätön. **-able** *a.* kykenemätön; *I am ~ to* en voi. **-abridged** lyhentämätön. **-acceptable** mahdoton hyväksyä. **-accommodating** myöntymätön, töykeä. **-accompanied** ilman seuraa, yksin; ilman säestystä. **-accountable** selittämätön, outo. **-accustomed** tottumaton; outo. **-acknowledged** *a.* tunnustamaton, vastauksetta jäänyt. **-acquainted:** *~ with* jstk tietämätön. **-adaptable** *a.* sopeutumaton.

unadvis|able epäviisas, ei suotava. **-ed** varomaton, harkitsematon.

un|**affected** a. teeskentelemätön,
luonnollinen; *he is ~ by* häneen ei
vaikuta, hän ei ole millänsäkään
(jstk). -**aided** ilman apua, avutta.
-**alterable** a. muuttumaton.
-**ambiguous** a. yksiselitteinen.
~-**American** a. epäamerikkalainen.
unanim|**ity** [ju:nɔ'nimiti] s.
yksimielisyys. -**ous** [ju(:)'nænimɔs] a.
yksimielinen.
un|**announced** kenenkään
ilmoittamatta. -**answerable**
kumoamaton. -**answered** vastauksetta
jäänyt. -**appreciative**
ymmärtämätön, jtk arvostamaton;
kiittämätön.
un|**approachable** luoksepääsemätön,
luotaantyöntävä. -**armed** aseeton.
-**ashamed** häpeämätön,
ujostelematon. -**asked** pyytämättä.
-**assailable** jonka kimppuun ei voi
hyökätä, kiistaton. -**assisted** omin
avuin. -**assuming** vaatimaton.
-**attached** ei sidottu, vapaa. -**attended**
vailla silmälläpitoa. -**attainable**
saavuttamaton. -**authorized**
valtuuttamaton, laiton. -**availing**
hyödytön, turha. -**avoidable**
väistämätön.
un**aware** ['ʌnɔ'weɔ] a. tietämätön *(of,
that* jstk). -**s** [-z] adv. äkkiarvaamatta;
tietämätön|än, -ni jne.; *take sb. ~*
yllättää jku.
un|**balanced** tasapainoton;
päättämätön (tili ym). -**bar** v. poistaa
telki, avata. -**bearable** sietämätön.
-**beaten** voittamaton, lyömätön.
-**becoming** epäpukeva, ei sopiva.
-**belief** s. epäusko. -**believable**
uskomaton. -**believing** epäuskoinen.
un**bend** v. oikaista, suoristaa; päästää
laukeamaan; suoristua; vapautua,
rentoutua. -**ing** a. taipumaton,
jäykkä, itsepintainen.
un|**bias(s)ed** ennakkoluuloton,
puolueeton. -**bidden** kutsumaton;
käskemättä, pyytämättä. -**bind**
irrottaa, avata (solmu). -**blemished**
tahraton, virheetön.
un**blushing** a. häpeämätön, röyhkeä.
un|**bolt** v. avata (salpa). -**born** a.
syntymätön. -**bosom** v. ilmaista
(jklle); ~ *oneself* avata sydämensä
(jklle). -**bounded** rajaton, ääretön;

hillitön.
un**bridled** a. hillitön.
un|**broken** a. murtumaton;
keskeytymätön, katkeamaton;
lyömätön (ennätys); kesyttämätön,
harjoittamaton. -**burden** v. vapauttaa
(taakasta); ~ *oneself (one's mind)*
purkaa sydämensä, keventää
sydäntään, uskoutua. -**businesslike** a.
epäasiallinen. -**button** v. aukaista
napeista. -**called-for** a. tarpeeton,
aiheeton. -**canny** [ʌn'kæni] a.
yliluonnollinen, salaperäinen,
kammottava. -**cared-for** a.
laiminlyöty, huonosti hoidettu.
-**ceasing** a. lakkaamaton,
taukoamaton. -**ceremonious** a.
kursailematon, luontena.
un**certain** a. epävarma; epäiltävä;
epävakainen. -**ty** s. epävarmuus,
epätietoisuus; epävakaisuus.
un**challenge|able** a. kiistaton,
epäämätön. -**d** a. = ed.; väittämättä
vastaan.
un**chang|ed** muuttumaton, entisellään.
-**ing** muuttumaton.
un**charitable** a. armoton,
kovasydäminen.
un|**charted** kartoittamaton. -**chaste**
siveetön. -**checked** esteetön, hillitön;
esteettä; tarkistamaton. -**christian**
epäkristillinen. -**civil** epäkohtelias;
(~**ized** barbaari-, sivistymätön).
un|**claimed** noutamatta jäänyt. -**clasp**
v. aukaista.
un**cle** ['ʌŋkl] s. setä, eno; sl.
panttilainaaja.
un**clouded** pilvetön; valoisa.
un**co** ['ʌŋkɔu] (Skotl.) outo;
erinomaisen.
un|**coil** v. suoristaa. -**comfortable** a.
epämukava; levoton, alla päin oleva;
nolo, epämiellyttävä. -**committed**
sitoutumaton; puolueeton. -**common**
a. epätavallinen, harvinainen; adv.
(puhek.) tavattoman. -**communicative**
harvapuheinen, umpimielinen.
-**companionable** seuraa karttava.
-**complaining** kärsivällinen.
-**complimentary** a. kaikkea muuta
kuin imarteleva. -**compromising** a.
taipumaton.
un**concern** s. välinpitämättömyys. -**ed**
a. väliäpitämätön, huoleton; *I am*

quite ~ *(in, with)* olen täysin ulkopuolinen.

un|conditional ehdoton; ~ *surrender* antautuminen ehdoitta. **-confirmed** vahvistamaton. **-congenial** eriluonteinen, epämieluinen, yhteen sopimaton, (ilmastosta) epäterveellinen. **-conquerable** voittamaton. **-conscionable** *a.* kohtuuton; ylettömän (pitkä ym).

unconscious *a.* tiedoton; *(~ of)* tietämätön jstk; tajuton; *the* ~ piilotajunta; *~ly* huomaamatta(an, -ni jne.); tietämättä(än, -ni jne.). **-ness** *s.* tietämättömyys *(of* jstk); tajuttomuus.

un|considered *a.* harkitsematon. **-constrained** *a.* vapaaehtoinen; vapaa, luonteva. **-controllable** *a.* hillitön, ei hallittavissa (oleva). **-conventional** epäsovinnainen, ennakkoluuloton. **-cork** *v.* avata (pullo). **-couple** *v.* irrottaa, päästää irti. **-couth** [ʌn'ku:θ] kömpelö, hiomaton, moukkamainen; eriskummallinen.

uncover *v.* nostaa pois (kansi); paljastaa (juoni); (vanh.) paljastaa päänsä. **-ed** *a.* avopäin; paljas.

un|critical *a.* arvostelukyvytön. **-crowned** *a.* kruunaamaton.

unct|ion [ʌn(k)ʃn] *s.* voitelu; voide; intoilu, hurskailu; *extreme* ~ viimeinen voitelu. **-uous** [ʌn(k)tjuəs] *a.* hurskasteleva.

un|cultivated viljelemätön. **-cultured** sivistymätön.

un|curl *v.* suoristua, oieta. **-damaged** vahingoittumaton. **-dated** päiväämätön. **-daunted** peloton, lannistumaton. **-deceive** *v.* poistaa harhaluulo, avata jkn silmät.

un|decided ratkaisematon; epävarma, epäröivä. **-decipherable** *a.* mahdoton lukea, selvittämätön. **-defiled** *a.* tahraton.

undefin|able mahdoton määritellä. **-ed** epämääräinen.

un|delivered perille toimittamaton. **-demonstrative** hillitty, pidättyvä. **-deniable** kieltämätön, epäämätön.

under [ʌndə] *prep. & adv.* alla, alle; alapuolella, -lle; jnk alaisena; jnk nojalla; *a.* ala-, ali-, alempi; *those* ~

him hänen alaisensa; ~ *age* alaikäinen; ~ *arms* aseissa; ~ *one's breath* hillityllä äänellä; ~ *the circumstances* näissä oloissa; ~ *consideration* harkittavana; ~ *control* ohjailtavissa, hallittavissa; ~ *pain of death* kuoleman uhalla; ~ *repair* korjauksen alaisena; ~ *sail* purjeitmassa; ~ *way* matkalla, menossa, käynnissä.

under [ʌndə-] *pref.* ali-, ala-. **-act** *v.* näytellä liian laimeasti. **-bid** *v.* tehdä halvempi tarjous. **-brush** *s.* aluskasvillisuus. **-carriage** *s.* laskuteline. **-clothes, -clothing** *s.* alusvaatteet. **-current** *s.* pohjavirta. **-cut** *s.* seläke, filee; *v.* tarjota t. myydä halvemmalla kuin. **-developed** *a.* alikehittynyt. **-dog** *s.* alakynnessä oleva, vähäväkinen. **-done** puolikypsä. **-employment** *s.* vajaatyöllisyys. **-estimate** *v.* aliarvioida; *s.* aliarviointi. **-exposed** alivalotettu (valok.). **-exposure** *s.* alivalotus. **-fed** *a.* aliravittu. **-foot** *adv.* jaloissa, maassa. **-go** *v.* kokea, joutua jnk alaiseksi; ~ *a change* muuttua; ~ *an operation* joutua leikkaukseen. **-graduate** [-'grædjuit] *s.* ylioppilas, opiskelija. **-ground** *adv.* maan alla t. alle; *a.* maanalainen; *the* ~ maanalainen rautatie. **-growth** *s.* aluskasvillisuus. **-hand** [' - - -] *a.* salainen, salakähmäi|nen; *(adv.* -sesti, salaa). **-handed** *a.* salakavala. **-hung** *a.* ulkoneva.

under|lie *v.* olla jnk perustana. **-line** *v.* alleviivata; korostaa. **-ling** *s.* käskyläinen. **-lying** *a.* allaoleva, perustana oleva. **-mine** *v.* kaivaa, uurtaa perustukset alta; heikentää, jäytää. **-most** *a.* alin, alhaisin. **-neath** *prep. & adv.* alla, alle, alapuolella, -lle. **-pass** *s.* alikäytävä. **-pay** *v.* maksaa liian vähän. **-pin** *v.* pönkittää. **-privileged** *a.* vähäväkinen. **-production** *s.* vajaatuotanto. **-rate** *v.* arvioida liian vähäiseksi, aliarvioida. **-score** *v.* all viivata. **~-secretary** *s.*: *U.-S. of State* alivaltiosihteeri. **-sell** *v.* myydä halvemmalla (kuin). **-signed** *a.*: *the* ~ allekirjoittanut. **-sized** *a.* lyhytkasvuinen. **-staffed** *a.*: *we are* ~ meillä on liian vähän henkilökuntaa.

understand [ʌndə'stænd] v. (ks. *stand*)
ymmärtää, käsittää; luulla tietävänsä,
saada jk käsitys, luulla tietävänsä; vrt.
-stood; I ~ that. .olen kuullut että;
that is understood. .on itsestään
selvää; *we were given to ~* saimme sen
käsityksen, meidän annettiin
ymmärtää; *am I to ~* [*that*]
tarkoitatko. **-able** a. ymmärrettävä.
-ably adv. ymmärrettävää kyllä. **-ing**
a. ymmärtäväinen; s. ymmärrys;
ymmärtämys; sopimus; yksimielisyys;
lack of ~ ymmärtämyksen puute;
reach (come to) an ~ sopia jstk; *on the
~ that* edellyttäen että.
under|state v. ilmoittaa liian
vähäiseksi. **-statement** s. alisanojen
käyttö, vähättelevä ilmaus. **-stood**
imp. & pp.; a. sovittu, tietty; *it is an
~ thing* on sanomattakin selvä.
-study s. varamies, sijainen (teatt.);
v. harjoitella toisen (näyttelijän)
osaa.
undertak|e [ʌndə'teik] v. (ks. *take*)
ottaa toimeksensa, ottaa
vastatakseen, ryhtyä jhk; sitoutua
jhk; taata. **-er** s.: ['ʌndə-] s.
hautajaisurakoitsija; *~ 's*
hautaustoimisto. **-ing** s. yritys;
['ʌndə-] hautaushuolto.
under|tone s.: *in an ~* hillityllä,
matalalla äänellä. **-took** imp. ks.
undertake. **-tow** [-təu] s. pohjavirta.
-value v. aliarvioida, väheksyä. **-vest**
s. ihopaita. **-wear** s. alusvaatteet.
-went imp. ks. *undergo*. **-world** s.
manala; alamaailma. **-write** v. (ks.
write) harjoittaa
merivakuutustoimintaa;
allekirjoittaa. **-writer** s. ks. ed.
undeserved a. ansaitsematon. **-edly**
adv. ansaitsematta. **-ing** a. ansioton.
undesigned a. harkitsematon.
undesirable a. ei suotava, ei toivottu.
un|determined a. ratkaisematon;
epävarma. **-deterred** a. peloton; *~ by*
jtk pelästymättä. **-developed** a.
kehittymätön. **-did** imp. ks. *undo*.
undies ['ʌndiz] s. (puhek.) naisten
alusvaatteet.
un|digested sulamaton. **-dignified**
arvoton, sopimaton. **-diminished**
vähentymätön.
un|disciplined kuriton, vallaton.

-disclosed salainen. **-disguisedly** adv.
peittelemättä. **-dismayed** peloton.
-disputed kiistämätön. **-distinguished**
peräti tavallinen, ei huomiota
herättävä, mitätön. **-disturbed**
häiritsemä|tön, -ttä.
un|do ['ʌnd'u:] v. tehdä
tekemättömäksi t. tyhjäksi, kumota;
purkaa, avata, irrottaa; tuhota, syöstä
turmioon. **-doing** ['ʌn'du(:)iŋ] s.
turmio, tuho. **-done** a. hukassa,
tuhottu; *he is ~* hän on mennyttä
miestä; *leave ~* jättää tekemättä.
un|doubted a. eittämätön,
kiistämätön; *~ly* epäilemättä.
-dreamed, -dreamt (-of) a.
aavistamaton, . . jota ei voi
kuvitellakaan.
undress v. riisua, riisuutua; s.
aamupuku, (sot.) kenttäpuku.
undue a. kohtuuton, asiaton.
undula|te ['ʌndjuleit] v. aaltoilla; **-ting**
m. kumpuileva. **-tion** [-'leiʃn] s.
aaltoilu, aaltoliike.
un|duly adv. kohtuuttomasti, liiaksi.
-dutiful velvollisuutensa unohtava,
tottelematon. **-dying** kuolematon,
katoamaton. **-earned** ansaitsematon.
-earth v. kaivaa esiin; vetää
päivänvaloon; ajaa esiin (pesästä).
-earthly a. ylimaallinen,
yliluonnollinen; kammottava.
un|easiness s. levottomuus, huoli. **-easy**
a. levoton, huolestunut; vaivautunut.
un|eatable a. syötäväksi kelpaamaton.
-economical a. epätaloudellinen.
-ending a.
loppumaton, ääretön. **-endowed**
(laitoksesta) ilman lahjoituksia
toimiva. **-endurable** sietämätön.
un-English a. epäenglantilainen.
un|enlightened valistumaton.
-enterprising saamaton.
unequ|al a. erilainen, epätasainen; *is ~
to* ei pysty jhk; *he is ~ to the task* hän
ei ole tehtävän tasalla. **-alled** a.
lyömätön, vertaansa vailla. **-ivocal** a.

täysin selvä, yksiselitteinen.
un|erring *a.* erehtymätön. **-essential**
epäolennainen. **-even** epätasainen;
rosoinen. **-eventful** yksitoikkoinen,
tapahtumista köyhä. **-exampled**
ainutlaatuinen, tavaton.
-exceptionable *a.* moitteeton.
-expected odottamaton,
aavistamaton. **-explored** tutkimaton.
-expressed ilmaisematon.
un|fading *a.* kuihtumaton,
katoamaton. **-failing** *a.* pettämätön;
ehtymätön.
unfair *a.* epäoikeudenmukainen,
kohtuuton, väärä; epärehellinen.
-ne s *s.* vääryys jne.
un|faithful *a.* uskoton. **-faltering** *a.*
järkkymätön. **-familiar** *a.* outo,
tuntematon, vieras; *be ~ with* ei
tuntea.
unfasten *v.* irrottaa.
un|fathomable *a.* mittaamaton,
pohjaton. **-favourable** *a.* epäsuotuisa;
epäedullinen. **-feeling** *a.* tunteeton,
sydämetön, kova. **-feigned** *a.* vilpitön.
unfetter *v.* päästä (kahleista),
vapauttaa.
un|filial *a.* pojalle (t. tyttärelle)
sopimaton. **-finished** *a.*
keskeneräinen.
unfit *a.* sopimaton, kelpaamaton,
kykenemätön; *v.* tehdä
kykenemättömäksi, sopimattomaksi.
-ness *s.* sopimattomuus,
soveltumattomuus. **-ted, -ting** *a.*
sopimaton.
unfix *v.* irrottaa.
un|flagging *a.* väsymätön,
hellittämätön. **-fledged** *a.*
höyhenetön, hento; kypsymätön.
-flinching *a.* horjumaton,
järkkymätön.
unfold *v.* kääriä auki, levittää; esittää,
ilmaista; levittäytyä, kehittyä,
kehkeytyä, ilmetä.
un|foreseen aavistamaton. **-forgettable**
unohtumaton.
unforgiv|able *a.* anteeksiantamaton.
-ing *a.* leppymätön, kova.
unfortunate *a.* onneton, valitettava. **-ly**
adv. onnettomuudeksi; valitettavasti,
ikävä kyllä.
un|founded *a.* perusteeton; perätön.
-frequented *a.* missä harvoin

käydään, yksinäinen.
unfriend|liness *s.* epäystävällisyys. **-ly**
a. epäystävällinen.
un|frock *v.* panna (pappi) viralta.
-fruitful *a.* hedelmätön; hyödytön.
-fulfilled *a.* täyttymätön,
toteutumaton. **-furl** *v.* kääriä auki,
levittää; levitä. **-furnished** *a.*
kalustamaton. **-gainly** *a.* kömpelö,
tökerö. **-generous** *a.* kitsas;
halpamainen.
ungentle *a.* tyly, kova, epäystävällinen.
-manly *a.* sivistyneelle miehelle
sopimaton, epähieno.
unget-at-able ['--'ætəbl] *a.*
luoksepääsemätön, saavuttamaton.
un|gird *v.* riisua (vyö). **-godly** *a.*
jumalaton.
ungovernable *a.* mahdoton hallita;
hillitön, raju.
un|graceful *a.* kömpelö, suloton.
-gracious *a.* epäystävällinen,
epäkohtelias. **-grammatical** *a.* ei
kieliopin mukainen. **-grateful** *a.*
kiittämätön; epäkiitollinen.
-grounded *a.* perusteeton, aiheeton.
-grudging *a.* aulis, antelias. **-guarded**
a. vartioimaton; varomaton,
ajattelematon.
unguent ['ʌŋgwənt] *s.* voide,
voiteluaine.
un|hallowed *a.* epäpyhä, jumalaton.
-hampered esteetön.
unhapp|ily *adv.* onnettomasti; pahaksi
onneksi. **-iness** *s.* onnettomuus. **-y** *a.*
onneton, kovaonninen, (joskus)
alakuloinen; epäonnistunut.
un|harmed *a.* vahingoittumaton.
-harness *v.* päästää valjaista. **-healthy**
a. sairaalloinen; epäterveellinen.
-heard *adv.* kuul(ustel)ematta; *~ of*
ennen kuulumaton.
unheed|ed *a.* huomaamatta jäänyt.
-ing *a.* varomaton, huomaamaton.
unhesitating *a.* ripeä, aikailematon,
siekailematon. **-ly** *adv.* empimättä,
arvelematta.
un|hinge *v.* nostaa saranoilta;
järkyttää, saattaa sekasorron tilaan.
-hitch *v.* irrottaa; riisua valjaista.
-holy *a.* epäpyhä, jumalaton; *~ row*
hirmuinen hälinä. **-hook** *v.* irrottaa
koukusta, aukaista hakasista.
-hoped-for *a.* odottamaton, .. jota ei

osattu toivoa. **-horse** v. heittää
satulasta. **-hurt** a. vahingoittumaton.
uni- ['ju:ni-] pref. yksi-. -corn s.
yksisarvinen (her.). **-fication**
[-fi'keiʃn] s. yhdistäminen.
uniform ['ju:nifɔ:m] a.
yhdenmukainen; samanlainen,
tasainen; s. virkapuku, univormu. **-ed**
a. virkapukuinen. **-ity** [-'fɔ:miti] s.
yhdenmukaisuus, samanlaisuus. **-ly**
adv. kauttaaltaan; yhtäläisesti.
uni|fy ['ju:nifai] v. yhdistää, sulattaa
yhteen. **-lateral** a. toispuolinen,
yksipuolinen.
unimagin|able a. jota ei voi kuvitella.
-ative a. mielikuvitukseton.
un|impaired a. vähentymätön,
heikentymätön; vahingoittumaton.
-impeachable a. moitteeton,
nuhteeton. **-impeded** esteetön.
-importance s. vähäinen merkitys.
-important vähäpätöinen, mitätön.
-improved ei parantunut, ennallaan;
viljelemätön (maa). **-informed**
tietämätön; asiaton (~ criticism).
-inhabited asumaton. **-inhibited**
estoton. **-initiated** (asiaan)
perehtymätön.
unintellig|ent heikkoälyinen. **-ible**
käsittämätön.
un|intentional vahingossa sattunut,
tahaton. **-interesting** a.
mielenkiinnoton, ikävä. **-interrupted**
keskeytymätön, yhtämittainen.
uninvit|ed kutsumaton. **-ing** a. ei
houkutteleva, epämiellyttävä.
union ['ju:njən] s. yhtyminen,
yhteenliittymä; liitto, -valtio; unioni;
yksimielisyys, sopu;
köyhäinhoitopiiri; trade ~
ammattiyhdistys; the U~ (m.)
Yhdysvallat; U~ Jack Britannian
kansallislippu. **-ist** [-ist] s.
ammattiyhdistyksen jäsen; unionisti
(valt.). **-ize** [-aiz] v. järjestä(yty)ä
ammattiliitoksi.
unique [ju:'ni:k] a. ainoa laatuaan,
ainutlaatuinen. **-ly** a. ainutlaatuisen,
verrattoman.
unison ['ju:nizn] s. yhteissointu;
sopusointu, yksimielisyys; in ~
yksiäänisesti; yhdessä (tuumin).
unit ['ju:nit] s. yksikkö; osa, elementti,
aggregaatti (tekn.); m. osasto; kitchen

~ s keittiökalusteet. **-arian** [-'tɛəriən]
a. unitaarinen.
unite [ju:'nait] v. yhdistää, liittää
yhteen; yhtyä, liittyä yhteen. **-d** [-id]
a. yhdistetty, yhtynyt; yksimielinen;
the ~ Kingdom Yhdistynyt
kuningaskunta (Iso-Britannia ja
Pohj. Irlanti); the ~ Nations
Yhdistyneet Kansakunnat; the ~
States Yhdysvallat. **-dly** [-idli] adv.
yhdessä, yhteisvoimin.
unity ['ju:niti] s. ykseys, yhteys,
yhtenäisyys; yksimielisyys,
sopusointu; ykkönen (mat.); the
dramatic unities toiminnan, ajan ja
paikan yhteys.
universal [ju(:)ni'və:sl] a. yleinen,
yleis-, yleis|maailmallinen, -pätevä;
vallitseva; a ~ language
maailmankieli. **-ity** [-və:'sæliti] s.
yleispätevyys, universaalisuus. **-ize**
[-aiz] v. yleistää. **-ly** adv. yleisesti,
poikkeuksetta, kaikkialla.
universe ['ju:nivə:s] s.
maailmankaikkeus, universumi.
university [ju:ni'və:siti] s. yliopisto,
korkeakoulu.
unjust a. epäoikeudenmukainen,
väärä; kohtuuton. **-ifiable** a. jota ei
voi puolustaa, anteeksiantamaton.
-ified a. aiheeton, epäoikeutettu. **-ly**
adv. väärydellä, väärin.
unkempt ['ʌn'kem(p)t] a.
kampaamaton, hoitamaton.
unkind a. epäystävällinen, kova, tyly,
ilkeä; huono (sää). **-ly** adv.
epäystävällisesti; a. = ed.
unknow|ing a. tietämätön. **-n** a.
tuntematon, outo, vieras; ~ to me
tietämättäni; the ~ warrior
tuntematon sotilas.
un|lace v. avata (kengän)nauhat. **-lade**
v. purkaa lasti, tyhjentää. **-ladylike** a.
sopimaton hienolle naiselle. **-latch** v.
avata säppi. **-lawful** a. laiton,
lainvastainen, luvaton.
unlearn v. unohtaa (oppimansa). **-ed**
[-id] a. oppimaton.
un|leash v. laskea valloilleen.
-leavened a. happamaton. **-less**
[ʌn'les, ən-] konj. ellei, jollei.
-lettered a. oppimaton. **-licensed** a.
valtuuttamaton; luvaton, sala-.
unlike a. erilainen; adv. toisin kuin.

-**lihood** s. epätodennäköisyys. -**ly** [ʌn'laikli] a. epätodennäköinen; vähän lupaava; *it is not at all* ~ on varsin mahdollista.

un|**limited** a. rajoittamaton, rajaton. -**lined** a. sisustamaton, vuoriton. -**load** v. purkaa (lasti); nostaa panos; keventää. -**lock** v. avata (lukko); irrottaa. -**locked** a. lukitsematon. -**looked-for** a. odottamaton, arvaamaton. -**loose** v. irrottaa, päästää auki.

unlov|**ely** a. epämiellyttävä. -**ing** a. kovasydäminen, tyly.

unluck|**ily** adv. pahaksi onneksi. -**y** a. onneton, kovaonninen.

un|**make** v. tuhota, tehdä tyhjäksi. -**man** v. masentaa jkn rohkeus; ~ned ilman miehistöä (oleva). -**manageable** a. kuriton, vaikea t. mahdoton käsitellä. -**manly** a. epämiehekäs. -**mannerly** a. sivistymätön, huonokäytöksinen. -**marked** a. huomaamatta jäänyt, merkitsemätön. -**married** a. naimaton. -**mask** v. riisua naamio, paljastaa. -**matched** a. verraton. -**meaning** a. tahaton; merkityksetön. -**mentionable** sopimaton (lausuttavaksi). -**merciful** armoton, säälimätön. -**merited** ansaitsematon. -**mindful** a.: ~ of jstk välinpitämätön. -**mistakable** a. ilmeinen, selvä. -**mitigated** lieventymätön. -**mixed** sekoittamaton. -**molested** häiritsemätön. -**moved** heltymätön; liikuttumatta. -**natural** luonnoton.

unnecessar|**ily** adv. tarpeettoma|n, -sti. -**y** a. tarpeeton, turha.

un|**nerve** v. lamaannuttaa, riistää jklta rohkeus. -**noticed** huomaamatta jäänyt. -**objectionable** harmiton. -**obliging** epäkohtelias. -**obtrusive** ei tungetteleva, vaatimaton. -**occupied** varaamaton, vapaa; asumaton. -**official** epävirallinen. -**pack** v. purkaa. -**palatable** vastenmielinen. -**paralleled** vertaa vailla (oleva). -**pardonable** anteeksiantamaton. -**paved** kiveämätön, kestopäällysteetön. -**perturbed** a. hermostumaton, tyyni. -**pick** v. ratkoa (sauma).

unpleasant a. epämiellyttävä, ikävä.

-**ness** s. harmi, ikävyys.

un|**polished** a. kiillottamaton, hiomaton. -**popular** (yleisön) epäsuosiossa oleva.

unpracti|**cal** epäkäytännöllinen. -**sed** a. kokematon, tottumaton, harjaantumaton.

un|**precedented** a. ennenkuulumaton. -**predictable** arvaamaton, oikullinen. -**prejudiced** ennakkoluuloton, puolueeton. -**premeditated** harkitsematon. -**prepared** valmistamaton, valmistumaton. -**prepossessing** a. ei puoleensa vetävä. -**presuming** a. vaatimaton. -**pretending,** -**pretentious** a. vaatimaton. -**principled** a. periaatteeton. -**printable** a. sopimaton painettavaksi. -**productive** a. hedelmätön, ei tuottava. -**professional** a. ei ammattimainen, harrastaja-. -**profitable** voittoa t. hyötyä tuottamaton, kannattamaton. -**promising** vähän lupaava. -**pronounceable** mahdoton ääntää. -**propitious** epäsuotuisa. -**protected** a. suojaton, turvaton. -**provided** a.: ~ for turvaton, huoltoa vailla. -**provoked** provosoimaton, aiheeton. -**punctual** epätäsmällinen. -**qualified** ehdoton, täydellinen; ~ (for) epäpätevä. -**quenchable** sammumaton.

unquestion|**able** kiistaton, epäämätön. -**ed** kieltämätön, eittämätön. -**ing** a. ehdoton, empimätön.

un|**ravel** [ʌn'rævl] v. selvittää (sotku), purkaa, purkautua; ratkaista.

unreal a. epätodellinen, kuviteltu. -**ity** s. epätodellisuus.

unreason|**able** a. kohtuuton. -**ing** a. järjetön.

un|**recognizable** a. mahdoton tuntea. -**recognized** a. (psyk.) tiedostamaton. -**recorded** muistiin merkitsemätön. -**redeemed** lunastamaton. -**refined** jalostamaton: hienostumaton. -**regenerate** a. uudesti syntymätön, turmeltunut. -**related** ei sukua oleva, ei jhk liittyvä, aivan muu. -**relenting** heltymätön, kova, armoton. -**reliable** epäluotettava. -**relieved** ilman vaihtelua oleva. -**remitting** lakkaamaton; uupumaton. -**repentant**

katumaton. **-requited** palkitsematon,
yksipuolinen. **-reserved** ehdoton,
varaukseton; avomielinen;
varaamaton. **-resolved** ratkaisematon.
-responsive välinpitämätön.

unrest s. levottomuus.

un|restrained hillitön. **-restricted**
rajoittamaton, rajaton. **-rewarding**
epäkiitollinen. **-righteous** väärä;
jumalaton. **-ripe** kypsymätön, raaka.
-rivalled vertaa vailla oleva. **-roll** v.
levittää auki, avata; avautua. **-ruffled**
tyven; rauhallinen. **-ruly**
niskoitteleva; kuriton. **-safe** a.
epävarma, vaarallinen. **-saleable** a.
mahdoton myydä.

unsatis|factory a. epätyydyttävä,
riittämätön. **-fied** a. tyydyttämätön;
tyytymätön.

un|savoury mauton, vastenmielinen.
-say v. peruuttaa (sanansa). **-scathed**
a. vahingoittumaton. **-screw** v. kiertää
auki t. irti. **-scrupulous** a.
häikäilemätön, tunnoton. **-seal** v.
murtaa sinetti, avata.

unseason|able a. vuodenajalle
sopimaton t. harvinainen, huonoon
aikaan tapahtuva. **-ably** adv.
sopimattomaan aikaan. **-ed** a.
maustamaton, höystämätön; kostea
(puutavara); karaistumaton, (to jhk)
tottumaton.

un|seat v. heittää satulasta; riistää
edustajanpaikka (parl.). **-seeing**
sokea. **-seemly** sopimaton, säädytön.
-seen a. näkemätön; the ~ näkymätön
maailma; ~ [translation]
valmistamatta suoritettu käännös.
-selfish epäitsekäs.

unsettle v. saattaa epäjärjestykseen,
järkyttää; hämmentää (järki). **-d** a.
levoton; epävakaa, vaihteleva;
ratkaisematon; maksamaton.

un|shaken järkkymätön, luja. **-shapely**
muodoton, ruma. **-sheathe** vetää
huotrasta, paljastaa. **-ship** purkaa
(laivasta). **-shrinking** a. peloton.
-sightly a. ruma, epämuotoinen.

unskil|ful a. taitamaton, pystymätön.
-led a. = ed ; ammattitaidoton; ~
worker sekatyömies; ~ labour
ammattitaidoton työvoima.

un|slaked sammuttamaton. **-sociable**
seuraa vierova. **-solved**

ratkaisematon. **-sophisticated**
teeskentelemätön, luonnollinen,
yksinkertainen. **-sound** a. epäterve,
sairaalloinen, turmeltunut,
pilaantunut; väärä; epäluotettava,
epävarma, kestämätön; of ~ mind
mielisairas. **-sparing** antelias,
tuhlaileva. **-speakable** sanomaton,
kuvaamaton. **-sporting** (puhek.)
epäreilu. **-sportsmanlike** a.
epäurheilijamainen; = ed. **-spotted**
tahraton, puhdas. **-stable** horjuva,
epävakainen. **-stamped** a.
leimaamaton; ilman postimerkkiä.
-steady epävakainen, horjuva;
säännötön. **-stinted** runsas, antelias.
-stop v. avata (tukoksista). **-strap** a.
avata (hihnat). **-stressed** painoton.

un|strung hermostunut. **-studied**
luonnollinen, vapaa. **-substantial**
heikko, hatara; epätodellinen,
kuviteltu. **-successful** epäonnistunut;
be ~ epäonnistua. **-suitable**
sopimaton. **-sullied** tahraton.
-surmountable voittamaton.
-suspecting pahaa aavistamaton,
hyväuskoinen. **-swerving**
järkkymätön. **-sympathetic**
myötätuntoa vailla (oleva),
välinpitämätön. **-tainted**
pilaantumaton. **-tamed** kesyttämätön,
hurja. **-taxed** veroton. **-teachable**
kankeaoppinen. **-tempered**
karkaisematon; hillitön. **-tenable**
kestämätön, paikkansa pitämätön.
-tenanted asumaton. **-tended**
hoitamaton.

unthink|able a. mahdoton kuvitella.
-ing ajattelematon, varomaton.

untidy huolimaton, siistimätön.

untie v. irrottaa, aukaista.

until [ən'til] prep. jhk asti; konj.
kunnes; ennen kuin; not ~ vasta kun.

un|timely a. (ajankohtaan) sopimaton;
ennenaikainen; adv. sopimattomaan
aikaan. **-tiring** a. väsymätön,
uupumaton.

unto ['ʌntu] prep. (vanh.) = to.

un|told a. lukematon, määrätön,
mittaamaton. **-touchable** kastiton.
-touched koskematon. **-toward**
[-'tə(u)əd] vastuksellinen, onneton,
ikävä. **-traceable** mahdoton löytää.
-trained kouluttamaton,

harjaantumaton. **-trammelled**
esteetön. **-translatable** a. mahdoton
kääntää. **-tried** koettelematon,
kokematon. **-trodden** a. tallaamaton;
raivaamaton. **-troubled**
häiritsemätön; tyyni. **-true** perätön,
valheellinen; uskoton. **-trustworthy**
epäluotettava.
untruth s. valheellisuus, valhe. **-ful** a.
valheellinen (henkilö).
un|turned a.: leave no stone ~
mullistaa taivaat ja maat, tehdä
kaikkensa. **-tutored** a.
kouluttamaton, oppimaton. **-twist** v.
kiertää auki; purkautua.
unus|ed a. käyttämätön; [-ju:st]
tottumaton (to jhk). **-ual** a.
harvinainen, epätavallinen.
un|utterable sanomaton, kuvaamaton.
-varied yksitoikkoinen. **-varnished**
vilpitön, koruton. **-varying**
muuttumaton.
unveil v. paljastaa.
un|voiced lausumaton; soinniton.
-wanted ei toivottu. **-warranted**
epäoikeutettu; laiton.
un|wary varomaton, ajattelematon.
-wavering horjumaton, luja.
-wearied, -wearying väsymätön,
uupumaton.
un|welcome a. ei tervetullut,
epämieluinen. **-well** a. pahoinvoipa,
huonovointinen. **-wholesome**
epäterveellinen. **-wieldy** kömpelö,
hankala käsitellä. **-willing** haluton,
vastahakoinen.
unwind v. (ks. wind 2) keriä auki;
kiertyä auki, aueta.
un|wise epäviisas. **-witting** a.
tietämätön; tietämättään,
tahtomattaan (m. ~ly). **-womanly**
epänaisellinen. **-wonted** [-wɔuntid]
harvinainen. **-workable** mahdoton
toteuttaa. **-worldly** ajallisista
piittaamaton. **-worthy** arvoton, (jtk)
ansaitsematon; kelvoton.
un|wrap v. aukaista (käärö). **-written**
a.: ~ law kirjoittamaton laki.
-yielding taipumaton, järkkymätön.
up [ʌp] adv. ylös, -päin, ylhäällä, -lle;
korkealle, -lla; pystyssä, pystyyn,
jalkeilla; lopussa, päättynyt; lomalla;
int. ylös! prep. ylöspäin, jtk ylös; v.
(leik.) hypähtää pystyyn; ~ there

tuolla ylhäällä; ~ and about jalkeilla;
~ and doing täydessä työssä; ~ and
down [the country] edestakaisin; time
is ~ aika on lopussa; what's ~ mitä on
tekeillä? mikä hätänä? burn ~ palaa
poroksi; get ~ nousta; go ~
(hinnoista) nousta; have sb. ~ for
haastaa oikeuteen jstk; speak ~ ! puhu
kovemmin! [we are] ~ against it
saamme ikävyyksiä; ~ at . . -ssa
opiskelemassa; [well] ~ in perehtynyt
jhk; ~ to jhk asti; what is he ~ to now
mitä (juonia) hänellä nyt on mielessä;
I don't feel ~ to en kykene, en jaksa; it
is ~ to us to do it meidän on tehtävä
se; it's ~ to you to choose sinun on
valittava; ~ to now tähän mennessä;
come ~ with saavuttaa; it is all ~ with
him hän on mennyttä miestä; ~ [the]
country sisämaassa, -maahan; ~ the
river jokea ylöspäin; an ~ train
Lontooseen menevä juna; ~s and
downs onnen vaiheet, myötä- ja
vastoinkäymiset; ~ -and-coming
yritteliäs.

up|braid [ʌp'breid] nuhdella, moittia
(with jstk.). **-bringing** ['---] kasvatus.
-country adv. sisämaahan (päin).
~-date v. saattaa ajan tasalle.
~-grade [ʌp'greid] v. korottaa; s. ['--]
nousu. **-heaval** [ʌp'hi:vl] s. mullistus.
-hill ['-'-] a. nouseva, kohoava;
vaivalloinen, raskas, vaikea; adv.
ylämäkeä.
uphold [ʌp'həuld] v. (ks. hold)
kannattaa, tukea; pitää yllä t.
voimassa; puolustaa. **-er** [-ə] s. tuki;
puolustaja.
upholster [ʌp'həulstə] v. pehmustaa,
verhoilla; sisustaa huone (verhoilla
ym). **-er** [-rə] s. verhoilija. **-y** [-ri] s.
verhoilijanammatti, verhoilu.
up|keep ['--] s. kunnossapito. **-land**
[-ənd] s. ylämaa (tav. ~s); a.
ylämaan-. **-lift** [ʌp'lift] v. kohottaa,
ylentää; s. ['--] maankohoaminen;
(mielen) ylennys.
upon [ə'pɔn, əpɔn] prep. päällä, -lle; =
on; depend ~ it! siitä voit olla varma;
~ my word kunniasanallani.
upper ['ʌpə] a. ylempi, ylä-;
korkeampi; s. pl. (kengän)
päällysnahka; ~ case isot kirjaimet;
~-class yläluokan; ~ room

yläkerroksen huone; *U~ House*
ylähuone (parl.); ~ *storey* yläkerta,
(sl.) pää; *the ~ ten* [*thousand*]
yläluokka, hienosto; *get the ~ hand*
saada yliote; *on one's ~ s* (sl.)
ahtaalla, vaikeuksissa. **-cut** *s.* koukku
(nyrkk.). **-most** *a.* ylin, korkein; *be ~*
olla ensi sijalla, päällimmäisenä.
uppish [ˈʌpiʃ] *a.* ylpeä, mahtaileva;
don't be too ~ älä ole liikaa olevinasi.
up|right [ˈʌprait] *a.* pysty, kohtisuora;
suora, rehellinen; *s.* pylväs; pianiino
(*~piano*); *adv.* [ʌpˈrait] pystyssä,
-yyn. **-rising** *s.* kansannousu.
uproar [ˈʌprɔ:] *s.* hämminki, meteli;
hälinä; *make an ~* (lapsista)
mekastaa. **-ious** [ʌpˈrɔ:riəs] *a.*
meluava.
uproot [ʌpˈru:t] *v.* kiskoa juurineen.
upset 1. [ʌpˈset] *v.* (ks. *set*) kaataa;
tehdä tyhjäksi; järkyttää, saattaa pois
tolaltaan; panna sekaisin t.
epäkuntoon (ruoansulatus); *s.*
kaatuminen, keikahdus; järkytys;
(urh.) yllätys; *~ting* hermostuttava
kuohuttava; [*be*] *~* (m.) kiihtynyt.
upset 2. [ˈʌpset] *a.: ~ price* (alin)
huutokauppahinta.
up|shot [ˈʌpʃɔt] *s.* lopullinen tulos,
päätös; *the ~ of the matter was* asia
päättyi siihen että. **-side down** *adv.*
ylösalaisin, skin sokin, mullin mallin.
-stairs [-ˈstɛəz] *adv.* yläkerrassa,
-kertaan; *a.* yläkerran. **-standing** *a.*
ryhdikäs, rehti. **-start** *s.* nousukas.
-stream *adv.* vastavirtaan. **-surge** *s.*
elpyminen. **-take** *s.* käsityskyky; *slow
in the ~* hidasälyinen. **-tight** *a.* kireä
(kuv.), jännittynyt; *don't get ~!* älä
hikeenny!
up-to-date [ˈʌptədeit] *a.*
ajanmukainen, uudenaikainen.
upward [ˈʌpwəd] *a.* ylöspäin
suunnattu; nouseva; *adv.* = seur. **-s**
[-z] *adv.* ylöspäin, ylös; enemmän;
and ~ ja siitä yli.
ur(a)emia [ju:ˈri:miə] *s.*
virtsamyrkytys.
Ural [ˈjuər(ə)l] *erisn.: the ~ s* Uralin
vuoristo.
uranium [juəˈreinjəm] *s.* uraani.
urban [ˈɔ:bən] *a.* kaupunki-. **-e**
[ɔ:ˈbein] *a.* hienostunut, kohtelias.
-ity [ɔ:ˈbæniti] *s.* hieno käytöstapa,

kohteliaisuus. **-ization** [-aiˈzeiʃn] *s.*
kaupungistuminen,
kaupunkilaistuminen. **-ize** [-aiz] *v.*
kaupungistaa; *become ~d*
kaupungistua, kaupunkilaistua.
urchin [ˈɔ:tʃin] *s.* poikaviikari.
urethra [u:ˈri:θrə] *s.* virtsaputki.
urg|e [ɔ:dʒ] *v.* jouduttaa, kiirehtiä,
kannustaa (*~ on*); yllyttää;
(vakavasti) kehottaa; *s.* pakottava
halu (kutsumus); vietti; *~ upon sb.*
tähdentää jklle, teroittaa jkn mieleen.
-ency [-(ə)nsi] *s.* pakko, kiireellisyys,
(kiireellinen) tarve; itsepintaisuus.
-ent [-(ə)nt] *a.* kiireellinen, tärkeä;
kiihkeä, itsepintainen; *in ~ need
of. .* kipeässä tarpeessa.
uric [ˈjuərik] *a.: ~ acid* virtsahappo.
urin|al [ˈjuərin|l] *s.* virtsalasi; käymälä,
pisoaari. **-ary** [-əri] *a.* virtsa-; *~ tract*
(t. *passages*) virtsatiet. **-ate** [-eit] *v.*
virtsata. **-e** [ˈjuərin] *s.* virtsa.
urn [ə:n] *s.* uurna, m. tuhkauurna
(*funeral ~*); teekeitin, kahvinkeitin.
urology [juəˈrɔlədʒi] *s.* urologia.
Ursa [ˈɔ:sə] *s.: ~ Major* Iso Karhu,
Otava; *~ Minor* Pikku Karhu.
Uruguay [ˈurugwai] *erisn.*
us [ʌs, əs] *pron.* objektimuoto ks. *we;*
meidät, meitä, meille; *all of ~* me
kaikki; *with ~* meidän kanssamme.
usable [ˈju:zəbl] *a.* käyttökelpoinen.
usage [ˈju:zidʒ] *s.* kohtelu, käsittely;
käyttö, m. kielenkäyttö; totuttu tapa,
käytäntö; *rough ~* kovakourainen
käsittely.
use 1. [ju:s] *s.* käyttö, käyttäminen;
käyttökelpoisuus, hyöty;
käyttöoikeus (vakiintunut) tapa; *be
in ~* olla käytännössä; *come into ~*
tulla käytäntöön; *make ~ of* käyttää
hyväkseen jtk; *put. .to a good ~*
käyttää hyvin; *directions for ~*
käyttöohjeet; *be of ~* olla hyödyksi;
have ~ for tarvita; *it is no ~ trying* ei
kannata yrittää; *what's the ~ of
talking* mitä hyödyttää puhua; *~ of
piano included* pianon käyttöoikeus
sisältyy vuokraan.
use 2. [ju:z] *v.* käyttää; käsitellä,
kohdella; kuluttaa; (vain imperf.) *~d
to* [ˈju:stə, -tu] oli tapana; *he ~d to say*
hänellä oli tapana sanoa; *they ~d to
live here* he asuivat ennen täällä; *~ up*

kuluttaa loppuun, uuvuttaa. **-d** [-d]
pp. käytetty jne.; ['juːst] tottunut; *get*
~ *to* tottua jhk.

use|ful ['juːsf(u)l] *a.* hyödyllinen;
käyttökelpoinen; tehokas, kätevä;
come in ~ olla hyvään tarpeeseen.
-fulness *s.* hyödyllisyys, hyöty. **-less** *a.*
hyödytön; käyttökelvoton; tarpeeton,
turha. **-lessly** *adv.* hyödyttömästi,
turhaan.

user ['juːzə] *s.* käyttäjä.

usher ['ʌʃə] *s.* paikannäyttäjä,
vahtimestari; juhlamenojen ohjaaja,
marsalkka; *v.* ohjata; ilmoittaa
(vieras); ~ *in* aloittaa, edeltää. **-ette**
[-'ret] *s.* paikannäyttäjä (tyttö).

usual ['juːʒuəl] *a.* tavallinen,
tavanmukainen; *as* ~ kuten
tavallisesti; *as is* ~ *with them* kuten
heidän tapansa on. **-ly** *adv.*
tavallisesti.

usufruct ['juːsjufrʌkt] *s.* nautintaoikeus
(lak.).

usur|er ['juːʒ(ə)rə] *s.* koronkiskuri.
-ious [juː'zjuəriəs] *a.* kiskuri-,
kiskonta-.

usurp [juː'zəːp] *v.* anastaa. **-ation**
[-'peiʃn] *s.* anastus. **-er** [-ə] *s.* (vallan)
anastaja.

usury ['juːʒuri] *s.* koronkiskonta;
(kiskuri)korko.

Utah ['juːtɑː] *erisn.*

utensil [juː(ː)'tensl] *s.* talousesine; *pl.*
välineet, tarvikkeet.

uter|ine ['juːtər|ain] *a.* kohtu- (lääk.).
-us [-əs] *s.* kohtu.

utilitarian [juːtili'tɛəriən] *s.*
utilitarismin kannattaja. **-ism** [-izm] *s.*
hyödyllisyysoppi, utilitarismi.

util|ity [juː(ː)'tiliti] *s.* hyödyllisyys,
hyöty; (halpa) käyttö(tavara); *public*
-ities sähkö-, vesi- ja kaasulaitos.
-ization [juːtilai'zeiʃn] *s.*
hyödyksikäyttö. **-ize** ['juːtilaiz] *v.*
käyttää hyödykseen, käyttää.

utmost ['ʌtməust] *a.* äärimmäinen;
mitä suurin; ylin, korkein; *at the* ~
korkeintaan; *to the* ~ viimeiseen
saakka; *do one's* ~ tehdä kaikkensa.

Utopia [juː'təupjə] *s.* Utopia, onnela.
-n [-n] *a.* utopistinen, kuviteltu; *s.*
utopisti.

utter 1. ['ʌtə] *a.* täydellinen, ehdoton.

utter 2. ['ʌtə] *v.* päästää (huuto ym),
lausua, sanoa; laskea liikkeelle; ~ *an*
oath kirota. **-ance** ['ʌt(ə)r(ə)ns] *s.*
ilmaus, lausuma, sanat; ääntäminen;
give ~ *to* ilmaista, tuoda ilmi.

utter|ly *adv.* täysin, kokonaan,
ehdottomasti. **-most** *a.* äärimmäinen
(et. kuv.); = *utmost.*

uvula ['juːvjulə] *s.* kitakieleke.

uxorious [ʌk'sɔːriəs] *a.* ylenpalttisesti
vaimoonsa kiintynyt.

V

V, v [viː] *s.* v-kirjain.
　Lyh.: **v.** *versus* vastaan, *(vide) see;* **Va.**
　Virginia; **vb** *verb;* **V.C.**
　Vice-Chancellor, Victoria Cross; **V.D.**
　veneral disease; **V E Day** *Victory in*
　Europe (8.5.1945); **Ven.** *Venerable;*
　v.g. *very good;* **V.H.F.** *very high*
　frequency metriaaltoalue (rad.);
　V.I.P. [ˈviːaiˈpiː] *very important*
　person; **viz.** *(videlicet) namely;* **vol.**
　volume; **vs.** *versus;* **vv.** *verses.*
vac [væk] (= *vacation*) loma.
vacan|cy [ˈveik(ə)nsi] *s.* tyhjyys (m.
　kuv.), tyhjä tila; avoin virka, vakans-
　si. **-t** [-(ə)nt] *a.* tyhjä, avoin; varaama-
　ton; vapaa, joutilas; ilmeetön, tylsä.
vaca|te [vəˈkeit] *v.* jättää tyhjäksi,
　tyhjentää; jättää, luopua. **-tion**
　[vəˈkeiʃn] *s.* loma, -aika;
　tyhjentäminen, jättäminen.
vaccin|ate [ˈvæksineit] *v.* rokottaa.
　-ation [-ˈneiʃn] *s.* rokotus. **-e**
　[ˈvæksiːn] *s.* rokote.
vacillat|e [ˈvæsileit] *v.* horjua, häilyä,
　epäröidä. **-ing** *a.* horjuva, epävarma.
　-ion [-ˈleiʃn] *s.* horjuminen, häilyvyys.
vacu|ity [væˈkjuː(ː)iti] *s.* tyhjyys;
　älyttömyys. **-ous** [ˈvækjuəs] *a.* tyhjä;
　älytön. **-um** [ˈvækjuəm] *s.* tyhjiö,
　tyhjö; tyhjä tila; alipaine; *v.*
　puhdistaa pölynimurilla, imuroida;
　~ *cleaner* pölynimuri; ~ *flask*
　termospullo; ~ *pitcher* termoskannu.
vade-mecum [ˈveidiˈmiːkəm] *s.*
　(tasku)käsikirja.
vagabond [ˈvægəbɔnd] *a.* kuljeskeleva,
　kiertelevä; *s.* kulkuri, maankiertäjä;
　tyhjäntoimittaja.
vagary [ˈveigəri] *s.* (omituinen)
　päähänpisto, oikku.
vagina [vəˈdʒainə] *s.* emätin.
vagr|ancy [ˈveigr(ə)nsi] *s.* irtolaisuus,
　kulkurielämä. **-ant** [-(ə)nt] *a.*

kuljeskeleva, kiertelevä; harhaileva;
　s. maankiertäjä, irtolainen.
vague [veig] *a.* epämääräinen,
　epäselvä, epävarma, hämärä. **-ness** *s.*
　epämääräisyys.
vain [vein] *a.* turha, tyhjä(npäiväinen);
　hyödytön, hukkaan mennyt;
　turhamainen; *in* ~ turhaan; *take* [*the*
　name of God] *in* ~ lausua turhaan.
　-glorious *a.* pöyhkeilevä,
　omahyväinen. **-glory** [-ˈ--] *s.*
　omahyväisyys, turhamaisuus. **-ly** *adv.*
　turhaan; turhamaisesti.
valance [ˈvæləns] *s.* poikkiverho,
　kappa, rimssu.
vale [veil] *s.* (run.) laakso; ~ *of tears*
　murheen laakso.
valedic|tion [væliˈdikʃn] *s.* hyvästijättö.
　-tory [-ˈdiktori] *a.* jäähyväis-. **-torian**
　s. päättäjäispuheen pitäjä, tav.
　priimus.
valentine [ˈvæləntain] *s.* (Pyhän
　Valentinin päivänä valittu) lemmitty;
　kortti t. lahja V:n päiväksi; *St.* V~'s
　day helmikuun 14. päivä.
Valera [vəˈlɛərə] *erisn.*
valet [ˈvælit] *s.* mies-, kamaripalvelija;
　v. olla (jkn) palvelijana.
valetudinarian [ˈvælitjuːdiˈnɛəriən] *a.*
　& s. kivulloinen, raihnas (henkilö),
　luulosairas.
valiant [ˈvæljənt] *a.* urhea.
valid [ˈvælid] *a.* (laillisesti) pätevä,
　sitova, lakivoimainen; hyvin
　perusteltu; *is* ~ *on* voimassa. **-ate**
　[-eit] *v.* laillistaa, vahvistaa. **-ity**
　[væˈliditi] *s.* pätevyys, lainvoimaisuus.
valise [vəˈliːz, Am. -iːs] *s.* (et. Am.)
　matkalaukku; (pieni) reppu.
valley [ˈvæli] *s.* laakso.
valorous [ˈvælərəs] *a.* urhoollinen,
　urhea.
valour, valor [ˈvælə] *s.* urhoollisuus,

rohkeus.

valua|ble ['væljuəbl] *a.* arvokas, kallisarvoinen; ~s kalleudet, arvoesineet. **-tion** [-'eiʃn] *s.* arviointi; (arvioitu) arvo.

value ['vælju:] *s.* arvo; merkitys; *v.* arvioida; pitää arvossa, arvostaa; *to the* ~ *of*. . n arvosta; ~ *received* arvo saatu; *of* ~ arvokas; *of no* ~ arvoton; *it gives good* ~ se on hintansa arvoinen; ~ *highly* pitää suuressa arvossa. **~-added tax** (lyh. *VAT*) lisäarvonvero. **-d** [-d] *a.* arvioitu; arvossapidetty. **-less** *a.* arvoton. **-r** [-ə] *s.* arviomies.

valv|e [vælv] *s.* venttiili, läppä (m. anat.); radioputki. **-ular** [-julə] *a.* läppä-.

vamoose [və'mu:s] *v.* Am. sl. pötkiä pakoon, häipyä.

vamp 1. [væmp] *s.* (kengän) päällisnahka; *v.* parannella, paikata (tav. ~ *up);* sepittää (säestys).

vamp 2. [væmp] *s.* vamppi, viettelijätär; *v.* vietellä, vampata.

vampire ['væmpaiə] *s.* verenimijä, vampyyri.

van 1. [væn] *s.* etujoukko, kärki(joukko).

van 2. [væn] *s.* pakettiauto, (umpinainen) kuljetusauto, muuttovaunut; asuntovaunu; *luggage* ~ matkatavaravaunu.

Vancouver [væn'ku:və] *erisn.*

Vandal ['vændl] *s.* vandaali. **v~ism** [-izm] *s.* vandalismi, hävitysvimma.

vane [vein] *s.* tuuliviiri; (potkurin, myllyn) siipi.

vanguard ['vænga:d] *s.* etujoukko, kärki(joukko).

vanilla [və'nilə] *s.* vanilja.

v nish ['væniʃ] *v.* kadota, häipyä, haihtua; ~*ing cream* päivävoide.

vanity ['væniti] *s.* turhamaisuus; turhuus; *V~ Fair* turhuuden markkinat.

vanquish ['væŋkwiʃ] *v.* voittaa, kukistaa.

vantage ['va:ntidʒ] *s.:* ~ *point,* ~ *ground* edullinen asema.

vapid ['væpid] *a.* väljähtynyt, lattea, hengetön.

vapor|ize ['veipər|aiz] *v.* muuttaa t. muuttua höyryksi, höyrystää, -tyä.

-ous [-əs] *a.* höyryinen, höyrymäinen; (vanh.) turha, kuviteltu.

vapour, vapor ['veipə] *s.* höyry; huuru, usva; *pl.* kuvittelut, (vanh.) raskasmielisyys.

variability [veəriə'biliti] *s.* vaihtelevuus, epävakaisuus.

varia|ble ['veəriəbl] *a.* muuttuva, vaihteleva; epävakainen; *s.* muuttuja (mat.). **-nce** [-əns] *s.* ristiriitaisuus, epäsopu, riita; *at* ~ epäsovussa, ristiriidassa. **-nt** [-ənt] *a.* poikkeava, erilainen; *s.* toisinto, muunnos. **-tion** [-'eiʃn] *s.* vaihtelu; muunnos; muunnelma (mus.).

varicose ['værikəus] *a.:* ~ *veins* suonikohjut.

varied ['veərid] *a.* vaihteleva; moninainen, sekalainen, kirjava.

variegated ['veərigeitid] *a.* kirjava, monivärinen.

variety [və'raiəti] *s.* vaihtelu; moninaisuus; laji, lajike; *a* ~ *of* monenlaisia, useita eri; ~ [*show*] varietee.

various ['veəriəs] *a.* eri, erilainen, monenlainen, moninainen; useat(a); *for* ~ *reasons* monesta eri syystä.

varmint ['va:mint] *s.* (vanh.) vintiö.

varnish ['va:niʃ] *s.* vernissa, lakka; ulkokiilto, pintakoreus; *v.* lakata, kaunistella.

varsity ['va:s(i)ti] *s.* (puhek.) = *university.*

vary ['veəri] *v.* vaihdella, tehdä vaihtelevaksi, muuttaa; olla erilainen, poiketa; *they varied in price from* . . niiden hinta vaihteli -sta . .

vascular ['væskjulə] *a.* suoni-.

vase [va:z, Am. veis] *s.* maljakko.

vaseline ['væsili:n] *s.* vaseliini.

vaso- ['veizəu-] *a.* verisuoni(a)-.

vassal ['væsl] *s.* vasalli; alamainen, orja. **-age** [-əlidʒ] *s.* vasallius.

vast [va:st] *a.* avara, valtava; suunnattoman suuri, ääretön. **-ly** *adv.* suunnattoman. **-ness** *s.* (suunnaton) laajuus.

vat [væt] *s.* iso allas, sammio.

Vatican ['vætikən] *s.: the* ~ Vatikaani.

Vaughan ['vo:n] *erisn.*

vault [vo:lt] *s.* holvi; hautaholvi; hyppy; *v.* holvata; hypätä (jnk yli, jhk); *pole* ~ seiväshyppy; ~*ing* [*ambition*]

ylenmääräinen. **-ed** *a.* holvattu. **-ing** *s.*
holvirakennus, holvisto. **-ing-horse**
(voim.) (hyppy)arkku.

vaunt [vɔ:nt] *v.* ylvästellä, kerskailla; *s.*
kerskailu.

veal [vi:l] *s.* vasikanliha.

veer [viə] *v.* muuttaa suuntaa; muuttaa
mielensä (us. ~ *round*).

vegeta|ble ['vedʒ|təbl] *a.* kasvi(s)-; *s.:*
~ *s* vihannekset, kasvikset; ~
kingdom kasvikunta; ~ *mould*
ruokamulta. **-l** [-itl] *a.* kasvi-. **-rian**
[-i'teəriən] *s.* kasvissyöjä; *a.* kasvis-.
-te [-iteit] *v.* kasvaa, elellä toimetonna
(ajatuksiaan rasittamatta). **-tion**
[-i'teiʃn] *s.* kasvillisuus. **-tive** [-itətiv]
a. vegetatiivinen.

vehem|ence ['vi:əməns] *s.* kiivaus,
rajuus, kiihko. **-ent** [-ənt] *a.* kiihkeä,
kiivas, raju; ankara, kova.

vehic|le ['viəkl] *s.* ajoneuvo,
kulkuneuvo; ilmaisukeino, väline;
liuote. **-ular** [vi'hikjulə] *a.* ajoneuvo-,
ajo-.

veil [veil] *s.* harso, huntu; peite, verho;
v. hunnuttaa; verhota, peittää, salata;
under the ~ *of* jnk varjolla; *take the* ~
ruveta nunnaksi.

vein [vein] *s.* laskimo; suoni; taipumus,
juonne; (geol.) juoni; *in the right* ~
oikeassa vireessä. **-ed** [-d] *a.*
suoninen; juovikas.

veldt [velt] *s.* (Et.-Afr.) ruohoaavikko.

vellum ['veləm] *s.*
(vasikannahka)pergamentti.

velocity [vi'lɔs(i)ti] *s.* nopeus.

velum ['vi:ləm] *s.* kitapurje.

velvet ['velvit] *s.* sametti; *a.* sametti-,
sametinpehmeä. **-een** [-'ti:n] *s.*
puuvillasametti. **-y** [-i] *a.*
samettimainen.

venal ['vi:nl] *a.* ostettavissa,
lahjottavissa (oleva). **-ity** [vi:'næliti] *s.*
lahjottavuus.

vend [vend] *v.* myydä. **-or** [-ɔ:] *s.*
myyjä, kaupustelija.

veneer [və'niə] *v.* päällystää
(jalommalla puulla); *s.* ohut
(jalopuu)kerros; pinta, pintakiilto.

venera|ble ['venrəbl] *a.*
kunnianarvoisa, kunnioitettava. **-te**
['venəreit] *v.* kunnioittaa. **-tion**
[-'reiʃn] *s.* kunnioitus.

venereal [vi'niəriəl] *a.* sukupuoli-,

veneerinen.

Venetian [vi'ni:ʃn] *a. & s.*
venetsialainen; ~ *blind* sälekaihdin.

Venezuela [venə'zweilə] *erisn.* **-n** [-n] *a.*
& s. Venezuelan, venezuelalainen.

vengeance ['vendʒəns] *s.* kosto; *with a*
~ perusteellisesti, (sateesta)
ryöppynä.

venial ['vi:njəl] *a.* anteeksiannettava,
vähäpätöinen.

Venice ['venis] *erisn.* Venetsia.

venison ['venzn] *s.* hirvenliha.

venom ['venəm] *s.* myrkky; ilkeys. **-ous**
[-əs] *a.* myrkyllinen.

venous ['vi:nəs] *a.* laskimo-; suoninen.

vent [vent] *s.* ilma-, henkireikä, aukko;
sankkireikä; purkautumistie; *v.*
päästää valloilleen; purkaa; *find* [*a*] ~
purkautua; *give* ~ *to* [*one's anger*]
purkaa.

ventila|te ['ventileit] *v.* tuulettaa;
käsitellä julkisesti, pohtia. **-tion**
[-'leiʃn] *s.* tuuletus, ilmanvaihto. **-tor**
[-ə] *s.* tuuletin.

ventri|cle ['ventrikl] *s.* ontelo,
(sydän)kammio. **-loquist**
[ven'triləkwist] *s.* vatsastapuhuja.

venture ['ventʃə] *s.* (uskalias) yritys,
uhkapeli; keinottelu; panos; *v.*
uskaltaa, uskaltautua, rohjeta;
vaarantaa; *at a* ~ umpimähkään.
-some [-səm] *a.* uskalias, uhkarohkea.

venue ['venju:] *s.* tapahtumapaikka,
kohtauspaikka.

Venus ['vi:nəs] *erisn.*

Vera ['viərə] *erisn.*

verac|ious [və'reiʃəs] *a.* totuudessa
pysyvä, tosi. **-ity** [və'ræsiti] *s.*
totuudenmukaisuus.

veranda(h) [və'rændə] *s.* (katettu)
veranta, kuisti.

verb [və:b] *s.* verbi. **-al** [-(ə)l] *a.* sana-,
sanallinen; suullinen;
sananmukainen; verbi-; ~ *ly*
suullisesti. **-atim** [və:'beitim] *adv.*
sanasta sanaan, sananmukaisesti.

verbena [və(:)'bi:nə] *s.* rautayrtti.

verb|iage ['və:biiʒ] *s.* monisanaisuus.
-ose [və:'bəus] *a.* monisanainen.
-osity [və:'bɔsiti] *s.* monisanaisuus.

verd|ancy ['və:d(ə)nsi] *s.* vehreys. **-ant**
[-(ə)nt] *a.* viheriöivä, vehreä;
kokematon.

verdict ['və:dikt] *s.* tuomio, ratkaisu,

päätös.

verdigris ['vɔːdigris] s. espanjanvihreä, vaskenruoste.

verdure ['vɔːdʒə] s. vehreys, vihanta.

verge [vɔːdʒ] s. ääri, reuna, parras, laita, raja; v.: ~ [up] on lähestyä, olla jnk rajalla; on the ~ of ruin perikadon partaalla; on the ~ of [80] .. kynnyksellä. **-r** [-ə] s. kirkonvahtimestari, suntio; (piispan ym) sauvankantaja.

verifi|able ['verifaiəbl] a. todistettavissa (oleva). **-cation** [-fi'keiʃn] s. varmennus, oikeaksi todistaminen.

veri|fy ['verifai] v. varmistaa, varmentaa; tarkistaa; todentaa, todistaa oikeaksi. **-ly** adv. totisesti. **-similitude** s. todennäköisyys. **-table** [-təbl] a. tosi, todellinen, oikea, aito. **-ty** [-ti] s. totuus.

vermi|celli [vɔːmiˈseli] s. lankamakaronit. **-form** ['- -] a. matomainen.

vermilion [vəˈmiljən] a. & s. helakanpunainen (väri).

vermin ['vɔːmin] s. (sg. = pl.) tuholaiset; syöpäläiset; roskaväki. **-ous** [-əs] a. syöpäläisiä täynnä oleva, syöpäläisten aiheuttama.

Vermont [vɔːˈmɔnt] erisn.

vermouth ['vɔːməθ, Am. vɔːˈmuːθ] s. vermutti.

vernacular [vəˈnækjulə] a. maan, kansan (kieli ym); s. kansankieli, -murre.

vernal ['vɔːnl] a. kevään, keväinen; ~ equinox kevätpäiväntasaus.

Verona [vəˈrəunə] erisn.

Veronica [vəˈrɔnikə] erisn.

versatil|e ['vɔːsətail] a. monipuolinen. **-ity** [-ˈtiliti] s. monipuolisuus.

vers|e [vɔːs] s. säe; runo; jae; säkeistö; runomuoto(inen); in ~ runomitalla. **-ed** [-t] a.: ~ in jhk perehtynyt, jssk taitava. **-ification** [-ifiˈkeiʃn] s. runoilu, runonsepittely. **-ifier** [-ifaiə] v. pukea runomuotoon; runoilla.

version ['vɔːʃn] s. käännös; versio, tulkinta; Authorized V~ v:n 1611 raamatunkäännös.

versus ['vɔːsəs] prep. vastaan (lyh. v.)

vertebr|a ['vɔːtibrə] s. (pl. -ae [-iː]) selkänikama. **-ate** [-it] a. & s.

selkärankainen.

vert|ex ['vɔːteks] s. (pl. -ices [-isiːz]) huippu; päälaki. **-ical** ['vɔːtik(ə)l] a. pystysuora; ~ line pystyviiva.

verti|ginous [vɔːˈtidʒinəs] a. pyörivä; huimaus-. **-go** ['vɔːtigəu] s. huimaus (lääk.).

verve [vɔːv] s. into, vauhti, lennokkuus.

very [veri] a. tosi, todellinen, oikea, juuri (sama), juuri se (oikea); yksinpä, pelkkä; adv. hyvin, sangen, varsin, erittäin; oikein; (superl. ed.) kaikkein; in the ~ act itse teossa; from the ~ beginning aivan alusta; at that ~ moment juuri sillä hetkellä; at the ~ end aivan lopussa; at the ~ latest viimeistään; our ~ thoughts jopa ajatuksemmekin; for my ~ own idiomakseni; ~ well erittäin hyvin; hyvä on! oh, ~ well [if . . olkoon menneeksi; not ~ ei erikoisen.

vesic|le ['vesikl] s. rakkula. **-ular** [veˈsikjulə] a. rakon-, rakkulanmuotoinen.

vesper ['vespə] s.: ~s iltajumalanpalvelus.

vessel ['vesl] s. astia; alus, laiva; blood ~ verisuoni; the weaker ~ heikompi astia.

vest [vest] s. ihokas, aluspaita; Am. (miesten) liivit; (puvun) etumus; v. antaa, uskoa jklle (with); be ~ ed in joutua jklle, kuulua jklle, olla jkn hallussa.

vestal ['vest] s. vestaali; a. neitseellinen.

vested ['vestid] a. vakiintunut, laillisesti saatu, lain myöntämä.

vestibule ['vestibjuːl] s. eteinen, eteishalli; ~ train (Am.) läpikuljettava juna.

vestige ['vestidʒ] s. jälki, merkki; hiven, rahtu.

vestment ['vestmənt] s. messupuku; virka-asu.

vestry ['vestri] s. sakaristo; kirkkoneuvosto. **-man** kirkkoneuvoston jäsen.

Vesuvius [viˈsuːvjəs] erisn.

vet [vet] s. (lyh.) eläinlääkäri; v. tutkia, tarkistaa.

vetch [vetʃ] s. virna.

veter n ['vetr(ə)n] s. sotavanhus,

veteraani; entinen rintamamies; *a.*
vanha ja kokenut.
veterinary ['vetrin(ə)ri] *a.*
eläinlääkintä, eläinlääkäri(n); *s.*
eläinlääkäri (m. ~ *surgeon*).
veto ['vi:tou] *s.* (pl. ~*es*) veto-oikeus;
v. (~*ed*) käyttää vetoaan (m. *cast
one's* ~), estää (päätöksen)
voimaantulo.
vex [veks] *v.* suututtaa, harmittaa;
kiusata. **-ation** ['-eiʃn] *s.* harmi, kiusa.
-atious ['-'eiʃəs] *a.* harmillinen,
kiusallinen; tuskastuttava. **-ed** [-t] *a.*
harmistunut, suuttunut; ~*ed question*
kiistakysymys; ~*ing* harmillinen,
kiusallinen.
via ['vaiə] *prep.* jnk kautta. **-duct**
[-dʌkt] *s.* maasilta.
viable ['vaiəbl] *a.* elinkykyinen.
vial ['vaiəl] *s.* pieni (lääke)pullo.
viands ['vaiəndz] *s. pl.* ruokatavarat.
vibra|nt ['vaibr(ə)nt] *a.* värähtelevä,
väräjävä. **-te** [vai'breit] *v.* värähdellä,
väristä. **-tion** [-'reiʃn] *s.* värähdys,
värähtely, heilahtelu.
vicar ['vikə] *s.* kirkkoherra; (katol.)
sijainen. **-age** [-ridʒ] *s.* pappila. **-ious**
[vi'kɛəriəs, Am. vai-] *a.* sijais-; toisen
sijasta kärsitty.
vice 1. [vais] *s.* pahe; (hevosen) paha
tapa.
vice 2. [vais] *s.* ruuvipuristin.
vice- 3. [vais] *pref.* vara-; *prep.* ['vaisi]
asemesta. ~**-chancellor** *s.* (yliopiston)
rehtori. **-gerent** [-'dʒernt] *s.*
käskynhaltija. ~**-president**
vara|puheenjohtaja, -presidentti.
-reine [-rein] *s.* varakuninkaan
puoliso. **-roy** [-rɔi] *s.* (Intian)
varakuningas.
vice versa ['vaisi'və:sə] *adv.*
päinvastoin.
vicinity [vi'siniti] *s.* läheisyys,
lähiseutu, ympäristö.
vicious ['viʃəs] *a.* paheellinen,
turmeltunut, huono; virheellinen;
äksy; kiukkuinen; ~ *circle*
noidankehä, kehäpäätelmä.
vicissitude [vi'sisitju:d] *s.* vaihe,
muutos; *pl.* vaiheet, vaihtelut.
victim ['viktim] *s.* uhrieläin; uhri; *fall a*
~ *to* joutua jnk uhriksi. **-ize** [-aiz] *v.*
ottaa uhrikseen; pettää.
victor ['viktə] *s.* voittaja. **-ia** [-'tɔ:riə] *s.*

kevyet nelipyöräiset vaunut; *the* V~
Cross Viktorian risti (Engl. korkein
sotilaskunniamerkki). **V ~ian**
[-'tɔ:riən] *a. & s.* kuningatar V:n
aikainen t. aikalainen. **-ious** [-'tɔ:riəs]
a. voitollinen, voittoisa. **-y** ['vikt(ə)ri]
s. voitto.
victual ['vitl] *s.:* ~*s* ruokatavarat,
muona; *v.* muonittaa. **-ler** [-ə] *s.*
muonanhankkija. **-ling** *s.* muonitus.
vicuna [vi'kju:nə] *s.* vikunja (laama).
vide ['vaidi(:)] *imp.* katso! (lyh. *v.*).
-licet [vi'di:liset] *adv.* nimittäin (tav.
lyh. *viz.*).
video ['vidiəu] *s.* Am. televisio; ~*tape*
kuvanauha; nauhoittaa.
vie [vai] *v.* (ppr. *vying*) kilpailla.
Vienn|a [vi'enə] *erisn.* Wien. **-ese**
[vie'ni:z] *a.* wieniläis-; *s.* wieniläinen.
Vietnam [vjet'næm] *erisn.* **-ese**
[-nə'mi:z] *a. & s.* vietnamilainen.
view [vju:] *s.* näky, näkö; näköala,
näkymä, maisema; silmäys; tarkastus;
näkökanta, käsityskanta, mielipide,
käsitys, kuva; silmämäärä, aikomus,
tarkoitus; *v.* katsella, silmäillä,
tarkastaa; *point of* ~ näkökanta; *be
lost to* ~ kadota näkyvistä; *in* ~
näkyvissä; *in* ~ *of* jhk katsoen, jtk
huomioonottaen; *in my* ~ minun
mielestäni; *have in* ~ pitää
silmämääränään, aikoa; *on* ~
näytteillä; *with a* ~ *to* jssk
tarkoituksessa. **-er** ['vju:ə] *s.*
(television ym) katselija; katselulaite.
~**-finder** etsin (valok.). **-point**
näkökanta, katsantokanta.
vigil ['vidʒil] *s.* juhlan aatto;
yöjumalanpalvelus; yövalvonta. **-ance**
[-əns] *s.* valppaus; ~ *committee*
valvontajärjestö (rikollisuuden
vastustamiseksi). **-ant** [-ənt] *a.* valpas;
~*es* valppausmiehet; ks. *-ance*
(v.-komitean jäsenet)
vignette [vi'njet] *s.* koristekuvio.
vigorous ['vig(ə)rəs] *a.* voimakas,
ponteva, elinvoimainen.
vigour, vigor ['vigə] *s.* voima,
pontevuus, tarmo.
viking ['vaikiŋ] *s.* viikinki.
vil|e [vail] *a.* kehno, kurja, viheliäinen,
alhainen, inhottava. **-ify** ['vilifai] *v.*
panetella, halventaa.
villa ['vilə] *s.* huvila. **-ge** [vilidʒ] *s.*

kylä. **-ger** ['vilidʒə] s. kyläläinen,
m alainen.

villain ['vilən] s. konna, roisto; lurjus.
-ous [-əs] a. roistomainen,
halpamainen; kurja. **-y** [-i] s.
roistomaisuus; konnankoukku.

vim [vim] s. tarmo, puhti.

vindica|te ['vindikeit] v. puolustaa;
osoittaa oikeaksi. **-tion** [-'keiʃn] s.
puolustus.

vindictive [vin'diktiv] a.
kostonhimoinen. **-ness** s. kostonhimo.

vine [vain] s. viiniköynnös, köynnös.

vinegar ['vinigə] s. etikka. **-y** [-ri] a.
etikanhapan.

vine|ry ['vainəri] s. viiniansari. **-yard**
['vinjəd] s. viinitarha.

vinous ['vainəs] a. viini-.

vint|age ['vintidʒ] s. viinisato;
viininkorjuu(aika); vuosikerta; ~
[wines] hyvää vuosikertaa olevat. **-ner**
['vintnə] s. viinikauppias.

vinyl ['vainil] s. vinyyli.

viol ['vaiəl] s. viola (mus.).

viola 1. [vi'əulə] s. alttoviulu.

viola 2. ['vaiələ] s. orvokki.

viol|ate ['vaiəleit] v. loukata, rikkoa;
tehdä väkivaltaa, raiskata. **-ation**
[-'leiʃn] s. loukkaaminen, loukkaus,
rikkominen; raiskaus. **-ence** [-(ə)ns] s.
rajuus, ankaruus; väkivalta(isuus);
crimes of ~ väkivaltarikokset; there
has been an outbreak of ~
levottomuuksia on sattunut. **-ent**
[-(ə)nt] a. raju, hurja, kiivas, kiihkeä,
väkivaltainen, ankara, voimakas; ~
death väkivaltainen kuolema; lay ~
hands upon tehdä väkivaltaa jklle.

violet ['vaiəlit] s. orvokki; a.
sinipunainen.

violin [vaiə'lin] s. viulu; ~-maker
viulunrakentaja. **-ist** ['vaiəlinist] s.
viulunsoittaja, viulutaiteilija.

violoncello [vaiələn'tʃeləu] s. sello.

viper ['vaipə] s. kyykäärme; käärme.
-ish a. myrkyllinen.

virago [vi'ra:gəu] s. (pl. ~s) syöjätär,
raivotar.

Virgil ['və:dʒil] erisn. Vergilius.

virgin ['və:dʒin] s. neitsyt; a.
neitseellinen, koskematon; the V~
Neitsyt Maria; ~ soil muokkaamaton
maa; ~ forest aarniometsä. **-al** [-l] a.
neitseellinen; s. eräänl. spinetti. **-ity**

[və:'dʒiniti] s. neitsyys.

Virginia [və'dʒinjə] erisn.; ~ creeper
villiviini.

viril|e ['virail] a. miehekäs, ryhdikäs.
-ity [vi'riliti] s. miehekkyys; miehuus.

virology [vai'rɔlədʒi] s. virusoppi.

virtual ['və:tʃuəl, 'və:tjuəl] a.
tosiasiallinen. **-ly** adv.
todellisuudessa, itse asiassa,
käytännöllisesti katsoen.

virtue ['və:tʃu:, 'və:tju:] s. hyve; siveys;
etu, hyvä puoli; teho; by ~ of jnk
nojalla.

virtu|osity [və:tju'ɔsiti] s. taituruus.
-oso [-'əuzou] s. taituri. **-ous**
['və:tjuəs] a. hyveellinen; siveä.

virul|ence ['viruləns] s. myrkyllisyys;
tarttuvuus. **-ent** [-ənt] a. myrkyllinen;
katkera, vihamielinen; tappava;
(lääk.) virulentti.

virus ['vaiərəs] s. virus; (kuv.) myrkky.

visa ['vi:zə] s. viisumi; v. (~ed)
viseerata (passi).

visage ['vizidʒ] s. kasvot.

vis-a-vis ['vi:zavi:, Am. vizə-] adv.
vastapäätä, jnk suhteen.

viscera ['visərə] s. pl. sisälmykset.

visc|id ['visid] a. tahmea, sitkeä. **-osity**
[vis'kɔsiti] s. tahmaisuus, sitkeys.

viscount ['vaikaunt] s. varakreivi. **-ess**
[-is] s. varakreivitär. **-cy** [-si] s.
varakreivin arvo.

viscous ['viskəs] a. tahmea, sitkeä.

vise [vais] s. Am. ruuvipuristin.

visé ['vi:zei] ks. visa.

visibility [vizi'biliti] s. näkyvyys.

visib|le ['vizəbl] a. näkyvä, näkyvissä
oleva; **-ly** silminnähtävästi, ilmeisen.

vision ['viʒ(ə)n] s. näkö, -kyky; näky;
harhanäky, haamu; näkemys;
avarakatseisuus; range of ~ näköpiiri.
-ary [-əri] a. näkyjä näkevä,
haaveellinen; näynomainen, haave-;
s. näkyjen näkijä, haaveilija.

visit ['vizit] v. käydä jssk t. jkn luona,
vierailla; käydä jssk; seurustella; pitää
tarkastus; (vanh.) koetella, rangaista
(jkta on); s. käynti, vierailu; oleskelu;
pay sb. a ~ vierailla, käydä jkn luona;
-ation [-'teiʃn] s. tarkastus;
koettelemus, vitsaus. **-ing** a.
vieraileva; ~-card käyntikortti; ~
hours vierailuaika; ~ nurse
(kotikäyntejä tekevä) terveyssisar.

-or [-ə] s. vieras, kävijä; ~ s' *book* vieraskirja.

visor ['vaizə] s. kypärän silmikko; (lakin) lippa.

vista ['vistə] s. näköala.

Vistula ['vistjulə] *erisn.: the* ~ Veiksel.

visual ['viʒuəl] a. näkö-; ~ *arts* kuvataiteet; ~ *field* näkökenttä. **-ize** [-aiz] v. muodostaa mielikuva, nähdä edessään, muistaa minkä näköinen jku on.

vital ['vaitl] a. elämän-, elin-; elintärkeä, ensiarvoinen; ~ *parts* elintärkeät elimet; ~ *power* elinvoima, ~ *statistics* väestötilasto; *of* ~ *importance* elintärkeä. **-ity** [vai'tæliti] s. elinvoima. **-ize** ['vaitəlaiz] v. elähdyttää. **-ly** *adv.* ensiarvoisen; ~ *important* elintärkeä. **-s** [-z] s. pl. elintärkeät elimet ym.

vitamin ['vitəmin, Am. 'vait-] s. vitamiini.

vitiate ['viʃieit] v. pilata, turmella; tehdä tyhjäksi.

viticulture ['vitikʌltʃə] s. viininviljely.

vitr|eous ['vitriəs] a. lasimainen, lasi-. **-ify** [-ifai] v. lasittua.

vitriol ['vitriol] s. vihtrilli; *blue* ~ kuparisulfaatti. **-ic** [-'ɔlik] a. myrkyllinen.

vitupera|te [vai'tju:pəreit] v. (ankarasti) moittia. **-tion** [-'reiʃn] s. ankara moite, solvaus.

vivac|ious [vi'veiʃəs] a. vilkas, eloisa. **-ity** [vi'væsiti] s. vilkkaus, eloisuus.

viva voce ['vaivə 'vousi] *adv.* suullisesti; s. suullinen tutkinto.

vivid ['vivid] a. vilkas, eloisa, elävä; kirkas, heleä. **-ness** s. elävyys, elokkuus.

vivi|fy ['vivifai] v. elävöittää, elvyttää. **-parous** [vi'vipərəs] a. eläviä poikasia synnyttävä. **-section** [-'sekʃn] s. vivisektio.

vixen ['viksn] s. naaraskettu; äkäpussi.

viz. lyh. (luetaan *namely*) nimittäin, ks. *videlicet*.

vizier [vi'ziə] s. visiiri.

vizor ks. *visor*.

vocabulary [və'kæbjuləri] s. sanasto, sanavarasto.

vocal ['vəuk(ə)l] a. ääni-; puhuttu, äänekäs; ~ *cords* ks. t.; ~ *music* laulumusiikki. **-ic** [və(u)'kælik] a.

vokaali-. **-ist** ['vəukəlist] s. laulaja, -tar. **-ize** ['vəukəlaiz] v. ääntää (soinnillisena); laulaa. **-ly** *adv.* suullisesti, laulaen.

vocation [və(u)'keiʃn] s. kutsumus; ammatti. **-al** [-ʃnl] a.: ~ *school* ammattikoulu; ~ *guidance* ammatinvalinnan ohjaus.

vocative ['vɔkətiv] s. vokatiivi.

vocifer|ate [vəu'sifəreit] v. huutaa, pauhata. **-ation** [-'reiʃn] s. huuto, rähinä. **-ous** [-f(ə)rəs] a. suuriääninen, meluava.

vodka ['vɔdkə] s. votka.

vogue [vəug] s. muoti; suosio; *in* ~ muodissa; *all the* ~ viimeistä huutoa.

voice [vɔis] s. (laulu-, puhe-)ääni; ilmaisu; sanan-, äänivalta, mielipide; pääluokka (kiel.) v. ilmaista; lausua soinnillisena; *give* ~ *to* purkaa ilmi; *I have no* ~ *in the matter* minulla ei ole mitään sanomista asiaan; *in a low* ~ hiljaa; *with one* ~ yksimielisesti. **-d** [-t] a. soinnillinen. **-less** a. soinniton.

void [vɔid] a. tyhjä, paljas, (~ *of*) jtk vailla, jtk puuttuva; mitätön, pätemätön (et. *null &* ~); s. tyhjyys, tyhjä paikka; v. julistaa pätemättömäksi, (vanh.) tyhjentää; ~ *of interest* mielenkiinnoton. **-ness** s. tyhjyys.

volatil|e ['vɔlətail] a. haihtuva; eloisa, epävakainen. **-ity** [vɔlə'tiliti] s. haihtuvuus; huikentelevuus. **-ize** [vɔ'lætilaiz] v. haihduttaa.

volcan|ic [vɔl'kænik] a. tuliperäinen. **-o** [vɔl'keinəu] s. (pl. ~ *es*) tulivuori.

vole [vəul] s. (pelto)myyrä.

volition [və(u)'liʃn] s. tahto; tahdonvoima. **-al** [-l] a. tahdon-.

volley ['vɔli] s. yhteislaukaus; ryöppy, tulva; lentolyönti (tennis); v. ampua yhteislaukaus; singota; lennättää. **-ball** s. lentopallo.

volplane ['vɔlplein] s. & v. (tehdä) liitolasku.

volt [vəult] s. voltti (sähk.). **-age** [-idʒ] s. jännite.

volte-face ['vɔlt'fa:s] s. täyskäännös (m. kuv.).

volub|ility [vɔlju'biliti] s. suulaus. **-le** ['vɔljubl] a. kielevä, suulas; sujuva.

volum|e ['vɔlju:m] s. nidos, osa; paljous; tilavuus; (äänen)

täyteläisyys; (rad.) äänen
voimakkuus; ~ s m. vuosikerrat; ~ s of
smoke savupilvet; .. in three ~ s
kolmiosainen. -inous [vəˈluːminəs] a.
laaja, iso, mittava; tuottelias.
voluntari|ly adv. vapaaehtoisesti. **-ness**
s. vapaaehtoisuus.
volunt|ary [ˈvɔlənt(ə)ri] a.
vapaaehtoinen; tahallinen,
tarkoituksellinen; tahdonalainen; s.
urkusoolo (jumalanpalveluksen
aikana). **-eer** [-ˈtiə] s. vapaaehtoinen;
v. tarjoutua vapaaehtoisesti, palvella
vapaaehtoisena; ~ [a remark] lausua
(oma-aloitteisesti t. pyytämättä).
voluptu|ary [vəˈlʌptʃuəri] s.
hekumoitsija. **-ous** [-əs] a.
hekumallinen, aistillinen.
volute [vəˈljuːt] s. (rak.) kierukka.
vomit [ˈvɔmit] v. oksentaa; s.
oksennus.
voodoo [ˈvuːduː] s. (neekerien)
noituus.
vorac|ious [vəˈreiʃəs] a. ahnas,
ahmatti. **-ity** [vəˈræsiti] s. ahneus.
vort|ex [ˈvɔːteks] s. (pl. m. -ices [-isiːz]
pyörre, pyörretuuli. **-ical** [ˈvɔːtik(ə)l]
a. pyörre-.
Vosges [vəuʒ] erisn.: the ~ Vogeesit.
votar|ess [ˈvəutəris] s. papitar. **-y** [-ri] s.
(Jumalan) palvelija, palvoja; harras
ihailija, kannattaja.
vot|e [vəut] s. ääni; äänestyslippu;
äänioikeus; v. äänestää; päättää
(äänestämällä), myöntää (varoja);
selittää, pitää jnak; a ~ was taken on
the question asiasta toimitettiin
äänestys; put to the ~ äänestää jstk; by
twenty ~ s to ten 20 äänellä 10 vastaan;

~ down äänestää kumoon; ~ for
äänestää jkta; ~ in valita jhk; I ~
[that] (puhek.) ehdotan että. **-er** [-ə] s.
äänestäjä. **-ing** s. äänestys.
votive [ˈvəutiv] a. lahja-, lupaus-; ~
offering uhrilahja; ~ tablet
muistotaulu.
vouch [vautʃ] v.: ~ for taata, mennä
takuuseen jstk. **-er** [-ə] s. (kirjallinen)
todiste, tosite; kuitti, vastamerkki;
todistaja; lahjakortti. **-safe** [-ˈseif] v.
suoda; alentua, suvaita.
vow [vau] s. juhallinen lupaus; v.
(juhlallisesti) luvata, vannoa; take a
~ antaa pyhä lupaus; was under a ~
oli juhlallisesti luvannut.
vowel [ˈvauəl] s. vokaali, ääntiö.
voyage [ˈvɔidʒ] s. (tav. pitkä)
merimatka; lentomatka; v. matkustaa
(vesitse). **-r** [-ə] s. matkailija.
vulcan|ite [ˈvʌlkənait] s. eboniitti. **-ize**
[-aiz] v. vulkanoida.
vulgar [ˈvʌlgə] a. rahvaanomainen,
karkea, vulgääri, sivistymätön. **-ism**
[-rizm] s. sivistymätön puhetapa;
rahvaanomaisuus. **-ity** [-ˈgæriti] s.
sivistymättömyys; pl. törkeydet. **-ize**
[-raiz] v. tehdä liian kansanomaiseksi.
Vulgate [ˈvʌlgit] s. Versio vulgata
(latinal. raamatunkäännös).
vulnera|bility [vʌlnərəˈbiliti] s.
haavoittuvuus. **-ble** [ˈvʌlnərəbl] a.
haavoittuva, arka.
vulpine [ˈvʌlpain] a. kettu-,
ketuntapainen, ovela.
vulture [ˈvʌltʃə] s. korppikotka;
haaskalintu.
vying [ˈvaiiŋ] a. ks. vie.

W

W, w [ˈdʌblju:] *s.* w-kirjain. Lyh.: **w.**
watt; **W.** West; **W.A.** *West Africa,*
Western Australia; **W.A.A.C.**
Women's Army Auxiliary Corps;
Wash. *Washington;* **W.C.** *west*
Central (London Postal District); **w.c.**
water closet; **Wed.** *Wednesday;*
WHO *World Health Organization;*
W.I. *West Indies;* **Wisc.** *Wisconsin;*
Wisd. *Wisdom of Solomon;* **Wm**
William; **W.O.** *War Office;* **w.p.**
weather permitting; **W.R.A.F.**
Women's Royal Air Force; **W.R.N.S.**
[renz] *Women's Royal Naval Service;*
Wt. *weight;* **W/T** *Wireless Telegraphy;*
Wyo. *Wyoming.*

wad [wɔd] *s.* tuppo, tukko; setelitukku;
(sot.) etupanos; *v.* pehmustaa,
täyttää, tilkitä; **-ding** *s.* pakkaustäyte,
pehmuste.

waddle [ˈwɔdl] *v.* taapertaa, lyllertää;
s. taaperrus.

wad|e [weid] *v.* kahlata (m. kuv.); ~
into sth. käydä (tarmolla) käsiksi jhk;
-ing bird kahlaaja. **-er** [-ə] *s.* kahlaaja;
~ *s* kahluusaappaat.

wafer [ˈweifə] *s.* vohvelikeksi; öylätti,
ehtoollisleipä; suulakka.

waffle [ˈwɔfl] *s.* vohveli; *v.* laverrella;
~ **-iron** vohvelirauta.

waft [wɑ:ft] *v.* kuljettaa (et. halki
ilman), lennättää; *s.* tuulahdus,
tuoksahdus.

wag [wæg] *v.* heiluttaa; huojuttaa,
keikuttaa, ravistaa (päätään); heilua;
s. heilautus; vekkuli, koiranleuka; ~
one's finger at heristää sormeaan
nuhtelevasti; *tongues began to* ~
kielenkannat irtosivat, juoruilu alkoi.

wage [weidʒ] *s.* (tav. *pl.*) palkka (et.
viikko-, päivä-); *v.* käydä (sotaa); ~
differentials palkkahaitari; ~ *sheet*
palkkalista. **~-earner**

palkkatyöläinen, palkannauttija.

wager [ˈweidʒə] *s.* vedonlyönti, veto; *v.*
lyödä vetoa (m. *lay a* ~)

wag|gery [ˈwægəri] *s.* veitikkamaisuus;
naljailu, kujeet. **-gish** [-iʃ] *a.*
veitikkamainen; kujeileva.

waggle [ˈwægl] *v.* heiluttaa.

waggon [ˈwægən] *s.* ks. seur.

wagon [ˈwægən] *s.* kuormarattaat,
vankkurit; tavaravaunu (rautat.); *on*
the ~ (sl.) »vesipoika». **-er** [-ə] *s.*
kuorma-ajuri.

wagtail [ˈwægteil] *s.* västäräkki.

waif [weif] *s.* koditon lapsi, kulkuri;
kulku|kissa t. -koira; ~ *s and strays*
koditttomat lapset.

wail [weil] *v.* valittaa, itkeä, surra; *s.*
valitus, parku.

wain [wein] *s.* vankkurit (et. run.).

wainscot [ˈweinskət] *s.* seinälaudoitus,
paneeli; *v.* paneloida. **-ing** *s.* paneeli.

waist [weist] *s.* vyötäiset, vyötärö;
miehusta; [*shirt-*] ~ pusero. **~-band**
vyötärönauha. **-coat** [ˈweiskət, Am.
wes-] liivit. **~-high** vyötäisiin asti.
-line vyötärö.

wait [weit] *v.* odottaa (*for* jkta);
tarjoilla, palvella; *s.* odotus; väijytys;
pl. joululaulajat; ~ *at table* tarjoilla
pöydässä; ~ [*up*]*on* tarjoilla, palvella,
(vanh.) käydä jkn luona
(tervehdyskäynnillä); *please* ~ *a*
minute! (odottakaa) hetkinen, olkaa
hyvä! ~ *for me, please!* ole hyvä ja
odota minua! [*you must*] ~ *your turn*
odottaa vuoroasi; ~ *up for* valvoa
kunnes . . tulee; *keep sb.* ~ *ing* antaa
jkn odottaa; ~ *a bit!* odota hetkinen!
don't ~ *dinner for me* älä odota minua
päivälliselle; *lie in* ~ *for* väijyä jkta.
-er [-ə] *s.* tarjoilija.

waiting *s.* odotus; tarjoilu; *lady-in-*~
(kuningattaren) kamarirouva.

~**-room** s. odotushuone.
waitress ['weitris] s. tarjoilija(tar).
waive [weiv] v. luopua. **-r** [-ə] s. (lak.)
luopuminen.
wake 1. [weik] v. imp. woke t. ~d; pp.
~d t. woke [n] (us. ~ up) herätä;
herättää, havahtua; s. (Irlannissa)
valvojaiset (vainajan ääressä); waking
valveilla olo.
wake 2. [weik] s. vanavesi.
wakeful ['weikf(u)l]a. uneton, valpas;
a ~ night valvottu yö. **-ness** s.
unettomuus, valppaus.
waken ['weikn] v. herättää, herätä.
wale [weil] s. ks. weal.
Wales [weilz] erisn.; the Prince of ~
Walesin prinssi.
walk [wɔːk] v. kävellä, kulkea (jalan);
kummitella; kulkea pitkin jtk;
kävelyttää, saattaa; panna astumaan
käymäjalkaa; s. käynti, astunta;
kävely(retki); kävely|paikka, -tie; (~
of life) ala, toimiala; ~ the boards olla
näyttelijä; ~ the streets olla katutyttö;
~ about kuljeskella; ~ away from
voittaa helposti; ~ into (s.) torua,
haukkua, käydä käsiksi (esim.
ruokaan), ahmia; ~ off mennä
tiehensä; kävelen ällä päästä jstk; ~
off with varastaa; ~ on olla statistina;
~ out on hylätä, jättää pulaan; ~ out
with seurustella; go for a ~, take a ~
mennä kävelylle. **-er** [-ə] s. kävelijä.
-ie-talkie s. kevyt radiopuhelin.
walking a. jalka-, kävely-; s. kävely; a
~ [on] part (mykkä) sivuosa. ~**-stick**
kävelykeppi. ~**-tour** kävelyretki,
jalkamatka.
walk|-out m. lakko, ulosmarssi,
mielenosoituksellinen poistuminen.
~**over** helppo voitto.
wall [wɔːl] s. seinä, muuri, valli; v.
rakentaa muuri jnk ympärille; W~
Street Yhdysvalt. rahamarkkinat,
pörssi; go to the ~ joutua alakynteen;
push sb. to the ~ panna seinää
vastaan; ~ up muurata umpeen; ~ed
muurien ympäröimä; ~-to~-
carpet(ing) kokolattiamatto.
wallaby ['wɔləbi] s. pieni kenguru.
Wallace ['wɔləs] erisn.
wallet [wɔlit] s. lompakko; laukku,
reppu (vanh.).
wallflower kultalakka (kasv.);

seinäkoriste (jota ei pyydetä tanssiin).
wallop ['wɔləp] v. löylyttää, rökittää.
-ing a. iso, paksu (valhe); s.
selkäsauna.
wallow ['wɔləu] v. kieriskellä, rypeä.
wall|-painting seinämaalaus. ~**-paper**
seinäpaperi, tapetti.
walnut ['wɔːlnət] s. saksanpähkinä,
-puu.
Walpole ['wɔːlpəul] erisn.
walrus ['wɔːlrəs] s. mursu.
waltz [wɔːls] s. valssi; v. tanssia valssia.
wan ['wɔn] a. kalpea, kalvakka,
riutunut.
wand [wɔnd] s. virkasauva, taikasauva;
tahtipuikko.
wander ['wɔndə] v. vaeltaa, harhailla,
kuljeskella, samota; mennä harhaan;
puhua sekavasti, hourailla; ~ from
poiketa (aiheesta). **-er** [-rə] s.
vaeltaja. **-ing** a. vaeltava, harhaileva;
s. pl. vaellusretket, hourailu.
wane [wein] v. vähetä, heiketä; s.
väheneminen; the moon is on the ~ on
alakuu.
wangle ['wæŋgl] v. puijata.
want [wɔnt] s. puute; hätä; tarve; v.
olla jtk vailla, tarvita, haluta; haluta
tavata jkta; puuttua, olla vajaa; kärsiä
puutetta; for ~ of jnk puutteessa; in ~
puutteessa; be in ~ of tarvita, olla jnk
puutteessa; [tell him] that I ~ him että
hän tulisi luokseni; do you ~ me?
onko teillä asiaa minulle? he ~s me to
hän haluaa että minä; it ~s a minute
to…kello on minuuttia vailla; W~ed
palvelukseen halutaan; ~ed by the
police etsintäkuulutettu; you ~ to be
careful sinun on oltava varovainen;
you are ~ed teitä kysytään; ~ for olla
jnk puutteessa **-ing** prep. ilman; be ~
puuttua; he is ~ in häneltä puuttuu;
he is a little ~ hän on hieman
heikkoälyinen; found ~ köykäiseksi
havaittu.
wanton ['wɔntən] a. leikillinen, raisu,
vallaton, oikullinen; rehevä;
kevytmielinen, siveetön; aiheeton,
tarpeeton; s. kevytkenkäinen nainen;
v. riehua, kisailla, (~ away) tuhlata.
-ly adv. vallattomasti jne; huvin
vuoksi, turhan päiten. **-ness** s.
kevytmielisyys jne.
war [wɔː] s. sota; v. sotia, käydä sotaa,

taistella; *art of ~* sotataito; *W ~
Office* sotaministeriö; *Secretary of
State for W ~* sotaministeri; *declare ~
[upon]* julistaa sota; *make (wage) ~
[upon]* käydä sotaa; *at ~ [with]*
sodassa, sotatilassa; *go to ~ against*
ryhtyä sotaan. **~-baby** (avioton)
sotalapsi.

warble ['wɔːbl] *v.* liverrellä, visertää; *s.*
livertely, viserrys. **-r** [-ə] *s.* laululintu;
garden ~ lehtokerttu.

war|-blinded *a.* sotasokea. **~-cry** *s.*
sotahuuto.

ward [wɔːd] *s.* holhokki, holhotti;
(kaupungin) piiri, alue; (sairaalan)
vuodeosasto; *v.: ~ off* torjua, väistää.
-en [-n] *s.* valvoja, isäntä; *(collegen
ym)* johtaja; *air-raid ~*
ilmasuojeluvalvoja; *traffic ~*
pysäköinnin valvoja. **-er** [-ə] *s.*
vanginvartija. **-robe** vaatekaappi,
vaatevarasto, vaatteet; *built-in ~*
vaatekomero. **-room** *s.* upseerin messi
(sotalaivassa).

-ward(s) [-wədz] *suff.* päin, kohti.

ware [wɛə] *s.* (tav. *pl.*) myyntitavara,
tavarat; *-tavara; (china ~* posliini.
-house varasto, makasiini; *v.* panna
makasiiniin; *bonded ~* tullivarasto.

war|fare ['wɔːfɛə] *s.* sota, sodankäynti.
-head ydinkärki *(nuclear ~)*.

wari|ly *adv.* varovaisesti. **-ness** *s.*
varovaisuus.

warlike *a.* sotainen, sotaisa; *~
preparations* sotavarustelut.

warm [wɔːm] *a.* lämmin, kuuma;
sydämellinen, innokas, vilkas;
kiihtynyt, kiivas; (puhek.) hyvissä
varoissa oleva; *v.* lämmittää, lämmetä
(us. *~ up);* innostua; *s.* (puhek.)
lämmittely, lämmitys; *~ to one's work*
innostua työhönsä; *~ oneself [at the
fire]* lämmitellä. **~-hearted**
lämminsydäminen. **-ly** *adv.*
lämpimästi. **-th** [-θ] *s.* lämpö,
sydämellisyys; into.

warmonger [-mʌŋɡə] *s.* sodanlietsoja.

warn [wɔːn] *v.* varoittaa; ennakolta
ilmoittaa; *~ off* kehottaa poistumaan;
I ~ed him not to skate [on thin ice]
varoitin häntä luistelemasta. **-ing** *a.*
varoittava; *s.* varoitus, varoittava
esimerkki; irtisanominen; *give ~*
sanoa, sanoutua irti (palveluksesta);

gale ~ myrskyvaroitus.

warp [wɔːp] *v.* vääntää kieroon;
käyristää, vääristää, tehdä kieroksi;
käyristyä; *s.* loimet, loimi;
hinausvarppi; kierous; *is ~ed* m. on
kieroutunut.

war|-paint sotamaalaus; täysi
juhla-asu. **~-path** sotapolku.

warrant ['wɔr(ə)nt] *s.* valtuutus,
valtakirja, vangitsemismääräys;
tosite; tae; *v.* oikeuttaa, puolustaa;
taata; *~ed pure silk* taatusti aitoa
silkkiä; *dividend ~* osinkolippu; *death
~* kuolemantuomio. **~-officer** *s.* l.v.
(mer.) sotilamestari. **-able** [-əbl] *a.*
oikeutettu. **-ed** [-id] *a.* taattu. **-or** [-ɔː]
s. takaaja. **-y** [-i] *s.* takuu.

warren ['wɔrin] *s.* kaniinitarha.

warring *a.* taisteleva; ristiriitainen,
vastakkainen.

warrior ['wɔriə] *s.* soturi.

Warsaw ['wɔːsɔː] *erisn.* Varsova.

war-ship *s.* sotalaiva.

wart [wɔːt] *s.* syylä; *~-hog* pahkasika.
-y [-i] *a.* syyläinen.

Warwick ['wɔrik] *erisn.*

wary ['wɛəri] *a.* varovainen.

was [wɔz, wəz] *imp.* ks. *be.*

wash [wɔʃ] *v.* pestä, huuhtoa; peseytyä,
huuhtoutua; pestä pyykkiä; sietää
pesua; *s.* pesu, peseminen, pyykki;
pesuvaseet; huuhtelu; loske;
vesivelli, (sian)litku; *(mouth ~)*
suuvesi; *does this ~ well?* sietääkö
tämä hyvin pesua? *~ away* pestä,
huuhtoa pois; *~ ashore* heittää
rantaan; *~ down* huuhdella alas
(ruoka); *~ off* pestä pois, lähteä
pesussa; *~ out* poistaa (tahra); *~ up*
pestä astioita; *~ed out* uupunut; *he's
all ~ed up* poissa pelistä; *have a ~*
peseytyä; *give the car a ~ [-down]*
pestä auto; *in the ~* pyykissä. **-able**
[-əbl] *a.* pesunkestävä. **~-basin**
pesuallas. **-er** [-ə] *s.* tiivistysrengas;
pesukone.

washing *s.* pesu, -vaatteet, pyykki;
huuhtelu; *~ day* pyykkipäivä; *~
machine* pesukone; *~ up* astiainpesu.

Washington ['wɔʃiŋtən] *erisn.*

wash|-out sl. täydellinen
epäonnistuminen, »pannukakku».
~-stand pesu|teline, -kaappi. **-y** [-i] *a.*
vetinen, vesimäinen, laimistunut,

haalistunut, väljähtynyt
(tyyli, tunne).
wasn't ['wɔznt] = was not.
wasp [wɔsp] s. ampiainen; ~ 's nest
ampiaispesä. **-ish** [-iʃ] a. terävä,
pahasisuinen.
wastage ['weistidʒ] s. hukka; tuhlaus.
waste [weist] a. autio, tuhottu;
viljelemätön; heite-, hylky-, jäte-; v.
kuluttaa, hukata; tuhlata, riuduttaa,
riutua (m. ~ away): hävittää, tuhota;
s. tuhlaus, haaskaus; jätteet,
jäteaineet; autio maa; ~ land
joutomaa; ~ paper jätepaperi,
keräyspaperi; lay ~ hävittää,
autioittaa; lie ~ olla
viljelemättömänä, kesantona; ~ time
hukata aikaa, vitkastella; a wasting
disease hivuttava tauti; be ~d mennä
hukkaan; ~ of time ajan hukka; go
(run) to ~ mennä hukkaan. **-ful** a.
tuhlaavainen; ~ly tuhlailevasti.
~-paper basket paperikori. **~-pipe**
poistoputki. **-r** [ə] s. tyhjäntoimittaja,
hylkiö. **~-water** jätevesi.
wastrel ['weistr(ə)l] s. tuhlari;
tyhjäntoimittaja, hylkiö.
watch [wɔtʃ] s. (tasku-, ranne)kello;
valvonta, vartiointi; vartio;
vartioaika, -vuoro, (mer.) vahti; v.
katsella; pitää silmällä, tarkata,
valvoa (sairasvuoteen ääressä); keep
~ vartioida; on ~ vartiossa; be on the
~ for vaania, tähystellä jtk; ~ one's
time odottaa oikeata hetkeä; ~ out, ~
one's step olla varuillaan. **~-dog**
vahtikoira. **-er** [-ə] katselija. **-ful** a.
valpas, tarkkaavainen, varovainen.
~-guard kellonperät. **-maker**
kelloseppä. **-man** vartija; yövartija.
~-spring kellonjousi. **~-tower**
vartiotorni. **-word** tunnussana;
iskusana.
water ['wɔ:tə] s. vesi; (~s) vesistö,
vedet; v. kastella, juottaa; täyttää
(kone) vedellä; laimentaa (m. ~
down); ottaa vettä; by ~ meritse,
vesiteitä; high (low) ~ nousu-,
laskuvesi; in low ~ vaikeuksissa,
rahapulassa; hold ~ pitää vettä, olla
luotettava; keep one's head above ~
pysytellä pinnalla (kuv.); pass ~
heittää vettä, virtsata; make ~ = ed.,
(laivasta) vuotaa, saada vuoto;

drink (take) the ~s juoda
terveysvettä, oleskella kylpylässä;
[spend. .] like ~ tuhlaillen; of the first
~ hienointa laatua; it made his mouth
~ vesi kihahti hänen kielelleen.
~-borne vesitse kuljetettu. **~-closet**
vesiklosetti. **~-colour**
vesiväri(maalaus). **~-course** väylä;
virta. **~-cress** vesikrassi. **~-cure**
vesiparannus. **~-diviner**
kaivonkatsoja. **-ed** [-d] a.: ~ silk
läikesilkki. **-fall** vesiputous. **-fowl**
vesilinnut. **~-front** ranta, satama-alue.
-ing-can ruiskukannu. **-ing-place**
kylpylä; juottopaikka. **~-lily** lumme.
~-line vesiviiva. **-logged** vesilastissa
oleva; vettynyt.
Waterloo [wɔ:tə'lu:] erisn.
water|man lautturi. **-mark** vesileima.
~-melon arbuusi. **~-pipe**
vesijohtoputki. **~-power** vesivoima.
-proof a. vedenpitävä; s. vedenpitävä
kangas, sadetakki. **-shed** vedenjakaja.
~-shoot vesikouru. **~-spout** vesipatsas.
~-supply vesihuolto. **~-tap** vesihana.
~-tight vedenpitävä; w.-t.
compartments vedenpitävät laipiot.
~-way vesiväylä. **~-works**
vesijohtolaitos; turn on the w.-w.
ruveta pillittämään. **~-worn** veden
kuluttama. **-y** [-ri] a. vesi-, vetinen,
laimea; väritön; kyyneleinen; sadetta
enteilevä.
watt [wɔt] s. vatti (sähk.).
wattle ['wɔtl] s. vitsapunos(aita);
heltta; australial. akaasiapuu; ~d
(oksista ym) punottu.
Waugh [wɔ:] erisn.
wave [weiv] v. liehua, aaltoilla;
huiskuttaa; heiluttaa; kähertää; s.
aalto, laine; heiluskutus, heilautus;
kampaus, käherrys; ~ aside torjua
(asiattomana); [her hair] ~s naturally
on luonnonkihara; on short ~ lyhyillä
aalloilla; on the medium ~ transmitters
keskipitkillä aalloilla. **~-length**
aallonpituus.
waver ['weivə] v. häilyä, horjua, olla
päättämätön, epäröidä. **-ing** a.
horjuva, epäröivä; s. horjunta,
epäröinti.
wavy ['weivi] a. aaltoileva,
aaltomainen.
wax 1. [wæks] v. (kuusta) enetä,

kasvaa; (vanh.) tulla jksk.
wax 2. [wæks] s. vaha; vaikku;
suksivoide; (sealing-~)
lakka; (cobbler's ~) suutarin piki; v.
vahata, kiillottaa. **~-cloth**
vahakangas. **-en** [-n] a., vahankalpea;
pehmeä. **-wing** tilhi. **~-work**
vahakuva; pl. vahakabinetti. **-y** [-i] a.
vahamainen; sl. kiukkuinen.
way [wei] s. tie, rata; matka, etäisyys;
tapa, menettely-, elämäntapa; suunta,
kulku, vauhti; keino; pl. telapölkyt; ~
in sisäänkäytävä; ~ out ulospääsy; the
~ there menomatka; ~s and means
keinot, mahdollisuudet; Committee of
W~s and Means l.v.
raha-asiainvaliokunta; ~ of life
elämäntapa; all the ~ koko matkan;
[can I help you] in any ~? millään
tavalla; in no ~ [remarkable] ei
missään suhteessa; one ~ or another,
some ~ or other tavalla tai toisella,
jollakin tapaa; rather the other ~
round pikemminkin päinvastoin; that
~ sillä tapaa; sitä tietä, sille taholle;
[I'll do it] the ~ I like niinkuin haluan;
ask sb. the ~ kysyä tietä; fight one's ~
ponnistella eteenpäin; find one's ~
löytää jnnek; find a ~ keksiä keino;
give ~ väistyä, antaa tilaa, (autosta)
väistää; myöntyä, antaa perään;
horjua, murtua; go a long ~ [towards]
edistää huomattavasti; go the ~ of all
flesh kuolla; have one's own ~ päästä
tahtonsa perille; she has a ~ with
children osaa käsitellä lapsia; know
one's ~ about tuntea tiet, selviytyä;
look this ~ [, please] katso tännepäin;
lose one's ~ eksyä; make ~ for
väistyä, antaa tilaa jklle; make one's
~ raivata itselleen tie, menestyä; I
don't see my ~ to en näe
mahdolliseksi; by the ~ sivumennen
(sanoen); by ~ of (jnk paikan) kautta;
by ~ of answer vastaukse|na, -ksi; by
~ of apology anteeksipyyntönä; not by
a long ~ ei lähimainkaan; in a ~
tavallaan; in a bad ~ huonossa tilassa,
huonolla kannalla; in every ~ joka
suhteessa, kaikin tavoin; in a small ~
pienessä mittakaavassa; is in a terrible
~ about it on kiihdyksissään siitä; in
that ~ sillä tavoin; in the ~ tiellä;
something new in the ~ of books

joitakin uusia kirjoja; get into the ~ of
tottua jhk; on the ~ matkalla; out of
the ~ syrjässä; syrjäinen; [he has
done] nothing out of the ~ ei mitään
erikoisen huomattavaa; go out of one's
~ [to] vaivautua, yrittää parhaansa;
over the ~ vastapäätä; under ~
matkalla, käynnissä, tekeillä; get
under ~ lähteä (matkaan). **-bill**
matkustajaluettelo, kuormauskirja.
-farer matkalainen. **-lay** v. olla
väijyksissä, hyökätä jkn kimppuun.
-side s. tienvieri; a. tien varrella
sijaitseva t. kasvava. **-ward** a.
itsepäinen, oikullinen.
we [wi:] pers. pron. me.
weak [wi:k] a. heikko; hölä, hauras;
voimaton; mieto, laimea; a ~ point
heikko puoli. **-en** [-n] v. heikentää,
-tyä; laimentaa, -tua. **-ling** s. heikko
raukka. **-ly** a. heikko, sairaalloinen.
~-minded heikko|älyinen,
-luonteinen. **-ness** s. heikkous; heikko
puoli, vika. **~-spirited** arka.
weal 1. [wi:l] s.: for the public (general)
~ yhteiseksi hyväksi.
weal 2. [wi:l] s. (ruoskan) jälki, viiru.
wealth [welθ] s. varallisuus, rikkaus;
runsaus, yltäkylläisyys. **-y** [-i] a. rikas,
varakas.
wean [wi:n] v. vieroittaa (lapsi),
totuttaa jstk luopumaan. **-ing** s.
vieroittaminen.
weapon ['wepən] s. ase. **-less** a.
aseeton.
wear [wɛə] wore, worn, v. käyttää, olla
yllään (t. päässään); kuluttaa,
hivuttaa, kalvaa, uuvuttaa; kulua;
kestää; jatkua verkalleen; kääntää
tuulen mukaan; s. käyttö; kulutus,
kuluminen; kestävyys, lujuus; puku,
asu; she ~s her hair short hänellä on
lyhyt tukka; ~ glasses käyttää
silmälaseja; [she] never ~s green ei
milloinkaan pukeudu vihreään; ~
well olla kestävä; ~ away kuluttaa,
kulua pois; kulua verkalleen; ~ down
kuluttaa; uuvuttaa, murtaa
(vastarinta); ~ off kuluttaa kulua
pois; hävittä; ~ on (ajasta) kulua
verkalleen, pitkittyä, jatkua; ~ out
kulua loppuun, kuluttaa loppuun,
uupua, uuvuttaa; he has worn out his
welcome hän on viipynyt

kyllästyttävän kauan; ~ *and tear*
kuluminen *(fair ~ and tear* normaali
k.); *for everyday* ~ arkikäyttöä
varten; *the worse for* ~ kulunut; *sports*
~ urheiluasu(steet).

weari|ed ['wiərid] *a.* väsynyt, uupunut,
raukea. **-ness** *s.* väsymys, uupumus.
-some *a.* väsyttävä, vaivalloinen,
ikävä.

weary ['wiəri] *a.* väsynyt, kyllästynyt;
väsyttävä; *v.* väsyttää, kyllästyttää,
ikävystyttää; vaivata; väsyä,
kyllästyä; ~ *for* kaivata.

weasel ['wi:zl] *s.* lumikko.

weather ['weðə] *s.* sää; *attr.*
tuulenpuoleinen; *v.* kestää, selviytyä
jstk (m. ~ *out);* rapauttaa, -utua;
kiertää (niemi) tuulen puolelta; ~
[*wood*] kuivattaa alttiiksi ilman
vaikutukselle; ~ *forecast* säätiedotus;
under the ~ huonossa kunnossa; *keep*
one's ~ *eye open* olla varuillaan; *make*
heavy ~ *of* pitää jtk vaikeana;
~-beaten tuulenpieksämä,
ahavoitunut. **~-boards**
vuorauslaudat. **~-chart** sääkartta.
-cock tuuliviiri. **-proof** tuulenkestävä,
joka sääin kestävä.

weav|e [wi:v] *wove woven, v.* kutoa
(kangasta); punoa, sepittää;
puikkelehtia (~ *one's way*).

web [web] *s.* kudos, kangas; seitti;
verkko; uimaräpylä. **-bed** [-d] *a.:* ~
foot räpyläjalka. **-bing** *s.*
reunavahviste.

we'd [wi:d] = *we had, we would.*

wed [wed] *wedded, wedded* t. pp. *wed,*
v. naida, mennä naimisiin; naittaa,
vihkiä; liittää yhteen. **-ded** [-id] *pp. &*
a. avio-; *be* ~ *to* olla jssk kiinni.

wedding ['wediŋ] *s.* häät, vihkiäiset.
~-ring vihkisormus. **~-trip** häämatka.

wedge [wedʒ] *s.* kiila; *v.* kiilata;
tunkea; *it is the thin end of the* ~ se on
vasta alkua. **~-shaped** *a.*
kiilanmuotoinen.

wedlock ['wedlɔk] *s.* avio|liitto, -sääty;
born in ~ aviolapsi.

Wednesday ['wenzdi] *s.* keskiviikko.

wee [wi:] *a.* pienen pieni, pikkuruinen;
a ~ *bit* pikku|isen, -riikkisen.

weed [wi:d] *s.* rikkaruoho; sl. sikari,
tupakka, sl.m. marijuana; ruipelo.
rääpäle; *v.* kitkeä, perata (us. ~ *out);*

[*my garden*] *is running to* ~ *s* työntää
rikkaruohoja. **-s** [wi:dz] *s. pl.* lesken
surupuku. **-y** [-i] *a.* rikkaruohoja
kasvava; hontelo, hintelä.

week [wi:k] *s.* viikko; *this* ~ tällä
viikolla; *ten pounds a* ~ 10 puntaa
viikossa; *day of the* ~ viikonpäivä;
tomorrow ~ huomisesta viikon
kuluttua. **-day** arkipäivä. **~-end**
viikonloppu; *v.* viettää v-loppua.
~-ender viikonlopun viettäjä. **-ly** *a.*
viikko-, viikoittain ilmestyvä; *adv.*
kerran viikossa; *s.* viikkolehti.

weep [wi:p] *wept wept, v.* itkeä,
vuodattaa kyyneleitä (~ *over);* ~ *for*
joy itkeä ilosta. **-ing** *a.* itkevä; *s.* i ku;
~ *birch* riippakoivu; ~ *willow*
itkupaju.

weevil ['wi:vil] *s.* kärsäkäs.

weft [weft] *s.* kude, kuteet.

weigh [wei] *v.* punnita; harkita; nostaa
(ankkuri); painaa, olla tärkeä,
painava, merkitä paljon; ~ *down*
painaa alas; ~*ed down with cares*
huolten painama; ~ *in* (urheilijasta)
käydä punnituksessa; ~ *in with* esittää
painokkaasti; ~ *out* punnita (osiin); ~
upon olla taakkana, rasittaa. **~-bridge**
siltavaaka. **-ing-machine** vaaka.

weight [weit] *s.* paino; punnus; taakka,
kuorma; (kellon) luoti; merkitys,
tärkeys, painavuus; (urh. m.) kuula;
sarja; *v.* painottaa, jyvittää; rasittaa,
raskauttaa; ~ *s and measures* painot ja
mitat; *net* = nettopaino; *over (under)*
~ yli-(ali)painoinen; *have* ~ olla
tärkeä, tähdellinen; *pull one's* ~ tehdä
oma osuutensa, kantaa kortensa
kekoon; *put on* ~ lihoa; *throw one's* ~
~ *about* rehennellä; *a matter of* ~
tärkeä asia; *carry* ~ olla tärkeä. **-iness**
s. painavuus, tärkeys. **~-lifting**
painonnosto. **-y** [-i] *a.* raskas,
painava; tärkeä, tähdellinen.

weir [wiə] *s.* pato; katiska-aita.

weird [wiəd] *a.* kohtalon(omainen);
kummallinen, käsittämätön,
yliluonnollinen; *the* ~ *sisters*
kohtalottaret, noidat.

welcome ['welkəm] *a.* tervetullut,
mieluinen; *s.* tervetulotoivotus,
ystävällinen vastaanotto; *v.* toivottaa
tervetulleeksi; tervehtiä ilolla; *int.*
tervetuloa *(to* jnnk); *bid sb.* ~

weld   498

toivottaa jku tervetulleeksi; *make sb.*
~ ottaa jku ystävällisesti vastaan; *you
are ~ to* saat(te) kernaasti, pidä
hyvänäsi! *you are ~!* ei kestä kiittää!
kaikin mokomin!
weld [weld] *v.* hitsata; liittää yhteen; *s.*
hitsiliitos. **-ing** *s.* hitsaus.
welfare ['welfɛə] *s.* jkn hyvä, paras,
hyvinvointi; huolto; *child ~*
lastenhuolto; *~ state*
hyvinvointivaltio; *~ work*
yhteiskunnallinen huoltotyö.
welkin ['welkin] *s.* (run.) taivas.
well 1. [wel] *s.* kaivo; lähde;
porausreikä; hissikuilu; syvennys
(mustepulloa varten); *v.* pulputa,
kummuta (jstk, us. *~ up, out, forth*).
well 2. [wel] *adv.* (*better, best*) hyvin;
oikein, viisaasti; tarkasti,
huolellisesti; runsaasti; melkoisesti;
oikeutetusti, syystä kyllä; *a.* (vain
predikatiivina) terve; hyvä, hyvin,
sopiva; *int.* no niin, no (jaa): *very ~!*
hyvä on! *~ then?* entä sitten? *well ~!*
kas, kas! *~ off* hyvissä varoissa; *~ on
in years* melko iäkäs; *~ over an hour*
runsaan tunnin; *~ up in the list*
luettelon yläpäässä; *do ~* [*for oneself*]
menestyä; *be doing ~* olla hyvässä
kunnossa; *as ~* yhtä hyvin; myös; *as
~ as* sekä — että; *it is all very ~ for
you to* kyllähän teidän kelpaa; *think ~
of* ajatella jksta hyvää; *I wish I were ~
out of* it kunpa selviäisin siitä
kunnialla. **~-advised** viisas,
varovainen. **~-balanced**
tasapainoinen. **~-behaved**
hyväkäytöksinen. **~-being**
hyvinvointi. **~-bred** sivistynyt, hyvin
kasvatettu. **~-connected** jolla on
hyviä (perhe)suhteita. **~-deserved**
hyvin ansaittu, oikeudenmukainen.
~-disposed suopea. **~-dressed** hyvin
pukeutunut. **~-founded** hyvin
perusteltu, oikeutettu. **~-groomed**
huoliteltu. **~-grounded** hyvät
pohjatiedot omaava.
well-head *s.* lähde.
well-informed *a.* asioista perillä oleva,
asiantunteva.
Wellington ['welintən] *erisn.; w~ s.*
pitkävartiset saappaat.
well-intentioned hyvää tarkoittava.
well|-known tunnettu. **~-meaning,**

~-**meant** hyvää tarkoittava. ~-**nigh**
lähes, melkein. ~-**proportioned**
sopusuhtainen. ~-**read** paljon
lukenut. ~-**stocked** hyvin varustettu.
~-**timed** oikeaan aikaan tehty, oikein
ajoitettu. ~-**to-do** varakas. ~-**wisher**
suosija, ystävä.
Welsh [welʃ] *a.* walesilainen; *s.* kymrin
kieli; *the ~* walesilaiset; *~ rabbit*
paahdettu juustovoileipä. **-man,**
-woman *s.* walesilainen;
walesilaisnainen.
welsh [welʃ] *v.* petkuttaa, luikkia
tiehensä.
welt [welt] *s.* (kengän) reunos.
welter ['weltə] *v.* piehtaroida, rypeä; *s.*
hämmennys, sekasorto. ~-**weight**
välisarja.
wen [wen] *s.* rasvakasvain.
wench [wen(t)ʃ] *s.* (maalais)tyttö, likka;
v. käydä naisissa (t. huorissa).
wend [wend] *v.: ~ one's way* suunnata
kulkunsa.
went [went] *imp.* ks. *go.*
wept [wept] *imp.* ks. *weep.*
were [wɛə, wə] *imp.* ks. *be; I wish I ~*
toivoisin olevani.
werewolf ['wə:wulf] *s.* ihmissusi.
west [west] *s.* länsi; *a.* läntinen, länsi-;
adv. länteen, lännessä; *to the ~ of* jnk
länsipuolella; *the W~* Länsi,
länsimaat; *the W~ End*
Länsi-Lontoo; *W~ Germany*
Länsi-Saksa; *the W~ Indies*
Länsi-Intia; *go ~* (leik.) kuolla,
kellahtaa. **-erly** [-əli] *a.* läntinen,
länsi(tuuli). **-ern** [-ən] *a.* läntinen,
länsi-; länsimainen; *s.* villin lännen
elokuva (kertomus ym) **-erner** [-ənə]
s. länsimaalainen. **-ernize** [-ənaiz] *v.*
länsimaistaa. **-ward(s)** [-wəd, -z] *adv.*
länteen päin.
Westminster ['wes(t)minstə] *erisn.*
wet [wet] *a.* märkä, kostea;
sateinen; . . jossa ei ole kieltolakia; *s.*
märkyys, kosteus; sadesää; *v.*
kostuttaa, kastaa, kastella; *~* [*dock*]
uiva; *~-nurse* imettäjä; *~ paint!*
maalattu! *~ through* läpimärkä; *get ~*
kastua.
wether [weðə] *s.* oinas.
wetness *s.* märkyys.
whack [(h)wæk] *v.* läimäyttää; *s.*
läimäys; *~ing* aimo; *a ~ing lie*

emävalhe. **-ed** [-t] *a.* (puhek.)
uupunut, lopussa, kuin rätti.
whale [(h)weil] *s.* valas; *v.* harjoittaa
valaanpyyntiä. **~-boat**
valaanpyyntivene. **-bone** valaanluu.
~-oil traani. **-r** [-ə] *s.*
valaanpyyntialus, valaanpyytäjä.
whaling *s.* valaanpyynti.
whang [(h)wæŋ] *v.* läimäyttää; *s.*
läiske; *int.* läiskis.
wharf [(h)wɔ:f] *s.* (pl. m. *wharves*)
(satama)laituri. **-age** [-idʒ] *s.*
laiturimaksu. **-inger** [-in(d)ʒə] *s.*
laiturimestari.
what [(h)wɔt] *inter. pron.* mikä, mitä,
mitkä; *relat. pron.* mikä, mitä; *konj.*
osittain . . osittain; ~ *is he like*
minkälainen, minkä näköinen hän on;
~ *time is it* paljonko kello on; ~ *about
going* [*there*] mitä arvelet;
menisimmekö? ~ *about him* entä hän;
~ *if . .* entä jos; ~ *though* entä sitten
vaikka; [*at*] ~ *time?* mihin aikaan? ~
a pity! kuinka ikävää! ~ *little he said*
se vähä mitä hän sanoi; *know* ~ *is* ~
olla perillä asioista; *I'll tell you* ~
sanonpa teille jotakin; *so* ~ *?* (ja t. no)
entä sitten? ~ *with one thing and
another* syystä tai toisesta; *and* ~ *not*
ja muuta sellaista; *well,* ~ *of it*
(puhek. *so* ~ *?*) entä sitten? **-ever**
[-'evə] *pron.* mikä, mitä hyvänsä,
kaikki mikä; mitään, lainkaan; ~
happens tapahtuipa mitä tahansa;
nothing ~ ei yhtään mitään; ~ *are you
thinking about?* mitä ihmettä sinä
ajattelet? **-not** *s.* hyllykkö, hyllypöytä.
-soever *pron.* ks. *whatever*.
wheat [(h)wi:t] *s.* vehnä. **-ear** kivitasku.
-en [-n] *a.* vehnä-.
wheedle [(h)wi:dl] *v.* houkute ta,
lirkutella, (leik.) vikitellä.
wheel [(h)wi:l] *s.* pyörä, ratas; ohjaus-,
polkupyörä; *v.* pyörittää, kierittää,
työntää, lykätä; kääntää ympäri,
kaartaa; pyöriä, kierrellä; tehdä
käännös; ajaa polkupyörällä. *~
spinning* ~ rukki; *at the* ~ ratissa,
peräsimessä; [*there are*] ~*s within* ~*s*
monta mutkaa, salaisia syitä. **-barrow**
työntökärryt. **~-chair** pyörätuoli. **-ed**
[-d] *a.* pyörillä varustettu, -pyöräinen.
-wright seppä.
wheez|**e** [(h)wi:z] *v.* kähistä, vinkua; *s.*

vinkuna. **-y** [-i] *a.* vinkuva (hengitys).
whelk [(h)welk] *s.* eräänl. simpukka.
whelp [(h)welp] *s.* koiranpentu,
penikka; nulikka; *v.* penikoida.
when [(h)wen] *adv.* milloin? koska?
jolloin; *konj.* kun, milloin, silloin kun,
jolloin; vaikka; ~ *speaking*
puhuessaan; ~ *there* sinne tultaessa;
~ *young* nuorena. **-ever** [-'evə] *konj.*
milloin hyvänsä, joka kerran kun,
aina kun. **-soever** [-'səu] *ks.* ed.
whence [(h)wens] *adv.* mistä?
where [(h)wɛə] *adv.* missä? mihin?
jossa, missä, johon, minne; *near* ~
jonka lähellä; ~ *does he come from*
mistä hän tulee? mistä hän on
kotoisin? ~ *are you going?* ~ *are you
off to?* minne menet? *is this* ~ *Mr A.
lives?* täälläkö herra A. asuu? ~ *shall
we be* [*if*] miten meidän käy; *that's* ~
you are mistaken siinäpä juuri olet
väärässä. **-abouts** [-rə'bauts] *adv.*
mihin (suunnilleen)? *s.* olinpaikka;
his present ~ *is unknown* hänen
nykyinen osoitteensa on tuntematon.
-as [-'ræz] *konj.* kun taas, kun sitä
vastoin, ottaen huomioon että; koska.
-at [-'ræt] *adv.* jolloin, jonka
johdosta. **-by** [-'bai] *adv.* jonka
avulla. **-fore** *adv.* (vanh.) minkä
tähden? miksi? *s.:* *the whys and* ~*s*
syyt. **-in** [-'rin] *adv.* missä? missä
suhteessa? **-of** [-'rɔv] *adv.* mistä?
josta. **-soever** ks. *wherever*. **-to** [-'tu:]
konj. mihin. **-upon** [-rə'pɔn] *adv.*
jonka jälkeen.
wherever [-'evə] *konj.* missä t. mihin
hyvänsä; [*from . .*] ~ *that may be*
missä se sitten mahtaneekin sijaita.
wherewith [-'wið] *adv. & konj.* (vanh.)
jolla, jolloin. **-al** [-wiðɔ:l] *s.:* *the* ~
(tarvittavat) varat.
whet [(h)wet] *v.* teroittaa, hioa;
kiihottaa.
whether ['(h)weðə] *konj.* -ko, -kö; ~ *. .
or* -ko (-kö) *. .* vai; ~ *or no* joka
tapauksessa.
whetstone *s.* kovasin.
whew [hju:] *int.* ohhoh! huh!
whey [(h)wei] *s.* hera.
which [(h)witʃ] *interr. pron.* mikä?
kuka? kumpi? *rel. pron.* mikä, joka; ~
of the boys kuka (kumpi) pojista; [*he
said he was there,*] ~ *was untrue* mikä

ei ollut totta; ~ *I did* minkä teinkin; *about* ~ josta; *after* ~ jonka jälkeen; *for* ~ josta; *in* ~ missä. **-ever** [-'evə] *pron.* mikä t. kumpi tahansa.

whiff [(h)wif] *s.* henkäys; tuprahdus, haiku; pieni sikari.

Whig [(h)wig] *s.* whig-puolueen jäsen.

while [(h)wail] *s.* tuokio, hetki(nen); *konj.* sillä aikaa kun; niin kauan kuin; samalla kun, kun taas; *v.:* ~ *away* kuluttaa; *a little* ~ *ago* hetki sitten; *not for a long* ~ ei pitkään aikaan; *the* ~ sillä välin; [*all*] *the* ~ kaiken aikaa; *between* ~*s* välillä; *for a* ~ vähäksi aikaa, jonkin aikaa; *in a little* ~ hetken kuluttua; *once in a* ~ silloin tällöin; *it is not worth* ~ se ei maksa vaivaa; ~ *in London* .. Lontoossa ollessani (-ani, -asi).

whilst [(h)wailst] *konj.* = ed.

whim [(h)wim] *s.* oikku, päähänpisto, mielijohde.

whimper ['(h)wimpə] *v.* uikuttaa, ulista; *s.* uikutus.

whimsical ['(h)wimzikl] *a.* oikullinen; eriskummainen, .. jolla on ihmeellisiä päähänpistoja. **-ity** [-'kæliti] *s.* oikullisuus; hulluttelevat tapa (käytös); **-ities** hassuttelu, kujeet.

whimsy ['(h)wimzi] *s.* oikku, päähänpisto, kujeilu.

whine [(h)wain] *v.* vikistä, vinkua, uikuttaa, valittaa; *s.* vikinä; ruikutus.

whinny ['(h)wini] *v.* hirnahtaa (hiljaa); *s.* hirnahdus.

whip [(h)wip] *v.* piiskata, ruoskia; pieksää; antaa selkään; vatkata; ommella yliluoden; (puhek.) voittaa; siepata, tempaista; rientää, livahtaa, kiitää; *s.* piiska, ruoska; piiskuri (parl.); piiskurin määräys; pikööri (ajometsästyksessä); *be* ~*ped* saada selkäänsä; *he* ~*ped off to France* hän lähti kiireesti Ranskaan; ~ *on* ruoskalla hoputtaa; ~ *round* toimittaa rahankeräys; *a* ~*-round* keräys. **-cord** piiskansiima. **~-hand:** *have the w.-h. of* olla yliote jksta. **~-lash** piiskansiima. **-per-in** *s.* pikööri. **-per-snapper** nulikka.

whippet ['(h)wipit] *s.* whippet, pieni vinttikoira.

whipping *s.* selkäsauna; vatkaaminen.

~**-boy** syntipukki. ~**-top** siimahyrrä.

whippoorwill ['(h)wippuəwil] *s.* (pohj.am.) kehrääjälintu, preeriakehrääjä.

whir, whirr [(h)wə:] *v.* suhista, surista; *s.* suhina, surina, viuhina.

whirl [(h)wə:l] *v.* pyöriä, kieppua; kieriä; kiitää, lentää; pyörittää, kiidättää; *s.* pyörre; *my thoughts are in a* ~ ajatukset pyörivät päässäni. **-igig** [-igig] *s.* hyrrä, karuselli; kiertokulku; *the* ~ *of time* onnen vaihtelut. **-pool** pyörre. **-wind** tuulenpyörre.

whisk [(h)wisk] *s.* huisku, vispilä; (hännän) huiskutus; *v.* huiskauttaa, huitaista; vatkata; temmata, lennättää, viilettää, livahtaa (m. ~ *away*, ~ *off*). **-er** [-ə] *s.:* ~*s* poskiparta, pulisongit; (kissan) kuonokarvat. **-ered** [-əd] *a.* poskipartaa käyttävä.

whisky ['(h)wiski] *s.* whisky, viski.

whisper ['(h)wispə] *v.* kuiskata, suhista, humista; *s.* kuiskaus, kuiske; suhina, humina; hiiskaus; ~ *abroad* levittää (huhua); *it is* ~*ed* [*that*] kuiskaillaan; *in a* ~ kuiskaten. **-ing** *s.* kuiskailu, kuiskuttelu.

whist [(h)wist] *s.* visti (korttip.).

whistle ['(h)wisl] *v.* viheltää, viuhua, suhista, vinkua; *s.* vihellys; viuhina, suhina; vihellyspilli; ~ *for* turhaan odottaa jtk; *wet one's* ~ kostuttaa kurkkuaan.

whit [(h)wit] *s.* rahtunen, hitunen; *not a* ~ ei rahtuakaan.

Whit [(h)wit] *s.:* ~ *Monday* toinen helluntaipäivä.

white [(h)wait] *a.* valkoinen, valko-; vaalea; kalpea; *s.* valkoinen (väri); valkoihoinen; munanvalkuainen (~ *of an egg*); silmänvalkuainen (~ *of the eye*); ~ *ant* termiitti; ~ *bread* vehnäleipä; ~*-collar worker* henkisen työn tekijä; ~ *frost* huurre; ~ *heat* valkohehkutus; ~ *horses* vaahtopäälaineet; ~ *lie* hätävalhe; ~ *man* valkoinen; ~ *night* uneton yö; ~ *tie* iltapuku (frakki); *the* ~*s* valkoihoiset. **-bait** pikkusilli. **-fish** Am. siika.

Whitehall *erisn.* katu Lontoossa; Britannian hallitus.

white|-hot valkohehkuinen. ~**-livered**

pelkurimainen.

white|n ['(h)waitn] v. valkaista;
vaaleta. **-ness** s. valkeus, valkoisuus.
-ning s. valkaisuaine. **-thorn**
orapihlaja. **-throat** pensaskerttu.
-wash v. kalkita, valkaista; (kuv.)
pestä puhtaaksi; s. valkaisu;
kalkkivesi, -väri. **-washing** s. valkaisu.

whither ['(h)wiðə] adv. (vanh.) mihin?
minne? jonne.

whit|ing ['(h)waitiŋ] s. kalkkiväri;
valkoturska. **-ish** [-iʃ] a. valkeahko.

whitlow ['(h)witləu] s. kynsinahan
tulehdus, sormiajos.

Whitsun '(h)witsn] = Whit. **-day** s.
helluntaipäivä. **-tide** s.
helluntai(pyhät t. -viikko).

whittle ['(h)witl] v. veistää, veistellä,
vuolla; ~ down typistää, pienentää.

whiz, whizz [(h)wiz] v. viuhua,
suhahtaa, pyrähtää, pyyhältää,
hurahtaa, viilettää; s. viuhina.

who [hu:] interr. pron. kuka, ketkä;
relat. joka; whom (puhek. who) did
you see? kenet näit t. tapasit? ~ did
you give it to? kenelle sen annoit?
Who's Who kuka kukin on; ~ever?
kuka ihmeessä? all of ~m jotka
kaikki; whose kenen.

whoa [wəu] int. ptruu!

whodunit [hu:'dʌnit] s. sl.
salapoliisiromaani, jännäri.

whoever [-'evə] relat. pron. kuka
tahansa joka; (jokainen) joka.

whole [həul] a. koko; kokonainen,
ehjä; koskematon; jakamaton,
vähentymätön; s. kokonainen,
kokonaisuus; [swallow sth.] ~
kokonaisena; ~ meal kokojyvä-; ~
milk kuorimaton maito; ~ number
kokonaisluku; with a ~ skin ehjin
nahoin; make ~ parantaa; the ~ of
kaikki, koko; on the ~ suurin piirtein,
ylimalkaan, kaikki huomioonottaen;
[taken] as a ~ kokonaisuutena
(katsoen). **-hearted** ehdoton,
kokosydäminen. **~-length:** w.-l.
picture kokovartalokuva. **-ness** s.
kokonaisuus. **-sale** a. tukkukauppa-,
tukku-; joukko-; sell [by] ~ myydä
tukuittain; ~ dealer (merchant)
tukkukauppias; ~ price tukkuhinta; a
~ slaughter joukkomurha. **-saler** s.
tukkukauppias. **-some** [-səm] a.

terveellinen; hyödyllinen. **~-time** a.
päätoiminen.

wholly ['həuli] adv. kokonaan,
täydellisesti; täysin.

whom [hu:m] pron. (obj. muoto, nyk.
us. who); both of ~ jotka molemmat.

whoop [hu:p] v. hinkua; huutaa; s.
hinkuminen; huuto, hihkaisu; ~ it up
(sl.) remuta, ottaa ilo irti elämästä.
-ee ['wu:pi:] s. remuava juhla; make
~ remuta. **-ing-cough** s. hinkuyskä.

whop [(h)wɔp] v. antaa selkäsauna,
piestä. **-per** [-ə] s. sl. emävalhe. **-ping**
a. sl. aikamoinen, emä-(valhe); a ~
big fish aika vonkale.

whore [hɔ:] s. portto.

whorl [(h)wə:l] s. kiehkura (kasv.);
(kierukan) kierre.

whortleberry ['(h)wə:tlberi] s.
mustikka.

who|se [hu:z] pron. (gen. ks. who)
kenen, keiden; jonka, joiden. **-soever**
[hu:sə(u)'evə] ks. whoever.

why [(h)wai] adv. miksi?
minkätähden? (relat.) jonka tähden,
miksi; int. hyvänen aika! no niin! no!
~, no! ei suinkaan! ~ not miksi ei; the
reasons why [he ..] syyt miksi; this is
~ I left tästä syystä lähdin.

wick [wik] s. (kynttilän ym) sydän.

wicked ['wikid] a. paha, huono,
syntinen, jumalaton, paheellinen;
ilkeä, häijy, katala, kurja;
pahanilkinen, ilkikurinen. **-ness** s.
pahuus, turmelus, häijyys.

wicker ['wikə] s. koripaju; ~ chair
korituoli. **~-work** kori|punonta, -työ.

wicket ['wikit] s. pieni ovi t. veräjä;
(krik.) portti. **~-keeper** maalivahti.

wide [waid] a. laaja, avara; väljä,
leveä; laajalle ulottuva; suuri;
harhaan osunut; adv. laajalle, -lla,
laajalti; kauas, kaukana; a ~
knowledge monipuoliset tiedot; the ~
world avara maailma; ~ of the mark
kauas maalista, päin seiniä; far and ~
joka taholla, kaikkialla; ~ apart
kaukana toisistaan; ~ awake täysin
hereillä; ~ open selkoselällään; ~ boy
(sl.) huijari(poika); with ~ eyes silmät
suurina; ~ screen laajakangas.
~-angle laajakulma (valok.).
~-awake a. (kuv.) valpas, valppaana.
-ly adv. laajalti, laajasti; suuresti;

differ ~ *in opinion* olla aivan eri mieltä; ~ *popular* laajoissa piireissä suosittu. **-n** [-n] *v.* laajentaa, suurentaa, leventää; avartaa; laajentua, levetä; *road* ~ *ing* tien levennys. **-ness** *s.* laajuus, leveys. **-spread** *a.* laaja(lle levinnyt).

widgeon ['widʒn] *s.* haapana.

widow ['widəu] *s.* leski(rouva). **-ed** [-d] *a.* leskeksi jäänyt, leski-. **-er** [-ə] *s.* leskimies. **-hood** *s.* leskeys.

width [widθ] *s.* laajuus, leveys; *of the same* ~ samanlevyinen.

wield [wi:ld] *v.* käsitellä, käyttää, pitää hallussaan; ~ *the pen* kirjoittaa; ~ *the sceptre* kantaa valtikkaa, hallita.

wife [waif] *s.* (pl. *wives*) vaimo, aviovaimo, (avio)puoliso; *old wives' tales!* akkojen loruja! **-like, -ly** [-li] *a.* aviovaimon.

wig [wig] *s.* tekotukka, peruukki; ~ *ging* läksytys. **-ged** [-d] *a.* peruukkipäinen.

wiggle ['wigl] *v.* nytkyttää, väännellä.

wight [wait] *s.* (vanh.) olento.

Wight [wait] *erisn.: the Isle of* ~ Wight-saari.

wigwam ['wigwəm] *s.* intiaanimaja, -teltta.

wild [waild] *a.* villi, autio, raivaamaton; raakalais-; kesytön, vauhko; hurja, raju, raivokas; ankara, hillitön, huimapäinen; mieletön, vimmattu; sekava; *adv.* hurjasti jne; umpimähkään, harkitsemattomasti; *s.* (tav. ~ *s*) erämaa(t), sydänmaa(t); ~ *life* villielämistö; [*this flower*] *grows* ~ *in* .. kasvaa luonnonvaraisena -ssa; ~ *flowers* luonnonvaraiset kukat; ~ *scheme* harkitsematon suunnitelma; ~ *shot* umpimähkään ammuttu laukaus; ~ *thought* päähänpisto; ~ *words* sekava t. tolkuton puhe; ~ *about sb.* hullaantunut jhk; ~ *with delight* suunniltaan ilosta; *get* ~ (m.) joutua suunniltaan, raivostua; *he has been* ~ *in his youth* hän on hurjistellut nuorena; *run* ~ villiintyä; juoksennella vapaana; karata tiehensä; *talk* ~ puhua sekavasti, hourailla. **-cat** *s.: ~ strike* korpilakko.

Wilde [waild], **-r** [-ə] *erisn.*

wildebeest ['wildibi:st] *s.* gnu.

wilderness ['wildənis] *s.* erämaa, korpi, salomaa; *a* ~ *of* loputon määrä jtk.

wild|-eyed *a.* hurja(sti tuijottava); uskomaton, mieletön. **-fire** *s.: [spread] like* ~ kuin kulovalkea'. **~-goose** *s.: be on a w.-g. chase* tavoitella mahdottomia. **-ly** *adv.* hurjasti, huimasti; *talk* ~ puhua tolkuttomia. **-ness** *s.* villeys jne; kesyttömyys.

wile [wail] *s.* (tav. *pl.)* juoni, juonet, vehkeily; *v.* houkutella; ~ *away* ks. *while away.*

wilful ['wilf(u)l] *a.* itsepäinen; tahallinen, tarkoituksellinen. **-ly** *adv.* tieten tahtoen. **-ness** *s.* itsepäisyys.

wiliness *s.* kavaluus, juonet.

will [wil] *apuv.* (imp. *would*) käytetään mm. futuuria muodostettaessa (et. 2. 3. pers.); *v. tr.* (*willed willed*) tahtoa; testamentissa määrätä; *s.* tahto; testamentti, jälkisäädös; *he* ~ *come* hän tulee (fut.); *I* ~ *do it* teen sen, aion tehdä sen; *pass the salt,* ~ *you?* ole hyvä ja ojenna suola; ~ *you come in?* tulkaa (t. käykää) sisään, olkaa hyvä; *that* ~ *do* se riittää; *boys* ~ *be boys* pojat ovat poikia; *such things* ~ *happen* sellaista sattuu (toisinaan); *she would sit idle for hours* hän saattoi istua tuntikausia jouten; *he* ~ *recover* hän paranee (fut.); *God* ~ *ing* jos Jumala suo; *have one's* ~ päästä tahtonsa perille; *if he had his* ~ jos hän saisi määrätä; *make one's* ~ tehdä testamenttinsa; *leave by* ~ määrätä testamentilla; *against her* ~ vastoin (hänen) tahtoansa; *at* ~ mielensä mukaan, vapaasti, esteettömästi; *of one's own free* ~ vapaasta tahdostaan; *with a* ~ sydämen pohjasta, tarmokkaasti. **-ed** [-d] *a.* (yhd.) -tahtoinen.

willing ['wiliŋ] *a.* halukas, aulis, taipuvainen; *be* ~ *to* kernaasti tahtoa, suostua, olla valmis jhk. **-ly** [-li] *adv.* kernaasti, mielellään, auliisti. **-ness** *s.* aulius, halukkuus.

will-o'-the-wisp ['wiləðəwisp] *s.* virvatuli.

Willoughby ['wiləbi] *erisn.*

willow ['wiləu] *s.* paju, raita. **-herb** *s.* horsma. **-y** [-i] *a.* norja, notkea, solakka.

will-power s. tahdonvoima.
willy-nilly ['wili'nili] adv. tahtoen tai tahtomattaan.
wilt 1. [wilt] (vanh.) 2. pers. sg. prees. ks. will.
wilt 2. [wilt] v. lakastua, kuihtua; kuihduttaa.
Wilts [wilts] lyh. = Wiltshire.
wily ['waili] a. salakavala.
wimple ['wimpl] s. (nunnan)huntu.
win [win] won won, v. voittaa; saavuttaa, saada osakseen; saada puolelleen; miellyttää, viehättää; s. voitto; we've won! me voitimme! ~ the day (field) päästä voittajaksi; ~ by a length voittaa yhdellä (hevosen t. veneen) mitalla; ~ over voittaa jku puolelleen; ~ through, ~ out selviytyä voittajana.
wince [wins] v. vavahtaa, sävähtää; s. vavahdus, sävähdys; without a ~ silmää räpäyttämättä.
winch [win(t)ʃ] s. kampi; vintturi.
wind 1. [wind] s. tuuli; hengitys, henki; vainu, vihi; (vatsan) kaasu, ilma(vaivat); kielenpieksäntä, jonninjoutava puhe; the ~ puhaltimet (mus.); v. [wind] ~ed ~ed vainuta, hengästyttää; lepuuttaa (hevosta); [waind] puhaltaa (imp. & pp. m. wound); there is no ~ today tänään ei tuule; sail close to the ~ purjehtia liki tuulta, (kuv.) hipoa säädyttömyyttä t. epärehellisyyttä; in the ~ tekeillä; the eye of the ~ myrskyn silmä; in the ~'s eye, in the teeth of the ~ vasten tuulta; cast (fling) to the ~s heittää tuulen teille, hylätä; break ~ pieraista, päästää kaasua; get ~ of saada vihiä jstk; get the ~ up (sl.) olla peloissaan; put the ~ up sb. (sl.) pelottaa; raise the ~ (sl.) hankkia rahoja.
wind 2. [waind] wound wound, v. kiertää, kietoa, keriä, puolata; vetää (kello, tav. ~ up;) kiertyä, kietoutua, kiemurrella, mutkitella; s. mutka; ~ up vetää (kello), (kaupp.) selvittää; päättää, lopettaa, loppua; jännittää; ~ing staircase kierreportaat.
wind|-bag [i] suunpieksijä. **~-cheater** tuulitakki. **-ed** a. hengästynyt. **-fall** pudonneet hedelmät; odottamaton perintö ym, onnenpotku. **~-flower** vuokko. **~-gauge** tuulenmittari. **-iness**

s. tuulisuus; pöyhistely, tyhjänpäiväisyys.
winding [ai] a. kiemurteleva, polveileva; s. mutka, polvi, kiertyminen; ~ stairs kierreportaat. **~-up** lopettaminen; selvitys.
wind|-instrument [i] puhallussoitin. **-jammer** [-dʒæmə] iso purjealus.
windlass ['windləs] s. vintturi.
windmill ['winmil] s. tuulimylly; tilt at ~s taistella tuulimyllyjä vastaan.
window ['windəu] s. ikkuna; show-näyteikkuna; ticket- lippuluukku; blind- valeikkuna; at the ~ ikkunassa, ikkunan ääressä; [look] out of the ~ ikkunasta. **~-box** kukkalaatikko. **~-dressing** (näyte)ikkunan somistus; mainostus. **~-frame** ikkunankehys. **~-pane** ikkunaruutu. **~-sill** ikkunalauta.
wind|pipe henkitorvi. **-screen** (auton) tuulilasi; ~-wiper tuulilasin pyyhkijä. **-shield** s. Am. = ed. **~-sock** s. tuulipussi (ilm.). **~-swept** tuulen pieksemä.
Windsor ['winzə] erisn.
windward ['windwəd] adv. tuulen puolella, -lle; a. tuulenpuolinen; s. tuulen puoli.
windy ['windi] s. tuulinen, tuulelle altis; tyhjänpäiväinen, monisanainen; (sl.) pelokas.
wine [wain] s. viini; over the ~ viinilasien ääressä. **~-bibber** (vanh.) ryyppymies. **~-card** viinilista. **-glass** viinilasi. **-press** viininpuserrin.
wing [wiŋ] s. siipi; siipirakennus; (sot.) sivusta, siipi; lentorykmentti; pl. sivukulissit; v. varustaa siivillä; kiidättää; lentää, kiitää; haavoittaa siipeen t. käsivarteen; left ~ vasen siipi, vasemmisto(-); add (lend) ~s to antaa siivet, siivittää; on the ~ lennossa; take ~ lähteä lentoon; ~ one's way suunnata lentonsa, lentää. **~-commander** (ilm.) everstiluutnantti. **-ed** [-d] a. siivekäs; siipeenammuttu. **~-span, ~-spread** siipien väli.
wink [wiŋk] v. vilkuttaa, räpyttää; iskeä silmää (at jklle); vilkkua; s. vilkutus, räpytys; vihjaus; uinahdus; ~ at sth. ummistaa silmänsä jllek, ei olla huomaavinaan; I did not sleep a ~

en ummistanut silmiäni; *forty ~s*
nokkaunet; *~ing lights* (auton)
vilkkuvalot.

winkle ['wiŋkl] *s.* rantakotilo; *v.: ~ out
the truth* tiukata totuus ilmi.

winn|er ['winə] *s.* voittaja. **-ing** *a.*
voittava; viehättävä, miellyttävä; *~s
voitto(summa).* **-ing-post** maalipylväs.

winnow ['winəu] *v.* pohtaa, viskata
eloa; seuloa, erotella.

winsome ['winsəm] *a.* miellyttävä,
viehättävä.

winter ['wintə] *s.* talvi; *attr.* talvi-,
talvinen; *v.* talvehtia, viettää talvea;
in [*the*] *~* talvella.

wintry ['wintri] *a.* talvinen, talvi-;
kylmä, kalsea.

wipe [waip] *v.* pyyhkiä, kuivata; *s.*
pyyhkäisy, sipaisu; sl. nenäliina; *~
one's eyes* pyyhkiä kyyneleensä; *~
one's nose* pyyhkiä nenäänsä; *~ away*
pyyhkiä pois; *~ out* pyyhkiä
puhtaaksi; tuhota, (sl.) tappaa. **-r** [-ə]
s. pyyhkijä, pyyhin.

wire ['waiə] *s.* metallilanka; (sähkö-
ym) johdin, puhelinlanka;
sähkösanoma; *v.* kääriä, kiinnittää,
vahvistaa metallilangalla; sähköttää;
barbed ~ piikkilanka; *~ gauze* hieno
metalliverkko; *~ rope* teräsköysi; *pull
the ~s* (kuv.) hoidella (pitää
käsissään) lankoja; *by ~* sähköteitse.
-cutters peltisakset. **~-haired**
karkeakarvainen. **-less** *a.* langaton; *s.*
radio; radiosanoma; *~ operator*
radiosähköttäjä; *~ set*
radio(vastaanotin). **~-netting**
rautalankaverkko. **~-puller**
näkymätön johtaja (joka pitelee
käsissään lankoja).

wir|ing *s.* sähköjohdot. **-y** ['waiəri] *a.*
sitkeä, jäntevä, luja.

Wisconsin [wis'konsin] *erisn.*

wisdom ['wizdəm] *s.* viisaus; *~ after the
event* jälkiviisaus. **~-tooth**
viisaudenhammas.

wise 1. [waiz] *s.* (vanh.) tapa, *in no ~* ei
suinkaan, ei mitenkään; *-wise* jnk
tavoin, jhk suuntaan; *cross~* ristissä,
-iin.

wise 2. [waiz] *a.* viisas,
ymmärtäväinen; järkevä; *a ~ guy*
(sl.) itserakas heppu; *the* [*three*] *W~
Men* tietäjät; *I was none the ~r for it*

en tullut siitä hullua hurskaammaksi;
~ to perillä jstk; *get ~ to* (sl.) hoksata;
put sb. ~ to valistaa; *~d up* (sl.)
perillä jstk. **-acre** [-eikə] *s.* rikkiviisas,
kaikkitietäväinen. **-crack** *s.* sutkaus;
v. sutkauttaa. **-ly** *adv.* viisaasti
(kyllä).

wish [wiʃ] *v.* toivoa, haluta, toivottaa;
s. toivomus, toive, halu, mielihalu;
toivotus; *~ sb. well* tahtoa jkn
parasta; *~ for* haluta, kaivata jtk;
good ~es onnentoivotukset; *best ~es
for a happy Christmas!* hyvää joulua!
get one's ~ päästä tahtonsa perille; *at
sb.'s ~* jkn pyynnöstä; *I ~ I were*
kunpa olisin. **-ed-for** *a.* toivottu,
kaivattu. **-ful** *a.* halukas, innokas; *~
thinking* toiveajattelu. **-(ing-)bone**
(linnun) hankaluu. **-y-washy** *a.* mieto,
latkuinen; laimea.

wisp [wisp] *s.* nippu, suortuva,
(savu)haituva, kiemura. **-y** [-i] *a.*
hapsottava.

wistaria [wis'tɛəriə] *s.* vistaria.

wistful [wistf(u)l] *a.* kaihoisa, haikea.
-ness *s.* kaiho(mielisyys).

wit [wit] *s.* (*sg.* t. *pl.*) äly, ymmärrys,
järki; älyniekka; *v.* (vanh.) tietää; *has
slow ~s* (-lla) on hidas käsityskyky; *I
am at my ~s' end* olen aivan
ymmälläni; *frightened out of his ~s*
suunniltaan pelosta; *be out of one's ~s*
olla järjiltään; *have one's ~s about
one* olla valppaana (t. pää kylmänä).

witch [witʃ] *s.* noita(-akka),
velho; lumooja(tar); *~ doctor*
poppamies; *~ hunt*
(poliittinen) noitavaino.
-craft noituus.

with [wið] *prep.* kanssa, kera, mukana,
seurassa, luona; (ilm. keinoa,
välinettä) jnk avulla, -lla, -llä (ilm. m.
tapaa, syytä); *we see ~ our eyes*
näemme silmillämme; *a coat ~ three
pockets* takki, jossa on kolme taskua;
increases ~ age lisääntyy iän
karttuessa; *he is staying ~ the Browns*
hän asuu Brownien luona; *a girl ~
blue eyes* sinisilmäinen tyttö; *he told
me ~ tears* hän kertoi kyynelsilmin; *~
ease* vaivattomasti, helposti; *~ child*
raskaana; *stiff ~ cold* jäykkänä
kylmästä; *angry ~* suuttunut jklle;
charge . . ~ syyttää jstk; *fight ~*

taistella jkta vastaan; *part* ~ erota
jksta; *I'm* ~ *you in .*. olen puolellasi;
~ *all his faults* [*I like him*] hänen
vioistaan huolimatta. **-al** [wi'ðɔ:l] *adv.*
(vanh.) samalla, myöskin, sen ohessa;
= *with.*

withdraw [wið'drɔ:] *v.* (ks. *draw*) vetää
takaisin t. pois; ottaa pois, poistaa
(ohjelmasta, liikkeestä ym);
peruuttaa; vetäytyä pois, poistua,
peräytyä; luopua, erota; ~ *one's
custom* lopettaa asiakassuhde. **-al**
[-(ə)l] *s.* takaisin vetäminen, pois
ottaminen, poistaminen;
peruuttaminen; luopuminen,
eroaminen. **-n** [-n] *a.* eristäytyvä,
sulkeutunut.

withe [waið] *s.* pajunvitsa.

wither ['wiðə] *v.* lakastua, kuihtua;
surkastua, kuivua (kokoon);
kuihduttaa (m. ~ *up);* musertaa
(kuv.). **-ed** [-d] *a.* kuihtunut,
lakastunut. **-ing** *a.* (kuv.) musertava,
murhaava.

withers ['wiðəz] *s.* (hevosen ym) säkä.

withhold [wið'həuld] *v.* (ks. *hold*)
pidättää, salata jklta; evätä; *I shall* ~
my consent en suostu.

within [wi'ðin] *prep.* sisäpuolella, -lle;
sisällä, -lle, sisässä, sisään; m. jnk
puitteissa, rajoissa; *adv.:* ~ *and
without* sisä- ja ulkopuolella; *live* ~
one's income elää varojensa mukaan;
~ *five years* viiden vuoden kuluessa;
~ *an hour* tunnin kuluessa; *anything*
~ *reason* kaikki mitä kohtuudella
voidaan vaatia; ~ *reach* ulottuvilla; ~
sight näkyvissä.

without [wi'ðaut] *prep.* ilman, vailla,
-tta, -ttä, -ton, -tön; (vanh.)
ulkopuolella, -lle; *adv.* (vanh.)
ulkopuolella; *from* ~ ulkoa päin; ~
fear pelotta, peloton; ~ *interruption*
keskeytymättä; ~ *knowing*
tietämättä(än); *do* ~ tulla toimeen
ilman jtk; *go* ~ olla ilman, vailla jtk; *it
goes* ~ *saying* on sanomattakin selvä.

withstand [wið'stænd] *v.* (ks. *stand*)
kestää, pitää puoliaan jtk vastaan,
vastustaa.

withy ['wiði] *s.* ks. *withe.*

witless *a.* typerä, älytön.

witness ['witnis] *s.* silminnäkijä,
todistaja; todistus; *v.* todistaa (m. jk

oikeaksi); olla jnk silminnäkijänä;
olla todistuksena t. osoituksena jstk;
bear ~ *to* todistaa; *call as a* ~ kutsua
todistajaksi; *in* ~ *of* jnk todistukseksi;
~*ed by* (jäljennöksen ym) oikeaksi
todistavat. **~-box** todistajan aitio.

wit|icism ['witisizm] *s.* sukkeluus.
-iness *s.* älykkyys, henkevyys. **-ingly**
['witiŋli] *adv.* tieten tahtoen, ehdoin
tahdoin. **-y** ['witi] *a.* älykäs, henkevä,
sukkela.

wives [waivz] *pl.* ks. *wife.*

wizard ['wizəd] *s.* noita, velho.

wizened ['wiznd] *a.* kurttuinen.

woad [wəud] *s.* värimorsinko; siniväri.

wobbl|e ['wɔbl] *v.* horjua (m. kuv.),
horjahtaa, heilua, epäröidä;
huojuttaa; *s.* heiluminen,
horjuminen. **-y** [-i] *s.* horjuva,
huojuva, epävarma.

woe [wəu] *s.* suru, murhe; kärsimys,
onnettomuus; *int.* voi! ~ *is me!* voi
minua! **-begone** [-bigɔn] *a.* surun
murtama, onneton, kurja. **-ful** *a.*
murheellinen; surkea.

wog [wɔg] *s.* egyptiläisen, arabin ym
pilkkanimi.

woke [wəuk] *imp.* ks. *wake.*

wold [wəuld] *s.* kumpuileva
kangasmaa.

wolf [wulf] *s.* (pl. *wolves*) susi; *she*~
naarassusi; *cry* ~ hälyttää turhaan;
keep the ~ *from the door* pitää nälkä
loitolla; *a* ~ *in sheep's clothing* susi
lammasten vaatteissa; ~ [*down*]
nielaista ahnaasti, hotkia. **~-cub**
sudenpentu (m. partiolainen). **-ish**
[-iʃ] *a.* ahnas.

wolverine ['wulvəri:n] *s.* ahma.

wolves [wulvz] *pl.* ks. *wolf.*

woman ['wumən] *s.* (pl. *women*)
nainen; *attr.* nais-; ~*doctor*
naislääkäri; ~ *driver* naisautoilija;
~*-hater* naistenvihaaja; ~ *friend*
ystävätär; *women's rights* naisasia.
-hood *s.* naisellisuus; *reach* ~ kypsyä
naiseksi. **-ish** [-iʃ] *a.* naismainen. **-izer**
[-aizə] *s.* naisten metsästäjä. **-kind** *s.*
naiset, naisväki. **-like, -ly** *a.* naisellinen.

womb [wu:m] *s.* kohtu. **-at** ['wɔmbət] *s.*
vompatti.

women ['wimin] *pl.* ks. *woman.* **-folk**
(koll.) naiset, naisväki.

won [wʌn] *imp. & pp.* ks. *win.*

wonder ['wʌndə] s. ihme; ihmettely, kummastus; v. ihmetellä, kummastella *(at* jtk); haluta tietää; *I ~ who he is* kuka hän mahtaa olla; *I ~ if you have*.. onkohan teillä.. . *I ~ if you could* [*help me*] voisitteko ystävällisesti.. ; *in ~* ihmetellen; *for a ~* kerran ihmeen vuoksi; *and small ~!* ja ihmekös tuo! *no ~ he*..eipä ihme että hän; *work ~ s* saada aikaan ihmeitä. **-ful** *a.* ihmeellinen. **-fully** *adv.* ihmeellisesti; ihmeen. **-land** ihme-, satumaa. **-ment** *s.* ihmettely.

wondrous ['wʌndrəs] *a.* ihmeellinen; *adv.* ihmeen.

wonky ['wɔŋki] *a.* sl. hatara, tutiseva.

won't [wcount] lyh. = *will not*.

wont [wcount] *s.* tottumus, tapa; *he was ~ to* hänellä oli tapana. **-ed** [-id] *a.* tavanmukainen.

woo [wu:] *v.* kosia, kosiskella; tavoitella.

wood [wud] *s.* metsä (m. *~s*); puu, puuaine, halot, tynnyri; *out of the ~* turvassa; [*wine*] *from the ~* tynnyristä laskettu. **~-anemone** valkovuokko. **-bine** kuusama. **-cock** lehtokurppa. **-craft** eränkäyntitaito. **-cut** puupiirros. **~-cutter** hakkuumies. **-ed** [-id] *a.* metsäinen. **-en** [-n] *a.* puinen, puu-; puiseva, kankea, ilmeetön; *~-headed* pölkkypäinen. **-land** *s.* metsämaa, metsä; *a.* metsä-. **~-louse** maasiira. **-man** metsänvartija; hakkuumies. **-pecker** tikka. **~-pulp** puuhioke. **-ruff** maratti (kasv.). **-s** [-z] *s.* pl. metsä. **-sman** eränkävijä. **-winds** puupuhaltimet (mus.). **-work** *s.* puutyö; veisto. **-y** [-i] *a.* metsäinen; puumainen.

woof [wu:f] *s.* kude.

wool [wul] *s.* villa, villat; villalanka, **-kangas**; *pure ~* täyttää villaa; *much cry, little ~* paljon porua, vähän villoja; *a ball of ~* villalankakerä; *dyed in the ~* »pesunkestävä»; *pull the ~ over sb.'s eyes* puijata. **-gathering** *s.* hajamielisyys; *a.* uneksiva, hajamielinen. **-len** [-in] *a.* villa-, villainen; *s.: ~ s, ~ goods* villatavarat. **-ly** [-i] *a.* villainen; untuva; epäselvä, epämääräinen; *s.* villa(neule)takki; *woollies* villaiset (alus)vaatteet. **-sack** *s.: the W~* lordikanslerin istuin

ylähuoneessa.

Woolwich ['wulidʒ] *erisn.*

woozy ['wu:zi] *a.* sl. sotkuinen, m. humalainen, kännissä.

wop [wɔp] *s.* (sl.) italialainen (pilkkanimi).

Worcester ['wustə] *erisn.*

word [wə:d] *s.* sana; *(pl.* m. puhe, keskustelu, sanakiista); viesti, tiedonanto; lupaus; käsky; tunnussana; *v.* sanoin ilmaista, antaa sanamuoto; *be as good as one's ~* pysyä sanassaan; *bring ~* tuoda sana, tieto; *give the ~ to fire* komentaa ampumaan; *have a ~ with* vaihtaa pari sanaa jkn kanssa; *have ~ s with* kinastella, joutua sanaharkkaan jkn kanssa; *put in a good ~ for* puhua jkn puolesta; *send ~* lähettää sana, tiedottaa; *take my ~ for it* usko minun sanoneen, voit luottaa minuun! *take sb. at his ~* luottaa jkn sanoihin; *~ for ~* sanasta sanaan, sananmukaisesti; *by ~ of mouth* suusanallisesti; *in a ~* sanalla sanoen; *tell* (sb.) *in so many ~ s* puhua asiat halki; [*a man*] *of few words* harvasanainen; *upon my ~* kunniasanallani; mitä ihmettä! todellako? **-ed** [-id] *a.* -sanainen. **-iness** *s.* monisanaisuus. **-ing** *s.* sanamuoto. **~-perfect** *a.: be w.-p.* osata sanasta sanaan. **~-play** sanaleikki.

Wordsworth ['wə:dzwəθ] *erisn.*

wordy ['wə:di] *a.* monisanainen.

wore [wɔ:] *imp.* ks. *wear.*

work 1. [wə:k] *s.* työ, työnteko; teos, tuote; *pl.* tehdas, laitos, laitteet, (kone)paja, *pl.* (kellon) koneisto; *pl.* linnoituslaitteet; *a ~ of art* taideteos; *a ~ on history* historiallinen teos; *I'll have my ~ cut out* [*for me*] minulla on aikamoinen urakka; *set to ~* ryhtyä, käydä käsiksi työhön; *at ~* työssä, käynnissä; *be hard at ~* [*upon*] työskennellä uutterasti; *look for ~* hakea työtä; *in* (out of) *~* työssä, työttömänä; *make short ~ of* selviytyä nopeasti jstk; *public ~ s* yleiset työt; *~ s council* tuotantokomitea; *the ~ s of Scott* S:n teokset; *give sb. the ~ s* (sl.) antaa löylytys.

work 2. *~ed ~ed* (joskus *wrought wrought*) *v.* tehdä työtä, olla jssk

työssä, työskennellä; olla käynnissä,
käydä, toimia; onnistua, tehota,
tepsiä, vaikuttaa; kuohua, (piirteistä)
vääntyä; ponnistella (eteenpäin);
käydä (juomista); pitää työssä,
teettää työtä; pitää käynnissä,
käyttää; hoitaa, harjoittaa;
aikaansaada; tunkea (vähitellen);
valmistella, käsitellä, muokata,
viljellä, vaivata (taikinaa); kirjoa,
ommella; tutkia, ratkaista; taivutella;
~ *the bellows* painaa palkeita, polkea
urkuja; ~ *havoc* tehdä paljon tuhoa,
tuhota; ~ *loose* irtautua, höltyä;
irrottaa; ~ *one's passage* maksaa
työllä matkansa; ~ *one's way* raivata
tiensä, tunkeutua, *(through university)*
suorittaa opintonsa ansiotyönä
ohella; ~ *at* olla jssk työssä, opiskella
jtk; ~ *away* ahertaa; ~ *down* luisua
alas; ~ *in* vähitellen tunkeutua sisään,
sovittaa; ~ *into* tunkeutua jhk; *he*
~*ed them* [*up*] *into enthusiasm* hän sai
heidät innostumaan; ~ *off* selvittää,
(työllä) purkaa jtk; ~ *on* jatkaa työtä;
(= ~ *upon*) vaikuttaa, tehota jhk; ~
out tunkeutua ulos t. näkyviin;
luonnistua; ratkaista, kehitellä;
käyttää loppuun; *the costs* ~ *out at £
50* kustannukset nousevat 50 puntaan;
it may ~ *out all right* ehkä asia selviää;
~ *over* muokata, parantaa; ~ *up*
kehittää, kehitellä; käsitellä, jalostaa,
saada aikaan, kiihottaa; vähitellen
kohota; *her wrought-up nerves* hänen
kiihtyneet hermonsa. **-able** [-əbl] *a.*
mahdollinen käsitellä, viljellä ym;
mahdollinen panna toimeen;
käyttökelpoinen. **-aday** [-ədei] *a.*
arkipäiväinen, ikävä. **-day** työpäivä,
arkipäivä. **-er** [-ə] *s.* työntekijä; ~ *bee*
työmehiläinen; *woman* ~
naistyöläinen. **-house** (vanh.)
köyhäintalo, Am. työlaitos.
working ['wə:kiŋ] *s.* työskentely, työ;
toiminta, käynti; käyttö; *pl.*
(kaivoksen) louhos, kaivos; *a.* työtä
tekevä; ~ *capital* käyttöpääoma; *the*
~ *classes* työväenluokka; *in* ~ *order*
käyttökunnossa; ~ *expenses*
käyttökustannukset; ~ *hours*
työaika; ~ *hypothesis*
työhypoteesi; *a* ~ *knowledge*
of käytännöllinen (esim.

kieli)taito; *a* ~ *majority* riittävä
enemmistö. ~**-day** työpäivä. ~**-man**
työmies. ~**-out** laskelma, kehittely;
toteutus.
work|man *s.* työmies, työläinen.
-manlike *a.* taitava. **-manship** *s.*
ammattitaito; suoritetun työn laatu;
of good ~ erinomaista työtä. **-out** *s.*
harjoitus. ~**-people** työläiset. **-place**
työpaikka. **-s** [-s] *s. pl.* tehdas; ~
council ks. *work 1; give sb. the* ~ ks.
work 1. ~**-shop** työpaja, verstas. ~**-shy**
työtä vieroksuva. ~**-study**
työntutkimus.
world [wə:ld] *s.* maailma; ääretön
joukko t. määrä; ~ *without end*
iankaikkisesti; *begin the* ~ aloittaa
uransa; *bring into the* ~ saattaa
maailmaan; *be thrown upon the* ~
jäädä oman onnensa nojaan; *a man of
the* ~ maailmanmies; *a* ~ *of*
äärettömän paljon, valtavasti; *not for
the* [*whole*] ~ ei mistään hinnasta; *for
all the* ~ *like* tarkalleen jkn näköinen;
how in the ~ *?* miten ihmeessä? *all the*
~ *and his wife* kaikki silmäntekevät;
~ *war* maailmansota. **-liness** *s.*
maailmallisuus, maailmanmielisyys.
-ling [-liŋ] *s.* maailmanlapsi. **-ly** [-li] *a.*
maallinen, aineellinen; = seur.;
(~**-minded** maailmallinen; ~**-wise**
maailmaa kokenut, viisastunut.)
world|-power maailmanvalta.
~**-renowned** maailmankuulu. ~**-wide**
koko maanpiirin käsittävä,
yleismaailmallinen; *w.-w. fame*
maailmanmaine.
worm [wə:m] *s.* mato (m. kuv.),
toukka; ruuvikierre, -kierteet; (~ *of
conscience*) kalvava tuska; *v.:* ~
oneself (one's way) luikerrella (esim.
jkn suosioon). ~**-eaten** madonsyömä.
~**-gear** kierukkapyörä. ~**-wood** mali
(kasv.), katkera nöyryytys. **-y** [-i] *a.*
matoja täynnä oleva, matoinen.
worn [wɔ:n] ks. *wear; a.* kulunut;
riutunut, uupunut *(with* jstk); ~ *down*
kulunut, nukkavieru. ~**-out** *a.* lopen
kulunut, uupunut.
worri|ed ['wari|d] *a.* levoton,
huolestunut; *be* ~ olla huolissaan. **-er**
[-ə] *s.* kiusanhenki.
worry ['wari] *v.* vaivata, huolestuttaa,
aiheuttaa huolta jklle; kiusata,

ahdistaa; olla levoton, olla huolissaan,
huolehtia; (koirasta ym) rääkätä; *s.*
huoli, kiusa, vaiva, harmi;
levottomuus; *don't ~!* älä ole levoton!
-ing *a.* huolestuttava, kiusallinen.
worse [wə:s] *komp.* ks. *bad*; *a.*
pahempi, huonompi; *adv.* pahemmin,
huonommin; *~ and ~* yhä huonompi
t. huonommin; *be ~ off* olla
huonommassa asemassa; *~ luck!* sitä
pahempi! *for better or ~* kävi miten
kävi; *to make matters ~* kaiken
kukkuraksi; *so much the ~ for him* sitä
pahempi hänelle; *[he] is none the ~ for
the accident* selvisi tapaturmasta
vammoitta; *the ~ for drink* humalassa;
the ~ for wear kulunut; *a change for
the ~* muutos huonompaan suuntaan;
from bad to ~ ojasta allikkoon. **-n** [-n]
v. pahentua, huonontua; pahentaa.
worship [wə:ʃip] *s.* palvonta;
jumalanpalvelus, hartaushetki,
hartaudenharjoitus; *v.* palvella;
palvoa, jumaloida; harjoittaa
hartautta, pitää jumalanpalvelusta;
hours of ~ jumalanpalveluksen
aika; *public ~* julkinen
jumalanpalvelus. **-per** [-ə] *s.* palvoja;
kirkkovieras.
worst [wə:st] *sup.* ks. *bad*; *a.* pahin,
huonoin; *adv.* pahimmin,
huonoimmin; *s.* pahin osa, asia jne; *v.*
voittaa, päästä voitolle jksta; *if the ~
comes to the ~* pahimmassa
tapauksessa; *get the ~ of it* joutua
tappiolle; *at[its, his] ~* pahimmillaan;
at ~ pahimmassa tapauksessa; *be ~ed*
[-id] saada selkäänsä.
worsted ['wustid] *s.* kampalanka.
-wort [wə:t] *s.* (yhd.) yrtti.
worth 1. [wə:θ] *a.* jnk arvoinen; *s.*
arvo, ansio(kkuus); *be ~* olla jnk
arvoinen, kannattaa; omistaa; *he is
~ . . a year* hänellä on . . -n vuositulot;
it is ~ noticing ansaitsee huomiota; *it
was ~ it (my while)* kannatti; *for what
it is ~* ilman takeita; *a man of ~*
ansiokas mies; *of great ~* hyvin
arvokas. **-ily** ['wə:ðili] *adv.*
arvokkaasti **-less** *a.* arvoton,
kelvoton, kehno. **-lessness** *s.*
arvottomuus, kelvottomuus. **~-while**
a. vaivan arvoinen, kannattava. **-y**
['wə:ði] *a.* arvokas, ansiokas; *s.*

huomattava henkilö; *~ of* jtk
ansaitseva, jnk arvoinen; *~ of
consideration* varteenotettava; *~ of
praise* kiitettävä.
wot [wɔt] *s.* (vanh.) ks. *wit.*
would [wud] *imp.* ks. *will; it ~ be
a pity* sepä olisi vahinko; *she ~ sit
there for hours* hän saattoi istua
siellä tuntikausia. **~-be:** *a ~
-be poet* runoilijan mainetta
havitteleva.
wound 1. [waund] *imp. & pp.* ks. *wind.*
wound 2. [wu:nd] *s.* haava (m. kuv.); *v.*
haavoittaa; loukata; *the ~ed*
haavoittuneet. **-ing** *a.* haavoittava,
loukkaava.
wove [wouv] *imp.* ks. *weave.* **-n** [-(ə)n]
pp. ks. *weave;* kudottu.
wow [wau] *int.* Am. sl. ohhoh; voi
veljet! *s.* jymymenestys.
wrack [ræk] *s.* rantaan ajautuneet
ruskolevät ym; *~ and ruin* ks. *rack.*
wraith [reiθ] *s.* haamu.
wrangle ['ræŋgl] *v.* riidellä, kinastella;
s. riita, tora. **-r** [-ə] *s.* (Cambr.)
matemaattisessa tutkinnossa
korkeimman arvosanan saanut.
wrap [ræp] *v.* kääriä, kietoa jhk
(us. . . ~ *up);* verhota, kätkeä; *s.*
(esim. ilta)viitta; huivi, huopa ym; *~
oneself up* kääriytyä, pukeutua
lämpimästi; *be ~ped up in* olla jhk
verhoutunut, uppoutua jhk;
omistautua jklle kokonaan, olla
syventynyt, syvästi kiintynyt jkh;
~ped up in herself itseensä
käpertynyt. **-per** [-ə] *s.* päällys,
(paperi)kääre; aamutakki. **-ping** *s.*
päällys, käärepaperi (m. *~ paper); gift
~* lahjapakkaus.
wrath [rɔ(:)θ, Am. ræθ] *s.* viha. **-ful** *a.*
vihastunut.
wreak [ri:k] *v.* purkaa (*one's fury upon*
vihansa jkh); *~ vengeance on* kostaa
jklle.
wreath [ri:θ] *s.* [pl. -ðz] seppele;
kiehkura; (savu)rengas, kiekura. **-e**
[ri:ð] *v.* kietoa, solmia, sitoa
(seppele): seppelöidä; kietoutua; *~d
in smiles* hymyilevä.
wreck [rek] *s.* haaksirikko;
(laiva)hylky; raunioläjä; (henkilöstä)
raunio; *v.* viedä haaksirikkoon;
tuhota; tuhoutua; [*the car was*] a mere

~ pelkkää romua; *be ~ed* haaksirikkoutua, kariutua. **-age** [-idʒ] *s.* hylkytavara, pirstaleet, jäännökset. **-er** [-ə] *s.* rantarosvo.

wren [ren] *s.* peukaloinen (eläint.).

wrench [ren(t)ʃ] *s.* kiskaisu; nyrjähdys; (eron tuottama) tuska, kipu; ruuviavain; *v.* vääntää (irti): kiskaista; nyrjähdyttää; vääristellä.

wrest [rest] *v.* vääntää (esim. jkn kädestä): kiristää (esim. suostumus): vääristää; ~ *a living* ansaita kovalla työllä niukka toimeentulo.

wrestl|e ['resl] *v.* painia, painiskella, taistella, ponnistella, *s.* painiskelu; taistelu. **-er** [-ə] *s.* painija. **-ing** *s.* paini; ~ *match* painiottelu.

wretch [retʃ] *s.* raukka, parka, kurja olento; heittiö, (leik.) veijari. **-ed** [-id] *a.* onneton, kurja, surkea; epätoivoinen; viheliäinen, kelvoton. **-edness** [-idnis] *s.* kurjuus, surkeus jne.

wrick [rik] *v.* venähdyttää, nyrjähdyttää.

wriggle ['rigl] *v.* kiemurrella, luikerrella; vääntelehtiä; kieputtaa; *s.* kiemurtelu.

wright [rait] *s.* (yhd.) -tekijä, -seppä, -rakentaja.

wring [riŋ] *wrung wrung*, *v.* väännellä; vääntää (kuivaksi) (m. ~ *out*); pusertaa, puristaa; *s.* puserrus; ~ *from* kiristää jklta jtk; *it wrung my heart* sydäntäni särki. **-er** [-ə] *s.* vääntöpuserrin, mankeli.

wrinkl|e ['riŋkl] *s.* ryppy, kurttu, poimu; vihje, metku; *v.* rypistää; rypistyä, vetäytyä kurttuun. **-ed** [-d], **-y** [-i] *a.* ryppyinen, kurttuinen.

wrist [rist] *s.* ranne; ~ *watch* r.-kello. **-band** ['ris(t)bænd] *s.* kalvosin. **-let** [-lit] *s.* rannerengas.

writ [rit] *s.* (vanh.) kirjoitus; (oikeuden) päätös, haaste, käskykirje; *the Holy* ~ Pyhä Raamattu; *serve a* ~ *on* antaa haaste jklle; ~ *large* (kuv.) suuressa mittakaavassa, silmäänpistävän selvästi.

write [rait] *wrote written*, *v.* kirjoittaa; sepittää, laatia; toimia kirjailijana; ~ *down* kirjoittaa, merkitä muistiin,

alentaa (arvo), *(sb. down as)* sanoa jksk; ~ *off* poistaa tileistä; jättää laskuista pois; ~ *out* kirjoittaa täydellisenä, jäljentää; ~ *out fair* kirjoittaa puhtaaksi; ~ *up* täydentää, saattaa ajan tasalle, ylistää. **-r** [-ə] *s.* kirjoittaja; kirjailija. **-off** *s.: a complete* ~ pelkkää romua. **~-up** *s.* (ylistävä) kuvaus.

writhe [raið] *v.* vääntelehtiä, kieritellä; kärsiä tuskaa.

writing *s.* kirjoitus, kirjoittaminen; kirjoitus|taito, -tyyli; käsiala; kirjailijantoimi; *pl.* teokset; *in* ~ kirjallisesti; *put in* ~ kirjoittaa.

written ['ritn] *pp.* ks. *write; a.* kirjoitettu, kirjallinen; ~ *test* kirjallinen koe; ~ *language* kirjakieli. **~-off** *a.: amount* ~ poisto.

wrong [rɔŋ] *a.* väärä, virheellinen, nurja; *adv.* väärin, virheellisesti; *s.* vääryys, väärä; *v.* tehdä (jklle) vääryyttä; loukata; tuomita väärin; *all* ~ aivan päin seiniä; *the* ~ *side* nurja puoli; ~ *side out* nurin päin; *on the* ~ *side of 40* 40:n huonommalla puolen; *[in] the* ~ *way* väärin, hullusti, takaperoisesti; *I am* ~ olen väärässä; *what is* ~ *with you* mikä sinua vaivaa? *there is something* ~ *with . .* -ssa on jotakin vikaa, . . on epäkunnossa; *my watch is* ~ kelloni käy väärin; *go* ~ mennä väärää tietä, eksyä, (kuv.) joutua harhateille; epäonnistua, mennä myttyyn, joutua epäkuntoon; *be in the* ~ olla väärässä; *put sb. in the* ~ saattaa jku väärään valoon. **-doer** [-duːə] *s.* väärintekijä, lainrikkoja. **-doing** *s.* rikkomus. **-ful** *a.* väärä, laiton, epäoikeudenmukainen. **-fully** *adv.* vääryydellä, väärin. **~-headed** *a.* jääräpäinen. **-ly** *adv.* väärin; epäoikeudenmukaisesti.

wrote [rəut] *imp.* ks. *write.*

wroth [rəuθ] *a.* (run. & leik.) vihastunut, julmistunut.

wrought [rɔːt] *imp. & pp.* ks. *work; ~ up* kiihtynyt; ~ *iron* meltoteräs; *has ~ great changes in* on saanut aikaan suuria muutoksia.

wrung [rʌŋ] *imp. & pp.* ks. *wring; ~ out* uupunut.

wry [rai] *a.* kieroon vääntynyt, vääristynyt; *make a* ~ *face* irvistää; *a*

~ smile väkinäinen hymy. **-neck** s.
käenpiika (eläint.).
Wyclif(fe) ['wiklif] erisn.

Wykehamist ['wikəmist] s. Winchester
Collegen oppilas.
Wyoming [wai'əumiŋ] erisn.

X

X, x [eks] s. x-kirjain.
Xanthippe [zæn'θipi] erisn.; s.
äkäpussi.
xenophobia [zenə'fəubjə] s. vieraan
pelko.

Xmas ['krisməs] lyh. = Christmas.
X-rays, x-rays ['eks'reiz] s.
röntgensäteet. **x-ray** v. ottaa
röntgenkuva jksta.
xylophone ['zailəfəun] s. ksylofoni.

Y

Y, y [wai] s. y-kirjain.
Lyh.; **yd** yard: **Y.H.A.** Youth Hostel
Association; **Y.M.C.A., Y.W.C.A.**
Young Mens's (Women's) Christian
Association; **yr(s)** years.
yacht [jot] s. (kilpa)purjevene; v.
purjehtia; luxury ~ huvipursi. **-club**
pursiseura. **-ing** s. purjehdus. **-sman** s.
purjehtija.
yahoo [jə'hu:] s. peto ihmishahmossa.
yak [jæk] s. jakki(härkä).
Yale [jeil] erisn.
yam [jæm] s. jamssi.
yank [jæŋk] nykäistä; tempaista.
Yank [jæŋk] s. sl. = seur. **-ee** [-i] s.
jenkki.
yap [jæp] v. luskuttaa, haukkua; s.
luskutus.
yard [ja:d] s. yardi (0,914 metriä);
raakapuu; piha, -maa; tarha; aitaus;
dock~ telakka; railway ~ ratapiha.
-man ratapihan työmies. ~**-measure**

(yardin) mittakeppi t. -nauha. **-stick**
(kuv.) mittapuu.
yarn [ja:n] s. lanka; merimiesjuttu; v.
tarinoida; ks. spin.
yarrow ['jærəu] s. siankärsämö.
yaw [jɔ:] v. (laivasta) ajautua
suunnasta.
yawl [jɔ:l] s. jooli, vene, jolla.
yawn [jɔ:n] v. haukotella; olla
ammollaan, ammottaa; s. haukotus.
yaws [jɔ:z] s. (trooppinen)
vaapukkasyylätauti.
ye [ji:] pron. (vanh.) te.
yea [jei] adv. (vanh.) kyllä, myöntävä
ääni.
year [jə:, jiə] s. vuosi; pl. ikä; every two
~ s joka toinen vuosi; last ~ viime
vuonna; next ~ ensi vuonna; the ~
before last toissa vuonna; twice a ~
kahdesti vuodessa; £ 100 a ~ sata
puntaa vuodessa; ~ after ~, ~ by ~,
~ in ~ out vuosi vuodelta, vuodesta

vuoteen; *all the ~ round* ympäri
vuoden; *for ~ s* vuosikausia, -kausiin,
moneen vuoteen; *from ~ to ~*
vuodesta toiseen; *in* [*the ~*] *1945*
vuonna 1945; *advanced in ~ s* iäkäs;
[*a boy*] *of ten ~ s* kymmenvuotias; [*he
died*] *at* 60 *~ s of age*
kuusikymmenvuotiaana. **-ling** [-liŋ] *s.*
yksivuotias eläin. **-long** *adv.* vuosia
kestänyt. **-ly** [-li] *a.* vuotuinen,
jokavuotinen, vuosi-; *adv.* vuosittain,
joka vuosi.

yearn [jə:n] *v.* kaivata, ikävöidä *(for
jtk)*. **-ing** *a.* kaihoisa, ikävöivä; *s.*
kaiho, kaipaus.

yeast [ji:st] *s.* hiiva. **-y** [-i] *a.* kuohuva,
vaahtoava.

Yeats [jeits] *erisn.*

yell [jel] *v.* kirkua, kiljua, ulvoa; *s.*
kiljaisu, kirkaisu, huuto.

yellow [ˈjeləu] *a.* keltainen; *s.*
keltainen väri; *v.* kellastua, -taa; *~
with envy* kateudesta vihreä, *~ fever*
keltakuume; *the ~ peril* keltainen
vaara; *the ~ press* roskalehdet; *~
streak* hiven pelkuruutta. **~-hammer**
keltasirkku. **-ish** *a.* kellertävä.

yelp [jelp] *v.* haukahtaa, ulvahtaa; *s.*
haukahdus; kiljahdus.

Yemen [ˈjemən] *erisn.* Jemen. **-i** [-i] *a.
& s.* jemeniläinen.

yen [jen] *s.* jen (japanil. raha); Am.
kiihkeä halu, hinku *(have a ~ for).*

yeoman [ˈjəumən] *s.* (pl. *-men*)
itsenäinen talonpoika, maanviljelijä;
~ of the guard
henkivartiokaartilainen. **-ry** [-ri] *s.*
vapaaehtoinen ratsuväki.

yes [jes] *adv.* kyllä, niin; *s.*
myöntösana; *say ~* myöntää,
suostua. [*Can you read this?*]
— *Yes.* osaan.

yester|day [ˈjestədi] *adv.* eilen; *s.*
eilispäivä; *~ morning* eilen aamulla;
the day before ~ toissapäivänä; *~ 's
paper* eilinen sanomalehti. **~-year** *a.
& adv.* viime vuosi (vuonna).

yet [jet] *adv.* (*not ~* ei) vielä; *konj.*
kuitenkin, kumminkin, mutta; *is he
home ~?* onko hän jo kotona? *need
you go ~?* täytyykö sinun jo mennä? *a
~ harder task* vieläkin vaikeampi
tehtävä; *strange and ~ true*
ihmeellistä mutta totta; *as ~*

toistaiseksi; *nor ~* eikä myöskään; [*he
promised, and*] *~ he didn't come*
kumminkaan hän ei tullut.

yew [ju:] *s.* marjakuusi.

yiddish [ˈjidiʃ] *s.* juutalaissaksa,
jiddiš.

yield [ji:ld] *v.* tuottaa (satoa, voittoa);
luovuttaa; luopua jstk; antaa myöten,
myöntyä, alistua, taipua; myöntää,
suoda; *s.* tuotto, sato; voitto; *~
oneself prisoner* antautua vangiksi; *~
the point* myöntyä jssak kohdassa; *~
to despair* heittäytyä epätoivoon; *~ to
force* väistyä, taipua pakon edessä; *~
to temptation* langeta kiusaukseen.
-ing *s.* taipuva, myöntyvä, pehmeä.

yodel [ˈjoudl] *v.* jodlata; *s.* jodlaus.

yog|a [ˈjougə] *s.* jooga. **-i** [-i] *s.* yogi
(joogan opettaja, taitaja).

yog(h)urt [ˈjogət, Am. ˈjougə:t] *s.*
jogurtti.

yoke [jəuk] *s.* ies; härkäpari; korento
(kantotanko); (puvun) kaarroke; *v.*
iestää, panna ikeeseen; panna saman
ikeen alle, kytkeä yhteen. **~-fellow** *s.*
kumppani, puoliso.

yokel [ˈjəuk(ə)l] *s.* maalaismoukka,
tollo.

yolk [jəuk] *s.* munankeltuainen.

yon [jɔn] *a.* (run.) = seur. **-der** [-də]
adv. tuolla (etäämpänä); *adv.* tuo.

yore [jɔ:] *s.: of ~* muinoin, ennen
vanhaan.

York [jɔ:k] *erisn.* **-s** [-s] lyh. = seur.
-shire [-ʃ(i)ə] *erisn.*

you [ju:; ju] *pron.* sinä, te, Te; sinut,
sinua; teidät, teitä; epäm. *pron.* =
one; ~ soon get used to it siihen tottuu
pian; *~ never know* ei voi koskaan
tietää.

young [jʌŋ] *a.* nuori; vasta-alkava,
kokematon; *s.* poikaset, pennut; *the
~ nuoret,* nuoriso; *~ children* pienet
lapset; *~ fellow* nuorukainen; *her ~
man* hänen mielitiettynsä; *~ people*
nuoret, nuoriso; *with ~* tiine. **-er** [-gə]
a. & s. nuorempi. **-ish** [-iʃ] *a.*
nuorehko. **-ster** [-stə] *s.* nuorukainen,
poika; *~ s* nuoret, nuoriso.

your [jɔ:; juə] *poss. pron.* sinun, -si;
teidän, Teidän, -nne; *you cannot
always have ~ own way* ei voi aina
tehdä niinkuin haluaa.

yours [jɔ:z, juəz] *poss. pron.* (itsenäinen

muoto) sinun, teidän ks. *your; a friend of* ~ eräs ystävä|si, -nne; *this is* ~ tämä on sinun; *Yours [sincerely]* Teidän, Sinun (kirjeen lopussa).

yourself [jɔ:'self] *pron.* (pl. *-selves*) (sinä, te) itse; itsesi, -nne, itseäsi, -änne; *you did it* ~ sinä itse sen teit; *[all] by* ~ yksinäsi, omin neuvoin; *you can see for* ~ voit(te) itse nähdä; *did you hurt* ~? loukkaannuitko?

youth [ju:θ, pl. -ðz] *s.* nuoruus;

nuorukainen; nuoriso; ~ *centre* nuorisokerho; ~ *hostel* retkeilymaja. **-ful** *a.* nuorekas; nuoruuden-. **-fulness** *s.* nuorekkuus.

yucca ['jʌkə] *s.* palmulilja.

Yugoslav ['ju:gə(u)slɑ:v] *s.* jugoslaavi. **-ia** [-jə] *erisn.* Jugoslavia. **-ian** [-jən] *a.* jugoslavialainen.

yuk [juk] *s. & v.* syyhy(ä); ~-~ (sl.) lörpöttely.

yule [ju:l] *s.:* ~*-tide* joulu, -npyhät. ~*-log* joulupölkky.

Z

Z, z [zed] *s.* z-kirjain.

Zaire [zɑ(:)'iə] *erisn.*

Zambia ['zæmbiə] *erisn.*

Zanzibar [zænzi'bɑ:] *erisn.*

zany ['zeni] *s.* pelle, narri.

zeal [zi:l] *s.* into, uutteruus; hartaus.

Zealand ['zi:lənd] *erisn.; New* ~ Uusi Seelanti.

zeal|ot ['zelət] *s.* intoilija, kiivailija. **-otry** [-ri] *s.* kiivailu. **-ous** ['zeləs] *a.* uuttera, innokas, harras, palava; intoileva.

zebra ['zi:brə] *s.* seepra; ~ *crossing* suojatie.

zebu ['zi:bu:] *s.* seebu.

zenith ['zeniθ] *s.* (taivaan) lakipiste; huippukohta.

zephyr ['zefə] *s.* länsituuli; leuto tuuli; sefiirilanka.

zeppelin ['zepəlin] *s.* ilmalaiva.

zero ['ziərəu] *s.* (pl. ~ [-e]s) nolla; nollapiste, jäätymispiste; ~ *hour* H-hetki, (hyökkäyksen) alkamishetki.

zest [zest] *s.* halu, innostus, antaumus; ~ *for life* elämänhalu; *entered into it with* ~ ryhtyi siihen innolla.

Zeus [zju:s] *erisn.*

zigzag ['zigzæg] *a.* ristiin rastiin kulkeva; *adv.* polvitellen; *s.*

vinkkuraviiva; *v.* polvitella, kulkea ristiin rastiin.

zinc [ziŋk] *s.* sinkki.

zinnia ['zinjə] *s.* zinnia.

Zion ['zaiən] *erisn.* Siion. **-ism** [-izm] *s.* sionismi. **-ist** [-ist] *s.* sionisti.

zip [zip] *s.* viuhina; tarmo, puhti; vetoketju; *v.* kiinnittää vetoketjulla; sulkea, avata v-ketju (~ *up,* ~ *down*); *jam the* ~ rikkoa vetoketju. ~ **-fastener** vetoketju. **-per** [-ə] *s.* = ed.

zither ['ziθə] *s.* sitra.

zodiac ['zəudiæk] *s.* eläinrata.

zombie ['zɔmbi] *s.* sl. hölmö, ääliö.

zonal ['zəunl] *a.* vyöhyke-.

zone [zəun] *s.* vyöhyke; alue; *v.* jakaa (alueisiin).

zoning (kaupungin) yleiskaava(n laatiminen).

Zoo [zu:] *s.* (lyh. = *zoological garden*) eläintarha.

zoolog|ical ['zə(u)ə'lɔdʒikl] *a.* eläintieteellinen. **-ist** [zə(u)'ɔlədʒi] *s.* eläintiede.

zoom [zu:m] *v.* (ilm.) nousta äkkiä; (valok.) käyttää liukuobjektiivia; *s.* suhahdus; (valok.) liukuobjektiivi.

Zulu ['zu:lu:] *s.* zulu, zulun kieli.

Zurich ['zjuərik] *erisn.*

zymotic [zai'mɔtik] *s.* käymis-.